Textbook Internet resources are just a click away!

STEP 1 ▶ Go to **glencoe.com**

STEP 2 ▶ Connect to resources by entering  codes.

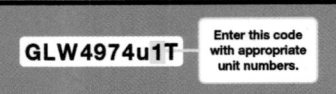   Enter this code with appropriate unit numbers.

STEP 3 ▶ Access your **Online Student Edition,** handheld downloads, games, and more:

Literature and Reading Resources

- Author Search
- Literature Classics
- Big Idea Web Quests
- Interactive Timelines and Being There Online
- Literary Elements eFlashcards and Games
- Interactive Reading Practice

Selection Resources

- Audio Summaries
- Selection Quizzes
- Selection Vocabulary eFlashcards and Games
- Reading-Writing Connection Activities

Vocabulary Resources

- Academic and Selection Vocabulary eFlashcards and Games
- Multi-Language Glossaries

Writing, Grammar, and Research Resources

- Interactive Writing Models
- Writing and Research Handbook
- Graphic Organizers
- Sentence-Combining Activities
- Publishing Options

Media Literacy, Speaking, Listening, and Viewing Resources

- Media Analysis Guides
- Project Ideas and Templates
- Presentation Tips and Strategies

Assessment Resources

- End-of-Unit Assessment
- ACT/SAT Vocabulary eFlashcards and Games
- Test-Taking Tips and Strategies

On the Cover:

Klee, Paul (1879-1940) © ARS, NY.

Castle and Sun, 1928.
Canvas.

Location: Private Collection,
Great Britain

TEACHER EDITION

Program Consultants

Jeffrey D. Wilhelm, Ph.D.
Douglas Fisher, Ph.D.
Beverly Ann Chin, Ph.D.
Jacqueline Jones Royster, DA

Acknowledgments

Grateful acknowledgment is given authors, publishers, photographers, museums, and agents for permission to reprint the following copyrighted material. Every effort has been made to determine copyright owners. In case of any omissions, the Publisher will be pleased to make suitable acknowledgments in future editions.

Acknowledgments continued on page R102.

 **Glencoe**

The McGraw·Hill Companies

Copyright © 2009 by the McGraw-Hill Companies, Inc. All rights reserved. Except as permitted under the United States Copyright Act, no part of this publication may be reproduced or distributed in any form or by any means, or stored in a database or retrieval system, without prior permission of the publisher.

TIME © Time, Inc. TIME and the red border design are trademarks of Time, Inc. used under license.

Send all inquiries to:
Glencoe/McGraw-Hill
8787 Orion Place
Columbus, OH 43240-4027

ISBN: (student edition) 978-0-07-845605-3
MHID: (student edition) 0-07-845605-3
ISBN: (teacher edition) 978-0-07-845497-4
MHID: (teacher edition) 0-07-845497-2

Printed in the United States of America.

2 3 4 5 6 7 8 9 10 027/043 13 12 11 10 09 08

Consultants

Senior Program Consultants

Jeffrey D. Wilhelm, PhD, a former middle and secondary school English and reading teacher, is currently Professor of Education at Boise State University. He is the author or coauthor of numerous articles and several books on the teaching of reading and literacy, including award-winning titles such as *You Gotta BE the Book* and *Reading Don't Fix No Chevys*. He also works with local schools as part of the Adolescent Literacy Project and recently helped establish the National Writing Project site at Boise State University.

Douglas Fisher, PhD, is Professor of Language and Literacy Education and Director of Professional Development at San Diego State University, where he teaches English language development and literacy. He also serves as Director of City Heights Educational Pilot, which won the Christa McAuliffe Award from the American Association of State Colleges and Universities. He has published numerous articles on reading and literacy, differentiated instruction, and curriculum design. He is coauthor of the book *Improving Adolescent Literacies: Strategies That Work* and coeditor of the book *Inclusive Urban Schools*.

Program Consultants

Beverly Ann Chin, PhD, is Professor of English, Director of the English Teaching Program, former Director of the Montana Writing Project, and former Director of Composition at the University of Montana in Missoula. She currently serves as a Member at Large of the Conference of English Leadership. Dr. Chin is a nationally recognized leader in English language arts standards, curriculum, and assessment. Formerly a high school teacher and an adult education reading teacher, Dr. Chin has taught in English language arts education at several universities and has received awards for her teaching and service.

Jacqueline Jones Royster, DA, is Professor of English and Senior Vice Provost and Executive Dean of the Colleges of Arts and Sciences at The Ohio State University. She is currently on the Writing Advisory Committee of the National Commission on Writing and serves as chair for both the Columbus Literacy Council and the Ohioana Library Association. In addition to the teaching of writing, Dr. Royster's professional interests include the rhetorical history of African American women and the social and cultural implications of literate practices. She has contributed to and helped to edit numerous books, anthologies, and journals.

Advisory Board

Special Consultants

Donald R. Bear, PhD.
Professor, Department of
Curriculum and Instruction
Director, E. L. Cord Foundation
Center for Learning and Literacy
at the University of Nevada,
Reno. Author of *Words Their
Way* and *Words Their Way with
English Learners.*

Jana Echevarria, PhD.
Professor, Educational
Psychology, California State
University, Long Beach.
Author of *Making Content
Comprehensible for English
Learners: the SIOP Model.*

FOLDABLES® **Dinah Zike, MEd,**
was a classroom teacher and
a consultant for many years
before she began to develop
Foldables®—a variety of easily
created graphic organizers. Zike
has written and developed more
than 150 supplemental books
and materials used in classrooms
worldwide. Her *Big Book of Books
and Activities* won the Teachers'
Choice Award.

The Writers' Express®
Immediate Impact. Lasting Transformation.   wex.org

Glencoe National Reading and Language Arts Advisory Council

Mary A. Avalos, PhD
Assistant Department Chair,
    Department of Teaching
    and Learning
Research Assistant Professor,
    Department of Teaching
    and Learning
University of Miami
Coral Gables, Florida

Wanda J. Blanchett, PhD
Associate Dean for Academic
    Affairs and Associate Professor
    of Exceptional Education
School of Education
University of Wisconsin–
    Milwaukee
Milwaukee, Wisconsin

William G. Brozo, PhD
Professor of Literacy
Graduate School of Education
College of Education and
    Human Development
George Mason University
Fairfax, Virginia

Nancy Drew, EdD
LaPointe Educational Consultants
Corpus Christi, Texas

Susan Florio-Ruane, EdD
Professor
College of Education
Michigan State University
East Lansing, Michigan

**Sharon Fontenot O'Neal,
PhD**
Associate Professor
Texas State University
San Marcos, Texas

Nancy Frey, PhD
Associate Professor of Literacy
    in Teacher Education
School of Teacher Education
San Diego State University
San Diego, California

**Victoria Ridgeway Gillis,
PhD**
Associate Professor
Reading Education
Clemson University
Clemson, South Carolina

Kimberly Lawless, PhD
Associate Professor
Curriculum, Instruction
    and Evaluation
College of Education
University of Illinois at Chicago
Chicago, Illinois

William Ray, MA
Lincoln-Sudbury Regional
    High School
Sudbury, Massachusetts

Janet Saito-Furukawa, MEd
English Language Arts Specialist
District 4
Los Angeles, California

Bonnie Valdes, MEd
Independent Reading Consultant
CRISS Master Trainer
Largo, Florida

Teacher Reviewers

The following teachers contributed to the review of *Glencoe World Literature*.

Bridget M. Agnew
St. Michael School
Chicago, Illinois

Monica Anzaldua Araiza
Dr. Juliet V. Garcia Middle School
Brownsville, Texas

Katherine R. Baer
Howard County Public Schools
Ellicott City, Maryland

Tanya Baxter
Roald Amundsen High School
Chicago, Illinois

Danielle R. Brain
Thomas R. Proctor Senior High
   School
Utica, New York

Yolanda Conder
Owasso Mid-High School
Owasso, Oklahoma

Gwenn de Mauriac
The Wiscasset Schools
Wiscasset, Maine

Courtney Doan
Bloomington High School
Bloomington, Illinois

Susan M. Griffin
Edison Preparatory School
Tulsa, Oklahoma

Cindi Davis Harris
Helix Charter High School
La Mesa, California

Joseph F. Hutchinson
Toledo Public Schools
Toledo, Ohio

Ginger Jordan
Florien High School
Florien, Louisiana

Dianne Konkel
Cypress Lake Middle School
Fort Myers, Florida

Melanie A. LaFleur
Many High School
Many, Louisiana

Patricia Lee
Radnor Middle School
Wayne, Pennsylvania

Linda Copley Lemons
Cleveland High School
Cleveland, Tennessee

Heather S. Lewis
Waverly Middle School
Lansing, Michigan

Sandra C. Lott
Aiken Optional School
Alexandria, Louisiana

Connie M. Malacarne
O'Fallon Township High School
O'Fallon, Illinois

Lori Howton Means
Edward A. Fulton Junior High
   School
O'Fallon, Illinois

Claire C. Meitl
Howard County Public Schools
Ellicott City, Maryland

Patricia P. Mitcham
Mohawk High School
   (Retired)
New Castle, Pennsylvania

Lisa Morefield
South-Western Career Academy
Grove City, Ohio

Kevin M. Morrison
Hazelwood East High School
St. Louis, Missouri

Jenine M. Pokorak
School Without Walls Senior
   High School
Washington, DC

Susan Winslow Putnam
Butler High School
Matthews, North Carolina

Paul C. Putnoki
Torrington Middle School
Torrington, Connecticut

Jane Thompson Rae
Cab Calloway High School of
   the Arts
Wilmington, Delaware

Stephanie L. Robin
N. P. Moss Middle School
Lafayette, Louisiana

Ann C. Ryan
Lindenwold High School
Lindenwold, New Jersey

Pamela Schoen
Hopkins High School
Minnetonka, Minnesota

Megan Schumacher
Friends' Central School
Wynnewood, Pennsylvania

Fareeda J. Shabazz
Paul Revere Elementary School
Chicago, Illinois

Molly Steinlage
Brookpark Middle School
Grove City, Ohio

Barry Stevenson
Garnet Valley Middle School
Glen Mills, Pennsylvania

Paul Stevenson
Edison Preparatory School
Tulsa, Oklahoma

Kathy Thompson
Owasso Mid-High School
Owasso, Oklahoma

Book Overview

Evening Snow on the Asuka Mountain, from 'Eight Views of Environs of Edo', c.1838.
Ando or Utagawa Hiroshige. Woodblock colour print. Brooklyn Museum of Art, New York.

Paisaje (Landscape). Juan Cardenas (Columbian b. 1939). Oil on linen, 50 x 65 cm. Private collection.

Contents

> "In a great effort he straightened up
> and was on his feet at one go—but
> the great bar of iron was twisted
> and had taken the form of a bow!"
>
> —Sundiata

▲▲

PART TWO

Modern AFRICA 1800–Present

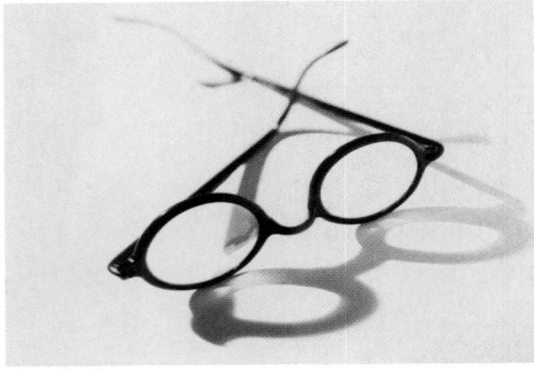

"As political prisoners they were
unlike the other prisoners in the
sense that they felt no guilt . . ."

—Bessie Head

UNIT TWO

ANCIENT GREECE AND ROME   1500 B.C.–A.D. 500

PART ONE

ANCIENT GREECE   1500 B.C.–1 B.C.

"With that he wrenched his bronze spear from the corpse, laid it aside and ripped the bloody armor off the back."

—Homer

PART TWO

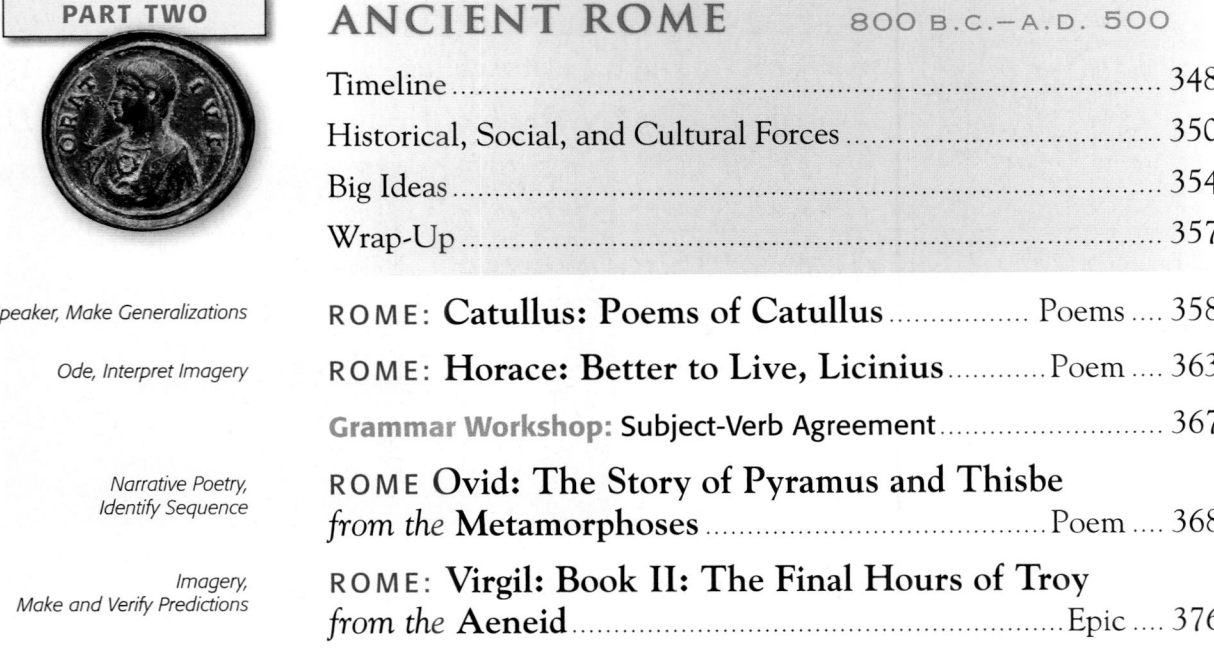

ANCIENT ROME   800 B.C.—A.D. 500

"Devouring fire whipped by the winds/ goes churning into the rooftops, flames surging/ over them, scorching blasts raging up the sky."

—Virgil

UNIT THREE

Southwest and South Central Asia   3500 B.C.—Present

PART ONE

Southwest Asia   3500 B.C.—Present

Epic Hero, Visualize

"Do not grieve for what is past;
When a thing is done, vex not yourself about it."

—*Rumi*

"Behind them the interior of the curtained wagon swelled with darkness and from the heart of that darkness shot out the nauseating stench which cut sharper than a sword . . ."

—Khalida Asghar

Red Townscape, 1961. Francis Newton Souza. Oil on canvas. Private collection.

UNIT FOUR

East Asia and the Pacific
2000 B.C.–Present

PART ONE

East Asia 2000 B.C.–Present

Maxim, Make Generalizations

Parallelism, Question

Tone, Visualize

Comparing Literature Across Time and Place

Imagery, Make Inferences About Theme

Mood, Interpret Imagery

Diary, Draw Conclusions About Author's Culture

"In time's assembly line
Night presses against night."

—Shu Ting

PART TWO

Southeast Asia and the Pacific
500 B.C.–Present

"Do you count me as a friend/ or am I the enemy in your eyes?"
—Nguyen Thi Vinh

Ham Rong Bridge,
1970. Vu Giang Huong.
Woodcut on rice paper,
12 x 16 7/8 in.
Collection of the Artist.

UNIT FIVE

EUROPE A.D. 400–PRESENT

PART ONE

EARLY EUROPE A.D. 400–1650

Description, Summarize

Epic, Evaluate Characters

Suspense,
Monitor Comprehension

> "He wept from his six eyes, and down three chins/ the tears ran mixed with bloody froth and pus."
>
> —Dante Alighieri

Father and Child, 1946. Ben Shahn. Tempera on cardboard, 39 7/8 x 30 in. Gift of James Thrall Soby. The Museum of Modern Art, NY.© VAGA, NY.

" 'Don't forget that you are in a concentration camp. In this place, it is every man for himself, and you cannot think of others.' "

—Elie Wiesel

THE AMERICAS 3000 B.C.–PRESENT

THE EARLY AMERICAS 3000 B.C.–A.D.1900

Skills and Standards

Myth, Clarify Meaning

Motif, Draw Conclusions About Culture

Journal, Recognize Bias

Setting, Analyze Cultural Context

"Broken spears lie in the roads/ we have torn our hair in our grief."

—*The Broken Spears*

PART TWO

THE MODERN AMERICAS 1800–PRESENT

Comparing Literature Across Time and Place

> " . . . suddenly he saw the red stone, shiny with the blood dripping off it, and the spinning arcs cut by the feet of the victim whom they pulled off . . ."
>
> —Julio Cortázar

Fire and Destruction, 1985. Juri Palm. Oil on canvas. Art Museum of Estonia, Tallinn.

Reference Section

Selections by Genre

Drama

Epic

Sacred Text

Nonfiction and Informational Text

Feature Article

Essay

Autobiography and Memoir

Diary

Speech

Features

The Art of Translation

Literary History

Independent Reading

Assessment

Skills Workshops

How to Use *Glencoe World Literature*

Organization

The literature you will read is organized geographically into six units spanning the globe.

Each unit contains the following:

A **PART INTRODUCTION** provides you with the background information to help make your reading experience more meaningful.

- The **TIMELINE** helps you keep track of major literary and historical events.

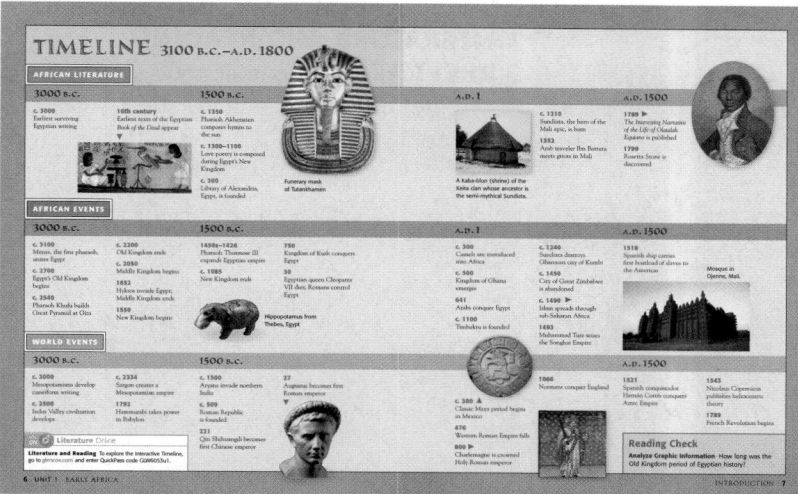

- **HISTORICAL, SOCIAL, AND CULTURAL FORCES** explain the influences that shape a specific literary period.

- **BIG IDEAS** target three concepts that you can trace as you read the literature.

LITERARY WORKS follow each Part Introduction. The selections are organized as follows.

Why do I need this book?

Glencoe World Literature is more than just a collection of stories, poems, nonfiction articles, and other literary works. Every part is built around **Big Ideas,** concepts that you will want to think about, talk about, and maybe even argue about. Big Ideas help you become part of an important conversation. You can join in lively discussions about who we are, where we have been, and where we are going.

Reading and Thinking

The main literary works in your textbook are arranged in three parts.

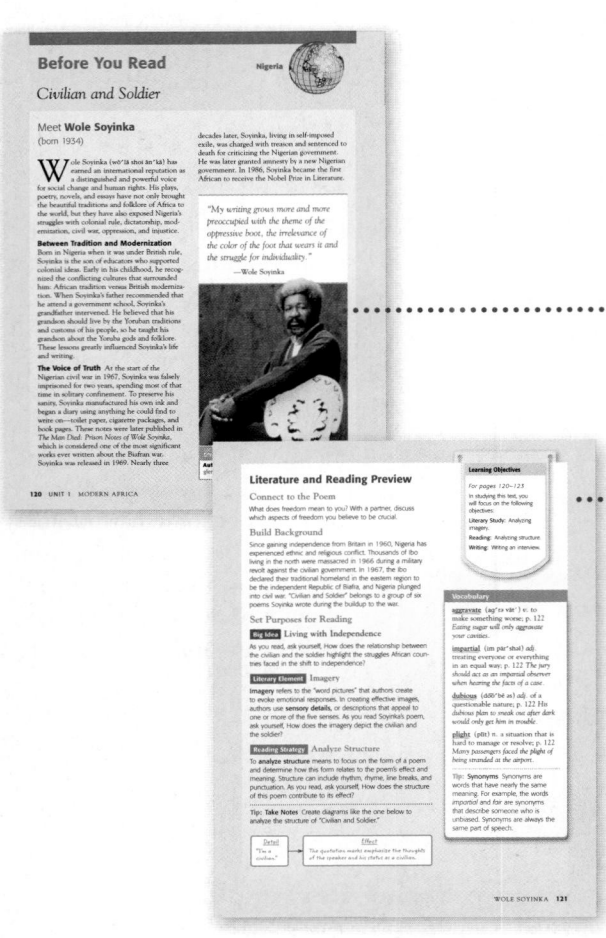

- Start with **BEFORE YOU READ**. Learn valuable background information about the literature and preview the skills and strategies that will guide your reading.

MEET THE AUTHOR presents a detailed biography of the writer whose work you will read and analyze.

LITERATURE AND READING PREVIEW lists the basic tools you will use to read and analyze the literary work.

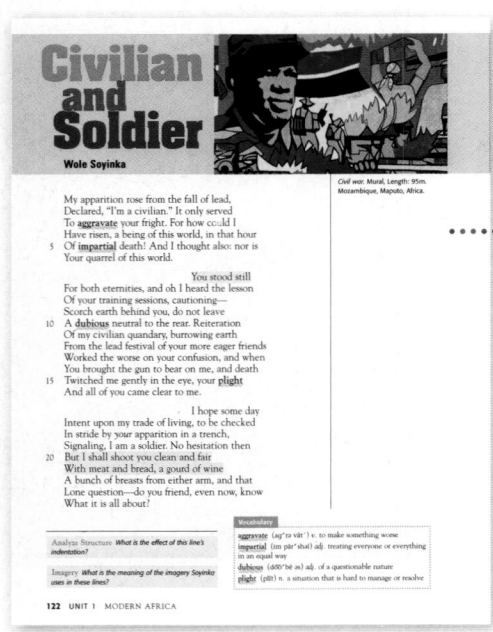

- Next, read the **LITERARY WORK**. As you flip through the selections, you will notice that parts of the text are highlighted in different colors. At the bottom of the page are color-coded questions that relate to the highlighted text. Yellow represents a *Big Idea*, magenta represents a *Literary Element*, and blue represents a *Reading Strategy*. These questions will help you gain a better understanding of the text.

- Wrap up the literature with **AFTER YOU READ**. Explore what you have learned through a wide range of reading, thinking, vocabulary, and writing activities.

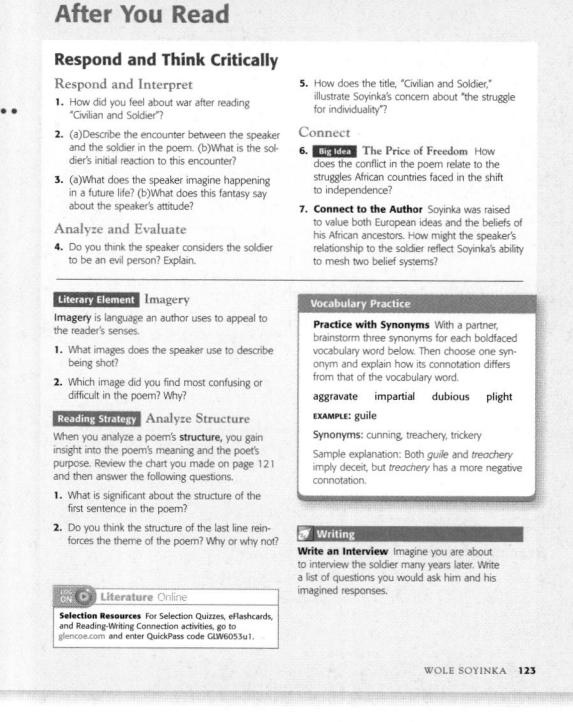

Vocabulary

VOCABULARY WORDS that may be new or difficult are chosen from most selections. They are introduced on the **BEFORE YOU READ** page. Each word is accompanied by its pronunciation, its part of speech, its definition, and the page number on which it appears. The vocabulary word is also used in a sample sentence. Vocabulary words are highlighted in the literary work.

VOCABULARY PRACTICE On the **AFTER YOU READ** pages, you will be able to practice using the vocabulary words in an exercise. This exercise will show you how to apply a vocabulary strategy to understand new or difficult words.

ACADEMIC VOCABULARY Many of the **AFTER YOU READ** pages will also introduce you to a word that is frequently used in academic work. You will be prompted to complete an activity based on that word.

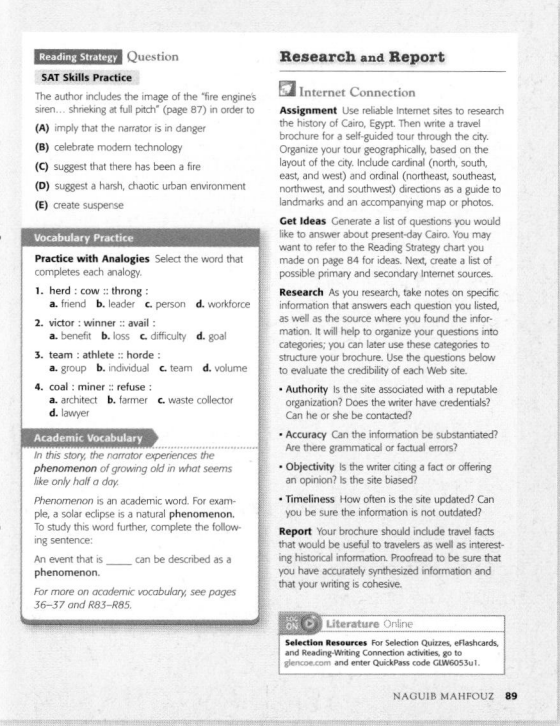

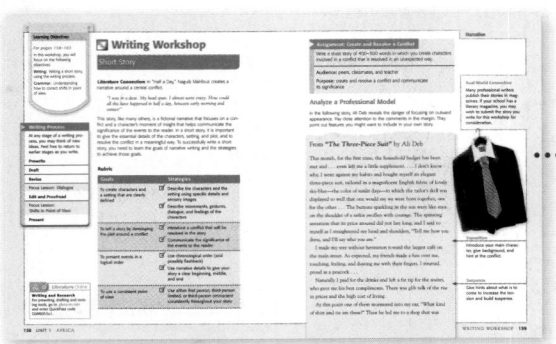

Writing Workshops

Each unit in *Glencoe World Literature* includes a Writing Workshop. The workshop walks you through the writing process as you work on an extended piece of writing related to the unit.

- You will create writing goals and apply strategies to meet them.

- You will pick up tips and polish your critical skills as you analyze professional and workshop models.

- You will focus on mastering specific aspects of writing, including organization, grammar, and vocabulary.

- You will use a rubric to evaluate your own writing.

Assessment

English–Language Arts

Reading: Fiction and Autobiography

Carefully read the following two passages. Use context clues to help you define any words with which you are unfamiliar. In each passage, pay close attention to the **author's purpose**, the **cultures** described, the **mood, tone,** and uses of **literary** or **rhetorical** devices. Then, on a separate sheet of paper, answer the questions on pages 172–173.

> **from *Things Fall Apart* by Chinua Achebe**
>
> The Feast of the New Yam was approaching and Umuofia was in a festival mood. It was an occasion for giving thanks to Ani, the earth goddess and the source of all fertility. Ani played a greater part in the life of the people than any other deity. She was the ultimate judge of morality and conduct. And what was more, she was in close communion with the departed fathers of the clan whose bodies had been committed to earth.
>
> The Feast of the New Yam was held every year before the harvest began, to honor the earth goddess and the ancestral spirits of the clan. New yams could not be eaten until some had first been offered to these powers. Men and women, young and old, looked forward to the New Yam Festival because it began the season of plenty—the new year. On the last night before the festival, yams of the old year were all disposed of by those who still had them. The new year must begin with tasty, fresh yams and not the shriveled and fibrous crop of the previous year. All cooking pots, calabashes and wooden bowls were thoroughly washed, especially the wooden mortar in which yam was pounded. Yam foo-foo and vegetable soup was the chief food in the celebration. So much of it was cooked that, no matter how heavily the family ate or how many friends and relatives they invited from neighboring villages, there was always a large quantity of food left over at the end of the day. The story was always told of a wealthy man who set before his guests a mound of foo-foo so high that those who sat on one side could not see what was happening on the other, and it was not until late in the evening that one of them saw for the first time his in-law who had arrived during the course of the meal and had fallen to on the opposite side. It was only then that they exchanged greetings and shook hands over what was left of the food.
>
> The New Yam Festival was thus an occasion for joy throughout Umuofia. And every man whose arm was strong, as the Ibo people say, was expected to invite large numbers of guests from far and wide. Okonkwo always asked his wives' relations, and since he now had three wives his guests would make a fairly big crowd.
>
> But somehow Okonkwo could never become as enthusiastic over feasts as most people. He was a good eater and he could drink one or two fairly big gourds of palm-wine. But he was always uncomfortable sitting around for days waiting for a feast or getting over it. He would be very much happier working on his farm.

170 UNIT 1 AFRICA

Assessment

At the end of each unit, you will be tested on the literature, reading, and vocabulary skills you have just learned. Designed to simulate standardized tests, this test will give you the practice you need to succeed while providing an assessment of how you have met the unit objectives.

FOLDABLES
Study Organizer
BOUND BOOK

Try using this organizer to explore your personal responses to the poetry, play and nonfiction.

Organizing Information

Graphic organizers—such as Foldables®, diagrams, and charts—help you keep your information and ideas organized.

Be Cyber Safe and Smart

Cyber Safety

As you explore the *Glencoe Literature* program, you will have many opportunities to go online. When you use the Internet at school or home, you enter a kind of community—the cyber world. In this online world, you need to follow safety rules and protect yourself. Here are some tips to keep in mind:

> ### Words to Know
>
> **cyber world** the world of computers and high-tech communications
> **cyber safety** actions that protect Internet users from harm
> **cyber ethics** responsible code of conduct for using the Internet
> **cyber bully** a person who uses technology to frighten, bother, or harm someone else
> **cyber citizen** a person who uses the Internet to communicate

☑ Be a responsible cyber citizen. Use the Internet to share knowledge that makes people's lives better. Respect other people's feelings and do not break any laws.

☑ Beware of cyber bullying. People can be hurt and embarrassed by comments that have been made public. You should immediately tell your teacher or counselor if you feel threatened by another student's computer postings.

☑ Do not give out personal information, such as your address and telephone number, without your parents' or guardians' permission.

☑ Tell your teacher, parent, or guardian right away if you find or read any information that makes you feel uneasy or afraid.

☑ Do not email your picture to anyone.

☑ Do not open email or text messages from strangers.

☑ Do not tell anyone your Internet password.

☑ Do not make illegal copies of computer games and programs, and software CDs.

LOG ON ▶ **Literature** Online

For more about internet safety and responsibility, go to glencoe.com

This chart provides an overview of the scope and sequence for *Glencoe World Literature*. For a detailed scope and sequence of skills, see the chart at the beginning of each unit in the Teacher Edition. Refer also to the Index of Skills in the Reference Section in the back of the book for a comprehensive listing of all skills and concepts taught in *Glencoe World Literature*.

✔ = Introduced   ✔ = Reviewed

	UNIT ONE	UNIT TWO	UNIT THREE	UNIT FOUR	UNIT FIVE	UNIT SIX
Literary Criticism						
Analyzing Literature in Context						
Literary Periods	✔	✔	✔	✔	✔	✔
Literary Genres						
Oral Tradition Forms						
Epic	✔	✔	✔	✔	✔	
Myth, Folklore, and Legend			✔	✔		✔
Fiction						
Short Story	✔		✔	✔	✔	✔
Nonfiction						
Autobiography or Memoir			✔		✔	
Speech		✔				
Poetry						
Epic					✔	
Free Verse					✔	
Narrative Poem		✔				
Ode		✔				
Sonnet					✔	
Drama						
Tragedy		✔				
Literary Elements						
Literary Structure						
Author's Purpose		✔	✔	✔	✔	✔
Characters	✔		✔	✔	✔	✔
Conflict			✔	✔		✔
Description					✔	
Narrator			✔		✔	✔

	UNIT ONE	UNIT TWO	UNIT THREE	UNIT FOUR	UNIT FIVE	UNIT SIX
Literary Elements *(cont.)*						
Parallelism		✔	✔			
Plot	✔		✔		✔	✔
Point of View	✔		✔	✔		✔
Setting	✔	✔	✔	✔		
Style		✔				✔
Suspense					✔	
Theme	✔	✔	✔	✔	✔	✔
Voice and Tone	✔	✔	✔	✔	✔	✔
Literary Language						
Diction	✔		✔	✔		
Figures of Speech				✔	✔	✔
Imagery	✔	✔	✔	✔		✔
Repitition	✔				✔	
Sound Devices			✔		✔	✔
Symbolism			✔	✔		✔
Reading Skills						
Strategies						
Analyzing	✔	✔	✔	✔	✔	✔
Applying Background Knowledge	✔	✔	✔	✔	✔	✔
Clarifying			✔	✔		✔
Compare and Contrast	✔	✔	✔	✔		✔
Connect to Personal Experience	✔	✔	✔	✔		✔
Determine Main Idea and Supporting Details		✔	✔	✔	✔	✔
Drawing Conclusions	✔			✔	✔	✔
Evaluating	✔	✔	✔	✔	✔	✔
Identifying	✔	✔	✔	✔	✔	✔
Making Inferences	✔		✔	✔	✔	✔
Making Predictions	✔		✔			✔
Monitoring Comprehension	✔	✔	✔		✔	✔
Paraphrasing		✔	✔			✔

SCOPE AND SEQUENCE

✔ = Introduced   ✔ = Reviewed

	UNIT ONE	UNIT TWO	UNIT THREE	UNIT FOUR	UNIT FIVE	UNIT SIX
Reading Skills (cont.)						
Previewing	✔	✔	✔	✔		✔
Questioning	✔		✔	✔		✔
Reading Independently	✔	✔	✔	✔	✔	✔
Recognizing Bias		✔				✔
Rereading		✔				
Review	✔					✔
Summarizing		✔	✔	✔	✔	✔
Synthesizing		✔	✔			✔
Visualizing	✔	✔	✔	✔	✔	✔
Vocabulary Development						
Academic Vocabulary	✔	✔	✔	✔	✔	✔
Analogies	✔		✔	✔	✔	✔
Antonyms	✔		✔		✔	✔
Context Clues	✔	✔	✔	✔	✔	✔
Denotation and Connotation		✔	✔	✔	✔	✔
Multiple-Meanig Words		✔				✔
Prefixes and Suffixes	✔	✔	✔	✔	✔	✔
Synonyms	✔	✔	✔	✔	✔	✔
Word Roots and Origins	✔	✔	✔	✔	✔	✔
Writing and Grammar						
Types of Writing						
Literary Criticism: Biographical or Historical Approach			✔			✔
Biographical Narrative			✔	✔	✔	
Description		✔	✔		✔	✔
Essay	✔	✔	✔	✔	✔	✔
Journal Entry	✔		✔			

Writing and Grammar (cont.)

	UNIT ONE	UNIT TWO	UNIT THREE	UNIT FOUR	UNIT FIVE	UNIT SIX
Letter		✔	✔	✔	✔	✔
Persuasive Speech	✔			✔		✔
Poem		✔	✔	✔	✔	✔
Research Report	✔	✔	✔	✔		✔
Review		✔				
Scene	✔		✔	✔	✔	✔
Short Story	✔		✔	✔	✔	✔

Writing Process

	UNIT ONE	UNIT TWO	UNIT THREE	UNIT FOUR	UNIT FIVE	UNIT SIX
Prewriting, Drafting, Revising, Editing and Proofreading, Presenting	✔	✔	✔	✔	✔	✔
Traits of Strong Writing	✔	✔	✔	✔	✔	✔

Grammar, Usage, and Mechanics

	UNIT ONE	UNIT TWO	UNIT THREE	UNIT FOUR	UNIT FIVE	UNIT SIX
Parts of Speech	✔		✔	✔	✔	✔
Capitalization and Punctuation	✔	✔	✔	✔	✔	✔
Sentence Structure	✔	✔	✔	✔	✔	✔

Speaking, Listening, and Viewing

	UNIT ONE	UNIT TWO	UNIT THREE	UNIT FOUR	UNIT FIVE	UNIT SIX
Debate	✔	✔	✔		✔	
Discussion	✔	✔	✔	✔	✔	✔
Interview		✔	✔			✔
Multimedia Presentation		✔	✔	✔	✔	✔
Oral Interpretation of a Short Story	✔	✔	✔	✔	✔	✔
Persuasive Speech	✔	✔	✔	✔		
Photo Essay		✔				
Presenting Literary Criticism						✔
Reading Aloud			✔		✔	✔
Reflective Presentation			✔			
Viewing Art	✔	✔	✔	✔	✔	✔

Teaching the Standards: World Literature Essential Course of Study

The following abbreviated curriculum is a suggestion for addressing those objectives that students commonly encounter on standardized tests. You may use it as a guide for prioritizing instruction in preparation for the tests.

Unit 1

Selections/Lessons	Pacing/Days	Genre	Where to Find Instruction	Commonly Tested Objectives
Egyptian poetry	1–3	Poetry	pp. 31–32	**Literary Study:** Imagery **Reading:** Analyzing diction
from **Sundiata**	2–6	Epic	pp. 59–63	**Literary Study:** Epic **Reading:** Making inference about characters
The Voter	2–6	Short Story	pp. 95–99	**Literary Study:** Motivation **Reading:** Activating prior knowledge
The Rain Came	2–6	Short Story	pp. 110–116	**Literary Study:** Setting **Reading:** Analyzing cultural context

Unit 2

Selections/Lessons	Pacing/Days	Genre	Where to Find Instruction	Commonly Tested Objectives
Lyric Poems	1–3	Poetry	pp. 243–245	**Literary Study:** Imagery **Reading:** Paraphrasing
Oedipus the King	3–12	Drama	pp. 253, 292–303	**Literary Study:** Irony **Reading:** Synthesizing
Pericles' Funeral Oration	2–6	Nonfiction	pp. 323–330	**Literary Study:** Argument **Reading:** Analyzing rhetorical devices
Better to Live, Licinius	1–3	Poetry	p. 365	**Literary Study:** Ode **Reading:** Interpreting imagery

Unit 3

Selections/Lessons	Pacing/Days	Genre	Where to Find Instruction	Commonly Tested Objectives
The Second Voyage of Sindbad the Sailor	1–3	Folktale	pp. 498–502	**Literary Study:** Point of View **Reading:** Identifying problem and solution
from the **Rubáiyát**	1–3	Poetry	pp. 507–508	**Literary Study:** Rhyme scheme **Reading:** Clarifying meaning
The Sound of Birds at Noon	1–3	Poetry	p. 522	**Literary Study:** Enjambment **Reading:** Recognizing author's purpose
The Kabuliwallah	2–6	Short Story	pp. 610–615	**Literary Study:** Characterization **Reading:** Analyzing cultural context
By Any Other Name	2–6	Nonfiction	pp. 627–632	**Literary Study:** Autobiography **Reading:** Connecting to contemporary issues

Unit 4

Selections/Lessons	Pacing/Days	Genre	Where to Find Instruction	Commonly Tested Objectives
from the Tao Te Ching	1–3	Sacred Text	pp. 691–692	**Literary Study:** Parallelism **Reading:** Questioning
Jade Flower Palace; Ozymandias; from Istanbul: Memories of the City	2–6	Poetry and Memoir	pp. 705, 707–710	**Literary Study:** Imagery **Reading:** Making inferences about theme
from The Pillow Book	2–6	Diary	pp. 718–720; 723–724	**Literary Study:** Diary **Reading:** Drawing conclusions about author's culture
Zen Parables	1–3	Parables	pp. 732–734	**Literary Study:** Parable **Reading:** Applying background knowledge
The Doll's House	1–3	Short Story	pp. 793–798	**Literary Study:** Symbol **Reading:** Analyzing sensory details

Unit 5

Selections/Lessons	Pacing/Days	Genre	Where to Find Instruction	Commonly Tested Objectives
from The Prose Edda	1–3	Myth	pp. 873–874	**Literary Study:** Description **Reading:** Summarizing
from the Inferno	4–12	Poetry	pp. 906–911	**Literary Study:** Allegory **Reading:** Analyzing sound devices
from Don Quixote	2–6	Novel Excerpt	pp. 942–944	**Literary Study:** Parody **Reading:** Make inferences about theme
from Candide	1–3	Novel Excerpt	pp. 963–966	**Literary Study:** Satire **Reading:** Applying background knowledge
The Myth of Sisyphus	2–6	Essay	pp. 1058–1060	**Literary Study:** Persuasion **Reading:** Determining main idea and supporting details

Unit 6

Selections/Lessons	Pacing/Days	Genre	Where to Find Instruction	Commonly Tested Objectives
from The Broken Spears	2–6	Nonfiction	pp. 1155–1158	**Literary Study:** Setting **Reading:** Analyzing cultural context
Two Countries	1–3	Poetry	p. 1171	**Literary Study:** Juxtaposition **Reading:** Analyzing figures of speech
TIME: The First Americans	2–6	Nonfiction	pp. 1173–1177	**Reading:** Determining main idea and supporting details
The Night Face Up	2–6	Short Story	pp. 1232–1238	**Literary Study:** Point of view **Reading:** Identifying sequence
Day of the Butterfly	2–6	Short Story	pp. 1266–1273	**Literary Study:** Dialect and idiom **Reading:** Analyzing characterization

Reference Section

Selections/Lessons	Pacing/Days	Genre	Where to Find Instruction	Commonly Tested Objectives
Functional Documents	2–6	Informational Text	pp. R22–R27	**Reading:** Analyzing expository texts
	Total: 46–150 days			

To Teachers

Welcome to the Teacher Edition of *Glencoe Literature*. We have created this teacher edition based on the standards developed by experienced teachers and educational consultants. Teaching suggestions, additional resources, and leveled activities for differentiated instruction are all labeled and wrapped around the student text for your convenience.

Unit Scope and Sequence

Every unit of *Glencoe Literature* is organized around a carefully researched scope and sequence that includes the reading skills and strategies, literary elements, writing skills, and listening, speaking and viewing skills that students need in order to successfully progress through the program.

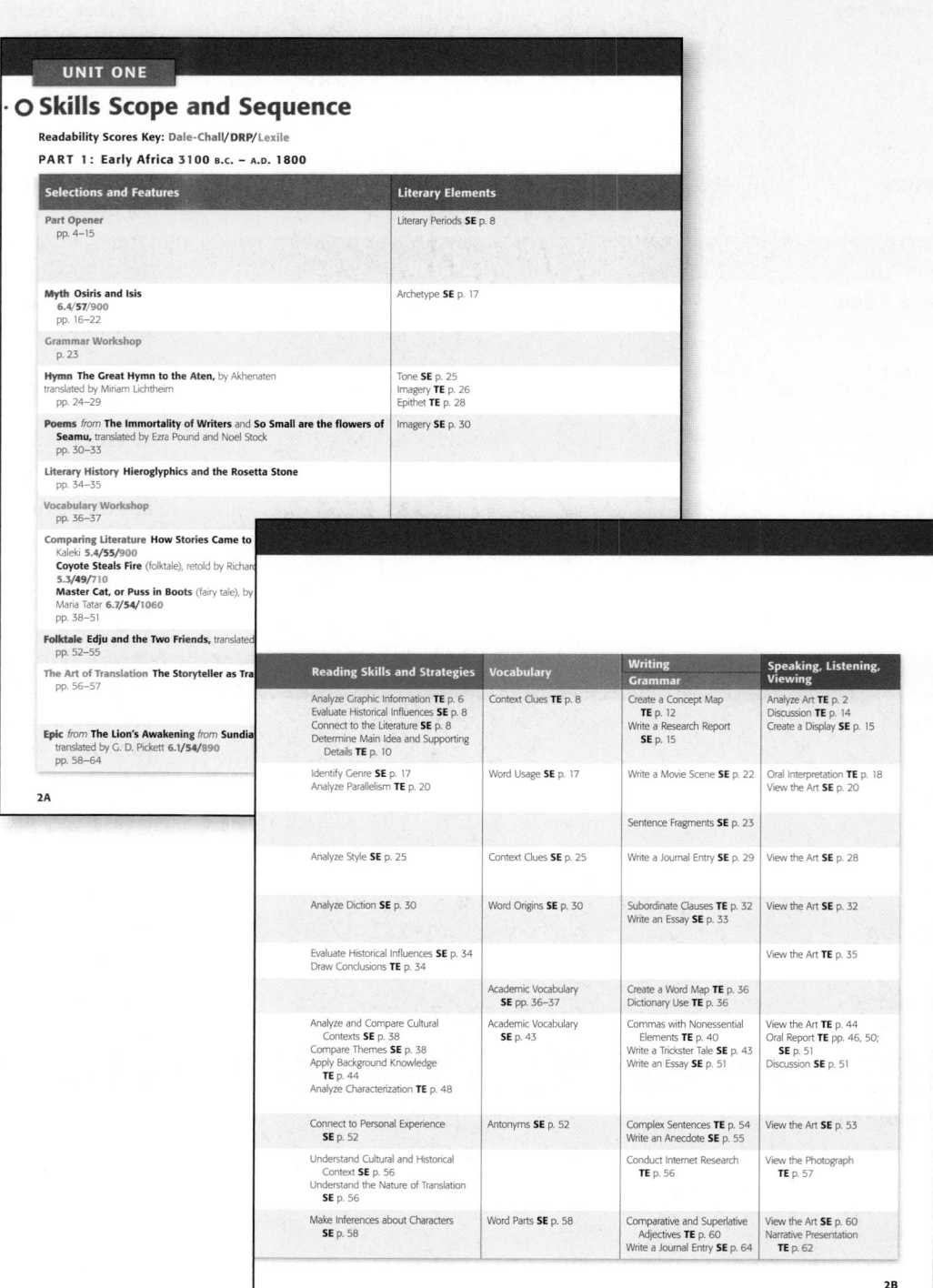

UNIT ONE
Skills Scope and Sequence

Readability Scores Key: Dale-Chall/**DRP**/Lexile

PART 1: Early Africa 3100 B.C. – A.D. 1800

Selections and Features	Literary Elements
Part Opener pp. 4–15	Literary Periods **SE** p. 8
Myth Osiris and Isis 6.4/**57**/900 pp. 16–22	Archetype **SE** p. 17
Grammar Workshop p. 23	
Hymn The Great Hymn to the Aten, by Akhenaten translated by Miriam Lichtheim pp. 24–29	Tone **SE** p. 25 Imagery **TE** p. 26 Epithet **TE** p. 28
Poems from **The Immortality of Writers** and **So Small are the flowers of Seamu,** translated by Ezra Pound and Noel Stock pp. 30–33	Imagery **SE** p. 30
Literary History Hieroglyphics and the Rosetta Stone pp. 34–35	
Vocabulary Workshop pp. 36–37	
Comparing Literature How Stories Came to Kaleki **5.4**/**55**/900 **Coyote Steals Fire** (folktale), retold by Richard **5.3**/**49**/710 **Master Cat, or Puss in Boots** (fairy tale), by Maria Tatar **6.7**/**54**/1060 pp. 38–51	
Folktale Edju and the Two Friends, translated pp. 52–55	
The Art of Translation The Storyteller as Tra pp. 56–57	
Epic from **The Lion's Awakening** from **Sundia** translated by G. D. Pickett **6.1**/**54**/890 pp. 58–64	

2A

Reading Skills and Strategies	Vocabulary	Writing Grammar	Speaking, Listening, Viewing
Analyze Graphic Information **TE** p. 6 Evaluate Historical Influences **SE** p. 8 Connect to the Literature **SE** p. 8 Determine Main Idea and Supporting Details **TE** p. 10	Context Clues **TE** p. 8	Create a Concept Map **TE** p. 12 Write a Research Report **SE** p. 15	Analyze Art **TE** p. 2 Discussion **TE** p. 14 Create a Display **SE** p. 15
Identify Genre **SE** p. 17 Analyze Parallelism **TE** p. 20	Word Usage **SE** p. 17	Write a Movie Scene **SE** p. 22	Oral Interpretation **TE** p. 18 View the Art **SE** p. 20
		Sentence Fragments **SE** p. 23	
Analyze Style **SE** p. 25	Context Clues **SE** p. 25	Write a Journal Entry **SE** p. 29	View the Art **SE** p. 28
Analyze Diction **SE** p. 30	Word Origins **SE** p. 30	Subordinate Clauses **TE** p. 32 Write an Essay **SE** p. 33	View the Art **SE** p. 32
Evaluate Historical Influences **SE** p. 34 Draw Conclusions **TE** p. 34			View the Art **TE** p. 35
	Academic Vocabulary **SE** pp. 36–37	Create a Word Map **TE** p. 36 Dictionary Use **TE** p. 36	
Analyze and Compare Cultural Contexts **SE** p. 38 Compare Themes **SE** p. 38 Apply Background Knowledge **TE** p. 44 Analyze Characterization **TE** p. 48	Academic Vocabulary **SE** p. 43	Commas with Nonessential Elements **TE** p. 40 Write a Trickster Tale **SE** p. 43 Write an Essay **SE** p. 51	View the Art **TE** p. 44 Oral Report **TE** pp. 46, 50; **SE** p. 51 Discussion **SE** p. 51
Connect to Personal Experience **SE** p. 52	Antonyms **SE** p. 52	Complex Sentences **TE** p. 54 Write an Anecdote **SE** p. 55	View the Art **SE** p. 53
Understand Cultural and Historical Context **SE** p. 56 Understand the Nature of Translation **SE** p. 56		Conduct Internet Research **TE** p. 56	View the Photograph **TE** p. 57
Make Inferences about Characters **SE** p. 58	Word Parts **SE** p. 58	Comparative and Superlative Adjectives **TE** p. 60 Write a Journal Entry **SE** p. 64	View the Art **SE** p. 60 Narrative Presentation **TE** p. 62

2B

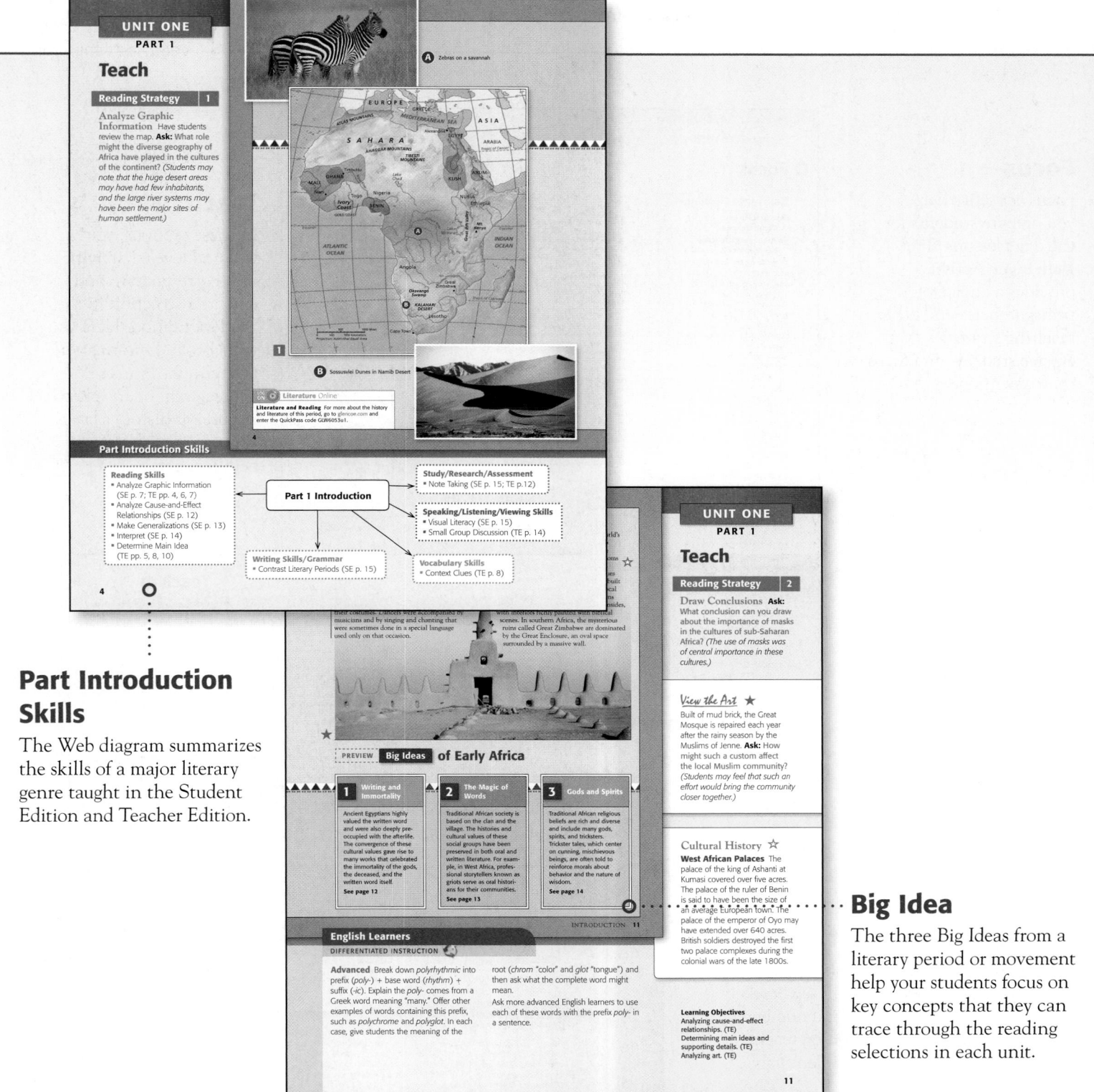

Part Introduction Skills

The Web diagram summarizes the skills of a major literary genre taught in the Student Edition and Teacher Edition.

Big Idea

The three Big Ideas from a literary period or movement help your students focus on key concepts that they can trace through the reading selections in each unit.

UNIT ONE — PART 1

Teach

Reading Strategy 1

Analyze Graphic Information Have students review the map. **Ask:** What role might the diverse geography of Africa have played in the cultures of the continent? (*Students may note that the huge desert areas may have had few inhabitants, and the large river systems may have been the major sites of human settlement.*)

A Zebras on a savannah

B Sossusvlei Dunes in Namib Desert

Literature Online
Literature and Reading For more about the history and literature of this period, go to glencoe.com and enter the QuickPass code GLW6053u1.

Part Introduction Skills

Reading Skills
- Analyze Graphic Information (SE p. 7; TE pp. 4, 6, 7)
- Analyze Cause-and-Effect Relationships (SE p. 12)
- Make Generalizations (SE p. 13)
- Interpret (SE p. 14)
- Determine Main Idea (TE pp. 5, 8, 10)

Part 1 Introduction

Writing Skills/Grammar
- Contrast Literary Periods (SE p. 15)

Study/Research/Assessment
- Note Taking (SE p. 15; TE p.12)

Speaking/Listening/Viewing Skills
- Visual Literacy (SE p. 15)
- Small Group Discussion (TE p. 14)

Vocabulary Skills
- Context Clues (TE p. 8)

UNIT ONE — PART 1

Teach

Reading Strategy 2

Draw Conclusions Ask: What conclusion can you draw about the importance of masks in the cultures of sub-Saharan Africa? (*The use of masks was of central importance in these cultures.*)

View the Art ★
Built of mud brick, the Great Mosque is repaired each year after the rainy season by the Muslims of Jenne. **Ask:** How might such a custom affect the local Muslim community? (*Students may feel that such an effort would bring the community closer together.*)

Cultural History ☆
West African Palaces The palace of the king of Ashanti at Kumasi covered over five acres. The palace of the ruler of Benin is said to have been the size of an average European town. The palace of the emperor of Oyo may have extended over 640 acres. British soldiers destroyed the first two palace complexes during the colonial wars of the late 1800s.

PREVIEW Big Ideas of Early Africa

1 Writing and Immortality
Ancient Egyptians highly valued the written word and were also deeply pre-occupied with the afterlife. The convergence of these cultural values gave rise to many works that celebrated the immortality of the gods, the deceased, and the written word itself.
See page 12

2 The Magic of Words
Traditional African society is based on the clan and the village. The histories and cultural values of these social groups have been preserved in both oral and written literature. For example, in West Africa, professional storytellers known as griots serve as oral historians for their communities.
See page 13

3 Gods and Spirits
Traditional African religious beliefs are rich and diverse and include many gods, spirits, and tricksters. Trickster tales, which center on cunning, mischievous beings, are often told to reinforce morals about behavior and the nature of wisdom.
See page 14

INTRODUCTION 11

English Learners
DIFFERENTIATED INSTRUCTION

Advanced Break down *polyrhythmic* into prefix (*poly-*) + base word (*rhythm*) + suffix (*-ic*). Explain the *poly-* comes from a Greek word meaning "many." Offer other examples of words containing this prefix, such as *polychrome* and *polyglot*. In each case, give students the meaning of the root (*chrom* "color" and *glot* "tongue") and then ask what the complete word might mean.

Ask more advanced English learners to use each of these words with the prefix *poly-* in a sentence.

Learning Objectives
Analyzing cause-and-effect relationships. (TE)
Determining main ideas and supporting details. (TE)
Analyzing art. (TE)

11

Three Part Lesson Plan

The Teacher Edition of *Glencoe Literature* is organized in a three-part structure: Focus, Teach, and Assess.

Focus

Focus activities help you prepare students for the day's lessons. The **Bellringer** Activity provides a choice of transparencies and other teaching strategies that engage students and focus their attention.

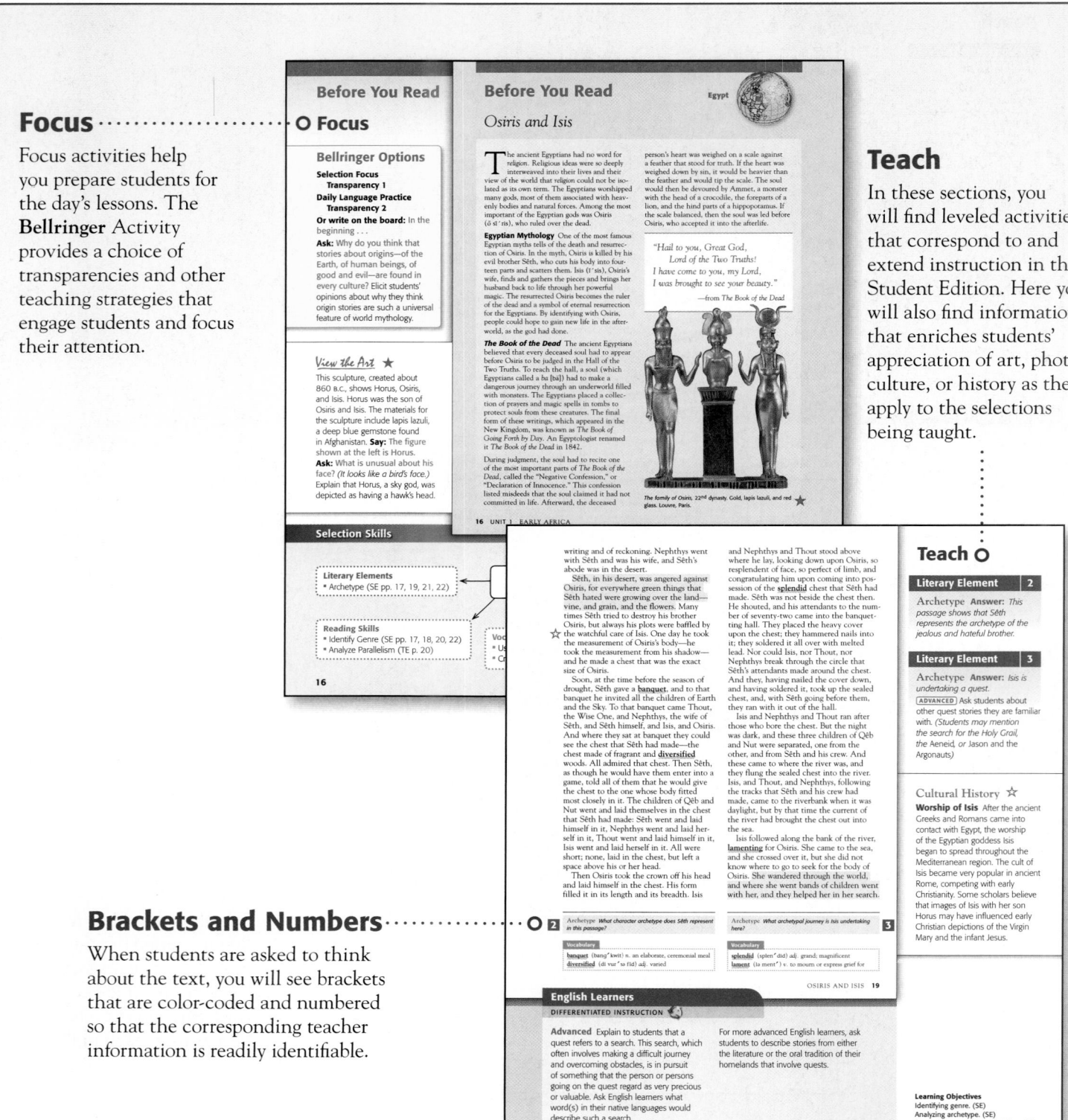

○ Focus

Bellringer Options

Selection Focus
   Transparency 1
Daily Language Practice
   Transparency 2
Or write on the board: In the beginning . . .
Ask: Why do you think that stories about origins—of the Earth, of human beings, of good and evil—are found in every culture? Elicit students' opinions about why they think origin stories are such a universal feature of world mythology.

View the Art ★
This sculpture, created about 860 B.C., shows Horus, Osiris, and Isis. Horus was the son of Osiris and Isis. The materials for the sculpture include lapis lazuli, a deep blue gemstone found in Afghanistan. **Say:** The figure shown at the left is Horus.
Ask: What is unusual about his face? *(It looks like a bird's face.)* Explain that Horus, a sky god, was depicted as having a hawk's head.

Selection Skills

Literary Elements
* Archetype (SE pp. 17, 19, 21, 22)

Reading Skills
* Identify Genre (SE pp. 17, 18, 20, 22)
* Analyze Parallelism (TE p. 20)

Before You Read

Egypt

Osiris and Isis

The ancient Egyptians had no word for religion. Religious ideas were so deeply interwoven into their lives and their view of the world that religion could not be isolated as its own term. The Egyptians worshipped many gods, most of them associated with heavenly bodies and natural forces. Among the most important of the Egyptian gods was Osiris (ō sī′ ris), who ruled over the dead.

Egyptian Mythology One of the most famous Egyptian myths tells of the death and resurrection of Osiris. In the myth, Osiris is killed by his evil brother Sëth, who cuts his body into fourteen parts and scatters them. Isis (ī′ sis), Osiris's wife, finds and gathers the pieces and brings her husband back to life through her powerful magic. The resurrected Osiris becomes the ruler of the dead and a symbol of eternal resurrection for the Egyptians. By identifying with Osiris, people could hope to gain new life in the afterworld, as the god had done.

The Book of the Dead The ancient Egyptians believed that every deceased soul had to appear before Osiris to be judged in the Hall of the Two Truths. To reach the hall, a soul (which Egyptians called a *ba* [bä]) had to make a dangerous journey through an underworld filled with monsters. The Egyptians placed a collection of prayers and magic spells in tombs to protect souls from these creatures. The final form of these writings, which appeared in the New Kingdom, was known as *The Book of Going Forth by Day*. An Egyptologist renamed it *The Book of the Dead* in 1842.

During judgment, the soul had to recite one of the most important parts of *The Book of the Dead*, called the "Negative Confession," or "Declaration of Innocence." This confession listed misdeeds that the soul claimed it had not committed in life. Afterward, the deceased person's heart was weighed on a scale against a feather that stood for truth. If the heart was weighed down by sin, it would be heavier than the feather and would tip the scale. The soul would then be devoured by Ammet, a monster with the head of a crocodile, the foreparts of a lion, and the hind parts of a hippopotamus. If the scale balanced, then the soul was led before Osiris, who accepted it into the afterlife.

"Hail to you, Great God,
Lord of the Two Truths!
I have come to you, my Lord,
I was brought to see your beauty."

—from *The Book of the Dead*

The family of Osiris, 22nd *dynasty. Gold, lapis lazuli, and red glass. Louvre, Paris.* ★

16 UNIT 1 EARLY AFRICA

Teach

In these sections, you will find leveled activities that correspond to and extend instruction in the Student Edition. Here you will also find information that enriches students' appreciation of art, photos, culture, or history as they apply to the selections being taught.

writing and of reckoning. Nephthys went with Sëth and was his wife, and Sëth's abode was in the desert.

   Sëth, in his desert, was angered against Osiris, for everywhere green things that Sëth hated were growing over the land—vine, and grain, and the flowers. Many times Sëth tried to destroy his brother Osiris, but always his plots were baffled by the watchful care of Isis. One day he took the measurement of Osiris's body—he took the measurement from his shadow—and he made a chest that was the exact size of Osiris.

   Soon, at the time before the season of drought, Sëth gave a **banquet**, and to that banquet he invited all the children of Earth and the Sky. To that banquet came Thout, the Wise One, and Nephthys, the wife of Sëth, and Sëth himself, and Isis, and Osiris. And where they sat at banquet they could see the chest that Sëth had made—the chest made of fragrant and **diversified** woods. All admired that chest. Then Sëth, as though he would have them enter into a game, told all of them that he would give the chest to the one whose body fitted most closely in it. The children of Qêb and Nut went and laid themselves in the chest that Sëth had made: Sëth went and laid himself in it, Nephthys went and laid herself in it, Thout went and laid himself in it, Isis went and laid herself in it. All were short; none, laid in the chest, but left a space above his or her head.

   Then Osiris took the crown off his head and laid himself in the chest. His form filled it in its length and its breadth. Isis and Nephthys and Thout stood above where he lay, looking down upon Osiris, so resplendent of face, so perfect of limb, and congratulating him upon coming into possession of the **splendid** chest that Sëth had made. Sëth was not beside the chest then. He shouted, and his attendants to the number of seventy-two came into the banqueting hall. They placed the heavy cover upon the chest; they hammered nails into it; they soldered it all over with melted lead. Nor could Isis, nor Thout, nor Nephthys break through the circle that Sëth's attendants made around the chest. And they, having nailed the cover down, and having soldered it, took up the sealed chest, and, with Sëth going before them, they ran with it out of the hall.

   Isis and Nephthys and Thout ran after those who bore the chest. But the night was dark, and these three children of Qêb and Nut were separated, one from the other, and from Sëth and his crew. And these came to where the river was, and they flung the sealed chest into the river. Isis, and Thout, and Nephthys, following the tracks that Sëth and his crew had made, came to the riverbank when it was daylight, but by that time the current of the river had brought the chest out into the sea.

   Isis followed along the bank of the river, **lamenting** for Osiris. She came to the sea, and she crossed over it, but she did not know where to go to seek for the body of Osiris. She wandered through the world, and where she went bands of children went with her, and they helped her in her search.

[2] Archetype *What character archetype does Sëth represent in this passage?*
Vocabulary
banquet (bang′ kwit) n. an elaborate, ceremonial meal
diversified (di vur′ sə fīd) adj. varied

Archetype *What archetypal journey is Isis undertaking here?* [3]
Vocabulary
splendid (splen′ did) adj. grand; magnificent
lament (lə ment′) v. to mourn or express grief for

OSIRIS AND ISIS **19**

Teach ○

Literary Element [2]
Archetype **Answer:** *This passage shows that Sëth represents the archetype of the jealous and hateful brother.*

Literary Element [3]
Archetype **Answer:** *Isis is undertaking a quest.*
ADVANCED Ask students about other quest stories they are familiar with. *(Students may mention the search for the Holy Grail, the Aeneid, or Jason and the Argonauts)*

Cultural History ★
Worship of Isis After the ancient Greeks and Romans came into contact with Egypt, the worship of the Egyptian goddess Isis began to spread throughout the Mediterranean region. The cult of Isis became very popular in ancient Rome, competing with early Christianity. Some scholars believe that images of Isis with her son Horus may have influenced early Christian depictions of the Virgin Mary and the infant Jesus.

English Learners
DIFFERENTIATED INSTRUCTION

Advanced Explain to students that a quest refers to a search. This search, which often involves making a difficult journey and overcoming obstacles, is in pursuit of something that the person or persons going on the quest regard as very precious or valuable. Ask English learners what word(s) in their native languages would describe such a search.

For more advanced English learners, ask students to describe stories from either the literature or the oral tradition of their homelands that involve quests.

Learning Objectives
Identifying genre. (SE)
Analyzing archetype. (SE)
Presenting an oral interpretation. (TE)

19

Brackets and Numbers

When students are asked to think about the text, you will see brackets that are color-coded and numbered so that the corresponding teacher information is readily identifiable.

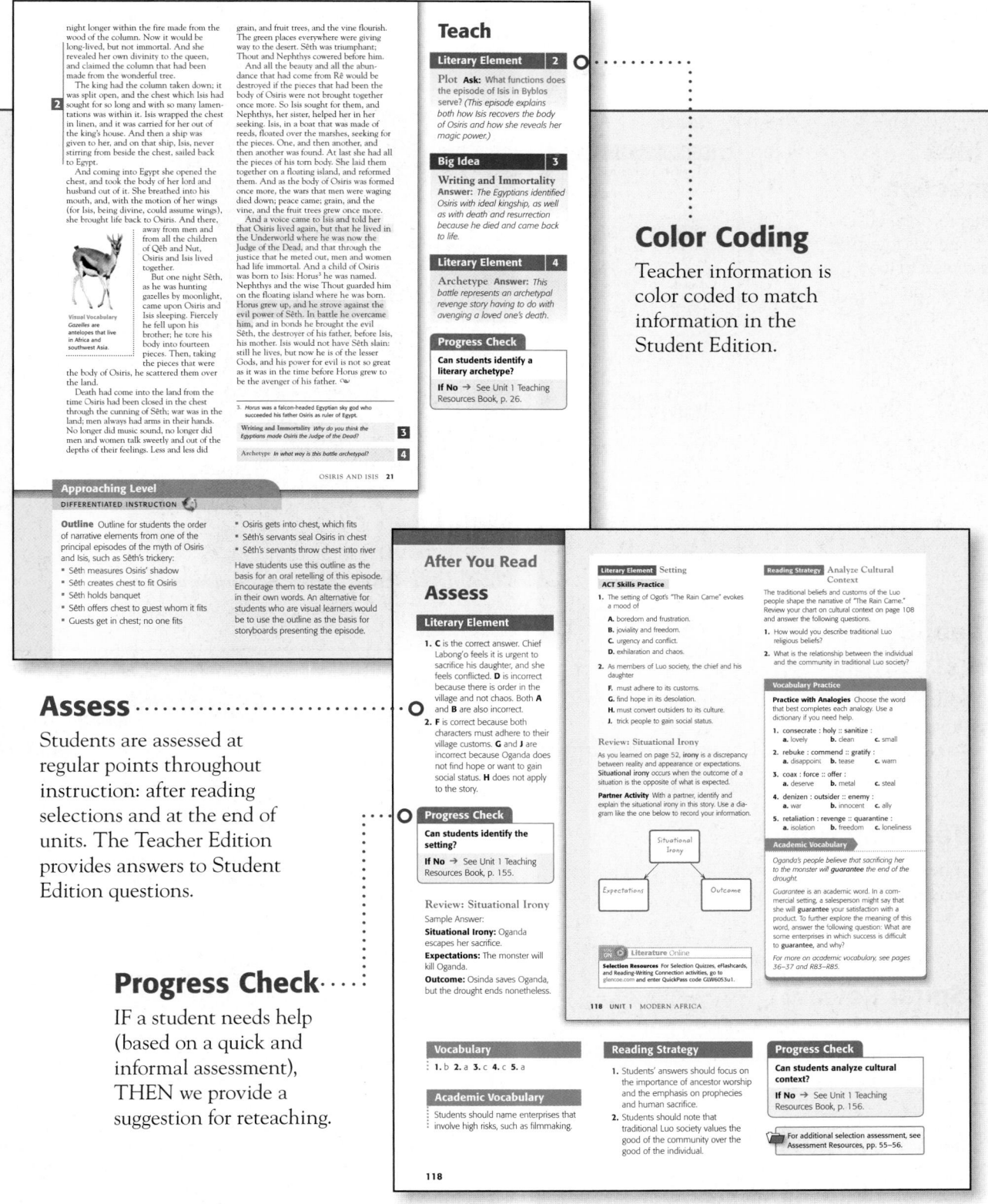

night longer within the fire made from the wood of the column. Now it would be long-lived, but not immortal. And she revealed her own divinity to the queen, and claimed the column that had been made from the wonderful tree.

2 The king had the column taken down; it was split open, and the chest which Isis had sought for so long and with so many lamentations was within it. Isis wrapped the chest in linen, and it was carried for her out of the king's house. And then a ship was given to her, and on that ship, Isis, never stirring from beside the chest, sailed back to Egypt.

And coming into Egypt she opened the chest, and took the body of her lord and husband out of it. She breathed into his mouth, and, with the motion of her wings (for Isis, being divine, could assume wings), she brought life back to Osiris. And there, away from men and from all the children of Qêb and Nut, Osiris and Isis lived together.

But one night Sêth, as he was hunting gazelles by moonlight, came upon Osiris and Isis sleeping. Fiercely he fell upon his brother; he tore his body into fourteen pieces. Then, taking the pieces that were the body of Osiris, he scattered them over the land.

Death had come into the land from the time Osiris had been closed in the chest through the cunning of Sêth; war was in the land; men always had arms in their hands. No longer did music sound, no longer did men and women talk sweetly and out of the depths of their feelings. Less and less did

Visual Vocabulary
Gazelles are antelopes that live in Africa and southwest Asia.

grain, and fruit trees, and the vine flourish. The green places everywhere were giving way to the desert. Sêth was triumphant; Thout and Nephthys cowered before him.

And all the beauty and all the abundance that had come from Rê would be destroyed if the pieces that had been the body of Osiris were not brought together once more. So Isis sought for them, and Nephthys, her sister, helped her in her seeking. Isis, in a boat that was made of reeds, floated over the marshes, seeking for the pieces. One, and then another, and then another was found. At last she had all the pieces of his torn body. She laid them together on a floating island, and reformed them. And as the body of Osiris was formed once more, the wars that men were waging died down; peace came; grain, and the vine, and the fruit trees grew once more.

And a voice came to Isis and told her that Osiris lived again, but that he lived in the Underworld where he was now the Judge of the Dead, and that through the justice that he meted out, men and women had life immortal. And a child of Osiris was born to Isis: Horus[3] he was named. Nephthys and the wise Thout guarded him on the floating island where he was born. Horus grew up, and he strove against the evil power of Sêth. In battle he overcame him, and in bonds he brought the evil Sêth, the destroyer of his father, before Isis, his mother. Isis would not have Sêth slain: still he lives, but now he is of the lesser Gods, and his power for evil is not so great as it was in the time before Horus grew to be the avenger of his father. ∽

3. *Horus was a falcon-headed Egyptian sky god who succeeded his father Osiris as ruler of Egypt.*

Writing and Immortality *Why do you think the Egyptians made Osiris the Judge of the Dead?* **3**

Archetype *In what way is this battle archetypal?* **4**

OSIRIS AND ISIS **21**

Approaching Level
DIFFERENTIATED INSTRUCTION

Outline Outline for students the order of narrative elements from one of the principal episodes of the myth of Osiris and Isis, such as Sêth's trickery:

- Sêth measures Osiris' shadow
- Sêth creates chest to fit Osiris
- Sêth holds banquet
- Sêth offers chest to guest whom it fits
- Guests get in chest; no one fits

- Osiris gets into chest, which fits
- Sêth's servants seal Osiris in chest
- Sêth's servants throw chest into river

Have students use this outline as the basis for an oral retelling of this episode. Encourage them to restate the events in their own words. An alternative for students who are visual learners would be to use the outline as the basis for storyboards presenting the episode.

Teach

Literary Element 2

Plot Ask: What functions does the episode of Isis in Byblos serve? *(This episode explains both how Isis recovers the body of Osiris and how she reveals her magic power.)*

Big Idea 3

Writing and Immortality Answer: *The Egyptians identified Osiris with ideal kingship, as well as with death and resurrection because he died and came back to life.*

Literary Element 4

Archetype Answer: *This battle represents an archetypal revenge story having to do with avenging a loved one's death.*

Progress Check

Can students identify a literary archetype?

If No → See Unit 1 Teaching Resources Book, p. 26.

Color Coding

Teacher information is color coded to match information in the Student Edition.

Assess

Students are assessed at regular points throughout instruction: after reading selections and at the end of units. The Teacher Edition provides answers to Student Edition questions.

Progress Check

IF a student needs help (based on a quick and informal assessment), THEN we provide a suggestion for reteaching.

After You Read

Assess

Literary Element

1. **C** is the correct answer. Chief Labong'o feels it is urgent to sacrifice his daughter, and she feels conflicted. **D** is incorrect because there is order in the village and not chaos. Both **A** and **B** are also incorrect.

2. **F** is correct because both characters must adhere to their village customs. **G** and **J** are incorrect because Oganda does not find hope or want to gain social status. **H** does not apply to the story.

Progress Check

Can students identify the setting?

If No → See Unit 1 Teaching Resources Book, p. 155.

Review: Situational Irony
Sample Answer:

Situational Irony: Oganda escapes her sacrifice.

Expectations: The monster will kill Oganda.

Outcome: Osinda saves Oganda, but the drought ends nonetheless.

Vocabulary
1. b 2. a 3. c 4. c 5. a

Academic Vocabulary
Students should name enterprises that involve high risks, such as filmmaking.

118

Literary Element Setting

ACT Skills Practice

1. The setting of Ogot's "The Rain Came" evokes a mood of
   A. boredom and frustration.
   B. joviality and freedom.
   C. urgency and conflict.
   D. exhilaration and chaos.

2. As members of Luo society, the chief and his daughter
   F. must adhere to its customs.
   G. find hope in its desolation.
   H. must convert outsiders to its culture.
   J. trick people to gain social status.

Review: Situational Irony

As you learned on page 52, **irony** is a discrepancy between reality and appearance or expectations. **Situational irony** occurs when the outcome of a situation is the opposite of what is expected.

Partner Activity With a partner, identify and explain the situational irony in this story. Use a diagram like the one below to record your information.

```
        Situational
          Irony
   /                  \
Expectations       Outcome
```

Literature Online

Selection Resources For Selection Quizzes, eFlashcards, and Reading-Writing Connection activities, go to glencoe.com and enter QuickPass code GLW6053u1.

118 UNIT 1 MODERN AFRICA

Reading Strategy Analyze Cultural Context

The traditional beliefs and customs of the Luo people shape the narrative of "The Rain Came." Review your chart on cultural context on page 108 and answer the following questions.

1. How would you describe traditional Luo religious beliefs?

2. What is the relationship between the individual and the community in traditional Luo society?

Vocabulary Practice

Practice with Analogies Choose the word that best completes each analogy. Use a dictionary if you need help.

1. consecrate : holy :: sanitize :
   a. lovely   b. clean   c. small

2. rebuke : commend :: gratify :
   a. disappoint   b. tease   c. warn

3. coax : force :: offer :
   a. deserve   b. metal   c. steal

4. denizen : outsider :: enemy :
   a. war   b. innocent   c. ally

5. retaliation : revenge :: quarantine :
   a. isolation   b. freedom   c. loneliness

Academic Vocabulary

Oganda's people believe that sacrificing her to the monster will **guarantee** the end of the drought.

Guarantee is an academic word. In a commercial setting, a salesperson might say that she will **guarantee** your satisfaction with a product. To further explore the meaning of this word, answer the following question: What are some enterprises in which success is difficult to **guarantee**, and why?

For more on academic vocabulary, see pages 36–37 and R83–R85.

Reading Strategy

1. Students' answers should focus on the importance of ancestor worship and the emphasis on prophecies and human sacrifice.

2. Students should note that traditional Luo society values the good of the community over the good of the individual.

Progress Check

Can students analyze cultural context?

If No → See Unit 1 Teaching Resources Book, p. 156.

For additional selection assessment, see Assessment Resources, pp. 55–56.

Teaching Support

Big Idea Connection

Thought-provoking questions prompt students to explore the Big Idea in context to the reading selection.

Readability Scores

Dale-Chall, DRP, and Lexiles are provided for every selection

Teaching Notes

These notes give you extra teaching hints and information.

Spiral Review

Because repetition and reinforcement are important for students' learning, we indicate when a skill is being reviewed.

Skills Support

Glencoe Literature provides addition support with the skills, such as reading, writing, literature, listening, speaking, and viewing, research, that provide the framework for all academic success.

Teach

Big Idea | 1

Living with Independence
Have students read the first paragraph of the story. **Ask:** What does this paragraph suggest about Africa's economic problems? (*Ambitious young men are abandoning village life to find employment in towns and cities.*)
APPROACHING Point out the narrator's observation that many young men had left the village seeking work, and ask what this indicates about the village's economic condition.

View the Art ★
Francks Francois Deceus (1966–) grew up in Haiti and later moved to New York City. His modernist painting style features simplified geometric forms, sharp angles, bold colors, and distorted perspectives.

For an audio recording of this selection, use Listening Library Audio CD-ROM.

Readability Scores
Dale-Chall: 6.4
DRP: 60
Lexile: 850

94

Moving on Up, 1999. Francks Deceus. Mixed media on canvas. Private collection. ★

The Voter
Chinua Achebe

94 UNIT 1 MODERN AFRICA

Grammar Practice

Use Semicolons Write these sentences from the story on the board: *Today he was Chief the Honorable; he had two long cars and had just built himself the biggest house anyone had seen in these par...* speeches; a... their whispe... that semicol... main clauses...

coordinating conjunction or that are joined by a conjunctive adverb, such as *however.* Have students write four sentences about the story using semicolons to join main clauses. Two of the sentences...

Teach

Reading Strategy | 1

Respond to Character
Direct students to lines 1001–1004. **Ask:** What words might you use to describe Oedipus's state? (*Possible answers: depressed, terrified, inconsolable.*)
ENGLISH LEARNERS Explain to students that the English idiom "beside oneself" means "in a state of extreme emotion, such as great elation or grief." Ask if there is a similar idiomatic expression from their native language and what it means literally.

For additional practice using the reading skill or strategy, see Unit 2 Teaching Resources Book, p. 104.

For an audio recording of this selection, use Listening Library Audio CD-ROM.

OEDIPUS THE KING

[*Enter JOCASTA from the palace, carrying a suppliant's branch wound in wool.*]

JOCASTA. Lords of the realm, it occurred to me,
just now, to visit the temples of the gods,
1000 so I have my branch in hand and incense too.

Oedipus is beside himself. Racked with anguish,
no longer a man of sense, he won't admit
the latest prophecies are hollow as the old—
he's at the mercy of every passing voice
1005 if the voice tells of terror.
I urge him gently, nothing seems to help,
so I turn to you, Apollo, you are nearest.

[*Placing her branch on the altar, while an old herdsman enters from the side, not the one just summoned by the King but an unexpected MESSENGER from Corinth.*]

I come with prayers and offerings . . . I beg you,
cleanse us, set us free of defilement!
1010 Look at us, passengers in the grip of fear,
watching the pilot of the vessel go to pieces.

MESSENGER. [*Approaching JOCASTA and the CHORUS.*]
Strangers, please, I wonder if you could lead us
to the palace of the king . . . I think it's Oedipus.
Better, the man himself—you know where he is?

1015 LEADER. This is his palace, stranger. He's inside.
But here is his queen, his wife and mother
of his children.

MESSENGER. Blessings on you, noble queen,
queen of Oedipus crowned with all your family—
blessings on you always!

1020 JOCASTA. And the same to you, stranger, you deserve it . . .
such a greeting. But what have you come for?
Have you brought us news?

MESSENGER. Wonderful news—
for the house, my lady, for your husband too.

292 UNIT 2 ANCIENT GREECE

Reading Practice

SPIRAL REVIEW
Visualize Point out to students that it is important to form mental pictures of scenes, characters, and events as they read. In many works of fiction, the writer provides visual details upon which to base such mental pictures. In visualizing *Oedipus the King,* where such details are largely absent, the reader may need to be creative.
Have students visualize how Oedipus or Jocasta might look if he or she lived at

the present time. How might his or her clothing reflect a particular personality? Tell students that they may choose pictures from magazines or draw their own pictures of the characters. Students should be prepared to explain why they think their pictures reflect the personalities of the characters they have chosen. Have students present their pictures to encourage class discussion.

292

Teach

Reading Strategy 1

Activate Prior Knowledge
Answer: *It implies the spreading of gossip, particularly gossip that is untrue or misleading. Students' examples from personal experience will vary.*

Literary Element 2

Figurative Language Point out to students that Achebe uses proverbs throughout this story to represent traditional wisdom.
Ask: How would you paraphrase the proverb of the iroko tree using American idiom or slang? (*Students' answers should express the proverb's central idea of taking full advantage of temporary opportunity.*)
ENGLISH LEARNERS Make sure that English learners grasp the basic meaning of the proverb. Ask them for examples of similar proverbs from the cultures of their homelands.

Literary Element 3

Motivation Answer: *Considering that they have been promised improvements for five years and have yet to receive them, they likely do not believe every word is true. Their loyalty is actually motivated by their desire to be paid for their votes.*

96

---

and went out to challenge his personal spirit. Marcus had christened his new house "Umuofia Mansions" in honor of his village, and he had slaughtered five bulls and countless goats to entertain the people on the day it was opened by the Archbishop.

Everyone was full of praise for him. One old man said: "Our son is a good man; he is not like the mortar which as soon as food comes its way turns its back on the ground." But when the feasting was over, the villagers told themselves that they had underrated the power of the ballot paper before and should not do so again. Chief the Honorable Marcus Ibe was not unprepared. He had drawn five months' salary in advance, changed a few hundred pounds

Visual Vocabulary
Jute (jōōt) is a flexible, glossy fiber made from one of two Asian plants.

into shining shillings and armed his campaign boys with eloquent little jute bags. In the day he made his speeches; at night his stalwarts conducted their whispering campaign. Roof was the most trusted of these campaigners.

"We have a Minister from our village, one of our own sons," he said to a group of elders in the house of Ogbuefi Ezenwa, a man of high traditional title. "What greater honor can a village have? Do you ever stop to ask yourselves why we should be singled out for this honor? I will tell you; it is because we are favored by the leaders of PAP. Whether or not we cast our paper for Marcus, PAP will continue to rule. Think of the pipe-borne water they have promised us . . ."

Activate Prior Knowledge: *What does the phrase "whispering campaign" imply about the kind of information campaign workers spread at night? Have you ever overheard a whispering campaign? If so, what was your reaction?* 1

96 UNIT 1 MODERN AFRICA

Besides Roof and his assistant there were five elders in the room. An old hurricane lamp with a cracked, sooty, glass chimney gave out yellowish light in their midst. The elders sat on very low stools. On the floor, directly in front of each of them, lay two shilling pieces. Outside beyond the fastened door, the moon kept a straight face.

"We believe every word you say to be true," said Ezenwa. "We shall, every one of us, drop his paper for Marcus. Who would leave an Ozo feast and go to a poor ritual meal? Tell Marcus he has our papers, and our wives' papers too. But what we do say is that two shillings is shameful." He brought the lamp close and tilted it at the money before him as if to make sure he had not mistaken its value. "Yes, two shillings is too shameful. If Marcus were a poor man—which our ancestors forbid—I should be the first to give him my paper free, as I did before. But today Marcus is a great man and does his things like a great man. We did not ask him for money yesterday; we shall not ask him tomorrow. But today is our day; we have climbed the iroko tree today and would be foolish not to take down all the firewood we need."

Roof had to agree. He had lately been taking down a lot of firewood himself. Only yesterday he had asked Marcus for one of his many rich robes—and had got it. Last Sunday Marcus's wife (the teacher that nearly got him in trouble) had objected (like the woman she was) when Roof pulled out his fifth bottle of beer from the refrigerator; she was roundly and publicly rebuked by her husband. To cap it all Roof had won a land case recently because, among other things, he had been chauffeur-

Motivation *Do you think the elders really believe every word is true? Why or why not? What actually motivates their loyalty to Roof?* 3

Writing Practice

PARTNERS **Character Analysis** Have students review the story to this point, recording information about the main character, Roof. Their notes should include information about both his behavior and his actions. Then have them write several paragraphs analyzing Roof's character. Suggest they answer questions such as the following:

What motivates Roof?
Why does he remain in his village rather than going elsewhere to look for work?
Why do the villagers approve of him?
After students have completed their analyses, have them exchange papers with a partner and do peer editing.

Resource Suggestions at Point-of-Use

Helpful suggestions for using *Glencoe Literature* ancillary material support and simplify instruction.

---

is Confucianism's most important virtue. Li means "ritual," "etiquette," or simply "good manners." In Confucian philosophy, relationships function smoothly when correct etiquette, or li, is observed.

Set Purposes for Reading

Big Idea Virtue and Wisdom

As you read, ask yourself, What emphasis does Confucius place on duty, morality, and respect?

Literary Element Maxim

A **maxim** is a short saying that contains a general truth or gives practical advice about how to behave and live morally. As you read, look for the maxims Confucius includes and ask yourself, What general truths or advice is he expressing?

Reading Strategy Make Generalizations

A **generalization** is a general statement or rule. When you make a generalization, you gather details from a text and then form a broad statement that can apply to life in general, or to several situations. As you read, ask yourself, How do Confucius's statements apply to life in general?

Tip: Convert Information Use a graphic organizer like the one below to record key details that reveal what is important to Confucius. Then convert those details into a generalization about how Confucius believes people should behave.

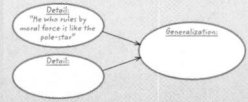

Vocabulary

homage (hom′ij) n. the honor or respect that is shown to another person; p. 687 *The priests paid homage to the Pope when they visited the Vatican.*

docile (dos′əl) adj. easily taught; obedient; p. 687 *The docile students listened attentively to the tour guide as he explained one of Picasso's paintings.*

dictates (dik′tāts) n. principles that must be followed; p. 687 *The dictates of society state that we should not steal.*

extent (iks tent′) n. amount or distance; p. 687 *The judge punished the thief to the greatest extent of the law.*

Tip: Synonyms Synonyms are words that have the same, or similar, meaning. They can often serve as context clues. For example, in the sentence *The docile students listened attentively to the guide, docile* must mean "easily taught" if the students listened attentively.

CONFUCIUS **685**

Advanced Learners/Pre-AP
DIFFERENTIATED INSTRUCTION

Conduct Research Ask students to conduct research on the role of Confucianism in Chinese society. They might focus on a single topic, such as the importance placed on Confucian texts in Chinese civil service exams from 124 B.C. to A.D. 1905. Tell students to examine the way Confucian beliefs figure into the secular realm of Chinese thought.

Approaching Level
DIFFERENTIATED INSTRUCTION

Close Reading Have students choose a sentence from the selection and review it word by word. Explain that a single word or phrase can include a range of ideas. Demonstrate this by taking one word or phrase, such as "moral force" and discussing its meaning. **Ask:** What do you think Confucius is trying to convey with the phrase "moral force"? (*Perhaps that morality has a physical force, like gravity.*)

685

Before You Read

Focus

Summary

The selected passages from the *Analects* present a dialogue between Tzu-yu and the master, Confucius, that stresses morality and compassion and underlines the importance of the teacher-student relationship. In these passages, Confucius emphasizes the importance of respecting one's parents and living simply. He also anticipates the golden rule by saying "Never do to others what you would not like them to do to you."

For summaries in languages other than English, see Unit 4 Teaching Resources Book, pp. 21–26.

Vocabulary

Multiple Definitions Organize students in a circle and pass around four pieces of paper, each with a vocabulary word at the top of the page. Have students write a one-sentence definition of the word and continue to fold over the paper so the previous sentence is not showing. When all four sheets of paper have circulated, read the definitions aloud and see how many match up. The students' definitions may veer away from the correct one, but reiterate the real definition while encouraging the students' creativity.

For additional vocabulary practice, see Unit 4 Teaching Resources Book, p. 29.

Grouping Icons

Flexible grouping is an effective way to provide instruction to a diverse classroom. These symbols suggest grouping options.

Differentiated Instruction

Activities for your diverse classrooms are clearly labeled.

Vocabulary Preteaching

Because vocabulary is a key component of reading success, we provide for the struggling students and English Learners in your classroom additional vocabulary preteaching activities.

Informational Text

The wide range of informational text in *Glencoe Literature* broadens the students' reading to include more than just poetry, short stories, and plays.

Perspectives

Award-winning book excerpts provide students with the in-depth information they need to explore the cultural, political, historical, and literary contexts of a reading selection.

Political Perspective
on *The Voter*

from
No Future
Without Forgiveness

Desmond Mpilo Tutu

Nobel Prize Winner

On the day of South Africa's first post-apartheid election, voters line up for miles waiting to cast their ballot.

Set a Purpose for Reading
Read to learn more about the political process in a newly democratic African nation.

Build Background
Desmond Tutu, the first black archbishop of Cape Town, South Africa, was awarded the Nobel Peace Prize in 1984 for his work to end apartheid, a devastating system of racial segregation. In the following excerpt from his memoir, Tutu describes the experience of voting in South Africa's first multiracial elections in 1994. The elections resulted in a victory for Nelson Mandela, who later appointed Tutu as chair of the Truth and Reconciliation Commission, a group designed to investigate human rights abuses that occurred during apartheid.

Reading Strategy Compare and Contrast Events

To **compare and contrast events** means to look for similarities and differences between events in two or more literary works. As you read, ask yourself, What events in this memoir can I compare and contrast with events in Chinua Achebe's "The Voter"?

I went to vote in Gugulethu, a black township[1] with its typical matchbox-type houses in row after monotonous row. There was a long queue[2] already waiting. People were in good spirits; they were going to need dollops of patience and good humor because they were in for a long wait. My first democratic vote was a media event, and many of our friends from overseas were present, acting as monitors to be able to certify whether the elections were fair and free. But they were doing a great deal more than that. They were really like midwives helping to bring to birth this new delicate infant—free, democratic, nonracial, nonsexist South Africa.

The moment for which I had waited so long came and I folded my ballot paper and cast my vote. Wow! I shouted, "Yippee!" It was giddy stuff. It was like falling in love. The sky looked blue and more beautiful. I

1. In South Africa under apartheid, a *township* was a poor urban area reserved for nonwhites.
2. A *queue* is a line.

DESMOND MPILO TUTU **103**

Learning Objectives

For pages 103–106
In studying this text, you will focus on the following objectives:

Literary Study: Making connections across literature.

Reading: Comparing and contrasting events. Analyzing informational text.

Political Perspective
on *The Voter*

Focus
Summary

Desmond Tutu, the former archbishop of Cape Town, South Africa, recounts his experience voting in South Africa's first multiracial election in 1994. He describes the election as a joyful event that gave a voice to the victims of apartheid and absolved the guilt of those who had enforced the system. Though the election was plagued by problems, including insufficient supplies and poor management, South Africans waited patiently in voting lines and cooperated with one another. To Tutu, this cooperation symbolized South Africans' willingness to look beyond race and recognize their "common humanity."

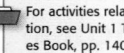
For activities related to this selection, see Unit 1 Teaching Resources Book, pp. 140–148.

For an audio recording of this selection, use Listening Library Audio CD-ROM.

Readability Scores
Dale-Chall: 8.4
DRP: 61
Lexile: 980

Approaching Level

DIFFERENTIATED INSTRUCTION

Analyze Figurative Language Tutu's frequent use of figurative language might make this selection difficult for some students. Have these students focus on one type of figurative language that Tutu uses—the simile. Remind them that a simile is a comparison that uses the word *like* or *as*. Explain that similes often compare two things that might not seem similar at first, as when Tutu says that voting is "like falling in love." Then have struggling students pair with more advanced students to identify and discuss other similes in the selection. *(Possible similes: It was like a festival; the memory of being treated like rubbish gnawing away at her very vitals like some corrosive acid; freedom that tasted like sweet nectar.)*

Some students may need more help understanding the concept of a simile.

Write the sentence *The election was like a festival* on the board. Then ask students what a festival is, and how one might feel at a festival. *(A festival is a fun, joyful party.)* Explain that Tutu says the election was "like a festival" because it was fun and joyful.

103

TIME Articles

Linked to the Big Idea, an author, or a reading selection, these articles deliver the facts on topical issues.

Learning Objectives

For pages 155–157
In studying this text, you will focus on the following objectives:

Reading:
Analyzing text structure.
Using text features.
Analyzing informational text.

Set a Purpose for Reading

Read to learn how one man journeyed from imprisonment to a career as an AIDS health-care worker. Consider how his story relates to the challenges facing Africans living with independence.

Preview the Article

"Heroes Among Us" profiles the life of Patrick Chamusso, whose imprisonment during apartheid in South Africa inspired him to help children with AIDS.

1. Examine the photograph and caption on page 156. What do they reveal?
2. Read the sentence below the title. What do you think is the focus of this article?

Reading Strategy Analyze Text Structure

When you analyze text structure, you recognize the pattern of organization. As you read, ask yourself, What are some causes and effects detailed in the article? Use a graphic organizer like this one to keep track of your answers.

Cause		Effect
Chamusso is arrested at oil refinery.	→	Chamusso becomes a freedom fighter.

TIME

HEROES Among Us

A former freedom fighter makes a home for kids orphaned by AIDS.

By SUSAN SCHINDEHETTE

ON A COOL AUTUMN AFTERNOON IN NEW YORK CITY, Patrick Chamusso gently traces a finger over photographs of his wife and children—not just his son and two daughters but also the dozens of AIDS orphans he considers his own. "It's too cold here," he says softly. "I am so homesick. I miss South Africa. Oh my, I miss you people."

That faraway country is the only real home Chamusso has ever known, from the poverty-stricken rural streets where he grew up to the threatening walls of the infamous Robben Island prison. Along with men like former South Africa President Nelson Mandela, Chamusso was imprisoned at Robben Island and held for a decade as an enemy of the apartheid government. (Under apartheid, a variety of laws allowed South Africa's ruling white minority to segregate people of African, Asian, and mixed race, denying them basic human and political rights for decades.)

Even 14 years after his release, as he traveled to promote *Catch a Fire*, the movie that tells the remarkable story of his life, it was still difficult for him to recall those days of unspeakable horror. "Whenever I start talking about it, I go right back to the room where they tortured me," he said. "They did awful, unbelievable things that I cannot begin to tell you about. It is like opening a wound on my heart."

Yet even more inspiring than the tale of Chamusso's survival is the story of what he has done with his hard-won freedom since. Released from Robben Island in 1992 during the fall of apartheid,

HEROES AMONG US **155**

Approaching Level

DIFFERENTIATED INSTRUCTION

Take Notes Copy the Main Idea Organizer on this page to the board. Ask students for the events and details that support the main idea and write these in the appropriate columns. Then, help them to summarize the article in a few sentences in the Conclusion column.

Main Idea: Patrick Chamusso's imprisonment during apartheid inspired him to help AIDS-affected children upon his release.

Supporting Detail	Supporting Detail	Supporting Detail

Conclusion:

TIME

Focus

Summary

South African Patrick Chamusso talks about what motivated him to become a health care worker for AIDS-affected orphans. While working at the Secunda refinery, he was wrongly accused of planting a bomb and conspiring with the African National Congress. After serving a short prison sentence, he became an ANC freedom fighter and committed acts of sabotage. Arrested and sentenced to 24 years in the Robben Island prison, he was released in ten years in 1992. He then learned that AIDS was plaguing his nation. Inspired, he took a course in health care, and in 1999, he built Two Sisters—a shelter for orphans in the village of Mganduzweni, where he and his wife, Conney Thibedi, assist AIDS-affected children.

For activities related to this selection, see Unit 1 Teaching Resources Book, pp. 226–234.

Readability Scores
Dale-Chall: 6.6
DRP: 56
Lexile: 1050

155

Guide to Readability

Throughout the teacher materials in your Teacher Edition, you will encounter DRP readability measures assigned to the reading selections in *Glencoe Literature*. You will also find readability scores based on the Lexile Framework® for Reading and the Dale-Chall Readability Formula. You can use these scores to select reading materials that are suitable for your entire class or for individual students.

Degrees of Reading Power® (DRP)

DRP values indicate the readability of prose text. The higher the value, the more difficult the text. The scale ranges from 1 to 100; commonly encountered English text tends to fall somewhere between 25 and 85. Although middle school texts have an average difficulty of 56, and high school texts have an average difficulty of 62, no single readability level is appropriate for each grade level. Rather, a typical classroom has materials with a range of readability levels available for use—some intended for less proficient readers, some for average readers, and some for stronger readers. The following chart shows the average DRP readability range for materials widely available for use at each grade. Some materials you might use, however, will certainly fall outside of the range for your particular grade.

Grade	DRP Readability Ranges
6	51–61
7	52–62
8	53–64
9	53–65
10	51–68
11	56–67
12	57–68

The Lexile® Framework

A Lexile measure assigned to a text is the specific number that describes the reading demands of the text. The typical Lexile Scale ranges from 200 to 1700 Lexiles. As with the DRP measures, there is not a direct translation from a specific Lexile measure to a specific grade level. Within any classroom, there will be a range of readers and a range of materials to be read. The levels shown on the following chart indicate the approximate range of Lexile scores for 50 percent of the materials found in a typical grade-level classroom. For example, the middle half of the instructional materials typically found in a sixth-grade classroom ranges in difficulty from about 850L to 1050L.

Grade	Text Measures (from Lexile Framework Map)
6	850L to 1050L
7	950L to 1075L
8	1000L to 1100L
9	1050L to 1150L
10	1100L to 1200L
11 and 12	1100L to 1300L

Dale-Chall Readability Formula

The Dale-Chall Formula is based on the average sentence length and the number of unfamiliar words in a passage. The idea behind this formula is that readers typically find it easier to read, process, and recall a passage if the words and sentences are familiar and grade appropriate. The Dale-Chall Formula assesses the difficulty of a passage by computing two different values from the text. The first measure is the average number of words per sentence. The second measure is the percentage of words in the passage not found on the grade appropriate Dale Word List. The following chart shows the average Dale-Chall readability scores for grades 5 thru 12.

Grade	Dale-Chall Readability Score
5-6th Grade	5.0 to 5.9
7-8th Grade	6.0 to 6.9
9-10th Grade	7.0 to 7.9
11-12th Grade	8.0 to 8.9

African American Vernacular English (AAVE)

Some of your students will be speakers of African American Vernacular English (AAVE). AAVE is a language system with well-formed rules for sounds, grammar, and meanings. Throughout the year you will help these students learn standard academic English by focusing on those places where AAVE differs from the standard and on those patterns that will have the most immediate impact on the students' reading and writing development.

These students will need help in understanding that what is appropriate in one setting is not appropriate in another, so they can shift easily and competently between varieties in different social contexts. Instruction will be more effective if it identifies nonstandard varieties of English as different, rather than inferior. All students should be taught standard English in a way that respects their home language.

Use the charts that follow to identify AAVE linguistic differences and instructional modifications that can help students as they learn to successfully and fluently speak, read, and write standard English. The modifications focus on the following:

- Providing students with clear enunciation examples during phonics and phonemic awareness lessons targeting difficult sounds. Then additional pronunciation practice is provided during small group phonics lessons.

- Using contrastive analysis during whole group and small group time in which students code switch between AAVE and standard English. The difference in each grammatical structure is highlighted and students are provided ample opportunities to practice standard English in speaking and writing. They are also taught the proper context for each usage.

- Using Discrimination Drills in which two sentences are read aloud or written on the board. One is standard English, the other reflects common AAVE structures. Students must determine which is standard English.

- Using Translation Drills in which students change an AAVE sentence into standard English.

Phonics Differences

English/Language Arts Skill	Linguistic Differences and Instructional Modifications
Digraph *th* **as in bathroom**	For many speakers of African American Vernacular English, the initial /th/ sound in function words such as *this* and *then* is often produced as a /d/ sound. In some words, such as *thing* and *through,* the /th/ sound is produced as a /t/ sound. At the ends of words and syllables, such as *bathroom* and *death,* the /th/ sound is replaced by the /f/ sound. This will affect students' spelling and speaking. Students will need additional articulation support prior to spelling these words.
Final Consonant *r*	Many speakers of African American Vernacular English drop the /r/ sound in words. For example, these students will say *sto'* for *store* or *do'* for *door.* Clearly pronounce these words, emphasizing the /r/ sound. Have students repeat several times, exaggerating the sound before spelling these words.
r-**Blends**	Many speakers of African American Vernacular English drop the /r/ in words with *r*-Blends. For example, these students will say *th'ow* for *throw.* Clearly pronounce these words in the lesson, emphasizing the sounds of the *r*-Blend. Have students repeat several times, exaggerating the sound.

Final Consonant /l/ and Final /l-Blends	Many speakers of African American Vernacular English drop the /l/ sound in words, particularly in words with *-ool* and *-oal* spelling patterns, such as *cool* and *coal*, and when the letter *l* precedes the consonants *p, t,* or *k* as in *help, belt,* and *milk.* These students will drop the *l* when spelling these words, as well. Provide additional articulation support prior to reading and spelling these words.
Final Consonant Blends	Many speakers of African American Vernacular English drop the final letter in a consonant blend (*e.g., mp, nt, nk, lo, lt, lk*). For example, they will say *des'* for *desk.* Clearly pronounce the final sound in these words and have students repeat several times, exaggerating the sound.
Plurals	When the letter *-s* is added to a word ending in a consonant blend, such as *test (tests),* many speakers of African American Vernacular English will drop the final sounds. Therefore they will say *tes'* or *tesses.* These students will need additional articulation support.
Contractions	Many speakers of African American Vernacular English drop the /t/ sound when pronouncing the common words *it's, that's,* and *what's.* These words sound more like *i's, tha's,* and *wha's.* These students will need additional articulation support in order to pronounce and spell these words.
Short Vowels *i* and *e*	When the /i/ and /e/ sounds appear before the consonants m or n in words, such as *pen/pin* and *him/hem,* many speakers of African American Vernacular English won't pronounce or hear the difference. Focus on articulation, such as mouth position for each vowel sound, during the lesson.
Inflectional Ending *-ing*	Many speakers of African American Vernacular English will pronounce words with *-ing* as /ang/. For example, they will say *thang* for *thing.* Emphasize the /i/ sound in these words to help students correctly spell and pronounce them.

Grammar, Usage, Mechanics Differences

English/Language Arts Skill	Linguistic Differences and Instructional Modifications
Subject-Verb Agreement (*he is , he goes*)	To acquire standard academic English speech and writing, speakers of African American Vernacular English need to learn to use *-s* with a verb and the third person and only there, as in *he is* and *he goes.* Many speakers of AAVE will leave out the -s or place it elsewhere, as in *he go* or *we goes.* Write a sentence from students' speech or writing. Then provide contrastive analysis work. Write the standard English form above that sentence. Discuss the key differences.
Subject-Verb Agreement (*do/does, have/has, was/were*)	Many speakers of African American Vernacular English have difficulties with subject-verb agreement when the verbs *do/does, have/has,* and *was/were* are used. Additional grammar instruction and practice will be needed. Write a sentence from students' speech or writing. Then provide contrastive analysis work. Write the standard English form above that sentence. Discuss the key differences.
Past Tense (*-ed*)	Many speakers of African American Vernacular English understand the use of *-ed* to form the past tense but leave it out or add sounds when pronouncing the word, as in *pick* or *pickted* for *picked.* Students will need additional work during small group time with *-ed* in order to know when and where to use it in writing.

Past Tense (simple past tense vs. past perfect tense)	Many speakers of African American Vernacular English will add *had* to the simple past tense, saying *We had picked* for *We picked.* The use of *had* indicates the past perfect tense in standard academic English. Other common nonstandard forms of irregular past-tense verbs include *He seen that* and *He had ran over there.*
The Verb "to be" (pronunciation)	In the first person present tense, many speakers of African American Vernacular English will properly use *I am* or *I'm*, but say it more like *"uhm."* Focus on pronunciation.
The Verb "to be" (writing)	To learn standard academic English, many speakers of African American Vernacular English will need to learn not to delete *is* and *are* when speaking and writing. For example, students might say *He my brother* or *She goin' over there.* Additional grammar instruction and practice will be needed. Use Discrimination and Translation Drills.
The Verb "to be" (speaking)	Many speakers of African American Vernacular English will use *was* in the singular and plural forms, as in *He was* and *They was.* Additional grammar instruction and practice will be needed.
The Verb "to be"	To learn standard academic English, many speakers of African American Vernacular English will need to learn to avoid using nonstandard forms, such as *He always be doing this,* in favor of *am, are,* and *is.* Also, additional instruction and practice will be needed to show the proper placement of the adverbs *always, never,* and *others.* For example, *He is always doing this* rather than *He always is doing this.* Write a sentence from students' speech or writing. Then provide contrastive analysis work. Write the standard English form above that sentence. Discuss the key differences.
Possessives ('s)	In standard academic English, *'s* is added to a noun to show possession. For many speakers of African American Vernacular English, the *'s* is absent. However, the *'s* is regularly added to mine, as in *This is mines.*
Possessive (whose)	The possessive pronoun whose is often not used by many speakers of African American Vernacular English. For example, students will say *I don't know who book this was.* Students will need additional instruction and practice to acquire this skill.
There is/There are	Many speakers of African American Vernacular English will need help in pronouncing *its* in standard academic English and in properly using the patterns *there is* and *there are.* In AAVE it is common to replace the word there with *it,* as in *It's a man at the door* rather than *There's a man at the door.* Use Discrimination and Translation Drills.
Plurals (nouns of measure)	Most speakers of African American Vernacular English correctly use the plural, except when it involves "nouns of measure," as in *It cost five dollars* or *She owe me five dollars.* However, the plural /s/ is often absent in writing, and students will need additional instruction and practice during small group time.
Negatives	Many speakers of African American Vernacular English will use several negatives in a sentence when only one is required, as in *Nobody never said nothing.* To master standard academic English, speakers of AAVE will need considerable practice to gain control of any, ever, and either after a negative word. Write a sentence from students' speech or writing. Then provide contrastive analysis work. Write the standard English form above that sentence. Discuss the key differences. In addition, use Discrimination and Translation Drills.

The Interaction Between English and Students' Primary Languages

By Jana Echevarria, PhD
California State University, Long Beach

Donald Bear, PhD
University of Nevada, Reno

It is important for teachers to understand why English Learners (ELs) use alternative pronunciations for some English words. Many English sounds do not exist or transfer to other languages, so English Learners may lack the auditory acuity to "hear" these English sounds and have difficulty pronouncing them. These students are not accustomed to positioning their mouth in a way the sound requires. The charts that appear on the following pages show that there is variation among languages, with some languages having more sounds in common and thus greater transfer to English than others.

For example, an English speaker may be able to pronounce the /r/ in the Spanish word pero ("but"), but not the /rr/ trill in perro ("dog"). The English speaker may also lack the auditory acuity to detect and the ability to replicate the tonal sounds of some Chinese words. Similarly, a Vietnamese speaker may have difficulty pronouncing /th/ in words such as thin or thanks.

Further, English Learners make grammatical errors due to interference from their native languages. In Spanish, the adjective follows the noun, so often English Learners say "the girl pretty" instead of "the pretty girl." While English changes the verb form with a change of subject (I walk. She walks.), some Asian languages keep the verb form constant across subjects. Adding /s/ to the third person may be difficult for some English Learners. Students may know the grammatical rule, but applying it consistently may be difficult, especially in spoken English.

When working with English Learners, you should also be aware of sociocultural factors that affect pronunciation. Students may retain an accent because it marks their social identity. Speakers of other languages may feel at a social distance from members of the dominant English-speaking culture.

English Learners improve their pronunciation in a nonthreatening atmosphere in which participation is encouraged. Opportunities to interact with native English speakers provide easy access to language models and give English Learners practice using English. However, students should not be forced to participate. Pressure to perform—or to perform in a certain way—can inhibit participation. In any classroom, teacher sensitivity to pronunciation differences contributes to a more productive learning environment.

Phonics, word recognition, and spelling are influenced by what students know about the sounds, word structure, and spelling in their primary languages. For example, beginning readers who speak Spanish and are familiar with its spelling will often spell short o with an a, a letter that in Spanish makes the short o sound. Similarly, English Learners who are unaccustomed to English consonant digraphs and blends (e.g., /ch/ and s-blends) spell /ch/ as sh because /sh/ is the sound they know that is closest to /ch/. Students learn about the way pronunciation influences their reading and spelling, beginning with large contrasts among sounds, then they study the finer discriminations. As vocabulary advances, the meaning of words leads students to the sound contrasts. For example, shoe and chew may sound alike initially, but meaning indicates otherwise. Students' reading and discussions of what they read advances their word knowledge as well as their knowledge in all language and literacy systems, including phonics, pronunciation, grammar, and vocabulary.

Phonics Transfers: Sound Transfers

This chart indicates areas where a positive transfer of sounds and symbols occurs for English Learners from their native languages into English. This symbol (✔) identifies a positive transfer. "Approximate" indicates that the sound is similar.

Consonants

Sound Transfers	Spanish	Cantonese	Vietnamese	Hmong	Korean	Khmer
/b/ as in bat	✔	approximate	approximate	approximate	approximate	✔
/k/ as in cake, kitten, peck	✔	✔	✔	✔	✔	✔
/d/ as in dog	✔	approximate	approximate	✔	approximate	✔
/f/ as in farm	✔	✔	✔	✔		
/g/ as in girl	✔	approximate	✔	approximate	approximate	
/h/ as in ham	✔	✔	✔	✔	✔	approximate
/j/ as in jet, page, ledge		approximate	approximate		approximate	
/l/ as in lion	✔	✔	✔	✔	✔	
/m/ as in mat	✔	✔	✔	✔	✔	✔
/n/ as in night	✔	✔	✔	✔	✔	✔
/p/ as in pen	✔	✔	✔	approximate	✔	✔
/kw/ as in queen	✔	approximate	✔		✔	✔
/r/ as in rope	approximate					✔
/s/ as in sink, city	✔	✔	✔	✔	✔	approximate
/t/ as in ton	✔	✔	approximate	approximate	✔	✔
/v/ as in vine	✔		✔	✔		
/w/ as in wind	✔	✔			✔	✔
/ks/ as in six	✔				✔	✔
/y/ as in yak	✔	✔		✔	✔	✔
/z/ as in zebra			✔	.		

Diagraphs

Sound Transfers	Spanish	Cantonese	Vietnamese	Hmong	Korean	Khmer
/ch/ as in cheek, patch	✔	approximate		✔	✔	✔
/sh/ as in shadow			✔	✔	✔	
/hw/ as in whistle					✔	✔
/th/ as in path	approximate		approximate			
/TH/ as in that	approximate					

Diagraphs (continued)

Sound Transfers	Spanish	Cantonese	Vietnamese	Hmong	Korean	Khmer
/ng/ as in sting	✔	✔	✔	✔	✔	approximate

Short Vowels

Sound Transfers	Spanish	Cantonese	Vietnamese	Hmong	Korean	Khmer
/a/ as in cat	approximate		approximate	✔	✔	
/e/ as in net	✔	approximate	approximate		✔	
/i/ as in kid	approximate	approximate			✔	
/o/ as in spot	approximate	approximate	approximate	approximate	approximate	✔
/u/ as in cup	approximate	approximate	✔		✔	✔

Long Vowels

Sound Transfers	Spanish	Cantonese	Vietnamese	Hmong	Korean	Khmer
/ā/ as in lake, nail, bay	✔	approximate	approximate	approximate	✔	✔
/ē/ as in bee, meat, cranky	✔	approximate	✔	✔	✔	✔
/ī/ as in kite, tie, light, dry	✔	approximate	✔	✔	✔	✔
/ō/ as in home, road, row	✔	approximate	approximate		✔	
/ū/ as in dune, fruit, blue	✔	approximate	✔	✔	✔	✔
/yü/ as in mule, cue	✔	approximate			✔	

r-Controlled Vowels

Sound Transfers	Spanish	Cantonese	Vietnamese	Hmong	Korean	Khmer
/är/ as in far	approximate	approximate				
/ôr/ as in corn	approximate	approximate				
/ûr/ as in stern, bird, suburb	approximate	approximate				
/âr/ as in air, bear						
/îr/ as in deer, ear						

Variant Vowels

Sound Transfers	Spanish	Cantonese	Vietnamese	Hmong	Korean	Khmer
/oi/ as in boil, toy	✔	approximate	approximate		✔	✔
/ou/ as in loud, down	✔	approximate	✔	approximate	✔	✔
/ô/ as in law	approximate	✔	✔	approximate	approximate	✔
/ô/ as in laundry	approximate	approximate	✔	approximate	approximate	✔
/ôl/ as in salt, call	approximate	approximate			approximate	✔
/ōō/ as in moon, drew	✔	approximate	approximate	✔	✔	✔
/oo/ as in look		approximate	approximate		approximate	✔
/ə/ as in askew			approximate		✔	

Phonics Transfers: Sound Symbol Match

Consonants						
Sound Transfers	**Spanish**	**Cantonese**	**Vietnamese**	**Hmong**	**Korean**	**Khmer**
/b/ as in bat	✔		✔			
/k/ as in cake	✔		✔			
/k/ as in kitten	✔		✔	✔		
/k/ as in peck						
/d/ as in dog	✔		✔	✔		
/f/ as in farm	✔			✔		
/g/ as in girl	✔		✔			
/h/ as in ham			✔	✔		
/j/ as in jet, page, ledge						
/l/ as in lion	✔		✔	✔		
/m/ as in mat	✔		✔	✔		
/n/ as in night	✔		✔	✔		
/p/ as in pen	✔		✔	✔		
/kw/ as in queen			✔			
/r/ as in rope	approximate					
/s/ as in sink, city	✔		✔			
/t/ as in ton	✔		✔	✔		
/v/ as in vine	✔		✔	✔		
/w/ as in wind	✔					
/ks/ as in six	✔					
/y/ as in yak	✔			✔		
/z/ as in zebra						

Diagraphs

Sound Transfers	Spanish	Cantonese	Vietnamese	Hmong	Korean	Khmer
/ch/ as in cheek, patch	✔					
/sh/ as in shadow						
/hw/ as in whistle						
/th/ as in path			✔			
/TH/ as in that						
/ng/ as in sting	✔		✔			

Short Vowels

/a/ as in cat			✔	✔		
/e/ as in net	✔		✔			
/i/ as in kid						
/o/ as in spot			✔	✔		
/u/ as in cup						

Long Vowels

/ā/ as in lake						
/ā/ as in nail						
/ā/ as in bay						
/ē/ as in bee						
/ē/ as in meat						
/ē/ as in cranky						
/ī/ as in kite, tie, light, dry						
/ō/ as in home, road, row						
/ū/ as in dune			✔	✔		
/ū/ as in fruit, blue						
/yü/ as in mule, cue						

r-Controlled Vowels

Sound Transfers	Spanish	Cantonese	Vietnamese	Hmong	Korean	Khmer
/är/ as in far	✔					
/ôr/ as in corn	✔					
/ûr/ as in stern	✔					
/ûr/ as in bird, suburb						
/âr/ as in air, bear						
/îr/ as in deer, ear						

Variant Vowels

Sound Transfers	Spanish	Cantonese	Vietnamese	Hmong	Korean	Khmer
/oi/ as in boil	✔		✔			
/oi/ as in toy	✔					
/ou/ as in loud						
/ou/ as in down						
/ô/ as in law						
/ô/ as in laundry						
/ôl/ as in salt	✔					
/ôl/ as in call						
/o͞o/ as in moon, drew						
/oo/ as in look						
/ə/ as in askew						

Grammar Transfers: Grammatical Form

This chart can be used to address common mistakes that some English Learners make when they transfer grammatical forms from their native languages into English.

Nouns

Grammatical Form	Transfer Mistakes in English	Native Language	Cause of Difficulty
Plural Marker -s	**Forgets plural marker -s** *I have 3 sister.*	Cantonese, Haitian Creole, Hmong, Korean, Vietnamese, Khmer	Native language does not use a plural marker.
Countable and Uncountable Nouns	**Confuses countable and uncountable nouns** *the homeworks* or *the informations*	Haitian Creole, Spanish	Countable and uncountable nouns are different in English and native language.
Possessives	**Uses prepositions to describe possessives** *the book of my brother* as opposed to *my brother's book*	Haitian Creole, Hmong, Spanish, Vietnamese	Possession is often described using a prepositional phrase.
	Avoids using 's *dog my father* as opposed to *my father's dog*	Haitian Creole, Vietnamese, Khmer	A noun follows the object in the native language.

Articles

Grammatical Form	Transfer Mistakes in English	Native Language	Cause of Difficulty
	Consistently omits articles *He has book. They want dog not cat.*	Cantonese, Haitian Creole, Hmong, Korean, Vietnamese, Khmer	There is no article in the native language or no difference between the and a.
	Overuses articles *The English is difficult. The soccer is popular in the Europe.*	Haitian Creole, Hmong, Spanish	Some languages use articles that are omitted in English.
a/an	**Mistakes one for a/an** *She is one nurse.*	Haitian Creole, Hmong, Vietnamese	The native language either does not use articles or uses articles differently.

Pronouns

Grammatical Form	Transfer Mistakes in English	Native Language	Cause of Difficulty
Gender-Specific Pronouns	**Uses pronouns with the inappropriate gender** *He is my sister.*	Cantonese, Haitian Creole, Hmong, Korean, Spanish, Khmer	The third person pronoun in the native language is gender free, or the personal pronoun is omitted.
	Uses inappropriate gender, particularly with neutral nouns *The day is sunny. She is beautiful.*	Spanish	Nouns have feminine or masculine gender in the native language, and the gender may be carried over into English.

Pronouns

Grammatical Form	Transfer Mistakes in English	Native Language	Cause of Difficulty
Object Pronouns	**Confuses subject and object pronouns** *Her talks to me.*	Cantonese, Hmong, Khmer	The same pronoun form is used for subject and object in the native language.
	Omits object pronouns *That girl is very rude, so nobody likes.*	Korean, Vietnamese	The native language does not use direct objects.
Pronoun and Number Agreement	**Uses the wrong number for pronouns** *I saw many red birds. It was pretty.*	Cantonese, Korean	The native language does not require number agreement.
Subject Pronouns	**Omits subject pronouns** *Mom isn't home. Is at work.*	Korean, Spanish	Subject pronouns may be dropped because in the native language the verb ending gives information about the number and/or gender.
Pronouns in Clauses	**Omits pronouns in clauses** *If don't do homework, they will not learn.*	Cantonese, Vietnamese	The native language does not need a subject in the subordinate clause.
Pronouns and Nouns	**Overuses pronouns with nouns** *This school, it very good.*	Hmong, Vietnamese	This is popular in speech in some languages. The speaker mentions a topic, then makes a comment about it.
	Avoids pronouns and repeats nouns *Carla visits her sister every Sunday, and Carla makes a meal.*	Korean, Vietnamese	In the native language, the speaker repeats nouns and does not use pronouns.
Pronoun one	**Omits the pronoun one** *I saw two dogs, and I like the small.*	Spanish	Adjectives can stand alone in the native language, but English requires a *noun* or *one*.
Possessive Forms	**Confuses possessive forms** *The book is my.*	Cantonese, Hmong, Vietnamese	Cantonese and Hmong speakers tend to omit the final *n* sound, which may create confusion between my and mine.

Verbs

Grammatical Form	Transfer Mistakes in English	Native Language	Cause of Difficulty
Present Tense	**Omits -s in present tense, third person agreement** *He like pizza.*	Cantonese, Haitian Creole, Hmong, Korean, Vietnamese, Khmer	Subject-verb agreement is not used in the native language.
Irregular Verbs	**Has problems with irregular subject-verb agreement** *Tom and Sue has a new car.*	Cantonese, Hmong, Korean, Khmer	Verbs' forms do not change to show the number of the subject in the native language.
Inflectional Endings	**Omits tense markers** *I study English yesterday.*	Cantonese, Haitian Creole, Hmong, Korean, Vietnamese, Khmer	The native language does not use inflectional endings to change verb tense.
Present and Future Tenses	**Incorrectly uses the present tense for the future tense** *I go next week.*	Cantonese, Korean	The native language may use the present tense to imply the future tense.
Negative Statements	**Omits helping verbs in negative statements** *Sue no coming to school.*	Cantonese, Korean, Spanish	The native language does not use helping verbs in negative statements.
Present-Perfect Tense	**Avoids the present-perfect tense** *Marcos live here for three months.*	Haitian Creole, Vietnamese	The native language does not use the present-perfect verb form.
Past-Continuous Tense	**Uses the past-continuous tense for recurring action in the past** *When I was young, I was talking a lot.*	Korean, Spanish	In the native language, the past-continuous tense is used but in English the expression used to or the simple past tense is used.
Main Verb	**Omits the main verb** *Talk in class not good.*	Cantonese	Cantonese does not require an infinitive marker when using a verb as a noun. Speakers may confuse the infinitive for the main verb.
Main Verbs in Clauses	**Uses two or more main verbs in one clause without any connectors** *I took a book went studied at the library.*	Hmong	In Hmong, verbs can be used consecutively without conjunctions or punctuation.
Linking Verbs	**Omits the linking verb** *He hungry.*	Cantonese, Haitian Creole, Hmong, Vietnamese, Khmer	In some languages, be is implied in the adjective form. In other languages, the concept is expressed with a verb.
Helping Verb in Passive Voice	**Omits the helping verb in the passive voice** *The homework done.*	Cantonese, Vietnamese	In Cantonese and Vietnamese, the passive voice does not require a helping verb.

Verbs

Grammatical Form	Transfer Mistakes in English	Native Language	Cause of Difficulty
Passive Voice	**Avoids the passive voice** *They speak English here.* *One speaks English here.* **English is spoken here.**	Haitian Creole	The passive voice does not exist in the native language.
Transitive Verbs	**Confuses transitive and intransitive verbs** *The child broke. The child broke <u>the plate</u>.*	Cantonese, Korean, Spanish	Verbs that require a direct object differ between English and the native language.
Phrasal Verbs	**Confuses related phrasal verbs** *I ate at the apple.* *I ate up the apple.*	Korean, Spanish	Phrasal verbs are not used in the native language, and there is often confusion over their meaning.
Have **and** *be*	**Uses have instead of be** *I have thirst. He has right.*	Spanish	Spanish and English have different uses for **have** and **be**.

Adjectives

Grammatical Form	Transfer Mistakes in English	Native Language	Cause of Difficulty
Word Order	**Places adjectives after nouns** *I saw a car red.*	Haitian Creole, Hmong, Spanish, Vietnamese, Khmer	Nouns often precede adjectives in the native language.
	Consistently places adjectives after nouns **This is a lesson new.**	Cantonese, Korean	Adjectives always follow nouns in the native language.
-er **and** *-est* **Endings**	**Avoids *-er* and *-est* endings** *I am more old than you.*	Hmong, Korean, Spanish, Khmer	The native language shows comparative and superlative forms with separate words.
-ing **and** *ed* **Endings**	**Confuses -ing and -ed forms** *Math is bored.*	Cantonese, Korean, Spanish, Khmer	Adjectives in the native language do not have active and passive meanings.

Adverbs

Grammatical Form	Transfer Mistakes in English	Native Language	Cause of Difficulty
Adjectives and Adverbs	**Uses an adjective where an adverb is needed** *Talk quiet.*	Haitian Creole, Hmong, Khmer	Adjectives and adverb forms are interchangeable in the native language.
Word Order	**Places adverbs before verbs** *He quickly ran.* *He ran quickly.*	Cantonese, Korean	Adverbs usually come before verbs in the native language, and this tendency is carried over into English.

Prepositions

Grammatical Form	Transfer Mistakes in English	Native Language	Cause of Difficulty
	Omits prepositions *I like come school.*	Cantonese	Cantonese does not use prepositions the way that English does.

How to Use the Grammar Transfer Charts

The grammar of many languages differs widely from English. For example, a student's primary language may use a different word order than English, may not use parts of speech in the same way, or may use different verb tenses. The Grammar Transfer Charts are designed to help you anticipate and understand possible student errors in speaking and writing standard English. With all grammar exercises, the emphasis is on oral communication, both as a speaker and listener.

1. Highlight Transferrable Skills

If the grammar skill transfers from the student's primary language to English, state that during the lesson. In many lessons an English Learner feature will indicate which skills do and do not transfer.

2. Preteach Non-Transferrable Skills

Prior to teaching a grammar lesson, check the chart to determine if the skill transfers from the student's primary language into English. If it does not, preteach the skill. Provide sentence frames and ample structured opportunities to use the skill in spoken English. Students need to talk, talk, and talk some more to master these skills.

3. Provide Additional Practice and Time

If the skill does NOT transfer from the student's primary language into English, the student will require more time and practice mastering it. Continue to review the skill using additional resources, such as the grammar lessons in the **Grammar and Language Workbook** in upcoming weeks.

4. Use Contrastive Analysis

Tell students when a skill does not transfer and include contrastive analysis work to make the student aware of how to correct their speaking and writing for standard English. For example, when a student uses an incorrect grammatical form, write the student sentence, then write the correct English form underneath. Explain the difference between the student's primary language and English. Have the student correct several other sentences using this skill.

5. Increase Writing and Speaking Opportunities

Increase the amount of structured writing and speaking opportunities for students needing work on specific grammatical forms. Sentence starters and paragraph frames, such as those found in the lessons, are ideal for both written and oral exercises.

6. Focus on Meaning

Always focus on the meanings of sentences in all exercises. As they improve and fine-tune their English speaking and writing skills, work with students on basic comprehension of spoken and written English.

To help students move to the next level of language acquisition and master English grammatical forms, recast their responses during classroom discussions or provide additional language for them to use as they respond further. Provide leveled-language sentence frames orally or in writing for students to use as they respond to questions and prompts. Below are samples.

English Learner Response Chart

Beginning (will respond by pointing or saying one word answers)	**Sample Frames** (simple, short sentences) *I see a _____.* *This is a _____.* *I like the _____.*
Early Intermediate (will respond with phrases or simple sentences)	**Sample Frames** (simple sentences with adjectives and adverbs added, and compound subjects or predicates) *I see a _____ _____.* *The _____ animal is _____.* *There are _____ and _____.*
Intermediate (will respond with simple sentences and limited academic language)	**Sample Frames** (harder sentences with simple phrases in consistent patterns; some academic language included) *The animal's prey is _____ because _____.* *The main idea is _____ because _____.* *He roamed the park so that _____.*
Early Advanced (will begin to use more sophisticated sentences and some academic language)	**Sample Frames** (complex sentences with increased academic language, beginning phrases and clauses, and multiple-meaning words) *When the violent storm hit, _____.* *As a result of the revolution, the army_____.* *Since most endangered animals are _____, they _____.*
Advanced (will have mastered some more complex sentence structures and is increasing the amount of academic language used)	Use the questions and prompts provided in the lessons for the whole group. Provide additional support learning and using academic language. These words are boldfaced throughout the lessons and sentence starters are often provided.

Classroom Resources: Print

Blackline Masters

Unit Teaching Resources

These blackline master booklets provide all the teaching materials you need to reinforce the content in each unit of *Glencoe Literature.* Worksheets include the following:

Unit Introduction
Big Idea Foldable
Big Idea School-to-Home Connection
- English
- Spanish
- Vietnamese
- Tagalog
- Cantonese
- Haitian Creole
- Hmong
Challenge Planner
Academic Vocabulary Development
Part Opener
Literary Focus
English Language Coach
Literary History
Comparing Literature Graphic Organizer
Grammar Workshop Practice
Media Workshop Practice
Selection Summaries
- English
- Spanish
- Vietnamese
- Tagalog
- Cantonese
- Haitian Creole
- Hmong
Literary Element
Reading Strategy
Selection Vocabulary Practice
Grammar Practice
Vocabulary Strategy
Selection Quick Check
- English
- Spanish
Spelling Practice
Writing Workshop Graphic Organizer
Writing Workshop Rubric
Speaking, Listening, and Viewing Activities
Speaking, Listening, and Viewing Workshop Rubric

Practice Books

Read and Write

INTERACTIVE These leveled consumable worktexts provide structured instruction and practice with selected readings from the anthology.

- On-Level provides fast-track instruction for on-level students.

- Approaching provides scaffolding for struggling or reluctant readers.

- English Learners helps students whose primary language is not English read and comprehend selection.

The Novel Companion

This worktext provides accelerated instruction for advanced students through novel study. With the tools for a detailed analysis of a novel and related reading for every unit of the anthology, students explore in more depth the Big Ideas around which the anthology is organized.

Spelling Power Workbook

Provides additional support for practice and mastery of spelling.

Writing

Glencoe Language Arts Writing Resources

This writing resource contains the following transparencies:

Writing Process Strategies Transparencies provide graphic organizers to help you guide your students through the various stages of the writing process.

Writing Practice Transparencies provide opportunities for students to practice writing in modes that are appropriate for their grade level including Narrative, Expository, and Persuasive Writing and Responding to Literary Texts.

Process of Revision Transparencies use base transparencies and corresponding overlays to show and explain actual revisions and edits. The set of revision transparencies guides students through the process of improving a sample essay. A blank Student Revision transparency is included so student volunteers can make their own revisions to improve the quality of an essay.

Writing Constructed Responses

This sourcebook with blackline masters helps students respond effectively to short essay questions.

Success in Writing: Research and Reports

These blackline masters reinforce and extend the coverage of research presented in the student edition.

Grammar and Language Workbook

This workbook provides full coverage of grammar, usage, and mechanics rules, examples, and practice exercises.

Grammar and Composition Handbook

This handbook is a handy desk reference tool providing full coverage of the writing process as well as rules and practice exercises for grammar, usage, and mechanics.

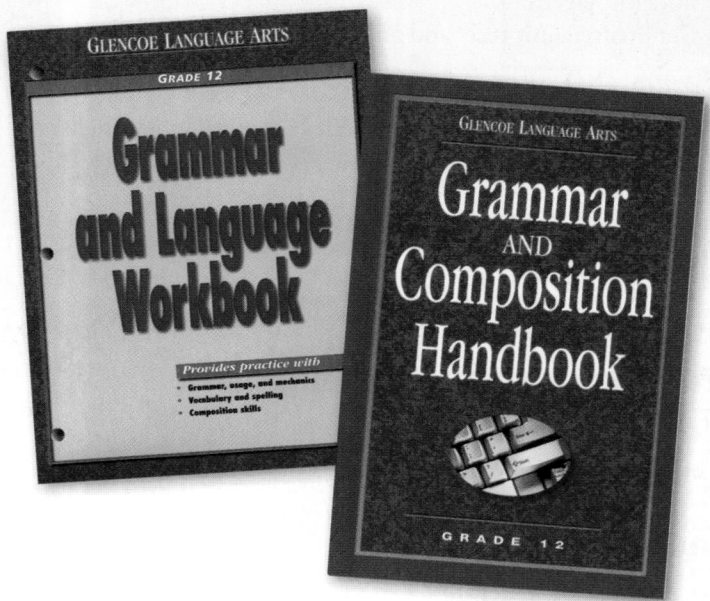

Grammar and Writing Transparencies

Help reinforce the skills taught in the grammar links and writing workshops.

Classroom Resources: Print

Assessment

Assessment Resources

This assessment tool provides three types of tests:

- Diagnostic assessment by learning objectives
- Formative tests and answer keys for selections
- Summative unit tests and answer keys

Standardized Test Prep and Practice

These materials feature exercises and activities that get students ready for standardized exams.

ACT/SAT Preparation and Practice Workbook

Fluency Practice and Assessment

English Language Development

English Language Coach

These worksheets provide extra support for English Learners.

Independent Reading

Ethnic Anthologies

The following anthologies offer students introductions to the richness and variety of literature written by African, Asian, Hispanic, and Native Americans. A Teacher's Guide for each anthology suggests answers to questions accompanying each selection to help further student discussion.

- *Glencoe African American Literature*
- *Glencoe Asian American Literature*
- *Glencoe Hispanic American Literature*
- *Glencoe Native American Literature*

InTIME Magazines

This lively collection of articles drawn from TIME helps students develop skills for reading informational text.

Transparencies

Bellringer Transparencies

include warm-up exercises to engage students and to provide a quick review of previously taught skills.

Fine Art Transparencies

enhance visual literacy and provide a strong humanities approach to literature.

Literary Elements Transparencies

help reinforce literary elements that are the focus of each lesson.

Read Aloud, Think Aloud Transparencies

model active reading

Classroom Resources: Technology

Classroom Planning, Management, and Instruction

TeacherWorks Plus CD-ROM

- Plan and manage daily lessons and activities
- Access all program resources
- Edit lesson plans and worksheets
- Track the standards taught in your classroom

Classroom Presentation Toolkit CD-ROM or DVD-ROM

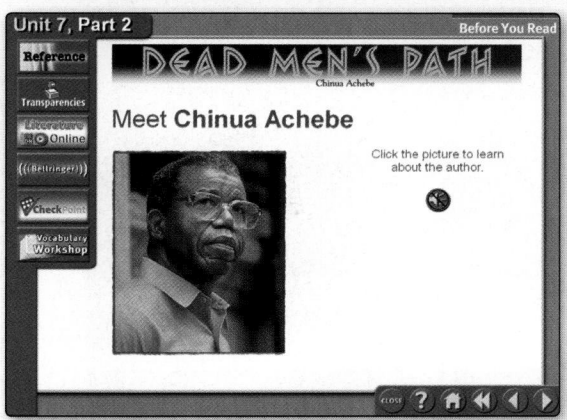

- Present customizable lessons via PowerPoint
- Launch transparencies, audio, video, and software at point-of-use during instruction

Digital Learning

Online Student Edition and StudentWorks Plus CD-ROM or DVD-ROM

- Full-text synced-audio selection read support
- Audio summaries in multiple languages
- Search, highlighting, and notes tools
- Multimedia links to video, activities, animations, and graphic graphic organizers
- Access student workbooks, Student Media Toolkit, and Student Presentation Builder
- Daily Assignments and Grade Log

Assessment and Progress Monitoring

ExamView Assessment Suite CD-ROM

- Administer ready-made diagnostic, formative, and summative assessments in English or Spanish

- Edit assessment items or create new items as needed
- Monitor student progress through a variety of reporting options
- Provides real assessment-driven remediation options

Progress Reporter Online Assessment

- Administer ready-made diagnostic, formative, and summative assessments online in English or Spanish
- Edit assessment items or create new items as needed
- Assessments administered online are scored automatically
- Essay questions are scored automatically
- Ready-made exams provide students with item rationales, explaining why each answer choice is correct or incorrect
- Automatically assigns reteaching and remediation based on student performance
- Monitor student progress by standard or by standard strand or through a variety of other reporting options

Literature Online: Assessment Resources

- End-of-Unit Assessment
- Test-taking Tips and Strategies

Literature and Reading

Literature Classics

- Choose from over 1,100 additional classic literature selections
- Search selections by author, title, date, genre, country, course/grade level, and Big Question or Big Idea
- Reinforce instruction with Genre Focus Lesson Plans and blackline masters
- Available on CD-ROM and access via glencoe.com

Classroom Resources: Technology

Listening Library CD

- Help students improve overall comprehension and reading fluency with engaging recordings of the selections in *Glencoe Literature*
- Assist English Learners with audio selection summaries in their native language
- Use the Listening Library CDs in conjunction with the Listening Library Sourcebook, a collection of standards-based strategies and activities, found on your TeacherWorks™ Plus CD-ROM

Literature Launchers: Pre-Reading Videos DVD

- Each of the engaging video segments on this DVD brings the literature to life, providing a visual context for every Unit and key selections
- Use this DVD in conjunction with the Literature Launchers Teacher Guide, found on your TeacherWorks™ Plus CD-ROM, which provides teaching strategies and video-specific blackline masters.
- English and Spanish subtitles

Literature Library Teacher Resources CD-ROM

- Access all Glencoe Literature Library Study Guides
- Develop vocabulary with Vocabulary Puzzlemaker
- Assess with ExamView Assessment Suite

BookLink K-12 CD-ROM

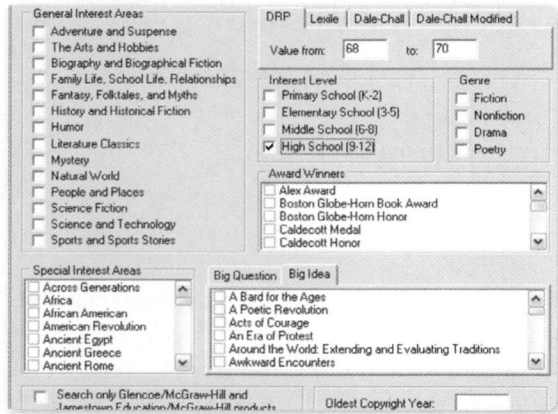

- Create customized reading lists for your students from a database of over 30,000 titles

- Search for award-winning titles and for books on state recommended reading lists
- Organize reading lists by students' reading level, author, genre, theme, or area of interest
- Find Degrees of Reading Power™ (DRP), Lexile™, and Dale-Chall scores for all selections in the Glencoe Literature program

Skill Level Up! A Skills-Based Language Arts Game CD-ROM

- Offers an innovative approach to Language Arts and Reading skills practice, assessment and remediation
- Skill Level Up!'s networkable game environment provides a context and purpose for learning by immersing students in an engaging adventure
- Features two access modes: the immersive story mode, which covers all the skills in the context of the adventure game play, or the skill-based assignment mode, which allows teachers to assign discrete activities according to their curriculum plan
- Adapts to each student's performance by offering remediation when necessary or enrichment activities when applicable
- Manage and track student performance using convenient assignment, tracking, and reporting functions featured in the program's management system
- Covers the following Reading Skills and Literary Elements:
  - Connecting
  - Questioning
  - Predicting
  - Point of View
  - Visualizing

- Rhyme
- Dialog
- Main Idea and Supporting Details/Paraphrasing and Summarizing
- Plot
- Conflict
- Interpreting
- Drawing Conclusions
- Setting
- Fact and Opinion
- Theme
- Author's Purpose and Perspective
- Voice, Style, Tone, Narrator
- Description, Imagery, Sensory Details
- Symbolism
- Inferring
- Figurative Language
- Analyzing Text Structure
- Meter and Rhythm
- Character and Characterization
- Sound Devices
- Genre
- Synthesizing

Literature Online: Literature, Reading, and Selection Resources (glencoe.com)

- Author and Artist Search
- Web Quest
- Selection Quizzes
- Selection Vocabulary eFlashcards
- Selection Reading-Writing Connection activities
- Reading Skills Review
- Interactive Reading Practice
- Literary Elements eFlashcards
- Fluency Practice
- Games

Vocabulary Development

Glencoe Interactive Vocabulary CD-ROM

- Generate flashcard sets from a visual glossary of selection, academic, content area, and social vocabulary terms
- Includes audio support in multiple languages for all terms
- Provides instructional modules and practice via an engaging game environment:

- signal words
- cognates/false cognates
- multiple meaning words
- synonyms and antonyms
- idioms
- analogies
- figures of speech
- context clues
- etymology
- troublesome words
- text features
- compound words
- homonyms

Vocabulary PuzzleMaker

- Create crossword puzzles, word search puzzles, and jumble puzzles in an instant
- Choose from selection and academic vocabulary (in both English and Spanish) and literary terms
- Available on CD-ROM and for download via glencoe.com

Skill Level Up! A Skills-Based Language Arts Game CD-ROM

- Using Context Clues
- Multiple Meaning Words
- Examining Words Origins
- Words with Special Meanings
- Denotation and Connotation
- Using Analogies
- Synonyms
- Antonyms
- Homonyms
- Word Parts/Structural Analysis: Base Words
- Word Parts/Structural Analysis: Prefixes
- Word Parts/Structural Analysis: Suffixes

Classroom Resources: Technology

Literature Online: Vocabulary and Spelling Resources (glencoe.com)

- Multi-Language Glossary
- Selection Vocabulary eFlashcards
- Academic Vocabulary eFlashcards
- Vocabulary Games
- Spelling Lessons
- Spelling Games

Writing

Glencoe Online Essay Grader powered by Bookette SkillWriter™ (glencoewriting.com)

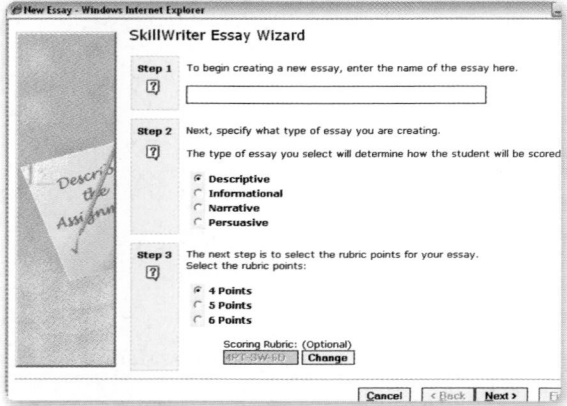

- Score student writing assignments and provide individualized feedback to each student automatically
- Assign prompts from Glencoe Literature Writing Workshops or create your own prompts!
- Manage demographic data, assign tests and run a variety of progress monitoring reports using the program's management system.

Literature Online: Writing and Research Resources (glencoe.com)

- Annotated Writing Models
- Interactive Writing Models
- Writing and Research Handbook
- Research Tips and Strategies
- Graphic Organizers
- Transition Bank
- Grammar Troubleshooter
- Sentence-Combining Practice

- Editing and Proofreading Marks
- Publishing Options

Speaking, Listening and Viewing

Skill Level Up! A Skills-Based Language Arts Game CD-ROM

- Analyzing Persuasive Techniques
- Listening Critically
- Examining Visuals in Literature and Media: Maps, Charts, Graphs
- Examining Visuals in Literature and Media: Visual Techniques

Student Presentation Builder

- Assign additional Unit-based multimedia presentation projects
- Includes a PowerPoint™ tutorial, a PowerPoint™ presentation template, and an image bank
- Available on StudentWorks Plus or via the Online Student Edition
- Teacher Guide is available on TeacherWorks Plus

Literature Online: Speaking, Listening, and Viewing Resources (glencoe.com)

- Project Ideas and Templates
- Presentation Tips and Strategies

Media Literacy

Glencoe Media Workshop DVD

- Engage students in the study and critical review of media from film footage of important events in history to analysis of commercials
- English and Spanish subtitles

Student Media Toolkit

- Provides additional interactive media analysis activities
- Includes media generator tools

Literature Online: Media Literacy Resources (glencoe.com)

- Media Analysis Guides
- Project Ideas

Library Resources

Glencoe Literature Library

Each *Glencoe Literature* Library volume consists of at least one complete extended-length reading accompanied by several related readings from a broad range of genres. A separate Study Guide for each book provides teaching notes and reproducible activity pages for students. Students may also find these activity pages at glencoe.com.

The Adventures of Huckleberry Finn by Mark Twain **DRP 54***

All Quiet on the Western Front by Erich Maria Remarque **DRP 52**

. . . And the Earth Did Not Devour Him by Tomas Rivera **DRP 52**

Animal Farm by George Orwell **DRP 60**

The Autobiography of Benjamin Franklin by Benjamin Franklin **DRP 64**

The Autobiography of Miss Jane Pittman by Ernest J. Gaines **DRP 49**

The Awakening by Kate Chopin **DRP 58**

Beowulf

Billy Budd by Herman Melville **DRP 68**

The Bridge of San Luis Rey by Thornton Wilder **DRP 55**

The Brothers Karamazov by Fyodor Dostoevsky **DRP 55**

The Canterbury Tales by Geoffrey Chaucer **DRP 59**

The Chosen by Chaim Potok **DRP 56**

A Country Doctor by Sarah Orne Jewett **DRP 59**

Cyrano de Bergerac by Edmond Rostand **DRP**

Ethan Frome by Edith Wharton **DRP 59**

Fallen Angels by Walter Dean Myers **DRP 47**

Frankenstein by Mary Shelley **DRP 64**

Great Expectations by Charles Dickens **DRP 60**

Gulliver's Travels by Jonathan Swift **DRP 67**

Hamlet by William Shakespeare

Heart of Darkness and *The Secret Sharer* by Joseph Conrad **DRP 58**

A House for Mr Biswas by V. S. Naipaul **DRP 58**

The House of the Seven Gables by Nathaniel Hawthorne **DRP 65**

The Importance of Being Earnest by Oscar Wilde **DRP**

Invisible Man by Ralph Ellison **DRP 57**

Jane Eyre by Charlotte Brontë **DRP 61**

Julius Caesar by William Shakespeare

The Jungle by Upton Sinclair **DRP 59**

The Mayor of Casterbridge by Thomas Hardy **DRP 60**

The Metamorphosis by Franz Kafka **DRP 57**

A Midsummer Night's Dream by William Shakespeare

My Ántonia by Willa Cather **DRP 57**

Narrative of the Life of Frederick Douglass by Frederick Douglass **DRP 62**

Nectar in a Sieve by Kamala Markandaya **DRP 56**

Night by Elie Wiesel **DRP 51**

One Day in the Life of Ivan Denisovich by Aleksandr Solzhenitsyn **DRP 56**

Our Town by Thornton Wilder

Picture Bride by Yoshiko Uchida **DRP 55**

Pride and Prejudice by Jane Austen **DRP 61**

A Raisin in the Sun by Lorraine Hansberry

The Red Badge of Courage by Stephen Crane **DRP 60**

The Return of the Native by Thomas Hardy **DRP 61**

The Scarlet Letter by Nathaniel Hawthorne **DRP 67**

Sense and Sensibility by Jane Austen **DRP 63**

A Separate Peace by John Knowles **DRP 59**

Silas Marner by George Eliot **DRP 55**

The Souls of Black Folk by W. E. B. Du Bois **DRP 66**

The Story of My Life by Helen Keller **DRP 59**

The Strange Case of Dr Jekyll and Mr Hyde by Robert Louis Stevenson **DRP 63**

A Tale of Two Cities by Charles Dickens **DRP 62**

The Tempest by William Shakespeare

Things Fall Apart by Chinua Achebe **DRP 56**

The Time Machine and *The War of the Worlds* by H. G. Wells **DRP 59**

To Kill a Mockingbird by Harper Lee **DRP 51**

Walden by Henry David Thoreau **DRP 62**

The Way to Rainy Mountain by N. Scott Momaday **DRP 55**

Wuthering Heights by Emily Brontë **DRP 61**

The Yearling by Marjorie Kinnan Rawlings **DRP 53**

*Degrees of Reading Power® DRP values indicate the readability of prose text. The higher the value, the more difficult the text. Though the scale ranges from 0 to 100, texts widely available for use at grades nine through twelve typically range from 53 to 68. Some materials, however, may certainly fall outside of this range.

Skills Scope and Sequence

Readability Scores Key: Dale-Chall/DRP/Lexile

PART 1: Early Africa 3100 B.C. – A.D. 1800

Selections and Features	Literary Elements
Part Introduction pp. 4–15	Literary Periods **SE** p. 8
Myth Osiris and Isis **6.4/57/900** pp. 16–22	Archetype **SE** p. 17
Grammar Workshop p. 23	
Hymn The Great Hymn to the Aten, by Akhenaten translated by Miriam Lichtheim pp. 24–29	Tone **SE** p. 25 Imagery **TE** p. 26 Epithet **TE** p. 28
Poems *from* **The Immortality of Writers** and **So Small are the flowers of Seamu,** translated by Ezra Pound and Noel Stock pp. 30–33	Imagery **SE** p. 30
Literary History Hieroglyphics and the Rosetta Stone pp. 34–35	
Vocabulary Workshop pp. 36–37	
Comparing Literature How Stories Came to Earth (folktale), retold by Kaleki **5.4/55/900** **Coyote Steals Fire** (folktale), retold by Richard Erdoes and Alfonso Ortiz **5.3/49/710** **Master Cat, or Puss in Boots** (fairy tale), by Charles Perrault, translated by Maria Tatar **6.7/54/1060** pp. 38–51	Anthropomorphism **SE** p. 39 Point of View **TE** p. 42
Folktale Edju and the Two Friends, translated by Paul Radin **4.1/48/640** pp. 52–55	Irony **SE** p. 52
The Art of Translation The Storyteller as Translator pp. 56–57	
Epic *from* **The Lion's Awakening** *from* **Sundiata,** retold by D. T. Niane, translated by G. D. Pickett **6.1/54/890** pp. 58–64	Epic **SE** p. 58

Reading Skills and Strategies	Vocabulary	Writing / Grammar	Speaking, Listening, Viewing
Analyze Graphic Information **TE** p. 6 Evaluate Historical Influences **SE** p. 8 Connect to the Literature **SE** p. 8 Determine Main Idea and Supporting Details **TE** p. 10	Context Clues **TE** p. 8	Create a Concept Map **TE** p. 12 Write a Research Report **SE** p. 15	Analyze Art **SE** p. 2 Discussion **TE** p. 14 Create a Display **SE** p. 15
Identify Genre **SE** p. 17 Analyze Parallelism **TE** p. 20	Word Usage **SE** p. 22	Write a Movie Scene **SE** p. 22	Oral Interpretation **TE** p. 18 View the Art **SE** p. 20
		Sentence Fragments **SE** p. 23	
Analyze Style **SE** p. 25	Context Clues **SE** p. 29	Write a Journal Entry **SE** p. 29	View the Art **SE** p. 28
Analyze Diction **SE** p. 30	Word Origins **SE** p. 30	Subordinate Clauses **TE** p. 32 Write an Essay **SE** p. 33	View the Art **SE** p. 32
Evaluate Historical Influences **SE** p. 34 Draw Conclusions **TE** p. 34			View the Art **TE** p. 35
	Academic Vocabulary **SE** pp. 36–37	Create a Word Map **TE** p. 36	
Analyze Cultural Contexts **SE** p. 39 Compare Themes **SE** p. 38 Apply Background Knowledge **TE** p. 44 Analyze Characterization **TE** p. 48	Academic Vocabulary **SE** p. 43	Commas with Nonessential Elements **TE** p. 40 Write a Trickster Tale **SE** p. 43 Write an Essay **SE** p. 51	View the Art **TE** p. 44 Oral Report **TE** pp. 46, 50; **SE** p. 51 Discussion **SE** p. 51
Connect to Personal Experience **SE** p. 52	Antonyms **SE** p. 55	Complex Sentences **TE** p. 54 Write an Anecdote **SE** p. 55	View the Art **SE** p. 53
Understand Cultural and Historical Context **SE** p. 56 Understand the Nature of Translation **SE** p. 56		Conduct Internet Research **TE** p. 56	View the Photograph **TE** p. 57
Make Inferences about Characters **SE** p. 58	Word Parts **SE** p. 64	Comparative and Superlative Adjectives **TE** p. 60 Write a Journal Entry **SE** p. 64	View the Art **SE** p. 60 Narrative Presentation **TE** p. 62

Reading Skills and Strategies	Vocabulary	Writing / Grammar	Speaking, Listening, Viewing
	Thesaurus Use **SE** p. 65 Synonyms **SE** p. 65		
Analyze Graphic Information **SE** p. 68 Evaluate Historical Influences **SE** p. 70 Connect to the Literature **SE** p. 71 Compare and Contrast **TE** p. 72 Distinguish Fact and Opinion **TE** p. 74	Word Parts **TE** p. 76	Create a Flow Chart **TE** p. 68 Commas with Appositives **TE** p. 70 Write a List **TE** p. 76 Write a Research Report **SE** p. 77	View the Art **TE** pp. 66, 68, 70, 73, 74 Panel Discussion **SE** p. 77
Monitor Comprehension **SE** p. 79	Context Clues **SE** p. 82	Write a Monologue **SE** p. 82	
Question **SE** p. 84 Review **TE** p. 84	Analogies **SE** p. 89 Academic Vocabulary **SE** p. 89	Demonstratives **TE** p. 86 Conduct Internet Research **SE** p. 89 Write a Travel Brochure **SE** p. 89	View the Photograph **TE** p. 87
		Sentence Combining **SE** p. 90 Prepositional, Appositive, and Participial Phrases **SE** p. 90 Coordinating and Subordinating Conjunctions **SE** p. 91 Semicolons **TE** p. 90	
Activate Prior Knowledge **SE** p. 93 Compare and Contrast **TE** p. 98	Word Parts **SE** p. 101 Academic Vocabulary **SE** p. 101	Semicolons **TE** p. 94 Write a Character Analysis **TE** p. 96 Apply Irony **SE** p. 101 Write an Expository Essay **SE** p. 101	View the Art **SE** p. 98
		Possessive Apostrophes **SE** p. 102 Its and It's **TE** p. 102	
Compare and Contrast Events **SE** p. 103 Analyze Informational Text **SE** p. 103	Loaded Words **TE** p. 106		Oral Report **TE** p. 104

Readability Scores Key: Dale-Chall/DRP/Lexile

PART 2: Modern Africa 1800–Present *(continued)*

Selections and Features	Literary Elements
Short Story The Rain Came, by Grace Ogot 6/55/730 pp. 107–119	Setting **SE** p. 108 Situational Irony (review) **SE** p. 118
Poem Civilian and Soldier, by Wole Soyinka pp. 120–123	Imagery **SE** p. 121
Short Story The Prisoner Who Wore Glasses, by Bessie Head 8.1/58/800 pp. 124–132	Character **SE** p. 125 Motivation (review) SE p. 131
Short Story The Return, by Ngugi wa Thiong'o 4.5/54/560 pp. 133–140	Personification **SE** p. 134
Drama Bones, by Sadru Kassam pp. 141–148	Satire **SE** p. 142
Short Story A House for Us, by Etidal Osman 6.0/55/920 pp. 149–154	Description **SE** p. 150
Informational Text TIME: Heroes Among Us, by Susan Schindehette 6.6/56/1050 pp. 155–157	
Writing Workshop pp. 158–165	
Speaking, Listening, and Viewing Workshop pp. 166–167	
Independent Reading pp. 168–169	Cultural Context **SE** p. 168
Assessment pp. 170–175	

Reading Skills and Strategies	Vocabulary	Writing / Grammar	Speaking, Listening, Viewing
Analyze Cultural Context **SE** p. 108 Question **TE** p. 108 Analyze Suspense **TE** p. 116	Analogies **SE** p. 118 Academic Vocabulary **SE** p. 118	Write a Character Sketch **TE** p. 112 Coordinating Conjunctions **TE** p. 114 Write a Research Report **SE** p. 119 Parentheses and Brackets **SE** p. 119	View the Art **TE** pp. 109, 113 Speech **TE** p. 110 Discussion **SE** p. 117
Analyze Structure **SE** p. 121	Synonyms **SE** p. 123	Adapt a Myth **TE** p. 122 Write an Interview **SE** p. 123	
Identify Assumptions **SE** p. 125 Make Predictions **TE** p. 126	Word Origins **SE** p. 132 Academic Vocabulary **SE** p. 132	Transitive and Intransitive Verbs **TE** p. 128 Write a List **SE** p. 132	View the Art **TE** p. 129 Debate **SE** p. 132
Make and Verify Predictions **SE** p. 134 Analyze Motivation **TE** p. 138	Antonyms **SE** p. 140	Note Taking **TE** p. 134 Past Perfect Tense **TE** p. 136 Write a Dialogue **SE** p. 140	Discussion **TE** p. 134 View the Art **SE** p. 138
Visualize **SE** p. 142	Word Usage **SE** p. 148	Adjectives **TE** p. 144 Apply Metaphor **TE** p. 146 Write an Editorial **SE** p. 148	View the Art **TE** p. 143
Make Inferences About Theme **SE** p. 150 Analyze Structure **TE** p. 152	Synonyms **SE** p. 154	Participles **TE** p. 150 Write a Description **SE** p. 154	
Analyze Text Structure **SE** p. 155 Preview **SE** p. 155		Write a Summary **SE** p. 157	
		Prewrite **SE** p. 162 Draft **SE** p. 162 Revise **SE** p. 164 Dialogue **SE** p. 164 Write a Short Story **SE** p. 165 Shifts in Point of View **SE** p. 165	
		Write Questions **SE** p. 167	Discussion **TE** p. 166 Oral Response **SE** p. 167
Read Literature Independently **SE** p. 168 Evaluate **TE** p. 168		Write a Review **SE** p. 169	
Preview **TE** p. 172	Word Origins **TE** p. 174	Write an Essay **SE** p. 173	Analyze Directions **TE** p. 170

Focus

Bellringer Options

Literature Launcher
  Pre-Reading Video Unit 1
Daily Language Practice
  Transparency 1
Or ask: What historical features do you associate with early Africa? *(Students might mention advanced civilizations, slavery, or colonies.)*

View the Art ★

Answer: *Answers will vary. Students may say that it conveys a sense of sorrow or hardship.* This mask was created by the Kuba (or Bakuba) people who live in the southeastern part of the Democratic Republic of the Congo (formerly Zaire).

 For school-to-home activities, see Unit 1 Teaching Resources Book, pp. 5–11.

 For students who would profit from independent novel study, see Novel Companion, pp. 7–50.

A Kuban mask of Ngaady aMwaash, Congo. *View the Art* Ngaady aMwaash, a renowned beauty, was the wife of Mwaash aMbooy, the first king of the Kuba, a group living in central Congo. She is often depicted with diagonal lines running beneath her eyes, which represent tears. What emotions does this mask convey? ★

2

Viewing Practice

Analyze Art Point out to students that all art, whatever its form, intends to communicate.

To grasp what a specific work of art communicates, students need to ask questions such as the following:

Why was this work of art created?
- Was it produced for everyday use?
- Was it created for religious or cultural purposes?
- Was it purely decorative?

What is the style of this work of art?
- Is it realistic? (Does it attempt to represent objects as they appear?)
- If not, how does it reshape the object it represents? (Does it idealize? Exaggerate? Distort? Simplify?)

What seems to be the artist's point of view?
- Does the work of art seem personal?
- If not, does it reflect some other point of view (such as a religion or culture)?

What is my response to this work of art?
- How does it make me feel?
- How would I express its "message"?

Pair students and have them ask each other several of these questions about the Kuban mask. Ask each pair to offer one insight or observation from their discussion.

AFRICA
3100 B.C.—Present

Kwa mwendwo gutiri irima.

On the way to one's beloved there are no hills. **1**

—Kikuyu proverb ☆

PART ONE
Early Africa..pages 4–65 **2**

PART TWO
Modern Africa.................................pages 66–175

3

Unit Resources

Print Materials
- Unit 1 Teaching Resources, pp. 1–262
- Interactive Read and Write
- Novel Companion, pp. 7–50
- Bellringer Option Transparencies: Selection Focus 1–21; Daily Language Practice 1–20
- Assessment Resources, Selection Assessment, pp. 37–66

Technology
- TeacherWorks Plus CD
- StudentWorks Plus CD
- Literature Launchers: Pre-Reading Videos DVD, Unit 1
- Literature Online
- Listening Library CD-ROM
- ExamView CD-ROM
- Skill Level Up! CD-ROM

Focus
Summary

Unit One is divided into two sections, Early Africa and Modern Africa. The year 1800 is set as the dividing line between the two eras. The introduction for Part 1 is on pages 4–15; the introduction for Part 2 is on pages 66–77.

Teach

Reading Strategy 1

Analyze Theme Ask: What is the meaning of this proverb? *(Love overcomes all obstacles.)* Have students research or create other proverbs or sayings that express a meaning similar to this Kikuyu proverb.

Text Element 2

Table of Contents Have students review the unit title, dates and the brief table of contents at the bottom of the page. **Ask:** What period does Unit One cover? *(from 3100 B.C. to the present)* **Ask:** Into what parts is Unit One divided? (Early Africa and Modern Africa)

Cultural History ☆

Kikuyus Living in the highlands of south-central Kenya, the Kikuyu people form the country's largest ethnic group. Having migrated from the northeast to their present homeland between the 1600s and 1800s, the Kikuyus now live by farming and raising livestock.

3

Teach

Reading Strategy | 1

Analyze Graphic Information Have students review the map. **Ask:** What role might the diverse geography of Africa have played in the cultures of the continent? *(Students may note that the huge desert areas may have had few inhabitants, and the large river systems may have been the major sites of human settlement.)*

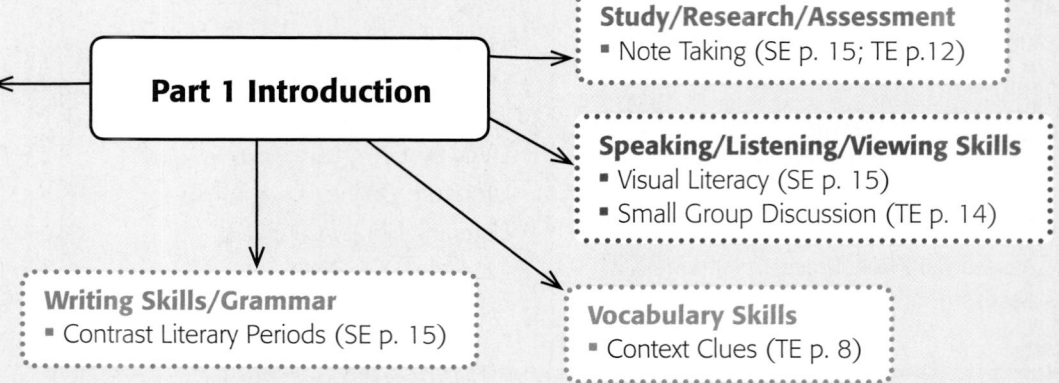

A Zebras on a savannah

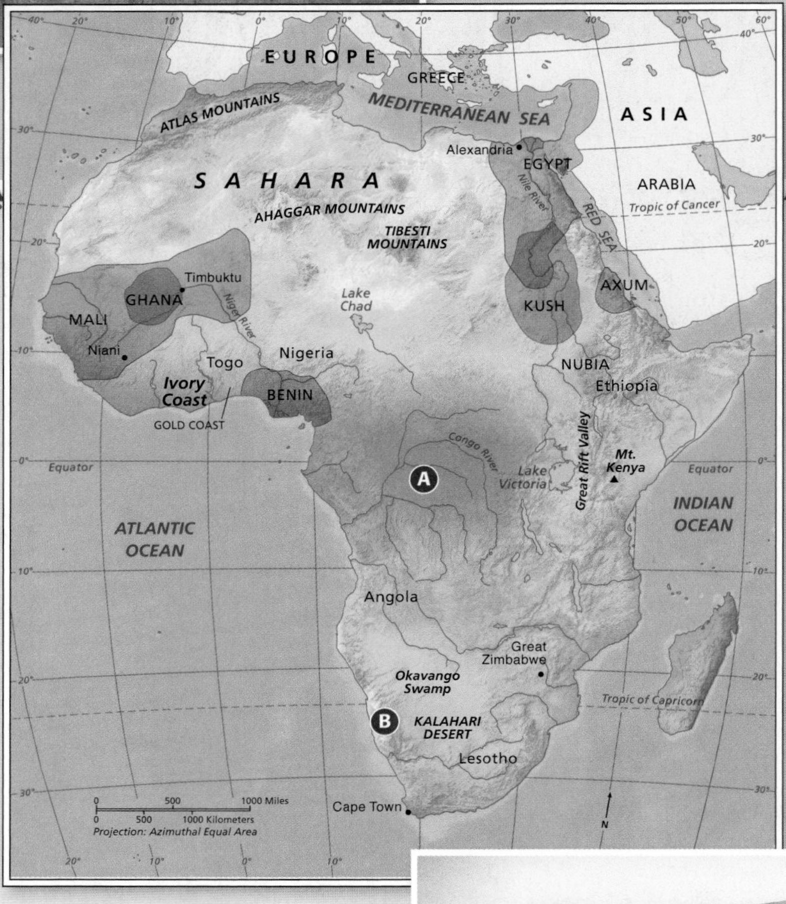

B Sossusvlei Dunes in Namib Desert

LOG ON ▶ **Literature** Online

Literature and Reading For more about the history and literature of this period, go to glencoe.com and enter the QuickPass code GLW6053u1.

4

Part Introduction Skills

Reading Skills
- Analyze Graphic Information (SE p. 7; TE pp. 4, 6, 7)
- Analyze Cause-and-Effect Relationships (SE p. 12)
- Make Generalizations (SE p. 13)
- Interpret (SE p. 14)
- Determine Main Idea (TE pp. 5, 8, 10)

Part 1 Introduction

Study/Research/Assessment
- Note Taking (SE p. 15; TE p.12)

Speaking/Listening/Viewing Skills
- Visual Literacy (SE p. 15)
- Small Group Discussion (TE p. 14)

Writing Skills/Grammar
- Contrast Literary Periods (SE p. 15)

Vocabulary Skills
- Context Clues (TE p. 8)

Early AFRICA
3100 B.C.—A.D. 1800

Male Allegorical Figure in 19th century military dress, possibly representing Gezo, the first ruler of Dahomey.

Being There

2 The continent of Africa is second only to Asia in size. As many as a thousand languages are spoken by different African ethnic groups, each of which has a distinct history, culture, and set of religious beliefs. Africa's earliest civilizations, Egypt and Kush, developed in the fertile Nile Valley in northeast Africa about 5,000 years ago. Between the eighth and the nineteenth centuries A.D., the trading states of Ghana, Mali, and Benin flourished in West Africa.

Looking Ahead

Ancient Egypt produced a rich written literature, from myths and hymns to love poetry. Across the Sahara in West Africa, oral storytellers known as griots preserved the literary traditions of heroes and kings. Throughout Africa, traditional village-based societies also created a wide variety of oral literature, including myths, folktales, poetry, and proverbs.

Keep the following questions in mind as you read:

▲ What were the most common types of ancient Egyptian literature?

▲ What roles did griots have in West African kingdoms such as Mali?

▲ What are the basic traits of the folklore figure known as the trickster?

5

Focus
Summary

This introduction gives an overview of the Nile Valley and West Africa before 1800. It discusses the civilization of ancient Egypt, the trading states of Ghana and Mali, the slave trade, and the traditional arts of Africa. Also covered are the function of writing in ancient Egyptian civilization, the characteristics of the oral cultures of sub-Saharan Africa, and the features of traditional African religious beliefs.

Teach

Reading Strategy **2**

Determine Main Idea Have students read the paragraph under Being There. **Ask:** What three basic points are being made about Africa, African culture, and African history? *(Africa is huge, is culturally complex, and has a long history.)*

ENGLISH LEARNERS Students may need help with key terms such as *continent, ethnic,* and *civilizations*.

Approaching Level
DIFFERENTIATED INSTRUCTION

Set a Purpose Point out to students that the questions at the bottom of page 5 are intended to help guide their reading of the Part 1 introduction and are specifically answered on pages 12, 13, and 14. Work with students to create other purpose-setting questions, such as the following:

▪ What were the most important features of ancient Egyptian civilization?

▪ How did oral tradition function in the societies of West Africa?

▪ What were the basic characteristics of traditional African religious beliefs?

Have them write down all these questions and answer them as they read the introduction to Part 1.

Teach

Reading Strategy | 1

Analyze Graphic Information Ask: Which literary work is more recent—the Egyptian *Book of the Dead* or the love poetry of the New Kingdom? *(love poetry)*

Reading Strategy | 2

Activate Prior Knowledge
Have students tell what they know about one African and one world event from this period. *(Students might mention African events such as the building of the Great Pyramid or the death of Cleopatra; world events such as the First Crusade or the Black Death.)*

[APPROACHING] Pair students and have the partners work together to find information about several events on the timeline.

View the Art ★

The Egyptian *Book of the Dead* was a collection of prayers and spells that was placed inside tombs to aid the souls of the deceased on their journey to the Afterlife.

For additional support for English Learners, see Unit 1 Teaching Resources Book, p. 19.

TIMELINE 3100 B.C.–A.D. 1800

AFRICAN LITERATURE

3000 B.C.

c. 3000
Earliest surviving Egyptian writing

16th century
Earliest texts of the Egyptian *Book of the Dead* appear ▼

1500 B.C.

c. 1350
Pharaoh Akhenaten composes hymns to the sun

c. 1300–1100
Love poetry is composed during Egypt's New Kingdom | 1 |

c. 300
Library of Alexandria, Egypt, is founded

Funerary mask of Tutankhamen

★

AFRICAN EVENTS | 2 |

3000 B.C.

c. 3100
Menes, the first pharaoh, unites Egypt

c. 2700
Egypt's Old Kingdom begins

c. 2540
Pharaoh Khufu builds Great Pyramid at Giza

c. 2200
Old Kingdom ends

c. 2050
Middle Kingdom begins

1652
Hyksos invade Egypt; Middle Kingdom ends

1550
New Kingdom begins

1500 B.C.

1450s–1426
Pharaoh Thutmose III expands Egyptian empire

c. 1085
New Kingdom ends

750
Kingdom of Kush conquers Egypt

30
Egyptian queen Cleopatra VII dies; Romans control Egypt

Hippopotamus from Thebes, Egypt

WORLD EVENTS

3000 B.C.

c. 3000
Mesopotamians develop cuneiform writing

c. 2500
Indus Valley civilization develops

c. 2334
Sargon creates a Mesopotamian empire

1792
Hammurabi takes power in Babylon

1500 B.C.

c. 1500
Aryans invade northern India

c. 509
Roman Republic is founded

221
Qin Shihuangdi becomes first Chinese emperor

27
Augustus becomes first Roman emperor ▼

LOG ON ▶ **Literature** Online

Literature and Reading To explore the Interactive Timeline, go to glencoe.com and enter QuickPass code GLW6053u1.

Reading Practice

Analyze Graphic Information
Remind students that a timeline is a chart that shows a sequence of events. Point out the three timelines on this chart. Then:

- Read the title of each timeline and explain the contents briefly.
- Show how events appear in time order, from left to right, with the earliest events on the far left.
- Show how events in a single time period, across all three categories of events, appear in columns.
- Check comprehension by asking questions about both sequential and contemporaneous events.
- Point out that when an exact date is not known for an event, *c.* or *circa* appears before the year.

A.D. 1

A Kaba-blon (shrine) of the Keita clan whose ancestor is the semi-mythical Sundiata.

c. 1210
Sundiata, the hero of the Mali epic, is born

1352
Arab traveler Ibn Battuta meets griots in Mali

A.D. 1500

1789 ▶
The Interesting Narrative of the Life of Olaudah Equiano is published

1799
Rosetta Stone is discovered

A.D. 1

c. 300
Camels are introduced into Africa

c. 500
Kingdom of Ghana emerges

641
Arabs conquer Egypt

c. 1100
Timbuktu is founded

c. 1240
Sundiata destroys Ghanaian city of Kumbi

c. 1450
City of Great Zimbabwe is abandoned

c. 1490 ▶
Islam spreads through sub-Saharan Africa

1493
Muhammad Ture seizes the Songhai Empire

A.D. 1500

1518
Spanish ship carries first boatload of slaves to the Americas

Mosque in Djenne, Mali.

c. 300 ▲
Classic Maya period begins in Mexico

476
Western Roman Empire falls

800 ▶
Charlemagne is crowned Holy Roman emperor

1066
Normans conquer England

A.D. 1500

1521
Spanish conquistador Hernán Cortés conquers Aztec Empire

1543
Nicolaus Copernicus publishes heliocentric theory

1789
French Revolution begins

Reading Check

Analyze Graphic Information How long was the Old Kingdom period of Egyptian history?

INTRODUCTION **7**

Approaching Level

DIFFERENTIATED INSTRUCTION

Connect to Personal Experience
Some students might need more help in grasping the concept of a timeline. Have them construct a personal timeline, divided into 24 hours, that charts how they spend a typical day. Have them key four or five ordinary activities (such as getting up, dressing, eating breakfast, and going to school) to the times when these events usually occur.

Advanced Learners/Pre-AP

DIFFERENTIATED INSTRUCTION

Research Have students select a particular period covered by the timeline (for example, A.D.1–1000) and research one additional event in the category of African literature, African history, or world history.

Teach

Reading Check

Answer: *The Old Kingdom period lasted about 500 years.*

Reading Strategy   **3**

Analyze Graphic Information Ask: What event occurred in the same year as the beginning of the French Revolution? *(the publishing of* The Interesting Narrative of the Life of Olaudah Equiano)

View the Art ★

The head of the emperor Charlemagne is surrounded with a halo, a symbol of holiness, in an image from a medieval prayer book. **Ask:** Why do you think Charlemagne is shown with a halo? *(to indicate divine approval of his reign)*

Learning Objectives
Analyzing graphic information. (SE)
Activating prior knowledge. (TE)
Analyzing art. (TE)

Teach

Reading Strategy **1**

Determine Main Idea

Ask: Why was the Nile River so important to the ancient Egyptians? *(The river provided a transportation route, and its floods deposited rich soil on the surrounding land.)*

Reading Strategy **2**

Identify Sequence

Ask: Into what periods is the history of ancient Egypt divided? *(Old Kingdom, Middle Kingdom, and New Kingdom)*

[**APPROACHING**] Point out to students that historical periods involve dates, so they should look for the dates in the paragraph to answer the question.

View the Art ★

This boat with sail and oars was painted on the wall of an Egyptian tomb. **Ask:** How did the Egyptians' style of painting relate to their hieroglyphic writing system? *(Both tend toward simplified depictions of real objects.)*

Learning Objectives

For pages 4–15

In studying this text, you will focus on the following objectives:

Literary Study: Analyzing literary periods.

Reading:
Evaluating historical influences.
Connecting to the literature.

Early AFRICA
3100 B.C.–A.D. 1800

Historical, Social, and Cultural Forces

The Gift of the Nile

The Nile River stretches 4,000 miles through Africa, flowing northward from south of the equator and emptying into the Mediterranean Sea. It is the longest river in the world. The ancient Egyptians called the Nile *Aur*, or "black," a reference to the rich soil left behind by the annual flooding of the river. The Nile was crucial to the formation of ancient Egyptian civilization; the soil left by the floods allowed the Egyptians to farm crops, while the river itself was used to transport people and merchandise. As ancient Greek historian Herodotus observed, Egypt is "the gift of the Nile." **1**

Egypt

The history of Egypt begins in about 3100 B.C., when Menes (mee′nēz) united Upper (southern)

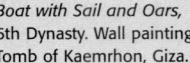
Boat with Sail and Oars, 6th Dynasty. Wall painting. Tomb of Kaemrhon, Giza. ★

Vocabulary Practice

Use Context Clues Remind students that they can determine the meaning of an unfamiliar word by examining the context—the words and phrases surrounding the word and text feature clues such as subheadings and artwork.

Ask: What context clue for *dynasty* is given in the paragraph under "Egypt"? *("family of rule")*

Ask students to identify another example of a context clue on page 9. *("papyrus, a paper made from the reeds that grew along the Nile")*

2 and Lower (northern) Egypt into a single kingdom. His reign began the first Egyptian dynasty, or family of rule, and the kings after him wore a double crown to mark the unification of their country. Modern historians have divided ancient Egyptian history into three major periods of stable rule, known as the Old Kingdom (2700–2200 B.C.), the Middle Kingdom (2050–1652 B.C.), and the New Kingdom (1550–1085 B.C.). Each of these periods is marked by unique rulers, historical events, and slightly varied cultural values. The periods between the kingdoms were marked by chaos and political instability.

Asante scorpion ring. African school. Gold. Ghana.

> "Hail to you, O Nile!
> Sprung from Earth,
> Come to nourish Egypt!"
>
> —Egyptian hymn to the Nile

Sacred Writing

Writing in Egypt emerged around 3100 B.C. The Greeks later called this earliest Egyptian writing hieroglyphics (hī′ ər ə glif′ iks), meaning "priest carvings" or "sacred writings." Hieroglyphics were used for formal inscriptions in stone. Later, a simplified version of the script was developed for business transactions, record keeping, and the general needs of daily life. This simplified script was written on papyrus (pə pī′ rəs), a paper made from the reeds that grew along the Nile. Most of the ancient Egyptian literature that exists was originally written on rolls of papyrus, which survived for thousands of years in the dry climate of Egypt.

Desert Caravans

While the Nile provided one way to traverse the Sahara desert, camel caravans provided an alternative means of transportation. About 1,700 years ago, Africans began using camels to carry people and goods across the desert. As a result, an extensive trade network developed between the people of North Africa and the kingdoms of the sub-Saharan region. Before the trade routes

began, people south of the desert lived in villages. The trade routes, however, gave rise to sizable towns, including the desert city of Timbuktu, which flourished as a center of learning as well as a commercial center.

Ghana and Mali

Trade across the Sahara gave rise to a series of West African empires, notably the powerful kingdoms of Ghana and Mali. Ghana, the first great trading empire in West Africa, emerged as early as A.D. 500. Ghana's wealth and power derived from its abundance of gold, which could be traded for salt and other products from North Africa. Ghana flourished for several hundred years until, weakened by various wars, it was defeated by Malian hero-king Sundiata (sōōn dyä′ tə) around 1240. Sundiata's victory solidified the Mali Empire, which flourished until the sixteenth century.

The Slave Trade

In 1518, a Spanish ship carried the first boatload of enslaved Africans directly from Africa to the Americas. During the next two centuries, the Atlantic trade in African slaves grew dramatically, reaching its peak in the 1700s, when more than six million Africans endured the Middle Passage, the brutal sea voyage from West Africa to the Americas. These slaves frequently died from malnourishment, epidemics, and mutinies while on the boats. Those who arrived in the Americas often died from diseases from which they had little or no immunity.

Teach

Reading Strategy	3

Analyze Cause-and-Effect Relationships Have students read and look for possible causes and effects on pages 8 and 9.

(Possible response: The expansion of caravan trade across the North African desert led to the development of large towns in sub-Saharan Africa.)

View the Art

Crafted by the Ashanti (or Asante) people of West Africa, this gold ring was shaped in the form of a scorpion. **Ask:** Why might an artisan give an ornament the shape of dangerous creature? *(Students may say that such an ornament might be regarded as a protection from danger.)*

English Learners

DIFFERENTIATED INSTRUCTION

Intermediate For students having difficulties with the Vocabulary Skills Practice on page 8, indicate the context of *papyrus* and ask them what the context indicates about the meaning of this word.

(The word paper *indicates that* papyrus *may have something to do with writing.)*

Learning Objectives
Determining main ideas. (TE)
Identifying sequence. (TE)
Understanding context clues. (TE)
Analyzing cause-and-effect relationships. (TE)
Analyzing art. (TE)

Teach

Analyze Cause-and-Effect Relationships Ask: How did geography influence the development of traditional African art? *(Materials available to the peoples of different regions influenced their choice of artistic forms.)*

View the Art ★

Played in Ethiopia and Eritrea, the five- or six-stringed lyre known as a *krar* can be either plucked or strummed.

Cultural History ☆

Call-and-Response African music has traditionally had conversational elements in that different instruments and voices seem to talk to one another, alternately entering and leaving the song. In call-and-response singing, a chorus repeats a lead singer's words in response. The call-and-response element of African tradition became part of African-American oral culture, influencing, for example, styles of preaching.

Visual Arts

Across the continent, early Africans created magnificent visual art for religious, ceremonial, and everyday uses. These artists, like many artists today, used the materials close at hand, such as specific metals or stones, to create their works. The geography of Africa is extremely varied, so traditional African arts were also very diverse. For example, people who lived near forests became accomplished wood-carvers, while those who worked with or near livestock tooled leather.

Music

After about A.D. 700, African people who lived north of the Sahara were influenced by the Arab traditions of music and dance. Musicians and dancers who lived south of the Sahara entertained at royal courts and performed at religious and ceremonial events. Musicians used a wide variety of instruments, including drums, harps, flutes, and xylophones, but the drum was usually considered most important. The West African "talking drum" was designed to change pitch to imitate speech patterns. Traditional African music is polyrhythmic; musicians and dancers created complex and interlocking rhythms by beating drums, striking bells, clapping hands, and stamping feet. ☆

Masked Dogon Funerary dancer at Bandiagara Escarpment, Mali.

◀ Lyre. African school. Wood, beadwork, leather. Horniman Museum, London.
★

> "We are the men of dance, whose feet regain vigor in striking the hard earth."
>
> —Léopold Sédar Senghor, from "Prayer to the Masks"

10 UNIT 1 EARLY AFRICA

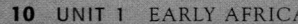

Reading Practice

Determine Main Idea and Supporting Details Remind students that a passage often contains one main idea and several details that support it. Note that the main idea of an individual paragraph is often expressed in a topic sentence, which may not always be the first sentence of the paragraph. Ask students to find and write down the topic sentences of the paragraphs headed "Visual Arts" and "Masked Dances" and list at least two details to support each topic sentence. Have partners compare the topic sentences and details they have identified.

Masked Dances

In West Africa and some parts of central Africa, masked dances were a major part of ceremonial life. Important ceremonial events included stages in the agricultural year, such as the first rains and harvesting; rights of passages marking birth, adulthood, marriage, and death; rituals of secret societies; and healing rituals. Masked dances were public, but only members of the masked dance societies were allowed to see the masks outside of performances and to observe dancers putting on their costumes. Dancers were accompanied by musicians and by singing and chanting that were sometimes done in a special language used only on that occasion.

Architecture

The ancient Egyptians were among the world's greatest architects. Egyptians used stone to create great, pillared temples as well as the famous pyramids. The West African kingdoms built great palaces that sometimes covered several acres and were decorated with statues and carvings. Muslim mosques were often built of sun-baked bricks, made according to local custom. In Ethiopia, the Coptic Christians produced churches carved into mountainsides, with interiors richly painted with biblical scenes. In southern Africa, the mysterious ruins called Great Zimbabwe are dominated by the Great Enclosure, an oval space surrounded by a massive wall.

PREVIEW **Big Ideas** of Early Africa

1 Writing and Immortality	**2** The Magic of Words	**3** Gods and Spirits
Ancient Egyptians highly valued the written word and were also deeply pre-occupied with the afterlife. The convergence of these cultural values gave rise to many works that celebrated the immortality of the gods, the deceased, and the written word itself. **See page 12**	Traditional African society is based on the clan and the village. The histories and cultural values of these social groups have been preserved in both oral and written literature. For example, in West Africa, professional storytellers known as griots serve as oral historians for their communities. **See page 13**	Traditional African religious beliefs are rich and diverse and include many gods, spirits, and tricksters. Trickster tales, which center on cunning, mischievous beings, are often told to reinforce morals about behavior and the nature of wisdom. **See page 14**

INTRODUCTION **11**

English Learners

DIFFERENTIATED INSTRUCTION

Advanced Break down *polyrhythmic* into prefix (*poly-*) + base word (*rhythm*) + suffix (*-ic*). Explain the *poly-* comes from a Greek word meaning "many." Offer other examples of words containing this prefix, such as *polychrome* and *polyglot*. In each case, give students the meaning of the root (*chrom* "color" and *glot* "tongue") and then ask what the complete word might mean.

Ask more advanced English learners to use each of these words with the prefix *poly-* in a sentence.

Teach

Reading Strategy 2

Draw Conclusions **Ask:** What conclusion can you draw about the importance of masks in the cultures of sub-Saharan Africa? *(The use of masks was of central importance in these cultures.)*

View the Art ★

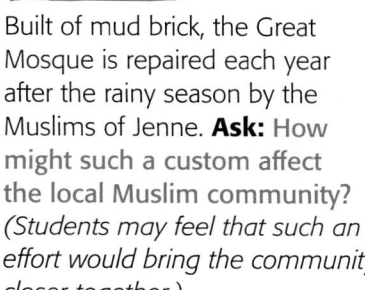

Built of mud brick, the Great Mosque is repaired each year after the rainy season by the Muslims of Jenne. **Ask:** How might such a custom affect the local Muslim community? *(Students may feel that such an effort would bring the community closer together.)*

Cultural History ☆

West African Palaces The palace of the king of Ashanti at Kumasi covered over five acres. The palace of the ruler of Benin is said to have been the size of an average European town. The palace of the emperor of Oyo may have extended over 640 acres. British soldiers destroyed the first two palace complexes during the colonial wars of the late 1800s.

Learning Objectives
Analyzing cause-and-effect relationships. (TE)
Determining main ideas and supporting details. (TE)
Analyzing art. (TE)

Teach

Reading Check

Answer: *Scribes enjoyed a privileged position because writing was a specialized skill that was essential to Egyptian society and government.*

Vocabulary	1

Context Clues Ask:

From the context, what is the meaning of the word *optimistic* in paragraph 1? *(tending to believe in a favorable outcome or result)*

ENGLISH LEARNERS Identify the context clues for *optimistic* and then ask students to indicate the word's probable meaning.

View the Art ★

In Egyptian mythology, the dead are reborn into the netherworld after they receive food and drink from the goddess Amentet. **Ask:** How did ancient Egyptians picture the existence of people after death? *(as very much like their earthly life)*

Big Idea 1
Writing and Immortality

The fertility of the Nile Valley provided the Egyptians with a dependable food supply, and the surrounding deserts and mountains usually protected them from invaders. These lucky circumstances gave the civilization of ancient Egypt an optimistic outlook on life.

Dead person drinking the waters at Amenti, west bank of the Nile. Chapter 59 of Book of the Dead. Ragab Papyrus Institute, Cairo. ★

A Timeless World

The ancient Egyptians believed that their circumstances were the result of blessings bestowed on them by their gods, and religion was a vital part of their daily lives. Among the greatest Egyptian gods were Osiris and his wife, Isis. Osiris was worshipped as the king of the dead, and the myth about his death (see pages 16–22) was the foundation of the Egyptians' elaborate beliefs about the afterlife.

About 1350 B.C., Egyptian ruler Amenhotep IV attempted to replace Egypt's numerous gods with a single deity named Aten, the god of the sun disk. The Aten represented immortality through his return each morning and his life-giving properties. The pharaoh renamed himself Akhenaten ("It is well with Aten") and made his religion mandatory in Egypt. Akhenaten created a new liturgy and even wrote hymns (see pages 24–29). His new religion did not last, however; after his death, Egyptians reverted to their old religious customs.

The Value of Learning

Scribes were masters of the art of hieroglyphics and also its teachers. Training to become a scribe took many years, and boys from the upper classes began school at the age of ten. Discipline was hard, but scribes enjoyed prominent status in society. The writings of the scribes allowed Egyptians to keep official documents and to record myths, songs, and poems. Hieroglyphics were also etched into tombs; the "The Great Hymn to the Aten" survives today because it was etched into the tomb of Akhenaten.

The Afterlife

The ancient Egyptians' optimism extended into the afterlife, which they conceived as a pleasurable continuation of their lives on earth. Ancient Egyptians made careful preparations for the life they expected to enjoy after death. The bodies of royal family members were preserved as mummies and placed in stone tombs. Their burial places contained images of all the things the dead people might need in the afterlife.

Reading Check

Analyze Cause-and-Effect Relationships Why do you think scribes enjoyed a privileged position in ancient Egypt?

Reading Practice

Take Notes To help students keep track of the ideas presented on page 12, have them make a concept map for each major heading. An example follows.

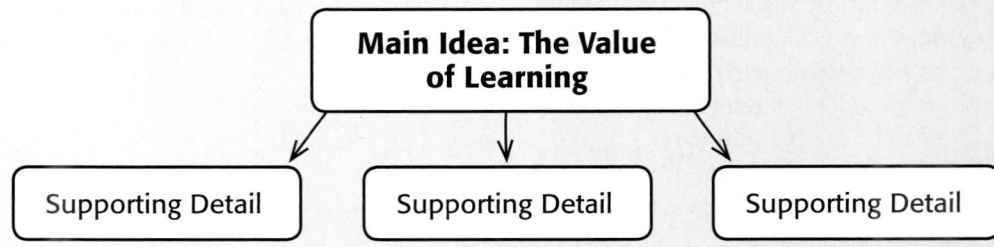

Main Idea: The Value of Learning

Supporting Detail | Supporting Detail | Supporting Detail

Big Idea 2
The Magic of Words

When we gather with our friends and families, we often entertain one another through storytelling, which helps us recount our shared past, share this past with others, and hear tales of earlier times. In this way, all of us participate in oral tradition, the passing on of stories, songs, sayings, and other material by word of mouth. In many early African societies, oral tradition served to define and preserve communities.

Family and Clan

Traditional African societies centered on small villages in the countryside. The people in these villages derived their sense of identity from their membership in an extended family and kinship group. The foundation of this group was the extended family, made of up parents, children, grandparents, and other family dependents. These extended families were in turn combined with larger communities, clans, or kinship groups whose members could all claim to be descended from a real or legendary common ancestor.

> *"Without us the names of kings would vanish into oblivion, we are the memory of mankind."*
>
> —Griot Djeli Mamoudou Kouyaté, from the *Sundiata, An Epic of Old Mali*

2 Oral Tradition and the Griot

Many stories in African literature have been passed on orally from one generation to another for thousands of years. African oral literature includes a variety of literary forms, including histories of ethnic and kinship groups, heroic legends, praise songs for chiefs and kings, trickster stories, animal fables, riddles, and proverbs. As in all oral literatures, the storyteller is free to change or elaborate on the story to suit local audiences. Oral literature has long served as a way to record the past, glorify current leaders, and teach morals and traditions to new generations.

In West Africa, professional oral storytellers called griots (grē′ōz) committed stories and family histories to memory and recited verses while playing a stringed instrument. Griots underwent special training from childhood to enable them to memorize the long, complex oral traditions of their communities. These storytellers were also oral historians who kept alive the past of their peoples. For example, generations of griots preserved much of what survives about the founder of the Mali Empire, Sundiata (see pages 58–64).

Memory Figure Sitting on a Stool. Akan Culture, Ghana. Terracotta. Private collection.

Reading Check
Make Generalizations What role did oral tradition have in early African societies?

English Learners
DIFFERENTIATED INSTRUCTION

Intermediate Point out that the verb *underwent* is a compound word formed from the prefix *under-* and the verb *go*. *Undergo* means "to experience" or "to suffer." The present tense of the verb is *undergo* or *undergoes*, the past tense is *underwent*, the present participle is *undergoing*, and the past participle is *undergone*. Point out that there are many verbs in English beginning with *under-*. In some cases, the meaning simply combines the meanings of the prefix and root, as in *underlie*, "to be located beneath." But more often there is an extended meaning, as, for example, in *underdress*, which means both "to wear too little clothing for the weather" and "to dress too informally for an occasion." Sometimes the meaning bears very little relation to the meanings of the components, as in *understand*, meaning "to grasp mentally."

Teach

Reading Check

Answer: *Oral tradition preserved the history and culture of early African societies.*

Reading Strategy | 2

Connect to Personal Experience Ask: What types of oral traditions are you familiar with from the social groups you belong to, such as your family, community, ethnic group, state or nation? *(Students will mention family sayings, jokes, anecdotes, counting-out rhymes, local legends, urban legends, ethnic folksongs and folklore, and other types of oral traditions.)*

APPROACHING Students may need help recalling examples of oral tradition. You might offer an example of a familiar counting-out rhyme or urban legend and ask students if they have ever heard it.

View the Art ★

Among the Ashanti people, stools—such as the one this figure is represented sitting on—are ritual objects rather than furniture.

Learning Objectives
Evaluating historical influences. (SE)
Using context clues. (TE)
Taking notes. (TE)
Connect to personal experience. (TE)

13

Teach

Reading Check

Answer: *Tricksters vividly and memorably expressed the unpredictable, chaotic elements of life.*

Reading Strategy   1

Make Generalizations

Ask: After reading this page, what generalizations can you make about traditional African religious beliefs? *(Students may say Africans traditionally believed that human events are affected by a variety of supernatural forces, including gods, spirits, and ancestors.)*

APPROACHING Ask students which of the subheadings show the most important elements of African religious beliefs. *("Gods" and "Ancestors"—note to students the importance of the use of the plurals.)*

View the Art

Crafted of wood, cowrie shells, and leather, this figure depicts Eshu, the chief Yoruba trickster god. **Ask:** What qualities are conveyed by this image? *(Students might feel that the figure conveys such qualities as energy, mystery, and humor.)*

Big Idea 3
Gods and Spirits

As we get older, we realize that many important life events are influenced by random occurrences, comic situations, and other circumstances beyond our control. Traditional African beliefs attributed these puzzling events to gods, ancestors, or mischievous spirits known as tricksters.

Gods

Across early Africa, there were hundreds of religious systems, each with its own gods, shrines, and ceremonies. Most African societies, however, shared some common religious ideas. One of these was a belief in a single creator god, such as the Yoruban god Olorun.

One way to communicate with the gods was through rituals, which were usually carried out by a special class of people called diviners. Diviners were believed to have the power to foretell events, typically by working with supernatural forces. Their ability to contact the gods was thought to guarantee a bountiful harvest or to protect the interests of the community or the kingdom.

Ancestors

Ancestors also played a key role in many early African religions. Each kinship group could trace itself back to a founding ancestor or group of ancestors. These forebears were thought to be closer to the gods, and ritual ceremonies were held in their honor. Their descendants believed the ancestors had the power to influence their lives, for good and for bad; many songs, myths, and stories reflect this belief.

The Trickster

Tricksters, common figures in African and Native American mythologies, are beings who are alternately cunning and foolish, playful and cruel, funny and brutal. They sometimes take animal forms and sometimes appear as humans. One

famous African trickster is Anansi the Spider (also spelled Ananse, see pages 39–43), whose stories are told by the Ashanti people of West Africa. The Ashanti, in fact, call all of their folktales *Anansesem*—"Spider stories"—even if Anansi does not appear in them. Another well-known West African trickster is Edju (also spelled Eshu, see pages 52–55), one of the Orishas, the gods of the Yoruba people. As he observes of himself, "Sowing dissension is my chief delight."

> *"Do they want sacrifice,*
> *do they want blood?*
> *Are they far,*
> *are they near?"*
>
> —"The Ancestors," traditional song of the
> Khoikhoi people of South Africa

Eshu figure, Yoruba Culture, Nigeria. Wood, cowries, and leather. Private collection.

★

Reading Check

Interpret Why do you think tricksters were popular characters in African oral literature?

Speaking Practice

SMALL GROUP **Conduct a Discussion** Point out to students that the trickster archetype, embodied in African figures such as Edju and Anansi, is one of the most universal figures in world mythology and folklore. The trickster also remains part of modern popular culture, in cartoon characters such as Bugs Bunny and Bart Simpson, for example. Have student volunteers hold a small group discussion exploring such questions as what the

trickster archetype represents in human nature and why this figure has remained so popular. Reserve time for the class to ask questions of the discussion group.

Wrap-Up

Legacy of the Period

The civilization of ancient Egypt, which developed at the crossroads of Asia, Africa, and Europe, had a profound influence on other cultures throughout these regions. For example, a simplified form of hieroglyphics contributed to the later development of the Phoenician alphabet, which is the basis for all modern alphabets. Egyptian sculpture deeply influenced the development of classical Greek sculpture.

The horrific slave trade across the Atlantic resulted in misery, human degradation, and the deaths of millions of people. One of its unforeseen results, however, was the spreading of African cultures to the Americas and other parts of the world.

Cultural and Literary Links

▲ The French expedition to Egypt under Napoleon from 1798 to 1801 stimulated a European interest in ancient Egyptian civilization. The results of this fascination can be seen in many works of literature and music, including Percy Shelley's

Chasuble, 1950-1952. Henri Matisse. Collezione d'Arte Religiosa Moderna, Vatican Museums, Vatican State. © ARS, NY.

poem "Ozymandias" and the opera *Aïda* by Italian composer Giuseppe Verdi.

▲ Stories about African tricksters traveled to the Americas with enslaved Africans. Among the Gullah people of the Sea Islands of South Carolina and Georgia, the name *Anansi* became "Aunt Nancy."

▲ Traditional African sculpture influenced the works of Pablo Picasso and Henri Matisse.

 Literature Online

Unit Resources For additional skills practice, go to glencoe.com and enter QuickPass code GLW6053u1.

Activities

 Use what you have learned about the region to do one of these activities.

1. **Follow Up** Go back to the Looking Ahead on page 5 and answer the questions.

2. **Contrast Literary Periods** The belief that spirits and ancestors influence everyday events is present not only in Africa, but in Central and South America as well. A literary movement that reflects this belief is **magic realism**. Research magic realism and write a short essay comparing and contrasting the ideas in the Gods and Spirits Big Idea with the mythical elements of magic realism.

3. **Build Visual Literacy** Collect and display examples of American popular culture (such as movies, advertising, comic books, and video

games) that use elements drawn from the civilization of ancient Egypt. Discuss with your classmates what common assumptions these materials reveal about ancient Egypt.

4. **Take Notes** You might try using this graphic organizer to keep track of the three Big Ideas in this part.

 THREE-TAB BOOK

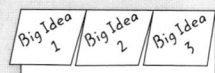

Advanced Learners/Pre-AP

DIFFERENTIATED INSTRUCTION

Research Probably the most distinctive feature of traditional African art is the mask. The existence of ancient rock paintings of masked figures shows that this artistic tradition is very old, and despite the influence of the modern world, mask-making and masked dancing continue to be practiced in Africa today. The art of African masks has also fascinated many important modern artists, including Pablo

Picasso and Henri Matisse. Have interested students review the material about masks in this introduction, conduct further research, and deliver a report on African masks in the modern world, presenting their continuing presence in Africa itself and their influence on the world of art.

Assess

Activities

1. **Follow Up** Students should answer questions with specific facts from the text.

2. **Contrast Literary Periods** Students should draw clear comparisons and contrasts between African beliefs and magic realism. The essays should reflect an understanding of African and Latin American cultures.

3. **Build Visual Literacy** Students may discuss films such as *Stargate* and *The Mummy*, which assume that the Egyptian gods were real. For example, in *The Mummy*, the gods' power remains active in modern times.

4. **Take Notes** Students' Foldables should be well organized, and their notes should have specific details about each Big Idea.

 **Study Organizer**

Have students make and label the bound book. Then have them use it to keep track of literary elements.

Focus

Bellringer Options

Daily Language Practice Transparency 2

Or write on the board: In the beginning . . .

Ask: Why do you think that stories about origins—of the Earth, of human beings, of good and evil—are found in every culture? Elicit students' opinions about why they think origin stories are such a universal feature of world mythology.

View the Art ★

This sculpture, created about 860 B.C., shows Horus, Osiris, and Isis. Horus was the son of Osiris and Isis. The materials for the sculpture include lapis lazuli, a deep blue gemstone found in Afghanistan. **Say:** The figure shown at the left is Horus.

Ask: What is unusual about his face? *(It looks like a bird's face.)* Explain that Horus, a sky god, was depicted as having a hawk's head.

Selection Skills

Before You Read

Egypt

Osiris and Isis

The ancient Egyptians had no word for *religion*. Religious ideas were so deeply interweaved into their lives and their view of the world that *religion* could not be isolated as its own term. The Egyptians worshiped many gods, most of them associated with heavenly bodies and natural forces. Among the most important of the Egyptian gods was Osiris (ō sī´ris), who ruled over the dead.

Egyptian Mythology One of the most famous Egyptian myths tells of the death and resurrection of Osiris. In the myth, Osiris is killed by his evil brother Sêth, who cuts his body into fourteen parts and scatters them. Isis (ī´sis), Osiris's wife, finds and gathers the pieces and brings her husband back to life through her powerful magic. The resurrected Osiris becomes the ruler of the dead and a symbol of eternal resurrection for the Egyptians. By identifying with Osiris, people could hope to gain new life in the afterworld, as the god had done.

The Book of the Dead The ancient Egyptians believed that every deceased soul had to appear before Osiris to be judged in the Hall of the Two Truths. To reach the hall, a soul (which Egyptians called a *ba* [bä]) had to make a dangerous journey through an underworld filled with monsters. The Egyptians placed a collection of prayers and magic spells in tombs to protect souls from these creatures. The final form of these writings, which appeared in the New Kingdom, was known as *The Book of Going Forth by Day.* An Egyptologist renamed it *The Book of the Dead* in 1842.

During judgment, the soul had to recite one of the most important parts of *The Book of the Dead,* called the "Negative Confession," or "Declaration of Innocence." This confession listed misdeeds that the soul claimed it had not committed in life. Afterward, the deceased person's heart was weighed on a scale against a feather that stood for truth. If the heart was weighed down by sin, it would be heavier than the feather and would tip the scale. The soul would then be devoured by Ammet, a monster with the head of a crocodile, the foreparts of a lion, and the hind parts of a hippopotamus. If the scale balanced, then the soul was led before Osiris, who accepted it into the afterlife.

> *"Hail to you, Great God,*
> *Lord of the Two Truths!*
> *I have come to you, my Lord,*
> *I was brought to see your beauty."*
>
> —from *The Book of the Dead*

The family of Osiris, 22nd dynasty. Gold, lapis lazuli, and red glass. Louvre, Paris. ★

Literary Elements
- Archetype (SE pp. 17, 19, 21, 22)

Osiris and Isis

Speaking/Listening/Viewing Skills
- Oral Interpretation (TE p. 18)

Reading Skills
- Identify Genre (SE pp. 17, 18, 20, 22)
- Analyze Parallelism (TE p. 20)

Vocabulary Skills
- Usage (SE p. 22)
- Creative Paragraphs (TE p. 17)

Writing Skills/Grammar
- Movie Scene (SE p. 22)

Literature and Reading Preview

Connect to the Myth

Have you ever had to sacrifice something to help someone in need? Freewrite for a few minutes about what this person required and why you decided to make that sacrifice.

Build Background

The Egyptians believed that humans had both a physical body and a spiritual body. This spiritual body, or life force, was called the *ka* (kä) and was distinct from the *ba*, or soul. They believed that if the physical body was preserved after death and the tomb furnished with the various objects of daily life, the *ka* could return.

Set Purposes for Reading

Big Idea **Writing and Immortality**

For the ancient Egyptians, magical writings could be the key to immortality. As you read "Osiris and Isis," ask yourself, How might writings such as this myth have influenced the Egyptians' understanding of immortality?

Literary Element **Archetype**

An **archetype** (ar′kə tīp′) is a symbol, an image, or a story pattern that recurs in literature and evokes strong responses, often based on subconscious memory. An ancient divine ruler, such as Osiris, who taught his people essential skills is an example of the archetype of the cultural hero. As you read "Osiris and Isis," ask yourself, What archetype does Sêth represent?

Reading Strategy **Identify Genre**

A **genre** is a category or a type of literature. Examples of genres include poetry, drama, fiction, and nonfiction. Each genre has specific characteristics. As you read this Egyptian myth, ask yourself, What details identify this as a myth?

Tip: **List Genre Characteristics** Create a chart like the one below, filling in details from "Osiris and Isis" that correspond to the characteristics of the myth genre listed on the left.

Genre Characteristics	Details from "Osiris and Isis"
Gods as characters Good and evil brothers Creation stories Origins of culture Quests	Osiris, Isis, Sêth, and other Egyptian gods

---

Learning Objectives

For pages 16–22

In studying this text, you will focus on the following objectives:

Literary Study: Analyzing archetype.

Reading: Identifying genre.

Writing: Writing a movie scene.

Vocabulary

banquet (bang′kwit) *n.* an elaborate, ceremonial meal; p. 19 *At the end of its successful season, the basketball team held a victory banquet.*

diversified (di vur′sə fīd) *adj.* varied; p. 19 *Because of immigration, the city had a diversified population.*

splendid (splen′did) *adj.* grand; magnificent; p. 19 *The new production of Aïda featured splendid Egyptian costumes.*

lament (lə ment′) *v.* to mourn or express grief for; p. 19 *The whole family lamented the untimely death of their young cousin.*

Tip: **Word Usage** When you encounter a new word, it might help you to answer a specific question about the word. For example, In what ways is a **banquet** a lavish event?

Advanced Learners/Pre-AP

DIFFERENTIATED INSTRUCTION

Deliver an Oral Presentation Remind students that Osiris, who according the Egyptian myth taught human beings how to raise food and practice various crafts, is an example of the mythological figure known as the *cultural hero* (or *culture hero*). Have interested students research some of the cultural heroes listed below and deliver an oral presentation for the class describing (1) the features these mythological figures have in common and (2) the specific characteristics of cultural heroes from different mythologies.

- Quetzalcoatl (Mesoamerican)
- Prometheus (Greek)
- Huangdi (Chinese)
- Maui (Polynesian)
- Raven (Northwest Coast)
- Anansi (Ashanti)

Before You Read

Focus

Summary

The Egyptian god Osiris; his wife, Isis; and his evil brother, Sêth, are among the divine children of the Earth and the Sky. Under the rule of Osiris, human beings experience a golden age without death or violence. Continually trying to destroy Osiris, Sêth tricks his brother into getting into a large chest, which Sêth throws into a river that carries it to the sea. Isis finds the chest that holds Osiris and restores him to life. Sêth again tries to destroy his brother by tearing his body in pieces and scattering them. Once again Isis brings Osiris back to life, but this time he lives on in the Underworld as the Judge of the Dead.

 For summaries in languages other than English, see Unit 1 Teaching Resources Book, pp. 20–25.

Teach

Vocabulary

Creative Paragraphs Divide the class into several teams and have the members of each team work together to produce a paragraph that uses all four vocabulary words creatively. When each team has presented its paragraph to the rest of the class, have the class vote on which group's paragraph displays the most creative—and correct—use of the vocabulary words.

 For additional vocabulary practice, see Unit 1 Teaching Resources Book, p. 29.

Teach

Reading Strategy | 1

Identify Genre **Answer:**
Students might recognize this as an example of a creation story.

📁 For additional practice using the reading skill or strategy, see Unit 1 Teaching Resources Book, p. 27.

 View the Art ★

This image of Osiris (left) as the Judge of the Dead in the Underworld comes from the Egyptian *Book of the Dead,* a collection of prayers and spells designed to protect the souls of the dead. In this copy, which dates from about 1000 B.C., the soul of a deceased person named Padiamenet, who had been the head baker on an estate, is shown burning incense to Osiris.

Ask: What does Padiamenet's status as a mere baker—rather than a noble or a priest—suggest about ancient Egyptian views concerning salvation in the afterlife? *(It suggests that the ancient Egyptians, at least by the time this copy of the* Book of the Dead *was created, had come to believe that salvation was available to ordinary Egyptians.)*

 For an audio recording of this selection, use Listening Library Audio CD-ROM.

Readability Scores

Dale-Chall: 6.4
DRP: 57
Lexile: 900

18

OSIRIS & ISIS

Retold by
Padraic Colum

Papyrus from the Book of the Dead of Pediamenet, c. 1000 BC. British Museum, London. ★

When Osiris reigned death was not in the land. Arms were not in men's hands; there were not any wars. From end to end of the land music sounded; men and women spoke so sweetly and out of such depth of feeling that all they said was oratory and poetry.

Osiris taught men and women wisdom and he taught them all the arts. He it was who first planted the vine; he it was who showed men how and when to sow grain, how to plant and tend the fruit-trees; he caused them to rejoice in the flowers also. Osiris made laws for men so that they were able to live together in harmony; he gave them knowledge of the Gods, and he showed them how the Gods might be honored.

And this was what he taught them concerning the Gods: In the beginning was the formless abyss, Nuu. From Nuu came Rê, the Sun. Rê was the first and he was the most divine of all beings. Rê created all forms. From his thought came Shu and Tefênet, the Upper and the Lower Air. From Shu and Tefênet came Qêb and Nut, the Earth and the Sky. The Earth and the Sky had been separated, the one from the other, but once they had been joined together. From the eye of Rê, made out of the essence that is in that eye, came the first man and the first woman.

And from Qêb, the Father, and Nut, the Mother, Osiris was born. When he was born a voice came into the world, crying, "Behold, the Lord of all things is born!"

And with Osiris was born Isis, his sister. Afterwards was born Thout,[1] the Wise One. Then there was born Nephthys. And, last, there was born Sêth. And Sêth tore a hole in his mother's side—Sêth the Violent One. Now Osiris and Isis loved each other as husband and wife, and together they reigned over the land. Thout was with them, and he taught men the arts of

1 Identify Genre *What type of myth does this passage illustrate?*

1. *Thout* (also called *Thoth*) was the Egyptian god of wisdom.

18 UNIT 1 EARLY AFRICA

Speaking Practice

Present an Oral Interpretation Have several students each briefly rehearse and then present for the class individual oral interpretations of the first paragraphs of this retelling of the myth of Osiris and Isis. Remind the students to keep the following guidelines for speaking in mind:

- Vary the volume of your voice as needed but speak loudly enough that everyone can hear you.
- Speak clearly, enunciating all the words.

- Let the punctuation in the passage guide your pacing. Pause briefly for semicolons and slightly longer for periods.
- Use your voice to stress important words and ideas.
- When each student has finished his or her presentation, ask the rest of the class to provide polite, constructive feedback on these oral interpretations.

writing and of reckoning. Nephthys went with Sêth and was his wife, and Sêth's abode was in the desert.

Sêth, in his desert, was angered against Osiris, for everywhere green things that Sêth hated were growing over the land—vine, and grain, and the flowers. Many times Sêth tried to destroy his brother Osiris, but always his plots were baffled by the watchful care of Isis. One day he took the measurement of Osiris's body—he took the measurement from his shadow—and he made a chest that was the exact size of Osiris.

Soon, at the time before the season of drought, Sêth gave a **banquet,** and to that banquet he invited all the children of Earth and the Sky. To that banquet came Thout, the Wise One, and Nephthys, the wife of Sêth, and Sêth himself, and Isis, and Osiris. And where they sat at banquet they could see the chest that Sêth had made—the chest made of fragrant and **diversified** woods. All admired that chest. Then Sêth, as though he would have them enter into a game, told all of them that he would give the chest to the one whose body fitted most closely in it. The children of Qêb and Nut went and laid themselves in the chest that Sêth had made: Sêth went and laid himself in it, Nephthys went and laid herself in it, Thout went and laid himself in it, Isis went and laid herself in it. All were short; none, laid in the chest, but left a space above his or her head.

Then Osiris took the crown off his head and laid himself in the chest. His form filled it in its length and its breadth. Isis

and Nephthys and Thout stood above where he lay, looking down upon Osiris, so resplendent of face, so perfect of limb, and congratulating him upon coming into possession of the **splendid** chest that Sêth had made. Sêth was not beside the chest then. He shouted, and his attendants to the number of seventy-two came into the banqueting hall. They placed the heavy cover upon the chest; they hammered nails into it; they soldered it all over with melted lead. Nor could Isis, nor Thout, nor Nephthys break through the circle that Sêth's attendants made around the chest. And they, having nailed the cover down, and having soldered it, took up the sealed chest, and, with Sêth going before them, they ran with it out of the hall.

Isis and Nephthys and Thout ran after those who bore the chest. But the night was dark, and these three children of Qêb and Nut were separated, one from the other, and from Sêth and his crew. And these came to where the river was, and they flung the sealed chest into the river. Isis, and Thout, and Nephthys, following the tracks that Sêth and his crew had made, came to the riverbank when it was daylight, but by that time the current of the river had brought the chest out into the sea.

Isis followed along the bank of the river, **lamenting** for Osiris. She came to the sea, and she crossed over it, but she did not know where to go to seek for the body of Osiris. She wandered through the world, and where she went bands of children went with her, and they helped her in her search.

---

2 Archetype *What character archetype does Sêth represent in this passage?*

Vocabulary

banquet (bang′kwit) *n.* an elaborate, ceremonial meal
diversified (di vur′sə fīd) *adj.* varied

Archetype *What archetypal journey is Isis undertaking here?* **3**

Vocabulary

splendid (splen′did) *adj.* grand; magnificent
lament (lə ment′) *v.* to mourn or express grief for

OSIRIS AND ISIS **19**

Literary Element	2

Archetype **Answer:** *This passage shows that Sêth represents the archetype of the jealous and hateful brother.*

Literary Element	3

Archetype **Answer:** *Isis is undertaking a quest.*
ADVANCED Ask students about other quest stories they are familiar with. *(Students may mention the search for the Holy Grail, the* Aeneid, *or* Jason and the Argonauts)

Cultural History ☆

Worship of Isis After the ancient Greeks and Romans came into contact with Egypt, the worship of the Egyptian goddess Isis began to spread throughout the Mediterranean region. The cult of Isis became very popular in ancient Rome, competing with early Christianity. Some scholars believe that images of Isis with her son Horus may have influenced early Christian depictions of the Virgin Mary and the infant Jesus.

English Learners

DIFFERENTIATED INSTRUCTION

Advanced Explain to students that a quest refers to a search. This search, which often involves making a difficult journey and overcoming obstacles, is in pursuit of something that the person or persons going on the quest regard as very precious or valuable. Ask English learners what word(s) in their native languages would describe such a search.

For more advanced English learners, ask students to describe stories from either the literature or the oral tradition of their homelands that involve quests.

Learning Objectives
Identifying genre. (SE)
Analyzing archetype. (SE)
Presenting an oral interpretation. (TE)

Teach

Reading Strategy | 1

Identify Genre Answer:
This passage reflects the supernatural use of fire, an element present in many myths; for example, it is used in the myth of Achilles' heel.

View the Art ★

Answer: *The significance may be that the headdress shows that Isis retained power over Sêth, even after he killed Osiris. Although she mourns her husband, her power and dedication ultimately allow her to restore his body.*

Cultural History ☆

Byblos to Bible The ancient seaport of Byblos, which was located on the Mediterranean Sea about 20 miles north of present-day Beirut, Lebanon, was a center for trade in Egyptian papyrus. The English word *bible*, meaning the Jewish and Christian scriptures once written on papyrus, has its origin in the name of this port.

The Goddess Isis lamenting the death of her husband Osiris. Painted wood. British Museum, London.

View the Art Isis was often depicted wearing the hieroglyphic sign for "throne" on her head, as she does in this sculpture. What might be the significance of her wearing this headdress as she mourns Osiris? ★

The chest that held the body of Osiris had drifted in the sea. A flood had cast it upon the land. It had lain in a thicket of young trees. A tree, growing, had lifted it up. The branches of the tree wrapped themselves around it; the bark of the tree spread itself around it; at last the tree grew there, covering the chest with its bark.

☆ The land in which this happened was Byblos.[2] The king and queen of the city, Melquart and Astarte, heard of the wonderful tree, the branches and bark of which gave forth a fragrance. The king had the tree cut down; its branches were trimmed off, and the tree was set up as a column in the king's house. And then Isis, coming to Byblos, was told of the wonderful tree that grew by the sea. She was told of it by a band of children who came to her. She came to the place: she found that the tree had been cut down and that its trunk was now set up as a column in the king's house.

She knew from what she heard about the wonderful fragrance that was in the trunk and branches of the tree that the chest she was seeking was within it. She stayed beside where the tree had been. Many who came to that place saw the queenly figure that, day and night, stood near where the wonderful tree had been. But none who came near was spoken to by her. Then the queen, having heard about the stranger who stood there, came to her. When she came near, Isis put her hand upon her head, and thereupon a fragrance went from Isis and filled the body of the queen.

The queen would have this majestical stranger go with her to her house. Isis went. She nursed the queen's child in the hall in which stood the column that had closed in it the chest which she sought.

She nourished the queen's child by placing her finger in its mouth. At night she would strip wood from the column that had grown as a tree, and throw the wood upon the fire. And in this fire she would lay the queen's child. The fire did not injure it at all; it burned softly around the child. Then Isis, in the form of a swallow, would fly around the column, lamenting.

One night the queen came into the hall where her child was being nursed. She saw no nurse there; she saw her child lying in the fire. She snatched the child up, crying out. Then Isis spoke to the queen from the column on which, in the form of a swallow, she perched. She told the queen that the child would have gained immortality had it been suffered to lie for a night and another

---

2. *Byblos* was a city in the ancient country of Phoenicia, located where Lebanon and Syria are today.

Identify Genre *What mythic element does this passage reflect?* | 1

Reading Practice

Analyze Parallelism Point out to students that **parallelism** is the use of a series of words, phrases, or sentences that have a similar structure. Parallelism is used to emphasize the relationship between ideas. Write this example on the board: "He it was who first planted the vine; he it was who showed men and women how and when to sow grain."

Ask: What are the parallel elements here? *("He it was who")*

Ask: What idea does this use of parallelism emphasize? *(the importance of Osiris and his contributions to humankind)*

Have students review the last few paragraphs of the story to find other examples of parallelism and to identify the ideas they emphasize.

night longer within the fire made from the wood of the column. Now it would be long-lived, but not immortal. And she revealed her own divinity to the queen, and claimed the column that had been made from the wonderful tree.

The king had the column taken down; it was split open, and the chest which Isis had sought for so long and with so many lamentations was within it. Isis wrapped the chest in linen, and it was carried for her out of the king's house. And then a ship was given to her, and on that ship, Isis, never stirring from beside the chest, sailed back to Egypt.

And coming into Egypt she opened the chest, and took the body of her lord and husband out of it. She breathed into his mouth, and, with the motion of her wings (for Isis, being divine, could assume wings), she brought life back to Osiris. And there,

Visual Vocabulary
Gazelles are antelopes that live in Africa and southwest Asia.

away from men and from all the children of Qêb and Nut, Osiris and Isis lived together.

But one night Sêth, as he was hunting gazelles by moonlight, came upon Osiris and Isis sleeping. Fiercely he fell upon his brother; he tore his body into fourteen pieces. Then, taking the pieces that were the body of Osiris, he scattered them over the land.

Death had come into the land from the time Osiris had been closed in the chest through the cunning of Sêth; war was in the land; men always had arms in their hands. No longer did music sound, no longer did men and women talk sweetly and out of the depths of their feelings. Less and less did

grain, and fruit trees, and the vine flourish. The green places everywhere were giving way to the desert. Sêth was triumphant; Thout and Nephthys cowered before him.

And all the beauty and all the abundance that had come from Rê would be destroyed if the pieces that had been the body of Osiris were not brought together once more. So Isis sought for them, and Nephthys, her sister, helped her in her seeking. Isis, in a boat that was made of reeds, floated over the marshes, seeking for the pieces. One, and then another, and then another was found. At last she had all the pieces of his torn body. She laid them together on a floating island, and reformed them. And as the body of Osiris was formed once more, the wars that men were waging died down; peace came; grain, and the vine, and the fruit trees grew once more.

And a voice came to Isis and told her that Osiris lived again, but that he lived in the Underworld where he was now the Judge of the Dead, and that through the justice that he meted out, men and women had life immortal. And a child of Osiris was born to Isis: Horus[3] he was named. Nephthys and the wise Thout guarded him on the floating island where he was born. Horus grew up, and he strove against the evil power of Sêth. In battle he overcame him, and in bonds he brought the evil Sêth, the destroyer of his father, before Isis, his mother. Isis would not have Sêth slain: still he lives, but now he is of the lesser Gods, and his power for evil is not so great as it was in the time before Horus grew to be the avenger of his father. ◥

---

3. *Horus* was a falcon-headed Egyptian sky god who succeeded his father Osiris as ruler of Egypt.

Writing and Immortality *Why do you think the Egyptians made Osiris the Judge of the Dead?* **3**

Archetype *In what way is this battle archetypal?* **4**

OSIRIS AND ISIS **21**

Teach

Literary Element 2

Plot **Ask:** What functions does the episode of Isis in Byblos serve? *(This episode explains both how Isis recovers the body of Osiris and how she reveals her magic power.)*

Big Idea 3

Writing and Immortality
Answer: *The Egyptians identified Osiris with ideal kingship, as well as with death and resurrection because he died and came back to life.*

Literary Element 4

Archetype **Answer:** *This battle represents an archetypal revenge story having to do with avenging a loved one's death.*

Progress Check

Can students identify a literary archetype?

If No → See Unit 1 Teaching Resources Book, p. 26.

Approaching Level

DIFFERENTIATED INSTRUCTION

Outline Outline for students the order of narrative elements from one of the principal episodes of the myth of Osiris and Isis, such as Sêth's trickery:

- Sêth measures Osiris' shadow
- Sêth creates chest to fit Osiris
- Sêth holds banquet
- Sêth offers chest to guest whom it fits
- Guests get in chest; no one fits

- Osiris gets into chest, which fits
- Sêth's servants seal Osiris in chest
- Sêth's servants throw chest into river

Have students use this outline as the basis for an oral retelling of this episode. Encourage them to restate the events in their own words. An alternative for students who are visual learners would be to use the outline as the basis for storyboards presenting the episode.

Learning Objectives
Identifying genre. (SE)
Analyzing archetype. (SE)
Analyzing parallelism. (TE)
Analyzing plot. (TE)

After You Read

Assess

1. Answers will vary. Sêth's murder of Osiris may recall Loki's murder of the good god Balder in Norse mythology. Isis's search for Osiris may recall the Greek goddess Demeter's search for her daughter Persephone.

2. (a) Sêth seals Osiris in a box. (b) Sêth is cunning and manipulative.

3. (a) Sêth's rule brings discord and death. (b) These details highlight how peaceful and happy Egypt was under Osiris.

4. (a) She places the child in a fire to make it immortal. (b) Isis is a powerful and compassionate magician.

5. (a) Grain, trees, and vines grow once again. (b) Osiris represented fertility.

6. (a) Osiris is king, then victim, and finally ruler of the dead; Sêth is desert god, then villain; Isis is wife, then savior. (b) Students may feel that Isis is the strongest because she has magical powers.

7. Answers will vary.

8. It offered the possibility of immortality.

9. Students may mention comic book superheroes or fictional heroes such as Peter Pan or King Arthur. These stories may remain popular because they depict courage in the face of adversity and also offer escape.

Literary Element

1. Unrelenting anger, a desire for power, cunning, and cruelty are all archetypal characteristics of villains.

2. Answers will vary. Students should support their comparison with relevant and precise details from the text.

Reading Strategy

1. The myth explains the origin of death.

2. The myth explains that Osiris taught farming and laws to humans and that writing and mathematics began with Thout (or Thoth).

⚡ Writing

Students' scripts should include appropriate dialogue and imaginative production details.

Vocabulary

1. Choices should reflect a lavish meal.

2. Pro: becoming well rounded; con: lack of focus.

3. Details should show magnificence.

4. Activities should reflect sadness.

After You Read

Respond and Think Critically

Respond and Interpret

1. What details in "Osiris and Isis" remind you of other myths and legends you have read?

2. (a) How does Sêth trick Osiris? (b) What do Sêth's actions convey about his character?

3. (a) How does Sêth's rule affect Egyptian civilization? (b) Why might details about Sêth's rule be included in the myth?

4. (a) What does Isis do with the child of Queen Astarte? (b) What does this episode reveal about Isis?

5. (a) What changes does the reformation of Osiris's body produce in the Egyptian landscape? (b) What does this indicate about the nature of Osiris in Egyptian belief?

Analyze and Evaluate

6. (a) How do the roles of Osiris, Isis, and Sêth shift throughout this myth? (b) In your view, which of the three emerges as the most powerful figure, and why?

7. What is your opinion of Isis's decision to spare Sêth?

Connect

8. **Big Idea** **Writing and Immortality** Why do you think the story of Osiris and Isis was central to Egyptian mythology?

9. **Connect to Today** Heroes with extraordinary abilities abound in popular culture. Who are some of these heroes, and why do you think they remain popular?

Literary Element Archetype

Archetypes such as heroes, villains, tricksters, and quests appear frequently in myths and legends.

1. What characteristics associated with Sêth indicate that he is an archetypal figure?

2. Think of another famous archetypal villain. What do this villain and Sêth have in common?

Reading Strategy Identify Genre

A **myth** is a traditional story that may explain a fact about the world, a custom, or a force of nature.

1. "Osiris and Isis" explains the origin of what fact of life?

2. What aspects of Egyptian civilization are explained?

LOG ON ▶ Literature Online

Selection Resources For Selection Quizzes, eFlashcards, and Reading-Writing Connection activities, go to glencoe.com and enter QuickPass code GLW6053u1.

Vocabulary Practice

Practice with Usage Respond to these items to better understand the vocabulary words.

1. Make a list of foods you would like to have served at a **banquet** held in your honor.

2. Identify some pros and cons of having a widely **diversified** set of hobbies.

3. Describe the most **splendid** building you have ever seen.

4. How might you **lament** the death of a pet?

📝 Writing

Write a Movie Scene Choose one scene from "Osiris and Isis" and adapt it into a movie script. Include stage directions and brief descriptions of the set. To get started, use a chart like the one on page 17 to list film conventions, such as dialogue and costumes, and note how you could use these features to illustrate archetypes and themes.

For additional assessment, see Assessment Resources, pp. 37–38.

Grammar Workshop

Sentence Fragments

Literature Connection A **sentence fragment** is a word or group of words that composes only part of a sentence and does not express a complete thought. Look at this sentence from "Osiris and Isis": "Isis followed along the bank of the river, lamenting for Osiris." Think about the effect if the author had instead written, "Isis followed along the bank of the river. Lamenting for Osiris." "Lamenting for Osiris" is a sentence fragment because it lacks a subject and a verb.

PROBLEM 1 Some sentence fragments lack either a subject or a verb (or both).

> *Tore his body into fourteen pieces.* [lacks a subject]

> *The land in which this happened.* [lacks a verb]

SOLUTION Add the missing subject and/or verb.

> *Sêth tore his body into fourteen pieces.*

> *The land in which this happened was Byblos.*

PROBLEM 2 Some sentence fragments are really subordinate clauses that have been mistaken for a complete sentence. Although they have a subject and a verb, subordinate clauses do not express a complete thought and cannot stand alone as a sentence.

> *If the pieces that had been the body of Osiris were not brought together once more.*

SOLUTION A Join the subordinate clause to a main clause.

> *Rê would be destroyed if the pieces that had been the body of Osiris were not brought together once more.*

SOLUTION B Remove the subordinating conjunction at the beginning of the clause.

> *The pieces that had been the body of Osiris were not brought together once more.*

Revise Use the strategies shown above to correct the sentence fragments in this paragraph.

> *Isis sought the chest. She wrapped the chest in linen. And carried it to the king's house. Given a ship, she sailed back to Egypt. Where she opened the chest. And took out the body of her husband.*

Learning Objectives

In this workshop, you will focus on the following objective:

Grammar: Understanding how to avoid sentence fragments.

Sentence Fragments

A **sentence fragment** is a word or group of words that composes only part of a sentence and does not express a complete thought.

Tip

One way to eliminate sentence fragments is to join two clauses, or ideas, with a subordinating conjunction. Some common subordinating conjunctions are *after, because, before, if, since, than, though, unless, when, where,* and *while.*

Language Handbook

For more about sentence fragments, see the Language Handbook, p. R40.

LOG ON **Literature** Online

Grammar For more grammar practice, go to glencoe.com and enter QuickPass code GLW6053u1.

English Learners

DIFFERENTIATED INSTRUCTION

Intermediate Pair beginning English learners with those with more advanced or fluent English skills, and have them match the related words in the columns at right to form simple sentences.

Write on the board:

subject + action verb + direct object = sentence

Subject	Action Verb	Direct Object
dogs	read	food
students	cook	holes
chefs	dig	books

After they have written their sentences, have the pairs of students brainstorm a list of other objects that would be appropriate in sentences containing subjects and verbs listed above.

Grammar Workshop

Sentence Fragments

Focus

Write on the board: Taught people how to farm. Ask students to identify the sentence part that is missing from the fragment *(the subject)* and have them add a word to make the fragment a complete sentence. Ask a volunteer to share his or her sentence with the class. *(Possible answer: Osiris taught people how to farm.)*

Teach

Identify Fragments

Point out to students that reading their writing aloud can help them discover sentence fragments. If they find a fragment, they can often correct it by joining it to a main clause that precedes or follows it, or by adding missing words.

Assess

Possible revision: Isis sought the chest. She wrapped the chest in linen and carried it to the king's house. Given a ship, she sailed back to Egypt, where she opened the chest and took out the body of her husband.

 For additional grammar practice, see Unit 1 Teaching Resources Book, p. 33.

Learning Objectives
Identifying sentence fragments. (SE)
Understanding how to avoid sentence fragments. (SE)
Revising sentence fragments into complete sentences. (SE)

The Great Hymn to the Aten

Before You Read

Bellringer Options

Daily Language Practice Transparency 3

Ask: If you were going to single out one feature of the natural world—such as the sun, moon, stars, seas, mountains, forests, deserts, animals, or seasons— for special praise, what feature would you choose and why? Elicit students' opinions about why they would single out a particular feature of the natural world for special praise.

Meet **Akhenaten**

(ruled 1353 B.C.–1336 B.C.)

Given the overwhelming power of the sun in Egypt, it is not surprising that the sun god Re (rā) was central to the ancient Egyptians' mythology. Re, who was also the creator god, was worshipped as the source of all life and was represented in many forms. The Egyptians depicted him as a sun-shaped disk, a human, a falcon, or a man with a falcon's head. From very early in Egypt's history, the pharaoh took the title "Son of Re," because the ruler was seen as an earthly form of the sun god.

The New Kingdom and Amen-Re Around 1550 B.C., Egyptian princes from the city of Thebes expelled invaders who had ruled Egypt for almost a century. These princes reunited the country and established the New Kingdom, during which Egypt would reach the height of its wealth and power. When Thebes became the capital of Egypt under the New Kingdom pharaohs, the Egyptians combined the worship of the Theban god Amen with that of their sun god Re, calling the new god Amen-Re. Amen-Re became the most important Egyptian god, and his priests eventually gained great power and wealth.

> "How many are your deeds,
> Though hidden from sight,
> O Sole God beside whom there is none!"
>
> —Akhenaten, from
> "The Great Hymn to the Aten"

The Rebel Pharaoh A new ruler named Amenhotep IV (ä′mən hō′tep) came to the throne of Egypt about 1370 B.C. To return

power to the pharaohs, Amenhotep closed the great temples of Amen-Re and dismissed the armies of temple workers. His most radical change, however, was the creation of a new religion based on the worship of only a single god, Aten (ät′n), god of the sun disk. The rebel pharaoh changed his own name to Akhenaten (ä′ke nät′n) (also spelled Akhenaton), which means "It is well with Aten." However, only his wife, Nefertiti (nef′ər tē′tē), his family, and his close advisers accepted this new religion.

Akhenaten moved his court from Thebes to a city he built about 250 miles north on the Nile. The pharaoh called his new city Akhetaten, "the Horizon of the Aten" (an archaeological site known today as Tell el-Amarna). Akhenaten and his court created a cultured, pleasant life in Akhetaten. The pharaoh himself composed a beautiful hymn to Aten to be used in temple services there. Found on a tomb wall at Tell el-Amarna, "The Great Hymn to the Aten" is the finest poetry surviving from ancient Egypt.

 **Literature** Online

Author Search For more about Akhenaten, go to glencoe.com and enter QuickPass code GLW6053u1.

Selection Skills

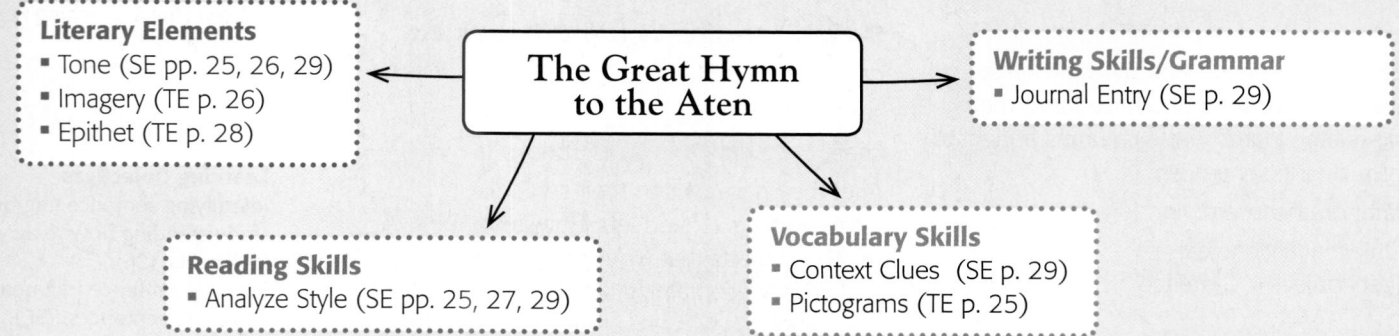

Literary Elements
- Tone (SE pp. 25, 26, 29)
- Imagery (TE p. 26)
- Epithet (TE p. 28)

The Great Hymn to the Aten

Writing Skills/Grammar
- Journal Entry (SE p. 29)

Reading Skills
- Analyze Style (SE pp. 25, 27, 29)

Vocabulary Skills
- Context Clues (SE p. 29)
- Pictograms (TE p. 25)

Literature and Reading Preview

Connect to the Hymn

What about the sun might be impressive enough to inspire worship? Discuss this question with a partner.

Build Background

Before Akhenaten came to power, Egypt had always been tolerant of multiple gods. Many Egyptians viewed Akhenaten's new religion as the destruction of their society. His religious revolution was undone soon after his death, however, by his successor, the boy-pharaoh Tutankhamen (tŏŏ´tängk ä´mən), who restored the old gods and the power of the priests.

Set Purposes for Reading

Big Idea Writing and Immortality

In Egyptian mythology, the god Re traveled in his sun-boat each night through the underworld, where monsters attacked him. His reappearance at dawn was a powerful symbol of immortality to the Egyptians. As you read "The Great Hymn to the Aten," ask yourself, How does Akhenaten depict the Aten's immortal role on earth?

Literary Element Tone

Tone is an author's attitude toward his or her subject matter or the audience. Tone is conveyed through elements such as word choice, punctuation, sentence structure, and figures of speech. As you read "The Great Hymn to the Aten," ask yourself, What is the author's attitude toward his subject?

Reading Strategy Analyze Style

Style refers to the expressive qualities that distinguish an author's work, including word choice, the use of figurative language and imagery, and the length and arrangement of sentences. These literary devices work together to evoke emotions in the reader. As you read, ask yourself, How do various literary elements contribute to the author's style?

Tip: Make a Style Chart Use a chart like the one below to record lines from the hymn and their effect on style.

Lines from Hymn	Effect on Style
"O living Aten, creator of life!" (line 2)	The starting "O" and the invocation of the god's name contribute to the formal style.

AKHENATEN **25**

Learning Objectives

For pages 24–29

In studying this text, you will focus on the following objectives:

Literary Study: Analyzing tone.

Reading: Analyzing style.

Writing: Writing a journal entry.

Vocabulary

radiant (rā´dē ənt) *adj.* glowing; beaming; p. 26 *The radiant bonfire illuminated the children's faces.*

hover (huv´ər) *v.* to hang in the air; p. 26 *We watched a hawk hover overhead, looking for prey.*

dispel (dis pel´) *v.* to drive off; p. 27 *The police tried to dispel the onlookers at the scene of the accident.*

Tip: Context Clues You can often figure out the meaning of new words by looking at their context, the words and sentences that surround them. For example, in the sentence *We watched a hawk hover overhead, looking for prey*, *hover* must mean "to hang in the air," since the hawk stayed in the air without landing.

Before You Read

Focus

Summary

The different sections of the hymn praise various aspects of the Aten's creative work:

(lines 1–12) the effect beauty and radiance of the rising sun;

(lines 13–23) the setting sun and the dangers that darkness brings;

(lines 24–44) the sun's effects on plants, animals, and human beings;

(lines 45–61) the Aten as the creator of the Nile and rain;

(lines 62–76) the Aten as bringer of the seasons;

(lines 77–83) the Aten as universal ruler;

(lines 84–103) the Aten as patron of the king.

For summaries in languages other than English, see Unit 1 Teaching Resources Book, pp. 34–39.

Vocabulary

Pictograms Remind students that many Egyptian hieroglyphics were *pictograms*, or symbols in which pictures are used to convey ideas. Show them several examples of Egyptian hieroglyphics and then have students create a pictogram in the style of an Egyptian hieroglyphic to express the meaning of each of the vocabulary words. (*Hover*, for example, might be expressed by a pictogram of a bird in flight; *radiant*, by a sun disk with projecting rays.)

For additional vocabulary practice, see Unit 1 Teaching Resources Book, p. 42.

Advanced Learners/Pre-AP

DIFFERENTIATED INSTRUCTION

Visual Presentation Have interested students research examples of both archaic Egyptian paintings and sculptures and the Amarna-style art inspired by Akhenaten, mentioned on page 28. Have students do a visual presentation for the class, showing the examples and comparing and contrasting the important characteristics of each style.

Approaching Level

DIFFERENTIATED INSTRUCTION

Compare and Contrast Art Have students work in groups to identify previously unexamined examples of Egyptian art as either traditional Egyptian art or Amarna-style art based on the characteristics that have been identified in the presentation. If the groups have trouble distinguishing the two styles, have the student presenters help them.

Teach

Literary Element   1

Tone Answer: *The hymn opens with a flattering adjective and a reference to Aten's place in the heavens and to his role as creator, establishing a reverent tone.*

APPROACHING If students have trouble identifying the tone, point to the words *splendid*, *living*, and *creator*, and then ask what these words indicate about the author's feelings toward the Aten.

> For additional literary element practice, see Unit 1 Teaching Resources Book, p. 40.

View the Art ★

Reliefs were popular art forms in ancient Egypt. In this relief, Akhenaten's disproportionate size helps create an impression of status and power.

> For an audio recording of this selection, use Listening Library Audio CD-ROM.

---

from
The Great Hymn
to the **Aten**

Akhenaten
Translated by Miriam Lichtheim

Splendid you rise in heaven's lightland,°
O living Aten, creator of life!
When you have dawned in eastern lightland,
You fill every land with your beauty.
5   You are beauteous, great, **radiant**,
High over every land;
Your rays embrace the lands,
To the limit of all that you made.
Being Re, you reach their limits,
10   You bend them <for> the son whom you love;
Though you are far, your rays are on earth,
Though one sees you, your strides are unseen.

When you set in western lightland,
Earth is in darkness as if in death;
15   One sleeps in chambers, heads covered,
One eye does not see another.
Were they robbed of their goods,
That are under their heads,
People would not remark it.
20   Every lion comes from its den,
All the serpents bite;
Darkness **hovers**, earth is silent,
As their maker rests in lightland.

1   **lightland:** the sky.

1   Tone *How does the opening of the hymn immediately establish the author's attitude toward the Aten?*

Vocabulary

radiant (rā′dē ənt) *adj.* glowing; beaming
hover (huv′ ər) *v.* to hang in the air

The Royal Family of Amenophis IV Akhenaten offers sacrifice to Aton, the sun god, ca. 1365-1349 BC. Stone relief. Egyptian Museum, Cairo. ★

26   UNIT 1   EARLY AFRICA

Literary Element Practice

Imagery Point out to students that imagery is descriptive language that appeals to one or more of the five senses: sight, hearing, touch, taste, and smell. The use of sensory detail helps create an emotional response in the reader. Have students identify the images in lines 13–23 and in lines 24–44 of Akhenaten's hymn and then contrast the emotional effects of the imagery in these two sections. *(Lines 13–23 depict sunset; lines 24–44 depict sunrise. Students should contrast the frightening effect created by the image of sunset and the pleasing effect created by the image of sunrise.)*

Earth brightens when you dawn in lightland,
25   When you shine as Aten of daytime;
       As you **dispel** the dark,
       As you cast your rays,
       The Two Lands° are in festivity.
       Awake they stand on their feet,
30   You have roused them;
       Bodies cleansed, clothed,
       Their arms adore your appearance.
       The entire land sets out to work,
       All beasts browse on their herbs;
35   Trees, herbs are sprouting,
       Birds fly from their nests,
       Their wings greeting your *ka*.°
       All flocks frisk on their feet,
       All that fly up and alight,
40   They live when you dawn for them.
       Ships fare north, fare south as well,
       Roads lie open when you rise;
       The fish in the river dart before you,
       Your rays are in the midst of the sea. . . .

45   How many are your deeds,
       Though hidden from sight,
       O Sole God beside whom there is none!
       You made the earth as you wished, you alone,
       All peoples, herds, and flocks;
50   All upon earth that walk on legs,
       All on high that fly on wings,
       The lands of Khor and Kush,°
       The land of Egypt.
       You set every man in his place.
55   You supply their needs;
       Everyone has his food,
       His lifetime is counted.
       Their tongues differ in speech,
       Their characters likewise;
60   Their skins are distinct,
       For you distinguished the peoples.

Analyze Style *What do these cumulative parallel images suggest about the Aten's power?* **2**

Vocabulary

dispel (dis pel´) *v.* to drive off

28 **Two Lands:** Upper Egypt and Lower Egypt, whose names are based on the northward flow of the Nile River. Upper Egypt was the southern (or upriver) part of the country; Lower Egypt was the northern (or downriver) part.

37 **ka:** the spiritual body or life force.

52 **Khor and Kush:** the Egyptian names for Syria and Nubia (the region south of Egypt).

Teach

Reading Strategy   2

Analyze Style Answer: *The parallel images show the broad scope of the Aten's power.*

 For additional practice using the reading skill or strategy, see Unit 1 Teaching Resources Book, p. 41.

Cultural History ☆

From Tutankhaten to Tutankhamen Tutankhamen, one of the most famous of all Egyptian rulers since the discovery of his tomb in 1922, was married to one of Akhenaten's daughters. Early in his brief reign, the boy-king changed his original name, Tutankhaten ("living image of Aten") to Tutankhamen. The new name reflected his abandonment of his father-in-law's religious revolution and the return of the old beliefs, particularly the worship of Amun, the king of the Egyptian gods.

Learning Objectives
Analyzing tone. (SE)
Analyzing style. (SE)
Analyzing imagery. (TE)

English Learners

DIFFERENTIATED INSTRUCTION

Intermediate Students may need help distinguishing both homonyms and homophones. Direct their attention to line 41, "Ships fare north, fare south as well."
Ask: What does *fare* mean here? Help students use context clues to understand that *fare* as a verb means "travel." Then write *fare* and *fair* on the board. Help students distinguish between the meanings of *fare* (noun meaning "money paid for travel"), *fair* (adjective meaning "impartial"), and *fair* (noun meaning "social event.")

Teach

Literary Element 1

Theme Ask: How do these lines sum up the theme of Akhenaten's hymn? *(They identify the Aten as the source of all life.)*

Reading Strategy 2

Analyze Style Ask: Why do you think Akhenaten introduces himself into the end of the hymn? *(The pharaoh is important because he is the earthly embodiment of the Aten.)*

[APPROACHING] Review the last section of the hymn with students, pointing out how Akhenaten stresses both his power and justice ("The King who lives by Maat").

View the Art ★

Answer: *The relief exemplifies the Amarna style by depicting the royal family in a casual domestic scene. The relief might reveal that Akhenaten wanted his subjects to relate to him as a person as well as a powerful ruler.*

Found at the archeological site of Tell el-Amarna, this work is a typical example of the naturalistic, informal Amarna style inspired by Akhenaten's religious revolution. Tell-el-Amarna is the site of the ruins of Akhenaten's capital, Akhetaten.

📁 To check students' understanding of the selection, see Unit 1 Teaching Resources Book, p. 44.

You made Hapy in *dat*,°
You bring him when you will,
To nourish the people,
65 For you made them for yourself.
Lord of all who toils for them,
Lord of all lands who shines for them,
Aten of daytime, great in glory!
All distant lands, you make them live,
70 You made a heavenly Hapy descend for them;
He makes waves on the mountains like the sea,
To drench their fields and their towns.
How excellent are your ways, O Lord of eternity!
A Hapy from heaven for foreign peoples,
75 And all lands' creatures that walk on legs,
For Egypt the Hapy who comes from *dat*.

Your rays nurse all fields,
When you shine they live, they grow for you;
You made the seasons to foster all that you made,
80 Winter to cool them, heat that they taste you.
You made the far sky to shine therein,
To behold all that you made;
You alone, shining in your form of living Aten,
Risen, radiant, distant, near.
85 You made millions of forms from yourself alone,
Towns, villages, fields, the river's course;
All eyes observe you upon them,
For you are the Aten of daytime on high. . . .
. . . . . . ———. . .

<Those on> earth come from your hand as you made them,
90 When you have dawned they live,
When you set they die;
You yourself are lifetime, one lives by you. **1**
All eyes are on <your> beauty until you set,
All labor ceases when you rest in the west;
95 When you rise you stir [everyone] for the King,
Every leg is on the move since you founded the earth.
You rouse them for your son who came from your body,
The King who lives by Maat,° the Lord of the Two Lands.
Neferkheprure, Sole-one-of-Re,
100 The Son of Re who lives by Maat, the Lord of crowns, **2**
Akhenaten, great in his lifetime;
(And) the great Queen whom he loves, the Lady of the Two Lands,
Nefer-nefru-Aten Nefertiti, living forever.

---

62 Hapy in dat: rain. The Egyptians believed the source of the Nile River (**Hapy**) was in the underworld (**dat**) and that rain was the river descending to earth.

Akhenaten and His Family, ca. 1345 BC. Painted limestone relief, 32.5 x 39 cm. Staatliche Museen zu Berlin, Germany.

View the Art During Akhenaten's reign, Egyptian artists moved away from the formal depictions of royalty that had been popular in earlier dynasties and began to depict the royal family in more natural poses and relaxed settings. This approach is now called the Amarna style. How does this relief exemplify the Amarna style, and what might it reveal about Akhenaten's reign? ★

98 Maat: the Egyptian goddess who personified truth and justice.

Literary Element Practice

Epithet Point out to students that an epithet is a brief phrase used to characterize a person. **Ask:** What American president was known as "Honest Abe" and "The Great Emancipator"? When you have elicited the correct response from students, ask them to give some examples of contemporary celebrities—such as athletes and movie stars—that are referred to by epithets. Then have students review the poem and find examples of epithets used to describe the following:

- Aten *(line 2, "living Aten" and "creator of life"; line 47, "Sole God")*
- Akhenaten *(line 97, "King who lives by Maat" and "Lord of the Two Lands"; line 100, "Son of Re")*
- Nefertiti *(line 102, "Lady of the Two Lands")*

After You Read

Respond and Think Critically

Respond and Interpret

1. How are the author's feelings about the sun in "The Great Hymn to the Aten" like and unlike your own?

2. (a)What events are associated with nightfall in the hymn? (b)What do these events suggest about the Aten's protective role toward humans?

3. (a)What does the poem say in lines 62–76 about the Aten's relationship to the Nile? (b)For the Egyptians, what significance would this relationship give to the Aten?

4. (a)According to the poem, what relationship exists between the Aten and Akhenaten? (b)How would this relationship affect the status of the pharaoh in the eyes of his subjects?

Analyze and Evaluate

5. (a)What kinds of living things are shown responding to the Aten? (b)What do these images reveal about the Aten's power?

6. What characteristics of this hymn might make it effective as an oral presentation?

Connect

7. **Big Idea** Writing and Immortality (a)In lines 89–93, what claim does the hymn make about the Aten? (b)How does this claim relate to Egyptian ideas of immortality?

8. **Connect to Today** "The Great Hymn to the Aten" praises the sun. In what ways do people today honor nature?

Literary Element Tone

An author's **tone** might convey a variety of attitudes such as sympathy, objectivity, or humor.

1. How might Akhenaten's chosen subject matter have influenced his tone?

2. What elements help create this tone?

Reading Strategy Analyze Style

Style can reveal an author's **purpose** in writing; for example, a carefree style may reveal that the author is writing to amuse readers.

1. What might be Akhenaten's purposes for writing this hymn?

2. How does the style of "The Great Hymn to the Aten" help convey these purposes?

Literature Online

Selection Resources For Selection Quizzes, eFlashcards, and Reading-Writing Connection activities, go to glencoe.com and enter QuickPass code GLW6053u1.

Vocabulary Practice

Practice with Context Clues Look back at pages 26–28 to find context clues for the vocabulary words below. Record your findings in a chart like the one here.

radiant   hover   dispel

EXAMPLE:

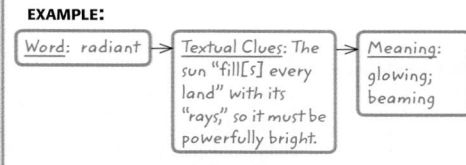

Word: radiant → Textual Clues: The sun "fill[s] every land" with its "rays," so it must be powerfully bright. → Meaning: glowing; beaming

Writing

Write a Journal Entry Imagine that you are one of Akhenaten's subjects. Write a journal entry in which you examine your feelings about his new religion. Imitate the tone Akhenaten used in his poem. Review the chart you made on page 25 for other aspects of his style that you might want to incorporate into your writing.

AKHENATEN **29**

After You Read

Assess

1. Answers will vary.

2. (a) Robbery and the appearance of dangerous beasts (b) The Aten's presence keeps these dangers away.

3. (a) The Aten created the Nile River and brings rain from the heavens. (b) It would show the supremacy of the sun god because the Nile restored the fertility of Egypt's fields.

4. (a) Akhenaten is Aten's son. (b) It would emphasize his role as god-king.

5. (a) Humans, beasts, trees, herbs, birds, and fish (b) The breadth and benevolence of the Aten's power

6. The poem's parallelism and repetition make it suitable for reading aloud.

7. (a) These lines identify the Aten as the source of all life. (b) This claim links the human life cycle and hope for immortality to the immortal cycle of the Aten.

8. In a variety of ways, including Arbor Day and Earth Day

Writing

Students' journal entries should reflect understanding of the subject, provide specific reasons for their feelings, and use elements of Akhenaten's style.

Literary Element

1. Akhenaten's tone derives from his reverence and adoration for his subject: the Aten, who Akhenaten worships and for whom he restructured Egyptian religion.

2. This tone is created through Akhenaten's many complimentary descriptions of the Aten and through powerful images of nature.

Reading Strategy

1. Expressing faith, creating a feeling of reverence, encouraging others to worship the Aten, and contributing to group worship.

2. It is formal, yet also exuberant and descriptive. This style conveys Akhenaten's reverence for the Aten and his excitement for the religion, while underscoring his hope that others will recognize the Aten's power.

Vocabulary

hover clue: Darkness "hovers" over the earth at nightfall; meaning: float above

dispel clue: Sunrise "dispel[s] the dark" at dawn; meaning: drive away

> For additional selection assessment, see Assessment Resources, pp. 39–40.

Bellringer Options

**Selection Focus
Transparency 1**

**Daily Language Practice
Transparency 4**

Or ask: What famous people from our time do you think will be remembered three thousand years from now? *(Students may identify artists, government leaders, scientists, or celebrities.)* **Or ask:** What do you think is the best way to ensure that people remember you in the future? Find out what students think is the most lasting contribution one can make, perhaps an invention, a technological innovation, or an artistic contribution.

Summary

This segment from "The Immortality of Writers" claims that books make their authors remembered long after they are dead, thus immortalizing writers. "So small are the flowers of Seamu" is a love poem that relates how the beloved enriches the speaker's life.

Selection Skills

Egyptian Poetry

Connect to the Poems

In what ways can people be remembered after they're gone? Discuss this question with a partner.

Build Background

"The Immortality of Writers" and "So small are the flowers of Seamu" date from the New Kingdom (around 1550–1085 B.C.), a period in which Egypt reached the height of its power. "The Immortality of Writers" is from a textbook used by boys learning to write hieroglyphs (see pages 34–35). "So small are the flowers of Seamu" is from a collection of love poems.

Set Purposes for Reading

Big Idea Writing and Immortality

The ancient Egyptians were very concerned with life after death. As you read "The Immortality of Writers," ask yourself, What kind of life after death does this poem suggest?

Literary Element Imagery

Imagery is language that appeals to the senses. For example, in "So small are the flowers of Seamu," the poet includes an image of "perfumed flowers". As you read these Egyptian poems, ask yourself, How do they use imagery to evoke readers' emotions?

Reading Strategy Analyze Diction

Authors use language carefully to convey meaning. Their choice of words is called **diction**. As you read, ask yourself, How does diction contribute to the message of these poems?

Tip: **Chart Diction** Make a chart to analyze how the diction differs in these poems. In the left column, list words that contribute to the message of "The Immortality of Writers"; in the right column, list words that contribute to the message of "So small are the flowers of Seamu."

"The Immortality of Writers"	"So small are the flowers of Seamu"
Decays	Flowers

Learning Objectives

For pages 30–33

In studying this text, you will focus on the following objectives:

Literary Study: Analyzing imagery.

Reading: Analyzing diction.

Writing: Writing an essay.

Vocabulary

decay (di kā´) *v.* to rot or decompose; p. 31 *The timbers of the sunken ship will decay over time.*

perish (per´ish) *v.* to die or cease to exist; p. 31 *We must work to save endangered species before they perish.*

tranquil (trang´kwəl) *adj.* calm; peaceful; p. 32 *The family enjoyed the tranquil mornings in the country.*

Tip: **Word Origins** Word origins, also called **etymologies**, are the history and development of words. They are often found in dictionary entries. For example, an entry for the word *tranquil* might include the following information: [ME *tranquill,* fr. L *tranquillus*]. This means that the modern word *tranquil* has a long history; it was derived from the Middle English (ME) word *tranquill,* which in turn was based on the Latin (L) word *tranquillus.*

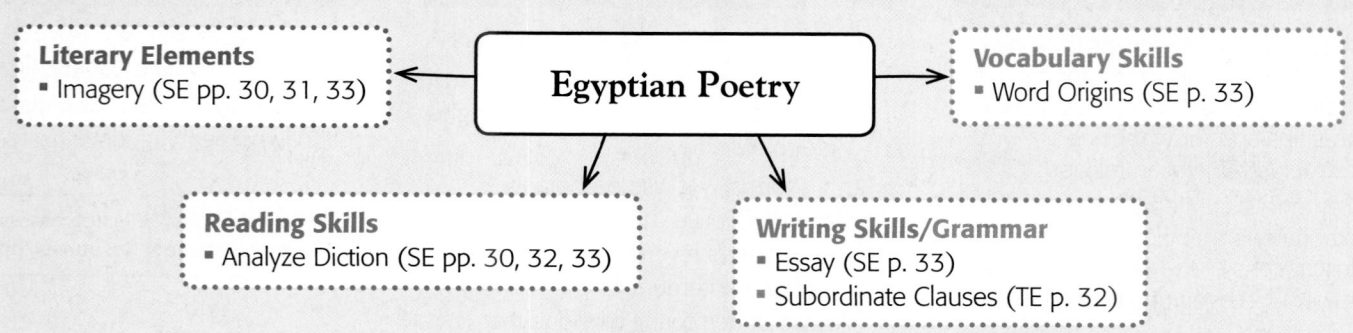

Literary Elements
- Imagery (SE pp. 30, 31, 33)

Egyptian Poetry

Vocabulary Skills
- Word Origins (SE p. 33)

Reading Skills
- Analyze Diction (SE pp. 30, 32, 33)

Writing Skills/Grammar
- Essay (SE p. 33)
- Subordinate Clauses (TE p. 32)

from
THE **IMMORTALITY** OF WRITERS

Man **decays**, his corpse is dust,
All his kin have **perished**;
☆ But a book makes him remembered,
Through the mouth of its reciter.
5 Better is a book than a well-built house,
Than tomb-chapels in the West;
Better than a solid mansion,
Than a stela[1] in the temple!

Is there one here like Hardedef?...[2]
10 Is there another like Ptahhotep?...[3]
Death made their names forgotten
But books make them remembered!

---

1. A *stela* (stē′lə) is a carved stone slab or pillar used for commemorative purposes.
2. *Hardedef* (har′dä def), an Egyptian prince, was buried in an elaborate underground tomb near the Great Pyramid of Khufu.
3. *Ptahhotep* (tä′hō tep′) wrote a work of philosophy dating back to 2800 B.C.

1 Imagery *What similarities exist between the objects in this line and the objects in lines 6–8?*

2 Writing and Immortality *What does this observation indicate about the value Egyptians placed on writing?*

Vocabulary

decay (di kā′) *v.* to rot or decompose
perish (per′ish) *v.* to die or cease to exist

Detail of the Book of the Earth, from the burial chamber of the Tomb of Rameses VI. Wall painting. Egypt.

Teach

Literary Element   1

Imagery Answer: *They are all things built to be long lasting.*

📁 For additional literary element practice, see Unit 1 Teaching Resources Book, p. 52.

Big Idea   2

Writing and Immortality
Answer: *This observation indicates that ancient Egyptians valued writing and writers highly.*

Literary History ☆

Artistic Immortality Present the Latin saying *Ars longa, vita brevis* ("art is long; life is short"). Tell students that this phrase was shortened from Hippocrates' aphorism *"Life is short, Art long, Occasion sudden and dangerous, Experience deceitful, and Judgment difficult."* Hippocrates, a physician of ancient Greece, was the founder of modern medicine. The Hippocratic Oath, the code doctors use as an ethical guide, is attributed to him.

📖 **Interactive Read and Write**
Other options for teaching this selection can be found in Interactive Read and Write for On-Level Learners, pp. 2–8.

Approaching Level

DIFFERENTIATED INSTRUCTION 🐾

Visual Literacy Instruct students to create a hieroglyphic (pictorial) representation of a simple story they know, perhaps a folktale or nursery rhyme, giving them help if necessary. Students can refer to the illustrations on pages 34–35 for ideas. Pair students and instruct them to tell their stories to each other aloud, using the hieroglyphics as a guide.

Advanced Learners/Pre-AP

DIFFERENTIATED INSTRUCTION 🐾

Research Have advanced students select a time period and culture to research. They can then use the Internet to investigate society's treatment of writers in their chosen era. Have them write a paragraph comparing and contrasting the role of the writer in the era they researched to that in ancient Egypt, as depicted in "The Immortality of Writers."

Learning Objectives
Analyzing imagery. (SE)
Analyzing diction. (SE)

Teach

Imagery Have the students read lines 3–4. **Ask:** How is being first among loves similar to a "freshly sprinkled garden"? *(The poet may mean that he or she feels reborn or revived as a result of being greatly loved.)*

(APPROACHING) Point out that grass that is "freshly sprinkled" has been watered recently. Ask them what that would do for a lawn that had not been watered in a long time.

Reading Strategy | 2

Analyze Diction Answer: *Words such as* pleasant *and* freshness *convey feelings of refreshment and pleasure.*

 For additional practice using the reading skill or strategy, see Unit 1 Teaching Resources Book, p .53.

View the Art ★

Answer: *You could infer that fashion was based on plenty of adornment, such as the bracelets, headdresses, and earrings worn by the women. Women also likely invested in beauty treatments and fragrance, based on the kohl-rimmed eyes, carefully-done nails and perfumed incense shown here. Finally, you could infer that the women here are wealthy, based on their lavish appearance.*

Ladies Chat at a Banquet, 18th dynasty. Paint on limestone from tomb of Nebamun. British Museum, London.

View the Art Much of what we know about ancient Egyptian dress comes from artwork, such as this tomb painting from the New Kingdom. What can you infer about Egyptian fashion in the 18th dynasty, based on the outfits of the women in this painting? What can you infer about their lifestyles?

So small are the flowers of Seamu

Translated by Ezra Pound and Noel Stock

So small are the flowers of Seamu
Whoever looks at them feels a giant.

1 I am first among your loves,
Like a freshly sprinkled garden of grass and perfumed flowers.

5 Pleasant is the channel you have dug
In the freshness of the north wind.

Tranquil our paths
When your hand rests on mine in joy.

Your voice gives life, like nectar.

10 To see you, is more than food or drink.

Analyze Diction *What feelings does the word choice in these lines convey?* **2**

Vocabulary

tranquil (trang′kwəl) *adj.* calm; peaceful

Grammar Practice

Use Subordinate Clauses Remind students that a subordinate clause is a group of words that has a subject and a predicate but cannot stand alone as a sentence. Subordinate clauses may act as adjectives, adverbs, or nouns. Write these sentences on the board: "So small are the flowers of Seamu / <u>Whoever looks at them</u> feels a giant," and "Tranquil our paths / <u>When your hand rests on mine in joy.</u>" Explain that the first underlined clause functions as the subject of another clause; thus, it is a noun clause. The second is an adverb clause; it tells when the action occurred.

Have students write three sentences about either poem, using a noun clause, an adverb clause, and an adjective clause. Have students identify the clauses and check their work.

After You Read

Respond and Think Critically

Respond and Interpret

1. What questions would you like to ask the speakers of these poems?

2. (a)How does "The Immortality of Writers" describe death? (b)According to the poem, what is one benefit people can derive from books?

3. (a)What are books compared with in "The Immortality of Writers"? (b)What is unexpected about the fact that a book is compared with these other things?

4. (a)Explain the last two lines in "So small are the flowers of Seamu." (b)What do these lines suggest about the speaker's attitude toward the beloved?

Analyze and Evaluate

5. What might be the significance of the people mentioned in "The Immortality of Writers"?

6. Analyze the rhythm of "So small are the flowers of Seamu." Does the rhythm of the translation seem musical (fluid) or rigid? Explain.

Connect

7. **Big Idea** **Writing and Immortality** What kinds of books help people be remembered?

8. **Connect to Today** Aside from books, what are some ways people today can be remembered after death?

Literary Element Imagery

Strong **imagery** is especially important in poetry, as poets often rely on brief, intense images to convey their message.

1. Select an image from "The Immortality of Writers." How does the image you selected contribute to the meaning of the poem?

2. How does the imagery in this poem differ from that in "So small are the flowers of Seamu"?

Reading Strategy Analyze Diction

Refer to the chart you created on page 30 and answer the following questions.

1. How does the diction in "So small are the flowers of Seamu" help convey the theme of the poem?

2. How does the diction of this poem differ from that of "The Immortality of Writers"?

 LOG ON **Literature** Online

Selection Resources For Selection Quizzes, eFlashcards, and Reading-Writing Connection activities, go to glencoe.com and enter QuickPass code GLW6053u1.

Vocabulary Practice

Practice with Word Origins Create a word map for each boldfaced vocabulary word. Refer to a dictionary for help.

decay   perish   tranquil

EXAMPLE:

- *Definition:* highest in authority or goodness
- *Etymology:* Latin *superus*, meaning "upper"
- supreme
- *Sample Sentence:* Amen-Re was considered the supreme being of the universe.

Writing

Write an Essay Reflect on the ideas about life and death that these two poems convey. Then write a brief expository essay describing the Egyptian worldview. Use quotations from the poems to support your claims.

EGYPTIAN POETRY **33**

Assess

1. Answers will vary. Possible question: Why is your culture so interested in immortality?

2. (a) With images of decay and dust (b) They can be remembered after death.

3. (a) Houses, tombs, a mansion, and a stela (b) A mere book outlasts things that seem more substantial.

4. (a) Love nourishes the speaker. (b) They suggest that the beloved is vital to the speaker.

5. They might be people who are still remembered after death because of books.

6. Most students will find the poem musical, noting the variety of line lengths and the general cadence.

7. Possible answers: historical accounts and works of literature

8. Possible answers: in photography or on film

Writing

Students' essays should address both similarities and differences between the two poems, incorporate background information about ancient Egypt, and be logically organized, with an introduction, a body, and a conclusion.

Literary Element

1. Students should choose a specific image and support their answer with examples.

2. The images in "The Immortality of Writers" are of death and sturdiness; the images in "So small are the flowers of Seamu" are of life, fragility, and youthfulness.

Reading Strategy

1. The poem includes words such as "pleasant," and "joy," which contribute to the theme that happiness is found in a loved one.

2. The diction in this poem presents the living world and a sense of joy; the diction in "The Immortality of Writers" presents a world of inanimate objects and a mood of defiance.

Vocabulary

Sample sentences will vary.

Word: <u>decay</u>; Definition: to rot or decompose; Etymology: Old North French *decair*, "to fall"

Word: <u>perish</u>; Definition: to die or cease to exist; Etymology: Latin *perire*, "to go through"

Word: <u>tranquil</u>; Definition: calm; peaceful; Etymology: Latin *trans* "over" + *quies* "rest"

33

Focus

Bellringer Options

Daily Language Practice Transparency 5

Write on the board:
alphabet—26 letters
hieroglyphics—700 symbols

Ask: What do you think the effects on U.S. education would be if we used a writing system as complex as Egyptian hieroglyphics? Elicit students' opinions about what effects employing a highly complex writing system would have on American education.

Reading Strategy

Analyze Cause-and-Effect Relationships Ask: Why did scribes often become government officials in ancient Egypt? *(Their knowledge of writing made scribes vital to government record-keeping and led to their becoming officials.)*

 For activities related to this selection, see Unit 1 Teaching Resources Book, pp. 58–59.

View the Photograph ★

The Rosetta Stone was carved in 196 B.C. The text is a decree of the Egyptian ruler Ptolemy V. The decree concerns the repeal of certain taxes and the creation of religious sculpture.

34

Learning Objectives

For pages 34–35

In studying this text, you will focus on the following objectives:

Reading:
Evaluating historical influences.
Connecting to contemporary issues.

Hieroglyphics and the Rosetta Stone

> *"Though I spend the day telling you 'Write,' it seems like a plague to you. Writing is very pleasant!"*
> —from an ancient Egyptian exercise book for scribes

Egyptian Writing Systems

The ancient Egyptians developed one of the world's first systems of writing. The earliest surviving examples of this script, known as "hieroglyphics" (from Greek words meaning "priest carvings," or "sacred writings"), date from about 3000 B.C. The complex hieroglyphic script includes pictures that represent words and more abstract forms that represent sounds. Learning and practicing the script took much time and skill. As a result, a highly simplified version of hieroglyphics, known as "hieratic" ("priestly") script, was developed. Hieratic script used the same principles as hieroglyphic writing, but the characters were simplified by using dashes, strokes, and curves rather than the more formal symbols. Much later, a third system, known as "demotic" ("of the people"), was also developed.

Papyrus

Hieroglyphics were used for official inscriptions on temple walls and tombs, which were meant to last for centuries. Hieratic and demotic scripts were used for everyday writing on papyrus, a material produced from the fibers of the papyrus plants that grow along the Nile River. (The English word *paper* comes from *papyrus*.) Papyrus scrolls were made by pressing together moistened layers of papyrus fibers. These sheets were then glued together to form scrolls that were sometimes up to 130 feet in length. In the dry Egyptian climate, papyrus was very durable; the earliest surviving papyrus dates from about 2600 B.C.

The Rosetta Stone, 196 BC. British Museum, London.

34 UNIT 1 EARLY AFRICA

Reading Practice

Draw Conclusions Point out to students that drawing a conclusion is making a general statement you can explain with reason or with supporting details from a text. Have students use the information in this article to draw a conclusion about the culture of the ancient Egyptians. Using a graphic organizer like this can help students keep track of the information they find in the article.

Subject
Culture of Ancient Egypt
Evidence
▪ Ancient Egypt developed one of the world's first writing systems.
▪
▪
Conclusion
▪

Hieroglyphic inscription in the tomb of Sety I, 19th Dynasty. Painted limestone from tomb in the Valley of the Kings at Thebes.

Scribal Schools

Because hieroglyphic script was difficult to master, a highly respected class of scribes came into existence. Scribes functioned as secretaries or clerks and were essential to the Egyptian state—scribes often became important government officials. At the age of ten, boys of the upper classes began attending schools run by scribes. There they learned hieroglyphics by laboriously copying texts, which usually celebrated the virtues of being a scribe. Discipline was strict, and boys were often punished severely.

The Rosetta Stone

Once alphabetical writing came into use in Egypt around the fourth century A.D., the ability to understand hieroglyphics soon faded away. The ancient symbols remained a mystery for hundreds of years. In 1799 in the Egyptian city of Rosetta, however, a French officer serving with Napoleon's expedition to Egypt discovered a large slab of granite covered with writing in three ancient scripts: hieroglyphics, demotic script, and Greek. This slab would prove to be the key to understanding hieroglyphics. The inclusion of Greek on the slab—later named the Rosetta Stone—meant the ancient scripts could be translated and better understood.

The British, who defeated the French in Egypt, seized the Rosetta Stone as a spoil of war. (It was presented to the British Museum in London in 1802 and remains there to this day.) By 1814 British scholar Thomas Young had successfully deciphered the Egyptian demotic inscription using the accompanying Greek text. Building on Young's work, French scholar Jean-François Champollion worked on the hieroglyphic text, which he deciphered by 1824. The Rosetta Stone allowed scholars to unlock the riches of ancient Egyptian civilization by providing the key to reading hieroglyphics. In recent years, Dr. Zawi Hawass, Secretary General of Egypt's Supreme Council of Antiquities, has demanded the return of the Rosetta Stone from Britain, describing it as "the icon of our Egyptian identity."

 Literature Online

Literature and Reading For more about hieroglyphics and the Rosetta Stone, go to glencoe.com and enter QuickPass code GLW6053u1.

Respond and Think Critically

1. What is your opinion on the issue of returning artifacts such as the Rosetta Stone to their country of origin?

2. How did the education of scribes in ancient Egypt differ from contemporary American education?

3. How did the difficulty of hieroglyphics affect the role of scribes in ancient Egypt?

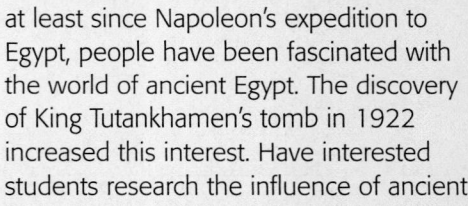

Advanced Learners/Pre-AP

DIFFERENTIATED INSTRUCTION

Research Point out to students that at least since Napoleon's expedition to Egypt, people have been fascinated with the world of ancient Egypt. The discovery of King Tutankhamen's tomb in 1922 increased this interest. Have interested students research the influence of ancient Egypt on some aspect of modern culture, such as literature, film, or design.

English Learners

DIFFERENTIATED INSTRUCTION

Intermediate Some students come from cultures where another script or writing system is employed. Bring in modern examples of languages that use another script or ask students familiar with them to show the class examples of alphabets or writing systems from their own cultures.

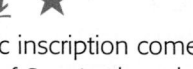

Teach

View the Art ★

This hieroglyphic inscription comes from the tomb of Sety I, who ruled from 1290 to 1279 B.C.

Ask: What words would you use to describe the effect created by this script? *(Students might use such words as* serious, formal, artistic, *or* mysterious.*)*

Assess

1. Many students may feel that artifacts rightfully belong to their country of origin and should be returned; others may feel that artifacts belong to those who currently have them.

2. Unlike contemporary American education, the education of scribes was limited to male students and was based on copying texts.

3. Their specialized learning gave scribes status in society; many became government officials, while others went on to become teachers.

Learning Objectives
Evaluating historical influences. (SE)
Connecting to contemporary issues. (SE)
Drawing conclusions. (TE)

Focus

Write on the board: joystick, four-wheel drive, downsize

Ask: What does each of these terms mean? *(joystick: a lever used to control a computer; four-wheel drive: a system that controls a car; downsize: reduce in number)* Explain to students that these terms are examples of *jargon,* or terminology specific to a particular trade, profession, or group. The word *joystick* might be used by a video game enthusiast; the term *four-wheel drive* might be used by an auto mechanic, and the word *downsize* might be used by a businessperson. **Say:** In order to succeed in any trade, you need to be familiar with that trade's jargon. Academic vocabulary is a specific type of jargon used by scholars and academics.

Learning Objectives

For pages 36–37

In this workshop, you will focus on the following objective:

Vocabulary: Understanding academic vocabulary.

For a complete list of academic vocabulary words, see pages R83–R85.

Test-Taking Tip

These key academic vocabulary words often appear on standardized tests.

Analyze: to systematically and critically examine all parts of an issue or an event

Compare: to show how things are alike

Contrast: to show how things are different

Describe: to present a sketch or an impression

Discuss: to systematically write about all sides of an issue or an event

Evaluate: to make a judgment and support it with evidence

Explain: to clarify or make plain

Vocabulary Workshop

Academic Vocabulary

What Is Academic Vocabulary? Words that are commonly used in academic texts, such as textbooks, directions, and tests, are called **academic vocabulary.** Learning academic vocabulary is important because these words will help you read, write, and research in many academic areas. These words will also help you succeed on standardized tests.

Different Kinds of Words Some words are specific to certain disciplines, or areas of study. For example, the words *onomatopoeia, free verse,* and *simile* pertain to literature. Other words, such as *analysis, definition,* and *estimate,* are used in many areas of study. The charts below show more examples of both kinds of words.

Discipline-Specific Words

Discipline	Words
Math	circumference, percentage, rectangle
Science	chlorophyll, genus, mitosis
Social Studies	antebellum, confederation, federalism

General Academic Vocabulary

area	evident
context	indicate
demonstrator	interpret
evaluate	structure

Academic Words in This Book You will learn about discipline-specific and general academic vocabulary words in this book. Words that are specific to literature and language arts will most often be introduced and explained in Literary Element and Reading Strategy features before and after you read literary works. You will encounter more general academic vocabulary words in features called Academic Vocabulary that appear after literature.

Multiple-Meaning Words Many academic vocabulary words, such as *approach,* have more than one meaning. The first meaning is a literal, more common definition that you may already be familiar with

Vocabulary Practice

Use Word Maps To help students further explore the meanings of the academic words listed in this workshop, have them use a dictionary or thesaurus to make four-square organizers like the one below.

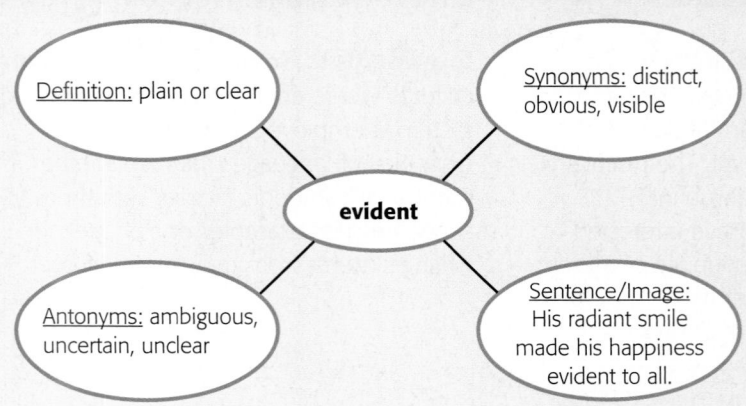

Definition: plain or clear

Synonyms: distinct, obvious, visible

evident

Antonyms: ambiguous, uncertain, unclear

Sentence/Image: His radiant smile made his happiness evident to all.

(*approach* means "to come near to"). The second definition is more academic and may be unfamiliar to you (*approach* also means "the method used in setting about a task"). These two definitions are often related, however. In the case of *approach,* the second, academic definition is connected to the common definition because "the method used in setting about a task" allows one to come closer to a goal. The chart below lists additional examples of academic words with more than one meaning.

Words	Definitions	Relationships
chart	*n.* a sheet giving information in tabular form *v.* to make a plan for	Both definitions involve organizing information.
exhibit	*v.* to show or display *n.* something displayed	Both definitions involve displaying
vehicle	*n.* a means of carrying or transporting something *n.* a medium through which something is expressed	Both definitions involve forms of carrying or transmitting

As you encounter academic vocabulary words in this book, you will master the words through various activities. You'll have a chance to practice some of these activities in the exercise below.

Practice Complete the following items.

1. *The Golden Age in Greece was a **dynamic** period marked by spectacular cultural and political achievement.*

   Dynamic is an academic word. In more casual conversation, someone might say the best player on a basketball team is a **dynamic** player. Using context clues, try to figure out the meaning of the word in the sentence about Greece above. Check your guess in a dictionary.

2. *"Of all the Socratic dialogues, the most influential was the Republic, which examines the **nature** of justice."*
   —from Meet Plato, page 334

   Nature has several meanings. Using context clues, try to figure out the meaning of *nature* in each sentence below and explain the difference between the two meanings.

   a. Brian loved hiking in the mountains; it made him feel connected to **nature.**

   b. The complex **nature** of this research project requires us to work long hours.

Test-Taking Tip

These key academic vocabulary words often appear on standardized tests.

Illustrate: to provide examples or to show with a picture or another graphic

Infer: to read between the lines or to use knowledge or experience to draw conclusions, make generalizations, or form predictions

Justify: to prove or to support a position with specific facts and reasons

Predict: to tell what will happen in the future based on an understanding of prior events and behaviors

State: to briefly and concisely present information

Summarize: to give a brief overview of the main points of an event or an issue

Literature Online

Vocabulary For more vocabulary practice, go to glencoe.com and enter QuickPass code GLW6053u1.

Vocabulary Workshop

Academic Vocabulary

Teach

Use Academic Vocabulary

Students might find it helpful to explore the meanings of academic words by using them to describe casual, everyday situations. Have students use the academic words *approach, exhibit* and *vehicle* to write questions they could ask about other students' everyday lives. Then have students divide into pairs and take turns answering one another's questions.

[APPROACHING] If necessary, pair more advanced students with students who are having difficulty using the academic words correctly, and have the partners work together to create a list of questions.

Assess

1. In this context, *dynamic* means "energetic." The context clue "spectacular cultural and political achievement" should lead students to this definition.

2. a. In this context, *nature* means "the external natural world." The context clue is "mountains."
   b. In this context, *nature* means "the inherent character of a thing." The context clue is "of this research project."

English Learners

DIFFERENTIATED INSTRUCTION

Advanced Many English learners may have difficulty with multiple-meaning academic words. Make sure students understand that dictionaries usually show the most common definition of a word first. Remind students that the correct definition of a word must be the one that fits the context.

Have students compare the definitions on page 37 with entries in a bilingual dictionary. Ask students which definitions are easiest to understand and which give the most information.

Learning Objectives
Understanding academic vocabulary. (SE)
Understanding multiple-meaning words. (SE)

Focus

Bellringer Options

**Daily Language Practice
Transparency 6**

**Literature Launcher
Prereading Video: Unit 1**

Show students the Literature Launcher Video. Introduce students to the practice of preserving history in the form of oral narratives. Remind students that these stories form an important part of many African peoples' cultural identity.

Or ask: How might having a strong oral history tradition have helped some African peoples to hand down their traditions to new generations? *(People would have been able to tell the same stories they had been told to their own children.)*

Compare Literature About Tricksters

Tricksters are mischievous and magical animal-humans who outwit their opponents. The trickster often functions as a hero, a creator, a fool, a destroyer, or a prankster. In the following tales, the trickster is embodied in the form of a spider, a coyote, and a cat.

COMPARE THE `Big Idea` **Gods and Spirits**

In each of these tales, tricksters use cunning, wit, and supernatural abilities for gains such as a box of stories, the ability to give fire to the world, and wealth. Some of these tricksters defy the gods, while others acquire godlike qualities. As you read, ask yourself, Are these tricksters trying to benefit only themselves or others as well?

COMPARE Trickster Tales

Trickster tales often follow similar narrative patterns, but they may vary in their outcomes. For example, while tricksters are ultimately successful, the result of their trickery may be negative or positive. As you read, ask yourself, Do the end results of the tricksters' actions justify their behavior?

COMPARE Cultures

To understand trickster tales, it is important to know their cultural context. "How Stories Came to Earth" originates from the Ashanti people (also spelled Asante), who live mainly in the villages of Ghana in Africa. "Coyote Steals Fire" comes from the Klamath, a Native American group who lost possession of their ancestral lands. "Master Cat, or Puss in Boots" was written in seventeenth-century France and reflects society under the reign of an absolute monarch. As you read, ask yourself, What aspects of these different cultures are apparent in the stories?

Learning Objectives

For pages 38–51

In studing these texts, you will focus on the following objectives:

Literary Study: Analyzing anthropomorphism.

Reading: Analyzing and comparing cultural contexts. Comparing themes.

Writing: Writing a trickster tale. Comparing trickster tales.

Linguist Staff (Okyeame), 20th century. Ghana (Asante), Guinea Coast. Gold foil, wood, nails, H x W x D: 156.5 x 14.6 x 5.7cm. The Metropolitan Museum of Art, NY.

LOG ON ▶ **Literature** Online

Author Search For more about Charles Perrault, go to glencoe.com and enter QuickPass code GLW6053u1.

Selection Skills

Literary Elements
- Analyze Anthropomorphism (SE pp. 39, 41, 43)
- Point of View (TE p. 42)

Reading Skills
- Analyze Cultural Context (SE pp. 39, 40, 42, 43)
- Apply Background Knowledge (TE p. 44)
- Analyze Characterization (TE p. 48)

Comparing Literature

Vocabulary Skills
- Academic Vocabulary (SE p. 43)
- Trickster Words (TE p. 39)

Speaking/Listening/Viewing Skills
- Compare Cultures (SE p. 51)
- Oral Report (TE pp. 46, 50)

Writing Skills/Grammar
- Trickster Tale (SE p. 43)
- Comma Usage (TE p. 40)

Before You Read

How Stories Came to Earth

Connect to the Folktale

Why might trickster tales be passed down from one generation to the next? Discuss this question with a partner.

Build Background

"How Stories Came to Earth" features Anansi the Spider, who is a central trickster in many West African folktales. In these tales, Anansi often opposes the sky god by stealing his stories or by bringing disease into the world. In trickster tales such as these, the trouble caused by the trickster often brings about a necessary change in society.

Set Purposes for Reading

Big Idea Gods and Spirits

The traditional religion of the Ashanti is based on an array of gods and spirits, including a distant supreme being. As you read, ask yourself, How does the Ashanti sky-god regard stories?

Literary Element Anthropomorphism

Anthropomorphism is the attribution of human characteristics to gods, animals, or inanimate objects. It is often a key element in tales in which animals are the main characters. Storytellers may use anthropomorphism to point out human flaws, such as greed, violence, and selfishness. As you read, ask yourself, How does anthropomorphism function in this story?

Reading Strategy Analyze Cultural Context

To **analyze cultural context** means to examine how a literary work reflects a specific culture and how the culture contributes to the meaning of the work. As you read, ask yourself, How does this story reflect the Ashanti culture?

Tip: Take Notes As you read, use a chart to record specific details that reveal something about Ashanti culture.

Stool with curved seat supported by a leopard from the Ashanti tribe of Ghana, Africa. Wood. Private collection.

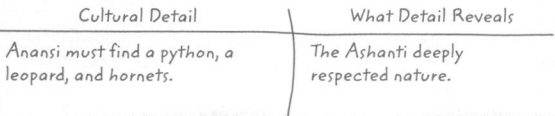

Cultural Detail	What Detail Reveals
Anansi must find a python, a leopard, and hornets.	The Ashanti deeply respected nature.

HOW STORIES CAME TO EARTH **39**

Focus

Summary

With his wife's help, Anansi the Spider uses his ability to fool others to pay the sky-god, Nyame, for the stories the god has kept to himself. By doing so, Anansi provides the people with stories, or knowledge of "the beginnings and endings of things."

> For summaries in languages other than English, see Unit 1 Teaching Resource Book, pp. 61–66.

Vocabulary

Trickster Words Draw students' attention to the language used to characterize First Spider. Anansi is said to be noble and wise as well as a trickster. **Say:** As you read, make a list of other words that could be used to describe the main character.

English Learners

DIFFERENTIATED INSTRUCTION

Intermediate Have students look up the list of words at right in a dictionary and write the definitions in their notebooks. Help students make the connection between the creatures named and the adjectives that are used to describe them. Ask students to use the names and adjectives to predict what will happen in the story.

Word List:

fearsome, elusive, python, leopard, hornets, swarm, fairy

Teach

Asante mask. Ghana. Gold. Private collection.

Big Idea — 1

Gods and Spirits Answer: *This passage might reveal that the Ashanti believed that stories were known first to the gods, could be locked away at will, and were valued most highly by the sky-god.*

Reading Strategy — 2

Analyze Cultural Context Answer: *Women were valued for their knowledge, and may have served as counsel to their families.*

 For additional practice using the reading skill or strategy, see Unit 1 Teaching Resources Book, p. 68.

 For an audio recording of this selection, use Listening Library Audio CD-ROM.

Readability Scores

Dale-Chall: 5.4
DRP: 55
Lexile: 900

How Stories Came to Earth

An Ashanti Legend
Retold by Kaleki

It was long ago in Africa, child, when there was First Spider, Kwaku Anansi. He went everywhere, throughout the world, travelling on his strong web strings—sometimes looking more like a wise old man than a spider.

In that long-ago time, child, there were no stories on Earth for anyone to tell. The sky-god kept all stories to himself, up high in the sky, and locked away in a wooden box.

These the spider wanted, as many creatures had before him, so that he could know the beginnings and endings of things. Yet all who had tried for the stories had returned empty-handed.

Now Anansi climbed up his web to the sky-god, Nyame, to ask for the sky-god's stories.

Child, when the powerful sky-god saw the thin, spidery, old man crawling up to his throne, he laughed at him, "What makes you think that you, of all creatures, can pay the price I ask for my stories?" Spider only wanted to know, "What is the price of the stories?"

"My stories have a great price, four fearsome, elusive creatures: Onini, the python that swallows men whole; Osebo, the leopard with teeth like spears; Mmoboro, the hornets that swarm and sting; and Mmoatia, the fairy who is never seen. Bring these to me."

Bowing, the spider quietly turned and crept back down through the clouds. He meant to capture the four creatures he needed as price for the stories. He first asked his wife, Aso, how he might capture Onini, the python that swallows men whole.

She told him a plan, saying, "Go and cut off a branch of the palm tree and cut some string-creeper as well. Take these to the stream where python lives."

As Anansi went to the swampy stream, carrying these things, he began arguing aloud, "This is longer than he; you lie, no; it is true; this branch is longer and he is shorter, much shorter."

---

1 **Gods and Spirits** *What might this passage reveal about the relationship between gods and stories in Ashanti belief?*

Analyze Cultural Context *Based on Aso's advice to her husband, what can you conclude about the role of women in Ashanti society?* **2**

Grammar Practice

Use Commas with Nonessential Elements Point out that a number of sentences in "How Stories Came to Earth" include nonessential elements. Explain that these elements, set off by commas, interrupt the flow of thought and provide new information. Inform students that participles, infinitives, infinitive phrases, adjective phrases, and appositives can all be nonessential elements, depending on the context.

Write on the board: Now Anansi climbed up his web to the sky-god, Nyame, to ask for the sky god's stories. Explain that this sentence contains a nonessential appositive *(Nyame)*. **Say:** To determine whether an element is essential to the meaning of the sentence, ask yourself if the element fundamentally changes the meaning of the sentence. If it does not, then set it off with commas.

Have students determine whether the underlined appositives in the example sentences are essential or nonessential and if they need to be set off with commas.

1. The trickster figure <u>Anansi</u> plays an essential role in Ashanti folklore. *(essential; doesn't need commas)*

2. A leopard <u>Osebo</u> is the next animal who Anansi tricks. *(nonessential; needs commas)*

The python was listening, and asked what spider was talking about, "What are you muttering, Anansi?"

"I tell you that my wife, Aso, is a liar, for she says that you are longer than this palm branch and I say that you are not."

Onini, the python, said, "Come and place the branch next to me and we will see if she is a liar."

And so, Anansi put the palm branch next to the python's body, and saw the large snake stretch himself alongside it. Anansi then bound the python to the branch with the string-creeper and wound it over and over—nwenene! nwenene! nwenene!—until he came to the head. Then the spiderman said to Onini, "Fool, I will now take you to the sky-god."

This Anansi did as he spun a web around the snake to carry him back through the clouds to the sky kingdom.

On seeing the gigantic snake, Nyame merely said, "There remains what still remains."

Spider came back to Earth to find the next creature, Osebo the leopard, with teeth like spears.

His wife, Aso, told him, "Go dig a large hole."

Anansi said, "I understand, say no more."

After following the tracks of the leopard, spider dug a very deep pit. He covered it over with the branches of the trees and came home. Returning in the very early morning, he found a large leopard lying in the pit.

"Leopard, is this how you act? You should not be prowling around at night; look at where you are! Now put your paw here, and here, and I will help you out."

The leopard put his paws up on the sticks that Anansi placed over the pit and began to climb up. Quickly, Anansi hit him over the head with a wooden knife— gao! Leopard fell back into the pit—fom! Anansi quickly spun the leopard to the sticks with his web string.

"Fool, I am taking you to pay for the sky-god's stories."

But the sky-god received the leopard saying, "What remains, still remains."

Next the spiderman went looking for Mmoboro, the hornets that swarm and sting. Spider told his wife, Aso, what he was looking for and she said, "Look for an empty gourd[1] and fill it with water."

This spider did and he went walking through the bush until he saw a swarm of hornets hanging there in a tree. He poured out some of the water and sprinkled it all over their nest. Cutting a leaf from a nearby banana tree, he held it up and covered his head. He then poured the rest of the water from the gourd all over himself. Then while he was dripping he called out to the hornets,

"The rain has come, do you see me standing here with a leaf to cover my head? Fly inside my empty gourd so that the rain will not beat at your wings."

---

1. A *gourd* (gôrd) is the hard-shelled fruit of any of a group of trailing or climbing vines of the gourd family, including the melon, squash, and pumpkin. They can be used as containers.

---

3 Anthropomorphism *What human characteristics do the python and Anansi exhibit?*

Anthropomorphism *What actions does Anansi take in this passage? How would you describe his behavior?* **4**

HOW STORIES CAME TO EARTH **41**

Teach

Literary Element   3

Anthropomorphism
Answer: *Anansi and the python can talk and reason with each other.*

Literary Element   4

Anthropomorphism
Answer: *He pours and sprinkles water, cuts a leaf from a tree, and covers his head. His behavior is human; his actions are well planned and sneaky.*

Cultural History ☆

Family Structure Aso's clever advice reflects the strong role of women in Ashanti society. For example, the Ashanti people are matrilineal—that is, they trace family descent through the female line of ancestors.

Learning Objectives
Analyzing cultural context. (SE)
Understanding anthropomorphism. (SE)
Using commas with nonessential elements. (TE)

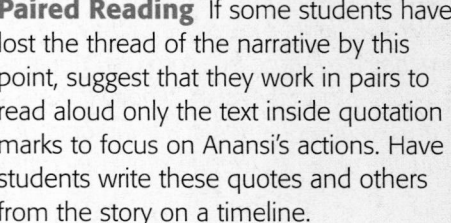

Approaching Level

DIFFERENTIATED INSTRUCTION

Paired Reading If some students have lost the thread of the narrative by this point, suggest that they work in pairs to read aloud only the text inside quotation marks to focus on Anansi's actions. Have students write these quotes and others from the story on a timeline.

English Learners

DIFFERENTIATED INSTRUCTION

Intermediate English learners may be confused by the use of *child* in the first sentence of the selection: *It was long ago in Africa,* <u>child</u>, *when there was the First Spider, Kwaku Anansi.* To grasp why the translator included this word, students should imagine a wise elder telling this story to a younger person. Point out that while in this sentence *child* is set off with commas and appears to be an appositive, it does not provide more information

about Africa. Instead, it is an address to the audience of the story. Discuss with students other conventional phrases from folktales, fairy tales, and other narratives, such as "Once upon a time, . . ." "They lived happily ever after," and so on.

Comparing Literature

Teach

Reading Strategy | 1

Analyze Cultural Context
Answer: *The Ashanti people may have believed in supernatural beings such as fairies and may also have believed that these beings lived in places such as the vicinity of the odum tree.*

Big Idea | 2

Gods and Spirits Answer:
The proclamation reveals that he is trustworthy and will keep his word, that he is generous, and that he is willing to acknowledge the accomplishments of others.

The hornets flew into the gourd, saying, "Thank you—hhhuuummm—Aku; thank you—hhhuuummm—Anansi."

Anansi stopped up the mouth of the gourd, and spinning a thick web around it, said, "Fools, I'm taking you to the sky-god as price for his stories."

The sky-god, Nyame, accepted Mmoboro, the hornets that swarm and sting, and said, "What remains, still remains."

Visual Vocabulary
An *Akua's Child* is a sculpture with a large head and an elongated neck that is sometimes used as a fertility doll in Ghana.

Anansi knew very well what remained—it was the fairy, Mmoatia, who is never seen. When the spider came back to Earth, he asked Aso what to do. And so, he carved an Akua's child, a wooden doll with a black, flat face, and covered it with sticky fluid from a tree.

Walking through the bush, he found the odum tree, where the fairies like to play. He then made eto, pounded yams, and put some in the doll's hand and even more of the yams into a brass basin at her feet—there by the odum tree. Anansi next hid in the bushes, with a vine creeper in his hands that was also tied to the doll's neck.

It wasn't long before the fairies came, two sisters, to play. They saw the doll with the eto and asked if they could have some. Anansi made the doll's head nod, "Yes," by pulling on the string-creeper. Soon the fairies had eaten all the eto and so, thanked the doll, but the doll did not reply. The fairies became angry.

One sister said, "When I thank her, she says nothing."

The other sister replied, "Then slap her in her crying place."

This the fairy did, she slapped it's cheek—"pa!"—but her hand stuck there. She slapped it with her other hand—"pa!"—and that hand stuck, too. She kicked it with both one foot, then the other, and both feet stuck to the sticky wooden doll. Finally, she pushed her stomach to it and that stuck.

Then Anansi came from his hiding place, and said, "Fool, I have got you, and now I will take you to the sky-god to buy his stories once and for all."

Anansi spun a web around the last of the four creatures and brought Mmoatia up to Nyame in the sky kingdom. The sky-god, seeing this last catch, called together all his nobles. He put it before them and told them that the spiderman had done what no one else had been able to do. He said in a loud voice that rang in the sky,

> "From now and forever, my sky-god stories belong to you—kose! kose! kose!—my blessing, my blessing, my blessing. We will now call these 'Spider Stories.'"

And so, child, stories came to Earth because of the great cunning of Kwaku Anansi, and his wife, Aso. When Anansi brought the wooden box of stories to his home, he and his wife eagerly learned each one of them. And you can still see today that Aku and Aso tell their stories. Everywhere you look, they spin their webs for all to see. ❧

1 **Analyze Cultural Context** *What might this passage reveal about Ashanti views of the supernatural?*

Gods and Spirits *Based on his proclamation, what character traits might be attributed to Nyame?* **2**

Literary Element Practice

SPIRAL REVIEW   SMALL GROUP

Point of View Divide students into small groups. Assign each group one of the following secondary characters from the story: Onini, Osebo, Mmoboro, and Mmoatia. Have each group rewrite the story from the point of view of their character. Each group should focus only on the part of the story involving their character. For example, the Onini group would rewrite from "As Anansi went to the swampy stream," to "through the clouds to the sky kingdom." (pp. 40–41). Encourage students to develop both positive and negative human qualities of the character, and have students explore the motivation behind their character's actions in the story. Have members of each group read or act out their section of the story in the order of the group numbers above. After each group has performed, **ask:** How did using animals rather than people as characters affect the way you wrote the story? *(Students may say that they felt that they had more freedom using animal characters than they would have if they had used human characters; the animals allow the writer to exaggerate a key trait.)*

After You Read

Respond and Think Critically

Respond and Interpret

1. Do you think Anansi's tricks are justified? Why or why not?

2. (a)What are some of Anansi's physical characteristics? (b)Why might Nyame laugh at Anansi because of these characteristics?

3. (a)What four creatures does the sky-god tell Anansi to capture? (b)What do these creatures have in common?

Analyze and Evaluate

4. (a)What is the significance of Anansi's capture of the other creatures? (b)Why might the tale incorporate both large creatures, such as the leopard, and small creatures, such as fairies?

5. (a)In your opinion, is Anansi a sympathetic character? Explain. (b)Which of his character traits support your opinion?

6. Why might the Ashanti have chosen the image of the web to describe stories?

Connect

7. **Big Idea** Gods and Spirits Why might the Ashanti have worshipped a god who they believed kept stories from them, when they value storytelling so highly?

8. **Connect to Today** (a)What famous examples of anthropomorphized animals exist in books or movies today? (b)Why might these types of animals continue to be popular?

Literary Element Anthropomorphism

Personification is similar to anthropomorphism but is usually confined to a figure of speech.

1. What are some human characteristics of Anansi?

2. What positive and negative human qualities does Anansi possess?

Reading Strategy Analyze Cultural Context

By reading "How Stories Came to Earth," you can make generalizations about the Ashanti culture.

Partner Activity With a classmate, reread the story, examining the skills and resources Anansi uses to outsmart each creature. Based on what you find, compile a list of the skills and resources most likely valued by the Ashanti people.

 Literature Online

Selection Resources For Selection Quizzes, eFlashcards, and Reading-Writing Connection activities, go to glencoe.com and enter QuickPass code GLW6053u1.

Academic Vocabulary

*Tricksters deceive people for the **benefit** of society as a whole.*

Benefit is an academic word. Using context clues, try to figure out the meaning of *benefit* in each sentence below.

1. The auction was held as a **benefit** to raise money for the American Red Cross.

2. One **benefit** of switching to public transportation is faster travel time.

For more on academic vocabulary, see pages 36–37 and R83–R85.

Writing

Write a Trickster Tale Using Anansi as a model, write a trickster tale featuring an animal character of your choice. Use the chart you made on page 39 to help you think about the cultural values you want to express in your tale.

HOW STORIES CAME TO EARTH **43**

After You Read

Assess

1. Answers will vary.

2. (a) Anansi is thin and old. (b) Nyame believes that he is too small and old to pay the price of the stories.

3. (a) A python, a leopard, hornets, and a fairy (b) All four creatures will be difficult to capture, and might be dangerous.

4. (a) It shows that his power lies in intelligence, manipulation, and careful planning. (b) To emphasize that Anansi's success is due to cunning rather than size

5. (a) Students who say he is sympathetic may note that his task is worthy. Those who disagree may note his manipulation and his arrogance. (b) Answers will vary.

6. Both stories and webs take time and skill to spin, are found everywhere, and are interconnected.

7. Despite the fact that he kept the stories for himself, Nyame is fair and generous.

8. (a) Answers will vary. (b) These animals may continue to be popular because they are often sympathetic.

Literary Element

1. Anansi can speak and reason.
2. Positive: loyal and hopes to give stories to Earth. Negative: manipulative and destructive.

Reading Strategy

Lists should include values and traditions important in the Ashanti culture.

Progress Check

Can students identify anthropomorphism?

If No → see Unit 1 Teaching Resource Book, p. 67.

 For grammar practice, see Unit 1 Teaching Resource Book, p. 69.

Academic Vocabulary

1. "an event held to raise money for a charitable cause"
2. "advantage"

Writing

Students' trickster tales should
- feature an animal character
- express a set of cultural values

43

Teach

View the Art ★

Coyote is an important character in Native American folklore in many parts of North America. The word *coyote* is derived from the Aztec word *coyotl.* In Aztec folklore, the coyote was a loyal companion of the god of war. This Aztec sculpture shows a coyote with feathers, which symbolize movement. **Ask:** Why might the Aztecs have considered the coyote to be a suitable companion for their god of war? *(Students may say that the coyote is a cunning predator that can strike suddenly.)*

Readability Scores

Dale-Chall: 5.3
DRP: 49
Lexile: 710

Reading Practice

Apply Background Knowledge Point out how Coyote takes advantage of the rage of his opponent to accomplish his goal. **Ask:** Do you know of any other stories in which the main character defeats an opponent who loses his or her temper?

Build Background

The trickster assumes many personas in Native American folktales, but Coyote is the most prevalent trickster of all. He is often portrayed as part animal and part human and possesses many human qualities, including greed, strength, weakness, heroism, and cowardice. In various stories, Coyote creates Earth, animals, and humans and brings fire and sunlight to people.

"Coyote Steals Fire" comes from the Native American oral tradition of the Klamath, who now live in south-central Oregon and northern California. Their territorial land is in the southern Cascade mountain range, where they were fishers and hunters. Traditionally, the Klamath lived in villages with leaders, shamans, and medicine men.

Feathered Coyote, c.1500. Aztec. Carved stone. Museo Nacional de Antropologia, Mexico City. ★

Coyote Steals Fire

Retold by Richard Erdoes and Alfonso Ortiz

There was a time when people had no fire. In winter they could not warm themselves. They had to eat their food raw. Fire was kept inside a huge white rock that belonged to Thunder, who was its caretaker. Thunder was a fearful being. Everybody was afraid of him. Even Bear and Mountain Lion trembled when they heard Thunder's rumbling voice.

Coyote was not afraid of Thunder. He was afraid of nothing. One day, Thunder was in an angry mood and roared and

(Students may mention "Jack and the Beanstalk.") What might be the moral of such a story? *(Students may say that the moral of the story is that self-control is an important virtue.)*

rumbled his loudest, so that the earth trembled and all animals went into hiding. Coyote decided that this was the time to get the fire away from Thunder. Coyote climbed the highest mountain on which Thunder lived. Thunder was at home. "Uncle," said Coyote, "let us play a game of dice. If you win, you can kill me. If I win, you have to give me fire."

"Let us play," said Thunder.

They played with dice made from the gnawing teeth of beavers and woodchucks. The beaver teeth were male dice. The woodchuck teeth were female dice. A design was carved on one side of these teeth. The teeth were thrown on a flat rock. If the male teeth came up with the carved sides, they counted two points. If the female teeth came up with the carved sides, they counted one. If the dice came up uneven, they did not count. There was a bundle of sticks for counting, for keeping track of the points scored.

Now, Coyote is the trickiest fellow alive. He is the master at cheating at all kinds of games. He continuously distracted Thunder so that he could not watch what Coyote was up to. Thunder was no match for Coyote when it came to gambling. Whenever Thunder took his eyes off Coyote's hands, even for just the tiniest part of a moment, Coyote turned his dice up so that they showed the carved sides. He turned Thunder's dice up so that they showed the blank sides. He distracted Thunder and made him blink. Then, quick as a flash, he took a counting stick away from Thunder's pile and added it to his own. In the end, Thunder was completely confused. Coyote had all the counting sticks, Thunder had none. "Uncle, I won," said Coyote. "Hand over the fire." Thunder knew that Coyote had cheated but could not prove it.

Coyote called upon all the animals to come up to the mountaintop to help him carry the big rock that contained the fire. That rock was huge and looked solid, but it was very fragile, as fragile as a seashell. So all the animals prepared to carry the rock away. "Not so fast," growled Thunder. "Coyote won the game and so I give him the fire. But he cheated, and for that I shall take his life. Where is he so that I can kill him?"

Now, Coyote had read Thunder's mind. He had anticipated what Thunder was up to. Coyote could pull the outer part of his body off, as if it were a blanket, so he put his skin, his pelt, his tail, his ears—all of his outside—close by Thunder, and with the inside of his body, his vitals, moved a distance away. Then he changed his voice so that it sounded as if it were coming not from a distance, but like from just a few feet away. "Here I am, Uncle," he cried. "Kill me if you can." Thunder picked up the huge rock containing fire and hurled it at what he thought was Coyote. But he hit only the skin and fur. The rock splintered into numberless pieces. Every animal took a little piece of the fire and put it under its armpit or under its wing, and they hurried all over the world, bringing fire to every tribe on earth. Coyote calmly put on his outer skin and fur again. "Good-bye, Uncle," he said to Thunder. "Don't gamble. It is not what you do best." Then he ran off.

> 💬 **Discussion Starter**
>
> "Coyote Steals Fire" is an example of a Native American trickster tale in which the trickster obtains a much-needed item for the inhabitants of Earth. Why does Coyote succeed when others are too afraid to confront Thunder? What might Coyote represent to the Klamath? Discuss these questions with a group.

COYOTE STEALS FIRE **45**

Assess

Discussion Starter

Coyote succeeds because he is unafraid to confront Thunder and is willing to cheat and use magic to obtain his goal. Moreover, he is patient—he waits until Thunder is angry to confront him. Coyote's human characteristics represent both good and bad aspects of human nature. The story shows how these aspects can work together to achieve a positive goal.

English Learners

DIFFERENTIATED INSTRUCTION

Intermediate Speakers of Romance languages may be led astray by false cognates. For example, in Spanish the word *embarazada* means *pregnant*. It is a false cognate for the English *embarrassed*. Have English learners whose first language has many such cognates think of other false cognates that they have come across while learning English. Students can create a two-column chart listing the words and

their meanings in English and the student's first language.

Focus

Summary

In this tale, a miller dies and leaves his mill, donkey, and cat to his eldest, middle, and youngest sons, respectively. The eldest has inherited the family business, which will support him. The second son to can also earn money with his donkey. But what can the youngest do with the family cat? At first heartbroken, the youngest son discovers that the cat has a plan. Once he is given a pair of boots, the cat proceeds to fool the king himself into making the young man's fortune.

Literary Element **1**

Anthropomorphism Remind students that though the lead character in this story is a cat, he is a cat that acts like a man and his actions may be compared to the actions of a man during this time period. Explain to students that boots were generally worn only by adult males, and might be given as a special present when a young man came of age. Boots were thus a symbol of power. **Ask:** What do you think such a symbol means in the story? What did it mean to the story's original audience that the cat asks for boots? Suggest to students that his stated reason, so he can move through the underbrush, seems unlikely because generally cats have little trouble with underbrush.

Readability Scores

Dale-Chall: 6.7
DRP: 54
Lexile: 1060

Build Background

Written in 1697, "Master Cat, or Puss in Boots" first appeared in Charles Perrault's compilation, *Tales of Mother Goose*. It mirrors the French society of Perrault's time, which was fond of pretentious behavior and opulent lifestyles under the reign of Louis XIV. Puss in Boots (Master Cat) gains favor for his manipulation of these values and uses trickery to change his master's social class.

The story applies the trickster motif to the fairy tale genre. Perrault wrote fairy tales to amuse children and added morals at the end of them. However, as in "Puss in Boots," these morals often served as social commentaries, rather than lessons.

Master Cat,
or Puss in Boots

Charles Perrault
Translated by Maria Tatar

A miller left to his three sons all his worldly possessions: a mill, a donkey, and a cat. The estate was divided up quickly. No one called in a notary[1] or an attorney, for they would have quickly consumed the paltry inheritance. The oldest son got the mill; the second son received the donkey; and the youngest got nothing but the cat.

The youngest son was heartbroken when he saw how little he had inherited. "My brothers can earn an honest living if they decide to join forces," he said. "But as for me, once I've eaten the cat and made a muff[2] from its skin, I will surely starve to death."

The cat listened to this speech but pretended not to hear it and said in a solemn and earnest manner: "Don't be upset, master. Just get me a pouch and have a pair of boots[3] made up so that I can get through the underbrush easily, and you'll see that you really don't have that bad a deal." **1**

Although the cat's master was not encouraged by this declaration, he had noticed that this cat was able to catch rats

---

1. A *notary* is a public officer authorized to administer oaths and certify documents.

2. A *muff* is a fluffy tube often made of fur designed so that one hand can be slipped in at each end for warmth.

3. In seventeenth-century France, a *pair of boots* was a sign of elegance.

46 UNIT 1 EARLY AFRICA

Speaking Practice

Present an Oral Report Draw students' attention to the mention of the cat's ability to catch rats and mice. Ask students to research the dangers of rats in medieval Europe. Have them report their findings orally to the class. Then outline the story of the Pied Piper of Hamelin. Point out to students that a culture plagued with vermin would have understood perfectly what a boon it would be to remove all the rats from a town or village.

Teach

 View the Art ★

Gustave Doré was born in 1832. At the age of 13 he began creating his first formal works of art, and by the time he was 14 he had his first collection of illustrations published, called *Les Travaux d'Hercules* (The Labors of Hercules). When he was 15 he began working as an illustrator for a magazine, and that same year he exhibited his first ink drawings and was greatly admired. From 1851 he illustrated, among others, the works of famous French writers, including Balzac and Rabelais; more fairy tales; the works of Edgar Allan Poe; and many Bible stories. He is noted for the fantastic imaginary landscapes he created, and for the impassioned Romanticism of the images.

Puss in Boots, 1883. Gustave Dore. Engraving. Private collection. ★

CHARLES PERRAULT **47**

Learning Objectives
Analyzing anthropomorphism. (TE)
Presenting an oral report. (TE)

Approaching Level
DIFFERENTIATED INSTRUCTION

Fluency Hearing and understanding fluent reading helps less-fluent readers to develop reading and speaking skills. Consider reading aloud some or all of "Puss In Boots" to such students, modeling expression and "fairy tale" style and tone. You might also read aloud, or ask more-proficient students to read aloud, other well-known fairy tales.

English Learners
DIFFERENTIATED INSTRUCTION

Intermediate Point out to students that one of the rabbits the cat catches is described as being "still wet behind the ears." Explain to English learners that this is an example of an idiom. Idioms are expressions that signify more than their literal meaning.

Explain that to say someone is "wet behind the ears" means that the person is "so uninformed and inexperienced that they

may as well have just been born." Note that the phrase derives from babies, who are born with moisture behind their ears.

Comparing Literature

Teach

Reading Strategy   1

Analyze Cultural Context

Let students know that the cat's gifts of rabbits and pheasants were gifts of food. The king would be expected to kill and eat the pheasants. Explain to students that the people in this story usually fed themselves by raising their own food, whether animal or vegetable. A gift of game such as the pheasants, which had to be trapped or shot, was a special treat. **Ask:** What gifts of food are a special mark of friendship and respect today? *(Students may mention cookies, a cake, or a meal at a restaurant.)*

Cultural History ☆

Titled Europe Point out that many fairy tales feature kings, princes, princesses, and other nobility. Students may be confused by some of the noble titles presented here. Tell them that a marquis was a kind of noble who ranked above a count but below a duke. The usual titles for men were king, prince, duke, marquis, earl, count, viscount, baron, baronet.

View the Art ★

Gustave Doré was best known for his engravings, two of which appear with this selection. These engravings were made by cutting grooves into a metal plate, inking the plate, and pressing the plate on paper to make a print.

and mice by playing clever tricks (hanging upside down by his paws or lying down in flour and playing dead), and so he saw a ray of hope in his miserable situation.

As soon as the cat was given what he had asked for, he brashly pulled on his boots, hung the pouch around his neck, held the strings with his forepaws, and raced over to a warren that housed a large number of rabbits. He put a little clover and lettuce into the pouch, lay down next to it, and played dead. Then he waited for one of the little rabbits, one inexperienced in the ways of the world, to crawl into the sack and try to eat what was in it.

Just as he was stretching out, he scented success: a young rabbit, still wet behind the ears, hopped into the sack. Master Cat pulled the strings in a flash, grabbed the bag, and, without feeling the least pity for his prey, killed it.

Proud of his prize, he raced straight to the king's palace and demanded an audience with him. He was ushered into the chambers of His Majesty, and, upon entering, bowed deeply to the king and said: "I am presenting you with a rabbit from my lord, the Marquis de Carabas (that was the name he had bestowed on his master). He has instructed me to present it to you on his behalf."

1 "Tell your master that I am grateful to him and that he has given me great pleasure."

Some time later, the cat hid in a field of wheat, keeping his pouch open. When two partridges entered it, he pulled the strings and caught both of them. Then he presented them to the king, just as he had done with the rabbits. The king accepted the two partridges gratefully and gave the cat a small token of his appreciation.

For two to three months, the cat continued presenting the king with game of one

kind or another, always "shot by his master." One day, he learned that the king was planning to go on an excursion along the riverbank with his daughter, the most beautiful princess in the world. He said to his master: "If you want to make your fortune, then take my advice. Just go over to the river and take a swim at the spot I will show you. Leave the rest to me."

The Marquis de Carabas did as the cat told him, without knowing exactly what good would come of it. While he was in the water, the king drove by, and the cat began to yowl at the top of his lungs: "Help! Help! My lord, the Marquis de Carabas, is drowning!"

Puss in Boots, 1868. Gustave Doré. Engraving. Private collection. ★

Reading Practice

Analyze Characterization Encourage students to note how the character of the cat develops. Point out that the cat becomes as lordly as any duke when he is speaking to the people working in the field. **Ask:** What do you think this change signals to the reader? *(It signals the cat's courage and growing power.)*

Students may say it also suggests that the cat's role in life is changing—just as he has become more than just a housecat, the hero may become someone more important and may move from one station in life to another.

At the sound of the yowling, the king stuck his head out the coach window, and when he recognized the cat that had brought him game so many times, he ordered his guards to hurry to the aid of the Marquis de Carabas.

While the guards were rescuing the poor Marquis de Carabas, the cat went up to the royal coach and told the king that thieves had stolen his master's clothing while he was swimming. He had done everything he could by shouting, "Stop the thieves!" but it was no use. In reality, the scoundrel had hidden the clothes under a rock.

The king ordered the officers of the royal wardrobe to fetch one of his finest suits for the Marquis de Carabas. The king paid him a thousand compliments. Since the fine clothes that the marquis was wearing flattered him (he was both handsome and statuesque), the king's daughter found him much to her liking. All the Marquis de Carabas had to do was to cast two or three respectful and somewhat tender glances in her direction to make her fall head over heels in love with him.

The king insisted that the marquis ride in his carriage and accompany them on their excursion. The cat, delighted to see that his plan was succeeding, ran on ahead. When he came across some peasants who were mowing a field, he said: "Listen to me, my good people. If you do not say that the fields you are mowing belong to the Marquis de Carabas, each and every one of you will be cut into little pieces until you look like chopped meat!"

The king did not fail to ask the mowers whose field they were mowing: "It belongs to our lord, the Marquis de Carabas," they all said in unison, for the cat had frightened them with his threats.

2 "You have a very substantial inheritance there," the king said to the Marquis de Carabas.

"You can see, Sire, that this field offers an abundant yield every year," the marquis replied.

Master Cat made a point of staying ahead of the coach. When he met some reapers, he said: "Listen to me, my good people. If you do not say that all of this wheat you are reaping belongs to the Marquis de Carabas, you will be cut into little pieces until you look like chopped meat." **2**

The king drove by a moment later and wanted to know who owned the wheat fields in the vicinity. "They belong to the Marquis de Carabas," the mowers all replied, and the king once more expressed his pleasure to the marquis.

Master Cat made a point of staying in front of the coach, and he said the same thing to everyone he met. The king was astonished at the vast amount of property owned by the Marquis de Carabas.

At last Master Cat arrived at a beautiful castle owned by an ogre who was renowned for his wealth.[4] All the lands through which the king had been traveling were in his domain. The cat, who had made a point of finding out who this ogre was and learning the extent of his powers, asked for an audience. He claimed that he could not possibly be so close to his castle **3** without paying his respects.

The ogre received him as politely as an ogre can and asked him to sit down.

"It has been said," the cat stated, "that you have the ability to transform yourself into any animal at all. I'm told that you can, for example, turn yourself into a lion or an elephant."

"It's true," replied the ogre brusquely, "and just to prove it, I will turn into a lion."

---

4. An *ogre who was renowned for his wealth* may refer to a character who symbolizes a feudal lord.

CHARLES PERRAULT **49**

Advanced Learners/Pre-AP

DIFFERENTIATED INSTRUCTION

Primogeniture Encourage students to research the history of the law of primogeniture—the practice of leaving everything to the first-born male child. Leaving entire estates to the firstborn male heir was the practice all over Europe for centuries. Ask them to present this information to the class.

English Learners

DIFFERENTIATED INSTRUCTION

Intermediate Encourage students who are learning English to form pairs and retell the story thus far to each other. You may wish to write a list of words on the board that indicate sequence, such as *first, next, then, meanwhile*, and *finally*. Have students write these words at appropriate intervals on a sheet of paper. Then have them list the story events in proper sequence.

Comparing Literature

Teach

Vocabulary **2**

Modifiers Remind students that a modifier describes, or modifies, another word: adjectives modify nouns, and adverbs tell about a verb, an adjective, or another adverb. Have students list the modifiers they find in this passage. (*Possible answers: substantial, abundant, little*) **Ask:** What do these words have in common? (*They describe amounts.*) Ask students to look in the remainder of the selection for more modifiers that describe amounts, and to list them.

Literary Element **3**

Anthropomorphism Explain to students that this passage, and the cat's statement, illustrate that the cat has continued to put on the airs of a gentleman. When he says that he could not pass the ogre's castle "without paying his respects," he imitates a country gentleman's behavior. This portrait of the cat as genteel caller is Perrault's joking portrait of the society he knew. **Ask:** What actions by the cat shows that it still retains some animal characteristics? (*the capture and devouring of the mouse*)

Learning Objectives
Analyzing cultural context. (TE)
Understanding modifiers. (TE)
Understanding anthropomorphism. (TE)
Analyzing characterization. (TE)

Comparing Literature

Assess

Quickwrite

Like all fairy tales, "Puss in Boots" was intended for both adults and children, though Perrault wrote them for his own children. Children would have been happy with a tale about a magic cat, and satisfied that the story rights the injustice done to the hero in his father's will. Adults would laugh at the cat's duplicity as well as enjoy the fantasy of a poor young man's rise to wealth. Some students may point out that adults would also have been aware that lying and cheating one's way to wealth has never been uncommon.

The cat was so terrified at seeing a lion before him that he instantly scurried up to the gutters on the roof, not without some pain and peril, for his boots were not made for walking on tiles.

A little later, when the cat saw that the ogre had turned back to his former state, he scampered back down and admitted that he had been terrified.

"It has also been said," the cat declared, "but I can hardly believe it, that you have the power to take the shape of small animals. I've heard, for example, that you can change into a rat or a mouse. I confess that it seems utterly impossible to me."

"Impossible?" the ogre replied. "Take a look."

At that moment, he transformed himself into a mouse, which ran across the floor. As soon as the cat saw it, he pounced on it and ate it up.

Meanwhile, the king, who could see the beautiful castle of the ogre from his coach, was hoping to enter it. The cat heard the sound of the coach rolling over the drawbridge, ran to meet it, and said to the king: "Your Majesty, welcome to the castle of the Marquis de Carabas!"

"What?" the king shouted. "Does this castle also belong to you, Monsieur Marquis? I have never seen anything as beautiful as this courtyard and the buildings surrounding it. Let's go inside, if you please."

The marquis took the hand of the young princess, and they followed the king, who went up the stairs. When they entered the grand hall, they discovered a magnificent repast[5] prepared by the ogre for his friends, who were supposed to see him that very day, but who did not dare enter, knowing that the king was there.

The king was as charmed by the many qualities of the Marquis de Carabas, as was his daughter, who remained head over heels in love with him. Realizing how much wealth he possessed, the king said to him, after having quaffed[6] five or six glasses of wine: "It's up to you whether you want to become my son-in-law or not, Monsieur Marquis."

The marquis, bowing deeply, accepted the honor conferred on him by the king. That very day he married the princess. The cat became a great lord and never again had to run after mice, except when he wanted to amuse himself.

Moral
However great the benefit
Of inheriting a tidbit
Handed down from father to son.
Young people with industry
Will prefer using ingenuity[7]
Even if the gains are hard-won.

Second Moral
If a miller's son can have success
In winning the heart of a fair
  princess
And drawing tender gazes from her,
Then watch how his manner,
  youth, and dress,
Inspire in her tenderness,
They count for something, you'll
  concur.[8]

---

6. *Quaffed* means "to have drunk deeply."
7. *Ingenuity* means "cleverness."
8. *Concur* means "to agree."

Quickwrite

Fairy tales are often intended for children and sometimes contain a lesson. What do you think the intended lesson of "Puss in Boots" was for people in seventeenth-century France? Is this a lesson for children or adults? Explain your answers in a paragraph.

---

5. A *repast* is a meal or a snack.

Speaking Practice

Present an Oral Report Tell students that Perrault was the originator of Mother Goose, and is best remembered for this collection of fairy stories, *Contes de ma mère l'oye* (Tales of Mother Goose, 1697). The stories, among them "Little Red Riding Hood," "The Sleeping Beauty," "Puss in Boots," and "Bluebeard," were written to amuse his children. Perrault's tales were modern versions of half-forgotten folk tales. Invite students to research the roots of the fairy tales Perrault used as sources, and present them to the class.

- *How Stories Came to Earth* retold by Kaleki

- *Coyote Steals Fire* retold by Richard Erdoes and Alfonso Ortiz

- *Master Cat, or Puss in Boots* by Charles Perrault

COMPARE THE [Big Idea] Gods and Spirits

Group Activity Tricksters often use supernatural powers to reach their goals. In "How Stories Came to Earth" and "Coyote Steals Fire," the tricksters use these powers to gain something from a god or a magical being. In "Puss in Boots," the cat uses his wits, rather than supernatural abilities, to gain wealth and status. In a small group, discuss the following questions. Cite evidence from the texts to support your points.

1. Do the tricksters in these three tales use their magical powers for good or bad purposes? Explain.

2. How do the tricksters and others in these tales regard Nyame the sky-god, Thunder, and the ogre?

3. How does "Puss in Boots" differ from the other two tales? Why do you think this story lacks a character that is either a god or a spirit?

COMPARE Trickster Tales

Writing The trickster in each of these tales makes a change that affects the community in which he lives. Some of these changes are for the good of society, while others are more selfish in nature. In a brief essay, compare the strategies each trickster uses to fulfill his goal. Discuss how these strategies are beneficial, destructive, or both. Finally, conclude your essay by discussing whether the outcomes achieved by the tricksters justify the means they used.

COMPARE Cultures

Speaking and Listening To some extent, these trickster tales reflect the cultural beliefs and values of the society from which they were derived or in which they were written. Research the Ashanti, Klamath, and French cultures that shaped these stories. Then give a brief oral presentation to the class about your findings, comparing and contrasting cultural similarities and differences.

Kukujumuku, 1992. John Goba. Painted wood and porcupine quills, 130 x 60 x 65 cm. The Pigozzi Collection, Geneva.

 Literature Online

Selection Resources For Selection Quizzes, eFlashcards, and Reading-Writing Connection activities, go to glencoe.com and enter QuickPass code GLW6053u1.

COMPARING LITERATURE **51**

Assess

Compare the Big Idea

1. The tricksters manipulate and even kill other creatures, actions that are generally considered negative. However, some of the creatures they trick are selfish or frightening to others.

2. Nyame, Thunder, and the ogre are all regarded as powerful and often fearsome creatures that must be defeated or manipulated. The trickster in each tale is the only character willing to stand up to these gods and magical beings without fear.

3. In "Puss in Boots," the final outcome is wealth for an individual, rather than something to benefit the world. This story may show that wealth is a purely human pursuit not influenced by gods and spirits. It lacks a god or spirit because it was written in a culture different from that of the Ashanti and Klamath people.

Compare Trickster Tales

Each trickster sets traps for his opponents. However, it is each creature's lack of suspicion that allows the trickster to trick the creature. Coyote cheats at dice and uses his ability to remove his outer skin to trick Thunder. Puss in Boots uses his charm and skills as a predator to trick humans. All three creatures are cunning and greedy, yet their actions are ultimately beneficial.

Compare Cultures

Students should note the specific ways in which each culture influenced its trickster tale. They should note similarities, such as the prevalence of magical animals in African and Native American mythologies, and differences, such as Perrault's use of animal characters to comment shrewdly on human society. Students may also note the all-encompassing worldview of Native American and African cultures, which include animals and natural phenomena in addition to human society.

Focus

Bellringer Options

Selection Focus Transparency 2

Daily Language Practice Transparency 7

Or ask: Have you ever had a fight with a friend for a reason that might have seemed ridiculous to an onlooker?

Find out what surprising or trivial arguments students have had.

Summary

To create dissension between two best friends, Edju walks between the fields where the two men work, dressed so that each man sees him differently. When the two friends go home, they argue about the appearance of Edju. They end up in a physical confrontation. When they are summoned to explain themselves, Edju admits that "sowing dissension" is his "chief delight."

 For summaries in languages other than English, see Unit 1 Teaching Resources Book, pp. 72–77.

Before You Read

Edju and the Two Friends

Connect to the Folktale

Think about a quarrel you once had with a friend. What was the outcome of the argument? Write a journal entry in which you reflect on the quarrel and its outcome.

Build Background

The following trickster tale features Edju (also spelled Eshu), one of the most important gods of the Yoruba people of Nigeria. At first glance, Edju does not seem to deserve much respect—he plays tricks on gods and humans alike and enjoys stirring up mischief. The Yoruba, however, view him as both a creative and a destructive force.

Set Purposes for Reading

Big Idea Gods and Spirits

Traditional African literature often explores the interactions between humans and gods or spirits. As you read the following folktale, ask yourself, What are Edju's motivations for his behavior?

Literary Element Irony

Irony is a contrast between reality and appearance or expectations. **Dramatic irony** occurs when the reader or audience knows something that a character does not know. As you read "Edju and the Two Friends," ask yourself, What are some examples of dramatic irony in this tale?

Reading Strategy Connect to Personal Experience

One way to connect to a literary work is to draw upon your personal background to create meaning. As you read the following folktale, ask yourself, How is the friends' quarrel similar to a quarrel I have had?

Tip: Compare Relationships Make a chart like the one below to record similarities and differences between the quarrel described in the story and your own experiences.

"Edju and the Two Friends"	My Own Experience
The two friends always dressed alike.	I bought a shirt that my friend also wanted.

Learning Objectives

For pages 52–55

In studying this text, you will focus on the following objectives:

Literary Study: Analyzing irony.

Reading: Connecting to personal experience.

Writing: Writing an anecdote.

Vocabulary

toil (toil) *n.* fatiguing work or effort; p. 54 *The long day's toil left the laborer exhausted.*

retort (ri tôrt´) *v.* to reply in kind, especially with anger or with a witty or an insulting response; p. 54 *Her comments often cause me to retort sarcastically.*

assailant (ə sā´lənt) *n.* attacker; p. 54 *The police officer captured the young woman's assailant after a foot chase.*

dissension (di sen´shən) *n.* disagreement; discord; p. 54 *The town meeting produced no solution to the problem and only increased dissension.*

Tip: Antonyms Antonyms are words that have opposite or nearly opposite meanings and are the same part of speech. For example, the words *toil* and *relaxation* are antonyms.

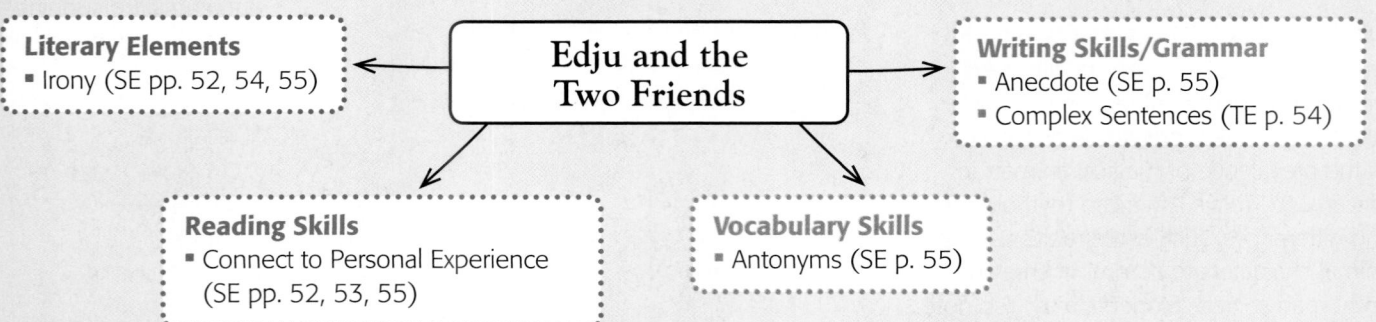

Literary Elements
- Irony (SE pp. 52, 54, 55)

Edju and the Two Friends

Writing Skills/Grammar
- Anecdote (SE p. 55)
- Complex Sentences (TE p. 54)

Reading Skills
- Connect to Personal Experience (SE pp. 52, 53, 55)

Vocabulary Skills
- Antonyms (SE p. 55)

Edju & the Two Friends

Translated by Paul Radin

Ayo, 1990. Agbagli Kossi (Togo). Painted wood. Height: 107cm. The Pigozzi Collection, Geneva.

View the Art This sculpture is an Ayo—a servant or an escort for a spirit, according to the Mamy Wata religion. An Ayo usually has three heads. How does this representation of an Ayo reflect the plot of "Edju and the Two Friends"? ★

Once upon a time, Olorun[1] first created Enja, or mortal man, and, after that, Edju, the god. Once there were a pair of friends. When they went out they were always dressed alike. Everyone said, "These two men are the best of friends." Edju saw them and said, "These men are very dear to each other. I will make them differ and that will be a fine beginning for a very big Idja [lawsuit]." The fields of these friends adjoined. A path ran between and separated them. Edju used to walk on it of a morning and then wore a "filla" or black cap.

Now, when Edju wanted to start this quarrel, he made himself a cap of green, black, red, and white cloth, which showed a different color from whatever side it was looked at. He put it on one morning on his walk abroad. Then he took his tobacco

---

1. **Olorun** is the original and supreme sky god who created hundreds of other lesser gods according to Yoruban belief.

Connect to Personal Experience *Based on your own experiences with friends, how would you describe the relationship between these two friends?* **1**

EDJU AND THE TWO FRIENDS **53**

Teach

Reading Strategy 1

Connect to Personal Experience **Answer:**
Students might use expressions such as "They're like brothers" or "They're really tight" to describe the closeness of the two friends' relationship.

📁 For additional practice using the reading skill or strategy, see Unit 1 Teaching Resources Book, p. 79.

View the Art ★
Answer: *Students might note that the Ayo looks like two people divided by a snake—the two people could be seen as the friends and the snake could be viewed as Edju. Alternatively, students might say that the Ayo is two-faced, as the friends prove to be toward one another.*

Readability Scores
Dale-Chall: 4.1
DRP: 48
Lexile: 640

Learning Objectives
Analyzing irony. (SE)
Connecting to personal experience. (SE)

Approaching Level

DIFFERENTIATED INSTRUCTION

Literary Conventions Explain to the class that fairy tales and folktales use common characteristics to signal readers to expect certain conventions, kinds of subjects, and kinds of themes. The opening phrase "Once upon a time" is a key element in signaling what will come. Have students work in small groups to develop a list of their expectations when they hear the phrase "Once upon a time."

Have groups share their conclusions with the rest of the class. When students have finished reading "Edju and the Two Friends," ask them which of their expectations was satisfied by the story. For students who need more support, divide them into small groups and instruct them to make a list of common characters, settings, and themes found in fairy tales and folk tales.

Advanced Learners/Pre-AP

DIFFERENTIATED INSTRUCTION

Write a Folktale Have advanced students use their knowledge of folktales to write a short anecdote featuring a trickster character, similar to "Edju and the Two Friends." Their folktales should include common features of the genre, such as the trickster's duping of other characters and a moral at the end of the tale.

Teach

Literary Element	1

Irony **Answer:** *This is an example of dramatic irony because the friends do not know what the reader knows: Edju has purposely tricked them.*

Big Idea	2

Gods and Spirits **Answer:** *Students might mention figures such as the African trickster Anansi and the Native American tricksters Raven and Coyote.*

Cultural History ☆

Blame It on the Gods? Inform your students that mythology and folklore tend to blame irrational acts on the interference of the gods. The Yoruba traditionally blame Edju when they experience trouble in their lives. The ancient Greeks blamed some irrational human behavior on dissension among the gods. According to myth, the Trojan War began because Hera, Aphrodite, and Athena forced Paris to judge a beauty contest. Paris awarded Aphrodite the prize when she promised him the most beautiful woman on earth, Helen of Troy (who was already Queen of Sparta).

pipe and put it, not, as usual, in his mouth, but at the nape[2] of his neck, as if he were smoking at the back of his head. And then he took his staff as usual, but, this time, carried it upside down, that is to say, so that it hung, not over his breast in front, but over his shoulder behind. Both the friends were at work in their fields. They looked up for a second. Edju called out, "Good morning!" They gave him the same and went on with their **toil.**

Then they went home together. One said to the other, "The old man (Edju) went the opposite road through the fields today. I noticed that by his pipe and stick." The other said, "You're wrong. He went the same way as usual, I saw it by the way his feet were going." The first said, "It's a lie; I saw his pipe and his staff much too plainly; and, besides, he had on a white instead of a black cap." The second one **retorted,** "You must be blind or asleep; his cap was red." His friend said, "Then you must have already had some palm-wine this morning, if you could see neither the color of his cap, nor the way he was walking." The other one answered him, "I haven't even seen a drop this morning, but you must be crazed." The other man said, "You are making up lies to annoy me." Then the other one said, "Liar yourself! And not for the first time by a good deal." One of them drew his knife and went for the other who got a wound. He also drew his knife and cut his **assailant.** They both ran away

---

2. *Nape* is the back of the neck.

1 **Irony** *Why is this passage an example of dramatic irony?*

Vocabulary

toil (toil) *n.* fatiguing work or effort
retort (ri tôrt´) *v.* to reply in kind, especially with anger or with a witty or an insulting response
assailant (ə sā´lənt) *n.* attacker

54 UNIT 1 EARLY AFRICA

bleeding to the town. The folk saw them and said, "Both these friends have been attacked. There will be war." One of them said, "No, this liar is no friend of mine." And the other one, "Don't believe a single word of his. When he opens his mouth, the lies swarm from it."

Meanwhile, Edju had gone to the King of the town. He said to the King, "Just ask the two friends what is the matter with them! They have cut each other's heads about with knives and are bleeding!" The King said, "What, the two friends, who always wear clothes alike have been quarreling? Let them be summoned!" So it was done. The King asked them, "You are both in sad case. What made you fall out?" They both said, "We could not agree as to what it was that went through our fields this morning." Then the King asked, "How many people went along your footpath?" "It was a man who goes the same way every day. Today he went in another direction, wearing a white cap instead of a black one," said one of the friends. "He lies," shouted the other; "the old man had on a red cap and walked along in the usual direction!" Then the King asked, "Who knows this old man?" Edju said, "It is I. These two fellows quarreled because I so willed it." Edju pulled out his cap and said, "I put on this cap, red on one side, white on the other, green in front, and black behind. I stuck my pipe in my nape. So my steps went one way while I was looking another. The two friends couldn't help quarreling. I made them do it. Sowing **dissension** is my chief delight." ∾

Gods and Spirits *What other figures from world mythology remind you of Edju?* **2**

Vocabulary

dissension (di sen´shən) *n.* disagreement; discord

Grammar Practice

Use Complex Sentences Remind students that a complex sentence has one main clause and one or more subordinate clauses. Explain that a subordinate clause has a subject and a verb but cannot stand alone as a sentence, whereas a main clause can. Write this sentence without the underlining on the board: Now, when Edju wanted to start this quarrel, he made himself a cap of green, black, red, and white cloth, which showed a different color from whatever side it was looked at. Ask students to identify the main clause (underlined) and the subordinate clauses (double underlined). Then have students identify three additional complex sentences in the story. Have them underline each main clause once and each subordinate clause twice.

After You Read

Respond and Think Critically

Respond and Interpret

1. Did you find this story humorous? Why or why not?

2. (a)What does Edju decide to do to the two friends? (b)Why does Edju choose these friends as his victims?

3. (a)What do the two friends see when Edju walks past them? (b)How does Edju's behavior set off a chain of events?

Analyze and Evaluate

4. (a)Why do you think Edju confesses his trickery? (b)What do you think will happen to him after his confession?

5. Do you think the two farmers were truly good friends before their quarrel, or was their friendship superficial? Explain.

6. What do you think is the lesson of "Edju and the Two Friends"?

Connect

7. **Big Idea** Gods and Spirits In your opinion, does the tale portray Edju as evil or merely mischievous? Use evidence from the story to support your answer.

8. **Connect to Today** (a)What are some examples of tricksters in film, television, or literature today? (b)Why do you think tricksters have a timeless appeal?

Literary Element Irony

Authors sometimes use dramatic irony for comic effect.

1. Do you think dramatic irony is intended for comedic effect in this story? Explain.

2. What might the dramatic irony of this story teach readers about friendship?

Reading Strategy Connect to Personal Experience

By connecting the events, emotions, and characters in a literary work to your own life, you will be able to better understand the text and to recall information you learned from it.

1. Do you think the account of the two friends' sudden quarrel was realistic? Why or why not?

2. In your experience, what are some of the most frequent causes of quarrels between friends?

 Literature Online

Selection Resources For Selection Quizzes, eFlash-cards, and Reading-Writing Connection activities, go to glencoe.com and enter QuickPass code GLW6053u1.

Vocabulary Practice

Practice with Antonyms With a partner, brainstorm three antonyms for each boldfaced vocabulary word below. Then discuss your choices with your classmates. Be prepared to explain why you chose your words.

toil   retort   assailant   dissension

EXAMPLE: haughty

Antonyms: approachable, humble, modest

Sample explanation: A haughty person behaves coldly toward others, but an approachable person behaves warmly.

 Writing

Write an Anecdote "Edju and the Two Friends" employs dramatic irony to describe a quarrel between friends. Think of a comedic or a dramatic event in your life when people around you had more information about the situation than you did. Write an anecdote providing insight into this experience. You may want to use a chart like the one on page 52 to identify examples of dramatic irony in your life.

Assess

1. Answers will vary.

2. (a) Edju decides to make them quarrel. (b) He chooses them because they are close friends.

3. (a) Each friend sees a different side of Edju and his outfit. (b) When the two friends discuss his appearance later, they quarrel about what they saw.

4. (a) He confesses because he delights in creating discord and is proud of it. (b) Edju's trickery is valued, so probably nothing will happen to him.

5. Many students may think that the quickness and violence of the friends' quarrel reveal long-standing resentments.

6. Students may say the lesson is "Never trust appearances."

7. Some students will say that Edju is evil. Others will say that Edju just played a practical joke.

8. (a) Answers will vary. (b) People seem to be continually intrigued by the ambivalent, mischievous nature of tricksters.

> **For additional assessment, see Assessment Resources, pp. 45–46.**

Writing

Students' anecdotes should clearly introduce characters and situations to the reader, describe a situation that involves dramatic irony, and include a conclusion that explains the significance of the event.

Vocabulary

toil: rest, leisure, idleness

retort: question, inquire, request

assailant: guardian, custodian, protector

dissension: agreement, harmony, consensus

Literary Element

1. Students may feel that Edju's actions and manner create a comedic use of dramatic irony. Others may feel that the quarrel and violence produce dramatic irony that is not humorous.

2. Readers might learn that friends should talk openly with one another and should give one another the benefit of the doubt.

Reading Strategy

1. Many students may feel that the account of the violent flare-up between the two friends was essentially true-to-life. Others may think that the quarrel was overdramatic and unrealistic.

2. Students may mention jealousy, competitiveness, and misunderstandings as common causes of quarrels.

Focus

Bellringer Options

**Daily Language
Transparency 8**

Or ask: What makes someone a good storyteller? (*Students might mention an engaging dramatic style, effective gestures, and an expressive voice.*)

Teach

Big Idea · 1

The Magic of Words

Ask: How are stories and legends passed along in contemporary America? Do we have an "oral tradition"? Students might mention books, television, and films, as well as oral traditions such as folk songs, urban legends, and jokes.

Cultural History ☆

Changing Traditions A living oral tradition often incorporates contemporary references. For example, the ritual formulas praising Shango, the Yoruba god of thunder, now include allusions to the speed and thundering sound of a locomotive. In southern Africa, men returning to the country from working in the cities may recount their experiences in the traditional "praise-song" format.

Learning Objectives

For pages 56–57

In studying this text, you will focus on the following objectives:

Reading: Understanding cultural and historical context. Understanding the nature of translation.

The Storyteller as Translator

AMONG THE MANDINGO PEOPLE OF WEST AFRICA, THE *SUNDIATA*—the epic of Mali—is a story that lives, grows, and changes. It is an enduring part of people's lives. From childhood on, many West Africans experience the story through the dynamic performances of a griot, a storyteller-musician who chants or sings the verses to music and acts out the dramatic parts. **1**

Griots perform the *Sundiata* at ceremonies and festivals in villages and towns throughout West Africa. Oral versions of the story can be traced to the thirteenth century, but not until the twentieth century did these oral versions start to be preserved through writing. As a result, there are hundreds of variations of the *Sundiata*; each version reflects the unique storytelling of a particular griot.

"My guitar, for me, is like a book. Once I start playing, I am inspired and everything comes into my mind."
—griot Djeli Baba Sissoko

Improvising an Epic

Each time an audience sees a griot perform the *Sundiata*, the experience is a little different. The griot takes the basic story and reworks it to fit the situation and the mood of the audience. For example, the griot may create a song that praises the host or patron or add an ancestor of the patron as a minor character. A griot may modernize the epic by referring to contemporary weapons or clothing, or historical figures. The epic may also be used to explain a village custom. If the audience is enjoying a particular scene, such as a battle, the griot may draw it out to entertain it. If the audience seems bored, the griot may condense a scene. The griot constantly adapts to the audience, who not only claps and sings, but also interjects questions and comments.

Griots relating people's history while looking at fox tracks.

56 UNIT 1 EARLY AFRICA

Research Practice

Conduct Internet Research Students will find a wealth of information on griots and the *Sundiata* on the Internet. They can read more of the epic, see a modern retelling of it, and hear griots tell tales accompanied by music. Suggest that students use a search engine and such keywords as *Sundiata, Mali, Ghana,* and *griot* in their research. Have students report on their discoveries to the class.

In essence, the griot translates the *Sundiata* by reshaping the basic story to make it relevant to the audience and location of each performance. The version you will read (see pages 58–64) was told by griot Djeli Mamoudou Kouyaté to historian D. T. Niane, who adapted it into prose. As you read, note how Kouyaté's version of Sundiata's first attempt to walk differs from this version by griot Bamba Suso:

> **2** "*When he had grasped the rods, they both broke. They said, "How will Sunjata [Sundiata] get up? He himself said to them, "Call my mother; When a child has fallen down, it is his mother who picks him up." When his mother came, He laid his hand upon his mother's shoulder, And he arose and stood up.*"

Becoming a Living Library

Griots have been called "living libraries" because they store the history, tales, songs, and traditions of the Mandingo people in their minds. They pass on this "library" from one generation to the next by reciting epics and other stories. A griot is both born into this role and trained for it. Mandingo society is organized by occupational castes, or classes, and to become a griot, a person must be born into the griot caste. However, not every child of a griot becomes a storyteller. Only children who show special talent become apprenticed to a master griot within their clan or extended family.

Griots looking at fox tracks in a sand grid to read the future. ★

In addition to learning the stories, apprentices learn to build, repair, and play musical instruments. Music is just as important to the griot as words. Apprentices study the tunes, rhythms, and words of all the stories in the repertoire of their master. As they practice storytelling, the master coaches them on how to use their voices and incorporate movements and gestures into their performances. Eventually, the apprentice pulls all this training together into the performance of an epic. However, it can take 50 years to become a master. Griots are proud of their knowledge and skill. Kouyaté claimed that the "warmth of the human voice" is superior to books, which cannot speak.

LOG ON ▶ **Literature** Online

Literature and Reading For more about storytellers and the translators in this book, go to glencoe.com and enter QuickPass code GLW6053u1.

Respond and Think Critically

1. Do you agree with Kouyaté's claim, which implies that it is better to hear a story told than to read it in a book? Why or why not?

2. How is each performance of the *Sundiata* a kind of translation?

3. How do birth and training contribute to the development of a griot?

Teach

Reading Strategy | **2**

Compare and Contrast Style Present students with these excerpts from the two versions of the *Sundiata: He laid his hand upon his mother's shoulder, / And he arose and stood up.* (Bamba Suso)

Sogolon Kedjou was all eyes and watched her son's legs which were trembling as though from an electric shock (D. T. Niane)

Ask students to compare the two styles of narration, and to comment on which excerpt represents a more "spoken" style. *(Niane's version contains sensory details and figurative language, while Bamba Suso's version is simpler. Bamba Suso's version seems more "spoken" because it is straightforward and rhythmic.)*

View the Photograph ★

In the Dogon tradition, the griot draws a grid in the sand and leaves it overnight. Foxes run across the grid during the night, and the next day the griot interprets the tracks and predicts the future. **Ask:** Why might a griot perform this function, in addition to telling stories? *(Possible answer: Griots help people connect with the future by telling "stories" about it.)*

Assess

1. Many students may agree with Kouyaté's claim and enjoy listening to the voice of a storyteller; others may express a preference for the quiet, personal experience of reading.

2. The griot adapts the basic story of the epic to fit the circumstances of the performance and the attitude of the audience.

3. All griots must be born into a traditional griot caste, and every griot undergoes a long, rigorous training process.

Learning Objectives
Understanding cultural and historical context. (SE)
Understanding the nature of translation. (SE)
Conducting Internet research. (TE)

Focus

Bellringer Options

**Selection Focus
    Transparency 3**

**Daily Language Practice
    Transparency 9**

Or ask: What are some benefits that can be gained by overcoming an obstacle? Ask students about what they have learned from specific obstacles they have overcome.

---

from Sundiata

Connect to the Epic

Who are your heroes? What qualities draw you to these men and women? Discuss these questions with a partner.

Build Background

The *Sundiata* (söön dyä′tə) is the epic of the Mandingo people, who live in present-day Mali and parts of coastal West Africa. It celebrates the founding of the ancient Mali Empire. A king named Sundiata appears in the epic as a mythical hero. Oral poets known as griots (grē′ōz) have performed the *Sundiata* for more than five centuries and continue to recite it today.

Set Purposes for Reading

Big Idea **The Magic of Words**

As you read, ask yourself, What aspects of Mandingo culture and history are preserved in this oral text?

Literary Element **Epic**

An **epic** is a long narrative poem about a larger-than-life hero who embodies the values of his or her people. Oral epics are passed from generation to generation. As you read, ask yourself, What elements indicate that this text is an epic?

Reading Strategy **Make Inferences About Characters**

To make **inferences about characters** means to come to conclusions based on the evidence about a character's traits, beliefs, or motivations. As you read, ask yourself, What details contribute to my inferences about each character?

Tip: Focus on Details Use a chart like the one below to record your inferences about the characters.

Details	Inferences About Characters
"... she kept a little garden in the open ground behind the village. It was there that she passed her brightest moments looking after her onions ..."	Sogolon is modest and enjoys the simple things in life.

58 UNIT 1 EARLY AFRICA

Learning Objectives

For pages 58–64

In studying this text, you will focus on the following objectives:

Literary Study: Analyzing epic.

Reading: Making inferences about characters.

Writing: Writing a journal entry.

Vocabulary

derisively (di rī′siv lē) *adv.* using ridicule or scorn; p. 61 *The old man spoke derisively of his family, which had moved away.*

affront (ə frunt′) *n.* a deliberate insult; p. 61 *The mayor felt that the reporter's question was an affront to his dignity.*

discreetly (dis krēt′lē) *adv.* unnoticeably; p. 61 *The girls discreetly passed out invitations for their friend's surprise birthday party.*

heedless (hēd′lis) *adj.* inconsiderate; thoughtless; p. 62 *We were heedless of our unwashed hands, eager to get to the dinner table.*

Tip: Word Parts Recognizing word parts can help you unlock the meaning of an unfamiliar word. For example, heedless is formed from the words *heed,* which means "to pay attention" and *less,* which means "not having."

Selection Skills

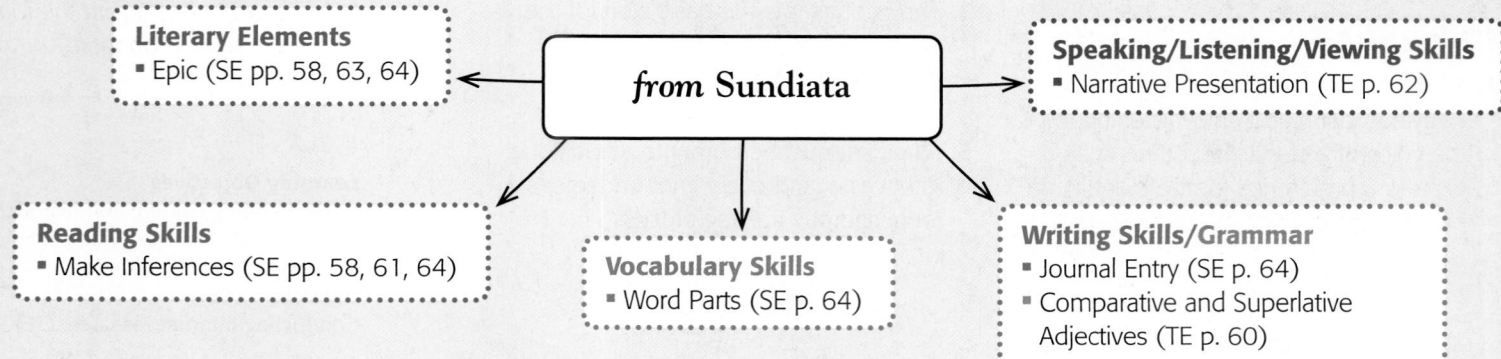

Literary Elements
- Epic (SE pp. 58, 63, 64)

Speaking/Listening/Viewing Skills
- Narrative Presentation (TE p. 62)

from **Sundiata**

Reading Skills
- Make Inferences (SE pp. 58, 61, 64)

Vocabulary Skills
- Word Parts (SE p. 64)

Writing Skills/Grammar
- Journal Entry (SE p. 64)
- Comparative and Superlative Adjectives (TE p. 60)

from The Lion's Awakening from Sundiata

Retold by D. T. Niane

Translated by G. D. Pickett

Characters

MARI DJATA (Also called Sundiata and Sogolon Djata) hero of the epic

SOGOLON KEDJOU Mari Djata's mother

SASSOUMA The Queen Mother

BALLA FASSÉKÉ Mari Djata's griot

FARAKOUROU Master Smith and soothsayer

SOGOLON DJAMAROU Mari Djata's sister

Even before he was born, Sundiata was destined for greatness. Acting on the instructions of a soothsayer, his father, the King of Mali, marries a hideous, hunchbacked woman named Sogolon. As foretold, the couple has a son. It seems, however, that the boy is unlikely to become a great leader as has been predicted. At the age of seven Sundiata is still unable to walk. He and his ugly mother are the object of cruel jokes and jealous abuse by the old king's first wife.

SUNDIATA **59**

Teach

Summary

This section of the *Sundiata* tells of Mari Djata's first steps toward his heroic destiny. His mother suffers insults because, although the child is seven years old, he cannot yet walk. Mari Djata vows to walk that very day and orders that a heavy iron rod be brought. When the rod, made by the current forge master's father, is brought to Mari Djata, he is miraculously able to stand and walk.

> **For summaries in languages other than English, see Unit 1 Teaching Resources Book, pp. 85–90.**

> **For an audio recording of this selection, use Listening Library Audio CD-ROM.**

> **Interactive Read and Write** Other options for teaching this selection can be found in Interactive Read and Write for On-Level Learners, pp. 9–18.

Readability Scores

Dale-Chall: 6.1
DRP: 54
Lexile: 890

Learning Objectives
Analyzing epic. (SE)
Making inferences about character. (SE)

English Learners

DIFFERENTIATED INSTRUCTION

Beginning On the board, draw a family tree consisting of boxes and circles. In each space, write a description of how one of the characters is related to another character. Have the students write the appropriate character's name in each box. Offer help when needed. Use a diagram like this one:

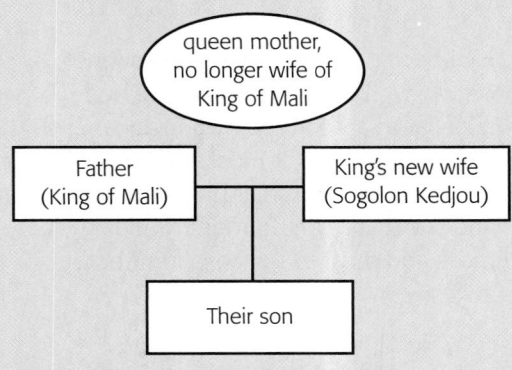

queen mother, no longer wife of King of Mali

Father (King of Mali) — King's new wife (Sogolon Kedjou)

Their son

Advanced Learners/Pre-AP

DIFFERENTIATED INSTRUCTION

Write a Character Sketch Have students write character sketches of Sogolon Kedjou and Sassouma, working from information in the selection. Instruct them to describe in detail the characters' physical and emotional traits. To add complexity to their descriptions, explain the idea of interior monologue and suggest that they include one in their sketches.

Teach

View the Art ★

Answer: *Sundiata sits helplessly on the ground because he cannot walk.*

This clay sculpture may have been created as far back as the 1300s, when the Mali Empire was at its height. Many sculptures from the region show human subjects in similar poses.

Seated figure. Segou, Mali region. Terracotta. Musee Barbier-Mueller, Geneva.

View the Art In what way does this figure remind you of Sundiata?

Grammar Practice

Comparative and Superlative Adjectives Remind students that modifiers have three degrees: The positive, or base form, cannot be used to make a comparison ("Help yourself, you <u>poor</u> woman"). The comparative form shows two things being compared ("Allah Almighty, you never created a <u>finer</u> day"). The superlative form shows three or more things being compared ("Through your fault, I have just suffered the <u>greatest</u> affront of my life").

Explain that for most adjectives of one or two syllables, the comparative and superlative are formed by adding *-er* and *-est* respectively. For most adjectives of more than two syllables, the comparative and superlative are formed by adding *more* and *most* to the base form of the adjective.

Finally, ask students to write a comparison-and-contrast paragraph in which they use the comparative and superlative forms of one or more adjectives.

Sogolon Kedjou and her children lived on the queen mother's leftovers, but she kept a little garden in the open ground behind the village. It was there that she passed her brightest moments looking after her onions and gnougous.[1] One day she happened to be short of condiments and went to the queen mother to beg a little baobab[2] leaf.

Visual Vocabulary
A *calabash* is a gourd whose hard shell is used as a utensil, such as a bottle or a dipper.

"Look you," said the malicious Sassouma, "I have a calabash full. Help yourself, you poor woman. As for me, my son knew how to walk at seven and it was he who went and picked these baobab leaves. Take them then, since your son is unequal to mine." Then she laughed **derisively** with that fierce laughter which cuts through your flesh and penetrates right to the bone.

Sogolon Kedjou was dumbfounded. She had never imagined that hate could be so strong in a human being. With a lump in her throat she left Sassouma's. Outside her hut Mari Djata, sitting on his useless legs, was blandly eating out of a calabash. Unable to contain herself any longer, **1** Sogolon burst into sobs and seizing a piece of wood, hit her son.

---

1. *Gnougous* (noo´gooz´) are vegetables similar to spinach.
2. A *baobab* (bā´ə bab´) is a tropical tree of the silk-cotton family. Its edible fruit resembles a gourd, and its bark can be used for making paper, cloth, and rope.

---

2 Make Inferences About Characters *Why do you think Sassouma focuses her insults on Mari Djata's inability to walk?*

Vocabulary

derisively (di rī´siv lē) *adv.* using ridicule or scorn to show contempt

---

"Oh son of misfortune, will you never walk? Through your fault I have just suffered the greatest **affront** of my life! What have I done, God, for you to punish me in this way?"

Mari Djata seized the piece of wood and, looking at his mother, said, "Mother, what's the matter?"

"Shut up, nothing can ever wash me clean of this insult."

"But what then?"

"Sassouma has just humiliated me over a matter of a baobab leaf. At your age her own son could walk and used to bring his mother baobab leaves."

"Cheer up, Mother, cheer up."

"No. It's too much. I can't."

"Very well then, I am going to walk today," said Mari Djata. "Go and tell my father's smiths to make me the heaviest possible iron rod. Mother, do you want just the leaves of the baobab or would you rather I brought you the whole tree?"

"Ah, my son, to wipe out this insult I want the tree and its roots at my feet outside my hut."

Balla Fasséké, who was present, ran to the master smith, Farakourou, to order an iron rod.

Sogolon had sat down in front of her hut. She was weeping softly and holding her head between her two hands. Mari Djata went calmly back to his calabash of rice and began eating again as if nothing had happened. From time to time he looked up **discreetly** at his mother who was murmuring in a low voice, "I want the whole tree, in front of my hut, the whole tree."

---

3 Make Inferences About Characters *What can you infer about Mari Djata from his offer to bring his mother the whole tree?*

Vocabulary

affront (ə frunt´) *n.* a deliberate insult
discreetly (dis krēt´lē) *adv.* unnoticeably

Teach

Respond to Plot **Ask:** Why do you think Sogolon hit her son? *(Students should realize that Sogolon was frustrated with her son for not walking.)*

Reading Strategy **2**

Make Inferences About Characters **Answer:** *Her son's inability to walk is the topic about which Sogolon is the most sensitive. A healthy son brings status to a woman in this society.*

Reading Strategy **3**

Make Inferences About Characters **Answer:** *Students should infer that Mari Djata has confidence and a sense of his own destiny.*

Learning Objectives
Making inferences about character. (SE)
Understanding comparative and superlative adjectives. (TE)
Analyzing art. (TE)

Advanced Learners/Pre-AP

DIFFERENTIATED INSTRUCTION

Research and Writing Explain that epic heroes often embody the values of their people. Have students work independently to research the Mandingo culture. Then ask them to write a short essay in which they make generalizations about the values of Mandingo culture as evidenced in this excerpt from the *Sundiata*.

Apply Background Knowledge Have students brainstorm the names of other heroes that they are familiar with in literature, film, or television. Then ask them to write a paragraph in which they discuss characteristics that all heroes share.

Teach

Political History ☆

The Real Sundiata According to oral tradition, Sundiata and his twelve brothers were heirs to the throne of the small kingdom of Kangaba, near the Mali-Guinea border. Sumanguru, the ruler of the neighboring state of Kangiage, murdered all of Sundiata's brothers. Sundiata was supposely spared because he was sickly and it seemed he would die soon. Then, as legend has it, Sundiata organized a private army and defeated Sumanguru at the Battle of Kirina. Tradition attributes the ruler's success in battle to his abilities as a magician.

All of a sudden a voice burst into laughter behind the hut. It was the wicked Sassouma telling one of her serving women about the scene of humiliation and she was laughing loudly so that Sogolon could hear. Sogolon fled into the hut and hid her face under the blankets so as not to have before her eyes this **heedless** boy, who was more preoccupied with eating than with anything else. With her head buried in the bedclothes Sogolon wept and her body shook violently. Her daughter, Sogolon Djamarou, had come and sat down beside her and she said, "Mother, Mother, don't cry. Why are you crying?"

Mari Djata had finished eating and, dragging himself along on his legs, he came and sat under the wall of the hut for the sun was scorching. What was he thinking about? He alone knew.

The royal forges were situated outside the walls and over a hundred smiths worked there. The bows, spears, arrows and shields of Niani's warriors came from there. When Balla Fasséké came to order the iron rod, Farakourou said to him, "The great day has arrived then?"

"Yes. Today is a day like any other, but it will see what no other day has seen."

The master of the forges, Farakourou, was the son of the old Nounfaïri, and he was a soothsayer like his father. In his workshops there was an enormous iron bar wrought by his father Nounfaïri. Everybody wondered what this bar was destined to be used for. Farakourou called six of his apprentices and told them to carry the iron bar to Sogolon's house.

When the smiths put the gigantic iron bar down in front of the hut the noise was so frightening that Sogolon, who was lying down, jumped up with a start. Then Balla

Vocabulary

heedless (hēd′lis) *adj.* inconsiderate; thoughtless

Musician playing a kora. Dogon sculpture. Wood. Brooklyn Museum, NY.

Speaking Practice

SMALL GROUP

Deliver a Narrative Presentation Have the class work in two separate groups to recreate the Sundiata tale as if they were griots, using contemporary language and even slang in their retelling. Suggest that they choose a story narrator and students to play the roles of some of the characters in this excerpt. Have them refer to the character list on page 59 to assign roles. You may want to prompt them to begin

their tale by covering some of these plot points:

- Sundiata is destined for greatness.
- The King of Mali marries Sogolon.
- The queen mother is jealous of them and insults Sogolon because Sundiata cannot walk.
- Sundiata grows determined to walk and asks for an iron bar.

Fasséké, son of Gnankouman Doua, spoke.

"Here is the great day, Mari Djata. I am speaking to you, Maghan, son of Sogolon. The waters of the Niger can efface the stain from the body, but they cannot wipe out an insult. Arise, young lion, roar, and may the bush know that from henceforth it has a master."

The apprentice smiths were still there, Sogolon had come out and everyone was watching Mari Djata. He crept on all fours and came to the iron bar. Supporting himself on his knees and one hand, with the other hand he picked up the iron bar without any effort and stood it up vertically. Now he was resting on nothing but his knees and held the bar with both his hands. A deathly silence had gripped all those present. Sogolon Djata closed his eyes, held tight, the muscles in his arms tensed. With a violent jerk he threw his weight on to it and his knees left the ground. Sogolon Kedjou was all eyes and watched her son's legs which were trembling as though from an electric shock. Djata was sweating and the sweat ran from his brow. In a great effort he straightened up and was on his feet at one go—but the great bar of iron was twisted and had taken the form of a bow!

Then Balla Fasséké sang out the "Hymn to the Bow," striking up with his powerful voice:

> "Take your bow, Simbon,
> Take your bow and let us go.
> Take your bow, Sogolon Djata."

When Sogolon saw her son standing she stood dumb for a moment, then suddenly she sang these words of thanks to God who had given her son the use of his legs:

> "Oh day, what a beautiful day,
> Oh day, day of joy;
> Allah Almighty, you never created a
> finer day.
> So my son is going to walk!"

Standing in the position of a soldier at ease, Sogolon Djata, supported by his enormous rod, was sweating great beads of sweat. Balla Fasséké's song had alerted the whole palace and people came running from all over to see what had happened, and each stood bewildered before Sogolon's son. The queen mother had rushed there and when she saw Mari Djata standing up she trembled from head to foot. After recovering his breath Sogolon's son dropped the bar and the crowd stood to one side. His first steps were those of a giant. Balla Fasséké fell into step and pointing his finger at Djata, he cried:

> "Room, room, make room!
> The lion has walked;
> Hide antelopes,
> Get out of his way."

Behind Niani there was a young baobab tree and it was there that the children of the town came to pick leaves for their mothers. With all his might the son of Sogolon tore up the tree and put it on his shoulders and went back to his mother. He threw the tree in front of the hut and said, "Mother, here are some baobab leaves for you. From henceforth it will be outside your hut that the women of Niani will come to stock up."

Sogolon Djata walked. From that day forward the queen mother had no more peace of mind.

---

1 The Magic of Words *Why might passages such as this be particularly effective when spoken aloud?*

Epic *What do you think is the significance of Balla Fasséké's exclamation and his reference to Djata as a lion?* **2**

SUNDIATA **63**

Teach

Big Idea   1

The Magic of Words
Answer: *Passages such as this were meant to be sung, which would have been an engaging way to reach listeners.*

Literary Element   2

Epic **Answer:** *Fasséké describes Mari Djata in terms that indicate Djata's coming dominance. The lion is a noble animal, predatory, and a symbol of strength and prowess.*

> For additional literary element practice, see Unit 1 Teaching Resources Book, p. 91.

Progress Check

Can students make inferences about characters?

If No → See Unit 1 Teaching Resources Book, p. 92.

Learning Objectives
Analyzing epic. (SE)
Delivering a narrative presentation. (TE)

English Learners

DIFFERENTIATED INSTRUCTION

Intermediate Students may have difficulty understanding the last sentence of the story. Discuss the idiom "peace of mind." **Ask:** What does "peace" mean? *(a state of quiet or harmony)* How would one feel if she had no peace of mind? *(worried, afraid, out of control)* Why would Mari Djata's strength cause Sassouma, the queen mother, to worry? *(She is the king's first wife. If Mari Djata* is weak, he will never become king. If he is strong, he will become a ruler and Sassouma could be punished for the way she has treated him and his mother.) To check for students' level of understanding, **ask:** What might happen next in the story? *(Students should be able to predict that Mari Djata will continue gaining strength and that Sassouma will become jealous of him)*

63

After You Read

Assess

1. Students may feel inspired by Mari Djata's triumph.
2. (a) That will walk that very day (b) Confident and calm
3. (a) He uses the iron rod for support as he pulls himself up. (b) The queen mother trembles because Mari Djata is now a threat to her and her son.
4. (a) He pulls up a baobab tree and places it before his mother's hut. (b) It suggests that she will be honored in the village.
5. (a) Sassouma thinks that Sogolon and Mari Djata threaten her position. (b) Students may say it is justified because Sassouma insults her honor.
6. His readiness to take on responsibility
7. A griot serves as a messenger when he conveys Mari Djata's request for an iron rod to the master smith. Traditionally, a griot would recite the story itself.
8. Some students may note that personal honor is still very important and mention leaders such as Nelson Mandela.

⚡ Writing

Students' journal entries should describe Mari Djata from Sassouma's viewpoint and reveal Sassouma's character.

After You Read

Respond and Think Critically

Respond and Interpret

1. In a short paragraph, describe your feelings about the main characters.
2. (a)What does Mari Djata declare when he learns about his mother's encounter with Sassouma? (b)How would you describe his attitude on this occasion?
3. (a)Describe how Mari Djata stands up. (b)Why do you think Sassouma trembles when she sees him in this position?
4. (a)What action does Mari Djata perform for his mother? (b)How do you interpret the last statement he makes in this episode?

Analyze and Evaluate

5. (a)Why do you think Sassouma treats Sogolon so unfairly? (b)In your opinion, was Sogolon's reaction to the treatment she received from Sassouma justified? Why or why not?
6. A **symbol** is an object or an action that stands for something else in addition to itself. What does Mari Djata's act of standing up symbolize?

Connect

7. **Big Idea** **The Magic of Words** How is the oral tradition of the griot represented in and by this work?
8. **Connect to Today** Is personal honor as important to people today as it is to the characters in the *Sundiata*? Explain.

Literary Element Epic

The *Sundiata* is called a **folk epic** because it arose through oral storytelling, from the collective experiences of a people.

1. What values do you think were important to the ancient Mandingo people?
2. Why do you think epics are important in many different cultures?

Reading Strategy Make Inferences About Characters

Readers can better understand the theme of a work by making **inferences** about the characters. Review the chart you made on page 58.

1. What inferences did you make about Mari Djata?
2. How did these inferences about Mari Djata help you understand the theme?

 **Literature** Online

Selection Resources For Selection Quizzes, eFlashcards, and Reading-Writing Connection activities, go to glencoe.com and enter QuickPass code GLW6053u1.

64 UNIT 1 EARLY AFRICA

Vocabulary Practice

Practice with Word Parts For each boldfaced vocabulary word, identify the word in the right column that shares a part or a root with it. Underline the part they share. Determine the meaning of the related word and explain how it is connected to the vocabulary word.

1. **derisively** ridiculous
2. **affront** doubtless
3. **discreetly** indiscernible
4. **heedless** confrontation

EXAMPLE: phil<u>anthrop</u>ic, <u>anthrop</u>ology

<u>Philanthropic</u> means "marked by a concern for humankind." <u>Anthropology</u> is the study of human beings. *Philanthropic* and *anthropology* both relate to humans.

⚡ **Writing**

Write a Journal Entry Imagine you are Sassouma. Write a journal entry that describes your feelings about Mari Djata and his sudden ability to walk.

Literary Element

1. Physical strength, patience, honor, devotion to parents, and social status
2. Epics can communicate a culture's values and celebrate its heritage.

 For additional assessment, see Assessment Resources, pp. 47–48.

Reading Strategy

1. Students' answers will vary. Many will infer that he is kind to his father's subjects, confident about his destiny, and noble.
2. Students may note that their inferences help them to understand the theme of great leaders who rise to power despite the obstacles they face.

Vocabulary

1. <u>deris</u>ively—"in a contemptuous manner"; <u>ridic</u>ulous—"laughable"
2. af<u>front</u>—"direct insult"; con<u>front</u>ation—"face-to-face meeting"
3. <u>dis</u>creetly—"unnoticeably"; in<u>dis</u>cernible—"unable to be seen"
4. heed<u>less</u>—"without attention"; doubt<u>less</u>—"without doubt"

Vocabulary Workshop

Thesaurus Use

Literature Connection

"When the smiths put the gigantic iron bar down in front of the hut the noise was so frightening that Sogolon, who was lying down, jumped up with a start."

In this passage from the *Sundiata*, D. T. Niane could have called the iron bar *big*, instead of *gigantic*. He could also have chosen the word *scary* rather than *frightening*. Niane chose precise words to convey meaning. You can do the same by using **synonyms**, or words with the same or similar meanings. While some synonyms are practically interchangeable, many have subtle differences in meaning or connotation.

Most dictionaries list and explain the differences among synonyms, but for many words you will need a thesaurus. A **thesaurus** is a specialized dictionary of synonyms and antonyms. Thesauruses (or thesauri) are organized either traditionally by concept or in dictionary order.

Traditional Organization Probably the best-known thesaurus is *Roget's Thesaurus,* which organizes large categories of words related to a general concept. To find a synonym for the verb *taste,* for example, browse the alphabetical index of categories until you find the category *senses,* which includes the subentry *taste.* The index will refer you to the page for the subentry, where you will find a list of synonyms.

Dictionary Organization This type of thesaurus presents words in alphabetical order, as a dictionary does.

Here is a sample entry for the word *gigantic.*

part of speech

gigantic *adj. Russia is a gigantic country, the largest in the world:* very large, huge, vast, enormous, immense, giant, colossal, mammoth, massive, tremendous, stupendous; mighty, unwieldy, ponderous, hulking, strapping, bulky, lumpish, lubberly, towering, voluminous, large-scale, prodigious, gargantuan, Herculean, titanic *Ant.* small, little, tiny, miniature, compact; infinitesimal, microscopic; feeble, puny, weak; petty, insignificant; dwarfish, pygmy.

example sentence

list of synonyms with the most common ones first

list of antonyms

Practice Using a thesaurus, find two synonyms for each word below. Then look up the definitions of these synonyms in a dictionary to identify the precise meaning for each one.

a. laugh   **b.** tenderly   **c.** sorrow   **d.** pity   **e.** mad

LOG ON ▶ **Literature** Online
Vocabulary For more vocabulary practice, go to glencoe.com and enter QuickPass code GLW6053u1.

Learning Objectives

In this workshop, you will focus on the following objectives:

Vocabulary: Understanding language resources. Understanding synonyms.

Synonyms

Synonyms are words with the same or similar meanings. A **thesaurus** is a reference guide used to find groups of synonyms.

Test-Taking Tip

To decide whether two words are synonyms, first identify the part of speech for each word. Synonyms are always the same part of speech.

Focus

Write on the board: The castle was very big. Looking at its big towers made me dizzy. **Ask:** What is wrong with these sentences? Explain to students that the sentences would be more vivid and interesting if the repeated word *big* were replaced with two different, precise adjectives. Have students use a thesaurus to suggest revisions.

Assess

Practice

Students' synonyms will vary. Encourage students to discuss the subtle differences in connotation. Possible synonyms include:

a. laugh *(giggle, guffaw)*
b. tenderly *(gently, softly)*
c. sorrow *(sadness, mournfulness)*
d. pity *(sympathy, compassion)*
e. mad *(angry, furious)*

Learning Objectives
Understanding language resources. (SE)
Understanding synonyms. (SE)

Approaching Level

DIFFERENTIATED INSTRUCTION

Create a Web Diagram Students may benefit from creating webs of simple synonyms on their own. Have students create webs like the one at right, using synonyms for words such as *happy, mad,* and *sad.* Some students may find it easier to use an image in the center of their web. To model this, draw the sample web on the board, but add a simple drawing in the center bubble.

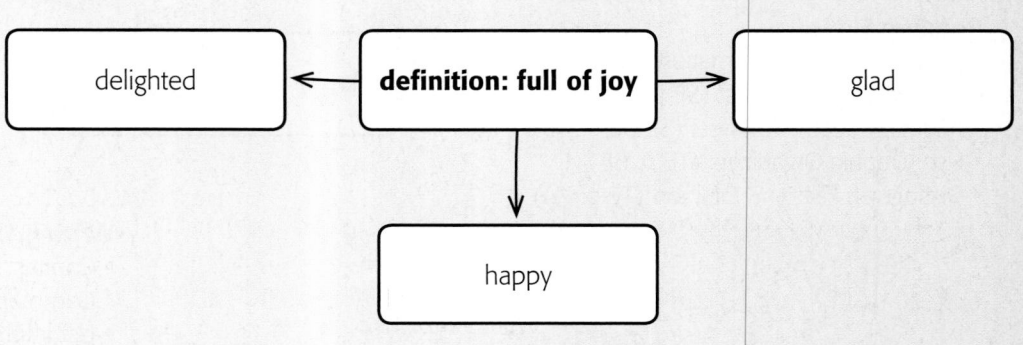

delighted ← **definition: full of joy** → glad
↓
happy

PART 2

Focus

Bellringer Options

**Literature Launchers
Pre-Reading Videos DVD
Daily Language Practice
Transparency 10**

Or ask: Do you think most Africans identify more closely with being citizens of a particular country—such as South Africa or Nigeria—or with being members of a particular ethnic group—such as the Zulu or the Ibo? Indicate to students that some of the major challenges facing modern African nations result directly or indirectly from two or more ethnic groups living together within the same country.

View the Art ★

Ethiopian emperor Haile Selassie (1892–1975) fires a machine gun at Italian warplanes attacking his country during Italy's invasion of Ethiopia in the mid 1930s. **Ask:** How is Haile Selassie presented in this painting? (*as a hero of the Ethiopian resistance*)

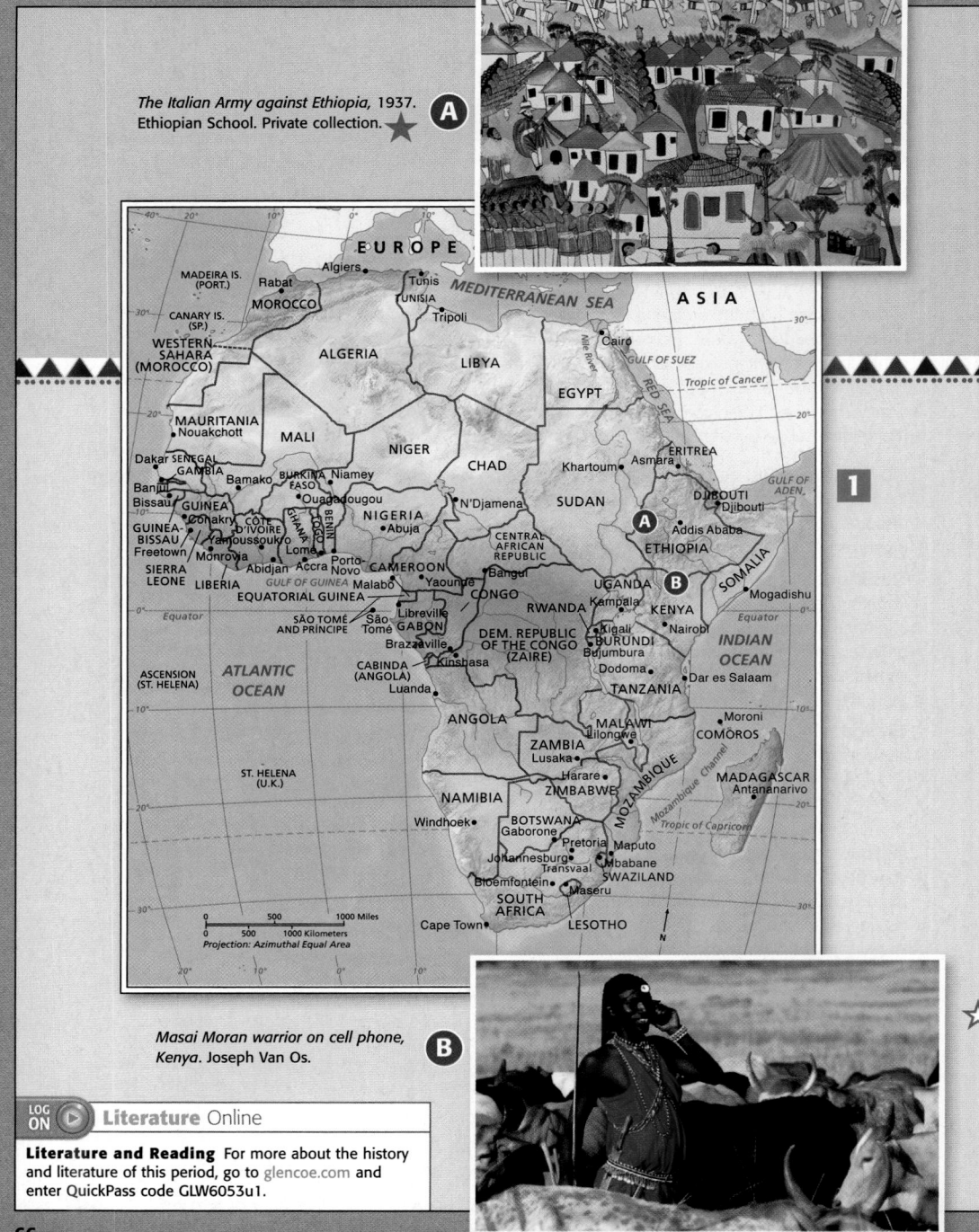

The Italian Army against Ethiopia, 1937. Ethiopian School. Private collection. ★ **A**

Masai Moran warrior on cell phone, Kenya. Joseph Van Os. **B**

LOG ON ▶ Literature Online

Literature and Reading For more about the history and literature of this period, go to glencoe.com and enter QuickPass code GLW6053u1.

66

Part Introduction Skills

Reading Skills
- Analyze Graphic Information (SE p. 69)
- Compare and Contrast (SE p. 74; TE p. 72)
- Analyze Cause and Effect (SE pp. 75, 76)
- Use Graphic Organizers (TE p. 68)
- Distinguish Fact and Opinion (TE p. 74)

Part 2 Introduction

Speaking/Listening/Viewing Skills
- Panel Discussion (SE p. 77)
- Analyze Art (TE pp. 66, 68, 70, 72–74)

Vocabulary Skills
- Word Parts (TE p. 76)

Writing Skills/Grammar
- Contrast Literary Periods (SE p. 77)
- Commas with Appositives (TE p. 70)
- List Information (TE p. 76)

Modern AFRICA
1800–Present

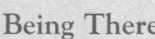

Figure of a Chokwe Chief, c.1850-1900. African school. Wood. Indianapolis Museum of Art, IN.

Being There

Contemporary African nations, like other nations throughout the world, have been deeply affected by political upheavals, rapid technological changes, and globalization. Yet many Africans still value the traditional customs and beliefs of their people. Oral storytellers continue to recount the stories of their ancestors, while tribes such as the Masai continue to wear traditional dress. Throughout the continent, Africans share a common goal: to preserve their heritages while facing the challenges of the modern world.

Looking Ahead

European colonization of Africa in the nineteenth and twentieth centuries left an indelible mark, stripping many African nations of freedom, equality, and traditional values. Modern African literature reflects the struggle of these countries to preserve their cultural values and to build independent nations in the postcolonial era.

Keep the following questions in mind as you read:

▲ How did Africans fight colonialism and racism in the twentieth century?

▲ What are the conflicts between traditional and modern African cultures?

▲ What are the major problems African nations face today?

67

Focus
Summary

This introduction gives an overview of the history and literature of Africa since 1800. It discusses the impact of European colonization, the rise of African nationalist movements in the mid-twentieth century, the emergence of new African nations beginning in the late 1950s, the challenges faced by contemporary Africa, and the interaction of tradition and innovation in modern African culture.

Reading Strategy | 1

Analyze Graphic Information Point out that the many straight boundary lines on the map of modern Africa are relics of the colonial period, when European nations carved the continent up into colonies. Because much of Africa was still unknown to the colonial powers, the borders they created did not reflect the territories occupied by different ethnic groups.

Ask: What problems might arise from foreign nations imposing borders? *(These borders might not reflect the ethnic geography of the region, which could contribute to future conflicts.)*

Approaching Level

DIFFERENTIATED INSTRUCTION

Set a Purpose Point out to students that the questions at the bottom of page 67 are intended to help guide their reading of the Part 2 introduction and are specifically answered on pages 74, 75, and 76. Work with small groups of students to create other purpose-setting questions, such as the following:

▪ Why did European countries create colonies in Africa?

▪ How did African nations become independent?

▪ How do Africans live today?

Have students write down their questions and answer them as they read the introduction to Part 2.

Cultural History ☆

Masai The Masai are a nomadic people of East Africa who raise livestock. Their basic food is the meat and milk of their cattle.

 For additional support for English Learners, see Unit 1 Teaching Resources Book, p. 99.

Teach

Reading Strategy | 1

Analyze Graphic Information Ask: Did Chinua Achebe publish *Things Fall Apart* before or after the outbreak of civil war in Nigeria? *(before)*

Reading Strategy | 2

Analyze Graphic Information Ask: Approximately how long a period elapsed between the rise of Zulu kingdom under Shaka and its fall following the Anglo-Zulu War? *(About 60 years)*

View the Art ★

The Yoruba wood carver who created this statue of Queen Victoria probably based it on a photograph. **Ask:** Which details of the statue seem European? Which details seem African? *(Students may feel that the facial features seem European, but the overall style seems African.)*

TIMELINE 1800–Present

AFRICAN LITERATURE

1800

1824
Jean-François Champollion completes translation of the Rosetta Stone

1842
German translator Karl Richard Lepsius publishes first collection of the *Book of the Dead*

1897
Mary Kingsley publishes *Travels in West Africa*

1934
Negritude movement is founded

Mary Kingsley

Figure of Queen Victoria, Yoruba, Nigeria ★

AFRICAN EVENTS

1800

1816–1828
Shaka establishes and rules the Zulu kingdom **2**

1822
Formerly enslaved people from the United States found Liberia

1837–1901
Queen Victoria reigns

1879
Anglo-Zulu War is fought

1884–1885
European colonialists divide Africa at the Berlin Conference

1900

1910
British and Dutch settlers form the Union of South Africa

1922
Egypt declares independence from Britain

1935
Italy invades Ethiopia

1948
South Africa establishes apartheid

WORLD EVENTS

1800

1807
Britain abolishes the slave trade

1815
Napoleon is defeated at Waterloo

1861
American Civil War begins

1900

◄ **1903**
Wright Brothers make first powered flight

1914 ►
World War I begins

1917
Russian Revolution begins

1929
Great Depression begins

1939
World War II begins

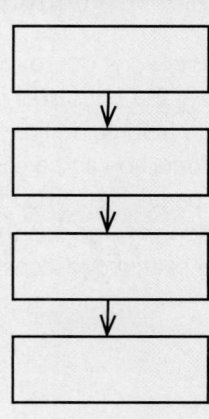

LOG ON ▶ Literature Online

Literature and Reading To explore the Interactive Timeline, go to **glencoe.com** and enter QuickPass code GLW6053u1.

Reading Practice

Use Graphic Organizers Explain that a timeline presents a sequence of events. A flow chart can also serve this function. Tell students that to construct a historical flow chart they need to arrange events in order. Then they can draw arrows between events to show how one event flows into another. Have them create a four-part flow chart using the following four statements. Emphasize that the first step is to determine the order of events.

Nelson Mandela is elected president of South Africa. *(4)*

Nelson Mandela is released from prison; apartheid begins to be dismantled. *(3)*

South Africa establishes apartheid. *(1)*

Nelson Mandela is arrested and imprisoned in South Africa. *(2)*

1950 | 1975

1956
Naguib Mahfouz publishes
Palace Walk

1958
1 Chinua Achebe publishes
Things Fall Apart

1960
Wole Soyinka's play
A Dance of the Forests
is produced

1966
Grace Ogot publishes
The Promised Land

1967
Ngugi wa Thiong'o
publishes *A Grain of Wheat*

1968
Bessie Head publishes
When Rain Clouds Gather

1986
3 Wole Soyinka wins the
Nobel Prize

1986
Mark Mathabane publishes
Kaffir Boy

1988
Naguib Mahfouz wins
the Nobel Prize

1991
Nadine Gordimer wins
the Nobel Prize

1950 | 1975

1960
Léopold Sédar Senghor
becomes the first president
of Senegal

1962
Nelson Mandela is
arrested and imprisoned
in South Africa

1967
Civil war breaks out
in Nigeria

1979
Idi Amin, ruler of Uganda,
is overthrown

1990
Nelson Mandela is
released from prison;
apartheid begins to
be dismantled

1994
Nelson Mandela is elected
president of South Africa;
Hutu kill 500,000 Tutsi
in Rwanda

1950 | 1975

1959
Fidel Castro comes to
power in Cuba

1966
Chinese Cultural
Revolution begins

Young Bhopal residents
paint a skull on the
enclosing wall of the
Union Carbide India Ltd

1975
Vietnam War ends

 1984
Bhopal disaster takes place
in India

1991
Soviet Union collapses,
ending the Cold War

2004
Massive tsunami
devastates southeast Asia

Reading Check
Analyze Graphic Information How long was
Nelson Mandela imprisoned in South Africa?

Advanced Learners/Pre-AP

DIFFERENTIATED INSTRUCTION

Research Have students select a specific
African episode covered by the timeline
(such as the Anglo-Zulu War or the Italian
invasion of Ethiopia) and do research to
prepare a timeline of this episode. Make
sure students include events leading up
to the episode as well as the events that
ensued. Encourage students to do picture
research and illustrate their timelines. Have
them present their timelines to the class.

Teach
Reading Check
Answer: *Mandela was imprisoned for twenty-eight years.*

Reading Strategy | 3

**Analyze Graphic Informa-
tion Say:** Wole Soyinka was
the first African to win the Nobel
Prize for Literature. **Ask:** How
many years passed between the
first distribution of the Nobel
Prizes in 1901 and the year of
Soyinka's award? *(85 years)*

Cultural History ☆
The Suez Canal and *Aïda*
A French construction company
began excavation of the Suez
Canal in 1859 and completed the
waterway ten years later. The canal
was opened with an elaborate ceremony on November 17, 1869.
Two years later, on December
24, 1871, *Aïda*, Giuseppe Verdi's
famous opera set in ancient Egypt,
had its premiere at Cairo's new
opera house.

Learning Objectives
Analyzing graphic information. (SE)
Analyzing art. (TE)

Teach

Reading Strategy　　1

Analyze Cause-and-Effect Relationships
Ask: How did conditions in Europe between 1880 and 1900 affect African history? *(Growing nationalism and economic rivalries among European nations led to competition for African colonies.)*

[ENGLISH LEARNERS] Explain to students that *nationalism* means several things, but in this context it refers to a high level of devotion to the interests and culture of a particular nation. Ask students born in other countries what effects of nationalism they observed in their homelands.

View the Art ★

Scenes of colonial life in British Nigeria about 1940 appear on this leatherwork panel. **Ask:** How does this leatherwork panel depict the roles of colonial people in British Nigeria? *(It depicts them as servants and soldiers.)*

Learning Objectives

For pages 66–77
In studying this text, you will focus on the following objectives:

Literary Study: Analyzing literary periods.

Reading: Evaluating historical influences.
Connecting to the literature.

Modern AFRICA
1800–Present

Historical, Social, and Cultural Forces

Leatherwork panel depicting colonial scenes, Hausa, Northern Nigeria, c.1940. ★

Colonialism in Africa

Before the nineteenth century, European knowledge of Africa was restricted primarily to the coastal regions. African merchants traded gold, copper, ivory, and timber for imported goods from Europe at trading stations on the coasts; therefore, Europeans did not need to travel to the interior of the continent for goods. Before 1880, Europeans were content to let African rulers and merchants represent European interests. However, between 1880 and 1900, intense rivalries involving nationalism and economics grew among Britain, France, Germany, Belgium, Italy, Spain, and Portugal. These European colonial powers met in Berlin, Germany, in 1884–1885 to settle their competing claims to territory in Africa. No African delegates were present at the Berlin Conference, and as a result, nearly all of Africa was placed under European control.

The age of colonialism lasted only 100 years, yet it had a profound and traumatic effect on the continent. Colonial regimes varied widely in their treatment of African people but were generally characterized by economic exploitation and racism. While some African countries gained independence earlier, many nations did not gain independence until World War II or later.

Grammar Practice

Use Commas with Appositives Have students notice the use of a comma to set off explanatory information at the end of a sentence:

"One of the poisonous legacies of colonialism in South Africa was apartheid, an extreme form of racial segregation."

Point out that commas are used both before and after such information when the appositive appears in the middle of a sentence:

Apartheid, an extreme form of racial segregation, was one of the poisonous legacies of colonialism in South Africa.

Ask students to use commas to set off the appositives in these sentences.

1. Nelson Mandela the first black president of South Africa had been imprisoned for opposing apartheid.

2. Mandela spent much of his nearly 30 years of imprisonment at Robben Island a maximum-security prison.

Rise of African Nationalism

As the twentieth century began, Africans became increasingly resentful of colonial powers. Across the continent, a new class of Africans educated in Europe began to organize political parties and movements seeking the end of foreign rule. Colonial powers often used force to end these efforts, but they also made minor reforms in an attempt to satisfy the demands of native citizens. These small concessions were inadequate, however, and by the 1930s, an increasing number of African leaders were calling for independence. In Kenya, Jomo Kenyatta, who had been educated in Britain, argued that British rule was destroying traditional African culture. Léopold Sédar Senghor, who had studied in France, organized an independence movement in Senegal.

The Transition to Independence

After World War II, Europeans began to realize that colonial rule in Africa was increasingly unnecessary. Many African nations finally won independence when Great Britain and France let go of their colonial empires in the late 1950s and the 1960s. In 1957, the Gold Coast, renamed Ghana, was the first former British colony to gain independence. By 1965, dozens more new African **2** nations had followed. After a series of brutal guerrilla wars, the Portuguese surrendered the colonies of Mozambique and Angola in the 1970s. For many African nations, independence precipitated a new series of problems, including economic stagnation, political corruption, ethnic violence, and overpopulation.

> *"The time for the healing of the wounds has come."*
>
> —Nelson Mandela, from his inauguration speech

Demonstrators celebrate the independence of Guinea-Bissau from Portuguese rule.

New Hopes

One of the poisonous legacies of colonialism in South Africa was apartheid, an extreme form of racial segregation. Apartheid faced criticism from around the world, but its most famous critic was Nelson Mandela, who, in 1994, became the first black South African president.

Mandela had been sentenced to life imprisonment in 1962 for his anti-apartheid activities. He served almost 26 years in maximum-security prisons but never wavered from the fight for equality. Worldwide opposition to apartheid finally led the white South African government to dismantle apartheid laws, and Mandela was released in 1990.

INTRODUCTION **71**

Reading Strategy | **2**

Make Inferences **Ask:** What can you infer about Portuguese colonial policy from this? *(You can infer that Portuguese colonial policy was harsh.)*

(APPROACHING) Explain to students that guerrilla warfare involves hit-and-run raiding tactics used by small groups of fighters against a stronger occupying force. **Ask:** Why would anti-colonialist fighters adopt guerrilla warfare tactics? *(Because they are weaker militarily than the colonial forces)*

Learning Objectives
Analyzing historical influences. (SE)
Analyzing cause-and-effect relationships. (TE)
Using commas with appositives. (TE)
Analyzing art. (TE)

English Learners

DIFFERENTIATED INSTRUCTION

Intermediate Point out to students that in a passage of historical background, such as pages 70–71, introductory adverbial phrases and clauses frequently provide information about time:

- *"After World War II,* Europeans began to realize that colonial rule in Africa was increasingly unnecessary."

- *"As the twentieth century began,* Africans became increasingly resentful of colonial powers."

Have students identify the adverbial phrases and clauses in the following sentences. (Do not include the underlining when writing the sentences on the board.)

1. Before the nineteenth century started, European knowledge of Africa was restricted primarily to the coastal regions.

2. Between 1880 and 1900, European nations divided most of African into colonies.

71

Teach

Determine Topic Sentence

Ask: What is the topic sentence of this paragraph? *("In modern Africa, traditional art forms are continually re-imagined in ways that reflect globalization and contemporary ideals.")*

Parentheses Point out that material within parentheses often provides information about an unfamiliar term. **Ask:** What is a kora? *(A stringed instrument made from a gourd)*

View the Art ★

Each symbol on this textile represents a quality of one of the kings of Abomey, an area that is now the country of Benin. For example, the ferocious fish represents King Behanzin and his fierce resistance to colonization.

Tradition and Innovation

1 Art often reflects the interests, personal values, and histories of the artists who create it. In modern Africa, traditional art forms are continually reimagined in ways that reflect globalization and contemporary ideals. For example, African musicians such as Ladysmith Black Mambazo and Youssou N'Dour are famous worldwide for their synthesis of traditional African sounds with pop music. Changes in traditional art are also reflected on a regional scale; for example, a hand-blocked West African cloth may have a political slogan, rather than a customary pattern.

3

> "Here we stand
> infants overblown,
> poised between two civilizations… "
>
> —Mabel Segun, from "Conflict"

Music

The convergence of traditional and modern types of music can be heard across Africa. In Algeria, traditional Arab-influenced songs are accompanied by synthesizers and digital drums. In South Africa, choirs combining Zulu and Christian church choral styles provided anthems for the liberation struggle. Many contemporary African musicians have worked with performers from other cultures. For example, kora (a stringed **2** instrument made from a gourd) players from Mali have recorded with Spanish guitar players and Arab percussionists to produce music that blends a ☆ variety of traditions.

Drummer salutes the Kabaka, (Bugandan People's King). Ssentema in Wakiso District, Uganda.

Symbols of the Kings of Abomey. Textile display. Abomey, Benin.
★

Reading Practice

Compare and Contrast Remind students that recognizing comparisons and contrasts is an essential reading skill. Have them note how the transition word *rather* signals a contrast in the following sentence:

"African artists have begun to produce masks and other traditional objects as works of art in themselves, <u>rather</u> than for their traditional purposes in rituals."

Have students identify what is being compared or contrasted in the following sentences and what transition word or phrase signals the comparison or contrast.

1. African artists once created rock art or face paintings, but today they often paint on canvas. *(contrast between artistic methods; but)*

2. Algerian musicians use synthesizers to accompany traditional Arabic song; in the same way, South African musicians combine Zulu and European choral styles. *(Comparison between cultural fusions; in the same way)*

Paintings and Prints

The art of painting has a long history in Africa. The tradition can be seen in prehistoric rock art, traditional ritual body and face painting, and the brightly decorated walls of contemporary African villages. Painting on canvas became increasingly popular throughout the twentieth century. For example, in the early 1970s, Nigerian painters called the Nsukka group began to use Ibo images to express modern themes.

Art in Context

Traditionally, African art was often intended to be seen only when in ceremonial use. Masks were meant to be viewed in motion, made mysterious by shadow and torchlight, rather than admired in an exhibit. However, as African art gained world-wide recognition, museums and galleries began collecting and selling it. African artists have begun to produce masks and other traditional objects as works of art in themselves, rather than for their traditional purposes in rituals.

Ndebele urban mural art. Esther Mahlangu. Mabhoko, South Africa.

 PREVIEW **Big Ideas** of Modern Africa

1 Tradition and Change	**2** The Price of Freedom	**3** Living with Independence
Modern Africa is a study in contrasts. Old and new, native and foreign exist side by side. Modern African authors have responded to these contrasts by exploring the connections between traditional and modern African ways of life. **See page 74**	Imperialism and the efforts of black Africans to gain independence and equal rights have dominated contemporary African history. African authors have explored and documented these issues and their effects on both white and black Africans. **See page 75**	Faced with problems such as ethnic violence and political corruption, many African countries have struggled since gaining independence. African authors have responded to these struggles in works that range from humorous to poignant. **See page 76**

INTRODUCTION **73**

English Learners

DIFFERENTIATED INSTRUCTION

Intermediate To help students with the Reading Practice on page 72, give them a list of words and phrases that signal comparisons and contrasts.

Comparisons

like, likewise, also, similarly, in the same way

Contrasts

but, however, in contrast, on the other hand, as opposed to

Advanced Learners/Pre-AP

DIFFERENTIATED INSTRUCTION

Comparison-and-Contrast Paragraph Have students write a paragraph in which they examine both what Africa's artistic traditions might gain and what they might lose as a result the worldwide recognition they have received in modern times. Remind students to use transition words and phrases to make their comparisons and contrasts clear.

Teach

Reading Strategy 3

Analyze Metaphor Ask: What does Mabel Segun mean by "poised between two civilizations"? *(She emphasizes the strong contrasts between old Africa and modern Africa.)*

[APPROACHING] Explain to students that a metaphor is a comparison between two unlike things that is not signaled by the word *like* or *as*.

Cultural History ☆

Kora This traditional African instrument consists of a large, round resonator—made from a gourd—and a long neck. The kora's twenty-one strings are arranged in two parallel rows from the neck to the sound-board of the resonator. Traditionally used to accompany vocal performances, the kora is now often played as a solo instrument.

View the Art ★

The Ndebele women of South Africa have traditionally painted the walls of their homes with geometric designs in bright colors. **Ask:** How does this painting depart from that tradition? *(The painting includes figures as well as geometric designs.)*

Learning Objectives
Analyzing historical influences. (SE)
Determining topic sentence. (TE)
Comparing and contrasting. (TE)
Analyzing metaphor. (TE)

Teach

Reading Check

Answer: *Negritude authors celebrated traditional African culture; opponents of negritude explored both good and bad aspects of traditional African society.*

ADVANCED **Ask:** Why might a form of cultural nationalism such as the negritude movement be necessary to colonial peoples? *(Such a movement might strengthen their cultural independence and help prepare the way for political independence.)*

View the Art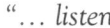

Wood is the best-known medium in traditional African sculpture.
Ask: How does this Yoruba sculpture reflect both tradition and change? *(The sculpture uses the traditional medium of woodcarving to interpret the modern figure of a man on a bicycle.)*

Big Idea 1
Tradition and Change

The tension between tradition and modern ideas is among the most powerful topics in contemporary African literature and society. This tension often arises when traditional ways of life collide with foreign ideas.

City and Countryside

In Africa, European colonialism was first and most firmly established in the cities. Many cities are direct products of colonial rule, including Dakar, Senegal; Lagos, Nigeria; Cape Town, South Africa; Brazzaville, Republic of the Congo; and Nairobi, Kenya. In rural areas, however, modern influence has had less of an effect. Millions of people throughout Africa live much as their ancestors did, in thatched dwellings without plumbing or electricity. People in rural communities often farm or hunt by traditional methods, wear regional clothing, and adhere to local customs and beliefs. Some people who live in the countryside believe that the cities are corrupting traditional African values and customs.

> "... listen
> To the deep pulse of Africa beating
> in the midst of forgotten villages."
>
> —Léopold Sédar Senghor, from
> "Night of Sine"

A Cultural Debate

An early response to colonial influence in African culture was the Negritude movement. Negritude was started in the early 1930s by a group of French-speaking African and Caribbean authors, led by poet Léopold Sédar Senghor (see pages 78–82). They rejected the notion of European superiority and asserted that Africa already had a

Man with Bicycle, 20th century. Yoruba people, Nigeria. Wood, Height: 35 3/4 in. Collection of The Newark Museum. ★

vibrant culture of its own. The name *Negritude* was chosen to suggest a common heritage shared by all black people.

English-speaking African authors began to criticize the Negritude movement in the 1950s and 1960s. These authors felt that Negritude idealized Africa and restricted the creative spirit. Authors such as Nigerian novelist Chinua Achebe (see pages 92–101) have explored both the positive and negative aspects of traditional African society. Achebe's fiction illustrates the problems faced by Africans who live amid conflicting cultural values.

Reading Check

Compare and Contrast What is the difference between the outlook of the Negritude movement and that of its critics?

Reading Practice

Distinguish Fact and Opinion Remind students that a fact is a statement that can be proved true from direct observation or by consulting an authoritative source, such as a reference book. For example: *The poet Léopold Sédar Senghor was born in 1906.* Point out that this fact can be verified by looking in an encyclopedia or a biographical dictionary.

An opinion is a statement that expresses an attitude or a judgment. For example:

The poet Léopold Sédar Senghor was the greatest African writer of the twentieth century. Point out that, unlike a fact, an opinion cannot be proved true; however, an opinion can be supported by facts.

Have students identify one fact and one opinion on pages 74–75. *(Possible fact: Negritude was started in the early 1930s by a group of French-speaking African and Caribbean authors; possible opinion: The tension between tradition and mod-*

ern ideas is among the most powerful topics in contemporary African literature and society.)

Big Idea 2
The Price of Freedom

Many black Africans fought in the British and French armies during World War I, hoping that their countries would be rewarded with independence when the war ended. These hopes were not realized.

African Protests

1 In the years following World War I, Africans became increasingly active in politics and the fight for independence. Soldiers who had fought in the armies of colonial countries had learned new ideas about freedom and nationalism. In Kenya, the Young Kikuyu Association organized a protest against British rule in 1921, resulting in the arrest of the group's leader. When an angry crowd stormed the jail and demanded his release, government authorities fired into the crowd and killed at least twenty people. In the early 1950s,

A protester carries a portrait of Nelson Mandela during funerals for victims of police repression. Cape Town, South Africa.

the Kenyan nationalist movement known as Mau Mau began an armed resistance against the British. By the time the Mau Mau rebels were defeated in 1956, more than 11,000 Kikuyu had been killed or put into detention camps. Among the victims were members of the family of Kenyan author Ngugi wa Thiong'o (see pages 133–140). Despite the Mau Mau defeat, the uprising did pave the way to Kenyan independence in 1963. Jomo Kenyatta, who had been jailed as a Mau Mau leader in 1953, became the new nation's first prime minister.

> *"Remember Sharpeville*
> *Remember bullet-in-the-back day"*
>
> —Dennis Brutus, from "Sharpeville"

Fighting Apartheid

In South Africa, black citizens formed the African National Congress (ANC) in 1912. The ANC sought reform, but its efforts met with little success. By the 1950s, South African whites had established apartheid, a system of legalized segregation. In 1960, police in Sharpeville fired on marchers protesting apartheid, killing 69 people. After Nelson Mandela was arrested in 1962, ANC members called for armed resistance. Despite this, after Mandela was elected president of South Africa in 1994, he asked Archbishop Desmond Tutu (see pages 103–106) to lead the Truth and Reconciliation Commission, which sought to review apartheid atrocities without resorting to violent retribution.

Reading Check
Analyze Cause-and-Effect Relationships How did World War I encourage the development of nationalist movements in Africa?

Teach
Reading Check

Answer: *Black Africans who had fought for Britain and France hoped their countries would be rewarded with independence. When this hope was not realized, many turned to political action to gain independence.*

Reading Strategy   **1**

Analyze Cause-and-Effect Relationships **Ask:** How did World War I encourage the rise of African nationalist movements? *(African soldiers who had fought in the armies of colonial countries learned new ideas about freedom and nationalism.)*

Cultural History ☆

Dennis Brutus Born in what is now Zimbabwe in 1924, South African poet Dennis Brutus spent 18 months in prison for his protests against apartheid. The South African government also banned him from teaching and writing. Brutus spent many years as a political exile, first in England and later in the United States.

Advanced Learners/Pre-AP
DIFFERENTIATED INSTRUCTION

Deliver an Oral Interpretation Have a group of students create a program of oral interpretations of anti-apartheid writings such as Dennis Brutus's poem "Sharpeville." Other South African writers whose works students might present as part of their program include Nadine Gordimer, Peter Abrahams, Richard Rive, Es'kia Mphahlele, Bloke Modisane, Alfred Hutchinson, and Steve Biko.

Learning Objectives
Analyzing cause-and-effect relationships. (SE)
Analyzing metaphor. (SE)
Distinguishing fact and opinion. (TE)

75

Teach

Reading Check

Answer: *European countries drew boundaries for African colonies that did not reflect the distribution of various ethnic groups. As a result, some independent African countries were home to several ethnic groups, which bred conflicts.*

Vocabulary | 1

Word Parts Ask: What is the root word of *authoritarian*? *(authority) How do you think an authoritarian government acts? (An authoritarian government enforces strict obedience to authority.*

ENGLISH LEARNERS Point out to English learners that the suffix *-arian* added to a word means "a person who" or "a thing that" or "pertaining to." Review the following examples of words with the *–arian* suffix: *antiquarian, humanitarian, libertarian, parliamentarian, utilitarian,* and *veterinarian.*

Cultural History ☆

Hotel Rwanda The award-winning 2004 film *Hotel Rwanda* tells the true-life story of Paul Rusesabagina, a hotel manager who sheltered more than a thousand Tutsi refugees fleeing from the Hutu militia in Rwanda.

Big Idea 3
Living with Independence

The hopes and dreams of African nationalists had been directed toward winning independence from Europe. However, for many countries, independence resulted in a number of unexpected economic and social problems.

Political Challenges

African nationalists had hoped that independence would lead to a stable political order based on democracy. Unfortunately, some democratic governments gave way to military regimes and one-party states. Many African authors have been forced to spend long periods in exile because of their criticism of authoritarian governments. Wole Soyinka (see pages 120–123), the first African to be awarded the Nobel Prize in Literature, spent several years in exile after being charged with treason by the military government of Nigeria.

In other countries, warring ethnic groups undermined the concept of nationhood. These conflicts were not surprising, given that European governments had often determined the boundaries of African nations with little regard for the ethnic differences of African people. Ethnic conflicts often resulted in war and bloodshed. During the early 1990s, conflict erupted between the Hutu and Tutsi peoples in the central African states of Burundi and Rwanda. In 1994, a Hutu rampage left some 500,000 Tutsi dead in Rwanda.

Economic and Health Problems

Independence did not bring economic prosperity to Africa. Most African nations still relied on exporting a single crop or natural resource. The efforts to create modern economies were also frustrated by high population growth. Additionally, droughts led to widespread starvation. As a result of these problems, poverty continues to affect many Africans, especially in rural areas.

African cities have grown tremendously and are often surrounded by enormous slums. This growth has overwhelmed sanitation and transportation systems, resulting in pollution and massive traffic jams. Another problem Africa faces is the epidemic of acquired immune deficiency syndrome (AIDS). By the end of the twentieth century, AIDS was the leading cause of death for Africans. The epidemic has resulted in splintered families, devastated communities, and economic hardships across the continent.

With the relaxing of apartheid laws, blacks can ride on white buses in South Africa.

Reading Check

Analyze Cause-and-Effect Relationships How did colonialism create conditions that led to ethnic violence in modern African nations?

Writing Practice

List Information Remind students that outlining—even in a simple form—is helpful in identifying the essential information presented in a passage. Direct students to use a list such as the one started below, to organize the material presented on page 76.

Political challenges

- hopes for stability and democracy
- reality of military regimes and one-party states
- authors exiled by authoritarian governments
- exile of Wole Soyinka

Wrap-Up

Legacy of the Period

The impact of European colonialism extends beyond Africa to countries around the world, including many in Asia and the Caribbean. The colonial powers reshaped local religious and cultural traditions while simultaneously stripping native citizens of basic human rights. In Africa, the absence of any African representatives at the Berlin Conference resulted in a continent run almost entirely by colonial rule for decades.

Throughout the twentieth century, African authors, artists, and intellectuals have explored the conflict between traditional ways of life and colonialism in a variety of ways. The works of these artists have given people outside Africa an appreciation of the importance of intercultural understanding and have shown what the influence of globalization may be in years to come.

Cultural and Literary Links

▲ Chinua Achebe's novel *Things Fall Apart* was partially inspired by his desire to refute the

Opportunity Magazine, cover, June 1926. Aaron Douglas. Schomburg Center for Research in Black Culture, The New York Public Library.

primitive impression of Africa given by Joseph Conrad's *Heart of Darkness*.

▲ The Negritude movement drew inspiration from the Harlem Renaissance, the cultural movement among African Americans in the Harlem neighborhood of New York City in the 1920s.

 Literature Online

Unit Resources For additional skills practice, go to glencoe.com and enter QuickPass code GLW6053u1.

Activities

Use what you have learned about the period to do one of these activities.

1. Follow Up Go back to Looking Ahead on page 67 and answer the questions.

2. Contrast Literary Periods In the United States, formerly enslaved people, such as Frederick Douglass, wrote slave narratives. Research slave narratives and write an essay comparing the concerns of the authors with those of African postcolonial authors.

3. Speaking/Listening Research the issues involved in the debate between the Negritude movement and the African authors who opposed it. Then hold a panel discussion exploring the relative merits of African tradition and Western culture.

4. Take Notes Use this organizer to explore your responses to the literary works in this part.

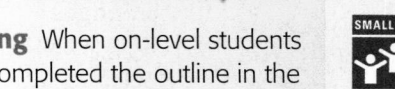 **BOUND BOOK**

Nonfiction
Short Stories
Poems
Reader-Response Journal

Assess

Activities

1. Follow Up Students should answer questions with specific facts from the text.

2. Contrast Literary Periods Students' essays should show that they have researched the topic and should draw clear parallels between the concerns of postcolonial African authors and those of formerly enslaved African Americans.

3. Speaking/Listening Encourage students to discuss how their perception of the debate changed through the course of their research.

4. Note Taking Students' Foldables should be well organized, and their notes should have specific responses to the literature.

Approaching Level
DIFFERENTIATED INSTRUCTION

Peer Mentoring When on-level students have correctly completed the outline in the Writing Practice on page 76, have them demonstrate the process to students who are struggling.

Advanced Learners/Pre-AP
DIFFERENTIATED INSTRUCTION

SMALL GROUP **Africa at a Glance** Have a group of students research statistical data relating to contemporary Africa, including such things as population growth, life expectancy, literacy rates, per capita income, resources, urbanization, and other key information. Have students present this information in whatever graphic form (such as a table, bar graph, or pie chart) makes it the easiest to grasp. Have the group present their information to the class.

Before You Read

Focus

Bellringer Options

Selection Focus
  Transparency 4

Daily Language Practice
  Transparency 11

Or ask: What are some very old cultural traditions that are still practiced in our society today? Students may mention religious rituals, secular holidays, or artistic practices. Have students discuss which traditions have changed over time, and which have remained the same.

Before You Read

Night of Sine

Meet **Léopold Sédar Senghor**
(1906–2001)

Poet, politician, philosopher, and teacher, Léopold Sédar Senghor (seng´hôr) was one of the most brilliant lights of Africa's postcolonial period. In 1960, Senghor became the first president of Senegal, a position he would retain for the next two decades. A leader in the struggle for independence from France, Senghor was also a leader in the effort to modernize and democratize the young country of Senegal, which remains one of the most stable nations in Africa.

> *"I leave matter to the engineers. To the Poet belongs the spirit."*
>
> —Léopold Sédar Senghor

Africa and the West The son of a wealthy planter and trader, Senghor spent his early years in a traditional Senegalese village in the Sine (sē´nā) region. He was educated in a Roman Catholic seminary with the aim of becoming a priest. By the time he turned twenty, however, Senghor had found that his calling lay elsewhere. After a brief time in Dakar, Senegal's capital, Senghor traveled to Paris, France, in 1928. While there, he completed his studies and began writing poems while working as a teacher. At the start of World War II, Senghor was drafted into the French army. In 1940, he was captured and held in Nazi concentration camps, where he continued to write poetry. After his release two years later, Senghor became active in the underground French Resistance fighting Nazi Germany's occupation.

From Liberation to Retirement As the war came to a close, Senghor became involved in politics, first as a member of the French Constituent Assembly and then as the mayor of Thiès, one of Senegal's largest cities. When Senegal was finally liberated from French rule in 1960, Senghor became the country's first president. Although a coup was attempted only two years into his first term, he remained in power until 1980, when he became the first African president to leave office voluntarily. Senghor's presidency was filled with many advances for Senegal, including the modernization of its agriculture and vast economic and trade reforms. The poet-president also wrote the lyrics to the country's national anthem. After retiring, Senghor returned to France, where he continued to write poetry and completed a memoir. In 1984, Senghor became the first African to be inducted into the French Academy—France's most prestigious, exclusive, and oldest literary organization.

As a poet, Senghor was influenced by black writers from the United States and the Caribbean as well as French poets such as Charles Baudelaire and Arthur Rimbaud.

LOG ON   **Literature** Online

Author Search For more about Léopold Sédar Senghor, go to glencoe.com and enter QuickPass code GLW6053u1.

Selection Skills

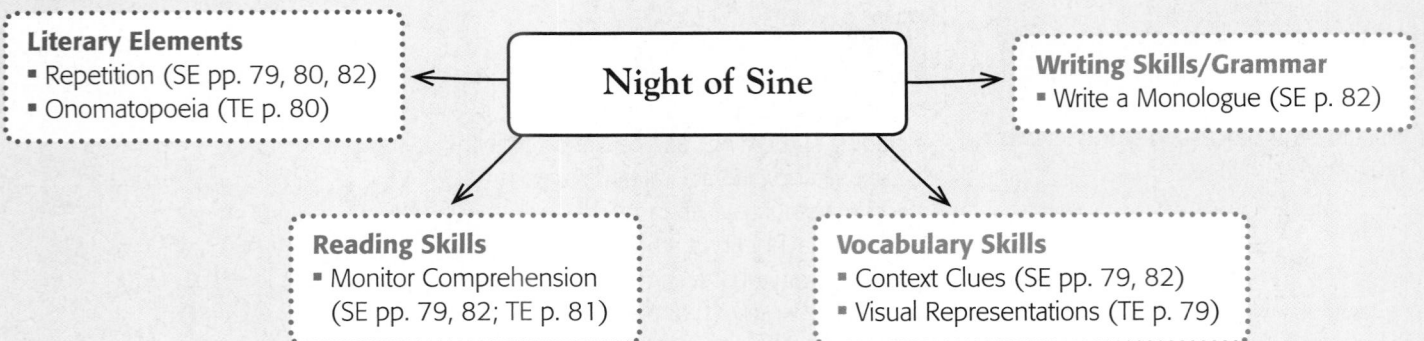

Literary Elements
- Repetition (SE pp. 79, 80, 82)
- Onomatopoeia (TE p. 80)

Night of Sine

Writing Skills/Grammar
- Write a Monologue (SE p. 82)

Reading Skills
- Monitor Comprehension (SE pp. 79, 82; TE p. 81)

Vocabulary Skills
- Context Clues (SE pp. 79, 82)
- Visual Representations (TE p. 79)

Literature and Reading Preview

Connect to the Poem

How do our native country and culture shape us? Write a journal entry in which you reflect on these influences and their effects on your life.

Build Background

In the 1930s, Senghor and other black intellectuals living in Paris formed the Negritude movement. They came together to explore their African heritage and to reclaim it as a source of cultural pride. In Senghor's poetry and the poetry of other Negritude authors, similar topics often recur: the beauty of the African landscape, the dignity of the African people, and the rejection of colonizers' assumptions of superiority.

Set Purposes for Reading

Big Idea **Tradition and Change**

As you read, ask yourself, What traditions did Africa lose as a result of colonialism?

Literary Element **Repetition**

Repetition is the recurrence of sounds, words, phrases, lines, or stanzas in a literary work. Repetition may be used to enhance the unity of a work. It can also create a musical or a rhythmic effect or emphasize an idea. As you read, ask yourself, How does repetition affect the meaning of this poem?

Reading Strategy **Monitor Comprehension**

When you monitor comprehension during reading, you make sure you understand what you are reading. The syntax of this poem can be difficult to follow and may require clarification. As you read, ask yourself, Do I understand this line or stanza? If not, reread it carefully.

Tip: Restate Passages When you encounter passages that are difficult to comprehend, it can be helpful to rewrite them using both language and a sequence that make sense to you. Use a chart like the one below.

Unclear Passage	My Rewrite
"Woman, lay on my forehead your perfumed hands, hands softer than fur."	"Woman, lay your perfumed hands, which are softer than fur, on my forehead."

Learning Objectives

For pages 78–82

In studying this text, you will focus on the following objectives:

Literary Study: Analyzing repetition.

Reading: Monitoring comprehension.

Writing: Writing a monologue.

Vocabulary

rustle (rus′əl) *v.* to make a succession of soft crackling sounds; p. 80 *The student's papers rustle in the light breeze.*

acrid (ak′rid) *adj.* strong, bitter, and often unpleasant in smell or taste; p. 81 *The hikers covered their noses to block out the acrid smell.*

torrent (tôr′ənt) *n.* a powerful flood or outpouring; p. 81 *Every meeting started with a torrent of information.*

....

Tip: Context Clues Context clues are words and sentences surrounding an unfamiliar term that can help you determine the meaning of the term. For example, in the sentence *The hikers covered their noses to block out the <u>acrid</u> smell,* the fact that the hikers "covered their noses" indicates that the smell was bad, or *acrid.*

Before You Read

Focus

Summary

The speaker of the poem, addressing an unnamed woman, describes a peaceful night in a village in the Sine region of Senegal. He observes palm trees swaying, the moon shining, a choir singing, and dancers dancing. He then retires to a hut and hears the voices of ancient spirits speaking as he falls asleep.

 For summaries in languages other than English, see Unit 1 Teaching Resources Book, pp. 100–105.

Teach

Vocabulary

Visual Representations

Write the vocabulary words on note cards, have a volunteer pick a card, and then sketch an image that represents that word on the board. Tell them to consider including images of words that rhyme with the vocabulary word or part of the vocabulary word. Have the rest of the class compete to see who can be the first to guess the word that the sketch represents.

 For additional vocabulary practice, see Unit 1 Teaching Resources Book, p. 108.

English Learners

DIFFERENTIATED INSTRUCTION

Intermediate Explain to all students that much of the beauty of Senghor's poem—and poetry in general—is created by sound and rhythm. Ask each English learner to bring in a short poem in his or her first language and read it aloud for the class.

Have students listen carefully to one another and pay attention to the sounds of the different languages.

Teach

Repetition Answer: *The repetition of the words* listen *and* beat *generates a rhythm and emphasizes the musical quality of the language.*

Literary History ☆

Negritude and the Harlem Renaissance Senghor's Negritude movement was strongly influenced by the Harlem Renaissance, an American literary and artistic movement that emerged in the 1920s among a group of black intellectuals in New York City. Senghor was particularly inspired by the work of a Jamaican-born writer named Claude McKay. Along with his fellow Negritude writers, Senghor embraced McKay's straightforward, candid representations of black life, going so far as to call McKay "the true inventor" of the values of negritude.

 For an audio recording of this selection, use Listening Library Audio CD-ROM.

Night of Sine

Léopold Sédar Senghor

Translated by John Reed & Clive Wake

> Woman, lay on my forehead your perfumed hands, hands
>   softer than fur.
> Above, the swaying palm trees **rustle** in the high night breeze
> Hardly at all. No lullaby even.
> The rhythmic silence cradles us.
> 5 Listen to its song, listen to our dark blood beat, listen
> To the deep pulse of Africa beating in the mist of
>   forgotten villages.

Baule dancers. African Ivory Coast. Gilded wood. Private collection.

---

1   Repetition *In your opinion, what is the effect of the repetition in these lines?*

Vocabulary

rustle (rus′əl) *v.* to make a succession of soft crackling sounds

Literary Element Practice

Onomatopoeia Explain to students that writers often tailor their writing to appeal to the senses. Many writers use onomatopoeia to help the reader hear the sound being described. Onomatopoeia is the use of a name or word that is formed by imitating the sound associated with that object or action. For example, Senghor writes, "the palm trees rustle." The word *rustle* is an example of onomatopoeia, because the word sounds like the sound it describes.

Have students work in pairs to complete the following sentences with appropriate onomatopoeia, and then have them read their answers out loud for the class.

1. The heavy crate fell off the high shelf with a startling _____.
(Possible answer: crash)

2. The raindrop bounced of the air conditioner with a _____.
(Possible answer: ping).

The butter _____ in the hot pan while I chopped the onions.
(Possible answer: sizzled)

See the tired moon comes down to her bed on the slack sea
The laughter grows weary, the story-tellers even
Are nodding their heads like a child on the back of its mother
10   The feet of the dancers grow heavy, and heavy the voice of
the answering choirs.

2   It is the hour of stars, of Night that dreams
Leaning upon this hill of clouds, wrapped in its long
milky cloth.
The roofs of the huts gleam tenderly. What do they say so
secretly to the stars?
Inside the fire goes out among intimate smells that are
acrid and sweet.

3   15   Woman, light the clear oil lamp, where the ancestors
gathered around may talk as parents talk when the children
are put to bed.
Listen to the voice of the ancients of Elissa.° Exiled like us
They have never wanted to die, to let the **torrent** of their
seed be lost in the sands.
Let me listen in the smoky hut where there comes a glimpse
of the friendly spirits
My head on your bosom warm like a *dang*° still steaming
from the fire.
20   Let me breathe the smell of our Dead, gather and speak out
again their living voice, learn to
Live before I go down, deeper than diver, into the high
profundities of sleep.

16 Elissa is a village in Guinea-Bissau, a country directly south of Senegal.

19 Dang is couscous that is cooked in broth.

---

4   Tradition and Change *What do the activities in lines 7–10 suggest about the culture's views on tradition?*

> **Vocabulary**
>
> **acrid** (ak′rid) *adj.* strong, bitter, and often unpleasant in smell or taste
> **torrent** (tôr′ənt) *n.* a powerful flood or outpouring

LÉOPOLD SÉDAR SENGHOR   **81**

Approaching Level

DIFFERENTIATED INSTRUCTION

Visualize Students having difficulty with the complex sentences in the poem may benefit from breaking them down into phrases that convey images and then creating illustrations for each image. Offer the following as ideas to those students having trouble selecting phrases to illustrate: "the swaying palm trees rustle," "the mist of forgotten villages," "the tired moon comes down," or "the roofs of the huts gleam tenderly."

For those students who need more help, write the following words on the board: palm trees, moon, sea, dancers, stars, hut Have students choose one of these words and create a drawing that illustrates it.

Teach

Big Idea   **2**

Tradition and Change Have students read the third stanza. **Ask:** Do you think the portrait of the village that Senghor has presented so far is realistic or idealized? Explain. *(Some students may feel that it is idealized, because it presents the village as a peaceful, harmonious place that seems separate from the modern world.)*

Reading Strategy   **3**

Monitor Comprehension Have students read the fourth stanza. **Say:** Summarize what the speaker says about the ancestors in this stanza. *(They live on. Their advice is to live well before death.)*

 For additional practice using the reading skill or strategy, see Unit 1 Teaching Resources Book, p. 107.

Big Idea   **4**

Tradition and Change
Answer: *The presence of the choir, along with the storytellers and dancers, suggests that some traditions have been kept, despite the influences of the modern world.*

Progress Check

Can students identify repetition?

If No ➔ See Unit 1 Teaching Resources Book, p. 106.

Learning Objectives
Analyzing repetition. (SE)
Monitoring comprehension. (SE)
Using onomatopoeia. (TE)

81

After You Read

Assess

1. Answers will vary.

2. (a) A woman (b) They are very close, possibly married.

3. (a) He wants to listen to the voices of the ancestors. (b) The ancestors can help him "learn to live" (lines 20–21).

4. (a) The tone is loving and intimate, sweet and soothing. (b) Answers will vary.

5. (a) Sight (the night sky, the roofs of huts), sound (rustling trees, the voice of choirs), and smell (smoky hut) (b) The images create vivid impressions.

6. (a) The values of community, respect for the past, and love of home and country (b) Students may share these values.

7. The story-tellers and choir, the relationship to nature, and the voices of ancestors represent traditional Africa.

8. Africa's past and present meld in this poem. The speaker hopes to learn how best to live from his ancestors but also seems content to live in the present.

✍ Writing

Students' monologues should be written in one of the voices mentioned in the poem, reflect an understanding of Senghor's style, and use repetition.

After You Read

Respond and Think Critically

Respond and Interpret

1. Do the images of night in this poem remind you of any personal memories? If so, which ones?

2. (a)Whom is the speaker addressing in the poem? (b)What is the relationship between the speaker and the person addressed?

3. (a)What does the speaker want to listen to in the hut? (b)Why might listening to this be important to him?

Analyze and Evaluate

4. (a)**Tone** is the attitude a speaker takes toward his or her subject. How would you describe the tone in this poem? (b)Does the tone seem appropriate? Why or why not?

5. (a)To what senses does the imagery in this poem appeal? (b)Do you think the images are effective? Explain.

6. (a)What cultural values does Senghor express in this poem? (b)In what way are these values similar to your own?

Connect

7. **Big Idea** **Tradition and Change** What elements of traditional Africa does this poem present?

8. **Connect to the Author** As the president of Senegal, Senghor tried to ensure that modernization did not destroy Africa's people and ideals. How does this poem reflect his vision?

Literary Element | Repetition

Alliteration is the repetition of consonant sounds at the beginnings of words.

1. Find an example of alliteration in this poem. What does it add to the poem?

2. What effect does the repetition of the word *listen* have throughout this poem?

Reading Strategy | Monitor Comprehension

Syntax, or word arrangement, can sometimes make a poem difficult to comprehend.

1. What line or stanza was most difficult for you to understand? Why did you find it confusing?

2. How did you rewrite this portion of the poem to improve your comprehension?

LOG ON ▶ **Literature** Online

Selection Resources For Selection Quizzes, eFlashcards, and Reading-Writing Connection activities, go to glencoe.com and enter QuickPass code GLW6053u1.

Vocabulary Practice

Practice with Context Clues Identify the context clues that help you determine the meaning of each boldfaced vocabulary word in the following sentences.

1. The branches softly **rustled** in the mild breeze.

2. The flowers in the vase no longer smelled mild and sweet; in fact, they were growing **acrid.**

3. A **torrent** of water swept over the town, crushing houses and cars.

✍ Writing

Write a Monologue The poem mentions several voices and speakers, such as the choir, the ancestors, and the roofs of the huts. Write a monologue from the perspective of one of these voices, using repetition to create a rhythmic effect. Refer to the comprehension chart you made on page 79 to clarify the different voices.

Literary Element

1. Examples include "blood beat," "slack sea," and "secretly to the stars." The alliteration adds to the poem's musicality.

2. The repetition unifies the poem in a way that is rhythmic and soothing, much like the repetition in lullabies. The word is also part of the poem's theme—listening to the wisdom of the ancestors.

Reading Strategy

1. Answers will vary. Students should have a specific example and articulate why they found the line or stanza confusing.

2. Students should have clarified the line or stanza without changing the meaning.

Vocabulary

1. *Softly* and *mild breeze* infer that *rustle* mens "to make a succession of soft crackling sounds."

2. The flowers smell the opposite of "mild and sweet," so one can infer that *acrid* means "strong and bitter."

3. *Swept* and *crushing* indicate that *torrent* means "a powerful flood."

Before You Read

Half a Day

Meet **Naguib Mahfouz**
(1911–2006)

When Naguib Mahfouz (nä zhēb´ mä fōōz´) was growing up, the novel had only a minor place in Arabic literature. Mahfouz loved fiction, however, so he learned his craft by focusing on the works of European authors. Mahfouz's major influences included French authors Honoré de Balzac, Gustave Flaubert, and Guy de Maupassant. After studying philosophy at the University of Cairo in Egypt, Mahfouz took a civil service job and wrote fiction in his spare time. He skillfully adapted Western literary techniques to portray Egyptian society and culture.

> *"If the urge to write should ever leave me, I want that day to be my last."*
>
> —Naguib Mahfouz

Literary Influences Born and raised in Cairo, Mahfouz was influenced by the social, political, and cultural history of his country. Three of his early novels focused on ancient Egypt. However, his novel *New Cairo* was a turning point for his work, and he became "preoccupied, almost without exception, with the present." He claimed that his novel *The Harafish* is partially based on his conversations among his friends in the underclass, about whom he remarked, "nobody had any genuine sympathy for us or understood our situation." The year 1967 marked a new phase in Mahfouz's literary career, and he began writing drama and extended fables. Drawing not only from politics and literature,

Mahfouz found inspiration in world cinema, Arabic music, and Islamic art and architecture.

A Range of Responses Mahfouz's writings earned him both acclaim and criticism. His 1947 novel *Midaq Alley* depicted life in a ghetto in Cairo and established him as a realistic writer. In *The Cairo Trilogy*, his most famous work, Mahfouz chronicles the period from World War I to the military coup that toppled the monarchy of King Farouk in 1952 and the rise of Gamal Abdel Nasser. An early supporter of Nasser's government, Mahfouz eventually expressed distaste for its later reforms. His 1967 novel *Children of Gebelawi*— a narrative about mankind and religion—was originally banned by Islamic fundamentalists, but it is now available in Egypt. Despite the controversy surrounding some of his works, Mahfouz was awarded the Nobel Prize in Literature in 1988, becoming the first Arabic author to win the prestigious award. The Swedish Academy, which grants the prize, hailed Mahfouz as an author who "has formed an Arabian narrative art that applies to all mankind."

Literature Online

Author Search For more about Naguib Mahfouz, go to glencoe.com and enter QuickPass code GLW6053u1.

Before You Read

Focus

Bellringer Options

**Selection Focus
   Transparency 5**
**Daily Language Practice
   Transparency 12**

Or ask: What does going to school mean to you? Elicit students' feelings about going to school, which may include seeing friends, learning, and preparing for the future. **Or ask:** What makes a city a nice place to live? What makes a city an unpleasant place to live? Elicit students' opinions about the advantages and disadvantages of living in a city. Students might mention entertainment, traffic, and pollution.

Selection Skills

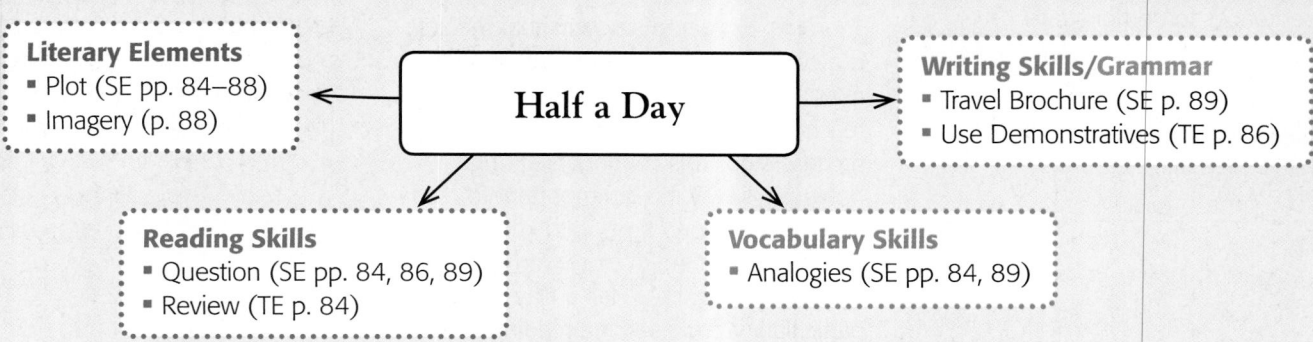

Literary Elements
- Plot (SE pp. 84–88)
- Imagery (p. 88)

Half a Day

Writing Skills/Grammar
- Travel Brochure (SE p. 89)
- Use Demonstratives (TE p. 86)

Reading Skills
- Question (SE pp. 84, 86, 89)
- Review (TE p. 84)

Vocabulary Skills
- Analogies (SE pp. 84, 89)

Before You Read

Focus

Summary

The narrator, a young boy, walks through the streets of Cairo with his father. It is the boy's first day of school. When they arrive, his father promises to pick him up that evening. The boy narrates events of his first day at school, which turns out to be better than he expected. When he leaves the school grounds, he notices that the city has changed. The gardens and trees are gone, replaced by crowds of people, tall buildings, and garbage. As he prepares to cross the street, a young lad offers to help, saying, "Grandpa, let me take you across." The narrator's life has passed in what seemed like only half a day. Meanwhile, the city he knew has become crowded and noisy.

> For summaries in languages other than English, see Unit 1 Teaching Resources Book, pp. 112–117.

Teach

Vocabulary

Brief Narrative Have students form pairs. Each pair should write a brief narrative that incorporates all four vocabulary words. Narratives should be just a few sentences to demonstrate understanding of the vocabulary.

> For additional vocabulary practice, see Unit 1 Teaching Resources Book, p. 120.

Literature and Reading Preview

Connect to the Story

What events have been rites of passage in your life? Write a journal entry about these events and how they affected the way in which you perceive the world.

Build Background

"Half a Day" is set in Cairo, the capital of Egypt. The older sections of Cairo contain medieval mosques and other historic architecture, which stand in contrast to the city's modern downtown. More than a thousand years old, Cairo grew rapidly during the twentieth century, leading to overcrowding and pollution. Mahfouz imaginatively portrays these changes.

Set Purposes for Reading

Big Idea **Tradition and Change**

As you read, ask yourself, How does the school in the story emphasize Egyptian traditions, and how does the passage of time cause changes in the environment?

Literary Element **Plot**

Plot is the sequence of events in a story. Most plots develop around a **conflict,** a struggle between opposing forces. A plot begins with **exposition,** which introduces the story's characters, setting, and situation. **Rising action** develops the conflict with complications. **Climax** is the emotional high point of the story. **Falling action** shows what happens after the climax, and the **resolution** shows how the conflict is resolved. As you read "Half a Day," ask yourself, What is the sequence of events in this story?

Reading Strategy **Question**

Questioning is a step you can take to check your understanding of a literary work or make predictions about what will happen in the text. As you read "Half a Day," ask yourself, What questions can I ask to clarify the events and conflict in this story?

Tip: Answer Your Questions Use a two-column chart to quiz yourself as you read.

Question	Answer
Why does the narrator say he was 'cast' into school?	Cast connotes being discarded. The boy feels he is being abandoned by his parents or punished for some wrongdoing.

Learning Objectives

For pages 83–89
In studying this text, you will focus on the following objectives:

Literary Study: Analyzing plot.

Reading: Questioning.

Researching: Conducting Internet research.

Vocabulary Preview

throng (throng) *n.* a crowd of many people; p. 86 *After the accident, a throng of reporters gathered to observe the situation.*

avail (ə vāl′) *n.* use or advantage; p. 86 *Her efforts to persuade her friend to join the volleyball team were to no avail.*

horde (hôrd) *n.* a teeming crowd or throng; p. 87 *She held her son's hand so she would not lose him in the horde of shoppers.*

refuse (ref′ūs) *n.* trash; garbage; p. 87 *As he cleaned his apartment, he discarded the refuse from each room.*

Tip: Analogies Analogies are comparisons that show similarities between two things that are otherwise dissimilar.

horde : individual :: fleet : ship

The relationship between these words is one of a part to a whole. An individual is part of a horde just as a ship is part of a fleet.

Reading Practice

Review Explain to students that reading is a constant process of predicting and revising predictions. Not until the reader reaches the end of a story does the process stop. This continual revising, however, is why it is so important to read literature a second time, with knowledge of the end in mind. A story with a surprise ending, like "Half a Day," benefits particularly from a second reading to allow the reader to recognize clues that lead to the ending.

Have students read the story a second time. Ask them how their understanding, appreciation, and perception of the story changed on a second reading.

Half a Day

Naguib Mahfouz

Translated by Denys Johnson-Davies

I proceeded alongside my father, clutching his right hand, running to keep up with the long strides he was taking. All my clothes were new: the black shoes, the green school uniform, and the red tarboosh. My delight in my new clothes, however, was not altogether unmarred, for this was no feast day but the day on which I was to be cast into school for the first time.

Visual Vocabulary
A *tarboosh* is a brimless red hat worn by some Muslims.

My mother stood at the window watching our progress, and I would turn toward her from time to time, as though appealing for help. We walked along a street lined with gardens; on both sides were extensive fields planted with crops, prickly pears, henna trees, and a few date palms.

"Why school?" I challenged my father openly. "I shall never do anything to annoy you."

Plot *What conflict is presented here?*

"I'm not punishing you," he said, laughing. "School's not a punishment. It's the factory that makes useful men out of boys. Don't you want to be like your father and brothers?"

I was not convinced. I did not believe there was really any good to be had in tearing me away from the intimacy of my home and throwing me into this building that stood at the end of the road like some huge, high-walled fortress, exceedingly stern and grim.

When we arrived at the gate we could see the courtyard, vast and crammed full of boys and girls. "Go in by yourself," said my father, "and join them. Put a smile on your face and be a good example to others."

I hesitated and clung to his hand, but he gently pushed me from him. "Be a man," he said. "Today you truly begin life. You will find me waiting for you when it's time to leave."

I took a few steps, then stopped and looked but saw nothing. Then the faces of boys and girls came into view. I did not know a single one of them, and none of them knew me. I felt I was a stranger who

NAGUIB MAHFOUZ **85**

Teach

Literary Element

Plot **Answer:** *The narrator is pleased with his clothes, but also nervous because he has to wear them in a new and unfamiliar setting.*

(ADVANCED) Point out that the narrator says that he will be "cast into school." **Ask:** What connotations does the verb *cast* have that relate to the boy's mood? *(Cast connotes being discarded. The boy feels he is being abandoned by his parents or punished for some wrongdoing.)*

 For an audio recording of this selection, use Listening Library Audio CD-ROM.

Readability Scores

Dale-Chall: 7.0
DRP: 54
Lexile: 730

Learning Objectives
Analyzing plot. (SE)
Reviewing. (TE)

English Learners

DIFFERENTIATED INSTRUCTION

Intermediate Have students create flash cards for each of the vocabulary words on page 84 prior to reading "Half a Day." In addition to the definitions, students should write a sentence using the word in context.

Point out to students that these words are all nouns. Ask for examples of adjectives that might go with each word. Have students write a sentence for each word, using an adjective to modify the noun.

Teach

Plot **Answer:** *The "rich variety" refers to the many friends he makes at school and the activities offered. These friends and activities are important because they show that school is much different from how the narrator envisioned it before he was a student.*

Question **Answer:** *The narrator uses the phrase "bade farewell," a mature choice for a young child. The phrase suggests a final parting, rather than an afternoon good-bye. It is also strange that the narrator makes so many friends and sweethearts in a single day.*

---

had lost his way. But glances of curiosity were directed toward me, and one boy approached and asked, "Who brought you?"

"My father," I whispered.

"My father's dead," he said quite simply.

I did not know what to say. The gate was closed, letting out a pitiable screech. Some of the children burst into tears. The bell rang. A lady came along, followed by a group of men. The men began sorting us into ranks. We were formed into an intricate pattern in the great courtyard surrounded on three sides by high buildings of several floors; from each floor we were overlooked by a long balcony roofed in wood.

"This is your new home," said the woman. "Here too there are mothers and fathers. Here there is everything that is enjoyable and beneficial to knowledge and religion. Dry your tears and face life joyfully."

We submitted to the facts, and this submission brought a sort of contentment. Living beings were drawn to other living beings, and from the first moments my heart made friends with such boys as were to be my friends and fell in love with such girls as I was to be in love with, so that it seemed my misgivings had had no basis. I had never imagined school would have this rich variety. We played all sorts of different games: swings, the vaulting horse, ball games. In the music room we chanted our first songs. We also had our first introduction to language. We saw a globe of the Earth, which revolved and showed the various continents and countries. We started learning the numbers. The story of the Creator of the universe was read to us, we were told of His present world and of His

> **Plot** *Read a little beyond this passage. What is the "rich variety" the narrator speaks of? Why is it important to the rising action of the plot?*   **1**

Hereafter, and we heard examples of what He said. We ate delicious food, took a little nap, and woke up to go on with friendship and love, play and learning.

As our path revealed itself to us, however, we did not find it as totally sweet and unclouded as we had presumed. Dust-laden winds and unexpected accidents came about suddenly, so we had to be watchful, at the ready, and very patient. It was not all a matter of playing and fooling around. Rivalries could bring about pain and hatred or give rise to fighting. And while the lady would sometimes smile, she would often scowl and scold. Even more frequently she would resort to physical punishment.

In addition, the time for changing one's mind was over and gone and there was no question of ever returning to the paradise of home. Nothing lay ahead of us but exertion, struggle, and perseverance. Those who were able took advantage of the opportunities for success and happiness that presented themselves amid the worries.

The bell rang announcing the passing of the day and the end of work. The **throngs** of children rushed toward the gate, which was opened again. I bade farewell to friends and sweethearts and passed through the gate. I peered around but found no trace of my father, who had promised to be there. I stepped aside to wait. When I had waited for a long time without **avail**, I decided to return home on my own. After I had taken a few steps, a middle-aged man passed by, and I realized at once that I knew him. He came toward me, smiling, and shook me by

> **Question** *What about this sentence suggests that time has passed differently than the reader might assume?*   **2**

> **Vocabulary**
>
> **throng** (throng) *n.* a crowd of many people
> **avail** (ə vāl′) *n.* use or advantage

Grammar Practice

Use Demonstratives Write these sentences from the story on the board: "<u>This</u> is your new home." "We submitted to the facts, and <u>this</u> submission brought a sort of contentment." "<u>Those</u> who were able took advantage of the opportunities for success and happiness that presented themselves amid the worries." Point out that the words *this, that, these,* and *those* are called demonstratives because they demonstrate, or point out, people or

things. Explain that a demonstrative can function as an adjective or a pronoun.

Have students identify how demonstratives function in the sentences on the board. *(The first and third are pronouns, and the second is an adjective.)* Students should generate two original sentences, one using a demonstrative as a pronoun and one using a demonstrative as an adjective.

the hand, saying, "It's a long time since we last met—how are you?"

With a nod of my head, I agreed with him and in turn asked, "And you, how are you?"

"As you can see, not all that good, the Almighty be praised!"

Again he shook me by the hand and went off. I proceeded a few steps, then came to a startled halt. Good Lord! Where was the street lined with gardens? Where had it disappeared to? When did all these vehicles invade it? And when did all these **hordes** of humanity come to rest upon its surface? How did these hills of **refuse** come to cover its sides? And where were the fields that bordered it? High buildings had taken over, the street surged with children, and disturbing noises shook the air. At various points stood conjurers[1] showing off their tricks and making snakes appear from baskets. Then there was a band announcing the opening of a circus, with clowns and weight lifters walking in front. A line of trucks carrying central security troops crawled majestically by. The siren of a fire engine shrieked, and it was not clear how the vehicle would cleave its way to reach the blazing fire. A battle raged between a taxi driver and his passenger, while the passenger's wife called out for help and no one answered. Good God! I was in a daze. My head spun. I almost went crazy. How could all this have happened in half a day, between early morning and sunset? I would find the answer at home with my father.

---

1. A *conjurer* is a person who practices magic.

 3 Plot *What is the climax of this story?*

Vocabulary

horde (hôrd) *n.* a teeming crowd or throng
refuse (ref´ūs) *n.* trash; garbage

Pedestrians walk down city street in Cairo. Sylvain Grandadam. Robert Harding Picture Library.

But where was my home? I could see only tall buildings and hordes of people. I hastened on to the crossroads between the gardens and Abu Khoda. I had to cross Abu Khoda to reach my house, but the stream of cars would not let up. The fire engine's siren was shrieking at full pitch as it moved at a snail's pace, and I said to myself, "Let the fire take its pleasure in what it consumes." Extremely irritated, I wondered when I would be able to cross. I stood there a long time, until the young lad employed at the ironing shop on the corner came up to me. He stretched out his arm and said gallantly, "Grandpa, let me take you across."

Tradition and Change *What has changed about the city from the beginning of the story to this point?* **4**

Plot *What is the resolution of the story?* **5**

NAGUIB MAHFOUZ **87**

English Learners

DIFFERENTIATED INSTRUCTION

Intermediate Review the meanings of the vocabulary words. Have the students name places where they might encounter the words. For instance, *I would find **refuse** in a garbage can.*

Teach

Literary Element | **3**

Plot **Answer:** *The narrator realizes that the cityscape has changed and is unfamiliar to him.*
[APPROACHING] Remind students that the climax is the emotional high point in a story and marks a turning point in the plot. **Ask:** Where does this turning point occur? *(When the narrator realizes that the city has changed.)*

Big Idea | **4**

Tradition and Change
Answer: *The opening scene is peaceful with fields of "crops, prickly pears, henna trees, and a few date palms." The city is now crowded with people and high-rise buildings.*

Literary Element | **5**

Plot **Answer:** *The narrator has grown old, and his life has passed quickly.*

View the Photograph ★

Ask: How does the photograph of Cairo reflect the themes of the story? *(Students may say that there is a mix of old and new. Some of the people wear modern clothing, but much of the architecture is traditional.)*

To check students' understanding of the selection, see Unit 1 Teaching Resources Book, p. 123.

Learning Objectives
Analyzing plot. (SE)
Clarifying meaning. (SE)
Using demonstratives. (TE)

After You Read

Assess

1. (a) Answers will vary. (b) Life passes quickly, things change.

2. (a) He says that it has been a long time since he has seen the narrator. (b) The man addresses the narrator as if they have known each other for awhile.

3. (a) A conjurer doing tricks and a fight between a taxi driver and his passenger (b) Preferred the quiet, garden-lined streets of his youth

4. (a) A lifetime that passed too quickly (b) The narrator learns to build relationships, to do hard work, and to persevere.

5. The quickness of Cairo's transformation is overwhelming.

6. The revelation that the narrator has aged by the end of the story depends on his perception of his own life.

7. The garden-lined streets have given way to vehicles, high-rises, and congestion. Traditions have become street entertainment for profit.

8. Mahfouz may have found that many changes created a noisy, congested city. However, his decision to remain in Cairo indicates that he probably found some benefits to city life.

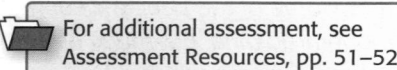

For additional assessment, see Assessment Resources, pp. 51–52.

After You Read

Respond and Think Critically

Respond and Interpret

1. (a) Did the resolution of the story surprise you? Explain. (b) What comment about life might this story be making?

2. (a) What does the middle-aged man say to the narrator when they meet? (b) How does this hint at the passage of time in the story?

3. (a) What events does the narrator witness that illustrate the changes in the city? (b) What does his irritation at these events reveal about the narrator?

Analyze and Evaluate

4. (a) A **symbol** is an object or an action that stands for something else in addition to itself. What do the narrator's day at school and the title of the story symbolize? (b) How does what the narrator learns in school parallel the lessons a person learns throughout his or her life?

5. What might the different descriptions of street life at the beginning and the end of the story reveal about the narrator?

6. A story told from the **first-person point of view** is narrated by one of the characters in the story. Why do you think Mahfouz used a first-person narrator for "Half a Day"?

Connect

7. **Big Idea** **Tradition and Change** How do you think the changes in Cairo, as described in the story, affected its traditional appearance and the traditions of its people? Support your answer with evidence from the story.

8. **Connect to the Author** Mahfouz spent most of his life living in and around Cairo and watched the city change firsthand. Based on this story and what you know about his life, what do you think Mahfouz thought about these changes?

Literary Element Plot

The plot of "Half a Day" has a **surprise ending,** or an unexpected twist at the end of the story. A surprise ending is most effective when it adds to the meaning of a story rather than merely overturning the reader's expectations.

1. Is the ending of "Half a Day" a complete surprise, or did Mahfouz provide clues throughout the story to suggest that years have passed? Explain.

2. (a) Do you think the ending of "Half a Day" is effective? Why or why not? (b) How else might Mahfouz have ended the story?

Review: Imagery

As you learned on page 30, **imagery** is the "word pictures" an author creates to evoke an emotional response. Authors use **sensory details** that appeal to one or more of the five senses to create effective imagery.

Partner Activity With a partner, review "Half a Day" and discuss imagery that you both feel is particularly strong. In a chart like the one below, list each image, which sense it appeals to, and the details that make the image effective. When you are done, discuss your choices with the class.

Image	Sense	What Makes Image Effective
"...this building that stood...like some huge, high-walled fortress, exceedingly stern and grim"	Sight	Adjectives such as "huge" and "high-walled" describe the building's appearance, while "stern and grim" capture a specific mood.

Literary Element

1. The narrator provided clues when describing the extensive amount of learning he did, the relationships he formed with his friends, and the hardships he faced while at school.

2. (a) Some students will say that the ending effectively conveys how quickly time seems to pass and the speed of change in the modern world. (b) Answers will vary. The author might have concluded with an "it was all a dream" ending.

Review: Imagery

Students' choices will vary. Each chart should list specific images, the senses to which each image appeals, and the reasons that the students found the images effective.

Progress Check

Can students identify the plot?

If No → See Unit 1 Teaching Resources Book, p. 118.

Reading Strategy | Question

SAT Skills Practice

The author includes the image of the "fire engine's siren… shrieking at full pitch" (page 87) in order to

(A) imply that the narrator is in danger

(B) celebrate modern technology

(C) suggest that there has been a fire

(D) suggest a harsh, chaotic urban environment

(E) create suspense

Vocabulary Practice

Practice with Analogies Select the word that completes each analogy.

1. herd : cow :: throng :
   a. friend **b.** leader **c.** person **d.** workforce

2. victor : winner :: avail :
   a. benefit **b.** loss **c.** difficulty **d.** goal

3. team : athlete :: horde :
   a. group **b.** individual **c.** team **d.** volume

4. coal : miner :: refuse :
   a. architect **b.** farmer **c.** waste collector
   d. lawyer

Academic Vocabulary

In this story, the narrator experiences the **phenomenon** *of growing old in what seems like only half a day.*

Phenomenon is an academic word. For example, a solar eclipse is a natural **phenomenon.** *To study this word further, complete the following sentence:*

An event that is _____ can be described as a **phenomenon.**

For more on academic vocabulary, see pages 36–37 and R83–R85.

Research and Report

 Internet Connection

Assignment Use reliable Internet sites to research the history of Cairo, Egypt. Then write a travel brochure for a self-guided tour through the city. Organize your tour geographically, based on the layout of the city. Include cardinal (north, south, east, and west) and ordinal (northeast, southeast, northwest, and southwest) directions as a guide to landmarks and an accompanying map or photos.

Get Ideas Generate a list of questions you would like to answer about present-day Cairo. You may want to refer to the Reading Strategy chart you made on page 84 for ideas. Next, create a list of possible primary and secondary Internet sources.

Research As you research, take notes on specific information that answers each question you listed, as well as the source where you found the information. It will help to organize your questions into categories; you can later use these categories to structure your brochure. Use the questions below to evaluate the credibility of each Web site.

- **Authority** Is the site associated with a reputable organization? Does the writer have credentials? Can he or she be contacted?

- **Accuracy** Can the information be substantiated? Are there grammatical or factual errors?

- **Objectivity** Is the writer citing a fact or offering an opinion? Is the site biased?

- **Timeliness** How often is the site updated? Can you be sure the information is not outdated?

Report Your brochure should include travel facts that would be useful to travelers as well as interesting historical information. Proofread to be sure that you have accurately synthesized information and that your writing is cohesive.

 Literature Online

Selection Resources For Selection Quizzes, eFlashcards, and Reading-Writing Connection activities, go to glencoe.com and enter QuickPass code GLW6053u1.

NAGUIB MAHFOUZ **89**

Reading Strategy

(D) is the correct answer. This image works with the others in the final paragraph to create the impression of a bustling, hectic city.

Progress Check

Can students use questioning effectively?

If No → See Unit 1 Teaching Resources Book, p. 119.

Vocabulary

1. c
2. a
3. b
4. c

Academic Vocabulary

phenomenon

Definition: a remarkable event or occurrence

Synonyms: spectacle, miracle

Antonyms: triviality, insignificance

Sentence: The emergence of a certain type of cicada every seventeen years is a fascinating phenomenon.

Research and Report

Students' brochures should

- be written as a guided tour
- describe important landmarks and their place in Cairo's history
- reflect accurate and reliable sources
- include a map or photos

 For grammar practice, see Unit 1 Teaching Resources Book, p. 122.

 To create custom assessments online, go to Progress Reporter Online Assessment.

Focus

Write on the board:

1. The score was tied.
2. The crowd was screaming.
3. There were only minutes left to play.

Ask students to combine these three simple sentences into one or more sentences and write down their rearrangements. Then ask volunteers to share the various ways they rearranged sentences with the class. Ask them why they combined sentences in the manner they chose. Did they wish to emphasize one point over another? (Possible answer: *With only minutes left to play in the fourth quarter, the score was tied and the crowd was screaming.*)

ADVANCED Have students create three or four related simple sentences. Then group them into pairs and instruct them to exchange sentences. Have them practice combining one another's simple sentences.

Teach

Develop Style

Have students look at a sample of their writing. **Ask:** Do most of your sentences contain a similar number of words? Do they usually open sentences the same way? Do most of your sentences contain the same rhythm? Point out that trying new patterns and combining sentences in different ways can help them stretch themselves and develop their own style.

90

Learning Objectives

For pages 90–91

In this workshop, you will focus on the following objectives:

Grammar: Understanding how to combine sentences.

Understanding how to use prepositional, appositive, and participial phrases.

Understanding how to use coordinating and subordinating conjunctions.

Drafting Tips

Try these strategies to combine sentences when you write.

- Read sentence variations aloud to yourself to decide which one sounds best.

- Use the context of a paragraph to decide how best to combine sentences.

- Work with a partner to get new ideas and compare sentences.

- Look for stylistic patterns in your writing.

- Take risks—they will help you develop your personal style.

Grammar Workshop

Sentence Combining

Literature Connection In this quotation from "Half a Day," Naguib Mahfouz combines two main clauses, *I hesitated and clung to his hand* and *he gently pushed me from him,* with the coordinating conjunction *but.*

> "I hesitated and clung to his hand, but he gently pushed me from him."

Combining sentences can dramatically improve the readability, variety, and style of your writing so that it does not sound choppy and repetitive. There are four general strategies for combining:

- deleting repeated words
- adding connecting words
- rearranging words
- changing the form of words

The example below shows one way of using some of these strategies to combine four choppy sentences.

Mahfouz is a masterful writer. ~~He~~ who uses descriptive words. ~~He uses~~ and[1] imagery. ~~to~~ ~~He~~[2] conveys[3] important themes.

1. Use connecting words. **2. Delete repeated words.**
3. Change the form of words.

More specific strategies for combining sentences appear below.

Phrases

You can use prepositional, appositive, or participial phrases to combine sentences.

Prepositional phrases clarify relationships, such as those involving space or time. They begin with words such as *in, about,* or *with.*

I read three books. The books were <u>about the colonization of Africa.</u>

I read three books <u>about the colonization of Africa.</u>

Appositive phrases explain unfamiliar nouns. They are often set off from the rest of the sentence by commas, dashes, a colon, or parentheses.

Abu Khoda serves as a key image in the story. Abu Khoda <u>is a busy street.</u>

Abu Khoda, <u>a busy street,</u> serves as a key image in the story.

Grammar Practice

Use Semicolons Point out to students that semicolons can be valuable tools for combining sentences. They are used to separate main clauses that are not joined by a coordinating conjunction. A semicolon implies a stronger connection between sentences than a period does. Semicolons also separate items that contain commas. On the board, **write:** "Her voice was hoarse; she had been to a football game the day before."

Point out that this sentence has both two main clauses and internal punctuation, but they are closely related.

Have students review a recent writing assignment, looking for three sentences that might have been joined by semicolons instead of separated by periods or conjunctions. Students should recopy the sentences with the new punctuation. Check the revisions for accuracy.

Participial phrases contain verbs that function as adjectives. These verbs, which are also known as **participles,** usually end in *–ing* or *–ed.* Make sure you position participial phrases to correctly modify the right word.

The narrator is searching for his home in Cairo. He is <u>growing confused.</u>

<u>*Growing confused,*</u> *the narrator searches for his home in Cairo.*

Conjunctions and Clauses

Try using coordinating or subordinating conjunctions to turn simple sentences into more complex ones.

Coordinating Conjunctions (such as *and, but, or, for,* or *yet*) help combine two sentences that contain equally important ideas. See the quotation from Mahfouz on page 90 for an example of combining sentences using the coordinating conjunction *but.*

Subordinating Conjunctions When two sentences are not equally important, you can add a subordinating conjunction to the beginning of one of the sentences to create an adverb clause or an adjective clause. These clauses typically add supplemental information or describe a relationship based on time, location, or cause and effect.

- **Adverb clauses** modify a verb, an adjective, or another adverb and include subordinating conjunctions such as *after, because,* or *since.*

  The narrator protests. <u>He thinks he is being punished.</u>

  The narrator protests <u>because he thinks he is being punished.</u>

- **Adjective clauses** modify a noun or a pronoun and typically include a subordinating conjunction such as *who, whose,* or *that.*

  Nelson Mandela became president in 1994. He <u>had been imprisoned during apartheid.</u>

  Nelson Mandela, <u>who had been imprisoned during apartheid,</u> became president in 1994.

Revise Apply the strategies described in this workshop to combine each group of sentences below.

1. "Half a Day" is a short story. I wanted to read "Half a Day" tonight. I lost the book.
2. The Sahara desert stretches across most of northern Africa. The Sahara is vast. It consists of sand dunes and oases.
3. British rule of Cairo ended. The number of foreigners living there declined. Cairo is Egypt's capital.

Revising Tips

Evaluate your sentence combining using these criteria.

- ☑ Do I vary long and short sentences?
- ☑ Do I vary sentence openers?
- ☑ Do I use parallel structures of words, phrases, and clauses?
- ☑ Do I create emphasis with commas, colons, semicolons, dashes, and parentheses?
- ☑ Do I use different patterns to emphasize key ideas?

Test-Taking Tip

If you are unsure how to combine two sentences on a test, write down several possible opening words or phrases, and then fill in the rest.

 Literature Online

Grammar For more grammar practice, go to glencoe.com and enter QuickPass code GLW6053u1.

Writer's Technique ☆

Combine for Style Point out that combining sentences is a way for students to identify their personal writing styles. Practice in sentence combining helps young writers see that sentences are flexible tools for thought, not rigid structures cast in concrete. The simple fact that they feel confident in moving sentence parts around will increase their control of revising and editing.

Assess

Possible answers:

1. I wanted to read the short story "Half a Day" tonight, but I lost the book.
2. Consisting of sand dunes and oases, the vast Sahara Desert stretches across most of northern Africa.
3. After British rule of Cairo, Egypt's capital, ended, the number of foreigners living there declined.

 For additional grammar practice, see Unit 1 Teaching Resources Book, p. 125.

Approaching Level

DIFFERENTIATED INSTRUCTION

Oral Reading Students who struggle with reading may benefit from hearing examples of sentence combinations read aloud. Have them record themselves reading first the simple sentences from the "Combining Sentences" activity. Then have them record themselves reading the revised, combined sentences. Tell them to listen to the tape they made and ask them how the second sentences sound different than the first.

Before You Read

Focus

Bellringer Options

Selection Focus
  Transparency 6
Daily Language Practice
  Transparency 13

Or ask: What is fair and what is unfair in an election campaign? Elicit students' opinions about what they consider to be legitimate campaign practices and what they consider to be wrong.

Or ask: Should people be allowed to contribute money to influence the outcomes of election campaigns? Elicit students' opinions on whether political campaign contributions and campaign spending should be restricted.

Before You Read

Nigeria

The Voter

Meet **Chinua Achebe**
(born 1930)

Chinua Achebe (chēn′wää chä′bā) believes that an author's function, particularly an African author's function, is a social one. In his novels, he criticizes both the dehumanizing effects of British imperialism on the Nigerian population and the destructive influences of Nigerian political corruption that plagued his country after achieving independence. Above all, his novels express his desire to destroy the myth of African inferiority and to inspire a more tolerant society.

> *"The worst thing that can happen to any people is the loss of their dignity and self-respect. The writer's duty is to help them regain it...."*
>
> —Chinua Achebe

Christian and Ibo Roots Born in Ogidi, Nigeria, when Nigeria was still a British colony, Achebe was raised in a Christian family that had converted from the traditional religion of their Ibo (also spelled Igbo) kinsfolk. In his autobiography, he describes his parents as strong in their Christian beliefs but not fanatical. "Their lives were ruled," he says, "as much by reason as by faith; as much by common sense and compassion as by doctrine." Achebe's experiences growing up in two different cultures and his observations of Nigeria under colonial rule and after independence instilled in him a strong belief in the values of objectivity, pragmatism, and tolerance.

Things Fall Apart After graduating from college, Achebe accepted a position as a producer for the Nigerian Broadcasting Corporation. During this period, he published several of the novels that have secured his literary reputation. The first of these, *Things Fall Apart*, is the story of a traditional Ibo community that disintegrates after the arrival of European missionaries. The book earned Achebe international recognition and is regarded by some historians as the most widely read and influential African novel ever written. Achebe's later novels portray Nigerian society during colonial times and following independence.

Award Winner In 2007, Achebe won the prestigious Man Booker International Prize, which is given once every two years to a living author for his or her body of fictional work. One of the judges, South African author Nadine Gordimer, commented that Achebe's "early work made him the father of modern African literature...."

LOG ON **Literature** Online

Author Search For more about Chinua Achebe, go to glencoe.com and enter QuickPass code GLW6053u1.

Selection Skills

Literary Elements
- Motivation (SE pp. 93, 95-97, 99, 100)
- Tone (SE p. 100)
- Figurative Language (TE p. 96)

Reading Skills
- Activate Prior Knowledge (SE pp. 93, 96, 97,101)
- Compare and Contrast (TE p. 98)

The Voter

Vocabulary Skills
- Word Parts (SE p. 101)

Speaking/Listening/Viewing Skills
- Analyze Art (SE p. 98)

Writing Skills/Grammar
- Apply Irony (SE p. 101)
- Character Analysis (TE p. 96)
- Use Semicolons (TE p. 94)

Literature and Reading Preview

Connect to the Story

In school elections, how do you decide which candidates to vote for? Freewrite for a few minutes about what qualities you look for in a candidate.

Build Background

Nigeria became an independent nation in 1960, but political corruption and cultural differences among ethnic groups have hampered its efforts to establish a democratic system. Following episodes of violence and a full-scale civil war, Nigeria came under the rule of military regimes at the end of the twentieth century. Achebe's story "The Voter" takes place in an Ibo village shortly after Nigerian independence.

Set Purposes for Reading

Big Idea Living with Independence

As you read, ask yourself, How does this story illustrate the political problems in Nigeria?

Literary Element Motivation

Motivation is the stated or implied reason or cause for a character's actions. As you read "The Voter," think about why the characters behave the way they do toward one another. Ask yourself questions such as, Why does Marcus Ibe host a feast for the villagers in honor of the completion of his new home?

Reading Strategy Activate Prior Knowledge

You can increase your understanding of a work of literature by drawing on knowledge you already have before reading the text. As you read "The Voter," ask yourself, What information do I have that can help me make predictions and better understand the events in this story?"

....

Tip: Use Personal Experience As you read, record details that remind you of your own experiences as well as details that are illuminated by what you have learned about Nigeria from the author biography on page 92 and the Build Background on this page. Use a chart like the one below.

Details Similar to Personal Experience	Details Illuminated by Background Knowledge
Marcus Ibe's feast reminds me of the time Bernie hosted a picnic to encourage us to vote for him.	Marcus Ibe's wealthy lifestyle illustrates the real political corruption in postcolonial Nigeria.

CHINUA ACHEBE **93**

Learning Objectives

For pages 92–101

In studying this text, you will focus on the following objectives:

Literary Study: Analyzing motivation.

Reading: Activating prior knowledge.

Writing: Applying irony.

Vocabulary

gratitude (grat´ə tōōd´) *n.* thankfulness; p. 95 *We expressed heartfelt gratitude for his generosity in our time of need.*

constituency (kən stich´ōō ən sē) *n.* voters in a district; a group of supporters; p. 95 *The crime novel bombed because its ad campaign did not target its core constituency: mystery fans.*

nonentity (non en´tə tē) *n.* a person or a thing of little or no importance; p. 95 *Sam's inexperience with computers made him a nonentity in the eyes of the tech job recruiter.*

defiance (di fī´əns) *n.* a refusal to recognize or obey someone or something; p. 97 *Nadia's refusal to join the conspiracy was apparent by the defiance in her eyes.*

mesmerize (mez´mə rīz´) *v.* to hypnotize; spellbind; p. 97 *The fun-house mirrors started to mesmerize me the more I looked at them.*

English Learners

DIFFERENTIATED INSTRUCTION

Intermediate Have English learners look up the following words in the dictionary prior to reading "The Voter." Point out to students that these words describe the story's main character, Roof. Based on these words, ask students to predict what type of character Roof might be.

energetic, enthusiasm, springy, jauntily

Before You Read

Focus

Summary

Rufus "Roof" Okeke is working to get Marcus Ibe reelected as minister of culture, but Roof's job is much harder than it was five years before. The people of his village are wiser about politics and know that they can expect to be paid for their votes, so Roof ends up paying more for votes of the village elders than he did in the previous election. Shortly after he buys the votes of elders, Roof himself is offered a large bribe to vote for the opposition candidate. After he accepts the money, his promised is sealed in the presence of an *iyi*, a religious idol that he fears to offend. When he finally gets into the voting booth, Roof resolves his dilemma by tearing his ballot in half and voting for both candidates.

 For summaries in languages other than English, see Unit 1 Teaching Resources Book, pp. 126–131.

Teach

Vocabulary

Mnemonic Device Have students create a drawing or a brief poem for each of the vocabulary words. Each mnemonic should convey the word's meaning in some way. Have students share their mnemonics with partners, and discuss which are most effective.

 For additional vocabulary practice, see Unit 1 Teaching Resources Book, p. 134.

Teach

Big Idea · 1

Living with Independence

Have students read the first paragraph of the story. **Ask:** What does this paragraph suggest about Africa's economic problems? *(Ambitious young men are abandoning village life to find employment in towns and cities.)*

[APPROACHING] Point out the narrator's observation that many young men had left the village seeking work, and ask what this indicates about the village's economic condition.

View the Art ★

Francks Francois Deceus (1966–) grew up in Haiti and later moved to New York City. His modernist painting style features simplified geometric forms, sharp angles, bold colors, and distorted perspectives.

Interactive Read and Write
Other options for teaching this selection can be found in Interactive Read and Write for On-Level Learners, pp. 19–30.

For an audio recording of this selection, use Listening Library Audio CD-ROM.

Readability Scores

Dale-Chall: 6.4
DRP: 60
Lexile: 850

Moving on Up, 1999. Francks Deceus. Mixed media on canvas. Private collection.

The Voter

Chinua Achebe

Grammar Practice

Use Semicolons Write these sentences from the story on the board: *Today he was Chief the Honorable; he had two long cars and had just built himself the biggest house anyone had seen in these parts. In the day he made his speeches; at night his stalwarts made their whispering campaign.* Explain that semicolons are used to separate main clauses that are not joined by a coordinating conjunction or that are joined by a conjunctive adverb, such as *however.*

Have students write four sentences about the story using semicolons to join main clauses, Two of the sentences should contain conjunctive adverbs, Have partners exchange papers for accuracy.

1 Rufus Okeke—Roof for short—was a very popular man in his village. Although the villagers did not explain it in so many words Roof's popularity was a measure of their **gratitude** to an energetic young man who, unlike most of his fellows nowadays had not abandoned the village in order to seek work, any work, in the towns.

And Roof was not a village lout either. Everyone knew how he had spent two years as a bicycle repairer's apprentice in Port Harcourt, and had given up of his own free will a bright future to return to his people and guide them in these difficult times. Not that Umuofia needed a lot of guidance. The village already belonged *en masse* to the People's Alliance Party, and its most illustrious son, Chief the Honorable Marcus Ibe, was Minister of Culture in the outgoing government (which was pretty certain to be the incoming one as well). Nobody doubted that the Honorable Minister would be elected in his **constituency**. Opposition to him was like the proverbial fly trying to move a dunghill. It would have been ridiculous enough without coming, as it did now, from a complete **nonentity**.

As was to be expected Roof was in the service of the Honorable Minister for the coming elections. He had become a real expert in election campaigning at all levels—village, local government or national. He could tell the mood and temper of the electorate at any given time. For instance he had warned the Minister months ago about the radical change that had come into the thinking of Umuofia since the last national election.

The villagers had had five years in which to see how quickly and plentifully politics brought wealth, chieftaincy titles, doctorate degrees and other honors some of which, like the last, had still to be explained satisfactorily to them; for in their naïveté they still expected a doctor to be able to heal the sick. Anyhow, these honors and benefits had come so readily to the man to whom they had given their votes free of charge five years ago that they were now ready to try it a different way.

Their point was that only the other day Marcus Ibe was a not too successful mission school teacher. Then politics had come to their village and he had wisely joined up, some said just in time to avoid imminent dismissal arising from a female teacher's pregnancy. Today he was Chief the Honorable; he had two long cars and had just built himself the biggest house anyone had seen in these parts. But let it be said that none of these successes had gone to Marcus's head as well they might. He remained devoted to his people. Whenever he could he left the good things of the capital and returned to his village which had neither running water nor electricity, although he had lately installed a private plant to supply electricity to his new house. He knew the source of his good fortune, unlike the little bird who ate and drank

---

2 Motivation *According to the villagers, what was Roof's motivation for leaving a promising career?*

Vocabulary

gratitude (grat′ə tōōd′) *n.* thankfulness

constituency (kən stich′ōō ən sē) *n.* voters in a district; a group of supporters

nonentity (non en′tə tē) *n.* a person or a thing of little or no importance

---

3 Living with Independence *How does the information in this passage mirror what you have learned about Nigeria after it achieved independence?*

4 Motivation *Do you think it is devotion to his people or something else that motivates Marcus to visit the village whenever he can? Explain.*

CHINUA ACHEBE **95**

Literary Element **2**

Motivation Answer: *The villagers believe he moved back to guide them through difficult times.*

Big Idea **3**

Living with Independence
Answer: *The villagers have seen how their leaders have acquired wealth, titles, and honors but are aware that this development has not benefited the villagers themselves. This situation mirrors the political corruption that has hindered democratic reforms in postcolonial Nigeria.*

Literary Element **4**

Motivation Answer: *It is more likely that currying favor for votes is Marcus's real reason for returning often to the village. If he were truly devoted to his people, he would find a way to provide water and electricity for the entire village, not just for his new house.*

Learning Objectives
Analyzing motivation. (SE)
Activating prior knowledge. (SE)
Using semicolons. (TE)

English Learners

DIFFERENTIATED INSTRUCTION

Advanced English language learners my miss the satiric tone of this story. Explain that Achebe's frank account of illegal actions is satirical. Writing the following on the board: *The villagers told themselves that they had underrated the power of the ballot paper and should not do so again.* The "power of the ballot" generally refers to the people's selection of their own leaders by voting, but Achebe refers to its power to bring money to the voters through bribes.

Have small mixed groups identify several satiric statements in the story. Have groups paraphrase the statements and then share them with the class.

Teach

Reading Strategy　1

Activate Prior Knowledge

Answer: *It implies the spreading of gossip, particularly gossip that is untrue or misleading. Students' examples from personal experience will vary.*

Literary Element　2

Figurative Language　Point out to students that Achebe uses proverbs throughout this story to represent traditional wisdom.

Ask: How would you paraphrase the proverb of the iroko tree using American idiom or slang? *(Students' answers should express the proverb's central idea of taking full advantage of temporary opportunity.)*

ENGLISH LEARNERS　Make sure that English learners grasp the basic meaning of the proverb. Ask them for examples of similar proverbs from the cultures of their homelands.

Literary Element　3

Motivation　Answer: *Considering that they have been promised improvements for five years and have yet to receive them, they likely do not believe every word is true. Their loyalty is actually motivated by their desire to be paid for their votes.*

and went out to challenge his personal spirit. Marcus had christened his new house "Umuofia Mansions" in honor of his village, and he had slaughtered five bulls and countless goats to entertain the people on the day it was opened by the Archbishop.

Everyone was full of praise for him. One old man said: "Our son is a good man; he is not like the mortar which as soon as food comes its way turns its back on the ground." But when the feasting was over, the villagers told themselves that they had underrated the power of the ballot paper before and should not do so again. Chief the Honorable Marcus Ibe was not unprepared. He had drawn five months' salary in advance, changed a few hundred pounds

Visual Vocabulary
Jute (jo͞ot) is a flexible, glossy fiber made from one of two Asian plants.

into shining shillings and armed his campaign boys with eloquent little jute bags. In the day he made his speeches; at night his stalwarts conducted their whispering campaign. Roof was the most trusted of these campaigners.

"We have a Minister from our village, one of our own sons," he said to a group of elders in the house of Ogbuefi Ezenwa, a man of high traditional title. "What greater honor can a village have? Do you ever stop to ask yourselves why we should be singled out for this honor? I will tell you; it is because we are favored by the leaders of PAP. Whether or not we cast our paper for Marcus, PAP will continue to rule. Think of the pipe-borne water they have promised us . . . "

1　**Activate Prior Knowledge**　*What does the phrase "whispering campaign" imply about the kind of information campaign workers spread at night? Have you ever overheard a whispering campaign? If so, what was your reaction?*

Besides Roof and his assistant there were five elders in the room. An old hurricane lamp with a cracked, sooty, glass chimney gave out yellowish light in their midst. The elders sat on very low stools. On the floor, directly in front of each of them, lay two shilling pieces. Outside beyond the fastened door, the moon kept a straight face.

"We believe every word you say to be true," said Ezenwa. "We shall, every one of us, drop his paper for Marcus. Who would leave an Ozo feast and go to a poor ritual meal? Tell Marcus he has our papers, and our wives' papers too. But what we do say is that two shillings is shameful." He brought the lamp close and tilted it at the money before him as if to make sure he had not mistaken its value. "Yes, two shillings is too shameful. If Marcus were a poor man—which our ancestors forbid—I should be the first to give him my paper free, as I did before. But today Marcus is a great man and does his things like a great man. We did not ask him for money yesterday; we shall not ask him tomorrow. But today is our day; we have climbed the iroko tree today and would be foolish not to take down all the firewood we need." **2**

Roof had to agree. He had lately been taking down a lot of firewood himself. Only yesterday he had asked Marcus for one of his many rich robes—and had got it. Last Sunday Marcus's wife (the teacher that nearly got him in trouble) had objected (like the woman she was) when Roof pulled out his fifth bottle of beer from the refrigerator; she was roundly and publicly rebuked by her husband. To cap it all Roof had won a land case recently because, among other things, he had been chauffeur-

---

Motivation　*Do you think the elders really believe every word is true? Why or why not? What actually motivates their loyalty to Roof?*　**3**

Writing Practice

PARTNERS

Character Analysis　Have students review the story to this point, recording information about the main character, Roof. Their notes should include information about both his behavior and his actions. Then have them write several paragraphs analyzing Roof's character. Suggest they answer questions such as the following:

What motivates Roof?

Why does he remain in his village rather than going elsewhere to look for work?

Why do the villagers approve of him?

After students have completed their analyses, have them exchange papers with a partner and do peer editing.

driven to the disputed site. So he understood the elders about the firewood.

"All right," he said in English and then reverted to Ibo. "Let us not quarrel about small things." He stood up, adjusted his robes and plunged his hand once more into the bag. Then he bent down like a priest distributing the host and gave one shilling more to every man; only he did not put it into their palms but on the floor in front of them. The men, who had so far not deigned to touch the things, looked at the floor and shook their heads. Roof got up again and gave each man another shilling.

"I am through," he said with a **defiance** that was no less effective for being transparently faked. The elders too knew how far to go without losing decorum. So when Roof added: "Go cast your paper for the enemy if you like!" they quickly calmed him down with a suitable speech from each of them. By the time the last man had spoken it was possible, without great loss of dignity, to pick up the things from the floor . . .

The enemy Roof had referred to was the Progressive Organization Party (POP) which had been formed by the tribes down the coast to save themselves, as the founders of the party proclaimed, from "total political, cultural, social and religious annihilation." Although it was clear the party had no chance here it had plunged, with typical foolishness, into a straight fight with PAP, providing cars and loudspeakers to a few local rascals and thugs to go around and make a lot of noise. No one knew for certain how much money POP had let loose in Umuofia but it was said to be very considerable. Their local campaigners would end up very rich, no doubt.

Vocabulary

defiance (di fī′əns) *n.* a refusal to recognize or obey someone or something

Up to last night everything had been "moving according to plan," as Roof would have put it. Then he had received a strange visit from the leader of the POP campaign team. Although he and Roof were well-known to each other, and might even be called friends, his visit was cold and business-like. No words were wasted. He placed five pounds[1] on the floor before Roof and said, "We want your vote." Roof got up from his chair, went to the outside door, closed it carefully and returned to his chair. The brief exercise gave him enough time to weigh the proposition. As he spoke his eyes never left the red notes on the floor. He seemed to be **mesmerized** by the picture of the cocoa farmer harvesting his crops.

"You know I work for Marcus," he said feebly. "It will be very bad . . . "

"Marcus will not be there when you put in your paper. We have plenty of work to do tonight; are you taking this or not?"

"It will not be heard outside this room?" asked Roof.

"We are after votes not gossip."

"All right," said Roof in English. **4**

The man nudged his companion and he brought forward an object covered with a red cloth and proceeded to remove the cover. It was a fearsome little affair contained in a clay pot with feathers stuck into it.

---

1. The *pound* is the basic unit of money in the United Kingdom.

Motivation *Considering the boldness of the campaign rival's offer, why does Roof stall for time instead of immediately turning it down?* **5**

Activate Prior Knowledge *What rationalization do the campaign worker's words imply? What everyday examples of rationalizations can you think of for doing or saying something you know is wrong?* **6**

Vocabulary

mesmerize (mez′mə rīz′) *v.* to hypnotize; spellbind

CHINUA ACHEBE **97**

Teach

Reading Strategy | 4

Question **Ask:** Why do you think Roof replies to the POP supporter in English? *(Probably so anyone listening who does not speak English will not know he has agreed to support the opposition.)*

Literary Element | 5

Motivation Answer: *He needs time to think about the offer. The lure of the large bribe is too tempting to turn down immediately.*

Reading Strategy | 6

Activate Prior Knowledge Answer: *The campaign worker is implying that Roof's vote will be entirely secret and therefore he need not worry about being disloyal. If students hesitate in providing examples, offer this example to stimulate their thinking: when people say,"What you don't know won't hurt you."*

Learning Objectives
Analyzing motivation. (SE)
Activating prior knowledge. (SE)
Analyzing figurative language. (TE)

Approaching Level

DIFFERENTIATED INSTRUCTION

Connect to Personal Experience The climax of the story comes when Roof agrees to sell his own vote. Students may find it difficult to grasp his dilemma. Roof has been buying votes for Marcus; now he has sworn to sell his own vote to Marcus's opponent and had this oath witnessed by a spirit known as an *iyi*. It may help if students try to connect this to some life experience of their own of divided loyalties.

Model for students how to connect Roof's dilemma to their personal life experiences by suggesting a parallel situation; for example: *"Roof's situation is something like a person who has been dating one person and then, in a weak moment, agrees to go out with another person."*

Teach

Reading Strategy 1

Make Inferences Ask:
What can you infer from Roof's reaction to the sight of the iyi? *(He believes that it has power to punish him for wrongdoing.)*

View the Art ★

Answer: *Marcus aspires to the kind of lifestyle the people in the painting seem to have.*

Cheri Samba (1956–) was born in the Congo and now resides in Paris part of the year. He is a well-known contemporary artist whose paintings often include text in French and in Lingala, an African language.

A Successful Life, 1995. Cheri Samba. Contemporary African Art Collection Limited.

View the Art Samba is known for his realistic brightly colored paintings. How does the lifestyle of the people in this painting compare with that of Marcus? ★

"The *iyi*[2] comes from Mbanta. You know what that means. Swear that you will vote for Maduka. If you fail to do so, this *iyi* take note."

1 Roof's heart nearly flew out when he saw the *iyi*; indeed he knew the fame of Mbanta in these things. But he was a man of quick decision. What could a single vote cast in secret for Maduka take away from Marcus's certain victory? Nothing.

"I will cast my paper for Maduka; if not this *iyi* take note."

"Das all," said the man as he rose with his companion who had covered up the object again and was taking it back to their car.

"You know he has no chance against Marcus," said Roof at the door.

2. An *iyi* is a tribal god.

"It is enough that he gets a few votes now; next time he will get more. People will hear that he gives out pounds, not shillings, and they will listen."

E lection morning. The great day every ☆ five years when the people exercise power. Weather-beaten posters on walls of houses, tree trunks and telegraph poles. The few that were still whole called out their message to those who could read. Vote for the People's Alliance Party! Vote for the Progressive Organization Party! Vote for PAP! Vote for POP! The posters that were torn called out as much of the message as they could.

As usual Chief the Honorable Marcus Ibe was doing things in grand style. He had hired a highlife band from Umuru and sta-

Reading Practice

Compare and Contrast Point out to students that this story is structured in two parts. In the first part Roof bribes the village elders; in the second part Maduka's man bribes Roof.

Ask: *How is Roof's bribing the elders like his being bribed by Maduka? How do the situations differ? (The situations are similar in that in both cases a vote is being sold for cash; they are different in that, in Roof's case, the bribe is much larger, he has a previous commitment to Ibe, and he asks the* iyi *to witness his agreement to vote for Maduka.)*

Divide students into small groups and have each group prepare a chart in which they delineate the similarities and differences in the two situations. Conclude the activity by having students speculate about Achebe's purpose in showing both.

tioned it at such a distance from the voting booths as just managed to be lawful. Many villagers danced to the music, their ballot papers held aloft, before proceeding to the booths. Chief the Honorable Marcus Ibe sat in the "owner's corner" of his enormous green car and smiled and nodded. One enlightened villager came up to the car, shook hands with the great man and said in advance, "Congrats!" This immediately set the pattern. Hundreds of admirers shook Marcus's hand and said "Corngrass!"

Roof and the other organizers were prancing up and down, giving last minute advice to the voters and pouring with sweat.

"Do not forget," he said again to a group of illiterate women who seemed ready to burst with enthusiasm and good humor, "our sign is the motor car . . ."

"Like the one Marcus is sitting inside."

"Thank you, mother," said Roof. "It is the same car. The box with the car shown on its body is the box for you. Don't look at the other with the man's head: it is for those whose heads are not correct."

This was greeted with loud laughter. Roof cast a quick and busy-like glance towards the Minister and received a smile of appreciation.

"Vote for the car," he shouted, all the veins in his neck standing out. "Vote for the car and you will ride in it!"

"Or if we don't, our children will," piped the same sharp, old girl.

The band struck up a new number: "Why walk when you can ride . . ."

In spite of his apparent calm and confidence Chief the Honorable Marcus was a relentless stickler for detail. He knew he would win what the newspapers called "a landslide victory" but he did not wish, even so, to throw away a single vote. So as soon as the first rush of voters was over he promptly asked his campaign boys to go one at a time and put in their ballot papers.

"Roof, you had better go first," he said.

Roof's spirits fell; but he let no one see it. All morning he had masked his deep worry with a surface exertion which was unusual even for him. Now he dashed off in his springy fashion towards the booths. A policeman at the entrance searched him for illegal ballot papers and passed him. Then the electoral officer explained to him about the two boxes. By this time the spring had gone clean out of his walk. He sidled in and was confronted by the car and the head. He brought out his ballot paper from his pocket and looked at it. How could he betray Marcus even in secret? He resolved to go back to the other man and return his five pounds . . . Five pounds! He knew at once it was impossible. He had sworn on that *iyi*. The notes were red; the cocoa farmer busy at work.

At this point he heard the muffled voice of the policeman asking the electoral officer what the man was doing inside. "Abi na pickin im de born?"

Quick as lightning a thought leapt into Roof's mind. He folded the paper, tore it in two along the crease and put one half in each box. He took the precaution of putting the first half into Maduka's box and confirming the action verbally: "I vote for Maduka."

They marked his thumb with indelible purple ink to prevent his return, and he went out of the booth as jauntily as he had gone in.

---

2 | **Living with Independence** *Why might Achebe have chosen a car to symbolize the PAP and a head to symbolize the POP?*

Motivation *Why does Roof put the first half of his ballot in Maduka's box and confirm this vote aloud?* | 3

Teach

Big Idea | 2

Living with Independence
Answer: *The car might symbolize material wealth. The head (where a person's brain is located) might symbolize a thinking man or a man of ideas. By choosing these symbols, Achebe reinforces the idea that the voters are choosing material wealth over the opportunity for genuine democratic reform.*

Literary Element | 3

Motivation Answer: *He genuinely fears the consequences of violating the oath that he swore on the* iyi *and wants to make sure that the gods of his religion hear his vote.*

Political History ☆
Nigerian Politics A recurring theme in Achebe's work is the problem of political leadership in a nation where the basis for government had always been the traditional village. Since the Biafran War (1967–1970), Nigeria has suffered from military coups and questionable election practices.

English Learners

DIFFERENTIATED INSTRUCTION

Advanced Point out to students that every culture has a rich repository of proverbs and offer some examples from contemporary American culture, such as "Think outside the box." Have students research a substantial number of proverbs from such sources as quotation dictionaries and the Internet. Encourage students to include proverbs from their own cultures. After completing their research, students should read their proverbs aloud in class.

After You Read

Assess

1. Some will argue that splitting his ballot was the only practical solution to his dilemma; others that it was his own duplicity that created the dilemma.

2. (a) He has left a job elsewhere to return to his village. (b) The village is poor and offers few job opportunities.

3. (a) They are impressed by Ibe's wealth and admire him for spending time in the village. (b) Students may feel this positive view is undeserved, because Ibe's attention to the village is for personal gain.

4. (a) To lay the groundwork for a future election victory by gaining votes in this election and spreading word of his party's generosity. (b) Roof convinces himself that he has not betrayed Ibe because Ibe will win without his vote.

5. (a) He decides to split his vote and tears his ballot in half. (b) His two votes will probably cancel each other out.

6. (a) He reminds them that Ibe comes from their village, and repeats Ibe's promise to bring running water there. (b) Offering bribes brings Roof's sincerity into question.

7. The story's main theme is that rampant political corruption thwarts the democratic process.

8. His torn ballot symbolizes his divided loyalties.

9. "The Voter" illustrates the corrupt political practices that plagued Nigeria after achieving independence.

10. Achebe may criticize Nigeria because he feels it has the potential to be a great nation.

100

After You Read

Respond and Think Critically

Respond and Interpret

1. In this story, Roof has to make a difficult decision about how to cast his vote. Do you agree with the way he resolves this dilemma? Why or why not?

2. (a) Why is Roof popular in his village? (b) What can you infer about the village's economic situation from the narrator's explanation of Roof's popularity?

3. (a) What do the villagers think of Marcus Ibe? (b) Do you think their opinion of him is deserved? Explain.

4. (a) Why does the leader of the opposition's campaign offer Roof a bribe? (b) Do you think Roof believes he is betraying Marcus Ibe by accepting the bribe? Explain.

5. (a) What decision does Roof make in the voting booth? (b) What do you think will be the result of Roof's vote?

Analyze and Evaluate

6. (a) Apart from offering the villagers bribes, what reasons does Roof give to convince the villagers to vote for Marcus Ibe? (b) Are his reasons sincere or mere campaign rhetoric? Support your answer with evidence from the story.

7. A **theme** is a central message or idea about life in a literary work. What is the main theme in "The Voter"?

8. A **symbol** is an object or an action that stands for something else in addition to itself. What might Roof's torn ballot symbolize?

Connect

9. **Big Idea** **Living with Independence** How do Roof's actions in this story parallel the problems Nigeria faced after gaining independence?

10. **Connect to the Author** Achebe is famous for his anti-imperialist views and his appreciation of Ibo culture. Despite this, "The Voter" is a harsh criticism of Nigeria and its politics. Why might Achebe have chosen to criticize his country in this story?

Literary Element Motivation

ACT Skills Practice

The passage "As he spoke... harvesting his crops" (page 97) suggests that Roof accepts the bribe primarily because

A. he knows that Marcus will still win the election

B. he is confident that his vote will be secret

C. he wants the money

D. he is scared of the POP leader

Review: Tone

As you learned on page 25, **tone** is an author's attitude toward his or her subject matter. Tone is conveyed through elements such as word choice, punctuation, sentence structure, and figures of speech.

Partner Activity Meet with a partner to analyze the tone of "The Voter" and answer the following questions.

1. How does Achebe's use of sentence fragments throughout the story contribute to the story's tone?

2. Do you think the tone of the "The Voter" is satiric? Explain your answer, using examples from the text to support your point.

Literary Element

(C) is the correct answer. "Mesmerized" suggests he is motivated by greed, but he tries to convince himself otherwise.

Progress Check

Can students identify motivation?

If No → See Unit 1 Teaching Resources Book, p. 132.

Review: Tone

1. The sentence fragments contribute to a conversational, relaxed tone.

2. The tone is satiric. An example includes "The villagers told themselves that they had underrated the power of the ballot paper and should not do so again." While the "power of the ballot" generally refers to the power of choosing a leader, here it refers to the power to bring money.

Reading Strategy: Activate Prior Knowledge

Activating prior knowledge includes drawing upon your personal experiences as well as recalling information learned through reading and listening. Review the chart you made on page 93.

1. What character behaviors in the story remind you of behaviors you have displayed or observed in others?

2. What background information pertaining to Nigeria and its problems helped you appreciate the events in the story? How did it help?

Vocabulary Practice

Practice with Word Parts For each bold-faced vocabulary word in the left column, identify the related word with a shared part in the right column. Write each pair and underline the part they have in common. Use a dictionary to look up the meaning of the related word. Then explain how it is related to the vocabulary word.

1. gratitude	nonevent
2. constituency	defile
3. nonentity	mesmeric
4. defiance	gratuitous
5. mesmerize	constitute

Academic Vocabulary

In Achebe's story, the POP does not pose a serious threat to the PAP **regime**.

Regime is an academic word. Nelson Mandela's Government of National Unity, which ruled South Africa in the 1990s, could be called a **regime**, although the word often carries a negative connotation. To further explore the meaning of this word, complete the sentence below.

A political regime that _____ might be characterized as unjust.

For more on academic vocabulary, see pages 36–37 and R83–R85.

Write with Style

 Apply Irony

Assignment Although Roof appears devoted to his political ideals, he is truly motivated by greed. This discrepancy between appearance and reality creates **irony** in the story. Write an expository essay about an ironic situation from the real world that details the motivations of a person or a group.

Get Ideas Brainstorm ironic situations from multiple sources, including your personal experience and background knowledge. For example, you might write about a time when a school group alleged that it supported one idea but behaved in a way that showed support for another idea. Create a three-column chart like the one below to clarify the irony in the situation.

Appearance	Reality	Irony
A group held a vigil to protest the development of a local meadow.	The group was so large that it disturbed wildlife and trampled vegetation.	The group harmed the meadow; its motivation seemed to be publicity instead of environmentalism.

Give It Structure Refer to the chart you made while generating ideas to organize your essay in a logical pattern. Be sure that each section of your essay clearly relates to your thesis and supports the points you want to make.

Look at Language Like short stories, expository essays can benefit from the use of figurative language and proverbs. These additions will give your writing personal style and make it more entertaining. It may be helpful to review Achebe's story for models of figurative language and proverbs.

Literature Online

Selection Resources For Selection Quizzes, eFlashcards, and Reading-Writing Connection activities, go to glencoe.com and enter QuickPass code GLW6053u1.

CHINUA ACHEBE **101**

After You Read

Assess

Reading Strategy

1. Students' examples will vary. Encourage students to frame their observations in a constructive way and to avoid comments that lay blame on others.

2. Students should be able to cite background information in the unit introduction and the author biography. Encourage them to cite specific examples from the story that they were able to connect to the background information.

Progress Check

Can students activate prior knowledge?

If No → See Unit 1 Teaching Resources Book, p. 133.

Vocabulary

Possible answers:

1. <u>grat</u>itude—"thankfulness"; <u>grat</u>uitous—"free." If something is gratuitous, one might show thankfulness.

2. <u>constitu</u>ency—"group represented"; <u>constitu</u>te—"form." The people in a congressional district constitute a representative's constituency.

3. <u>non</u>entity—"not existing"; <u>non</u>event—"not taking place." A nonevent and a nonentity both have little importance.

4. <u>defi</u>ance—"refusal to obey"; <u>defi</u>le—"make unclean." Defiling a statue is one way of showing defiance to a leader.

5. <u>mesmer</u>ize—"to hypnotize"; <u>mesmer</u>ic—"fascinating." It can be mesmeric to watch a mesmerized person.

Academic Vocabulary

Possible answer: A political regime that treats citizens violently might be characterized as unjust.

 For additional assessment, see Assessment Resources, pp. 53–54.

Writing

Students' essays should:

- describe and explain a specific ironic situation
- follow a clear organizational pattern that supports the thesis
- effectively use proverbs and figurative language

Grammar Workshop

Focus

Write on the board:
- The children's playground.
- The dog's were hungry.

Ask: Which uses an apostrophe correctly? (*The first phrase uses an apostrophe correctly in a possessive, while the second uses an apostrophe incorrectly in a plural.*)

Teach

On separate lines on the board, **write:** singular noun, plural noun ending in *s*, indefinite pronoun. Have students write, on the board, examples of how to make possessives of each. If they have trouble with the term *indefinite pronoun,* write *it* as an example.

Assess

1. **a.** ballots' **b.** witness's
   c. someone's **d.** pounds'
2. **a.** The children's future was at stake. **b.** The village elders' knowledge of politics had increased over time. **c.** C

 For additional grammar practice, see Unit 1 Teaching Resources Book, p. 139.

Grammar Practice

Its* and *It's Tell students that many people confuse the possessive pronoun *its* with the contraction *it's*. Explain that *its* is a third-person singular pronoun. On the board, write the following sentence:

The city of Buenos Aires, Argentina, gets its name from the Spanish words for "fair winds."

Point out to students that the antecedent of the pronoun *its* is *Buenos Aires.*

Then write this sentence:

102

Learning Objectives

In this workshop, you will focus on the following objective:

Grammar: Understanding how to use possessive apostrophes.

Possessive Nouns

A **possessive noun** shows possession, ownership, or the relationship between two nouns.

Tip

To decide whether a noun needs an apostrophe only or an apostrophe and an -*s*, decide what kind of noun it is. Plural nouns ending in -*s*, such as *countries,* do not take an -*s* after an apostrophe to make them possessive (*countries',* not *countries's*).

Language Handbook

For more on apostrophes, see Language Handbook, p. R40.

 **Literature** Online

Grammar For more grammar practice, go to glencoe.com and enter QuickPass code GLW6053u1.

Grammar Workshop

Possessive Apostrophes

Literature Connection As the following quote from "The Voter" by Chinua Achebe shows, an important use of the apostrophe is to make nouns and some pronouns possessive.

> *"Although the villagers did not explain it in so many words Roof's popularity was a measure of their gratitude . . ."*

To form the possessive, add either an apostrophe or an apostrophe and an -*s,* as in *Roof's.*

To make the possessive form of a singular noun ending in -*s,* add an apostrophe and an -*s.*

> Marcus wife was a teacher.
> Marcus's wife was a teacher.

If a plural noun ends in -*s,* make it possessive by adding only an apostrophe.

> The man answered the voters questions.
> The man answered the voters' questions.

If a plural noun does not end in -*s,* add an apostrophe and an -*s.*

> The people votes were important to Roof.
> The people's votes were important to Roof.

Form the possessive of an indefinite pronoun (for example, *someone* or *everybody*) by adding an apostrophe and an -*s.* Apostrophes are not used with possessive pronouns, such as *hers* and *theirs.*

> Roof used bribes to secure everyones votes.
> Roof used bribes to secure everyone's votes.

Revise Complete the following items using what you know about possessive apostrophes.

1. On a separate sheet of paper, rewrite the following words as possessive.
   a. ballots   **b.** witness   **c.** someone   **d.** pounds
2. For each sentence below, if the sentence is correct, write *C* on a separate sheet of paper. If the sentence is incorrect, rewrite it correctly.
   a. The childrens' future was at stake.
   b. The village elders knowledge of politics had increased over time.
   c. Roof's mission was to win the election for Marcus Ibe.

Buenos Aires has a large port; it's one of the busiest ports in the world.

Note that *it's* is a contraction of *it is.* Explain to students that one of the best ways to figure out whether to use *its* or *it's* in a sentence is to see if *it is* can be substituted. Whenever *it is* can be used, *it's* is the correct choice.

Have students choose *its* or *it's* for these sentences:

Do you know the capital of Alaska? _____ Juneau. *(It's)*

Alaska is known for _____ salmon. *(its)*

from
No Future
Without Forgiveness

Desmond Mpilo Tutu

 Nobel Prize Winner

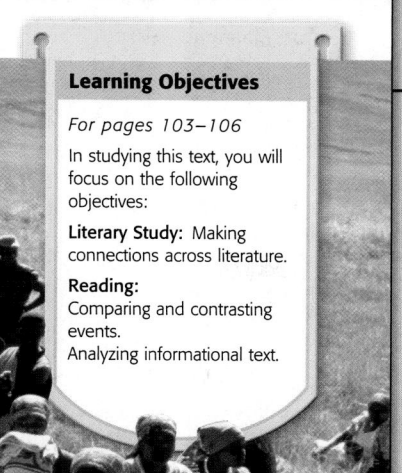

Learning Objectives

For pages 103–106
In studying this text, you will focus on the following objectives:

Literary Study: Making connections across literature.

Reading:
Comparing and contrasting events.
Analyzing informational text.

On the day of South Africa's first post-apartheid election, voters line up for miles waiting to cast their ballot.

Set a Purpose for Reading

Read to learn more about the political process in a newly democratic African nation.

Build Background

Desmond Tutu, the first black archbishop of Cape Town, South Africa, was awarded the Nobel Peace Prize in 1984 for his work to end apartheid, a devastating system of racial segregation. In the following excerpt from his memoir, Tutu describes the experience of voting in South Africa's first multiracial elections in 1994. The elections resulted in a victory for Nelson Mandela, who later appointed Tutu as chair of the Truth and Reconciliation Commission, a group designed to investigate human rights abuses that occurred during apartheid.

Reading Strategy Compare and Contrast Events

To **compare and contrast events** means to look for similarities and differences between events in two or more literary works. As you read, ask yourself, What events in this memoir can I compare and contrast with events in Chinua Achebe's "The Voter"?

I went to vote in Gugulethu, a black township[1] with its typical matchbox-type houses in row after monotonous row. There was a long queue[2] already waiting. People were in good spirits; they were going to need dollops of patience and good humor because they were in for a long wait. My first democratic vote was a media event, and many of our friends from overseas were present, acting as monitors to be able to certify whether the elections were fair and free. But they were doing a great deal more than that. They were really like midwives helping to bring to birth this new delicate infant—free, democratic, non-racial, nonsexist South Africa.

The moment for which I had waited so long came and I folded my ballot paper and cast my vote. Wow! I shouted, "Yippee!" It was giddy stuff. It was like falling in love. The sky looked blue and more beautiful. I

---

1. In South Africa under apartheid, a *township* was a poor urban area reserved for nonwhites.
2. A *queue* is a line.

DESMOND MPILO TUTU **103**

Focus
Summary

Desmond Tutu, the former archbishop of Cape Town, South Africa, recounts his experience voting in South Africa's first multiracial election in 1994. He describes the election as a joyful event that gave a voice to the victims of apartheid and absolved the guilt of those who had enforced the system. Though the election was plagued by problems, including insufficient supplies and poor management, South Africans waited patiently in voting lines and cooperated with one another. To Tutu, this cooperation symbolized South Africans' willingness to look beyond race and recognize their "common humanity."

 For activities related to this selection, see Unit 1 Teaching Resources Book, pp. 140–148.

 For an audio recording of this selection, use Listening Library Audio CD-ROM.

Readability Scores
Dale-Chall: 8.4
DRP: 61
Lexile: 980

Approaching Level

DIFFERENTIATED INSTRUCTION

Analyze Figurative Language Tutu's frequent use of figurative language might make this selection difficult for some students. Have these students focus on one type of figurative language that Tutu uses—the simile. Remind them that a simile is a comparison that uses the word *like* or *as*. Explain that similes often compare two things that might not seem similar at first, as when Tutu says that voting is "like falling in love." Then have struggling students pair with more advanced students to identify and discuss other similes in the selection. *(Possible similes: It was like a festival; the memory of being treated like rubbish gnawing away at her very vitals like some corrosive acid; freedom that tasted like sweet nectar.)*

Some students may need more help understanding the concept of a simile.

Write the sentence *The election was like a festival* on the board. Then ask students what a festival is, and how one might feel at a festival. *(A festival is a fun, joyful party.)* Explain that Tutu says the election was "like a festival" because it was fun and joyful.

103

Political Perspective
on *The Voter*

Teach

Text Element	1

Footnote Have students read footnote 3. **Ask: Who has been changed or transformed?** *(the South African people)*

Political History ☆

Life Under Apartheid During apartheid, South Africa's brutal system of racial segregation, blacks were forced to live on bleak reservations known as homelands, where there were no jobs and little money. Some black South Africans managed to move to townships, poor settlements on the periphery of urban centers. Though conditions in the townships were squalid, there was at least the small possibility of finding work.

saw the people in a new light. They were beautiful, they were transfigured.[3] I too was transfigured. It was dreamlike. You were scared someone would rouse you and you would awake to the nightmare that was apartheid's harsh reality. Someone referring to that dreamlike quality had said to his wife, "Darling, don't wake me. I like this dream."

After voting, I went outside and the people cheered and sang and danced. It was like a festival. It was a wonderful vindication for all of those who had borne the burden and the heat of repression, the little people whom apartheid had turned into the anonymous ones, faceless, voiceless, counting for nothing in their motherland, whose noses had been rubbed daily in the dust. They had been created in the image of God but their dignity had been callously trodden underfoot daily by apartheid's minions and those who might have said they were opposed to apartheid but had nonetheless gone on enjoying the privileges and huge benefits that apartheid provided them—just because of an accident of birth, a biological irrelevance, the color of their skin.

I decided to drive around a bit to see what was happening. I was appalled by what I saw. The people had come out in droves, standing in those long lines which have now become world famous. They were so vulnerable. The police and the security forces were probably stretched but they were hardly a conspicuous presence. It would have taken just a few crazy extremists with AK-47s to sow the most awful mayhem and havoc. It did not happen. And virtually everywhere there was a hitch of one sort or the other. Here it was insufficient ballot papers, there it was not enough ink pads, elsewhere the officials had not yet turned up hours after the polls

were due to have opened. The people were quite amazing in their patience. It was a comprehensive disaster waiting to happen. And it did not happen.

It was an amazing spectacle. People of all races were standing together in the same queues, perhaps for the very first time in their lives. Professionals, domestic workers, cleaners and their madams—all were standing in those lines that were snaking their way slowly to the polling booth. What should have been a disaster turned out to be a blessing in disguise. Those lines produced a new and peculiarly South African status symbol. Afterward people boasted, "I stood for two hours to vote." "I waited for four hours!"

Those long hours helped us South Africans to find one another. People shared newspapers, sandwiches, umbrellas, and the scales began to fall from their eyes. South Africans found fellow South Africans—they realized what we had been at such pains to tell them, that they shared a common humanity, that race, ethnicity, skin color were really irrelevancies. They discovered not a Colored, a black, an Indian, a white. No, they found fellow human beings. What a profound scientific discovery that blacks, Coloreds (usually people of mixed race), and Indians were in fact human beings, who had the same concerns and anxieties and aspirations. They wanted a decent home, a good job, a safe environment for their families, good schools for their children, and almost none wanted to drive the whites into the sea. They just wanted their place in the sun.

Everywhere else elections are secular political events. Ours was more than this, much, much more. It was a veritable[4] spiritual experience. It was a mountaintop

---

1   3. *Transfigured* means "changed" or "transformed."

4. *Veritable* means "true."

Speaking Practice

Present an Oral Report Students might gain a better understanding of "The Voter" and Tutu's memoir by researching voting procedures and controversies in African countries following independence. Have students choose either Nigeria or South Africa and brainstorm a list of questions about the modern voting process in their chosen country. Remind students to keep in mind that these two countries have very different

political histories. Then have them use a variety of reputable sources, including encyclopedias, books, newspapers, and magazines, to find answers to their questions. Students should present their research to the class and explain how their findings affect their understanding of the selections. They may wish to display media from recent elections such as photographs, radio reports, or news footage to help illustrate their points.

Man casting his ballot in first post-apartheid election.

Teach

Big Idea   2

Living with Independence
Have students recount specific details from Tutu's description of the elections. **Ask:** Based on what you know about the problems that African countries have faced following independence, does Tutu's perspective on the South African elections seem balanced? Explain. *(Some students may think that his view of the election as a "spiritual experience" is a bit unrealistic, in light of the corruption that has plagued the political process in so many countries. Others may point out that he also mentions the problems with the election, but chooses to focus on the positive step it represents for South Africa.)*

experience. The black person entered the booth one person and emerged on the other side a new, transfigured person. She entered weighed down by the anguish and burden of oppression, with the memory of being treated like rubbish gnawing away at her very vitals like some corrosive acid. She reappeared as someone new, "I am free," as she walked away with head held high, the shoulders set straighter, and an elastic spring in her step. How do you convey that sense of freedom that tasted like sweet nec-

tar for the first time? How do you explain it to someone who was born into freedom? It is impossible to convey.

The white person entered the voting booth burdened by the load of guilt for having enjoyed the fruits of oppression and injustice. He emerged as somebody new. He too cried out, "The burden has been lifted from my shoulders, I am free, transfigured, made into a new person." He walked tall, with head held high and shoulders set **2** square and straight.

DESMOND MPILO TUTU   **105**

English Learners

DIFFERENTIATED INSTRUCTION

Intermediate Point out the following sentence on this page: "She entered weighed down by the anguish and burden of oppression, with the memory of being treated like rubbish gnawing away at her very vitals like some corrosive acid." Clarify for students that the woman was not literally weighed down by a heavy object and that rubbish did not literally gnaw her. Explain that Tutu is using figurative

language to describe her emotional condition. Have students look up the word oppression, and tell them that the word vitals means "vital organs," such as the heart and stomach. Ask them to use this information to determine the meaning of the phrase. *(Students should convey that the woman had been emotionally damaged by apartheid.)*

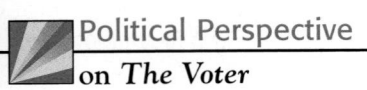

Political Perspective
on *The Voter*

Assess

1. Summaries should mention the effects of voting on the voters and their sense of unity.

2. Students' answers will vary. Some students may be surprised that Tutu calls voting a "spiritual experience."

3. (a) The people are patient, peaceful, and in good spirits. (b) Waiting to vote helps unite the population as people recognize their "common humanity."

4. (a) Tutu compares their situation to that of two convicts manacled together who can make their way out of a ditch only by working together. (b) This comparison is effective because it illustrates that South Africa can achieve progress only if blacks and whites cooperate.

5. (a) This change is shown in descriptions of people's confident postures after voting. Examples include a "head held high" and "shoulders set square." (b) Black South Africans were freed from oppression, and white South Africans from their guilt.

6. (a) Tutu's experience is joyful; he is optimistic about the future of his country and feels united with his fellow voters. The experience of the characters in "The Voter" is less satisfying; they lose their freedom through bribery and are resigned to the election outcome before they even vote. (b) The South African elections signaled freedom from apartheid and resulted in Mandela's presidency, so it is unsurprising that Tutu views them in a positive light. Nigeria's independence resulted in ethnic strife and violence, so it is understandable that Achebe has a less positive outlook.

106

White people found that freedom was indeed indivisible.[5] We had kept saying in the dark days of apartheid's oppression that white South Africans would never be truly free until we blacks were free as well. Many thought it was just another Tutu slogan, irresponsible as all his others had been. Today they were experiencing it as a reality. I used to refer to an intriguing old film *The Defiant Ones*, in which Sidney Poitier was one of the stars. Two convicts escape from a chain gang. They are manacled[6] together, the one white, the other black. They fall into a ditch with slippery sides. The one convict claws his way nearly to the top and out of the ditch but cannot make it because he is bound to his mate, who has been left at the bottom in the ditch. The only way they can make it is together as they strive up and up and up together and eventually make their way over the side wall and out.

So too I would say we South Africans will survive and prevail only together, black and white bound together by circumstance and history as we strive to claw our way out of the morass[7] that was apartheid racism. Up and out together, black and white together. Neither group on its own could or would make it. God had bound us, manacled us, together. In a way it was to live out what Martin Luther King, Jr., had said, "Unless we learn to live together as brothers [and sisters] we will die together as fools." ❧

---

5. *Indivisible* means "unable to be separated."
6. *Manacled* means "shackled together, as with handcuffs."

7. In this context, *morass* means "a difficult or an overwhelming situation."

Respond and Think Critically

Respond and Interpret

1. Write a brief summary of the main ideas in this excerpt before you answer the following questions. For help on writing a summary, see page 1147.

2. Were you surprised by the way Tutu describes the experience of voting? Explain.

3. (a) How do the people behave while waiting in line to vote? (b) According to Tutu, what effect does waiting to vote have on the population?

Analyze and Evaluate

4. (a) At the end of the excerpt, to what does Tutu compare the situation of black and white South Africans? (b) What is this comparison meant to illustrate? Is it effective? Explain.

5. (a) According to Tutu, voting "transfigures" both black and white voters. What images does Tutu use to describe this change? (b) Given what you know about the history of South Africa, why might voting have this effect?

Connect

6. (a) Contrast Tutu's experience of voting with the experience of voting described in Chinua Achebe's "The Voter." (b) Considering the histories of South Africa and Nigeria, why might these two authors portray voting differently?

Vocabulary Practice

Recognize Loaded Words Explain to students that authors and orators often use "loaded words"—words that express strong opinions or emotions—to make their writing and speeches more powerful.

Point out Tutu's use of the words *oppression* and *racism*. Explain that these words are powerful labels that convey Tutu's own feeling about South African politics.

Have students work in groups to identify other loaded words in the selection and discuss how they help Tutu achieve his purpose.

Before You Read

The Rain Came

Kenya

Meet Grace Ogot
(born 1930)

Grace Ogot (ō´gōt) was born in western Kenya's Nyanza district, which lies along the shores of Lake Victoria. She is a member of the Luo people, an African ethnic group that resides in parts of Kenya, Tanzania, and Uganda. Much of Ogot's fiction is set against the background of the Lake Victoria region and is based on the customs, legends, and history of the Luo. Their ancestors were nomadic herders who moved southward hundreds of years ago from Sudan to the areas they occupy today. One of the largest ethnic groups in Kenya, the Luo participated actively in the struggle for Kenyan independence from Great Britain in the 1950s and early 1960s. Ogot came of age as an author during this time, and she has often written about conflicts between the Luo and the British.

A Diverse Career Ogot's fascination with storytelling stems from her childhood, when she would eagerly listen to her grandmother recite folktales. Later, Ogot would loosely base many of her short stories on the Luo tales she heard from her grandmother. As a young woman, Ogot trained as a nurse and a midwife in both Uganda and England. Ogot's work as a nurse later allowed her to write about the conflict between traditional healing methods and modern Western medicine. While training as a midwife, she met and married Professor Bethwell Allan Ogot, a Luo and a prominent African historian. In addition to writing fiction, Grace Ogot has served as a member of Kenya's parliament, held positions in broadcasting and public relations, and represented her country at the United Nations and at UNESCO (United Nations Educational, Scientific, and Cultural Organization).

Banana Fields, Kenya, 2001. John Newcomb. Watercolor. Private collection.

"There are more tragic incidents in life than there are comic ones."

—Grace Ogot

Themes of Sacrifice Grace Ogot began publishing her fiction in the late 1960s. When she submitted her first manuscript to a Kenyan publisher, the manager complained that her stories were not very uplifting. Still, Ogot persisted in writing about the subjects that interested her, including sacrifice, one of her major topics. She often portrays characters who are willing to give up personal happiness for the sake of family or community. Ogot has become perhaps the best-known woman writer in Kenya, publishing works in both English and Luo.

 Literature Online

Author Search For more about Grace Ogot, go to glencoe.com and enter QuickPass code GLW6053u1.

GRACE OGOT **107**

Before You Read

Focus

Bellringer Options

**Selection Focus
  Transparency 7**
**Daily Language Practice
  Transparency 14**

Or ask: Who are some people you know of who have made sacrifices for the good of others? Allow students to describe selfless individuals who they have heard of or known personally. **Or:** Pass around magazine and newspaper articles about individuals who have made sacrifices for their communities. Have students discuss what these individuals sacrificed, and their reasons for doing so.

Selection Skills

Literary Elements
- Setting (SE pp. 108, 111–114, 118)
- Situational Irony (SE p. 118)

The Rain Came

Speaking/Listening/Viewing Skills
- Discuss Proverbs (SE p. 117)
- Deliver a Speech (TE p. 110)

Writing Skills/Grammar
- Research Report (SE p. 119)
- Character Sketch (TE p. 112)
- Use Coordinating Conjunctions (TE p. 114)

Reading Skills
- Analyze Cultural Context (SE pp. 108–114, 118)
- Question (TE pp. 108, 115)
- Draw Conclusions (TE p. 110)
- Review (TE p. 118)

Vocabulary Skills
- Understand Analogies (SE p. 118)
- Pantomime (TE p. 108)

Before You Read

Focus

Summary

Chief Labong'o must sacrifice his only daughter, Oganda, to save the land and the Luo people from drought and starvation. Oganda accepts her destiny and travels to a lake in the sacred land where she must drown herself as the sun sets on the appointed day. As she approaches the lake, Oganda feels she is being pursued. She runs for the lake, but faints before she reaches the water. When she awakes, Osinda, one of her two suitors, is with her. He persuades her to run away from her fate, and as they leave the sacred land, the rain comes down in torrents.

 For summaries in languages other than English, see Unit 1 Teaching Resources Book, pp. 149–154.

Vocabulary

Pantomime Hand out cards with instructions to act out scenarios using the vocabulary words (Sample card: *Pretend to coax a cat out of a tree.*) Have students silently pantomime the actions on the cards. Classmates should try to guess the words.

Reading Practice

 SMALL GROUP **Question** Explain to students that this story portrays a culture and a system of values that are quite different from those of Western culture. Students should make every effort to ask questions actively as they read and not to glide over cultural differences. Explain that the more questions they ask, the more likely they are to appreciate the story. Have students work in small groups to write questions about the life and value system of the Luo using headings like the ones that follow.

Passage

The words of Ndithi, the medicine man, still echoed in his ears. "Podho, the ancestor of the Luo, appeared to me in a dream last night."

Questions

- What are the functions of a medicine man?

- How is a medicine man different from a Western doctor?

Have groups share their questions with the rest of the class. Ask students to answer the questions they can, and research answers for the others.

Literature and Reading Preview

Connect to the Story

What is the greatest sacrifice you have ever made? List the reasons you made the sacrifice and how this sacrifice benefited others.

Build Background

Ancestor worship is common in traditional African societies. People worship the spirits of the dead through prayer, sacrifice, and celebrations involving storytelling and dance. Usually the worshippers view their ancestors as beneficial spirits who can stop illness or drought, encourage the fertility of crops, help couples have children, and intervene with the gods on behalf of their descendants.

Set Purposes for Reading

Big Idea **Tradition and Change**

As you read, ask yourself, Why might the village in the story continue to follow traditional Luo values?

Literary Element **Setting**

Setting is the time and place in which the events of a literary work occur. The elements of setting may include geographical location, historical period, season of the year, time of day, and the beliefs and customs of a society. "The Rain Came" is set in a Luo village in Kenya during a drought. As you read, ask yourself, How are the seasonal circumstances integral to this story's plot?

Reading Strategy **Analyze Cultural Context**

To **analyze cultural context** means to examine the values, ideas, and traditions that are apparent in a text to better understand the culture in which that text was written. As you read "The Rain Came," ask yourself, What details illustrate the cultural context that shapes this story?

···

Tip: Take Notes As you read, use a chart like the one below to record details from the story and what they indicate about Luo culture.

Detail	Cultural Context
p. 110, "A young woman whispered to her co-wife . . !"	In Luo society, a man can have more than one wife.

Vocabulary

consecrate (kon′sə krāt′) *v.* to elevate into a sacred position through a religious rite; p. 110 *The bishop came to consecrate several new priests.*

rebuke (ri būk′) *v.* to criticize sharply; p. 110 *The librarian rebuked the noisy children.*

coax (kōks) *v.* to persuade by means of gentle urging or flattery; p. 112 *My sister tried to coax me into attending her rehearsal by telling me she wanted my opinion of her acting.*

denizen (den′ə zən) *n.* an inhabitant; p. 114 *The denizens of the swamp included alligators, opossums, and turtles.*

retaliation (ri tal′ē ā′shən) *n.* revenge; p. 116 *His witty retaliation for his friends' Halloween prank made everyone laugh.*

The Rain Came

Grace Ogot

Girl in Red, 1992. Tilly Willis. Oil on canvas. Private collection.

English Learners

DIFFERENTIATED INSTRUCTION

Advanced Write these words from the story on the board: <u>sacri</u>*ficing*, *con<u>secr</u>ated*. Point out that the root *sacri-* comes from the Latin *sacer*, which means "holy." In the story, a sacrifice is an offering to a deity, a holy being. This root with a slightly different spelling forms the word *consecrate*, which means "to make or declare something sacred or holy." Other words in English with this root include *sacred, sacrament, sacrilegious,* and *sacrosanct.* Have students look up the four words listed above and restate the definitions in their own words.

Have more advanced English speakers use each of the four words in a sentence and share their sentences with one another.

Teach

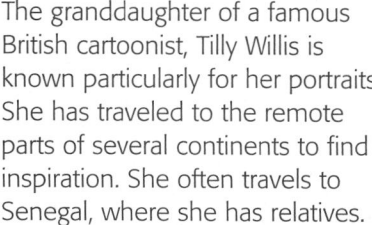

View the Art ★

The granddaughter of a famous British cartoonist, Tilly Willis is known particularly for her portraits. She has traveled to the remote parts of several continents to find inspiration. She often travels to Senegal, where she has relatives.

Ask: What seems to be the mood of the girl in the portrait? *(Students may say that she appears to be deep in thought and at peace with her surroundings.)*

Cultural History ☆

The Luo With a population of more than three million, the Luo is Kenya's third-largest ethnic group. This ethnic group has traditionally lived by farming and fishing. In today's Kenya, Luo men often travel to cities to find work while the women work on the farms.

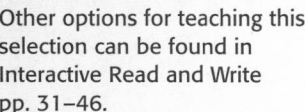

Interactive Read and Write
Other options for teaching this selection can be found in Interactive Read and Write pp. 31–46.

For an audio recording of this selection, use Listening Library Audio CD-ROM.

Readability Scores

Dale-Chall: 6.0
DRP: 55
Lexile: 730

Learning Objectives
Analyzing cultural context. (SE)
Analyzing art. (TE)

109

Teach

Reading Strategy | 1

Analyze Cultural Context
Answer: *The passage indicates that the ancestors are intermediaries between their descendants and God.*

 For additional practice using the reading skill or strategy, see Unit 1 Teaching Resources Book, p. 156.

Reading Strategy | 2

Draw Conclusions Explain to students that this paragraph includes details that reveal Labong'o's more general ideas about leadership. **Ask:** What does Labong'o feel his role is? What does a chief owe his people? *(The chief has pledged to lay down his life and the lives of his family for his people; he places the good of the group over his personal needs.)*

Reading Strategy | 3

Analyze Cultural Context
Answer: *Self-control and bravery seem to be qualities of the Luo chief.*

The chief was still far from the gate when his daughter Oganda saw him. She ran to meet him. Breathlessly she asked her father, "What is the news, great Chief? Everyone in the village is anxiously waiting to hear when it will rain." Labong'o held out his hands for his daughter but he did not say a word. Puzzled by her father's cold attitude Oganda ran back to the village to warn the others that the chief was back.

The atmosphere in the village was tense and confused. Everyone moved aimlessly and fussed in the yard without actually doing any work. A young woman whispered to her co-wife, "If they have not solved this rain business today, the chief will crack." They had watched him getting thinner and thinner as the people kept on pestering him. "Our cattle lie dying in the fields," they reported. "Soon it will be our children and then ourselves. Tell us what to do to save our lives, oh great Chief." So the chief had daily prayed with the Almighty through the ancestors to deliver them from their distress.

Instead of calling the family together and giving them the news immediately, Labong'o went to his own hut, a sign that he was not to be disturbed. Having replaced the shutter, he sat in the dimly lit hut to contemplate.

It was no longer a question of being the chief of hunger-stricken people that weighed Labong'o's heart. It was the life of his only daughter that was at stake. At the time when Oganda came to meet him, he saw the glittering chain shining around her waist. The prophecy was complete. "It is Oganda, Oganda, my only daughter, who must die so young." Labong'o burst into tears before finishing the sentence.

---

1 **Analyze Cultural Context** *What does this passage reveal about the role of ancestors in Luo religion?*

110 UNIT 1 MODERN AFRICA

The chief must not weep. Society had declared him the bravest of men. But Labong'o did not care any more. He assumed the position of a simple father and wept bitterly.

He loved his people, the Luo, but what were the Luo for him without Oganda? Her life had brought a new life in Labong'o's world and he ruled better than he could remember. How would the spirit of the village survive his beautiful daughter? "There are so many homes and so many parents who have daughters. Why choose this one? She is all I have." Labong'o spoke as if the ancestors were there in the hut and he could see them face to face. Perhaps they were there, warning him to remember his promise on the day he was enthroned when he said aloud, before the elders, "I will lay down life, if necessary, and the life of my household, to save this tribe from the hands of the enemy." "Deny! Deny!" he could hear the voice of his forefathers mocking him.

When Labong'o was **consecrated** chief he was only a young man. Unlike his father, he ruled for many years with only one wife. But people **rebuked** him because his only wife did not bear him a daughter. He married a second, a third, and a fourth wife, but they all gave birth to male children. When Labong'o married a fifth wife she bore him a daughter. They called her Oganda, meaning "beans," because her skin was very fair. Out of Labong'o's twenty children, Oganda was the only girl. Though she was the chief's favorite, her mother's co-wives swallowed their jealous feelings

---

3 Analyze Cultural Context *Based on this passage, what qualities must a chief in Luo society have?*

Vocabulary

consecrate (kon′sə krāt′) *v.* to elevate into a sacred position through a religious rite
rebuke (ri būk′) *v.* to criticize sharply

Speaking Practice

PARTNERS **Deliver a Speech** On the board, write out Labong'o's brief speech on page 111, second column: "One whom we love and treasure must be taken away from us. Oganda is to die. The ancestors have chosen her to be offered as a sacrifice to the lake monster in order that we may have rain." This short speech is an excellent model for delivering bad news: Labong'o prepares the people for the news in general terms; then he tells them specifically what will happen; finally he explains why the action must take place.

Have students work in pairs. Give each person a slip of paper on which is written a simple "bad news" scenario. *(Example: Your partner has lost a close race for president of the class because he or she offended some students by suggesting in a campaign speech that they were apathetic.)* Using Labong'o's model, have each student prepare and deliver the bad news to his or her partner. Partners should be prepared to evaluate each other's delivery style.

110

and showered her with love. After all, they said, Oganda was a female child whose days in the royal family were numbered. She would soon marry at a tender age and leave the enviable position to someone else.

Never in his life had he been faced with such an impossible decision. Refusing to yield to the rainmaker's request would mean sacrificing the whole tribe, putting the interests of the individual above those of the society. More than that. It would mean disobeying the ancestors, and most probably wiping the Luo people from the surface of the earth. On the other hand, to let Oganda die as a ransom for the people would permanently cripple Labong'o spiritually. He knew he would never be the same chief again.

The words of Ndithi, the medicine man, still echoed in his ears. "Podho, the ancestor of the Luo, appeared to me in a dream last night, and he asked me to speak to the chief and the people," Ndithi had said to the gathering of tribesmen. "A young woman who has not known a man must die so that the country may have rain. While Podho was still talking to me, I saw a young woman standing at the lakeside, her hands raised, above her head. Her skin was as fair as the skin of young deer in the wilderness. Her tall slender figure stood like a lonely reed at the river bank. Her sleepy eyes wore a sad look like that of a bereaved mother. She wore a gold ring on her left ear, and a glittering brass chain around her waist. As I still marveled at the beauty of this young woman, Podho told me, 'Out of all the women in this land, we have chosen this one. Let her offer herself as a sacrifice to the lake monster! And on that day, the rain will come down in torrents. Let everyone stay at home on that day, lest he be carried away by the floods.'"

Outside there was a strange stillness, except for the thirsty birds that sang lazily on the dying trees. The blinding mid-day heat had forced the people to retire to their huts. Not far away from the chief's hut, two guards were snoring away quietly. Labong'o removed his crown and the large eagle-head that hung loosely on his shoulders. He left the hut, and instead of asking Nyabog'o the messenger to beat the drum, he went straight and beat it himself. In no time the whole household had assembled under the siala tree where he usually addressed them. He told Oganda to wait a while in her grandmother's hut.

When Labong'o stood to address his household, his voice was hoarse and the tears choked him. He started to speak, but words refused to leave his lips. His wives and sons knew there was great danger. Perhaps their enemies had declared war on them. Labong'o's eyes were red, and they could see he had been weeping. At last he told them. "One whom we love and treasure must be taken away from us. Oganda is to die." Labong'o's voice was so faint, that he could not hear it himself. But he continued, "The ancestors have chosen her to be offered as a sacrifice to the lake monster in order that we may have rain."

They were completely stunned. As a confused murmur broke out, Oganda's mother fainted and was carried off to her own hut. But the other people rejoiced. They danced around singing and chanting, "Oganda is the lucky one to die for the people. If it is to save the people, let Oganda go."

In her grandmother's hut Oganda wondered what the whole family were discussing about her that she could not hear. Her grandmother's hut was well away from the

---

4 Tradition and Change *How might a decision to ignore the rainmaker's request affect Luo tradition?*

5 Setting *What elements of the setting highlight the problem the Luo face?*

Teach

Big Idea 4

Tradition and Change
Answer: *Luo tradition would be affected because the chief would have ignored his people's belief that the good of the community comes before that of the individual; other people may follow this example. His decision may also undermine the rainmaker's role in the community.*

Literary Element 5

Setting Answer: *The "thirsty birds," "dying trees," and "blinding" heat highlight the effects of the drought.*

Cultural History

Lake Victoria The Luo live on the eastern side of Lake Victoria, the largest lake in Africa. The lake's flat, bare northern coast stretches across Uganda and into western Kenya. This may be the lake referred to in the story.

Learning Objectives
Analyzing cultural context. (SE)
Analyzing setting. (SE)
Drawing conclusions. (TE)
Delivering a speech. (TE)

Advanced Learners/Pre-AP

DIFFERENTIATED INSTRUCTION

Research and Report The offering of human life to gods has been practiced across several different cultures and time periods. Some students may wish to conduct research to learn more about the reasons for this practice. Have them present their findings in a written report in which they compare and contrast the rituals surrounding human sacrifice, as well as the purposes behind it, across several cultures. Remind students of the importance of using a variety of unbiased, reputable sources in their research.

Teach

Reading Strategy   1

Analyze Cultural Context
Answer: *It indicates that—at least for women—a marriage partner is chosen by the individual's family.*

[APPROACHING] Some students may find it difficult to relate to the constraints of Oganda's situation. Ask them if their families have ever tried to control whom they were friends with, and why.

Literary Element   2

Setting Answer: *The single exit in the hut may symbolize that Oganda now has a single option for leaving her village: self-sacrifice.*

chief's court and, much as she strained her ears, she could not hear what was said. "It must be marriage," she concluded. It was an accepted custom for the family to discuss their daughter's future marriage behind her back. A faint smile played on Oganda's lips as she thought of the several young men who swallowed saliva at the mere mention of her name.

There was Kech, the son of a neighboring clan elder. Kech was very handsome. He had sweet, meek eyes and a roaring laughter. He would make a wonderful father, Oganda thought. But they would not be a good match. Kech was a bit too short to be her husband. It would humiliate her to have to look down at Kech each time she spoke to him. Then she thought of Dimo, the tall young man who had already distinguished himself as a brave warrior and an outstanding wrestler. Dimo adored Oganda, but Oganda thought he would make a cruel husband, always quarreling and ready to fight. No, she did not like him. Oganda fingered the glittering chain on her waist as she thought of Osinda. A long time ago when she was quite young Osinda had given her that chain, and instead of wearing it around her neck several times, she wore it round her waist where it could stay permanently. She heard her heart pounding so loudly as she thought of him. She whispered, "Let it be you they are discussing, Osinda, the lovely one. Come now and take me away . . . "

The lean figure in the doorway startled Oganda, who was rapt in thought about the man she loved. "You have frightened me, Grandma," said Oganda laughing. "Tell me, is it my marriage you are discussing? You can take it from me that I won't marry any of

them." A smile played on her lips again. She was **coaxing** the old lady to tell her quickly, to tell her they were pleased with Osinda.

In the open space outside the excited relatives were dancing and singing. They were coming to the hut now, each carrying a gift to put at Oganda's feet. As their singing got nearer Oganda was able to hear what they were saying: "If it is to save the people, if it is to give us rain, let Oganda go. Let Oganda die for her people, and for her ancestors." Was she mad to think that they were singing about her? How could she die? She found the lean figure of her grandmother barring the door. She could not get out. The look on her grandmother's face warned her that there was danger around the corner. "Mother, it is not marriage then?" Oganda asked urgently. She suddenly felt panicky like a mouse cornered by a hungry cat. Forgetting that there was only one door in the hut Oganda fought desperately to find another exit. She must fight for her life. But there was none.

She closed her eyes, leapt like a wild tiger through the door, knocking her grandmother flat to the ground. There outside in mourning garments Labong'o stood motionless, his hands folded at the back. He held his daughter's hand and led her away from the excited crowd to the little red-painted hut where her mother was resting. Here he broke the news officially to his daughter.

For a long time the three souls who loved one another dearly sat in darkness. It was no good speaking. And even if they tried, the

---

Setting *How might the setting here symbolize Oganda's dilemma?*   2

Vocabulary

coax (kōks) *v.* to persuade by means of gentle urging or flattery

---

Analyze Cultural Context *In the paragraph that follows, what does Oganda's assessment of possible husbands indicate about Luo marriage customs?*   1

Writing Practice

Write a Character Sketch Call students' attention to this passage: "There was Kech, the son of a neighboring clan elder. Kech was very handsome. He had sweet, meek eyes and a roaring laughter. He would make a wonderful father, Oganda thought." Point out that this passage could be the beginning of a character sketch, a brief description of a character's personality, values, and motivations. Authors often write character sketches in order to develop and explore the characters they will later use in a story. Have students use the details from the story to write a character sketch of either Labong'o or Oganda. Remind students that, while their character sketches should include physical descriptions whenever possible, they should focus primarily on the character's inner qualities.

Bobo Butterfly Mask, Early 20th century. BWA People, Burkina Faso. Pigment on wood, width: 245.1 cm. Collection of Thomas G. B. Wheelock. ★

words could not have come out. In the past they had been like three cooking stones, sharing their burdens. Taking Oganda away from them would leave two useless stones which would not hold a cooking-pot.

Visual Vocabulary
Cooking stones are rocks that support a cooking pot.

News that the beautiful daughter of the chief was to be sacrificed to give the people rain spread across the country like wind. At sunset the chief's village was full of relatives and friends who had come to congratulate Oganda. Many more were on their way coming, carrying their gifts. They would dance till morning to keep her company. And in the morning they would prepare her a big farewell feast. All these relatives thought it a great honor to be selected by the spirits to die, in order that the society may live. "Oganda's name will always remain a living name among us," they boasted.

But was it maternal love that prevented Minya from rejoicing with the other women? Was it the memory of the agony and pain of childbirth that made her feel so sorrowful? Or was it the deep warmth and understanding that passes between a suckling babe and her mother that made Oganda part of her life, her flesh? Of course it was an honor, a great honor, for her daughter to be

chosen to die for the country. But what could she gain once her daughter was blown away by the wind? There were so many other women in the land, why choose her daughter, her only child! Had human life any meaning at all—other women had houses full of children while she, Minya, had to lose her only child!

In the cloudless sky the moon shone brightly, and the numerous stars glittered with a bewitching beauty. The dancers of all age-groups assembled to dance before Oganda, who sat close to her mother, sobbing quietly. All these years she had been with her people she thought she understood them. But now she discovered that she was a stranger among them. If they loved her as they had always professed why were they not making any attempt to save her? Did her people really understand what it felt like to die young? Unable to restrain her emotions any longer, she sobbed loudly as her age-group got up to dance. They were young and beautiful and very soon they would marry and have their own children. They would have husbands to love and little huts for themselves. They would have reached maturity. Oganda touched the chain around her waist as she thought of Osinda. She wished Osinda was there too, among her friends. "Perhaps he is ill," she thought gravely. The chain comforted

---

3 | Analyze Cultural Context *How will Oganda's relatives benefit from her death?*

Tradition and Change *In this passage, how do the traditions of her people affect Oganda's perception of her community?* **4**

GRACE OGOT **113**

Approaching Level

DIFFERENTIATED INSTRUCTION

Shifting Perspective Some students may have difficulty with the way that the narrator switches between the perspectives of multiple characters. Explain to students that third-person narrators have the power to "zoom" in and out, like movie cameras, in order to show the same story from different points of view. Have students identify passages that use this technique to express the inner thoughts and feelings of Labong'o and Oganda.

Teach

Reading Strategy	**3**

Analyze Cultural Context
Answer: *Her relatives will benefit from their blood ties to a community heroine.*

Big Idea	**4**

Tradition and Change
Answer: *The feast, the belief in the honor of her death, and the traditional dances make Oganda question the loyalty and friendships of her people. They adhere to traditions but show little sadness or grief in response to her sacrifice.*

View the Art ★

The Bwa people of Burkina Faso and Mali use wooden masks to honor the nature spirits that affect their daily lives. The concentric circles on the wings probably represent water holes. **Ask: What might this mask represent to its wearer?** *(The mask might represent a connection to the natural world.)*

Learning Objectives
Analyzing setting. (SE)
Analyzing cultural context. (SE)
Writing a character sketch. (TE)

113

Teach

Reading Strategy 1

Analyze Cultural Context
Answer: *The chief wears a "mourning skin" and no shoes. Based on his description as a "simple father," this seems to be a customary mourning outfit, regardless of a person's rank in the community.*

ENGLISH LEARNERS It may help English learners to compare Labong'o's dress and behavior with the ways that people from their own cultures and in the United States express mourning.

Literary Element 2

Setting Answer: *The drought is pervasive as she walks through the "thin dry trees in the forest."*

Reading Strategy 3

Analyze Cultural Context
Answer: *The age-group seems to have some special responsibility for decisions relating to its members.*

Oganda—she would die with it around her waist and wear it in the underground world.

In the morning a big feast was prepared for Oganda. The women prepared many different tasty dishes so that she could pick and choose. "People don't eat after death," they said. Delicious though the food looked, Oganda touched none of it. Let the happy people eat. She contented herself with sips of water from a little calabash. The time for her departure was drawing near, and each minute was precious. It was a day's journey to the lake. She was to walk all night, passing through the great forest. But nothing could touch her, not even the **denizens** of the forest. She was already anointed with sacred oil. From the time Oganda received the sad news she had expected Osinda to appear any moment. But he was not there. A relative told her that Osinda was away on a private visit. Oganda realized that she would never see her beloved again.

In the afternoon the whole village stood at the gate to say good-bye and to see her for the last time. Her mother wept on her neck for a long time. The great chief in a mourning skin came to the gate barefooted, and mingled with the people—a simple father in grief. He took off his wrist bracelet and put it on his daughter's wrist saying, "You will always live among us. The spirit of our forefathers is with you."

Tongue-tied and unbelieving Oganda stood there before the people. She had nothing to say. She looked at her home once more. She could hear her heart beating so painfully within her. All her childhood plans were coming to an end. She felt

like a flower nipped in the bud never to enjoy the morning dew again. She looked at her weeping mother, and whispered, "Whenever you want to see me, always look at the sunset. I will be there."

Oganda turned southwards to start her trek to the lake. Her parents, relatives, friends and admirers stood at the gate and watched her go.

Her beautiful slender figure grew smaller and smaller till she mingled with the thin dry trees in the forest. As Oganda walked the lonely path that wound its way in the wilderness, she sang a song, and her own voice kept her company.

> The ancestors have said Oganda must die
> The daughter of the chief must be
>   sacrificed,
> When the lake monster feeds on my flesh.
> The people will have rain.
> Yes, the rain will come down in torrents.
> And the floods will wash away the sandy
>   beaches
> When the daughter of the chief dies in
>   the lake.
> My age-group has consented
> My parents have consented
> So have my friends and relatives.
> Let Oganda die to give us rain.
> My age-group are young and ripe,
> Ripe for womanhood and motherhood
> But Oganda must die young,
> Oganda must sleep with the ancestors.
> Yes, rain will come down in torrents.

The red rays of the setting sun embraced Oganda, and she looked like a burning candle in the wilderness.

---

1 Analyze Cultural Context *What Luo custom is noted in this passage, and what seems to be its significance?*

Vocabulary
denizen (den'ə zən) n. an inhabitant

Setting *What characteristics of the setting stand out as Oganda leaves the village?* **2**

Analyze Cultural Context *What role does the "age-group" seem to have in Luo society?* **3**

Grammar Practice

Use Coordinating Conjunctions
Remind students that a coordinating conjunction is a word used to connect similar parts of a sentence, such as subjects, predicates, modifiers, and clauses. *And, but, or, nor, for, yet,* and *so* are coordinating conjunctions. Write this sentence on the board: *Her voice was now hoarse <u>and</u> painful, <u>but</u> there was no need to worry any more.* Ask students to identify the elements connected by

the underlined conjunctions. *(predicate adjectives, independent clauses)*

Have students find three additional instances of coordinating conjunctions used in the story. For each conjunction, students should identify what is being joined—words, independent clauses, or phrases.

The people who came to hear her sad song were touched by her beauty. But they all said the same thing: "If it is to save the people, if it is to give us rain, then be not afraid. Your name will forever live among us."

At midnight Oganda was tired and weary. She could walk no more. She sat under a big tree, and having sipped water from her calabash, she rested her head on the tree trunk and slept.

When Oganda woke up in the morning the sun was high in the sky. After walking for many hours, she reached the *tong'*, a strip of land that separated the inhabited part of the country from the sacred place (*kar lamo*). No layman could enter this place and come out alive—only those who had direct contact with the spirits and the Almighty were allowed to enter this holy of holies. But Oganda had to pass through this sacred land on her way to the lake, which she had to reach at sunset.

A large crowd gathered to see her for the last time. Her voice was now hoarse and painful, but there was no need to worry any more. Soon she would not have to sing. The crowd looked at Oganda sympathetically, mumbling words she could not hear. But none of them pleaded for life. As Oganda opened the gate, a child, a young child, broke loose from the crowd, and ran towards her. The child took a small earring from her sweaty hands and gave it to Oganda saying, "When you reach the world of the dead, give this earring to my sister. She died last week. She forgot this ring." Oganda, taken aback by the strange request, took the little ring, and handed her precious water and food to the child. She did not need them now. Oganda did not know whether to laugh or cry. She had heard mourners sending their love to their sweethearts, long dead, but this idea of sending gifts was new to her.

Nighttime Landscape 1. Wendy L. Goldberg-Hammon. Getty collection.

Oganda held her breath as she crossed the barrier to enter the sacred land. She looked appealingly at the crowd, but there was no response. Their minds were too preoccupied with their own survival. Rain was the precious medicine they were longing for, and the sooner Oganda could get to her destination the better.

A strange feeling possessed Oganda as she picked her way in the sacred land. There were strange noises that often startled her, and her first reaction was to take to her heels. But she remembered that she had to fulfill the wish of her people. She was exhausted, but the path was still winding. Then suddenly the path ended on sandy land. The water had retreated miles away from the shore leaving a wide stretch of sand. Beyond this was the vast expanse of water. **4**

Oganda felt afraid. She wanted to picture the size and shape of the monster, but fear would not let her. The society did not talk about it, nor did the crying children who were silenced by the mention of its name. The sun was still up, but it was no longer hot. For a long time Oganda walked ankle-deep in the sand. She was exhausted and longed desperately for her calabash of water. As she moved on, she had a strange feeling **5**

GRACE OGOT **115**

Literary Element 4

Setting Have students read the description of the lake. **Ask:** How does the description of the lake reinforce the need for Oganda to sacrifice herself? *(Because of the drought, the lake is nearly dry; the water has retreated "miles away from the shore.")*

Reading Strategy 5

Question Have students read the final paragraph on the page.
Ask: What is the significance of Oganda's having to go alone through inhospitable country to drown herself? *(It demonstrates that her sacrifice is freely chosen and not compelled by others.)*

Learning Objectives
Analyzing cultural context. (SE)
Analyzing setting. (SE)
Using coordinating conjunctions. (TE)
Questioning. (TE)

Approaching Level

DIFFERENTIATED INSTRUCTION

PARTNERS **Adjust Reading Rate** Struggling readers may find it helpful to pause frequently while reading and review what has just happened. Model this process by giving the following summary of the story's ending: *As Oganda travels through the sacred land, she senses that a "creature" is following her. She begins to run, but the creature catches up to her and grabs her. She faints. When she* wakes up, she realizes that the creature was really one of her suitors, Osinda. Osinda convinces Oganda to escape with him, and as they flee the sacred land, it finally begins to rain. Have struggling students pair with more advanced students and have the pairs work together to summarize other parts of the story.

Advanced Learners/Pre-AP

DIFFERENTIATED INSTRUCTION

Writing Ask more advanced students to try writing an alternative ending for the story. Encourage them to imagine what would have happened if Osinda had not followed Oganda, or if the rain never came to the village. Students should try to imitate Ogot's style in their writing.

Teach

Big Idea   1

Tradition and Change

Answer: *His love for Oganda provokes Osinda to leave his community, persuade Oganda to disobey the rainmaker, and find ways to hide from the ancestors. Oganda means more to him than tradition.*

Literary History ☆

Abraham and Isaac There is a striking similarity between the ending of this story and that of the Biblical story in which God asks Abraham to sacrifice his son, Isaac. In the Bible, God stops Abraham's hand just as he is about to kill his son, revealing that the request was actually a test of Abraham's willingness to obey. Similarly, in "The Rain Came," it appears that Oganda's willingness to sacrifice herself satisfies the Luo deity.

 To check students' understanding of the selection, see Unit 1 Teaching Resources Book, p. 160.

Reading Practice

Analyze Suspense Remind students that suspense is the tension or excitement that a reader feels about what will happen next in a story. Writers often create suspense by raising questions in the reader's mind about the outcome of a conflict. Suspense helps keep readers interested in a story and is especially important in the plots of adventure or mystery stories.

---

that something was following her. Was it the monster? Her hair stood erect, and a cold paralyzing feeling ran along her spine. She looked behind, sideways and in front, but there was nothing, except a cloud of dust.

Oganda pulled up and hurried but the feeling did not leave her, and her whole body became saturated with perspiration.

The sun was going down fast and the lake shore seemed to move along with it.

Oganda started to run. She must be at the lake before sunset. As she ran she heard a noise from behind. She looked back sharply, and something resembling a moving bush was frantically running after her. It was about to catch up with her.

Oganda ran with all her strength. She was now determined to throw herself into the water even before sunset. She did not look back, but the creature was upon her. She made an effort to cry out, as in a nightmare, but she could not hear her own voice. The creature caught up with Oganda. In the utter confusion, as Oganda came face to face with the unidentified creature, a strong hand grabbed her. But she fell flat on the sand and fainted.

When the lake breeze brought her back to consciousness, a man was bending over her. ". . . . . !" Oganda opened her mouth to speak, but she had lost her voice. She swallowed a mouthful of water poured into her mouth by the stranger.

"Osinda, Osinda! Please let me die. Let me run, the sun is going down. Let me die, let them have rain." Osinda fondled the glittering chain around Oganda's waist and wiped the tears from her face.

"We must escape quickly to the unknown land," Osinda said urgently. "We

must run away from the wrath of the ancestors and the **retaliation** of the monster."

"But the curse is upon me, Osinda, I am no good to you any more. And moreover the eyes of the ancestors will follow us everywhere and bad luck will befall us. Nor can we escape from the monster."

Oganda broke loose, afraid to escape, but Osinda grabbed her hands again.

"Listen to me, Oganda! Listen! Here are two coats!" He then covered the whole of Oganda's body, except her eyes, with a leafy attire made from the twigs of *Bwombwe.* "These will protect us from the eyes of the ancestors and the wrath of the monster. Now let us run out of here." He held Oganda's hand and they ran from the sacred land, avoiding the path that Oganda had followed.

The bush was thick, and the long grass entangled their feet as they ran. Halfway through the sacred land they stopped and looked back. The sun was almost touching the surface of the water. They were frightened. They continued to run, now faster, to avoid the sinking sun.

"Have faith, Oganda—that thing will not reach us."

When they reached the barrier and looked behind them trembling, only a tip of the sun could be seen above the water's surface.

"It is gone! It is gone!" Oganda wept, hiding her face in her hands.

"Weep not, daughter of the chief. Let us run, let us escape."

There was a bright lightning. They looked up, frightened. Above them black furious clouds started to gather. They began to run. Then the thunder roared, and the rain came down in torrents. ❧   ☆

---

1 **Tradition and Change** *How might Oganda's possible death have changed the way Osinda views tradition?*

Vocabulary

retaliation (ri tal´ē ā´shən) *n.* revenge

Ask students what suspense they felt early on in "The Rain Came." (*Most students will have felt tension about whether Labong'o will sacrifice Oganda and whether Oganda will agree to the sacrifice.*) Then have students work in pairs to look back over the part of the story that begins when Oganda enters the sacred land. Have them identify the devices that Ogot uses to heighten suspense in the final section of the story.

(*Oganda's feelings of fear heighten suspense, as does her sense of being followed. Suspense is also heightened by her perception that the lake shore is retreating; no matter how fast she runs, she seems to make no progress.*)

Respond and Think Critically

Respond and Interpret

1. What was your reaction to the outcome of the story?

2. (a)According to the medicine man's prophecy, what is the only way to end the drought in Oganda's village? (b)Why does Labong'o obey the prophecy?

3. (a)How do the villagers react when Labong'o tells them about the prophecy? (b)Why does Oganda feel like a stranger among her people during the feast held in her honor?

4. (a)How does Oganda react when she realizes what is planned for her? (b)Do you think Oganda's feelings about her fate change as the story unfolds? Explain.

Analyze and Evaluate

5. (a)An **internal conflict** is a struggle within a character's mind. Describe one internal conflict in "The Rain Came." (b)Is this conflict resolved convincingly? Explain.

6. (a)A **symbol** is an object or an action that stands for something else in addition to itself. What does the brass chain around Oganda's waist symbolize? (b)Do you think this is an effective symbol? Explain.

Connect

7. **Big Idea** **Tradition and Change** What view of Luo tradition does "The Rain Came" offer the reader? Explain.

8. **Connect to Today** What kinds of sacrifices do people today make for the good of their communities?

Daily Life & Culture

Proverbs from Kenya

The oral traditions of African peoples are rich in **proverbs.** These short, vivid sayings express a truth about life or contain a bit of popular wisdom. The following proverbs are from the Luo and Kikuyu peoples, two of the largest ethnic groups in Kenya.

Luo Proverbs

A cowardly hyena lives for many years.

An eye that you treat is the one that turns against you.

The fierce white ants cause the death of the kind and harmless ants.

Kikuyu Proverbs

To get the warmth of fire one must stir the embers.

Darkness caused to dance even him who cannot.

Group Activity Discuss the following questions with your classmates. Refer to the proverbs.

1. The Luo proverb about the ants refers to two species that live together: destructive termites and a species the Luo value as food. What do you think the proverb means?

2. What proverbs do you know that are similar to any of the ones here?

GRACE OGOT **117**

Daily Life & Culture

1. Possible answer: In life, punishing the guilty often involves punishing the innocent as well.

2. Possible answers:
- *A cowardly hyena lives for many years.* ("Better a live dog than a dead lion.")
- *A little, contemptible path is sometimes the one that leads you to the highway.* ("Great oaks from little acorns grow.")
- *To get the warmth of fire one must stir the embers.* ("No pain, no gain.")
- *Darkness caused to dance even him who cannot.* ("In the night all cats are gray.")

After You Read

Assess

1. Many students will be surprised and relieved because Oganda's death seemed inevitable.

2. (a) A young woman who wears a chain around her waist must be sacrificed to the lake monster to bring rain. (b) Labong'o believes that the ancestors require the sacrifice, and he has sworn to sacrifice himself or his family for the good of the people.

3. (a) They rejoice because they will be saved, and they say Oganda is honored to be chosen to die for her people. (b) Oganda's feelings about her sacrifice differ greatly from those of the villagers.

4. (a) She panics and tries to escape. (b) Her gradual acceptance of being sacrificed can be seen in her reaction to the child who gives her a gift for a dead sister and her parting words to her mother.

5. (a) Possible answer: Labong'o is torn between his love for Oganda and his duty as chief (b) Students will probably feel that both these conflicts are resolved convincingly within the context of Luo culture.

6. (a) The chain symbolizes the love between Oganda and Osinda, as well as her link to her people. (b) Most students will probably say that the chain is an effective symbol of Oganda's ties to Osinda and her people.

7. The narrator seems respectful of most Luo traditions but questions the tradition of human sacrifice and its repercussions.

8. Possible answers: Soldiers risk possible death for their country; police officers, firefighters, and rescue workers often take risks to benefit others; people volunteer time to work on community projects.

After You Read

Assess

Literary Element

1. **C** is the correct answer. Chief Labong'o feels it is urgent to sacrifice his daughter, and she feels conflicted. **D** is incorrect because there is order in the village and not chaos. Both **A** and **B** are also incorrect.

2. **F** is correct because both characters must adhere to their village customs. **G** and **J** are incorrect because Oganda does not find hope or want to gain social status. **H** does not apply to the story.

Progress Check

Can students identify the setting?

If No → See Unit 1 Teaching Resources Book, p. 155.

Review: Situational Irony

Sample Answer:

Situational Irony: Oganda escapes her sacrifice.

Expectations: The monster will kill Oganda.

Outcome: Osinda saves Oganda, but the drought ends nonetheless.

Literary Element Setting

ACT Skills Practice

1. The setting of Ogot's "The Rain Came" evokes a mood of
   - **A.** boredom and frustration.
   - **B.** joviality and freedom.
   - **C.** urgency and conflict.
   - **D.** exhilaration and chaos.

2. As members of Luo society, the chief and his daughter
   - **F.** must adhere to its customs.
   - **G.** find hope in its desolation.
   - **H.** must convert outsiders to its culture.
   - **J.** trick people to gain social status.

Review: Situational Irony

As you learned on page 52, **irony** is a discrepancy between reality and appearance or expectations. **Situational irony** occurs when the outcome of a situation is the opposite of what is expected.

Partner Activity With a partner, identify and explain the situational irony in this story. Use a diagram like the one below to record your information.

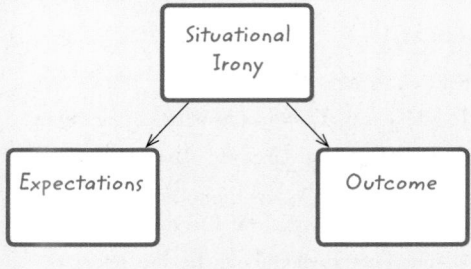

LOG ON ▶ **Literature** Online

Selection Resources For Selection Quizzes, eFlashcards, and Reading-Writing Connection activities, go to glencoe.com and enter QuickPass code GLW6053u1.

118 UNIT 1 MODERN AFRICA

Reading Strategy Analyze Cultural Context

The traditional beliefs and customs of the Luo people shape the narrative of "The Rain Came." Review your chart on cultural context on page 108 and answer the following questions.

1. How would you describe traditional Luo religious beliefs?

2. What is the relationship between the individual and the community in traditional Luo society?

Vocabulary Practice

Practice with Analogies Choose the word that best completes each analogy. Use a dictionary if you need help.

1. consecrate : holy :: sanitize :
   - **a.** lovely   **b.** clean   **c.** small

2. rebuke : commend :: gratify :
   - **a.** disappoint   **b.** tease   **c.** warn

3. coax : force :: offer :
   - **a.** deserve   **b.** metal   **c.** steal

4. denizen : outsider :: enemy :
   - **a.** war   **b.** innocent   **c.** ally

5. retaliation : revenge :: quarantine :
   - **a.** isolation   **b.** freedom   **c.** loneliness

Academic Vocabulary

Oganda's people believe that sacrificing her to the monster will **guarantee** *the end of the drought.*

Guarantee is an academic word. In a commercial setting, a salesperson might say that she will **guarantee** your satisfaction with a product. To further explore the meaning of this word, answer the following question: What are some enterprises in which success is difficult to **guarantee,** and why?

For more on academic vocabulary, see pages 36–37 and R83–R85.

Vocabulary

1. b **2.** a **3.** c **4.** c **5.** a

Academic Vocabulary

Students should name enterprises that involve high risks, such as filmmaking.

Reading Strategy

1. Students' answers should focus on the importance of ancestor worship and the emphasis on prophecies and human sacrifice.

2. Students should note that traditional Luo society values the good of the community over the good of the individual.

Progress Check

Can students analyze cultural context?

If No → See Unit 1 Teaching Resources Book, p. 156.

 For additional selection assessment, see Assessment Resources, pp. 55–56.

Respond Through Writing

Research Report

Investigate Setting A severe drought plays a key role in "The Rain Came." Using this setting as a springboard, research the agriculture, geography, and climate of Kenya and how these factors affect the Luo people. Prepare a research report of 1,500 words or more exploring this topic, using primary and secondary sources for reference.

Understand the Task Primary sources are firsthand accounts, such as diaries or eyewitness news articles. **Secondary sources** are materials written by people who did not influence or experience an event but have studied it.

Prewrite Plan carefully before you begin to research by writing four or five questions about the topic. Then gather the information you need to answer those questions from primary and secondary sources. To help structure your report, make an outline similar to the one below.

I. Lake Victoria and Kenya

   A. Part of the arid and flat East African Rift System

   B. Setting of many of Ogot's stories

II. The Luo people

   A. Agricultural heritage

   B. Participated in Kenya's struggle for independence

Draft Gather evidence to support your thesis from the questions and answers you wrote, making sure to convey information accurately and coherently. Also, be sure to use technical terms such as "East African Rift System" correctly. You should anticipate readers' potential misunderstandings of these terms by including brief explanations.

Revise As you incorporate the information from your notes, evaluate whether the information is relevant. Exchange your paper with a partner and create a checklist to review organization, clarity, and use of language.

Edit and Proofread Proofread your paper, correcting any errors in spelling, grammar, and punctuation. Review the Grammar Tip in the side column for information on how to use parentheses and brackets.

GRACE OGOT **119**

Learning Objectives

In this assignment, you will focus on the following objectives:

Writing: Writing a research report.

Grammar: Using parentheses and brackets

Grammar Tip

Parentheses and Brackets

Parentheses are used to distinguish in-text citations in research papers. They are also used to mark supplemental information in a sentence, as in the following example.

The Owen Falls Dam (now called the Nalubaale Dam) was completed in 1954.

Brackets can be used to provide clarifying information within a quotation, as in the sentence below.

Ogot writes, "He loved his people, the Luo [an ethnic group in western Kenya], but what were the Luo for him without Oganda?"

After You Read

Assess

Respond Through Writing

Students' research reports should

- have a clear thesis supported with evidence from primary and secondary sources
- follow a clear organizational pattern
- use technical terms correctly and anticipate readers' potential misunderstandings of these terms

A student who meets all of these criteria should receive the equivalent of a 4-point response.

A student who fully meets two or partially meets three of these criteria should receive the equivalent of a 3-point response.

A student who fully meets one or partially meets two of these criteria should receive the equivalent of a 2-point response.

A student who partially meets one of these criteria should receive the equivalent of a 1-point response.

 For grammar practice, see Unit 1 Teaching Resources Book, p. 159.

 To create custom assessments online, go to Progress Reporter Online Assessment.

 To create custom assessments using software, use ExamView Assessment Suite.

English Learners

DIFFERENTIATED INSTRUCTION

Intermediate English language learners may find it daunting to conduct research for their reports in English. Help them to select appropriate sources, and suggest that they take notes in their native languages. They may also want to conduct Internet research using sources in their native languages. Help them to determine which parts of the research process would be easier to conduct in their native languages.

Focus

Civilian and Soldier

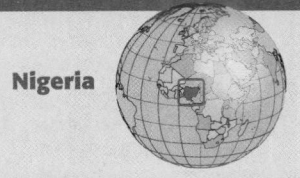

Bellringer Options

**Selection Focus
Transparency 8**

**Daily Language Practice
Transparency 15**

Or ask: What would you do if you could get revenge against a person who had wronged you? Elicit opinions about whether students would get revenge or be forgiving.

Literary History ☆

Reexamining Mythology
Soyinka's childhood education in mythology led him to write later in life about folklore. In the essays that make up *Myth, Literature, and the African World*, he studies the part the artist plays in the mythology of the Yoruban people. In 1973, Soyinka wrote two studies of Greek mythology: the novel *Season of Anomy*, which compares the myth of Orpheus and Eurydice with Yoruban mythology, and the play *The Bacchae of Euripides*, an African adaptation of Euripides' tragedy about the god Dionysus.

Meet **Wole Soyinka**

(born 1934)

Wole Soyinka (wō′lā shoi ān′kä) has earned an international reputation as a distinguished and powerful voice for social change and human rights. His plays, poetry, novels, and essays have not only brought the beautiful traditions and folklore of Africa to the world, but they have also exposed Nigeria's struggles with colonial rule, dictatorship, modernization, civil war, oppression, and injustice.

Between Tradition and Modernization
Born in Nigeria when it was under British rule, Soyinka is the son of educators who supported colonial ideas. Early in his childhood, he recognized the conflicting cultures that surrounded him: African tradition versus British modernization. When Soyinka's father recommended that he attend a government school, Soyinka's grandfather intervened. He believed that his grandson should live by the Yoruban traditions and customs of his people, so he taught his grandson about the Yoruba gods and folklore. These lessons greatly influenced Soyinka's life and writing.

The Voice of Truth At the start of the Nigerian civil war in 1967, Soyinka was falsely imprisoned for two years, spending most of that time in solitary confinement. To preserve his sanity, Soyinka manufactured his own ink and began a diary using anything he could find to write on—toilet paper, cigarette packages, and book pages. These notes were later published in *The Man Died: Prison Notes of Wole Soyinka*, which is considered one of the most significant works ever written about the Biafran war. Soyinka was released in 1969. Nearly three decades later, Soyinka, living in self-imposed exile, was charged with treason and sentenced to death for criticizing the Nigerian government. He was later granted amnesty by a new Nigerian government. In 1986, Soyinka became the first African to receive the Nobel Prize in Literature.

> "My *writing grows more and more preoccupied with the theme of the oppressive boot, the irrelevance of the color of the foot that wears it and the struggle for individuality.*"
>
> —Wole Soyinka

LOG ON ▶ **Literature** Online

Author Search For more about Wole Soyinka, go to glencoe.com and enter QuickPass code GLW6053u1.

Selection Skills

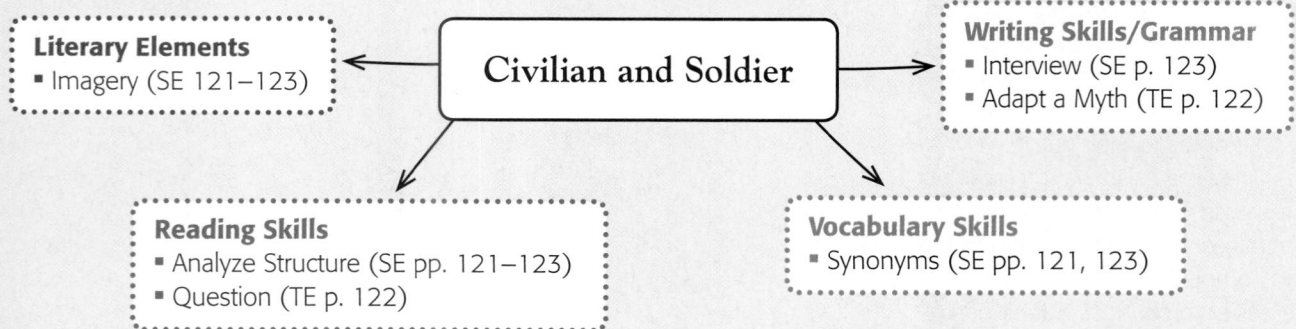

Literary Elements
- Imagery (SE 121–123)

← **Civilian and Soldier** →

Writing Skills/Grammar
- Interview (SE p. 123)
- Adapt a Myth (TE p. 122)

Reading Skills
- Analyze Structure (SE pp. 121–123)
- Question (TE p. 122)

Vocabulary Skills
- Synonyms (SE pp. 121, 123)

Literature and Reading Preview

Connect to the Poem

What does freedom mean to you? With a partner, discuss which aspects of freedom you believe to be crucial.

Build Background

Since gaining independence from Britain in 1960, Nigeria has experienced ethnic and religious conflict. Thousands of Ibo living in the north were massacred in 1966 during a military revolt against the civilian government. In 1967, the Ibo declared their traditional homeland in the eastern region to be the independent Republic of Biafra, and Nigeria plunged into civil war. "Civilian and Soldier" belongs to a group of six poems Soyinka wrote during the buildup to the war.

Set Purposes for Reading

Big Idea **Living with Independence**

As you read, ask yourself, How does the relationship between the civilian and the soldier highlight the struggles African countries faced in the shift to independence?

Literary Element **Imagery**

Imagery refers to the "word pictures" that authors create to evoke emotional responses. In creating effective images, authors use **sensory details,** or descriptions that appeal to one or more of the five senses. As you read Soyinka's poem, ask yourself, How does the imagery depict the civilian and the soldier?

Reading Strategy **Analyze Structure**

To **analyze structure** means to focus on the form of a poem and determine how this form relates to the poem's effect and meaning. Structure can include rhythm, rhyme, line breaks, and punctuation. As you read, ask yourself, How does the structure of this poem contribute to its effect?

Tip: Take Notes Create diagrams like the one below to analyze the structure of "Civilian and Soldier."

Detail	Effect
"I'm a civilian."	The quotation marks emphasize the thoughts of the speaker and his status as a civilian.

Learning Objectives

For pages 120–123

In studying this text, you will focus on the following objectives:

Literary Study: Analyzing imagery.

Reading: Analyzing structure.

Writing: Writing an interview.

Vocabulary

aggravate (ag′rə vāt′) *v.* to make something worse; p. 122 *Eating sugar will only aggravate your cavities.*

impartial (im pär′shəl) *adj.* treating everyone or everything in an equal way; p. 122 *The jury should act as an impartial observer when hearing the facts of a case.*

dubious (do͞o′bē əs) *adj.* of a questionable nature; p. 122 *His dubious plan to sneak out after dark would only get him in trouble.*

plight (plīt) *n.* a situation that is hard to manage or resolve; p. 122 *Many passengers faced the plight of being stranded at the airport.*

Tip: Synonyms Synonyms are words that have nearly the same meaning. For example, the words *impartial* and *fair* are synonyms that describe someone who is unbiased. Synonyms are always the same part of speech.

Before You Read

Focus

Summary

The ghost of a recently killed civilian addresses the soldier who shot him. As he dies, the civilian thinks of how, if their roles were to be reversed someday, he would "shoot" the soldier with food, drink, and hospitality.

 For summaries in languages other than English, see Unit 1 Teaching Resources Book, pp. 162–167.

Vocabulary

Synonyms Divide your class into groups of four. Instruct them to, for each vocabulary word, go around in a circle, allowing each student ten seconds to come up with a synonym for the word until one of the group's members is unable to think of one which has not yet been said. Then have them write down the best synonyms their group came up with and present them to the class.

For additional vocabulary practice, see Unit 1 Teaching Resources Book, p. 170.

WOLE SOYINKA **121**

Advanced Learners/Pre-AP
DIFFERENTIATED INSTRUCTION

Apply Form Give advanced students copies of poems that have regular metrical structures and end-stopped lines. Tell them to rearrange the poem, using Soyinka's as a model, to give it new meaning without changing its content. They may alter the line endings, play with spacing, break up stanzas, or do anything else they might think of, so long as they do not change the poem's content.

Approaching Level
DIFFERENTIATED INSTRUCTION

Read Aloud In order to help students identify the distinguishing structural elements of the poem, have them read it aloud as a group, with each student reading one line. Ask students if there were any moments where the switch from reader to reader seemed odd. Have students identify those moments and ask why Soyinka might have chosen to place a line break there. Did the unusual breaks affect the students in any particular way?

Teach

Reading Strategy 1

Question Have students read the first stanza of the poem.

Ask: Who is the speaker and who is being addressed? (*The civilian speaks. The soldier is being addressed.*)

(**ADVANCED**) For advanced learners, ask from which point of view the poem is told. (*The poem is told from the first-person point of view.*)

Reading Strategy 2

Analyze Structure
Answer: *The indentation focuses the reader's attention on the action of the soldier and gives it more importance.*

Progress Check

Can students analyze structure?

If No → See Unit 1 Teaching Resources Book, p. 169.

Literary Element 3

Imagery Answer: *Soyinka depicts a nonviolent encounter by inverting images of violence to show how the hospitable civilian will "shoot" with food and drink.*

View the Art ★

The southeast African nation of Mozambique endured a devastating civil war from the mid-1970s into the 1990s. Point out that the actual width of this mural is 95 meters. Ask students to name a familiar object that is about this same width. (*a football or soccer field*)

122

Civilian and Soldier

Wole Soyinka

Civil war. Mural, Length: 95m. Mozambique, Maputo, Africa. ★

1
My apparition rose from the fall of lead,
Declared, "I'm a civilian." It only served
To **aggravate** your fright. For how could I
Have risen, a being of this world, in that hour
5 Of **impartial** death! And I thought also: nor is
Your quarrel of this world.

              You stood still
For both eternities, and oh I heard the lesson
Of your training sessions, cautioning—
Scorch earth behind you, do not leave
10 A **dubious** neutral to the rear. Reiteration
Of my civilian quandary, burrowing earth
From the lead festival of your more eager friends
Worked the worse on your confusion, and when
You brought the gun to bear on me, and death
15 Twitched me gently in the eye, your **plight**
And all of you came clear to me.

              I hope some day
Intent upon my trade of living, to be checked
In stride by *your* apparition in a trench,
Signaling, I am a soldier. No hesitation then
20 But I shall shoot you clean and fair
With meat and bread, a gourd of wine
A bunch of breasts from either arm, and that
Lone question—do you friend, even now, know
What it is all about?

2 **Analyze Structure** *What is the effect of this line's indentation?*

3 **Imagery** *What is the meaning of the imagery Soyinka uses in these lines?*

122 UNIT 1 MODERN AFRICA

Vocabulary

aggravate (ag′rə vāt′) *v.* to make something worse
impartial (im pär′shəl) *adj.* treating everyone or everything in an equal way
dubious (dōō′bē əs) *adj.* of a questionable nature
plight (plīt) *n.* a situation that is hard to manage or resolve

Writing Practice

Adapt a Myth After being released from prison, Soyinka wrote his own adaptation of Euripides' tragedy about Dionysus and his followers, *Bacchae*. Soyinka's play places the plot of the classical Greek drama into the setting of Africa. In his play, he relates another culture's mythology to his own cultural background and experience.

Have students research folktales from other cultures using a library or the Internet. Instruct them to choose a folktale or myth from a culture outside their own and write a short adaptation of it in which they place the myth in their own cultural setting.

Respond and Think Critically

Respond and Interpret

1. How did you feel about war after reading "Civilian and Soldier"?

2. (a)Describe the encounter between the speaker and the soldier in the poem. (b)What is the soldier's initial reaction to this encounter?

3. (a)What does the speaker imagine happening in a future life? (b)What does this fantasy say about the speaker's attitude?

Analyze and Evaluate

4. Do you think the speaker considers the soldier to be an evil person? Explain.

5. How does the title, "Civilian and Soldier," illustrate Soyinka's concern about "the struggle for individuality"?

Connect

6. **Big Idea** **The Price of Freedom** How does the conflict in the poem relate to the struggles African countries faced in the shift to independence?

7. **Connect to the Author** Soyinka was raised to value both European ideas and the beliefs of his African ancestors. How might the speaker's relationship to the soldier reflect Soyinka's ability to mesh two belief systems?

Literary Element **Imagery**

Imagery is language an author uses to appeal to the reader's senses.

1. What images does the speaker use to describe being shot?

2. Which image did you find most confusing or difficult in the poem? Why?

Reading Strategy **Analyze Structure**

When you analyze a poem's **structure,** you gain insight into the poem's meaning and the poet's purpose. Review the chart you made on page 121 and then answer the following questions.

1. What is significant about the structure of the first sentence in the poem?

2. Do you think the structure of the last line reinforces the theme of the poem? Why or why not?

LOG ON ▶ **Literature** Online

Selection Resources For Selection Quizzes, eFlashcards, and Reading-Writing Connection activities, go to glencoe.com and enter QuickPass code GLW6053u1.

Vocabulary Practice

Practice with Synonyms With a partner, brainstorm three synonyms for each boldfaced vocabulary word below. Then choose one synonym and explain how its connotation, or implied meaning, differs from that of the vocabulary word.

aggravate   impartial   dubious   plight

EXAMPLE: guile

Synonyms: cunning, treachery, trickery

Sample explanation: Both *guile* and *treachery* imply deceit, but *treachery* has a more negative connotation.

Writing

Write an Interview Imagine you are about to interview the soldier many years later. Write a list of questions you would ask him and his imagined responses.

---

1. Answers may vary. Some students find it depressing.

2. (a) The soldier shot and killed the civilian, who has risen from his body to speak to the soldier. (b) The soldier is frightened and stands still.

3. (a) He envisions sharing food and drink with the soldier. (b) He is forgiving and peaceful.

4. No, since he offers to break bread with him and questions whether he really understands the fight.

5. The poem depicts how war can dehumanize people.

6. It highlights the way civilians were often caught up in military and political struggles.

7. The speaker also believes that differences in opinion can be overcome.

Literary Element

1. "You brought the gun to bear on me, and death/Twitched me gently in the eye."

2. Students' answers may vary; many students may have read the first and second stanzas more than once to understand the imagery.

Progress Check

Can students identify imagery?

If No → See Unit 1 Teaching Resources Book, p. 168.

Writing

Students' interviews should
- ask clear, direct questions
- have thoughtful, imaginative responses

Reading Strategy

1. It splits at "the fall of lead," focusing on how the "apparition" died; the next line begins with "Declared," which highlights the poem's supernatural elements.

2. Answers will vary; students should recognize that isolating the civilian's question draws focus to it and highlights its importance.

Vocabulary

Sample answers; explanations will vary:

aggravate: enhance, inflame, increase

impartial: unbiased, just, neutral

dubious: debatable, questionable, suspicious

plight: predicament, situation, dilemma

📁 **For additional selection assessment, see Assessment Resources, pp. 57–58.**

Bellringer Options

**Selection Focus
 Transparency 9**
**Daily Language Practice
 Transparency 16**

Or ask: What were some similarities and differences between apartheid in South Africa and segregation in the United States? Discuss with students the similarities of government sanctioned racial divisions and the more punitive nature of the apartheid system.
Or ask: Do prisoners have the right to be treated justly? Why or why not? Ask students to support their arguments with evidence from outside examples from the news media.

Before You Read

Botswana

The Prisoner Who Wore Glasses

Meet **Bessie Head**
(1937–1986)

From her own troubled life, Bessie Head discovered a means of conveying racial oppression and sexist discrimination in a way that was deeply personal rather than overtly political. In fact, her themes extend past the borders of South Africa and Botswana to become enduring, universal messages about freedom and equality, alienation, the individual's responsibility to society, and the abuse of power and authority. Head noted that "Every story or book starts with something just for myself. Then from that small me it becomes a panorama—the big view that has something for everyone."

"We black Africans did not know who or what we were, apart from objects of abuse and exploitation."

—Bessie Head

A Difficult Beginning Head was born in a South African mental hospital to an upper-class white woman who had been declared "insane" because of her relationship with Head's father, a black servant. Their relationship was illegal under apartheid, a system designed to maintain white dominance by segregating the black community, which was three-quarters of South Africa's population. As a result, Head grew up in a foster family and later in an orphanage, where she was trained to be a teacher. She disliked teaching, however, and became a journalist for the African magazine *Drum*. In 1964, she decided she could no longer live under the oppression of apartheid, and she and her infant son moved north to Botswana, where they were declared political refugees. She eventually found a sense of peace in the refugee community, despite living in poverty and feeling alienated.

A Life's Work Head used African oral traditions, folklore, and aspects of village life for inspiration. While examining apartheid and exile in her work, Head also considered the power of love and the potential for good in the face of evil. She believed "that love is really good . . . and . . . that it is important to be an ordinary person. More than anything else I want to be noble."

In her short life, Head wrote three novels and numerous short stories, articles, and essays, culminating in a personal glimpse into South African apartheid and African life.

 Literature Online

Author Search For more about Bessie Head, go to glencoe.com and enter QuickPass code GLW6053u1.

Skills Practice

Literary Elements
- Character (SE pp. 125, 128, 130, 131)
- Motivation (SE p. 131)

Reading Skills
- Identify Assumptions (SE pp. 125, 127, 132)

The Prisoner Who Wore Glasses

Vocabulary Skills
- Word Origins (SE p. 132)
- Academic Vocabulary (SE p. 132)

Speaking/Listening/Viewing Skills
- Debate (SE p. 132)

Writing Skills/ Grammar
- Use Transitive and Intransitive Verbs (TE p. 128)

Literature and Reading Preview

Connect to the Story

Have you ever seen someone treat others unfairly? Freewrite for a few minutes about this injustice.

Build Background

In the 1600s, a Dutch colony was established in what is now South Africa. Dutch descendants known as Afrikaners instituted the forced segregation policy of apartheid, which lasted until 1990. "The Prisoner Who Wore Glasses" takes place during apartheid and is based on a true story Head heard from a South African refugee.

Set Purposes for Reading

Big Idea The Price of Freedom

As you read, ask yourself, How do the prisoners uphold their beliefs against a racist, unjust government?

Literary Element Character

Literary **characters** can be classified as round or flat, and as dynamic or static. A **round character** shows varied and sometimes contradictory traits, whereas a **flat character** reveals only one personality trait. A **dynamic character** changes during a story, but a **static character** remains basically the same. As you read, ask yourself, What types of characters are Brille and Hannetjie?

Reading Strategy Identify Assumptions

When you **identify assumptions,** you recognize the beliefs held by the author or characters and how those beliefs impact the story. As you read, ask yourself, What assumptions does Head make about the relationship between prisoners and guards, and what assumptions do Brille and Hannetjie make about each other?

Tip: Track Assumptions Use a chart like the one below to track assumptions and evaluate their validity and importance.

Assumption	Validity	Importance
Hannetjie assumes that guards can easily intimidate prisoners.	The guards intimidated most prisoners.	Brille will not let the guards intimidate him.

Learning Objectives

For pages 124–132

In studying this text, you will focus on the following objectives:

Literary Study: Analyzing character.

Reading: Identifying assumptions.

Listening and Speaking: Conducting a debate.

Vocabulary

obscure (əb skyoor′) *v.* to hide from view; p. 126 *The high rows of hedges obscure the house.*

assertive (ə sur′tiv) *adj.* bold; forceful in a confident way; p. 127 *She was so assertive that she could approach anyone without feeling shy.*

bedlam (bed′ləm) *n.* a state of uproar or confusion; p. 128 *With six children, the bedlam in the house never ceased.*

cunningly (kun′ing lē) *adv.* cleverly; sneakily; p. 130 *John cunningly tricked Ted into thinking he wasn't late by telling him his watch was fast.*

Tip: Word Origins Understanding a word's origin can help you learn the meaning of a new word or phrase. For example, *cunningly* comes from the base word *cunning,* which derives from the Middle English word *connen,* meaning "to know."

Before You Read

Focus

Summary

Brille, a political prisoner in a South African prison and a member of Span One, is a small and unassuming man. When he encounters the brutal new guard, Jacobus Hannetjie, however, he shows extraordinary courage. Hannetjie makes life miserable for Span One. After catching Hannetjie stealing fertilizer, Brille reports him for theft. Eventually, Hannetjie becomes the best guard the prisoners have ever had, with some coercion from Brille, and Span One works hard for Hannetjie.

 For summaries in languages other than English, see Unit 1 Teaching Resources Book, pp. 174–179.

Vocabulary

Cue and Respond Ask students to read the words and their definitions on page 125. Then ask them to work in pairs with one person listening and the other responding to cues; they should switch roles with each cue. Give them these cues:

- Deliver an <u>assertive</u> statement.
- Make an <u>obscure</u> reference.
- Act <u>cunningly</u>.
- Describe how the class would behave in a state of <u>bedlam</u>.

 For additional vocabulary practice, see Unit 1 Teaching Resources Book, p. 182.

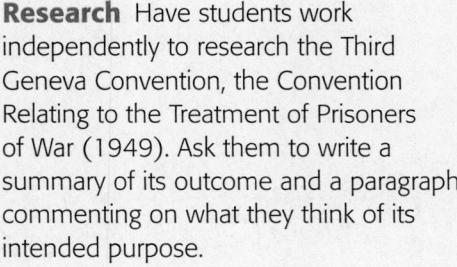

Advanced Learners/Pre-AP

DIFFERENTIATED INSTRUCTION

Research Have students work independently to research the Third Geneva Convention, the Convention Relating to the Treatment of Prisoners of War (1949). Ask them to write a summary of its outcome and a paragraph commenting on what they think of its intended purpose.

Teach

Literary Element | 1

Style Have students read the first paragraph of the story.
Ask: What does the author's word choice and use of imagery in these sentences reveal about the attitude, or tone, she takes toward her subject and characters? *(The author is building a contrast between a serene picture of nature and the lives of prisoners in a working camp situation. She also paints a picture of the prisoner who wore glasses as an anomaly amongst the prisoners because he has hope.)* ADVANCED

 For an audio recording of this selection, use Listening Library Audio CD-ROM.

Readability Scores

Dale-Chall: 8.1
DRP: 58
Lexile: 800

Reading Practice

Make Predictions Explain to students that the use of clues by the author to prepare readers for events that will happen in a story is foreshadowing. Ask them to reread the passages on this page. As they read, have them identify phrases that give them clues about what might happen next. Copy the graphic organizer below to the board. Complete it with their predictions about the story's plot and character development.

The Prisoner Who Wore Glasses

Bessie Head

1 Scarcely a breath of wind disturbed the stillness of the day and the long rows of cabbages were bright green in the sunlight. Large white clouds drifted slowly across the deep blue sky. Now and then they **obscured** the sun and caused a chill on the backs of the prisoners who had to work all day long in the cabbage field. This trick the clouds were playing with the sun eventually caused one of the prisoners who wore glasses to stop work, straighten up and peer shortsightedly at them. He was a thin little fellow with a hollowed out chest and comic knobbly knees. He also had a lot of fanciful ideas because he smiled at the clouds.

"Perhaps they want me to send a message to the children," he thought, tenderly, noting that the clouds were drifting in the direction of his home some hundred miles away. But before he could frame the message, the warder[1] in charge of his work span shouted: "Hey, what do you think you're doing, Brille?"

The prisoner swung round, blinking rapidly, yet at the same time sizing up the enemy. He was a new warder, named Jacobus Stephanus Hannetjie. His eyes were the color of the sky but they were

Vocabulary

obscure (əb skyoor´) *v.* to hide from view

_____

1. A *warder* is a prison guard.

Clues	Predictions

frightening. A simple, primitive, brutal soul gazed out of them. The prisoner bent down quickly and a message was quietly passed down the line: "We're in for trouble this time, comrades."

"Why?" rippled back up the line.

"Because he's not human," the reply rippled down and yet only the crunching of the spades as they turned over the earth disturbed the stillness.

This particular work span was known as Span One. It was composed of ten men and they were all political prisoners. They were grouped together for convenience as it was one of the prison regulations that no black warder should be in charge of a political prisoner lest this prisoner convert him to his view. It never seemed to occur to the authorities that this very reasoning was the strength of Span One and a clue to the strange terror they aroused in the warders. As political prisoners they were unlike the other prisoners in the sense that they felt no guilt nor were they outcasts of society. All guilty men instinctively cower, which was why it was the kind of prison where men got knocked out cold with a blow at the back of the head from an iron bar. Up until the arrival of Warder Hannetjie, no warder had dared beat any member of Span One and no warder had lasted more than a week with them. The battle was entirely psychological. Span One was **assertive** and it was beyond the scope of white warders to handle assertive black men. Thus, Span One had got out of control. They were the best thieves and liars in the camp. They

lived all day on raw cabbages. They chatted and smoked tobacco. And since they moved, thought and acted as one, they had perfected every technique of group concealment.

Trouble began that very day between Span One and Warder Hannetjie. It was because of the shortsightedness of Brille. That was the nickname he was given in prison and is the Afrikaans[2] word for someone who wears glasses. Brille could never judge the approach of the prison gates and on several occasions he had munched on cabbages and dropped them almost at the feet of the warder and all previous warders had overlooked this. Not so Warder Hannetjie.

"Who dropped that cabbage?" he thundered.

Brille stepped out of line.

"I did," he said meekly.

"All right," said Hannetjie. "The whole Span goes three meals off."

"But I told you I did it," Brille protested.

The blood rushed to Warder Hannetjie's face.

"Look 'ere," he said. "I don't take orders from a kaffir.[3] I don't know what kind of kaffir you think you are. Why don't you say Baas.[4] I'm your Baas. Why don't you say Baas, hey?"

Brille blinked his eyes rapidly but by contrast his voice was strangely calm.

"I'm twenty years older than you," he said. It was the first thing that came to mind but the comrades seemed to think it a huge joke. A titter swept up the line. The

---

2 Identify Assumptions *What assumptions does Head make about political prisoners?*

Vocabulary

assertive (ə sur′tiv) *adj.* bold; forceful in a confident way

---

2. *Afrikaans* is a language derived from Dutch that is spoken by Afrikaners. It is one of the official languages of South Africa.
3. Usually used disparagingly, *kaffir* (kaf′ ər) is a term for a black South African.
4. *Baas* is a form of address meaning "master" or "boss."

BESSIE HEAD **127**

Teach

Reading Strategy | 2

Identify Assumptions
Answer: *Head assumes that political prisoners do not feel guilty or ashamed for being in prison. She also assumes that they are unlike other types of criminals in that they are not viewed as outcasts by society.*

Cultural History ☆
Cultural Oppression By narrowly defining race and grouping people according to blanket identity labels, apartheid oppressed the distinct cultural heritage of many different types of people. It defined racial groups as the following: "Blacks," or indigenous San, Zulu, and Khoekhoe people; "Coloreds," or mixed-raced people; ethnic Asians; and "Whites," or Caucasian people of mainly Dutch or British descent.

Learning Objectives
Identifying assumptions. (SE)
Understanding style. (TE)
Making predictions. (TE)

English Learners

DIFFERENTIATED INSTRUCTION

Beginning Explain the term *Afrikaners,* or Dutch descendants. Help students to identify which characters are black and which characters are white Afrikaners. Have them create a graphic showing the warder and the ten prisoners of Span One, along with the race of each. Then have students work with partners to develop brief character descriptions of Hannetjie and Brille.

Advanced Learners/Pre-AP

DIFFERENTIATED INSTRUCTION

Writing Ask students to work independently to write essays comparing apartheid in South Africa with segregation in the United States. Focus each student on one perspective of the topic, such as history, legal aspects, social aspects, political aspects, impact on individuals, or current status.

127

Teach

Big Idea   1

The Price of Freedom

Answer: *They have accepted that they are united by their beliefs and their imprisonment together. Imprisonment is the price they must pay for fighting for freedom.*

Literary Element   2

Character **Answer:** *This background provides the reader with information about Brille's thoughts and experiences to give him more depth and make him a round character.*

Big Idea   3

The Price of Freedom

Answer: *Brille questions whether his decisions in politics were the right ones. His message suggests that his children's lives will be easier if they comply and be good rather than fight all the time.*

Visual Vocabulary
A *knobkerrie* is a short, wooden club with a heavy round knob at one end. It is used as a weapon in South Africa, particularly by the Zulu people.

next thing Warder Hannetjie whipped out a knobkerrie and gave Brille several blows about the head. What surprised his comrades was the speed with which Brille had removed his glasses or else they would have been smashed to pieces on the ground.

That evening in the cell Brille was very apologetic.

"I'm sorry, comrades," he said. "I've put you into a hell of a mess."

"Never mind, brother," they said. "What happens to one of us, happens to all."

"I'll try to make up for it, comrades," he said. "I'll steal something so that you don't go hungry."

Privately, Brille was very philosophical about his head wounds. It was the first time an act of violence had been perpetrated against him but he had long been a witness of extreme, almost unbelievable human brutality. He had twelve children and his mind traveled back that evening through the sixteen years of **bedlam** in which he had lived. It had all happened in a small drab little three-bedroomed house in a small drab little street in the Eastern Cape, and the children kept coming year after year because neither he nor Martha ever managed the contraceptives the right way, and a teacher's salary never allowed moving

to a bigger house, and he was always taking exams to improve his salary only to have it all eaten up by hungry mouths. Everything was pretty horrible, especially the way the children fought. They'd get hold of each other's heads and give them a good bashing against the wall. Martha gave up somewhere along the line so they worked out a thing between them. The bashings, biting and blood were to operate in full swing until he came home. He was to be the bogeyman[5] and when it worked he never failed to have a sense of godhead at the way in which his presence could change savages into fairly reasonable human beings.

Yet somehow it was this chaos and mismanagement at the center of his life that drove him into politics. It was really an ordered beautiful world with just a few basic slogans to learn along with the rights of mankind. At one stage, before things became very bad, there were conferences to attend, all very far away from home.

"Let's face it," he thought ruefully. "I'm only learning right now what it means to be a politician. All this while I've been running away from Martha and the kids."

And the pain in his head brought a hard lump to his throat. That was what the children did to each other daily and Martha wasn't managing and if Warder Hannetjie had not interrupted him that morning he would have sent the following message: "Be good comrades, my children. Cooperate, then life will run smoothly."

---

5. A *bogeyman* is a terrifying or dreaded person.

---

1   **The Price of Freedom** *What have the members of Span One accepted about their choices and their fate?*

Vocabulary

bedlam (bed′ləm) *n.* a state of uproar or confusion

Character *Why do you think Head describes Brille's life before he was a prisoner?*   **2**

The Price of Freedom *What reason might Brille have for wanting to send this message to his children?*   **3**

Grammar Practice

Transitive and Intransitive Verbs
Explain that when an action verb conveys action to a direct object, it is transitive. When an action verb has no direct object, it is intransitive. Write these sentences on the board: "The next day Warder Hannetjie caught this old man of twelve children stealing grapes from the farm shed." "Brille smiled." Explain that *caught* is transitive because it takes a direct object—in this case *old man*. *Smiled* is

intransitive because it has no direct object. Ask students to find three more examples of each kind of verb in the story. For each transitive verb, ask them to identify both the verb and its direct object.

The next day Warder Hannetjie caught this old man of twelve children stealing grapes from the farm shed. They were an enormous quantity of grapes in a ten gallon tin and for this misdeed the old man spent a week in the isolation cell. In fact, Span One as a whole was in constant trouble. Warder Hannetjie seemed to have eyes at the back of his head. He uncovered the trick about the cabbages, how they were split in two with the spade and immediately covered with earth and then unearthed again and eaten with split-second timing. He found out how tobacco smoke was beaten into the ground and he found out how conversations were whispered down the wind.

For about two weeks Span One lived in acute misery. The cabbages, tobacco and conversations had been the pivot of jail life to them. Then one evening they noticed that their good old comrade who wore the glasses was looking rather pleased with himself. He pulled out a four ounce packet of tobacco by way of explanation and the comrades fell upon it with great greed. Brille merely smiled. After all, he was the father of many children. But when the last shred had disappeared, it occurred to the comrades that they ought to be puzzled. Someone said: "I say, brother. We're watched like hawks these days. Where did you get the tobacco?"

"Hannetjie gave it to me," said Brille.

There was a long silence. Into it dropped a quiet bombshell.

4 "I saw Hannetjie in the shed today," and the failing eyesight blinked rapidly. "I caught him in the act of stealing five bags of fertilizer and he bribed me to keep my mouth shut."

There was another long silence.

Dogon pendant of a seated prisoner. Mali. Bronze. Private collection.

"Prison is an evil life," Brille continued, apparently discussing some irrelevant matter. "It makes a man contemplate all kinds of evil deeds."

He held out his hand and closed it.

"You know, comrades," he said. "I've got Hannetjie. I'll betray him tomorrow."

Everyone began talking at once.

"Forget it, brother. You'll get shot."

Brille laughed.

"I won't," he said. "That is what I mean about evil. I am a father of children and I saw today that Hannetjie is just a child and stupidly truthful. I'm going to punish him severely because we need a good warder."

The Price of Freedom *Do you think Brille is justified in going back on his word to Hannetjie? Why or why not?* **5**

BESSIE HEAD **129**

Teach

Literary Element   4

Situational Irony Explain that the conflict between reality and appearance or expectations is irony. Define situational irony as when what actually happens is the opposite of what is expected. **Ask:** What in this passage reveals situational irony, and why? (*Hannetjie, who enforces the law, was caught breaking the law. In order to protect himself, he takes part in a bribe.*)

Big Idea   5

The Price of Freedom
Answer: *Most students will probably say Brille's actions are justified because he has been treated poorly and is trying to ensure that he and the other inmates of Span One are treated fairly.*

View the Art

The Dogon people of the central Mali plateaus have rich traditions of art and mythology. **Ask:** What event in the story might this sculpture best represent? (*Brille's time in an isolation cell*)

English Learners
DIFFERENTIATED INSTRUCTION

Intermediate Identify idiomatic and figurative phrases on this page, including "have eyes at the back of his head," "We're watched like hawks these days," and "I caught him in the act of stealing." Invite volunteers to interpret what these phrases mean. Prompt them with such questions or statements as "What could you do if you had eyes in the back of your head?" "How do hawks watch their prey?" or "Think about what the words *caught* and *act* mean."

Advanced Learners/Pre-AP
DIFFERENTIATED INSTRUCTION

Research Have students investigate the issue of political prisoners—prisoners held for their dissident political opinions. Each student should work independently to find an article in a magazine or a newspaper, or on the Internet, about political prisoners somewhere in the world. Have each student summarize an article and then make some general comments about what they think about political imprisonment.

Learning Objectives
Analyzing character. (SE)
Analyzing situational irony. (TE)
Using transitive and intransitive verbs. (TE)

Teach

Literary Element | 1

Character Answer:
Hannetjie loses his nerve after Brille gets him into trouble with the commander. He realizes that he and Brille cannot keep antagonizing each other and talks to Brille about a solution. Hannetjie is a round, dynamic character.

Progress Check

Can students identify types of characters?

If No → See Unit 1 Teaching Resources Book, p. 180.

 To check students' understanding of the selection, see Unit 1 Teaching Resources Book, p. 185.

The following day, with Brille as witness, Hannetjie confessed to the theft of the fertilizer and was fined a large sum of money. From then on Span One did very much as they pleased while Warder Hannetjie stood by and said nothing. But it was Brille who carried this to extremes. One day, at the close of work Warder Hannetjie said: "Brille, pick up my jacket and carry it back to the camp."

"But nothing in the regulations says I'm your servant, Hannetjie," Brille replied coolly.

"I've told you not to call me Hannetjie. You must say Baas," but Warder Hannetjie's voice lacked conviction. In turn, Brille squinted up at him.

"I'll tell you something about this Baas business, Hannetjie," he said. "One of these days we are going to run the country. You are going to clean my car. Now, I have a fifteen year old son and I'd die of shame if you had to tell him that I ever called you Baas."

Warder Hannetjie went red in the face and picked up his coat.

On another occasion Brille was seen to be walking about the prison yard, openly smoking tobacco. On being taken before the prison commander he claimed to have received the tobacco from Warder Hannetjie. Throughout the tirade from his chief, Warder Hannetjie failed to defend himself but his nerve broke completely. He called Brille to one side.

"Brille," he said. "This thing between you and me must end. You may not know it but I have a wife and children and you're driving me to suicide."

"Why don't you like your own medicine, Hannetjie?" Brille asked quietly.

"I can give you anything you want," Warder Hannetjie said in desperation.

"It's not only me but the whole of Span One," said Brille, **cunningly**. "The whole of Span One wants something from you."

Warder Hannetjie brightened with relief.

"I think I can manage if it's tobacco you want," he said.

Brille looked at him, for the first time struck with pity, and guilt.

He wondered if he had carried the whole business too far. The man was really a child.

"It's not tobacco we want, but you," he said. "We want you on our side. We want a good warder, because without a good warder we won't be able to manage the long stretch ahead."

Warder Hannetjie interpreted this request in his own fashion and his interpretation of what was good and human often left the prisoners of Span One speechless with surprise. He had a way of slipping off his revolver and picking up a spade and digging alongside Span One. He had a way of producing unheard of luxuries like boiled eggs from his farm nearby and things like cigarettes, and Span One responded nobly and got the reputation of being the best work span in the camp. And it wasn't only take from their side. They were awfully good at stealing certain commodities like fertilizer which were needed on the farm of Warder Hannetjie. ∾

Character *What causes Hannetjie's final transformation into a good person? What type of character is he?* **1**

Vocabulary

cunningly (kun′ing lē) *adv.* cleverly; sneakily

Assessment Practice

Process of Elimination Remind students that a key strategy for answering multiple-choice questions on standardized tests is the ability to eliminate incorrect answers. Have them practice this strategy by using the following multiple choice question:

What is a key theme of "The Prisoner Who Wore Glasses"?

A. A clever mind can overcome great obstacles.

B. Hannetjie is a brutal warder who continually beats the prisoners.

C. The theft of fertilizer was a major problem during apartheid.

D. Political prisoners suffered more than other kinds of prisoners in South Africa.

Ask students why **B, C,** and **D** can be eliminated. *(B—there is only one mention of beating; C—there is no information that any South African other than Hannetjie stole fertilizer; D—conditions at other prisons are not discussed)*

Respond and Think Critically

Respond and Interpret

1. What new insights into human nature did Brille's actions give you?

2. (a)How were political prisoners treated differently from other prisoners before Warder Hannetjie's arrival at the camp? (b)How did the political prisoners view themselves?

3. (a)What violence had Brille witnessed at home before he became a prisoner? (b)How do his memories of this violence and his home life give him insight into Warder Hannetjie's character?

4. (a)What deal do the prisoners of Span One strike with Warder Hannetjie? (b)Why might Hannetjie's interpretation of their deal surprise the prisoners of Span One?

Analyze and Evaluate

5. (a)Why are the warders intimidated by the political prisoners? (b)Why don't the members of Span One relent and become submissive when Hannetjie arrives at camp and treats them brutally?

6. **Irony** is a contrast between what is expected and what actually exists or occurs. What is ironic about Brille's eyesight?

7. **Foreshadowing** occurs when an author provides hints about what will happen in a story. How does the story foreshadow Brille's transformation of Warder Hannetjie into a "good warder"?

8. Early in the story, Brille says that Hannetjie is not human. Do you think Brille changes his mind by the end of the story? Explain.

Connect

9. **Big Idea** **The Price of Freedom** Do you think the story expresses optimism or pessimism about the future of South Africa? Explain.

10. **Connect to the Author** Head left South Africa in 1964 and became a political refugee in Botswana. What similarities might there be between her exile and the imprisonment of the political prisoners in this story?

Literary Element **Character**

A **round character** displays a variety of personality traits, while a **flat character** is dominated by a single personality trait. A **dynamic character** changes significantly in a story, whereas a **static** character undergoes very little change.

1. (a)Is Brille a round or a flat character? (b)What character traits does he display?

2. Would you classify Warder Hannetjie as a static or a dynamic character? Explain.

Review: Motivation

As you learned on page 93, **motivation** is the stated or implied reason or cause for a character's actions. A character's motivation affects how he or she interacts with other characters, how the story unfolds, and how conflicts are resolved.

Partner Activity With a partner, review the text and look for specific passages that reveal Brille's and Hannetjie's motivations.

1. (a)What do both men want emotionally? (b)What do they want materially?

2. (a)How do their motivations initially affect their choices and actions? (b)How do these motivations affect the resolution of the story?

BESSIE HEAD **131**

Review: Motivation

1. (a) Brille wants respect and equality. Hannetjie wants respect and control. (b) Brille wants some comforts, such as food and tobacco. Hannetjie wants fertilizer and materials for his farm.

2. (a) Brille's refusal to be controlled by the warder initially gets him beaten and put in solitary confinement. Hannetjie initially beats Brille in an effort to prove he is in charge.

(b) Brille's desire for equality makes him wait for the opportunity to prove he is Hannetjie's equal. Hannetjie's motivation to keep his job and get materials for his farm and family makes him take the deal Brille offers him. Both men's motivations result in a better situation for both sides.

Assess

1. Answers will vary.

2. (a) They weren't beaten; they were allowed to steal food, smoke, and chat. (b) They felt no guilt and knew they were not outcasts of society.

3. (a) His children beat up one another. (b) They make him realize that because Hannetjie behaves like a child, he must punish him like one.

4. (a) They get him to look out for their interests. (b) He helps them dig and brings them eggs.

5. (a) The political prisoners are united behind a cause. (b) They do not want brutal treatment to become the norm.

6. Despite his poor vision, he is more observant than others.

7. Brille recalls how his presence at home could change his children from "savages" into "fairly reasonable human beings."

8. Students may say that Brille changes his mind because he starts to feel guilty about the way he has treated Hannetjie.

9. Students may say it expresses optimism because it shows the possibility of cooperation.

10. Head and the prisoners both left their former lives behind, either due to choice or coercion. Additionally, their actions partially redefine their identities, Head as "refugee" and the men in Span One as "prisoners."

Literary Element

1. (a) round (b) Possible answers: pride, consideration, imagination, resourcefulness.

2. Dynamic; he starts out cruel and rigid but learns to cooperate with the prisoners and treat them kindly.

After You Read

Reading Strategy

(B) is the correct answer. Hannetjie first assumes that the men of Span One are just like the other prisoners and can be easily controlled and intimidated, but Brille's defiant behavior shows him otherwise.

Progress Check

Can students identify assumptions?

If No → See Unit 1 Teaching Resources Book, p. 181.

Vocabulary

Sample sentences will vary.

obscure

Definition: to hide from view

Etymology: Latin <u>obscurus</u>, meaning "dark"

assertive

Definition: bold; forceful in a confident way

Etymology: Latin <u>asserere</u>, meaning "to join"

bedlam

Definition: a state of uproar or confusion

Etymology: the name of a London insane asylum (the Hospital of St. Mary of Bethlehem)

cunningly

Definition: cleverly; sneakily

Etymology: Middle English <u>can</u>, meaning "know"

 For additional selection assessment, see Assessment Resources, pp. 59–60.

Reading Strategy Identify Assumptions

SAT Skills Practice

Hannetjie's assumptions about the prisoners of Span One are most strongly refuted by

(A) Brille's imaginative nature

(B) Brille's refusal to submit to Hannetjie

(C) Brille's discovery that Hannetjie has been stealing

(D) the prisoners' bad behavior

(E) the regulations that govern this prison

Vocabulary Practice

Practice with Word Origins Create a word map like the one below to study the word origins for each of the boldfaced vocabulary words. Use a dictionary for help.

obscure   assertive   bedlam   cunningly

EXAMPLE:

Definition
a state of over-powering emotion

Etymology
Greek <u>ékstasis</u>, meaning "displacement" or "trance"

ecstasy

Sample Sentence
His enemy's taunts sent him into an ecstasy of rage.

Academic Vocabulary

*The political prisoners of Span One fight for **legal** rights, including equality and freedom.*

Legal is an academic word. The **legal** system interprets laws. To further explore the meaning of this word, answer the following question. What **legal** rights were denied to black South Africans under apartheid?

For more on academic vocabulary, see pages 36–37 and R83–R85.

Academic Vocabulary

Among other things, black South Africans were denied the legal rights to vote, to receive an education equal to that of white South Africans, and to live where they pleased.

 To create custom assessments using software, use ExamView Assessment Suite.

Listening and Speaking

Debate

Assignment Do Hannetjie and the prisoners come to like and trust one another by the end of the story, or do they cooperate only because it is in their best interest? Divide into two teams to conduct a debate on whether Hannetjie and the prisoners become allies or remain adversaries.

Prepare Look at the chart you made on page 125 to review the characters' assumptions and behavior. Write a list of clear arguments that support your team's thesis. Organize your arguments and evidence in a chart to make sure you include all the important points.

Argument	Evidence
Hannetjie begins to treat the prisoners humanely.	He helps with the work and brings the prisoners boiled eggs.

Then research the cultural attitudes and practices of the apartheid era to find information to strengthen and support your arguments.

Debate In the debate, use logical, emotional, and ethical appeals to argue your side and to convince the audience. These appeals should be supported with specific evidence from the text and from your research.

Evaluate Create a pro-and-con chart to evaluate the strengths and weaknesses of your peers' performances in the debate. Consider the content of their appeals, the evidence they used to support them, and their use of oral delivery techniques.

LOG ON ▶ **Literature** Online

Selection Resources For Selection Quizzes, eFlashcards, and Reading-Writing Connection activities, go to glencoe.com and enter QuickPass code GLW6053u1.

Listening and Speaking

Students' debates should

- be supported with evidence from the text
- show that team members cooperated and built on one another's ideas
- reflect that the teams listened to each other carefully and could present thoughtful counterarguments

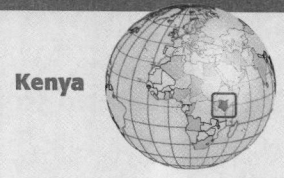

Before You Read

The Return

Meet **Ngugi wa Thiong'o**
(born 1938)

Ngugi wa Thiong'o (ng ōō´gē wä tē ōn´ gō) is one of East Africa's most important novelists. His political outlook and literary ambitions were greatly influenced by his poverty-stricken childhood and his experiences growing up under the brutal British colonial government.

Colonialism and Resistance Ngugi is a member of the Kikuyu (or Gikuyu) people, Kenya's largest ethnic group. The Kikuyu began fighting for Kenyan independence as early as the 1920s. This resistance sparked a violent backlash from the British authorities, which led to the deaths of more than 11,000 people.

Ngugi earned two bachelor's degrees, first at Makerere University in Uganda and then later at the University of Leeds in England. Around this time, Ngugi's family was swept up in the anticolonial movement known as the Mau Mau (mou´mou´) rebellion. During the conflict, his stepbrother was killed and his mother was tortured. Ngugi's first novel, *Weep Not, Child*, published in 1964, is set during the rebellion. Two later novels, *The River Between* (1965) and *A Grain of Wheat* (1967), also explore issues of independence, colonialism, and cultural conflict.

☆ **Radicalism, Arrest, and Exile** In the 1970s, Ngugi became increasingly pro-African and anticolonial. He began composing novels and plays in his native Kikuyu language.

After the performance of a radical, politically charged play he coauthored, *I Will Marry When I Want*, Ngugi was held for a year by the Kenyan government in a maximum-security prison. During his imprisonment, Ngugi wrote

"*I belong to Kenyan people, African people, Third World people, all peoples struggling against economic exploitation and social oppression, those in the world struggling for human dignity.*"

—Ngugi wa Thiong'o

Devil on the Cross, the first modern novel composed in Kikuyu.

After his release, he left Kenya and eventually moved to the United States. In 2004, Ngugi returned to Kenya to promote *Wizard of the Crow*, his latest novel. His prolific and observant writings have both documented and examined life in modern Kenya.

Literature Online

Author Search For more about Ngugi wa Thiong'o, go to glencoe.com and enter QuickPass code GLW6053u1.

NGUGI WA THIONG'O **133**

Before You Read

Focus

Bellringer Options

Selection Focus
 Transparency 10
Daily Language Practice
 Transparency 17

Or ask: What kinds of experiences can change people forever? Students might mention war, death of a loved one, a traumatic accident, or anything else that irrevocably changes someone.

Literary History ☆

Devil on the Cross Ngugi wa Thiong'o went against the grain when he decided to publish his book in Kikuyu, the Bantu language native to his people, instead of in English, as is commonly done. Of this choice, he said, "Only by a return to the roots of our being in the languages and cultures and heroic histories of the Kenyan people can we rise up to the challenge of helping in the creation of a Kenyan patriotic national literature and culture that will be the envy of many foreigners and the pride of Kenyans."

Selection Skills

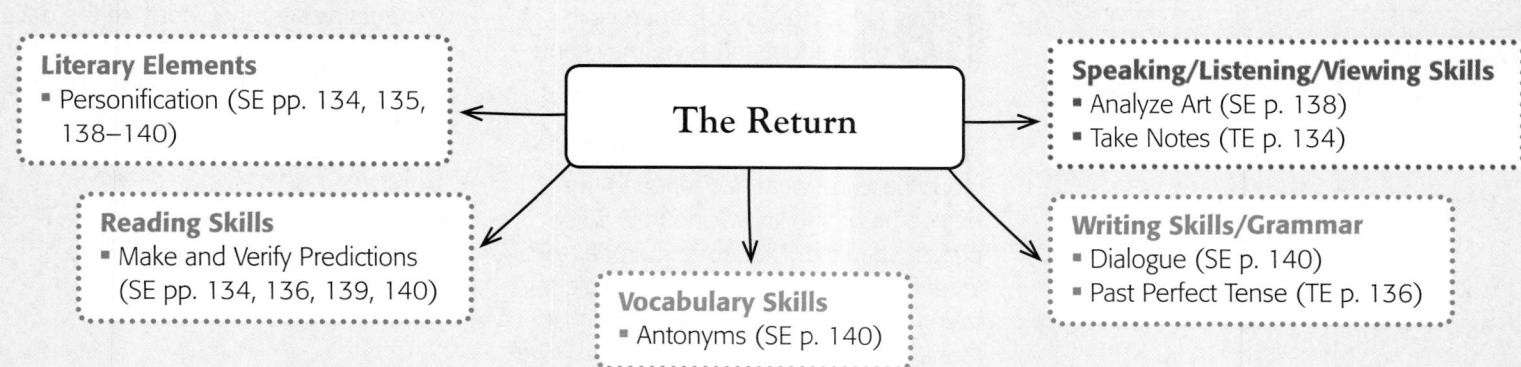

Literary Elements
- Personification (SE pp. 134, 135, 138–140)

Reading Skills
- Make and Verify Predictions (SE pp. 134, 136, 139, 140)

The Return

Vocabulary Skills
- Antonyms (SE p. 140)

Speaking/Listening/Viewing Skills
- Analyze Art (SE p. 138)
- Take Notes (TE p. 134)

Writing Skills/Grammar
- Dialogue (SE p. 140)
- Past Perfect Tense (TE p. 136)

Before You Read

Focus

Summary

Kamau returns to his village after five years in a detention camp. The people he used to know treat him with indifference or fear; even his own father does not recognize him. Kamau learns that Karanja, a comrade, told the village that Kamau had died in the camp. Karanja also courted and won Kamau's wife and took her away. Kamau is heartbroken, but as he stands near the Honia River, he accepts the fact that life has gone on without him.

 For summaries in languages other than English, see Unit 1 Teaching Resources Book, pp. 187–192.

Vocabulary

Memory Game Put students in pairs. One partner should look up the vocabulary words in a dictionary or thesaurus and find an antonym for each word. Then he or she should make eight cards with one word on each card (four will be from the selection and four will be antonyms). The student should lay the cards out on the floor; then the partner flips over two cards every turn to make matches. A vocabulary word and its antonym are a matching pair.

 For additional vocabulary practice, see Unit 1 Teaching Resources Book, p. 195.

Literature and Reading Preview

Connect to the Story

In general, why do people resist change? Why is the future sometimes frightening? Discuss these questions with a partner.

Build Background

"The Return" is set in Kenya in the 1950s during the Mau Mau rebellion. The Kikuyu people, who led the uprising, were angry because British colonists had taken large tracts of their land. The Mau Mau advocated the violent overthrow of the British authorities. In 1950, the organization was banned, and in 1952, the British imprisoned tens of thousands of Kikuyu. Although the Mau Mau rebellion failed, it helped convince the British government to grant independence to Kenya in 1963.

Set Purposes for Reading

Big Idea **The Price of Freedom**

As you read, ask yourself, What details in this story hint at the struggle Kenyans faced in the rebellion?

Literary Element **Personification**

Personification is a figure of speech in which an animal, an object, a force of nature, or an idea is given human qualities. As you read, ask yourself, What are examples of personification in this story?

Reading Strategy **Make and Verify Predictions**

When you **make a prediction,** you make an educated guess about what will happen. As you read, ask yourself, What predictions can I make about the outcome of this story?

....

Tip: **Take Notes** Use a graphic organizer like the one below to make, verify, and adjust your predictions.

> _Prediction:_ Kamau will be greeted like a returning hero.

> ↓

> _Verifying Evidence:_ "Again they looked at him. They stared at him with cold, hard looks; like everything else, they seemed to be deliberately refusing to know or own him."

> ↓

> _Actual Outcome:_ Things have changed a great deal in the village since Kamau's departure.

Listening Practice

SMALL GROUP **Take Notes** Ask students to think about someone they know who changed as the result of a difficult experience. Assign students to small groups and have each member of the group describe what happened to the person he or she knew, and how that person changed. The group member to the left of each speaker is responsible for taking notes and then reading them back to the speaker to check for accuracy. Have volunteers present their notes to the class in the form of a short narration. Then as a class discuss the challenges of conveying other people's thoughts accurately.

Learning Objectives

For pages 133–140

In studying this text, you will focus on the following objectives:

Literary Study: Analyzing personification.

Reading: Making and verifying predictions.

Writing: Writing a dialogue.

Vocabulary

animosity (an′ə mos′ə tē) _n._ ill will or resentment; p. 135 _The students expressed animosity toward their unfair teacher._

desist (di zist′) _v._ to cease; to stop; p. 136 _It has been made clear that personal calls during work hours must desist._

flout (flout) _v._ to treat with disdain or contempt; scoff at; p. 137 _It is not a good idea to flout the authorities in this situation._

incessant (in ses′ənt) _adj._ continuing without interruption; p. 139 _The birds' chirping was incessant throughout the morning._

....

Tip: **Antonyms** Antonyms are words that have opposite or nearly opposite meanings. They are always the same part of speech. For example, _animosity_ and _affection_ are antonyms.

THE RETURN

Ngugi wa Thiong'o

El-Molo young woman from Lake Turkana, Kenya.

Teach

Literary Element

Personification Answer: *The dust is being personified. Most students will agree that this is an effective use of personification. It adds to the mood and suggests Kamau's feelings.*

(APPROACHING) Ask students to list the instances of personification they can find on the first page of the story. *(The dust is angry. The road has a grudge. The countryside is weary. Kamau worries that the river might not recognize him.)*

 For an audio recording of this selection, use Listening Library Audio CD-ROM.

Readability Scores
Dale-Chall: 4.5
DRP: 54
Lexile: 560

Learning Objective
Identifying personification. (SE)

The road was long. Whenever he took a step forward, little clouds of dust rose, whirled angrily behind him, and then slowly settled again. But a thin train of dust was left in the air, moving like smoke. He walked on, however, unmindful of the dust and ground under his feet. Yet with every step he seemed more and more conscious of the hardness and apparent **animosity** of the road. Not that he looked down; on the contrary, he looked straight ahead as if he

would, any time now, see a familiar object that would hail him as a friend and tell him that he was near home. But the road stretched on.

He made quick, springing steps, his left hand dangling freely by the side of his once white coat, now torn and worn out. His right hand, bent at the elbow, held onto a string tied to a small bundle on his slightly drooping back. The bundle, well wrapped with a cotton cloth that had once been printed with red flowers now faded out, swung from side to side in harmony with the rhythm of his steps. The bundle held the bitterness and hardships of the years spent in detention camps. Now and then he looked at the sun on its homeward journey. Sometimes he darted quick side-

---

Personification *What is being personified in this sentence? Is this an effective use of personification? Explain.*

Vocabulary

animosity (an´ ə mos´ ə tē) *n.* ill will or resentment

NGUGI WA THIONG'O **135**

English Learners

DIFFERENTIATED INSTRUCTION

Beginnning Ask students who were born in another country to describe some differences between the place they used to live and the place where they live now. Ask students who were born in this country what their parents say about their country of origin.

To relate the discussion to the selection, have students make a chart with two columns, "What Kamau expects" and "What Kamau finds." As they read, students should fill in the chart with details of what Kamau expects to encounter when he returns to his village, and what he actually finds.

135

Teach

Reading Strategy | 1

Make and Verify Predictions Answer: *This passage suggests Kamau's uneasiness about his return. He is unsure how he will be received. This might suggest that he will not be greeted with a "hero's welcome."*

Reading Strategy | 2

Compare and Contrast Guide students to consider the differences in the experiences of the prisoners and their families.

Ask: How might prisoners feel about the villages and the people they left? How are they likely to feel about the change? Will the people left in the villages feel the same way? *(The prisoners live on memories, which remain idealized but basically unchanged. Those at home focus more on the here and now, and they have adjusted to the changes as they occurred.)*

glances at the small hedged strips of land which, with their sickly-looking crops, maize,[1] beans, and peas, appeared much as everything else did—unfriendly. The whole country was dull and seemed weary. To Kamau, this was nothing new. He remembered that, even before the Mau Mau emergency, the overtilled Gikuyu[2] holdings wore haggard looks in contrast to the sprawling green fields in the settled area.

A path branched to the left. He hesitated for a moment and then made up his mind. For the first time, his eyes brightened a little as he went along the path that would take him down the valley and then to the village. At last home was near and, with that realization, the faraway look of a weary traveler seemed to desert him for a while. The valley and the vegetation along it were in deep contrast to the surrounding country. For here green bush and trees thrived. This could only mean one thing: Honia River still flowed. He quickened his steps as if he could scarcely believe this to be true till he had actually set his eyes on the river. It was there; it still flowed. Honia, where so often he had taken a bath, plunging stark naked into its cool living water, warmed his heart as he watched its serpentine movement around the rocks and heard its slight murmurs. A painful exhilaration passed all over him, and for a moment he longed for those days. He sighed. Perhaps the river would not recognize in his hardened features that same boy to whom the riverside world had meant everything. Yet as he approached Honia,

he felt more akin to it than he had felt to anything else since his release.

A group of women were drawing water. He was excited, for he could recognize one or two from his ridge. There was the middle-aged Wanjiku, whose deaf son had been killed by the Security Forces just before he himself was arrested. She had always been a darling of the village, having a smile for everyone and food for all. Would they receive him? Would they give him a "hero's welcome"? He thought so. Had he not always been a favorite all along the ridge? And had he not fought for the land? He wanted to run and shout: "Here I am. I have come back to you." But he **desisted**. He was a man.

"Is it well with you?" A few voices responded. The other women, with tired and worn features, looked at him mutely as if his greeting was of no consequence. Why! Had he been so long in the camp?[3] His spirits were damped as he feebly asked: "Do you not remember me?" Again they looked at him. They stared at him with cold, hard looks; like everything else, they seemed to be deliberately refusing to know or own him. It was Wanjiku who at last recognized him. But there was neither warmth nor enthusiasm in her voice as she said, "Oh, is it you, Kamau? We thought you—" She did not continue. Only now he noticed something else—surprise? fear? He could not tell. He saw their quick glances dart at him and he knew for certain that a secret from which he was excluded bound them together.

---

1. Here, *maize* is a grain.
2. *Gikuyu* (gē kōō′yōō), more commonly Kikuyu, are the most numerous ethnic group in Kenya.

 Make and Verify Predictions *Based on this passage, what prediction can you make about the reception Kamau will receive at home?*

3. *Camp* refers to "Operation Anvil," the colonial government's final effort to end the Mau Mau rebellion in 1954. The government screened the entire Kikuyu population and forced thousands of Kikuyu into detention camps.

Vocabulary

desist (di zist′) *v.* to cease; to stop

Grammar Practice

Past Perfect Tense Write these sentences from the story on the board: "Yet as he approached Honia, he felt more akin to it than he <u>had felt</u> to anything else since his release." (page 136) "He left them, feeling embittered and cheated. The old village <u>had</u> not even <u>waited</u> for him." (page 137) Point out that these verbs are in the past perfect tense, a tense used to name an action that happened before another action in

the past. The story itself is written in the past tense, and when the author wants to refer to the more distant past, he uses the past perfect tense. The past perfect tense consists of the helping verb *had* and the past participle of the main verb.

Have students write down three other sentences from the story that use the past perfect tense. To help them understand the change in time reference, have them circle the action that happened first.

"Perhaps I am no longer one of them!" he bitterly reflected. But they told him of the new village. The old village of scattered huts spread thinly over the ridge was no more.

2 He left them, feeling embittered and cheated. The old village had not even waited for him. And suddenly he felt a strong nostalgia for his old home, friends and surroundings. He thought of his father, mother and—and—he dared not think about her. But for all that, Muthoni, just as she had been in the old days, came back to his mind. His heart beat faster. He felt desire and a warmth thrilled through him. He quickened his step. He forgot the village women as he remembered his wife. He had stayed with her for a mere two weeks; then he had been swept away by the colonial forces. Like many others, he had been hurriedly screened and then taken to detention without trial. And all that time he had thought of nothing but the village and his beautiful woman.

The others had been like him. They had talked of nothing but their homes. One day he was working next to another detainee from Muranga. Suddenly the detainee, Njoroge, stopped breaking stones. He sighed heavily. His worn-out eyes had a faraway look.

"What's wrong, man? What's the matter with you?" Kamau asked.

"It is my wife. I left her expecting a baby. I have no idea what has happened to her."

Another detainee put in: "For me, I left my woman with a baby. She had just been delivered. We were all happy. But on the same day, I was arrested . . ."

And so they went on. All of them longed for one day—the day of their return home. Then life would begin anew.

Kamau himself had left his wife without a child. He had not even finished paying the bride price.[4] But now he would go, seek work in Nairobi, and pay off the remainder to Muthoni's parents. Life would indeed begin anew. They would have a son and bring him up in their own home. With these prospects before his eyes, he quickened his steps. He wanted to run—no, fly to hasten his return. He was now nearing the top of the hill. He wished he could suddenly meet his brothers and sisters. Would they ask him questions? He would, at any rate, not tell them all: the beating, the screening and the work on roads and in quarries with an askari always nearby ready to kick him if he relaxed. Yes. He had suffered many humiliations, and he had not resisted. Was there any need? But his soul and all the vigor of his manhood had rebelled and bled with rage and bitterness. One day these wazungu[5] would go!

One day his people would be free! Then, then—he did not know what he would do. However, he bitterly assured himself no one would ever **flout** his manhood again.

Visual Vocabulary
An *askari* is an indigenous soldier who serves in the troops of a colonial power.

---

4. A *bride price* can be either money or material assets that a prospective husband pays to the bride's parents for allowing the marriage.
5. A *wazungu* (wä zōō′ ngōō) is a white person.

The Price of Freedom What does Kamau's anger here reveal about the toll that oppression has taken on him? **3**

Vocabulary

flout (flout) *v.* to treat with disdain or contempt; scoff at

NGUGI WA THIONG'O **137**

Big Idea **3**

The Price of Freedom
Answer: *The oppression has given him a negative outlook. He has developed a hatred for colonialism.*

(ADVANCED) Ask students how Kamau's mood affects his first sight of the village. *(His view reflects his gloomy mood. The village is partially obscured by smoke and mist, and the sun is as red as blood.)*

Learning Objectives
Making and verifying predictions (SE)
Understanding past perfect tense. (TE)
Comparing and contrasting. (TE)

Approaching Level

DIFFERENTIATED INSTRUCTION

Summarize Remind students that Kamau has been away from home for a long time, and now he is returning to see his wife and family again. **Ask:** How does Kamau feel as he draws closer to his village? *(He feels excited to go home and he expects to be welcomed joyfully.)*

Teach

Literary Element | 1

Personification Answer:
The huts are being personified. Students' explanations will vary. Some might say that the word crouching *indicates that the villagers and the huts have been subjected to frightening events.*

View the Art ★

Answer: *It seems that because so many people are crowded into one small space, much like a town, they must learn to live side by side, or else chaos will ensue, destroying relationships and ultimately the entire town.*

Georges Lilanga D. Nyama comes from a region of southern Africa where dance and sculpture are highly valued. He learned to sculpt as a boy and later studied other art forms.

He mounted the hill and then stopped. The whole plain lay below. The new village was before him—rows and rows of compact mud huts, crouching on the plain under the fast-vanishing sun. Dark blue smoke curled upward from various huts, to form a dark mist that hovered over the village. Beyond, the deep, blood-red sinking sun sent out fingerlike streaks of light that thinned outward and mingled with the gray mist shrouding the distant hills.

In the village, he moved from street to street, meeting new faces. He inquired. He found his home. He stopped at the entrance to the yard and breathed hard and full. This was the moment of his return home. His father sat huddled up on a three-legged stool. He was now very aged and Kamau pitied the old man. But he had been spared—yes, spared to see his son's return—

"Father!"

The old man did not answer. He just looked at Kamau with strange vacant eyes. Kamau was impatient. He felt annoyed and irritated. Did he not see him? Would he behave like the women Kamau had met by the river?

In the street, naked and half-naked children were playing, throwing dust at one another. The sun had already set and it looked as if there would be moonlight.

"Father, don't you remember me?" Hope was sinking in him. He felt tired. Then he saw his father suddenly start and tremble like a leaf. He saw him stare with unbelieving eyes. Fear was discernible in those eyes. His mother came, and his brothers too. They crowded around him. His aged mother clung to him and sobbed hard.

Mji Ni Watu Si Mji Na Sisi Hapa Tulipo Ni Watu Kama Wewe (A Town Is Composed of People. Without People It Is No Longer a Town. We Are Here as People Just Like You.), 1992. George Lilanga D. Nyama. Acrylic on Plywood, 242 x 122 c.m. The Pigozzi Collection, Geneva.

View the Art This painting, which is filled with bodies in motion, offers a powerful vision of the spiritual cohesiveness of traditional communities. How does this painting reflect its title? ★

"I knew my son would come. I knew he was not dead."

"Why, who told you I was dead?"

"That Karanja, son of Njogu."

And then Kamau understood. He understood his trembling father. He understood

---

1 | **Personification** *What is being personified in this sentence? How does this personification mirror the occupants of the village?*

Reading Practice

SMALL GROUP

Analyze Motivation When you read, you make judgments about characters' actions and decisions. Students should ask themselves, What do I think of that action? Would I have done the same thing? What were the alternatives?

Have students break into groups of three or four to discuss characters' motivations in the story. They should consider the behavior of Karanja and Muthoni, and Kamau's reaction to the news that his wife is gone. Ask what Kamau might do, given his situation. Whose actions were justifiable? Whose actions were questionable?

the women at the river. But one thing puzzled him: he had never been in the same detention camp with Karanja. Anyway he had come back. He wanted now to see Muthoni. Why had she not come out? He wanted to shout, "I have come, Muthoni; I am here." He looked around. His mother understood him. She quickly darted a glance at her man and then simply said:

"Muthoni went away."

Kamau felt something cold settle in his stomach. He looked at the village huts and the dullness of the land. He wanted to ask many questions but he dared not. He could not yet believe that Muthoni had gone. But he knew by the look of the women at the river, by the look of his parents, that she was gone.

"She was a good daughter to us," his mother was explaining. "She waited for you and patiently bore all the ills of the land. Then Karanja came and said that you were dead. Your father believed him. She believed him too and keened[6] for a month. Karanja constantly paid us visits. He was of your Rika,[7] you know. Then she got a child. We could have kept her. But where is the land? Where is the food? Ever since land consolidation, our last security was taken away. We let Karanja go with her. Other women have done worse—gone to town. Only the infirm and the old have been left here."

He was not listening; the coldness in his stomach slowly changed to bitterness. He felt bitter against all, all the people including his father and mother. They had betrayed him. They had leagued against him, and Karanja had always been his rival.

---

6. To *keen* is "to lament or mourn loudly."
7. *Rika* (re ka´) is Swahili for age group or generation.

 Make and Verify Predictions *Why do you think Karanja lied about Kamau's death?*

Five years was admittedly not a short time. But why did she go? Why did they allow her to go? He wanted to speak. Yes, speak and denounce everything—the women by the river, the village and the people who dwelled there. But he could not. This bitter thing was choking him.

"You—you gave my own away?" he whispered.

"Listen, child, child . . ."

The big yellow moon dominated the horizon. He hurried away bitter and blind, and only stopped when he came to the Honia River.

And standing at the bank, he saw not the river, but his hopes dashed on the ground instead. The river moved swiftly, making ceaseless monotonous murmurs. In the forest the crickets and other insects kept up an **incessant** buzz. And above, the moon shone bright. He tried to remove his coat, and the small bundle he had held on to so firmly fell. It rolled down the bank and before Kamau knew what was happening, it was floating swiftly down the river. For a time he was shocked and wanted to retrieve it. What would he show his—Oh, had he forgotten so soon? His wife had gone. And the little things that had so strangely reminded him of her and that he had guarded all those years, had gone! He did not know why, but somehow he felt relieved. Thoughts of drowning himself dispersed. He began to put on his coat, murmuring to himself, "Why should she have waited for me? Why should all the changes have waited for my return?"

Personification *How does personification here contribute to the story's mood?* **3**

Vocabulary

incessant (in ses´ənt) *adj.* continuing without interruption

NGUGI WA THIONG'O **139**

Teach

Reading Strategy | **2**

Make and Verify Predictions Answer: *Karanja lied about Kamau so he could marry Muthoni.*

(ADVANCED) Have advanced learners consider how Kamau alters his expectations on arriving home, now that he knows that Karanja lied. (*He might try to track down Karanja and ask his wife to come back to him. Or he might accept what has happened, and try to move on.*)

Literary Element | **3**

Personification Answer: *The images of "hopes dashed" and the river "making ceaseless monotonous murmurs" contribute to the bleak and hopeless mood.*

Progress Check

Can students identify personification?

If No → See Unit 1 Teaching Resources Book, p. 193.

To check students' understanding of the selection, see Unit 1 Teaching Resources Book, p. 198.

Approaching Level

DIFFERENTIATED INSTRUCTION

Context Clues Write this sentence from the story on the board: *The big yellow moon dominated the horizon.* Have students use context clues to determine the meaning of *dominated.* (*The moon is big; it sounds like the moon is the only thing you can see on the horizon. Something that dominates something else is the most important aspect of that thing.*)

Learning Objectives
Making and verifying predictions. (SE)
Identifying personification. (SE)
Analyzing motivation. (TE)

After You Read

Assess

1. Students may feel sorry for Kamau or be relieved that he is able to accept change.

2. (a) Kamau was held in a camp for participating in a rebellion. (b) He is excited to go home.

3. (a) He learns that the old village was destroyed and that the residents have moved to a new village. (b) He feels nostalgic.

4. (a) The bundle symbolizes his life with Muthoni and his dream of home. (b) This is an effective symbol. It is literal and figurative "baggage."

5. The prisoners live on idealized memories.

6. The colonizers had taken all the good land; Kamau's recollection of the detention camp reveals that the Kikuyu were oppressed.

7. Ngugi may have chosen this perspective because of his own experiences as a prisoner. Also, the protester has seen injustice both in prison and at home and may have a broader view of the situation than do the villagers.

Literary Element

1. He hopes to see a familiar object that will "hail him as a friend."

2. He is eager to be in familiar territory and be welcomed home by his village.

Reading Strategy

1. Students' answers will vary. Make sure the details they present are useful for making predictions about the plot.

2. Students' answers will vary. Many will be surprised by the greeting of the village women and Kamau's change of heart at the end of the story.

140

After You Read

Respond and Think Critically

Respond and Interpret

1. What emotions did you experience at the end of the story?

2. (a)Why has Kamau been away from the village? (b)How would you describe his feelings as he approaches the village?

3. (a)What does Kamau learn from the women at the river? (b)How would you describe his emotions after learning this information?

Analyze and Evaluate

4. (a)A **symbol** is an object or an action that stands for something else in addition to itself. What might Kamau's bundle symbolize? (b)Do you think it is an effective symbol? Why or why not?

5. Consider the conversation between the detainees regarding their families. How might the prisoners feel about the people and villages they left behind?

Connect

6. **Big Idea** **The Price of Freedom** What details in this story suggest why Kamau and other Kikuyu men revolted against colonial rule?

7. **Connect to the Author** Ngugi witnessed the great injustice perpetrated on the Kikuyu. Why might he have chosen to write about a returning protester, rather than the villagers who stayed behind?

Literary Element Personification

Authors often use **personification** to reinforce the mood of a literary work and to suggest the unspoken feelings of their characters.

1. In the first paragraph, what does Kamau hope to see, and how does he personify it?

2. What does this personification reveal about Kamau's emotions as he approaches home?

Reading Strategy Make and Verify Predictions

As you read, you **make predictions** about what will happen next. Review the chart you made on page 134 and answer these questions.

1. What details helped you predict the ending of "The Return"?

2. Which turn in the plot most surprised you?

LOG ON ▶ **Literature** Online

Selection Resources For Selection Quizzes, eFlashcards, and Reading-Writing Connection activities, go to glencoe.com and enter QuickPass code GLW6053u1.

140 UNIT 1 MODERN AFRICA

Vocabulary Practice

Practice with Antonyms With a partner, match each boldfaced vocabulary word below with its antonym. Use a thesaurus or a dictionary to check your answers. You will not use all the answer choices.

1. animosity   a. unpleasant   e. continue

2. desist   b. goodwill   f. obey

3. flout   c. intermittent

4. incessant   d. celebrate

 Writing

Write a Dialogue Imagine that Kamau and Muthoni run into each other at a later time. Write a brief description of where they meet, using personification. Then, write a dialogue, imagining the conversation they have.

Progress Check

Can students make logical predictions and verify them?

If No → See Unit 1 Teaching Resources Book, p. 194.

Vocabulary

1. b **2.** e **3.** f **4.** c

 Writing

Students' writing should

- be consistent with the characterization in the story
- use personification

140

Before You Read

Bones

Kenya

Meet **Sadru Kassam**

(born 1941)

Like many fellow African writers and artists, Sadru Kassam (sä drōō′ kä säm′) has developed an art form that is both inspired and complicated by the changes Africa has faced in modern times. Kassam, who wrote and performed for the Free Travelling Theatre, uses modern group theater to help Africans from a variety of cultures, regions, and languages better understand the common problems they will encounter as Africa continues to embrace independence.

> "[W]ith the Free Travelling Theatre, performance in the open air would give birth to a huge 'cast' of three hundred, four hundred, and more people because all the villagers used to join in. . . ."
>
> —Micere Githae Mũgo,
> Kenyan playwright and poet

Theater and Satire Kassam was born in Mombasa, the second-largest city in Kenya. He became involved with the Free Travelling Theatre while studying English at Makerere University in Uganda. Professors and students formed the Free Travelling Theatre to bring theater to rural villages and towns, and it served as an important testing ground for new African drama.

Kassam originally wrote *Bones* in Swahili, one of Kenya's two official languages (along with English). He performed the lead role of the butcher with exaggerated comic gestures.

Magie-de-Nuit, 1992. Francks Deceus. Oil on canvas. Private collection.

According to one of the founders of the Free Travelling Theatre, the play was "unfailingly a tumultuous success." Audiences from different cultures identified with the social problems that Kassam satirized in his play.

Spotlight on Swahili Swahili (also called *kiSwahili* or *Kiswahili*) is a Bantu language spoken mainly on the east coast of Africa, from Kenya to southern Tanzania. Although the people of this region speak a variety of languages and dialects, Swahili is common among many of them. Swahili was greatly influenced by Arabic. In fact, the name *Swahili* comes from the Arabic word *sawahili,* meaning "of the coast." The Arabic influence resulted from centuries of trading between Arabians and the inhabitants of Africa's east coast. As a result of the Arab influence, Swahili became the common language among several close Bantu-speaking tribal groups along the coast. The spread of Arab ivory and slave caravans into Congo and Uganda during the nineteenth century furthered the spread of Swahili westward. While the oldest preserved Swahili literature is written in Arabic script, Swahili is now written in the Roman alphabet.

Literature Online

Author Search For more about Sadru Kassam, go to glencoe.com and enter QuickPass code GLW6053u1.

SADRU KASSAM **141**

Bellringer Options

Selection Focus
Transparency 11
Daily Language Practice
Transparency 18

Or ask: Are you confident that the food you eat is fresh and safe? Discuss measures that individuals and government can take to promote food safety.

Or ask: Have you ever bribed or persuaded someone to get what you wanted, only to have it backfire? Elicit students' experiences of such situations.

Selection Skills

Literary Elements
- Satire (SE pp. 142, 145, 147, 148)
- Metaphor (TE p. 146)

Bones

Speaking/Listening/Viewing Skills
- Analyze Art (TE p. 143)

Reading Skills
- Visualize (SE pp. 142, 144–146, 148)
- Make Inferences (TE pp. 143, 145)

Vocabulary Skills
- Usage (SE p. 148)

Writing Skills/Grammar
- Editorial (SE p. 148)
- Identify Adjectives (TE p. 144)

Before You Read

Focus

Summary

A butcher's shop fails a health inspection, and the butcher must figure out what to do to have his trading license reinstated within a week. He asks his friend Kanubhai how to pass the inspection, and Kanubhai tells him to give the inspector "bones." The butcher is puzzled until he realizes that "bones" is Kanubhai's way of suggesting a bribe. Even though the butcher gets his license by bribing the inspector, he loses a regular customer because he has let his shop get dirty.

 For summaries in languages other than English, see Unit 1 Teaching Resources Book, pp. 200–205.

Vocabulary

Charades Group students of different levels together in pairs. Instruct the pairs to decide which of the two shall go first. Tell these students to choose a vocabulary word and act it out without using words, trying to make their partners guess the word. They can embody the word, mime a scenario in which the word is applicable, or sound the word out. When the partner has guessed the word, have them trade and repeat the exercise until all of the words have been enacted and guessed.

 For additional vocabulary practice, see Unit 1 Teaching Resources Book, p. 208.

Literature and Reading Preview

Connect to the Play

When might it be acceptable to use your position, influence, or wealth to make a change? When would it be inappropriate? Discuss these questions with a partner.

Build Background

In Kenya, as in most African countries, a number of languages are spoken. Thus, the actors in the Free Travelling Theatre, which was popular nationwide, had to learn to perform in several languages, including Runyoro, Luganda, English, and Swahili.

Set Purposes for Reading

Big Idea **Living with Independence**

As you read *Bones,* ask yourself, How do these characters respond to the complexities of independence?

Literary Element **Satire**

A **satire** ridicules human flaws, ideas, social customs, or institutions in order to effect change in society. The ultimate purpose of satire is to persuade, although satires can be effective only if they also entertain. As you read, ask yourself, What details in this drama indicate that it is a satire?

Reading Strategy **Visualize**

To **visualize** means to picture an author's ideas or descriptions in your mind's eye. Visualizing can help you "see," "hear," and interpret the action of a play in your mind. As you read, ask yourself, How can I visualize this scene to help me better understand how it might be staged?

Tip: Interpret Characters As you read, use a chart like the one below to record the characters' actions you visualize, and interpret what each action reveals about him or her.

Character:	Character's Action:	Interpretation:
Butcher	The butcher drops a meat joint and then just brushes it off instead of throwing it away.	The butcher is unconcerned with cleanliness.

Learning Objectives

For pages 141–148

In studying this text, you will focus on the following objectives:

Literary Study: Analyzing satire.

Reading: Visualizing.

Writing: Writing an editorial.

Vocabulary

vigorously (vig′ər əs lē) *adv.* energetically; p. 143 *Tom vigorously shook the blanket to get the dust out.*

endorse (en dôrs′) *v.* to inscribe with one's signature to show legal or official approval; p. 145 *She didn't want to endorse the check because she knew it might bounce.*

pester (pes′tər) *v.* to harass or annoy with petty irritations; p. 145 *If Paul bought candy, his younger brothers would pester him until he gave them some.*

fumble (fum′bəl) *v.* to grope or handle clumsily; p. 147 *Eagle High School had a winning baseball season thanks in part to its star shortstop, who would never fumble the ball.*

Reading Practice

Visualize Point out to students that reading a play is usually less pleasurable than watching one. So much of the enjoyment of drama comes from the staging—what the actors look and sound like, the set design, music, movement—even being a part of the audience changes the experience. Getting the most from reading a play requires picturing the scene fully and "hearing" the actors' voices in one's imagination. Reading a play more slowly and deliberately than a short story helps.

Suggest to students that they try the technique of acting out parts of the play in their heads. They should picture the scene in detail and imagine exactly what each character looks like, how their voices sound, and how they might behave. The idea is to put back into silent reading some of what they would see in a performance.

Bones

Sadru Kassam
Translated by the Author

Teach

Reading Strategy   1

Make Inferences Have students read the character descriptions of the Butcher and Dongo.

Ask: Based on these character descriptions, what do you think the relationship is between the Butcher and Dongo? *(Dongo is probably going to be inspecting the Butcher's store.)*

 For additional practice using the reading skill or strategy, see Unit 1 Teaching Resources Book, p. 207.

1 CHARACTERS

THE BUTCHER

DONGO: a health inspector

KANUBHAI: a Hindu trader

A WOMAN ⎫
         ⎬ customers
A GIRL ⎭

SCENE: *A butcher's shop. A sign reads:* "SALEH BIN AWADH, *The Big Butcher, P. O.* MAJI MOTO, *Coast Region.*" *On one wall is a painting of a bull, and on another a picture of the* BUTCHER *slaughtering another bull. There are notices reading:* "FRASH MEAT" *and* "WEL-COME."

NOTE: *It is intended that each scene shall open with an extended mime by the* BUTCHER, *which can be developed from the outlines in the stage directions.*

SCENE 1

[*The shop is tolerably clean and tidy. The* BUTCHER *wears an almost white coat and his hair is combed. He sings as he arranges his meat to conceal its shortcomings. A joint tumbles to the ground: he looks to see if anyone is around, then picks it up and brushes it before replacing it, clean side upwards. He spits and scratches himself* **vigorously**. *He starts dividing some meat into smaller sections with a large knife, swinging the blade dangerously.*

> **Vocabulary**
>
> **vigorously** (vig′ər əs lē) *adv.* energetically

SADRU KASSAM   **143**

View the Art ★

The illustrations that appear on pages 143–147 were created by Sue Todd specifically for "Bones." A graduate of an art school in Toronto, Todd combines traditional and modern media in her work. She begins by carving images into pieces of linoleum. Then she photographs the designs and scans them into a computer software program. She uses the software to colorize the images. Have students skim the illustrations. **Ask:** What sort of mood do these illustrations create? *(Students may say that they create a lighthearted mood.)*

Approaching Level

DIFFERENTIATED INSTRUCTION

Preview Place students in small, mixed groups. Instruct students having difficulty to read the opening stage directions of the play, picking out details Kassam gives describing the butcher shop. Have the groups discuss what these details tell them about the store.

English Learners

DIFFERENTIATED INSTRUCTION

Beginning Have English learners draw the play's set based on the list of details their groups have compiled. The design should show all the elements noted in the description of the shop. Ask students to look up any unfamiliar terms. Encourage them to be creative with their set designs and vary from the visual interpretations in the illustrations in this book.

 For an audio recording of this selection, use Listening Library Audio CD-ROM.

Learning Objectives
Making inferences. (TE)
Analyzing art. (TE)

Teach

Reading Strategy 1

Visualize Answer: *Students will likely say the stage directions help them envision the butcher's appearance, his disregard for cleanliness, and his mannerisms.*

[ENGLISH LEARNERS] For English learners, explain words from the stage directions with which they might not be familiar, such as *vigorously, shrieks,* and *prances.* Ask them what emotional state these words suggest.

Big Idea 2

Living with Independence
Answer: *Even in an independent society, the threat of cheating and corruption exists. People still need to be wary and look out for themselves.*

At length he cuts himself, shrieks, prances around, tends his bleeding finger, wipes the blood off on a piece of meat and sucks the wound. The WOMAN is heard singing as she approaches. She enters, wearing a khanga.[1]]

WOMAN. Eee, banakuba![2] How are you?

BUTCHER. Me? Very well, mama, very well. You want meat?

WOMAN. Yes, banakuba, I want meat. How's your meat? Is it good?

BUTCHER. Very good, mama. Good and fresh. Can't you see me in the picture there slaughtering a bull?

WOMAN. From what part will you give me?

BUTCHER. Any part you want, mama. Whatever you ask for, I'm here to serve you.

[He sharpens his knife on his file.]

WOMAN. I want some of that. I hope it's fresh.

BUTCHER. Completely fresh, mama: numberi[3] one. How much do you want?

WOMAN. Aaaah! A shilling's worth only—unless you want to give me more on credit.

BUTCHER. No, no, no, not today.

[The BUTCHER cuts a small piece from the meat the WOMAN has chosen, and then begins to cut larger pieces from another joint.]

WOMAN. A-a-a-a, I want off that only.

BUTCHER. Yes, but you want good and fresh meat, isn't it? This is very good. See . . . excellent! Numberi one! I tell you.

WOMAN. [Violently.] I don't want it.

BUTCHER. O.K. . . . your wish. Was it this one you wanted?

WOMAN. That's it. Now you know it.

[He puts some meat on the scales, and is about to add several bones.]

WOMAN. What's that you're doing there? I didn't ask for stones. I don't want them. Remove them at once.

BUTCHER. Mama, they aren't stones. They are very good bones with plenty of meat on them. See . . . excellent! Grade one!

WOMAN. And what am I to do with bones? I'm not a dog.

[He finishes weighing the meat and wraps it. The WOMAN takes out a small pouch and offers money which she draws back as the BUTCHER tries to snatch it, so that he pitches across his counter before she gives it to him.]

BUTCHER. Here it is, mama, your meat.

WOMAN. And here's your money . . . unless you don't want it.

BUTCHER. Eh, why not? Thank you, mama, thank you very much. God help you.

WOMAN. O.K., banakuba, good-bye.

---

1. A *khanga* (КНän′gä) is a loincloth worn by women in East Africa. Khangas are usually decorated and are often inscribed with slogans or proverbs.
2. *Eee, banakuba* (ē bä nä kōō′bä) is a Swahili slang term of respect meaning "hey, big man."
3. *Numberi* (nōōm bä′rē) means "number."

1 Visualize *How do the stage directions help you envision the butcher before he says a word?*

2 Living with Independence *What do the butcher's actions suggest about life after independence?*

Grammar Practice

Identify Adjectives Remind students that adjectives modify or describe nouns or pronouns. Write these sentences on the board and ask students to identify the adjectives and the words they modify:

"Yes, but you want <u>good</u> and <u>fresh</u> meat, isn't it? (adjectives: *good, fresh;* noun: *meat*)

"I'm going to the <u>next</u> butcher, to a <u>cleaner</u> shop." (adjective: *next;* noun: *butcher;* adjective: *cleaner;* noun: *shop*)

Have students identify all the adjectives (excluding articles) on page 144. They should make a chart, with all the adjectives in the left hand column, and the words they modify in the right hand.

[A GIRL *enters, dressed in a dirty, tattered* *frock*[4] *and carrying a kikapu.*[5]]

GIRL. Get me half a pound of meat, please. Nice—like you!

[*As the* WOMAN *is going out she bumps into* DONGO *as he enters.*]

3 **DONGO.** Good morning, mama.

WOMAN. Good morning, brother.

DONGO. What's the quarrel with the butcher?

WOMAN. Aaaa, nothing.

DONGO. Weren't you complaining of ill-treatment? I heard you shouting.

WOMAN. No, no, no. I was just joking with him. That butcher is a very nice man, you know.

DONGO. I see. O.K. Good-bye.

WOMAN. Good-bye. [*Exit.*]

GIRL. Give me very good meat, and no bones, please.

BUTCHER. No, no, no. No bones. Just a little one for your father.

GIRL. No. My father has no teeth.

BUTCHER. Oh, I see. [DONGO *has been clearing his throat loudly to attract the* BUTCHER's *attention.*] Dongo, Mr. Dongo! Just come over here, please. I'm delighted to see you. How are you?

DONGO. Excellent, thank you. And you?

BUTCHER. Aaaa, not well at all, because you know you still haven't **endorsed** my trading license. Please do it just now. Only a week is left before the closing date.

---

4. A *frock* is a woman's dress.
5. A *kikapu* (kē kä′poo) is a basket.

Vocabulary

endorse (en dôrs′) *v.* to inscribe with one's signature to show legal or official approval

[DONGO *stands as if ready to receive a gift.* *He looks away, pauses, then looks back at his* *hand as if surprised to see it empty.*]

DONGO. Your trading license? Hasn't anyone taught you how to get it? [*The* BUTCHER *shakes his head.*] Just look at your shop! [DONGO *sweeps a pile of scraps from the counter onto the floor.*] See, the whole floor is littered with scraps and bones. When did you last sweep it? [DONGO *wipes his hands, now covered in blood from the meat, on the* BUTCHER's *apron.*] And why is your apron so dirty? Where is your file? [DONGO *takes the file and breaks it in two.*] Why is it broken? [*He runs his hands through the* BUTCHER's *hair, ruffling it.*] And why have you not combed your hair? Who made you a big butcher? Look, you must get things in order before **pestering** me to endorse your license. Do you understand that?

 Visualize *What does this stage direction suggest about Dongo and his job?* **4**

 Satire *How is Dongo's response to the butcher satirical? What is Kassam satirizing here?* **5**

Vocabulary

pester (pes′tər) *v.* to harass or annoy with petty irritations

SADRU KASSAM **145**

English Learners

DIFFERENTIATED INSTRUCTION

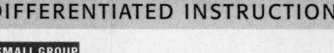 **SMALL GROUP** **Intermediate** Group students in mixed-level groups of five, each student taking on a role from the play. Have them read the play aloud while seated. They should use suitable facial expressions and gestures. English learners will benefit particularly from practicing speaking.

Advanced Learners/Pre-AP

DIFFERENTIATED INSTRUCTION

Leadership Instruct the advanced students to act as "directors" of the groups' readings. If the English learners have difficulties with words or phrases, the advanced students should help explain or say the lines aloud, having the English learner repeat them. They can also help explain to non-native speakers why certain lines and interchanges are humorous.

Teach

Reading Strategy **3**

Make Inferences Tell students to reread Dongo's exchange with the Woman. **Ask:** What can you infer from Dongo's question to the woman as he enters the store? *(He seems to be looking for reasons to criticize the Butcher.)*

Reading Strategy **4**

Visualize Answer: *Dongo's gesture suggests he expects to be bribed and is surprised when the butcher neglects to give him anything. He must be accustomed to receiving bribes without having to drop hints.*

(APPROACHING) For students who have difficulties visualizing this, have two volunteers act out the exchange to clarify it.

Literary Element **5**

Satire Answer: *Dongo is saying the shop is dirty, but he is making it dirty by pushing scraps onto the floor. Despite his comments, Dongo's behavior reveals that the granting of trading licenses has little to do with cleanliness. Kassam uses humor and exaggeration to satirize corrupt government practices.*

Learning Objectives
Visualizing. (SE)
Analyzing satire. (SE)
Making inferences. (TE)
Identifying adjectives. (TE)

145

Teach

Big Idea   1

Living with Independence
Have the students read the Butcher's line after the Girl exits.
Ask: How does the Girl's action show another side to the difficulties of independence?
(The customer is taking advantage of the shop owner. This suggests that corruption can go both ways, and that in independent societies, each person has to look out for himself or herself.)

Reading Strategy   2

Visualize Answer: *Kanubhai is trying to show that Dongo is a "dog"; that is, he is swayed by money the way a dog is swayed by a bone.*

APPROACHING For students having difficulties, point out that Kassam uses the word *snarling* in the stage direction where Kanubhai compares Dongo to a dog. **Ask:** Does it seem that he's saying Dongo is friendly and loyal like a pet dog? What kind of dog is he like? *(a vicious dog)*

BUTCHER. I . . . I . . . I'm sorry. I didn't know about these things. If . . . if you return next week, I promise everything will be in order. But please, I must have the license endorsed by next Monday.

DONGO. That's your business. I'm warning you, if everything is not ready by next week, you won't get your license, is that clear?

BUTCHER. Yes, yes. Everything will be in order next week. I promise.

DONGO. Your business. [*Exit.*]

GIRL. Come on, where's my meat?

1 BUTCHER. Oh, dear, yes. I'm sorry. I won't be a minute. Here it is. [*She exits. The* BUTCHER *surveys his shop in despair.*] What's to be done? And that girl, she didn't pay me. Which way did she go? Too late: she's made off. [*Enter* KANUBHAI, *a Hindu trader, in dhoti and cap. He holds his nose in disgust as he passes the* BUTCHER's *shop.*] Kanubhai! Oh, Kanubhai! Just come over here please, quick.

Visual Vocabulary
A *dhoti* (thō′te) is a loincloth worn by Hindu men.

KANUBHAI. Come near your stinking meat? No, no, no, never!

BUTCHER. Ah, this old man! [*He comes from his shop and crosses to* KANUBHAI.] Kanubhai, please help me. You know that health inspector, he's refusing to endorse my trading license. I whitewashed[6] my shop and I bought a new apron, but still he comes and asks me why my shop's dirty, and why my hair is not stylishly done, and what not. What am I to do?

KANUBHAI. That man! I know him. He's a dog. He's hungry.

---

6. *Whitewashed* means "applied a mixture of lime and water to whiten a surface."

146 UNIT 1 MODERN AFRICA

BUTCHER. Hungry?

KANUBHAI. Yes, hungry. He wants some bones. [*He pretends to snarl.*]

BUTCHER. Bones?

KANUBHAI. Yes, bones. You still don't understand? [*He takes out some coins, jingles them, and pretends to eat them, snarling as he does so.*] He wants bones, bones!

BUTCHER. Oh, bones, bones! Yes, I see, he wants some bones.

[*As* KANUBHAI *exits, the* BUTCHER *leaps joyfully into the air, claps his hands, and returns purposefully to his shop.*]

SCENE 2 ◆◆◆◆◆◆◆◆◆◆◆◆◆◆◆

[*The same scene a week later. The floor is littered with rubbish. The* BUTCHER's *apron is filthy. Rusty knives and broken implements lie around.*]

ANNOUNCER. The same scene. One week later.

[*The* BUTCHER *stretches, yawns, scratches himself, spits on the floor, kicks at the rubbish. Enter* DONGO; *he coughs. The* BUTCHER *works at his counter, pretending not to have seen* DONGO, *who strolls with exaggerated casualness up to the shop. The* BUTCHER *looks up, pretending surprise.*]

BUTCHER. Oh, Dongo! Good morning. How are you?

DONGO. Mmm! Not so well.

BUTCHER. Not well? I'm very sorry. Anyway, I hope you've come to endorse my license.

DONGO. Endorse your license? Just like that? With such a dirty shop?

BUTCHER. Oh, by the way, Mr. Dongo, I

Visualize *Why does Kanubhai take out coins, pretend to eat them, and snarl? What is he trying to show?* **2**

Literary Element Practice

Metaphor When Kanubhai says of Dongo, "He's a dog," he uses a metaphor. A metaphor is a figure of speech that compares seemingly unlike things without using the word *like* or *as*. Kanubhai does not mean that Dongo is literally a dog; he is comparing Dongo to a dog because of their shared characteristic of hunger: a dog's hunger for bones and Dongo's for money.

Tell students that to create their own metaphors, they should think of a person they know (not a member of the class). Then they can think of something they are similar to, but are not literally like. This may be, for instance, an animal, an object, or a meteorological occurrence. Then craft the metaphor into a sentence without using the word *like* or *as*. Example: "My

baby brother is a fire alarm; my family is exhausted because he cried all last night."

146

almost forgot: I have something for you. I thought you might like a few bones to take home.

[*The butcher hands dongo a small package.*]

DONGO. Bones? Bones? What should I want with bones? [*As he **fumbles** with the package, a couple of coins fall out. He chases after them, and then slips the package in his pocket.*] Oh, bones, bones! That's very thoughtful of you. They will come in very handy. [*He smiles broadly.*] Mr. Awadh, your shop looks really clean today. See, no cobwebs, a clean scale, a new broom, a dustbin outside. It's the way we want it. Don't you worry about your hair. Come on, give me those forms. [*The BUTCHER hands him the forms. DONGO takes out a pen, goes to sign, but finds the nib[7] is broken.*] Just lend me your pen, please. Something's gone wrong with mine.

BUTCHER. Certainly, certainly. I'm at your service.

[*The BUTCHER hands over his pen, which DONGO examines admiringly.*]

DONGO. Eh, you've bought a new pen. [*He finishes signing and slips the pen into his own pocket.*] Well that's done. Now you'll be all right. O.K., Mr. Awadh, kwaheri.[8]

BUTCHER. Thank you. Kwaheri, kwaheri.

DONGO. Kwaheri.

BUTCHER. Kwaheri.

[*DONGO goes out and then returns for his hat, which he had put on the counter while signing.*]

DONGO. Ah, my hat, there it is. Kwaheri, kwaheri.

BUTCHER. Kwaheri. [*DONGO goes out. The BUTCHER returns to his work. Enter the WOMAN. She surveys the shop, screws up her face, holds her nose, and walks past with her head in the air.*] Hello, mama! Good morning. [*She eyes him sourly.*] Aren't you coming to buy meat today?

WOMAN. Just look at your shop! And at yourself! Dirty and stinking! I'm not going to buy meat from you anymore. I'm going to the next butcher, to a cleaner shop. [*Exit.*]

BUTCHER. But mama, mama, I have my license. Listen. [*He reads.*] "Certified clean and fit to sell meat for human consumption." Mama! Mama! ❧

Curtain.

---

7. A *nib* is a pen point.
8. *Kwaheri* (kwä hä′rē) is Swahili for "good-bye."

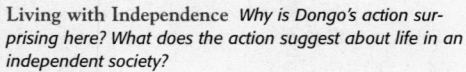

3 **Living with Independence** *Why is Dongo's action surprising here? What does the action suggest about life in an independent society?*

Vocabulary

fumble (fum′bəl) *v.* to grope or handle clumsily

Satire *Why is the woman's sudden refusal to buy the butcher's meat satirical?* **4**

SADRU KASSAM **147**

Advanced Learners/Pre-AP

DIFFERENTIATED INSTRUCTION

Writing Have advanced learners write their own short satirical play. The plays should have about five roles and should comment on human nature or society in an entertaining, comic manner. Have students exchange their plays with one another and make suggestions for improvement.

Teach

Big Idea **3**

Living with Independence
Answer: *Dongo's theft of the pen is surprising because he has just been paid off by the butcher and should be satisfied. The action suggests that corrupt people are completely unreasonable.*

Literary Element **4**

Satire **Answer:** *The woman realizes that the license is meaningless and that the shop is filthy. Her unwillingness to buy the butcher's meat after he receives the license reveals that his work ethic has become corrupted as well as his relationship with the inspector.*
(ADVANCED) Ask advanced students what the message in the final lines of the play is. (*A certificate gained through bribery has no value.*)

Progress Check

Can students analyze satire?

If No → See Unit 1 Teaching Resources Book, p. 206.

Learning Objectives
Visualizing. (SE)
Analyzing satire. (SE)
Applying metaphor. (TE)
Analyzing irony. (TE)

After You Read

Assess

1. Most students will probably say the butcher is most amusing.

2. (a) He says that Dongo is a hungry dog who wants some bones. (b) Most students will say the metaphor is appropriate, because the term *dog* here implies begging and underhandedness.

3. (a) The shop is relatively clean in scene 1 but very dirty in scene 2. (b) The butcher no longer cares about even basic cleanliness because he now knows that only a bribe will get him a license.

4. (a) He is polite, but he tries to cheat his customer. (b) Answers will vary.

5. Many students will say Dongo is more dishonest.

6. Possible answer: when the butcher gets the license, his shop is so filthy that customers no longer want to shop there.

7. (a) Corruption and cheating can continue. (b) Citizens do not benefit equally from independence when at the mercy of corrupt officials.

8. Most students will say that such a shop would not stay open in their community.

✍ Writing

Students' editorials should

- address why corruption occurs and whether it can be justified
- offer suggestions for reforms
- be written in an appropriate style and tone

Literary Element

1. (a) Kassam satirizes corrupt government practices. (b) He uses humor, exaggeration, and irony.

2. The tone is fairly gentle and good-natured. Evidence will vary.

148

After You Read

Respond and Think Critically

Respond and Interpret

1. Which character in the play did you find the most amusing? Explain.

2. (a) A **metaphor** is a comparison between two seemingly unlike things. What metaphor does Kanubhai use to explain to the butcher how to get a license? (b) Is the metaphor appropriate? Explain.

3. (a) How does the cleanliness of the butcher shop in scene 2 compare to that in scene 1? (b) What might be the reason for this change?

Analyze and Evaluate

4. (a) What are some of the butcher's positive and negative traits? (b) Are any of his negative traits justifiable? Explain.

5. Who do you think is more dishonest in the play, Dongo or the butcher? Explain.

6. **Irony** is a contrast between what is expected and what actually exists or occurs. Identify an example of irony in the play.

Connect

7. **Big Idea** Living with Independence
A country's newfound independence is generally considered beneficial to all its citizens. (a) Based on the play, what flaws are there in this reasoning? (b) Do all citizens benefit equally from independence?

8. **Connect to Today** Do you think a shop such as the butcher's would be allowed to remain open in your community? Explain.

Literary Element Satire

Authors use **satire** to expose human flaws and questionable social customs and institutions in an entertaining way.

1. (a) What does Kassam satirize in *Bones*? (b) What literary devices does he use?

2. How would you describe the tone of Kassam's satire? Support your response with evidence from the text.

Reading Strategy Visualize

Review the chart you made on page 142.

1. How do the stage directions in *Bones* contribute to your visualization of the butcher?

2. From an actor's perspective, what might be the benefit of having no stage directions?

LOG ON ▶ **Literature** Online

Selection Resources For Selection Quizzes, eFlashcards, and Reading-Writing Connection activities, go to glencoe.com and enter QuickPass code GLW6053u1.

Vocabulary Practice

Practice with Usage Respond to these statements to help you explore the meanings of vocabulary words from the play.

1. Describe a time when you worked **vigorously** to achieve one of your goals.

2. List some documents that one might need to **endorse**.

3. Give an example of a time when you were **pestered** by a family member or a friend.

4. List some things that might cause someone to **fumble**.

✍ Writing

Write an Editorial Imagine that the butcher and his shop are in your town and you have just learned about his bribery. Write a brief editorial in which you address the problem of corrupt businesses in your community.

Reading Strategy

1. The stage directions describe his coat, hair, filthy habits, and clumsiness.

2. Without directions, an actor can interpret the character freely and perhaps more creatively.

 For additional selection assessment, see Assessment Resources, pp. 63–64.

Vocabulary

1. Students should describe an activity to which they applied energy and zeal.

2. Answers will vary.

3. Students might describe an interaction with a sibling.

4. Answers will vary.

Before You Read

A House for Us

Egypt

Meet **Etidal Osman**
(born 1942)

E tidal Osman (e ti′däl o͞os′män) belongs to a group of contemporary women authors from Cairo, Egypt, who experiment with language and literary techniques. Although Osman wrote extensively as a teenager, she did not begin publishing her work until she was more than 40 years old. Since then, she has published collections of stories and critical essays. Before moving to the United Arab Emirates, Osman was the managing editor of *Sutoor*, an Egyptian cultural magazine.

> *"Etidal Osman is interested in making language itself the main character of her stories."*
>
> —Marilyn Booth, from *My Grandmother's Cactus: Stories by Egyptian Women*

North African Women Authors In many North African countries, women find it difficult to pursue writing careers because of cultural and religious restrictions. Egyptian women authors face similar obstacles, but they have established a strong literary tradition that dates to the late nineteenth century. Women from earlier generations usually wrote in a realistic style and focused on issues such as gender discrimination in education, employment, and politics. Osman's writing is more experimental and somewhat more abstract, yet it still successfully explores the region's history and the social and political issues critical to the future of North Africa and the Middle East. Her belief in the value of creative freedom is underscored by her

Cairo Night, 1996. Lucy Willis. Watercolor on paper. Private collection.

membership in International PEN, an organization that "stands for the principle of unhampered transmission of thought within each nation and between all nations."

Spotlight on Egypt Egypt is in the northeast corner of Africa. Since Egypt's emergence as a republic in 1953, its government has demonstrated both dictatorial and democratic tendencies. In many ways, its political life has been a steady reaction to regional conditions and international conflicts. Clashes with Israel, pan-Arabism (a movement to unite Arab people and countries and reject colonialism), the Cold War, socialism, and Islamic extremism have all played a role in Egypt's development. Osman's short story "A House for Us" highlights some of the political and religious conflicts of the region.

Osman is now an instructor of Arabic language and literature at Zayed University in Dubai, although she remains a member of the Supreme Council of Culture in Egypt. Her works include *Sun Tattoo, Short Stories* (1992) and *Illuminating the Text, Readings in Modern Arabic Poetry* (1988).

 Literature Online

Author Search For more about Etidal Osman, go to glencoe.com and enter QuickPass code GLW6053u1.

ETIDAL OSMAN **149**

Before You Read

Focus

Bellringer Options

Selection Focus Transparency 12

Daily Language Practice Transparency 19

Or ask: What might make two friends drift apart? Students might say that friends drift apart due to physical distance, developing different interests, or an argument.

Or ask: How do you measure maturity? Students might say that the ability to accept consequences and the acceptance of differing views are signs of maturity.

Selection Skills

Literary Elements
• Description (SE pp. 150–152, 154)

Reading Skills
• Make Inferences about Theme (SE pp. 150, 153, 154)

A House for Us

Vocabulary Skills
• Synonyms (SE p. 154)
• Memory Game (TE p. 150)

Speaking/Listening/Viewing Skills
• Analyze Art (TE p. 151)

Writing Skills/Grammar
• Description (SE p. 154)
• Participles (TE p. 150)

Before You Read

Focus

Summary

A childish spat mirrors the conflict over whether the city of Bethlehem belongs to Christians, Jews, or Muslims. After fighting over a lead marble, Rami tells the narrator that his city, Bethlehem, belongs to the Christians and that God's house is there. The narrator says that God is everywhere. They separate in anger. For days, the narrator draws pictures of a house that resembles the one that Rami described. The narrator says she does not know how to draw the Lord's house, but she can draw a house for herself and Rami.

 For summaries in languages other than English, see Unit 1 Teaching Resources Book, pp. 213–218.

Vocabulary

Memory Game Put students in pairs. One partner should look up the vocabulary words in a dictionary or thesaurus and find a synonym for each word. Then he or she should make eight cards with one word on each card (four will be from the selection and four will be synonyms). The student should lay the cards out on the floor; then the partner flips over two cards every turn to make matches. A vocabulary word and its synonym are a matching pair.

 For additional vocabulary practice, see Unit 1 Teaching Resources Book, p. 221.

Literature and Reading Preview

Connect to the Story

Can friendships survive major differences of opinion? Write a journal entry about this question.

Build Background

Possession of the city of Bethlehem—a sacred place for Christians, Jews, and Muslims—has been a controversial issue. In 1967, Israel gained control of the West Bank, where Bethlehem is situated, and ordered the demolition of many Palestinian homes, claiming they had been built illegally. Palestinians believed that Israel had made it nearly impossible for them to obtain legal building permits. Egypt and Israel went to war several times over this and other issues before signing a peace agreement in 1979. In 1995, Israel placed Bethlehem and other areas under Palestinian self-rule, but problems continue. One of the characters in Osman's story is a member of the Christian Palestinian minority, a refugee from Bethlehem.

Set Purposes for Reading

Big Idea **Living with Independence**

As you read, ask yourself, How do the characters in the story cope with the political difficulties and religious differences faced by their newly independent countries?

Literary Element **Description**

Description is writing that creates a clear image of a feeling, an action, or a scene in the reader's mind. The use of figurative language and precise verbs, adjectives, and adverbs can also help make description vivid. As you read, ask yourself, What are some effective descriptive details in this story?

Reading Strategy **Make Inferences About Theme**

When you **make inferences about theme,** you make a reasonable guess about the message of a literary work. As you read "A House for Us," ask yourself, What inferences can I make to determine the story's theme?

Tip: Take Notes Use a chart like the one below to record inferences you make from the details in the story.

Detail	Inference

Learning Objectives

For pages 149–154

In studying this text, you will focus on the following objectives:

Literary Study: Analyzing description.

Reading: Making inferences about theme.

Writing: Writing a description.

Vocabulary

coincide (kō´in sīd´) *v.* to occupy the same place in space or time; p. 151 *The lunar eclipse will coincide with the start of winter.*

taut (tôt) *adj.* having no give or slack; tightly drawn; p. 152 *The taut kite line loosened as the wind died down.*

stifled (stī´fəld) *adj.* muffled or repressed; p. 153 *She could hear the young girls hiding behind the curtain, despite their stifled laughter.*

submerge (səb murj´) *v.* to go under water; p. 153 *The old, decayed fishing boat eventually submerged in the lake.*

Tip: Synonyms Synonyms are words that have the same or similar meanings. They are always the same part of speech. For example, *submerge* and *immerse* have about the same meaning.

Grammar Practice

Participles Explain that present and past participles of many verbs can be adjectives. Usually, present participles end in –*ing* and past participles end in –*d* or –*ed.* Write these sentences and ask students to identify the participles: I heard a muffled voice. (*muffled*) A growing child eats a lot. (*growing*)

Have students write three sentences about the story, using a participle in each. Have pairs exchange papers to identify each principle.

Literary Element

Description **Answer:** *The description is effective because Osman uses imagery and similes to capture the colors and texture of the marbles.*

> For additional literary element practice, see Unit 1 Teaching Resources Book, p. 219.

Stormy Day, Aqaba, 1984. Nicholas Egon. Watercolour and pastel on handmade paper. Collection of HM King Hussein of Jordan.

A House for Us

Etidal Osman   Translated by Marilyn Booth

Rami and me, me and Rami . . . always together, except on Sunday mornings and Christian holidays, which fall at times other than our Lesser and Greater Feasts and never even **coincide** with the Prophet's Birthday.

Together, we feel our love for the sea when it is right there at our balcony and when its white birds circle overhead. They come from afar, from Rami's country which lies beyond the sea.

When the sun grows hot we play in the shade of my room. We divide up the colored crystal marbles: the blue ones, the color of the sea, are for you; the green ones, green as the plants around us, are mine.

Vocabulary

coincide (kō´ in sīd´) *v.* to occupy the same place in space or time

---

Description *What literary elements in this passage make the description effective?*

ETIDAL OSMAN **151**

View the Art

Nicholas Egon (1921–) was born in Czechoslovakia to an aristocratic family. He showed artistic promise at an early age and taught painting in England while still in his 20s. He then settled in Greece. Although best known for his portraits, Egon has also done many watercolors of landscapes and seascapes, such as this one of the famous Jordanian seaport of Aqaba. Ask students to keep this image in mind as they read the selection and to think of ways in which it connects with the text.

English Learners

DIFFERENTIATED INSTRUCTION

Intermediate Explain to students what happens in the beginning of the story: Rami and the narrator enjoy playing marbles together. They always fight over one special marble. The narrator gets upset when she loses the game, and Rami gives her all the marbles to comfort her.

Ask: What does this episode tell us about the relationship between the two friends? *(They enjoy playing together, and even when they fight, they make up soon.)*

Readability Scores

Dale-Chall: 6.6
DRP: 55
Lexile: 920

Learning Objectives
Analyzing description. (SE)
Using participles. (TE)

Teach

Literary Element   1

Description Answer: *The description captures feelings associated with anger and indicates that the narrator is upset by Rami's statement; it is clear a disagreement may arise.*

Literary History ☆

Sindbad The friends are probably reading from *The Thousand and One Nights.* This is a medieval Arabic collection of tales: Queen Scheherazade tells her husband a story every night, always leaving the ending for the next night so he must postpone her execution another day. The frame story is set in Central Asia, but the tales have origins in the Near East, Middle East, and India. Some of the tales, such as those of Aladdin and Sindbad the Sailor, have become part of Western culture.

Every time, we fight over a lone, lead-toned marble, its grayness a lustrous, silvery gleam. Your little hand always takes that marble first, folding over it tightly, clasping it forcefully. For a moment you gaze at something before you, something I cannot see. You speak to someone other than me, when there is no one but us in the room: "I know this lead."

I feel the wings of a white bird fluttering in my heart, and I'm content to let you be the first to take aim. And always . . . always, the marbles run into your row. No matter what I do, I lose every round. I change the position from which I will shoot; I come closer or move further away, or I veer into a corner. I look carefully, consider everything minutely, and adjust the position of my hand until it is just right. I incline my body as far as I possibly can until I am nearly prostrate[1] on the camel-wool rug; or else I crouch down on my knees and hold my breath before the lead-gray marble shoots off from between my fingers and misses the other marbles. You win, getting the larger share.

I'm so angry that I practically burst into tears. As I sit on the floor facing the wall, fuming and waiting, you come to my side, the marbles cupped in your palms, and you put them in my lap.

"They're all for you."

In the late afternoons we open books, lots of them, bright with pictures. We travel together to the land of marvels. You ☆ read to me, I read to you: about Sindbad who rode the high seas and came back with a bird in a cage, its feathers of silver and gold. And about Sitt el-Husn and el-Shatir Hasan, the seas between them, and the haunted house with the thousand windows and thousand rooms, all of them open but one. And about the djinni[2] who guards that room and has not slept for a thousand thousand years.

You are reading. Suddenly you stop and say, "In Bethlehem there's a house that belongs to us."

The words take me by surprise—as if I have forgotten that you, like the seabirds, come from far away. You go on, as if to assure me with further words.

"Bethlehem is our city, and it's the city of the Lord's House, and of grapevine trellises and olive trees."

I was sitting next to you on the large sofa that is draped in a heavy cotton weave of tiny, interwined stars and circles. Between us was a heavy cushion, flattened, the cushion-cover **taut**, on which we rested the book. I found that the patterns in the weaving were becoming blurred. My head was growing hot and my cheeks started to burn. I

Visual Vocabulary
A *trellis* (trel′ is) is a latticework frame used to support climbing plants.

---

2. A *djinni* (jē′ nē) is one of a class of supernatural spirits that, according to Muslim belief, can take different forms and wield various powers. A *genie* in a lamp is an example of these spirits.

Description *How does the description of the narrator's reaction advance the plot of the story?*   1

Vocabulary

taut (tôt) *adj.* having no give or slack; tightly drawn

---

1. *Prostrate* means "lying flat."

Reading Practice

Analyze Structure The structure of a story is just as important as characterization and plot. Have students review the sequence of events in the story. **Ask: How does the structure influence the narrative? How might the tone of the story change if things were switched around?**

Have students write an outline of a different version of the story, using the same events in Osman's story but rearranging their order. For instance, the narrative could begin with Rami explaining that his house was destroyed. Students should explain how the tone of the switched-around story would differ from Osman's.

heard a **stifled** voice, not mine, coming from between my lips: "God is in the heavens, and everywhere. He doesn't have a house."

You gazed at me, astonished, seeking to understand. Your almond-shaped eyes, wide in silent distress yet tearless, gave off a brownish flash. It vanished only to return with a stubbornness that pierced my chest. My heart no longer fluttered on a pair of wings.

I was afraid of my own confusion and anger, and of the darkness that now attacked us, and of the stubborn light radiating outwards to **submerge** itself in the sea. You spoke in a calm but insistent masculine voice years older than yourself.

"Our house was made of white stones. It was built on a small hill and it had a little set of stairs outside, five steps. The last one was split on one edge, the crack would be on my left when I was going down the steps to the narrow flagstone path that led to the beginning of the street . . . to the city of the Lord's House . . . I saw our house turn into a heap of rubble, and my father was underneath it, still holding his Mauser rifle. There were four leads in it, I counted them with him, and there's a fifth one with me . . . in my pocket, it never leaves me . . . here it is, look, just like the leaden marble except it's pointed."

I didn't look. I remained silent, afraid, my face towards the wall, the cushion between us. I wasn't expecting that Rami would push the cushion away to put something in my lap.

The next moment his mother's voice was calling from beneath the balcony. "Rami, Rami . . . it's nearly evening . . . come on down now."

Rami went. And for many days thereafter I felt angry with the balcony and the sea and refused to go near them, and I forgot Rami. I withdrew into a corner of my room, with my many-colored books and lots of blank, white paper on which I drew a hill and a house made of large stones; a house that had five steps. And the sun was getting ready to begin its journey, taking from the flowers along the house's flagstone path a dark purplish hue that shone on crystal windows, all of them closed but one. From that one open window a single eye gazed out: an eye lit up with brown rays, shining forth, stubborn like the eye of a haunted lighthouse guarding the sea, ever sleepless.

I drew and drew but I didn't know, and I still don't know, how to draw a calm masculine voice, coming from the depths, the voice of a youth who never grew old. And I don't know how to draw the house of the Lord which I will never see. Yet I do draw, often, a house for us.

---

2   **Living with Independence** *How might Rami's experience reflect the experiences of others living in this region?*

Make Inferences About Theme *What can you infer about the theme from the story's final sentences?*   3

Vocabulary

stifled (stī′fəld) *adj.* muffled or repressed
submerge (səb murj′) *v.* to go under water

ETIDAL OSMAN   **153**

Approaching Level

DIFFERENTIATED INSTRUCTION

Paraphrase To help approaching-level students answer the inference question in the side column on this page, have them paraphrase the last paragraph of the selection. Begin by asking them to skim the previous paragraphs on this page to find out who has "a calm masculine voice." *(Rami)* **Ask:** In what city is "the house of the Lord"? *(Bethlehem)* Who used to live in Bethlehem? *(Rami)* To whom

does the word *us* refer? *(Rami and the narrator)* Why might the narrator draw "a house for us"? *(The narrator misses Rami.)*

Teach

Big Idea   2

Living with Independence
Answer: *Many people continue to experience violence as a result of political, religious, and ethnic conflicts in this region.*

[APPROACHING] Explain to learners having difficulty that Rami is a member of the Christian Palestinian minority. His house was destroyed by forces from Israel, the Jewish state. Egypt and Palestine were allied against Israel, so although Rami and the narrator are of different religions, they are allowed to play together.

Reading Strategy   3

Make Inferences About Theme Answer: *Students might infer that the theme centers on how people should work to overcome their differences and get along, even if they sometimes strongly disagree with one another.*

Progress Check

Can students make inferences about the theme?

If No → See Unit 1 Teaching Resources Book, p. 220.

To check students' understanding of the selection, see Unit 1 Teaching Resources Book, p. 224.

Learning Objectives
Analyzing description. (SE)
Making inferences about theme. (SE)
Analyzing structure. (TE)

153

After You Read

Assess

1. Students may be surprised that the narrator was so angry and withdrawn, given the friendship and what Rami had suffered.

2. (a) They are friends. (b) Rami is more mature; he has been exposed to violence, and the narrator has not.

3. (a) It was destroyed while his father was inside. (b) He wants the narrator to understand his feelings.

4. (a) The narrator is silent and afraid. (b) The narrator is scared and lacks full comprehension of Rami's loss.

5. (a) Possible answers: the sea is the friendship between the children, the bullet is the violence of Rami's past, and the narrator's drawing is an attempt to understand Rami. (b) Answers will vary.

6. (a) The story begins in the present tense to describe the friends' ongoing activities, and switches to the past tense to describe a specific incident. (b) This change establishes that the narrator is examining the incident years later.

7. Free societies must learn to tolerate many viewpoints.

8. Osman portrays Rami's situation sympathetically. The struggles in the Middle East may have inspired Osman to handle her subjects with sensitivity.

After You Read

Respond and Think Critically

Respond and Interpret

1. Did the narrator's reaction to Rami's story surprise you? Explain.

2. (a)How would you describe the relationship between the children before Rami tells the narrator his story? (b)What factors create conflict between Rami and the narrator?

3. (a)What happened to Rami's house in Bethlehem? (b)Why do you think he tells this story to the narrator?

4. (a)How does the narrator react to Rami's story? (b)Why do you think the narrator reacts this way?

Analyze and Evaluate

5. (a)A **symbol** is an object or an action that stands for something else in addition to itself. What symbols appear in the story? (b)Do you think these symbols are effective? Why or why not?

6. (a)Why do you think the author shifts from the present tense to the past tense midway through the story? (b)What does this shift contribute to the story?

Connect

7. **Big Idea** **Living with Independence** How does the children's conflict reflect some of the issues related to countries that are newly independent?

8. **Connect to the Author** Osman's country, Egypt, fought Israel over the destruction of Palestinian homes. How might Egypt's struggle have affected the way Osman wrote this story?

 **Literary Element** Description

Effective **description** can make a scene more believable and make characters more vivid.

1. Why is the description of Rami's house in Bethlehem crucial to the plot?

2. Which words in Osman's description of the marble game help you picture the children's movements?

Reading Strategy Make Inferences About Theme

Refer to the chart you made on page 150.

1. (a)Is the theme of "A House for Us" directly stated or implied? (b)How can you tell?

2. What is this story's theme? Support your claim with evidence from the text.

LOG ON  **Literature** Online

Selection Resources For Selection Quizzes, eFlashcards, and Reading-Writing Connection activities, go to glencoe.com and enter QuickPass code GLW6053u1.

Vocabulary Practice

Practice with Synonyms With a partner match each boldfaced vocabulary word below with its synonym. Use a thesaurus or dictionary to check your answers. You will not use all the answer choices.

1. coincide	a. sink	e. smothered
2. taut	b. tight	f. correspond
3. stifled	c. loose	
4. submerge	d. released	

Writing

Write a Description Write a description of a confrontation you once had with another person, narrating from that person's perspective. What might that person have wanted you to understand about his or her perspective? What larger issues were at stake? Use figurative language to describe the misunderstanding.

Literary Element

1. It is the catalyst for the disagreement between the children. Additionally, it allows readers to imagine the house in Bethlehem and underscores Rami's refugee status.

2. Possible answers: *veer, incline, prostrate, crouch.*

Reading Strategy

1. (a) The theme is implied. (b) Osman never states any theme directly in the text.

2. The theme is that people must learn to accept those with beliefs different from their own. Students might point to the story's end, in which the narrator is drawing a house that can hold both Rami and the narrator.

Vocabulary

1. f 2. b 3. e 4. a

Writing

Students' descriptions should be written from the perspective of the other person, illustrate the larger issues underlying the conflict, and employ figurative language and specific details

Learning Objectives

For pages 155–157

In studying this text, you will focus on the following objectives:

Reading:
Analyzing text structure.
Using text features.
Analyzing informational text.

Set a Purpose for Reading

Read to learn how one man journeyed from imprisonment to a career as an AIDS health-care worker. Consider how his story relates to the challenges facing Africans living with independence.

Preview the Article

"Heroes Among Us" profiles the life of Patrick Chamusso, whose imprisonment during apartheid in South Africa inspired him to help children with AIDS.

1. Examine the photograph and caption on page 156. What do they reveal?

2. Read the sentence below the title. What do you think is the focus of this article?

Reading Strategy Analyze Text Structure

When you analyze text structure, you recognize the pattern of organization. As you read, ask yourself, What are some causes and effects detailed in the article? Use a graphic organizer like this one to keep track of your answers.

Cause		Effect
Chamusso is arrested at oil refinery.	→	Chamusso becomes a freedom fighter.

TIME

HEROES Among Us

A former freedom fighter makes a home for kids orphaned by AIDS.

By SUSAN SCHINDEHETTE

O N A COOL AUTUMN AFTERNOON IN NEW YORK CITY, Patrick Chamusso gently traces a finger over photographs of his wife and children—not just his son and two daughters but also the dozens of AIDS orphans he considers his own. "It's too cold here," he says softly. "I am so homesick. I miss South Africa. Oh my, I miss you people."

That faraway country is the only real home Chamusso has ever known, from the poverty-stricken rural streets where he grew up to the threatening walls of the infamous Robben Island prison. Along with men like former South Africa President Nelson Mandela, Chamusso was imprisoned at Robben Island and held for a decade as an enemy of the apartheid government. (Under apartheid, a variety of laws allowed South Africa's ruling white minority to segregate people of African, Asian, and mixed race, denying them basic human and political rights for decades.)

Even 14 years after his release, as he traveled to promote *Catch a Fire*, the movie that tells the remarkable story of his life, it was still difficult for him to recall those days of unspeakable horror. "Whenever I start talking about it, I go right back to the room where they tortured me," he said. "They did awful, unbelievable things that I cannot begin to tell you about. It is like opening a wound on my heart."

Yet even more inspiring than the tale of Chamusso's survival is the story of what he has done with his hard-won freedom since. Released from Robben Island in 1992 during the fall of apartheid,

HEROES AMONG US **155**

TIME

Focus

Summary

South African Patrick Chamusso talks about what motivated him to become a health care worker for AIDS-affected orphans. While working at the Secunda refinery, he was wrongly accused of planting a bomb and conspiring with the African National Congress. After serving a short prison sentence, he became an ANC freedom fighter and committed acts of sabotage. Arrested and sentenced to 24 years in the Robben Island prison, he was released after serving ten years in 1992. He then learned that AIDS was plaguing his nation. Inspired, he took a course in health care, and in 1999, he built Two Sisters—a shelter for orphans in the village of Mganduzweni, where he and his wife, Conney Thibedi, assist AIDS-affected children.

 For activities related to this selection, see Unit 1 Teaching Resources Book, pp. 226–234.

Approaching Level

 DIFFERENTIATED INSTRUCTION

Take Notes Copy the Main Idea Organizer on this page to the board. Ask students for the events and details that support the main idea and write these in the appropriate columns. Then, help them to summarize the article in a few sentences in the Conclusion column.

Main Idea: Patrick Chamusso's imprisonment during apartheid inspired him to help AIDS-affected children upon his release.

Supporting Detail	Supporting Detail	Supporting Detail

Conclusion:

Readability Scores

Dale-Chall: 6.6
DRP: 56
Lexile: 1050

TIME

Teach

Big Idea   1

The Price of Freedom Have students identify tactics of the African National Congress.

Ask: What does this article reveal about the movement to resist apartheid in South Africa? *(Members of the ANC sometimes resorted to terrorism in their struggles with the government.)*

(APPROACHING) For students having difficulty, explain the meaning of *sabotage* and *terrorism*. Ask students to discuss why the conditions of apartheid would lead some people to react with violence.

Political History ☆

Opposition to Apartheid One of the first organizations opposed to apartheid was the African National Congress. The ruling National Party of South Africa outlawed the ANC in 1960. As a result, the ANC committed acts of sabotage and guerilla warfare. Many of the ANC's leaders, including Nelson Mandela, received long prison sentences.

Khali Mazraawi–AFP/GETTY

ALL HIS CHILDREN "I was worried what would happen to me, and Patrick saved me," says Sandile Ndlovu (front row, in beige T-shirt, with Chamusso, Conney, and some of the children at the Two Sisters shelter in 2005).

Chamusso soon learned about a new affliction in his homeland: AIDS. "We had fought so hard for freedom," he says. "And now there was this sickness that was making so many of us prisoners of disease."

Spurred to action by that crisis, in 1999 Chamusso founded Two Sisters, a modest shelter for orphans in the village of Mganduzweni. There, with small donations and his $260 monthly pension, he and his wife, Conney Thibedi, struggle to provide shelter, food, care, and love to a group of children who have been affected by the disease. Named for two HIV-positive girls the couple took in who later died, Two Sisters is a full-time home for 15 children who have lost one or both parents to AIDS. It's a second home for about 110 more who live with relatives or foster families in the village and come to Two Sisters during the day to eat, bathe, play, and be taken to school or a nearby medical clinic for treatment. "These are all my children," says Chamusso. "I love them as much as if I was their real father. I love each one as my own."

In an area hit hard by poverty and the AIDS epidemic, the four-room shelter is a rare safety net. Sincedile Malatji began coming after her father died of AIDS. "There was no food at home," says Malatji, whose mother worked harvesting bark from trees. Chamusso and Conney "gave me clothes to wear and made it a welcoming place," she says. It can also be a sad one. Some of the children have HIV or AIDS themselves. "Whenever a child dies, Patrick measures the child, and because coffins are so expensive to buy, makes one from planks and then buries them," says Conney. "It breaks his heart every time."

More than 40 years ago, Chamusso was himself a poor teenager struggling to make ends meet. After his father abandoned him, he was trained as a boilermaker and a housepainter and in 1976 won a highly valued job as a foreman in the Secunda oil refinery. Then, in 1980, members of the anti-apartheid African National Congress (ANC) staged a bombing at Secunda in an attempt to disrupt the country's economy. Though innocent, Chamusso was arrested and tortured. "They smashed my teeth and pulled out my fingernails. They tied my hands behind my back and used a machine to lift me off the ground.

1

Reading Practice

Analyze Text Structure Ask: What was the chronology of events in Patrick Chamusso's life? On the board, write an outline of Chamusso's life with bullet points for the following: boyhood, first job, first arrest, joining the ANC, imprisonment, release from prison, and becoming an AIDS health care provider. Have students identify dates and excerpts from the article to complete the bullets to this outline.

Then ask: Why do you think the events of Chamusso's life are not discussed in chronological order in the article? Guide students to identify how one event in Chamusso's life was caused by another event in his life. Have them discuss the purpose of cause-effect structure in writing.

Day after day they said, 'Confess, confess!' But I didn't know the truth," he says quietly. "I didn't know anything."

Months later, Chamusso was released—a changed man: "I thought, if they can beat an innocent man like this, they can do anything to anyone." His experience inspired Chamusso to work for revolutionary change, and he trained to become an ANC freedom fighter. "Now, I thought, even if I am arrested and killed, I would have suffered and died for a reason," he says. In 1982, after planting several bombs at the Secunda refinery, he was found guilty of terrorism and sentenced to 24 years in prison. "I dreamed of vengeance," he says. "But the older prisoners said, 'No, we must show them that we are not what they think we are.' Forgiveness was the biggest lesson I learned on Robben Island." Ten years later, Chamusso was released: "Being on that boat leaving the island was the most beautiful day of my life."

His joy faded when he first learned about the little-understood disease that was sweeping his country. Determined to make a difference, Chamusso took a course in health care. He educated himself about how AIDS is treated and how the virus that causes the disease spreads and began providing home-based care for the sick. "So many people were being shunned and left in the street to die," he says. "There were orphans everywhere. No one would help the children whose parents had died."

> ❝ These are all my children. I love them as much as if I was their real father. I love each one as my own. ❞
>
> —Patrick Chamusso

Chamusso did. Battling ignorance and fear, he built the house that now serves as Two Sisters. Today, even as he struggles to raise the money needed "for so many things: fresh eggs for the children, medicine, schoolbooks," he seems a man focused on forgiveness—and the future. His grand dream is to build a soccer field for his kids in a country where that sport is almost a religion. "Sometimes, I ask the children, 'Do you want to play as well as [David] Beckham [the world-famous professional soccer player]?'" he says. "And they reply, 'No, we want to play better than him. We want to be the best players in the world.'"

Chamusso is inspired by his kids' goals. He thinks that "Black kids in South Africa dreaming of being the best in the world at something—and not being afraid to say it out loud" is a sort of miracle. "For me, that is true victory. It is everything I fought for."

—Reported by Steve Erwin/
New York City; Pete Norman/
Mganduzweni

Respond and Think Critically

Respond and Interpret

1. Write a brief summary of the main ideas in this article before you answer the following questions. For help on writing a summary, see page 1147.

2. In your opinion, what is one of Chamusso's most striking character traits?

3. (a)What happened to Chamusso during his boyhood? (b)How did this influence his adult life?

4. (a)When was Chamusso first arrested? (b)How did this lead him to fight against apartheid?

Analyze and Evaluate

5. (a)How might apartheid have contributed to the spread of AIDS in South Africa? (b)What parallel does Chamusso see between apartheid and the spread of AIDS?

6. In what ways might the name of Chamusso's orphanage be significant?

7. (a)What lesson did Chamusso learn on Robben Island, and how did he learn it? (b)Why do you think this lesson is important in his life now?

Connect

8. How does Chamusso's life reflect the realities that people face in postcolonial Africa?

HEROES AMONG US **157**

English Learners

DIFFERENTIATED INSTRUCTION

Advanced Have students identify compound adjectives used in the article. Some examples include "poverty-stricken," "hard-won," "HIV-positive," "anti-apartheid," "little-understood," and "home-based." Have them discuss how an adjective changes meaning when it is hyphenated with a noun. **Ask:** What is the difference between apartheid and anti-apartheid? Or, why would an author choose to write "poverty-stricken rural streets," instead of "rural streets where there is poverty"?

Explain that when a compound adjective follows a noun, it is not hyphenated. For example, *"hard-won freedom"* versus "Their freedom was hard won."

TIME

Assess

1. Summaries will vary but should mention Chamusso's childhood, his arrest and torture, his fight against apartheid, and his work with children who have AIDS.

2. Students may say he is resilient and compassionate and has strong convictions.

3. (a) Chamusso was abandoned by his father. (b) His experience gave him empathy for children who weren't raised by their parents.

4. (a) When the African National Congress staged a bombing at the Secunda oil refinery (b) Despite his innocence, Chamusso was arrested and tortured. These injustices made him determined to fight against apartheid.

5. (a) Apartheid created a class of poor and uneducated black South Africans who did not understand the disease. (b) Both are impediments to freedom in South Africa.

6. Answers may vary. The name alludes to the sense of family created in the orphanage and the idea that the orphans, like the two sisters, are not alone.

7. (a) After sharing his hopes for vengeance with older prisoners, Chamusso learned instead to forgive those who had wronged him. (b) By practicing forgiveness, Chamusso can give to others and not stay bitter.

8. Chamusso's life reflects the efforts of people throughout Africa to help their countries and their people after independence.

Focus

Bellringer Options

Daily Language Practice Transparency 20

Or write on the board: The last human sat alone in a room. There was a knock at the door.

Ask: Is this a complete story? Elicit from students what they feel is the essence of narrative. *(Students might mention elements such as characters, plot, and conflict.)* Encourage students to debate why they believe one element of a story is more important than another.

 For Writing Workshop graphic organizer and rubric, see Unit 1 Teaching Resources Book, pp. 236–238.

Learning Objectives

For pages 158–165
In this workshop, you will focus on the following objectives:

Writing: Writing a short story, using the writing process.

Grammar: Understanding how to correct shifts in point of view.

▶ **Writing Process**

At any stage of a writing process, you may think of new ideas. Feel free to return to earlier stages as you write.

Prewrite

Draft

Revise

Focus Lesson: Dialogue

Edit and Proofread

Focus Lesson:
Shifts in Point of View

Present

 **Literature** Online

Writing and Research
For prewritng, drafting and revising tools, go to glencoe.com and enter QuickPass code GLW6053u1.

Writing Workshop

Short Story

Literature Connection In "Half a Day," Naguib Mahfouz creates a narrative around a central conflict.

> *"I was in a daze. My head spun. I almost went crazy. How could all this have happened in half a day, between early morning and sunset?"*

This story, like many others, is a fictional narrative that focuses on a conflict and a character's moment of insight that helps communicate the significance of the events to the reader. In a short story, it is important to give the essential details of the characters, setting, and plot, and to resolve the conflict in a meaningful way. To successfully write a short story, you need to learn the goals of narrative writing and the strategies to achieve those goals.

Rubric

Goals	Strategies
To create characters and a setting that are clearly defined	☑ Describe the characters and the setting using specific details and sensory images ☑ Describe movements, gestures, dialogue, and feelings of the characters
To tell a story by developing the plot around a conflict	☑ Introduce a conflict that will be resolved in the story ☑ Communicate the significance of the events to the reader
To present events in a logical order	☑ Use chronological order (and possibly flashback) ☑ Use narrative details to give your story a clear beginning, middle, and end
To use a consistent point of view	☑ Use either first person, third-person limited, or third-person omniscient consistently throughout your story

---

Workshop Resources

Print Materials

- Unit 1 Teaching Resources pp. 237–238
- Writing Kit
- Success in Writing: Research and Reports

Technology

- Literature Online: Writing Resources and Grammar Resources, glencoe.com
- Online Essay Grader, glencoe.com
- Student Presentation Builder on StudentWorks Plus CD-ROM
- Media Workshop DVD
- Online Student Edition

Assignment: Create and Resolve a Conflict

Write a short story of 400–500 words in which you create characters involved in a conflict that is resolved in an unexpected way.

Audience: peers, classmates, and teacher

Purpose: create and resolve a conflict and communicate its significance

Analyze a Professional Model

In the following story, Ali Deb reveals the danger of focusing on outward appearance. Pay close attention to the comments in the margin. They point out features you might want to include in your own story.

From *"The Three-Piece Suit"* by Ali Deb ☆

This month, for the first time, the household budget has been met and . . . even left me a little supplement. . . . I don't know why, I went against my habits and bought myself an elegant three-piece suit, tailored in a magnificent English fabric of lovely sky-blue—the color of sunlit days—in which the tailor's skill was displayed so well that one would say we were born together, one for the other . . . The buttons sparkling in the sun were like stars on the shoulder of a sailor swollen with courage. The spinning sensation that its price aroused did not last long, and I said to myself as I straightened my head and shoulders, "Tell me how you dress, and I'll say who you are."

I made my way without hesitation toward the largest café on the main street. As expected, my friends made a fuss over me, touching, feeling, and dusting me with their fingers. I strutted, proud as a peacock . . .

Naturally I paid for the drinks and left a fat tip for the waiter, who gave me his best compliments. There was glib talk of the rise in prices and the high cost of living.

At this point one of them murmured into my ear, "What kind of shirt and tie are these?" Then he led me to a shop that was

Real-World Connection

Many professional writers publish their stories in magazines. If your school has a literary magazine, you may wish to submit the story you write for this workshop for consideration.

Exposition

Introduce your main character, give background, and hint at the conflict.

Suspense

Give hints about what is to come to increase the tension and build suspense.

WRITING WORKSHOP **159**

English Learners

DIFFERENTIATED INSTRUCTION

Intermediate Students who are learning English may benefit from an opportunity to speak about their story ideas before they begin to write. Have them form groups in which they discuss settings they are considering. Suggest that students from other countries choose settings for their stories from their homelands.

Advanced Learners/Pre-AP

DIFFERENTIATED INSTRUCTION

Setting Remind students that writers can use setting to establish tone. **Ask:** What is the typical setting for a horror story? *(Students might answer that the setting for a horror story is often dark and gloomy.)* Have students look out the window. **Ask:** Is it cloudy, sunny, windy, or calm? What type of story best fits the current setting? Have students write two opening sentences of a story by describing the view.

Teach

Big Idea

Tradition and Change

Remind students that traditional African oral literature did not have a literary form like the modern short story. Introduced into Africa by Europeans during the colonial period, the short story has been adapted by modern African writers to interpret the history and culture of Africa. **Ask:** How does the short story reflect the interaction of tradition and change in modern Africa? *(The short story had its origins in European literature and has been adapted by African writers to address conditions in Africa.)*

Writing Process

Journal Point out that writers often record ideas for future stories in journals. Emphasize that such story ideas can be very brief—for example: "Two people meet who are opposites in every way but still become close friends." Have students start a writer's journal to collect notes for future stories.

Literary History ☆

Ali Deb Ali Deb was born in 1941 in the North African country of Tunisia. Deb is known mostly for his poetry, but he has also published short stories, plays, and nonfiction.

Learning Objectives
Writing a short story. (SE)
Using the writing process. (SE)
Writing a journal entry. (TE)

Teach

Writing Skills

Logical Order Point out that a narrative is composed of a series of events. Many writers choose to present these events in chronological order; that is, in the order in which they took place.

Writing Skills

Point of View Point out to students that once they have a story idea, they may find that a particular point of view will seem right. For example, if they are using an autobiographical incident as the basis for their story, they may find it most natural to tell the story from a first-person point of view.

Logical Order

Tell the events of your story in chronological order.

Narrative Details

Give precise details and use transitions to explain what happens when.

Point of View

Choose one perspective from which to tell your story.

---

celebrated for the high quality of its merchandise and for its voraciousness. His good taste and affability were such that my pockets were emptied, and it was only with great difficulty that I managed to pay the ticket home.

For one whole week, I concentrated on straightening out my accounts and forced myself to exactitude and strict austerity. I was thus obliged to forgo luxury and excess such as eggs and butter. I also reduced by half my consumption of meat . . . and pretended to lack the time for entertainment with my friends. . . . I managed somehow or other to put my accounts back in order, while still not forgetting to trim my mustache, smooth my face with a close shave, and spray myself with aftershave.

There I was, strolling about, puffed up with pride, on the main street, taking care to pass by the women's soaks since their tastes are more refined and assured and their eyes are sharper. . . . I heard as though a murmur in my ear, "The flaw is in your shoes." I turned and noticed a light blush on the face of a young girl. I counted the age of my shoes on my fingers. Goodness, how quickly the months had flown by. "Only a pair of shoes stands between me and perfection!" I chose a pair on Liberty Avenue, then returned to my friends. They directed their entire repertoire of flattering expressions my way, and I was literally overcome by a delicious peace that was troubled only by the price of a cup of coffee. I almost proposed another spot in which to drink it but gave up; this café was better suited to my attire. My only recourse was a long, discreet sigh.

On the way home, the weather took a sudden turn, and fine little drops fell on my oh-so-proud-nose. "Abominable sky," and I bought an umbrella that saved me, in spite of its poor quality.

On Barcelona Square, I was accosted by young beggars. Their sullen faces, extended hands, and supplications surrounded me to the point of suffocation. There were three of them, I handed fifty millimes to each one and, rid of their harassment, I gave a sigh of relief, but their leader came after me, repeating, "You're worth

---

Writing Practice

Use a Character Web Have students use a web like the one here to help organize their ideas about the traits of the main characters in their stories.

```
                    ┌─────────────────────┐
                    │ Background—family,   │
                    │ home, social class   │
                    └─────────────────────┘
                              │
┌──────────────────┐  ┌──────────────┐  ┌──────────────────┐
│ Appearance—age,  │──│ Character's  │──│ Behavior—speech  │
│ height, dress    │  │ name         │  │ and actions      │
└──────────────────┘  └──────────────┘  └──────────────────┘
                              │
                    ┌─────────────────────┐
                    │ Thoughts—goals,      │
                    │ dreams, secrets      │
                    └─────────────────────┘
```

much more," showing the coin to all the passersby. I bought his silence for double the amount . . .

I walked prudently, taking the sidewalk, avoiding the dust on carts and jostling pedestrians. I fled the crowd and buses and never forgot to polish my shoes and iron my shirts carefully, often using the fire to dry them faster. The January cold suddenly came to mind, and I anticipated the need to buy a coat and change my suit when winter had passed. Should I hold out my hand for a loan or draw directly form the company's cash box? Finally, I got on the train. I breathed in the fetid breath of the passengers. I leaned on the armrest of a seat; a lady grumbled and said to her neighbor, "They're even contesting our second-class seats." So I slipped into the first class where a seat and a supplementary fee of some consequence awaited me. I went into the local supermarket. It had been quite some time since I had taken care of my shopping. Upon seeing me, a neighbor literally shrieked for joy, shook my hand and then, raising his flat voice, asked me for a loan that I would have naturally refused him if I had not been wearing my suit.

I bought several items and held them in my arms against my chest. The salesgirl greeted me and unhooked a suitable basket. I had no other alternative but to deposit my purchases inside, and since the proper sort of people, my sort, buy without consideration for the price, I did not even bother to look at the cash register total. When I had returned home, my blood pressure was at its peak, my head was literally boiling, my tongue was twisted, and my chest heaving. I no longer saw where I walked or where I threw my jacket, vest, and trousers. I clenched my teeth and gritted them as I cursed the traps of this century and the folly of fools. I finally went back to being my old self, and since that day no one has troubled me anymore.

Narration

Dialogue
Use dialogue to reveal characters' personalities and background.

Sensory Details
Describe sights, sounds, smells, tastes, and textures vividly.

Setting
Give details about the setting that help emphasize the conflict or the theme.

Resolution
Present the final outcome or consequences of the conflict. Make the significance of the events clear to the reader.

Short Story

Teach

Writing Skills

Dialogue Encourage students to use dialogue to make their story believable. They should use dialogue to explain what is happening and to make their characters seem real and identifiable to the reader. Explain that direct quotations, such as "You're worth much more," create a stronger effect than indirect quotations, such as "The beggar told me I was worth much more."

Writing Skills

Climax Explain to students that each event in a story's plot should be more intense than the one that comes before it, until the rising action finally reaches its peak in the climax, or point of highest emotional intensity. The climax then gives way to the failing action as the main character succeeds in solving the conflict, which leads to the resolution.

Approaching Level

DIFFERENTIATED INSTRUCTION

Transitional Statements Help students grasp how a writer signals time order by pointing out the transitions in "The Three-Piece Suit" ("This month, for the first time," "For one whole week," "On the way home," "When I had returned home," "since that day").

Have students create a timeline that presents the events of "The Three-Piece Suit" in chronological order. Next to each point on the timeline, have them indicate the transitional phrase that shows its chronological order. For example:

Time: Sometime in the current month ("This month")

Event: Narrator buys suit

Learning Objectives
Writing a short story. (SE)
Using the writing process. (SE)
Identifying short story elements. (SE)
Using a character web. (TE)

161

Writing Workshop

Short Story

Teach

Writing Process

Prewrite Encourage students to freewrite to discover what they would really like to write about. Explain that when writing this way, it is usually best to write whatever comes to mind without worrying about structure, grammar, or punctuation. After students finish, they can read through their freewrites and retain whatever they judge is useful.

Literary History ☆

Flash Fiction Tell students that one popular contemporary form of short fiction is the short-short story, sometimes also called flash fiction, micro-fiction, or sudden fiction. Short-short stories generally fall within the limit of 250 to 1,000 words. Traditional short stories—which usually range between 2,000 and 20,000 words—are intended to be read in one sitting. By contrast, short-short stories require only several minutes of reading time.

Prewrite

Gather Ideas You might try thinking about people, places, and experiences in your own life to help you generate story ideas. Use your imagination to add details and develop a unique and engaging narrative.

Imagine Characters Whom is your story about? Choose your main character and the necessary minor characters. Consider what the characters will look like, how they will speak, move, and behave, and what they will try to achieve.

Create Setting Where and when does your story take place? Use vivid details to establish your setting.

Develop Plot Once you think of a possible character or situation, consider some *what ifs* to help you formulate the plot: What if your character got lost? What if your character is not the person everyone thinks he or she is? Keep the plot simple and focus on a conflict the main character faces. The conflict can be **external** (between a character and an outside force) or **internal** (inside a character's head). Before you begin writing, fill out a plot diagram like the one below to plan your short story.

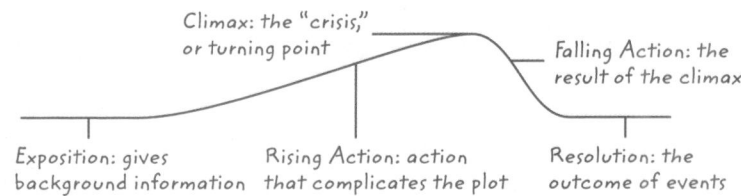

Build Suspense

Suspense is the tension a reader feels about what will happen next in a story. To create suspense, you might use an eerie setting, slow the pace at a crucial moment, use flashbacks, or change the scene. Keep in mind that suspense is a balancing act: too many hints might spoil the surprise, but too few might confuse the reader.

Avoid Plagiarism

As you work on your story, you might remember the words of another writer who perfectly captured a scene or an idea you want to convey. Copying these words, however, is wrong unless you give credit to the source. If one of your characters is quoting a literary work, for example, you must attribute the source of the quotation and use quotation marks appropriately.

Choose a Point of View Point of view is the perspective from which a story is told. You can use **first-person point of view** if you want to tell the story from the narrator's standpoint using *I* and *me*. Or, you can use **third-person point of view** to tell the story through the eyes of a narrator who stands outside the action.

Show Your Style Use figurative language, irony, symbols, and imagery to help develop your characters, setting, and themes.

Reading-Writing Connection Think about the writing techniques you just encountered and try them out in the short story you write.

Draft

Get Going As you draft, use your plot diagram as a guide, but if you find yourself getting stuck, try altering some aspects of the plot. You can add or delete details when you revise later.

162 UNIT 1   AFRICA

Writing Practice

Use Vivid Verbs and Adverbs Remind students of the importance of using verbs and adverbs that give the reader a clear sense of action. Point out the differing effects of the following two sentences:

I looked at the pile of dirty dishes.
I stared glumly at the pile of dirty dishes.

Write the following sentences on the board and have students rewrite them by substituting specific verbs for general ones

and adding vivid adverbs.

Sharon raised her hand.
Eduardo spoke to his brother.
The cat ate its dinner.

(Possible rewrites:
Sharon thrust her hand up defiantly.
Eduardo whispered slyly to his brother.
The cat greedily devoured its dinner.)

162

Analyze a Workshop Model

Here is a final draft of a short story. Read the story and answer the questions in the margin. Use the answers to these questions to guide you as you write.

Rush

"Hey, Pop," I said as I rushed in through the back door of our restaurant. My father hardly shifted his gaze from the stove.

"Here, slice these," he said, handing me two onions. "*Thin* slices. Not those big chunks." I grabbed a cutting board. "Are you taking the test soon?" he asked. He meant my driver's test. I had had my learner's permit since May, but I had practiced driving only once. I nodded, trying not to look at him. My father threw three plates of fettuccini on the counter, yelling, "Order up!" Just then my brother Stanley slid into the kitchen. He loaded his tray, swung it over his shoulder, and waltzed out. Stanley never got frazzled at work. But none of this translated to the road.

When I got my learner's permit in May, Stanley took me driving. During our first lesson, he panicked every time I got near another car. I was horrified. As the test got closer, my stomach was in knots. So, I called the DMV and canceled.

After Stanley took the fettuccini out, my father checked the calendar. "The test was today!" he cried. "How did it go?" I was caught off guard. "Fine," I lied, finishing the onions.

The next night my brother went home sick. Then during the dinner rush, we ran out of bread. "Here," said my father throwing me his keys. "Go get some." I stood there, staring at the car keys.

"Hey, Pop," I muttered. "I can't." My father slowly turned toward me. The kitchen seemed to stop. I saw his forehead beaded with sweat and creases line his brow. He looked so old. "I never took the test," I said, handing him back the keys.

That night after we closed up, my father let me drive on the back roads in the country. "It's worth it, isn't it?" he asked. "For this alone it's worth it." "It is," I said. It was.

Narration

Writing Frames

As you read the workshop model, think about the writer's use of the following dialogue frames.

- "_____," I said as I _____.
- "_____," he said, _____.

Exposition
How does this story's opening make the exposition more interesting?

Dialogue
How does the dialogue in this conversation help distinguish the characters?

Descriptive Details
How do descriptive details in this paragraph reveal Stanley's character?

Flashback
How does this flashback help advance the plot?

Point of View
Is this paragraph told from a consistent point of view? Explain.

Rising Action
What makes this part of the story the rising action?

Climax
How does the writer create suspense during the climax?

Resolution
How does the writer reveal the significance of events?

WRITING WORKSHOP **163**

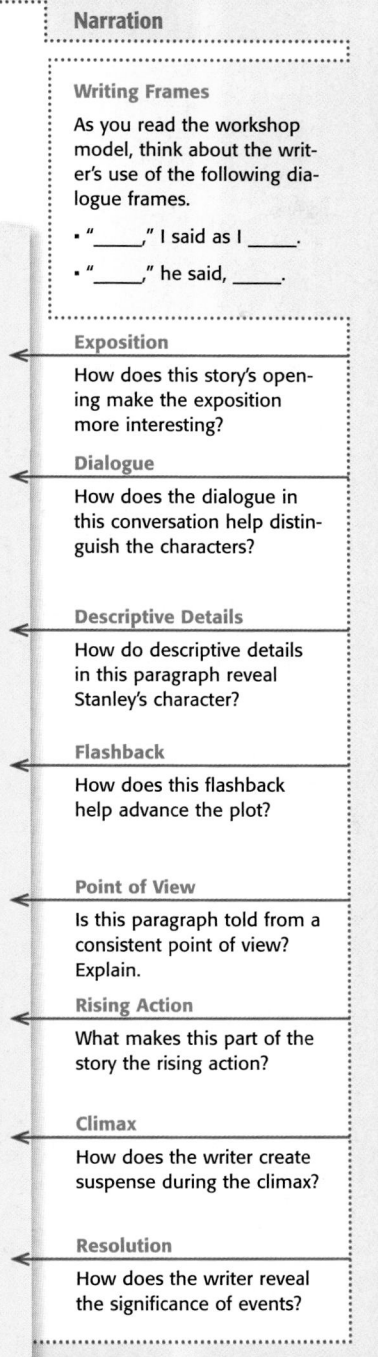

Writing Workshop

Short Story

Teach

Writing Skills

Exposition Answer: *The opening starts right in the middle of the action.*

Dialogue Answer: *The father's dialogue reveals an urgency and authority, whereas the narrator's dialogue is more youthful and casual ("Hey, Pop").*

Descriptive Details Answer: *Details such as "slid" and "waltzed" show Stanley to be smooth and agile.*

Flashback Answer: *The flashback helps develop the conflict between the narrator and the fear of driving.*

Point of View Answer: *The point of view is consistent; the narrator's comments reflect only what he or she sees and feels.*

Rising Action Answer: *The father's request increases the tension.*

Climax Answer: *The writer delays the action at this point.*

Resolution Answer: *The writer conveys the significance by emphasizing the relaxing, liberating, and bonding effects of driving.*

Approaching Level

DIFFERENTIATED INSTRUCTION

Retell To help students get a feeling for constructing a narrative, have them retell a familiar folktale or fable orally in their own words. When they have finished, point out the basic elements of fiction in their narratives, particularly the conflict, main characters, and setting.

Learning Objectives
Writing a short story. (SE)
Analyzing short story elements. (SE)
Using the writing process. (SE)
Using vivid verbs and adverbs. (TE)

Short Story

Teach

Writing Process

Revise Suggest to students that they take some time when revising their stories to add more details where appropriate to enrich their characters. Have them review the character webs they created for their main characters to make sure any additional details are consistent with the basic outline they created for each character.

Writer's Technique ☆

Revising Power Share with students author Naomi Shihab Nye's perspective on the revision process: "If a teacher told me to revise, I thought that meant my writing was a broken-down car that needed to go to the repair shop. I felt insulted. I didn't realize the teacher was saying, 'Make it shine. It's worth it.' Now I see revision as a beautiful word of hope. It's a new vision of something. It means you don't have to be perfect the first time. What a relief!"

Traits of Strong Writing

Follow these traits of strong writing to express your ideas effectively.

Ideas message or theme and the details that develop it

Organization arrangement of main ideas and supporting details

Voice writer's unique way of using tone and style

Word Choice vocabulary a writer uses to convey meaning

Sentence Fluency rhythm and flow of sentences

Conventions correct spelling, grammar, usage, and mechanics

Presentation the way words and design elements look on a page

For more information on using the Traits of Strong Writing, see pages R28–R30.

Word Choice

Here are some steps to follow as you write dialogue.

- Write your dialogue in words and phrases appropriate to each character.

- Make your dialogue easy to follow by using clear attributions ("he said," for example) and correct paragraphing.

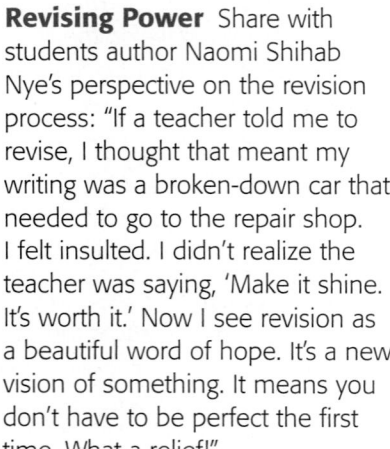

LOG ON ▶ **Literature** Online

Writing and Research For editing and publishing tools, go to glencoe.com and enter QuickPass code GLW6053u1.

Revise

Peer Review When you finish your draft, meet with a partner to exchange papers and discuss ways to improve your story. Make sure the story includes a conflict that is resolved in a meaningful way. Use the checklist below to evaluate and strengthen your story.

Checklist

☑ Do you use descriptive details to create a setting and characters that are clearly defined?

☑ Do you introduce and resolve a conflict and communicate its significance?

☑ Do you use narrative details and present events in chronological order?

☑ Do you maintain a consistent point of view?

 **Focus Lesson**

Dialogue

Dialogue, or the conversation between characters, brings characters in a story to life. Use dialogue to advance the plot, help establish conflict, or reveal character.

Draft:

"Hello Dad," I said as I rushed in through the back door of our restaurant. . . .

"Hello, son. Here are some onions to slice," he said, handing me two onions. "Cut thin slices instead of big chunks."

Revision:

"Hey, Pop,"¹ I said as I rushed in through the back door of our restaurant. . . .

"Here, slice these,"² he said, handing me two onions. "Thin slices. Not those big chunks."³

1: Write dialogue that reflects a character's age and background.

2: Mimic the disconnected flow of real speech.

3: Use fragments and emphasis to make dialogue sound natural.

Writing Practice

Punctuate Dialogue Point out to students that when writing dialogue they should keep the following rules in mind:

- Capitalize the first word in dialogue.
- Do not capitalize the first word after interruption in the dialogue.
- Enclose end punctuation within quotation marks.
- Indent each new line of dialogue.

Example:

"Why are you so late?" asked Jay's mother.

"I came home earlier," Jay explained, "but you were not here."

Have students work together in small groups to create dialogue in which they demonstrate each of these rules. Write their dialogue on the board.

Edit and Proofread

Get It Right When you have completed the final draft of your story, proofread it for errors in grammar, usage, mechanics, and spelling. Refer to the Language Handbook, pages R40–R59, as a guide.

> **Focus Lesson**
>
> ### Shifts in Point of View
>
> After revising your draft, make sure the point of view is consistent. Use the pronoun *I* for first-person narrators and *he, she, it,* or *they* for third person.

Original: The narrative switches from first-person to third-person point of view.

When I got my learner's permit in May, Stanley took him driving.

Improved: Pronoun shifts to maintain a consistent point of view.

When I got my learner's permit in May, Stanley took me driving.

Original: The first-person narrator gives details about the father's actions and feelings that he or she could not know.

My father slowly turned toward me. The kitchen seemed to stop. I saw his forehead beaded with sweat and creases line his brow. He felt much older than he was.

Improved: Edit so that the first-person narrator tells only what he or she could know and experience.

My father slowly turned toward me. The kitchen seemed to stop. I saw his forehead beaded with sweat and creases line his brow. He looked so old.

Present/Publish

The Final Touch Before you turn in your story, make sure it is free of errors and is 400–500 words. If you typed your story on a computer, make sure the margins, tabs, and spacing are set correctly. If you wrote your story by hand, make sure it is neat and legible.

Peer Review Tips

If you review a classmate's story, take notes as you read so you can give constructive feedback. Use the following questions as a guide.

- Are the characters and conflict clearly presented?
- Is the sequence of events easy to follow?
- Is the setting clearly described?
- Does the story have a satisfying ending?

Word-Processing Tip

If you are typing your story on a computer, make sure you use an appropriate font and size. Choose a font that is easy to read and not too ornate or distracting. Many word-processing programs automatically default to a 12-point size, which is usually adequate.

Writer's Portfolio
Place a clean copy of your short story in your portfolio to review later.

English Learners

DIFFERENTIATED INSTRUCTION

Advanced Show students examples of first-person narration, pointing out the pronouns *I, me, my, mine, we,* or *our.* Then show them examples of third-person narration, pointing out the pronouns *he, him, his, she, her, it, its, they, their,* or *them.* Explain that a story told from the third-person point of view might still have first-person pronouns in dialogue.

For students who master this activity, give them a passage of first-person narration and have them rewrite it in the third person. Then give them a passage of third-person narration and have them rewrite it in the first person. Have them review both versions to make sure they have consistently maintained a point of view.

⚡ Writing Workshop

Short Story

Teach

Writing Process

Edit and Proofread Encourage students to use the Proofreading Checklist on the inside back cover of their texts. Students can begin by checking any direct quotations in their short stories for incorrect punctuation marks. When finished, students should check their work for errors in grammar, usage, mechanics, and spelling.

Writing Process

Present Encourage students to submit their stories to literary magazines or short story contests. Make them aware that some contests require an entry fee. Students should make sure that they have formatted their stories to satisfy any required standards set by a magazine or contest.

(**ADVANCED**) Suggest that students illustrate their stories. Have them select a type of illustration appropriate to the tone of their stories. For example, if the tone is humorous, a cartoon-style illustration might be appropriate.

Learning Objectives
Writing a short story. (SE)
Using the writing process. (SE)
Using quotation marks in dialogue. (TE)

Focus

Summary

In this workshop, students will learn techniques for planning and presenting a group discussion of a short story to the class.

Teach

Literary History ☆

Word Spinners In a conversation in 1998, Wole Soyinka attributed his story-telling ability to growing up surrounded by an extended family of "word-spinners": "I was constantly surrounded, I recall, by aunts, uncles, my father's intellectual companions, all of them raconteurs of some sort or the other. They recounted episodes involving themselves, battles, conflicts. I grew up in an atmosphere where words were an integral part of culture."

 For help with creating presentations, see Student Presentation Builder on StudentWorks Plus.

 For Speaking, Listening, and Viewing activities and rubric, see Unit 1 Teaching Resources Book, pp. 239–242.

Learning Objectives

For pages 166–167
In this workshop, you will focus on the following objective:

Listening and Speaking: Presenting an oral interpretation.

Know Your Audience

Keep in mind that your audience consists of people who have already read the story. Therefore, you do not need to summarize the plot when delivering your interpretation. Instead, focus on making connections between your ideas and elements from the story.

Speaking, Listening, and Viewing Workshop

Oral Response to Literature

Literature Connection Many people interpret literature in their own ways. Wole Soyinka said, "My father used to tell me stories before I fell ☆ asleep. When the children would gather, at a certain point, I had a tendency to make up my own elementary variations on stories I had heard, or to invent totally new ones."

After reading a short story, it is helpful to discuss your thoughts and interpretations with a group. When you deliver an oral interpretation of literature, you share your responses to the story with others, making connections between your ideas and the text.

> **Assignment** **Discuss a Short Story** In groups, discuss and respond to the major themes present in a short story from Unit One.

Prepare

Assign roles, such as facilitator and recorder, to members in your group. Each group member is to be equally responsible for discussion. This rubric will help you understand these roles.

Leader/Facilitator	Group Participants (All)	Recorder
☑ Introduces the discussion topic	☑ Form ideas and questions about the literature before the discussion	☑ Helps the group leader form conclusions based on the discussion
☑ Invites each participant to speak	☑ Contribute throughout the discussion	☑ Keeps track of the most important points
☑ Keeps the discussion focused and interactive	☑ Support any opinions with facts	☑ Helps summarize the discussion
☑ Keeps track of the time	☑ Listen carefully to other group members	
☑ Helps participants arrive at a consensus	☑ Avoid repeating what has been said earlier	
	☑ Evaluate and respect the opinions of others	

Listening Practice

Compare and Contrast Point out that an effective way of participating in a group discussion of a literary work is to compare and contrast the interpretations presented by the other participants. Advise students to pay particular attention to similarities and differences of all members' interpretations of the story. Suggest that students prepare graphic organizers with a column for each group member. Have students use these charts to keep track of the interpretations of each of their fellow participants in the group discussion.

Gather Evidence

When delivering an oral interpretation of literature, you are making a series of judgments about a story. For others to understand your views, you need to support your ideas with evidence from the text. You must first ask yourself what point you want to make about the story. Then, you must connect your ideas to quotations, facts, and other information pulled directly from the story.

Listen Effectively

You can gain valuable insights about a text from listening to the opinions of other group members. When you listen well, you understand, evaluate, and remember what you hear so that you are better able to respond to a speaker's message. Use the techniques below to improve your listening skills.

- Prepare to listen. Clear you mind of other thoughts and focus on the speaker, keeping eye contact. Do not glance around the room, look through papers, or let your mind wander.

- Note the topic and recall what you already know about it. It is easier to understand and remember information about a subject with which you are familiar. Connect the subject to information you have read about or discussed previously.

- Ask questions, aloud or silently. If you don't understand a point a speaker is trying to make, ask questions. Even when you do understand, ask yourself silent questions to evaluate what you hear.

> **Speaking Frames**
> As you discuss interpretations, think about using some of the following frames to get started.
>
> - The author implies _____ by saying _____.
>
> - The author uses details such as _____ and _____ to create _____.
>
> - I really like the point _____ made about _____, because _____.

 Literature Online

Speaking, Listening, and Viewing For project ideas, templates, and presentation tips, go to glencoe.com and enter QuickPass code GLW6053u1.

Techniques for Delivering an Oral Interpretation of a Short Story

Verbal Techniques	Nonverbal Techniques
☑ **Pace** Allow each group member enough time to voice his or her opinion before moving on.	☑ **Listen** Remain quiet until it is your turn to speak.
☑ **Discuss** Try to ask questions that have no right or wrong answer to promote discussion.	☑ **Poise** Maintain eye contact and upright posture to show that you are listening and understand what the speaker is saying.
☑ **Volume** Speak loudly and clearly so that the rest of the group can hear what you are saying. However, do not distract any nearby discussion groups.	☑ **Gestures** Avoid nervous habits and other movements that may distract the speaker.

Teach

Speaking Skills

Prepare for a Discussion Invite students to select a specific passage from the story, ranging from a phrase to a paragraph, to bring to the small group discussion. If students are having difficulty entering the discussion, introducing an excerpt from the passage they have already selected can be less intimidating.

Listening Skills

Respond Remind students that effective listening combines both passive and active characteristics. They should listen quietly to fellow participants until they finish and not interrupt speakers with comments or questions.

Learning Objectives
Delivering an oral response to a story. (SE)
Participating in a discussion. (SE)
Comparing and contrasting. (TE)
Listening actively. (TE)

English Learners

DIFFERENTIATED INSTRUCTION

SMALL GROUP **Intermediate** Have students work in small pre-discussion groups to develop strategies for participating more fully in the final group discussions of the story. In these pre-discussion groups, students can try out and clarify their ideas about the story to be discussed. Have one student look up dictionary definitions of words in the story that group members do not understand.

Focus

Summary

The purpose of this feature is to interest students in reading additional literature by African writers. Classic fiction and nonfiction by modern writers of the region are represented in the profiled works.

Teach

Literary History ☆

Laye and Negritude The idyllic picture of traditional African life that Camara Laye presents in the early chapters of *The Dark Child* is typical of the outlook of the literary movement known as Negritude. Founded by French-speaking black writers from Africa and the Caribbean in the mid-1930s, the Negritude movement celebrated African heritage and values and protested European political domination. Another prominent writer of the Negritude movement was Léopold Sédar Senghor.

Reading Practice

Evaluate Development Point out to students the value of periodically evaluating their development as independent readers. Have them review how much they read on their own, what types of books they read, and how the pattern of their reading has changed (if at all) in the past twelve months. Prompt them by asking questions such as the following:

Independent Reading

Literature of the Region

ONE OF THE MOST ENDURING CULTURAL LEGACIES OF AFRICA'S COLONIAL past is the European languages—usually English or French—spoken by many Africans today. Modern African authors must often decide in what language to write. This is not a simple decision; to some authors, writing in a European language implies an endorsement of colonialism. Writing in an African language, however, may significantly limit an author's audience. To enable their works to reach an international audience, as well as a broad African one, many authors in Africa today write in Arabic or in a European language. Recently, some African authors have begun publishing first in their own African languages and then translating the work for a larger audience.

The Dark Child ☆

Camara Laye

Born into the Malinke people in what was then the colony of French Guinea, Camara Laye left his homeland when he was eighteen for further schooling in France. He was working in a factory in Paris when he wrote his first book, *L'Enfant Noir (The Dark Child)*, an autobiographical novel describing his childhood and youth. A lyrical, nostalgic lament for the passing of a traditional way of life, *The Dark Child* (1953) presents one of Laye's pivotal topics, the contrast between a village upbringing and a modern education.

Burger's Daughter ☆

Nadine Gordimer

Nobel Prize–winning author Nadine Gordimer grew up in South Africa when apartheid was its official policy of racial segregation. Her stories and novels explore the negative consequences of the system. In *Burger's Daughter* (1979), Rosa Burger must come to terms with her anti-apartheid family history after the death of her parents. Under the watchful eye of the government, Rosa realizes how the political environment of South Africa affects her daily life and has made her who she is.

- How many works of fiction have you read on your own in the past year?
- What type(s) of fiction do you prefer reading now?
- Have your tastes in fiction changed over the past year?
- What type(s) of nonfiction are you reading currently?
- What is your favorite kind of reading now?

- How does this preference compare with last year's?

Give students time to jot down their responses. Then either ask volunteers to discuss how their reading habits have changed over the past year or have all students write a one-paragraph evaluation of their independent reading over the past year.

GLENCOE LITERATURE LIBRARY

Things Fall Apart

Chinua Achebe

One of the most influential African novels ever written, *Things Fall Apart* is set at the beginning of the twentieth century as Britain's imperial ambitions extend deeper into Africa. The traditional Ibo village where the novel takes place succumbs to the influence of missionaries who ignore local customs, causing a centuries-old way of life to vanish. Tension with the villagers escalates into violence, and Okonkwo, the larger-than-life protagonist, meets his moving, tragic end.

An honest account of what happens when cultures clash, the novel explores a variety of topics, including the role of women in society, human dignity, the nature of racism, and justification for violence.

 Write a Review

Read one of the books listed on these pages and write a review of it for your classmates. Be sure to summarize the characters, plot, and major themes and explain why other students might enjoy the book. Present your review to the class.

CRITICS' CORNER

"Using his African background, [Soyinka] explores the human condition. . . . He makes the fullest use of Yoruba mythology, the Nigerian landscape—mountain, stream and forest— as well as its steel bridges, power stations, night clubs, and tenement houses. The local pantheon of deities, the shrines in which they were and are worshiped, the animals, the plants, the rocks, all form the environment against which Soyinka treats his essential subject, homo sapiens, in his constant struggle of adjustment to the changing environment."

—Eldred D. Jones, from *Introduction to Nigerian Literature*

Aké: The Years of Childhood

Wole Soyinka

Nobel Prize–winning playwright and poet Wole Soyinka was born in Nigeria when it was a British colony. Yoruban culture has been an important element in his writing, but Soyinka has been an outspoken opponent of the Afrocentrist cultural movement known as Negritude. In his memoir *Aké: The Years of Childhood*, Soyinka vividly recalls the village where he grew up, his parents, and his education in Yoruban traditions.

English Learners

DIFFERENTIATED INSTRUCTION

Advanced Review the profiled books with students, pointing out their key subjects and themes. For example, **Say:** Both Camara Laye's *The Dark Child* and Wole Soyinka's *Ake: The Years of Childhood* are accounts of growing up in traditional African cultures. **Ask:** Do these books remind you of any other books you have read? When students offer examples, ask them to describe the books and their responses to them.

Teach

Write a Review

Students' reviews should
- summarize the characters, plot, and themes of the book
- explain why other students might like the book

Glencoe Literature Library

Glencoe Literature Library offers an extensive collection of hardcover books that help you encourage your students to read independently. Choose among the more than 120 full-length literary works—novels, novellas, plays, and nonfiction. Each book includes related readings from a broad range of genres. Go to glencoe.com for more information.

 For access to all study guides for the Glencoe Literature Library, see the Literature Library Teacher Resources CD-ROM.

To create customized reading lists from a database of more than 30,000 titles, use BookLink K–12 CD-ROM.

Literary History ☆

Gordimer on Writing
Gordimer is widely admired for the courage of her convictions. She once said, "The writer is of service to humankind only insofar as the writer uses the word even against his or her own loyalties."

Learning Objectives
Reading literature independently. (SE)
Writing a review. (SE)

Focus

Bellringer Options

Daily Language Practice
Transparency 21

Or **say:** "You will take many tests in your life, from those you take in school to ones for getting a driver's license or job certification. Many strategies apply to a range of test-taking situations. **Ask:** Which strategies have worked for you?" Have students discuss test-taking strategies that have worked for them in the past.

Teach

Assessment

Tell students that the Assessment will provide reinforcement in general test-taking strategies. Students will read two selections and will answer context, comprehension, and inference questions. Then they will respond to a short essay item. Finally, they will choose answers for sentence-completion items and sentence-improvement items.

 To create custom assessments online, go to Progress Reporter Online Assessment.

 To create custom assessments using software, use ExamView Assessment Suite.

Reading: Fiction and Autobiography

1 Carefully read the following two passages. Use context clues to help you define any words with which you are unfamiliar. In each passage, pay close attention to the **author's purpose,** the **cultures** described, the **mood, tone,** and uses of **literary** or **rhetorical devices.** Then, on a separate sheet of paper, answer the questions on pages 172–173.

2

from *Things Fall Apart* by Chinua Achebe

The Feast of the New Yam was approaching and Umuofia was in a festival mood. It was an occasion for giving thanks to Ani, the earth goddess and the source of all fertility. Ani played a greater part in the life of the people than any other deity. She was the ultimate judge of morality and conduct. And what was more, she was in close communion with the departed fathers of the clan whose bod-
5 ies had been committed to earth.

The Feast of the New Yam was held every year before the harvest began, to honor the earth goddess and the ancestral spirits of the clan. New yams could not be eaten until some had first been offered to these powers. Men and women, young and old, looked forward to the New Yam Festival because it began the season of plenty—the new year. On the last night before the festival, yams of
10 the old year were all disposed of by those who still had them. The new year must begin with tasty, fresh yams and not the shriveled and fibrous crop of the previous year. All cooking pots, calabashes and wooden bowls were thoroughly washed, especially the wooden mortar in which yam was pounded. Yam foo-foo and vegetable soup was the chief food in the celebration. So much of it was cooked that, no matter how heavily the family ate or how many friends and relatives they invited
15 from neighboring villages, there was always a large quantity of food left over at the end of the day. The story was always told of a wealthy man who set before his guests a mound of foo-foo so high that those who sat on one side could not see what was happening on the other, and it was not until late in the evening that one of them saw for the first time his in-law who had arrived during the course of the meal and had fallen to on the opposite side. It was only then that they exchanged
20 greetings and shook hands over what was left of the food.

The New Yam Festival was thus an occasion for joy throughout Umuofia. And every man whose arm was strong, as the Ibo people say, was expected to invite large numbers of guests from far and wide. Okonkwo always asked his wives' relations, and since he now had three wives his guests would make a fairly big crowd.
25 But somehow Okonkwo could never become as enthusiastic over feasts as most people. He was a good eater and he could drink one or two fairly big gourds of palm-wine. But he was always uncomfortable sitting around for days waiting for a feast or getting over it. He would be very much happier working on his farm.

170 UNIT 1 AFRICA

Listening Practice

Analyze Directions Explain to students that instructors often give special instructions for test taking orally. Ask students to listen carefully as you read aloud the test directions at the top of page 170. Ask volunteers to restate the directions in their own words. Tell students that restating or paraphrasing information is a listening strategy for checking comprehension. Preview the directions on pages 174–175.

Provide clarification, especially for the directions on page 175, after you have read them aloud.

30   The festival was now only three days away. Okonkwo's wives had scrubbed the walls and the huts with red earth until they reflected light. They had then drawn patterns on them in white, yellow and dark green. They then set about painting themselves with cam wood and drawing beautiful black patterns on their stomachs and on their backs. The children were also decorated, especially their hair, which was shaved in beautiful patterns. The three women talked excitedly about the relations who
35   had been invited, and the children reveled in the thought of being spoiled by these visitors from the motherland.

from *Aké: The Years of Childhood* by Wole Soyinka

They were all strangers. I had seen none of the faces before. I wondered if they were passers-by who had climbed the steps leading up to the gate for an even clearer view. I thought they looked at me in some rather uncertain way, but, they made way for me to come to the front and we ignored each other's presence at the sight of the police band, the cause of the excitement. They had on bright
5 sashes, bright red fez caps with dangling tassels and what looked like embroidered waistcoats. The drum which was strapped to the man in front was unbelievable in its size; at every step I expected him to topple over, but he pounded its white skin with complete mastery, his gaze set rigidly to the front. His arms made flourishes in the air, giving the heavy-ended drumsticks a twirl, then dashing them against the sides. The man in the lead juggled an enormous mace, threw it in the air, spun
10 around and caught it as it descended. Once, he even caught it backwards, earning a roar from the crowd. A gleaming brass funnel rose between the players; the face which blew into it looked as if it would burst. It gave off notes which were nearly as deep as the big drum but the strain on the player's face far exceeded that of the drummers.
  I had a strange sensation. Each time the big drum was hit, it seemed that the vibrations entered
15 my stomach, echoed around its walls, then went out again to re-join the drum. I listened and *felt* each time the *boom* came and I was left in no doubt about it; obviously it was the way of the big drum, I had no doubt that it affected everyone the same way. I noticed little boys following the band, some walked directly behind, imitating the march of the policemen, others walked alongside, at the extreme edges of the road. They seemed not much bigger than I, and I soon joined them. Unlike the
20 strangers at the gate, none of them seemed to notice me. I stayed with the group at the back, taking care however not to mimic the swagger of the others. It did not seem a decorous thing to do and the policemen looked stern enough to take offence.

Advanced Learners/Pre-AP

DIFFERENTIATED INSTRUCTION

Test Preparation Explain to students that when they see two different texts in one section of a test, they may be asked to compare and contrast the texts. As students begin to read the second selection, encourage them to note similarities to and differences from the first selection. Providing students with a Venn diagram before reading will help them track their observations.

Or, students could create a T-chart with the title of each selection at the top of the column. If they note details from each selection as they read, they can draw conclusions from their notes when they have finished reading the selections.

Assessment
English-Language Arts

Teach

Reading Strategy   1

Take Notes Encourage students to take notes on the passages they read for a test. One good technique is to outline, or "map," a passage, noting the main points and sequence of events. Then, when questions are asked about a specific topic, the student will know where to look.

Reading Strategy   2

Make Inferences Before students begin reading, explain that standardized reading tests ask students to make inferences about the text. As they read, students should note clues in the text which signal the author's attitude toward the topic. Word choice, punctuation, and syntax can help the reader understand the author's attitude. For example, in the opening lines of Passage 1, the author uses the words *judge, morality,* and *communion,* when describing the feast, suggesting that it is a serious and important tradition. In Passage 2, the author uses the words *stranger, wondered,* and *uncertain,* suggesting that the event is unexpected and unknown to the narrator.

Learning Objectives
Using context clues. (SE)
Analyzing directions. (TE)
Taking notes. (TE)
Making inferences. (TE)

171

Assess

1. B is the correct answer. The paragraph does not suggest that all of the gods are of a single gender or that the deities worshipped in Umuofia take human forms, so **C**, **D**, and **E** are incorrect. ⟨DOK 4⟩

2. D is the correct answer. *Powers* clearly refers to the earth goddess Ani and the clan's ancestors because the previous sentence mentions honoring these spirits. **A**, **B**, and **C** are not honored beings, so they are incorrect. **E** is incorrect because the ancestors are not included. ⟨DOK 1⟩

3. A is the correct answer. The importance of the yam to the community suggests that the region is not urban, so **B** is incorrect. The festival is important to the community, so **C** is incorrect. The paragraph never suggests that yams are the only source of nutrition, so **D** is incorrect. Beef and pork are not mentioned, so **E** is incorrect. ⟨DOK 2⟩

4. A is the correct answer. Okonkwo's apathy toward the festival is brought up later in the story, so **B** is incorrect. Achebe does not try to persuade the reader, suggest that the festival is outdated, or justify the festival's existence, so **C**, **D**, and **E** are incorrect. ⟨DOK 2⟩

5. E is the correct answer. In lines 30–34, Achebe mentions Okonkwo's three wives. ⟨DOK 1⟩

Use the passage from *Things Fall Apart* (pages 170–171) to help you answer questions 1–5.

1. The statement in lines 2–3 ("Ani played… deity") suggests that
   (A) the people of Umuofia worship only one god
   (B) the people of Umuofia worship more than one god
   (C) all the deities worshipped in Umuofia are male
   (D) all the deities worshipped in Umuofia are female
   (E) all the deities worshipped in Umuofia take human forms

2. In line 8, *powers* most nearly means
   (A) the harvest
   (B) all the people of Umuofia
   (C) the Feast of the New Yam
   (D) Ani and the clan's ancestors
   (E) the earth goddess

3. Which answer best represents the community of Umuofia as it is presented in lines 6–11?
   (A) Umuofia is primarily an agricultural community.
   (B) Umuofia is primarily an urban community.
   (C) Festivals are unimportant to people in Umuofia.
   (D) Yams are the sole source of food for people in Umuofia.
   (E) Beef and pork are the chief foods in the Umuofia festival.

4. The primary purpose of the first two paragraphs is to
   (A) explain the traditions associated with the New Yam Festival
   (B) highlight why Okonkwo is apathetic toward the New Yam Festival
   (C) persuade the reader to visit the New Yam Festival
   (D) suggest that the New Yam Festival is outdated
   (E) justify the existence of the New Yam Festival

5. The information about domestic life in Umuofia in lines 23–24 ("Okonkwo always… crowd") suggests that
   (A) religion plays an important role in daily life
   (B) families are very small
   (C) families are very large
   (D) women are free to divorce their husbands
   (E) men may have more than one spouse

Use the passage from *Aké: The Years of Childhood* (page 171) to help you answer questions 6–10.

6. The narrator's observation in lines 2–4 ("I thought…excitement") is made in a tone of
   (A) personal triumph
   (B) utter confusion
   (C) joking nonchalance
   (D) dark cynicism
   (E) mild uncertainty

7. Soyinka uses descriptive language in lines 4–5 ("They had…waistcoats") primarily to
   (A) highlight the comedy of the situation
   (B) de-emphasize the narrator's unease
   (C) show that the people were strangers
   (D) offer a vivid picture of the police band
   (E) underscore the confidence of the band

8. In line 8, *dashing* most nearly means
   (A) spirited
   (B) running
   (C) striking
   (D) spinning
   (E) touching

172 UNIT 1   AFRICA

Assessment Practice

Set a Purpose Point out to students that in an test situation, their reading purpose must be to answer the test questions correctly. Tell them that previewing the questions before reading the passage will help them read effectively and efficiently. Have students read through the questions on pages 172–173 and note the kinds of information they require, such as the words to be defined.

9. The "gleaming brass funnel" (line 11) refers to
   (A) the twirling drumsticks
   (B) a brass instrument
   (C) the mace
   (D) the tassels on the police band hats
   (E) a metal bandstand

10. From line 19 ("They seemed…them"), it can be inferred that the speaker is
    (A) generally very unhappy
    (B) elderly
    (C) a child
    (D) an orphan
    (E) wealthy

Use the passages from *Things Fall Apart* and *Aké: The Years of Childhood* to help you answer questions 11 and 12.

11. Which statement best characterizes the overall relationship between the two passages?
    (A) Passage 2 is a first-person account of the events of Passage 1.
    (B) Passage 1 and Passage 2 both tell about some kind of festival.
    (C) Passage 1 has a decidedly darker tone than Passage 2.
    (D) Passage 1 has no discernible relationship to Passage 2.
    (E) Passage 1 and Passage 2 both tell the story of a young African boy.

12. Based on these two passages, with which statement would both Achebe and Soyinka agree?
    (A) Festivals are unimportant distractions.
    (B) Nothing is more important than community festivals.
    (C) Unpleasant commotion fills African village life.
    (D) African village life is lively and complex.
    (E) Food is an integral part of any festival.

Essay

Think carefully about the following quotation and assignment.

> The role of community is of key importance in our modern world. It relates to…the need for a sense of connection and meaning within our lives.
>
> —F. David Peat, physicist and writer

Assignment: Do you agree with F. David Peat about the importance of community in the modern world? On a separate sheet of paper, write a brief essay in which you discuss whether you think a sense of community and community celebrations are important. Support your opinion with reasons and examples from literature or your own life.

As you write, keep in mind that your essay will be checked for **ideas, organization, voice, word choice, sentence fluency, conventions,** and **presentation.**

Assess

6. **E** is the correct answer. The narrator is slightly unsure of the import of his interaction. **DOK 4**

7. **D** is the correct answer. Soyinka uses descriptive language to give the reader a vivid picture of the police band. **DOK 4**

8. **C** is the correct answer. From the context it is clear that the intended meaning of the word is "striking." **DOK 1**

9. **B** is the correct answer. From the context it is clear that a musician is blowing into the brass funnel, meaning it must be a brass instrument. **DOK 1**

10. **C** is the correct answer. It is clear from this statement that the speaker is a child, so **C** must be correct. **DOK 4**

11. **B** is the correct answer. Both passages describe a festival. **DOK 2**

12. **D** is the correct answer. Given the liveliness and complexity of the festivals described, the reader can infer that **D** is correct. **DOK 2**

Essay

In their essays, students should address the quote by F. David Peat regarding the importance of community in the modern world. Students may consider how cultural heritage is evident in a community's celebrations. Students should include examples to support their positions. **DOK 3**

Intermediate Point out that standardized tests often ask students to write an essay in response to a writing prompt in a specified amount of time. Using the prompt on page 173, show students how to identify key words that indicate what needs to be covered in the essay. Model this skill by doing a think-aloud. **Say:** *Agree* means I need to give my opinion about whether I think something is true or not. The topic about which I'm to give an opinion is "whether [I] think a sense of community and community celebrations are important." And, I am to support my opinion with "reasons and examples from literature or [my] own life."

Assessment
English-Language Arts

Assess

1. D is the correct answer. *Throngs, bedlam,* and *hordes* all make sense in the first part, but only *tranquil* makes sense in the second. $\boxed{\text{DOK 2}}$

2. A is the correct answer. Only *rebuked* makes sense in the context. $\boxed{\text{DOK 2}}$

3. D is the correct answer. Only *flout* and *perish* make sense in the context. $\boxed{\text{DOK 2}}$

4. C is the correct answer. *Vigorously* makes the most sense in the context. $\boxed{\text{DOK 2}}$

5. B is the correct answer. Only *endorse* makes sense in the context. $\boxed{\text{DOK 2}}$

6. E is the correct answer. Only *denizens* and *lament* make sense in the context. $\boxed{\text{DOK 2}}$

7. C is the correct answer. Only *diversified* makes sense in the context. $\boxed{\text{DOK 2}}$

8. C is the correct answer. Only *gratitude* and *plight* make sense in the context. $\boxed{\text{DOK 2}}$

Vocabulary Skills: Sentence Completion

For each item in the Vocabulary Skills section, choose the word or words that best complete the sentence. Write your answers on a separate sheet of paper.

1. The _____ of workers who were constructing the Great Pyramid at Giza disrupted the _____ ambience of the desert.
   - **(A)** throngs…acrid
   - **(B)** bedlam…radiant
   - **(C)** constituency…splendid
   - **(D)** hordes…tranquil
   - **(E)** torrents…stifled

2. The international community has repeatedly _____ President Mugabe of Zimbabwe for his country's poor human rights record.
   - **(A)** rebuked
   - **(B)** obscured
   - **(C)** pestered
   - **(D)** availed
   - **(E)** submerged

3. If poachers continue to _____ the law, the African elephant may well _____ in the coming decades.
   - **(A)** hover…decay
   - **(B)** desist…coincide
   - **(C)** rustle…dispel
   - **(D)** flout…perish
   - **(E)** fumble…flout

4. Many politicians, activists, and celebrities have campaigned _____ to end hunger and poverty in sub-Saharan Africa.
   - **(A)** cunningly
   - **(B)** discreetly
   - **(C)** vigorously
   - **(D)** derisively
   - **(E)** tautly

5. The government could not _____ the documents until a lawyer had reviewed them.
   - **(A)** consecrate
   - **(B)** endorse
   - **(C)** lament
   - **(D)** coax
   - **(E)** retort

6. The Mbuti people, _____ of the Ituri rain forest in the Democratic Republic of the Congo, _____ the destruction of their homeland by logging companies, settlers, and poachers.
   - **(A)** assailants…aggravate
   - **(B)** affronts…mesmerize
   - **(C)** banquets…dispel
   - **(D)** torrent…retort
   - **(E)** denizens…lament

7. As more African nations create _____ economies, the African continent will play a greater role in the global marketplace.
   - **(A)** stifled
   - **(B)** heedless
   - **(C)** diversified
   - **(D)** impartial
   - **(E)** acrid

8. In 2001, the Nobel Foundation showed its _____ for United Nations Secretary-General Kofi Annan, awarding him the Nobel Peace Prize for, among other things, his effort to address the _____ of poor Africans infected by HIV/AIDS.
   - **(A)** toil…refuse
   - **(B)** defiance…denizen
   - **(C)** gratitude…plight
   - **(D)** dissension… animosity
   - **(E)** nonentity…bedlam

Vocabulary Practice

Analyze Word Origins Emphasize to students that knowledge of word origins can help them with vocabulary tests. Point out that *disrupt* comes from the Latin verb *rumpere*, "to break." Work with students to identify some of the English words that are created by adding various prefixes or suffixes to the Latin root *rupt* (from the past participle of *rumpere*). These include *abrupt, corrupt, erupt, interrupt,* and *rupture*. Give students the root word of *retort* (Latin *torquere*, "to twist"). Have students identify other English words formed by adding prefixes or suffixes to the Latin root *tort* (from the past participle of *torquere*). These include *contort, distort, extort,* and *torture*.

Assessment
English-Language Arts

Grammar and Writing Skills:
Sentence Improvement

Read the following sentences carefully. Then, on a separate sheet of paper, write the letter of the answer that correctly fixes each underlined portion.

1. Global warming has become such a hot-button <u>issue, but politicians</u> have had to reconsider their positions on it.
   (A) issue, but
   (B) issue that
   (C) issue, that
   (D) issue, also
   (E) issue when

2. Because many cargo ships are too large to pass through the Panama Canal, <u>the Panamanian government planning to widen the waterway.</u>
   (A) the Panamanian government planning to widen the waterway
   (B) the Panamanian government plans to widen the waterway
   (C) the waterway is widened by the Panamanian government
   (D) the Panamanian government is plans to widen the waterway
   (E) the Panama Canal has widen

3. Among the most beautiful cities in the United States, <u>San Francisco benefits from its location on a peninsula and its hilly terrain.</u>
   (A) San Francisco benefits from its location on a peninsula and its hilly terrain
   (B) San Francisco benefits as a hilly peninsula
   (C) the hilly terrain and peninsula location benefit San Francisco
   (D) the benefit of San Francisco is its hilly peninsula
   (E) as San Francisco benefits from its location on a peninsula and its hilly terrain

4. Cultures that lack written language often have strong oral traditions <u>which stories are passed down by word of mouth.</u>
   (A) which stories are passed down by word of mouth
   (B) by which word-of-mouth is passed down in stories
   (C) that stories are passed down by word of mouth
   (D) however, stories are passed down by word of mouth
   (E) in which stories are passed down by word of mouth

5. <u>*The Tale of Genji* often considered the world's first novel, was written</u> in the early eleventh century.
   (A) *The Tale of Genji* often considered the world's first novel, was written
   (B) *The Tale of Genji* often considered the world's first novel was written
   (C) *The Tale of Genji*, often considered the world's first novel, was written
   (D) Considered the world's first novel *The Tale of Genji* was written
   (E) *The Tale of Genji*—often considered the world's first novel, was written

6. Many jobs require long hours in front of a computer, <u>or many workers have developed carpal tunnel syndrome.</u>
   (A) or many workers have developed carpal tunnel syndrome
   (B) because many workers have carpal tunnel syndrome
   (C) however many workers have developed carpal tunnel syndrome
   (D) and many workers have developed carpal tunnel syndrome
   (E) so develops carpal tunnel syndrome

 Literature Online

Assessment For additional test practice, go to glencoe.com and enter QuickPass code GLW6053u1.

ASSESSMENT **175**

Assess
Grammar

1. **B** is the correct answer. The restrictive modifying clause should not be set off by a comma. [DOK 1]
2. **B** is the correct answer. The main clause requires a verb. [DOK 1]
3. **A** is the correct answer. No change is needed. [DOK 1]
4. **E** is the correct answer. A preposition is needed to introduce the modifying clause. [DOK 1]
5. **C** is the correct answer. The nonrestrictive modifying clause needs to be set off with commas. [DOK 1]
6. **D** is the correct answer. The conjunction needed to connect the two clauses is *and*. [DOK 1]

Approaching Level
DIFFERENTIATED INSTRUCTION

Think Aloud Explain to students that a critical test-taking skill is eliminating incorrect responses. Eliminating one or more possibilities will considerably increase their chances of choosing the correct answer from the remaining ones. Model a think-aloud using one of the items from page 175. **Say:** In item 3, the phrase that starts the sentence describes San Francisco, so it would be incorrect to have it modify either "the hilly terrain and peninsula" in answer C or "the benefit" in answer D. So the correct answer must be either A, B, or E.

Once you have modeled this procedure, ask a group of students to demonstrate it by trying think-alouds using other test items.

Skills Scope and Sequence

Readability Scores Key: Dale-Chall/DRP/Lexile

PART 1: Ancient Greece 1500 B.C.–1 B.C.

Selections and Features	Literary Elements
Part Introduction pp. 176–189	Literary Periods **SE** p. 182
Literary History The Homeric Epics pp. 190–191	Literary Genres **SE** p. 190
Epic Book I: The Rage of Achilles *from* the **Iliad,** by Homer, translated by Robert Fagles pp. 192–209	Epic Hero **SE** p. 193
Epic Book XXII: The Death of Hector *from* the **Iliad,** by Homer, translated by Robert Fagles pp. 210–231	Epic Simile **SE** p. 210 Setting **TE** p. 212 Imagery **TE** p. 228 Epic Hero (review) **SE** p. 230
The Art of Translation Homer Through the Ages pp. 232–233	
Historical Perspective *from* **Echoes of the Heroic Age,** by Caroline Alexander **8.7/63/1380** pp. 234–240	
Poems Most Beautiful of All the Stars, In My Eyes He Matches the Gods, For My Mother Said, and **Some Say Thronging Cavalry** by Sappho, translated by Jim Powell pp. 241–247	Imagery **SE** p. 242 Personification (review) **SE** p. 246
Literary History Classical Greek Drama pp. 248–249	Literary Genres **SE** p. 248
Drama Oedipus the King, Part 1, by Sophocles, translated by Robert Fagles pp. 250–273	Chorus **SE** p. 251

Reading Skills and Strategies	Vocabulary	Writing / Grammar	Speaking, Listening, Viewing
Evaluate Historical Influences **SE** p. 182 Activate Prior Knowledge **TE** p. 188 Connect to the Literature **SE** p. 189	Connotation and Denotation **TE** p. 186	Parallelism **TE** p. 182 Primary and Secondary Sources **TE** p. 184	View the Art **SE** p. 176 Discussion **SE** p. 189 Create a Display **SE** p. 189
Evaluate Historical Influences **SE** p. 190 Connect to the Literature **SE** p. 191			Oral Report **TE** p. 190
Evaluate Credibility **SE** p. 193	Synonyms **SE** p. 209	Write an Interior Monologue **TE** p. 206 Write a Character Sketch **SE** p. 209	Oral Interpretation **TE** p. 196 View the Art **SE** pp. 199, 204; **TE** p. 206 Debate **TE** p. 202
Analyze Cultural Context **SE** p. 210 Compare and Contrast Characters **TE** p. 220 Analyze Cause-and-Effect Relationships **TE** p. 224	Multiple-Meaning Words **TE** p. 214 Denotation and Connotation **SE** p. 230 Academic Vocabulary **SE** p. 230	Write a Description **TE** p. 216 Write a Research Report **TE** p. 222 Write an Expository Essay **SE** p. 231	View the Art **SE** pp. 220, 226
Understand Cultural and Historical Context **SE** p. 232 Understand the Nature of Translation **SE** p. 233			
Analyze and Evaluate Informational Text **SE** p. 234 Evaluate Evidence **SE** p. 234 Connect to Contemporary Issues **SE** p. 234		Write a Description **TE** p. 238 Write a Summary **SE** p. 240	Photo-Essay **TE** p. 234
Paraphrase **SE** p. 242	Synonyms **SE** p. 247 Academic Vocabulary **SE** p. 247	Dashes **TE** p. 244 Apply Imagery in a Poem or Narrative Sketch **SE** p. 247	View the Art **SE** p. 244
Evaluate Historical Influences **SE** p. 248 Connect to the Literature **SE** p. 249		Note Taking **TE** p. 248 Write a Summary **TE** p. 248 Write an Outline **TE** p. 248	
Apply Background Knowledge **SE** p. 251 Summarize **TE** p. 254 Synthesize **TE** p. 272	Word Parts **TE** p. 266 Denotation and Connotation **SE** p. 273	Write an Expository Essay **TE** p. 260 Noun Clauses **TE** p. 270 Write a Letter **SE** p. 273	View the Art **SE** pp. 252, 267, 270 Oral Report **TE** pp. 256, 268 Visual Interpretation **TE** p. 264

PART 1: Ancient Greece 1500 B.C.–1 B.C. *(continued)*

Selections and Features	Literary Elements
Drama Oedipus the King, Part 2, by Sophocles, translated by Robert Fagles pp. 274–290	Tragedy **SE** p. 274
Drama Oedipus the King, Part 3, by Sophocles, translated by Robert Fagles pp. 291–318	Irony **SE** p. 291 Tragedy (review) **SE** p. 317
Vocabulary Workshop p. 319	
Speech Pericles' Funeral Oration *from* **History of the Peloponnesian War 8/59/1240,** by Thucydides, translated by Rex Warner pp. 320–332	Argument **SE** p. 321 Tone (review) **SE** p. 331
Vocabulary Workshop p. 333	
Nonfiction *from* the **Dialogues** *from* the **Apology,** by Plato, translated by Benjamin Jowett **9/59/1050** pp. 334–341	Formal Speech **SE** p. 335 Setting (review) **SE** p. 340
Informational Text **TIME: All the Right Questions,** by Anita Hamilton **8.6/63/1140** pp. 342–345	

PART 2: Ancient Rome 800 B.C.–A.D. 500

Part Introduction pp. 346–357	Literary Periods **SE** p. 350
Poems Poems of Catullus, by Catullus, translated by Carl Sesar pp. 358–362	Speaker **SE** p. 359
Poem Better to Live, Licinius, by Horace, translated by Joseph P. Clancy pp. 363–366	Ode **SE** p. 364
Grammar Workshop p. 367	

Reading Skills and Strategies	Vocabulary	Writing / Grammar	Speaking, Listening, Viewing
Analyze Argument **SE** p. 274 Identify Problem and Solution **TE** p. 276	Synonyms **SE** p. 290	Write a Research Paper **TE** pp. 278, 282 Write an Essay **SE** p. 290	Readers' Theater **TE** p. 284
Synthesize **SE** p. 291 Visualize **TE** p. 292 Monitor Comprehension **TE** p. 300 Analyze Plot **TE** p. 306 Analyze Literary Technique **TE** p. 308	Word Origins **SE** p. 317 Academic Vocabulary **SE** p. 317	Dashes **TE** p. 296 Write a Narrative **TE** p. 298 Create a Character Web **TE** p. 312 Write an Expository Essay **SE** p. 318 Ellipsis Points **SE** p. 318	Storytelling **TE** p. 294 View the Photograph **TE** p. 300 View the Art **SE** pp. 295, 305 Discussion **SE** p. 317; **TE** p. 304 Critical Viewing **TE** p. 314
	Jargon **SE** p. 319		
Analyze Rhetorical Devices **SE** p. 321 Compare and Contrast **TE** p. 324 Connect to the Literature **TE** p. 330	Analogies **SE** p. 332 Academic Vocabulary **SE** p. 332	Parallelism **SE** p. 332 Write a Speech **SE** p. 332	View the Art **SE** p. 327 Speech **TE** p. 322; **SE** p. 332
	Dictionary Use **SE** p. 333		
Analyze Persuasion **SE** p. 335	Word Parts **SE** p. 341 Academic Vocabulary **SE** p. 341	Write a Speech **TE** p. 336	View the Art **SE** p. 337 Debate **SE** p. 341
Distinguish Fact from Opinion **SE** p. 342 Preview **SE** p. 342		Write a Press Release **TE** p. 342 Write a Summary **SE** p. 345	Discussion **TE** p. 344
Evaluate Historical Influences **SE** p. 350 Connect to the Literature **SE** p. 357	Word Origins **TE** p. 350 Connotation and Denotation **TE** p. 351	Write a Research Report **TE** p. 348 Italics **TE** p. 356 Write an Essay **SE** p. 357	Create a Display **SE** p. 357 View the Art **TE** pp. 346–350, 352, 354, 356
Make Generalizations **SE** p. 359 Recognize Author's Purpose **TE** p. 360	Academic Vocabulary **SE** p. 362	Write a Poem **SE** p. 362	
Interpret Imagery **SE** p. 364 Determine Main Idea and Supporting Details **TE** p. 364	Word Usage **SE** p. 366	Write a Letter **SE** p. 366	View the Art **TE** p. 365
		Subject-Verb Agreement **SE** p. 367	

PART 2: Ancient Rome 800 B.C.–A.D. 500 *(continued)*

Reading Skills and Strategies	Vocabulary	Writing Grammar	Speaking, Listening, and Viewing
Identify Sequence **SE** p. 369 Analyze Sensory Details **TE** p. 374	Denotation and Connotation **SE** p. 375	Appositive Phrases **TE** p. 370 Write a Summary **SE** p. 375	View the Art **SE** p. 373

Make and Verify Predictions **SE** p. 377
Activate Prior Knowledge **TE** p. 384
Summarize **TE** p. 390
	Context Clues **SE** p. 397
	Academic Vocabulary
	    SE p. 397
		Write an Expository Essay
		    SE p. 398
		Comparative and Superlative
		    Forms **SE** p. 398
			View the Art **SE** pp. 385, 393
			Literature Group **TE** p. 386
			Interview **TE** p. 388

	Word Origins **SE** p. 399		

Compare Cultural Contexts **SE** p. 400
Recognize Bias **SE** p. 402
Analyze Point of View **TE** p. 402
Apply Background Knowledge
    TE p. 404
	Word Origins **SE** p. 407	Write a Mission Statement
		    SE p. 407
		Write a Description **TE** p. 410
		Write a Poem **TE** p. 412
		Write an Essay **SE** p. 415
			Discussion **SE** pp. 412, 415;
			    TE p. 408
			View the Art **TE** p. 413
			Visual Display **SE** p. 415

Analyze Text Structure **TE** p. 418		Write a Biographical Narrative **SE** p. 416 Prewrite **SE** p. 419 Draft **SE** p. 420 Revise **SE** p. 422 Verb Tense **SE** p. 423	
			Effective Speaking **TE** p. 422 Photo-Essay **SE** p. 424
Read Literature Independently **SE** p. 426		Write a Review **SE** p. 427	
Reread **TE** p. 432		Write an Essay **SE** p. 433	

Focus

Bellringer Option

**Literature Launcher
    Pre-Reading Video**
**Daily Language Practice
    Transparency 22**

Or ask: What characteristics do you associate with the words classic or classical? *(Students might mention characteristics such as high quality, historical importance, artistic seriousness, and critical reputation.)*
Point out to students that the literature and art they will encounter in Unit Two are key products of the original classical civilizations—ancient Greece and Rome.

 For school-to-home activities, see Unit 2 Teaching Resources Book, pp. 5–11.

 For students who would profit from independent novel study, see Novel Companion, pp. 51–118.

View the Art ★

Possible answers: *The ancient Greeks were interested in realistic sculptures of human forms; Greek artists were careful about details, as shown by the natural draping of the sculptured fabrics; ancient Greece flourished a long time ago because this sculpture is weathered and broken.*

The frieze of the Parthenon is a long, narrow, horizontal band of sculpture carved in low relief on the outer wall of an inner room. These three figures from the frieze depict Poseidon, god of the sea; Apollo, sun-god and patron of poets; and Artemis, goddess of the moon and of the hunt.

Poseidon, Apollo, and Artemis (detail). Phidias. Parthenon frieze. Acropolis Museum, Athens.
 The sculptor Phidias supervised, or created himself, the statues of the Parthenon. What do these figures suggest about ancient Greece? ★

176

Viewing Practice

Analyze Greek Sculpture Point out to students that these figures represent the development of Greek sculpture, from the stiffly poised figures of the earlier Archaic style to a fluid, balanced, natural depiction of the human body. Have groups of students discuss the images, and answer questions such as the following:

- What do the postures of the figures express? *(grace, serenity, and dignity)*

- How does the arrangement of the figures contribute to the overall composition? *(lines of limbs echo each other)*

- What effect is created by the different textures of skin and fabric? *(texture of fabric accentuates the smoothness of skin)*

- What seems to be the artist's point of view toward the subject? *(reverence, admiration)*

ANCIENT GREECE AND ROME

1500 B.C.—A.D. 500

🔲🔲🔲🔲🔲🔲🔲🔲🔲🔲🔲🔲🔲🔲🔲🔲🔲🔲🔲🔲🔲🔲🔲🔲🔲🔲🔲🔲

Μνάσεσθαί τινά φαμι καὶ ὕστερον ἀμμέων

Someone, I tell you, will remember us.

—Sappho, Fragment 138 **1**

PART ONE

PART TWO

177

Focus

Summary

Unit Two is divided into two sections: Ancient Greece and Ancient Rome. The introduction for Part 1 is on pages 178–189; the introduction for Part 2 is on pages 346–357.

Teach

Reading Strategy | 1

Identify Theme **Ask:** What concern is reflected in this fragment of ancient Greek poetry? *(that the works of the poet will be forgotten)*

Cultural History ☆

Survival of Ancient Writings
Point out that what survives today of the works of ancient Greek and Roman writers is only a small portion of what once existed. Much of Sappho's work, for example, was lost during the early Middle Ages. Only one complete poem and about one hundred fragments were preserved.

For diagnostic and end-of-unit assessment, see Assessment Resources, pp. 7–12, 255–256.

Unit Resources

Print
- Unit 2 Teaching Resources, pp. 1–244
- Interactive Read and Write, On Level
- Novel Companion, pp. 51–118
- Bellringer Option Transparencies: Selection Focus 13–21; Daily Language Practice 22–30
- Literary Element Transparencies

- Assessment Resources, Unit Assessment, pp. 255–256
- Assessment Resources, Selection Assessment, pp. 67–92

Technology
- TeacherWorks Plus CD
- StudentWorks Plus CD
- Literature Launchers: Pre-Reading Videos DVD
- Literature Online
- Listening Library CD-ROM
- ExamView CD-ROM
- Skill Level Up! CD-ROM

Focus

A *The Acropolis.* Reed Kaestner. Athens, Greece. ★

View the Art ★

The Greek word *acropolis* means "city at the top." The term refers to the high ground around which most ancient Greek cities developed. **Ask:** Why do you think most Greek cities were constructed around an acropolis? *(to make them more defensible against attackers)*

📁 For students who would profit from independent novel study, see Novel Companion pp. 51–118.

B *Cape Matapan.* Schmitz-Söhnigen. Photograph. Mani, Laconia, Greece.

LOG ON ▶ **Literature** Online

Literature and Reading For more about the history and literature of this period, go to glencoe.com and enter QuickPass code GLW6053u2.

178

Part Introduction Skills

Reading Skills
- Analyze Graphic Information (SE p. 181)
- Make Generalizations (SE p. 186)
- Compare and Contrast (SE p. 187)
- Analyze Cause-and-Effect Relationships (SE p. 188; TE p. 183)

← **Part 1 Introduction** →

Speaking/Listening/Viewing Skills
- Panel Discussion (SE p. 189; TE p. 183)
- Analyze Art (SE pp. 176; TE pp. 180–182, 184)

Vocabulary Skills
- Connotation and Denotation (TE p. 186)
- Word Roots (TE p. 182)

Writing Skills/Grammar
- Write a Description (TE p. 181)
- Use Parallelism (TE p. 182)

ANCIENT GREECE

1500 B.C.–1 B.C.

Running girl, 520-500 BC. Greek.
Bronze figure. British Museum, London.

Being There

Ancient Greek civilization developed on a rugged peninsula and many islands scattered throughout the surrounding sea. Much of Greece consists of small plains and river valleys surrounded by high mountain ranges. Separated by natural barriers, the Greeks developed small, fiercely independent communities, or city-states. The area's challenging landscape was matched by its history. Early centuries were marked by waves of destructive invasions. Later, the Greeks were threatened by their mighty neighbor, the Persian Empire.

2 Looking Ahead

History and geography combined to form the Greek character. Greek civilization valued the individual human being. In art, history, and philosophy, Greeks focused on the human body and mind. Ancient Greek literature explored an ideal of heroism, a concept of the good life, and a tragic sense of human destiny.

Keep the following questions in mind as you read:

- What was the ancient Greek ideal of heroism?

- How did the Greeks explore concepts of the good life?

- What social and cultural functions did drama serve in ancient Athens?

179

English Learners

DIFFERENTIATED INSTRUCTION

SMALL GROUP **Intermediate** Have students bring in maps and photographs of their homelands to share in small mixed groups. Each student should present the items along with a description of the climate, the major geographic features, and any other interesting facts about the region. Allow groups time to ask questions about each student's presentation.

Approaching Level

DIFFERENTIATED INSTRUCTION

SMALL GROUP  **Set a Purpose** Point out to students that the questions at the bottom of page 179 are intended to help guide their reading of the Part 1 introduction. Work with small groups of students to create other purpose-setting questions, such as:

- How did Athens and Sparta differ?

Have students write down their questions and answer them as they read.

Focus

Summary

This introduction gives an overview of historical, social, and cultural forces in ancient Greece between 1500 and 1 B.C. It discusses the impact of geography on the development of Greece; the rise of the two preeminent Greek city-states, Athens and Sparta; the struggle between the Greeks and the Persian Empire that led to the golden age of Athens; and some of the characteristic forms of Greek civilization.

Teach

Reading Strategy | 1

Analyze Graphic Information Have students examine the map of ancient Greece and the surrounding areas. **Ask:** How might the fact that Greece is surrounded by water have affected culture? *(Students may note that access to the sea would have encouraged trade with other countries, thus bringing the ancient Greeks into contact with other cultures.)*

Reading Strategy | 2

Analyze Cultural Context Have students read the paragraph under Looking Ahead. **Ask:** Why do you think the ancient Greeks valued individual humans? *(Students may feel that the small scale of Greek city-states and the challenges of Greek history emphasized the importance of the individual.)*

Teach

Text Element | 1

Timeline Remind students that in the B.C. time scale later dates have smaller numbers than earlier dates. **Ask:** What is the date of the earliest event in the Part One timeline? *(1479 B.C.)* **Ask:** What is the date of the latest event in the Part One timeline? *(100 B.C.)*

Reading Strategy | 2

Analyze Graphic Information **Ask:** Did Pericles deliver his funeral oration before or after Sophocles won his first victory in dramatic competition? *(after)*

View the Art ★

This bronze statue shows a charioteer at the moment of his triumph at ancient Greek games held in honor of Apollo. The victor presented the statue to Apollo's shrine at Delphi in gratitude for the god's help. **Ask:** How would you describe the attitude of the charioteer? *(Students will probably feel that the charioteer seems very modest in victory, perhaps in recognition of the divine aid he has received.)*

TIMELINE 1500 B.C.– 1 B.C.

GREEK LITERATURE

1500   **800**

Vessel depicting scene from Homer's *Iliad*

◀ **c. ninth century**
Homer composes the *Iliad* and the *Odyssey*

c. 610–570
Lyric poet Sappho flourishes

The Charioteer of Delphi

GREEK EVENTS

1500   **800**

1450
Minoan civilization on Crete begins to collapse

eighth century
Apollo's oracle is established at Delphi

1300
Mycenaean civilization flourishes

776
First Olympic Games are held

c. early 12th century
The Trojan War begins (according to ancient Greek tradition)

c. 700
Athens becomes unified city-state

WORLD EVENTS

1500 **1**   **800**

1479–1426
Egyptian Empire flourishes under Thutmose III

c. 1350
Akhenaten institutes sun worship in Egypt

970
Solomon becomes King of Israel

▲
586
Jews are exiled to Babylon

559
Cyrus the Great founds the Persian Empire

◀ **551**
Chinese philosopher Confucius is born

LOG ON ▶ **Literature** Online

Literature and Reading To explore the Interactive Timeline, go to glencoe.com and enter QuickPass code GLW6053u2.

180 UNIT 2   ANCIENT GREECE

Reading Practice

Making Connections Point out that a timeline is a sampling of significant events that took place during a specific period. Broad connections between some of the events have already been made: (a) All the events in the top panel relate to Greek literature. (b) All the events in the middle panel relate to Greek history. Further examination will reveal other links.

Have students research the links between one of the following pairs of entries:

399 Socrates is executed in Athens.

c. 387 Plato founds Academy at Athens.

586 Jews are exiled to Babylon.

559 Cyrus the Great founds the Persian Empire.

480 Siddhartha Gautama, founder of Buddhism, dies.

c. 274 Asoka becomes ruler of India.

500 **100**

468
Sophocles wins his
first victory in dramatic
competition

Bust of Socrates

c. 430
Pericles delivers his
funeral oration

2

399
Socrates is executed
in Athens

411
Thucydides leaves
his *Peloponnesian War*
incomplete

c. 387
Plato founds his Academy
in Athens

100

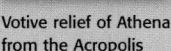
Votive relief of Athena
from the Acropolis

445
Athenian Empire expands

3 432
Parthenon is completed

405
Athenian Empire
is destroyed

326
Alexander the Great
reaches India

c. 500
Golden Age of
Athens begins

431–404
Peloponnesian War between
Athens and Sparta

490
Greeks defeat Persians
at Marathon

500 **100**

480
Siddhārtha Gautama,
founder of Buddhism, dies

100
Europe and China
are linked through the
Silk Road **4**

c. 400
Olmec civilization
declines in Mexico

▲
c. 220
Construction of the Great
Wall of China is begun

c. 274
Asoka becomes ruler
of India

Reading Check

Analyze Graphic Information About how many
years passed between the Golden Age of Athens
and its collapse?

INTRODUCTION **181**

Teach

Reading Check

Answer: *About 105 years passed.*

Reading Strategy | 3

Analyze Graphic Information **Ask:** Was the Parthenon completed before or after the start of the Peloponnesian War? *(before)*

Reading Strategy | 4

Analyze Graphic Information **Ask:** Could early European visitors to China via the Silk Road have seen portions of the Great Wall? *(yes)*

View the Art ★

Athena, goddess of wisdom and war, is usually shown wearing a soldier's helmet and often carries a spear. In this relief from the Athenian Acropolis, she leans on her spear with its point facing downward. **Ask:** What emotion is conveyed by this sculpture? *(Students will probably feel that the goddess seems thoughtful or sad.)*

Advanced Learners/Pre-AP

DIFFERENTIATED INSTRUCTION

Descriptive Writing Have students use pairs of timeline entries as the basis for writing a description of a historical person, a place, or an event by an imaginary persona. Here are some possibilities:

- a description of Cyrus the Great by an exiled Jew in Babylon
- a description of the Great Wall by an early European visitor to China via the Silk Road

- a recollection of the battle of Marathon by an Athenian of the Golden Age

Encourage students to stay within the limits of their imaginary personas.

Learning Objectives
Analyzing graphic information. (SE)
Analyzing art. (TE)

Word Roots Point out that the Greek word *polis*, "city," is not only the root of such English words as *politics*, but also of *police* and *policy*. **Ask:** What English word is formed from the Greek roots *polis* and *meter*, "mother"? (*metropolis*, "mother city")

Summarize Ask: How would you summarize Athenian democracy? (*Free male citizens were able to participate fully in Athenian democracy, but Athenian women, slaves, and former slaves had few political rights or none.*)

ADVANCED Explain to students that Athens was a direct democracy, meaning that a vote of all male citizens determined public issues. **Ask:** How does this differ from democracy in the United States? (*The United States is a representative democracy; citizens elect representatives who make laws.*)

APPROACHING Review for students the distinction between direct democracy and representative democracy.

Learning Objectives

For pages 178–189
In studying this text, you will focus on the following objectives:

Literary Study: Analyzing literary periods.

Reading: Evaluating historical influences.
Connecting to the literature.

ANCIENT GREECE

1500 B.C.–1 B.C.

Historical, Social, and Cultural Forces

The Greek World

Greece is a land of islands, mountains, and peninsulas. Rocky hilltops separate parts of the territory from each other and make the soil difficult to farm. White limestone cliffs drop off into the blue and ever-present sea. Most parts of Greece are within 50 miles of saltwater, and this rugged, maritime landscape has affected Greece's history from its beginning. The rough terrain meant settlements were isolated and self-sufficient, and

Hoplites and cavaliers. Princeton Painter. Attic black figure amphora. Louvre, Paris. ⭐

the proximity to the sea encouraged trade and provided access to other cultures. The Greeks eventually developed a type of community they called a *polis*, or city-state. (*Polis* is the root of such English words as *politics* and *political*.) The polis was a city, a town, or even a village that controlled the surrounding countryside. The most powerful of the ancient Greek city-states were Athens and Sparta. Although they were fiercely independent, these city-states shared a common language, religion, and social organization.

Athens

Athens grew over the centuries from a small city-state to become the center of one of the most successful and cultured societies in the history of the world. By the fifth century B.C., history's first democratic government had taken hold there. Free Athenian men spent much of their time in public outdoor spaces, discussing philosophy and politics. Wealth from nearby silver mines, from other cities paying tribute, and from trade allowed Athenians ample time to pursue learning. While citizens enjoyed freedom and opportunity, however, most people in Athens were not citizens. Scholars estimate at least forty percent of the Athenian population was enslaved. Although enslaved people could often buy their freedom, they could never gain full rights as citizens. Free women could not participate openly in politics and were expected to spend their time at home.

Writing Practice

✐ Use Parallelism Point out the use of parallelism in the quote from Thucydides on page 183.

Remind students that parallelism is the use of a series of words, phrases, clauses, or sentences that have similar grammatical form.

Have students rewrite the following sentences to maintain parallel structure.

1. Greek geography, its politics, and the history of Greece all encouraged an emphasis on the individual. (*Greek geography, Greek politics, and Greek history all encouraged an emphasis on the individual.*)

2. Athens was famous for its flourishing culture; military strength made Sparta famous. (*Athens was famous for its flourishing culture; Sparta was famous for its military strength.*)

View the Art ⭐

The Greek foot soldiers painted on this vase were known as *hoplites*. **Ask:** What is suggested about ancient Greek infantry tactics by the way these hoplites are depicted? (*In battle, Greek hoplites stood close together with their shields overlapping to present a wall to enemy troops.*)

Sparta

While Athens was known for its democratic government and flourishing culture, Sparta was known for its military strength. The Spartan government believed the lives of its citizens should center on the military. For this reason, young boys were taken away from their parents and housed in dormitories while they underwent rigorous physical training. Girls were trained in all-female groups. From the age of twenty until the age of 60, men belonged to the army. Although they were allowed to marry, only after 30 could they live with their wives.

> *"'Our love of what is beautiful does not lead to extravagance; our love of the things of the mind does not make us soft.'"*
>
> —Thucydides, *The Peloponnesian War*

The Challenge of Persia

As the Greek city-states developed, they came into conflict with the vast and powerful Persian Empire to the east. In 490 B.C., an invading Persian force landed on the Plain of Marathon, only 26 miles from Athens. Badly outnumbered, the Athenians decisively defeated the Persian army. According to legend, a messenger from Marathon raced to Athens with news of the Persian defeat and uttered only the word *Nike* ("victory") before dropping dead of exhaustion.

Ten years later, 300 Spartan soldiers delayed a second and even larger Persian invasion, holding back 180,000 Persian troops at the pass of Thermopylae while fighting to the last man. The onslaught of the enemy forces threatened the Athenians; they abandoned their city, which the Persians burned. In a sea battle off the island of Salamis, however, the Greek fleet, though outnumbered, outmaneuvered the Persian fleet and defeated it. The defeat of Persia allowed Athens to assume the leadership of Greece and reach the height of political power and cultural brilliance.

Bust of Pericles, 2nd century BC. Roman. Marble. British Museum, London.

The Age of Pericles

Under Pericles (per′ə klēz′), the leader who dominated Athenian politics from 461 to 429 B.C., Athens became the center of Greek culture. The Persians had destroyed much of the city during the Persian Wars, but Pericles set in motion a vast rebuilding program. New temples and statues soon symbolized the greatness of Athens. Art, architecture, and philosophy flourished. The greatest symbol of Periclean Athens is the Parthenon (pär′thə nän′), the beautiful temple of the city's patroness Athena, goddess of wisdom. This temple displays grace and harmony, the ideals of classical art.

3

4

Teach

Reading Strategy 3

Analyze Cause-and-Effect Relationships Ask: How did the Persian Wars help shape the architecture of Athens during the Golden Age? *(The Persians had destroyed much of the city, which was rebuilt under Pericles.)*

Reading Strategy 4

Connect to Personal Experience Point out to students that classical architecture has had a great influence on the design of many structures in the United States, including government offices, courts, libraries, colleges, museums, art galleries, banks, and other public buildings. Offer an example of a neoclassical structure from your community. **Ask:** What qualities does the design of this building stress? *(Most neoclassical buildings stress simplicity, dignity, and a respect for tradition.)*

ENGLISH LEARNERS Ask students who have come from other countries to bring photographs of public buildings from their homelands and discuss how they are like and unlike neoclassical buildings in the United States.

Approaching Level

DIFFERENTIATED INSTRUCTION

Graphic Organizer Suggest that students use a simple graphic organizer such as the two-column chart here to keep track of the characteristics of the rival Greek city-states of Athens and Sparta.

Athens	Sparta
▪ celebrated for its culture	▪ respected for military strength

Advanced Learners/Pre-AP

DIFFERENTIATED INSTRUCTION

Panel Discussion Have a group of students do research and then hold a panel discussion on the question of whether it would have been better for an ancient Greek woman to live in Athens or in Sparta.

Learning Objectives
Analyzing historical influences. (SE)
Analyzing word roots. (TE)
Summarizing. (TE)
Using parallelism. (TE)
Analyzing art. (TE)

183

Reading Strategy | 1

Determine Main Idea
Ask: What is the topic sentence of this paragraph? ("Athletics was highly valued in ancient Greece.")

Reading Strategy | 2

Analyze Cultural Context
Ask: How did the ancient Olympics reflect the Greek ideal of arête, or all-around excellence? (*The competitions were not only in athletics, but also in poetry and music.*)

View the Art ★
Contrapposto is an Italian word meaning "opposite." Placing the weight of the body on one leg shifts the position of the hips and shoulders. **Ask:** What effect does the use of contrapposto create in this statue? (*The posture of the statue seems more relaxed and life-like.*)

Sculpture

Greek sculptors usually presented human forms. They used symmetry and proportion to create a new kind of beauty. Initially, Greek sculptures showed figures with their weight balanced equally on both legs. However, Greek sculptors soon began experimenting with a more natural, asymmetrical style in which the weight of the figure rests primarily on one leg. Sculptors studied how muscles and bones work together, and their realistic sculptures reflected this new knowledge.

The Olympics

1 Athletics was highly valued in ancient Greece. The best athletes trained for years to participate in the Olympic Games, the premier competition of the time. Held every four years in the Greek city of Olympia, the games were elaborate festivals **2** that focused on religion, poetry, and music as well as on sports. The first Olympics featured only one event, a foot race across the distance of the stadium. In later years more races and other events were added. Only men could compete in the Olympics, and usually only wealthy men had time to train, practice, and travel to Olympia. While there were no official cash prizes, cities often rewarded their champions with large sums.

Sophocles, c. 340-30 BC. Museo Gregoriano Profano, Vatican Museums, Vatican State. ★

Running hoplite, 520-510 BC. Skythos Painter. Interior of a red-figured cup from Tanagra. Louvre, Paris.

> "*Beauty of style and harmony and grace and good rhythm depend on simplicity.*"
>
> —Plato, from *The Republic*

Reading Practice

Distinguish Primary and Secondary Sources Point out to students that primary sources are firsthand accounts, records, or artifacts of a person, an event, or a culture. For example, the quote from Plato's *Republic* on page 184 is a primary source for ancient Greek culture.

A secondary source is an account or record created by someone not immediately acquainted with the person, present at the event, or part of the culture. For example, the work of the classical historian H.D.F. Kitto quoted on page 186 is a secondary source for ancient Greek culture.

Have students determine whether each of the following is a primary or a secondary source for ancient Greek culture.

1. a poem by Sappho (*primary*)

2. a modern biography of Socrates (*secondary*)

3. an ancient Greek account of the battle of Marathon (*primary*)

4. a Greek statue (*primary*)

5. a scholar's introduction to Homer's *Iliad* (*secondary*)

Architecture

Although Greek people lived in humble houses, they constructed magnificent public buildings. Each city-state had an acropolis, or a fortified area at the highest point in the city, where temples were built. The Acropolis of Athens includes the Parthenon, the temple of the goddess Athena that symbolizes classical Greek architecture. The Athenian Acropolis contains examples of the three main styles, or "orders," of Greek architecture.

- The Doric order, which is plain, severe, and dignified, was the earliest style. The Parthenon exemplifies the Doric order.

- The Ionic order, which is more light, delicate, and complex, came into wide use about a century after the Doric order.

- The Corinthian order was the last and most elaborate style, featuring decorations of leaves and scrolls.

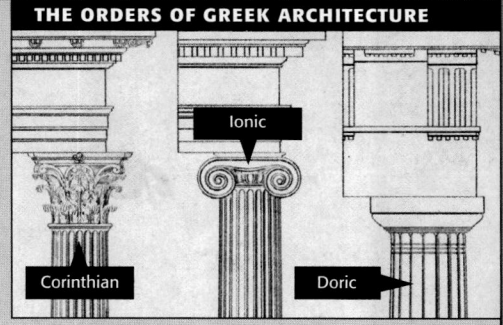

THE ORDERS OF GREEK ARCHITECTURE

Ionic

Corinthian

Doric

⭐ *Facade of the Parthenon, 447–432 BC. Callicrates and Ictinus. Acropolis, Athens.* ▶

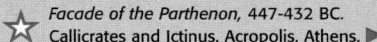

PREVIEW **Big Ideas** **of Ancient Greece**

1 The Heroic Ideal	**2** The Good Life	**3** The Tragic Vision
Although Greece was organized into small, fiercely independent city-states, the Greeks shared a cultural heritage. One of the key elements of this heritage was the literature of Homer. His epic poems provided models of heroic behavior. **See page 186**	Greek civilization sought to discover what constitutes the good life. Introducing personal values into literature, Greek lyric poets such as Sappho explored what mattered personally to them. Greek philosophers such as Socrates questioned traditional values in an attempt to determine how individuals should behave. **See page 187**	The Greeks of Athens invented drama, which they used to explore vital social and religious questions. Athenian dramatists such as Sophocles created powerful, darkly beautiful visions of human destiny, as well as tragic heroes, whose character flaws partly contribute to their downfall. **See page 188**

Reading Strategy 3

Analyze Cultural Context

Ask: What does the contrast between private simplicity and public splendor indicate about Greek cultural values? *(Many students may feel that it indicates a high degree of civic pride.)*

(ADVANCED) **Ask:** How does this contrast in ancient Greek society compare with the private and public display of wealth in modern American society? *(Students will probably feel that there is much greater emphasis on the display of private wealth in American society.)*

Cultural History ⭐

The Parthenon The Greek word *parthenon* means "maiden's room." In a Greek home, the *parthenon* was the room in which a girl lived before she left her family as a bride. (One of the epithets, or descriptive names, that the Athenians had for their city's patron goddess was Athena Parthenos, "the girl.") When Athens decided to build a great new temple for the goddess on the city's Acropolis, they called it the Parthenon.

 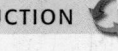
Primary and Secondary Sources To help students with the Reading Practice on page 184, offer them an everyday example illustrating the distinction between primary and secondary sources. **Say:** Suppose you were writing a report on the early history of your town. Primary sources might include town records, letters and diaries by first settlers. Secondary sources might include a recent history of the town.

Research Have students select one of the topics below (or a topic of their choosing about an aspect of ancient Greece) and then research and assemble three primary sources and three secondary sources for an essay on the topic.

- the Parthenon
- the Battle of Thermopylae
- the ancient Olympic Games
- the oracle of Delphi

Learning Objectives
Analyzing historical influences. (SE)
Determining topic sentence. (TE)
Distinguishing primary and secondary sources. (TE)

185

Teach

Reading Check

Answer: *To the Greeks, arête meant excellence in whatever ways a human might excel. This might include physical power, intellectual ability, and moral strength (such as bravery and endurance).*

Vocabulary   1

Word Usage Point out that the word *mercenary* has its origin in a Latin word meaning "wages" or "price." **Ask:** What has this word come to mean in common usage? *(motivated solely by money)*

[APPROACHING] Make sure students understand the distinction between a mercenary, a professional soldier who serves primarily for wages, and the citizen-soldier who serves primarily as a patriotic duty.

Reading Strategy   2

Analyze Tone Ask: What attitude toward the soldier's life does Archilochus express? *(realistic, matter-of-fact, uncomplaining, stoic)*

View the Art ★

The subjects depicted on ancient Greek red-figure pottery include both episodes from Greek myth and legend and scenes of everyday life. **Ask:** How does the painter convey a feeling of movement in this image? *(by depicting one of the figure's feet slightly elevated)*

Big Idea 1
The Heroic Ideal

Different societies develop different concepts of the hero. Some cultures value a simple heroic ideal, such as that of the warrior or the saint; other cultures celebrate a complex and multifaceted ideal of heroism, such as that of the "Renaissance man," an individual known for excellence in several different fields. The Greek heroic ideal was based on the aristocratic warrior but valued all-round excellence, the ability to do well at whatever was required, from sailing a ship to delivering a speech.

Homeric Epics

At the foundation of Greek literature stand the epic poems of Homer (see page 192), set in a legendary "Heroic Age" and retelling stories of war and adventure. To the ancient Greeks, Homer was not only the greatest poet and the authority for their early history, but also their moral teacher. The *Iliad* and the *Odyssey* were used in schools to teach Greek students the values of loyalty, courage, and honor. These ideals influenced the following lines from Archilochus, a Greek poet who was also a mercenary soldier.

Ulysses as Archer, c.450–440 BC. Penelope Vasepainter. Red figured Attic skyphos. Antikensammlung, Staatliche Museen zu Berlin, Germany. ★

> "Throw forward your chest
> To the enemy;
> Keep close in the attack;
> Move back not an inch.
> But never crow in victory,
> Nor mope hangdog in loss."
>
> —Archilochus,
> from *"Soul, Soul"*

The Pursuit of Excellence

A Greek hero strove to realize his human potential to achieve personal excellence, which the Greeks called *arête*. *Arête* could mean different things in different contexts. In a racehorse, *arête* meant speed; in a cart-horse, strength; in a hero, complete development of qualities such as physical strength, intellectual ability, and moral force (such as bravery and endurance). As the classical historian H. D. F. Kitto observes, Homer's hero Odysseus "is a great fighter, a wily schemer, a ready speaker, a man of stout heart and broad wisdom who knows that he must endure without too much complaining what the gods send." Similarly, in the *Iliad*, Achilles develops his potential to the highest degree. This hero, noble of soul, is a skillful speaker, a great fighter, and a swift runner.

Heroes typically displayed *arête* in a struggle or contest on the athletic field or in battle. Through his willingness to fight, the hero protected his family and friends, preserved his honor, and earned his reputation.

Reading Check

Make Generalizations How would you summarize the ancient Greeks' meaning of *arête*?

Writing Practice

⚡ Use Connotation and Denotation

Remind students that the denotation of a word is its literal, or dictionary, meaning. The connotation of a word is the meaning or association that the word has beyond its literal meaning. The connotations of a word often create positive or negative feelings.

Point out that one of the literal meanings of *mercenary* is "a person who works primarily for wages." Indicate that this word has acquired strongly negative connotations, suggesting that someone described as *mercenary* is "money-grubbing." Have students determine whether the connotations of each of the following words are positive or negative.

1. gaunt *(negative)*
2. ambitious *(positive)*
3. obedient *(positive)*
4. audacity *(negative)*
5. devious *(negative)*

Big Idea 2
The Good Life

What can humans do to create better lives for themselves? Is happiness found in family life, in passion, in the natural world, or in the pursuit of wisdom or art? The ancient Greeks sought to discover what constitutes the good life.

Greek Lyric Poetry

3 The Homeric epics are objective and impersonal in that the poet seldom introduces personal feelings into the narrative. Later Greek poets such as Sappho (sa′fō) (see pages 241–247), however, created a different kind of poetry which dealt with the concerns of individuals and everyday life. Sappho's lyric poetry celebrates the beauty of the world, the pleasures (and pains) of love, the joys of family life, and the power of art to transcend death.

Greek Philosophy

4 The Greek emphasis on the human experience gave rise to systematic questioning and observation of the world at large. As a result, the Greeks made great advances in science, medicine, and philosophy. Philosophy is the methodical use of reason to discover the truth. The term derives from a Greek word meaning "love of wisdom."

The Sophists were an influential group of ancient Greek philosophers who taught that there was no absolute right or wrong. Many Greeks viewed the Sophists as dangerous, especially to young people, because of their moral relativism.

> "*The unexamined life is not worth living.*"
>
> —Plato, the *Apology*

Seated Girl with Dove, 2nd half 4th century BC. Late Classical Greek. Terracotta, height:. 21.4 cm. Antikensammlung, Staatliche Museen zu Berlin, Germany.

Among the critics of the Sophists was the philosopher Socrates (sok′rə tēz). Because he left no writings, we know about him primarily through the works of his pupil, Plato (plā′tō). Socrates' teaching approach, known as the Socratic method, used a question-and-answer format to lead pupils to discover the truth. Socrates believed individuals could discover the truth within themselves through rational inquiry.

Besides Socrates and Plato, other notable Greek thinkers include

- Hippocrates (hi pok′rə tēz), who trained doctors to look into the causes of disease.

- Aristotle (ar′is tot′əl), who systematized the study of science.

- Herodotus (hə rod′ə təs), who established the idea that history could be studied as a collection of true facts, rather than a series of legends.

Reading Check

Compare and Contrast How did Socrates differ from the Sophists?

English Learners

DIFFERENTIATED INSTRUCTION

Advanced To help English learners understand denotation and connotation, show them sets of ordinary words and phrases, where one term has no strong connotations, one term has positive connotations, and one term has negative connotations. For example:

practical (neutral)
thrifty (positive)
penny-pinching (negative)

fast (neutral)
swift (positive)
hasty (negative)

Teach
Reading Check

Answer: *The Sophists denied the reality of absolute truth. Socrates pursued absolute truth as his ultimate quest.*

Reading Strategy | 3

Compare and Contrast
Ask: What is the basic difference between Greek epic and lyric poetry? *(Greek epic poetry is objective and impersonal; Greek lyric poetry is subjective and personal.)*

ADVANCED **Ask:** What is the relationship between the speaker and the poet in Greek lyric poetry? *(The speaker in a Greek lyric poem can often be identified with the poet.)*

Vocabulary | 4

Word Origins Point out that the suffix *–phile,* "one who loves or prefers," comes from the Greek word *philos,* meaning "loving." This suffix is often used to describe people with a love of particular national cultures; for example, *Anglophile, Francophile.* The opposite tendency is also described using a suffix with a Greek root, *-phobe,* from *phobos,* "fear": *Anglophobe, Francophobe.* **Ask:** How would you describe someone who likes technology? *(technophile)* Or dislikes it? *(technophobe)*

Learning Objectives
Making generalizations. (SE)
Comparing and contrasting. (SE)
Identifying tone. (TE)

Teach

Reading Check

Answer: *Drama inspired audiences to examine their own lives, to define their beliefs, and to cleanse their emotions of pity and terror.*

Reading Strategy	1

Connect to Personal Experience **Ask:** Do we cause most of our miseries through our misdeeds and foolishness, or are they simply the result of bad luck? Elicit students' opinions on this question before they read page 188.

Reading Strategy	2

Make Generalizations

Ask: What were the religious and social purposes of ancient Greek drama? *(Greek drama explored the relationship between humans and the gods and encouraged people to question their behavior.)*

Cultural History ☆

The *Oresteia* In the first play of this trilogy, King Agamemnon is murdered by his wife after he has sacrificed their daughter. In the second play, Agamemnon's son Orestes avenges his father by killing his mother. Orestes stands trial for his deed in the third play. When the jury splits six to six, the goddess Athena intervenes and casts the deciding vote in favor of mercy. The moral of the trilogy is that the law of the community, not personal revenge, should decide punishment.

Big Idea 3
The Tragic Vision

1 **W**hat contributes most to human unhappiness? Do evil deeds bring about suffering, or is misery primarily the result of an error in judgment? The ancient Greek dramatists pondered these questions.

Athenian Drama

2 One of the great Greek achievements was drama, created by the Athenians. In Athens, tragedies were performed at religious festivals and often explored the relationship between humans and the gods. In the process, they raised important questions about life. The first Greek tragedies were presented in a trilogy, or a set of three plays, that explored a common theme. For example, Aeschylus (es′kə ləs) composed the *Oresteia*, a trilogy that relates the fate of Agamemnon and

his family after his return from the Trojan War. In these plays, evil breeds more evil and greater suffering. Yet in the end, reason triumphs over the forces of blood-guilt and revenge.

> *"Count no man happy till he dies, free of pain at last."*
>
> —Sophocles, *Oedipus the King*

Sophocles (sof′ə klēz) (see pages 250–318), another Athenian playwright, composed *Oedipus the King*. In this timeless tragedy, a plague sent by the gods ravages the people of Thebes. Oedipus, the king of Thebes, diligently tries to relieve his people of the plague but in the process discovers a horrifying truth about himself.

The Nature of Tragedy

Central to Greek tragedy is the fall of a great man (or woman, though in ancient Greece her part would have been acted by a man)—the tragic hero, whose fate is partly brought about by a flaw within his or her own character. The tragic hero's aim was to inspire audiences to examine their own lives, to define their beliefs, and to cleanse their emotions of pity and terror through compassion for the character. Greek tragedies were so insightful and complex that they continue to be relevant today. They have profoundly influenced the Western literary tradition.

Oedipus visiting the Sphinx, 5th century BC. Attic red figure kylix (drinking cup). Museo Gregoriano Etrusco, Vatican Museums, Vatican State.

Reading Check

Analyze Cause-and-Effect Relationships How did the experience of drama help the ancient Greeks deal with their problems?

Reading Practice

Activate Prior Knowledge Point out that the Greeks invented the two basic forms of Western drama—comedy and tragedy. Explain that Aristophanes, the greatest Greek writer of comedy, created highly imaginative social satires in which he poked fun at important people and commented humorously on social issues.

Before they read page 188, have students write definitions of both comedy and tragedy based on their previous understand-

ing of the terms. When they have read page 188, have them write a new definition of the term *tragedy* and compare it with what they wrote earlier.

WRAP-UP

Legacy of the Period

3 The ancient Greeks laid the intellectual and cultural foundations of Western civilization. They debated basic questions about the nature of the universe, the purpose of life, and the meaning of truth. The Greeks not only strove to answer these questions but also created a logical method for exploring them—philosophy.

The Greeks were the first to use reason to explain natural phenomena. In other words, they were the first scientists. The Greek philosopher Aristotle wrote on a number of scientific subjects, including astronomy, geology, biology, and physics. Until the seventeenth century, science in the Western world remained largely based on Aristotle's ideas.

In general, the Greeks established one of the bedrock values of Western civilization—the importance of the individual. Athenians founded democracy, proclaiming the right of ordinary individuals to govern themselves.

Kelly Holmes celebrates as she crosses the finish line to win the Olympics women's 1500 metres, 2004. Mike Blake. Athens.

Cultural and Literary Links

 Greek mythology has provided a rich treasury of narratives and characters for Western art and literature. Even some scientific concepts, such as the Oedipus complex and the Gaia hypothesis, are named after Greek myths.

 Homer remains one of the most influential authors in world literature. His epic poems have inspired countless works, from the *Aeneid* by the Roman poet Virgil to *Omeros* by the Caribbean Nobel Prize laureate Derek Walcott.

 In A.D. 393, the Romans banned the ancient Olympic Games. In the summer of 1896, however, the first modern Olympics took place in Athens.

 **Literature** Online

Unit Resources For additional skills practice, go to glencoe.com and enter QuickPass code GLW6053u2.

Activities

Use what you have learned about the period to do one of these activities.

1. **Follow Up** Go back to Looking Ahead on page 179 and answer the questions.

2. **Contrast Literary Periods** Working with other students, hold a panel discussion about how one of this period's Big Ideas still influences American culture today. You can use examples from literature, fine art, music, movies, or other kinds of artistic expression.

3. **Build Visual Literacy** Create a display of images of modern buildings that reflect the influence of Greek architecture.

4. **Take Notes** You might try using this graphic organizer to keep track of the three Big Ideas in this part.

FOLDABLES Study Organizer **THREE-POCKET BOOK**

Big Idea 1 / Big Idea 2 / Big Idea 3

Advanced Learners/Pre-AP

DIFFERENTIATED INSTRUCTION

The Greek Legacy Have students write a brief essay supporting the following thesis: "The ancient Greeks laid the intellectual and cultural foundations of Western civilization." In defending this thesis, suggest that they use the Big Ideas presented in the introduction—the Heroic Ideal, the Good Life, and the Tragic Vision—to help organize their essay.

UNIT TWO

PART 1

Teach

Vocabulary   3

Word Origins Point out that many English words have their origins in Greek tradition. Offer these examples:

- *draconian*, which means "severe" or "cruel," refers to the harsh measures enacted by the Athenian lawgiver Draco;

- *laconic*, which means "using few words" or "terse," refers to Laconia, the region around Sparta, and to the fact that Spartans were encouraged to use short, direct statements rather than to study oratory as in other Greek city-states.

Assess

Activities

1. **Follow Up** Students should support their answers with details from this introduction.

2. **Contrast Literary Periods** You might divide the class into three groups and have each group explore the relevance of one of the Big Ideas in the United States today.

3. **Build Visual Literary** Students may choose to annotate their images or create captions.

4. **Take Notes** After students finish each selection, have them list details in the graphic organizer that relate the selection to one of the Big Ideas.

Learning Objectives
Analyzing cause-and-effect relationships. (SE)
Connecting to personal experience. (TE)
Making generalizations. (TE)
Activating prior knowledge. (TE)

Focus

Bellringer Options

Daily Language Transparency 23

Or ask: What accomplishments by famous people today might be good topics for a long, epic poem? *(Students may suggest scientific discoveries, sports victories, political triumphs, or artistic achievements.)*

Teach

Reading Strategy ▏1

Connect to Personal Experience Ask: Have you heard any slam poetry? Does slam poetry have anything in common with epic poetry? *(Students who have heard slam poetry will recognize that its use of personal narrative and enthusiastic expression may be seen as similar, but that slam poetry would likely resist anything as restrictive as "formula.")*

 For an audio recording of this selection, use Listening Library Audio CD-ROM.

 For an activity related to this selection, see Unit 2 Teaching Resources Book, pp. 20–21.

Learning Objectives

For pages 190–191

In studying this text, you will focus on the following objectives:

Literary Study: Analyzing literary genres.

Reading:
Evaluating historical influences.
Connecting to the literature.

The Homeric Epics

> *"Well let me die—*
> *but not without some struggle, not without glory, no,*
> *in some great clash of arms that even men to come*
> *will hear of down the years!"*
>
> —Homer, from the *Iliad*

DOOMED BY THE GODS, THE TROJAN HERO Hector speaks these words. He imagines his deeds will live on, perhaps in the immortal lines of a poet. The oral poets of ancient Greece composed narratives of heroic deeds, chanting them to musical accompaniment. The greatest of these oral poets was Homer. The Greeks attributed to him two of the earliest surviving epic poems—the *Iliad* and its sequel the *Odyssey*—which celebrated the heroes of the Trojan War.

The Art of the Bard

How did an oral poet such as Homer compose his poems? In some ways, he was like a musician who starts with a well-known tune and plays variations on it every time he performs. Just as a musician plays to a steady rhythm, so Homer had a steady rhythm in his words. The long and short syllables alternated in a regular pattern.

Composing poetry in front of an audience without "drawing a blank" may seem like an arduous task, but the fact that Homer performed to a rhythm simplified the job. It meant certain phrases worked better than others because they fit rhythmically into a line of poetry. Homer used those phrases again and again. For example, he repeatedly referred to the goddess Athena as "gray-eyed Athena" and mentioned Dawn's "fingertips of rose." He also recycled longer passages that described routine actions, such as a character's way of entering a room, donning armor, or saying good-bye.

Marble seated harp player, Ca. 2800-2700 BC. Marble, H. with harp 11 1/2 in. The Metropolitan Museum of Art, NY.

This use of repetition helped Homer and pleased his audience. The poet did not have to memorize or make up every word. Though the story may have been somewhat different in each retelling, the repeated phrases remained like handles for the poet to grip. Homer's audience looked forward to these repetitions, as listeners today look forward to the ▏1▕ chorus of a song.

Speaking Practice

Present an Oral Report Point out that in addition to the epic, there are many other types of oral literature. These include riddles, folk tales, myths, legends, ballads, nursery rhymes, hymns, and spirituals. Have students select an oral form of literature (other than epic) and use encyclopedias and Internet resources to do research for a short report. Students' reports should include the characteristics of the form, the specific ways in which this oral tradition conveys content from generation to generation, and geographic regions in which this particular oral form has flourished.

Attic red-figure hydria, c. 440-420 BC. Greek. Ceramic. Ashmolean Museum, University of Oxford, UK.

2 Epic Poetry

Homer's *Iliad* and *Odyssey* have been read for centuries as **epic poems**. Since Homer's time, epic poetry has been considered a subgenre, or type, of literature. An epic poem has the following characteristics:

- It is a long narrative poem built around heroic adventures.

- The setting is vast. It may include the sea, a palace, and the abode of the gods.

- The main character is a legendary hero who usually embodies the goals and virtues of an entire culture.

- The action includes extraordinary or superhuman deeds. Typically, the epic hero struggles with natural and supernatural obstacles and antagonists, which test his bravery, wits, and physical prowess.

- Gods or supernatural beings take part in the action, protecting, advising, and sometimes punishing epic heroes.

3 - The purpose is not only to entertain, but to teach values and ideals, inspiring the audience with models of heroic behavior.

Epic Narration

An epic poem is narrated in predictable ways:

- In an invocation, the poet-narrator states the subject and prays for inspiration to a muse, a goddess of poetry.

- The narrator begins the tale in the "middle of things," describing what is happening after certain important events have already occurred.

- The narrative includes speeches by the principal characters—including gods and antagonists of the epic hero—which reveal their personalities.

- The language is elevated, and the style is formal rather than conversational.

- The use of figurative language makes the narrative vivid and exciting, maintaining a dignified tone. Figurative language includes epic similes, which are longer and more elaborate than ordinary similes.

The *Iliad*, the epic you are about to read, is a monumental artistic achievement. It presents the climactic events of a long, brutal war. Because of Homer's superb depiction of both the glory and the horror of battle, the *Iliad* still moves readers today nearly 3,000 years after its creation.

LOG ON **Literature** Online

Literature and Reading For more about the Homeric epics, go to glencoe.com and enter QuickPass code GLW6053u2.

Respond and Think Critically

1. Why do you think Homer's epics are still enjoyed today?

2. How did the composition method of ancient Greek oral poets resemble that of a musician?

3. What purposes did Homer's epics serve for the ancient Greeks?

English Learners

DIFFERENTIATED INSTRUCTION

Intermediate Ask English learners to name some epic poets in other cultures and to talk about the subjects and sources of their poems. Make sure students understand that the term "epic poetry" is applied to an entire genre of literature. Tell students that epic poems were originally long oral stories—hence the use of formulas and repetition. Have students use the checklists they compiled to compare the characteristics of epics in other cultures to those in ancient Greece.

Ask: Are they similar, or are there significant differences? Have students discuss the possible reasons for such similarities or differences.

Teach

Reading Strategy   2

 Synthesize Organize the class into small groups. Have students review these pages and prepare a checklist of the elements of epic poetry and epic narration that they can use as they read. Have them leave space after each element in the list. As they read the *Iliad*, they can check off each element as they encounter it in the text. Have students save the checklists for review.

Big Idea   3

The Heroic Ideal Ask: Why do you think the most popular ancient Greek literature was largely about war? *(Students may feel that the continual conflict between city-states led to a national literature that was mostly about war. They may also feel that war gave people more opportunities to behave heroically.)*

Assess

1. Students may say these poems tell exciting stories, celebrate mighty heroes, provide glimpses of life in ancient times, and offer timeless lessons about living.

2. Like a musician, the ancient Greek oral poets used a familiar theme as the basis for improvisation.

3. For the Greeks, Homer's epics provided both entertainment and moral instruction.

Learning Objectives
Understanding the characteristics of the epic poem. (SE)
Connecting to the historical context of the literature. (SE)
Presenting an oral report. (TE)

191

from the *Iliad*

Ancient Greece

Bellringer Options

Selection Focus
Transparency 13
Daily Language Practice
Transparency 24

Or ask: What kinds of honors and rewards do you think are appropriate for soldiers who have behaved courageously in battle? Allow students to discuss the ways in which soldiers should be rewarded for courage in battle.

Literary History ☆

More About Homer The literacy of Homer was taken for granted until the 1600s. Also, some scholars have questioned whether he actually wrote the works attributed to him. Some scholars point out that none of the characters in the *Iliad* or the *Odyssey* are literate and also mention the difficult writing system that was in use at the time of the epics' composition. The doubt of his literacy led to the separatist belief that Homer was not the sole author of the poems. The issue is still debated today.

Meet **Homer**

(c. ninth century B.C.)

Homer is given credit for the two great epics on which all Greek literature is founded: the *Iliad* (il′ē əd) and the *Odyssey* (od′ə sē). Homer probably lived in Ionia, in what is now western Turkey, and recited or sang his verses to the accompaniment of a lyre. Some scholars have argued that the *Iliad* and the *Odyssey* developed over an extended period, with many poets contributing toward the final version. Today most experts believe Homer composed at least one, if not both, of these epics, which reflect a deep understanding of traditional storytelling techniques.

Homer's *Iliad* Homer used these techniques to create epic poems of unprecedented length and beauty. The *Iliad*, for example, runs nearly 16,000 lines. The name of this epic comes from the word *Ilion*, another name for the city of Troy, located in Asia Minor. Around the early twelfth century B.C., the Greeks fought against Troy in a great war. Homer composed the *Iliad*, which tells the story of the Trojan War, around 350 years later.

Following the epic tradition of *in medias res* (Latin for "in the middle of things"), Homer plunges the reader into the tenth year of the Trojan War. He interweaves Greek and Trojan history as background for the battles that mostly take place over just a few days. Homer probably created the *Iliad* orally, dictating it later to a scribe. For centuries prior, Greek poets improvised songs without benefit of writing. Homer drew upon this oral tradition for narrative details and literary techniques. The *Iliad* contains many formulaic, or fixed, expressions that made verses easier to remember. Most noticeable are the epithets, such as "the swift runner Achilles."

> "Read Homer once, and you can read no more; For all books else appear so mean, so poor. . ."
>
> —John Sheffield,
> Duke of Buckingham and Normandy

Homer's Legacy By 400 B.C. Homer's *Iliad* and *Odyssey* had become classics in Greece. Homer's influence gradually spread throughout the world. Rome's greatest poet, Virgil, drew on Homer's epics in creating the *Aeneid* (see pages 376–398). Later, Homer's epics profoundly affected Renaissance thought and inspired countless artistic works, including Shakespeare's play *Troilus* and *Cressida*. James Joyce's novel *Ulysses*, published in 1922, is based on the *Odyssey*, as is the recent film *O Brother, Where Art Thou?* (2000). In fact, much of the literary heritage of the Western world derives from Homer's epics.

LOG ON **Literature** Online

Author Search For more about Homer, go to glencoe.com and enter QuickPass code GLW6053u2.

Selection Skills

Literary Elements
- Epic Hero (SE pp. 193–209)
- Author's Purpose (TE p. 206)

Reading Skills
- Evaluate Credibility (SE pp. 193, 196–209)
- Make and Verify Predictions (TE p. 202)

Assessment Practice
- Multiple-Choice Questions (TE p. 208)

The Rage of Achilles

Speaking/Listening/Viewing Skills
- Present an Oral Interpretation (TE p. 196)
- Present an Oral Report (TE p. 198)

Writing Skills/Grammar
- Write a Character Sketch (SE p. 209)
- Write a Dialogue (TE p. 200)

Vocabulary Skills
- Understand Synonyms (SE p. 209)

Book I: The Rage of Achilles from the *Iliad*

Connect to the Epic
What causes war? Discuss this question with a partner.

Build Background
According to Homer, the Trojan War began when Paris, a Trojan prince, abducted Helen, the beautiful queen of Sparta, in Greece. For nine years the Greeks attacked Troy, with the Trojans at first resisting them. Suddenly, in the tenth year of the war, an unforeseen event triggered a bitter quarrel between Agamemnon, the leader of the Greek forces, and Achilles, the greatest of the Greek warriors. It is at this point the *Iliad* begins.

Set Purposes for Reading

Big Idea The Heroic Ideal

The ancient Greeks believed the heroic ideal consisted of qualities esteemed by warriors: physical prowess, courage, intelligence, self-control, endurance, and honor. As you read, ask yourself, What actions in the epic reflect the heroic ideal?

Literary Element Epic Hero

An **epic hero** is a larger-than-life figure of high social status who embodies the ideals of his or her people. As you read, ask yourself, Who is the epic hero of the *Iliad*, and why?

Reading Strategy Evaluate Credibility

When you **evaluate credibility**, you make a judgment about whether a character is knowledgeable and truthful. The characters in Book I offer opinions and advice that have a direct bearing on the events that unfold. As you read, ask yourself, Are the characters' statements convincing?

....

Tip: Use a Checklist Use a checklist like the one below to evaluate the characters' credibility.

- ☑ Does the character have something to hide or anything to gain?
- ☑ Can the statement be corroborated by events or by other characters?
- ☑ Does the statement make sense?
- ☑ Are the character's opinions biased?

Learning Objectives

For pages 192–209

In studying this text, you will focus on the following objectives:

Literary Study: Analyzing epic hero.

Reading: Evaluating credibility.

Writing: Writing a character sketch.

Vocabulary

droves (drōvz) *n.* large numbers of animals or people, moving along together; crowd; p. 195 *Horses stampeded across the plain in droves.*

appease (ə pēz′) *v.* to satisfy insistent demands; p. 197 *The offer to remove the graffiti from the bleacher wall appeased the principal.*

commandeer (kom′ən dēr′) *v.* to take arbitrary or forceful possession of; p. 198 *The pirate crew commandeered the ship, seizing its precious cargo.*

enlist (en list′) *v.* to join or give help; convince (someone) to join or to give help; p. 203 *To finish loading the van before dark, we will have to enlist our neighbor's help.*

ignominious (ig′nə min′ē əs) *adj.* marked or characterized by disgrace or shame; p. 205 *The players were stunned by their ignominious loss to a weak opponent.*

HOMER **193**

Before You Read

Focus

Summary
Agamemnon has taken the daughter of Chryses as a war prize. Chryses, a priest of Apollo, offers Agamemnon a great treasure for the return of his daughter, but Agamemnon refuses. Chryses enlists the aid of the enraged Apollo to bring a plague upon the Greeks. The plague is to be removed only when Chryses' daughter is returned, but Agamemnon refuses to comply with the ultimatum. Achilles and the seer convince Agamemnon to return their hostage; Agamemnon demands that Achilles give him his war prize, Briseis. Achilles then appeals to his mother, the sea-goddess Thetis, to ask Zeus to aid the Trojans against the Greeks.

> **For summaries in languages other than English, see Unit 2 Teaching Resources Book, pp. 22–27.**

Vocabulary

Charades Have students work in groups of five. Each student should write one of the vocabulary words on a slip of paper and put the paper in a box. Then students should take turns drawing a word out of the box and acting it out while the rest of the group tries to guess the word.

English Learners
DIFFERENTIATED INSTRUCTION

Intermediate Have English learners look up the following words in a dictionary before reading the epic:

rage, clashed, fury, fatal, ransom, plunder, brutal, piercing, ranks, muster

Ask: What do these words have in common? *(They are all related to various aspects of war.)* Suggest that students add to their list of war-related words as they read.

Advanced Learners/Pre-AP
DIFFERENTIATED INSTRUCTION

Research Inform advanced learners that the word *epithet* originated from the Greek word *epitithenai*, which means "to put on." Have them look for additional examples of epithets in the *Iliad*, and suggest that they conduct research to discover other epithets from history (such as "Alexander the Great" and "Ivan the Terrible") and literature (such as "the Swan of Avon" and "the Wasp of Twickenham").

Reading Strategy   **1**

Evaluate Credibility
Answer: *Answers may vary. Students may say that, as a loving father, Chryses may be willing to sacrifice the welfare of Troy to ensure the safe return of his daughter. However, Chryses may be willing to say anything if it helps get his daughter back.*

Literary History ☆

The Origins of the *Iliad* There are records of official recitations of the Iliad in the sixth century B.C. Alexandrian scholars in the fourth and fifth centuries B.C. wrote commentaries on the poem, which were recorded on rolls of papyrus. The rolls may have numbered 24, which would explain the division of the books of the *Iliad*. The handwritten copies were passed down, as books evolved from papyrus rolls to the bound form we now use. The first printed edition of the *Iliad* appeared in 1488 in Florence. Since then, many editions and translations have been published.

For an audio recording of this selection, use Listening Library Audio CD-ROM.

FROM THE ILIAD

from Book I:

THE RAGE OF ACHILLES

☆

Homer

Translated by Robert Fagles

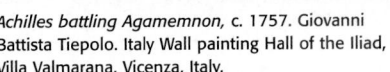
Achilles battling Agamemnon, c. 1757. Giovanni Battista Tiepolo. Italy Wall painting Hall of the Iliad, Villa Valmarana, Vicenza, Italy.

> Rage—Goddess, sing the rage of Peleus' son Achilles,
> murderous, doomed, that cost the Achaeans countless losses,
> hurling down to the House of Death so many sturdy souls,
> great fighters' souls, but made their bodies carrion,
> 5   feasts for the dogs and birds,
> and the will of Zeus was moving toward its end.
> Begin, Muse, when the two first broke and clashed,
> Agamemnon lord of men and brilliant Achilles.
>
>   What god drove them to fight with such a fury?
> 10   Apollo the son of Zeus and Leto. Incensed at the king
> he swept a fatal plague through the army—men were dying
> and all because Agamemnon spurned Apollo's priest.
> Yes, Chryses approached the Achaeans' fast ships
> to win his daughter back, bringing a priceless ransom
> 15   and bearing high in hand, wound on a golden staff,
> the wreaths of the god, the distant deadly Archer.°
> He begged the whole Achaean army but most of all
> the two supreme commanders, Atreus' two sons,
> "Agamemnon, Menelaus—all Argives° geared for war!
> 20   May the gods who hold the halls of Olympus° give you
> Priam's city to plunder, then safe passage home.
> Just set my daughter free, my dear one . . . here,
> accept these gifts, this ransom. Honor the god
> who strikes from worlds away—the son of Zeus, Apollo!"

10–16 Incensed at the king . . . deadly Archer (Apollo): In a raid on Thebes, a Trojan ally, the Greeks captured Chryseis, daughter of Chryses, Apollo's high priest. Agamemnon claimed her as his share of the plunder.

19 Argives: natives of the city-state of Argos; Greeks.

20 Olympus: highest mountain in Greece; in mythology, the home of the deities.

---

1   Evaluate Credibility *Is Chryses sincere in this speech? Do you think Agamemnon believes him? Explain.*

194   UNIT 2   ANCIENT GREECE

Reading Practice

Preview Ask students what they know about Greek mythology. On the board, make a list of deities and heroes mentioned. Discuss the remaining characters. Make sure students can answer the following questions:

- Which are men and which are women?
- Which are gods and which are mortals?
- What are the family relationships?

As an aid in remembering the characters, have students copy and organize their own lists. Have them create a key and mark their lists with, for example, different colored highlighters to represent gender, immortality, and familial relationships.

25   And all ranks of Achaeans cried out their assent:
"Respect the priest, accept the shining ransom!"
But it brought no joy to the heart of Agamemnon.
The king dismissed the priest with a brutal order
ringing in his ears: "Never again, old man,
30   let me catch sight of you by the hollow ships!°
Not loitering now, not slinking back tomorrow.
The staff and the wreaths of god will never save you then.
The girl—I won't give up the girl. Long before that,
old age will overtake her in *my* house, in Argos,
35   far from her fatherland, slaving back and forth
at the loom, forced to share my bed!
                        Now go,
don't tempt my wrath—and you may depart alive."

    The old man was terrified. He obeyed the order,
turning, trailing away in silence down the shore
40   where the battle lines of breakers crash and drag.
And moving off to a safe distance, over and over
the old priest prayed to the son of sleek-haired Leto,
lord Apollo, "Hear me, Apollo! God of the silver bow
who strides the walls of Chryse and Cilla sacrosanct—
45   lord in power of Tenedos—Smintheus,° god of the plague!
If I ever roofed a shrine to please your heart,
ever burned the long rich bones of bulls and goats
on your holy altar, now, now bring my prayer to pass.
Pay the Danaans back—your arrows for my tears!"

50   His prayer went up and Phoebus° Apollo heard him.
Down he strode from Olympus' peaks, storming at heart
with his bow and hooded quiver slung across his shoulders.
The arrows clanged at his back as the god quaked with rage,
the god himself on the march and down he came like night.
55   Over against the ships he dropped to a knee, let fly a shaft
and a terrifying clash rang out from the great silver bow.
First he went for the mules and circling dogs but then,
launching a piercing shaft at the men themselves,
he cut them down in **droves**—
60   and the corpse-fires burned on, night and day, no end in sight.

30 ships: The Greek camp was on the beaches before the city of Troy. The 1,000-ship navy that carried them there lay at anchor offshore.

44–45 Chryse, Cilla, Tenedos: places near Troy that **Smintheus** (another name for Apollo) considers sacrosanct, or sacred.

50 Phoebus: literally means "bright"; a reference to Apollo's role as the sun god.

---

2 | **The Heroic Ideal** *What does this response suggest about Agamemnon?*

Vocabulary

droves (drōvz) *n.* large numbers of animals or people, moving along together; crowd

HOMER **195**

Advanced Learners/Pre-AP
DIFFERENTIATED INSTRUCTION

Research Health Students may be interested in researching the effects of anger on the human body and mind. Suggest that they conduct research online or at a library. They may focus on the mental effects, such as the loss of rationality, or on the physical effects, such as the increase of heart rate and blood pressure. Have students present their findings to the class.

English Learners
DIFFERENTIATED INSTRUCTION

Intermediate Point out the word *will* in line 6, and remind students that many words have multiple meanings. They are probably familiar with the verb form of this word, but here it is used as a noun. Point out that the articles *a, an,* and *the* always signal that a noun is coming up. Ask students to name some synonyms of the noun *will* (*desire, wish, intention, determination*).

Teach

Big Idea | **2**

The Heroic Ideal **Answer:**
Students may say Agamemnon's response is cruel, haughty, and spiteful.

(**APPROACHING**) Have learners approaching level review lines 9–37 and restate the events briefly.

(Possible answer: The Greeks are suffering a plague because they hold Chryses' daughter. Chryses comes to the Greeks and unsuccessfully begs for her return.)

View the Art ★

This painting shows the goddess Athena grabbing Achilles by his hair to keep him from attacking Agamemnon. It is one of many wall paintings that Giovanni Battista Tiepolo created to decorate palaces and churches. Tiepolo included columns and a monumental structure in the background, though the scene actually takes place in the Greek camp. **Ask:** How does the depiction of Athena compare with that of the mortal figures in the painting? *(Athena is a muscular figure who appears just as substantial as Achilles and the other mortals.)*

Learning Objectives
Evaluating credibility. (SE)
Analyzing art. (SE)
Previewing Greek mythology. (TE)

Teach

The Heroic Ideal **Answer:**
Achilles cares about his comrades and seeks a means to better their situation.

Nine days the arrows of god swept through the army.°
On the tenth Achilles called all ranks to muster—
the impulse seized him, sent by white-armed Hera
grieving to see Achaean fighters drop and die.
65   Once they'd gathered, crowding the meeting grounds,
the swift runner Achilles rose and spoke among them:
"Son of Atreus, now we are beaten back, I fear,
the long campaign is lost. So home we sail . . .
if we can escape our death—if war and plague
70   are joining forces now to crush the Argives.
But wait: let us question a holy man,
a prophet, even a man skilled with dreams—
dreams as well can come our way from Zeus—
come, someone to tell us why Apollo rages so,
75   whether he blames us for a vow we failed, or sacrifice.
If only the god would share the smoky savor of lambs
and full-grown goats, Apollo might be willing, still,
somehow, to save us from this plague."
                                        So he proposed
and down he sat again as Calchas rose among them,
80   Thestor's son, the clearest by far of all the seers°
who scan the flight of birds.° He knew all things that are,
all things that are past and all that are to come,
the seer who had led the Argive ships to Troy
with the second sight° that god Apollo gave him.
85   For the armies' good the seer began to speak:
"Achilles, dear to Zeus . . .
you order me to explain Apollo's anger,
the distant deadly Archer? I will tell it all.
But strike a pact with me, swear you will defend me
90   with all your heart, with words and strength of hand.
For there is a man I will enrage—I see it now—
a powerful man who lords it over all the Argives,
one the Achaeans must obey . . . A mighty king,
raging against an inferior, is too strong.
95   Even if he can swallow down his wrath today,
still he will nurse the burning in his chest
until, sooner or later, he sends it bursting forth.
Consider it closely, Achilles. Will you save me?"

And the matchless runner reassured him: "Courage!
100   Out with it now, Calchas. Reveal the will of god,
whatever you may know. And I swear by Apollo

51–61 Down he strode . . . swept through the army: Apollo causes a plague to break out in the Greek camp. Homer uses imagery (Apollo as "deadly archer") to convey the effect of the disease.

80 seers: individuals with extraordinary moral and spiritual insight. The Greeks believed that seers had mystical powers given to them by the gods.

81 scan the flight of birds: The examination of animal behavior and their internal organs helped seers make predictions or interpret the will of the deities.

84 second sight: the ability to see remote or future objects or events.

1 **The Heroic Ideal** *What do Achilles' first words in the poem reveal about him?*

Speaking Practice

Present an Oral Interpretation
Explain that some people may find this selection difficult because of the many unusual phrases and descriptions. The reason for this is that poetry often uses grammatical constructions that are unfamiliar to the average speaker. Have pairs of students review pages 196 and 197, looking for difficult phrases and passages to restate in their own words. Students should take turns speaking and listening to each other.

dear to Zeus, the power you pray to, Calchas,
when you reveal god's will to the Argives—
        no one,
not while I am alive and see the light on earth,
        no one
105 will lay his heavy hands on you by the
        hollow ships.
None among all the armies. Not even if you
        mean
Agamemnon here who now claims to be, by far,
the best of the Achaeans."
                        The seer took heart
and this time he spoke out, bravely: "Beware—
110 he casts no blame for a vow we failed, a sacrifice.
The god's enraged because Agamemnon spurned
        his priest,
he refused to free his daughter, he refused the
        ransom.
That's why the Archer sends us pains and he will
        send us more
and never drive this shameful destruction from the
        Argives,
115 not till we give back the girl with sparkling eyes
to her loving father—no price, no ransom paid—
and carry a sacred hundred bulls to Chryse town.°
Then we can calm the god, and only then **appease** him."

        So he declared and sat down. But among them rose
120 the fighting son of Atreus, lord of the far-flung kingdoms,
Agamemnon—furious, his dark heart filled to the brim,
blazing with anger now, his eyes like searing fire.
With a sudden, killing look he wheeled on Calchas first:
"Seer of misery! Never a word that works to my advantage!
125 Always misery warms your heart, your prophecies—
never a word of profit said or brought to pass.
Now, again, you divine° god's will for the armies,
bruit° it about, as fact, why the deadly Archer

Achilles. Attic red figure amphora. Museo Gregoriano Etrusco, Vatican Museums, Vatican State.

117 carry a sacred hundred bulls to Chryse town: sacrifice a hundred bulls on the altar to Apollo at Chryse.

127 divine: to discover hidden knowledge; here, to interpret the will of a god.
128 bruit (br o͞ o t): to make known loudly and publicly.

---

2 The Epic Hero *What values does Achilles reflect in these lines?*

3 Evaluate Credibility *Why might the Greeks view Calchas as a credible informant?*

Vocabulary

appease (ə pēz´) *v.* to satisfy insistent demands

HOMER **197**

Epic Hero **Answer:** *Achilles reflects bravery, loyalty, and self-confidence.*

For additional literary element practice, see Unit 2 Teaching Resources Book, p. 28.

Reading Strategy **3**

Evaluate Credibility
Answer: *Calchas has the reputation of being "the clearest" of the seers, having received "second sight" from the god Apollo.*

View the Art

The Greeks used a two-handled clay jar called an *amphora* to hold wine or olive oil. Some of these jars were decorated with red-figure paintings such as the one shown here. The figure was formed from the natural color of the clay set against a black glaze background. **Ask:** Which of Achilles' qualities do you think this artist wanted to express? *(The painting suggests Achilles' physical strength and commanding presence.)*

Approaching Level

DIFFERENTIATED INSTRUCTION

Monitor Comprehension
Students who are unfamiliar with Greek mythology often find it difficult to keep track of the characters and the different sides of the battle. To help students comprehend the story, encourage them to actively question the events in the text. Follow these steps:

- Have small groups work together to write a list of questions concerning the events up to this point in the story.
- Have groups trade questions and supply answers.

If groups have difficulty answering some of the questions, review them as a class and determine whether reading further will provide the answers.

Learning Objectives
Analyzing art. (SE)
Evaluate credibility. (SE)
Present an oral interpretation. (TE)

Teach

Big Idea | 1

The Heroic Ideal Answer:
Agamemnon demands a war prize to replace Chryseis; otherwise, as leader of the Greek army, he will be deprived of an honor enjoyed by many of his subordinates.

Reading Strategy | 2

Evaluate Credibility
Answer: *Achilles' advice is reasonable. He promises Agamemnon he will be compensated for the loss of Chryseis when Troy is taken. He reminds Agamemnon that taking another warrior's treasure would be a grave insult. Achilles has faithfully served his leader in the past, so there is no reason to believe his promise is insincere.*

130 multiplies our pains: because I, I refused
that glittering price for the young girl Chryseis.
Indeed, I prefer *her* by far, the girl herself,
I want her mine in my own house! I rank her higher
than Clytemnestra, my wedded wife—she's nothing less
135 in build or breeding, in mind or works of hand.
But I am willing to give her back, even so,
if that is best for all. What I really want
is to keep my people safe, not see them dying.
But fetch me another prize, and straight off too,
else I alone of the Argives go without my honor.
140 That would be a disgrace. You are all witness,
look—*my* prize is snatched away!"

But the swift runner
Achilles answered him at once, "Just how, Agamemnon,
great field marshal . . . most grasping man alive,
how can the generous Argives give you prizes now?
145 I know of no troves of treasure, piled, lying idle,
anywhere. Whatever we dragged from towns we plundered,
all's been portioned out. But collect it, call it back
from the rank and file? *That* would be the disgrace.
So return the girl to the god, at least for now.
150 We Achaeans will pay you back, three, four times over,
if Zeus will grant us the gift, somehow, someday,
to raze° Troy's massive ramparts to the ground."

But King Agamemnon countered, "Not so quickly,
brave as you are, godlike Achilles—trying to cheat *me*.
155 Oh no, you won't get past me, take me in that way!
What do you want? To cling to your own prize°
while I sit calmly by—empty-handed here?
Is that why you order me to give her back?
No—if our generous Argives *will* give me a prize,
160 a match for my desires, equal to what I've lost,
well and good. But if they give me nothing
I will take a prize myself—your own, or Ajax'°
or Odysseus' prize—I'll **commandeer** her myself

152 **raze:** to destroy completely.

156 **To cling to your own prize:** After a raid on the city of Lyrnessos, Achilles had chosen, as his share of the plunder, the young woman named Briseis.

162 **Ajax:** The Greek army had two great warriors named Ajax. Ajax, the son of Telamon, was considered second only to Achilles in skill and courage.

1 **The Heroic Ideal** *The ancient Greeks believed acquiring a war prize was an honor for a warrior, and losing one was a disgrace. How does this help explain Agamemnon's response?*

2 **Evaluate Credibility** *Is Achilles' advice reasonable? Is his promise sincere? Explain.*

Vocabulary

commandeer (kom′ ən dēr′) *v.* to take arbitrary or forceful possession of

198 UNIT 2 ANCIENT GREECE

Speaking Practice

Present an Oral Report Students may be interested in learning about the lives, religious beliefs, and traditions of the ancient Greeks. Encourage them to conduct research on a topic that interests them. Remind students to limit the breadth of their topic to a manageable size. They might, for example, choose any one of these topics:

- holidays the ancient Greeks celebrated
- the ways they worshipped a specific god
- the role education played in their lives
- temple architectural styles
- the history of the Olympic games

Have students conduct research on their topics and prepare oral reports to present to the class. Remind listeners of their responsibility to listen attentively while someone is speaking.

The Abduction of Helen. Zenone Veronese. Oil on canvas, 44 x 112 in. Private collection.

 View the Art The abduction of Helen of Troy by the Trojan prince Paris triggered the Trojan War. In this painting, the artist portrays Paris carrying Helen to the ships waiting to set sail for Troy. How would you describe the way the artist presents Helen's departure from Sparta?

and let that man I go to visit choke with rage!
165 Enough. We'll deal with all this later, in due time.
Now come, we haul a black ship down to the bright sea,
gather a decent number of oarsmen along her locks
and put aboard a sacrifice, and Chryseis herself,
in all her beauty . . . we embark her too.
170 Let one of the leading captains take command.
Ajax, Idomeneus, trusty Odysseus or you, Achilles,
you—the most violent man alive—so you can perform
the rites for us and calm the god yourself."
                                        A dark glance
and the headstrong runner answered him in kind:
    "Shameless—
175 armored in shamelessness—always shrewd with greed!
How could any Argive soldier obey your orders,
freely and gladly do your sailing for you
or fight your enemies, full force? Not I, no.
It wasn't Trojan spearmen who brought me here to fight.
180 The Trojans never did *me* damage, not in the least,
they never stole my cattle or my horses, never
in Phthia° where the rich soil breeds strong men
did they lay waste my crops. How could they?
Look at the endless miles that lie between us . . .
185 shadowy mountain ranges, seas that surge and thunder.
No, you colossal, shameless—we all followed you,
to please you, to fight for you, to win your honor

182 Phthia (thē´ ə): a small kingdom in Greece ruled by Peleus, the father of Achilles.

HOMER **199**

Teach

View the Art ★

Answer: *He presents her departure as a dramatic, decisive moment.*

In their narrative paintings, Renaissance artists often dressed ancient Greek figures in contemporary clothing. Zenone Veronese followed this custom in his portrayal of Helen's abduction. The ships in the harbor are typical of those in Veronese's day.

Literary History ☆

Clytemnestra Clytemnestra was Agamemnon's wife. Their daughter was Iphigenia, whom Agamemnon "slew for a charm / Against the Thracian winds." (Earlier, lack of wind had stopped the fleet, and Calchas had said that the sacrifice of Iphigenia was what the goddess Artemis required before she started the winds again. This explains why Agamemnon uses the word *again* in line 127 and why he is so angry with Calchas.) When Agamemnon finally returned home after battle, Clytemnestra killed Agamemnon to avenge her daughter's death.

Approaching Level

DIFFERENTIATED INSTRUCTION

 SMALL GROUP **Act Out Scenes** Some readers may find it difficult to follow the dialogue in this story. Students might benefit from acting out the scenes and paraphrasing the speech of the characters.

Divide students into groups of mixed reading levels. Have each group choose a different scene from the text to act out. Students should first review the text and paraphrase the dialogue, making it more contemporary and, thus, easier to understand. Then groups should take turns presenting their scenes to the class. Encourage students to use gestures and facial expressions, along with any props that might help them express the ideas in the text.

Learning Objectives
Evaluating credibility. (SE)
Analyzing art. (SE)
Presenting an oral report. (TE)

Teach

Vocabulary 1

Word Origins The verb *plunder* comes from the German noun *plundern*, which originally meant "household goods" but evolved to mean "to rob of household goods."

(ADVANCED) Have advanced learners make a list of five synonyms of *plunder* and use each one in a sentence. They can list nouns as well as verbs. *(Examples: pillage, despoil, sack, steal, robbery, booty, loot)*

Literary Element 2

Epic Hero Answer: *Homer reveals Achilles is no more willing to give up his prize than Agamemnon is. Achilles is offended because Agamemnon is threatening to punish him to appease Apollo. His behavior is selfish rather than heroic.*

Big Idea 3

The Heroic Ideal Answer: *Agamemnon is clearly envious of Achilles and states, probably unwittingly, why—the gods have favored Achilles with physical prowess that surpasses that of any other warrior.*

---

back from the Trojans—Menelaus and you, you dog-face! ☆
What do *you* care? Nothing. You don't look right or left.°
190 And now you threaten to strip me of my prize in person—
the one I fought for long and hard, and sons of Achaea
handed her to me.
          My honors never equal yours,
whenever we sack some wealthy Trojan stronghold—
my arms bear the brunt of the raw, savage fighting,
195 true, but when it comes to dividing up the plunder [1]
the lion's share is yours, and back I go to my ships,
clutching some scrap, some pittance that I love,
when I have fought to exhaustion.
             No more now—
back I go to Phthia. Better that way by far,
200 to journey home in the beaked ships° of war.
I have no mind to linger here disgraced,
brimming your cup and piling up your plunder."

    But the lord of men Agamemnon shot back,
"*Desert*, by all means—if the spirit drives you home!
205 I will never beg you to stay, not on *my* account.
Never—others will take my side and do me honor,
Zeus above all, whose wisdom rules the world.
You—I hate you most of all the warlords
loved by the gods. Always dear to your heart,
210 strife, yes, and battles, the bloody grind of war.
What if you are a great soldier? That's just a gift of god.
Go home with your ships and comrades, lord it over your
    Myrmidons!°
You *are* nothing to me—you and your overweening° anger!
But let this be my warning on your way:
215 since Apollo insists on taking my Chryseis,
I'll send her back in my own ships with *my* crew.
But I, I will be there in person at your tents
to take Briseis in all her beauty, your own prize—
so you can learn just how much greater I am than you
220 and the next man up may shrink from matching words
    with me,
from hoping to rival Agamemnon strength for strength!"

---

2 The Epic Hero *What does Homer reveal about Achilles in these lines? Does his behavior seem heroic? Explain.*

3 The Heroic Ideal *What is ironic about Agamemnon's admission that he hates Achilles for being "a great soldier"?*

200 UNIT 2 ANCIENT GREECE

189 You don't look right or left: You are completely self-centered.

200 beaked ships: ships with a metal-pointed beam that projected from the bow, or front, of an ancient ship. The beak was used to pierce an enemy ship's hull.

212 Myrmidons: warriors who followed Achilles to Troy.

213 overweening: arrogant; presumptuous; overstepping proper bounds.

Writing Practice

Write a Dialogue Point out that the dialogue spoken by characters is one way authors can give their characters personality and keep them recognizable and distinct from one another throughout a work. Have students imagine Achilles and Agamemnon in a modern setting. **Ask:** What grievances might they have with each other? How would they talk about them? *(Answers will vary.)* Have students write a dialogue between the two characters in which the personality of each shines through. To organize their thoughts before writing, have students create a chart like this one.

	Achilles	Agamemnon
personality traits		
what he wants		
how he speaks		

He broke off and anguish gripped Achilles.
The heart in his rugged chest was pounding, torn . . .
Should he draw the long sharp sword slung at his hip,
225   thrust through the ranks° and kill Agamemnon now?—
or check his rage and beat his fury down?
As his racing spirit veered back and forth,
just as he drew his huge blade from its sheath,
down from the vaulting heavens swept Athena,
230   the white-armed goddess Hera sped her down:
Hera loved both men and cared for both alike.
Rearing behind him Pallas seized his fiery hair—
only Achilles saw her, none of the other fighters—
struck with wonder he spun around, he knew her at once,
235   Pallas Athena! the terrible blazing of those eyes,
and his winged words went flying: "Why, why now?
Child of Zeus with the shield of thunder,° why come now?
To witness the outrage Agamemnon just committed?
I tell you this, and so help me it's the truth—
240   he'll soon pay for his arrogance with his life!"

    Her gray eyes clear, the goddess Athena answered,
"Down from the skies I come to check your rage
if only you will yield.
The white-armed goddess Hera sped me down:
245   she loves you both, she cares for you both alike.
Stop this fighting, now. Don't lay hand to sword.
Lash him with threats of the price that he will face.°
And I tell you this—and I *know* it is the truth—
one day glittering gifts will lie before you,
250   three times over to pay for all his outrage.
Hold back now. Obey us both."
                                    So she urged
and the swift runner complied at once: "I must—
when the two of you hand down commands, Goddess,
a man submits though his heart breaks with fury.
255   Better for him by far. If a man obeys the gods
they're quick to hear his prayers."
                                    And with that
Achilles stayed his burly hand on the silver hilt
and slid the huge blade back in its sheath.
He would not fight the orders of Athena.

225   **thrust through the ranks:**
push past Agamemnon's
bodyguards.

237   **shield of thunder:** Zeus is the
god of thunder and lightning. He
often hurled thunderbolts as an
expression of his anger.

247   **Lash him with threats of the
price that he will face:** Warn
Agamemnon that his arrogance will
cost him your support and that
Achilles and the Myrmidons will
withdraw from the war.

---

4   The Epic Hero   *How might Achilles' impulse to attack Agamemnon be viewed as
both heroic and unheroic?*

HOMER   **201**

Epic Hero   **Answer:** *Achilles'
behavior can be viewed as heroic
because Agamemnon's threat is
a gross insult to Achilles' honor,
an offense worth fighting for. His
behavior is unheroic in that by
reacting impulsively to the insult,
Achilles is blind to the fact he is
about to harm an ally.*

Political History ☆

The Trojans The Trojans were
the inhabitants of the city of Troy
in northwestern Anatolia. This
ancient walled city was positioned
strategically, guarding the southern
entrance to the Dardanelles (a
narrow strait that links the Black
Sea with the Aegean Sea) and
also controlling a land route to
Europe. Troy probably forced
trading vessels and other travelers
to pay tolls to use these routes,
which might in fact have been the
Greeks' real purpose in waging war
against them.

Learning Objectives
Analyzing epic hero. (SE)
Participating in a debate. (TE)

English Learners

DIFFERENTIATED INSTRUCTION

Intermediate Explain to students that
line 227, "As his racing spirit veered
back and forth," is a figurative way of
saying that Achilles was trying to decide
between killing Agamemnon and accepting
Agamemnon's decision.

Advanced Learners/Pre-AP

DIFFERENTIATED INSTRUCTION

Analyze Cultural Context Have
students consider the scene in which
Pallas Athena intervenes to stop Achilles
from killing Agamemnon. Remind students
that the Greeks thought of the gods
and goddesses as real, not as symbols.
Ask students to consider the following
questions: What does Homer's explanation
of Achilles' quick change of mind reveal
about his culture's view of the universe and
people's place in it? What other explanation
for Achilles' behavior might a modern
reader offer? *(Homer's explanation
reveals that the Greeks saw the gods as
a ubiquitous presence and themselves
as worthy of interacting with the gods. A
modern reader might say that Achilles
simply decided to control his temper.)*

Teach

Reading Strategy   1

Make and Verify Predictions **Ask:** Do you think Nestor will be successful in calming Agamemnon and Achilles? Explain. *(Students will probably predict that Nestor will be successful, since he is called "the man of winning words.")*

Literary Element   2

Inversion Point out that in this line, the usual word order has been reversed, a literary device called *inversion*. Writers use inversion for emphasis and variety, to maintain rhyme scheme or meter, or to emphasize certain words and images. **Ask:** What would be the normal word order for this line? *(The voice flowed on and on, sweeter than honey from his tongue.)*

Big Idea   3

The Heroic Ideal **Answer:** *Agamemnon is portrayed as both cowardly and greedy, using his rank to avoid the dangers of actual combat and stealing the prizes of warriors who criticize him. This behavior is at odds with the heroic ideal.*

---

260   Soaring home to Olympus, she rejoined the gods
      aloft in the halls of Zeus whose shield is thunder.

      But Achilles rounded on Agamemnon once again,
      lashing out at him, not relaxing his anger for a moment:
      "Staggering drunk, with your dog's eyes, your fawn's heart!°
265   Never once did you arm with the troops and go to battle
      or risk an ambush packed with Achaea's picked men—
      you lack the courage, you can see death coming.
      Safer by far, you find, to foray° all through camp,
      commandeering the prize of any man who speaks against you.
270   King who devours his people! Worthless husks, the men you
        rule—
      if not, Atrides, this outrage would have been your last.
      I tell you this, and I swear a mighty oath upon it . . .
      by this, this scepter,° look,
      that never again will put forth crown and branches,
275   now it's left its stump on the mountain ridge forever,
      nor will it sprout new green again, now the brazen° ax
      has stripped its bark and leaves,° and now the sons of Achaea
      pass it back and forth as they hand their judgments down,
      upholding the honored customs whenever Zeus commands—
280   This scepter will be the mighty force behind my oath:
      someday, I swear, a yearning for Achilles will strike
      Achaea's sons and all your armies! But then, Atrides,
      harrowed° as you will be, *nothing* you do can save you—
      not when your hordes of fighters drop and die,
285   cut down by the hands of man-killing Hector! Then—
      then you will tear your heart out, desperate, raging
      that you disgraced the best of the Achaeans!"
                           Down on the ground
      he dashed the scepter studded bright with golden nails,
      then took his seat again. The son of Atreus smoldered,
290   glaring across at him, but Nestor rose between them,   **1**
      the man of winning words, the clear speaker of Pylos . . .
 2   Sweeter than honey from his tongue the voice flowed on
        and on.
      Two generations of mortal men he had seen go down by now,
      those who were born and bred with him in the old days,
295   in Pylos' holy realm, and now he ruled the third.
      He pleaded with both kings, with clear good will,
      "No more—or enormous sorrow comes to all Achaea!

---

3   **The Heroic Ideal** *Based on this portrayal of Agamemnon, do you think he fulfills the heroic ideal? Explain.*

264 your dog's eyes, your fawn's heart: expressions meant to suggest that Agamemnon is a coward.

268 foray: to plunder.

273 scepter (sep´tər): a staff borne by a ruler as an emblem or symbol of authority.

274–277 that never again . . . stripped its bark and leaves: having been cut and carved from a living tree, the staff is dead wood.

276 brazen: Here, the adjective has a double meaning: figuratively— bold, defiant; literally—the blade of the ax may have been made from brass.

283 harrowed: under constant attack.

Listening Practice

Conduct a Debate By debating issues, students learn the importance of supporting a position with examples, details, and interpretations of factual information. Explain the format of a formal debate:

- Two teams, usually of two members each, argue for and against a resolution.

- Each team receives equal time—a first period to present its side and a shorter period to rebut the opposing team.

- Affirmative side speaks first.

Organize the class into two groups, one supporting and one opposing the following resolution: "Resolved: Achilles should be allowed to keep his prize." Have students review the selection for reasons to support their side. They should also anticipate what the other side might say and be prepared to rebut the opposing side. Allow time for groups to discuss their findings. Then, have students elect two representatives from their side to debate the issue in front of the class. Remind students that only one person should speak at a time and that effective listening skills are essential to forming a rebuttal to an argument.

How they would exult, Priam and Priam's sons
and all the Trojans. Oh they'd leap for joy
300 to hear the two of you battling on this way,
you who excel us all, first in Achaean councils,
first in the ways of war.
                     Stop. Please.
Listen to Nestor. You are both younger than I,
and in my time I struck up with better men than you,
305 even you, but never once did they make light of me.
I've never seen such men, I never will again . . .
men like Pirithous, Dryas, that fine captain,
Caeneus and Exadius, and Polyphemus, royal prince,
and Theseus,° Aegeus' boy, a match for the immortals.°
310 They were the strongest mortals ever bred on earth,
the strongest, and they fought against the strongest too,
shaggy Centaurs,° wild brutes of the mountains—
they hacked them down, terrible, deadly work.
And I was in their ranks, fresh out of Pylos,
315 far away from home—they **enlisted** me themselves
and I fought on my own, a free lance, single-handed.
And none of the men who walk the earth these days
could battle with those fighters, none, but they,
they took to heart my counsels, marked my words.
320 So now you listen too. Yielding is far better . . .
Don't seize the girl, Agamemnon, powerful as you are—
leave her, just as the sons of Achaea gave her,
his prize from the very first.°
And you, Achilles, never hope to fight it out
325 with your king, pitting force against his force:
no one can match the honors dealt a king, you know,
a sceptered king to whom great Zeus gives glory.°
Strong as you are—a goddess was your mother—
he has more power because he rules more men.
330 Atrides, end your anger—look, it's Nestor!
I beg you, cool your fury against Achilles.
Here the man stands over all Achaea's armies,
our rugged bulwark° braced for shocks of war."

307–309 Pirithous . . . Theseus:
The individuals named are all
heroes of Nestor's generation.

**309 Aegeus' boy, a match for the
immortals:** Theseus of Athens is the
hero of many adventure tales.

312 Centaurs: a race of savage
creatures, fabled to be half man and
half horse, who lived in the
mountains of Greece.

**322–323 leave her . . . his prize
from the very first:** Let her remain
with Achilles, since the Greek army
agreed that she should be his
reward for valor in battle.

**326–327 no one can match . . .
great Zeus gives glory:** No one has
the right to defy a king who rules by
the will of the gods.

333 bulwark (bool´wərk): a
solid wall-like structure raised for
defense; a strong support or
protection. Here, it refers to Achilles'
position of strength among the
Greek army.

 4 **Evaluate Credibility** *What argument does Nestor use to try to persuade Agamemnon and Achilles to stop quarreling? Is his argument based on sound reasoning? Explain.*

5 **The Epic Hero** *Read the side note about the word bulwark. What do Nestor's lines suggest about Achilles?*

Vocabulary

enlist (en list´) *v.* to join or give help; convince (someone) to join or to give help

---

Reading Strategy   **4**

Evaluate Credibility
Answer: *Nestor reminds them
the Trojans would be overjoyed
to learn the Greek leaders are
squabbling among themselves
instead of working together to
defeat them. By reminding the
two warriors of the Trojans' likely
reaction, Nestor makes them
aware of both the destructiveness
of what they are doing and
the foolishness of inadvertently
abetting the Trojan cause.*

Literary Element   **5**

Epic Hero **Answer:** *Nestor
suggests Achilles represents
the main source of the Greeks'
strength by describing him as the
Greeks' bulwark.*

Learning Objectives
Evaluating credibility. (SE)
Analyzing epic hero. (SE)
Writing a dialogue. (TE)
Making and verifying predictions. (TE)
Recognizing inversion. (TE)

Approaching Level

DIFFERENTIATED INSTRUCTION

Review and Paraphrase To maintain
students' attention and enhance their
comprehension, try breaking down this
selection into smaller, more manageable
parts.

Have students work in pairs to paraphrase
the argument between Agamemnon and
Achilles.

Achilles' side	Agamemnon's side

Advanced Learners/Pre-AP

DIFFERENTIATED INSTRUCTION

Present an Art Show Many painters
and sculptors have used the characters
and events of the *Iliad* as their subjects.
Have advanced students search the
Internet or the library for artistic depictions
of the characters introduced in this
selection. They can print out pages from
Web sites and bring in books to share their
findings with the class.

203

Teach

Review Refer students to Achilles' speech starting on line 342 and ending on line 355.
Ask: What is Achilles willing to fight for? What does he refuse to fight for? (*He is willing to fight for all of his possessions, except for his war prize, Briseis.*)

But King Agamemnon answered him in haste.
335 "True, old man—all you say is fit and proper—
but this soldier wants to tower over the armies,
he wants to rule over all, to lord it over all,
give out orders to every man in sight. Well,
there's one, I trust, who will never yield to
  him!
340 What if the everlasting gods have made a
  spearman of him?
Have they entitled him to hurl abuse at *me?*"

"Yes!"—blazing Achilles broke in quickly—
"What a worthless, burnt-out coward I'd be
  called
if I would submit to you and all your orders,
345 whatever you blurt out. Fling them at others,
don't give me commands!
1 Never again, *I* trust, will Achilles yield to *you.*
And I tell you this—take it to heart, I warn you—
my hands will never do battle for that girl,
350 neither with you, King, nor any man alive.
You Achaeans gave her, now you've snatched her back.
But all the rest I possess beside my fast black ship—
not one bit of it can you seize against my will, Atrides.
Come, try it! So the men can see, that instant,
355 your black blood gush and spurt around my spear!"

Once the two had fought it out with words,
battling face-to-face, both sprang to their feet
and broke up the muster° beside the Argive squadrons.
Achilles strode off to his trim ships and shelters,
360 back to his friend Patroclus and their comrades.
Agamemnon had a vessel hauled down to the sea,
he picked out twenty oarsmen to man her locks,
put aboard the cattle for sacrifice to the god
and led Chryseis in all her beauty amidships.°
365 Versatile Odysseus took the helm as captain.

  All embarked,
the party launched out on the sea's foaming lanes
while the son of Atreus told his troops to wash,
to purify themselves from the filth of plague.
They scoured it off, threw scourings in the surf
370 and sacrificed to Apollo full-grown bulls and goats
along the beaten shore of the fallow barren sea
and savory smoke went swirling up the skies.

Achilles and Ajax playing dice. Attic black-figure amphora, 540-530 BC. Exekias. H: 61 cm. Museo Gregoriano Etrusco, Vatican Museums, Vatican State.
View the Art An amphora was an ancient Greek jar with a narrow neck, an oval body, and two handles. Why do you think the artist might have chosen to depict Achilles and Ajax in the midst of a game?

358 muster: here, an assembly, specifically a formal military gathering.

364 amidships: midway between the bow and the stern; most stable part of the ship, and, therefore, the location of the best living quarters.

Grammar Practice

Avoid Run-on Sentences Remind students that a run-on sentence is two or more independent clauses strung together as a single sentence without the use of a comma and a coordinating conjunction to join them or appropriate punctuation to separate them. Sometimes poets use this ungrammatical sentence form for effect, as in this example: "Fling them at others, don't give me commands!" Write these corrected versions on the board:

- Fling them at others. Don't give me commands!
- Fling them at others—don't give me commands!
- Fling them at others; don't give me commands!
- Fling them at others, but don't give me commands!

Have students find two more examples of run-on sentences in the selection and write corrected versions of those sentences. For example, they might choose to correct the following sentences:

- "You Achaeans gave her, now you've snatched her back."
- "They were afraid, they held the king in awe and stood there, silent."

So the men were engaged throughout the camp.
But King Agamemnon would not stop the quarrel,
375   the first threat he hurled against Achilles.
He called Talthybius and Eurybates briskly,
his two heralds, ready, willing aides:
"Go to Achilles' lodge. Take Briseis at once,
his beauty Briseis by the hand and bring her here.
380   But if he will not surrender her, I'll go myself,
I'll seize her myself, with an army at my back—
and all the worse for him!"
                                    He sent them off
with the strict order ringing in their ears.
Against their will the two men made their way
385   along the breaking surf of the barren salt sea
and reached the Myrmidon shelters and their ships.
They found him beside his lodge and black hull,
seated grimly—and Achilles took no joy
when he saw the two approaching.
390   They were afraid, they held the king in awe
and stood there, silent. Not a word to Achilles,
not a question. But he sensed it all in his heart,
their fear, their charge,° and broke the silence for them:
"Welcome, couriers!° Good heralds of Zeus and men,
395   here, come closer. You have done nothing to me.
You are not to blame. No one but Agamemnon—
he is the one who sent you for Briseis.
Go, Patroclus, Prince, bring out the girl
and hand her to them so they can take her back.
400   But let them both bear witness to my loss . . .
in the face of blissful gods and mortal men,
in the face of that unbending, ruthless king—
if the day should come when the armies need *me*
to save their ranks from **ignominious**, stark defeat.
405   The man is raving—with all the murderous
     fury in his heart.
He lacks the sense to see a day behind,
     a day ahead,
and safeguard the Achaeans battling by the ships."

393 their charge: the instructions they had been given; their orders or mission.

394 couriers: a member of the armed forces whose duties include carrying mail, information, or supplies.

---

2 **The Heroic Ideal** *Why might the two heralds react this way to their assigned task?*

3 **The Epic Hero** *What can you infer about Achilles from his treatment of the two heralds?*

Vocabulary

ignominious (igʹnə minʹē əs) *adj.* marked or characterized by disgrace or shame

HOMER   **205**

Teach

Big Idea   **2**

The Heroic Ideal Answer:
The two heralds are reluctant to execute Agamemnon's orders. They probably admire Achilles, recognize the insult to his honor, and perhaps fear the prospect of continuing the war without Achilles' support.

Literary Element   **3**

Epic Hero Answer: *By absolving the two heralds of responsibility for their actions and indicating his argument is not with them, Achilles rises above the pettiness he displayed toward Agamemnon. He acts sympathetically toward them.*

View the Art ★

Answer: *He wanted to portray the human side of the characters during a lull in the fighting, but even at rest, they are ready to return to battle.*

Exekias, one of the foremost artists of the sixth century B.C., often signed his pots with the inscription *Exekias epoiesen me* ("Exekias made me"). The scene depicted on this amphora shows Achilles (wearing a helmet) and Ajax absorbed in a game but ready to spring back into battle.

Advanced Learners/Pre-AP

DIFFERENTIATED INSTRUCTION

Translations Robert Fagles, the translator of the selection presented here, has added a new dimension to the translations of ancient works—he has presented these epics in language that makes them more accessible to modern readers. Advanced learners might find it interesting to do further research into the art of translation.

Have students research the work of Robert Fagles, a Princeton University professor of comparative literature. Students may focus on his translation of the *Iliad*, ancient Greek plays, or the *Odyssey*. Have students describe why, and possibly how, he translated these works. Have students compile their findings in a written report.

Learning Objectives
Analyzing epic hero. (SE)
Analyzing art. (SE)
Reviewing exposition. (TE)
Avoiding run-on sentences. (TE)

Teach

Author's Purpose Ask:
Why do you think Homer shows Achilles crying? *(Students may observe that showing him crying makes the reader more sympathetic to his character.)*

Epic Hero Answer: *Most students will argue that it enhances his stature because it illustrates courage in putting himself at risk in a war in which he is fated to die.*

View the Art ★

Wall paintings were a common form of interior decoration in ancient Rome. Most of the examples that have survived come from Pompeii and nearby towns in southern Italy, which were buried under volcanic ash when Mount Vesuvius erupted in A.D. 79. In the painting shown here, Achilles glances over his shoulder as Patroclus leads Briseis to Agamemnon's men. **Ask: How do you interpret Achilles' expression in this painting?** *(Students might respond that he appears sorrowful or disturbed.)*

Patroclus obeyed his great friend's command.
He led Briseis in all her beauty from the lodge
410　and handed her over to the men to take away.
And the two walked back along the Argive ships
while she trailed on behind, reluctant, every step.
But Achilles wept, and slipping away from his companions,
1　far apart, sat down on the beach of the heaving gray sea
415　and scanned the endless ocean. Reaching out his arms,
again and again he prayed to his dear mother:
"Mother!
You gave me life, short as that life will be°
so at least Olympian Zeus, thundering up on high,
should give me honor—but now he gives me nothing.
420　Atreus' son Agamemnon, for all his far-flung kingdoms—
the man disgraces me, seizes and keeps my prize,
he tears her away himself!"
　　　　　　　So he wept and prayed
and his noble mother heard him, seated near her father,
the Old Man of the Sea° in the salt green depths.
425　Suddenly up she rose from the churning surf
like mist and settling down beside him as he wept,
stroked Achilles gently, whispering his name, "My child—
why in tears? What sorrow has touched your heart?
3　Tell me, please. Don't harbor it deep inside you.
We must share it all."
430　　　　　　　And now from his depths
the proud runner groaned: "You know, you know,
why labor through it all? You know it all so well . . .
We raided Thebe once, Eetion's° sacred citadel,
we ravaged° the place, hauled all the plunder here
435　and the armies passed it round, share and share alike,
and they chose the beauty Chryseis for Agamemnon.
But soon her father, the holy priest of Apollo
the distant deadly Archer, Chryses approached
the fast trim ships of the Argives armed in bronze
440　to win his daughter back, bringing a priceless ransom
and bearing high in hand, wound on a golden staff,
the wreaths of the god who strikes from worlds away.°

The surrender of Briseis. Roman fresco. Museo Archeologico Nazionale, Naples, Italy. ★

417 short as that life will be: The Fates, goddesses who determine human affairs, prophesied that Achilles would die in the war if he joined the expedition against Troy.

424 the Old Man of the Sea: Nereus, a sea god.

433 Eetion: king of Thebes, slain by Achilles.

434 ravaged: devastated destructively and violently.

442 the god who strikes from worlds away: Apollo, god of archery, whose arrows are deadly.

2　**The Epic Hero** *Does Achilles' knowledge of his early death enhance his stature as an epic hero? Why or why not?*

Writing Practice

Write an Interior Monologue Achilles shows anger when he confronts Agamemnon and the other fighters. However, when he is alone, he expresses his hurt and frustration about the situation. Tell students that one way to work through problems is to write down feelings and emotions. This allows one to work through the frustration in a private way. It also permits one to step back from the problem and review the different sides.

Have students imagine that they are in Achilles' place. They are hurt and angered about the situation. Have them spend a few minutes writing an interior monologue in their journals about the situation. Choose volunteers to read their monologues aloud. Then, discuss with students whether they think writing an interior monologue could help them with problems of their own.

He begged the whole Achaean army but most of all
the two supreme commanders, Atreus' two sons,
445 and all ranks of Achaeans cried out their assent,
'Respect the priest, accept the shining ransom!'
But it brought no joy to the heart of Agamemnon,
our high and mighty king dismissed the priest
with a brutal order ringing in his ears.
450 And shattered with anger, the old man withdrew
but Apollo heard his prayer—he loved him, deeply—
he loosed his shaft° at the Argives, withering plague,
and now the troops began to drop and die in droves,
the arrows of god went showering left and right,
455 whipping through the Achaeans' vast encampment.
But the old seer who knew the cause full well
revealed the will of the archer god Apollo.
And I was the first, mother, I urged them all,
'Appease the god at once!' That's when the fury
460 gripped the son of Atreus. Agamemnon leapt to his feet
and hurled his threat—his threat's been driven home.
One girl, Chryseis, the fiery-eyed Achaeans
ferry out in a fast trim ship to Chryse Island,
laden with presents for the god. The other girl,
465 just now the heralds came and led her away from camp,
Briseus' daughter, the prize the armies gave me.
But you, mother, if you have any power at all,
protect your son! Go to Olympus, plead with Zeus,
if you ever warmed his heart with a word or any action . . .

470   Time and again I heard your claims in father's halls,
boasting how you and you alone of all the immortals
rescued Zeus, the lord of the dark storm cloud,
from ignominious, stark defeat . . .
That day the Olympians tried to chain him down,
475 Hera, Poseidon lord of the sea, and Pallas Athena—
you rushed to Zeus, dear Goddess, broke those chains,
quickly ordered the hundred-hander° to steep Olympus,
that monster whom the immortals call Briareus
but every mortal calls the Sea-god's son, Aegaeon,
480 though he's stronger than his father. Down he sat,
flanking Cronus' son,° gargantuan in the glory of it all,

452 **loosed his shaft:** shot his arrow.

477 **hundred-hander:** Briareus, a monster with one hundred hands who warred with the gods until he was banished to the infernal regions.

481 **Cronus' son:** Zeus.

 4 Evaluate Credibility *Review lines 436–466. Has Achilles given his mother a credible account of the quarrel with Agamemnon? Explain.*

Reading Strategy 3

Compare and Contrast Tone Have students compare the passage in which Achilles' mother speaks to him with the previous passages in which Achilles has been addressed. **Ask:** How does the tone of the passages differ? How do they affect your view of Achilles? *(Students should note that when his mother talks to Achilles, she addresses him as a child, not as a great warrior. Students may suggest that his mother's point of view gives them a more human perspective of him.)*

Reading Strategy 4

Evaluate Credibility
Answer: *Achilles' account is somewhat biased. He does not mention that Agamemnon must not only return Chryseis but also add treasure to the gift. He also does not connect the way Agamemnon feels about returning the prize to the way Achilles feels about losing Briseis.*

Learning Objectives
Analyzing epic hero. (SE)
Analyzing author's purpose. (TE)
Writing an interior monologue. (TE)
Comparing and contrasting tone. (TE)

English Learners

DIFFERENTIATED INSTRUCTION

Intermediate English learners might find it difficult to write an interior monologue about their feelings because of limited vocabulary related to those feelings. Encourage them to use a thesaurus to find synonyms for words related to various emotions, such as anger, outrage, embarrassment, frustration, resentment, and discouragement.

Advanced Learners/Pre-AP

DIFFERENTIATED INSTRUCTION

Write a Dramatic Monologue Remind students that a dramatic monologue is a form of poetry in which a speaker addresses a silent listener at a critical moment. Advanced learners might wish to turn their interior monologue into a dramatic monologue, which they may then share with the class.

Teach

Reading Strategy

Evaluate Credibility
Answer: *Students may say Achilles' deep love for Briseis motivated his quarrel with Agamemnon.*

Progress Check

Can students evaluate credibility?

If No → See Unit 2 Teaching Resources Book, p. 29.

Cultural History ☆

More About Achilles Greek mythology relates that Achilles was fated to die in Troy, so his mother disguised him as a girl and sent him to live with Lycomedes, the king. Odysseus found him there and enlisted him to fight in the Greek army against the Trojans.

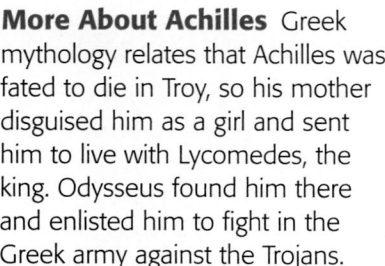
To check students' understanding of the selection, see Unit 2 Teaching Resources Book, p. 33.

and the blessed gods were struck with terror then,
they stopped shackling Zeus.
                        Remind him of that,
now, go and sit beside him, grasp his knees . . .
485 persuade him, somehow, to help the Trojan cause,
to pin the Achaeans back against their ships,
trap them round the bay and mow them down.
So all can reap the benefits of their king—
so even mighty Atrides can see how mad he was
490 to disgrace Achilles, the best of the Achaeans!"

    And Thetis answered, bursting into tears,
"O my son, my sorrow, why did I ever bear you?
All I bore was doom . . .°
Would to god you could linger by your ships
495 without a grief in the world, without a torment!
Doomed to a short life, you have so little time.
And not only short, now, but filled with heartbreak too,
more than all other men alive—doomed twice over.
Ah to a cruel fate I bore you in our halls!
500 Still, I shall go to Olympus crowned with snow
and repeat your prayer to Zeus who loves the lightning.
Perhaps he will be persuaded.
                      But you, my child,
stay here by the fast ships, rage on at the Achaeans,
just keep clear of every foray° in the fighting.
505 Only yesterday Zeus went off to the Ocean River°
to feast with the Aethiopians,° loyal, lordly men,
and all the gods went with him. But in twelve days
the Father returns to Olympus. Then, for your sake,
up I go to the bronze floor, the royal house of Zeus—
I'll grasp his knees, I think I'll win him over."
510   With that vow
his mother went away and left him there, alone,
his heart inflamed for the sashed and lovely girl
they'd wrenched away from him against his will. . . ☆

493 All I bore was doom: a reference to the fact that Achilles' life is to be short and unhappy.

504 foray: in this use, a raid or sudden attack.

505 the Ocean River: The Greeks believed that the oceans of the world were one body of water that surrounded the earth.

506 Aethiopians: to the ancient Greeks, residents of Aethiopia (Ethiopia), the lands in Africa south of Egypt and close to the Ocean River.

Evaluate Credibility *Based on these lines, what do you think is the real cause of Achilles' quarrel with Agamemnon?*

Assessment Practice

Analyze Multiple-Choice Questions
Remind students of the importance of reading each question very carefully to ensure understanding. It is also important to read all the answer choices before making a selection. Words such as *most, least,* and *except* can be clues to the correct answer. Have students identify the key words in these questions and then choose the correct answers.

1. The adjective least likely to be applied to Achilles is
   a. courageous
   b. humble
   c. headstrong
   d. angry

2. The prize Achilles values the most is
   a. a scepter
   b. a shield
   c. Briseis
   d. Chryseis
   (Key words are least *and* most; *answers are b and c.)*

After You Read

Respond and Think Critically

Respond and Interpret

1. Both Agamemnon and Achilles behave badly in this episode. Whom did you sympathize with more and why?

2. (a)Why has a plague struck the Greek camp? (b)Why is the prophet Calchas reluctant to explain the plague's cause?

3. (a)On what condition will Agamemnon give back Chryseis to her father? (b)Why does Achilles take offense at this condition?

4. (a)How does Agamemnon intend to punish Achilles for arguing with him? (b)Why does Achilles accept this punishment?

5. (a)How does Achilles intend to get even with Agamemnon for seizing Briseis? (b)Why does he call upon his mother for help?

Analyze and Evaluate

6. In your opinion, when did tension between Agamemnon and Achilles actually begin? Explain.

7. How would you characterize the Greek gods and their relationship with humans?

8. An **internal conflict** is a struggle within a character's mind. Describe at least one internal conflict in Book I of the *Iliad*.

Connect

9. **Big Idea** **The Heroic Ideal** Based on this excerpt from the *Iliad*, how are the actions of the heroes important to their society?

10. **Connect to Today** How are Homer's characters much like people today?

Literary Element The Epic Hero

The traditional **epic hero** is a larger-than-life figure—a courageous, noble, and confident warrior.

1. How is Achilles a larger-than-life figure?

2. Most of Homer's characters have both strengths and weaknesses. Does Homer show Achilles as entirely admirable? Explain.

Reading Strategy Evaluate Credibility

Review the checklist you made on page 193 and then answer the following questions.

1. Is Nestor credible as he attempts to mediate the dispute between Achilles and Agamemnon? Explain.

2. Why does his attempt fail?

LOG ON **Literature** Online

Selection Resources For Selection Quizzes, eFlashcards, and Reading-Writing Connection activities, go to glencoe.com and enter QuickPass code GLW6053u2.

Vocabulary Practice

Practice with Synonyms With a partner, match each boldfaced vocabulary word below with its synonym. Use a thesaurus or dictionary to check your answers. You will not use all the answer choices.

1. droves
2. appease
3. commandeer
4. enlist
5. ignominious

a. unsightly
b. shameful
c. seize
d. superior
e. mollify

f. throng
g. recruit

Writing

Write a Character Sketch Write a brief character sketch of Achilles, using details from the epic to support your points. To get started, consider Michael Grant's comment on Achilles: "Savage, sulky, and vindictive, at times, but also the most handsome, eloquent, courteous, generous, wise, and cultured of all the heroes."

HOMER **209**

After You Read

Assess

1. Answers will vary.

2. (a) Apollo is punishing the Greeks because Agamemnon refuses to return Chryseis, his war prize, to her father, a priest of Apollo. (b) Calchas knows Agamemnon will be angry.

3. (a) He must receive a different prize. (b) He knows there is no more treaure.

4. (a) He plans to take Achilles' prize, Briseis. (b) Because Hera and Athena beg him not to harm Agamemnon

5. (a) He decides to leave the battlefield with his men. (b) So that Zeus will help the Trojans defeat Agamemnon.

6. Achilles cites all the times he has fought for Agamemnon without reward, and Agamemnon reveals he envies Achilles' physical prowess and favor with the gods.

7. The gods possess many human qualities, they interfere in the affairs of humans, and they have favorites among them.

8. Achilles is conflicted about whether to draw his sword on Agamemnon.

9. Students may say the actions of heroes preserve values important to their society.

10. Students may say people today and Homer's characters can be both fearful and brave, sometimes lack self-control, and react aggressively to insults.

Writing

Students' character sketches should
- describe the qualities that distinguish Achilles
- use details from the selection to support their points

Literary Element

1. He is brave and is a great warrior. His mother is a goddess.

2. His need for revenge and his pride are two of his weaknesses.

Vocabulary

1. f 2. e 3. c 4. g 5. b

Reading Strategy

1. Nestor is credible. He is old, experienced in battle, and respected as a seer. The Greeks admire him and value his judgment.

2. His attempt fails because Agamemnon will not listen to him.

 For additional assessment, see Assessment Resources, pp. 67–68.

209

Before You Read

Focus

Bellringer Options

Daily Language Practice Transparency 25

Or ask: Why might a victor treat a fallen enemy with disrespect? Students may say that a victor might be tempted to treat a fallen enemy with disrespect if that enemy had caused great harm or fought unfairly, but it would still be wrong.

Summary

To avenge the death of his best friend, Patroclus, Achilles faces battle with Hector. At the last minute, Hector loses his nerve and begins fleeing the intimidating warrior. Eventually Zeus gives Athena permission to help Achilles. She assumes the form of Hector's brother and convinces Hector to fight Achilles. Achilles is victorious. Ignoring Hector's plea that his body be returned to his family, Achilles drags the corpse around the city in public view.

Book XXII: The Death of Hector from the *Iliad*

Build Background

After Achilles and the Myrmidons withdraw from the war, the Trojan army drives the Greeks back to the edge of the sea. Patroclus, Achilles' best friend, cannot endure the slaughter of his comrades. He wears Achilles' armor, leading the Myrmidons into combat, but is slain by Hector. The death of Patroclus enrages Achilles, who returns to the battlefield in search of Hector. The Trojan army flees into the city, leaving Hector alone to await his rival.

Set Purposes for Reading

Big Idea **The Heroic Ideal**

As you read, ask yourself, What actions in Book XXII either reflect or violate the heroic ideal?

Literary Element **Epic Simile**

An **epic simile** (sometimes called a Homeric simile) extends a comparison with elaborate descriptive details that can fill several lines of verse. As you read, ask yourself, How does Homer's use of epic similes evoke readers' emotions?

Reading Strategy **Analyze Cultural Context**

When you **analyze cultural context,** you think about how the values of the people living in a particular time and place might have influenced a literary work. The ancient Greeks believed the universe consisted of mortals and gods who sometimes intervened in human affairs. As you read, ask yourself, How does the *Iliad* reflect this belief?

Tip: Determine Influences As you read, list examples of the gods' influence on events.

God or Goddess	Action
Apollo	Lines 9–21: tricks Achilles into chasing him, allowing the Trojans to escape.

Learning Objectives

For pages 210–231

In studying this text, you will focus on the following objectives:

Literary Study: Analyzing epic similes.

Reading: Analyzing cultural context.

Writing: Writing an expository essay.

Vocabulary

bereft (bi reft′) *adj.* deprived or robbed; p. 213 *After losing her husband, the widow was bereft of her best friend.*

glistening (glis′ən′ing) *adj.* glittering; twinkling; p. 216 *Glistening in the rain, the street seemed strangely beautiful.*

barbaric (bär bar′ik) *adj.* crude; wild in taste, style, or manner; p. 222 *He shoveled food into his mouth with his hands in a barbaric manner.*

gloat (glōt) *v.* to regard with malignant satisfaction; p. 224 *Terry's opponent sneered and gloated over his error.*

Tip: Denotation and Connotation The **denotation** of a word is its literal meaning; the **connotation** of a word is its implied meanings. For example, the word *gloat* evokes negative feelings.

210 UNIT 2   ANCIENT GREECE

Selection Skills

Literary Elements
- Epic Simile (SE pp. 210–230)
- Epic Hero (SE p. 230)

The Death of Hector

Writing Skills/Grammar
- Write an Expository Essay (SE p. 231)
- Use Descriptive Language (TE p. 216)
- Write a Research Report (TE p. 222)

Reading Skills
- Analyze Cultural Context (SE pp. 210–230)
- Compare and Contrast Characters (TE p. 220)
- Analyze Cause-and-Effect Relationships (TE p. 224)

Vocabulary Skills
- Denotation and Connotation (SE p. 230)
- Academic Vocabulary (SE p. 230)
- Multiple-Meaning Words (TE pp. 213–214)

The Fury of Achilles. Charles-Antoine Coypel. Hermitage, St. Petersburg, Russia.

FROM THE ILIAD

from Book XXII: The Death of

HECTOR

Homer

Translated by Robert Fagles

So all through Troy the men who had fled like panicked fawns
were wiping off their sweat, drinking away their thirst,
leaning along the city's massive ramparts now
while Achaean troops, sloping shields to shoulders,
5   closed against the walls. But there stood Hector,
shackled fast by his deadly fate,° holding his ground,
exposed in front of Troy and the Scaean Gates.°
And now Apollo turned to taunt Achilles:
"Why are you chasing *me?*° Why waste your speed?—
10 son of Peleus, you a mortal and I a deathless god.
You still don't know that I am immortal, do you?—
straining to catch me in your fury! Have you forgotten?
There's a war to fight with the Trojans you stampeded,
look, they're packed inside their city walls, but you,
15 you've slipped away out here. You can't kill *me*—
I can never die—it's not my fate!"
                                      Enraged at that,
Achilles shouted in mid-stride, "You've blocked my way,
you distant, deadly Archer, deadliest god of all—
you made me swerve away from the rampart there.

6 by his deadly fate: Hector had told his wife, Andromache, that he knew in his heart he would die in the war and Troy would fall.

7 Scaean (skē′ən) Gates: one of the main gates in the wall around Troy.

9 "Why are you chasing me?": Apollo had disguised himself as a Trojan leader, tempting Achilles into pursuing him. This gave the Trojan army time to flee.

The Heroic Ideal *What traits set Hector apart from the other Trojans?*

HOMER **211**

Teach

Big Idea

The Heroic Ideal Answer:
Courage, honor, and perseverance set Hector apart from his comrades. He stands his ground alone, while they "are drinking away their thirst" inside the walls of Troy.

View the Art

This painting shows the wrathful Achilles being guided by Athena (wearing a helmet), Poseidon (emptying a water vessel), and other gods. The artist, a failed playwright, was known for the highly dramatic quality of his paintings. **Ask:** Why might *The Fury of Achilles* be an apt title for the painting? *(Students may say the swirling patterns in the composition of the painting suggest the power of Achilles' unleashed fury.)*

For an audio recording of this selection, use Listening Library Audio CD-ROM.

Learning Objective
Analyzing art. (TE)

English Learners
DIFFERENTIATED INSTRUCTION

Beginning Some students may lack the vocabulary to summarize events concisely. Explain that transitional words—such as *first, next, then,* and *after*—are useful because they place the events sequentially. Have English learners work with partners to summarize "The Rage of Achilles." They should first list the major events. Then, partners should summarize orally. Finally, have the students prepare a one-paragraph written summary.

Advanced Learners/Pre-AP
DIFFERENTIATED INSTRUCTION

Analyze Archetypes Remind students that an archetype is a recurring symbol, image, or story pattern that occurs frequently in literature and evokes an emotional response. The underdog who faces a superior foe is an archetypal figure, represented here by Hector as he stands up to the far more powerful Achilles. Students might wish to investigate this common literary archetype and report to the class on other examples, such as the story of David and Goliath in the Old Testament, Caliban in Shakespeare's *The Tempest,* and Joseph K. in Kafka's *The Trial.*

211

Teach

Reading Strategy 1

Analyze Cultural Context

Answer: *Achilles lacks the power to battle Apollo, a god. Though his mother is a goddess, Achilles is still mortal and, thus, inferior to Apollo.*

Literary Element 2

Epic Simile **Answer:** *Homer compares Achilles to a champion stallion. This simile emphasizes Achilles' strength, speed, and efficiency.*

(ADVANCED) Advanced students might enjoy creating additional similes to emphasize these qualities of Achilles. Have them share their ideas with the class.

20 Else what a mighty Trojan army had gnawed the dust
    before they could ever straggle through their gates!
    Now you've robbed me of great glory, saved their lives
    with all your deathless ease. Nothing for you to fear,
    no punishment to come. Oh I'd pay you back
25 if I only had the power at my command!"

    No more words—he dashed toward the city,
    heart racing for some great exploit, rushing on
    like a champion stallion drawing a chariot full tilt,
    sweeping across the plain in easy, tearing strides—
30 so Achilles hurtled on, driving legs and knees.

    And old King Priam was first to see him coming,
    surging over the plain, blazing like the star
    that rears at harvest,° flaming up in its brilliance,—
    far outshining the countless stars in the night sky,
35 that star they call Orion's° Dog—brightest of all
    but a fatal sign emblazoned on the heavens,
    it brings such killing fever down on wretched men.
    So the bronze flared on his chest as on he raced—
    and the old man moaned, flinging both hands high,
40 beating his head and groaning deep he called,
    begging his dear son who stood before the gates,
    unshakable, furious to fight Achilles to the death.
    The old man cried, pitifully, hands reaching out to him,
    "Oh Hector! Don't just stand there, don't, dear child,
45 waiting that man's attack—alone, cut off from friends!
    You'll meet your doom at once, beaten down by Achilles,
    so much stronger than you—that hard, headlong man.
    Oh if only the gods loved him as much as I do . . .°
    dogs and vultures would eat his fallen corpse at once!—
50 with what a load of misery lifted from my spirit.
    That man who robbed me of many sons, brave boys,
    cutting them down or selling them off as slaves,
    shipped to islands half the world away . . .
    Even now there are two, Lycaon and Polydorus—°
55 I cannot find them among the soldiers crowding Troy,
    those sons Laothoë° bore me, Laothoë queen of women.
    But if they are still alive in the enemy's camp,
    then we'll ransom them back with bronze and gold.

32–33 the star that rears at harvest: Sirius, the dog star, which first appears in the fall and was thought to bring disease.

35 Orion: a mighty hunter who was placed among the stars as a constellation by Artemis, goddess of the hunt.

48 if only the gods loved him as much as I do: an example of irony—the real meaning of the statement is the opposite of the surface meaning. Priam then explains his hatred for Achilles.

54 Lycaon and Polydorus: sons of Priam slain by Achilles in battle.

56 Laothoë: one of Priam's wives; daughter of Altes, a wealthy king.

1 Analyze Cultural Context *What prevents Achilles from taking revenge on Apollo?*

2 Epic Simile *To what does Homer compare Achilles in these lines? What aspects of Achilles' character does this emphasize?*

212 UNIT 2 ANCIENT GREECE

Reading Practice

Analyze Setting Students may benefit from analyzing the setting and spatial relationships in the text by looking for directional words and phrases. Have students identify words and phrases on page 211 that tell the reader where the action is taking place. Then ask them to complete a chart like this one, describing the settings as they appear in the account.

Location	In the city of Troy	
Action	The troops are hiding from the Greeks and Achilles.	
Directional words and phrases	"So all through Troy the men . . ."	

We have hoards inside the walls, the rich dowry
60   old and famous Altes presented with his daughter.
But if they're dead already, gone to the House of Death,
what grief to their mother's heart and mine—
      we gave them life.
For the rest of Troy, though, just a moment's grief
unless you too are battered down by Achilles.
65   Back, come back! Inside the walls, my boy!
Rescue the men of Troy and the Trojan women—
don't hand the great glory to Peleus' son,
bereft of your own sweet life yourself.
                    Pity me too!—
still in my senses, true, but a harrowed, broken man
70   marked out by doom—past the threshold of old age . . .
and Father Zeus will waste me with a hideous fate,
and after I've lived to look on so much horror!
My sons laid low,° my daughters dragged away
and the treasure-chambers looted, helpless babies
75   hurled to the earth in the red barbarity of war . . .
my sons' wives hauled off by the Argives' bloody hands!
And I, I last of all—the dogs before my doors
will eat me raw, once some enemy brings me down
with his sharp bronze sword or spits° me with a spear,
80   wrenching the life out of my body, yes, the very dogs
I bred in my own halls to share my table, guard my gates—
mad, rabid at heart° they'll lap their master's blood
and loll before my doors.
                    Ah for a young man
all looks fine and noble if he goes down in war,
85   hacked to pieces under a slashing bronze blade—
he lies there dead . . . but whatever death lays bare,
all wounds are marks of glory. When an old man's killed
and the dogs go at the gray head and the gray beard
and mutilate the genitals—that is the cruelest sight
90   in all our wretched lives!"
                    So the old man groaned
and seizing his gray hair tore it out by the roots
but he could not shake the fixed resolve of Hector.
And his mother wailed now, standing beside Priam,
weeping freely, loosing her robes with one hand

73 laid low: slain.

79 spits: here, pierces with
something pointed; impales. [3]

82 rabid at heart: extremely
violent; exhibiting the behavior of an
animal suffering from rabies.

---

[4]   **The Heroic Ideal** *What aspect of the heroic ideal does Priam reference in these lines?*

Vocabulary

bereft (bi reft´) *adj.* deprived or robbed

HOMER   **213**

Vocabulary   **3**

Multiple-Meaning Words
One meaning of the verb *spit*, as
mentioned in the footnote, is "to
impale." When functioning as a
noun, *spit* can refer to "a slender
pointed rod for holding meat
over a fire." **Ask:** What other
meanings of the word *spit* do
you know? *(Possible answers: to
eject saliva, to utter with a spitting
sound or scornful expression, to
rain or snow very lightly)*

Big Idea   **4**

The Heroic Ideal **Answer:**
*Priam, who has lost several sons
to Achilles and the Greeks already,
fears Hector also will be killed. If
Hector is slain, Priam is afraid his
city and his own life will be lost.*

Learning Objectives
Analyzing cultural context. (SE)
Analyzing epic simile. (SE)
Understanding multiple-meaning
words. (TE)
Analyzing imagery. (TE)
Analyzing setting. (TE)

Approaching Level

DIFFERENTIATED INSTRUCTION

Read Footnotes Understanding the
many allusions in the text adds another
dimension to comprehending the story
fully, but visually impaired students may
find it difficult to decipher the footnotes
connected to the text. To assist these
students, read or have a student read
several passages aloud, pausing to read
footnotes as they are cited. Then suggest
that visually impaired students read the
passage silently to themselves. Ask them
to compare their levels of comprehension
before and after having read the footnotes.

Teach

Literary Element 1

Imagery Point out Priam's use of vivid word pictures to express his vision of the future. Remind students that imagery uses language that engages the senses. Have students find other examples of imagery on pages 214 and 215.

Literary Element 2

Epic Simile Answer: *This comparison conveys the intensity of Hector's commitment to stand his ground.*

95 and holding out her bare breast with the other,
her words pouring forth in a flight of grief and tears:
"Hector, my child! Look—have some respect for *this*!
Pity your mother too, if I ever gave you the breast
to soothe your troubles, remember it now, dear boy—
100 beat back that savage man from safe inside the walls!
Don't go forth, a champion pitted against him—
merciless, brutal man. If he kills you now,
1 how can I ever mourn you on your deathbed?—
dear branch in bloom, dear child I brought to birth!—
105 Neither I nor your wife, that warm, generous woman . . .
Now far beyond our reach, now by the Argive ships
the rushing dogs will tear you, bolt your flesh!"

So they wept, the two of them crying out
to their dear son, both pleading time and again
110 but they could not shake the fixed resolve of Hector.
No, he waited Achilles, coming on, gigantic in power.
As a snake in the hills, guarding his hole, awaits a man—
bloated with poison, deadly hatred seething inside him,
glances flashing fire as he coils round his lair . . .
115 so Hector, nursing his quenchless fury, gave no ground,
leaning his burnished shield against a jutting wall,
but harried still, he probed his own brave heart:
"No way out. If I slip inside the gates and walls,
Polydamas° will be first to heap disgrace on me—
120 he was the one who urged me to lead our Trojans
back to Ilium° just last night, the disastrous night
Achilles rose in arms like a god. But did I give way?
Not at all. And how much better it would have been!
Now my army's ruined, thanks to my own reckless pride,
125 I would die of shame to face the men of Troy
and the Trojan women trailing their long robes . . .
Someone less of a man than I will say, 'Our Hector—
staking all on his own strength, he destroyed his army!'
So they will mutter. So now, better by far for me
130 to stand up to Achilles, kill him, come home alive
or die at his hands in glory out before the walls.
But wait—what if I put down my studded shield
and heavy helmet, prop my spear on the rampart
and go forth, just as I am, to meet Achilles,

Greek warrior with a shield in hand. Hellenistic reliefs from frieze on the tomb of a Lycian prince. Kunsthistorisches Museum, Vienna, Austria

119 Polydamas: a cautious Trojan leader; a rival who often opposes Hector's military strategy.

121 Ilium: another name for the city of Troy.

---

2 Epic Simile *What does this comparison convey about Hector?*

Vocabulary Practice

Multiple Meaning Words
Remind students that many words have multiple meanings. Have students find each of the following words in the text on page 215 and define the word based on the context.

rest (line 142)	holds (line 142)	hide (line 144)	stores (line 145)	show (line 147)	rock (line 152)	like (line 153)

might (line 154)	right (line 159)	nerve (line 163)	ground (line 163)	fast (line 165)	quarry (line 169)

135　noble Prince Achilles . . .
　　　why, I could promise to give back Helen, yes,
　　　and all her treasures with her, all those riches
　　　Paris once hauled home to Troy in the hollow ships—
　　　and they were the cause of all our endless fighting—
140　Yes, yes, return it all to the sons of Atreus now
　　　to haul away, and then, at the same time, divide
　　　the rest with all the Argives, all the city holds,
　　　and then I'd take an oath for the Trojan royal
　　　　council
　　　that we will hide nothing! Share and share alike the hoards
145　our handsome citadel stores within its depths and—
　　　Why debate, my friend? Why thrash things out?
　　　I must not go and implore him. He'll show no mercy,
　　　no respect for me, my rights—he'll cut me down
　　　straight off—stripped of defenses like a woman
150　once I have loosed the armor off my body.
　　　No way to parley° with that man—not now—
　　　not from behind some oak or rock to whisper,
　　　like a boy and a young girl, lovers' secrets
　　　a boy and girl might whisper to each other . . .
155　Better to clash in battle, now, at once—
　　　see which fighter Zeus awards the glory!"
　　　　　　　　　　　　　　　　So he wavered,
　　　waiting there, but Achilles was closing on him now
　　　like the god of war, the fighter's helmet flashing,
　　　over his right shoulder shaking the Pelian ash spear,°
160　that terror, and the bronze around his body° flared
　　　like a raging fire or the rising, blazing sun.
　　　Hector looked up, saw him, started to tremble,
　　　nerve gone, he could hold his ground no longer,
　　　he left the gates behind and away he fled in fear—
165　and Achilles went for him, fast, sure of his speed
　　　as the wild mountain hawk, the quickest thing on wings,
　　　launching smoothly, swooping down on a cringing dove
　　　and the dove flits out from under, the hawk screaming
　　　over the quarry, plunging over and over, his fury

151 parley: to discuss terms.

159 Pelian ash spear: Achilles' spear was carved from an ash tree on Mount Pelion. Chiron, wisest of the Centaurs, gave it to him and taught him to use it.

160 the bronze around his body: his armor.

3　The Heroic Ideal *What do these lines suggest about Hector?*

4　Analyze Cultural Context *According to Hector, what role will the gods play in this conflict?*

5　Epic Simile *To what birds does Homer compare Achilles and Hector? What might these birds represent?*

Teach

| Big Idea | 3 |

The Heroic Ideal Answer: *Hector acknowledges Achilles would lose respect for him if he doffed his armor and tried to sue for peace. This alludes to the Greeks' admiration for warriors who show courage in battle.*

| Reading Strategy | 4 |

Analyze Cultural Context Answer: *The gods will favor and protect one of the combatants, but no one knows whom.*

| Literary Element | 5 |

Epic Simile Answer: *Homer compares Achilles to a wild mountain hawk, a fierce bird of prey, and Hector to a dove, a traditional symbol of peace.*

Learning Objectives
Analyzing epic simile. (SE)
Analyzing cultural context. (SE)
Analyzing imagery. (TE)
Undertanding multiple-meaning words. (TE)

Advanced Learners/Pre-AP

DIFFERENTIATED INSTRUCTION

Oral Tradition Explain to students that long before the *Iliad* was written, it was recited. This affected the form of the epic. The storyteller included many repetitive phrases, or epithets, such as "Hector breaker of horses," to make the story easier to remember. Also, rhythm and meter played an important part. The translator, Robert Fagles, has remained as true as possible to the poem's original beat. Have volunteers take turns reading aloud parts of the story to the class. Students reading the poem should spend a few minutes reviewing their passage to enable them to capture the feeling of telling a story as opposed to reading one aloud. Discuss the effect of hearing the story as opposed to reading it.

Literary Element | 1

Epithet Review with students the definition of *epithet* and ask them to identify the epithet used here. *(The epithet "breaker of horses" is used to identify Hector.)*

Political History ☆

The River God Scamander

In Greek mythology, Scamander was a river god. During the Trojan War, he fought on the side of the Trojans as the personification of the Scamander River that flowed near the city of Troy. Called Xanthus by the gods, Scamander tried to stop Achilles from slaughtering the Trojans by drowning him, but the goddess Hera and her son intervened on Achilles' behalf.

170 driving him down to beak and tear his kill—
so Achilles flew at him, breakneck on in fury
with Hector fleeing along the walls of Troy,
fast as his legs would go. On and on they raced,
passing the lookout point, passing the wild fig tree
175 tossed by the wind, always out from under the ramparts
down the wagon trail they careered° until they reached ☆
the clear running springs where whirling Scamander°
rises up from its double wellsprings bubbling strong—
and one runs hot and the steam goes up around it,
180 drifting thick as if fire burned at its core
but the other even in summer gushes cold
as hail or freezing snow or water chilled to ice . . .
And here, close to the springs, lie washing-pools
scooped out in the hollow rocks and broad and smooth
185 where the wives of Troy and all their lovely daughters
would wash their **glistening** robes in the old days,
the days of peace before the sons of Achaea came . . .
Past these they raced, one escaping, one in pursuit
and the one who fled was great but the one pursuing
190 greater, even greater—their pace mounting in speed
since both men strove, not for a sacrificial beast
1 or oxhide trophy, prizes runners fight for, no,
they raced for the life of Hector breaker of horses.°
Like powerful stallions sweeping round the post for trophies,
195 galloping full stretch with some fine prize at stake,
a tripod, say, or woman offered up at funeral games
for some brave hero fallen—so the two of them
whirled three times around the city of Priam,
sprinting at top speed while all the gods gazed down,
200 and the father of men and gods broke forth among them now:
"Unbearable—a man I love, hunted round his own city walls
and right before my eyes. My heart grieves for Hector.
Hector who burned so many oxen in my honor, rich cuts,
now on the rugged crests of Ida, now on Ilium's heights.°
205 But now, look, brilliant Achilles courses him round
the city of Priam in all his savage, lethal speed.
Come, you immortals, think this through. Decide.
Either we pluck the man from death and save his life
or strike him down at last, here at Achilles' hands—
210 for all his fighting heart."
                    But immortal Athena,

176 careered: went at top speed, especially in a headlong manner.

177 Scamander (skə manʹ dər): chief river near the city of Troy.

193 breaker of horses: Hector was famed for his ability to tame horses.

203–204 Hector who burned . . . heights: Hector sacrificed oxen to Zeus on Mount Ida, overlooking Troy.

Vocabulary

glistening (glisʹ ən´ ing) *adj.* glittering; twinkling

Writing Practice

⚡ Use Descriptive Language

Discuss with students the importance of using vivid imagery in writing. Explain that vivid detail and descriptive language that appeals to the senses help stories come to life for readers. Point out that similes and metaphors, which compare two seemingly unlike things, produce strong visual images.

Have students choose a scene to describe—from the *Iliad* or from their own lives. Students should write a description of the scene in one or two paragraphs, employing vivid, descriptive detail and similes. They might wish to complete a chart like this one, listing words and phrases that engage the senses. Have students share their descriptions with the class.

Sight	Hearing	Taste	Smell	Touch

her gray eyes wide, protested strongly: "Father!
Lord of the lightning, king of the black cloud,
what are you saying? A man, a mere mortal,
his doom sealed long ago?° You'd set him free
215 from all the pains of death?
                              Do as you please—
but none of the deathless gods will ever praise you."

And Zeus who marshals the thunderheads replied,
"Courage, Athena, third-born of the gods, dear child.
Nothing I said was meant in earnest, trust me,
220 I mean you all the good will in the world. Go.
Do as your own impulse bids you. Hold back no more."

So he launched Athena already poised for action—
down the goddess swept from Olympus' craggy peaks.

And swift Achilles kept on coursing Hector, nonstop
225 as a hound in the mountains starts a fawn from its lair,
hunting him down the gorges, down the narrow glens
and the fawn goes to ground,° hiding deep in brush
but the hound comes racing fast, nosing him out
until he lands his kill. So Hector could never throw
230 Achilles off his trail, the swift racer Achilles—
time and again he'd make a dash for the Dardan Gates,
trying to rush beneath the rock-built ramparts, hoping
men on the heights might save him, somehow, raining spears
but time and again Achilles would intercept him quickly,
235 heading him off, forcing him out across the plain
and always sprinting along the city side himself—
endless as in a dream . . .
when a man can't catch another fleeing on ahead
and he can never escape nor his rival overtake him—
240 so the one could never run the other down in his speed
nor the other spring away. And how could Hector have fled
the fates of death so long? How unless one last time,
one final time Apollo had swept in close beside him,
driving strength in his legs and knees to race the wind?

---

214 his doom sealed long ago:
his fate: all humans are mortal and
doomed to die from birth.

227 goes to ground: tries to avoid
notice by remaining motionless.

---

2 Analyze Cultural Context *What apparent contradiction regarding the ancient
Greeks' attitude toward fate is illustrated in Athena's remarks?*

3 Epic Simile *How does this simile echo the one in lines 165–167?*

Teach

Reading Strategy   2

Analyze Cultural
Context **Answer:** *Athena,
who is allied with the Greeks,
reminds Zeus that fate has
decreed Hector must die. The
ancient Greeks believed fate
controlled the destiny of humans
but that the gods could intervene
to try to save the life of a doomed
mortal.*

(ADVANCED) Ask advanced learners
to research the role of the Three
Fates (the Moirai) in Greek
mythology and report on their
findings to the class.

Literary Element   3

Epic Simile **Answer:** *By
comparing Achilles to a hound
and Hector to a fawn, Homer
reinforces their roles as predator
and victim depicted in the simile of
the hawk and the dove.*

Learning Objectives
Analyzing epic simile. (SE)
Analyzing cultural context. (SE)
Analyzing epithet. (TE)
Using descriptive language. (TE)

Approaching Level

DIFFERENTIATED INSTRUCTION

Make and Verify Predictions
Less-proficient readers can benefit from
predicting what will happen next. This
forces them to focus their attention on the
motivation and actions of the characters.
Explain that to make informed predictions,
they must do the following:

▪ First, review what they know about the
characters and the plot.
▪ Next, examine the action up to a given
point.
▪ Finally, make an educated guess about
what will happen next.

Have students work in small groups to
review the action in this selection up to
page 216. What do they think will happen
next? Have groups share their predictions
and explain their reasoning. Remind
students that they may have to revise their
predictions as they continue to read.

Teach

Literary Element | 1

Repetition Point out the repeated initial consonant sounds in the phrases "great glory" and "distant deadly." Remind students that repetition of initial consonant sounds, or alliteration, is an effective literary device that can call attention to particular ideas. Have students look for other examples of repetition (of sounds, words, or phrases) in the selection.

Reading Strategy | 2

Analyze Cultural Context **Answer:** *Zeus holds up the scales of judgment, placing Achilles' fate in one scale and Hector's in the other. This passage suggests the gods, regardless of their preferences, abide by the decrees of fate.*

Big Idea | 3

The Heroic Ideal **Answer:** *Athena wants to make sure Hector faces Achilles so Achilles has the opportunity to kill him, thus winning glory and avenging Patroclus.*

245 And brilliant Achilles shook his head at the armies,
never letting them hurl their sharp spears at Hector—
someone might snatch the glory, Achilles come in second.
But once they reached the springs for the fourth time,
then Father Zeus held out his sacred golden scales:
250 in them he placed two fates of death that lays men low—
one for Achilles, one for Hector breaker of horses—
and gripping the beam mid-haft° the Father raised it high
and down went Hector's day of doom, dragging him down
to the strong House of Death—and god Apollo left him.°
255 Athena rushed to Achilles, her bright eyes gleaming,
standing shoulder-to-shoulder, winging orders now:
"At last our hopes run high, my brilliant Achilles—
Father Zeus must love you—
we'll sweep great glory back to Achaea's fleet,
260 we'll kill this Hector, mad as he is for battle!
No way for him to escape us now, no longer—
not even if Phoebus the distant deadly Archer
goes through torments, pleading for Hector's life,
groveling over and over before our storming Father Zeus.
265 But you, you hold your ground and catch your breath
while I run Hector down and persuade the man
to fight you face-to-face."
       So Athena commanded
and he obeyed, rejoicing at heart—Achilles stopped,
leaning against his ashen spearshaft barbed in bronze.
270 And Athena left him there, caught up with Hector at once,
and taking the build and vibrant voice of Deiphobus
stood shoulder-to-shoulder with him, winging orders:
"Dear brother, how brutally swift Achilles hunts you—
coursing you round the city of Priam in all his lethal speed!
275 Come, let us stand our ground together—beat him back."

 "Deiphobus!"—Hector, his helmet flashing, called
   out to her—
"dearest of all my brothers, all these warring years,
of all the sons that Priam and Hecuba produced!
Now I'm determined to praise you all the more,

249–254 Zeus held out . . . Apollo left him: Fate determined that Hector would lose this battle. Apollo, realizing that further help was futile, returned to Olympus.

252 gripping the beam mid-haft: holding the scales impartially so as not to favor one side or the other.

---

2 Analyze Cultural Context *What does this passage suggest about the gods and fate?*

3 The Heroic Ideal *Why doesn't Athena kill Hector herself, thus sparing Achilles the effort?*

218 UNIT 2 ANCIENT GREECE

Grammar Practice

Use Dashes Review with students these functions of dashes:

- To introduce or set off a word or group of words you want to emphasize
- To indicate a sudden break or shift in thought
- To indicate an unfinished statement or word
- To indicate the omission of letters and words

Have students identify the reason for the dashes in these lines from the selection:

1. "'Do as you please—but none of the deathless gods will ever praise you.'" (*a group of words to emphasize*)
2. "So he launched Athena already poised for action—down the goddess swept from Olympus' craggy peaks." (*sudden shift in thought*)

Have students find additional examples of the use of dashes and identify the reason the author uses them in each case.

218

280   you who dared—seeing me in these straits—
      to venture out from the walls, all for *my* sake,
      while the others stay inside and cling to safety."

         The goddess answered quickly, her eyes blazing,
      "True, dear brother—how your father and mother both
285   implored me, time and again, clutching my knees,
      and the comrades round me begging me to stay!
      Such was the fear that broke them, man for man,
      but the heart within me broke with grief for you.
      Now headlong on and fight! No letup, no lance spared!
290   So now, now we'll *see* if Achilles kills us both
      and hauls our bloody armor back to the beaked ships
      or *he* goes down in pain beneath your spear."

         Athena luring him on with all her immortal cunning—
      and now, at last, as the two came closing for the kill
295   it was tall Hector, helmet flashing, who led off:
      "No more running from you in fear, Achilles!
      Not as before. Three times I fled around
      the great city of Priam—I lacked courage then
      to stand your onslaught. Now my spirit stirs me
300   to meet you face-to-face. Now kill or be killed!
      Come, we'll swear to the gods, the highest witnesses—
      the gods will oversee our binding pacts. I swear
      I will never mutilate you—merciless as you are—
      if Zeus allows me to last it out and tear your life away.
305   But once I've stripped your glorious armor, Achilles,
      I will give your body back to your loyal comrades.
      Swear you'll do the same."
                                 A swift dark glance
      and the headstrong runner answered, "Hector,
         stop!
      You unforgivable, you . . . don't talk to me of
         pacts.
310   There are no binding oaths between men and
         lions—
      wolves and lambs can enjoy no meeting of the
         minds—
      they are all bent on hating each other to the death.

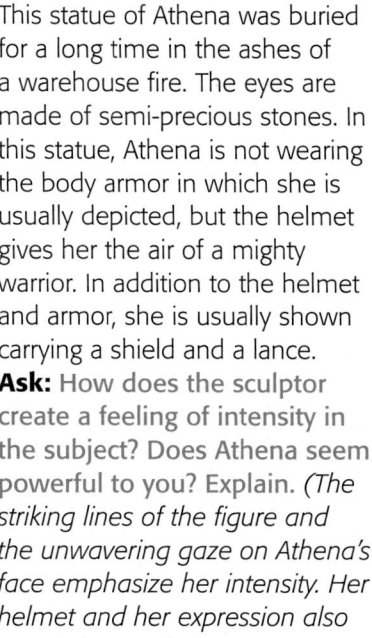

 Statue of Athena. Ancient Greece The National Museum, Athens.

Advanced Learners/Pre-AP

DIFFERENTIATED INSTRUCTION

Reading Further Advanced learners can benefit from a more thorough understanding of the work. They will attain a more comprehensive view of the literature, as well as a better understanding of the characters, by reading more of the epic on their own. Challenge them to read Books II–XXI, the books of the *Iliad* that fall between this selection and the previous one. They may also wish to finish the entire epic by reading Books XXIII and XXIV. Then have them share their insights with the rest of the class in oral reports.

Teach

View the Art ★

This statue of Athena was buried for a long time in the ashes of a warehouse fire. The eyes are made of semi-precious stones. In this statue, Athena is not wearing the body armor in which she is usually depicted, but the helmet gives her the air of a mighty warrior. In addition to the helmet and armor, she is usually shown carrying a shield and a lance.
Ask: How does the sculptor create a feeling of intensity in the subject? Does Athena seem powerful to you? Explain. *(The striking lines of the figure and the unwavering gaze on Athena's face emphasize her intensity. Her helmet and her expression also suggest power.)*

Learning Objectives
Analyzing cultural context. (SE)
Using dashes. (TE)
Recognizing repetition. (TE)
Analyzing art. (TE)

Teach

The Heroic Ideal Answer:
Achilles is loyal to Athena. To defeat Hector, Achilles still must display superior fighting skills, so his glory is not diminished even though he receives divine help.

View the Art ★

Answer: *Rubens portrays the fallen Hector striving to defend himself as Achilles prepares to drive his spear through his opponent's throat.*

This painting by Peter Paul Rubens shows the vivid and voluptuous dimensions for which Rubens is famous. Many consider his powerful style the epitome of Baroque art of the 1600s. **Ask:** Who is hovering overhead in this painting? What role does she seem to be playing? Explain. *(Students may note that the being floating overhead is Athena, based on her involvement in the battle between Hector and Achilles in the text. They may say that she is overseeing the fighting or helping Achilles.)*

Achilles defeating Hector. Peter Paul Rubens. Oil on wood, 1.08 x 1.27 m. Musee des Beaux-Arts, Pau, France.

View the Art Recognized as one of the greatest of painters, Peter Paul Rubens fused the realism of Flemish painting with the classical themes of the Italian Renaissance. His baroque style emphasized color, movement, and energy. How does Rubens make his painting of the killing of Hector a dynamic scene? ★

So with you and me. No love between us. No truce
till one or the other falls and gluts with blood
315 Ares° who hacks at men behind his rawhide shield.
Come, call up whatever courage you can muster.
Life or death—now prove yourself a spearman,
a daring man of war! No more escape for you—
Athena will kill you with my spear in just a moment.
320 Now you'll pay at a stroke for all my comrades' grief,
all you killed in the fury of your spear!"
                                        With that,
shaft poised, he hurled and his spear's long shadow flew
but seeing it coming glorious Hector ducked away,
crouching down, watching the bronze tip fly past
325 and stab the earth—but Athena snatched it up
and passed it back to Achilles
and Hector the gallant captain never saw her.°

314–315 gluts with blood Ares: spills so much blood that even Ares, the god of war, becomes nauseated.

325–327 Athena . . . never saw her: The deities can hide their presence and their movements from certain people.

1 **The Heroic Ideal** *Why does Achilles accept Athena's help? In your opinion, does Athena's help diminish Achilles' glory? Explain.*

Reading Practice

Compare and Contrast Characters
Draw students' attention to the exchange between Hector and Achilles in lines 301–321. **Ask:** What does this exchange reveal about each man's values? How do their attitudes compare regarding the relationship between enemies? Which one has a more civilized attitude regarding the treatment of an enemy's body? *(Possible answers: Hector values loyalty and honor in battle, whereas Achilles will hate to the end. Achilles is less civilized in battle and holds no regard for an enemy, alive or dead.)* To organize their thoughts, students can use a Venn diagram. In the outer sections, they can write what is unique about each warrior. In the intersecting area, they can write what they have in common.

He sounded out a challenge to Peleus' princely son:
"You missed, look—the great godlike Achilles!

330　So you knew nothing at all from Zeus about my death—
and yet how sure you were! All bluff,° cunning° with words,
that's all you are—trying to make me fear you,
lose my nerve, forget my fighting strength.
Well, you'll never plant your lance in my back

335　as I flee *you* in fear—plunge it through my chest
as I come charging in, if a god gives you the chance!
But now it's for you to dodge *my* brazen spear—
I wish you'd bury it in your body to the hilt.
How much lighter the war would be for Trojans then

340　if you, their greatest scourge, were dead and gone!"

　　　Shaft poised,° he hurled and his spear's long shadow flew
and it struck Achilles' shield—a dead-center hit—
but off and away it glanced and Hector seethed,
his hurtling spear, his whole arm's power poured

345　in a wasted shot. He stood there, cast down . . .
he had no spear in reserve. So Hector shouted out
to Deiphobus bearing his white shield—with a ringing shout
he called for a heavy lance—
　　　　　　　　but the man was nowhere near him,
vanished—°
　　　　yes and Hector knew the truth in his heart

350　and the fighter cried aloud, "My time has come!
At last the gods have called me down to death.
I thought he was at my side, the hero Deiphobus—
he's safe inside the walls, Athena's tricked me blind.
And now death, grim death is looming up beside me,

355　no longer far away. No way to escape it now. This,
this was their pleasure after all, sealed long ago—
Zeus and the son of Zeus, the distant deadly Archer—
though often before now they rushed to my defense.
So now I meet my doom. Well let me die—

360　but not without struggle, not without glory, no,
in some great clash of arms that even men to come
will hear of down the years!"
　　　　　　　And on that resolve

330–331 you knew nothing . . . All bluff: You were lying when you said the gods were on your side.

331 cunning: here, wily; tricky.

341 Shaft poised: the long handle of the spear held in the proper position for throwing it.

348 the man . . . vanished: Athena had cast off her disguise as his brother and deserted him.

---

2 Analyze Cultural Context　*Why is Hector certain his time has come?*

3 The Heroic Ideal　*In what sense has Hector returned to where he began as a heroic figure?*

Reading Strategy　2

Analyze Cultural Context
Answer: *Hector concludes the gods have doomed him to die upon suddenly realizing Athena has tricked him by posing as his brother Deiphobus.*

Big Idea　3

The Heroic Ideal　Answer:
At the beginning of the episode, Hector stands his ground alone, determined to face Achilles courageously. But when Achilles approaches, Hector panics and flees from Achilles. Now Hector boldly acknowledges he will die, but not without glory. He accepts his forthcoming death bravely, refusing to give up without a fight.

Learning Objectives
Analyzing cultural context. (SE)
Analyzing art. (SE)
Comparing and contrasting characters. (TE)

English Learners

DIFFERENTIATED INSTRUCTION

Advanced Write the word *determined* on the board. **Say:** There are many words in English that are similar in Spanish and in other languages. These are called cognates. Sometimes you can use your knowledge of Spanish and other languages to figure out what words mean. **Ask:** Do you know a word in Spanish that looks or sounds like *determined*? (*determinado*) Ask

a student to write the word in Spanish on the board next to the English word. **Say:** What does that mean? Notice how similar the two words are. If you know a word in a different language that looks similar to an English word, it might mean the same thing. Repeat this activity for the following words: *venture (aventurarse), implore (implorar), comrades (comaradas, compañeros,*

compadres), spirit (espíritu), and *pacts (pactos).* Students might be able to find other examples on these pages.

221

Cultural History ☆

The Evening Star Also known as Hesperus, the evening star is actually the planet Venus. In Greco-Roman mythology, he is the son or brother of Atlas and is also identified with the morning star, Phosphorus, the bringer of light. Hesperus is also referred to in the poetry of Sappho included in this unit.

---

he drew the whetted° sword that hung at his side,
tempered,° massive, and gathering all his force
365   he swooped like a soaring eagle
launching down from the dark clouds to earth
to snatch some helpless lamb or trembling hare.

1 So Hector swooped now, swinging his whetted sword
and Achilles charged too, bursting with rage, **barbaric**,°
370   guarding his chest with the well-wrought blazoned° shield,
head tossing his gleaming helmet, four horns strong
and the golden plumes shook that the god of fire°
drove in bristling thick along its ridge.
Bright as that star amid the stars in the night sky,
375   star of the evening, brightest star that rides the heavens, ☆
so fire flared from the sharp point of the spear Achilles
brandished high in his right hand, bent on Hector's death,
scanning his splendid body—where to pierce it best?
The rest of his flesh seemed all encased in armor,
380   burnished, brazen—*Achilles' armor that Hector stripped
from strong Patroclus when he killed him—true,
but one spot lay exposed,
where collarbones lift the neckbone off the shoulders,°
the open throat, where the end of life comes quickest—*there
385   as Hector charged in fury brilliant Achilles drove his spear
and the point went stabbing clean through the tender neck
but the heavy bronze weapon failed to slash the windpipe—
Hector could still gasp out some words, some last reply . . .
he crashed in the dust—

                    godlike Achilles gloried over him:
390   "Hector—surely you thought when you stripped Patroclus' armor
that you, you would be safe! Never a fear of me—
far from the fighting as I was—you fool!
Left behind there, down by the beaked ships
his great avenger waited, a greater man by far—
395   that man was I, and I smashed your strength! And you—
the dogs and birds will maul you, shame your corpse
while Achaeans bury my dear friend in glory!"

   Struggling for breath, Hector, his helmet flashing,

---

363 **whetted:** sharpened.
364 **tempered:** hardened by reheating and cooling in oil; strengthened.

369 **barbaric:** This word choice is ironic because barbaric originally meant anyone not belonging to one's cultural group, which to a Greek would be a non-Greek.
370 **well-wrought:** fashioned with great effort and artistry. **blazoned:** in this use, adorned with ornate symbolic inscriptions and artwork.

372 **god of fire:** Hephaestus (hi fes′təs), son of Zeus, god of fire and metalworking (blacksmithing). At Thetis's request, he had made armor for Achilles.

378–383 **scanning . . . off the shoulders:** Since the armor had once been his own, Achilles knew where to look for its one vulnerable spot.

---

2 Epic Simile *What does this simile convey about Hector's attack?*

Vocabulary

barbaric (bär bar′ik) *adj.* crude; wild in taste, style, or manner

Writing Practice

Write a Research Report In today's world, personal battles such as the one described in the *Iliad* rarely occur. However, many conflicts do arise between nations. Often each side must compromise to reach an agreement. Have students research two countries or groups with a long history of conflict. Possibilities include Protestants and Catholics in Northern Ireland, Israelis and Palestinians, and Croatians and Serbians. Students should investigate how nations resolved conflicts in the past and how they deal with them today. Have students present their findings in a written report.

said, "I beg you, beg you by your life, your parents—
400 don't let the dogs devour me by the Argive ships!
Wait, take the princely ransom of bronze and gold,
the gifts my father and noble mother will give you—
but give my body to friends to carry home again,
so Trojan men and Trojan women can do me honor
405 with fitting rites of fire° once I am dead."

Staring grimly, the proud runner Achilles answered,
"Beg no more, you fawning dog—begging me by my parents!
Would to god my rage, my fury would drive me now
to hack your flesh away and eat you raw—
410 such agonies you have caused me! Ransom?
No man alive could keep the dog-packs off you,
not if they haul in ten, twenty times that ransom
and pile it here before me and promise fortunes more—
no, not even if Dardan Priam should offer to weigh out
415 your bulk in gold! Not even then will your noble mother
lay you on your deathbed, mourn the son she bore . . .
The dogs and birds will rend you—blood and bone!"

At the point of death, Hector, his helmet flashing, **3**
said, "I know you well—I see my fate before me.
420 Never a chance that I could win you over . . .
Iron inside your chest, that heart of yours.
But now beware, or my curse will draw god's wrath
upon your head, that day when Paris and lord Apollo—
for all your fighting heart—destroy you at the
Scaean Gates!"°

425 Death cut him short. The end closed in around him.
Flying free of his limbs
his soul went winging down to the House of Death, ☆
wailing his fate, leaving his manhood far behind,
his young and supple strength. But brilliant Achilles
430 taunted Hector's body, dead as he was, "Die, die!
For my own death, I'll meet it freely—whenever Zeus
and the other deathless gods would like to bring it on!"

With that he wrenched his bronze spear from the corpse,
laid it aside and ripped the bloody armor off the back.
435 And the other sons of Achaea, running up around him,

405 **fitting rites of fire:** proper religious funeral services that included cremation of the body.

422–424 **beware . . . Scaean Gates:** Hector predicts the place and circumstances of Achilles' own death.

---

4 Analyze Cultural Context *According to Hector, what factors will bring about Achilles' death?*

HOMER **223**

English Learners

DIFFERENTIATED INSTRUCTION

Intermediate Have students read lines 374–378. **Ask:** What strategies can you use to figure out what *brandished* means? *(Answers: reread, ask themselves what they know about the unfamiliar word, activate prior knowledge, read ahead, use context clues)* Have students discuss with a partner what they think the word means and why. Ask volunteers to share their responses. Then reiterate to students the different strategies they can use to determine the meanings of unfamiliar words.

Teach

Vocabulary 3

Word Origins The English word *fate* originally comes from the Latin word *fari*, meaning "to speak." In ancient Rome the word *fatum*, which evolved from *fari*, meant that the gods or an oracle had spoken. *Fate* has come to mean "destiny."

(**ENGLISH LEARNERS**) Ask English learners if the culture they come from has a word for *fate*. Have them share the attitude of their culture toward the concept of fate.

Reading Strategy 4

Analyze Cultural Context
Answer: *Hector identifies his own curse, the Trojan hero Paris, and the god Apollo as factors that will contribute to Achilles' death.*

Cultural History ☆

The House of Death The ancient Greeks believed that a person's soul went to the House of Death, or the Underworld, which was ruled by Hades and Persephone. Sometimes the Underworld is presented as divided into Tartarus, the more remote section, and Erberus, the place souls pass through immediately after death.

Learning Objectives
Analyzing epic simile. (SE)
Analyzing cultural context. (SE)
Responding to literature. (TE)
Writing a research report. (TE)
Identifying word origins. (TE)

Teach

The Heroic Ideal Answer:
Achilles acknowledges Hector has caused the Greeks more agony than all the other Trojan warriors, and wonders whether the loss of their greatest warrior will demoralize the Trojans.

crowded closer, all of them gazing wonder-struck
at the build and marvelous, lithe beauty of Hector.
And not a man came forward who did not stab
    his body,
glancing toward a comrade, laughing: "Ah, look
    here—
440   how much softer he is to handle now, this
    Hector,
than when he gutted our ships with roaring fire!"

            Standing over him, so they'd **gloat** and
                            stab his body.
But once he had stripped the corpse the proud
    runner Achilles
took his stand in the midst of all the Argive troops
445   and urged them on with a flight of winging orders:
"Friends—lords of the Argives, O my captains!
Now that the gods have let me kill this man
who caused us agonies, loss on crushing loss—
more than the rest of all their men combined—
450   come, let us ring their walls in armor, test them,
see what recourse the Trojans still may have in mind.
Will they abandon the city heights with this man fallen?
Or brace for a last, dying stand though Hector's gone?
But wait—what am I saying? Why this deep debate?
455   Down by the ships a body lies unwept, unburied—
Patroclus . . . I will never forget him,
not as long as I'm still among the living
and my springing knees will lift and drive me on.
Though the dead forget° their dead in the House of Death,
460   I will remember, even there, my dear companion.
                                    Now,
come, you sons of Achaea, raise a song of triumph!
Down to the ships we march and bear this corpse on high—
we have won ourselves great glory. We have brought
magnificent Hector down, that man the Trojans
465   glorified in their city like a god!"

                        So he triumphed
and now he was bent on outrage, on shaming noble Hector.

Achilles dragging the body of Hector, c. 520–510 BC. attributed to The Anitope Group, Ancient Greece. Black-figure vase, height: 56 cm, diameter: 33 cm. Museum of Fine Arts, Boston. ★

459 the dead forget: a mental state oblivious to emotions, such as love or sorrow, was a characteristic of the dead in Greek mythology.

---

1 **The Heroic Ideal** *What compliment does Achilles pay Hector in lines 447–453?*

Vocabulary
gloat (glōt) *v.* to regard with malignant satisfaction

Reading Practice

 SMALL GROUP **Analyze Cause-and-Effect Relationships** Explain to students that events usually result from one or more causes. **Say:** Cause-and-effect relationships can occur in three ways: as a sequence of events, with one event causing many effects, or with several events causing one effect. To demonstrate the sequential chain, write the following analysis of Book 1 on the board:

| Agamemnon takes Chryseis as a war prize. | → | A plague is inflicted on the Greeks. | → | Agamemnon gives Chryseis back but takes Bryseis from Achilles. | → | Achilles vows not to fight for the Greeks. | → | The Trojans advance on the Greeks and are winning the war. |

Have students work in groups to analyze the cause-and-effect relationships in Book 22 of the *Iliad*, presenting a chart like the one for Book 1. Tell students to include only major causes and effects.

Piercing the tendons,° ankle to heel behind both feet,
he knotted straps of rawhide through them both,
lashed them to his chariot, left the head to drag
470 and mounting the car, hoisting the famous arms aboard,
he whipped his team to a run and breakneck on they flew,
holding nothing back. And a thick cloud of dust rose up
from the man they dragged, his dark hair swirling round
that head so handsome once, all tumbled low in the dust—
475 since Zeus had given him over to his enemies now
to be defiled in the land of his own fathers.

So his whole head was dragged down in the dust.
And now his mother began to tear her hair . . .
she flung her shining veil to the ground and raised
480 a high, shattering scream, looking down at her son.
Pitifully his loving father groaned and round the king
his people cried with grief and wailing seized the city—
for all the world as if all Troy were torched and smoldering
down from the looming brows of the citadel to her roots.
485 Priam's people could hardly hold the old man back,
frantic, mad to go rushing out the Dardan Gates.
He begged them all, groveling in the filth,
crying out to them, calling each man by name,
"Let go, my friends! Much as you care for me,
490 let me hurry out of the city, make my way,
all on my own, to Achaea's waiting ships!
I must implore that terrible, violent man . . .
Perhaps—who knows?—he may respect my age,
may pity an old man. He has a father too,
495 as old as I am—Peleus sired him once,
Peleus reared him to be the scourge of Troy
but most of all to me—he made my life a hell.
So many sons he slaughtered, just coming into bloom . . .
but grieving for all the rest, one breaks my heart the most
500 and stabbing grief for him will take me down to Death—
my Hector—would to god he had perished in my arms!
Then his mother who bore him—oh so doomed,
she and I could glut ourselves with grief."

So the voice of the king rang out in tears,
505 the citizens wailed in answer, and noble Hecuba
led the wives of Troy in a throbbing chant of sorrow:

---

3 Analyze Cultural Context *What do these lines suggest about Zeus and the gods?*

467 **Piercing the tendons:** ironic, because a wound in the tendon of the heel, his only vulnerable spot, will kill Achilles.

2

Teach

Reading Strategy 2

Evaluate Style Have students evaluate the description of the grief of the Trojans in this passage. **Ask:** Do you think the description is effective? Why or why not? *(Many students will say the description is effective because Homer uses vivid language and sensory imagery, as well as dialogue, to portray the Trojans' grief.)*

Reading Strategy 3

Analyze Cultural Context
Answer: *Zeus and the gods seem indifferent to flagrant cruelty by permitting Achilles to desecrate Hector's body.*

Learning Objectives
Analyzing cultural context. (SE)
Analyzing cause-and-effect relationships. (TE)
Evaluating style. (TE)

English Learners

DIFFERENTIATED INSTRUCTION

Intermediate Some students may find the idiomatic references in this selection difficult to understand. Explain that many of the expressions are not used in everyday speech but can be analyzed to reveal their meanings. Write the following phrase on the board: "in the land of his own fathers." **Say:** This phrase means "in his native country," because his father and father's father were born in this land.

Have English learners work with proficient English speakers to interpret such phrases as "wailing . . . for all the world to see," "from the looming brows of the citadel to her roots," "coming into bloom," and "breaks my heart."

Teach

Multiple-Meaning Words

The word *loom* can refer to a machine for weaving, as it is used here. However, *loom* can also mean "to take shape as an impending occurrence." **Ask:** How does this second meaning apply to the selection? (*The news of Hector's death loomed before his wife.*)

Reading Strategy   2

Analyze Cultural Context

Answer: *It suggests the ancient Greek heroes accomplished their deeds with divine help or divine consent.*

V̲i̲e̲w̲ ̲t̲h̲e̲ ̲A̲r̲t̲ ★

Answer: *The painting shows Hector's corpse being dragged away by Achilles' horse, rather than by a chariot. Di Antonio may have chosen to use more modern European styles to help his viewers relate to the devastation of the incident.*

With the perfection of the printing press in the middle of the fifteenth century, many Italian artists were able to read the literature of ancient Greece and Rome. Their familiarity with these works led artists to illustrate works of Greek and Roman mythology.

The Siege of Troy: The Death of Hector, c. 1490. Biagio di Antonio. Oil on panel, 47 x 161 cm. Fitzwilliam Museum, University of Cambridge, UK.

V̲i̲e̲w̲ ̲t̲h̲e̲ ̲A̲r̲t̲ Although this narrative painting represents the siege of Troy, the warriors wear Renaissance armor and the buildings reflect medieval and Renaissance architecture. What incident related to Hector's death is represented here? Why might di Antonio have chosen to portray this incident as he did? ★

> "O my child—my desolation! How can I go on living?
> What agonies must I suffer now, now *you* are dead and gone?
> You were my pride throughout the city night and day—
> 510 a blessing to us all, the men and women of Troy:
> throughout the city they saluted you like a god.
> You, you were their greatest glory while you lived—
> now death and fate have seized you, dragged you down!"
>
> Her voice rang out in tears, but the wife of Hector
> 515 had not heard a thing. No messenger brought the truth
> of how her husband made his stand outside the gates.
> **1** She was weaving at her loom, deep in the high halls,
> working flowered braiding into a dark red folding robe.
> And she called her well-kempt women through the house
> 520 to set a large three-legged cauldron over the fire
> so Hector could have his steaming hot bath
> when he came home from battle—poor woman,
> she never dreamed how far he was from bathing,
> struck down at Achilles' hands by blazing-eyed Athena.
> 525 But she heard the groans and wails of grief from the
>   rampart now
> and her body shook, her shuttle° dropped to the ground,
> she called out to her lovely waiting women, "Quickly—
> two of you follow me—I must see what's happened.
> That cry—that was Hector's honored mother I heard!
> 530 My heart's pounding, leaping up in my throat,

526 **shuttle:** a device used in weaving for passing thread through the loom.

2 Analyze Cultural Context *What does this line suggest about how the ancient Greeks viewed the relationship between gods and humans?*

Grammar Practice

Use Appositives and Appositive Phrases Remind students that an appositive is a noun, a noun phrase, or a pronoun that is placed next to another noun or pronoun to identify or give additional information. An appositive phrase is an appositive plus any words that modify the appositive.

Write the following examples on the board: "Hector's wife, <u>Andromache</u>, was weaving at her loom." "Andromache heard the cry of Hecuba, <u>the mother of Hector</u>, and she guessed the truth." Have students identify the words that are modified by the appositives. (*wife, Hecuba*).

Ask students to identify five appositives from the story. To prevent their mistaking a clause for an appositive, remind them that appositives do not contain verbs. Review students' answers for accuracy.

the knees beneath me paralyzed—Oh I know it . . .
something terrible's coming down on Priam's children.
Pray god the news will never reach my ears!
Yes but I dread it so—what if great Achilles
535 has cut my Hector off from the city, daring Hector,
and driven him out across the plain, and all alone?—
He may have put an end to that fatal headstrong pride
that always seized my Hector—never hanging back
with the main force of men, always charging ahead,
540 giving ground to no man in his fury!"
                                            So she cried,
dashing out of the royal halls like a madwoman,
her heart racing hard, her women close behind her.
But once she reached the tower where soldiers massed
she stopped on the rampart, looked down and saw it all—
545 saw him dragged before the city, stallions galloping,
dragging Hector back to Achaea's beaked warships—
ruthless work. The world went black as night
before her eyes, she fainted, falling backward, **3**
gasping away her life breath . . .
550 She flung to the winds her glittering headdress,
the cap and the coronet,° braided band and veil,
all the regalia° golden Aphrodite gave her once,
the day that Hector, helmet aflash in sunlight,
led her home to Troy from her father's house
555 with countless wedding gifts to win her heart.
But crowding round her now her husband's sisters
and brothers' wives supported her in their midst,
and she, terrified, stunned to the point of death,
struggling for breath now and coming back to life,
560 burst out in grief among the Trojan women: "O Hector—
I am destroyed! Both born to the same fate after all!
You, you at Troy in the halls of King Priam—
I at Thebes, under the timberline of Placos,°
Eetion's° house . . . He raised me as a child,
565 that man of doom, his daughter just as doomed—
would to god he'd never fathered *me*!
                                        Now you go down
to the House of Death, the dark depths of the earth,
and leave me here to waste away in grief, a widow
lost in the royal halls—and the boy only a baby,
570 the son we bore together, you and I so doomed.

551 **coronet:** a small crown.
552 **regalia** (ri gā′ lē ə): emblems or symbols indicating royalty.

563 **Placos:** mountain which dominates the landscape near Thebes.
564 **Eetion:** Andromache's father, king of Thebes, killed by Achilles during the sacking of that city.

4 The Heroic Ideal *Based on what you know about Hector, is Andromache's assessment of her husband accurate? Explain.*

HOMER **227**

Teach

Reading Strategy **3**

Visualize Read the passage that begins here and ends at line 566. Have students close their eyes as you read and visualize the images described. Have students then discuss the descriptive language used to produce the image of Andromache in her grief. (*Possible answers: "falling backward, gasping away her life breath," "flung . . . her glittering headdress," "she, terrified, stunned to the point of death."*)

(APPROACHING) To help those learners who are approaching level visualize this scene, have a group of students act it out as you read the passage aloud.

Big Idea **4**

The Heroic Ideal Answer: *Andromache recognizes not only her husband's strengths, such as courage and daring, but also his flaws, such as pride and fury.*

Learning Objectives
Analyzing cultural context. (SE)
Analyzing art. (SE)
Identifying multiple-meaning words. (TE)
Using appositives and appositional phrases. (TE)
Visualizing. (TE)

English Learners

DIFFERENTIATED INSTRUCTION

Advanced Students learning English may have trouble distinguishing between homonyms and homophones. Direct their attention to line 509, "You were my pride throughout the city night and day." **Ask:** What does *pride* mean here? Help students use context clues to understand that Hector's mother is saying she was very proud of her son and that she delighted in his accomplishments. Then write *pride* and *pried* on the board. Help students distinguish between the meanings of *pride* (noun meaning "someone or something one is proud of"), *pride* (noun meaning "a group of lions"), and *pried* (verb meaning "raised, moved, or forced through leverage"). Have students write context sentences showing the correct use of *pride* (each meaning) and *pried*.

Teach

Reading Strategy | 1

Make Inferences **Ask:** Why do you think Andromache is convinced that the fate of her son will be horrible? *(Students may say that his father was disgraced, so he, too, will be disgraced.)*

Reading Strategy | 2

Analyze Cultural Context
Answer: *The passage suggests burial rites held a position of extreme importance in ancient Greek culture.*

> To check students' understanding of the selection, see Unit 2 Teaching Resources Book, p. 46.

View the Art ★

After long periods of exposure to the elements, bronze sculptures form a tinted crust or film called a patina. Modern sculptors can simulate the appealing effect of a patina by chemically treating the bronze. This contemporary sculpture by Carol Miller has a green patina.

Carol Miller has had more than sixty exhibits of her work since 1960. She is a lecturer and author.

Ask: How does the feeling conveyed by the figure's posture compare with your response to Andromache's emotions? *(The sculpture conveys a feeling of utter anguish, just as students might be saddened by Andromache's loss.)*

Hector, what help are you to him, now you are dead?—
what help is he to you? Think, even if he escapes
the wrenching horrors of war against the Argives,
pain and labor will plague him all his days to come.
575 Strangers will mark his lands off, stealing his estates.
The day that orphans a youngster cuts him off from friends.
And he hangs his head low, humiliated in every way . . .
his cheeks stained with tears, and pressed by hunger
the boy goes up to his father's old companions,
580 tugging at one man's cloak, another's tunic,
and some will pity him, true,
and one will give him a little cup to drink,
enough to wet his lips, not quench his thirst.
But then some bully with both his parents living
585 beats him from the banquet, fists and abuses flying:
'You, get out—you've got no father feasting with us here!'
And the boy, sobbing, trails home to his widowed mother . . .
Astyanax!
              And years ago, propped on his father's knee,
he would only eat the marrow, the richest cuts of lamb,
590 and when sleep came on him and he had quit his play,
cradled warm in his nurse's arms he'd drowse off,
snug in a soft bed, his heart brimmed with joy.
Now what suffering, now he's lost his father—
                                                    Astyanax!

The Lord of the City, so the Trojans called him,
595 because it was you, Hector, you and you alone
who shielded the gates and the long walls of Troy.
But now by the beaked ships, far from your parents,
glistening worms will wriggle through your flesh,
once the dogs have had their fill of your naked corpse—
600 though we have such stores of clothing laid up in the halls,
fine things, a joy to the eye, the work of women's hands.
Now, by god, I'll burn them all, blazing to the skies!
No use to you now, they'll never shroud your body—
but they will be your glory
605 burned by the Trojan men and women in your honor!"

Her voice rang out in tears and the women wailed in answer.

Andromache, 1980. Carol Miller. Bronze with dark green patina, Height: 49.5 cm. Private collection. ★

2 Analyze Cultural Context *What does this passage suggest about the ancient Greeks' beliefs about death?*

228 UNIT 2 ANCIENT GREECE

Reading Practice

Analyze Imagery Remind students that imagery is sensory language that creates word pictures in the reader's mind and helps evoke an emotional response. Imagery appeals to one or more of the five senses. Have students reread Andromache's words in lines 588–593 and in lines 597–606 and then contrast the emotional effects of the imagery in these two sections.

After You Read

Respond and Think Critically

Respond and Interpret

1. What was your reaction to Hector's death? Share your reaction with your classmates.

2. (a)What happens when Achilles approaches Hector at the gates? (b)In your opinion, does Hector behave cowardly when Achilles approaches him for battle? Why or why not?

3. (a)How does Athena help Achilles in his attack on Hector? (b)What emotions does Hector display when he realizes the gods are acting against him?

4. (a)What request does Hector make after he is mortally wounded by Achilles? (b)Why does Achilles deny Hector's final request?

Analyze and Evaluate

5. Why are Priam and Hecuba important?

6. A **symbol** is an object or action that stands for something else in addition to itself. Reread lines 540–566. What object(s) or action is a symbol for Andromache's mourning of Hector?

Connect

7. **Big Idea** **The Heroic Ideal** What kinds of behavior exemplify the heroic ideal? Support your views with examples from this episode.

8. **Connect to Today** Think of a time when you mourned the death of a public figure. How would you compare your grief to that of the Trojans for Hector?

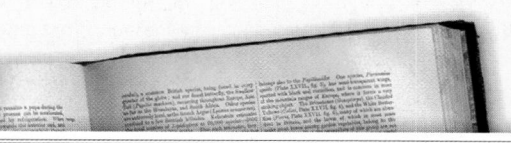

You're the Critic

Different Viewpoints

For the ancient Greeks, the warriors in Homer's poems provided models of heroic conduct. Achilles and Hector are two heroes with important similarities and marked differences. The following passages by literary critics explore one key difference.

"Unlike his great enemy Hector, the outsider Achilles is rootless. He has no family near him and no friends, except for one close friend. We see him leave the war, then rejoin the war, as the individualist hero par excellence. . . ."
—M. S. Silk, from *Homer: The Iliad*

"Unlike Achilles, [Hector] has always remained identified with the values and rituals of his society. Throughout the Iliad, Hector and the other Trojans provide a different perspective on heroism from the Greeks, as they fight around and for their own city, battling for the survival of their homes and families, rather than for the glory to be won in a foreign expedition."
—Sheila Murnaghan, from the Introduction to *Iliad*, translated by Stanley Lombardo

Group Activity Discuss the following questions with your classmates.

1. From the perspective of ancient Greek values, who is the greater hero? Explain.

2. From the perspective of contemporary American values, who is the greater hero?

You're the Critic

1. Students should support their answers with evidence from the poem, considering each hero's accomplishments and sense of honor.

2. Students may consider the importance of the victor and the underdog in contemporary American values.

After You Read

Assess

1. Opinions will vary.

2. (a) Hector loses his nerve and flees. (b) Hector appears to act cowardly because he runs from Achilles. However, common sense may have told him he was in danger of being killed (being alone and facing "godlike" Achilles), and may have prompted him to retreat to gain an advantage later.

3. (a) Athena assumes the form of Hector's brother, come to help, to persuade him to confront Achilles. (b) Students may say Hector shows disillusionment, resignation, bravery, and defiance.

4. (a) He begs Achilles to return his body to his family for proper burial. (b) Achilles still hates Hector for having killed his friend, Patroclus.

5. Before the battle, Hector's parents heighten suspense by imploring their son not to face Achilles' unleashed fury. After Hector is slain, their inconsolable grief confirms his stature as a hero.

6. Andromache throws off her wedding headdress and vows to burn the clothing stored in Troy because it cannot cover his corpse.

7. Possible answer: The heroic ideal includes pursuing excellence in all endeavors, assuming responsibility for protecting one's family and community, and displaying physical prowess and courage on the battlefield. Both Achilles and Hector display these qualities in Book XXII: Achilles is dedicated to his best friend, Patroclus; Hector faces the battle he is almost sure to lose.

8. Answers will vary. Students should mention the Trojans are distraught, because they fear the loss of Hector means Troy itself is doomed.

After You Read

Assess

Literary Element

1. Students may mention the epic similes in lines 31–37, 111–115, 194–199, or others.

2. Epic similes make an extended comparison and paint a more detailed picture than most other similes.

Progress Check

Can students identify epic similes?

If No → See Unit 2 Teaching Resources Book, p. 41.

Review: Epic Hero

1. Students may say Achilles and Hector reflect courage, honor, determination, and respect for the gods.

2. Students may say they admire Hector more because he is not half-divine.

3. Students may say political officials, sports stars, and movie stars attract similar attention.

Reading Strategy

(E) is the correct answer. In this passage, Andromache is saying her grief for her husband is aggravated by the realization his corpse will be ravaged by worms and dogs, rather than buried with honor.

Progress Check

Can students analyze cultural context?

If No → See Unit 2 Teaching Resources Book, p. 42.

230

Literary Element Epic Simile

An **epic simile** extends over several lines. For example, in lines 165–170, Homer develops a detailed comparison of Achilles to a "wild mountain hawk" and Hector to a "cringing dove":

> and Achilles went for him, fast, sure of his
>   speed
> as the wild mountain hawk, the quickest thing
>   on wings,
> launching smoothly, swooping down on a
>   cringing dove
> and the dove flits out from under, the hawk
>   screaming
> over the quarry, plunging over and over, his
>   fury
> driving him down to beak and tear his kill—

1. Find another example of an epic simile in this book of the epic. Identify the elements the simile compares.

2. How does your experience of reading an epic simile differ from that of reading a regular simile?

Review: Epic Hero

As you learned on page 193, **epic heroes** are larger-than-life figures who reflect the values of their cultures. In the *Iliad*, both Achilles and Hector function as epic heroes.

Partner Activity Working with a partner, review the events in this book of the epic. Then answer the following questions.

1. What values do Achilles and Hector reflect?

2. Do you admire Hector or Achilles more? Support your response with details from the text.

3. The Greeks and Trojans closely followed the exploits of their heroes. What figures in today's society attract similar attention from ordinary citizens?

LOG ON ▶ **Literature** Online

Selection Resources For Selection Quizzes, eFlashcards, and Reading-Writing Connection activities, go to glencoe.com and enter QuickPass code GLW6053u2.

Reading Strategy Analyze Cultural Context

SAT Skills Practice

Reread lines 598–599 ("glistening worms . . . corpse"). These lines suggest the Trojans

(A) believed the body could feel pain even after death

(B) did not draw a clear distinction between earthly life and the afterlife

(C) were indifferent to the decay of the body

(D) worshipped the earth and its natural cycles

(E) placed importance on the preparation and burial of bodies

Vocabulary Practice

Practice with Denotation and Connotation Denotation is the literal meaning of a word, while **connotation** is its implied meaning. For example, *aroma* has a positive connotation and *stench* has a negative connotation. Next to each vocabulary word below is a word with a similar denotation. Choose the word that has a more positive connotation.

1. bereft   without

2. glistening   shiny

3. gloat   rejoice

4. barbaric   unrefined

Academic Vocabulary

Hector asked Achilles to respect his body; **nevertheless**, *Achilles tied it to the chariot.*

Nevertheless is an academic word. More familiar words similar in meaning are *yet, still, but,* and *however.* To study this word further, complete the sentence below.

It rained on Saturday; **nevertheless**, my best friend and I were able to _____.

For more on academic vocabulary, see pages 36–37 and R83–R85.

Vocabulary

1. without
2. glistening
3. rejoice
4. unrefined

Academic Vocabulary

To complete the sentence, students should describe an activity the rain failed to prevent.

Respond Through Writing

Expository Essay

Analyze Cause and Effect At the climax of the *Iliad*, Achilles and Hector meet in battle to determine the fate of Troy. Why does this event happen? Write an essay in which you analyze the cause-and-effect relationships that lead up to this decisive battle.

Understand the Task Cause and effect describes the relationship between an action and its consequence. The **effect**, or consequence, is a direct result of the **cause**, or action.

Prewrite To help organize your essay, list cause-and-effect relationships in a chart like the one below. Add as many rows as you need. Remember that just because one event precedes another does not mean the first event is the cause of the other. To help assess the gods' role in the battle, review the chart you made on page 210. Finally, write a thesis sentence to state your idea about cause-and-effect relationships.

Cause	Effect
Hector slays Patroclus.	Achilles vows revenge.

Draft Using the cause-and-effect relationships listed in your chart, determine how each one supports your thesis. The following frame may help you write your body paragraphs.

Apollo says, "There's a war to fight with the Trojans you stampeded, / look, they're packed inside their city walls, but you, / you've slipped away out here." In saying this, Apollo causes _____ by inciting _____.

Revise Exchange papers with a partner and evaluate each other's essays. Does the writer support a thesis? Are cause-and-effect relationships clearly explained? Provide comments for your partner and revise your essay according to his or her comments.

Edit and Proofread Proofread your paper, correcting any errors in grammar, spelling, and punctuation. Use the Grammar Tip in the side column to help you with participles.

Learning Objectives

In this assignment, you will focus on the following objectives:

Writing: Writing an expository essay.

Grammar: Understanding participles.

> **Grammar Tip**

Participles

A **participle** is a verb form that can function as an adjective. Identify the participle in the following sentence.

Resolved, Hector stands his ground.

Resolved, a verb form that describes Hector, is a participle. Present participles always end in *-ing (losing)*. Past participles often end in *-ed (wounded)*.

Participles may be used in phrases with prepositions and objects, as in the example below.

Priam watched Achilles hurtling over the plain.

Hurtling over the plain is a **participial phrase** that describes Achilles.

After You Read

Assess

Respond Through Writing

Students' essays should

- clearly state the thesis and support it with relevant textual evidence
- establish clear connections between causes and effects
- apply appropriate strategies to evaluate and revise the draft

A student who meets all of these criteria should receive the equivalent of a 4-point response.

A student who fully meets two or partially meets three of these criteria should receive the equivalent of a 3-point response.

A student who fully meets one or partially meets two of these criteria should receive the equivalent of a 2-point response.

A student who partially meets one of these criteria should receive the equivalent of a 1-point response.

 For additional assessment, see Assessment Resources, pp. 69–70.

 For grammar practice, see Unit 2 Teaching Resource Book, p. 45.

 To create custom assessments online, go to Progress Reporter Online Assessment.

 To create custom assessments using software, use ExamView Assessment Suite.

Approaching Level

DIFFERENTIATED INSTRUCTION

Participles Remind approaching level students that a participle is a word that has the functions of both a verb and an adjective. Like a verb, it has tense (past or present), can take an object, and can be modified by an adverb. Like an adjective, it can modify a noun.

Have students review parts of "The Death of Hector" and find examples of participles and participial phrases. Have them

identify the noun that is modified by each example.

(Examples: **panicked** *in line 1 modifies* **fawns***;* **Enraged at that** *in line 17 modifies* **Achilles***;* **flinging both hands high** *in line 39 modifies* **man***.)*

Focus

Bellringer Options

Daily Language Practice Transparency 26

Or ask: What challenges do modern audiences face in reading ancient epics like those of Homer? Students may respond that the language and style of these epics may be difficult for modern readers or that the customs and beliefs of the characters may be unfamiliar. Point out that part of a translator's work is to render ancient works accessible to modern audiences.

Teach

Text Element   1

Bullet Points Have students read the four bulleted items.

Ask: Why are bullet points an effective organizational strategy here? *(Possible answer: Four distinct ideas are being presented one after another. The bullet points allow the reader to distinguish clearly between the four points.)*

APPROACHING Explain to less proficient readers that bullet points are used to mark each item in a list. Point out that bullet points give readers a way of visualizing the organization of a piece of writing.

For pages 232–233

In studying this text, you will focus on the following objectives:

Reading:

Understanding cultural and historical context.

Understanding the nature of translation.

Homer Through the Ages

HOMER IS ONE OF THE MOST WIDELY TRANSLATED AUTHORS IN HISTORY. Today the *Iliad* appears in many different languages and literary forms. Almost every generation has seen a new translation of the *Iliad* and the *Odyssey* in English since the first complete translation of both epics was made by George Chapman in 1611 and 1616, respectively.

The Challenges of Translating

Why do translators feel the need to create these new versions, and what purpose do they serve? Before trying to answer these questions, it is necessary to consider some of the difficulties that arise when attempting to translate a piece of literature.

1

- A word might have the same meaning (denotation) in another language, but not the same associations and feelings (connotation).
- Idiomatic expressions—such as "he's pulling your leg"—are unique to their original language, and their meanings have little to do with the literal meaning of the words.
- Sentence structure and grammar vary from one language to another.
- Every translator will have a different idea of the author's meaning and intentions.

These challenges, the changes the English language has undergone over time, and the change in writing styles and taste of a given period give a sense of the many possible reasons translators might interpret the ancient works of Homer for readers of their time.

Translating Homer

The British poet Matthew Arnold noted that a good Homeric translation must try to capture the key elements of Homer's work: fast-paced storytelling, plainness and directness of expression and idea, and a highly noble style. Throughout the ages, translators have emphasized each of these qualities to differing degrees based on their own interests and the interests of their audiences.

232 UNIT 2 ANCIENT GREECE

Achilles at the Court of King Lycomedes with his Daughters, 1746. Pompeo Girolamo Batoni. Oil on canvas. Galleria degli Uffizi, Florence.

Iliad, Book I, lines 1–5

LITERAL TRANSLATION

Sing, O Goddess (Muse), (the) destroying anger
of Achilles, son of Peleus, which placed
　　innumerable woes
to the Achaeans but (and) prematurely-sent many
　　brave
souls of heroes to Hades and made them prey
to dogs and all birds of prey.

Literary Element Practice

Meter Remind students that **meter** is a regular pattern of stressed (marked ′) and unstressed (marked ˘) syllables in poetry. Each repeating unit of meter in a line of syllables is called a **foot**. Demonstrate to students how to analyze a poem's metrical pattern by writing the line *Achilles' wrath, to Greece the direful spring* on the board. Then write the scansion ˘ ′ ˘ ′ ˘ ′ ˘ ′ ˘ ′

above the text. Point out that the line has five iambic feet (˘ ′). Have students work in groups to analyze the meter of the Chapman and Pope excerpts by following this model. Encourage them to read the excerpts out loud to help them determine which syllables are stressed and which are unstressed.

George Chapman's Translation, 1611

Achilles' baneful wrath resound, O Goddess, that
   imposed
Infinite sorrows on the Greeks, and many brave
   souls losed
From breasts heroic; sent them far to that invisible
   cave
That no light comforts; and their limbs to dogs and
   vultures gave.

Alexander Pope's Translation, 1720

Achilles' wrath, to Greece the direful spring
Of woes unnumber'd, heav'nly Goddess, sing!
That wrath which hurl'd to Pluto's gloomy reign
The souls of mighty chiefs untimely slain;
Whose limbs, unburied on the naked shore,
Devouring dogs and hungry vultures tore.

Richmond Lattimore's Translation, 1951

Sing goddess, the anger of Peleus'
   son Achilleus
and its devastation, which put pains
   thousandfold upon the Achaians
hurled in their multitudes to the
   house of Hades strong souls
of heroes, but gave their bodies to
   be the delicate feasting
of dogs, of all birds.

A word-for-word translation gives the reader a sense of Homer's directness—his use of just a few words to establish that the poem is about human weakness and tragedy. But the awkwardness of the literal version fails to capture Homer's spirit and powerful

Hector and Andromache, 1924. Giorgio de Chirico. Oil on canvas, 89.5 x 60.3 cm. Private collection © Foundation Giorgio de Chirico/Licensed by VAGA, New York.

images. George Chapman and Alexander Pope chose to render Homer's style in rhyming couplets, the most elevated poetic form of their times. However, both these versions seem somewhat stilted to modern readers, who favor straightforward translations that read as if the works were originally written in English. Modern translators such as Richmond Lattimore and Robert Fagles have replaced the long similes used by Homer with quick, direct phrases.

 Literature Online

Literature and Reading For more about the *Iliad* and the translators in this book, go to glencoe.com and enter QuickPass code GLW6053u2.

Respond and Think Critically

1. What do you consider the greatest challenge in translating Homer?

2. Robert Fagles translated the excerpts from the *Iliad* that you read earlier in this book. How would you compare his translation of the opening passage with the translations in this feature?

3. Choose a passage from Fagles's translation that you particularly admire. What examples of word choice and "quick, direct phrases" do you find particularly impressive, and why?

THE ART OF TRANSLATION **233**

English Learners

DIFFERENTIATED INSTRUCTION

Intermediate Students learning English may have a better appreciation of the art of translation because they have to translate their own thoughts. This appreciation can be shared with those students who speak only English. Have students work in groups that include English learners. Have English learners present an everyday phrase in their first language. Then have these students provide several translations, first a literal translation and then an English equivalent. Discuss the differences between the meanings and connotations of the translations.

Teach

Big Idea   2

The Heroic Ideal Have students read the four translations.
Ask: In your opinion, which translation most effectively conveys the image of heroic warriors? Remind students to provide specific reasons for their answers.

Assess

1. Students may identify challenges such as rendering Homer's meaning accurately and approximating the effect his verse made while using informal language.

2. By opening with the emphatic word *rage*, which he then repeats in the first line, Fagles creates a bolder and stronger effect.

3. Choice of passages and answers will vary.

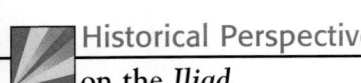

Historical Perspective

on the *Iliad*

Focus

Summary

In this excerpt, Caroline Alexander connects Homer's *Iliad* to archaeological research. She comments on German archaeologist Heinrich Schliemann's early excavations of the cities of Troy and Mycenae, relating artifacts from the digs to details in the epic. She then discusses the work of an international team of archaeologists under the direction of German Manfred Korfmann, who continued their work after Korfmann's death in 2005. His team's work accounts for the discovery of nine layers of Troy.

Teach

Cultural History ☆

The Spoils of Troy Beginning work in 1871, Heinrich Schliemann dug through a man-made mound in northwestern Turkey; he had hoped to reach its lowest level. Unable to do so, he discovered a treasure of gold jewels within fortifications and remains of the lost city of Troy. Believing he had found the spoils of King Priam, he smuggled the jewels out of Turkey. In February 1874, when he returned to his work, he faced a lawsuit from the Ottoman government concerning the division of the treasure.

Readability Scores

Dale-Chall: 8.7
DRP: 63
Lexile: 1380

Historical Perspective

on the *Iliad*

Learning Objectives

For pages 234–240

In studying this text, you will focus on the following objectives:

Reading:
Analyzing and evaluating informational text. Connecting to contemporary issues.

from
Echoes of the **Heroic Age**

Library Journal Best Books of the Year Winner   **Caroline Alexander**

Set a Purpose for Reading

Read to learn about possible connections between archaeological discoveries and the *Iliad*.

Build Background

Inspired by Homer's *Iliad*, Heinrich Schliemann in the late nineteenth century made one of the greatest finds in the history of archaeology: the sites of the ancient cities of Troy and Mycenae. In this excerpt from the magazine article "Echoes of the Heroic Age," Caroline Alexander discusses the relationship between the Trojan War and the excavations conducted by Heinrich Schliemann and Manfred Korfmann. Though Korfmann died in 2005, his team still continues his work at Troy.

Reading Strategy **Evaluate Evidence**

When you **evaluate evidence,** you judge the strength of the facts and details that support an argument. As you read, ask yourself, What are the claims, or main points, and the supporting evidence that the author provides? Use a two-column chart like the one below to list your findings.

Claims	Supporting Evidence

For Greeks of antiquity the *Iliad* related events from their own past; the Trojan War was taken as historical fact. Some believed they were descendants of Homer's heroes; Alexander the Great,[1] who slept with a copy of the *Iliad*, traced his maternal ancestry back to Achilles. But the reality is far more complex. The *Iliad* is not a "true story," nor does it offer a realistic picture of life in Greece's late Bronze Age—about 1600 to 1100 B.C.

Indeed, the *Iliad* was not composed in this period, known to historians as the Mycenaean Age,[2] but is the end result of an inspired oral poetic tradition spanning 500 years. Between the 13th century B.C., the height of the Mycenaean Age, and the age of Homer in the eighth century B.C., lie five centuries during which generations of unknown professional poets passed down

---

1. *Alexander the Great,* king of Macedonia from 336 to 323 B.C., defeated the Persian Empire and spread Greek culture to his conquered lands.
2. *Mycenaean Age* (mī sə nē´ ən) refers to a period during the late Bronze Age, from 1600 B.C. to 1100 B.C. Mycenae (mī sē´ nē) was a Greek city in the Peloponnese, the peninsula that forms the southern part of mainland Greece.

Viewing Practice

Present a Photo-Essay Explain that a photo essay is a group of photographs arranged to explore a theme or tell a story. Ask students to preview the photographs and their captions in this article. Have them work in small groups to create their own photo essay of the remains of Troy and Mycenae. Ask them to use the Internet or library resources such as art books. They should order their photographs chronologically or by subject matter to help illustrate the story of these "lost cities." Suggest that they explore artifacts such as jewelry, weaponry, and sculpture; or the remains of warships, tombs, or palaces.

the epic-in-the-making. Each added something of his own genius, and the taste of the successive audiences who kept the *Iliad* in demand must have been of the same high standard as the skill of the bards themselves. The Greeks credited the final composition of this masterpiece to a poet they called *theios Homeros*—"divine Homer"—and we, as they, know nothing more about this person than his supposed name.

Most archaeologists and scholars study the late Bronze Age for its own sake, not because they seek to shed light on the *Iliad*. "I don't *care* about Homer!" an archaeologist in Greece said to me, exasperated by the popular view that she was searching for the Trojan War. Nonetheless, sophisticated modern studies of this period continue to yield unmistakably Homeric details, proving that the *Iliad*, though not a Bronze Age work, has preserved shards of Bronze Age history. Like the archaeologist, I was not in search of the Trojan War, but I was deeply interested in all those shards of history that give the *Iliad* its rich texture: The land around Troy itself in northwestern Turkey, the giant walls of Mycenae and its fabled gold, warships of the Bronze Age, weaponry and armaments, scraps of Mycenaean, the language of the Greek Bronze Age—these relics were my quest.

In a sense the *Iliad* is a tale of two cities: Troy, or "windy Ilion," the wealthy Asiatic city commanding the Dardanelles,[3] and "Mycenae of much gold," the city leading the united Greek invasion across the Aegean Sea to the gates of Troy. For centuries the wealth of these legendary cities was thought to exist only in the realm of imagination. But between 1870 and 1890 Heinrich Schliemann, an ambitious and ruthless businessman from Germany, put the "lost" cities on the map. Acting on the advice of a local amateur archaeologist (whom he did not bother to credit), Schliemann revealed the ruins of Troy, then found the gold of Mycenae.

The *Iliad*'s every description of Mycenae speaks of its power. And from the base of the rocky acropolis on which Homer's "strong-founded citadel" stands, I looked up to discover that these descriptions still hold true. Even in decay the great fortress remains imperious, still commanding, as it did centuries ago, the mountain-ringed plain of Argos,[4] now a blur of purple-gold in the hazy heat. Making my way up the entrance ramp, I paused before the citadel's famous Lion Gate—posts and a lintel[5] of colossal stone overarched by two weathered heraldic lions. . . .

As an epic, the *Iliad* is mostly interested in the fate of kings and warriors, not of the common man. And while archaeologists have uncovered traces of the small timber and mud-brick dwellings of humble people, it is the relics of Mycenae's rich and powerful that are most in evidence. The massive walls enclosed a palatial administrative complex—houses, sanctuaries, storerooms, and royal courts with colorful frescoes and sculpted stone. Wandering through the vacant citadel, past walls that had collapsed into rubble, across a floor of beaten earth that had once been decorated with painted stucco and gypsum slabs, I felt a lingering air of regal might.

In the *Iliad* the king of Mycenae, Agamemnon, is also commander in chief of the Greek forces—not on account of any special qualifications but because he has

---

3. The *Dardanelles* (Hellespont) is a narrow strait that links the Black Sea with the Aegean Sea by way of the Sea of Marmara.

4. *Argos* is a city in the northeastern Peloponnese of Greece.
5. A *lintel* is a horizontal piece that spans an opening and is supported by two posts.

CAROLINE ALEXANDER **235**

Historical Perspective
on the *Iliad*

Teach

Big Idea	1

The Heroic Ideal **Ask:**
What about the Bronze Age captivated Alexander? *(Students should recognize that Alexander was interested in comparing details from Homer's epic with the discovered relics of ships, walls, jewels, and weapons. She was also interested in the geography of the* Iliad's *actual setting.)*

For an activity related to this selection, see Unit 2 Teaching Resources Book, pp. 48–56.

Learning Objectives
Evaluating evidence. (SE)
Analyzing and evaluating informational text. (SE)
Presenting a photo-essay. (TE)

English Learners

DIFFERENTIATED INSTRUCTION

Beginning Paraphrase the first few paragraphs of this article. Then explain that the Iliad is a story of Troy passed down by poets to the eighth century B.C. and that archaeologists discovered the real Troy of the Bronze Age (1600 B.C.–1100 B.C.).

Help students to understand the progression of the B.C. dates by writing on the board a timeline like the one below.

The Bronze Age   **Homer's** *Iliad*

3500 B.C. 1600 B.C. 1100 B.C.   900 B.C.   1 B.C.   100 A.D. 1950 A.D. 2009 A.D.

Teach

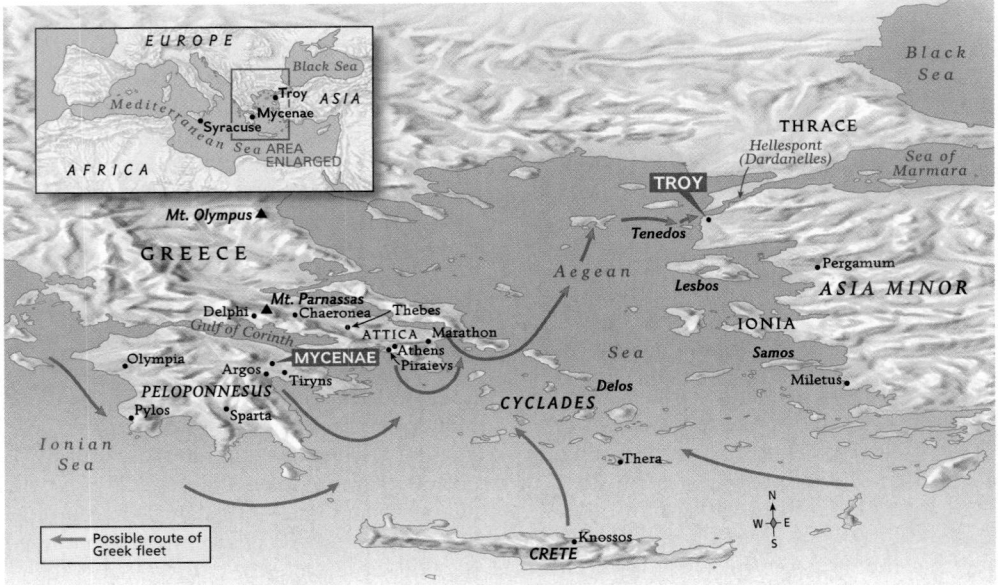

Big Idea   1

The Heroic Ideal Ask:
Based on the descriptions of Mycenae's remains and the author's commentary, how would you describe the cultural values of the real Mycenae? *(Most students will describe the real Mycenae as a culture that valued wealth, regality, fine architecture, worship, and military strength.)*

Reading Strategy   2

Identify Assumptions and Ambiguities Explain that when you identify assumptions and ambiguities you examine arguments that may not be foolproof or seem vague. **Ask:** Do the author's arguments about Ajax's "wall-like" shield include any assumptions or ambiguities? Why or why not? *(Some may say it is necessary for the author to make assumptions in order to prove her thesis. Others may think an image of a "wall-like" shield on a gold ring is a vague association to a line of text from Homer's epic.)*

inherited Mycenae's wealth and power from his father, Atreus. The historical Mycenae dominated the Argolid, the important and wealthy region of the northeast Peloponnese that in turn controlled much Aegean trade. . . .

The story turns mainly on a single application of Mycenae's broad power—that of leading united Greeks into war against the Trojans. . . .

Among the grave goods found by Schliemann at Mycenae on display in the National Archaeological Museum in Athens is a small gold ring dating from the 16th century B.C. Its carved face shows a miniature battle scene with a man taking refuge behind a shield that covers his entire body—the kind of shield Homer describes the Greek hero Ajax[6] carrying before him

"like a wall." From later representations we know that this type of shield fell out of use some centuries later, in the 13th century B.C. The *Iliad*'s knowledge of Ajax's "wall-like" shield, therefore, must be a genuine memory preserved from early Mycenaean times.

Similarly, in one dark scene the *Iliad* describes with careful detail a helmet Odysseus wears for a night ambush—a cap with "the shining teeth of a white-tusked boar . . . close joined one after another." Archaeologists have unearthed evidence of boar's tusk helmets from several Mycenaean graves, as well as depictions of warriors wearing such helmets on ivory carvings and frescoes. Bronze shin guards, called greaves, have counterparts in the *Iliad*, as do 16th- and 15th-century B.C. swords with silver rivet caps. In this last case Homer's phrase for the "silver-studded sword"—*phasganon arguroelon*—is pure Mycenaean. . . .

---

6. In Greek legend, *Ajax* was the son of Telamon, the king of Salamis. In the *Iliad,* he is considered to be second only to Achilles for strength in combat.

236   UNIT 2   ANCIENT GREECE

Reading Skills

Recognize Bias Explain that when you recognize an author's bias, you discover that author's inclination toward a certain opinion about a topic. Engage students in a discussion of why Alexander might be biased in her interpretation of archaeological research. They should be able to point to statements from the excerpt that show her bias.

Trojan Horse and Greek soldiers, 640 BC. Relief from the neck of an earthenware amphora. From Mykonos. Overall height 120 cm.

Today remains of Troy's walls still stand where Homer described the city, near the Dardanelles, overlooking a plain crossed by two rivers lined with willows, the *Iliad's* Simois and Scamander.[7] Once at the fallen city I slowly followed the subtle curve of the high sloping walls of Troy VI, one of two excavated levels that overlap the critical "Homeric" 13th-

century B.C. level. Fortunately I had timed my visit for late evening, when the setting sun made the walls glow gold and set fire to the Dardanelles, called by Homer the Hellespont, "where fish swarm."

Heinrich Schliemann's excavation of Troy was, by modern standards, impatient and brutal. Sinking deep trenches to bedrock, where he was sure Homer's Ilion must lie, he destroyed intervening layers of history. Today an international team of archaeologists under

[3] 7. *Simois,* is a small river, a tributary of the *Scamander.*

CAROLINE ALEXANDER **237**

English Learners

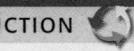

DIFFERENTIATED INSTRUCTION

Beginning Write the following words and phrases on the board: *palatial, sanctuary,* and *fresco.* Draw an image on the board of a large stately building to help them visualize the word *palatial.* Suggest that the White House could be considered palatial. Then explain that a sanctuary is a place where people worship, or pray. Have them identify other types of sanctuaries. If possible, show them a picture of a building with a fresco.

Advanced Learners/Pre-AP

DIFFERENTIATED INSTRUCTION

Write a Summary Have students prepare a summary of how the field of archaeology developed. Ask them to focus primarily on the techniques of archaeological discovery rather than focusing on how archaeologists interpret their research. Remind students to use reliable and varied sources and to apply a chronological structure to their summary.

Teach

Text Element | 3

Footnotes Have students read the footnotes in the article. **Ask:** How can you use footnotes effectively as you read? *(Students should respond that glancing at a footnote as they read is effective, but then rereading the sentence after they understand the footnote improves overall comprehension.)*

Reading Strategy | 4

Visualize What are some words and phrases you would use to describe Troy and Mycenae? *(Some answers may be agrarian, regal, lush, rugged, and trade routes.)*

View the Art

A Greek vessel, an amphora is a pot with two handles and a neck that is narrower than its body. There are two types of amphoras: one with the neck that meets the body at an angle, and one with the neck that meets the body at a curve. Their height varies from 12 inches to 5 feet. These vessels were used for storage of olives, cereal, oil, and wine.

Learning Objectives
Identifying assumptions and ambiguities. (TE)
Analyzing footnotes. (TE)
Visualizing. (TE)
Recognizing bias. (TE)
Analyzing art. (TE)

Teach

View the Art ★

The middle of three main sections of a work that rests on a capital is known as a frieze in classical Greek and Roman architecture. It may have also referred to a long, narrow, horizontal panel that was used for decoration in pottery, on the walls of a room, or on the outside of a building. This frieze is from the north wall of the Treasury of Sifnos in Delphi, Greece. It depicts fighting in the Trojan War.

the direction of Manfred Korfmann of Germany's Tübingen University in partnership with the University of Cincinnati is reexcavating the entire site. The object of their scrutiny is not just Hisarlik, the hill on which the ruins of Troy stand, but also the coastal area and surrounding plain, where according to the *Iliad* the Greeks beached their curved ships and the war was waged. Troy's many levels—nine in all—range from 3000 B.C. to the Roman city of New Ilium in the early sixth century A.D.

According to one version of Greek tradition the Trojans were the descendants of the hero Teucer, who came from Crete, seeking a place to settle. The historical Trojans, however, may have been Luvians, an Anatolian[8] people who became vassals of the Hittites.[9] Animal bones show that the Trojans kept sheep, cattle, pigs, and horses, while carbonized seeds indicate that they cultivated barley in marshy valleys. The city had a thriving wool industry and traded throughout Central Asia, receiving horses from the steppes beyond the Black Sea, tin from Afghanistan. Whether or not Troy ever went to war with Mycenae, there certainly was trading contact between the two peoples. Mycenaean pottery at Troy dates as far back as 1500 B.C.

In the past, visitors to Troy have been struck by the smallness of the site, wondering how so insignificant a place could have entered legend. But directing me through high grass and cotton fields well beyond Schliemann's citadel, Korfmann pointed out a line of trenches that reveal one of his team's most exciting discoveries—the outer defenses of an entire lower town below the citadel. Here Korfmann's team located

Fighting in the Trojan War, c. 525 BC. Relief, frieze, from north wall of Treasury of Sifnos, Delphi, Greece.

evidence of an encircling trench—some ten feet wide and eight feet deep—1,300 feet beyond the citadel walls. Increasing the known area of Troy VI by as much as 50 acres, the reconfigured city is almost ten times as large as Schliemann's citadel, containing a population of at least 6,000.

"Hittite documents refer to Taruisa," Korfmann told me. Taruisa has been identified by scholars with Troy. "*Tara* may be Luvian for 'wooden'—the city's name is perhaps a reference to the wooden houses of the lower town, which would have been conspicuous."

Yet the *Iliad* refers only to Troy's "well built walls" of stone such as Schliemann found on the citadel itself. These walls—and the damage done to them—have given archaeologists the most reliable key to the fate of the city.

---

8. *Anatolian* refers to the people of Anatolia, a peninsula that today is the Asian part of Turkey.
9. The *Hittites* were Indo-Europeans who lived in Anatolia around 2000 B.C. By 1340, they were a dominant power in the Middle East.

Writing Practice

Write a Description Ask students to imagine what the ancient Greek civilization must have been like for its citizens, who lived more modestly than the ruling class. Ask them to research how herders, farmers, and people in the trades lived in the Bronze Age. Then have them write a description of a day in the life of a humble Greek citizen. Emphasize that they should use sensory details. Suggest they structure their descriptions by the order of events as they occur in a person's day. Have them include what the thoughts of a Greek citizen might have been during that time.

Cracks and fire marks indicate that an earthquake destroyed the first Homeric candidate, Troy VI, around 1250 B.C. Soon afterward the same people who fled the earthquake returned to repair their city, creating a second settlement, Troy VIIa. The remains of small, cramped houses indicate that a larger population than before crowded inside the protective walls, while buried storage jars suggest to some scholars preparations for a siege. Flame-damaged walls indicate that about 70 years later a fierce fire destroyed this settlement. Was this the ☆ Troy, weakened by earthquake, that the invading Greeks finally sacked? Or had the Greeks attacked but not destroyed Troy VI in the wake of a natural disaster? Or was the fall of Troy entirely unrelated to the Homeric legend? . . .

The reconstruction below shows Mycenae's fortress in the late thirteenth century B.C., at the peak of its power.

Whether or not they played any role in Troy's destruction, the Mycenaeans did not long survive the city's fall. Why the apparently thriving Mycenaean civilization collapsed remains one of the most baffling questions of Bronze Age history. Pylos, Mycenae, Tiryns, Midea—nearly all the great palaces fell sometime around 1200 B.C. Some scholars have sought the cause in natural disasters, citing an earthquake such as destroyed Troy VI or even climatic change. Another theory has it that the Mycenaean economy, highly centralized and bureaucratic, became over-extended and collapsed under its own weight. The downfall of Mycenaean palaces occurs at about the same time as the fall of numerous cities throughout the Aegean and eastern Mediterranean, and although there is no archaeological evidence of foreign invasion, a revolutionary change in fighting tactics may have given barbarian raiders a new advantage. Most scholars suggest there **1**

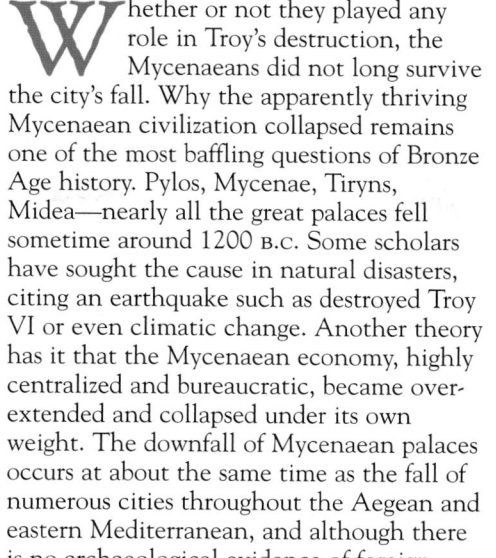

MYCENAE

Citadel

Lion Gate

Grave circle

Cult center

CAROLINE ALEXANDER **239**

Historical Perspective
on the *Iliad*

Teach

Reading Strategy   1

Review What are some theories about Mycenae's demise? *(Students should recognize that earthquakes, climate change, an overextended economy, or a vulnerability to barbarian attacks are all theories of Mycenae's demise.)*

Writer's Technique ☆
Exploring Sentence Style
Explain that how a writer combines sentences is an aspect of his or her style. Alexander varies the structure of her sentences by using introductory clauses on occasion—and by sometimes tucking information in the middle of the sentence. She also poses questions to the audience to interrupt the narrative and emphasize her thesis. Ask students to note her sentence length, variety, and structure.

Advanced Learners/Pre-AP
DIFFERENTIATED INSTRUCTION

Mapping Ancient Greece Have students work in small groups to research the geography of ancient Greece. Ask them to make a copy of a current map of Europe and the Middle East. Then have them attempt to outline the borders of the Greek empire in the Bronze Age and to identify the location of the cities of Troy and Mycenae on their map.

Learning Objectives
Evaluating evidence. (SE)
Reviewing. (TE)
Analyzing art. (TE)
Writing a description. (TE)

239

Assess

1. Summaries should include a statement of Alexander's claim that the *Iliad* "has preserved shards of Bronze Age history" as well as details about what the excavations at Troy have uncovered.

2. The ancient Greeks regarded the *Iliad* as a true account of their own past, but modern scholars regard it primarily as a fictional creation that includes fragments of historical truth.

3. (a) According to Alexander, storytellers from fallen Mycenaean towns transmitted legends about the Trojan War orally for several centuries during a period known as "the dark age of Greece." Then at the close of the eighth century B.C., Homer appeared. To him the Greeks attributed the final composition of the *Iliad*. (b) The epic depicts the titanic struggle between the city of Troy and the united cities of Greece, led by Mycenae.

4. Artifacts include a gold ring, dating from the sixteenth century B.C., that shows a battle scene with a warrior behind a large shield; boar's tusk helmets; bronze shin guards; and swords with silver rivet caps.

5. (a) Nine levels (b) Troy VIIa is the second settlement rebuilt after Troy VI was damaged by an earthquake. The flame-damaged walls suggest that a fire ravaged the second settlement. "The remains of small, cramped houses" may suggest that a large population huddled inside the city walls, and buried storage jars may suggest preparations to withstand a siege.

240

---

was a protracted decline, a slow trickling away of the population. . . .

The collapse of the Mycenaean world marked the beginning of several centuries traditionally known as the dark age of Greece, a period of shrinking populations, poverty, and cultural decline. Gone were the rich palaces with their colorful frescoes and imported luxuries. All the sophisticated arts of palace civilization were lost— monumental architecture, painting, metalwork, literacy. Yet it is this period of apparent cultural vacuum that transmitted two of the world's literary masterworks: the *Iliad* and the *Odyssey*. And while the *Iliad* bears evidence of its Mycenaean roots, it was the unknown poets of the dark age, centuries removed from the events they described, who fostered the great epic.

It is not difficult to imagine wayfarers from the fallen Mycenaean towns carrying their storytelling traditions with them during the 11th century B.C. As the generations passed, successive storytellers may have transformed a minor trade skirmish in Anatolia—or elsewhere—into an epic clash between Asiatic Troy and a unified force of Greek-speaking warriors, much as Britons[10] wistfully re-created the history of their clashes with invading Anglo-Saxons[11] into the legends of King Arthur.

The close of the eighth century B.C. revealed an entirely new human landscape. Everywhere populations had rebounded. Isolated settlements had given way to small city-states. Perhaps the characterization of the independent-minded hero Achilles and the *Iliad's* interest in different types of leadership reflect associated political change. Trade had revived and overseas colonization flourished. Above all, the new era revealed the epic poems attributed to Homer.

---

10. *Britons* refers to the Celtic people who inhabited Britain before the Anglo-Saxon invasions.
11. *Anglo-Saxons* refers to Germanic tribes who invaded England in the fifth century A.D. and controlled it until the Norman Conquest in A.D. 1066.

Respond and Think Critically

Respond and Interpret

1. Write a brief summary of the main ideas in this article before you answer the following questions. For help on writing a summary, see page 1147.

2. How would you compare the way ancient Greeks regarded the *Iliad* with the way modern scholars regard it?

3. (a)How does Alexander explain the origins of the *Iliad*? (b)Why does she call this epic poem "a tale of two cities"?

4. What artifacts discovered at Mycenae resemble items described by Homer in the *Iliad*?

5. (a)How many levels of Troy have been excavated? (b)What evidence suggests that Troy VIIa might be Homer's Troy? Refer to your chart from page 234 as you answer this question.

Analyze and Evaluate

6. What do you find most impressive about the discoveries of Schliemann and Korfmann? Explain.

7. (a)What claims does Alexander make about the historical Trojans? (b)How well does she support these claims?

8. Which of the theories about the collapse of the Mycenaean civilization seems most convincing? Explain.

Connect

9. How has your understanding of the *Iliad* changed as a result of reading this excerpt?

---

6. Answers will vary.

7. (a) Alexander asserts that the Trojans raised livestock, cultivated barley, developed a wool industry, and traded with Mycenae in Greece and cities throughout central Asia. (b) She provides facts to support these claims, such as the discovery of animal bones, carbonized seeds, and Mycenaean pottery in Troy.

8. Students may say that the theory that the Mycenaean civilization fell victim to a natural disaster or climatic change seems most convincing because Troy VI was destroyed by an earthquake.

9. Students' answers will vary. Some may say they can better visualize the Greek warriors and the Trojan community described in the *Iliad*. Others may say they now appreciate the *Iliad* as the final product of centuries of oral tradition.

Before You Read

Lyric Poems

Meet **Sappho**
(c. 610–570 B.C.)

In the seventh century B.C., lyric poetry, a type of poetry with a highly individual voice, appeared in Greece. One of the earliest and greatest of the ancient Greek lyric poets was Sappho (sa′fō).

Greek Lyric Poet Sappho lived on Lesbos, a Greek island off the coast of what is now Turkey. Of noble birth, she had a daughter and at least two brothers whom she sometimes addressed in her poems. Some scholars believe that Sappho was in charge of a school that educated young noblewomen in the arts. Due to political disturbances on Lesbos, it seems likely she and her family went into exile in Sicily, where Greek colonists had founded the city of Syracuse. She later returned to Lesbos, where she died.

> "I do not expect my fingers
> to graze the sky"
>
> —Sappho, from Fragment 4

Greek lyric poets usually performed their work in private for friends and invited guests. They often sang or chanted their poetry, accompanying themselves on a harp-like instrument they called a *lyra*. In the dialect of Lesbos, Sappho composed both highly personal poems and more formal hymns and wedding songs. Her style was closer to everyday speech than to the more established literary style of her time. Though Lesbos produced several famous lyric poets, Sappho was early recognized as the greatest.

Legacy After her death, Sappho became famous throughout the Mediterranean world. She was honored with public statues. Greek and Roman authors imitated her poems, and Greek scholars collected her poetry in nine volumes. A poem attributed to the Greek philosopher Plato pays Sappho the ultimate tribute, classifying her among the goddesses of poetry: "Some say there are nine Muses: but they're wrong. Look at Sappho of Lesbos; she makes ten."

Unfortunately, much of Sappho's work was lost during the early Middle Ages. Only one complete poem and about 100 fragments were preserved as quotations in the works of other authors. Additional fragments have been discovered on archaeological digs in the twentieth century, including one fragment that appeared on a strip of papyrus removed from a mummified crocodile.

Sappho's poetry provides a rare glimpse of ancient Greece from a woman's perspective. Though only fragments of her work have survived, her intense, controlled verses have earned her a place as one of the world's greatest lyric poets.

 Literature Online

Author Search For more about Sappho, go to glencoe.com and enter QuickPass code GLW6053u2.

SAPPHO **241**

Before You Read

Focus

Bellringer Options

Selection Focus
   Transparency 14

Daily Language Practice
   Transparency 27

Or ask: Is there a specific saying or piece of advice that has influenced you? What people in your life have played an essential role in shaping your identity? Have students describe a particular instance where they recall being instructed or advised. Let them elaborate on people that have influenced them in important ways.

Or: Write some familiar sayings on the board, such as "The early bird gets the worm" and ask students to respond to the validity of each saying using personal examples.

Writer's Technique ☆

Literary Style Sappho's poetry revolves around intimate relationships and the role of women in Greek society. Such personal subjects distance her from many other writers of her time, who focused heavily on political life.

Selection Skills

Literary Elements
- Imagery (SE pp. 242, 243, 246)
- Personification (SE p. 246)

Poems by Sappho

Speaking/Listening/Viewing Skills
- Analyze Art (SE p. 244)

Reading Skills
- Paraphrase (SE pp. 242, 245, 247)

Vocabulary Skills
- Synonyms (SE p. 247)
- Academic Vocabulary (SE p. 247)
- Link-up (TE p. 242)

Writing Skills/Grammar
- Apply Imagery (SE p. 247)
- Use Dashes (TE p. 244)

Before You Read

Focus

Summary

In "Most Beautiful of All the Stars," a star, Hesperus, exemplifies the night restoring order to the world. In "In My Eyes He Matches the Gods" Sappho compares her lover to a God. "Some Say Thronging Cavalry" highlights the temperament of Helen as a beauty on the outside, but less so in the inside, and goes on to compare her to Anactoria, the speaker's lover. This poem argues that whatever one loves the best is the most beautiful. The speaker in "For My Mother Said" describes her mother's method for tying back hair.

 For summaries in languages other than English, see Unit 2 Teaching Resource Book, pp. 57–62.

> **Interactive Read and Write**
> Other options for teaching this selection can be found in Interactive Read and Write for On-Level Learners, pp. 47–54.

Vocabulary

Link-up Write the vocabulary words and a simple definition for each in two separate lists on the board. Have students close their books and match up the word with the correct definition.

 For additional vocabulary practice, see Unit 2 Teaching Resource Book, p. 65.

Literature and Reading Preview

Connect to the Poems

What makes a person or thing look beautiful to you? Freewrite for a few minutes, explaining why you consider someone or something beautiful.

Build Background

Sappho's poems express intense personal feelings—love, anger, sorrow, and joy. She frequently used a verse form that came to be called the "sapphic stanza." It consists of four lines—three long and one shorter.

Set Purposes for Reading

Big Idea The Good Life

As you read, notice what Sappho's poetry reveals about the ancient Greeks' thoughts on the good life. Ask yourself, What matters personally to Sappho?

Literary Element Imagery

Imagery refers to the "word pictures" that authors create to evoke an emotional response. In creating effective images, authors use **sensory details**, or descriptions that appeal to one or more of the five senses: sight, hearing, touch, taste, and smell. As you read, ask yourself, How do the images in these poems contribute to the mood, or overall feeling?

Reading Strategy Paraphrase

When you **paraphrase**, you put something into your own words. Unlike a summary, a paraphrase is usually about the same length as the original passage. As you read, ask yourself, How does paraphrasing help you figure out the message of each poem?

....

Tip: Use a Paraphrase Chart Use a chart like the one below to record your paraphrase of each poem. Paraphrase each stanza of the longer poems.

Author's Words	My Paraphrase
"Most Beautiful of All the Stars"	Lovely evening star, at nightfall you send home the animals and children that have been away since dawn.

Reading Practice

Clarify Ask students to discuss the use of first person in the poems. How does the viewpoint affect their understanding of the poem? Does it make it more or less difficult to draw meaning from the text? Explain the difference between the author (Sappho) and the speaker (I), emphasizing that one is not necessarily synonymous with the other.

Learning Objectives

For pages 241–247

In studying this text, you will focus on the following objectives:

Literary Study: Analyzing imagery.

Reading: Paraphrasing.

Writing: Applying imagery.

Vocabulary

subtle (sut′əl) *adj.* hard to detect; p. 243 *The message of the poem was subtle and indirect.*

fasten (fas′ən) *v.* to attach firmly; p. 244 *He fastened the poster to the wall with masking tape.*

surpass (sər pas′) *v.* to exceed; p. 245 *We hope the results of the fund-raiser surpass those of previous years.*

....

Tip: Synonyms Synonyms are words that have nearly the same meaning. To determine whether two words are synonyms, see if one word can replace the other in a sentence. For example, in the sentence *The message of the poem was subtle and indirect*, the word *elusive* can replace *subtle*. Therefore, *elusive* and *subtle* are synonyms.

Lyric *Poetry*

Sappho
Translated by Jim Powell

Most Beautiful of All the Stars

Most beautiful of all the stars
O Hesperus,° bringing everything
the bright dawn scattered:
you bring the sheep, you bring the goat,
you bring the child back to her mother.

In My Eyes He Matches the Gods

In my eyes he matches the gods, that man who
sits there facing you—any man whatever—
listening from closeby to the sweetness of your
    voice as you talk, the

5 sweetness of your laughter: yes, that—I swear it—
sets the heart to shaking inside my breast, since
once I look at you for a moment, I can't
    speak any longer,

but my tongue breaks down, and then all at once a
10 **subtle** fire races inside my skin, my
eyes can't see a thing and a whirring whistle
    thrums at my hearing,

cold sweat covers me and a trembling takes
ahold of me all over: I'm greener than the
15 grass is and appear to myself to be little
    short of dying.

---

1 The Good Life *What matters to the speaker personally?*

2 Imagery *What sense(s) do these images primarily appeal to?*

Vocabulary

subtle (sut´ əl) *adj.* hard to detect

2 **Hesperus:** name for the planet Venus, the evening star, prominent in the western sky shortly after sunset.

Teach

Big Idea   **1**

The Good Life Answer:
Students may say the nurturing of innocent and vulnerable creatures matters to the speaker.

(**APPROACHING**) For students having difficulty, pull specific examples from the text and ask them to draw simple conclusions about what the speaker might feel. For the first one, read a line from a poem and give students options of what she may feel according to her writing.

Literary Element   **2**

Imagery Answer: *These images primarily appeal to the sense of touch.*

Progress Check

Can students analyze imagery?

If No → See Unit 2 Teaching Resources Book, p. 63.

For an audio recording of this selection, use Listening Library Audio CD-ROM.

Learning Objectives
Analyzing imagery. (SE)
Clarifying. (TE)

Advanced Learners/Pre-AP

DIFFERENTIATED INSTRUCTION

Recognize Author's Purpose Ask students to make inferences as to why Sappho wrote the poem "Most Beautiful of All the Stars." **Ask:** What kinds of things could have happened to Sappho that would cause her to write such a poem? *(Students may say that this poem is a response to connecting with nature and attempting to make sense of the infinite feeling of the universe.)* For students wishing to go further, compile a list of words and ideas following the themes presented in Sappho's poems to guide students in writing their own poem. Some examples include stars, animals, love, and myth. Let their poems take any direction.

Teach

View the Art ★

Answer: *Students may respond that Moreau's Sappho experiences deep feelings as do the speakers of her poems.*

Sappho inspired several works by Gustave Moreau (1826–1898). He modeled the robe in this painting on Japanese costumes. According to Moreau, the robe evokes Sappho's grace, severity, and imagination.

Sappho. **Gustave Moreau. Watercolor, 18.4 x 12.4 cm. Victoria & Albert Museum, London.**

View the Art
In this watercolor, Gustave Moreau, a French symbolist painter, portrays Sappho in a melancholy moment. How does this image of Sappho match the one you get from her poems? ★

For My Mother Said

for my mother said

that when she was a girl if you
bound the locks of your hair in back,
gathered there in a circlet of plaited purple,°

5   that was truly a fine adornment,
but for blondes with hair yellower
than a torch it is better to **fasten** it

with fresh garlands of flowers in bloom,
and more recently there were headbands
10 decorated in Sardis,° elaborately
embroidered . . .°

4 **circlet of plaited purple:** circular ornament of woven or braided strands made from purple material. Purple was the most prized color of the ancient Mediterranean world.

10 **Sardis:** the capital of Lydia.
11 **embroidered:** decorated with ornamental needlework.

Vocabulary

fasten (fas´ ən) *v.* to attach firmly

244 UNIT 2   ANCIENT GREECE

Grammar Practice

Use Dashes In verse, dashes are used to indicate a break in thought or as a form of elaboration. In "My Eyes," for example, the dash clarifies that the speaker is talking not about a specific man, but "any man whatever." Have students read aloud the sentences in the poems that make use of dashes, paying close attention to where they orally put emphasis. Ask them to think of other forms of punctuation that could replace the dash in these instances—perhaps a comma or a colon.

Some Say Throng Cavalry

Some say thronging cavalry, some say foot soldiers,
others call a fleet the most beautiful of
sights the dark earth offers, but I say it's what-
      ever you love best.

5 And it's easy to make this understood by
everyone, for she who **surpassed** all human
kind in beauty, Helen,° abandoning her
      husband—that best of

men—went sailing off to the shores of Troy and
10 never spent a thought on her child or loving
parents: when the goddess seduced her wits and
      left her to wander,

she forgot them all, she could not remember
anything but longing, and lightly straying
15 aside, lost her way. But that reminds me
      now: Anactória,

she's not here, and I'd rather see her lovely
step, her sparkling glance and her face than gaze on
all the troops in Lydia° in their chariots and
20   glittering armor.

7 Helen: known as *Helen of Troy;* the wife of Menelaus, king of Sparta. Her abduction by Paris, a prince of Troy, triggered the Trojan War.

19 Lydia: wealthy kingdom in Asia Minor (present-day Turkey) in the sixth and seventh centuries B.C.

Paraphrase *Paraphrase the last stanza of this poem.*

Vocabulary

surpass (sər pas´) *v.* to exceed

SAPPHO **245**

Teach

Reading Strategy

Paraphrase **Answer:** *I would prefer the sight of my absent friend's face to the sight of a great army bedecked in splendor.*

To check students' understanding of the selection, see Unit 2 Teaching Resource Book, p. 67.

Cultural History ☆

Helen of Troy In Greek myth, Helen of Troy was considered the most beautiful woman in the world. Paris, Prince of Troy, kidnapped her and this abduction led to the Trojan War. Helen has since become the epitome of ultimate beauty. In his play *Doctor Faustus*, Christopher Marlowe calls her "the face that launched a thousand ships." In this poem, Sappho uses Helen to exemplify a universal truth.

English Learners

DIFFERENTIATED INSTRUCTION

Intermediate Clarify for English learners the military terms used in the first stanza above. *Cavalry* refers to soldiers on horseback. *Foot soldiers,* also called infantry, are soldiers who march into battle. A fleet is a large group of warships. Ask students to use information from their reading of the *Iliad* to shed additional light on their understanding of "Some Say Thronging Cavalry."

After You Read

Assess

1. Answers will vary.
2. (a) She praises Hesperus because it brings together those whose daily activities separate them. (b) The mood is tender, affectionate, and protective.
3. (a) The speaker is a person experiencing feelings associated with passionate love, including jealousy and desire. (b) The speaker in "For My Mother Said" is perhaps a child, but probably an adult recalling her mother's reminiscences.
4. (a) The speaker says when Helen fell in love she left her husband without a thought for him, her child, or her parents. (b) Students may say she is sympathetic toward Helen and cite lines 11–15.
5. Students may say people often love other people or things because of their own motivations and feelings and this love endows what is loved with an aura of beauty.
6. (a) Sappho speaks of how beauty relates to what and whom she loves, even when those people are absent. (b) Perhaps she feels closer to these people and things by writing about them.
7. Students may say "For My Mother Said" seems most incomplete because it begins in the middle of the same long sentence.
8. Responses may include time to reflect, memories of childhood, deep personal relationships, and the appreciation of beauty.
9. Students may mention any person admired for beauty and fame but unwise in love.

246

After You Read

Respond and Think Critically

Respond and Interpret

1. What memories do these poems stir in you?
2. The **speaker** of a poem is the voice that talks to the reader. (a)In "Most Beautiful of All the Stars," why does the speaker consider Hesperus the most beautiful of all the stars? (b)How would you describe the **mood**, or overall feeling, of this poem?
3. (a)How would you describe the speaker of "In My Eyes He Matches the Gods"? (b)How does this speaker differ from the one in "For My Mother Said"?
4. (a)In "Some Say Thronging Cavalry," what does the speaker say about Helen of Troy? (b)Do you think the speaker is sympathetic toward Helen or critical of her? Support your opinion.

Analyze and Evaluate

5. In "Some Say Thronging Cavalry," the speaker says whatever one loves best is the most beautiful of sights. Do you agree? Explain.
6. (a)How would you describe the subject matter of Sappho's poems? (b)Why do you think she chose to write about these subjects?
7. Almost all of Sappho's surviving poems are fragments. Which of the poems here seems most incomplete to you? Explain why.

Connect

8. **Big Idea** **The Good Life** On the basis of these lyric poems, how might Sappho describe what constitutes the good life?
9. **Connect to Today** If Sappho were writing for a modern audience, whom might she substitute for Helen of Troy in "Some Say Thronging Cavalry"? Why?

Literary Element **Imagery**

SAT Skills Practice

1. The images in lines 11–12 of "In My Eyes He Matches the Gods" appeal primarily to the sense of
   - **(A)** sight
   - **(B)** hearing
   - **(C)** smell
   - **(D)** taste
   - **(E)** touch

2. In "For My Mother Said," Sappho uses the image "bound the locks" (line 3) to suggest
   - **(A)** freshness and youth
   - **(B)** abuse or mistreatment
   - **(C)** quiet contentment
   - **(D)** old-fashioned formality
   - **(E)** wealth and luxury

246 UNIT 2 ANCIENT GREECE

Review: Personification

As you learned on page 134, **personification** is a figure of speech in which a nonhuman thing is given human characteristics. The use of personification makes descriptions vivid and can help intensify the drama of a work of literature.

Partner Activity Meet with a partner to find examples of personification in "Most Beautiful of All the Stars" and "In My Eyes He Matches the Gods." Then discuss what Sappho gains by using this technique.

 **Literature** Online

Selection Resources For Selection Quizzes, eFlashcards, and Reading-Writing Connection activities, go to glencoe.com and enter QuickPass code GLW6053u2.

Literary Element

1. **(B)** is the correct answer. The lines describe the sound of a whistle.
2. **(D)** is the correct answer. The poem contrasts hair adornments popular when the speaker's mother was a child with more recent styles.

 For additional assessment, see Assessment Resources, pp. 71–72.

Review: Personification

In "Most Beautiful of All the Stars," examples of personification are found in lines 4 and 5, in which the evening star is compared to a herdsman or a guardian. In "In My Eyes He Matches the Gods," an example of personification is found in line 10, in which fire is compared to a runner. By using this technique, Sappho intensifies the drama of the images she creates.

Reading Strategy — Paraphrase

When **paraphrasing** long, complex sentences or passages, you may find it helpful to search for the simple subject and simple predicate in a sentence. Review the chart you made on page 242 and then answer the following questions.

1. What are the simple subjects and predicates of the four clauses in lines 9–11 of "In My Eyes He Matches the Gods"?

2. What insights into the poems' meanings have you gained from paraphrasing passages?

Vocabulary Practice

Practice with Synonyms With a partner, brainstorm three synonyms for each boldfaced vocabulary word below. Then discuss your choices with your classmates.

subtle   fasten   surpass

EXAMPLE: *introverted*

Synonyms: *shy, withdrawn, timid*

Explanation: An introverted person, like a timid person, would likely be afraid to talk to strangers.

Academic Vocabulary

In her love poetry, Sappho sometimes comments on the **variables** *involved in the perception of beauty.*

Variables is an academic word that can be used in different contexts. For example, a wedding planner knows all about the **variables** of a wedding day. Use context clues to figure out the meaning of *variables* in each sentence below.

1. I had trouble finding the **variable**, x, in the mathematical expression $3x + 5 = 17$.

2. There are two kinds of **variable** stars, or stars whose brightness fluctuates.

For more on academic vocabulary, see pages 36–37 and R83–R85.

Write with Style

 Apply Imagery

Assignment Rather than directly stating ideas and feelings in her poems, Sappho often uses imagery to suggest them. **Images** are details that appeal to one or more of the five senses: sight, hearing, touch, taste, and smell. Write a brief poem or narrative sketch in which you use imagery as Sappho does.

Get Ideas Look at paintings and photographs; listen to music; and observe the sights, sounds, and smells of the natural world. Then jot down verbs, adjectives, and nouns that describe these sensory experiences. What characters, feelings, or events do the images suggest to you?

Give It Structure Once you have created a few images, choose a logical order in which to present them. For example, you might start by introducing one image and then contrasting it with another, as Sappho does in "For My Mother Said." If you are writing a narrative, think about how to incorporate your images into a clear sequence of events.

Look at Language As you write your first draft, strive for accuracy in your imagery, but don't worry too much about the coherence of the whole. Take risks with language, and let the images flow naturally from one to another. As you revise, try to make your images "pop" by replacing vague words with vivid, precise ones.

EXAMPLE:

I heard the wagon ~~rolling down the street~~.

I heard the wagon clattering over the cobblestones.

Remember, too, that a simple image can be more powerful than a sequence of adjectives. Notice that in the following sentence, only a few words are needed to appeal to the reader's sense of touch.

EXAMPLE:

The ~~hard, rough~~ bark ~~scratched and~~ scraped the child's ~~sensitive,~~ soft palms.

The bark scraped the child's soft palms.

Write with Style

Students' poems or narratives should

- use precise, concrete images that appeal to the senses
- present the images in a logical order and convey a unified idea or feeling
- use fresh language and avoid wordiness

 To create custom assessments online, go to Progress Reporter Online Assessment.

 To create custom assessments using software, use ExamView Assessment Suite.

After You Read

Assess

Reading Strategy

1. Simple subjects: *tongue, fire, eyes,* and *whistle.* Simple predicates: *breaks down, races, can't see,* and *thrums.*

2. Students' responses should indicate how restating passages in their own words helps increase their understanding of the texts.

Progress Check

Can students paraphrase?

If No → See Unit 2 Teaching Resources Book, p 64.

Vocabulary

subtle Synonyms: sly, clever, delicate
Sample explanation: If something is described as subtle, it means it is not obvious. For example, something that you hardly notice can be subtle.

fasten Synonyms: tighten, connect, secure
Sample explanation: To fasten something means to make it secure. It most often refers to a physical object, such as a seatbelt.

surpass Synonyms: outdo, outshine, top
Sample explanation: If you surpass someone, you perform in a superior manner. In other words, you top him or her.

Academic Vocabulary

1. In the context of this sentence about mathematics, a **variable** is a figure that assumes a set of values.

2. Because the stars' brightness fluctuates, *variable* means "tending to change."

Focus

Bellringer Options

Daily Language Practice Transparency 28

Or write the following statement on the board:

Films have replaced theatrical dramas. **Ask:** Do you agree or disagree with this statement? *(Students may say that movies have taken much of the audience from the theater, but that both still exist as distinct art forms.)* **Ask:** Can you identify similarities and differences between theater and film? *(Similarities: players acting out a story; sets; dialogue. Differences: drama is live; movies can use complex special effects. Advanced students may note that the differences are almost all technological; good screenwriting still produces catharsis.)*

Teach

Reading Strategy

Identify Genre Say: The Greek root of the word *drama* suggests that the Greeks believed that plays were an art form in which a story is "done"—that is, performed—for the audience, not told to them. **Ask:** Which other forms of art might be said to be "told"? Which art forms can be seen as being "done"? *(Visual arts, literature, and music are "told" art forms. Drama, dance, performance, and interactive art are "done." Film could be considered a fusion of the two.)*

Learning Objectives

For pages 248–249

In studying this text, you will focus on the following objectives:

Literary Study: Analyzing literary genres.

Reading: Evaluating historical influences.

Connecting to the literature.

Classical Greek Drama

THEATER MEANT FAR MORE THAN ENTERTAINMENT FOR THE PEOPLE of ancient Greece. It was part of their religion, a way of displaying loyalty to their city-state, and a method of honoring local heroes. It was also a major social event, a thrilling competition, and a place where important philosophical issues could be aired.

"The Athenian citizen took his drama seriously, not only because it was a part of a great religious festival, but because he loved talk and display and the tales the poets told."

—Vera Mowry Roberts,
from *On Stage: A History of Theatre*

Greek drama is one of the oldest forms of drama we know. In ancient Greece, plays grew out of religion and myths. From the sixth century B.C., religious festivals featured a chorus, or group of actors, that danced and sang hymns to Dionysus (dī ə nē′ səs), the god of wine. In about 534 B.C., the lyric poet Thespis introduced the use of a single actor, separate from the chorus. (Actors today are still called thespians.) The chorus voiced the attitudes of the community while the actor delivered speeches, answered the chorus, and performed the story. In the early fifth century, the great dramatist Aeschylus (c. 524–456 B.C.) added a second actor to the stage; within a few years, his rival, Sophocles (496–406 B.C.), added a third. With these changes, drama—from the Greek word for *doing*, rather than *telling*—was born.

Reproductions of ancient Greek theater masks.

At the Theater

What would you have seen from the benches of an ancient Greek amphitheater? Up to 15,000 spectators might throng the Theater of Dionysus in Athens. Seated in the upper rows, a spectator was more than 55 yards from the stage below. The actors' gestures had to be exaggerated and dramatic, for no one in the back row could have interpreted slight movements.

Only men were allowed to perform. All the actors wore masks made of wool, linen, wood, or plaster. In the mid-fifth century B.C., the time of Sophocles, masks were fairly realistic representations of human faces. In later centuries, masks grew in size and became less realistic, featuring deep eye sockets and wide, gaping mouths, making actors appear larger against the background. Typically, tragic actors wore striking, richly decorated robes that set them apart from the audience. Chorus members wore more conventional costumes, which identified the roles they were playing: soldiers, priests, mourners, or even—in the case of comedies—frogs, birds, or wasps.

Ancient Greek theaters were open-air, so the lighting was natural. There were very few props. A hunter might carry a bow; an elderly man, a stick; a soldier,

Reading Practice

Take Notes Have students use note cards to take notes on the Literary History feature on pages 248–249. Guide them to look for the names of significant dramatic features and ideas in the text. Have them note the names of important playwrights and their contributions to Greek drama. Have them write a summary of the qualities of a tragic hero or heroine and make a connection between the downfall of the tragic figure and Greek drama's goal of provoking pity and terror in the audience. After they take notes, have them write an extended outline of the selection, filling in details from their research.

a sword and shield. These props served more as symbols to identify the character's role in the play than to imitate life. The violence—murder, suicide, and battles—almost always occurred offstage. Typically, a messenger would appear after the event and describe in gory detail what just happened.

The Golden Age

During the fifth century B.C., drama grew to be a vital part of life in Athens. The festival of Dionysus, the most important Greek religious festival, introduced a drama competition. The four greatest Greek dramatists—Aeschylus, Sophocles, Euripides (c. 480–406 B.C.), and Aristophanes (c. 448–c. 385 B.C.)—presented their plays at these festivals.

These dramatists—all from Athens—wrote plays in verse, based on themes familiar to their audiences. They retold myths, rewrote history, and ridiculed politicians. Aristophanes, the sole comic writer among the four Athenian masters, landed himself in legal trouble for boldly and uproariously satirizing society, politics, and even the gods. However, his three great contemporaries were all tragic poets, whose plays capture humankind's timeless struggle to find meaning and self-understanding.

Central to the tragedy is the fall of a great man (or woman, though her part would have been acted by a man). According to the Greek philosopher Aristotle, the tragic hero should be neither very good nor very bad. The hero's downfall is brought about by a flaw within his or her own character. In this way, the downfall of a hero would encourage audiences to examine their own lives, to define their beliefs, and to cleanse their emotions of pity and terror through compassion for the character.

 Literature Online

Literature and Reading For more about classical Greek drama, go to glencoe.com and enter QuickPass code GLW6053u2.

Restored seats in Theater of Dionysus. Athens.

Respond and Think Critically

1. In your opinion, what is the most significant difference between ancient Greek theater and modern American theater? Consider any American plays you have seen or read.

2. How did the purpose of Greek comedy differ from that of tragedy?

3. Why do you think Aristotle argued that the tragic hero should be a person neither especially good nor especially bad?

LITERARY HISTORY **249**

English Learners

DIFFERENTIATED INSTRUCTION

Advanced Students from non-Western cultures may not be familiar with the importance of Greek drama to the development of a Western dramatic tradition. Have students locate Greece on a world map. Discuss some of the more common conventions of Greek drama (the flawed tragic hero or heroine, the chorus, the occurrence of violence offstage) and Greek stagecraft (masks, costumes, props). These dramatic elements differ widely from many Asian or Native American dramatic traditions, for example. Ask English learners who are willing to discuss the traditional roots of dramatic and artistic performance in their own cultures and the significance of performance to those societies. Ask them to share similarities and differences between these dramatic traditions and those of ancient Greece.

Teach

Big Idea

The Tragic Vision Say: Keep the following question in mind as you read: How might a tragic hero's or heroine's nobility figure into his fall? *(Noble loyalty to a potentially damaging belief or personal commitment to a good-person-gone-bad could bring about the fall. An excessive faith in his or her own nobility could be the hero's or heroine's fatal flaw.*

 For an activity related to this selection, see Unit 2 Teaching Resources Book, p. 69–70.

Assess

1. Students' answers might focus on the ancient Greeks' attending theater as a civic duty as the most significant difference, or they might point to the differences in performance style between ancient and modern theater.

2. Greek comedy was topical, satirizing contemporary issues; Greek tragedy addressed broader, more universal human issues.

3. The downfall of a very good person would be shocking and that of a very bad person would seem simply just. An audience is much better able to recognize and learn from a person who possesses a mixture of good and bad qualities, just as the audience members do.

Bellringer Options

Daily Language Practice Transparency 29

Or ask: What does it mean to be an outcast in society? How do you think an outcast feels? You may want to define *outcast*: "a person or thing cast out or rejected by a group of people." Students may agree that most outcasts would feel lonely without connections to any community. **Or:** What are some things that cause people to become outcasts in society? Allow students to discuss crimes or antisocial behaviors that result in people being shunned or exiled by ordinary people.

Interactive Read and Write

Other options for teaching this selection can be found in Interactive Read and Write for On-Level Learners, pp. 55–78.

Oedipus the King

Meet **Sophocles**
(c. 496–406 B.C.)

Sophocles lived in the fifth century B.C. during the Golden Age of Greece—a time of spectacular cultural and political achievement. Few authors have ever been as warmly embraced by their fellow citizens.

Sophocles was born to a wealthy family from Colonus, a village near Athens. Handsome, athletic, and skilled in music, the young man was groomed for stardom. His teachers included the noted philosopher Archelaus, and Lamprus, the most acclaimed musician of his time. Sophocles also studied tragedy, musical composition, and choreography based on the influence of Aeschylus, the great writer of tragedy.

A Dramatist for All Time At 28 Sophocles entered a prestigious drama competition held annually in Athens to honor Dionysus, the god of wine and fertility. Competing against the established and brilliant Aeschylus, Sophocles won first prize. During the next 62 years, he wrote more than 120 plays, about 24 of which won first prize at the Dionysia, the great dramatic festival in Athens. Unfortunately, only seven of his plays survive intact. Of them, *Oedipus the King* is often singled out as the finest play of the classical period.

Theatrical Innovations Sophocles brought new possibilities to drama by adding a third actor to the stage, and he is said to have introduced the use of painted scenery to the theater. He also invented the *deus ex machina* (literally, "god from a machine"), in which an actor was lowered on a crane as a god from the sky to provide a last-minute plot twist. His choral odes, remarkable for their beautiful language and depth of meaning, were integral to the action of his plays.

Later Years and Legacy In his life, as in his art, Sophocles remained energetic and productive to the end. He loved Athens and volunteered to serve in military campaigns. Late in life, he was given the honor of serving as one of ten *probouloi*, or chosen commissioners, to govern Athens.

Sophocles is widely regarded as one of the greatest dramatists of all time. His insight into human suffering was profound. Focusing on individual characters, he wrote tragedies that explored timeless issues such as the struggle for self-knowledge and the interplay of fate and free will in human life.

> *"The keenest sorrow is to recognize ourselves as the sole cause of all our adversities."*
>
> —Sophocles

LOG ON ▶ **Literature** Online

Author Search For more about Sophocles, go to glencoe.com and enter QuickPass code GLW6053u2.

Selection Skills

Literary Elements
- Chorus (SE pp. 251, 259–261, 264, 268, 272, 273)
- Stage Directions (TE p. 253)

Reading Skills
- Background Knowledge (SE pp. 251, 255, 267, 269, 271, 273)
- Read Aloud with Fluency (TE p. 252)

Oedipus the King (part 1)

Vocabulary Skills
- Practice with Connotation and Denotation (SE p. 273)
- Analyze Word Structure (TE p. 266)

Speaking/Listening/Viewing Skills
- Analyze Art (SE pp. 252, 267, 270; TE pp. 255, 258)
- Perform a Visual Interpretation (TE p. 264)

Writing Skills/Grammar
- Letter (SE p. 273)
- Expository Essay (TE p. 260)

Literature and Reading Preview

Connect to the Play

Is it always better to know the truth, no matter what the consequences? Respond to this question in your journal.

Build Background

According to legend, when Oedipus arrived at Thebes, the Sphinx, a winged creature with a lion's body and a woman's head, was terrorizing the city. She killed anyone who could not solve this riddle: What walks on four legs in the morning, on two at noon, and on three in the evening? Oedipus correctly answered "man," who crawls as a baby, stands in maturity, and walks with a stick in old age. Upon hearing this answer, the Sphinx killed herself. Oedipus then became king and married the widowed queen Jocasta.

Set Purposes for Reading

Big Idea The Tragic Vision

As you read the play, ask yourself, What noble qualities and character flaws does Oedipus reveal?

Literary Element Chorus

In Greek theater, the **chorus** danced and chanted between scenes in a circular space, known as the orchestra. The chorus's songs comment on the action that has just occurred and express social and religious views of the time. As you read, ask yourself, How does Sophocles use the chorus in this play?

Reading Strategy Apply Background Knowledge

Background knowledge refers to what you already know about the historical, social, and cultural forces that help shape a literary work. As you read, ask yourself, How can I apply what I already know about Sophocles and ancient Greek culture to better understand this text?

....

Tip: Take Notes As you read, record inferences and predictions you make based on your background knowledge. Use a chart like the one below.

Background	Inference/Prediction
Sophocles believed people must take moral responsibility for their own lives.	Oedipus will have to take responsibility for his actions.

Learning Objectives

For pages 250–273

In studying this text, you will focus on the following objectives:

Literary Study: Analyzing chorus.

Reading: Applying background knowledge.

Writing: Writing a letter.

Vocabulary

dignity (dig′nə tē) *n.* worthiness; the quality of being worthy of honor; p. 254 *Seated on his throne, the king was a figure of dignity.*

vengeance (ven′jəns) *n.* revenge; the return of a harmful deed for a harmful deed; p. 255 *The prince demanded vengeance for his brother's murder.*

denounce (di nouns′) *v.* to inform against; accuse publicly; p. 262 *He planned to denounce the student for cheating on the test.*

dire (dīr) *adj.* terrible; bad enough to arouse dread; p. 265 *He feared dire consequences after he was caught stealing.*

....

Tip: Denotation and Connotation A word's **denotation** is its dictionary meaning; its **connotation** is the emotional association it evokes. For example, the word *dignity* has a positive connotation because it suggests respectability.

SOPHOCLES **251**

Approaching Level

DIFFERENTIATED INSTRUCTION

Main Idea Remind students that for the Greeks, attending the theater was akin to a religious experience. They went to hear beautiful poetry, thrillingly recited or sung, and to see a well-known story brought to life once more, both relying on language and dialogue more than action. Suggest that students try to find the main idea in each long speech or scene. By understanding these, they will strengthen their understanding of the play.

Before You Read

Focus

Summary

Many years earlier, Oedipus left Corinth to avoid the prophesy of the Delphic oracle: that he would murder his father and marry his mother. On his journey out of Corinth, he got into an argument with an old man, whom he eventually killed. Approaching Thebes, Oedipus solved the riddle of the Sphinx, freeing Thebes from the Sphinx. As a reward, he became king of Thebes and married Jocasta.

The play begins with Oedipus reigning over Thebes, which has been stricken by a plague. The Delphic oracle reveals that the plague will not end until the murder of Jocasta's first husband, King Laius, is avenged. Oedipus is determined to find Laius's murderer and begins the investigation.

 For summaries in languages other than English, see Unit 2 Teaching Resources Book, pp. 71–76.

Vocabulary

Flash Cards Suggest that students make up sets of flash cards for the vocabulary words in Parts 1, 2, and 3 of *Oedipus the King*. Each card should contain: the vocabulary word, the page on which it appears, a definition, and either a visual representation or a mnemonic device to help in learning and reviewing the word.

 For additional vocabulary practice, see Unit 2 Teaching Resources Book, p. 79.

Teach

View the Art ★

Answer: *Students may say that the play will involve eyes or violence.*

Gottlieb organized the painting on page 252 in a grid format. Each section is filled with an image from the Oedipus story. Have students note how the eyes merge into bird wings at the top and upper-right sections. Gottlieb was attracted to the Oedipus story because he believed that artists should focus on "tragic and timeless" subject matter. **Ask:** Which images can you find repeated in this painting? *(Images of eyes, birds, hands, crowns, and faces are repeated.)*

 For an audio recording of this selection, use Listening Library Audio CD-ROM.

Eyes of Oedipus, 1945. Adolph Gottlieb. Oil on canvas. The Israel Museum, Jerusalem.

View the Art Adolph Gottlieb is known for his pictograph style of painting in which shapes—often inspired by mythology—appear in a gridlike pattern. Based on the images in this painting, what do you think this play is about? ★

252 UNIT 2 ANCIENT GREECE

Reading Practice

Read Aloud with Fluency Explain that this translation is written in blank verse—unrhymed iambic pentameter—with many deviations from a strict five-beat meter. The translator, Robert Fagle, probably chose this verse form as a way to suggest to English-speaking readers the effect of the original ancient Greek poetic form. The meter is what accounts for certain lines being overly indented (for example: "Speak up, old man . . ." in line 9). To read this kind of verse, suggest that students ignore the line breaks, but read for the sense of each sentence or speech, letting punctuation be their guide.

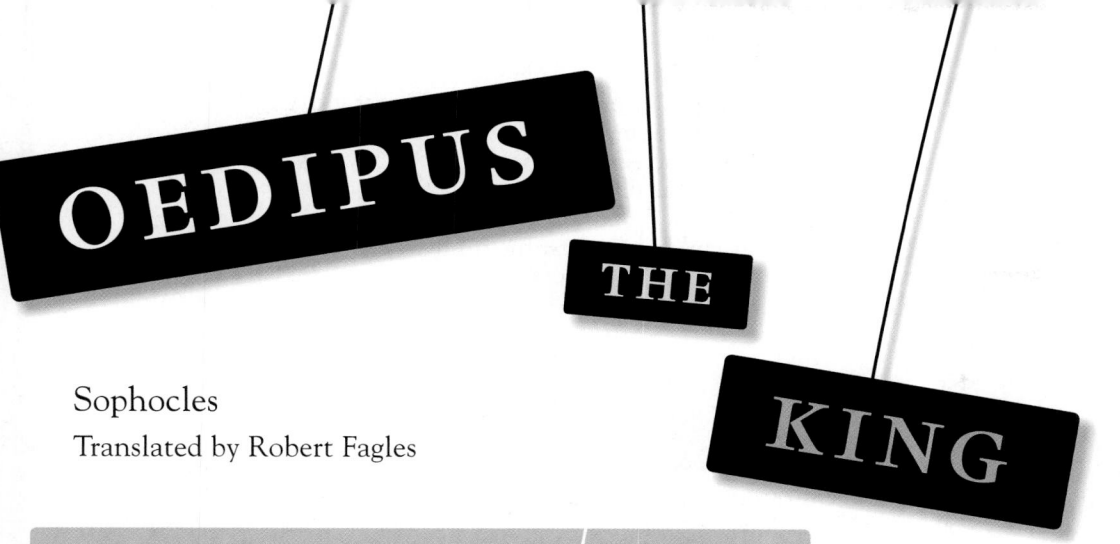

OEDIPUS THE KING

Sophocles
Translated by Robert Fagles

CHARACTERS

OEDIPUS: king of Thebes

A PRIEST: of Zeus

CREON: brother of Jocasta

A CHORUS: of Theban citizens and their LEADER

TIRESIAS: a blind prophet

JOCASTA: the queen, wife of Oedipus

A MESSENGER: from Corinth

A SHEPHERD

A MESSENGER: from inside the palace

ANTIGONE, ISMENE: daughters of Oedipus and Jocasta

GUARDS AND ATTENDANTS

PRIESTS OF THEBES

TIME AND SCENE: *The royal house of Thebes. Double doors dominate the façade; a stone altar stands at the center of the stage.*

Many years have passed since OEDIPUS *solved the riddle of the Sphinx and ascended the throne of Thebes, and now a plague has struck the city. A procession of* PRIESTS *enters; suppliants,° broken and despondent, they carry branches wound in wool° and lay them on the altar.*

The doors open. GUARDS *assemble.* OEDIPUS *comes forward, majestic but for a telltale limp, and slowly views the condition of his people.*

suppliants: people humbly asking a monarch to grant a request.
branches wound in wool: symbolic goodwill offerings to the gods.

SOPHOCLES **253**

Teach

Literary Element

Stage Directions **Ask:** How do the stage directions function on these pages? *(Stage directions often describe the setting. They also describe the action taking place so that actors will know what to do and readers can visualize the events.)*

Learning Objectives
Analyzing art. (SE)
Interpreting stage directions. (TE)
Reading aloud with fluency. (TE)

English Learners

DIFFERENTIATED INSTRUCTION

Intermediate Some students may find the vocabulary in this selection especially difficult. As they read, have them fill in a chart with these headings: Unfamiliar Word or Phrase, My Guess at Its Meaning, and What It Means. After they have guessed at meanings, students can consult dictionaries to find definitions.

Approaching Level

DIFFERENTIATED INSTRUCTION

Read for Meaning If students find the number of unfamiliar words overwhelming, instruct them to skip over some words. Suggest that they read to get the overall sense of each speech. They can fill in their vocabulary charts with selected words and highlight words appearing repeatedly. Begin a class list of important words to know and their definitions on the board or on a poster so students can verify meaning while they read.

Pantomime Have two students demonstrate the meaning of *dignity* by moving across the front of the room in a dignified manner without speaking.

Literary Element | 2

Exposition Remind students that the background a viewer or reader needs to understand a literary work is called *exposition*. Here, lines 16–50 provide important exposition, explaining the current state of Thebes. In *Oedipus the King*, such exposition is not all provided at the beginning; instead, it is distributed throughout the play and becomes the source of many of Oedipus's terrible discoveries. Have students record further examples of exposition as they read.

Big Idea | 3

The Tragic Vision
Answer: *Oedipus offers to do anything to help relieve the suffering people of his kingdom.*

OEDIPUS. Oh my children, the new blood of ancient Thebes,
why are you here? Huddling at my altar,
praying before me, your branches wound in wool.
Our city reeks with the smoke of burning incense,
5   rings with cries for the Healer° and wailing for the dead.
I thought it wrong, my children, to hear the truth
from others, messengers. Here I am myself—
you all know me, the world knows my fame:
I am Oedipus.

[*Helping a* PRIEST *to his feet.*]

                            Speak up, old man. Your years,
10 **1** your **dignity**—you should speak for the others.
Why here and kneeling, what preys upon you° so?
Some sudden fear? some strong desire?
You can trust me; I am ready to help,
I'll do anything. I would be blind to misery
15   not to pity my people kneeling at my feet.

2 PRIEST. Oh Oedipus, king of the land, our greatest power!
You see us before you, men of all ages
clinging to your altars. Here are boys,
still too weak to fly from the nest,
20   and here the old, bowed down with the years,
the holy ones—a priest of Zeus° myself—and here
the picked, unmarried men, the young hope of Thebes.
And all the rest, your great family gathers now,
branches wreathed, massing in the squares,
25   kneeling before the two temples of queen Athena°
or the river-shrine where the embers glow and die
and Apollo sees the future in the ashes.°
                                Our city—
look around you, see with your own eyes—
our ship pitches wildly, cannot lift her head
30   from the depths, the red waves of death . . .
Thebes is dying. A blight° on the fresh crops
and the rich pastures, cattle sicken and die,
and the women die in labor, children stillborn,
and the plague, the fiery god of fever hurls down

5 **the Healer:** Apollo, god of sunlight, healing, prophecy, and archery.

11 **preys upon you:** troubles your mind.

21 **Zeus:** the chief Greek god.

25 **Athena:** also Pallas Athena, goddess of wisdom and the arts and sciences.
26–27 **river-shrine . . . in the ashes:** a nearby shrine where Apollo's priests read the future in the ashes left by burnt offerings.

31 **blight:** a disease that kills plants.

---

3 The Tragic Vision   *One of the qualities of a tragic hero is nobility. How does Oedipus demonstrate this quality here?*

Vocabulary

dignity (dig′nə tē) *n.* worthiness; the quality of being worthy of honor.

Reading Practice

SMALL GROUP

Summarize Long selections such as this one pose a challenge to students' comprehension. Having students break the selection into shorter, more digestible sections to summarize will improve students' understanding of the play as a whole. Explain that the key to summarizing is to focus on the main ideas or events.

Have students work in small groups to summarize, scene by scene, the events of the play thus far. For purposes of this activity, consider that a new scene begins whenever a character enters or leaves the stage.

Evaluate group summaries as they are shared with the class. Repeat the activity at intervals throughout the play. Tell students that their summaries will be a useful device for reviewing the play when they come to the end.

35 on the city, his lightning slashing through us—
4 raging plague in all its **vengeance**, devastating
      the house of Cadmus! And Black Death luxuriates°
      in the raw, wailing miseries of Thebes.

      Now we pray to you. You cannot equal the gods,
40   your children know that, bending at your altar.
      But we do rate you first of men,
      both in the common crises of our lives
      and face-to-face encounters with the gods.
      You freed us from the Sphinx; you came to Thebes
45   and cut us loose from the bloody tribute we had paid
      that harsh, brutal singer. We taught you nothing,
      no skill, no extra knowledge, still you triumphed.
      A god was with you, so they say, and we believe it—
      you lifted up our lives.
                              So now again,
50   Oedipus, king, we bend to you, your power—
      we implore you, all of us on our knees:
      find us strength, rescue! Perhaps you've heard
      the voice of a god or something from other men,
      Oedipus . . . what do you know?
55   The man of experience—you see it every day—
      his plans will work in a crisis, his first of all.

      Act now—we beg you, best of men, raise up our city!
      Act, defend yourself, your former glory!
      Your country calls you savior now
60   for your zeal, your action years ago.
      Never let us remember of your reign:
      you helped us stand, only to fall once more.
      Oh raise up our city, set us on our feet.
      The omens were good that day you brought us joy—
65   be the same man today!
      Rule our land, you know you have the power,
      but rule a land of the living, not a wasteland.
      Ship and towered city are nothing, stripped of men
      alive within it, living all as one.

37 **house of Cadmus:** Thebes;
Cadmus founded the city.
luxuriates: indulges in pleasure;
grows abundantly.

Tiresias, 1946. Mark Rothko.
Oil on canvas, 79 3/4 x 40in.
Collection of Christopher
Rothko. ©ARS, NY.

---

5 Apply Background Knowledge *How did Oedipus save Thebes from the Sphinx?*

Vocabulary

vengeance (ven′ jəns) n. revenge; the return of a harmful deed for a harmful deed

SOPHOCLES **255**

Real-Life Context Have
students work in small groups
to construct webs listing some
reasons a person might want to
seek *vengeance* against another
person.

Reading Strategy **5**

**Apply Background
Knowledge Answer:** *Oedipus
correctly answers the Sphinx's
riddle. Enraged, the Sphinx kills
herself, and the people of Thebes
are saved.*

For additional practice using the
reading skill or strategy, see Unit
2 Teaching Resource Book, p. 78.

View the Art ★

Mark Rothko (1903–1970) was
a self-taught painter. Born in
Dvinsk, Russia, he moved to the
United States at age ten. In the
1930s Rothko began his career by
painting realistic images, but by the
1940s his paintings had become
more abstract.

During World War II, Rothko turned
to mythological subjects. He was
especially inspired by Greek tragic
drama. Instead of illustrating the
myths themselves, he tried to
express the human feelings and
desires embodied in them. **Ask:**
What might the dark spot on the
head of this figure represent?
(Students may say it represents a
blind eye of Tiresias.)

Learning Objectives
Applying background knowledge. (SE)
Analyzing art. (TE)
Summarizing. (TE)

English Learners

DIFFERENTIATED INSTRUCTION

Intermediate The word *tribute* (line 45)
has many meanings. Have students use
a dictionary to list these meanings and
then examine the context for the most
appropriate one ("a forced payment").
Ask: What, specifically, was the tribute
the Sphinx demanded from passersby?
*(Their lives: she killed those who could not
answer her riddle.)*

Advanced Learners/Pre-AP

DIFFERENTIATED INSTRUCTION

Build Vocabulary Have students
suggest synonyms for the Sphinx's *tribute*
that have counterparts in our society.
*(Possible responses: extortion, bribery,
pay-off, kick-back, abduction, kidnapping
for ransom, terrorism)*

Teach

The Tragic Vision Answer:
He is empathetic to his people and committed to finding the remedy for the plague.

View the Art ★

The red-figured pottery depicted here was created in Athens around 430 B.C. This painting on a drinking cup, or kylix, shows the Delphic Oracle at work. At the oracle, divine messages were transmitted through a woman known as the Pythia. She is shown seated on a sacred tripod in the room where she received prophecies. In her left hand she holds the leaves of the laurel (Apollo's sacred tree), which she either shook or chewed during the ritual.

Have students guess what the Pythia might be holding in her other hand. Then explain that it is a dish containing water from a sacred stream.

Cultural History ☆

Apollo A son of Zeus, Apollo is also known as the Archer, the Healer, the god of light, and the god of truth. The Greeks believed that Apollo was the source of the divine messages transmitted at the Oracle of Delphi.

Athenian red-figure kylix depicting Aegeus, King of Athens, consulting the Delphic Oracle. Staatliche Museen, Berlin. ★

OEDIPUS.   My children,
70   I pity you. I see—how could
     I fail to see
   what longings bring you
     here? Well I know
   you are sick to death,
     all of you,
   but sick as you are,
     not one is sick as I.
   Your pain strikes
     each of you alone,
     each
75   in the confines of
     himself, no other.
   But my spirit
   grieves for the city, for
     myself and all of you.
   I wasn't asleep, dreaming.
     You haven't wakened me—
   I've wept through the nights, you
     must know that,
   groping, laboring over many paths of thought.
80   After a painful search I found one cure:
   I acted at once. I sent Creon,
   my wife's own brother, to Delphi—°
   Apollo the Prophet's oracle—° to learn
   what I might do or say to save our city.

85   Today's the day. When I count the days gone by
   it torments me . . . what is he doing?
   Strange, he's late, he's gone too long.
   But once he returns, then, then I'll be a traitor
   if I do not do all the god makes clear.

90   PRIEST.   Timely words. The men over there
   are signaling—Creon's just arriving.

   OEDIPUS.   [*Sighting* CREON, *then turning to the altar.*] Lord
     Apollo,
   let him come with a lucky word of rescue,
   shining like his eyes!

   PRIEST.   Welcome news, I think—he's crowned, look,
95   and the laurel wreath is bright with berries.°

   OEDIPUS.   We'll soon see. He's close enough to hear—

82 Delphi: site of a shrine to Apollo; Delphi was the most famous oracle in ancient Greece.
83 oracle: a shrine at which questions might be answered about the hidden past or the future; the term *oracle* can also refer to the answer itself or to the priestess who gives the answer.

94–95 crowned . . . with berries: A crown of laurel was given as a prize for victory or excellence.

---

1   The Tragic Vision *What qualities does Oedipus exhibit in lines 77–79?*

Speaking Practice

Present an Oral Report Oedipus was different from most kings in that he was given the throne by the people of the city instead of inheriting it. However, he was still responsible for the well-being of his country.

Ask students to research the responsibilities of the king or queen in a specific monarchy (for example: Denmark, the Netherlands, Jordan, Great Britain). Have students present oral reports to the class.

As an alternative, have students work in small groups to discuss and list the skills and personality traits a person must have in order to make an effective leader. A spokesperson for the group can present an oral report on the group's deliberations.

[*Enter* CREON *from the side; his face is shaded with a wreath.*]

> Creon, prince, my kinsman, what do you bring us?
> What message from the god?

CREON.   Good news.
> I tell you even the hardest things to bear,
> 100 if they should turn out well, all would be well.

OEDIPUS. Of course, but what were the god's *words?*° There's no hope
> and nothing to fear in what you've said so far.

CREON. If you want my report in the presence of these . . .

[*Pointing to the* PRIESTS *while drawing* OEDIPUS *toward the palace.*]

> I'm ready now, or we might go inside.

OEDIPUS.   Speak out,
> 105 speak to us all. I grieve for these, my people,
> far more than I fear for my own life.

CREON.   Very well,
> I will tell you what I heard from the god.
> Apollo commands us—he was quite clear—
> "Drive the corruption from the land, **2**
> 110 don't harbor° it any longer, past all cure,
> don't nurse it in your soil—root it out!"

OEDIPUS. How can we cleanse ourselves—what rites?°
> What's the source of the trouble?

CREON. Banish the man, or pay back blood with blood.
> Murder sets the plague-storm on the city.

115 OEDIPUS.   Whose murder?
> Whose fate does Apollo bring to light?

CREON.   Our leader,
> my lord, was once a man named Laius,°
> before you came and put us straight on course.

OEDIPUS.   I know—
> or so I've heard. I never saw the man myself.

120 CREON. Well, he was killed, and Apollo commands us
> now—
> he could not be more clear,
> "Pay the killers back—whoever is responsible."

3 OEDIPUS. Where on earth are they? Where to find it now,
> the trail of the ancient guilt so hard to trace?

101 the god's words: Apollo; it was believed that the god spoke through the voice of the priestess at the oracle.

110 harbor: to give shelter to; to conceal.

112 rites: religious ceremonies; symbolic acts often required to atone for a wrongdoing.

117 Laius: the king who immediately preceded Oedipus; first husband of Jocasta.

4 The Tragic Vision *How would you rate Oedipus as a leader so far?*

Teach

| Vocabulary | 2 |

Synonyms Have students brainstorm as many synonyms for *corruption* as they can individually before getting together with a partner or small group to compare notes.

| Reading Strategy | 3 |

Connect to Personal Experience Ask students how they think Oedipus must feel about the seemingly impossible task of finding and punishing Laius's murderer. **Ask:** How would you feel if you were told to do the same in order to save your country? *(Students may say that Oedipus must feel overwhelmed and frightened for himself and his people.)*

| Big Idea | 4 |

The Tragic Vision Answer: *Oedipus seems compassionate, putting the needs of his people ahead of his own.*

English Learners

DIFFERENTIATED INSTRUCTION

Advanced Some students have trouble with English idioms because their meanings are often metaphorical or go beyond the words' literal meanings. Explain that "root it out" in line 111 is an expression meaning "get rid of it" as one would get rid of a weed by tearing it up by its roots. Ask why students think Creon's choice of words is appropriate here. *(The corruption has taken firm root; it needs to by uprooted completely.)*

Extend this activity by having students suggest as many English idioms meaning "get rid of it" as they know.

Learning Objectives
Connecting to personal experience. (TE)
Analyzing art. (TE)
Presenting an oral report. (TE)

Teach

Reading Strategy 1

Evaluate Style Comment that throughout the play, Oedipus is collecting clues to the mystery, much as a detective does today. **Ask:** What details in this scene might be clues? *(Students will discover that every character who enters brings new clues. Here, Creon reports that the eyewitness claimed that a band of thieves killed Laius.)*

Reading Strategy 2

Evaluate Argument Have students evaluate Oedipus's statement that a thief would not be so daring as to kill a king unless paid to do so. **Ask:** Do you think this is necessarily true? Why or why not? *(Students should recognize that the murderer may not have known that Laius was a king.)*

Big Idea 3

The Tragic Vision Answer: *Oedipus regards himself as the crusader for his people and Apollo.*

125   CREON. "Here in Thebes," he said.
      Whatever is sought for can be caught, you know,
      whatever is neglected slips away.

      OEDIPUS.   But where,
1   in the palace, the fields or foreign soil,
      where did Laius meet his bloody death?

130   CREON. He went to consult an oracle, he said,
      and he set out and never came home again.

      OEDIPUS. No messenger, no fellow-traveler saw what
         happened?
      Someone to cross-examine?

      CREON.   No,
      they were all killed but one. He escaped,
135   terrified, he could tell us nothing clearly,
      nothing of what he saw—just one thing.

      OEDIPUS.   What's that?
      One thing could hold the key to it all,
      a small beginning give us grounds for hope.

      CREON. He said thieves attacked them—a whole band,
      not single-handed, cut King Laius down.

140   OEDIPUS.   A thief,
2   so daring, so wild, he'd kill a king? Impossible,
      unless conspirators paid him off in Thebes.

      CREON. We suspected as much. But with Laius dead
      no leader appeared to help us in our troubles.

145   OEDIPUS. Trouble? Your *king* was murdered—royal blood!
      What stopped you from tracking down the killer
      then and there?

      CREON.   The singing, riddling Sphinx.
      She . . . persuaded us to let the mystery go
      and concentrate on what lay at our feet.

      OEDIPUS.   No,
150   I'll start again—I'll bring it all to light myself!
      Apollo is right, and so are you, Creon,
      to turn our attention back to the murdered man.
      Now you have *me* to fight for you, you'll see:
      I am the land's avenger by all rights°
155   and Apollo's champion° too.
      But not to assist some distant kinsman, no,

154 land's avenger by all rights: As king, Oedipus has the authority to punish crimes.

155 champion: one who defends a worthy person or a just cause.

---

3   The Tragic Vision *What do these lines reveal about Oedipus?*

258   UNIT 2   ANCIENT GREECE

Viewing Practice

SMALL GROUP

Analyze Art Present students with several paintings or renditions of the god Apollo, such as the ones on pages 261 and 281, or have them research visual representations of Apollo on the Internet. After they have had a chance to study several representations, have them work in small groups to discuss the following questions:

1. What differences are there in the ways Apollo is depicted by different cultures or in different centuries?

2. Which representation seems to fit with the descriptions of Apollo in *Oedipus the King?*

3. Do you see Apollo more as a god of destruction or as a beneficent god who tries to help the Thebans rid themselves of the plague?

for my own sake I'll rid us of this corruption.
Whoever killed the king may decide to kill me too,
with the same violent hand—by avenging Laius
I defend myself.

[*To the* PRIESTS.]

160   Quickly, my children.
Up from the steps, take up your branches now.

[*To the* GUARDS.]

One of you summon the city here before us,
tell them I'll do everything. God help us,
we will see our triumph—or our fall.

☆ [OEDIPUS *and* CREON *enter the palace, followed by the* GUARDS.]

165   PRIEST. Rise, my sons. The kindness we came for
Oedipus volunteers himself.
Apollo has sent his word, his oracle—
Come down, Apollo, save us, stop the plague.

[*The* PRIESTS *rise, remove their branches and exit to the side.*]

[*Enter a* CHORUS, *the citizens of Thebes, who have not heard the news that* CREON *brings. They march around the altar, chanting.*]

CHORUS.   Zeus!
Great welcome voice of Zeus,° what do you bring?
170   What word from the gold vaults of Delphi
comes to brilliant Thebes? I'm racked with terror—
                  terror shakes my heart
and I cry your wild cries, Apollo, Healer of Delos°
I worship you in dread . . . what now, what is your price?
175   some new sacrifice? some ancient rite from the past
come round again each spring?—
              what will you bring to birth?°
Tell me, child of golden Hope
      warm voice that never dies!

180   You are the first I call, daughter of Zeus
deathless Athena—I call your sister Artemis,°
heart of the market place enthroned in glory,
                 guardian of our earth—
I call Apollo, Archer astride the thunderheads° of
      heaven—
185   O triple shield against death,° shine before me now!

---

169 **voice of Zeus:** Apollo, as the god of prophecy, spoke for his father, Zeus.

173 **Delos:** island birthplace of Apollo and a famous center of his worship.

174–177 **worship you in dread . . . bring to birth:** They fear what sacrifice the gods will demand from them to end the plague.

181 **Artemis:** goddess of the hunt and of the moon.

184 **Archer:** Apollo was sometimes referred to as "the distant deadly Archer," whose arrows caused disease or death. **astride the thunderheads:** riding atop storm clouds.
185 **triple shield against death:** Athena, Artemis, and Apollo.

 4   Chorus *What group of people do you think the chorus represents?*

SOPHOCLES   **259**

Teach

Literary Element   **4**

Chorus **Answer:** *The chorus represents the citizens of Thebes.*

Cultural History ☆

The Greek Theater Because of the physical design of Greek theaters, scenery could not be changed physically; all scenes took place in front of the universal setting of the scene building, with no curtain or lighting effects to signal transitions. Here, Oedipus and Creon go in the palace simply to leave the stage clear for the Chorus.

Learning Objectives
Analyzing chorus. (SE)
Evaluating style. (TE)
Evaluating argument. (TE)

Approaching Level

DIFFERENTIATED INSTRUCTION 🐾

Question All students benefit from actively questioning the text during reading. Beginning and less-proficient readers can improve their comprehension by questioning what is unclear. For example: How did the Sphinx "persuade" the people to "let the mystery [of Laius's murder] go"? *(She was a more immediate danger; they simply had too much on their minds.)*

Advanced Learners/Pre-AP

DIFFERENTIATED INSTRUCTION 🐾

SMALL GROUP 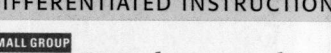 **Paraphrase and Interpret**
Explain that the chorus in Greek tragedies can serve different purposes. The chorus can move the action of the play forward, provide foreshadowing, or represent the values of the Greek people. Assign student groups ten line sections of the chorus's speech in lines 169–244 to paraphrase. Ask the groups to read their paraphrases aloud in the correct order. Discuss the role of the chorus in this section of the play.

Teach

Literary Element | 1

Simile **Ask:** What is compared to "seabirds winging west" in line 201? *(The comparison is to dead souls flying toward the land of the dead, located beyond the western horizon.)*

Literary Element | 2

Chorus **Answer:** *The plague is destroying all life in Thebes. Citizens young and old are stricken. Cattle are dying, the crops are blighted, and babies are expiring in the womb.*

Cultural History ☆

Greeks and Their Gods

In lines 180–244, the chorus calls for the help of the gods. The ancient Greeks believed in a number of gods, and they believed that the gods played an active role in their lives, dictating their fate. The only way to avoid the anger of a god or goddess was to appease him or her with a sacrifice of some sort or to call upon another god to intercede. **Ask:** How many gods does the chorus call upon in this scene, and which gods seem most important to them? *(They call upon Athena, Artemis, Apollo, Zeus, and Dionysus. No one god seems more important here; the chorus calls on them to act in concert.)*

If ever, once in the past, you stopped some ruin
launched against our walls
        you hurled the flame of pain
far, far from Thebes—you gods
    come now, come down once more!
190   No, no
the miseries numberless, grief on grief, no end—
too much to bear, we are all dying
O my people . . .
    Thebes like a great army dying
195 and there is no sword of thought° to save us, no
and the fruits of our famous earth, they will not ripen
no and the women cannot scream their pangs to birth—
screams for the Healer, children dead in the womb°
       and life on life goes down
200   you can watch them go
  like seabirds winging west,° outracing the day's fire
down the horizon,° irresistibly
       streaking on to the shores of Evening
                      Death
so many deaths, numberless deaths on deaths, no end—
205 Thebes is dying, look, her children
stripped of pity . . .
    generations strewn on the ground
unburied, unwept, the dead spreading death
and the young wives and gray-haired mothers with them
210 cling to the altars, trailing in from all over the city—
Thebes, city of death, one long cortege°
      and the suffering rises
               wails for mercy rise
   and the wild hymn for the Healer blazes out
215 clashing with our sobs our cries of mourning—
    O golden daughter of god,° send rescue
radiant as the kindness in your eyes!
Drive him back!—the fever, the god of death
           that raging god of war
220 not armored in bronze, not shielded now, he burns me,
battle cries in the onslaught burning on—°
O rout him from our borders!
Sail him, blast him out to the Sea-queen's chamber
            the black Atlantic gulfs°
225   or the northern harbor, death to all
where the Thracian surf° comes crashing.

195 sword of thought: keen insight.

197–198 women . . . womb: The plague in Thebes causes not only the earth not to bring forth fruit, but affects Theban women as well, for their infants are stillborn.

201 winging west: The west, where the sun sets, was thought to be where the dead resided.
201–202 outracing . . . horizon: moving faster than the setting sun.

211 cortege: funeral procession.

216 golden daughter of god: Athena.
218–221 the fever . . . burning on: The plague is compared with a battle raging inside the body.

223–24 blast him . . . Atlantic gulfs: send winds to carry the plague westward to the Atlantic Ocean.
226 Thracian surf: Thrace was a region northeast of Thebes.

> **2**   **Chorus** *Why is the chorus lamenting?*

Writing Practice

⚡ Write an Expository Essay

The citizens of Thebes are stricken with a plague, supposedly because they are harboring a murderer. However, the real source of plagues can often be traced to unsanitary conditions or to rodents or insects that carry disease.

Have students research, in books or on the Internet, a plague or major public health disaster, finding the cause(s), the carriers, the effects on the community, and what steps were taken, if any, to prevent its recurrence. Then have them write brief essays presenting their findings, with citations.

Chariot of the Sun Driven by Apollo, ca.1600. Antonio Maria Viani. Fresco. Galleria e Museo di Palazzo Ducale, Mantua, Italy.

Now what the night spares he comes by day and kills—
the god of death.

        O lord of the stormcloud,
you who twirl the lightning, Zeus, Father,
230   thunder Death to nothing!

Apollo, lord of the light, I beg you—
    whip your longbow's golden cord
showering arrows on our enemies—shafts of power
champions strong before us rushing on!

235   Artemis, Huntress,
torches flaring over the eastern ridges—
      ride Death down in pain!

God of the headdress gleaming gold, I cry to you—
your name and ours are one, Dionysus—°
240   come with your face aflame with wine
      your raving women's cries°
your army on the march! Come with the lightning
come with torches blazing, eyes ablaze with glory!
Burn that god of death that all gods hate!

[OEDIPUS enters from the palace to address the CHORUS, as if addressing the entire city of Thebes.]

239 your name . . . Dionysus: Thebes was the first city to celebrate the rites of Dionysus, god of wine and vegetation. His father was Zeus, and his mother was a Theban woman.
241 raving women's cries: The Maenads, female attendants, helped Dionysus punish enemies.

3 Chorus *What does the chorus want from Athena?*

SOPHOCLES **261**

Teach

| Literary Element | **3** |

Chorus **Answer:** *The chorus wants Athena to drive back the god of death and save the people from the plague.*

View the Art ★

Antonio Maria Viani (1555?–1629?) was born in the Italian city of Cremona, where he studied under the Campi, a famous family of painters. Paintings done by the Cremonese school are known for their elegance and rich colors.
Ask: How did the artist create a feeling of forward movement in this painting? *(Students may mention the horses' raised front legs, Apollo's raised right arm, and the harnesses and the clouds stretching across the fresco horizontally.)*

Learning Objectives
Analyzing chorus. (SE)
Interpreting similes. (TE)
Writing an expository essay. (TE)

English Learners

DIFFERENTIATED INSTRUCTION

Advanced Point out that when the chorus addresses the gods, they call them by other names (epithets) that are attributes or qualities associated with the particular gods. For example, they call Zeus "Father" (line 229) because he is the chief god and actually the father of some of the other gods. Often, such epithets are appositives, set off by commas, to the gods' names. Have students list such addresses as they appear in this scene and then identify the god who is being addressed. *(Some examples: "Child of golden Hope"—Apollo; "daughter of Zeus"—Athena; "God of the headdress" —Dionysus)* Advanced learners might be interested in researching one or more of the gods to find out how they earned their epithets.

261

Teach

Literary Element 1

Irony **Ask:** How are lines 247–251 particularly *ironic*? *(Oedipus was not only present at the time, but he himself is the cause of the crime and the solution to the mystery.)*

Vocabulary 2

Demonstrate Have a volunteer rise and *denounce* an imaginary fellow student for having violated an important school rule.

View the Art ★

Egyptian mythology gives the first mention of the creature known as the sphinx. It had a lion's body and a human head. In ancient Greek and Asian literature, a sphinx often also had wings, as is the case with Sphinx of Thebes, shown in the relief. **Ask:** Why might the sphinx have one claw raised toward Oedipus? *(Students may say it is prepared to kill Oedipus if he gives the wrong answer to the riddle.)*

---

245   OEDIPUS.   You pray to the gods? Let me grant your prayers.
     Come, listen to me—do what the plague demands:
     you'll find relief and lift your head from the depths.
     I will speak out now as a stranger to the story,
     a stranger to the crime. If I'd been present then,
250   there would have been no mystery, no long hunt
     without a clue in hand. So now, counted
     a native Theban years after the murder,
     to all of Thebes I make this proclamation:
     if any one of you knows who murdered Laius,
255   the son of Labdacus, I order him to reveal
     the whole truth to me. Nothing to fear,
     even if he must **denounce** himself,
     let him speak up
     and so escape the brunt of the charge—
260   he will suffer no unbearable punishment,
     nothing worse than exile, totally
     unharmed.

[OEDIPUS *pauses, waiting for a reply.*]

                          Next,
     if anyone knows the murderer is a stranger,
     a man from alien soil, come, speak up.
     I will give him a handsome reward, and lay up
265   gratitude in my heart for him besides.

[*Silence again, no reply.*]

     But if you keep silent, if anyone panicking,
     trying to shield himself or friend or kin,
     rejects my offer, then hear what I will do.
     I order you, every citizen of the state
270   where I hold throne and power: banish this man—
     whoever he may be—never shelter him, never
     speak a word to him, never make him partner
     to your prayers, your victims burned to the gods.
     Never let the holy water touch his hands.
275   Drive him out, each of you, from every home.
     He is the plague, the heart of our corruption,

Oedipus and the Sphinx. Relief of Hellenistic sarcophagus. Ancient Art & Architecture Collection Ltd. ★

> **Vocabulary**
>
> **denounce** (di nouns′) *v.* to inform against; accuse publicly

---

Vocabulary Practice

Understand Denotation and Connotation Today, the word *curse* is often used as a synonym for bad language. However, in other times and other cultures, a curse was very serious business indeed. Essentially, a curse is a prayer or invocation to a god or spirit expressing a wish that great misfortune—death, disease, or serious injury—be visited upon another person. By its nature, a curse lies within the domain of religion or magic. Whether curses worked or not may have depended on the extent to which the victim believed in its power.

Ancient Greek curses were somewhat formal and official. Sometimes they were written on tablets and buried in places where they were most likely to affect the victims.

Suggest that students use the Internet to research notorious curses in history. Students can give brief oral reports on their findings.

as Apollo's oracle has revealed to me
just now. So I honor my obligations:
I fight for the god and for the murdered man.

280 Now my curse on the murderer. Whoever he is,
a lone man unknown in his crime
or one among many, let that man drag out
his life in agony, step by painful step—
I curse myself as well . . . if by any chance
285 he proves to be an intimate of our house,
here at my hearth, with my full knowledge,
may the curse I just called down on him strike me!

These are your orders: perform them to the last.
I command you, for my sake, for Apollo's, for this country
290 blasted root and branch by the angry heavens.
Even if god had never urged you on to act,
how could you leave the crime uncleansed so long?
A man so noble—your king, brought down in blood—
you should have searched. But I am the king now,
295 I hold the throne that he held then, possess his bed
and a wife who shares our seed . . . why, our seed
might be the same, children born of the same mother
might have created blood-bonds between us
if his hope of offspring hadn't met disaster—°
300 but fate swooped at his head and cut him short.
So I will fight for him as if he were my father,
stop at nothing, search the world
to lay my hands on the man who shed his blood,
the son of Labdacus descended of Polydorus,
305 Cadmus of old and Agenor,° founder of the line:
their power and mine are one.
                              Oh dear gods,
my curse on those who disobey these orders!
Let no crops grow out of the earth for them—
shrivel their women,° kill their sons,
310 burn them to nothing in this plague
that hits us now, or something even worse.
But you, loyal men of Thebes who approve my actions,
may our champion, Justice, may all the gods
be with us, fight beside us to the end!

296–299 our seed . . . disaster: If Laius had fathered children before his death, Oedipus would be their stepfather.

305 Agenor: father of Cadmus.

309 shrivel their women: keep them from bearing any more children and carrying on the family line.

---

3 The Tragic Vision *In what ways might this speech foretell the tragic hero's downfall?*

4 The Tragic Vision *What does this passage suggest about Oedipus's fate?*

SOPHOCLES **263**

Teach

Big Idea	**3**

The Tragic Vision Answer:
Oedipus always desires to see the truth, which unwittingly may be his curse if the murderer should turn out to be a member of the royal household or perhaps even Oedipus himself.

Big Idea	**4**

The Tragic Vision Answer:
Oedipus's fate might have something to do with the fact that he and Laius, the slain king, shared the same woman, Jocasta, as a wife.

ADVANCED The Greek notion of tragic flaw included hamartia, (hä′mär-tě′ə) an injury committed in ignorance; in this case, Oedipus didn't know that the stranger was his father and Jocasta his mother.

Learning Objectives
Understanding irony. (TE)
Analyzing art. (TE)
Understanding denotation and connotation. (TE)

Approaching Level

DIFFERENTIATED INSTRUCTION

Understand Irony Some students might have difficulty understanding the concept of irony, which is important to this play. Review the definition of *irony* in the Handbook on page R9. Have students supply examples of verbal irony. *(Example: Saying "What a beautiful day!" when it is pouring rain.)* Then point out Oedipus's claim in line 301: "So I will fight for him as if he were my father." **Ask: Why is this an example of dramatic irony?** *(The audience knows what Oedipus doesn't: Laius really was his father.)* **Ask: What other example of dramatic irony appears in this scene?** *(Oedipus curses the murderer: himself.)*

Teach

Literary Element | 1

Chorus Answer: *He speaks for himself because he uses the singular pronoun, but he also speaks as a representative of the people whose sentiments he reflects.*

ENGLISH LEARNERS Remind students that the chorus is made up of the people of Thebes. Here, the Leader steps out as a separate character. Review the uses of the first-person singular (*I, me, my*) and plural (*we, us, our*) pronouns.

Cultural History ☆

Tiresias The ironic figure of Tiresias, blind seer of Thebes, drifts in and out of literary tradition. In the *Odyssey*, Tiresias maintains the gift of prophecy even in Hades, and Oedipus seeks his help there to dodge the wrath of the sea god, Poseidon. Even in twentieth-century literature, Tiresias plays a starring role in T. S. Eliot's masterpiece, *The Waste Land*. Much legend surrounds Tiresias's blindness and gift of prophecy. One version is that he happened upon the goddess Athena while she was bathing, and in her anger she blinded him; then in an afterthought of mercy, she awarded him the gift of prophecy.

315 LEADER. In the grip of your curse, my king, I swear
I'm not the murderer, cannot point him out.
As for the search, Apollo pressed it on us—
he should name the killer.

OEDIPUS.   Quite right,
but to force the gods to act against their will—
no man has the power.

320 LEADER.   Then if I might mention
the next best thing . . .

OEDIPUS.   The third best too—
don't hold back, say it.

LEADER.   I still believe . . .
Lord Tiresias sees with the eyes of Lord Apollo.°
325 Anyone searching for the truth, my king,
might learn it from the prophet, clear as day.

OEDIPUS. I've not been slow with that. On Creon's cue
I sent the escorts, twice, within the hour.
I'm surprised he isn't here.

LEADER.   We need him—without him
we have nothing but old, useless rumors.

330 OEDIPUS. Which rumors? I'll search out every word.

LEADER. Laius was killed, they say, by certain travelers.

OEDIPUS. I know—but no one can find the murderer.

LEADER. If the man has a trace of fear in him
he won't stay silent long,
335 not with your curses ringing in his ears.

OEDIPUS. He didn't flinch at murder,
he'll never flinch at words.

☆ [*Enter* TIRESIAS, *the blind prophet, led by a boy with escorts in attendance. He remains at a distance.*]

LEADER. Here is the one who will convict him, look,
they bring him on at last, the seer, the man of god.
The truth lives inside him, him alone.°

340 OEDIPUS.   O Tiresias,
master of all the mysteries of our life,
all you teach and all you dare not tell,
signs in the heavens, signs that walk the earth!°
Blind as you are, you can feel all the more

323 sees with the eyes of Lord Apollo: knows information hidden from other mortals.

339 The truth lives . . . alone: Only the seer Tiresias can reveal what happened so long ago.

343 signs . . . the earth: the will of the gods as shown in the movement of celestial bodies and in animal behavior.

---

1 **Chorus** *Does the leader of the chorus speak for himself or the group? Explain.*

Viewing Practice

SMALL GROUP

Perform a Visual Interpretation Greek drama made much use of formal, stylized movement and dance. Climaxes or moments of heightened drama might be emphasized by tableaux, or pictures in which all the actors on stage held frozen positions, rather like still photographs. Have students work in small groups to choose such moments and to plan and stage their own tableaux. Each group can choose one especially dramatic moment and position their bodies so as to tell the story. Invite the audience to identify the moment and to identify the characters represented.

345 what sickness haunts our city. You, my lord,
     are the one shield, the one savior we can find.
     We asked Apollo—perhaps the messengers
     haven't told you—he sent his answer back:
     "Relief from the plague can only come one way.

350 Uncover the murderers of Laius,
     put them to death or drive them into exile."
     So I beg you, grudge us nothing now, no voice,
     no message plucked from the birds,° the embers
     or the other mantic° ways within your grasp.°

355 Rescue yourself, your city, rescue me—
     rescue everything infected by the dead.
     We are in your hands. For a man to help others
     with all his gifts and native strength:
     that is the noblest work.

TIRESIAS.   How terrible—to see the truth
360 when the truth is only pain to him who sees!
     I knew it well, but I put it from my mind,
     else I never would have come.

OEDIPUS. What's this? Why so grim, so **dire**?

TIRESIAS. Just send me home. You bear your burdens,
365 I'll bear mine. It's better that way,
     please believe me.

OEDIPUS.   Strange response . . . unlawful,
     unfriendly too to the state that bred and raised you;
     you're withholding the word of god.

TIRESIAS.   I fail to see
     that your own words are so well-timed.
370 I'd rather not have the same thing said of me . . .

OEDIPUS. For the love of god, don't turn away,
     not if you know something. We beg you,
     all of us on our knees.

TIRESIAS.   None of you knows—
     and I will never reveal my dreadful secrets,
375 not to say your own. ☆

OEDIPUS. What? You know and you won't tell?
     You're bent on betraying us, destroying Thebes?

352–354 grudge us nothing . . . within your grasp: do not hold back any of your power to help us
353 message plucked from the birds: mystery revealed by studying internal organs of dead birds or the flight of living ones.
354 mantic: relating to divination, the discovery or interpretation of divine will.

Vocabulary

dire (dīr) *adj.* terrible; bad enough to arouse dread

Teach

Vocabulary

Examples Have volunteers describe situations (they can be fictional, even exaggerations) that might look *dire*.

Cultural History ☆

Augury (ô′gyə-rē) is the practice of divination, or telling the future. In ancient times, seers such as Tiresias would make predictions based on omens, rune stones, and the flight patterns of birds. These seers are comparable to modern-day psychics who make predictions based on astrology, crystal balls, and tarot cards.

Learning Objectives
Analyzing chorus. (SE)
Performing a visual interpretation. (TE)

Approaching Level

DIFFERENTIATED INSTRUCTION

Review Pause and review what has happened so far. If you had students write summaries (see Reading Practice, p. 254), go back over them now. **Ask: Why has Oedipus sent for Tiresias? What does he expect to learn from him?** *(Tiresias is a seer, or prophet. Oedipus hopes that he can reveal the name of Laius's murderer.)*

Advanced Learners/Pre-AP

DIFFERENTIATED INSTRUCTION

Interpret Dialogue Have students choose a line or lines from the play to interpret. A good example is lines 359–360, "How terrible—to see the truth when the truth is only pain to him to sees!" Have students write the quote at the top of the page. Ask students to write a paragraph about what they think the quote means by first paraphrasing the quote, then explaining in their own words what

they think the words mean. Ask students to share and discuss their interpretations with the class or with a small group.

Teach

Big Idea | **1**

The Tragic Vision **Answer:**
Oedipus cannot understand why Tiresias refuses to reveal what he knows about Laius's murder.

Big Idea | **2**

The Tragic Vision **Answer:**
Fury is a flaw in a leader because it clouds thinking and may erupt into violence.

View the Art ★

Answer: *Students may respond that they suggest humility, yet also wisdom or confidence.*

Glyn Philpot (1884–1937) was an English painter and sculptor who studied in Paris before returning to England to become a trustee of the Tate Art Gallery in the 1920s. Many of his paintings depict religious and mythological scenes. Philpot is best known for his paintings and sculptures of African men.

TIRESIAS. I'd rather not cause pain for you or me.
So why this . . . useless interrogation?
You'll get nothing from me.

380 OEDIPUS.   Nothing! You,
you scum of the earth, you'd enrage a heart of stone!
You won't talk? Nothing moves you?
Out with it, once and for all!

TIRESIAS. You criticize my temper . . .° unaware
385 of the one *you* live with, you revile° me.

OEDIPUS. Who could restrain his anger hearing you?
What outrage—you spurn the city!

TIRESIAS. What will come will come.
Even if I shroud it all in silence.

390 OEDIPUS. What will come? You're bound to *tell* me that.

TIRESIAS. I'll say no more. Do as you like, build your anger
to whatever pitch you please, rage your worst—

OEDIPUS. Oh I'll let loose, I have such fury in me—
now I see it all. You helped hatch the plot,
395 you did the work, yes, short of killing him
with your own hands—and given eyes° I'd say
you did the killing single-handed!

TIRESIAS.   Is that so!
I charge you, then, submit to that decree
you just laid down: from this day onward
400 speak to no one, not these citizens, not myself.
You are the curse, the corruption of the land!

OEDIPUS. You, shameless—
aren't you appalled to start up such a story?
You think you can get away with this?

TIRESIAS.   I have already.
405 The truth with all its power lives inside me.

OEDIPUS. Who primed you° for this? Not your
prophet's trade.

TIRESIAS. You did, you forced me, twisted it out of me.

OEDIPUS. What? Say it again—I'll understand it better.

TIRESIAS. Didn't you understand, just now?

---

384 temper: Here, *temper* refers to character; the qualities that determine how a person behaves.
385 revile: abuse verbally.

396 and given eyes: (ironic) if I had knowledge of the past.

406 primed you: instructed you beforehand in what to say.

1 The Tragic Vision *Why does Oedipus suddenly turn against Tiresias?*

2 The Tragic Vision *Is fury a desirable quality in a leader, or is it a flaw? Explain.*

266 UNIT 2 ANCIENT GREECE

Vocabulary Practice

Analyze Word Structure In line 418, Tiresias warns that Oedipus and his loved ones "live together in *infamy*." Work on the board or on an overhead projector as students analyze the structure of this word. Suggest that they consult a dictionary for any word parts they are unsure of.

- *In-* prefix meaning "not; without"
- *Fam* root word from the Latin *fama,* "fame; reputation"
- *-y* noun-forming suffix

Now suggest that students go further to consider the connotation: *infamy* means "without fame or reputation," but not in the sense that one's neighbor has no fame in comparison, say, to a movie star. Instead, it suggests a very bad reputation, notoriety, or dishonor. A person of great wickedness might be accused of *infamy*. Have students suggest other synonyms they know that suggest a similar degree of badness. (*disgrace, disrepute, ignominy*)

410   Or are you tempting me to talk?

   OEDIPUS. No, I can't say I grasped your meaning.
    Out with it, again!

   TIRESIAS. I say you are the murderer you hunt.

   OEDIPUS. That obscenity, twice—by god, you'll pay.

415 TIRESIAS. Shall I say more, so you can really rage?

   OEDIPUS. Much as you want. Your words are nothing—futile.

3   TIRESIAS. You cannot imagine . . . I tell you,
    you and your loved ones live together in infamy,
    you cannot see how far you've gone in guilt.

420 OEDIPUS. You think you can keep this up and never suffer?

   TIRESIAS. Indeed, if the truth has any power.

   OEDIPUS.   It does
    but not for you, old man. You've lost your power,
    stone-blind, stone-deaf—senses, eyes blind as stone!

   TIRESIAS. I pity you, flinging at me the very insults
    each man here will fling at you so soon.

425 OEDIPUS.   Blind,
    lost in the night, endless night that nursed you!
    You can't hurt me or anyone else who sees the
    light—
    you can never touch me.

   TIRESIAS.
        True, it is not your fate
    to fall at my hands. Apollo is quite enough,
430   and he will take some pains to work this
    out.

4   OEDIPUS. Creon! Is this conspiracy his
    or yours?

   TIRESIAS. Creon is not your downfall,
    no, you are your own.

   OEDIPUS.
            O power—
    wealth and empire, skill
      outstripping skill
    in the heady° rivalries of life,
435   what envy lurks inside you!° Just

---

5 Apply Background Knowledge *Who are Oedipus's loved ones?*

433–435 O power . . . lurks inside you: competition for power leads to jealousy.
434 heady: intoxicating; dizzying.

Oedipus replying to the Sphinx, 1931. Glyn Philpot. Bronze, height: 84 cm Tate Gallery, London.
View the Art What do you think the sculpture's hand gestures and facial expression suggest about Oedipus? ★

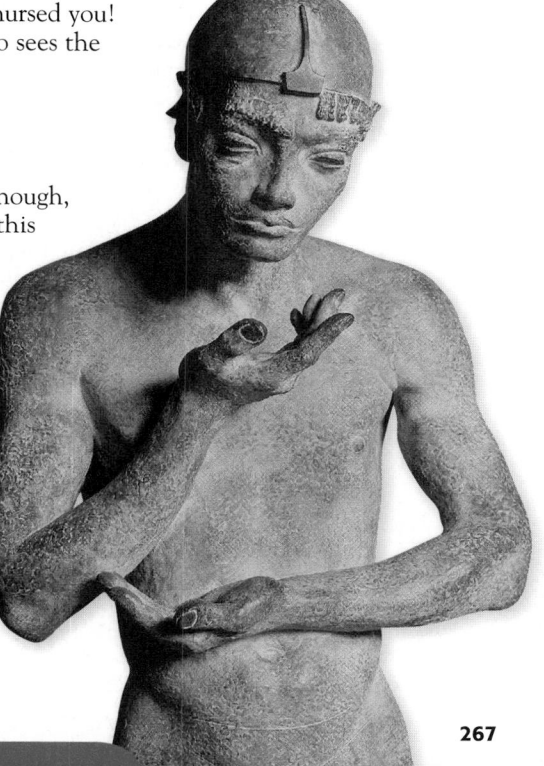

267

Teach

Reading Strategy | 3

Review Have students review their previous evaluations of Oedipus's character. **Ask:** In lines 415–425, what information do you learn about Oedipus's character? *(He is quick to anger and to judgment.)*

Reading Strategy | 4

Draw Conclusions

Oedipus accuses Creon or Tiresias—or both—of conspiracy. **Ask:** In line 431, is Oedipus jumping to a conclusion, or does he have evidence for this accusation? *(He has no evidence; he is speaking in anger.)*

Reading Strategy | 5

Apply Background Knowledge **Answer:**
Oedipus's loved ones are his wife Jocasta and his four children.

Learning Objectives
Activating background knowledge. (SE)
Reviewing character. (TE)
Drawing conclusions. (TE)
Analyzing word structure. (TE)

Advanced Learners/Pre-AP

DIFFERENTIATED INSTRUCTION

SMALL GROUP
Compare and Contrast Point out the changes that seem to take place in Oedipus's character. **Ask:** Does he seem like the sympathetic king who greeted his subjects in the beginning, or does he seem more like a tyrant? (If necessary, discuss the meaning of *tyrant.*) *(Most students will agree he now seems more like a tyrant.)*

Have students work in small groups to compare and contrast Oedipus's behavior at the beginning with his behavior at this point. They can use a simple two-column chart to list acts that make him seem a benevolent ruler and those that make him seem a tyrant. Have groups share any conclusions with the class.

Benevolent King	Tyrant

Teach

Big Idea   1

The Tragic Vision Answer:
Oedipus has an exalted opinion of himself because only he could solve the riddle of the Sphinx. Pride in his intelligence might prove to be a character flaw if it leads him to think he alone is always right.

Literary Element   2

Chorus Answer: *The chorus's leader is the voice of reason and moderation. He tries to persuade both Oedipus and Tiresias to calm down and focus on the problem at hand—identifying Laius's murderer.*

for this,
the crown the city gave me—I never sought it,
they laid it in my hands—for this alone, Creon,
the soul of trust, my loyal friend from the start
steals against me . . . so hungry to overthrow me

440 he sets this wizard on me, this scheming quack,
this fortune-teller peddling lies, eyes peeled
for his own profit—seer blind in his craft!

Come here, you pious fraud. Tell me,
when did you ever prove yourself a prophet?

445 When the Sphinx, that chanting Fury° kept her
    deathwatch here,
why silent then, not a word to set our people free?
There was a riddle, not for some passer-by to solve—
it cried out for a prophet. Where were you?
Did you rise to the crisis? Not a word,

450 you and your birds, your gods—nothing.
No, but I came by, Oedipus the ignorant,
I stopped the Sphinx! With no help from the birds,
the flight of my own intelligence hit the mark.

And this is the man you'd try to overthrow?

455 You think you'll stand by Creon when he's king?
You and the great mastermind—
you'll pay in tears, I promise you, for this,
this witch-hunt.° If you didn't look so senile
the lash° would teach you what your scheming means!

460 LEADER. I would suggest his words were spoken in anger,
Oedipus . . . yours too, and it isn't what we need.
The best solution to the oracle, the riddle°
posed by god—we should look for that.

TIRESIAS. You are the king no doubt, but in one respect,

465 at least, I am your equal: the right to reply.
I claim that privilege too.
I am not your slave. I serve Apollo.
I don't need Creon to speak for me in public.
                                                    So,
you mock my blindness? Let me tell you this.

445 Fury: The Furies were three avenging spirits who punished crimes that were beyond the reach of human justice. This reference is used loosely by Oedipus; the Sphinx was not one of the Furies.

458 witch-hunt: false accusation; search for evidence that does not exist.
459 lash: whip.

462 solution to the . . . riddle: The precise meaning of an oracle was often vague or ambiguous (open to different interpretations).

1 **The Tragic Vision** *How would you describe Oedipus's opinion of himself? Could this be problematic? Explain.*

2 **Chorus** *What can you infer about the attitude of the chorus's leader?*

268 UNIT 2   ANCIENT GREECE

Speaking Practice

Deliver an Informative Presentation
Explain to students that drama and poetry of ancient Greece was often accompanied by music. The members of the chorus did not merely chant their lines, they sang them, at the same time moving back and forth in the circular orchestra area in formalized dance patterns.

Have students investigate the music played during ancient Greek performances and contemporary performances of ancient classics. Suggest that they check Web sites that contain sound or video clips of contemporary performances. Have students present their findings to the class in an informative presentation.

470 You with your precious eyes,
     you're blind to the corruption of your life,
     to the house° you live in, those you live with—
     who *are* your parents? Do you know? All unknowing
     you are the scourge of your own flesh and blood,
475 the dead below the earth and the living here above,
     and the double lash of your mother and your father's curse
     will whip you from this land one day, their footfall
     treading you down in terror,° darkness shrouding°
     your eyes that now can see the light!
                                        Soon, soon
480 you'll scream aloud—what haven won't reverberate?°
     What rock of Cithaeron° won't scream back in echo?
     That day you learn the truth about your marriage,
     the wedding-march that sang you into your halls,
     the lusty voyage home to the fatal harbor!°
485 And a load of other horrors you'd never dream
     will level you with yourself and all your children.

     There. Now smear us with insults—Creon, myself
     and every word I've said. No man will ever
     be rooted from the earth as brutally as you.

490 OEDIPUS. Enough! Such filth from him? Insufferable—°
     what, still alive? Get out—
     faster, back where you came from—vanish!

     TIRESIAS. I'd never have come if you hadn't called me here.

     OEDIPUS. If I thought you'd blurt out such absurdities,
495   you'd have died waiting before I'd had you summoned.

     TIRESIAS. Absurd, am I? To you, not to your parents:
         the ones who bore you found me sane enough.

     OEDIPUS. Parents—who? Wait . . . who is my father?

     TIRESIAS. This day will bring your birth and your
         destruction.

500 OEDIPUS. Riddles—all you can say are riddles, murk
         and darkness.

     TIRESIAS. Ah, but aren't you the best man alive at
         solving riddles?

---

472 house: in this use, a family including ancestors, descendants, and close relatives.

477–478 footfall . . . in terror: memory of what occurred will haunt you.
478 shrouding: covering; ironic, because a shroud is also used to cover the dead.
480 you'll scream . . . reverberate: you will find no escape from the horror.
481 Cithaeron: a remote mountain range.

484 lusty voyage . . . harbor: refers to the consummation of Oedipus's marriage to Jocasta.

490 Insufferable: unbearable; intolerable.

---

4 The Tragic Vision *Why does Oedipus ask for Tiresias's help and then refuse it?*

5 Apply Background Knowledge *How does Tiresias turn Oedipus's reputation for solving riddles against him?*

Literary Element 3

Foreshadowing Point out that the words of Tiresias in lines 480–486 foreshadow the doom to come for Oedipus. **Ask:** How do you think Tiresias's prediction will come to pass? (*Students will probably agree that Tiresias's prediction will come true; how that will happen may be the source of some imaginative guesswork.*)

Big Idea 4

The Tragic Vision
Answer: *Tiresias has identified Oedipus as the killer he seeks, and Oedipus is not ready to think of himself as guilty of murder.*

Reading Strategy 5

Apply Background Knowledge Answer: *Tiresias is saying in effect, "You were clever enough to solve the Sphinx's riddle; you should be able to solve this riddle as well."*

English Learners

DIFFERENTIATED INSTRUCTION

Beginning Students who have difficulty reading the play may be able to understand better by seeing it. First have students write down several questions about the reading. Then show a videotape or DVD of selected scenes from a production of *Oedipus the King*. Tell students to watch for how the characters relate to each other. Have them try to follow the basic events as they unfold.

Then discuss the questions that students have written and any new questions that may have arisen.

If no recorded version is available, you might consider asking theater students to stage a modified readers-theater version. Books in hand, they should stage entrances and exits and use what gestures seem appropriate.

Learning Objectives
Analyzing chorus. (SE)
Applying background knowledge. (SE)
Analyzing foreshadowing. (TE)
Deliver an informative presentation. (TE)

269

Teach

Literary Element | 1

Theme Exchanging riddles with strangers is a common theme in world literature. The hero's fate usually depends on giving the correct answers to the riddle. In Giacomo Puccini's opera *Turandot*, Princess Turandot executes any suitor who cannot answer her riddles. In J.R.R. Tolkien's fantasy *The Hobbit*, Bilbo's life is at stake as he exchanges riddles with Gollum. **Ask:** How do riddles figure prominently in the Oedipus legend? *(Oedipus answers the riddle of the Sphinx to save Thebes and become king. Now he is trying to solve another riddle to save Thebes once again.)*

View the Art ★

Answer: *The old man seated on the right has probably requested a prophecy because he is the least involved in the ritual.*

George Edward Robertson painted landscapes as well as portraits of contemporary and historical figures. In this fanciful painting, the Pythia is burning laurel leaves to prepare herself for receiving a prophecy from Apollo. Other figures are holding lyres—stringed instruments strongly associated with Apollo.

The Oracle. George Edward Robertson (b. 1864). Oil on canvas, 145.5 x 250.2 cm. Private collection.

View the Art In this painting, Robertson depicts three people holding lyres—stringed instruments associated with Apollo. Which figure in this painting do you think has come, like Creon, to request a prophecy from the oracle? How can you tell? ★

---

1 OEDIPUS. Mock me for that, go on, and you'll reveal
    my greatness.

  TIRESIAS. Your great good fortune, true, it was your ruin.

  OEDIPUS. Not if I saved the city—what do I care?

  TIRESIAS. Well then, I'll be going.

[*To his* ATTENDANT.]

505   Take me home, boy.

  OEDIPUS. Yes, take him away. You're a nuisance here.
    Out of the way, the irritation's gone.

[*Turning his back on* TIRESIAS, *moving toward the palace.*]

  TIRESIAS.   I will go,
    once I have said what I came here to say.
    I'll never shrink from the anger in your eyes—

Grammar Practice

Identifying Noun Clauses

Tell students that a noun clause is a subordinate clause used as a noun. A noun clause can be used as a subject, a direct object, an indirect object, an object of a preposition, or a predicate nominative. Words that introduce noun clauses include *how, that, what, when, where,* and *who.* Write the following on the board and ask students to identify the noun clauses and their functions:

I have said <u>what I came here to say</u>. *(direct object)*

<u>Whoever murdered King Laius</u> must leave Thebes. *(subject)*

Tiresias knew the details about <u>what had happened</u>. *(object of the preposition)*

Have students write sentences with noun clauses used in at least three of the functions mentioned above.

510   you can't destroy me. Listen to me closely:
          the man you've sought so long, proclaiming,
          cursing up and down, the murderer of Laius—
          he is here. A stranger,°
          you may think, who lives among you,
515   he soon will be revealed a native Theban
          but he will take no joy in the revelation.
          Blind who now has eyes, beggar who now is rich,
          he will grope his way toward a foreign soil,
          a stick tapping before him step by step.

      [OEDIPUS *enters the palace*.]

520   Revealed at last, brother and father both
          to the children he embraces, to his mother
          son and husband both—he sowed the loins
          his father sowed,° he spilled his father's blood!

          Go in and reflect on that, solve that.
525   And if you find I've lied
          from this day onward call the prophet blind.

      [TIRESIAS *and the* BOY *exit to the side*.]

      CHORUS.   Who—
          who is the man the voice of god denounces
          resounding out of the rocky gorge of Delphi?
            The horror too dark to tell,
530   whose ruthless bloody hands have done the work?
          His time has come to fly
       to outrace the stallions of the storm
                     his feet a streak of speed—
          Cased in armor, Apollo son of the Father°
535   lunges on him, lightning-bolts afire!
          And the grim unerring Furies
                closing for the kill.
                           Look,
          the word of god has just come blazing
          flashing off Parnassus'° snowy heights!
540   That man who left no trace—
          after him, hunt him down with all our strength!
          Now under bristling timber
            up through rocks and caves he stalks
                 like the wild mountain bull—

513 stranger: in its original sense, a stranger was a foreigner or a person in another's house as a guest or as an intruder.

522–523 sowed the loins . . . sowed: had children with the same woman with whom his father had children.

534 the Father: Zeus.

539 Parnassus: twin-peaked mountain near Delphi, sacred to Apollo and Dionysus.

 Apply Background Knowledge *Under what circumstances did Oedipus marry Jocasta?*

Teach

Literary Element   **2**

Metaphor Point out, in line 532, the metaphor "the stallions of the storm." **Ask:** What do you think this metaphor means? Why is it appropriate? *(A stallion is a powerful, swift force, like a storm. The metaphor is appropriate because it would be impossible to outrun or escape either force.)*

Reading Strategy   **3**

Apply Background Knowledge **Answer:** *When Oedipus arrived in Thebes after destroying the Sphinx, he was acclaimed as the savior of the people and offered the throne, along with the hand of Jocasta, recently widowed because of Laius's death.*

Learning Objectives
Applying background knowledge. (SE)
Analyzing art. (TE)
Analyzing theme. (TE)
Identifying noun clauses. (TE)
Analyzing metaphor. (TE)

English Learners

DIFFERENTIATED INSTRUCTION

Advanced Ask students to review what questions Oedipus set out to answer and to list the answers that have come so far from various sources. **Ask:** How has Oedipus responded to the information he has found out? *(He has denied the truth of much of it and has accused Tiresias and Creon of conspiracy for daring to suggest that he, Oedipus, might be at fault.)*

Advanced Learners/Pre-AP

DIFFERENTIATED INSTRUCTION

Predict Have students review the evidence that Oedipus has collected so far to solve the mystery of Laius's murder. **Ask:** Why isn't the play over? What's left to happen? *(Oedipus insists on finding proof for the accusations against him.)* Remind students that Greek audiences would have come to this play knowing Oedipus's story. They were not so much concerned with the solution to the mystery as with *how* that solution is revealed and how the characters react to what they learn.

271

Teach

Reading Strategy | 1

Make Inferences Read lines 556–560 aloud to students.

Ask: From this passage, how do you infer the citizens of Thebes feel about their king? *(They are loyal to him; they refuse to believe that Oedipus killed Laius without proof to support Tiresias's statement.)*

Literary Element | 2

Chorus **Answer:** *The chorus reveres the prophet Tiresias but cannot believe his accusation that Oedipus killed Laius.*

Progress Check

Can students analyze chorus?

If No → See Unit 2 Teaching Resources Book, p. 77.

 To check students' understanding of the selection, see Unit 2 Teaching Resource Book, p. 82.

545   cut off from men, each step an agony, frenzied, racing
        blind
      but he cannot outrace the dread voices of Delphi
      ringing out of the heart of Earth,°
          the dark wings° beating around him shrieking doom
                      the doom that never dies, the terror—
550   The skilled prophet scans the birds and shatters me with
        terror!
      I can't accept him, can't deny him, don't know what to
        say,
      I'm lost, and the wings of dark foreboding beating—
      I cannot see what's come, what's still to come . . .
      and what could breed a blood feud between
555   Laius' house and the son of Polybus?°
   1 I know of nothing, not in the past and not now,
      no charge to bring against our king, no cause
      to attack his fame that rings throughout Thebes—
          not without proof—not for the ghost of Laius,
560   not to avenge a murder gone without a trace.

      Zeus and Apollo know, they know, the great masters
              of all the dark and depth of human life.
      But whether a mere man can know the truth,
      whether a seer can fathom° more than I—
565   there is no test, no certain proof
          though matching skill for skill
      a man can outstrip a rival. No, not till I see
      these charges proved will I side with his accusers.
      We saw him then, when the she-hawk° swept against him,
570   saw with our own eyes his skill, his brilliant triumph—
          there was the test—he was the joy of Thebes!°
          Never will I convict my king, never in my heart.

                            ⳹

2 | Chorus *What dilemma is troubling the chorus?*

547 **the heart of Earth:** a sacred, egg-shaped stone in the temple at Delphi was said to mark the center of the earth.
548 **dark wings:** The Furies are often depicted as winged monsters.

555 **son of Polybus:** Oedipus; Polybus was the king of Corinth who raised Oedipus.

563–571 **whether a mere man . . . joy of Thebes:** They will not believe that the hero who saved Thebes can be guilty without positive proof.
564 **fathom:** here, understand a mysterious or complex matter.

569 **she-hawk:** the Sphinx.

Reading Practice

SMALL GROUP

Synthesize For students to understand a literary work fully, it is important that they know how to synthesize outside information with their reading. Present this quotation from Aristotle's *Poetics:*

"The plot, then, is the first principle, and as it were the soul of a tragedy: character holds the second place."

Remind students that Aristotle was not creating rules for writing Greek drama; he was analyzing Greek drama—including *Oedipus the King*—that he had seen.

Have students work in small groups to discuss the quotation in terms of the play. Do they think the characters and the changes they go through are as vital as the plot? How would the play be different

with different character development? *(Answers will vary, but have students provide textual support for their opinions.)* Students should share the main points of their discussions with the class.

After You Read

Respond and Think Critically

Respond and Interpret

1. What did you find most surprising in this section of the play? Explain.

2. (a)Why do the Theban citizens come to Oedipus at the beginning of the play? (b)How would you describe Oedipus's response to them?

3. (a)According to Apollo's oracle, why has the plague struck Thebes? (b)What does this explanation suggest about ancient Greek beliefs?

4. (a)How does Oedipus react to Tiresias's accusation? (b)What might this suggest about his character?

Analyze and Evaluate

5. A **symbol** is something that stands both for itself and something in addition to itself. (a)What might Tiresias's blindness symbolize? (b)Do you think this is an effective symbol? Explain.

6. How would you describe the **mood**, or overall feeling, of the play? Explain.

Connect

7. **Big Idea** **The Tragic Vision** How does *Oedipus the King* so far reflect Sophocles' vision of human destiny as "darkly beautiful"?

8. **Connect to Today** How does *Oedipus the King* resemble a modern detective story?

Literary Element Chorus

In ancient Greek drama, the **chorus** expressed traditional social and religious views many audience members shared.

1. How do the lines of the chorus differ from other speeches in the play?

2. How does Sophocles involve the chorus in the play's action?

Reading Strategy Apply Background Knowledge

Applying what you know to what you are reading helps you make connections that increase your understanding of a drama.

Partner Activity Review the chart you made on page 251 and then answer this question with a partner. Which pieces of background information did you find most useful, and why?

Literature Online

Selection Resources For Selection Quizzes, eFlashcards, and Reading-Writing Connection activities, go to glencoe.com and enter QuickPass code GLW6053u2.

Vocabulary Practice

Practice with Denotation and Connotation
Work with a partner to complete a graphic organizer like the one below for each vocabulary word. Write the vocabulary word in one box and a word with a similar denotation in the next. Then explain which of the two words has stronger positive or negative connotations.

dignity   vengeance   denounce   dire

EXAMPLE:

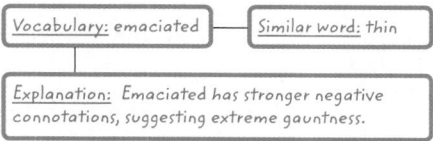

Writing

Write a Letter Imagine you are traveling through ancient Greece. When you arrive in Thebes, you find the city in turmoil because of the plague. Describe this crisis in a letter to a friend. Express your opinion of the Thebans and make sure to base your description on information in the play.

SOPHOCLES **273**

After You Read

Assess

1. Answers will vary.

2. (a) to save the city from the plague (b) He offers to do whatever he can.

3. (a) The city is harboring the murderer of its former king. (b) The gods use natural disasters to punish crimes.

4. (a) Oedipus is outraged and accuses Tiresias of plotting with Creon to seize the throne. (b) Oedipus is quick to anger.

5. (a) inner sight and wisdom (b) Some students may say blindness as a symbol for wisdom is too common in literature to be effective for modern readers.

6. The mood seems ominous.

7. The belief that the gods punish crimes is "darkly beautiful." Oedipus's determination to find the killer of Laius is admirable.

8. There is a murder (the killing of Laius), a detective (Oedipus), an investigation, and a suspect (Oedipus).

Writing

Students' letters should express opinions of the Thebans and their leaders, include descriptions based on information from the play, and follow the format of a personal letter.

Vocabulary

dignity—self-respect; dignity has stronger positives, suggesting a physical as well as emotional bearing.

vengeance—retaliation; vengeance has stronger negatives, suggesting a violent way of getting even.

denounce—accuse; denounce has stronger negatives, suggesting a public attack.

dire—terrible; dire has stronger negatives, suggesting inescapable fate.

Literary Element

1. The lines seem directed to the audience, they are sung, and they are presented by a group.

2. The leader of the chorus interacts with Oedipus.

Reading Strategy

Students may say their knowledge of the riddle of the Sphinx helped them understand why Oedipus is so eager to solve Laius's murder.

Before You Read

Focus

Summary

Oedipus accuses Creon of conspiring against him, and Creon denies his charges angrily. Jocasta tries to mediate their quarrel and, to prove that oracles cannot be trusted, tells how Laius had their son killed so that he could not kill his father, as predicted. Oedipus then tells how he left Corinth to avoid his own predicted fate and how he killed a stranger who attacked him. They await the testimony of the sole eyewitness to that event.

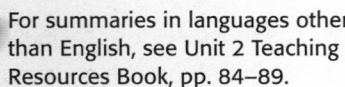

For summaries in languages other than English, see Unit 2 Teaching Resources Book, pp. 84–89.

Vocabulary

Cartoon Depictions
Suggest that students draw sketches or cartoons to depict situations suggested by each of the vocabulary words. They can display their artwork and challenge classmates to name the vocabulary words.

274

Before You Read

Oedipus the King

Build Background

Greek dramas were based on myths and legends known and loved by Athenians. Favorite subjects included the Trojan War and such legendary figures as Oedipus, Agamemnon, and the Greek gods and goddesses. Because the audience already knew the ending of Oedipus's story, Sophocles could focus on developing character and creating dialogue rich in meaning and tinged with irony.

Literary Element · Tragedy

A **tragedy** is a literary work in which the main character, or hero, is a person of great ability who experiences a downfall primarily because of a **tragic flaw:** a fault within his or her character. Excessive pride, or *hubris* (hyü′brəs), is the most common flaw. Ambition, jealousy, self-doubt, and anger are other weaknesses that can defeat the tragic hero. Even though he or she suffers defeat, and often death, the tragic hero ultimately gains some kind of insight into himself or herself. As you read, ask yourself, What tragic qualities does *Oedipus the King* reflect?

Reading Strategy · Analyze Argument

Argument is a form of persuasion in which logic or reason is used to try to influence someone's ideas or actions. Logical reasoning may be either inductive or deductive. **Inductive** reasoning moves from the specific to the general; **deductive** reasoning moves from the general to the specific. As you read this section of *Oedipus the King*, ask yourself, What arguments do the characters construct and what reasons do they cite for acting and thinking as they do?

Tip: Examine Reasoning Use a chart like the one below to record the thesis statements and evidence the characters present.

Thesis	Evidence

Learning Objectives

For pages 274–290

In studying this text, you will focus on the following objectives:

Literary Study: Analyzing tragedy.

Reading: Analyzing argument.

Writing: Writing an essay.

Vocabulary

sullen (sul′ən) *adj.* showing resentment and ill humor by sulky withdrawal; p. 280 *My little brother was sullen because he was grounded.*

foreboding (fôr bō′ding) *n.* a feeling something bad or harmful will happen; p. 285 *Caroline had a foreboding the plane would crash.*

gauge (gāj) *v.* to estimate; judge; p. 286 *Actors try to gauge the audience's reactions to their lines.*

crucial (krōō′shəl) *adj.* essential; decisive; p. 287 *She made the crucial decision to become a writer.*

retract (ri trakt′) *v.* take back or deny; p. 287 *Harry realized it was too late to retract his cruel words.*

Tip: Synonyms Synonyms are words that have nearly the same meaning. For example, *glum* is a synonym of *sullen* because it is an adjective that also describes something that shows ill humor.

Selection Skills

Literary Elements
- Tragedy (SE pp. 274, 276, 279, 280, 283, 285, 290)
- Irony (TE p. 277)
- Sequence (TE p. 283)

Vocabulary Skills
- Practice with Synonyms (SE p. 290)
- Understand Idiom (TE p. 279)
- Understand Synonyms and Antonyms (TE p. 287)

Oedipus the King (part 2)

Speaking/Listening/Viewing Skills
- Analyze Art (TE p. 281)
- Present an Oral Interpretation (TE p. 284)

Reading Skills
- Analyze Argument (SE pp. 274, 278, 280, 283, 288, 290; TE p. 286)
- Evaluate Characters (TE pp. 275, 276, 280)
- Identify Problem and Solution (TE p. 276)
- Review (TE p. 285)

Writing Skills/Grammar
- Essay (SE p. 290)
- Research Report (TE p. 278)
- Informational Document (TE p. 282)
- Emphatic Verbs (TE p. 288)

274

OEDIPUS THE KING

[*Enter* CREON *from the side*.]

CREON. My fellow-citizens, I hear King Oedipus
levels terrible charges at me. I had to come.
575 I resent it deeply. If, in the present crisis,
he thinks he suffers any abuse from me,
anything I've done or said that offers him
the slightest injury, why, I've no desire
to linger out this life, my reputation a shambles.
580 The damage I'd face from such an accusation
is nothing simple. No, there's nothing worse:
branded a traitor in the city, a traitor
to all of you and my good friends.

1 LEADER.   True,
but a slur might have been forced out of him,
585 by anger perhaps, not any firm conviction.

CREON. The charge was made in public, wasn't it?
I put the prophet up to spreading lies?

LEADER. Such things were said . . .
I don't know with what intent, if any.

590 CREON. Was his glance steady, his mind right
when the charge was brought against me?

LEADER. I really couldn't say. I never look
to judge the ones in power.

[*The doors open.* OEDIPUS *enters*.]

                                   Wait,
2 here's Oedipus now.

OEDIPUS.   You—here? You have the gall
595 to show your face before the palace gates?
You, plotting to kill me, kill the king—
I see it all, the marauding° thief himself
scheming to steal my crown and power!

597 **marauding:** roaming about in search of loot.

3 The Tragic Vision *Why has Oedipus reached this conclusion? What does his behavior suggest about his character?*

SOPHOCLES **275**

Teach

Reading Strategy   1

Evaluate Characters
Direct students to lines 583–585.

Ask: Do you agree with the leader or think that Oedipus really believes Creon is plotting against him? (*Answers will vary, but have students support their answers.*)

Vocabulary   2

Multiple-Meaning Words
Point out *gall* in line 594. Have students use a dictionary to list the many meanings this word has and then use context to determine the appropriate meaning here. (*Possible answers: rudeness; boldness; audacity.*)

Big Idea   3

The Tragic Vision
Answer: *Oedipus concludes Creon is plotting to overthrow him because Creon suggested that Oedipus summon Tiresias, who then accused Oedipus of murdering Laius. Oedipus is disturbed and is acting irrationally.*

Approaching Level

DIFFERENTIATED INSTRUCTION

 SMALL GROUP

Paraphrase The poetic style of this translation may be difficult for some students to understand. Explain that poetic or dramatic translators often employ unusual sentence order to create a particular sound, mood, or rhythm. Have students identify passages they find difficult and then discuss the passages in small groups. Suggest that they paraphrase speeches or try to put them in more literal form to help their comprehension.

English Learners

DIFFERENTIATED INSTRUCTION

SMALL GROUP

Intermediate For English learners having difficulty, examine the text to find key sentences. Copy them and add a paraphrase or more literal translation for each. Ideally, your collection of key sentences should provide highlights that will help students understand the plot. Distribute copies, have students locate the quotations in the text, and discuss them in small groups.

Learning Objectives
Evaluating characters. (TE)
Understanding multiple-meaning words

Teach

Vocabulary | 1

Idiom Ask: Look at the phrase "a wicked way with words" in line 610. Using context, what do you think it means? *(cleverness in using words)* Have students supply other idioms or familiar phrases with *wicked*. *(Possible responses: wicked temper, wicked fastball, wicked ways)*

Reading Strategy | 2

Evaluate Character
Direct students to lines 627–629. **Ask:** Do you think Oedipus makes a valid point about Tiresias's failure to accuse him at the time of the murder? *(Some students may say that Oedipus's point seems valid. Others, however, may say that the prophet would not be aware of the information at the time if the gods did not want him to be.)*

Literary Element | 3

Tragedy Answer: *Oedipus's pride is clouding his judgment, preventing him from even considering what others tell him.*

For additional literary element practice, see Unit 2 Teaching Resource Book, p. 90.

                                                        Tell me,
600   in god's name, what did you take me for,
       coward or fool, when you spun out your plot?
       Your treachery—you think I'd never detect it
       creeping against me in the dark? Or sensing it,
       not defend myself? Aren't you the fool,
       you and your high adventure. Lacking numbers,
605   powerful friends, out for the big game of empire—
       you need riches, armies to bring that quarry° down!

       CREON. Are you quite finished? It's your turn to listen
       for just as long as you've . . . instructed me.
       Hear me out, then judge me on the facts.

610   OEDIPUS. You've a wicked way with words, Creon, **1**
       but I'll be slow to learn—from you.
       I find you a menace, a great burden to me.

       CREON. Just one thing, hear me out in this.

       OEDIPUS.   Just one thing,
       don't tell me you're not the enemy, the traitor.

615   CREON. Look, if you think crude, mindless stubbornness
       such a gift, you've lost your sense of balance.

       OEDIPUS. If you think you can abuse a kinsman,
       then escape the penalty, you're insane.

       CREON. Fair enough, I grant you. But this injury
620   you say I've done you, what is it?

       OEDIPUS. Did you induce me, yes or no,
       to send for that sanctimonious° prophet?

       CREON. I did. And I'd do the same again.

       OEDIPUS. All right then, tell me, how long is it now
       since Laius . . .

       CREON.   Laius—what did *he* do?

625   OEDIPUS.   Vanished,
       swept from sight, murdered in his tracks.

       CREON. The count of the years would run you far back . . .

       OEDIPUS. And that far back, was the prophet at his trade?

2 CREON. Skilled as he is today, and just as honored.

       OEDIPUS. Did he ever refer to me then, at that time?

630   CREON.   No,
       never, at least, when I was in his presence.

606 quarry: something pursued or hunted; prey.

622 sanctimonious: exhibiting false virtue; hypocritical.

3 Tragedy *Why does Oedipus display such stubbornness here?*

276 UNIT 2 ANCIENT GREECE

Reading Practice

Identify Problem and Solution Review with students that problems often have various possible solutions and that it is important to explore all of the solution options before deciding on one. Oedipus is faced with a plague tormenting his city.

Have small groups of students discuss the solutions Oedipus explores and create other possible solutions not mentioned in the text. Suggest that groups analyze

one problem at a time and record each possible solution. They can use a simple two-column chart like the following.

Problem	Possible Solution

When students have concluded their discussion, they should recommend the solution they think is best and explain the reasons for their conclusions.

276

OEDIPUS. But you did investigate the murder, didn't you?

CREON. We did our best, of course, discovered nothing.

OEDIPUS. But the great seer never accused me then—
why not?

635 CREON. I don't know. And when I don't, *I* keep quiet.

OEDIPUS. You do know this, you'd tell it too—
if you had a shred of decency.

CREON.   What?
If I know, I won't hold back.

OEDIPUS.   Simply this:
if the two of you had never put heads together,
640 we'd never have heard about *my* killing Laius.

CREON. If that's what he says . . . well, you know best.
But now I have a right to learn from you
as you just learned from me.

OEDIPUS.   Learn your fill,
you never will convict me of the murder.

645 CREON. Tell me, you're married to my sister, aren't you?

4 OEDIPUS. A genuine discovery—there's no denying that.

CREON. And you rule the land with her, with equal power?

OEDIPUS. She receives from me whatever she desires.

CREON. And I am the third, all of us are equals?°

650 OEDIPUS. Yes, and it's there you show your stripes—
you betray a kinsman.

CREON.   Not at all.
Not if you see things calmly, rationally,
as I do. Look at it this way first:
who in his right mind would rather rule
655 and live in anxiety than sleep in peace?
Particularly if he enjoys the same authority.
Not I, I'm not the man to yearn for kingship,
not with a king's power in my hands. Who would?
No one with any sense of self-control.
660 Now, as it is, you offer me all I need,
not a fear in the world. But if I wore the crown . . .
there'd be many painful duties to perform,
hardly to my taste.
                              How could kingship
please me more than influence, power
665 without a qualm? I'm not that deluded yet,

649 all of us are equals:
As the queen's brother, Creon is
a member of the royal family
with great influence and power.

SOPHOCLES **277**

Teach

Literary Element   4

Irony Point out Oedipus's
comment "A genuine discovery"
in line 646. **Ask:** What is this
special form of irony? What is its
effect? *(Students should recognize
it as sarcasm. Its effect is to
negate what is said.)*

Learning Objectives
Analyzing tragedy. (SE)
Evaluating character. (TE)
Identify irony. (TE)
Identify problem and solution. (TE)

Advanced Learners/Pre-AP

DIFFERENTIATED INSTRUCTION

Connect to Personal Experience
Students may be able to empathize
with Oedipus and his reactions to the
accusations. Discuss how he must feel,
convinced as he is that his brother-in-law
is working against him, his city is in a state
of destruction, and he has been accused
of murder.

Have students spend several minutes
writing in their journals about a time when
they have either been wrongfully accused
of doing something or have tried to get
away with something. They should explore
the emotions they had at the time and
their reactions.

277

Teach

Reading Strategy · 1

Apply Background Knowledge **Ask:** Why does Creon tell Oedipus to go to Delphi in line 676? *(The oracle of Apollo at Delphi was where Creon got the message that the unpunished murder of Laius was destroying Thebes, which set about all the plot events.)*

Reading Strategy · 2

Analyze Argument **Answer:** *Creon's argument is convincing. He uses deductive reasoning. He states a general principle, that no one would want the anxiety of being king when he can have power and influence without the crown, and argues that, living by that principle, he has no motive for conspiring to overthrow Oedipus.*

Big Idea · 3

The Tragic Vision **Answer:** *Jumping to conclusions might lead one to make unfounded accusations or to act rashly without considering the consequences.*

to reach for anything but privilege outright,
profit free and clear.
Now all men sing my praises, all salute me,
now all who request your favors curry mine.°
670 I'm their best hope: success rests in me.
Why give up that, I ask you, and borrow trouble?
A man of sense, someone who sees things clearly
would never resort to treason.
No, I've no lust for conspiracy in me,
675 nor could I ever suffer one who does.

1 Do you want proof? Go to Delphi yourself,
examine the oracle and see if I've reported
the message word-for-word. This too:
if you detect that I and the clairvoyant°
680 have plotted anything in common, arrest me,
execute me. Not on the strength of one vote,
two in this case, mine as well as yours.
But don't convict me on sheer unverified surmise.°

How wrong it is to take the good for bad,
685 purely at random, or take the bad for good.
But reject a friend, a kinsman? I would as soon
tear out the life within us, priceless life itself.
You'll learn this well, without fail, in time.
Time alone can bring the just man to light;
690 the criminal you can spot in one short day.

LEADER.   Good advice,
my lord, for anyone who wants to avoid disaster.
Those who jump to conclusions may be wrong.

OEDIPUS. When my enemy moves against me quickly,
plots in secret, I move quickly too, I must,
695 I plot and pay him back. Relax my guard a moment,
waiting his next move—he wins his objective,
I lose mine.

CREON.   What do you want?
You want me banished?

OEDIPUS.   No, I want you dead.

669 curry mine: seek my approval, especially through flattery.

679 clairvoyant (klār voi′ənt): a seer, one who is able to apprehend what is not apparent to the five senses; psychic.

683 surmise: speculation; suspicion.

2 Analyze Argument *Is Creon's argument convincing? Explain.*

3 The Tragic Vision *Why might jumping to conclusions be considered a character flaw?*

278 UNIT 2 ANCIENT GREECE

Writing Practice

Write a Research Report Point out to students that in the United States, an accused person must be proven guilty "beyond a reasonable doubt" in order to be convicted of a crime.

Have students research the definition of "beyond a reasonable doubt." Students might look on the Internet for historical or fictional accounts of jury deliberations and the processes that the jurors had to go through to determine a person's guilt or innocence.

As an alternative, students might research historical periods (such as the witchcraft trials of the 1500s–1600s or the McCarthy era of the 1940s–1950s) in which such a concept was not respected.

Finally, have students write paragraphs in which they describe their findings and cite their sources.

CREON. Just to show how ugly a grudge can . . .

OEDIPUS. So,
700   still stubborn? you don't think I'm serious?

CREON. I think you're insane.

OEDIPUS. Quite sane—in my behalf.

CREON. Not just as much in mine?

OEDIPUS. You—my mortal enemy?

CREON. What if you're wholly wrong?

OEDIPUS. No matter—I must rule.

CREON. Not if you rule unjustly.

OEDIPUS. Hear him,° Thebes, my city!

705   CREON. My city too, not yours alone!

LEADER. Please, my lords.

[Enter JOCASTA from the palace.]

Look, Jocasta's coming,
   and just in time too. With her help
   you must put this fighting of yours to rest.

JOCASTA. Have you no sense? Poor misguided men,
710   such shouting—why this public outburst?
   Aren't you ashamed, with the land so sick,
   to stir up private quarrels?

[To OEDIPUS.]

   Into the palace now. And Creon, you go home.
   Why make such a furor over nothing?

715   CREON. My sister, it's dreadful . . . Oedipus, your husband,
   he's bent on a choice of punishments for me,
   banishment from the fatherland or death.

OEDIPUS. Precisely. I caught him in the act, Jocasta,
   plotting, about to stab me in the back.   **4**

720   CREON. Never—curse me, let me die and be damned
   if I've done you any wrong you charge me with.

JOCASTA. Oh god, believe it, Oedipus,
   honor the solemn oath he swears to heaven.
   Do it for me, for the sake of all your people.

[The CHORUS begins to chant.]

725   CHORUS. Believe it, be sensible

704 Hear him: Oedipus suggests that Creon is advocating usurpation—the unlawful seizing of the throne from the rightful king.

5   Tragedy *What quality does Oedipus reveal in his response to Creon?*

Teach

Vocabulary   **4**

Idiom The phrase "stab in the back" (as in line 719) has come to mean a person's being maligned without realizing it. It also implies that someone is trying to harm another by taking actions to insure that he or she does not get ahead in life.

Literary Element   **5**

Tragedy **Answer:** *Oedipus reveals hubris, or excessive pride, insisting on exercising authority even if he is wrong.*

Learning Objectives
Analyzing argument. (SE)
Analyzing tragedy. (SE)
Applying background knowledge. (TE)
Analyzing idioms. (TE)
Writing a research report. (TE)

English Learners

DIFFERENTIATED INSTRUCTION

Intermediate The argument between Oedipus and Creon is becoming quite heated when Jocasta enters to try to put a stop to it. **Ask:** What does Jocasta do in this scene? What role or function does she serve? *(She acts as a mediator, or go-between, to try to get the men to discuss the situation calmly—and in private.)*

Have students suggest contemporary situations they know of in which a mediator or go-between might be useful. **Ask:** By what different names are these people called? What do they do? *(Possible responses are lawyer or family counselor. Answers will vary.)*

Teach

Reading Strategy   1

Evaluate Characters
Ask: The chorus gives two reasons in lines 727–728 for Oedipus not to condemn Creon. Are they valid reasons? *(Students may agree that the Chorus's reasons are sensible and valid.)*

Vocabulary   2

Pantomime Have one or two volunteers pantomime being in a *sullen* mood.

Reading Strategy   3

Analyze Argument
Answer: *No. Oedipus is offended by Creon's accusation, which prevents him from thinking logically.*

Literary Element   4

Tragedy Answer: *Creon alludes to Oedipus's great pride.*

---

    give way, my king, I beg you!

OEDIPUS. What do you want from me, concessions?°

CHORUS. Respect him—he's been no fool in the past
    and now he's strong with the oath he swears to god.

OEDIPUS. You know what you're asking?

CHORUS.   I do.

730 OEDIPUS.   Then out with it!

CHORUS. The man's your friend, your kin, he's under oath—
    don't cast him out, disgraced
    branded with guilt on the strength of hearsay only.

OEDIPUS. Know full well, if that's what you want
735   you want me dead or banished from the land.

CHORUS.   Never—
    no, by the blazing Sun, first god of the heavens!
    Stripped of the gods, stripped of loved ones,
    let me die by inches if that ever crossed my mind.
    But the heart inside me sickens, dies as the land dies
740   and now on top of the old griefs you pile this,
    your fury—both of you!

OEDIPUS.   Then let him go,
    even if it does lead to my ruin, my death
    or my disgrace, driven from Thebes for life.
    It's you, not him I pity—your words move me.
745   He, wherever he goes, my hate goes with him.

CREON. Look at you, **sullen** in yielding, brutal in your rage—
    you'll go too far. It's perfect justice:
    natures like yours are hardest on themselves.

OEDIPUS. Then leave me alone—get out!

CREON.   I'm going.
750   You're wrong, so wrong. These men know I'm right.

[*Exit to the side. The* CHORUS *turns to* JOCASTA.]

CHORUS. Why do you hesitate, my lady
    why not help him in?

727 **concessions:** actions that yield or give in to the demands of another.

---

3   Analyze Argument   *Is Oedipus thinking logically when he makes this statement? Explain.*

4   Tragedy   *To what flaw in Oedipus does Creon allude?*

Vocabulary

sullen (sul′ ən) *adj.* showing resentment and ill humor by sulky withdrawal

---

Grammar Practice

Identify Irregular Verbs Remind students that an irregular verb forms its past tense and past participle in ways other than by adding *-ed* to the base form. Write the following words on the board and have students supply the past tense and past participle of each: *do* (did, done); *drive* (drove, driven); *seek* (sought, sought); *shrink* (shrank, shrunk); *give* (gave, given).

Have students identify five other irregular verbs in the selection and provide the base form, past tense, and past participle of each. They can use a simple chart like the following.

Verb Base	Past Tense	Past Participle

(Possible answers: strike, struck, stricken; leave, left, left; has, had, had)

Apollo. Pietro Vannucci Perugino. Fresco. Salla Del Cambio, Perugia, Italy.

"I have a **terrible** *fear*

the *blind* seer *can* **see**."

SOPHOCLES **281**

Teach

View the Art ★

Pietro Vannucci Perugino (1450?–1523) was an Italian Renaissance painter who once worked in the shop where Leonardo da Vinci was apprenticed. Perugino was famous for his frescoes (such as this detail showing Apollo), which are murals painted on wet plaster. Pope Sixtus IV commissioned Perugino to paint frescoes in the Sistine Chapel, but they were destroyed by Michelangelo, who needed the space to complete his famous fresco of the *Last Judgment*.

Apollo is usually represented as an archer rather than a charioteer. However, he became associated with the sun god Helios, who drove a chariot across the sky each day. Perugino appropriately painted this picture of flight on a ceiling. **Ask:** How does this portrayal of Apollo compare with your idea of what a Greek god might look like? (*Students may say that Apollo looks more like a human than like their idea of a Greek god.*)

Advanced Learners/Pre-AP

DIFFERENTIATED INSTRUCTION

SMALL GROUP **Synthesize** Have students adapt the action in lines 734–751 to a modern setting. Assign students to groups. Ask them to rewrite the dialogue using contemporary language. Tell them to include stage directions specifying setting and costume design. They should also include directions specifying the movements of the characters. Have groups perform their scenes in front of the class. Afterwards, have each group evaluate how true their adaptations remained to the original material, citing examples to support their points.

Learning Objectives
Analyzing argument. (SE)
Analyzing tragedy. (SE)
Evaluating character. (TE)
Identifying irregular verbs. (TE)
Analyzing art. (TE)

281

Teach

Reading Strategy | 1

Metaphor **Ask:** What metaphors appear in lines 760–770? *(the storm-tossed and shattered land; the good helmsman)*

ENGLISH LEARNERS Clarify for English Learners that the chorus is describing the troubles of Thebes and the leadership of Odysseus with these metaphors. Then have them look up *helm* and use that context to infer the definition of *helmsman.*

JOCASTA. Tell me what's happened first.

CHORUS. Loose, ignorant talk started dark suspicions
755   and a sense of injustice cut deeply too.

JOCASTA. On both sides?

CHORUS.   Oh yes.

JOCASTA.   What did they say?

CHORUS. Enough, please, enough! The land's so racked already
   or so it seems to me . . .
   End the trouble here, just where they left it.

760 OEDIPUS. You see what comes of your good intentions now?
   And all because you tried to blunt my anger.

CHORUS.   My king,
   I've said it once, I'll say it time and again—
   I'd be insane, you know it,
   senseless, ever to turn my back on you.
765   You who set our beloved land—storm-tossed, shattered—
   straight on course. Now again, good helmsman,
   steer us through the storm!

[*The* CHORUS *draws away, leaving* OEDIPUS *and* JOCASTA *side by side.*]

JOCASTA.   For the love of god,
   Oedipus, tell me too, what is it?
   Why this rage? You're so unbending.

770 OEDIPUS. I will tell you. I respect you, Jocasta,
   much more than these . . .

[*Glancing at the* CHORUS.]

   Creon's to blame, Creon schemes against me.

JOCASTA. Tell me clearly, how did the quarrel start?

OEDIPUS. He says *I* murdered Laius—I am guilty.

775 JOCASTA. How does he know? Some secret knowledge
   or simple hearsay?

OEDIPUS.   Oh, he sent his prophet in
   to do his dirty work. You know Creon,
   Creon keeps his own lips clean.

JOCASTA.   A prophet?
   Well then, free yourself of every charge!

Writing Practice

SMALL GROUP

Write an Informational Document Explain to students that dramas such as *Oedipus the King* were presented in large theaters during the Festival of Dionysus. Playwrights would compete for a prize by presenting a *tetralogy,* or series of four plays. The tetralogy usually included three tragedies and a comedy.

Have students research the history of the Festival of Dionysus and the drama contests that took place during the festivals. Students may focus on the playwrights that participated or the events that occurred during the festival.

Have students write one-page reports on their findings and share their reports with small groups.

780   Listen to me and learn some peace of mind:
      no skill in the world,
      nothing human can penetrate the future.
      Here is proof, quick and to the point.

      An oracle came to Laius one fine day
785   (I won't say from Apollo himself
      but his underlings, his priests) and it said
      that doom would strike him down at the hands of a son,
2   our son, to be born of our own flesh and blood. But Laius,
      so the report goes at least, was killed by strangers,
790   thieves, at a place where three roads meet . . . my son—
      he wasn't three days old and the boy's father°
      fastened his ankles, had a henchman° fling him away
      on a barren, trackless mountain.
                                    There, you see?
      Apollo brought neither thing to pass. My baby
795   no more murdered his father than Laius suffered—
      his wildest fear—death at his own son's hands.
      That's how the seers and all their revelations
      mapped out the future. Brush them from your mind.
      Whatever the god needs and seeks
800   he'll bring to light himself, with ease.

OEDIPUS.   Strange,
      hearing you just now . . . my mind wandered,
      my thoughts racing back and forth.

JOCASTA. What do you mean? Why so anxious, startled?

OEDIPUS. I thought I heard you say that Laius
805   was cut down at a place where three roads meet.

JOCASTA. That was the story. It hasn't died out yet.

OEDIPUS. Where did this thing happen? Be precise.

JOCASTA. A place called Phocis,° where two branching roads,
      one from Daulia,° one from Delphi,
810   come together—a crossroads.

3   OEDIPUS. When? How long ago?

JOCASTA. The heralds no sooner reported Laius dead
      than you appeared and they hailed you king of Thebes.

791 **the boy's father:** Laius.
792 **henchman:** assistant.

808 **Phocis:** territory in central Greece.
809 **Daulia:** a city near Delphi.

---

4 Tragedy *What do you predict will happen when Jocasta shares this memory?*

5 Analyze Argument *What does Jocasta try to prove? Is she convincing? Explain.*

SOPHOCLES   **283**

Advanced Learners/Pre-AP

DIFFERENTIATED INSTRUCTION

Write a Biography Sophocles presents Oedipus as a pawn of fate; however, Oedipus deals with situations by lashing out in anger, and, therefore, contributes to sealing his own future.

Challenge students to write a biographical sketch of Oedipus's life, keeping in mind the question of whether his fate was inevitable or whether he brought it on himself. Remind students that a biography should include retellings of specific incidents in the subject's life as well as a presentation of the subject's character. Tell students that their sketches should capture the most important personality traits of Oedipus.

Teach

Literary Element **2**

Exposition Point out that Jocasta is supplying vital information about what happened in the past. Tell students to note what conclusions she draws and how this information fits into the overall picture.

Literary Element **3**

Sequence Ask: In lines 810–813, why is Oedipus so concerned with putting together the exact sequence of events? *(He is beginning to realize that his appearance in Thebes immediately following Laius's death was no coincidence.)*

Literary Element **4**

Tragedy Answer: *Students may predict Oedipus will make the connection between himself and King Laius's murder.*

Reading Strategy **5**

Analyze Argument
Answer: *She argues that since the oracle was wrong in predicting Laius would be killed by his son, its other predictions are not to be trusted. Her argument seems logical.*

Learning Objectives
Analyzing tragedy. (SE)
Analyzing argument. (SE)
Identifying metaphors. (TE)
Analyzing exposition. (TE)
Identifying sequence. (TE)
Writing an informational document. (TE)

Reading Strategy | 1

Question Direct students to lines 834–840. **Ask:** Why do you think the servant asked to be sent away? *(He had witnessed Oedipus murder Laius.)*

Big Idea | 2

The Tragic Vision **Answer:**
He realizes Tiresias's statements are probably true based on Jocasta's account of the murdered man and the circumstances of the murder.

OEDIPUS. My god, my god—what have you planned
    to do to me?

JOCASTA. What, Oedipus? What haunts you so?

815 OEDIPUS.   Not yet.
    Laius—how did he look? Describe him.
    Had he reached his prime?

JOCASTA.   He was swarthy,°
    and the gray had just begun to streak his temples,
    and his build . . . wasn't far from yours.

OEDIPUS.   Oh no no,
820   I think I've just called down a dreadful curse
    upon myself—I simply didn't know!

JOCASTA. What are you saying? I shudder to look at you.

OEDIPUS. I have a terrible fear the blind seer can see.°
    I'll know in a moment. One thing more—

JOCASTA.   Anything,
825   afraid as I am—ask, I'll answer, all I can.

OEDIPUS. Did he go with a light or heavy escort,
    several men-at-arms, like a lord, a king?

JOCASTA. There were five in the party, a herald
    among them, and a single wagon carrying Laius.

OEDIPUS.   Ai—
830   now I can see it all, clear as day.
    Who told you all this at the time, Jocasta?

JOCASTA. A servant who reached home, the lone survivor.

OEDIPUS. So, could he still be in the palace—even now?

JOCASTA. No indeed. Soon as he returned from the scene
835   and saw you on the throne with Laius dead and gone,
    he knelt and clutched my hand, pleading with me

[1]   to send him into the hinterlands,° to pasture,
    far as possible, out of sight of Thebes.
    I sent him away. Slave though he was,
840   he'd earned that favor—and much more.

OEDIPUS. Can we bring him back, quickly?

JOCASTA. Easily. Why do you want him so?

OEDIPUS.   I'm afraid,
    Jocasta, I have said too much already.
    That man—I've got to see him.

817 swarthy: having a dark or suntanned complexion.

823 the blind seer can see: can reveal hidden truths.

837 hinterlands: remote regions lying inland from the coast.

[2] The Tragic Vision *Why does Oedipus now realize that the seer "sees"?*

284 UNIT 2 ANCIENT GREECE

Speaking Practice

Present an Oral Interpretation This play lends itself to a readers' theater performance because the dialogue is charged with emotional language. Have students work in small groups to prepare a reader's theater presentation of chosen scenes or sections of the play.

Reader's theater is typically performed with the actors standing or seated on stools, facing the audience, holding their books or resting them on music stands.

Actors address their reading toward the audience and do not turn to look at each other except at special moments. Physical gestures are limited. Actors do, however, make full use of intonation and inflection to portray the emotions of the characters. After groups have had time to practice, have them perform their scenes for the class.

JOCASTA.   Then he'll come.
845   But even I have a right, I'd like to think,
         to know what's torturing you, my lord.

         OEDIPUS.   And so you shall—I can hold nothing back from
              you,
         now I've reached this pitch of dark **foreboding**. **3**
         Who means more to me than you? Tell me,
850   whom would I turn toward but you
         as I go through all this?

         My father was Polybus, king of Corinth.
         My mother, a Dorian,° Merope. And I was held
         the prince of the realm among the people there,
855   till something struck me out of nowhere,
         something strange . . . worth remarking perhaps,
    4 hardly worth the anxiety I gave it.
         Some man at a banquet who had drunk too much
         shouted out—he was far gone, mind you—
860   that I am not my father's son. Fighting words!
         I barely restrained myself that day
         but early the next I went to mother and father,
         questioned them closely, and they were enraged
         at the accusation and the fool who let it fly.
865   So as for my parents I was satisfied,
         but still this thing kept gnawing at me,   **5**
         the slander° spread—I had to make my move.
                                                  And so,
         unknown to mother and father I set out for Delphi,
         and the god Apollo spurned me, sent me away
870   denied the facts I came for,
         but first he flashed before my eyes a future
         great with pain, terror, disaster—I can hear him cry,
         "You are fated to couple with° your mother,
              you will bring
         a breed of children into the light no man can
              bear to see—
875   you will kill your father, the one who gave you life!"
         I heard all that and ran. I abandoned Corinth,

853 **Dorian:** one of four cultural groups that occupied ancient Greece; the Dorians founded the city of Corinth.

867 **slander:** false speech meant to damage another's reputation.

873 **couple with:** marry.

---

6 Tragedy *How did Oedipus react to this prophecy before the play began? What was the result of his actions?*

Vocabulary

foreboding (fôr bō′ ding) n. a feeling that something bad or harmful will happen

SOPHOCLES   **285**

Impromptu Have several volunteers voice their *forebodings* of terrible things that may happen in the next few days. (They can be wildly exaggerated and humorous, or they can be serious.) *(Possible answers: Our cross-country team will be attacked by wild boars; a tornado will hit our town.)*

Literary Element   4

Foreshadowing Point out that lines 855–860 give a clue as to how the story will unfold. **Ask:** How do you think Oedipus will come to the realization that the man has spoken the truth? *(Students may suggest that Oedipus will learn from the servant who witnessed the murder.)*

Reading Strategy   5

Review Discuss with students the role of fate in this play. **Ask:** How important do you think the oracle's prophecy will be to the plot? *(Students should note that given the importance of fate in the lives of ancient Greeks, the prophecy will most likely dictate the plot of the play.)*

Literary Element   6

Tragedy Answer: *He left his supposed father and mother at Corinth and made his way toward Thebes, where he killed Laius. He later destroyed the Sphinx and was awarded the throne and the widowed queen.*

Learning Objectives
Analyzing tragedy. (SE)
Questioning. (TE)
Analyzing foreshadowing. (TE)
Reviewing. (TE)
Presenting an oral interpretation. (TE)

285

Approaching Level

DIFFERENTIATED INSTRUCTION

Monitor Comprehension Help approaching-level students to understand that as Oedipus continues to collect evidence about his past, none of the evidence proves he is innocent of the murder of his father. **Ask:** How did Oedipus find out that Polybus and Merope might not be his real mother and father? *(A guest at a banquet who had too much to drink said that Oedipus was not his father's son.)* How did Oedipus try to show that what the man said was untrue? *(He went to Delphi to ask the famous oracle there.)* Did the oracle at Delphi tell Oedipus that Polybus was his father? *(No)* Instead, what does the oracle say about Oedipus and his father? *(Oedipus will kill his father.)*

Examples Have students work with partners to list a number of things that might be *gauged* and how they might go about gauging them. They can then share their examples with the class.

from that day on I **gauged** its landfall only   **1**
by the stars,° running, always running
toward some place where I would never see

880   the shame of all those oracles come true.
And as I fled I reached that very spot
where the great king, you say, met his death.
Now, Jocasta, I will tell you all.
Making my way toward this triple crossroad

885   I began to see a herald, then a brace° of colts
drawing a wagon, and mounted on the bench . . . a man,
just as you've described him, coming face-to-face,
and the one in the lead and the old man himself
were about to thrust me off the road—brute force—

890   and the one shouldering me aside, the driver,
I strike him in anger!—and the old man, watching me
coming up along his wheels—he brings down
his prod, two prongs straight at my head!
I paid him back with interest!

895   Short work, by god—with one blow of the staff
in this right hand I knock him out of his high seat,
roll him out of the wagon, sprawling headlong—
I killed them all—every mother's son!

Oh, but if there is any blood-tie

900   between Laius and this stranger . . .
what man alive more miserable than I?
More hated by the gods? *I* am the man
no alien, no citizen welcomes to his house,
law forbids it—not a word to me in public,

905   driven out of every hearth° and home.
And all these curses I—no one but I
brought down these piling° curses on myself!
And you, his wife, I've touched your body with these,
the hands that killed your husband cover you with blood.

910   Wasn't I born for torment? Look me in the eyes!
I am abomination°—heart and soul!
I must be exiled, and even in exile
never see my parents, never set foot
on native earth° again. Else I'm doomed

915   to couple with my mother and cut my father down . . .

877–878 **gauged . . . the stars:** never went near Corinth.

885 **brace:** matched pair.

905 **hearth:** fireplace; in ancient Greece, the most important part of the home.
907 **piling:** mounting.

911 **abomination:** something disgusting or loathsome; wickedness.

913–914 **set foot . . . native earth:** return to Corinth.

Vocabulary

gauge (gāj) *v.* to estimate; judge

Analyze Argument Have students compare the information given by Oedipus in lines 883–894 with the information given by Jocasta in lines 788–790 and lines 828–829. **Ask:** What information is similar in these two accounts of a killing? *(Both Jocasta and Oedipus mention a crossroads of three roads, a herald, and a wagon; Oedipus says that Jocasta's description of Laius matches the appearance of one* of the men in the wagon.) What effect is this information having on Oedipus's argument that he did not kill Laius? *(Oedipus is doubting his argument now.)* Why does Oedipus use the term *stranger* in line 901, and to whom is he referring? *(In line 789 Jocasta said that Laius was killed by strangers; Oedipus believes he himself may be the "stranger" who killed Laius.)*

Polybus who reared me, gave me life.

But why, why?
Wouldn't a man of judgment say—and wouldn't he
   be right—
some savage power has brought this down upon my head?

920   Oh no, not that, you pure and awesome° gods,
      never let me see that day! Let me slip
      from the world of men, vanish without a trace
      before I see myself stained with such corruption,
      stained to the heart.

LEADER.   My lord, you fill our hearts with fear.
925   But at least until you question the witness,
         do take hope.

OEDIPUS.   Exactly. He is my last hope—
      I am waiting for the shepherd. He is **crucial**. **2**

JOCASTA.   And once he appears, what then? Why so urgent?

OEDIPUS.   I'll tell you. If it turns out that his story
930   matches yours, I've escaped the worst.

JOCASTA.   What did I say? What struck you so?

OEDIPUS.   You said *thieves*—
      he told you a whole band of them murdered Laius.
      So, if he still holds to the same number,
      I cannot be the killer. One can't equal many.
935   But if he refers to one man, one alone,
      clearly the scales come down on me:°
      I am guilty.

JOCASTA.   Impossible. Trust me,
      I told you precisely what he said,
      and he can't **retract** it now; **3**
940   the whole city heard it, not just I.
      And even if he should vary his first report
      by one man more or less, still, my lord,
      he could never make the murder of Laius

919 **awesome**: in this use, deserving of fear and worship.

936 **scales**: an instrument of measurement made from two trays of equal weight on either side of a balanced center beam. **scales come down on me**: the weight of the evidence is against me.

---

4   The Tragic Vision *What does Oedipus mean by "some savage power"?*

Vocabulary

crucial (krōō′shəl) *adj.* essential; decisive
retract (ri trakt′) *v.* take back or deny

Teach

Vocabulary   2

Impromptu Have two students stage an impromptu news conference in which a reporter asks an official why he or she accused an opponent of some underhanded deed and the official *retracts* the accusation.

Vocabulary   3

Synonyms and Antonyms Have students compile lists of synonyms and antonyms for *crucial*, using simple two-column charts. (They can use dictionaries or thesauri if necessary.) Then construct a master class chart on the board.

Big Idea   4

The Tragic Vision Answer: *Oedipus means some inscrutable force, such as fate, maliciously thwarted his efforts to elude its decrees.*

Learning Objectives
Identifying synonyms and antonyms. (TE)
Analyzing argument. (TE)

English Learners

DIFFERENTIATED INSTRUCTION

Intermediate Remind students that they can often learn and remember a word better when they are aware of the word's origin. Point out the word *abomination* in line 911. Explain that it derives from the Latin *abominatus*, "to regard as an ill omen." Then use the board to break the word into its parts:

ab- "from, from off, down"
omen "a thing or happening supposed to foretell a future event"
-ation noun-forming suffix meaning "the condition of being"

Have a volunteer walk through the process of putting the parts together to form the word. Finally, have students suggest examples of things that might be considered abominations.

Teach

Reading Strategy | 1

Analyze Argument Answer:
The murder of Laius did not fulfill the prophecy because his son, who was already dead, could not have killed him.

Progress Check

Can students analyze argument?

If No → See Unit 2 Teaching Resources Book, p. 91.

Big Idea | 2

The Tragic Vision Answer:
The members of the chorus believe destiny—fate or the gods—controls their lives.

View the Art ★

This relief is on a sarcophagus, an elaborately carved burial coffin. Its name means "body eater" (derived from the Greek words *sarx*, "flesh," and *phagein*, "eat").

This scene from the Oedipus legend may have been considered for a Roman sarcophagus because it concerns death.

---

945   truly fit the prophecy. Apollo was explicit:
my son was doomed to kill my husband . . . my son,
poor defenseless thing, he never had a chance
to kill his father. They destroyed him first.

So much for prophecy. It's neither here nor there.
From this day on, I wouldn't look right or left.

950   OEDIPUS. True, true. Still, that shepherd,
someone fetch him—now!

JOCASTA. I'll send at once. But do let's go inside.
I'd never displease you, least of all in this.

[OEDIPUS *and* JOCASTA *enter the palace.*]

CHORUS. Destiny° guide me always
955   Destiny find me filled with reverence
pure in word and deed.
Great laws tower above us, reared on high
born for the brilliant vault of heaven—
Olympian° Sky their only father,
960   nothing mortal, no man gave them birth,
their memory deathless, never lost in sleep:
within them lives a mighty god, the god does not
grow old.°

Oedipus kills Laertes on chariot, 3rd century AD. Marble relief from a Roman sarcophagus. Vatican Museums, Vatican State. ★

954 Destiny: refers to a future that has been determined in advance and the outcome of which is inevitable.

957–962 Great laws . . . grow old: The gods have decreed certain unchanging laws that cannot be disobeyed.
959 Olympian: of or relating to Olympus, the highest mountain in Greece and home of the gods.

1 Analyze Argument *What is Jocasta's main point?*

2 The Tragic Vision *What do these lines suggest about the tragic vision of the play?*

288 UNIT 2 ANCIENT GREECE

Grammar Practice

SMALL GROUP
Use Emphatic Verb Forms
Remind students that the emphatic form of a verb combines the auxiliary *do* or *did* with the base form of the verb to place emphasis on the verb. Explain that the emphatic form occurs only in the present and past tenses (and only with active verbs, not verbs of being). Write the following examples on the board:

Let's go inside.
Do let's go inside. (from line 952)
You said thieves. (from line 931)
You did say thieves.

Do or *did* makes each statement seem more urgent by emphasizing the verb.

Have students write five sentences about the play using the emphatic form. Then ask students to trade papers with partners who are to write the sentences without using the emphatic forms. Partners can discuss the difference in the meanings.

288

Pride° breeds the tyrant
violent pride, gorging, crammed to bursting
965   with all that is overripe and rich with ruin—
clawing up to the heights, headlong pride
crashes down the abyss—sheer doom!
    No footing helps, all foothold lost and gone.°
But the healthy strife° that makes the city strong—
970   I pray that god will never end that wrestling:
god, my champion, I will never let you go.

But if any man comes striding, high and mighty
    in all he says and does,
no fear of justice, no reverence
975   for the temples of the gods—
    let a rough doom tear him down,
repay his pride, breakneck, ruinous pride!
If he cannot reap his profits fairly
    cannot restrain himself from outrage—
980   mad, laying hands on the holy things untouchable!

Can such a man, so desperate, still boast
he can save his life from the flashing bolts of god?
    If all such violence goes with honor now
    why join the sacred dance?°

985 | Never again will I go reverent to Delphi,
    | the inviolate° heart of Earth
3 | or Apollo's ancient oracle at Abae
    | or Olympia° of the fires—
    | unless these prophecies all come true
990   for all mankind to point toward in wonder.
King of kings, if you deserve your titles
    Zeus, remember, never forget!
You and your deathless, everlasting reign.

They are dying, the old oracles sent to Laius,
995   now our masters strike them off the rolls.°
    Nowhere Apollo's golden glory now—
    the gods, the gods go down.

---

963 Pride: here, the Greek concept of *hubris*; pride that goes beyond acceptable limits and brings on divine punishment.

966–968 clawing up . . . lost and gone: Hubris can make the mighty overreach and bring about their own doom.
969 strife: competition.

983–984 If all such . . . why join the sacred dance: If actions such as these go unpunished, why should anyone show reverence for the gods?
986 inviolate: pure.
987–988 Abae or Olympia: other famous shrines.

995 rolls: official records.

---

4 The Tragic Vision *How do the citizens of Thebes feel at this point in the play? Explain.*

Teach

Reading Strategy 3

Analyze Cause-and-Effect Relationships Direct students to lines 985–989. **Ask:** What is the effect of all these events on the Chorus? What do they claim they will never do again? Why? *(They will no more pay reverence to the oracles if these prophecies do not come true.)*

Big Idea 4

The Tragic Vision Answer: *They feel confused. They have looked to Oedipus as infallible, and he now appears guilty. They are still reeling from the horrors of the plague. Finally, if the prophecies of the oracle prove false, then belief in the gods is destroyed.*

Learning Objectives
Analyzing argument. (SE)
Analyzing cause-and-effect relationships. (TE)
Using emphatic verb forms. (TE)

Advanced Learners/Pre-AP

DIFFERENTIATED INSTRUCTION

Draw Conclusions The chorus concludes Part 2 of *Oedipus the King* by singing:

"Nowhere Apollo's golden glory now—the gods, the gods go down."

Ask: If you were a member of the Greek audience at the premier of this play, how would you react to this statement? Tell students to keep in mind the number of gods in the ancient Greek religion, how

the common people related to their gods, and that the very performance of this play was part of a religious ceremony. *(Students will likely respond that they would feel shocked, outraged, or saddened.)*

Have students pretend to be Greek citizens and write letters to family members describing their reactions. Their letters might include the scene in which the speech is set; the lines and what students

think they mean; and the students' feelings of shock, sadness, or outrage over what might be interpreted as an attack on their religion.

289

After You Read

Assess

1. Most students will say their opinions changed when they discovered Oedipus's past deeds and increasing arrogance.

2. (a) Oedipus has accused him of plotting to steal the throne. (b) The chorus leader believes Oedipus is a good person, and the leader intends to calm Creon.

3. (a) She says the seer predicted wrongly Laius would be killed by his child. (b) Oedipus remembers the setting and the situation she describes.

4. (a) He left to avoid killing his father and marrying his mother. (b) He killed travelers, including King Laius.

5. Oedipus's argument with Creon shows excessive pride.

6. Jocasta describes her husband's murder and Oedipus recalls a similar incident

7. Killing one's father and committing incest with one's mother were (and are) strong taboos, violations of the laws of gods and men. That Oedipus unwittingly commits these crimes is indeed tragic.

8. Answers will vary.

> For additonal selection assessment, see Assessment Resources, pp. 75–76.

Literary Element

1. One knows it will not end well.

2. His horrible destiny, his having been a good ruler, and his having gone to great lengths not to commit the crime prophesied.

Vocabulary

1. e 2. c 3. a 4. f 5. b

290

After You Read

Respond and Think Critically

Respond and Interpret

1. Has your opinion of Oedipus changed since reading this section of the play? Share your feelings about him with your classmates.

2. (a)Why is Creon upset at the beginning of this section? (b)Why might the leader of the chorus respond as he does to Creon's questions?

3. (a)What reason does Jocasta offer for not believing Tiresias? (b)Why does her speech fail to calm Oedipus?

4. (a)Why did Oedipus leave his home in Corinth? (b)What happened on his way to Thebes?

Analyze and Evaluate

5. In the ode at the end of this section, the chorus says "Pride breeds the tyrant." Do you think Oedipus shows excessive pride? Explain.

6. **Rising action** refers to the part of a plot when complications develop. What is the most significant complication in this section of the play?

Connect

7. **Big Idea** The Tragic Vision The heart of this tragedy lies in the oracle's prophecy (lines 873–875). Explain why these actions, carried out, would prove so tragic to Greek audiences.

8. **Connect to Today** Think of a modern leader who was accused of committing a crime. What steps were taken to investigate the leader?

Literary Element Tragedy

In Greek **tragedy**, the main character's downfall is often caused by an error in judgment.

1. How did knowing this play is a tragedy influence your expectations about it?

2. Despite his tragic flaws, what might encourage you to feel sympathy or admiration for Oedipus?

Reading Strategy Analyze Argument

Review the chart you made on page 274 and answer the following questions.

1. Which character do you think makes a stronger case, Oedipus or Creon? Why?

2. Does Creon use deductive or inductive reasoning in his argument? Explain.

LOG ON ▶ **Literature** Online

Selection Resources For Selection Quizzes, eFlashcards, and Reading-Writing Connection activities, go to glencoe.com and enter QuickPass code GLW6053u2.

Vocabulary Practice

Practice with Synonyms With a partner, match each boldfaced vocabulary word below with its synonym. Use a thesaurus or dictionary to check your answers. You will not use all the answer choices.

1. **sullen**	a. measure	f. critical
2. **foreboding**	b. withdraw	g. stubborn
3. **gauge**	c. portent	
4. **crucial**	d. question	
5. **retract**	e. gloomy	

🚀 Writing

Write an Essay Write an essay analyzing two conflicts that develop in this section of the play. Explain whether each conflict is internal or external and how it is resolved. If they are not resolved, offer predictions about how they might be resolved in the future.

Reading Strategy

1. Students may say that Creon's argument is logical and convincing whereas Oedipus's is accusatory.

2. Deductive reasoning: Creon moves from a general statement to a specific instance. He states a principle, that no one would prefer kingship when he can enjoy almost unlimited power and influence without it, and concludes that he could not be conspiring to overthrow Oedipus.

📝 Writing

Students' analyses should

- explain the ways in which the conflicts are internal or external
- include explanations or predictions about the resolutions

Oedipus the King

Build Background

According to the ancient Greek critic and philosopher Aristotle, witnessing a tragedy on stage is healthy for the spectators' emotions. Tragedy evokes pity for the sufferer and terror because of his or her great misfortunes. These emotions undergo a cleansing, or *catharsis* (kə thar′səs), during the play. It gradually dawns on the audience that the hero's sufferings, though seemingly undeserved, are fitting in a mysterious way. The audience leaves the theater with greater sympathy and less fear.

Literary Element Irony

Irony is a contrast or discrepancy between appearance and reality. **Verbal irony** occurs when the meaning of a statement is the reverse of what is said. **Situational irony** exists when the outcome of a situation is the opposite of what is expected. **Dramatic irony** occurs when readers or viewers know something the characters in a literary work do not. As you read, ask yourself, What examples of irony are in this play?

Reading Strategy Synthesize

To **synthesize** means to combine various details or simple ideas to come to a conclusion. Synthesizing information helps you reach a deeper understanding of a literary work. As you read, ask yourself, What conclusions can I draw by synthesizing information?

Tip: Take Notes In a graphic organizer like the one below, record key details and relevant background information from the play. Synthesize the information and details to gain new insights into *Oedipus the King*.

Learning Objectives

For pages 291–318
In studying this text, you will focus on the following objectives:

Literary Study: Analyzing irony.

Reading: Synthesizing.

Writing: Writing an expository essay.

Vocabulary

random (ran′dəm) *n.* lack of careful choice or plan; p. 294 *Contestants were selected at random from the studio audience.*

oblivion (ə bliv′ē ən) *n.* state of having been forgotten; p. 303 *That story once was popular but is now relegated to oblivion.*

inflict (in flikt′) *v.* to give or cause; p. 305 *The hurricane inflicted terrible damage on the city.*

horrendous (hô ren′dəs) *adj.* horrible; frightful; p. 310 *The prisoners of war endured horrendous experiences.*

vulnerable (vul′nər ə bəl) *adj.* weak; unable to defend oneself; p. 314 *Alone in the woods at night, I felt vulnerable to attack.*

Tip: Word Origins Knowing a word's origin can lead you to its meaning. Knowing that *vulnerable* derives from the Latin *vulnus*, meaning "wound," may help you remember that *vulnerable* means "capable of being wounded."

SOPHOCLES **291**

Focus

Summary

A messenger arrives from Corinth with news that Polybus the king is dead. Believing Polybus to be his father, Oedipus is initially relieved by news that seemingly voids the prophecy, but then he learns that Polybus was not his father and a shepherd knows the secret of Oedipus's birth. Horrified by what she now realizes, Jocasta flees into the palace. The shepherd reveals that Oedipus is the son of Laius and Jocasta. Oedipus also flees into the palace, from which a messenger comes to reveal that Jocasta has hanged herself and Oedipus has blinded himself. After a brief reunion with his daughters, the blind Oedipus departs into exile.

Vocabulary

Context Narrative Have students work in groups of four. Two students in each group should write a brief narrative in which they creatively use all five vocabulary words, providing sufficient context to indicate each word's meaning. Then the other two students should write definitions of the vocabulary words based on the context provided in the narrative.

Selection Skills

Vocabulary Skills
- Word Origins (SE p. 317)
- Academic Vocabulary (SE p. 317)

Writing Skills/Grammar
- Expository Essay (SE p. 318)
- Ellipsis Points (SE p. 318)
- Narrative (TE p. 298)
- Analysis of Literary Technique (TE p. 308)
- Demonstrative Pronouns (TE p. 310)

Oedipus the King (part 3)

Literary Elements
- Irony (SE pp. 291, 295, 296, 298, 299, 301, 303, 317)
- Tragedy (SE p. 317; TE p. 307)

Speaking/Listening/Viewing Skills
- Storytelling (TE p. 294)
- Analyze Art (SE pp. 295, 305)
- Critical Viewing (TE p. 314)

Reading Skills
- Synthesize (SE pp. 291, 293, 297, 302, 303, 307, 309–311, 313, 314, 317)
- Visualize (TE pp. 292, 300)

Teach

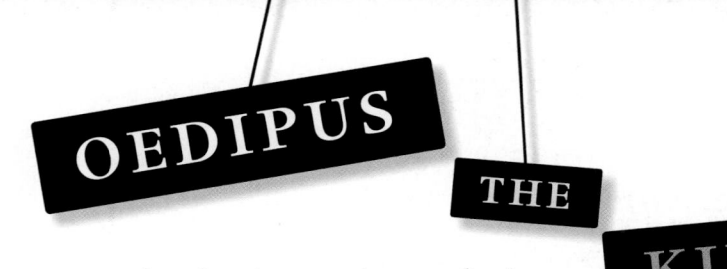

Reading Strategy 1

Respond to Character

Direct students to lines 1001–1004. **Ask:** What words might you use to describe Oedipus's state? *(Possible answers: depressed, terrified, inconsolable.)*

[ENGLISH LEARNERS] Explain to students that the English idiom "beside oneself" means "in a state of extreme emotion, such as great elation or grief." Ask if there is a similar idiomatic expression from their native language and what it means literally.

 For additional practice using the reading skill or strategy, see Unit 2 Teaching Resources Book, p. 104.

 For an audio recording of this selection, use Listening Library Audio CD-ROM.

[*Enter* JOCASTA *from the palace, carrying a suppliant's branch wound in wool.*]

    JOCASTA. Lords of the realm, it occurred to me,
       just now, to visit the temples of the gods,
1000   so I have my branch in hand and incense too.

1 Oedipus is beside himself. Racked with anguish,
       no longer a man of sense, he won't admit
       the latest prophecies are hollow as the old—
       he's at the mercy of every passing voice
1005   if the voice tells of terror.
       I urge him gently, nothing seems to help,
       so I turn to you, Apollo, you are nearest.

[*Placing her branch on the altar, while an old herdsman enters from the side, not the one just summoned by the King but an unexpected* MESSENGER *from Corinth.*]

       I come with prayers and offerings . . . I beg you,
       cleanse us, set us free of defilement!
1010   Look at us, passengers in the grip of fear,
       watching the pilot of the vessel go to pieces.

    MESSENGER. [*Approaching* JOCASTA *and the* CHORUS.]
       Strangers, please, I wonder if you could lead us
       to the palace of the king . . . I think it's Oedipus.
       Better, the man himself—you know where he is?

1015 LEADER. This is his palace, stranger. He's inside.
       But here is his queen, his wife and mother
       of his children.

    MESSENGER.   Blessings on you, noble queen,
       queen of Oedipus crowned with all your family—
       blessings on you always!

1020 JOCASTA. And the same to you, stranger, you deserve it . . .
       such a greeting. But what have you come for?
       Have you brought us news?

    MESSENGER.   Wonderful news—
       for the house, my lady, for your husband too.

292 UNIT 2 ANCIENT GREECE

Reading Practice

SPIRAL REVIEW

Visualize Point out to students that it is important to form mental pictures of scenes, characters, and events as they read. In many works of fiction, the writer provides visual details upon which to base such mental pictures. In visualizing *Oedipus the King*, where such details are largely absent, the reader may need to be creative.

Have students visualize how Oedipus or Jocasta might look if he or she lived at the present time. How might his or her clothing reflect a particular personality? Tell students that they may choose pictures from magazines or draw their own pictures of the characters. Students should be prepared to explain why they think their pictures reflect the personalities of the characters they have chosen. Have students present their pictures to encourage class discussion.

JOCASTA.   Really, what? Who sent you?

MESSENGER.   Corinth.
1025   I'll give you the message in a moment.
            You'll be glad of it—how could you help it?—
            though it costs a little sorrow in the bargain.

JOCASTA.   What can it be, with such a double edge?

MESSENGER.   The people there, they want to make your
                Oedipus
1030   king of Corinth, so they're saying now.

JOCASTA.   Why? Isn't old Polybus still in power?

MESSENGER.   No more. Death has got him in the tomb.

JOCASTA.   What are you saying? Polybus, dead?—dead?

MESSENGER.   If not,
            if I'm not telling the truth, strike me dead too.

1035   JOCASTA.   [To a SERVANT.] Quickly, go to your master, tell
            him this!

            You prophecies of the gods, where are you now?
            This is the man that Oedipus feared for years,
            he fled him, not to kill him—and now he's dead,
            quite by chance, a normal, natural death,
1040   not murdered by his son.

OEDIPUS.   [Emerging from the palace.] Dearest,
            what now? Why call me from the palace?

JOCASTA.   [Bringing the MESSENGER closer.] Listen to him, see
                for yourself what all
            those awful prophecies of god have come to.

OEDIPUS.   And who is he? What can he have for me?

1045   JOCASTA.   He's from Corinth, he's come to tell you
            your father is no more—Polybus—he's dead!

OEDIPUS.   [Wheeling on the MESSENGER.] What? Let me have
            it from your lips.

MESSENGER.   Well,
            if that's what you want first, then here it is:
            make no mistake, Polybus is dead and gone.

1050   OEDIPUS.   How—murder? sickness?—what? what killed him?

---

2   Synthesize   *Recall the oracle's prophecy. Why was Oedipus afraid of Polybus?*

Advanced Learners/Pre-AP

DIFFERENTIATED INSTRUCTION

SMALL GROUP

Performance Assessment
Point out that when a society is confronted by a type of emergency, such as a natural disaster or terrorism, it turns to its leaders for guidance. One of the key responsibilities of those who govern is disaster or emergency management. Oedipus, as king of Thebes, is responsible for leading his people in their search for relief from the plague.

Have a group of students review the text of the play as the basis for a performance assessment of Oedipus's skills in emergency management. In their assessment they should determine how well he functions in (1) gathering information about the plague, (2) initiating steps to end the plague, and (3) working with others—such as Creon—who participate in the government of Thebes.

Teach

Reading Strategy   2

Synthesize   Answer: *Oedipus thought he was fated to kill his father, whom he believed to be Polybus.*

APPROACHING   If students have trouble remembering the prophecy, have them review lines 873–875.

Cultural History   ☆

Corinth   Located on the narrow Isthmus of Corinth that connects mainland Greece to the Peloponnesian peninsula, the ancient city of Corinth grew wealthy from trade. A stone ramp was used to haul ships between the Gulf of Corinth and the Saronic Gulf, which flank the isthmus.

Learning Objectives
Synthesizing. (SE)
Responding to character. (TE)
Visualizing. (TE)

The Tragic Vision **Answer:**
She says chance, rather than a beneficent providence, rules human life

(ADVANCED) **Ask:** In what way is the tragic vision linked to a belief in an underlying order and purpose in the universe? In other words, if the universe is ruled by chance, how is tragedy possible? *(Some students may feel that a random, meaningless universe invalidates the idea of tragedy; others may feel that even in a universe ruled by chance, the possibility of tragedy—of human suffering having meaning—still exists.)*

Cultural History ☆

Hell Point out that this is not the Christian place of fiery punishment for sinners. The ancient Greeks believed that nearly all of the dead went to the underworld, a dismal, region ruled by the god Hades. (A few favored souls were granted immortality in Elysium, the Greek paradise.) Although the underworld is bleak and joyless, only a few of the dead are actually tormented there for their deeds in life.

MESSENGER. A light tip of the scales can put old bones to rest.°

OEDIPUS. Sickness then—poor man, it wore him down.

MESSENGER.   That,
  and the long count of years he'd measured out.

OEDIPUS.   So!
  Jocasta, why, why look to the Prophet's hearth,
1055 the fires of the future? Why scan the birds
  that scream above our heads? They winged me on
  to the murder of my father, did they? That was my doom?
  Well look, he's dead and buried, hidden under the earth,
  and here I am in Thebes, I never put hand to sword—
1060 unless some longing for me wasted him away,
  then in a sense you'd say I caused his death.
  But now, all those prophecies I feared—Polybus
  packs them off to sleep with him in hell! ☆
  They're nothing, worthless.

JOCASTA.   There.
1065 Didn't I tell you from the start?

OEDIPUS. So you did. I was lost in fear.

JOCASTA. No more, sweep it from your mind forever.

OEDIPUS. But my mother's bed, surely I must fear—

JOCASTA.   Fear?
  What should a man fear? It's all chance,
1070 chance rules our lives. Not a man on earth
  can see a day ahead, groping through the dark.
  Better to live at **random**, best we can.
  And as for this marriage with your mother—
  have no fear. Many a man before you,
1075 in his dreams, has shared his mother's bed.
  Take such things for shadows, nothing at all—
  Live, Oedipus,
  as if there's no tomorrow!

1051 **A light tip . . . to rest:** refers to the frailty of old age, in which a minor illness can be fatal.

---

1 The Tragic Vision *How does Jocasta's speech reflect the tragic vision of the ancient Greeks?*

Vocabulary

random (ran′dəm) n. lack of careful choice or plan

Speaking Practice

SMALL GROUP
Storytelling Most plays in ancient Greek drama are based on myths and legends that were very familiar to their audiences. The story of Oedipus was featured in three of the seven surviving plays of Sophocles, in a tragedy written by Aeschylus, and in one by Euripides. Ask students why Greek audiences might want to see these familiar tales enacted over and over.

Have small groups retell a familiar story.

Before planning the presentation, students should consider how to make the familiar seem "new." After groups have time to prepare, have them share their retelling of stories with the rest of the class.

OEDIPUS.
                              Brave words,
    and you'd persuade me if mother
        weren't alive.
1080 But mother lives, so for all your
        reassurances
    I live in fear, I must.

JOCASTA.
                      But your father's death,
    that, at least, is a great blessing,
        joy to the eyes!

OEDIPUS. Great, I know . . . but I fear
    her—she's still alive.

MESSENGER. Wait, who is this woman,
    makes you so afraid?

1085 OEDIPUS. Merope, old man. The wife of
    Polybus.

MESSENGER. The queen? What's there to
    fear in her?

OEDIPUS. A dreadful prophecy, stranger,
    sent by the gods.

MESSENGER. Tell me, could you? Unless it's forbidden
    other ears to hear.

OEDIPUS.   Not at all.
1090 Apollo told me once—it is my fate—
    I must make love with my own mother,
    shed my father's blood with my own hands.
    So for years I've given Corinth a wide berth,
    and it's been my good fortune too. But still,
1095 to see one's parents and look into their eyes
    is the greatest joy I know.

MESSENGER.   You're afraid of that?
    That kept you out of Corinth?

OEDIPUS.   My father, old man—
    so I wouldn't kill my father.

MESSENGER.   So that's it.
    Well then, seeing I came with such good will, my king,
1100 why don't I rid you of that old worry now?

OEDIPUS. What a rich reward you'd have for that.

---

2 Irony *What is ironic about Jocasta's reaction to Polybus's death?*

Oedipe et le Berger (Oedipus and the Shepherd). Honoré Daumier. 65.5 x 50 cm. Private collection.

 View the Art This painting of Oedipus as an infant shows Honoré Daumier's talent for capturing movement and light. What feelings does the shepherd seem to have for the baby Oedipus? What details in the painting lead you to this conclusion? ★

Teach

Literary Element **2**

Irony **Answer:** *Ordinarily the death of a father is heartbreaking news, but Jocasta is joyful because she thinks Polybus's death means the prophecy concerning Oedipus cannot come true.*

View the Art ★

Answer: *The way the shepherd cradles Oedipus in his arm and the serene light suggests that the shepherd has tender feelings for the infant.*

During his lifetime, Honoré Daumier was known primarily for his witty drawings and cartoons satirizing nineteenth-century French politics and society. He also created a great many paintings based on mythology and classical literature. Daumier was one of the first to paint in the style that would later be called Impressionism, emphasizing the effect of light on objects.

Learning Objectives
Analyzing irony. (SE)
Analyzing art. (SE)
Retelling a story. (TE)

English Learners

DIFFERENTIATED INSTRUCTION

Beginning Encourage students to select stories they have heard since childhood to retell. Have them deliver their retelling to small groups.

Advanced Learners/Pre-AP

DIFFERENTIATED INSTRUCTION

SMALL GROUP

Storytelling Point out that famous myths and legends such as Oedipus often exist in several versions. Homer tells the story of Oedipus, for example, but in his version there is no riddle of the Sphinx and Oedipus remains king of Thebes. Have a group of students select a tale—such as a familiar folktale or heroic legend—and research different versions. Have them do a presentation for the class outlining the differences.

Teach

Reading Strategy 1

Predict **Ask:** After reading line 1111, do you think that Oedipus will be happy about the news that Polybus is not his biological father? *(Students will probably feel that the news will renew Oedipus's fears.)*

Literary Element 2

Irony **Answer:** *Oedipus finds out the man whom he loved as a father was not related to him; moreover, he realizes he has not escaped his fate.*

(APPROACHING) Remind students that situational irony occurs when what actually happens is the opposite of what is expected. Ask them to draw on their own experience to give an example of situational irony.

MESSENGER. What do you think I came for, majesty?
   So you'd come home and I'd be better off.

OEDIPUS. Never, I will never go near my parents.

1105 MESSENGER. My boy, it's clear, you don't know what
   you're doing.

OEDIPUS. What do you mean, old man? For god's
   sake, explain.

MESSENGER. If you ran from *them*, always dodging home . . .

OEDIPUS.   Always, terrified Apollo's oracle might
   come true—

MESSENGER. And you'd be covered with guilt, from both
   your parents.

1110 OEDIPUS. That's right, old man, that fear is always with me.

MESSENGER. Don't you know? You've really nothing to fear. **1**

OEDIPUS. But why? If I'm their son—Merope, Polybus?

MESSENGER. Polybus was nothing to you, that's why,
   not in blood.

OEDIPUS. What are you saying—Polybus was not my father?

1115 MESSENGER. No more than I am. He and I are equals.

OEDIPUS.   My father—
   how can my father equal nothing? You're nothing to me!

MESSENGER. Neither was he, no more your father than I am.

OEDIPUS. Then why did he call me his son?

MESSENGER.   You were a gift,
   years ago—know for a fact he took you
   from my hands.

1120 OEDIPUS.   No, from another's hands?
   Then how could he love me so? He loved me, deeply . . .

MESSENGER. True, and his early years without a child
   made him love you all the more.

OEDIPUS.   And you, did you . . .
   buy me? find me by accident?

MESSENGER.   I stumbled on you,
   down the woody flanks of Mount Cithaeron. ☆

1125 OEDIPUS.   So close,
   what were you doing here, just passing through?

---

2 **Irony** *Why is this passage an example of situational irony?*

Grammar Practice

Use Dashes Remind students that a dash is used to signal a change in thought or to emphasize a parenthetical comment. Draw students' attentions to these examples from the play.

"What are you saying—Polybus was not my father?" (line 1114)

"You were a gift, years ago—know for a fact he took you." (lines 1118–1119)

Point out that a good test of the correct use of dashes is to delete the information that the dashes set off. If the remaining sentence retains its basic meaning, then the dashes were properly used. If the remaining sentence has lost crucial information, then the dashes were improperly used. Have students determine whether dashes in the following sentences are used correctly or incorrectly.

1. Every role in ancient Greek drama was performed—by male actors. *(incorrect)*

2. Actors wore masks—as in Japanese No drama—to identify what type of character they were playing. *(correct)*

3. Greek drama was not just entertainment—as our theater basically is. *(correct)*

MESSENGER. Watching over my flocks, grazing them
     on the slopes.

OEDIPUS. A herdsman, were you? A vagabond, scraping
     for wages?

MESSENGER. Your savior too, my son, in your worst hour.

OEDIPUS.   Oh—
1130   when you picked me up, was I in pain? What exactly?

MESSENGER. Your ankles . . . they tell the story. Look at
     them.

OEDIPUS. Why remind me of that, that old affliction?

MESSENGER. Your ankles were pinned together; I set you free.

OEDIPUS. That dreadful mark—I've had it from the cradle.

1135 MESSENGER. And you got your name from that
     misfortune too,
     the name's still with you.°

OEDIPUS.   Dear god, who did it?—
     mother? father? Tell me.

MESSENGER.   I don't know.
     The one who gave you to me, he'd know more.

OEDIPUS. What? You took me from someone else?
     You didn't find me yourself?

1140 MESSENGER.   No sir,
     another shepherd passed you on to me.

OEDIPUS. Who? Do you know? Describe him.

MESSENGER. He called himself a servant of . . .
     if I remember rightly—Laius.

     [JOCASTA turns sharply.] **3**

1145 OEDIPUS. The king of the land who ruled here long ago?

MESSENGER. That's the one. That herdsman was *his* man.

OEDIPUS. Is he still alive? Can I see him?

MESSENGER. They'd know best, the people of these parts.

     [OEDIPUS and the MESSENGER turn to the CHORUS.]

OEDIPUS. Does anyone know that herdsman,
1150   the one he mentioned? Anyone seen him
     in the fields, in town? Out with it!

---

4 Synthesize *How is Jocasta's speech in lines 790–793 connected to the
messenger's remark?*

> 1135–1136 **you got your
> name . . . still with you:** One
> meaning of the word *Oedipus* is
> "swollen foot."

SOPHOCLES **297**

Approaching Level

DIFFERENTIATED INSTRUCTION

Body Language Remind students
that communication is not limited to
speech—our body language reveals a great
deal about our thoughts and reactions. For
example, people who are nervous may
chew their fingernails or play with their hair.
Confident people tend to gesture as they
speak. Shy people often slouch or avoid
eye contact.

Have students work in pairs to choose
an emotion to represent through body
language. Students may view videotapes
of mime performances to gather ideas of
ways to express emotions. Allow students
to practice their interpretations before
they present them to the class. Audience
members should be able to guess which
emotions are portrayed.

Teach

Reading Strategy 3

Respond to Character
Direct students to the stage
direction after line 1144.
Ask: What has happened to
Jocasta? *(She is beginning
to connect the story of her
abandoned child with that of
Oedipus.)*

Reading Strategy 4

Synthesize Answer: *Jocasta
revealed that before her baby
was exposed, Laius "fastened
his ankles." Now the messenger
mentions Oedipus's ankles were
pinned together, and Oedipus
acknowledges that "dreadful
mark."*

Cultural History ☆

Cithaeron In addition to the
association with Oedipus, Mount
Cithaeron in central Greece is
also famous as the scene of the
myths of Actaeon and Pentheus
and of one of the deeds of
Hercules. The Greeks' victory at
Plataea, the climactic battle of their
war with the Persians, took place
on the slopes of Mount Cithaeron
in 79 B.C.

Learning Objectives
Analyzing irony. (SE)
Synthesizing. (SE)
Predicting. (TE)
Using dashes. (TE)
Responding to character. (TE)

Teach

Reading Strategy   1

Question Direct students to lines 1158–1159. **Ask:** Why does Jocasta tell Oedipus to ignore the shepherd? (*She is now terrified that the old shepherd will reveal the truth about who Oedipus is.*)

Literary Element   2

Irony **Answer:** *He thinks she would be offended to find herself married to a slave. Oedipus does not realize Jocasta has discovered she is his mother.*

(ADVANCED) **Ask:** Why do you think Oedipus seems relatively unconcerned at the prospect of discovering he might be of low birth? (*Students might feel it is because he is to considerable extent, a "self-made man." He owes his present status as king of Thebes to his ability to answer the riddle of the Sphinx rather than to the right of inheritance.*)

Big Idea   3

The Tragic Vision **Answer:** *Tiresias earlier called Oedipus "blind," and Oedipus still does not want to acknowledge what he fears might be true.*

The time has come to reveal this once for all.

LEADER. I think he's the very shepherd you wanted to see,
  a moment ago. But the queen, Jocasta,
  she's the one to say.

1155 OEDIPUS.   Jocasta,
  you remember the man we just sent for?
  Is *that* the one he means?

JOCASTA.   That man . . .
  why ask? Old shepherd, talk, empty nonsense,
  don't give it another thought, don't even think—

1160 OEDIPUS. What—give up now, with a clue like this?
  Fail to solve the mystery of my birth?
  Not for all the world!

JOCASTA.   Stop—in the name of god,
  if you love your own life, call off this search!
  My suffering is enough.

OEDIPUS.   Courage!
1165 Even if my mother turns out to be a slave,
  and I a slave, three generations back,
  you would not seem common.

JOCASTA.   Oh no,
  listen to me, I beg you, don't do this.

OEDIPUS. Listen to you? No more. I must know it all,
  see the truth at last.

1170 JOCASTA.   No, please—
  for your sake—I want the best for you!

OEDIPUS. Your best is more than I can bear.°

JOCASTA.   You're doomed—
  may you never fathom who you are!

OEDIPUS. [*To a* SERVANT.] Hurry, fetch me the herdsman,
  now!
1175 Leave her to glory in her royal birth.

JOCASTA. Aieeeeee—
      man of agony—
  that is the only name I have for you,
  that, no other—ever, ever, ever!

1171 Your best . . . I can bear:
Not knowing the truth is unbearable.

---

2   **Irony** *How does Oedipus misread Jocasta's anxiety? What is ironic here?*

3   **The Tragic Vision** *Why do you suppose Oedipus has not yet solved the mystery of his identity?*

Writing Practice

Write a Narrative Remind students that narrative writing shares many elements with drama—characters, plot, setting, and theme. Drama is told primarily through dialogue, however, and is interpreted for the audience by the actors. Narrative writing relies more heavily on description. Have students select an episode from the play to adapt to narrative form. Remind students of the importance of setting the scene and making the characters come to life through both dialogue and description. When students have finished, have them share their narratives with the rest of the class.

[*Flinging through the palace doors. A long, tense silence follows.*]

LEADER. Where's she gone, Oedipus?
1180   Rushing off, such wild grief . . .
    I'm afraid that from this silence
    something monstrous may come bursting forth.

OEDIPUS. Let it burst! Whatever will, whatever must!
    I must know my birth, no matter how common
1185   it may be—must see my origins face-to-face.
    She perhaps, she with her woman's pride
    may well be mortified by my birth,
    but I, I count myself the son of Chance,
    the great goddess, giver of all good things—
1190   I'll never see myself disgraced. She is my mother!°
    And the moons have marked me out, my blood-brothers,
    one moon on the wane, the next moon great with
      power.°
    That is my blood, my nature—I will never betray it,
    never fail to search and learn my birth!

1195 CHORUS. Yes—if I am a true prophet
           if I can grasp the truth,
      by the boundless skies of Olympus,°
    at the full moon of tomorrow, Mount Cithaeron
    you will know how Oedipus glories in you—
1200   you, his birthplace, nurse, his mountain-mother!
    And we will sing you, dancing out your praise—
    you lift our monarch's heart!
      Apollo, Apollo, god of the wild cry
        may our dancing please you!
                    Oedipus—
1205   son, dear child, who bore you?
    Who of the nymphs° who seem to live forever
    mated with Pan,° the mountain-striding Father?
    Who was your mother? who, some bride of Apollo
    the god who loves the pastures spreading toward the sun?
1210   Or was it Hermes,° king of the lightning ridges?
    Or Dionysus, lord of frenzy, lord of the barren peaks—
    did he seize you in his hands, dearest of all his lucky
      finds?—
      found by the nymphs, their warm eyes dancing, gift
    to the lord who loves them dancing out his joy!°

---

4   Irony *How is Oedipus's claim an example of dramatic irony?*

SOPHOCLES **299**

1188–1190 I count myself . . . She is my mother: Oedipus believes that he has always had good fortune and therefore has nothing to fear.
1191–1192 the moons . . . great with power: What has seemed to be misfortune has always led to triumph.

1197 by . . . Olympus: by all that is holy.

1205–1214 who bore you . . . dancing out his joy: In mythology, mysterious children often turn out to be the offspring of gods. The Chorus imagines this might be the case with Oedipus.
1206 nymphs: minor female deities who lived in forests, on hills, or in rivers.
1207 Pan: god of fields, forests, and herdsmen, who often was involved romantically with woodland nymphs.
1210 Hermes: god of science, travelers, and vagabonds; pictured with winged helmet and sandals, he was the messenger of the gods.

Teach

Literary Element	4

Irony Answer: *The audience knows what Oedipus does not know, namely whose son he truly is.*

Cultural History ☆

Nymphs In Greek mythology, nymphs were minor nature goddesses closely identified with particular natural settings, such as forests, mountains, and bodies of water. Forest nymphs were known as *dryads*, mountain nymphs as *oreads*, and water nymphs as *naiads*. Nymphs were not immortal like the Olympian gods, but were extremely long-lived.

Learning Objectives
Analyzing irony. (SE)
Questioning. (TE)
Writing a narrative. (TE)

Approaching Level

DIFFERENTIATED INSTRUCTION

SMALL GROUP **Ethical Dilemmas** Discuss with students that sometimes a person might say one thing and mean another in order to protect someone else. For example, when Jocasta says, "Old shepherd, talk, empty nonsense . . ." She discounts him because she fears what he has to say will destroy Oedipus.

Have groups of students discuss the issue of not being entirely honest in order to protect someone else. **Ask:** When would such a situation arise? Is it ever acceptable not to be completely honest?

Advanced Learners/Pre-AP

DIFFERENTIATED INSTRUCTION

SMALL GROUP **Debate** Have a group of students debate whether Jocasta would have been justified in suppressing the truth about the identity of Oedipus.

299

Teach

Visualize Ask: What does the shepherd's slow, reluctant entrance suggest about the news he brings? *(His reluctance signifies that he is the bearer of bad news.)*

(ENGLISH LEARNERS) English learners may need help with the word *reluctant*. Give them a context sentence, "Most of us are reluctant to go to the dentist."

View the Photograph ★

The Olivier Theatre is the largest of the three theatres that make up London's National Theatre. Named for its finest artistic director—the famed British actor Sir Laurence Olivier—the Olivier Theatre is modeled on the ancient Greek theater at Epidaurus. Point out to students that the actors are wearing theatrical masks as in ancient Greek drama. **Ask: What is the effect of such masks? Is it appropriate to the story?** *(Students might feel that the masks give the play a remote, otherworldly quality suitable to the mythic subject matter.)*

Oedipus and the Shepherd. Olivier Theatre.

[*OEDIPUS strains to see a figure coming from the distance. Attended by* PALACE GUARDS, *an old* SHEPHERD *enters slowly, reluctant to approach the king.*]

1215 OEDIPUS. I never met the man, my friends . . . still,
    if I had to guess, I'd say
    that's the shepherd,
    the very one we've looked for all along.
    Brothers in old age, two of a kind,
    he and our guest here.
    At any rate
1220   the ones who bring him in
    are my own men,
    I recognize them.

[*Turning to the* LEADER.]

             But you
    know more than I,
    you should, you've seen the man before.

    LEADER. I know him, definitely. One of Laius' men,
    a trusty shepherd, if there ever was one.

1225 OEDIPUS. You, I ask you first, stranger,
    you from Corinth—is this the one you mean?

    MESSENGER. You're looking at him. He's your man.

    OEDIPUS. [*To the* SHEPHERD.] You, old man, come over here—
    look at me. Answer all my questions.
    Did you ever serve King Laius?

1230 SHEPHERD.   So I did . . .
    a slave, not bought on the block though,
    born and reared in the palace.

    OEDIPUS. Your duties, your kind of work?

    SHEPHERD. Herding the flocks, the better part of my life.

1235 OEDIPUS. Where, mostly? Where did you do your grazing?

Reading Practice

Monitor Comprehension To make sure that students are following the action in the story, introduce the idea of a small-group review.

Have small groups review the last three pages of the play and compile a list of five questions that require both literal recall of the events and interpretation of the text. Then have groups exchange lists of questions and provide answers. After groups have finished, discuss any questions that remain unanswered.

SHEPHERD.   Well,
   Cithaeron sometimes, or the foothills round about.

OEDIPUS. This man—you know him? ever see him there?

SHEPHERD. [*Confused, glancing from the* MESSENGER *to the King.*]
   Doing what?—what man do you mean?

OEDIPUS. [*Pointing to the* MESSENGER.] This one here—ever
   have dealings with him?

1240 SHEPHERD. Not so I could say, but give me a chance,
   my memory's bad . . .

MESSENGER. No wonder he doesn't know me, master.
   But let me refresh his memory for him.
   I'm sure he recalls old times we had
1245 on the slopes of Mount Cithaeron;
   he and I, grazing our flocks, he with two
   and I with one—we both struck up together,
   three whole seasons, six months at a stretch
   from spring to the rising of Arcturus° in the fall,
1250 then with winter coming on I'd drive my herds
   to my own pens, and back he'd go with his
   to Laius' folds.°

[*To the* SHEPHERD.]
                       Now that's how it was,
   wasn't it—yes or no?

2
SHEPHERD.   Yes, I suppose . . .
   it's all so long ago.

MESSENGER.   Come, tell me,
1255 you gave me a child back then, a boy, remember?
   A little fellow to rear, my very own.

SHEPHERD. What? Why rake up that again?

MESSENGER. Look, here he is, my fine old friend—
   the same man who was just a baby then.

1260 SHEPHERD. Damn you, shut your mouth—quiet!

OEDIPUS. Don't lash out at him, old man—
   you need lashing° more than he does.

SHEPHERD.   Why,
   master, majesty—what have I done wrong?

OEDIPUS. You won't answer his question about the boy.

1265 SHEPHERD. He's talking nonsense, wasting his breath.

---

3 Irony *Why is the shepherd's response to the messenger so vehement?*

1249 **Arcturus:** a star in the northern sky; its rising, or reappearance, in mid-September signaled the end of summer.
1252 **folds:** enclosure or pen for livestock.

1261–1262 **lash out . . . lashing:** a play on words; **lash out** means "verbally abuse" while **lashing** refers to a whipping.

SOPHOCLES **301**

Teach

| **Literary Element** | **2** |

Dialogue Ask: How does the dialogue in lines 1253-1254 imitate the rhythms of natural speech? (*It imitates natural speech by adding pauses marked by ellipses.*)

[ADVANCED] **Ask:** What is the hesitation in the old shepherd's speech meant to convey? (*It conveys both his reluctance to reveal what he knows to be a horrible revelation and his natural shyness in the presence of his king.*)

| **Literary Element** | **3** |

Irony Answer: *The shepherd does not want the truth to come out: namely, he gave away Laius's infant many years ago.*

Learning Objectives
Analyzing irony. (SE)
Visualizing. (TE)
Monitoring comprehension. (TE)
Analyzing dialogue. (TE)

English Learners

DIFFERENTIATED INSTRUCTION

Intermediate Point out to students that many words in English have multiple meanings. Draw their attention to the word *pens* in line 1251. Students may be familiar with *pen* meaning "writing instrument," but may have never encountered it meaning "enclosure for livestock."

Have students use a dictionary to identify three meanings for each of the following words.

1. flight (*act of flying, series of stairs, escape*)

2. shift (*change in position, people working during a specific period, a type of dress*)

3. bound (*to leap, a limit, headed for*)

4. title (*name of a book or work of art, a championship, right of ownership*)

5. sound (*noise, healthy, to test depth of*)

301

Teach

Reading Strategy | 1

Synthesize Answer: *In the past, Oedipus has resorted to violence when frustrated. He admits to striking the old stranger (Laius) in anger and then killing most of the men in his party. His anger also exploded when Tiresias refused to reveal the truth about Laius's murder.*

(APPROACHING) If students have trouble, have them review these passages: Oedipus and Tiresias (lines 393–416; Oedipus and Laius (lines 886–898).

Big Idea | 2

The Tragic Vision Answer: *Oedipus may be keeping in mind his promise to Thebes to expose Laius's murderer. He may also be pursuing the truth of his identity because the mystery of his birth has haunted him for many years.*

OEDIPUS. So, you won't talk willingly—
    then you'll talk with pain.

[*The* GUARDS *seize the* SHEPHERD.]

SHEPHERD. No, dear god, don't torture an old man!

OEDIPUS. Twist his arms back, quickly!

SHEPHERD.   God help us, why?—
1270   what more do you need to know?

OEDIPUS. Did you give him that child? He's asking.

SHEPHERD. I did . . . I wish to god I'd died that day.

OEDIPUS. You've got your wish if you don't tell the truth.

SHEPHERD. The more I tell, the worse the death I'll die.

1275 OEDIPUS. Our friend here wants to stretch things out,°
    does he?

[*Motioning to his men for torture*.] ☆

SHEPHERD. No, no, I gave it to him—I just said so.

OEDIPUS. Where did you get it? Your house? Someone else's?

SHEPHERD. It wasn't mine, no, I got it from . . . someone.

OEDIPUS. Which one of them?

[*Looking at the citizens*.]

                              Whose house?
SHEPHERD.   No—
1280   god's sake, master, no more questions!

OEDIPUS. You're a dead man if I have to ask again.

SHEPHERD. Then—the child came from the house . . .
    of Laius.

OEDIPUS.   A slave? or born of his own blood?

SHEPHERD.   Oh no,
    I'm right at the edge, the horrible truth—I've got to say it!

1285 OEDIPUS. And I'm at the edge of hearing horrors, yes, but I
    must hear!

SHEPHERD. All right! His son, they said it was—his son!
    But the one inside, your wife,
    she'd tell it best.

1275 **stretch things out:** a play on words; in one sense, it means "delay," and in another, it refers to torture—stretching limbs to unnatural limits, as on a rack.

---

1 Synthesize *Is Oedipus's treatment of the shepherd out of character? Explain.*

2 The Tragic Vision *Why does Oedipus insist on hearing the truth, no matter how horrible it might be?*

Grammar Practice

Use Prepositional Phrases Remind students that a prepositional phrase is a group of words that begins with a preposition and ends with the object of the preposition. A prepositional phrase shows the relationship between people or objects (*books on the desk, wind in the trees, man across the street*). Prepositional phrases usually function as adjectives or adverbs.

Write the following example on the board: The plays of Sophocles [adjective modifying *plays*] were performed in outdoor theaters [adverb modifying *performed*].

Have students identify three other prepositional phrases on page 302 and identify the words they modify and their functions in the sentences. (*Possible answers: line 1279, of them, adjective*

modifying one; line 1282, from the house, adverb modifying came; line 1283, of his own blood, adverb modifying born)

OEDIPUS. My wife—
1290 *she* gave it to you?

SHEPHERD. Yes, yes, my king.

OEDIPUS. Why, what for?

SHEPHERD. To kill it.

OEDIPUS. Her own child,
1295 how could she?

SHEPHERD. She was afraid—
frightening prophecies.

OEDIPUS. What?

SHEPHERD.   They said—
he'd kill his parents.

1300 OEDIPUS. But you gave him to this old man—why?

SHEPHERD. I pitied the little baby, master,
hoped he'd take him off to his own country,
far away, but he saved him for this, this fate.
If you are the man he says you are, believe me,
you were born for pain.

1305 OEDIPUS.   O god—
all come true, all burst to light!
O light—now let me look my last on you!°
I stand revealed at last—
cursed in my birth, cursed in marriage,
1310 cursed in the lives I cut down with these hands!

[*Rushing through the doors with a great cry. The Corinthian*
MESSENGER, *the* SHEPHERD *and* ATTENDANTS *exit slowly to the side.*]

CHORUS. O the generations of men
the dying generations—adding the total
of all your lives I find they come to nothing . . .
          does there exist, is there a man on earth
1315 who seizes more joy than just a dream, a vision?
And the vision no sooner dawns than dies
blazing into **oblivion**.

1307 **O light . . . on you:** let me die now; it also foreshadows his own torment.

3 Irony *What is ironic about the shepherd's simple act of kindness long ago?*

4 Synthesize *How has the prophecy been fulfilled?*

Vocabulary

oblivion (ə bliv′ ē ən) n. state of having been forgotten

SOPHOCLES **303**

Literary Element	3

Irony Answer: *The baby whom he spared would grow up to kill Laius and marry Jocasta.*

Reading Strategy	4

Synthesize Answer: *Oedipus and the people of Thebes realize he has killed his father and married his mother.*

Political History

Torture The use of torture was common in many ancient societies, including Greece, particularly when slaves or people of low social class were being questioned. The Greeks believed that the use of torture made the testimony of such people more reliable.

Learning Objectives
Synthesizing. (SE)
Analyzing irony. (SE)
Using prepositional phrases. (TE)

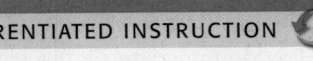

Advanced Learners/Pre-AP

DIFFERENTIATED INSTRUCTION

Dramaturgy Point out to students that a dramaturg is a special consultant who provides specific in-depth knowledge and literary resources to a director, producer, or theater company. Dramaturgs have been around since the 1800s, but it is only in the last 25 years that they have become really important. In the complex environment of contemporary theater, a dramaturg provides directors and producers with a more efficient way to sort through and evaluate the great mass of literature and background information available.

Have interested students research the specific functions of the dramaturg in theatrical companies today and report to the class.

Teach

Synthesize Ask: Why does Sophocles have the chorus mention the Sphinx again in lines 1323–1325? *(At the moment of Oedipus's downfall, the chorus recalls the act that began his rise to power in Thebes: solving the riddle of the Sphinx.)*

[ADVANCED] Remind students that it was solving the riddle of the Sphinx that brought Oedipus to the kingship of Thebes. **Ask:** What two riddles has Oedipus now solved? *(He has solved the riddle of the Sphinx and the riddle of his own identity.)*

Reading Strategy 2

Respond to Characters
What is your reaction to the sympathetic response of the citizens of Thebes in lines 1328–1331? How do you think people would respond today? *(Students may be surprised by the sympathetic response of the Thebans and believe that people today would be less understanding.)*

Big Idea 3

The Tragic Vision Answer: *The chorus feels both pity and revulsion for Oedipus.*

[ENGLISH LEARNERS] Help students understand the contrast between the words *pity* and *revulsion*. **Ask:** What is a synonym for pity? *(concern, sympathy, compassion)* **Ask:** What is a synonym for revulsion? *(disgust, distaste, repugnance)*

You are my great example, you, your life,
your destiny, Oedipus, man of misery—
I count no man blest.°

1320   You outranged all men!
Bending your bow to the breaking-point
you captured priceless glory, O dear god,
and the Sphinx came crashing down,
            the virgin, claws hooked
1325 like a bird of omen singing, shrieking death—
like a fortress reared in the face of death
you rose and saved our land.

From that day on we called you king
we crowned you with honors, Oedipus, towering over all—
1330 mighty king of the seven gates of Thebes.
But now to hear your story—is there a man more
    agonized?
More wed to pain and frenzy? Not a man on earth,
the joy of your life ground down to nothing
O Oedipus, name for the ages—
1335   one and the same wide harbor served you
                  son and father both
son and father came to rest in the same bridal chamber.
How, how could the furrows your father plowed
bear you, your agony, harrowing° on
in silence O so long?

1340   But now for all your power
Time, all-seeing Time has dragged you to the light,
judged your marriage monstrous from the start—
the son and the father tangling, both one—
O child of Laius, would to god
1345   I'd never seen you, never never!
Now I weep like a man who wails the dead
and the dirge comes pouring forth with all my heart!
I tell you the truth, you gave me life
my breath leapt up in you
1350 and now you bring down night upon my eyes.°

[*Enter a* MESSENGER *from the palace.*]

    MESSENGER. Men of Thebes, always first in honor,

1311–1320 O the generations . . . I count no man blest: The human struggle is pointless, and happiness is just a fleeting illusion; the fate of Oedipus is a perfect example.

1338 harrowing: a play on words; in one sense, it means "cultivating soil," and in another, it means "vexing or tormenting."

1348–1350 you gave me . . . upon my eyes: You saved Thebes, and now you have caused its ruin.

---

3 The Tragic Vision *How does the chorus feel about Oedipus's downfall?*

Speaking Practice

Conduct a Group Discussion

Students can obtain ideas and varied viewpoints from discussing elements of a literary work. Their listening and speaking skills will also benefit from their participation in oral discourse.

Write the word *honor* on the board and have students discuss its meaning and importance in the play. Ask students what they think it means to be honorable in today's society. How are the two meanings similar? How do they differ? If the play were set in today's society, would Oedipus be considered honorable? Why or why not? Discuss these and other questions that arise and help students apply the discourse to their reading of the play.

Reading Strategy | 4

Connect to Personal
Experience **Ask:** What is
your opinion of the observation
in lines 1360–1361? (*Students
may agree that feelings such as
guilt or regret, which we impose
on ourselves, are very difficult to
bear.*)

what horrors you will hear, what you will see,
what a heavy weight of sorrow you will shoulder . . .
if you are true to your birth, if you still have
1355   some feeling for the royal house of Thebes.
I tell you neither the waters of the Danube
nor the Nile can wash this palace clean.
Such things it hides, it soon will bring to light—
terrible things, and none done blindly now,
1360   all done with a will. The pains
we **inflict** upon ourselves hurt most of all. **4**

LEADER.   God knows we have pains enough already.
What can you add to them?

MESSENGER.   The queen is dead.

LEADER.   Poor lady—how?

1365   MESSENGER.   By her own hand. But you are spared the worst,
you never had to watch . . . I saw it all,
and with all the memory that's in me
you will learn what that poor woman suffered.

Once she'd broken in through the gates,
1370   dashing past us, frantic, whipped to fury,

*Oedipus abandoned on
Mount Cithaeron by the
shepherd.* 3rd century AD.
Ancient Rome. Marble relief
from a sarcophagus. Catican
Museums, Vatican State.

View the Art This relief
was used to decorate a
sarcophagus, a type of coffin
that was popular with upper-
class members of Greco-
Roman society. What is the
mood of this relief, and how
does it parallel the mood at
this point in the play?

Vocabulary

inflict (in flikt′) *v.* to give or cause

View the Art ★

Answer: *The shepherd's gestures
of pity for the boy parallel the
Chorus's expressions of pity for
Oedipus after he discovers his
awful fate.*

The first sarcophagi, made out of
stone, were used by Egyptians
around 2650 B.C. The sarcophagi
used in ancient Rome after 300
B.C. were made of terra cotta,
stone, or marble and often
featured carved figures of the
deceased on their lids.

Learning Objectives
Synthesizing. (SE)
Analyzing art. (SE)
Responding to characters. (TE)
Connecting to personal experience. (TE)
Conducting a group discussion (TE)

SOPHOCLES   **305**

Advanced Learners/Pre-AP

DIFFERENTIATED INSTRUCTION

Offstage Violence Point out to students
that one of the conventions of ancient
Greek drama was that violence was not
shown on stage. Greek plays are full of
horrible acts, but the audience never
sees these dreadful deeds. Instead, they
hear about them through the report of
a character. Have small, heterogeneous
groups of students discuss how this affects
the impact of a play.

Approaching Level

DIFFERENTIATED INSTRUCTION

Scaffold Questions If some students
are in the groups are having trouble
participating, suggest they respond to
some of the following questions:

- How does the messenger's description
of violent acts differ from showing the
acts themselves?

- How would the atmosphere of the play
be different if Oedipus blinded himself
on stage?

- If Jocasta's suicide occurred on stage,
how would it affect the focus on
Oedipus as the tragic hero?

Teach

Reading Strategy 1

Respond Direct students to lines 1395–1400. **Ask:** What is your response to the messenger's description of Oedipus's discovery of Jocasta's body? What do you think he feels? *(Students may say that Oedipus not only feels pain in losing Jocasta, but may also feel responsible for her death.)*

ripping her hair out with both hands—
straight to her rooms she rushed, flinging herself
across the bridal-bed, doors slamming behind her—
once inside, she wailed for Laius, dead so long,
1375 remembering how she bore his child long ago,
the life that rose up to destroy him, leaving
its mother to mother living creatures
with the very son she'd borne.
Oh how she wept, mourning the marriage-bed
1380 where she let loose that double brood—monsters—
husband by her husband, children by her child.
                                          And then—
but how she died is more than I can say. Suddenly
Oedipus burst in, screaming, he stunned us so
we couldn't watch her agony to the end,
1385 our eyes were fixed on him. Circling
like a maddened beast, stalking, here, there,
crying out to us—
                    Give him a sword! His wife,
no wife, his mother, where can he find the mother earth
that cropped two crops at once, himself and all his
        children?
1390 He was raging—one of the dark powers pointing the way,
none of us mortals crowding around him, no,
with a great shattering cry—someone, something leading
        him on—
he hurled at the twin doors and bending the bolts back
out of their sockets, crashed through the chamber.
1395 And there we saw the woman hanging by the neck,
cradled high in a woven noose, spinning,

1 swinging back and forth. And when he saw her,
giving a low, wrenching sob that broke our hearts,
slipping the halter° from her throat, he eased her down,
1400 in a slow embrace he laid her down, poor thing . . .
then, what came next, what horror we beheld!

1399 halter: rope or strap.

He rips off her brooches, the long gold pins
holding her robes—and lifting them high,
looking straight up into the points,
1405 he digs them down the sockets of his eyes, crying, "You,
you'll see no more the pain I suffered, all the pain
    I caused!

Reading Practice

Use a Plot Diagram Remind students that plot of a literary work moves through a series of stages. The **exposition** introduces the characters, setting, and conflict; the **rising action** develops the conflict with complications; the **climax** is the emotional high point of the plot; the **falling action** is created by the events following the climax, and the **resolution** shows how the conflict is settled. Draw a triangular plot diagram on the board and put these labels on it. Have students copy the diagram on a separate sheet of paper and work in pairs to position the following events on the diagram up through the climax.

- Jocasta hangs herself *(climax)*
- Thebans beg Oedipus to stop the plague *(exposition)*
- Tiresias identifies Oedipus as the murderer *(rising action)*
- messenger reveals that Polybus is not Oedipus's father *(rising action)*
- Oedipus blinds himself *(climax)*
- Apollo indicates Laius's murderer as the cause of plague *(rising action)*
- shepherd reveals that Oedipus is the child of Laius *(climax)*

When they have completed the chart, have them retain it to note down the events of the falling action and the resolution.

Too long you looked on the ones you never should
    have seen,°
blind to the ones you longed to see, to know!° Blind
from this hour on! Blind in the darkness—blind!"

1410 His voice like a dirge, rising, over and over
raising the pins, raking them down his eyes.
And at each stroke blood spurts from the roots,
splashing his beard, a swirl of it, nerves and clots—
black hail of blood pulsing, gushing down.

1415 These are the griefs that burst upon them both,
coupling man and woman. The joy they had so lately,
the fortune of their old ancestral house
was deep joy indeed. Now, in this one day,
wailing, madness and doom, death, disgrace,

1420 all the griefs in the world that you can name, **2**
all are theirs forever.

LEADER.   Oh poor man, the misery—
    has he any rest from pain now?

[*A voice within, in torment.*]

MESSENGER.   He's shouting,
    "Loose the bolts, someone, show me to all of Thebes!
    My father's murderer, my mother's—"

1425 No, I can't repeat it, it's unholy.
Now he'll tear himself from his native earth,°
not linger, curse the house with his own curse.
But he needs strength, and a guide to lead him on.
This is sickness more than he can bear.

[*The palace doors open.*]

                         Look,
1430 he'll show you himself. The great doors are opening—
you are about to see a sight, a horror
even his mortal enemy would pity.

[*Enter* OEDIPUS, *blinded, led by a boy. He stands at the palace steps,
as if surveying his people once again.*]

CHORUS.   O the terror—
    the suffering, for all the world to see,
    the worst terror that ever met my eyes.
1435 What madness swept over you? What god,

3 Synthesize *Who called Oedipus blind earlier in the play? What might Oedipus gain though he has lost his physical sight?*

1407 the ones you never should have seen: Laius as his victim and Jocasta as his wife.
1408 the ones you longed . . . to know: Laius and Jocasta as his parents.

1426 tear . . . his native earth: leave Thebes.

Teach

| **Literary Element** | **2** |

Tragedy Discuss with students the role of fate—or the will of the gods—in Greek tragedy, explaining that the inevitability of the hero's downfall heightened the sense of tragedy for the ancient Greeks.

Ask: How does this quality of inescapable fate affect your reaction to Oedipus's downfall? (*Most students will probably feel that that it makes Oedipus seem more of a victim and hence more pitiable.*)

| **Reading Strategy** | **3** |

Synthesize Answer: *Tiresias called Oedipus blind to his own corruption in line 471. Oedipus might gain wisdom and have spiritual sight as does Tiresias.*
(ADVANCED) **Ask:** How is Sophocles using blindness as an ironic symbol at this point in the play? (*Oedipus finally "sees" the truth only when he loses his physical sight.*)

Learning Objectives
Synthesizing. (SE)
Responding to description. (TE)
Using a plot diagram. (TE)
Analyzing tragedy. (TE)

English Learners

DIFFERENTIATED INSTRUCTION

Intermediate Working with this diagram should help English learners with the literary vocabulary associated with plot. Reinforce this learning by giving them further definition and a context sentence for the words *exposition, climax,* and *resolution.*

- **Exposition** means "a detailed explanation" ("The scientist gave a lengthy <u>exposition</u> on nuclear power.")

- **Climax** means "point of greatest intensity" ("The <u>climax</u> of the game was a grand slam home run in the seventh inning.")

- **Resolution** means "solution" or "settlement" ("An agreement between the owners and the union brought a <u>resolution</u> of the strike.")

Advanced Learners/Pre-AP

DIFFERENTIATED INSTRUCTION

Comparison and Contrast Point out to students that the stage direction after line 1432 (*"Enter OEDIPUS, blinded, led by a boy"*) echoes that for the entrance of Tiresias after line 337 (*"Enter TIRESIAS, the blind prophet, led by a boy"*). Have a group of students discuss how the situation of the blinded Oedipus is like and unlike that of Tiresias.

Teach

Big Idea 1

The Tragic Vision **Answer:**
Sophocles uses images of drowning and stabbing to convey Oedipus's suffering.

[ADVANCED] **Ask:** What previous action do the images of stabbing recall? *(Oedipus blinding himself with the pins from Jocasta's brooches.)*

Cultural History ☆

Greek Psychology The ancient Greeks often attributed irrational, self-destructive human behavior to the influence of the gods. Greek mythology included a goddess named Ate (ä'tē) who was believed to incite humans to rash, acts that lead to suffering.

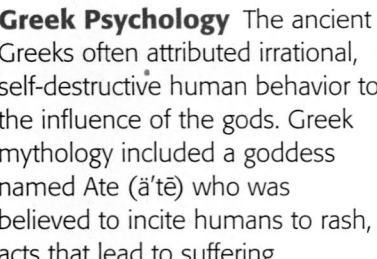

what dark power leapt beyond all bounds,
beyond belief, to crush your wretched life?—
godforsaken, cursed by the gods!
I pity you but I can't bear to look.
1440   I've much to ask, so much to learn,
so much fascinates my eyes,
but you . . . I shudder at the sight.

OEDIPUS.   Oh, Ohh—
the agony! I am agony—
where am I going? where on earth?
1445   where does all this agony hurl me?
where's my voice?—
     winging, swept away on a dark tide—
My destiny, my dark power, what a leap you made!

CHORUS.   To the depths of terror, too dark to hear, to see.

1450 OEDIPUS.   Dark, horror of darkness
my darkness, drowning, swirling around me
crashing wave on wave—unspeakable, irresistible
     headwind, fatal harbor! Oh again,
the misery, all at once, over and over
1455   the stabbing daggers, stab of memory
raking me insane.

CHORUS.   No wonder you suffer
twice over, the pain of your wounds,
the lasting grief of pain.

OEDIPUS.   Dear friend, still here?
Standing by me, still with a care for me,
1460   the blind man? Such compassion,
     loyal to the last. Oh it's you,
I know you're here, dark as it is
I'd know you anywhere, your voice—
it's yours, clearly yours.

CHORUS.   Dreadful, what you've done . . .
1465   how could you bear it, gouging out your eyes?
What superhuman power drove you on?

OEDIPUS.   Apollo, friends, Apollo— ☆
he ordained my agonies—these, my pains on pains!
But the hand that struck my eyes was mine,
1470   mine alone—no one else—

---

1 **The Tragic Vision** *What images does Sophocles use in these lines to convey Oedipus's overwhelming suffering?*

Writing Practice

Analyze Literary Technique
Students may benefit from analyzing the techniques Sophocles uses to bring about the climax of his play. Introduce students to the term *deus ex machina* (from a Latin phrase meaning "god from a machine"). Explain that this term refers to the common practice in Greek and Roman drama of having a god (played by an actor lowered on a crane or "machine") come on stage at the close of a play to provide explanations or resolve difficulties. A deus ex machina has come to mean "a person or thing appearing suddenly to provide a contrived solution."

Have students write a paragraph evaluating the messenger from Corinth as a deus ex machina figure. Have them consider the plausibility of his appearance and the timing of Polybus's death. Students' essays should also discuss whether Sophocles' use of this technique makes the tragedy more effective or less effective.

I did it all myself!
What good were eyes to me?
Nothing I could see could bring me joy.

CHORUS. No, no, exactly as you say.

OEDIPUS.   What can I ever see?
1475   What love, what call of the heart
        can touch my ears with joy? Nothing, friends.
            Take me away, far, far from Thebes,
            quickly, cast me away, my friends—
this great murderous ruin, this man cursed to heaven,
1480   the man the deathless gods hate most of all!

CHORUS. Pitiful, you suffer so, you understand so much . . .
        I wish you'd never known.

OEDIPUS.   Die, die—
        whoever he was that day in the wilds
        who cut my ankles free of the ruthless pins,
1485   he pulled me clear of death, he saved my life
        for this, this kindness—
                            Curse him, kill him!
        If I'd died then, I'd never have dragged myself,
        my loved ones through such hell.

CHORUS. Oh if only . . . would to god.

1490 OEDIPUS.   I'd never have come to this,
        my father's murderer—never been branded
        mother's husband, all men see me now! Now,
            loathed by the gods, son of the mother I defiled
            coupling in my father's bed, spawning lives in the loins
1495   that spawned my wretched life. What grief can crown this
        grief?
            It's mine alone, my destiny—I am Oedipus!

CHORUS. How can I say you've chosen for the best?
        Better to die than be alive and blind.

OEDIPUS. What I did was best—don't lecture me,
1500   no more advice. I, with *my* eyes,
        how could I look my father in the eyes
        when I go down to death? Or mother, so abused . . .
        I have done such things to the two of them,
        crimes too huge for hanging.
                            Worse yet,

 Synthesize *Whom does Oedipus curse?*

SOPHOCLES **309**

Teach

| Reading Strategy | 2 |

Synthesize **Answer:** *Oedipus curses the shepherd who saved him as an infant.*

APPROACHING If students are having difficulty, review lines 1129–1134 with them. **Ask:** What was ironic about the shepherd's kind act? *(He would later be cursed by Oedipus for his kindness.)*

Learning Objectives
Synthesizing. (SE)
Analyzing literary technique. (TE)

Approaching Level

DIFFERENTIATED INSTRUCTION

Designing a Mask Students have seen examples of theatrical masks in the photograph on page 300. Have students create their own masks to be worn by one of the principal characters in the play, such as Oedipus, Jocasta, Creon, or Tiresias. Remind students that such a mask should both convey the character's age and sex and also be appropriate to the performance of a tragedy. Students can limit their project to designing a mask or they can carry through creating a three-dimensional mask in a medium such as plaster bandages or papier mâché.

Advanced Learners/Pre-AP

DIFFERENTIATED INSTRUCTION

Using a Mask Ask students who have designed and created actual masks to deliver one of their character's speeches wearing the mask.

Teach

Literary Element | 1

Personification Explain to students that personification is the assigning of human traits to non-human things.

Ask: What is personified in lines 1531–1537? *(Oedipus personifies the crossroads, addressing the spot as a person, stating that it "drank," "remembered," and "saw.")*

(ENGLISH LEARNERS) Use the word *personify* as a starting point to help English learners with the suffixes *-fy* and *-ify*. Point out that these suffixes mean "cause to become."

Ask: What does *personify* mean? (cause to become a person). Have students use a dictionary to find the meanings of these words: *magnify, qualify, quantify, and indemnify.*

Reading Strategy | 2

Synthesize Answer: *Oedipus promised to expose and banish the murderer of Laius, and now he is doing so.*

1505
the sight of my children, born as they were born,
how could I long to look into their eyes?
No, not with these eyes of mine, never.
Not this city either, her high towers,
the sacred glittering images of her gods—

1510
I am misery! I, her best son, reared
as no other son of Thebes was ever reared,
I've stripped myself, I gave the command myself.°
All men must cast away the great blasphemer,°
the curse now brought to light by the gods,

1515
the son of Laius—I, my father's son!

Now I've exposed my guilt, **horrendous** guilt,
could I train a level glance on you,° my countrymen?
Impossible! No, if I could just block off my ears,
the springs° of hearing, I would stop at nothing—

1520
I'd wall up my loathsome body like a prison,
blind to the sound of life, not just the sight.
Oblivion—what a blessing . . .
for the mind to dwell a world away from pain.

O Cithaeron, why did you give me shelter?

1525
Why didn't you take me, crush my life out on the spot?
I'd never have revealed my birth to all mankind.

O Polybus, Corinth, the old house of my fathers,
so I believed—what a handsome prince you raised—
under the skin, what sickness to the core.

1530
Look at me! Born of outrage, outrage to the core.

1 O triple roads—it all comes back, the secret,
dark ravine, and the oaks closing in
where the three roads join . . .
You drank my father's blood, my own blood

1535
spilled by my own hands—you still remember me?
What things you saw me do? Then I came here
and did them all once more!
                              Marriages! O marriage,
you gave me birth, and once you brought me into

1512 I've stripped . . . command myself: Oedipus issued the proclamation that decreed the murderer's punishment.
1513 blasphemer: one who has shown contempt for something sacred.

1517 train a level glance on you: look you in the eye.

1519 springs: here, source.

2 Synthesize *How has Oedipus kept the promise he made to his people at the beginning of the play?*

Vocabulary

horrendous (hô ren′dəs) *adj.* horrible; frightful

310 UNIT 2 ANCIENT GREECE

Grammar Practice

Use Demonstrative Pronouns
Remind students that demonstrative pronouns (*this, that, these,* and *those*) point out specific persons, places, things, or ideas. A demonstrative pronoun functions as a noun—as a subject, a direct object, an indirect object, or the object of a preposition. Write the following sentence on the board, and have students identify the function of the demonstrative pronoun *this*.

To avoid this, Oedipus flees from, Corinth. (direct object of the verb *avoid*)
Have students write four sentences about the play, using each of the demonstrative pronouns. Students should identify the function of each pronoun. Warn students to avoid using the words as adjectives, as in "This play . . . "

(Possible answers:
This is the theme of Oedipus the King.— subject
When Oedipus said that, Creon grew angry. —direct object
Several of these are brought by messengers. —object of a preposition
The actors wore those to play the parts of the chorus.—direct object)

310

the world
you brought my sperm rising back, springing to light
1540 fathers, brothers, sons—one murderous breed—
brides, wives, mothers. The blackest things
a man can do, I have done them all!

              No more—
it's wrong to name what's wrong to do. Quickly,
for the love of god, hide me somewhere,
1545 kill me, hurl me into the sea
where you can never look on me again.

[*Beckoning to the* CHORUS *as they shrink away.*]

                  Closer,
it's all right. Touch the man of sorrow.
Do. Don't be afraid. My troubles are mine
and I am the only man alive who can sustain° them.

[*Enter* CREON *from the palace, attended by palace* GUARDS.]

1550 LEADER. Put your requests to Creon. Here he is,
just when we need him. He'll have a plan, he'll act.
Now that he's the sole defense of the country
in your place.

OEDIPUS.   Oh no, what can I say to him?
How can I ever hope to win his trust?
1555 I wronged him so, just now, in every way.
You must see that—I was so wrong, so wrong.

CREON. I haven't come to mock you, Oedipus,
or to criticize your former failings.

[*Turning to the* GUARDS.]

                You there,
have you lost all respect for human feeling?
1560 At least revere the Sun, the holy fire
that keeps us all alive. Never expose a thing
of guilt and holy dread so great it appalls
the earth, the rain from heaven, the light of day!
Get him into the halls—quickly as you can.
1565 Piety° demands no less. Kindred alone
should see a kinsman's shame. This is obscene.

OEDIPUS. Please, in god's name . . . you wipe my fears away,
coming so generously° to me, the worst of men.
Do one thing more, for your sake, not mine.

1549 sustain: here, suffer; Oedipus is suggesting that his troubles are not contagious and cannot be transmitted to others by touch.

3

1565 Piety: loyalty to natural or fundamental obligations, often used with respect to religious devotion.

1568 coming so generously: Creon's kindness goes beyond what Oedipus has any right to expect.

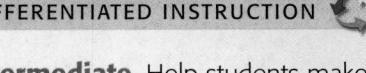 **4** Synthesize *Why does the kingship now pass to Creon?*

SOPHOCLES **311**

Teach

Reading Strategy   **3**

Make Inferences Ask: What can you infer about Creon's character from his reaction in lines 1557–1566? (*Creon shows his compassionate, forgiving nature by trying to protect Oedipus.*)

Reading Strategy   **4**

Synthesize Answer: *As the brother of Jocasta, the dead queen, Creon is next in line for the throne.*

(ADVANCED) **Ask:** What does this indicate about the custom of succession to the kingship in Thebes? (*It indicates that the Theban kingship does not pass to the eldest son of the ruler, as in many monarchies.*)

Learning Objectives
Synthesizing. (SE)
Analyzing personification. (TE)
Using demonstrative pronouns. (TE)
Making inferences. (TE)

English Learners

DIFFERENTIATED INSTRUCTION

Intermediate Help students make the distinction between demonstrative pronouns and demonstrative adjectives by having them rewrite their sentences from the Skills Practice on page 310. For example:

<u>This statement</u> is the theme of Oedipus the King. (modifies subject)

When Oedipus made <u>that remark</u>, Creon grew angry. (modifies direct object)

Advanced Learners/Pre-AP

DIFFERENTIATED INSTRUCTION

Further Reading Point out to students that *Oedipus the King* is the first of three plays Sophocles wrote about Oedipus and his children. In the second play, *Oedipus at Colonus,* Oedipus has been exiled for many years and is taken in by the village of Colonus, near Athens. In the third play,

Antigone, Creon, now ruler of Thebes, comes into conflict with Antigone, the daughter of Oedipus. Interested students may want to read one or the other of these plays and share oral summaries with the class.

Teach

Reading Strategy   1

Respond to Character

Remind students that a tragic hero is a good person with a serious flaw. **Ask:** How does the response to Creon in lines 1583–1585 indicate both the good and bad in Oedipus? *(Students may feel that his concern that Jocasta be decently buried shows his basic goodness, but his tendency to command— even after his downfall—displays his tragic weakness of pride.)*

Big Idea   2

The Tragic Vision   Answer:
Oedipus, who has spent most of his life trying to avoid his fate, finally embraces his destiny.

(ADVANCED) **Ask:** How might Oedipus's sense of "something great and terrible, something strange" awaiting him in the future be related to his blindness? *(Students may feel that his blindness has given him a prophetic sense, like that of Tiresias.)*

1570   CREON. What do you want? Why so insistent?

OEDIPUS. Drive me out of the land at once, far from sight,
    where I can never hear a human voice.

CREON. I'd have done that already, I promise you.
    First I wanted the god to clarify my duties.

1575   OEDIPUS. The god? His command was clear, every word:
    death for the father-killer, the curse—
    he said destroy me!

CREON. So he did. Still, in such a crisis
    it's better to ask precisely what to do.

1580   OEDIPUS. You'd ask the oracle about a man like me?°

CREON. By all means. And this time, I assume,
    even you will obey the god's decrees.

1   OEDIPUS.   I will,
    I will. And you, I command you—I beg you . . .
    the woman inside, bury her as you see fit.
1585   It's the only decent thing,
    to give your own the last rites. As for me,
    never condemn the city of my fathers
    to house my body, not while I'm alive, no,
    let me live on the mountains, on Cithaeron,
1590   my favorite haunt, I have made it famous.
    Mother and father marked out that rock
    to be my everlasting tomb—buried alive.
    Let me die there, where they tried to kill me.

    Oh but this I know: no sickness can destroy me,
1595   nothing can. I would never have been saved
    from death—I have been saved
    for something great and terrible, something strange.
    Well let my destiny come and take me on its way!

    About my children, Creon, the boys at least,
1600   don't burden yourself. They're men;°
    wherever they go, they'll find the means to live.
    But my two daughters, my poor helpless girls,
    clustering at our table, never without me
    hovering near them . . . whatever I touched,
1605   they always had their share. Take care of them,
    I beg you. Wait, better—permit me, would you?

1580 ask the oracle . . . me: refers to the practice of consulting oracles only for matters of utmost importance. Oedipus now thinks he is unworthy; ironic, because the oracle has already played a large role in Oedipus's life.

1600 They're men: refers to the boys' gender and the opportunities open to males in ancient Greek society; it is not a reference to their age.

2   The Tragic Vision   *How has Oedipus's attitude toward his fate changed?*

Reading Practice

Use a Character Web Point out that Sophocles takes legendary figures from Greek myth and creates rich, complex dramatic characters. Using a character web is a way of organizing the information about a character presented in a literary work. Have students use a character web like the one started below to analyze the traits of one of the main characters in the play, such as Oedipus, Jocasta, or Creon. Draw the web on the board and have them copy it on a separate sheet of paper. Have them use it to note down character traits.

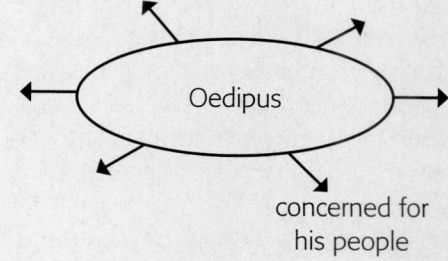

Oedipus

concerned for his people

Just to touch them with my hands and take
our fill of tears. Please . . . my king.
Grant it, with all your noble heart.
1610 If I could hold them, just once, I'd think
I had them with me, like the early days
when I could see their eyes.

[ANTIGONE and ISMENE, two small children, are led in from the palace by a nurse.]

                            What's that?
O god! Do I really hear you sobbing?—
my two children. Creon, you've pitied me?
1615 Sent me my darling girls, my own flesh and blood!
Am I right?

CREON.   Yes, it's my doing.
I know the joy they gave you all these years,
the joy you must feel now.

OEDIPUS.   Bless you, Creon!
May god watch over you for this kindness,
better than he ever guarded me.
1620   Children, where are you?
Here, come quickly—

[Groping for ANTIGONE and ISMENE, who approach their father cautiously, then embrace him.]

             Come to these hands of mine,
your brother's hands, your own father's hands°
that served his once bright eyes so well—
that made them blind. Seeing nothing, children,
1625 knowing nothing, I became your father,
I fathered you in the soil that gave me life.

How I weep for you—I cannot see you now . . .
just thinking of all your days to come, the bitterness,
the life that rough mankind will thrust upon you.
1630 Where are the public gatherings you can join,
the banquets of the clans? Home you'll come,
in tears, cut off from the sight of it all,
the brilliant rites unfinished.
And when you reach perfection, ripe for marriage,
1635 who will he be, my dear ones? Risking all
to shoulder the curse that weighs down my parents,
yes and you too—that wounds us all together.

1622 **your brother's . . . father's hands:** because Oedipus married his mother and had children with her, these children are both sisters and daughters to him.

3 **Synthesize** *How might Sophocles' audience, who would have known the future misfortune of Oedipus's daughters, have responded to these lines?*

Teach

Reading Strategy   **3**

Synthesize **Answer:** *They would have responded with deeper feelings of pity and terror for the tragic fates yet to unfold.*

Literary History ☆

Antigone and Haemon
According to Greek legend, Antigone later fell in love with Haemon, the son of Creon. The two great Greek tragedians Sophocles and Euripides imagined very different fates for the lovers. In his *Antigone,* Sophocles has both Antigone and Haemon commit suicide. In Euripides's version, however, Antigone and Haemon survive and marry.

Learning Objectives
Synthesizing. (SE)
Responding to character. (TE)
Using a character web. (TE)

English Learners

DIFFERENTIATED INSTRUCTION

Advanced Point out to students that the reasons for leaving one's home country vary greatly. While some, like Oedipus, might be forced out, others might be seeking a greater opportunity. Have students develop a list of reasons for moving to a new country. For each reason, identify the positive and negative effects of moving.

Have students predict what Oedipus's life outside of Thebes might be like.

Teach

Reading Strategy | 1

Synthesize Answer: *They are essentially powerless. They depend upon fathers or husbands for their identities and their livelihoods.*

Political History ☆

Exile in Athens Athenian democracy included a system called ostracism. Each year, citizens could write the name of an undesirable politician on a piece of baked clay called an ostracon. If a person's name appeared on 6,000 ostraca, he could be exiled. An ostracized politician had to leave Athenian territory within ten days and stay away for ten years.

What more misery could you want?
Your father killed his father, sowed his mother,
1640   one, one and the selfsame womb sprang you—
he cropped the very roots of his existence.°

Such disgrace, and you must bear it all!
Who will marry you then? Not a man on earth.
Your doom is clear: you'll wither away to nothing,
single, without a child.

[Turning to CREON.*]*

1645   Oh Creon,
you are the only father they have now . . .
we who brought them into the world
are gone, both gone at a stroke—
Don't let them go begging, abandoned,
1650   women without men. Your own flesh and blood!
Never bring them down to the level of my pains.
Pity them. Look at them, so young, so **vulnerable**,
shorn of everything—you're their only hope.
Promise me, noble Creon, touch my hand.

[Reaching toward CREON, *who draws back.]*

1655   You, little ones, if you were old enough
to understand, there is much I'd tell you.
Now, as it is, I'd have you say a prayer.
Pray for life, my children,
live where you are free to grow and season.°
1660   Pray god you find a better life than mine,
the father who begot you.

CREON.   Enough.
You've wept enough. Into the palace now.

OEDIPUS.   I must, but I find it very hard.

CREON.   Time is the great healer, you will see.

1665   OEDIPUS.   I am going—you know on what condition?

CREON.   Tell me. I'm listening.

OEDIPUS.   Drive me out of Thebes, in exile. ☆

CREON.   Not I. Only the gods can give you that.

1641 cropped . . . existence: fathered children by his own mother.

1659 season: mature; age properly.

---

1   **Synthesize** *What does this plea suggest about the position of women in ancient Greek society?*

Vocabulary

vulnerable (vul′nər ə bəl) *adj.* weak; unable to defend oneself

Viewing Practice

View Critically Explain to students that when they critically view a play they should pay attention to the director's interpretation of roles as well as the overall tone of the production. Doing this will allow them to analyze and respond to interpretations other than their own and will give them the opportunity to evaluate those interpretations.

Present a videotape of *Oedipus the King* to the class. Suggest that students make a chart like this one to fill in as they watch the production.

Elements	Comments	Evaluation
Setting		
Mood		
Overall Presentation		

OEDIPUS. Surely the gods hate me so much—

CREON. You'll get your wish at once.

1670 OEDIPUS.   You consent?

CREON. I try to say what I mean; it's my habit.

OEDIPUS. Then take me away. It's time.

CREON. Come along, let go of the children.

OEDIPUS.   No— don't take them away from me, not now! No no no!

[Clutching his daughters as the GUARDS wrench them loose and take them through the palace doors.]

1675 CREON. Still the king, the master of all things? No more: here your power ends. None of your power follows you through life.

[Exit OEDIPUS and CREON to the palace. The CHORUS comes forward to address the audience directly.]

CHORUS. People of Thebes, my countrymen, look on Oedipus. He solved the famous riddle with his brilliance,
1680 he rose to power, a man beyond all power. Who could behold his greatness without envy? Now what a black sea of terror has overwhelmed him. Now as we keep our watch and wait the final day,° count no man happy till he dies, free of pain at last.°

[Exit in procession.]

---

 2 The Tragic Vision *Why do you think Sophocles includes this final detail about Oedipus?*

3 The Tragic Vision *In what way do the chorus's final lines summarize the tragic vision?*

Head of Oedipus, 2nd-3rd century AD. Relief on a Roman mausoleum.

Rheinisches Landesmuseum, Trier, Germany.

1683 watch: period of time during which a person is employed to protect someone or something. **keep . . . final day:** try to live our lives in keeping with honor and duty.
1684 count no man . . . at last: Do not call any man happy until he dies, because up until that point his fate is unknown and no one can predict what the future holds in store.

SOPHOCLES **315**

Teach

Big Idea	2

The Tragic Vision Answer: *This final detail arouses sympathy for Oedipus, a broken father whose daughters are taken from him. The detail also suggests Oedipus has not fully learned he is not in control.*

Big Idea	3

The Tragic Vision Answer: *One can escape pain and suffering of life only through death.*

Learning Objectives
Synthesizing. (SE)
Viewing critically. (TE)

Advanced Learners/Pre-AP

DIFFERENTIATED INSTRUCTION

Justice in Ancient Greece *Oedipus the King* offers examples of how criminal justice functions in Sophocles's imaginary Thebes. In lines 245–287, for example, Oedipus outlines the punishment for the criminal who killed Laius. Some students might be interested in examining the historical reality of criminal justice in ancient Greece.

Have interested students research the criminal justice system that existed in Athens at the time of Sophocles. This should include both how trials were conducted and what types of punishments were used.

After You Read

Assess

1. Some students may answer they were surprised by the horror of the tragedy.

2. (a) The messenger tells Oedipus Polybus was not his real father. (b) Oedipus fears he might be the son of slaves.

3. (a) Jocasta does not want Oedipus to learn the truth about his birth. (b) She kills herself out of horror and shame as the truth finally comes to light.

4. Oedipus says he could not look upon anything that would make him happy, and he could not bear to see more sorrow.

5. Some students may say the coincidences should have led him to the conclusion earlier. Others will note he believed Polybus and Merope to be his real parents.

6. Some students will say his blinding himself was punishment enough. Others will say his banishment fulfills the condition set by the oracle for the removal of the plague.

7. Students may say Thebes will never recover from the tragedy.

8. Possible responses: when the shepherd reveals the truth to Oedipus; when Oedipus blinds himself.

9. Possible responses: Some students may say Oedipus is responsible because he angrily killed Laius and then married his widow. Later he displayed excessive pride in investigating the murder of the king. Others may say he is a victim because he left his home in Corinth to prevent the horrid prophecy from coming true.

316

After You Read

Respond and Think Critically

Respond and Interpret

1. What was your reaction to the end of the play?

2. (a) What does the messenger tell Oedipus about his birth? (b) At this point, what is the worst outcome Oedipus foresees?

3. (a) Why does Jocasta try to prevent Oedipus from questioning the shepherd? (b) Why do you think Jocasta kills herself?

4. How does Oedipus explain his decision to blind himself?

Analyze and Evaluate

5. Do you think Oedipus should have figured out the truth about his past sooner? Explain.

6. In your opinion, should Oedipus be banished from Thebes? Explain.

7. What do you predict will happen to Thebes after Oedipus's fall from power?

8. In a dramatic work, the **climax** is the point of greatest interest or emotional intensity. What is the climax of *Oedipus the King*?

Connect

9. **Big Idea** **The Tragic Vision** In your opinion, is Oedipus responsible for his downfall, or is he a victim of fate? Explain.

10. **Connect to Today** How might the experiences of a modern audience at a performance of *Oedipus the King* differ from those of Sophocles' original audience?

Daily Life & Culture

The Delphic Oracle

The ancient Greeks believed the gods revealed the future in mysterious ways. The most important shrine of the gods was the oracle at Delphi, sacred to Apollo. An oracle was a priest or priestess who reported the responses of a god to human petitioners. (The word *oracle* also referred to the response itself and to the shrine of the god.) Delphi, now a famous archaeological site, is located on the lower plateau of Mount Parnassus in central Greece. Apollo was thought to convey his messages to a priestess, known as the Pythia, while she experienced an ecstatic trance. An official interpreter wrote down her frenzied prophecies, which were cryptic and open to conflicting interpretations.

Consulting the god Apollo at Delphi, vase fragment, 4th century BC. Classical Greek. Museo Nazionale Taranto, Italy.

Group Activity Discuss the following questions in a small group.

1. To what extent are the actions and reactions of the characters in this play dependent on oracular prophesies?

2. What are some examples of prophecy in today's society?

10. Sophocles' original audience regarded drama as a religious experience rather than mere entertainment, was more familiar with the mythical background of the play, watched the performance in a huge amphitheater, and was accustomed to seeing male actors in masks portray the characters.

Daily Life & Culture

1. Most of the characters—Laius and Jocasta, Oedipus, and Creon—seek advice from an oracle and act upon it, while Tiresias himself serves as a prophet.

2. Students may mention daily horoscopes, tabloid prophecies, and the popularity of palm readers and tarot card readers.

Literary Element | Irony

ACT Skills Practice

Why is it ironic that Oedipus forces the shepherd to speak?

A. Jocasta tries to prevent Oedipus from doing it.

B. The shepherd is unwilling to tell what he knows.

C. The shepherd's revelations will destroy Oedipus.

D. The chorus warns Oedipus not to do it.

Review: Tragedy

As you learned on page 274, a **tragedy** is a play in which the main character is brought to ruin or suffers a great sorrow. The **tragic hero** is typically a person of dignified or heroic stature whose downfall is at least partly caused by a flaw or an error in judgment.

Partner Activity Meet with another classmate to discuss how you would rate each statement below. Use this rating system:

strongly disagree ★ | disagree ★★ | agree ★★★ | strongly agree ★★★★

Support your ratings with evidence from the play.

1. Oedipus should have remained in Corinth.

2. Oedipus should never have murdered anyone.

3. Oedipus's tragic flaw is excessive pride, or *hubris*.

LOG ON ▶ **Literature** Online

Selection Resources For Selection Quizzes, eFlash-cards, and Reading-Writing Connection activities, go to glencoe.com and enter QuickPass code GLW6053u2.

Reading Strategy | Synthesize

Synthesizing details, sidenote information, biographical and cultural information, and your own prior knowledge can help you interpret a drama. Review the chart you made on page 291 and answer the following questions.

1. When were the seeds of Oedipus's downfall originally sown?

2. Violent events in classical Greek drama almost always occurred offstage. How would the effect of Oedipus's blinding have been different for the audience if it had been shown on stage?

Vocabulary Practice

Practice with Word Origins Create a word map, like the one below, for each boldfaced vocabulary word. Use a dictionary for help.

random   oblivion   inflict
horrendous   vulnerable

EXAMPLE:

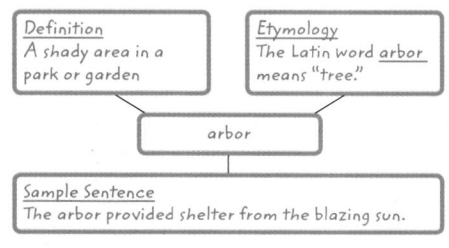

Definition
A shady area in a park or garden

Etymology
The Latin word *arbor* means "tree."

arbor

Sample Sentence
The arbor provided shelter from the blazing sun.

Academic Vocabulary

Based on a **hypothesis** *he forms, Oedipus accuses Creon of conspiracy.*

Hypothesis is an academic word. Familiar words that are similar in meaning include *theory* and *assumption*. To further explore the meaning of this word, answer the following question: If you were a detective trying to solve a crime, how might you develop a **hypothesis**?

For more on academic vocabulary, see pages 36–37 and R83–R85.

After You Read

Assess

Literary Element

1. C is correct. **A** and **B** are true but not ironic; **D** is not true.

Progress Check

Can students analyze irony?

If No → See Unit 2 Teaching Resource Book, p. 103.

Review: Tragedy

Students' ratings will vary but should be supported with evidence from the play.

Reading Strategy

1. They were sown with the original prophecy that Laius would be killed by his son.

2. Students may say the spectacle of the blinding would have riveted the audience, taking attention away from the significance of the event.

Vocabulary

Word—**random;** Definition—lack of careful choice or plan; Etymology—from Old High German *rinnan*, "to run"; Sample sentence—The members of the teams were chosen at random.; Word—**oblivion;** Definition—state of having been forgotten; Etymology—from Latin *oblivisci*, "to forget"; Sample sentence—Oblivion had overtaken the writing system of the ancient

civilization.; Word—**inflict;** Definition—to give or cause; Etymology—from prefix *in-* + Latin *fligere*, "to strike"; Sample sentence—The terrorist attack inflicted great loss of life.; Word—**horrendous;** Definition—horrible; frightful; Etymology—from Latin *horrere*, "to tremble"; Sample sentence—The effect of the avalanche on the mountain village was horrendous.; Word—**vulnerable;** Definition—weak; unable to defend oneself; Etymology—from Latin *vulnus*,

"wound"; Sample sentence—The peasants were vulnerable to attacks by bandits.

Academic Vocabulary

Students should cite tasks that would help them make a reasonable guess, such as dusting for fingerprints, interviewing eyewitnesses, and performing background checks.

After You Read

Assess

Respond Through Writing

Students' essays should

- clearly state a thesis about the overall effect of dramatic irony in the play
- analyze Sophocles' use of dramatic irony
- support the thesis with relevant textual evidence

A student who meets all of these criteria should receive the equivalent of a 4-point response.

A student who fully meets two or partially meets three of these criteria should receive the equivalent of a 3-point response.

A student who fully meets one or partially meets two of these criteria should receive the equivalent of a 2-point response.

A student who partially meets one of these criteria should receive the equivalent of a 1-point response.

⚡ Respond Through Writing

Expository Essay

Analyze Irony Sophocles' mastery of dramatic irony is evident in *Oedipus the King*, a timeless tragedy. In an essay, analyze Sophocles' use of dramatic irony and describe its overall effect. Support your ideas with examples from the text.

Understand the Task **Dramatic irony** occurs when the reader or audience knows something important a character does not know.

Prewrite Before you begin to write, fill out a chart like the one below. Add as many rows as you need.

Example	Ironic Meaning	Effect on Reader
"Oedipus . . . what do you know?" (line 54)	The chorus asks Oedipus for knowledge, but he doesn't even know who he is.	The reader senses the people of Thebes are in terrible danger.

Draft Formulate a clear thesis, supported by valid and relevant evidence. Develop an engaging introduction, a body, and a conclusion. Use smooth transitions to build coherence. Your body paragraphs should provide examples of dramatic irony and describe their effect on the reader. You may find it helpful to use sentence frames as you write. For example, you might state your thesis as follows.

In Oedipus the King, *Sophocles' use of dramatic irony creates an overall effect of* _____.

Revise Exchange papers with a classmate and evaluate each other's essays. Does the writer clearly state and support a thesis? Are there accurate and detailed references to the text? Provide comments for your partner and revise your essay according to his or her comments.

Edit and Proofread Proofread your paper, correcting any errors in grammar, spelling, and punctuation. Use the Grammar Tip in the side column to help you with using ellipsis points in quoted material.

Learning Objectives

In this assignment, you will focus on the following objectives:

Writing: Writing an expository essay.

Grammar: Understanding ellipsis points.

▶ Grammar Tip

Ellipsis Points

Ellipsis points, or a series of three spaced periods, indicate the omission of material from a quotation. For example, notice the ellipses in the following quotation from lines 150–159 of the play:

"I'll bring it all to light myself! . . . by avenging Laius / I defend myself."

The ellipses sharpen the focus of the quotation, highlighting the irony.

Use three ellipsis points if the omitted material occurs at the beginning of a sentence. If the omitted material is in the middle or at the end of a sentence, use any necessary punctuation plus the ellipsis points.

 For additional selection assessment, see Assessment Resources, pp. 71–72.

 To create custom assessments online, go to Progress Reporter Online Assessment.

 To create custom assessments using software, use ExamView Assessment Suite.

Vocabulary Workshop

Jargon

Literature Connection In the following quotation from *The Poetics*, Aristotle uses Oedipus as an example of the ideal type of tragic hero, whose downfall is the result of what he calls *hamartia*.

> *"There remains, then, the intermediate kind of personage, a man not eminently virtuous and just, whose misfortune, however, is brought upon him not by wickedness or worthlessness but through some* hamartia."

What does the term *hamartia* mean? Context clues can provide some help. In the above sentence, *hamartia* is contrasted with "wickedness" and "worthlessness"; therefore the word does not refer to immorality. If you check in a dictionary, you will see *hamartia* is often translated as "tragic flaw" or "tragic mistake."

Such technical terms specific to a particular trade or field are called **jargon**. Because Aristotle's study of tragedy has been very influential, *hamartia* has become an important term in dramatic criticism. When you first encounter such technical terms in a passage, you will often be provided with an appositive definition. For example, *"Greek theater had its origin in the* dithyramb, *a hymn sung in honor of the god Dionysus."*

Law and medicine are two fields that use jargon.

Jargon

Jargon is the specialized or technical language of a trade.

Test-Taking Tip

When you encounter unfamiliar jargon in a text, first check to see if an appositive definition is provided. Then look for clues in the subject of the text and the context of the sentence.

Legal Jargon	Medical Jargon
sidebar—conference between opposing lawyers and the judge during a trial	**meds**—medications or drugs
nolo—short for nolo contendere, plea by which a defendant admits guilt	**crash cart**—wheeled hospital cart with basic equipment necessary to save someone's life in an emergency

Practice Identify the jargon pertaining to drama in each of the following sentences. Then write what you think each of these technical terms might mean. Check your guesses in a dictionary.

1. Oedipus, the protagonist of Sophocles' play, is king of Thebes.
2. Like many tragic heroes, the proud, reckless Oedipus suffers from hubris.
3. Behind the acting area was the skene, which served as the permanent setting for all plays.

Literature Online

Vocabulary For more vocabulary practice, go to glencoe.com and enter QuickPass code GLW6053u2.

VOCABULARY WORKSHOP **319**

Approaching Level

DIFFERENTIATED INSTRUCTION

Restating Some students may be overwhelmed by texts that contain frequent technical terms and jargon. Encourage these students to select difficult passages and then work in pairs to "translate" unfamiliar terms into language they can understand. Have them read the passages out loud, substituting their simple translations for the more difficult words.

Advanced Learners/Pre-AP

DIFFERENTIATED INSTRUCTION

Writing More advanced students may wish to create a glossary of jargon from an area with which they are familiar—perhaps sports or music. Remind these students to use simple, accessible language. They should be careful to avoid using additional jargon in their definitions.

Focus

Activity

Write on the board: I post my thoughts about current events in my blog.

Ask: What is a *blog*? *(an online diary or journal)* Point out to students that *blog* (short for *weblog*) is a relatively new word, created specifically for use in the field of computer technology. Ask students to give other examples of computer-specific terms. Then explain that these terms are all examples of *jargon*, or language that is specific to a particular trade or field.

Teach

Multiple Meanings Point out that, while some jargon is newly created, other jargon is adopted from common parlance and altered in meaning to suit a particular field. Examples include the word *bug*, which is used in computer technology to mean "an error in a computer program"; and the word *minor*, which is used in higher education to mean "a secondary course of study."

Assess

1. The <u>protagonist</u> is the principal character in a drama.
2. <u>Hubris</u> is excessive pride or rashness.
3. The <u>skene</u> is the building behind the main acting area.

Bellringer Options

Daily Language Practice Transparency 30

Or ask: What do you think is a fitting tribute to those who have died in service of their country? Find out if students think national monuments, days of observance, speeches, or other tributes are suitable remembrances.

Language History ☆

Strategy Tell students that the English word "strategy" has its origin in the Greek term *strategos* (the singular of *strategoi*). In ancient Greece, a *strategos* was the elected leader of a military regiment. Nowadays, the word "strategy" refers to skillful, warlike planning used to obtain a goal. Ask students what the term *strategoi*, as described in the text, has in common with the previously mentioned definition of the word "strategy." (*Both are related to warfare.*)

Before You Read

Ancient Greece

Pericles' Funeral Oration

Meet **Thucydides**
(c. 460–c. 404 B.C.)

One of the greatest historians of the Western world was also one of the first—Thucydides (thoo sid´ə dēz´). Little is known about his life; even the dates of his birth and death must be inferred from references in his writing. He was likely born in or near Athens to a wealthy, upper-class family. In 424 B.C., Thucydides was elected one of the ten *strategoi*, or high-ranking military leaders, of the year. He was put in command of the Athenian fleet based in the northern Aegean Sea. His responsibility was to defend the city of Amphipolis. When the Spartans captured the city, Thucydides was sent into exile. He returned to Athens after the war ended and is believed to have died shortly thereafter.

> "I shall be content if [the History of the Peloponnesian War] is judged useful by those inquirers who desire an exact knowledge of the past as an aid to the interpretation of the future . . ."
>
> —Thucydides from Book I,
> *History of the Peloponnesian War*

His Life's Work Thucydides' *History of the Peloponnesian War*, his life's work, narrates the conflict between Athens and Sparta in the fifth century B.C. At that time Greece was a collection of city-states, each with its own government and sphere of influence. The struggle ended with the defeat of Athens in 404 B.C. and the eclipse of Athenian civilization.

Thucydides, who began this work just before 431 B.C., told his readers he believed the war would be "more worthy of relation than any that had preceded it." In his attempt to present an accurate account, he interviewed participants and eyewitnesses from both sides, sifted through statements others had made, and presented his results in concise, chronological order. He often reported the exact words of significant political speeches, including Pericles' funeral oration. Thucydides is celebrated as the first historian to apply truly rigorous standards of accuracy to his work.

Thucydides never completed the *History*: his account stops abruptly more than six years before the war ended. This abruptness has led to speculation that he may have died suddenly—and perhaps violently—a victim of social upheaval after the war.

LOG ON ▶ **Literature** Online
Author Search For more about Thucydides, go to glencoe.com and enter QuickPass code GLW6053u2.

Selection Skills

Literary Elements
- Argument (SE pp. 321, 324–326, 329–331)
- Tone (SE p. 331)

Reading Skills
- Analyze Rhetorical Devices (SE pp. 321, 324, 327, 329, 332)
- Compare and Contrast Speeches (TE p. 324)
- Connect (TE p. 330)

Pericles' Funeral Oration

Vocabulary Skills
- Analogies (SE pp. 332)
- Word Origins (TE p. 321)

Speaking /Listening/Viewing Skills
- Deliver a Speech (SE p. 332)
- Analyze Art (SE p. 327)

Writing Skills/Grammar
- Historical Analysis (TE p. 326)

Literature and Reading Preview

Connect to the Speech

Why do some speeches continue to inspire people through the ages? Write a journal entry in which you describe the qualities of a memorable speech you have heard or read.

Build Background

The most powerful city-state in Greece in the fifth century B.C. was Athens. The enduring achievements of Athens owe much to the leadership of Pericles, who was elected more than fifteen times to the office of general. Shortly after the outbreak of the war with Sparta in 431 B.C., Pericles delivered this eulogy to honor those slain in battle.

Set Purposes for Reading

Big Idea The Heroic Ideal

As you read, notice how Pericles' eulogy reflects the heroic ideal of the ancient Greeks. Ask yourself, What qualities does Pericles consider heroic?

Literary Element Argument

Argument is a type of persuasive writing or speaking in which reason is used to influence ideas or actions. Pericles includes several arguments in his eulogy to the Athenian war dead. As you read, ask yourself, What is his purpose for including them?

Reading Strategy Analyze Rhetorical Devices

Rhetoric is the art of using language to present facts and ideas to persuade an audience. **Rhetorical devices** are techniques speakers and authors use to evoke an emotional response in the audience. Rhetorical devices include the use of repetition, connotative words, parallelism, and emotional appeals.

....

Tip: Take Notes In a chart like the one below, identify examples of rhetorical devices as you read the eulogy.

Example	Rhetorical Devices	Purpose
the words "honor," "courage," and "valiant/valiantly"	Connotative words and repetition	To reinforce the idea of Athenian nobility and the justness of its cause

Learning Objectives

For pages 320–332

In studying this text, you will focus on the following objectives:

Literary Study: Analyzing argument.

Reading: Analyzing rhetorical devices.

Listening and Speaking: Delivering a speech.

Vocabulary

incredulous (in krej′ə ləs) *adj.* doubting; skeptical; p. 323 *The incredulous crowd doubted the speaker's foolish claims.*

versatility (vur′sə til′ə tē) *n.* ability to do many things well; p. 326 *The athlete showed versatility by excelling in several sports.*

tangible (tan′jə bəl) *adj.* real; actual; definite; p. 326 *The guard saw tangible evidence of damage.*

consummation (kon′sə mā′ shən) *n.* end; completion; p. 327 *The author's consummation of his life's work was a trilogy of novels.*

commiserate (kə miz′ə rāt′) *v.* sympathize with; pity; p. 329 *I can commiserate with you during this difficult time.*

THUCYDIDES **321**

Before You Read

Focus

Summary

In this selection, Thucydides, a Greek historian and general, is reporting the speech the great Greek statesman and general, Pericles gave at the annual public funeral held in 431 B.C. Pericles lauds the greatness of Athens, praises the honor and bravery of the dead soldiers, and offers comfort to the bereaved and advice to his listeners on ways to maintain Athens's greatness.

 For summaries in languages other than English, see Unit 2 Teaching Resource Book, pp. 110–115.

Vocabulary

 Word Origins
Divide students into groups of five, with each student responsible for one vocabulary word. Instruct students to research their word's etymology, or origins. Have each student write down three statements about the origin of his or her word; one of the statements should be the real one, and the other two should be invented. Then have each student share his or her statements within the small group, with the other students in the group writing down guesses as to which statement contains the word's true origins. When all the other group members have recorded their guesses, have the student who wrote the three statements reveal which is correct.

 For additional vocabulary practice, see Unit 2 Teaching Resource Book, p. 118.

English Learners

DIFFERENTIATED INSTRUCTION

Advanced Students learning English might find this selection's vocabulary words intimidating or difficult to remember. Have them look up the vocabulary words in a thesaurus and write down several synonyms for each word, perhaps choosing shorter or more common words with which they feel more comfortable.

Instruct them to choose one synonym of each vocabulary word and then use the synonym in a sentence. Then pair students together and instruct them to read their sentences aloud to one another. When they feel comfortable with these synonyms, have them insert the selection's vocabulary words into the sentences in place of their synonyms, making any adjustments necessary to make them fit. Then have students read the sentences with the vocabulary words aloud to one another.

Teach

Reading Strategy   1

Question Thucydides states that the bones of the dead soldiers from each tribe were buried in one coffin. Do you think this practice honors the dead more than having an individual burial would?

(ADVANCED) Ask advanced learners what this practice tells them about ancient Athenian values. *(Athenians value good citizenship and membership to the tribe more than they value individuality.)*

Interactive Read and Write

Other options for teaching this selection can be found in

Interactive Read and Write for On-Level Learners, pp. 79–100.

Readability Scores

Dale-Chall: 8
DRP: 59
Lexile: 1240

Combat scene, 560-550 BC. Cleimachos. Black-figured hydria. Louvre, Paris.

Pericles'
FUNERAL ORATION

from History of the Peloponnesian War

Thucydides
Translated by Rex Warner

Speaking Practice

Deliver a Speech In this selection, Pericles delivers a speech honoring those slain in battle. Have students prepare and deliver their own short (one to two minute) orations. In this case, however, have the students choose subjects which would not normally be honored publicly. Perhaps they might choose to praise Bobby "Boris" Pickett, singer of the song "Monster Mash"; exalt the city of Cork, Ireland, and its world record for the largest Irish dance; or laud London's Ken Edwards, who ate 36 cockroaches in one minute in 2001. Tell students to try to persuade their audience of their subject's greatness by citing specific examples, using rhetorical devices, and employing heightened language. They can also incorporate multimedia, such as photographs, in-class demonstrations, or audio and video aids. Be sure to tell them to use appropriate eye contact, body language, and vocal inflections when giving their speeches.

In the same winter the Athenians, following their annual custom, gave a public funeral for those who had been the first to die in the war. These funerals are held in the following way: two days before the ceremony the bones of the fallen are brought and put in a tent which has been erected, and people make whatever offerings they wish to their own dead. Then there is a funeral procession in which coffins of cypress wood are carried on wagons. There is one coffin for each tribe, which contains the bones of members of that tribe. One empty bier[1] is decorated and carried in the procession: this is for the missing, whose bodies could not be recovered. Everyone who wishes to, both citizens and foreigners, can join in the procession, and the women who are related to the dead are there to make their laments at the tomb. The bones are laid in the public burial-place, which is in the most beautiful quarter outside the city walls. Here the Athenians always bury those who have fallen in war. The only exception is those who died at Marathon,[2] who, because their achievement was considered absolutely outstanding, were buried on the battlefield itself.

When the bones have been laid in the earth, a man chosen by the city for his intellectual gifts and for his general reputation makes an appropriate speech in praise of the dead, and after the speech all depart. This is the procedure at these burials, and all through the war, when the time came to do so, the Athenians followed this ancient custom. Now, at the burial of those who

were the first to fall in the war Pericles, the son of Xanthippus,[3] was chosen to make the speech. When the moment arrived, he came forward from the tomb and, standing on a high platform, so that he might be heard by as many people as possible in the crowd, he spoke as follows:

"Many of those who have spoken here in the past have praised the institution of this speech at the close of our ceremony. It seemed to them a mark of honor to our soldiers who have fallen in war that a speech should be made over them. I do not agree. These men have shown themselves valiant in action, and it would be enough, I think, for their glories to be proclaimed in action, as you have just seen it done at this funeral organized by the state. Our belief in the courage and manliness of so many should not be hazarded on the goodness or badness of one man's speech. Then it is not easy to speak with a proper sense of balance, when a man's listeners find it difficult to believe in the truth of what one is saying. The man who knows the facts and loves the dead may well think that an oration tells less than what he knows and what he would like to hear: others who do not know so much may feel envy for the dead, and think the orator over-praises them, when he speaks of exploits that are beyond their own capacities. Praise of other people is tolerable only up to a certain point, the point where one still believes that one could do oneself some of the things one is hearing about. Once you get beyond this point, you will find people becoming jealous and **incredulous**.

---

1. Here, *bier* means "coffin."
2. *Marathon* was the site of the Greek victory over the Persians in 490 B.C., after which a Greek runner ran from the battlefield to Athens (about 26 miles) to bring news of the victory.

 The Heroic Ideal *How do Athenian burial customs reflect the heroic ideal?*

---

3. *Xanthippus* (zan thi´ pēs) was a Greek statesman from an established Athenian family.

Vocabulary

incredulous (in krej´ ə ləs) *adj.* doubting; skeptical

THUCYDIDES **323**

Teach

 Big Idea   2

The Heroic Ideal
Answer: *The ancient Greeks believed their fallen heroes possessed the attributes of the heroic ideal. The elaborate funeral rites served as a tribute to their everlasting glory.*

ENGLISH LEARNERS Ask English learners if the cultures they come from have any particular practices to honor heroes who have died. Have students tell the class about their cultures' practices regarding honoring heroes.

For an audio recording of this selection, use Listening Library Audio CD-ROM.

Learning Objectives
Deliver a speech. (TE)
Question. (TE)

English Learners

DIFFERENTIATED INSTRUCTION

Advanced Some students may have difficulties delivering a speech in English. If students find this challenging, pair them up with more advanced English learners or native English speakers and have them work one-on-one to become more comfortable giving their speeches. You can have the more advanced students take notes on pronunciation while their partners rehearse.

Advanced Learners/Pre-AP

DIFFERENTIATED INSTRUCTION

Give a Historical Speech Advanced learners might want to select historical subjects for their speeches. Have them research and perform speeches about figures and moments in history which are not ordinarily viewed as worthy of praise, such as astronomer James Challis, who

is famous because he failed to discover Neptune due to laziness, or the Ford Edsel, a famous automotive failure. They might want to interview someone of another generation to generate ideas for topics. Advise them to employ irony in the praise of their subjects.

Teach

Literary Element 1

Argument Answer: *He would prefer that actions, not words, pay tribute to the courage of the heroic warriors.*

Reading Strategy 2

Analyze Rhetorical Devices Answer: *He compliments them for their courage and virtues, which have kept Athens free.*

Literary Element 3

Argument Answer: *Power is in the hands of all the people, not just a privileged minority. All citizens are equal under the law and free to hold office regardless of social class.*

[APPROACHING] For approaching level students, ask how the political structure of Athens, as Pericles describes it, is similar to that of the United States.

Our constitution is called a democracy because power is in the hands

not of a minority but of the whole people.

However, the fact is that this institution was set up and approved by our forefathers, and it is my duty to follow the tradition and do my best to meet the wishes and the expectations of every one of you.

'I shall begin by speaking about our ancestors, since it is only right and proper on such an occasion to pay them the honor of recalling what they did. In this land of ours there have always been the same people living from generation to generation up till now, and they, by their courage and their virtues, have handed it on to us, a free country. They certainly deserve our praise. Even more so do our fathers deserve it. For to the inheritance they had received they added all the empire we have now, and it was not without blood and toil that they handed it down to us of the present generation. And then we ourselves, assembled here today, who are mostly in the prime of life, have, in most directions, added to the power of our empire and have organized our State in such a way that it is perfectly well able to look after itself both in peace and in war.

'I have no wish to make a long speech on subjects familiar to you all: so I shall say nothing about the warlike deeds by which we acquired our power or the battles in which we or our fathers gallantly[4] resisted our enemies, Greek or foreign. What I want to do is, in the first place, to discuss the spirit in which we faced our trials and also our constitution and the way of life which has made us great. After that I shall speak in praise of the dead, believing that this kind of speech is not inappropriate to the present occasion, and that this whole assembly, of citizens and foreigners, may listen to it with advantage.

'Let me say that our system of government does not copy the institutions of our neighbors. It is more the case of our being a model to others, than of our imitating anyone else. Our constitution is called a democracy because power is in the hands not of a minority but of the whole people. When it is a question of settling private disputes, everyone is equal before the law; when it is a question of putting one person before another in positions of public responsibility, what counts is not membership of a particular class, but the actual ability which the man possesses. No one, so long as he has it in him to be of service to the state, is kept in political obscurity because of poverty. And, just as our political life is free and open, so is our day-to-day life in our relations with each other. We do not get into a state with our next-door neighbor if he enjoys himself in his own way, nor do we give him the kind of black looks which, though they do no real harm, still do hurt people's feelings. We are free

---

4. *Gallantly* means "nobly or bravely."

1 Argument *Why is Pericles reluctant to deliver the funeral oration?*

2 Analyze Rhetorical Devices *How does Pericles appeal to his audience in this passage?*

Argument *What reasons support the claim that the Athenian government is a model to others?* **3**

Reading Practice

Compare and Contrast Speeches

Have students find the text of another historical eulogy. Instruct them to read the speech they have chosen and make a two-column chart comparing and contrasting it to "Pericles' Funeral Oration," shown here. They should use the chart below as a model. Tell them to look with care at the rhetorical devices, diction, and tone the speakers use.

Similarities to Pericles' Funeral Oration	Differences from Pericles' Funeral Oration

and tolerant in our private lives; but in public affairs we keep to the law. This is because it commands our deep respect.

'We give our obedience to those whom we put in positions of authority, and we obey the laws themselves, especially those which are for the protection of the oppressed, and those unwritten laws which it is an acknowledged shame to break.

'And here is another point. When our work is over, we are in a position to enjoy all kinds of recreation for our spirits. There are various kinds of contests and sacrifices regularly throughout the year; in our own homes we find a beauty and a good taste which delight us every day and which drive away our cares. Then the greatness of our city brings it about that all the good things from all over the world flow in to us, so that to us it seems just as natural to enjoy foreign goods as our own local products.

'Then there is a great difference between us and our opponents, in our attitude towards military security. Here are some examples: Our city is open to the world, and we have no periodical deportations in order to prevent people observing or finding out secrets which might be of military advantage to the enemy. This is because we rely, not on secret weapons, but on our own real courage and loyalty. There is a difference, too, in our educational systems. The Spartans, from their earliest boyhood, are submitted to the most laborious training in courage; we pass our lives without all these restrictions, and yet are just as ready to face the same dangers as they are. Here is a proof of this: When the Spartans invade our land, they do not come by themselves, but bring all their allies with them; whereas we, when we launch an attack abroad, do the job by ourselves, and, though fighting on foreign soil, do not often fail to defeat opponents who are fighting for their own

hearths and homes. As a matter of fact none of our enemies has ever yet been confronted with our total strength, because we have to divide our attention between our navy and the many missions on which our troops are sent on land. Yet, if our enemies engage a detachment of our forces and defeat it, they give themselves credit for having thrown back our entire army; or, if they lose, they claim that they were beaten by us in full strength. There are certain advantages, I think, in our way of meeting danger voluntarily, with an easy mind, instead of with a laborious training, with natural rather than with state-induced courage. We do not have to spend our time practicing to meet sufferings which are still in the future; and when they are actually upon us we show ourselves just as brave as these others who are always in strict training. This is one point in which, I think, our city deserves to be admired. There are also others:

'Our love of what is beautiful does not lead to extravagance; our love of the things of the mind does not make us soft. We regard wealth as something to be properly used, rather than as something to boast about. As for poverty, no one need be ashamed to admit it: the real shame is in not taking practical measures to escape from it. Here each individual is interested not only in his own affairs but in the affairs of the state as well: even those who are mostly occupied with their own business are extremely well-informed on general politics—this is a peculiarity of ours: we do not say that a man who takes no interest in politics is a man who minds his own business; we say that he has no business here at all. We Athenians, in our own persons, take our decisions on policy or submit them to proper

---

 Argument *Reread this paragraph. Why does Pericles consider Athens better militarily than other city-states?* **4**

THUCYDIDES **325**

Literary Element	4

Argument Answer: *No one can be deported from Athens lest he reveal military secrets. Athenians value courage more than secret weapons. Their courage is natural rather than induced by rigorous training.*

Cultural History ☆
Athena Athens is named after Athena, Greek goddess of reason and war. In contrast to the brutal Ares, the other Greek god of war, Athena was representative of intellectual, civilized, skillful warfare. In peacetime, she was thought of as a goddess of skilled crafts, such as weaving and spinning. Ask students if this portrait of the city's patron goddess fits or does not fit with the portrait of Athens that Pericles paints in his speech.

Learning Objectives
Analyzing argument. (SE)
Comparing and contrast speeches. (TE)

Approaching Level
DIFFERENTIATED INSTRUCTION

Clarify Meaning Some students might have difficulties following the meaning of Pericles' speech. If so, instruct them to reread the speech aloud slowly. Each time they identify a point, they should write it down in their own words as an item in a bulleted list. When finished, they can look back at the list they have made and review the main points of Pericles' speech to clarify its meaning.

Advanced Learners/Pre-AP
DIFFERENTIATED INSTRUCTION

Present an Oral Report Have advanced students research the background of the Peloponnesian War. They may use the Internet but should also go to a library to find information about the conflict. You can also assign them more specific topics within the larger subject of the war if you wish. Then have students present an oral report to the class about their findings. Urge them

to use appropriate body language, eye contact, and tone of voice, as well as to include visual aids in their presentations. Knowing more about the historical context surrounding Pericles' oration will give the entire class a greater understanding of the selection.

Teach

Big Idea | **1**

The Heroic Ideal

Answer: *True heroism is the courage to take risks while fully aware of the danger involved.*

(ADVANCED) Ask advanced students to cite examples they have previously encountered— from history, literature, or contemporary culture—of this kind of courage.

Literary Element | **2**

Argument Answer: *Athens is the only city that does good deeds to other cities and nations without expecting anything in return.*

Literary Element | **3**

Argument Answer: *Pericles implies Athenians owe it to the memory of those who have courageously fought to protect the city.*

discussions: for we do not think that there is an incompatibility between words and deeds; the worst thing is to rush into action before the consequences have been properly debated. And this is another point where we differ from other people. We are capable at the same time of taking risks and of estimating them beforehand. Others are brave out of ignorance; and, when they stop to think, they begin to fear. But the man who can most truly be accounted brave is he who best knows the meaning of what is sweet in life and of what is terrible, and then goes out undeterred to meet what is to come.

'Again, in questions of general good feeling there is a great contrast between us and most other people. We make friends by doing good to others, not by receiving good from them. This makes our friendship all the more reliable, since we want to keep alive the gratitude of those who are in our debt by showing continued goodwill to them: whereas the feelings of one who owes us something lack the same enthusiasm, since he knows that, when he repays our kindness, it will be more like paying back a debt than giving something spontaneously. We are unique in this. When we do kindnesses to others, we do not do them out of any calculations of profit or loss: we do them without afterthought, relying on our free liberality. Taking everything together then, I declare that our city is an education to Greece, and I declare that in my opinion each single one of our citizens, in all the manifold⁵ aspects of life, is able to show himself the rightful lord and owner of his

own person, and do this, moreover, with exceptional grace and exceptional **versatility**. And to show that this is no empty boasting for the present occasion, but real **tangible** fact, you have only to consider the power which our city possesses and which has been won by those very qualities which I have mentioned. Athens, alone of the states we know, comes to her testing time in a greatness that surpasses what was imagined of her. In her case, and in her case alone, no invading enemy is ashamed at being defeated, and no subject can complain of being governed by people unfit for their responsibilities. Mighty indeed are the marks and monuments of our empire which we have left. Future ages will wonder at us, as the present age wonders at us now. We do not need the praises of a Homer, or of anyone else whose words may delight us for the moment, but whose estimation of facts will fall short of what is really true. For our adventurous spirit has forced an entry into every sea and into every land; and everywhere we have left behind us everlasting memorials of good done to our friends or suffering inflicted on our enemies.

'This, then, is the kind of city for which these men, who could not bear the thought of losing her, nobly fought and nobly died. It is only natural that every one of us who survive them should be willing to undergo hardships in her service. And it was for this reason that I have spoken at such length about our city, because I wanted to make it clear that for us there is more at stake than

---

5. *Manifold* means "of many kinds or parts; many and various."

1 **The Heroic Ideal** *What does Pericles consider true heroism?*

2 **Argument** *According to Pericles, why is Athens "an education to Greece"?*

Argument *Why should Athenians be willing to sacrifice for Athens?* | **3**

Vocabulary

versatility (vur´ sə til´ ə tē) *n.* ability to do many things well
tangible (tan´ jə bəl) *adj.* real; actual; definite

Writing Practice

Historical Analysis Explain that literature has much to teach readers about not only human nature but also history. Analyzing the historical underpinnings of a work can enhance readers' understanding of both the work and the culture from which it sprang.

Ask students to write expository essays in which they explain what the selection teaches about Athenian values and leadership. Encourage students to further discuss the positives and negatives they see in ancient Athenian culture.

Combat scene, 5th century BC. Marble relief. British Museum, London.

View the Art Why do you think the soldiers in this relief are taking the man on the horse away? How does their action reflect Pericles' view on Athenians?

there is for others who lack our advantages; also I wanted my words of praise for the dead to be set in the bright light of evidence. And now the most important of these words has been spoken. I have sung the praises of our city; but it was the courage and gallantry of these men, and of people like them, which made her splendid. Nor would you find it true in the case of many of the Greeks, as it is true of them, that no words can do more than justice to their deeds.

'To me it seems that the **consummation** which has overtaken these men shows us the meaning of manliness in its first revelation and in its final proof. Some of them, no doubt, had their faults; but what we ought to remember first is their gallant conduct against the enemy in defence of their native land. They have blotted out evil with good, and done more service to the commonwealth than they ever did harm in their private lives. No one of these men weakened because he wanted to go on enjoying his wealth: no one put off the awful day in the

---

4 | Analyze Rhetorical Devices *What idea, introduced at the beginning of the speech, does Pericles echo here? What purpose might this repetition serve?*

Vocabulary

consummation (kon´sə mā´shən) n. end; completion

THUCYDIDES **327**

English Learners

DIFFERENTIATED INSTRUCTION

Advanced In his speech, Pericles speaks persuasively to the Romans about their responsibilities as citizens. Have students learning English write a paragraph-long journal entry about the responsibilities that come with one of the roles they take on in life. For example, they might write about their responsibilities as a student, friend, or family member. They should write several sentences about the duties and obligations that come with that role. Write this sentence frame on the board and tell students they can start their entries with it:

As a _____, I have many responsibilities.

Teach

Reading Strategy | **4**

Analyze Rhetorical Devices **Answer:** *Pericles echoes the idea that speaking about the courage of the fallen warriors is not sufficient. This repetition reinforces an important theme of his eulogy: Athenians must support the war against Sparta through action, not just words.*

(**ADVANCED**) Ask advanced students how they react to Pericles' using his speech to make the point that words are ineffectual. *(The students will probably find the statement ironic.)*

View the Art ★

Answer: *The soldier on the horse is probably dead. Pericles touts the honor of the Athenians; carrying away a dead soldier in battle is an honorable action.*

Learning Objectives
Analyzing argument. (SE)
Analyzing rhetorical devices. (SE)
Analyzing art. (SE)
Writing an elegy. (TE)

327

Teach

Literary Element | 1

Personification Ask: What literary technique does Pericles use here in his representation of Athens? *(Personification)*

ENGLISH LEARNERS Ask English learners to point out which words in this statement show that Pericles is referring to Athens as a woman. *("she," "her")*

View the Art ★

This helmet was made in the ancient region of Thrace, which existed in the modern area of the southeastern Balkans. Thracians were known as excellent warriors, but frequent political problems stopped them from becoming a powerful region. **Ask:** Why might a helmet have engraved figures and designs on it? *(Students might say that the designs and figures represent things that were important to the culture.)*

Helmet, 4th century BC. Greek school. Silver with repousse, chased and engraved decoration. The Detroit Institute of Arts, MI. ★

Viewing Practice

Analyze Persuasive Techniques Point out to students that many television shows and radio programs feature examples of speakers employing arguments. Examples of such shows include courtroom dramas, talk shows, political debates, and news programs. In these shows, a speaker or group tries to persuade the audience of their proposition or point of view.

Have students watch and analyze a discussion on a television news show in which panelists try to persuade their audience of something. Tell students to take notes on the persuasive techniques, reasoning, and proof that the panelists use to argue their viewpoints. Then invite students to share their observations and analyses of the discussion with the class.

hope that he might live to escape his poverty and grow rich. More to be desired than such things, they chose to check the enemy's pride. This, to them, was a risk most glorious, and they accepted it, willing to strike down the enemy and relinquish everything else. As for success or failure, they left that in the doubtful hands of Hope, and when the reality of battle was before their faces, they put their trust in their own selves. In the fighting, they thought it more honorable to stand their ground and suffer death than to give in and save their lives. So they fled from the reproaches of men, abiding with life and limb the brunt of battle; and, in a small moment of time, the climax of their lives, a culmination of glory, not of fear, were swept away from us.

'So and such they were, these men—worthy of their city. We who remain behind may hope to be spared their fate, but must resolve to keep the same daring spirit against the foe. It is not simply a question of estimating the advantages in theory. I could tell you a long story (and you know it as well as I do) about what is to be gained by beating the enemy back. What I would prefer is that you should fix your eyes every day on the greatness of Athens as she really is, and should fall in love with her. When you realize her greatness, then reflect that what made her great was men with a spirit of adventure, men who knew their duty, men who were ashamed to fall below a certain standard. If they ever failed in an enterprise, they made up their minds that at any rate the city should not find their courage lacking to her, and they gave to her the best contribution that they could. They gave her their lives, to her and to all of us, and for

their own selves they won praises that never grow old, the most splendid of sepulchres—not the sepulchre in which their bodies are laid, but where their glory remains eternal in men's minds, always there on the right occasion to stir others to speech or to action. For

Visual Vocabulary
A sepulchre (also spelled sepulcher) is a structure that holds human remains or sacred relics. The word also means "tomb" or "grave."

famous men have the whole earth as their memorial: it is not only the inscriptions on their graves in their own country that mark them out; no, in foreign lands also, not in any visible form but in people's hearts, their memory abides and grows. It is for you to try to be like them. Make up your minds that happiness depends on being free, and freedom depends on being courageous. Let there be no relaxation in face of the perils of the war. The people who have most excuse for despising death are not the wretched and unfortunate, who have no hope of doing well for themselves, but those who run the risk of a complete reversal in their lives, and who would feel the difference most intensely, if things went wrong for them. Any intelligent man would find a humiliation caused by his own slackness more painful to bear than death, when death comes to him unperceived, in battle, and in the confidence of his patriotism.

'For these reasons I shall not **commiserate** with those parents of the dead, who are

---

Argument What reason does Pericles give for insisting the Athenians continue to be courageous in the war? **3**

Vocabulary

commiserate (kə miz′ ə rāt′) v. sympathize with; pity

---

 2 **Analyze Rhetorical Devices** *In this passage, Pericles uses connotation as a rhetorical device. What does the phrase "culmination of glory" suggest to you?*

Advanced Learners/Pre-AP

DIFFERENTIATED INSTRUCTION

Write an Interior Monologue Instruct advanced learners to reread the speech, imagining themselves to be someone attending the funeral, listening to the speech at the time it was originally given. This character should be personally connected to the events of the day; perhaps the character might be the parent, spouse, or child of one of the soldiers Pericles honors in his eulogy. Then have

students write a paragraph or two depicting their character's interior monologue while listening to the speech. Are they inspired by it? Appalled? Grief-stricken? Make sure students include their characters' emotional states in the monologue as well as direct references to Pericles' speech.

Teach

Reading Strategy **2**

Analyze Rhetorical Devices Answer: *The phrase "culmination of glory" suggests the pinnacle of honor.*

Literary Element **3**

Argument Answer: *He says it would be humiliating not to be courageous, an indication of cowardice and lack of patriotism.*

Learning Objectives
Analyzing rhetorical devices. (SE)
Analyzing argument. (SE)
Analyzing personification. (TE)
Analyzing persuasive techniques. (TE)

Teach

Reading Strategy **1**

Respond to Argument
Ask students how they feel about Pericles' argument here. Do they think a politician would make a statement like this in a public speech today?

(ADVANCED) Ask advanced students what this statement shows them about gender roles in ancient Greece. *(Women were thought of as being inferior to men.)*

Literary Element **2**

Argument Answer: *Pericles' argument is convincing. He argues that the sons and brothers of the fallen warriors will always be considered less heroic because the dead invariably receive more honor than do the living. He uses a general truth to explain a specific circumstance.*

When one is alive, one is always liable to the jealousy of one's competitors, but when one is out of the way, the honor one receives is

sincere and unchallenged.

present here. Instead I shall try to comfort them. They are well aware that they have grown up in a world where there are many changes and chances. But this is good fortune—for men to end their lives with honor, as these have done, and for you honorably to lament them: their life was set to a measure where death and happiness went hand in hand. I know that it is difficult to convince you of this. When you see other people happy you will often be reminded of what used to make you happy too. One does not feel sad at not having some good thing which is outside one's experience: real grief is felt at the loss of something which one is used to. All the same, those of you who are of the right age must bear up and take comfort in the thought of having more children. In your own homes these new children will prevent you from brooding over those who are no more, and they will be a help to the city, too, both in filling the empty places, and in assuring her security. For it is impossible for a man to put forward fair and honest views about our affairs if he has not, like everyone else, children whose lives may be at stake. As for those of you who are now too old to have children, I would ask you to count as gain the greater part of your life, in which you have been happy, and remember that what remains is not long, and let your hearts be lifted up at the thought of the fair fame of the dead. One's sense of honor is the only thing that does not grow old, and the last pleasure, when one is worn out with age, is not, as the poet said, making money, but having the respect of one's fellow men.

'As for those of you here who are sons or brothers of the dead, I can see a hard struggle in front of you. Everyone always speaks well of the dead, and, even if you rise to the greatest heights of heroism, it will be a hard thing for you to get the reputation of having come near, let alone equalled, their standard. When one is alive, one is always liable[6] to the jealousy of one's competitors, but when one is out of the way, the honor one receives is sincere and unchallenged.

'Perhaps I should say a word or two on the duties of women to those among you who are now widowed. I can say all I have to say in a short word of advice. Your great glory is not to be inferior to what God has made you, and the greatest glory of a woman is to be least talked about by men, whether they are praising you or criticizing you. I have now, as the law demanded, said what I had to say. For the time being our offerings to the dead have been made, and for the future their children will be supported at the public expense by the city, until they come of age. This is the crown and prize which she offers, both to the dead and to their children, for the ordeals which they have faced. Where the rewards of valor are the greatest, there you will find also the best and bravest spirits among the people. And now, when you have mourned for your dear ones, you must depart.' ❧

---

6. *Liable* means "subject to the possibility; susceptible."

Argument *Is Pericles' argument here convincing? Explain.* **2**

Reading Practice

Connect Connecting personally to the selection will help students become more involved in the reading of it. Ask students to close their eyes and imagine that they are in the crowd listening to Pericles' eulogy. Read Tacitus' introduction to the speech aloud so that they can visualize the setting. Then ask them how they would feel hearing this speech if they were a family member of the departed. Would Pericles' words comfort or anger them?

After You Read

Respond and Think Critically

Respond and Interpret

1. What passages in this speech impressed you most, and why?

2. (a)Why does Pericles disapprove of the custom of giving a solemn public speech to honor the Athenian war dead? (b)According to Pericles, why do these dead possess the grandest of all sepulchres?

3. (a)How do the Athenians and Spartans differ in their military training? (b)Why do you think Pericles emphasizes these differences?

4. (a)What is the Athenian attitude toward wealth and poverty? (b)Toward participation in public life?

Analyze and Evaluate

5. Ancient Greek culture often promoted the ideal of the "golden mean," referring to moderation and balance in all aspects of life. As described by Pericles, how might the Athenian lifestyle be regarded as an example of this ideal? Cite several examples from the speech.

6. What do Pericles' comments on the women and children in the audience suggest about family life in ancient Athens?

7. Why does Pericles devote so much space in his speech to describing the virtues of Athenians and their city? Explain.

Connect

8. **Big Idea** **The Heroic Ideal** How does Pericles' description of courage and honor illustrate the ancient Greek concept of the heroic ideal?

9. **Connect to Today** How would you compare Pericles' description of Athenian democracy with American democratic government today? Explain.

Literary Element Argument

SAT Skills Practice

According to Pericles, which of the following elements make Athenian society and culture superior?

(A) Athenian government, lifestyle, education, lack of militarism, and philosophy

(B) Athenian government, lifestyle, education, and lack of militarism

(C) Athenian government, lifestyle, education, and architecture

(D) Athenian lifestyle, education, and lack of militarism

(E) Athenian lifestyle, education, and athletics

Review: Tone

As you learned on page 25, **tone** is a reflection of an author's attitude toward his or her subject. Tone may reflect a variety of attitudes, such as sympathy, objectivity, seriousness, bitterness, or humor. Several elements—including diction, imagery, and figures of speech—help convey tone.

Partner Activity Meet with a partner to determine Pericles' tone toward Athens in his funeral oration. Use a web like the one below to identify the elements that help convey the tone.

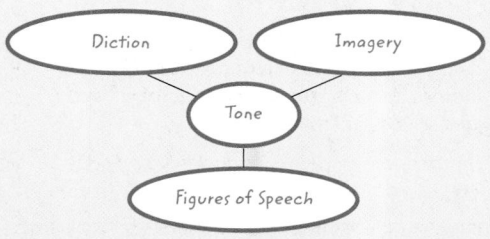

THUCYDIDES **331**

Review: Tone

Pericles' tone is one of love and respect. Examples: "it is only right and proper on such an occasion to pay them the honor"; "the most splendid of sepulchres"; "bear up and take comfort"

Progress Check

Can students analyze argument?

If No → See Unit 2 Teaching Resources Book, p. 116.

Assess

1. Answers will vary.

2. (a) The merit of the dead should not depend on a speech. (b) They live in people's minds everywhere.

3. (a) The Spartans toil in pursuit of courage; the Athenians face danger when it arises. (b) He wants to belittle the enemy and bolster Athenian confidence.

4. (a) Wealth is an opportunity for achievement; poverty is not degradation if there is an effort to overcome it. (b) Participation in public affairs is a duty for all citizens.

5. He points out that Athenians balance work with play, love beauty without extravagance, and cultivate both the mind and the body.

6. Families mourned the loss of loved ones, but it was the city-state that took financial responsibility for the children of the fallen soldiers.

7. Pericles wants to inspire pride, patriotism, and self-sacrifice in the audience.

8. The ancient Greeks believed courage and honor went hand in hand and that courage entailed standing one's ground regardless of the consequences. These are the qualities that Pericles extols in the fallen warriors.

9. Answers will vary. Students may say interest in public affairs was greater in ancient Athens than it is in modern America.

Literary Element

(B) is the correct answer. All the others omit key factors and/or include factors Pericles does not mention.

After You Read

Assess

Reading Strategy

1. (a) *valiant, gallant, gallantly* (b) *honor, virtue, worthy, heroism, glory, manliness, tolerant, greatness*

2. Key repeated words include *courage, honor, gallant, valiant, heroism,* and *glory.* A repeated idea that is courage involves standing one's ground, or pressing on, in the face of peril.

3. His references to the greatness of Athenian ancestry, the greatness of the city, and the moral superiority of Athenians appeal to the patriotism of his audience, reinforcing his position that Athenians have a duty to support the war against Sparta.

Progress Check

Can students analyze rhetorical devices?

If No → See Unit 2 Teaching Resources Book, p. 117.

Reading Strategy Analyze Rhetorical Devices

Rhetorical devices are techniques authors use to manipulate language for effect or to evoke an emotional response in the reader. Review the chart you made on page 321 and then answer the following questions.

1. (a) What synonyms for *courage* can you identify in the oration? (b) What other words with highly positive connotations does Pericles use to describe Athenian character traits?

2. What examples of repetition (either of words or ideas) can you find?

3. What emotional appeals does Pericles make?

Vocabulary Practice

Practice with Analogies Choose the word that best completes each analogy. Use a dictionary if you need help.

1. **incredulous : trusting :: loyal :**
   a. faithful   **b.** treacherous   **c.** honorable

2. **versatility : adaptability :: courage :**
   a. dependability   **b.** ability   **c.** bravery

3. **tangible : definite :: vague :**
   a. exact   **b.** unclear   **c.** solid

4. **consummation : achievement :: breakdown :**
   a. failure   **b.** fulfillment   **c.** completion

5. **commiserate : ignore :: applaud :**
   a. acclaim   **b.** question   **c.** criticize

Academic Vocabulary

*Pericles speaks of the **intrinsic** worth of Athens in his funeral oration.*

Intrinsic is an academic word. If people are naturally gifted, their talents are said to be **intrinsic** to their nature. Name a quality that is intrinsic to all mammals.

For more on academic vocabulary, see pages 36–37 and R83–R85.

Listening and Speaking

Speech

Assignment Pericles identifies Athenian values he believes are worth fighting for—and, if necessary, dying for. Write and deliver a speech on the values you believe are important to our society.

Prepare Before drafting your speech, review the chart you filled out on page 321 to identify the rhetorical devices used in "Pericles' Funeral Oration." Consider which devices you might use in your speech. For example, you might decide to use parallelism—a series of words, phrases, or sentences that have similar grammatical form—to link key ideas and make them memorable for your audience.

Formulate a clear thesis with credible, valid, and relevant evidence to support it. Develop an engaging introduction, convincing body paragraphs, and an effective conclusion. Use transitions to weave your ideas together. You may find it helpful to use sentence frames as you draft your speech. For example, your thesis might be stated as follows:

Though I agree that _____, I still maintain that _____.

Your body paragraphs may contain statements to address counterarguments, such as the following:

While it is true that _____, that does not necessarily mean that _____.

Create note cards and visual aids as needed to support your presentation.

Deliver Make eye contact with your audience when you give your speech. Speak loudly and clearly so everyone can hear you. Maintain good posture to reflect confidence and use gestures as appropriate, such as when emphasizing a point.

Evaluate Write a paragraph evaluating your speech. Refer to page 843 for a rubric to help with your evaluation.

 Literature Online

Selection Resources For Selection Quizzes, eFlash-cards, and Reading-Writing Connection activities, go to glencoe.com and enter QuickPass code GLW6053u2.

Vocabulary

1. b **2.** c **3.** b **4.** a **5.** c

Academic Vocabulary

Answers will vary. Sample answer: *All mammals have hair or fur.*

 For additional selection assessment, see **Assessment Resources, pp. 79–80.**

Listening and Speaking

Students' speeches should
- include a clear thesis supported by evidence
- use rhetorical devices effectively
- address potential counterarguments

 For grammar practice, see Unit 2 Teaching Resources Book, p. 120.

Vocabulary Workshop

Dictionary Use

Literature Connection Sometimes you can skim over an unfamiliar word as you read and still understand it. But at other times, the meaning of a passage hinges on the definition of a word. The sentence below concludes a long paragraph in "Pericles' Funeral Oration" by Thucydides.

> *"But the man who can most truly be accounted brave is he who best knows the meaning of what is sweet in life and of what is terrible, and then goes out undeterred to meet what is to come."*

This sentence is clearly about bravery. But what does *undeterred* mean? This is where readers reach for a dictionary.

Looking for a Word Looking up a word sometimes involves a little detective work. For example, you will not find *undeterred* in the average dictionary. But notice that *undeterred* begins with *un-*, meaning *not*, one of the most common prefixes in English. Take away the prefix and the *-ed* suffix and you are left with *deter*. Paring down the word led you to its dictionary entry.

The Main Entry A main entry tells you far more about a word than its definition. Here is what one dictionary says about *deter*.

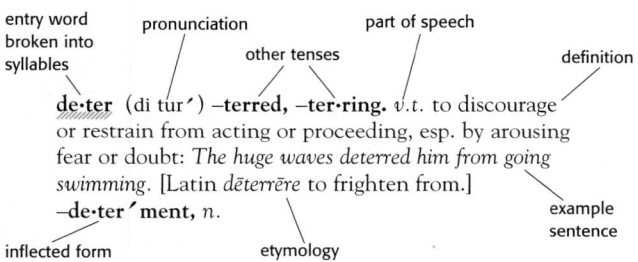

entry word broken into syllables   pronunciation   other tenses   part of speech   definition

de·ter (di tur′) **–terred, –ter·ring.** *v.t.* to discourage or restrain from acting or proceeding, esp. by arousing fear or doubt: *The huge waves deterred him from going swimming.* [Latin *dēterrēre* to frighten from.]
—**de·ter′ment,** *n.*

inflected form   etymology   example sentence

Etymology

Etymology is the history and origin of a word. Not all print dictionaries contain etymologies, but they are often available in online dictionaries.

Test-Taking Tip

Homographs are words that are spelled the same but have different etymologies and meanings (e.g. *sole*, meaning "alone," and *sole*, "a flat fish"). Homographs have separate entries in a dictionary and are marked by small raised numbers immediately before or after the entry word.

Practice Use the dictionary entry shown above to answer the following questions.

1. What two pieces of information does the pronunciation provide?
2. Why is it useful to see how the past and present participles of *deter* are spelled?
3. What aspect of the definition does the example sentence emphasize?
4. What word could you use in place of *undeterred* in the sentence from "Pericles' Funeral Oration" at the top of the page?

 Literature Online

Vocabulary For more vocabulary practice, go to glencoe.com and enter QuickPass code GLW6053u2.

VOCABULARY WORKSHOP **333**

English Learners

DIFFERENTIATED INSTRUCTION

Intermediate It may be helpful for English learners to further break down the word *undeterred*. Point out that the word *deter* is formed by combining the prefix *de-* with the Latin root *terre*, which means "frighten." Ask students if they can think of another English word that contains the root *terre* and means "frightened" or "fright." *(Terrified, terror)*

Advanced Learners/Pre-AP

DIFFERENTIATED INSTRUCTION

Misleading Roots Caution students that two words may appear to have similar roots, but might in fact be very different in meaning. For example, the Latin root *terre* ("frighten") looks quite similar to the Latin root *terr* ("land" or "earth"), which is found in words such as *terrestrial*. Have advanced students use dictionaries to come up with lists of other words that have misleadingly similar roots.

Focus

Write on the board: In what situations have you used a dictionary in the past? Students will probably respond that they have used a dictionary to find the definitions and spellings of new words. Remind them that a dictionary also provides information on how to pronounce a word and add suffixes to it correctly. In addition, most dictionaries give information on a word's origin and history.

Teach

Multiple-Meaning Words
Remind students that, unlike homographs, multiple-meaning words are words that have several related definitions listed within a single dictionary entry. For example, the word *cry* can be a verb meaning "to weep," or a noun meaning "a loud scream."

Assess

Dictionary Use

1. It shows how to sound the letters and how to accent the syllables.
2. In both cases the letter *r* is doubled.
3. The "huge waves" suggest the element of fear and doubt in *deter*.
4. Possible answers: *undiscouraged, resolute*

Before You Read

Focus

Bellringer Options

**Selection Focus
    Transparency 15**
**Daily Language Practice
    Transparency 31**
Ask: What are some of your convictions? Encourage students to discuss how far they would go to defend their convictions.

Literary History

The Theories of the Early Dialogues Three philosophical theories run through Plato's early dialogues. One is the theory of knowledge as recollection—that the soul not only survives the death of the body but also exists before birth. Another is the conception of the tripartite soul, which means the soul is made up of reason, appetite, and spirit (or will.) The final one is the theory of Forms, which holds that Forms such as Beauty and Justice are to be held in higher regard than the things of this world.

Before You Read

from the *Apology*

Meet **Plato**
(c. 427–347 B.C.)

Born into a distinguished family in Athens, Plato (plā′tō) was groomed for a career in politics. He put aside that life, however, to follow Socrates (470–399 B.C.), a philosopher who claimed that a divine voice led him to challenge the statements of people who pretended to be wise. For Socrates, true wisdom meant recognizing that one was ignorant. His probing questions and nontraditional approach eventually got him in trouble with the authorities.

In 399 B.C., during a period of political turmoil in Athens, some leaders accused Socrates of undermining Athenian patriotism. At the age of 70, he was charged with ignoring the gods and corrupting the youth of Athens and was sentenced to death by poison. His ideals and wisdom continue to live on largely because of the writings of Plato.

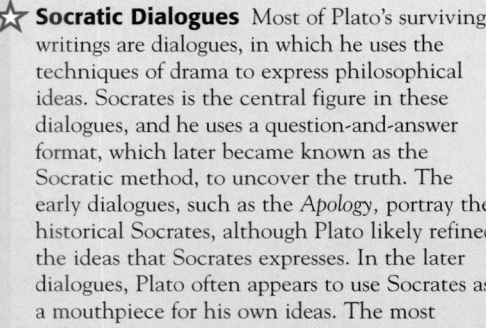

> *"God orders me to fulfill the philosopher's mission of searching into myself and other men."*
>
> —Socrates, in Plato's *Apology*

 Socratic Dialogues Most of Plato's surviving writings are dialogues, in which he uses the techniques of drama to express philosophical ideas. Socrates is the central figure in these dialogues, and he uses a question-and-answer format, which later became known as the Socratic method, to uncover the truth. The early dialogues, such as the *Apology*, portray the historical Socrates, although Plato likely refined the ideas that Socrates expresses. In the later dialogues, Plato often appears to use Socrates as a mouthpiece for his own ideas. The most influential of the Socratic dialogues was the *Republic*, which examines the nature of justice.

Philosopher for the Ages Deeply distraught over Socrates' execution, Plato knew his fellow Athenians had acted out of ignorance. He concluded that what they needed was an education in philosophy. To achieve that goal, Plato established the Academy, a large, park-like school. With its open spaces and shaded walkways, the Academy offered an idyllic setting where students and teachers could exchange and discuss ideas.

Like his mentor Socrates, Plato was committed to using reason in a relentless search to discover the truth. Many of the basic concepts of Western philosophy can be traced to him. A brilliant literary stylist and a profound thinker, he has inspired authors and philosophers for more than 2,000 years. As the nineteenth–century American thinker Ralph Waldo Emerson observed, "Plato is philosophy, and philosophy Plato."

 Literature Online

Author Search For more about Plato, go to glencoe.com and enter QuickPass code GLW6053u2.

Literary Elements
• Formal Speech
  (SE pp. 335, 336, 338, 340)

from Plato's Apology

Speaking/Listening/ Viewing Skills
• Debate (SE p. 341)

Reading Skills
• Analyze Persuasion (SE p. 335, 336, 338, 341)
• Analyze Rhetorical Devices (TE p. 336)

Vocabulary Skills
• Practice with Word Parts (SE p. 341)

Writing Skills/Grammar
• Write a Speech (TE p. 336)
• Use Comparative and Superlative Adjectives (TE p. 338)

Literature and Reading Preview

Connect to the Speech

Who is the wisest person you have known? With a partner, discuss what it means to be wise.

Build Background

The *Apology* (a formal explanation for actions or beliefs) is a collection of speeches that Socrates made in his defense. After he was found guilty, the jury asked him to propose an alternative punishment. Socrates replied that Athens should reward him with a pension for his services as a gadfly, or pest. The following excerpt is from the speech Socrates gave to the jury after it sentenced him to death.

Set Purposes for Reading

Big Idea The Good Life

In this speech, Socrates shares his views about the Athenian people, government, and life and death. As you read, ask yourself, What values does Socrates consider worth living—and dying—for?

Literary Element Formal Speech

In a **formal speech**, the speaker tries to influence the audience's behavior, beliefs, and attitudes. The main purpose of a formal speech is to persuade, although it can also inform and entertain. As you read, ask yourself, What views does Socrates express, and how does he support them?

Reading Strategy Analyze Persuasion

When you **analyze persuasion**, you identify and examine the techniques that speakers or authors use to sway the audience. These techniques may include defending an idea, refuting the opposition, promoting a new idea, or inspiring listeners to take action. As you read, ask yourself, What persuasive techniques does Socrates use?

Tip: **Chart Persuasive Techniques** As you read the excerpt from the *Apology*, use a chart to list examples of defending an idea, refuting the opposition, promoting a new idea, and inspiring listeners to take action.

Defending	Refuting	Promoting	Inspiring

Learning Objectives

For pages 334–341

In studying this text, you will focus on the following objectives:

Literary Study: Analyzing formal speech.

Reading: Analyzing persuasion.

Listening and Speaking: Conducting a debate.

Vocabulary

detractor (di trak′ tər) *n.* one who speaks ill of someone or something; p. 336 *Many detractors criticized the mayor's proposed tax increases.*

acquittal (ə kwit′ əl) *n.* a setting free from a criminal charge by verdict, sentence, or other legal process; p. 336 *No one expects an acquittal in the trial of the alleged murderer.*

censure (sen′ shər) *v.* to find fault with and criticize; p. 338 *The manager censured the athletes for breaking curfew.*

intimation (in′ tə mā′ shən) *n.* an indirect suggestion; p. 338 *There were intimations that the team would soon move to a new city.*

PLATO **335**

Before You Read

Focus

Summary

Socrates has been sentenced to death for his beliefs and his challenging of the government. This selection covers the speech he makes to his followers before the sentence is carried out. He shares his views on the Athenian people, the government, and death.

 For summaries in languages other than English, see Unit 2 Teaching Resources Book, pp. 123–128.

Vocabulary

Mnemonic Device Have students come up with phrases that help them remember the definition for each of the vocabulary words. Allow them to use slang or colloquialisms. For example, a detractor disrespects. Have students share their mnemonics with partners, and discuss which are most effective.

 For additional vocabulary practice, see Unit 2 Teaching Resources Book, p. 131.

Approaching Level

DIFFERENTIATED INSTRUCTION

False Accusations Engage students in a conversation about false accusations. Ask them if they have ever been wrongly accused of something. How did they respond? Were they able to defend themselves? Then explain that some ancient Greeks in Athens believed Socrates had spoken against their city. In the *Apology*, Socrates defended his stance even though the Athenians wanted to execute him. Ask students if they would always stand by their viewpoints, even during trying times, as Socrates did.

Advanced Learners/Pre-AP

DIFFERENTIATED INSTRUCTION

The Socratic Method Explain that the Socratic method is a philosophical method of systematic doubt and questioning of another to elicit a clear expression of a truth supposed to be implicitly known by all rational beings. Have students research its origins and applications. Challenge volunteers to demonstrate the Socratic method for the class.

Teach

Reading Strategy `1`

Analyze Persuasion
Answer: *He refutes the opposition by stating what his opponents think and then demonstrating that they have misjudged him.*

Literary Element `2`

Formal Speech Answer:
Socrates gives details showing how a man can avoid death in battle if he is willing to sacrifice his honor. Socrates also says that one can escape death by saying the "right" thing or by betraying one's own beliefs.

 For an audio recording of this selection, use Listening Library Audio CD-ROM.

Readability Scores

Dale-Chall: 5.6
DRP: 57
Lexile: 970

from the

APOLOGY

from the Dialogues

PLATO ❧ Translated by Benjamin Jowett

Not much time will be gained, O Athenians, in return for the evil name which you will get from the **detractors** of the city, who will say that you killed Socrates, a wise man; for they will call me wise, even although I am not wise, when they want to reproach you. If you had waited a little while, your desire would have been fulfilled in the course of nature. For I am far advanced in years, as you may perceive, and not far from death. I am speaking now not to all of you, but only to those who have condemned me to death. And I have another thing to say to them: You think that I was convicted because I had no words of the sort which would have procured my **acquittal**—I mean, if I had thought fit to leave nothing undone or unsaid. Not so; the deficiency which led to my conviction was not of words—certainly not. But I had not the boldness or impudence or inclination to address you as you would have liked me to do, weeping and wailing and lamenting, and saying and doing many things which you have been accustomed to hear from others, and which, as I maintain, are unworthy of me. I thought at the time that I ought not to do anything common or mean when in danger: nor do I now repent of the style of my defense; I would rather die having spoken after my manner, than speak in your manner and live. For neither in war nor yet at law ought I or any man to use every way of escaping death. Often in battle there can be no doubt that if a man will throw away

---

Analyze Persuasion *Which persuasive technique does Socrates use here?* `1`

Formal Speech *Formal speeches contain topic sentences and details to support them. How does Socrates support this statement in the next few lines?* `2`

Vocabulary

detractor (di trak′ tər) *n.* one who speaks ill of someone or something
acquittal (ə kwit′ əl) *n.* a setting free from a criminal charge by verdict, sentence, or other legal process

336 UNIT 2 ANCIENT GREECE

Writing Practice

📝 **Write a Speech** Give students the following writing prompt: Imagine that students in an animal rights group at your school want to put posters up in the hallway about why it is wrong to eat meat. The teachers in your school feel that those students' viewpoints do not represent all students and that they should not be allowed to advertise their opinions in school hallways. Write a speech that either sides with the students in the animal rights group or with the teachers. Speak about your topic with the conviction that Socrates shows in his argument before the Athenians. As you write, apply parallel structure, repetition, and figurative language to persuade your audience.

The Death of Socrates, 1650. Charles Alphonse Dufresnoy. Oil on canvas, 122 x 155 cm. Galleria Palatina Palazzo Pitti, Florence.

View the Art In this painting, Socrates' disciples express their grief as he carries out his death sentence by drinking hemlock. How do the attitudes of the subjects influence the mood of the painting? ★

his arms, and fall on his knees before his pursuers, he may escape death; and in other dangers there are other ways of escaping death, if a man is willing to say and do anything. The difficulty, my friends, is not to avoid death, but to avoid unrighteousness; for that runs faster than death. I am old and move slowly, and the slower runner has overtaken me, and my accusers are keen and quick, and the faster runner, who is unrighteousness, has overtaken them. And now I depart hence[1] condemned by you to suffer the penalty of death,—they too go their ways condemned by the truth to suffer the penalty of villainy and wrong; and I must abide by my award—let them abide by theirs. I suppose that these things may be regarded as fated,—and I think that they are well.

And now, O men who have condemned me, I would fain[2] prophesy to you; for I am about to die, and in the hour of death men are gifted with prophetic power. And I prophesy to you who are my murderers, that immediately after my departure punishment far heavier than you have inflicted on me will surely await you. Me you have killed because you wanted to escape the accuser, and not to give an account of your lives. But that will not be as you suppose:

---

1. Here, *hence* means "from this world or life."

3 The Good Life *What can you infer about Socrates' values in life?*

---

2. *Fain* means "willingly" or "with pleasure."

PLATO **337**

The Good Life Answer: *Socrates believes that it is essential to remain true to his beliefs even if it costs him his life.*

View the Art ★

Answer: *Students may say that the mood is grim or sad.*

Charles Alphonse Dufresnoy was born in Paris and studied under Simon Vouet before moving in 1633 to Italy, where he lived for twenty years. Dufresnoy's style was influenced by classical art, which he studied while living in Rome. Behind Socrates in the painting stands the prison guard who prepared the poison.

Learning Objectives
Analyzing persuasion. (SE)
Analyzing formal speech. (SE)
Analyzing art. (SE)
Writing a speech. (TE)

English Learners

DIFFERENTIATED INSTRUCTION

SMALL GROUP **Intermediate** English language learners may not understand Plato's use of synonyms. Write on the board *boldness* or *impudence*. Explain that both words signify having confidence; however, impudence means you have confidence to the point of showing disrespect. Then have groups of students use a dictionary to compare and contrast the meanings of *weeping*, *wailing*, and *lamenting*. Ask them to define each word by using a sentence frame like the one below:

When you weep, you _____.

Advanced Learners/Pre-AP

DIFFERENTIATED INSTRUCTION

Research the Dialogues Have advanced learners work with other students to introduce another aspect of Plato's *Dialogues*. Advanced learners should research another one of the dialogues and explain its theme to other students. Then the entire group should engage in a conversation about what political, ethical, or social objective Plato was trying to demonstrate in that dialogue.

337

Teach

Reading Strategy   1

Analyze Persuasion

Answer: *Socrates states his young followers will be so enraged by his death they will speak out against his accusers. Thus, Socrates' murderers have not solved their problems by sentencing to death one who censured them for their wicked lives.*

Literary Element   2

Formal Speech   **Answer:**
Most students will say Socrates makes the point effectively. He supports his view that death is a good thing by arguing death brings about good consequences: either a state of utter nothingness or the migration of the soul to another place where he can continue his search into true and false knowledge.

Cultural History ☆

The Greeks and the Concept of Virtue In this passage, Socrates exhorts the Athenians work toward "improving" themselves. The Greeks believed that acting with virtue benefited the individual as well as the community. In Greek society, it was more important to live virtuously than to acquire material wealth.

---

far otherwise. For I say that there will be more accusers of you than there are now; accusers whom hitherto I have restrained: and as they are younger they will be more inconsiderate with you, and you will be more offended at them. If you think that by killing men you can prevent someone from **censuring** your evil lives, you are mistaken; that is not a way of escape which is either possible or honorable; the easiest and the noblest way is not to be disabling others, but to be improving yourselves. This is the prophecy which I utter before my departure to the judges who have condemned me.

Friends, who would have acquitted me, I would like also to talk with you about the thing which has come to pass, while the magistrates are busy, and before I go to the place at which I must die. Stay then a little, for we may as well talk with one another while there is time. You are my friends, and I should like to show you the meaning of this event which has happened to me. O my judges—for you I may truly call judges—I should like to tell you of a wonderful circumstance. Hitherto the divine faculty[3] of which the internal oracle[4] is the source has constantly been in the habit of opposing me even about trifles, if I was going to make a slip or error in any matter; and now as you see there has come upon me that which may be thought, and is generally believed to be, the last and worst evil. But the oracle made no sign of

opposition, either when I was leaving my house in the morning, or when I was on my way to the court, or while I was speaking, at anything which I was going to say; and yet I have often been stopped in the middle of a speech, but now in nothing I either said or did touching the matter in hand has the oracle opposed me. What do I take to be the explanation of this silence? I will tell you. It is an **intimation** that what has happened to me is a good, and that those of us who think that death is an evil are in error. For the customary sign would surely have opposed me had I been going to evil and not to good.

Let us reflect in another way, and we shall see that there is great reason to hope that death is a good; for one of two things—either death is a state of nothingness and utter unconsciousness, or, as men say, there is a change and migration of the soul from this world to another. Now if you suppose that there is no consciousness, but a sleep like the sleep of him who is undisturbed even by dreams, death will be an unspeakable gain. For if a person were to select the night in which his sleep was undisturbed even by dreams, and were to compare with this the other days and nights of his life, and then were to tell us how many days and nights he had passed in the course of his life better and more pleasantly than this one, I think that any man, I will not say a private man, but even the great king will not find many such days or nights, when compared with the others. Now if death be of such a nature, I say that

---

3. *Faculty* means "an inherent or natural ability."
4. Socrates uses *internal oracle* as a metaphor for the human conscience.

1   **Analyze Persuasion** *How does Socrates refute the opposition in this prophecy?*

Vocabulary

censure (sen′ shər) *v.* to find fault with and criticize

Formal Speech *Read the rest of this paragraph. Does Socrates effectively argue the point made in this topic sentence? Explain.*   **2**

Vocabulary

intimation (in′ tə mā′ shən) *n.* an indirect suggestion

338   UNIT 2   ANCIENT GREECE

Grammar Practice

Use Comparative and Superlative Adjectives Remind students that comparative adjectives compare two nouns or pronouns and superlative adjectives compare more than two. For most one- and two- syllable adjectives, add *-er* to form the comparative and *-est* to form the superlative. For adjectives of three or more syllables, use *more* or *less* for the comparative and *most* or *least* for the superlative. Ask students the

effect of the phrases on this page such as "more inconsiderate," "more offended," "the noblest way," and "worst evil." How do these forms of the adjectives help Socrates convey his point? *(Sample answer: The phrase "the noblest way" suggests there is only one path to acting ethically.)*

to die is gain; for eternity is then only a single night. But if death is the journey to another place, and there, as men say, all the dead abide, what good, O my friends and judges can be greater than this? If indeed when the pilgrim arrives in the world below, he is delivered from the professors of justice in this world, and finds the true judges who are said to give judgment there, Minos and Rhadamanthus and Aeacus[5] and Triptolemus,[6] and other sons of God who were righteous in their own life, that pilgrimage will be worth making. What would not a man give if he might converse with Orpheus[7] and Musaeus and Hesiod and Homer?[8] Nay, if this be true, let me die again and again. I myself, too, shall have a wonderful interest in there meeting and conversing with Palamedes, and Ajax the son of Telamon, and any other ancient hero who has suffered death through an unjust judgment; and there will be no small pleasure, as I think, in comparing my own sufferings with theirs. Above all, I shall then be able to continue my search into true and false knowledge; as in this world, so also in the next; and I shall find out who is wise, and who pretends to be wise, and is not. What would not a man give, O judges, to be able to examine the

leader of the great Trojan expedition; or Odysseus[9] or Sisyphus,[10] or numberless others, men and women too! What infinite delight would there be in conversing with them and asking them questions! In another world they do not put a man to death for asking questions: assuredly not. For besides being happier than we are, they will be immortal, if what is said is true.

Wherefore, O judges, be of good cheer about death, and know of a certainty, that no evil can happen to a good man, either in life or after death. He and his are not neglected by the gods; nor has my own approaching end happened by mere chance. But I see clearly that the time had arrived when it was better for me to die and be released from trouble; wherefore the oracle gave no sign. For which reason, also, I am not angry with my condemners, or with my accusers; they have done me no harm, although they did not mean to do me any good; and for this I may gently blame them.

Still I have a favor to ask of them. When my sons are grown up, I would ask you, O my friends, to punish them; and I would have you trouble them, as I have troubled you, if they seem to care about riches, or anything, more than about virtue; or if they pretend to be something when they are really nothing,—then reprove them, as I have reproved you, for not caring about that for which they ought to care, and thinking that they are something when they are really nothing. And if you do this, both I and my sons will have received justice at your hands.

The hour of departure has arrived, and we go our ways—I to die, and you to live. Which is better God only knows. ☙

---

5. *Minos, Rhadamanthus,* and *Aeacus* were rulers known for their wisdom and fairness. After their deaths, they became judges in Hades, the underworld.
6. *Triptolemus* taught agriculture and was known for his compassion.
7. In Greek mythology, *Orpheus* was a musician so gifted that his melodies could charm animals, trees, and rocks.
8. *Musaeus, Hesiod,* and *Homer* were renowned Greek poets.
9. *Palamedes, Ajax,* and *Odysseus* were Greek warriors famed for their heroic exploits during the Trojan War.
10. *Sisyphus* was a crafty king who tried to trick death. For his deceitfulness, he was condemned in the underworld to roll a huge stone uphill forever. Each time it reached the crest, the stone rolled back down, forcing Sisyphus to begin again.

The Good Life *What does this passage indicate about Socrates' vision of the good life?* **3**

Teach

Big Idea   **3**

The Good Life **Answer:** *It indicates that Socrates' vision of the good life is based on seeking virtue and knowledge.*

Cultural History ☆

The Greeks and the Underworld In this passage, Socrates comments that "death is a journey to another place." The Greeks believed that when people died, the demon Charon rowed them on a ferry across the River Styx to the Underworld. In the Underworld, Hades and his wife Persephone rule over the "shades" of the deceased.

Learning Objectives
Analyzing persuasion. (SE)
Analyzing formal speech. (SE)
Using comparative and superlative adjectives. (TE)

Approaching Level

DIFFERENTIATED INSTRUCTION

Use Footnotes Approaching-level students may have difficulty following the text on this page due to the number of allusions that are footnoted. Point out that Socrates is noting the positive attributes of the people and characters to whom he is alluding. As students read, ask them to use a phrase about the characteristics of the person or group of people to whom Socrates is alluding, to help them

understand Socrates' meaning. For example:
"If indeed when the pilgrim arrives in the world below, he is delivered from the professors of justice in this world, and find the true judges who are said to give judgment there, the rulers known for wisdom and fairness, and other sons of God . . ."

Advanced Learners/Pre-AP

DIFFERENTIATED INSTRUCTION

Research Rhetoric Have students research classical rhetoric as it developed from the ancient Greeks to the Romans. Have one group of students investigate Aristotle's text *Rhetoric* and another group investigate *Institutio oratoria* ("The Training of an Orator"), written by the Roman Quintilian. Then have the two groups compare what they have learned about some of the general principles of these two rhetoricians.

After You Read

Assess

1. Answers will vary.

2. (a) Socrates could have saved himself if he had pleaded with his accusers and renounced his beliefs. (b) His life is less important to him than his principles are.

3. (a) Socrates predicts they will be more tormented by his followers than they were by him. (b) Socrates may have wanted them to realize they were making a mistake.

4. (a) Socrates has remained virtuous, so he has nothing to fear from death. (b) Students may suggest his remarks are based more on faith because the afterlife is in the realm of the unknown.

5. His theory that he may meet with other great figures in history seems to be Socrates' preference. He believes that when he is surrounded by other wise people his beliefs will receive the credit they deserve.

6. (a) It seems to indicate he wants his philosophy to live on in his sons. (b) It suggests he is truly dedicated to his beliefs.

7. (a) Socrates values virtue. (b) Answers will vary.

8. Answers will vary.

Progress Check

Can students analyze formal speech?

If No → See Unit 2 Teaching Resources Book, p. 129.

340

After You Read

Respond and Think Critically

Respond and Interpret

1. Which idea in this speech struck you most forcefully? How does it relate to your life?

2. (a)According to Socrates, how could he have saved himself? (b)Why might Socrates consider it unworthy of him to try to save himself?

3. (a)What prophecy does Socrates make regarding those who condemned him? (b)In your opinion, why might Socrates have revealed his prophecy to them?

Analyze and Evaluate

4. (a)Why is Socrates convinced he acted properly in court and has nothing to fear from death? (b)How would you characterize Socrates' remarks about death? Explain whether you think his remarks are based more on faith or on reason.

5. Of the two theories about death in the speech, which do you think Socrates would prefer were true? Why?

6. (a)In your opinion, why does Socrates make his final request? (b)What does this request suggest about him?

Connect

7. **Big Idea** **The Good Life** (a)Socrates states it is more important to avoid unrighteousness than death. What does Socrates value most in life? (b)What would you have done in Socrates' place?

8. **Connect to Today** Compare Socrates with a modern leader who was imprisoned or executed for his or her ideas. What traits did they share?

Literary Element **Formal Speech**

There are four types of **formal speech**: legal, political, ceremonial, and religious. Legal speeches are usually delivered to win a conviction or acquittal, but they can also have a larger political or moral significance. In ancient Athens, people had to defend themselves if they were put on trial. This law made it important for ordinary citizens to develop good speaking skills.

1. How does Socrates try to influence his audience in the *Apology*?

2. How does Socrates make his argument personal?

Review: Setting

As you learned on page 108, **setting** refers to the time and place the events of a literary work occur. The setting can include not only physical surroundings, but also the ideas, customs, values, and beliefs of the people who live there. Setting often helps influence a work's mood.

Partner Activity Work with a partner to create a web diagram like the one below listing details (such as the political climate or Socrates' final request) that evoke the setting. Then discuss why the setting is important for this philosophical work.

Setting
Place: ancient Athens
Time: following Socrates' conviction, preceding his execution.

Literary Element

1. He tries to persuade his audience that one's beliefs are worth dying for.

2. He is willing to accept death rather than recant.

Review: Setting

Students may say the setting affects this work by providing the final occasion for Socrates to address others.

Reading Strategy | Analyze Persuasion

SAT Skills Practice

Socrates' argument beginning with "Hitherto the divine faculty . . ." and ending with the question "What do I take to be the explanation of this silence?" on page 338 serves primarily to

(A) show the court that his conscience is completely clear

(B) cast doubt on the existence of the gods

(C) present new definitions of good and evil

(D) convince the court he has divine powers

(E) relate an amusing tale

Vocabulary Practice

Practice with Word Parts For each bold-faced vocabulary word in the left column, identify the related word that has a shared word part in the right column. Use a printed or online dictionary to look up the definition of the related word. Then explain how it is related to the vocabulary word.

1. detractor   quietus

2. acquittal   censorship

3. censure   attract

4. intimation   interior

Academic Vocabulary

Although his accusers brought false charges against him, Socrates remained true to his own **code** *of ethics.*

In the sentence above, *code* means "a collection of principles and rules." What would your own **code** of ethics be? Write a list of the values and ideals by which you live.

For more on academic vocabulary, see pages 36–37 and R83–R85.

Listening and Speaking

Debate

Assignment Today, there is an ongoing debate over what ideas should be expressed in public. Divide into two teams. Conduct a debate in which one team argues for freedom of speech and the other for limitations.

Prepare Work with your group to create a list of arguments that support your side. For each of your main arguments, make a web like the one below. You may want to model your persuasive techniques on the ones you recorded in the chart on page 335.

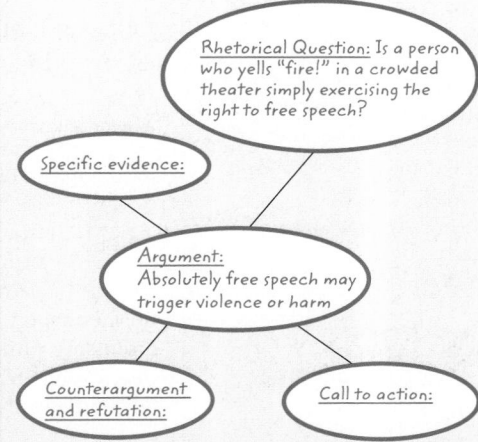

Debate During the debate, listen carefully to your team members' ideas so you can build on them when it is your turn to speak. Also listen to the opposing team's arguments so you can effectively challenge them. Remember to use evidence from real life to support your logical arguments.

Evaluate Create a rubric with criteria for evaluating your team's performance in the debate.

 Literature Online

Selection Resources For Selection Quizzes, eFlashcards, and Reading-Writing Connection activities, go to glencoe. com and enter QuickPass code GLW6053u2.

After You Read

Assess

Reading Strategy

(A) is the correct answer. The passage argues if Socrates had done something wrong, his conscience would bother him—but it does not.

Progress Check

Can students analyze persuasion?

If No → See Unit 2 Teaching Resources Book, p. 130.

Vocabulary

1. attract; to *attract* means "to draw through physical force or by appealing to the senses or emotions." A detractor attracts negative attention toward someone or something.

2. quietus; a *quietus* is something that serves to suppress or eliminate. An acquittal removes one from legal proceedings

3. censorship; *censorship* is the act of censoring or removing objectionable material. *Censure* means to "find fault with."

4. interior; *interior* means "of the inside". An *intimation* is an indirect suggestion that gets at a deeper meaning.

Academic Vocabulary

Students might mention religious tenets or moral beliefs, such as treating others the way they would wish to be treated or forgiving others' wrongs.

Listening and Speaking

Students' debates should

- allow everyone to have an equal chance to speak
- involve cooperation and collaboration among team members
- involve careful listening and thoughtful response to counterarguments

Focus

Summary

Former journalist and teacher Christopher Phillips explains how and why he started philosophical discussion groups known as Socrates Cafés. After starting one of the groups at a bookstore, Phillips went on to form groups across the United States, and now they exist in cafés, homeless shelters, Native American reservations, and senior centers. International groups now meet in such places as Finland, Spain, and Afghanistan.

Teach

Readability Scores

Dale-Chall: 8.6
DRP: 63
Lexile: 1140

 For an activity related to this selection, see Unit 2 Teaching Resources Book, pp. 136–144.

 For an audio recording of this selection, use Listening Library Audio CD-ROM.

Learning Objectives

For pages 342–345

In studying this text, you will focus on the following objectives:

Reading:
Distinguishing fact from opinion.
Using text features.
Analyzing informational text.

Set a Purpose for Reading

Read to learn how the teachings of Socrates are being applied in today's world.

Preview the Article

1. Read the **deck,** the large type after the title. What sorts of issues do you predict these groups discuss?

2. What do you already know about Socrates and the Socratic method?

Reading Strategy

Distinguish Fact from Opinion

A **fact** is a statement that can be proven with evidence. An **opinion** is a personal judgment that cannot be proven true or false. As you read this article, ask yourself, What is the relationship between stated facts and the opinions of individuals? Use a chart like the one below to record your findings.

Facts	Opinion

All the Right QUESTIONS

Discussion groups based on the teachings of Socrates are reviving the art of conversation.

By ANITA HAMILTON

THERE'S A BUZZ IN THE AIR AT THE EL DIABLO COFFEE CO. in Seattle, Washington, and it's not just coming from the aroma of the shop's Cuban-style espresso drinks. On a recent Wednesday evening, as most patrons sat quietly reading books or tapping away on their laptop computers, about 15 people gathered in a circle discussing philosophy. "When is violence necessary?" asked one. "What is a well-lived life?" asked another, as the group enjoyed a well-caffeinated, intellectual debate.

Known as a Socrates Café, the group at El Diablo is just one of 150 or so that meet in coffee shops, bookstores, libraries, churches and community centers across the country. Founded by Christopher Phillips, a former journalist and teacher, the cafés are designed to get people talking about philosophical issues. Using a kind of Socratic method, the cafés encourage people to develop their views by asking questions, being open to challenges, and considering alternative answers. Adhering to Socrates' belief that the unexamined life is not worth living, the cafés focus on exchanging ideas, not using them to compete with or belittle other participants. "Instead of just yelling back and forth, we take a few steps back and examine people's underlying values. People can ask why to their heart's content," says Phillips.

While a modern-day discussion group based on the teachings of a thinker from the 5th century B.C. may seem outdated, Socrates Cafés have found a surprisingly large and diverse following.

✍ Write a Press Release

Help students identify the format of a press release. See the example below as a guide. Instruct them to write a press release for a new group they would like to see meet at school after hours. Guide them to include in the first paragraph the "5 W's—who, what, when, where, and why. Then encourage them to look at their press release from the perspective of their audience, or other students.

EXAMPLE:

January 10, 2008 (date)

Indianapolis, IN—Sports Enthusiast Group (Location followed by headline)

Students form sports enthusiast group after hours at North Central High School to discuss some of their favorite sports moments and stories from that week. (byline)

(Begin article)

Contact Information:
Joseph Smith
North Central High School
Indianapolis, IN
jsmith@school.edu

In Seattle, participants meet and talk in a local coffeehouse.

Ann States

Meetings have been held everywhere from a Navajo Nation reservation in Ganado, Arizona, to an airplane terminal in Providence, Rhode Island. Ongoing groups have formed in prisons, senior centers, and homeless shelters. International groups have even popped up in Afghanistan, Finland, and Spain. What's the attraction? "People who get off on ideas come to this," says Fred Korn, a retired philosophy professor, who attends the Wednesday night meetings at El Diablo. "Outside of college, there's not a lot of opportunity to get together with people who want to talk about ideas," he says.

For Phillips, the dialogue groups are about much more than good conversation. "It's grassroots

> "The whole idea is not that we have to find a final answer; it's that we keep thinking."
>
> —Christopher Phillips
> Founder, Socrates Café

democracy," he says. "It's only in a group setting that people can hash out their ideas about how we

should act not just as an individual but as a society." To avoid divisive dead-end arguments, the cafés frequently turn current events into broader philosophical questions. For example, rather than asking whether the U.S. and its allies should have invaded Iraq, a group asked, "What is a just war?"

Phillips first came up with the idea for such sessions while studying political philosophy at the College of William and Mary in Williamsburg, Virginia. Several days a week after class, he and other students would meet with a favorite professor at a local restaurant in order to discuss philosophical issues. Often other

ALL THE RIGHT QUESTIONS **343**

TIME

Teach

Big Idea | 1

The Heroic Ideal **Ask:** How does the Greek concept of arête, or the drive to achieve personal excellence, apply to the Socrates Café discussion groups? *(The group strives to better its members' understanding of their own consciences through an open exchange of ideas with others.)*

Reading Strategy | 2

Synthesize Explain to students that the Socratic method of Socrates' time involved the questioner's asking the responder a series of questions that made the responder contradict himself or herself and lose an argument. **Ask:** How is the Socratic method of Socrates' time similar to or different from the Socratic method used at the Socrates Cafés? *(Students should realize that modern Socratic method hopes to create a dialogue rather than to demonstrate the participants' ignorance of philosophical concepts.)*

Advanced Learners/Pre-AP

DIFFERENTIATED INSTRUCTION

The Nature of Oppression Have students work in pairs to investigate cultures from other parts of the world that do not allow freedom of speech for their citizens. Ask them to write a summary of the following points:

- the type of government system that rules the country
- the specific law that bans free speech

- an example of a person or group of people who have been oppressed by that government system

Then ask all advanced learners to have a small group discussion about the nature of oppression and what its costs are to individual citizens.

Learning Objectives
Previewing a magazine article. (SE)
Distinguishing fact from opinion. (SE)
Writing a press release. (TE)
Synthesizing information. (TE)

Teach

Cultural History ☆

The Philosopher's Club

Christopher Phillips has expanded his idea of creating Socrates Cafés to young people. Today, Phillips helps initiate Philosopher's Clubs with groups of young people. The meetings are facilitated by teachers or adult volunteers and strive to teach children what Phillips calls "the fourth R"—the ability to reason. The clubs hope to enable children to answer these three questions: "Who am I?" "What am I capable of?" and "Who can I become?"

Photo Caption TK

Portrait statuette of Socrates, c. 200 AD. British Museum, London.

344 UNIT 2 ANCIENT GREECE

people would overhear their heated discussions and join in. "I thought, 'Wouldn't it be wonderful just to have these great conversations all the time?'" he says.

After quitting work as a writer, Phillips held his first Socrates Café at a Borders bookstore in Wayne, New Jersey, in the summer of 1996. Within a month, he met a woman named Cecilia, who was the only person to show up at one meeting. "We held a dialogue on the question What is love? and fell in love," he says. Married in 1998, the couple put their belongings in storage and travel year-round helping form new groups around the country.

The mood, tone and topic of discussion for each café vary greatly, depending on the participants. Typically, the topic is decided by group vote, and anyone can suggest an idea. At El Diablo, the mostly middle-aged crowd (ages 25 to 66) settled on a tough one: Do countries with greater power have a greater responsibility to act fairly? "Is any act that a nation makes in its own self-interest ever moral?" asked Matt Waller, a technical writer. "I say no." "Well, what's the nature of self-interest?" responds housepainter Steve Crawford. "Nations don't exist in a vacuum, certainly not in today's world." After two hours of discussion, no conclusion was reached, but that's not the point. "It's exercise of the mind," says Margaret Friedman, a writer and real estate agent who took part in the exchange.

At a Chicago, Illinois, homeless shelter for women called Deborah's Place, the discussion turns deeply

Speaking Practice

Participate in a Discussion Group

Have students work in two groups to hold an open discussion about the importance of freedom of the press and freedom of expression to a democratic government. These freedoms are not necessarily guaranteed by the United States Constitution, but they are often considered fundamentals of democracy. Ask them to begin their discussion with

a Socratic question, such as "What is the meaning of democracy?" Then guide them to be open to ideas by using the following sentence frames:

- I really like that point _____ made about _____, because _____.

- I take your point that _____, but I still think _____.

- I agree with you that _____, but disagree that _____, because _____.

personal with the question What's the role of courage in love? A woman replies, "The courage to walk away." Another says, "To walk away and not become a stalker. When I was 21 and in love with someone who was 19, that was the hardest thing I ever had to do." Launched three years ago with the question Why do bad things happen to good people?, the café at the shelter has been going strong ever since. "Just listening and participating made me grow a lot and care about myself when before I didn't," says Jackie Grayer, a Deborah's Place resident who regularly attends meetings.

While Phillips believes the cafés can benefit anyone, one of his favorite groups is children. One morning he met with seven kids ranging in age from 6 to 16 at Children's Hospital in Oakland, California. Wearing multicolored hospital gowns and fuzzy slippers, the children were bashful about answering direct questions at first. But Phillips was determined to begin a conversation. After making jokes about his own "uncool" haircut and asking a couple of easy questions like "What's four plus three?" and "Do you like to draw?", he finally got his audience warmed up and eased them on to the heavier topic of truth, lies, and secrets. "When is it not better to tell the truth?" Phillips asked his now rapt audience. "When is it good to lie?" Mariela, who has severe asthma, replied, "When you're trying to help somebody escape from something like slavery."

Philosophy is important for kids of all ages, Phillips says later, because "it gives them this great chance to sculpt their moral code, to figure out clearly who they are and who they want to be . . . The whole idea is not that we have to find a final answer; it's that we keep thinking about these things." One question at a time.

—With reporting by Laura A. Locke/Oakland, Eli Sanders/ Seattle and Leslie Whitaker/ Chicago

Respond and Think Critically

Respond and Interpret

1. Write a brief summary of this article's main ideas before you answer the following questions. For help on writing a summary, see page 1147.

2. (a)How do the Socrates Café groups approach philosophical discussion? (b)How do the groups approach current political issues?

3. (a)Where are some of the places Socrates Café groups have formed? (b)How are the groups different from one another? How are they similar?

Analyze and Evaluate

4. (a)Describe how two different people mentioned in the article support the philosophical opinions they put forth. Do they use facts? Explain. (b)Do you agree with their opinions? Explain.

5. (a)Do you think there are criteria you can use to determine whether one opinion is more valid than another? Explain. (b)Do you think it is possible for people to reach consensus on the types of questions mentioned in this article? Explain.

Connect

6. After reading the *Apology* and this article, do you think Socrates' philosophical methods are as relevant today as they were in ancient Greece? Explain.

---

5. (a) Some students may say opinions supported by facts are more valid; however, students should recognize two people can interpret the same facts in very different ways. (b) Some students will say consensus is not possible, because people are deeply influenced by their own feelings and experiences.

Connect

6. Some students may say Socrates' philosophical methods are as relevant today as they were in ancient Greece. Others may feel that in today's world, we need practical political solutions rather than philosophical discussions.

After You Read

Assess

1. Students' summaries will vary, but should mention the main points about Socrates Cafés from the article.

2. (a) The groups approach philosophical discussion by posing questions and considering alternative answers. (b) The groups approach current political issues indirectly, by asking related philosophical questions.

3. (a) Groups have formed in places including coffee shops, homeless shelters, prisons, senior centers, and a children's hospital. (b) The topics of discussion vary depending on the participants; some discussions are more academic, while others are based mainly on personal experience. The method of questioning, however, is similar in all the groups.

4. (a) Possible answer: One woman supports her opinion that "to walk away" is what defines courage in love by referencing her own experience. The girl at the children's hospital uses her knowledge of the history of slavery to support her opinion that lying can sometimes be good. The woman speaks from personal experience, while the girl would probably be able to use concrete historical evidence to back up her opinion. (b) Students should provide evidence from their own personal experience to support their answers.

Focus

Bellringer Options

**Daily Language Practice
Transparency 28**

Or write on the board: "The glory that was Greece and the grandeur that was Rome"
—Edgar Allan Poe

Ask: Why do you think Poe linked Rome with "grandeur"? *(Students may mention such factors as Rome's huge and long-lasting empire and impressive architectural monuments.)*

View the Art ★

El Jem is the modern Tunisian town occupying the site of the ancient Roman city of Thysdrus.

Ask: What does the great size of the amphitheater indicate about the economy of this part of the Roman Empire? *(Roman Africa was wealthy.)*

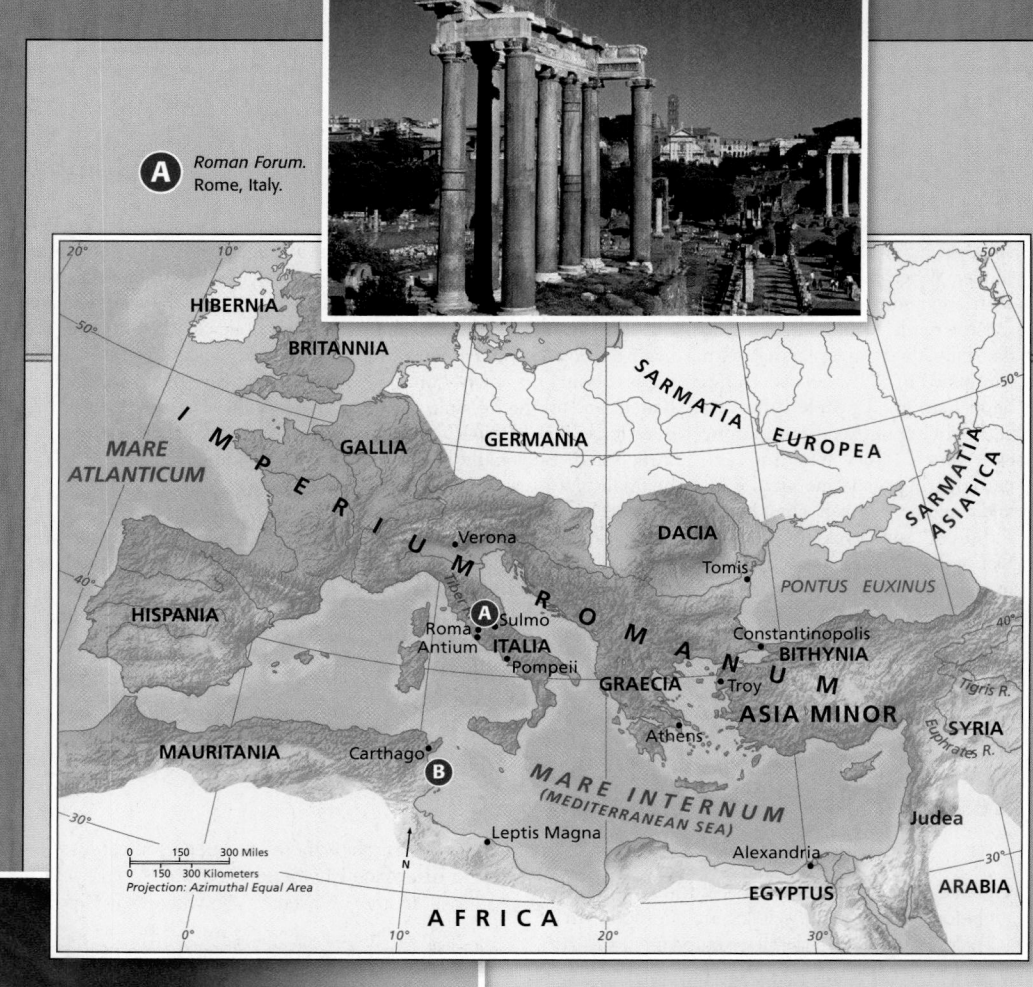

A Roman Forum. Rome, Italy.

B El Jem, Roman amphitheatre ★

LOG ON ▶ **Literature** Online

Literature and Reading For more about the history and literature of this period, go to glencoe.com and enter QuickPass code GLW6053u2.

346

Part Introduction Skills

Text Elements
- Captions (TE p. 348)

Reading Skills
- Analyze Graphic Information (SE p. 349; TE pp. 346–349)
- Compare and Contrast (SE p. 354)
- Make Generalizations (SE p. 355)
- Analyze Cause-and-Effect Relationships (SE p. 356; TE p. 350)

Part 2 Introduction

Vocabulary Skills
- Word Roots (TE p. 350)

Study Skills/Research/Assessment
- Take Notes (SE p. 357)

Speaking/Listening/Viewing Skills
- Visual Literacy (SE p. 357)
- Public Speaking (TE p. 349)
- Analyze Art (TE pp. 346–350, 352, 354)

Writing Skills/Grammar
- Comparison Essay (SE p. 357)
- Investigate History (TE p. 348)

ANCIENT ROME

800 B.C.–A.D. 500

Being There

Although only a small farming town in the beginning, Rome had great natural advantages. The seven hills on which it was built offered protection from its more powerful neighbors. Its location fifteen miles up the Tiber River offered easy access to the sea, and its position at the crossing of several trade routes brought foreign goods and ideas. As Rome expanded, Romans improved the lands they gained. They paved roads, constructed great aqueducts to carry water, built cities, encouraged trade, and applied the rule of law. Rome developed from a city-state into one of the largest empires in history.

The Knucklebone Player, late 2nd century AD. Roman school. Marble, height: 70 cm. Antikensammlung, Staatliche Museen zu Berlin, Germany.

Looking Ahead

In literature, as in other areas, the Romans learned from the Greeks. They adapted poetic forms the Greeks had established, such as the epic, ode, and lyric. Roman authors, however, also developed poetic forms of their own, such as satire, which mocks the follies of the time.

Keep the following questions in mind as you read:

- How did Greek philosophy help shape Roman thought?
- What were the basic features of Roman religion?
- What were living conditions like in imperial Rome?

347

Focus

Summary

This introduction gives an overview of historical, social, and cultural forces in ancient Rome between 800 B.C. and A.D. 500. It discusses the impact of geography on the development of Rome; the rise of the Roman Republic; the expansion and gradual decline of the Roman Empire; and the characteristic forms of Roman civilization.

View the Art

This girl is playing a game with knucklebones, toys originally made from the anklebones of sheep or other animals. **Ask:** What do this girl's dress and hairstyle suggest about her social class? *(Her elaborate dress and carefully braided hair suggest that she is an upper-class child.)*

> For additional support for English Learners, see Unit 2 Teaching Resources Book, p. 146.

Approaching Level

DIFFERENTIATED INSTRUCTION

Geography Students' comprehension of the introduction and general geographical knowledge will improve from an in-depth study of the regions of the Roman Empire.

Have groups of students study the map on page 346. Then present them with a modern map of the same geographic area. Students should compare the two maps, noting the number of current countries that were once under Roman rule. Have

students answer the following questions:
1. What is the modern name of the Pontus Euxinus? *(Black Sea)*
2. What two Roman provinces were located in what is now Turkey? *(Bithynia and Asia Minor)*
3. What modern countries occupy the region of Hibernia? *(Ireland and Northern Ireland)*
4. What modern country occupies most of the Roman province of Dacia? *(Romania)*

Point out to students that the questions at the bottom of page 347 are intended to help guide their reading of the Part 2 introduction and are specifically answered on pages 354, 355, and 356.

Teach

Text Element | 1

Captions Remind students that in the B.C. section of the timeline, later dates have *lower* numbers than earlier dates, while in the A.D. section they have *higher* numbers. **Ask:** What is the date of the earliest Roman event in the Part Two timeline? *(753 B.C.—Legendary date of Rome's founding)* **Ask:** What is the date of the latest Roman event in the Part Two timeline? *(A.D 476— Western Roman Empire ends)*

Reading Strategy | 2

Analyze Cause-and-Effect Relationships Ask: What was the cause-and-effect relationship between the Assyrians, the Babylonians, and the Persian ruler Cyrus the Great? *(The Assyrians were conquered by the Babylonians, who in turn were conquered by Cyrus the Great.)*

View the Art ★

In this mosaic, the Roman poet Virgil is flanked by (left) Clio, the Muse of history, and (right) Melpomene, the Muse of Tragedy. The Muses are the nine goddesses who inspire art and thought.
Ask: Why is Virgil shown sitting between these goddesses? *(They are inspiring him in the creation of his poetry.)*

TIMELINE 800 B.C.–A.D. 500

ROMAN LITERATURE

800 B.C.

Virgil and the Muses from Sousse ★

300 B.C.

c. 254
Comic playwright Plautus is born

70
Epic poet Virgil is born

◄ **51**
Julius Caesar publishes his *Gallic Wars*

38
Lyric poet Horace meets Maecenas, his patron

▲ **23**
Horace publishes the first three books of his *Odes*

19
Virgil dies, leaving the *Aeneid* unfinished

ROMAN EVENTS

800 B.C.

753
Legendary date of Rome's founding

616
Etruscans rule Rome

509
Rome becomes a republic

450
The Twelve Tables, the basis of Roman law, is codified

312
Appian Way, first Roman road, is built

300 B.C.

264 ▶
First Punic War begins

216
Hannibal defeats Romans at Cannae

146
Rome destroys Carthage

73
Spartacus leads a slave revolt

44
Julius Caesar is assassinated **3**

27
Octavian is named emperor

WORLD EVENTS

800 B.C.

612
Babylonians conquer the Assyrian Empire **2**

539
Cyrus the Great conquers the Babylonian Empire **2**

▲
sixth century
Lao-tzu, founder of Taoism, dies

c. 500
Nok culture emerges in western Africa

300 B.C.

141
Han emperor Wu Ti comes to the throne in China

Head from Nok, Nigerian culture

LOG ON ▶ Literature Online

Literature and Reading To explore the Interactive Timeline, go to glencoe.com and enter QuickPass code GLW6053u2.

Writing Practice

⚡ **Investigate History** Have students identify events on the timeline that they would like to learn more about. Discuss appropriate resources for the information they would like to find and how to credit their sources. Share this example for an online encyclopedia entry with students:

"Pliny the Elder." Encyclopædia Britannica. 2007. Encyclopædia Britannica Online. 4 Sept. 2007 <http://www.britannica.com/eb/article-9060423>.

Have students write short research papers about the events they have chosen. Guide them in proper documentation of their work.

A.D. 1

8
Augustus banishes Ovid

14
Augustus Caesar dies;
Golden Age of Latin
literature ends

79
Naturalist Pliny the
Elder dies during eruption
of Mt. Vesuvius

A.D. 300

c. 120
Historian Tacitus dies

A.D. 1

c. 30
Jesus is crucified in
Jerusalem

64
Fire destroys much
of Rome

79
Eruption of Mt. Vesuvius
destroys Pompeii

122
Construction of Hadrian's
Wall begins **3**

180
Marcus Aurelius dies;
Pax Romana ends

A.D. 300

313
Emperor Constantine
legalizes Christianity **4**

330
Constantine makes
Constantinople the
imperial capital

380
Theodosius makes
Christianity Rome's
state religion **4**

410
Visigoths sack Rome

476
Western Roman
Empire ends

A.D. 300

320
Chandra Gupta founds
Gupta dynasty in India

c. 400 ▲
Hopewell culture begins
decline in the Ohio River
Valley

Reading Check

Analyze Graphic Information About how many
years elapsed between Rome's founding and the
end of the Roman Empire?

Teach

Reading Check **Answer:**
About 654 years

Reading Strategy   **3**

**Analyze Graphic
Information** **Ask:** Could
Julius Caesar have seen
Hadrian's Wall? *(no)*

Reading Strategy   **4**

**Analyze Graphic
Information** **Ask:** How long
after Constantine legalized
Christianity did Theodosius
make it Rome's state religion?
(67 years)

View the Art ★

A wall painting from Pompeii
shows a wealthy Roman matron
holding a cithara, a stringed
instrument. **Ask:** What does this
image indicate about Roman
painting? *(This wall painting
displays recognizable portraits
of its subjects, the woman and
child. It indicates that the Romans
valued realism in painting.)*

Advanced Learners/Pre-AP

DIFFERENTIATED INSTRUCTION

SMALL GROUP

How-to Presentation Point
out that the Romans were the
greatest engineers of the ancient world.
They applied their engineering know-how
in constructing roads, bridges, aqueducts,
and huge public buildings such as the
Colosseum and the Pantheon. Have a
group of students research materials for
a visual how-to presentation detailing
the steps involved in a typical Roman
engineering project, such as building a
road. Have them include some of the
following visual aids to help the rest of
the class follow the process they are
describing:

- illustrations
- diagrams
- models
- computer simulations

Learning Objectives
Analyzing graphic information. (SE)
Analyzing text features. (TE)
Analyzing art. (TE)
Writing a research report. (TE)

Teach

Vocabulary | 1

Word Roots Point out that the geographical term *peninsula*, meaning "a piece of land that projects into a body of water," comes from the Latin words *paene*, "almost," and *insula*, "island." **Ask:** What other English words have *insula* as a root? *(insulate, insular)*

APPROACHING Direct students' attention to the outline of Italy on the map on page 334 to help them understand the meaning of *peninsula*. Then have them identify other peninsulas in the Roman Empire. *(Hispania, Graecia)*

Reading Strategy | 2

Summarize Ask: How would you summarize the process by which the Roman Republic changed into an empire? *(Roman political leaders struggled for power; Julius Caesar seized control, but was assassinated; his heir Octavian defeated rivals for power and was named emperor by the Senate.)*

View the Art ★

The Great Cameo of France is a famous sardonyx (a type of onyx) cameo depicting many ancient Roman rulers, including Tiberius and Caesar Augustus. **Ask:** What does such a cameo indicate about the Romans' attitude toward their leaders? *(The Romans probably had a great deal of respect and admiration for their leaders to commemmorate them this way.)*

Learning Objectives

For pages 346–357

In studying this text, you will focus on the following objectives:

Literary Study: Analyzing literary periods.

Reading: Evaluating historical influences. Connecting to the literature.

ANCIENT ROME

800 B.C.–A.D. 500

Historical, Social, and Cultural Forces

The Great Cameo of France, 1st century AD. Roman. Agate. Bibliotheque Nationale, Paris. ★

The Land of Italy

Italy is a long, narrow peninsula that juts into the Mediterranean Sea. Divided by a mountain range running down its length, Italy still has large fertile plains ideal for farming. One of these is the plain of Latium, on which the city of Rome is located. The Latin-speaking peoples who inhabited this region had migrated into the peninsula sometime between about 1500 and 1000 B.C. After about 800 B.C., other peoples, including the Etruscans and the Greeks, began settling in Italy. The Etruscans ruled the early Romans from about 616 to 509 B.C.

The Roman Republic

In 509 B.C. the Romans overthrew the last Etruscan king and established a republic. For the next 200 years, the city strove to control the rest of Italy. Later, in the Punic Wars, the Romans fought against the city of Carthage in Northern Africa for control of the Mediterranean. In 146 B.C., the Romans set fire to Carthage and sold its people into slavery.

As Rome expanded its conquests, civil war erupted because its political leaders vied for power.

Reading Practice

Analyze Cause-and-Effect Relationships The material in this introduction provides many opportunities to practice identifying causes and effects. Begin with the section titled "The Land of Italy." **Ask:** What cause-and-effect relationships can you identify in this paragraph? *(Students may say that the presence of large fertile plains in Italy* caused such groups as the Latin-speaking peoples and the Etruscans to immigrate there.)*

Have students take notes in a cause-and-effect chart as they read the rest of the material in the introduction. Remind them that one cause can have multiple effects and that one effect can result from multiple causes.

The greatest of these leaders was Julius Caesar, a brilliant soldier who used his military success as a springboard to seize control of Rome. In 44 B.C., Caesar was assassinated. Octavian, his nephew and adopted son, later defeated the forces of Mark Antony and Cleopatra at the Battle of Actium in 31 B.C. Four years later, the Roman Senate awarded Octavian the title of *Augustus* ("revered one") and named him *imperator* (the source of the English word *emperor*), or commander in chief.

Augustus ushered in an era of peace and prosperity, known as the *Pax Romana*, "Roman peace." During this period, which lasted almost two centuries, literature, art, and architecture flourished.

> *"I came. I saw. I conquered."*
>
> —Julius Caesar, describing one of his victories

The Roman Empire

At its greatest extent, early in the second century, the Roman Empire extended from northern Britain to what is now Iraq and included a population estimated at more than 50 million. The Romans were open to the cultures of the peoples they conquered. In particular, they admired the intellectual achievements of the Greeks and spread Greek culture throughout their lands.

After the death of the successful ruler Marcus Aurelius in A.D. 180, a series of inept or cruel leaders used military strength to seize the imperial throne. However, beginning in A.D. 284, the emperors Diocletian and then Constantine helped restore order and stability to the empire. Rome remained the capital of the Western Roman Empire; Byzantium, renamed Constantinople (modern Istanbul), became the capital of the Eastern Roman Empire. The Western Roman Empire suffered increasing pressure as Germanic barbarian hordes invaded its frontiers. Finally, in A.D. 476, with the deposition of the Roman emperor, the Western Roman Empire came to an end.

Italian warrior, reconstruction. 4th century BC. Private collection.

Teach

Vocabulary | 3

Connotation and Denotation Point out that the English word *barbarian* has its origin in a Greek word simply meaning "non-Greek." (The Greek word is probably onomatopoeic in origin, imitating foreign speech that sounded like babble to the ancient Greeks.) The Romans followed the Greeks in applying the Latin term *barbarus* to the non-Mediterranean peoples they encountered, such as Celts and Germans, whom they regarded as uncivilized. Point out that this is the current meaning of the word *barbarian*. **Ask:** Based on the primary denotation of "uncivilized," what type of connotations has *barbarian* acquired? *(strong negative connotations conveying "savage" and "cruel")*

Learning Objectives
Analyzing historical influences. (SE)
Analyzing word roots. (TE)
Summarizing information. (TE)
Analyzing cause-and-effect relationships. (TE)
Analyzing art. (TE)

English Learners

DIFFERENTIATED INSTRUCTION

Intermediate Point out to students that rhetoric was essential to the education of an ancient Roman who intended to have a career in public life.

Have students work with partners to practice oral presentations. Students may choose a famous speech or discuss a current topic of interest. Have partners take turns presenting and evaluating each other's speeches.

Advanced Learners/Pre-AP

DIFFERENTIATED INSTRUCTION

 SMALL GROUP **Roman Oratory** Have several students research the art of public speaking as it was practiced in ancient Rome and then do a presentation for the class. The presentation might include the following:

- the education of a Roman orator
- the careers of famous Roman orators (such as Cicero and Quintilian)

- a passage from a famous speech (such as Cicero's oration against Catiline) delivered in the Roman fashion

351

Teach

Reading Strategy · 1

Compare and Contrast

Ask: What was the basic difference between Greek and Roman art? *(Greek art expressed ideal beauty; Roman art presented realism.)*

[APPROACHING] Students may need help making a distinction between ideal forms and Realism. Point out that the creation of ideal forms in painting or sculpture means presenting an image of something—such as a human body—as a perfect form, rather than with the imperfections that exist in actual human bodies. Realism means presenting objects as close as possible to the way they actually appear. **Ask:** What are some examples of the creation of ideal forms in contemporary American culture? *(Students might mention the use of computer technology to remove the imperfections in images of fashion models and movie stars.)*

View the Art ★

The Romans used structures such as the Pont du Gard to carry aqueducts across low ground. Built to bring water to the Roman provincial city of Nemausus (present-day Nîmes) in what is now southern France, the Pont du Gard was constructed entirely without mortar. **Ask:** What was the key structural element used by Roman builders here? *(the arch)*

Visual Arts

Roman art was heavily influenced by that of Greece. Many Roman artists were Greeks themselves or had trained in Greece. There was some difference in emphasis, however: whereas Greek artists had stressed ideal forms, the Romans were more interested in realism. The Roman government supported the arts, and many original Roman statues portrayed generals, senators, and emperors. Wealthy Romans were also patrons of the arts. Their homes had central courtyards for light and air but few outside windows, so they hired artists to paint frescoes on the large walls. To make a fresco, artists painted directly on a thin wet layer of plaster. These paintings, which include cityscapes, vistas of gardens, and scenes of everyday life, often appear as if they were viewed through a window. Today the surviving paintings provide a window back through time, revealing the kinds of clothes, architecture, and activities common to Roman life.

> "I found Rome a city of bricks and left it a city of marble."
>
> —Augustus

The Campana Relief (detail). Roman. Relief sculpture. British Museum, London.

Architecture

Above all, the Romans were builders. Theaters, temples, and public buildings sprang up all along the roads they built, from the rainy lowlands of Scotland to the arid deserts of Iraq. The city of Rome itself became the most magnificent anyone had ever seen. Although the styles of architecture were largely those that originated in Greece, the Romans made important advances in building techniques. They used rounded forms, such as arches, vaults, and domes, more frequently. In addition, they invented cement, built the first apartment houses in Eurasia, and piped hot air under bathing rooms to keep them warm.

Pont du Gard, ca. 50 AD. Languedoc-Roussillon, France. ★

352 UNIT 2 ANCIENT ROME

Reading Practice

Determine Main Ideas and Supporting Details Point out that each paragraph in the body of an essay should have a topic sentence. Remind students that structuring their paragraphs in this way will make writing easier. Read aloud the topic sentence of the paragraph under the heading "Architecture": "Above all, the Romans were builders."

Ask: How does the writer support this topic sentence? *(The writer presents details showing that the Romans built widely, built on a grand scale, and developed new building techniques.)*

Have students analyze other paragraphs of the introduction to analyze the topic sentence and supporting details.

Public Activities

The fact that Rome's grandest buildings included bathhouses, arenas, and amphitheaters shows how important bathing and entertainment were to social life in Rome. Many people visited the public baths every day, not only to use their hot and cold baths but also to enjoy the gymnasiums, libraries, gardens, and other recreational spaces bathhouses provided. Up to 3,000 people at a time might visit these massive structures, which were lavishly decorated with marble and gold.

Romans of all economic classes also attended the many public entertainments sponsored by the government. The largest Roman arena was the Circus Maximus, which seated about 150,000 people. Spectators would throng this arena to watch races in which two or four horses would pull chariots around the track at breathtaking speeds. Other entertainment was more violent. On holidays, crowds piled into amphitheaters such as the Colosseum to watch gladiatorial combats (the "games"). Such life-or-death struggles, which had originated among the Etruscans as

Circus gladiators fighting with animals. Roman. Relief sculpture. Museo Teatrale alla Scala, Milan, Italy.

sacred rituals, came to be considered crowd-pleasing entertainment. Even though many educated Romans condemned the games, they appealed to the masses who packed the amphitheaters in Rome and other cities throughout the empire.

PREVIEW **Big Ideas** of Ancient Rome **2**

1 Seize the Day	**2** Roman Myth	**3** The Imperial City
As Rome's power expanded, wealth poured into the city, fostering a cultured lifestyle. The Latin phrase *carpe diem* (literally "seize the day"), or "live for the moment," captured the spirit of this lifestyle. Building on the tradition of Greek poetry, Roman poets explored a variety of human concerns, including the passion of love and the quest for wisdom. **See page 354**	As Rome's empire grew, the Romans often associated their myths with those of the peoples they conquered. To celebrate the emperor Augustus and the divine destiny of the Roman Empire, the epic poet Virgil created a mythical past for Rome linked to the Greek legend of the Trojan War. **See page 355** **3**	As the center of a huge and powerful empire, Rome became an overcrowded capital, divided by extremes of wealth and poverty. Roman historians such as Tacitus vividly recorded what life was like in the imperial city during the early Roman Empire. **See page 356**

Advanced Learners/Pre-AP

DIFFERENTIATED INSTRUCTION

Architecture Roman architects carefully planned the public buildings they constructed. For example, the Colosseum had 80 entrances for spectators.

Have students work in small groups to design a stadium for their high school. In creating their proposal for the new stadium, each group should consider the following questions:

- How will the design of the stadium fit in with the character of the school?
- How many spectators need to be accommodated?
- What should be the number and the position of the exits?
- What type of facilities (such as locker rooms, snack bars, and restrooms) need to be included?

Text Element 2

Boxes Point out to students that the boxed and numbered elements at the bottom of page 353 identify "Big Ideas"—important features of Roman civilization—that will help them to better understand the literature in Part 2. **Ask:** What does the Latin phrase *carpe diem* mean? *("seize the day" or "live for the moment")*

Reading Strategy 3

Preview Ask: Previewing Big Idea 2, what do you expect the subject of Virgil's epic poem the *Aeneid* will be? *(Students should be able to anticipate that Virgil's epic will be related to the Trojan War.)*

Cultural History ☆

The Colosseum Begun around A.D. 70, this huge amphitheater took ten years to build. The amphitheater's name did not refer to its massive size; it was a reference to an enormous statue of the emperor Nero, called the Colossus, which once stood nearby. Dedicated in A.D. 80 with ten days of games, the Colosseum was used for fights between gladiators and other forms of combat.

Learning Objectives
Analyzing historical influences. (SE)
Comparing and contrasting. (TE)
Determining main idea and supporting details. (TE)

Teach

Reading Check

Answer: *Both Epicureanism and Stoicism stressed the importance of a virtuous life. The two philosophies differed in that Epicureanism emphasized the pursuit of personal pleasure while Stoicism stressed fulfilling one's duty and mastering emotions.*

Reading Strategy | 1

Connect to Personal Experience Have students read the first paragraph. **Ask:** Based on your own experience, is reason, experience, or instinct the best guide in making decisions?

ENGLISH LEARNERS Help students to understand the expression "throw caution to the wind." *(take a chance; do something although it is risky)*

View the Art ★

This mosaic of a skeleton carrying wine jugs probably came from the dining-room floor of a house in Pompeii. Skulls and skeletons were popular Roman design motifs.
Ask: How does this image relate to the idea of *carpe diem*? *(It reminds the viewer of death.)*

Big Idea 1
Seize the Day

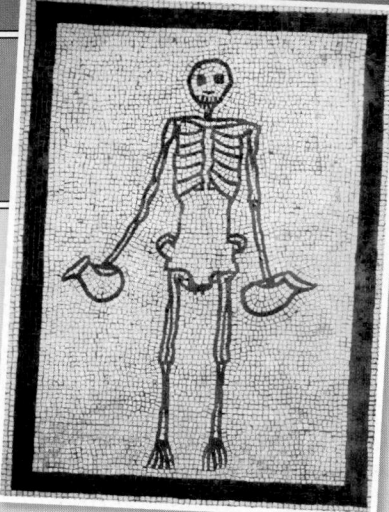

Human skeleton, 1st century AD. Roman. Mosaic pavement. Musée Archéologique, Naples. ★

1 **W**hat principles should guide human life? Should people primarily observe social traditions, seek insight in religion, or cultivate the use of reason? Is it better to throw caution to the wind in an attempt to live fully in the present moment? The ancient Romans addressed these questions and others like them.

Epicureanism

Two important influences on Roman thought were Epicureanism and Stoicism, schools of philosophy that developed in Greece around 300 B.C. Epicureanism (e pi kyū′rē ə ni zəm) took its name from its founder, Epicurus, who taught that the purpose of life is personal happiness, or the pursuit of pleasure. To achieve pleasure and freedom from anxiety, one must live prudently and virtuously. The greatest expression in Latin literature of Epicurus's ideas was the philosophical poem *De rerum natura* ("On the Nature of Things") by the Roman poet Lucretius.

> *"Even as we speak, envious time has passed:*
> *Seize the day, putting as little trust as possible in tomorrow!"*
>
> —Horace, from *Odes*, Book I, 11

The Golden Mean and *Carpe Diem*

Epicureanism also influenced the Roman poet Horace (see pages 363–366). In his poems, he urged readers to live virtuously by following the "golden mean"—that is, by steering a middle course and thereby avoiding extremes of behavior such as rashness and cowardice. Horace coined the phrase *carpe diem*, or seize the day, to capture the sweetness and brevity of human life—and the importance of living in the here and now. As Horace observed in a letter to a friend, "Amid hopes and cares, amid fears and passions, believe that every day that has dawned is your last."

Stoicism

Stoicism (stō ə si′zəm), a school of Greek philosophy opposed to Epicureanism, also influenced Roman thought. The name derives from the Greek word *stoa* (or "porch"), a reference to the site in the marketplace of Athens where Zeno, the founder of this school, taught his followers. Stoicism emphasized the importance of doing one's duty, living according to nature, and mastering emotions. It preached indifference to everything but virtue. This philosophy, which reinforced traditional Roman values such as self-control, family loyalty, and love of country, influenced many Roman writers, including the emperor Marcus Aurelius.

Reading Check

Compare and Contrast What are the similarities and differences between Epicureanism and Stoicism?

Reading Practice

Use Graphic Organizers
Point out that students can create graphic organizers suited to the particular type of information presented in the material they are reading. For example, the material on page 342 presents information about Epicureanism and Stoicism, the two dominant schools of philosophy in ancient Rome. A two-column table like the one started here, listing the main features of each school side by side, would be a good way to grasp the essential features of the two philosophies and their primary differences. Have students copy and complete the chart.

Epicureanism	Stoicism

Big Idea 2
Roman Myth

The earliest Roman religious practices involved rituals in the home presided over by the paterfamilias, the father of the family. These rituals centered on the worship of the guardian spirits, including family ancestors and minor divinities known as the household gods.

State Religion

Augustus restored traditional festivals to revive the state religion, which focused on the public worship of gods and goddesses, including Jupiter, Juno, Venus, and Mars. In addition, beginning with Augustus, the Roman Senate sometimes declared emperors to be divine, thus linking religion and patriotism.

To honor Augustus and proclaim the destiny of Rome, Virgil (see pages 376–398) composed his epic poem, the *Aeneid*. It traced the ancestry of the Romans to Aeneas, a Trojan prince who sailed to Italy after Troy fell to the Greeks. His descendants were Romulus and Remus, twins who, according to legend, founded Rome in 753 B.C.

Kore or Hera enthroned sprinkling the peplos and nuptial diadem. 5th century BC. Terracotta. Museo Archeologico, Taranto, Italy.

Like the Greeks, the Romans believed in many gods. They assumed the peoples whom they conquered worshipped the same gods, only under different names. For example, the Romans took the Greek Zeus as their own Jupiter.

The Romans believed their success in establishing an empire was a manifestation of divine favor. As the Roman statesman Cicero asserted in the first century B.C., "We have overcome all the nations of the world, because we have realized that the world is directed and governed by the gods." At the same time, the Romans generally tolerated other religions.

> "Rome shall extend her empire to earth's end, her ambition to the sky...."
>
> —Virgil, from the *Aeneid*, Book VI

Christianity

An exception to this policy of religious tolerance was Christianity. Ironically, early Christians often were accused of atheism, since they denied the existence of the pagan gods. Eventually, however, Christians gained respect for their work in feeding the poor and tending the sick. And the virtues they taught—piety, hard work, courage—were those the Romans had always admired. By the time the emperor Constantine legalized Christianity, it had already become widespread. In A.D. 380, Theodosius declared Christianity the official religion of the Roman Empire. **2**

Reading Check

Make Generalizations How did the Romans respond to the religions of other peoples?

English Learners

DIFFERENTIATED INSTRUCTION

Intermediate Point out that many English words are related to the names of Roman gods. For example *Jove*, an alternative form of Jupiter, is the origin of the word *jovial*, meaning "good-humored" or "cheerful." Have students use a dictionary to identify the meaning of each of the following words and the name of the Roman god that is related to it.

1. martial *(relating to war; Mars, god of war)*
2. volcanic *(powerfully explosive; Vulcan, god of fire)*
3. saturnine *(gloomy, Saturn, harvest god)*
4. mercurial *(quick, changeable; Mercury, messenger of the gods)*
5. cupidity *(desire for wealth; Cupid, god of love)*

UNIT TWO
PART 2

Teach

Reading Check

Answer: *Romans were generally tolerant of other religions, allowing the worship of native gods and goddesses throughout their provinces. One major exception to this was Christianity, which Romans saw as harmful to the Roman state because Christians refused to worship the state gods and emperors.*

Reading Strategy   2

Analyze Cultural Context **Ask:** How were state religion and patriotism linked in Roman culture? *(The emperor was given divine status, and emperor-worship became a patriotic observance.)* **Ask:** How did this link between religion and patriotism affect Roman attitudes toward the early Christians? *(The Christians' refusal to practice emperor-worship caused the Romans to regard them as disloyal to the empire.)*

APPROACHING You might use a diagram to help students grasp this cultural relationship. *(Roman emperor viewed as divine > Roman state religion includes emperor-worship > Christians refuse to practice emperor-worship > Romans view Christians as disloyal to empire)*

Learning Objectives
Comparing and contrasting. (SE)
Using graphic organizers. (TE)
Analyzing cultural context. (TE)

Teach

Reading Check

Answer: *Fire was a constant threat in Roman apartment buildings because of the use of moveable stoves, torches, candles, and lamps within the rooms.*

Connect to Contemporary Issues As they read the material on page 356, have students consider how Rome's problems resembled those of contemporary American society. **Ask:** Which problems of ancient Rome do Americans face today? *(Students may mention such problems as crowded cities, income inequality, widespread poverty, and large-scale disasters.)*

View the Art ★

Chariot races were the main events of the public games staged at Rome's Circus Maximus, a huge amphitheater that could seat 250,000 spectators. Roman chariots were light, two-wheeled vehicles drawn by teams of swift horses. In a typical race, four to six chariots sped seven times around the track at the Circus. Collisions were frequent, and serious or fatal injuries often resulted. **Ask:** What technique is employed to give a three-dimensional realism to the image of the horse? *(Different colors of stones create effects of highlights and shadows, heightening the illusion of rounded forms.)*

Big Idea 3
The Imperial City

At the center of the vast Roman Empire was the ancient city of Rome. Truly a capital city, Rome had the largest population of any city in the empire—nearly one million people by the time of Augustus. Rome was the place to be for anyone with ambition. As a result, people from all parts of the empire thronged to this city.

Living Conditions

Like any huge city, Rome had its problems. Because of the congestion, cart and wagon traffic was banned from city streets during the day. At night, however, the noise from these vehicles often disturbed sleep. Walking in Rome at night was not without risks; although Augustus had organized a police force, people were still assaulted or robbed.

> *"All degraded and shameful practices collect and flourish in the capital."*
>
> —Tacitus, from the *Annals*

An enormous gulf divided a rich minority from the masses of poor people. The rich lived in comfortable villas; the poor were crowded into tenements called *insulae* (Latin for "islands"), which might tower six stories high. These timber-frame buildings were potential firetraps because of the use of moveable stoves, torches, candles, and lamps. In A.D. 64, as the historian Tacitus describes in his *Annals* (see pages 401–407), fire destroyed most of the city.

Bread and Circuses

Rome boasted public buildings unequaled anywhere in the empire. Its temples, markets, baths, theaters, government buildings, and amphitheaters gave the city an aura of grandeur and magnificence. Still, beneath the surface glitter, poverty was widespread. During Augustus's reign, about three-fourths of the million people living in Rome were impoverished. From that time on, the emperors provided free grain merely to help the urban poor survive.

According to the satirist Juvenal, the Roman masses craved only two things: "Bread and circuses." In addition to free grain, the emperors also provided public spectacles as part of the great religious festivals in the city. These festivals featured three types of entertainment: horse and chariot races, which attracted hundreds of thousands at the Circus Maximus; dramatic performances staged in the theaters; and the most popular of the Roman public spectacles, the gladiatorial games.

Chariot Coachman and Horse. Roman. Mosaic.

Reading Check

Analyze Cause-and-Effect Relationships How did living conditions in ancient Rome contribute to the fire in A.D. 64?

Grammar Practice

Use Italics Remind students that italic type is used with titles of books, magazines, newspapers, and works of art; names of specific ships, trains, planes, and other vehicles; foreign words; and words introduced as vocabulary.

Have students select which words and phrases in the following sentences should be in italic type and why the word or phrase should be italicized.

1. The Latin phrase carpe diem means "seize the day." (carpe diem; *foreign term*)

2. Virgil's Aeneid is an epic about the mythical origin of Rome. (Aeneid; *title of literary work*)

3. The mythical hero Jason sailed in the Argo to find the Golden Fleece. (Argo; *name of ship*)

WRAP-UP

Legacy of the Period 2

Roman achievements in language, law, and government greatly influenced modern civilization. This legacy is so pervasive that, in a cultural sense, Rome never really "fell." The Latin language of the empire survives in the Romance languages, including Italian, French, Spanish, and Portuguese. Although English is not a Romance language, much of its vocabulary derives from Latin. The Roman alphabet is still used for writing languages throughout the world. Another monumental contribution to the modern world was the Roman legal system. Some of the fundamental principles of modern law, including the right to trial by jury, were part of the Roman system. Representative government also has its roots in ancient Rome.

Rome greatly influenced subsequent European civilizations. The cultural movement known as Neoclassicism, which dominated European art, architecture, and literature in the late 1700s, used Roman civilization as its standard for excellence.

A Funny Thing Happened on the Way to the Forum. Mitchell Gerber. Manhattan, NY.

Cultural and Literary Links

- William Shakespeare based two of his greatest tragedies, *Julius Caesar* and *Antony and Cleopatra*, on events from Roman history.

- The discovery of the buried Roman cities of Pompeii and Herculaneum in the mid-1700s contributed to the development of archaeology.

- For the title of his play *Arms and the Man*, Irish playwright George Bernard Shaw used the famous opening lines of Virgil's *Aeneid*, "Arma virumque cano" ("I sing of arms and the man").

- The 1962 musical *A Funny Thing Happened on the Way to the Forum* was based on the comedies by the Roman playwright Plautus.

LOG ON ▶ **Literature** Online

Unit Resources For additional skills practice, go to glencoe.com and enter QuickPass code GLW6053u2.

Activities

Use what you have learned about the period to do one of these activities.

1. **Follow Up** Go back to Looking Ahead on page 347 and answer the questions.

2. **Contrast Literary Periods** In England during the early seventeenth century, the Cavalier Poets were inspired by Roman authors such as Horace. Research one of the Cavalier Poets, such as Robert Herrick, and write an essay comparing his treatment of the theme of *carpe diem* with that of a Roman poet.

3. **Build Visual Literacy** Collect images of modern buildings showing the influence of Roman architec-

ture. Create a visual display showing elements of Roman architecture (the arch, vault, and dome).

4. **Take Notes** Use this graphic organizer to keep track of the literary elements you learn in this part.

 FOLDABLES Study Organizer   **BOUND BOOK**

Nonfiction
Short Stories
Poems
Reader-Response Journal

INTRODUCTION **357**

Connect to Personal Experience Point out to students that if they have ever sat in a domed stadium or voted in a student election, they have benefited from Roman innovations in engineering and government.

Ask: What other legacies of the Roman world are still with us? *(Students might offer such as examples as the names of the planets, signs of the Zodiac, and the months of the year).*

(APPROACHING) If students need help, draw their attention to a calendar or show them the Latin motto on an American coin.

(ENGLISH LEARNERS) Ask students from other countries to offer examples of the legacy of Rome in their homelands.

Activities

1. **Follow Up** Students should support their answers with details from this introduction.

2. **Contrast Literary Periods** Encourage students to provide several points of comparison.

3. **Build Visual Literacy** Suggest that students annotate the images they present, identifying Roman elements found in modern buildings.

4. **Take Notes** After students finish each selection, have them list details in the graphic organizer that relate to the selection's literary element.

Learning Objectives
Analyzing cause-and-effect relationships. (SE)
Connecting to contemporary issues. (TE)
Analyzing art. (TE)

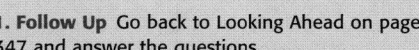
Approaching Level

DIFFERENTIATED INSTRUCTION 🐾

 SMALL GROUP
Roman Situation Comedy Some students may find it difficult to focus on and comprehend the historical and cultural background presented in the introduction. These students may be helped using activities that stimulate their interest and focus their attention.

Have small mixed groups brainstorm a list of what they know about ancient Roman life. Then, using their lists, have groups

plan a situation comedy that might have aired in ancient Rome. What issues would drive the plot? Where would the action take place? What kind of costumes and props would the cast need? Have groups share their plans with the class.

Focus

Bellringer Options

Selection Focus
   Transparency 16
Daily Language
   Transparency 29

Or ask: What is your favorite type of poetry? If students are reluctant to choose a favorite type of poetry, encourage them to describe which forms of art or media they prefer.

Literary History

Displeasing Caesar In Suetonius's biography, *Life of Julius Caesar*, he relates the story of Catullus and Caesar. He says that Catullus, in his writings, had the nerve to ridicule Caesar and his close associates. Caesar believed these comments were so damaging to his image that they would tarnish history's memory of him. Catullus was forced to apologize to the future dictator; Caesar accepted the apology immediately by inviting the poet to dinner.

The Poems of Catullus

Meet **Catullus**
(c. 84–54 B.C.)

Gaius Valerius Catullus (kə tul′əs) was the first great lyric poet of ancient Rome. Although little is known about him, it is possible—mostly on the basis of his poems—to sketch an outline of his life. He came from a wealthy and elite family in Verona, a city in northern Italy. Catullus spent much of his short life in Rome but traveled to Bithynia (a Roman province on the southern shore of the Black Sea) to briefly serve on the staff of the Roman governor there.

> "Lesbia, let us live and love,
> And think what crabbed old men
>   resent
> With all their talk, not worth a cent."
>
> —Catullus

New Style of Poetry At the time Catullus began writing, Roman poetry was largely devoted to long, serious poems on patriotic themes. Catullus's poetry, however, was in the style of the *neoteroi*. Members of this literary circle scorned poets who blindly followed tradition. Instead, they valued innovation in subject matter and technique. They especially admired the Greek poets of Alexandria for their sophistication and craftsmanship.

Catullus was strongly influenced by the short personal lyrics written by Sappho (see pages 241–247). His highly polished and witty short poems are like personal letters. Their fluid style gives the impression that he simply poured his thoughts and feelings onto his writing tablet. Catullus wrote about love affairs, described playful encounters with friends, repeated gossip, and mocked those who aroused his disapproval—even the formidable Julius Caesar, his father's friend.

Rapture and Agony Catullus's simple, direct style earned him acclaim as a lyric poet of uncommon individuality. He had a major influence on the work of later Roman authors such as Horace, Virgil, and Ovid. He is remembered today for the immediacy and passion of his love poetry. The classical historian Edith Hamilton observed that Catullus "put love's rapture and agony into words so direct, they seem to leave no veil between the reader and the poet's heart."

LOG ON ▶ **Literature** Online

Author Search For more about Catullus, go to glencoe.com and enter QuickPass code GLW6053u2.

Selection Skills

Literary Elements
- Speaker (SE pp. 359, 361–362)
- Paradox (TE p. 360)

← **Poems of Catullus** →

Writing Skills/Grammar
- Poem (SE p. 362)

Reading Skills
- Make Generalizations (SE pp. 359, 361–362)
- Recognize Author's Purpose (TE p. 360)

Vocabulary Skills
- Academic Vocabulary (SE p. 362)

Literature and Reading Preview

Connect to the Poems

Have you ever had mixed feelings about someone? Write a journal entry about this person, providing examples of his or her behavior to help explain your conflicting feelings.

Build Background

Catullus's best-known poems are about a woman he calls "Lesbia." This pseudonym apparently pays homage to Lesbos, the birthplace of Sappho. The real "Lesbia" was probably Clodia, sister of Clodius, a notorious political gangster. Although the speaker sometimes describes moments of happiness with her, in most of the poems he expresses anguish over her behavior and wishes he could overcome his obsessive love.

Set Purposes for Reading

Big Idea Seize the Day

The Latin motto *carpe diem* ("seize the day") characterizes the spirit of the Romans' cultured lifestyle. As you read, ask yourself, How do Catullus's poems reflect this spirit?

Literary Element Speaker

The **speaker** of a poem is the voice that talks to the reader or to the person addressed by the poem. Sometimes the speaker's voice is that of the poet. Other times, poets create characters who may express concerns or emotions that the poet does not share. As you read, ask yourself, How would you characterize the speaker of these poems?

Reading Strategy Make Generalizations

When you **make generalizations**, you draw conclusions based on specific details. To make generalizations, ask yourself questions such as the following: What does the author suggest about the speaker or life in general? How do these poems relate to my prior knowledge and background information?

....

Tip: Take Notes As you read, list your questions and generalizations in a chart like the one below.

Questions	Generalizations
What does the author suggest about the speaker?	

Learning Objectives

For pages 358–362

In studying this text, you will focus on the following objectives:

Literary Study: Analyzing speaker.

Reading: Making generalizations.

Writing: Writing a poem.

Marriage Scene. Relief from Roman Funerary Altar. Museo Nazionale Romano, Rome, Italy.

CATULLUS **359**

Before You Read

Focus

Summary

In these poems, the speaker speaks of his love for Lesbia and the agony it causes him. Though she hurts him and he doubts her sincerity, he cannot help but love her.

 For summaries in languages other than English, see Unit 2 Teaching Resources Book, pp. 147–152.

Literary History

Manuscripts in Peril Although the works of Catullus were well regarded during his lifetime, from the late second century through the twelfth century his works were largely unstudied and therefore went out of circulation. The only existing manuscript was discovered in 1300 and copied twice before it was lost. One of those copies was in turn copied twice, only to be lost as well. Therefore, there are three surviving copies of the poems, one each in the Bodleian Library at Oxford, the Bibliothèque Nationale in Paris, and the Vatican Library in Rome. The copies vary, however, due to human errors during the process of transcription. Using elements from all three, scholars have reconstructed an "archetype"— their best guess at Catullus's originals.

English Learners

DIFFERENTIATED INSTRUCTION

Advanced Ask English learners if they know of any art forms from their cultures comparable to lyric poetry. Perhaps they know folk songs, myths, or modern poetry that relates the idea of the happiness and sadness of love. Have students translate examples of them or explain them to the class.

Advanced Learners/Pre-AP

DIFFERENTIATED INSTRUCTION

Write a Poem Have advanced students write their own poem about someone for whom they have strong feelings, romantic or otherwise. Tell them that, like Catullus's poems, theirs do not need to be long or complicated in order to be effective. Urge them to use simple language to convey strong points, and let them know that they can create an alias for the subject of their poem, as Catullus does.

Teach

Literary Element   1

Paradox Ask: What about this statement is paradoxical? *(The fact that the speaker loves Lesbia and dislikes her at the same time is paradoxical.)*

ADVANCED For advanced learners, **ask:** What can you infer from this paradox about the emotional state of the speaker? *(The speaker feels confused and conflicted about his feelings for Lesbia.)*

For additional literary element practice, see Unit 2 Teaching Resources Book, p. 153.

Big Idea   2

Epicureanism and Stoicism
Ask: Do you think the speaker of these poems would be a Stoic or an Epicurean? Why? *(Most students will say he would be an Epicurean. He wishes to pursue pleasure in loving Lesbia, like an Epicurean, and is not seeking to master his emotions as a Stoic would.)*

View the Art ★

Answer: *Neara's dress, the type of bench she sits on, the scroll she is holding, and the artwork behind her all indicate that the scene takes place in antiquity.*

Neaera Reading a Letter from Catullus, 1894 Henry J. Hudson. Oil on canvas 155.5 x 104.5 cm. Bradford City Art Gallery & Museum, England.

 **View the Art** In this painting, Henry Hudson, a nineteenth-century painter of portraits and figures, may have wanted to suggest an imaginary love affair between Catullus and the nymph Neaera, who appears in the *Odyssey*. What are some of the details the artist uses to indicate his subject is from ancient Rome?

Reading Practice

 Recognize Author's Purpose
Explain to students that recognizing an author's purpose often provides insight into a work. Discuss with students the different purposes for writing. For example, many narratives are written to tell a story and to entertain an audience. Ask students what they think is the main purpose of lyric poetry.

Have students work in small groups to review the poems and discuss their content. Ask students to suggest possible purposes the author may have had in writing the poems. Make sure groups cite examples from the poems to support their suggestions.

Poems of Catullus

Translated by Carl Sesar

My woman says there's nobody she'd rather marry
than me, not even Jupiter[1] himself if he asked her.
She says, but what a woman says to a hungry lover
you might as well scribble in wind and swift water.

My mind's sunk so low, Lesbia, because of you,
wrecked itself on your account so bad already,
1 I couldn't like you if you were the best of women,
or stop loving you, no matter what you do.

I hate her and I love her. Don't ask me why. **2**
It's the way I feel, that's all, and it hurts.

---

1. *Jupiter*, also called Jove, is the chief Roman god. He is the god
   of light, the sky, and the weather. In Greek mythology, he is known
   as Zeus.

3 Speaker *What idea does the speaker convey with the word*
scribble *in this image?*

4 Make Generalizations *What generalization might you make
about the speaker's personality based on this statement?*

CATULLUS **361**

Teach

Literary Element | 3

Speaker Answer: *The speaker
does not believe what his woman
says. The word* scribble *suggests
something scrawled in haste and
not worth keeping.*

Reading Strategy | 4

**Make Generalizations
Answer:** *The speaker seems
prone to feeling extreme
emotions.*

Literary History ☆

Lesbia Catullus's "Lesbia" is
commonly believed to be one of
the three Clodia sisters of Publius
Clodius Pulcher. The sisters were
widely gossiped about because
of various scandals surrounding
them. Most likely, "Lesbia" was the
Clodia married to the governor of
Cisalpine Gaul, the region Catullus
was from. After her husband died,
Clodia was courted by Marcus
Caelius Rufus—probably the
Rufus whom Catullus accuses
of betraying his friendship and
stealing his love's affection in poem
LXXVII. Clodia later brought charges
against Caelius for attempting
to poison her, but Caelius was
acquitted.

English Learners

DIFFERENTIATED INSTRUCTION

Intermediate Remind students learning
English that reflexive pronouns are formed
by adding -*self* or -*selves* to certain
personal and possessive pronouns.

Write on the board: **myself, ourselves,
yourself, yourselves, himself, herself,
itself, themselves**

Explain that a reflexive pronoun refers to
a noun or another pronoun. Pair students
together and have them write two
sentences each using reflexive pronouns.
Then have them trade sentences and
identify what each reflexive pronoun
refers to.

Learning Objectives
Analyzing speaker. (SE)
Making generalizations. (SE)
Analyzing paradox. (TE)
Recognizing author's purpose. (TE)

After You Read

Assess

1. Answers will vary.
2. (a) She would marry him even over the god Jupiter. (b) He does not put much stock in what the woman says. He thinks she is fickle.
3. The speaker loves Lesbia but also resents her for the torment she has put him through.
4. The tone, which is anguished and passionate, reflects the speaker's emotional turmoil.
5. He obviously loves the woman whom he discusses, but he finds women somewhat cruel and flighty.
6. His style is straightforward; he expresses emotions in direct and simple language.
7. The speaker pursues a passionate, romantic relationship in the present with little concern for the future.
8. Students should describe the character's feelings and the way he or she resolved a conflict.

Literary Element

1. Students are likely to suggest that all three poems have the same speaker because the emotions presented are connected.
2. Students may suggest *lovelorn, infatuated, smitten,* or *obsessed.*

Reading Strategy

1. (a) First poem: The speaker doubts his lover's sincerity. Second and third poems: The speaker is depressed and emotionally torn. (b) The details suggest that the speaker is conflicted and filled with passion.
2. Possible generalization: Romantic relationships are overwhelmingly passionate and painful.

362

After You Read

Respond and Think Critically

Respond and Interpret

1. What emotions did these poems stir in you?
2. (a)What does the speaker say the woman professes in the first poem? (b)Does it seem as if the speaker believes what the woman says? Explain.
3. An **internal conflict** is a struggle within a character. What internal conflict does the speaker reveal in the second poem?
4. **Tone** is the attitude an author or speaker takes toward a subject. What does the tone of the third poem reveal about the speaker's attitude toward his subject?

Analyze and Evaluate

5. What attitude does the speaker in these poems appear to have toward women? Explain.
6. How would you describe Catullus's style and use of poetic techniques?

Connect

7. **Big Idea** **Seize the Day** How does the speaker of these poems live for the moment?
8. **Connect to Today** Can you think of a character in modern literature, film, or television who, like the speaker in these poems, has conflicting emotions about someone? How does the character resolve the conflict?

Literary Element | Speaker

Understanding the **speaker** and his or her attitude can help you understand a poem's meaning more fully.

1. Do you think all three of these poems by Catullus have the same speaker? Why or why not?
2. What adjectives would you use to describe the speaker or speakers of these poems?

Reading Strategy | Make Generalizations

You can **make generalizations** by drawing conclusions about themes and ideas in Catullus's poems. Review the chart you filled in on page 359.

1. (a)What details do you find in each poem? (b)What connections do you see among them?
2. What generalization can you make about Catullus's views on romantic relationships?

LOG ON **Literature** Online

Selection Resources For Selection Quizzes, eFlash-cards, and Reading-Writing Connection activities, go to glencoe.com and enter QuickPass code GLW6053u2.

362 UNIT 2 ANCIENT ROME

Academic Vocabulary

*Catullus's poems, though short, suggest a **series** of events between the speaker and his beloved Lesbia.*

The word *series* has different meanings in different contexts. Using context clues, try to figure out the meaning of *series* in each sentence below and explain the difference between the two meanings.

1. One of my happiest memories is when the Red Sox won the World **Series**.
2. I was amazed when my uncle began to play a **series** of notes on the bagpipe.

For more on academic vocabulary, see pages 36–37 and R83–R85.

Writing

Write a Poem Write a poem in response to one of the poems by Catullus. If you wish, you may speak in your own voice, or you may use Lesbia as the speaker of your poem. Read the poem aloud to the class when you are finished. Explain why you decided to use a particular speaker in your poem.

Progress Check

Can students make generalizations?

If No → See Unit 2 Teaching Resources Book, p. 154.

Academic Vocabulary

1. a group of games
2. a succession of related things

Writing

Students' poems should
- express feelings that make the identity of the speaker apparent.
- respond to one of Catullus's poems.

Before You Read

Better to Live, Licinius

Meet **Horace**

(65–8 B.C.)

Horace knew from experience that life could take sudden and strange turns. His father, a freed slave, sent him to Rome and later to Athens to study Greek philosophy and poetry. While Horace was in Athens, he was caught up in the civil war that erupted after Julius Caesar's assassination. Horace helped command one of Brutus's legions against the forces of Octavian and Mark Antony. Unfortunately for Horace, Brutus's troops were defeated in the battle of Philippi. When an amnesty permitted Horace to return to Rome, he found his father had died and his father's land had been confiscated. Suddenly penniless, Horace worked as a government clerk and began writing poetry.

Finding a Patron Horace's poetry soon caught the eye of the poet Virgil, who recommended him to Maecenas (mi sē′nəs), a wealthy statesman and patron of the arts. Horace and Maecenas became close friends, and through him Horace met Octavian—who later became the emperor Augustus Caesar. With Maecenas's and the emperor's support, Horace became one of Rome's leading poets, occasionally writing patriotic verse for the government.

Lasting Influence Horace's *Odes* are considered his masterpieces. They explore topics such as love, patriotism, peace, and friendship. Though patterned on earlier Greek models, Horace's odes are shorter and less formal, yet more sensitive and personal. According to critic Grant Showerman, Horace's work "is the eloquent record of the life of Rome in an age which for intensity is unparalleled in the annals of the ancient world." In addition to providing snapshots of daily life under Augustus, these odes reflect a personality that is wise, witty, and warm.

Horace's purpose for writing poetry was twofold: to teach and to delight. In his poems he often praised "golden moderation," or the "golden mean." Horace also taught the value of living for the moment. He coined the expression *carpe diem*, or "seize the day," to capture this idea, which has inspired countless authors.

> "The poet's aim is either to profit
> or to please,
> Or to blend in one the delightful
> and the useful."
>
> —Horace

 Literature Online

Author Search For more about Horace, go to glencoe.com and enter QuickPass code GLW6053u2.

HORACE **363**

Before You Read

Focus

Bellringer Options

Selection Focus
    Transparency 17

Daily Language Practice
    Transparency 30

Or ask: What is the difference between courage and foolishness? Ask students to give examples, such as running into a burning home to save a child (courageous) versus a computer (foolish). Explore whether students think the difference is motivation, the amount of risk involved, or something else.

Interactive Read and Write
Other options for teaching this selection can be found in Interactive Read and Write for On-Level Learners, pp. 101–108.

Selection Skills

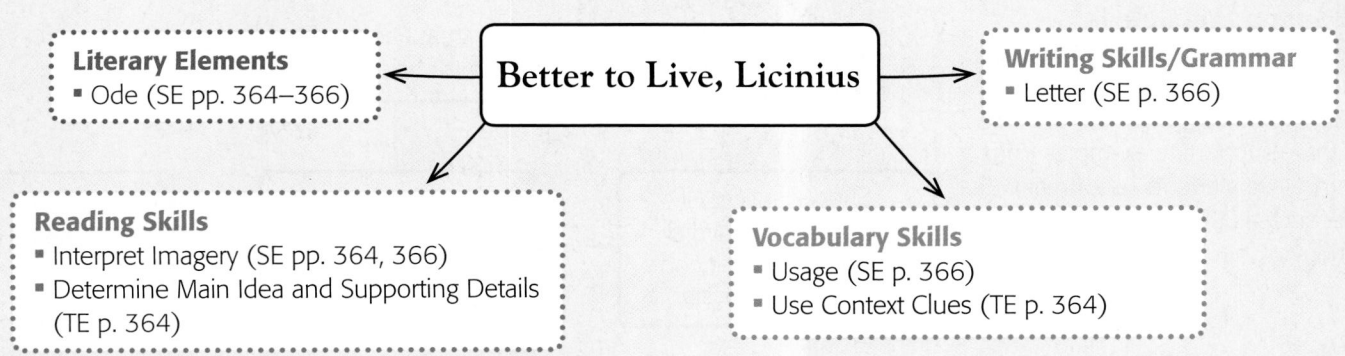

Literary Elements
- Ode (SE pp. 364–366)

Better to Live, Licinius

Writing Skills/Grammar
- Letter (SE p. 366)

Reading Skills
- Interpret Imagery (SE pp. 364, 366)
- Determine Main Idea and Supporting Details (TE p. 364)

Vocabulary Skills
- Usage (SE p. 366)
- Use Context Clues (TE p. 364)

Before You Read

Focus

Summary

In the ode "Better to Live, Licinius," Horace promotes a life of balance, according to his belief in "golden moderation." Horace believes that a wise person neither exults in times of peace nor despairs in times of uncertainty.

 For summaries in languages other than English, see Unit 2 Teaching Resources Book, pp. 157–162.

Vocabulary

Use Context Clues Have students write sentences with context clues for each vocabulary word. Have them leave a blank for the vocabulary word and ask a partner to use the context clues to guess the correct word. Encourage students to use a variety of types of context clues, such as cause-effect, synonym, contrast, definition, and example. Have students identify their best sentences to share with the class.

 For additional vocabulary practice, see Unit 2 Teaching Resources Book, p. 165.

Literature and Reading Preview

Connect to the Poem

What is the best piece of practical advice you have ever received? Freewrite for a few minutes about these "words of wisdom" and explain why you consider them important.

Build Background

The ode "Better to Live, Licinius" is probably addressed to the brother-in-law of Maecenas, Horace's patron. Aulus Terentius Varro Murena (formerly known as Licinius Murena) rose to the consulship, Rome's highest official position, in 23 B.C. The emperor Augustus soon had him removed from office because of his outspoken political views. Murena was executed the following year for allegedly conspiring against Augustus.

Set Purposes for Reading

Big Idea Seize the Day

In Horace's time, Romans led a cultured lifestyle reflected in the theme "seize the day." As you read, ask yourself, What connections do you see between this poem and that theme?

Literary Element Ode

An **ode** is a lyric poem, or a song, with an elevated style and exalted or enthusiastic tone. Before Horace, most odes were written to glorify public figures or to commemorate important events. Horace developed a more meditative and personal type of ode. As you read, ask yourself, What characteristics of an ode does this poem reflect?

Reading Strategy Interpret Imagery

Imagery refers to the word pictures that authors create to evoke emotional responses. In creating imagery, authors use sensory details that appeal to sight, hearing, touch, taste, or smell. When you **interpret** imagery, you analyze these word pictures and determine the emotional responses they evoke in the reader. As you read, ask yourself, What do the images in this poem mean?

Tip: Take Notes As you read the poem, use a chart like the one below to make associations between images.

Image (line)	Appeals to Sense of . . . (line)	Emotional Response

364 UNIT 2 ANCIENT ROME

Learning Objectives

For pages 363–366

In studying this text, you will focus on the following objectives:

Literary Study: Analyzing ode.

Reading: Interpreting imagery.

Writing: Writing a letter.

Vocabulary

moderation (mod′ə rā′shən) *n.* avoiding or limiting excesses or extremes; self-control; p. 365 *His limited income forced him to practice moderation when he went shopping.*

stern (sturn) *adj.* harsh or severe in manner; firm or unyielding; p. 365 *His stern look revealed his disapproval of our conduct.*

swell (swel) *v.* to increase in size or volume; expand; p. 365 *Pumping air into the tire caused it to swell.*

Tip: Word Usage When you encounter a new word, it might help you to ask a question about that word. For example, What jobs might require a **stern** attitude?

Reading Practice

 SMALL GROUP

Determine Main Idea and Supporting Details

After students finish reading the poem, have them reread it in small groups. Ask each group to paraphrase the main idea and list three supporting examples from the poem. Have students use a main idea organizer such as the one here.

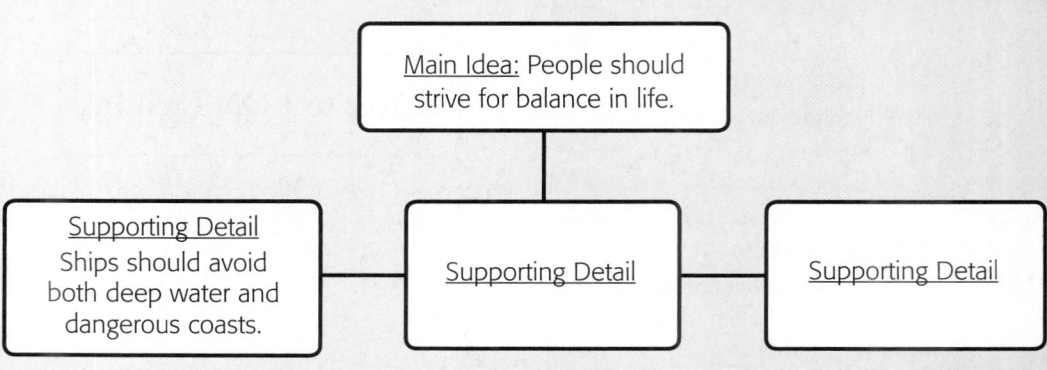

Main Idea: People should strive for balance in life.

Supporting Detail: Ships should avoid both deep water and dangerous coasts.

Supporting Detail

Supporting Detail

364

Better to Live, Licinius

Horace
Translated by Joseph P. Clancy

Better to live, Licinius, not always
rushing into deep water, and not, when fear
of storms makes you shiver, pushing too close to
the dangerous coast.

5 A man who prizes golden **moderation**
stays safely clear of the filth of a run-down
building, stays prudently out of a palace
others will envy.

The giant pine is more often troubled by the
10 wind, and the tallest towers collapse with a
heavier fall, and bolts of lightning strike the
tops of the mountains.

Hopeful in the bad times, fearful in the good times,
that is the man who has readied his heart for
15 the turn of the dice. Jupiter brings back foul
winters; he also

takes them away. No, if things are bad now, they
will not remain that way: sometimes Apollo
wakes the silent Muse with his lyre° and is not
20   always an archer.

When troubles come, show that you have a stout heart
and a **stern** face: but see that you have the good sense
to take in sail° when it **swells** in a wind that's
a little too kind.

A Boat, 2nd century AD. Roman relief from a stone sarcophagus. Museo della Civilta Romana, Rome.

18–19 Apollo: god of sunlight, prophecy, archery, music, and poetry, was also guardian of the **Muses**, who presided over the arts. As god of music he is often shown playing a **lyre**, a harp-like instrument.

23 to take in sail: to roll up the sail on a boat to reduce speed.

1 **Seize the Day** *Why does Horace admire this type of person?*

2 **Ode** *Why might these references to Apollo and the Muse be fitting in this poem?*

Vocabulary

moderation (mod′ə rā′shən) *n.* avoiding or limiting excesses or extremes; self-control

stern (sturn) *adj.* harsh or severe in manner; firm or unyielding

swell (swel) *v.* to increase in size or volume; expand

HORACE **365**

Teach

Big Idea   1

Seize the Day **Answer:** *This type of person is prepared to respond to whatever challenges or opportunities life offers.*

(ADVANCED) Ask advanced learners to relate the term *carpe diem* to Augustus, whom Horace held in high regard. (*As Rome's first emperor, Augustus used his power to transform Roman life and maintain a long peace.*)

Literary Element   2

Ode **Answer:** *Odes are written in a lofty style. A reference to the gods is fitting in an ode.*

For additional literary element practice, see Unit 2 Teaching Resources Book, p. 163.

View the Art

Ask: What part of the poem does this image relate to? (*It relates to the first stanza and the last two lines.*)

Learning Objectives
Analyzing ode. (SE)
Determining main idea and supporting details. (TE)

English Learners

DIFFERENTIATED INSTRUCTION

Intermediate Encourage students to deepen their understanding of the ode by paraphrasing each stanza. Have students use a thesaurus to search for appropriate synonyms, rearrange sentences, shorten sentences, replace imagery with their own examples, and so on to make the ode reflect the students' own voices. Then have them share their paraphrases in small groups. Provide an example for the first stanza, such as "A good way to live, Licinius, is to not always jump into a fire. Or when storms scare you, don't run outside."

Advanced Learners/Pre-AP

DIFFERENTIATED INSTRUCTION

Readers' Theater Encourage advanced learners to perform the ode for the class. Have students work in groups of six, one for each stanza, and annotate the poem with words they want to emphasize, places where they should insert long pauses, and places where they want to shift emotion. Have groups discuss annotations for each stanza and practice performing their parts. Then have them present the ode.

After You Read

Assess

1. Answers will vary.
2. Do not make rash decisions or take great risks.
3. One should steer a middle course and avoid extremes.
4. (a) They are more likely to be troubled by wind, to fall, and to be struck by lightning, respectively. (b) Possible answer: Those who rise to the greatest heights are often the least secure.
5. (a) A person is compared with a ship. (b) The metaphor returns in the last line when the poet advises Licinius to "take in sail."
6. The tone seems to be fatherly, wise, and prudent.
7. Fate is uncontrollable but cyclical.
8. Students may say that his advice refutes the theme because living in moderation may prevent one from enjoying each moment.
9. Answers will vary.

Literary Element

1. He may have been addressing a friend, or he may have chosen to write this way in order to make the message more personal.
2. Some students may say preaching moderation in an exalted style seems somewhat inappropriate.

Progress Check

Can students interpret imagery?

If No → See Unit 2 Teaching Resources Book, p. 164.

 For additional selection assessment, see Assessment Resources Book, pp. 85–86.

366

After You Read

Respond and Think Critically

Respond and Interpret

1. How do you feel about the speaker's advice in this poem?
2. How would you summarize the first stanza of the poem?
3. According to the speaker, how should one live if one prizes "golden moderation"?
4. (a) What happens to the giant pine, the tallest towers, and the tops of mountains? (b) What idea about people do these images suggest?

Analyze and Evaluate

5. (a) What comparison is made in stanza 1? (b) How is this metaphor extended later in the poem?

Literary Element Ode

Most **odes** are poems of address, in which the speaker speaks directly to someone or something.

1. Why might Horace have chosen to address "Better to Live, Licinius" to a specific person?
2. Does the subject of this poem seem appropriate for an ode? Explain.

Reading Strategy Interpret Imagery

To understand Horace's poem, you must decide what the "word pictures" and sensory details mean. Review the chart you filled in on page 364 as you read the poem.

1. Which images in the poem did you find most powerful? Why?
2. What examples of contrasting images can you identify in the poem?

 Literature Online

Selection Resources For Selection Quizzes, eFlashcards, and Reading-Writing Connection activities, go to glencoe.com and enter QuickPass code GLW6053u2.

366 UNIT 2 ANCIENT ROME

---

6. **Tone** is the attitude that an author or speaker takes toward a subject. How would you describe the speaker's tone in addressing Licinius?
7. What view of fate is suggested in this poem? Explain.

Connect

8. **Big Idea** **Seize the Day** Does Horace's advice of golden moderation support or refute the idea of living for the moment? Explain.
9. **Connect to the Author** Horace's purpose for writing poetry was to teach and to delight. Did he fulfill his twofold purpose in writing this poem? Explain.

Vocabulary Practice

Practice with Usage Respond to each statement or question below to help you explore the meanings of vocabulary words from the poem.

1. Name some types of people who do not practice **moderation** in their lives.
2. Identify an issue on which your parents or guardians might take a **stern** stance.
3. If membership in a club were to **swell**, what would that indicate?

 **Writing**

Write a Letter Write a letter to someone who does not practice "golden moderation"—perhaps a person who is overly ambitious or in need of motivation. Use "word pictures," as Horace does, to persuade him or her to consider steering a middle course.

Reading Strategy

1. Answers will vary.
2. In the first stanza, the images of "rushing into deep water" and "pushing too close to / the dangerous coast" contrast. In stanza 5, the image of Apollo playing on a lyre contrasts with the image of him as an archer.

Vocabulary Practice

1. Answers will vary.
2. Students should name an important issue, such as drug use.
3. The club is becoming very popular.

Writing

Students' letters should include sensory details and convey the benefits of practicing moderation.

Grammar Workshop

Subject-Verb Agreement

Literature Connection In every sentence and clause, the subject and verb must agree. For example, look at the lines from Horace's "Better to Live, Licinius" below. The subject of the singular verb *makes* is the singular noun *fear* and not the plural noun *storms*, which is the object of the preposition *of*.

> *"Better to live, Licinius, not always*
> *rushing into deep water, and not, when fear*
> *of storms makes you shiver, pushing too close to*
> *the dangerous coast."*

You can avoid subject-verb agreement errors in your own writing by following the guidelines below.

PROBLEM 1 A predicate nominative differs in number from the subject.

> *Peace and order <u>was</u> the goal of the emperor Augustus.*

SOLUTION Ignore the predicate nominative and make the verb agree with the subject, in this case, *peace* and *order*.

> *Peace and order <u>were</u> the goal of the emperor Augustus.*

PROBLEM 2 A compound subject is joined by *or* or *nor*.

> *Neither "Better to Live, Licinius" nor Horace's other odes <u>is</u> as formal as Greek odes.*

SOLUTION Make the verb agree with the part of the compound subject that is closer to it.

> *Neither "Better to Live, Licinius" nor Horace's other odes <u>are</u> as formal as Greek odes.*

PROBLEM 3 An indefinite pronoun is the subject.

> *Everyone <u>have heard</u> Horace's famous maxim "seize the day."*

SOLUTION Determine whether the indefinite pronoun is singular or plural and make the verb agree with it.

> *Everyone <u>has heard</u> Horace's famous maxim "seize the day."*

Proofread For each sentence below, choose the correct form of the verb.

1. A love of country scenes (mark, marks) Horace's poetry.
2. Horace and Virgil (was, were) part of the circle of Maecenas.
3. Neither Nancy nor the other students (find, finds) it easy to translate Horace's Latin.

Learning Objective

In this workshop, you will focus on the following objective:

Grammar: Understanding how to correct subject-verb agreement.

Subject-Verb Agreement

A **subject** is the "who or what" of a sentence. The **verb** describes the action. When you have **subject-verb agreement**, you have formed a correct sentence in which the verb form matches the subject.

Tip

When a collective noun refers to a group as a whole, it requires a singular verb (*The* **chorus sings** *beautifully*). When a collective noun refers to each member of a group individually, it requires a plural verb (*The* **chorus have** *separate parts to learn*).

Language Handbook

For more about **subject-verb agreement**, see Language Handbook, p. R40.

 Literature Online

Grammar For more grammar practice, go to glencoe.com and enter QuickPass code GLW6053u2.

Advanced Learners/Pre-AP

 DIFFERENTIATED INSTRUCTION

Stump Your Classmates Instruct advanced learners to compose a sentence with unusual subject-verb agreement which they think will stump their classmates. Then have them write their sentence on the board. They should not include the verb in the sentence, but leave a space for it and state its infinitive form at the end, like this:

The audience _____ expressing their opinions about the play. (to be)

Ask the other students to fill in the verb and state why they chose the form they did.

Focus

Compound Subjects

Write on the board: Prudence and self-control are the basis of "golden moderation."

Have students point out the predicate nominative in this sentence (*the basis*).

Say: A predicate nominative is a noun or pronoun that follows a linking verb and points back to the subject to identify it further.

Ask: Why does this sentence contain the word "are" instead of the word "is"? (*"To be" is the verb and "prudence and moderation," the subject, must agree with it.*)

Teach

Test-Taking Tip

Suggest to students that when they write for a test, they check for subject-verb agreement as a separate step in the proofreading process.

Assess

1. marks
2. were
3. find

 For an activity related to thiis workshop, see Unit 2 Teaching Resources Book, p. 169.

Before You Read

Bellringer Options

Selection Focus
Transparency 18
Daily Language Practice
Transparency 31

Or ask: Which stories of doomed love have you previously encountered? Students might mention *Romeo and Juliet, Titanic,* or other narratives from various genres.
Or ask: Do families have the right to keep young people apart? Start a discussion about the degree of control that parents or guardians should have in choosing whom their children should be with.

Literary History ☆

Ovid in Exile Ovid was relegated—a lesser form of banishment—to Tomis in the spring of A.D. 9. Ovid's time there was difficult because almost no one in Tomis spoke Latin and there was little civilized society there. Ovid began to write poetry to his wife, friends, and, most importantly, the emperor. In his writings, Ovid begged them to allow him to return to Rome.

Before You Read   Ancient Rome

The Story of Pyramus and Thisbe from the *Metamorphoses*

Meet **Ovid**

(43 B.C.–A.D. 17)

☆ For most of his life, Ovid (ov′id) enjoyed the social privileges and pleasures of the cultivated world of Rome. Yet he eventually died in lonely exile from the city he loved.

Ovid came from an upper-class family in present-day Sulmona, Italy. His father groomed him to become a public official, sending him to Rome to study law and rhetoric. Ovid held a few minor government positions in his twenties but soon gave up politics to devote himself to writing poetry. His witty, elegant style and gift for imaginative storytelling soon brought him popular success. He became renowned for his brilliant love poetry, particularly the *Art of Love,* a collection of poems giving advice, and the *Heroides,* a series of fictitious love letters from famous women in mythology.

> *"My intention is to tell of bodies changed to different forms . . ."*
>
> —Ovid, from *Metamorphoses*

Metamorphoses Ovid considered the *Metamorphoses* (met′ə mor′fə sēs) his masterpiece. This great narrative poem retells more than 200 ancient Greek and Roman legends and myths. Most of the stories feature a character that undergoes some type of metamorphosis, or transformation—often changing into a thing in nature. The tales are told in chronological order, from the creation of the universe to the founding of the Roman Empire. Ovid describes the adventures of both gods and mortals with wit and humor.

The tone of the *Metamorphoses* is generally playful, yet Ovid's imaginative retellings can also be very moving. His real focus is on the characters' emotions, which he portrays with compassion and insight. "Above all, Ovid was interested in passion," observed British poet Ted Hughes. "Or rather, in what a passion feels like to the one possessed by it."

Timeless Legacy Ovid's life took a disastrous turn shortly before the *Metamorphoses* was published. In A.D. 8, the emperor Augustus exiled him for unknown reasons. Ovid was sent from Rome to Tomis, a bleak outpost on the Black Sea, where he remained for the rest of his life.

From Ovid's time to the present, authors and artists have mined the rich subject matter of his tales. In particular, the *Metamorphoses* greatly influenced the literature of the Middle Ages and Renaissance, inspiring Dante Alighieri (1265–1321, see page 898), Geoffrey Chaucer (c. 1340–1400), and William Shakespeare (1564–1616).

 Literature Online

Author Search For more about Ovid, go to glencoe.com and enter QuickPass code GLW6053u2.

Selection Skills

Literary Elements
- Narrative Poetry (SE pp. 369, 370, 372, 373, 375)

The Story of Pyramus and Thisbe

Writing Skills/Grammar
- Summary (SE p. 375)
- Use Appositive Phrases (TE p. 370)
- Use Participles and Participial Phrases (TE p. 372)

Reading Skills
- Identify Sequence (SE pp. 369, 372, 375)
- Analyze Sensory Details (TE p. 374)

Vocabulary Skills
- Denotation and Connotation (SE pp. 369, 375)
- Illustrate Vocabulary (TE p. 369)

Literature and Reading Preview

Connect to the Poem

Why do people sometimes make false assumptions? Discuss this question with a small group.

Build Background

Ovid's favorite subject was love. In "The Story of Pyramus and Thisbe," he tells about two lovers who are determined to be together. They live in ancient Babylon—the "brick-walled city" mentioned in the first line of the poem—located between the Tigris and Euphrates Rivers in what is now Iraq.

Set Purposes for Reading

Big Idea Seize the Day

As you read, ask yourself, In what ways does this poem reflect the theme of living for the moment?

Literary Element Narrative Poetry

Narrative poetry is verse that tells a story. Narrative poems have characters, settings, and narrators who describe a series of events. Many narrative poems also include figurative language and dialogue. As you read, ask yourself, What narrative elements appear in this poem?

Reading Strategy Identify Sequence

When you **identify sequence,** you find the logical order of ideas or events in a text. In "The Story of Pyramus and Thisbe," Ovid narrates the events in **chronological order,** the order in which they occur. As you read, ask yourself, What is the sequence of events, and how does it affect the plot?

Tip: Complete a Sequence Chain Use a sequence chain like the one started below to record the key events in the poem. Add as many boxes as you need.

Pyramus and Thisbe talk to each other through a chink in the wall. → One morning they agree to run off together. →

Learning Objectives

For pages 368–375

In studying this text, you will focus on the following objectives:

Literary Study: Analyzing narrative poetry.

Reading: Identifying sequence.

Writing: Writing a summary.

Vocabulary

suppress (sə pres′) *v.* keep in or hold back; p. 370 *To avoid an argument, the old man suppressed his anger.*

detect (di tekt′) *v.* discover or determine; p. 370 *Examining the gem, the jeweler detected a flaw.*

futile (fū′til) *adj.* useless; worthless; ineffectual; p. 371 *Without adequate food or supplies, it would be futile to attempt this journey.*

sly (slī) *adj.* clever; wily; secretive; p. 371 *The burglar used a sly maneuver to open the lock.*

Tip: Denotation and Connotation
A word's **denotation** is its literal definition; its **connotations** are its suggested or implied meanings. To explore connotations, think of your own associations with a word, especially the positive or negative feelings it stirs in you. For example, the word *sly* suggests skill in concealing underhanded methods and therefore evokes negative feelings in most readers.

Before You Read

Focus

Summary

Pyramus and Thisbe are in love. After their parents forbid them to see each other, they decide to run away. As Thisbe waits at the designated meeting place, a lion comes by. Thisbe flees, dropping her veil, which the lion tears to pieces. When Pyramus arrives and sees the bloodied veil, he thinks that the lion has killed Thisbe, and he commits suicide. When Thisbe returns, she finds his body and takes her own life.

For summaries in languages other than English, see Unit 2 Teaching Resources Book, pp. 170–175.

Vocabulary

Illustrate Vocabulary Have students write a sentence for each vocabulary word; the action of each sentence should show the meaning of the word. For instance, for the word *tumble,* they might write "Louis tumbled down the stairs." Then have students draw a picture that illustrates this sentence, displaying the meaning of the word through their drawings.

English Learners

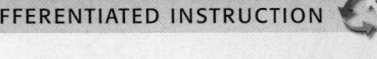
DIFFERENTIATED INSTRUCTION

Intermediate Explain to students that taking the time to paraphrase each stanza will improve their comprehension.

You might also have English learners read the first stanza and note any words or phrases they find confusing. Then pair them with fluent English speakers to clarify the confusion. Partners can then paraphrase the action in the stanza.

Advanced Learners/Pre-AP

DIFFERENTIATED INSTRUCTION

Write a Short Story Have advanced learners take the plot of "The Story of Pyramus and Thisbe" and write a short story based on it. They may keep the story in its original setting if they would like, or they can reset it in a different time and place. They should, however, make sure to follow the basic story elements of the narrative poem. Pair students together and have them exchange stories to compare

their them. Instruct them to discuss why they made the choices they did as well as how their stories are similar to one another and how they are different.

Teach

Big Idea · 1

Roman Myth Ovid often wrote on mythological themes and characters. The *Metamorphoses* is extremely important in its representations of ancient mythology, particularly Greek mythology. Ovid's poem is the main source for many of the Greek myths that scholars study today. His telling of the story of Pygmalion has served as the basis for numerous pieces of art, such as Jean-Léon Gérôme's painting *Pygmalion and Galatea* and George Bernard Shaw's play *Pygmalion*.

Literary Element · 2

Narrative Poetry Answer: *The elements are setting and character.*

Literary Element · 3

Narrative Poetry Answer: *Though they are happy to speak to each other, they feel very frustrated because the wall prevents them from embracing.*

 For an audio recording of this selection, use Listening Library Audio CD-ROM.

THE STORY OF
Pyramus AND *Thisbe*

1 *from the* **Metamorphoses**

Ovid

Translated by Rolfe Humphries

"Next door to each other, in the brick-walled city
Built by Semiramis, lived a boy and girl,
Pyramus, a most handsome fellow, Thisbe,
Loveliest of all those Eastern° girls. Their nearness
5 Made them acquainted, and love grew, in time,
So that they would have married, but their parents
Forbade it. But their parents could not keep them
From being in love: their nods and gestures showed it—
You know how fire **suppressed** burns all the fiercer.
10 There was a chink° in the wall between the houses,
A flaw the careless builder had never noticed,
Nor anyone else, for many years, **detected**,
But the lovers found it—love is a finder, always—
Used it to talk through, and the loving whispers
15 Went back and forth in safety. They would stand
One on each side, listening for each other,
Happy if each could hear the other's breathing,
And then they would scold the wall: 'You envious barrier,
Why get in our way? Would it be too much to ask you
20 To open wide for an embrace, or even
Permit us room to kiss in? Still, we are grateful,
We owe you something, we admit; at least

4 Eastern: The Roman Empire extended from the Atlantic Ocean on the west to the eastern rim of the Mediterranean Sea. To ancient Romans, people who lived in southwest Asia were *Eastern*.

10 chink: a small slit or opening in a wall.

2 Narrative Poetry *What elements of a short story does Ovid introduce at the beginning of the poem?*

3 Narrative Poetry *What does the dialogue in these lines tell you about the characters?*

Vocabulary

suppress (sə pres′) *v.* keep in or hold back
detect (di tekt′) *v.* discover or determine something

Grammar Practice

Use Appositive Phrases An **appositive** is a noun or pronoun that is placed next to another noun or pronoun to identify or give additional information about it. An **appositive phrase** is an appositive plus any words that modify the appositive. The phrase "Pyramus, <u>a most handsome fellow</u>," contains an appositive phrase. If an appositive is not essential to the meaning of a sentence, it should be set off using commas.

Write the following sentences on the board and have students insert commas to set off the nonessential appositive phrases.

- I was born in Madison the capital of Wisconsin. (*I was born in Madison, the capital of Wisconsin.*)
- Jenny my friend is a champion fencer. (*Jenny, my friend, is a champion fencer.*)
- A historic city New Orleans was originally settled by the French. (*A historic city, New Orleans was originally settled by the French.*)

You let us talk together.' But their talking
Was **futile**, rather; and when evening came
25 They would say Good-night! and give the good-night kisses
That never reached the other.
                                                    "The next morning
Came, and the fires of night burnt out, and sunshine
Dried the night frost, and Pyramus and Thisbe
Met at the usual place, and first, in whispers,
30 Complained, and came—high time!—to a decision.
That night, when all was quiet, they would fool
Their guardians, or try to, come outdoors,
Run away from home, and even leave the city.
And, not to miss each other, as they wandered
35 In the wide fields, where should they meet? At Ninus'
Tomb,° they supposed, was best; there was a tree there,
A mulberry-tree,° loaded with snow-white berries,
Near a cool spring. The plan was good, the daylight
Was very slow in going, but at last
40 The sun went down into the waves,° as always,
And the night rose, as always, from those waters.

And Thisbe opened her door, so **sly**, so cunning,
There was no creaking of the hinge, and no one
Saw her go through the darkness, and she came,
45 Veiled, to the tomb of Ninus, sat there waiting
Under the shadow of the mulberry-tree.
Love made her bold. But suddenly, here came something!—
A lioness, her jaws a crimson froth
With the blood of cows, fresh-slain, came there for water,
50 And far off through the moonlight Thisbe saw her
And ran, all scared, to hide herself in a cave,
And dropped her veil as she ran. The lioness,
Having quenched her thirst, came back to the woods,
    and saw
The girl's light veil, and mangled it and mouthed it
55 With bloody jaws. Pyramus, coming there
Too late, saw tracks in the dust, turned pale, and paler
Seeing the bloody veil. 'One night,' he cried,
'Will kill two lovers, and one of them, most surely,

36 Ninus' Tomb: Ninus was an
Assyrian king and the husband of
Semiramis (sə mir´ə mis). He
founded the Assyrian capital,
Nineveh. After his death, Semiramis
erected a temple on the outskirts of
Babylon—Ninus' tomb.
37 mulberry trees: Asian trees
cultivated as ornamental trees and
for their sweet, edible fruits.
**40 The sun went down into the
waves:** refers to the horizon on
which the sun appears to set.
Babylon was located between the
Tigris and Euphrates Rivers.

4 Seize the Day *Do the lovers live for the moment, or not? Explain.*

Vocabulary

futile (fū´til) *adj.* useless; worthless; ineffectual
sly (slī) *adj.* clever; wily; secretive

Big Idea	**4**

Seize the Day Answer:
*Their decision to run off together
suggests that they value living in
the moment. They do not pause to
consider an alternative plan.*

Learning Objectives
Analyzing narrative poetry. (SE)
Using appositive phrases. (TE)

English Learners

DIFFERENTIATED INSTRUCTION

SMALL GROUP

Beginning Insufficient
vocabulary skills may make it
difficult for English language learners to
comprehend the poem. By analyzing
descriptions and visualizing images,
these students can both enhance
their vocabulary skills and improve
comprehension.

Students should note any confusing
descriptions as they read and then share

them in groups. Suggest that students
paraphrase the descriptions in simple
language, consulting a dictionary if needed.
Then have groups represent the images
by finding magazine photographs or by
drawing the images.

Advanced Learners/Pre-AP

DIFFERENTIATED INSTRUCTION

Retell a Myth Instruct advanced learners
to research a classical myth, and then
write a short narrative poem or short story
retelling this myth. They should add details
to the myth to make it vivid for the reader.
They can change the particulars of the
myth slightly for the sake of storytelling, so
long as the general idea and themes of the
myth remain.

Teach

Literary Element　1

Narrative Poetry Answer:
Pyramus's speech reveals both the intensity of his love for Thisbe and his anguish over what he believes has happened to her. The speech adds suspense to the story, making the reader wonder what Pyramus will do next.

[APPROACHING] Ask learners approaching level what predictions they made while reading this passage. What did they think Pyramus would do next? *(Answers will vary.)*

 For additional literary element practice, see Unit 2 Teaching Resources Book, p. 176.

Reading Strategy　2

Identify Sequence
Answer: *Had Thisbe returned sooner, she might have prevented Pyramus's suicide.*

[ENGLISH LEARNERS] Ask English learners what they think would have happened if Thisbe had returned sooner. *(Possible answers: they would have run away together, they would have been caught by their parents, or they would have been eaten by the lion.)*

Deserved a longer life. It is all my fault,
60　I am the murderer, poor girl; I told you
To come here in the night, to all this terror,
And was not here before you, to protect you.
Come, tear my flesh, devour my guilty body,
Come, lions, all of you, whose lairs lie hidden
65　Under this rock! I am acting like a coward,
Praying for death.' He lifts the veil and takes it
Into the shadow of their tree; he kisses
The veil he knows so well, his tears run down
Into its folds: 'Drink my blood too!' he cries,
70　And draws his sword, and plunges it into his body,
And, dying, draws it out, warm from the wound.
As he lay there on the ground, the spouting blood
Leaped high, just as a pipe sends water spurting
Through a small hissing opening, when broken
75　With a flaw in the lead,° and all the air is sprinkled.
The fruit of the tree, from that red spray, turned crimson,
And the roots, soaked with the blood, dyed all the berries
The same dark hue.
　　　　　　　　　　"Thisbe came out of hiding,
Still frightened, but a little fearful, also,
80　To disappoint her lover. She kept looking
Not only with her eyes, but all her heart,
Eager to tell him of those terrible dangers,
About her own escape. She recognized
The place, the shape of the tree, but there was something
85　Strange or peculiar in the berries' color.
Could this be right? And then she saw a quiver
Of limbs on bloody ground, and started backward,
Paler than boxwood,° shivering, as water
Stirs when a little breeze ruffles the surface.
90　It was not long before she knew her lover,
And tore her hair, and beat her innocent bosom
With her little fists, embraced the well-loved body,
Filling the wounds with tears, and kissed the lips
Cold in his dying. 'O my Pyramus,'
95　She wept, 'What evil fortune takes you from me?
Pyramus, answer me! Your dearest Thisbe
Is calling you. Pyramus, listen! Lift your head!'

75 a flaw in the lead: compares the way water issues from a broken pipe to how blood spurts from a wound.

88 boxwood: a shrub used for hedges and borders.

1 **Narrative Poetry** *What does Pyramus's speech reveal about his character? What else does the speech add to the story?*

2 **Identify Sequence** *What might have been prevented had Thisbe returned sooner to the tomb?*

Grammar Practice

Use Participles and Participial Phrases A participle is a verb form that can also function as an adjective. Present participles always end in *-ing*. Past participles often end in *-ed*, although they can take other forms as well. When they are not essential to the meaning of a sentence, participles and participial phrases are set off by commas, as in: "She came, <u>veiled,</u> to the tomb of Ninus." Sometimes they introduce sentences, such as: <u>Looking for Pyramus,</u> Thisbe comes out of hiding.

Have students review "The Story of Pyramus and Thisbe," looking for participles and participial phrases set off by commas. When they find a sentence that contains one, have them copy the entire sentence. Then have them identify its essential parts as well as the participle or participial phrase to help clarify its meaning.

Night and Sleep, 1878. Evelyn de Morgan. Oil on canvas. De Morgan Foundation, London.

View the Art Evelyn de Morgan (1855–1919) was one of the few female English Pre-Raphaelite painters. These painters strove to attain a naturalistic style of art. What is the mood of this painting? What part of the story does it reflect? ★

He heard the name of Thisbe, and he lifted
His eyes, with the weight of death heavy upon them,
100 And saw her face, and closed his eyes.
                                    "And Thisbe
Saw her own veil, and saw the ivory scabbard°
With no sword in it, and understood. 'Poor boy,'
She said, 'So, it was your own hand,
Your love, that took your life away. I too
105 Have a brave hand for this one thing, I too
Have love enough, and this will give me strength
For the last wound. I will follow you in death,
Be called the cause and comrade of your dying.
Death was the only one could keep you from me,
110 Death shall not keep you from me. Wretched parents
Of Pyramus and Thisbe, listen to us,

101 **scabbard:** a sheath for a sword or dagger.

3 | Narrative Poetry *What does Thisbe's speech reveal about her?*

4 | Seize the Day *Why does Thisbe decide to take her life?*

OVID **373**

Approaching Level

DIFFERENTIATED INSTRUCTION

SMALL GROUP
Write and Perform a Skit
Divide students into small groups and have them write a skit based on Ovid's telling of the story of Pyramus and Thisbe. They should write it in the form of a drama (they can look at Sophocles' *Oedipus* beginning on page 250 as an example). They should use the action of their skit to make the sequence of events of the narrative poem clear to themselves as well as to the audience. They can also simplify

the language used in the poem to clarify its meaning. They should develop a set which will have all the necessary pieces (wall with chink, mulberry tree, etc.) to tell the story and should include characters explicit in the text (Pyramus, Thisbe, lion) and possibly those not explicit (parents, narrator).

Then have them rehearse the skit and perform it for the class. Ask students if the skit helped them to better understand the poem.

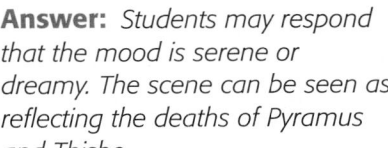

Narrative Poetry **Answer:**
Thisbe's speech reveals the intensity of her love and the courage it gives her.

(APPROACHING) Ask students approaching level what word or phrase is repeated in this speech. *("I too have")*

Big Idea | **4**

Seize the Day **Answer:**
Thisbe would rather be with Pyramus in death than live without him.

View the Art ★

Answer: *Students may respond that the mood is serene or dreamy. The scene can be seen as reflecting the deaths of Pyramus and Thisbe.*

Like the paintings of her Pre-Raphaelite counterparts, Evelyn de Morgan's paintings often express mythological and classical themes; several of her paintings depict characters from Greek mythology. De Morgan, who felt that any time not spent painting was wasted, was among the first female students to enter the Slade School of Art. She began exhibiting her art when she was only twenty. In this allegorical work, Night supports Sleep as the two float across the sky. The red flowers are those of the poppy plant, which is sometimes associated with sleep.

Learning Objectives
Analyzing narrative poetry. (SE)
Identifying sequence. (SE)
Using participles and participial phrases. (TE)

373

Teach

View the Art ★

Lucas Cranach the Elder was one of the most important German artists of the sixteenth century. The people in this painting are, as is usual in his paintings, almost impossibly slender and arrayed in dress and jewelry fashionable at the time of the painting, but inaccurate for the historical setting of the poem.

Pyramus and Thisbe, 1472 Lucas Cranach the Elder. Oil on canvas. Neue Residenz, Bamberg, Germany. ★

Listen to both our prayers, do not begrudge us,
Whom death has joined, lying at last together
In the same tomb. And you, O tree, now shading
115   The body of one, and very soon to shadow
The bodies of two, keep in remembrance always
The sign of our death, the dark and mournful color.'
She spoke, and fitting the sword-point at her breast,
Fell forward on the blade, still warm and reeking
120   With her lover's blood. Her prayers touched the gods,
And touched her parents, for the mulberry fruit
Still reddens at its ripeness, and the ashes
Rest in a common urn."°

123 urn: a vessel, typically an ornamental vase on a pedestal. Urns are often used for preserving the ashes of the dead after cremation.

374 UNIT 2   ANCIENT ROME

Literary Element Practice

Sensory Details Have students make a two-column chart—like the one here—which they can use to identify the sensory details in "The Story of Pyramus and Thisbe." In the first column, have them list quotes containing the sensory details they find in the poem. In the second column, have them make notes of what these details show the reader.

Example:

Sensory Detail	Notes
"You know how fire suppressed burns all the fiercer."	The things that separate Pyramus and Thisbe only intensify their love.

After You Read

Respond and Think Critically

Respond and Interpret

1. Were you surprised by the outcome of this poem? Explain.

2. (a)Why must Pyramus and Thisbe talk through a chink in a wall? (b)What does the narrator suggest with the remark, "You know how fire suppressed burns all the fiercer"?

3. (a)Why does Thisbe run off after she arrives at the tomb of Ninus? (b)Why does Pyramus blame himself for Thisbe's "death"?

4. (a)Identify an assumption in "The Story of Pyramus and Thisbe" that has tragic consequences. (b)What leads the character to make the incorrect assumption?

Analyze and Evaluate

5. In your opinion, what factors led to the deaths of Pyramus and Thisbe?

6. **Myths** often explain some aspect of nature. In what way does the end of the poem function as a myth?

Connect

7. **Seize the Day** What does Ovid's poem suggest about love? (b)How does the poem reflect the theme of living for the moment? Support your answer with details from the poem.

8. **Connect to Today** If you were updating the story of Pyramus and Thisbe, what elements would you change?

Literary Element Narrative Poetry

A **narrative poem** has a plot that centers on a conflict.

1. What is the main conflict in "The Story of Pyramus and Thisbe"?

2. A **lyric poem** is a brief, songlike poem expressing personal thoughts and feelings. How would you compare the experience of reading a lyric poem with that of reading a narrative poem?

Reading Strategy Identify Sequence

Review the sequence chain you filled in on page 369. Then answer the following questions.

1. Which events, if their sequence were different, would change the outcome of the plot?

2. How might this poem be different if it were told in reverse, rather than chronological, order?

 **Literature** Online

Selection Resources For Selection Quizzes, eFlash-cards, and Reading-Writing Connection activities, go to glencoe.com and enter QuickPass code GLW6053u2.

Vocabulary Practice

Practice with Denotation and Connotation
Although the words *cheap* and *inexpensive* have similar denotations, the word *cheap* has negative connotations but *inexpensive* generally does not. In each pair of words below, choose the one with negative connotations.

1. suppress   curb
2. detect   expose
3. futile   impractical
4. sly   clever

Writing

Write a Summary Write a brief summary of "The Story of Pyramus and Thisbe." Before writing, look back at your sequence chain on page 369 to review the important events. In your summary, use signal words such as *then, next, later,* and *finally* to show the order of events.

Reading Strategy

1. If Pyramus had arrived at the tomb before Thisbe, or if Thisbe had returned to the tomb before Pyramus.

2. Students may suggest that the dramatic irony would be enhanced in reverse.

Progress Check

Can students identify sequence?

If No → See Unit 2 Teaching Resources Book, p. 177.

Vocabulary

1. suppress   **3.** futile
2. expose   **4.** sly

After You Read

Assess

1. Answers will vary.

2. (a) Their parents will not let them see one another. (b) Their limited opportunities to meet heighten their desire to be together.

3. (a) A lioness approaches. (b) He believes Thisbe was killed because he was not there to protect her.

4. (a) Pyramus assumes that a lion has killed Thisbe and this assumption ultimately leads to their deaths. (b) The bloodied veil leads him to think this.

5. Possible answers: the parents' decision to keep the lovers apart, the lovers' decision to run away, and Pyramus's mistake in assuming Thisbe was dead.

6. The ending suggests something in nature (berries) takes its color from the effects of the event.

7. Possible answers: (a) Love cannot be suppressed or love knows no bounds. (b) Love overwhelms Pyramus and Thisbe, prompting them to act without careful forethought.

8. Students may suggest replacing the mulberry tree with a more common landmark.

Literary Element

1. Their parents prevent the young lovers from marrying.

2. Possible answer: narrative poetry is more satisfying because it tells a story.

Writing

Students' summaries should

- recount the events in the order in which they occur in the poem
- include the important elements of the story—plot, characters, and conflict

375

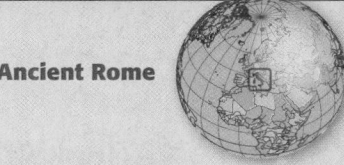

Bellringer Options

Selection Focus
Transparency 19

Daily Language Practice
Transparency 32

Or ask: Aeneas is a fictional cultural hero, the very first Roman. Why do you think Virgil made him the son of a goddess? Why do you think he decided to have Aeneas face both tremendous victories and horrible tragedies? Elicit students' opinions. You might suggest that having an immortal parent made Aeneas larger than life, somewhat like a classical superhero. Having him face tremendous victories formed a tribute to the power of Rome; having him face horrible tragedies made him a more sympathetic, romantic character.

Meet **Virgil**
(70–19 B.C.)

Virgil, ancient Rome's greatest poet, grew up on a farm in northern Italy, near what is now the town of Mantua. Shy and gentle, he preferred the peace of the countryside to the bustle of the city and celebrated rural life in many of his poems. Virgil attended school in Cremona and Milan and later went to Rome to study mathematics, medicine, and rhetoric (the art of persuasion).

Rome's Honored Poet The assassination of Julius Caesar in 44 B.C. triggered civil war in Rome. To escape the turmoil, Virgil moved to Naples, where he lived in a house Maecenas, his wealthy patron, had given him. Thanks to Maecenas, Virgil was able to devote himself to philosophy and literary pursuits.

Virgil's connection with Maecenas proved fortunate in another way. His patron was a close adviser to Octavian, who later became the emperor Augustus. Probably prompted by Maecenas, Octavian took an interest in the young poet. After Octavian had defeated his rivals and seized control of the Roman Empire, he urged Virgil to compose a patriotic poem to honor Rome. To glorify the city and its new ruler, Virgil wrote the *Aeneid*, a twelve-book epic in Latin.

The National Epic Modeling the *Aeneid* on the Homeric epics the *Iliad* and the *Odyssey*, Virgil drew upon the ancient legend of Troy. Virgil's hero is Aeneas, a Trojan prince who escapes from Troy and visits Carthage in North Africa, where he falls in love with Queen Dido. He then travels to Italy, where he conquers the Latins and establishes a new nation. Aeneas's descendants are destined to found Rome and create a worldwide empire. Although the *Aeneid* celebrates Rome's long tradition of military conquest, Virgil does not overlook the tragic side of warfare.

Virgil began writing the Aeneid at age 40. In 19 B.C. he set out on a voyage to Greece with the intention of revising the poem he spent eleven years composing, but he became gravely ill. On his deathbed he requested his unrevised manuscript be burned. Fortunately, Emperor Augustus ordered the poem be published. The *Aeneid* secured Virgil's literary reputation and has profoundly influenced Western culture through the ages.

"At the heart of things there are tears."

—Virgil, the *Aeneid*

LOG ON ▶ **Literature** Online

Author Search For more about Virgil, go to glencoe.com and enter QuickPass code GLW6053u2.

Selection Skills

Literary Elements
- Analyze Imagery (SE pp. 377–397)
- Epic Hero (SE p. 397)
- Identify Narrator (TE p. 379)

Reading Skills
- Make and Verify Predictions (SE pp. 377–397)
- Visualize (TE p. 378)

Vocabulary Skills
- Context Clues (SE p. 397)
- Academic Vocabulary (SE p. 397)
- Act It Out! (TE p. 377)

from the Aeneid

Speaking/Listening/Viewing Skills
- Participate in a Literature Group (TE p. 386)
- Role-Playing (TE p. 388)

Writing Skills/Grammar
- Expository Essay (SE p. 398)
- Write Descriptions (TE p. 392)

Literature and Reading Preview

Connect to the Epic

What does it mean to be a hero? Write a journal entry about someone you consider heroic and why.

Build Background

Aeneas is the son of Venus, the goddess of love and beauty, and Anchises, a mortal. At a feast in his honor, Aeneas reluctantly agrees to tell Queen Dido the story of Troy's destruction, the event that prompted his search for a new homeland.

Set Purposes for Reading

Big Idea Roman Myth

Virgil created a mythical past for Italy linked to Aeneas, whom he portrays as the ideal Roman hero. As you read, ask yourself, What qualities of a hero does Aeneas embody?

Literary Element Imagery

Imagery refers to the "word pictures" authors create to evoke an emotional response. In creating effective images, authors use sensory details, or descriptions that appeal to one or more of the five senses: sight, hearing, touch, taste, and smell. As you read, ask yourself, What images does Virgil create to help you visualize Aeneas's experiences?

Reading Strategy Make and Verify Predictions

When you **make predictions**, you make educated guesses about what will happen later in a literary work. You then **verify predictions** by looking for textual evidence that confirms their accuracy. As you read, ask yourself, What predictions can I make about the outcomes of events in this epic?

Tip: Take Notes Use a chart like the one below to make and verify predictions as you read.

Prediction	Evidence for Prediction	Verification

Learning Objectives

For pages 376–398

In studying this text, you will focus on the following objectives:

Literary Study: Analyzing imagery

Reading: Making and verifying predictions

Vocabulary

dupe (do͞op) *v.* to deceive or delude; p. 381 *He duped her into giving away all her money.*

impel (im pel′) *v.* to urge forward as if through moral pressure; p. 384 *She was impelled to tell her parents the truth.*

defile (di fīl′) *v.* to make unclean; p. 386 *The vandals defiled the holy shrine, scrawling hateful messages on the walls.*

suppliant (sə′plē′ənt) *n.* one who asks humbly and earnestly; p. 386 *The suppliant pleaded with the court to hear his testimony.*

Tip: Context Clues When you come across an unfamiliar term, pay close attention to the surrounding words. For example, in the sentence *The vandals defiled the holy shrine, scrawling hateful messages on the walls,* *defiled* must mean "to make unclean" because "vandals" wrote "hateful messages."

VIRGIL **377**

Before You Read

Focus

Summary

In this excerpt, Aeneas relates the story of the destruction of Troy. He tells how he and his countrymen fought to save the city. He witnessed the murder of King Priam and the Greeks' destruction of the city. Fleeing the city with his family, he became separated from his wife. When he found that she had died, he left with no hope of return. He became the leader of other Trojans to be exiled, including his father and his son.

 For summaries in languages other than English, see Unit 2 Teaching Resources Book, pp. 182–187.

Vocabulary

Act It Out! Give a volunteer a slip of paper on which you have written one of the vocabulary words. Have the volunteer "act out" the word while classmates try to guess its identity. For example, for *suppliant*, the volunteer might ask for a favor in a humble way; for *defile,* he or she might scribble all over the chalkboard. Repeat until all vocabulary words have been used.

 For additional vocabulary practice, see Unit 2 Teaching Resources Book, p.190.

Advanced Learners/Pre-AP

DIFFERENTIATED INSTRUCTION

Research Have interested students use the library or reliable Internet sources to learn more about Augustus Caesar and his leadership of Rome. Then, as they read this excerpt from the *Aeneid*, have them discuss why Augustus refused to burn the poem—what made him value it so highly? What did it offer to him and to the people of Rome? What does it offer to modern readers?

Approaching Level

DIFFERENTIATED INSTRUCTION

Structure and Form Remind students to pay attention to punctuation marks as they read, and to reread any sentences that seem unclear. You might pause from time to time to explain the meanings of difficult passages. Additionally, encourage students to use context clues and footnotes as guides to meaning. Some students might also benefit from working with reading partners.

Teach

View the Art

Giovanni Battista Tiepolo was once described as "full of spirit . . . of infinite fire, dazzling color, and astonishing speed." Tiepolo was one of the most popular artists in Venice during the eighteenth century, adorning palaces and churches with frescoes and paintings that depicted scenes from mythology, Roman history, and Christianity. His rapid brushwork helped bring a sense of energy and drama to the crowd scenes he painted. **Ask: How would you describe the crowd's reaction to the Trojan horse in this painting?** *(Students might respond that the crowd seems joyous or ecstatic.)*

For an audio recording of this selection, use Listening Library Audio CD-ROM.

Reading Practice

Visualize Based on what students have read about ancient Greece and Rome, and the content of the selection summary, ask them to answer the following questions:

- How do you visualize the physical appearance and apparel of a Roman warrior? *(Answers will vary.)*

- How do your visualizations of the citizens compare with the people in the painting on this page? *(Some* *students may note that the people in the painting seem to be wearing togas, which may match students' visualizations.)*

As students begin reading the selection, encourage them to use details in the text to visualize the characters and events.

378

---

from **Book Two:**

THE FINAL HOURS OF TROY FROM THE AENEID

VIRGIL TRANSLATED BY ROBERT FAGLES

Procession of the Trojan Horse into Troy, 1727. Giovanni Battista Tiepolo. Oil on canvas. National Gallery, London.

IN THE TENTH YEAR OF THE TROJAN WAR, *the Greeks built a large wooden horse, which they claimed was an offering to ensure their safe passage home. After hiding warriors inside the horse's belly, the Greek forces pretended to sail away. Some Trojans wanted to bring the horse into their city, but others urged caution. The debate was interrupted by a captured Greek named Sinon* (sī′nən), *whose lies convinced the Trojans to drag the horse inside. Under cover of darkness, Sinon set free the hidden Greeks, who then dropped out of the horse and opened Troy's gates to their fellow warriors. Aeneas was asleep at the time, dreaming that the dead Trojan hero Hector told him to take his household gods and abandon the city. (The Romans believed household gods, or Penates* (pə nā′tēz), *protected the pantry, and their images were worshipped in every household.) Aeneas awoke to the sound of battle.*

378 UNIT 2 ANCIENT ROME

                              "But now.

chaos—the city begins to reel with cries of grief,
louder, stronger, even though father's palace
stood well back, screened off by trees, but still
the clash of arms rings clearer, horror on the attack.
5 I shake off sleep and scrambling up to the pitched roof
I stand there, ears alert, and I hear a roar like fire
assaulting a wheatfield, whipped by a Southwind's fury,
or mountain torrent in full spate,° flattening crops,
leveling all the happy, thriving labor of oxen,
10 dragging whole trees headlong down in its wake—
and a shepherd perched on a sheer rock outcrop
hears the roar, lost in amazement, struck dumb.
No doubting the good faith of the Greeks now,
their treachery plain as day.
15   "Already, there,
the grand house of Deiphobus° stormed by fire,
crashing in ruins—
                  "Already his neighbor Ucalegon°
up in flames—
                "The Sigean straits° shimmering back the blaze,
the shouting of fighters soars, the clashing blare of trumpets.
Out of my wits, I seize my arms—what reason for arms?
20 Just my spirit burning to muster troops for battle,
rush with comrades up to the city's heights,
fury and rage driving me breakneck on
as it races through my mind
what a noble thing it is to die in arms!
                       "But now, look,
25 just slipped out from under the Greek barrage of spears,
Panthus, Othrys' son, a priest of Apollo's° shrine
on the citadel—hands full of the holy things,
the images of our conquered gods—he's dragging along
his little grandson, making a wild dash for our doors.
30 'Panthus, where's our stronghold? our last stand?'—
words still on my lips as he groans in answer:
'The last *day* has come for the Trojan people,
no escaping this moment. Troy's no more.
Ilium,° gone—our awesome Trojan glory.
35 Brutal Jupiter° hands it all over to Greece,

---

8 **spate:** here, a flood.

15 **Deiphobus** (dē´ ə phō´ bəs): a son of Priam.

16 **Ucalegon** (ū kal´ ə gən): a Trojan elder.

17 **Sigean straits:** waterways near Troy.

26 **Panthus:** Trojan elder. **Apollo:** god of sunlight, healing, prophecy, archery, music, and poetry. He favored the Trojans.

34 **Ilium** (il´ ē əm): Troy.

35 **Jupiter:** chief god and the god of the sky and weather; he favored Troy but knew it could not be saved.

---

2   Imagery *What senses does Virgil appeal to in this description?*

Literary Element	1

Narrator Remind students that the epic is told in the first-person point of view because Aeneas is relating the story to Dido. **Ask:** Who is the narrator? (*Aeneas, as narrator, relates what he experienced in the battle to Dido.*) Make sure students understand that Aeneas is a Trojan prince. In this opening scene, he is awakened by the clamor of the Greek attack.

Literary Element	2

Imagery Answer: *Virgil appeals to the senses of hearing and sight.*

Advanced Learners/Pre-AP

DIFFERENTIATED INSTRUCTION

Visualize Some students may have difficulty understanding the descriptive vocabulary. Point out that Aeneas is awakened by the sound of battle. Have students visualize the scene, and have more proficient English speakers help them by describing in their own words the details—*cries of grief, clash of arms, a roar like fire assaulting a wheat field,* and so forth.

English Learners

DIFFERENTIATED INSTRUCTION

Intermediate Have students find and read a prose account of the fall of Troy. (An excellent version appears in Edith Hamilton's classic work, *Mythology*.) Doing so will provide a useful context for the characters and events described in this excerpt from the *Aeneid*. For example, characters appearing on this page include Hector, Aeneas and his father, Deiphobus (son of Priam), and Ucalegon.

Learning Objectives
Analyzing imagery. (SE)
Visualizing. (TE)
Identifying narrator. (TE)

Teach

Literary Element | 1

Imagery Answer: *Virgil compares the Trojans with a "wolfpack out for blood." The comparison emphasizes the ferocity of the Trojans at bay.*

ADVANCED Advanced learners might enjoy suggesting additional similes and metaphors to describe the Trojans' feelings and actions in response to the Greek attack and the ongoing destruction of their city.

Greeks are lording over our city up in flames.
The horse stands towering high in the heart of Troy,
disgorging its armed men, with Sinon in his glory,
gloating over us—Sinon fans the fires.
40   The immense double gates are flung wide open,
Greeks in their thousands mass there, all who ever
sailed from proud Mycenae.° Others have choked
the cramped streets, weapons brandished now
in a battle line of naked, glinting steel
45   tense for the kill. Only the first guards
at the gates put up some show of resistance,
fighting blindly on.'

                                                                "Now
like a wolfpack out for blood on a foggy night,
driven blindly on by relentless, rabid hunger,
50   leaving cubs behind, waiting, jaws parched—
so through spears, through enemy ranks we plow
to certain death, striking into the city's heart,
the shielding wings of the darkness beating round us.
Who has words to capture that night's disaster,
55   tell that slaughter? What tears could match
our torments now? An ancient city is falling,
a power that ruled for ages, now in ruins.
Everywhere lie the motionless bodies of the dead,
strewn in her streets, her homes and the gods' shrines
60   we held in awe. And not only Trojans pay the price in
      blood—
at times the courage races back in their conquered hearts
and they cut their enemies down in all their triumph.
Everywhere, wrenching grief, everywhere, terror
and a thousand shapes of death…

42 Mycenae (mī sē´ nē): capital of the kingdom ruled by Agamemnon.

MISTAKEN FOR GREEKS, *Aeneas and his companions are able to destroy a Greek faction. Then, encouraged by their victory, they try a new strategy. They disguise themselves in Greek armor and continue fighting.*

                                                                "But, oh
65   how wrong to rely on gods dead set against you!
Watch: the virgin daughter of Priam, Cassandra,°

66 Priam (prī´ əm): King of Troy and father of Hector and many others.
Cassandra (kə săn´ drə): prophetess whose predictions, though always true, were never believed.

1 **Imagery** *Virgil uses a simile to create an image of the Trojans. What does he compare them with?*

Reading Practice

Paraphrase Make sure students understand the thinking behind Aeneas's question and Panthus's reply (lines 34–37). To monitor comprehension, have them paraphrase the dialogue. *(Aeneas asks for the location where they will be able to give their strongest defense ("last stand"). He assumes they will fight and ultimately defeat the Greeks. Panthus replies that there is no "last stand." There is only the "last day." He foresees the fall of Troy.)*

Ask students which point of view they connect to: Aeneas's determination to fight to the finish, or Panthus's more realistic view that the battle has already been lost.

Cassandra, 1898. Evelyn De Morgan. Oil on canvas, 97.7 x 48.2 cm. The De Morgan Centre, London. ★

torn from the sacred depths of Minerva's° shrine,
dragged by the hair, raising her burning eyes
to the heavens, just her eyes, so helpless,
70   shackles kept her from raising her gentle hands.
Coroebus° could not bear the sight of it—mad with rage
he flung himself at the Greek lines and met his death.
2 Closing ranks we charge after him, into the thick of battle
and face our first disaster. Down from the temple roof
75   come showers of lances hurled by our own comrades there,
duped by the look of our Greek arms, our Greek crests
that launched this grisly slaughter. And worse still,
the Greeks roaring with anger—we had saved Cassandra—
attack us from all sides! Ajax,° fiercest of all and
80   Atreus' two sons and the whole Dolopian° army,
wild as a rampaging whirlwind, gusts clashing,

67 Minerva (mi nur´və): goddess of wisdom and the arts and sciences.

71 Coroebus (kər ō´ə bəs): Trojan ally who loves Cassandra.

79 Ajax: Ajax the Lesser, a great warrior in the Greek army.
80 Atreus' two sons: Agamemnon and Menelaus. **Dolopian:** referring to a kingdom ruled by Achilles' father.

Vocabulary

dupe (dōōp) v. to deceive or delude

VIRGIL **381**

Analyze Cause-and-Effect Relationships Make sure students understand the sequence of causes and effects that follow. **Ask:** What causes Coroebus to charge the Greek warriors? What happens to him as a result? What do Aeneas and his men do as a result? What horrible mistake follows, and why? (*He loves Cassandra, and tries to rescue her. He is killed. Aeneas and his men charge the Greek lines. However, because they have disguised themselves as Greeks, their own men (Trojans) hurl lances at them. Meanwhile, the Greeks attack on all sides.*)

View the Art ★

Evelyn De Morgan is best known for her portraits of famous women from literature, who are usually shown covered in draped garments. In this work, Cassandra pulls at her red hair as Troy burns in the background. The Trojan Horse appears at the far left of the painting. **Ask:** What does Cassandra's gesture in this painting suggest about her state of mind? (*Her pulling of her hair suggests that she feels anguish over the destruction of Troy.*)

Approaching Level

DIFFERENTIATED INSTRUCTION

Prior Knowledge Students who have difficulty visualizing the battle scene might benefit from a discussion of similar battles in history, modern stories, or familiar movies. Point out that the Trojans are now so desperate that they are ripping off the roof tiles and tearing out the golden beams of the building ("the inlaid glory of all our ancient fathers") and using them as weapons.

Advanced Learners/Pre-AP

DIFFERENTIATED INSTRUCTION

Cultural Context

Discuss how the gilded beams represent "the inlaid glory of all our ancient fathers." The Trojans are destroying not only their buildings, but tributes to, and records of, their culture. Discuss how this might affect history, and why, in Virgil's mind, it might have eventually led Aeneas to establish the new culture of Rome.

Learning Objectives
Making and verifying predictions. (SE)
Analyzing imagery. (SE)
Analyzing cause-and-effect relationships. (TE)

Teach

Reading Strategy   1

Analyze Plot Make sure that students understand and can visualize what Aeneas does.

Ask: Why does Aeneas take some men through the secret door? Where does it lead? Why do they attack the tower? *(He wants to sneak into Priam's palace and get up to the roof, to the tower. They pry the tower loose and let it fall upon the Greek army.)*

Literary Element   2

Imagery Answer: *The image of a tortoise shell of shields is used in this description. Students will probably say they visualize a huge tortoise advancing against the enemy.*

---

the West- and the South- and Eastwind riding high
on the rushing horses of the Dawn, and the woods howl
and Nereus, thrashing his savage trident,° churns up
85   the sea exploding in foam from its rocky depths.
And those Greeks we had put to rout,° our ruse
in the murky night stampeding them headlong on
throughout the city—back they come, the first
to see that our shields and spears are naked lies,
90   to mark the words on our lips that jar with theirs.

    "And there, I tell you, a pitched battle flares!
You'd think no other battles could match its fury,
nowhere else in the city were people dying so.
Invincible Mars° rears up to meet us face-to-face
95   with waves of Greeks assaulting the roofs, we see them
choking the gateway, under a tortoise-shell of shields,
and the scaling ladders cling to the steep ramparts—
just at the gates the raiders scramble up the rungs,
shields on their left arms thrust out for defense,
100   their right hands clutching the gables.°
Over against them, Trojans ripping the tiles
and turrets° from all their roofs—the end is near,
they can see it now, at the brink of death, desperate
for weapons, some defense, and these, these missiles they
     send
105   reeling down on the Greeks' heads—the gilded beams,
the inlaid glory of all our ancient fathers.
Comrades below, posted in close-packed ranks,
block the entries, swordpoints drawn and poised.
My courage renewed, I rush to relieve the palace,
110   brace the defenders, bring the defeated strength.

    "There was a secret door, a hidden passage
linking the wings of Priam's house—remote,
far to the rear. Long as our realm still stood,
Andromache,° poor woman, would often go this way,
115   unattended, to Hector's° parents, taking the boy
Astyanax° by the hand to see grandfather Priam.
I slipped through the door, up to the jutting roof
where the doomed Trojans were hurling futile spears.
There was a tower soaring high at the peak toward the sky,
120   our favorite vantage point for surveying all of Troy

84 Nereus: (nēr′ē əs): sea god; the old man of the sea. **trident:** three-pronged spear carried by the sea god.
86 put to rout: to defeat or to force to retreat.

94 Mars: god of war.

100 gables: triangular architectural sections.

102 turrets: small tower-shaped projections on a building.

114 Andromache (an drom′ə kē): Hector's wife.
115 Hector: Troy's greatest hero, killed by Achilles.
116 Astyanax (as tī′ə naks): the young son of Hector and Andromache.

2   Imagery *What image is used in this description? What do you visualize as you read this passage?*

Writing Practice

 Summarize

SMALL GROUP Point out the forceful fighting and desperate feelings described in this passage. Then point out that the writer's use of vivid verbs throughout the battle adds to the force of the descriptions. As examples, point out *block* (line 113) and *rush* (line 115). Then ask students to find others

(hurling, soaring, rocked, wrenched, heaved, grind, assaulting, etc.) You might also point out that *springs* (line 135) is particularly effective, because it suggests that just after Aeneas and his men launch their strongest defense (the toppling of the tower), Pyrrhus suddenly appears out of nowhere, a mighty new threat to face.

Have students work with partners or in small groups to write a report from the point of view of Pyrrhus: what he saw when he arrived at the front gate, what he felt as a response, and what he planned to do. Encourage them to use vivid verbs in their writing.

and the Greek fleet and camp. We attacked that tower
with iron crowbars, just where the upper-story planks
showed loosening joints—we rocked it, wrenched it free
of its deep moorings and all at once we heaved it toppling
125 down with a crash, trailing its wake of ruin to grind
the massed Greeks assaulting left and right. But on
came Greek reserves, no letup, the hail of rocks,
the missiles of every kind would never cease.

   "There at the very edge of the front gates
130 springs Pyrrhus, son of Achilles, prancing in arms,
aflash in his shimmering brazen° sheath like a snake
buried the whole winter long under frozen turf,
swollen to bursting, fed full on poisonous weeds
and now it springs into light, sloughing° its old skin
135 to glisten sleek in its newfound youth, its back slithering,
coiling, its proud chest rearing high to the sun,
its triple tongue flickering through its fangs.
Backing him now comes Periphas, giant fighter,
Automedon too, Achilles' henchman, charioteer
140 who bore the great man's armor—backing Pyrrhus,
the young fighters from Scyros° raid the palace,
hurling firebrands at the roofs. Out in the lead,
Pyrrhus seizes a double-axe and batters the rocky sill
and ripping the bronze posts out of their sockets,
145 hacking the rugged oaken planks of the doors,
makes a breach, a gaping maw,° and there, exposed,
the heart of the house, the sweep of the colonnades,°
the palace depths of the old kings and Priam lie exposed
and they see the armed sentries bracing at the portals.

150   "But all in the house is turmoil, misery, groans,
the echoing chambers ring with cries of women,
wails of mourning hit the golden stars.
Mothers scatter in panic down the palace halls
and embrace the pillars, cling to them, kiss them hard.
155 But on he comes, Pyrrhus with all his father's force,
no bolts, not even the guards can hold him back—
under the ram's repeated blows the doors cave in,
the doorposts, prised° from their sockets, crash flat.

131 **brazen:** made of brass.

134 **sloughing:** shedding an outer layer of dead skin.

141 **Scyros** (skī′ rəs): island in the Aegean Sea off Greece; birthplace of Pyrrhus.

146 **maw:** an opening.
147 **colonnades:** a series of columns placed at intervals.

158 **prised:** forced loose.

---

3 Imagery *What does this image suggest about Pyrrhus?*

4 Make and Verify Predictions *What do you predict Pyrrhus will do after breaking into the palace?*

VIRGIL **383**

Teach

Literary Element	**3**

Imagery Answer: *The image of Pyrrhus as a snake suggests he will be a deadly, pitiless enemy.*

Reading Strategy	**4**

Make and Verify Predictions Answer: *Students may say that Pyrrhus will probably go on a murderous rampage, killing anyone in sight. He may even go after the king.*

Cultural History ☆
Ancient Weapons

Explain that Pyrrhus and his soldiers use a battering ram to smash through the doors. This was a large tree trunk, often mounted on wheels, that was repeatedly thrust toward walls or doors to smash through them. Sometimes the thrusting end was covered with a metal shield. Other times, the thrusting end was set on fire to burn as well as smash through wooden walls and doors.

Learning Objectives
Analyzing imagery. (SE)
Making and verifying predictions. (SE)
Summarizing. (TE)

Approaching Level

DIFFERENTIATED INSTRUCTION

Paraphrase and Visualize Have students work in groups or with more proficient partners to paraphrase the entrance of Pyrrhus, and Priam's preparations for his last battle. Make sure students understand that Priam is very old, but extremely dedicated to his city and his people, and is preparing for a heroic, yet futile, "last stand." Students might draw pictures to show this dramatic scene.

Advanced Learners/Pre-AP

DIFFERENTIATED INSTRUCTION

Movie Scene Students might enjoy working together to create a script for a movie scene based on the advance of Pyrrhus and his men, the raging fire, the preparation of Priam to defend his city, and Hecuba's words of warning. Urge them to include dialogue, sound effects, set descriptions, and stage directions.

Teach

Reading Strategy **1**

Review Review with students the character of Hector. Ask students who he is and what happened to him. *(He was the son of Priam and was killed by Achilles in the* Iliad.*)*

Force makes a breach and the Greeks come storming
　　through,
160　butcher the sentries, flood the entire place with men-at-
　　arms.
　　No river so wild, so frothing in spate, bursting its banks
　　to overpower the dikes, anything in its way, its cresting
　　tides stampeding in fury down on the fields to sweep
　　the flocks and stalls across the open plain.
165　I saw him myself, Pyrrhus crazed with carnage
　　and Atreus' two sons just at the threshold—
　　　　　　　　　　　　　　　　　　　　　　"I saw
　　Hecuba° with her hundred daughters and daughters-in-law,
　　saw Priam fouling with blood the altar fires
　　he himself had blessed.
　　　　　　　　　　　　"Those fifty bridal-chambers
170　filled with the hope of children's children still to come,
　　the pillars proud with trophies, gilded with Eastern gold,
　　they all come tumbling down—
　　and the Greeks hold what the raging fire spares.

　　"Perhaps you wonder how Priam met his end.
175　When he saw his city stormed and seized, his gates
　　wrenched apart, the enemy camped in his palace depths,
　　the old man dons his armor long unused, he clamps it
　　round his shoulders shaking with age and, all for nothing,
　　straps his useless sword to his hip, then makes
180　for the thick of battle, out to meet his death.
　　At the heart of the house an ample altar stood,
　　naked under the skies,
　　an ancient laurel° bending over the shrine,
　　embracing our household gods within its shade.
185　Here, flocking the altar, Hecuba and her daughters
　　huddled, blown headlong down like doves by a black storm—
　　clutching, all for nothing, the figures of their gods.
　　Seeing Priam decked in the arms he'd worn as a young man,
　　'Are you insane?' she cries, 'poor husband, what **impels** you
190　to strap that sword on now? Where are you rushing?
　　Too late for such defense, such help. Not even

1　my own Hector, if *he* came to the rescue now . . .
　　Come to me, Priam. This altar will shield us all
　　or else you'll die with us.'

167　**Hecuba** (hek′yə bə): Priam's wife.

183　**laurel:** evergreen shrub or tree.

Vocabulary

impel (im pel′) *v.* to urge forward as if through moral pressure

---

Reading Practice

Activate Prior Knowledge Discuss with students the facts that are contained in the dialogue between Pyrrhus and Priam that echo the characters and events in the *Iliad*. Work with them to create family trees, showing the relationships between the Greeks (Achilles and Pyrrhus) and between the Trojans (Priam, Hector, and Polites). Use the diagrams to point out the underlying roles of revenge and honor. Compare and contrast the honor with which Achilles treated the corpse of Hector with the brutal way in which Pyrrhus butchers Polites. Remind students that the events in this account are described by Virgil's hero, Aeneas. Ask them how Virgil's purpose for writing (to glorify Rome) might have colored his version of the events. If necessary, remind them that Virgil intended to emphasize the Roman values of piety, respect, honor, duty, and self-denial.

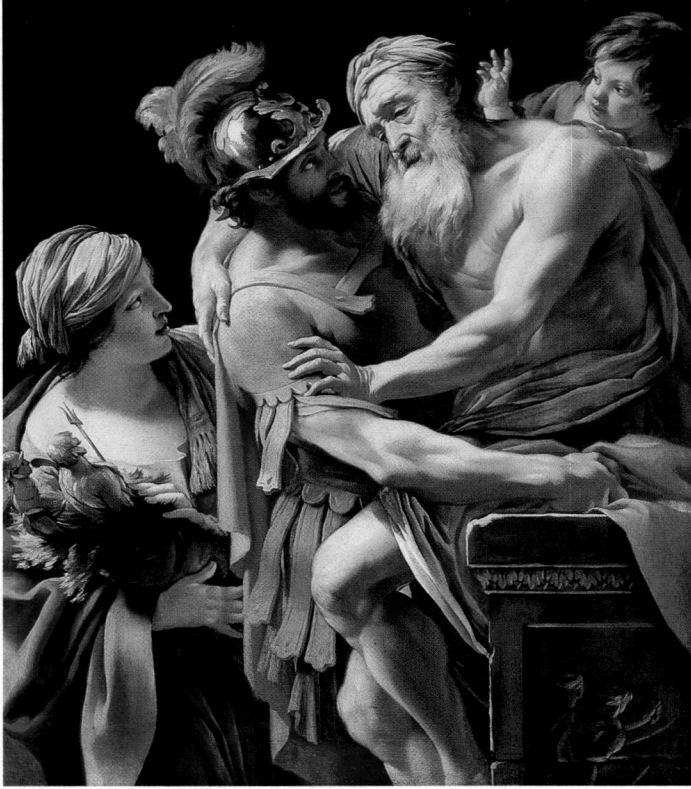

Aeneas and his Father Fleeing Troy, c. 1635. Simon Vouet. Oil on canvas, 140.3 x 110 cm. San Diego Museum of Art, CA.

View the Art This painting shows Aeneas's wife (clutching the household gods) and son watching as Aeneas lifts Anchises onto his shoulders. What does the painting suggest about the relationship between Aeneas and his father?

"With those words,
195   drawing him toward her there, she made a place
for the old man beside the holy shrine.
                  "Suddenly,
look, a son of Priam, Polites,° just escaped
from slaughter at Pyrrhus' hands, comes racing in
through spears, through enemy fighters, fleeing down
200   the long arcades and deserted hallways—badly wounded,
Pyrrhus hot on his heels, a weapon poised for the kill,
about to seize him, about to run him through and pressing
home as Polites reaches his parents and collapses,
vomiting out his lifeblood before their eyes.
205   At that, Priam, trapped in the grip of death,
not holding back, not checking his words, his rage:

197 Polites (pə lī′ tēz): young Trojan warrior.

---

2 Make and Verify Predictions *Pyrrhus murders Polites before Priam's very eyes. What do you predict Priam will do now?*

VIRGIL **385**

Teach

Reading Strategy	2

Make and Verify Predictions Answer: *Students may say Priam will try to avenge his son's death by killing Pyrrhus.*

(**ENGLISH LEARNERS**) If students have difficulty understanding the idiom *hot on his heels*, point out that it means "running close behind him."

View the Art

Answer: *Aeneas shows affection and concern for his father.*

Simon Vouet was born in Paris, but he lived and painted in Italy for fifteen years. He returned to France only after King Louis XIII told him that he would name him his "first," or most important, painter. Vouet was influential in introducing the Italian Baroque style of painting to France, and he was commissioned to paint nearly every important painting in France for fifteen years after his return from Italy. His skill in creating sharp contrasts of light and shadow can be seen in this painting.

Learning Objectives
Making and verifying predictions. (SE)
Activating prior knowledge. (TE)

Approaching Level
DIFFERENTIATED INSTRUCTION

Visual Aids Some students may comprehend the text better if given the opportunity to see the action and the characters visually represented. Search the Internet or a library for visual depictions of the events and characters in the *Aeneid*.

You might use paintings or sculptures, or illustrations from other versions of the epic. Have students identify the events and characters. Then have them express how these visual depictions are similar to, or different from, their own visualizations.

Advanced Learners/Pre-AP
DIFFERENTIATED INSTRUCTION

Literary Comparison Have students look at Percy Bysshe Shelley's sonnet, "Ozymandias" on page 707. Have students work with partners or in small groups to analyze this poem and then compare the life and fate of Ozymandias with that of Priam.

Teach

Imagery Answer: *Helpful images include* he drags the old man straight to the altar, slicks of his son's blood, twisting Priam's hair, a flash of steel, *and* he buries it hilt-deep in the king's flank.

APPROACHING If students have difficulty understanding these images, help them by describing the actions in simpler terms.

Literary History ☆

Helen of Troy According to myth, the Greek woman Helen had such beauty that the Trojan prince Paris fell in love with her instantly and took her away to Troy. Her Greek husband Menelaus reacted by declaring war. The Greek army immediately sailed a large fleet to attack Troy. Hence, Helen has traditionally been blamed for causing the Trojan War. Several authors and poets, including William Butler Yeats, have used her as a symbol of irresistible but treacherous beauty. In his 16th-century play *Doctor Faustus*, the British writer Christopher Marlowe coined the now-famous phrase "the face that launched a thousand ships" in reference to Helen's beauty.

Listening Practice

SMALL GROUP
Participate in a Literature Group Find examples of paintings and illustrations of Helen of Troy. Try to find examples from different eras, in order to exemplify how "beauty" was defined at different times. Remind students that according to ancient legends, the Trojan War was a result of this woman's extraordinary beauty. Have students view and discuss the various pictures of Helen. Then have them work in small groups to discuss this question: *Do you believe that it is realistic that nations would go to war over a beautiful woman?* Use the discussion to point out the similarity between ancient legends and more modern folk tales or fables ("The Emperor's New Clothes," "The Boy Who Cried Wolf," "Jack and the Beanstalk," etc.), in which simple, romantic, or foolish events or people lead to dramatic consequences.

'You!' he cries, 'you and your vicious crimes!
If any power on high recoils at such an outrage,
let the gods repay you for all your reckless work,
210 grant you the thanks, the rich reward you've earned.
You've made me see my son's death with my own eyes,
defiled a father's sight with a son's lifeblood.
You say you're Achilles' son? You lie! Achilles
never treated his enemy Priam so. No, he honored
215 a **suppliant's** rights, he blushed to betray my trust,
he restored my Hector's bloodless corpse for burial,
sent me safely home to the land I rule!'
                                        "With that
and with all his might the old man flings his spear—
but too impotent now to pierce, it merely grazes
220 Pyrrhus' brazen shield that blocks its way
and clings there, dangling limp from the boss,
all for nothing. Pyrrhus shouts back: 'Well then,
down you go, a messenger to my father, Peleus'° son!
Tell him about my vicious work, how Neoptolemus°
225 degrades his father's name—don't you forget.
Now—die!'
"That said, he drags the old man
straight to the altar, quaking, slithering on through
slicks of his son's blood, and twisting Priam's hair
in his left hand, his right hand sweeping forth his sword—
230 a flash of steel—he buries it hilt-deep in the king's flank.
    "Such was the fate of Priam, his death, his lot on earth,
with Troy blazing before his eyes, her ramparts down,
the monarch who once had ruled in all his glory
the many lands of Asia, Asia's many tribes.
235 A powerful trunk is lying on the shore.
The head wrenched from the shoulders.
A corpse without a name.
                            "Then, for the first time
the full horror came home to me at last. I froze.
The thought of my own dear father filled my mind
240 when I saw the old king gasping out his life

223 Peleus (pē′ lē əs): father of Achilles.
224 Neoptolemus: (nē op tôl′ə məs′): another name for Pyrrhus.

---

1 Imagery *What images help you visualize Priam's death?*

Vocabulary

defile (di fīl′) *v.* to make unclean
suppliant (sə′ plē′ ənt) *n.* one who asks humbly and earnestly

with that raw wound—both men were the same age—
and the thought of my Creusa,° alone, abandoned,
our house plundered, our little Iulus'° fate.
I look back—what forces still stood by me?
245 None. Totally spent in war, they'd all deserted,
down from the roofs they'd flung themselves to earth
or hurled their broken bodies in the flames.
                                    ["So,
at just that moment I was the one man left
and then I saw her, clinging to Vesta's° threshold,
250 hiding in silence, tucked away—Helen of Argos.
Glare of the fires lit my view as I looked down,
scanning the city left and right, and there she was . . .
terrified of the Trojans' hate, now Troy was overpowered,
terrified of the Greeks' revenge, her deserted husband's
    rage—
255 that universal Fury, a curse to Troy and her native land
and here she lurked, skulking, a thing of loathing
cowering at the altar: Helen. Out it flared,
the fire inside my soul, my rage ablaze to avenge
our fallen country—pay Helen back, crime for crime.

260   " 'So, this woman,' it struck me now, 'safe and sound
she'll look once more on Sparta, her native Greece?
She'll ride like a queen in triumph with her trophies?
Feast her eyes on her husband, parents, children too?
Her retinue fawning round her, Phrygian° ladies, slaves?
265 That—with Priam put to the sword? And Troy up in flames?
And time and again our Dardan° shores have sweated blood?
Not for all the world. No fame, no memory to be won
for punishing a woman: such victory reaps no praise
but to stamp this abomination out as she deserves,
270 to punish her now, they'll sing my praise for that.
What joy, to glut° my heart with the fires of vengeance,
bring some peace to the ashes of my people!'

    "Whirling words—I was swept away by fury now]
when all of a sudden there my loving mother stood

---

242 **Creusa** (krē ū′sə): wife of Aeneas.
243 **Iulus** (ū′ləs): son of Aeneas and Creusa, also called Ascanius.

249 **Vesta**: goddess of the hearth and household activities.

264 **retinue**: retainers who accompany a high-ranking individual. **Phrygian** (frij′ē ən): people from a region near Troy.
266 **Dardan**: Trojan.

271 **glut**: to fill beyond capacity, or satiate.

---

2   Roman Myth   *What qualities of the ideal Roman hero does Aeneas possess?*

3   Make and Verify Predictions   *Do you think Aeneas will kill Helen? Explain.*

VIRGIL **387**

Advanced Learners/Pre-AP

DIFFERENTIATED INSTRUCTION

Find the Facts After discussing the romantic notion of Greece and Troy's going to war over the beauty of a woman, students might enjoy researching the facts about ancient Greece and Troy to find more realistic reasons that might have led to war. To stimulate thought, you might suggest that they explore facts regarding geographical location and trade routes. Have them present their findings to the class.

Approaching Level

DIFFERENTIATED INSTRUCTION

Main Idea Help readers understand that Venus's main purpose for appearing to Aeneas is to persuade him that he should not waste time or energy punishing Helen or Paris because it is the wrath of the gods that has caused the destruction of Troy. Once students understand Venus's purpose, work with them to rephrase her speech in modern prose.

Teach

| **Big Idea** | | | 2 |

Roman Myth Answer:
Aeneas's love of family is reflected in these lines. He deeply loves his father, his wife, and his son.

| **Reading Strategy** | | 3 |

Make and Verify Predictions Answer: *Some students may say that Aeneas is so incensed he will not be able to restrain himself from killing Helen, who he believes is the cause of Troy's destruction. Others may say Aeneas's role as the ideal Roman hero would preclude such a shameful deed.*

Literary History

Aeneas's Mother Aeneas's mother was Venus, the Roman counterpart of Aphrodite, the Greek goddess of love. This is ironic, because according to Greek myth, Aphrodite had a major role in bringing on the Trojan War. She, Athena, and Hera competed to win the title of the fairest goddess. They decided on Paris as the judge. Then each goddess offered him a bribe. Hera would make him ruler of the world, Athena would make him victorious in battle, and Aphrodite would give him the most beautiful woman in the world. He chose Aphrodite. Her gift of Helen led to the war.

Learning Objectives
Analyzing imagery. (SE)
Making and verifying predictions. (SE)
Participating in a literature group. (TE)

387

Teach

Literary Element 1

Imagery Answer: *She describes the destruction as a storm unleashed by Neptune, the god of the sea.*

APPROACHING Help students to understand the participation of the other gods and goddesses (Juno, Pallas, Athena, and Jove) in the destruction of Troy. Then remind students that often, ancient myths and legends explained disastrous historical events by blaming them on the gods.

275 before my eyes, but I had never seen her so clearly,
      her pure radiance shining down upon me through the night,
      the goddess in all her glory, just as the gods behold
      her build, her awesome beauty. Grasping my hand
      she held me back, adding this from her rose-red lips:
280 'My son, what grief could incite such blazing anger?
      Why such fury? And the love you bore me once,
      where has it all gone? Why don't you look first
      where you left your father, Anchises, spent with age?
      Do your wife, Creusa, and son Ascanius still survive?
285 The Greek battalions are swarming round them all,
      and if my love had never rushed to the rescue,
      flames would have swept them off by now or
      enemy sword-blades would have drained their blood.
      Think: it's not that beauty, Helen, you should hate,
290 not even Paris,° the man that you should blame, no,
      it's the gods, the ruthless gods who are tearing down
      the wealth of Troy, her toppling crown of towers.
      Look around. I'll sweep it all away, the mist
      so murky, dark, and swirling around you now,
295 it clouds your vision, dulls your mortal sight.
      You are my son. Never fear my orders.
      Never refuse to bow to my commands.
                                    " 'There,
      yes, where you see the massive ramparts shattered,
      blocks wrenched from blocks, the billowing smoke and
        ash—
300 it's Neptune° himself, prising loose with his giant trident
      the foundation-stones of Troy, he's making the walls quake,
      ripping up the entire city by her roots.
                                    " 'There's Juno,°
      cruelest in fury, first to commandeer the Scaean Gates,°
      sword at her hip and mustering comrades, shock troops
305 streaming out of the ships.
                                    " 'Already up on the heights—
      turn around and look—there's Pallas° holding the fortress,
      flaming out of the clouds, her savage Gorgon° glaring.
      Even Father himself, he's filling the Greek hearts
      with courage, stamina—Jove in person spurring the gods
310 to fight the Trojan armies!

290 **Paris:** the prince of Troy whose kidnapping of Helen triggered the Trojan War.

300 **Neptune:** the god of the sea.

302 **Juno:** chief goddess and protector of marriage; wife of Jupiter, she favored the Greeks.
303 **Scaean Gates** (skē´ ən): set of gates in the walls surrounding Troy.

306 **Pallas:** Athena, the Greek goddess of war and wisdom.
307 **Gorgon:** refers to Medusa, a monster whose appearance turned beholders to stone. Here, her head is attached to Pallas's shield.

---

1 Imagery *What image does Venus use to describe the destruction of Troy?*

Speaking Practice

Role-Play Have students practice their speaking and listening skills, and become more actively engaged in the literature, by having partners role-play interviews between Aeneas's father and a news reporter. Students taking the role of the father should study his speech (lines 335–350) to discover his motivation for staying in the city. Students taking the role of the interviewer should ask questions about his thoughts and feelings during the destruction of his city, his attitudes toward the Greeks and the Trojans, and his feelings for his family. Call on volunteers to act out their interviews for the class.

                    " 'Run for your life, my son.
Put an end to your labors. I will never leave you,
I will set you safe at your father's door.'

        "Parting words. She vanished into the dense night.
And now they all come looming up before me,
315   terrible shapes, the deadly foes of Troy,
the gods gigantic in power.
                            "Then at last
I saw it all, all Ilium settling into her embers,
Neptune's Troy, toppling over now from her roots
like a proud, veteran ash on its mountain summit,
320   chopped by stroke after stroke of the iron axe as
woodsmen fight to bring it down, and over and
over it threatens to fall, its boughs shudder,
its leafy crown quakes and back and forth it sways
till overwhelmed by its wounds, with a long last groan
325   it goes—torn up from its heights it crashes down
in ruins from its ridge . . .
Venus leading, down from the roof I climb
and win my way through fires and massing foes.
The spears recede, the flames roll back before me.

330   "At last, gaining the door of father's ancient house,
my first concern was to find the man, my first wish
to spirit him off, into the high mountain range,
but father, seeing Ilium razed from the earth,
refused to drag his life out now and suffer exile.
335   'You,' he argued, 'you in your prime, untouched by age,
your blood still coursing strong, you hearts of oak,
you are the ones to hurry your escape. Myself,
if the gods on high had wished me to live on,
they would have saved my palace for me here.
340   Enough—more than enough—that I have seen
one sack of my city, once survived its capture.
Here I lie, here laid out for death. Come say
your parting salutes and leave my body so.
I will find my own death, sword in hand:
345   my enemies keen for spoils will be so kind.
Death without burial? A small price to pay.
For years now, I've lingered out my life,
despised by the gods, a dead weight to men,

---

2 Imagery *What word picture does Virgil create here?*

Literary Element	2

Imagery Answer: *He creates a word picture of an old, towering ash tree being chopped down.*

[APPROACHING] **Ask:** Why does he make a comparison between Troy and a mighty tree? *(Both were once strong and at "the top"; both have now fallen.)*

Learning Objectives
Analyzing imagery. (SE)
Role-playing. (TE)

Approaching Level

DIFFERENTIATED INSTRUCTION

Make Connections Students having difficulty understanding the conflicts facing Aeneas and his family may benefit from taking turns reading lines 376–380 aloud. Model the reading, using an emotional voice to ask the short, staccato questions. Then have students read them. Emphasize that their reading of the lines should show an accurate portrayal of Aeneas's feelings.

Teach

Reading Strategy · 1

Make and Verify Predictions **Answer:** *Some students may say Anchises will refuse to leave his palace because he is so attached to his city that he cannot imagine living without it. Others may say the pleas of his family will touch his heart and make him yield to their wishes.*

Big Idea · 2

Roman Myth **Answer:** *This passage suggests that despite the terrible odds facing him, the honor of a Roman warrior is extremely important; courage is more important than life.*

ever since the Father of Gods and King of Mortals
350   stormed at me with his bolt and scorched me with its fire.'

    "So he said, planted there. Nothing could shake him now.
But we dissolved in tears, my wife, Creusa, Ascanius,
the whole household, begging my father not to pull
our lives down with him, adding his own weight
355   to the fate that dragged us down.
He still refuses, holds to his resolve,
clings to the spot. And again I rush to arms,
desperate to die myself. Where could I turn?
What were our chances now, at this point?
360   'What!' I cried. 'Did you, my own father,
dream that I could run away and desert you here?
How could such an outrage slip from a father's lips?
If it please the gods that nothing of our great city
shall survive—if you are bent on adding your own death
365   to the deaths of Troy and of all your loved ones too,
the doors of the deaths you crave are spread wide open.
Pyrrhus will soon be here, bathed in Priam's blood,
Pyrrhus who butchers sons in their fathers' faces,
slaughters fathers at the altar. Was it for this,
370   my loving mother, you swept me clear of the weapons,
free of the flames? Just to see the enemy camped
in the very heart of our house, to see my son, Ascanius,
see my father, my wife, Creusa, with them, sacrificed,
massacred in each other's blood?
                'Arms, my comrades,
375   bring me arms! The last light calls the defeated.
Send me back to the Greeks, let me go back
to fight new battles. Not all of us here
will die today without revenge.'
               "Now buckling on
my sword again and working my left arm through
380   the shieldstrap, grasping it tightly, just as I
was rushing out, right at the doors my wife, Creusa,
look, flung herself at my feet and hugged my knees

---

1   Make and Verify Predictions *Do you predict Anchises will leave with Aeneas or remain in his palace? Explain.*

2   Roman Myth *What does this passage suggest about the Roman attitude toward the role of the warrior and the importance of courage?*

390   UNIT 2   ANCIENT ROME

Reading Practice

 SMALL GROUP

Summarize
Remind students that an effective way to make sure they understand what they read is to stop periodically to summarize the main ideas. Write the following questions (with line references) on the chalkboard. Have students work with partners or in small groups to answer each question by summarizing the main ideas.

1. (lines 404–408) What two choices does Creusa suggest to Aeneas?

2. (lines 414–419) What strange sight appears on the head of Aeneas's son?

3. (lines 420–425) How does Anchises interpret this strange sight, and what does he decide to do?

4. (lines 431–443) What is Aeneas's plan, for his wife and son, his father, and the servants?

and raised our little Iulus up to his father.
'If you are going off to die,' she begged,
385 'then take us with you too,
to face the worst together. But if your battles
teach you to hope in arms, the arms you buckle on,
your first duty should be to guard our house.
Desert us, leave us now—to whom? Whom?
390 Little Iulus, your father and your wife,
so I once was called.'
⠀⠀⠀⠀⠀⠀⠀⠀⠀"So Creusa cries,
her wails of anguish echoing through the house
when out of the blue an omen strikes—a marvel!
Now as we held our son between our hands
395 and both our grieving faces, a tongue of fire,
watch, flares up from the crown of Iulus' head,
a subtle flame licking his downy hair, feeding
around the boy's brow, . . .

IN ADDITION TO THE MAGIC FLAME *that illuminates Iulus's hair, a shooting star streaks across the sky and lands in the forests near Mount Ida. These supernatural signs deeply move Anchises.*

Won over at last, my father rises to his full height
400 and prays to the gods and reveres that holy star:
'No more delay, not now! You gods of my fathers,
now I follow wherever you lead me, I am with you.
Safeguard our house, safeguard my grandson Iulus!
This sign is yours: Troy rests in your power.
405 I give way, my son. No more refusals.
I will go with you, your comrade.'
⠀⠀⠀⠀⠀⠀⠀⠀⠀"So he yielded
but now the roar of flames grows louder all through Troy
and the seething floods of fire are rolling closer.
'So come, dear father, climb up onto my shoulders!
410 I will carry you on my back. This labor of love
will never wear me down. Whatever falls to us now,

3 Imagery *What senses do these details appeal to?*

Teach

Literary Element 3

Imagery Answer: *They appeal to the senses of sight, hearing, and touch.*

Cultural History ☆

Household Gods When Aeneas in line 422 asks his father to carry the "hearth-gods," he refers to the Penates, the "little gods" of the home. In Latin, their name is a combination of "cupboard" and "food." In ancient Greece and Rome, each family built a small altar in their home, on which they placed statues of gods. They adorned the altars with flowers and candles, and prayed to these "household gods" for protection. Fleeing his home, Aeneas shows the Roman values of piety and respect by making sure that these "sacred vessels" are not left behind. Wherever their flight takes them, the family will have their gods with them to establish a new, secure household.

Learning Objectives
Analyzing imagery. (SE)
Summarizing. (TE)
Comparing and contrasting. (TE)

Approaching Level
DIFFERENTIATED INSTRUCTION

What Went Wrong? To make sure students understand the disappearance of Creusa, have them summarize the plan that Aeneas set up for his family's safe escape from the city. Then have them reread and discuss what happens as the plan unfolds. What went wrong, and why? *(Creusa was to follow Aeneas through the city to a shrine. But she never gets there, apparently having lost her way and died.)*

Advanced Learners/Pre-AP
DIFFERENTIATED INSTRUCTION

Connect to Social Studies Explain to students that one of the tragic results of war—in ancient and in modern times—is the displacement of people from their cities, their homes, and their livelihoods. Discuss how Aeneas and his family members might have felt as they looked back on their burning city and fled for their lives. Then have students work with partners or in small groups to research facts about modern war refugees. You might assign each group to a specific conflict, such as World War II, the Vietnam War, Darfur, and the Iraq War.

391

Teach

Reading Strategy | 1

Compare and Contrast

Ask: What time of day is it now? *(night)* How does Aeneas characterize his usual attitude toward battle? *(He is never afraid of enemy soldiers.)* How are his current feelings different from that usual attitude? *(He is fearful of every sound.)* Why? *(He feels responsible for the welfare of the child and his elderly father.)* Encourage students to make connections with his feelings. **Ask:** Do you grow more cautious or conservative if you are responsible for someone else's welfare? Have students offer specific examples.

Big Idea | 2

Roman Myth **Answer:** *The Roman attitude toward the gods was one of piety. Aeneas refuses to touch the images of the gods because his hands are unclean, still bloody from battle.*

---

we both will share one peril, one path to safety.
Little Iulus, walk beside me, and you, my wife,
follow me at a distance, in my footsteps.
415 Servants, listen closely . . .
Just past the city walls a grave-mound lies
where an old shrine of forsaken Ceres° stands
with an ancient cypress growing close beside it—
our fathers' reverence kept it green for years.
420 Coming by many routes, it's there we meet,
our rendezvous. And you, my father, carry
our hearth-gods now, our fathers' sacred vessels.
I, just back from the war and fresh from slaughter,
I must not handle the holy things—it's wrong—
425 not till I cleanse myself in running springs.'
                                        "With that,
over my broad shoulders and round my neck I spread
a tawny lion's skin for a cloak, and bowing down,
I lift my burden up. Little Iulus, clutching
my right hand, keeps pace with tripping steps.
430 My wife trails on behind. And so we make our way
along the pitch-dark paths, and I who had never flinched
at the hurtling spears or swarming Greek assaults—
now every stir of wind, every whisper of sound
alarms me, anxious both for the child beside me
435 and burden on my back. And then, nearing the gates,
thinking we've all got safely through, I suddenly
seem to catch the steady tramp of marching feet
and father, peering out through the darkness, cries:
'Run for it now, my boy, you must. They're closing in,
440 I can see their glinting shields, their flashing bronze!'

   "Then in my panic something strange, some enemy power
robbed me of my senses. Lost, I was leaving behind
familiar paths, at a run down blind dead ends
when—
         "Oh dear god, my wife, Creusa—
445 torn from me by a brutal fate! What then,
did she stop in her tracks or lose her way?
Or exhausted, sink down to rest? Who knows?
I never set my eyes on her again.

---

417 forsaken Ceres: the goddess of grain, whose daughter Proserpina was stolen by Pluto and taken to the underworld.

2 **Roman Myth** *What does this passage suggest about the Roman attitude toward the gods?*

Writing Practice

Write Descriptions Discuss with students the importance of using clear description to create mental pictures in readers' minds. Explain that one way of writing descriptively is to use imagery, as Virgil does in the *Aeneid*. Discuss the different means of presenting imagery, such as through simile and metaphor.

Have students choose someone or something to describe in two or three paragraphs into which they incorporate imagery, such figures of speech as simile and metaphor, and strong verbs and precise adjectives. Have them share their descriptions in small groups.

Aeneas Carrying His Father Anchises from the Blazing City of Troy. Daniel Van Heil. Oil on copper, 18.2 x 25.4 cm. Private collection.

 View the Art This painting was done on a copper plate, a medium that allows painters to create rich, glowing colors. What impression do the color and lighting create in this painting?

> I never looked back, she never crossed my mind—
> 450 Creusa, lost—not till we reached that barrow
> sacred to ancient Ceres where, with all our people
> rallied at last, she alone was missing. Lost
> to her friends, her son, her husband—gone forever.
> Raving, I blamed them all, the gods, the human race—
> 455 what crueler blow did I feel the night that Troy went down?
> Ascanius, father Anchises, and all the gods of Troy,
> entrusting them to my friends, I hide them well away
> in a valley's shelter, don my burnished gear
> and back I go to Troy . . .

3   Roman Myth   *What can you infer about the ideal Roman hero from this passage?*

Big Idea   **3**

Roman Myth Answer: *The ideal Roman hero cared deeply about his loved ones and wasn't afraid to express his emotions. Aeneas, mad with grief over the loss of his wife, holds nothing back.*

View the Art

Answer: *The color and lighting give a strong impression of the fire's heat and ferocity.*

In the sixteenth century, artists began to make oil paintings on copper plates. This technique is usually limited to small paintings, because the weight of the copper makes larger ones impractical.

Learning Objectives
Analyzing art. (SE)
Connecting to personal experience. (TE)
Understanding multiple-meaning words. (TE)

English Learners

DIFFERENTIATED INSTRUCTION

Intermediate Students learning English may have difficulty with multiple-meaning words. Therefore, during the Vocabulary Practice activity, you might lend extra assistance to them by having them work with language-proficient partners. Have the pairs identify and practice pronouncing any multiple-meaning words that have several different pronunciations.

Teach

Reading Strategy   1

Connect to Personal Experience Ask students how Aeneas must be feeling as he desperately searches for his wife, and how they might feel under similar circumstances. *(Students will probably mention fear and despair.)*

APPROACHING Some students might need assistance understanding Aeneas's plight. Work with them to paraphrase the lines that describe the horrors that Aeneas sees as he desperately searches for her—the fire, the deserted palace, and the stacks of plunder. Use those images to help them understand his feelings.

Reading Strategy   2

Make and Verify Predictions Answer: *Students may say Creusa's ghost will tell her husband that the gods willed her death and that he must carry on and take care of their child, Iules.*

Progress Check

Can students make and verify predictions?

If No → See Unit 2 Teaching Resources Book, p. 189.

460   my mind steeled to relive the whole disaster,
      retrace my route through the whole city now
      and put my life in danger one more time.
                                    "First then,
      back to the looming walls, the shadowy rear gates
      by which I'd left the city, back I go in my tracks,
465   retracing, straining to find my footsteps in the dark,
      with terror at every turn, the very silence makes me cringe.
      Then back to my house I go—if only, only she's gone
          there—
      but the Greeks have flooded in, seized the entire place.
      All over now. Devouring fire whipped by the winds
470   goes churning into the rooftops, flames surging
      over them, scorching blasts raging up the sky.
      On I go and again I see the palace of Priam
      set on the heights, but there in colonnades
      deserted now, in the sanctuary of Juno, there
475   stand the elite watchmen, Phoenix,° ruthless Ulysses°
      guarding all their loot. All the treasures of Troy
      hauled from the burning shrines—the sacramental tables,
      bowls of solid gold and the holy robes they'd seized
      from every quarter—Greeks, piling high the plunder.
480   Children and trembling mothers rounded up
      in a long, endless line.
                              "Why, I even dared fling
      my voice through the dark, my shouts filled the streets
      as time and again, overcome with grief I called out
      'Creusa!' Nothing, no reply, and again 'Creusa!'
485   But then as I madly rushed from house to house,
      no end in sight, abruptly, right before my eyes
      I saw her stricken ghost, my own Creusa's shade.
      But larger than life, the life I'd known so well.
      I froze. My hackles° bristled, voice choked in my throat,
490   and my wife spoke out to ease me of my anguish:
      'My dear husband, why so eager to give yourself
      to such mad flights of grief? It's not without
      the will of the gods these things have come to pass.
      But the gods forbid you to take Creusa with you,
495   bound from Troy together. The king of lofty Olympus°
      won't allow it. A long exile is your fate . . .
      the vast plains of the sea are yours to plow

475 Phoenix (fē´niks): a Greek leader who had been Achilles' tutor.
475 Ulysses (ū´lis´ēz): Odysseus, the king of Ithaca; Greek leader known for his stratagems.

489 hackles: hairs on the back of the neck.

495 Olympus: Mount Olympus, the highest mountain in Greece and the home of the gods.

2 **Make and Verify Predictions** *What do you predict Creusa's ghost will say to her husband?*

Vocabulary Practice

Understand Multiple-Meaning Words Remind students that many words have more than one meaning. As examples, write these words on the chalkboard: *rest, right, bow.* Call on volunteers to take turns using a dictionary to find different meanings of each word, read the definition aloud, and use the word in a sentence showing its specific

meaning. Then draw attention to the following words in the text. Have students find each word in the dictionary and use context clues in the text to decide which meaning the poet/translator intended. Have them write the correct definition and use the word in an original sentence.

back (line 467)	shade (line 487)
place (line 468)	mad (line 492)
over (line 469)	will (line 493)
over (line 471)	bound (line 495)
quarter (line 479)	rich (line 499)

until you reach Hesperian land, where Lydian Tiber°
flows with its smooth march through rich and loamy fields,
500 a land of hardy people. There great joy and a kingdom
are yours to claim, and a queen to make your wife.
Dispel your tears for Creusa whom you loved.
I will never behold the high and mighty pride
of their palaces, the Myrmidons,° the Dolopians,
505 or go as a slave to some Greek matron, no, not I,
daughter of Dardanus° that I am, the wife of Venus' son.
The Great Mother of Gods detains me on these shores.
And now farewell. Hold dear the son we share,
we love together.'
                  "These were her parting words
510 and for all my tears—I longed to say so much—
dissolving into the empty air she left me now.
Three times I tried to fling my arms around her neck,
three times I embraced—nothing . . . her phantom
sifting through my fingers,
515 light as wind, quick as a dream in flight.
                        "Gone—
and at last the night was over. Back I went to my people
and I was amazed to see what throngs of new companions
had poured in to swell our numbers, mothers, men,
our forces gathered for exile, grieving masses.
520 They had come together from every quarter,
belongings, spirits ready for me to lead them
over the sea to whatever lands I'd choose.
And now the morning star was mounting above
the high crests of Ida,° leading on the day.
525 The Greeks had taken the city, blocked off every gate.
No hope of rescue now. So I gave way at last and
lifting my father, headed toward the mountains."

---

3 Imagery *What do the similes in this passage suggest about Aeneas's actions?*

4 Roman Myth *How does the ideal Roman hero respond to adversity?*

498 Hesperian: (he sper′ē ən): of the land to the west where the sun sets, known as the "land of the evening"; Italy, the peninsula on which Rome is located. **Tiber** (tī′ bər): the river that flows through Rome, Italy: at that time, controlled by Etruscans, who may have come from Lydia (li′ dē ə), in Asia Minor.
504 Myrmidons: the followers of Achilles.
506 Dardanus: thought to be the founder of Troy.

524 Ida: mountain near Troy.

Teach

Literary Element   3

Imagery Answer: *The similes "light as wind" and "quick as a dream in flight" suggest the futility of trying to embrace a phantom.*

Progress Check

Can students analyze imagery?

If No → See Unit 2 Teaching Resources Book, p. 188.

Big Idea   4

Roman Myth Answer: *No matter what misfortunes and challenges he faces, the ideal Roman hero embraces his duty and fulfills his mission.*

 To check students' understanding of the selection, see Unit 2 Teaching Resources Book, p. 193.

Approaching Level

DIFFERENTIATED INSTRUCTION

Paraphrase and Visualize To make sure that students approaching level understand the final scene, work with them to paraphrase each sentence. After each one, call on volunteers to describe what they visualize in their minds. Lead students to understand that in the light of a new day, Aeneas, carrying his father on his back, led the surviving people of Troy off to find a new land.

After You Read

Assess

1. Students should give explanations for what made their chosen passages exciting.

2. Students may suggest that pride, loyalty, and bravery motivate him.

3. (a) Priam is trying to avenge his slain son when Pyrrhus kills him. (b) Aeneas emphasizes the injustice and horror of the murder, as well as the greatness of Priam's reign.

4. Aeneas is a loyal and loving son.

5. (a) He runs ahead, and she gets lost while they are fleeing the Greeks. (b) They seem to care deeply about each other.

6. Venus wants Aeneas to realize the gods, not Helen, are responsible for Troy's fall, and to come with her to protect his family.

7. Although both fight fiercely against their adversaries, Aeneas is more admirable because he is fighting to defend his homeland. In addition, Pyrrhus is shown butchering Polites, a young warrior, and Priam, the decrepit king.

8. Aeneas represents bravery, perseverance, devotion to family, and piety.

9. Students might mention the killing of civilian populations and the destruction of communities in many recent conflicts around the world.

After You Read

Respond and Think Critically

Respond and Interpret

1. What passage in this excerpt did you find most exciting? Explain why the passage made an impression on you.

2. Even as he prepares to attack the Greeks, Aeneas realizes he doesn't have a chance. What motivates him to fight?

3. (a) What are the circumstances of Priam's death? (b) What does Aeneas emphasize about the king's death?

4. How would you characterize Aeneas's attitude toward his father?

5. (a) How does Aeneas become separated from his wife? (b) What impression do you have of Aeneas's relationship with his wife?

Analyze and Evaluate

6. Why does Venus reveal the actions of the gods to her son Aeneas?

7. A **foil** is a character whose attitudes, beliefs, and behavior differ significantly from those of another character. How would you compare Aeneas's actions with those of his foil Pyrrhus?

Connect

8. **Big Idea** Roman Myth An epic hero represents the ideals of his or her society. What ideals does Aeneas represent?

9. **Connect to Today** Virgil portrays the suffering and chaos that result from Troy's fall. What modern event does this remind you of? Why?

Primary Visual Artifact

Depicting the Trojan Horse

In describing the fall of Troy, Aeneas gives Dido few concrete details about the appearance of the Trojan horse other than that it was huge, hollow, and made of wood. Perhaps because Virgil's description is so limited, artists have freely used their imaginations in portraying the Trojan horse. As a result, depictions of it have varied widely. The image here is a German pen and ink and watercolor done in 1464.

Group Activity Discuss the following questions with your classmates. Refer to the image and cite evidence from the *Aeneid*.

1. What words would you use to describe the style of this image? Explain.

2. How would you compare this image with other images of the Trojan horse in art and movies?

Primary Visual Artifact

1. Students might use such words as *primitive* or *childish*. It includes such unrealistic details as wheels and windows through which the heads of Greek warriors can be seen. It is not drawn to scale.

2. It seems less sophisticated than many other images.

Literary Element Imagery

SAT Skills Practice

1. The description of Cassandra in lines 66–70 is introduced to show the

   (A) trickery of the Greeks
   (B) courage of the Trojans
   (C) failure of divine help
   (D) weakness of Trojan women
   (E) inevitability of fate

2. The image of the ash tree in lines 319–326 most emphasizes

   (A) the overthrow of Troy
   (B) the Trojans' stubborn resistance
   (C) Troy's hilltop setting
   (D) the persistence of the Greeks
   (E) the destruction of former majesty

Review: Epic Hero

As you learned on page 193, an **epic hero** is usually someone of high social status who embodies the ideals of his people.

Partner Activity Meet with a classmate and discuss the differences between Achilles or Hector, Homer's epic heroes in the *Iliad* (see page 192), and Aeneas, Virgil's epic hero in the *Aeneid*. What ideals does each hero reflect? In your discussion, consider the following comment about the *Aeneid* by classical historian Michael Grant.

> *"Victory … is no longer seen as a triumphant, Homeric affair; Virgil knows all too well the weariness, frustration, and harrowing pathos that fighting and winning wars involve … He saw the true victory, it appears, not so much in military conquest as in the human spirit's conquest of itself."*

 **Literature** Online

Selection Resources For Selection Quizzes, eFlashcards, and Reading-Writing Connection activities, go to glencoe.com and enter QuickPass code GLW6053u2.

Reading Strategy Make and Verify Predictions

As you read the epic poem, you **made predictions** about what would happen. Look back at the chart you made on page 377. Now review your incorrect predictions. Were there clues that you missed? Based on what you know from reading this excerpt, consider what the future might hold for Aeneas.

1. What do you think will eventually happen to Aeneas?

2. What clues support your prediction?

Vocabulary Practice

Practice with Context Clues Look back at pages 378–395 to find context clues for the boldfaced vocabulary words below. Record your findings in a graphic organizer like the one shown here.

dupe impel defile suppliant

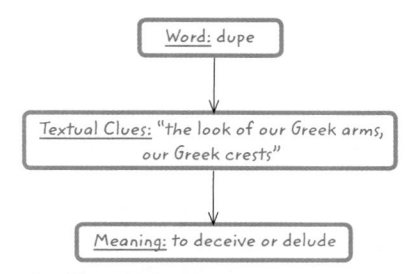

Word: dupe

↓

Textual Clues: "the look of our Greek arms, our Greek crests"

↓

Meaning: to deceive or delude

Academic Vocabulary

At the end of this excerpt, Aeneas faces the **prospect** of leaving Troy with a band of refugees.

Prospect is an academic word meaning "a mental idea of a future possibility." What **prospect** do the captured Trojan women and children now face? Write your expectations of what life will be like for them, citing evidence from the *Aeneid*.

For more on academic vocabulary, see pages 36–37 and R83–R85.

VIRGIL **397**

Vocabulary

Word: impel
Textual Clues: "See Priam decked in the arms"; "strap that sword on"
Meaning: to urge forward as if through moral pressure
Word: defile
Textual Clues: "made me see my son's death"
Meaning: to make unclean

Word: suppliant
Textual Clues: "honored . . . rights"; "blushed to betray my trust"
Meaning: one who asks humbly and earnestly

After You Read

Assess

Literary Element

1. **C** is the correct answer. Cassandra is a priestess of Minerva and the goddess's failure to help her shows the gods have turned against Troy.

2. **A** is the correct answer. The fall of the tree most clearly depicts the final overthrow of the city.

Review: Epic Hero

Students may say Homer glorifies war and victory far more than Virgil does. Homer writes extensively about the spoils of war and describes in graphic detail Achilles' decisive battle with Hector. Aeneas, on the other hand, overcomes his desire to kill Helen and to fight the Greeks so he might rescue his family and flee Troy with them.

Reading Strategy

1. Aeneas will lead his father, his son, and the Trojan refugees across the Mediterranean Sea and will establish a settlement in Italy.

2. The ghost of Creusa, Aeneas's wife, tells her husband "the vast plains of the sea are yours to plow / until you reach Hesperian land."

Academic Vocabulary

Students should describe a terrible future for captured Trojan women and children, involving enslavement in foreign lands.

After You Read

Assess

Respond Through Writing

Students' essays should

- use a clear thesis statement
- show how the imagery contributes to the power and total effect of Virgil's poem
- identify a pattern of images

A student who meets all of these criteria should receive the equivalent of a 4-point response.

A student who fully meets two or partially meets three of these criteria should receive the equivalent of a 3-point response.

A student who fully meets one or partially meets two of these criteria should receive the equivalent of a 2-point response.

A student who partially meets one of these criteria should receive the equivalent of a 1-point response.

 For grammar practice, see Unit 2 Teaching Resources Book, p. 192.

 For additional selection assessment, see Assessment Resources, pp. 89–90.

 To create custom assessments online, go to Progress Reporter Online Assessment.

 To create custom assessments using software, use ExamView Assessment Suite.

398

 Respond Through Writing

Expository Essay

Analyze Imagery Virgil's poetry is known for its powerful visual imagery, or word pictures. In an essay of 1,500 words, analyze the imagery used to describe the fall of Troy in Book Two of the *Aeneid*. Build your essay around a thesis that states the overall effect the imagery creates.

Understand the Task The **thesis** states your paper's main idea or what you're trying to prove or support.

Prewrite Virgil often uses figurative language to create images. Use a chart like the one below to note passages containing figurative comparisons. Once you have identified several of these passages, look for patterns in the imagery.

Passage	Comparison	Type of Imagery
"I hear a roar like fire … and a shepherd perched on a sheer rock outcrop." (lines 6–11)	The sound of fighting is compared with a grassfire and a flood	Violent forces in nature

Draft Formulate a clear thesis and provide valid and relevant evidence to support it. Develop an introduction, a body, and a conclusion. Use transitional words and phrases to achieve coherence. You may find it helpful to use sentence frames as an organizational tool while drafting your essay. For example, the thesis statement might follow this format:

In Book Two of the Aeneid, *Virgil uses visual imagery to create an overall pattern of _____.*

Revise In your revision, identify and address complexities within the *Aeneid*. For example, you may need to account for any images that do not fit neatly into the pattern identified in your thesis. Use the rubric on page 1292 to check other elements of your essay.

Edit and Proofread Proofread your paper, correcting any errors in spelling, grammar, and punctuation. Use the Grammar Tip in the side column to help you with the comparative and superlative degrees of adjectives and adverbs.

Learning Objectives

In this assignment, you will focus on the following objectives:

Writing: Writing an expository essay.

Grammar: Understanding how to use comparative and superlative forms.

Grammar Tip

Comparative and Superlative Degrees of Adjectives and Adverbs

Adjectives such as *strong* and adverbs such as *forcefully* are in the **positive** form. These forms change to reflect the number of things compared.

The **comparative** form of an adjective (*stronger*) or an adverb (*more forcefully*) shows two things being compared:

The Greek army moves more forcefully than a flooded river.

The **superlative** form of an adjective (*strongest*) or an adverb (*most forcefully*) shows three or more things being compared:

Ajax is the strongest of all the Greeks.

Grammar Practice

Use Active Voice Before students begin revising the drafts of their essays, review the differences between active and passive voice.

Active voice: action performed *by* the verb's subject

Example: The arrow hit the target.

Passive voice: action performed *upon* the verb's subject

Example: The target was hit by the arrow.

Point out that active voice is more forceful than passive voice. Encourage students to read over their drafts to find any sentences in the passive voice. Urge them to change such sentences to the active voice.

Vocabulary Workshop

Greek and Latin Word Origins

Literature Connection The *Aeneid* includes references to many Roman deities, which highlight the fact that ancient Rome did not have a monotheistic belief system. *Monotheistic*, meaning "having one God," comes from the Greek root *mono (mon)*, meaning "one, single, or alone." Many words related to fields such as political science and medicine have Greek and Latin origins. Becoming familiar with a few common roots can help you determine the meanings of unfamiliar words.

Word	Definition	Origin	Discipline
agoraphobia	fear of open spaces	Greek, *phobia*, "fear; aversion"	Medicine
flexor	muscle that bends a limb	Latin, *flect (flex)*, "bend"	Medicine
fracture	break or crack	Latin, *fract (frag)*, "break"	Medicine
hypothermia	below normal body temperature	Greek, *hypo*, "under"	Medicine
macrocosm	larger world; universe	Greek, *macro*, "large"	Political science
microsurgery	surgery performed with microscopes and tiny instruments	Latin, *micro*, "small"	Medicine
regicide	act of killing a king	Latin, *cide*, "killing"	Political science

Practice Using a dictionary and the chart above, find the origin and meaning of the root and the definition of each of the following words.

1. hypoglycemia
2. claustrophobia
3. genocide
4. polytheism
5. creed

LOG ON **Literature** Online

Vocabulary For more vocabulary practice, go to glencoe.com and enter QuickPass code GLW6053u2.

Learning Objectives

In this workshop, you will focus on the following objective:

Vocabulary: Understanding word origins.

Etymology

Etymology is the history of a word. A word **root** is the original basis for a word.

Test-Taking Tip

When you encounter an unfamiliar term on a test, try to identify the root. It may help you determine the meaning of the word.

Focus

Latin Prefix

Write on the board: Bacteria are <u>microorganisms</u> that exist in any natural environment. **Ask:** Based on what you know about word origins, what do you think *microorganism* means? Students should look in the origin chart to see that *micro* means "small," and should realize that a "microorganism" is a very small organism.

Teach

Find Words with Common Origins For each word in the Practice, have students find three words that share its root. Below are possible answers:

1. hypoglycemia *(hypochondria, hypocrite, hypothesis)*
2. claustrophobia *(hydrophobia, arachnophobia, xenophobia)*
3. genocide *(fratricide, homicidal, suicide)*
4. polytheism *(polygamy, polyglot, polygon)*
5. creed *(incredulous, credo, credulity)*

Assess

1. Greek, *hypo*, "under"; *hypoglycemia*, "low level of sugar in the blood"
2. Greek, *phobia*, "fear; aversion"; *claustrophobia*, "fear of enclosed spaces"
3. Latin, *cide*, "killing"; *genocide*, "killing of a racial, political, or cultural group"
4. Greek, *poly*, "many"; *polytheism*, "belief in many gods"
5. Latin, *credo*, "belief"; *creed*, "set of beliefs"

English Learners

DIFFERENTIATED INSTRUCTION

Intermediate Reviewing Greek and Latin root words may provide English learners the opportunity to connect their first languages to English through common roots.

Ask English learners whose first languages are Latin-based to review the root words presented on this page and to list several words from their first language that contain these roots. Then have them work in small mixed groups to identify the connections between the words they have listed and the English translations of those words. Discuss the similarities between the languages.

Focus

Bellringer Options

Selection Focus
Transparency 20
Daily Language Practice
Transparency 33

Or ask: Is it possible to compare the attack on New York City on September 11, 2001, to the burning of ancient Rome? How are the disasters similar or different? How are the cultures similar or different? Did the disaster change the way the United States responds to other cultures around the world?

(Students may say that Rome's disaster was not the result of an attack, though both caused terrible fires. Students may say that the United States has become warier of other cultures.)

Connect to the Reading Selections

Have students brainstorm a list of disasters. Encourage them to compare the impact of disasters of various proportions.

Selection Skills

Comparing Literature
Across Time and Place

Compare Literature About Disasters

Disasters evoke our deepest fears and expose our hidden frailties. The three authors compared here—Tacitus, Takashi Nagai, and Wisława Szymborska—vividly describe disasters that occurred in different times and places.

COMPARE THE | Big Idea | **The Imperial City**

These three literary works focus on a city in the throes of a disaster. Tacitus reveals the conditions in ancient Rome that led to a fire spreading out of control, Nagai describes the chaos in Nagasaki immediately after an atomic explosion, and Szymborska explores the thoughts of a famous biblical character as the city of Sodom is destroyed. As you read, ask yourself, What details do the authors reveal about these three cities?

COMPARE Style

Each of these authors uses different styles and literary techniques to re-create a calamity and reflect on its meaning. As you read, ask yourself, What literary techniques contribute to the style of each work?

COMPARE Cultures

Tacitus in ancient Rome, Nagai in Japan near the end of World War II, and Szymborska in modern Poland—these authors represent different cultures. As you read, ask yourself, What cultural values and beliefs do these authors reflect in their work?

The Destruction of Sodom and Gomorrah. **Attributed to Joachim Patinir. Oil on panel. Ashmolean Museum, University of Oxford, UK.**

 Literature Online

Author Search For more about Tacitus, Takashi Nagai, and Wisława Szymborska, go to glencoe.com and enter QuickPass code GLW6053u2.

Learning Objectives

For pages 400–415

In studying these texts, you will focus on the following objectives:

Literary Study:
Comparing themes.
Analyzing author's purpose.

Reading:
Comparing cultural contexts.
Recognizing bias.

Writing: Writing a mission statement.

Literary Elements
- Recognize Author's Purpose (SE pp. 402, 403, 407)

Reading Skills
- Recognize Bias (SE pp. 402, 404, 407)
- Apply Background Knowledge (TE p. 404)
- Analyze Cultural Context (TE p. 409)
- Recognize Author's Purpose (TE pp. 408, 411)

Comparing Literature

Vocabulary Skills
- Word Origins (SE p. 407)

Speaking/Listening/Viewing Skills
- Group Discussion (SE p. 415)
- Visual Display (SE p. 415)

Writing Skills/Grammar
- Comparison Essay (SE p. 415)
- Mission Statement (SE p. 407)
- Understand Prepositional Phrases (TE p. 414)

Before You Read

The Burning of Rome

Ancient Rome

Meet **Tacitus**

(c. A.D. 56–c. 120)

Although he was a successful politician and lawyer, Tacitus (tas'i təs), is best known as the historian of the early Roman Empire. He lived during a turbulent time in Rome, when the democratic rule of the republic was replaced by the absolute rule of the Roman emperor. Having experienced emperors who abused their power, Tacitus found himself confronting their evil deeds more than singing their praises in his histories.

Born into a wealthy family, Tacitus rose to political prominence during Emperor Domitian's reign (A.D. 81–96). He saw many fellow senators destroyed by this tyrannical emperor, which no doubt influenced his view of imperialism. Despite his pessimism, however, Tacitus rose to the position of governor of Asia, Rome's most important province.

Role of the Historian Tacitus's first major work was the *Histories*. Of the original fourteen volumes, only four complete books remain. This work, which covers the period from A.D. 69 to the assassination of Emperor Domitian in A.D. 96, is one of the most detailed histories in Greek and Roman literature.

His second major work is the sixteen-volume *Annals*, which covers the years A.D. 14–68, from the death of Augustus to the death of Nero. In this historical and literary masterpiece, Tacitus portrays the fire that ravaged Rome in A.D. 64 as vividly as an eyewitness, although in fact he relied on sources such as public records and earlier historical accounts. He recorded virtuous and evil actions, rumors and first-hand accounts,

> "It seems to me a historian's foremost duty to ensure that merit is recorded, and to confront evil deeds and words with the fear of posterity's denunciations."
>
> —Tacitus, from the *Annals*

believing his words would punish the bad, reward the good, and instruct future generations.

Today, Tacitus's works continue to be valued for their vivid pictures of imperial Rome. His friend Pliny the Younger accurately predicted, "Your histories will be immortal."

 Literature Online

Author Search For more about Tacitus, go to glencoe.com and enter QuickPass code GLW6053u2.

Comparing Literature

Before You Read

Focus

Literary History ☆

Nero the Firefighter Several accounts of the burning of Rome in A.D. 64 show a very different Nero than the one portrayed by Tacitus. One account says Nero rushed home from Antium upon news of the fire and actually helped to fight the fire himself.

Reading Strategy

Connect to Contemporary Issues Tacitus clearly felt it was important to record the major events of Roman history for posterity. **Ask:** Who is responsible for recording history today? Who will be this age's Tacitus? *(Students will likely name some contemporary writers who write about historical events. Some students may point out that because many contemporary events are recorded for broadcast, a written record like Tacitus's is unnecessary.)*

English Learners

DIFFERENTIATED INSTRUCTION

Advanced English learners and more fluent English speakers alike can benefit from sharing stories about disasters from different cultural histories. In addition, English learners will gain speaking skills when given the opportunity to share such stories with the class. Have English learners prepare a retelling of a major historical event from another country's history.

Advanced Learners/Pre-AP

DIFFERENTIATED INSTRUCTION

Research Tell students that Benjamin Franklin founded the United States' first fire company. Have interested students research the instances of fire in Philadelphia, where Franklin lived, and what led him to conclude that the community should organize a means to respond to reports of fire. **Ask:** Why didn't the Romans practice such a remedy? *(Students may say that Rome was too big,*

complex, and corrupt to organize such societies, or they may observe that there is little evidence to suggest that authorities had citizens' best interests at heart).

Before You Read

Focus

Summary

Tacitus presents a historical record of the burning of Rome during the reign of the Emperor Nero. He describes the actual fire as well as the suspicions that arose concerning the likelihood of Nero's having set the fire. Tacitus also describes how the city was rebuilt.

 For summaries in languages other than English, see Unit 2 Teaching Resources Book, pp. 196–201.

Vocabulary

Word Parts Have students review the vocabulary words. **Say:** Each of these words has a root that helps you understand its meaning. When you encounter new words that use these roots, you will be better able to understand their meaning.

ENGLISH LEARNERS English learners who are native speakers of Romance languages may recognize the roots of these vocabulary words. Ask these students to help their classmates to discover how word roots contribute to a word's meaning.

Reading Practice

Analyze Point of View Explain to students that when they read histories, they should be aware that the author includes opinion as well as fact. Some readers of ancient history may find it difficult to distinguish opinion from fact, and bias from each of these. *(Point out that Tacitus uses the phrases "a rumor had spread that" and "the people believed that" to indicate that opinions or bias are being expressed, either by others or by himself.)*

402

Literature and Reading Preview

Connect to the History

Think of a disaster that occurred recently. What effect did it have on you? Discuss this question with a small group.

Build Background

In this excerpt, Tacitus tells about the fire that ravaged Rome in A.D. 64. Many Romans suspected the emperor, Nero (A.D. 37–68), had started the fire to clear space for a huge construction project. His rebuilding plans fueled this rumor; he proposed a new palace that would have covered a third of the city.

Set Purposes for Reading

Big Idea **The Imperial City**

The capital of a huge and powerful empire, ancient Rome was a city divided by extremes of wealth and poverty. As you read, ask yourself, What does Tacitus reveal about this imperial city?

Literary Element **Author's Purpose**

Authors write with a **purpose** in mind—to inform, persuade, narrate, describe, explore ideas, or to entertain or move readers. Although complex works may have several purposes, usually one is most important. As you read, ask yourself, What is Tacitus's purpose for writing this historical account?

Reading Strategy **Recognize Bias**

When you **recognize bias**, you discover an author's inclination toward an opinion or a position. To detect bias, you must read carefully to separate facts from opinions. As you read, ask yourself, What biases does Tacitus reveal in this excerpt?

Tip: **Identify Biased Statements** In a chart like the one below, record any examples of bias you find in this excerpt and your inferences about the beliefs they reflect.

Examples	Bias
"Perhaps they had received orders. Or they may just have wanted to plunder unhampered."	Tacitus believes that some people exploit disasters for personal gain.

Vocabulary

demolition (dem´ ə lish´ ən) *n.* an act of tearing down or breaking to pieces; destruction; p. 405 *A wrecking ball completed the demolition of the tower.*

precipitous (pri sip´ ə təs) *adj.* having very steep sides; p. 405 *The precipitous slopes of that hill were great places for sledding.*

munificence (mū nif´ ə səns) *n.* great generosity; p. 406 *A rich patron's munificence enabled the gallery to buy a number of new paintings.*

sinister (sin´ is tər) *adj.* singularly evil; menacing; p. 406 *A sinister figure wielding a club lurked in the fog.*

depraved (di prāvd´) *adj.* marked by evil; p. 406 *His depraved conduct made him unwelcome in the community.*

Tip: **Word Origins** Knowing a word's etymology, or origin, often provides a clue to its meaning. For example, knowing that *munificence* derives from the Latin word *munus,* which means "gift," may help you remember that *munificence* means "generosity."

Have students work in small groups to make a chart with two columns, one labeled *Opinion or Bias* and the other *Clues.* Have students review the selection, listing the opinions or biases stated. Then have them list the words or phrases that signaled the presence of bias or opinion to them as they read.

The Burning of Rome

from the *Annals*

Tacitus

Translated by
Michael Grant

Hadrian Arch, 0 AD. Ruins of the ancient Roman city, Jerash (Kerash).

1 Now started the most terrible and destructive fire which Rome had ever experienced. It began in the Circus,[1] where it adjoins the hills. Breaking out in shops selling inflammable goods, and fanned by the wind, the conflagration instantly grew and swept the whole length of the Circus. There were no walled mansions or temples, or any other obstruc-

tions which could arrest it. First, the fire swept violently over the level spaces. Then it climbed the hills—but returned to ravage the lower ground again. It outstripped every countermeasure. The ancient city's narrow winding streets and irregular blocks encouraged its progress.

Terrified, shrieking women, helpless old and young, people intent on their own safety, people unselfishly supporting invalids or waiting for them, fugitives and lingerers alike—all heightened the confusion. When people looked back, menacing flames sprang up before them or outflanked them. When they escaped to a neighboring quarter, the fire followed—even districts believed remote proved to be

---

1. Originally, a *circus* was a large arena enclosed by tiers of seats and used for sports or spectacles. Ancient Rome had several. Tacitus may be referring to the Circus Maximus, the oldest such structure, which was located between the Palatine and Aventine hills.

2 Author's Purpose *Why does Tacitus begin his account with these details?*

TACITUS **403**

Comparing Literature

Teach

Reading Strategy | 1

Question The opening sentence vividly describes the fire. **Ask:** How do you think the author could be certain that this fire was worse than any other? *(Let students know that Tacitus consulted other histories of the city. He may have spoken with other historians.)*

Literary Element | 2

Author's Purpose Answer: *He wants to inform the reader about how the fire began and spread.*

Readability Scores

Dale-Chall: 10.0
DRP: 67
Lexile: 1010

Advanced Learners/Pre-AP

DIFFERENTIATED INSTRUCTION

Research Ask advanced learners to research how San Francisco recovered after the Loma Prieta earthquake of 1989. **Ask:** What damage did the earthquake do? What changes to the city plan did Californians introduce in their rebuilding effort? Can California's experience be compared with Rome's? *(Students will discover that numerous architectural and urban planning changes were put in place to make the city safer after the earthquake. Students will observe that the earthquake was a natural disaster, while the fire Tacitus describes may have been the result of arson.)*

Teach

Big Idea   1

The Imperial City Remind students of another Big Idea, "Seize the Day," that they examined earlier in this unit. **Ask:** How might Nero's behavior, as described by Tacitus, exemplify this idea? *(Students should observe that, even if he did not set fire to the city himself, Nero certainly seized the opportunity to put his building ambitions into practice.)*

Reading Strategy   2

Recognize Bias **Answer:** *Although Tacitus says the men may or may not have acted under orders, he suspects the fire was deliberately set, even though he cannot prove it.*

View the Art ★

Hubert Robert painted so many landscapes of Roman ruins that his fellows nicknamed him "Robert des Ruines" ("Robert of the Ruins"). **Ask:** How does this painting convey the mood of fear and dread that would accompany the destruction of a great city? *(The painting shows terror in the faces of figures in the foreground and the frantic gestures of others on the bridge and in the background.)*

The Burning of Rome. Robert Hubert. Oil on canvas, 76 x 93 cm. Musée des Beaux-Arts André Malraux, Le Havre, France.

involved. Finally, with no idea where or what to flee, they crowded on to the country roads, or lay in the fields. Some who had lost everything—even their food for the day—could have escaped, but preferred to die. So did others, who had failed to rescue their loved ones. Nobody dared fight the flames. Attempts to do so were prevented by menacing gangs. Torches, too, were openly thrown in, by men crying that they acted under orders. Perhaps they had received orders. Or they may just have wanted to plunder unhampered.

1 Nero was at Antium.[2] He only returned to the city when the fire was approaching the mansion he had built to link the Gardens of Maecenas to the Palatine. The flames could not be prevented from overwhelming the whole of the Palatine, including his palace. Nevertheless, for the relief of the homeless, fugitive masses he threw open the Field of Mars,[3] including Agrippa's public buildings, and even his own Gardens. Nero also constructed emergency accommodation for the destitute multitude. Food was brought from Ostia and neighboring towns, and the price of corn was cut. Yet these measures, for all their popular character, earned no gratitude. For a rumor had spread that, while the city was burning, Nero had gone to his private stage and, comparing modern calamities with ancient, had sung of the destruction of Troy.[4]

---

2. *Antium* (now Anzio) is an ancient coastal city about 30 miles south of Rome. It was Nero's birthplace.

2 Recognize Bias *What does Tacitus suspect is the cause of the fire? Explain.*

3. The *Field of Mars* was a grassy area used for athletic and military events honoring Mars, the Roman god of war.

4. *Troy* was an ancient city of Asia Minor. Its destruction by the Greeks is told in the *Aeneid,* an epic poem by Virgil.

404 UNIT 2   ANCIENT ROME

Reading Practice

Apply Background Knowledge Draw students' attention to Tacitus's account of the Romans' efforts to enlist the gods' aid on their behalf. **Say:** You remember that the Romans worshipped an array of different gods. **Ask:** Why do you think the Romans prayed to these particular gods during the fire? *(Students should note that Vulcan was the god who governed fire, Ceres and Proserpina protected the harvest, and Juno oversaw hearth and home.)*

Point out that these gods and goddesses might seem to be good ones to pray to, in the hopes of stemming the fire and protecting the Romans' well-being and livelihood.

By the sixth day enormous **demolitions** had confronted the raging flames with bare ground and open sky, and the fire was finally stamped out. But before panic had subsided, or hope revived, flames broke out again in the more open regions of the city. Here there were fewer casualties; but the destruction of temples and pleasure arcades was even worse. This new conflagration caused additional ill feeling because it started on Tigellinus'[5] estate. For people believed that Nero was ambitious to found a new city to be called after himself.

Of Rome's fourteen districts only four remained intact. Three were leveled to the ground. The other seven were reduced to a few scorched and mangled ruins. To count the mansions, blocks, and temples destroyed would be difficult. They included shrines of remote antiquity, the precious spoils of countless victories, Greek artistic masterpieces, and authentic records of old Roman genius. All the splendor of the rebuilt city did not prevent the older generation from remembering these irreplaceable objects. It was noted that the fire had started on July 19th, the day on which the Senonian Gauls[6] had captured and burned the city.

But Nero profited by his country's ruin to build a new palace. Its wonders were not so much customary and commonplace luxuries like gold and jewels, but lawns and lakes and faked rusticity—woods here,

open spaces and views there. With their cunning, impudent artificialities, Nero's architects and contractors outbid Nature.

They also fooled away an emperor's riches. For they promised to dig a navigable canal from Lake Avernus to the Tiber estuary,[7] over the stony shore and mountain barriers. The only water to feed the canal was in the Pontine marshes. Elsewhere, all was **precipitous** or waterless. Moreover, even if a passage could have been forced, the labor would have been unendurable and unjustified. But Nero was eager to perform the incredible; so he attempted to excavate the hills adjoining Lake Avernus. Traces of his frustrated hopes are visible today.

In parts of Rome unfilled by Nero's palace, construction was not—as after the burning by the Gauls—without plan or

Visual Vocabulary
A *colonnade* is a series of columns set at regular intervals that usually supports a roof.

demarcation. Street fronts were of regulated dimensions and alignment, streets were broad, and houses spacious. Their height was restricted, and their frontages protected by colonnades. Nero undertook to erect these at his own expense, and also to clear debris from building sites before transferring them to their owners. He announced bonuses, in

---

5. *Tigellinus* was a close adviser and friend of Nero.
6. The *Gauls* were Celtic-speaking peoples who lived in modern-day northern Italy, France, and Germany. The *Senonian Gauls* captured and burned Rome in 390 B.C.

3 Author's Purpose *What do these details reveal about Tacitus's purpose for writing?*

Vocabulary

demolition (dem′ ə lish′ ən) *n.* an act of tearing down or breaking to pieces; destruction

---

7. The *Tiber estuary* is the section of the Tiber River—which flows through Rome—that meets the sea.

Recognize Bias *What does this passage suggest about Tacitus's opinion of Nero?* **4**

Vocabulary

precipitous (pri sip′ ə təs) *adj.* having very steep sides

TACITUS **405**

Comparing Literature

Teach

Literary Element **3**

Author's Purpose **Answer:**
His purpose is to inform.

Progress Check

Can students identify author's purpose?

If No → See Unit 2 Teaching Resources Book, p. 202.

Reading Strategy **4**

Recognize Bias **Answer:**
Words such as "eager to perform the incredible" and "attempted" suggest that Tacitus believed Nero was selfish, foolish, and unconcerned about either the plight of the workers or the effect of his schemes on Rome.

Learning Objectives
Recognizing bias. (SE)
Analyzing author's purpose. (SE)
Applying background knowledge. (TE)
Analyzing art. (TE)

Advanced Learners/Pre-AP

DIFFERENTIATED INSTRUCTION

Research Tacitus describes the rebuilding efforts after the fire as "not . . . without plan or demarcation," as they had been after the invasion of the Gauls. Advanced students might research what happened when the barbarian Gauls burned Rome. What was that rebuilding effort like, and what does Tacitus mean when he says it was "without plan or demarcation"?

(Students may conclude that the rebuilding effort after the Gauls' invasion consisted of unplanned overbuilding of wooden structures, which became a fire hazard.)

English Learners

DIFFERENTIATED INSTRUCTION

Advanced Tacitus says in this passage that Nero's builders and planners "fooled away" Nero's wealth. Clarify that here, the word *fooled* does not mean "tricked" or "deceived." Instead, Tacitus wishes to tell the reader that the architects and engineers spent the emperor's money foolishly.

405

Teach

Reading Strategy

Question **Ask:** What other precautions might a government require of its citizens in the name of safety? *(Students may point out that United States law requires citizens to have certain kinds of insurance, to wear certain kinds of protective gear such as seat belts, and to provide fire exits in homes and public buildings. Students will suggest other examples.)*

Big Idea

The Imperial City Answer: *Tacitus views the city as a corrupting influence.*

---

proportion to rank and resources, for the completion of houses and blocks before a given date. Rubbish was to be dumped in the Ostian marshes by corn ships returning down the Tiber.

A fixed proportion of every building had to be massive, untimbered stone from Gabii or Alba (these stones being fire-proof). Furthermore, guards were to ensure a more abundant and extensive public water supply, hitherto diminished by irreg-ular private enterprise. Householders were obliged to keep firefighting apparatus in an accessible place; and semi-detached houses were forbidden—they must have their own walls. These measures were welcomed for their practicality, and they beautified the new city. Some, however, believed that the old town's configuration had been health-ier, since its narrow streets and high houses had provided protection against the burn-ing sun, whereas now the shadowless open spaces radiated a fiercer heat.

So much for human precautions. Next came attempts to appease heaven. After consultation of the Sibylline[8] books, prayers were addressed to Vulcan, Ceres, and Proserpina.[9] Juno, too, was propitiated. But neither human resources, nor imperial **munificence**, nor appeasement of the gods, eliminated **sinister** suspicions that the fire had been instigated. To suppress this rumor, Nero fabricated scapegoats—and

---

8. Sibyls were priestesses who interceded with the gods on behalf of those who wanted to appease the deities. *Sibylline* is the adjective form of the word.
9. *Vulcan* is the god of the destructive, devouring fire. *Ceres* is the goddess of growth, crops, and vegetation. *Proserpina*, daughter of Jupiter and Ceres, is queen of the underworld.

Vocabulary

munificence (mū nif′ ə səns) *n.* great generosity
sinister (sin′ is tər) *adj.* singularly evil; menacing

---

punished with every refinement the noto-riously **depraved** Christians[10] (as they were popularly called). Their originator, Christ, had been executed in Tiberius'[11] reign by the governor of Judaea, Pontius Pilate.[12] But in spite of this temporary setback the deadly superstition had broken out afresh, not only in Judaea (where the mischief had started) but even in Rome. All degraded and shameful practices collect and flourish in the capital.

First, Nero had self-acknowledged Chris-tians arrested. Then, on their information, large numbers of others were con-demned—not so much for incendiarism[13] as for their antisocial tendencies. Their deaths were made farcical. Dressed in wild animals' skins, they were torn to pieces by dogs, or crucified, or made into torches to be ignited after dark as substitutes for day-light. Nero provided his Gardens for the spectacle, and exhibited displays in the Circus, at which he mingled with the crowd—or stood in a chariot, dressed as a charioteer. Despite their guilt as Christians, and the ruthless punishment it deserved, the victims were pitied. For it was felt that they were being sacrificed to one man's brutality rather than to the national interest. ∾

---

10. Christians, of course, denied the divinity of Jupiter and the other deities of the state religion. This made them atheists in the eyes of most Romans, and as such they were suspected of all kinds of immoral activities.
11. *Tiberius* was the Roman emperor from A.D. 14–37.
12. *Pontius Pilate* was the Roman official who governed Judea—what is now southern Palestine—at the time of Christ's crucifixion.
13. *Incendiarism* means the act of deliberately setting fire to a building or other property.

The Imperial City *What is Tacitus's view of Rome?*

Vocabulary

depraved (di prāvd′) *adj.* marked by evil

---

406 UNIT 2 ANCIENT ROME

Grammar Practice

Commas in a Series Remind students to use commas to separate three or more words, phrases, or clauses in a series—including one before the conjunction that precedes the last item listed. Write the following example from the selection on the board: *Prayers were addressed to Vulcan, Ceres, and Proserpine.*

Write the following sentences on the

board without commas and have students copy them and insert commas where needed.

- *The fire destroyed the circus, the palatine, and many other buildings.*
- *Lawns, lakes, and woods were built around Nero's new palace.*

After You Read

Respond and Think Critically

Respond and Interpret

1. What details or information did you find most surprising in this excerpt?

2. (a)What factors led to the fire spreading quickly through Rome? (b)Why did some Romans not try to escape the fire?

3. (a)The fire left many citizens homeless. What measures did Nero take to help them? (b)Why did Nero's efforts fail to win the victims' gratitude?

4. (a)How was Rome altered when it was rebuilt after the fire? (b)What do the new laws governing construction in Rome suggest about Nero?

Analyze and Evaluate

5. Why might Nero have blamed the fire on the Christians and not some other group?

6. (a)How would you describe the tone of Tacitus's writing? (b)What details create this tone?

Connect

7. **Big Idea** **The Imperial City** What does Tacitus's description of the fire reveal about life in ancient Rome?

8. **Connect to Today** Which modern historical leader reminds you of Nero? What qualities do they have in common?

Literary Element **Author's Purpose**

An **author's purpose** influences his or her choice of techniques. For example, a persuasive editorial might use strong connotations, but such word choices would be inappropriate for an objective news article.

1. What purpose or purposes can you identify in "The Burning of Rome"?

2. How might Tacitus's purpose have influenced his choice of words and other writing strategies?

Reading Strategy **Recognize Bias**

Bias reveals an author's opinions, values, and personal perspectives. Review the chart you made on page 402 before you answer these questions.

1. Do you think Tacitus's account of the fire is objective? Why or why not?

2. How would you characterize Tacitus's attitude toward the Christians? Explain your answer.

 **Literature** Online

Selection Resources For Selection Quizzes, eFlashcards, and Reading-Writing Connection activities, go to glencoe.com and enter QuickPass code GLW6053u2.

Vocabulary Practice

Practice with Word Origins Create a word map like the one below for each boldfaced vocabulary word. Use a dictionary for help.

demolition   precipitous   munificence
sinister   depraved

EXAMPLE

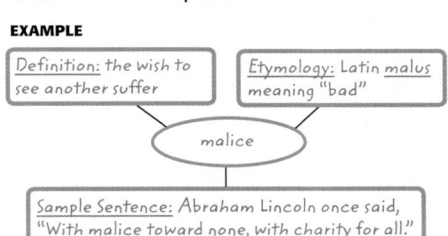

Definition: the wish to see another suffer

Etymology: Latin *malus* meaning "bad"

malice

Sample Sentence: Abraham Lincoln once said, "With malice toward none, with charity for all."

Writing

Write a Mission Statement Tacitus's account explains the conditions in ancient Rome that helped the fire spread out of control. Think of unsafe conditions in your community. Write a mission statement an organization might use to promote improvement of these conditions.

TACITUS   **407**

Literary Element

1. to inform and persuade.
2. His descriptions might have been less emotional if he were writing strictly to inform.

Reading Strategy

1. Students should support their responses.
2. He is hostile toward them.

Vocabulary Practice

Word: **demolition**; Etymology: Latin root: *demoliri:* deconstruct; Word: **precipitous**; Etymology: Latin root: *precipitium;* a precipice; Word: **munificence**; Etymology: Latin root: *munificentia;* generous, from *munus*, gift; Word: **sinister**; Etymology: Latin root: *sinister;* on the left side; Word: **depraved**; Etymology: Latin root: *depravare;* to pervert

---

Assess

1. Answers will vary.

2. (a) flammable goods, the wind, narrow streets, confused citizens, and gangs who hampered the fire-fighting efforts. (b) They had lost everything and preferred to die.

3. (a) He opened the Field of Mars and constructed emergency accommodations. He had food brought in, and he reduced the price of corn. (b) Nero's slowness to return to Rome and rumors concerning his singing made victims believe he welcomed the fire or was even responsible for setting it.

4. (a) The streets were wider, the houses were unattached, more fire-resistant materials were used, and the public water supply was increased. (b) They suggest Nero was a responsible leader in at least some respects.

5. They were already hated, so they made convenient scapegoats.

6. (a) critical, serious, sarcastic, and cynical. (b) Details will vary.

7. His description reveals Nero's abuse of power and his megalomania. It also reveals how the Romans rebuilt their city.

8. Students should give reasons for their responses.

Progress Check

Can students recognize bias?

If No → See Unit 2 Teaching Resources Book, p. 203.

Writing

Students' statements should have a clear purpose supported by reasons.

407

Comparing Literature

Focus

Summary

At the end of World War II, the United States dropped an atomic bomb on the Japanese city of Nagasaki. Thousands died on the spot, and many more died in the horrific fires that followed. Among the survivors were Dr. Takashi Nagai, a professor at the University of Nagasaki's medical school, and a small band of doctors, nurses, and students. Nagai tells how he and this small group struggled against unimaginable odds to save lives and to treat the wounded and dying.

Teach

Reading Strategy | 1

Recognize Author's Purpose Let students know that Dr. Nagai wrote this account while he lay dying of leukemia, which he developed as a result of his exposure to radiation from the bomb. **Ask: How might knowing this have affected his purpose in writing The Bells of Nagasaki?** *(It may have prompted him to include the observation that many others also died of sicknesses resulting from radiation.)*

Readability Scores

Dale-Chall: 7.2
DRP: 56
Lexile: 930

Build Background

Near the end of World War II, the United States dropped atomic bombs over the cities of Hiroshima and Nagasaki in Japan. In the following excerpt, Dr. Takashi Nagai—a physician who specialized in radiology—describes his experience helping victims of the Nagasaki attack. Nagai was born in 1908 and worked at the Nagasaki Medical College, located only 700 meters from the area directly beneath the explosion. Several months after the explosion, Nagai was diagnosed with leukemia—the result of his exposure to radiation from the bombing—and died in 1951. **1**

From *The Bells of* NAGASAKI

Takashi Nagai
Translated by William Johnston

On August 9, 1945, at two minutes past eleven in the morning, a plutonium atomic bomb exploded at an altitude of some five hundred meters over Matsuyama in the center of the Urakami district of Nagasaki.[1] Tremendous energy was released. And this energy, a tempestuous blast of air traveling at a rate of two thousand meters per second, smashed, pulverized, and blew apart anything in its path. The void created at the center of the explosion sucked up everything on the ground, carrying it high into the sky, and hurled it back violently against the earth. The heat of 9000° Fahrenheit burned the surrounding area. Fragments of incandescent metal rained down in balls of fire immediately setting everything alight.

It is estimated that thirty thousand people lost their lives and that more than one hundred thousand received light or serious wounds, while countless others were afflicted with atomic diseases caused by radiation. In some cases the symptoms of these diseases appeared immediately; in others they appeared much later.

The cloud of smoke in the sky, caused by the bomb and the debris that had been sucked up, hid the rays of the sun, bringing a total darkness like an eclipse. After about three minutes, however, as this immense cloud of smoke and dirt grew bigger, it scattered and became less dense. And once again light and heat filtered down to the earth.

As I have already said, I myself was buried beneath a heap of debris. But finally I managed to extricate myself by my own efforts and make my way to the photography room where I found Professor Fuse with Nurse Hashimoto, the chief nurse, and the others. They all ran to me. "Oh, good! Good!" they kept shouting as they threw their arms around me joyfully.

I looked at their faces one by one. How precious life is, I reflected. How good that you are alive!

---

1. *Matsuyama* is a port city on Shikoku Island, east of Kyushu, Nagasaki's island. The *Urakami district* of Nagasaki was an industrial zone named after the Urakami River, on which Nagasaki is situated.

408 UNIT 2 ANCIENT ROME

Speaking Practice

Conduct a Group Discussion The use of atomic weapons by the United States has always aroused debate. As a class, discuss whether the United States should have used the bomb to end the war. *(Answers will vary. Some students will say that the American lives saved by cutting the war short were worth the total devastation of Nagasaki and the deaths of thousands of civilians. Other will feel that the horrible effects of the bomb should have precluded its use under any circumstances.)*

"But people are missing," I said. "What about Yamashita? What about Inoue? What about Umezu? Let's look for the others and help them. Come back here in five minutes." And with that we left the room and scattered in all directions.

Professor Fuse and Shiro went to the developing room. Pulling away pieces of rubble and looking underneath, they kept shouting: "Hey! Hey!" and strained their ears. But there was no answer. "Moriguchi, are you alive?" roared Shiro. But all was silent.

Choro brought back Umezu seriously wounded. He had found him amidst the instruments in the radiotherapy room. Covered with blood, Umezu threw himself down in the corridor. "I've lost my eyes," he whimpered.

"Don't talk nonsense! Your eyes are all right," said Choro, examining the wound. Above his eyes was a deep gash and there were cuts all over his body.

"It's all right, it's all right," said the chief nurse encouragingly as she applied iodine, put some gauze on the wound, and skillfully bandaged it.

I took Umezu's pulse and gave some instructions about how we should treat the wounded.

"Doctor, help me!"
"Give me medicine!"
"Look at this wound!"
"Doctor, I'm cold. Give me clothes!"

A strange group of naked human beings crowded around us, all shouting. These were the people who somehow survived when everybody and everything was swept into the air and hurled in all directions by the explosion.

Since the bomb had fallen just when the outpatients were coming in great numbers for consultation, this part of the corridor

2 and the waiting room were littered with an enormous number of fallen people. Their clothes had been torn off; their skin was cut and peeling away. Covered with dirt and smoke, they were gray like phantoms, and it was difficult to believe they were human or that they belonged to this world.

"I looked at their faces one by one. How precious life is, I reflected."

Some, in whom a spark of life remained, extricated themselves from the vast and motionless heap of dead flesh and crawled up to me. Clinging to my feet, they cried: "Doctor, help me! Doctor, help me!" Someone held up a wrist from which blood was pouring profusely. "Mommy! Mommy!" screamed a little girl as she ran this way and that. And mothers, writhing in agony, kept calling the names of their children. "Where's the exit?" roared a big man as he ran around. "Stretcher! Stretcher!" shouted agitated students. And the whole place fell into deeper and deeper turmoil and confusion.

We began emergency treatment. But we quickly ran out of bandages and had to tear shirts, using the strips to bind the wounds.

No sooner had we treated ten or twenty victims than from behind came more and more shouting, "Help me! Help me!" On and on they came and it seemed there was no limit to their number. Since I had to keep one hand pressed tightly against my own wounded forehead, I found it difficult to work. Whenever I removed this hand in order to attend to a patient's wound, the blood would spurt out like red ink from a water pistol, splattering the wall and the

TAKASHI NAGAI **409**

Comparing Literature

Reading Strategy | 2

Analyze Cultural Context Let students know that, like Rome, Nagasaki was a large and crowded city. **Ask:** How should cities respond when a catastrophe takes place? *(Students will point out that cities should have well-established evacuation plans in case of catastrophe. Ask students whether they have made plans with their families for an emergency.)*

Cultural History ☆

The War Effort Tell students about the shortage of bandages, iodine, and other vital supplies in Japan. Note that at the same moment in the United States, huge drives were being held to collect materials to help the United States win the war. Women gave up wearing silk stockings, so that the silk could be used to make parachutes. People collected empty cans for the metal in them, old tires for the rubber, and old newspapers to make wadding for artillery shells.

Clarify Because much of this text is dialogue, and appears inside quotation marks, students may lose the thread of events. Clarify for students that the short, broken sentences in the text above are actually the exclamations of the victims of the bomb; in this selection, Dr. Nagai is reporting what he remembers.

Intermediate You may wish to clarify for English learners the United States' role in World War II. Explain that the United States had been attacked at Pearl Harbor in Hawaii, where Japanese airplanes bombed and sank ships at anchor in peacetime, killing many American servicemen. Shortly after this event, the United States declared war on Japan. Emphasize that President Truman made the decision to use the atomic bomb because he believed that to do so would end the war much sooner and would save many more lives than the only alternative course—an invasion of Japan by American forces.

Comparing Literature

Reading Strategy | 1

Identify Sequence Draw attention to Dr. Nagai's believing at the time that more bombs would fall, that the country would be invaded, and that the city would soon be under siege from the sea. He is trying to plan how he will respond to these events. Let students know that Japan surrendered almost immediately after the Nagasaki bomb was dropped.

View the Photograph ★

The destruction of Nagasaki was so complete it was difficult to determine how many people died. In many instances there were no "bodies" to count. Historians have estimated that 60,000 to 80,000 people were killed. About 40,000 people died that day, and the rest died later from radiation poisoning, burns, or injuries. **Ask: What feelings does this image evoke?** *(Students will probably say it evokes feelings of desolation or despair.)*

Remains of the Nagasaki Medical College, August 1945. Japan.

shoulder of the chief nurse. An artery in my temple had been cut. But since it was a small artery, I thought my body would hold out for about three hours. Sometimes I felt my own pulse and then went on treating the patients. . . .

I did some serious thinking. The place had become a bloody field of battle. We were the ambulance corps. Our real work was just beginning; we must stand with determination. Doubtless the enemy would continue to drop these bombs. Within a week he would invade our shores and fighting would break out. This was no time for wavering. If we fell into confusion, we would be able to do nothing. We must assemble the core staff members and get organized. We must make sure we had sufficient supplies of medicine and food. We must prepare a camp. After that, we had to establish an efficient system of communi-

cations and choose a suitable place in the country for a hospital. Sooner or later Nagasaki would be bombarded from the sea. We must get the patients quickly away and reassemble in a nearby valley.

I looked out the window. I could see nothing but a forest of fire. The whole neighborhood had become one great mass of flames. The fire had even spread to one corner of the building in which we were, and now we could hear the crackling of the approaching flames. . . .

Already twenty minutes had elapsed since the explosion, and Urakami had become a flaming landscape. From the center of the hospital, flames were spreading through the whole campus. The only place free from fire was the hill on the east side of the hospital. Pumps, hoses, water tanks, energetic people—anything or

Writing Practice

Apply Description Have students review Dr. Nagai's use of description in this selection and point out that his writing is crowded with incident. While many students will be troubled by the vivid details in this passage, explain how Dr. Nagai's reportage from ground zero in Nagasaki provides a unique account of

the event—the observations of someone who survived the nuclear blast, an event that many people experienced only from long-range images of a mushroom cloud or from pictures of desolate land.

Ask students to use this selection as a model to write a 250-word description

about a disaster. Suggest students write about something they experienced firsthand or that they have read about. Encourage them to include people's response to the event, rather than simply describing a series of devastating events, and to show how people attempted to help each other survive and cope with the disaster.

anyone capable of quenching those flames had vanished in a moment. Only one possibility remained: to allow the flames to spread and spread.

Even the survivors were penetrated by powerful radioactive rays. Their clothes were torn and many of them were completely naked. From downtown they ran, climbing the mountain with tottering steps in an effort to escape the flames. Two children passed by dragging their father. A young woman ran clutching a headless child. An aged couple, hand in hand, slowly climbed the mountain. As she ran, a girl's clothes burst into flames and she fell writhing in a ball of fire. On top of a roof that was enveloped in flames, I saw a man dancing and singing wildly: he was out of his mind. Some people kept looking back, looking back as they ran; others did not even turn their heads. A girl was scolding her little sister who lagged behind, but the little one begged her to wait. And from behind the flames pressed on.

About one in ten people had had the good fortune to survive. The others lay charred and dead beneath the wreckage of their burned houses.

As the fire roared on, the direction of the wind changed and from far and near it **2** carried the sound of voices incessantly crying for help. I stood aghast, with folded arms, contemplating the spectacle. Never in my life had I felt so deeply my own impotence. Was there no way of helping these suffering people who were rushing to death before my very eyes? . . .

Was it not for today that we practiced with those stretchers and gave all those **3** lectures on relief work? And now we were confronted with total failure. Like a mosquito whose legs have been plucked off, like a crab whose claws have been torn

away, we faced a multitude of wounded people, helpless and empty-handed. It was really primitive medicine that we were now reduced to. Our knowledge, our love, our hands—we had only these with which **3** to save the people. Crestfallen and depressed, I climbed the steps and, standing in the entrance, surveyed the whole situation once more.

Discouraged though I was, I knew that around me stood doctors and nurses and students—about twenty people in all—who would work till they dropped. The groups of two who had gone from room to room to pick up the wounded now returned and put them in the coal shed beside the entrance. This was the only place that was safe from falling sparks.

I stood helplessly in the middle of them, doing nothing. The fire was becoming more and more violent. Black smoke swirled round and round in the sky; and the thick cloud, reflecting the color of the fire, glowed with an ominous red light. It was an utterly disheartening scene. . . .

Dr. Nagai and the other survivors carry the wounded to safety outdoors, but are unable to save the school and its resources.

The university had become one big ball of fire. It was indeed the end. The president, Professor Tsuno, had suffered serious wounds. No one had seen the director of the hospital, Professor Naito, and it was presumed that he had met the same fate as the hospital itself. According to the students' reports, only Professors Koyano and Cho were safe. Almost all the others had vanished, though someone reported that Professors Kitamura and Hasegawa had been rescued by hospital workers and had been seen covered with blood climbing the hill at the back. Eighty per cent of the

TAKASHI NAGAI **411**

Comparing Literature

Reading Strategy 2

Recognize Bias **Ask:** Can you detect any bias in Nagai's account? *(Students should notice the highly objective, unbiased nature of Nagai's account. His only concern seems to have been for his coworkers and for the wounded.)*

Reading Strategy 3

Recognize Author's Purpose **Say:** Clearly this author's purpose is to inform people of what an atomic attack is like. He also describes his terrible helplessness in the face of all the horror. **Ask:** Do you think Dr. Nagai's account will affect people in a way that another type of account would not? *(Students will likely say yes, there would be much less chance of a bomb ever being dropped again if everyone read this account.)*

Advanced Learners/Pre-AP

DIFFERENTIATED INSTRUCTION

Compare Have advanced learners compare Tacitus's account of the burning of Rome to Dr. Nagai's account of the bombing of Nagasaki. **Ask:** What differences do you notice between these two accounts of a city on fire? *(Students should note that Dr. Nagai's account is more immediate and affecting, because he was actually present and saw the disaster firsthand.)* Invite the class as a whole to compare and contrast the two accounts.

Learning Objectives
Identifying sequence. (TE)
Applying description. (TE)
Recognizing bias. (TE)
Recognizing author's purpose. (TE)
Analyzing art. (TE)

Comparing Literature

Comparing Literature

View the Photograph ★

Let students know that the people in the photograph built the shelter they are sitting in out of debris from the explosion. **Ask: Is this an image of hope or despair?** *(Answers will vary, but students should note the efforts someone has made to resume routine tasks such as laundry.)*

Mother and Son Living in Nagasaki Ruins, September 14, 1945. Nagasaki, Japan. ★

Cultural History ☆

The Showa Era Japanese history is broken into eras. Historians use these names to designate the time periods in which events took place. The Showa ("Bright Peace") era lasted from 1926 to 1989. During this period Japan was ruled by a single Emperor, Hirohito. This period came to an end when Hirohito died. Dr. Nagai's use of this term must be seen as ironic. Emperor Hirohito's son, Akihito, has called his reign Heisei, or "Achieving Peace."

students and nurses had died. Among those who survived, many were seriously wounded. Combining my group, consisting mainly of people from the surgery department, and another group from the dermatology and pediatrics departments working at the rear entrance area, the total number of survivors was about fifty.

Since we despaired of any survivors from the rooms of fundamental medicine, we had to admit that in terms of personnel and equipment the university was utterly destroyed. We who were standing on the hill looking at the last traces of that burning university, we were the heroic soldiers of the era of Showa.[2]

From one of the hospital rooms, Dr. Okura brought out a big white sheet. Taking a handful of the blood that was

dripping from my chin, I traced a huge circular sun on the sheet, which now became a Japanese flag. Attaching this "Rising Sun" to a bamboo pole, we lifted it up and watched it flutter loudly as the hot wind blew all around.

With sleeves rolled up and a white band around his head, young Nagai grasped the pole with both hands and raised the flag high in the air. And then he moved slowly forward carrying the bloody Rising Sun up that hill covered with black smoke. And we all followed in solemn and silent procession. It was five o'clock in the afternoon.

Thus our Nagasaki School of Medicine lost the battle and was reduced to ashes. ✍

---

2. In Japanese history, the *Showa* period (meaning "Bright Peace") lasted for the duration of the reign of emperor Hirohito (1926–1989). The early Showa period lasted from 1926 until the end of World War II in 1945.

💬 Discussion Starter

In a small group, discuss what world leaders might learn from reading Dr. Nagai's account of the Nagasaki bombing. How did reading this memoir increase your knowledge of the devastation caused by a nuclear explosion?

412 UNIT 2 ANCIENT ROME

Writing Practice

 **Write a Poem** Ask students to write a haiku from the point of view of one of the victims at Nagasaki. They should try to use the traditional 5-7-5 syllable form. Encourage students to learn more about haiku by looking at pages 738–742 in this book. Tell students that this art form is particularly meaningful to the Japanese people and is greatly valued for its ability to capture delicate shades of meaning and experience.

Build Background

According to Genesis 19 in the Bible, Sodom and Gomorrah were the twin cities of sin. God's angels found only one virtuous man living in Sodom—Lot. The angels told him to flee with his family and not look back at Sodom, a city doomed to fiery destruction. Disregarding the angels' warning, Lot's wife looked back at the burning city and was transformed into a pillar of salt. In the following poem, Wisława Szymborska (vis lä′vä   shim bôr′skä) imagines this biblical character examining her motives for looking back.

Lot's Wife

Lot's Wife Looks Back (Burning), 1991. Albert Herbert. Oil on board. Private collection.

Wisława Szymborska
Translated by Adam Czerniawski

I looked back supposedly curious.
But besides curiosity I might have had other reasons.
I looked back regretting the silver dish.
Through carelessness—tying a sandal strap.
5 In order not to keep staring at the righteous nape[1]
of my husband, Lot.
Because of sudden conviction that had I died
he wouldn't have stopped.
Being humble yet disobedient.

---

1. The *nape* is the back of the neck.

WISŁAWA SZYMBORSKA   **413**

English Learners

DIFFERENTIATED INSTRUCTION

Advanced To help English learners understand the poem, aid them in clarifying what the speaker is doing. Encourage English learners to rephrase the lines of Szymborska's poem in their first languages. They need not try to write a poem. The result should be a list of "reasons" for looking back that Lot's wife offers the reader, along with her descriptions of her flight from Sodom. When students have their lists, have them meet in small groups to discuss the poem and share their lists.

Comparing Literature

Focus

Summary

The speaker, in the character of Lot's wife, delivers a litany of observations and reasons for having looked behind her, ranging from nostalgia for her home to being distracted by animals in her path. Eventually the reader understands that there is no final answer, that perhaps she looked back simply because she was human.

Teach

Reading Strategy | 1

Compare and Contrast
Say: Look at the speaker's description of possible motives for having looked back at Sodom as she ran. Compare her actions with those of the people from Nagasaki described by Dr. Nagai on page 411—"Some people kept looking back, looking back, as they ran." **Ask:** Can you compare the people fleeing Nagasaki with Lot's wife? *(Students may say Szymborska's description and Dr. Nagai's seem very similar in some respects.)*

View the Art ★

Albert Herbert is known for painting biblical scenes in a contemporary style. **Ask:** Based on this painting, what do you think Lot's wife looks back on? *(Students will probably mention that she looks back on her home and the people she left behind.)*

Reading Strategy   1

Compare and Contrast Tone **Say:** The three authors you have just read use very different tones in their writing. **Ask:** How would you describe the tone each author uses? *(Students should quickly identify the tone Tacitus uses as critical and suspicious. Students will note that Dr. Nagai's tone is controlled and factual, even detached; his own possible emotional reaction does not appear in the text. You may need to help students recognize the tone of Szymborska's speaker as bemused and ironic, even fractured as she offers one possible motive after another—some contradictory—for disobeying the angel.)*

Quickwrite

Students should cite specific passages from the poem to support their views as to why Lot's wife's disregarded the angel's warning.

10 Listening for pursuers.
Touched with silence, hoping God had changed His mind.
Our two daughters were already disappearing beyond the hilltop.

I felt my age. Distance,
futility of wandering. Drowsiness.
15 I looked back when setting down the bundle.
I looked back in terror where to step next.
My path suddenly teeming with snakes,
spiders, field mice and baby vultures.
Now neither good nor evil—just everything living
20 crawled and hopped in crowded panic.
I looked back in desolation.[2]
Ashamed of running away in stealth.[3]
Wanting to scream, to turn back.
Or only when a gust of wind
25 untied my hair and lifted up my skirts.

I had a feeling they were watching from the walls of Sodom
with bursts of hearty laughter again and again.
I looked back in anger.
To savor their perdition.[4]
30 I looked back willessly.
It was only a rock slipping, growling beneath me.
It was a crevice suddenly cut my way off.
A hamster trotted on the edge on two paws
and then it was we both looked back.

35 No, no. I ran on,
I crawled and I soared
until darkness crashed from heaven
and with it hot gravel and dead birds.
Losing breath I often swerved.
40 If anyone saw me, would have thought I was dancing.
Conceivably, my eyes were open. **1**

2. When describing emotions, *desolation* names a grief so deep that it leaves a person feeling empty and lost.
3. *In stealth* means "in secret."
4. *Perdition* means complete destruction and suggests eternal damnation.

Quickwrite

In this poem, Lot's wife explores her motives for looking back at Sodom as it is destroyed. Which of her explanations seems most plausible to you? Write a paragraph supporting your opinion, using specific evidence from the poem.

Grammar Practice

Prepositional Phrases Remind students that a prepositional phrase can act as an adjective or an adverb. Used as an adjective, a prepositional phrase modifies a noun or a pronoun. Used as an adverb, it modifies a verb, an adjective, or an adverb.

Write the following sentences on the board and have students identify the function of each prepositional phrase.

1. The gust <u>of wind</u> untied by hair. *(adjective, modifying the noun* gust*)*
2. My path was suddenly teeming <u>with snakes.</u> *(adverb, modifying the verb* was teeming.*)*
3. Our daughters disappeared <u>beyond the hilltop.</u> *(adverb, modifying the verb* disappeared*)*

Wrap-Up: Comparing Literature

Across Time and Place

- **The Burning of Rome** by Tacitus
- **from The Bells of Nagasaki** by Takashi Nagai
- **Lot's Wife** by Wisława Szymborska

COMPARE THE **Big Idea** The Imperial City

Group Activity Tacitus, Nagai, and Szymborska vividly describe the destruction of different cities. Tacitus gives a harrowing account of the fire that burned large sections of Rome in A.D. 64; Nagai tells of the disastrous effects of the atomic bomb that was dropped on Nagasaki, Japan, on August 9, 1945; and Szymborska speculates about why Lot's wife turned to witness the destruction of Sodom in biblical times. With a small group, discuss the following questions, citing evidence from the texts to support your views.

1. How is the urban setting important in each of these three literary works?

2. What can people in modern cities learn from reading these works?

COMPARE Style

Writing Each of these authors describes a catastrophic event. Write a brief essay comparing and contrasting the styles and literary techniques each author uses to convey the terror and desolation caused by the disaster. Consider how elements such as genre, word choice, imagery, and point of view contribute to the style of each work. You might also add your thoughts about how well each style fits the author's subject.

COMPARE Cultures

Visual Display Tacitus, Nagai, and Szymborska grew up in different cultures that shaped their perspectives. Research the three authors' cultures—ancient Rome for Tacitus, World War II–era Japan for Nagai, and modern Poland for Szymborska. Then create a collage of images that reflect these cultures. Consider incorporating contemporary photographs, fine art from or about each period, or some of your own art work.

A mushroom cloud towers 20,000 feet above Nagasaki, Japan, August 9, 1945.

Assess

Compare the Big Idea

1. Possible answers: In Tacitus's "The Burning of Rome," urban overcrowding, narrow streets, and tenement buildings made of wood contribute to the spread of the raging fire. In Dr. Nagai's memoir, the scope of the disaster is greatly increased because the bomb exploded in an urban setting where a large number of people lived and worked. In Szymborska's poem, Lot's wife realizes countless people whom she left behind are suffering inside Sodom.

2. Students might mention recent disasters, such as the tsunami in Southeast Asia or Hurricane Katrina in New Orleans. Possible answers: by reading these accounts, people in modern cities can understand the vulnerability of any city to disaster and should consider what they might do if they found themselves in similar life-threatening situations.

Compare Style

Students might compare the points of view (third-person for Tacitus, first-person for Nagai and Szymborska), diction, and imagery. For instance, Tacitus moralizes and passes judgments, Dr. Nagai describes the compassion a disaster can evoke in survivors, and Szymborska focuses on the conflicting emotions a woman might feel if she were forced to abandon her native city.

Compare Cultures

Students should research art from the three cultures. Students should explain the connections between the images they chose in their collages and the details presented in the selections.

Writing Workshop

Biographical Narrative

Focus

Bellringer Options

Daily Language Practice Transparency 34

Or ask: Which do you enjoy reading more, fiction or nonfiction? Have students provide reasons for their choices. *(Some may prefer fiction because it is less dry and factual; others may prefer nonfiction because they are interested in real-world events.)*

Summary

In this workshop students will write and present a biographical narrative. Students will follow the stages of the writing process: prewriting, drafting, revising, and editing. In addition, mini-lessons on using action verbs and correcting verb tense are provided.

📁 For Writing Workshop graphic organizer and rubric, see Unit 2 Teaching Resources Book, pp. 210–212.

Learning Objectives

For pages 416–423

In this workshop, you will focus on the following objectives:

Writing: Writing a biographical narrative using the writing process.

Grammar:

Understanding how to use action verbs.

Understanding how to correct verb tense.

▶ **Writing Process**

You may think of new ideas at any stage of a writing process. Feel free to return to earlier stages as you write.

Prewrite

Draft

Revise

Focus Lesson: Action Verbs

Edit and Proofread

Focus Lesson: Verb Tense

Present

 **Literature** Online

Writing and Research For prewriting, drafting, and revising tools, go to glencoe.com and enter QuickPass code GLW6053u2.

 # Writing Workshop

Biographical Narrative

Literature Connection In "The Burning of Rome," Tacitus reveals the infamous character of the Roman emperor Nero.

"For a rumor had spread that, while the city was burning, Nero had gone to his private stage and, comparing modern calamities with ancient, had sung of the destruction of Troy."

Similar to a fictional narrative, Tacitus's story contains a specific setting, point of view, plot, and characters. Yet the narrative is nonfiction because the people and events are historical. As in any narrative, imagery, vivid details, and realistic dialogue bring the characters of a biographical narrative to life. To write a successful biographical narrative, you will need to learn the goals of narrative writing and the strategies to achieve those goals.

Rubric

Goals	Strategies
To narrate a significant incident in a person's life	☑ Explore the meaning of a particular incident
To use specific details to describe the person and the experience	☑ Describe appearances, movements, sensory images, personal feelings, shifts in perspective, and settings in concrete detail
	☑ Use dialogue to bring a character to life
To narrate the events and actions in a logical order	☑ Use narrative details to narrate the events in chronological order
	☑ Pace the action to match changes in time, space, or mood
To connect with an audience	☑ Use a thoughtful, but natural, style
	☑ Capture the audience's interest and imagination

Workshop Resources

Print Materials

- Unit 2 Teaching Resources pp. 210–212
- Writing Kit
- Success in Writing: Research and Reports

Transparencies

- Writing Workshop Transparencies 11–15

Technology

- Literature Online: Writing Resources and Grammar Resources, glencoe.com
- Online Essay Grader, glencoe.com
- Student Presentation Builder on StudentWorks Plus CD-ROM
- Media Workshop DVD
- Online Student Edition

Assignment: Write a Profile

Write a biographical narrative of at least 1,000 words about a true story or series of events involving a friend, family member, historical figure, or another real person to reveal his or her unique character.

Audience: your school or community

Purpose: to reveal the unique personality of a familiar person or public figure

Analyze a Professional Model

In the excerpt below, Mary Renault recounts Alexander the Great's conquest of the Sogdian Rock, a fortress in central Asia. Renault's use of precise narrative and descriptive details reveals the unique character of Alexander. The comments in the margin point out features you might want to include in your own biographical narrative.

Real-World Connection

You may be required to use nonfiction narrative skills to tell facts about your life when you apply to college or for a job. The main points you present about your experiences and your character, along with the supporting details, may be used to judge your merits as a future student or an employee.

from *The Nature of Alexander* by Mary Renault

Everything of importance fell on [Alexander]. He could not delegate to an establishment he was in process of constructing as he went.

He was founding more cities, deeply concerned with them both as viable communities, and as his own memorials. Kandahar still echoes his name. On choice of site hung the settlers' welfare, even their lives. . . .

The country was full of precipitous cliffs and summits, fortified from remote antiquity in the perennial cycles of blood feud and tribal war. From time to time some especially sensational and ingenious siege gets detailed description. It was impossible for Alexander to hear that a strongpoint was impregnable without regarding it as a personal challenge. This showed a perceptive grasp of war psychology in Sogdiana, where courage, strength and success were essentials of status and of survival.

The most notorious of such pinnacles was the Sogdian Rock; high, sheer, and riddled at the top with caves well stocked with

Introduction

Capture your reader's interest in the subject's character and experiences.

Setting

Use details of setting to help the reader visualize your subject's world.

Personal Feelings

Make your subject come alive by revealing his or her feelings.

Approaching Level

DIFFERENTIATED INSTRUCTION

Restating Some students may have difficulty with Renault's unusual sentence structure, or syntax. Write the following sentence on the board: On choice of site hung the settlers' welfare, even their lives. **Say:** If you are having difficulty understanding a sentence, try rearranging the words in a more familiar order. Model this process by rewriting the sentence as follows: The settlers' welfare, and even their lives, hung on choice of site. Then, have students work in pairs to rewrite the following sentences:

- The most notorious of such pinnacles was the Sogdian Rock.
- Political expediency has been suggested but does not convince.

Teach

Big Idea

The Heroic Ideal After students have read the professional model, point out that the ancient Greeks mythologized Alexander even in his own lifetime. Similarly, Alexander looked to legendary heroes such as Achilles, Heracles, and Dionysus as models for his actions. **Ask:** What qualities does Alexander share with some of the heroes you have encountered in Greek literature? *(He is a successful military leader, as well as being adventurous, strong-willed, and passionate.)*

Writing Skills

Sentence Length Advise students that alternating between long and short sentences will add elegance, variety, and interest to their writing. Point out that Renault follows the short sentence "Everything of importance fell on [Alexander]" with longer sentences, elaborating on her main point.

Learning Objectives
Writing a biographical narrative. (SE)
Using the writing process. (SE)
Varying sentence length. (TE)

417

Teach

Writing Skills

Setting Students not only should describe the setting of their biographical narratives but should also try to explain the relevance of the setting to the narratives. Point out that the first sentence of the fourth paragraph is an excellent example of this technique. Renault gives a visual image of the setting as "precipitous cliffs and summits," and then notes that this was the site of "perennial cycles of blood feud and tribal war," establishing the relevance of the setting to Alexander's journey.

Writing Skills

Adverbs Point out that Renault uses vivid adverbs, such as *quixotically* and *disastrously*, to convey specific details. Encourage students to do the same, but caution them that adverbs should be used sparingly, as using too many can interrupt the flow of a narrative or make it seem too wordy.

[APPROACHING] Remind students that an adverb is a word that modifies a verb, an adjective, or another adverb. Explain that you can often identify an adverb by looking for the suffix *–ly*.

Sensory Details
Add sensory details to help the reader visualize scenes.

Descriptive Details
Include concrete details to create a clear picture.

Conclusion
Discuss how the episode you have presented reveals your subject's character.

---

food and water. Its chieftain, Oxyartes, was away raising the countryside, leaving his family and garrison in the charge of his son. The single path to the top was entirely commanded from above. The area was under snow.

Alexander offered a parley [conference]. Two envoys climbed down, laughed in his face, and told him not to waste his time unless his men had wings. That settled the matter. He called for volunteers who were expert climbers, and got 300. At night, helped by the snow which would have etched out all the ledges, they were to ascend the steepest, unguarded face, a "very severe." The first man up would get 12 talents, a sum on which to be comfortable for life; the next 11; and so through the first twelve. Iron tent pegs for pitons, mallets, and ropes got them up, in spite of snow-numbed fingers, with a loss of one in ten. In Sogdiana, to have conceded failure might have cost lives by the thousand.

Stunned at dawn by the sight of an unknown force above him, the chief's son surrendered, and everyone was spared. A feast was offered, at which the ladies of the family performed a dance for the conqueror. Among them was the chief's daughter, Roxane. Alexander fell in love with her at first sight. Quixotically renouncing the right of capture which neither friend nor foe would have questioned, he asked for her hand in marriage.

Political expediency has been suggested, but does not convince. No doubt had she been disastrously unsuitable—married for instance—he would have mastered his feelings; but everything points to an authentic *coup de foudre* [love at first sight]. . . . It would seem that falling in love with a woman was a new and exhilarating experience, and, ever the explorer, he was eager to pursue it without delay.

Reading-Writing Connection Think about the writing techniques you just encountered and try them out in the biographical narrative you write.

418 UNIT 2   ANCIENT GREECE AND ROME

Reading Practice

SMALL GROUP

Analyze Text Structure
Students can gain insight into Renault's organizational technique by creating an outline of her narrative. Model this process by outlining the second paragraph on the board as follows:

2. Alexander's concern with building viable cities

  a. Kandahar as memorial

  b. Importance of choice of site

  c. Delegation of duties to Hephaestion

Point out to students that the numbered item gives the paragraph's main idea, while the lettered items list the supporting points. Then have students work in pairs to outline the rest of Renault's narrative. Encourage them to create similar outlines to plan their own narratives.

Prewrite

Choose a Subject As you consider a person you might write about, ask yourself which particular traits stand out and make that person unique. Then think of an incident that helped you see or understand your subject in a new way.

Reveal Character Like a fictional narrative, your biographical narrative should involve specific characters, have a specific setting, and be told from a particular point of view. Try to reveal the personality of your character through his or her actions and interactions with others, rather than simply explaining what that person is like. Use conversation, or dialogue, to make your characters more lifelike. In addition, dialogue lets readers form their own opinions about a character as they "listen in" to the conversation.

Use a Cluster Diagram Use a cluster diagram like the one below to help you plan your narrative. Start by putting your subject's name in the center, and then list general events in his or her life. Move outward to more specific aspects of these events.

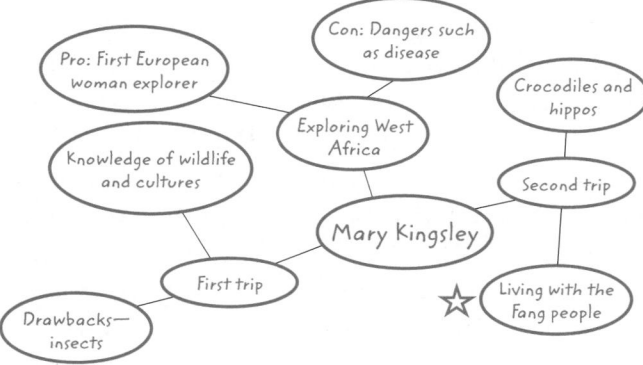

Round Out Your Character You are familiar with the character you are writing about, but your audience may need additional background information to feel the full impact of your narrative. Select details that will help capture your audience's interest and imagination.

Share Your Ideas Meet with a partner to help develop your writing voice. Take turns telling each other the most vivid details about your character and the incident you will write about. As you write, aim for a natural, highly descriptive voice to narrate your experience.

Narration

Use Vivid Description

Avoid general descriptions or vague characterizations, such as "Claudia is loud and brash." Instead, *demonstrate* your character's nature through specific observations and precise language.

Avoid Plagiarism

As you work on your narrative, you might conduct research about a historical figure. Remember it is wrong to copy directly from another source and present another person's work as your own. Make sure you credit a quotation properly if you wish to incorporate one in your essay.

For more on avoiding plagiarism, see pages R33–R34.

Teach

![icon] Writing Skills

Sequence of Events Explain to students that they do not necessarily have to write their biographical narratives in chronological order. Instead, they may want to organize their narratives by key character traits or points about their subject. Encourage those who narrate chronologically to start their essays with an attention-grabbing anecdote or detail, instead of simply starting with what happened first.

(APPROACHING) Some students might benefit from mapping the sequence of events in their narratives on a simple timeline. Have them use the distances between the points on their timelines to represent longer and shorter increments of time.

Cultural History ☆

The Fang People The Fang are a Bantu-speaking people living in modern-day Cameroon, Equatorial Guinea, and Gabon. Fine warriors and hunters, the Fang historically built up a reputation as cannibals in order to intimidate outsiders. Today, the Fang have gained a good degree of political influence, particularly in Gabon.

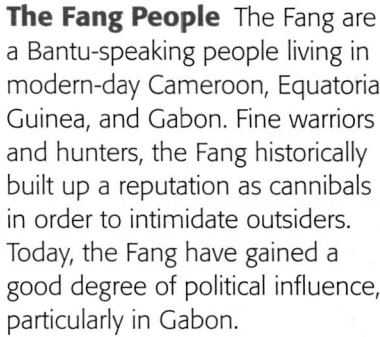

Learning Objectives
Writing a biographical narrative. (SE)
Using the writing process. (SE)
Analyzing text structure. (TE)

Advanced Learners/Pre-AP
DIFFERENTIATED INSTRUCTION

Compare Sources Encourage advanced students to choose historical subjects about whom several biographies or autobiographies have been written. In their narratives, have them compare and contrast what they learn from the different accounts, considering whether their subjects perceive themselves differently than outsiders do.

English Learners
DIFFERENTIATED INSTRUCTION

Intermediate Conducting research in English may be daunting for English learners. Encourage students to write about a friend or family member about whom they will not need to do much research. While other students are conducting research, work with English learners to brainstorm lists of verbs and adjectives that describe their subjects.

419

Writing Workshop

Teach

Writing Skills

Introduction

Answer: *The writer presents the sharp contrast between Kingsley's early life and later career as an explorer.*

Background Information

Answer: *The first paragraph describes Kingsley's confined early life and explains how the deaths of her parents freed her from these limitations.*

Shift in Perspective

Answer: *The ambition to be the first European woman to explore West Africa changes Kingsley's view of her life.*

Chronological Order

Answer: *Chronological terms clarify the order of events in the narrative.*

Writing Frames

As you read the workshop model, think about the writer's use of the following frames.

• First _____, until _____. Then _____.

• One of _____'s goals was to _____.

Consider using frames such as these in your biographical narrative.

Introduction

How does the writer introduce the subject and create interest?

Background Information

What background information does the first paragraph supply? How does it help the reader understand Mary Kingsley?

Shift in Perspective

How does the writer show a shift in the subject's perspective?

Chronological Order

How do transitional phrases help the reader follow the writer's ideas?

Draft

Think Organization Remember that each of your body paragraphs should be about one main idea or event. If the paragraph retells an event, arrange your details in chronological order.

Analyze a Workshop Model

Here is a final draft of a biographical narrative. Read the narrative and answer the questions in the margin. Use the answers to these questions to guide you as you write.

Crocodiles and Cannibals

For a proper Victorian lady who, before she was 30, had gone almost nowhere, Mary Kingsley packed a lot of adventure into the remainder of her short life. Kingsley was born in London in 1862. She taught herself to read and fed her thirst for adventure by reading travel books in her father's library. Kingsley was not able to go on journeys of her own, however, until the deaths of both her parents in 1892 freed her from her household duties.

Kingsley's first journey was a brief trip to the Canary Islands, off the western coast of Africa. She had read about West Africa in her father's library, and she decided to visit this mysterious region. No European woman had ever explored this part of the world, but Kingsley intended to be the first despite the danger. European visitors exposed to the hot climate and tropical diseases frequently became ill and often died.

First Kingsley sailed down the West African coast until she reached Angola in August 1893. Then she journeyed into the interior. The strange sights and sounds of the vast tropical forest, and the lives of its animals and people, enchanted Kingsley. Striding along or paddling a dugout canoe, she explored northward until she reached present-day Nigeria. As she had been warned, there *were* drawbacks. Among the most unpleasant kinds of African wildlife she encountered were the insects—enormous things she described as looking like "flying lobsters."

Writing Skills

SMALL GROUP **Write a Dialogue** Explain to students that in most cases, when writing a biographical narrative, they will not actually have experienced the events they are relating firsthand. As writers they need to re-imagine the events, filling in details based on what they know about their subject's life and personality. One way to bring your narrative to life is by incorporating dialogue.

Pass around slips of paper with descriptions of interactions on them. (Sample description: My grandmother often begged my grandfather to replace his old truck with a newer model, but he always refused.) Have students work in pairs to write brief dialogues that dramatize the scenes, using the example from the workshop model as a guide.

She returned to England in January 1894 with specimens and a growing knowledge of the cultures of West Africa. Kingsley had also gained something far more unusual for a European of her time—sympathy and respect for African peoples. She could not stop thinking about her first journey. She had to go back.

Kingsley traveled to southern Nigeria in December 1894. One of her most memorable encounters on this trip was with a crocodile. When the animal tried to crawl aboard her dugout canoe, Kingsley recalled, "I had to . . . fetch him a clip on the snout with a paddle." Another time she found herself sharing a tiny island with a hippopotamus, which she finally convinced to leave by poking it with her umbrella.

One of Kingsley's goals on this trip was to study a people known as the Fang, who were rumored to be cannibals. Trying to sleep in a Fang hut one night, Kingsley was troubled by a terrible smell coming from small bags hanging from the ceiling. She took them down and emptied the contents into her hat only to discover a human hand, three big toes, four eyes, two ears, and some other body parts! Despite her surprise, Kingsley, as always, was a calm, careful observer. "The hand was fresh," she noted. On her return to England she lectured about her adventures and wrote a book, *Travels in West Africa*, which became a best seller.

On Kingsley's next trip, she went to South Africa, where the British were fighting a war with the Boers, descendants of Dutch colonists who had settled the region. Kingsley nursed Boer prisoners until she caught a fever and died, on June 3, 1900. The British author Rudyard Kipling, was mystified by Mary Kingsley's courage: "Being human, she must have feared some things, but one never arrived at what they were."

Large Fang mask. Gabon, Africa. Private collection.

Narration

Quotations
How does the use of a quotation reveal Kingsley's character?

Descriptive Details
How do these details help the reader visualize Kingsley as an explorer?

Conclusion
How does the writer sum up the subject's character?

WRITING WORKSHOP **421**

Teach

Writing Skills

Quotations
Answer: *The quotation shows that Kingsley is curious and clinical in her observations.*

Descriptive Details
Answer: *These details present vivid pictures of Kingsley's experiences during her African travels.*

Conclusion
Answer: *The writer concludes by focusing on Kingsley's fearlessness—the trait that enabled her to accomplish what she did.*

View the Art

The art of the Fang people is characterized by elegant simplicity. Masks, worn during hunting and other ceremonies, are one of the most common forms of decorative art. Like the one shown here, masks are usually painted white, with facial features outlined in black. **Ask:** Does this mask remind you of anything? If so, what? *(Students may say the mask reminds them of an animal—perhaps a crocodile.)*

Learning Objectives
Writing a biographical narrative. (SE)
Using the writing process. (SE)
Writing a dialogue. (TE)

English Learners

DIFFERENTIATED INSTRUCTION

Advanced Students may have difficulty picking up on the lighthearted, often humorous tone of the workshop model. Write this sentence on the board: One of her most memorable encounters on this trip was with a crocodile. When the animal tried to crawl aboard her dugout canoe, Kingsley recalled, "I had to . . . fetch him a clip on the snout with a paddle." Explain that Kingsley's word choice is humorous. Remind students that they should try to match the tone of their biographical narrative—whether humorous or somber—to their subject. Then have students work in groups to identify other examples of humor in the workshop model.

 **Writing Workshop**

Biographical Narrative

Teach

 Writing Process

Revising Encourage students to point out clichés—stale, overused expressions—in their partner's writing. Common clichés include *brief stint, through thick and thin, live life to the fullest,* and *rude awakening.* Remind students that clichés—while once vivid, effective expressions—have lost their appeal through overuse. Clichés may be tempting to use, but they reveal unoriginal thinking on the part of the writer.

Writer's Technique ☆

Passive Voice While the active voice usually makes a stronger impression, many writers use the passive voice if they want to deemphasize the performer of an action. Writers also use the passive voice if the performer of an action is unknown, as in the sentence *The door was locked.* In addition, academics frequently write in the passive voice. However, in narratives, the active voice is usually considered more effective.

Writing Skills

 Develop Coherent Paragraphs

Remind students that each of their paragraphs should have a main idea, to which all the sentences in the paragraph should be linked. In addition, students should include transitions, such as *after a while, moreover,* or *in fact,* to show how ideas are related to one another.

Have students exchange papers and underline the main ideas in each other's paragraphs. Then have them underline any sentences that do not support the main ideas in a different color. Finally, have them underline transitions in a third color and mark any places where transitions are missing.

Traits of Strong Writing

Include these traits of strong writing to express your ideas effectively.

Ideas

Organization

Voice

Word Choice

Sentence Fluency

Conventions

Presentation

For more information on using the Traits of Strong Writing, see pages R28–R30.

Word Choice

The following academic vocabulary word is used in the student model.

encounter (en koun′tər) *n.* an unexpected or casual meeting; *One of her most memorable encounters on this trip was with a crocodile.*

Using academic vocabulary may help strengthen your writing. Try to use one or two academic vocabulary words in your essay. See the complete list on pages R83–R85.

Revise

Peer Review After you complete your draft, read it aloud for a partner. Use the checklist below to evaluate and strengthen each other's biographical narrative.

Checklist

☑ Do you present main points about your subject's life?

☑ Does your essay have a clear beginning, middle, and end?

☑ Do you narrate events in chronological order and/or tell main ideas in a logical order?

☑ Do you use descriptive details and other precise language?

☑ Do you supply any necessary background information readers need?

☑ Do you write in a conversational tone that allows your voice to come through?

▶ Focus Lesson

Action Verbs

Action verbs tell what someone or something does. When the subject of the sentence performs the action, the action verb is in the active voice. Keep your writing in the active voice as often as possible. Avoid the passive voice, which consists of a form of *to be* plus the past participle. ☆

Draft:

Then she continued her journey into the interior. The strange sights and sounds of the vast tropical forest, and the lives of its animals and human inhabitants, were very interesting to Kingsley. Walking or using a dugout canoe, she moved northward until she reached present-day Nigeria.

Revision:

Then she journeyed[1] into the interior. The strange sights and sounds of the vast tropical forest, and the lives of its animals and people, enchanted[2] Kingsley. Striding[3] along or paddling[3] a dugout canoe, she explored[3] northward until she reached present-day Nigeria.

1 Replace wordy verb constructions with precise verbs.
2 Use active voice whenever possible.
3 Avoid vague writing by using precise action verbs.

Edit and Proofread

Get It Right When you have completed the final draft of your narrative, proofread it for errors in grammar, usage, mechanics, and spelling. Refer to the Language Handbook, pages R40–R59, as a guide.

> **Focus Lesson**
>
> ### Verb Tense
>
> As you edit your biographical narrative, make sure that your verb tenses are formed correctly and that any shifts in tense are accurate.
>
> **Original:** There is an incorrect shift in tense.
>
> *Kingsley nursed Boer prisoners until she catches a fever and dies, on June 3, 1900.*
>
> **Improved:** Make sure the tenses of verbs in the same sentence match each other.
>
> *Kingsley nursed Boer prisoners until she caught a fever and died, on June 3, 1900.*
>
> **Original:** The tense of the sentence does not show that events occurred at different times.
>
> *She read about West Africa in her father's library, and she decided to visit this mysterious region.*
>
> **Improved:** Shift from the past tense to the past perfect tense to show that her reading took place before her decision to go to Africa.
>
> *She had read about West Africa in her father's library, and she decided to visit this mysterious region.*

Present/Publish

Make a Good Impression After you finish editing and proofreading, look over your essay one last time. Make sure the paper is typed and double-spaced with readable fonts and appropriate margins. Give it an interesting title and check with your teacher about any additional presentation guidelines.

Peer Review Tips

A classmate may ask you to read his or her narrative. Take notes as you read so you can give constructive feedback. Use the following questions to get started.

- Do you get a clear sense of the subject?
- Is the tone engaging?
- Are there vivid details?

Word-Processing Tip

If you are typing your narrative on a computer, make sure you use appropriate margin sizes. Half an inch for all margins is usually adequate. Margins too wide or too narrow can be distracting for readers.

Writer's Portfolio

Place a clean copy of your biographical narrative in your portfolio to review later.

 **Literature** Online

Writing and Research For editing and publishing tools, go to glencoe.com and enter QuickPass code GLW6053u2.

WRITING WORKSHOP **423**

Advanced Learners/Pre-AP

DIFFERENTIATED INSTRUCTION

Writing Encourage students to write several more brief biographical narratives about individuals whose lives are connected to their original subject's life in some way. Have students present their biographical sketches as a collection and have them include an introductory paragraph that reflects on the relationship between the individual narratives. For example, a collection of narratives about historical figures from a particular time period might reveal general trends of the era, or a collection of narratives about different family members might reveal the values of the family as a whole.

 **Writing Workshop**

Biographical Narrative

Teach

Writing Skills

Verb Tense Remind students that when writing about real events that happened in the past, they should always use the past tense. This differs from the technique they may have learned for writing essays about fictional works. **Ask:** What tense does one use when referring to events in a poem or piece of fiction? *(One uses the present tense to refer to events, even if the work is narrated in the past tense.)*

ENGLISH LEARNERS English learners may have difficulty with the second example in the Verb Tense focus lesson because the past participle of the verb *read* looks identical to the present form of the verb but is pronounced differently. Explain that this is one of many irregular verbs in English. Review the two pronunciations and explain that context clues can help them determine which form of the verb is intended.

Writing Process

Presenting Students may have discovered interesting photographs or portraits of their subjects while researching. Encourage students to write captions for these images and include them with their final drafts.

Learning Objectives
Writing a biographical narrative. (SE)
Using the writing process. (SE)
Developing coherent paragraphs. (TE)

423

Speaking, Listening, and Viewing Workshop

Photo-Essay

Focus

Summary

In this workshop, students will learn techniques for planning, rehearsing, and presenting a photo-essay to the class.

Teach

View the Art ★

This marble bust of Alexander dates from the Hellenistic period of Greek art, during which sculptors represented their subjects in states of lively action and emotion. **Ask:** Judging by the sculpture's title, what emotions do you think the sculptor intended to convey? *(Students might mention pain or despair.)*

 For Speaking, Listening, and Viewing activities and rubric, see Unit 2 Teaching Resources Book, pp. 213–216.

Speaking Practice

SMALL GROUP **Develop Voice** Remind students that the spoken component of their presentation does not need to be formally scripted; rather, it should sound natural, reflecting their own unique speaking style. After students have researched their subjects and assembled collections of images, have them divide into pairs and take turns talking about their subjects and their images. Have the partners listen carefully and jot down phrases that are characteristic of each other's speaking style. Then have them offer feedback to their partners about words or phrases that were particularly effective. Partners should also point out any speaking habits that are ineffective or distracting, such as frequent use of "filler" words, including *um* or *like*.

424

Do Your Research

Before creating a photo- or art-essay, research art and photo exhibits. What is it about these exhibits that speaks to the audience and stands out above everyday images? You should incorporate these elements into your presentation.

Speaking, Listening, and Viewing Workshop

Photo-Essay

Literature Connection

"You will find him depicted as one of the four kings on the standard French pack of playing cards; you will find the map of his empire on every Greek school map, and every taverna wall; he's on Sicilian carnival carts, Ethiopian bridal cloths, Byzantine church murals, and on paintings from Moghul India."

Alexander the Great has been the subject of an extraordinary variety of artwork, as shown in the quotation above by Michael Wood from *In the Footsteps of Alexander the Great*. Examine the image below. What does it reveal about the artist's view of Alexander?

You can collect and combine art or photographs to present the significance of a historical figure in a photo-essay.

Assignment	**Present a Photo- or Art-Essay**

Plan and deliver a photo- or art-essay on a historical figure.

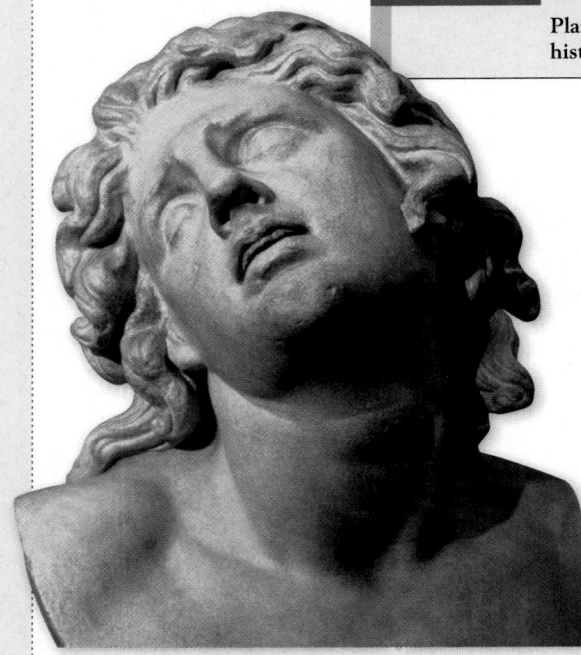

The Dying Alexander the Great, 356-323 BC. ★
Marble. Ancient Art and Architecture Collection Ltd.

Plan Your Presentation

Just like written essays, your photo- or art-essay needs to have a main idea. Choose a historical person you would like to represent and decide what you want to express about that individual. For example, if you decide to present legends about Alexander the Great, you might collect medieval images showing him flying through air or exploring underwater. Your presentation should be compelling and interesting to gain and keep your audience's attention. Follow these guidelines when presenting an art- or photo-essay.

- **Research the topic well.** You should be prepared to answer any questions the audience may have about your historical figure and each image you present.

- **Allow enough time to prepare.** Think about how many pieces you would like to have in your essay, as well as what kinds of images would best suit your purpose.

- **Decide how you will showcase your work.** Will you use an easel, poster board, a slide projector, or a computer presentation?

Create Meaning in Visual Media

It is often said a picture is worth a thousand words. Your pictures need to be able to "speak" to the audience, or convey emotion and feeling.

Presentation Tips

Use the following checklist to evaluate your presentation.

- Did you remember not to block the visuals?

- Did you face the audience and not the visuals?

- Did you vary the tone of your visuals, incorporating both humor and serious images when appropriate?

Techniques for Presenting a Photo- or Art-Essay

Verbal Techniques	Nonverbal Techniques
☑ **Volume** Speak loudly and clearly so your audience can understand any background information you provide.	☑ **Eye Contact** Make frequent eye contact with the audience. However, you should also look at the photographs or art to draw attention to important details.
☑ **Pace** Allow the audience enough time to view and react to each image before moving on to the next one.	☑ **Gestures** Point out key details in your art, but be careful not to block your essay when presenting.
☑ **Tone** The tone of your speech should match the tone of your photo- or art-essay. If your essay is of a serious nature, you should speak in a dignified, serious tone. More light-hearted essays can be presented with a more informal tone.	☑ **Display** Use an easel or poster board to display your images. The art and photographs should be presented in such a way that your entire audience can view them.

 Literature Online

Speaking, Listening, and Viewing For project ideas, templates, and presentation tips, go to glencoe.com and enter QuickPass code GLW6053u2.

Teach

Viewing Skills

Evaluate Images Remind students that some images are more reputable, compelling, or original than others. Encourage students to ask themselves questions like the following when selecting images for their photo-essay: Is the image effective on its own, or does it need lengthy explanation? Does it reveal a unique insight into the character of the subject?

Listening Skills

Question Remind students that they should actively assess the presenters' interpretations of images. As each image is presented, students should listen carefully, consider their own reactions to the image, and then jot down their responses and questions for the presenter.

Learning Objectives
Presenting a photo-essay. (SE)
Developing voice. (TE)

Approaching Level

DIFFERENTIATED INSTRUCTION

Compare Images Students who are having difficulty organizing their images into a cohesive presentation may benefit from comparing and contrasting two images at a time. Have these students select a pair of images and answer the following questions: *What aspects of the historical figure's appearance are the same in both images? What aspects are different? In which image does the historical figure seem more likeable? In which does he or she seem more realistic?* Have students plan their presentations around their answers to these questions.

Advanced Learners/Pre-AP

DIFFERENTIATED INSTRUCTION

Cultural Context Encourage students to conduct additional research on artistic movements and trends from particular time periods. Invite them to consider the cultural and historical context of the images they present, reflecting on what each image reveals about its time.

Focus

Summary

The purpose of this feature is to interest students in reading additional literature about ancient Greece and Rome. Profiled works include plays by Greek tragedians, a Shakespearean drama about Roman politics, an English epic, and a scholarly introduction to mythology.

Teach

Literary History ☆

A Cinematic *Odyssey* Students who found Homer's *Iliad* interesting may enjoy watching *O Brother, Where Art Thou?* a film by Joel and Ethan Coen based on the plot of Homer's *Odyssey*. The comedy is set in the Depression-era South and features three convicts who have escaped from a chain gang. The movie offers a creative and entertaining adaptation of the epic poem. The film is rated PG-13 for violence and language.

Reading Practice

Analyze Historical Context Point out to students that being informed about the historical context of a work of literature will help to deepen their understanding of and insight into the works they read independently. Advise them to take a few minutes before they begin independently reading a new text to research its historical context. They can use this rubric to help them analyze the historical context:

426

Independent Reading

Literature of the Region

THE AUTHORS OF ANCIENT GREECE AND ROME INHERITED AND PASSED ON A RICH TRADITION of great narratives: their mythology. These stories, populated by gods and heroes, inspired many Greek and Roman poets and playwrights. The tales of the Greek gods (who later became fused with the Roman gods), the larger-than-life deeds of early heroes, the saga of the Trojan War, the wanderings of Odysseus—all these myths are among the most precious legacies of ancient Greece and Rome.

Mythology

Edith Hamilton

"A people's literature is the great textbook for real knowledge of them," observed Edith Hamilton, one of the most influential classical scholars of her time. Hamilton reveals many essential features of ancient Greek and Roman civilization in her enduringly popular book *Mythology* (1942), an engaging introduction to classical myths and legends of ancient Greece and Rome that vividly retells the stories of gods and heroes. Hamilton's book presents detailed, engrossing accounts of the major narrative cycles of classical mythology.

The Oresteia

Aeschylus

Generally regarded as the "father of tragedy," Aeschylus was the first noted dramatist to grapple with the painful and unanswerable questions of life and to create characters who were grand in their suffering. His masterpiece is the *Oresteia* (458 B.C.), a cycle of three plays based on the fate of the family of Agamemnon, king of Mycenae and leader of the Greek expedition against Troy. Robert Fagles's version of the trilogy is the finest modern translation of these powerful dramatic works.

- Read about the author's life, works, and his or her cultural and political involvement
- Learn where the author lived when he or she wrote the piece
- Read about what was happening in the world at the time that the piece was written
- Research what was happening in the area where the author lived while he or she wrote the work

- Look up references from the text with which you are not familiar
- Read about how the piece has been received throughout the years

Explain to students that these points will help them better understand and enjoy their independent reading.

GLENCOE LITERATURE LIBRARY

Beowulf ☆

Beowulf is the first great epic in English literature. Written centuries ago by an anonymous author, it tells the story of the legendary hero Beowulf and his battles against monsters such as the vicious Grendel and a formidable dragon. The epic emphasizes courage in the face of death and the search for a measure of immortality through heroic deeds. Along with Achilles and Hector, Beowulf stands as one of the world's most famous epic heroes.

The Tragedy of Julius Caesar

William Shakespeare

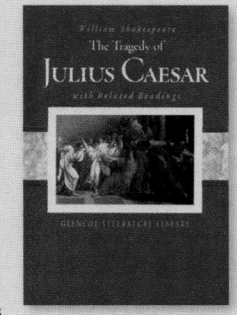

Set during Rome's transition from a republic to an empire, *Julius Caesar* (c. 1599) relates the story of the emperor Caesar's murder and the intrigues and ambitions of his supporters and enemies. Like Oedipus, Caesar is an impressive but flawed leader who ignores signs of impending danger despite many warnings. It has been said the drama is more about the story of Brutus and Antony (conspirators against Caesar) than of the murdered emperor, since Caesar is killed early in the play; but Caesar's enduring presence, if not the man himself, is at the center of the drama's conflicts.

CRITICS' CORNER

"Medea's mad monomania [single-minded obsession] is undoubtedly a Euripidean discovery. Monomania singles Medea out, separates and cuts her off from the real world. Through her monomania Medea is alone. Heroes of tragedy have to be alone."

—Jan Kott, from "Medea at Pescara"
in *The Eating of the Gods:
An Interpretation of Greek Tragedy*

Medea and Other Plays

Euripides

Euripides (c. 484 B.C. – 406 B.C.) was critical of convention, sensitive to suffering, and skeptical of the gods. Unlike Aeschylus and Sophocles, he was less concerned with large questions of religion and morality and more concerned with the emotions of individual characters. An excellent recent translation by James Morwood collects several of the greatest plays of Euripides, including *Medea*, a compelling study of the ferocious passions of a woman scorned by the Greek hero Jason.

Write a Review

Read one of the books listed on these pages and write a review of it for your classmates. Be sure to summarize the characters, plot, and major themes and explain why other students might enjoy the book. Present your review to the class.

Teach

Write a Review

Students' reviews should

- focus on one book presented in this feature
- summarize the characters, plot, and themes of the book
- explain why other students might like the book

Literary History ☆

A Graphic *Beowulf* Students who enjoy comic books may like reading one of the several graphic novels recently published which depict the epic of *Beowulf*. Based on both the A. J. Church and the Francis Gummere translations, Gareth Hinds's graphic novel concentrates on the action of the epic story, depicting Beowulf as a near-superhero. James Rumford's *Beowulf: A Hero's Tale Retold* is a more text-centered graphic novel, which focuses on the normal life of the Danish court.

Glencoe Literature Library

Glencoe Literature Library offers an extensive collection of hardcover books that help you encourage your students to read independently. Choose among the more than 120 full-length literary works—novels, novellas, plays, and nonfiction. Each book includes related readings from a broad range of genres. Go to glencoe.com for more information.

Learning Objectives
Reading literature independently. (SE)
Writing a review. (SE)
Analyzing historical context. (TE)

Approaching Level

DIFFERENTIATED INSTRUCTION

High-Interest Reading Students who are struggling with the texts included in this unit may find some of these independent reading recommendations more suitable. Hamilton's organized, concise presentation of Greek and Roman mythology makes *Mythology* appropriate for less-proficient readers. The graphic-novel retelling of *Beowulf* may also help such students follow the text of the epic.

Advanced Learners/Pre-AP

DIFFERENTIATED INSTRUCTION

Works with Nuance More advanced students may benefit from reading Thornton Wilder's novel *The Ides of March*, which uses fictional letters between historical figures to tell of the escalating drama of the months leading up to Julius Caesar's assassination. Aristophanes's *The Frogs* is an ancient comedy in which the god Dionysus must decide if Aeschylus or Euripides is the greatest poet.

Assessment

English-Language Arts

Focus

Bellringer Options

Daily Language Transparency 35

Students often go into test-taking situations with a little anxiety, if not outright fear. Encourage students to take more control of the situation. **Ask:** What can you do to have more confidence when you face a testing situation? *(Get plenty of sleep the night before; study; arrive early.)* Generate a list of strategies on the board and discuss with students.

Teach

Assessment

Tell students that the Assessment section will provide reinforcement in general test-taking strategies and will test them on the skills and vocabulary taught in this unit. Students will read a nonfiction selection and will answer context, comprehension, and inference questions. Then, they will choose answers for ten sentence-completion items and ten paragraph-improvement items. Finally, they will be asked to write a short essay based on a prompt.

 To create custom assessments online, go to Progress Reporter Online Assessment.

 To create custom assessments using software, use ExamView Assessment Suite.

428

Assessment

English–Language Arts

Reading: Nonfiction

Carefully read the following passage. Use context clues to help you define any words with which you are unfamiliar. Pay close attention to credibility, cultural context, the author's purpose, and his use of literary devices. Then, on a separate sheet of paper, answer the questions on pages 429–433.

from *Julius Caesar* by Suetonius

Now Caesar's approaching murder was foretold to him by unmistakable signs. . . . Shortly before his death, as he was told, the herds of horses which he had dedicated to the river Rubicon when he crossed it, and had let loose without a keeper, stubbornly refused to graze and wept copiously. Again,
5 when he was offering sacrifice, the soothsayer Spurinna warned him to beware of danger, which would come not later than the Ides of March. On the day before the Ides of that month, a little bird called the king-bird flew into the Hall of Pompey with a sprig of laurel, pursued by others of various kinds from the grove hard by, which tore it to pieces in the hall. In fact the
10 very night before his murder he dreamt now that he was flying above the clouds, and now that he was clasping the hand of Jupiter; and his wife Calpurnia thought that the pediment of their house fell, and that her husband was stabbed in her arms; and on a sudden the door of the room flew open of its own accord.
15 Both for these reasons and because of poor health he hesitated for a long time whether to stay at home and put off what he had planned to do in the Senate; but at last, urged by Decimus Brutus not to disappoint the full meeting, which had for some time been waiting for him, he went forth almost at the end of the fifth hour; and when a note revealing the plot was handed
20 him by someone on the way, he put it with others which he held in his left hand, intending to read them presently. Then, after many victims had been slain, and he could not get favorable omens, he entered the Senate in defiance of portents, laughing at Spurinna and calling him a false prophet, because the Ides of March were come without bringing him harm. Spurinna
25 replied that they had of a truth come, but they had not gone.
As he took his seat, the conspirators gathered about him as if to pay their respects, and straightway Tillius Cimber, who had assumed the lead, came nearer as though to ask something; and when Caesar with a gesture put him off to another time, Cimber caught his toga by both shoulders; then as

428 UNIT 2 ANCIENT GREECE AND ROME

Reading Practice

Transitional Words and Phrases

Explain that transitional words and phrases provide coherence and flow within a text. Often they can be effective in providing clues to relationships between ideas in a work as well as indicating the sequence of events. Ask students to give examples of transitional words and phrases. *(Possible answers: however, then, next, therefore, first, moreover, on the other hand)*.

When testing, look for transitional words to signal relationships and changes in sequence. When possible during tests, mark the margin when a transitional word or phrase appears.

30 Caesar cried, "Why, this is violence!" one of the Cascas stabbed him from one side just below the throat. Caesar caught Casca's arm and ran it through with his stylus, but as he tried to leap to his feet, he was stopped by another wound. When he saw that he was beset on every side by drawn daggers, he
35 muffled his head in his robe, and at the same time drew down its lap to his feet with his left hand, in order to die more decently, with the lower part of his body also covered. And in this way he was stabbed with three and twenty wounds, uttering not a word, but merely a groan at the first stroke, though some have written that when Marcus Brutus rushed at him, he said in Greek,
40 "You too, my child?" All the conspirators made off, and he lay there lifeless for some time, until finally three common slaves put him on a litter and carried him home, with one arm hanging down. And of so many wounds none turned out to be mortal, in the opinion of the physician Antistius, except the second one in the breast.

1. In the opening paragraph, what warning does Caesar receive of his approaching death?
   A. One of the conspirators informs Caesar.
   B. Strange events suggest something bad will happen.
   C. Caesar's friends warn him in person.
   D. Caesar receives a letter from a friend.

2. Suetonius introduces the horses in lines 2–4 to show that:
   F. Caesar loves animals.
   G. Caesar is generous.
   H. the animals sense Caesar's impending death.
   J. Caesar believes deeply in the Roman gods.

3. As it is used in line 5, the word *soothsayer* most nearly means:
   A. doctor.
   B. fortune-teller.
   C. bodyguard.
   D. murderer.

4. The accounts of Caesar and Calpurnia in lines 9–14 suggest that:
   F. Calpurnia is going to be an accomplice in Caesar's murder.
   G. Spurinna's warnings have a positive effect on Caesar.
   H. Caesar and his wife have premonitions of his death.
   J. Caesar knows how he is going to die.

5. The discussion of the days leading up to Caesar's assassination in paragraph 1 suggests that the Romans:

   I. were apathetic toward their animals.
   II. were always thinking about death.
   III. believed in omens and fortune-telling.

   A. II only
   B. III only
   C. I and III only
   D. II and III only

Assessment
English-Language Arts

Assess

1. **B** is the correct answer. The narrator explicitly says Caesar's death was "foretold him by unmistakable signs." **DOK 1**

2 **H** is the correct answer. The narrator introduces the horses as one of the omens foretelling Caesar's murder. **DOK 4**

3. **B** is the correct answer. Spurinna is not described as a doctor, bodyguard, or murderer, so **A**, **C**, and **D** are incorrect. He is described as warning Caesar of future danger. **DOK 2**

4. **H** is the correct answer. Caesar and his wife both have premonitions in lines 12–18. Calpurnia's visions do not implicate her in the crime, so **F** is incorrect. Spurinna's warnings have a negative effect on Caesar, so **G** is incorrect. Caesar never knows exactly how he is going to die, so **J** is incorrect. **DOK 1**

5. **B** is the correct answer. The discussion of the days leading up to Caesar's assassination suggest that omens and fortune-telling were highly regarded in Rome. **DOK 2**

Approaching Level
DIFFERENTIATED INSTRUCTION

"Self Talk" Frequently the anxiety of students who are nervous about taking a test is self-defeating. Encourage students to write down any negative thoughts they have previously encountered while preparing for and taking tests. Then tell them to counter these negative thoughts with positive statements about themselves. They should repeat positive statements often to help reprogram their minds to concentrate on their strengths and successes instead of weaknesses and failures. When they become anxious or frustrated during a test, taking a moment to repeat these positive thoughts can help them focus on the task at hand.

Assessment

English-Language Arts

Assess

6. F is the correct answer. Failing to read the letter that warns of the plot did not cause Caesar to meet with the Senate, so **G** is incorrect. Caesar's poor health caused him to avoid company, not seek it out, so **H** is incorrect. Caesar has no luck attaining a good omen so he decides to disregard the omens and Spurinna the soothsayer. This does not mean he no longer believes in omens, so **J** is incorrect. [DOK 1]

7. D is the correct answer. The context associates the word *portents* with omens. [DOK 2]

8. F is the correct answer. **G**, **H**, and **J** do not make sense in the context. [DOK 1]

9. A is the correct answer. The fact that Caesar ran through Cascas's arm with it, indicated that the stylus could not be any of the other items. [DOK 2]

10. J is the correct answer. Caesar tries to brush off Tillius Cimber just before Cimber grabs his toga by the shoulders. [DOK 1]

11. C is the correct answer. The narrator explicitly says Caesar pulled down his robe to cover the lower part of his body "in order to die more decently." [DOK 1]

12. F is the correct answer. Suetonius states that Caesar let out "a groan at the first stroke." [DOK 1]

13. B is the correct answer. The reader does not have enough information to know whether Caesar knows all the conspirators, so **A** is incorrect. **C** and **D** are not supported by the passage. [DOK 4]

6. Caesar eventually decides to meet with the Senate because:
   F. Decimus Brutus convinces him the Senate has been waiting long enough.
   G. he fails to read the letter that warns of the plot.
   H. he is in poor health and prefers to be with others.
   J. he no longer believes in omens of any sort.

7. As it is used in line 23, the word *portents* most nearly means:
   A. enemies.
   B. victims.
   C. prophets.
   D. forewarnings.

8. Caesar scoffs at Spurinna and calls him a false prophet because:

   I. the Ides of March have arrived without incident.
   II. Caesar wants to give an impression of confidence.
   III. none of Spurinna's prophecies ever came true.

   F. I only
   G. III only
   H. I and II only
   J. I, II, and III

9. As it is used in line 32, the word *stylus* most nearly means:
   A. a sharp-pointed pen
   B. a sandal
   C. a long robe
   D. a heavy club

10. At what point does Caesar try to dismiss one of the senators?
    F. after he cries "Why, this is violence!"
    G. before the conspirators gathered about him
    H. after the first attack
    J. before Tillius Cimber grabs his toga

11. Why does Caesar draw his toga to his feet?
    A. to protect his legs from wounds
    B. to keep from being cold
    C. to die with dignity
    D. to avoid falling

12. When does Caesar let out a groan?
    F. as the first wound is inflicted
    G. after the twenty-third wound was inflicted
    H. after Marcus Brutus rushed at him
    J. after he muffled his head in his robe

13. After reading Suetonius's account, what generalization can you make about Caesar?
    A. He knows all of the conspirators intimately.
    B. He is proud and stoic.
    C. He has great respect for the physician Antistius.
    D. He often disagrees with his wife Calpurnia.

14. What is the author's primary purpose in this passage?
    F. to entertain
    G. to inform
    H. to persuade
    J. to express feelings

15. According to the physician Antistius, what is the cause of Caesar's death?
    A. his inability to fight back
    B. only some of the 23 blows
    C. Caesar's failure to heed bad omens
    D. the second wound in Caesar's breast

14. G is the correct answer. Suetonius does not attempt to prove a point, so **H** is incorrect. He does not express any personal feelings, so **J** is also incorrect. He does not seek to entertain, so **F** is incorrect. [DOK 4]

15. D is the correct answer. Suetonius clearly states in lines 53–55, "And of so many wounds none turned out to be mortal, in the opinion of the physician Antistius, except the second one in the breast." [DOK 1]

Vocabulary Skills: Sentence Completion

For each item in the Vocabulary Skills section, choose the word or words that best complete the sentence. Write your answers on a separate sheet of paper.

1. Seeking _____, the Persians once again invaded Greece ten years after the culmination of the battle at Marathon.
   A. vengeance
   B. munificence
   C. moderation
   D. demolition

2. For a Greek soldier, leaving weapons and armor in the hands of the enemy was considered _____ behavior, likely to be _____ by fellow Greeks.
   F. ignominious...denounced
   G. incredulous...dignity
   H. stern...intimation
   J. tangible...versatility

3. The Greek poet Sappho hoped her writings would be remembered rather than fall into _____.
   A. foreboding
   B. droves
   C. detractor
   D. oblivion

4. Athens _____ all other Greek city-states in the brilliance of its civilization.
   F. appeased
   G. inflicted
   H. surpassed
   J. retracted

5. Theater was a _____ and _____ element of the culture of ancient Athenians, who used it to explore everything from religious experiences to social questions.
   A. horrendous...ignominious
   B. sullen...incredulous
   C. crucial...tangible
   D. random...vulnerable

6. In their struggle with Carthage, the Romans _____ help from other peoples of Italy.
   F. swelled
   G. enlisted
   H. surpassed
   J. censured

7. The assassins surrounded Julius Caesar and _____ 23 wounds, leaving him dead and his supporters and family _____.
   A. appeased...suppliant
   B. fastened...sinister
   C. enlisted...horrendous
   D. inflicted...bereft

8. Breaking out on July 18, A.D. 64, the Great Fire of Rome had _____ results, bringing the city to the brink of disaster.
   F. vulnerable
   G. subtle
   H. dire
   J. futile

9. Epicureanism _____ people to avoid pain and to seek wisdom in seclusion, withdrawing from public life.
   A. impelled
   B. defiled
   C. detected
   D. suppressed

10. Roman gladiatorial combats were fights to the death, never _____ as too violent by their bloodthirsty audiences.
   F. duped
   G. denounced
   H. detected
   J. gloated

Assess

1. **A** is the correct answer. **B**, **C**, and **D** make no sense in this context. Having been defeated, the Persians would most likely be seeking vengeance. (DOK 2)

2. **F** is the correct answer. **G**, **H**, and **J** make no sense in this context. (DOK 2)

3. **D** is the correct answer. **A**, **B**, and **C** make no sense in this context. The unknown word is contrasted with "remembered." (DOK 2)

4. **H** is the correct answer. **F**, **G**, and **J** make no sense in this context. (DOK 2)

5. **C** is the correct answer. **A**, **B**, and **D** make no sense in this context. (DOK 2)

6. **G** is the correct answer. **F**, **H**, and **J** make no sense in this context. (DOK 2)

7. **D** is the correct answer. **A**, **B**, and **C** make no sense in this context. (DOK 2)

8. **H** is the correct answer. **F**, **G**, and **J** make no sense in this context. (DOK 2)

9. **A** is the correct answer. **B**, **C**, and **D** make no sense in this context. (DOK 2)

10. **G** is the correct answer. **F**, **H**, and **J** make no sense in this context. (DOK 2)

Approaching Level

DIFFERENTIATED INSTRUCTION

Sentence Completion When doing the sentence-completion part of a test, students should consider these three simple steps:

1. **Look ahead:** Read the sentence and predict an answer.

2. **Make your choice:** Decide which answer choice best fits the blank or blanks.

3. **Read the sentence back:** Verify your answer by reading it aloud with the word in the sentence.

Assessment

English-Language Arts

Assess

1. **B** is the correct answer. The sentence incorrectly makes the verb agree with the predicate nominative rather than the subject. `DOK 1`

2. **G** is the correct answer. The sentence incorrectly uses commas in a series. `DOK 1`

3. **D** is the correct answer. No other answers make sense in the context. `DOK 1`

4. **H** is the correct answer. Because the writer is discussing the feats of a historical figure, both verbs should be in the past tense. `DOK 1`

5. **C** is the correct answer. The dash is the correct mark of punctuation needed here. `DOK 1`

Reading Practice

Rereading Tell students that paragraph-improvement exercises are like puzzles. They will have to read the passage more than once to figure out the most logical sequence of sentences. To help students become more comfortable with these exercises, provide practice models that they can work on during their free time. You might take a passage from a book that the class is reading and rearrange the sentences.

432

Grammar and Writing Skills: Sentence Improvement

Read carefully through the following passage from the first draft of a student's essay. For question 1–8, choose the best alternative for each word or phrase that is underlined and numbered. If you think the original version is best, choose "NO CHANGE." Then answer Questions 9 and 10. Write your answers on a separate sheet of paper.

[1]

The defeat and destruction of Rome <u>was</u> the lifelong goal of the Carthaginian general Hannibal. <u>Brave brilliant, cunning, resourceful and relentless</u>, he was the most dangerous enemy the Romans ever faced. When Hannibal was a child, his father made him swear before the gods that he would never stop fighting Rome. That promise Hannibal kept <u>under</u> all his victories and his final defeat.

[2]

<u>When he grew up, Hannibal first seizes</u> one of Rome's allied cities in Spain, an act of war. His next move was even <u>bolder; to attack Italy itself.</u> Leading 40,000 soldiers and about forty elephants, Hannibal marched out of Spain. He <u>crossed southern Gaul and reached</u> the foot of the Alps in the fall of 218 B.C. <u>Before, he reached northern Italy, cold, ice, hunger, sickness, and attacks</u> by mountain peoples killed half of Hannibal's army and most of his elephants.

[3]

[1] Although the Carthaginians were usually outnumbered, Hannibal led his troops to a series of victories against Roman armies. [2] Determined to stop him, Rome's leaders sent out the most powerful force they had ever assembled, an army estimated to have been as large as 100,000 men. [3] Luring his enemies into a trap, Hannibal surrounded and destroyed nearly the entire Roman army. [4] In early August 216 B.C., the Romans met <u>Hannibal's troops near the town of Cannae in southeastern Italy.</u> [5] Roman armies were organized into units known as legions, centuries, and cohorts.

1. **A.** NO CHANGE
   B. were
   C. had been
   D. are

2. **F.** NO CHANGE
   G. Brave, brilliant, cunning, resourceful, and relentless
   H. Brave and brilliant, cunning, resourceful, and relentless
   J. Brave, brilliant, cunning, resourceful, relentless

3. **A.** NO CHANGE
   B. over
   C. into
   D. through

4. **F.** NO CHANGE
   G. When he grows up, Hannibal will first seize
   H. When he grew up, Hannibal first seized
   J. Growing up, Hannibal first seized

5. **A.** NO CHANGE
   B. bolder, to attack Italy itself.
   C. bolder—to attack Italy itself.
   D. bolder to attack Italy itself.

6. **F.** NO CHANGE
    G. crossed southern Gaul, and reached
    H. crosses southern Gaul, and reaches
    J. had crossed southern Gaul and reaches

7. **A.** NO CHANGE
    B. Before he reached northern Italy, cold, ice, hunger, sickness, and attacks
    C. Before, he reached northern Italy cold, ice, hunger, sickness, and attacks
    D. Before he reached northern Italy, cold ice, hunger sickness, and attacks

8. **F.** NO CHANGE
    G. Hannibal's troops near the town of Cannae, in southeastern Italy
    H. Hannibal troops near the town of Cannae in southeastern Italy
    J. Hannibals troops near the town of Cannae in Southeastern Italy

9. Which of the following sequences of sentences will make Paragraph 3 most logical?
    A. 1, 2, 4, 5, 3
    B. 2, 1, 3, 4, 5
    C. 3, 4, 1, 2, 3
    D. 1, 2, 5, 4, 3

Question 10 refers to the preceding passage as a whole.

10. The writer has been asked to write an essay that includes an introduction, a body, and a conclusion about what motivated Hannibal. Would this essay fulfill that assignment?
    F. Yes; the writer explains Hannibal's motivations and includes an introduction, a body, and a conclusion.
    G. No; the writer does not discuss Hannibal's motivations.
    H. No; the writer does not include an introduction.
    J. No; the writer discusses what motivated Hannibal but does not include a conclusion.

Essay: Writing Situation

Which of the individuals you encountered in this unit seems the most heroic?

Directions for Writing

Remember that the Greek heroic ideal stressed all-around excellence, including physical power, intellectual ability (often viewed as cunning), and moral strength (such as bravery and endurance). Select one of the figures from this unit, either a real person (such as Socrates) or an imaginary character (such as Oedipus), and analyze how this individual reflects or departs from the Greek heroic ideal.

Remember to:

- Write about the assigned topic.
- Make your writing thoughtful and interesting.
- Make sure each sentence you write contributes to your composition as a whole.
- Make sure your ideas are clear and easy for the reader to follow.
- Write about your ideas in depth so the reader is able to develop a good understanding of what you are saying.

- Proofread your writing to correct errors in spelling, capitalization, punctuation, grammar, and sentence structure.

 Literature Online

Assessment For additional test practice, go to glencoe.com and enter QuickPass code GLW6053u2.

ASSESSMENT **433**

Assess

6. F is the correct answer. The sentence is correct as written. `DOK 1`

7. B is the correct answer. As written, the sentence contains an unnecessary comma after *Before*. `DOK 1`

8. F is the correct answer. The sentence is correct as written. `DOK 1`

9. D is the correct answer. Sentence 5, a statement about the organization of the Roman army, logically follows the estimate of the size of the army. Sentence 3 must follow Sentence 4 because it describes what happened after the Romans met Hannibal's army. `DOK 4`

10. J is the correct answer. The writer sufficiently describes what motivated Hannibal. The essay includes an introduction and a body, but lacks a conclusion. `DOK 4`

Essay

Allow students to review the pages of their textbook that discuss the Greek heroic ideal. This will help them with the first step in writing their essays. `DOK 3`

English Learners

DIFFERENTIATED INSTRUCTION

Intermediate Students may struggle to use active verbs in their essays. Using active verbs will make their essays more polished and persuasive. In order to identify instances in which they could use active verbs, instruct students to review their essays. Every time they find a "being" verb—*be, was, were, am, are, is*—they should circle it.

They should read the sentences they have found with the "being" verbs and use a thesaurus to find active verbs they could use instead. They should work individually to edit their essays, replacing the "being" verbs with the active verbs they have found.

Approaching Level

DIFFERENTIATED INSTRUCTION

Craft a Thesis Statement Advise students to craft a thesis statement by answering and rephrasing the essay prompt. Write the thesis statement they would use with this prompt on the board:

_____ [character/historical figure] seems the most heroic individual in this unit.

433

Skills Scope and Sequence

Readability Scores Key: Dale-Chall/DRP/Lexile

PART 1: Southwest Asia 3500 B.C.–Present

Selections and Features	Literary Elements
Part Introduction pp. 434–447	Literary Periods **SE** p. 440
Epic *from* **Gilgamesh** n/a/**56**/980 pp. 448–466	Epic Hero **SE** p. 449 Setting (review) **SE** p. 465
Grammar Workshop p. 467	
Literary History Sacred Texts pp. 468–469	Literary Genres **SE** p. 468
Sacred Text Genesis 6–9: The Flood, *from the* **King James Version of the Bible,** *from the* **Hebrew Bible** 8.6/**61**/1000 pp. 470–476	Theme **SE** p. 471
Sacred Text The Book of Ruth, *from the* **King James Version of the Bible,** *from the* **Hebrew Bible** 8.1/**61**/1000 pp. 477–485	Parallelism **SE** p. 477 Theme (review) **SE** p. 484
Parable The Parable of the Prodigal Son, *from the* **King James Version of the Bible,** *from* **The New Testament** 7.5/**54**/860 pp. 486–490	Parable **SE** p. 487
Sacred Text *from the* **Qur'an,** translated by N. J. Dawood pp. 491–495	Antithesis **SE** p. 492
Short Story The Second Voyage of Sindbad the Sailor, *from* **The Thousand and One Nights,** translated by N. J. Dawood 8.5/**62**/1110 pp. 496–504	Point of View **SE** p. 497 Imagery (review) **SE** p. 503
Poems *from the* **Rubáiyát,** by Omar Khayyám pp. 505–510	Rhyme Scheme **SE** p. 506 Speaker (review) **SE** p. 509
Poem The Counsels of the Bird, *from* **The Masnavi,** by Rumi pp. 511–515	Maxim **SE** p. 512

Reading Skills and Strategies	Vocabulary	Writing / Grammar	Speaking, Listening, Viewing
Summarize **TE** p. 438 Evaluate Historical Influences **SE** p. 440 Connect to the Literature **SE** p. 441	Technical Words **TE** p. 442	Write a Journal Entry **TE** p. 444 Write a Comparison-Contrast Essay **SE** p. 447	View the Art **SE** p. 434; **TE** pp. 440–446 Visual Display **SE** p. 447
Visualize **SE** p. 449 Summarize **TE** p. 454 Make Predictions **TE** p. 458	Word Origins **SE** p. 465 Academic Vocabulary **SE** p. 465	Write a Movie Scene **TE** p. 452 Write an Expository Essay **SE** p. 466	Oral Interpretation **TE** p. 450 Presentation **TE** p. 450 View the Art **SE** p. 452 Discussion **SE** p. 464
		Pronoun-Antecedent Agreement **SE** p. 467	
Evaluate Historical Influences **SE** p. 468 Connect to the Literature **SE** p. 469		Write a Summary **TE** p. 468	View the Art **TE** pp. 468, 469
Question **SE** p. 471	Synonyms **SE** p. 476	Adverb Clauses **TE** p. 474 Write a Narrative **SE** p. 476	View the Art **TE** p. 472 Speech **TE** p. 472
Respond to Characters **SE** p. 477 Paraphrase **TE** p. 480	Denotation and Connotation **SE** p. 484 Academic Vocabulary **SE** p. 484	Write a Persuasive Essay **SE** p. 485 Infinitives and Infinitive Phrases **SE** p. 485	View the Art **SE** p. 481 Discussion **SE** p. 483
Make Inferences About Theme **SE** p. 487 Compare and Contrast **TE** p. 488	Academic Vocabulary **SE** p. 490	Write a Parable **SE** p. 490	View the Art **SE** p. 489
Interpret Imagery **SE** p. 492 Synthesize **TE** p. 494	Context Clues **SE** p. 495	Write a Memo **SE** p. 495	View the Art **TE** p. 493
Identify Problem and Solution **SE** p. 497 Analyze Cause-and-Effect Relationships **TE** p. 498	Analogies **SE** p. 504 Academic Vocabulary **SE** p. 504	Write a Poem **TE** p. 502 Write a Research Report **SE** p. 504	Connect to Art **SE** p. 504
Clarify Meaning **SE** p. 506 Analyze Persuasive Techniques **TE** p. 508	Word Usage **SE** p. 510 Academic Vocabulary **SE** p. 510	Write Literary Criticism **SE** p. 510	Oral Report **SE** p. 510
Make Generalizations About Characters **SE** p. 512	Antonyms **SE** p. 515	Write a Maxim **SE** p. 515	View the Art **TE** p. 513

PART 1: Southwest Asia 3500 B.C.–Present *(continued)*

Selections and Features	Literary Elements
Poem Elegy for a Woman of No Importance, by Nāzik al-Malā'ikah, translated by Chris Knipp and Mohammad Sadiq pp. 516–519	Personification **SE** p. 517 Imagery **TE** p. 518
Poem The Sound of Birds at Noon, by Dahlia Ravikovitch, translated by Chana Bloch and Ariel Bloch pp. 520–523	Enjambment **SE** p. 521 Personification **TE** p. 522
Poem The Diameter of the Bomb, by Yehuda Amichai, translated by Chana Bloch and Stephen Mitchell pp. 524–527	Diction **SE** p. 525
Poem Butterflies, by Fawziyya Abu Khalid pp. 528–531	Simile **SE** p. 529
Graphic Novel The Letter *from* **Persepolis: The Story of a Childhood,** by Marjane Satrapi pp. 532–541	Symbol **SE** p. 533
Informational Text **TIME:** **Regarding Rania,** by Scott MacLeod **9.8/64/1200** pp. 542–545	

PART 2: South Central Asia 2500 B.C.–Present

Selections and Features	Literary Elements
Part Introduction pp. 546–557	Literary Periods **SE** p. 554
Sacred Text *from* **The Rig-Veda: Creation Hymn,** translated by Wendy Doniger O'Flaherty **6.3/55/n/a** pp. 558–562	Paradox **SE** p. 559
Epic Hundred Questions *from* **The Mahabharata,** retold by R. K. Narayan **8.3/60/840** pp. 563–573	Epic Hero **SE** p. 564 Theme (review) **SE** p. 572
The Art of Translation **The Mahabharata As Shadow Play** pp. 574–575	
Cultural Perspective *from* **Homer in India,** by William Dalrymple **9.2/58/1340** pp. 576–581	

Readability Scores Key: Dale-Chall/DRP/Lexile

PART 2: South Central Asia 2500 B.C.–Present *(continued)*

Reading Skills and Strategies	Vocabulary	Writing / Grammar	Speaking, Listening, and Viewing
Monitor Comprehension **SE** p. 583 Foreshadowing **TE** p. 584 Analyze Diction **TE** p. 586	Denotation and Connotation **SE** p. 593 Academic Vocabulary **SE** p. 593	Create a Graphic Organizer **SE** p. 593 Write a Summary **SE** p. 593 Write an Evaluation **SE** p. 593	View the Art **SE** p. 591 Literature Group **SE** p. 593
Compare Cultural Contexts **SE** p. 594 Preview **SE** p. 596 Connect to Contemporary Issues **TE** p. 600 Analyze Rhyme Scheme **TE** p. 602 Make Predictions **TE** p. 604	Word Parts **SE** p. 599	Verb Tense **TE** p. 596 Write a Song **TE** p. 598 Write a Fable **SE** p. 599 Write an Essay **SE** p. 606	View the Art **SE** pp. 598, 603 Discussion **SE** pp. 601, 603, 606 Oral Report **SE** p. 606
Analyze Cultural Context **SE** p. 608 Analyze Motivation **TE** p. 610 Compare and Contrast Characters **TE** p. 614	Word Origins **SE** p. 617 Academic Vocabulary **SE** p. 617	Write a Reflective Essay **SE** p. 618 Em Dashes and En Dashes **SE** p. 618	View the Art **SE** p. 615 Discussion **SE** p. 616
Activate Prior Knowledge **SE** p. 620	Context Clues **SE** p. 624	Write an Anecdote **SE** p. 624	
Connect to Contemporary Issues **SE** p. 626 Analyze Setting **TE** p. 628 Analyze Plot **TE** p. 632	Antonyms **SE** p. 634 Academic Vocabulary **SE** p. 634	Write a Speech **SE** p. 634	View the Art **SE** p. 630 Debate **TE** p. 630 Speech **SE** p. 634
	Homonyms and Homophones **SE** p. 635		
Identify Ambiguities **SE** p. 637 Visualize **TE** p. 646	Context Clues **SE** p. 650 Academic Vocabulary **SE** p. 650	Write a News Story **TE** p. 648 Write an Editorial **SE** p. 651 Colons **SE** p. 651	Interview **TE** p. 640 View the Art **SE** p. 647 Discussion **SE** p. 649
Analyze Tone **TE** p. 654		Prewrite **SE** p. 654 Draft **SE** p. 655 Revise **SE** p. 658 Write a Reflective Essay **SE** p. 659	View the Photograph **TE** p. 656
		Write Note Cards **SE** p. 661	Reflective Presentation **SE** p. 660 Read Aloud **TE** p. 660
Read Literature Independently **SE** p. 662		Write a Letter **TE** p. 662	Visual Display **SE** p. 663
Clarify Meaning **TE** p. 664		Write an Essay **SE** p. 669	

Focus

Bellringer Options

**Literature Launchers:
    Pre-Reading Videos DVD,
    Unit 3**

**Daily Language Practice
    Transparency 36**

Southwest Asia encompasses
the area often referred to as the
Middle East. South Central Asia
consists primarily of India. **Ask:**
What literature of the Middle
East and India are you already
familiar with? *(Students may say
that they are familiar with religious
texts from the regions, the* Arabian
Nights, *or the* Ramayana.)

View the Art ★

Answer: *Hanuman displays courage, determination, and leadership.*
Malwa paintings, sometimes known
as Central Indian paintings, come from
the 17th century-school of Rajasthani
miniature painting. These miniatures
are known for their flat composition and black and chocolate-brown
backgrounds. Figures are typically
shown against solid color patches. The
appealing facets of Malwa painting
include childlike vision and charm.

 For school-to-home activities, see
Unit 3 Teaching Resources Book,
pp. 5–11.

 For students who would profit
from independent novel study, see
Novel Companion, pp. 119–162.

Hanuman, King of the Monkeys Goes to Ceylon, 17th century. Hindu miniature. National Museum, New Delhi, India.

View the Art Popular among the Hindus, Hanuman is the only character who appears in both the *Ramayana* and
the *Mahabharata* (famous Indian epics). A trickster god, he led the monkey army and helped Rama rescue his wife
Sita from the demon Ravana on the island of Lanka. What heroic qualities does Hanuman display in this miniature?

Speaking Practice

Put on a Skit Organize students into
small groups. Then tell them that they are
going to write and perform a short skit that
shows the meaning of the quotation. Allow
students to use objects in the classroom as
props.

Tell groups to first write the lines of the skit.
Make sure each group member is involved
in the writing and acting of the skit. After
students have written their skits, allow
them time to practice them. Have groups
perform their skits for the class. After they
have finished, have them explain how their
skit shows the meaning of the quotation.

Southwest and South Central Asia

3500 B.C.–Present

چون بادِ بهار عشق جنبان گردد
هر شاخ که خشک نیست رقصان گردد

When the spring breeze of love begins to swirl,
Any branch that is not dead will dance.

—Rumi **1**

PART ONE

PART TWO

435

Unit Resources

Print Materials

- Unit 3 Teaching Resources, pp. 1–335
- Interactive Read and Write
- Novel Companion, pp. 119–162
- Bellringer Option Transparencies: Selection Focus 22–40; Daily Language Practice 36–57
- Assessment Resources, Selection Assessment, pp. 93–134

Technology

- TeacherWorks Plus CD
- StudentWorks Plus CD
- Literature Launchers: Pre-Reading Videos DVD, Unit 3
- Literature Online
- Listening Library CD-ROM
- ExamView CD-ROM
- Skill Level Up! CD-ROM

Focus

Reading Strategy | 1

Monitor Comprehension
Have a volunteer read aloud the quotation from Rumi **Ask:** How would you summarize Rumi's thoughts? *(Students may say the quotation is about the power of love and its positive effects on all living things.)*

 For diagnostic and end-of-unit assessment, see Assessment Resources, pp. 13–18, 257–258.

Focus

Reading Strategy

Have students research communication routes in the area. They might divide into groups to investigate ancient trade routes, sea routes, desert travel, travel on the Tigris and Euphrates rivers, and other topics.

View the Art ★

Ask: What sort of unique shapes do you see in the Dubai skyline? *(Students' responses will vary, but they may note spirals, triangles, spires, and cylinder shaped buildings.)*

 For additional support for English Learners, see Unit 3 Teaching Resources Book, pp. 19–20.

A *Skyline.* Jose Fuste Raga. Dubai Emirate, United Arab Emirates. ★

B An Israeli woman shops for tomatoes at a produce stand of an Arab vendor at a market in Jerusalem, Israel.

LOG ON ▶ **Literature** Online

Literature and Reading For more about the history and literature of this period, go to glencoe.com and enter QuickPass code GLW6053u3.

436

Part Introduction Skills

Reading Skills
- Analyze Graphic Information (SE p. 439)
- Make Generalizations (SE p. 444)
- Analyze Cause-and-Effect Relationships (SE pp. 445, 446)
- Identify Sequence (TE p. 446)

Part 1 Introduction

Vocabulary Skills
- Technical Words (TE p. 442)

Speaking/Listening/Viewing Skills
- Visual Literacy (SE p. 447)
- Analyze Art (TE pp. 440–446)

Writing Skills/Grammar
- Compare-and-Contrast Essay (SE p. 447)
- Summary (TE p. 438)
- Journal Entry (TE p. 444)

PART ONE

Southwest Asia

3500 B.C.–Present

Being There

The western edge of southwest Asia borders the Mediterranean Sea. To the north and the east, the land rises into rugged, snowcapped mountain ranges. Vast deserts occupy much of the southern part of the region. In the center lies the valley of the Tigris and the Euphrates rivers, known in the ancient world as Mesopotamia. The people of southwest Asia have a long and rich cultural history.

Looking Ahead

Some of the world's earliest civilizations arose in Mesopotamia more than 5,000 years ago. Later, three major religions—Judaism, Christianity, and Islam—originated in the region. Religion remains an important and often divisive force in contemporary southwest Asia. The region is primarily Muslim, with the exception of the Jewish state of Israel and some small Christian communities.

Keep the following questions in mind as you read:

- How did the sacred scriptures of Judaism, Christianity, and Islam develop?

- How did Persian poetry develop, and what are some of its main themes?

- How have recent political and cultural events affected the contemporary literature of southwest Asia?

437

Focus

Summary

This introduction gives an overview of the history, culture, religion, art, and literature of southwest Asia from 3500 B.C. to the present. It describes the various empires that ruled the area, such as Babylonia and Persia. The introduction also describes the major religions of the region and how these religions influenced art, dance, and architecture. It also explains the many conflicts over land rights and religious and cultural movements that have dominated the area.

Being There

Reading a Map Have students look at a map of southwest Asia. Point out the Mediterranean Sea and the Tigris and Euphrates rivers. Draw students' attention to the desert area of the region. You may wish to keep this map out as students read the literature in Part 1.

Advanced Learners/Pre-AP

DIFFERENTIATED INSTRUCTION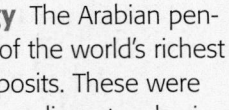

Investigate Geology The Arabian peninsula contains some of the world's richest oil and natural gas deposits. These were built up in the region's sedimentary basins over thousands of years.

Have students investigate the geological factors associated with the concentration of fossil fuels in this area. They may concentrate on the formation of the deposits, on the process of exploring for deposits, on the similarities and differences between the geology of this area and those of other oil-producing areas, or other related topics.

Teach

Reading Strategy 1

Use the Timeline Help students read the timeline and relate key events in southwest Asian literary history to southwest Asian events. **Ask:** What event occurs around the same time that cuneiform is invented? *(Powerful city-states arise in Sumer.)*

Cultural History ☆

The Dead Sea Scrolls In 1947, a shepherd found some manuscripts in a cave on the shore of the Dead Sea. These manuscripts were named the Dead Sea Scrolls. More manuscripts were found in other sites. These pieces of writing deal with subjects such as history and religion. Some scholars believe the scrolls to be the remains of an ancient library.

Timeline 3500 B.C.–Present

SOUTHWEST ASIAN LITERATURE

3500 B.C.

c. 3000
Cuneiform writing is developed

c. 2500
Gilgamesh epic is composed

1500 B.C.

c. 1000
David becomes king of Israel

970
Solomon becomes king of Israel

c. 250
First five books of the Hebrew Bible are translated into Greek

SOUTHWEST ASIAN EVENTS

3500 B.C.

c. 3000
Powerful city-states arise in Sumer

c. 2334
Sargon creates a Mesopotamian empire

1792 ▶
Hammurabi takes power in Babylon

1500 B.C.

612–609
Assyrian Empire falls

c. 586–538
Jews exiled to Babylonia

550
Cyrus the Great founds the Persian Empire

334–330
Alexander the Great conquers the Persian Empire

c. 4
Birth of Jesus

WORLD EVENTS

3500 B.C.

c. 3100
Menes, the first pharaoh, unites Egypt

1500 B.C.

c. 1500
Aryans invade India

◀ **551**
Chinese philosopher Confucius is born

c. 483
Siddhartha Gautama, founder of Buddhism, dies

27
Augustus becomes first Roman emperor

LOG ON ▶ **Literature** Online

Literature and Reading To explore the Interactive Timeline, go to glencoe.com and enter QuickPass code GLW6053u3.

Confucius Vase with Two Bwo gunners and Waterbirds, Late Classic, 550-800

Writing Practice

Summarize Have students select one of the timelines to summarize. Instruct them to come up with a main idea for the timeline. Then they can use details in the timeline to support their main ideas. You may wish to have students work with a partner to complete the summary.

Allow students enough time to complete their summaries. After they have finished, ask volunteers to share their summaries with the class. Make sure you have a volunteer for each timeline. If you do not have a timeline covered, have the class summarize it together. Discuss the similarities and differences between the summaries.

Qur'an with Naskh script, 1468. Persian School. Vellum. © The Trustees of the Chester Beatty Library, Dublin.

A.D. 1

40
Earliest portions of the New Testament are written

c. 632
Zayd ibn Thabit begins compiling written version of the Qur'an

800s
Story collection that became *The Thousand and One Nights* is begun

A.D. 1500

1010
Firdusi completes the Persian epic the *Shah Nameh*

1048
Omar Khayyám is born

1207
Rumi is born

1257–1258
Sa'di composes the *Bustan* and the *Gulistan*

1704–1717
French translation of *The Thousand and One Nights* is published

1947 ▶
Dead Sea Scrolls are discovered ☆

2000
Yehuda Amichai dies

A.D. 1

6
Judaea becomes a Roman province

70
Romans destroy Jewish temple in Jerusalem

632
Muhammad dies

c. 650
Arabs conquer Persia

A.D. 1500

1099
First Crusade captures Jerusalem ☆

1258
Mongols capture Baghdad

1453 ▶
Ottoman Turks capture Constantinople

1923
Republic of Turkey is established

1932
Saudi Arabia is established

A CONSTANTINOPLI II

1948
State of Israel is established

1980
Iran-Iraq War begins

2003
United States and Great Britain invade Iraq

A.D. 1

c. 300
Mayan civilization begins in Mexico

476
Western Roman Empire falls

1066
Normans conquer England

A.D. 1500

1347–1351
Black Death spreads through Europe

1492
Christopher Columbus reaches the Caribbean islands

1776
American Declaration of Independence is signed

1914
World War I begins

1939
World War II begins

1991
Soviet Union collapses, ending the Cold War

Reading Check

Analyze Graphic Information About how long after the death of Muhammad was the written text of the Qur'an begun?

INTRODUCTION **439**

UNIT THREE

PART 1

Teach

Reading Check

Answer: *The official text was begun the same year he died.*

Reading Strategy

Recognize Author's Purpose **Ask:** What do you think is the purpose of these timelines? *(Students may suggest that the purpose is to describe the events in southwest Asia's literature and history. The timelines also provide background knowledge for the literature that follows.)*

Political History ☆

The Crusades In the 11th and 14th centuries, European Christians led a series of wars against the Muslims. The goal of the European Christians was to take back the Holy Land. During the First Crusade, approximately 80,000 people helped the cause.

Approaching Level

DIFFERENTIATED INSTRUCTION

Timeline Questions Have students write five questions about the timeline that are similar to the Reading Check question. Encourage them to use events from the literature timeline along with events from one of the other two timelines. Then, organize students into pairs. Have each student exchange his or her questions with his or her partner's. Each partner should answer the questions.

Advanced Learners/Pre-AP

DIFFERENTIATED INSTRUCTION

Timeline Research Have students select one event, person, or piece of literature from one of the timelines that interests them. Then, instruct them to use Internet and print sources to research the event or topic. Have students share their findings with the class. Students can share their findings in the form of an oral presentation or a poster.

Learning Objectives
Analyzing literary periods. (SE)
Evaluating historical influences. (SE)
Analyzing graphic information. (SE)
Writing a summary. (TE)

439

Teach

Make Inferences **Ask:** What inference can you make about why so many empires tried to take control of Mesopotamia? *(Mesopotamia's location near the Tigris and Euphrates rivers made the area desirable to the other empires.)*

View the Art ★

Ramadan takes place in the ninth month of the Muslim year; the holiday is a holy month of fasting. Devout Muslims make a haji (pilgrimage) to Mecca and the Haram Mosque, or the Great Mosque. The mosque's architecture has been embellished over time and the site is extremely large, accommodating as many as one million worshippers at a time. **Ask:** Why do you think so many people go to Mecca to worship during Ramadan? *(Students may say it is because the prophet Muhammad was born there, and they worship at the Haram Mosque to pay respect.)*

Evaluate Historical Influences Point out to students that the Mesopotamians produced many technical and intellectual achievements that affected the world today. **Ask:** What are some of Mesopotamia's technical and intellectual achievements? *(Their achievements include the plow, the wheel, the sailboat, the sixty-minute hour, and the world's first system of writing.)*

Learning Objectives

For pages 436–447

In studying this text, you will focus on the following objectives:

Literary Study: Analyzing literary periods.

Reading: Evaluating historical influences.
Connecting to the literature.

Southwest Asia

3500 B.C.—Present

Historical, Social, and Cultural Forces

Ancient Mesopotamia

Ancient Mesopotamian farmers benefited greatly from the fresh water provided by the Tigris and the Euphrates rivers. This water allowed them to grow a surplus of food, which fed a growing population—including the rulers, the priests, and the scribes who eventually created and organized the world's first city-states, around 3000 B.C. The technical and intellectual achievements of the ancient Mesopotamians included the plow, the wheel, the sailboat, the 60-minute hour, and the world's first writing system.

As the city-states of ancient Mesopotamia grew, they came into conflict with one another. Around 2334 B.C., a ruler named Sargon conquered Mesopotamia and created the world's first empire. Over the next 3,000 years, a long series of empires—Babylonian, Assyrian, Persian, Macedonian, Parthian, and Sassanid—rose and fell in this region.

Judaism and Christianity

The Jewish people emerged as a distinct cultural group between 1200 B.C. and 1000 B.C. They established the ancient kingdom of Israel on the Mediterranean coast and practiced the faith known today as Judaism. At the time, Judaism was unique among the religions of southwest Asia because of its tenet that there is only one God. Because of this, the ancient Jews had to struggle to preserve both their religion and their political independence from powerful neighbors such as the Babylonians and the Assyrians. By the first century A.D., Israel had become part of the Roman Empire. Under Roman rule, a Jewish prophet named Jesus, who stressed the importance of tolerance, love, and charity, was crucified as a revolutionary. His followers, who believed Jesus to be the son of God, became known as Christians (from *Christos*, "anointed one," a Greek title for Jesus).

Laylat al-Qadr Celebrated. Kazuyoshi Nomachi. Mecca, Saudi Arabia. ★

Lead a discussion about how these advancements may have affected the area's literary history. Guide the discussion by asking the following questions:

- How might technical advancements, such as the plow and wheel, have affected the topics or characters in literature?
- How might the achievement of the sailboat have affected the spread of literature to other areas?

- How did a system of writing affect the oral tradition?

Islam

Islam became the predominant religion throughout southwest Asia after the Islamic empire expanded in the seventh century A.D. Muhammad, the founder of Islam (*Islam* is Arabic for "submission"), was born about A.D. 570 in the city of Mecca on the Arabian Peninsula. Muslims believe that Muhammad was a prophet through whom Allah (God) revealed himself as he had done earlier through Jewish prophets such as Moses and Jesus. Muhammad taught that Islam was a more fundamental unifying force than nationality or kinship. Muslim power in southwest Asia remained strong until the 1700s, when it began a long decline that would continue into modern times.

> "There is no god but God;
> Muhammad is the messenger
> of God."
>
> —Islamic profession of faith

2 Islamic Civilization

The early Arab empire was prosperous and was supported by an extensive trade network. It was home to flourishing cities, including Cairo and Baghdad. The Abassids, a line of Muslim rulers, built Baghdad to be their capital city. Under their rule, Arab civilization reached a cultural high point. They were great patrons of the arts and made Baghdad one of the most splendid cities in the world. Muslim scholars preserved ancient works while making new contributions to history, literature, philosophy, and science. In the mid-thirteenth century, Mongol invaders overran the Abbasid Empire, capturing and destroying Baghdad in 1258. As a result, the new center of Islamic civilization became Cairo, Egypt. Later, the Ottoman and Persian empires dominated southwest Asia.

Modern Islam 3

After World War I, the Arabic provinces of the Ottoman Empire came under British and French control. By the late 1940s, all these areas had regained their independence. In the former Ottoman province of Palestine, Jewish settlers established the State of Israel in 1948. Since then, there has been nearly continual tension between Israel and its Arab neighbors, punctuated by several wars. Southwest Asia has also been troubled by conflicts between various Muslim states, such as the Iran-Iraq War of the 1980s.

Abbasid Plaque, 12th century. Iraq or Iran. Ivory. Louvre, Paris.

Approaching Level

DIFFERENTIATED INSTRUCTION

Create an Organizer Students may find it useful to create a three-column chart or a Venn diagram that shows the similarities and differences among the three main monotheistic religions: Judaism, Christianity, and Islam. Students can use what they have learned about each religion to fill in their organizers. You may wish to have students complete their organizers with a partner or small group.

Advanced Learners/Pre-AP

DIFFERENTIATED INSTRUCTION

World War I Point out the effects of World War I on the provinces of Turkey. Have students research other effects of World War I. Tell students to use reliable sources to research the effects. Explain that they can compile a list of the effects of World War I. Then have them present their findings to the class.

UNIT THREE

PART 1

Teach

Reading Strategy 2

Draw Conclusions about Culture Ask: Based on the details under "Islamic Civilization," what do you think the Abbasids valued? *(They valued the arts and people who made strides in science and philosophy.)*

Reading Strategy 3

Connect to Contemporary Issues After students have read the paragraph called "Modern Islam," discuss recent events that have taken place in that region.
Ask: In what ways is modern Islam similar to or different from ancient Islam? *(Students may say that the religion itself is the same, but new conflicts over it arise all the time. Others may say that such conflicts occur with all religions due to social changes around the world.)*

View the Art ★

Reliefs, such as the Abbasid Plaque, are typical of the art of the Middle East. Artists chose to use ivory because it was considered a luxurious article. **Ask:** Why might ivory reliefs such as the one shown be important to Islamic civilization? *(Students may respond that they were important because under early Arab rule, civilizations reached a cultural peak during which the arts were supported.)*

Learning Objectives
Evaluating historical influences. (TE)
Making inferences. (TE)

Teach

Determine Main Idea **Ask:** What is the main idea of the section "Islamic Art"? *(As a result of Muhammad's teachings, Islamic art does not contain pictures of people or animals.)*

Evaluate Text Structure
Ask: How has the author set up this introduction? *(The author uses subheads to separate the information in the introduction.)*
Ask: Do you think this type of structure is effective? *(Students may suggest that the structure makes the information easy to find and understand.)*

ADVANCED Have advanced learners consider how they would have structured this introduction. Lead a discussion about what they would do differently.

View the Art ★

Early Islamic art consisted of a variety of arabesques. Geometric shapes and intertwining plants characterized this style of art. For Muslim artists, the arabesque became very formalized, and for religious reasons no human or animal figures were included. **Ask:** What figures are depicted in the bowl on this page? *(figures of people and fish)*

Islamic Art 1

An early collection of Muhammad's sayings warned against any attempt to imitate God by creating pictures of living beings. As a result, from early times, no depictions of humans or animals appear in Islamic art, and no representation of the prophet Muhammad ever adorns a mosque, or an Islamic house of worship. Instead, most Islamic art consists of Arabic letters, shapes derived from plants and flowers, and abstract figures. These motifs are repeated in geometric patterns called *arabesques* that cover the surfaces of objects and buildings. Arts and crafts, such as pottery, metalwork, and carpet weaving, are much appreciated and given high status. Calligraphy, the creation of beautiful handwriting, became a high art in Islamic civilization.

Bowl, 13th century. Persian School. Stone-paste with lustre over glaze. Ashmolean Museum, University of Oxford, UK.

Whirling Dervish Performing. Hans Georg Roth. Istanbul, Turkey. ▶

The miniature, a pictorial tradition developed in Persia, was an exception to the avoidance of portraying people and animals in Islamic art. Persian miniature painting was usually done to illustrate works of literature. Persian artists used rich, jewel-like colors to paint elaborate pictures showing scenes from epic poems, romances, fables, and other works.

> "I came in like a cloud, and I left like a wind."
>
> —Rumi

Vocabulary Practice

Analyze Technical Words Point out to students that they may often come across technical vocabulary words as they read. These types of words are specific to a subject. For example, *miniatures, frescoes, calligraphy, arabesque,* and *mosaics* are all terms used by people to describe kinds of art. Students may also find technical vocabulary in articles about science or computers.

Have students look up definitions of any art terms above that they do not know. Students can use dictionaries, encyclopedias, or Internet sources. If possible, have students make sketches or bring in pictures of examples to share with the class.

Religious Dance 2

In Islam, dance is not considered appropriate religious expression. The one exception is the tradition of dancing practiced by Sufi dervishes. (*Sufis* got their name from the Arabic word *suf*, or "wool," which refers to the woolen cloaks worn by early dervishes as a sign of their poverty—*dervish* is Persian for "beggar.") Sufism is a religious movement that seeks to attain a direct experience of God through contemplation and other practices. One of these practices is a whirling dance whose goal is to put dervishes into a trance in which they can experience a mystical union with God. For seven centuries, this tradition has been kept alive by the order of Mevlevi (or Mawlawi) dervishes, founded by the great Sufi poet Rumi (see pages 511–515) in the thirteenth century.

Religious Architecture 3

Many of the most beautiful buildings in southwest Asia were built for religious use. Cities such as Aleppo in Syria and Esfahān in Iran contain magnificent mosques and shrines. There are also beautiful Christian churches (notably in Istanbul, Turkey), which often feature Byzantine artwork, such as frescoes and mosaics. The region also contains great surviving temples of the ancient world, such as Baalbek in Lebanon.

Hagia Sophia. Murat Taner. Istanbul, Turkey. ★

PREVIEW **Big Ideas** of Southwest Asia

1 The Secret of Life	**2** The Search for Wisdom	**3** The Violence of Change
Southwest Asia was the birthplace of three great world religions, Judaism, Christianity, and Islam. The sacred texts of these faiths often explore and reveal different ideas about the secrets of life. **See page 444**	Medieval Persia gave rise to an extraordinarily rich collection of literature, including the skeptical poetry of Omar Khayyám and the mystical writings of Jalal al-Din Rumi. In their works, these poets explore wisdom and how it is achieved. **See page 445**	In the twentieth century, southwest Asia became a focus of great political, social, and economic change, which has led to violent conflicts among Muslims, Israelis, and Westerners that continue to this day. **See page 446**

INTRODUCTION **443**

Advanced Learners/Pre-AP

DIFFERENTIATED INSTRUCTION

Religious Dance Have students research the Sufi dervishes. Tell students to find more information about their dance and other rituals. Also, have them discover how Sufism is different from Islam.

If researching Sufi dervishes does not appeal to students, have them instead research other sects or religions that have a tradition of dance as a part of sacred ritual.

Have students convey their findings in a short report. Encourage them to include pictures or photographs that illustrate their points. After students have finished, lead a discussion about the interesting facts they discovered.

UNIT THREE
PART 1

Teach

Reading Strategy 3

Determine Supporting Details **Ask:** What are some of the details that show the influence of Islam on art and dance? *(No depiction of humans or animals appears in art because of Islamic tradition. There is very little dance. Pottery, calligraphy, and architecture are important because they do not rely on human and animal figures.)*

View the Art ★

From an architectural point of view, the word "basilica" denoted a large roofed building. As time went on, basilicas were limited to a form consisting of a rectangular walled structure, with side aisles set off by colonnades, and an open hall extending from end to end. The Hagia Sophia (Church of Holy Wisdom) in Istanbul, Turkey, was built in only six years and many claim the basilica's dome is the most beautiful in the world. **Ask:** Why is Hagia Sophia considered a great work of Byzantine architecture? *(Students may say the large dome, rectangular walled structure, and vivid colors makes Hagia Sophia a great work of Byzantine architecture.)*

Learning Objectives
Making generalizations. (SE)
Analyzing technical words. (TE)

443

Teach

Reading Check

Answer: *Jews, Christians, and Muslims are known as "people of the book" because their faiths are based on sacred scriptures.*

Reading Strategy   1

Determine Main Idea

Guide students in identifying the main idea of the section titled The First Literature. **Ask: What is cuneiform and who used it?** *(Cuneiform is a system of writing that was used by merchants and scribes.)*

View the Art ★

Hebrew literature has been written from the early 12th century B.C. From 1200 B.C. to c. A.D. 200 the people of Palestine spoke Hebrew, first as biblical Hebrew, then as a later dialect called Mishnaic Hebrew. Prints and drawings, such as the page from the Hebrew Bible with birds, have been created over the centuries by many cultures. The quality of such prints is influenced by the quality of the paper upon which they are created. **Ask: Why might it be important for art historians to treat the page of the Hebrew bible carefully?** *(Students may respond that the page from the Hebrew bible is very old and the manuscript should be protected in order to enable people to continue to learn about Hebrew literature from original pieces of art printed on paper.)*

Big Idea 1
The Secret of Life

Page from a Hebrew Bible with birds, 1299. Instituto da Biblioteca Nacional, Lisbon, Portugal. ★

What is the most essential function of writing? For many cultures, it has been the recording of religious tenets and traditions. Sacred texts form a basic element of the literature of southwest Asia, dating back to some of the earliest written records in the world. From the beginning, these religious writings spoke to fundamental human concerns, such as how the world was created and what happens to the soul after death.

The First Literature 1

The first writing to appear in Mesopotamia—and possibly in the world—probably took the form of pictographs (pictures representing ideas or words). As part of an ancient record-keeping system, merchants marked wedge-shaped symbols representing different goods onto wet clay tablets. By 3000 B.C., Mesopotamian scribes were using a writing system based on these symbols. Modern scholars refer to this script as *cuneiform* ("wedge-shaped"). Archaeologists have discovered thousands of cuneiform tablets. Among them is the world's oldest literary masterpiece, the epic of *Gilgamesh* (see pages 448–466), which relates the quest of a legendary Mesopotamian king for the secret of eternal life.

> *"He went on a long journey, was weary, worn out with labor, and returning engraved on a stone the whole story."*
>
> —from *Gilgamesh*

People of the Book

Judaism, Christianity, and Islam share a belief in one God and a basis in sacred texts believed to be revealed by God. One of these texts, the Islamic

Qur'an (kô rän´), describes Jews, Christians, and Muslims as "people of the book." The traditions of the Jewish people are preserved in their sacred text, the Tanakh, or Hebrew Bible (see pages 470–485). The Jews believed that God gave a code of laws, the Ten Commandments, to Moses. By obeying these laws, an individual can establish a personal relationship with God.

Jesus, the Jewish founder of Christianity, taught that to achieve salvation, people needed not only to obey God's laws, but also to be transformed by love for one another. Accounts of the life and the teachings of Jesus, along with other religious texts, circulated among early Christian communities and were later gathered together as the New Testament (see pages 486–490), the second part of the Christian Bible. (Parts of the Hebrew Bible form the first part, known to Christians as the Old Testament.) Muslims believe that those who desire to achieve salvation and life after death must subject themselves to the will of Allah as revealed in the Qur'an (see pages 491–495), Islam's sacred text.

Reading Check

Make Generalizations Why are Jews, Christians, and Muslims known as "people of the book"?

Writing Practice

Write a Journal Entry Have students imagine that they are scribes or merchants living in Mesopotamia. In a journal entry, have students record the events of one day in their lives in Mesopotamia. Instruct students to comment on cuneiform. Perhaps they see flaws in the system of writing or they have ideas about how to improve it. Or, perhaps they are writing the epic of *Gilgamesh*.

Allow students enough time to write their journal entries. Encourage them to be creative and use what they have read about ancient life in Mesopotamia. After they have finished, ask volunteers to share their journal entries with the class. Point out the similarities and differences between the students' entries.

Big Idea 2
The Search for Wisdom

Farhad carrying Shirin and her horse. Miniature from *Khusrau u Shirin.* Victoria & Albert Museum, London.

What is wisdom? Is it simply shrewdness and common sense? Is it based on a mature understanding of human limits and the fleeting nature of happiness? Or is it a profound insight into the underlying reality of things? Medieval Persian literature explores wisdom in all its forms.

Islamic Persia

Muslim armies conquered Persia within twenty years of Muhammad's death in 632. Because Islam requires that believers read the Qur'an in Arabic, many Arabic words entered the Persian language after the Muslim conquest. The Persians preserved their own language, however, unlike many conquered peoples who adopted Arabic. By the middle of the tenth century, the Muslim empire had grown weak. Native princes regained control of Persia, and nationalist feeling reawakened. One result of this shift in power was a revival of Persian literature.

> "The Moving Finger writes; and, having writ,
> Moves on: nor all your Piety nor Wit
> Shall lure it back to cancel half a Line,
> Nor all your Tears wash out a Word of it."
> —from the *Rubáiyát*

Persian Literature

Persians regarded poetry as the highest form of literature. Therefore, it is not surprising that a poet was largely responsible for the revival of Persian literature. This poet, Firdusi, was born

about 935. He combined traditional Persian myth, legend, and history in an epic poem, the *Shah Nameh* (Persian for "Book of Kings"). In short, rhyming couplets, Firdusi told the story of Persia from the time of its mythical kings, through the conquests of Alexander the Great, and up to the Arab conquest. The *Shah Nameh* became the Persian national epic and the inspiration for many masterpieces of Persian miniature painting.

Some of the works of Islamic literature that are most familiar to Western readers were produced in Persia during the Middle Ages. Among them is the famous collection known as the *Rubáiyát* (Persian for "quatrains") by Persian poet, scientist, and mathematician Omar Khayyám (see pages 505–510). Another well-known medieval Persian poet is thirteenth-century Sufi mystic Rumi (see pages 511–515), author of *The Masnavi*, a large collection of Sufi sermons and fables in verse. Many of the stories in the vast collection of tales known as *The Thousand and One Nights* (see pages 496–504) are also Persian in origin.

Reading Check

Analyze Cause-and-Effect Relationships How did the weakening of Muslim control in Persia lead to a revival of Persian literature?

INTRODUCTION **445**

Teach

Reading Check

Answer: *Native princes regained control of Persia, and nationalist feeling reawakened. One result was a revival of Persian literature.*

APPROACHING Organize students into small groups. Have each group member take turns reading aloud one paragraph on the page. Tell students to continue in this fashion until each group member has read a portion of the text. Compliment students on their ability to speak fluently.

View the Art ★

Calligraphy is a word deriving from the Greek words "good" and "beautiful." Masters called this type of writing the art of fair writing. In Western culture the simpler Latin and Greek alphabets made calligraphy "everybody's art." However, in a few instances, especially after the Renaissance, some writing aimed to match the importance of earlier calligraphy. **Ask:** How might calligraphy contribute to the revival of Persian literature? *(Students may say that writers using calligraphy to write poems, stories, or epics were using one form of art to revive another form of art by creating pieces of literature.)*

Advanced Learners/Pre-AP

DIFFERENTIATED INSTRUCTION

Wisdom in Fables Point out that Rumi wrote fables that explored wisdom. Have students think of fables that they have read or heard. For example, students may be familiar with "The Tortoise and the Hare" or "The Lion and the Mouse." Ask students to describe the fables they know and what wisdom the fables impart.

Tell students to make a captioned drawing representing both the fable and the wise lesson it contains. Provide students with materials they may need, such as paper, crayons, or colored pencils. After students have finished, have them share their drawings with the class. Lead a discussion about whether students think fables are a good medium in which to impart wisdom.

Learning Objectives
Making generalizations. (SE)
Analyzing cause-and-effect relationships. (SE)
Determining main idea. (TE)

Teach

Reading Check

Answer: *One cause of the conflicts is the formation of the State of Israel in 1948. Another cause is religious and ethnic movements in the region.*

Reading Strategy

Analyze Cause-and-Effect Relationships **Ask:** What were the effects of the Industrial Revolution? *(European nations gained economic and military power over Muslim nations.)* What is the effect of religious and cultural movements? *(The effect is conflict, such as the Iran-Iraq War.)*

View the Art ★

Arikha is a renowned Israeli-French artist and art historian. Until the mid-1960s, he painted abstract works, but after that point he began drawing from life. **Ask:** How many figures are holding flags in this painting? *(Students should see three figures.)*

Reading Practice

Identify Sequence Have students create a sequence chart that contains the information found on this page. On the board, draw a sample chart for students to mimic. For example, you could draw three boxes and place them next to each other horizontally. Then, draw an arrow from one box to the next.

Explain that students should write one event in each box. Students can add as many boxes to the chart as they need. Instruct students to start their charts with the Industrial Revolution. After they have finished, have students share their charts with a small group. Have students add any events that they may have missed.

446

Big Idea 3
The Violence of Change

The Flag Bearer, 1955. Avigdor Arikha. Oil on canvas. Israel Museum, Jerusalem. ★

Periods of rapid political and cultural change are difficult for those who experience them, whether the changes are ultimately positive or not. When such periods are accompanied by violence and the outcome remains uncertain, they can be almost unendurable.

A Region of Conflict

The Industrial Revolution, which began in the 1700s, made European nations very powerful. Using their economic and military strength, they gained power over the Muslim peoples of southwest Asia. In the decades following World War II, Muslim nations regained their independence, and some states became enriched by oil revenues. Persistent political problems trouble the region, however, and many Muslims resent what they see as the West's hostility toward traditional Islamic values. These political and cultural conflicts have often erupted into violence.

The creation of the Jewish state of Israel in 1948 and disputes over land rights have also led to many conflicts. Since Israel's formation, Israelis have fought several wars with neighboring Muslim countries. Palestinian Arabs displaced by the Israelis have staged violent protest movements known as *intifadas* (Arabic for "uprisings") against Israel. Additionally, religious and cultural movements and ethnic disputes have led to conflicts such as the Iran-Iraq War, which lasted from 1980 to 1988. Finally, Muslim nations and groups have fought with some Western countries, as evidenced by the two American-led wars against Iraq.

> *"Put it on record.*
> *I am an Arab.*
> *I am a name without a title . . ."*
> —Mahmoud Darwish, from "Identity Card"

A Literature of Conflict

The modern literature of southwest Asia is permeated with themes that derive from the region's conflicts. This is especially true of the poetry written by Hebrew poets Yehuda Amichai (see pages 524–527) and Dahlia Ravikovitch (see pages 520–523). Both of these poets received international acclaim for their explorations of the physical and emotional repercussions of war. A prominent voice of Palestinian resistance to Israel, Mahmoud Darwish spent many years living in exile before returning to the Palestinian territory of the West Bank in 1996. In her acclaimed graphic novel *Persepolis*, Iranian illustrator and author Marjane Satrapi (see pages 532–541) has explored her own recollections of the Iranian Revolution and the ways in which it changed Iran and impacted her friends and family.

Reading Check

Analyze Cause-and-Effect Relationships What is one cause of the recent conflicts in southwest Asia?

Wrap-Up

Legacy of the Region

Some of the most influential cultural and religious ideas in the world originated in southwest Asia. The ancient Mesopotamians developed what was probably the world's first system of writing and used it to produce a rich literary tradition, including the world's oldest literary masterpiece, *Gilgamesh*. Judaism, Christianity, and Islam all arose in southwest Asia. Their beliefs, values, traditions, and sacred scriptures have had an extraordinary impact on world history.

Islam became the driving force and the cultural basis for an empire that—at its greatest extent around A.D. 750—stretched from Spain to the borders of China. Islamic civilization both preserved and transformed the cultures of the peoples within the Muslim empire. One of the greatest of these cultures was Persia's, which gave rise to poets Omar Khayyám and Rumi and was the source of many of the tales in *The Thousand and One Nights*.

Since World War II, southwest Asia has been the scene of violent protests, acts of terrorism, and wars. Bitter conflicts continue to plague the region.

They have been transported swiftly, from *The Arabian Nights,* 1939. Roger Broders. Colour engraving. Private collection.

Cultural and Literary Links

 The Hebrew Bible and the Christian New Testament have profoundly influenced Western civilization.

 After *The Thousand and One Nights* was translated into European languages, characters such as Sindbad the Sailor, Ali Baba, and Aladdin took their place among the most popular of all fairy-tale figures.

 The *Rubáiyát* became popular outside Persia after Edward FitzGerald translated it in the nineteenth century.

LOG ON ► **Literature** Online

Unit Resources For additional skills practice, go to glencoe.com and enter QuickPass code GLW6053u3.

Activities

🔘 **Use what you have learned about the region to do one of these activities.**

1. **Follow Up** Go back to Looking Ahead on page 437 and answer the questions.

2. **Contrast Literary Periods** In the United States, the Civil War era gave rise to classic works, including *The Red Badge of Courage* and *Incidents in the Life of a Slave Girl*. Compare and contrast the causes of the Civil War with the sources of conflict authors in southwest Asia have explored.

3. **Build Visual Literacy** Create a visual display showing how different illustrators have depicted tales from *The Thousand and One Nights*.

4. **Take Notes** Use this study organizer to keep track of the literary elements you learn in this part.

FOLDABLES Study Organizer   **BOUND BOOK**

Reader-Response Journal

Assess

Activities

1. **Follow Up** Students should answer questions with specific facts from the text.

2. **Contrast Literary Periods** Students' essays should draw clear parallels and contrasts between the causes of the Civil War and the conflicts that authors in southwest Asia have explored.

3. **Build Visual Literacy** Students' displays should have different types of illustrations based on *The Thousand and One Nights*. Students should discuss what they found and how these styles highlight certain themes, characters, or events in the text.

4. **Take Notes** Students' Foldables should be well organized, and their notes should relate to specific literary elements.

Advanced Learners/Pre-AP

DIFFERENTIATED INSTRUCTION

Create a Game Organize students into small groups. Have each group create a game that tests the information found in the Part 1 Introduction. Students may follow the format of existing board games or television game shows. Or, they can create their own new game. Be sure to provide students with any necessary materials, such as construction paper, cardboard, markers, or colored pencils.

After students have finished creating the game, instruct them to play it to make sure it works. Students may find that they need to work out kinks or that they are missing something. After the game is finalized, have groups exchange the games with other groups. Students can play the games and test their knowledge of the Part 1 Introduction.

Before You Read

Focus

Bellringer Options

Selection Focus
   Transparency 21
Daily Language
   Transparency 37

Or bring to class a copy of the *Iliad, The Hobbit,* or another book with a quest theme. Tell students that they will be reading the story of Gilgamesh, one of the oldest quest stories in the world.

Ask: Why are quest stories so popular in so many times and places? Which is your favorite? (*Students may note the popularity of heroes, action, and adventure. Others may say that a quest is a universal topic because everyone experiences his or her own quest of searching for meaning in the world.*)

Before You Read

from *Gilgamesh*

The epic of *Gilgamesh* is the greatest surviving literary work of ancient Mesopotamia (a region centered in what is now Iraq). Mesopotamia was home to a series of important ancient cultures, including the Sumerians', the Babylonians', and the Assyrians'. Each of these cultures played a role in the development and preservation of the *Gilgamesh* epic.

History and Myth *Gilgamesh* is a series of separate tales that describe the exploits of the epic hero Gilgamesh. Although the epic projects him into the realm of myth, Gilgamesh was an actual person who ruled the ancient Sumerian city-state of Uruk around 2700 B.C. Historians believe that Sumerian storytellers began to recount tales of Gilgamesh's adventures and accomplishments soon after his death. However, these stories may not have been written down for nearly 1,000 years. Sometime between 2000 and 1600 B.C., the tales were recorded in Akkadian, the language of the Babylonian Empire, which had conquered the Sumerian city-states.

A Lost Epic By the seventh century B.C., the Assyrians dominated the Mesopotamian region. Assyrian emperor Ashurbanipal had the tales recorded on clay tablets and stored in his library at the palace at Nineveh. Assyria was destroyed soon after his rule, and the tablets were lost for nearly 2,500 years. They were unearthed in the mid-1800s by archaeologist Hormuzd Rassam. This discovery brought international recognition to one of the oldest and most important epics in the world. Since the nineteenth century, many other tablets and fragments of *Gilgamesh* have been discovered.

> *"Humans are born, they live, then they die,*
> *this is the order that the gods have decreed."*
>
> —from *Gilgamesh*

The Story of the Epic Exposed to the dangers of flood, drought, and warfare, the Mesopotamians seem to have believed that earthly life was fleeting and fraught with peril. In the epic, Gilgamesh is strong and handsome, but he is also a tyrant. After his subjects beg the gods to end his oppression, the gods create a powerful man named Enkidu to conquer Gilgamesh. Although they battle at first, the two men become friends and eventually succeed in killing a monster named Humbaba on a dangerous mission to a sacred forest. They then incur the wrath of the gods, who send a dream to Enkidu as he lies sick in bed. The dream shows that misery and sorrow are the fate of healthy men. Gilgamesh watches over his friend for twelve days, but Enkidu dies. The excerpt you are about to read begins as Gilgamesh is grieving for his friend.

Selection Skills

Literary Elements
- Epic Hero (SE pp. 449, 451, 454, 458, 460, 465)
- Setting (SE p. 465)

from Gilgamesh

Speaking/Listening/Viewing Skills
- Analyze Art (TE pp. 452, 455, 457, 461, 462)
- Give an Oral Presentation (TE p. 450)

Reading Skills
- Visualize (SE pp. 449, 453, 457, 465)
- Summarize (TE p. 454)
- Analyze Literary Influences (TE p. 456)

Vocabulary Skills
- Word Origins (SE p. 465)

Writing Skills/Grammar
- Expository Essay (SE p. 466)
- Avoid Run-on Sentences (TE p. 460)

Literature and Reading Preview

Connect to the Epic

With a partner, discuss what qualities you look for in a friend. How might these qualities contribute to a lasting friendship?

Build Background

The influence of oral tradition on *Gilgamesh* is evident in many features of the epic's style, such as repetition. For example, Utnapishtim is often called "the Distant One." Oral storytellers use repetition to remember details about characters and places.

Set Purposes for Reading

Big Idea The Secret of Life

As you read *Gilgamesh*, ask yourself, What does this epic convey about the meaning of life?

Literary Element Epic Hero

An **epic hero** is a courageous person (usually a man) of high social status who embodies the ideals of his people. His story is told in an **epic,** a long narrative poem that recounts his adventures, which often entail a quest and supernatural beings. As you read the epic, ask yourself, How does Gilgamesh fit the definition of an epic hero?

Reading Strategy Visualize

When you **visualize,** you picture characters, scenes, and actions in your mind. You use the sensory details described by the author to imagine how various items in the text, such as flowers or food, might smell, look, or taste.

....

Tip: Make a Sketch Using a chart like this one, make sketches of various characters and other details from the epic.

Text	Sketch
"Two scorpion people were posted at the entrance . . ."	

Learning Objectives

For pages 448–466

In studying this text, you will focus on the following objectives:

Literary Study: Analyzing epic hero.

Reading: Visualizing.

Vocabulary

ravaged (rav′ijd) *adj.* devastated; ruined; p. 454 *The continued warfare left the city in a ravaged state.*

treacherous (trech′ər əs) *adj.* hazardous; dangerous; p. 458 *We barely survived the treacherous drive through the blizzard.*

prevail (pri vāl′) *v.* to gain ascendancy through strength or superiority; to triumph; p. 459 *The runner knew she would prevail if she focused on the finish line.*

antidote (an′ti dōt′) *n.* something that relieves, prevents, or counteracts; p. 462 *Alex found yoga to be an antidote to stress.*

....

Tip: Word Origins Word origins are the history and development of words. Also called **etymologies,** they are often included in dictionary entries. For example, the entry for *prevail* states: [ME, fr. L *praevalēre,* fr. *prae-* pre + *valēre* to be strong]. This means that *prevail* came from a Middle English (ME) word that derived from Latin (L).

Before You Read

Focus

Summary

After the death of his friend Enkidu, Gilgamesh journeys to Utnapishtim, the only mortal saved by the gods from the great flood. Utnapishtim challenges Gilgamesh to a test. If Gilgamesh can stay awake for six days and seven nights, Utnapishtim will assemble the gods to seek eternal life for Gilgamesh. Gilgamesh fails the test, but Utnapishtim tells him where to find a plant that restores youth. Gilgamesh loses the plant and returns home to endure the fate of all mortals.

 For summaries in languages other than English, see Unit 3 Teaching Resources Book, pp. 21–26.

Vocabulary

Word Origin Flash Cards
Have students create flash cards with each vocabulary word's origin. Students can challenge one another to guess the word by looking at its origin and to guess the origin by looking at the word. Point out to students that they will frequently encounter certain words and word parts, particularly those with Greek or Latin origins.

English Learners

DIFFERENTIATED INSTRUCTION

Advanced Explain to students that the tales of *Gilgamesh* have been found in several different languages, indicating their movement from one area to another over time. Have students consider how the story might have traveled before the existence of printing presses, radio or television networks, or the Internet.

Have students form small, mixed-level groups to share ideas on how stories could have spread among peoples who spoke different languages. Students might refer to their own experiences in absorbing or sharing such aspects of culture as stories, music, and food. Have groups share their ideas with the class, and encourage a class discussion of the ideas.

Advanced Learners/Pre-AP

DIFFERENTIATED INSTRUCTION

More of *Gilgamesh* Suggest that students delve deeper into the Gilgamesh story by reading other sections of the epic, such as The Death of Enkidu. Invite students to create a presentation that describes events in the tale that precede and follow the selection. Students should report on what surprised them about the new part of the epic.

Teach

Reading Strategy   1

Visualize **Ask:** What does the description of the Twin Peaks help you visualize? *(very tall mountains that reach heaven above and the underworld below)*

For additional practice using the reading skill or strategy, see Unit 3 Teaching Resources Book, p. 28.

For an audio recording of this selection, use Listening Library Audio CD-ROM.

Readability Scores

Dale-Chall: 5.7
DRP: 61
Lexile: 1000

Gate guardian in the form of a lion, c. 1800 BC. Middle Euphrates, Neo-Sumerian.Bronze. Louvre, Paris.

PROPER NAMES IN THE EPIC

Characters

ENKIDU (en´kē dōo): Created by the gods to challenge Gilgamesh's authority. Originally lived with the beasts of the forests as a wild or natural man; later becomes Gilgamesh's friend

GILGAMESH (gil´gə mesh´): King of Uruk and the hero of the epic; son of the goddess Ninsun and the mortal King Lugulbanda; named in a Sumerian list of kings as the fifth monarch after the flood

HUMBABA (hum bä´bə): Monster who guards the Cedar Forest; slain by Gilgamesh and Enkidu

ISHTAR (ish´tär): Goddess of love, fertility, and war, as well as patron of the city of Uruk, where she had an important temple; falls in love with Gilgamesh but is spurned by him

SHAMASH (shä´mäsh): God of the sun; also a judge and a lawgiver

SHIDURI (sə dōo´rē): Winemaker for the gods

URSHANABI (er´shə nä bē): Ferryman across the Waters of Death

UTNAPISHTIM (ōot nə pēsh´tēm): Survivor of the flood, he narrates the story of the deluge to Gilgamesh and is the only mortal to be given eternal life by the gods.

Places

EANNA TEMPLE: A temple tower with terraced pyramids in receding stories built in the district of Eanna in Mesopotamia

1   **TWIN PEAKS:** Two mountains that guard the rising and setting sun

URUK (ōo´rook): City of Gilgamesh

Speaking Practice

Present an Oral Interpretation
Encourage students to present orally portions of the epic that they think will excite an audience. Point them to scenes containing interesting characters or dramatic dialogue, such as the one in which Gilgamesh encounters the scorpion people. Explain that students may choose the tone of their scene—for example, dramatic or humorous.

Presentations Arrange students in groups of two or three and tell them to choose an actor for each character. Allow time for rehearsal and preparation of props or costumes. If possible, record the presentations on either video or audio media and play them back for the class. Discuss each group's interpretation and whether it represented the particular mood of the scene.

FROM Gilgamesh

Translated by Stephen Mitchell

The Search for Everlasting Life

Gilgamesh wept over Enkidu his friend,
bitterly he wept through the wilderness.
"Must I die too? Must I be as lifeless
as Enkidu? How can I bear this sorrow
5   that gnaws at my belly, this fear of death
that restlessly drives me onward? If only
I could find the one man whom the gods made immortal,
I would ask him how to overcome death."

So Gilgamesh roamed, his heart full of anguish,
10   wandering, always eastward, in search
of Utnapishtim, whom the gods made immortal.

Finally he arrived at the two high mountains
called the Twin Peaks. Their summits touch
the vault of heaven, their bases reach down
15   to the underworld, they keep watch over
the sun's departure and its return.
Two scorpion people were posted at the entrance,
guarding the tunnel into which the sun
plunges when it sets and moves through the earth
20   to emerge above the horizon at dawn.
The sight of these two inspired such terror
that it could kill an ordinary man.

3   Epic Hero *How does the description of the scorpion people indicate that Gilgamesh is an epic hero?*

GILGAMESH **451**

Teach

Literary Element   **2**

Epic Hero **Ask:** What heroic feats has Gilgamesh performed? *(He is the first person to travel over the imposing mountains and deserts.)*

[APPROACHING] Point out to struggling readers that we only know of these feats because the scorpion man has described them.

Literary Element   **3**

Epic Hero **Answer:** *Like other epic heroes, Gilgamesh is more daring and strong willed than an "ordinary man." He cannot be frightened to death.*

Learning Objectives
Analyzing epic hero. (SE)
Visualizing. (TE)
Presenting an oral interpretation. (TE)

English Learners

DIFFERENTIATED INSTRUCTION

Intermediate Point out the pronouns *he* and *they* in lines 12–15 and the possessive pronouns *their* and *its.* Explain that pronouns, including possessive pronouns, should agree in number with their antecedents—the nouns to which they refer. Explain to students that the antecedent should appear before the pronoun, usually in the same sentence but sometimes in the previous sentence. Ask students to

identify the antecedents for *he* and *they.* *(Gilgamesh and the Twin Peaks)*

Then ask students to identify the antecedents for *their* and *its*—that is, *whose* summits and *whose* return. *(the Twin Peaks' summits and the sun's return)* Tell students to pause as they read to determine antecedents and improve their comprehension.

Advanced Learners/Pre-AP

DIFFERENTIATED INSTRUCTION

Legendary Mountains Invite students to research mountains in myths and legends. Challenge students to find out whether the Twin Peaks of *Gilgamesh* are thought to be specific mountains in Iraq. Students may also research the role that mountains play in other tales and how they represent a challenge to epic heroes in those cultures. Encourage students to bring in maps and share their discoveries with the class.

451

Teach

Literary History ☆

Stories of Gilgamesh In addition to the long epic of *Gilgamesh*, five shorter poems have been found that feature this Mesopotamian hero. They are titled "Gilgamesh and Huwawa," "Gilgamesh and the Bull of Heaven," "Gilgamesh and Agga of Kish," "Gilgamesh, Enkidu, and the Netherworld," and "The Death of Gilgamesh." These were written in Sumerian rather than the Akkadian language of the 12-tablet epic.

View the Art ★

Answer: *This man appears to be fearless. Students might say that Gilgamesh seems fearless.*

Relief comes from the Italian word *relievare,* meaning, "to raise." Artwork in which figures project from a plane surface can be classified as a relief. The relief shown features Ashurbanipal, known for his athleticism and hunting abilities.

Their auras shimmered over the mountains.
When Gilgamesh saw them, he was pierced with dread, ☆
25   but he steadied himself and headed toward them.

The scorpion man called out to his wife,
"This one who approaches—he must be a god."

The scorpion woman called back to him,
"He is two-thirds divine and one-third human."

30   The scorpion man said, "What is your name?
How have you dared to come here? Why
have you traveled so far, over seas and mountains
difficult to cross, through wastelands and deserts
no mortal has ever entered? Tell me
35   the goal of your journey. I want to know."
"Gilgamesh is my name," he answered,
"I am the king of great-walled Uruk ☆
and have come here to find my ancestor

Ashurbanipal on a Horse, Hunting Lion, c. 668-627 BC. Sumeria. Relief from the North Palace at Nineveh.

View the Art This relief is from Ashurbanipal's throne-room suite at the Palace of Nineveh. The reliefs disovered there are some of the finest existing Assyrian sculpture. How might the man on the horse remind you of Gilgamesh? ★

452   UNIT 3   SOUTHWEST ASIA

Writing Practice

Write a Movie Scene Invite students to write a movie scene of the events at Shiduri's tavern. Students should describe cinematic elements such as the set, props, camera angles, or special effects as well as the information for the actors, including actions, movements, and dialogue.

Have students review dramatic selections to familiarize themselves with stage directions. Challenge students with artistic ability to make storyboards for their scenes, or plan each camera angle and shot. Encourage students to share their ideas with the class. As a class, cast each part, considering the physical and emotional make-up of each character in the scene.

Utnapishtim, who joined the assembly
40 of the gods, and was granted eternal life.
He is my last hope. I want to ask him
how he managed to overcome death."

The scorpion man said, "No one is able
to cross the Twin Peaks, nor has anyone ever
45 entered the tunnel into which the sun
plunges when it sets and moves through the earth.
Inside the tunnel there is total darkness:
deep is the darkness, with no light at all."

The scorpion woman said, "This brave man,
50 driven by despair, his body frost-chilled,
exhausted, and burnt by the desert sun—
show him the way to Utnapishtim."

The scorpion man said, "Ever downward
through the deep darkness the tunnel leads.
55 All will be pitch black before and behind you,
all will be pitch black to either side.
You must run through the tunnel faster than the wind.
You have just twelve hours. If you don't emerge
from the tunnel before the sun sets and enters,
60 you will find no refuge from its deadly fire.
Penetrate into the mountains' depths,
may the Twin Peaks lead you safely to your goal,
may they safely take you to the edge of the world.
The gate to the tunnel lies here before you.
65 Go now in peace, and return in peace." . . .

Before him the garden of the gods appeared,
with gem-trees of all colors, dazzling to see.
There were trees that grew rubies, trees with lapis
lazuli° flowers, trees that dangled
70 gigantic coral clusters like dates.
Everywhere, sparkling on all the branches,
were enormous jewels: emeralds, sapphires,
hematite, diamonds, carnelians,° pearls.
Gilgamesh looked up and marveled at it all.

69 lapis lazuli: (lap´ is laz´ ə lē)
a deep blue semiprecious stone.

73 hematite: (hem´ ə tīt´) a
reddish-brown to black mineral.
carnelians: (kär nēl´ yəns) red or
reddish-orange semiprecious stones
often set in jewelry.

---

1 Visualize *What mood do the sensory details create in this passage?*

2 Visualize *What details in this stanza help you visualize the scene? To what sense do these images appeal?*

GILGAMESH **453**

Teach

Reading Strategy | 1

Visualize **Answer:** *They create a mood of urgency and terror.*

Reading Strategy | 2

Visualize **Answer:** *The details of the gem-trees and of dazzling colors help the reader visualize the scene. They appeal to the sense of sight.*

Historical Note ☆

Uruk Uruk, an ancient city in Mesopotamia, was located on the Euphrates River. This Sumerian city dated back to the fifth millennium B.C. In the city were sanctuaries of the goddesses Anu and Inanna, making the city an important religious center.

Learning Objectives
Visualizing. (SE)
Analyzing epic hero. (TE)
Writing a movie scene. (TE)

Approaching Level

DIFFERENTIATED INSTRUCTION

Paraphrase Remind students that to paraphrase is to restate a text in one's own words. Have students paraphrase the scorpion man's directions to Gilgamesh. Encourage students to change sentence structure to help them avoid plagiarizing the original poem. *(Possible answer: Go down into the dark passage. It will be very dark in front and in back of you, and on both sides. You should run through the passage as fast as you can. You have to do it in twelve hours. If you can't come out of the tunnel before dusk, you will burn forever in its heat. Go into the center of the mountains. They will help you succeed. I hope they will help you far in your journey. Good luck.)*

Advanced Learners/Pre-AP

DIFFERENTIATED INSTRUCTION

Gemstones The garden of the gods in *Gilgamesh* is made up of gemstones and minerals. Have students research to learn the appearance, quality, and value of the various stones. Also encourage students to discover whether these stones are still found in the part of the world where *Gilgamesh* originates.

453

Teach

Epic Hero Answer: *He is proud, fearless, and superhuman.*

(APPROACHING) Direct approaching-level students to Gilgamesh's dialogue. **Ask:** What does Gilgamesh say to introduce himself? Why do you think he chooses those words? *(Gilgamesh boasts that he is a king and describes his defeated enemies. He probably wants to impress Shiduri with his strength and bravery.)*

75   At the edge of the ocean, the tavern keeper
     Shiduri was sitting. Her face was veiled,
     her golden pot-stand and brewing vat
     stood at her side. As Gilgamesh came
     toward her, worn out, his heart full of anguish,
80   she thought, "This desperate man must be
     a murderer. Why else is he heading
     straight toward me?" She rushed into her tavern,
     locked the door, then climbed to the roof.
     Gilgamesh heard the noise, he looked up
85   and saw her standing there, staring at him.
     "Why did you lock yourself in?" he shouted.
     "I want to enter now. If you don't let me,
     I will smash your locks and break down your door."

     Shiduri answered, "You seemed so wild
90   that I locked my door and climbed to the roof.
     Tell me your name now. Where you are going?"

     "Gilgamesh is my name," he said. ☆
     "I am the king of great-walled Uruk.
     I am the man who killed Humbaba
95   in the Cedar Forest, I am the man
     who triumphed over the Bull of Heaven."°

     Shiduri said, "Why are your cheeks so hollow
     and your features so **ravaged**? Why is your face
     frost-chilled, and burnt by the desert sun?
100 Why is there so much grief in your heart?
     Why are you worn out and ready to collapse,
     like someone who has been on a long, hard journey?"

     Gilgamesh said, "Shouldn't my cheeks
     be hollow, shouldn't my face be ravaged,
105 frost-chilled, and burnt by the desert sun?
     Shouldn't my heart be filled with grief?
     Shouldn't I be worn out and ready to collapse?
     My friend, my brother, whom I loved so dearly,
     who accompanied me through every danger—

---

1 Epic Hero *What qualities of an epic hero does Gilgamesh possess?*

Vocabulary

ravaged (rav′ijd) *adj.* devastated; ruined

454 UNIT 3 SOUTHWEST ASIA

96 Bull of Heaven: this bull was unleashed on Uruk by Ishtar's father, the sky god Anu, after Gilgamesh refused to become Ishtar's lover. The bull killed hundreds of people, but Enkidu and Gilgamesh eventually killed it.

Reading Practice

Summarize Remind students that a summary briefly describes the main idea and important details of a text. Have students summarize Shiduri's ideas about what constitutes a good life and Gilgamesh's response. Then, explain that most organizations have a mission statement, which is a brief, explicit listing of their goals and priorities.

Say: If Shiduri had written a mission statement, it might be something like, "Eat, drink, and be merry!"

Challenge students to write a "mission statement" for their own lives. Short, clear, and simple statements work best. Encourage students to share their statements with the class, and discuss how many students produced something close to Shiduri's philosophy.

Gilgamesh, having learnt the whereabouts of the Plant of Life which confers immortality, sets out to find it, 1924. Artist unknown.

110　Enkidu, my brother, whom I loved so dearly,
　　　who accompanied me through every danger—
　　　the fate of mankind has overwhelmed him.
　　　For six days I would not let him be buried,
　　　thinking, 'If my grief is violent enough,
115　perhaps he will come back to life again.'
　　　For six days and seven nights I mourned him,
　　　until a maggot fell out of his nose.
　　　Then I was frightened, I was terrified by death,
　　　and I set out to roam the wilderness.
120　I cannot bear what happened to my friend—
　　　I cannot bear what happened to Enkidu—
　　　so I roam the wilderness in my grief.
　　　How can my mind have any rest?

　　　My beloved friend has turned into clay—
125　my beloved Enkidu has turned into clay.
　　　And won't I too lie down in the dirt
　　　like him, and never arise again?"

---

2 The Secret of Life *What does this passage reveal about the ancient Mesopotamian attitude toward death?*

GILGAMESH **455**

Teach

Big Idea　　　　**2**

The Secret of Life Answer:
The Mesopotamians fear death and grieve openly when loved ones die. **Ask:** How does this attitude compare with modern attitudes toward death? *(Students may say that people do not grieve as openly now. Others may say that to modern people, death seems a natural process and another part of life.)*

Cultural History ☆

Horzmuzd Rassam Horzmuzd Rassam (1826–1910), a noted scholar who studied Assyrian civilization, built his reputation by excavating some of the finest Assyrian and Babylonian antiquities now at the British Museum. Among his achievements is the uncovering of cuneiform tablets at Nineveh and Sippar (in Iraq). Rassam joined famed British scholar Austen Henry Layard in the excavation at Nineveh (1849–1851) and discovered the remainder of the royal library that housed the tablets on which were written most of the epic of *Gilgamesh*.

View the Art ★

Ask: How would you describe the style of this painting? *(Students may say primitive, childlike, or flat.)*

Approaching Level

DIFFERENTIATED INSTRUCTION

Rhetorical Questions Less-proficient readers may not understand the use of rhetorical questions in lines 103–107. Point out that Gilgamesh does not expect a literal answer to his questions beginning "Shouldn't my . . .". He is really emphasizing, through repetition, that his feelings are natural.

Advanced Learners / Pre-AP

DIFFERENTIATED INSTRUCTION

Symbolism Encourage advanced learners to investigate the symbolism of day and night in this epic, especially the significance of six days and seven nights. Ask students to research other traditional tales that use these elements and to find out how this particular period of time is used to challenge a hero. Encourage students to share their discoveries with the class.

Learning Objectives
Analyzing epic hero. (SE)
Summarizing. (TE)

Teach

The Secret of Life Answer:
It reveals that Mesopotamians valued the ordinary pleasures of life.

Ask: Is this philosophy a good one for modern life? *(Some students may say that it is sensible to enjoy and appreciate life. Others may say that if everyone believed this philosophy, nothing would ever get done, and serious but important matters like justice would be ignored.)*

Literary History ☆

Mesopotamian Myths Myths in addition to *Gilgamesh* have originated in Mesopotamia. Several of them, such as the Myth of Adapa and the story of Etana, the King of Kish, also have themes related to death and immortality. Other common topics are the cycle of fertility, the destruction of cities, and the suffering of humans before the gods.

Shiduri said, "Gilgamesh, where are you roaming?
You will never find the eternal life
130 that you seek. When the gods created mankind,
they also created death, and they held back
eternal life for themselves alone.
Humans are born, they live, then they die, ☆
this is the order that the gods have decreed.
135 But until the end comes, enjoy your life,
spend it in happiness, not despair.
Savor your food, make each of your days
a delight, bathe and anoint° yourself,
wear bright clothes that are sparkling clean,
140 let music and dancing fill your house,
love the child who holds you by the hand,
and give your wife pleasure in your embrace.
That is the best way for a man to live."

Gilgamesh cried out, "What are you saying,
145 tavern keeper? My heart is sick
for my friend who died. What can your words mean
when my heart is sick for Enkidu who died?
Show me the road to Utnapishtim.
I will cross the vast ocean if I can. If not,
150 I will roam the wilderness in my grief."

Shiduri said, "Never has there been a path
across the vast ocean, nor has there ever
been any human who was able to cross it.
Only brave Shamash as he climbs the sky
155 can cross the vast ocean—who else can do it?
The crossing is harsh, the danger is great,
and midway lie the Waters of Death,
whose touch kills instantly. Even if you manage
to sail that distance, what will you do
160 when you reach the Waters of Death? The one
man who can help you is Urshanabi,
Utnapishtim's boatman. He is trimming
pine branches down in the forest, and he has
the Stone Men with him. Go to him. Ask.
165 If he says yes, you can cross the vast ocean.
If he says no, you will have to turn back." . . .

138 **anoint:** (ə noint´) smear with an oily liquid.

---

1   The Secret of Life *What does this stanza reveal about ancient Mesopotamian views concerning what is valuable in life?*

Reading Practice

Analyze Literary Influences Explain to students that literature does not exist in a vacuum. That is, nearly all literature is influenced by other literature that precedes it, or by cultural or societal incidents or changes. In turn, what is written now will influence later writers. Have students list familiar elements from this tale that they have encountered in other contexts.

(Students are likely to list biblical elements such as seven days and a flood, or elements from other myths such as crossing a dangerous body of water.) Discuss with students the influences that *Gilgamesh* may have had on literature that followed it; also discuss the influences that other literature may have had on the authors of *Gilgamesh*.

Encourage students to consider why certain elements are found in stories across cultures.

The Stone Men work for the ferryman Urshanabi and help people across the Waters of Death. Gilgamesh smashes the Stone Men to pieces with his ax. He then learns from Urshanabi that he destroyed Urshanabi's crew.

Gilgamesh went deep into the forest,
he cut down three hundred punting poles,° each
a hundred feet long, he stripped them, made grips,
170   and brought them to Urshanabi the boatman.
They boarded the boat and sailed away.

They sailed, without stopping, for three days and nights,
a six weeks' journey for ordinary men,
until they reached the Waters of Death.
175   Urshanabi said, "Now be careful,
take up the first pole, push us forward,
and do not touch the Waters of Death.
When you come to the end of the first pole, drop it,
take up a second and a third one, until
180   you come to the end of the three-hundredth pole
and the Waters of Death are well behind us."

When all three hundred poles had been used,
Gilgamesh took Urshanabi's robe.
He held it as a sail, with both arms extended,
185   and the little boat moved on toward the shore.

Alone on the shore stood Utnapishtim,
wondering as he watched them approach.
"Where are the Stone Men who crew the boat?
Why is there a stranger on board?
190   I have never seen him. Who can he be?"

Gilgamesh landed. When he saw the old man,
he said to him, "Tell me, where can I find
Utnapishtim, who joined the assembly
of the gods, and was granted eternal life?"

195   Utnapishtim said, "Why are your cheeks
so hollow? Why is your face so ravaged,
frost-chilled, and burnt by the desert sun?
Why is there so much grief in your heart?"

168 **punting poles:** long poles used to propel a boat through shallow water.

Head of an Akkadian ruler (Naramsin or Sargon), ca. 2334-2154 BC. Bronze cast, height 36 cm, width 20cm. Iraq Museum, Baghdad.

3   Visualize *How do the details in these lines help you visualize Gilgamesh's task?*

Approaching Level
DIFFERENTIATED INSTRUCTION

Bridging Passages Point out the bridging passage between lines 166 and 167. Explain that this passage is used to summarize a longer segment of the poem that has been omitted. **Ask:** Why does Gilgamesh cut down the poles? *(He smashed Urshanabi's stone helpers, so he has to do work himself in order to get across the ocean.)*

Advanced Learners/Pre-AP
DIFFERENTIATED INSTRUCTION

Water as Death Many myths speak of water as the boundary between life and death. Have students research the Greek myth of the River Styx and compare and contrast it with the ocean that Gilgamesh must cross. **Ask:** How do the two myths differ? How are they similar? How does an epic hero conquer each challenge? Invite students to share their discoveries with the class.

Teach

Literary Element   2

Epic Hero Refer students to lines 172–185. **Ask:** What epic feats of strength does Gilgamesh perform while crossing the ocean? *(He sails without stopping for three days and nights. Then he holds up a sail made from Urshanabi's robe to complete the journey.)* **Ask:** What supernatural help does Gilgamesh receive? *(He receives help from Urshanabi the boatman.)*

Reading Strategy   3

Visualize **Answer:** *They show his superhuman strength and the enormity of his task. For example, Gilgamesh does not just cut down poles; he cuts down 300 poles, which is arduous work.*

View the Art ★

Sargon was a ruler of the Akkadian dynasty. According to legend, his mother bore him in secret. She placed him in a basket and set him afloat on a river. Aqqui, drawer of water, found and raised the infant. **Ask:** Why is water so important both for the legend of Sargon and in the epic of Gilgamesh? *(Students may suggest water is important because it represents life; if Sargon's mother had not put him in the water, the infant would not have been found by Aqqui. In contrast, in Gilgamesh water is equated with great danger and even death.)*

Learning Objectives
Visualizing. (SE)
Analyzing epic hero. (TE)
Making predictions. (TE)

| Literary Element | 1 |

Epic Hero Answer: *He has overcome obstacles on a great quest and has persevered when an ordinary man would have given up.*

| Big Idea | 2 |

The Secret of Life Answer: *They believed that human life is fleeting and under the control of the gods.* **Ask:** How does Utnapishtim say humans feel about the fragility of life? *(They go on about their daily living as if they will last forever.)*

200 Why are you worn out and ready to collapse,
like someone who has been on a long, hard journey?" . . .

Gilgamesh said,
"I must find Utnapishtim,"
whom men call 'The Distant One.' I must ask him
how he managed to overcome death.
I have wandered the world, climbed the most **treacherous**
205 mountains, crossed deserts, sailed the vast ocean,
and sweet sleep has rarely softened my face.

I have worn myself out through ceaseless striving,
I have filled my muscles with pain and anguish.
I have killed bear, lion, hyena, leopard,
210 tiger, deer, antelope, ibex,° I have eaten
their meat and have wrapped their rough skins around me.
And what in the end have I achieved?
When I reached Shiduri the tavern keeper,
I was filthy, exhausted, heartsick. Now let
215 the gate of sorrow be closed behind me,
and let it be sealed shut with tar and pitch." . . .

Utnapishtim said,
"Yes: the gods took Enkidu's life.
But man's life *is* short, at any moment
it can be snapped, like a reed in a canebrake.°
220 The handsome young man, the lovely young woman—
in their prime, death comes and drags them away.
Though no one has seen death's face or heard
death's voice, suddenly, savagely, death
destroys us, all of us, old or young.
225 And yet we build houses, make contracts, brothers
divide their inheritance, conflicts occur—
as though this human life lasted forever.
The river rises, flows over its banks
and carries us all away, like mayflies

210 ibex: (ī′ bex) wild mountain goat with curving horns that is native to Europe, Asia, and northern Africa.

219 canebrake: thicket of cane.

1 **Epic Hero** *How does the description in lines 204–208 characterize Gilgamesh as an epic hero?*

2 **The Secret of Life** *What does this stanza reveal about the Mesopotamian view of death?*

Vocabulary

treacherous (trech′ ər əs) *adj.* hazardous; dangerous

Reading Practice

Make Predictions Tell students that they can use prior knowledge or experiences plus clues from a text to make predictions about plot development or characters' actions. In this case, students should use what they already know about legends, mythology, and epic heroes to make predictions about what will happen to Gilgamesh later in the tale.

Ask: What can you predict will happen to Gilgamesh from the line "sweet sleep has rarely softened my face" (line 206)? *(Students should note that his boasting may foreshadow a future challenge. In spite of his strengths, he still needs to sleep like all humans.)*

230 floating downstream: they stare at the sun,
then all at once there is nothing.

"The sleeper and the dead, how alike they are!
Yet the sleeper wakes up and opens his eyes,
while no one returns from death. And who
235 can know when the last of his days will come?
When the gods assemble, they decide your fate,
they establish both life and death for you,
but the time of death they do not reveal."

Gilgamesh said to Utnapishtim,
240 "I imagined that you would look like a god.
But you look like me, you are not any different.
I intended to fight you, yet now that I stand
before you, now that I see who you are,
I can't fight, something is holding me back.
245 Tell me, how is it that you, a mortal,
overcame death and joined the assembly
of the gods and were granted eternal life?"
Utnapishtim said, "I will tell you
a mystery, a secret of the gods. . . ."

*Utnapishtim describes a time when the gods decided to
send a flood. Ea, the god of wisdom, told him to build a ship
out of his house to save his life and take examples of every
living creature aboard the ship. The god Enlil boarded the ship
and touched the forehead of both Utnapishtim and his wife
and made them immortal. Enlil sent them to the mouth of the
rivers to live.*

The Return

250 "Now then, Gilgamesh, who will assemble
the gods for *your* sake? Who will convince them
to grant you the eternal life that you seek?
How would they know that you deserve it?
First pass this test: Just stay awake
3 255 for seven days. **Prevail** against sleep,
and perhaps you will prevail against death."

Vocabulary

prevail (pri vāl´) *v.* to gain ascendancy through strength or superiority;
to triumph

Literary Element | 3

Epic Hero Ask: What heroic feat must Gilgamesh perform to gain immortal life? *(He must stay awake for seven days.)*

Cultural History

Death in Mesopotamia
Attitudes toward death were harsh in Mesopotamia. Sickness and death were considered punishment for sins. There was no belief in an afterlife that would compensate a person for having led a good life. Instead of judgment of souls, a common fate awaited everyone, good and evil. Given this belief system, it is understandable that Gilgamesh fears death to such an extent that he feels his only recourse is to achieve immortality.

Learning Objectives
Analyzing epic hero. (SE)
Analyzing literary influences. (TE)

English Learners

DIFFERENTIATED INSTRUCTION

Intermediate Remind students that a simile is a type of figurative language that compares two seemingly unrelated things using the word *like* or *as*. Direct students' attention to lines 228–231, and explain that a mayfly is a type of fly that hatches, mates, and dies in one day.

Point out that the author compares humans to mayflies in this simile. **Ask:** Why is Utnapishtim saying that humans are like mayflies? *(Students should note how both mayflies and humans live for only a short period of time compared with the eternity of nature.)*

Advanced Learners/Pre-AP

DIFFERENTIATED INSTRUCTION

Analyze Traditional Characters Ask students to consider how Utnapishtim resembles another character in traditional literature. He was originally a mortal, but has been granted eternal life. Gilgamesh imagines that he should look like a god. **Ask:** What other person in literature does he resemble? *(Noah)* What qualities might a reader assume he shares with Noah? *(righteousness).*

Teach

Reading Strategy | 1

Visualize **Ask:** To what senses do the descriptions of the bread appeal? *(the senses of sight, touch, and possibly smell)*

Literary Element | 2

Epic Hero **Ask:** How is Gilgamesh unlike an epic hero in this scene? *(He fears death and he has lost his courage.)*

Literary Element | 3

Epic Hero **Answer:** *It shows that he is susceptible to normal human weaknesses.* **Ask:** What does this moment mean in terms of his quest? *(He has failed the test and will not achieve his goal.)*

So Gilgamesh sat down against a wall
to begin the test. The moment he sat down,
sleep swirled over him, like a fog.

260 Utnapishtim said to his wife,
"Look at this fellow! He wanted to live
forever, but the very moment he sat down,
sleep swirled over him, like a fog."

His wife said, "Touch him on the shoulder, wake him,
265 let him depart and go back safely
to his own land, by the gate he came through."

Utnapishtim said, "All men are liars.
When he wakes up, watch how he tries to deceive us.
So bake a loaf for each day he sleeps,
1 270 put them in a row beside him, and make
a mark on the wall for every loaf."

She baked the loaves and put them beside him,
she made a mark for each day he slept.
The first loaf was rock-hard, the second loaf
275 was dried out like leather, the third had shrunk,
the fourth had a whitish covering, the fifth
was spotted with mold, the sixth was stale,
the seventh loaf was still on the coals
when he reached out and touched him. Gilgamesh
280 woke with a start and said, "I was almost
falling asleep when I felt your touch."

Utnapishtim said, "Look down, friend,
count these loaves that my wife baked and put here
while you sat sleeping. This first one, rock-hard,
285 was baked seven days ago, this leathery one
was baked six days ago, and so on for all
the rest of the days you sat here sleeping.
Look. They are marked on the wall behind you."

Gilgamesh cried out, "What shall I do,
2 290 where shall I go now? Death has caught me,
it lurks in my bedroom, and everywhere I look,
everywhere I turn, there is only death."

---

3 Epic Hero *How does this action contrast with Gilgamesh's earlier heroic feats?*

Grammar Practice

Avoid Run-on Sentences Explain that a run-on sentence is a sentence made of two or more sentences that have been incorrectly blended into a single sentence. Draw students' attention to the sentence in lines 296–298. Explain to students that poetry sometimes contains incorrect sentence construction and grammar, but that run-on sentences are not generally accepted in other types of writing.

Explain that to correct the problem, students should punctuate the independent clauses as separate sentences, add conjunctions, or rewrite one or more independent clauses as dependent clauses. Ask students how this sentence could be rewritten to avoid a run-on. *(Possible answers: As for this man, he is filthy and tired, his hair is matted, and animal skins have obscured his beauty.)*

Have students identify and rewrite other run-on sentences in the poem.

Nile Mosaic (detail). Late 2nd century BC. Museo Archeologico Prenestino, Palestrina, Italy. ★

Utnapishtim said to the boatman,
"This is the last time, Urshanabi,
295 that you are allowed to cross the vast ocean
and reach these shores. As for this man,
he is filthy and tired, his hair is matted,
animal skins have obscured his beauty.
Bring him to the tub and wash out his hair,
300 take off his animal skin and let
the waves of the ocean carry it away,
moisten his body with sweet-smelling oil,
bind his hair in a bright new headband,
dress him in fine robes fit for a king.
305 Until he comes to the end of his journey
let his robes be spotless, as though they were new."
He brought him to the tub, he washed out his hair,
he took off his animal skin and let
the waves of the ocean carry it away,
310 he moistened his body with sweet-smelling oil,
he bound his hair in a bright new headband,
he dressed him in fine robes fit for a king.

5   Visualize *To what senses does this image appeal?*

Advanced Learners/Pre-AP

DIFFERENTIATED INSTRUCTION

Metaphors Review metaphors with students, and explain that they are a comparison of two things in which the author says that one thing *is* another. Point out the metaphors the poet uses to describe the loaves of bread. Remind students that saying that something is moldy is not a metaphor but merely a description.

However, saying that a loaf *is* mold is a metaphor. Challenge students to create a series of seven metaphors to describe the condition of the seven loaves of bread. For example, the first loaf might be compared to petrified wood. Then, challenge students to create metaphors to describe Gilgamesh and the other characters of this scene.

Teach

Literary Element   4

Epic Hero Ask: Does Gilgamesh look like an epic hero early in this scene? Explain. *(Students are likely to say that Gilgamesh doesn't look like a hero because he is filthy and ragged.)*

Reading Strategy   5

Visualize Answer: *The image appeals to touch ("moistened"), smell ("sweet-smelling"), and sight ("bright new headband" and "fine robes").* **Ask:** What does this transformation in Gilgamesh's appearance suggest about his status? *(Although he has failed in his quest, the gods still want to reward him for his efforts.)*

View the Art ★

A mosaic is composed of closely set, variously colored, small pieces of materials such as glass, tile, or shell, which decorate a surface with a design. Because of the form of its individual pieces, a mosaic cannot be reassembled if it is taken apart. During the Hellenistic period (3rd–1st century B.C.), glass appeared among mosaic materials.

Ask: In the mosaic featured, what colors are used? *(reds, blues, black, brown, and white)*
Ask: How does this mosaic of a man steering a boat up the Nile relate to the story of Gilgamesh? *(Students may say the mosaic depicts a scene similar to what Gilgamesh would have experienced in his journey across the ocean.)*

Learning Objectives
Analyzing epic hero. (SE)
Visualizing. (TE)
Avoiding run-on sentences. (TE)

461

Teach

Big Idea `1`

The Secret of Life Answer:
Gilgamesh seeks everlasting life and youth. **Ask:** Which is more desirable, youth or immortality? *(Some students may say that immortality would not be a blessing if it included perpetual aging. Others may say that finding the secret of youth prevents a person from growing wise.)*

View the Art ★

In an earlier part of the epic, Gilgamesh and his friend Enkidu go to the Cedar Forest where they kill the monster Humbaba.
Ask: What other monsters can you think of that were killed by mythical heroes? *(Students may mention monsters from Greek mythology such as Medusa (killed by Perseus) or the Hydra (killed by Heracles).)*

Then Gilgamesh and Urshanabi
boarded, pushed off, and the little boat
315 began to move away from the shore.

But the wife of Utnapishtim said, "Wait,
this man came a very long way, he endured
many hardships to get here. Won't you
give him something for his journey home?"

320 When he heard this, Gilgamesh turned the boat
around, and he brought it back to the shore.
Utnapishtim said, "Gilgamesh,
you came a very long way, you endured
many hardships to get here. Now
325 I will give you something for your journey home,
a mystery, a secret of the gods.
There is a small spiny bush that grows
in the waters of the Great Deep, it has sharp spikes
that will prick your fingers like a rose's thorns.

330 If you find this plant and bring it to the surface,
you will have found the secret of youth."

Gilgamesh dug a pit on the shore
that led down into the Great Deep. He tied
two heavy stones to his feet, they pulled him
335 downward into the water's depths.
He found the plant, he grasped it, it tore
his fingers, they bled, he cut off the stones,
his body shot up to the surface, and the waves
cast him back, gasping, onto the shore.

340 Gilgamesh said to Urshanabi,
"Come here, look at this marvelous plant,
the **antidote** to the fear of death.
With it we return to the youth we once had.
I will take it to Uruk, I will test its power
345 by seeing what happens when an old man eats it.
If that succeeds, I will eat some myself
and become a carefree young man again."

Humbaba, demon, genie and guardian of the cedar forests of the Lebanon range, 20th-16th century BC. Terracotta. Louvre, Paris. ★

`1` **The Secret of Life** *What is the goal of Gilgamesh's quest?*

Vocabulary

antidote (an′ti dōt′) *n.* something that relieves, prevents, or counteracts

462 UNIT 3 SOUTHWEST ASIA

Reading Practice

Analyze Cause and Effect Explain that a cause-and-effect relationship is a chain of events in which one event causes another, and that effect can cause an additional effect. **Ask:** What causes Gilgamesh to plan to give a leaf of the plant to an old man? *(He wants to test the plant.)* What effect does he hope for? *(He hopes the old man will survive and become young again.)*

What effect will the old man's surviving then cause? *(It will cause Gilgamesh to believe the plant safe, and then he will eat some of it.)* Encourage students to follow cause-and-effect relationships in their reading, especially when the author has not explicitly explained a character's motivation.

At four hundred miles they stopped to eat,
at a thousand miles they pitched their camp.
350 Gilgamesh saw a pond of cool water.
He left the plant on the ground and bathed.
A snake smelled its fragrance, stealthily
it crawled up and carried the plant away.
As it disappeared, it cast off its skin.

355 When Gilgamesh saw what the snake had done,
he sat down and wept. He said to the boatman,
"What shall I do now? All my hardships
have been for nothing. O Urshanabi,
was it for this that my hands have labored,
360 was it for this that I gave my heart's blood?
I have gained no benefit for myself
but have lost the marvelous plant to a reptile.
I plucked it from the depths, and how could I ever
manage to find that place again?
365 And our little boat—we left it on the shore."

At four hundred miles they stopped to eat,
at a thousand miles they pitched their camp.
When at last they arrived, Gilgamesh
said to Urshanabi, "This is
370 the wall of Uruk, which no city on earth can equal.
See how its ramparts gleam like copper in the sun.
Climb the stone staircase, more ancient than the mind can
   imagine
approach the Eanna Temple, sacred to Ishtar,
a temple that no king has equaled in size or beauty,
375 walk on the wall of Uruk, follow its course
around the city, inspect its mighty foundations,
examine its brickwork, how masterfully it is built,
observe the land it encloses: the palm trees, the gardens,
the orchards, the glorious palaces and temples, the shops
380 and marketplaces, the houses, the public squares."

---

2 **The Secret of Life** *What is the lesson of Gilgamesh's journey?*

3 **Visualize** *What does the description of Uruk in lines 369–372 imply about Gilgamesh and his city?*

English Learners

DIFFERENTIATED INSTRUCTION

Intermediate One of the vocabulary words, *antidote*, includes the prefix *anti-*, which means "against." Tell students not to confuse it with the prefix *ante-*, which means "before," as in the word *antecedent*. Students should list and define words with the prefixes *anti-* and *ante-*. Then they can consider these prefixes' opposites, the prefixes *pro-* (for) and *post-* (after).

Advanced Learners/Pre-AP

DIFFERENTIATED INSTRUCTION

Eternal Youth Have students research other myths and legends about the quest for eternal youth. Note that real people, such as Ponce de Leon, have tried to find mythical sources of eternal youth or immortality, such as the Fountain of Youth. Discuss why people are so eager to believe that myths of eternal youth are real. Have students consider medical advances such as plastic surgery or hormone injections as a modern quest for eternal youth.

Teach

Big Idea   2

The Secret of Life **Answer:** *He should value life and accept aging, rather than seeking immortality.*

Reading Strategy   3

Visualize **Answer:** *It implies that the city, its ruler, and its people are grand and unrivaled.*

Ask: Why is the return to Uruk significant? *(Gilgamesh is returning to everyday life after his encounters with the supernatural.)*

Political History ☆

Uruk In addition to serving as an important religious center, Gilgamesh's home city of Uruk (also called Erech) was a prosperous city. Its ruins have been found in Iraq and excavated by archaeologists. It has revealed more about early urban life than any other site in the world. Uruk was known for its many fine ziggurats, or temples, and precious metals worked with great skill. The city was surrounded by six miles of brick walls.

Learning Objectives
Visualizing. (SE)
Analyzing epic hero. (TE)
Analyzing cause-and-effect relationships. (TE)

After You Read

Assess

1. (a) Students will probably have expected Gilgamesh to achieve immortality. (b) Answers will vary.

2. (a) The scorpion man says that no man has ever gone into the tunnel. Shiduri reminds Gilgamesh that the gods allotted death to humankind during creation. (b) Gilgamesh watched Enkidu suffer and die and now fears his own death.

3. (a) Urshanabi is the ferryman over the Waters of Death. (b) His character may represent the journey people take between life and death.

4. (a) The gods decide when mortals live and die. (b) Gilgamesh wants to control his life and avoid suffering.

5. (a) Sleep probably symbolizes death, the fate of all humans. (b) The ability to stay awake may symbolize eternal life.

6. In spite of his efforts, Gilgamesh loses the gift and is unable to change his fate.

7. People should accept death as an inevitable part of life and enjoy life.

8. Answers will vary. Students might note the prevalence of plastic surgery and the variety of magazine articles on how to feel and look younger.

Daily Life and Culture

1. The landscape is depicted as extreme and stark. Gilgamesh's appearance also reflects the harsh weather; his face is described as "frost-chilled, and burnt by the desert sun."

2. People in such an environment likely would have deities that are, like the weather, capricious and uncaring.

464

After You Read

Respond and Think Critically

Respond and Interpret

1. (a) How did you expect Gilgamesh's quest to end? (b) Did the ending meet your expectations? Explain.

2. (a) Which two characters try to persuade Gilgamesh to give up his journey to find Utnapishtim, and what argument does each present? (b) In your opinion, why does Gilgamesh refuse to give up?

3. (a) What is Urshanabi's job? (b) What might his character represent?

4. (a) What do the gods decide for mortals? (b) Why does Gilgamesh find this hard to accept?

Analyze and Evaluate

5. (a) What might sleep symbolize, or represent, in Utnapishtim's challenge to Gilgamesh? (b) What might the ability to stay awake represent?

6. **Irony** is a contrast between what is expected and what actually happens. What is ironic about the outcome of Utnapishtim's gift to Gilgamesh?

Connect

7. **Big Idea** **The Secret of Life** What is the theme, or main idea about life, of this epic?

8. **Connect to Today** Many people in modern society still appear to be on a quest for the "secrets of youth." How do popular media, including films, books, and magazines, reflect this quest?

Daily Life & Culture

Harsh Climate—Harsh Outlook

Read the following description of the environment of the Tigris-Euphrates valley, the setting for the Gilgamesh epic.

The same rivers that bring life can also bring disaster. The winters may be too cold or rainless, the summer winds too dry. . . . Confronted with these manifestations of supernatural forces, the Mesopotamian felt bewildered and helpless. . . . His own life, the life of his family, the produce of his field and of his cattle, the rhythm and measure of the river floods. . . and indeed the very existence of the universe were constantly at stake.
—Georges Roux, from *Ancient Iraq*

Group Activity Discuss the following questions with your classmates. Refer to Roux's quotation and *Gilgamesh* to support your answers.

1. How does *Gilgamesh* reflect the Mesopotamian environment?

2. Do you think people living in such an environment would believe in benevolent supernatural beings, or would their gods be willful and uncaring? Explain.

 For additional selection assessment, see Assessment Resources, pp. 93–94.

Literary Element | Epic Hero

ACT Skills Practice

1. The portrayal of Gilgamesh in this epic shows that the Mesopotamians admired the quality of:

    A. argumentativeness.

    B. deception.

    C. wisdom.

    D. harshness.

2. As an epic hero, Gilgamesh embodies the quality of:

    F. loyalty.

    G. diversity.

    H. vindictiveness.

    J. friendliness.

Review: Setting

As you learned on page 108, the **setting** is the time and place in which the events of a literary work take place. Setting also includes the cultural background of that time and place.

Partner Activity With a partner, discuss how the changes in setting in the epic reflect the development of the story. Complete a sequence chain like the one below. Include a description of each setting and an explanation of what Gilgamesh learns.

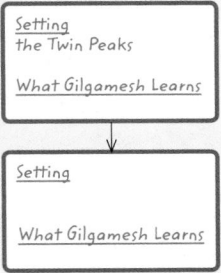

Setting
the Twin Peaks

What Gilgamesh Learns

↓

Setting

What Gilgamesh Learns

 Literature Online

Selection Resources For Selection Quizzes, eFlashcards, and Reading-Writing Connection activities, go to glencoe.com and enter QuickPass code GLW6053u3.

Reading Strategy | Visualize

When you **visualize** a scene, it helps to imagine how it would feel to be there in person. What would you see, hear, feel, smell, and taste? Refer to the chart you made on page 449 and answer the following questions.

1. (a)Identify a section of *Gilgamesh* that has sensory details. (b)Explain how specific details help you visualize the scene.

2. Why is it important to visualize the scenes described in a literary work?

Vocabulary Practice

Practice with Word Origins You can better understand the meaning of a word if you study its **origin**, or history. Create a word map like the one below for each of the boldfaced vocabulary words. Use a dictionary for help.

ravaged   treacherous   prevail   antidote

EXAMPLE:

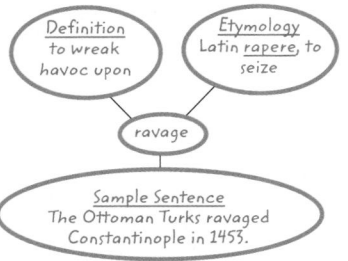

Definition
to wreak
havoc upon

Etymology
Latin *rapere*, to
seize

ravage

Sample Sentence
The Ottoman Turks ravaged
Constantinople in 1453.

Academic Vocabulary

*Gilgamesh hoped to attain eternal life **via** consumption of a plant.*

Via is an academic word. In more casual conversation, people might say they get to work **via** public transportation. To further explore the meaning of this word, complete the sentence below.

A mailed package reaches its destination **via** _____.

For more on academic vocabulary, see pages 36–37 and R83–R85.

After You Read

Assess

Literary Element

1. **C** is the correct answer. **A, B,** and **D** are incorrect because they were negative qualities for the Mesopotamians.

2. **F** is the correct answer. **G** is incorrect and is not required of legendary heroes, as they may represent only their own culture. **H** would be considered a negative quality. **J** is incorrect; it is acceptable for a hero to sacrifice friendliness in favor of strength and courage.

Progress Check

Can students identify epic hero?

If No → See Unit 3 Teaching Resources Book, p. 27.

Review: Setting

Charts should include settings such as the Twin Peaks, where Gilgamesh learns how to cross the mountains; the edge of the ocean, where he learns from Shiduri that Urshanabi can help him across the Waters of Death; and the underworld, where he learns he will be unable to achieve immortality.

Reading Strategy

1. (a) Students should identify a specific scene with vivid sensory details. *(Possible response: The scene that describes the loaves of bread.)* (b) They should note the individual details that help them visualize and explain how these details appeal to the senses.

2. Visualizing makes reading more enjoyable and increases comprehension.

Vocabulary Practice

Word: treacherous; **Definition:** hazardous; dangerous; **Etymology:** Middle English *treacherous* means "to deceive"; **Sample Sentence:** They made the treacherous climb up Mt. Everest.

Word: prevail; **Definition:** to triumph; **Etymology:** Latin *prae-* (pre-) + *valere,* "to be strong"; **Sample Sentence:** In the end, we will prevail.

Word: antidote; **Definition:** something that relieves or prevents; **Etymology:** Greek *anti-* + *didonai,* "to give"; **Sample Sentence:** The snakebite victim needed an antidote immediately.

Academic Vocabulary

Possible answer: A mailed package reaches its destination via the postal service, freight trains, or airmail.

After You Read

Assess

Respond Through Writing

Students' expository essays should compare and contrast Gilgamesh with contemporary pop culture heroes, offer credible and relevant evidence to support the thesis, use transitions to signal comparisons and contrasts, and conclude by evaluating whether Gilgamesh is a hero by modern standards.

A student who meets all of these criteria should receive the equivalent of a 4-point response.

A student who fully meets two or partially meets three of these criteria should receive the equivalent of a 3-point response.

A student who fully meets one or partially meets two of these criteria should receive the equivalent of a 2-point response.

A student who partially meets one of these criteria should receive the equivalent of a 1-point response.

Grammar Tip

Often, students believe that using interrogative and exclamatory sentences makes for more dramatic writing. Encourage students to use highly emotional sentences sparingly.

Respond Through Writing

Expository Essay

Analyze Epic Hero In an expository essay of at least 1,500 words, analyze the heroic qualities Gilgamesh displays and compare and contrast these qualities with those of the costumed crime fighters and other heroes of modern popular culture. In your conclusion, evaluate whether Gilgamesh is a hero by today's standards.

Understand the Task When you **compare** and **contrast** two things, you identify similarities and differences between them.

Prewrite To begin organizing your thoughts, create a Venn diagram like the one below to note Gilgamesh's heroic qualities, the qualities of pop culture heroes, and the qualities they share.

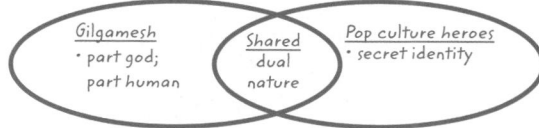

Gilgamesh
• part god;
  part human

Shared
dual
nature

Pop culture heroes
• secret identity

Draft As you begin writing, evaluate the quality of your sources and make sure you convey information from these sources accurately and coherently. Review the story and your research notes to gather evidence to support your thesis.

Revise As you revise, be sure to use transitional words and phrases to clearly signal comparisons (*likewise*) and contrasts (*but, however*). Also, check to ensure that you have used literary terms, such as epic hero, accurately and that you have addressed any potential misunderstandings your readers may have. Use the rubric on page 1292 to check other elements of your review.

Edit and Proofread Proofread your paper, correcting any errors in spelling, grammar, and punctuation. Use the word count feature on your computer to determine whether your paper is at least 1,500 words. Review the Grammar Tip in the side column for information on sentence types.

Learning Objectives

In this workshop, you will focus on the following objectives:

Writing: Writing an expository essay.

Grammar: Understanding sentence types.

Grammar Tip

Sentence Types

English has four types of sentences, classified according to the kinds of messages they express.

A **declarative sentence** makes a statement.

Gilgamesh was a legendary king of Uruk.

An **imperative sentence** gives a command or makes a request.

Please feast and rejoice.

An **interrogative sentence** asks a question.

Where are you going?

An **exclamatory sentence** expresses strong feeling or emotion.

"Despair is in my heart!"

As you write, try to use a variety of these sentence types.

Reading Practice

Connect to Contemporary Issues
When students are brainstorming for their expository essays, encourage them to consider the word *hero* in contemporary culture. **Ask:** What characteristics make someone a hero? *(Students are likely to say that bravery and patriotism are heroic characteristics.)* Discuss possible contemporary situations that might cause someone to be identified as a hero.

Ask: Who are heroes in our culture? *(Students may identify historical figures, soldiers, fire fighters, and athletes.)* Encourage students to consider people they know who act heroically, even in small ways. Ask students to consider how they can connect Gilgamesh's quest for immortality to contemporary issues. *(Students may mention the behind-the-scene heroics of scientific researchers and doctors who study fatal diseases.)*

Grammar Workshop

Pronoun-Antecedent Agreement

Literature Connection In the sentence "Humans are born, they live, then they die" from *Gilgamesh,* the pronoun *they* refers to *humans.* This pronoun is plural because its antecedent is plural. **Incorrect pronoun shifts** occur when a writer uses a pronoun of one person or number and then illogically shifts to a pronoun in another person or number. Another type of agreement problem occurs when a pronoun has no clearly stated antecedent.

PROBLEM 1 A pronoun does not agree with its antecedent in person.

Shiduri asks <u>Gilgamesh</u> why <u>you</u> look so ravaged.

SOLUTION Replace the incorrect pronoun with a pronoun that agrees with its subject in person.

Shiduri asks <u>Gilgamesh</u> why <u>he</u> looks so ravaged.

PROBLEM 2 A pronoun does not agree with its antecedent in number.

<u>Gilgamesh</u> faces many obstacles in <u>their</u> quest for immortality.

SOLUTION Replace the incorrect pronoun with a pronoun that agrees with its subject in number.

<u>Gilgamesh</u> faces many obstacles in <u>his</u> quest for immortality.

PROBLEM 3 A pronoun has no clearly stated antecedent.

Gilgamesh mourns for Enkidu, <u>which</u> leads to his decision to seek Utnapishtim.

SOLUTION Replace the incorrect pronoun with an appropriate noun.

Gilgamesh mourns for Enkidu, and his <u>grief</u> leads to his decision to seek Utnapishtim.

Proofread For each sentence below, write the correct form of the pronoun or the correct rephrasing of the sentence on a separate sheet of paper.

1. Gilgamesh was a legendary king of the Sumerians who was famous for (his, their) strength and courage.
2. Ancient scribes wrote the stories of Gilgamesh on clay tablets, and (your, these records) survived.
3. Gilgamesh meets Shiduri, who says (him, he) should try to enjoy life.

Learning Objectives

In this workshop, you will focus on the following objective:

Grammar: Understanding correct pronoun-antecedent agreement.

Pronouns and Antecedents

A **pronoun** is a word that takes the place of a noun, a group of words acting as a noun, or another pronoun. The word or group of words a pronoun refers to is called its **antecedent.**

Tip

Use gender-neutral language, such as *his* or *her* and *he* or *she,* when the gender of an antecedent is unknown. For example, *A doctor faces many challenges in his or her lifetime.* You can also make the pronoun and antecedent plural: *Doctors face many challenges in their lifetimes.*

Language Handbook

For more on pronouns, see the Language Handbook, p. R40.

 Literature Online

Grammar For more grammar practice, go to glencoe.com and enter QuickPass code GLW6053u3.

GRAMMAR WORKSHOP **467**

English Learners

DIFFERENTIATED INSTRUCTION

Intermediate To give students more practice in pronoun-antecedent agreement, have student pairs write paragraphs that contain at least two different pronouns and their corresponding antecedents. First, have each pair decide on a topic for their paragraphs. Then ask them to make a list of pronouns. They can choose pronouns from this list to include in their stories. Pairs should work together to write the paragraphs.

After pairs have finished, instruct them to rewrite the paragraphs, leaving blank spaces in place of each pronoun. Then, have them create a word bank of the missing pronouns. Have each pair switch their story with another pair's. Students can then work together to fill in the missing pronouns.

Focus

Pronoun Number

Write on the board: Singular Pronouns: I, you, he, she, it

Plural Pronouns: we, you, they

Review the singular and plural pronouns with students. Remind them that *you* can be a singular pronoun when it refers to an individual or it can be plural when it refers to several people. Explain that it is important for pronouns—singular or plural—to match or agree with their antecedents.

Teach

Checking Pronoun-Antecedent Agreement

Tell students that it can be easy to make errors in pronoun-antecedent agreement when writing. Recommend that students underline the antecedent for each pronoun. Then they can make sure that a pronoun matches its antecedent.

Assess

1. his
2. these records
3. he

For additional grammar practice, see Unit 3 Teaching Resources Book, p. 34.

Learning Objective
Understanding correct pronoun-antecedent agreement. (SE)

Focus

Bellringer Option

Ask: What stories in your family have been passed down from generation to generation? Why do you think these stories continue on this way? *(Some may suggest these stories are passed down because they reveal family traditions or heritage and help the family understand and define itself.)*

Teach

Reading Strategy

Question Ask: In which five religions do sacred texts play a vital role? *(Judaism, Christianity, Islam, Hinduism, and Buddhism)*

Ask: How are these sacred texts different? *(The lengths of the texts differ as well as the type of writing found in them.)*

View the Art ★

This woodcut is taken from the Gutenberg Bible. **Ask:** Why do you think there are so many pieces of art that depict scenes from sacred texts? *(Students may say that since sacred texts relate religious tradition to its people it is natural for art to portray these stories, sermons, and parables because of their great religious importance.)*

Learning Objectives

For pages 468–469

In studying this text, you will focus on the following objectives:

Literary Study: Analyzing literary genres.

Reading:

Evaluating historical influences.

Connecting to the literature.

Sacred Texts

SACRED TEXTS ARE WRITINGS THAT ARE CLOSELY LINKED WITH A specific religion or religious tradition. These texts, which include poetry, epics, parables, songs, and sermons, are often revered as holy.

Many sacred texts, such as the Bible, are regarded as divine revelations, directly communicated from God to humans. Other sacred texts are the written records of an oral teaching or a sermon given by a religious leader. Sacred texts have also originated from oral tradition; these texts developed over time until they were written down. For many religions, the oral dimension of sacred texts remains important and is still incorporated into religious rituals through reciting, chanting, and singing.

Sacred texts compiled centuries ago continue to play a vital role in Judaism, Christianity, Islam, Hinduism, and Buddhism, the five major religions of the modern world. However, such scriptures are not characteristic of all religions. For example, ancient Greeks and Romans had hundreds of myths based on their gods, but these stories tended to be told orally, rather than written down.

The Tanakh

The Tanakh, or Hebrew Bible, consists of three books: the Torah, the Nevi'im, and the Ketuvim. These books are seen as a repository of the laws, rituals, and history of Israel. The Torah consists of the first five books of the Bible and is the book of Hebrew law. The Nevi'im is a collection of visions and sermons of Jewish prophets, including Samuel, Joshua, and Ezekiel. The Ketuvim is a collection of psalms, proverbs, and history.

Moses and the Plague of Locusts. **German woodcut from the Gutenberg Bible. Victoria & Albert Museum, London.** ★

468 UNIT 3 SOUTHWEST ASIA

> *"In the beginning God created the heaven and the earth. And the earth was without form, and void; and darkness was upon the face of the deep."*
>
> —from the book of Genesis, in the Bible

The Christian Bible

The Bible (from Greek *biblia*, "books") is said to be the most widely read book in the world. Christianity is rooted in Judaism, so the Christian Bible contains the Tanakh, called the Old Testament by Christians, as well as additional books called the New Testament. The New Testament (see page 486) includes books on the life, death, and teachings of Christianity's central figure, Jesus Christ. The four primary books of the New Testament are called the Gospels.

Reading Practice

Summarize To help students manage the content of this page, ask them to summarize the information under each subhead. Remind students that a summary includes the main idea of a passage and its supporting details, and omits extra, unnecessary information.

If students have trouble writing their summaries, remind them that the main idea of a section is often found in the first sentence. After they have found the main idea, have them make a list of the most important details in the section. Then, have them turn their list into paragraph form.

The Qur'an

The Qur'an (kô rän´) (see pages 491–495) is the holy book of Islam. Muslims believe that the contents of the Qur'an are the actual words of God (in Arabic, *Allah*) as they were revealed to the prophet Muhammad from A.D. 610 to A.D. 632. The word *Qur'an* (also spelled *Koran*) is Arabic for "recitation" or "oral reading." The written text of the Qur'an was standardized within 30 years of Muhammad's death. Today, the Qur'an helps guide the lives of more than 1.3 billion Muslims around the globe.

> *"Praise be to God, Lord of the Universe,*
> *The Compassionate, the Merciful,*
> *Sovereign of the Day of Judgement!"*
> —from "The Exordium," in the Qur'an

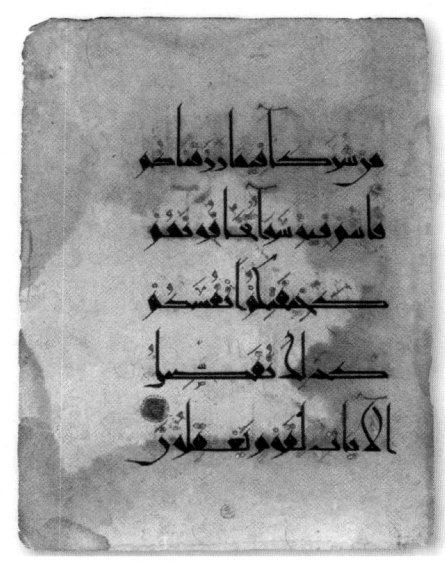

Koran, Surah al-Rum, verses 24 and 25, 11th century. Persian. Kufic writing. Victoria and Albert Museum, London.

The Vedas

Unlike Judaism, Christianity, and Islam, Hinduism, the traditional religion of India, acknowledges a number of gods and goddesses. The oldest sacred texts of Hinduism are called the Vedas (from Sanskrit, meaning "knowledge"). They are believed by Hindus to be the eternal truth as it was revealed to ancient seers. The Vedas contain four collections of hymns and verses composed by various authors from about 1500 B.C. to 1000 B.C. The oldest and most revered of the four collections is the Rig-Veda (see pages 558–562), which contains more than 1,000 hymns. Another important sacred Hindu text is the Bhagavad Gita, a philosophical dialogue that appears within the epic poem the *Mahabharata*.

Buddhist Texts

Buddhism has hundreds of sacred texts, some of which were initially passed on orally, rather than written down. The texts are primarily written in Pali, a dialect considered the Buddha's own language. The sacred texts of Buddhism include the *Dhammapada*, a popular work on Buddhist doctrine; the *Suttanipata*, a collection of 55 poems; and the *Theragatha* and the *Therigatha*, hymns written by senior monks and nuns.

LOG ON ▶ **Literature** Online

Literature and Reading For more about sacred texts, go to glencoe.com and enter QuickPass code GLW6053u3.

Respond and Think Critically

1. How do sacred texts vary from stories passed down through oral tradition?

2. What are some similarities among the sacred texts of these five major religions?

3. Based on your knowledge of sacred texts and world cultures, what might be the benefits of reading the sacred texts of different world religions?

LITERARY HISTORY **469**

Teach

Big Idea

The Secret of Life
Ask: What do you think motivates people to read sacred texts? *(They read the texts to explore the meaning of life; they hope to understand life's secrets.)*

View the Art ★

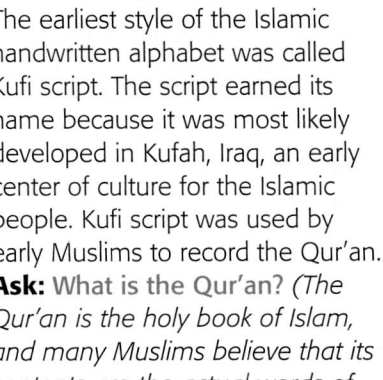

The earliest style of the Islamic handwritten alphabet was called Kufi script. The script earned its name because it was most likely developed in Kufah, Iraq, an early center of culture for the Islamic people. Kufi script was used by early Muslims to record the Qur'an. **Ask:** What is the Qur'an? *(The Qur'an is the holy book of Islam, and many Muslims believe that its contents are the actual words of God.)*

Assess

1. Sacred texts are often believed to be divinely inspired or transmitted by God to a particular person, unlike stories in most oral traditions.

2. They have a history that extends over centuries, they are tied to religious rituals and customs, and some are believed to be written by divine inspiration.

3. It helps people understand different cultures and value systems, grasp allusions and references in literary texts, and understand world history and art.

Advanced Learners/Pre-AP

DIFFERENTIATED INSTRUCTION

Research a Religion Have students select one of the religions on these two pages to investigate. Then, tell them to use Internet and print resources to research more about the religion. Students can learn about the religion's origins, followers, and fundamental beliefs.

Have students present their findings in an oral presentation. Encourage them to use visual aids or props and to organize their information for the audience. Allow time to practice their presentations with a partner.

Bellringer Options

Selection Focus
Transparency 22
Daily Language
Transparency 38

Or ask: How do people today prepare for natural disasters such as storms and floods? (*Students may mention stocking up on food and water and developing an emergency plan.*) Point out that natural disasters may seem like the end of the world for people who experience them. Ask students how a disaster such as a flood might cause someone to re-examine his or her priorities in life.

Before You Read

Israel

from the *Hebrew Bible*

The Bible is a collection of historical and legal writings, stories, songs, proverbs, sermons, prophecies, and letters that compose the sacred text of Judaism and Christianity. The Hebrew Bible, also called the Tanakh, is the sacred text of Judaism. The Christian Bible includes most of the same texts as the Hebrew Bible, as well as 27 additional books called the New Testament.

The Tanakh and the Old Testament The word *Tanakh* is an acronym composed of the first letters of the Hebrew words for the three sections of the Hebrew Bible: *T* for *Torah* ("Law"), *N* for *Nevi'im* ("Prophets"), and *K* for *Ketuvim* ("Writings"). Scholars believe that the Torah was originally passed down through oral tradition and was developed in written form beginning around 1000 B.C. Almost all of the Tanakh was originally written in Hebrew. Around the mid-200s B.C., Jewish scholars translated the Torah into Greek. This translation, combined with later Greek translations of the rest of the Tanakh, was called the Septuagint. The early Christians, most of whom spoke Greek, used the Septuagint as their sacred text. Later, after the books of the New Testament were written and added to the Christian Bible, the Septuagint was renamed the Old Testament.

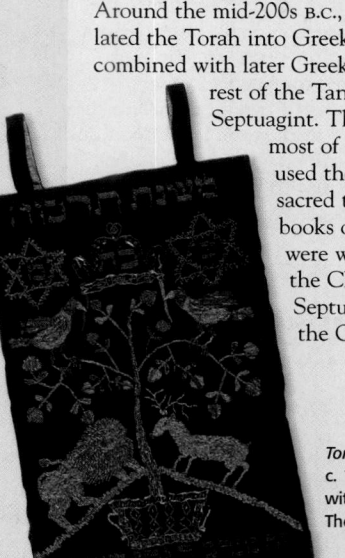

Torah Mantle. Eastern Europe, c. 1870. Velvet, embroidered with beads and metallic thread. The Jewish Museum, NY.

> *"And the rain was upon the earth forty days and forty nights."*
>
> —from Genesis

The Torah's Five Books The Torah, the first section of the Tanakh, contains five books commonly referred to as the books of Moses: Genesis, Exodus, Leviticus, Numbers, and Deuteronomy. These books include the story of the creation, the origins and history of the Israelites (the ancestors of the Jewish people), and many of the religious laws and teachings of Judaism. The story of the Flood appears in Genesis, the first book of the Torah. These five books, in the same order, also begin the Old Testament of the Christian Bible.

The King James Bible The texts you are about to read come from the King James Bible, also called the English Bible. In 1604, England's King James commissioned a group of 47 scholars to create a new English Bible. The scholars worked from both the original Hebrew and Greek texts of the Bible and the first English translations of the Bible that had emerged from the Protestant Reformation of the 1500s. The most influential of these translations was completed by William Tyndale in 1525. At that time, the Christian Bible was traditionally read in Latin, and Tyndale was executed for heresy.

Literary Elements
- Theme (SE pp. 471, 473, 476; TE p. 475)

Reading Skills
- Question (SE pp. 471, 473, 474–476)

Genesis 6–9: The Flood

Vocabulary Skills
- Practice with Synonyms (SE p. 471, 476)

Speaking/Listening/Viewing Skills
- Analyze Art (TE p. 472)
- Deliver a Speech (TE p. 472)

Writing Skills/Grammar
- Narrative (SE p. 476)
- Adverb Clauses (TE p. 474)

Literature and Reading Preview

Connect to the Sacred Text

Whom do you know who is generally considered to be a fair-minded and moral person? Write a journal entry about the actions or the ideas that led to this person's honorable reputation.

Build Background

Mount Ararat, an extinct volcano in Turkey, is traditionally considered the final resting place of Noah's ark. Since 1829, when Johann Jacob von Parrot became the first person known to reach its summit, a number of explorers and climbers have claimed to see remnants of the ark on this mountain. However, the name Ararat, as it is used in the Bible, actually translates in Hebrew to *Urartu*, an early Mesopotamian civilization.

Set Purposes for Reading

Big Idea **The Secret of Life**

As you read, ask yourself, What tenets of Judaism and Christianity are illustrated in the story of the Flood?

Literary Element **Theme**

The **theme** of a literary work is its central message about life. In some works, the theme is directly expressed. In most works, however, the **theme** is **implied**, or revealed gradually through events, dialogue, or descriptions. Be careful not to confuse *theme* with *topic*. The **topic** of a work might be love, but the theme is the message the author conveys about love. As you read, ask yourself, What details reveal the theme?

Reading Strategy **Question**

When you **question** the information in a literary work, you evaluate different events or ideas to determine their significance. As you read, ask yourself, What is the significance of the events in each chapter?

....

Tip: Take Notes Use a chart like the one below to list questions about events in the story.

Events	Questions
"Sons of God" take human wives.	Who are these "sons of God"?

Learning Objectives

For pages 470–476

In studying this text, you will focus on the following objectives:

Literary Study: Analyzing theme.

Reading: Questioning.

Writing: Writing a narrative.

Vocabulary

corrupt (kə rupt′) *adj.* morally unsound; evil; p. 472 *The journalist's article attacked the corporation's corrupt business practices.*

covenant (kuv′ə nənt) *n.* an agreement; a pact; p. 473 *The long-standing covenant between the workers and the factory owners served the interests of both groups.*

abate (ə bāt′) *v.* to lessen or decrease; p. 474 *We took shelter under a tree and waited for the storm to abate.*

Tip: Synonyms Words that have nearly the same meaning are synonyms. For example, a synonym of *abate* is *subside*, a verb that means "to lessen."

Before You Read

Focus

Summary

To punish widespread wickedness, God decides to destroy all his creations except for the family of Noah, a righteous man, and a pair of every type of animal. Noah builds an ark and survives a long period of flooding. God establishes a covenant, promising never to flood the earth again.

 For summaries in languages other than English, see Unit 3 Teaching Resources Book, pp. 37–42.

Vocabulary

Practice with Synonyms

Have student groups practice finding synonyms with a matching game. For each vocabulary word, have students write the word, at least one possible synonym, and at least one incorrect synonym on separate index cards. Have groups play each other's games by turning over the index cards. Students should take turns choosing pairs of index cards until they find a vocabulary word and its matching synonym.

 For additional vocabulary practice, see Unit 3 Teaching Resources Book, p. 45.

English Learners

DIFFERENTIATED INSTRUCTION

Beginning Explain that the story of a great flood occurs not only in the Hebrew Bible and in the epic of *Gilgamesh* but also in the literature of other cultures. For example, ancient Greek myths tell of a flood sent by the god Zeus to destroy the people of the Bronze Age.

Ask students to share their knowledge of ancient flood stories from their own traditions. Ask students to listen for similarities among the stories. Discuss why people in different cultures might have told or written stories about floods. Ask students to suggest the lessons that some people might learn from hearing the flood stories.

Teach

Reading Strategy 1

Predict Ask: Why is God angry with humans? What does God regret? *(God feels that humans are evil in their thoughts and actions. God regrets creating humans and animals.)* Have students predict the significance of this information. Tell them to consider how God might react to these feelings.

> For additional practice using the reading skill or strategy, see Unit 3 Teaching Resources Book, p. 44.

View the Art

The mosaics that decorate the church of San Marco in Venice were completed by a succession of artists over three centuries. Depicting major biblical figures and scenes, the mosaics form, in the words of art historian Otto Demus, "a cosmic panorama." *Noah Releasing the White Dove* is one of fifteen mosaics that portrays the life and death of the Old Testament patriarch. **Ask:** What might Noah's thoughts have been as he released the dove? *(Students may answer that Noah might have hoped that the dove would not return, signifying that it had found a place to land.)*

> For an audio recording of this selection, use Listening Library Audio CD-ROM.

Readability Scores

Dale-Chall: 8.6
DRP: 57
Lexile: 960

Genesis 6–9:

The Flood

from the King James *version of the* Bible

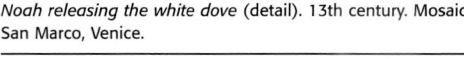
Noah releasing the white dove (detail). 13th century. Mosaic. San Marco, Venice. ★

Chapter 6

And it came to pass, when men began to multiply on the face of the earth, and daughters were born unto them, that the sons of God saw the daughters of men that they were fair; and they took them wives of all which they chose. And the Lord said, "My Spirit shall not always strive with man, for that he also is flesh: yet his days shall be an hundred and twenty years." There were giants in the earth in those days; and also after that, when the sons of God came in unto the daughters of men, and they bare children to them, the same became mighty men which were of old, men of renown.

1 And God saw that the wickedness of man was great in the earth, and that every imagination of the thoughts of his heart was only evil continually. And it repented the Lord that he had made man on the earth, and it grieved him at his heart. And the Lord said, "I will destroy man whom I have created from the face of the earth; both man, and beast, and the creeping thing, and the fowls of the air; for it repenteth me that I have made them." But Noah found grace in the eyes of the Lord.

These are the generations of Noah: Noah was a just man and perfect in his generations, and Noah walked with God. And Noah begat three sons, Shem, Ham, and Japheth.

The earth also was **corrupt** before God, and the earth was filled with violence. And God looked upon the earth, and, behold, it was corrupt; for all flesh had corrupted his way upon the earth. And God said unto Noah, "The end of all flesh is come before me; for the earth is filled with violence through them; and, behold, I will destroy them with the earth. Make thee an ark of gopher wood; rooms shalt thou make in the ark, and shalt pitch it within and without

> **Vocabulary**
>
> **corrupt** (kə rupt′) *adj.* morally unsound; evil

472 UNIT 3 SOUTHWEST ASIA

Speaking Practice

Write and Deliver a Speech
In Chapter 6 Noah receives momentous news about the fate of the world and his own family. He must relay this news to his family. Point out to students that how he decides to share this news will affect their reactions. For example, if his tone is negative and panicked, his listeners may be frightened and unable to act.

Have students work in small groups to discuss how Noah might have communicated his news in a calming and inspiring way. Students should consider elements such as word choice, tone, and pacing. Have student groups compose and deliver speeches that communicate Noah's news.

with pitch.[1] And this is the fashion which thou shalt make it of: The length of the ark shall be three hundred cubits,[2] the breadth[3] of it fifty cubits, and the height of it thirty cubits. A window shalt thou make to the ark, and in a cubit shalt thou finish it above; and the door of the ark shalt thou set in the side thereof; with lower, second, and third stories shalt thou make it.

"And, behold, I, even I, do bring a flood of waters upon the earth, to destroy all flesh, wherein is the breath of life, from under heaven; and every thing that is in the earth shall die. But with thee will I establish my **covenant;** and thou shalt come into the ark, thou, and thy sons, and thy wife, and thy sons' wives with thee. And of every living thing of all flesh, two of every sort shalt thou bring into the ark, to keep them alive with thee; they shall be male and female. Of fowls after their kind, and of cattle after their kind, of every creeping thing of the earth after his kind, two of every sort shall come unto thee, to keep them alive. And take thou unto thee of all food that is eaten, and thou shalt gather it to thee; and it shall be for food for thee, and for them." Thus did Noah according to all that God commanded him, so did he.

Chapter 7

And the Lord said unto Noah, "Come thou and all thy house into the ark; for thee have I seen righteous before me in this generation. Of every clean beast[4] thou shalt take to thee by sevens, the male and his female: and of beasts that are not clean by two, the male and his female. Of fowls also of the air by sevens, the male and the female; to keep seed alive upon the face of all the earth. For yet seven days, and I will cause it to rain upon the earth forty days and forty nights; and every living substance that I have made will I destroy from off the face of the earth." And Noah did according unto all that the Lord commanded him.

And Noah was six hundred years old when the flood of waters was upon the earth. And Noah went in, and his sons, and his wife, and his sons' wives with him, into the ark, because of the waters of the flood. Of clean beasts, and of beasts that are not clean, and of fowls, and of every thing that creepeth upon the earth. There went in two and two unto Noah into the ark, the male and the female, as God had commanded Noah. And it came to pass after seven days, that the waters of the flood were upon the earth.

In the six hundredth year of Noah's life, in the second month, the seventeenth day of the month, the same day were all the fountains of the great deep broken up, and the windows of heaven were opened.

And the rain was upon the earth forty days and forty nights. In the selfsame day entered Noah, and Shem, and Ham, and Japheth, the sons of Noah, and Noah's wife, and the three wives of his sons with

---

1. *Pitch* is a black, tarlike substance that was used as a waterproofing compound.
2. A *cubit* equals about eighteen inches.
3. *Breadth* is another word for *width*.

2 | Theme *How does this sentence underscore the theme of the story?*

Vocabulary

covenant (kuv′ə nənt) *n.* an agreement, a pact

4. According to Jewish religious law, *clean beasts* are beasts that are fit to eat and are acceptable to be used for sacrifices—this excludes pigs, reptiles, amphibians, rodents, carnivorous animals, most insects, and all shellfish.

Question *What is confusing about God's instructions here, given what he told Noah earlier?* **3**

Question *How does this information conflict with information at the beginning of the story? How might you explain the apparent contradiction?* **4**

THE FLOOD **473**

Advanced Learners/Pre-AP

DIFFERENTIATED INSTRUCTION

The Flood in Art Explain that the biblical flood and Noah's ark have been depicted in many famous works of art. Have students visit museum Web sites or look through art history books to find portrayals of this iconic event. Ask each student to choose a piece and analyze how well the artwork portrays the information in Genesis.

Approaching Level

DIFFERENTIATED INSTRUCTION

Paraphrasing Students may have difficulty with the narrative's language and style. Encourage them to paraphrase each paragraph with a partner. Remind students that paraphrasing is using their own words to describe a text. To help students find their own words, suggest that they imagine they are telling a friend or family member about what they are reading.

Teach

Literary Element | **2**

Theme Answer: *Noah has always followed God's will, which is why he and his family are spared—this underscores the theme that those who obey God and live righteously will be rewarded.*

Reading Strategy | **3**

Question Answer: *The reference to seven pairs is confusing because earlier God instructed Noah to take one pair of each type of animal.*

Reading Strategy | **4**

Question Answer: *God initially decreed that humans should not live longer than 120 years. Noah might have been allowed to live longer because he was righteous.*

Cultural History

Clean and Unclean Beasts The terms "clean" and "unclean" refer to Jewish laws about what items are acceptable (kosher) for ritual or dietary use. The word *kosher* means "fit," and the word *terefah* means "unfit." For example, shellfish is considered unfit to eat. The laws also specify that dairy products and meat should never be served at the same meal or with the same plates and utensils. Fruits and vegetables, on the other hand, may be eaten at any time.

Learning Objectives
Analyzing theme. (SE)
Asking questions. (SE)
Delivering a speech. (TE)

Teach

The Secret of Life   Answer: *They would learn that God remembers God's people and keeps promises.*

Language History ☆

Cubits The cubit was a unit of length used in many ancient and medieval civilizations, including Egypt. The length of a cubit could vary from 18 to 21 inches. Just as the word *foot* implies that the measurement is based on a body part, a cubit was supposed to be the distance from the elbow to the end of the middle finger. Palms and spans are other units of measurement used by ancient peoples.

---

them, into the ark; they, and every beast after his kind, and all the cattle after their kind, and every creeping thing that creepeth upon the earth after his kind, and every fowl after his kind, every bird of every sort. And they went in unto Noah into the ark, two and two of all flesh, wherein is the breath of life. And they that went in, went in male and female of all flesh, as God had commanded him: and the Lord shut him in.

And the flood was forty days upon the earth; and the waters increased, and bare up the ark, and it was lift up above the earth. And the waters prevailed, and were increased greatly upon the earth; and the ark went upon the face of the waters. And the waters prevailed exceedingly upon the earth; and all the high hills, that were under the whole heaven, were covered. Fifteen ☆ cubits upward did the waters prevail; and the mountains were covered. And all flesh died that moved upon the earth, both of fowl, and of cattle, and of beast, and of every creeping thing that creepeth upon the earth, and every man: all in whose nostrils was the breath of life, of all that was in the dry land, died. And every living substance was destroyed which was upon the face of the ground, both man, and cattle, and the creeping things, and the fowl of heaven; and they were destroyed from the earth: and Noah only remained alive, and they that were with him in the ark. And the waters prevailed upon the earth an hundred and fifty days.

Chapter 8

And God remembered Noah, and every living thing, and all the cattle that was with him in the ark: and God made a wind to pass over the earth, and the waters assuaged;

the fountains also of the deep and the windows of heaven were stopped, and the rain from heaven was restrained; and the waters returned from off the earth continually: and after the end of the hundred and fifty days the waters were abated. And the ark rested in the seventh month, on the seventeenth day of the month, upon the mountains of Ararat. And the waters decreased continually until the tenth month: in the tenth month, on the first day of the month, were the tops of the mountains seen.

And it came to pass at the end of forty days, that Noah opened the window of the ark which he had made: and he sent forth a raven, which went forth to and fro, until the waters were dried up from off the earth. Also he sent forth a dove from him, to see if the waters were **abated** from off the face of the ground. But the dove found no rest for the sole of her foot, and she returned unto him into the ark; for the waters were on the face of the whole earth: then he put forth his hand, and took her, and pulled her in unto him into the ark. And he stayed yet another seven days; and again he sent forth the dove out of the ark; and the dove came in to him in the evening; and, lo, in her mouth was an olive leaf plucked off: so Noah knew that the waters were abated from off the earth. And he stayed yet other seven days; and sent forth the dove; which returned not again unto him any more.

And it came to pass in the six hundredth and first year, in the first month, the first day of the month, the waters were dried up from off the earth: and Noah removed the covering of the ark, and looked, and, behold, the face of the ground was dry. And in the second month, on the seven and twentieth day of the month, was the earth dried.

1   **The Secret of Life** *What reassuring lesson would readers of the Bible learn from this passage?*

Vocabulary

abate (ə bāt´) *adj.* to lessen or decrease

Grammar Practice

Adverb Clauses **Write on the board:** And <u>when the waters had swelled on the earth one hundred and fifty days</u>, God remembered Noah and all that were with him. Explain that the underlined portion is an adverb clause. An adverb clause can modify a verb, an adjective, or an adverb in the main clause. An adverb clause begins with a subordinating conjunction such as *after, although, because, if, since, when,* or *where.*

Have students combine sentences using adverb clauses.

1. Our team warmed up at one end of the gym. Our opponents warmed up at the other. *(Possible response: As our team warmed up at one end of the gym, our opponents warmed up at the other.)*

2. We were playing at home. That meant we had support from the crowd. *(Since we were playing at home, we had support from the crowd.)*

And God spake unto Noah, saying, "Go forth of the ark, thou, and thy wife, and thy sons, and thy sons' wives with thee. Bring forth with thee every living thing that is with thee, of all flesh, both of fowl, and of cattle, and of every creeping thing that creepeth upon the earth; that they may breed abundantly in the earth, and be fruitful, and multiply upon the earth." And Noah went forth, and his sons, and his wife, and his sons' wives with him: every beast, every creeping thing, and every fowl, and whatsoever creepeth upon the earth, after their kinds, went forth out of the ark.

And Noah builded an altar unto the Lord; and took of every clean beast, and of every clean fowl, and offered burnt offerings on the altar. And the Lord smelled a sweet savor;[5] and the Lord said in his heart, I will not again curse the ground any more for man's sake; for the imagination of man's heart is evil from his youth: neither will I again smite[6] any more every thing living, as I have done. While the earth remaineth, seedtime and harvest, and cold and heat, and summer and winter, and day and night shall not cease.

Chapter 9

And God blessed Noah and his sons, and said unto them, "Be fruitful, and multiply, and replenish the earth. And the fear of you and the dread of you shall be upon every beast of the earth, and upon every fowl of the air, upon all that moveth upon the earth, and upon all the fishes of the sea; into your hand are they delivered. Every moving thing that liveth shall be meat for you; even as the green herb have I given you all things. But flesh with the life thereof, which is the blood thereof, shall ye

not eat. And surely your blood of your lives will I require; at the hand of every beast will I require it, and at the hand of man; at the hand of every man's brother will I require the life of man. Whoso sheddeth man's blood, by man shall his blood be shed: for in the image of God made he man. And you, be ye fruitful, and multiply; bring forth abundantly in the earth, and multiply therein.

And God spake unto Noah, and to his sons with him, saying, "And I, behold, I establish my covenant with you, and with your seed after you; and with every living creature that is with you, of the fowl, of the cattle, and of every beast of the earth with you; from all that go out of the ark, to every beast of the earth. And I will establish my covenant with you; neither shall all flesh be cut off any more by the waters of a flood; neither shall there any more be a flood to destroy the earth."

And God said, "This is the token of the covenant which I make between me and you and every living creature that is with you, for perpetual generations: I do set my bow in the cloud, and it shall be for a token of a covenant between me and the earth. And it shall come to pass, when I bring a cloud over the earth, that the bow shall be seen in the cloud: and I will remember my covenant, which is between me and you and every living creature of all flesh; and the waters shall no more become a flood to destroy all flesh. And the bow shall be in the cloud; and I will look upon it, that I may remember the everlasting covenant between God and every living creature of all flesh that is upon the earth.

---

5. A *savor* is a smell or an odor.
6. *Smite* means "strike down" or "attack."

2 Question *What does the size of Noah's sacrifice indicate?*

THE FLOOD **475**

3

2

Teach

Reading Strategy 2

Question **Answer:** *The enormity of his sacrifice indicates the solemnity of the moment and the gratitude Noah feels toward God for sparing him and his family.*

Literary Element 3

Theme Have students read the words that God speaks to Noah and his sons. **Ask:** What do the details about the covenant suggest about the theme? *(The covenant supports the theme of rewarding good people. God makes a covenant with Noah because Noah has trusted in God and been a good person.)*

Progress Check

Can students identify the story's theme?

If No → See Unit 3 Teaching Resources Book, p. 43.

 To check students' understanding of the selection, see Unit 3 Teaching Resources Book, p. 48.

Learning Objectives
Asking questions. (SE)
Analyzing theme. (TE)
Using adverb clauses. (TE)

English Learners

DIFFERENTIATED INSTRUCTION

Intermediate Explain that the endings of verbs indicate the tense and number of the verb. For example, the *–s* in *moves* indicates that it is a present tense, third-person verb. Explain that when the King James Bible was written, the present tense, third-person ending was *–eth*. Review the past tense ending in *–d* or *–ed*. Point out

that some past tenses that are irregular in modern English *(build/built)* are "regular" in this passage *(builded)*.

Approaching Level

DIFFERENTIATED INSTRUCTION

Reading Fluency Have students work on fluency in mixed-ability groups by taking turns reading aloud the sentences in Chapter 9. Allow them to practice pronouncing unfamiliar words, using dictionaries as needed. For more difficult sentences, suggest that students work with separate clauses before reading aloud whole sentences.

After You Read

Assess

1. Answers will vary.

2. (a) Noah is a righteous man. (b) God punishes the wicked and rewards the righteous.

3. (a) He sends forth a raven and then a dove to search for land. (b) Doves symbolize peace or reconciliation. This derives from their use as "messengers" of the end of the Flood, or the reconciliation between God and humankind.

4. (a) He builds an altar and sacrifices some of the animals. (b) He is grateful to God.

5. (a) They are responsible for replenishing the earth, and are forbidden from eating the lifeblood of animals or shedding the blood of humans. (b) They committed these sins.

6. (a) Most students will associate rainbows with hope. (b) The rainbow is an effective symbol of the optimism suggested by the covenant.

7. They would learn that God punishes wickedness, rewards virtue, will never again flood the earth, and forbids them from eating the lifeblood of animals or shedding the blood of humans.

8. Students may recognize that some people find solace in believing that a higher power is watching over them.

After You Read

Respond and Think Critically

Respond and Interpret

1. If you had had the opportunity to interview Noah after the Flood, what questions would you have asked him?

2. (a) Why does God spare Noah and his family? (b) What lesson does this contain for followers of Judaism and Christianity?

3. (a) What test does Noah devise to determine whether the waters have receded? (b) What do doves often symbolize in the modern world? Explain how that symbolism might relate to this story.

4. (a) What does Noah do after leaving the ark? (b) What do his actions reveal about his character?

Analyze and Evaluate

5. (a) What responsibilities does God place on Noah and his descendants? (b) What does this suggest about humankind before the Flood?

6. (a) What ideas or feelings do you associate with rainbows? (b) In your opinion, is the rainbow an effective **symbol**, or representation, of God's covenant? Explain.

Connect

7. **Big Idea** **The Secret of Life** What spiritual lessons would followers of Judaism learn from this story?

8. **Connect to Today** How does religious faith help some people face terrifying ordeals or disasters in today's world?

Literary Element Theme

Review the story and consider its message, noting the dialogue and the events that take place.

1. What do you think is the theme of this story?

2. (a) What does water often symbolize in literature and art? (b) How does this symbol relate to the theme of this text?

Reading Strategy Question

Review your chart on page 471, and then answer the following questions.

1. What events or details did you find confusing in the story?

2. What effect, if any, did these confusing events have on your appreciation of the story? Explain.

Vocabulary Practice

Practice with Synonyms With a partner, match each boldfaced vocabulary word below with its synonym. Use a thesaurus or a dictionary to check your answers. You will not use all the answer choices.

1. corrupt   **a.** diminish

2. covenant   **b.** promise

3. abate   **c.** unethical

                d. insincere

Writing

Write a Narrative Imagine what life was like on Noah's ark for one of the animals. Choose either third-person or first-person point of view and write a narrative about that animal's experiences. Your narrative should suggest a theme that relates to God's covenant with Noah. Use figurative language to vividly capture the animal's experience and to express your personal style.

LOG ON ▶ **Literature** Online

Selection Resources For Selection Quizzes, eFlash-cards, and Reading-Writing Connection activities, go to glencoe.com and enter QuickPass code GLW6053u3.

Literary Element

1. God punishes the wicked, rewards and protects the righteous, and has an unbreakable covenant with those who trust in God.

2. (a) It often symbolizes rebirth and renewal. (b) Humankind is "reborn" through the Flood. God floods the earth to wash away the sinful and gives humanity another chance.

Reading Strategy

1. Students may cite the various periods of rain, the difficulty of fitting all the animals on the ark, the discrepancy in the number of pairs of animals, and the huge animal sacrifice that Noah offers to God after the Flood.

2. Encourage students to support their opinions with sound reasoning and examples from the story.

Vocabulary

1. c **2.** b **3.** a

Writing

Students' narratives should have a clear theme and a consistent point of view, comment on the relationship of the animal to God and Noah, and use figurative language.

Before You Read

The Book of Ruth from the Hebrew Bible

Connect to the Sacred Text

Do you look forward to new situations, or are you apprehensive about them? Freewrite for a few minutes about your reactions to new experiences.

Build Background

The Israelites consider Ruth an outsider because her homeland is Moab, a neighboring kingdom of idol worshippers. Furthermore, because Ruth is a childless widow with no property rights, she is in urgent need of shelter and protection.

Set Purposes for Reading

Big Idea **The Secret of Life**

As you read, ask yourself, What can I learn about Judaism from the book of Ruth?

Literary Element **Parallelism**

Parallelism is the use of words, phrases, or sentences that have similar grammatical structures. **Repetition,** the recurring use of the same words, phrases, or sentences, is closely related to parallelism. As you read, ask yourself, What are examples of parallelism and repetition in this text?

Reading Strategy **Respond to Characters**

When you **respond to characters,** you react to what you like, dislike, or find surprising about the characters in a work. As you read, ask yourself, What do I think about each character?

Tip: Make a Web Use a character web like the one below to organize details about Naomi, Ruth, and Boaz.

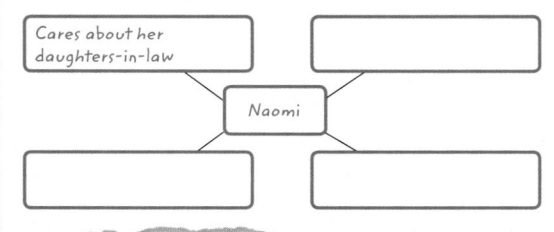

Learning Objectives

For pages 477–485

In studying this text, you will focus on the following objectives:

Literary Study: Analyzing parallelism.

Reading: Responding to characters.

Vocabulary

sojourn (sō´jurn) v. to stay or reside temporarily; p. 478 *After sojourning briefly in France, I returned home to the United States.*

glean (glēn) v. to gather what's left by reapers; to gather slowly, bit by bit; to discover or find out slowly; p. 479 *The cows gleaned the grain the harvesters had left behind.*

winnow (win´ō) v. to remove by exposing to air currents; to free from lighter particles; to sift; to separate; p. 480 *The inspectors winnowed out the misshapen pieces of candy.*

redeem (ri dēm´) v. to buy back, as with property; p. 482 *After many years of hard work, my father redeemed his mortgage.*

Before You Read

Focus

Summary

There is a famine in Judah, and so Naomi and her husband travel to Moab to find food. Their sons marry Moabite women but die ten years later. Naomi, also widowed, and her daughter-in-law Ruth return to Judah. Ruth works in the fields of Boaz, a kinsman of her late husband, Elimelech. Boaz treats Ruth kindly, marries her, and welcomes Naomi into his household. Naomi becomes foster mother to Ruth's first son, from whose line the future king David will descend.

 For summaries in languages other than English, see Unit 3 Teaching Resources Book, pp. 50–55.

Vocabulary

Practice with Connotations Have students find each vocabulary word in the selection. Ask them if each word has a positive, negative, or neutral connotation.

 For additional vocabulary practice, see Unit 3 Teaching Resources Book, p. 58.

Selection Skills

Literary Elements
- Parallelism (SE pp. 477, 478, 482, 484; TE p. 480)
- Theme (SE p. 484)

Reading Skills
- Respond to Characters (SE pp. 477, 479–480, 484; TE p. 482)
- Paraphrase (TE p. 480)

The Book of Ruth

Vocabulary Skills
- Denotation and Connotation (SE p. 484; TE p. 477)

Speaking/Listening/Viewing Skills
- Analyze Art (SE p. 481)

Writing Skills/Grammar
- Persuasive Essay (SE p. 485)
- Apply Parallelism (TE p. 478)
- Graphic Story (TE p. 482)

Teach

Big Idea | 1

The Secret of Life **Answer:** *She hopes that God will give them new husbands.*

Literary Element | 2

Parallelism **Answer:** *"Turn again, my daughters," a repeated phrase, illustrates both parallelism and repetition.*

 For an audio recording of this selection, use Listening Library Audio CD-ROM.

Readability Scores

Dale-Chall: 8.1
DRP: 52
Lexile: 820

The Book of Ruth

from the King James *version of the* Bible

Chapter 1

Now it came to pass in the days when the judges ruled, that there was a famine in the land. And a certain man of Bethlehem-Judah went to **sojourn** in the country of Moab, he, and his wife, and his two sons. And the name of the man was Elimelech, and the name of his wife Naomi,[1] and the name of his two sons Mahlon and Chilion, Ephrathites[2] of Bethlehem-Judah. And they came into the country of Moab, and continued there.

And Elimelech Naomi's husband died; and she was left, and her two sons. And they took them wives of the women of Moab; the name of the one was Orpah, and the name of the other Ruth: and they dwelled there about ten years. And Mahlon and Chilion died also both of them; and the woman was left of her two sons and her husband.

Then she arose with her daughters-in-law, that she might return from the country of Moab: for she had heard in the country of Moab how that the Lord had visited his people in giving them bread. Wherefore she went forth out of the place where she was, and her two daughters-in-law with her; and they went on the way to return unto the land of Judah.

And Naomi said unto her two daughters-in-law, "Go, return each to her mother's house: the Lord deal kindly with you, as ye have dealt with the dead, and with me. The Lord grant you that ye may find rest, each of you in the house of her husband." Then she kissed them; and they lifted up their voice, and wept. And they said unto her, "Surely we will return with thee unto thy people."

And Naomi said, "Turn again, my daughters: why will ye go with me? Are there yet any more sons in my womb, that they may be your husbands? Turn again, my daughters, go your way; for I am too old to have a husband. If I should say, I have hope, if I should have a husband also tonight, and should also bear sons; would ye tarry[3] for them till they were grown?

---

1. In Hebrew, *Naomi* means "beautiful," "pleasant," or "delightful."
2. *Ephrathites* are citizens of Bethlehem.

Vocabulary

sojourn (sō′jurn) *v.* to stay or reside temporarily

---

3. *Tarry* means "wait" or "remain."

The Secret of Life *What hope does Naomi express for her daughters-in-law by instructing them to turn back?* | **1**

Parallelism *Identify an example of both parallelism and repetition in these lines.* | **2**

Writing Practice

Apply Parallelism Review the definition of parallelism with students. Point out the parallelism in the selection's first paragraph: "And the name of the man was Elimelech, and the name of his wife Naomi, and the name of his two sons Mahlon and Chilion, Ephrathites of Bethlehem-Judah." Explain that "and the name of" is an example of parallelism.

Have students write a paragraph that utilizes at least one or two sentences with parallelism. After they have finished, have them exchange paragraphs with a partner. Have each partner check for correct use of parallelism. Then, ask several volunteers to share their paragraphs with the class.

Would ye stay for them from having husbands? Nay, my daughters; for it grieveth me much for your sakes that the hand of the Lord is gone out against me."

And they lifted up their voice, and wept again: and Orpah kissed her mother-in-law; but Ruth clave[4] unto her. And she said, "Behold, thy sister-in-law is gone back unto her people, and unto her gods: return thou after thy sister-in-law." And Ruth said, "Entreat me not to leave thee, or to return from following after thee: for whither thou goest, I will go; and where thou lodgest, I will lodge: thy people shall be my people, and thy God my God: where thou diest, will I die, and there will I be buried: the Lord do so to me, and more also, if ought but death part thee and me." When she saw that she was steadfastly minded to go with her, then she left speaking unto her. So they two went until they came to Bethlehem.

And it came to pass, when they were come to Bethlehem, that all the city was moved about them, and they said, "Is this Naomi?" And she said unto them, "Call me not Naomi, call me Mara:[5] for the Almighty hath dealt very bitterly with me. I went out full, and the Lord hath brought me home again empty: why then call ye me Naomi, seeing the Lord hath testified against me, and the Almighty hath afflicted me?"

So Naomi returned, and Ruth the Moabitess, her daughter-in-law, with her, which returned out of the country of Moab: and they came to Bethlehem in the beginning of barley harvest.

---

4. *Clave* is an archaic form of the verb *cleaved*, meaning "adhered or clung to."
5. *Mara* means "bitter."

3 | Respond to Characters *How did you respond to Ruth when you read her plea to Naomi? What does this plea reveal about Ruth?*

Chapter 2

And Naomi had a kinsman of her husband's, a mighty man of wealth, of the family of Elimelech; and his name was Boaz.[6]

And Ruth the Moabitess said unto Naomi, "Let me now go to the field, and **glean** ears of corn after him in whose sight I shall find grace." And she said unto her, "Go, my daughter." And she went, and came, and gleaned in the field after the reapers: and her hap[7] was to light on a part of the field belonging unto Boaz, who was of the kindred of Elimelech.

And, behold, Boaz came from Bethlehem, and said unto the reapers, "The Lord be with you." And they answered him, "The Lord bless thee." Then said Boaz unto his servant that was set over the reapers, "Whose damsel is this?" And the servant that was set over the reapers answered and said, "It is the Moabitish damsel that came back with Naomi out of the country of Moab: And she said, 'I pray you, let me glean and gather after the reapers among the sheaves': so she came, and hath continued even from the morning until now, that she tarried a little in the house."

Then said Boaz unto Ruth, "Hearest thou not, my daughter? Go not to glean in another field, neither go from hence, but abide here fast by my maidens: Let thine eyes be on the field that they do reap, and go thou after them: have I not charged the young men that they shall not touch thee? And when thou art athirst, go unto

4

---

6. In Hebrew, the name *Boaz* is associated with the word for strength. *Boaz* is also the name of a pillar in a great temple built by Solomon, the son and successor of King David.
7. *Hap* means "luck" or "lot."

Vocabulary

glean (glēn) *v.* to gather what's left by reapers; to gather slowly, bit by bit; to discover or find out slowly

THE BOOK OF RUTH **479**

Approaching Level

DIFFERENTIATED INSTRUCTION

Use Farming Vocabulary Explain that farming and agriculture, like other types of work, have a specialized vocabulary. Many of their terms are used to enhance everyday language.

Write the following sentences on the board and have students use the literal definition of each underlined term to figure out its everyday meaning.

1. Each fall we have another <u>crop</u> of new movies. *(group; batch)*
2. Frank tried to <u>sow</u> suspicion among Sherry's friends in order to turn them against her. *(plant)*
3. It was time, thought Carla, to <u>reap</u> the rewards for all the favors she had done. *(collect; gather)*

Teach

Reading Strategy | **3**

Respond to Characters
Answer: *Some students may think Ruth should be more independent. Others may respond positively, since her plea reveals her loyalty, courage, and obedience.*

📁 For additional practice using the reading skill or strategy, see Unit 3 Teaching Resources Book, p. 57.

Reading Strategy | **4**

Respond to Characters
Ask: Were you surprised by Boaz's kindness to Ruth in the field? Why or why not? *(Some may suggest that they are surprised that Boaz is so kind to her. Others may note that he was a friend of her husband's.)*

Cultural History ☆

Gleaning According to Jewish law, the poor were entitled to whatever food the reapers dropped. In Leviticus 19:9–10 for example, it says, "When thou reapest the corn of thy land, thou shalt not cut down all that is on the face of the earth to the very ground: nor shalt thou gather the ears that remain. Neither shalt thou gather the bunches and grapes that fall down in thy vineyard: but shalt leave them to the poor and the strangers to take."

Learning Objectives
Analyzing parallelism. (SE)
Responding to characters. (SE)
Applying parallelism in a paragraph. (TE)

479

Teach

Literary Element   1

Parallelism **Ask:** What repeated word in the paragraph beginning "So she gleaned" creates parallelism? *(The repetition of the word* gleaned *creates parallelism in the paragraph.)*

Big Idea   2

The Secret of Life **Answer:** *Boaz's reference is to Ruth's conversion to Judaism, the faith of Naomi and Boaz.*

Reading Strategy   3

Respond to Characters **Answer:** *He displays compassion and generosity. Readers are supposed to respond positively to him.*

---

the vessels, and drink of that which the young men have drawn."

Then she fell on her face, and bowed herself to the ground, and said unto him, "Why have I found grace in thine eyes, that thou shouldest take knowledge of me, seeing I am a stranger?"

And Boaz answered and said unto her, "It hath fully been shewed me, all that thou hast done unto thy mother-in-law since the death of thine husband and how thou hast left thy father and thy mother, and the land of thy nativity, and art come unto a people which thou knewest not heretofore. The Lord recompense[8] thy work, and a full reward be given thee of the Lord God of Israel, under whose wings thou art come to trust."

Then she said, "Let me find favor in thy sight, my lord; for that thou hast comforted me, and for that thou hast spoken friendly unto thine handmaid, though I be not like unto one of thine handmaidens."

And Boaz said unto her, "At mealtime come thou hither, and eat of the bread, and dip thy morsel in the vinegar." And she sat beside the reapers: and he reached her parched corn, and she did eat, and was sufficed, and left.

And when she was risen up to glean, Boaz commanded his young men, saying, "Let her glean even among the sheaves, and reproach her not: And let fall also some of the handfuls of purpose for her, and leave them, that she may glean them, and rebuke her not."

1   So she gleaned in the field until even, and beat out that she had gleaned: and it

was about an ephah[9] of barley. And she took it up, and went into the city: and her mother-in-law saw what she had gleaned: and she brought forth, and gave to her that she had reserved after she was sufficed. And her mother-in-law said unto her, "Where hast thou gleaned today? And where wroughtest thou? Blessed be he that did take knowledge of thee." And she shewed her mother-in-law with whom she had wrought, and said, "The man's name with whom I wrought today is Boaz."

And Naomi said unto her daughter-in-law, "Blessed be he of the Lord, who hath not left off his kindness to the living and to the dead." And Naomi said unto her, "The man is near of kin unto us, one of our next kinsmen." And Ruth the Moabitess said, "He said unto me also, 'Thou shalt keep fast by my young men, until they have ended all my harvest.'" And Naomi said unto Ruth her daughter-in-law, "It is good, my daughter, that thou go out with his maidens, that they meet thee not in any other field." So she kept fast by the maidens of Boaz to glean unto the end of barley harvest and of wheat harvest; and dwelt with her mother-in-law.

Chapter 3

Then Naomi her mother-in-law said unto her, "My daughter, shall I not seek rest for thee, that it may be well with thee? And now is not Boaz of our kindred, with whose maidens thou wast? Behold, he **winnoweth** barley tonight in the threshing floor. Wash thyself therefore, and anoint thee, and put

---

8. *Recompense* (rek′əm pens′) means "repay."

2   **The Secret of Life** *Explain the meaning of this reference as it applies to Ruth's faith.*

3   **Respond to Characters** *What character traits does Boaz reveal in these instructions to his workers? How do you think readers are meant to respond to Boaz?*

480   UNIT 3   SOUTHWEST ASIA

9. An *ephah* is a Hebrew unit of measure that equals a little more than a bushel.

Vocabulary

winnow (win′ō) *v.* to remove by exposing to air currents; to free from lighter particles; to sift; to separate

---

Reading Practice

Paraphrase Point out to students that while the original Hebrew language of the Tanakh has never changed, there have been various translations over time. In some of these versions, the translators have tried to use more modern language, though not always to everyone's satisfaction.

Working together as a class, have each student select a paragraph or two of the selection. Ask each student to paraphrase the passage in a way that reflects his or her understanding. Then have students work together to make a single version that all parties find acceptable.

thy raiment[10] upon thee, and get thee down to the floor: but make not thyself known unto the man, until he shall have done eating and drinking. And it shall be, when he lieth down, that thou shalt mark the place where he shall lie, and thou shalt go in, and uncover his feet, and lay thee down; and he will tell thee what thou shalt do." And she said unto her, "All that thou sayest unto me I will do."

And she went down unto the floor, and did according to all that her mother-in-law bade her. And when Boaz had eaten and drunk, and his heart was merry, he went to lie down at the end of the heap of corn: and she came softly, and uncovered his feet, and laid her down. And it came to pass at midnight, that the man was afraid, and turned himself: and, behold, a woman lay at his feet.

And he said, "Who art thou?" And she answered, "I am Ruth thine handmaid: spread therefore thy skirt over thine handmaid; for thou art a near kinsman."

And he said, "Blessed be thou of the Lord, my daughter: for thou hast shewed more kindness in the latter end than at the beginning, inasmuch as thou followedst not young men, whether poor or rich. And now, my daughter, fear not; I will do to thee all that thou requirest: for all the city of my people doth know that thou art a virtuous woman. And now it is true that I am thy near kinsman: howbeit there is a kinsman nearer than I. Tarry this night, and it shall be in the morning, that if he will perform unto thee the part of a kinsman, well; let him do the kinsman's part: but if he will not do the part of a kinsman to thee, then will I do the part of a kinsman to thee, as the Lord liveth: lie down until the morning."

---

10. *Raiment* (rā′mənt) is another word for clothing.

4 The Secret of Life *What might be one secret to a good life, according to this passage?*

Ruth parting from Naomi, 1803. William Blake. Wash, pencil, coloured chalk. Southampton City Art Gallery, Hampshire, UK.

View the Art Poet William Blake was one of England's greatest religious artists. This watercolor depicts Naomi, Ruth, and Orpah. How would you describe the contrast between Ruth and Orpah?

And she lay at his feet until the morning: and she rose up before one could know another. And he said, "Let it not be known that a woman came into the floor." Also he said, "Bring the vail that thou hast upon thee, and hold it." And when she held it, he measured six measures of barley, and laid it on her: and she went into the city.

And when she came to her mother-in-law, she said, "Who art thou, my daughter?" And she told her all that the man had done to her. And she said, "These six measures of barley gave he me; for he said to me, 'Go not empty unto thy mother-in-law.'" Then said she, "Sit still, my daughter, until thou know how the matter will fall: for the man will not be in rest, until he have finished the thing this day."

Big Idea | **4**

The Secret of Life Answer:
Virtuous behavior is often noticed, appreciated, and rewarded.

View the Art

Answer: *Ruth is passionate. Her head is bowed as she clings to her mother-in-law. Orpah departs with a hurried step as though ashamed of leaving Naomi.*

Poet William Blake (1757–1827) was also known as an English engraver and one of England's greatest religious artists. Blake enrolled in the Royal Academy of Arts in 1779 and concentrated on using watercolors on paper to paint objects from the Bible and British history. In Blake's lifetime he was considered mad and was often overlooked; however, in the early twenty-first century he was renowned as the first and most original of the Romantic poets.

Learning Objectives
Responding to characters. (SE)
Analyzing parallelism. (TE)
Paraphrasing a passage. (TE)

English Learners

DIFFERENTIATED INSTRUCTION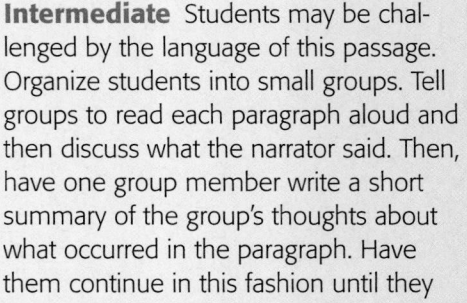

Intermediate Students may be challenged by the language of this passage. Organize students into small groups. Tell groups to read each paragraph aloud and then discuss what the narrator said. Then, have one group member write a short summary of the group's thoughts about what occurred in the paragraph. Have them continue in this fashion until they have finished each paragraph on the page.

Approaching Level

DIFFERENTIATED INSTRUCTION

Mime To help students gain a better grasp of the events of the story, have them work with a small group to mime the actions on this page. Tell students to use gestures and facial expressions to reveal the feelings of the characters. Allow students time to practice. Remind them that pantomimes have no speaking or sound. Have groups perform their mimes for the class.

Teach

| Reading Strategy | 1 |

Respond to Characters
Ask: Are readers supposed to be happy for Naomi? *(The birth of Ruth's son and the blessings of the other women reveal that readers should be happy for Naomi.)*

| Literary Element | 2 |

Parallelism Answer: *The repetition of the word* begat *creates parallelism. The simplicity of this parallelism and repetition helps the reader understand the ancestral line that led to King David.*

Literary History ☆

King David Naomi's great grandson is David. Most people know David from his victory over the giant, Goliath. David killed Goliath with a stone and a sling. Later, David became king of Israel.

To check students' understanding of the selection, see Unit 3 Teaching Resources Book, p. 61.

Chapter 4

Then went Boaz up to the gate, and sat him down there: and, behold, the kinsman of whom Boaz spake came by; unto whom he said, "Ho, such a one! turn aside, sit down here." And he turned aside, and sat down. And he took ten men of the elders of the city, and said, "Sit ye down here." And they sat down.

And he said unto the kinsman, "Naomi, that is come again out of the country of Moab, selleth a parcel of land, which was our brother Elimelech's: and I thought to advertise thee, saying, 'Buy it before the inhabitants, and before the elders of my people. If thou wilt **redeem** it, redeem it: but if thou wilt not redeem it, then tell me, that I may know: for there is none to redeem it beside thee; and I am after thee.'" And he said, "I will redeem it." Then said Boaz, "What day thou buyest the field of the hand of Naomi, thou must buy it also of Ruth the Moabitess, the wife of the dead, to raise up the name of the dead upon his inheritance." And the kinsman said, "I cannot redeem it for myself, lest I mar mine own inheritance: redeem thou my right to thyself; for I cannot redeem it."

Now this was the manner in former time in Israel concerning redeeming and concerning changing, for to confirm all things; a man plucked off his shoe, and gave it to his neighbor: and this was a testimony in Israel. Therefore the kinsman said unto Boaz, "Buy it for thee." So he drew off his shoe. And Boaz said unto the elders, and unto all the people, "Ye are witnesses this day, that I have bought all that was Elimelech's, and all that was Chilion's and Mahlon's, of the hand of Naomi. Moreover Ruth the Moabitess, the wife of Mahlon, have I purchased to be my wife, to raise up the name of the dead upon his inheritance,

that the name of the dead be not cut off from among his brethren, and from the gate of his place: ye are witnesses this day."

And all the people that were in the gate, and the elders, said, "We are witnesses. The Lord make the woman that is come into thine house like Rachel and like Leah,[11] which two did build the house of Israel: and do thou worthily in Ephratah, and be famous in Bethlehem: And let thy house be like the house of Pharez, whom Tamar bare unto Judah, of the seed which the Lord shall give thee of this young woman."

So Boaz took Ruth, and she was his wife: and when he went in unto her, the Lord gave her conception, and she bare a son. And the women said unto Naomi, "Blessed be the Lord, which hath not left thee this day without a kinsman, that his name may be famous in Israel. And he shall be unto thee a restorer of thy life, and a nourisher of thine old age: for thy daughter-in-law, which loveth thee, which is better to thee than seven sons, hath borne him."

And Naomi took the child, and laid it in her bosom, and became nurse unto it. And the women her neighbors gave it a name, saying, "There is a son born to Naomi; and they called his name Obed: he is the father of Jesse, the father of David."

Now these are the generations of Pharez: Pharez begat Hezron, and Hezron begat Ram, and Ram begat Amminadab, and Amminadab begat Nahshon, and Nahshon begat Salmon, and Salmon begat Boaz, and Boaz begat Obed, and Obed begat Jesse, and Jesse begat David.[12] ∽

1
☆

---

11. *Rachel* and *Leah* were two of the wives of Jacob (or Israel) and are therefore ancestors of the Jewish people.
12. *David* was one of the most revered kings of Israel. He ruled from c. 1000 B.C. to c. 962 B.C.

Parallelism *Identify the parallelism and repetition in the passage that follows. What purpose do they serve?* **2**

Vocabulary

redeem (ri dēm′) *v.* to buy back, as with property

Writing Practice

 **Write a Graphic Story**
Have students turn this excerpt from the Book of Ruth into a graphic story. Tell students that graphic stories rely more on pictures than words to tell a story. For an example, have students turn to the excerpt from Marjane Satrapi's *Persepolis* on pages 532–541.

Allow students to create their stories in either black and white or color. Tell them to include the most important events of the story in the correct order. After students have finished, ask volunteers to share their graphic stories with the class. Lead a discussion about the similarities and differences between the stories.

After You Read

Respond and Think Critically

Respond and Interpret

1. Which character in the story did you most admire? Explain.

2. (a)What tragedy befalls Naomi and her daughters-in-law in Moab? (b)Why do you think Naomi asks people to call her *Mara* after the tragedy?

3. (a)What happens to Ruth and Naomi at the end? (b)How does Naomi's attitude toward God change during the course of the story?

4. (a)What happens to the property owned by Naomi's husband? (b)In your opinion, why does Boaz remind the redeemer of the particulars of Bethlehem's property laws?

Analyze and Evaluate

5. How does dialogue help develop the main characters in the story?

6. How might Boaz's name **symbolize,** or represent, his character?

7. How does concluding with King David's lineage help illuminate two purposes of the story?

Connect

8. **Big Idea** **The Secret of Life** (a)How is Naomi's faith in God rewarded? (b) What might this reveal about the secret of life?

9. **Connect to Today** How does the status of women in ancient Hebrew culture compare with the status of women in modern Western society?

You're the Critic: Point/Counterpoint

Is the Book of Ruth a Feminist Work?

Each of the following passages offers a different view on the question above.

Ruth harvesting.
Bible of Borso d'Este.

"None of Ruth's characters are warriors, priests, prophets, or kings. It is entirely a domestic tale of two women—Naomi and her daughter-in-law Ruth, the reversals they suffer, and how they manage to salvage their fortunes by their own wits."
—Virginia Stem Owens

"The story of Ruth . . . is remembered primarily because Ruth provides the womb through which the line of King David can flourish . . . I doubt Ruth's story would have been canonized had it been only about women's loyalties."
—Vanessa L. Ochs

Group Activity Discuss the following questions with classmates. Refer to the passages above and cite evidence from the book of Ruth for support.

1. What elements in the book of Ruth do you think support a feminist interpretation of the story?

2. What elements argue against a feminist interpretation?

You're the Critic

1. Students might describe the narrative's focus on well-defined, appealing female characters; Ruth's success in gleaning barley; and the deep affection between women.

2. Students might note the patriarchal character of ancient Judaic society; Ruth's humble behavior in the presence of Boaz; and the value of the male line of descent.

 For additional selection assessment, see Assessment Resources, pp. 95–96.

After You Read

Assess

1. All three main characters have admirable traits. Students are likely to choose the one with whom they most closely identify.

2. (a) They are all widowed and vulnerable. (b) Her new name reflects the bitterness of her situation.

3. (a) Ruth marries Boaz, and he takes care of her and Naomi. Naomi becomes their child's foster mother. (b) At first, she cannot understand why God has made her suffer. Later, she praises God for his blessings.

4. (a) It is passed on to Boaz after being offered first to a kinsman. (b) He probably does this to discourage him. Boaz wants to marry Ruth.

5. It reveals the characters' thoughts, feelings and personalities to make them seem more like real people.

6. His name symbolizes a strong and noble character on which a future dynasty will be built.

7. It draws attention to his ancestry and makes a plea for acceptance of outsiders (as Ruth was not originally from Judah).

8. (a) Although she does not understand why God has improved her life, she adheres to her faith and appreciates her blessings. (b) One secret of life might be that God will continue to watch over his people, even if they are suffering.

9. Ancient Hebrew women were limited to domestic work. They rarely owned property and usually depended on male family members for financial support and social status. Women in modern Western society can chose their own professions, support themselves, own property, and create their own social lives.

After You Read

Assess

Literary Element

1. **(C)** is the correct answer. The quotation contains two clauses.
2. **(A)** is the correct answer. **(B), (C),** and **(D)** are incorrect; **(E)** is correct but describes the parallel structure less exactly than **(A)**.

Progress Check

Can students identify parallelism?

If No → See Unit 3, Teaching Resources Book, p. 56.

Review: Theme

1. Possible answers: Loyalty and love can overcome many obstacles. Faith in God will be rewarded. Outsiders can be loyal and loving.
2. Ruth's loyalty to Naomi brings her happiness. Boaz's loyalty to his family obligations and his love for Ruth bring him happiness. Ruth's conversion to Naomi's religion brings her the respect and love of Boaz. Ruth's loyalty and love for Naomi and Boaz is rewarded.

SAT Skills Practice

1. Ruth's response to Naomi, "thy people shall be my people, and thy God my God," is best described as an example of parallel

   (A) words
   (B) metaphors
   (C) clauses
   (D) similes
   (E) sentences

2. Naomi's blessing of her daughters-in-law, "the Lord deal kindly with you, as ye have dealt with the dead, and with me," is best described as an example of parallel

   (A) tenses
   (B) sentences
   (C) clauses
   (D) images
   (E) words

Review: Theme

As you learned on page 471, the **theme** of a literary work is its main insight or central message about life. As a sacred text, the story of Ruth is meant to teach a lesson or present a central idea about Judaism.

Partner Activity With a partner, discuss the theme of the book of Ruth. Then answer the following questions.

1. What do you think is the central idea or lesson to be learned in the book of Ruth?
2. What evidence from the story can you cite to support your opinion?

LOG ON ▶ **Literature** Online

Selection Resources For Selection Quizzes, eFlashcards, and Reading-Writing Connection activities, go to glencoe.com and enter QuickPass code GLW6053u3.

---

484 UNIT 3 SOUTHWEST ASIA

When you **respond** to characters, you note your initial reactions to them, as well as details that linger in your mind. Refer to the chart you made on page 477 and then answer these questions.

1. (a) What qualities does Naomi demonstrate? What qualities does Boaz demonstrate? (b) What words or actions reveal these qualities?
2. Was your response to Ruth favorable or unfavorable? Explain.

Vocabulary Practice

Practice with Denotation and Connotation
The **denotation** of a word is its literal definition. A word's **connotations**, or implied meanings, are often related to the intensity of a word's meaning. With a partner, identify connotations by completing a graphic organizer for each boldfaced vocabulary word.

sojourn   glean   winnow   redeem

EXAMPLE:

Vocabulary word: grieve	→	Similar word: mourn

Explanation: *Grieve* has stronger connotations. While both words imply sadness over a loss, *mourn* connotes a lingering sadness, while *grieve* connotes a powerful, overwhelming despair.

Academic Vocabulary

*Naomi and Ruth become poor when they are widowed; Boaz marries Ruth and **restores** the living conditions of the two women.*

Restore is an academic word. In more casual conversation, you may hear someone say that a judge **restored** order in a court. Using context clues in the sentence above, try to figure out the meaning of this word.

For more on academic vocabulary, see pages 36–37 and R83–R85.

Reading Strategy

1. (a) Naomi demonstrates ingenuity, loyalty, and kindness. Boaz demonstrates strength, loyalty, and compassion. (b) Students can cite Naomi's interest in the welfare of her daughters-in-law, her willingness to help Ruth win Boaz's favor, and Boaz's kind treatment of Ruth.
2. Answers will vary.

484

Vocabulary

Sample answers:

Vocabulary word: sojourn; Similar word: travel; Explanation: *sojourn* has the stronger connotation; Vocabulary word: glean; Similar word: discover; Explanation: *Glean* has the stronger connotation. Vocabulary word: winnow; Similar word: remove; Explanation: *winnow* has the stronger connotation; Vocabu-

lary word: redeem; Similar word: buy; Explanation: *redeem* has the stronger connotation

Academic Vocabulary

Restore means to return someone or something to its original state, or to renew.

Respond Through Writing

Persuasive Essay

Argue a Position When Ruth moved to Judah with Naomi, she became an immigrant who needed help to survive in her new community. Imagine you are Ruth, and in a persuasive essay, convince your fellow Judeans to provide the resources you need as a newcomer. Present arguments and evidence in favor of your position.

Understand the Task An **argument** is a logical statement supported by evidence that is used to defend a position in persuasive writing.

Prewrite Before you draft your paper, research possible resources you might benefit from as an immigrant. Record and organize your research in a chart like the one below. Then use your research to create logical arguments.

Ruth's Needs	Resources
Instruction in local customs	

Draft Formulate a clear thesis, with credible and relevant evidence to support it. Refer to your experiences (as Ruth) in your essay. Make sure your arguments are structured logically and that they anticipate opposing arguments or biases your readers may have. Sometimes it is helpful to use sentence frames as you write. For example, your introduction will include your thesis, which might be stated as follows:

Like me, immigrants in your community want to fit in, but may need _____ to help them do so.

Revise As you revise, make sure you have used persuasive techniques, such as appeals to ethics or emotions, to convince your readers.

Edit and Proofread Proofread your paper, correcting any errors in spelling, grammar, and punctuation. Review the Grammar Tip in the side column for information on infinitives and infinitive phrases.

Learning Objectives

In this assignment, you will focus on the following objectives:

Writing: Writing a persuasive essay.

Grammar: Understanding infinitives and infinitive phrases.

> ### Grammar Tip
>
> **Infinitives and Infinitive Phrases**
>
> An **infinitive** is a verb form that begins with the word *to* and functions as a noun, an adjective, or an adverb. An **infinitive phrase** contains the infinitive plus its complements and modifiers.
>
> In the sentence that follows, the infinitive "to succeed" is essential to the meaning:
>
> *Newcomers to our community often need help to succeed.*
>
> In the following sentence, the infinitive phrase "to be fair" is not essential.
>
> *To be fair, newcomers in a community often have special needs.*
>
> Use commas to set off infinitives and infinitive phrases that are not essential to the meaning of the sentence.

After You Read

Assess

 ## Respond Though Writing

Students' persuasive essays should have a clear thesis supported by evidence, develop logical arguments to support the position, appeal to ethics or emotion, and refer to Ruth's experience.

A student who meets all of these criteria should receive the equivalent of a 4-point response.

A student who fully meets three of these criteria should receive the equivalent of a 3-point response.

A student who fully meets two of these criteria should receive the equivalent of a 2-point response.

A student who fully or partially meets one of these criteria should receive the equivalent of a 1-point response.

> For grammar practice, see Unit 3 Teaching Resources Book, p. 60.

Approaching Level
DIFFERENTIATED INSTRUCTION

Addressing Opposing Arguments
As students begin to form their arguments, have them consider any opposing arguments that may arise. Point out that issues such as cost, time, and location are often mentioned in opposing arguments. Tell students to imagine that they are on the other side of the argument. What objections might they have? This will help them address any issues in their essays.

Advanced Learners/Pre-AP
DIFFERENTIATED INSTRUCTION

Persuasive Speech Have students adapt their persuasive essays into speeches. Tell students to imagine that they will be addressing a neighborhood committee about the issue in their essay. Point out that they will not be able to simply read their essay aloud. They will need to manipulate the text in order to make it sound as if should be read aloud.

Before You Read

Focus

Bellringer Options

**Daily Language
    Transparency 39**

Or, ask: Have you ever had a friend or family member leave your town? How did you feel? (*Some may suggest that they felt upset.*) Ask students whether this person ever comes home. How do they feel when this happens?

 For an audio recording of this selection, use Listening Library Audio CD-ROM.

Before You Read   Palestine

The Parable of the Prodigal Son from *The New Testament*

The Christian Bible is composed of two parts: the Old Testament, which was originally a Greek translation of the Hebrew Bible, and the New Testament, which covers the life, death, and teachings of Jesus Christ. The 27 books of the New Testament were written over an extended period, roughly between A.D. 40 and A.D. 150. These books include the four Gospels, the Acts of the Apostles, the Epistles (letters) written by Paul and other disciples, and the book of Revelation. The books of the New Testament are arranged in a narrative order based on Jesus's life, rather than in the order in which they were written, beginning with the four Gospels.

The Gospels give various accounts and lessons centered on Jesus's life and teachings. The Gospels precede the Acts of the Apostles, which presents the history and spread of the early church. Following the Acts are the Epistles, which offer instruction in the Christian faith and are widely believed to be the earliest books of the New Testament. Finally, the book of Revelation presents a vision of the future and the fulfillment of God's plan for humanity.

The Authors of the Gospels The word *gospel* derives from the Old English word *godspel*, meaning "good news." The "good news" is God's new covenant with humanity through Jesus, which Christians believe was prophesied in the Old Testament. The true authors of the Gospels are unknown. Traditionally, the Gospels of Matthew and John are believed to have been written by Jesus's apostles Matthew and John, but many scholars doubt this is true. Scholars have speculated that Mark was written by a follower of the apostle Peter and that Luke was written by a physician friend of the apostle Paul. The Gospel of Luke is usually considered to be the most skillfully written of the four Gospels.

St. Luke with his symbol, from the Lindisfarne Gospels, 710-721 AD.

> "The disciples came, and said to him, 'Why do you speak to them in parables?'"
>
> —Gospel of Matthew 13:10

The Synoptic Gospels The Gospels of Matthew, Mark, and Luke contain a number of parables, or simple stories that teach a moral lesson and have both literal and metaphorical meanings. In fact, these three Gospels share so many similarities, they are referred to as the "synoptic Gospels," from the Greek *synoptikos*, meaning "seen together." The synoptic Gospels seem to have derived their content from the same or similar original sources, and many parables are repeated from one Gospel to another. The Gospel of John presents the teachings of Jesus in the form of longer narratives, and much of its content is unique.

Selection Skills

Literary Elements
- Parable (SE p. 487, 488, 490)

The Parable of the Prodigal Son

Speaking/Listening/Viewing Skills
- Analyze Art (SE p. 489)

Reading Skills
- Make Inferences About Theme (SE p. 487, 488, 490)
- Compare and Contrast (TE p. 488)

Vocabulary Skills
- Academic Vocabulary (SE p. 490)

Writing Skills/Grammar
- Parable (SE p. 490)

Literature and Reading Preview

Connect to the Parable

Has there ever been a time when you behaved badly but were forgiven or left unpunished? In your journal, discuss your actions and how this forgiveness made you feel.

Build Background

In ancient Palestine, practices and laws regarding inheritance suggest it was uncommon for sons to receive their inheritances while the father was still living, with the exception of gifts to sons who married. Laws protected a father's right to the income from an inheritance until his death, and it would have been considered disrespectful for a son to request his inheritance.

Set Purposes for Reading

Big Idea **The Secret of Life**

Jesus's parables reveal moral lessons in a simple yet effective manner—in fact, these stories are often told to children. As you read, ask yourself, What moral lesson does this parable offer, and how might this lesson be a guide to a more fulfilling life?

Literary Element **Parable**

A **parable** is a very short and simple story that teaches a religious or a moral lesson. Parables function on both a literal and a metaphorical level, describing details and scenarios from everyday life while teaching a deeper lesson. As you read, ask yourself, Why might parables teach lessons or ideas effectively?

Reading Strategy **Make Inferences About Theme**

A **theme** is the main idea or insight about life conveyed in a work of literature. Usually, the theme is implied rather than directly stated. The reader must make **inferences,** or educated guesses, about the theme based on information the author gives—for example, by analyzing events or dialogue in the work. As you read, ask yourself, What inferences can I make about the theme?

....

Tip: **Chart Questions** Using a chart like the one below, take notes to help you infer the theme of the parable.

Question	Answer	Inference
Why is the younger son's departure significant?	It shows his selfishness and lack of forethought.	Selfishness or bad behavior may be an important part of the theme.

Musical scene. The pleasures of the prodigal son. Paul Coecke van Aelst. Museo Correr, Venice.

Learning Objectives

For pages 486–490

In studying this text, you will focus on the following objectives:

Literary Study: Analyzing parable.

Reading: Making inferences about theme.

Writing: Writing a parable.

Focus

Summary

In this parable, Jesus tells the story of a man with two sons. The younger son asks for his inheritance early, and wastes the money on wild living. He returns to his father, offering to be just a household servant. The father forgives him and welcomes him back lavishly, but the older brother is resentful.

 For summaries in languages other than English, see Unit 3 Teaching Resources Book, pp. 63–68.

Cultural History ☆

Animal Sacrifices When the father decides to slaughter a calf in celebration of his son's return, he performs an act that has a long history in many cultures. Sacrifices were performed to ask for assistance from the gods, to remember a battle or other event, or to celebrate a blessing. While animals or other objects were often burnt or buried in the ground, the fatted calf in this parable is eaten during the family's feast.

Approaching Level

DIFFERENTIATED INSTRUCTION

Using Background Knowledge Have students describe other works they know, such as fables, fairy tales, or poems, that teach a lesson. Have them explain how characteristics of the genre help the writer to share a lesson. Lead a discussion about how these genres are similar or different. Have students keep their ideas in mind as they read the parable.

Finding Parables Have students research other parables that are found in the King James version of the Bible. Tell students to write brief summaries of the parables and their lessons. Lead a discussion about the similarities and differences between the parables. Do students notice any pattern?

Teach

Literary Element | 1

Parable Ask: Based on the fact that the son squanders all of his money, what kind of lesson might the parable address? (*The lesson may deal with behaving responsibly.*)

Literary Element | 2

Parable Answer: *It will probably be about a family. This is an effective topic because most people can identify with it.*

Progress Check

Can students identify a parable?

If No → See Unit 3 Teaching Resources Book, p. 69.

Reading Strategy | 3

Make Inferences About Theme Answer: *It shows that the theme centers on forgiveness and compassion, rather than on anger or retribution.*

For additional practice using the reading skill or strategy, see Unit 3 Teaching Resources Book, p. 70.

Readability Scores

Dale-Chall: 7.5
DRP: 54
Lexile: 860

The Parable of the Prodigal Son

from the King James *version of the* Bible

And he[1] said, "A certain man had two sons: and the younger of them said to his father, 'Father, give me the portion of goods that falleth to me.' And he divided unto them his living. And not many days after the younger son gathered all together, and took his journey into a far country, and there wasted his substance with riotous living. And when he had spent all, there arose a mighty famine in that land; and he began to be in want. And he went and joined himself to a citizen of that country; and he sent him into his fields to feed swine.[2] And he would fain[3] have filled his belly with the husks that the swine did eat: and no man gave unto him.

"And when he came to himself, he said, 'How many hired servants of my father's have bread enough and to spare, and I perish with hunger! I will arise and go to my father, and will say unto him,

---

1. Here, *he* refers to Jesus Christ.
2. *Swine* (or pigs) are considered unclean animals in Jewish belief.
3. *Fain* means "willingly" or "gladly."

---

2 **Parable** *Based on this opening sentence, what might be the topic of this parable? Why might this be an effective topic to use to teach a lesson?*

"Father, I have sinned against heaven, and before thee, and am no more worthy to be called thy son: make me as one of thy hired servants." '

"And he arose, and came to his father. But when he was yet a great way off, his father saw him, and had compassion, and ran, and fell on his neck, and kissed him. And the son said unto him, 'Father, I have sinned against heaven, and in thy sight, and am no more worthy to be called thy son.' But the father said to his servants, 'Bring forth the best robe, and put it on him; and put a ring on his hand, and shoes on his feet: and bring hither the fatted calf, and kill it; and let us eat, and be merry: for this my son was dead, and is alive again; he was lost, and is found.' And they began to be merry.

"Now his elder son was in the field: and as he came and drew nigh to the house, he heard music and dancing. And he called one of the servants, and asked what these things meant. And he said unto him, 'Thy brother is come; and thy father hath killed the fatted calf, because he hath received

---

Make Inferences About Theme *What might the father's reaction to his son's return reveal about the theme?* **3**

488 UNIT 3 SOUTHWEST ASIA

Reading Practice

 SMALL GROUP

Compare and Contrast Explain that comparing and contrasting means seeing how two or more things are alike and different. Point out that using a graphic organizer is a good way to compare and contrast two characters in a narrative, or the actions and feelings of one character before and after a story event.

In small groups, have students prepare a two-column chart or Venn diagram. Half of the groups should compare and contrast the two brothers. The rest should compare and contrast the younger son at the beginning of the parable and when all his money is gone. Use the students' graphic organizers as a source for discussion.

The return of the Prodigal Son, 1773. Pompeo Batoni. Oil on canvas, 173 x 122 cm. Kunsthistorisches Museum, Vienna, Austria.

View the Art Batoni was renowned in eighteenth-century Rome for his ornate depictions of mythological and historical subjects. How does his portrayal of the prodigal son and his father compare with how you imagine these men looked and dressed? ★

him safe and sound.' And he was angry, and would not go in: therefore came his father out, and intreated[4] him. And he answering said to his father, 'Lo, these many years do I serve thee, neither transgressed I at any time thy commandment: and yet thou never gavest me a kid,[5] that I might make merry with my friends: but as soon as this thy son was come, which hath devoured thy living with harlots, thou hast killed for him the fatted calf.' And he said unto him, 'Son, thou art ever with me, and all that I have is thine. It was meet that we should make merry, and be glad: for this thy brother was dead, and is alive again; and was lost, and is found.' " ❧

---

4. *Intreated* is a variant spelling of *entreated,* which means "begged" or "pleaded."
5. A *kid* is a young goat.

The Secret of Life *What might be the metaphorical and religious meaning of the father's statement to his older son?* **4**

THE PARABLE OF THE PRODIGAL SON **489**

English Learners

DIFFERENTIATED INSTRUCTION

Advanced Explain that in biblical times, there were very different expectations of family members, servants, and slaves. Discuss with students what obligations and rights each character in the parable has toward the others. Then, have students compare these expectations with the expectations of their own family or culture.

Approaching Level

DIFFERENTIATED INSTRUCTION

Readers' Theater Students may better understand the story if they perform a Readers' Theater. Organize students into groups of four. Have them read the parts of the father, the two sons, and the narrator. Provide hard copies of the story so that students can highlight their lines. Have groups read through the story several times to better grasp its meaning.

Teach

Big Idea	4

The Secret of Life

Answer: *It shows that God the father loves all of his children equally and shares his riches with them.*

(ADVANCED) Ask students whether they think the father made a good decision when he welcomed the son with a feast and new clothing.

View the Art ★

Answer: *Answers will vary. Students may say that, despite the father's wealth, they did not imagine he would look so regal or be dressed in expensive fabrics and gold jewelry. They may also say they pictured the son in tattered clothes, rather than half-dressed in rags.*

Italian painter Pompeo Girolamo Batoni (1708–1787) was known as an artist of historical subjects. His painting of the return of the Prodigal Son is an example of the Baroque style of art. During this period, the Roman Catholic Church displayed pieces of art showing scenes that relied heavily on expressive and dramatic gestures and movements.

Learning Objectives
Making inferences about theme. (SE)
Analyzing parable. (SE)
Comparing and contrasting characters. (TE)

489

After You Read

Assess

1. Answers will vary.
2. (a) The youngest son asks for his inheritance. (b) The reaction reveals the father' generosity. trust, and patience.
3. (a) The youngest son takes a job feeding swine. (b) Jewish people believe that swine are unclean animals; it would have been considered shameful to feed them.
4. (a) The father reassures his older son that he is always in his thoughts and that all the father owns belongs to the older son. (b) The father loves and accepts both of his sons.
5. Some may think the older brother behaved properly, while others will claim that he is ungenerous.
6. "Wasteful" applies to the son because he spends all his money. "Overly generous" applies to the father because he continues to give to the son.
7. The parable shows the importance of caring and forgiving.
8. It teaches universal values of compassion, forgiveness, and unconditional love.

Writing

Students' parables should include characters and a conflict that can be interpreted literally and symbolically.

Literary Element

1. The story functions on both a literal level (what happens in the family) and a metaphorical level (the relationship between God and his followers). It teaches a moral lesson.
2. (a) True love is unconditional and family is the strongest bond. (b) The father's feelings represent God's limitless love and forgiveness.

Reading Strategy

1. (a) The younger son has a conflict when he leaves his family, squanders his inheritance, and is near starvation. The older son has a conflict when his younger brother is welcomed home. (b) The first conflict is resolved when the younger son receives his father's forgiveness. The second is resolved when the father reassures the older son that he loves him.

2. Literally, finding something lost is joyful. Symbolically, the return of lost souls is an occasion for celebration.

Academic Vocabulary

Students will most likely answer that the United States Constitution is the framework of the government.

490

After You Read

Respond and Think Critically

Respond and Interpret

1. Did the ending of the parable surprise you? Why or why not?
2. (a)What request does the younger son make to his father? (b)What does the father's response to this request reveal about the father?
3. (a)What is the younger son forced to do when he runs out of money? (b)What is particularly humiliating about his situation?
4. (a)How does the father respond to his older son's comments? (b)What point do you think the father is making?

Analyze and Evaluate

5. Do you think the older son's reaction to the welcoming festivities is justified? Why or why not?
6. *Prodigal* has several meanings, including "wasteful" and "overly generous." Considering these definitions, how might *prodigal* describe both the father and the younger son?

Connect

7. **Big Idea** The Secret of Life What lessons about family and other close relationships does this parable teach?
8. **Connect to Today** Why might this parable continue to influence readers today?

Literary Element Parable

Review the **parable**, paying attention to its structural elements. Then answer the questions below.

1. What elements of this story help identify it as a parable?
2. (a)What lesson does the father teach the older son? (b)How might you interpret this lesson symbolically?

Reading Strategy Make Inferences About Theme

When you **make inferences about theme**, you identify an insight about life that is implied through the events in a text. Refer to the chart you made on page 487 and answer the following questions.

1. (a)Describe the conflicts that unfold in the parable. (b)How are the conflicts resolved?
2. What insights about life are implied in the story?

LOG ON ▶ **Literature** Online

Selection Resources For Selection Quizzes, eFlashcards, and Reading-Writing Connection activities, go to glencoe.com and enter QuickPass code GLW6053u3.

Academic Vocabulary

The framework of "The Parable of the Prodigal Son" is one of repentance and forgiveness.

In the sentence above, *framework* means "the basic structure of ideas." For example, the *framework* of a new law is based on constitutional rights. To further explore the meaning of this word, answer this question: What is the **framework** of the United States government?

For more on academic vocabulary, see pages 36–37 and R83–R85.

Writing

Write a Parable Write a short **parable** that teaches a lesson about modern life. Develop a plot in which the characters and the conflict can be interpreted on both literal and symbolic levels. After you draft your parable, exchange papers with a peer and review each other's work, offering comments for revision.

Before You Read

from the *Qur'an*

The Qur'an (kô rän´) is the holy book of Islam, believed by Muslims to be the sacred word of Allah, or God. According to Muslim belief, Allah revealed the Qur'an to Muhammad ("the Glorified One"), the prophet who founded Islam. Muhammad was born in A.D. 570 to a merchant family in Mecca (also spelled Makkah), a thriving city on one of the major caravan trade routes across Arabia. He was orphaned by the age of six and was raised by family members, eventually becoming a manager on a caravan trade route, a husband, and a father.

The Word of God Muhammad's sense of justice and devotion to prayer were renowned. He sometimes retreated into the desert and the hills to pray. According to Muslim tradition, during one such retreat around A.D. 610, Allah sent the angel Gabriel to Muhammad and told him to recite what Gabriel said. The Qur'an, whose title means "recitation" in Arabic, came out of these revelations over 23 years. Muhammad's followers eventually wrote them down.

A New Religion Gabriel's messages called on Muhammad to forsake the gods of his people and start a new religion marked by devotion to a single deity, pious conduct, and submission to the will of Allah. Muhammad came to believe that Allah had already revealed himself in part through Moses and Jesus—and thus through the traditions of Judaism and Christianity. He believed, however, that the final revelations of Allah were now being given to him. While Muhammad was able to convert some followers, he also met with much opposition. For the rest of his life, both in Mecca and in the city of Yathrib (now called Medina), Muhammad worked to spread the word of Allah. In the century after Muhammad's death in A.D. 632, Islam spread rapidly, and the Islamic Empire expanded until it stretched from Spain to the borders of India.

> "To God belong the East and the West;
> whithersoever you turn, there is the
>   Face of God;
> God is All-embracing,
> All-knowing. . . ."
>
> —from the Qur'an

A Difficult Masterpiece Within 30 years after Muhammad's death, the Qur'an was compiled into a standard written text. The book consists of 114 chapters (called *suras*), which vary in length from hundreds of verses to only one or two lines. Except for the brief opening sura—"The Exordium" (or introduction)—these chapters are arranged approximately according to length, beginning with the longer ones. Notoriously difficult to translate, the Qur'an established the classical form of the Arabic language and is regarded as a literary masterpiece.

QUR'AN **491**

Before You Read

Focus

Bellringer Options

Selection Focus
    Transparency 23
Daily Language
    Transparency 40

Or ask: What rules guide your life? What advice might you give to others who want to know how to live their lives? Discuss students' responses. They may describe how it is important to treat others fairly or respect their elders.

 For an audio recording of this selection, use Listening Library Audio CD-ROM.

Selection Skills

Literary Elements
- Antithesis (SE p. 492, 494, 495)

from the Qu'ran

Speaking/Listening/Viewing Skills
- Analyze Art (TE p. 493)

Reading Skills
- Interpret Imagery (SE p. 492, 495; TE p. 493)
- Apply Background Knowledge (TE p. 492)
- Synthesize (TE p. 494)

Vocabulary Skills
- Use Context Clues (SE p. 492, 495)

Writing Skills/Grammar
- Memo (SE p. 495)

Before You Read

Focus

Summary

The first selection praises Allah and asks him to help guide true believers to righteousness. The second selection emphasizes the loving care of Allah, and advises the reader to treat other people with that same compassion and understanding.

 For summaries in languages other than English, see Unit 3 Teaching Resources Book, p. 74–79.

Vocabulary

Use Context Clues On the board, write three sentences, each one containing one of the vocabulary words and appropriate context clues. Ask volunteers to come to the board and underline the context clues in the sentence that help reveal the meaning of each vocabulary word.

 For additional vocabulary practice, see Unit 3 Teaching Resources Book, p. 82.

Reading Practice

Apply Background Knowledge Have students recall the information they read about Islam on pages 440–443 in the Part 1 Introduction. Tell them to summarize the information they learned in a paragraph, a bulleted list of facts, or a web.

Have students use this information to prepare for reading the excerpts from the Qur'an. Lead a discussion about what types of information students would expect to find in the Qur'an. After students have read the selections, have them supplement their paragraphs, lists, or webs with any new information.

Literature and Reading Preview

Connect to the Sacred Text

Why might a person choose to live compassionately? In your journal, reflect on this question.

Build Background

Set forth in the Qur'an, the fundamental doctrines of Muslim religious belief are known as "the five pillars of Islam": acknowledging Allah as the only God, praying five times a day, fasting from dawn to dusk during the holy month of Ramadan, giving alms to the poor, and making a pilgrimage to Mecca at least once in a lifetime, if the believer has the means.

Set Purposes for Reading

Big Idea The Secret of Life

Sacred texts often reveal how one can attain fulfillment and enlightenment. As you read this sacred text, ask yourself, What Islamic ideas on how to live well does it reveal?

Literary Element Antithesis

Antithesis is the balanced contrast of two phrases or ideas, as illustrated in lines 7–8 of "The Exordium":

> The path of those whom You have favored,
> Not of those who have incurred Your wrath…

In this passage, "those whom you have favored" is the opposite of "those who have incurred your wrath." As you read "Daylight," ask yourself, What is an example of antithesis, and how does it contribute to the verse?

Reading Strategy Interpret Imagery

Imagery refers to descriptive language that appeals to one or more of the five senses: sight, hearing, touch, taste, and smell. When you **interpret imagery,** you examine how it contributes to the underlying ideas in the text. As you read, ask yourself, What are some examples of images, and what do they mean?

Tip: Take Notes Use a chart like the one below to help you interpret images.

Image	Sensory Response	Meaning
"the straight path"	a well-marked trail leading to your destination	Following Allah's word will lead one toward a righteous lifestyle.

Learning Objectives

For pages 491–495

In studying this text, you will focus on the following objectives:

Literary Study: Analyzing antithesis.

Reading: Interpreting imagery.

Writing: Writing a memo.

Vocabulary

incur (in kur´) *v.* to bring upon oneself; p. 494 *She incurred large library fines by failing to return her books on time.*

abhor (ab hôr´) *v.* to detest; p. 494 *His bad attitude led many people to abhor the basketball player.*

chide (chīd) *v.* to scold; p. 494 *The babysitter had to chide the girls for making so much noise.*

Tip: Context Clues You can often figure out the meaning of words by looking at their **context,** the words and sentences that surround them. For example, in the sample sentence above for *chide,* the phrase "making so much noise" suggests that *chide* means "scold."

Page from the Qur'an, 17th century, Turkey. Museé Conde, Chantilly, France.

from the Qur'an

Translated by N. J. Dawood

View the Art ★

Artists work closely with calligraphers to design the magnificent illuminations that decorate handmade copies of the Qur'an. Ink was made from soot; pigments, from gold leaf, powdered lapis lazuli, and other precious metals and stones. Note the symmetry of the design and the use of circles and rectangles. Islamic art often reflects the ancient Arab interest in mathematical principles. **Ask:** How do you think the person who decorated these pages felt about the text? *(Students may say the person decorating the pages of the text may have felt feelings of devotion, awe, and reverence. Additionally he or she may have felt a duty to provide something beautiful to honor Allah.)*

English Learners

DIFFERENTIATED INSTRUCTION

Advanced Direct students' attention to the various names or titles for Allah in the selection. Explain that other leaders or religious figures often have multiple titles or designations as well. Have students work in small groups to compile lists of titles for Jesus or for Hindu gods.

Advanced Learners/Pre-AP

DIFFERENTIATED INSTRUCTION

Analyze Tone Have students analyze the tone of "The Exordium." **Ask:** What kinds of feelings or attitudes does the language evoke? *(Students may suggest reverence, awe, submission, or supplication.)* Lead a discussion about whether this was the type of tone that students expected to find in the Qur'an. Have them explain their responses.

493

Teach

Big Idea   1

The Secret of Life Answer: *It suggests that Muslims believe life begins and ends with Allah. It also suggests that Muslims value compassion.*

Literary Element   2

Antithesis Answer: *The contrast is between someone who has no one to nurture them and those who are saved by Allah. It emphasizes Allah's compassion.*

Progress Check

Can students identify antithesis?

If No → See Unit 3 Teaching Resources Book, p. 80.

Language History ☆

The Arabic Language There are 28 basic letters in the Arabic alphabet, all of which represent consonants. In addition, the language has a limited number of vowels—three long and three short. Every Arabic word begins with one consonant followed by a vowel. Unlike English, Arabic is written from right to left.

The *E*xordium

*In the Name of God
the Compassionate the Merciful*

Praise be to God, Lord of the Universe,
The Compassionate, the Merciful,
Sovereign of the Day of Judgement!
You alone we worship, and to You alone
we turn for help.
Guide us to the straight path,
The path of those whom You have favored,
Not of those who have **incurred** Your wrath,
Nor of those who have gone astray.

*D*aylight

*In the Name of God,
the Compassionate, the Merciful*

By the light of day, and by the dark of night, your Lord
has not forsaken you, nor does He **abhor** you.
The life to come holds a richer prize for you than this
present life. You shall be gratified with what your Lord will
give you.
  Did He not find you an orphan and give you shelter?
  Did He not find you in error and guide you?
  Did He not find you poor and enrich you?
  Therefore do not wrong the orphan, nor **chide** away the
beggar. But proclaim the goodness of your Lord.

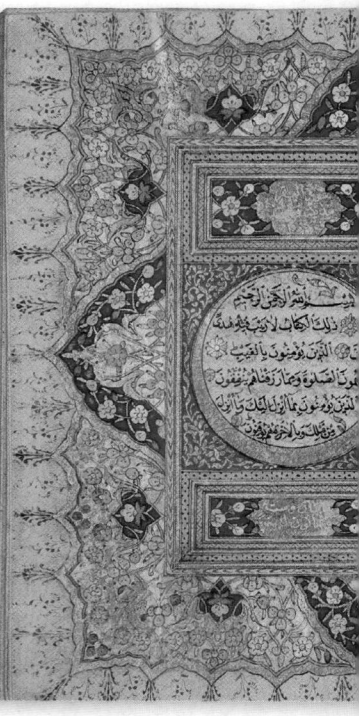

---

1   **The Secret of Life** *What does this description of God suggest about the Islamic view of life?*

2   **Antithesis** *What antithesis is presented here? What quality of God's does this antithesis emphasize?*

Vocabulary

incur (in kur′) *v.* to bring upon oneself
abhor (ab hôr′) *v.* to detest
chide (chīd) *v.* to scold

494   **UNIT 3**   SOUTHWEST ASIA

Reading Practice

Synthesize Explain to students that when they synthesize they combine elements or ideas to extend their understanding of something or to create something new. Point out that "The Exordium" and "Daylight" both present important tenets of the Islamic religion.

Organize students into pairs. Tell pairs to take whatever they have learned about Islam from "The Exordium" and "Daylight" and combine them into a single synthesizing statement of one to three sentences. After students have finished, have them share their statements with a class. Lead a discussion about the similarities and differences among students' statements.

After You Read

Respond and Think Critically

Respond and Interpret

1. What insights into Islam have you gained by reading these suras?

2. (a)In lines 6–9 of "The Exordium," who has not followed the "straight path"? (b)What does the straight path represent?

3. (a)What two images are in the first line of "Daylight"? (b)Why might these images begin the sura, and what is their significance?

4. (a)What promise is given to the faithful in lines 3–5 of "Daylight"? (b)Who seems to be the intended audience for this sura?

Analyze and Evaluate

5. What kind of **tone**, or attitude toward the subject matter, does "The Exordium" set for the Qur'an as a whole? Use evidence from the text to support your response.

6. How would you state the **theme**, or main message, of "Daylight"?

Connect

7. **Big Idea** **The Secret of Life** How is a Muslim life best lived according to these two suras?

8. **Connect to Today** "Daylight" maintains that people should respect one another, especially those who are less fortunate. How does modern society demonstrate this value?

Literary Element Antithesis

Authors often emphasize important ideas through the use of **antithesis,** or the balanced contrast of two phrases or ideas.

1. What important idea in "The Exordium" is emphasized through the use of antithesis?

2. In what lines of "Daylight" is antithesis used?

Reading Strategy Interpret Imagery

The pattern of **imagery** in a literary work can help convey the meaning of that work. Refer to your chart from page 492 and then answer the following questions.

1. What is the dominant image in "The Exordium"?

2. Why does "Daylight" provide contrasting images such as *orphan* and *shelter* and *poor* and *rich*?

LOG ON ▶ **Literature** Online

Selection Resources For Selection Quizzes, eFlashcards, and Reading-Writing Connection activities, go to glencoe.com and enter QuickPass code GLW6053u3.

Vocabulary Practice

Practice with Context Clues Read the following sentences and identify the context clues that help you determine the meaning of each boldfaced vocabulary word.

1. David **incurred** large debt because of his poor money management skills and expensive tastes.

2. Always the opposite of her sister, Jenna loved the headlining band, while Gina **abhorred** it.

3. His coach would **chide** him every time he made a mistake, so Eric lost his confidence.

Writing

Write a Memo How well do your classmates get along with one another? Think about this question and write a memo to your class with ideas on how to improve interpersonal relationships. Try to mirror the ideas conveyed in "Daylight" and use **antithesis** to emphasize key ideas.

QUR'AN **495**

After You Read

Assess

1. Answers will vary.

2. (a) Those who have angered God have gone astray. (b) The straight path represents a religious way of life that leads to God, as followed by his "favored" ones.

3. (a) Images of the light of day and fall of night open the sura. (b) The imagery highlights God's power over the world. It describes how the message of the sura is relevant at all times.

4. (a) Devoted believers will be rewarded with a blessed afterlife. (b) The sura is written for people who may doubt God.

5. The tone is reverential, solemn, or joyous, as shown by religious language like "Praise be to God" and "You alone we worship."

6. God takes care of his people, so his believers should trust him and respect one another.

7. One should respect other people, be devoted to God, grateful for his generosity, and aware of a satisfying afterlife.

8. Answers will vary.

⚡ Writing

Students' memos should offer suggestions that reflect an understanding of the ideas in "Daylight" and use antithesis.

Literary Element

1. The antithesis between God's favored treatment of those who are faithful and his wrath toward those who have gone astray emphasizes the idea that religious observance is rewarded.

2. Lines 6–8 use antithesis to show specific examples of ways in which God has blessed the faithful.

Reading Strategy

1. the straight path

2. The images remind Muslims that God has helped them and that they should, in turn, offer help to people who are less fortunate or in need.

Vocabulary Practice

1. David's "poor money management skills and expensive tastes" imply he brought on, or **incurred**, the debt.

2. Jenna and Gina are "opposites," so if Jenna "loves" the band, Gina must hate, or **abhor**, it.

3. Eric's "mistakes" cause the coach to scold, or **chide**, him in a way that makes him lose confidence.

Before You Read

Focus

Bellringer Options

**Daily Language
    Transparency 41**

Or bring to class a selection of travel books, guidebooks, memoirs, and true adventure stories. Allow students to examine them.
Ask: Which of these books would be most useful if you were planning a trip? *(Students may say that the factual guidebook is most useful for planning, but the first-person memoir of a trip is likely to be more interesting to read. Students may point out that the memoir covers important information that the guidebook does not discuss, such as the subtleties of local communication and body language.)*

Before You Read

Persia

The Second Voyage of Sindbad the Sailor

T he *Thousand and One Nights*, also known as *The Arabian Nights*, is one of the most famous and beloved collections of legends and folktales in the world. The stories, most of which are believed to be Persian, Indian, or Arabian in origin, probably evolved over centuries of oral storytelling before they were written down. The earliest known collection was originally written in Persian and was translated into Arabic during the ninth century. *The Thousand and One Nights* became popular in Europe after the publication of Antoine Galland's twelve-volume French translation between 1704 and 1717. The first English translation of Galland's version appeared as early as 1708.

Stories Within a Story The stories in *The Thousand and One Nights* are connected by a frame narrative about Scheherazade (shə her′ə zäd′), a brave, clever woman who has been condemned to die by her husband, a cruel sultan named Shahriyar (shä′rē yär′). Shahriyar's first wife had been unfaithful to him, and he had her put to death in retaliation. This betrayal led him to hate all women, so he began marrying a new wife every day only to have each one executed the next morning. Scheherazade, the daughter of Shahriyar's vizier (or prime minister), eventually devises a plan to stop the bloodshed. She willingly marries the sultan and begins telling him a spellbinding story on their wedding night, cleverly leaving the story unfinished. Enthralled with the story, Shahriyar lets her live another day so she can tell him how the story ends. Night after night, she continues to spin her stories, including "Ali Baba and the Forty Thieves," "Aladdin and the Magic Lamp," and "The Seven Voyages of Sindbad the Sailor." After the cycle has been repeated for 1,001 nights, the sultan lifts Scheherazade's death sentence, and they remain happily married.

Sinbad embarking, illustration for 'Sinbad the Sailor', from 'The Arabian Nights', 1895

> "We are all like Scheherazade's husband, in that we want to know what happens next."
>
> —E. M. Forster, from *Aspects of the Novel*

Enduring Popularity Galland's enormously popular translation of *The Thousand and One Nights* introduced the text to a new audience and helped the stories become beloved classics. *The Thousand and One Nights* continues to capture the attention of people worldwide and to inspire writers, filmmakers, and artists. Its pervasive influence can be seen in many works of Romantic literature, such as Samuel Taylor Coleridge's famous poem *Kubla Khan*. As Argentine author Jorge Luis Borges observed of *Nights's* widespread effects on culture, "It is a book so vast that it is not necessary to have read it."

Selection Skills

Literary Elements
- Point of View (SE pp. 497, 498, 503)
- Imagery (SE p. 503)

Reading Skills
- Identify Problem and Solution (SE pp. 497–504)

The Second Voyage of Sindbad the Sailor

Vocabulary Skills
- Practice with Analogies (SE pp. 497, 504)

Speaking/Listening/Viewing Skills
- Analyze Art (TE p. 498)

Writing Skills/Grammar
- Report (SE p. 504)
- Personal Essay (TE p. 500)
- Poem (TE p. 502)

Literature and Reading Preview

Connect to the Story

Think of a time when you devised an effective solution to a problem you faced. Discuss this incident with a partner.

Build Background

One of the best-known series of tales in *The Thousand and One Nights* recounts the adventures of Sindbad (also spelled Sinbad) the Sailor. Forming a frame story within the larger frame of Scheherazade, the first tale opens with Sindbad the Porter, a poor man who stops to rest outside a palace, wondering why the man inside is so much richer than he. The rich man, Sindbad the Sailor, overhears him and invites him in. The sailor then tells the porter the stories of his seven voyages, each one fraught with danger. At the end, the porter agrees that Sindbad deserves his wealth, and Sindbad shares some of his riches with the porter.

Set Purposes for Reading

Big Idea **The Search for Wisdom**

As you read, ask yourself, What do Sindbad's adventures reveal about how to obtain knowledge and use it effectively?

Literary Element **Point of View**

Point of view is the perspective from which a story is told. Sindbad narrates this story, using first-person pronouns to refer to himself. As you read, ask yourself, How does first-person point of view contribute to the impact of the story?

Reading Strategy **Identify Problem and Solution**

When you **identify problems and solutions** in a literary work, you consider a character's problems and then evaluate his or her solutions for solving them. As you read, ask yourself, What solution does Sindbad devise for each problem he faces?

....

Tip: Track Results In a chart like the one below, list Sindbad's problems and solutions, and track the results of those solutions.

Problem	Sindbad's Solution	Result
Sindbad is stuck on a deserted island.	He ties himself to the talons of a roc.	The roc deposits him near a snake-infested valley.

Learning Objectives

For pages 496–504

In studying this text, you will focus on the following objectives:

Literary Study: Analyzing point of view.

Reading: Identifying problem and solution.

Writing: Connecting literature to art.

Vocabulary

thicket (thik′ it) *n.* a dense growth of shrubs, underbrush, or small trees; p. 498 *The deer disappeared into the thicket.*

fruitless (fro͞ot′ lis) *adj.* unproductive; useless; sure to end in failure; p. 499 *My efforts to open the window were fruitless because it was painted shut.*

confound (kən found′) *v.* to confuse or bewilder; p. 499 *I was confounded by his poor grades because he always studied hard.*

tumult (to͞o′ məlt) *n.* commotion or noisy confusion; p. 501 *The tumult in the street woke all the neighbors.*

....

Tip: Analogies To complete an analogy, apply the relationship represented by the first pair of words to the second pair of words, as in the following example:

   fruitless : futile :: obvious : blatant

Fruitless and *futile* are synonyms, as are *obvious* and *blatant*.

Before You Read

Focus

Summary

Sindbad the mariner sets out on a second voyage, only to find himself left behind after a stopover on a strange island. Exploring the island, he finds a huge egg and ties himself to the giant mother bird's leg. The bird lifts him from the island, setting him down near a deep valley covered with diamonds. Sindbad takes some of the diamonds for himself and saves himself again by tying himself to an animal. He returns home a wealthy man and shares his riches.

For summaries in languages other than English, see Unit 3 Teaching Resources Book, pp. 87–92.

Vocabulary

Practice with Analogies

Have students use the vocabulary words to write analogies. Tell them to write the first pair of words on one side of a card and the answer pair on the other side. Have students use these cards to practice their knowledge of analogies and the vocabulary words.

For additional vocabulary practice, see Unit 3 Teaching Resources Book, p. 95.

Interactive Read and Write
Other options for teaching this selection can be found in Interactive Read and Write for On-Level Learners, pp. 109–120

English Learners

DIFFERENTIATED INSTRUCTION

Advanced Writing in the first-person point of view creates suspense and gives a story a feeling of immediacy. The reader finds out what happens right along with the narrator. Point out to students that the story they are about to read is written in the first-person point of view. Explain that students are likely to see pronouns such as *I* and *me*.

Advanced Learners/Pre-AP

DIFFERENTIATED INSTRUCTION

Travel Tales Have students think of other stories they have read or television shows or movies they have seen where a character takes a journey or travels to an unknown place. Discuss how the character reacted to the new environment. Did they adapt easily? What conflicts did they face?

Teach

Literary Element | 1

Point of View Answer: *The narrator uses the first-person pronouns* I *and* my *to refer to himself.*

For additional literary element practice, see Unit 3 Teaching Resources Book, p. 93.

Reading Strategy | 2

Identify Problem and Solution Answer: *Sindbad falls asleep on the island without letting anyone know his location; his crew does not check for him before leaving.* **Ask:** How does Sindbad react to his difficulty? *(At first, he panics and despairs, then he begins to look around for solutions.)*

View the Art

The illustrations in this selection are based on original drawings by Arabian-born Zakariya ibn Muhammad ibn Mahmud Abu Yahya, also known as al-Kazwini (1203–1283), from his large volume on cosmology, titled the *Wonders of Creation and Oddities of Existence.* **Ask:** Do these images seem realistic? Why or why not? *(Students will say the images seem fanciful because men don't hang from birds' legs and enormous mythological creatures don't exist.)*

For an audio recording of this selection, use Listening Library Audio CD-ROM.

Readability Scores

Dale-Chall: 8.5
DRP: 62
Lexile: 1110

498

The Second Voyage of
Sindbad the Sailor

from The Thousand and One Nights

Translated by N. J. Dawood

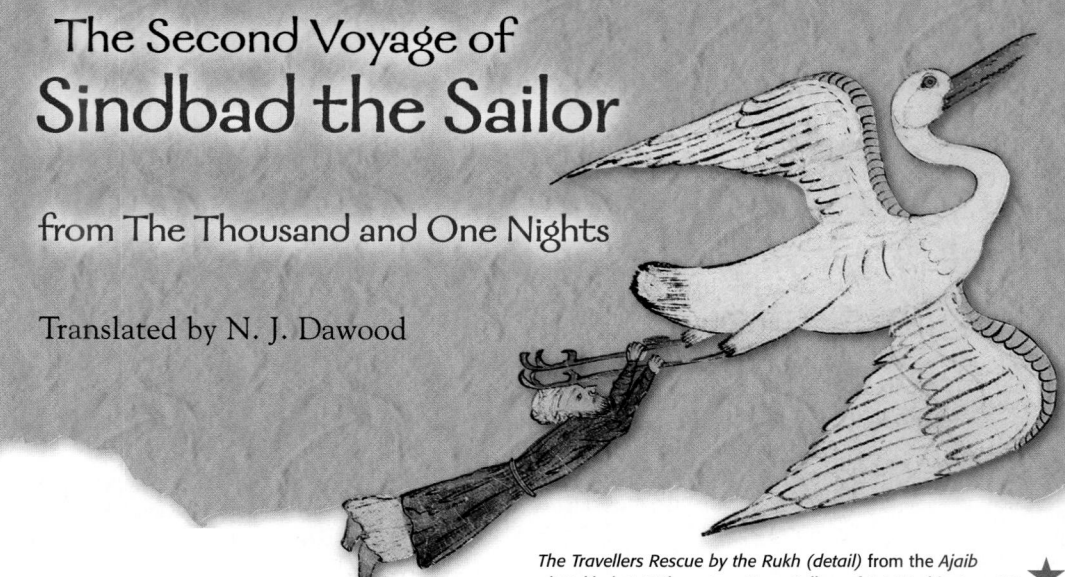

The Travellers Rescue by the Rukh (detail) from the *Ajaib al-Makhukat,* 14th century. Freer Gallery of Art, Washington, DC. ★

For some time after my return to Baghdad I continued to lead a joyful and carefree life, but it was not long before I felt an irresistible longing to travel again about the world and to visit distant cities and islands in quest of profit and adventure. So I bought a great store of merchandise and, after making preparations for departure, sailed down the Tigris to Basrah.[1] There I embarked, together with a band of merchants, in a fine new vessel, well-equipped and manned by a sturdy crew, which set sail the same day.

Aided by a favorable wind, we voyaged for many days and nights from port to port and from island to island, selling and bartering our goods, and haggling with merchants and officials wherever we cast anchor. At length Destiny carried our ship to the shores of an uninhabited island, rich in fruit and flowers, and jubilant with the singing of birds and the murmur of crystal streams.

Here passengers and crew went ashore, and we all set off to enjoy the delights of the island. I strolled through the green meadows, leaving my companions far behind, and sat down in a shady **thicket** to eat a simple meal by a spring of water. Lulled by the soft and fragrant breeze which blew around me, I lay upon the grass and presently fell asleep.

I cannot tell how long I slept, but when I awoke I saw none of my fellow-travelers, and soon realized that the ship had sailed away without anyone noticing my absence.

---

1. In Sindbad's time, Baghdad was a thriving city whose merchants traded in many kingdoms. To set out on a trading expedition, sailors traveled down the Tigris River from Baghdad to *Basrah,* a port near where the Tigris and the Euphrates rivers meet.

1 **Point of View** *What details in this sentence indicate that the story will be told from the first-person point of view?*

Identify Problem and Solution *What factors lead to Sindbad's problem?* **2**

Vocabulary

thicket (thik′it) *n.* a dense growth of shrubs, underbrush, or small trees

498 UNIT 3 SOUTHWEST ASIA

Reading Practice

Analyze Cause and Effect Have students create a chart that shows the cause-and-effect relationship between the events on the page. For example, students may draw a series of boxes with arrows leading from one box to another. This chart would show the cause-and-effect relationships of the events.

After students have designed a chart that works for them, have them fill it in with events from the page. You may want to use the following questions to guide students' charts:

- Why does Sindbad take a second voyage?
- Why did the sailors stop at the uninhabited island?
- Why is Sindbad alone on the island?

I ran in frantic haste towards the sea, and on reaching the shore saw the vessel, a white speck upon the vast blue ocean, dissolving into the far horizon.

Broken with terror and despair, I threw myself upon the sand, wailing: "Now your end has come, Sindbad! The jar that drops a second time is sure to break!" I cursed the day I bade farewell to the joys of a contented life and bitterly repented my folly in venturing again upon the hazards and hardships of the sea, after having so narrowly escaped death in my first voyage.

At length, resigning myself to my doom, I rose and, after wandering about aimlessly for some time, climbed into a tall tree. From its top I gazed long in all directions, but could see nothing save the sky, the trees, the birds, the sands, and the boundless ocean. As I scanned the interior of the island more closely, however, I gradually became aware of some white object looming in the distance. At once I climbed down the tree and made my way towards it. Drawing nearer, I found to my astonishment that it was a white dome of extraordinary dimensions. I walked all round it, but could find no door or entrance of any kind; and so smooth and slippery was its surface that any attempt to climb it would have been **fruitless**. I walked round it again, and, making a mark in the sand near its base, found that its circumference measured more than fifty paces.

Whilst I was thus engaged the sun was suddenly hidden from my view as by a great cloud and the world grew dark around me. I lifted up my eyes towards the sky, and was **confounded** to see a gigantic bird with enormous wings which, as it flew through the air, screened the sun and hid it from the island.

The sight of this prodigy[2] instantly called to my mind a story I had heard in my youth from pilgrims and adventurers—how in a far island dwelt a bird of monstrous size called the roc, which fed its young on elephants; and at once I realized that the white dome was no other than a roc's egg. In a twinkling the bird alighted upon the egg, covering it completely with its wings and stretching out its legs behind it on the ground. And in this posture it went to sleep. (Glory to Him who never sleeps!)

Rising swiftly, I unwound my turban from my head, then doubled it and twisted it into a rope with which I securely bound myself by the waist to one of the great talons of the monster. "Perchance this bird," I thought, "will carry me away to a civilized land; wherever I am set down, it will surely be better than a solitary island."

Visual Vocabulary
A *turban* is a headdress made of a long cloth wound about the head.

I lay awake all night, fearing to close my eyes lest the bird should fly away with me while I slept. At daybreak the roc rose from the egg, and, spreading its wings, took to the air with a terrible cry. I clung fast to its talon as it winged its flight through the void and soared higher and higher until it almost touched the heavens. After some

---

 3 The Search for Wisdom *What does Sindbad's action here reveal about his ability to search out new information?*

Vocabulary

fruitless (frōōt′lis) *adj.* unproductive; useless; sure to end in failure

---

2. Here, *prodigy* means "an event or a thing so rare or extraordinary as to inspire wonder."

Vocabulary

confounded (kən found′) *v.* to confuse or bewilder

THE SECOND VOYAGE OF SINDBAD THE SAILOR **499**

Teach

Big Idea	3

The Search for Wisdom
Answer: *It reveals that he is willing to use prior knowledge—such as how to measure a circumference and remembering to mark where he began—to search out new wisdom, such as what the object might be.*

Literary History ☆

The Roc This giant, mythical, and legendary bird appears in the collection of tales known as *The Thousand and One Nights* and in the writings of the famed Venetian traveler, Marco Polo. According to Marco Polo, Kublai Khan (the founder of the Mongol dynasty in China) heard that the bird could be found on Madagascar and other islands off the coast of eastern Africa. He wanted to learn more about the roc, and his curiosity was rewarded with what was supposed to be a roc's feather. In reality, it was probably a palm frond.

Learning Objectives
Analyzing point of view. (SE)
Analyzing problems and solutions. (SE)
Analyzing cause-and-effect relationships. (TE)

English Learners

DIFFERENTIATED INSTRUCTION

Intermediate Have students read through the page and record any unfamiliar words. Then, organize students into small groups. Have group members work together to discover the meaning of their words. Before they use dictionaries, have students use context clues in the text to try to figure out the words' meanings.

Advanced Learners/Pre-AP

DIFFERENTIATED INSTRUCTION

Frame Stories Although it is not apparent from this excerpt, Sindbad is part of a frame story. A frame story is a larger work that uses a structure or framework to connect fictional narratives being told by a storyteller, in this case Scheherezade. Have students write their own frame stories. Suggest they work on the "inner" story first, then consider who might be telling this story and why.

499

Teach

Reading Strategy 1

Identify Problem and Solution Answer: *Sindbad's new problem is worse because there doesn't appear to be food or water and he is stranded on a precipice.*

Big Idea 2

The Search for Wisdom

Answer: *Answers may vary. Some students may say that his religious beliefs, his reliance on Allah, and his willingness to keep vigil are evidence of wisdom. Others may think that since he fell asleep on the first island, keeping vigil alone may be unwise.*

Draco (detail) (constellation of the Northern Hemisphere) from the Ajaib al-Makhukat *, 14th century. Freer Gallery of Art, Washington, DC.*

time it began to drop, and sailing swiftly downwards came to earth on the brow of a steep hill.

Trembling with fear, I hastened to untie my turban before the roc became aware of my presence. Scarcely had I released myself when the monster darted off towards a great black object lying near and, clutching it in its fearful claws, took wing again. As it rose in the air I was astonished to see that this was a serpent of immeasurable length; and with its prey the bird vanished from sight.

Looking around, I found myself on a precipitous hillside overlooking an exceedingly deep and vast valley. On all sides towered craggy mountains whose beetling[3] summits no man could ever scale. I was stricken with fear and repented my rashness. "Would I had remained in that island!" I thought to myself. "There at least I lacked neither fruit nor water, while these barren steeps offer nothing to eat or drink. No sooner do I escape from one peril than I find myself in another more grievous. There is no strength or help save in Allah!"

When I had made my way down the hill I marvelled to see the ground thickly cov-

ered with the rarest diamonds, so that the entire valley blazed with a glorious light. Here and there among the glittering stones, however, coiled deadly snakes and vipers, dread keepers of the fabulous treasure. Thicker and longer than giant palm-trees, they could have swallowed whole elephants at one gulp. They were crawling back into their sunless dens, for by day they hid themselves from their enemies the rocs and the eagles and moved about only at night.

Overwhelmed with horror, and oblivious of hunger and fatigue, I roamed the valley all day searching with infinite caution for a shelter where I might pass the night. At dusk I came upon a narrow-mouthed cave, into which I crawled, blocking its entrance from within by a great stone. I thought to myself: "Here I shall be safe tonight. When tomorrow comes, let Destiny do its worst."

Scarcely had I advanced a few steps, when I saw at the far end of the cave an enormous serpent coiled in a great knot round its eggs. My hair stood on end and I was transfixed with terror. Seeing no way of escape, however, I put my trust in Allah and kept vigil all night. At daybreak I rolled back the stone and staggered out of the cave, reeling like a drunken man.

---

3. *Beetling* means "overhanging" or "projecting."

1 **Identify Problem and Solution** *Why is Sindbad's new problem worse than his original one?*

The Search for Wisdom *Do you think Sindbad's decision here is wise? Explain.* **2**

500 UNIT 3 SOUTHWEST ASIA

Writing Practice

Write a Personal Essay Although students have never experienced adventures like Sindbad's, they may still have experienced some unique or interesting events in their lives. Have students write a personal essay that describes one of their own adventures. Suggest that students think back to when they were children. At that age, many events may have seemed like an adventure.

Tell students to go into detail in their essays. They should describe the setting, events, and other people involved in their experiences. Point out that imagery can help bring a piece of writing alive for readers. After students have finished, ask volunteers to share their essays with the class. Point out any similarities or differences between the students' adventures and Sindbad's.

As I thus stumbled along I noticed a great joint of flesh come tumbling down into the valley from rock to rock. Upon closer inspection I found this to be a whole sheep, skinned and drawn. I was deeply perplexed at the mystery, for there was not a soul in sight; but at that very moment there flashed across my mind the memory of a story I had once heard from travelers who had visited the Diamond Mountains—how men obtained the diamonds from this treacherous and inaccessible valley by a strange device. Before sunrise they would throw whole carcasses of sheep from the top of the mountains, so that the gems on which they fell penetrated the soft flesh and became embedded in it. At midday rocs and mighty vultures would swoop down upon the mutton and carry it away in their talons to their nests in the mountain heights. With a great clamor the merchants would then rush at the birds and force them to drop the meat and fly away, after which it would only remain to look through the carcasses and pick out the diamonds.

As I recalled this story a plan of escape formed in my mind. I selected a great quantity of priceless stones and hid them all about me, filling my pockets with them and pressing them into the folds of my belt and garments. Then I unrolled my turban, stuffed it with more diamonds, twisted it into a rope as I had done before, and, lying down below the carcass, bound it firmly to my chest. I had not remained long in that position when I suddenly felt myself lifted from the ground by the talons of a huge vulture which had tightly closed upon the meat. The bird climbed higher and higher and finally alighted upon the top of a mountain. As soon as it began to tear at the flesh there arose from behind the neighboring rocks a great **tumult**, at which the bird took fright and flew away. At once I freed myself and sprang to my feet, with face and clothes all bloody.

I saw a man come running to the spot and stop in alarm as he saw me. Without uttering a word he cautiously bent over the carcass to examine it, eyeing me suspiciously all the while; but finding no diamonds, he wrung his hands and lifted up his arms, crying: "O heavy loss! Allah, in whom alone dwell all power and majesty, defend us from the wiles of the Evil One!"

Before I could explain my presence the man, shaking with fear, turned to me and asked: "Who are you, and how came you here?"

"Do not be alarmed, sir," I replied, "I am no evil spirit, but an honest man, a merchant by profession. My story is an extraordinary one, and the adventure which has brought me to these mountains surpasses in wonder all the marvels that men have seen or heard of. But first pray accept some of these diamonds, which I myself gathered in the fearful valley below." [4]

I took some splendid jewels from my pocket and offered them to him, saying: "These will bring you all the riches you can desire."

The owner of the bait was overjoyed at the unexpected gift; he warmly thanked me and called down blessings upon me. Whilst we were thus talking, several other merchants came up from the mountain-side. They crowded round us, listening in amazement to my story, and congratulated me, saying: "By Allah, your escape was a miracle; for no man has ever set foot in that valley and returned alive. Allah alone be praised for your salvation."

---

[3] **Identify Problem and Solution** *What role might the diamonds play in solving Sindbad's problems?*

Vocabulary

tumult (tōō′məlt) *n.* commotion or noisy confusion

Reading Strategy [3]

Identify Problem and Solution Answer: *Sindbad wants a bird to take him to the merchants who set out the meat; the diamonds may help him pay for food and drinks, shelter, and a way back home.*

Big Idea [4]

The Search for Wisdom
Ask: How does Sindbad help others on their search for wisdom? *(Sindbad gladly shares his adventures and knowledge with others.)*

Learning Objectives
Identifying problem and solution. (SE)
Analyzing point of view. (SE)
Writing a personal essay. (TE)

English Learners

DIFFERENTIATED INSTRUCTION

Intermediate Write the following sentence on the board: "Do not be alarmed, sir." Point out the comma before *sir*, explaining that it is a comma of direct address. When someone is addressed by name or title, that word is set off by commas.

Write the following sentences on the board. Have students copy them, adding the commas of direct address where needed.

1. Ladies and gentlemen please stand for the national anthem. *(Ladies and gentlemen,)*
2. You are welcome Madame President to our country. *(, Madame President,)*
3. What's your opinion of the new movie complex sir? *(, sir)*

Advanced Learners/Pre-AP

DIFFERENTIATED INSTRUCTION

Mythic Beasts Students may enjoy researching the mythical and real beasts that Sindbad encounters. Have students produce portraits and descriptions of the mythical karkadan and actual elephant or buffalo. Rocs would also make good subjects for illustration and description. After students have finished, have them share their descriptions and portraits with the class.

Teach

Big Idea | 1

The Search for Wisdom
Answer: *People consulted travelers to foreign lands for news and information about the world.*
Ask: What may have been good and bad about relying on travelers' tales for information about the world? *(People could hear firsthand accounts of actual events in exotic places they would never visit. On the other hand, the stories might be exaggerated, inaccurate, or completely fictitious, giving an incorrect view of the world.)*

Cultural History ☆

Alms When Sindbad gives away diamonds and jewels to people he meets and to the poor of the city, he is not just being a generous person, but a good Muslim. Giving alms is one of the five basic principles (the Pillars of Islam) by which the faithful are supposed to live. These religious requirements include ritual prayer, fasting during the holy month of Ramadan, and a pilgrimage to Mecca, in addition to distributing alms.

Capricornus (detail) from the *Ajaib al-Makhukat of al-Kawzwini,* 14th century. Freer Gallery of Art, Washington DC.

The merchants then led me to their tent. They gave me food and drink and there I slept soundly for many hours. Early next day we set out from our tent and, after journeying over a vast range of mountains, came at length to the seashore. After a short voyage we arrived in a pleasant, densely wooded island, covered with trees so huge that beneath one of them a hundred men could shelter from the sun. It is from these trees that the aromatic substance known as camphor[4] is extracted. The trunks are hollowed out, and the sap oozes drop by drop into vessels which are placed beneath, soon curdling into a crystal gum.

In that island I saw a gigantic beast called the karkadan, or rhinoceros, which grazes in the fields like a cow or buffalo. Taller than a camel, it has a single horn in the middle of its forehead, and upon this horn Nature has carved the likeness of a man. The karkadan attacks the elephant and, impaling it upon its horn, carries it aloft from place to place until its victim dies. Before long, however, the elephant's fat melts in the heat of the sun and, dripping down into the karkadan's eyes, puts out its sight, so that the beast blunders

---

4. *Camphor* is used in lotions and medicines.

502 UNIT 3 SOUTHWEST ASIA

helplessly along and finally drops dead. Then the roc swoops down upon both animals and carries them off to its nest in the high mountains. I also saw many strange breeds of buffalo in that island.

I sold a part of my diamonds for a large sum and exchanged more for a vast quantity of merchandise. Then we set sail and, trading from port to port and from island to island, at length arrived safely in Basrah. After a few days' sojourn there I set out upstream to Baghdad, the City of Peace.

Loaded with precious goods and the finest of my diamonds, I hastened to my old street and, entering my own house, rejoiced to see my friends and kinsfolk. I gave them gold and presents, and distributed alms[5] among the poor of the city. ☆

I soon forgot the perils and hardships of my travels and took again to sumptuous living. I ate well, dressed well, and kept open house for innumerable gallants and boon[6] companions.

From far and near men came to hear me speak of my adventures and to learn the news of foreign lands from me. All were astounded at the dangers I had escaped and wished me joy of my return. Such was my second voyage.

Tomorrow, my friends, if Allah wills, I shall relate to you the extraordinary tale of my third voyage.

The famous mariner ended. The guests marvelled at his story.

When the evening feast was over, Sindbad the Sailor gave Sindbad the Porter a hundred pieces of gold, which he took with thanks and many blessings, and departed, lost in wonderment at all he had heard. ❧

---

5. *Alms* are money, food, or other items given to aid the poor.
6. *Boon* describes people who are sociable and make good company.

The Search for Wisdom *Based on this sentence, how did people during this time learn about the world?* | 1 |

Writing Practice

⚡ **Write a Poem** Have students turn this voyage of Sindbad into a poem. Students should relay the events of the adventure and describe Sindbad's feelings about his experiences. Tell students that rhyming their lines is optional.

Encourage students to use literary devices in their poems such as figurative language, imagery, and repetition. For example, students could have a pair of repeating lines that occur each time Sindbad finds himself in a dangerous situation. Or perhaps they could use a simile to describe the roc. After students have finished, have them share their poems in small groups.

After You Read

Respond and Think Critically

Respond and Interpret

1. Which parts of the story did you find most entertaining? Why?

2. (a)Briefly describe the roc and its egg. (b)How do Sindbad's descriptions help create suspense?

3. (a)How does Sindbad escape from the roc's island? (b)What does his plan of escape suggest about his character?

4. (a)How do merchants obtain diamonds from the Diamond Mountains? (b)How does their method help Sindbad escape?

5. (a)What does Sindbad do with his riches when he returns home? (b)What do his actions reveal about him?

Analyze and Evaluate

6. **Irony** occurs when something is the opposite of what is expected. What is ironic about Sindbad's situation after the roc deposits him in the Diamond Mountains?

7. (a)**Hyperbole** is exaggeration or overstatement for effect. What are some examples of hyperbole in the story? (b)What effects does this literary device have on the tale?

Connect

8. **Big Idea** **The Search for Wisdom** What does this story reveal about the ways in which people gain information and the sources to which they turn for knowledge and inspiration?

9. **Connect to Today** What elements of Sindbad's story are common in contemporary adventure books and stories?

Literary Element **Point of View**

"The Second Voyage of Sindbad the Sailor" is told from the **first-person** point of view. Other points of view include the **third-person omniscient,** in which an outside narrator is all knowing, and the **third-person limited,** in which the events are described as only one character perceives them.

1. What effect does the first-person point of view have on "The Second Voyage of Sindbad the Sailor"?

2. How would the story be different if it had been told from the third-person point of view?

Review: Imagery

As you learned on page 242, **imagery** is language that creates "word pictures" in the reader's mind and evokes emotional responses. Imagery appeals to one or more of the five senses and can enhance the reader's enjoyment of a literary work.

Partner Activity With a partner, find examples of imagery in the story. Work together to create a chart like the one below. For each of the five senses listed, find corresponding imagery in the text that appeals to that sense.

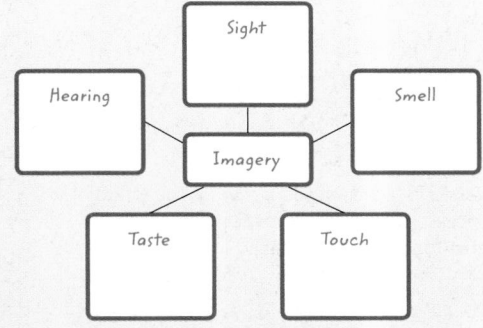

After You Read

Assess

1. Answers will vary.

2. (a) The roc is a huge bird; its wings block the sun from view. The egg is a huge white dome. (b) Sindbad's vivid descriptions build suspense by capturing the initial mystery of the egg and the enormity and the power of the roc.

3. (a) He ties himself to a talon of the bird with his turban. (b) He is brave and resourceful.

4. (a) They toss sheep carcasses into the valley, where diamonds adhere to them. When rocs and vultures later carry the carcasses away, the merchants scare the birds away and retrieve the diamonds. (b) Sindbad attaches himself to one of the carcasses and is lifted to safety.

5. (a) Sindbad shares his wealth but also lives well. (b) He is generous but practical.

6. It is ironic that Sindbad escapes the roc's island only to be set down in what seems to be a worse situation.

7. (a) Instances of hyperbole include the descriptions of the sizes of the trees, the snakes, and the vipers and the karkadan's battle with the elephant. (b) The hyperbole makes the story enjoyable.

8. People gain information and inspiration from other people, books and stories, and religion.

9. Elements include an independent hero, a terrifying adversary, setbacks along the way, and a successful conclusion.

Literary Element

1. The point of view allows the reader to see the events as Sindbad sees them and to feel the immediacy and danger of his adventures. The reader can also understand his motivations and his feelings.

2. The story would be different because the reader would have a limited understanding of events.

Review: Imagery

Possible answers:

<u>Sight:</u> "green meadows" (p. 498)

<u>Hearing:</u> "singing of birds and murmur of crystal streams" (p. 498)

<u>Smell:</u> "fragrant breeze" (p. 498)

<u>Taste:</u> "rich in fruit" (p. 498)

<u>Touch:</u> "felt myself lifted from the ground" (p. 501)

After You Read

Assess

Reading Strategy

Identify Problem and Solution **C** is the correct answer because the context indicates that Sindbad is attempting to determine the size of the egg. **A**, **B**, and **D** are not solutions to this problem.

Progress Check

Can students identify problem and solution?

If No → See Unit 3 Teaching Resources Book, p. 94.

Vocabulary Practice

1. a **2.** b **3.** c **4.** a

Academic Vocabulary

Possible answer: An inspection of a crime scene would include gathering evidence, dusting for fingerprints, and photographing the area.

Connect to *Art*

Students' reports should reflect the use of effective research strategies, connect the pictorial style of Persian miniatures to the narrative style of *The Thousand and One Nights*, and use the preferred form for citations.

 For additional selection assessment, see Assessment Resources, pp. 103–104.

Reading Strategy Identify Problem and Solution

ACT Skills Practice

Sindbad makes a mark in the sand at the base of the roc's egg to:

A. claim the egg later as his property.

B. leave some memento of his stay on the island.

C. determine the egg's circumference.

D. be able to identify the egg later.

Vocabulary Practice

Practice with Analogies Choose the correct word to complete each analogy.

1. beach : sand :: thicket :
  a. shrubs   **c.** lumber
  b. nests   **d.** fruit

2. enormous : massive :: fruitless :
  a. meaningful   **c.** chaotic
  b. pointless   **d.** priceless

3. peace : calm :: tumult :
  a. mob   **c.** din
  b. party   **d.** crime

4. thrill : entertain :: confound :
  a. confuse   **c.** discover
  b. join   **d.** destroy

Academic Vocabulary

*In this story, Sindbad's careful **inspection** of his surroundings helps him escape.*

Inspection is an academic word. The Board of Health might conduct **inspections** to ensure that food is handled safely. To further explore this word, complete the sentence below.

An inspection of a crime scene would include _____, _____, and _____.

For more on academic vocabulary, see pages 36–37 and R83–R85.

Connect to *Art*

Write a Report

Assignment Persian miniatures are vivid paintings that were used to illustrate Persian manuscript books in the Middle Ages. Research this art form and write a brief report on the style and the subjects of the miniatures. In your report, compare the pictorial style of the miniatures with the narrative style of *The Thousand and One Nights*.

Investigate Develop a research plan, such as deciding what search terms—for example, "Iranian painting"—may be helpful. Generate ideas from multiple sources, such as art history books and the Internet. Keep a record of the bibliographical information about your sources and use a chart like the one below to record your notes.

Painting	Subject	Style
Illustration from Persian epic the Shah-nama ("Book of Kings")	Combat between warrior heroes Sohrab and Rustum	Bright colors, flat (little perspective), every area filled with ornamental detail

Create Illustrate your report with specific examples of the Persian miniatures about which you are writing. Photocopy or scan the images you want to use or download examples you find on the Internet.

Report Compile the information you have gathered and write your report, making sure to incorporate relevant historical and cultural background. Include a works cited list, or bibliography, using your teacher's preferred form for citations.

LOG ON **Literature** Online

Selection Resources For Selection Quizzes, eFlashcards, and Reading-Writing Connection activities, go to glencoe.com and enter QuickPass code GLW6053u3.

Writing Practice

Write an Editorial
Have students imagine that one of the Persian miniatures they researched was used in an article in their local newspaper. Tell students to write an editorial in which they give their opinion of the miniature. You may wish to bring in a few editorials for students to look at as a guide.

Students can give their opinions about the miniature's color, artistry, or its cultural history. Allow students enough time to write the editorial. After they have finished, have students switch editorials with partners in order to look for spelling, grammar, and punctuation mistakes. After they have revised any errors, have volunteers share their editorials with the class.

Before You Read

from the *Rubáiyát*

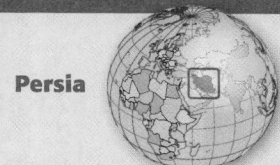

Meet **Omar Khayyám**
(1048–1131)

Ironically, Omar Khayyám, the best-known Persian poet in the Western world, was famous in his own lifetime as an astronomer and a mathematician. The word *khayyám* means "tent maker," but Khayyám—whose name may have been derived from his father's occupation—was a brilliant scholar versed in philosophy, medicine, and astronomy.

A Man of Many Talents The details of Khayyám's life are vague, but modern scholars believe he was born in the Persian city of Nishapur (now Neyshabur in Iran), which was the intellectual capital of Islam at the time. While in his twenties, Khayyám wrote a scholarly work on algebra that caught the attention of Sultan Malik-shah, who asked him to join a learned group that was reforming the Islamic calendar. Their work resulted in the Jalali calendar, which remains the most accurate calendar in the world.

Despite his impressive accomplishments in mathematics and astronomy, Khayyám's fame in the West rests largely on a collection of four-line poems he wrote using a popular medieval Persian poetic form called the *rubá'i* (*rubá'i* means "quatrain"; the plural form is *rubáiyát*). Typically, the first two lines of a rubá'i introduce a problem or a situation, the third creates tension or surprise, and the fourth offers resolution, sometimes with an unexpected slant or twist.

A Rediscovered Poet Khayyám's poetry, which never developed a significant audience during his lifetime, remained largely unknown to readers outside of Persia for hundreds of years. In the mid-1800s, however, copies of Khayyám's verses were discovered in the Bodleian Library at Oxford University in England. Struck by the

Omar Khayyám, Persian Astronomer-poet (detail). Sir Frank Brangwyn. Oil on canvas. Private collection.

> "Ah, make the most of what we yet may spend,
> Before we too into the Dust descend . . ."
>
> —from *The Rubáiyát of Omar Khayyám*

beauty and emotional depth of the poems, British poet Edward FitzGerald (1809–1893) translated them into English and published them as *The Rubáiyát of Omar Khayyám* in 1859. Although it was little noticed at first, the *Rubáiyát* gradually found an enthusiastic readership. FitzGerald's translation increased in popularity, and he later published several revised and expanded editions.

In the late nineteenth and early twentieth centuries, publishers all over the world created illustrated editions of the *Rubáiyát*. These editions helped make Khayyám a world-renowned poet more than 700 years after his death.

LOG ON ▶ **Literature** Online

Author Search For more about Omar Khayyám, go to glencoe.com and enter QuickPass code GLW6053u3.

OMAR KHAYYÁM **505**

Before You Read

Focus

Bellringer Options

Selection Focus
Transparency 24
Daily Language
Transparency 42

Or ask: Do you feel it is better to live for the moment or to plan for the future? *(Students may say that the world is changing so fast that it is difficult to predict the future. Others may say that if they do not enjoy themselves now, they may regret it later.)* Ask students whether they think living for the moment is more characteristic of younger people or of older people, and why.

View the Art ★

Ironically, Omar Khayyám, the best-known Persian poet in the Western world, was known during his own lifetime as a mathematician, not as a poet. Khayyám's verse was not known in the West until the mid-1800s. **Ask:** Why might Khayyám's poetry not have been known in the West until after he died? *(Students may say that people instead focused on his stature as a prominent mathematician.)*

Selection Skills

Literary Elements
- Rhyme Scheme (SE pp. 506, 507–509)

Reading Skills
- Clarify Meaning (SE pp. 506, 507, 510)
- Recognize Author's Purpose (TE p. 506)
- Analyze Persuasive Techniques (TE p. 508)

from the **Rubáiyát**

Vocabulary Skills
- Usage (SE pp. 506, 510)
- Ask Questions (TE p. 506)

Speaking/Listening/Viewing Skills
- Analyze Art (TE pp. 507, 508)

Writing Skills/Grammar
- Literary Criticism (SE p. 510)

Before You Read

Focus

Summary

These verses are quatrains, or four-line poems, selected from the *Rubáiyát*. Each four-line verse probably was originally meant to stand alone, as a complete poem. Many of the verses have similar themes, such as the fleeting nature of beauty and pleasure, so translator Edward FitzGerald numbered and grouped them in an order he thought suitable to emphasize those themes.

 For summaries in languages other than English, see Unit 3 Teaching Resources Book, pp. 100–105.

Vocabulary

Ask Questions Organize students in pairs. Have each pair ask each other questions using the vocabulary words *waive* and *conspire*.

Literature and Reading Preview

Connect to the Poems

Why might people believe that certain pleasures in life should be denied or enjoyed only moderately? Write a journal entry about your thoughts on this question.

Build Background

FitzGerald wanted modern readers to be able to respond emotionally to the *Rubáiyát*. To accomplish this, he often incorporated contemporary images that differed from the original Persian. He also arranged the quatrains so that they appear to be an account of a single day, although it is unlikely that Khayyám intended this arrangement.

Set Purposes for Reading

Big Idea The Search for Wisdom

As you read, ask yourself, Does it seem wise to always seek refuge in pleasure and to live for the moment?

Literary Element Rhyme Scheme

Rhyme scheme is the pattern that end rhymes form in a stanza or a poem. Rhyme scheme is designated by the assignment of a different letter of the alphabet for each rhyme. As you read the verses from the *Rubáiyát*, ask yourself, What is the rhyme scheme of each *ruba'i*?

Reading Strategy Clarify Meaning

To **clarify meaning** as you read, it often helps to reread difficult passages or to read more slowly if you are confused. When reading poetry, you should follow the syntax, or arrangement, of the lines to track complete thoughts. As you read, ask yourself, Do I understand the meaning of this line or quatrain?

Tip: Track Word Order Pay particular attention to lines that do not follow normal word-order patterns. Use a chart like this to track inverted, or reverse, word order in Khayyám's verses.

Khayyám's Word Order	Normal Word Order
"Myself when young did eagerly frequent"	"When I was young I eagerly frequented"

506 UNIT 3 SOUTHWEST ASIA

Learning Objectives

For pages 505–510
In studying this text, you will focus on the following objectives:

Literary Study: Analyzing rhyme scheme.

Reading: Clarifying meaning.

Writing: Reporting on literary criticism.

Vocabulary

waive (wāv) v. to reject, decline, or give up; p. 507 *The suspect wanted to defend himself, so he chose to waive his right to be silent.*

conspire (kən spīr′) v. to join in agreement; to plot; p. 508 *The younger siblings decided to conspire against their self-absorbed older brother.*

Tip: Word Usage When you encounter a new word, it might help you to ask yourself a question about it. For example, when might you *conspire* with a friend?

Reading Practice

Recognize Author's Purpose Remind students that they have learned about four kinds of sentences: declarative, which make a statement; imperative, which give a command; interrogative, which ask a question; and exclamatory, which express strong emotion. Tell students that a poet's choice of sentence type might reveal clues about his or her purpose for writing.

Have students examine poems I, VII, XII, and XIII of the *Rubáiyát* and indicate what kind of sentence begins each one. *(I, VII, and XIII are imperative; XII is exclamatory.)* Why do students think the poet begins these poems this way? *(Possibly he hopes to appeal to the emotions of the person to whom he is addressing these lines.)*

from the Rubáiyát

Omar Khayyám
Translated by Edward FitzGerald

Shah Abbas I and a Courtier (detail). Persian school. Fresco. Chehel Sotun Isfahan, Iran.

I

Awake! for Morning in the Bowl of Night°
Has flung the Stone° that puts the Stars to Flight:
    And Lo! the Hunter of the East has caught
The Sultán's Turret° in a Noose of Light.

VII

Come, fill the Cup, and in the Fire of Spring
The Winter Garment of Repentance fling:
    The Bird of Time has but a little way
To fly—and Lo! the Bird is on the Wing.

XII

"How sweet is mortal Sovranty!"°—think some:
Others—"How blest the Paradise to come!"
    Ah, take the Cash in hand and **waive** the Rest;
Oh, the brave Music of a *distant* Drum!

XIII

Look to the Rose that blows about us—"Lo,
Laughing," she says, "into the World I blow:
    At once the silken Tassel of my Purse
Tear, and its Treasure on the Garden throw."

XVII

They say the Lion and the Lizard keep
The Courts where Jamshy´d° gloried and drank deep;
    And Bahrám,° that great Hunter—the Wild Ass
Stamps o'er his Head, and he lies fast asleep.

I, 1 Bowl of Night: the night sky.
I, 2 Stone: the rising sun.

I, 4 Turret: a small, often ornamental, tower projecting from a larger structure.

XII, 1 Sovranty: freedom from external control (spelled *sovereignty* in Standard English).

XVII, 2 Jamshy´d: In Persian mythology, he was a king of celestial beings condemned to live as a mortal being.
XVII, 3 Bahrám: legendary king who was killed while hunting an ass.

1 Rhyme Scheme *Which three lines in this verse rhyme?*

2 Clarify Meaning *How might you rearrange this line to follow a more standard sentence structure?*

Vocabulary
waive (wāv) *v.* to reject, decline, or give up

English Learners

DIFFERENTIATED INSTRUCTION

Advanced Have students work in small groups to develop simple four-line poems. Give each group a topic such as "Day and Night" or "Summer and Winter." You might also provide them with a bank of common rhyming words, or allow them to find this information online.

Approaching Level

DIFFERENTIATED INSTRUCTION

Main Ideas Have students read each quatrain on this page. Have students work in small groups to first determine the main idea of each one and then to decide what the title of each might be if it was separate from the others.

Teach

Literary Element   1

Rhyme Scheme Answer:
Lines 1 (Night), 2 (Flight), and 4 (Light) rhyme.

ADVANCED Ask: Why might the poet have made only one line unrhymed? *(Students may say that he made the line unrhymed because he wanted to draw attention to it. Because it does not follow the pattern of the other three lines, it stands out.)*

For additional literary element practice, see Unit 3 Teaching Resources Book, p. 106.

Reading Strategy   2

Clarify Meaning Answer:
Students may rearrange the line as follows: Some think, "How sweet is mortal Sovranty!"

View the Art

Shah Abbas I was shah of Persia from 1588 to 1629. During his reign the arts reached a pinnacle.
Ask: What are the people in this painting doing? *(Students should recognize that the people are eating and drinking.)*

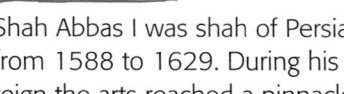 For an audio recording of this selection, use Listening Library Audio CD-ROM.

Interactive Read and Write
Other options for teaching this selection can be found in Interactive Read and Write for On-Level Learners, pp. 121–128.

Learning Objectives
Analyzing rhyme scheme. (SE)
Clarifying meaning. (SE)
Recognizing author's purpose. (TE)

Teach

Big Idea 1

The Search for Wisdom

Answer: *It suggests that the well-educated should be consulted but that they do not always contribute to the search for wisdom.*

Literary Element 2

Rhyme Scheme Answer: *All four lines rhyme.*

Literary History ☆

Quatrains Quatrains are any poems of exactly four lines. The alternating quatrain is simply *abab*. An envelope stanza rhymes *abba*. Two envelope stanzas in a row are called an Italian octave, which is used in sonnets. The in memoriam stanza is an envelope stanza written in a specific meter (iambic tetrameter). It gets its name from a poem written in that form by Tennyson. Other types of quatrains are the Italian and Sicilian quatrains, the hymnal stanza, and the pantoum.

View the Art ★

This nineteenth-century Persian painting shows the influence of European art forms. The medium —oil on canvas—is purely European, as is the artist's attempt to create perspective by painting fruit in the foreground. The subject matter, essentially a flat figure, and careful attention to decorative detail are, however, distinctly Persian. **Ask:** What type of music might this girl play or dance to? *(The girl is holding a tambourine, and therefore would be playing or dancing to music with a strong beat.)*

508

A Dancing Girl with a Tambourine. Qajar school. Oil on canvas. Private collection. ★

XXVII
Myself when young did eagerly frequent
Doctor and Saint, and heard great Argument
About it and about: but evermore
Came out by the same Door as in I went.

XXVIII
With them the Seed of Wisdom did I sow,
And with my own hand labor'd it to grow:
   And this was all the Harvest that I reap'd—
"I came like Water, and like Wind I go."

LXVIII
We are no other than a moving row
Of Magic Shadow-shapes that come and go
   Round with the Sun-illumined Lantern held
In Midnight by the Master of the Show.

LXIX
But helpless Pieces of the Game He plays
Upon this Checker-board of Nights and Days;
   Hither and thither moves, and checks, and slays,
And one by one back in the Closet lays.

LXXI
And much as Wine has play'd the Infidel,
And robb'd me of my Robe of Honor—well,
   I often wonder what the Vintners° buy
One half so precious as the Goods they sell.

XCIX
Ah, Love! could you and I with Him **conspire**
To grasp this sorry Scheme of Things entire,
   Would not we shatter it to bits—and then
Re-mold it nearer to the Heart's Desire!

LXXI, 3. **Vintners:** sellers of wine and liquor.

1 **The Search for Wisdom** *What does this verse suggest about the role of well-educated people in the search for wisdom?*

2 **Rhyme Scheme** *How does the rhyme scheme in this verse differ from the usual ruba'i pattern?*

Vocabulary

conspire (kən spīr´) *v.* to join in agreement; to plot

508 UNIT 3 SOUTHWEST ASIA

Reading Practice

SMALL GROUP **Analyze Persuasive Techniques** Explain that some poets use their powers of expression to get readers to believe something or to do something. The poet of the *Rubáiyát* is directing his ideas to someone. Have students explore what he is trying to persuade that person to do.

Arrange the class in small groups, and assign each group one or two of the poems. Have groups paraphrase their poems to determine what the poet is asking or stating. What techniques is he using to persuade? Is he convincing? Why or why not? Have each group discuss with the rest of the class how its poem contributes to the overall theme of the *Rubáiyát*.

After You Read

Respond and Think Critically

Respond and Interpret

1. What images linger in your mind after reading these verses?

2. (a)What time of day is **personified**, or given human characteristics, in ruba'i I? (b)What part of the human life cycle might this time of day represent?

3. (a)In ruba'i VII, what does the speaker urge readers to do? (b)What reason does the speaker give?

4. (a)What is the **theme**, or overall message, of ruba'i XVII? (b)What image develops this theme?

Analyze and Evaluate

5. (a)Does the speaker agree with the beliefs of others whom he quotes in ruba'i XII? (b)What does his response to these beliefs suggest about him?

6. (a)What image does Khayyám create in ruba'i LXVIII? (b)What does this image suggest about the speaker's view of human life?

Connect

7. **Big Idea** **The Search for Wisdom** Critics have said that the knowledge that death is inevitable drives the love of life displayed in the *Rubáiyát*. In your opinion, is this view accurate? Explain.

8. **Connect to the Author** Omar Khayyám was a brilliant scholar educated in a variety of subjects. How might his broad education have contributed to the verses of the *Rubáiyát* excerpted here?

Literary Element Rhyme Scheme

Poems are often structured around a particular **rhyme scheme**, or a regular pattern of rhyme. Rhyme schemes are analyzed by assigning a different letter of the alphabet to each rhyme, beginning with the letter *a*, as in the following example from the *Rubáiyát:*

Awake! for Morning in the Bowl of <u>Night</u> *a*

Has flung the Stone that puts the Stars to <u>Flight</u>: *a*

And Lo! the Hunter of the East has <u>caught</u> *b*

The Sultán's Turret in a Noose of <u>Light</u>. *a*

1. What rhyme scheme appears most frequently in the *Rubáiyát?*

2. Do you think the verses would be more or less effective if all the lines rhymed with one another? Explain.

Review: Speaker

As you learned on page 359, a poem's **speaker** is the person or being who is speaking, similar to a narrator in a work of prose. The speaker is sometimes the poet but can also be a fictional person or even an object. The speaker communicates a particular **tone**, or attitude, in the poem by using specific word choice, or **diction**.

1. Choose a verse from the *Rubáiyát* and explain how the **diction** contributes to the speaker's tone.

2. Review the chart you made on page 506 to restate inverted word order in normal English. How do your restatements affect the tone of the lines?

3. What are three or four adjectives you might use to describe the speaker of the *Rubáiyát?*

After You Read

Assess

1. Answers will vary.

2. (a) The morning is personified. (b) The morning, or beginning of the day, might represent birth, the beginning of life, or childhood.

3. (a) The speaker urges readers to "fill the Cup" and fling away the "Winter Garment of Repentance." (b) His reason is that time is always passing quickly, so repentance is not worthwhile.

4. (a) Even those who were great are now gone, so the time to enjoy life is now. (b) The image of animals stamping over the head of a great hunter helps convey the theme.

5. (a) He does not agree with these beliefs. (b) His response suggests that he values earthly riches over heavenly ones and finds courage in living by his own rules, rather than depending on the "Music of a *distant* Drum."

6. (a) He creates the image of life as a stage performance in which humans are only a row of shadows lit by the lantern of the "Master." (b) It suggests that he sees human life as fleeting and inconsequential in the grand scheme of the universe.

7. Some students may say that because we know we will die, it is critical to experience life and love while we can.

8. Answers will vary. Students may note that his education in astronomy is evident in his references to the sun and stars, that his understanding of sciences may have led to his skepticism about a heavenly reward in the afterlife, and that his knowledge of many subjects is evident in his confidence at sowing a "Seed of Wisdom."

Literary Element

1. The rhyme scheme used most frequently is *aaba*.

2. Students may note that having each line rhyme would allow less variety in words and images and would detract from the energy of the poems.

Review: Speaker

1. Students should identify specific imagery and figurative language that shapes the tone of the poem they choose.

2. Answers will vary.

3. Students might choose adjectives such as *melancholy, disillusioned, romantic,* and *thoughtful.*

After You Read

Assess

Reading Strategy

B is the correct answer. **A** and **C** are only partly correct; **D** is true but irrelevant; **E** is wrong.

Progress Check

Can students clarify meaning?

If No → See Unit 3 Teaching Resources Book, p. 107.

Vocabulary Practice

1. Students should note the benefits of free speech and its contributions to democracy.
2. Students should indicate acts such as civil disobedience.

Academic Vocabulary

Students should note a thing they had reservations about doing.

Research and Report

Students' reports should respond to a credible work of literary criticism, use valid evidence to support claims, and be presented using verbal and nonverbal techniques.

Reading Strategy Clarify Meaning

SAT Skills Practice

The speaker introduces Jamshy'd and Bahrám in ruba'i XVII to

(A) celebrate their power and glory

(B) emphasize the passing of fame

(C) evoke the greatness of the past

(D) create a desert landscape

(E) evoke a mood of despair

Vocabulary Practice

Practice with Usage Respond to the statements below to gain a better understanding of the meaning of each boldfaced vocabulary word from the verses.

1. Why might a country refuse to **waive** the right to free speech?
2. How might citizens **conspire** to overthrow a tyrant?

Academic Vocabulary

The speaker of the Rubáiyát *believes that people should live without* **inhibitions** *and should enjoy life fully.*

Inhibition is an academic word. In more casual conversation, you might say that a person who is afraid to dance in front of people has an **inhibition.** To further explore the meaning of this word, complete the sentence below.

My inhibitions prevented me from _____.

For more on academic vocabulary, see pages 36–37 and R83–R85.

LOG ON ▶ **Literature** Online

Selection Resources For Selection Quizzes, eFlashcards, and Reading-Writing Connection activities, go to glencoe.com and enter QuickPass code GLW6053u3.

Research and Report

📝 Literary Criticism

Assignment Evaluate a passage of literary criticism that comments on the outlook on life expressed in Khayyám's poetry. Write a short response in which you explain whether you agree or disagree with the critic, using evidence from the *Rubáiyát.* Present your response to the class in a report.

Prepare Use the Internet and the library to research credible literary criticism that has been written on Khayyám's poetry. Choose an appropriate passage to evaluate and then formulate a thesis you can support with valid, relevant evidence from the text. Use a chart like the one below to match different points made by the critic with your opinions and the evidence you will use to support them.

Critic's Statement	My Opinion	Evidence
"In spite of the labels which some commentators have tried to pin on him, Omar was not a mystic." (Louis Untermeyer)	I agree	Khayyám notes that people should not take refuge in paradise but instead should "… take the Cash in hand and waive the Rest."

Report Make sure your report includes logical arguments that will inform and persuade your listeners. When you present the report, make eye contact, speak loudly and clearly, and maintain good posture. Use appropriate tones of voice to clarify logical appeals and to enhance emotional ones.

Evaluate In a short paragraph, evaluate your delivery of the report. Consider the quality of your research and your use of verbal and nonverbal techniques.

Writing Practice

📝 **Research and Report** Tell students that the foundation of a research report is the thesis statement, or the main point of a paper. When writing a thesis statement, students should consider the position they will explore in their papers. For this assignment, they should ask: What is the critic's opinion of an aspect of Khayyám's poetry, and do I agree or disagree with it?

Have student pairs share their thesis statements, using the following questions as a guide for evaluation.

1. Does the thesis statement present the literary critic's opinion and the student's position on it?
2. Is the thesis statement too broad or too narrow? It needs to be specific, but broad enough to allow students to fully explore it in the body of their reports.

3. Does the thesis statement use strong, specific words? Can students think of other words that might make more of an impact on readers?

Allow students time to discuss their reviews and then edit their thesis statements, if necessary. Students should then review their papers to make sure they fully address and support the position specified in the thesis statement.

Before You Read

The Counsels of the Bird

Meet **Rumi**

(1207–1273)

According to Islamic tradition, when the famous Persian poet Farid ud-Din Attar was very old, he met Jalal al-Din Rumi (rü′mē), who was then only a child, and proclaimed that Rumi would become a great leader. Although this story may be a myth, Rumi did become an exceptionally influential Islamic poet and mystic. His poetry has inspired Muslims and non-Muslims alike from the thirteenth century to the present.

Early Life Rumi was born in 1207 in the city of Balkh (now a part of northern Afghanistan). He and his family fled westward when the Mongol armies of Genghis Khan invaded the area. The family eventually settled in the city of Konya (in present-day Turkey), where the king had invited Rumi's father to teach at a madrassa, or religious school. When his father died in 1231, Rumi filled his position at the madrassa, and gained acclaim as a teacher of Sufism, an Islamic mystical movement.

Spiritual Friendship In 1244, Rumi's life changed permanently when he met a wandering mystic named Shams al-Din Tabrizi. Shams's religious teachings and spirituality inspired Rumi, and the men became inseparable. This friendship caused jealousy in the Sufi community, especially when Rumi began to neglect his Sufi disciples and his family. In 1248, Shams vanished mysteriously—modern historians agree he was murdered, likely by men jealous over his relationship with Rumi. Distraught by his friend's disappearance, Rumi began to write thousands of verses of poetry that expressed feelings of love and loss. He signed these poems in Shams's name—a Sufi gesture that signified the spiritual bond between the two men.

> "Beyond this world and life we know there is Someone watching over us. To know Him is not in our power. But once in a glimpse I saw that we are His shadow and our shadow is the world."
>
> —Rumi

The Masnavi Rumi's most famous work is *The Masnavi* ("couplets" in Arabic), a huge collection of Sufi sermons and fables in verse. *The Masnavi* is regarded by some as Islam's most important spiritual literature after the Qur'an. It asserts that God is present in everything—all people, places, and objects—yet also describes the difficulty many people have experiencing a personal relationship with God. Poet and translator Jonathan Star observed of Rumi, "…his every word came from a place of love and inspiration, a place where the soul and its Creator are one."

 Literature Online

Author Search For more about Rumi, go to glencoe.com and enter QuickPass code GLW6053u3.

Before You Read

Focus

Bellringer Options

Selection Focus
   Transparency 25
Daily Language
   Transparency 43

Or read to the class one of Aesop's fables, such as "The Fox and the Grapes" or "The Fox and the Crow." **Ask:** Why do so many of these kinds of stories feature talking animals? What are the stories really about? *(Students may say that the stories are really about human beings and their thoughts, words, and actions. Putting the words in an animal's mouth makes the tale funnier and gives a message without insulting humans.)*

Selection Skills

Literary Elements
- Maxim (SE pp. 512, 514, 515; TE p. 512)

The Counsels of the Bird

Speaking/Listening/Viewing Skills
- Analyze Art (TE p. 513)

Reading Skills
- Make Generalizations About Characters (SE pp. 512, 513, 515)
- Activate Prior Knowledge (TE p. 514)

Vocabulary Skills
- Practice with Antonyms (SE pp. 512, 515)

Writing Skills/Grammar
- Maxim (SE p. 515)

Before You Read

Focus

Summary

In this poem, a man captures a bird who promises three pieces of good advice in exchange for his freedom. The bird's advice is indeed good, but the man does not act on the advice and the bird becomes exasperated.

 For summaries in languages other than English, see Unit 3 Teaching Resources Book, pp. 111–116.

Vocabulary

Practice with Antonyms

Organize students in pairs. Have each pair make an antonym crossword puzzle based on the vocabulary words. For example, students might list possible antonyms as clues and the vocabulary words as answers. If time allows, have students add other words from the text and their antonyms. Ask pairs to exchange work and solve each other's puzzles.

 For additional vocabulary practice, see Unit 3 Teaching Resources Book, p. 119.

Literary Element Practice

Maxim Tell students that maxims are found in countries and cultures all over the world. Ask students to share maxims they know from other cultures, and write their ideas on the board. How did students hear of the maxim? Was it something they heard friends or family members say? Was it something they read?

Have students compare and contrast the maxims listed on the board. Do students think the sayings can be applied universally? Why or why not? *(Students may note that some maxims are universal because people around the world share many of the same beliefs about morality and behavior.)*

Literature and Reading Preview

Connect to the Poem

Have you ever ignored a piece of advice? Freewrite for a few minutes about this advice and why you ignored it.

Build Background

Sufis sought to find truth and knowledge through a personal experience with God. They embraced poverty and wore *sufs,* or patched cloaks of rough wool, as a sign of their unworldliness. Rumi founded the Mevlevi order of Sufis, whose ritual prayer (called *dhikr*) involves spinning dances set to music. This garnered them the nickname "whirling dervishes" (*dervish* is Persian for "beggar").

Set Purposes for Reading

Big Idea **The Search for Wisdom**

As you read, ask yourself, How does the bird in the poem use wisdom to gain his freedom?

Literary Element **Maxim**

A **maxim** is a short saying that contains a general truth, a fundamental principle, or a rule of conduct about morality, personal behavior, or human experience. Such statements existed throughout history—for example, in the works of the philosopher Confucius, the biblical book of Proverbs, and the oral traditions of Africa. As you read, ask yourself, What maxims does the bird offer the man?

Reading Strategy **Make Generalizations About Characters**

When you **make generalizations about characters,** you draw conclusions about them based on details in the text. As you read, ask yourself, What generalizations can I make about the bird and the man based on their words and actions?

Tip: Track Words and Actions In a chart like the one below, track the words and actions of the bird and the man.

Character	Words and Actions	Generalization
Man	Captured bird by wiles and snares	Man is cunning enough to trap bird

---

Learning Objectives

For pages 511–515

In studying this text, you will focus on the following objectives:

Literary Study: Analyzing maxims.

Reading: Making generalizations about characters.

Writing: Writing a maxim.

Vocabulary

deem (dēm) *v.* to regard in a certain way; p. 514 *She did not deem him worthy of her attention.*

assertion (ə sur′shən) *n.* a forceful or confident statement of fact or belief; p. 514 *The alumni believed the coach's assertion that the team would win the championship.*

prosperity (pros per′ə tē) *n.* the state of being successful; p. 514 *Her prosperity was due to her dedicated work ethic and high-paying job.*

Tip: Antonyms Antonyms are words with opposite meanings. For example, *poverty,* or the lack of money and material possessions, is an antonym of *prosperity.* Antonyms are always the same part of speech.

A Bird. Persian Miniature.

The **Counsels** *of the* **Bird**
from The Masnavi

Rumi
Translated by E. H. Winfield

A man captured a bird by wiles and snares;
The bird said to him, "O noble sir,
In your time you have eaten many oxen and sheep,
And likewise sacrificed many camels;
5   You have never become satisfied with their meat,
So you will not be satisfied with my flesh.
Let me go, that I may give you three counsels,
Whence you will see whether I am wise or foolish.
The first of my counsels shall be given on your wrist,
10 The second on your well-plastered roof,
And the third I will give you from the top of a tree.

---

1 Make Generalizations About Characters *Think about the locations the bird mentions. What generalization can you make about the bird from what he proposes here?*

Teach

Reading Strategy   1

Make Generalizations About Characters **Answer:**
A person could make the generalization that the bird is very cunning because he will deliver each counsel farther away from the man.

📁 For additional practice using the reading skill or strategy, see Unit 3 Teaching Resources Book, p. 118.

View the Art

After Rumi's close friend Shams al Din died, Rumi's grief led him to specialize in *ghazals*. This genre of lyric poem in Islamic literature is short, graceful, and deals with themes of love. **Ask:** How might the poem "The Counsels of the Bird" fit into the *ghazal* genre? *(Students may answer that by not listening to the bird's counsels, the man is forced to look at the things he has lost, which may have led him to gain things he could love.)*

Approaching Level
DIFFERENTIATED INSTRUCTION

Readers' Theater Have student pairs act out the exchange between the man and the bird. Tell students to focus on acting out the general idea of the story: that a man catches a bird and receives three pieces of advice from it. Encourage students to use their own words during the performance.

Advanced Learners/Pre-AP
DIFFERENTIATED INSTRUCTION

Write a Children's Fable Have students work in small groups to create fables intended for younger students. Remind students that the fable must have a maxim or moral that is clear and age-appropriate for the audience. Suggest that students assign each team member a particular aspect of the book (writing, art, cover, etc.). If possible, have groups read their fables to elementary school students.

Learning Objectives
Making generalizations about characters. (SE)
Analyzing maxims. (TE)

Teach

Literary Element | 1

Maxim Have students read lines 14–18. **Ask: What are the first two pieces of advice that the bird gives the man?** *(The first is that he should not believe "foolish assertions." The second is that he should not worry about things that have already been done.)* **Ask: Do you think this is good advice? Why or why not?** *(Students will likely agree that this is good advice. People should not believe the foolish statements of others or waste time worrying about things they cannot change.)*

Big Idea | 2

The Search for Wisdom
Answer: *The man has learned nothing, since he has already forgotten the first two pieces of advice.*

Literary Element | 3

Maxim Answer: *It is useless to give advice to a person who is too dull and foolish to listen.*

Cultural History

Birds as Symbols Animal motifs are found not just in Persian storytelling, but also in Persian rugs. Along with other symbolic items such as trees and other animals, Persian weavers include eagles, doves, and other birds in their art. Different kinds of birds represent different qualities. The dove, for example, means peace, while the peacock signifies the gods' protection. An eagle represents good fortune, and a phoenix, immortality.

On hearing all three you will **deem** yourself happy.
As regards the counsel on your wrist, 'tis this,—
'Believe not foolish **assertions** of any one!' "
15 When he had spoken this counsel on his wrist, he flew
Up to the top of the roof, entirely free.
Then he said, "Do not grieve for what is past;
When a thing is done, vex not yourself about it."
He continued, "Hidden inside this body of mine
20 Is a precious pearl, ten drachms° in weight.
That jewel of right belonged to you,
Wealth for yourself and **prosperity** for your children.
You have lost it, as it was not fated you should get it,
That pearl whose like can nowhere be found."
25 Thereupon the man, like a woman in her travail,°
Gave vent to lamentations and weeping.
The bird said to him, "Did I not counsel you, saying, ☆
'Beware of grieving over what is past and gone?'
When 'tis past and gone, why sorrow for it?
30 Either you understood not my counsel or are deaf.
The second counsel I gave you was this, namely,
'Be not misguided enough to believe foolish assertions.'
O fool, altogether I do not weigh three drachms,
How can a pearl of ten drachms be within me?"
35 The man recovered himself and said, "Well then,
Tell me now your third good counsel!"
The bird replied, "You have made a fine use of the others,
That I should waste my third counsel upon you!
To give counsel to a sleepy ignoramus
40 Is to sow seeds upon salt land.
Torn garments of folly and ignorance cannot be patched.
O counselors, waste not the seed of counsel on them!"

20 **drachm:** about half an ounce.

25 **a woman in her travail:** a woman in labor.

---

2 **The Search for Wisdom** *What do you think the man has learned from the counsels of the bird?*

3 **Maxim** *What general truth does this maxim reveal?*

Vocabulary

deem (dēm) *v.* to regard in a certain way
assertion (ə sur′shən) *n.* a forceful or confident statement of fact or belief
prosperity (pros per′ə tē) *n.* the state of being successful

Reading Practice

 SMALL GROUP

Activate Prior Knowledge Explain that recalling familiar stories about clever animals that fool their adversaries will help students better understand this story. Ask students to describe the bird in this selection. Record their thoughts on the board. Have students work in small groups to develop a list of animal characters from literature and popular entertainment to which the same descriptions might apply.

Ask students to compare and contrast the clever tricksters in the stories they have recalled. Suggest that students use a graphic organizer, such as a chart or Venn diagram. Ask groups to share their findings in a class discussion. *(Students may compare and contrast such similar characters as Anansi, Raven, and Coyote.)*

After You Read

Respond and Think Critically

Respond and Interpret

1. Did the ending of the poem surprise you? Explain why or why not.

2. (a)What advice does the bird give when he is on the man's wrist? (b)Why might the bird have given this advice first?

3. How does the man react to the loss of the pearl?

Analyze and Evaluate

4. **Irony** is a contrast between expectations and reality. What irony do you see in the conclusion of the poem?

Literary Element Maxim

Maxims are most effective when they state truths with wit, fresh imagery, and penetrating insight.

1. Reread the maxim in lines 17–18. What general truth does it teach?

2. Restate the third counsel of the bird (lines 39–41) in your own words. What, if anything, is lost by rewording it? Explain.

Reading Strategy Make Generalizations About Characters

When you **make generalizations about characters,** you will better understand them.

1. (a)What generalizations can you make about the bird's character? (b)What or whom might the bird represent?

2. (a)What generalizations can you make about the man's character? (b)What or whom might he represent?

LOG ON ▶ **Literature** Online

Selection Resources For Selection Quizzes, eFlashcards, and Reading-Writing Connection activities, go to glencoe.com and enter QuickPass code GLW6053u3.

---

5. What is the **theme,** or message, of the poem?

Connect

6. **Big Idea** The Search for Wisdom Translators Jonathan Star and Shahram Shiva observe that with Rumi's verse, "one must always be aware of the meaning behind the meaning, and the veils behind the veils." How do meanings hide behind meanings in "The Counsels of the Bird"?

7. **Connect to the Author** Rumi was well known as a teacher, particularly of Islamic mysticism. How might his career as a teacher have influenced the way he wrote this poem?

Vocabulary Practice

Practice with Antonyms With a partner, brainstorm three antonyms for each boldfaced vocabulary word below. Then discuss your choices with your classmates. Be prepared to explain why you chose your antonyms.

deem	assertion	prosperity

EXAMPLE: evade
Antonyms: participate; join; contribute
Sample explanation: A person who *evades* avoids taking part in something, while a person who *contributes* does take part.

Writing

Write a Maxim What truths have you learned through experience? Write a list of five or more maxims that express these truths, using the maxims in "The Counsels of the Bird" as models. Try to use metaphors to make your maxims memorable. Make sure the details in your maxims relate to broad truths by creating a graphic organizer similar to the one you filled out on page 512.

RUMI **515**

After You Read

Assess

1. Answers will vary.

2. (a) The bird advises the man not to believe foolish statements, no matter who says them. (b) The bird probably gives this advice first to teach the man to be skeptical before he accepts the bird's other statements.

3. The man cries because he believes the bird.

4. That the bird tricks the man is an ironic reversal of the man's having captured the bird. The outcome is ironic because the man has not received the third counsel, yet he has lost the bird.

5. Possible answer: Do not accept advice if you are not going to follow it.

6. The man disregards the first two counsels but is eager to hear the third one; the man's behavior illustrates the wisdom of the bird's counsels.

7. Possible answer: Rumi's ability to teach truths about life may have stemmed from his years of teaching.

Progress Check

Can students identify maxims?

If No → See Unit 3 Teaching Resources Book, p. 117.

Literary Element

1. It teaches that there is no use in grieving over the past, which cannot be changed.

2. Students may say that their rewordings are less memorable because the original makes its point through metaphor.

Reading Strategy

1. (a) The bird is clever and understands human nature. (b) The bird could represent a wise teacher who has learned through experience.

2. (a) The man is inattentive and greedy. He is not clever or a good listener. (b) He might represent society's materialism and laziness or people who are unwilling to listen to others.

Vocabulary

Explanations will vary. Sample answers:
Word: deem; Antonyms: learn; hear about; Word: assertion; Antonyms: denial, refutation, contradiction; Word: prosperity; Antonyms: poverty, paucity, dearth

Writing

Students' maxims should use metaphors and relate to broad truths.

515

Focus

Elegy for a Woman of No Importance

Bellringer Options

Selection Focus
Transparency 26

Daily Language
Transparency 44

Or ask: How would you like people to remember you when you are gone? Have students share the qualities they possess or the deeds they have done that they would like people to remember. Point out any similarities or differences between students' responses.

Meet **Nāzik al-Malā'ikah**

(1922–2007)

Nāzik al-Malā'ikah (nä'zēk äl'mäl i'khä), a poet and a literary critic, was one of the most notable women authors in the Middle East. Al-Malā'ikah began to challenge the traditional structure of Arabic poetry with the publication of her first volume of free-verse poetry, *The Lover of Night,* in 1947.

Al-Malā'ikah was born in Baghdad, the capital of Iraq, in 1923 and was the first of her parents' seven children. Her mother was a poet who wrote under the pseudonym Um Nizar, and her father was a grammar teacher, a poet, and the editor of a twenty-volume encyclopedia. Her parents inspired al-Malā'ikah's love of literature and language at an early age; she wrote her first classical Arabic poem at the age of ten, under her father's guidance. Al-Malā'ikah graduated from a college in Baghdad and went on to study at Princeton University and the University of Wisconsin in the United States. Al-Malā'ikah's earliest published poems, which were printed while she was in college, revealed her inclination toward modernist poetics.

Cultural Influences Al-Malā'ikah was strongly influenced by her society and often responded to current events. One of her best-known poems, "Cholera," centers on the effects of a cholera epidemic that struck Egypt in 1947. Al-Malā'ikah later said of the poem, "I woke up and lay in bed listening to the broadcaster on the radio, who said that the number of the dead in Egypt had reached 1,000. I was overwhelmed by a profound sadness and deep distress. I jumped out of bed, took out a pen and paper . . . and began to compose 'Cholera'. . ."

> "Why do we fear words?
> Some words are secret bells,
>   the echoes
> of their tone announce the start
>   of a magic
> And abundant time"
>
> —Nāzik al-Malā 'ikah,
> from "Love Song for Words"

"Cholera" was one of al-Malā'ikah's first free-verse poems. Although she defended the free-verse movement, she believed that poems should retain some form of meter and often a rhyme scheme. She remained a prominent figure in Arabic modernism throughout the 1950s, but by the late 1960s, her poetry became less experimental. She spent 40 years teaching in Iraqi schools and universities but left Iraq in 1970 after Saddam Hussein came to power and spent the rest of her life in exile in Kuwait and Egypt. Al-Malā'ikah published several volumes of poetry, including *Splinters and Ashes, Bottom of the Wave,* and *The Sea Changes its Colors.*

 Literature Online

Author Search For more about Nāzik al-Malā'ikah, go to glencoe.com and enter QuickPass code GLW6053u3.

Selection Skills

Literary Elements
- Personification (SE pp. 517–519)
- Imagery (TE p. 518)

Elegy for a Woman of No Importance

Speaking/Listening/Viewing Skills
- Analyze Art (TE p. 518)

Reading Skills
- Analyze Tone (SE pp. 517, 519)

Vocabulary Skills
- Synonyms (SE pp. 517, 519)

Writing Skills/Grammar
- Write an Elegy (SE p. 519)

Literature and Reading Preview

Connect to the Poem

Imagine you are considered to be a person of no importance. What would your emotions be? How would the goals of your life change? Respond to these questions in a journal entry.

Build Background

The following poem is an **elegy**, a poem mourning a death or another great loss. The elegy, which is named after an ancient Greek metrical form, is one of the most enduring forms of poetry. Although elegies originally dealt with famous people, al-Malā'ikah mourns the loss of a woman no one will miss.

Set Purposes for Reading

Big Idea The Violence of Change

As you read, ask yourself, What kind of society do the images in the poem portray?

Literary Element Personification

Personification is the attribution of human qualities or thoughts to an animal, an object, or an idea. Poets often use personification to bring energy to a poem, to help readers visualize and relate to the events, or to establish the mood and tone of the work. As you read, ask yourself, How does personification reinforce the indifferent reaction to the woman's death?

Reading Strategy Analyze Tone

When you **analyze** the **tone** of a poem, you look for the literary elements that help you understand the author's or speaker's attitude toward the subject. These elements include word choice, imagery, and figures of speech. As you read, ask yourself, What do the literary elements contribute to the tone?

Tip: Note Literary Elements Use a chart like the one below to identify literary elements and describe their effects.

Passage	Literary Element	Effect
"No face turned pale, no lips trembled"	Imagery	Suggests loneliness

Learning Objectives

For pages 516–519

In studying this text, you will focus on the following objectives:

Literary Study: Analyzing personification.

Reading: Analyzing tone.

Writing: Writing an elegy.

Vocabulary

vague (vāg) *adj.* unclear; without form; indistinct; p. 518 *The driving instructor gave vague, confusing instructions on how to parallel park.*

murmur (mur′mər) *v.* to say something in an indistinct voice; to say something quietly and cautiously; p. 518 *The crowd began to murmur when the guest speaker did not appear on stage.*

shrill (shrill) *adj.* high-pitched; p. 518 *The shrill ringing of the fire alarm startled everyone.*

Tip: Synonyms Synonyms are words with similar meanings. For example, the words *shrill* and *piercing* are synonyms. Replacing a word with a synonym can make the meaning more precise, but not all synonyms can be used to replace one another.

NĀZIK AL-MALĀ'IKAH **517**

Before You Read

Focus

Summary

This poem expresses the reactions—or rather, non-reactions—of a community toward a woman who died. The poem uses sensory images to help the reader visualize the scene and share in the speaker's feelings.

 For summaries in languages other than English, see Unit 3 Teaching Resources Book, pp. 124–129.

Vocabulary

List Synonyms Have students list as many synonyms as they can for each of the vocabulary words. Try replacing the vocabulary words in the sample sentences with the synonyms. Do each of the sentences still work?

 For additional vocabulary practice, see Unit 3 Teaching Resources Book, p. 132.

Advanced Learners/Pre-AP

DIFFERENTIATED INSTRUCTION

Connecting Point out that it is possible to learn about a society's attitude toward death by comparing those attitudes with our own views.

Have students use Internet or print resources to research the death rituals of various cultures. Tell them to print out or create images that represent these ceremonies and rites.

Ask students to share their findings in an oral presentation. They should present their information and images in a clear, organized manner. After the presentations, discuss the following:

- What are the cultural and religious similarities and differences?
- How do these views relate to your own views about death?

Teach

Big Idea   1

The Violence of Change
Ask: What change does the poet seem to suggest in her poem? *(She suggests that women should be viewed differently.)*

Literary Element   2

Personification   Answer:
The author personifies the news of the woman's death as stumbling down an alley without finding shelter. This emphasizes the irrelevance of the news, as no one cares that the woman died.

View the Art ⭐

Watercolor is a medium in which pigment ground in gum is applied with water and a brush, typically to paper. Instead of building up paint, a watercolorist approach leaves paint out, relying on the white paper to create whites. **Ask: What techniques do you think the artist has employed in *Solitude*?** *(Students may say that while the painting is a watercolor, the artist in many places used very little water to create darker colors.)*

Progress Check

Can students identify personification?

If No → See Unit 3 Teaching Resources Book, p. 130.

Learning Objectives
Analyzing personification. (SE)
Analyzing imagery. (TE)

518

Elegy for a Woman of
No Importance

Nāzik al-Malā'ikah
Translated by Chris Knipp and Mohammad Sadiq

Solitude, 1991. Al-Adhamy, Firyal.
Watercolour on paper. Private collection.

When she died no face turned pale, no lips trembled
doors heard no retelling of her death
no curtains opened to air the room of grief
no eyes followed the coffin to the end of the road—
5 only, hovering in the memory, a **vague** form
        passing in the lane

The scrap of news stumbled in the alleyways
its whisper, finding no shelter,
lodged obscurely in an unseen corner.
The moon **murmured** sadly.

10 Night, unconcerned, gave way to morning
light came with the milk cart and the call to fasting°
with the hungry mewing of a cat of rags and bones
the **shrill** cries of vendors in the bitter streets
the squabbling of small boys throwing stones
15 dirty water spilling along the gutters
smells on the wind
which played about the rooftops
playing in deep forgetfulness
playing alone   **1**

> **11 call to fasting:** begins each day during Ramadan, the month during which Muslims fast from sunrise to sunset.

2 Personification *What is the author personifying in these lines? What effect does this create?*

Vocabulary

vague (vāg) *adj.* unclear; without form; indistinct
murmur (mur′mər) *v.* to say something in an indistinct voice; to say something quietly and cautiously
shrill (shrill) *adj.* high-pitched

Literary Element Practice

Imagery Tell students that imagery is the use of descriptions that appeal to the five senses—sight, sound, taste, touch, and smell. Have students identify examples of imagery in the poem. Then have them identify the sense that each example appeals to. For example, the imagery in line 12 appeals to the sense of sound.

Explain to students that writers use imagery to make their writing come alive for readers. Have students write a short paragraph that includes examples of imagery. Tell them to write examples that appeal to at least three of the five senses. After they have finished, ask volunteers to share their paragraphs with the class. Have the other students identify the examples of imagery in the volunteers' paragraphs.

After You Read

Respond and Think Critically

Respond and Interpret

1. How did you feel about the woman's death after reading the poem?

2. (a)According to lines 1–5, how does the woman's neighborhood react to her death? (b)What do these lines suggest about the woman's status in the neighborhood?

3. (a)Based on lines 11–15, what do you think the setting of the poem might be? (b)How does the setting contribute to the meaning of the poem?

Analyze and Evaluate

4. (a)What images of loneliness does al-Malā'ikah use in the poem? (b)Why might this imagery be an effective way to convey the mood of the poem?

5. Why might the poet have chosen not to name the woman or to give details of her life?

6. What is the speaker truly mourning? Explain.

7. In your opinion, would the author agree that the woman was "of no importance"? Explain.

Connect

8. **Big Idea** **The Violence of Change** What type of society does this poem reflect?

9. **Connect to the Author** Al-Malā'ikah was well known for her free-verse poetry that does not follow a regular rhythm or rhyme scheme. How does this style influence the effect of the poem?

Literary Element **Personification**

Poets often use **personification** to highlight an idea or create a striking description.

1. Identify at least four examples of personification in this poem.

2. How do these examples reinforce the ideas of solitude and indifference?

Reading Strategy **Analyze Tone**

Tone is a reflection of the author's or speaker's attitude toward the subject—for example, sympathy, amusement, or superiority.

1. What is the tone of the poem?

2. What literary elements create this tone?

 Literature Online

Selection Resources For Selection Quizzes, eFlash-cards, and Reading-Writing Connection activities, go to glencoe.com and enter QuickPass code GLW6053u3.

Vocabulary Practice

Practice with Synonyms A synonym is a word that has the same or nearly the same meaning as another word. With a partner, match each boldfaced vocabulary word below with its synonym. Use a thesaurus or a dictionary to check your answers. You will not use all the answer choices.

1. vague	**a.** sing	**d.** mumble
2. murmur	**b.** mock	**e.** muted
3. shrill	**c.** uncertain	**f.** blaring

Writing

Write an Elegy Write an elegy about a loss you have suffered. Include images that express your feelings and set an appropriate mood. Use personification to help readers better visualize your imagery. To get ideas for other literary elements to use, look at the chart you filled out on page 517.

After You Read

Assess

1. Students may feel regret and sorrow for the woman.

2. (a) The neighborhood is indifferent—no face turns pale and no eyes follow the coffin down the street. (b) She had little to no status in her neighborhood.

3. (a) The poem is set in a dirty and depressing part of the city. (b) The dreary urban setting ("hungry mewing of a cat of rags and bones," "shrill cries," "bitter streets," and "dirty water spilling along the gutters") underscores the sorrow of the woman's life and death.

4. (a) Images include the doors that hear no retelling of the death, the moon murmuring sadly, and the night giving way to morning "unconcerned." (b) This imagery echoes the loneliness and isolation of the woman.

5. Keeping her anonymous makes her a universal figure of loneliness.

6. The speaker mourns the humble position of women in this society and the countless people of "no importance" who die alone.

7. The author does not agree; she clearly thinks the woman's death is a tragedy.

8. The poem reflects a bleak and uncaring society.

9. The tone and mood are crafted by images and ideas, rather than by specific poetic forms.

Literary Element

1. Examples include doors that might hear retellings (line 2); a scrap of news that stumbles in alleyways (line 6); the moon murmurs (line 9); and the night is unconcerned (line 10).

2. With the exception of the moon, each object ignores the woman's death, just as the people do.

Reading Strategy

1. The tone is mournful and somber.

2. Personification and imagery help create this tone.

Vocabulary Practice

1. c **2.** d **3.** f

Writing

Elegies should focus on a specific loss and use imagery and personification.

Before You Read

Focus

Bellringer Options

Selection Focus
  Transparency 27
Daily Language
  Transparency 45
Or ask: What sounds do you hear in a park or a forest? Do you find these sounds peaceful? Why or why not? *(Students may suggest that they hear birds, animals, trees blowing in the wind, and insects.)*

For an audio recording of this selection, use Listening Library Audio CD-ROM.

Before You Read

Israel

The Sound of Birds at Noon

Meet **Dahlia Ravikovitch**
(1936–2005)

"*I tell you, even rocks crack, and not because of age.*"

—Dahlia Ravikovitch

Dahlia Ravikovitch is considered Israel's most prominent woman poet. She was also a gifted teacher and a dedicated peace activist. In her writing, she often used deceptively straightforward imagery and language to convey complex ideas.

Early Sorrow Ravikovitch was born in 1936 in Ramat Gan, a suburb of Tel Aviv, in what was then Palestine. Israel became an independent nation twelve years later. Her father was killed by a hit-and-run driver when she was just six years old, and her grief over his death gave her insight into human suffering. Ravikovitch developed a deep empathy for other people, a trait that would remain constant over the course of her life.

After studying at the Hebrew University of Jerusalem, Ravikovitch worked as a journalist and then as a high school teacher. However, she discovered her true calling when she began to write. She went on to publish fiction, children's books, and several collections of poetry, including *The Love of an Orange* and *The Window*.

Antiwar Activist For many years, Ravikovitch was an activist in the grassroots movement for peace in the Middle East, where tensions between Israel and Arab countries often erupt into war. She dedicated herself to campaigning for the rights of the Palestinian people who were displaced by the creation of Israel and its later expansion. Ravikovitch—who once stated that "everyone wants peace, but everyone thinks someone else should bring it"—tried to set an example through actions such as arranging for a Palestinian Boy Scout troop to spend a day visiting with Israeli teenagers.

Ravikovitch's poetry frequently addresses the conflicts within and around her homeland. Her antiwar poems vividly convey the suffering of those who have been victims of acts of violence. In her more personal poems, such as "The Sound of Birds at Noon," the tensions between nations play a less prominent but still unmistakable role.

Moments of Insight Ravikovitch is known for writing intensely lyrical poems that reach their emotional peak in an epiphany, or a sudden, unexpected moment of insight. She composed her poems in Hebrew and preferred to use everyday language and a relaxed, conversational tone. In 1998, she was awarded the Israel Prize, her country's highest honor, in recognition of her achievement as a poet. The citation for the prize noted, "Her poetic style is distinguished by its skillful synthesis of a rich literary language with the colloquial idiom, and of her personal outcry with that of the collective."

 Literature Online
Author Search For more about Dahlia Ravikovitch, go to glencoe.com and enter QuickPass code GLW6053u3.

Selection Skills

Literary Elements
- Enjambment (SE pp. 521–523)
- Personification (TE p. 522)

Reading Skills
- Recognize Author's Purpose (SE pp. 521, 523)

The Sounds of Birds at Noon

Vocabulary Skills
- Use Context Clues (SE pp. 521, 523)

Speaking/Listening/Viewing Skills
- Analyze Art (TE p. 522)

Writing Skills/Grammar
- Poem (SE p. 523)

Literature and Reading Preview

Connect to the Poem

What images come to mind when you think of birds? With a partner, discuss how birds are typically described and what they often symbolize for people.

Build Background

In 1982, Israel invaded southern Lebanon to destroy the Palestinian forces based there. The war in Lebanon outraged Ravikovitch, who began to express a new urgency in her work and more forcefully stress the need for peace and understanding. In colloquial and sometimes harsh language, she described the atrocities and moral dilemmas of wartime life.

Set Purposes for Reading

Big Idea The Violence of Change

As you read, ask yourself, Why might Ravikovitch have used peaceful images from nature to criticize the violence in and around her homeland?

Literary Element Enjambment

Enjambment is the continuation of a sentence from one line of a poem to another. This is the opposite of an **end-stopped line,** which expresses a complete thought and ends with a period, a semicolon, or sometimes a comma. As you read "The Sound of Birds at Noon," ask yourself, What are some examples of enjambment in this poem?

Reading Strategy Recognize Author's Purpose

An **author's purpose** is his or her intent for writing a literary work. Authors typically write to persuade, to inform, to explain, to entertain, or to describe. To recognize an author's purpose, look for the fundamental ideas expressed by the details in the text. As you read, ask yourself, What might have been Ravikovitch's purpose for writing this poem?

Tip: Link Ideas Use a chart like the one below to link the behaviors of birds to those of humans to help you better understand the purpose of the poem.

Birds	People
Easily share branches	Fight over the ownership and control of land

Learning Objectives

For pages 520–523

In studying this text, you will focus on the following objectives:

Literary Study: Analyzing enjambment.

Reading: Recognizing author's purpose.

Writing: Writing a poem.

Vocabulary

malicious (mə lish′əs) *adj.* marked by a desire to cause pain, injury, or distress to another; p. 522 *Although Maria's remarks hurt Sonia's feelings, Sonia could tell the intent was not malicious.*

rare (rār) *adj.* distinctive or seldom seen; p. 522 *Many rare plants grow only in rain forests.*

compassion (kəm pash′ən) *n.* sympathetic awareness of another's distress; p. 522 *Stephen's compassion made him a very effective doctor.*

Tip: Context Clues You can often find clues to a word's meaning by looking at its context, or the other words and sentences that surround it. For example, in the sentence for the word *rare* above, the fact that the plants *grow only in rain forests* is a context clue that tells you the plants are seldom seen, or *rare.*

DAHLIA RAVIKOVITCH **521**

Before You Read

Focus

Summary

The speaker of this poem comments on the positive qualities of birds. He or she says that birds are not malicious or heavy-hearted. All birds, no matter the species, are full of grace.

 For summaries in languages other than English, see Unit 3 Teaching Resources Book, pp. 136–141.

Vocabulary

Context Clues Write the following sentences on the board:

1. At the library, Cara read a book about a _____ species of insect that lives only in rain forests. *(rare)*
2. Colin's _____ for dogs in shelters led to his adopting two dogs of his own. *(compassion)*
3. Everyone witnessed Jeffrey's _____ behavior when he yelled at his friend in the hallway. *(malicious)*

Tell students to fill in each sentence with one of the vocabulary words. After they have filled in the blanks correctly, ask them to point out the context clues in the sentences that helped them figure out the correct vocabulary word.

 For additional vocabulary practice, see Unit 3 Teaching Resources Book, p. 144

 Interactive Read and Write
Other options for teaching this selection can be found in Interactive Read and Write for On-Level Learners, pp. 129–134.

English Learners

DIFFERENTIATED INSTRUCTION

Beginning Ask students what they know about birds. Guide the discussion by asking what birds look like, what they sound like, what they eat, and where they live. Write their responses on the board. Then, ask students what their opinions of birds are. Do they like them? Why? Have them keep their thoughts in mind as they read the ideas of the speaker in the poem.

Advanced Learners/Pre-AP

DIFFERENTIATED INSTRUCTION

Poetic Form Have students take the sentences that make up the poem and rewrite them in paragraph form. Discuss how the line breaks in the poem change the strength and impact of the words. Point out that the line breaks force the reader to stop at certain places. Have students consider why the author chose to put her thoughts into the form of a poem.

Teach

Reading Strategy · 1

Recognize Author's Purpose **Ask:** What details in the poem reveal that the author may be writing about people and their behavior? *(The word* malicious *refers to a human emotion. The phrase "the seed of Abraham" makes the reader think of people in the Middle East. The birds sing "without giving us a thought," which points the reader in the direction of thinking about people.)*

Literary Element · 2

Enjambment **Answer:** *It emphasizes the slow passage of time by breaking after the word* years, *thus drawing the reader's attention to the passing of years while the reader pauses before the next line.*

Progress Check

Can students identify enjambment?

If No → See Unit 3 Teaching Resources Book, p. 142.

View the Art ★

Have students view the photograph of the group of birds sitting on a branch. Point out that the birds are all sitting very close to one another and do not seem to be disturbing each other. **Ask:** Which lines of the poem does this photograph represent? *(Lines 15–16.)* **Ask:** How are these birds sharing their space? Why might they be different from people sharing a small space? *(Students may say the birds are sharing the branch in harmony, while people may become territorial.)*

522

This chirping
is not in the least **malicious.**
They sing without giving us a thought
and they are as many
5   as the seed of Abraham.[1]
They have a life of their own,
they fly without thinking.
Some are **rare,** some common,
but every wing is grace.
10   Their hearts aren't heavy
even when they peck at a worm.
Perhaps they're light-headed.
The heavens were given to them
to rule over day and night
15   and when they touch a branch,
the branch too is theirs.
This chirping is entirely free of malice.
Over the years
it even seems to have
20   a note of **compassion.** **1**

---

1. The *seed of Abraham* refers to Genesis 22:17, in which God promises that Abraham's descendants will be "as numerous as the stars in the sky and the grains of sand on the seashore."

2 **Enjambment** *How does this line break affect your understanding of the poem's time frame?*

522   UNIT 3   SOUTHWEST ASIA

The Sound of Birds at Noon

Dahlia Ravikovitch

Translated by Chana Bloch and Ariel Bloch

Vocabulary

malicious (mə lish′əs) *adj.* marked by a desire to cause pain, injury, or distress to another
rare (rār) *adj.* distinctive or seldom seen
compassion (kəm pash′ən) *n.* sympathetic awareness of another's distress

Literary Element Practice

Personification Point out to students that many pieces of literature use animals to comment on human nature. Two such works are George Orwell's *Animal Farm* and *Aesop's Fables*.

Explain that authors often give human qualities to animals. This is called personification.

Have students write a short story that uses animals and personification to comment on an aspect of human nature. For example, perhaps they could write a story about a turtle that only cares about itself. Allow students enough time to write their stories. Then, ask volunteers to share their stories with the class.

After You Read

Respond and Think Critically

Respond and Interpret

1. What images in the poem do you find most striking or memorable? Explain.

2. (a)In lines 1–2, how does the speaker characterize the song of the birds? (b)Why might this characterization surprise readers?

3. (a)What two things are compared in lines 4–5? (b)What impression does this simile create?

Analyze and Evaluate

4. (a)In lines 6–11, which of the birds' qualities impress the speaker? (b)Why might the speaker admire these particular qualities?

5. (a)How does line 17 echo lines 1–2? (b)In your opinion, what effect does this echo create?

Connect

6. **Big Idea** **The Violence of Change** Based on the last lines of the poem, do you think the speaker would advocate a change brought about by violence? Explain.

7. **Connect to the Author** Ravikovitch once joked that ". . . a slice of bread with butter and honey on an oilcloth-covered breakfast table solves any problem better than an elusive poem." What does this quotation suggest about her reasons for writing antiwar poetry?

Literary Element Enjambment

Enjambment allows the poet to break lines at points where people would normally pause in conversation and also to emphasize ideas and images.

1. In what lines of "The Sound of Birds at Noon" does Ravikovitch use enjambment?

2. How do the line breaks give the poem a conversational quality?

Reading Strategy Recognize Author's Purpose

To recognize an author's purpose, look for clues to help you infer if the author wrote to persuade, inform, explain, describe, or entertain.

1. How might lines 10–11 reveal Ravikovitch's purpose?

2. Why do you think Ravikovitch ended the poem with the words "a note of compassion"?

 Literature Online

Selection Resources For Selection Quizzes, eFlashcards, and Reading-Writing Connection activities, go to glencoe.com and enter QuickPass code GLW6053u3.

Vocabulary Practice

Practice with Context Clues Identify the context clues in the following sentences that help you determine the meaning of each boldfaced vocabulary word.

1. Alex's babysitter quit because she was tired of his **malicious** comments and cruel tricks.

2. As natural resources grow scarce, there may come a day when oil is considered a **rare** treasure.

3. The nurse's **compassion,** or awareness of another's distress, led her to treat the patient gently.

Writing

Write a Poem Write a descriptive poem that compares a particular animal behavior with a specific human interaction. As you write, use sensory details to describe the distinctive characteristics of your subject. Use **enjambment** to create a rhythm that mimics everyday speech. Create a graphic organizer like the one on page 521 to help you link the details in your poem to a larger statement about society.

DAHLIA RAVIKOVITCH **523**

After You Read

Assess

1. Answers will vary.

2. (a) The song of the birds is "not in the least malicious." (b) Bird songs are not usually malicious, so it might surprise readers that Ravikovitch uses this word.

3. (a) The number of birds is compared with the number of descendants of the biblical patriarch Abraham. (b) The simile implies that there are an incalculable number of birds.

4. (a) The birds' independence (line 6), effortlessness (line 7), grace (line 9), and freedom from care (lines 10–11) impress the speaker. (b) The speaker may value these qualities because the human world is not carefree, he or she does not feel truly independent, and human life is often not effortless or graceful.

5. (a) The phrase "free of malice" (line 17) echoes "not in the least malicious" (line 2). (b) The echo emphasizes the fact that, unlike humans, the birds harbor no ill will toward one another.

6. The speaker would likely not advocate a change brought about by violence, because he or she seems to value compassionate interactions.

7. The quotation suggests that Ravikovitch believed in the power of poetry to effect change, even if it can't offer immediate solutions.

Literary Element

1. 1–2, 3–5, 10–11, 13–15, 18–20.
2. The line breaks mimic the pauses a speaker might use in a conversation.

Writing

Students' poems should clearly compare an animal behavior with a human interaction, use sensory details, and use enjambment.

Reading Strategy

1. Lines 10–11 reveal her purpose by highlighting that the birds do not live with heavy hearts, as people often do, even when faced with burdensome tasks. Her purpose was to underscore aspects of bird life that humans might do well to emulate.

2. By ending with these words, she drew the reader's focus to hope.

Vocabulary Practice

1. That his tricks were "cruel" indicates that the comments were intended to cause harm, or were **malicious**.
2. The word *scarce* signals that **rare** has a similar meaning.
3. **Compassion** is defined in the sentence.

Focus

The Diameter of the Bomb

Israel

Bellringer Options

Selection Focus
Transparency 28
Daily Language
Transparency 46

Or play a recording of an anti-war protest song from the 1960s, such as Bob Dylan's "Blowin' in the Wind." Explain that people have often used art to protest war and violence. **Ask:** Why is a poem or a song an effective way to make a point about a controversial issue? *(Students may say that the rhythm, rhyme, and imagery of poetry make it memorable, so the message can spread from person to person.)* Point out that poems and songs can be performed many times, which reinforces their message.

 For an audio recording of this selection, use Listening Library Audio CD-ROM.

Meet **Yehuda Amichai**
(1924–2000)

The life and writings of Yehuda Amichai (yə hoō´də ä´mi khī) have been deeply influenced by the history of Israel and the political issues it has faced. Amichai was born in Germany to Orthodox Jewish parents and was taught to speak both Hebrew and German. Their ancestors had lived in southern Germany since the Middle Ages, but the Amichai family moved to Palestine in 1935 after the Nazis came to power. This move saved them from the horrors of the Holocaust, but many of their friends and relatives perished in Nazi concentration camps. These losses haunted Amichai for the rest of his life.

Soldier and Poet Palestine was a British-controlled area when Amichai and his family immigrated there in the 1930s. Amichai served with the British army during World War II and then joined the underground movement for the creation of a Jewish state. This goal was achieved when the United Nations partitioned Palestine into an Arab and a Jewish state, and Israel proclaimed its independence on May 14, 1948. Amichai also served with the Israeli Defense Forces during the Arab-Israeli war of 1948, which immediately followed the establishment of Israel. He believed that modern poetry must deal with current issues, so the warfare that impacted his life and country deeply influenced his poetry. After he fought in the Arab-Israeli war, Amichai studied biblical and Hebrew literature at the Hebrew University of Jerusalem. He later taught these subjects in Israel and abroad.

A Versatile Style Amichai's first volume of poetry, *Now and in Other Days*, was published in 1955. By the 1960s, he had earned a reputation

> "My personal history has coincided with a larger history. For me it's always been one and the same."
>
> —Yehuda Amichai

as Israel's leading poet. British and American readers first took note of Amichai in the 1970s when he collaborated with British poet Ted Hughes on translations of two of Amichai's books. Amichai's use of a variety of language styles, from classical Hebrew to modern colloquialisms, soon earned him a reputation as the "poet who plays with words."

Amichai's use of everyday language and his ability to capture the rhythms of conversation show the influence of poets such as Robert Frost and W. H. Auden. In 1982, Amichai was awarded the prestigious Israel Prize for poetry and was praised for the "revolutionary change in poetry's language" that his work had effected. Amichai's work has been translated into 37 other languages, including English, French, and Spanish.

LOG ON ▶ **Literature** Online

Author Search For more about Yehuda Amichai, go to glencoe.com and enter QuickPass code GLW6053u3.

Selection Skills

Literary Elements
- Diction (SE pp. 525–527)

The Diameter of the Bomb

Speaking/Listening/Viewing Skills
- Analyze Art (TE p. 526)

Reading Skills
- Analyze Cause-and-Effect Relationships (SE pp. 525–527)

Vocabulary Skills
- Analogies (SE pp. 525, 527)

Writing Skills/Grammar
- Write an Essay (SE p. 527)
- Write a Personal Response (TE p. 526)

Literature and Reading Preview

Connect to the Poem

How can people solve arguments without resorting to violence? Discuss this question with a partner.

Build Background

Terrorism, as it is currently defined, is the use of violence against nonmilitary targets without warning. Early terrorists, such as those in czarist Russia, attacked government representatives. More recently, terrorists have targeted civilians.

Set Purposes for Reading

Big Idea The Violence of Change

As you read this poem, ask yourself, What point is it making about the changes the bomb causes?

Literary Element Diction

Diction is an author's choice of words. Depending on vocabulary and style, diction can be described in a variety of ways: formal or informal, old-fashioned or modern, friendly or detached. As you read, ask yourself, How does Amichai's diction affect the **tone,** or attitude, of the poem?

Reading Strategy Analyze Cause-and-Effect Relationships

A **cause-and-effect relationship** exists when one event causes another event to happen. Understanding cause-and-effect relationships is an important part of logical thinking. To analyze causes and effects, ask yourself these questions.

- *Why* does something happen (the cause)?
- *What* happens as a result (its effect)?
- What words and phrases, such as *because, as a result,* and *consequently,* hint at causes and effects?

Tip: Make a Flowchart Create a flowchart like the one below to track the cause-and-effect relationships in the poem.

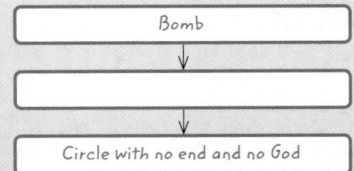

Bomb
↓
[ ]
↓
Circle with no end and no God

YEHUDA AMICHAI **525**

Learning Objectives

For pages 524–527

In studying this text, you will focus on the following objectives:

Literary Study: Analyzing diction.

Reading: Analyzing cause-and-effect relationships.

Writing: Writing an essay.

Vocabulary

range (rānj) *n.* the full extent over which something moves or is seen, heard, effective, etc.; scope; p. 526 *The government faced a range of problems, including health care and the economy.*

considerably (kən sid′ər ə blē) *adv.* greatly; by a large amount; p. 526 *Diana's painting style was considerably influenced by Impressionism.*

solitary (sol′ə ter′ē) *adj.* characterized by loneliness or lack of companions; lonely; p. 526 *Each morning, the same solitary woman occupied the corner table of the coffeehouse.*

Tip: Analogies Analogies compare words based on the relationship between each pair's meaning. For example, in the analogy *tiny : massive :: solitary : crowded,* the relationship between the words is that they are **antonyms,** or words with opposite meanings.

Before You Read

Focus

Summary

This poem tells about the far-reaching, destructive effects of a terrorist bomb and considers possible ways to measure those effects.

 For summaries in languages other than English, see Unit 3 Teaching Resources Book, pp. 148–153.

Vocabulary

Analogies Let students practice with analogies by having pairs write analogies for the vocabulary words, leaving the answer blank. Remind students that their analogies should consist of four words and that each pair of words should have the same relationship. Ask pairs to complete each other's analogies.

 For additional vocabulary practice see Unit 3 Teaching Resources Book, p. 156

English Learners

DIFFERENTIATED INSTRUCTION

Beginning Tell students that this poem uses the term *diameter,* which is often encountered in math and science. Draw a sketch to help students understand the meaning of a circle's *diameter* (the distance across it), *radius* (the distance from its center to its edge), and *circumference* (the length of the line that forms the circle, or its outside edge).

Approaching Level

DIFFERENTIATED INSTRUCTION

Measurements Point out to students that measurements in this poem are given in centimeters, meters, and kilometers. Bring a meter stick to class, and show students the actual lengths of a centimeter, thirty centimeters, and a meter. Tell students that a mile is about the same length as one and a half kilometers.

Teach

Reading Strategy   1

Analyze Cause-and-Effect Relationships Answer: *The images reflect the physical and emotional effects the bomb had on individuals and on society. The images of the hospital and the graveyard call attention to the people who were injured or killed and those who mourn for them.*

 For additional practice using the reading skill or strategy, see Unit 3 Teaching Resources Book, p. 155.

Literary Element   2

Diction Answer: *The repetition links God and the incomplete circle. The effect is distressing; it is a profound idea stated in a simple manner.*

Progress Check

Can students identify diction?

If No → See Unit 3 Teaching Resources Book, p. 154

View the Art ★

Ask: How might this painting be associated with Amichai's poems? *(Students may respond that the painting is grim and dark and seems related to mourning.)*

THE DIAMETER OF THE BOMB

Yehuda Amichai

Translated by Chana Bloch and Stephen Mitchell

Eulogy, 1996. Nissan Engel. Mixed media. Private collection. ★

The diameter of the bomb was thirty centimeters
and the diameter of its effective **range** about seven meters,
with four dead and eleven wounded.
And around these, in a larger circle
5 of pain and time, two hospitals are scattered
and one graveyard. But the young woman
who was buried in the city she came from,
at a distance of more than a hundred kilometers,
enlarges the circle **considerably**,
10 and the **solitary** man mourning her death
at the distant shores of a country far across the sea
includes the entire world in the circle.
And I won't even mention the crying of orphans
that reaches up to the throne of God and
15 beyond, making
a circle with no end and no God.

1 Analyze Cause-and-Effect Relationships *How does this image reflect the changes caused by the terrorists?*

2 Diction *Why might Amichai have repeated the word* no *in this line? What is its effect?*

Vocabulary

range (rānj) *n.* the full extent over which something moves or is seen, heard, effective, etc.; scope
considerably (kən sid′ər ə blē) *adv.* greatly; by a large amount
solitary (sol′ə ter′ē) *adj.* characterized by loneliness or lack of companions; lonely

526   UNIT 3   SOUTHWEST ASIA

Writing Practice

⚡ **Write a Personal Response**
Explain to students that, in addition to careful reading and discussion, writing a personal response to a poem can help clarify ideas and increase comprehension.

Have students write a personal response to "The Diameter of the Bomb." Use these questions to help them respond:

- What did you find interesting or surprising about the poem?
- How did the poem make you feel?
- Did you find any parts of the poem particularly profound or meaningful?
- Did the poem make you think about something in a new way?
- Did you disagree with anything in the poem?

Remind students that they should clearly explain their response by addressing specific words, phrases, or lines of the poem.

After You Read

Respond and Think Critically

Respond and Interpret

1. (a)Based on the title, what did you expect the poem to be about? (b)Did the poem meet your expectations? Explain.

2. (a)What specific facts about the bombing does the poem's speaker present in lines 1–3? (b)How do these details contrast with the details in lines 4–16?

3. (a)What is included as the circle grows in lines 4–12? (b)What is the effect of the **imagery** in these lines?

4. (a)Who and what are included in the circle by the end of the poem? (b)How do lines 13–16 provide the emotional climax, or a high point, to the poem?

Analyze and Evaluate

5. The image of an ever-widening circle unifies the poem. In your opinion, is this image appropriate for the subject matter? Explain.

6. (a)How does the speaker feel about the people's suffering? (b)Based on the speaker's attitude, what is the theme of the poem?

Connect

7. **Big Idea** **The Violence of Change** (a)What might cause a person or a group to use violence? (b)What advice might you give to someone who says violence brings change?

8. **Connect to Today** Recall another act of terrorism that you know about. How does the theme of this poem apply to that incident?

Literary Element Diction

Authors often vary their **diction**. For example, a scientist would use more technical diction with scientists than with the general public.

1. (a)What is the tone of lines 1–3? (b)Which words and phrases contribute to this tone?

2. (a)What is the tone of lines 4–16? (b)How does the diction help build this tone?

Reading Strategy Analyze Cause-and-Effect Relationships

Remember that a single cause may have several effects, and one effect may have multiple causes.

1. List three effects caused by the bomb.

2. (a)How do the effects of the bomb expand throughout the world? (b)In your opinion, which effect is most devastating?

 Literature Online

Selection Resources For Selection Quizzes, eFlash-cards, and Reading-Writing Connection activities, go to glencoe.com and enter QuickPass code GLW6053u3.

Vocabulary Practice

Practice with Analogies For each of these analogies, determine the relationship between the first pair of words. Apply that relationship to the second pair to complete the analogy.

1. expansion : enlargement :: range :
   a. danger   **b.** depth   **c.** path   **d.** limit

2. completely : partially :: considerably :
   a. largely   **b.** scarcely   **c.** easily   **d.** slowly

3. religious : minister :: solitary :
   a. hermit   **b.** musician   **c.** farmer   **d.** soldier

Writing

Write an Essay Write an expository essay about the effects of terrorism in one part of the world. Consider the graphic organizer you filled out on page 525 as you examine the cause-and-effect relationships associated with terrorist acts. As you write, pay close attention to your diction.

After You Read

Assess

1. Answers will vary.

2. (a) the size of the bomb, its effective range, and the number of people killed and wounded (b) These details are factual and impersonal, whereas the details in the rest of the poem carry more emotional weight.

3. (a) Two hospitals, a graveyard, and the entire world are included. (b) The imagery of two hospitals that are "scattered" draws attention to the chaos of the scene, while the graveyard highlights the isolation and grief caused by the bomb.

4. (a) It includes orphaned children, the throne of God, and "beyond." (b) They illustrate that the circle is boundless; it has no diameter and no God.

5. Most students will say the image is appropriate because it suggests the outward-moving shock waves of an explosion.

6. (a) The speaker empathizes with the people's suffering. (b) The harm terrorism inflicts is incalculable.

7. (a) Someone might turn to violence out of desperation or because their earlier demands have not been met. (b) Students should promote a peaceful solution.

8. Answers will vary.

Literary Element

1. (a) detached (b) "Diameter," "thirty centimeters," "effective range," "seven meters," and "four dead and eleven wounded" contribute to the tone.

2. (a) emotional involvement (b) "Pain," "graveyard," "young woman," "solitary man mourning her death," "crying of orphans," and "throne of God" help build this tone.

Reading Strategy

1. Four people died, seven people were wounded, and orphans cried.

2. (a) The effects expand through the continued suffering of survivors and mourners. (b) Answers will vary.

 For additional assessment, see Assessment Resources, pp. 113–114.

Vocabulary Practice

1. d **2.** b **3.** a

Writing

Students' essays should explain the causes and effects of terrorism in a region of the world, discuss ideas for addressing terrorism, and use appropriate diction.

527

Before You Read

Focus

Bellringer Options

Selection Focus
  Transparency 29
Daily Language
  Transparency 47

Or discuss with students their friends or close family members.

Ask: Why are you close to this person? What helped create the bond or connection between you? Have students discuss how long they have been close to this person or persons. Tell them to consider how the bond or connection with this person has changed over time.

View the Art ★

Al-Adhamy is an Iraqi artist who is greatly inspired by traditional Arab and Islamic art forms, such as textiles, jewelry, and wood carvings.
Ask: What mood does this piece convey? (*Students may say the painting conveys a mood of loneliness or sadness.*)

Selection Skills

Before You Read

Butterflies

 **Saudi Arabia**

Meet **Fawziyya Abu Khalid**
(born 1955)

Fawziyya Abu Khalid (fô´ zē yä´ ä boo´khä´ lēd) published her first collection of verse when she was only eighteen years old. This was a remarkable accomplishment, given that she had been raised in Saudi Arabia during the 1950s and 1960s, when traditional Islamic values and customs governed Saudi women's lives. Abu Khalid was one of the relatively few Saudi women of her generation to be educated; the first Saudi school for girls opened in 1956, the year after she was born. She is known for writing controversial poetry that confronts the conservative culture of her country. Her willingness to challenge these cultural ideas is evident in her poem "To a Man," in which she writes, "For myself, / I have torn up all heir's contract with the past."

Head of a Woman, 2005. Firyal Al-Adhamy. Acrylic on canvas. Private collection. ★

"Without paper or pen
into your heart I reach
Listening is more poignant
than any speech."

—Fawziyya Abu Khalid, "Poem"

A Traditional World Saudi Arabia occupies about three-fourths of the Arabian Peninsula, the homeland of both the Arab people and the religion of Islam. It continues to be a very religious and culturally conservative society, where girls and boys are educated in separate schools. Abu Khalid was born in the Saudi capital of Riyadh to a family of traditional Bedouin nomads. She studied sociology at both the American University of Beirut in Lebanon and Lewis & Clark College in Oregon. After completing her courses in the United States, Abu Khalid returned to Riyadh and earned a master's degree from King Saud University, where she became a lecturer. She has published hundreds of articles on social, political, and literary subjects in newspapers and magazines in Saudi Arabia and throughout the Arab world.

A Controversial Poet Abu Khalid's poems were first published in a local newspaper while she was still in her early teens. When her first book of poems was published in Lebanon in 1973, it was attacked by critics there and banned in Saudi Arabia. However, Abu Khalid continued to write poetry, and her second collection, *Secret Reading in the History of Arab Silence,* was published in 1985. According to poet and editor Nathalie Handal, Abu Khalid's poetry "interrogates Arab culture and history, the relationship between the sexes, between poetry and religion, between Islamic society and Western society, while demonstrating a profound insight into a woman's mind and consciousness."

LOG ON ▶ **Literature** Online

Author Search To learn more about Fawziyya Abu Khalid, go to glencoe.com and enter QuickPass code GLW6053u3.

528 UNIT 3 SOUTHWEST ASIA

Literary Elements
• Simile (SE pp. 529–531; TE p. 530)

→ **Butterflies** →

Speaking/Listening/Viewing Skills
• Analyze Art (TE pp. 528, 530)

Reading Skills
• Connect to Personal Experience (SE pp. 529–531)

Vocabulary Skills
• Academic Vocabulary (SE p. 531)

Writing Skills/Grammar
• Write a Personal Essay (SE p. 531)

Literature and Reading Preview

Connect to the Poem

How would you feel if your best friend moved away and you lost contact with each other? Write a journal entry addressing this question.

Build Background

The Bedouins are Arabic-speaking nomads of southwest Asia and North Africa. Until quite recently, the Bedouin way of life remained much the same as it had for a thousand years. During the hot, dry months, the clans congregated in large groups around water sources. During the cooler months, they migrated in small groups into the desert on horseback or camelback with their herds of animals.

Set Purposes for Reading

Big Idea **The Violence of Change**

As you read, ask yourself, Can significant changes in a person's life occur without violent emotional upheaval?

Literary Element **Simile**

A **simile** is a figure of speech that uses *like* or *as* to compare seemingly unlike things to suggest an underlying similarity. Poets often use similes to integrate vivid images into their work while simultaneously suggesting important themes and ideas. As you read "Butterflies," ask yourself, What is the simile in this poem, and what does it suggest?

Reading Strategy **Connect to Personal Experience**

When you **connect** a poem to your personal experience, you gain a deeper understanding of the speaker's meaning. As you read, reflect on experiences that are similar to those in the work. Then ask yourself, How do the insights I gained from my experiences help me appreciate the meaning of this poem?

....

Tip: Use a Venn Diagram In a diagram like the one below, compare and contrast your thoughts with those of the speaker.

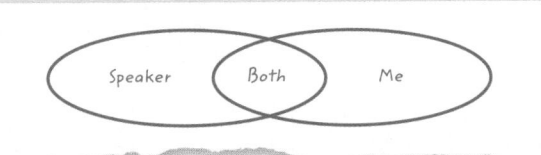

Learning Objectives

For pages 528–531

In studying this text, you will focus on the following objectives:

Literary Study: Analyzing simile.

Reading: Connecting to personal experience.

Writing: Writing an essay.

Bedouin Great Sand Sea, Lybian desert, Siwa Oasis. Egypt.

FAWZIYYA ABU KHALID **529**

Before You Read

Focus

Summary

The speaker in "Butterflies" expresses his or her feelings about being separated from someone.

 For summaries in languages other than English, see Unit 3 Teaching Resources Book, pp. 160–165.

 For an audio recording of this selection, use Listening Library Audio CD-ROM.

Advanced Learners/Pre-AP

DIFFERENTIATED INSTRUCTION

Poems About Loss Have students think of poems or song lyrics that address the topic of losing someone. Then, lead a discussion with the following questions:

- Do the poems or lyrics express whether the loss is temporary or permanent?
- How does the poet or songwriter use language to express the loss?
- Do the poem or lyrics suggest that the person can recover from the loss?

Have students write their own poems or song lyrics about loss. They can follow the form of an existing poem or song, or they can create their own. Encourage students to use figurative language in their poems to express the feelings of loss. After students have finished, invite volunteers to share their poems or lyrics with the class.

Teach

Reading Strategy   1

Connect to Personal Experience Answer: *The poem should be accessible to those outside of Saudi culture because it describes a situation that can happen in any culture. A reader may not know much about Bedouins but should be able to relate to the type of people who have an instinctive understanding of things they have lost and can therefore trace them.*

 For additional practice using the reading skill or strategy, see Unit 3 Teaching Resources Book, p. 167.

Progress Check

Can students identify simile?

If No → See Unit 3 Teaching Resources Book, p. 166.

View the Art ★

The artist Suad Al-Attar was born in Iraq in 1942 and now lives in London. Her work has been exhibited in Europe, the United States, and the Middle East. In 1984 she was the recipient of a gold medal and the first prize at the International Biennial of Cairo. Her work has also been featured on UNICEF's 1975 and 1993 New Year's cards. **Ask: How might the poet Fawziyya Abu Khalid and the artist Suad Al-Attar be similar?** *(Students may suggest the poet and the artist may be similar in that they both came from the Middle East where women often struggle for success. Both women are similar in that they are artists who have accomplished great achievements.)*

530

BUTTERFLIES

Fawziyya Abu Khalid

The Waiting Horseman, 1990. Suad Al-Attar. Oil on canvas. Private collection. ★

When you abandoned me,
I didn't need an elegy°
because you had planted
a flight of butterflies in my heart
whose path I follow
like a bedouin who knows
how to perfectly trace the footsteps
    of his truant mare.°

2 elegy: a song or a poem that expresses sadness and grief, usually for a person who has died.

8 truant mare: a female horse that has strayed.

1 Connect to Personal Experience *In your opinion, does this reference to a Bedouin make the poem inaccessible to readers unfamiliar with Saudi culture? Explain.*

Literary Element Practice

Simile Remind students that a simile is a figure of speech that compares two unlike things using the word *like* or *as.* You might want to point out that the words *like* and *as* are key in identifying a simile. Explain that a metaphor also compares two unlike things; however, it does not use *like* or *as.*

Give students practice in writing their own similes. Tell them to select five objects from the classroom. Then, tell them to write a simile that describes each object. Allow students to brainstorm ideas with partners. After they have finished, have volunteers share their similes with the class. If time permits, have students try to write some metaphors as well.

After You Read

Respond and Think Critically

Respond and Interpret

1. Would you recommend this poem to other readers? Why or why not?

2. (a)According to the first line of the poem, what has happened to the speaker? (b)What do you think the speaker means by "I didn't need an elegy"?

3. (a)What has been planted in the speaker's heart? (b)What feelings might this metaphor express?

Analyze and Evaluate

4. (a)Can you tell whether the speaker in "Butterflies" is a man or a woman? Explain. (b)Do you need to know the speaker's gender to understand the poem? Why or why not?

5. How would you describe the tone of the poem? Support your answer with details from the text.

6. How does the poet's **diction**, or word choice, affect your perception of the speaker's feelings?

Connect

7. **Big Idea** The Violence of Change (a)What change has taken place in the speaker's life? (b)In what way does the speaker's reaction to this change indicate that dramatic upheavals can have positive effects?

8. **Connect to the Author** Abu Khalid left Saudi Arabia to study in the United States but eventually returned home. What ideas about departure and return are evident in "Butterflies"?

Literary Element Simile

Poets use **similes**, a type of **figurative language**, to create vivid images and suggest meaning.

1. What is the **simile**, or comparison, in lines 4–8?

2. What does this simile suggest about the speaker's relationship with the person addressed?

Reading Strategy Connect to Personal Experience

Connecting events, emotions, and characters to your own life can help you explore a literary work more deeply. Refer to the Venn diagram you made on page 529 and then answer these questions.

1. Do you and the speaker have anything in common? Explain.

2. Rewrite the last three lines of the poem, using a simile that relates to your own life.

 **LOG ON** **Literature** Online

Selection Resources For Selection Quizzes, eFlash-cards, and Reading-Writing Connection activities, go to glencoe.com and enter QuickPass code GLW6053u3.

Academic Vocabulary

In "Butterflies," the speaker addresses a person who has **abandoned** her.

Abandon is an academic word. Synonyms include *desert, forsake,* and *leave.* To study this word further, fill out a graphic organizer like the one below.

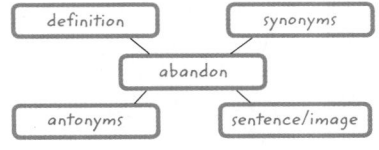

For more on academic vocabulary, see pages 36–37 and R83–R85.

Writing

Write an Essay Reflect on an event that was particularly emotional for you, such as the end of a friendship. Write an essay describing this event, how you felt, and what you learned. Use a **simile** in your essay to add interest and enliven the style.

FAWZIYYA ABU KHALID   **531**

After You Read

Assess

1. Answers will vary.

2. (a) The speaker has been "abandoned." (b) The speaker is saying he or she does not need to be mourned or consoled.

3. (a) a "flight of butterflies" (b) Students may say the metaphor expresses feelings of fragility, love, and uncertainty.

4. (a) You cannot tell, because the poem does not include any references that indicate the speaker's gender. (b) You do not need to know, because the emotions he or she describes are universal.

5. Answers will vary. Some students may think the tone is melancholy and nostalgic; others will think it is positive.

6. Students may suggest that the poet's direct style indicates strength and resignation, or they may say that her sparse diction betrays intense emotions.

7. (a) The speaker has been abandoned by a loved one. (b) Students may note that the speaker does not "need an elegy" and is positive enough to appreciate the relationship.

8. The speaker highlights the permanence of some departures as well as the possibility that returns can be facilitated by those who know where to look.

Literary Element

1. The speaker compares how he or she follows the butterflies' path to how a Bedouin skillfully follows the tracks of a mare that has strayed.

2. It suggests that the speaker and the person being addressed were very close. The speaker understands the person innately and could trace his or her footsteps if need be.

Reading Strategy

1. Students may say they have also been left behind by a friend or a loved one.

2. Rewrites will vary. Students should use similes that relate to their own lives.

For additional assessment, see Assessment Resources, pp. 115–116.

Academic Vocabulary

Definition: to leave without intending to return; Synonyms: forsake, desert; Antonyms: return, join; Sentence: The mother bear abandoned her cub.

Writing

Students' personal essays should reflect on a specific event and include details and an original simile.

Before You Read

Focus

Bellringer Options

Daily Language Transparency 48

Or bring in a graphic novel, a comic book, and a bound book. Discuss their similarities and differences with the class. Ask students to try to define serious literature. **Then ask:** Can any one of these be serious literature? Explain. *(Students who are unfamiliar with graphic novels and comic books may think that the genres do not qualify as serious literature.)* Point out that all three genres have stories that can be considered serious literature. In addition, emphasize that each genre can tackle serious subjects.

Before You Read

Iran

The Letter from *Persepolis:*
The Story of a Childhood

Meet **Marjane Satrapi**

(born 1969)

"❝I like black and white better than anything," observes graphic novelist Marjane Satrapi, "because there's no bluff in black and white." Satrapi has used a simple but vigorous black and white drawing style to present memoirs of her life, as well as to tell stories from the lives of her friends and family.

Revolution and War Satrapi was born in Iran (formerly Persia) in 1969, the only child of prosperous, idealistic parents. They instilled a fierce sense of independence in their bright, troublesome daughter, whom they enrolled in a progressive French school. Satrapi was still a child when widespread unrest began to threaten the government of Iran's monarch, Mohammad Reza Shah Pahlavi. His leadership and the revenue gained from oil had helped Iran become a rich country, but devout Muslims opposed the shah and believed that modern Iranian culture was based on greed and materialism. Ayatollah Ruholla Khomeini (kō′mā nē) , a member of the Muslim clergy, led the opposition against the shah, eventually overthrowing him in 1979 and establishing an Islamic republic.

> *"Violence today has become something so normal, so banal . . . black and white makes it abstract and more meaningful."*
>
> —Marjane Satrapi

A Memoir in Pictures Satrapi spent her early adolescence living with repression and war. A beloved uncle was executed by the Islamic regime, and a neighbor's family was killed by an Iraqi missile that destroyed their home during the Iran-Iraq War (1980–1988). Fearing for the safety of their defiant, outspoken daughter in a fundamentalist Iran, Satrapi's parents sent her to high school in Austria. After attending college in Iran, Satrapi returned to Europe, where she studied illustration. Settling in Paris, she shared a studio with a group of young French graphic artists, to whom she told stories about her life in Iran and the Iranian Revolution of 1978–1979. They encouraged Satrapi to turn the story of her childhood into a comic, and the result was the award-winning graphic novel *Persepolis*. (The title refers to the capital of the ancient Persian Empire.)

Distinct illustrations, narrative clarity, and a keen sensitivity to universal emotions have gained *Persepolis* solid critical reviews. "Satrapi's drawing style is graceful and unfussy . . ." observed Lisa McLaughlin in a *Time* review. "By telling her own story in lean, simple strokes, she also tells the complicated modern history of her country."

LOG ON ▶ **Literature** Online

Author Search For more about Marjane Satrapi, go to glencoe.com and enter QuickPass code GLW6053u3.

Selection Skills

Literary Elements
- Symbol (TE pp. 534, 536, 538, 539, 541)

Reading Skills
- Identify Genre (TE pp. 533–535, 537, 539–541)
- Identify Problem and Solution (TE p. 536)

The Letter

Vocabulary Skills
- Synonyms (SE p. 541; TE p. 533)

Speaking/Listening/Viewing Skills
- Conduct an Interview (TE p. 538)

Writing Skills/Grammar
- Graphic Story (SE p. 541)
- Use Quotation Marks (TE p. 534)
- Write a Letter (TE p. 540)

Literature and Reading Preview

Connect to the Graphic Novel

Have you ever been angered over a decision made by your school, the government, or a corporation? Freewrite about why you disagreed with this decision.

Build Background

In the 1960s and 1970s, Ayatollah Ruholla Khomeini incited many Iranians against the corruption and Western secularism that characterized the reign of Mohammad Reza Shah Pahlavi. In 1978, street demonstrations broke out in every major Iranian city. "The Letter" touches briefly on Black Friday, September 8, 1978. On that day, Iranian soldiers fired upon more than 20,000 demonstrators, killing hundreds.

Set Purposes for Reading

Big Idea **The Violence of Change**

As you read "The Letter," ask yourself, How does Satrapi's involvement with political changes in Iran affect her family life?

Literary Element **Symbol**

A **symbol** is a person, a place, or a thing that exists on a literal level but also stands for something else, usually something abstract. As you read, ask yourself, What things in this story symbolize aspects of Iranian society?

Reading Strategy **Identify Genre**

When you **identify genre,** you recognize the characteristic elements of a particular type of literature. An increasingly popular genre is the **graphic novel,** or a lengthy story in comic book form. Elements of the graphic novel include **images,** the pictures that present the visual narrative; **panels,** the grid that establishes the narrative sequence of the images; and **word (or speech) balloons,** which contain the words or thoughts of the characters. As you read, ask yourself, What identifies this story as an excerpt from a graphic novel?

Tip: Take Notes As you read, use a chart to note how the elements of the graphic novel work together to create meaning.

Elements	Effects
Panels	• Setting changes frequently
	• Plot advances quickly

Learning Objectives

For pages 532–541

In studying this text, you will focus on the following objectives:

Literary Study: Analyzing symbol.

Reading: Identifying genre.

Writing: Writing a graphic story.

Vocabulary

clandestine (klan des′tin) *adj.* secret; p. 534 *The spies used clandestine tactics to gather information.*

devoted (di vō′tid) *adj.* dedicated; feeling strong attachment; p. 536 *The actor was devoted to his art and often spent hours rehearsing.*

demonstrate (dem′ən strāt′) *v.* to participate in a public display of group opinion; to rally or march; p. 539 *The citizens gathered to demonstrate against the war.*

Tip: Synonyms Synonyms are words with the same or similar meanings. For example, a synonym for *demonstrate* is *protest,* a verb that means "to express an objection."

MARJANE SATRAPI **533**

Before You Read

Focus

Summary

Marji, a young girl from a wealthy Iranian family, has a maid named Mehri who falls in love with a neighbor. Marji helps their romance by writing letters for Mehri, who is illiterate. Marji's father learns of the romance and tells the neighbor that Mehri is a maid. He rejects her because she comes from a lower class. To protest against the social class system, Marji and Mehri go to a demonstration against the government. Many people are killed, and Marji's mother is angry when the girls come home late.

 For summaries in languages other than English, see Unit 3 Teaching Resources Book, pp. 170–175.

Vocabulary

Synonym Match Have students write each vocabulary word on a separate index card. As you read aloud possible synonyms, have students hold up the matching vocabulary card. Include words that are not synonyms for any of the vocabulary words.

 For additional vocabulary practice, see Unit 3 Teaching Resources Book, p. 178

Advanced Learners/Pre-AP

DIFFERENTIATED INSTRUCTION

Social Class in Literature Tell students that conflict between social classes is a common topic in literature. Ask students to share short stories and novels they have read that addressed this topic. *(Students may share short stories such as Guy de Maupassant's "The Necklace" and novels such as those by Jane Austen.)*

Ask students why conflict between social classes might be a common subject in literature. *(Students may point out that class differences exist in different cultures, countries, and time periods. It can be a source of conflict, especially when people from different classes become friends or fall in love.)* As students read "The Letter," have them look for similarities and differences between the other works they discussed.

Teach

Reading Strategy | 1

Identify Genre Have students read the first page of "The Letter."
Ask: How is this story like a comic book? How is it different? *(The graphic novel is similar to a comic book because it tells its story with pictures in panels, as well as with words. This graphic novel is not like a comic book because it is black and white and a full-length memoir.)*

Literary Element | 2

Symbol Point out the three panels at the bottom of the page.
Ask: What does the car symbolize, and why does Marji feel ashamed? *(The car symbolizes the family's wealth and social position. Marji is ashamed because she does not believe there should be different social classes.)*

THE LETTER 1

I'D NEVER READ AS MUCH AS I DID DURING THAT PERIOD.

MY FAVORITE AUTHOR WAS ALI ASHRAF DARVISHIAN, A KIND OF LOCAL CHARLES DICKENS. I WENT TO HIS CLANDESTINE BOOK-SIGNING WITH MY MOTHER.

FER ME FRIEND KOUROSH.

WHY DOES HE SPEAK LIKE THAT?

IT'S JUST HIS KURDISH ACCENT.

HE TOLD SAD BUT TRUE STORIES: REZA BECAME A PORTER AT THE AGE OF TEN.

LEILA WOVE CARPETS AT AGE FIVE.

HASSAN, THREE YEARS OLD, CLEANED CAR WINDOWS.

GET DOWN FROM THERE, STUPID!

I FINALLY UNDERSTOOD WHY I FELT ASHAMED TO SIT IN MY FATHER'S CADILLAC.

THE REASON FOR MY SHAME AND FOR THE REVOLUTION IS THE SAME: THE DIFFERENCE BETWEEN SOCIAL CLASSES.

BUT NOW THAT I THINK OF IT... WE HAVE A MAID AT HOME !!!

2

534 UNIT 3 SOUTHWEST ASIA

Grammar Practice

Quotation Marks Tell students that in graphic novels, dialogue balloons indicate speech. Traditional literature, however, uses quotation marks to indicate when a character is speaking.

Write the following sentence on the board to demonstrate proper use of quotation marks: *"Hey, Shane!" Regina called from the back of the bus. "Do you know what time it is?" Shane checked his watch. "Yes, it's almost noon."*

For each of the following sentences, have students add quotation marks to indicate direct speech. Tell them that some sentences contain thoughts or indirect speech; students should be sure not to add quotation marks to these.

1. Deena said, ["]Joshua is my lab partner.["]
2. Sasha says that his sister was at the party.

3. ["]So did you decide yet what you're going to do after graduation?["] asked Brandy.
4. Did you ask if you could bring the potato salad?
5. ["]I can't believe he said that!["] exclaimed Cole.
6. Joelle said that she was running late.

HER →

THIS IS MEHRI.

SHE WAS EIGHT YEARS OLD WHEN SHE HAD TO LEAVE HER PARENTS' HOME TO COME TO WORK FOR US. JUST LIKE REZA, LEILA AND HASSAN.

WE HAVE TOO MANY CHILDREN, 14 OR 15 INCLUDING HER.

SHE WILL EAT WELL AT YOUR HOUSE.

WE WILL TAKE CARE OF HER.

SHE WAS JUST TEN YEARS OLD WHEN I WAS BORN...SHE TOOK CARE OF ME.

SHE PLAYED WITH ME.

AND SHE ALWAYS FINISHED MY FOOD.

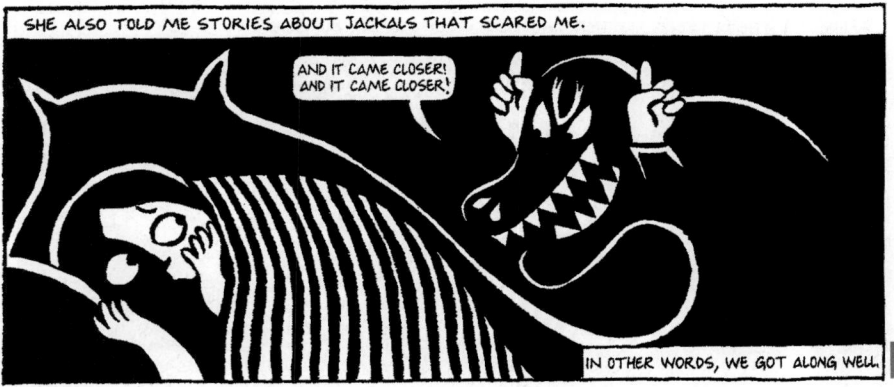

SHE ALSO TOLD ME STORIES ABOUT JACKALS THAT SCARED ME.

AND IT CAME CLOSER! AND IT CAME CLOSER!

IN OTHER WORDS, WE GOT ALONG WELL. **3**

MARJANE SATRAPI **535**

English Learners

DIFFERENTIATED INSTRUCTION

Beginning Students will likely enjoy the graphic format of "The Letter." To help them further connect with the story, tell them to examine the characters' expressions in the panels. Suggest that they use self-stick notes to indicate when a character experiences a change in emotion. Students can refer to the notes for reinforcement as they read the text.

Approaching Level

DIFFERENTIATED INSTRUCTION

The Narrator Make sure that students understand the conventions of dialogue and thought balloons. Explain that the speaker is indicated by a "tail" on the balloon pointing at the person who is talking. A dialogue box without a "tail" operates like the narrator of a story, making comments on events and people.

Teach

Reading Strategy   3

Identify Genre Direct students' attention to the last panel on the page. **Ask:** How is the art in this panel different from the earlier panels? Why is it different? *(Mehri is telling a frightening story, so the art suggests a dark and frightening setting. The art in the previous panels has not been frightening.)* Then **ask:** What does this change in artistic style add to the story? *(Students may suggest that the change adds an undercurrent of fear and danger to the story.)*

Political History ☆

Iran Before the Revolution
Before the Iranian Revolution began in 1978, Iran had a political system in which the only real power was held by the Shah. Trying to be a modern leader, he attempted land reform and modernization but did not allow the Iranian people to participate in the government. The Shah's brutal secret police, called SAVAK, shut down political dissent and spied on, censored, and tortured people from both the left and right. Failed economic policies and widespread corruption led to protest against the Shah's regime.

Learning Objectives
Identifying genre. (TE)
Analyzing symbols. (TE)
Using quotation marks in dialogue. (TE)

Teach

Symbol Ask students to summarize what is happening between Mehri and her sister. *(Mehri's sister begins to fall in love with Hossein, too. Out of jealousy, she tells a family member about Mehri's relationship.)* **Ask:** What might Hossein represent for Mehri and her sister? *(Students should see that for Mehri and her sister, both members of a lower working class, he represents both economic opportunity and oppression.)*

Literary History ☆

Graphic Novels Graphic novels were popular in Europe and Japan long before they became accepted in the United States. In 1978, Will Eisner published what is usually considered to be the first graphic novel. As graphic novels appear more frequently in libraries and bookstores and as film adaptations, they are beginning to attract more attention in the United States. They account for only a tiny percentage of the book business, but they are a fast-growing market.

536 UNIT 3 SOUTHWEST ASIA

Reading Practice

Identify Problem and Solution Tell students that identifying problems and solutions in a text can help them connect to the characters. After students read this page, **ask:** What is Mehri's problem? How does Marji help her solve it? *(Mehri falls in love but cannot read or write love letters. Marji helps her by writing and reading Mehri's letters for her.)*

Then ask: How does this change Mehri and Marji's relationship? *(Marji is doing favors and errands for her servant.)* Ask students what other problems this change might cause. *(Students might suggest that Marji and Mehri could get in trouble with Marji's parents.)*

1

2

MARJANE SATRAPI **537**

Reading Strategy 2

Identify Genre Have students read the panels on this page. **Ask:** How is this graphic novel similar to and different from a traditional novel? *(The use of plot, characters, conflict, dialogue, and rising action are similar. The format is different; it uses a combination of words and images to tell the story. It also uses far fewer words than a traditional novel, and it conveys dialogue through balloons.)*

Cultural History ☆

Social Class Theories about social class, or groups of people at different socioeconomic levels, have been discussed since the nineteenth century. After the Industrial Revolution, class was no longer dependent solely on one's genealogy, but on one's property and wealth. There are generally considered to be three social classes in modern industrial society: upper, middle, and lower (or working) class. In most countries, people are able to move upward or downward among these classes.

Advanced Learners/Pre-AP
DIFFERENTIATED INSTRUCTION

Analyze Style Ask artistically inclined students to evaluate the style of art used in this graphic novel. Students might respond to one or more of the following questions.

▪ Does the art add to or detract from the story? How?

▪ Would the art be more or less effective if it were in color? Why?

▪ How well does the art convey different characters and their emotions?

▪ Does the art give readers a clear sense of the story's setting? Explain.

▪ How well does Satrapi use shadow and shading?

Ask students to discuss their opinions in small groups.

Learning Objectives
Identifying genre. (TE)
Analyzing symbols. (TE)
Identifying problem and solution. (TE)

Teach

Big Idea   1

The Search for Wisdom

Direct students' attention to the last panel on the page. **Ask:** Which character seems to be the most advanced in his or her thinking? How can you tell? *(Marji is the most advanced. She realizes the inherent unfairness of the social class system.)*

Literary Element   2

Symbol   **Ask:** What does the bed in the last panel symbolize? *(The bed symbolizes the closeness of the girls' relationship regardless of their different social classes. Their friendship makes them equals.)*

APPROACHING If approaching-level learners struggle to analyze symbols in the story, remind them that symbols mean more than their basic definitions. For example, here a bed is not just a place to sleep; for Marji and Mehri, it is a place where they can share their feelings. The bed offers them a refuge from the judgmental outside world.

Speaking Practice

Conduct an Interview Organize students in pairs. Have each pair of students choose to interview one of the characters in the story. You might wish to check students' choices to ensure that all the characters are covered. Tell students to work together to develop a list of questions they would like to ask the character.

Then, students should write possible answers that the character would give. Remind students that their answers should stay true to how the character is portrayed in the story.

After students finish writing their interview, have them perform the exchange for the class. One student should take the part of the character, and one student should take the part of the interviewer.

MARJANE SATRAPI **539**

Teach

Reading Strategy | 3

Identify Genre Direct students' attention to the last two panels on this page. **Ask:** How does the artist use simple black-and-white forms to create the impression of a violent demonstration? *(In the next-to-last panel, the artist shows identical repeated figures with their fists raised to suggest the anonymity of a large crowd. In the next panel, the artist shows individual faces with expressions of anger.)*

Literary Element | 4

Symbol Ask: What does the demonstration symbolize for Marji and Mehri? *(The demonstration symbolizes their feelings about the failed relationship between Mehri and Hossein. It allows them to voice the anger they feel toward a system that keeps apart people of different social classes.)*

Progress Check

Can students analyze symbol?

If No → See Unit 3 Teaching Resources Book, p. 176.

Approaching Level

DIFFERENTIATED INSTRUCTION

Tracking Panels Students may struggle to read the panels in the correct sequence. First use a page of the story to model reading the panels in order. Then provide students with photocopies of the story, and guide them in numbering the panels or drawing arrows to indicate the order in which students should read.

Advanced Learners/Pre-AP

DIFFERENTIATED INSTRUCTION

Create Storyboards Tell students that graphic novels are similar to storyboards, a series of panels used while planning an animated or action film. Have students take a familiar children's story such as "Goldilocks and the Three Bears" and draw the plot using as few storyboard panels as possible. Tell students to use "The Letter" as a guide for style and format.

Learning Objectives
Analyzing symbols. (TE)
Identifying genre. (TE)
Conducting an interview. (TE)

Teach

Big Idea

The Violence of Change
Have students read the first two panels. **Ask:** How has the demonstration impacted Mehri and Marji? *(They seem exhilarated and energized by it. They do not want to leave.)* Discuss with students what Marji might hope to gain from participating in the demonstration. *(Students will likely say that Marji might hope to change her country's class system.)*

Reading Strategy

Identify Genre Have students read the final two panels. **Ask:** What purposes do the words and pictures serve here? *(The words give historical information about the demonstration. The pictures show the people who died on Black Friday and the imprints of slaps on the girls' faces.)*

Progress Check

Can students identify genre?

If No → See Unit 3 Teaching Resources Book, p. 177.

  To check students' understanding of the selection, see Unit 3 Teaching Resources Book, p. 181.

540 UNIT 3 SOUTHWEST ASIA

Writing Practice

Write a Letter Ask students where "The Letter" leaves Marji at the end. *(Her mother is angry that she attended the demonstration. Her country has just experienced a day of massive violence.)* Have students write a letter to Marji, advising her on what she should do next—about her mother, Mehri, and her feelings about social classes.

Ask students to consider the volatile political climate of Marji's country. What other ways can she safely express her disagreement with her country's class system? Can she affect change in her own household? What can she do to ease her mother's anger and help heal Mehri's heartbreak? Ask volunteers to share their letters with the class.

After You Read

Respond and Think Critically

Respond and Interpret

1. What was your immediate response to Satrapi's graphic style? Explain.

2. What realization does Satrapi have about her shame and the revolution?

3. What aspect of oppression in Iran is represented by Mehri's job and her age when she took it?

4. (a)How does Satrapi react when the neighbor rejects Mehri? (b)What does her reaction reveal about her feelings for Mehri? Explain.

Analyze and Evaluate

5. (a)How does Satrapi graphically convey the emotions and violence of the demonstrations? (b)Do you think these images are effective? Explain.

6. (a)Why do you think Satrapi makes the imprint of slaps remain on her face and on Mehri's face on page 540? (b)What statement do you think Satrapi is making about violence?

Connect

7. **Big Idea** **The Violence of Change** Based on "The Letter," how would you describe the time of the Iranian Revolution?

8. **Connect to the Author** Satrapi states that she prefers drawing in black and white because "there is no bluff" in it. What do you think her statement means?

Literary Element **Symbol**

Some **symbols** have well-known meanings. Other symbols may be created by an author based on what he or she values and is trying to convey.

Partner Activity With a partner, discuss what the letter in this excerpt symbolizes. Consider the role social class plays in the excerpt.

Reading Strategy **Identify Genre**

Satrapi, like many other graphic novelists, uses her medium to meld humor with social commentary.

1. How do the elements of the graphic novel help advance the plot throughout the "The Letter"?

2. Do you think this graphic novel would be more or less effective if it were told as a conventional narrative without illustrations? Explain.

 LOG ON ▶ **Literature** Online

Selection Resources For Selection Quizzes, eFlash-cards, and Reading-Writing Connection activities, go to glencoe.com and enter QuickPass code GLW6053u3.

Vocabulary Practice

Practice with Synonyms With a partner, brainstorm three synonyms for each boldfaced vocabulary word below. Be prepared to explain your choices.

clandestine   devoted   demonstrate

EXAMPLE: inquire
Synonyms: ask, question, query

Sample explanation: When you inquire about a product, you ask about it.

📝 Writing

Write a Graphic Story *Persepolis* shows how key events in Satrapi's life changed her perspective on the world. Using her work as a model, create a short graphic novel, using images, panels, speech balloons, and symbols to tell a story from your life. Look at the graphic organizer you filled out on page 533 as you consider how to apply this genre's elements.

Literary Element

The letter represents the differences in class status, since Mehri cannot write it herself and Hossein accepts it only because he thinks she is from a higher class. It also symbolizes the potential for interaction between the classes, when people do not realize or recognize class differences.

Reading Strategy

1. These elements help convey the action and the characters' emotions.

2. Possible answer: The story would not be as effective because the emotions of the characters might not be as apparent and the narration might seem flat without the illustrations.

After You Read

Assess

1. Answers will vary.

2. by driving in an expensive car she is part of the system that discriminates by class

3. child labor, just as with Reza, Leila, and Hassan

4. (a) Satrapi is nearly as upset as Mehri. (b) Her reaction indicates her love and devotion as well as her feelings of sympathy for Mehri's social standing.

5. (a) The emotions are captured in the characters' facial expressions and in the mass of people chanting. The violence is captured in the drawing of corpses. (b) Answers will vary.

6. (a) This illustration shows both the physical and the emotional impact of the slaps. (b) Violence is not easily forgotten. Its effects remain long after the actual violence has stopped.

7. Students may note that the time period was full of passion, fear, and violence. "The Letter" shows how people tried to change the system but also contributed to it.

8. Satrapi might mean that it allows her to focus on the fundamentals of the story.

Vocabulary Practice

Explanations will vary. Sample answers:

Word: clandestine; Synonyms: covert, secret, furtive; Word: devoted; Synonyms: loyal, faithful, constant; Word: demonstrate; Synonyms: protest, speak out, dissent

📝 Writing

Students' graphic stories should correctly use the elements of the graphic novel genre and use symbolism.

TIME

Focus

Summary

Throughout Southwest Asia, the status of women has been controversial. In most Middle Eastern nations, women have had few rights and little status. Jordan's Queen Rania is breaking out of the existing stereotypes to work for change. She is encouraging women to take a more active part in public life, and promoting programs for education and civil rights for girls and women.

> For summaries in languages other than English, see Unit 3 Teaching Resources Book, pp. 183–188.

Teach

Reading Strategy   1

Connect to Contemporary Issues The struggle for women's rights is not a problem unique to Southwest Asia. Even in countries such as the United States, there is much that needs to be done. **Ask: What issues regarding women's rights are controversial in the United States today?** *(Women in the United States face issues of combining family and work, and gaining greater representation in the political process.)*

> For additional practice using the reading skill or strategy, see Unit 3 Teaching Resources Book, p. 189.

Readability Scores

Dale-Chall: 9.8
DRP: 64
Lexile: 1200

542

Learning Objectives

For pages 542–545

In studying this text, you will focus on the following objectives:

Reading: Connecting to contemporary issues.

Using text features.

Analyzing informational text.

Set a Purpose for Reading

Read to learn about how one Arab woman is fighting for the rights of women in her society.

Preview the Article

1. Read the deck—the brief text beneath the article's title—and view the photographs on pages 543 and 544. What impression of Rania do these features give you?

2. Skim the entire article, reading the first sentence of each paragraph. What conflicts might the article address?

Reading Strategy   Connect to Contemporary Issues

When you **connect to contemporary issues,** you relate what you read to what you already know about current events and ideas. As you read, ask yourself:

- How does this information fit with what I already know about the Middle East?

- What new information does this article teach me about current events, ideas, and conflicts?

TIME

Regarding
RANIA

Blazing a trail for Arab women, Jordan's stylish queen has redefined her role to become an agent of political change. But in the face of traditionalist opposition, she can push women's issues only so far. **1**

By SCOTT MACLEOD

STEPPING OUT OF HER GUNMETAL-GRAY SUV AND striding into the compound of Kamalia School for Girls in Amman, Jordan, Rania al Abdullah doesn't fit the prim, cautious image of an Arab queen. For one thing, she's wearing a tight-fitting metallic gold top, matching pants, and two-inch heels, and her glossy brown hair brushes across her shoulders as she walks. For another, rather than standing around exchanging pleasantries, she's walking briskly to her appointment like the busy head of a corporation heading to a board meeting. Nor could she seem more unlike the audience that awaits her inside the school: 28 teenage girls in drab blue uniforms, half of them with their hair fully covered with scarves in the tradition of conservative Muslims.

The Jordanian queen's exposed hair and modern style are social and political statements, of course, advertising her belief that the veil worn by many Muslim women as a part of their religious beliefs should be a matter of personal choice. Rania usually chooses not to. But she isn't at the school to lecture anybody about fashion or faith. She's marking the start of Human Rights Day at one of many events being held in schools across the kingdom of Jordan. The nationwide observance—never before held in an Arab world famous for its violations of basic freedoms—was Rania's idea, just

---

Reading Practice

Identify Author's Purpose The *Time* magazine article is a nonfiction piece of writing. In nonfiction as well as in fiction, various literary techniques can help an author convey his or her purpose for writing. Point out that authors may write to entertain, to describe, to explain, to inform, or to persuade.

Tell students that the topic of a piece of writing may provide clues to the author's purpose. Also, an author's word choice and tone also reveal his or her purpose. Ask students what they think is the author's purpose for writing this piece. Tell them to support their responses with examples from the text.

one of many modernizing notions and programs she works for.

2 After greeting the students, Rania reads aloud a passage about the rights of women, drawn from the United Nations' Universal Declaration of Human Rights. "Freedom means no discrimination on the basis of race, language, religion, politics, or origin, with no differences between men and women," she says in a teacherly way. "Everyone is equal." To the queen's delight, one of the girls responds by quoting Islam's prophet Muhammad on women's equality. Others throw up their hands in a competition to join in. Long after Rania has left, the girls still have stars in their eyes. "She talks to us about freedom, that nobody can take it away from us," beams Rula Nasser. The 10th grader pauses for a moment, then adds: "She's amazing!"

No Western queen or first lady would get such a glowing review just for reading from a legal document. But in the Arab world, where most rulers' wives follow the conservative line in dress and behavior, Rania is a rarity: a powerful woman who uses that power to push a forward-looking, modern agenda. While other Arab wives typically limit their public profile to supporting uncontroversial charities, Rania uses her influence on controversial issues that have brought her praise from modernists, criticism from traditionalists—and attention from well beyond the borders of tiny Jordan. "She's a mover and shaker," says one of the Arab press's leading commentators, Abdul Rahman al Rashid, columnist for the London, England–based *Asharq al Awsat*. "She's not a woman who

INSPIRATION Posing with starstruck students at Amman's Kamalia School for Girls on Human Rights Day

Khalil Mazraawi—AFP/Getty

wants media attention, but one who wants to deliver a program. It is not easy to change things, but she is making noise and delivering what she promises."

The secret to Rania's transformative approach to the monarchy may be her background. She was not raised to be a queen. Her parents are Palestinian—her father was a children's doctor—and she earned a living as part of Amman's middle class, working as a marketing executive for Apple Computer before meeting and marrying then Prince Abdullah in 1993. After becoming queen in 1999 she turned into an international fashion symbol (Italian designer Giorgio Armani said she "has the body of a model, and she holds herself like the queen she is—what more could you want?"). But recently she has evolved into someone even more impressive and hard to define. After a recent earthquake reduced the Iranian town of Bam to rubble, she supervised the loading of

relief supplies onto a Jordanian transport plane and then rode on it to Iran to comfort the victims. She's on the governing board of **3** the World Economic Forum (WEF), the only Arab helping to guide that group of global political and business leaders.

Rania and her husband, King Abdullah II, teamed up with the WEF and U.S. tech company Cisco Systems to launch the Jordan Education Initiative, which teaches people in the Middle East how to learn with the Internet. Her favorite part of the project is Jordan's 10 Cisco Networking Academies. There, high-tech skills are taught to 600 students— almost two-thirds of them women. And thanks to Rania's urging, Arab satellite channels now broadcast public-service ads aimed at boosting women's participation in public life.

3 Rania's most controversial work is done behind the scenes in Amman, where she quietly urges the king and leading Jordanian

REGARDING RANIA **543**

English Learners

DIFFERENTIATED INSTRUCTION

Advanced Explain to students that Jordan is a constitutional monarchy. This means that a king rules the country. The king, who currently is King Abdullah II, creates a cabinet and has a prime minister to act in his name. Invite students to explain the form of government in their native countries. Have them describe the governments to the class.

Advanced Learners/Pre-AP

DIFFERENTIATED INSTRUCTION

Compare and Contrast Invite students to learn more about Queen Noor by researching her accomplishments on the Internet. Then, have them prepare a summary, display chart, or other medium to show the similarities and differences between Queen Noor and Queen Rania. Students can compare and contrast the women's actions, achievements, and backgrounds.

TIME

Teach

Reading Strategy **2**

Connect to Contemporary Issues Ask: When girls do not participate in the educational process, what is the effect on society? (*Lack of education leads to lack of social, economic, and political power. Women are limited in the jobs they can do and have little chance of advancement.*)

Big Idea **3**

The Violence of Change Violence is not usually associated with the women's movement. Point out that passive resistance and work for change from within the system have been more common approaches. **Ask:** How have Queen Rania's efforts to improve the lives of women avoided violent change? (*Rania leads by example and stresses the positive aspect of women's rights, such as better education. Rather than confronting those in power, Rania lets her own life and actions make her points.*)

Political History ☆

Queen Noor The queen of Jordan before Rania was Queen Noor. Much of her charitable work was in the field of empowering children through education, promotion of Jordanian culture, and humanitarian issues.

Learning Objectives
Connecting to contemporary issues. (TE)
Identifying author's purpose. (TE)

TIME

Teach

| Reading Strategy | 1 |

Connect to Contemporary Issues

Point out to students that Rania, like Princess Diana of England, has earned a place in the public eye due to her appearance and her humanitarian aid projects. **Ask:** How is Rania able to use the power of her celebrity to aid others? (*Rania knows that she will receive media attention, so she purposely makes both fashion and political statements by not wearing traditional Arab dress. Like Diana, she uses the media to get attention for causes that are important to her.*)

Political History ☆

Women in the Military Women have been part of Jordan's military forces since the 1950s. All of them volunteer for service, and many serve as teachers and medical personnel. Recent initiatives have resulted in Jordanian military women filling roles as military police and military intelligence.

QUEEN RANIA attends the Red Cross gala evening during her visit to London in June.

Salah Malkawi–Getty; Royal Palace/Balkis Press,/ABACA

politicians to establish social and political reforms, many of them aimed at improving the circumstances of women. In 2003, her promptings helped lead to an increase in the number of women holding leadership positions in Jordanian politics. The following year six seats were reserved for women in the newly elected 110-seat Chamber of Deputies. The king had also appointed seven women to the 55-seat Senate and ☆ included three women in his government's 21-member cabinet. "She comes and pushes the case," says Abdullah. "She'll say, 'I'm just reminding you, if we are going to give women more of a role, for them to feel a stronger part of society, how about trying to push the envelope?'"

There's plenty of pushing left to be done. In a series of interviews with TIME, Rania described a Middle East where many women's lives remain disadvantaged by inequality. "One of the main obstacles preventing the Arab world from advancing is the exclusion of women," she says. "Sometimes people ask, 'Do you have an agenda?' Yes, I do have a gender agenda. The more you include women, the more people will get used to the fact that yes they are capable, yes they are part of the scene."

But the same traditions that suppress Arab women also place limits on what Rania can achieve. Jordan's conservative politicians have struck many of her modernizing programs down. Also in 2003,

parliament rejected proposals she supported to equalize divorce rights and increase the marrying age of girls from 15 to 18. Rania has also tried and failed to persuade politicians to end a regulation that prevents Jordanian mothers from handing down citizenship to their children. Without citizenship, which can be passed down only by fathers in Jordan, children cannot get state-sponsored education and medical care.

Officials close to the queen say that the setbacks in parliament have taught her not to expect overnight success. "My disappointments," Rania says, "have come mainly from my own impatience. [Reform] requires changes from within society. If society still believes that a woman's place is in the home, you are not going to get change." Even so, she is firmly convinced that "now is the time to confront these issues."

She has already witnessed plenty of change. Rania al Yasin was born in Kuwait in August 1970. Her family remained in Kuwait until Iraq invaded the tiny oil-rich nation in 1990. The Yasins left and never went back. Rania earned a business degree from the American University in Cairo, Egypt, before joining her parents in Amman in 1991. She worked in marketing, first for Citibank, then for Apple. She met Abdullah, oldest son of Jordan's then King Hussein, at a dinner party in 1992, and they married the following year.

She was not expected to become queen. On his deathbed, King Hussein decided to pass over his brother Hassan, who had been next in line for the throne, and instead make Abdullah his heir.

544 UNIT 3 SOUTHWEST ASIA

Reading Practice

Main Idea and Supporting Details

Say: To find the main idea in an informational text, examine how the author organizes ideas. Have students first look at the first paragraph on page 542. **Ask:** What is the main idea of this article? (*Rania is different from most Arab women.*) What details in the next paragraph support the main idea? (*her lack of a veil, her modern style, and her overt political beliefs*)

That decision caught Rania—and all of Jordan—by surprise. "A whole new life and responsibility was suddenly placed on my shoulders," she recalls. "You start feeling insecure. You feel you have to prove yourself."

The traditional role of the Arab wife would have required the new queen to limit herself to the raising of their three children. Instead, the king asked her to develop programs on human rights, women's rights, children's rights, education, and health. As a result, Rania set up a separate office, which has a staff of 20, including researchers, speechwriters, schedulers, and media advisers. Many of the people who work in the office are modern young Jordanian women like herself. Although she rarely states her political positions in public, Abdullah says he frequently asks for Rania's advice. "I come home at night, and I have a problem with education or health, and I need somebody to [discuss them with]," he says.

If her discussions with Abdullah have become political, Rania's early public image was centered on her looks and her wardrobe. There were comparisons to former U.S. First Lady Jacqueline Kennedy and Great Britain's Princess Diana, and she became a favorite of celebrity interviewers, gossip columnists, and fashion magazines on both sides of the Atlantic. The media attention led to some criticism in Amman, where Rania's fondness for designer dresses and expensive European vacations is considered inappropriate for the queen of a poor country. The gossips call her "the handbag queen," and even serious commentators in Jordan complain about the costly lifestyle of the royal family. She calls the criticism "part of the turf," but adds: "If the gossip gets out of hand, I may have to look at myself and ask, Am I doing something wrong?"

She has done a lot that is right. Shortly after Abdullah's coronation, she agreed to become a spokeswoman for the global finance movement, which seeks to give power to Third World women by providing them with loans to start small businesses. She has since traveled the globe promoting the Washington, D.C.-based Foundation of International Community Assistance, holding lunches with women in Washington and Hollywood and delivering aid to women in battle zones like Kosovo.

These days, Rania is entirely at home in a room filled with powerful world leaders. When she was invited to address the Economic Forum in Saudi Arabia—where discrimination against women is so pervasive that they are barred from most occupations—she boldly accepted. When the day came, Jordan's queen presented a blunt message. Instead of a speech on business, Rania wanted to talk about something "a little more relevant": the need to include Arab women in all aspects of life. "We must face up to hard truths," she said from the podium. "It will not help to wring our hands, point fingers, or clench our fists. First, we must *all* participate." For women across the Arab world, it was a call to action from one of their own.

—Updated 2007, From TIME Atlantic

Respond and Think Critically

Respond and Interpret

1. Write a brief summary of the main ideas in this article before you answer the following questions. For help on writing a summary, see page 1147.

2. (a)What are some of Rania's political accomplishments? (b)What obstacles has she faced in trying to institute reforms?

3. (a)How are Rania's politics and public persona untraditional? (b)What criticisms has she faced in Jordan?

Analyze and Evaluate

4. How might Rania's background have influenced her political opinions?

5. (a)Why do you think Rania has gained international attention? (b)Why might she be viewed differently in the West than in the Middle East?

Connect

6. How does the description of gender conflict in this article relate to the other literature you have read in Unit 3, Part 1?

REGARDING RANIA **545**

Assess

1. Students' summaries will vary but should mention the fact that Rania is effecting change in the Middle East, despite some setbacks.

2. (a) Rania has increased the number of women involved in Jordanian politics and has helped bring Internet-based learning to the Middle East. (b) The conservative parliament has rejected many of her initiatives.

3. (a) Rania's politics are untraditional because she has lobbied for women's rights and other progressive causes. Her public persona is untraditional because she does not always wear a veil, she is outspoken, and she is actively involved in politics. (b) Besides facing opposition from conservative politicians, Rania has been criticized for her expensive lifestyle.

4. Her professional experience may have shaped her belief that women can be independent and successful outside the home. Her observations of the social injustices faced by Arab women and other human rights concerns in the Middle East may have sparked her interest in politics.

5. (a) Rania has gained international attention for her aggressive political agenda, her public appearances around the world, and her fashionable style. (b) Possible answer: Outspoken, powerful women are more accepted in Western culture; Rania also fits the glamorous Western image of a celebrity.

6. Answers will vary. Students may mention that it reflects al-Malā'ikah's concern that the needs of Middle Eastern women—and people of all races and creeds—can be forgotten or ignored.

Learning Objectives
Connecting to contemporary issues. (TE)
Determining main idea and supporting details. (TE)

545

Bellringer Options

Daily Language Transparency 49

Or on the board, **write:** south central Asia. **Ask:** What do you know about south central Asia's history, culture, or geography? (*Students may mention the colonization of India, Hinduism, Islam, and the Himalayas*).

Reading Strategy

Read the Map **Ask:** How do you think the location of the Indian subcontinent has contributed to its cultural diversity? (*Students may suggest that the surrounding seas encourage trade and migration.*)

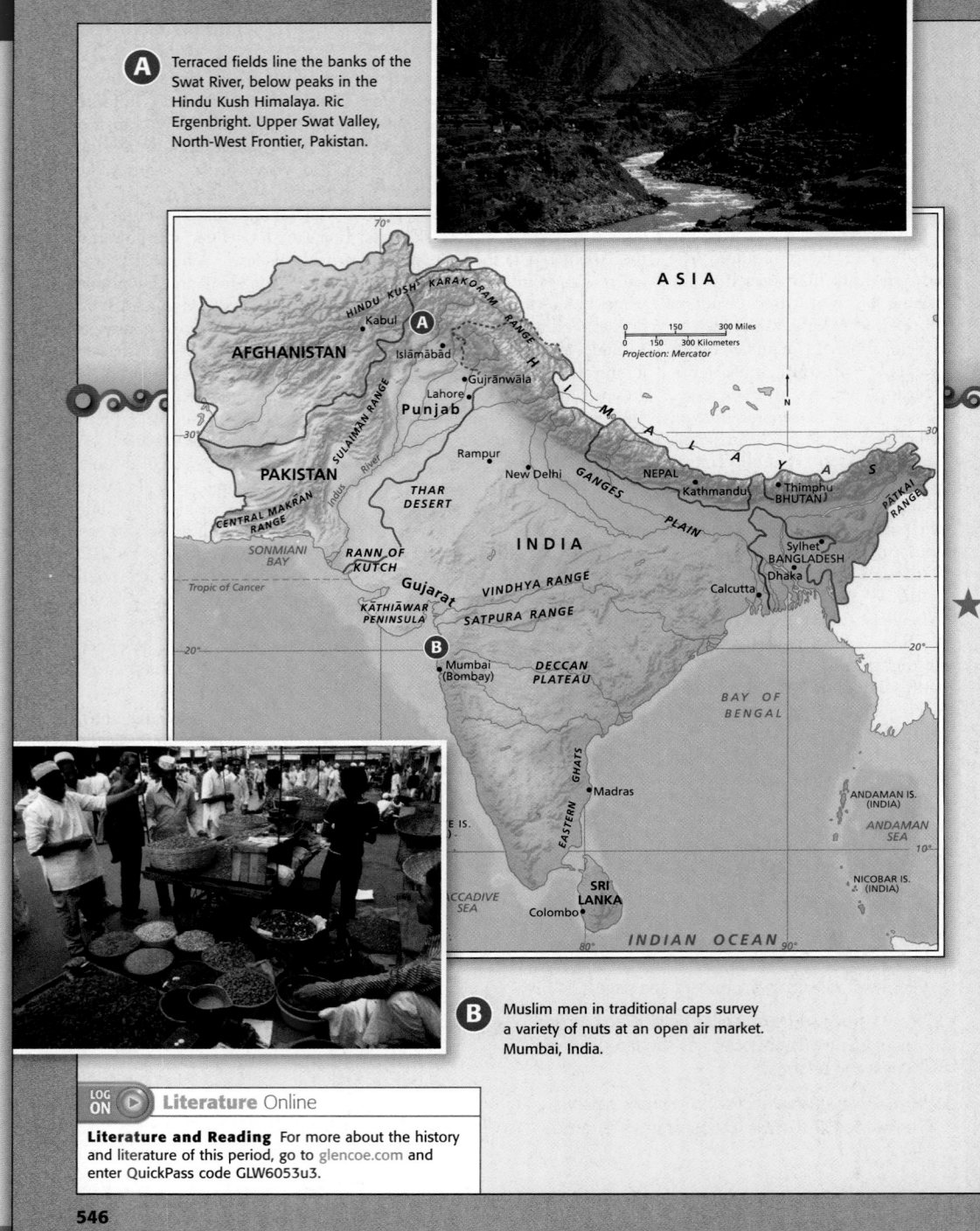

A Terraced fields line the banks of the Swat River, below peaks in the Hindu Kush Himalaya. Ric Ergenbright. Upper Swat Valley, North-West Frontier, Pakistan.

B Muslim men in traditional caps survey a variety of nuts at an open air market. Mumbai, India.

LOG ON ▶ **Literature** Online

Literature and Reading For more about the history and literature of this period, go to glencoe.com and enter QuickPass code GLW6053u3.

546

Part Introduction Skills

Reading Skills
- Analyze Graphic Information (SE p. 549)
- Make Generalizations (SE p. 554)
- Analyze Cause-and-Effect Relationships (SE pp. 555, 556; TE p. 550)

Part 2 Introduction

Speaking/Listening/Viewing Skills
- Small-Group Discussion (SE p. 557)
- Analyze Art (TE pp. 550, 551, 553–556)

Study Skills/Research/Assessment
- Timeline (TE p. 548)
- Use Graphic Organizers (TE p. 554)

Writing Skills/Grammar
- Compare-and-Contrast Essay (SE p. 557)
- Description (TE p. 552)

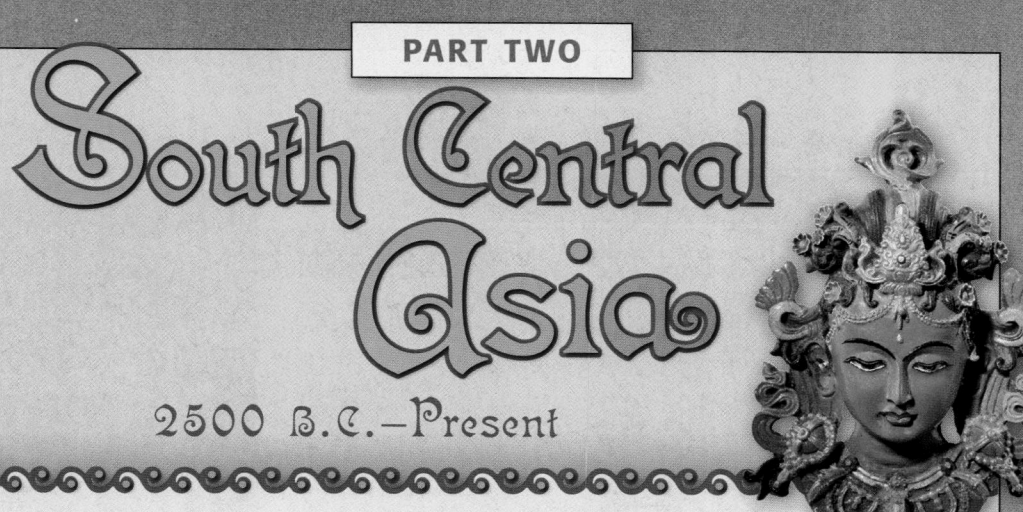

South Central Asia

2500 B.C.–Present

Sculpture of Hindu God Shiva.

Being There

South central Asia is one of the most diverse regions on earth. It stretches from the snow-capped Himalayas to tropical islands, deserts, and fertile river valleys. Because of its enormous size, it is often referred to as a subcontinent. The region is currently home to one-fifth of the world's population, living in areas as varied as the villages of Nepal and the crowded streets of Delhi, India.

Looking Ahead

One of the world's oldest civilizations, the Indus, began in south central Asia about 4,500 years ago. The rich farmland and mineral resources in India have long attracted invaders, from the Indo-European tribes who arrived 3,500 years ago to the British, who left in 1947. All of these occupiers contributed—both positively and negatively—to the cultural heritage of the region.

Keep the following questions in mind as you read:

- What were some of the contributions of the Indo-European peoples to the ancient culture of south central Asia?

- How were women's lives limited by traditional south central Asian culture?

- How does language contribute to the cultural complexity of modern south central Asia?

547

Advanced Learners/Pre-AP

DIFFERENTIATED INSTRUCTION

Research Geography Ask students to choose a geographic feature--such as the Himalayas, one of the many rivers that run through the region, or a climate pattern--and research its effect on the history of south central Asia. Invite students to present their findings to the class in oral or written reports. Encourage them to include maps, photographs, and other visuals.

Focus

Summary

This introduction gives an overview of the history, culture, religion, and literature of south central Asia from 3000 B.C. to the present. It describes the rise of empires after the instability of invasions, the time of British colonial rule, and the separation of the colonies into India and Pakistan. The introduction also describes the culture of the region, including art, music, and dance, as well as the importance of Hinduism and spirituality. It also touches on the more difficult issues of gender discrimination and the caste system.

Cultural History ☆

The Himalayas The Himalayan Mountains form the northern border of the Indian subcontinent. Stretching 1,500 miles from east to west and 200 miles from north to south, the mountain chain is capped by at least 50 peaks more than five miles high. The tallest is Mount Everest, on the border between Nepal and Tibet. **Ask:** How do you think this mountain range has impacted cultural exchange? (Students will probably guess that it has impeded exchange to some extent.)

> For additional support for English learners, see Unit 3 Teaching Resources Book, p. 193.

Teach

Reading Strategy

Using the Timeline Have students examine the timeline and relate any key events in south central Asian literature to world history as well as to the history of the region. **Ask:** What connection can you make between invasions in the B.C. era and the development of literature in south central Asia? (*Students will most likely note that the earliest* Vedas *followed the first occupation of North India by Indo-European tribes and that the* Ramayana *followed Alexander the Great's invasion.*)

Timeline 2500 B.C.–Present

SOUTH CENTRAL ASIAN LITERATURE

3000 B.C.

1000 B.C.

c. 1500
Earliest Vedas appear

c. 750–550
Upanishads are compiled

c. 563 ▶
Siddhārtha Gautama
(the Buddha) is born
in India

500
Classical Sanskrit begins
to develop

c. 300
Ramayana is composed

SOUTH CENTRAL ASIAN EVENTS

3000 B.C.

1000 B.C.

c. 2600
First Indus Valley cities
are established

c. 1500
Indo-European tribes
occupy northern India

326
Alexander the Great
invades India

c. 1700
Indus Valley cities are
abandoned

◀ **c. 265–238**
Emperor Aśoka promotes
Buddhism

WORLD EVENTS

3000 B.C.

1000 B.C.

c. 3000
Cuneiform writing
is developed

c. 2589–2566
Pharaoh Khufu builds
Great Pyramid at Giza

c. 509
Roman Republic
is founded

221
Ch'in Shih Huang Ti
becomes first Chinese
emperor
▼

1450s–c. 1425
Pharaoh Thutmose III
expands Egyptian Empire

LOG ON ▶ **Literature** Online

Literature and Reading To explore the Interactive
Timeline, go to glencoe.com and enter QuickPass code
GLW6053u3

Reading Practice

Timeline Explain that a timeline is a chart that shows a sequence of events. Name the three timelines on this chart and point out that events from 3000 B.C. to the present appear in a double-wide column across the three timelines.

Ask: How many years passed between the formation of the Indian National Congress and India's partition? (*62 years*) Ask students to list events that happened within the same 50- to 100-year span across all three timelines. Encourage students to consider whether there is a connection between these events.

100 Years of Indian Cinema
Celebrated on Postage Stamps

a.d. 1   **a.d. 1000**   **a.d. 2000**

c. 400
Present text of
Mahabharata takes form

☆ **1440**
Mystical poet Kabir is born

c. 1529
Bābur writes his memoirs

1913
Rabindranath Tagore wins
the Nobel Prize in
Literature

1935
R. K. Narayan publishes
the first of his Malgudi
fiction

2005
Poet and novelist Amrita
Pritam dies

a.d. 1   **a.d. 2000**

c. 380–415
Candra Gupta II rules
northern India

712
Muslims invade India

Mughal Flask
(metalwork)

1498 ▲
Portuguese explorer Vasco
da Gama reaches India

1526
Bābur establishes Mogul
Empire

1653
Shāh Jāhan completes
the Taj Mahal

1885
Indian National Congress
is formed

1947
British India is partitioned
into India and Pakistan

1948 ▶
Mohandas Gandhi is
assassinated

1984
Union Carbide disaster
takes place in Bhopal,
India

2004
Tsunami devastates Indian
Ocean coastal areas

a.d. 1   **a.d. 1000**   **a.d. 2000**

313
Constantine I legalizes
Christianity in Rome

552
Buddhism is introduced
to Japan

c. 610
Muhammad, founder of
Islam, begins preaching

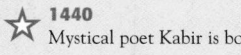

1517
Martin Luther posts
95 theses in Germany
▼

1762
Catherine the Great
becomes ruler of Russia

1945
World War II ends

Reading Check

Analyze Graphic Information About how long
after Babur formed the Mogul Empire did he write
his memoirs?

UNIT THREE
PART 2

Teach

Reading Check

Answer: *Babur wrote his memoirs about three years after he formed the Moghul Empire.*

Reading Strategy

Make Inferences **Ask:** Based on what you have read, what can you infer about the years immediately following the partitioning of British India into India and Pakistan in 1947? (*This was a violent and unpredictable time in India, as shown by Mohandas Gandhi's assassination in 1948.*)

APPROACHING For approaching-level students, turn the question around. **Ask:** What does Mohandas Gandhi's assassination in 1948 help you infer about the year after the separation of British India into two separate countries?

Literary History ☆

Kabir An orphan raised as a Muslim, Kabir created his own religion called *sahaja-yoga* ("simple union"), in which he rejected the caste system but embraced the karma of Hinduism while accepting a single god of Islam. Kabir's poetry lacked proper grammar and elegance. As a result, common people responded well to it. Some of his hymns were included in the sacred book of the Sikhs, the *Adi Granth*.

Learning Objectives
Analyzing graphic information. (SE)
Making inferences. (TE)

Approaching Level

DIFFERENTIATED INSTRUCTION

Students may still be overwhelmed by the three timelines that cover more than 5,000 years of history. Have students select one event from the middle timeline. Ask students to find one event in the top timeline that preceded the selected event and one event in the bottom timeline that followed the selected event. Students can take these three events and draw a small timeline of their own for visual support.

Advanced Learners/Pre-AP

DIFFERENTIATED INSTRUCTION

Have students create a four-level timeline—starting at the year of their birth—that includes events from their own lives as well as world events, south central Asian events, and highlights in south central Asian literature.

549

Teach

Reading Strategy

Draw Conclusions **Ask:** Based on the information about the Gupta and Mughal empires, what conclusion can you draw about the influence of efficient rulers and government on society? (*Stable government leads to advances in art and literature.*)

Language History ☆

Naming a Country The ancient Persians used the term *India* to describe the lands east of their empire, through which a mighty river—the *Indus*—flowed. The people who lived in what is now India referred to their land as *Bharata*, which may have been the name of a great warrior. When the constitution of India was enacted in 1950, lawmakers adopted *Bharat* as the country's alternative name.

View the Art ★

Under the mounds of Mohenjo-Daro ("the mound of the dead") lie the remains of what was once the Indus civilization's largest city. Thousands of steatite seals have been found in the remains; this seal is believed to show a unicorn. The tiles contain lettering that no one has been able to decipher. **Ask:** What might the untranslated symbols indicate about the Indus civilization? (*Students may say that the mysterious language indicates that the Indus civilization was more advanced than might be first assumed.*)

550

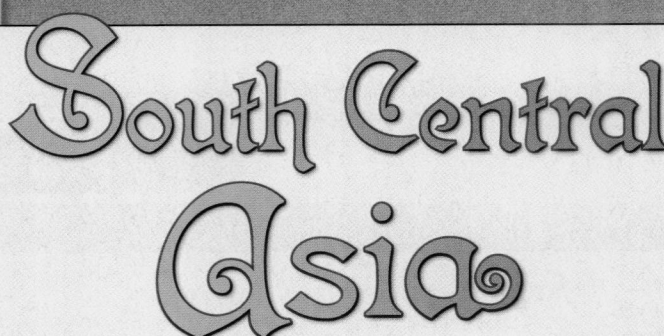

South Central Asia

Learning Objectives

For pages 546–557

In studying this text, you will focus on the following objectives:

Literary Study: Analyzing literary periods.

Reading: Evaluating historical influences. Connecting to the literature.

3500 B.C.–Present

Historical, Social, and Cultural Forces

The Indus Civilization ☆

Between 3000 B.C. and 1500 B.C., the valleys of the Indus River system in present-day Pakistan supported a flourishing civilization that stretched from the Himalaya mountain range to the coast of the Arabian Sea. Archaeologists have found the remains of more than 1,000 settlements in this region. The well-planned cities of the Indus

civilization indicate a highly organized society. Eventually, however, natural disasters, a shift in the course of the Indus River, and climate change weakened the Indus civilization, whose cities seem to have been largely abandoned by 1700 B.C.

The Indo-Europeans

What remained of the Indus Valley civilization was destroyed in about 1500 B.C. by migrating peoples (now referred to as the Indo-Europeans or Aryans) who had crossed the Hindu Kush mountain range from their homelands on the plains of central Asia. The Indo-Europeans were herders with a strong warrior tradition. They gradually abandoned herding for farming as they extended their control over most of India. Their early literature, which includes hymns and heroic legends, reveals that between 1500 B.C and 400 B.C., India was plagued by continual warfare. Various tribal leaders, known as *rajas* ("kings" in Sanskrit), carved out small states and fought one another, attacking fortresses and seizing women, cattle, and treasure.

Seal depicting a mythological animal and pictographic symbols, 3000-1500 BC. Stone. Mohenjo-Daro, Indus Valley, Pakistan.

Reading Practice

Analyze Cause-and-Effect Relationships Have students read the text on this spread. **Ask:** What was the cause of the weakening of the Indus civilization? (*natural disasters, climate change, and a shift in the Indus River's course*) **Ask:** What was the effect of the Indo-Europeans' emigrating from Central Asia into what is now India? (*The previous civilization in the Indus Valley was destroyed, and the Indo-Europeans took control of most of India.*)

Explain that when one cause leads to an effect, that effect is often the cause of another effect, thus creating a chain of cause-and-effect relationships. In groups, have students create cause-and-effect charts using other events from the information in this spread.

Invaders and Empire-Builders

Alexander the Great crossed the Indus River in 326 B.C. after he had heard of the riches of India. He defeated some native rulers in fierce battles, but his soldiers grew weary of fighting and refused to advance farther into the region, forcing him to withdraw. Alexander's conquests set the stage for India's first empire-builders, the Mauryan dynasty. At its height under Aśoka, who ruled from 265 B.C. to 238 B.C., the Mauryan Empire included most of India. After Aśoka's death, the Mauryan Empire declined and was succeeded for centuries by warring kingdoms.

In A.D. 321, a prince named Candragupta created a new state in the central Ganges Valley. His successors, the Guptas, expanded their rule into an empire. Under a series of efficient rulers—especially Candra Gupta II, who reigned from 380 to 415—the Gupta Empire marked a golden age of Indian civilization. The great Sanskrit poet Kalīdāsa lived during the Gupta dynasty. The famous murals of the Ajanta Caves in western India also date from the Gupta period.

> "The mighty army of Delhi was laid in the dust in the course of half a day."
>
> —Bābur describing his victory over the Indians in his *Autobiography*

The last great conqueror to establish an Indian empire was Bābur, who defeated the sultan of Delhi at the battle of Panipat in 1526. Bābur was a descendent of the Mongol conqueror Genghis Khan, and the line of rulers he established is known as the Mogul (Persian, for "Mughul") dynasty. The greatest Mogul emperor was Bābur's grandson Akbar, who ruled from 1556 to 1605. A great soldier, Akbar was also a wise and humane ruler who established a policy of religious toleration that helped reconcile the many sects in his empire.

Maharana Raj Singh I of Mewar, c.1670. Indian School. Gouache with gold on paper. Ashmolean Museum, University of Oxford, UK.

British Rule and Modern India

By the early 1700s, the power of the Mogul rulers was waning. The arrival of the British hastened the decline of the Mogul Empire. British authority in India was exercised by the East India Company, a private company empowered by the British crown to act on its behalf for more than two centuries. By the mid-nineteenth century, the company controlled much of India, hiring Indian soldiers, known as sepoys, to protect its interests. A rebellion by the sepoys prompted Britain to tighten its control by establishing direct rule of India.

The British created a modern infrastructure in south central Asia, building railroads, a court system, hospitals, and schools, but they also exploited the region economically and treated the people they ruled as social and cultural inferiors. In 1885, a small group of Indians formed the Indian National Congress, which demanded that Indians share in the governing process. After World War I, political leader Mohandas Gandhi began using nonviolent methods of civil disobedience to protest British rule. By the 1940s, the Muslim League had begun to believe in the need for the creation of a separate Muslim state. In 1947, British India was divided into two independent nations: India (officially secular with a Hindu majority) and Pakistan (officially Muslim).

INTRODUCTION **551**

Reading Strategy

Summarize Ask: How would you summarize what you have learned about Great Britain's involvement in India? (*Great Britain came to rule much of India by the 1900s because of the East India Company, which had been established 200 years earlier. Although Great Britain helped modernize south central Asia, its actions concerning the region's resources and people led to the people's seeking independence.*)

View the Art ★

Painting styles in India's history can often be linked to specific courts or rulers. Early Mewar paintings focused on religious or mythic subjects. As portraiture took hold in the seventeenth century, rulers and court life became popular subjects; however, the lack of communication between the Mewar and Mughal rulers during this time resulted in Mewar illustration that lacked a naturalistic style. **Ask:** How would you describe the energy or lack thereof in this painting? (*Students are likely to say that the painting is stiff and formal, with all of the faces in profile.*)

English Learners

DIFFERENTIATED INSTRUCTION

Intermediate Explain that some advanced vocabulary words have more than one meaning. In groups, have students use a dictionary to look up the various definitions of words on this spread, including *plagued, height, succeed,* and *inferior.* Groups should come to a consensus on which definition is being used in the context of the sentence.

Advanced Learners/Pre-AP

DIFFERENTIATED INSTRUCTION

Have students imagine that they are living in India during British rule. Tell them to use details from the text to create a journal entry for their imagined selves. For example, a student could imagine that he or she is a sepoy. The student could write about his or her daily activities working for the British.

Learning Objectives
Evaluating historical influences. (SE)
Drawing conclusions. (TE)
Summarizing. (TE)
Analyzing Cause-and-Effect Relationships. (TE)

Teach

Reading Strategy

Preview and Make Inferences Have students read the subheads on this spread. **Ask:** What information will you expect to read about on these pages? (*Students are likely to say that they expect to read about music, dance, and art.*) Then, have students read the main caption of the art. **Ask:** What can you infer about the importance of dance in Hindu culture? (*Students are likely to say that the representation of one of Hinduism's greatest gods as "Lord of the Dance" indicates that dance is especially important in Hindu culture.*)

Cultural History ☆

Sitar The sitar is a musical instrument that is popular in India, Bangladesh, and Pakistan. The word *sitar* comes from the Persian *sehtar*, meaning "three stringed," though a sitar may have as many as nineteen strings. Popular since the 1500s, sitars have evolved into their current shape; similar in form to a guitar, sitars are usually four feet long and have a pear-shaped body, although different schools use sitars of different sizes and shapes.

The Arts

The art of south central Asia reflects the influence of Hinduism and Buddhism, and much of it adorns the elaborate temples of the region. Although the area has its own distinctive artistic styles, its artists have been open to influences from outside—including Greek sculpture, Arabic calligraphy, and Persian miniature painting. The film industry in India—called Bollywood—produces more than 1,000 films annually. Bollywood films are characterized by their vibrant colors, song-and-dance scenes, and internationally famous stars.

> "*The man who knows nothing of literature, music, or art, is nothing but a beast without the beast's tail and horns.*"
>
> —ancient Indian proverb

Sitar. Bengali School. Wood, silver, and ivory. Horniman Museum, London. ☆

Traditional Music

The traditional musical form of India is called the *raga*; northern and southern India have their own variations on this style. The raga, which is named after the Sanskrit word for "color," is based on a musical scale with a given set of notes. The raga musician improvises as he plays each song and stresses melody rather than harmony. The musical ensemble might include plucked or bowed string instruments, drums, and wind and reed instruments. Drone instruments repeat a single note or series of notes to provide the basic background.

Indian Musical Instruments, plate 23 from *Oriental Drawings,* published 1806. Aquatint. Stapleton Collection, UK.

Writing Practice

Write a Description Have students write a description of one of the musical instruments on this page. Students may include details about the instrument's appearance or the colors and textures in the picture. Instruct students to use sensory details in their descriptions. Remind them that sensory details are details that appeal to a reader's five senses—sight, hearing, smell, touch, and taste.

Allow students enough time to write their descriptions. After they have finished, have students exchange their descriptions with a partner's. Partners should make sure that sensory details have been included in the description. They should also look for errors in grammar, spelling, and punctuation. Students should then revise their descriptions based on their partner's feedback.

Classical Dance

Dance is especially important in Hindu culture. Modern dancers and their teachers still consult a 2,000-year-old text, the *Natya-sastra*, for information on dance styles and gestures. Classical dances portray religious stories and mythological episodes using elaborate hand and body gestures. Folk dance is also an important part of Hindu religious festivals, occasionally lasting late into the night. In both the folk and the classical traditions, musicians and dancers maintain close communication with one another, reacting to changes in one another's rhythms. Audiences respond to the familiar stories by counting out rhythms and shouting their approval.

Young Woman Performing Indian Bharat Natyam Dance. ★

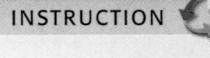 **Big Ideas** of South Central Asia

1 The Search for Enlightenment

The civilization of south central Asia has been defined by several religious traditions—particularly Hindu and Buddhist—that offer many paths to spiritual salvation. The sacred literature of these traditions includes hymns, religious epics, and fables.

See page 554

2 A Place in Society

The caste system, an inherited social hierarchy, defined the lives of Indians for generations. This system is evident in much of the literature of the region. Modern authors have also explored the limited roles to which women have traditionally been restricted.

See page 555

3 A Complex Heritage

South central Asia has a complicated cultural heritage, resulting from its mixture of ethnic and religious traditions and its long experience under British rule. Modern authors of the region often address diverse issues ranging from personal integrity to environmental problems.

See page 556

INTRODUCTION **553**

Teach

Literary Element

Recognize Author's Purpose Ask: What is the author's purpose for including the highlighted quote on the previous page? (*The author wishes to encourage readers to become educated about literature, music, and art.*) **Ask:** What does the author appeal to in this quote by comparing humans with animals? (*The author appeals to readers' egos and sense of superiority to animals.*)

View the Photograph ★

Bharat Natyam (or Bharatanatyam) is based on an ancient style of dance in India. Once performed in temples, classical dance nearly died out under British rule in the nineteenth century, only to be rediscovered and gain popularity after independence in the mid-twentieth century. **Ask:** How is this dancer similar to and different from traditional Western dancers, such as ballet dancers? (*Students may say that this dancer's costume and jewelry are much more elaborate than any ballet dancer's, but that her art depends on intricate movements and expression, similar to a ballet dancer.*)

English Learners

DIFFERENTIATED INSTRUCTION

Intermediate Have students start a glossary of words that they will most likely encounter in the rest of the unit, such as *Shiva* and *raga*. Students should list the words and their definitions to help themselves later as they read selections.

Advanced Learners/Pre-AP

DIFFERENTIATED INSTRUCTION

Have students delve further into Indian music and dance by performing research on the subject in small groups. Students can use Internet or print sources to discover information about Indian music and dance. Groups can present oral presentations on their findings. Each group member should play a role in the presentation.

Learning Objectives
Analyzing literary periods. (TE)
Evaluating historical influences. (TE)
Writing a Description. (TE)

Teach

Reading Check

Answer: *The spiritual goal of Hinduism is to escape the cycle of reincarnation and unite the individual soul, or atman, with the universal spirit, or Brahman.*

Reading Strategy | 1

Determine Main Idea and Supporting Details **Ask:**
What is the main idea of the first Big Idea? (*Religion influences all aspects of life in south central Asia.*) **Ask:** What details in the final paragraph support the main idea? (*Hinduism influenced literature from the thirteenth century through the seventeenth century in south central Asia.*)

View the Art ★

In Hindu mythology, Krishna, an incarnation of the Hindu god Vishnu, was raised by cowherds; as a young man, he attracted the attention of the cowherds' daughters and wives (*gopis*), and loved one in particular—Radha. To commemorate his marriage in the late eighteenth century, the ruler of Kangra had a series of paintings of Krishna and Radha made, to which this painting's lush, romantic style is similar. **Ask:** What is the relationship between love and nature in this painting? (*Students may say that the lush, colorful vegetation seems to be embracing Krishna and Radha, indicating nature's acceptance and even encouragement of their love.*)

Big Idea 1
The Search for Enlightenment

Religion dominates all aspects of life in south central Asia. Hindus make up about 80 percent of the population, while Muslims account for about 10 percent. India is the birthplace of Jainism, which stresses spirituality through discipline, and Sikhism, which began as a Hindu movement. Although India is also the birthplace of Siddhārtha Gautama, the founder of Buddhism, Sri Lanka and Bhutan are the only Buddhist countries in south central Asia today.

Hinduism

Hindus worship many gods, whom they believe to be the various forms of Brahman, a single, universal, and divine spirit. The most important forms of Brahman are the three gods that form the "Hindu trinity": Brahma, the creator; Vishnu, the preserver; and Shiva, the destroyer. Hindus believe the soul goes through a series of rebirths, each based on a person's actions in the previous life. The force that is generated by these actions and that determines how that person will be reborn is called *karma*. Karma, in turn, is ruled by *dharma*, the divine law that requires all people to fulfill the duties of their station in life. Eventually, a person who lives well and fulfills his or her dharma can break out of this cycle, and the person's *atman*, or soul, will unite with the universal spirit.

Radha and Krishna embrace in a grove of flowering trees, c.1780. Watercolor on paper. Victoria & Albert Museum, London. ★

Classical Literature

The earliest literature of south central Asia—the Vedas, the *Mahabharata*, and the *Ramayana*—was first composed and transmitted through oral tradition and later written down in Sanskrit, the classical language of India. The Vedas, which contain four collections of hymns, are the most important sacred texts in Hinduism. The *Mahabharata* is an epic that tells the story of a set of cousins who battle over a kingdom in northern India. In one section of this vast narrative, the Hindu god Krishna delivers a sermon on moral duty. This sermon, known as the Bhagavad Gita, or "Song of God," is the most famous poem in Indian literature. The second great Sanskrit epic, the *Ramayana*, tells the story of the god-king Rama, whose dharma is to defeat the demon Ravana.

> *"The Eternal in man cannot kill: the Eternal in man cannot die."*
>
> —from the Bhagavad Gita

An increased emphasis on spirituality within Hinduism in the thirteenth to seventeenth centuries inspired many fine poets such as Tulsīdās, who translated the *Ramayana* into Hindi (a language descended from Sanskrit); the blind poet Surdas; and the Rajput princess and mystical poet Mirabai. Another mystical poet was Kabir, a Muslim who sought to combine the spiritual elements of Islam and Hinduism and urged people to overcome the prejudices of the caste system. **1**

Reading Check

Make Generalizations What is the spiritual goal of Hinduism?

Reading Practice

Use Graphic Organizers Have students reread the information about Hinduism on this page. The description of the three gods of the "Hindu Trinity" can be difficult to understand. To help students visualize this connection between Hindu gods, have them create a graphic organizer of three circles connected by arrows within a larger circle.

After students understand that the actions of each of the three gods are connected, encourage them to create their own graphic organizers to visualize the Hindu concepts that they will encounter in this unit. You may wish to provide them with some basic organizer ideas, such as charts, webs, and Venn diagrams.

Big Idea 2
A Place in Society

Women carry vessels containing water in the village of Kundaliya.

For generations, Indian society has been defined by the caste system, which classifies people based on the social group into which they are born. Until recently, people's jobs, homes, and spouses were determined by this inherited status. For Indian women, religious beliefs have also led to strictly defined roles and rules of conduct.

The Caste System

The invasion of India by the Indo-Europeans resulted in a system of class divisions that separated the conquerors from the conquered. Over time, these divisions developed into the traditional Hindu caste system. The castes were divided by occupation: priests (Brahmans), rulers and soldiers (Kshatriyas), merchants and farmers (Vaishyas), and peasants and laborers (Sudras). At the bottom were the "untouchables," who were made to do tasks other Indians would not accept, such as handling dead bodies. The degrading aspects of the caste system were ruled illegal when newly independent India adopted its constitution in 1950, although the castes themselves still exist. More social mobility exists now than ever before, fueled in part by economic growth and by people who have obtained higher education.

Village Life

While the caste system is not as pervasive as it once was, it still continues in many places, particularly rural areas. Despite the growth of urban districts, many people in south central Asia live in villages and farm or herd animals. Families of the same caste tend to live near one another, with the lowest castes at the fringes of the villages. In the past, families often created alliances with families of other castes and traded specialized services, such as carpentry, barbering, or officiating at religious rites. These hereditary alliances could be traced back over many generations.

> "A woman must never
> be independent."
>
> —The Laws of Manu

Family Life

Traditionally, three or four generations of one family lived in a single home. These households typically included a man and wife, their sons and their sons' wives, unmarried daughters, and the children of their sons. In some urban centers today, the nuclear family is the more standard arrangement.

Religious beliefs have defined the lives and roles of Indian women throughout history. The Laws of Manu, which are followed by many traditional Hindus, state that a woman is always subject to her father, husband, or son. Some Indian women have also followed *purdah,* a belief that began in Islam but was adopted by many Hindus. Purdah requires women to live mostly in seclusion and to wear veils in the presence of nonfamily members. In recent times, however, Indian women have become increasingly active in many professions, including medicine and business.

Reading Check

Analyze Cause-and-Effect Relationships How have modern political and social conditions affected the caste system?

INTRODUCTION **555**

English Learners

DIFFERENTIATED INSTRUCTION

Intermediate Encourage students to use context clues to ascertain the meanings of difficult words. Tell students that context clues are words or phrases in sentences that help readers with difficult vocabulary words. For example, writers sometimes use antonyms to help readers understand a word's meaning, such as the word *urban*. In other cases, a writer will use explanation to define a word, such as the word *nuclear*.

Advanced Learners/Pre-AP

DIFFERENTIATED INSTRUCTION

Castes Have students research more information about the traditional Hindu caste system. Tell them to use Internet and print sources to discover more information about the dress, duties, and responsibilities of each caste.

After students have finished researching, tell them to write a short story that involves at least two of the castes.

Teach

Reading Check

Answer: *The degrading aspects of the caste system were ruled illegal when newly independent India adopted its constitution. Social mobility—fueled by education and economic growth—now permits more freedom from caste.*

Reading Strategy | 2

Make Inferences Ask: Based on how the author has ordered the castes in the text, what can you infer about the levels of the castes? (*The Brahmans [priests] were the highest caste, and the Sudras [peasants and laborers] and "untouchables" were the lowest.*)

APPROACHING Explain that authors will usually list items in either ascending or descending order of importance. Draw the levels of the caste system on the board for students still having difficulty.

View the Photograph

Ask: What can you infer about the lives of rural women from this photograph? (*Students may say that women in rural areas of India have difficult lives because they don't have running water; others may say that, regardless of the lack of running water, the women's colorful clothing indicates an appreciation for beauty.*)

Learning Objectives
Making generalizations. (SE)
Analyzing cause-and-effect relationships. (SE)
Using graphic organizers. (TE)

555

Teach

Reading Check

Answer: *There are so many major languages in south central Asia that people from different language backgrounds use English— the language introduced by the British—as a common language.*

Reading Strategy

Determine Main Idea

Ask: What is the main idea of the section titled Modern South Asian Literature? *(The British influence in south central Asian literature resulted in the authors of the regions turning their attention from poetry to short stories and novels, as well as their writing in English.)*

View the Art ★

The capital of West Bengal, Calcutta is not only one of India's most populated cities but also its largest at 533 square miles.
Ask: What differences in social status are visible in this photo? *(Some people ride in rickshaws, some walk, and others ride in cars; some, such as the rickshaw drivers, are dressed poorly while others seem dressed for office jobs.)*

Big Idea 3
A Complex Heritage

What would it be like to live in a country with 22 official state and national languages? That is only one aspect of modern India's cultural complexity.

South Central Asia Today

Like other regions around the world, south central Asia has undergone a number of positive changes over the past few decades. India, for example, has achieved extraordinary technological development and the noticeable growth of a middle class. However, there are also serious problems, including overpopulation, poverty, and ethnic and religious conflict. Unlike its neighbor India, Pakistan was a completely new nation when it attained independence in 1947. Its early years were marked by internal conflicts, particularly the hostility between East and West Pakistan. In 1971, East Pakistan declared its independence and, after a bloody civil war, became the new nation of Bangladesh. Both Pakistan (as West Pakistan is now known) and Bangladesh, however, have had difficulty establishing stable governments.

The Languages of a Subcontinent

More than twenty major languages are spoken in south central Asia, along with hundreds of other languages and dialects. Sanskrit was the dominant language until about A.D. 1000 and is the language of Hindu sacred literature. The official national language of India (Hindi) and that of Pakistan (Urdu) are both descended from Sanskrit. English, introduced by the British, is also widely spoken in south central Asia, particularly between people of different language backgrounds.

Modern South Asian Literature

Poetry was the major form of literature in south central Asia until the British introduced modern European literary forms such as the novel and the short story. Rabindranath Tagore, who won the Nobel Prize in 1913, and Prem Chand, who wrote novels and short stories about rural life, were among the first Indian authors to explore these new forms. Hindi and Urdu are the most widely read languages of south central Asia, but each of the region's other languages—some spoken by millions of people—have their own literatures. English is not identified with a specific ethnic group, but offers writers a worldwide audience. Several major authors, such as R. K. Narayan, wrote in English. Tagore wrote his work in Bengali (the language of Bangladesh), but often translated his works into English himself.

Rickshaws jostling for work. Thierry Prat. Calcutta, India. ★

Reading Check

Analyze Cause-and-Effect Relationships
Why does English continue to be used in south central Asia?

Reading Practice

Connect to Contemporary Issues
Have students read the information about language and literature in south central Asia. **Ask:** What issues might an author who does not speak or write in English face in south central Asia? *(These authors will have a smaller audience for their writing.)* Have students consider the many languages that are spoken in the United States. **Ask:** What problems might a non-English speaker face in the United States? *(Students may suggest that everyday activities, such as grocery shopping and taking public transportation, may be difficult for non-English speakers.)* Then, have students brainstorm how stores and other places of business try to accommodate non-English speakers. *(Students may suggest that places such as airports and restaurants offer instructions and menus in several different languages.)*

Legacy of the Region

India's ancient civilization had a great effect on other cultures. Since monks originally carried it to China, Korea, Southeast Asia, and Japan, Buddhism has remained active in all four areas. More than 375 million people worldwide practice some form of it today, making Buddhism the world's fourth-largest religion.

Indian nationalist Mohandas Gandhi's nonviolent resistance to political oppression has had a powerful influence on civil rights and on human rights leaders around the world, including Martin Luther King Jr., Nelson Mandela of South Africa, and Aung San Suu Kyi of Myanmar.

Cultural and Literary Links

 The fables of the *Panchatantra* were among the sources used by seventeenth-century French author Jean de La Fontaine (see page 602).

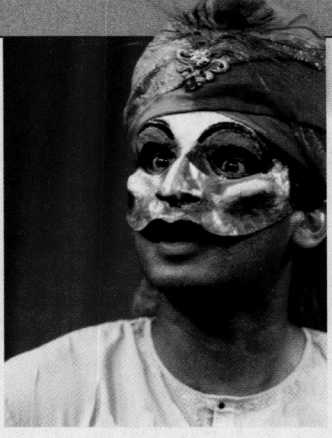

Actor Jacob Rajan in *Krishnan's Diary*. Robbie Jack. Edinburgh, Scotland.

 The *Mahabharata* was the basis for a nine-hour theatrical version (and a five-hour film) created by British director Peter Brook.

 The conventions of classical Sanskrit drama, with its emphasis on music and dancing, have greatly influenced the modern Indian Bollywood movies that are becoming popular with Western audiences.

> **LOG ON** ▶ **Literature** Online
>
> **Unit Resources** For additional skills practice, go to glencoe.com and enter QuickPass code GLW6053u3.

Activities

 **Use what you have learned about the region to do one of these activities.**

1. Follow Up Go back to Looking Ahead on page 547 and answer the questions.

2. Contrast Literary Periods During the seventeenth- and eighteenth-century European movement known as the Enlightenment, authors and scholars explored how reason could be used to achieve knowledge and contentment. Research an author from this period and write an essay comparing and contrasting his or her arguments with what you have learned about the search for enlightenment in south central Asia.

3. Speaking/Listening Tragedy was not permitted in classical Indian drama, in which the imitation of

defeat and death was not seen as providing a catharsis for the audience as in Western tragedy. Working with other students, research classical Indian theater and discuss how it is like and unlike Western theater.

4. Take Notes You might try using this organizer to explore your responses to the literary works in this part.

 FOLDABLES Study Organizer **BOUND BOOK**

Nonfiction / Short Stories / Poems
Reader-Response Journal

Advanced Learners/Pre-AP

DIFFERENTIATED INSTRUCTION

Compare and Contrast Cultures Have students use what they have learned to compare south central Asian literature, music, dance, and art with those aspects of early American culture. Tell students to use Internet and print sources to research the culture of the early United States. You might suggest that they focus on a specific time period.

After students have completed their research, have them write an essay comparing the United States and south central Asia. Students should note and similarities and differences between the two cultures. You may want students to exchange essays with partners to help with the revision process. Make sure students have correctly credited their sources.

Teach

Legacy of the Region

Refer students to the second paragraph, which talks about non-violent resistance. **Ask:** How has this type of protest evolved or changed in recent history? *(Students may describe entertainment as protest, such as Live 8 or Live Earth, or online activist groups.)*

Cultural Links

As students read the part, encourage them to consider how Western culture and literature have been influenced by south central Asia.

Assess

Activities

1. **Follow Up** Students should answer questions with specific facts from the text.

2. **Contrast Literary Periods** Students should draw clear comparisons and contrasts between the arguments of the Enlightenment author they chose and the search for enlightenment in south central Asia. The essays should reflect a grasp of how each culture interprets enlightenment.

3. **Speaking/Listening** Suggest that students describe how Indian theater makes up for its lack of the tragic elements familiar to Western theater.

4. **Take Notes** Students' Foldables should be well organized, and their notes should have specific responses to the literature.

Before You Read

Focus

Bellringer Options

Selection Focus
   Transparency 30

Daily Language
   Transparency 50

Or ask: What does the word *hymn* make you think of? What topics are generally found in hymns? As students share their answers, write their responses on the board.

Before You Read

Creation Hymn from the *Rig-Veda*

The Vedas are the oldest sacred writings of Hinduism, the predominant religion in India. These texts consist of four collections of hymns that were composed in Sanskrit, beginning about 1500 to 1200 B.C. The Rig-Veda is considered the earliest and most sacred of the four Vedas, which are older than the sacred texts of any other major religion. Hindus believe the Vedas contain eternal truths (*veda* means "knowledge") that were divinely revealed to ancient prophets, and they revere the scriptures as *shruti*, or "that which is heard."

Oral Preservation Priests known as Brahmans (also spelled Brahmins) preserved the Vedas by using special memorization techniques, which included group chanting. As historian A. L. Basham observed, "Thanks to the brilliant feats of memory of many generations of Brahmans, and the extreme sanctity which the hymns were thought to possess, they have survived to the present day in a form which, from internal evidence, appears not to have been seriously tampered with for nearly three thousand years."

Vedism Although the Vedas are the sacred texts of Hinduism, they derived originally from an earlier religion called Vedism. This religion involved elaborate sacrifices to a number of gods, among them the fire god Agni and the warrior god Indra. The hymns of the Rig-Veda were composed for these sacrificial ceremonies, which Brahmans led. Hinduism gradually evolved from Vedism, and Hindu priests still recite Vedic verses as part of religious rituals and ceremonies.

Hinduism Because Hindus believe the divine is in everything, they revere life in all its forms. Observant Hindus do not eat meat because they do not wish to have an animal killed to provide them with food. To Hindus, behavior is more important than religious doctrine. A central

belief of Hinduism is reincarnation, or the idea that all living beings participate in a cosmic cycle of death and rebirth and are reborn into higher or lower forms of life based on their behavior in the previous life. Life on earth is seen as a temporary burden, and the goal is to be released from the cycle of death and rebirth to enter the indescribable state of *moksha* (liberation).

> *"Indra, bestow on us the best of treasures, the spirit of ability and fortune…"*
>
> —from the Rig-Veda

Vishnu, seated on the Serpent Sesha, holding a shell, mace, disc, and lotus, c 19th century. Indian school. Ivory. Freud Museum, London.

Selection Skills

Literary Elements
- Paradox (SE pp. 559, 562)

***from the* Rig-Veda**

Speaking/Listening/Viewing Skills
- Analyze Art (SE p. 560; TE p. 561)

Reading Skills
- Analyze Connotation (SE p. 559, 561, 562)
- Paraphrase (TE p. 560)

Vocabulary Skills
- Analogies (SE p. 562)
- Synonyms and Antonyms (TE p. 559)

Writing Skills/Grammar
- List (SE p. 562)

Literature and Reading Preview

Connect to the Hymn

What creation myths are you familiar with? With a partner, discuss these myths and the elements they have in common.

Build Background

The Rig-Veda (meaning "knowledge of verses") includes more than 1,000 verse hymns that pay homage to the many gods of Vedism. Although the text of this collection runs as long as the *Iliad* and the *Odyssey* combined, the Rig-Veda was passed on orally for more than 3,000 years. The Rig-Veda is a classic of world literature and an invaluable source of historical information about religious and cultural development in early India.

Set Purposes for Reading

Big Idea **The Search for Enlightenment**

As you read, ask yourself, How does the view of creation in this hymn vary from that in other creation stories I have read?

Literary Element **Paradox**

A **paradox** is a statement that seems contradictory but reveals an unexpected truth. Authors often use paradox to draw attention to a point they want to emphasize. As you read, ask yourself, What are some examples of paradox in the hymn, and what truth lies behind each one?

Reading Strategy **Analyze Connotation**

When you **analyze connotation,** you consider the ideas or emotions associated with a word beyond its dictionary definition, or **denotation.** As you read, ask yourself, How do the connotations of key words contribute to the meaning?

....

Tip: Chart Connotation Use a chart like the one below to keep track of the connotations of key words in the hymn.

Word	Connotation
realm	governed, stately, large territory

Learning Objectives

For pages 558–562

In studying this text, you will focus on the following objectives:

Literature Study: Analyzing paradox.

Reading: Analyzing connotation.

Writing: Writing a list.

Vocabulary

distinguishing (dis ting′gwish ing) *adj.* marking as different; characterizing; p. 560 *The distinguishing beauty mark on Isabel's cheek helps people tell her apart from her twin.*

impulse (im′puls) *n.* a sudden desire or feeling that makes one want to act; p. 560 *An impulse to help the storm victims prompted Tyler's volunteer work.*

proclaim (prə klām′) *v.* to announce publicly; to make known; to declare; p. 561 *The king walked onto the balcony to proclaim that his navy had won the battle at sea.*

Tip: Analogies Analogies are comparisons based on relationships between words and ideas. Some analogies are based on synonyms, as in the analogy *proclaim : announce :: destroy : ruin.*

Before You Read

Focus

Summary

This excerpt of a hymn describes the beginning of the universe as a time during which neither existence nor death exists; in the darkness, there is only water and heat. The end of the hymn questions the origin of creation and whether any being knows its source.

 For summaries in languages other than English, see Unit 3 Teaching Resources Book, pp. 194–199.

Vocabulary

Synonyms and Antonyms
Organize students into pairs, and have them look up synonyms and antonyms for each new vocabulary word. Then, have students test one another to guess the vocabulary word by its synonym or antonym.

 For additional vocabulary practice, see Unit 3 Teaching Resources Book, p. 202.

English Learners

DIFFERENTIATED INSTRUCTION

Advanced Have English learners look up the following words in a dictionary prior to reading the excerpt. Students should record each word's etymology as well as its definition.

existence, immortality, distinguishing, whence, arisen

To determine students' comprehension, have the students use each word correctly in a sentence. Then, ask students to explain why these words might be used in a hymn that describes the creation of the world.

Teach

Literary Element | 1

Paradox Answer: *It would initially seem that if there was no non-existence, then there would have to be existence. The paradox seems to suggest that whatever there was at the time of creation, it cannot be defined by human terms such as* existence.

APPROACHING Make sure that approaching-level students understand the concept of a paradox. To simplify it for them, replace *existence* and *non-existence* with other terms such as *death* and *life* or *night* and *day*.

Progress Check

Can students identify paradox?

If No → See Unit 3 Teaching Resources Book, p. 200.

View the Art ★

Possible Answer: *tranquility, wisdom*

Known as the "king of the gods" in early Hindu mythology, Indra conquers enemies and brings rain to the people. This wall painting shows an Iranian influence, likely the result of an ancient transcontinental trading route. The stylized triangular flames near Indra's left shoulder and the round gold crown are Iranian symbols of royalty.

Readability Scores

Dale-Chall: 6.3
DRP: 55
Lexile: NA

560

---

from the Rig-Veda

Translated by Wendy Doniger O'Flaherty

Indra, 7th-8th century. Wall painting. National Museum of India, New Delhi.

View the Art Indra, god of thunder and war, was the supreme ruler of the Vedic gods. He was the defender of gods and humans against the forces of evil. What qualities might you associate with Indra, based on this painting?

★

Creation Hymn (Nāsadīya)

1 There was neither non-existence nor existence then; there was neither the realm of space nor the sky which is beyond. What stirred? Where? In whose protection? Was there water, bottomlessly deep?

2 There was neither death nor immortality then. There was no **distinguishing** sign of night nor of day. That one breathed, windless, by its own **impulse**. Other than that there was nothing beyond.

3 Darkness was hidden by darkness in the beginning; with no distinguishing sign, all this was water. The life force that was covered with emptiness, that one arose through the power of heat.

---

1 Paradox *Explain the paradox in this line.*

Vocabulary

distinguishing (dis ting′gwish ing) *adj.* marking as different; characterizing
impulse (im′puls) *n.* a sudden desire or feeling that makes one want to act

560 UNIT 3 SOUTH CENTRAL ASIA

Reading Practice

 SMALL GROUP **Paraphrase** Paraphrasing, like translating, conveys the same information using one's own words. Point out that paraphrasing is different from summarizing. When one summarizes, one only includes the main idea and most important details. When one paraphrases, one puts every sentence or idea in a passage into one's own words.

Explain to students that paraphrasing a complex thought is a good way to remember important ideas and to monitor comprehension.

Have students work in pairs. Ask them to read each stanza together and then paraphrase it. Bring students together to present their interpretations to the class. Encourage students to evaluate their understanding of the ideas presented in the hymn.

4 Desire came upon that one in the beginning; that
  was the first seed of mind. Poets seeking in their
  heart with wisdom found the bond of existence in
  non-existence.

5 Their cord was extended across. Was there below?
  Was there above? There were seed-placers; there were
  powers. There was impulse beneath; there was giving-
  forth above.

6 Who really knows? Who will here **proclaim** it?
  Whence was it produced? Whence is this creation?
  The gods came afterwards, with the creation of this
  universe. Who then knows whence it has arisen?

7 Whence this creation has arisen—perhaps it formed
  itself, or perhaps it did not—the one who looks down
  on it, in the highest heaven, only he knows—or
  perhaps he does not know.

---

2 Analyze Connotation *Which words and phrases in this passage are associated with fertility and growth? How do these words help clarify the speaker's view of creation?*

Vocabulary

proclaim (prə klām′) *v.* to announce publicly; to make known; to declare

Vishnu sleeping between the two periods of cosmic evolution, 17th century. Rajasthan, India. Painting on paper, 30 x 24 cm. National Gallery, Prague.

RIG-VEDA **561**

Teach

Reading Strategy 2

Analyze Connotation

Answer: *The words and phrases associated with fertility and growth are "seed," "seed-placers," "impulse beneath," and "giving-forth above." They help clarify that the view of creation here is tied to agriculture—the giving forth of life through planting and nurturing.*

Progress Check

Can students analyze connotation?

If No → See Unit 3 Teaching Resources Book, p. 201.

View the Art ★

In the painting, the Hindu god Vishnu and Lakshmi (goddess of fortune) are lying on the serpent Ananta, who represents eternity.
Ask: What does this painting tell you about Vishnu? *(Students may say that Vishnu appears like an indulgent being, content to lazily float along and smell flowers.)*

Learning Objectives
Analyzing paradox. (SE)
Analyzing connotation. (SE)
Analyze art. (SE)
Paraphrasing. (TE)

Advanced Learners/Pre-AP

DIFFERENTIATED INSTRUCTION

Analyzing Rhetorical Questions
Explain that rhetorical questions are questions that an author asks to make a point. Often, the author does not expect an answer, or the answer is obvious. Students have most likely seen rhetorical questions in persuasive pieces.

Have student groups discuss and analyze the questions in the hymn. Ask students to explain whether the author of the Rig-Veda expected to ever find an answer to these questions or whether the questions are used to make a point. Have students expand their answers to describe the point the author was trying to make with each question.

(Students may say that the author of the Rig-Veda did not expect to get an answer to the questions but used them to spur other people on their own path to enlightenment. For example, the question "Who really knows?" is unanswerable; its very nature as a rhetorical question prompts readers or listeners to admit that there is no way to truly know.)

After You Read

Assess

1. Answers will vary.
2. (a) The speaker says nothing existed, except perhaps water, and that the life force arose through the power of heat. (b) Hindus believe water and heat were more essential to creation than a creator god.
3. (a) The speaker says the gods came after the act of creation. (b) This indicates that the gods weren't responsible for creation.
4. (a) The speaker concludes that creation is a puzzle no one can solve. (b) This suggests that Hindus are not receptive toward dogma in religion.
5. (a) The cord is the bond of existence forged by the poets as they sought wisdom. (b) It suggests that oral tradition is highly esteemed by Hindus.
6. (a) You could infer that Hindus do not believe that one person or belief system holds the answers to the questions of life. (b) to draw attention to the mysteries that surround us
7. It suggests that the search for enlightenment requires a willingness to question everything.
8. It suggests that people should be willing to ask important questions.

After You Read

Respond and Think Critically

Respond and Interpret

1. Did the story of creation offered in this hymn surprise you? Explain.
2. (a)In stanza 3, how does the speaker describe conditions before creation? (b)What do these conditions reveal about the Hindu understanding of creation?
3. (a)How does the speaker describe the relationship of the gods to creation? (b)What does this imply about the gods and their involvement in creation?
4. (a)What conclusions does the speaker draw about creation? (b)What does this tell you about the Hindu attitude toward dogma (absolute belief) in religion?

Analyze and Evaluate

5. (a)What is the "cord" mentioned in stanza 5? (b)What does this image suggest about Hindu views of oral tradition?
6. (a)What can you infer about Hinduism from the questions asked in stanza 6? (b)What might be the purpose of this stanza?

Connect

7. **Big Idea** **The Search for Enlightenment** What is the value of a creation hymn that questions the origin of the universe?
8. **Connect to Today** Critical thinking is a crucial skill used in countless professions in contemporary society. What lessons does this hymn offer about the value of critical thinking?

Literary Element Paradox

A **paradox** states an apparent contradiction that actually reflects reality. For example, the statement "You must be cruel to be kind" sounds contradictory, but sometimes unkind words may benefit someone.

Partner Activity With a partner, identify examples of paradox in "Creation Hymn" and explain them.

Reading Strategy Analyze Connotation

By examining the **connotations**, or implied meanings, of key words in a literary work, you can better explore its main ideas. Review the chart you made on page 559 and then answer these questions.

1. What are the connotations of the word *poet*?
2. Why might "poets" be mentioned in "Creation Hymn?"

LOG ON ▶ **Literature** Online

Selection Resources For Selection Quizzes, eFlashcards, and Reading-Writing Connection activities, go to glencoe. com and enter QuickPass code GLW6053u3.

Vocabulary Practice

Practice with Analogies Choose the word that best completes each analogy.

1. similar : akin :: distinguishing :
   a. separating c. noble
   b. expensive d. merging
2. conviction : reservation :: impulse :
   a. energetic c. surprising
   b. sudden   d. premeditation
3. enact : law :: proclaim :
   a. whisper   c. shout
   b. announcement d. dialogue

Writing

Write a List Think about the big questions that people ponder, and then list three or more that you would like answered. Include a paradox in one question; for example, you might frame a question as: How can _____ be both _____ and _____?

Literary Element

Examples of paradox include: "There was neither non-existence nor existence then," "there was neither the realm of space nor the sky which is beyond," and "There was neither death nor immortality then." Each paradox suggests that humans have no idea what there was before creation and may be incapable of defining it.

Reading Strategy

1. Students may include words such as *creative, inventive, gifted, inquisitive, sensitive,* and *intuitive.*
2. Poets are often thought of as especially creative people who pose questions and search for the truth. For these reasons it makes sense to associate the poetic/storytelling impulse with creation.

Vocabulary

1. a 2. d 3. b

 Writing

Students' lists should
- pose insightful questions
- include a paradox

562

Before You Read
Hundred Questions from the *Mahabharata*

India

The *Mahabharata* (mə hä′bär′ə tə), one of India's most revered epics, is approximately seven times the length of the *Iliad* and the *Odyssey* combined, making it one of the longest literary works in the world. It is of great religious, philosophical, and historical importance to Indian culture. The epic describes a feud between two rival groups of cousins, the Pandavas and the Kauravas, who are descendants of King Bharat (*Mahabharata* is a Sanskrit word meaning "great epic of the Bharata dynasty").

In the epic, the five Pandava (pän dä′vä) brothers lose their kingdom in northern India and all their wealth to the Kauravas (kôr ä′vəs), who cheat them by using loaded dice in a game of chance. The Pandavas are exiled for twelve years, after which time they battle the Kauravas to regain their kingdom. In the end, the Pandavas win, but the destruction is so great that their victory is hollow.

Tales Within a Tale The feud between the cousins is the main story within the epic, but many episodes and digressions, including myths, legends, stories, and religious ideas, are interwoven with the tale. The most famous of the digressions is the Bhagavad Gita (bä′gə väd′ gē′tə), the most important Hindu religious text, which emphasizes aspects of Hindu philosophy. The central focus of the *Mahabharata* is the Hindu concept of *dharma* (där′mə), which is a sacred code of conduct and duty. Hindus believe that people preserve the natural order of the universe by fulfilling their responsibilities according to their station in life.

> "What is found here, may be found elsewhere. What is not found here, will not be found elsewhere."
>
> —the *Mahabharata*

The Creation of the *Mahabharata* Hindu tradition maintains that a wise man named Vyasa dictated the Sanskrit verses of the *Mahabharata* to Ganesha, the god of wisdom, who wrote them down. Compiled in its present form about A.D. 400, the *Mahabharata* contains about 100,000 verses and is divided into books called *parvas*. "Hundred Questions" is an episode from the third book, *Aranya-parva* ("Forest"), in which the Pandava brothers have nearly completed their twelve-year exile in a forest.

For many generations, the epic was preserved through oral tradition, although it is unlikely that any one storyteller ever told the entire epic in one sitting. The following version is from the prose retelling of the epic by the modern Indian author R. K. Narayan.

MAHABHARATA **563**

Before You Read
Focus

Bellringer Options

Selection Focus
   Transparency 31
Daily Language
   Transparency 51
Or ask: What stories have you read or heard that teach lessons or morals? *(Students may cite biblical or other religious stories, fables, myths, or legends.)* As students name the stories, ask them to describe the lessons the stories teach.

Selection Skills

Literary Elements
- Epic Hero (SE pp. 564, 568, 570, 572)
- Theme (SE p. 572)

from the **Mahabharata**

Speaking/Listening/Viewing Skills
- Visual Literacy (SE p. 571)
- Oral Presentation (TE p. 564)

Reading Skills
- Apply Background Knowledge (SE pp. 564, 566, 568, 572)
- Analyze Plot (TE p. 566)
- Analyze Conflict (TE p. 568)

Vocabulary Skills
- Antonyms (SE p. 572)
- Academic Vocabulary (SE p. 572)

Writing Skills/Grammar
- Research Report (SE p. 573)
- Character Sketch (TE p. 570)

563

Before You Read

Focus

Summary

The five Pandava brothers are on a mission to retrieve stolen articles of prayer, and they are growing tired and thirsty. From the top of a tree, one brother sights a clear pond. The first brother approaches the water to drink. He is challenged by the voice of a yaksha, an invisible but semi-divine being, who insists that the young man answer a series of questions before he can drink. Refusing, the brother is struck dead. Three other brothers, in turn, die after refusing to answer the questions. This continues until the last brother, Yudhistira, arrives. He alone accepts the challenge, answers all the rapid-fire questions, and lives. The yaksha—who is really Yudhistira's father—then revives all the young men.

 For summaries in languages other than English, see Unit 3 Teaching Resources Book, pp. 207–212.

Vocabulary

Flash Cards Have students create five flash cards, each with a vocabulary word written on one side and its antonym written on the other. Student pairs can test one another, using the antonym to guess the vocabulary word.

 For additional vocabulary practice, see Unit 3 Teaching Resources Book, p. 215

Literature and Reading Preview

Connect to the Epic

What questions would you pose to test a person's wisdom and character? Discuss your questions with a partner.

Build Background

Until recent times, Indian society was organized according to a caste system, which divided people based on their inherited social status. The Brahmans (also spelled Brahmins), or priests, were the highest rank; the Kshatriyas (cha′trē ə), who were rulers or warriors, were the second rank; and the Vaishyas, or commoners, were the third rank. Below all of these were the Sudras, the peasants. The "untouchables" were below even the Sudras.

Set Purposes for Reading

Big Idea **The Search for Enlightenment**

As you read, ask yourself, What do the yaksha's questions and the answers given by Yudhistira suggest about enlightenment?

Literary Element Epic Hero

An **epic hero** is traditionally a man of high social status who embodies the ideals of his people. He is usually of historical or legendary importance. Epic plots often involve journeys, supernatural events, or life-and-death struggles. As you read, ask yourself, What heroic qualities does Yudhistira embody?

Reading Strategy Apply Background Knowledge

To better understand a literary work, think about how the historical and cultural background of the work may have influenced its creation and themes. As you read, ask yourself, How can the background information I have learned about India and the *Mahabharata* help me understand this excerpt?

Tip: Chart Background Review the information in the chart below. As you read, fill in actions or dialogue that you were better able to understand because you knew this information.

Background	Action or Dialogue
Religion dominates all aspects of life in south central Asia.	"'The Creator Brahma makes the sun rise, and his dharma causes the sun to set. . . .'"
War was common in ancient India.	
Traditionally, the epic is believed to have been dictated by a wise man and written down by Ganesha.	

Vocabulary

austerity (ôs ter′ə tē) n. a morally strict act; p. 566 *Peter thought fasting for his religion was an austerity that proved his faith.*

poignancy (poin′yən sē) n. the quality of painfully affecting one's feelings; p. 567 *The poignancy of the sick child's request deeply touched him.*

inordinate (in ôr′də nit) adj. excessive; p. 568 *The military police were accused of an inordinate use of force in extracting confessions from suspects.*

fatuous (facħ′ o̅o̅ əs) adj. silly; foolish; p. 569 *Mrs. Roberts thought her neighbor was being fatuous when he said her hedge was too tall.*

avarice (av′ər is) n. greed; p. 569 *King Midas's avarice resulted in his turning his own daughter into gold.*

Tip: Antonyms Words that are the same parts of speech and have opposite meanings are antonyms. For example, an antonym for *avarice* is *generosity*.

Literary Element Practice

Epic Heroes from Other Traditions

Students may be familiar with traditional tales about heroes with supernatural powers that struggle against dangerous foes. Students may also be familiar with tales about brothers or sisters whose characters are tested when each confronts the same situation. Often, these tales highlight cultural values or offer a moral or lesson.

Invite students to share tales with which they are familiar that involve epic heroes facing dangerous situations or that involve the testing of character in siblings. Encourage students to identify common virtues—such as bravery, wisdom, compassion, or humility—in the heroes of these tales and present their findings in an oral report.

564

Hundred Questions

Combat with arches and swords with four people, 19th century. Paithan school. Illustration of the Mahabharata. Gouache on paper, 30 x 42 cm. Musee des Arts Asiatiques-Guimet, Paris.

from the Mahabharata

Retold by R. K. Narayan

Literary Element

Epic Hero Have students read the descriptions of the Pandava brothers in the character list on the next page closely. **Ask:** What qualities do Yudhistira's brothers Bhima and Arjuna have? *(Bhima is the strongest character of the epic, and Arjuna is the greatest warrior of the epic.)* Point out that Yudhistira is the hero of the epic.

View the Art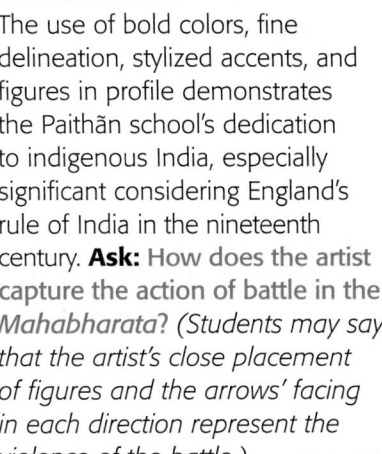

The use of bold colors, fine delineation, stylized accents, and figures in profile demonstrates the Paithãn school's dedication to indigenous India, especially significant considering England's rule of India in the nineteenth century. **Ask:** How does the artist capture the action of battle in the *Mahabharata*? *(Students may say that the artist's close placement of figures and the arrows' facing in each direction represent the violence of the battle.)*

For an audio recording of this selection, use Listening Library Audio CD-ROM.

Advanced Learners/Pre-AP

DIFFERENTIATED INSTRUCTION

Epic Heroes Then and Now Lead a discussion about the evolution of the epic hero as an archetype. Have students consider whether the idea of the epic hero has changed from ancient eras to now. **Say:** Think about who could be regarded as epic heroes in contemporary literature, television, and film. **Ask:** What values do these heroes represent?

Have students select an "epic hero" from a contemporary piece of literature, a television show, or a film. Then, have them write an essay that explains what makes this contemporary character "epic." Students should also explain the values that the character embodies. *(Students may select a hero from a popular action movie and explain that the hero embodies bravery, selflessness, and quick thinking.)*

Readability Scores

Dale-Chall: 8.3
DRP: 60
Lexile: 840

Learning Objectives
Applying background knowledge. (SE)
Analyzing epic hero. (TE)

Teach

Literary Element | 1

Epic Hero **Ask:** What details in the beginning of this tale reveal that it has an epic plot? *(A deer of extraordinary size steals a brahmin's religious items and runs away.)*

[APPROACHING] For students having difficulty, explain that stories with epic plots frequently begin with a supernatural situation or event.

Reading Strategy | 2

Apply Background Knowledge **Answer:** *Yudhistira is a kshatriya, or a member of the ruler/warrior class, which is beneath the Brahmin caste. Thus, he must follow his dharma, which requires that he help the Brahmin.*

For additional practice using the reading skill or strategy, see Unit 3 Teaching Resources Book, p. 214

Political History ☆

Brahmin Influence Brahmins held the highest place in the caste system, and they were in charge of all Indian scholarship. As a result of their social status, they were placed in positions of power and influence as government advisers.

CHARACTERS IN THE EPIC

Pandava Brothers

YUDHISTIRA (yōō dē′stē rə) eldest brother and hero of the epic

BHIMA (bē′mə) second brother and strongest character in the epic

ARJUNA (är′jōō nə) third brother and greatest warrior of the epic

NAKULA (nä′k ōō lə) one of the twins born to Madri

SAHADEVA (sä hä dā′və) second twin born to Madri

Others

BRAHMA one of the major gods of Hinduism

DURYODHANA (dōōr yō′də nə) eldest of the 100 Kaurava brothers, cousins and rivals of the Pandavas

KUNTHI mother of Yudhistira, Bhima, and Arjuna

MADRI mother of Nakula and Sahadeva

YAMA god of justice, father of Yudhistira

The Pandavas were in a hopeful mood when they came back to their original starting point, Dwaitavana, after their prolonged pilgrimage. Dwaitavana was rich in fruits and roots, and the Pandavas lived on sparse diets, performing **austerities** and practicing rigid vows.

They managed to live, on the whole, a tranquil life—until one day a brahmin arrived in a state of great agitation. He had lost a churning staff and two faggots[1] of a special kind, with which he produced the fire needed for his religious activities. All his hours were normally spent in the performance of rites. But that day, he wailed, "A deer of extraordinary size, with its antlers spreading out like the branches of a tree, dashed in unexpectedly, lowered its head, and stuck the staff and the faggots in its horns, turned round, and vanished before I could understand what was happening. I want your help to recover those articles of prayer, for without them I will not be able to perform my daily rites. You can see its hoof marks on the ground and follow them."

As a kshatriya, Yudhistira felt it his duty to help the brahmin, so with his brothers, he set out to chase the deer. They followed its hoof marks and eventually spotted it, after a long chase. But when they shot their arrows, the deer sprang away, tempted them to follow it here and there, and suddenly vanished without a trace. They were by

1. A *faggot* is a bundle of sticks.

Vocabulary

austerity (ôs ter′ə tē) *n.* a morally strict act

Apply Background Knowledge *Based on the background information you have read, why do think Yudhistira helps the brahmin?* 2

Reading Practice

 SMALL GROUP **Analyze Plot** Point out that many tales have repeated plot patterns that allow the reader to predict what might happen next. Ask students to identify the repeated pattern in "Hundred Questions." *(Each brother comes to the pond and is challenged to answer questions before he can drink.)*

Ask small groups of students to brainstorm a list of stories in which there is a repeated plot pattern. Then have them share several from their list. *(Students may suggest* The Thousand and One Nights, *"Goldilocks and the Three Bears," and the epic of* Gilgamesh.*)*

Invite students to compare these tales and ask them to discuss reasons why many stories have repeated plot elements. *(Possible reasons include its being easier to pass along tales orally when the tales have a repeated pattern, which helps the storyteller to remember plot developments.)*

this time drawn far into the forest and, feeling fatigued and thirsty, they sat under a tree to rest.

Yudhistira told his youngest brother, Nakula, "Climb this tree and look for any sign of water nearby."

Presently, Nakula cried from the top of the tree, "I see some green patches and also hear the cries of cranes . . . must be a water source." He came down and proceeded towards a crystal-clear pond, sapphire-like, reflecting the sky. He fell down on his knees and splashed the water on his face. As he did this, a loud voice, which seemed to come from a crane standing in the water, cried, "Stop! This pond is mine. Don't touch it until you answer my questions. After answering, drink or take away as much water as you like." Nakula's thirst was so searing that he could not wait. He bent down and, cupping his palms, raised the water to his lips. He immediately collapsed, and lay, to all purposes, dead.

After a while, Yudhistira sent his brother, Sahadeva, to see what was delaying Nakula's return. He too rushed forward eagerly at the sight of the blue pond, heard the warning, tasted the water, and fell dead.

Arjuna followed. On hearing the voice, he lifted his bow, shot an arrow in the direction of the voice, and approached the water's edge. The voice said, "Don't be foolhardy. Answer me first before you touch the water."

Arjuna, surveying with shock and sadness the bodies of his younger brothers, replied, "When you are silenced with my arrows, you will cease to question. . . ." Driven to desperation with thirst and enraged at the spectacle of his dead brothers, he sent a rain of arrows in all directions. As the voice continued to warn, "Don't touch," he stooped and took the water to his lips and fell dead.

Next came Bhima. He saw his brothers lying dead, and swung his mace and cried back when he heard the voice, "O evil power, whoever you may be, I will put an end to you presently, but let me first get rid of this deadly thirst. . . ." Turning a deaf ear to the warning, he took the water in the cup of his palm and with the first sip fell dead, the mace **3** rolling away at his side.

Yudhistira himself presently arrived, passing through the forest where no human being had set foot before except his brothers. He was struck by the beauty of the surroundings—enormous woods, resonant with the cry of birds, the occasional grunt of a bear, or the light tread of a deer on dry leaves— and then he came upon the magnificent lake, looking as if made by heavenly hands. There on its bank he saw his brothers.

He wept and lamented aloud. Both the **poignancy** and the mystery of it tormented him. He saw Arjuna's bow and Bhima's mace lying on the ground, and reflected, "Where is your promise to split Duryodhana's thigh?[2] What was the meaning of the gods' statement at Arjuna's birth that no one could vanquish him?" How was he to explain this calamity to Kunthi?

Visual Vocabulary
A *mace* is a spiked club used as a weapon.

---

2. Bhima promised to *split Duryodhana's thigh* after the Pandavas had lost everything to their cousins in the game of dice.

Vocabulary

poignancy (poin′yən sē) *n.* the quality of painfully affecting one's feelings

MAHABHARATA **567**

Literary Element | **3**

Epic Hero Ask: How do Yudhistira's four brothers' actions show that they are not the epic heroes of this tale? *(Their actions show them to be rash, inconsiderate, and even foolhardy. They do not listen to the warnings, and they let their thirst triumph over caution. They even threaten the phantom voice.)*

Cultural History ☆
Hindu Death Rituals

As a Hindu person is about to die, family members pour water into the person's mouth along with a tulsi leaf. The water is taken from the place where the Ganges and Yamuna rivers meet. The dying person's forehead is covered with white clay and, after he or she has died, the body is wrapped in clean cloth. Finally, following Hindu tradition, family members cremate the body as an offering to the god of fire.

Learning Objectives
Applying background knowledge. (SE)
Analyzing epic hero. (SE)
Analyzing plot. (TE)

English Learners
DIFFERENTIATED INSTRUCTION

Intermediate Tell students that a participle is a verb form that is used as an adjective. Present participles end in *-ing* and most past participles end in *-ed, -d, -n, -en,* or *-t.*
Participial phrases are groups of words that contain a participle and its modifiers. Explain that participial phrases describe the noun or pronoun that they are closest to in a sentence.

Have students reread this sentence on page 567: "Turning a deaf ear to the warning, he took the water in the cup of his palm and with the first sip fell dead, the mace rolling away at his side." Point out that the participial phrase "Turning a deaf ear to the warning" describes "he," or Bhima.

Have students find other examples of participial phrases in the tale and identify the nouns that they describe. *(Possible examples include "surveying with shock and sadness the bodies of his younger brothers," which describes Arjuna on page 567; and "packed with layers of significance," which describes the yaksha's questions on page 569.)*

Teach

Reading Strategy | 1

Apply Background Knowledge Answer: *Yudhistira suspects Duryodhana because he is the eldest of the Kaurava brothers, who are the enemies of the Pandavas.*

Literary Element | 2

Epic Hero Answer: *He shows responsibility, self-restraint, and reverence for religious subjects.*

Big Idea | 3

The Search for Enlightenment Ask: How does Yudhistira's answer to the yaksha's first two questions reflect Yudhistira's beliefs?

(Yudhistira's answers illustrate his religious beliefs in Brahma, a part of the divine spirit, and dharma, the divine law that requires all beings to fulfill the duties associated with their station in life.)

View the Art ★

Answer: *Students might agree that the brothers seem united and solid in their sameness. The artist may have wanted to represent them this way to show their loyalty to one another.*

On a symbolic level, the epic battle described in the *Mahabharata* represents a struggle between different religious creeds. During the battle, the Pandavas are protected by Krishna, an avatar of Vishnu, while the Kauravas are protected by Indra, ancient god of the heavens.

Pancha Pandava, the five hero brothers of the Mahabharata. India. Painted stone relief. Surya Temple, Somnath, Mumbai.

View the Art This relief was created for Surya Temple—in Hinduism, Surya is both the sun and the sun god. He is also believed to be the father of Manu, the forefather of the human race. Why might the artist of this relief have chosen to represent the Pandavas almost identically? ★

A little later he said to himself, "This is no ordinary death. I see no marks of injury on any of them. What is behind it all?" Could it be that Duryodhana had pursued them, and had his agents at work? He observed the dead faces; they bore no discoloration or sign of decay. He realized that his brothers could not have been killed by mortals, and concluded that there must be some higher power responsible. Resolving not to act hastily, he considered all the possibilities, and stepped into the lake to perform the rites for the dead.

The voice now said, "Don't act rashly; answer my questions first and then drink and take away as much water as you like. If you disregard me, you will be the fifth corpse here. I am responsible for the deaths of all these brothers of yours; this lake is mine and whoever ignores my voice will die. Take care!"

Yudhistira said humbly, "What god are you to have vanquished these invincible brothers of mine, gifted and endowed with **inordinate** strength and courage? Your feat is great and I bow to you in homage, but please explain who you are and why you have slain these innocent slakers of thirst? I do not understand your purpose, my mind is agitated and curious. Please tell me who you are."

At this request he saw an immense figure materializing beside the lake, towering over the surroundings. "I am a yaksha.[3] These brothers of yours, though warned, tried to force their way in and have paid for it with their lives. If you wish to live, don't drink this water before you answer my questions."

Yudhistira answered humbly, "O yaksha, I will not covet what is yours. I will not touch this water without your sanction, in spite of my thirst. I will answer your questions as well as I can."

The yaksha asked, "What makes the sun rise? . . . What causes him to set?"

---

1 Apply Background Knowledge *Why does Yudhistira suspect Duryodhana and his agents?*

2 Epic Hero *How are Yudhistira's actions consistent with those of an epic hero?*

3. A *yaksha* is a spirit that guards the world's wealth. The feminine spelling is *yakshi.*

Vocabulary

inordinate (in ôr′ də nit) *adj.* excessive

Reading Practice

Analyze Conflict Explain that conflicts can be internal or external. An internal conflict is a struggle that a character has within himself or herself. An external conflict is a struggle that a character has with an outside force, such as another character, nature, society, or fate.

Ask: What external conflict is Yudhistira facing? *(He has to answer all of the yaksha's questions.)* **Ask:** What internal conflict may he be facing? *(He may be worried that his answers are not sufficient for the yaksha. He may also be worrying about how to save his brothers.)*

3 Yudhistira answered, "The Creator Brahma makes the sun rise, and his dharma causes the sun to set. . . ."

Yudhistira had to stand a gruelling test. He had no time even to consider what to say, as the questions came in a continuous stream. Yudhistira was afraid to delay an answer or plead ignorance. Some of the questions sounded **fatuous**, some of them profound, some obscure but packed with layers of significance. Yudhistira was constantly afraid that he might upset the yaksha and provoke him to commit further damage, although one part of his mind reflected, "What worse fate can befall us?"

Without giving him time to think, the questions came, sometimes four at a time in one breath. Their range was unlimited, and they jumped from one topic to another.

"What is important for those who sow? What is important for those who seek prosperity?" Before Yudhistira could complete his sentence with "Rain," he also had to be answering the next question with "Offspring. . . ."

The yaksha went on to ask, "What is weightier than the earth?"

"Mother."

"Higher than the heavens?"

"Father."

"Faster than the wind?"

"Mind."

"What sleeps with eyes open?"

"Fish."

"What remains immobile after being born?"

"Egg."

"Who is the friend of the exile?"

"The companion on the way."

4 "Who is the friend of one about to die?"

"The charity done in one's lifetime."

"Who is that friend you could count as God given?"

"A wife."

"What is one's highest duty?"

"To refrain from injury."

To another series of questions on renunciation, Yudhistira gave the answers: "Pride, if renounced, makes one agreeable; anger, if renounced, brings no regret; desire, if renounced, will make one rich; **avarice**, if renounced, brings one happiness. True tranquility is of the heart. . . . Mercy may be defined as wishing happiness to all creatures. . . . Ignorance is not knowing one's duties. . . . Wickedness consists in speaking ill of others."

"Who is a true brahmin? By birth or study or conduct?"

"Not by birth, but by knowledge of the scriptures and right conduct. A brahmin born to the caste, even if he has mastered the Vedas,[4] must be viewed as of the lowest caste if his heart is impure."

There were a hundred or more questions in all. Yudhistira felt faint from thirst, grief, and suspense, and could only whisper his replies. Finally, the yaksha asked, "Answer four more questions, and you may find your brothers—at least one of them—revived. . . . Who is really happy?"

"One who has scanty means but is free from debt; he is truly a happy man."

"What is the greatest wonder?"

"Day after day and hour after hour, people die and corpses are carried along, yet the onlookers never realize that they are also to die one day, but think they will live forever. This is the greatest wonder of the world."

---

4. The *Vedas*—sacred Hindu writings—are believed to contain eternal truths that were divinely revealed.

Vocabulary

fatuous (fach′ oo əs) *adj.* silly; foolish

Vocabulary

avarice (av′ ər is) *n.* greed

MAHABHARATA **569**

Approaching Level

DIFFERENTIATED INSTRUCTION

Following Dialogue Explain to students that when two characters are speaking to each other, an author often drops the identifying tags, such as "he said" or "she answered." Tell students that when they come across a long passage in which two characters trade lines of dialogue, they can go back to the beginning of the conversation to determine which character is speaking each line of dialogue.

One way that students can more easily follow the conversation is to assign a number or letter to each character; students can mark the lines of dialogue that each character speaks with the corresponding letter or number. You may wish to copy a paragraph onto the board so that students can freely mark up the dialogue.

Teach

Literary Element | 4

Epic Hero Ask: The yaksha asks Yudhistira to identify the friend of one about to die. What does Yudhistira's answer reveal about the values of the Hindu people? *(Yudhistira answers that the friend of someone about to die is the charity that that person has performed in his or her lifetime. His answer reveals that the Hindu people value kind actions and people who help others.)*

APPROACHING Some students may have difficulty understanding Yudhistira's answers. Direct them to reread "Tales Within a Tale" on the Before You Read page to reacquaint themselves with the concept of dharma.

Cultural History ☆

Family and Kinship Family life is of utmost importance to many Indians. The head of the family unit is the eldest male, usually a father. Women do not hold the same social status as men. Traditionally, many marriages are arranged, and the wife becomes part of the husband's family.

Learning Objectives
Applying background knowledge. (SE)
Analyzing epic hero. (SE)
Analyzing conflict. (TE)

569

Teach

The Search for Enlightenment

Answer: *He seems to believe there is no definitive guidebook on how to live an enlightened life; he must follow his dharma and live according to Hindu principles as best he can.*

Literary Element	2

Epic Hero

Answer: *The qualities that enable him to save himself and his brothers include reverence, self-restraint, and thoughtfulness. Yudhistira's qualities please the yaksha enough that he revives the brothers.*

View the Art ★

Babur, emperor of the Mughal dynasty from 1526–1530 and a descendant of Genghis Khan, tried several times to recapture Samarqan, the city of another ancestor Timur (Tamerlane). This painting, from Babur's memoirs *Baburnamah*, is from the court of Babur's descendant, Akbar; the Akbari style of Mughal painting combines Persian traditions, such as attention to detail, with India's love of vibrant colors and of nature. **Ask: Which figure in the painting is Babur? How can you tell?** *(Students may say that Babur is the figure to the left on the blue-gray horse; this man is in the lead of the race, and the figure is in the center of the painting, all indicating that he is the emperor.)*

> 📁 To check students' understanding of the selection, see Unit 3 Teaching Resources Book, p. 218.

Babur racing with two companions during the flight from Samarqan (detail), ca. 1590-1592. The Pierpont Morgan Library, New York. ★

"What is the Path?"

"The Path is what the great ones have trod. When one looks for it, one will not find it by study of scriptures or arguments, which are contradictory and conflicting."

At the end of these answers, the yaksha said, "From among these brothers of yours, you may choose one to revive."

Yudhistira said, "If I have only a single choice, let my young brother, Nakula, rise."

The yaksha said, "He is after all your stepbrother. I'd have thought you'd want Arjuna or Bhima, who must be dear to you."

"Yes, they are," replied Yudhistira. "But I have had two mothers. If only two in our family are to survive, let both the mothers have one of their sons alive. Let Nakula also live, in fairness to the memory of my other mother Madri."

The yaksha said, "You have indeed pleased me with your humility and the judiciousness of your answers. Now let all your brothers rise up and join you."

The yaksha thereafter revived all his brothers and also conferred on Yudhistira the following boon:[5] "Wherever you may go henceforth, with your brothers and wife, you will have the blessing of being unrecognized." The yaksha was none other than Yama, the God of Justice, and father of Yudhistira, who had come to test Yudhistira's strength of mind and also to bless him with the power to remain incognito—[6] a special boon in view of the conditions laid down for the last year of exile. ✑

---

5. A *boon* is a blessing.
6. If someone is *incognito*, he or she can escape notice.

> **The Search for Enlightenment** *Based on Yudhistira's answer here, what does he seem to believe about enlightenment?*   **1**

> **Epic Hero** *Which of Yudhistira's qualities enabled him to save himself and his brothers?*   **2**

Writing Practice

🖊 **Character Sketch** After students finish reading the story, have them write a character sketch of Yama. Explain that a character sketch is a brief glimpse of what a character is like. Students should give readers a feeling of Yama's character by describing the negative and positive characteristics that Yama displays through his actions and words in this excerpt.

(Students will most likely say that Yama seems cruel to kill his sons; students may also describe him as distant and someone with very high expectations. Students may suggest that, on a positive note, Yama shows fairness when he brings all of Yudhistira's brothers back to life and that he is generous when he bestows a boon on Yudhistira).

After You Read

Respond and Think Critically

Respond and Interpret

1. Which of the yaksha's questions surprised you most? Why?

2. (a)What happens to the first four Pandava brothers at the pond? (b)How would you characterize their actions?

3. (a)What happens to Yudhistira at the pond? (b)What do his actions reveal about him?

4. (a)What kinds of questions does the yaksha ask Yudhistira? (b)What seems to be the yaksha's intent in asking these questions?

Analyze and Evaluate

5. (a)Why is the yaksha pleased with Yudhistira? (b)How does the yaksha's offer to reward Yudhistira constitute a final test of Yudhistira's character?

6. (a)Why does Yudhistira save his stepbrother Nakula? (b)What does this decision reveal about Yudhistira's character?

7. What do you think is the most important question the yaksha poses to Yudhistira? Explain.

Connect

8. **Big Idea** The Search for Enlightenment How does this excerpt from the *Mahabharata* reflect Hindu religious beliefs?

9. **Connect to Today** What kinds of tests of character does modern life pose? Describe a situation from your own experience that tested your character.

Visual Literacy

Graphic Organizer

To better understand "Hundred Questions," use a graphic organizer to arrange your notes based on the three paths to salvation, according to Hindu belief.

- The path of duty requires the proper performance of religious and ethical duties.
- The path of knowledge involves the study of philosophical texts and the practice of contemplation.
- The path of devotion involves mystical self-surrender to deities.

You can organize your notes on specific events and dialogue according to which path they exemplify. Complete a chart like this one.

The Path of Duty	The Path of Knowledge	The Path of Devotion
Yudhistira's duty as a kshatriya is to help the brahmin chase the deer.		

Group Activity Discuss the following questions with classmates. Refer to your chart and cite evidence from the excerpt.

1. Do your classmates agree with the way you classified events and dialogue? If not, discuss why your classifications differ and see whether you can reach a consensus.

2. Working together, think of other actions the Pandavas might take to fulfill each path.

MAHABHARATA **571**

Visual Literacy

1. Students should give logical reasons for their classifications.

2. Each action students think of should clearly fulfill one of the three paths.

 For additional selection assessment, see Assessment Resources, pp. 121–122.

After You Read

Assess

1. Answers will vary.

2. (a) They ignore the voice's warning not to drink the water until they answer his questions. When they drink the water, each appears to die. (b) Their actions are rash, self-serving, and foolish.

3. (a) Unlike his brothers, Yudhistira listens and obeys the voice and answers all the questions. (b) Yudhistira's actions reveal that he is cautious and humble.

4. (a) The yaksha poses riddles and asks questions about the nature of life and morality. (b) He seems to be testing Yudhistira's character and religious convictions.

5. (a) The yaksha is pleased because Yudhistira acts humbly, answers all his questions judiciously, and proves his selflessness. (b) The yaksha's offer tests Yudhistira's character by revealing whether the criteria Yudhistira will use to decide whom to save will be as thoughtful as his other answers.

6. (a) Yudhistira saves Nakula so that Yudhistira's stepmother, Madri, will have one child of her own spared. (b) Yudhistira's decision reveals his selflessness. He considers the feelings and the happiness of his stepmother before his own feelings.

7. Answers will vary.

8. The Pandava brothers find the pond while they are fulfilling their duty to a religious man, the Brahmin. Many of the yaksha's questions—and Yudhistira's answers—are based on Hinduism and the concept of dharma.

9. Answers will vary according to students' experiences.

After You Read

Assess

Literary Element

1. **C** is the correct answer. **A** is incorrect because the gods treat Yudhistira as a human. **B** is incorrect because Yudhistira exhibits compassion by asking for Nakula to be revived. **D** is incorrect because Yudhistira tries not to act too hastily.

2. **G** is the correct answer. **F** is incorrect because Yudhistira comments that purity of the heart is more important than religious study alone. **H** is incorrect because he feels confident in his ability to answer the yaksha's questions. **J** is incorrect because he does not rely only on strength in decision making.

Progress Check

Can students identify epic heroes?

If No → See Unit 3 Teaching Resources Book, p. 213.

Review: Theme
Possible theme: People who act virtuously, thoughtfully, and perceptively will be rewarded for their behavior. This is demonstrated by the fact that Yudhistira is able to rescue his dead brothers because he acts wisely and selflessly.

Reading Strategy

Possible answer: The dominance of religion helps explain Yudhistira's eagerness to perform rites for the dead, his assumption that the voice he hears is that of a god, and the Hindu ideals behind his answers. The constant warfare of the time helps explain Arjuna's violence and Yudhistira's suspi-

572

Literary Element Epic Hero

ACT Skills Practice

1. What is the main insight suggested by the paragraph on page 568 that begins "A little later he said to himself . . ."?

   A. Yudhistira is spared by the gods because he is considered to be divine.

   B. Yudhistira lacks compassion for his family members.

   C. Yudhistira is the most perceptive and thoughtful of all of the brothers.

   D. Yudhistira is obsessed with performing the funeral rites quickly.

2. In the paragraph on page 569 that begins "Not by birth, but by knowledge of the scriptures . . ." Yudhistira demonstrates that he:

   F. is more dedicated to study than to action.

   G. has a reasoned understanding of religious principles.

   H. is unsure of himself.

   J. is strong only in his physical stature.

Review: Theme

As you learned on page 471, the **theme** of a literary work is its central idea about life. Some works have a **stated theme**, which the author expresses directly, but most works have an **implied theme**, which the author reveals gradually through events, dialogue, or description.

Partner Activity With a partner, discuss what might be the theme of "Hundred Questions." Consider how the events in the story demonstrate the theme.

LOG ON ▶ **Literature** Online

Selection Resources For Selection Quizzes, eFlashcards, and Reading-Writing Connection activities, go to glencoe.com and enter QuickPass code GLW6053u3.

572 UNIT 3 SOUTH CENTRAL ASIA

Reading Strategy Apply Background Knowledge

The meaning of a literary work becomes more apparent when you **apply background knowledge** to your reading. For example, applying the background knowledge you have learned about Hinduism can help you better understand the meanings of "Hundred Questions."

Partner Activity Review the three background facts given in the Reading Strategy chart on page 564. With a partner, discuss how each fact gives you insight into the story.

Vocabulary Practice

Practice with Antonyms With a partner, match each boldfaced vocabulary word below with its antonym. Use a thesaurus or a dictionary to check your answers. You will not use all the answer choices.

1. austerity	a. solemn
2. poignancy	b. sensible
3. inordinate	c. moderate
4. fatuous	d. indifference
5. avarice	e. self-indulgence
	f. generosity
	g. dryness

Academic Vocabulary

In the Mahabharata, *the Pandava brothers have no* **alternative** *but to help the brahmin chase the deer, since he is from a higher caste.*

Alternative is an academic word. In more casual conversation, someone might say certain types of music are an **alternative** to what is frequently played on the radio. To further explore the meaning of this word, answer the question below.

What are two examples of **alternative** energy sources?

For more on academic vocabulary, see pages 36–37 and R83–R85.

---

cion that a rival clan is responsible for his brothers' deaths. The tradition helps explain the value of the *Mahabharata* for Hindus and the importance of its teachings and philosophies.

Vocabulary

⋮ **1.** e **2.** d **3.** c **4.** b **5.** f

Academic Vocabulary

⋮ Possible answers: Wind, water, or solar power may be alternative sources of energy.

Respond Through Writing

Research Report

Investigate the Epic Investigate how the ideas of the *Mahabharata* are interpreted in modern India by researching how the epic is depicted in a variety of forms, such as movies, plays, and art. Write a research report of 1,500 words or more on this topic.

Understand the Task When you **investigate**, you research background information and uncover insights from multiple sources.

Prewrite As you begin researching multiple sources and compiling notes, consider moving from handwritten notes to an electronic spreadsheet. This way, you can use various software features to sort information and make it easier to find when you begin drafting. Create a classification chart like the one below to organize your research notes.

Music	Theater	Film	Art
The epic describes types of folk music that are common in Indian society today. Dancing such as bhangra is an outgrowth of this music.			

Draft As you write, support your thesis with evidence from "Hundred Questions" and from credible primary and secondary sources. Be sure to convey information accurately and coherently. Anticipate potential misunderstandings by providing cultural context for terms that might be unfamiliar to your reader, such as *dharma*.

Revise To complement your report, try including photos of art or dance related to the epic. After you finish your draft, exchange papers with a partner and evaluate each other's work, checking for clarity, organization, and supporting evidence.

Edit and Proofread Proofread your paper, correcting any errors in spelling, grammar, and punctuation. Use the Grammar Tip in the side column to help you correct any problems with italics.

> **Grammar Tip**

Italics

Writers often use italics (characters set in type that slants to the right) to highlight or emphasize certain words or thoughts in a text. Using italics is appropriate in a number of situations.

foreign words: *dharma*

special emphasis: Rather than physical strength, it is the *moral* strength of Yudhistira that inspires Hindus.

titles of books, plays, artworks, longer musical compositions, and longer poems: *Mahabharata*

After You Read

Assess

Respond Through Writing

Students' reports should

- explain how modern Indian culture reflects the main ideas of the *Mahabharata*
- reflect the use of appropriate organizational strategies, such as graphic organizers
- include evidence from primary and secondary sources

A student who meets all of these criteria should receive the equivalent of a 4-point response.

A student who fully meets two or partially meets three of these criteria should receive the equivalent of a 3-point response.

A student who fully meets one or partially meets two of these criteria should receive the equivalent of a 2-point response.

A student who partially meets one of these criteria should receive the equivalent of a 1-point response.

Grammar Tip

Explain that students should be careful to use italics sparingly in their writing. When italics are used too often, important words and concepts lose their impact.

Approaching Level

DIFFERENTIATED INSTRUCTION

Paraphrasing Direct Quotes Students may have difficulty avoiding plagiarism. Explain that they should paraphrase someone else's quote by restating all of it in their own words. Students can use a thesaurus to look up synonyms to use for their paraphrases. Have students practice reordering the construction of a quoted sentence so that their paraphrases differ from the original.

Advanced Learners/Pre-AP

DIFFERENTIATED INSTRUCTION

Creating a Glossary Students can create a glossary to accompany their reports. Have students list the unfamiliar terms they have used in their report—including Hindu and Indian words. Their glossary should be in alphabetical order and should include pronunciation guides, a definition of each term, and an accompanying visual if available.

Focus

Bellringer Option

Say: In Indonesia, shadow plays bring the ancient stories of the *Mahabharata* to life. The plays are not only visually appealing but they are also orally entertaining with sound effects, singing, and musical accompaniment. **Ask:** What movies or plays have you seen that are based on books? Which version of the story do you prefer and why?

Teach

Reading Strategy | 1

Analyze Cultural Context

Ask: What does the popularity of shadow plays reveal about the values of Indonesians?
(The people of Indonesia value traditional stories as well as visual and musical arts.)

Learning Objectives

For pages 574–575
In studying this text, you will focus on the following objectives:

Reading:
Analyzing cultural context.
Analyzing historical context.
Making connections across literature.

The *Mahabharata* as Shadow Play

IN A VILLAGE HOME ON THE INDONESIAN ISLAND OF JAVA AT MIDNIGHT, a few dozen people sit in front of a long screen lit from behind, watching vibrant shadow images of the Pandava brothers as they fight a bloody battle against their cousins, the Kauravas.

These Indonesian villagers know the stories of the *Mahabharata* well, although most of them do not know Sanskrit and have never read the epic. Instead, they have learned the *Mahabharata* from watching *wayang kulit*—Indonesian shadow puppet plays. The name of this performing art derives from the Javanese words for "shadow" (*wayang*) and "skin" (*kulit*), which refers to the water buffalo leather from which the puppets are crafted. *Wayang kulit* is considered to be the most prestigious performing art in Indonesia.

Wayang shadow puppets, 2002. Bali Province, Indonesia.

Staging a Shadow Play

Staging a shadow puppet performance of the *Mahabharata* is no simple task. A performance may last for eight or nine hours, beginning around nine in the evening and continuing until dawn. The performance often takes place in the home of a wealthy sponsor in a rural village, where shadow plays are often commissioned for weddings and other special occasions. In urban areas, the plays are frequently performed at local auditoriums.

> *"The* wayang *plays retain a ceremonial, mystical aspect which suggests that originally they may have been a religious ritual performed by the head of the family to invoke the aid and advice of ancestral spirits."*
>
> —Bil Baird, *The Art of the Puppet*

The key figure of the *wayang kulit* is the *dalang*, a skilled artist who functions as the storyteller, the puppeteer, a singer, the sound effects technician, and the director. For the entire performance, the dalang sits cross-legged on the floor and works the leather puppets, which have been intricately carved and painted to indicate particular characters and their personalities. These puppets are animated by sticks—one for the body and one for each arm.

Writing Practice

Write an Advice Column Have students imagine that they are in charge of the advice column of their local newspaper. Tell them that an anonymous person has written in to ask their advice on staging a shadow play. Students should use the information that they have read to write a response to the anonymous writer. You may wish to have students compose the anonymous person's letter as well.

Allow students enough time to complete the writing assignment. After they have finished, ask volunteers to share their advice with the class.

(Students' columns may offer advice on stories that would fit well as shadow plays, what props or materials you would need to stage a play, and what kind of music or auditory effects could be added.)

The puppets are kept in a large wooden chest that doubles as a sound effects box. The dalang holds one hammer between the toes of his right foot and another in his left hand and strikes the wood or a small bronze plate on the chest to set a rhythm or to punctuate dramatic moments. The dalang is accompanied by singers and, often, by an Indonesian gamelan orchestra that includes drums, gongs, and a variety of other percussion instruments.

Bringing a Story to Life

In addition to manipulating the puppets and creating sound effects, the dalang narrates the story and sings lines of classical poetry or songs. The dalang speaks all the parts and interprets the characters by giving them distinctive voices and ways of moving. For example, Arjuna, the greatest warrior in the epic, might move fluidly across the stage, while his wife Draupadi takes small, dainty steps. During battle scenes, Arjuna shoots a bow, while his brother Bhima, the strongest character in the epic, strikes opponents with a big club. The dalang also imitates the chatter of monkeys, the grunts of pigs, and the neighing of horses.

Although parts of every shadow play are standardized, much of the dalang's work involves improvisation. Working without a script, the dalang creates dialogue, weaves subplots into the main story, and injects jokes and slapstick into the story. If there is an orchestra, it plays music throughout the performance. The dalang chooses from a repertoire of more than 100 musical selections that fit certain types of scenes, characters, or other elements of drama.

Wayang kulit is second in popularity only to televised soccer matches among forms of entertainment in Indonesia. Contemporary Indonesians often refer to characters from the *Mahabharata*; an Indonesian might say another

person is "like Bhima"—that is, honest, brave, and strong. Through the magic of *wayang kulit*, the story, the characters, and the moral messages of the *Mahabharata* have become ingrained in the culture of Indonesia.

Javanese Shadow Puppet Maker. Yogyakarta, Java, Indonesia.

 Literature Online

Literature and Reading For more about the *Mahabharata* as shadow play and the translators in this book, go to glencoe.com and enter QuickPass code GLW6053u3.

Respond and Think Critically

1. How would watching a shadow puppet performance of the *Mahabharata* differ from reading the epic?

2. What do you think is the most challenging aspect of the dalang's performance?

3. Why do you think *wayang kulit* continues to be popular in Indonesia?

THE ART OF TRANSLATION **575**

Teach

Big Idea 2

The Search for Enlightenment **Ask:** How do shadow plays of the *Mahabharata* help people in their search for enlightenment? *(The shadow plays of the* Mahabharata *help teach viewers about aspects of the Hindu path, such as moral duty.)*

Assess

1. Students may respond that reading is a more private experience than watching a shadow puppet play. Shadow plays allow people to share an emotional experience and to be entertained collectively. Reading, however, allows people to envision scenes on their own.

2. Answers will vary. Some students may feel that the improvisational aspect of the dalang's performance would be the most challenging to master.

3. Students may feel that the continuing popularity of *wayang kulit* is due to its broad appeal as an art form—it can be enjoyed by both children and adults. Additionally, the artistry behind each performance is unique, so audiences can experience the stories in many ways.

Learning Objectives
Understanding cultural and historical context. (SE)
Understanding the nature of translation. (SE)
Writing an advice column. (TE)

Advanced Learners/Pre-AP

 DIFFERENTIATED INSTRUCTION

Art and Religion Explain to students that the arts are especially valued in Asia, where they are often closely interwoven with the religions of various cultures. Students may enjoy the challenge of tracing the relationships between religions and art forms.

Have students choose one of the major religions of south central Asia—Buddhism, Islam, Hinduism—and research one artistic expression of that belief system. The possibilities include sculpture, music, painting, dance, and drama. Have them present an illustrated written report that includes students' well-researched theories as to why the religion chooses a particular art form for expression.

Focus

Summary

William Dalrymple worries that the oral tradition in India is dying as it has in other cultures. He discovers that a group of lower-caste villagers, called *bhopas*, have become the keepers of this art. Through an acquaintance, Dalrymple is invited to a performance of a story that includes singing, a vibrant painting of mythical deities and ancient Indian life, and musical accompaniment. When speaking with the *bhopa*, Dalrymple discovers that the oral tradition is alive in India because it has become a religious ritual through which the villagers of India connect to the divine.

 For activities related to this selection, see Unit 3 Teaching Resources Book, pp. 220–228.

Teach

Literary History ☆

Homer and the Oral Tradition
Little is known about Homer beyond his existence in Greece in the ninth or eighth century B.C. as a poet who has been linked to the epics the *Iliad* and the *Odyssey*. Vitally influential on Western literature for centuries, the *Iliad* and the *Odyssey* are part of a tradition in which the verses were passed down orally. In fact, *aoidos*, or "singer," is the ancient Greek word Homer used to describe poets.

Readability Scores

Dale-Chall: 9.2
DRP: 58
Lexile: 1340

576

Learning Objectives

For pages 576–581
Reading:
Analyzing cultural context.
Making connections across literature.
Analyzing informational text.

from Homer in India

William Dalrymple

Thomas Cook Travel Book Award Winner

Set a Purpose for Reading
Read to learn about the function of storytellers and the oral epic tradition in modern India.

Build Background
Scottish author and historian William Dalrymple is known for skillfully combining travel memoir with historical investigation. From 1989 to 1995, Dalrymple lived in Delhi, a city in northern India. While there, he wrote his critically acclaimed book *City of Djinns: A Year in Delhi*. Ten years later, he returned and became interested in the culture of the *bhopas*, traditional storytellers in the Indian state of Rajasthan who retell the *Mahabharata* and other ancient epics from memory. In the following excerpt from an article in the *New Yorker* magazine, Dalrymple describes this unique oral tradition.

Reading Strategy Analyze Cultural Context

When you **analyze cultural context,** you look closely at how a particular culture shaped the form, style, and themes of a literary tradition or text. In this article, Dalrymple examines a unique oral tradition to reveal insights about the history, beliefs, and daily life of the people who value it. As you read, keep track of how this excerpt reveals various aspects of Rajasthani culture.

576 UNIT 3 SOUTH CENTRAL ASIA

While I was staying at Rohet,[1] I heard about what seemed to be the most remarkable survival of all: the existence of several orally transmitted epic poems. Unlike the ancient epics of Europe—the *Iliad*, the *Odyssey*, *Beowulf*, and the *Nibelungenlied* (the basis of Wagner's "Ring Cycle"[2])—which were now the province only of academics and literature classes, the epics of Rajasthan were still very much alive. They were preserved by a caste of wandering *bhopas*—shamans and bards—who travelled from village to village, staging performances.

"The *bhopa* is a normal villager until the god Pabuji comes to him," one of the aunts explained. "Then he has great power. People bring him the possessed, and Pabuji cures them."

"How?" I asked.

---

1. *Rohet* refers to Rohet Garh, an early seventeenth-century fortress. While in Rajasthan, Dalrymple stays with the family who lives at Rohet Garh, including two elderly aunts.
2. Richard *Wagner* (1813–1883) was a German composer. One of his most famous works is *The Ring of the Nibelung,* or the *Ring Cycle*.

Reading Practice

Make Inferences Tell students that to make an inference is to guess or assume what an author has suggested but has not directly said. Students can make inferences by using clues from a text paired with their own knowledge or experience. Have students reread the aunt's description on this page of a *bhopa's* actions when dealing with a possessed person.

Or ask: What can you infer about the culture's spiritual beliefs from this description? *(Students may infer that this culture believes deeply in the ability of a spirit to possess a human. Furthermore, the culture believes that the spiritual world is powerful, as it accepts physical harm as a way to rid someone of an evil spirit.)*

"Sometimes the *bhopa* just says a mantra over them. He tries to make the spirit speak—to reveal who he is. But," she added ominously, "sometimes he has to beat the possessed person with his rods, or cut him and draw blood."

One afternoon, during a long walk through the desert, I met a *bhopa*. He was very old and dressed in a tatty white kurtadhoti.[3] He had a cataract in his left eye, and he parted his great fan of beard outward at the center of his chin. This man worked as a village exorcist,[4] but I had heard that there were still many other *bhopas*, out in the wild places of the desert, whose job it was to recite the great epics, some of them many thousands of stanzas long. . . .

While the *Mahabharata* is today the most famous of the Indian epics, it was originally only one of a large number. During the Mogul period, for example, one of the most popular was the Muslim epic *Dastan-i Amir Hamza*, or the *Story of Hamza*. The brave and chivalrous Hamza, the paternal uncle of the Prophet, journeys from Iraq to Sri Lanka, via Mecca, Tangiers, and Byzantium, on the way falling in love with various beautiful Persian and Greek princesses, and all the while avoiding the traps laid for him by his terrible foe, the dastardly magician Zumurrud Shah.

Over the centuries, the factual underpinning of the story was covered in layers of fantastic subplots and a cast of dragons, giants, and sorcerers—in one of its most popular forms, the tale encompassed three hundred and sixty stories. Today, however, while children in Persia, Pakistan, and parts of India may be acquainted with some

episodes, the *Story of Hamza* as a whole no longer really exists as an oral epic. There are fears that the *Mahabharata* and other Hindu epics could share that fate in the twenty-first century, surviving in written or recorded forms only.

Given all this, it seemed extraordinary to find in modern Rajasthan performers who were still the guardians of an entire self-contained oral culture. Apart from anything else, I longed to know how the *bhopas*, who were always simple villagers—ploughmen, cowherds, and so on—and often illiterate, could remember such colossal quantities of verse. Recently, having moved back to Delhi after an absence of ten years, I decided to go in search of the *bhopas* who had preserved this ancient tradition. It would, I felt, be a little like meeting Homer in the flesh.

There were several full-fledged Rajasthani epic poems that the *bhopas* performed, but two were especially popular. One told the tale of the deeds, feuds, life, death, and avenging of Pabuji, a semi-divine warrior and incarnate[5] god who died protecting a goddess's cattle against demonic rustlers. The other—four times its size, much more ambitious, and with similarities to both the *Iliad* and "Once Upon a Time in the West"—was the tale of a humble cattle herder named Sawai Bhoj, of the Bagravat clan; he eloped with an incarnate goddess, who had taken the form of a beautiful young wife of an elderly Rajput raja, and so sparked a monumental caste war. This ultimately led to the bloody death of Sawai Bhoj and twenty-two of his twenty-three brothers—deaths that were avenged, Sicilian style, by Sawai Bhoj's son, Dev Narayan, the legend's hero. Both epics—like the *Dastan-i Amir Hamza* and the *Mahabharata*—seemed to be

---

3. A *kurtadhoti* is a traditional outfit worn by Hindu men. It consists of a knee-length, loose shirt and a long, draped loincloth that looks like baggy pants.
4. An *exorcist* is a person who frees others from possession by evil spirits.

---

5. Something *incarnate* has a bodily form.

WILLIAM DALRYMPLE   **577**

Cultural Perspective
on the *Mahabharata*

Teach

Big Idea | 1

A Place in Society **Ask:**
How do the *bhopas* undermine the caste system? *(The heroes of the* bhopas' *tales are likely based on real people; they have become mythologized and deified, which threatens the Brahmins' hold on religious power.)*

Learning Objective
Making inferences. (TE)

Approaching Level

DIFFERENTIATED INSTRUCTION

Analyze Cultural Heroes Help students understand that the actions of famous people often evolve through the years into legendary stories that we still know today. More familiar legends, such as those featuring King Arthur, are likely based on real people. The identity of the real person may have been lost to time, and the adventures have become greatly exaggerated.

Explain to students that exaggerated elements include details such as magic and special powers. **Ask:** What effect do you think exaggerated elements have on tales such as the Story of Hamza? *(Students may say that the exaggerated elements make the stories more entertaining and memorable.)* Point out that exaggerated stories may be more likely to be thought of and retold through the years.

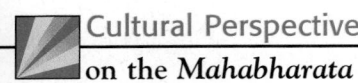

Cultural Perspective
on the *Mahabharata*

Teach

Literary History ☆

Rani Laxmi Kumari Chundawat Lacking a formal education and married when still a teenager, Rani Laxmi Kumari Chundawat became one of the most famous names in Rajasthani literature. For her work on the *Dev Narayan*, she was awarded the Padma Shri in 1984. The award, established in 1954, recognizes those who have served India with distinction.

based on a kernel of historical truth and revolved around figures who may once have lived, before the mythological process began to elaborate their stories and turn them into gods. Significantly, the divinity of both figures is not usually accepted by the Hindu priestly caste, the Brahmins, and the gods' priests and *bhopas* are drawn from among villagers of the lower castes.

According to the Rohet aunts, the Dev Narayan epic—which, recited in full, could take almost a month of eight-hour, night-long performances—had been written down only some thirty years ago. The person who did this was a distant neighbor and friend of the aunts, an elderly but feisty-sounding Rajasthani rani (or princess) named Laxmi Kumari Chundawat. I discovered that Laxmi Chundawat was still living in Jaipur, and we arranged to meet there, in her family's town house. . . . ☆

"The area where the story of Dev Narayan was set was in my father's principality and in my own constituency," she said. It was during her time in the assembly that she became interested in the epic, but she also became increasingly fearful that it was under threat from television and the cinema. "When I realized that the epic about him was beginning to die out," she added, "I determined to do something about it."

In the early nineteen-seventies, the Rani began inquiring if any of the local *bhopas* still knew the entire saga by heart. Many knew the outlines, she discovered, and some knew parts in detail, but none seemed to know the entire story. Eventually, however, she was directed to a village near Jaipur where an old gray-bearded *bhopa* named Lakshminarayan lived. She persuaded him to come to her house, along with another *bhopa* ("to encourage him"), while she went to Delhi and bought a tape recorder.

"He came to stay with me for ten or twelve weeks," she said. "He used to sing and I used to write. We did nothing else except this, six or seven hours at a time. It is astonishing that any individual could remember such a long work. In my printed edition, it takes six hundred and twenty-six pages.

"The *bhopa* told me he was only four years old when his father began to teach him to learn it by heart," the Rani continued. "Every day, he had to learn ten or twenty lines by rote. His father gave him buffalo milk so that his memory would improve.

"Anyway," she added, "I've arranged a performance of the Pabuji epic for you tonight. Mohan Bhopa is coming here at seven. So you can ask him all about it then."

That night, when I returned to Rani Chundawat's mansion, the courtyard had been transformed. Lamps had been hung around the arches, amid tangling bougainvillea. Thin white mattresses had been laid out on the ground, along with round silk bolsters to lean on, and at the end of the cloister, stretched between two poles, a long painted hanging had been unfurled.

It was like a fresco transferred to textile: a vibrant, apparently chaotic seventeen-foot-long panorama of medieval India—women, horses, peacocks, carts, archers, battles, washermen and fishermen, kings and queens, huge gray elephants and herds of white cows, many-armed demons and blue-skinned gods, all arranged around the central outsized figures of Pabuji, his magnificent black mare, and his four brothers-in-arms. This, I knew, must be the *phad*.

"The *bhopas* use the *phad* as part of their performance," the Rani had explained. "It's a very ancient tradition. If you look at the paintings from the caves in Central Asia,

578 UNIT 3 SOUTH CENTRAL ASIA

Reading Practice

Identify Sequence Tell students that in expository as well as narrative writing, authors use clues to help readers follow the sequence of events. Explain that while some clues are obvious, such as the words *then, after,* and *before,* others are more subtle. Shifts in verb tense can help students determine when in a sequence a certain event takes place.

Ask: What happens before Laxmi Chundawat and her guests arrive? *(Mohan and his wife raise their hands in reverence to the deity of the* phad *scroll.)*

Ask: What clues help you determine the sequence of these two events? *(The author uses the description "before long" to indicate that Laxmi Chundawat arrives after the ritual.)*

Ask: What clue helps you determine that Laxmi Chundawat explained the use of the *phad* before Dalrymple went to the performance at her mansion? *(He changes verb tense and says that she "had explained" the use of the* phad *to him; this indicates that she spoke to him before he ever saw the painting.)*

Hamzanama, 16th century. India school. Ink, watercolor, and gold on cotton, Height: 70.8 cm Width: 54.9 cm.
The Metropolitan Museum of Art, NY.

WILLIAM DALRYMPLE **579**

View the Art ★

The folios from the *Hamzanama* portray the exploits of the hero Hamza, who is based on Amir Hamza, one of Muhammad's uncles. His adventures as he spread the word of Islam around the world became the stuff of legends. These paintings were done for Emperor Akbar (1542–1605). He commissioned 1,400 paintings that took fifteen years to finish.
Ask: What seems to be happening in the foreground of this painting? *(Students will probably note that people seem to be exchanging or offering food.)*

Cultural History ☆

Colorful Gods In Indian mythological paintings, deities can be identified by the items they carry or by the color of their skin. Krishna, considered the eighth incarnation of Vishnu, is recognizable by his blue skin. Krishna's half-brother, Balarama, is usually painted with fair skin, and Yama, the lord of death, is green.

Advanced Learners/Pre-AP

DIFFERENTIATED INSTRUCTION

Multimedia Presentation Have students do research to find a filmed or illustrated (graphic novel) version of a story mentioned in this article, such as the *Mahabharata* or the story of Sawai Bhoj. Students can show part of a movie to the class or create a presentation that describes the media used to introduce the tale to new viewers or readers.

Teach

Big Idea   **1**

A Place in Society   Ask:

How do women participate in the performances? *(Women seem to have a relatively equal role in the performance as evidenced by Patasi taking turns singing with her husband.)*

Reading Strategy   **2**

Analyze Cultural Context

Ask: Based on Mohan Bhopa's description, what do the villagers he performs for seem to value most? *(They value their animals and livestock.)* **Ask:** How might technological progress affect the tradition of the bhopas? *(Students may say that technological progress would more closely connect the rural villages with the outside world. Medical advances might result in the* bhopas' *receiving less value and respect.)*

(APPROACHING) If Approaching Level learners struggle with the previous question, tell them to consider what learning about advanced medicine might do to the villagers and their reliance on *bhopas* to heal their livestock.

Bhopa Family Dancing, New Delhi, India.

such as those at Dunhuang, you'll see images of itinerant monks and storytellers with the scrolls they used then. The *phads* are the last survival of that tradition. The *bhopas* like to say that the *phad* of Dev Narayan is so full of bravery that when you tell the tale the grass gets burned around it." . . .

At first, I didn't notice the *bhopa* and his family, squatting in the shadows. Mohan Bhopa was a tall, dark-skinned man of about sixty, with a bristling gray handlebar mustache. He wore a long red robe and a tightly tied red turban. He was barefoot and there were bells attached to his ankles. Beside Mohan was his wife, Patasi, her face shrouded in a red peaked veil. As Mohan supervised, she swept the ground around the *phad* and sprinkled it with water. Then she prepared the wick of an oil lamp and both of them raised their palms in reverence to the deity of the scroll.

Before long, Laxmi Chundawat arrived with her guests, and she gave the signal for Mohan to begin. He picked up his fiddle—an instrument called a *ravanhattha*—as his wife held up the lamp to illuminate the *phad*. Mohan played an instrumental overture, then, accompanied by his son on the *dholak* (a drum), he began to sing in a voice full of solemnity and sadness. Every so often, as Patasi held up the lamp, he would stop, point with his bow to an illustration on the *phad*, and then recite a line of explanatory verse, all the while plucking at the string with his thumb.

At the end of each *sloka*, Patasi would step forward, fully veiled, and sing the next stanza, before handing the song back to her **1** husband. As the story unfolded, and the husband and wife passed the *slokas* back and forth, the tempo increased, and Mohan began to whirl and dance, jiggling his hips and stamping his feet so as to ring the bells, and shouting out, "Aa-ha! Hai! Wa-hai!"

During the performance, I asked another guest, who understood Mewari, one of the five major dialects of Rajasthan, if he could check Mohan Bhopa's rendition against a transcription by John D. Smith, of Cambridge University, of a version performed in a different part of Rajasthan in the nineteen-seventies. Give or take a couple of turns of phrase, the two versions were identical, he said. And there was nothing homespun about Mohan Bhopa's language, he added. It was delivered in a fine and courtly diction. . . .

After Mohan had sung for a couple of hours, there was a break while the Rani's guests headed off for dinner. I asked Mohan whom he normally performed for—the local landowners, perhaps? No, he said, it was usually cowherds and his fellow-villagers. Their motives, as he described them, were less to hear the poetry than to use him **2** as a sort of supernatural veterinary service.

Reading Practice

Expository Texts Tell students to use the following strategies when reading this and other expository texts.

Vary Reading Rate Slow down when encountering difficult concepts, new vocabulary, or passages with much information.

Monitor Comprehension Question yourself as you read, and then reread, review, or read on to clarify what is unclear.

Track Information List key ideas as you read.

"People call me in whenever their animals fall sick," he said. "Camels, sheep, buffalo, cows—any of these. Pabuji is very powerful at curing sickness in beasts. He is also good at curing any child who is possessed by a djinn."[6]

"So does Pabuji enter you while you perform?"

"How can I do it unless the spirit comes?" Mohan said. "You are educated. I am not, but I never forget the words, thanks to Pabuji. As long as I invoke him at the beginning, all will be well. Wherever we perform, the demons run away. No ghosts, no spirits can withstand the power of this story." . . .

This, it seemed to me, was the key, and the answer to the question of how it was that the Rajasthani epics were still living in a way that the *Iliad* and the other epics of the West were not. The poems remained religious rituals, and the *bhopas* were still receptacles for the messages of the gods, able to penetrate the wall—in India always a fairly porous wall—between the divine and the mundane.

Moreover, the gods in question were not impossibly distant and metaphysical beings but deified locals with whom the herders could relate and who could understand their needs. The Gujars[7] certainly took care to propitiate[8] the great "national" gods, like Shiva and Vishnu, whom they understood as controlling the continuation of the wider cosmos. For everyday needs, however, they prayed to the less remote, less awesome figures of their local herder gods and heroes who—along with the almost numberless pantheon of sprites and godlings, tree spirits and water nymphs that are worshipped and propitiated in every Indian village—know the things that the great gods cannot: the till and soil of the local fields and the sweet water of the wells, the needs and thirsts of the cattle and the goats; and they are believed to guard and regulate the ebb and flow of daily life.

---

6. A *djinn* is a spirit with supernatural power over humans.

7. The *Gujars* are a Rajasthani herding caste.
8. *Propitiate* means "appease" or "pacify."

Respond and Think Critically

Respond and Interpret

1. Write a brief summary of the main ideas in this article before you answer the following questions. For help on writing a summary, see page 1147.

2. (a)Summarize the duties of the *bhopas*. (b)Would you characterize the *bhopas'* function as practical, spiritual, or both? Explain.

3. (a)Who does Mohan Bhopa say is his primary audience? (b)How would you describe the social status of the *bhopas?*

Analyze and Evaluate

4. (a)A **bias** is an assumption that stems from one's cultural values or prejudices. Which of his own biases does Dalrymple reveal as he speaks to Mohan Bhopa? (b)How do Dalrymple's findings prove his biases to be false? Explain.

5. According to Dalrymple, how does the close relationship between the divine and the mundane help explain the survival of the Rajasthani epic tradition?

6. According to Dalrymple, why do European epics lack popular appeal?

Connect

7. Does having read Dalrymple's article enhance your understanding of the "Hundred Questions"? Explain.

WILLIAM DALRYMPLE **581**

Assess

1. Students' summaries will vary but should include information about the *bhopas* and their performance techniques.

2. (a) The *bhopas* recite epics, perform exorcisms, and cure sick animals. (b) The *bhopas'* function is both practical and spiritual: people believe the *bhopas* can harness spiritual powers to cure the sick.

3. (a) Mohan Bhopa says his primary audience is made up of cowherds and local villagers. (b) The *bhopas* are usually ordinary villagers.

4. (a) Possible answer: Dalrymple implies that he expected the "local landowners" to be the typical audience for oral epics, indicating that he associates the epic tradition with a privileged social class. (b) This bias is proved false by the fact that local villagers usually make up the audiences.

5. The gods in the epics have practical functions that villagers can connect with, so the epics have remained relevant.

6. People no longer worship the gods found in European epics, and the epics have no practical connection to daily life.

7. Students may say that because Dalrymple highlights the interconnectedness of spirituality and daily life in India, they understand why the yaksha's appearance does not alarm Yudhistira.

English Learners

DIFFERENTIATED INSTRUCTION

Intermediate Students may be familiar with quotation marks when used with direct quotations or in the titles of short stories or poems. Explain that sometimes writers use quotation marks for special emphasis or to call out a term that is not particularly official or accurate. On the last page of the article, the author writes that Shiva and Vishnu are "national" gods.

By placing quotation marks around the word *national*, the author of the article is saying that these gods are especially important to Hindu culture and Indian life; however, there is no designation of a god as the official god of India.

Before You Read

Focus

Bellringer Options

Daily Language Transparency 52

Or ask: In contemporary society, what duties are most people expected to fulfill? *(Students may say that people are expected to finish their education, help others, be loyal to their families and countries, and be productive members of society.)* Write the duties on the board as students list them, and then discuss how these duties may change depending on people's ages or social status.

Before You Read

Rama and Ravana in Battle from the *Ramayana*

One of the great epic poems of India, the *Ramayana* ("Romance of Rama") is the story of Rama, a human form of the god Vishnu, who wages a great battle against the forces of evil. Like the *Mahabharata* and the *Bhagavad Gita*, the epic teaches the philosophies and ideas of Hinduism in an exciting and popular form.

> *"The* Ramayana *pervades our cultural life in one form or another at all times."*
>
> —R. K. Narayan

The Legend According to Hindu belief, Ravana was a giant demon with ten heads and twenty arms who ruled the kingdom of Lanka (believed by some to be modern Sri Lanka). The gods were unable to kill Ravana, so he believed himself immortal and overlooked the possibility that a human could kill him instead. Ravana ruled Lanka through terror and eventually threatened to enslave both gods and humans. To end Ravana's reign, Vishnu, one of the greatest Hindu gods, incarnated into human form as Rama, the son of King Dasaratha, who ruled the kingdom of Ayodhya (modern-day Oudh, in north central India). However, as Rama is about to ascend to the throne, his father is deceived and exiles him, his wife, Sita, and his half brother Lakshmana for fourteen years. While they are in exile, Ravana kidnaps Sita, and Rama must fulfill his dharma, or duties in life, by killing Ravana to save his wife and reclaim his kingdom.

The Poet and the Poem Traditionally, the epic is attributed to Indian poet and sage Valmiki. The *Ramayana* was composed in Sanskrit, the classical language of India, and consists of some 24,000 couplets divided into seven books, each based on a different period in Rama's life. The stories of the *Ramayana* center on themes about duty and morality and teach that evil will eventually be defeated.

The Legacy The *Ramayana* is familiar to almost everyone in contemporary India. It is told and discussed in many ways, ranging from bedtime stories for children to scholarly lectures. It is adapted into dramas or dances for the stage and plays for shadow puppets. The epic is also the subject of many films. In northern India, an annual pageant called the Ram Lila celebrates the life and exploits of Rama. The story is also well known beyond India, especially by people in Cambodia, Indonesia, and Thailand.

582 UNIT 3 SOUTH CENTRAL ASIA

Selection Skills

Literary Elements
- Conflict (SE pp. 583, 585, 586, 590, 592; TE p. 588)
- Epic (SE p. 592)

from the **Ramayana**

Reading Skills
- Monitor Comprehension (SE pp. 583, 584, 586, 587, 589, 593; TE pp. 588, 590)
- Analyze Diction (TE p. 586)

Vocabulary Skills
- Denotation and Connotation (SE p. 593)

Speaking/Listening/Viewing Skills
- Literature Groups (SE p. 593)
- Analyze Art (SE p. 591; TE pp. 584, 587)

Writing Skills/Grammar
- Alternative Ending (TE p. 590)

Literature and Reading Preview

Connect to the Epic

What are considered "fair" and "unfair" ways of fighting in modern warfare? With a partner, discuss these tactics and why they are labeled accordingly.

Build Background

Rama must find Sita and kill Ravana to fulfill his dharma, the rule of conduct that guides his life. An individual's dharma is based on his or her social class and station in life. Dharma is the basis of Hindu laws, which are compiled in the *dharmasutra*, which consists of more than 5,000 titles.

Set Purposes for Reading

Big Idea The Search for Enlightenment

As you read, ask yourself, How does Rama strive to fulfill his dharma?

Literary Element Conflict

In a literary work, the struggle between two opposing forces is a **conflict**. An **internal conflict** is a struggle that occurs within the mind of a character who is torn between opposing feelings, desires, or goals. An **external conflict** is a struggle between a character and an outside force. The plot of a work is often based on a combination of internal and external conflicts. As you read, ask yourself, What internal conflicts does Rama face?

Reading Strategy Monitor Comprehension

When you **monitor your comprehension,** you make sure you understand each part of a literary work as you read it. If you have trouble understanding a difficult passage, review the passage and try to summarize it. You can also create a graphic organizer to arrange information in a way that is easier for you to follow. As you read the excerpt, ask yourself, Do I understand the actions and the dialogue in this passage?

Tip: Take Notes In a chart like the one below, record the kinds of weaponry that Rama and Ravana use.

Character	Physical Weapons	Supernatural Weapons
Rama	bow and arrows	Danda (capable of pursuing and pulverizing its target)
Ravana		

Learning Objectives

For pages 582–593

In studying this text, you will focus on the following objectives:

Literary Study: Analyzing conflict.

Reading: Monitoring comprehension.

Listening and Speaking: Participating in a literature group.

Vocabulary

magnitude (mag′nə tōōd′) *n.* great size or importance; p. 585 *The magnitude of the destruction shocked the rescue workers.*

intermittently (in′tər mit′ənt lē) *adv.* on and off again; coming at intervals; p. 588 *I could hear Sharon's voice only intermittently on my cell phone because the signal was weak.*

primordial (prī môr′dē əl) *adj.* original; existing from the beginning; p. 589 *Earth's primordial atmosphere was inhospitable to many life forms.*

pristine (pris′tēn) *adj.* pure; unspoiled; p. 590 *The tourists gasped in awe at the pristine beauty of the Alaskan national park.*

Tip: Denotation and Connotation The denotation of a word is its literal meaning. The connotation of a word is the impression it suggests. For example, the connotation of *intermittently* is usually neutral, since the word does not convey strong feelings.

English Learners

DIFFERENTIATED INSTRUCTION

Beginning English learners may have a difficult time with the names of the characters in this tale, especially the main characters whose names both begin with "R." Have students keep a list of characters, writing a description of each as he or she is introduced. Also, encourage students to list weapon names.

Advanced Learners/Pre-AP

DIFFERENTIATED INSTRUCTION

Name Research Students may find the names of some characters and weapons interesting, especially the names that read like compound constructions that include the names of Hindu deities. Invite students to do some further research to find the characteristics of these particular Hindu gods. Then, students can use their information to determine the meanings of the character or weapon names.

Before You Read

Focus

Summary

In this excerpt from the *Ramayana*, the demon Ravana and Rama, an incarnation of Vishnu, battle to the end. Ravana takes his chariot and rushes toward Rama, hoping to finally vanquish the hero; however, the gods have intervened, giving Rama a magical chariot. The battle rages, with each side using supernatural weapons. In the end, however, Rama is able to defeat Ravana. Upon seeing Ravana's lifeless form, Rama believes that he has killed a retreating enemy. After he learns that this is not the case, Rama is able to fulfill his dharma and reclaim his kingdom.

 For summaries in languages other than English, see Unit 3 Teaching Resources Book, pp. 229–234.

Vocabulary

Denotation and Connotation Have students use a thesaurus to find synonyms of the vocabulary words. After students compile a list, they can work in pairs to assign a positive or negative connotation to each word.

 For additional vocabulary practice, see Unit 3 Teaching Resources Book, p. 237.

Teach

Reading Strategy | 1

Monitor Comprehension

Answer: *The monkey hordes support Rama. Their work is "too much" for Ravana to watch, which indicates they are working against him.*

[ENGLISH LEARNERS] Explain to English learners that *reveled* means "to take intense pleasure or satisfaction" in something. Ask students to describe activities that they revel in.

View the Art ★

The *Bala Kanda* is one of seven books of the *Ramayana*, believed to be written by the sage Valmiki. Although the Mewar school of Indian painting had begun to wane by the turn of the seventeenth to eighteenth century, this painting's style and subject matter belongs to the phase during which the court painters depicted the *Ramayana* and other epics in elaborate detail.
Ask: What elements of battle does this painting convey? *(This painting conveys the confusion and violence of hand-to-hand combat.)*

Readability Scores

Dale-Chall: 5.6
DRP: 57
Lexile: 970

Rama's army in battle with monkeys, 1713. British Library, London.

Rama and Ravana in Battle
from the Ramayana

Translated by R. K. Narayan

Every moment, news came to Ravana of fresh disasters in his camp. One by one, most of his commanders were lost. No one who went forth with battle cries was heard of again. Cries and shouts and the wailings of the widows of warriors came over the chants and songs of triumph that his courtiers arranged to keep up at a loud pitch in his assembly hall. Ravana became restless and abruptly left the hall and went up on a tower, from which he could obtain a full view of the city. He surveyed the scene below but could not stand it. One who had spent a lifetime in destruction, now found the gory spectacle intolerable. Groans and wailings reached his ears with deadly clarity; and he noticed how the monkey hordes[1] reveled in their bloody handiwork. This was too much for him. He felt a terrific rage rising within him, mixed with some admiration for Rama's valor. He told himself, "The time has come for me to act by myself again."

---

1. *Hordes* are large groups or crowds.

Monitor Comprehension *Do the monkey hordes support Rama or Ravana? How do you know?* **1**

584 UNIT 3 SOUTH CENTRAL ASIA

Literary Element Practice

Foreshadowing Explain that foreshadowing is an author's use of clues to prepare readers for what will happen in a story. Foreshadowing helps draw readers into the story. **Ask:** How does the author foreshadow that a battle will soon begin? *(Ravana puts on his armor, says special prayers, and goes to his chariot.)*
What do Ravana's thoughts about Sita and Mandodari foreshadow? *(They foreshadow Ravana's or Rama's death*

in battle) What does the gods' gift of the chariot to Rama foreshadow? *(The gods' gift foreshadows a dangerous and difficult battle ahead for Rama.)* Discuss with students other clues in the beginning of the story that foreshadow future plot events. *(Ravana orders his horses to speed ahead, while Rama sits back and waits calmly. Ravana won't accept help from Mahodora, while Rama asks others for advice.)*

He hurried down the steps of the tower, returned to his chamber, and prepared himself for the battle. He had a ritual bath and performed special prayers to gain the benediction[2] of Shiva;[3] donned his battle dress, matchless armor, armlets, and crowns. He had on a protective armor for every inch of his body. He girt his sword-belt and attached to his body his accoutrements[4] for protection and decoration.

When he emerged from his chamber, his heroic appearance was breathtaking. He summoned his chariot, which could be drawn by horses or move on its own if the horses were hurt or killed. People stood aside when he came out of the palace and entered his chariot. "This is my resolve," he said to himself:

"Either that woman Sita, or my wife Mandodari, will soon have cause to cry and roll in the dust in grief. Surely, before this day is done, one of them will be a widow."

The gods in heaven noticed Ravana's determined move and felt that Rama would need all the support they could muster. They requested Indra[5] to send down his special chariot for Rama's use. When the chariot appeared at his camp, Rama was deeply impressed with the **magnitude** and brilliance of the vehicle. "How has this come to be here?" he asked.

---

2. A *benediction* is a blessing.
3. *Shiva* is the Hindu god of destruction and reproduction.
4. *Accoutrements* (ə kōō´trə mənts) are equipment and accessories.
5. *Indra* is one of the chief Hindu gods, associated with rain and thunderbolts.

2 The Search for Enlightenment *Why is Shiva an appropriate god for Ravana to pray to at this time?*

3 Conflict *What indicates that the conflict between Rama and Ravana is nearing its climax?*

Vocabulary

magnitude (mag´nə tōōd´) *n.* great size or importance

"Sir," the charioteer answered, "my name is Matali. I have the honor of being the charioteer of Indra. Brahma, the four-faced god and the creator of the Universe, and Shiva, whose power has emboldened Ravana now to challenge you, have commanded me to bring it here for your use. It can fly swifter than air over all obstacles, over any mountain, sea, or sky, and will help you to emerge victorious in this battle."

Rama reflected aloud, "It may be that the rakshasas[6] have created this illusion for me. It may be a trap. I don't know how to view it." Whereupon Matali spoke convincingly to dispel the doubt in Rama's mind. Rama, still hesitant, though partially convinced, looked at Hanuman[7] and Lakshmana and asked, "What do you think of it?" Both answered, "We feel no doubt that this chariot is Indra's; it is not an illusory creation."

Rama fastened his sword, slung two quivers full of rare arrows over his shoulders, and climbed into the chariot.

The beat of war drums, the challenging cries of soldiers, the trumpets, and the rolling chariots speeding along to confront each other, created a deafening mixture of noise. While Ravana had instructed his charioteer to speed ahead, Rama very gently ordered his chariot-driver, "Ravana is in a rage; let him perform all the antics he desires and exhaust himself. Until then be calm; we don't have to hurry forward. Move slowly and calmly, and you must strictly follow my instructions; I will tell you when to drive faster."

Ravana's assistant and one of his staunchest supporters, Mahodara—the giant among giants in his physical appearance—begged Ravana, "Let me not be a

---

6. *Rakshasas* are demons capable of changing their forms at will.
7. *Hanuman* is the leader of the army of monkeys fighting on Rama's side.

RAMAYANA **585**

English Learners

DIFFERENTIATED INSTRUCTION

Intermediate Explain that *illusory* is an adjective that means "deceptive" or "based on illusion." It is related to the noun *illusion*, which means "a misleading visual image." Explain to students that they can sometimes decipher the meaning of unfamiliar words by identifying similar words or words with similar spellings. Invite students to keep a log of these types of word relationships.

Approaching Level

DIFFERENTIATED INSTRUCTION

Follow Plot Students may have difficulty following the action in this tale, especially because of confusion between the main characters' names and the fast action of the battle. Have students create a graphic organizer of two columns, one for Rama and one for Ravana. Each column should have a row for describing the man's followers, his weapons, and his actions.

Teach

Big Idea | **2**

The Search for Enlightenment Answer: *Shiva is the god of destruction—since Ravana hopes to "destroy" Rama, Shiva is an appropriate god to pray to.*

Literary Element | **3**

Conflict Answer: *In this line, Ravana vows to fight Rama to the death.*

(ADVANCED) **Ask:** What compels Ravana more here—an internal or external conflict? Explain. *(Students may say that Ravana is compelled more by the internal conflict of wanting to prove he is the best warrior; others may say that the external conflict of the fight with Rama is more motivating.)*

> For additional literary element practice, see Unit 3 Teaching Resources Book, p. 235.

Cultural History ☆

Indra Indra, the chief of the Vedic gods, is the god of rain and war. The weapons that he uses are thunderbolts and lightning. According to myth, Indra defeated the dragon Vritra that was blocking the monsoon, which is vital to India's crops.

Learning Objectives
Analyzing conflict. (SE)
Monitoring comprehension. (SE)
Analyzing foreshadowing. (TE)

Teach

Reading Strategy 1

Monitor Comprehension

Answer: *Mahodara wants the glory of killing Rama, so he ignores Ravana's command to leave Rama to him and dashes toward Rama's chariot. Rama kills him as he approaches.*

Literary Element 2

Conflict **Answer:** *His internal conflict seems to be his hope that Ravana can be saved, despite evidence to the contrary. Rama would rather not fight Ravana, despite the fact that it is part of his dharma.*

Ask: Why might Rama be experiencing this conflict? *(Students may say that Rama feels that no good can result from fighting.)*

Political History ☆

Elephants in Battle Because of their great size and fearlessness when facing men and horses, elephants were a part of warfare in India. Although no longer used in battle, elephants are still employed in India, where they are trained to do heavy work or carry tourists.

---

mere spectator when you confront Rama. Let me have the honor of grappling with him. Permit me to attack Rama."

"Rama is my sole concern," Ravana replied. "If you wish to engage yourself in a fight, you may fight his brother Lakshmana."

Noticing Mahodara's purpose, Rama steered his chariot across his path in order to prevent Mahodara from reaching Lakshmana. Whereupon Mahodara ordered his chariot-driver, "Now dash straight ahead, directly into Rama's chariot."

The charioteer, more practical-minded, advised him, "I would not go near Rama. Let us keep away." But Mahodara, obstinate and intoxicated with war fever, made straight for Rama. He wanted to have the honor of a direct encounter with Rama himself in spite of Ravana's advice; and for this honor he paid a heavy price, as it was a moment's work for Rama to destroy him, and leave him lifeless and shapeless on the field. Noticing this, Ravana's anger mounted further. He commanded his driver, "You will not slacken[8] now. Go." Many ominous signs were seen now—his bow-strings suddenly snapped; the mountains shook; thunders rumbled in the skies; tears flowed from the horses' eyes; elephants with decorated foreheads moved along dejectedly. Ravana, noticing them, hesitated only for a second, saying, "I don't care. This mere mortal Rama is of no account, and these omens do not concern me at all." Meanwhile, Rama paused for a moment to consider his next step; and suddenly turned towards the armies supporting Ravana, which stretched away to the horizon, and destroyed them.

---

8. To *slacken* means "to let up or grow weaker."

1 | Monitor Comprehension *Summarize how Mahodara meets his end.*

586 UNIT 3 SOUTH CENTRAL ASIA

He felt that this might be one way of saving Ravana. With his armies gone, it was possible that Ravana might have a change of heart. But it had only the effect of spurring Ravana on; he plunged forward and kept coming nearer Rama and his own doom.

Rama's army cleared and made way for Ravana's chariot, unable to stand the force of his approach. Ravana blew his conch[9] and its shrill challenge reverberated through space. Following it another conch, called "Panchajanya," which belonged to Mahavishnu[10] (Rama's original form before his present incarnation), sounded of its own accord in answer to the challenge, agitating the universe with its vibrations. And then Matali picked up another conch, which was Indra's, and blew it. This was the signal indicating the commencement of the actual battle. Presently Ravana sent a shower of arrows on Rama; and Rama's followers, unable to bear the sight of his body being studded with arrows, averted their heads. Then the chariot horses of Ravana and Rama glared at each other in hostility, and the flags topping the chariots—Ravana's ensign of the Veena[11] and Rama's with the whole universe on it—clashed, and one heard the stringing and twanging of bow-strings on both sides, overpowering in volume all other sound. Then followed a shower of arrows from Rama's own bow. Ravana stood gazing at the chariot sent by Indra and swore, "These gods, instead of supporting me, have gone to the support of this petty human being. I will teach them a lesson. He is not fit to be killed with my

---

9. A *conch* is a seashell used as a horn.
10. *Mahavishnu* is another name for Vishnu.
11. A *veena* (also spelled *vina*) is a stringed musical instrument.

2 | Conflict *What internal conflict does Rama seem to be having?*

Reading Practice

Analyze Diction Diction is an author's choice of words. Authors choose words that appropriately and effectively convey a particular meaning. Diction can be described with one word, such as formal, natural, simple, complex, poetic, or flowery.

Have students read the dialogue on this page. **Ask:** How would you describe the diction of the dialogue? *(Students are likely to say that it's formal.)*

Ask: What makes the dialogue sound formal? *(There are few contractions, the characters speak in full sentences, and they use no slang.)* How does the diction convey the feeling of an ancient time? *(Students are likely to say that the formal, old-fashioned, and serious tone of the diction reveal the time period tale.)*

Invite students to rewrite the dialogue in the tale using more contemporary diction. Have them decide how to make Rama and Ravana sound different from each other while still displaying the characteristics that they have in the tale. Have students share their new versions of the dialogue with the class.

586

arrows but I shall seize him and his chariot together and fling them into high heaven and dash them to destruction." Despite his oath, he still strung his bow and sent a shower of arrows at Rama, raining in thousands, but they were all invariably shattered and neutralized by the arrows from Rama's bow, which met arrow for arrow. Ultimately Ravana, instead of using one bow, used ten with his twenty arms, multiplying his attack tenfold; but Rama stood unhurt.

Ravana suddenly realized that he should change his tactics and ordered his charioteer to fly the chariot up in the skies. From there he attacked and destroyed a great many of the monkey army supporting Rama. Rama ordered Matali, "Go up in the air. Our young soldiers are being attacked from the sky. Follow Ravana, and don't slacken."

There followed an aerial pursuit at dizzying speed across the dome of the sky and rim of the earth. Ravana's arrows came down like rain; he was bent upon destroying everything in the world. But Rama's arrows diverted, broke, or neutralized Ravana's. Terror-stricken, the gods watched this pursuit. Presently Ravana's arrows struck Rama's horses and pierced the heart of Matali himself. The charioteer fell. Rama paused for a while in grief, undecided as to his next step. Then he recovered and resumed his offensive. At that moment the divine eagle Garuda was seen perched on Rama's flagpost, and the gods who were watching felt that this could be an auspicious[12] sign.

After circling the globe several times, the duelling chariots returned, and the fight continued over Lanka. It was impossible to be very clear about the location of the battleground as the fight occurred here, there, and everywhere. Rama's arrows pierced Ravana's armor and made him

---

12. *Auspicious* (ôs pish´ əs) means "favorable; predictive of success."

Rama on Hanuman fighting Ravana, c. 1820. Tamil Nadu. Album painting on paper. British Museum, London.

wince. Ravana was so insensible to pain and impervious to attack that for him to wince was a good sign, and the gods hoped that this was a turn for the better. But at this moment, Ravana suddenly changed his tactics. Instead of merely shooting his arrows, which were powerful in themselves, he also invoked several supernatural forces to create strange effects: He was an adept in the use of various asthras[13] which could be made dynamic with special incantations.[14] At this point, the fight became one of attack with supernatural powers, and parrying of such an attack with other supernatural powers.

---

13. *Asthras* are special weapons with supernatural powers.
14. *Incantations* are chants and magic spells.

Monitor Comprehension *How has the physical conflict escalated at this point?* **3**

RAMAYANA **587**

Monitor Comprehension
Answer: *The antagonists stop using conventional weapons, such as bows and arrows, and start using supernatural weapons.*
APPROACHING To help Approaching Level students monitor the change in the battle, **ask:** What weapons did Rama and Ravana use at the beginning of the battle? *(arrows)* Now what are they using? *(supernatural weapons)*

View the Art ★

Possibly influenced by the simplicity of the Vijayanagara wall paintings in Tamil Nadu temples, Rama and Hanuman are shown here in profile, heavily outlined and decorated with unvarying shades of flat green and yellow, while Ravana, whom they battle, is traditionally characterized with his many heads. The monkey Hanuman is worshipped in the Hindu world, often in dedicated temples, and was even the superhero subject of a popular Indian comic book. **Ask:** According to this painting, who seems to be winning the battle between Rama and Ravana? Explain. *(Students may say that Ravana seems to be winning; he takes up more space in the painting and has forced the figures of Rama and Hanuman beyond the frame of the painting.)*

English Learners

DIFFERENTIATED INSTRUCTION

Intermediate Explain to students that the suffix *-eer* is added to words to describe someone who performs a certain profession or makes a certain product. The suffix is added to *chariot* to create *charioteer,* a word that means "someone who drives a chariot." Ask students for any other words they might know with this suffix.

Advanced Learners/Pre-AP

DIFFERENTIATED INSTRUCTION

Create a Battlefield Invite students to create a mock-up of the battle. Students can draw a map of the battlefield where Rama and Ravana meet. Have them create icons for each character, the followers, and even the weapons. Students should position these icons on the battlefield as described by the text. Have them move the icons as the location of fighting changes.

Learning Objectives
Analyzing conflict. (SE)
Monitoring comprehension. (SE)
Analyzing diction. (TE)

Teach

Reading Strategy 1

Monitor Comprehension
Ask: What has happened to Matali? *(Rama has revived him.)* What does this tell you about Rama? *(He has some sort of supernatural powers.)*

Literary Element 2

Conflict Ask: How does Rama solve the conflict created by "Maya"? *(He uses "Gnana" to get rid of the imaginary army.)*

Language History ☆

Maya *Maya*, the Sanskrit word for "illusion" or "wizardry," originally described the power of a god to make humans believe an illusion. The meaning of the word evolved, however, and now it represents the greater cosmic force that presents the illusion that the world is real.

Ravana realized that the mere aiming of shafts with ten or twenty of his arms would be of no avail because the mortal whom he had so contemptuously thought of destroying with a slight effort was proving formidable, and his arrows were beginning to pierce and cause pain. Among the asthras sent by Ravana was one called "Danda," a special gift from Shiva, capable of pursuing and pulverizing its target. When it came flaming along, the gods were struck with fear. But Rama's arrow neutralized it.

Now Ravana said to himself, "These are all petty weapons. I should really get down to proper business." And he invoked the one called "Maya"—a weapon which created illusions and confused the enemy.

With proper incantations and worship, he sent off this weapon and it created an illusion of reviving all the armies and its leaders—Kumbakarna and Indrajit[15] and the others—and bringing them back to the battlefield. Presently Rama found all those who, he thought, were no more, coming on with battle cries and surrounding him. Every man in the enemy's army was again up in arms. They seemed to fall on Rama with victorious cries. This was very confusing and Rama asked Matali, whom he had by now revived, "What is happening now? How are all these coming back? They were dead." Matali explained, "In your original identity you are the creator of illusions in this universe. Please know that Ravana has created phantoms to confuse you. If you make up your mind, you can dispel them immediately." Matali's explanation was a great help. Rama at once invoked a weapon called "Gnana"— which means "wisdom" or "perception." This was a very rare weapon, and he sent it forth. And all the terrifying armies who

---

15. *Kumbakarna* and *Indrajit* are the brother and son of Ravana, respectively.

---

seemed to have come on in such a great mass suddenly evaporated into thin air.

Ravana then shot an asthra called "Thama," whose nature was to create total darkness in all the worlds. The arrows came with heads exposing frightening eyes and fangs, and fiery tongues. End to end the earth was enveloped in total darkness and the whole of creation was paralyzed. This asthra also created a deluge of rain on one side, a rain of stones on the other, a hailstorm showering down **intermittently**, and a tornado sweeping the earth. Ravana was sure that this would arrest Rama's enterprise. But Rama was able to meet it with what was named "Shivasthra." He understood the nature of the phenomenon and the cause of it and chose the appropriate asthra for counteracting it.

Ravana now shot off what he considered his deadliest weapon—a trident endowed with extraordinary destructive power, once gifted to Ravana by the gods. When it started on its journey there was real panic all round. It came on flaming toward

Visual Vocabulary
A *trident* is a three-pronged spear.

Rama, its speed or course unaffected by the arrows he flung at it.

When Rama noticed his arrows falling down ineffectively while the trident sailed towards him, for a moment he lost heart. When it came quite near, he uttered a certain mantra[16] from the depth of his being and while he was breathing out that

---

16. A *mantra* is a chant or a prayer.

Vocabulary

intermittently (in′ tər mit′ ənt lē) *adv.* on and off again; coming at intervals

---

Reading Practice

Analyze Antagonist and Protagonist Explain to students that the protagonist of a story is the central character around whom the conflict revolves. The antagonist is the character or force that opposes the protagonist. Generally, readers side with the protagonist. Tell students that they can remember the "good guy" by the prefix *pro–* which means "favoring."

Organize students into small groups, and tell them to discuss Rama's status as the protagonist and Ravana's as the antagonist. Have groups answer these questions:

- What characteristics make Rama the protagonist?
- Has Ravana displayed any sympathetic characteristics that could cause you to question his status as the antagonist?

- Is there room in literature for protagonists that are not all good and antagonists that are not all bad?

Come back together as a class and discuss the groups' responses. If necessary, review the characters of familiar stories from class or even television shows or movies to investigate the complexity of the concept of protagonist vs. antagonist.

incantation, an esoteric[17] syllable in perfect timing, the trident collapsed. Ravana, who had been so certain of vanquishing Rama with his trident, was astonished to see it fall down within an inch of him, and for a minute wondered if his adversary might not after all be a divine being although he looked like a mortal. Ravana thought to himself, "This is, perhaps, the highest God. Who could he be? Not Shiva, for Shiva is my supporter; he could not be Brahma, who is four faced; could not be Vishnu, because of my immunity from the weapons of the whole trinity.[18] Perhaps this man is the **primordial** being, the cause behind the whole universe. But whoever he may be, I will not stop my fight until I defeat and crush him or at least take him prisoner."

With this resolve, Ravana next sent a weapon which issued forth monstrous serpents vomiting fire and venom, with enormous fangs and red eyes. They came darting in from all directions.

Rama now selected an asthra called "Garuda" (which meant "eagle"). Very soon thousands of eagles were aloft, and they picked off the serpents with their claws and beaks and destroyed them. Seeing this also fail, Ravana's anger was roused to a mad pitch and he blindly emptied a quiverful of arrows in Rama's direction. Rama's arrows

---

17. *Esoteric* (es´ə ter´ik) means "secret; understood by only a few."
18. *Trinity* here refers to the three gods Shiva, Brahma, and Vishnu.

3 The Search for Enlightenment *What does Ravana begin to suspect at this point? Why does he begin to suspect it?*

4 Monitor Comprehension *Summarize the kinds of weapons the two adversaries have used against each other so far.*

Vocabulary

primordial (prī môr´dē əl) *adj.* original; existing from the beginning

met them half way and turned them round so that they went back and their sharp points embedded themselves in Ravana's own chest.

Ravana was weakening in spirit. He realized that he was at the end of his resources. All his learning and equipment in weaponry were of no avail and he had practically come to the end of his special gifts of destruction. While he was going down thus, Rama's own spirit was soaring up. The combatants were now near enough to grapple with each other and Rama realized that this was the best moment to cut off Ravana's heads. He sent a crescent-shaped arrow which sliced off one of Ravana's heads and flung it far into the sea, and this process continued; but every time a head was cut off, Ravana had the benediction of having another one grown in its place. Rama's crescent-shaped weapon was continuously busy as Ravana's heads kept cropping up. Rama lopped off his arms but they grew again and every lopped-off arm hit Matali and the chariot and tried to cause destruction by itself, and the tongue in a new head wagged, uttered challenges, and cursed Rama. On the cast-off heads of Ravana devils and minor demons, who had all along been in terror of Ravana and had obeyed and pleased him, executed a dance of death and feasted on the flesh.

Ravana was now desperate. Rama's arrows embedded themselves in a hundred places on his body and weakened him. Presently he collapsed in a faint on the floor of his chariot. Noticing his state, his charioteer pulled back and drew the chariot aside. Matali whispered to Rama, "This is the time to finish off that demon. He is in a faint. Go on. Go on."

But Rama put away his bow and said, "It is not fair warfare to attack a man who is in a faint. I will wait. Let him recover," and waited.

RAMAYANA **589**

Big Idea **3**

The Search for Enlightenment

Answer: *Ravana begins to suspect that Rama may not be just a "mere mortal" after all but may have powers Ravana had not anticipated. He wonders this because of Rama's abilities with supernatural weapons.*

Reading Strategy **4**

Monitor Comprehension

Answer: *Both Rama and Ravana have used bows and arrows and have attacked each other in flying chariots. Ravana has used magical asthras to pursue and pulverize, create illusions, create total darkness, expose frightening eyes and fangs and fiery tongues, shoot a destructive trident, and issue monstrous serpents. Rama has used weapons that neutralized all of Ravana's asthras.*

Learning Objectives
Monitoring comprehension. (SE)
Analyzing conflict. (TE)
Analyzing protagonist and antagonist. (TE)

Approaching Level

DIFFERENTIATED INSTRUCTION

Analyze Emotional Responses Place students in groups with similarly leveled students. Have students list the animals introduced in the tale up to this point in the reading, and tell them to debate whether the animals are good or evil. Students should discuss the emotional response most people have to certain animals. **Ask:** Are eagles considered positive or negative? Monkeys? Explain.

Advanced Learners/Pre-AP

DIFFERENTIATED INSTRUCTION

Analyze Character Traits Point out that Ravana's character traits lead him into battle with Rama. Organize advanced learners into small groups, and have them identify Ravana's character traits. Tell them to discuss how these traits may affect the outcome of his battle with Rama. *(Students may suggest that Ravana is rash, impatient, cruel, and bad-tempered. These traits may lead to his destruction in battle.)*

Teach

Reading Strategy   1

Monitor Comprehension
Ask: What happens to Ravana?
(He dies when Rama's weapon pierces his heart.)

Big Idea   2

The Search for Enlightenment Answer: *His layers of anger, conceit, cruelty, lust, and egotism have burned off, and his true self shows through as his appearance takes on serenity and peace.* **Ask:** Whom do you think this tale is more about, Rama or Ravana? Explain. *(Students may say that Rama is the main character because the tale is about his fulfilling his dharma; others may say that it is more about Ravana because of the change he undergoes upon his death.)*

Literary Element   3

Conflict Answer: *Rama is worried that his victory was achieved through an "unfair" tactic: striking an enemy from behind.*

When Ravana revived, he was angry with his charioteer for withdrawing, and took out his sword, crying, "You have disgraced me. Those who look on will think I have retreated." But his charioteer explained how Rama suspended the fight and forebore[19] to attack when he was in a faint. Somehow, Ravana appreciated his explanation and patted his back and resumed his attacks. Having exhausted his special weapons, in desperation Ravana began to throw on Rama all sorts of things such as staves, cast-iron balls, heavy rocks, and oddments he could lay hands on. None of them touched Rama, but glanced off and fell ineffectually. Rama went on shooting his arrows. There seemed to be no end of this struggle in sight.

Now Rama had to pause to consider what final measure he should take to bring this campaign to an end. After much thought, he decided to use "Brahmasthra," a weapon specially designed by the Creator Brahma on a former occasion, when he had to provide one for Shiva to destroy Tripura, the old monster who assumed the forms of flying mountains and settled down on habitations and cities, seeking to destroy the world. The Brahmasthra was a special gift to be used only when all other means had failed. Now Rama, with prayers and worship, invoked its fullest power and sent it in Ravana's direction, aiming at his heart rather than his head; Ravana being vulnerable at heart. While he had prayed for indestructibility of his several heads and arms, he had forgotten to strengthen his heart, where the Brahmasthra entered and ended his career.

1

Rama watched him fall headlong from his chariot face down onto the earth, and that was the end of the great campaign. Now one noticed Ravana's face aglow with a new quality. Rama's arrows had burnt off the layers of dross,[20] the anger, conceit, cruelty, lust, and egotism which had encrusted his real self, and now his personality came through in its **pristine** form—of one who was devout and capable of tremendous attainments. His constant meditation on Rama, although as an adversary, now seemed to bear fruit, as his face shone with serenity and peace. Rama noticed it from his chariot above and commanded Matali, "Set me down on the ground." When the chariot descended and came to rest on its wheels, Rama got down and commanded Matali, "I am grateful for your services to me. You may now take the chariot back to Indra."

Surrounded by his brother Lakshmana and Hanuman and all his other war chiefs, Rama approached Ravana's body, and stood gazing on it. He noted his crowns and jewelery scattered piecemeal on the ground. The decorations and the extraordinary workmanship of the armor on his chest were blood-covered. Rama sighed as if to say, "What might he not have achieved but for the evil stirring within him!"

At this moment, as they readjusted Ravana's blood-stained body, Rama noticed to his great shock a scar on Ravana's back and said with a smile, "Perhaps this is not an episode of glory for me as I seem to have killed an enemy who was turning his back and retreating. Perhaps I was wrong in

---

19. To *forbear* means "to refrain from; to hold oneself back." *Forebore* (or *forbore*) is the past tense of the word.

---

20. *Dross* means "waste matter; surface scum."

The Search for Enlightenment *What indicates that Ravana has at last achieved enlightenment?*   **2**

Conflict *Why does Rama seem unsure about the glory of having won the conflict as he did?*   **3**

Vocabulary

pristine (pris′tēn) *adj.* pure; unspoiled

Writing Practice

Alternative Ending Discuss with students how they predict this story will end. Then ask them to imagine another way that the story could end. **Ask:** At what point can you imagine the story changing course? What would you have the characters do differently? Would you want the battle to go on longer or end quickly?

Tell students to rewrite the ending of the story. Have them choose a particular spot in the story as their "starting point" and include a sentence or two of the original story in their retelling. Remind students that their new endings have to make sense in the larger story. Point out that the original story contains dialogue. Tell students to include some dialogue in their endings. Invite students to share their endings with the class.

Lakshmana Consulting the Heads of the Monkey Armies, 19th century. Indian school. Gouache on paper. Private collection.

 View the Art How do the monkey hordes in this painting compare with how you visualize them?

shooting the Brahmasthra into him." He looked so concerned at this supposed lapse on his part that Vibishana, Ravana's brother, came forward to explain. "What you have achieved is unique. I say so although it meant the death of my brother."

"But I have attacked a man who had turned his back," Rama said. "See that scar."

Vibishana explained, "It is an old scar. In ancient days, when he paraded his strength around the globe, once he tried to attack the divine elephants that guard the four

directions. When he tried to catch them, he was gored in the back by one of the tuskers and that is the scar you see now; it is not a fresh one though fresh blood is flowing on it."

Rama accepted the explanation. "Honor him and cherish his memory so that his spirit may go to heaven, where he has his place. And now I will leave you to attend to his funeral arrangements, befitting his grandeur." ∾

4 The Search for Enlightenment *According to Hinduism, why does Ravana deserve a place in heaven?*

RAMAYANA **591**

To check students' understanding of the selection, see Unit 3 Teaching Resources Book, p. 240.

Advanced Learners/Pre-AP

DIFFERENTIATED INSTRUCTION

Connecting Literature Across Cultures Have students consider themes, characters, and even objects in this tale that are similar to those in tales, myths, and legends from other cultures. Ask students to consider the role that gods play in the *Ramayana*, and have them compare it with the role of gods in Greek and Roman mythology.

Have students also compare the supernatural weapons that Ravana and Rama have with the special weapons in the myths of King Arthur, Beowulf, and other tales. Invite students to choose a certain aspect of the *Ramayana* and compare it to another culture's myth in a short comparison and contrast essay.

Teach

Big Idea 4

The Search for Enlightenment **Answer:** *After being purified, everyone deserves a place in heaven, even a demon such as Ravana.*

View the Art ★

Answer: *Students may say the monkeys in the painting seem much calmer than the fighting monkey hordes in this excerpt.* Although there have been a number of artistic schools of style throughout the regions and history of India, there is a strong unity of design and form that is instantly recognizable, as evidenced by the paintings accompanying this tale. Here, Lakshmana and the monkey army are depicted by heavily outlined and flat, repetitive forms, bright and unvarying colors, and a stylized landscape.

Learning Objectives
Analyzing conflict. (SE)
Monitoring comprehension. (TE)
Applying dialogue to a retelling of a story ending. (TE)

591

After You Read

Assess

1. Answers will vary.
2. (a) He decides that the war is not going well and he must join. (b) He has a ritual bath and prays to Shiva.
3. (a) The gods send Rama a magnificent chariot that can fly, because they feel he needs all the help he can get. (b) The chariot is a gift of the gods, which indicates that they are on Rama's side and that he embodies their values and the values of their people.
4. (a) Ravana wants to fight Rama himself. (b) Ravana is a leader who realizes when he must take charge. He sees that his troops are overwhelmed and he must join the fight. He also seeks the glory of killing Rama.
5. (a) Ravana's bowstrings snap, the mountains shake, thunder rumbles, horses cry, and elephants move dejectedly. (b) Ravana is arrogant about his powers and primed for battle.
6. (a) Rama approaches the battle slowly and calmly. He prefers to fight "fairly," refusing to strike Ravana when he is in a faint. He later worries that he has struck Ravana from behind. Ravana has no such qualms; he uses ten bows when Rama has one, and he starts using every supernatural weapon he can muster. (b) Rama demonstrates that he is honorable, just, and good, while Ravana, who is evil, fights to win any way he can.
7. (a) Rama uses the Brahmasthra and hits Ravana in the heart. (b) The Brahmasthra was "a special gift to be used only when all other means had failed."
8. One of the tenets of Hinduism is that good will ultimately prevail over evil, as Rama prevails over Ravana.

592

After You Read

Respond and Think Critically

Respond and Interpret

1. Which parts of the epic did you enjoy most? Explain.
2. (a) Why does Ravana join the battle at the beginning of this excerpt? (b) How does Ravana prepare for the battle to come?
3. (a) What do the gods send to aid Rama in the battle? Why? (b) What does this gift demonstrate about Rama's status as an epic hero?
4. (a) Why does Ravana tell Mahodara not to attack Rama? (b) What does this suggest about Ravana's character and his motivations?
5. (a) What omens appear after the death of Mahodara? (b) Why does Ravana ignore these omens?

Analyze and Evaluate

6. (a) What actions demonstrate the differences between Rama's and Ravana's fighting styles? (b) What do these differences suggest about the contrast between their characters?
7. (a) How does Rama finally win the battle? (b) Why do you suppose Rama doesn't apply his winning tactic earlier?

Connect

8. **Big Idea** The Search for Enlightenment How do this battle and its outcome demonstrate the beliefs of Hinduism?
9. **Connect to Today** Modern readers are often drawn to written accounts of war. Why do you think readers continue to be drawn to war stories? What can be learned from them?

Literary Element Conflict

An **external conflict** takes place between two characters or between a character and an abstract force such as society or fate. An **internal conflict** takes place within the mind of a character who is torn between opposing desires or goals. Usually, the central conflict of a story reaches a climax and is resolved at the end.

1. What external conflicts prompt Ravana to join the battle?
2. What internal conflict does Rama contend with after the battle?

Review: Epic

As you learned on page 58, an **epic** is a long narrative poem about the adventures and the exploits of a hero. Epics were often passed down over centuries through oral tradition.

Partner Activity With a partner, discuss the elements of the *Ramayana* that make it an epic. Working with your partner, create a web diagram like the one below. Then fill it in with details from the *Ramayana*.

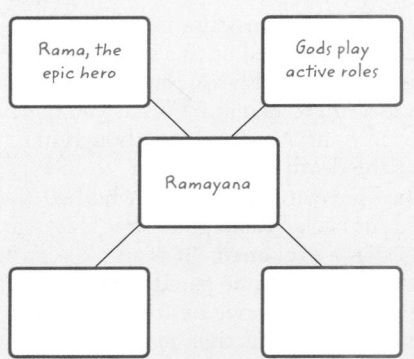

---

9. Answers will vary. Students may point out that readers are likely drawn to war stories because reading is one way people can better understand the causes, outcomes, and lessons of war.

Review: Epic

Possible answers: great armies in battle, supernatural weapons, high stakes (good *versus* evil), omens, descriptions of fierce fighting, good prevails

---

Literary Element

1. His commanders have all been killed, and the monkey hordes are killing off his army.
2. Rama worries that he may have inadvertently struck Ravana in the back, thus negating his glory.

Reading Strategy

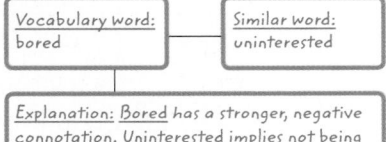

Reading Strategy Monitor Comprehension

SAT Skills Practice

What causes Ravana's demise before the paragraph on page 590 that begins "Rama watched him fall headlong from his chariot . . . "?

(A) The Brahmasthra enters Ravana's heart.

(B) Matali deceived Ravana.

(C) Ravana renounces the goddess Kali.

(D) Shiva overpowers Ravana.

(E) Rama gives Ravana a gold bracelet.

Vocabulary Practice

Practice with Denotation and Connotation Work with a partner to complete a graphic organizer like the one below for each boldfaced vocabulary word. Include the vocabulary word in one box and a word that has a similar denotation in another. Then explain which word has a stronger connotation.

magnitude   intermittently   primordial   pristine

EXAMPLE:

> Vocabulary word:
> bored
>
> Similar word:
> uninterested
>
> Explanation: Bored has a stronger, negative connotation. Uninterested implies not being engaged, while bored implies growing restless due to lack of interest.

Academic Vocabulary

*The **outcome** of the battle between Rama and Ravana is the victory of good over evil.*

Outcome is an academic word. More familiar synonyms include *result, ending,* and *effect.* To study this word further, answer the following question: What is one *outcome* of a war in modern history?

For more on academic vocabulary, see pages 36–37 and R83–R85.

Listening and Speaking

Literature Groups

Assignment The focus of this excerpt from the *Ramayana* is the extended battle between Rama and Ravana. With a small group, discuss the value of this and other battle scenes you have read or seen.

Prepare Review the graphic organizer on weaponry you filled out on page 583. Then create an organizer like the one below to refine your understanding of the battle in the epic. Compare and contrast that battle with other battle scenes.

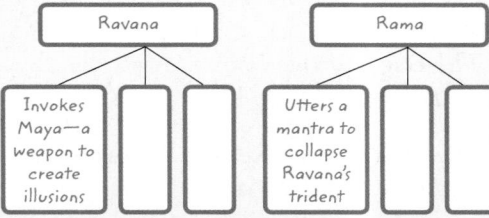

Ravana — Invokes Maya—a weapon to create illusions

Rama — Utters a mantra to collapse Ravana's trident

Set a purpose before you begin discussion. For example, your purpose may be to reach an agreement on a particular issue, such as whether a battle between good and evil is necessary in an epic.

Discuss Listen closely to what your peers say and try to build off their ideas. You might consider the following questions to jumpstart your discussion.

- In descriptions of battle scenes, is more better? Or is there a limit to the number of incidents that you care to see or read about?

- In battle, how can you tell who is good or bad?

Report Write a brief summary of your discussion. Format it as a bulleted list.

Evaluate Write a paragraph to assess your own contribution to the discussion and to identify communication skills you could improve.

LOG ON **Literature** Online

Selection Resources For Selection Quizzes, eFlashcards, and Reading-Writing Connection activities, go to glencoe.com and enter QuickPass code GLW6053u3.

RAMAYANA **593**

Reading Strategy

(A) is the correct answer. **(B)** is incorrect as Matali does not harm Ravana. **(C)** is incorrect as the goddess Kali is not mentioned in this episode. **(D)** is incorrect because it is Vishnu who is incarnated as Rama, not Shiva. **(E)** is wrong.

Progress Check

Can students monitor comprehension?

If No → See Unit 3 Teaching Resources Book, p. 236.

Vocabulary Practice

Explanations will vary. Sample answers:

Vocabulary word: magnitude; Similar word: size; Explanation: *magnitude* has the stronger connotation.

Vocabulary word: intermittently; Similar word: sporadically; Explanation: *sporadically* has the stronger connotation.

Vocabulary word: primordial; Similar word: elemental; Explanation: *primordial* has the stronger connotation.

Vocabulary word: pristine; Similar word: clean; Explanation: *pristine* has the stronger connotation.

Academic Vocabulary

Possible answer: One outcome of a modern war is the creation of nuclear weapons.

> For additional selection assessment, see Assessment Resources, pp. 123–124.

Approaching Level

DIFFERENTIATED INSTRUCTION

Using Recall Encourage students to ask themselves some questions about battle scenes before they begin the group assignment on p. 593. Here are some questions they could ask themselves:

- Who fought in the last battle scene you viewed?

- Who won?

- Was the battle the main focus of the story?

Listening and Speaking

Students' discussions should

- reflect careful organization, such as note taking and the use of a graphic organizer

- show cooperation among students

- include a summary of the arguments and the main ideas of the discussion

- be followed by a written evaluation of the students' participation and skills in the discussion

Focus

Comparing Literature

Across Time and Place

Bellringer Options

Selection Focus
 Transparencies 32–34

Daily Language
 Transparency 53

Display a collection of sayings or axioms, such as "Beggars can't be choosers" and "Don't count your chickens before they hatch." Challenge students to explain what the sayings mean, especially the more obscure ones like "A stitch in time saves nine."

Connecting to the Reading Selections

Have students discuss advice they have received from elders in their families or communities and decide whether it is advice that is timeless or just old-fashioned.

Learning Objectives

For pages 594–606

In studying these texts, you will focus on the following objectives:

Literary Study:
Comparing themes.
Analyzing moral.

Reading:
Comparing cultural contexts.
Previewing.

Writing: Writing a fable.

Compare Literature About Lessons

Fables—which are common to almost all cultures—teach lessons about human behavior. The following fables were written hundreds of years apart from one another in India, Greece, France, and the United States, yet each one contains a lesson on common sense.

COMPARE THE Big Idea **The Search for Enlightenment**

These fables feature characters, both human and nonhuman, who believe they have attained wisdom. The fates of these characters prompt readers to question their own behavior and enlightenment. As you read, ask yourself, What can I learn from the fates of these characters?

COMPARE Fables

The stories in the *Panchatantra* and Aesop's fables began as oral tales. La Fontaine (lə fon tān′) and Thurber wrote fables for a highly sophisticated audience. As you read, ask yourself, What is the style of each fable?

COMPARE Cultures

A fable reflects the culture in which it was created. The four cultures represented in the following fables have different values, social customs, and intellectual ideas, yet the lesson in each fable is universal. As you read, ask yourself, What cultural values and beliefs does each fable reflect?

A peri (fantastic creature) holding an effigy of the sun rides a composite Lion. Indian miniature on paper. The Pierpont Morgan Library, NY.

LOG ON ▶ **Literature** Online

Author Search For more about Aesop, Jean de la Fontaine, and James Thurber, go to glencoe.com and enter QuickPass code GLW6053u3.

Selection Skills

```
Literary Elements
• Moral (SE pp. 596, 598, 599)
```

```
Reading Skills
• Preview (SE pp. 596, 599)
• Connect to Contemporary Issues
  (TE p. 600)
• Analyze Rhyme (TE p. 602)
• Make Predictions (TE p. 604)
```

Comparing Literature

```
Vocabulary Skills
• Word Parts (SE p. 599; TE p. 596)
```

```
Speaking/Listening/Viewing Skills
• Oral Presentation (SE p. 606)
• Analyze Art (SE pp. 598, 603)
```

```
Writing Skills/Grammar
• Literary Analysis (SE p. 606)
• Use Correct Verb Tense (TE p. 596)
• Write a Song (TE p. 598)
```

Before You Read

The Lion-Makers
from the *Panchatantra*

India

The *Panchatantra* (pun´ chə tän´trə) is a collection of ancient Indian fables or stories that contain lessons about living wisely. The Sanskrit words *pancha tantra* mean "five chapters," which describes the way the collection is arranged. Each of the five chapters in the collection contains a variety of brief fables told within a single frame story.

> *"In what can wisdom not prevail?*
> *In what can resolution fail?*
> *What cannot flattery subdue?*
> *What cannot enterprise put through?"*
>
> —*Panchatantra*

Moral Tales *The Lion-Makers* is set within the frame story of a king who asks a learned Brahman, or Hindu priest, to teach his three foolish sons about interpersonal relationships and the art of ruling. The Brahman, named Vishnusharman (vish´nōō shär´mən), teaches the boys with stories that are instructive and entertaining. Most of them are animal fables or fables involving both humans and animals.

An Ancient Collection The stories of the *Panchatantra* were probably first collected and written down around 200 B.C. Many of the stories in the collection were originally passed down through oral tradition for much longer. As the stories were collected, they were classified into five chapters, each with a different theme: losing friends, winning friends, handling international relations, losing profits and possessions, and the consequences of hasty actions.

Warriors fighting a lion-griffin, 5th century AD. Stone relief. Museum, Sarnath, Uttar Pradesh, India.

The *Panchatantra* Outside India Over time, the fables of the *Panchatantra* spread through Asia and Europe, inspiring storytellers in many lands. They were translated into Persian as early as the sixth century and into Arabic, Greek, Hebrew, Latin, German, and Italian during the Middle Ages. In 1570, the *Panchatantra* became the first Indian work to be translated into English. Related stories of some of the tales can be found in many other works of world literature, including *The Thousand and One Nights* (see page 496), Aesop's fables (see page 600), Geoffrey Chaucer's *The Canterbury Tales*, and Giovanni Boccaccio's *Decameron* (see page 926).

Before You Read

Focus

Summary

Four men—three who have great scholarship but lack common sense and one who has only common sense—set out to make their fortune. Coming across the remains of a dead lion, the three scholars decide—against the advice of the sensible man—to bring the lion back to life. The sensible man hides in a tree. When the lion is brought to life, it kills the three scholars. Only the sensible man survives.

 For summaries in languages other than English, see Unit 3 Teaching Resources Book, pp. 243–248.

Advanced Learners/Pre-AP

DIFFERENTIATED INSTRUCTION

Interpreting Explain to students that familiar axioms, or morals, are often presented in story form to make them more interesting, memorable, and palatable. Occasionally, the moral is difficult to understand because of how it is presented or the language used. Tell students that interpreting the morals, or restating the lesson in their own words, is a powerful aid to understanding.

Ask students to read and paraphrase the following axioms from Benjamin Franklin's *Poor Richard's Almanack*, a collection of sayings published in 1732.

1. Clean your finger before you point at my spots. *(Be sure you are guiltless before you accuse me.)* **Ask:** What is another saying with a similar message? *(People who live in glass houses shouldn't throw stones.)*

2. He that pursues two hares at once does not catch one and lets the other go. *(If you try to do too much at once, you won't do well in anything.)* Have students try to find a more familiar saying with a similar message.

Comparing Literature

Before You Read

Focus

Vocabulary

Building Words Using Word Parts Divide the class into three teams. Give each team a vocabulary word from the list and have the team break the word into its parts. Then, without a dictionary each team should think up as many other words as they can that use any of the word parts. Let groups compete to see which team can come up with the most words.

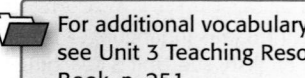
> **For additional vocabulary practice, see Unit 3 Teaching Resources Book, p. 251.**

Literature and Reading Preview

Connect to the Fable

Do you think common sense is as valuable as formal education? Discuss this question with a partner.

Build Background

The verse proverbs of the *Panchatantra* can be easily memorized, and the collection was intended as a *niti-shastra* (ni′tē shä strə), or a "textbook on the wise conduct of life." The word *niti* means "worldly wisdom,"and to achieve this state, a person needs to be determined, physically secure, free from want, intelligent, and in possession of good friends. A person with *niti* uses cleverness and wit, rather than force.

Set Purposes for Reading

Big Idea **The Search for Enlightenment**

As you read, ask yourself, How can people gain enlightenment through observing the world around them?

Literary Element **Moral**

A **moral** is a practical lesson about right or wrong conduct taught in a fable or a parable. In some fables, the author states the moral explicitly; in others, the reader must infer the moral from what happens in the story. Sometimes, the moral is written as an **epigram**, a short, pointed verse or saying. As you read, ask yourself, How do the events in this fable lead to the moral?

Reading Strategy **Preview**

You can **preview** a work of literature by noting the title and the subtitle and by looking ahead to any subheads, illustrations, and conclusions. Previewing can help you recognize the topic of a work, its organization, and sometimes its theme. Before you begin "The Lion-Makers," ask yourself, How can I preview this story to better understand it when I begin reading?

....

Tip: Predict An **epigraph** is a quotation at the beginning of a literary work that often provides a hint of what is to come. Use the checklist below to preview the fable and make predictions.

☑ Preview this fable. What might the story be about, based on the title and the illustrations?

☑ According to the epigraph, what will this fable be about?

Vocabulary

scholarship (skol′ər ship′) *n.* academic achievement or knowledge; p. 597 *Claude was known for his scholarship—he was well read in many subjects.*

attainment (ə tān′mənt) *n.* accomplishment; p. 597 *Ms. Lowndes, who started a business, was proud of this attainment.*

nullity (nul′ə tē) *n.* a mere nothing; something insignificant; p. 598 *Many religions hold that no living thing is a nullity and that all life is sacred.*

....

Tip: Word Parts You can often determine the meanings of unfamiliar words by examining their parts. For example, a *scholar* is a person who studies. The suffix *-ship* refers to a status level. Therefore, *scholarship* can mean the status of a person who is well studied, or "academic achievement."

Grammar Practice

Verb Tense Explain to students that past perfect tense refers to actions begun and ended before another past action began. Write this sentence on the board and underline accordingly: "When they <u>had gone</u> a little way, the eldest of them spoke up." Point out that the underlined verb is an example of past perfect tense.

Have students look for other examples of past perfect tense in the fable, and ask them to explain how the past perfect tense is used in these instances. *(Examples: "When this had been done" means that the lion was assembled before it was brought to life; "after the lion had gone elsewhere" means that the lion leaves before the fourth Brahman comes out of the tree.)*

from the
Panchatantra

Translated by Arthur W. Ryder

Lion at Rest, ca. 1585. India school. Ink, colors, silver, and gold on paper, Overall: 20.3 x 15.2 cm. The Metropolitan Museum of Art, NY.

Political History ☆

Brahman Influence Members of the Brahman caste had political influence in Hindu society for a long time. In some respects, the Brahmans were higher in status than the king. One such priest, Divakarapandita, was a close advisor to three Cambodian kings; he is commemorated at the temple of Angkor Wat.

The Lion-Makers

Indeed, there is wisdom in the saying:

*Scholarship is less than sense;
Therefore seek intelligence:
Senseless scholars in their pride
Made a lion; then they died.*

"How was that?" asked the wheel-bearer. And the gold-finder told the story of

In a certain town were four Brahmans ☆ who lived in friendship. Three of them had reached the far shore of all scholarship, but lacked sense. The other found scholarship distasteful; he had nothing but sense.

One day they met for consultation. "What is the use of **attainments**," said they, "if one does not travel, win the favor of kings, and acquire money? Whatever we do, let us all travel."

Vocabulary

scholarship (skol′ər ship′) *n.* academic achievement or knowledge

Vocabulary

attainment (ə tān′mənt) *n.* accomplishment

PANCHATANTRA **597**

Readability Scores
Dale-Chall: 7.1
DRP: 54
Lexile: 480

Learning Objective
Using correct verb tense. (TE)

English Learners

DIFFERENTIATED INSTRUCTION

Advanced Draw students' attention to the *wheel-bearer* and *gold-finder* at the beginning of the fable. Explain to students that these unnamed characters are only known by an *epithet*, a brief phrase used to characterize someone, but that throughout history people have been named after their occupations. Describe the meanings of last names in English, such as Miller, Cooper, and Smith.

Approaching Level

DIFFERENTIATED INSTRUCTION

Tracking Multiple Characters Struggling readers may have a difficult time keeping track of what the four Brahmans are each saying or doing. This may be particularly hard as none of the Brahmans are named, and the dialogue runs together. Have students create a four-column chart, one column per Brahman, and describe each character's words and actions in the fable.

Comparing Literature

Teach

Comparing Literature

Big Idea 1

The Search for Enlightenment **Answer:** *The Brahman believes that only scholarly enlightenment will gain the attention of kings.*

Literary Element 2

Moral **Answer:** *It is set apart at the end in quotation marks, and the phrase "And that is why I say" signals that it is the teaching of the storyteller.*

Progress Check

Can students identify moral?

If No → See Unit 3 Teaching Resources Book, p. 249.

View the Art ★

Answer: *Students may say that even though both the painting and the fable deal with a life-threatening event, the attack of a lion, both have the playful mood of a fairy tale.*

Prince Salim (Jahangir, or "World Siezer") assumed the throne after Akbar the Great's death (1605). Salim was a connoisseur of the arts. The miniature of Salim may have been an illumination for his memoirs, *Jahangirnama*.

But when they had gone a little way, the eldest of them said: "One of us, the fourth, is a dullard,[1] having nothing but sense. Now nobody gains the favorable attention of kings by simple sense without scholarship. Therefore we will not share our earnings with him. Let him turn back and go home."

Then the second said: "My intelligent friend, you lack scholarship. Please go home." But the third said: "No, no. This is no way to behave. For we have played together since we were little boys. Come along, my noble friend. You shall have a share of the money we earn."

With this agreement they continued their journey, and in a forest they found the bones of a dead lion. Thereupon one of them said: "A good opportunity to test the ripeness of our scholarship. Here lies some kind of creature, dead. Let us bring it to life by means of the scholarship we have honestly won."

Then the first said: "I know how to assemble the skeleton." The second said: "I can supply skin, flesh, and blood." The third said: "I can give it life."

So the first assembled the skeleton, the second provided skin, flesh, and blood. But while the third was intent on giving the breath of life, the man of sense advised against it, remarking: "This is a lion. If you bring him to life, he will kill every one of us."

"You simpleton!" said the other, "it is not I who will reduce scholarship to a **nullity**." "In that case," came the reply,

---

1. A *dullard* is someone with no imagination or intelligence.

1 **The Search for Enlightenment** *What opinion about enlightenment does this statement express?*

Vocabulary

nullity (nul′ə tē) *n.* a mere nothing; something insignificant

598 UNIT 3 SOUTH CENTRAL ASIA

Prince Salim surprised by lion while hunting, c.1595-1600, Mughal. Christie's Images.

View the Art Prince Salim, the future Jahangir, or "World-Conqueror," ruled the Mogul Empire from 1605 until his death in 1627. This painting shows a lion leaping at Prince Salim, who defends himself with a staff. How does the mood of this painting compare with the mood of the fable? ★

"wait a moment, while I climb this convenient tree."

When this had been done, the lion was brought to life, rose up, and killed all three. But the man of sense, after the lion had gone elsewhere, climbed down and went home.

"And that is why I say:
*   Scholarship is less than sense, . . .*
and the rest of it." ❧

Moral *How can you tell that this is the moral of the fable?* **2**

Writing Practice

⚡ **Write a Song** Have students write a song about the fable of the lion-makers, using either of the epithets as the chorus. Challenge students to write a song that runs at least four verses of four lines each, not including the chorus. Tell students that the song must include the moral of the fable.

To get students started, **ask:** Whose point of view will you use to tell the story? (The lion? The sensible Brahman? One of the other Brahmans?) Will the wheel-bearer or the gold-finder have a role in the song? Will you tell the fable in chronological order? Encourage students to set their songs to music and perform them for the class.

After You Read

Respond and Think Critically

Respond and Interpret

1. What was your reaction to this fable? Explain.

2. (a)What do the Brahmans seek on their travels? (b)Why do the first two Brahmans want to exclude the fourth Brahman from their travels?

3. (a)What do the Brahmans discover in the forest, and what do the first three decide to do? (b)Why does the fourth Brahman disagree with their plan?

Analyze and Evaluate

4. (a)Do you think the first three Brahmans are most disadvantaged by their education, their lack of common sense, or their pride? Explain. (b)Do you think the fourth Brahman is saved by his *lack* of education? Explain.

5. In your opinion, does this fable mean that people should *not* try to educate themselves? Explain.

Connect

6. **Big Idea** **The Search for Enlightenment** Who is truly enlightened in this story? What does this say about how enlightenment is achieved?

7. **Connect to Today** Do you think the moral of "The Lion-Makers" is relevant to contemporary society? Explain.

Literary Element Moral

A **moral** is the equivalent of a theme, or main idea.

1. Where is the moral of "The Lion-Makers" explicitly stated?

2. State the moral in your own words.

Reading Strategy Preview

When you preview a text, you form a mental picture of what the work is about and how it is organized. Review the chart you made on page 596.

Partner Activity Skim the "The Lion-Makers" and look for elements that stand out, such as the title, the epigraph, the subheads, and the illustrations. List these elements and discuss what they might lead a reader to expect from the fable.

 Literature Online

Selection Resources For Selection Quizzes, eFlash-cards, and Reading-Writing Connection activities, go to glencoe.com and enter QuickPass code GLW6053u3.

Vocabulary Practice

Practice with Word Parts For each boldfaced vocabulary word, identify the word with a shared word part in the right column. Write each word and underline the part both words share. Then explain how the words are related.

1. scholarship purity

2. attainment school

3. nullity accomplishment

EXAMPLE: re<u>ced</u>e pro<u>ceed</u>

Recede means "to go back"; *proceed* means "to go forward."

Writing

Write a Fable Using "The Lion-Makers" as a model, write a fable that presents a moral. In your fable, use elements of the *Panchatantra,* such as nonhuman characters, describe a specific setting, and include figurative language.

PANCHATANTRA **599**

Assess

1. Answers will vary.

2. (a) They seek to win the favor of kings and to acquire money. (b) They want to exclude the fourth because they think his lack of education means he has nothing to contribute to their quest; also, they do not want to share their money with him.

3. (a) They discover the bones of a lion and decide to bring it back to life. (b) because the revived lion could kill them

4. (a) Students may think that a lack of common sense combined with pride is what puts the scholars at a disadvantage. (b) He is saved not so much by his lack of education as by his common sense.

5. Nothing suggests that education in itself is a bad thing; instead, the fable suggests that educa-tion without common sense can be destructive.

6. The fourth Brahman is truly enlightened because he uses common sense to save himself. It might say that enlightenment is achieved when people use reason and careful observation.

7. Students should recognize that people still fare better in life when they use common sense.

Literary Element

1. The moral is explicitly stated in the first two lines of the epigraph and in the epigram at the end.

2. Answers might vary, but the moral can be stated along the lines of *education has more to do with common sense that with formal training.*

Reading Strategy

Students should explain how each element they identified would help a reader understand the story.

Writing

Students' fables should teach a moral, have a specific setting, and use literary devices to express personal style.

Vocabulary

1. <u>schol</u>arship, <u>schol</u>; *Scholarship* means "learning"; *school* is an institu-tion where one learns.

2. attain<u>ment</u>, accomplish<u>ment</u>; *Attain-ment* is the act of achieving; *accom-plishment* is the act of accomplishing.

3. nul<u>lity</u>, pur<u>ity</u>; both words are states of being.

Comparing Literature

Focus

Summary

In this fable, a dog invites a starving wolf to come home with him, where he will be fed in return for work. When the wolf realizes that part of the deal is to wear a collar, he leaves, stating that he would rather be free and hungry than a well-fed slave.

Literary History ☆

Aesop's Influence While there is no concrete evidence that a person named Aesop ever existed, the name *Aesop* has become forever linked with the word *fable*. First collected in the fourth century B.C., Aesop's fables survived to be collected again in the first century. It was this collection that influenced later authors, including Jean de La Fontaine.

Build Background

Aesop (ē′sop) was supposedly a Greek slave in the sixth century B.C. who was famous for telling witty and powerful fables. These fables expressed values that were widely held among ancient Greeks, many of which are still held by people today. Aesop's tales continue to delight and instruct people of all ages and many common phrases can be traced to them, including "sour grapes," "a wolf in sheep's clothing," and "killing the goose that laid the golden egg." ☆

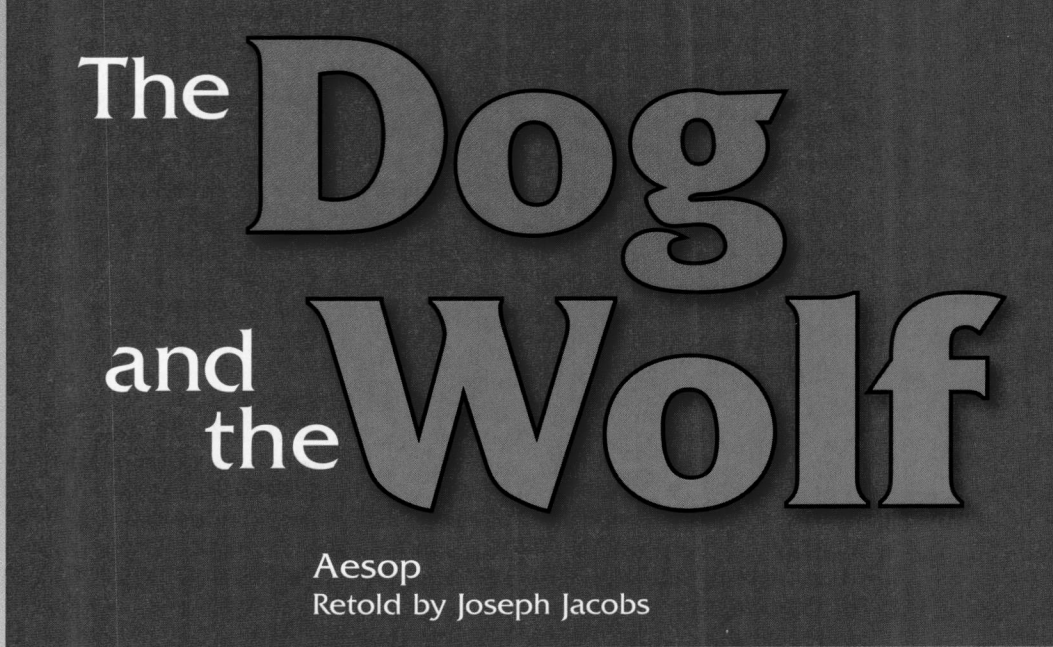

The Dog and the Wolf

Aesop
Retold by Joseph Jacobs

A gaunt Wolf was almost dead with hunger when he happened to meet a Housedog who was passing by. "Ah, Cousin," said the Dog, "I knew how it would be; your irregular life will soon be the ruin of you. Why do you not work steadily as I do, and get your food regularly given to you?"

"I would have no objection," said the Wolf, "if I could only get a place."

"I will easily arrange that for you," said the Dog; "come with me to my master and you shall share my work."

So the Wolf and the Dog went towards the town together. On the way there the Wolf noticed that the hair on a certain part of the Dog's neck was very much worn away, so he asked him how that had come about.

Reading Practice

Connect to Contemporary Issues Discuss with students the longevity of Aesop's fables and ask why students think they are still read today. Invite students to consider how such ancient tales can connect to contemporary issues. **Ask:** Why might the moral of this fable still be relevant today? (*Students are likely to say that in contemporary American society freedom is of vital importance.*)

Have students consider contemporary issues that connect to this ancient fable, and write a short essay describing one such connection. Students may write about a larger political issue, such as immigration, or a more local one, such as a movement toward shorter work weeks. Encourage students to share their essays with the class.

Aesop Hund und Wolf (Dog and Wolf), 15th century. Illuminated manuscript.

Teach

Literary Element | 1

Moral **Ask:** How would you understand the moral without the statement at the end? *(The dog describes the collar, and the wolf leaves after calling him "Master Dog." The wolf's comment sums up his opinion and the moral of fable.)*

Discussion Starter

Students should recognize that animals can be seen as exaggerated symbols of particular human qualities. With simplified characters, Aesop could teach clear-cut moral lessons. Students should be able to list a variety of animals and their associated qualities in contemporary culture, such as dogs (loyalty), sheep (gentleness and conformity), foxes (cunning), bees (industriousness), and owls (wisdom). Point out to students that animals represent different qualities in different cultures.

"Oh, it is nothing," said the Dog. "That is only the place where the collar is put on at night to keep me chained up; it chafes a bit, but one soon gets used to it."

"Is that all?" said the Wolf. "Then good-bye to you, Master Dog."

1 *"Better starve free than be a fat slave."*

> 💬 **Discussion Starter**
>
> "The Dog and the Wolf" is a **beast fable,** one that features animals that behave like humans. Why might Aesop have used animals to teach lessons about human behavior? How are animals used in contemporary culture to represent human behavior? Discuss these questions with a group.

AESOP **601**

English Learners

DIFFERENTIATED INSTRUCTION

Intermediate Explain to English learners that the word *only* should appear next to the word or group of words it modifies. A sentence's meaning may be unclear if *only* is positioned incorrectly. Write the following sentences on the board and discuss with students how the placement of *only* changes each sentence's meaning.

That is the *only* place where the collar is put on at night. *(only modifies place)*
That is the place where the collar is put on only at night. *(only modifies a time)*

Readability Scores

Dale-Chall: 5.8
DRP: NA
Lexile: 620

Learning Objectives
Analyzing moral. (TE)
Connecting to contemporary issues. (TE)

601

Comparing Literature

Focus

Summary

In this fable, an oak tree pities a reed's weakness and vulnerability to the wind and sun. The reed, on the other hand, tells the oak tree not to pity it, for the oak is vulnerable as well. A storm rolls in, and while the reed bends in the strong wind, the oak falls.

Teach

Reading Strategy | 1

Preview **Ask:** How does the form of this fable differ from that of the previous two? *(It is a poem.)* How might this affect how you will read the fable? *(Students are likely to say that they will read this poem more slowly or carefully.)*

Big Idea | 2

The Search for Enlightenment **Ask:** Who is more truly enlightened in this fable? *(the reed)* What is the dark side of false enlightenment? *(arrogance that leads to a downfall)*

Reading Practice

Analyze Rhyme Scheme Explain that while some rhyme schemes are simple, such as AABB or ABAB, others are much more complex. Have students reread the fable, finding rhymes and labeling them using the same letter for each set of rhyming words. *(Students may find this in the first ten lines: AABCBCDDEE. This same pattern does not repeat for the rest of the poem.)*

Build Background

In seventeenth-century France, fables were considered a minor literary form, unworthy of sophisticated readers. Jean de la Fontaine (zhän də lä fon tān´) challenged this notion in the three collections of fables he published over a 26-year period. He enhanced the dramatic impact of these brief tales through subtle characterization and rich imagery. Within a single fable, he could shift from tragic to comic styles. La Fontaine often suggested rather than stated the morals of his fables, allowing readers to draw their own conclusions.

The Oak and the Reed

Jean de la Fontaine

Translated by James Michie

1
One day the oak said to the reed:
"You have good cause indeed
To accuse Nature of being unkind.
To you a wren[1] must seem
5 An intolerable burden, and the least puff of wind
That chances to wrinkle the face of the stream
Forces your head low; whereas I,
Huge as a Caucasian peak,[2] defy
Not only the sun's glare, but the worst the weather can do.
10 What seems a breeze to me is a gale for you.
Had you been born in the lee[3] of my leaf-sheltered ground,
You would have suffered less, I should have kept you warm;
But you reeds are usually found
On the moist borders of the kingdom of the storm.
15 It strikes me that to you Nature has been unfair."
"Your pity," the plant replied, "springs from a kind heart.
But please don't be anxious on my part.
Your fear of the winds ought to be greater than mine.
I bend, but I never break. You, till now, have been able to bear
20 Their fearful buffets[4] without flexing your spine.
But let us wait and see." Even as he spoke,

1. A *wren* is a very small European bird.
2. *Caucasian peak* refers to the Caucasus mountains, which lie between Russia, Turkey, and Iran, and contain the highest mountains in Europe.
3. The *lee* is the side (as of a tree) that is sheltered from the wind.
4. *Buffets* (buf´ əts) means "blows."

602 UNIT 3 SOUTH CENTRAL ASIA

Ask: What effect does this complex pattern have on the readability of the poem? Does it make it more difficult to read? Explain. *(Students may say that the poem's complex rhyme scheme does not make it harder to read; in fact, the poem reads much like regular dialogue, yet the rhyming words lend it a musical quality.)*

Ask: What statements are emphasized by rhyming end lines? *(The oak's arrogance is strengthened in lines 7 and 8; the reed's confidence is highlighted by the rhyme in lines 16 and 17; and the oak's downfall is underlined in the rhyme in lines 29 and 30.)*

The Great Piece of Turf, 1503. Albrecht Dürer. Watercolor. Albertina Graphic Collection, Vienna.

View the Art Albrecht Dürer, painter and printmaker, was a central figure of the German Renaissance. His careful observation of nature in this watercolor is characteristic of Renaissance art. How does he portray the beauty of ordinary things? Which character in "The Oak and the Reed" does this watercolor suggest? Explain. ★

From the horizon's nethermost gloom
The worst storm the north had ever bred in its womb
    Furiously awoke.
25 The tree stood firm, the reed began to bend.
The wind redoubled[5] its efforts to blow—
    So much so
    That in the end
It uprooted the one that had touched the sky with its head,
30 But whose feet reached to the region of the dead.

5. *Redoubled* means "intensified."

> **Discussion Starter**
>
> A Chinese proverb states, "A wise man adapts himself to circumstances, as water shapes itself to the vessel that contains it." How might this proverb relate to the theme of "The Oak and the Reed"? How might it relate to the themes of "The Lion-Makers" and "The Dog and the Wolf"? Discuss these questions in a group.

JEAN DE LA FONTAINE **603**

Comparing Literature

Assess
Discussion Starter
Like the proverb, "The Oak and the Reed" teaches that there is wisdom in adaptability—the reed "shapes itself" to its circumstances and does not break. Students may point out that the fourth Brahman in "The Lion-Makers" is wise because he is adaptable: he recognizes that he is in a dangerous situation and adjusts his behavior accordingly. In contrast, the wolf in Aesop's fable demonstrates wisdom because he refuses to "get used to" unfavorable circumstances.

View the Art ★

Answer: *The artist conveys the beauty of ordinary things by portraying in careful detail a clump of weeds. The weeds suggest the reed, which appears weak but is flexible and can endure the fiercest storms.*

Albrecht Dürer (1471–1528) is famous for his woodcuts as well as his paintings. A trip he made to Italy in the 1490s led to a series of watercolor landscape paintings, of which this piece is likely a part.

Approaching Level
DIFFERENTIATED INSTRUCTION

Filling in Missing Words Students may have difficulty understanding the meaning of sentences with elliptical adverb clauses. Explain to students that elliptical adverb clauses have missing words. Write the following example from the poem: **Your fear of the winds ought to be greater than mine.** Point out the elliptical adverb clause (*than mine*), and supply the omitted words (*my fear of the winds*).

Point out that the word *than*, which indicates a comparison, is a clue that students are dealing with an elliptical adverb clause. Once students understand how to fill in the blanks left by this type of clause, they can more easily understand a sentence's meaning.

Encourage students to fill in the missing words when they find elliptical clauses.

Learning Objectives
Previewing. (TE)
Analyzing rhyme. (TE)

603

Focus

Summary

In this fable, an African elephant battles with all of the other animals and proclaims himself Ace of Beasts. The other animals, now enslaved, are forced to build the elephant a great wooden palace. A message arrives, challenging the elephant to a battle in his basement; however, when no one shows up to fight, the elephant is enraged and swears never to return to the basement. The next day, the house trembles and falls in, trapping the elephant in the basement. He soon learns that he has been bested by a termite.

Build Background

Twentieth-century American author and illustrator James Thurber commented that "Every writer is fascinated by the fable form; it's short, concise and can say a great deal about life." However, Thurber's fables do not include clear-cut prescriptions for moral behavior. Instead, they often parody well-known sayings—for example, "There is no safety in numbers, or in anything else" and "You can fool too many of the people too much of the time."

The Elephant
Who Challenged the World

James Thurber

An elephant who lived in Africa woke up one morning with the conviction that he could defeat all the other animals in the world in single combat, one at a time. He wondered that he hadn't thought of it before. After breakfast he called first on the lion. "You are only the King of Beasts," bellowed the elephant, "whereas I am the Ace!" and he demonstrated his prowess by knocking the lion out in fifteen minutes, no holds barred. Then in quick succession he took on the wild boar, the water buffalo, the rhinoceros, the hippopotamus, the giraffe, the zebra, the eagle, and the vulture, and he conquered them all. After that the elephant spent most of his time in bed eating peanuts, while the other animals, who were now his slaves, built for him the largest house any animal in the world had ever had. It was five stories high, solidly made of the hardest woods to be found in Africa. When it was finished, the Ace of Beasts moved in and announced that he could pin back the ears of any animal in the world. He challenged all comers to meet him in the basement of the big house, where he had set up a prize ring ten times the regulation size.

Several days went by and then the elephant got an anonymous letter accepting his challenge. "Be in your basement tomorrow afternoon at three o'clock," the message read. So at three o'clock the next day the elephant went down to the basement to meet his mysterious opponent, but there was no one there, or at least no one he could see. "Come out from behind whatever you're behind!" roared the elephant. "I'm not behind anything," said a tiny voice. The elephant tore around the basement, upsetting barrels and boxes, banging his head against the furnace pipes, rocking the house on its foundations, but he could not find his opponent. At the end of an hour the elephant roared that the whole business was a trick and a deceit—probably ventriloquism—and that

Reading Practice

Make Predictions Explain to students that they can make predictions by using prior knowledge. Because this is the final fable in this set, students should have a basic understanding of fables and their messages. **Ask:** Using the title and your prior knowledge of fables, how can you predict things will go for the elephant?

(Students are likely to say that things will not go well for the elephant.) **Ask:** Why? *(Students may say that the word* challenged *in the title indicates a challenge but not a victory.)* Have students read the first paragraph of this fable. **Ask:** What can you predict will happen to the elephant based on what you know about the moral lessons in fables?

(Students are likely to say that the elephant, who is arrogant and bossy, will live to learn the error of his ways.)

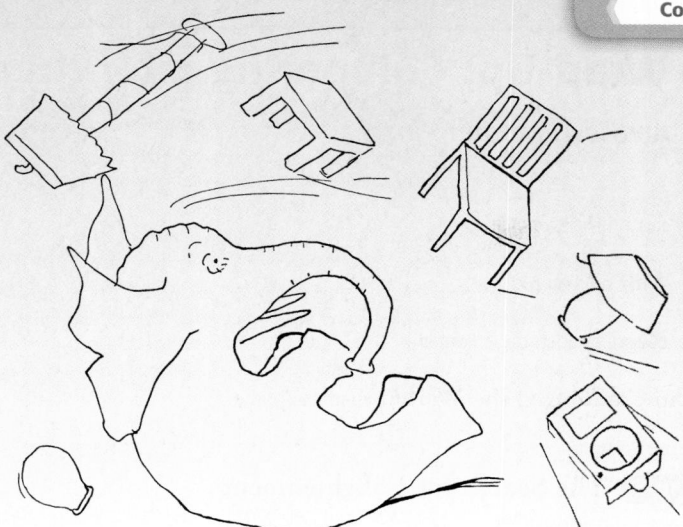

The Elephant Who Challenged the World. James Thurber. Illustration.

he would never come down to the basement again. "Oh, yes you will," said the tiny voice. "You will be down here at three o'clock tomorrow and you'll end up on your back." The elephant's laughter shook the house. "We'll see about that," he said.

The next afternoon the elephant, who slept on the fifth floor of the house, woke up at two-thirty o'clock and looked at his wristwatch. "Nobody I can't see will ever get me down to the basement again," he growled, and went back to sleep. At exactly three o'clock the house began to tremble and quiver as if an earthquake had it in its paws. Pillars and beams bent and broke like reeds, for they were all drilled full of tiny holes. The fifth floor gave way completely and crashed down upon the fourth, which fell upon the third, which fell upon the second, which carried away the first as if it had been the floor of a berry basket. The elephant was precipitated into the basement, where he fell heavily upon the concrete floor and lay there on

his back, completely unconscious. A tiny voice began to count him out. At the count of ten the elephant came to, but he could not get up. "What animal are you?" he demanded of the mysterious voice in a quavering tone which had lost its menace. "I am the termite," answered the voice.

The other animals, straining and struggling for a week, finally got the elephant lifted out of the basement and put him in jail. He spent the rest of his life there, broken in spirit and back. **1**

Moral: The battle is sometimes to the small, for the bigger they are the harder they fall. ∾

> **Quickwrite**
>
> How does Thurber's use of humor compare with the use of humor in the other fables you have read? What might be the advantages and the disadvantages of using humor in a fable? Write a paragraph or two addressing these questions. Use evidence from the fables to support your response.

JAMES THURBER **605**

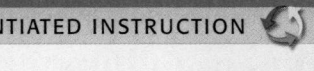

Advanced Learners/Pre-AP

DIFFERENTIATED INSTRUCTION

Compare and Contrast Invite students to compare and contrast "The Oak and the Reed" with "The Elephant Who Challenged the World." Have students compare the similarities in the morals of each fable. Tell students to compose an argument describing which fable they think is more successful in teaching a moral lesson and why. Invite students to argue their points in front of the class.

English Learners

DIFFERENTIATED INSTRUCTION

Advanced English learners might not understand some of the terms in this fable. Explain that the *King of Beasts* is what English speakers call the lion. The fable also contains fighting or boxing terms, such as "no holds barred," "pin back the ears," and "count him out." Encourage students to look these terms up and share similarly themed terms from their native languages.

Comparing Literature

Teach

Big Idea | **1**

The Search for Enlightenment **Ask:** Would the elephant have found enlightenment if not for the termite? **Explain.** (*Students may say that the elephant would have found enlightenment because he would have gotten old one day and been unable to beat everyone else; other students may say that the elephant would not have found enlightenment because none of the other animals could beat him, and he needed to be beat in order to see the light.*)

Quickwrite

Students' responses should

- contrast the use of subtle irony in the other fables with Thurber's overtly humorous dialogue and narration
- address advantages of humor, such as the power to entertain audiences, and disadvantages, such as the risk of treating serious subjects too lightly
- cite evidence from the selections to support their conclusions

Readability Scores

Dale-Chall: 6.8
DRP: 58
Lexile: 1100

Learning Objective
Making predictions. (TE)

605

Assess

Compare the Big Idea

1. In "The Lion-Makers," the fourth Brahman is the most enlightened because he uses common sense. In "The Dog and the Wolf," the wolf is the most enlightened because he sees that freedom is more important than having his material needs met. In "The Oak and the Reed," the reed is the most enlightened because it knows that flexibility is the key to endurance. In "The Elephant Who Challenged the World," the termite is the most enlightened because it outwits a stronger creature using cleverness.

2. In "The Lion-Makers," "The Oak and the Reed," and "The Elephant Who Challenged the World," foolishness is equated with arrogance. The Brahmans, the oak, and the elephant meet their ends because they are too prideful and set in their ways. The dog in Aesop's fable is not overtly arrogant, but he seems sure that his way of life is best—and suffers for it.

3. Students may notice that "The Dog and the Wolf" presents a different view of human nature than the other three tales. The other three underscore how people tend to become arrogant when they have achieved a measure of success and show that they would do well to be adaptable and humble. In contrast, "The Dog and the Wolf" shows that humans tend to give up their personal integrity and suggests they should take more pride in their principles.

- ***The Lion-Makers*** from the *Panchatantra*
- ***The Dog and the Wolf*** by Aesop
- ***The Oak and the Reed*** by Jean de la Fontaine
- ***The Elephant Who Challenged the World*** by James Thurber

COMPARE THE Big Idea **The Search for Enlightenment**

Group Activity Fables often impart insight into human behavior by presenting characters who embody foolishness, rather than wisdom. In a group, discuss the following questions. Cite evidence from the fables to support your points.

1. Which character in each of the fables is the most "enlightened" and why?

2. How are the portrayals of foolishness in these four fables similar?

3. What do the representations of wisdom and foolishness in these fables reveal about the authors' views of human nature?

COMPARE Fables

Writing The fables presented here are written in a range of styles—some use simple language and imagery, while others use detailed imagery and dialogue to convey a message. Write a brief essay in response to one of the following questions. Cite evidence from the fables to support your points.

1. How does the tone of "The Lion-Makers" compare with that of "The Elephant Who Challenged the World"?

2. How would you compare the author's use of dialogue in "The Dog and the Wolf" with that in "The Oak and the Reed"?

COMPARE Cultures

Speaking and Listening How might these fables reflect the values of each author's culture? Research the cultural values that underpin each fable and give a brief oral report to the class summarizing your findings. Use quotations from the fables, such as the epigrams and epitaphs, as starting points for your research.

The Dog and the Wolf. Georges Fraipont. Colour engraving. Private collection.

Literature Online

Selection Resources For Selection Quizzes, eFlashcards, and Reading-Writing Connection activities, go to glencoe.com and enter QuickPass code GLW6053u3.

Compare Fables

1. The author's tone in "The Lion-Makers" is detached, objective, and subtly ironic. The author's tone in "The Elephant Who Challenged the World" is also ironic, but it is more playful.

2. The dialogue in "The Dog and the Wolf" is formal and subtly ironic. The dialogue in "The Oak and the Reed" is more elaborate. It dramatizes the conditions of the oak and the reed.

Compare Cultures

Students should draw on their knowledge of the *Panchatantra*, ancient Greek values, and contemporary American values. They should discuss some or all of the following: the value of humbleness, practicality, personal integrity and autonomy, and the idea that even "small" people can get ahead if they are skilled and motivated.

Before You Read

The Kabuliwallah

India

Meet **Rabindranath Tagore**
(1861–1941)

Rabindranath Tagore (rə bēn′drə nät tə gôr′) was born in Calcutta (now Kolkata), India, into an upper-caste Hindu family with strong religious and artistic convictions. These convictions helped him grow into a beloved, world-renowned author. In 1915, Tagore was knighted by the British crown, one of the highest honors bestowed by Great Britain, in recognition of his contributions to world literature. However, he renounced his knighthood four years later, in protest against the Amritsar Massacre, in which British troops killed hundreds of demonstrators in Amritsar, India. This decision was representative of the social consciousness he exhibited throughout his life.

The Spirit of Creation Tagore's father was a philosopher and a religious reformer as well as a landowner and a businessman. Tagore was a gifted child with a wide range of talents and intellectual interests. "Our home was permeated with the spirit of creation," he wrote. He published his first poem at the age of thirteen and his first collection of poems at seventeen. In 1878, his father sent him to school in England to prepare him for a career in the Indian Civil Service. While in England, Tagore became familiar with the work of many Romantic and Victorian poets and dramatists.

An Awakened Social Conscience In 1890, Tagore's father put him in charge of the family's estates in eastern Bengal (modern Bangladesh). Tagore took his position seriously and worked efficiently. However, he also developed a deep awareness of the poverty and other hardships faced by many Indians. He became a strong supporter of human rights and immersed himself in

"Every child comes with the message that God is not yet discouraged of man."
—Rabindranath Tagore

social concerns, such as education. He wrote many of his best short stories, including "The Kabuliwallah," while working at the estates.

A Versatile Artist In 1913, Tagore became the first Asian author to be awarded the Nobel Prize in Literature. The prize brought Tagore international acclaim. He traveled around the world and gave lectures on India's spiritual traditions and the necessity for Indian independence from British rule. He wrote more than 1,000 poems as well as two dozen plays, eight novels, and several collections of short stories and essays. Tagore also composed some 2,000 songs and became a renowned painter when he was almost 70 years old. He introduced new literary forms and styles into the literature of Bengal and is considered by many to be the greatest modern India author. When he died, he might well have built a life, in his own words, "where tireless striving stretches its arms toward perfection."

LOG ON ▶ **Literature** Online

Author Search For more about Rabindranath Tagore, go to glencoe.com and enter QuickPass code GLW6053u3.

RABINDRANATH TAGORE **607**

Bellringer Options

Selection Focus
Transparency 35
Daily Language
Transparency 54

Ask: How do people today stay in touch with one another? How have new technologies affected communication between people? *(Students may suggest that people stay in touch with others through letters, e-mails, and telephone calls. New technologies, such as the Internet and cell phones, allow people to stay in touch with others no matter how far away they are located.)*

Selection Skills

Literary Elements
- Characterization (SE pp. 608, 610, 612, 614, 615, 617)
- Irony (SE p. 617)
- Analyze Motivation (TE p. 610)

The Kabuliwallah

Speaking/Listening/Viewing Skills
- Analyze Art (SE p. 615; TE p. 609)

Reading Skills
- Analyze Cultural Context (SE pp. 608, 611, 613, 615, 617)
- Comparing and Contrasting Characters (TE p. 614)

Vocabulary Skills
- Understand Word Origins (SE pp. 608, 617; TE p. 608)

Writing Skills/Grammar
- Reflective Essay (SE p. 618)
- Movie Scene (TE p. 612)

Before You Read

Focus

Summary

The Kabuliwallah, a peddler from Kabul, becomes fast friends with the narrator's five-year-old daughter Mini. When the peddler is jailed for attacking a man who owes him money, both the narrator and Mini forget about him. Eight years later, released from jail, the Kabuliwallah returns on Mini's wedding day. Neither she nor the Kabuliwallah's own child, a thousand miles away in Afghanistan, is as the peddler remembers. The narrator feels compassion for what both he and the Kabuliwallah have lost, the precious youth of their daughters.

 For summaries in languages other than English, see Unit 3 Teaching Resources Book, pp. 256–261.

Vocabulary

Etymology Matching Game Have students write each vocabulary word on a separate card. Then, have them write each word's etymology on a separate card. Instruct student pairs to scramble the cards and place them face down on a desk or table. Students can take turns trying to match words to their etymologies.

 For additional vocabulary practice, see Unit 3 Teaching Resources Book, p. 264

Literature and Reading Preview

Connect to the Story

Have you ever judged another person based on superficial reasons, such as appearance? Freewrite about that judgment and any personal biases that may have influenced you.

Build Background

The Hindi word *wallah* means "a person connected with a particular thing or function." A *Kabuliwallah* is a peddler from Kabul, the capital of Afghanistan. These peddlers, who sold fruits, nuts, and other merchandise door-to-door, were common in Calcutta in the late 1800s. Because they were outsiders, Kabuliwallahs were often feared or looked down upon. They were rarely seen in the company of people from the upper castes.

Set Purposes for Reading

Big Idea **A Place in Society**

As you read, ask yourself, How does the caste system define the lives of these characters and influence their behavior?

Literary Element **Characterization**

The methods an author uses to reveal the personality of a character are called **characterization**. In **direct characterization**, the author makes explicit statements about characters. In **indirect characterization**, the author reveals characters through their thoughts and actions, and through what other characters think about them. As you read, ask yourself, How does Tagore use these methods to reveal the personalities of his characters?

Reading Strategy **Analyze Cultural Context**

You can better understand the actions and motivations of literary characters if you **analyze the cultural context** in which they live. As you read, ask yourself, What does the characters' society value, and how does it influence interpersonal relationships?

....

Tip: **Track Cultural Effects** Construct a chart like the following to show the effects that culture has on the events in the story.

608 UNIT 3 SOUTH CENTRAL ASIA

Learning Objectives

For pages 607–617

In studying this text, you will focus on the following objectives:

Literary Study: Analyzing characterization.

Reading: Analyzing cultural context.

Vocabulary

demur (di mur′) *n.* a hesitation or an objection; p. 611 *He made no demur to the extravagant compliment but accepted it graciously.*

formidable (fôr′mi də bəl) *adj.* tending to inspire awe, wonder, or alarm; p. 612 *Todd faced his formidable wrestling opponent calmly.*

arid (ar′id) *adj.* excessively dry; p. 612 *During the Dust Bowl of the 1930s, huge areas of arid farmland blew away in great dust storms.*

fettered (fe′tərd) *adj.* chained; tied up; p. 613 *The suspect, fettered to a table leg, offered no further resistance to the police officers.*

sordid (sôr′did) *adj.* dirty; squalid; wretched; p. 614 *Dickens's novel* Oliver Twist *is set among the sordid slums of London, England.*

....

Tip: **Word Origins** Word origins, or etymologies, are the history and development of words. The origins for the word *sordid* are listed in its dictionary entry: [L *sordidus,* fr. *sordes* dirt], which means the origin of *sordid* is a Latin word (L) that came from (fr) the Latin word for *dirt.*

Reading Practice

Author's Purpose Explain to students that authors write for a purpose. For example, an author may write a story to inform, to explain, to entertain, or to persuade. Often, writers have multiple purposes for writing. Tell students that background knowledge about a writer can often help the reader discover the writer's purpose for writing.

Discuss with students Rabindranath Tagore's beliefs, as described on the Before You Read pages. **Ask:** What does Tagore's giving up his knighthood tell you about his beliefs and personality? (*Tagore stood up for what he believed in. He was compassionate and concerned with the suffering of others, especially Indians under British rule.*)

Encourage students to remember Tagore's actions while they read "The Kabuliwallah," and have them consider his purpose for writing the story.

The Kabuliwallah

Rabindranath Tagore
Translated by Sister Nivedita

Ramchandra Sabjiwala, 1983.
Shanti Panchal. Watercolour on
paper. Private collection.

View the Art

Contemporary Indian artist Shanti Panchal merges traditional Indian and Hindu figure styles with Western coloring and line, as seen in this heavily worked watercolor from 1983. Isolated figures, reserved emotions, and cultural themes characterize Panchal's work and encourage viewers to question their own place in the wider community. **Ask:** How might the unification of Western and Eastern painting styles in Panchal's work reflect modern India? (*Students may say that the combination of styles in Panchal's work reflect India's quest for modernization and its growing connection to the wider world.*)

Readability Scores

Dale-Chall: 7.4
DRP: 58
Lexile: 840

Learning Objectives
Identifying etymology. (TE)
Analyzing art. (TE)

Approaching Level

DIFFERENTIATED INSTRUCTION

Word Choice Tell students that a writer's word choice may provide clues about characters. Ask the following questions to help students understand how word choice reveals information about characters. **Ask:** In the first paragraph, what words does the narrator and his wife use to describe Mini's constant talking? (chattering *and* prattle)

Ask: How do the connotation of these words differ? (You may need to define connotation.) (*Students may say that* chattering *has a happy, cheerful connotation, and* prattle *has a negative, annoying connotation.*) **Ask:** What does this difference tell you about the narrator's opinion and his wife's opinion of Mini's talking? (*The narrator enjoys his daughter's chattiness and the mother does not.*)

Advanced Learners/Pre-AP

DIFFERENTIATED INSTRUCTION

Research In this story, students will learn about one man's relationship with his daughter; however, the status of girls in India, as well as other cultures, has a troubled history. Students can research how the lives of Indian girls during the time of the story differ from the lives of Indian girls today.

Teach

Literary Element 1

Characterization **Answer:**
They reveal that she loves talking and is rarely quiet. The narrator may characterize her so early because her talkativeness may play a role in the story's events.
[APPROACHING] Have approaching students reread the opening paragraph. Point out that the narrator describes Mini's actions; readers learn about her through indirect characterization.

Big Idea 2

A Place in Society
Answer: *The phrase "of his people" suggests that his clothing and turban are different from the clothes worn by natives of the area. His clothes are soiled, suggesting his poor living conditions away from home, and his wares establish him as an itinerant peddler. He is a stranger and doesn't really have an accepted place in this society.*

Political History ☆

The Frontier The area now known as the North West Frontier Province holds the Khyber Pass, the easiest route from Afghanistan to the Indian subcontinent. Sikhs controlled the area in the early 1800s, and then the British annexed the area to India in the mid-1800s. In 1947, the North West Frontier Province joined Pakistan.

Interactive Read and Write
Other options for teaching this selection can be found in Interactive Read and Write for On-Level Learners, pp. 135–148.

610

My five years' old daughter Mini cannot live without chattering. I really believe that in all her life she has not wasted a minute in silence. Her mother is often vexed at this, and would stop her prattle, but I would not. To see Mini quiet is unnatural, and I cannot bear it long. And so my own talk with her is always lively.

One morning, for instance, when I was in the midst of the seventeenth chapter of my new novel, my little Mini stole into the room, and putting her hand into mine, said: "Father! Ramdayal the door-keeper calls a crow a krow! He doesn't know anything, does he?"

Before I could explain to her the differences of language in this world, she was embarked on the full tide of another subject. "What do you think, Father? Bhola says there is an elephant in the clouds, blowing water out of his trunk, and that is why it rains!"

And then, darting off anew, while I sat still making ready some reply to this last saying, "Father! what relation is Mother to you?"

"My dear little sister in the law!" I murmured involuntarily to myself, but with a grave face contrived to answer: "Go and play with Bhola, Mini! I am busy!"

The window of my room overlooks the road. The child had seated herself at my feet near my table, and was playing softly, drumming on her knees. I was hard at work on my seventeenth chapter, where Protrap Singh, the hero, had just caught Kanchanlata, the heroine, in his arms, and was about to escape with her by the third story window of the castle, when all of a sudden Mini left her play, and ran to the window, crying, "A Kabuliwallah! a Kabuliwallah!"

Sure enough in the street below was a Kabuliwallah, passing slowly along. He wore the loose soiled clothing of his people, with a tall turban; there was a bag on his back, and he carried boxes of grapes in his hand.

I cannot tell what were my daughter's feelings at the sight of this man, but she began to call him loudly. "Ah!" I thought, "he will come in, and my seventeenth chapter will never be finished!" At which exact moment the Kabuliwallah turned, and looked up at the child. When she saw this, overcome by terror, she fled to her mother's protection, and disappeared. She had a blind belief that inside the bag, which the big man carried, there were perhaps two or three other children like herself. The peddler meanwhile entered my doorway, and greeted me with a smiling face.

So precarious was the position of my hero and my heroine, that my first impulse was to stop and buy something, since the man had been called. I made some small purchases, and a conversation began about Abdurrahman, the Russians, the English, and the Frontier Policy. ☆

As he was about to leave, he asked: "And where is the little girl, sir?"

And I, thinking that Mini must get rid of her false fear, had her brought out.

She stood by my chair, and looked at the Kabuliwallah and his bag. He offered her nuts and raisins, but she would not be tempted, and only clung the closer to me, with all her doubts increased.

This was their first meeting.

One morning, however, not many days later, as I was leaving the house, I was startled to find Mini, seated on a bench near

---

1 **Characterization** *What do these opening lines reveal about Mini? Why might the narrator characterize her so early in the story?*

610 UNIT 3 SOUTH CENTRAL ASIA

A Place in Society *What does this description tell you about the Kabuliwallah and his place in society?* **2**

Literary Element Practice

Analyze Motivation Motivation is the reason or reasons behind a character's actions. Sometimes a character's motivation is directly stated; other times, readers have to infer a character's motivation from story details. **Ask:** Why does the narrator tell Mini to go play at the beginning of the story? (*He wants to work on his novel.*)

Organize students into groups, and have them discuss the narrator's motivations for his interactions with the Kabuliwallah. Have them consider how the narrator's motivation changes. (*Students may suggest that the narrator wants to quickly get rid of the Kabuliwallah so he can continue writing. Later, however, the narrator wants the Kabuliwallah to stay so that Mini will realize the Kabuliwallah is not a threat.*)

the door, laughing and talking, with the great Kabuliwallah at her feet. In all her life, it appeared, my small daughter had never found so patient a listener, save her father. And already the corner of her little *sari* was stuffed with almonds and raisins, the gift of her visitor. "Why did you give her those?" I said, and taking out an eight-anna bit,[1] I handed it to him. The man accepted the money without **demur**, and slipped it into his pocket.

Visual Vocabulary
A *sari* is a garment worn by women of southern Asia. It is made from several yards of lightweight cloth draped so that one end forms a skirt and the other a shoulder or head covering.

Alas, on my return an hour later, I found the unfortunate coin had made twice its own worth of trouble! For the Kabuliwallah had given it to Mini, and her mother catching sight of the bright round object, had pounced on the child with: "Where did you get that eight-anna bit?"

"The Kabuliwallah gave it to me," said Mini cheerfully.

"The Kabuliwallah gave it you!" cried her mother much shocked. "Oh, Mini! how could you take it from him?"

I, entering at the moment, saved her from impending disaster, and proceeded to make my own inquiries.

It was not the first or second time, I found, that the two had met. The Kabuliwallah had overcome the child's first terror by a judicious bribery of nuts and almonds, and

the two were now great friends.

They had many quaint jokes, which afforded them much amusement. Seated in front of him, looking down on his gigantic frame in all her tiny dignity, Mini would ripple her face with laughter, and begin: "O Kabuliwallah, Kabuliwallah, what have you got in your bag?"

And he would reply, in the nasal accents of the mountaineer: "An elephant!" Not much cause for merriment, perhaps; but how they both enjoyed the witticism! And for me, this child's talk with a grown-up man had always in it something strangely fascinating.

Then the Kabuliwallah, not to be behindhand, would take his turn: "Well, little one, and when are you going to the father-in-law's house?"[2]

Now most small Bengali maidens have heard long ago about the father-in-law's house; but we, being a little new-fangled, had kept these things from our child, and Mini at this question must have been a trifle bewildered. But she would not show it, and with ready tact replied: "Are *you* going there?"

Amongst men of the Kabuliwallah's class, however, it is well known that the words *father-in-law's house* have a double meaning. It is a euphemism for *jail*, the place where we are well cared for, at no expense to ourselves. In this sense would the sturdy peddler take my daughter's question. "Ah," he would say, shaking his fist at an invisible policeman, "I will thrash my father-in-law!" Hearing this, and picturing the poor discomfited relative, Mini would

---

1. An *eight-anna bit* is a small coin.

Vocabulary

demur (di mur′) *n.* a hesitation or an objection

---

2. Traditionally, when women in India marry, they go to live with their husband's family, or to their *father-in-law's house.*

Analyze Cultural Context *Why do you think the narrator and his wife chose not to tell Mini about the father-in-law's house?*

RABINDRANATH TAGORE **611**

Teach

Literary Element 3

Characterization Ask: How is Mini characterized as almost superior to the Kabuliwallah? *(She is seated so that she may look down at him. The narrator says that she has a "tiny dignity.")*

Reading Strategy 4

Analyze Cultural Context
Answer: *The narrator and his wife consider themselves modern and may be influenced by European ideas, which were common among higher-caste Indians under British rule. Based on the narrator's behavior toward the Kabuliwallah, the narrator does not always follow local custom.*

For additional practice using the reading skill or strategy, see Unit 3 Teaching Resources Book, p. 263.

Learning Objectives
Analyzing cultural context. (SE)
Analyzing characterization. (TE)
Analyzing motivation. (TE)

English Learners

DIFFERENTIATED INSTRUCTION

Advanced English language learners may have some difficulty with the syntax and word choice of this selection. Write the following on the board, underlining as indicated: *She was underlined on the full tide of another subject. The Kabuliwallah had overcome the child's first terror by a judicious bribe of nuts and almonds.*

To help students understand the underlined phrases, **ask** them the following questions: How is Mini's conversation like a ship sailing out on full tide? *(It moves nonstop.)* How does the judicious, or practical, bribery succeed? *(It overcomes the child's terror.)* Explain that the first step to understanding the author in these cases is to look up unknown words, such as *embarked* or

judicious.

Organize students into small groups, and have them find other instances of difficult syntax in the selection. Group members should take turns looking up unknown words in a dictionary. As a member looks up a word, the rest of the group should investigate nearby words or phrases that may help them understand the author's meaning.

Teach

Literary Element   1

Characterization   Answer:
He characterizes himself as a dreamer. Based on his description, his "vegetable existence" leads him to be highly imaginative, as both a daydreamer and a writer of romantic fiction (see his comments about the hero Protrap Singh and heroine Kanchanlata).

Big Idea   2

A Place in Society   Ask:
How do the narrator's thoughts about the Kabuliwallah's life reveal the rigidity of the caste system? *(By imagining living life in the rugged mountains, the narrator almost wishes to be part of the Kabuliwallah's caste. The Kabuliwallah's life style is one that the narrator will never be able to experience.)*

[APPROACHING] Students may have difficulty understanding the narrator's envy. **Ask:** What does the narrator think is good about the Kabuliwallah's life? *(The Kabuliwallah lives freely in nature and does not have to deal with the day-to-day annoyances of city life.)*

Cultural History ☆

Malaria Malaria is a sometimes fatal disease caused by a parasite transmitted through mosquito bites. This disease is common in Central America, Southeast Asia, and sub-Saharan Africa.

go off into peals of laughter, in which her **formidable** friend would join.

These were autumn mornings, the very time of year when kings of old went forth to conquest; and I, never stirring from my little corner in Calcutta, would let my mind wander over the whole world. At the very name of another country, my heart would go out to it, and at the sight of a foreigner in the streets, I would fall to weaving a network of dreams,—the mountains, the glens, and the forests of his distant home, with his cottage in its setting, and the free and independent life of far-away wilds. Perhaps the scenes of travel conjure themselves up before me, and pass and repass in my imagination all the more vividly, because I lead such a vegetable existence, that a call to travel would fall upon me like a thunderbolt. In the presence of this Kabuliwallah, I was immediately transported to the foot of **arid** mountain peaks, with narrow little defiles twisting in and out amongst their towering heights. I could see the string of camels bearing the merchandise, and the company of turbaned merchants, carrying some of their queer old firearms, and some of their spears, journeying downward towards the plains. I could see—but at some such point Mini's mother would intervene, imploring me to "beware of that man."

Mini's mother is unfortunately a very timid lady. Whenever she hears a noise in the street, or sees people coming towards the house, she always jumps to the conclusion that they are either thieves, or

1 Characterization *How does the narrator characterize himself in this passage?*

Vocabulary

formidable (fôr′mi də bəl) *adj.* tending to inspire awe, wonder, or alarm

arid (ar′id) *adj.* excessively dry

drunkards, or snakes, or tigers, or malaria or ☆ cockroaches, or caterpillars, or an English sailor. Even after all these years of experience, she is not able to overcome her terror. So she was full of doubts about the Kabuliwallah, and used to beg me to keep a watchful eye on him.

I tried to laugh her fear gently away, but then she would turn round on me seriously, and ask me solemn questions.

Were children never kidnapped?

Was it, then, not true that there was slavery in Kabul?

Was it so very absurd that this big man should be able to carry off a tiny child?

I urged that, though not impossible, it was highly improbable. But this was not enough, and her dread persisted. As it was indefinite, however, it did not seem right to forbid the man the house, and the intimacy went on unchecked.

Once a year in the middle of January Rahmun, the Kabuliwallah, was in the habit of returning to his country, and as the time approached he would be very busy, going from house to house collecting his debts. This year, however, he could always find time to come and see Mini. It would have seemed to an outsider that there was some conspiracy between the two, for when he could not come in the morning, he would appear in the evening.

Even to me it was a little startling now and then, in the corner of a dark room, suddenly to surprise this tall, loose-garmented, much bebagged[3] man; but when Mini would run in smiling, with her, "O! Kabuliwallah! Kabuliwallah!" and the two friends, so far apart in age, would subside into their old laughter and their old jokes, I felt reassured.

One morning, a few days before he had

---

3. A *bebagged man* is one who is carrying many bags.

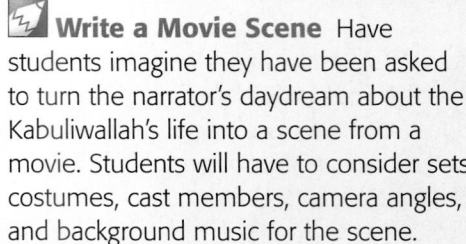

Writing Practice

⚡ **Write a Movie Scene** Have students imagine they have been asked to turn the narrator's daydream about the Kabuliwallah's life into a scene from a movie. Students will have to consider sets, costumes, cast members, camera angles, and background music for the scene.

To get students started, **ask:** Where is the narrator when he imagines the Kabuliwallah's life? What does the Kabuliwallah's native land look like? What props will each character need? What music best portrays the mood of the daydream?

Allow students enough time to complete their scenes. After they have finished, ask volunteers to share their scenes with the class.

made up his mind to go, I was correcting my proof sheets in my study. It was chilly weather. Through the window the rays of the sun touched my feet, and the slight warmth was very welcome. It was almost eight o'clock, and the early pedestrians were returning home, with their heads covered. All at once, I heard an uproar in the street, and, looking out, saw Rahmun being led away bound between two policemen, and behind them a crowd of curious boys. There were blood-stains on the clothes of the Kabuliwallah, and one of the policemen carried a knife. Hurrying out, I stopped them, and enquired what it all meant. Partly from one, partly from another, I gathered that a certain neighbor had owed the peddler something for a Rampuri shawl,[4] but had falsely denied having bought it, and that in the course of the quarrel, Rahmun had struck him. Now in the heat of his excitement, the prisoner began calling his enemy all sorts of names, when suddenly in a verandah of my house

Visual Vocabulary
A *verandah* is a porch, a balcony, or a roofed open area used for sitting outdoors.

appeared my little Mini, with her usual exclamation: "O Kabuliwallah! Kabuliwallah!" Rahmun's face lighted up as he turned to her. He had no bag under his arm today, so she could not discuss the elephant with him. She at once therefore proceeded to the next question: "Are you going to the father-in-law's

4. A *Rampuri shawl* is a shawl from the city of Rampur in northern India.

3 Analyze Cultural Context *Based on this passage, how might residents of Calcutta have treated people like the Kabuliwallah? Why do you think they behaved this way?*

house?" Rahmun laughed and said: "Just where I am going, little one!" Then seeing that the reply did not amuse the child, he held up his **fettered** hands. "Ah," he said, "I would have thrashed that old father-in-law, but my hands are bound!"

On a charge of murderous assault, Rahmun was sentenced to some years' imprisonment.

Time passed away, and he was not remembered. The accustomed work in the accustomed place was ours, and the thought of the once-free mountaineer spending his years in prison seldom or never occurred to us. Even my light-hearted Mini, I am ashamed to say, forgot her old friend. New companions filled her life. As she grew older, she spent more of her time with girls. So much time indeed did she spend with them that she came no more, as she used to do, to her father's room. I was scarcely on speaking terms with her.

Years had passed away. It was once more autumn and we had made arrangements for our Mini's marriage. It was to take place during the Puja Holidays.[5] With Durga returning to Kailas,[6] the light of our home also was to depart to her husband's house, and leave her father's in the shadow.

The morning was bright. After the rains,

---

5. *Puja* (pōō´jä) *Holidays* are Hindu rites or religious festivals.
6. *With Durga returning to Kailas* refers to the goddess Durga returning to Mount Kailas in the Himalayas, where her husband, the god Shiva, lives. Shiva is one of the most important gods in the Hindu pantheon.

A Place in Society *Why do you think the Kabuliwallah was "not remembered" by the narrator's household during his years in prison?* **5**

Vocabulary

fettered (fe´ tərd) *adj.* chained; tied up

English Learners

DIFFERENTIATED INSTRUCTION

Intermediate Explain to students that the word *companions* comes from the same family as the word *company*. When students come across an unfamiliar word, they can think of other words from the word's family. Thinking of other words in the same family can help students discover the meaning of unfamiliar words. Tell students to find other words in the selection that come from the same family.

Advanced Learners/Pre-AP

DIFFERENTIATED INSTRUCTION

Research Have students research the wedding rituals for Hindus and other social groups from south central Asia. Students should investigate whether the families arrange the marriages, how the wedding date is set, where weddings take place, and what is the ritual attire. Ask students to write a short essay comparing and contrasting the ceremonies of two religions or cultures.

Teach

Reading Strategy **3**

Analyze Cultural Context
Answer: *Residents of Calcutta might have treated such people scornfully and unfairly. Students' explanations will vary, but they may note that people often try to take advantage of those they feel are beneath them.*

Literary Element **4**

Characterization **Ask:** Mini sees the Kabuliwallah as he is being arrested. What does the Kabuliwallah's reaction reveal about him? *(Students may say that the Kabuliwallah is more worried for Mini than himself.)*

Big Idea **5**

A Place in Society
Answer: *Possible response: The Kabuliwallah was only an occasional visitor and a traveling peddler, not a close friend or a family member.*

Cultural History

Wedding Rituals Weddings can be rather opulent in Hindu society; however, some aspects of the ceremony are the same no matter how much money is spent. On the wedding day, the groom is welcomed as a guest at the bride's house. There, the new couple holds hands while they take seven steps around a ritual fire before going together to their new home.

Learning Objectives
Analyzing cultural context. (SE)
Analyzing characterization. (SE)
Writing a movie scene. (TE)

Teach

Reading Strategy 1

Analyze Cultural Context
Ask: What does the narrator's reaction to the Kabuliwallah's crime reveal about the values of their culture? *(The narrator is upset by the Kabuliwallah's crime; one can assume that the narrator's culture values nonviolence.)*

Literary Element 2

Characterization Answer:
He is, in his own way, also a doting father. Although he does not make much money peddling, he nevertheless wants to be generous to Mini, who reminds him of his own daughter.

there was a sense of ablution[7] in the air, and the sun-rays looked like pure gold. So bright were they that they gave a beautiful radiance even to the **sordid** brick walls of our Calcutta lanes. Since early dawn today the wedding-pipes had been sounding, and at each beat my own heart throbbed. The wail of the tune, Bhairavi, seemed to intensify my pain at the approaching separation. My Mini was to be married tonight.

From early morning noise and bustle had pervaded the house. In the courtyard the canopy had to be slung on its bamboo poles; the chandeliers with their tinkling sound must be hung in each room and verandah. There was no end of hurry and excitement. I was sitting in my study, looking through the accounts, when someone entered, saluting respectfully, and stood before me. It was Rahmun the Kabuliwallah. At first I did not recognize him. He had no bag, nor the long hair, nor the same vigor that he used to have. But he smiled, and I knew him again.

"When did you come, Rahmun?" I asked him.

"Last evening," he said, "I was released from jail."

The words struck harsh upon my ears. I had never before talked with one who had wounded his fellow, and my heart shrank within itself, when I realized this, for I felt that the day would have been better-omened had he not turned up.

"There are ceremonies going on," I said, "and I am busy. Could you perhaps come another day?"

At once he turned to go; but as he reached the door he hesitated, and said: "May I not see the little one, sir, for a moment?" It was his belief that Mini was

still the same. He had pictured her running to him as she used, calling "O Kabuli-wallah! Kabuliwallah!" He had imagined too that they would laugh and talk together, just as of old. In fact, in memory of former days he had brought, carefully wrapped up in paper, a few almonds and raisins and grapes, obtained somehow from a country-man, for his own little fund was dispersed.

I said again: "There is a ceremony in the house, and you will not be able to see anyone today."

The man's face fell. He looked wistfully at me for a moment, said "Good morning," and went out.

I felt a little sorry, and would have called him back, but I found he was returning of his own accord. He came close up to me holding out his offerings and said: "I brought these few things, sir, for the little one. Will you give them to her?"

I took them and was going to pay him, but he caught my hand and said: "You are very kind, sir! Keep me in your recollection. Do not offer me money!—You have a little girl, I too have one like her in my own home. I think of her, and bring fruits to your child, not to make a profit for myself."

Saying this, he put his hand inside his big loose robe, and brought out a small and dirty piece of paper. With great care he unfolded this, and smoothed it out with both hands on my table. It bore the impression of a little hand. Not a photograph. Not a drawing. The impression of an ink-smeared hand laid flat on the paper. This touch of his own little daughter had been always on his heart, as he had come year after year to Calcutta, to sell his wares in the streets.

Tears came to my eyes. I forgot that he was a poor Kabuli fruit-seller, while I was—

---

7. *Ablution* (əblōō´shən) **means "cleansing."**

Vocabulary

sordid (sôr´did) *adj.* dirty; squalid; wretched

Characterization *What does this revelation add to your understanding of the Kabuliwallah's character?* **2**

Reading Practice

Compare and Contrast Characters
One type of organizer that is perfect for comparing and contrasting characters is a Venn diagram. A Venn diagram consists of intersecting circles that show how ideas, objects, characters, or events are different and how they are alike.

Have students list the narrator's and the Kabuliwallah's character traits. Then, have students draw a Venn diagram and enter the distinctive traits for each character in the outer portions of the circles. Students should then note what the two men have in common in the intersecting area. Use students' diagrams to spur discussion about a comparison of the two men.

but no, what was I more than he? He also was a father.

That impression of the hand of his little *Pārbati*[8] in her distant mountain home reminded me of my own little Mini.

I sent for Mini immediately from the inner apartment. Many difficulties were raised, but I would not listen. Clad in the red silk of her wedding-day, with the sandal paste on her forehead, and adorned as a young bride, Mini came, and stood bashfully before me.

The Kabuliwallah looked a little staggered at the apparition. He could not revive their old friendship. At last he smiled and said: "Little one, are you going to your father-in-law's house?"

But Mini now understood the meaning of the word "father-in-law," and she could not reply to him as of old. She flushed up at the question, and stood before him with her bride-like face turned down.

I remembered the day when the Kabuliwallah and my Mini had first met, and I felt sad. When she had gone, Rahmun heaved a deep sigh, and sat down on the floor. The idea had suddenly come to him that his daughter too must have grown in this long time, and that he would have to make friends with her anew. Assuredly he would not find her, as he used to know her. And besides, what might not have happened to her in these eight years?

The marriage-pipes sounded, and the mild autumn sun streamed round us. But Rahmun sat in the little Calcutta lane,

and saw before him the barren mountains of Afghanistan.

I took out a bank-note, and gave it to him, saying: "Go back to your own daughter, Rahmun, in your own country, and may the happiness of your meeting bring good fortune to my child!"

Having made this present, I had to curtail some of the festivities. I could not have the electric lights I had intended, nor the military band, and the ladies of the house were despondent at it. But to me the wedding feast was all the brighter for the thought that in a distant land a long-lost father met again with his only child. ❧

First Marriage, 1988. Shanti Panchal. Watercolor on paper. Bradford Art Galleries and Museums, West Yorkshire, UK.

 View the Art Shanti Panchal is well known for his multihued, watercolor images of Indian life. How do the two figures in the foreground, or front, of the painting reflect Mini and the narrator and their reactions to the Kabuliwallah at the end of the story? ★

RABINDRANATH TAGORE **615**

8. *Pārbati* (par bä′ tē) is another name for the goddess Durga in a reincarnated form; *her distant mountain home* refers to Mount Kailas.

3 Analyze Cultural Context *What does this description reveal about Indian marriage customs? What might be the significance of Mini's appearance for the Kabuliwallah?*

4 Characterization *How has Mini changed since she was a small girl? To what do you attribute this change?*

Advanced Learners/Pre-AP

DIFFERENTIATED INSTRUCTION

Using Fragments for Emphasis
Although writing a sentence fragment in an assignment will usually result in a bad mark, understanding how to use a fragment can give strength to fiction writing. Writers often use fragments to create suspense, to show a character's emotion, or to reveal a character's personality.

Point out the author's use of fragments in this selection, especially in the description of the handprint that the Kabuliwallah carries. Then, have students rewrite one of the paragraphs in the selection using fragments for emphasis.

Teach

Reading Strategy | 3

Analyze Cultural Context
Answer: *It reveals that Indian brides wear bright colors and have their faces marked with paste. Her appearance might be significant for the Kabuliwallah because not only has she grown up, but her outfit shows that she is about to become a wife in a different household—likewise, his daughter may now be married.*

Literary Element | 4

Characterization Answer:
She has lost her childlike spontaneity and enthusiasm, and now behaves like a modest young woman. Some of this is due to her maturity, but much of it comes from her being socialized and taught the proper behavior for an Indian woman of her caste.

View the Art ★

Answer: *Answers will vary. Students may note that the male figure seems confident and determined, much like the narrator is when he demands Mini greet the Kabuliwallah. They may also note that the female figure seems shy, yet resigned, as Mini does when she speaks with Rahmun.*

Award-winning Shanti Panchal was born in India and went to art school in Bombay and London. He achieves his vibrant effect by layering colors in his paintings.

Learning Objectives
Analyzing characterization. (SE)
Analyzing cultural context (SE)
Comparing and contrasting characters (TE)

After You Read

Assess

1. Answers will vary.

2. (a) One day Mini calls the Kabuliwallah from the window of her house, but then she becomes shy and runs away from him. He gradually gains her friendship by giving her gifts of fruits and nuts, talking and joking with her, and listening to her patiently. (b) Their relationship is unusual because of the difference in their ages and social classes.

3. (a) She is suspicious and fearful and wants the relationship to end. (b) The narrator is tolerant of the Kabuliwallah and seems amused by the relationship.

4. (a) He reveals that Mini reminds him of his own daughter. (b) The narrator realizes that the Kabuliwallah is also a father and that he, the narrator, is not superior to him.

5. Possible answers: (1) Despite differences in social class and culture, all people have the same basic feelings. (2) Although people are aware of the passage of time, the changes it brings often surprise them.

6. Some students may say the central character is the Kabuliwallah because the plot revolves around him and the story takes its title from him. Others may say the narrator is the central character because he is the one who changes and learns from his experience.

7. In befriending the Kabuliwallah, Mini ignores her place in society. The Kabuliwallah knows his place but defies it because Mini charms him. By the day of her wedding, Mini has become thoroughly socialized and cannot bring herself to talk to the Kabuliwallah or look him in the

616

After You Read

Respond and Think Critically

Respond and Interpret

1. Which character in this story did you find most appealing? Why?

2. (a) How does the friendship between the Kabuliwallah and Mini develop? (b) What is unusual about their friendship?

3. (a) How does Mini's mother react to the relationship between Mini and the Kabuliwallah? Why? (b) How does the narrator's reaction to the Kabuliwallah differ from that of his wife?

4. (a) After his return, what does the Kabuliwallah reveal to the narrator about his interest in Mini? (b) Why does the narrator send for his daughter after he first refused to do so?

Analyze and Evaluate

5. The **theme** of a story is its message about life. Stories often have more than one theme. What are two **themes** of "The Kabuliwallah"?

6. Who do you think is the central character in this story, the Kabuliwallah or the narrator? Explain.

Connect

7.  **Big Idea** **A Place in Society** How do their respective places in society influence the behavior of Mini and the Kabuliwallah, both before and after his imprisonment?

8. **Connect to the Author** Tagore was known for his interest in human rights and social issues. Do you think these concerns influenced the themes and events in this story? Explain.

Daily Life & Culture

Indian Traditions

Calcutta (*Kalikata* in Bengali) is the third-largest city in India and was the British capital in India until 1912. The caste system flourished in Calcutta during the 1800s, the period in which "The Kabuliwallah" is set. This system helped determine a person's home, occupation, clothing, and acquaintances. People often entered arranged marriages as teenagers. It was a tradition for a bride to live with her husband's parents, so several generations of a family often lived together in a household.

Group Activity Discuss the following questions with your classmates.

1. Why might people live their lives according to strict rules, such as a caste system?

2. What are potential advantages and disadvantages of living with one's extended family?

Port of the Hooghly River, ca. 1870-1880. Samuel Bourne. Calcutta, India.

---

eye. The Kabuliwallah again defies his place, hoping that their earlier friendship will be remembered.

8. Students should note that these social concerns are likely the reason for Tagore's sympathetic portrayal of the Kabuliwallah and his relationship to Mini.

Daily Life & Culture

1. Possible answer: Many people have

no choice because the rules are an integral part of their society or are dictated by those in political control. Also, those who benefit from the rules likely want to keep them in place.

2. Possible answers: Advantages: One is never alone and has love, company, and support from family members. Disadvantages: One never has privacy and must constantly defer to older family members.

Literary Element Characterization

ACT Skills Practice

1. On page 611, Mini and the Kabuliwallah have an exchange in which Mini asks him "what have you got in your bag?" His response indicates that, at this point, their relationship is:

   A. vulnerable and untrustworthy.

   B. friendly and jovial.

   C. separated by caste.

   D. constantly guarded by Mini's mother.

2. On page 612, the paragraph beginning "These were autumn mornings, the very time of year when kings of old went forth to conquest" reveals that the narrator is:

   F. suspicious of foreigners.

   G. imaginative.

   H. reluctant to accept reality.

   J. longing to travel.

Review: Irony

As you learned on page 291, **irony** is a discrepancy between appearance and reality. **Situational irony** exists when an outcome is the opposite of expectations. **Verbal irony** occurs when the meaning of a statement is the opposite of what is said.

Partner Activity With a partner, discuss the following question: How does the expression "going to the father-in-law's house" become a source of irony in this story? Is it verbal irony, situational irony, or both? Explain.

LOG ON **Literature** Online

Selection Resources For Selection Quizzes, eFlash-cards, and Reading-Writing Connection activities, go to glencoe.com and enter QuickPass code GLW6053u3.

Reading Strategy Analyze Cultural Context

When you **analyze cultural context,** you think about how the society in which the characters live influences their relationships and interactions. Refer to the chart you created on page 608 and answer the questions below.

1. What might the narrator's references to Hindu holidays and gods reveal about him?

2. In your opinion, is the caste system purely negative or are there positive aspects to it? Explain.

Vocabulary Practice

Practice with Word Origins Create a word web, like the one below, for each vocabulary word from the story. Use a dictionary for help.

demur formidable arid fettered sordid

EXAMPLE:

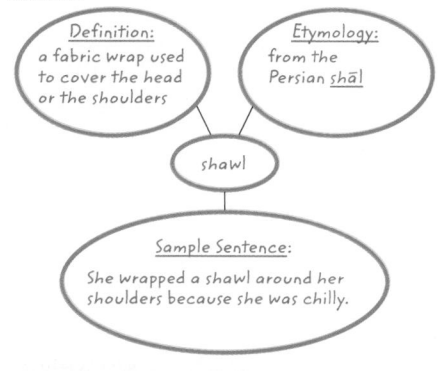

Academic Vocabulary

In many **instances,** *the Kabuliwallah shows his understanding of children.*

Instance is an academic word. Other words that are similar in meaning are *situation, occasion,* or *case.* To further explore the meaning of *instance,* answer this question: What is an **instance** that made you laugh?

For more on academic vocabulary, see pages 36–37 and R83–R85.

RABINDRANATH TAGORE **617**

After You Read

Literary Element

1. **B** is the correct answer. **A, C,** and **D** are not exemplified in the exchange on page 611.

2. **G** is the correct answer. **F** is incorrect because the narrator trusts the Kabuliwallah in the beginning of the story. **H** is incorrect because the narrator accepts that he is in a separate caste from the Kabuliwallah. **J** is incorrect because this passage does not indicate the desire to travel.

Progress Check

Can students identify characterization?

If No → See Unit 3 Teaching Resources Book, p. 262.

Review: Irony

The expression "going to the father-in-law's house" is an example of verbal irony because it can refer to two different things—getting married and going to jail. Mini's marriage and the Kabuliwallah's imprisonment are ironic because these events make what was originally a shared joke a reality.

Reading Strategy

1. It reflects that he is a religious man whose beliefs are a part of everyday life. His easy references to the gods may reflect not only his own religious beliefs, but those of other Hindus as well.

2. Students may mention that the limitations prevent people from realizing their dreams or aspirations by forcing them into jobs and social roles; on the other hand, the limitations allow people to know their place and what is expected of them.

617

Vocabulary Practice

Sample sentences will vary.

Word: demur; Definition: hesitation or objection; Etymology: Latin *-de* + *morari,* "to linger." Word: formidable; Definition: tending to inspire awe or alarm; Etymology: Latin *formidabilis,* "causing fear." Word: arid; Definition: excessively dry; Etymology: Latin *arere,*

"to be dry." Word: fettered; Definition: chained, tied up; Etymology: OE *fot,* "foot." Word: sordid; Definition: dirty, squalid; Etymology: Latin *sordes,* "dirt."

Academic Vocabulary

Answers will vary.

After You Read

Assess

Respond Through Writing

Students' essays should

- compare two events that reflect how students' ideas or values changed over time
- connect specific ideas to generalizations about life
- reflect the revisions and suggestions made by a peer reviewer

A student who meets all of these criteria should receive the equivalent of a 4-point response.

A student who fully meets two or partially meets three of these criteria should receive the equivalent of a 3-point response.

A student who fully meets one or partially meets two of these criteria should receive the equivalent of a 2-point response.

A student who partially meets one of these criteria should receive the equivalent of a 1-point response.

Grammar Tip

Explain to students the differences between a hyphen (-), an en dash (–) and an em dash (—). A hyphen is most often used to connect two words together, such as a compound modifier (a worst-case scenario). An en dash is usually used with numbers, such as when writing a series of years (1999–2001). An em dash is used to create a long pause in a sentence.

 For grammar practice, see Unit 3 Teaching Resources Book, p. 266.

Respond Through Writing

Reflective Essay

Compare Events When Mini is a young girl, the Kabuliwallah and she share jokes about going to the father-in-law's house. On her wedding day, the Kabuliwallah tries to revive their old joke, but Mini no longer finds it funny. Compare two events in your life that reflect how an idea or a value you once had changed over time. As you write, use narration, exposition, and description to explore this shift.

Understand the Task When you **reflect,** you look back at a specific experience to better understand its larger meaning.

Prewrite To choose two events that reflect how your perceptions changed, review old journal entries, flip through photo albums, or talk to friends. Create a Venn diagram like the one below to see how you can use an event from "The Kabuliwallah" as a springboard to craft your own reflection.

Mini getting ready to leave home after her marriage

- looking forward to independence
- saying good-bye to old friends
- fear of meeting new people

leaving home for summer camp

Draft As you write your reflection, pay attention to your word choice, sentence structure, and tone. Your writing should connect the events and the ideas you discuss to broader generalizations about life; for example, you might draw on the idea that people often learn valuable lessons through a coming-of-age experience. Your writing should reflect the significance and the emotions of your experience.

Revise Be sure that you have drawn clear comparisons between the two events and your old and new perceptions. Trade papers with a partner and ask him or her if the connections you made between your ideas and a broader generalization about life are apparent in your writing.

Edit and Proofread Proofread your paper, correcting any errors in grammar, spelling, and punctuation. Use the Grammar Tip in the side column to help you use dashes.

Learning Objectives

In this assignment, you will focus on the following objectives:

Writing: Writing a reflective essay.

Grammar: Understanding dashes.

Grammar Tip

Em Dashes and En Dashes

Em dashes (—) can indicate an abrupt break or change in thought.

They got along like old friends—at least when they first met.

Em dashes can also be used to set off a parenthetical statement.

The Fourth of July party lasted for three hours—only one of which included fireworks—in the state park.

Remember that an em dash is different from an en dash (–), which indicates a range of numbers, including dates, times, pages, and so on. In this usage the dash means "through" or "to." For example:

The Vietnam War (1954–75)

Literary Element Practice

Setting The setting of a piece of literature can impact the story or message. By setting a vibrant scene, writers bring their readers into the action. Ask students to consider the settings of the scenes of "The Kabuliwallah" and how these settings influence the mood of the story.

Have students describe the time of year, the place, the sounds, and other identifying items for each scene of the selection. **Ask:** How does the setting influence the mood of each scene? *(Students may say that, for instance, the autumn light and the wail of the marriage pipes cast a somber mood on the interaction between the narrator and the Kabuliwallah.)*

Have students remember the effect of setting on the mood when they are writing their reflective essays. Setting a descriptive scene will help them bring their important moments to life.

Before You Read

Like the Sun

Meet **R. K. Narayan**
(1906–2001)

R. K. Narayan was born in the southern Indian city of Madras (now called Chennai) to a family of the Brahman caste, the highest-ranking social class in India. Although he loathed the English schools he was forced to attend, he learned to love the English language, and it eventually became his language of choice when writing. Narayan believed that English is "a very adaptable language . . . [that] can take on the tint of any country." He taught for a short time but eventually decided to become a writer, relying on newspaper and magazine writing to earn a living while he wrote his novels. He set many of his works in a fictional village called Malgudi, which was based upon Mysore, the village where he grew up.

A Favor from an Admirer At first, Narayan had a difficult time getting his writing published because there was little support at the time for Indian authors who wrote in English. He had little luck with publishers in India, and English publishers initially rebuffed him. Narayan gave the manuscript of his first novel to a friend who was studying at Oxford University in England, and his friend passed the manuscript along to acclaimed British novelist Graham Greene. Greene so admired Narayan's prose that he personally recommended it to publisher Hamish Hamilton, who published the novel, renamed *Swami and Friends*, in 1935. The book became a critical success. One review in the British press lauded the novel as "an entirely delightful story" that depicts life in an Indian school and provides a vivid glimpse into Indian life and culture.

> "*For human beings the greatest source of strength lies in each other's presence.*"
>
> —R. K. Narayan

Tragedy and Transcendence In 1939, Narayan's wife, Rajam, died of typhoid. Narayan sank into a period of profound depression and believed he would never write again. By caring for the couple's daughter, Narayan eventually recovered. His acclaimed, mostly autobiographical novel *The English Teacher*, published in 1945, describes this turning point in his life. Narayan went on to become one of the most respected fiction authors in India. His legacy includes an impressive group of novels and short story collections, essays, memoirs, and prose retellings of two Indian epics, the *Mahabharata* (see pages 563–573) and the *Ramayana* (see pages 582–593). His work for publications such as the *New Yorker* magazine and his unique brand of storytelling earned him an international audience.

 Literature Online

Author Search For more about R. K. Narayan, go to glencoe.com and enter QuickPass code GLW6053u3.

R. K. NARAYAN **619**

Before You Read

Focus

Bellringer Options

Selection Focus
Transparency 36

Daily Language
Transparencies 55

Or say: A famous saying from Benjamin Franklin is "Honesty is the best policy." **Ask:** How important is it that people always tell the truth? *(Students may say that honesty is always important.)*
Ask: Is there ever a time when honesty is not helpful? Explain. *(Answers may vary.)* Write students' answers on the board and discuss their opinions.

Selection Skills

Literary Elements
- Analogy (SE pp. 620–622, 624)

Like the Sun

Speaking/Listening/Viewing Skills
- Analyze Art (TE pp. 621, 623)

Reading Skills
- Activate Prior Knowledge (SE pp. 620–622, 624)

Vocabulary Skills
- Use Context Clues (SE p. 624; TE pp. 620, 623)

Writing Skills/Grammar
- Anecdote (SE p. 624)
- Commas in a Series (TE p. 622)

Before You Read

Focus

Summary

Sekhar, a teacher, vows to spend one day telling the complete truth. In the process, he insults his wife's cooking and his headmaster's musicianship. He finds that it is hard for people to look truth, as with the sun, straight in the face. Because of his honest words, his wife sulks, and the headmaster insists that Sekhar grade one hundred papers overnight. Still, Sekhar concludes that the luxury of telling the untempered truth is worth the punishment.

 For summaries in languages other than English, see Unit 3 Teaching Resources Book, pp. 269–274.

Vocabulary

Context Clues Have students write out the sample sentences in the Vocabulary Preview. Then, have students underline words in each sentence that relate to the vocabulary word's definition or work as either a synonym or an antonym to help the student determine the word's meaning.

 For additional vocabulary practice, see Unit 3 Teaching Resources Book, p. 277.

Readability Scores

Dale-Chall: 6.1
DRP: 55
Lexile: 640

Literature and Reading Preview

Connect to the Story

What reasons might someone have for withholding his or her true opinions or feelings from someone else? Discuss this question with a partner.

Build Background

Classical Indian music is generally arranged around a melody pattern called a *raga*. The word *raga* derives from a Sanskrit word meaning "color" or "passion." A raga is based on an established scale and set of notes, but the performer improvises by playing only certain notes or by emphasizing only certain segments of the scale. For example, the musician might choose notes based on the mood he or she hopes to create.

Set Purposes for Reading

Big Idea A Complex Heritage

As you read, ask yourself, Why might people sometimes prefer to hear white lies instead of sincere comments?

Literary Element Analogy

An **analogy** creates a comparison between two things that are otherwise dissimilar. An analogy can clarify an unfamiliar idea or help you understand a familiar concept in a new way. As you read "Like the Sun," ask yourself, What insights do the analogies in the story clarify?

Reading Strategy Activate Prior Knowledge

When you **activate prior knowledge,** you use information you already know and apply it to the literary work you are reading. As you read "Like the Sun," ask yourself, How do my experiences and the insights I have gained from them help me better understand this story?

Tip: Chart Predictions You can often use your prior knowledge to predict what will happen next in a story. As you read, record your predictions in a chart like the one below. When you finish the story, check the chart to see if your predictions were correct.

Background Information	Event	My Prediction
Sekhar decides to tell nothing but the truth for a whole day.	His wife asks him how he likes the breakfast she made.	

Learning Objectives

For pages 619–624

In studying this text, you will focus on the following objectives:

Literary Study: Analyzing analogy.

Reading: Activating prior knowledge.

Writing: Writing an anecdote.

Vocabulary

shirk (shurk) *v.* to evade or avoid one's duty; p. 621 *Todd's parents made it clear that he could no longer shirk his chores.*

stupefied (stōō′pə fīd) *adj.* stupid, groggy, or insensible; p. 623 *The stupefied audience waited for the end of the long, dull lecture.*

increment (ing′krə mənt) *n.* something gained or added in a series, usually at regular intervals; p. 623 *The scientist filled the beaker by increments and watched the chemical mixture change color.*

scrutinize (skrōōt′ən īz′) *v.* to examine with close attention to detail; p. 623 *She had to scrutinize his shirt to see the coffee stain.*

Tip: Context Clues You can often determine the meaning of a new word by examining other words in the same sentence. For example, in the sentence *The stupefied audience waited for the end of the long, dull lecture,* the words "long" and "dull" indicate that the audience may be groggy or *stupefied.*

Literary Element Practice

Similes Write the following sentences on the board: *He croaks like a dozen frogs. He is bellowing like a buffalo. Now he sounds like loose window shutters in a storm.* Have students discuss what the author is trying to say. Point out that the sentences are similes, meaning they use the word *like* or *as* to compare two different things.

Remind students that using similes to make comparisons is one way that writers help us understand an experience.

Make a chart on the board. Label the first column *POSITIVE* and the second column *NEGATIVE.* Invite students to share other similes from English that would help readers understand how badly—or how well—someone sings.

620

Like the Sun

R. K. Narayan

Body of Summer. Michael Rothenstein. Lithograph. Fry Art Gallery, Saffron Walden, Essex, UK.

Truth, Sekhar reflected, is like the sun. I suppose no human being can ever look it straight in the face without blinking or being dazed. He realized that, morning till night, the essence of human relationships consisted in tempering truth so that it might not shock. This day he set apart as a unique day—at least one day in the year we must give and take absolute Truth whatever may happen. Otherwise life is not worth living. The day ahead seemed to him full of possibilities. He told no one of his experiment. It was a quiet resolve, a secret pact between him and eternity.

The very first test came while his wife served him his morning meal. He showed hesitation over a tidbit, which she had thought was her culinary masterpiece. She asked, "Why, isn't it good?" At other times he would have said, considering her feelings in the matter, "I feel full-up, that's all." But today he said, "It isn't good. I'm unable to swallow it." He saw her wince and said to himself, Can't be helped. Truth is like the sun.

His next trial was in the common room[1] when one of his colleagues came up and said, "Did you hear of the death of so and so? Don't you think it a pity?" "No," Sekhar answered. "He was such a fine man—" the other began. But Sekhar cut him short with: "Far from it. He always struck me as a mean and selfish brute."

During the last period when he was teaching geography for Third Form A, Sekhar received a note from the headmaster: "Please see me before you go home." Sekhar said to himself: It must be about these horrible test papers. A hundred papers in the boys' scrawls; he had **shirked** this work for weeks, feeling all the time as if a sword were hanging over his head.

---

1. The *common room* is the teacher's lounge.

Activate Prior Knowledge *Based on your experiences, how do you think Sekhar's colleagues might have reacted to this statement?* **2**

Vocabulary

shirk (shurk) *v.* to evade or avoid one's duty

R. K. NARAYAN **621**

1 **Analogy** *What is the meaning of the analogy in these sentences?*

Teach

Literary Element 1

Analogy Answer: *The meaning of the analogy is that truth, like the sun, is beneficial in small doses but can cause harm when it is too strong and direct.*

Reading Strategy 2

Activate Prior Knowledge
Answer: *Students may say his colleagues were probably shocked at his statement, since people usually speak well of the dead.*

Language History ☆
British Education System
Explain that the British education system uses terms different from those of the U.S. education system. The term *third form* is for students who are thirteen to fourteen years old; it is the equivalent of eighth grade in the United States. A *headmaster* is similar to a principal.

View the Art ★
This image by Michael Rothenstein (1908–1993) is a lithograph. Rather than painting directly on canvas or board, an artist makes a lithograph by creating an image on a stone or metal plate—with paint, ink, or another medium—and pressing it to a second.

Learning Objectives
Analyzing analogy. (SE)
Activating prior knowledge. (SE)
Analyzing art. (TE)

Approaching Level

DIFFERENTIATED INSTRUCTION

Identify Different Speakers Students may have difficulty with R. K. Narayan's writing style, especially when he runs together dialogue spoken by two different characters or places dialogue spoken aloud next to the narrator's internal thoughts. Explain that some authors choose to break the traditional rule of starting each character's dialogue on a new line.

Additionally, some authors place internal thoughts in italics, but others do not; this can make it difficult to determine when a thought is spoken aloud. Have students read aloud the second, third, and fourth paragraphs of the story, coming to a full stop at the end of each sentence. Students should ask themselves the identity of each speaker.

Teach

Reading Strategy 1

Activate Prior Knowledge
Answer: *Responses will vary, but students may say that nervousness or fear of retribution affected their ability to be honest.*

Big Idea 2

A Complex Heritage Ask:
What details from the scenes in the headmaster's office and house indicate complex rules of conduct in Indian society? *(Sekhar is forced to go home with the headmaster, indicating the importance of following a superior's wishes; however, the headmaster fawns all over Sekhar once they are home, indicating the importance of treating guests well.)*

Literary Element 3

Analogy Answer: *The overall impression is that his singing is unpleasant and uncontrolled.*

Progress Check

Can students identify analogy?

If No → See Unit 3 Teaching Resources Book, p. 275.

Cultural History ☆

Incense The long history of incense reaches back to religious rituals in ancient Egypt. In Hindu society, incense is often used in the worship of a person's chosen god as a part of *bhakti*, or devotion.

The bell rang and the boys burst out of the class.

Sekhar paused for a moment outside the headmaster's room to button up his coat; that was another subject the headmaster always sermonized about.

He stepped in with a very polite "Good evening, sir."

The headmaster looked up at him in a very friendly manner and asked, "Are you free this evening?"

Sekhar replied, "Just some outing which I have promised the children at home—"

"Well, you can take them out another day. Come home with me now."

"Oh . . . yes, sir, certainly . . ." And then he added timidly, "Anything special, sir?"

"Yes," replied the headmaster, smiling to himself . . . "You didn't know my weakness for music?"

"Oh, yes, sir . . ."

"I've been learning and practicing secretly, and now I want you to hear me this evening. I've engaged a drummer and a violinist to accompany me—this is the first time I'm doing it full-dress and I want your opinion. I know it will be valuable."

Sekhar's taste in music was well known. He was one of the most dreaded music critics in the town. But he never anticipated his musical inclinations would lead him to this trial. . . . "Rather a surprise for you, isn't it?" asked the headmaster. "I've spent a fortune on it behind closed doors. . . ." They started for the headmaster's house. "God hasn't given me a child, but at least let him not deny me the consolation of music," the headmaster said, pathetically, as they walked. He incessantly chattered about music: how he began one day out of

sheer boredom; how his teacher at first laughed at him, and then gave him hope; how his ambition in life was to forget himself in music.

At home the headmaster proved very ingratiating. He sat Sekhar on a red silk carpet, set before him several dishes of delicacies, and fussed over him as if he were a son-in-law of the house. He even said, "Well, you must listen with a free mind. Don't worry about these test papers." He added half humorously, "I will give you a week's time."

"Make it ten days, sir," Sekhar pleaded.

"All right, granted," the headmaster said generously. Sekhar felt really relieved now—he would attack them at the rate of ten a day and get rid of the nuisance.

The headmaster lighted incense sticks. "Just to create the right atmosphere," he explained. A drummer and a violinist, already seated on a Rangoon mat, were waiting for him. The headmaster sat down between them like a professional at a concert, cleared his throat, and began an alapana,[2] and paused to ask, "Isn't it good Kalyani?"[3] Sekhar pretended not to have heard the question. The headmaster went on to sing a full song composed by Thyagaraja[4] and followed it with two more. All the time the headmaster was singing, Sekhar went on commenting within himself, He croaks like a dozen frogs. He is bellowing like a buffalo. Now he sounds like loose window shutters in a storm.

The incense sticks burnt low. Sekhar's head throbbed with the medley of sounds that had assailed his eardrums for a couple of hours now. He felt half

1 Activate Prior Knowledge *Have you ever been asked to critique the work of someone in a position of authority or someone you admire? Did your relationship with the person affect your ability to be honest? Explain.*

2. An *alapana* is a musical improvisation.
3. *Kalyani* means "music."
4. *Thyagaraja* (thyä΄gä rä zhä) was an Indian composer (1767–1847) known for his devotional songs.

3 Analogy *What overall impression can you form about the headmaster's singing based on these analogies?*

Writing Practice

Commas in a Series Tell students that when a sentence contains a series (three or more elements), a comma should appear after every item in the series except for the last item. Explain that a series can be simple, as in "We bought carrots, spinach, and broccoli." A series can also be more complex, as in "We bought vegetables at the grocery, filled the car with gas, and returned home in time for the football game."

Write the following sentence on the board, and ask students to place the serial commas: "He sat Sekhar on a red silk carpet[,] set before him several dishes of delicacies[,] and fussed over him as if he were a son-in-law of the house." Have students practice using serial commas by writing sentences about the story, with the sentences containing three or more elements.

4 **stupefied**. The headmaster had gone nearly hoarse, when he paused to ask, "Shall I go on?" Sekhar replied, "Please don't, sir, I think this will do. . . ." The headmaster looked stunned. His face was beaded with perspiration. Sekhar felt the greatest pity for him. But he felt he could not help it. No judge delivering a sentence felt more pained and helpless. Sekhar noticed that the head-master's wife peeped in from the kitchen, with eager curiosity. The drummer and the violinist put away their burdens with an air of relief. The headmaster removed his spec-tacles, mopped his brow, and asked, "Now, come out with your opinion."

"Can't I give it tomorrow, sir?" Sekhar asked tentatively.

"No. I want it immediately—your frank opinion. Was it good?"

"No, sir . . ." Sekhar replied.

"Oh! . . . Is there any use continuing my lessons?"

"Absolutely none, sir . . ." Sekhar said with his voice trembling. He felt very unhappy that he could not speak more soothingly. Truth, he reflected, required as much strength to give as to receive.

All the way home he felt worried. He felt that his official life was not going to be smooth sailing hereafter. There were ques-tions of **increment** and confirmation and so on, all depending upon the headmaster's goodwill. All kinds of worries seemed to be in store for him. . . . Did not Harischandra[5] lose his throne, wife, child, because he would speak nothing less than the absolute Truth whatever happened?

At home his wife served him with a sul-len face. He knew she was still angry with

Flute Player. Lincoln Seligman. Oil on canvas. Private collection.

him for his remark of the morning. Two casualties for today, Sekhar said to himself. If I practice it for a week, I don't think I shall have a single friend left.

He received a call from the headmaster in his classroom next day. He went up apprehensively.

"Your suggestion was useful. I have paid off the music master. No one would tell me the truth about my music all these days. Why such antics at my age! Thank you. By the way, what about those test papers?"

"You gave me ten days, sir, for correcting them."

"Oh, I've reconsidered it. I must positively have them here tomorrow. . . ." A hundred papers in a day! That meant all night's sit-ting up! "Give me a couple of days, sir . . ."

"No. I must have them tomorrow morn-ing. And remember, every paper must be thoroughly **scrutinized**."

"Yes, sir," Sekhar said, feeling that sitting up all night with a hundred test papers was a small price to pay for the luxury of practicing Truth. ∾

---

5. *Harischandra* (hə′ rē shän′ drä) was a king who sacrificed his kingdom for the *Sat Panth,* or the Path of Truth.

Vocabulary

stupefied (stōō′ pə fīd) *adj.* stupid, groggy, or insensible
increment (ing′ krə mənt) *n.* something gained or added in a series, usually at regular intervals

A Complex Heritage *Do you think Sekhar's personal philosophy differs from the social norms in his culture? Explain.* **5**

Vocabulary

scrutinize (skrōōt′ ən īz′) *v.* to examine with close attention to detail

R. K. NARAYAN **623**

English Learners

DIFFERENTIATED INSTRUCTION

Intermediate Draw students' attention to the ellipses used in the story. Explain that ellipses are often used to represent missing words in academic writing, such as when paraphrasing a source. However, authors of fiction often use ellipses to indicate an uncomfortable pause, often when a character wishes to avoid saying something that may be offensive.

Advanced Learners/Pre-AP

DIFFERENTIATED INSTRUCTION

Research Draw students' attention to the mention of Harischandra on this page. Explain that the theme of obsession at the expense of one's livelihood or even life runs through the literature of many cultures. Ask students to find another tale or myth that focuses on a character who will not give up on a goal, no matter what price he or she pays.

Teach

Vocabulary | **4**

Context Clues Model the use of context clues to find the meaning of the word *stupefied*. **Say:** Sekhar describes how he feels after lis-tening to the music for hours; he has a headache from the sounds and the incense has burnt low, meaning that much time has passed. I can guess that *stupefied* means "to feel groggy or tired."

Big Idea | **5**

A Complex Heritage

Answer: *Based on the reactions of his wife, his colleagues, and his boss, it seems that his personal philosophy about absolute honesty does differ from the social norms of his culture.*

View the Art ★

Pausing momentarily, a single musician dressed and surrounded in cold white save for the dramatic orange of his turban poses with his flute—a simple yet significant instrument from indigenous Indian culture. Although simple in construc-tion with no more than eight holes, flutes are known by many names in India; in northern India, musi-cians play a flute called a bansuri, and the flute of southern India is a venu. **Ask:** How does this image contrast with the physical descrip-tion in the story of the evening spent at the headmaster's house? *(This simple, crisp image is in direct contrast to the headmaster's red silk carpet, incense, and musical accompaniment.)*

Learning Objectives
Analyzing analogy. (SE)
Activating prior knowledge. (SE)
Using context clues. (TE)
Using commas in a series. (TE)

623

After You Read

Assess

1. Answers will vary.
2. (a) Tempering the truth to avoid shocking people (b) The "absolute Truth" allows a person to be his or her true self, unrestricted by social norms.
3. (a) He is unable to swallow the breakfast she has prepared. (b) Her feelings are hurt.
4. (a) He is shocked and angered, but he believes Sekhar is correct. (b) He gives up his music, but he also punishes Sekhar.
5. (a) He values personal satisfaction over duty. (b) It reveals that his motivation, which put his happiness before that of other people, is not unique to this day of his life.
6. The social hierarchy is sharply delineated, and social interactions are fairly formal.
7. The "tint" of India is captured in details such as Sekhar's name and references to the Indian composer Thyagaraja and King Harischandra.

Writing

Students' anecdotes should
- narrate a brief sequence of events about giving an honest opinion
- include an analogy

After You Read

Respond and Think Critically

Respond and Interpret

1. What was your reaction to Sekhar's moments of truthfulness? Explain.
2. (a)What does Sekhar think is the essence of human relationships? (b)Why might he believe that life is not worth living unless a person experiences "absolute Truth"?
3. (a)What does Sekhar tell his wife about her "culinary masterpiece"? (b)Why do you think she reacts the way she does?

Analyze and Evaluate

4. (a)How do you think the headmaster feels about Sekhar's criticism of his musical ability? (b)What details create this impression?

5. (a)What does Sekhar's delay in grading his students' papers suggest about him? (b)What might this delay reveal about his motivation for having a day of truth?

Connect

6. **Big Idea** **A Complex Heritage** How do the social codes of Sekhar's culture make it difficult for him to maintain strict personal integrity in the form of absolute truthfulness?
7. **Connect to the Author** Narayan said English could "take on the tint of any country." How does he use English to capture the "tint" of India in this story?

Literary Element Analogy

The title "Like the Sun" highlights the main analogy in the story.

1. How does the first paragraph develop the analogy between truth and the sun?
2. How do the events in the story help support Sekhar's analogy?

Reading Strategy Activate Prior Knowledge

Draw on your prior knowledge and experiences to answer the following questions.

1. Do you think it is appropriate for the headmaster to ask an employee to judge his musical abilities? Explain.
2. Should the headmaster give up his dream based on the opinion of one person? Explain.

LOG ON ▶ **Literature** Online

Selection Resources For Selection Quizzes, eFlashcards, and Reading-Writing Connection activities, go to glencoe.com and enter QuickPass code GLW6053u3.

Vocabulary Practice

Practice with Context Clues Look back at pages 621–623 to find context clues for the boldfaced vocabulary words below. Record your findings in a chart like the one here.

shirk stupefied increment scrutinize

EXAMPLE:

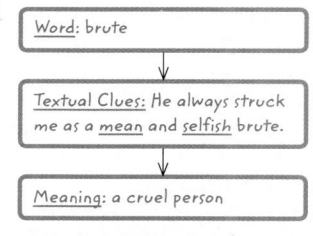

Word: brute

↓

Textual Clues: He always struck me as a mean and selfish brute.

↓

Meaning: a cruel person

Writing

Write an Anecdote An anecdote is a short, slice-of-life account that makes a witty observation, often about society. Write an anecdote about an experience that required you to give an honest opinion, despite misgivings you may have had.

Literary Element

1. It explains that just as one cannot look straight at the sun, one cannot face the truth without being hurt.
2. Sekhar's wife and the headmaster are hurt when he tells them the truth. Like the sun, the truth "burns" Sekhar and the headmaster, increasing Sekhar's workload and damaging the headmaster's pride.

Reading Strategy

1. Students may feel that the headmaster's position of power makes it unfair for him to ask Sekhar's judgment.
2. Students may note that Sekhar is a "known" critic, so it makes sense for the headmaster to stop wasting his time. Others may say that the headmaster should continue his musical studies, if only for his own enjoyment.

Vocabulary Practice

Sample answer:
Word: stupefied
Textual Clues: "Sekhar's head throbbed with the medley of sounds that had assailed his eardrums for a couple of hours now."
Meaning: groggy; insensible

Before You Read

By Any Other Name

Meet **Santha Rama Rau**

(born 1923)

Santha Rama Rau (sän´tä rä´mä rou) was born in Madras (now Chennai), India, while the country was still under British colonial rule. She attended schools in India, England, and the United States, and has traveled extensively. Her writings reflect a lifetime of experiences enriched by cultural diversity.

> "*Really, in the end, the only thing that can make you a writer is the person that you are, the intensity of your feeling, the honesty of your vision, the unsentimental acknowledgment of the endless interest of the life around and within you.*"
>
> —Santha Rama Rau

Global Traveler Rau's father was a high-ranking government official whose work required his family to travel frequently. By the time Rau arrived in the United States as a freshman at Wellesley College in Massachusetts, she had lived in many parts of India and in England and South Africa. After India became independent in 1947, her father was appointed India's first ambassador to Japan and later became the ambassador to the United States.

Rau's travels formed the basis for many of her books and articles in a variety of genres. She was fascinated by the interaction between people from differing cultures, a subject that runs throughout her work, particularly in her first book, *Home to India* (1945). This autobiography achieved both critical and popular success. Another autobiography, *East of Home* (1950), chronicles her experiences in postwar Japan, China, and other parts of the Far East, which inspired her to reflect on her identity as an Indian. Her first novel, *Remember the House* (1956), tells the story of an Indian woman who must navigate an arranged marriage, despite her investment in the idea of romantic love.

Acclaimed Dramatist In 1960, Rau dramatized E. M. Forster's novel *A Passage to India* for a critically acclaimed stage production in London. In an article published in the *New York Times* in July 1960, Rau praised Forster's novel, citing it as a rare work of fiction that "introduces us most thoughtfully and penetratingly to some Indians—educated Indians, at that." Rau has regularly contributed articles, essays, and reviews to the *New York Times*, the *New Yorker*, and other publications. The excerpt you are about to read is from *Gifts of Passage* (1961), a collection of mostly autobiographical stories.

 Literature Online

Author Search For more about Santha Rama Rau, go to glencoe.com and enter QuickPass code GLW6053u3.

SANTHA RAMA RAU **625**

Before You Read

Focus

Bellringer Options

Selection Focus
    Transparency 37
Daily Language
    Transparency 56

Ask: What stereotypes or discrimination have you encountered recently, either through the media or in real life? *(Students should explain any stereotypes or discrimination they've encountered in the recent past. Types of discrimination may vary—racial, gender, age, etc.)* Discuss why certain ideas are stereotypes and what people can do to help eradicate discrimination.

Selection Skills

Literary Elements
- Autobiography (SE pp. 626, 628, 632, 633; TE p. 629)
- Imagery (SE p. 633)

By Any Other Name

Speaking/Listening/Viewing Skills
- Speech (SE p. 634)
- Analyze Art (TE pp. 627, 630)

Reading Skills
- Connect to Contemporary Issues (SE pp. 626, 628, 631, 634; TE p. 632)
- Analyze Setting (TE p. 628)

Vocabulary Skills
- Antonyms (SE p. 634; TE p. 626)
- Word Parts (TE p. 629)

Before You Read

Focus

Summary

The narrator of this memoir recalls when she and her sister were sent to a school run by the British in India during colonial times. Without making any effort to learn the children's real names, the head-mistress gives both girls English names. The Indian children at the school are treated as if they are inferior. They are assigned seats in the last row and are assumed to be cheaters. This last indignity leads the older sister to march her sister home, never to return to the school.

 For summaries in languages other than English, see Unit 3 Teaching Resources Book, pp. 282–287.

Vocabulary

Crossword Puzzles Have students use the dictionary or a thesaurus to compile a list of antonyms for the vocabulary words. Then have students create a blank crossword puzzle; the puzzle clues will be the antonyms and the answers will be the vocabulary words. Students can trade papers with a classmate and try to solve his or her partner's puzzle.

 For additional vocabulary practice, see Unit 3 Teaching Resources Book, p. 290.

 Interactive Read and Write
Other options for teaching this selection can be found in Interactive Read and Write for On-Level Learners, pp. 149–160.

Literature and Reading Preview

Connect to the Story

How are the traditions of different ethnic groups reflected in American society? Do you think preserving these cultural heritages is important? Discuss these questions with a partner.

Build Background

Under British colonial rule, many Indians—particularly those who were members of the higher Indian castes—were sent to Western-style schools. The British hoped to create a class of Indians who could help interpret British policies for the rest of the population. Many Western-educated Indians became government administrators, political leaders, and professionals.

Setting Purposes for Reading

Big Idea **A Complex Heritage**

As you read, ask yourself, How does this story illustrate the cultural identity crises faced by many Indians under British colonial rule?

Literary Element **Autobiography**

An **autobiography** is the story of a person's life written by that person. Autobiographies can give insights into the author's view or himself or herself and the society in which he or she lived. As you read, ask yourself, What insights does this story convey about the author and her society?

Reading Strategy **Connect to Contemporary Issues**

When you **connect**, you link what you read to events in your own life or in the world around you. As you read, ask yourself, What elements of this story relate to contemporary issues?

Tip: Track Connections Use a chart like the one below to keep track of the ways Rau's story connects to contemporary issues.

Story Event	Contemporary Issue	Shared Significance
A girl in Santha's class tries to fit in by wearing a cotton dress.	Schools in England recently banned Muslim girls from wearing full-faced veils to school.	People are sometimes forced to reject their traditions to accommodate the cultural values of others.

Learning Objectives

For pages 625–634

In studying this text, you will focus on the following objectives:

Literary Study: Analyzing autobiography.

Reading: Connecting to contemporary issues.

Listening and Speaking: Delivering a speech.

Vocabulary

provincial (prə vin′shəl) *adj.* belonging or peculiar to a particular province; local; lacking sophistication or polish; p. 628 *The student came from a provincial town and had difficulty coping with the challenges of urban living.*

insular (in′sə lər) *adj.* isolated; narrow-minded; p. 628 *His wealthy, insular upbringing made him indifferent to the problems faced by homeless people.*

incomprehensible (in′kom pri hen′sə bəl) *adj.* unintelligible; indiscernible; not understood; p. 629 *Her sloppy handwriting made the letter incomprehensible.*

sedately (si dāt′lē) *adv.* in a dignified or serious manner; calmly; solemnly; p. 631 *The president walked sedately to the podium.*

tepid (tep′id) *adj.* lukewarm; halfhearted; p. 631 *The soft drink tasted tepid because it had been left on the counter for an hour.*

Reading Practice

Make Connections to Literature Explain to students that assimilation is the process of becoming absorbed into a culture. People who move to new places—countries, states, or even cities—find that they often must assimilate in some ways in order to find security, jobs, and friends in their new home. Assimilation includes learning a new language and rules of a society.

Have students consider ways that they or their family members have had to change in order to get along in a new place. **Ask:** What new rules or laws have you had to learn about? What new foods, holidays, or traditions have you adopted? Encourage students to share their experiences of assimilation with the class.

Head Mistress, 2005. Lincoln Seligman. Acrylic. Private collection.

By Any Other Name

Santha Rama Rau

At the Anglo-Indian day school in Zorinabad to which my sister and I were sent when she was eight and I was five and a half, they changed our names. On the first day of school, a hot, windless morning of a north Indian September, we stood in the headmistress's study and she said, "Now you're the new girls. What are your names?"

My sister answered for us. "I am Premila, and she"—nodding in my direction—"is Santha."

The headmistress had been in India, I suppose, fifteen years or so, but she still smiled her helpless inability to cope with Indian names. Her rimless half-glasses glittered, and the precarious bun on the top of her head trembled as she shook her

---

1 **A Complex Heritage** *What difficulties might students face at an "Anglo-Indian" school?*

SANTHA RAMA RAU **627**

Advanced Learners/Pre-AP

DIFFERENTIATED INSTRUCTION

Research Names Students can research the names of their friends and family members. Have students make a list of names, and then look up the names in books to find the origin and meaning of each. Students can then evaluate each name and determine whether the name's meaning matches its owner.

Have students to identify additional names that match the personalities of the classmates on their lists. Encourage students to share their research with the class or bring in the resources they used in their search.

Teach

Big Idea 1

A Complex Heritage
Answer: *Students might have to navigate both British and Indian customs and get along with people who have a different cultural heritage.*

View the Art ★

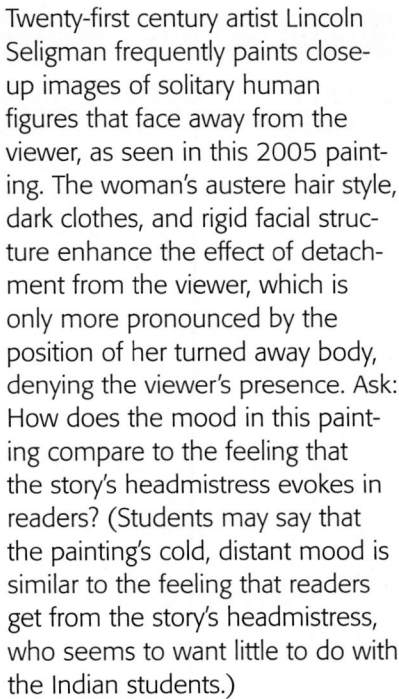

Twenty-first century artist Lincoln Seligman frequently paints close-up images of solitary human figures that face away from the viewer, as seen in this 2005 painting. The woman's austere hair style, dark clothes, and rigid facial structure enhance the effect of detachment from the viewer, which is only more pronounced by the position of her turned away body, denying the viewer's presence. Ask: How does the mood in this painting compare to the feeling that the story's headmistress evokes in readers? (Students may say that the painting's cold, distant mood is similar to the feeling that readers get from the story's headmistress, who seems to want little to do with the Indian students.)

Readability Scores
Dale-Chall: 7.8
DRP: 58
Lexile: 970

Learning Objectives
Analyzing autobiography. (SE)
Connecting to contemporary issues. (TE)

627

Teach

Literary Element 1

Autobiography Answer: *It indicates that Santha feels shy and intimidated. She does not want to challenge the headmistress.*

(APPROACHING) For approaching students, **ask: How might someone who is proud speak?** *(He or she might use a voice that sounds strong and confident.)*

Reading Strategy 2

Connect to Contemporary Issues Answer: *Based on this passage, one can infer that the British assumed that Indian schools were inadequate. Answers about modern American society will vary; students may note that people sometimes discriminate against those whose first language is not English.*

(ENGLISH LEARNERS) Explain to English learners that *valid* means "accepted as authentic or legal." Also, explain that in America some credits from one high school or college may not be valid at another school.

Literary Element 3

Autobiography Answer: *She feels that "Cynthia" is a different person and that her true identity lies elsewhere. The headmistress's treatment of her may have already taught her that Indian culture is not highly regarded at the school.*

head. "Oh, my dears, those are much too hard for me. Suppose we give you pretty English names. Wouldn't that be more jolly? Let's see, now—Pamela for you, I think." She shrugged in a baffled way at my sister. "That's as close as I can get. And for *you*" she said to me, "how about Cynthia? Isn't that nice?"

My sister was always less easily intimidated than I was, and while she kept a stubborn silence, I said, "Thank you," in a very tiny voice.

We had been sent to that school because my father, among his responsibilities as an officer of the civil service, had a tour of duty to perform in the villages around that steamy little **provincial** town, where he had his headquarters at that time. He used to make his shorter inspection tours on horseback, and a week before, in the stale heat of a typically postmonsoon day,[1] we had waved goodbye to him and a little procession—an assistant, a secretary, two bearers,[2] and the man to look after the bedding rolls and luggage. They rode away through our large garden, still bright green from the rains, and we turned back into the twilight of the house and the sound of fans whispering in every room.

Up to then, my mother had refused to send Premila to school in the British-run establishments of that time, because, she

---

1. A *postmonsoon day* is a day that occurs just after a monsoon, or heavy rainfall.
2. *Bearers* are porters who carry the equipment and supplies for a journey.

1 | Autobiography *What does the description of her voice indicate about Santha's emotional state at this point?*

Vocabulary

provincial (prə vin′shəl) *adj.* belonging or peculiar to a particular province; local; lacking sophistication or polish

628 UNIT 3 SOUTH CENTRAL ASIA

used to say, "you can bury a dog's tail for seven years and it still comes out curly, and you can take a Britisher away from his home for a lifetime and he still remains **insular.**" The examinations and degrees from entirely Indian schools were not, in those days, considered valid. In my case, the question had never come up, and probably never would have come up if Mother's extraordinary good health had not broken down. For the first time in my life, she was not able to continue the lessons she had been giving us every morning. So our Hindi books were put away, the stories of the Lord Krishna[3] as a little boy were left in midair, and we were sent to the Anglo-Indian school.

That first day at school is still, when I think of it, a remarkable one. At that age, if one's name is changed, one develops a curious form of dual personality. I remember having a certain detached and disbelieving concern in the actions of "Cynthia," but certainly no responsibility. Accordingly, I followed the thin, erect back of the headmistress down the veranda to my classroom feeling, at most, a passing interest in what was going to happen to me in this strange, new atmosphere of School.

The building was Indian in design, with wide verandas opening onto a central courtyard, but Indian verandas are usually whitewashed, with stone floors. These, in the tradition of British schools, were

---

3. *Lord Krishna* is an incarnation of the Hindu god Vishnu.

2 | Connect to Contemporary Issues *What cultural biases are revealed here? Do biases like this exist in modern American society? Explain.*

3 | Autobiography *Why do you think Santha feels only a passing interest in what will happen to her at school?*

Vocabulary

insular (in′sə lər) *adj.* isolated; narrow-minded

Reading Practice

Analyze Setting The author describes the setting of the school in great detail. The way an author describes a character's surroundings can help readers understand more about a place than just what it looks like. **Ask: What details of the school building stood out to the author?**

(Although the building is Indian in design, the décor inside is British. The room appeared dark and felt hot.)

Ask: How does the setting in the school help the author emphasize the theme of cultural alteration? *(The author strengthens the theme of cultural alteration by describing the British insistence on changing a foreign place to feel more like home, even at the risk of being uncomfortable.)*

painted dark brown and had matting on the floors. It gave a feeling of extra intensity to the heat.

I suppose there were about a dozen Indian children in the school—which contained perhaps forty children in all—and four of them were in my class. They were all sitting at the back of the room, and I went to join them. I sat next to a small, solemn girl who didn't smile at me. She had long, glossy-black braids and wore a cotton dress, but she still kept on her Indian jewelry—a gold chain around her neck, thin gold bracelets, and tiny ruby studs in her ears. Like most Indian children, she had a rim of black kohl around her eyes. The cotton dress should have looked strange, but all I could think of was that I should ask my mother if I couldn't wear a dress to school, too, instead of my Indian clothes.

Visual Vocabulary
Kohl is a cosmetic that women in southwest and south central Asia use to darken the edges of their eyelids.

I can't remember too much about the proceedings in class that day, except for the beginning. The teacher pointed to me and asked me to stand up. "Now, dear, tell the class your name."

I said nothing.

"Come along," she said, frowning slightly. "What's your name, dear?"

"I don't know," I said, finally.

The English children in the front of the class—there were about eight or ten of them—giggled and twisted around in their chairs to look at me. I sat down quickly and opened my eyes very wide, hoping in that way to dry them off. The little girl with the braids put out her hand and very lightly touched my arm. She still didn't smile.

Most of that morning I was rather bored.

I looked briefly at the children's drawings pinned to the wall, and then concentrated on a lizard clinging to the ledge of the high, barred window behind the teacher's head. Occasionally it would shoot out its long yellow tongue for a fly, and then it would rest, with its eyes closed and its belly palpitating, as though it were swallowing several times quickly. The lessons were mostly concerned with reading and writing and simple numbers—things that my mother had already taught me—and I paid very little attention. The teacher wrote on the easel blackboard words like "bat" and "cat," which seemed babyish to me; only "apple" was new and **incomprehensible**.

When it was time for the lunch recess, I followed the girl with braids out onto the veranda. There the children from the other classes were assembled. I saw Premila at once and ran over to her, as she had charge of our lunchbox. The children were all opening packages and sitting down to eat sandwiches. Premila and I were the only ones who had Indian food—thin wheat chapatties,[4] some vegetable curry, and a bottle of buttermilk. Premila thrust half of it into my hand and whispered fiercely that I should go and sit with my class, because that was what the others seemed to be doing.

The enormous black eyes of the little Indian girl from my class looked at my food longingly, so I offered her some. But she only shook her head and plowed her way solemnly through her sandwiches.

---

4. *Chapatties* (chä pät′ēz) are pancake-shaped, unleavened breads common to northern India.

A Complex Heritage *Why do you think the Indian girl declines Santha's offer?* **6**

Vocabulary
incomprehensible (in′kom pri hen′sə bəl) *adj.* unintelligible; indiscernible; not understood

SANTHA RAMA RAU **629**

Teach

Literary Element 4

Autobiography **Ask:** Why do you think the author shows how bored Santha is in class? *(Students may say that the author describes Santha's boredom to make a point of how uninvolved the teacher is with the Indian children in the class.)*

Vocabulary 5

Understand Word Parts
Explain that prefixes and suffixes can be used to create antonyms. The prefix *in–* means "not." So *incomprehensible* is the antonym of *comprehensible*. Ask students to name other prefixes or suffixes that do the same thing. *(examples include -less and un-)*

Big Idea 6

A Complex Heritage
Answer: *The Indian girl has already adjusted in part to the influence of Western culture at school, perhaps to get along with the other students.*

Cultural History ☆

Butter in Hindu Culture Butter is vital to Hindu rituals and daily life in India. Clarified butter (called *ghee*) is made by cooking butter until the water boils off; the *ghee* is the clear butterfat that is left behind. Ghee from cows, which is considered superior to ghee from buffalo, is used in Hindu religious ceremonies and is considered to be medicinally beneficial.

Learning Objectives
Connecting to contemporary issues. (SE)
Analyzing autobiography. (SE)
Analyzing setting. (TE)
Understanding word parts. (TE)

629

English Learners

DIFFERENTIATED INSTRUCTION

Intermediate Explain that adverbs are used to describe verbs, adjectives, or other adverbs. Adverbs often end in *-ly*. Have students find and list the adverbs on this page and note the word or words the adverb describes. *(Examples include: lightly touched, briefly looked.)* Explain that understanding how adverbs modify a character's actions can help students gain insight into the mood or feeling of a scene.

Advanced Learners/Pre-AP

DIFFERENTIATED INSTRUCTION

Switching Point of View Have students imagine the scene between Santha and the little Indian girl with the braids. Tell them to think about the scene from the little girl's point of view. **Ask:** What do the little girl's actions tell you about what she is feeling or thinking in this scene? Have students write a short internal monologue of the scene from the little girl's point of view.

Teach

Big Idea　　1

A Complex Heritage

Ask: What mixed message does Santha receive during the game of tag? *(Santha discovers that letting a smaller child win is not acceptable. The others thought of her as "not being a good sport.")*

Cultural History ☆

Tea in India Tea was an important part of the East India Company's trade in the eighteenth century. Some black teas, such as Assam and Darjeeling are grown in India. The popularity of tea in Britain resulted in there being 4,000 tea estates in India by 1900.

View the Art ★

Answer: *Students will probably note that the children in the painting seem more carefree than Premila and Santha.*

Slide, Mysore, 2001. Andrew Macara. Oil on canvas. Private collection.

View the Art Macara considers himself to be a self-taught artist. How does the mood of this painting compare with the mood of the excerpt? ★

I was very sleepy after lunch, because at home we always took a siesta. It was usually a pleasant time of day, with the bedroom darkened against the harsh afternoon sun, the drifting off into sleep with the sound of Mother's voice reading a story in one's mind, and, finally, the shrill, fussy voice of the ayah[5] waking one for tea.

At school, we rested for a short time on low, folding cots on the veranda, and then we were expected to play games. During the hot part of the afternoon we played indoors, and after the shadows had begun to lengthen and the slight breeze of the evening had come up we moved outside to the wide courtyard.

I had never really grasped the system of competitive games. At home, whenever we played tag or guessing games, I was always allowed to "win"—"because," Mother used to tell Premila, "she is the youngest, and we have to allow for that." I had often heard her say it, and it seemed quite reasonable to me, but the result was that I had no clear idea of what "winning" meant.

When we played twos-and-threes that afternoon at school, in accordance with my training, I let one of the small English boys catch me, but was naturally rather puzzled when the other children did not return the courtesy. I ran about for what seemed like hours without ever catching anyone, until it was time for school to close. Much later I learned that my attitude was called "not being a good sport," and I stopped allowing myself to be caught, but it was not for years that I really learned the spirit of the thing.

---

5. An *ayah* is a governess or a nanny.

Listening and Speaking Practice

Participate in a Debate Ask: Is it necessary to play by the rules, or is it appropriate, at times, to let someone win? Students can take sides on the topic of playing by the rules versus letting someone smaller or younger win. Assign a side of the argument to each half of the class. In groups, students can list reasons supporting their point. Tell students to remember to consider counterarguments, or arguments that refute the opposing side's points.

After each side has determined its argument and counterarguments, the groups can debate as a class or choose representatives to debate the issues. Before the debate, establish ground rules to keep the class in order. As students debate, keep track of the arguments by writing them on the board. Decide a winner at the end.

When I saw our car come up to the school gate, I broke away from my classmates and rushed toward it yelling, "Ayah! Ayah!" It seemed like an eternity since I had seen her that morning—a wizened, affectionate figure in her white cotton sari, giving me dozens of urgent and useless instructions on how to be a good girl at school. Premila followed more **sedately**, and she told me on the way home never to do that again in front of the other children.

⭐ When we got home we went straight to Mother's high, white room to have tea with her, and I immediately climbed onto the bed and bounced gently up and down on the springs. Mother asked how we had liked our first day in school. I was so pleased to be home and to have left that peculiar Cynthia behind that I had nothing whatever to say about school, except to ask what "apple" meant. But Premila told Mother about the classes, and added that in her class they had weekly tests to see if they had learned their lessons well.

I asked, "What's a test?"

Premila said, "You're too small to have them. You won't have them in your class for donkey's years." She had learned the expression that day and was using it for the first time. We all laughed enormously at her wit. She also told Mother, in an aside, that we should take sandwiches to school the next day. Not, she said, that *she* minded. But they would be simpler for me to handle.

That whole lovely evening I didn't think about school at all. I sprinted barefoot across the lawns with my favorite playmate, the cook's son, to the stream at the end of the garden. We quarreled in our usual way, waded in the **tepid** water under the lime trees, and waited for the night to bring out the smell of the jasmine. I listened with fascination to his stories of ghosts and demons, until I was too frightened to cross the garden alone in the semidarkness. The ayah found me, shouted at the cook's son, scolded me, hurried me in to supper—it was an entirely usual, wonderful evening.

It was a week later, the day of Premila's first test, that our lives changed rather abruptly. I was sitting at the back of my class, in my usual inattentive way, only half listening to the teacher. I had started a rather guarded friendship with the girl with the braids, whose name turned out to be Nalini (Nancy, in school). The three other Indian children were already fast friends. Even at that age it was apparent to all of us that friendship with the English or Anglo-Indian children was out of the question. Occasionally, during the class, my new friend and I would draw pictures and show them to each other secretly.

The door opened sharply and Premila marched in. At first, the teacher smiled at her in a kindly and encouraging way and said, "Now, you're little Cynthia's sister?"

Premila didn't even look at her. She stood with her feet planted firmly apart and

---

2 | **A Complex Heritage** *Does Premila really believe it would be simpler to take sandwiches to school, or does she have another reason for requesting them? Explain.*

Vocabulary

sedately (si dāt′lē) *adv.* in a dignified or serious manner; calmly; solemnly

Connect to Contemporary Issues *Why might this division be readily apparent to the Indian children? How does this passage relate to issues students face in school today?* **3**

Vocabulary

tepid (tep′id) *adj.* lukewarm; halfhearted

SANTHA RAMA RAU **631**

Teach

Big Idea | 2

A Complex Heritage
Answer: *Premila is not concerned about the ease of carrying sandwiches. What she really wants is for Santha to fit in and not draw attention to her Indian identity.*

Reading Strategy | 3

Connect to Contemporary Issues
Answer: *Being placed at the back of the classroom and forced to take another name has exposed the Indian children to the British culture's attitude of superiority. For the Indian children, this attitude may indicate that friendship is impossible. Students may mention issues such as assimilation in today's schools.*

Learning Objectives
Connecting to contemporary issues. (SE)
Analyzing autobiography. (SE)
Participating in a debate. (TE)

Approaching Level

DIFFERENTIATED INSTRUCTION

Follow Plot Explain to struggling readers that the plot of a story moves from one event to the next, culminating in a climactic moment. Use a flow chart to help struggling readers see how events in the story build on one another and lead to the climax. Have students answer the following questions and record their answers in the flow chart to indicate plot progression.

Ask: What was the first thing that happened when the girls arrived at school? *(The headmistress changed their names.)* Where was Santha seated in the classroom? *(in the last row with other Indian children)* What does Premila do when she comes to Santha's classroom? *(She tells Santha that they are leaving and going home.)*

Have students continue filling out the flow chart as they read the rest of the story. Then, help students recognize the turning point, or climax, of the story.

Teach

Reading Strategy   1

Connect to Contemporary Issues Ask: What events in twentieth century American history connect to the incident in Premila's classroom? *(seg-regation of African Americans in schools and other public places)*

[ENGLISH LEARNERS] Explain to English learners that before the Civil Rights movement of the 1960s, most African American students were sent to separate schools until desegregation was put into action.

Literary Element   2

Autobiography Answer: *She uses the third person to acknowledge that the person called "Cynthia" is someone else. In other words, she disowns the identity the school has imposed on her.*

Literary History ☆

Siestas The word *siesta* is used in Spanish-speaking countries to describe the time after lunch when most people take naps or otherwise rest. In Bangladesh, this time is called the "rice-sleep," or *bhat-gum*.

To check students' understanding of the selection, see Unit 3 Teaching Resources Book, p. 293.

Learning Objectives
Connect to contemporary issues. (SE)
Analyze autobiography. (SE)
Analyze plot. (TE)

her shoulders rigid, and addressed herself directly to me. "Get up," she said. "We're going home."

I didn't know what had happened, but I was aware that it was a crisis of some sort. I rose obediently and started to walk toward my sister.

"Bring your pencils and your notebook," she said.

I went back for them, and together we left the room. The teacher started to say something just as Premila closed the door, but we didn't wait to hear what it was.

In complete silence we left the school grounds and started to walk home. Then I asked Premila what the matter was. All she would say was "We're going home for good."

It was a very tiring walk for a child of five and a half, and I dragged along behind Premila with my pencils growing sticky in my hand. I can still remember looking at the dusty hedges, and the tangles of thorns in the ditches by the side of the road, smelling the faint fragrance from the euca-lyptus trees and wondering whether we would ever reach home. Occasionally a horse-drawn tonga[6] passed us, and the women, in their pink or green silks, stared at Premila and me trudging along on the side of the road. A few coolies[7] and a line of women carrying baskets of vegetables on their heads smiled at us. But it was nearing the hottest time of day, and the road was almost deserted. I walked more and more slowly, and shouted to Premila, from time to time, "Wait for me!" with increasing peevishness. She spoke to me only once, and

---

6. A *tonga* is a horse-drawn, two-wheeled vehicle for two to four people.
7. *Coolies* are unskilled laborers or porters who work for low wages. The term is considered derogatory today.

---

that was to tell me to carry my notebook on my head, because of the sun.

When we got to our house the ayah was just taking a tray of lunch into Mother's room. She immediately started a long, worried questioning about what are you children doing back here at this hour of the day.

Mother looked very startled and very concerned, and asked Premila what had happened.

Premila said, "We had our test today, and she made me and the other Indians sit at the back of the room, with a desk between each one."   **1**

Mother said, "Why was that, darling?"

"She said it was because Indians cheat," Premila added. "So I don't think we should go back to that school."

Mother looked very distant, and was silent a long time. At last she said, "Of course not, darling." She sounded displeased.

We all shared the curry she was having for lunch, and afterward I was sent off to the beautifully familiar bedroom for my siesta. I could hear Mother and Premila ☆ talking through the open door.

Mother said, "Do you suppose she under-stood all that?"

Premila said, "I shouldn't think so. She's a baby."

Mother said, "Well, I hope it won't bother her."

Of course, they were both wrong. I understood it perfectly, and I remember it all very clearly. But I put it happily away, because it had all happened to a girl called Cynthia, and I never was really particularly interested in her. ∾

Autobiography *Why does Santha refer to herself in the third person here?*   **2**

Reading Practice

Analyze Plot Remind students that the plot of a story includes exposition, rising action, climax, falling action, and resolu-tion. Autobiographies and memoirs often follow this same pattern. Tell students that sometimes it is difficult to identify the climax, or turning point of a plot. Explain that the climax rarely comes at the very end of a story.

Have students create and fill in a plot chart. **Ask: What is the climax of the story?** *(when Premila comes to Santha's classroom and takes her away)* **Ask: What makes this the climax of the story?** *(It is the most surprising part of the plot, and it marks the point at which a major change takes place.)*

632

After You Read

Respond and Think Critically

Respond and Interpret

1. Do you think Premila's decision to pull herself and her sister out of school is appropriate? Explain.

2. (a)How are the Indian students treated at the school? (b)What does this treatment reveal about the teachers' attitude toward them?

3. (a)Until the day of the test, how does Premila behave at school? (b)Why might she behave this way?

4. (a)On the day of the test, why does Premila leave school and take Santha with her? (b)What does this action reveal about Premila's character?

5. (a)What does Santha understand at the end of the story? (b)What reason does Santha give for claiming that she put the incident "happily away"?

Analyze and Evaluate

6. An **allusion** is a reference to something from history or from another work of literature, music, or art. The title of this story alludes to lines from William Shakespeare's play *Romeo and Juliet*: "What's in a name? that which we call a rose / By any other name would smell as sweet." (a) What do these lines mean? (b)How does this meaning apply to Rau's story?

7. (a)Why does the girls' mother worry that Santha understood Premila's reason for leaving school? (b)What does this reveal about the way Santha and Premila were raised?

Connect

8. **Big Idea** **A Complex Heritage** Can you think of any other ethnic groups whose cultural traditions were deeply affected by colonial powers? Explain.

9. **Connect to the Author** What insights does Rau's autobiography give into her personality and values? Support your answer with evidence from the text.

Literary Element Autobiography

SAT Skills Practice

The primary purpose of the first four paragraphs of the text is to

(A) inform the reader about the benefits of colonial education in India

(B) entertain the reader with an anecdote about childhood

(C) persuade the reader to empathize with Santha and Premila

(D) describe the thoughts of the headmistress

(E) show the playfulness of the children

Review: Imagery

As you learned on page 377, **imagery** is the "word pictures" authors create to evoke particular emotional responses. To create effective imagery, authors use **sensory details**—descriptions that appeal to one or more of the five senses (sight, hearing, touch, taste, and smell).

Partner Activity With a partner, review the text and answer the following questions.

1. Find words and phrases that describe the physical appearance of the headmistress. What do these descriptions suggest about Rau's view of her?

2. Find words and phrases that describe the climate and the weather conditions. How do these descriptions contribute to the tone and the mood of the story?

3. What images does Rau use to describe her life at home? What tone and mood do these images convey?

SANTHA RAMA RAU **633**

After You Read

Assess

1. Answers will vary.

2. (a) The students are given English names and are called cheaters. (b) They are prejudiced.

3. (a) She tries to fit in and encourages Santha to do the same. (b) She may think life at school will be easier if that way.

4. (a) She is told that Indians are cheaters. (b) There is a limit to the amount of bad treatment that she will accept.

5. (a) She and her sister will not return to the school because they were treated badly. (b) The incident happened to "Cynthia," a person different from herself.

6. (a) They mean that the essence of a thing is the same no matter what it is called. (b) Despite being given British names, Santha and Premila continued to embrace their Indian identity.

7. (a) Santha's mother does not yet want a little girl to know the pains of discrimination. (b) They were likely raised to believe that Indians are not inferior to the British.

8. Students may mention African ethnic groups or Native Americans.

9. She seems sensitive, perceptive, and family oriented. Students should support their choices with evidence from the text.

Review: Imagery

1. The rimless half-glasses; the trembling, precarious bun; and the thin, erect back might suggest a temperamental authoritarian figure. Students will likely think that Rau has an unfavorable view of her.

2. Students should be able to cite numerous descriptions of the oppressive heat. These descriptions reinforce the unpleasant, oppressive feeling of Rau's school experience.

3. Among other things, she describes her mother's high, white bedroom; enjoying the sights and smells of the garden on a lovely evening; and her own bedroom. Her descriptions of home convey warmth, love, security, and happiness.

> For additional selection assessment, see **Assessment Resources, pp. 131–132.**

Literary Element

(C) is the correct answer. **(A)**, **(B)**, **(D)**, and **(E)** are incorrect because they are not discussed in Rau's account.

Progress Check

Can students identify autobiography?

If No → See Unit 3 Teaching Resources Book, p. 288.

After You Read

Assess

Reading Strategy

1. (a) She leaves the school and takes Santha with her. (b) Some students may say they would do the same thing. Others may suggest that they would stay in the class but would report the incident to their parents later.

2. (a) Examples include learning about different religious or ethnic customs, learning an appreciation for different foods or types of music, and learning not to discriminate based on ethnicity. (b) Examples include having classes that teach English as a second language, being sensitive to different religious holidays or customs, and teaching in a way that many students can understand.

Progress Check

Can students connect the selection to contemporary issues?

If No ➔ See Unit 2 Teaching Resources Book, p. 289.

Vocabulary

1. a **2.** e **3.** b **4.** d **5.** c

Academic Vocabulary

Possible answer:

<u>definition:</u> something that connects two separate things

<u>synonyms:</u> connection, bond, association

<u>antonyms:</u> split, break

<u>sentence/image:</u> She used pliers to affix the last link to the chain necklace.

634

Reading Strategy Connect to Contemporary Issues

Review the chart you made on page 626 and then answer these questions.

1. (a) What does Santha's sister do when she is accused of being a cheater? (b) What would you do in a similar situation?

2. (a) In what ways do classes that have students from diverse ethnic backgrounds offer educational and social enrichment? (b) What challenges do schools face in meeting the needs of all students?

Vocabulary Practice

Practice with Antonyms With a partner, match each boldfaced vocabulary word below with its antonym. Use a thesaurus or a dictionary to check your answers. You will not use all the answer choices.

1. provincial	**a.** cosmopolitan
2. insular	**b.** understandable
3. incomprehensible	**c.** cool
4. sedately	**d.** playfully
5. tepid	**e.** broad-minded
	g. disgusted

Academic Vocabulary

*This excerpt from Rau's autobiography shows the **link** between her name and her identity.*

Link is an academic word. Words similar in meaning include *connection, bond,* and *tie.* To study *link* further, fill out the graphic organizer below.

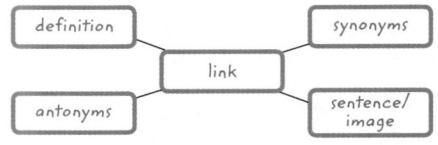

For more on academic vocabulary, see pages 36–37 and R83–R85.

Listening and Speaking

 Speech

Assignment In "By Any Other Name," Rau highlights the negative aspects of the Anglo-Indian school she attended. Write and deliver a speech about a change you would like to see made in your school. In your speech, connect local issues to issues that are relevant to education across the United States.

Prepare Review the graphic organizer you filled out on page 626 for ideas on how to relate your thesis to contemporary issues. Then, expand your ideas into an engaging introduction, a substantive body, and a conclusion, making sure to use logical, ethical, and emotional appeals. To support your argument and express personal style, try using literary elements such as rhetorical questions, figurative language, and concrete details. A visual aid, such as a photograph, may help support one of your key points.

Deliver When you deliver your speech, be sure to use appropriate body language and tone of voice and make eye contact with your audience. Respond to counterarguments by using a sentence frame like the one below:

Some students may object to this change I propose because _____.

Evaluate Write a paragraph evaluating your speech. Be honest with yourself and think about whether your ideas were clearly organized and whether you supported your thesis with ample evidence. Did you persuade the audience that the problem you talked about is worth fixing?

 **Literature** Online

Selection Resources For Selection Quizzes, eFlashcards, and Reading-Writing Connection activities, go to glencoe.com and enter QuickPass code GLW6053u3.

Listening and Speaking

Students' speeches should

- be based on a clear and well-supported thesis
- reflect the use of literary elements such as figurative language
- incorporate appropriate verbal and non-verbal techniques

 To create custom assessments online, go to Progress Reporter Online Assessment.

 To create custom assessments using software, use ExamView Assessment Suite.

Vocabulary Workshop

Homonyms and Homophones

Literature Connection Words that sound alike and are spelled alike but have different meanings are called **homonyms.** For example, *bun* can mean both a baked good and a roll of hair. In the sentence "... the precarious bun on the top of her head trembled as she shook her head," from "By Any Other Name," Santha Rama Rau describes the headmistress's appearance. Since it would make no sense for her to have a baked good on her head, *bun* refers to a hairstyle.

Homophones are words that sound alike but are spelled differently and have different meanings. For example, *hoarse,* meaning "rough-voiced," and *horse,* an animal, are homophones. Some common homonyms and homophones appear in the chart below.

Word	Type	Meaning	Example
bow	homonym	to bend in submission; the forward part of a ship	You should **bow** in front of the king. The **bow** of the boat was covered with ice.
bank	homonym	raised ground bordering a body of water; an institution that lends and safeguards money, among other financial activities	The turtle likes to sit on the **bank** of the river. I have to get money from my **bank.**
alter	homophone	change	Please don't **alter** my work without permission.
altar		raised structure where sacred rites are performed	The church has an **altar** at the front.
bear	homophone	an animal	The **bear** came close to the tent.
bare		lacking clothing	It's not safe to walk around with **bare** feet.

Practice Use context clues to determine the meaning of each homonym or choose the correct homophone below.

1. Sekhar read the <u>note</u> (brief letter/musical tone) from the headmaster.
2. Sekhar could not <u>bear</u> (to endure/an animal) to listen to the headmaster's awful singing.
3. Sekhar does not want to (lie/lye) about his lack of talent.
4. Sekhar realizes it's sometimes best not (to/too) be honest.

Learning Objective

In this workshop, you will focus on the following objectives:

Vocabulary:
Understanding homonyms and homophones. Understanding context clues.

Homonyms and Homophones

Homonyms are words that are pronounced and spelled the same yet have different meanings. **Homophones** are words that are pronounced the same but are spelled differently and have different meanings.

Test-Taking Tip

When you are unsure of the meaning of a homonym or a homophone in a passage, look for context clues to help you determine the meaning of the word and its part of speech.

 **Literature** Online

Vocabulary For more vocabulary practice, go to glencoe.com and enter QuickPass code GLW6053u3.

English Learners

DIFFERENTIATED INSTRUCTION

Intermediate Have students keep a log of homonyms and homophones. As they come across the words in their reading, students can add them to their log. Homonym entries should include the multiple definitions of the word. Homophone entries should include the different spellings and definitions of the words as well as a pronunciation key.

Advanced Learners/Pre-AP

DIFFERENTIATED INSTRUCTION

Homonym/Homophone Mixup
Encourage students to test themselves and their classmates. Have students write paragraphs about a topic covered in this unit, such as British colonialism or a Hindu deity. Tell them to include a mix of homonyms and homophones in their writing. Then, organize students into pairs. Have each pair swap their papers. Students can underline examples of homonyms and homophones.

Vocabulary Workshop

Homonyms and Homophones

Focus

Activity

Write the following sentences on the board: *At present, I have opened one birthday present. I dropped the bag of flower on the table and it got all over the vase of flours.* **Ask:** Which words in the first sentence are homonyms, and how is each word used? (present/present: *The first instance means* currently, *and the second instance means a gift.*) Ask students what is wrong with the second sentence. (*Flower should be* flour *and* flours *should be* flowers.) Point out that these words are homophones.

Teach

Homophones

Remind students that homophones may sound alike, but they are not spelled alike. This means that it is important that students be aware of the different spellings of homophones. For example, when they use word-processing software to compose an assignment, the spell-check software will not catch the wrong word as long as it is spelled correctly. Therefore, students need to read assignments closely to make sure they have included the correct homophone.

Assess

1. brief letter
2. to endure
3. lie
4. to

Before You Read

Focus

Bellringer Options

Selection Focus
    Transparency 38
Daily Language
    Transparency 57

Or ask: What do you find scarier when watching frightening movies: seeing the monster or not seeing the monster? Explain. *(Students may say that seeing the monster is scarier because the visual image of a monster is difficult to get rid of. Other students may say that the idea of knowing that something is there but being unable to see it is more frightening.)* Ask students to list titles of books or movies that contain horror and discuss their powers to scare.

Before You Read

The Wagon

Pakistan

Meet **Khalida Asghar**
(born 1938)

Technology creates the potential for both unprecedented achievement and unfathomable disaster. Khalida Asghar (kä lē′ dä ash′ gär) explores the consequences of modern technology in her highly original and imaginative fiction.

A Newly Formed Country Asghar was born in Lahore in a region of India that later became a Pakistani province. However, at the time of Asghar's birth, Pakistan was not a separate country. Pakistan was created when the partition of 1947 divided the Indian subcontinent along religious lines—Pakistan for the Muslim population and India for the Hindu one. At first, Pakistan was divided into East Pakistan and West Pakistan, which were separated by 1,000 miles of Indian territory. In 1971, after a nine-month civil war, East Pakistan became the independent nation of Bangladesh.

> "'The Wagon' . . . is an abstractly psychological story that has a powerfully hallucinatory effect on the reader even in translation."
>
> —Vinay Dharwadker

An Interrupted Career During the early 1960s, Asghar began to compose short stories in Urdu, the national language of Pakistan. "The Wagon," a short story she wrote early in her career, is considered a modern classic of Urdu

Gabba woollen mat (detail of woman making gabba). Pakistani school.

literature. In this story, Asghar uses a surrealistic approach and an eerie tone to address the problems that can stem from technological advances and human ambivalence. Asghar got married in 1965 and proceeded to publish very few stories for more than a decade. She resumed her career in 1981 with a book of short fiction. Since then, she has published two more short story collections and a short novel, *Kaghazi Ghat*. Some translations of her stories have appeared in anthologies such as *Hoops of Fire: Fifty Years of Fiction by Pakistani Women*; *The Tale of the Old Fisherman*; *Modern Literatures of the Non-Western World: Where the Waters Are Born*; and *Global Voices: Contemporary Literature from the Non-Western World*. In her more recent fiction, she often examines the place of women in Pakistani society, which men have traditionally dominated. Asghar began her career writing under her maiden name but has since written under the name Khalida Husain.

LOG ON ▶ **Literature** Online

Author Search For more about Khalida Asghar, go to glencoe.com and enter QuickPass code GLW6053u3.

Selection Skills

Literary Elements
- Narrator (SE pp. 637, 639, 642, 645, 647, 650)
- Plot (SE p. 650)

Reading Skills
- Identify Ambiguities (SE pp. 637, 639, 640, 643, 646, 648, 650)
- Visualize (TE p. 646)

The Wagon

Vocabulary Skills
- Context Clues (SE p. 650; TE pp. 637, 639)

Speaking/Listening/Viewing Skills
- Visual Literacy (SE p. 649)
- Analyze Art (SE p. 647)
- Conduct an Interview (TE p. 640)

Writing Skills/Grammar
- Editorial (SE p. 651)
- Using Commas with Parenthetical Expressions (TE p. 638)
- Write a News Story (TE p. 648)

Literature and Reading Preview

Connect to the Story

How would it feel to live in a place that was no longer healthy or pleasant because of an environmental hazard? Write a journal entry imagining how you might feel and what you might do in this situation.

Build Background

When Asghar wrote "The Wagon" in the early 1960s, fear of a nuclear holocaust was at an all-time high. Additionally, the effects of industry and manmade chemicals on the environment were starting to be better understood. "The Wagon" eerily foreshadows some of the environmental and nuclear disasters that were to come. One of the most tragic of these disasters occurred in Bhopal, India, in December 1984, when an insecticide plant leaked, killing 3,000 people almost immediately and between 15,000 and 20,000 people over time.

Set Purposes for Reading

Big Idea A Complex Heritage

As you read, ask yourself, What details in the story reveal how technology has changed the modern world?

Literary Element Narrator

The **narrator** is the person who tells a story. The narrator may be a character in the story or may be outside the story. The narrator may speak in the first person (using the pronoun *I*) or in the third person. As you read the story, ask yourself, What clues does the narrator reveal about his state of mind?

Reading Strategy Identify Ambiguities

When you **identify ambiguities**, you look for details in a literary work that cannot be explained in a single, clear way. Monitoring such ambiguities can help you discover hidden meanings in a text. As you read "The Wagon," ask yourself, Why might the ambiguities in this story be significant?

....

Tip: Track Details Use a chart to record your best explanations for the ambiguities in the story. In your chart, set up the details as questions and your explanations as answers.

Question	Answer #1	Answer #2
Why do the men's faces look "curiously alike"?	They are related.	They have similar concerns and habits.

Learning Objectives

For pages 636–650

In studying this text, you will focus on the following objectives:

Literary Study: Analyzing narrator.

Reading: Identifying ambiguities.

Vocabulary

impervious (im pur′vē əs) *adj.* not easily affected or disturbed; p. 639 *The comedian seemed impervious to the bad reviews.*

inexorable (i nek′sər ə bəl) *adj.* relentless; unyielding; p. 639 *The inexorable effects of aging had begun to slow Thomas down.*

pungent (pun′jənt) *adj.* having a sharp or stinging quality, especially affecting the sense of taste or smell; p. 643 *The pungent odor left by the skunk stung our nostrils.*

surge (surj) *n.* a strong, sudden increase or flow; p. 648 *She was getting tired, but a surge of energy enabled her to finish her long swim.*

Tip: Context Clues When you read an unfamiliar word, pay close attention to the context, or setting, in which it appears. For example, in the sentence *The pungent odor left by the skunk stung our nostrils,* you can determine that *pungent* means "having a sharp quality" because the odor "stung our nostrils."

KHALIDA ASGHAR **637**

Focus

Summary

A man sees three strange men on a bridge watching the sunset. The men reluctantly show him how the blood-red sky blazes even at nightfall. Then the city experiences waves of a pungent smell, which are thought to be from wagonloads of garbage passing through the city. One day the three villagers draw back the curtains of the wagon to see the source of the stench. Struck dumb with horror, they flee, never to be seen again. The stench abates, but the narrator waits for the next horror to be revealed.

 For summaries in languages other than English, see Unit 3 Teaching Resources Book, pp. 295–300.

Vocabulary

Context Clues Have students read the sentences supplied with the vocabulary words. Then, have students identify the context clues within the sentences that help them determine the words' meanings. Students should identify context clues as synonyms, antonyms, or explanations of unknown words.

 For additional vocabulary practice, see Unit 3 Teaching Resources Book, p. 303.

Advanced Learners/Pre-AP

DIFFERENTIATED INSTRUCTION

Connect to Contemporary Issues
Students may find some similarities between the natural phenomenon in "The Wagon" and dire predictions about our own climate changes. Encourage students to choose an ecosystem on Earth such as the ocean or a desert that is threatened by humans through pollution. Then, have students research the ecosystem to find out about its climate, natural resources, and animal life. Students should also research the effect that human interaction is having on the habitat. Have students write a short report describing the sources of environmental damage. Students should connect their findings to the glow in the sky and the smell that the narrator experiences in "The Wagon." Encourage students to share their findings with the class.

Teach

Literary Element | 1

Narrator **Ask:** What does the story's starting in the middle of the action tell you about the narrator's place in the action? *(Students are likely to say that the narrator seems to be little more than an observer who is there to narrate the story rather than cause the action.)*

[APPROACHING] A story that begins without much exposition might confuse struggling readers. **Ask:** What do you know about the narrator so far? *(Students will be unsure of the narrator's gender; they can answer that the narrator lives in a city and possibly doesn't own a car.)*

View the Art ★

Ask: What mood is created by this painting? *(Students may say that the fiery colors and the dramatic use of light create an ominous, oppressive mood.)*

Readability Scores

Dale-Chall: 6.7
DRP: 56
Lexile: 770

THE WAGON

Khalida Asghar

Translated by Muhammad Umar Memon

At the sunset, 2004. Ignacio Auzike. Oil on canvas. ★

638   UNIT 3   SOUTH CENTRAL ASIA

Writing Practice

Commas with Parenthetical Expressions Parenthetical expressions are words or phrases that interrupt the flow of a sentence. Parenthetical expressions can come at the beginning, middle, or end of a sentence. Explain that because the information is nonessential, it is set off from the sentence by commas. The information in the parenthetical expression isn't necessary to understand the meaning of the sentence.

Write the following sentences on the board: Will, do you have your homework? You said that you would turn it in tomorrow, didn't you? My assignment, not yours, is the more difficult one. Point out to students the parenthetical expressions in each sentence. Then, have students find any parenthetical expressions on page 639.

(Students may point out the following example from the first paragraph: There they were, three of them, leaning over the bridge's guard rails and gazing straight into the sunset.*)* Ask students why the information is not essential to the meaning of the sentence. *(Readers do not need to know the number of people present to understand what they were doing.)*

638

1 In a rush to get back to the city, I quickly crossed the dirt road and walked onto the Ravi bridge, looking indifferently at the blazing edge of the sun steadily falling into the marsh. I had a queer feeling, as though I saw something. I spun around. There they were, three of them, leaning over the bridge's guard rails and gazing straight into the sunset. Their deathly concentration made me look at the sunset myself, but I found nothing extraordinary in the scene; so I looked back at them instead. Their faces, although not at all similar, still looked curiously alike.

Their outfits suggested that they were well-to-do villagers, and their dust-coated shoes that they had trudged for miles just to watch the sun as it set over the marshes of the receding Ravi. **Impervious** to the traffic on the bridge, they went on staring at the marshes which were turning a dull, deep red in the sun's last glow.

I edged closer to them. The sun had gone down completely; only a dark red stripe remained on the far horizon. Suddenly the three looked at each other, lowered their heads, and silently walked away, toward the villages outside the city. For some time I stood watching their tired figures recede into the distance. Soon the night sounds coming to life in the city reminded me that it was getting late and I'd better rush home. I quickened my pace and walked on under the blue haze of the night sky, pierced here and there by the blinking lights of the city ahead.

The next evening when I reached the bridge, the sunset was a few minutes away. I suddenly recalled the three men and stopped to watch the sunset even though I knew Munna would be waiting on the front porch for sweets and Zakiya, my wife, would be ready for us to go to the movies. I couldn't budge. An **inexorable** force seemed to have tied me to the ground. Through almost all the previous night I'd wondered what it was about the marsh and the sunset that had engrossed those strange men so entirely. **3**

And then, just as the blazing orange disc of the sun tumbled into the marsh, I saw the three walk up the road. They were coming from villages outside the city limits. They wore identical clothes and resembled each other in their height and gait. Again they walked up to the bridge, stood at the same spot they had the previous evening and peered into the sunset with their flaming eyes filled with a dull sadness. I watched them and wondered why, despite their diverse features, they looked so much alike. One of them, who was very old, had a long, bushy snow-white beard. The second, somewhat lighter in complexion than the other, had a face that shone like gold in the orange glow of sunset. His hair hung down to his shoulders like a fringe, and he had a scar on his forehead. The third was dark and snub-nosed.

The sun sank all the way into the marsh. As on the previous day, the men glanced at each other, let their heads drop and, without exchanging a word, went their way.

That evening I felt terribly ill at ease. In a way I regretted not asking them about their utter fascination with the sunset. What could they be looking for in the sun's fading light?—I wondered. I told Zakiya about the strange threesome. She just

2 Identify Ambiguities *What are two ambiguities in this passage?*

Vocabulary

impervious (im pur′vē əs) *adj.* not easily affected or disturbed

Narrator *What information does this sentence provide about the narrator? What might be the significance of this information?* **4**

Vocabulary

inexorable (i nek′sər ə bəl) *adj.* relentless; unyielding

KHALIDA ASGHAR **639**

Teach

Reading Strategy **2**

Identify Ambiguities
Answer: *One ambiguity is why the narrator sees nothing extraordinary in a scene that greatly interests the three men. Another is that the men, although their faces are not similar, look "curiously alike."*

Vocabulary **3**

Context Clues Point out the word *inexorable* on this page.
Ask: What context clues can you find before and after the word? *("couldn't budge," "tied me to")* What do these clues tell you about the force? *(It can't be fought.)*

Literary Element **4**

Narrator Answer: *It reveals that he has a family who must usually be able to rely on him but that he is interested enough in the sunset to delay his return home. This action foreshadows his eventual obsession with the phenomenon.*

Cultural History ☆

Ravi River During part of its 450-mile course, the Ravi River runs along the Pakistan-India border. The river was the subject of disputes between India and Pakistan until 1960.

Learning Objectives
Analyzing narrator. (SE)
Identifying ambiguities. (SE)
Using context clues. (TE)
Using commas with parenthetical expressions. (TE)

English Learners

DIFFERENTIATED INSTRUCTION

Advanced English learners may have some difficulty with figurative language the narrator uses to describe his surroundings. Write the following on the board, underlining as indicated: *And then, just as the <u>blazing orange disc</u> of the sun <u>tumbled into</u> the marsh, I saw the three walk up the road.*

To help students understand the underlined phrases, **ask:** How is the sun a blazing disc? *(It is flat and circular, and it burns brightly as it sets.)* What does the word *tumble* help you visualize? *(the sun falling or rolling)* Discuss with students how the figurative language makes ordinary items more interesting.

Teach

Literary Element 1

Narrator Ask: Why might the narrator call the men "brothers" and ask them where they're from the first time he speaks to them? *(He probably wants them to trust him so that he can get information from them.)*

Reading Strategy 2

Identify Ambiguities
Answer: *The ambiguity is the aura, which the narrator only says is "weird." He cannot make Zakiya understand because it is some indefinable quality that makes the men so odd.*

laughed and said, "Must be peasants, on their way to the city to have a good time."

An air of strangeness surrounded these men. Zakiya, of course, could not have known it: one really had to look at them to feel the weird aura.[1]

The next day I waited impatiently for the evening. I walked to the bridge, expecting them to show up. And they did, just as the daylight ebbed away. They leaned over the bridge and watched the sun go down, indifferent to the sound of traffic. Their absorption in the scene made it impossible to talk to them. I waited until the sun had gone down completely and the men had started to return. This would be the time to ask them what it was they expected to find in the vanishing sun and the marshes of the receding river.

When the sun had sunk all the way, the men gave one another a sad, mute look, lowered their heads and started off. But, instead of returning to the village, they took the road to the city. Their shoes were covered with dust and their feet moved on rhythmically together.

1 I gathered my faltering courage and asked them, "Brothers! what village do you come from?"

The man with the snub nose turned around and stared at me for a while. Then the three exchanged glances, but none of them bothered to answer my question.

"What do you see over there . . . on the bridge?" I asked. The mystery about the three men was beginning to weigh heavily upon me now. I felt as though molten lead had seeped into my legs—indeed into my whole body, and that it was only a matter

---

1. An *aura* is a distinctive character or atmosphere surrounding a person or thing.

2 **Identify Ambiguities** *What is the ambiguity here? Why can't the narrator make Zakiya understand the men's strangeness?*

of time before I'd crumble to the ground reeling from a spell of dizziness.

Again they did not answer. I shouted at them in a choking voice, "Why are you always staring at the sunset?"

No answer.

We reached the heavily congested city road. The evening sounds grew closer. It was late October, and the air felt pleasantly cool. The sweet scent of jasmine wafted in, borne by the breeze. As we passed the octroi post,[2] the old man with snow-white hair suddenly spoke, "Didn't you see? Has nobody in the city seen . . . ?"

"Seen what?"

"When the sun sets, when it goes down all the way . . . ?" asked the hoary[3] old man, rearranging his mantle over his shoulders.

Visual Vocabulary
A *mantle* is a loose, sleeveless piece of clothing.

"When the sun goes down all the way?" I repeated. "What about it? That happens every day!"

I said that very quickly, afraid that the slightest pause might force them back into their impenetrable silence.

"We knew that, we knew it would be that way. That's why we came. That other village, there, too . . ." He pointed toward the east and lowered his head.

"From there we come . . ." said the snub-nosed man.

"From where?" I asked, growing impatient. "Please tell me clearly."

The third man peered back at me over his shoulder. The scar on his forehead suddenly seemed deeper than before. He said,

---

2. An *octroi* is a local customs tax, payable on goods moved within a country; it is collected at an *octroi post*.
3. *Hoary* means "gray or white with age."

Listening and Speaking Practice

Conduct an Interview Tell students that sometimes an interview isn't as easy as it seems because the person being interviewed either doesn't want to share information or doesn't have information to share. Have students conduct interviews with one another, taking turns being the interviewer. One student, when interviewed, will pretend to be the narrator; the other will be one of the three men.

To get pairs started, have them decide which student will be the narrator and which will be one of the villagers. Then, **ask:** What questions would you ask the three men? What are you most curious to know? What follow-up questions would you ask if you didn't get an answer the first time? Encourage students to keep their interviews brief and to the point.

Red Townscape, 1961. Francis Newton Souza. Oil on canvas. Private collection.

"We didn't notice, nor, I believe, did you. Perhaps nobody did. Because, as you say, the sun rises and sets every day. Why bother to look? And we didn't, when day after day, there, over there," he pointed in the direction of the east, "the sky became blood-red and so bright it blazed like fire even at nightfall. We just failed to notice . . ." He stopped abruptly, as if choking over his words. "And now this redness," he resumed after a pause, "it keeps spreading from place to place. I'd never seen such a phenomenon before. Nor my elders. Nor, I believe, did they hear their elders mention anything quite like that ever happening."

Meanwhile the darkness had deepened. All I could see of my companions were their white flowing robes; their faces became

visible only when they came directly under the pale, dim light of the lampposts. I turned around to look at the stretch of sky over the distant Ravi. I was stunned: it was glowing red despite the darkness.

"You are right," I said, to hide my puzzlement, "we really did fail to notice that." Then I asked, "Where are you going?"

"To the city, of course. What would be the point of arriving there *afterwards*?"

4

A sudden impulse made me want to stay with them, or to take them home with me. But abruptly, they headed off on another road, and I remembered I was expected home soon. Munna would be waiting on the front porch for his daily sweets and Zakiya must be feeling irritated by my delay.

The next day I stopped at the bridge to watch the sunset. I was hoping to see those three men. The sun went down completely, but they didn't appear. I waited impatiently

---

3 A Complex Heritage *What does this statement indicate about the culture of the three men? What does it indicate about the nature of the phenomenon?*

KHALIDA ASGHAR **641**

A Complex Heritage
Answer: *It indicates that they take history and the words of the elders seriously, perhaps more so than residents of the city, who ignore the phenomenon at first. The fact that elders have never experienced a similar phenomenon indicates that something new caused it.*

Reading Strategy   4

Identify Ambiguities   **Ask:**
What effect does the ambiguity of the word "afterwards" have? *(Students may say that this word strengthens the suspense and causes them to wonder what happened before.)*

(ENGLISH LEARNERS) Explain that italics in text signify importance.

View the Art ★

Francis Newton Souza (1924–2002) was influenced by the geometric contours made famous by his contemporary, Pablo Picasso, and by the disturbing and disjointed quality recognized in the Expressionism of the early twentieth century. **Ask:** What mood does this painting convey? How do these emotions compare to those in the story? *(Students may say that the painting conveys a disturbing, confusing, and disjointed mood that is similar to the emotions that the story's narrator experiences.)*

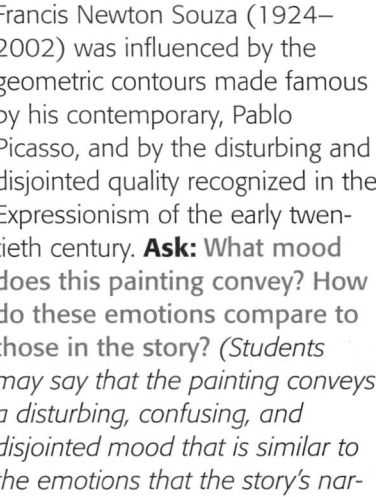

Learning Objectives
Identifying ambiguities. (SE)
Conducting an interview. (TE)

Advanced Learners/Pre-AP

DIFFERENTIATED INSTRUCTION

Research Students may enjoy discovering some of the reasons behind light phenomena in the sky. Invite students to research the aftereffects of a nuclear explosion on the atmosphere. Have students try to find out the colors the sky takes on, how the weather changes, and how long the effects last. Encourage students to share their findings with the class.

Teach

Literary Element | 1

Narrator Answer: *It reveals that he is generous but afraid to confront people directly with questions, since he has apparently not asked for his money or asked why they will not speak to him. It indicates that his hesitation to ask the three men details about the phenomenon is not out of character.*

Language History ☆

Sahib The term *sahib,* meaning "master," is found in both Hindi and Urdu (Pakistan's native language). Often used as when addressing someone of importance in colonial India, the term can also be found in the Sikh religion. There it is found in the name of the sacred scripture of Sikhism, the *Guru Granth Sahib,* and one of the religion's most important pilgrimage sites, Darbar Sahib.

for them to show up. Soon, however, I was entranced by the sunset's last magical glow.

The entire sky seemed covered with a sheet soaked in blood, and it scared me that I was standing all alone underneath it. I felt an uncanny presence directly behind me. I spun around. There was nobody. All the same, I felt sure there was someone— standing behind my back, within me, or perhaps, somewhere near.

Vehicles, of all shapes and sizes, rumbled along in the light of the street lamps. Way back in the east, a stretch of evening sky still blazed like a winding sheet of fire, radiating heat and light far into the closing darkness. I was alarmed and scurried home. Hastily I told Zakiya all I'd seen. But she laughed off the whole thing. I took her up to the balcony and showed her the red and its infernal bright glow against the dark night sky. That sobered her up a little. She thought for a while, then remarked, "We're going to have a storm any minute—I'm sure."

The next day in the office, as I worked, bent over my files, I heard Mujibullah ask Hafiz Ahmad, "Say, did you see how the sky glows at sunset these days? Even after it gets dark? Amazing, isn't it?"

All at once I felt I was standing alone and defenseless under that bloodsheet of a sky. I was frightened. Small drops of sweat formed on my forehead. As the evening edged closer, a strange restlessness took hold of me. The receding Ravi, the bridge, the night sky and the sun frightened me; I wanted to walk clear out of them. And yet, I also felt irresistibly drawn toward them.

I wanted to tell my colleagues about the three peasants who in spite of their distinctly individual faces somehow looked alike; about how they had come to the city accompanying this strange redness, had drawn my attention to it, and then dropped out of sight; and about how I'd searched in vain for them everywhere. But I couldn't.

Mujibullah and Hafiz Ahmad, my office-mates, had each borrowed about twenty rupees from me some time ago, which they conveniently forgot to return, and, into the bargain, had stopped talking to me ever since.

On my way home when I entered the bridge, a strange fear made me walk briskly, look away from the sun, and try to concentrate instead on the street before me. But the blood-red evening kept coming right along. I could feel its presence everywhere. A flock of evening birds flew overhead in a "V" formation. Like the birds, I too was returning home. Home—yes, but no longer my haven against the outside world; for the flame-colored evening came pouring in from its windows, doors, even through its walls of solid masonry.

I now wandered late in the streets, looking for the three peasants. I wanted to ask them where that red came from. What was to follow? Why did they leave the last settlement? What shape was it in? But I couldn't find them anywhere. Nobody seemed to care.

A few days later I saw some men pointing up to the unusual red color of the evening. Before long, the whole city was talking about it. I hadn't told a soul except Zakiya. How they had found out about it was a puzzle to me. Those three peasants must be in the city—I concluded. They have got to be.

The red of evening had now become the talk of the town.

Chaudhri Sahib, who owns a small bookshop in Mozang Plaza, was an old acquaintance of mine. People got together at his shop for a friendly chat every evening. Often, so did I. But for some time now, ☆

Narrator *What does this passage reveal about the narrator's willingness to talk to others? How might it contribute to a better understanding of his relationship with the three men?* **1**

Writing Practice

Write a Simile and a Metaphor
Review with students the differences between a simile and a metaphor. A simile uses *like* or *as* to compare two things; a metaphor says that one thing is another. Have students reread the narrator's experience with the pungent smell. Then, ask students to compose a simile and a metaphor describing the smell.

To add difficulty, tell students that they cannot write the simile and metaphor comparing the smell to another. Encourage students to try and imagine what the narrator is experiencing. To get students started, **ask:** What is the worst thing you have ever smelled? How would you describe it in words?

Show struggling students examples of simple metaphors and similes. Encourage them to start with the easier concept of similes before moving on to metaphors.

Coming from Rajasthan, 1984. Balraj Khanna. Acrylic on canvas. Arts Council Collection, Hayward Gallery, London. ★

since my first encounter with those mantle-wrapped oracular[4] figures, I had been too preoccupied with my own thoughts to go there. No matter where I went, home or outside, I felt restless. At home, an inexorable urge drove me outdoors; outdoors, an equally strong urge sent me scrambling back home, where I felt comparatively safer. I became very confused

---

4. *Oracular* means "prophetic."

Narrator *What conclusions can you draw about the physical and mental state of the narrator? What may be causing his behavior?*

2

about where I wanted to be. I began to feel heavy and listless.

All the same, I did go back to the bookshop once again that evening. Most of the regulars had already gathered. Chaudhri Sahib asked, "What do you think about it, fellows? Is it all due to the atomic explosions as they say? The rumor also has it that pretty soon the earth's cold regions will turn hot and the hot ones cold and the cycle of seasons will also be upset."

I wanted to tell them about my encounter with the three villagers but felt too shy to talk before so many people. Just then a **pungent** smell, the likes of which I'd never smelled before, wafted in from God knows where. My heart sank and a strange, sweet sort of pain stabbed my body. I felt nauseous, unable to decide whether it was a stench, a pungent aroma, or even a wave of bittersweet pain. I threw the newspaper down and got up to leave.

"What's the matter?" asked Chaudhri Sahib.

"I must go. God knows what sort of smell that is."

"Smell? What smell?" Chaudhri Sahib sniffed the air.

I didn't care to reply and walked away.

That offensive smell, the terrifying wave of pain, followed me all the way home. It

---

Identify Ambiguities *How might you account for the discrepancy in reactions to the stench the narrator notices?*   **3**

Vocabulary

pungent (pun'jənt) *adj.* having a sharp or stinging quality, especially affecting the sense of taste or smell

KHALIDA ASGHAR **643**

Teach

Literary Element   2

Narrator Answer: *Students may conclude that the narrator is experiencing a nervous breakdown of sorts. The mystery and foreboding created by the three men and the glowing sky seem responsible for this.*

Reading Strategy   3

Identify Ambiguities
Answer: *The narrator might be ill and therefore more susceptible to the odor; the narrator's focus on the phenomenon may make him more open to its effects; different people might have different levels of tolerance.*

View the Art ★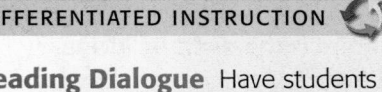

Shanti Panchal (1951–) was born in India and moved to Britain in 1978. The brilliant red color of the background and earth-tone colors of the foreground in *Contemplation* are typical of his work. He counts El Greco and William Blake among his influences. **Ask:** What might the subject of this painting have in common with the narrator of the story? *(Students may say that the man appears troubled and overwhelmed.)*

Approaching Level

DIFFERENTIATED INSTRUCTION

Reading Dialogue Have students work in pairs to read the dialogue on this spread between the narrator and his wife and between the narrator and his officemates. Students should take turns reading aloud in a manner that expresses the narrator's rising emotions. Have students try different modes of vocal delivery, including rising volume and varied inflection.

Advanced Learners/Pre-AP

DIFFERENTIATED INSTRUCTION

Analyze Cause and Effect Encourage students to investigate the ambiguous nature of the cause-and-effect relationship the author has created. Have students list the events that seem to lead to a strengthening of the odor or other effects on the narrator. Then, ask students to write a paragraph describing the effects such ambiguous cause-and-effect relationships have on the story and reader.

Learning Objectives
Analyzing narrator. (SE)
Identifying ambiguities. (SE)
Writing a simile and a metaphor. (TE)

Teach

View the Art ★

Fiery Night shows a balance of opposites: the right contains a brushstroke of cool blue and grey water that rushes through cubist buildings down to sweeping greens. The left contains the warm yellows and reds of a tall-reaching fire, lying against a backdrop of infinite darkness. The stable geometric buildings show the influences of Cubism while the sweeping movements and contrasting colors of water and fire indicate a Futurist influence. **Ask:** Which is more representative of the action in the story: the menace of the fire or the bleakness of the buildings? *(Some students may choose the fire because it connects with the pungent smells and feeling of danger; others may choose the buildings because their bleakness represent the narrator's negative outlook.)*

Fiery Night, 1997. Millie Basu Roy. Oil on board. Private collection. ★

made me giddy. I thought I might fall any minute. My condition frightened Zakiya, who asked, "What's the matter—you look so pale?"

"I'm all right. God knows what that smell is," I said, wiping sweat off my brow, although it was the month of November.

Zakiya also sniffed the air, then said, "Must be coming from the house of Hakim Sahib. Heaven knows what strange herb concoctions they keep making day and night. Or else it's from burnt food. I burnt some today accidentally."

"But it seems to be everywhere . . . in every street and lane . . . throughout the city."

"Why, of course. The season's changed. It must be the smell of winter flowers," she said inattentively, and became absorbed in her knitting.

With great trepidation I again sniffed the air, but couldn't decide whether the sickening odor still lingered on or had subsided. Perhaps it had subsided. The thought relieved me a bit. But there was no escape from its memory, which remained fresh in my mind, like the itching that continues for some time even after the wound has healed. The very thought that it might return gave me the chills.

By next morning I'd forgotten all about that rotten, suffocating smell. In the office, I found a mountain of files waiting for me. But Mujibullah and Hafiz Ahmad went on noisily discussing some movie. I couldn't concentrate on the work and felt irritated. So I decided to take a break. I called our office boy and sent him to the cafeteria for a cup of tea. Meanwhile I pulled out a pack of cigarettes from my pocket and lit up.

Just then I felt a cracking blow on my head, as if I had fallen off a cliff and landed on my head, which fused everything before my eyes in a swirling blue and yellow streak. It took my numbed senses some time to realize that I was being assaulted once again by the same pain, the same

644 UNIT 3 SOUTH CENTRAL ASIA

Reading Practice

Identify Ambiguities After students have finished reading this page, ask them to return to the quotation on page 636. Review with them the meaning of the word abstract, focusing on its sense as not dealing directly with its subject. Explain that the author reveals the psychology of the narrator not by a direct description but by providing examples of his thoughts. Return to the quotation and **ask:** From what noun is the word hallucinatory derived? *(hallucination)* On page 644, what examples can you find of thoughts that give the impression of being hallucinations? *(the narrator's not being sure if the odor is still present, the feeling of a cracking blow on the head)* Ask students to look for other examples of hallucinatory feelings as they continue to read.

terrible stench. It kept coming at me in waves, and it was impossible to know its source. I found myself frantically shutting every single window in the office, while both Mujibullah and Hafiz Ahmad gawked at me uncomprehendingly.

"Let the sun in! Why are you slamming the windows?" asked Hafiz Ahmad.

"The stench . . . the stench! My God, it's unbearable! Don't you smell it?"

Both of them raised their noses to the air and sniffed. Then Hafiz Ahmad remarked. "That's right. What sort of stench . . . or fragrance is that? It makes my heart sink."

Soon, many people were talking about the stink-waves which came in quick succession and then receded, only to renew their assault a little while later. At sundown they became especially unbearable.

Within a few weeks the stinking odor had become so oppressive that I often found it difficult to breathe. People's faces, usually quite lively and fresh, now looked drained and wilted. Many complained of constant palpitation[5] and headaches. The doctors cashed in. Intellectuals hypothesized that it must be due to nuclear blasts, which were producing strange effects throughout the world, including this foul odor in our city, which attacked people's nerves and left them in a mess. People scrambled to buy tranquilizers, which sold out instantly. Not that the supply was inadequate, but a sudden frenzy to stock up and horde had seized people. Even sleeping pills fetched the price of rare diamonds.

I found both tranquilizers and sleeping pills useless. The stench cut sharper than a sword and penetrated the body like a laser.

---

5. Here, a *palpitation* is a rapid heartbeat.

 Narrator *How does the reaction of other people compare with that of the narrator? What might this reveal about society and about the narrator?*

The only way to guard against it was to get used to it—I thought; and people would do well to remember that. But I was too depressed to tell them myself. Within a few weeks, however, they themselves came to live with the stench.

Just the same, the stench struck terror in the city. People were loath to admit it, but they could not have looked more tense: their faces contorted from the fear of some terrible thing happening at any moment. Nor was their fear unreasonable, as a subsequent event showed a few weeks later.

On a cold mid-December evening, I was returning home from Chaudhri Sahib's. The street was full of traffic and jostling crowds. The stores glittered with bright lights, and people went about their business as usual. Every now and then a stench-wave swept in, made me giddy, and receded. I would freeze in my stride the instant it assailed me and would start moving again as soon as it had subsided. It was the same with others. An outsider would surely have wondered why we suddenly froze, closed our eyes, stopped breathing, then took a deep breath and got started again. But that was our custom now.

That December evening I'd just walked onto the bridge when I felt as if a lance had hit me on the head. My head whirled and my legs buckled. Reeling, I clung on to a lamppost and tried to support my head with my hands. There was no lance, nor was there a hand to wield it. It was that smell—that same rotten smell—I realized with terror. In fact, it seemed that the source of the oppressive stench had suddenly moved very close to me, between my shoulder blades, near my back, immediately behind me—so close that it was impossible to think of it as apart from me.

It was then that my eyes fell on the strange carriage, rambling along in front of

KHALIDA ASGHAR **645**

Teach

Literary Element | 1

Narrator Answer: *Other people immediately rush to medicate themselves into a stupor, whereas the narrator remains painfully aware of what is happening around him. This reveals how people in society often reach for a quick solution, rather than taking the time to figure out the true cause of the problem and how it can be fixed. This in turn reveals how perceptive the narrator might be.*

Learning Objectives
Analyzing narrator. (SE)
Analyzing art. (TE)
Identifying ambiguities. (TE)

Advanced Learners/Pre-AP

DIFFERENTIATED INSTRUCTION

Analyze Symbolism Students may benefit from analyzing the story for symbolism. Encourage students to reread the story, noting particularly strong colors, instances of threes, and places that are used often in traditional literature to symbolize larger ideas. Students can research color symbolism, being careful to note that some colors in South Central Asian culture have different connotations than in the United States.

To get students started, **ask:** In what place does the narrator begin his strange experiences, and what might it symbolize? *(a bridge; moving from one experience or state of being to the next)* What colors does the narrator describe most often, and what might they symbolize? *(red, black, and white; blood, death, and spirits)*

Ask students to create a short presentation for the class that describes examples of symbolism in the story.

Teach

Reading Strategy   1

Identify Ambiguities

Answer: *The reader, like the narrator, does not know what the cage holds or why it has black curtains or "swaying walls" concealing its contents. This contributes to the suspense of the story by using frightening, dark imagery to deepen the mystery.*

Cultural History ☆

Sacred Cows In Hinduism, the cow is considered sacred, especially milk-producing cows; the milk is turned to butter, from which *ghee*, a sacred substance, is produced. Although the slaughter of cows is a political issue in India today, bulls and oxen were sacrificed in ancient times.

---

me. It was an oversized wagon pulled by a pair of scrawny white oxen with leather blinders over their eyes and thick ropes strung through their steaming nostrils. A wooden cage sat atop the base of the wagon, its interior hidden behind black curtains—or were they just swaying walls of darkness?

Two men, sitting outside the cage enclosure in the front of the wagon, drove the two emaciated, blindfolded animals. I couldn't make out their faces, partly because of the darkness, but partly also because they were buried in folds of cloth thrown loosely around them. Their heads drooped forward and they seemed to have dozed off, overcome by fatigue and sleep.

Behind them the interior of the curtained wagon swelled with darkness and from the heart of that darkness shot out the nauseating stench which cut sharper than a sword . . . Before I knew it, the wagon had creaked past me, flooding my senses with its cargo of stink. My head swirled. I jumped off the main road onto the dirt sidewalk . . . and vomited.

I had no idea whether the people in the city had also seen the eerie wagon. If they had, what must have they endured? I had the hardest time getting home after what I had seen. Once inside the house, I ran to my bed and threw myself on it. Zakiya kept asking me what had happened, but a blind terror sealed my lips.

A few days later a small news item appeared in the local papers. It railed against the local Municipal Office for allowing garbage carts to pass through busy streets in the evening. Not only did muck-wagons pollute the air, they also hurt the fine olfactory sense of the citizenry.

> **1**   Identify Ambiguities *How do these ambiguous details about the wagon contribute to the suspense of the story?*

I took a whole week off from work. During those seven days, though hardly fit to go out and observe firsthand the plight of the city, I was nonetheless kept posted of developments by local newspapers. Groups of concerned citizens demanded that the municipal authorities keep the city clear of the muck-wagons or, if that was impossible, assign them routes along less busy streets.

On the seventh day I ventured out. A change was already visible. Wrecked by insomnia and exhaustion, people strained themselves to appear carefree and cheerful, but managed only to look painfully silly. Suddenly I recalled that in the morning I had myself looked no different in the mirror.

About this time, the number of entertainment programs and movies shot up as never before. People swarmed to box offices—often hours before a show—where they formed long lines and patiently waited to be let in, and then filed out from the entertainment still looking pale and ridiculous.

In the office, no matter how hard I tried, I couldn't concentrate on work. Intermittently, the image of the muck-wagon lumbering down the streets flashed across my mind. Was it really one of those municipal dump-carts? No. It couldn't be. Municipal dump-carts never looked like that eerie wagon, with its sleepy drivers, a pair of blindfolded bony oxen, black curtains and the outrageously nauseating smell. What on earth could give off such an odd smell—at once fragrant and foul!

An insane desire suddenly overwhelmed me: to rush up to the wagon, lift up those swaying curtains, and peek inside. I must discover the source of the stench!

Reading Practice

Visualize Tell students that visualizing a scene includes not only imagining what the people, places, and events look like, but also what they sound, feel, taste, and smell like. Have students create a graphic organizer with five columns labeled See, Touch, Taste, Hear, and Smell. Ask students to reread the scene in which the narrator first encounters the wagon.

Then have students fill out their charts with information about each sense. To encourage a deeper reading of the scene, ask students to try to record information for each sentence they read. Also remind them that the narrator's imaginings are part of the visualization of the scene. It might help struggling students to be paired with advanced students for this activity.

The Couple, 1984. Hind Nasser (Jordan). Oil on canvas, 90 x 100 cm. Collection of the Mango Family.

View the Art How do the colors in this painting affect your response to it? How does color affect the characters in the story? ★

Coming to the bridge my feet involuntarily slowed down. There was still some time before sunset and the waves of the pain-filled odor came faster and stronger. I leaned over the bridge, an unknown fear slowly rising in my throat. The bottomless swamp, its arms ominously outstretched, seemed to be dragging me down toward it. I was afraid I might jump into the swamp, sink with the sun and become buried forever in that sprawling sheet of blood.

I became aware of something approaching me—or was I myself drawing closer to something? . . . Something awaited by all

2

men—those before and those after us. My whole body felt as though it was turning into a piece of granite, with no escape from the bridge, the miasma,[6] the sun, for now they all seemed inseparable from my being. Helplessly, I looked around myself and almost dropped dead.

The three men were coming towards me from the direction of the countryside. As before, they were wrapped in their flowing white robes and walked with their amazingly identical gait. I kept staring at them with glassy eyes until they walked right up to me and stopped. The hoary old man was

3 Narrator *How has the narrator changed since the beginning of the story?*

6. A *miasma* is a heavy vaporous emanation or atmosphere.

KHALIDA ASGHAR **647**

English Learners

DIFFERENTIATED INSTRUCTION

Intermediate To help English learners with their understanding of word parts, write on the board the words *involuntarily* and *inseparable,* which appear on this page. **Ask:** How does adding the prefix in- to a word change the word's meaning? *(Students should note that it makes the meaning opposite. If any students seem to be struggling with this concept, use* correct *and incorrect as an example.)* Point out that both *involuntarily* and *inseparable* begin with the prefix *in-.* Have students look in a dictionary to find definitions of *voluntarily* and *separable.* Then have them apply all of the information they have just learned to explain the meaning of the sentences in which *involuntarily* and *inseparable* appear.

Teach

Reading Strategy   2

Identify Ambiguities Ask: What do you think this ambiguous "something awaited by all men" could be? *(Students may identify the "something" as death.)*

Literary Element   3

Narrator Answer: *He has changed from a man who brought sweets to his child and went to the movies with his wife to someone who is simultaneously terrified of the events that are happening and obsessed with them.*

Progress Check

Can students analyze narrator?

If No → See Unit 3 Teaching Resources Book, p. 301.

View the Art ★

Answer: *The color in the painting seems nearly overwhelming, just as it overwhelms the narrator.*

Hind Nasser (1940–) was born in Jordan. She is "an abstract artist whose painted forms give the illusion and energy of three-dimensional sculpture," according to critic Anne Mullin Burnham. Nasser studied painting with one of Turkey's most famous female artists, Princess Fahr El Nissa Zeid. In recent years Nasser has creating weavings based on her paintings.

Learning Objectives
Identifying ambiguities. (SE)
Analyzing narrator. (SE)
Visualizing. (TE)

Teach

Reading Strategy 1

Identify Ambiguities **Ask:** How might the three men being unable to speak be a message about curiosity and knowledge? *(Students may say that the men's curiosity, and subsequent gaining of knowledge, has brought them harm. Because of their injury, they cannot share what they have learned; this may mean that the only knowledge people can truly have is that which they experience themselves.)*

[ENGLISH LEARNERS] Explain to English learners that the adjective *dumb* in this context means "mute."

Reading Strategy 2

Identify Ambiguities
Answer: *Students may say that given the stench and the black shroud over the cage, the wagon contains the bodies of people who have died as a result of the nameless threat.*

Progress Check

Can students identify ambiguities?

If No → See Unit 3 Teaching Resources Book, p. 302.

Writing Practice

Write a News Story Have students write a short news story based on the events in "The Wagon." They can use the skills they have practiced earlier, including visualization and interviewing. Explain to students that because of the ambiguities of the story, they will have to "conduct" interviews with characters as part of their news report.

Remind students that news stories should include an explanation of *who, what, when, where, why,* and *how.* Encourage students to focus on an attention-grabbing lead that quickly summarizes the main points of the events of "The Wagon." Have students publish their news stories, including a headline and illustration, to share with the class.

---

crying, and his snow-white beard was drenched in tears. The other two couldn't look up; their eyes were lowered mournfully, their teeth clenched and their faces withered by a deathly pallor.

"Where were you hiding all these days?" I said between gasps and stammers. "I searched for you everywhere. Tell me, please, what's happening to the city?"

1 "We were waiting. Trying to hold ourselves back. We had tied ourselves with ropes. Here, look!" They spread their arms before me and bared their shoulders and backs, revealing the deep marks of the rope.

"We did not want to come . . ." the old man said, drowned out by a fit of sobs.

"But there was no choice . . ." the second man said. Before he had finished, he doubled over. His companions also doubled over, as if unable to control a sudden **surge** of pain. The same wave of pain-filled stench stabbed the air about us, cutting us into halves, flooding our senses, as it scrambled past us.

"There! Look!" said the old man, pointing in the direction of the distant villages and turning deathly pale.

In the distance, I saw the wagon come up the road from behind a cloud of dust. The drowsing coachmen had wrapped their faces because of their nearness to the cutting stench.

A cold shiver ran through my spine. The eyes of the three men suddenly became dull. They were approaching their end—perhaps.

The wagon rumbled close—the stench from it draining the blood from our bodies—and then passed us. Its sinister, jet-black curtains, fluttering in the gentle breeze, appeared, oddly enough, entirely motionless.

Vocabulary
surge (surj) *n.* a strong, sudden increase or flow

The three men ran after the wagon, caught up to it and lifted the curtains. A split second later, a nonhuman scream burst from their gaping mouths. They spun around and bolted toward the distant fields.

"What was it? What did you see?" I asked, running after them. But they did not reply and kept running madly. Their eyes had frozen in a glazed stare.

I followed them until we had left the city several miles behind us, then grabbed the old man's robe and implored, "Tell me! Please tell me!"

He turned his deathly gaze and threw open his mouth. His tongue had got stuck to his palate.

All three had become dumb.

My head whirled, and I collapsed. The three men continued to run, soon disappearing in the distance behind a spiraling cloud of dust. Slowly the dust settled and I returned home.

For months now I have searched in vain for those men. They have vanished without a trace. And the wagon . . . from that fateful evening, it too has changed its route. It no longer passes through the city. After crossing the bridge, it now descends onto the dirt trail leading to villages in the countryside.

The cityfolk are no longer bothered by the slashing stench. They have become immune to it and think it has died, like an old, forgotten tale.

But it continues to torment my body, and day and night a voice keeps telling me, "Now, your turn! Now you shall *see!*"

And this evening I find myself on the bridge, waiting for the wagon . . . waiting. ∾

Identify Ambiguities *What do you think the wagon contains?* **2**

After You Read

Respond and Think Critically

Respond and Interpret

1. How did you feel as you read about the mysterious occurrences? Explain.

2. (a)As the story opens, whom does the narrator see on the Ravi bridge, and what are these individuals doing? (b)What does the narrator's interest in their behavior suggest about him?

3. (a)What change occurs in the sky? (b)What evidence indicates that the narrator is not hallucinating?

4. (a)How do Zakiya and other people in the city react to the changes in the environment? (b)What do these reactions suggest about human nature?

Analyze and Evaluate

5. (a)How is the strange odor described? (b)To what do other people attribute the odor? Do you agree with them? Why or why not?

6. (a)By the end of the story, the three villagers have vanished. What might their disappearance symbolize, or represent? (b)How effectively does the author develop these villagers as symbols? Explain.

7. (a)Why might Asghar have chosen not to reveal the actual cause of the phenomena? (b)In your opinion, would the story be better if she had? Explain.

Connect

8. **Big Idea** **A Complex Heritage** What might the presence of the three men indicate about the complex heritages of the people in the story?

9. **Connect to Today** Fiction and nonfiction horror stories continue to be immensely popular. Why might Asghar have chosen this style of writing to convey her theme?

Visual Literacy: Photography

Responding to Catastrophe

Study this photograph of a man standing in front of the wall that encloses the Union Carbide pesticide plant. Review the Build Background on page 637 about the disaster that took place at this plant.

Group Activity Discuss the following questions with your classmates. Refer to the photograph and cite evidence from "The Wagon" to support your answers.

1. How does this image parallel ideas in "The Wagon" and the narrator's response to them?

2. What does the wall painting in the photo reveal about opinions of the Bhopal residents who protested against Union Carbide?

Visual Literacy

1. The image parallels the idea that environmental hazards caused by technology and industry can have disastrous consequences. The man in the picture looks haunted and deeply upset, much like the narrator.

2. It reveals that they see the company as a "killer" interested only in profit (the dollar signs in the eye of the figure).

9. Asghar may have written the story as a horror story to underscore how truly awful it is that the potential for these disasters exists.

 For additional selection assessment, see Assessment Resources, pp. 133–134.

After You Read

Assess

1. Answers will vary.

2. (a) Three mysterious men are staring at the sunset. (b) He is very aware of the actions and emotions of other people, and that he is curious.

3. (a) The sky takes on a mysterious red glow that lingers after sunset. (b) Other people confirm the narrator's observations.

4. (a) Zakiya tries to explain away the phenomena. Other people take tranquilizers and go to movies. (b) Students may say that people try to explain or deny unpleasant situations.

5. (a) "pungent," "rotten," and "suffocating" (b) garbage carts passing through city streets; students may say that the stench seems too great to be caused by garbage carts.

6. (a) the loss of hope for any explanation or solution to the threat (b) Students may say effectively, because of the memorable images created by showing how concerned and saddened they are about the mysterious situation.

7. (a) to render the story a universal cautionary tale about the dangers of technology. (b) Answers will vary.

8. The men's approach to the problem contrasts sharply with that of the city residents, who accept easy explanations, take tranquilizers, and go to the movies. The presence of the men in the story may suggest the difference between people who are still tied to family and the environment and people who have become so desensitized by the modern world that they are apathetic about their environment.

After You Read

Assess

Literary Element

1. Students may agree that what he saw could not have been an ordinary dump-cart because of the reaction of the three villagers when they looked inside. They might also cite the narrator's claim that "Municipal dump-carts never looked like that eerie wagon."

2. Answers will vary.

Review: Plot

Exposition: The narrator talks about the three mysterious villagers, the blood-red sky, the stench, the reactions of other townspeople, and the appearance of the eerie cart.

Rising Action: The narrator becomes increasingly obsessed with the strange phenomena.

Climax: The three mysterious villagers look into the cart and let out an inhuman scream.

Falling Action: The narrator catches up to the men and asks what they saw. They cannot talk.

Resolution: There is no resolution. The narrator is still waiting for the men and the wagon to come back. Some students may enjoy the sense of mystery and the sense of dread the ending creates, while others will feel "left hanging" and perturbed.

Whether the narrator speaks in the first person or the third person, you need to ask yourself, Can I trust what this narrator tells me? A **reliable narrator** is one who can be trusted. An **unreliable narrator** is one whose point of view the reader distrusts—perhaps because the narrator reveals clues that he or she is unstable, dishonest, naïve, or otherwise questionable.

1. At one point in the story, the narrator seems haunted by the memory of the "muck-wagon" and begins to question his own perceptions. Do you agree with the narrator that what he saw could not have been an ordinary municipal dump-cart? Support your answer with evidence from the story.

2. Do you think the narrator is reliable or unreliable? Explain.

Review: Plot

As you learned on page 84, **plot** is the sequence of events in a work of fiction. The plot begins with **exposition,** which introduces the story's characters, setting, and conflict, then leads to **rising action** (which develops the conflict), a **climax,** and ends with **falling action** and **resolution.**

Partner Activity With a partner, discuss the various plot elements of this story. Then fill in a plot diagram like the one below with a description of each plot element in this story. Discuss how you feel about the ending. Is there a true resolution?

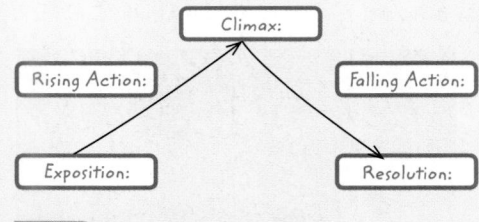

Climax:

Rising Action: Falling Action:

Exposition: Resolution:

LOG ON ▶ **Literature** Online

Selection Resources For Selection Quizzes, eFlashcards, and Reading-Writing Connection activities, go to glencoe.com and enter QuickPass code GLW6053u3.

SAT Skills Practice

On page 639, the passage "Their outfits suggested that they were well-to-do villagers, and their dust-coated shoes that they had trudged for miles just to watch the sun as it set over the marshes of the receding Ravi" creates ambiguity by:

(A) identifying the Ravi but not the time of day.

(B) noting that the men walked far but giving an odd reason for their journey.

(C) creating a contrast between the men's clothing and their shoes.

(D) using nonspecific adjectives.

(E) placing the villagers in unfamiliar territory.

Vocabulary Practice

Practice with Context Clues Look back at pages 638–648 to find context clues for the vocabulary words below. Record your findings in a graphic organizer like the one here.

impervious   inexorable   pungent   surge

EXAMPLE:

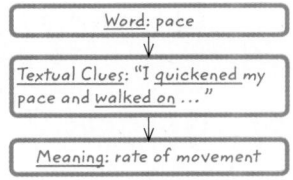

Word: pace

↓

Textual Clues: "I quickened my pace and walked on ... "

↓

Meaning: rate of movement

Academic Vocabulary

"The Wagon" suggests the serious effects that *technology* can have on the environment.

Technology is an academic word. In more casual conversation, a person might say that consumers look forward to advances in computer **technology.** To further explore the meaning of the word, answer this question: What is a career that involves developing new **technologies?**

For more on academic vocabulary, see pages 36–37 and R83–R85.

Reading Strategy

B is the correct answer. **A** is incorrect because the time of day is described. **C** is incorrect because these details do not create ambiguity. **D** is incorrect because adjectives such as "well-to-do" and "dust-coated" are specific. **E** is incorrect because nothing indicates the villagers do not know where they are.

Vocabulary Practice

Word: impervious; Clue: "Impervious to the traffic . . . they went on staring"; Meaning: not easily disturbed.

Word: inexorable; Clue: "An inexorable force seemed to have tied me to the ground"; Meaning: unyielding

Word: pungent; Clue: "a pungent smell . . . wafted in. . . . I felt nauseous"; Meaning: having a sharp quality

Word: surge; Clue: "His companions also doubled over, as if unable to control a sudden surge of pain"; Meaning: a strong, sudden flow

Academic Vocabulary

Students may mention engineering or computer science.

Respond Through Writing

Editorial

Offer a Solution Imagine you live in the city depicted in "The Wagon" and are fed up with the ambiguous stench. Write an editorial that offers a solution to the community's indifference to this pollution. Make an appeal to reason in your editorial that is supported by concrete details from the story and by your own inferences about this mysterious problem.

Understand the Task An **editorial** is an article that expresses the personal ideas and opinions of the writer. In an editorial, you **appeal to reason,** or use facts and evidence to convince your readers of a rational conclusion.

Prewrite Develop your editorial around a main point; for example, you could issue a call to action such as a protest or a letter-writing campaign. Write down your ideas as you brainstorm, and note the pros and cons of each idea. For inspiration, read editorials from a variety of newspapers and magazines. You will want to create an engaging opening, which journalists call the "lead."

Draft As you write, maintain a coherent link between problems in the village and the solutions you propose. Be sure your arguments are arranged logically and are supported with convincing evidence. It may be helpful to review details from the story to speculate on the cause of the problem and what can be done to solve it. Organize your notes in a graphic organizer like the one below.

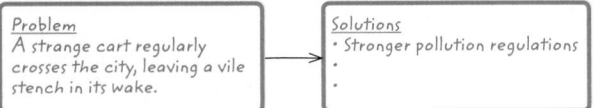

Problem
A strange cart regularly crosses the city, leaving a vile stench in its wake.

Solutions
· Stronger pollution regulations
·
·

Revise As you revise, pretend you are someone who disagrees with your viewpoint. Consider the flaws that person might see in your argument and address these concerns in your revision. Also, make sure to use direct quotations from the story and provide corresponding attributions.

Edit and Proofread Proofread your paper, correcting any errors in grammar, spelling, and punctuation. Use the Grammar Tip in the side column to help you use colons.

Learning Objectives

In this assignment, you will focus on the following objectives:

Writing: Writing an editorial.

Grammar: Using colons.

Grammar Tip

Colons

Colons can help introduce a list.

The sanitation department needs resources: laptop computers, infrared sensors, and more workers.

Colons can also be used to introduce material that illustrates, explains, or restates the preceding material.

The cause of the riot was apparent: people were fed up with the unsanitary conditions.

Finally, a colon can be used to introduce long or formal quotations and is often preceded by such words as *this, these, the following,* or *as follows.*

After You Read

Assess

Respond Through Writing

Students' editorials should

- propose a clear solution
- make an appeal to reason
- cite evidence from the text
- use colons correctly

A standard 4-point scoring guide might look as follows:

A student who meets all of these criteria should receive the equivalent of a 4-point response.

A student who fully meets two or partially meets three of these criteria should receive the equivalent of a 3-point response.

A student who fully meets one or partially meets two of these criteria should receive the equivalent of a 2-point response.

A student who partially meets one of these criteria should receive the equivalent of a 1-point response.

 For grammar practice, see Unit 3 Teaching Resources Book, p. 305

Approaching Level

DIFFERENTIATED INSTRUCTION

Make Inferences To help students with their editorials, review with them how to make inferences. Explain that an inference is a guess or an assumption that students make by using clues in the text paired with their experiences. **Ask:** What is one inference you can make about where the smell is coming from? *(Students may say the wagon.)*

Have students support their inferences by asking for support. **Ask:** What details from the text support this inference? *(The smell is stronger when the narrator nears the wagon.)* What experience supports this inference? *(Farm animals, such as cows or oxen, and muck carried in this type of wagon have a strong smell.)*

English Learners

DIFFERENTIATED INSTRUCTION

Advanced Show English learners examples of editorials from a local or national paper. Explain that newspaper editorials are often written in response to a controversy and that editorial writers usually take one side or another in an issue. Have students take the time to review the editorials before starting to write their own.

Focus

Bellringer Option

Discuss the moments of realization, or epiphanies, that the characters in "The Kabuliwallah," "Like the Sun," and "By Any Other Name" experienced. **Ask:** How would you describe their moments of realization? What did the characters experience? What kind of perspective did the characters gain?

Encourage students to understand that a significant moment of realization is not dependent upon an earth-shattering or tragic situation.

Summary

In this workshop, students will write a reflective essay in which they will describe a significant personal experience or observation. They will follow the stages of the writing process, including prewriting, drafting, revising, editing, and presenting. Two mini-lessons supporting an understanding of using sensory details and avoiding unclear pronoun references are also provided.

Workshop Resources

Print Materials

- Unit 3 Teaching Resources pp. 309–315
- Writing Kit
- Success in Writing: Research and Reports

Technology

- Literature Online: Writing Resources and Grammar Resources, glencoe.com
- Online Essay Grader, glencoe.com
- Student Presentation Builder on Student-Works Plus CD-ROM
- Media Workshop DVD
- Online Student Edition

652

Learning Objectives

For pages 652–659

In this workshop, you will focus on the following objectives:

Writing:
Writing a reflective essay using the writing process.

Understanding how to use sensory details.

Grammar: Understanding how to correct unclear pronoun references.

Writing Process

At any stage of a writing process, you may think of new ideas. Feel free to return to earlier stages as you write.

Prewrite

Draft

Revise

Focus Lesson:
Sensory Details

Edit and Proofread

Focus Lesson: Unclear
Pronoun References

Present

 **Literature** Online

Writing and Research For prewriting, drafting, and revising tools, go to glencoe.com and enter QuickPass code GLW6053u3.

 **Writing Workshop**

Reflective Essay

Literature Connection

*"They have a life of their own,
they fly without thinking.
Some are rare, some common,
but every wing is grace."*

In these lines from Dahlia Ravikovitch's poem "The Sound of Birds at Noon," the speaker's observations of birds lead her to reflect on human behavior. Authors use many forms of writing—poems, autobiographies, memoirs, and short essays—to reflect, or provide interpretations and explanations of the significance of an experience or an observation. A good reflective essay can make your audience feel the impact of even a small or an ordinary incident in your life. To write a successful reflective essay, you will need to meet the goals and learn the strategies listed below.

Rubric

Goals	Strategies
To present a meaningful experience from your life	☑ Reflect on a memorable experience or observation from your past.
To present a clear setting and sequence of events	☑ Give background details on the setting and your role in the incident.
	☑ Narrate the events in a logical order.
To make the experience seem real to the reader	☑ Describe appearances, movements, sensory images, and personal feelings in concrete detail.
	☑ Use action verbs and precise nouns.
To connect with an audience	☑ Use the first-person point of view.
	☑ Use a tone appropriate to the experience or the observation you describe.

Assignment: Reflect on an Observation

Write a reflective essay of at least 1,000 words about an observation you have made or an experience you have had. As you move through the stages of writing, keep your audience and purpose in mind.

Audience: classmates and peers

Purpose: to explore the meaning and the effect of a personal observation or experience

Analyze a Professional Model

The Taj Mahal is a white marble mausoleum, or tomb, in northern India. Built by a seventeenth-century emperor, it is one of the most magnificent structures in the world. In the following excerpt, author Salman Rushdie reflects on his experience of seeing the monument for the first time. Using vivid descriptions, he shows how the observation led him to an unexpected insight about the power of reality over imitation. As you read, note the comments in the margin; they point out features you might want to include in your own reflective essay.

1

from *"The Taj Mahal"* by Salman Rushdie

When you arrive at the outer walls of the gardens in which the Taj is set, it's as if every hustler and hawker in Agra is waiting for you to make the familiarity-breeds-contempt problem worse, peddling imitation Mahals of every size and price. This leads to a certain amount of shoulder-shrugging disenchantment. Recently, a British friend who was about to make his first trip to India told me that he had decided to leave the Taj off his itinerary because of its over-exposure. If I urged him not to, it was because of my own vivid memory of pushing my way for the first time through the jostling crowd, not only of imitation-vendors but also of prescribed readings, past all the myriad hawkers of meaning and interpretation, and into the presence of the *thing-in-itself*, which utterly overwhelmed me and made all my notions about its devaluation feel totally and completely redundant.

Exposition / Description

Real-World Connection

You may be required to retell a personal experience when you apply to college or for a job. Your ability to present your experience and reflect upon its significance may be used to judge your merits as a student or an employee.

Narrative Elements

Include elements of narrative, such as setting, in your reflection.

Tone

Match your tone to your subject. An ironic tone can draw your reader in and reveal the more humorous aspects of your experience.

WRITING WORKSHOP **653**

Focus

Big Idea   1

The Search for Enlightenment Remind students that observation and facing the truth of a situation are essential in the search for enlightenment. **Ask:** How does the reflective essay represent a step in the search for enlightenment? (*Students may say that the reflective essay affords someone a way to gain a deeper understanding of how he or she observes and experiences the world, which is a step on the road to enlightenment.*)

Literary History

Sir Salman Rushdie An Anglo-Indian writer, Salman Rushdie (1947–) published his first novel in 1975, but he is famous—or, to some, infamous—for his novel *The Satanic Verses*. Members of the Muslim community took offense at parts of this novel; subsequently, a *fatwa* was issued against him, forcing him to go into hiding for almost a decade to avoid execution. In 2007, he was knighted by the British crown.

English Learners

DIFFERENTIATED INSTRUCTION

SMALL GROUP
Beginning English language learners would benefit from discussing their thoughts before they begin to write. In small groups, have students take turns describing their understanding of reflective essays, including any topics they may be considering. Suggest that students ask one another questions about what makes a particular observation or experience significant.

Approaching Level

DIFFERENTIATED INSTRUCTION

Following Point of View Have students reread "The Taj Mahal" and underline or otherwise note the author's use of *I*, *me*, *my*, or *myself*. Explain to students that it is not necessary when writing a personal essay to use *I* in every sentence because it is understood that the author is describing actions from his or her point of view.

Learning Objectives
Writing a reflective essay. (SE)
Analyzing a professional model. (SE)
Understanding point of view. (TE)

Writing Workshop

Reflective Essay

Teach

Writing Skills

Setting Remind students that setting can play as important a part in their essays as the event or observation itself. Tell students that they have to describe the time and place of the event to people who were not there; even if a reader has had a similar experience, he or she did not experience it the same way as the student writing the essay. Draw students' attention to "The Taj Mahal" and note that the author has not described every part of the building, yet readers are able to set the scene with details such as "outer walls," "garden," "jostling crowd," "glowingly," and "beautiful."

> **For Writing Workshop graphic organizer and rubric, see Unit 3 Teaching Resources, pp. 309–311.**

First-Person Point of View

Write your reflection from the first-person point of view.

Background Information

Explain what occurred or how you felt before the incident to help the reader more fully understand the significance of your experience.

Descriptive Details

Try to *show* your reader what happened, rather than simply telling.

Conclusion

Use your current perspective to reflect on the meaning of the observation or the experience.

I had been skeptical about the visit. One of the legends of the Taj is that the hands of the master masons who built it were cut off by the emperor, so that they could never build anything lovelier. Another is that the mausoleum was constructed in secrecy behind high walls, and a man who tried to sneak a preview was blinded for his interest in architecture. My personal imagined Taj was somewhat tarnished by these cruel tales.

The building itself left my skepticism in shreds, however. Announcing itself as itself, insisting with absolute force on its sovereign authority, it simply obliterated the million million counterfeits of it and glowingly filled, once and forever, the place in the mind previously occupied by its simulacra [superficial representations].

And this, finally, is why the Taj Mahal must be seen: to remind us that the world is real, that the sound is truer than the echo, the original more forceful than its image in a mirror. The beauty of beautiful things is still able, in these image-saturated times, to transcend imitations. And the Taj Mahal is, beyond the power of words to say it, a lovely thing, perhaps the loveliest of things.

Reading-Writing Connection Think about the writing techniques you just encountered and try them out in the reflective essay you write.

Prewrite

Choose a Topic As you brainstorm topics, break down your life into different periods and think about which experiences you remember most vividly from each period. Ask yourself which experiences had the most meaning or significance, and choose the one that is most interesting to you and that you feel comfortable sharing.

Describe Vividly Your goal in writing a reflective essay is to make the experience or the observation seem real for your reader. Make a list of details that you remember from the experience you chose. Then look over your list and replace general or vague descriptions with language that *shows* the details to the reader: vivid and specific nouns and verbs, sensory details, and comparisons.

Reading Practice

Analyze Tone Review tone with students, explaining that it is an author's attitude toward his or her subject matter. Students can identify an author's tone by analyzing word choice, figures of speech, and even punctuation and sentence structure. Have students reread "The Taj Mahal" and pay close attention to the author's attitude toward his friend, the building, and his own past self.

Have students list the words that Rushdie uses to describe his surroundings and feelings during the moment when he first glimpses the Taj Mahal. (*vivid, jostling, thing-in-itself, overwhelmed, notions, redundant*) **Ask:** What tone does he take toward his younger self? Explain. (*He seems to think he was foolish before, as he describes his "notions" about the building being unworthy of adoration.*)

Encourage students to consider tone when writing their reflective essays. They should work to observe their younger selves with an open mind, admitting immature notions and attitudes.

Make an Outline Your next step is to organize your ideas for the beginning, the middle, and the end of your essay. You may find it helpful to narrate your experience in chronological order, or you may wish to skip back and forth between your past experience and your present reflections, as Rushdie does. Use a graphic organizer like the one below to arrange your essay.

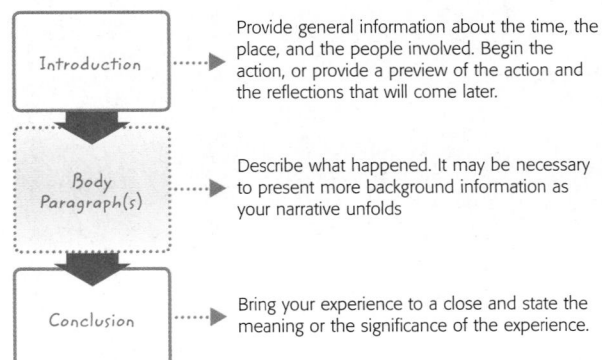

Introduction → Provide general information about the time, the place, and the people involved. Begin the action, or provide a preview of the action and the reflections that will come later.

Body Paragraph(s) → Describe what happened. It may be necessary to present more background information as your narrative unfolds

Conclusion → Bring your experience to a close and state the meaning or the significance of the experience.

Share Ideas Meet with a partner to discuss your topic. To help develop your writing voice, listen to your speaking voice as you describe the significance of the experience you chose. Write down words and phrases that capture your voice.

Draft

Structure Your Essay As you write, remember that your essay should have a clear beginning, middle, and end. Depending on your topic, you may need only three paragraphs, one for each part of the essay. Some topics may call for several middle paragraphs that include both narration and reflection. For topics that require lengthier narration, use transitional words such as *first, next,* and *then* to connect parts of the narration.

Analyze a Workshop Model

On the next page, you will read a final draft of a reflective essay. Read the essay and answer the questions in the margin. Use the answers to these questions to guide you as you write.

Focus on Significance

Remember that the goal of a reflective essay is not to simply recount an exciting or unusual event, but to reflect on the larger significance or meaning of an incident. To decide whether an event would make a good topic for your essay, ask yourself, How has the event changed my ideas or outlook?

Avoid Plagiarism

As you work on your essay, you might remember the words of another writer who perfectly captured an idea you want to convey. Copying these words, however, is wrong unless you give credit to the source.

 Writing Workshop

Reflective Essay

Teach

 Writing Skills

Sensory Details Encourage students to try and describe every part of a moment, even if they did not necessarily taste or smell something during a certain event. For example, during prewriting, students can describe what the grass or dirt would taste like on a playing field if a player fell face-first, or what an old living room couch would smell like to someone who was lying down on it. By describing all aspects of a moment, the student will open himself or herself to the whole experience rather than just a step-by-step account of events.

Learning Objectives
Analyzing a reflective essay. (SE)
Describing sensory details. (TE)
Analyzing tone. (TE)

English Learners

DIFFERENTIATED INSTRUCTION

Beginning English language learners may benefit from reviewing the words that describe the five senses. Have students list the verbs *see, smell, hear, taste,* and *touch.* Invite them to use a thesaurus to find other ways of describing these actions. For further practice, students can look up alternate words for the body parts that perform these actions.

Advanced Learners/Pre-AP

DIFFERENTIATED INSTRUCTION

Investigating Memoir Memoir has become a popular genre in recent years, and memoirs of the famous and not-so-famous line bookstore and library shelves. Encourage students to find a published memoir by someone who perhaps has a similar background to the student or whose experience closely resembles the one the student will write about.

Have students report on the memoir, noting how the author relates a personal experience that gives readers the feeling that they were there and experienced it too.

655

Teach

Writing Skills

First-Person Point of View
Answer: *The pronoun* I *tells the reader this.*

Background Information
Answer: *The facts about the butterfly sanctuary show the reader that this is a unique and an impressive phenomenon.*

View the Art ★

While the monarch butterfly can be found mainly in North, Central, and South America, it is also found as far away as Australia and India. Those that spend winter in California or Mexico can travel as much as 1,800 miles to their destinations.
Ask: How does this photograph visually match the essay author's description? (*The photograph shows masses of butterflies stacked atop one another, obscuring the tree branches beneath them, which visually matches what the author describes.*)

Writing Frames
As you read the workshop model, think about the writer's use of the following frames.

• The most memorable part was _____.

• At first, _____.

• I gained an appreciation for _____.

Consider using frames such as these in your reflective essay.

First-Person Point of View
Which pronoun tells the reader the essay is written from the first-person point of view?

Background Information
How does the background information in the second paragraph help you understand the writer's experience?

Monarch Madness ★

Last year during February vacation, my family and I went to visit my grandmother, who lives in Toluca, a city just west of Mexico City. This was my first time in Mexico. Having lived in Los Angeles all my life, I was fascinated by Mexico's landscape and its natural beauty. The most memorable part of the visit was a trip we took to a nearby place called Angangueo. There we saw the greatest show on Earth: the migration of the monarch butterflies.

Before we went, Grandma gave us a little bit of background. She told us Angangueo is the home of a monarch butterfly sanctuary. Every winter, butterflies make the long journey to Angangueo from North America. Some travel as far as 1,800 miles. Perhaps even more amazing, every year the butterflies come back to the very same place. Most of these butterflies live two years, which means they make this trip twice.

Our trip to the sanctuary began with a ride in a flatbed truck up a rural mountainside. Several trucks and buses were also making the trip up the bumpy, narrow road. We sat in the truck with several other Mexican families. Everyone seemed happy and expectant. Still, none of us were prepared for the great thrill that awaited us.

Writing Practice

 SMALL GROUP **Use Transitions** Remind students to use clear transitions to connect the sentences and paragraphs in their reflective essays. Encourage them to work together to create a master list of common transitional words and expressions. Divide the class into four groups and assign each group one of the four following categories of transitions to brainstorm:

(1) words and phrases that mean *and*;
(2) words and phrases that mean *but*;
(3) words and phrases that mean *so*;
(4) words and phrases that point out sequence, such as *first* and *next*. Have groups share their lists, or, if possible, compile a master list for students to keep. Encourage students to add to their lists when they come across new transitions.

Once we got within a quarter-mile of the sanctuary, we became part of a whole army of people hiking the final distance to the sanctuary at the top of the mountain. The last part of the climb took us through a congested area of stands where busy merchants were selling butterfly souvenirs, frying fragrant meats, and making spicy tamales and empanadas. We saw a vendor selling ice-cold green and pink drinks. They were too tantalizing to resist, because we had all become thirsty from our long journey in the hot sun.

At first, we spotted a few small groups of monarchs flying in the air overhead, clustering on the grass, or sitting together in a bush. Never having seen as many as five or ten monarchs together, we thought this was a big deal. But by the time we had climbed just ten feet higher into the sanctuary, we began to see a vast sea of orange. Butterflies covered entire trees, weighing down their branches. They filled the sky—a blizzard of butterflies. They landed on tourists' arms and heads, including my own, and were crushed under our feet, despite everyone's best efforts to avoid stepping on them.

My binoculars brought into focus whole tree trunks and boughs that were covered on every square inch with monarchs. Individual butterflies would have come into close view, except for the fact that the monarchs were all on top of one another, the way bees swarm in a hive or termites form a dense mass of insect bodies in a nest. As I looked through my binoculars, I repeatedly found myself exclaiming out loud—and often to no one! My family was scattered on all parts of the trail, oohing and aahing.

If I had to guess how many monarchs I saw in just that one day, I would say millions. I would guess, though I do not know this, that some trees held ten thousand or more. And I would say that seeing those monarchs was just as thrilling and memorable as seeing a million sparkling diamonds. I was more awed by the butterflies that day than by earthquakes and thunderstorms that I have experienced. From the trip to Angangueo, I gained an appreciation for more delicate natural spectacles.

Exposition / Description

Narrative Elements

What elements of narration, or storytelling, do you find in this paragraph?

Sensory Details

What senses does the writer appeal to in this paragraph?

Descriptive Details

Which nouns, verbs, and phrases in this paragraph help you imagine the scene?

Tone

How would you describe the writer's tone? What does it tell you about the experience?

Conclusion

How do you know that this experience was significant to the writer?

Writing Workshop

Reflective Essay

Teach

Narrative Elements
Answer: *The writer describes the events in chronological order, establishes a clear setting, and introduces the characters.*

Sensory Details
Answer: *The writer appeals to sight, smell, taste, and touch.*

Descriptive Details
Answer: *Possible responses: "clustering on the grass," "a vast sea of orange," "a blizzard of butterflies."*

Tone
Answer: *The writer's tone is enthusiastic. It tells you that this was an enjoyable experience.*

Conclusion
Answer: *The writer gained a deeper appreciation for nature.*

Advanced Learners/Pre-AP

DIFFERENTIATED INSTRUCTION

"Filming" a Reflective Essay Students may enjoy developing a reflective essay through screenplay rather than paragraph-focused prose. Thinking about the reflective essay as a visual product may give students more insight into their topics. Invite students to investigate the guidelines to writing a screenplay and filming a movie; they should review stage directions, camera angles, and even storyboards.

Have students use either "Monarch Madness" or their own reflective essay to turn into screenplay format. Students who choose the "Monarch Madness" essay will find themselves in a challenging role, writing a screenplay for an event that they did not experience themselves. Tell students to consider ways to express the significance of the moment without a voiceover.

Learning Objectives
Analyzing a reflective essay. (SE)
Identifying sensory and descriptive details. (SE)
Use transitions. (TE)
Using the writing process. (TE)

657

Teach

Writing Process

Revising Because of the nature of writing and rewriting an essay, writers often fail to "see" what they have written, which leads to an uninspired revision. Have students use highlighters to mark their essays, using different colors for adjectives, verbs, and transition words. By being able to "see" what they have written, students can more easily discover where they need a more vibrant action word or description.

Traits of Strong Writing

Follow these traits of strong writing to express your ideas effectively.

Ideas

Organization

Voice

Word Choice

Sentence Fluency

Conventions

Presentation

For more information on using the Traits of Strong Writing, see pages R28–R30.

Word Choice

The following academic vocabulary word is used in the student model.

individual (in´də vij´ o͞o əl) *adj.* single; distinct; *The writer had trouble focusing on individual butterflies because so many were clustered together.*

Using academic vocabulary may help strengthen your writing. Try to use one or two academic vocabulary words in your essay. See the complete list on pages R83–R85.

> **LOG ON** ▶ **Literature** Online
>
> **Writing and Research** For editing and publishing tools, go to glencoe.com and enter QuickPass code GLW6053u3.

Revise

Peer Review After you complete your draft, have a peer reviewer read it. Have him or her identify which parts are most memorable and interesting, and which parts seem vague or unclear. Ask your partner to make suggestions about where to add background information, sensory details, or reflection. Remember to refer to the traits of strong writing and consider how they apply to your essay. Use the checklist below to evaluate your writing.

Checklist

☑ Do you reflect, or look back, on a meaningful experience?

☑ Do you use the first-person point of view throughout your essay?

☑ Do you narrate events in a logical order ?

☑ Do you have an introduction that sets up the topic and a conclusion that summarizes your reflections?

☑ Do you use sensory details, precise nouns, and action verbs?

☑ Do you make the significance of your experience clear?

☑ Is your tone appropriate for your topic?

> ### Focus Lesson

Sensory Details

Sensory details are words or phrases that appeal to one of the five senses. Well-chosen sensory details help your readers feel they are experiencing the scenes you describe. Notice how the sensory details added to the passage below contribute to the narrative and to the overall impression the writer is trying to create.

Draft:

The last part of the climb took us through a congested area of stands where merchants were selling souvenirs and food.

Revision:

The last part of the climb took us through a congested area of stands where busy merchants were selling butterfly souvenirs, frying fragrant meats,[1] and making spicy tamales and empanadas.[2] We saw a vendor selling ice-cold green and pink drinks.[3]

1: Appeals to Smell   **2: Appeals to Taste**   **3: Appeals to Touch and Sight**

Writing Practice

SMALL GROUP

Revising Point out that maintaining a critical eye for one's own writing is possible when students allow themselves time between the stages in the writing process. Encourage students to give every stage of their writing a cooling-off period. Explain to students that by leaving a draft alone for a few days, a week, or even longer if possible, writers get a sense of perspective about their work.

Select volunteers to submit copies of their essays for peer review. Suggest that each reviewer write a short commentary on each of these four aspects of the essay: whether the writer conveyed the significance of the event; how well the writer led the reader through the story; which descriptions particularly stand out and which do not; and how effectively the writer used sensory details.

So students gain some perspective, hand back only one of the four peer commentaries per day. Students will have to take their time focusing on one aspect of the essay, while leaving other issues for the next day.

Edit and Proofread

Get It Right When you have completed the final draft of your reflective essay, proofread it for errors in grammar, usage, mechanics, and spelling. Refer to the Language Handbook, pages R40–R59, as a guide.

> ### Focus Lesson
>
> ## Unclear Pronoun References
>
> A pronoun must always refer to a noun or a pronoun that appears earlier in the piece of writing. Make sure each of your pronouns refers to the closest noun or pronoun before it. Below are examples of how to correct unclear pronoun references.
>
> **Original:** The sentence contains an unclear pronoun reference.
>
> The author intends the pronoun *They* to refer to *ice-cold green and pink drinks,* but as it is used, it refers to the antecedent *spicy tamales and empanadas.*
>
> *The last part of the climb took us through a congested area of stands where busy merchants were selling butterfly souvenirs, frying fragrant meats, selling ice-cold green and pink drinks, and making spicy tamales and empanadas. They were too tantalizing to resist, because we had all become thirsty from our long journey in the hot sun.*
>
> **Improved:** Replace the pronoun with the exact noun to which it refers.
>
> *. . . selling ice-cold green and pink drinks, and making spicy tamales and empanadas. The drinks were too tantalizing to resist, . . .*

Present/Publish

Final Check After you have finished editing and proofreading, make sure your essay is double-spaced with an appropriate font and margins. Give it an interesting title and check to see if your teacher has any additional presentation guidelines.

Peer Review Tip

A classmate may ask you to read his or her essay. Take notes as you read so you can give constructive feedback. Use the following questions to get started.

- Do you get a clear sense of the subject and its significance?
- Are there vivid details?

Word-Processing Tip

If you are typing your story on a computer, make sure you use an appropriate font and size. Choose a font that is easy to read and not too ornate or distracting. Many word-processing programs default to a 12-point size, which is usually adequate.

<u>Writer's</u> Portfolio

Place a clean copy of your reflective essay in your portfolio to review later.

Writing Workshop

Reflective Essay

Teach

Writing Process

Editing and Proofreading

Share with students some tricks to finding mistakes in one's own papers when editing and proofreading. Some writers like to read their work aloud. When we read silently, we often read very quickly, but reading aloud forces us to slow down; this way, it is easier to hear run-on sentences or detect missing words. Another trick, especially effective for students performing a final pass on a paper that they have nearly memorized, is to read the essay backwards, one sentence at a time. This way, the student will not automatically know what comes next and can look at each sentence as an individual entity.

Learning Objectives
Editing and proofreading compositions. (SE)
Reviewing a peer's work. (SE)
Revising compositions. (TE)
Using visual aids. (TE)

Approaching Level

DIFFERENTIATED INSTRUCTION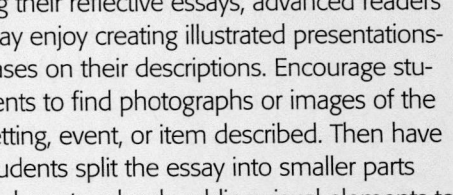

Reading Aloud in Peer Review
Approaching-level readers may lack the self-confidence to offer helpful criticism to their peers. Encourage them to judge the clarity of any exposition by how well they understand it. Pair readers of varied reading abilities, and make sure that each student has two copies of his or her reflective essay.

Have one student read his or her reflective essay aloud while the other student follows along silently on the second copy. To check for clarity, ask students to summarize the main ideas in partners' essays, ask questions, and offer helpful suggestions on parts that need revision. Then have the other partner take a turn reading and receiving constructive criticism.

Advanced Learners/Pre-AP

DIFFERENTIATED INSTRUCTION

Illustrated Presentations After finishing their reflective essays, advanced readers may enjoy creating illustrated presentations-bases on their descriptions. Encourage students to find photographs or images of the setting, event, or item described. Then have students split the essay into smaller parts and create a book, adding visual elements to each page before adding the essay to their portfolios.

659

Focus

Summary

In this workshop, students will learn techniques for planning and presenting their reflective essays orally and visually.

Teach

Viewing Skills

Effective Visual Aids There are many types of visual aids that students can use. When they are determining which aids to use, have them use the following questions as a guide:

- Will this image be large and clear to the audience?

- Will this image be colorful and interesting?

- Will this image be appropriate to the essay and understandable as an accompaniment to it?

 For help with creating presentations, see Student Presentation Builder on StudentWorks Plus.

Learning Objectives

For pages 660–661

In this workshop, you will focus on the following objective:

Listening and Speaking: Delivering a reflective presentation.

Focus on Main Points

Your audience cannot go back and reread parts of your presentation, as they can with an essay, so you will want to reinforce your most important ideas throughout the presentation. Look through your script and cut any details that are not related to your main points. Come back to your main ideas at the end of your presentation and restate them for your audience.

Speaking Frames

As you prepare your reflection, think about using some of the following frames to get started.

- I'd always felt that _____, until I _____.

- Like _____ [character/author], I have had the experience of _____.

 Literature Online

Speaking, Listening, Viewing For project ideas, templates, and presentation tips, go to glencoe.com and enter QuickPass code GLW6053u3

Speaking, Listening, and Viewing Workshop

Reflective Presentation

Literature Connection Salman Rushdie uses an impassioned tone in his essay on the Taj Mahal, writing that the building itself "simply obliterated the million million counterfeits of it." Imagine how reading these words aloud could add to their emotional charge. An oral presentation can make your written reflections come alive for your audience. Visual aids—for example, a large, glossy photograph—are another way to show your audience what you experienced. In this workshop, you will learn how to use an oral presentation and visuals to express the significance of the events in your reflective essay.

> **Assignment** **Deliver a Reflective Essay** Adapt your reflective essay into an oral presentation that uses appropriate voice, gestures, and visual aids.

Plan Your Presentation

Think of your presentation not as simply a spoken version of your essay, but as a chance to share your most important ideas with a live audience.

- Start by reading your essay aloud, keeping your audience in mind. Which parts of your essay sound best read aloud? Which seem to reflect your speaking style? Which images or incidents are most captivating?

- Next, go through your essay and highlight the parts you think will lend themselves best to oral delivery. Focus on the most important highlights instead of trying to present each idea.

- Adapt your essay into a script. Use the script as a study guide for remembering ideas and particularly effective phrases.

- Make note cards that include a few words and phrases that will remind you of your main points.

Reading Practice

SPIRAL REVIEW **Read Aloud with Fluency** Give students practice in **reading fluently** before they give their presentations. Select several passages from one or more of the selections in this unit. Make sure that the passages contain a variety of punctuation and sentence types.

Read aloud one passage for students. Be sure to model proper phrasing, inflection, and pausing. Then have the entire class read the passage aloud.

Read a second passage aloud to the class. Then organize the class in mixed-ability groups. Have each group member take turns reading paragraphs in the passage. You may wish to have one student read and then another echo. Students can continue in this fashion until they have finished the passage. Have groups read the passage several times until each member is fluently reading the text.

Create Your Visuals

Visual aids can be a powerful way to reach your audience. Look through your script and identify images that will help your audience connect to your experience. You can use photographs or even video clips to show your audience places or things that might otherwise be difficult to visualize. Use a graphic organizer like the one below to plan your visual aids. Be sure to discuss your visuals in your presentation, and write prompts on your note cards that cue you to display each image at the correct time.

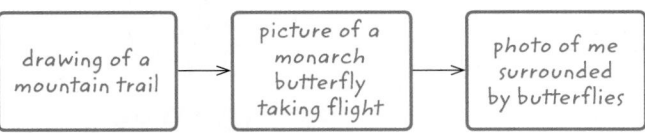

drawing of a mountain trail → picture of a monarch butterfly taking flight → photo of me surrounded by butterflies

Rehearse

After you have rehearsed on your own, present your reflection to a friend or a family member. If your teacher has given your presentation a time limit, ask the friend or the family member to time you—you may need to cut parts of your presentation to stay within the limit. Ask your friend or your family member to provide suggestions about how you could improve each of the techniques listed in the chart below.

Techniques for Presenting a Reflection

Verbal Techniques	Nonverbal Techniques
☑ **Tone** Match your tone to your subject, whether it is light or serious.	☑ **Eye Contact** Make frequent eye contact with your audience.
☑ **Pace** Speak slowly enough so the audience can react to your ideas.	☑ **Posture** Avoid leaning or slouching.
☑ **Volume** Speak loudly and clearly so your audience can understand you.	☑ **Gestures** Make natural gestures, but do not move so much that it becomes distracting.
☑ **Emphasis** Vary your emphasis, stressing important words and ideas.	☑ **Visual Aids** Present your visuals prominently, and be sure not to block them while you speak.

Presentation Tips

Use the following checklist to evaluate your presentation.

- Did you vary your tone and use natural gestures?
- Did you make eye contact with the audience?
- Did you remember not to block the visuals?
- Did you face the audience and not the visuals?

Teach

Speaking Skills

Pace Most students will begin rehearsing their presentations by speaking too fast. Tell them to set up their note cards in a way that helps them keep a slow pace. For example, have them list each main idea or point on a separate card. When they are giving the presentation, they will know to pause at each new card, or new thought.

Listening Skills

Peer Assessment Ask students to respond to each presentation, using the following criteria:

- Did the speaker engage the audience?
- Did the speaker use effective pacing, volume, and eye contact?
- Was the topic effectively supported by the visual aids?
- Did the presentation make a strong impact?

Learning Objectives
Delivering a presentation. (SE)
Reading aloud fluently. (TE)
Using topic sentences. (TE)

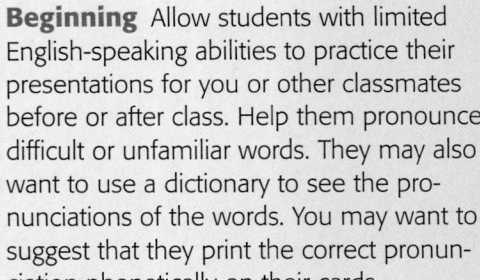

English Learners

DIFFERENTIATED INSTRUCTION

Beginning Allow students with limited English-speaking abilities to practice their presentations for you or other classmates before or after class. Help them pronounce difficult or unfamiliar words. They may also want to use a dictionary to see the pronunciations of the words. You may want to suggest that they print the correct pronunciation phonetically on their cards.

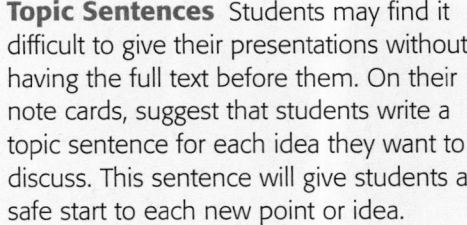

Approaching Level

DIFFERENTIATED INSTRUCTION

Topic Sentences Students may find it difficult to give their presentations without having the full text before them. On their note cards, suggest that students write a topic sentence for each idea they want to discuss. This sentence will give students a safe start to each new point or idea.

Focus

Summary

The purpose of this spread is to encourage students to read novels of the time period they have read about in this unit. The suggested novels will help students build on the knowledge they have gained from the works they have read.

Teach

Literary History ☆

Herman Hesse Herman Hesse is a German writer who was born in 1877. At the onset of World War I, Hesse moved to Switzerland, where he became a Swiss citizen in 1932. Hesse has published multiple novels and poems. Some of his work includes *The Glass Bead Game, Poems*, and *If the War Goes on. . .* In 1946, he won a Nobel Prize in Literature.

Independent Reading

Literature of the Region

THE TRADITIONAL LITERATURES OF SOUTHWEST AND SOUTH CENTRAL ASIA HAVE HAD A profound and far-reaching effect on the world from ancient times to the present. The stories of the Bible, the tales of *The Thousand and One Nights*, the fables of the *Panchatantra*, and other traditional narratives from this region have spread throughout the world, providing wisdom, inspiration, and entertainment.

Shahnameh

Ferdowsi

The national epic of Iran, the *Shahnameh*, or "Book of Kings" (1010), is a vast narrative that presents Iranian history from the creation of the world until Muslim Arab armies conquered Persia in the seventh century A.D. Writing several centuries after the Muslim conquest, the poet Ferdowsi (also spelled Firdowsi) collected and transmitted in verse form the myths and legends of his country. Though historical in nature, the epic contains many episodes and beings from the realm of fantasy including curses, supernatural creatures, and enormous birds.

Siddhartha

Hermann Hesse ☆

German author Hermann Hesse was a prolific novelist who focused on the idea that humans could find their true selves only by unfettering themselves from the confines of society. Hesse's interest in Eastern philosophy heavily influenced his most critically acclaimed work of fiction, *Siddhartha* (1922). The novella tells the story of a young Indian mystic who gives up everything he knows and sets off on a quest to find the true meaning of life. In one sense, this is a detective story in which Siddhartha searches for clues to unravel the mystery of self.

Writing Practice

SPIRAL REVIEW **Write a Letter** Have students select one of the authors from the suggested reading titles to write a letter to (even if the author is deceased). Tell students to tell the author why they think their work sounds interesting. Students may wish to include some of the knowledge they have gained from reading the selections in this unit. Allow students enough time to finish their letters. After they have finished, instruct students to exchange their letters with a partner's. Tell students to look for any spelling, punctuation, or grammar errors in the letter. Then have students revise their letters based on their partner's comments. Invite several volunteers to share their letters with the class.

GLENCOE LITERATURE LIBRARY

Nectar in a Sieve
Kamala Markandaya

With strength and dignity, an Indian peasant woman, Rukmani, survives many hardships in life, including monsoons, drought, and famine, as India embarks upon modernization in the second half of the twentieth century.

A House for Mr. Biswas
V. S. Naipaul ☆

Set in Trinidad in the mid-twentieth century, *A House for Mr. Biswas* draws from the author's childhood experiences as a Hindu Indian living in what was then a British colony.

Shabanu: Daughter of the Wind
Suzanne Fisher Staples

A Newbery Honor Book, Staples's first novel describes a young woman's experience growing up in the traditional nomadic culture of Pakistani desert dwellers.

CRITICS' CORNER

" . . . [T]he Nights not only celebrates the power of stories, but offers a vision of the very act of story-telling itself as nothing less than an art form which offers both its practitioners and its listeners an opportunity to order, comprehend, define, and delimit (at least temporarily) an otherwise chaotic and incomprehensible world of experience. It is by telling stories and by hearing stories told, the Nights seems to say, that we come to know our world, each other, and— ultimately—our own selves."

—Robert L. Mack, from the Introduction to *Arabian Nights' Entertainments*

The Thousand and One Nights

Perhaps the most famous collection of tales in all world literature, *The Thousand and One Nights* (c. 700s–1500s) has no author. It is often referred to as *The Arabian Nights*, but many of its tales come from Persia and India. The frame narrative tells of Scheherazade, a brave and clever woman who outwits a brutal sultan by telling him stories night after night to prevent him from killing her.

Create a Visual Display

Read one of the books listed on these pages and create a visual display about the book for your classmates. Find or create images that represent the characters, plot, and setting. Present your display to the class.

INDEPENDENT READING **663**

English Learners

DIFFERENTIATED INSTRUCTION

Advanced Some of the literature described here might be difficult for English learners. In addition to an English version, encourage students to look for a translation of the selected book in their native language. Then have students read the English version, using the native-language version only when they find that they do not understand a particular passage.

As students read, they should take note of the more difficult passages or terms. Encourage them to try to decipher the English-language version of the book by using the dictionary or other resources; they should only use the native-language version of the book when absolutely necessary. Have students write short summaries of difficult passages.

Literary History ☆

V. S. Naipaul Vidiadhar Surajprasad Naipaul was born in Trinidad to Hindu Indian parents. In 1950, Naipaul moved to England to study at the University of Oxford. Subsequently, he published various works, including *The Suffrage of Elvira, In a Free State,* and *A Way in the World.* Naipaul's talent earned him a knighthood in 1989 and the Nobel Prize for Literature in 2001.

Create a Visual Display

Students' displays should

- focus on one book presented in this feature
- include images that represent the characters, plot, and setting of the book

 For access to all study guides for the Glencoe Literature Library, see the Literature Library Teacher Resources CD-ROM.

 To create customized reading lists from a database of more than 30,000 titles, use BookLink K-12 CD-ROM.

Learning Objectives
Reading literature independently. (SE)
Creating a visual display. (SE)
Writing a letter. (TE)

Bellringer Option

Ask: What are your fears during and after taking a test? *(Students are likely to describe a fear of failing or forgetting what they studied.)* List the fears on the board as students describe them. Then have students brainstorm on studying and test-taking strategies that can help them avoid or overcome these fears.

Assessment

English–Language Arts

Reading: Fiction and Poetry

Carefully read the following two passages. Use context clues to help you define any words with which you are unfamiliar. Pay close attention to the **author's purpose, themes,** and use of **literary devices** in each text. Then, on a separate sheet of paper, answer the questions on page 666.

from *"The Raj Seal"* by Rabindranath Tagore

The elder brother of the new family was its guiding light. Everyone at home and in the neighborhood revered his opinions on all matters. He was a BA[1] and had a capable mind, but a fat salary and a position of authority did not appeal to him, neither did the whole business of contacts and patronage;
5 the British kept their distance from him, and he, likewise, preferred to keep them at arm's length. Thus, though his presence dazzled his domestic circle, he exerted little influence further afield.

Earlier, he had spent three years away in England. The courtesy of English people there had so captivated him that he had forgotten the humiliating
10 condition of his country and had returned home suited and booted in the English style.

His family had been a bit embarrassed at first, but soon they began to say that no one wore sahib's clothes as well as their elder brother. In due course, the glory of English dress penetrated to their very hearts.

15 The brother's own idea when he came back was: "I shall set the first example of how to be on equal terms with the British." By always bowing and scraping when we meet them, he maintained, we simply make ourselves inferior and at the same time do the sahibs an injustice.

He had brought back many cordial testimonials from important figures
20 in England, and so in Bengal he managed to attain some slight position in the councils of the British. Accompanied by his wife, he partook of English tea, dinner, sports and humor. His success made his blood tingle and go to his head.

It was around this time, on the occasion of the opening of a new railway
25 line, that some respectable native gentlemen, a favored few, were invited by the company to travel along the new track with the lieutenant-governor. The elder brother of the family was among them.

On the way back a railway sergeant insulted the party by compelling them to leave their special carriage. The brother, dressed in his usual English attire,

---

1. A *BA* is a person who has a bachelor of arts degree.

Reading Practice

SPIRAL REVIEW **Clarify Meaning by Rereading** Often students will rush through a reading selection when taking a test, assuming that they should spend more time on the questions. Tell students that taking their time to reread an unfamiliar selection presented in a test is a smart use of time. The first run-through is simply an introduction to the selection. The second read, however, will help students absorb the material. Tell students to pay attention to the plot, characters, and setting the first time they read a story. When finished, they should have a general idea of "what happened." When they reread the story, however, students should look for character motivation, foreshadowing, theme, and other literary devices. Express to students that rereading a story during a test will allow them to more easily answer the questions as well as identify the section of a story that a question is asking about.

30   was about to get out when the official politely said, "Why are you getting up?
    You may stay."

      The privilege puffed him up a little, to begin with. But as the carriage rolled
    on and the arid ashen-colored fields of Bengal rolled by, the dying glow of
    the sun setting on the western horizon seemed like a shameful stain across

35   the whole country; the mind of the lonely passenger, observing it unwinkingly,
    felt abashed. The thought of his Motherland cleft his whole heart and made
    his eyes sting with tears.

      An old story came to his mind. An ass was pulling a temple car along the
    sacred way, and the passers-by, prostrating themselves in the dust before it

40   were offering their *pranams.*[2] "They are all worshipping me," the foolish
    ass thought.

      "There's only one small difference between that ass and me," the elder
    brother told himself. "I have at last realized that it is not my person the British
    sahibs respect, but the jacket weighing on my shoulders."

45   As soon as he reached home, he called everyone together, lit a fire and
    cast into it all his English clothes, one by one, as sacrificial offerings.

---

2. *Pranams* are respectful gestures of greeting.

"Clockwork Doll" by Dahlia Ravikovitch
Translated by Chana Bloch and Ariel Bloch

    That night, I was a clockwork doll
    and I whirled around, this way and that,
    and I fell on my face and shattered to bits
    and they tried to fix me with all their skill.

5   Then I was a proper doll once again
    and I did what they told me, poised and polite.
    But I was a doll of a different sort,
    an injured twig that dangles from a stem.

    And then I went to dance at the ball,
10   but they left me alone with the dogs and cats
    though my steps were measured and rhythmical.

    And I had blue eyes and golden hair
    and a dress all the colors of garden flowers,
    and a trimming of cherries on my straw hat.

Teach

Assessment

Explain to students that Test Preparation and Practice is intended to reinforce their general test-taking strategies, as well as to test the skills and vocabulary covered in the unit. They will first be asked to read a fiction selection and a poem and answer comprehension, context clue, literary device, and theme questions. Then they will be asked to answer ten sentence-completion exercises and then paragraph-improvement questions. Finally, they will be asked to write a short analytical essay on a story from this unit.

 To create custom assessments online, go to Progress Reporter Online.

 To create custom assessments using software, use ExamView Assessment Suite.

English Learners

DIFFERENTIATED INSTRUCTION

Intermediate Explain to English learners that they can often determine the meaning of unfamiliar terms by separating the word into its basic parts. This is especially true when dealing with compound words, or words made of two combined words. Point out that the word *clockwork* is a compound word, made of the words *clock* and *work*.

A clock is a mechanical tool used to tell time; work can be thought of as action. Combining these definitions with the description on the first two lines of the poem can help students understand that a clockwork doll is a doll with mechanized parts.

Assessment
English-Language Arts

Assess

1. B is the correct answer. The brother was in England for several years and had forgotten the squalor and the customs of his native India. **DOK 1**

2. D is the correct answer. The context suggests that people typically respond to a sahib with signs of submission. **DOK 1**

3. C is the correct answer. These lines do describe the landscape, but that is not their chief concern, so **A** is incorrect. They do not explain why the English like Bengal, so **B** is incorrect. They show that the brother is sensitive, but these are details, not the main idea, so **D** and **E** are incorrect. **DOK 4**

4. B is the correct answer. In the context, *abashed* describes how the brother felt about seeing "a shameful stain across the whole country," so it can be inferred that abashment is related to shame. **DOK 1**

5. B. is the correct answer. In lines 45–46, Tagore says, "he called everyone together, lit a fire and cast into it all his English clothes, one by one." **DOK 1**

6. C is the correct answer. The tale does not mention the fair treatment of animals or the similarities between animals and people, so **A** and **D** are incorrect. **B** is a fact implied by the tale, but it is not a central lesson, so **B** is incorrect. The lesson in **E** does not apply to this story, so **E** is incorrect. **DOK 2**

7. C is the correct answer. None of the images in the poem suggest freedom or gifts, so **A** and **B** are incorrect. Though the speaker is "injured," there is no evidence that she is physically

injured or that another person inflicted the injury, so **D** is incorrect. The other people in the poem try to control the speaker's behavior. They also leave her "alone with the dogs and cats" instead of encouraging her to enjoy the ball. This is clearly not fair treatment, so **E** is incorrect. **DOK 2**

8. E is the correct answer. The author simply details the situation in straightforward language. **DOK 4**

9. D is the correct answer. The context of the phrase "injured twig" suggests that the author is referring to the speaker as "a doll of a different sort." **DOK 4**

10. B is the correct answer. Both selections feature characters who dress and act according to the expectations of those in power—though for different reasons. Neither ultimately gains respect or personal fulfillment from doing so. **DOK 2**

Items 1–6 apply to the passage from "The Raj Seal."

1. The statement in lines 8–11 ("The courtesy... style") suggests that the elder brother returns from England wearing English clothing because
   (A) he wants to show his power over his family
   (B) he has forgotten the customs of his country
   (C) he abhors the fashion of his own country
   (D) he has a strong desire to mock the English
   (E) he has long wanted to return to his homeland

2. In line 8, "sahibs" most nearly means
   (A) servants
   (B) family members
   (C) friends
   (D) masters
   (E) distant cousins

3. The primary purpose of the author's use of highly descriptive language in lines 32–37 is to
   (A) offer details about the landscape of Bengal
   (B) explain why the English love India
   (C) link the brother's passionate emotional reactions to his love for his homeland
   (D) show that the brother is a very sensitive young man
   (E) highlight the brother's loneliness

4. In line 36, "abashed" most nearly means
   (A) proud
   (B) ashamed
   (C) annoyed
   (D) startled
   (E) ignored

5. What does the brother do once he realizes the English value his clothes, not his character?
   (A) He throws away his English clothes.
   (B) He burns his English clothes one piece at a time.
   (C) He says his *pranams*.
   (D) He spends more time with his family.
   (E) He thinks of all the time he has wasted.

6. Which statement best expresses the moral of the story of the ass and the temple car (lines 38–41)?
   (A) It is important to respect animals.
   (B) Beauty leads to popularity.
   (C) One should not mistake the admiration of possessions for true respect.
   (D) People and animals are very similar.
   (E) One should never feel embarrassed.

Items 7–10 apply to "Clockwork Doll."

7. Which statement best describes how others treat the speaker?
   (A) They give her freedom.
   (B) They buy her gifts.
   (C) They try to control her behavior.
   (D) They physically injure her.
   (E) They treat her fairly.

8. What is the tone in lines 1–3?
   (A) hopeful
   (B) lively
   (C) angry
   (D) peaceful
   (E) straightforward

9. The "injured twig" in line 8 refers to
   (A) the speaker as a proper doll
   (B) the speaker as a clockwork doll
   (C) the speaker's feelings
   (D) the speaker as a doll of a different sort
   (E) a girl with blue eyes

10. Which of the following themes do the excerpt from "The Raj Seal" and the poem "Clockwork Doll" share?
    (A) People should not treat other humans like animals.
    (B) Conforming to expectations will not necessarily bring respect.
    (C) Physical appearance is never important.
    (D) Isolation is an unavoidable experience.
    (E) Solving problems requires a group effort.

Vocabulary Skills: Sentence Completion

For each item in the Vocabulary Skills section, choose the word or words that best complete the sentence. Write your answers on a separate sheet of paper.

1. Mohandas Gandhi's nonviolent resistance movement posed a _____ threat to British rule in India.
   (A) devoted
   (B) formidable
   (C) fatuous
   (D) stupefied
   (E) clandestine

2. Colonial schools offered Indian students the chance to pursue Western-style education; however, prejudiced teachers often _____ their students inferior.
   (A) demonstrated
   (B) deemed
   (C) waived
   (D) incurred
   (E) confounded

3. Many have_____ the caste system, focusing on the "untouchables" and their inability to break free of their _____ position.
   (A) incurred…arid
   (B) demonstrated…rare
   (C) ravaged…range
   (D) scrutinized…fettered
   (E) prevailed…treacherous

4. A(n)_____ characteristic of ancient Sumerian cities was their thick walls, which made them _____ to intruders.
   (A) inexorable…inordinate
   (B) primordial…pungent
   (C) fruitless…pristine
   (D) pristine…stupefied
   (E) distinguishing…impervious

5. According to Jewish tradition, the Israelites made a _____ with God, promising, in exchange for divine blessing, not to _____ their religious duties.
   (A) covenant…shirk
   (B) prosperity…prevail
   (C) demur…conspire
   (D) nullity…waive
   (E) austerity…sojourn

6. The years since Israel_____ itself an independent nation have been marked by unrest and _____between Israelis and Arabs.
   (A) proclaimed…tumult
   (B) abhorred…thicket
   (C) chided…compassion
   (D) demonstrated…poignancy
   (E) redeemed…magnitude

7. The ancient Mesopotamians gained economic _____ by irrigating the _____ lands of southwest Asia.
   (A) impulse…rare
   (B) prosperity…arid
   (C) increment…inordinate
   (D) demur…shrill
   (E) range…primordial

8. Impatient for religious freedom, activists _____ for the formation of a Muslim state.
   (A) demonstrated
   (B) proclaimed
   (C) shirked
   (D) deemed
   (E) murmured

Advanced Learners/Pre-AP

DIFFERENTIATED INSTRUCTION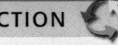

Reading Beyond the Classroom In addition to reading for their assignments, encourage students to read for pleasure as well as. Explain that reading magazines, books, poetry, and newspapers will introduce them to new vocabulary words and show them how familiar words are used in different contexts. Invite students to write in the books they own, underlining unfamiliar words to look up in the dictionary.

In addition to building vocabulary, reading for pleasure will help students become better writers; they will become more comfortable with variations in plot structure, dialogue, and even literary devices. Also encourage students to try crossword puzzles, which will challenge their memory and introduce them to words and ideas with which they might not have been familiar.

Assessment
English-Language Arts

Assess

1. **B** is the correct answer. Gandhi's nonviolent resistance movement posed a *formidable*, or powerful, threat to British rule. `DOK 2`

2. **B** is the correct answer. Prejudiced teachers *deemed*, or judged, their students to be inferior. `DOK 2`

3. **D** is the correct answer. Many critics have *scrutinized*, or examined, the caste system. The untouchables were *fettered*, or trapped, in their unfortunate situation. `DOK 2`

4. **E** is the correct answer. The walls of ancient Sumerian cities set the Sumerians apart, or *distinguished* them, from their enemies. The walls were *impervious*, or impenetrable. `DOK 2`

5. **A** is the correct answer. The Israelites made a *covenant*, or a pact, with God. They promised not to *shirk*, or avoid, their religious duties. `DOK 2`

6. **A** is the correct answer. Israel *proclaimed*, or declared, itself independent. The second blank requires a word similar in meaning to *unrest*, such as *tumult*. `DOK 2`

7. **B** is the correct answer. The Mesopotamians gained economic *prosperity*, or well-being, by irrigating *arid*, or dry, lands. `DOK 2`

8. **A** is the correct answer. The activists *demonstrated*, or protested, for the creation of a Muslim state. `DOK 2`

Assess

1. **E** is the correct answer. The sentence is correct as written. [DOK 1]

2. **C** is the correct answer. The present-tense verb *know* should be replaced with the past participle *known*. [DOK 1]

3. **A** is the correct answer. In this sentence, *that* should be replaced with *which*. The adjective clause "which originated in Mexico and Guatemala" is nonessential, and therefore *which* is the correct relative pronoun. [DOK 1]

4. **D** is the correct answer. In this sentence, *his* should be replaced with *their*. The possessive pronoun *his* refers to Frank Gehry, when it should refer to the subject of the sentence— "postmodern architects"—which takes a plural possessive pronoun. [DOK 1]

5. **B** is the correct answer. A comma should be placed after "sleeping bags." [DOK 1]

Grammar and Writing Skills: Paragraph Improvement

Read the following sentences carefully. Pay close attention to **pronouns**, **sentence types**, **punctuation**, and **introductory phrases**. Then, on a separate sheet of paper, choose the letter of the section that shows a grammatical mistake or choose E if there is no error.

1. Biotechnology <u>is</u> an emerging industry in India, <u>whose</u> economic <u>growth rate</u> continues <u>to</u> increase each year. <u>No error</u>
    A — whose, B — growth rate, C — to, D — increase, E — No error

2. Jean Piaget <u>was</u> a <u>Swiss</u> philosopher and developmental psychologist <u>know</u> primarily for his <u>work with children</u>. <u>No error</u>
    A — was, B — Swiss, C — know, D — work with children, E — No error

3. The avocado, <u>that</u> originated in Mexico and Guatemala, became a <u>profit-turning</u> crop for California farmers in the <u>1970s</u> when Americans began a <u>love affair</u> with guacamole that continues today. <u>No error</u>
    A — that, B — profit-turning, C — 1970s, D — love affair, E — No error

4. <u>Without</u> talented structural engineers, <u>postmodern</u> architects such as Frank Gehry would not <u>be able to</u> create <u>his</u> revolutionary buildings. <u>No error</u>
    A — Without, B — postmodern, C — be able to, D — his, E — No error

5. <u>As</u> materials for tents, <u>sleeping bags and</u> <u>backpacks</u> become more <u>lightweight</u>, pack weights for hikers and backpackers continue <u>to</u> drop. <u>No error</u>
    A — As, B — sleeping bags and, C — backpacks / lightweight, D — to, E — No error

6. Giuseppe Garibaldi, a revolutionary leader who <u>help</u> unify Italy in the 1860s, <u>has been</u> vilified by some <u>historians</u> and celebrated <u>by</u> others. <u>No error</u>
    A — help, B — has been, C — historians, D — by, E — No error

7. Internet banks <u>are</u> able to offer investors higher interest rates <u>then</u> traditional banks because they <u>employ</u> fewer workers and do not have to pay rent for <u>branch locations</u>. <u>No error</u>
    A — are, B — then, C — employ, D — branch locations, E — No error

8. *Moai*, the giant stone statues <u>on</u> Easter Island in the <u>South Pacific</u>, <u>are</u> carved from <u>volcanic</u> ash sometime after A.D. 1000. <u>No error</u>
    A — on, B — South Pacific, C — are, D — volcanic, E — No error

9. From <u>1967 to 1976</u>, when the dunk was <u>banned</u> in college basketball, centers such as Lew Alcindor and Bill Walton had to develop <u>shots</u> <u>like the sky hook</u> to make use of <u>his</u> height. <u>No error</u>
    A — 1967 to 1976, B — banned, C — like the sky hook / shots, D — his, E — No error

10. The <u>antelope</u> jackrabbit, an inhabitant of the Sonoran and Chihuahuan deserts, <u>uses</u> its large ears to radiate heat from <u>its</u> body, a process <u>that</u> regulates its body temperature. <u>No error</u>
    A — antelope, B — uses, C — its, D — that, E — No error

Grammar Practice

Pronoun-Antecedent Agreement Review with students pronoun-antecedent agreement. Point out that compound antecedents are the source of many pronoun-antecedent agreement mistakes. Tell students to stop and first identify all of the nouns in a complex sentence. Then they can determine the correct pronoun by identifying the number of antecedents and their connector. Write the following formulas on the board:

(1) Singular antecedent + *or/nor* + singular antecedent = singular personal pronoun. (*Neither Hannah nor Karen will be allowed to bring her kitten to school for show-and-tell.*) (2) Singular or plural antecedent + *or/nor* + plural antecedent = plural personal pronoun. (*After the dogs and the cat come inside, make sure to clean their paws.*)

(1) Antecedent + *and* + antecedent = plural personal pronoun. (*My brother and my sister took their final exams yesterday.*)

Explain that there is an exception to the third rule when dealing with ownership. A plural pronoun should be used if both antecedents own something jointly; A singular pronoun should be used if only one of the antecedents owns an item.

Essay

Think carefully about the following excerpt and the writing assignment below.

"Tears came to my eyes. I forgot that he was a poor Kabuli fruit-seller, while I was—but no, what was I more than he? He also was a father."

—Rabindranath Tagore, from "The Kabuliwallah"

Assignment: Write an essay in which you analyze the relationship between the narrator of "The Kabuliwallah" and the Kabuliwallah. In your essay, consider how social classes and economic divisions affect the characters. Present your ideas in a logical order and use evidence from the story to support your views. As you write, keep in mind that your essay will be checked for **ideas, organization, voice, word choice, sentence fluency, conventions,** and **presentation.**

Remember to:

- Write about the assigned topic.
- Make your writing thoughtful and interesting.
- Make sure each sentence you write contributes to your composition as a whole.
- Make sure your ideas are clear and easy for the reader to follow.
- Write about your ideas in depth so the reader is able to develop a good understanding of what you are saying.
- Proofread your writing to correct errors in spelling, capitalization, punctuation, grammar, and sentence structure.

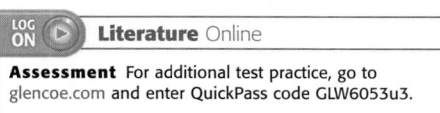

LOG ON ▶ **Literature** Online

Assessment For additional test practice, go to glencoe.com and enter QuickPass code GLW6053u3.

ASSESSMENT **669**

Assess

6. A is the correct answer. Because the sentence is about a historical figure from the 1860s, the present-tense verb *help* should be replaced with the past-tense verb *helped.* `DOK 1`

7. B is the correct answer. The adverb *then* should be replaced with the conjunction *than.* `DOK 1`

8. C is the correct answer. The present-tense verb *are* should be replaced with the past-tense verb *were* because the *moai* were carved many years ago. `DOK 1`

9. D is the correct answer. In this sentence, *his* should be replaced with *their.* The possessive pronoun *his* refers to one of the centers, when it should refer to both Lew Alcindor and Bill Walton. `DOK 1`

10. E is the correct answer. The sentence is correct as written. `DOK 1`

Essay

Students' essays should

- analyze the relationship between the two characters
- consider social and economic factors
- include evidence from the story
`DOK 3`

Analyzing Relationships Encourage approaching level students not to confuse analysis of a literary work with comparing and contrasting elements. Tell students that while differences and similarities are often found in an analysis, students should avoid simply making lists of how characters are similar and different. Encourage students to quickly compose a compare-contrast list to use as the starting point for an analytical essay.

Analyzing Point of View Remind students when writing an analytical essay on relationships between characters to remember the story's point of view. A first-person narrator will only give his or her own thoughts and will assume the feelings and thoughts of others. This perspective will influence the narrator's attitude of social class and economic divisions in a manner of which the narrator might not even be aware.

Skills Scope and Sequence

Readability Scores Key: Dale-Chall/DRP/Lexile

PART 1: East Asia 2000 B.C.–500 B.C.

Selections and Features	Literary Elements
Part Introduction pp. 670–683	Literary Periods **SE** p. 678
Sacred Text *from* **The Analects,** by Confucius, translated by Arthur Waley **5.5**/**55**/**n/a** pp. 684–688	Maxim **SE** p. 685
Sacred Text *from* **The Tao Te Ching,** by Lao-tzu, translated by Stephen Mitchell **7.9**/**54**/**n/a** pp. 689–693	Parallelism **SE** p. 690
Poem The River Merchant's Wife: A Letter, by Li Po, translated by Ezra Pound pp. 694–699	Tone **SE** p. 695 Setting (review) **SE** p. 698
The Art of Translation Creating a Work of Beauty pp. 700–701	
Comparing Literature Jade Flower Palace (poem), by Tu Fu, translated by Kenneth Rexroth **Ozymandias** (poem), by Percy Bysshe Shelley *from* **Istanbul: Memories and the City** (memoir), by Orhan Pamuk, translated by Maureen Freely **8.7**/**58**/**1360** pp. 702–711	Cultural Context **SE** p. 702 Theme **SE** p. 702 Imagery **SE** p. 704 Diction **TE** p. 704
Tanka When I Went to Visit, by Ki no Tsurayuki, **Forsaking the Mists,** by Lady Ise, **Was It That I Went to Sleep,** by Ono no Komachi, and **Trailing on the Wind,** by Saigyō, translated by Geoffrey Bownas and Anthony Thwaite pp. 712–715	Mood **SE** p. 713
Diary *from* **The Pillow Book,** by Sei Shōnagon, translated by Ivan Morris **7.4**/**60**/**880** pp. 716–728	Diary **SE** p. 717 Author's Purpose (review) **SE** p. 727

Reading Skills and Strategies	Vocabulary	Writing Grammar	Speaking, Listening, Viewing
Evaluate Historical Influences **SE** p. 676 Compare and Contrast **SE** p. 680 Analyze Cause-and-Effect Relationships **SE** p. 681 Make Generalizations **SE** p. 682 Connect to the Literature **SE** p. 683 Analyze Dialogue **TE** p. 686	Use Context Clues **TE** p. 676 Suffixes **TE** p. 677 Word Origins **TE** p. 680 Synonyms **TE** p. 682	Use Date Abbreviations **TE** p. 674 Write a Haiku **TE** p. 682 Write a Research Report **SE** p. 683	View the Art **SE** p. 670; **TE** p. 672, 677, 679 Panel Discussion **TE** p. 680 Visual Display **SE** p. 683
Make Generalizations **SE** p. 685	Synonyms **SE** p. 688	Write Guidelines **SE** p. 688	
Question **SE** p. 690 Analyze Structure **TE** p. 692	Analogies **SE** p. 693	Write a Blog **SE** p. 693	Debate **TE** p. 690 View the Art **TE** p. 692
Visualize **SE** p. 695	Academic Vocabulary **SE** p. 699	Write an Evaluation **SE** p. 699 Apply Form **TE** p. 696	Oral Interpretation **SE** p. 699
Analyze Cultural and Historical Context **SE** p. 700 Understand the Nature of Translation **SE** p. 701			
Make Inferences About Theme **SE** p. 704 Analyze Description **TE** p. 708 Analyze Cause-and-Effect Relationships **TE** p. 710	Academic Vocabulary **SE** p. 706	Write a Short Story **SE** p. 706 Write a Comparison-Contrast Essay **SE** p. 711	Discussion **SE** pp. 707, 711 Oral Report **SE** p. 711
Interpret Imagery **SE** p. 713 Make Inferences About Theme **TE** p. 714	Academic Vocabulary **SE** p. 715	Write a Tanka **SE** p. 715	
Draw Conclusions About Author's Culture **SE** p. 717 Compare and Contrast Tone **TE** p. 722	Denotation and Connotation **SE** p. 727 Academic Vocabulary **SE** p. 727	Write a Haiku **TE** p. 720 Write an Autobiographical Narrative **SE** p. 728 Gerunds **SE** p. 728	Dramatic Adaptation **TE** p. 724 View the Art **SE** p. 725 Discussion **SE** p. 726

Readability Scores Key: Dale-Chall/DRP/Lexile

PART 1: East Asia 2000 B.C.–500 B.C. *(continued)*

Reading Skills and Strategies	Vocabulary	Writing / Grammar	Speaking, Listening, Viewing
		Commas with Interjections and Parenthetical Expressions **SE** p. 729	
Apply Background Knowledge **SE** p. 731 Recognize Author's Purpose **TE** p. 732	Word Usage **SE** p. 735	Write a Parable **SE** p. 735	
Make Connections Across Literature **SE** p. 736 Connect to the Literature **SE** p. 737		Write a Scenario **TE** p. 736	
Analyze Imagery **SE** p. 739 Clarify Meaning **TE** p. 740	Academic Vocabulary **SE** p. 742	Apply Diction in a Descriptive Essay **SE** p. 742	
Evaluate Historical Influences **SE** p. 743 Interpret Meaning **TE** p. 746		Dashes **TE** p. 744 Write a Summary **SE** p. 747	View the Art **TE** p. 745
Analyze Historical Context **SE** p. 749 Paraphrase **TE** p. 750	Word Origins **SE** p. 752	Write a Speech **SE** p. 752	View the Photograph **SE** p. 751
Review **SE** p. 754 Identify Sequence **TE** p. 754	Word Origins **SE** p. 760 Academic Vocabulary **SE** p. 760	Write an Expository Essay **SE** p. 761 Coordinating Conjunctions **SE** p. 761	Discussion **SE** p. 759
Analyze Speaker **SE** p. 763	Academic Vocabulary **SE** p. 765	Apply Apostrophe **TE** p. 764 Write a Letter **SE** p. 765	
Analyze Diction **SE** p. 767	Word Usage **SE** p. 769	Write an Essay **SE** p. 769	Performance **TE** p. 768
Identify Problem and Solution **SE** p. 770 Preview **SE** p. 770	Adjectives **TE** p. 770	Write a Research Report **TE** p. 772 Write a Summary **SE** p. 773	View the Photograph **SE** p. 772

Readability Scores Key: Dale-Chall/DRP/Lexile

PART 2: Southeast Asia and the Pacific 500 B.C.–Present

Reading Skills and Strategies	Vocabulary	Writing Grammar	Speaking, Listening, and Viewing
Evaluate Historical Influences **SE** p. 778 Compare and Contrast **SE** p. 783 Connect to the Literature **SE** p. 785	Context Clues **TE** p. 778	Create a Graphic Organizer **TE** p. 776 Verb Tense **TE** p. 782 Write Questions **SE** p. 785	Panel Discussion **SE** p. 785 Visual Display **SE** p. 785
Analyze Structure **SE** p. 787	Academic Vocabulary **SE** p. 789	Write a Poem **SE** p. 789	Illustration **TE** p. 788
Analyze Sensory Details **SE** p. 791 Interpret Imagery **TE** p. 794	Context Clues **SE** p. 800 Academic Vocabulary **SE** p. 800	Write an Essay **TE** p. 798 Write a Short Story **SE** p. 801	Oral Interpretation **TE** p. 792 View the Art **SE** p. 797 Discussion **SE** p. 799
Clarify Meaning **SE** p. 803	Word Usage **SE** p. 805	Write a Proposal **SE** p. 805	
Connect to Personal Experience **SE** p. 807	Denotation and Connotation **SE** p. 809	Write an Internal Monologue **SE** p. 809	Oral Interpretation **TE** p. 808
Summarize **SE** p. 811 Analyze Tone **TE** p. 812	Academic Vocabulary **SE** p. 813	Write an Expository Essay **SE** p. 813	
Activate Prior Knowledge **SE** p. 815 Visualize **TE** p. 816	Synonyms **SE** p. 818	Write a Letter **SE** p. 818	View the Art **TE** p. 816
Question **SE** p. 820	Word Parts **SE** p. 827 Academic Vocabulary **SE** p. 827	Write a News Story **TE** p. 824 Write a Scene **SE** p. 827 Write an Evaluation **SE** p. 827	View the Art **SE** p. 825 Performance **SE** p. 827
	Denotation and Connotation **SE** p. 828		
Recognize Author's Purpose **SE** p. 830 Compare and Contrast **TE** p. 830	Analogies **SE** p. 833	Write a Poem **TE** p. 832 Create a Brochure **SE** p. 833	
		Write a Persuasive Speech **SE** p. 841	
Evaluate Evidence **TE** p. 842		Write Note Cards **SE** p. 842	Persuasive Presentation **SE** p. 843
Analyze Media Messages **SE** p. 844		Write an Advertising Slogan **TE** p. 844 Write a Summary **SE** p. 845	Discussion **SE** p. 846
Read Literature Independently **SE** p. 848		Write a Review **SE** p. 849	Presentation **SE** p. 849
Skim **TE** p. 850		Write a Persuasive Essay **SE** p. 855	

Focus

Bellringer Option

Literature Launcher DVD
  Pre-Reading Video Unit 4
Daily Language Practice
  Transparency 57
Or write on the board:
reciprocity

Ask: What does *reciprocity* mean? Elicit from students that the word *reciprocity* refers to a mutual exchange of rights and duties. (Some students may be familiar with the term *reciprocal* from their math classes.) Point out that reciprocity is a key concept in Confucianism, a traditional moral philosophy of China. Quote one of the classic expressions of Confucian reciprocity: "Do not do to others what you would not want others to do to you."

 *View the Art* ★

Answer: *There are numerous people and boats. The workers seem to be working in a large area.*
Yang Ti was a great builder, constructing huge palaces and the Grand Canal, which linked the rice-growing areas of southern China with the north. More than 1,000 miles long, the canal is the world's longest artificial waterway.

 For school-to-home activities, see Unit 4 Teaching Resources Book, pp. 5–11.

 For students who would profit from independent novel study, see Novel Companion pp. 163–206.

Emperor Yang Ti on his boat on the Grand Canal China, 18th century. Painting on silk. Bibliothèque Nationale, Paris.
View the Art Emperor Yang Ti (569–618) planned and constructed a series of waterways that united north and south China. More than five million people worked on the construction of the Grand Canal. How does the artist convey the immensity of Yang Ti's project? ★

Assessment Practice

Timed Writing Point out to students that standardized tests often ask students to write a response to a prompt in a limited period of time. Have students practice with timed writing by taking twenty minutes to develop a paragraph giving their opinion of the point that the Samoan proverb makes in the quotation on page 671. Have them follow these steps:

- Read over the quote several times to grasp what the proverb means and to formulate a response.
- Create a simple outline of the points to be made.
- Write an introductory sentence clearly stating an opinion.
- Present the remaining points and add a conclusion.
- Read over the paragraph, correcting errors in grammar and punctuation.

East Asia and the Pacific

2000 B.C.–Present

E pala ma'a, 'ae le pala 'upu.

Stones rot, but words last forever.

—Samoan proverb ☆

PART ONE
East Asia ....pages 672–773

PART TWO
Southeast Asia and the Pacific......pages 774–855

671

Unit Resources

Print Material

- Unit 4 Teaching Resources, pp. 1–313
- Interactive Read and Write for On-Level Learners
- Novel Companion, pp. 167–206
- Bellringer Option Transparencies: Selection Focus 39–51; Daily Language Practice 57–79
- Literary Element Transparencies
- Assessment Resources, Unit Assessment, pp. 259–261

- Assessment Resources, Selection Assessment, pp. 135–174

Technology

- TeacherWorks Plus CD
- StudentWorks Plus CD
- Literature Launchers: Pre-Reading Videos DVD, Unit 4
- Literature Online
- Listening Library CD-ROM
- ExamView CD-ROM
- Skill Level Up! CD-ROM

Focus

Summary

Unit Four is divided into two sections. Part 1 covers East Asia; Part 2 covers Southeast Asia and the Pacific. The introduction for Part 1 is on pages 672–683; the introduction for Part 2 is on pages 768–779.

Text Element   1

Headings Have students review the unit title and dates. **Ask:** What are some countries in East Asia? *(China, Japan, Korea)* **Ask:** How many years does Unit Four cover? *(about 4000 years)*

Political History ☆

Samoa The Samoan Islands lie in the South Pacific Ocean. They include the Independent State of Samoa, a country closely allied with New Zealand, and American Samoa, a territory of the United States. Originally settled by peoples from Southeast Asia in about 1000 B.C., Samoa came under the control of Germany and the United States in the early 1900s. New Zealand took control of the German section of Samoa during World War I. In American Samoa, American sports are popular, especially football. In the rest of Samoa, most people prefer rugby and cricket.

 For diagnostic and end-of-unit assessment, see Assessment Resources, pp. 19–24, 259–261.

671

Teach

Reading Strategy | 1

Analyze Graphic Information Have students examine the map of China, Korea, and Japan. **Ask:** Why might a Korean proverb describe the country as "a shrimp between whales"? *(Korea forms a peninsula on the east coast of Asia, extending south toward the western tip of Japan. Thus it acts as a bridge between its two powerful neighbors, the "whales" China and Japan.).*

View the Art ★

The geometric forms and patterns of China's terraced rice paddies are not only visually striking but also make efficient use of water resources and of hilly regions where farming would otherwise be nearly impossible. **Ask:** How might the necessity of such agricultural practices affect the Chinese response to landscape? *(Students might feel that intensive farming such as this would make the Chinese more sensitive to landscape.)*

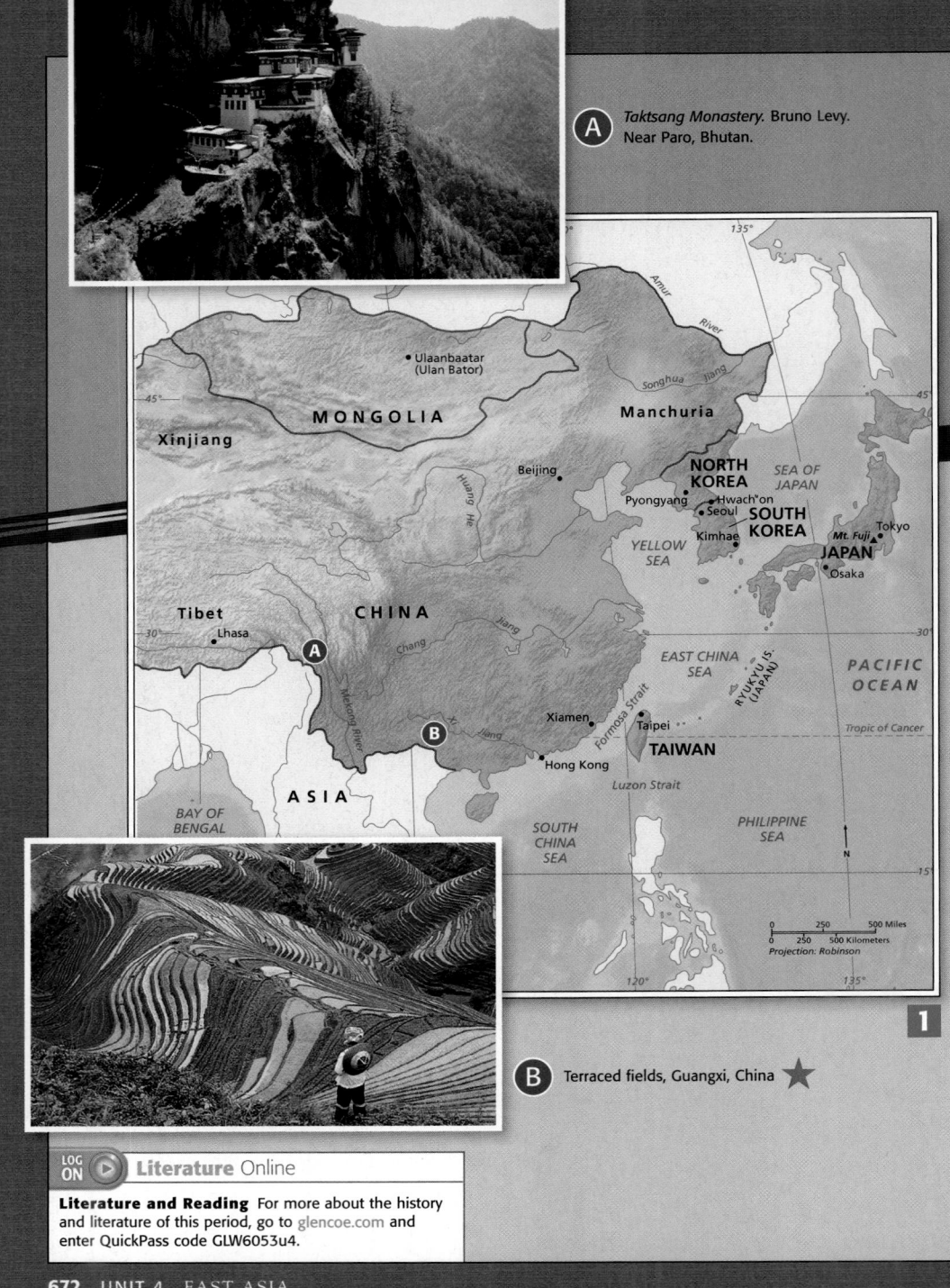

Ⓐ *Taktsang Monastery.* Bruno Levy. Near Paro, Bhutan.

Ⓑ Terraced fields, Guangxi, China ★

LOG ON ▶ **Literature** Online

Literature and Reading For more about the history and literature of this period, go to glencoe.com and enter QuickPass code GLW6053u4.

Part Introduction Skills

Reading Skills
- Analyze Graphic Information (SE p. 675; TE pp. 672, 675)
- Compare and Contrast (SE p. 680; TE p. 676)
- Analyze Cause-and-Effect Relationships (SE p. 681; TE pp. 676, 678)
- Make Generalizations (SE p. 682)
- Note Taking (SE p. 683)
- Use Graphic Organizers (TE p. 678)

Part 1 Introduction

Vocabulary Skills
- Context Clues (TE p. 676)
- Suffixes (TE p. 677)
- Word Origins (TE p. 680)

Speaking/Listening/Viewing Skills
- Visual Literacy (SE p. 683)
- Analyze Art (SE p. 670; TE pp. 672, 675, 677, 679, 681)
- Panel Discussion (TE p. 680)

Writing Skills/Grammar
- Date Abbreviations (TE p. 674)
- Haiku (TE pp. 682, 683)

East Asia

2000 B.C.–Present

Terracotta Army, Qin Dynasty, 210 BC; horses and carriage

Being There

East Asia stretches from the windswept plains of Mongolia and the lofty plateau of Tibet, through the rich agricultural lands of eastern China, across the Yellow Sea to the mountainous peninsula of Korea, and finally to the island country of Japan. The diverse countries in the region have been bound together for centuries by culture and history. China's most fertile land is found in the eastern third of the country, where the majority of the people live. Today, South Korea is one of Asia's most technologically developed countries. Though densely populated, Japan is the most prosperous nation in Asia.

Looking Ahead

China, one of the world's oldest civilizations, has greatly influenced the culture and history of East Asia. Much of this influence stems from the philosophies of Confucianism and Taoism. From very early times, Korea **2** and Japan followed Chinese models in government, the arts, and other areas, including familial and social structures. ☆

Keep the following questions in mind as you read:

- How did the worldviews of Confucianism and Taoism differ?
- How did the institution of the family shape East Asian cultures?
- How have East Asian cultures responded to change?

INTRODUCTION **673**

Approaching Level

DIFFERENTIATED INSTRUCTION

Identify Landforms Point out that this map shows dry areas with yellow-brown tones, fertile areas with green tones, and mountains with shading. Have students use the word *dry, mountainous,* or *fertile* (or some combination) to describe these areas:

1. Mongolia (*mountainous and dry*)
2. China near the Yellow Sea (*fertile*)
3. Southern China (*mountainous and fertile*)

Advanced Learners/Pre-AP

DIFFERENTIATED INSTRUCTION

Research the Silk Road Point out to students that the Silk Road, a network of trade routes over which caravans transported silk and other goods, began at the Pacific coast of China and ended at various ports on the Mediterranean Sea. Have interested students research the geography of the Silk Road to make a visual presentation to the class using resources like maps, works of art, and photographs.

Focus

Summary

This introduction gives an overview of historical, social, and cultural forces in China from the rise of the Shang dynasty in approximately 1766 B.C to the end of the Ming dynasty (A.D. 1644); the development of Japanese culture; the flowering of aristocratic Heian court life, and the shaping of Japan's militaristic feudal society; and the social, political, and technological changes of modern China. The introduction also describes several characteristic forms of East Asian culture, including Korean ceramics, East Asian theater, and the Japanese tea ceremony.

Reading Strategy   2

Analyze Cultural Context
Ask: What are two spiritual traditions that influenced East Asia? (*Confucianism and Taoism*)
Point out that Confucianism and Taoism are primarily philosophies or codes of ethics.

Cultural History ☆
Confucianism and Taoism
Unlike many other religious systems, spiritual traditions in East Asia are not exclusive. People sometimes follow different traditions at different times of their lives or even practice several at once.

For additional support for English Learners, see Unit 4 Teaching Resources Book, p. 20.

Teach

Text Element | 1

Timeline Remind students that in the B.C. section of the time scale, later dates have lower numbers than earlier dates and in the A.D. section later dates have higher numbers. **Ask:** Was the Han dynasty founded in China before or after the birth of Christ? *(before)* **Ask:** Is the date of the birth of the Chinese poet Bei Dao B.C. or A.D.? *(A.D.)*

Reading Strategy | 2

Analyze Graphic Information Ask: Did Buddhism reach China before or after it reached Japan? *(before)*

Cultural History ☆

Book of Songs Originally collected by the Chinese philosopher Confucius, the 305 poems of the *Shih-ching* ("Book of Songs") make up one of the Five Classics, the traditional texts that Confucius saw as the basis of all learning.

Timeline 2000 B.C.–Present

EAST ASIAN LITERATURE

2000 B.C.

c. 1400 ▶
Earliest known Chinese written records are developed

1000 B.C.

c. 1000
Chinese begin poems in the *Book of Songs* ☆

c. 759
Japanese compile massive poetry anthology the *Man'yo-shu* ("Collection of Ten Thousand Leaves")

6th century
Lao-tzu, founder of Taoism, lives

551
Confucius is born in China

213
Chinese emperor Qin Shihuangdi orders the destruction of most books

c. 105
Chinese invent paper

EAST ASIAN EVENTS

2000 B.C.

1900
First Chinese cities are founded

c. 1766 ▶
Shang, first historical Chinese dynasty, comes to power

1600
Chinese discover how to make bronze

Shang Dynasty Elephant-Shaped Zun. Bronze. Hunan Provincial Museum, Changsha City, China.

1000 B.C.

220 ▶
Chinese emperor Qin Shihuangdi orders the building of the Great Wall

206
Han dynasty is founded in China **1**

WORLD EVENTS

2000 B.C.

1792–1750
Hammurabi establishes code of law in Babylon

c. 1500 ▶
Olmec civilization begins in Mexico

1000 B.C.

432
Parthenon is completed in Greece

LOG ON ▶ **Literature** Online

Literature and Reading To explore the Interactive Timeline, go to glencoe.com and enter QuickPass code GLW6053u4.

674 UNIT 4 EAST ASIA

Grammar Practice

Use Date Abbreviations Remind students that the abbreviation B.C. is placed after the date to which it refers; A.D. is placed before the date. Both letters in these abbreviations are capitalized and a period generally follows each letter. Use only one period if the abbreviation occurs at the end of a sentence that would ordinarily take a period of its own. For example:

Confucius was born in China in 551 B.C.

If an abbreviation occurs at the end of a sentence that ends with a question mark or an exclamation point, use the period *and* the second mark of punctuation. For example:

Did you know that Confucius was born in China in 551 B.C.?

Have students determine whether the abbreviations are correctly used in the following sentences; if incorrect, have them indicate the necessary correction.

1. Did the Chinese invent paper in about 105 B.C.? *(correct)*
2. The Parthenon was completed in Greece in 432 B.C. *(correct)*
3. Olmec civilization began in Mexico in about B.C. 1500. *(incorrect; 1500 B.C.)*
4. The Chinese poet Tu Fu was born in 712 A.D. *(incorrect; A.D. 712)*

A.D. 1

701
Chinese poet Li Po is born

712
Chinese poet Tu Fu is born

868
Earliest printed book is made in China

990s
Sei Shōnagon writes *The Pillow Book* in China

A.D. 1000

1644
Japanese poet Matsuo Bashō is born

1949
Chinese poet Bei Dao is born

1968
Yasunari Kawabata becomes first Japanese author to win the Nobel Prize in Literature ▶

2000
Gao Xingjian becomes first Chinese author to win the Nobel Prize in Literature

A.D. 1

c. 65
Buddhism is introduced to China from India

552
Buddhism is introduced to Japan **2**

794
Japan's capital is moved to Heian (later Kyoto)

1260–1294
Mongol empire reaches its peak under Kublai Khan

1592–1598
Koreans fight off Japanese invasions

1854
Commodore Perry opens Japan to the West

1905
Japan defeats Russia in Russo-Japanese War **3**

1945
Korea is divided into North and South Korea

1949
Communists take control in China

1997
Hong Kong reverts to mainland China rule

A.D. 1

476
Western Roman Empire falls

c. early ninth century
First Maori arrive in New Zealand ▼

A.D. 1000

1099
Crusaders capture Jerusalem

1521
Spanish conquer Aztec Empire

1869
Suez Canal is completed in Egypt

1901
First Nobel Prizes are awarded

1948
State of Israel is formed ▲

1994
Nelson Mandela becomes president of South Africa

Reading Check

Analyze Graphic Information How many years after the Nobel Prizes were established was the first prize in literature awarded to a Japanese author? to a Chinese author?

INTRODUCTION **675**

UNIT FOUR

PART 1

Teach

Reading Check

Answer: *Japanese writer—67 years; Chinese writer—99 years.*

Reading Strategy	3

Analyze Graphic Information **Ask:** Was Commodore Perry's trip to Japan a result of the Russo-Japanese War? *(no; it happened before the war.)*

View the Art ★

Kublai Khan was the first great emperor of the Yuan, or Mongol, dynasty. A grandson of the Mongol conqueror Genghis Khan, he ruled from A.D. 1260 to 1294. He extended Mongol rule beyond China's border, conquering Korea and part of Southeast Asia. The famous medieval traveler Marco Polo described the splendors of the Khan's court.

Learning Objectives
Analyzing graphic information. (SE)
Analyzing art. (TE)
Using date abbreviations. (TE)

Advanced Learners/Pre-AP

DIFFERENTIATED INSTRUCTION

Zen Buddhism Buddhism was first introduced from China to Japan in A.D. 552. Zen, one of the best known forms of Buddhism, had a significant effect on Japan's cultural life for centuries and later generated a great deal of interest in the United States beginning in the 1960s. Robert Pirsig's book *Zen and the Art of Motorcycle Maintenance,* published in 1974, was immensely popular and

spawned a number of imitators, and "Zen and the Art of . . . " became a popular catchphrase.

Have interested students research the history of Zen Buddhism in the United States. Then have them consider what aspects of this tradition they think have made it particularly appealing to contemporary Americans. **Ask:** How have American interpreters changed the

traditional doctrines and practices of Zen Buddhism? Have students present their research to the class.

675

Teach

Reading Strategy | **1**

Analyze-Cause-and Effect Relationships **Ask:** How did China's geography affect its cultural development? (*China's isolation limited contact with the outside world and encouraged a single Chinese culture to develop.*)

Reading Strategy | **2**

Compare and Contrast **Ask:** How would you contrast Qin Shihuangdi's good and bad policies? (*good—uniform writing system and code of laws; bad— destruction of books and execution of scholars*)

[ADVANCED] **Ask:** Why might Qin have believed the destruction of books would contribute to his plan to unify China? (*Students might feel that Qin believed that by destroying books he could control what people knew about both the present and the past.*)

Learning Objectives

For pages 672–683
In studying this text, you will focus on the following objectives:

Literary Study: Analyzing literary periods

Reading: Evaluating historical influences.
Connecting to the literature.

East Asia
2000 B.C.–Present

Guardian of the Qin dynasty, ca. 221-206 BC. Museo Missionario Etnologico, Vatican Museums, Vatican State.

Historical, Social, and Cultural Forces

Early China

China's geographical isolation and lack of outside contact allowed it to develop one culture across many regions and preserve a strong sense of national identity. From the beginning of its recorded history until the early 1900s, China was governed by dynasties, or lines of rulers from the same family. The Shang, China's first dynasty, came to power around 1766 B.C.

Perhaps the most important cultural contribution of early China was the creation and development of the Chinese written language. By Shang times, the Chinese had developed a simple script that is the ancestor of the highly complex written language of today.

Warring States

The Shang rulers were succeeded around 1045 B.C. by the Zhou dynasty, which lasted for almost 800 years. During its final centuries, Zhou China fragmented into a number of small states that challenged the Zhou ruler. This decline led to a long and bloody conflict known as the "Period of Warring States," which began in 475 B.C. This disorder ended when the ruler of the state of Qin (chin) conquered his rivals in 221 B.C. and became

Qin Shihuangdi (chin′shir′hwäng′dē′), China's first emperor. A tireless, ruthless ruler, Qin Shihuangdi exercised both great vision and great brutality in his effort to strengthen and unify China. He instituted a uniform writing system and code of laws, but he also ordered the destruction of most books and executed scholars who opposed his policies.

> *"The King of Qin has the heart of a tiger or a wolf. Once he really has his way, he will hold the whole world captive."*
>
> —Sima Qian,
> from *The Records of the Grand Historian*

Vocabulary Practice

Use Context Clues Remind students that they can often figure out the meaning of an unfamiliar word by examining the clues in its context—the other words and sentences that surround it. Point out that one common type of context clue is a synonym or an explanation of an unfamiliar word. Draw students' attention to the following sentence on this page.

"From the beginning of its recorded history until the early 1900s, China was governed by dynasties, or lines of rulers from the same family."

Ask: What is the meaning of *dynasties*? (*lines of rulers from the same family*)

Have students identify the definitions of the underlined words and phrases in the following sentences.

1. Located five hundred miles from the Chinese mainland, Japan is an archipelago, a large group of islands. (*a large group of islands*)

2. The autocrat Shihuangdi, who built the Great Wall, was a ruler with unlimited power. (*a ruler with unlimited power*)

3. Filial piety, or children's respect for their parents and elders, is one of the basic virtues in Confucianism. (*children's respect for their parents and elders*)

The Golden Age of China

The period from the T'ang dynasty (A.D. 618–907) through the Ming dynasty (1368–1644) was a golden age of Chinese literature and art. The invention of printing during the T'ang dynasty helped to make literature more readily available and popular. The T'ang dynasty is viewed as the great age of poetry in China. The poets Li Po (see pages 694–699) and Tu Fu (see pages 703–706) were both prolific during this period.

Japan

As with China, geography significantly influenced the development of Japan. Isolated on their island chain, the ancient Japanese were close enough to the mainland to conduct a kind of cultural exchange with the mainland, but far enough away to retain their political and cultural independence. From China, the Japanese absorbed Buddhism, the Chinese writing system, and T'ang poetry. These influences combined with Japan's native religious system of Shinto ("the way of the gods"), which focuses on harmony with nature and reverence for deities and spiritual elements of nature.

By about A.D. 400, the leader of the Yamato clan established the first unified Japanese state. Over the succeeding centuries, emperors became largely ceremonial figureheads, and the heads of various ruling clans exercised the real political power. In 794 the imperial capital was moved to the city of Heian, which was later called Kyoto. The aristocrats of the Heian court created a culture that still reflected Chinese influence but was increasingly Japanese in character. This period was Japan's golden age of literature.

Beginning in 1156, a series of civil wars broke out between two great clans that lasted for more than 30 years. When it was over, the emperor bestowed on the head of the victorious clan the title of **3** *shogun*, or "general," which became hereditary. Japan remained a feudal society governed by a series of shogunates until the mid-1860s.

Under this feudal system, powerful lords governed large territories. Military retainers called samurai, who lived according to a strict code of honor and behavior called the Bushido ("The Way of the Warrior"), supported the lords. Besides the development of military skills, the Bushido emphasized such virtues as loyalty, courage, honor, frugality, and self-discipline.

Modern East Asia

In the twentieth century, China, Korea, and Japan underwent massive social, political, and technological changes. During the first half of the century, China endured revolution, civil war, and occupation by the Japanese during World War II. In 1949 the People's Republic of China was established, ruled by communist leader Mao Tse-tung (mau′dzə′doong′). Mao's government achieved some important social reforms; Chinese women, for example, gained new freedoms. Attempts in the 1950s to improve farming, however, led to famine, and the Cultural Revolution—Mao's effort to renew a revolutionary spirit throughout the country in the 1960s and 1970s—resulted in widespread abuses and stifled creativity. Since Mao's death in 1976, modified capitalist techniques have been used to encourage growth in industry and agriculture.

Shojiro with a sword, 1924. Natori Shunsen. Colour woodblock print. Private collection.

677

Teach

Vocabulary | 3

Suffixes Point out that *shogunate* is formed from the Japanese title *shogun* and the suffix *–ate*, meaning "government by" or "realm of." **Ask:** What are some other words that are formed by adding the *-ate* suffix to a title? *(Possible answers: emirate, caliphate)*

ENGLISH LEARNERS **Ask:** What does *shogunate* mean? *(government by a shogun)*

Cultural History

Shinto In early Japan, separate clans ruled their own regions. Clan members practiced a form of animism, or nature worship, called Shinto. The clan worshipped a common ancestor, often said to have been an animal or god, as its special *kami*, or spirit. Practitioners of Shinto believe that kami dwell within people, animals, and even nonliving things such as rocks and streams. To honor these kami, they hold rituals and festivals.

View the Art ★

This portrait depicts a famous Japanese actor, Sawada Shojiro, in the role of a samurai warrior. **Ask:** What qualities are conveyed by this portrait? *(Students may say that the portrait conveys such qualities as fierceness, intensity, and menace.)*

English Learners

DIFFERENTIATED INSTRUCTION

Advanced Invite students who speak Asian languages to teach their classmates about these languages. They should prepare an oral presentation describing the aspects of their language that differ the most from English; for example, the use of a pictographic script and tonal qualities to distinguish words, as in Chinese. Encourage students to research if needed.

Advanced Learners/Pre-AP

DIFFERENTIATED INSTRUCTION

Asian Languages Have interested students partner with students who speak Asian languages to create a demonstration displaying the differences between a specific Asian language and English.

Learning Objectives
Analyzing historical influences. (SE)
Using context clues. (TE)

Teach

Reading Strategy   1

Analyze Cause-and-Effect Relationships **Ask:** How did the Chinese influence the development of Korean ceramics? *(The Koreans adapted Chinese techniques of making porcelain.)*

Cultural History ☆

East Asian Dance Both folk dancing and classical court dancing are an important part of East Asian culture. In China, classical dancing has for centuries been regarded primarily as a component of "Peking Opera" style performances; these operas themselves developed from early dance rituals. The "Lion Dance" associated with Chinese New Year festivities is known worldwide. In Japan, dance was the foundation of both Noh and Kabuki drama, while folk dances were a vital part of rural agricultural festivals. In Korea, dance remained primarily a performance art in its own right. In all these countries, dances tend to emphasize arm and hand movements, often with little movement of the dancers' feet.

Reading Practice

Use Graphic Organizers Point out to students that creating a graphic organizer is a good way to keep track of the characteristics of the different types of East Asian theater. Have them create a table, such as the one started here, and use it to organize the information about East Asian theater on pages 678 and 679.

Type of Theater	Country of Origin	Dramatic Subjects	Theatrical Style
Peking Opera	China	Traditional stories	Dancing, singing, and acrobatics; colorful costumes and makeup

Korean Ceramics

1 Pottery and ceramics were perfected in all three East Asian countries. Korea's strength lay in the production of simple, yet beautiful, natural pottery. Between the eleventh and the thirteenth centuries, the Koreans learned Chinese techniques of producing high-fired porcelains and used them to create porcelain with a distinctive green glaze, called celadon (se′lə dän). Celadon is frequently decorated with carvings filled with a contrasting color of clay, often white or brown.

East Asian Theater

Although there are many styles of opera in China, the best known is referred to in the West as "Peking Opera" because it is associated with the capital Peking (or Beijing). Chinese opera tells traditional stories using a variety of theatrical effects, including dancing, singing, and acrobatics, all performed in colorful costumes and makeup. The most popular operas retell stories from hundreds of years ago.

Japan has two highly stylized forms of theater—Noh and Kabuki (see pages 736–737). The Noh dance-drama developed about 700 years ago for the nobility and the samurai. Performers do not act out the stories, but suggest them with references to scenes and stories with which the audience is familiar. Kabuki originated around 1600 as theater for the common people. The heroes of these plays were often people of lower classes who resisted oppression by the samurai. Performers repeatedly interact with the audience in Kabuki.

Puppet Theater

Puppet theater is an important part of the East Asian tradition. In China, several types of puppet theater are performed, but one of the liveliest uses glove puppets. This simple presentation is used to convey retellings of old folktales and versions of Peking Opera performances. Productions today often use dry ice, laser lighting, and other effects.

The Puppets, c. 1824-1827. Mlle. Formentin. Lithograph. Stapleton Collection, UK.

Traditional Peking Opera Performance. Marc Garanger. Beijing, China.
▼

In Korea, Kkoktukaksi (kok tōō′käk sē) puppet plays have been performed for centuries. The performers often improvise a satirical commentary on current affairs. These plays are still performed by actors who travel throughout the countryside.

Japanese *bunraku* (bən rä′m zōō) puppets act out traditional plays dating from the late seventeenth century. These lifelike three-foot-high puppets are treated almost as miniature actors. In fact, the traditional Kabuki acting style was influenced by the movements and gestures of *bunraku* puppets.

The Japanese Tea Ceremony

In the twelfth century, Chinese Buddhist monks introduced tea to Japan. The beverage became the focus of a time-honored ceremony that focuses on the appreciation of beauty. The ceremony takes place in a simple bamboo-and-wood construction that suggests the fragility of things. Tearooms typically contain a fireplace, floral arrangements, and an artwork for contemplation. To enter, guests stoop through a door, an act suggesting humility. The host gracefully combines powdered green tea leaves with hot water. This ceremony reflects the Japanese spirit of tranquility and serenity.

> "*Teaism is a cult founded on the adoration of the beautiful among the sordid facts of everyday existence.*"
>
> —Kakuzo Okakura, from *The Book of Tea*

▲ Performing Tea Ceremony in Court Dress.
Frank Leather. Japan.

PREVIEW **Big Ideas** **of East Asia**

1 Virtue and Wisdom	**2** Family and Tradition	**3** Moments of Reflection
Two contrasting philosophical traditions have shaped Chinese civilization: Confucianism and Taoism. Confucianism stresses moral duty; Taoism stresses spontaneity. Both philosophies emphasize virtuous behavior and wisdom. **See page 680**	The institution of the family and the traditions of royal courts underpin East Asian culture. Writings that explore these social structures express conflicting desires to uphold traditional values and free the individual from excessive obligations. **See page 681**	The traditional cultures of China and Japan convey a deep sense of the briefness of human life and the fragile, fleeting loveliness of nature. This is often presented through imagery or narratives that highlight beauty and loss, describing ruined palaces, doomed loves, or the passing of the seasons. **See page 682**

INTRODUCTION **679**

UNIT FOUR

PART 1

Teach

Reading Strategy | 2

Determine Main Idea
Remind students that a topic sentence can occur anywhere in a paragraph—the first sentence, the last sentence, or any of the intervening sentences. **Ask:** What is the topic sentence of this paragraph? *(the last sentence)*

ADVANCED **Ask:** Why is this the topic sentence? *(because it expresses the main idea, which is that the tea ceremony is devoted to the creation of serenity)*

View the Art
The tea ceremony remains a popular cultural form in contemporary Japan, and it is still practiced as it was hundreds of years ago. **Ask:** What does the persistence of such a tradition indicate about Japanese culture? *(Students will probably feel that it shows a desire for beauty and a reverence for the past.)*

Learning Objectives
Analyzing historical influences. (SE)
Using graphic organizers. (TE)

Approaching Level

DIFFERENTIATED INSTRUCTION

 **Puppet Theater** Point out that highly developed traditions of puppet theater, such as Japanese *bunraku* or the Korean puppet play *Kkoktukaksi*, exist around the world.

Have groups of students from different levels learn more about different forms of puppet theater. (You might direct students' attention to two forms of puppet "shadow plays," the Turkish Karagöz and Indonesian Wayang traditions.) Ask students to consider the following questions: What types of puppets are there? What methods of controlling puppets are used? What types of plays are performed? When groups have done their research, they should select a particular type of puppet theater and prepare a presentation about it for the class, including a simple demonstration of the performance techniques used.

English Learners

DIFFERENTIATED INSTRUCTION

Intermediate If students are familiar with the puppet theater traditions of their homelands, invite them to talk to the class about these cultural forms.

Teach

Reading Check

Answer: *Confucianism stressed proper conduct and societal roles. Taoism stressed spontaneity and inaction.*

Vocabulary	1

Word Origins Point out that the word *mandate* has its origin in the Latin word *mandatum,* meaning "ordered" or "commanded." **Ask:** What other English word has its origin in this same Latin root? *(mandatory)*

Reading Strategy	2

Recognize Author's Purpose **Ask:** What response to the universe is Lao-tzu urging in these lines? *(passive acceptance)*

Big Idea 1
Virtue and Wisdom

The Chinese often draw from a variety of traditions in responding to life. As an old Chinese proverb says, "The wise become Confucian in good times, Buddhist in bad times, and Taoist in old age."

Confucianism

Born in 551 B.C., Confucius (see pages 684–688) was deeply troubled by the violence and moral decay of his time. He presented a series of ideas, known as Confucianism, to restore social order. This philosophy became the backbone of Chinese culture. According to Confucianism, the key to life was to behave in harmony with the *Tao* (dou) or "Way," the principle of order in the universe. Five basic relationships, each with its own code of ethics, encapsulate this order: parent and child, husband and wife, old and young, friend and friend, ruler and subject.

1 According to Confucianism, rulers had a duty to be virtuous and subjects had a duty to be loyal. The Chinese believed their rulers governed according to the "Mandate of Heaven." If rulers were fair and effective, they received a divine mandate, or authority to rule. If rulers did not govern properly—as indicated by poor crops or losses in battle—they lost the mandate to someone else who then started a new dynasty.

Taoism

In Chinese tradition, Lao-tzu (see pages 689–693), or the "Old Master," was a contemporary of Confucius. Scholars cannot confirm if Lao-tzu actually existed, but the ideas associated with him became known as Taoism (dou′iz′əm) and gained popularity in the fifth and fourth centuries B.C. A belief in the *Tao Te Ching* links Taoism and Confucianism, yet each philosophy defines it in sharply contrasting ways. Taoism encourages people to ignore the dictates of society, live spontaneously, and not interfere with nature. To

Jade carving of Immortal with Crane holding Ling Zhi Fungus, 18th century. Oriental Museum, Durham University, UK.

the Taoist, wisdom is represented by the principle of *wu wei* (wōō′wā′), meaning "nonaction" or "letting things take their natural course."

> "The world is sacred.
> It can't be improved.
> If you tamper with it, you'll ruin it.
> If you treat it like an object, you'll
>   lose it."
>
> —Lao-tzu, from the *Tao Te Ching* **2**

Buddhism

When Buddhism was introduced to China from India during the first century A.D., it mixed with the indigenous philosophies of Confucianism and Taoism. Buddhism later spread to Korea and Japan. The fundamental principle of Buddhist *dharma,* or doctrine, is that a person should live a pure and upright life without becoming attached to worldly desires.

Reading Check

Compare and Contrast How do Confucianism and Taoism differ in their approach to the *Tao*?

Speaking and Listening Practice

Panel Discussion Point out to students that the golden age of Chinese philosophy, which lasted from about 550 to 250 B.C., is known as the Age of the Hundred Schools. Many different philosophical systems, including Confucianism and Taoism, developed during this period. The surviving philosophical texts often feature arguments or debates between philosophers representing different schools.

Have one group of students research the basic principles of Confucianism and other group research the basic principles of Taoism. Then have the two groups hold a panel discussion exploring which philosophical school would offer a better approach to some contemporary political or social issue, such as health care or global warming. Have the rest of the class serve as an audience and determine which group makes the better case.

Big Idea 2
Family and Tradition

The first group most of us experience is the family, and our ideas about what society will expect are based on values learned at home. The family was the most important social unit in ancient China and became the foundation for traditional Chinese values. In Japan, tradition also manifested itself in the royal court.

Filial Piety

As in most agricultural societies, the ancient Chinese viewed the family as the basic economic and social unit. However, the family took on an almost sacred quality as a symbol of the entire social order. Confucianism, China's most influential philosophical tradition, was one of the major factors that contributed to the central position of the family. At the heart of Confucianism was the idea of "filial piety," the duty of family members to subordinate their needs and desires to those of the male head of the family. Male supremacy was a key element in the social system of ancient China.

> "The duty of children to their parents is the foundation from which all virtues spring."
>
> —Confucius, from *The Analects*

The World of the Courtier

Beginning in the early seventh century A.D., the rulers of Japan sent cultural missions to China to further adopt Chinese styles and customs. A century after the imperial court was established at Heian in 794, the Japanese decided to end these missions. In the period that followed, an elite group of about 3,000 Japanese aristocrats, calling themselves "dwellers among the clouds," created Heian culture. Although these aristocrats still deeply admired Chinese culture, Japanese elements began to predominate in Heian court life, whose focus was a quest for beauty.

The Heian court's cultivation of the beautiful pervaded all activities, from elegantly wrapping a gift to carefully choosing the colors of the garments courtiers wore. People devoted hours each day to writing letters in pristine script, as beautiful calligraphy was believed to display the writer's character. During this period the women who wrote diaries, journals, essays, letters, and fiction produced much of Japan's earliest prose literature. These include Sei Shōnagon's journal, *The Pillow Book* (see pages 716–728), and the world's first novel, *The Tale of Genji* by Murasaki Shikibu—a masterpiece of Japanese literature.

A courtesan writing, 1770. Suzuki Harunobu. British Library, London.

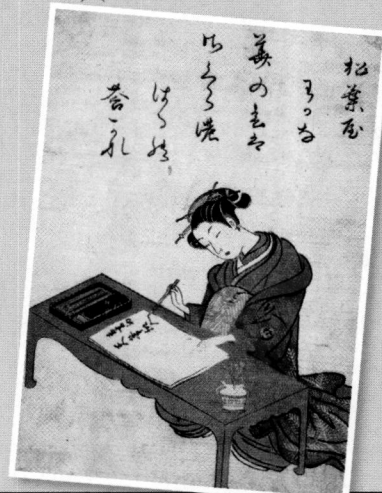

Reading Check

Analyze Cause-and-Effect Relationships How did the end of the Japanese cultural missions to China affect the development of Heian culture?

Teach

Reading Check

Answer: *By distancing themselves from the influence of Chinese culture, Heian aristocrats were able to develop a culture more distinctly Japanese.*

View the Art ★

Suzuki Harunobu was one of the earliest artists of the *Ukiyo-e* ("pictures of the floating world") movement, who used the medium of wood-block prints to depict the urban world of Edo (now Tokyo), often choosing such subjects as geishas and kabuki actors. **Ask:** What do you think the artist is trying to convey about his subject? *(Students will probably feel that the artist is trying to show this young woman's beauty, grace, and cultivation.)*

Learning Objectives
Comparing and contrast. (SE)
Analyzing cause-and-effect relationships. (SE)
Holding a panel discussion. (TE)

English Learners

DIFFERENTIATED INSTRUCTION

Intermediate Draw students' attention to the word *calligraphy*, which means "handwriting as an art form." Point out that this word is formed from a Greek word meaning "beautiful" plus the suffix *–graphy*, which means "writing." There are many English words using this suffix, which can have different meanings:

-graphy, meaning "image-making"
  photography "making images with light"
  cartography "making maps"
-graphy, meaning "study of a particular subject"
  biography "study of a person's life"
  oceanography "study of the oceans"

Have students use a dictionary to find the meanings of the following words.

1. cryptography *(study of codes)*
2. orthography *(study of spelling)*
3. stenography *(shorthand)*
4. ithography *(graphic art involving drawing on stone)*
5. geography *(study of the earth's surface)*

Teach

Reading Check

Answer: *Nature is typically characterized as delicate and related to the fleetingness of human life.*

Reading Strategy   1

Analyze Tone Ask: How would you describe the poet's attitude toward autumn in this poem? *(Students might feel that the poet's attitude seems very serious, almost depressed.)*

Vocabulary   2

Synonyms Ask: What does *transience* mean? *(the quality of lasting only a short time)*

Cultural History ☆

Ki no Tsurayuki and Kana One of the greatest Heian poets, Tsurayuki helped create the *Kokin-shu*, an influential anthology collected for the Japanese emperor about A.D. 905. In his prose introduction to this collection, he pioneered the use of *kana*, a graceful syllabic script later used so creatively by the women of the Heian court that it came to be known as *onna-de*, meaning "woman's hand."

Big Idea 3
Moments of Reflection

D epictions of nature in Western cultures tend to portray timelessness, power, danger, and mystery. In contrast, Chinese and Japanese literature emphasize the delicacy and fleetingness of natural beauty.

> On a withered branch
> a crow has settled—
> autumn nightfall
>
> —Bashō,
> translated by Harold G. Henderson **1**

Snowfall over Ukimodo Shrine at Katata, from *Eight Views of Omi*, 1918. Ito Shinsui. Colour woodblock print. British Library, London, UK.

Nature and Feeling

This famous haiku by Bashō vividly conveys the passing of the seasons. Its mood is reflective and melancholy, suggesting the fleeting nature of life. The natural imagery and universal theme of this haiku relate to a cultural touchstone. As Professor Yuriko Saito observes of Japan, "This frequent association between transience of nature and transience of human life stems from the conviction that nature and man are essentially the same, rooted in the same principle of existence." **2**

From the Heian period to the present, Japanese poets have used two very brief poetic forms, the tanka (see pages 712–715) and the haiku (see pages 738–742) to capture glimpses of nature that express how swiftly all things pass. These reflections have cultural underpinnings in Shintoism and Buddhism, including Zen Buddhism, which convey the interrelation of nature and human life. Ki no Tsurayuki, a Japanese author of the Heian period, noted that this type of poetic reflection strikes people "when they [are] startled into thoughts on the brevity of their lives by seeing the dew on the grass or the foam on the water."

Traditional Chinese poetry similarly employs natural imagery to express human frailty. In a lyric by the great T'ang poet Tu Fu, for example, he compares himself to a tiny shore-bird dwarfed by the vastness of its surroundings: "Flitting, flitting, what am I like / But a sand-snipe in the wide, wide world!"

Time and Memory

The emphasis in traditional Chinese and Japanese poetry on the transitory nature of human life coexists with the frequent use of dreams, personal memories, and meditations on the distant past. For instance, in Tu Fu's "Jade Flower Palace" (see pages 703–706), the speaker reflects on the ruins of an ancient palace. These writings often set the span of a human life against the backdrop of the natural world, including the relative longevity of such things as mountains and the slow, relentless effects of erosion. In other instances, this literature focuses on the brief lifespan of flora and fauna in relation to humans. Both approaches create poignant views on the passage of time and elegant reflections on the beauty and brevity of life.

Reading Check

Make Generalizations How would you characterize the depiction of nature in traditional Chinese and Japanese literature?

Writing Practice

 Write a Haiku Point out to students that the haiku form continues to be widely used in Japan and has also achieved great popularity around the world.

Have students try their hands at writing a haiku. Suggest that they follow these steps:

- Decide on a poetic image. (Point out to that traditional haiku—such as Bashō's poem about the autumn nightfall—are built around a single image.)

- Jot down ideas associated with this image. (Point out that these ideas might be a memory associated with this image or a feeling aroused by it.)

- Arrange these ideas into three lines. (Point out that this can be done very roughly at first.)

- Cut out any unnecessary words. (Point out that the goal is to have only five syllables in the first line, seven in the second, and five in the third.)

Wrap-Up

Legacy of the Periods

Confucian ideals remain essential to the Chinese, despite communist attacks on "old ideas" during the Cultural Revolution of the late 1960s. Like Confucianism, Taoism continues to influence the Chinese worldview. The Chinese often draw from both traditions in responding to life.

The literature of the Heian court, particularly *The Tale of Genji*, has helped define Japanese culture. Episodes from *The Tale of Genji* are as familiar to the Japanese as scenes from Shakespeare's plays are to Westerners.

The view that both nature and human life are fleeting is essential to the cultures of East Asia.

Cultural and Literary Links

 The writings of Confucius and his disciple Mencius were favorite reading of the nineteenth-century American authors known as the Transcendentalists, particularly Ralph Waldo Emerson and Henry David Thoreau.

Irish poet W. B. Yeats modeled two of his later plays on Japanese Noh drama, to which the American poet Ezra Pound introduced him.

Scene from the Tale of Genji, 16th century. Japanese school. Ink colour and gold leaf on paper. Brooklyn Museum of Art, NY.

 Early twentieth-century British and American poets known as the Imagists wrote brief, concrete lyrics inspired by Japanese haiku.

LOG ON ▶ **Literature** Online

Unit Resources For additional skills practice, go to glencoe.com and enter QuickPass code GLW6053u4.

Activities

Use what you have learned about the period to do one of these activities.

1. **Follow Up** Go back to the Looking Ahead on page 673 and answer the questions.

2. **Contrast Literary Periods** Research American Transcendentalism and compare its views about virtue and wisdom with those presented in this introduction.

3. **Build Visual Literacy** Research ancient and modern illustrations for *The Tale of Genji*. Create a visual display exhibiting the different styles artists have used in interpreting the characters and episodes.

4. **Take Notes** You might try using this study organizer to keep track of the Big Ideas in this part.

 **THREE-TAB BOOK**

Big Idea 1 | Big Idea 2 | Big Idea 3

Teach

Cultural History ☆

Imagists and Haiku The American poet Ezra Pound's famous Imagist lyric "In a Station of the Metro" is a classic example of haiku-inspired compression. Pound deleted many words to condense a first draft of thirty lines into a final poem of two lines of fourteen words that strikingly associates two vivid images—faces in a crowd and rain-soaked petals. He believed that the poet should "use no superfluous word, no adjective that does not reveal something."

Assess

Activities

1. **Follow Up** Students should support their answers with details from this introduction.

2. **Contrast Literary Periods** Transcendentalism shares with Taoism an emphasis on individuality and respect for nature.

3. **Visual Literacy** Students should describe how certain elements of the illustrations relate to characterization.

4. **Note Taking** Students' Foldables® should be well organized and their notes should have specific details about each Big Idea.

English Learners

DIFFERENTIATED INSTRUCTION

Advanced Suggest that students learning English first compose their haiku in their native language and then translate it into English.

Approaching Level

DIFFERENTIATED INSTRUCTION

Visual Haiku Suggest that students create a visual equivalent of a haiku by selecting or creating several images that when placed together create the effect of a haiku.

Focus

from the *Analects*

Meet **Confucius**
(551 B.C.–479 B.C.)

Bellringer Options

Selection Focus
   Transparency 39
Daily Language Practice
   Transparency 58

Or ask: Who in your life has affected your morals? Have students think about people (family, friends, role models) who have influenced their ethical stance.
Or: Read the following sentence from the *Analects* aloud: "I never enlighten anyone who has not been driven to distraction by trying to understand a difficulty or has not gotten into a frenzy trying to put his ideas into words" (VII.8) **Then ask:** What does this quotation suggest about Confucius's teachings? *(The quote suggests Confucius teachings are most valuable for people who are passionate about knowledge.)* Encourage students to discuss topics or activities they are passionate about and ways in which they could acquire more knowledge about them.

No individual has had a greater influence on Chinese culture and thought than the philosopher and teacher Confucius (kən fū′shəs). Until the early twentieth century, his collection of teachings, the *Analects*, was required reading for Chinese government officials. For more than 2,000 years, the Chinese Empire felt the influence of his emphasis on duty and responsibility.

> "*I am not one who was born in the possession of knowledge; I am one who is fond of antiquity, and earnest in seeking it there.*"
>
> —Confucius

The Master Confucius was born in eastern China in 551 B.C. during a period of great upheaval. War had broken out, and the social order had broken down. Though his birth name was K'ung Qiu, he later became known by the title "Master K'ung" (K'ung-fu-tzu), which was Westernized as "Confucius." Although Confucius was born into poverty, he was well-educated. Consumed with a desire for knowledge, he eagerly learned everything he could, and by age fifteen he considered himself a scholar.

In his early thirties, Confucius began teaching his philosophies, and he went on to devote his entire life to education and scholarship. He believed preserving traditions and practicing moderation and benevolence was the only way to save Chinese society. He is regarded as the first person in China to believe that education should be available to all people, not just the wealthy or noble classes.

Spreading the Word During his forties and fifties, Confucius traveled throughout China in an attempt to gain an important government position through which he could integrate his philosophies and spur social change. Though he was appointed magistrate and served in a few minor positions, he could not convince any rulers to accept his philosophies of reform. When he was 67, Confucius returned home to teach his philosophies to his followers, who numbered well into the thousands.

Confucius died at the age of 73, leaving no records of his sayings and beliefs. His followers collected his teachings and published them posthumously, and they continued to spread his philosophies throughout the world.

LOG ON ▶ **Literature** Online

Author Search For more about Confucius, go to glencoe.com and enter QuickPass code GLW6053u4.

Selection Skills

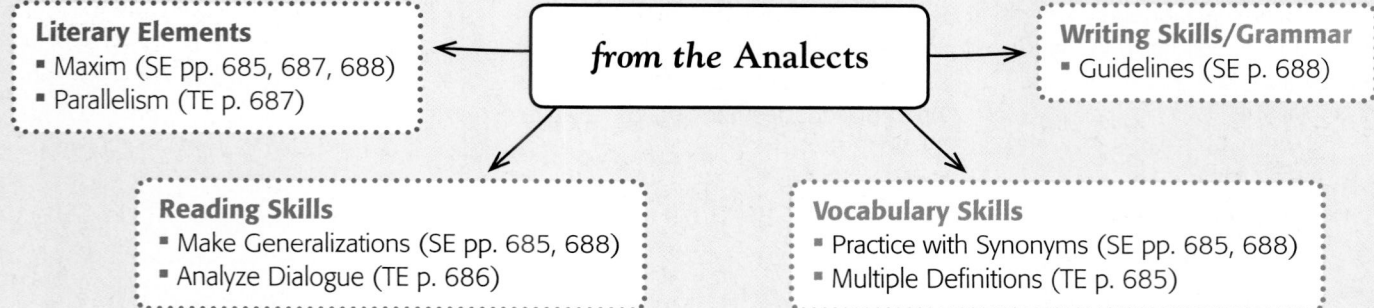

Literary Elements
- Maxim (SE pp. 685, 687, 688)
- Parallelism (TE p. 687)

from the Analects

Writing Skills/Grammar
- Guidelines (SE p. 688)

Reading Skills
- Make Generalizations (SE pp. 685, 688)
- Analyze Dialogue (TE p. 686)

Vocabulary Skills
- Practice with Synonyms (SE pp. 685, 688)
- Multiple Definitions (TE p. 685)

Literature and Reading Preview

Connect to the Sacred Text

In this excerpt, Confucius states, "Never do to others what you would not like them to do to you." What does this saying mean to you? Discuss this question with a partner.

Build Background

At the core of Confucianism are the concepts of *jen* and *li*. *Jen*, meaning "love," "goodness," "humanness" or "benevolence," is Confucianism's most important virtue. *Li* means "ritual," "etiquette," or simply "good manners." In Confucian philosophy, relationships function smoothly when correct etiquette, or *li*, is observed.

Set Purposes for Reading

Big Idea Virtue and Wisdom

As you read, ask yourself, What emphasis does Confucius place on duty, morality, and respect?

Literary Element Maxim

A **maxim** is a short saying that contains a general truth or gives practical advice about how to behave and live morally. As you read, look for the maxims Confucius includes and ask yourself, What general truths or advice is he expressing?

Reading Strategy Make Generalizations

A **generalization** is a general statement or rule. When you make a generalization, you gather details from a text and then form a broad statement that can apply to life in general, or to several situations. As you read, ask yourself, How do Confucius's statements apply to life in general?

....

Tip: Convert Information Use a graphic organizer like the one below to record key details that reveal what is important to Confucius. Then convert those details into a generalization about how Confucius believes people should behave.

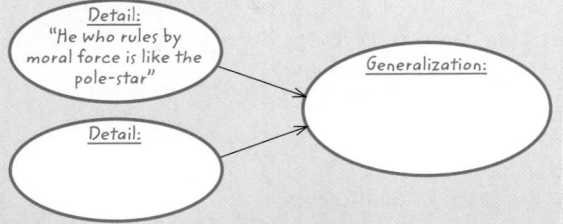

Learning Objectives

For pages 684–688

In studying this text, you will focus on the following objectives:

Literary Study: Analyzing maxims.

Reading: Making generalizations.

Writing: Writing guidelines.

Vocabulary

homage (hom′ij) *n.* the honor or respect that is shown to another person; p. 687 *The priests paid homage to the Pope when they visited the Vatican.*

docile (dos′əl) *adj.* easily taught; obedient; p. 687 *The docile students listened attentively to the tour guide as he explained one of Picasso's paintings.*

dictates (dik′tāts) *n.* principles that must be followed; p. 687 *The dictates of society state that we should not steal.*

extent (iks tent′) *n.* amount or distance; p. 687 *The judge punished the thief to the greatest extent of the law.*

....

Tip: Synonyms Synonyms are words that have the same, or similar, meaning. They can often serve as context clues. For example, in the sentence *The docile students listened attentively to the guide*, *docile* must mean "easily taught" if the students listened attentively.

CONFUCIUS **685**

Advanced Learners/Pre-AP

DIFFERENTIATED INSTRUCTION

Conduct Research Ask students to conduct research on the role of Confucianism in Chinese society. They might focus on a single topic, such as the importance placed on Confucian texts in Chinese civil service exams from 124 B.C. to A.D. 1905. Tell students to examine the way Confucian beliefs figure into the secular realm of Chinese thought.

Approaching Level

DIFFERENTIATED INSTRUCTION

Close Reading Have students choose a sentence from the selection and review it word by word. Explain that a single word or phrase can include a range of ideas. Demonstrate this by taking one word or phrase, such as "moral force" and discussing its meaning. **Ask:** What do you think Confucius is trying to convey with the phrase "moral force"? *(Perhaps that morality has a physical force, like gravity.)*

Before You Read

Focus

Summary

The selected passages from the *Analects* present a dialogue between Tzu-yu and the master, Confucius, that stresses morality and compassion and underlines the importance of the teacher-student relationship. In these passages, Confucius emphasizes the importance of respecting one's parents and living simply. He also anticipates the golden rule by saying "Never do to others what you would not like them to do to you."

 For summaries in languages other than English, see Unit 4 Teaching Resources Book, pp. 21–26.

Vocabulary

Multiple Definitions Organize students in a circle and pass around four pieces of paper, each with a vocabulary word at the top of the page. Have students write a one-sentence definition of the word and continue to fold over the paper so the previous sentence is not showing. When all four sheets of paper have circulated, read the definitions aloud and see how many match up. The students' definitions may veer away from the correct one, but reiterate the real definition while encouraging the students' creativity.

For additional vocabulary practice, see Unit 4 Teaching Resources Book, p. 29.

Teach

Literary Element | 1

Parallelism **Ask:** What instances of parallelism can you find in the maxim in the third paragraph? *(The phrase "At [a given age]," followed by a statement about the Master's mental state at that age, occurs several times in the maxim.)*

Cultural Note ☆

Confucianism Unlike many religions or philosophies, Confucianism harmoniously coexists with other religious traditions. Confucianism is viewed more as a way of life rather than as a religion. For instance, an individual can classify himself or herself as both a Muslim *and* as a Confucian. Confucius valued past cultural values and traditions and sought to conserve, revitalize, and promote them.

 For an audio recording of this selection, use Listening Library Audio CD-ROM.

Readability Scores

Dale-Chall: 5.5
DRP: 55
Lexile: not available

686

---

from the
Analects

Confucius
Translated by Arthur Waley

Portrait of Confucius, 17th century. Scroll with color on paper. Bibliotheque Nationale, Paris.

686 UNIT 4 EAST ASIA

Reading Practice

Analyze Dialogue Point out to students that the *Analects* has a unique point of view. Though it is not written in the first person, the text often includes the word *I* when quoting Confucius's dialogue. Sometimes this word set off by quotation marks and sometimes not.

Have that students review the text and identify where Confucius is quoted using quotation marks and moments where he is quoted without the use of quotation marks. Then have students discuss how this affects their reading of the *Analects.* *(An example of this shift occurs in the second stanza. The Master speaks, but only "Let there be no evil in your thoughts" is written as dialogue. This makes the reader question what role the Master has in giving such advice.)*

"Let there be no evil in your thoughts."

T he Master said, He who rules by moral force is like the pole-star,[1] which remains in its place while all the lesser stars do **homage** to it. (II, 1)

The Master said, If out of the three hundred *Songs*[2] I had to take one phrase to cover all my teaching, I would say "Let there be no evil in your thoughts." (II, 2)

1 The Master said, At fifteen I set my heart upon learning. At thirty, I had planted my feet firm upon the ground. At forty, I no longer suffered from perplexities.[3] At fifty, I knew what were the biddings[4] of Heaven. At sixty, I heard them with **docile** ear. At seventy, I could follow the **dictates** of my own heart; for what I desired

no longer overstepped the boundaries of right. (II, 4)

Tzu-yu asked about the treatment of parents. The Master said, "Filial[5] sons" nowadays are people who see to it that their parents get enough to eat. But even dogs and horses are cared for to that **extent**. If there is no feeling of respect, wherein lies the difference? (II, 7)

The Master said, He who seeks only coarse food to eat, water to drink and a bent arm for pillow, will without looking for it find happiness to boot. Any thought of accepting wealth and rank by means that I know to be wrong is as remote from me as the clouds that float above. (VII, 15)

Tzu-kung asked saying, Is there any single saying that one can act upon all day and every day? The Master said, Perhaps the saying about consideration: "Never do to others what you would not like them to do to you." (XV, 23) ◌

---

1. The *pole-star* is the North Star, used to tell direction.
2. The *three hundred Songs* refers to an anthology of the earliest Chinese poems, regarded as a source of wisdom.
3. *Perplexities* are confusing or complicated issues.
4. *Biddings* means "commands" or "orders."

2 Maxim *Restate this maxim in your own words. What does this passage suggest about Confucius?*

Vocabulary

homage (hom′ij) *n.* the honor or respect that is shown to another person

docile (dos′əl) *adj.* easily taught; obedient

dictates (dik′tāts) *n.* principles that must be followed

---

5. *Filial* means "befitting a son"; in this use, it refers to dutiful offspring who take care of their parents' material needs.

Vocabulary

extent (iks tent′) *n.* amount or distance

CONFUCIUS **687**

Teach

Literary Element **2**

Maxim **Answer:** *Possible restatement: Avoid thinking evil thoughts, as they often lead to evil actions. The passage suggests he is a spiritual leader.*

Cultural History ☆

Confucianism Today When the Communists came to power in China in 1949, Confucianism was declared counterrevolutionary; during the Cultural Revolution (1966–1976), the *Analects* was banned from schools. Today, China is once again learning from ancient Chinese traditions such as Confucianism. The Chinese book *Yu Dan's Reflections on "The Analects"* is a cultural sensation that has sold more than four million copies. The book uses the *Analects* to teach the people of today how to achieve happiness. Yu Dan argues that the text should and does have a place in modern society.

Learning Objectives
Analyzing maxims. (SE)
Analyzing dialogue. (TE)

Advanced Learners/Pre-AP

DIFFERENTIATED INSTRUCTION

Connect Across Cultures Have students select a maxim from the selection. Then have them find passages from other cultures that convey similar morals. Students may find it helpful to start with familiar, often-quoted figures such as Benjamin Franklin or Abraham Lincoln, moving gradually to lesser-known cultural figures in whom they might have an interest. Ask students to think about

the different environments surrounding the writers from whom they found quotes and consider what might have led them to create similar maxims.

Compare Translations Challenge interested students to locate and read a different translation of the *Analects*. Ask them to write a short essay comparing and contrasting the two translations. In their essays, students should state which translation they prefer, supporting their belief with evidence from the texts.

687

After You Read

Assess

1. Answers will vary.
2. (a) He compares a moral ruler to the pole-star. (b) Possible answer: moral leadership is constant and unchanging.
3. Possible answer: many sons care no more for their parents than they do for animals.
4. (a) Those who look for only life's bare necessities will find happiness. (b) He disdains it. (c) Answers will vary.
5. (a) Confucius says people should always treat people as they would wish to be treated. (b) All the other sayings support it.
6. (a) He believes wanting few possessions will allow people to concentrate their energies on more important and spiritual things. (b) He is implying that material possessions lead to greed and away from happiness.
7. Students may refer to the Golden Rule or the Ten Commandments.
8. Most students will agree these ideas continue to be relevant, as people still must behave morally.

Literary Element

1. "Let there be no evil in your thoughts."
2. Confucius may be suggesting action is motivated by thought; thus good thoughts are the first steps toward good actions.

Progress Check

Can students identify maxims?

If No → Use Unit 4 Teaching Resources Book, p. 27.

After You Read

Respond and Think Critically

Respond and Interpret

1. Which of Confucius's maxims did you find most memorable or intriguing? Explain.
2. (a) What simile does Confucius use in the first saying? (b) How do you interpret this simile?
3. What do you think Confucius means when he compares some sons' treatment of their parents to their treatment of dogs and horses?
4. (a) In the fifth saying, what kind of person does Confucius say will find happiness? (b) How does he view ill-gotten wealth? (c) Do you agree or disagree with his views? Explain.

Analyze and Evaluate

5. (a) How does Confucius say people should behave every day? (b) How is this saying central to his philosophy?
6. (a) Why do you think Confucius teaches that a simple life will lead to happiness? (b) What is he implying about people and their values?

Connect

7. **Big Idea** **Virtue and Wisdom** What proverbs or sayings have you heard that express sentiments similar to those of Confucius?
8. **Connect to Today** Do you think Confucius's ideas about people and society are still relevant today? Why or why not?

Literary Element **Maxim**

Many of the ideas contained in the *Analects* are conveyed as **maxims**. Throughout the centuries, philosophers and writers have often used maxims to offer instruction on morality and behavior.

1. What maxim is included in the second saying?
2. Why might Confucius say this maxim represents his teachings better than his other sayings?

Reading Strategy **Make Generalizations**

Refer to the web diagram you made on page 685 as you answer the following questions.

1. What generalization can you make about Confucius's views on society?
2. (a) What generalization can you make about the way people behaved at the time? (b) Does this differ from how people behave today? Explain.

LOG ON ▶ **Literature** Online

Selection Resources For Selection Quizzes, eFlashcards, and Reading-Writing Connection activities, go to glencoe.com and enter QuickPass code GLW6053u4.

688 UNIT 4 EAST ASIA

Vocabulary Practice

Practice with Synonyms With a partner, match each boldfaced vocabulary word below with its synonym. Use a thesaurus or dictionary to check your answers.

1. homage — a. rules
2. docile — b. reverence
3. dictates — c. degree
4. extent — d. passive

 Writing

Write Guidelines To establish a productive and fair environment, many groups create guidelines, or a code of conduct, that explain how people should behave and treat one another. Using Confucius's sayings as a model, write guidelines for a group of classmates, co-workers, or teammates. Feel free to diverge from Confucius's views when you disagree with them and present a few of your points as **maxims**.

Reading Strategy

1. Confucius seems to view society as needing guidance and reform.
2. (a) Students may say they think people were selfish or disrespectful or that leaders were cruel. (b) Most students will probably say people today behave similarly to how they acted then.

Vocabulary

1. b 2. d 3. a 4. c

Writing

Students' guidelines should
- refer to a specific group
- state what to do and what not to do
- include maxims

Before You Read

from the *Tao Te Ching*

China

Meet **Lao-tzu**
(sixth century B.C.)

> "Manifest plainness,
> Embrace simplicity,
> Reduce selfishness,
> Have few desires."
>
> —Lao-tzu,
> from Verse 19 of the *Tao Te Ching*

The life of Lao-tzu (lou´dzu´), the legendary author of the *Tao Te Ching* (dou´tä´ching´), is shrouded in mystery. Some scholars question whether he lived at all, and if he did, whether he was the author of the *Tao Te Ching*. To many followers of Taoism (dou´i´zəm), which is a way of approaching life based on the *Tao Te Ching*, Lao-tzu was a mythical figure who could adopt different personalities and who lived more than 200 years. Modern followers of Taoism embrace the philosophy credited to Lao-tzu: living a peaceful life of nonaction in harmony with nature.

A Legendary Meeting According to a biography written around 100 B.C. by the ancient Chinese historian Ssu-ma Ch'ien, Lao-tzu lived around 600 B.C. and served as a *shih* (a scholar of astrology and divination) to the kingdom of Chou (jō). In the biography, Ssu-ma Ch'ien says that while Lao-tzu was at the royal court, he met with Confucius (see pages 684–688) and criticized him for his pride and ambition. Ssu-ma Ch'ien goes on to say the chastened younger philosopher was so impressed by Lao-tzu he later spoke to his followers admiringly of him. While modern scholars doubt such a meeting took place, the story speaks to the relationship between Confucianism and Taoism in China.

Recording the Tao Another celebrated story in Ssu-ma Ch'ien's biography describes a trip Lao-tzu embarked on late in life. According to the biography, Lao-tzu left the royal court and rode off to the west, eventually coming to a gate in the wall at the edge of the kingdom. There the keeper of the gate asked him to write down his knowledge. Lao-tzu complied, recording his ideas in the 81-verse *Tao Te Ching* ("classic of the way of power"). Scholars, however, believe the *Tao Te Ching* was compiled by followers of Taoism in the fourth and third centuries B.C. Regardless of the authorship of the *Tao Te Ching*, its profound influence on Chinese culture and the cultures of many other Asian nations is undisputed.

Taoism spread as both a religion and a philosophy. Some religious Taoists sought to gain longevity, wealth, and even immortality through various mystical practices. However, it is as a philosophy, a way of approaching and understanding the world, that Taoism has had its greatest influence.

LOG ON ▶ **Literature** Online

Author Search For more about Lao-tzu, go to glencoe.com and enter QuickPass code GLW6053u4.

Before You Read

Focus

Bellringer Options

Selection Focus
Transparency 40

Daily Language Practice
Transparency 59

Or ask: When do you think war is justified? Be sure to pose this question objectively. Ask students to think about what war is and how it affects countries and individuals.

Cultural History ☆

Taoism Although Taoism is often linked with Buddhism and Confucianism, the ultimate goal of the Taoist is to achieve immortality. Taoists believe that there is an accepting and joyful way of life; the purpose of living is to find that way and exist within it. Lao-Tzu exemplified the Taoist life.

Interactive Read and Write
Other options for teaching the selection can be found in Interactive Read and Write for On-Level Learners, pp. 161–168.

Selection Skills

Literary Elements
- Parallelism (SE pp. 690, 692–693)

Tao Te Ching

Speaking/Listening/Viewing Skills
- Analyze Art (TE pp. 691–692)
- Participate in a Debate (TE p. 690)

Reading Skills
- Question (SE pp. 690, 692–693; TE p. 692)
- Analyze Structure (TE p. 692)

Vocabulary Skills
- Analogies (SE p. 693)
- Make Vocabulary Creative (TE p. 690)

Writing Skills/Grammar
- Blog (SE p. 693)
- Reflective Essay (TE p. 691)

Before You Read

Focus

Summary

This selection highlights important characteristics of leadership: verse 31 categorizes weapons as tools of violence that decent men do not employ. Verse 33 discusses the power of self-knowledge, self-fulfillment, and mastering death by accepting it. Verse 29 discusses why the world is unchangeable and how a good leader already knows such a fact.

 For summaries in languages other than English, see Unit 4 Teaching Resources Book, pp. 34–39.

Vocabulary

Make Vocabulary Creative

Split the class into four groups and assign one vocabulary word to each group. Ask students to work as a team to find out, in five minutes, everything they possibly can about their word. (Suggest starting with the word's etymology, definition, synonyms, and antonyms.) Then, have students write for five minutes about their particular word. Challenge them not to pick their pen up for the entire time and to let their thoughts flow.

 For additional vocabulary practice, see Unit 4 Teaching Resources Book, p. 42.

Literature and Reading Preview

Connect to the Sacred Text

Is violence ever necessary? If so, under what circumstances? Freewrite for a few minutes about this question.

Build Background

Taoism arose in response to the same conditions—war, chaos, and corruption—that produced Confucianism. But while Confucius hoped to reform society by promoting a strict code of social behavior, Lao-tzu recommended living in harmony with the natural world. At the heart of his philosophy is the principle of *wu wei* (wōō′wā′), meaning "nonaction" or "letting things take their natural course." Rather than inaction, *wu wei* stresses living free from worldly desires and in accordance with the underlying harmony of nature.

Set Purposes for Reading

Big Idea Virtue and Wisdom

As you read, ask yourself, What ideas in the *Tao Te Ching* illustrate the Taoist belief in nonaction and letting things take their natural course?

Literary Element Parallelism

Parallelism is the use of a series of words, phrases, or lines that have similar grammatical structure. Authors employ this technique in a literary work to emphasize an idea or emotion, to convey a sense of unity or balance, or to create a musical effect. As you read, look for examples of parallelism and ask yourself, What purposes might these uses of parallelism serve?

Reading Strategy Question

When you **question**, you ask yourself regularly whether you are comprehending what you read. It is similar to a running dialogue you conduct with yourself that helps you understand a text and connect it to your own experiences. As you read, ask yourself, Do I understand each section of the text?

Tip: Take Notes Use a chart like the one shown to record the questions that occur to you and your answers to them.

Questions	Answers
Why are weapons tools of fear?	People use them to defend themselves when they are afraid of being attacked.

Learning Objectives

For pages 689–693

In studying this text, you will focus on the following objectives:

Literary Study: Analyzing parallelism.

Reading: Questioning.

Writing: Writing a blog.

Vocabulary

detest (di test′) *v.* dislike intensely; hate; p. 691 *Used to doing as he pleased at home, the boy detested his aunt's rules.*

endure (en door′) *v.* continue to exist; last; p. 692 *If you take good care of yourself, you have a better chance of enduring for a long time.*

tamper (tam′pər) *v.* meddle improperly; p. 692 *To trick their mother into letting them stay up late, the children tampered with the settings on the clock.*

Tip: Analogies To complete an analogy, decide on the relationship represented by the first pair of words. Then apply that relationship to the second pair of words. For example, in the analogy *endure : continue :: terminate : end*, both sets of words are synonyms.

Listening and Speaking Practice

Participate in a Debate Ask students to think about what Lao-tzu means when he says the world "can't be improved" (verse 29). Divide the class into two groups, one responsible for arguing that the world can indeed be improved, and the other arguing in agreement with the text. Have them prepare and debate this topic using photographs, quotes, and other forms of media. Encourage students to support their thoughts with evidence from the text.

from the

TAO TE CHING

Lao-tzu
Translated by Stephen Mitchell

31

Weapons are the tools of violence;
all decent men **detest** them.

Weapons are the tools of fear;
a decent man will avoid them
5   except in the direst[1] necessity
and, if compelled, will use them
only with the utmost restraint.
Peace is his highest value.
If the peace has been shattered,
10 how can he be content?
His enemies are not demons,
but human beings like himself.
He doesn't wish them personal harm.
Nor does he rejoice in victory.
15 How could he rejoice in victory
and delight in the slaughter of men?

He enters a battle gravely,
with sorrow and with great compassion,
as if he were attending a funeral.

---

1. *Direst* (dīr′est) refers to an extreme condition of urgency
   or desperation.

Virtue and Wisdom *How do these lines illustrate Taoist beliefs?*

Vocabulary

detest (di test′) *v.* dislike intensely; hate

Bronze Horseman with Spears. Eastern
Han Dynasty, 2nd century A.D. Height: 53 cm.
National Museum, Beijing, China.

LAO-TZU   **691**

Teach

Big Idea

Virtue and Wisdom
Answer: *They are consistent with
the Taoist reluctance to interfere
with the natural order of things or
do harm.*

Cultural History ☆

Ruling Handbooks The Tao Te
Ching was originally written as a
guidebook for rulers; however, it
has been adapted into mainstream
education and society and now
functions a character guide for all
people. Another famous handbook
for rulers was *The Prince* by the
Italian writer Niccolò Machiavelli in
about 1500.

For an audio recording of this
selection, use Listening Library
Audio CD-ROM.

Readability Scores

Dale-Chall: 7.9
DRP: 54
Lexile: Not available

Learning Objective
Participating in a debate. (TE)

Approaching Level

DIFFERENTIATED INSTRUCTION

Add Specifics Some students might find
it difficult to draw meaning from a text as
ambiguous as Lao-tzu's *Tao Te Ching*. If so,
take the time to closely examine each sentence or phrase and make sure students
can identify the key ideas within the text.
For example, read the sentence "Knowing
others is intelligence" and flesh out what
Lao-tzu is trying to convey. Explain that
Lao-tzu says that when a person interacts
with others, he or she gains knowledge
through experience, yet it does not give
him or her the most important wisdom.
Some of the main ideas in the selected
passages may seem straightforward, but
encourage students to elaborate on *why*
this ideal is included in the Tao Te Ching.

For students who have trouble grasping
the ideas presented in the Tao Te Ching,
have them write a personal response to
what they have read. Ask them to read
each stanza a few times and write what
they think about it, even if they don't think
they understand it, and how it makes them
feel. Emphasize that personal response is a
valuable way to understand text.

Teach

Literary Element 1

Parallelism Answer:
"Knowing others is," "knowing yourself is," "Mastering others is," and "mastering yourself is."

Reading Strategy 2

Question Possible Answer:
The master is any follower of Taoism. The center of the circle is harmony with the natural world. Residing at the center is living a harmonious life.

View the Art ★

This painting's bold, head-on perspective invites the viewer to look across the surface of the water and into the bulging eyes of the brightly colored goldfish. The expressive style of this nineteenth-century painting reflects the experimentation over several centuries of a succession of artists who broke away from earlier traditions of painting. The artist, Xugu, was a monk-painter who, after deserting from the imperial army, lived and worked in Shanghai.

Ask: What is unusual or striking about this scroll? *(Answers may vary. Many will note the perspective.)*

33

Knowing others is intelligence;
knowing yourself is true wisdom.
Mastering others is strength;
mastering yourself is true power.

5 If you realize that you have enough,
you are truly rich.
If you stay in the center
and embrace death with your whole heart,
you will **endure** forever.

29

Do you want to improve the world?
I don't think it can be done.

The world is sacred.
It can't be improved.
5 If you **tamper** with it, you'll ruin it.
If you treat it like an object, you'll lose it.

There is a time for being ahead,
a time for being behind;
a time for being in motion,
10 a time for being at rest;
a time for being vigorous,
a time for being exhausted;
a time for being safe,
a time for being in danger.

15 The Master sees things as they are,
without trying to control them.
She lets them go their own way,
and resides at the center of the circle.

Wisteria and Goldfish, Qinq dynasty (mid-nineteenth century). Xu Gu. Hanging scroll; color on paper, 147.3 x 80.7 cm. Gift of Florence Ayscough and Harley Farnsworth MacNair, The Art Institute of Chicago. ★

1 Parallelism *Identify an example of parallel structure in these lines.*

2 Question *Who is the Master? What is the center of the circle?*

Vocabulary

endure (en door´) *v.* continue to exist; last
tamper (tam´ pər) *v.* meddle improperly

692 UNIT 4 EAST ASIA

Reading Practice

Analyze Structure Ask students to think about why the passage is written in a verse format as opposed to prose. Encourage them to delve into the ways in which the form corresponds with the content. **Ask:** How would your reading of the text change if the visual form were different? *(If the* Tao Te Ching *were written in prose, for example, the* contemplative nature and built-in pauses would be eliminated.) Use examples of other poetry, such as that of E. E. Cummings, where the form and the content are tightly connected.

After You Read

Respond and Think Critically

Respond and Interpret

1. Do you agree or disagree with the ideas expressed by Lao-tzu? Explain.

2. (a)According to Lao-tzu, how should a decent person view enemies? (b)What does Lao-tzu imply about people who are not decent?

3. (a)In verse 29, what word does Lao-tzu use to describe the world? (b)In your own words, describe his views on tampering with the world.

Analyze and Evaluate

4. (a)According to verse 33, how does knowing and mastering others differ from knowing and mastering oneself? (b)Why do you think Lao-tzu makes this distinction?

5. (a)What generalization can you make about the situations Lao-tzu lists in lines 7–14 of verse 29? (b)What point do you think he is making about these situations?

Connect

6. **Big Idea** **Virtue and Wisdom** Why do you think people find the ideas expressed in the *Tao Te Ching* appealing? Give reasons for your answer.

7. **Connect to Today** Imagine trying to live your life according to Lao-tzu's philosophy. Do you think his views are compatible with life in the modern world? Explain.

Literary Element Parallelism

Authors use **parallel structure** for a variety of reasons: to emphasize ideas, to convey unity or balance, or to create a musical effect.

1. (a)What purpose do you think the parallelism in lines 1–4 of verse 31 serves? (b)What purpose does the parallelism in verse 33 serve?

2. (a)What use of extended parallel structure exists in verse 29? (b)What purposes does it serve?

Reading Strategy Question

Questioning is an active, continuous way to check your comprehension of a piece of literature.

1. Did your chart from page 690 help you answer the questions above? Explain.

2. If you were given the opportunity to interview Lao-tzu, what questions would you ask?

 **LOG ON** **Literature** Online

Selection Resources For Selection Quizzes, eFlashcards, and Reading-Writing Connection activities, go to glencoe. com and enter QuickPass code GLW6053u4.

Vocabulary Practice

Practice with Analogies Choose the word that best completes each analogy. Use a dictionary if you need help.

1. detest : love :: leave :
  a. depart   **b.** delay   **c.** arrive

2. endure : survive :: trample :
  a. squash   **b.** fade   **c.** pain

3. tamper (with) : mend :: advance :
  a. retreat   **b.** attack   **c.** move

Writing

Write a Blog Blogs offer a growing record of how individuals respond to the world. What do you think Lao-tzu would write if he were alive today? Write a blog entry from the perspective of Lao-tzu, imagining he could spend time to learn about current issues. Use **parallelism** in a section of your entry.

LAO-TZU **693**

Literary Element

1. (a) Parallelism shows how the two ideas complement each other. (b) It helps to convey the importance of the two ideas in relation to each other.

2. (a) Most lines of the third stanza are parallel. (b) The structure unites the ideas, and creates a steady rhythm.

Progress Check

Can students identify parallelism?

If No → See Unit 4 Teaching Resources Book, p. 40.

Vocabulary

1. c **2.** a **3.** a

After You Read

Assess

1. Answers will vary. Students should provide support from the text.

2. (a) with compassion, as fellow humans (b) They rejoice in defeating their enemies and doing them harm.

3. (a) *sacred* (b) A person shouldn't try to change the world or control it; it cannot be improved. People who try will ruin it or lose it.

4. (a) Knowing and mastering oneself is even more important than knowing and mastering others. (b) to emphasize the importance of self-control

5. (a) They all represent situations people are likely to experience in the course of life. (b) One should accept all the things that will inevitably happen in life.

6. Students may say people find the ideas appealing because they relate to the ideas about growth and spiritual development and about living a peaceful, harmonious life.

7. Some students may feel his views provide a helpful coping device. Others may feel the pace of modern life and its technology make leading a serene, natural life difficult.

Reading Strategy

1. Review any questions that students found confusing or difficult.

2. Students may seek to clarify their understanding of Taoist ideas.

Writing

Students' blogs should

- show a grasp of Lao-tzu's beliefs
- relate to the contemporary world
- include parallelism

Before You Read

Focus

Bellringer Options

Selection Focus
    Transparency 41
Daily Language Practice
    Transparency 60

Or ask: What makes a good letter? *(Students might say that a good letter includes vivid details and expresses emotions).*

View the Art ★

Most portraits of Li Po depict the poet wearing a scholar's cap. Chinese men of differing ranks or status wore similar caps. The "feet" of the cap were stiffened with wire or bamboo so that they could be made to stay straight, curved, or crossed. A cap worn with its feet straight out to the sides indicated the wearer's high status. A cap worn with curved or crossed feet indicated the wearer's lower rank.

Selection Skills

Before You Read

China

The River Merchant's Wife: A Letter

Meet **Li Po**
(701–762)

Li Po's (lē′ pō′) vast talent, personal charisma, and eccentric lifestyle made his life the stuff of legend. One story, likely true, says the poet died when he fell out of a boat and drowned while trying to grasp the moon's reflection in the water, an appropriately poetic story for such a colorful character.

A Vagabond Life Li Po grew up in the southwestern province of Szechwan (sech′wän′). A well-educated young man from a good family, he chose not to take the test for imperial service most young men in his position took. Having shown an early talent for writing poetry, he probably could have had a career as a court poet, but he had other plans.

When Li Po was about 24 years old, he set out on his own. He lived as a hermit for a time, spending several years practicing Taoism in the mountains. Then he began a series of journeys that took him all over China. A colorful and intriguing personality, he made many friends during his travels. Among his friends were government officials, other hermits, and fellow poets, including Tu Fu (see page 703).

Skilled Swordsman, Banished Poet As he traveled, Li Po served as a wandering knight and honed his skill as a swordsman. During this time, his fame as a poet grew, and even the emperor came to admire him. When he was in his early forties, Li Po joined a group of distinguished court poets in Ch'ang-an, the T'ang dynasty capital. He kept this position for two years, until his wild behavior prompted his hosts to dismiss him.

> "[Li Po is] an immortal banished from heaven."
>
> —Ho Chih-chang, contemporary of Li Po ★

In his mid-fifties, Li Po served as an unofficial poet laureate with the military expedition of Prince Lin, the emperor's sixteenth son. After the prince came under suspicion for wanting to set up an independent kingdom, Li Po abandoned him, and the prince was later executed. Because of his association with the prince, Li Po was arrested and imprisoned for a short time, and by the summer of 758, he was banished from the province. However, the sentence was revoked as he was on his way into exile, and he returned to eastern China.

Li Po's work was praised both during and after his lifetime for its lyrical style, rich imagery, and expression of emotion. His work endures for its moving reflections on nature, friendship, solitude, and the passage of time.

 Literature Online

Author Search For more about Li Po, go to glencoe.com and enter QuickPass code GLW6053u4.

Literary Elements
- Tone (SE pp. 695, 697–698)
- Setting (SE p. 698)

The River-Merchant's Wife: A Letter

Speaking/Listening/Viewing Skills
- Oral Interpretation (SE p. 699)

Reading Skills
- Visualize (SE pp. 695, 697, 699)
- Make and Verify Predictions (TE p. 696)

Writing Skills/Grammar
- Apply Form (TE p. 696)

Literature and Reading Preview

Connect to the Poem

How would you feel if someone you loved had been gone for five months? Write a journal entry exploring this question.

Build Background

Many believe China's greatest poetry was written during the T'ang dynasty (A.D. 618–907), when Li Po lived. Two common types of T'ang verse are the "occasion poem" and the "character poem." Poets wrote occasion poems when extending an invitation or after seeing a friend. Character poems, such as "The River-Merchant's Wife: A Letter," describe character types of the period.

Set Purposes for Reading

Big Idea **Family and Tradition**

As you read the poem, ask yourself, How are ancient Chinese traditions, such as arranged marriages and loyalty, portrayed?

Literary Element **Tone**

The **tone** of a literary work is the author's or speaker's attitude toward his or her audience or subject. A work's tone can usually be described with a single adjective, such as sympathetic or critical, formal or informal, silly or serious, angry or calm. An author uses word choice, punctuation, sentence structure, and figures of speech to convey tone. As you read the poem, ask yourself, What clues indicate the speaker's attitude toward the subject matter?

Reading Strategy **Visualize**

Imagine a friend is describing her vacation—the bright sunshine of a clear fall afternoon, the foothills ablaze with crimson-leafed maple trees. You can picture the scene even though you've never been there because you're **visualizing** what your friend saw, or forming a mental picture of what she's describing. To visualize when you read, pay attention to concrete nouns, sensory details, adjectives, and active verbs. As you read the poem, ask yourself, What would this scene look like?

....

Tip: Focus on Details Create a chart like this one to keep track of the details that help you visualize the characters and the setting.

Stanza	Character Details	Setting Details
1	Hair cut straight across forehead	Near front gate, pulling flowers

Learning Objectives

For pages 694–699

In studying this text, you will focus on the following objectives:

Literary Study: Analyzing tone.

Reading: Visualizing.

Listening and Speaking: Presenting an oral interpretation.

Sakasai Ferry, plate 67 from the series *One Hundred Famous Views of Edo,* 1857. Ando or Utagawa Hiroshige. Woodblock print. Brooklyn Museum of Art, NY.

Before You Read

Focus

Summary

A young woman addresses her husband, a merchant, who has been gone for five months. She recalls how the two met as children and married as teenagers. Though she was bashful and uncertain at first, the speaker grew to love her husband. Now she mourns his absence as she observes falling leaves, paired butterflies, and other reminders of the passage of time.

> 📁 **For summaries in languages other than English, see Unit 4 Teaching Resources Book, pp. 47–52.**

Approaching Level

DIFFERENTIATED INSTRUCTION

Visualizing Some students may have difficulty grasping the poem's emotional depth. Explain to students that emotions in the poem are conveyed through subtle images, rather than through direct statements. Encourage them to pause while reading to create sketches of images in the poem, such as *lowering my head, I looked at the wall* and *The leaves fall early this autumn, in wind.*

Advanced Learners/Pre-AP

DIFFERENTIATED INSTRUCTION

Tang Arts Poetry was one great achievement of the Tang dynasty culture, but the era is also known for its music, painting, pottery, and architecture. Have advanced learners create visual presentations that focus on one of these aspects of the Tang dynasty. Encourage them to use photos, slides, or illustrations from Web sites in their presentations.

Teach

Reading Strategy   1

Make and Verify Predictions Have students read the first stanza. **Ask:** Based on this stanza, what do you think the future holds for these "two small people"? *(Joined at the outset, they will probably be so in the future.)*

APPROACHING Some students may find it difficult to understand the circumstances by which the two children become a couple. Explain that their marriage was arranged by their families, rather than chosen freely. As children, they play "without dislike or suspicion," never guessing that they will one day be married.

View the Art ★

During the Song dynasty (960–1279), a copper shortage forced artisans to work with clay, and pottery making flourished. In its balance, elegance, and purity of form, this vase is characteristic of Song pottery.

The River-Merchant's Wife: A Letter

Li Po
Translated by Ezra Pound

Mei-p'ing with Wave Design, 13th century, Southern Song dynasty, China. Stoneware, height: 26.3 cm, Diam. 16.7 cm. The Cleveland Museum of Art, OH. ★

696 UNIT 4 EAST ASIA

Writing Practice

Apply Form Point out that stanzas two through four have similar structures and show the progression of the young woman's attitude toward her marriage. At the beginning of each of these stanzas, the speaker announces her age, and then goes on to describe what occurred at that time. Have students apply this form to an autobiographical poem of their own. The following stanza frame may help them get started:

At _____, I _____.

I _____.

_____.

_____.

Students may wish to describe consecutive years of their lives, or to skip over several years to cover a longer span of time. Encourage them to focus on a specific event or image from each year that illustrates who they were at the time.

While my hair was still cut straight across my forehead
1 Played I about the front gate, pulling flowers.
You came by on bamboo stilts, playing horse,
You walked about my seat, playing with blue plums.
5 And we went on living in the village of Chokan:°
Two small people, without dislike or suspicion.

At fourteen I married My Lord you.
I never laughed, being bashful.
Lowering my head, I looked at the wall.
10 Called to, a thousand times, I never looked back.

At fifteen I stopped scowling,
I desired my dust to be mingled with yours
Forever and forever and forever.
Why should I climb the look out?

15 At sixteen you departed,
You went into far Ku-to-yen,° by the river of
    swirling eddies,
And you have been gone five months.
The monkeys make sorrowful noise overhead.

You dragged your feet when you went out.
20 By the gate now, the moss is grown, the different mosses,
Too deep to clear them away!
The leaves fall early this autumn, in wind.
The paired butterflies are already yellow with August
Over the grass in the West garden;
25 They hurt me. I grow older.
If you are coming down through the narrows of the
    river Kiang,°
Please let me know beforehand,
And I will come out to meet you
                As far as Cho-fu-Sa.°

5 Chokan: (chō´kän) a village in eastern China now called Changkan.

16 Ku-to-yen: (kōō´tō yən) a dangerous part of the Chang Jiang River.

26 Kiang: (kyäng´), now known as the Chang Jiang, is one of China's greatest rivers.

29 Cho-fu-Sa: (chō´fōō sä), a village 200 miles from Changkan now known as Chang Feng Sha.

2 Visualize *What details in this passage help you visualize the two characters as children?*

3 Tone *How would you describe the speaker's attitude toward her subject?*

Teach

Reading Strategy   2

Visualize Answer: *The narrator's hair is cut in a child's style, and the two characters are playing.*

Literary Element   3

Tone Answer: *The speaker's attitude is sorrowful.*

Literary History ☆

Li Po's Form Many poets of Li Po's time wrote in highly regulated verse forms with specific tonal patterns and numbers of syllables for each line. Li Po deliberately avoided these strict forms, choosing less formal styles to suit his topics, which ranged from the pleasures of wine to the joys of friendship.

Learning Objectives
Visualizing. (SE)
Analyzing tone. (SE)
Making and verifying predictions. (TE)
Applying form. (TE)

LI PO **697**

Approaching Level
DIFFERENTIATED INSTRUCTION

Footnotes Explain to students that the footnotes identify place names. Point out the last footnote. Explain that it is helpful to know that Cho-fu-Sa is 200 miles away, because this reveals that the speaker is willing to travel long distances to meet her husband. **Ask: Without this footnote, would you have been able to guess that Cho-fu-Sa was very far away? Explain.** *(Students may say yes, based on the speaker's devotion to her husband.)*

English Learners
DIFFERENTIATED INSTRUCTION

Intermediate Write the following sentence on the board: You came by on bamboo stilts, <u>playing horse</u>. Remind students that participial phrases are phrases that contain verbs that function as adjectives. These verbs, known as participles, usually end in –ing or –ed. Explain that *playing horse* is a participial phrase that modifies the noun *You*. Then have English learners work in pairs with more proficient English speakers to identify other participial phrases in the poem. *(Pulling flowers, playing with blue plums, being bashful, lowering my head, called to)*

697

After You Read

Assess

1. Answers and explanations will vary.

2. (a) nervous and uncertain (b) Eventually she came to love her husband and experience joy.

3. (a) five months (b) He was not eager to go; he "dragged [his] feet" when he left.

4. (a) the passing of time (b) Because they are in pairs, the butterflies remind her that her husband is gone.

5. (a) travel to Cho-fu-Sa, a village two hundred miles away, to meet him
(b) She is devoted and will go to great trouble to see him.

6. (a) sweetly sorrowful (b) The swirling eddies, autumn leaves, and paired butterflies

7. It reveals that arranged marriages were common and love was believed to grow out of such unions.

8. (a) In the United States, people expect to fall in love before, rather than after, marriage. However, the feeling of missing an absent spouse is still the same as it was in eighth-century China. (b) Advantages of arranged marriage: family approval, no need for long period of dating unsuitable partners; disadvantage: lack of love.

Literary Element

1. **(C)** is the correct answer. The speaker remembers the time as very happy, in contrast with her present loneliness.

2. **(A)** is the correct answer. The transition between short, simple sentences loaded with meaning makes the reader feel the speaker's detachment.

698

After You Read

Respond and Think Critically

Respond and Interpret

1. What images or lines from this poem did you find particularly memorable? Explain.

2. (a) According to lines 7–10, how did the speaker feel after she first married? (b) According to lines 11–14, how did her feelings change over time?

3. (a) How long has the speaker's husband been gone? (b) Was he eager to leave? Cite passages from the poem to support your response.

4. (a) What do the moss, falling leaves, and butterflies signify to the speaker? (b) Why might the butterflies hurt her?

Analyze and Evaluate

5. (a) In lines 26–29, what does the speaker say she will do? (b) What do these lines reveal about her feelings toward her husband?

6. (a) How would you describe the overall **mood**, or feeling, of this poem? (b) Which images in the poem help convey that mood?

Connect

7. **Big Idea** **Family and Tradition** What does this poem reveal about ancient Chinese traditions regarding love and marriage?

8. **Connect to Today** (a) How are the social customs and habits described in this poem different from or similar to those in the United States today? (b) What advantages and disadvantages do you see in each system?

Literary Element Tone

SAT Skills Practice

1. The word choice in lines 1–6 gives the first stanza a tone of

   (A) regretfulness
   (B) playfulness
   (C) nostalgia
   (D) sorrowfulness
   (E) jubilation

2. The sentence structure in line 25 ("They hurt me. I grow older.") reflects the speaker's

   (A) detachment
   (B) bitterness
   (C) annoyance
   (D) hopefulness
   (E) disappointment

698 UNIT 4 EAST ASIA

Review: Setting

As you learned on page 108, **setting** is the time and place in which the events of a poem or story take place. The setting includes the physical surroundings as well as the ideas, customs, values, and beliefs of the people who live there.

Partner Activity Meet with a classmate and discuss the setting of this poem. With your partner, complete a chart like the one below. Fill it in with details from the poem and what those details suggest about the setting.

Detail	Setting
Bamboo stilts	Bamboo suggests China; stilts as a child's toy suggest the past
Narrator is married at age fourteen to a man she calls "My Lord."	

Progress Check

Can students identify tone?

If No → See Unit 4 Teaching Resources Book, p. 53.

Review: Setting

Possible response: The nature images suggest a lonely, somewhat rural setting in autumn. The narrator's getting married at fourteen and calling her husband "My Lord" suggests a society where wives are subservient to their husbands. The references to river travel suggest an economy in which merchants travel long distances and are gone for long periods, creating uncertainty for their families.

Reading Strategy | Visualize

Reread lines 19–25, and **visualize** the young woman who has fallen in love with her husband and misses him in his absence. How does she appear to you? How is she dressed? How is her hair arranged? Does she look sad, tired, or upset? As you visualize the scene, you can add details the author has not included.

1. Make a list of concrete nouns, sensory details, adjectives, and other words that help you visualize these lines.

2. Make a storyboard, or a series of sketches, that illustrates what you visualize when you read these lines.

Academic Vocabulary

*Li Po **displays** the passage of time in his poem through such imagery as moss growing by the gate and leaves falling.*

Display is a commonly used academic word. In more familiar usage, a store seeking an employee might **display** a "Help Wanted" sign in its window. To further explore the meaning of this word, answer the following question: In what sort of situation have you been called upon to **display** leadership skills?

For more on academic vocabulary, see pages 36–37 and R83–R85.

Silk embroidery panel with flowers and ducks found in Dunhuang caves, China, 9th-10th century. British Museum, London.

Listening and Speaking

Oral Interpretation

Assignment Poets write for both the ear and the eye. With this in mind, read "The River-Merchant's Wife: A Letter" aloud and explain your interpretation of it.

Prepare Reread the poem to make sure you grasp its meaning. Take notes and keep in mind the details you recorded in your chart on page 695 to help your audience visualize the poem.

Perform Type your own copy of the poem, re-creating it exactly. Use this copy as your script; highlight key words you want to emphasize, mark where you should pause, and note the tone you want to use.

EXAMPLE:

You came by on bamboo stilts, playing horse, *playful tone*

You walked about my seat, playing with blue plums. ← *pause*

Follow your script as you recite, and try to reflect the tone of the poem in your vocal and physical presentation. When you finish reading, explain your interpretation of the poem and how you tried to express it through your reading.

Evaluate Write a paragraph assessing the effectiveness of your oral interpretation and describe if and how you better understand the poem's meaning and style after this experience. Look at the rubric on page 167 to help rate your presentation.

> **LOG ON** ▶ **Literature** Online
>
> **Selection Resources** For Selection Quizzes, eFlashcards, and Reading-Writing Connection activities, go to glencoe.com and enter QuickPass code GLW6053u4.

 For additional selection assessment, see Assessment Resources, pp. 139–140.

 To create custom assessments online, go to Progress Reporter Online Assessment.

 To create custom assessments using software, use ExamView Assessment Suite.

Reading Strategy

1. dragged, feet, gate, moss, deep, leaves, autumn, wind, paired butterflies, yellow, August, grass, garden, hurt, grow older

2. Students may choose to sketch something akin to a multi-panel painting, a popular format in Chinese painting. One panel might show the merchant leaving, another the moss-covered gate, yet another signs of autumn, and a fourth the sorrowful wife.

Progress Check

Can students visualize the key images in the poem?

If No → See Unit 4 Teaching Resources Book, p. 54.

Academic Vocabulary

Students might mention a group project, sports team, or school government position they have held.

Listening and Speaking

Students' oral interpretations should

- present an interpretation of the poem

- embody the tone of the poem and help the audience visualize its world

- explain the interpretation after reading and describe how the student tried to present that interpretation in the reading

Focus

Bellringer Options

Do you think it is ever possible for a translation of a poem to be better than the original? Explain. Students may say that a translation could be better than an original if the translator had a better feel for poetic language than the original author. **Then ask:** Should a creative translation really be considered a translation, or does it constitute an original work? Elicit students' responses.

Teach

Text Element	1

Chart Have students examine the chart on page 700. **Ask:** What does this chart compare? (*The chart compares Li Po's original Chinese characters, their romanized forms, Fenollosa's literal English translations, and Pound's poetic translations.*)

Learning Objectives

For pages 700–701
In studying this text, you will focus on the following objectives:

Reading:
Analyzing cultural and historical context.
Understanding the nature of translation.

Creating a Work of Beauty

"THE RIVER MERCHANT'S WIFE: A LETTER" IS EZRA POUND'S translation—the most beloved translation—of Li Po's poem "The Song of Ch'ang-Kan." Yet many scholars would call it a new work, not a translation, because Pound did not render Li Po's lines word-for-word. He also made a number of changes in the grammar, structure, and meaning of the original. Others consider Pound's version to be a translation of superior quality, believing it best captures the spirit and formal beauty of Li Po's original Chinese. A translator's decision whether to mirror the original text or depart from it is one aspect of the art of translation.

Approaches to Translation

The poet and translator W. S. Merwin has written that when he first began to translate poetry as a student, he sought advice from Ezra Pound. Pound urged Merwin to "get as close to the original as possible" and to focus on "the seed," not "the leaves," of the work. Sometimes getting close to the original source means not interpreting it literally, but rather encapsulating its spirit, or seed. One can see this paradox at work in Pound's translation of Li Po's poem.

1	Li Po	藍	藍	河	旁	草
	Chinese	Sei	Sei	Ka	Han	So
	Fenollosa	blue	blue	river	bank side	grass
	Pound	Blue, blue is the grass about the river				

Knowing virtually no Chinese, Pound based his translation on notes acquired from the American scholar Ernest Fenollosa (1853–1908). In various notebooks, Fenollosa had written lines from Chinese poems, the equivalent English words, and explanatory notes. Pound transformed these jottings into lines of exquisite beauty.

As the example below suggests, though Pound did not render the Chinese poem word-for-word, he managed to convey its essential meaning. Pound's mastery of poetry guided his work, enabling him, for instance, to capture the modest and naive voice of a young Chinese woman in "The River Merchant's Wife: A Letter." It also helped him—despite his ignorance of Chinese—to convey the clear, concise style and fresh imagery of Li Po's poem.

Sound and Sense

A good translator must not only understand other cultures, but have a feel for the music of language. One translation may be more accurate than others, but if it lacks the music of the original, it may not be the best. Wai-lim Yip's version of Li Po's poem, for example, is closer to the original than Pound's, but it lacks the musical phrasing of Pound's translation. Pound often ignored the literal meaning of a Chinese character—for instance, writing "blue plums" where other translators wrote "green plums"—to achieve a softer, more melodious effect. By making such choices, he created a work of elegance and beauty. Three translations of the beginning of Li Po's poem follow.

Reading Practice

Compare and Contrast Divide students into three groups and assign each group to one of the translations on page 701. Then have them compare their assigned translation with Pound's, using Venn diagrams like the one at the right. They should place words and phrases that both translations share in the center of the diagram, and words and phrases that are unique to each translation on either side.

Afterwards, have them discuss how the omission or inclusion of certain words and phrases changes the meaning of each translation.

<u>Pound</u>   <u>Shared</u>   <u>Bynner</u>

- cut straight across
- stilts
- walked about my seat
- blue

- hair
- forehead
- plums

- hardly covered
- my lover
- trotting in circles
- green

Witter Bynner

My hair had hardly covered my forehead.
I was picking flowers, playing by my door,
When you, my lover, on a bamboo horse,
Came trotting in circles and throwing green plums.
We lived near together on a lane in Ch'ang-kan,
Both of us young and happy-hearted.

Wai-lim Yip

My hair barely covered my forehead.
I played in front of the gate, plucking flowers,
You came riding on a bamboo-horse
And around the bed we played with green plums.
We were then living in Ch'ang-kan.
Two small people, no hate nor suspicion.

Florence Ayscough and
Amy Lowell

When the hair of your Unworthy One first began
 to cover her forehead.
She picked flowers and played in front of the door.
Then you, my Lover, came riding a bamboo horse.
We ran round and round the bed, and tossed about
 the sweetmeats of green plums.
We both lived in the village of Ch'ang Kan.
We were both very young, and knew neither
 jealousy nor suspicion.

Untitled (A Chinese girl seated looking out of the window), 18th century. attr. to Lam Qua. Oil on canvas. Private collection.

LOG ON ▶ **Literature** Online

Literature and Reading For more about translations of Li Po's poem and the translators in this book, go to glencoe.com and enter QuickPass code GLW6053u4.

Respond and Think Critically

1. Why might focusing too much on "the leaves" of a poem—the accuracy of individual words—create a less effective translation?

2. Compare Pound's translation of the opening lines of Li Po's poem on page 697 with the versions above. In your opinion, which translation is most like Pound's? Explain.

3. How is Pound's translation unique?

4. What poetic devices does Pound use to lend a musical quality to his translation?

Assess

1. Possible answer: The English words will sound different than the originals when combined, and by focusing too much on the individual words, the translator may forget to consider the poem's overall sound.

2. Answers will vary. Students should support their responses with reasons.

3. Pound's translation is unique in its images of the boy on stilts and of blue plums rather than green. He is the only translator who includes the image of hair "cut straight across" the girl's forehead.

4. Pound uses alliteration (*b*'s and *p*'s), assonance (long *a* sounds), consonance (*i* sounds), and repetition (*played* and *playing*).

Approaching Level

DIFFERENTIATED INSTRUCTION

In Other Words Students may come to better appreciate the art of translation by exploring the need for "translation" from one generation to another. Have students work in groups to list everyday terms they use that they think their parents or guardians might not understand. They should use each term in a sentence and then provide a translation of the sentence into standard English.

English Learners

DIFFERENTIATED INSTRUCTION

Intermediate Write this sentence on the board: We knew neither jealousy <u>nor</u> suspicion. Remind students that *nor* is a word used in negative phrases to introduce subsequent items in a list, similar to the way *or* is used in positive phrases. Have students work in groups to choose whether the word *or* or the word *nor* belongs in each of the following sentences:

I want to join either the band _____ the orchestra. *(or)*

Despite his illness, he felt neither frustration _____ despair. *(nor)*

The race will not be canceled for rain, _____ for snow. *(nor)*

Focus

Comparing Literature
Across Time and Place

Bellringer Options

Selection Focus
Transparency 42

Daily Language Practice
Transparency 61

Have students find images of an abandoned building, the more formally imposing the better. A decaying mansion or antebellum plantation would be ideal. Have students work in small groups to share their responses to the images. **Ask:** What kind of buildings do you think these were? What do you think happened in them? (*Answers will vary.*)

Connect to the Reading Selections

Ask students what associations they have with the word *glory*.
Ask: Is glory something an individual can earn? (*Students may say certain achievements, such as those in sports or in battle, could be seen as glorious.*)
Ask: How might a civilization or an empire be glorious? (*Students may mention military triumphs or cultural achievements.*)

Comparing Literature About Fallen Glory

How do you envision the empires of the past? Some authors see decadent palaces frozen in time, while others meditate on the decline and fall from the glory days. In the following literary works, Tu Fu, Percy Bysshe Shelley, and Orhan Pamuk reflect on the remains and effects of glorious empires that have vanished.

Jade Flower Palace by Tu Fu ....poem 703
CHINA, c. 757

Ozymandias by Percy Bysshe Shelley...........................poem 707
ENGLAND, 1818

from Istanbul: Memories and the City
by Orhan Pamuk...memoir 708
TURKEY, 2003

Spring Morning In The Palace Of Han (detail).

COMPARE THE **Big Idea** **Moments of Reflection**

These literary works reflect on the temporary nature of cities, empires, and rulers. Tu Fu depicts the ruins of an ancient palace in "Jade Flower Palace," Shelley describes a traveler's visit to a fallen monument of an Egyptian ruler in "Ozymandias," and Pamuk examines the people of Istanbul and how they respond with both melancholy and dignity to poverty, pollution, and overcrowding amid the ruins of a glorious past. As you read, ask yourself, How does each author reflect on fallen glory?

COMPARE Style

Such elements as imagery, figurative language, sentence structure, and word choice reveal an author's style. The authors here are a meditative ancient Chinese poet, a master of English Romanticism, and a contemporary Nobel laureate from Turkey. As you read, ask yourself, What stylistic elements contribute to the effect of each text?

COMPARE Historical Context

When you compare historical contexts, you compare the social and historical forces that influenced the writing of different literary works. As you read, ask yourself, How does each author link his historical context to past civilizations?

Learning Objectives

For pages 702–711
In studying these texts, you will focus on the following objectives:

Literary Study: Comparing historical contexts. Comparing themes. Analyzing imagery.

Reading: Making inferences about theme.

Writing: Writing a story.

 Literature Online

Author Search For more about Tu Fu, Percy Bysshe Shelley, and Orhan Pamuk, go to glencoe.com and enter QuickPass code GLW6053u4.

Selection Skills

Literary Elements
- Analyze Imagery (SE pp. 704–705; TE p. 709)

Reading Skills
- Make Inferences About Theme (SE pp. 704, 706; TE p. 705)
- Analyze Diction (TE p. 704)

Comparing Literature

Vocabulary Skills
- Academic Vocabulary (SE p. 706)

Speaking/Listening/Viewing Skills
- Oral Report on Historical Context (SE p. 711)

Writing Skills/Grammar
- Story (SE p. 706)
- Compare Style (SE p. 711)
- Apply Description (TE p. 708)

Before You Read

Jade Flower Palace

China

Meet Tu Fu
(712–770)

"Considering what bitter things happened to me, ordinary people must be truly in dire straits."

—Tu Fu

"I will not rest until my verses astound and awe people," Tu Fu once wrote. One of China's greatest poets, Tu Fu lived during the T'ang dynasty (618–907), a period when poetry and art flourished. Yet his work, which includes more than 1,500 poems, was virtually ignored during his lifetime.

Thwarted Ambitions Tu Fu came from a politically well-connected family: his mother was related to China's emperors, and his father came from a family of high-ranking court officials. After receiving a traditional education, young Tu Fu spent about five years wandering through the Yangtze and Yellow River regions of China. Around the age of 23, Tu Fu moved to the capital Ch'ang-an with the hope of securing an official post in the emperor's court. To qualify for such a position, he first had to take the imperial examination—in effect, a civil-service test. Unfortunately, Tu Fu was unable to pass the test. Disappointed, he took to the road again.

In 744 he met the famed poet Li Po (see pages 694–699) in Loyang, and the two men became

close friends. Many of Tu Fu's early poems were inspired by this relatively carefree period in his life. But Tu Fu had not given up on attaining an imperial position. In 746 he returned to Ch'ang-an to retake the examination and failed once again. He stayed there, however, until he was granted a minor post in the emperor's court in the early 750s. Despite his talent, Tu Fu's poetry was not highly regarded by the court. When an uprising against the emperor broke out in 755, rebels captured Tu Fu. He later escaped and lived a nomadic life until 757, when he was allowed to return to the emperor's court as a censor. Soon thereafter he developed the dangerous habit of giving the emperor unsolicited (and unappreciated) advice. As a result, Tu Fu was banished from the court.

A Wandering Poet Tu Fu spent the next nine years wandering through Szechwan writing poetry. A tireless perfectionist, he rewrote his poems again and again. The result was a series of technically brilliant and innovative poems that both vividly describe his personal experiences and critique larger social problems of the day. A sense of despair runs through these works, many of which focus on the sorrows and hardships of war. In his later work, Tu Fu often focused on the loneliness and alienation he endured as a homeless traveler growing older. He also continued to write poems of social protest. One of his favorite techniques was to contrast the impoverished lifestyle of common people with the lavish life at the imperial court. His verses remain powerful today because of their deep compassion and their thematic universality.

TU FU **703**

English Learners

DIFFERENTIATED INSTRUCTION

SMALL GROUP

Beginning Have students in small groups use the art and other images that appear on these pages to make predictions about what the poem will be about. Have them write their predictions and indicate what evidence they used to make their predictions. After they have read the selection, students should work in groups to review their predictions.

Advanced Learners/Pre-AP

DIFFERENTIATED INSTRUCTION

Research Have students use the Internet to research China during Tu Fu's time. How common were palaces? Who built them? How many people lived in them? What were their functions? What eventually happened to the palaces and the people? Have students present their research to the class, discussing how their findings changed their expectations about the poem.

Before You Read

Focus

Reading Strategy   1

Analyze Historical Context Draw students' attention to the characterization of Tu Fu's professional ambitions as having been thwarted. **Ask:** Given that Tu Fu's experience with the court was one of continual frustration, what expectations do you have of his poem about a palace? *(Students may say they might expect his poetry to reflect his professional disappointments in some way.)*

View the Art ★

Explain to students that this portrait was created long after Tu Fu had died and that are no known images of the poet made during his lifetime. Tu Fu almost certainly did not look much like this picture; the picture was intended to show who he was with regard to the culture more than how he looked. **Ask:** What impression of Tu Fu is the artist trying to create in this portrayal? *(Some students may say the poet looks wise and distinguished. Others may point out that his clothes and the implements he holds suggest that he served at the imperial court.)*

> **Interactive Read and Write**
> Other options for teaching these selections can be found in Interactive Read and Write for On-Level Learners, pp. 169–178.

Comparing Literature

Before You Read

Focus

Summary

The poem's speaker describes a desolate, stormy scene of a once-magnificent palace now empty and decayed by the passage of many years. The speaker describes rats scuttling over broken pavement and the roar of the storm, and he invokes the ghostly presence of the palace's former inhabitants, such as an unnamed prince's long-dead dancing girls. Viewing this melancholy scene, the speaker tries to write a poem, but he is overcome with feelings of pity for the vanished prince and his court.

 For summaries in languages other than English, see Unit 4 Teaching Resources Book, pp. 58–63.

Cultural History ☆

China's Palaces Whatever desolation Tu Fu encountered at his Jade Flower Palace, modern China now takes very good care of its palaces. Many of the palaces lie within the Forbidden City in Beijing, and their size and delicate decorative elements suggest just how luxurious life must have been in them. Students may wish to discuss what images these carefully preserved palaces may bring up for the Chinese.

Literature and Reading Preview

Connect to the Poem

What can the past suggest about the future? Discuss this question with a partner.

Build Background

In his early poetry, Tu Fu praises natural beauty and laments the passage of time, but in his later work, he criticizes warmongering nobles and satirizes the imperial court for its self-indulgent luxuriousness.

Set Purposes for Reading

Big Idea **Moments of Reflection**

As you read, ask yourself, What statement does the poem make about the passage of time and the nature of human existence?

Literary Element **Imagery**

Imagery refers to the "word pictures" authors create to evoke emotional responses. In creating effective imagery, authors use sensory details, or descriptions that appeal to one or more of the five senses. As you read, ask yourself, What images suggest aging, decay, loneliness, and the past?

Reading Strategy **Make Inferences About Theme**

When you **make inferences**, you use reasoning and your own experience to guess what an author means but does not come right out and say. Descriptive details, events, and changes in an author's style can often help you make inferences about the **theme**, or message about life, of a literary work.

Tip: Induce and Deduce When you make inferences, you either **induce**—make a general statement based on details—or **deduce**—make a guess about unstated details, based on general principles. Use a graphic like the one below when you use inductive reasoning to infer the underlying meaning expressed in "Jade Flower Palace."

Details		Inference
• broken tiles • shattered pavements	→	

704 UNIT 4 EAST ASIA

Birds and Flowers of the Four Seasons (detail). Kano Soshu. Pen and ink, colour, gold paper on panel. Private collection.

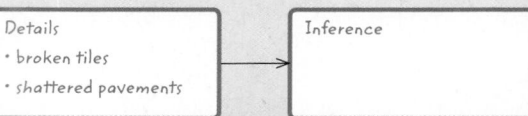
Reading Practice

Analyze Diction Have students carefully examine Tu Fu's word choice, especially his use of connotation and denotation. For example, point out the effect of using the word *shattered* rather than *broken*. Have students list the words that seem to them to have strong connotations. **Ask:** What effect does Tu Fu achieve with his word choices? *(Students may say the poet chooses words such as* moans, shattered, *and* crumbled, *which help to make the poem sad and elegiac.)*

Jade Flower Palace

Tu Fu

Translated by Kenneth Rexroth

The stream swirls. The wind moans in
The pines. Gray rats scurry over
Broken tiles. What prince, long ago,
Built this palace, standing in
5 Ruins beside the cliffs? There are
Green ghost fires in the black rooms.
The shattered pavements are all
Washed away. Ten thousand organ
Pipes whistle and roar. The storm
10 Scatters the red autumn leaves.
His dancing girls are yellow dust.

Their painted cheeks have crumbled
Away. His gold chariots
And courtiers are gone. Only
15 A stone horse is left of his
Glory. I sit on the grass and **2**
Start a poem, but the pathos of
It overcomes me. The future
Slips imperceptibly away.
20 Who can say what the years will
bring?

1 Imagery *What emotions do the images in these lines evoke?*

Moments of Reflection *What does this passage suggest about human existence?* **3**

Blue and Green Landscapes. Li Qing (China, d. 1853). Ink and color on paper, 10 x 11 in. Private collection.

Teach

Literary Element **1**

Imagery Answer: *The images evoke a sense of loneliness and desolation.*

Reading Strategy **2**

Make Inferences About Theme Ask: Why is the poet so overcome by pathos in the scene that he cannot finish his poem? *(The desolate scene causes him to think about his own attempts to create something lasting. He feels uncertain about his own future and ability to weather the years.)*

Progress Check

Can students make inferences about theme?

If No → See Unit 4 Teaching Resources Book, p. 65.

Big Idea **3**

Moments of Reflection Answer: *It suggests human existence is not only brief but also unreliable.*

Learning Objectives
Analyzing imagery. (SE)
Making inferences about theme. (SE)
Analyzing diction. (TE)

English Learners

DIFFERENTIATED INSTRUCTION

Intermediate Remind students that an adjective is a word that modifies a noun or pronoun by limiting its meaning. An adjective may describe a noun or pronoun by answering one of these questions: What kind? Which one? How many? How much? Have students identify all the adjectives in the poem in a list, indicating after each adjective which of the questions it answers.

Advanced Learners/Pre-AP

DIFFERENTIATED INSTRUCTION

Write a Dramatic Monologue Have students tell what emotions the images in lines 1–3 are intended to evoke. *(Students should say that the images seem intended to evoke a sense of loneliness and desolation.)* Suggest that students write a dramatic monologue expressing the speaker's thoughts as he regards the scene described in the poem. You may wish to review with students the style used in writing drama.

After You Read

Assess

1. Answers will vary.
2. The people deserted it long ago.
3. extravagant
4. Possible answer: The sense of desolation in the poem effectively expresses his pathos.
5. The images of broken tiles and the dancing girls that have turned to dust show the limited value of opulence.
6. Even as the speaker contemplates the future, it is quietly turning into the present and will then become the past.
7. The prince and the ruined palace can be connected to contemporary persons and institutions that have lost fame, wealth, or the respect of the people.

Literary Element

1. (a) the moaning wind, the scurrying rats, and the whistling and roaring pipe organs (b) These images create a sense of desolation.
2. Possible answers: (a) Lightning causes a fire-like appearance in the room. (b) The word *ghost* reminds the reader that the only inhabitants of the palace are the remnants of its former residents' belongings.

Progress Check

Can students analyze imagery?

If No → See Unit 4 Teaching Resources Book, p. 64.

After You Read

Respond and Think Critically

Respond and Interpret

1. After reading lines 1–19, how did you respond to the question at the end of the poem?
2. What does the condition of the palace tell you about the people who lived there?
3. How would you characterize the prince's lifestyle, based on lines 11–16?

Analyze and Evaluate

4. In your opinion, how well does the poem evoke a sense of compassion?

5. Tu Fu wrote many poems criticizing imperial opulence and power. Do you think this is one of them? Cite examples from the poem to support your answer.

Connect

6. **Big Idea** Moments of Reflection What do you think the speaker means by the words "The future / Slips imperceptibly away"?
7. **Connect to Today** What connections can you make between the prince and his ruined palace and a contemporary situation or person?

Literary Element Imagery

Tu Fu uses **imagery** to help readers visualize and experience a palace in a state of ruin. The imagery also helps fuel the **mood**, or overall feeling, of the poem.

1. (a)Which images in the poem appeal to your sense of hearing? (b)How do these images contribute to the poem's mood?
2. (a)How do you interpret the image of "green ghost fires" in line 6? (b)How might it relate to the rest of the poem?

Reading Strategy Make Inferences About Theme

When you **infer** you make a calculated guess about what an author wants the reader to take away from the details in a literary work.

1. What can you infer about the poem's theme from the description of the ruined palace?
2. (a)Do you think the speaker eventually completed the poem mentioned in line 17? Explain. (b)What can you infer about the poem's theme from this detail?

Academic Vocabulary

*In this poem, Tu Fu reflects on the **termination** of a palace's era of glory.*

Termination is an academic word. In a business context, dismissing an employee is often referred to as **termination**. To further explore the meaning of this word, answer the following question: What do you look forward to at the **termination** of the school year?

For more on academic vocabulary, see pages 36–37 and R83–R85.

Writing

Write a Story How do you imagine the prince described in the poem? Based on Tu Fu's details, write a story about his life. Use imagery to show what the palace might have been like when it was new. Present specific details that lead the reader to a broader statement about life and time. Refer to the chart you made on page 704 for help.

LOG ON **Literature** Online

Selection Resources For Selection Quizzes, eFlashcards, and Reading-Writing Connection activities, go to glencoe.com and enter QuickPass code GLW6053u4.

Reading Strategy

1. Students may say the theme is imperial wealth and power are ultimately hollow.
2. (a) Answers will vary (b) Students may say that we all must succumb to the ravages of time.

📁 **For additional selection assessment, see Assessment Resources, pp. 141–142.**

Academic Vocabulary

Students may say they look forward to sleeping in or summer camp.

Writing

Students' stories should include sensory details, create a vivid picture of the prince's life in the palace when it was new, and lead the reader to a broad statement about life and time.

Build Background

Percy Bysshe Shelley (1792–1822) is one of the greatest English Romantic poets. The Romantics valued imagination above all else and often wrote about past eras. "Ozymandias" alludes to King Ramses II, who ruled Egypt during the thirteenth century B.C. and was dubbed "the Great." He built his own funerary temple, the Ramesseum, on the west bank of the Nile. Today, all that remains of the temple are fragments of a 57-foot statue of Ramses II and carvings showing war scenes.

Ozymandias

Percy Bysshe Shelley

I met a traveler from an antique land
Who said: Two vast and trunkless legs of stone
Stand in the desert . . . Near them, on the sand,
Half sunk, a shattered visage[1] lies, whose frown,
5 And wrinkled lip, and sneer of cold command,
Tell that its sculptor well those passions read
Which yet survive, stamped on these lifeless things,
The hand[2] that mocked[3] them, and the heart[4] that fed:
And on the pedestal these words appear:
10 "My name is Ozymandias, king of kings:
Look on my works, ye Mighty, and despair!"
Nothing beside remains. Round the decay
Of that colossal wreck, boundless and bare
The lone and level sands stretch far away.

The head of a massive granite statue of the seated Ramses II sits on the ground at the Ramesseum, the pharoah's mortuary temple on the west bank of the Nile River at Thebes.

1. A *visage* is a face.
2. Here, *hand* refers to the hand of the sculptor.
3. *Mocked* means "imitated" or "derided."
4. *Heart* refers to the heart of Ozymandias.

> 💬 **Discussion Starter**
>
> The England of Shelley's time was a rapidly industrializing, blossoming empire that reached its peak near the end of the nineteenth century. How might living in this era have influenced Shelley in writing "Ozymandias"? What do you think the poem is saying about heroes? Discuss these questions with a small group.

PERCY BYSSHE SHELLEY **707**

English Learners

DIFFERENTIATED INSTRUCTION

Advanced English learners are very likely to have difficulty with word order and sentence structure in this poem. Let students know that poets in this period often inverted word order, or otherwise changed ordinary English grammar and syntax to achieve certain effects. Tell them that in "Ozymandias" the effect the poet is aiming for is one of profundity, or being deeply serious and significant. Model for students how to begin to untangle this poetic syntax. Have them treat difficult passages (such as lines 3–5, "Near them, on the sand, half sunk, a shattered visage lies") as though they were a sentence. First ask them to find the subject of the sentence, and follow with the modifying phrase and verb. "A shattered visage, half sunk in the sand, lies near them." Use the same technique to rephrase the rest of the poem, and then ask students to write the poem as though it were a prose sentence.

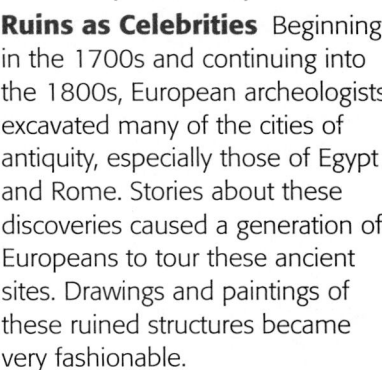

Comparing Literature

Focus
Summary

The speaker quotes a traveler who described the ancient ruin of a monument to Ozymandias, an ancient Egyptian pharaoh. The statue is inscribed with the king's order to behold his great works. All that remains of his great works is the crumbled ruin in the desert.

Teach

Literary History ☆

Ruins as Celebrities Beginning in the 1700s and continuing into the 1800s, European archeologists excavated many of the cities of antiquity, especially those of Egypt and Rome. Stories about these discoveries caused a generation of Europeans to tour these ancient sites. Drawings and paintings of these ruined structures became very fashionable.

Assess

Discussion Starter

Shelley may have been commenting on how leaders such as Ozymandias meet their demise—just like everyone else—and even the fame and monuments of kings have a limited life. Students may note that Shelley might have been alluding to the power of the British Empire, suggesting that it was finite too.

Comparing Literature

Before You Read

Focus

Summary

In this autobiographical account, Pamuk describes his deep melancholy, a kind of existential sadness for the fall of the Ottoman Empire that he believes he acquired during his childhood in Istanbul, and to which he gives the Turkish name *hüzün*. He takes the reader on an imaginary tour of the city, pointing out the evidence of a more glorious past and of a present marked by widespread poverty and urban decay. Although he says this melancholy is widespread among the people of Istanbul, he insists it is "ultimately as life-affirming as it is negating." He claims that *hüzün* teaches endurance and the ability to look at the passage of time as a journey to a better future, which may be borne as a kind of honor.

Teach

Reading Strategy   1

Make Inferences About Theme Have students gather and record details from the selection that they consider to be significant. **Ask:** What theme or themes can you suggest that would include all of these details? *(Students' inferences should recognize that the writer's theme is one of sorrow at the ravages time has wrought on once-glorious Istanbul.)*

Readability Scores

Dale-Chall: 8.7
DRP: 58
Lexile: 1360

708

Build Background

Nobel Prize winner Orhan Pamuk (born 1952) writes intricate, sweeping novels about Turkish identity, history, and politics. The setting of several of Pamuk's works, the city of Istanbul was in ancient times Constantinople—a Christian center and capital of the Byzantine Empire (the eastern part of the Roman Empire). In 1453, the Ottoman Turks conquered the city, brought Islam to it, and made it the capital of their empire. The Ottoman Empire lasted until 1922, and in 1923 Kemal Ataturk ushered in a new government and founded the Republic of Turkey. Pamuk's memoir, *Istanbul: Memories and the City*, focuses on the changes that have occurred in the city since the fall of the empire and on the sense of faded glory and melancholy (*hüzün* in Turkish) that seem to pervade the city.

FROM ISTANBUL:

MEMORIES AND THE CITY

by Orhan Pamuk

Translated by Maureen Freely

1 If I am to convey the intensity of the *hüzün* that Istanbul caused me to feel as a child, I must describe the history of the city following the destruction of the Ottoman Empire and—even more important—the way this history is reflected in the city's "beautiful" landscapes and its people. The *hüzün* of Istanbul is not just the mood evoked by its music and its poetry, it is a way of looking at life that implicates us all, not only a spiritual state but a state of mind that is ultimately as life-affirming as it is negating. . . .

But what I am trying to describe now is **2** not the melancholy of Istanbul but the *hüzün* in which we see ourselves reflected, the *hüzün* we absorb with pride and share as a community. To feel this *hüzün* is to see the scenes, evoke the memories, in which the city itself becomes the very illustration, the very essence, of *hüzün*. I am speaking of the evenings when the sun sets early, of the fathers under the streetlamps in the back streets returning home carrying plastic bags. Of the old Bosphorus ferries moored to deserted stations in the middle

708 UNIT 4 EAST ASIA

Writing Practice

Apply Description Point out to students that what makes Pamuk's work interesting and evocative is the concrete, specific detail he uses to make his writing vivid. As an example, point out Pamuk's description of "a cobblestone staircase with so much asphalt poured over it that its steps have disappeared."

Have students write a list of details about a place with which they have strong associations. They should use the details to evoke the essence of that place.

St. Sophia Mosque. Underwood & Underwood. Istanbul, Turkey. ☆

ORHAN PAMUK   **709**

Teach

Literary Element	2

Imagery Remind students that prose can contain as much imagery as poetry can. Have students note the list of successive images that Pamuk presents in this passage. **Ask:** What effect does Pamuk's use of imagery from the streets of Istanbul have on the reader? (*Students may note that his images create a powerful sense of defeat and sadness.*)

Cultural History ☆

The Ottoman Empire and Istanbul Istanbul is the largest city in Turkey and it has been a cultural and commercial crossroads for hundreds of years. The Ottoman Empire at one time included much of North Africa and the Middle East, as well as a considerable part of Southeastern Europe. The Ottoman Empire's wealth was immense, and some of the most beautiful and architecturally important buildings in the world were built in Istanbul. In the latter half of the twentieth century, however, Istanbul's population increased so quickly that its infrastructure could not support it. Today, Istanbul struggles with pollution, overcrowding, and unreliable city services. Yet it remains a fascinating city, with a rich cultural and historical heritage.

English Learners

DIFFERENTIATED INSTRUCTION

Beginning Encourage students to use the Internet to learn more about Istanbul's history and geography. Make sure maps of Istanbul and surrounding areas are available to students. Have them find pictures of the bridges and other features of Istanbul that Pamuk discusses in the selection. You may wish to post such pictures in the classroom and have students caption them with relevant passages from the selection.

Approaching Level

DIFFERENTIATED INSTRUCTION

Internet Research Pamuk's writing style uses many words with which English learners are likely to be unfamiliar. Encourage English learners to use a dictionary whenever they are in doubt about a vocabulary word. You may wish to provide access to online dictionaries.

Learning Objectives
Making inferences about theme. (TE)
Writing vivid descriptions. (TE)
Analyzing imagery. (TE)

Comparing Literature

Assess

Quickwrite

Pamuk connects Istanbul's history to its modern state by noting how its landscape has been transformed. For example, once-glorious fountains now lie in ruins, their faucets stolen; the *tekkes* of the dervishes have crumbled; and the boathouses along the Bosphorus are now empty. Aspects of the excerpt that reflect an industrialized society include television, asphalt, and buildings with knitting and sewing machines.

of winter, where sleepy sailors scrub the decks, pail in hand and one eye on the black-and-white television in the distance; of the old booksellers who lurch from one financial crisis to the next and then wait shivering all day for a customer to appear; of the barbers who complain that men don't shave as much after an economic crisis; of the children who play ball between the cars on cobblestoned streets; of the covered women who stand at remote bus stops clutching plastic shopping bags and speak to no one as they wait for the bus that never arrives; of the empty boathouses of the old Bosphorus villas; of the teahouses packed to the rafters with unemployed men; . . . of the city walls, ruins since the end of the Byzantine Empire; of the markets that empty in the evenings; of the dervish lodges, the *tekkes*, that have crumbled; of the seagulls perched on rusty barges caked with moss and mussels, unflinching under the pelting rain; of the tiny ribbons of smoke rising from the single chimney of a hundred-year-old mansion on the coldest day of the year; . . . of a cobble-stone staircase with so much asphalt poured over it that its steps have disappeared; of marble ruins that were for centuries glorious street fountains but now stand dry, their faucets stolen; of the apartment buildings in the side streets where during my childhood middle-class families—of doctors, lawyers, teachers, and their wives and children—would sit in their apartments listening to the radio in the evenings, and where today the same apartments are packed with knitting and button machines and young girls working all night long for the lowest wages in the city to meet urgent orders; of the view of the Golden Horn, looking toward Eyüp from the Galata Bridge; of the *simit* vendors on the pier who gaze at the view as they wait for customers; of everything being broken, worn out, past its prime; of the storks flying south from the Balkans and northern and western Europe as autumn nears, gazing down over the entire city as they waft over the Bosphorus and the islands of the Sea of Marmara; . . . I speak of them all.

It is by seeing *hüzün*, by paying our respects to its manifestations in the city's streets and views and people, that we at last come to sense it everywhere. On cold winter mornings, when the sun suddenly falls on the Bosphorus and that faint vapor begins to rise from the surface, the *hüzün* is so dense you can almost touch it, almost see it spread like a film over its people and its landscapes. . . .

Hüzün teaches endurance in times of poverty and deprivation; it also encourages us to read life and the history of the city in reverse. It allows the people of Istanbul to think of defeat and poverty not as a historical end point but as an honorable beginning, fixed long before they were born. So the honor we derive from it can be rather misleading. But it does suggest that Istanbul does not bear its *hüzün* as an incurable illness that has spread throughout the city, as an immutable poverty to be endured like grief, or even as an awkward and perplexing failure to be viewed and judged in black and white; it bears its *hüzün* with honor. ∾

> ### Quickwrite
> Pamuk refers to Istanbul's past as he describes its current poverty and overcrowding. How does he connect Istanbul's history to its modern state? What aspects of the excerpt reflect an industrialized society? Write a paragraph responding to these questions.

Reading Practice

Analyze Cause-and-Effect Relationships Ask: Does Pamuk's text provide any evidence for the cause of the melancholy, the *hüzün*, that so pervades Istanbul and its people? (*Students should observe that Pamuk mentions economic crises and urban decay.*)

Then ask: What do you think the author's purpose is in writing this memoir? (*Students may say the author wants to reflect on his feelings about Istanbul and examine the mood that the city creates in him.*)

Wrap-Up: Comparing Literature

Across Time and Place

- *Jade Flower Palace* by Tu Fu

- *Ozymandias* by Percy Bysshe Shelley

- from *Istanbul: Memories and the City* by Orhan Pamuk

COMPARE THE Big Idea **Moments of Reflection**

Group Activity All three authors use specific images to reflect on the meaning of life and the power of time. In a small group, discuss the following questions. Cite evidence from the texts to support your points.

1. What images stand out in each of these works? Which do you think are most effective, and why?

2. Compare and contrast the speakers in each of these works. Which do you think most effectively reflect on the past and present? Why?

3. What do you find similar about the content of Shelley's and Tu Fu's poems? How is Pamuk's reflection different?

COMPARE Style

Writing How do the styles of these three literary works differ? Write a brief essay discussing how the style of each text contributes to its effect. Consider elements such as word choice, sentence structure, imagery, and tone.

COMPARE Historical Context

Speaking and Listening Historical context plays a key role in each of these works. Tu Fu and Shelley both comment on vanished leaders or civilizations, while Pamuk describes the mood of people living in contemporary Istanbul in the shadow of a glorious former empire. Review the author biography information on page 703 and the Build Background notes on page 707 and 708. Research the cultures of each author. Prepare an oral report for the class about the historical context of each work.

A guide stands beside one of the two Colossi of Memnon. The Colossi stand over 60 feet high. Luxor, Egypt.

LOG ON ▶ **Literature** Online

Selection Resources For Selection Quizzes, eFlashcards, and Reading-Writing Connection activities, go to glencoe.com and enter QuickPass code GLW6053u4.

COMPARING LITERATURE **711**

Compare Historical Context

Students may report that, like other ancient Chinese poets, Tu Fu meditated on the fragility and transitory nature of time. This is sharply viewed in the final line of his poem, "Who can say what the years will bring?" The Build Background for Shelley's "Ozymandias" reveals Ramses II was considered a great ruler in his time. Shelley shows a ruler of the past is barely remembered in the present. Regarding Pamuk, a key piece of information is that Istanbul is a city dating back to the Roman Empire. Now the city faces the problems of an industrial nation, as it has become more Westernized. Pamuk comments that *hüzün* "allows the people of Istanbul to think of defeat and poverty not as a historical end point but as an honorable beginning, fixed long before they were born."

Assess

Compare the Big Idea

1. Students should cite specific images from the selections and identify the word choice and sensory details that make them effective.

2. In "Jade Flower Palace," the speaker may be Tu Fu himself, commenting on Chinese ruins. In "Ozymandias," Shelley uses a persona to describe the broken monument. *Istanbul* combines elements of memoir with prosaic descriptions. Students should be able to discuss which speaker reflects on the past and present best.

3. Possible response: Both Shelley's and Tu Fu's poems are about fallen figures from a distant past. Pamuk's reflection is based on the author's own memories of the people and mood in his city.

Compare Styles

Student might mention that Tu Fu appeals to all five senses in "Jade Flower Palace." Shelley also uses rich sensory details and provides narration in his poem. Pamuk often uses inversion. He also runs phrases together in a stream-of-consciousness style.

Before You Read

Focus

Bellringer Options

Daily Language Practice Transparency 62

Or ask: Have you had any particular experience that you want to make sure that you remember? Encourage students to think not just about concrete events but also about feelings or things that initially may seem unimportant. Emphasize the importance of finding the extraordinary in the everyday and point out how such a theme features prominently in these poems and in much other poetry.

Cultural History ☆

Mount Fuji Famous for its size and cultural significance, Mount Fuji acts as a religious shrine for many Japanese. Formed more than a thousand years ago, it is assumed by many to be a single volcano, yet the peak is actually composed of three unconnected volcanoes. Temples and shrines surround Mount Fuji and thousands of pilgrims make the trek to the summit each year.

Before You Read

Tanka

Meet **the Poets**

During the Heian period of Japanese history (A.D. 794–1185), tanka, an unrhymed verse form whose name means "short songs," was an integral part of courtly life. Aristocrats in the royal courts amused themselves by writing these short poems. Lovers communicated through verse—a prince might write a tanka to his beloved, and she would write her response in the same form. These poems frequently focus on the natural world. Poets of the Heian period wrote about the changing seasons to reflect upon nature's beauty and to express sorrow over the passage of time.

> *"[P]oetry, without effort, moves heaven and earth, . . . smoothes the relations of men and women, and calms the hearts of fierce warriors."*
>
> —Ki no Tsurayuki
> (from the preface to the *Kokinshū*)

Ki no Tsurayuki (c. 872–c. 945) One of the most important anthologies of Japanese verse is the *Kokinshū* (kō kēn´shoō), a collection gathered in 905 for Japan's emperor. Ki no Tsurayuki (kē nō tsoō rä yoō´kē), an official in the imperial court and a celebrated poet, critic, and diarist, was largely responsible for compiling this anthology. His opinions about poetry helped define Japanese verse for years to come.

Ono no Komachi (mid-ninth century) and Lady Ise (c. 875–c. 938) Two prominent women poets of this time were Ono no Komachi (ō´nō´ nō kō mä´chē) and the novelist Lady Ise (ē sā´). Komachi was a legendary

Representation of Ono-no-Komachi, from the Fashionable Beauties series. Kikukawa Eizan. Victoria & Albert Museum, London. ★

figure, both for her poetry and for her beauty. Named in the preface to the *Kokinshū*, she is honored as one of the Six Immortals of Poetry. Lady Ise served as a lady-in-waiting at the Heian court during the reigns of two emperors. Like Komachi, she wrote passionate poetry and is said to have been a great beauty.

Saigyō (1118–1190) The poet Saigyō (sä´ē gyō) was born the son of a samurai at a time when the imperial court was quite prosperous. A guardian of the imperial palace, he renounced court life at the age of 23 to become a Buddhist monk. He traveled throughout Japan, often living in the mountains as a recluse. His poems reflect his devotion to Buddhism and to nature.

Tanka's Reign From the eighth century until the sixteenth century, the tanka was the dominant form of Japanese poetry. Poets viewed the tanka as ideal for capturing a fleeting emotion or experience. As the poet Ishikawa Takuboku wrote, "Although a sensation may last only a second, it is a second that will never return again. I refuse to let such moments slip by."

 Literature Online

Author Search For more about tanka poets, go to glencoe.com and enter QuickPass code GLW6053u4.

Selection Skills

Literary Elements
- Mood (SE p. 713–715)

Tanka

Speaking/Listening/Viewing Skills
- Analyzing Art (TE p. 714)

Reading Skills
- Interpret Imagery (SE pp. 713, 715)
- Make Inference About Theme (TE p. 714)

Vocabulary Skills
- Academic Vocabulary (SE p. 715)

Writing Skills/Grammar
- Tanka (SE p. 715)

Literature and Reading Preview

Connect to the Poems

What scenes from nature have evoked strong emotions in you? Write a journal entry in response to this question.

Build Background

The tanka form consists of five lines. The first and third lines have five syllables each; the other lines have seven syllables each. The rigid 31-syllable form is usually not preserved in English translations; instead, translators try to capture the mood and imagery of the original poems.

Set Purposes for Reading

Big Idea Moments of Reflection

As you read, ask yourself, How do the poems use images from nature to suggest the passage of time and the fleeting nature of human life?

Literary Element Mood

Mood is the emotional quality a literary work conveys. To create mood, authors use devices such as imagery, evocative word choice, and vivid description. As you read, ask yourself, What devices do the poets use to create a specific mood?

Reading Strategy Interpret Imagery

When you **interpret imagery,** you first consider the literal meaning of an image. Then you apply your own understanding of the world to interpret the figurative or symbolic meanings. As you read, ask yourself, How do the images in these poems function on a literal and figurative level?

Tip: Make Imagery Equations Use equations to interpret the imagery in these poems. Set up your equations as shown below.

Imagery		Prior Knowledge		Interpretation
"The smoke from Mount Fuji Melts into the sky."	+	Mount Fuji was an active volcano then; smoke continually rose from it and drifted away.	=	The poet is comparing his thoughts to the smoke. Both rise and "melt," but they may reemerge in other forms.

Learning Objectives

For pages 712–715

In studying this text, you will focus on the following objectives:

Literary Study: Analyzing mood.

Reading: Interpreting imagery.

Writing: Writing a tanka.

Flying Geese and Full Moon, c. early 1900s. Koson Ohara. Colour woodblock print. UCL Art Collections, University College, London.

Before You Read

Focus

Summary

The selected tanka use simple but compelling imagery to reflect the universal power of isolated moments. Ki no Tsurayuki's poem describes the hardship of a journey the speaker made to visit a beloved. Lady Ise's poem details the experience of wild geese. Ono no Komachi's poem explores the division between dreams and waking life. Saigyo's poem compares the poet's thoughts to smoke rising from Mount Fuji.

> For summaries in languages other than English, see Unit 4 Teaching Resources Book, pp. 68–72.

View the Art ★

Beginning in the early sixteenth century, genre painting—often featuring elegant and beautiful women pursuing leisurely activities—became popular with the growing middle class. The demand for these images continued into the Edo period, when they were mass-produced by the technique of woodblock printing. During this time, the woodblock carver's art flourished. The painting on page 712 represents the poet Ono no Komachi as a "Fashionable Beauty" playing an instrument.

Advanced Learners/Pre-AP

DIFFERENTIATED INSTRUCTION

Brainstorm Synonyms As a way for students to interact with the text, have them go through the poems and make a list of key nouns and verbs. Then, for each word they have listed, have them brainstorm several synonyms that they think are more vivid. For example, instead of using *visit* in the first poem, students could suggest *reunite,* or instead of *crying, weeping* or *howling.* Remember to stress that a tanka should conform to a fairly strict syllabic structure.

Approaching Level

DIFFERENTIATED INSTRUCTION

Question For students who are struggling to draw meaning from the tanka, have them discuss questions they would ask the poets. The questions may refer to any aspect of the poem, such as diction, style, or form. Encourage students to offer possible answers to one another's questions, citing evidence from the text.

(ADVANCED) Ask advanced students to brainstorm other images that suggest the fleeting nature of life. Then have them create similes or metaphors based on the images. *(Time passes, just as water evaporates. Life is a shooting star.)* Guide students to discuss how the poem's tone in describing the fleeting quality of life includes both a reverence for the connection between nature and humanity and a lament for the brevity of human life. **Ask:** In your opinion, do you think Saigyo's poem creates a reflection on life that is primarily negative or primarily positive? Suggest that while thoughts may dissolve and "melt," they may also reemerge in other forms and other "unknown" contexts. Tell students to review the background provided in the Big Idea 3: Moments of Reflection essay in the Part 1 introduction as they consider this question.

Tanka

Translated by Geoffrey Bownas and Anthony Thwaite

When I Went to Visit
Ki no Tsurayuki

When I went to visit
The girl I love so much,
That winter night
The river blew so cold
That the plovers were crying.

Forsaking the Mists
Lady Ise

Forsaking the mists
That rise in the spring,
Wild geese fly off.
They have learned to live
In a land without flowers.

Mount Fuji Reflected in Lake Misaica. From the series '36 Views of Mount Fuji'. Woodblock print. Leeds Museums and Art Galleries, UK.

Was It That I Went to Sleep
Ono no Komachi

Was it that I went to sleep
Thinking of him,
That he came in my dreams?
Had I known it a dream
I should not have wakened.

Trailing on the Wind
Saigyō

Trailing on the wind,
The smoke from Mount Fuji
Melts into the sky.
So too my thoughts—
Unknown their resting place.

1 Mood *What mood does this image suggest to you?*

Moments of Reflection *How does this image suggest the fleeting nature of life?* **2**

Reading Practice

Make Inferences About Theme Remind students that a writer will often avoid stating his or her meaning directly but will provide clues and details that imply or suggest the meaning. Tell students that skilled readers notice these subtle clues, and remind them that an inference is an educated guess based on the available evidence in a text and on the reader's own knowledge and experience.

Tell students that an inference is a more complex judgment than a paraphrase, which is a restatement of a passage, or an interpretation, which is an explanation of the meaning of something that is stated in the text.

Have students analyze each of the four tanka for ideas or meanings that are implied but not directly stated. Student should write one inference about each tanka.

(Sample responses:

- *"When I Went to Visit": Maintaining relationships is difficult.*
- *"Forsaking the Mists": People are creatures of habit.*
- *"Was It That I Went to Sleep": The speaker is separated from the person she saw in the dream.*
- *"Trailing on the Wind": Human life is ephemeral.)*

After You Read

Respond and Think Critically

Respond and Interpret

1. What images or lines in these poems did you find most appealing? Explain.

2. (a)Who is the speaker visiting in Tsurayuki's poem? (b)What do the last two lines suggest about the outcome of his visit?

3. (a)In "Forsaking the Mists," where does the speaker say the geese have learned to live? (b)What do you think the speaker means by this?

4. (a)In Komachi's poem, what does the speaker wish she had not done? (b)Why do you think she feels this way?

5. (a)In Saigyō's poem, to what does the speaker compare his thoughts? (b)What might this imply about the speaker's state of mind?

Analyze and Evaluate

6. (a)What emotions are evoked in the last two lines of "Forsaking the Mists"? (b)What do you think this poem might be suggesting about people?

7. What, in your opinion, are the benefits and limitations of the tanka form?

Connect

8. **Big Idea** **Moments of Reflection** What attitude do these poems convey about change and the passage of time?

9. **Connect to the Author** How might "Trailing on the Wind" reflect Saigyō's experiences as a wandering monk?

Literary Element Mood

An author's choice of images and words helps to create mood.

1. How do the images in Tsurayuki's poem contribute to the mood?

2. What mood does Saigyō's tanka evoke?

Reading Strategy Interpret Imagery

Imagery refers to language that appeals to one or more of the senses. Review the imagery equations you made on page 713.

1. List three examples of imagery in these tanka, and explain to which sense each one appeals.

2. How do these images help you determine the symbolic meanings of the poems?

LOG ON **Literature** Online

Selection Resources For Selection Quizzes, eFlash-cards, and Reading-Writing Connection activities, go to glencoe.com and enter QuickPass code GLW6053u4.

Academic Vocabulary

In "Forsaking the Mists," spring **coincides** with hope and adventure as the geese fly away.

Coincide is an academic word. In more casual conversation, someone might say two friends whose birthdays **coincide** should celebrate together. Using context clues, try to figure out the meaning of *coincide* in the sentence above about the tanka.

For more on academic vocabulary, see pages 36–37 and R83–R85.

Writing

Write a Tanka Recall a time when you were struck by a thought, sensation, or emotion you didn't want to forget. Write a tanka that captures that moment. Use word choice and imagery that contribute to the **mood** you want to establish. Review the tanka form before you begin.

TANKA **715**

Literary Element

1. Winter imagery emphasizes the depth of his passion and evokes a feeling of melancholy in the reader.

2. Possible answers include tranquility and contentment.

Academic Vocabulary

Students should note the two events happen at the same time.

Reading Strategy

1. Possible answer: The crying of the plovers (sense of hearing), mists (sense of sight), and smoke (senses of sight and smell).

2. Students should apply their own experience of these phenomena to the images to determine the emotional response they evoke.

After You Read

Assess

1. Answers will vary.

2. (a) the girl he loves (b) The girl received the speaker coldly, she doesn't love him, and he is unhappy about it.

3. (a) in "a land without flowers" (b) The geese have grown accustomed to winter.

4. (a) awakened (b) If she were still dreaming, she could continue to be with her lover.

5. (a) the smoke from Mount Fuji (b) It is drifting or at peace.

6. (a) Possible answer: sadness and hardship (b) Possible answer: Human beings can learn to live bravely even in sad, desolate circumstances.

7. Possible answer: Because it is so short, it is well suited to capturing moments of emotion, but it may not be well suited for describing complex situations.

8. They convey the attitude that the passage of time and the element of change are inevitable and that human beings cannot hold on to the moments they hold dear.

9. Possible answer: His wanderings may have encouraged peaceful, unfocused thoughts.

Writing

Students' tankas should

- be five lines long, with the first and third lines having five syllables and all other lines having seven

- create a mood complimentary to the moment about which they write

- contain imagery the reader is likely to interpret in the manner intended

Before You Read

Focus

Bellringer Options

Selection Focus
 Transparency 43
Daily Language Practice
 Transparency 63
Or ask: What habits or behaviors of other people do you find annoying or enjoyable? Elicit students' opinions, stressing that they should not discuss teachers or classmates. Then have them read to discover what habits and behaviors the author finds annoying or enjoyable.

Cultural History ☆

The Divine Emperor Officially, the emperor ruled at the top of the Japanese government; however, he was considered to be divine, a direct descendant of the Shinto Sun Goddess, Amaterasu. Because of the belief in the emperor's divinity, the line of descent from one generation to the next has remained unbroken from ancient times to modern-day Japan. In the present day, his power is merely symbolic and ritualistic.

Before You Read

from *The Pillow Book*

Meet **Sei Shōnagon**
(c. 966–c. 1025)

When Sei Shōnagon (saʹē shōʹnä gōnʹ) became lady-in-waiting to Japan's Empress Sadako (säʹdäʹkōʹ), she feared she would be unable to perform her duties and stood in awe of the other ladies-in-waiting. "When I first went into waiting at Her Majesty's Court," she wrote, "so many different things embarrassed me that I could not even reckon them up and I was always on the verge of tears. As a result, I tried to avoid appearing before the Empress except at night, and even then I stayed behind a three-foot curtain of state."

A Literary Family Sei Shōnagon was born into a family in Japan known for its literary talent. Her father and her grandfather were famous poets. Very little is known of Sei Shōnagon's personal life, apart from what she reveals about herself in her writings. Even the name by which she is famous is not her own. According to court custom, she was called *Sei*, which derives from the Kiyohara clan, and *Shōnagon*, which means "minor counselor," a court post held by one of her relatives.

Life in Service When Shōnagon joined the court in the capital city of Heian-kyo in about 991, the Empress Sadako was still a teenager. During the peaceful Heian period, culture flourished in Japan, and the aesthetic life of the court was centered in the empress's apartments. The imperial court's function was purely symbolic, so ceremony and ritual were of the highest importance. A mistake in a ceremony could mean the end of a career. Nevertheless, Shōnagon soon overcame her initial embarrassment and became a highly regarded member of court, where she served until the empress died

in childbirth in 1000. According to some sources, Shōnagon was married and had at least one child, but what became of her after she left the court in 1001 remains a mystery.

Unique Work *The Pillow Book* is part diary and part journal, conveying Shōnagon's impressions of court life during the ten years she spent there. In it she demonstrates intelligence, wit, and keen powers of observation. She also demonstrates snobbery, a judgmental nature, and a lack of restraint that angered some of her contemporaries. Today, her work gives insight into aristocratic life in tenth-century Japan.

> *"You and you alone can see what feelings hide within my heart."*
>
> —Sei Shōnagon

Murasaki Shikbu. Korin. Private collection.

LOG ON ▶ **Literature** Online

Author Search For more about Sei Shōnagon, go to glencoe.com and enter QuickPass code GLW6053u4.

Selection Skills

Literary Elements
- Diary (SE pp. 717, 718, 720, 724, 727)
- Author's Purpose (SE p. 727)

Reading Skills
- Draw Conclusions About Author's Culture (SE pp. 717, 719, 722, 727)

from The Pillow Book

Writing Skills/Grammar
- Autobiographical Narrative (SE p. 728)
- Haiku (TE p. 720)

Vocabulary Skills
- Denotation and Connotation (SE p. 727)
- Riddles (TE p. 717)

Literature and Reading Preview

Connect to the Diary

Have you ever made lists of things you love or hate? Discuss this question with a small group. Consider what personal tastes can reveal about a person.

Build Background

After centuries of a predominant Chinese culture, the development of a Japanese script called *kana* triggered, in part, Japan's development of its own distinctive culture in the late ninth century. Although Japanese men usually wrote in Chinese, women generally wrote in their native language. As a result, the most important early literature in Japanese was written by women.

Set Purposes for Reading

Big Idea **Family and Tradition**

As you read, ask yourself, What role did court tradition, with its rituals and ceremonies, play in the lives of people at court?

Literary Element **Diary**

A **diary** is a daily record of personal impressions, thoughts, or anecdotes not written for publication. A **journal** is also a daily record of events, but a journal is usually less intimate, emphasizing events rather than emotions. As you read, ask yourself, Which passages are like a diary, and which are like a journal?

Reading Strategy **Draw Conclusions About Author's Culture**

When you **draw a conclusion** you use a number of pieces of information to make a broad statement. You should back up your conclusions with supporting details. As you read, ask yourself, What conclusions can I draw about Shōnagon's culture?

···

Tip: Classify Details Grouping or classifying details can help you understand and remember information. Classify details about such categories as court life and Shōnagon's preferences. Use these notes to help you draw conclusions about her culture.

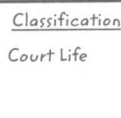 

Classification		Details		Conclusion
Court Life	+	• Cat was pampered and treated "with the greatest care" • Attendants help the empress bathe.	=	

Learning Objectives

For pages 716–727

In studying this text, you will focus on the following objectives:

Literary Study: Analyzing diary.

Reading: Drawing conclusions about author's culture.

Vocabulary

gesticulate (jes tik′yə lāt′) *v.* to make gestures, especially when speaking; p. 719 *If you gesticulate so broadly, you might knock your notes off the speaker's stand.*

inquisitive (in kwiz′ə tiv) *adj.* curious about the world or the affairs of others; p. 720 *My niece is at the age when she is naturally inquisitive and asks "Why?" about everything.*

trivial (triv′ē əl) *adj.* commonplace; of little importance; p. 720 *Martin was trying to train himself not to get upset over small, trivial things.*

chastise (chas tīz′) *v.* to punish, reprimand, or discipline severely; p. 721 *Katie's mother sent her to her room to chastise Katie for her bad behavior.*

banish (ban′ish) *v.* to drive away or remove by authority; p. 721 *What could Eli and Sam possibly have done at the restaurant that caused the manager to banish them?*

Before You Read

Focus

Summary

In *The Pillow Book*—so named because, at the time, such diaries were kept in sleeping quarters—Sei Shōnagon writes about life in the court of the emperor of Japan. In the process, she reveals much about her own character and values. Her topics are varied, ranging from "Hateful Things" and "Embarrassing Things" to the story of a dog banished for attacking the emperor's cat.

 For summaries in languages other than English, see Unit 4 Teaching Resources Book, pp. 78–83.

Vocabulary

Riddles Have students work with partners to create riddles based on the vocabulary words. For example, **ask:** When John reads a science article, he always goes to the Internet to find out more facts on the topic. What word best describes John? *(inquisitive)* Provide time for volunteers to challenge classmates to answer their riddles.

 For additional vocabulary practice, see Unit 4 Teaching Resources Book, p. 86.

Approaching Level

DIFFERENTIATED INSTRUCTION

Shades of Meaning Some students may need extra help grasping the concept of denotations and connotations. Use the phrases *shades of meaning* and *good or bad* to help them with connotations. For example, point out that *curious* and *inquisitive* have good shades of meaning, whereas *nosy*, which has a similar denotation, has a bad shade of meaning. Work with them to use "good" and "bad" words in sentences to emphasize the differing connotations. Examples might include *slender, skinny; sip, gulp; grin, sneer; large, bulky;* and *proud, boastful.*

Advanced Learners/Pre-AP

DIFFERENTIATED INSTRUCTION

Heian Culture Draw attention to the Life in Service passage on page 716. Have interested students find specific examples of how culture flourished in Japan during the Heian period. Have them find out what types of art and literature were produced and what types of ceremonies and rituals were popular. Have them report their findings to the class.

717

Teach

Literary Element | 1

Diary **Answer:** She may have numerous reasons, such as getting the complaints off her chest or recording her sense of propriety.

Literary History ☆

Rival Authors and Ladies of the Court Sei Shōnagon was not the only talented female writer in the imperial court. Murasaki Shikibu was also there. (See "Primary Source Quotation" on page 726 of the student edition.) She is famous for writing the novel *Genji monogatari* ("The Tale of Genji"). These two women are now considered to have been the leading writers of the Heian period. They were also bitter rivals who disliked each other intensely. Their rivalry as writers may have been the leading reason for their disputes, but they were in the service of ladies who were themselves rivals at court. Whereas Sei Shōnagon was a lady-in-waiting to Empress Sadako, Murasaki Shikibu was a lady-in-waiting to Empress Joto mon'in. Discuss how these facts may have influenced the thinking behind this particular "hateful thing."

from
The Pillow Book

Sei Shōnagon
Translated by Ivan Morris

Hateful Things

One is in a hurry to leave, but one's visitor keeps chattering away. If it is someone of no importance, one can get rid of him by saying, "You must tell me all about it next time"; but, should it be the sort of visitor whose presence commands one's best behavior, the situation is hateful indeed.

One finds that a hair has got caught in the stone on which one is rubbing one's inkstick, or again that gravel is lodged in the inkstick, making a nasty, grating sound.

Someone has suddenly fallen ill and one summons the exorcist.[1] Since he is not at home, one has to send messengers to look for him. After one has had a long fretful wait, the exorcist finally arrives, and with a sigh of relief one asks him to start his incantations.[2] But perhaps he has been exorcizing too many evil spirits recently; for hardly has he installed himself and begun praying when his voice becomes drowsy. Oh, how hateful!

A man who has nothing in particular to recommend him discusses all sorts of subjects at random as though he knew everything.

An elderly person warms the palms of his hands over a brazier[3] and stretches out the wrinkles. No young man would dream of behaving in such a fashion; old people can really be quite shameless. I have seen some dreary old creatures actually resting their feet on the brazier and rubbing them against the edge while they speak. These are the kind of people who in visiting someone's house first use their fans to wipe away the dust from the mat and, when they finally sit on it, cannot stay still but are forever spreading out the front of their hunting costume or even tucking it up under their knees. One might suppose that such behavior was restricted to people of humble station; but I

---

1. An *exorcist* is someone who expels evil spirits.
2. *Incantations* are verbal charms spoken or sung as part of a ritual of magic.

Diary *Why do you think Shōnagon writes down these annoyances even though she knows her diary will not make the situations change?*

---

3. A *brazier* (brā′zhər) is a pan that holds burning coals.

718 UNIT 4 EAST ASIA

Reading Practice

Connect to Personal Experiences
Point out that an inkstick was a stick that was blackened through burning. To make ink, a person would rub the stick against a stone. As black particles separated from the stick, the person would gradually mix in water, creating a black ink. Then the person would use a fine brush to write with the ink.

Ask students to paraphrase the "hateful" events described in the second paragraph of "Hateful Things." (*As the writer is grinding her ink, she finds a hair caught in it, and something in the inkstick is making an annoying noise.*)

Then ask: What similar frustrations might modern-day artists or writers experience? Has anything similar happened to you? Have students describe experiences and explain how they are similar to those described by the narrator. (*Students might mention hearing annoying noises when they are trying to write or having a painting get smudged.*)

Girl with a Mirror, c. 1790 Kitagawa Utamaro. Colour woodblock print. British Library, London.

have observed it in quite well-bred people, including a Senior Secretary of the Fifth Rank in the Ministry of Ceremonial and a former Governor of Suruga.

I hate the sight of men in their cups[4] who shout, poke their fingers in their mouths, stroke their beards, and pass on the wine to their neighbors with great cries of "Have some more! Drink up!" They tremble, shake their heads, twist their faces, and **gesticulate** like children who are singing, "We're off to see the Governor." I have seen really well-bred people behave like this and I find it most distasteful.

To envy others and to complain about one's own lot; to speak badly about people;

---

4. The phrase *in their cups* means they have had too much to drink.

Draw Conclusions About Author's Culture *What conclusion can you draw about the organization of the court from this secretary's official title?*

Vocabulary

gesticulate (jes tik′yə lāt′) *v.* to make gestures, especially when speaking

SEI SHŌNAGON **719**

Teach

Reading Strategy | **2**

Draw Conclusions About Author's Culture Answer: *There are many bureaucratic levels in court life.*

View the Art ★

The Japanese printmaker Utamaro is known for his portrayals of girls and women. His prints do not merely record a woman's beauty but often reflect a psychological insight revealed during a private moment.

For an audio recording of this selection, use Listening Library Audio CD-ROM.

Readability Scores

Dale-Chall: 7.4
DRP: 60
Lexile: 880

Learning Objectives
Analyzing diary. (SE)
Drawing conclusions about author's culture. (SE)
Connecting to personal experience. (TE)

Approaching Level

DIFFERENTIATED INSTRUCTION

Modern Comparisons Work with students to help them make personal connections to some of Shōnagon's "hateful things" and to paraphrase others into modern language and situations. Begin with the crying baby and the mosquito. Ask them if they have ever had similar experiences. How did they feel? Then ask them what modern situation might be similar to the carriage passing with the "nasty, creaking noise."

English Learners

DIFFERENTIATED INSTRUCTION

Intermediate Draw attention to the footnoted definition for the idiom *in their cups.* Remind students that English has many idioms—phrases and expressions that have meanings that are different from the literal meanings of the words themselves. For example, the men are not really inside the cups; this expression means that they have had too much to drink. Help students understand the meanings of the following idioms that appear on pages 719–720:

- "in such a fashion" *(in this way)*
- "people of humble station" *(poor people)*
- "to worm out some facts" *(to slyly make people tell you secrets)*
- "butts in" *(interrupts)*
- "makes a great fuss of them" *(spoils them)*
- "laying down the law" *(making the rules)*

Teach

Literary Element | 1

Diary Answer: *The impressions are personal and emotional.*

Reading Strategy | 2

Make Generalizations Ask students what generalizations they can make about Shōnagon's feelings concerning beauty. *(She is particularly affected by contrasts, and she appreciates color. She finds beauty in movement [of the geese] and sounds [of autumn evenings]).*

> **Interactive Read and Write**
> Other options for teaching this selection can be found in Interactive Read and Write for On-Level Learners, pp. 179–188.

to be **inquisitive** about the most **trivial** matters and to resent and abuse people for not telling one, or, if one does manage to worm out some facts, to inform everyone in the most detailed fashion as if one had known all from the beginning—oh, how hateful!

One is just about to be told some interesting piece of news when a baby starts crying.

A flight of crows circle about with loud caws.

One has gone to bed and is about to doze off when a mosquito appears, announcing himself in a reedy voice. One can actually feel the wind made by his wings and, slight though it is, one finds it hateful in the extreme.

A carriage passes with a nasty, creaking noise. Annoying to think that the passengers may not even be aware of this! If I am traveling in someone's carriage and I hear it creaking, I dislike not only the noise but also the owner of the carriage.

One is in the middle of a story when someone butts in and tries to show that he is the only clever person in the room. Such a person is hateful, and so, indeed, is anyone, child or adult, who tries to push himself forward.

One is telling a story about old times when someone breaks in with a little detail that he happens to know, implying that one's own version is inaccurate—disgusting behavior!

Very hateful is a mouse that scurries all over the place.

Some children have called at one's house. One makes a great fuss of them and gives them toys to play with. The children become accustomed to this treatment and

> **Vocabulary**
>
> **inquisitive** (in kwiz′ ə tiv) *adj.* curious about the world or the affairs of others
> **trivial** (triv′ ē əl) *adj.* commonplace; of little importance

start to come regularly, forcing their way into one's inner rooms and scattering one's furnishings and possessions. Hateful!

A certain gentleman whom one does not want to see visits one at home or in the Palace, and one pretends to be asleep. But a maid comes to tell one and shakes one awake, with a look on her face that says, "What a sleepyhead!" Very hateful.

A newcomer pushes ahead of the other members in a group; with a knowing look, this person starts laying down the law and forcing advice upon everyone—most hateful.

In Spring It Is the Dawn

In spring it is the dawn that is most beautiful. As the light creeps over the hills, their outlines are dyed a faint red and wisps of purplish cloud trail over them.

In summer the nights. Not only when the moon shines, but on dark nights too, as the fireflies flit to and fro, and even when it rains, how beautiful it is!

In autumn the evenings, when the glittering sun sinks close to the edge of the hills and the crows fly back to their nests in threes and fours and twos; more charming still is a file of wild geese, like specks in the distant sky. When the sun has set, one's heart is moved by the sound of the wind and the hum of the insects. | 2

In winter the early mornings. It is beautiful indeed when snow has fallen during the night, but splendid too when the ground is white with frost; or even when there is no snow or frost, but it is simply very cold and the attendants hurry from room to room stirring up the fires and bringing charcoal, how well this fits the season's mood! But as noon

> **Diary** *In what way are these impressions appropriate to the diary genre?* | 1

Writing Practice

Write a Haiku From poetry anthologies or literary websites, find and copy examples of haiku, the traditional Japanese form of poetry that has three lines and a total of seventeen syllables. Read and discuss them with students, leading students to see that haiku are usually about nature and usually contain vivid imagery that evokes strong emotions. Then have students review Shōnagon's prose in "In Spring It Is the Dawn."

Work with them to create, as a class, a haiku expressing the thoughts that Shōnagon presents in a specific passage. Then challenge students to write their own original haiku based on other passages in the selection. Provide time for volunteers to share their haiku with the class.

Cat on windowsill, from the series "100 views of Edo", 1857 Ando Hiroshige. Color woodblock print. Private collection.

approaches and the cold wears off, no one bothers to keep the braziers alight, and soon nothing remains but piles of white ashes.

The Cat Who Lived in the Palace

The cat who lived in the Palace had been awarded the headdress of nobility and was called Lady Myōbu. She was a very pretty cat, and His Majesty saw to it that she was treated with the greatest care.

One day she wandered on to the veranda, and Lady Uma, the nurse in charge of her, called out, "Oh, you naughty thing! Please come inside at once." But

the cat paid no attention and went on basking sleepily in the sun. Intending to give her a scare, the nurse called for the dog, Okinamaro.

"Okinamaro, where are you?" she cried. "Come here and bite Lady Myōbu!" The foolish Okinamaro, believing that the nurse was in earnest, rushed at the cat, who, startled and terrified, ran behind the blind in the Imperial Dining Room, where the Emperor happened to be sitting. Greatly surprised, His Majesty picked up the cat and held her in his arms. He summoned his gentlemen-in-waiting. When Tadataka, the Chamberlain,[5] appeared, His Majesty ordered that Okinamaro be **chastised** and **banished** to Dog Island. The attendants all started to chase the dog amid great confusion. His Majesty also reproached Lady Uma. "We shall have to find a new nurse for our cat," he told her. "I no longer feel I can count on you to look after her." Lady Uma bowed; thereafter she no longer appeared in the Emperor's presence.

The Imperial Guards quickly succeeded in catching Okinamaro and drove him out of the Palace grounds. Poor dog! He used to swagger about so happily. Recently, on the third day of the Third Month, when the Controller First Secretary paraded him through the Palace grounds, Okinamaro was adorned with garlands of willow leaves, peach blossoms on his head, and cherry blossoms round his body. How could the

---

5. A *chamberlain* is the chief office in the emperor's household.

Family and Tradition *What does Lady Uma's behavior tell you about life at court?*

Vocabulary

chastise (chas tīz´) *v.* to punish, reprimand, or discipline severely

banish (ban´ish) *v.* to drive away or remove by authority

Big Idea | **3**

Family and Tradition
Answer: *People of the court lived a life of leisure and spent their days in idle activities and in following protocol. It seems that Lady Uma's sole job was to care for the cat. When she failed, she lost her court position.*

View the Art ★

This print is part of a series, one of the last tributes to the "floating world" of the Edo period. Many of the sites featured in the series have historical, aesthetic, or literary associations; many, like this one, make poignant statements. Any human figures are far in the distance, observed by a solitary cat sitting on a sill on which someone has left remnants of his or her existence.

Learning Objectives
Analyzing diary. (SE)
Making generalizations. (TE)
Classifying details. (TE)

Advanced Learners/Pre-AP

DIFFERENTIATED INSTRUCTION

Different Points of View Point out that Shōnagon has added exaggerated details and events to the story of the dog, but that she maintains a sympathetic point of view. Ask students how the story might be different if it were written from the point of view of the Emperor, the Empress, Tadataka, the dog, or the cat. Have students choose one of these characters and rewrite the story from his or her point of view.

Approaching Level

DIFFERENTIATED INSTRUCTION

Social Criticism Students may have difficulty with the cruelty and abuse in this story. Point out that the story contains an underlying criticism of the trivial amusements of the emperors and their attendants. Because the emperor loves his cat, he is furious that a dog would dare to bite it. He expects total obedience and assumes that a dog can understand such demands. Then, after the dog is banished, it returns, a crime for which human beings would have faced beatings. Again, the emperor assumes that the dog knows the consequences of offending the emperor. Stress the absurdity of this reasoning. Then point out that Shōnagon remains sympathetic to the dog. Ask students if they think she might have exaggerated the story as a way of criticizing the trivial, self-centered point of view and lifestyle of the emperor.

Teach

Draw Conclusions About Author's Culture **Answer:** *The dog shakes, trembles, and weeps when the women talk about him. Obviously they think he reveals his true identity either because he understands what they are saying or because he has the depth of human feelings.*

Reading Strategy | **2**

Analyze Cause-and-Effect Relationships Have students review the last two paragraphs of "The Cat Who Lived in the Palace." **Ask:** Why did Shōnagon send a message to Tadataka saying that "it was not the same dog after all"? *(Tadataka was one of the men who had beaten the dog. Shōnagon wanted to protect the dog from further injury.)*

---

dog have imagined that this would be his fate? We all felt sorry for him. "When Her Majesty was having her meals," recalled one of the ladies-in-waiting, "Okinamaro always used to be in attendance and sit opposite us. How I miss him!"

It was about noon, a few days after Okinamaro's banishment, that we heard a dog howling fearfully. How could any dog possibly cry so long? All the other dogs rushed out in excitement to see what was happening. Meanwhile a woman who served as a cleaner in the Palace latrines ran up to us. "It's terrible," she said. "Two of the Chamberlains are flogging a dog. They'll surely kill him. He's being punished for having come back after he was banished. It's Tadataka and Sanefusa who are beating him." Obviously the victim was Okinamaro. I was absolutely wretched and sent a servant to ask the men to stop; but just then the howling ceased. "He's dead," one of the servants informed me. "They've thrown his body outside the gate."

That evening, while we were sitting in the Palace bemoaning Okinamaro's fate, a wretched-looking dog walked in; he was trembling all over, and his body was fearfully swollen.

"Oh dear," said one of the ladies-in-waiting. "Can this be Okinamaro? We haven't seen any other dog like him recently, have we?"

We called to him by name, but the dog did not respond. Some of us insisted that it was Okinamaro, others that it was not. "Please send for Lady Ukon," said the Empress, hearing our discussion. "She will certainly be able to tell." We immediately went to Ukon's room and told her she was wanted on an urgent matter.

"Is this Okinamaro?" the Empress asked her, pointing to the dog.

"Well," said Ukon, "it certainly looks like him, but I cannot believe that this loathsome creature is really our Okinamaro. When I called Okinamaro, he always used to come to me, wagging his tail. But this dog does not react at all. No, it cannot be the same one. And besides, wasn't Okinamaro beaten to death and his body thrown away? How could any dog be alive after being flogged by two strong men?" Hearing this, Her Majesty was very unhappy.

When it got dark, we gave the dog something to eat; but he refused it, and we finally decided that this could not be Okinamaro.

On the following morning I went to attend the Empress while her hair was being dressed and she was performing her ablutions.[6] I was holding up the mirror for her when the dog we had seen on the previous evening slunk into the room and crouched next to one of the pillars. "Poor Okinamaro!" I said. "He had such a dreadful beating yesterday. How sad to think he is dead! I wonder what body he has been born into this time. Oh, how he must have suffered!"

At that moment the dog lying by the pillar started to shake and tremble, and shed a flood of tears. It was astounding. So this really was Okinamaro! On the previous night it was to avoid betraying himself that he had refused to answer to his name. We were immensely moved and pleased. "Well, well, Okinamaro!" I said, putting down the mirror. The dog stretched himself flat on the floor and yelped loudly, so that the Empress beamed with delight. All the ladies gathered round, and Her Majesty summoned Lady Ukon. When the Empress

---

6. The phrase *performing her ablutions* means that she was bathing.

Draw Conclusions About Author's Culture *Why do the members of the court come to this conclusion about Okinamaro's identity?* **1**

Reading Practice

Compare and Contrast Tone Point out that some of Shōnagon's "Embarrassing Things" are somewhat similar to her "Hateful Things." Draw attention to her finding men who drink too much both "hateful" and "embarrassing." **Ask:** What is similar and what is different about these two situations—why is one tale of drunkenness hateful and the other merely embarrassing? *(The "hateful" men are carousing and talking loudly; there is no sense of loudness in her description of the man who repeats himself. Perhaps the largest difference, however, is that the drunken man who is merely "embarrassing" is a loved one. Discuss with students how people might have one standard for strangers and another for loved ones or friends.)*

explained what had happened, everyone talked and laughed with great excitement.

The news reached His Majesty, and he too came to the Empress's room. "It's amazing," he said with a smile. "To think that even a dog has such deep feelings!" When the Emperor's ladies-in-waiting heard the story, they too came along in a great crowd. "Okinamaro!" we called, and this time the dog rose and limped about the room with his swollen face. "He must have a meal prepared for him," I said. "Yes," said the Empress, laughing happily, "now that Okinamaro has finally told us who he is."

2 The Chamberlain, Tadataka, was informed, and he hurried along from the Table Room. "Is it really true?" he asked. "Please let me see for myself." I sent a maid to him with the following reply: "Alas, I am afraid that this is not the same dog after all." "Well," answered Tadataka, "whatever you say, I shall sooner or later have occasion to see the animal. You won't be able to hide him from me indefinitely."

Before long, Okinamaro was granted an Imperial pardon and returned to his former happy state. Yet even now, when I remember how he whimpered and trembled in response to our sympathy, it strikes me as a strange and moving scene; **3** when people talk to me about it, I start crying myself.

Embarrassing Things

While entertaining a visitor, one hears some servants chatting without any restraint in one of the back rooms. It is embarrassing to know that one's visitor can overhear. But how to stop them?

A man whom one loves gets drunk and keeps repeating himself.

To have spoken about someone not knowing that he could overhear. This is embarrassing even if it be a servant or some other completely insignificant person.

To hear one's servants making merry. This is equally annoying if one is on a journey and staying in cramped quarters or at home and hears the servants in a neighboring room.

Parents, convinced that their ugly child is adorable, pet him and repeat the things he has said, imitating his voice.

An ignoramus who in the presence of some learned person puts on a knowing air and converses about men of old.

A man recites his own poems (not especially good ones) and tells one about the praise they have received—most embarrassing.

Lying awake at night, one says something to one's companion, who simply goes on sleeping.

Visual Vocabulary
A *zither* is a stringed instrument that is placed horizontally and is plucked with the fingers.

In the presence of a skilled musician, someone plays a zither just for his own pleasure and without tuning it.

A son-in-law who has long since stopped visiting his wife runs into his father-in-law in a public place.

Pleasing Things

Finding a large number of tales that one has not read before. Or acquiring the second volume of a tale whose first volume one has enjoyed. But often it is a disappointment.

Family and Tradition *What sort of court or society traditions would lead Shōnagon to make such a statement?* **4**

SEI SHŌNAGON **723**

Teach

Reading Strategy | 3

Classify Details After students have read the story about Okinamaro, have them analyze it carefully. **Ask:** Which details are probably true, and which might be exaggerations or inventions? *(The bare outlines of the story are probably true: the dog bit the cat, was sent away and beaten, and, though injured, still came back, though injured. That the dog bit the cat on command, that he died and came back to life, that he withheld his identity, and that he then openly wept are probably exaggerations or inventions.)* Discuss how these features of the story make it similar to a tall tale. *(Though based in reality, it becomes legendary and acquires aspects of the supernatural through exaggeration and retelling.)*

Big Idea | 4

Family and Tradition
Answer: *Apparently court tradition held that servants should never call attention to themselves in any way, physically or verbally, but instead quietly perform their duties.*

Learning Objectives
Drawing conclusions about author's culture. (SE)
Analyzing diary. (SE)
Analyzing cause-and-effect relationships. (TE)

Advanced Learners/Pre-AP

DIFFERENTIATED INSTRUCTION

Defining Beauty Draw attention to the women pictured in the art on pages 719 and 725. Explain that in tenth-century Japan, beauty was defined in far different ways than it is in our culture. Very pale faces were considered beautiful, so women often powdered themselves snowy white. Plump, round bodies were considered far more attractive than slender ones. White teeth were considered unattractive, so women blacked their teeth with soot or tar. Have students research other facts about the definitions of beauty in physical appearance and clothing—for both males and females. Have them share their findings with the class. Then **ask:** What is the true and lasting definition of beauty? *(Students might mention inner beauty, kindness, or virtue.)*

Teach

Literary Element   1

Diary Answer: *She may feel safe confiding to her diary, or perhaps it feels good to admit her somewhat unworthy feelings.*

Progress Check

Can students analyze a diary?

If No → See Unit 4 Teaching Resources Book, p. 84.

Big Idea   2

Family and Tradition
Answer: *It is working for her. When the Empress calls her, the other women have to defer to her. Shōnagon is gloating over having been singled out.*

 To check students' understanding of the selection, see Unit 4 Teaching Resources Book, p. 89.

Someone has torn up a letter and thrown it away. Picking up the pieces, one finds that many of them can be fitted together.

One has had an upsetting dream and wonders what it can mean. In great anxiety one consults a dream-interpreter, who informs one that it has no special significance.

A person of quality is holding forth about something in the past or about a recent event that is being widely discussed. Several people are gathered round him, but it is oneself that he keeps looking at as he talks.

A person who is very dear to one has fallen ill. One is miserably worried about him even if he lives in the capital and far more so if he is in some remote part of the country. What a pleasure to be told that he has recovered!

I am most pleased when I hear someone I love being praised or being mentioned approvingly by an important person.

A poem that someone has composed for a special occasion or written to another person in reply is widely praised and copied by people in their notebooks. Though this is something that has never yet happened to me, I can imagine how pleasing it must be.

A person with whom one is not especially intimate refers to an old poem or story that is unfamiliar. Then one hears it being mentioned by someone else and one has the pleasure of recognizing it. Still later, when one comes across it in a book, one thinks, "Ah, this is it!" and feels delighted with the person who first brought it up.

I feel very pleased when I have acquired some Michinoku paper, or some white, decorated paper, or even plain paper if it is nice and white.

A person in whose company one feels awkward asks one to supply the opening or closing line of a poem. If one happens to recall it, one is very pleased. Yet often on such occasions one completely forgets something that one would normally know.

I look for an object that I need at once, and I find it. Or again, there is a book that I must see immediately; I turn everything upside down, and there it is. What a joy!

When one is competing in an object match (it does not matter what kind), how can one help being pleased at winning?

I greatly enjoy taking in someone who is pleased with himself and who has a self-confident look, especially if he is a man. It is amusing to observe him as he alertly waits for my next repartee;[7] but it is also interesting if he tries to put me off my guard by adopting an air of calm indifference as if there were not a thought in his head.

I realize that it is very sinful of me, but I cannot help being pleased when someone I dislike has a bad experience.

It is a great pleasure when the ornamental comb that one has ordered turns out to be pretty.

I am more pleased when something nice happens to a person I love than when it happens to myself.

Entering the Empress's room and finding that ladies-in-waiting are crowded round her in a tight group, I go next to a pillar which is some distance from where she is sitting. What a delight it is when Her Majesty summons me to her side so that all the others have to make way! ❧

---

7. *Repartee* is an interchange of witty remarks.

Diary *If she feels it is sinful, why do you think Shōnagon makes such an admission?*   **1**

Family and Tradition *Is court tradition working in Shōnagon's favor, or against her? Explain.*   **2**

Speaking and Listening Practice

SMALL GROUP

Dramatic Adaptation Have groups of students adapt some of the incidents in this excerpt from "The Pillow Book." They can base their dramatic adaptation on popular television shows, or create an original series. Allow students to choose between adapting either the narrative episodes from this excerpt or the general descriptions of hateful things, embarrassing things, or pleasing things.

Students should work together to create a script and then assign roles. Consider allowing them to design costumes and create props.

After each group performs its adaptation, have the class identify the part of the excerpt that served as the source of the material. Then discuss what made the adaptation effective.

Woman surrounded by Calligraphy. Utagawa Kunisada (Japan, 1786-1864). Color woodblock print. Private collection.

 View the Art During the eighteenth century in Japan, many courtesans who were celebrated for their artistic compositions were depicted in woodblock prints. How is the woman in the painting like the narrator? ★

SEI SHŌNAGON **725**

View the Art ★

Answer: *The woman's elaborate robe reflects her affluence and status. The numerous manuscripts suggest her love of reading and her curiosity, which extends to other people's private matters.*

During the eighteenth century in Japan, a group of scholars revitalized the role of women in the arts. Literacy became more widespread, and women from all classes of society were encouraged to study *waka*, a traditional form of Japanese poetry.

Learning Objectives
Analyzing diary. (SE)
Analyzing art. (SE)
Creating a dramatic adaption. (TE)

Approaching Level

DIFFERENTIATED INSTRUCTION

Paraphrase Work with students to paraphrase the more difficult passages, restating them in simple, accessible language. For example, you might paraphrase the paragraph beginning "A person of quality . . ." as follows:

An important person is speaking out on a popular issue. Lots of people are watching and listening, but he keeps looking at me as he talks.

After You Read

Assess

1. Answers may vary.

2. (a) Answers will vary. Students might mention a visitor who chatters when one is in a hurry, drunken men, envious people, and buzzing mosquitoes.
(b) Students may find that she is impatient, oversensitive, and proud.

3. (a) She prefers dawn in spring because of the colors, night in summer because of its beauty, evening in fall because of the sounds, and early morning in winter because of the white snow. (b) She has a great passion for nature and is a careful observer of natural phenomena.

4. (a) After Okinamaro rushes at the royal cat, he is banished to Dog Island, returns to the palace where he is beaten and left for dead, appears before the ladies-in-waiting and the Empress, and finally receives an imperial pardon. (b) It seems regimented, hierarchical, and concerned with trivialities.

5. (b) She is easily annoyed by children and thinks people of lower rank are "of no significance." (b) Most students will probably say her attitude is heavily influenced by her regal surroundings. Some students may note, however, that her environment is not an excuse for her snobbish beliefs.

6. (a) She mentions reading tales one hasn't read before, having one's poem widely praised, and being reminded of an old poem or story. (b) Reading and writing are very important to her. She lists books among her favorite things and aspires to writing poetry that others will praise.

7. Answers will vary.

After You Read

Respond and Think Critically

Respond and Interpret

1. What is your overall impression of Sei Shōnagon? Is she likable? Explain.

2. (a) Name several things Shōnagon finds hateful. (b) How would you characterize Shōnagon's personality, based on her list of hateful things?

3. (a) Which parts of the day does Shōnagon prefer in each of the four seasons? Why? (b) What do her choices reveal about her?

4. (a) Summarize what happens to Okinamaro after he rushes at the royal cat in "The Cat Who Lived in the Palace." (b) What, in your opinion, does this anecdote reveal about court life?

Analyze and Evaluate

5. (a) What do Shōnagon's comments reveal about her attitude toward children and people of lower rank? (b) Can her attitude be attributed to her environment? Explain.

6. (a) What pleasing things does Shōnagon mention that relate to reading or the act of writing? (b) How important do you think reading and writing are to Shōnagon? Explain.

7. Choose an item from Shōnagon's lists you think displays her best qualities and one that displays her worst. Explain your choices.

Connect

8. **Big Idea** Family and Tradition Cite two or three details of court life Shōnagon mentions that you feel give you special insight into the court and its traditions. Explain your choices.

9. **Connect to Today** Describe an experience of your own that fits one of Shōnagon's lists.

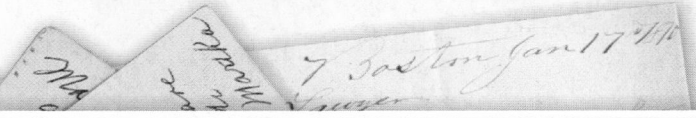

Primary Source Quotation

"Her Future Will Be a Hard One"

Murasaki Shikibu (mōō′rä sä′kē shē′kē bōō) known as Lady Murasaki, is the author of the novel *The Tale of Genji*, a masterpiece of Japanese literature that focuses on life at the court of the Japanese emperor. Sei Shōnagon and Lady Murasaki were contemporaries—and rival ladies-in-waiting in the court. About Shōnagon, Murasaki said the following.

"Someone who makes such an effort to be different from others is bound to fall in people's esteem, and I can only think that her future will be a hard one. She is a gifted woman, to be sure. Yet, if one gives free rein to one's emotions even under the most inappropriate circumstances. . . people are bound to regard one as frivolous."

Group Activity Discuss the following question with classmates: In your opinion, is it possible for a person's rival in art or society to offer an honest assessment of that person's achievements? Apply your reasoning to Murasaki's description of Shōnagon.

Ishiyama Moon, 1889. Yoshitoshi. Woodblock print. Private collection.

8. Answers will vary. Students may mention "The Cat Who Lived in the Palace" for its emphasis on ritual and proper behavior, bureaucracy, idleness, and superficiality. "Embarrassing Things" may suggest overly sensitive feelings of propriety and what should or shouldn't be heard and seen at court.

9. Answers will vary but should be hateful, embarrassing, or pleasing.

Primary Source Quotation

1. Students may feel that although Murasaki acknowledges Shōnagon's abilities, she does so rather grudgingly.

2. Answers will vary. Students may feel that Murasaki feels herself too much a rival of Shōnagon's to be truly honest about her.

Literary Element Diary

Diaries present a window into the writer's culture and an insightful view of the writer's psychology.

1. What elements of this work indicate Shōnagon did not intend it to be published?

2. Cite some elements of the diary that reflect the personal nature of Shōnagon's writing.

3. Do you think Shōnagon is completely honest in her diary? Support your answer with details from the text.

Review: Author's Purpose

As you learned on page 402, **author's purpose** is an author's intent in writing a literary work. Typically, authors write to persuade, to inform, to explain, to entertain, or to describe. Because diarists usually write with themselves as their sole audience, they often write for self-expression. Their purpose could be to vent frustrations or understand themselves better by recording key events and striking thoughts. Some diarists also anticipate that their work may eventually be published. Shōnagon, for instance, knew the impressions she recorded would be circulated among her peers at the court.

Partner Activity Meet with a classmate to discuss these questions.

1. In your opinion, what was Shōnagon's main purpose for keeping this diary?

2. Cite some examples from *The Pillow Book* you think Shōnagon would probably not have included if she had been writing for publication. What do you think was her purpose for including them?

LOG ON ▶ **Literature** Online

Selection Resources For Selection Quizzes, eFlashcards, and Reading-Writing Connection activities, go to glencoe.com and enter QuickPass code GLW6053u4.

Reading Strategy Draw Conclusions About Author's Culture

ACT Skills Practice

Judging by Shōnagon's diary, the court valued:

A. family and domesticity.

B. elegance and manners.

C. justice and democracy.

D. hard work and perseverance.

Vocabulary Practice

Practice with Denotation and Connotation Denotation is the literal meaning of a word. **Connotation** is its implied meaning. For example, the words *glad* and *ecstatic* have a denotation of "being happy," but *ecstatic* has the stronger connotation. Each of the boldfaced vocabulary words below is paired with a word with a similar denotation. Choose the word with a stronger connotation.

1. gesticulate   move

2. inquisitive   intrusive

3. trivial   meaningless

4. chastise   punish

5. banish   eject

Academic Vocabulary

In "Hateful Things," Shōnagon comments on drunk men's lack of **discretion**.

Discretion is an academic word. In more familiar usage, a mother might leave it to her child's **discretion** to decide what to wear to school. To further explore the meaning of this word, answer the following question: What type of behavior do you think Shōnagon would consider lacking **discretion**?

For more on academic vocabulary, see pages 36–37 and R83–R85.

SEI SHŌNAGON   **727**

Reading Strategy

B is the correct answer. Most of Shōnagon's observations relate to propriety and social graces. **A** is incorrect, as Shōnagon is quite critical of parents and children. **C** is incorrect, as the society Shōnagon describes is very hierarchical and bureaucratic. **D** is incorrect, as life at court is characterized by the lazy self-indulgence of people of elevated status.

Progress Check

Can students draw conclusions about the author's culture?

If No ➔ See Unit 4 Teaching Resources Book, p. 85.

Literary Element

1. The informal structure indicates Shōnagon wrote this work in a random way, with little or no planning. The very personal nature of many of the entries also suggests the diary was for her personal use only.

2. The items Shōnagon finds hateful, pleasing, or embarrassing are all personal in nature. Admissions about herself that she feels could be interpreted as sinful are also personal.

3. Answers will vary.

Review: Author's Purpose

1. Some students may say she kept it to show off her wit. Others may say she kept it for her own satisfaction.

2. Students may cite embarrassing things, such as summoning someone who does not want to be bothered, or pleasing things," such as someone she dislikes having a bad experience. She may have included them to release her feelings.

 For additional selection assessment, see Assessment Resources, pp. 145–146.

Vocabulary

1. gesticulate   4. chastise
2. intrusive   5. banish
3. meaningless

Academic Vocabulary

Students should mention actions referred to negatively in *The Pillow Book*, such as gossiping servants.

After You Read

Assess

Respond Through Writing

Students' narratives should:

- relate lists of things that provoke strong responses in the writer
- arrange these things into a coherent narrative with a logical organization
- elaborate upon their lists with details, particularly sensory details that vividly describe settings, characters, and actions

A four-point response addresses all three points fully.

A three-point response fully addresses two points and partially addresses a third point.

A two-point response fully addresses one point and partially addresses two points.

A one-point response partially addresses one point.

 For grammar practice, see Unit 4 Teaching Resources Book, p. 88.

Respond Through Writing

Autobiographical Narrative

Apply Description Write an autobiographical narrative, using *The Pillow Book* as a model. Apply Shōnagon's style to your narrative by presenting vivid descriptions and observations relating to the culture you live in and your attitude toward your environment.

Understand the Task When you **apply**, you use an author's form or style as a model for your own writing.

Prewrite Generate lists to organize your thoughts before writing your narrative. Consult the diagram you made on page 717 and use a chart like the one below to record your impressions; you can use the categories listed or create your own. List specific objects or situations that provoke strong responses in you, as Shōnagon does.

Hateful Things	Embarrassing Things	Pleasing Things	Scary Things
loud chewing	tripping on the sidewalk	popping bubble wrap	shark movies

Then refine and filter your initial thoughts into a coherent whole, eliminating items that do not provoke a strong emotional response or do not lend themselves to description.

Draft Use your chart to create a sequential outline for your narrative. Remember that in this narrative, you are both describing events and commenting on their cultural significance. Pace the action to show changes in time and mood.

Revise Review your writing to ensure your scenes and incidents take place in specific, vivid settings. Also be sure you have portrayed your characters and elaborated your descriptions with concrete and sensory details. Trade papers with a partner and ask him or her to describe a scene based on your draft. If your partner's description falls short of your experience, revise your narrative to make it more vivid and specific.

Edit and Proofread Proofread your paper, correcting any errors in spelling, grammar, and punctuation. Review the Grammar Tip in the side column to help you use gerunds.

Learning Objectives

In this assignment, you will focus on the following objectives:

Writing: Writing an autobiographical narrative.

Grammar: Understanding gerunds.

Grammar Tip

Gerunds

In the sentence *Rehearsing exhausts me, exhausts* is the verb. While *rehearsing* appears to be a verb, it is actually a gerund, or a verb form ending in *-ing* functioning as a noun. In the sentence *Crossing the school parking lot can be difficult, crossing* is the gerund and *crossing the school parking lot* is the complete gerund phrase, which functions as the subject.

You might use gerunds in your autobiographical narrative to name things you describe, such as swimming, eating, gossiping, and so on.

Writing Practice

Apply Description Point out to students that what makes Shōnagon's work so interesting a thousand years later is the concrete, specific detail she uses to make her writing vivid and lively. Explain that a modern version of Shōnagon's "Pleasing Things" list is the song "My Favorite Things" from *The Sound of Music*. If possible, write the song lyrics on the board. Discuss with students the wonderful specificity of detail that allows people to "see" each item—not just rain drops, but "raindrops on roses"; not just packages, but "brown paper packages tied up with strings." Using these two contrasts as examples, have students turn the following drab descriptions into lively ones, using concrete, specific modifying words and phrases.

1. snowflakes
2. a strong wind
3. a red flower
4. a car
5. an athlete
6. a baby
7. a bad dream
8. an old house

Grammar Workshop

Commas with Interjections and Parenthetical Expressions

Literature Connection In this passage from *The Pillow Book*, Sei Shōnagon uses the interjection "Ah" to express delight.

> *"Still later, when one comes across it in a book, one thinks, 'Ah, this is it!' and feels delighted with the person who first brought it up."*

Interjections are words that express emotion or exclamation, such as *ah, oh, ouch,* and *oh well.* Most interjections occur at the beginning of a sentence. Because these expressions have no grammatical connection to other words in the sentence, they should be set off with a comma.

Similarly, authors can set off **parenthetical expressions**—side thoughts—with commas. Here is an example from *The Pillow Book*: "And besides, wasn't Okinamaro beaten to death and his body thrown away?" "And besides" is a parenthetical expression. Parenthetical expressions include phrases such as *in fact, on the contrary,* and *by the way.*

PROBLEM 1 A comma is missing with an interjection.

Oh what happened to poor Lady Uma?

SOLUTION *Oh, what happened to poor Lady Uma?*

PROBLEM 2 Commas are missing with a parenthetical expression at the beginning of a sentence.

In fact Sei Shōnagon had strong opinions.

SOLUTION *In fact, Sei Shōnagon had strong opinions.*

PROBLEM 3 Commas are missing with a parenthetical expression in the middle of a sentence.

Lady Murasaki on the other hand felt Sei Shōnagon acted improperly.

SOLUTION *Lady Murasaki, on the other hand, felt Sei Shōnagon acted improperly.*

Revise Rewrite the following sentences, adding commas where needed.

1. After all the ladies-in-waiting could be highly competitive.
2. The palace cat on the other hand lived a life of leisure.
3. Ah I see that Sei Shōnagon came from a literary family.

Learning Objective

In this workshop, you will focus on the following objective:

Grammar: Understanding how to use commas with interjections and parenthetical expressions.

Interjections and Parenthetical Expressions

Interjections express emotion or exclamation. **Parenthetical expressions** are side thoughts that add information. Both need commas to separate them from the rest of a sentence.

Tip

Overuse of interjections and parenthetical expressions can make your writing appear overly casual and informal, so use them sparingly when writing for a test or an assignment.

Language Handbook

For more on **commas**, see the Language Handbook, p. R40.

 **Literature** Online

Grammar For more grammar practice, go to glencoe.com and enter QuickPass code GLW6053u4.

Grammar Workshop

Commas with Interjections and Parenthetical Expressions

Focus

Write these sentences on the board:

1. Wow was I surprised!
2. His laugh was in fact contagious.
3. On the contrary we were glad to hear the news.

Ask students to punctuate the sentences. (*1. Wow, was I surprised! 2. His laugh was, in fact, contagious. 3. On the contrary, we were glad to hear the news.*)

Teach

Write Sentences

Emphasize that interjections and parenthetical expressions are set off with commas. Give several examples and have students write sentences of their own.

Assess

1. After all, the ladies-in-waiting could be highly competitive.
2. The palace cat, on the other hand, lived a life of leisure.
3. Ah, I see that Sei Shōnagon came from a literary family.

English Learners

DIFFERENTIATED INSTRUCTION

Intermediate Students new to the United States may be unfamiliar with English interjections, many of which are slang. Note that interjections often show surprise or express emotions. Discuss appropriate use of interjections, including *oh, ah, ouch, well, gee, hey, excuse me, yikes,* and *hi.*

Pair English learners with native English speakers to explain the interjections above and give examples of interjections as used in everyday speech. Instruct English learners to repeat the examples back to the native English speakers.

Approaching Level

DIFFERENTIATED INSTRUCTION

Cloze Sentences Write the sentences below on the board. Have students fill in the blanks with interjections. Answers will vary.

1. _____, I'm glad that test is over. *(Phew; Whew; Well)*
2. _____! What a gorgeous view! *(Wow; Gee; Oh my)*
3. _____! Where are you going with my bicycle? *(Hey; Wait; Stop)*

Before You Read

Focus

Bellringer Options

Daily Language Practice Transparency 64

Or ask: Have you ever been taught a lesson in an unorthodox manner? Have students share stories of lessons they have learned in unusual manners.

Or ask: What does one have to do to master an art? See if students think it takes practice, talent, willpower, or other actions and attributes to achieve success.

Before You Read

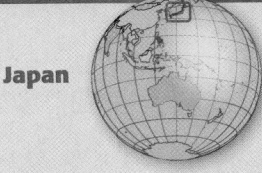

Zen Parables

In Buddhist legend, Bodhidharma, the monk credited with founding Zen Buddhism, stared at a wall for nine years to achieve enlightenment. Besides promoting the virtue of patience, this legend illustrates one of the core principles of Zen—that one must look beyond the logic of everyday life to attain enlightenment. Zen, a Japanese school of Buddhism, asserts each individual has the potential to reach an enlightened state characterized by tranquility, fearlessness, and spontaneity.

The Rise of Zen Bodhidharma (bō di där′mə) is said to have traveled from India to China during the sixth century. In China, his ideas mixed with Taoist philosophy to create the *Ch'an* school of Buddhism. Ch'an was introduced to Japan in 1191 and developed into what is now called Zen.

Unlike religions that emphasize worship or the study of scripture, Zen focuses on guidance toward *satori* (sä tō′rē), or enlightenment—total self-realization and liberation from ignorance and worldly desires. Zen Buddhists believe that people who achieve satori have reached a higher state of awareness.

Parables and Koans Zen masters do not teach their students by telling them facts and testing them on their knowledge. Instead, they use parables, or short stories that illustrate Zen principles. Some Zen masters use riddle-like questions called *koans* (kō′änz′) to stimulate their search for enlightenment. Famous koans include "What did your face look like before you were born?" and "What is the sound of one hand clapping?" Because such questions have no logical answers, contemplating them forces students to move beyond reason.

"Zen has entered internally into every phase of the cultural life of the people."

—Daisetz T. Suzuki, from *Zen and Japanese Culture*

The Impact of Zen The Zen values of discipline and fearlessness influenced the samurai culture that developed in the twelfth century. Samurai adopted the Zen art of swordsmanship, which emphasizes unity of the mind, body, and spirit. To this day, the Zen ideal of simplicity permeates Japanese arts as diverse as architecture, dance, and gardening.

Selection Skills

Literary Elements
- Parable (SE pp. 731, 734, 735)
- Irony (TE p. 732)

Zen Parables

Writing Skills/Grammar
- Parable (SE p. 735)

Reading Skills
- Apply Background Knowledge (SE pp. 731, 734, 735)
- Recognize Author's Purpose (TE p. 732)
- Identify Genre (TE p. 734)

Vocabulary Skills
- Word Usage (SE p. 735)

Literature and Reading Preview

Connect to the Parables

Do you believe you should always follow certain rules, or does correct behavior vary from situation to situation? Freewrite for a few minutes in response to this question.

Build Background

Buddhists believe people who achieve satori have tapped into a deeper part of their intuition that signifies a profound "waking up" of the individual's consciousness. However, the most direct way to attain enlightenment is through a form of sitting meditation called *zazen* (*za*: "sitting," *zen*: "absorption"). In practicing zazen, the sitter remains alert, but refrains from clinging to any thought, keeping the mind perfectly clear.

Set Purposes for Reading

Big Idea Virtue and Wisdom

As you read, ask yourself, How do these parables define virtue and wisdom? What principles do they share with Taoism?

Literary Element Parable

A **parable** is a brief story that illustrates a moral or lesson. Parables often contain a **paradox,** an apparent contradiction of logic that actually reveals an underlying truth. As you read the parables, ask yourself, How is paradox used to prompt the reader to question conventional thinking?

Reading Strategy Apply Background Knowledge

When you **apply background knowledge,** you use what you've learned about a subject or time period to gain a deeper understanding of a text. Your background knowledge includes information about the cultural forces that underpin a piece of literature. As you read, ask yourself, How can I use what I know about Zen Buddhism to interpret these parables?

Tip: Track Details In a chart like the one below, keep track of how you use background knowledge to interpret details in the parables.

Background Knowledge	Detail	Interpretation
Zen Buddhists believe in nonattachment.	Banzo tells Matajuro never to speak of fencing or touch a sword.	Matajuro can master swordsmanship only by freeing his mind.

ZEN PARABLES **731**

Learning Objectives

For pages 730–735

In studying this text, you will focus on the following objectives:

Literary Study: Analyzing parable.

Reading: Applying background knowledge.

Writing: Writing a parable.

Vocabulary

intersection (in′tər·sek′shən) *n.* a place where roads cross one another; p. 732 *When the light turned green, I drove through the busy intersection.*

anticipate (an tis′ə pāt′) *v.* expect; consider in advance; p. 734 *If there is an accident on the highway, drivers should anticipate delays.*

seldom (sel′dəm) *adv.* rarely; p. 734 *Michael seldom went to the movies, preferring to stay at home and read.*

Tip: Word Usage When you encounter a new word, it might be useful to answer a specific question about the word. For example, What kind of road does not have **intersections**?

Before You Read

Focus

Summary

In the first parable, Tanzan, a monk, carries a young woman across a muddy street. His fellow monk, Ekido, rebukes him for having touched a woman. Tanzan replies that he, who touched the girl, has forgotten her, whereas Ekido, who followed the rules, is still dwelling on her. In the second parable, Matajuro wishes to learn sword fighting from Banzo, a master. Matajuro is made to do chores and never think about swords. After three years of this, Banzo begins attacking him at random with a wooden sword. With this training, Matajuro soon becomes "the greatest swordsman in the land."

 For summaries in languages other than English, see Unit 4 Teaching Resources Book, pp. 92–97.

Vocabulary

Create Sentences Divide students up into small groups. Instruct each student to write one sentence that uses all of the selection's vocabulary words. Then have each share his or her sentence with the small group. Students should then collectively choose the most creative sentence in their group. The chosen sentences should then be written on the board.

 For additional vocabulary practice, see Unit 4 Teaching Resources Book, p. 100.

Approaching Level

DIFFERENTIATED INSTRUCTION

Rewrite a Moral Students approaching level may have difficulties grasping the morals of these parables as they are phrased in the selection. Have them work in pairs, discussing the lessons these parables are meant to teach. Each pair should then develop its own versions of the stories' morals, ones that are clear and understandable to them. Have the pairs share their morals with the group. Discuss with the class how the morals vary from group to group.

Advanced Learners/Pre-AP

DIFFERENTIATED INSTRUCTION

Write a Report Advanced learners might be interested in researching the practices of Zen Buddhism. They should use the Internet as well as a library to conduct research on a certain aspect of the practices of Zen Buddhism—perhaps meditation or the martial arts—and then write a short report on it. Advise students to research and write about whatever they find most interesting about Zen Buddhism.

Teach

Literary Element   1

Irony **Ask:** What is ironic about Ekido's statement? (*He follows the rules in not touching the young woman, but that does not stop him from noticing her physical attractiveness.*)

Big Idea   2

Virtue and Wisdom
Answer: *Ekido believes it is virtuous to follow strict rules of conduct, while Tanzan believes in being unattached to worldly emotions.*

[APPROACHING] Ask approaching-level students which monk's belief the story presents as the "right" one. (*Tanzan's*)

Interactive Read and Write
Other options for teaching this selection can be found in Interactive Read and Write for On-Level Learners, pp. 189–196.

Readability Scores

Dale-Chall: 6.6
DRP: 55
Lexile: 570

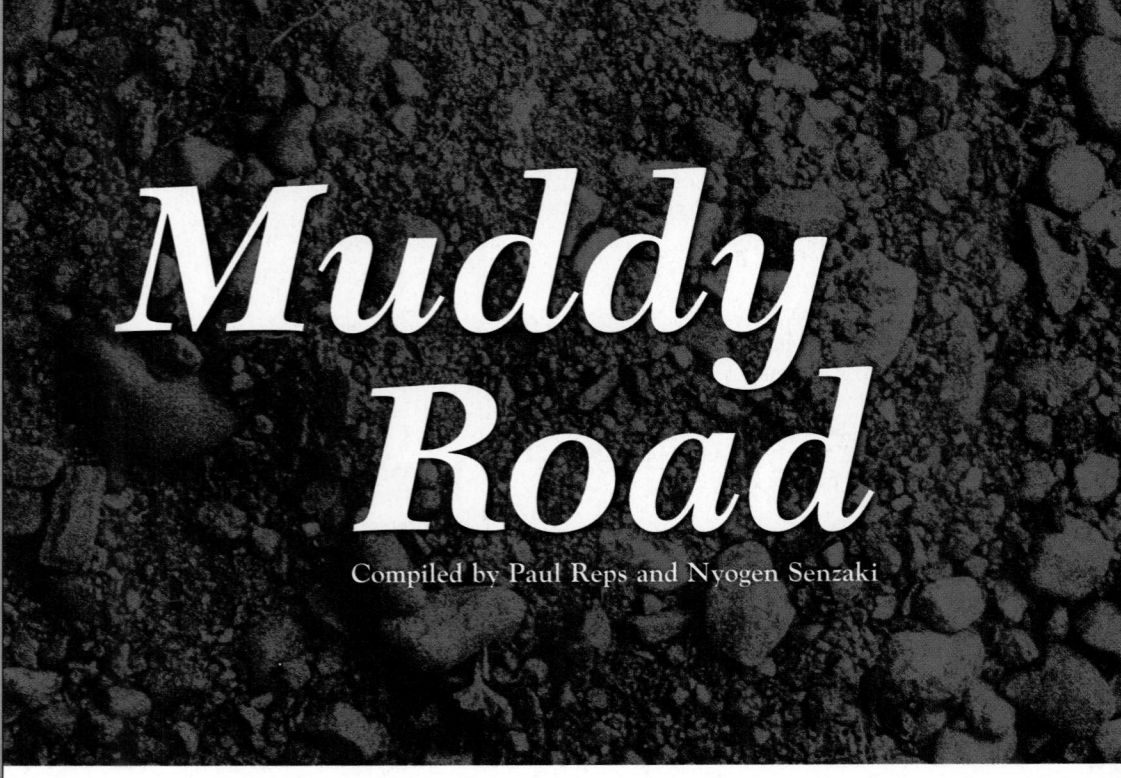

Muddy Road

Compiled by Paul Reps and Nyogen Senzaki

Tanzan and Ekido were once traveling together down a muddy road. A heavy rain was still falling. Coming around a bend, they met a lovely girl in a silk kimono and sash, unable to cross the **intersection**.

"Come on, girl," said Tanzan at once. Lifting her in his arms, he carried her over the mud.

Ekido did not speak again until that night when they reached a lodging temple. Then he no longer could restrain himself. "We monks don't go near females," he told Tanzan, "especially not young and lovely ones. It is dangerous. Why did you do that?" **1**

"I left the girl there," said Tanzan. "Are you still carrying her?" ∾

> **Vocabulary**
> **intersection** (in´tər sek´shən) *n.* a place where roads cross one another

Virtue and Wisdom *How does Tanzan's concept of virtue differ from Ekido's?* **2**

732   UNIT 4   EAST ASIA

Reading Practice

 SMALL GROUP
Recognize Author's Purpose
Remind students that an author's purpose is his or her reason for creating a literary work. Ask students what they think the author's purpose in writing these parables was. Then ask them how they think the parables would have been different had the author had a different purpose in mind.

Divide the students into small groups and have them work together to write a short retelling of one of the stories, assigning them the purpose of entertaining instead of enlightening.

732

Samurai warrior on the battlefield. Artist unkown. Japanese print.

The Taste of
Banzo's Sword

Compiled by Paul Reps and Nyogen Senzaki

Teach

Cultural History ☆

Zen and the Martial Arts Like Samurai sword fighting, East Asian martial arts are greatly influenced by both Zen Buddhism and Taoism. Martial arts such as judo, karate, and kung fu emphasize the necessity for a suspension of rationalization and calculation in their practitioners. The goal is to allow the mind and body to be unified, thereby allowing one's self to react immediately to anything in any given situation.

Learning Objectives
Applying background knowledge. (SE)
Analyzing irony. (TE)
Recognizing author's purpose. (TE)

Approaching Level

DIFFERENTIATED INSTRUCTION

Make a Timeline Using visuals can help less proficient readers track the events and characters in a story. This technique helps them to focus attention on the sequence of events and the process of review and discussion.

Have students chart the action of "The Taste of Banzo's Sword" using a timeline. They should place the first event of the story on the left hand side of the timeline.

The final event in the story should be placed on the far right hand side. In the middle, students should fill in the story's events in the chronological order in which they occur. The spacing of the events on the timeline should also reflect the time elapsed between events.

Advanced Learners/Pre-AP

DIFFERENTIATED INSTRUCTION

 Analyze Archetype
SMALL GROUP
Have students gather in small groups. Instruct them to use their prior knowledge to brainstorm a list of characters in literature and popular culture who fit the archetype of the wise, mysterious mentor. For each character they think of, they should discuss his or her similarities to and differences from Banzo.

733

Teach

Reading Strategy `1`

Apply Background Knowledge Answer: His responses are meant to confuse, challenge, and ultimately enlighten his pupil.

 For additional practice using the reading skill or strategy, see Unit 3 Teaching Resources Book, p. 99.

Reading Strategy `2`

Respond to Character

Ask: What was your reaction to Banzo's suddenly hitting Matajuro? *(Many students will think his actions were humorous. Some might have been surprised or perplexed by his sudden change in behavior.)*

Literary Element `3`

Parable Answer: *It shows that by patiently serving his master, Matajuro is able to achieve his goal of becoming a swordsman.*

(APPROACHING) Ask students approaching level if they believe that this method of teaching would actually work. *(Some may believe it; others will doubt it.)*

Progress Check

Can students identify parable?

If No → See Unit 4 Teaching Resources Book, p. 98.

Readability Scores

Dale-Chall: 6.2
DRP: 54
Lexile: 570

734

Matajuro Yagyu was the son of a famous swordsman. His father, believing that his son's work was too mediocre to **anticipate** mastership, disowned him.

So Matajuro went to Mount Futara and there found the famous swordsman Banzo. But Banzo confirmed the father's judgment. "You wish to learn swordsmanship under my guidance?" asked Banzo. "You cannot fulfill the requirements."

"But if I work hard, how many years will it take me to become a master?" persisted the youth.

"The rest of your life," replied Banzo.

"I cannot wait that long," explained Matajuro. "I am willing to pass through any hardship if only you will teach me. If I become your devoted servant, how long might it be?"

"Oh, maybe ten years," Banzo relented.

"My father is getting old, and soon I must take care of him," continued Matajuro. "If I work far more intensively, how long would it take me?"

"Oh, maybe thirty years," said Banzo.

"Why is that?" asked Matajuro. "First you say ten and now thirty years. I will undergo any hardship to master this art in the shortest time!"

"Well," said Banzo, "in that case you will have to remain with me for seventy years. A man in such a hurry as you are to get results **seldom** learns quickly."

"Very well," declared the youth, understanding at last that he was being rebuked for impatience, "I agree."

Matajuro was told never to speak of fencing and never to touch a sword. He cooked for his master, washed the dishes, made his bed, cleaned the yard, cared for the garden, all without a word of swordsmanship.

Three years passed. Still Matajuro labored on. Thinking of his future, he was sad. He had not even begun to learn the art to which he had devoted his life.

But one day Banzo crept up behind him and gave him a terrific blow with a wooden sword. `2`

The following day, when Matajuro was cooking rice, Banzo again sprang upon him unexpectedly.

After that, day and night, Matajuro had to defend himself from unexpected thrusts. Not a moment passed in any day that he did not have to think of the taste of Banzo's sword.

He learned so rapidly he brought smiles to the face of his master. Matajuro became the greatest swordsman in the land. ◑

`1` **Apply Background Knowledge** *How are Banzo's responses typical of a Zen master?*

Vocabulary

anticipate (an tis′ ə pāt′) *v.* expect; consider in advance

seldom (sel′ dəm) *adv.* rarely

`3` **Parable** *How does the parable illustrate the Zen principle of patience?*

734 UNIT 4 EAST ASIA

Reading Practice

Identify Genre Place students in small groups. Instruct them to develop their own definition of a parable based on the stories from this selection. Have them discuss questions such as: What is typical of a parable? How might one, reading an unfamiliar story, tell if it is a parable or not?

Instruct groups to refine their definitions until they are as clear and specific as possible. Then have each group share its definition with the class. Discuss as a class the differences between the groups' definitions.

After You Read

Respond and Think Critically

Respond and Interpret

1. What was your reaction to the ending of "Muddy Road"?

2. (a)In "Muddy Road," what does Tanzan do to upset Ekido? (b)Why does it upset him?

3. In "The Taste of Banzo's Sword," how does Banzo respond to Matajuro's promises to work hard?

4. (a)What does Banzo have Matajuro do for the first three years of his training? (b)Why might Banzo require this?

Analyze and Evaluate

5. (a)What does Tanzan mean by his question at the end of "Muddy Road"? (b)What general lesson might this question convey?

Literary Element Parable

Zen parables often use **paradoxes,** or apparent contradictions, to teach lessons.

1. (a)How does Tanzan's question at the end of "Muddy Road" contradict logic? (b)In what deeper sense are his words true?

2. Identify a paradox in "The Taste of Banzo's Sword."

Reading Strategy Apply Background Knowledge

Your **background knowledge** can help you interpret characters' actions in a literary work.

1. What principle of Zen Buddhism might Tanzan demonstrate by carrying the girl across the road? Explain.

2. Relate the legend about Bodhidharma on page 730 to "The Taste of Banzo's Sword."

LOG ON ▶ **Literature** Online

Selection Resources For Selection Quizzes, eFlashcards, and Reading-Writing Connection activities, go to glencoe.com and enter QuickPass code GLW6053u4.

6. (a)In "The Taste of Banzo's Sword," what qualities must Matajuro develop to become the greatest swordsman in the land? (b)Why do you think Banzo's teaching methods are successful?

Connect

7. **Big Idea** Virtue and Wisdom (a)What message about virtue does "Muddy Road" convey? (b)What message about attaining wisdom does "The Taste of Banzo's Sword" convey?

8. **Connect to Today** In your opinion, do the lessons of these parables apply to today's world? Explain.

Vocabulary Practice

Practice with Word Usage Respond to these statements to help you explore the meanings of the vocabulary words from the parables.

1. Make a list of things besides roads that can form an **intersection.**

2. Describe a situation in which you had to **anticipate** an occurrence or event.

3. Give an example of something that **seldom** occurs.

Writing

Write a Parable Write a parable of your own that expresses a Zen principle. Look back at the chart you filled out on page 731 to review the background information you'll need to keep in mind as you write. Then think of a modern situation to which a Zen principle might apply.

After You Read

Assess

1. Answers will vary. Many students may find it surprising.

2. (a) Tanzan carries a lovely girl across the mud. (b) As a monk, Tanzan is not supposed to have contact with females.

3. He responds by increasing the time it will take for Matajuro to master swordsmanship.

4. (a) He tells Matajuro never to speak of swordsmanship and has him do chores. (b) He is trying to teach Matajuro patience and to clear his mind of thoughts of swordsmanship.

5. (a) While Tanzan has let go of all thoughts of the girl, Ekido is still holding on to them. (b) Possible answer: A person's inner state is more important than his or her deeds.

6. (a) He must achieve patience and discipline and clear his mind of distractions. (b) Possible answer: The methods change Matajuro's attitude.

7. (a) Virtue consists more in having a pure mind than in behaving correctly. (b) Wisdom comes with time and patience.

8. Answers will vary.

Literary Element

1. (a) Ekido could not literally be carrying the girl, because they left her at the intersection. (b) Ekido is still carrying thoughts of the girl with him.

2. Possible answer: Banzo says it will take ten years for Matajuro to become a swordsman, but thirty years if he works harder.

⚡ Writing

Students' parables should

- clearly illustrate a Zen principle
- include a paradox

Reading Strategy

1. Possible answer: He demonstrates spontaneity, because his act is not in accordance with expectations or rules.

2. Both show the need for patience. Just as Bodhidharma gazed at the wall for nine years before reaching enlightenment, Matajuro worked for three years as a servant before even beginning to learn swordsmanship.

Vocabulary

1. Students might mention lines on a chart or spokes in a bike wheel.

2. Students should mention something they had to consider in advance—perhaps taking a driver's test or trying out for a sports team.

3. Students might mention an eclipse or a leap year.

Focus

Bellringer Options

Write on the board: Drama in the West is never written for only rich and powerful people.
Ask: Do you agree or disagree with this statement? *(Students may agree that this is largely true of Western drama after the twentieth century. However, some students may note that earlier European dramas including that of Shakespeare, were often written for the nobility, and sometimes commissioned by them.)*

Teach

Reading Strategy | 1

Analyze Cultural Context
Ask: How do you think Noh and Kabuki plays matter to modern Japan? Why are they still performed? *(Students may say that tradition is very important to the Japanese people, and that Noh and Kabuki plays are an important part of traditional Japanese art. Some students may recognize that other older forms of art are still relevant and meaningful to modern Western audiences.)*

Learning Objectives

For pages 736–737
In studying this text, you will focus on the following objectives:
Literary Study: Analyzing literary genres.
Reading:
Evaluating historical influences.
Connecting to the literature.

Japanese Drama: Noh and Kabuki

STILL PERFORMED TODAY, NOH AND KABUKI PLAYS PROVIDE A GLIMPSE into traditional Japanese culture. Noh, the elaborate classical theater of Japan, evolved more than 600 years ago from ancient religious rituals. Both Noh (also spelled No) and Kabuki, which developed later, involve rich, all-day spectacles of music, dance, and mime that show the influence of the Japanese court tradition.

Noh mask of jealous woman. Hanya.

And I spent my heart on the glimpse of a moon that slipped through the boughs of an autumn tree.
—Seami Motokiyo, from *The Damask Drum*

Noh Plays

Noh, the traditional theater of Japanese nobility, developed its permanent form in the fourteenth century. The form grew out of Zen Buddhist religious festivals and retains a strong spiritual element, using powerful gestures and meditative silences to tell stories. A typical Noh play has only three or four roles, all performed by men on a small, bare stage. The actors, in contrast, wear elaborate costumes and masks. A Noh play usually tells the tale of a restless ghost. The main character is a spirit, or *shite* (shē′tā), often in human form, who is tortured by memories from a troubled life. A secondary character, called a *waki* (wä′kē), asks questions of the *shite*. Throughout the play, a chorus echoes the words of the main characters, who dance and gesture **1** to the music of a flute player and drummers. Most action in a Noh play is symbolic. For example, a character may take only a few steps to indicate he is on a long journey. Noh drama has influenced such authors as the Irish poet and dramatist W. B. Yeats, who wrote a number of plays in this form, including *Four Plays for Dancers* (1921).

Seami Motokiyo

The most famous of the Noh actor-playwrights, Seami Motokiyo (1363–1443), wrote about 90 of the approximately 230 Noh plays typically performed today. According to Seami, among the most important aspects of Noh drama are the moments of "no action," in which actors captivate their audiences by conveying a sense of spiritual or mental

736 UNIT 4 EAST ASIA

Writing Practice

Write a Scenario Encourage students to write a scenario for their own modern Noh or Kabuki dramas. If they wish they may research more Noh and Kabuki dramas to use as models, but the students' plots and characters should be set in the present day.

Remind students that the dramas may be based upon mythic, legendary, or historical scenes. They may be tragic or they may not. Encourage students to

determine first how their drama will begin and end, and how many scenes and speeches will appear in it. Students might also include notes about staging and costume.

strength. Describing such moments, Seami wrote, "In the art of the Noh . . . the different types of miming are artificial things. What holds the parts together is the mind." In one of Seami's best-known plays, *The Damask Drum*, a beautiful princess tells an aged gardener if he beats a drum in a garden so hard it can be heard in her palace, she will visit him. When the old man realizes the futility of the task, he drowns himself. With its tragic outcome, stylized gestures, and mystical time shifts, this play is typical of the Noh aesthetic.

Kabuki Theater

Kabuki, a theater created for the common people, arose around 1600, eventually replacing Noh as Japan's most popular dramatic form. A group of female performers originated the style. However, the government viewed Kabuki as excessively provocative and banned women from performing in 1629. Today, Kabuki, like Noh, exists as an all-male art form. Unlike Noh plays, Kabuki plays are extravagant and unrestrained. They usually have a historical or domestic focus and feature lower-class heroes who resist oppression by the nobility. For example, the famous *Chushingura* (1748) tells the story of a band of samurai who revenge the death of their lord. Like Noh, Kabuki makes use of dance, music, and stylized gestures. However, Kabuki performers wear no masks and constantly interact with the audience. A Kabuki stage has passageways projecting into the audience on the left and right, which means the actors can encircle the audience. Kabuki programs continue from morning to night, accompanied by a continuous coming and going of the audience. Sometimes performers stop and address the crowd directly. Occasionally members of the audience break into the performance to praise a favorite scene or to call out the name of a favorite performer.

Contemporary Renditions

Twentieth-century playwright Mishima Yukio (1925–1970), reacting to what he saw as a deadening in modern Japanese culture, wrote his own version of *The Damask Drum*, in which he used the central image from the Seami play in a modern setting. Today's international performances of Noh and Kabuki range from classical renderings of Seami to Kabuki versions of Shakespeare plays. Recent productions of *Kabuki Othello* (1986) and *Kabuki Lady Macbeth* (2005) illustrate the appeal of these forms in the West.

Japanese Kabuki actor Kankuro Nakamura (foreground) performs with his sons Kantaro and Hichinosuke.

 **Literature** Online

Literature and Reading For more about Noh and Kabuki, go to glencoe.com and enter QuickPass code GLW6053u4.

Respond and Think Critically

1. How are Noh and Kabuki dramas similar? How do they differ?

2. Why might Seami have believed "no action" was one of the most powerful elements of Noh?

3. Review the information on Greek drama on pages 248–249. How does Noh drama compare with Greek tragedy?

4. What do the conventions and subjects of Noh and Kabuki dramas reflect about Japanese culture?

Advanced Learners/Pre-AP

DIFFERENTIATED INSTRUCTION

Visualize Invite advanced learners to read a Noh drama such as *The Damask Drum*. One important ability skilled readers possess is the ability to picture the characters and actions in a literary work. This ability is particularly valuable when reading drama, because a play is meant to be seen. As an aid to visualizing a play's action, students can chart the characters' movement on stage. Have students work in small groups to examine the text of the play and develop flow charts for the movement of the play's characters. Since there are no stage directions, students will have to use textual clues to determine appropriate movement. Have volunteer groups stage their versions of the Noh play for the class.

Assess

1. Both Noh and Kabuki dramas use elaborate costumes, gestures, and music. However, while Noh was created for the nobility, Kabuki was created for the common people. Noh plays address spiritual matters, while Kabuki plays usually have historical or domestic subjects. Kabuki actors do not wear masks and have more interaction with audiences than Noh actors.

2. Students may mention the power silence has to convey meaning. They may feel the visual elements of Noh drama, such as masks and costumes, would also be powerful and meaningful in and of themselves.

3. Noh includes many elements typical of Greek drama, including tragic plots, male performers, masks, a chorus, dancing, and music. In Noh drama, however, plots are less complex and actions are more symbolic.

4. Students may say the conventions and subjects of Noh and Kabuki dramas reflect the strict social hierarchy that existed in medieval Japan. They might also say the styles reflect the elaborate aesthetics of the Japanese court.

Before You Read

Focus

Bellringer Options

**Selection Focus
Transparency 44**

**Daily Language Practice
Transparency 65**

Or draw a blank web diagram on the board with the word "spring-time" in the center bubble. **Ask:** What moods or feelings do you associate with springtime? Fill in the outer bubbles of the diagram with students' responses.

Literary History ☆

Haiku's Popularity The haiku form has become popular around the world, and today, haiku are written in many different languages. In the early twentieth century, the Imagists, a group of British and American writers, popularized the form. By adopting the simple, clear images of haiku, they rejected what they saw as the sentimentality and excess of Victorian poetry. More recently, forums for sharing haiku have proliferated on the Internet, where subjects range from traditional to modern.

Before You Read

Haiku

Meet **the Poets**

The **haiku** (hī´kōō) is a Japanese poetic form consisting of seventeen syllables arranged in three lines. Because they are so short, haiku rely heavily on the power of suggestion. Words in a haiku are chosen for the associations they create in the reader's mind.

> *"Don't follow in the footsteps of the old poets, seek what they sought."*
>
> —Matsuo Bashō

Bashō, the Master (1644–1694) Matsuo Bashō (mät sōō´ō bä´shō) is known as Japan's master of the haiku, and he lived a wandering life that matched his poetic principles. Bashō began to follow his father's footsteps by leading the life of a samurai, adopting the samurai name Matsuo Munefusa. When his master died suddenly, Bashō changed paths, leaving his samurai training to travel and pursue writing, eventually moving to the capital of Japan, Edo (now Tokyo). There his writing attracted attention and a group of students built the poet a simple hut with a banana tree next to it. The satisfied poet then took his pen name, Bashō, from the Japanese word for "banana plant." His style—influenced by Chinese poetry and Zen Buddhism—revitalized the haiku form, which Bashō felt had become too rigid and focused on trivial themes. Many of Bashō's poems deal with finding ecstasy in the solitude of watching a dramatic snowstorm or a clear moon.

Yosa Buson (1716–1784) and Kobayashi Issa (1763–1828) Yosa Buson (yō sa´ōō sōn´) was born into a rich family but abandoned his wealth to study painting and poetry in Edo.

Matsuo Basho. Painted portrait. Osaka, Japan.

Though he became an accomplished painter, Buson is best known for his haiku, which display a fascination with color and visual detail. The life of Kobayashi Issa (kō bä yä´shē ē´sä), another great haiku poet, was marked by tragedy. He lost his mother at age two and later, his wife and children. His poems reflect the pain from these losses.

The Rise of Haiku The haiku developed from a Japanese poetic form called the **renga**. To create a renga, one poet would write the first three lines of a **tanka** (in which the first and third lines have five syllables each; the three other lines have seven syllables each), and a second poet would complete the poem. Another poet would then begin the next tanka, or link, in the renga. In the hands of Bashō and his contemporaries, the first three lines, or *hokku* (ho´kōō), of the renga became an independent verse form eventually known as the haiku. Traditionally, the first and third lines of a haiku have five syllables each and the middle line has seven. However, Bashō often departed from these syllable counts, although he retained the longer second line and the shorter first and third lines. The compressed form of the haiku required Bashō, Buson, and Issa to carefully choose and arrange their words.

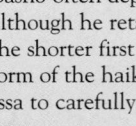

Literature Online

Author Search For more about Bashō, Buson, and Issa, go to glencoe.com and enter QuickPass code GLW6053u4.

Selection Skills

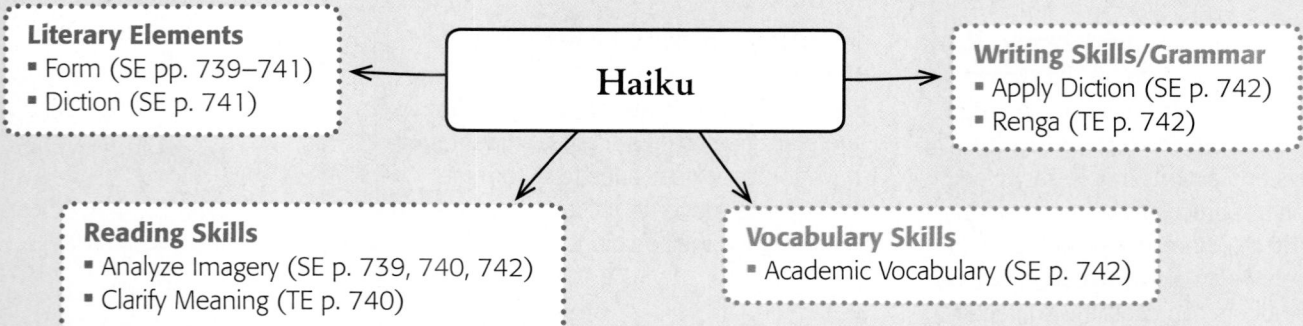

Literary Elements
- Form (SE pp. 739–741)
- Diction (SE p. 741)

Haiku

Writing Skills/Grammar
- Apply Diction (SE p. 742)
- Renga (TE p. 742)

Reading Skills
- Analyze Imagery (SE p. 739, 740, 742)
- Clarify Meaning (TE p. 740)

Vocabulary Skills
- Academic Vocabulary (SE p. 742)

Literature and Reading Preview

Connect to the Poems

What emotions do you associate with each of the four seasons? Discuss this question with a partner.

Build Background

Traditional haiku were written according to strict guidelines. Poems were considered incomplete without a *kigo* (kē′ gō)—a word or an image pertaining to a season. For example, haiku readers understood that cherry blossoms suggested spring, evening showers suggested summer, and snowfall suggested winter. ☆

Set Purposes for Reading

Big Idea Moments of Reflection

As you read, ask yourself, How do the poets use nature imagery to reflect on universal themes?

Literary Element Form

Form refers to the structure of a poem. For example, the traditional haiku form consists of three lines with the syllable pattern 5-7-5. Form can also consist of other structural elements such as a **caesura**, or pause, which often signals a change of subject. As you read, ask yourself, How does the haiku form contribute to the meanings of the poems?

Reading Strategy Analyze Imagery

When you **analyze imagery**, you examine individual images in a poem to help you understand the meaning of the whole poem. One element to look for is an **implied comparison**, or a comparison made by connecting two images in a new or unexpected way rather than by stating that one image is another (metaphor) or is *like* another (simile). As you read, look for examples of implied comparison in the poems and ask yourself, What ideas do the comparisons evoke?

Tip: Use a Web As you read the haiku, use a web like the one below to diagram the ideas you associate with the images in the poems.

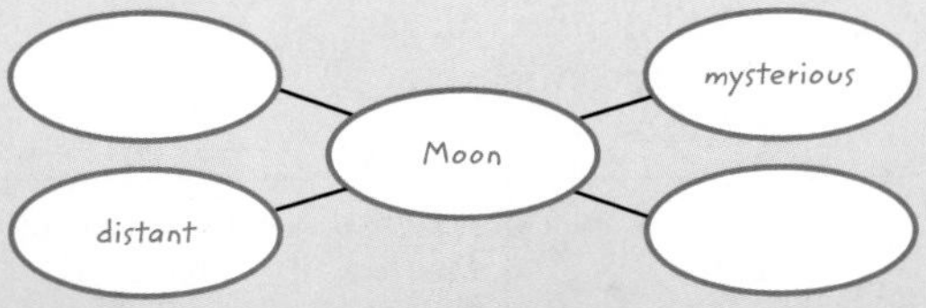

Learning Objectives

For pages 738–741

In studying this text, you will focus on the following objectives:

Literary Study: Analyzing form.

Reading: Analyzing imagery.

Writing: Applying diction.

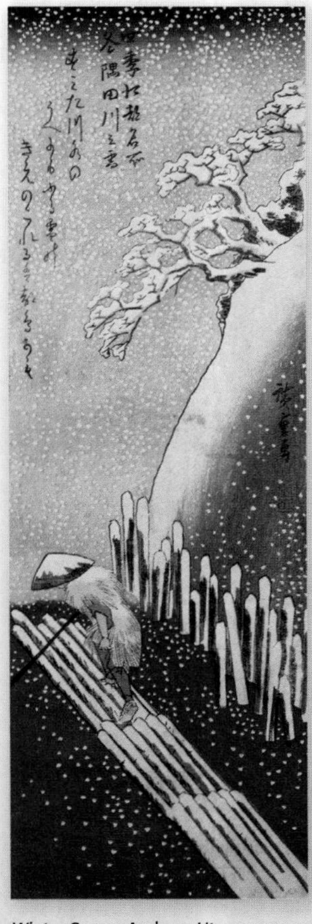

Winter Scene. Ando or Utagawa Hiroshige. Colour woodblock print. Victoria & Albert Museum, London.

Before You Read

Focus

Summary

In the first haiku by Bashō, a poor child pauses in his work to gaze at the moon; in the second, spring flowers turn to follow the path of the sun. In the first haiku by Buson, people with straw capes and umbrellas walk through a spring rainstorm; in the second, a child's ball, forgotten on a roof, soaks in the rain. In the first haiku by Issa, morning dew rapidly disappears; in the second, children run outside to play as the snow melts.

For summaries in languages other than English, see Unit 4 Teaching Resources Book, pp. 107–112.

Cultural History ☆

Japan's Climate References to rain and snow are common in Japanese haiku, which is not surprising since the country's climate is characterized by frequent precipitation. The rainiest season occurs in June and July, and is known as the *baiu*, or plum rain, because it coincides with the ripening of plums.

English Learners

DIFFERENTIATED INSTRUCTION

Intermediate Encourage English learners to use context clues to clarify the meaning of unfamiliar words as they read the haiku. Demonstrate this process with the word *hollyhocks*, in the second haiku by Bashō. **Model:** I'm not sure what hollyhocks are, but I know that haiku are usually about the natural world, so hollyhocks are probably a natural thing, like a plant or an animal. The poem says they "turn toward" the path of the sun, and I know that flowering plants grow toward the sun, so hollyhocks are probably a type of flower.

Teach

Literary Element | 1

Form Answer: *It uses a kigo, or season word.*

ENGLISH LEARNERS Phrases that suggest "spring" to certain students may not suggest that season to those who come from other regions of the world. Group together English learners and have them make lists of the natural phenomena that suggest "spring" in their home countries.

Progress Check

Can students analyze form?

If No → See Unit 4 Teaching Resources Book, p. 113.

Reading Strategy | 2

Analyze Imagery Answer: *Children run out to play as the sun begins to melt the snow.*

Progress Check

Can students analyze imagery?

If No → See Unit 4 Teaching Resources Book, p. 114.

View the Art ★

The image on this page, a calendar print for the year 1765, is like a *haiku* in that it captures a moment in a sudden rainstorm. The artist, Suzuki Haranobu, often portrayed images of the fleeting moments of everyday life.

To check students' understanding of the selection, see Unit 4 Teaching Resources Book, p. 115.

740

Haiku

Young Woman in a Summer Shower, 1765. Suzuki Haranobu (Japanese, 1724–1770). Woodblock print, 28.6 x 22 cm. Clarence Buckingham Collection, The Art Institute of Chicago, IL. ★

Matsuo Bashō
Translated by Harold G. Henderson

Poverty's child—
    he starts to grind the rice,
      and gazes at the moon.

The sun's way:
    hollyhocks turn toward it
      through all the rain of May.

Yosa Buson
Translated by Geoffrey Bownas
and Anthony Thwaite

Spring rain:
Telling a tale as they go,
Straw cape, umbrella.

Spring rain:
Soaking on the roof
A child's rag ball.

Kobayashi Issa
Translated by Geoffrey Bownas and
Anthony Thwaite

The world of dew is
A world of dew . . . and yet,
And yet . . .

Melting snow:
And on the village
Fall the children.

1 Form *Review the background information on page 739. How is this opening line typical of the haiku form?*

Analyze Imagery *What action does this image convey?* **2**

Reading Practice

 SMALL GROUP

Clarify Meaning Students may find that their comprehension of haiku is enhanced by spending some time filling in what has been left out because of the strictures of the form. Demonstrate with the first of the Buson haiku by writing the following on the board:

I look out my window in the spring rain and see two friends walking together, telling a tale as they go. One is wearing a straw cape; the other is holding an umbrella. They make a lovely picture. Have small groups elaborate on the other five haiku. Have each group share some elaborations. Point out that elaborating on the poems can help students understand them more fully, but it also robs the poems of some of their purity and simplicity.

740

After You Read

Respond and Think Critically

Respond and Interpret

1. What do you think of the haiku form? Do you find it puzzling or enjoyable? Explain.

2. (a)What images in Buson's poems follow the words "Spring rain"? (b)What moods or emotions do these images suggest?

3. (a)What can you infer about the life of the boy in the first poem by Bashō? (b)What might cause him to gaze at the moon?

4. (a)Where do the hollyhocks turn in the second poem by Bashō? (b)What do you think is the significance of their action?

Analyze and Evaluate

5. **Connotations** are the associations a word brings to mind beyond its dictionary definition.

Describe all the connotations that words in one of the haiku have for you.

6. (a)What *kigo,* or season word, is present in the second poem by Buson? (b)In light of your associations with this season, did you find the poem surprising? Explain.

7. (a)Do you find the last line of the second poem by Issa surprising? Explain. (b)What does this line reveal about the speaker's attitude toward the subject matter?

Connect

8. **Big Idea** **Moments of Reflection** What universal themes about nature do these haiku reflect?

9. **Connect to the Author** Do you think Issa's poems reflect the sorrows he experienced in his life? Explain.

Literary Element Form

Poets use **form**, such as the haiku's arrangement of lines, to enhance the emotional and thematic effects of their poems.

1. (a)Where do the **caesuras**, or pauses, occur in the two haiku by Bashō? (b)What are the effects of the caesuras?

2. What is the effect of the break between the second and third lines of the second haiku by Issa?

3. What do you think might be gained or lost by rewriting these haiku as longer, free-verse poems?

Review: Diction

As you learned on page 525, **diction** is an author's word choice. In a short poem such as a haiku, the poet must select each word very carefully, considering its meanings and connotations. Translators of haiku also must select words carefully to preserve

the spirit of the original. Two translators of the same poem may interpret it very differently.

Partner Activity Meet with a partner to read and compare these two different translations of a haiku by Bashō. Then discuss the following questions.

Poverty's child—
    he starts to grind the rice,
        and gazes at the moon.
                    —Harold G. Henderson translation

The young farm-child
interrupts rice husking to
gaze up at the moon
                    —Sam Hamill translation

1. (a)How would you describe the diction in each of these translations? (b)What effects does the diction in each create? Support your response with examples from the translations.

2. Which translation do you prefer? Explain.

After You Read

Assess

1. Answers will vary.

2. (a) A straw cape, an umbrella, and a child's rag ball (b) Comfort and safety in the first poem, melancholy in the second

3. (a) It is difficult; he works hard, even at night. (b) It may help him see beyond the harsh reality of his life.

4. (a) Toward the sun (b) It shows the power of the sun and may suggest the hollyhocks' faith that summer will come.

5. Answers will vary.

6. (a) *Spring* (b) Students who associate spring with happiness may be surprised by the poem's melancholy feeling. Others may anticipate this mood from the word *rain.*

7. (a) It is unexpected because one does not expect children to "fall" on the village. (b) It playfully reverses expectations; the speaker has an amused attitude about the children's bursting out of their homes.

8. Possible answer: Even as we are admiring natural beauty, time passes and nature changes.

9. While the first poem hints at the transience of life, the second poem rejoices in the happiness of children.

Literary Element

1. (a) After the first line (b) In the first poem, the pause gives the reader time to contemplate the idea of "poverty's child" before the poet gives an elaborating image. In the second poem, the caesura separates two distinct images. In both, the pauses create stillness and tension.

2. The line break creates a pause,

enhancing the elements of surprise and humor in the last line.

3. Possible answer: Doing so would allow one to describe the images more completely, but it would also rob the poems of some of their spare, pure quality.

Review: Diction

1. (a) The first translation's diction is more poetic and suggestive of a

melancholy mood, while the second translation's diction is more stilted and literal sounding. (b) Possible response: Henderson's use of "poverty's child" in place of "farm-child" creates a sadder picture.

2. Students may prefer Henderson's translation for its vivid language and powerful punctuation. Others may enjoy the style and sense of mystery Hamill's translation creates.

After You Read

Assess

Reading Strategy

C is the correct answer. Issa shows a link between nature and human beings in showing how children come tumbling out to play when the weather turns warm and the snow begins to melt. The poem doesn't suggest fragility or death, so **A** and **B** are incorrect. The poem doesn't comment on children's opinion of winter, so **D** and **E** are incorrect.

Academic Vocabulary

Students should complete the sentence with actions or qualities that signify goodness. They might mention being responsible, obeying rules, or volunteering.

Write with Style

Students' essays should
- describe an experience with nature
- include both prose and haiku
- present an overall impression through specific details
- use diction that contributes to the overall impression
- use sentences of varying lengths

Reading Strategy · Analyze Imagery

SAT Skills Practice

Issa compares imagery of melting snow and children to

A. emphasize how fragile human life is

B. highlight the impermanence of natural beauty

C. show the interconnectedness of humans and nature

D. suggest that children like winter more than summer

E. prove that rural children enjoy winter

Academic Vocabulary

Haiku often present a **paradigm** *of interconnectedness between humans and the natural world, linking human life to the passage of time and the seasons.*

Paradigm is a word often used in academic settings. Classical Greek democracy was the **paradigm** for the government of the United States. To study this word further, finish the sentence below. If you need help, look up the word in a dictionary.

Someone who is a paradigm of virtue might _____, _____, or _____.

For more on academic vocabulary, see pages 36–37 and R83–R85.

Haiku View of Mt. Fuji (detail). **Katsushika Hokusai (1760–1849). Color woodblock print. Chester Beatty Library and Gallery of Oriental Art, Dublin.**

742 UNIT 4 EAST ASIA

Write with Style

 Apply Diction

Assignment Haiku masters such as Bashō labored over each word to create brief, crystal clear descriptions that reflect broad thematic ideas. Apply this careful diction and form to your own descriptive essay reflecting on an experience with nature you have had.

Get Ideas In addition to haiku, Bashō wrote *haibun*—travelogues that intersperse haiku with prose descriptions of his journeys. Read the following excerpt from Bashō's *Narrow Road to the Interior* (translated by Sam Hamill) to gain a deeper context for his method of recording his experiences from nature in prose and haiku. Notice how Bashō evokes complex themes through simple diction. Use this example as a model for your essay. You can also gather ideas using an imagery web like the one on page 739.

Monks at the foot of the mountain offered rooms, then we climbed the ridge to the temple, scrambling up through ancient gnarled pine and oak, gray smooth stones and moss. The temple doors, built on rocks, were bolted. I crawled among boulders to make my bows at shrines. The silence was profound. I sat, feeling my heart begin to open.

Lonely stillness—
a single cicada's cry
sinking into stone.

Give It Structure Be sure to have in mind an overall impression you want your reader to gain from your description. Strive to make every element of your description contribute to this overarching impression. Include both prose and haiku in your description as Bashō does.

Look at Language Check the variety of your sentences. Try using a short sentence to highlight a key description, such as Bashō's sentence "The silence was profound." Use a thesaurus to find the ideal adjectives for your description.

 LOG ON ▶ **Literature** Online

Selection Resources For Selection Quizzes, eFlashcards, and Reading-Writing Connection activities, go to glencoe.com and enter QuickPass code GLW6053u4.

Writing Practice

Renga Remind students that the haiku form developed out of the first three lines of a *renga*—a type of collaborative poem in which multiple tanka are linked together. Have students reread the information about the tanka form on page 713 and the information about the renga form on page 738.

Then have them split into groups of three and write rengas of their own. Students should agree upon a length for their renga before they begin. Have one student write the first three lines of the first tanka in the renga, and the second write the final two lines of the first tanka. Have the third student write the first three lines of the next tanka, the first student write the final three lines, and so forth. They should rotate in this manner until the renga reaches the desired length. Encourage them to focus more on the continuity and flow of the lines than on strict syllable counts as they write.

 For additional selection assessment, see Assessment Resources, pp. 149–150.

Literary Perspective

on *Haiku*

FROM

THE ESSENTIAL *Haiku*

Robert Hass

National Book Critics Circle Award Winner

Learning Objectives

For pages 743–747

In studying this text, you will focus on the following objectives:

Literary Study:
Analyzing literary traditions.
Making connections across literature.
Analyzing informational text.

Set a Purpose for Reading

Read to appreciate and understand more about the haiku form.

Build Background

Robert Hass is a former poet laureate of the United States who has produced acclaimed translations of the haiku of Bashō, Buson, and Issa. Hass's own poetry has been strongly influenced by Japanese haiku. In the following excerpt from the introduction to *The Essential Haiku*, Hass discusses how Japanese views of nature and spirituality influenced the development of haiku.

Reading Strategy **Evaluate Historical Influences**

When you **evaluate historical influences**, you examine background information related to the writing of literary works. As you read, take notes on how historical Japanese literary conventions shaped the haiku of Bashō, Buson, and Issa. Use a two-column chart like the one below.

Aspect of Japanese Literary Tradition	Effect on Haiku Form

I t is a truism of Japanese literary criticism that the[se] three men represent three types of the poet—Bashō the ascetic and seeker, Buson the artist, Issa the humanist—and their differences are clear at a glance when you read them. Here is a fall poem that has Bashō's poignant calm and spiritual restlessness:

> Deep autumn—
> my neighbor,
> how does he live, I wonder?

And this winter poem was Buson's painterly mix of precision and strangeness:

> Tethered horse;
> snow
> in both stirrups.

And here is a summer poem of Issa's, with its pathos and humor:

> Don't worry, spiders,
> I keep house
> casually.

ROBERT HASS **743**

Literary Perspective

on *Haiku*

Focus

Summary

Hass traces the emergence of the haiku form. He argues that the haiku of Bashō, Buson, and Issa were more influenced by the poets' individual personalities than by the Japanese literary tradition. He notes, however, that the seasonal references in these haiku convey deeply traditional themes about nature and human life. Hass also praises the haiku form's mysterious ability to capture fleeting moments in time.

Teach

Literary History

Sabi Bashō coined the term *sabi* to describe what he believed to be an essential quality of haiku. The term, which he derived from a Japanese word meaning "loneliness," refers to an awareness of the fleeting, transient nature of earthly things, as well as a sense of quiet melancholy.

For activities related to this selection, see Unit 4 Teaching Resources Book, pp. 117–125.

Advanced Learners/Pre-AP

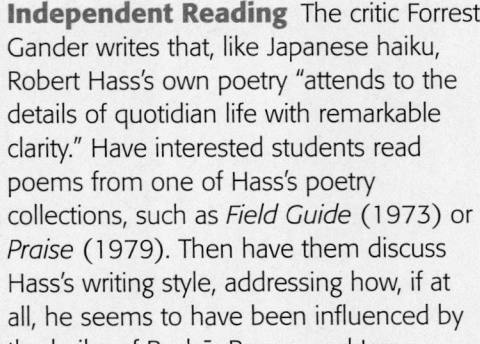

DIFFERENTIATED INSTRUCTION

Independent Reading The critic Forrest Gander writes that, like Japanese haiku, Robert Hass's own poetry "attends to the details of quotidian life with remarkable clarity." Have interested students read poems from one of Hass's poetry collections, such as *Field Guide* (1973) or *Praise* (1979). Then have them discuss Hass's writing style, addressing how, if at all, he seems to have been influenced by the haiku of Bashō, Buson, and Issa.

Learning Objectives
Evaluating historical influences. (SE)

Teach

Big Idea 1

Moments of Reflection

Read the following quotation from Bashō aloud: "The old verse can be about willows. Haikai requires crows picking snails on a rice paddy." **Ask:** What strikes you about these two images? *(Possible answer: One is classically beautiful; the other is unconventional, specific, and not necessarily beautiful.)* **Ask:** Which of these images is easier to visualize? *(Students will probably choose the second image.)* **Ask:** How does the comparison of these two images help you understand what was "new" about the haiku form? (Possible answer: Unlike the classical poets, who used timeless, general nature imagery, haiku poets used images that were fleeting, original, and specific.)*

Readability Scores

Dale-Chall: 11
DRP: 65
Lexile: 1240

Their careers span the great flowering of the haiku form. Bashō lived in the latter half of the seventeenth century, Buson in the middle of the eighteenth, Issa at the end of the eighteenth and the beginning of the nineteenth. Much of what has been done with this small form, they did. . . .

The *hokku,* as it was called in Bashō's time, emerged, almost accidentally, from the practice of linked verse. It was, from the beginning, very attentive to time and place. It tended to begin with a theme from classical poetry—the poetry of the Heian court—that was associated with a season of the year. It then added an image that seemed to penetrate to the essence of the classical theme. The spirit of haiku required that the language be kept plain. "The function of haikai," Bashō once said, "is to rectify common speech." It also demanded accurate **1** and original images, drawn mostly from common life. "The old verse can be about willows," Bashō also said, "Haikai requires crows picking snails in a rice paddy." He insisted on poetry as a serious calling. One of the fascinations of his life is that it amounted to years of immensely subtle thinking about how to give resonance and depth to the image, which he worked out in practice in his own work and with his friends and students. "A poet," he said, "needs to discipline himself every day."

2 The insistence on time and place was crucial for writers of haiku. The seasonal reference was called a *kigo* and a haiku was thought to be incomplete without it. In Bashō's poem quoted above, for example, the phrase *aki fukaki,* "deep autumn" or "autumn deepens" is traditional and had accumulated resonances and associations from earlier poetry as well as from the Japanese way of thinking about time and change. So does the reference to snow—

yuki, which can also mean "snowfall"— in Buson's poems. It is always connected to a sense of exposure to the elements, for which there is also a traditional phrase, *fuyuzare,* which means "winter bareness." The practice was sufficiently codified and there was even a rule that the seasonal reference should always appear either in the first or third unit of the three phrase poem. Buson's poem—it is typical of him— violates that rule and an attentive reader might be led to ask what the connection is between the unexpected snow in the second line and the tethered horse or the rather mysterious snow in both stirrups. In the same way, the spiders in Issa's poem were a traditional mid-summer theme.

These references were conventional and widely available. They were the first way readers of the poems had of locating themselves in the haiku. Its traditional themes— deep autumn, a sudden summer shower, the images of rice seedlings and plum blossoms, of spring and summer migrants like the mountain cuckoo and the bush warbler, of the cormorant-fishermen in summer, and the apprentices on holiday in the spring—gave a powerful sense of a human place in the ritual and cyclical movement of the world.

If the first level of a haiku is its location in nature, its second is almost always some implicit Buddhist reflection on nature. One of the striking differences between Christian and Buddhist thought is that in the Christian sense of things, nature is fallen,[1] and in the Buddhist sense it isn't. Another is that, because there is no creator-being in Buddhist cosmology, there

---

1. The Christian doctrine of the Fall says ever since the time humans first sinned and were banished from an earthly paradise, the natural world has been harsh, imperfect, and distant from God.

Skills Practice

SMALL GROUP

Use Dashes Write on the board:

Deep autumn—
my neighbor,
how does he live, I wonder?

Buson's poem—it is typical of him— violates that rule.

Remind students that em dashes (—) can be used to indicate an abrupt break or change in a sentence, as in the first example, or to set off a parenthetical statement,

as in the second example. Have them work in groups to punctuate the following sentences with em dashes:

There was only one tree in the field a twisted, withered elm. *(There was only one tree in the field—a twisted, withered elm.)*

The bird a small warbler perched on the windowsill. *(The bird—a small warbler—perched on the windowsill.)*

Don't go I need your help. *(Don't go—I need your help.)*

Evening Snow on the Asuka Mountain, from *Eight Views of Environs of Edo,* c.1838. Ando or Utagawa Hiroshige. Woodblock colour print. Brooklyn Museum of Art, New York. ★

is no higher plane of meaning to which nature refers. At the core of Buddhist metaphysics are three ideas about natural things: that they are transient; that they are contingent; and that they suffer. Though the melancholy of autumn is as traditional an experience in European poetry as it is Japanese, it is not fundamentally assimilated into the European system of thought. English poets had a word for these feelings, they called them "moods." When Wordsworth or Keats[2] writes about being "in pensive or in wayward mood," you know that they're doing one of the jobs of the artist, trying to assimilate psychological states for which

the official culture didn't have a language. Bashō's Japan did. The old Japanese phrase that sums up the transience of things, "swirling petals, falling leaves," was a religious thought.

Bashō's "Deep autumn" is a poem about the transience of things, and Bashō has connected it to a particular expression of spiritual loneliness. Buson's "Tethered horse" would, for Japanese readers, connect it through the image of a snowstorm to our mortal bareness, and the horse's tether would lead a reader to think quite naturally that suffering is a condition of creatures. Issa's busy spiders make their webs in a

2. William Wordsworth (1770–1850) and John Keats (1795–1821) were English Romantic poets.

ROBERT HASS **745**

Literary Perspective
on *Haiku*

Teach

Literary Element | 2

Setting Note to students that this emphasis on time and place in haiku can be related to the concept of setting in prose. **Ask:** What restrictions are put on time within the haiku form? *(The time aspect should focus on one of the four seasons.)* **Ask:** Are there any restrictions put on place? *(Students may say that natural environments are emphasized.)*

View the Art ★

Have students compare this woodblock print with the one on page 739. **Ask:** What are some similar elements in the two prints? *(Students may mention the trees and the human figures.)* **Ask:** What are some different elements? *(Students may say that it appears to be snowing harder in the first scene, which focuses more on the human activity and includes a body of water. The second print focuses more on the landscape.)*

English Learners

DIFFERENTIATED INSTRUCTION

Advanced English learners may have difficulty with Hass's sentences, which contain many subordinate clauses and parenthetical phrases. Encourage students to break down sentences, omitting clauses and parenthetical phrases. For example, the sentence "The *hokku,* as it was called in Bashō's time, emerged, almost accidentally, from the practice of linked verse" could be read as "The

hokku emerged from the practice of linked verse." Then, once students have grasped the core meaning of each sentence, have them reintroduce the clauses and phrases and think about the meaning of the sentence as a whole. Remind them to look up any unfamiliar words in a dictionary.

Learning Objectives
Evaluating historical influences. (SE)
Analyzing setting. (SE)
Using dashes. (TE)

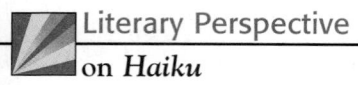

Literary Perspective
on *Haiku*

Teach

Literary History ☆

"Images Haunt" Robert Hass has written extensively on the effect of images on the imagination. "Images haunt," he writes in his 1984 prose collection *Twentieth Century Pleasures*. He continues, "We all live our lives in the light of . . . sets of images that get us up in the morning and move us about our days. I do not think anybody can live without one, for very long, without suffering intensely from deadness or futility."

Flowers and insects. Painting, hanging scroll. The Trustees of the Chester Beatty Library, Dublin.

world peculiarly contingent on the whims of housekeepers with their own notions of useful activity, and they happened to be spared by the moods of summer, which in turn make the argument for a kind of compassion. All three poems represent quite traditional Japanese ways of thinking about being.

But what has fascinated all readers about them is that they are also something more, or other, than that. They have a quality of actuality, of the moment seized on and rendered purely, and because of this they seem to elude being either traditional images of nature or ideas about it. The formal reason for this mysteriousness is that they don't

Reading Practice

Interpret Meaning The second paragraph on page 744 contains the following quotation from Bashō: "The function of haikai [haiku] is to rectify common speech." Review with students the meaning of *rectify,* and then discuss the possible meaning of the quotation. **Ask: What is there about "common speech" that might need to be rectified?** *(Students may mention lack of precision and clarity.)* **Ask: What process might a** **writer of haiku use to rectify common speech.** *(Students may say that the writer might try to uncover the basic meaning of the speech and express it in concise, elegant verse..)* Point out that one difference between classical forms of poetry and modern forms is that some modern poets, such as Walt Whitman and William Carlos Williams, sought to celebrate common speech in their poetry rather than to alter it.

usually generalize their images. When the *hokku* became detached from linked verse, it also cast off the room the *tanka* provided for drawing a moral (though not all *tanka* do moralize, of course) and what was left was the irreducible mysteriousness of the images themselves. . . .

So much has been written by western commentators about the connection between haiku and Zen that I'm not inclined to say much about it here. A short version would be to say that Zen provided people training in how to stand aside and leave the meaning-making activity of the ego to its own devices. Not resisting it, but seeing it as another phenomenal thing, like bush warblers and snow fall, though more intimate to us. Trying to find this quality in every haiku, however, romanticizes them

and the culture they came from. It tends to make one rush to their final mysteriousness and silence. I know that for years I didn't see how deeply personal these poems were or, to say it another way, how much they have the flavor—Bashō might have said "the scent"—of a particular human life, because I had been told and wanted to believe that haiku were never subjective.... Better to sink down through the levels of these poems—their attention to the year, their ideas about it, the particular human consciousness the poems reflect, Bashō's profound loneliness and sense of suffering, Buson's evenness of temper, his love for the materials of art and for the color and shape of things, Issa's pathos and comedy and anger. One returns to their mysteriousness anyway. ◐

Respond and Think Critically

Respond and Interpret

1. Write a brief summary of the main ideas in this excerpt before you answer the following questions. For help in writing a summary, see page 1147.

2. (a)What is a *kigo*? (b)Why is it helpful to know about Japanese literary tradition in order to fully understand the meaning of a *kigo*?

3. (a)According to Hass, what are the three main Buddhist ideas about nature? (b)What does Hass mean when he says "there is no higher plane of meaning to which nature refers" in Buddhist thought?

4. (a)What is the relationship between the haiku form and the tanka form? (b)How does Hass use this relationship to explain the effects of haiku?

Analyze and Evaluate

5. Hass writes that looking for the Zen influence "in every haiku . . . romanticizes them and the culture they came from." What does this suggest about Hass's attitude toward using generalizations to understand literature?

6. (a)Which does Hass seem to think is a more important influence on these poets' work—their individual personalities, or their cultural traditions? Explain. (b)Which of these elements do you think is more important to take into account when interpreting literature? Explain.

Connect

7. Did Hass's individual characterizations of Bashō, Buson, and Issa change your understanding of the haiku on page 740? Explain.

ROBERT HASS **747**

Assess

1. Answers will vary.

2. (a) A *kigo* is the seasonal reference in a haiku. (b) *Kigo* have emotional and spiritual associations from their earlier use in Japanese literature.

3. (a) In the Buddhist view, natural things are transient, they are contingent, and they suffer. (b) He means Buddhists do not believe in a god who created nature, so they do not read nature as reflecting truths about God.

4. (a) The haiku form developed "almost accidentally" out of the tanka form. Haiku follows the same pattern as the first three lines of a tanka. (b) Hass says detaching the haiku from the tanka left no room to moralize or generalize and kept the focus on imagery.

5. It suggests he believes readers should look at each piece of literature individually, rather than trying to identify how it fits a generalization.

6. (a) Students may say he seems to think both are equally important. (b) Students should give logical reasons for their choices.

7. Answers will vary. Students should use specific passages from the essay and the poems to support their answers.

Advanced Learners/Pre-AP

DIFFERENTIATED INSTRUCTION

Fragments Students may notice that in the final paragraph Hass uses sentence fragments. Explain to students that this is a technique that professional writers use to add a conversational, varied quality to their writing. Have interested students identify the fragments. *(One begins "Not resisting it . . ."; another begins "Better to sink down . . ..")* Then have them discuss the effects of the fragments and why Hass may have

chosen to use them in these particular places. Encourage them to experiment with fragments in their own writing, but caution them that fragments should be used only where they sound natural and should be avoided in more formal writing.

Bellringer Options

**Selection Focus
  Transparency 45**
**Daily Language Practice
  Transparency 66**
Or: What are different ways one can change society? Discuss students' ideas about working within versus working against society to make a change.

Political History ☆

Cultural Revolution In 1966, Mao Zedong initiated the Cultural Revolution, a movement to suppress what he perceived as a growing acceptance of traditional "bourgeois" values, an increasing division of social classes, and a deterioration of communist ideals. Mao incited high school and university students to form an extremist paramilitary arm. The Red Guard, as it was called, terrorized, jailed, and tortured those perceived to be against Mao and communism. The Red Guard created chaos in urban areas; it eventually disbanded in the mid-1970s after years of internal strife.

Meet **Bei Dao**
(born 1949)

"In the world I am / Always a stranger," Bei Dao once wrote. "I do not understand its language / It does not understand my silence." However, through his words this revolutionary Chinese author has helped call people to action in his country.

Turning Against the Red Guards Bei Dao (bā dou′) was born in Beijing just two months before Mao Tse-tung made China a communist nation. As a boy, Bei attended one of Beijing's finest schools, which was open only to the elite. While at school, he enlisted in the Red Guards, the youth organization Mao charged with upholding the Communist Party's principles during the Cultural Revolution of the 1960s. Instead of revitalizing Chinese culture and society, the Red Guards soon devolved into a quasi-military group that violently persecuted intellectuals, artists, and teachers. Bei became disillusioned, turned his back on the Red Guards, and began to write poetry.

The Voice of a Generation Bei Dao earned his reputation as a poet during the 1970s. Partly in response to his disillusionment with the Cultural Revolution, he filled his poems with bold political statements and vivid imagery. He also rejected the idea that literature should promote communist ideology. Instead, Bei created verses that praised the power and the necessity of individual expression. His poems questioned everything, including the motives and the goals of the ruling party. In an attempt to discredit Bei and other dissident authors, critics labeled them the "Misty Poets," implying that their poems were vague and obscure. Yet despite critical opposition, the number of dissident poets continued to grow—and so did their audience.

"Freedom is only the distance between the hunter and his prey."

—Bei Dao

The Fight for Democracy In 1976 a new wave of discontent swept through China. In response Bei wrote his famous poem "Answer," which became the rallying cry of Chinese youth for democracy and social change. When he was 29, he began to publish an underground literary magazine, which the Chinese government eventually banned. In 1989 Bei was traveling in Europe when the Chinese government opened fire on a pro-democracy demonstration in Beijing's Tiananmen Square, killing several hundred unarmed protesters. At that point, Bei knew he was no longer safe in China. Since then, he has lived in exile in Europe and the United States. Despite the political thrust of much of his writing, Bei says, "You can't change society with poetry."

LOG ON ▶ **Literature** Online

Author Search For more about Bei Dao, go to glencoe.com and enter QuickPass code GLW6053u4.

Selection Skills

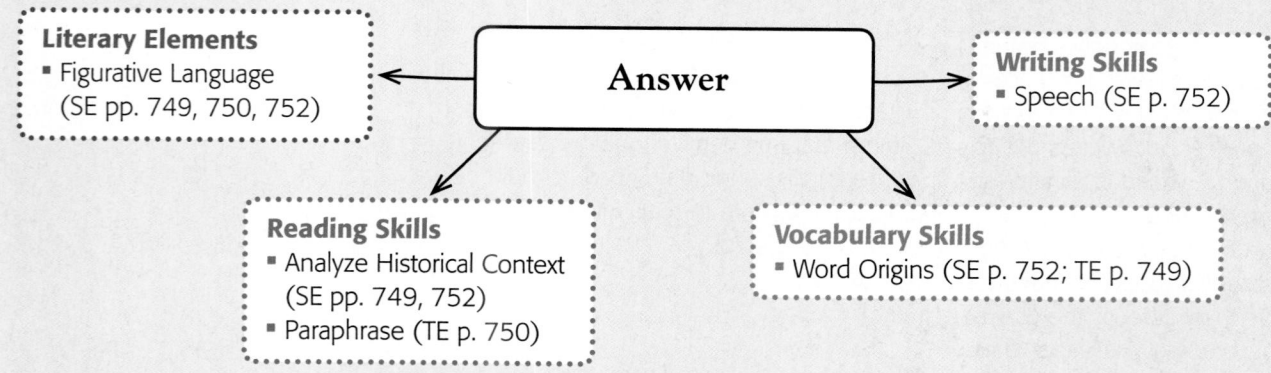

Literary Elements
- Figurative Language (SE pp. 749, 750, 752)

Answer

Writing Skills
- Speech (SE p. 752)

Reading Skills
- Analyze Historical Context (SE pp. 749, 752)
- Paraphrase (TE p. 750)

Vocabulary Skills
- Word Origins (SE p. 752; TE p. 749)

Literature and Reading Preview

Connect to the Poem

What historical figures have stood up against oppressive governments? Write a journal entry about someone who resisted an unjust government.

Build Background

During Mao Tse-tung's Cultural Revolution, radicals and moderates in the Chinese government vied for power. On April 5, 1976, large numbers of people began demonstrations in Beijing and other cities in support of the moderates. Bei Dao took part in this protest movement, called the April Fifth Movement. Police broke up the demonstrations, and the government condemned the protests as being "counterrevolutionary." Bei Dao wrote "Answer" in response.

Set Purposes for Reading

Big Idea Virtue and Wisdom

As you read, ask yourself, What has been the impact of social change in a nation founded on the ancient traditions of Confucianism and Taoism?

Literary Element Figurative Language

Figurative language is language used for descriptive effect to convey ideas or emotions. Figurative expressions include **similes** (comparisons using *like* or *as*) and **metaphors** (comparisons not using *like* or *as*). Figurative expressions are not literally true but express some truth beyond the literal level. As you read the poem, ask yourself, What phrases suggest ideas and truths beyond their literal meanings?

Reading Strategy Analyze Historical Context

When you **analyze historical context**, you examine the key issues of the time during which or about which a literary work was written. As you read "Answer," ask yourself, How does it reflect the time of the April Fifth Movement?

Tip: Link Details to Context As you read, use a chart to note details in the poem that relate to the historical context.

Details	Context
"The scoundrel carries his baseness around like an ID card."	

Learning Objectives

For pages 748–752

In studying this text, you will focus on the following objectives:

Literary Study: Analyzing figurative language.

Reading: Analyzing historical context.

Writing: Writing a speech.

Vocabulary

undulant (un´jə lənt) *adj.* having a wavy form or motion; p. 750 *The canoe rocked on the undulant surface of the lake.*

trample (tram´pəl) *v.* to walk upon and damage by crushing or bruising; to stomp; p. 750 *He had to run quickly so that the runaway steer would not trample him.*

reprisal (ri prī´zəl) *n.* the act of using force in retaliation for damage or loss suffered; p. 750 *The football team prepared for reprisal against their league rivals.*

glittering (glit´ər ing) *adj.* marked by a sparkling quality or brilliance; p. 751 *The night sky was filled with glittering stars.*

Tip: Word Origins You can find the origin of a word, or its etymology, in a dictionary. You can use word origins to help you unlock the meaning of unfamiliar words. For example, the word *undulant* derives from the Latin word *undula*, meaning "small wave."

BEI DAO **749**

Approaching Level

DIFFERENTIATED INSTRUCTION

Word Parts Explain to students that breaking a word into its word parts can help them remember the word's meaning and pronunciation. Encourage students to keep a vocabulary notebook. Have them write the vocabulary terms in their notebook and use a dictionary to help them circle the prefixes and suffixes in each word and underline the root. Then have students write the definition of each word part.

English Learners

DIFFERENTIATED INSTRUCTION

Intermediate Have students practice saying and using the vocabulary terms by making a story string in a small group. To help students get started, write a prompt on the board that uses the first vocabulary term, such as "Rick's boat swayed violently on the undulant sea." Then have students take turns using a different vocabulary term to explain what happens next in the story. Have them continue until they have each used every vocabulary term at least once.

Before You Read

Focus

Summary

In the poem "Answer," Bei Dao uses imagery and figurative language to condemn the oppressive regime behind communist China and the Cultural Revolution. In the first two stanzas, Dao exposes the pride with which government supporters tyrannize protesters, and the death sentence that protesters carry for believing in "truth." He compares China to the ice age and wonders why death (government) is chosen over hope (change). In the next three stanzas, he identifies himself as an enemy of the government and reveals his relentless distrust of it. In the last two stanzas, Bei establishes that he would fight to the death to see his country free and has faith that change will come.

📁 For summaries in languages other than English, see Unit 4 Teaching Resources Book, pp. 126–131.

Vocabulary

Word Origins Have students work with a partner to find the etymology of each vocabulary term. Have them use online resources or references in the library, such as a word history book, to find one interesting fact about the origin of each word. Have them create flash cards, writing each fact on one side of an index card and the corresponding word on the other side. Then ask students to take turns quizzing another team of partners.

📁 For additional vocabulary practice, see Unit 4 Teaching Resources Book, p. 134.

Teach

Figurative Language

Answer: *The speaker may be saying that contemporary times are backward, that his society is frozen in a single mindset, or that government is cold and heartless.*

For additional literary element practice, see Unit 4 Teaching Resources Book, p. 132.

Virtue and Wisdom

Answer: *The question might have been "Whose side are you on?" "Are you loyal to the party?" or "Do you believe in the cause?"*

(APPROACHING) For students who are having difficulty comprehending the Big Idea, explain that doing what you believe is right sometimes means standing up and fighting for what you believe in, even when many others think you are wrong. **Ask:** Why would someone not believe in a communist government? (*Communist governments limit individual freedoms and expression.*)

For an audio recording of this selection, use Listening Library Audio CD-ROM.

Reading Practice

Paraphrase Say: Since the poem consists mainly of figurative language, its overall meaning relies heavily on your interpretation of the figurative language. There are no lines that directly state the meaning of the poem. Tell students that paraphrasing, or retelling, each stanza can help improve their comprehension of the poem. Encourage students to work with a partner to rewrite the poem in their own words. Begin by having partners read the entire poem again. Then have them read one stanza at a time and discuss how to paraphrase it. Have students paraphrase the poem, write a one-sentence theme statement, and read their work aloud to the class.

750

ANSWER

Bei Dao

Translated by Donald Finkel with Chen Xueliang

The scoundrel carries his baseness around like an ID card.
The honest man bears his honor like an epitaph.
Look—the gilded° sky is swimming
with **undulant** reflections of the dead.

5   They say the ice age ended years ago.
Why are there icicles everywhere?
The Cape of Good Hope° has already been found.
Why should all those sails contend on the Dead Sea?

I came into this world with nothing
10 but paper, rope, and shadow.
Now I come to be judged,
and I've nothing to say but this:

Listen. *I don't believe!*
OK. You've **trampled**
15 a thousand enemies underfoot. Call me
a thousand and one.

I don't believe the sky is blue.
I don't believe what the thunder says.
I don't believe dreams aren't real,
20 that beyond death there is no **reprisal**.

3 gilded: deceptively attractive. A meaning no longer in use is "smeared with blood."

7 Cape of Good Hope: a rocky outcrop at the southernmost point in Africa.

---

1 Figurative Language *Why do you think the speaker compares his own time to the ice age?*

2 Virtue and Wisdom *If this poem serves as the speaker's "answer," what do you think the question was?*

Vocabulary

undulant (un′jə lənt) *adj.* having a wavy form or motion

trample (tram′pəl) *v.* to walk upon and damage by crushing or bruising; to stomp

reprisal (ri prī′zəl) *n.* the act of using force in retaliation for damage or loss suffered

Tien An Men Square Peaceful Protesters Carry the Statue of Democracy. Jacques Langevin. Beijing, China.

View the Photograph ★

The 1989 student protest at Tiananmen Square is captured in this photograph. A government-sanctioned violent halt of the protest resulted in the deaths of hundreds of student demonstrators. **Ask:** What does the statue represent, and how does it relate to the protesters' demands? *(It is an adaptation of the Statue of Liberty and reveals that the protesters demanded a democratic government.)*

To check students' understanding of the selection, see Unit 4 Teaching Resources Book, p. 136.

Progress Check

Can students analyze historical context?

If No → See Unit 4 Teaching Resources Book, p. 133.

If the sea should break through the sea-wall,
let its brackish° water fill my heart.
If the land should rise from the sea again,
we'll choose again to live in the heights.

25 The earth revolves. A **glittering** constellation
pricks the vast defenseless sky.
Can you see it there? that ancient ideogram—°
 the eye of the future, gazing back.

22 **brackish:** salty.

26 **ideogram:** a character or a symbol representing an idea. It is one type of pictograph.

Vocabulary

glittering (glit′ ər ing) *adj.* marked by a sparkling quality or brilliance

BEI DAO **751**

DIFFERENTIATED INSTRUCTION

Research Have students research the Tiananmen Square uprising of 1989 and create presentations. Tell them to find both primary and secondary sources in a variety of media, including print and online sources. Encourage the use of images. Have them focus on the causes and effects of the event. Consider introducing the assignment by displaying the famous photo of a single man standing and blocking the approach of a tank to Tiananmen Square.

After You Read

Assess

1. Answers wil vary.
2. (a) Counting the speaker, 1001 (b) The speaker stands with those who have been abused and against the authorities.
3. Hope for reprisal and continued resistance against the powers that be
4. (a) "I don't believe" (b) The repetition increases the poem's defiant power.
5. (a) The government should be swept away by the sea; from the flood, the people would rise up once again and life would be better. (b) They show that he is willing to endure anything, including death, for his beliefs.
6. Students may think the speaker's response does demonstrate wisdom because he is unwilling to blindly accept what the government mandates.
7. Students may mention the civil rights movement and peace marches.

Literary Element

1. In line 1, "like an ID card" signifies something the scoundrel is proud of. In line 2, "like an epitaph" suggests death and the danger of being honest in a dishonest or cowardly society.
2. The heights of human dignity or of unrestricted thought

Reading Strategy

1. Party members embrace their baseness; honesty may be punishable by death.
2. (a) The Cape of Good Hope and the Dead Sea (b) A political system that might allow hope and prosperity for the people and a stagnant and regimented system

752

After You Read

Respond and Think Critically

Respond and Interpret

1. Which lines in the poem do you find most memorable or striking?
2. (a)How many enemies does the poem say have been "trampled underfoot?" (b)What does this suggest about the speaker's relationship with the authorities?
3. According to line 20, what will the speaker have when he leaves the world?

Analyze and Evaluate

4. (a)What line does the speaker repeat several times? (b)Why do you think it is repeated?

5. (a)How would you paraphrase the statement the speaker makes in lines 21–24? (b)How do these lines illustrate the speaker's commitment to his beliefs?

Connect

6. **Big Idea** Virtue and Wisdom Do you think the speaker's response to the values of communist China demonstrates wisdom? Why or why not?

7. **Connect to Today** What are some contemporary examples, in the United States or elsewhere, of people fighting against the status quo to achieve a better political or social system?

Literary Element Figurative Language

A **simile** is a figure of speech that uses *like* or *as* to compare two things. A **metaphor** is a figure of speech that makes a comparison between two seemingly unlike things without using *like* or *as*.

1. Identify two similes in the poem and explain their meanings.
2. What "heights" is the speaker living in in line 24?

Reading Strategy Analyze Historical Context

Bei Dao compares opposing images to illuminate his point about the unfairness of his country's government.

1. What is the speaker suggesting in lines 1–2 about members of the Chinese Communist Party and the role of honesty in this society?
2. (a)In lines 7–8, what things does the poet contrast? (b)What larger comparison does this suggest?

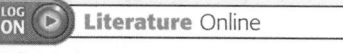 **Literature** Online

Selection Resources For Selection Quizzes, eFlashcards, and Reading-Writing Connection activities, go to glencoe.com and enter QuickPass code GLW6053u4.

Vocabulary Practice

Practice with Word Origins Create a word map like the one below for each of these vocabulary words. Use a dictionary for help.

undulant   trample   reprisal   glittering

EXAMPLE:

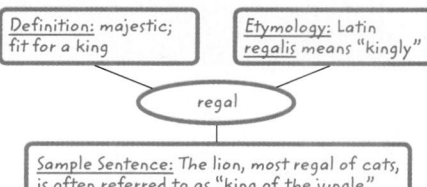

Definition: majestic; fit for a king

Etymology: Latin *regalis* means "kingly"

regal

Sample Sentence: The lion, most regal of cats, is often referred to as "king of the jungle."

Writing

Write a Speech Bei Dao makes bold statements in response to an unstated question. The question could ask a number of things, such as, Do you believe our version of the truth? Think of such a question that would provoke a strong response in you and then write a speech replying to that question. Use **figurative language** and review the chart you made on page 749 to see how you can shape your work with historical context.

Vocabulary

Sample responses:

undulant: <u>Definition:</u> having a wavy form or motion; <u>Etymology:</u> Latin <u>undula</u> means "small wave"; <u>Sample sentence:</u> The undulant mirrors in the fun house distorted my shape.

trample: <u>Definition:</u> to walk upon and damage by crushing; <u>Etymology:</u> Middle English <u>trampen</u> means "to tramp";

<u>Sample sentence:</u> When the dogs ran through our garden, they trampled many of our flowers.

Writing

Students' speeches should
- respond clearly to a question
- include figurative language

Before You Read

The Jay

Meet **Yasunari Kawabata**
(1899–1972)

Yasunari Kawabata's (kä wä bä′ tä) first piece of important writing was *Diary of My Sixteenth Year*, which he claimed he composed during twelve days in 1914. The diary was not published until 1925, however. Kawabata commented, "The strangest thing was that I had not the least recollection of the events described in the diary."

A Difficult Childhood By the time he turned sixteen, Kawabata's father, mother, and only sibling, a sister, had died, as had a grandmother and a grandfather with whom he had lived since becoming an orphan. These early experiences with tragedy may have contributed to Kawabata's desire to escape into the world of reading. Before he left elementary school, he had read every volume in the school library, including *The Tale of Genji* by Murasaki Shikibu and *The Pillow Book* by Sei Shōnagon (see page 716), books that he claimed had an enormous influence on his later writing.

A Budding Career While attending elite First High School in Tokyo and Tokyo Imperial University, Kawabata studied Japanese literature and translated some Russian and British short stories. His first published story, "A View of the Yasukuni Festival," won him favorable attention from important figures in the Japanese literary world. He also had work published in the literary magazine, *Bungei Shunju*, the first of many literary and critical publications to which Kawabata contributed. His first major success was a short story, "The Izu Dancer," based on his youthful attraction to a dancer.

> *"Many writers, in their youth, write poetry; I, instead of poetry, wrote the palm-of-the-hand stories . . . the poetic spirit of my young days lives on in them."*
>
> —Yasunari Kawabata

Finding His Voice Kawabata married, and in 1927, his wife gave birth to a daughter, who died in infancy. The couple agreed not to have more children. Kawabata expressed his unease about parenting, describing it as an "audacious experiment." Like many characters in his novels, Kawabata seemed to distance himself from close family relationships. Some critics have suggested that Kawabata's lonely childhood contributed to this view of life.

Kawabata also wrote many short stories, most of which he called "palm-of-the-hand stories" for their brevity. The stories have been compared to haiku because they create striking observations in few words. In 1968, he became the first Japanese author to win the Nobel Prize in Literature.

LOG ON ▶ **Literature** Online

Author Search For more about Yasunari Kawabata, go to glencoe.com and enter QuickPass code GLW6053u4.

Before You Read

Focus

Bellringer Options

Selection Focus
Transparency 46

Daily Language Practice
Transparency 67

Or ask: How would feel if you were about to meet someone whose first impression of you was very important? *(Students may say that they would be nervous or anxious.)* How would you prepare to meet him or her? *(Students may say that they would wear nice clothes and be polite.)*

Literary History ☆

Kawabata's Imagery When he was young, Kawabata wanted to be a painter. His love of and interest in art had a profound influence on his writing, which is marked by rich imagery. Color plays an especially important role in his striking descriptions; he often uses it to set particular moods in his stories or to create thematic associations.

Selection Skills

Literary Elements
- Conflict (SE pp. 754–756, 758, 760)
- Mood (SE p. 760)

The Jay

Writing Skills/Grammar
- Expository Essay (SE p. 761)
- Demonstrative Pronouns (TE p. 756)
- Participial Phrases (TE p. 758)

Reading Skills
- Review (SE pp. 754, 758, 760)
- Chart Sequence (TE p. 754)

Vocabulary Skills
- Word Origins (SE p. 760)
- Charades (TE p. 754)

Before You Read

Focus

Summary

As Yoshiko prepares to meet her estranged father and stepmother, as well as her future mother-in-law, she notices a jay searching for its lost chick. A marriage proposal has been arranged by Yoshiko's father, who moved away in anger when her brother mentioned a forbidden subject— his first wife, their mother. Before the guests' arrival, Yoshiko finds the baby bird and reunites it with its mother, mirroring the reconciliation she hopes to achieve by accepting her father's carefully negotiated proposal.

 For summaries in languages other than English, see Unit 4 Teaching Resources Book, pp. 138–143.

Vocabulary

 Charades Hand out cards with the vocabulary words written on them. Instruct students to embody the vocabulary word on their card without using words. The goal is to have classmates guess the word.

 For additional vocabulary practice, see Unit 4 Teaching Resources Book, p. 146.

Literature and Reading Preview

Connect to the Story

In your opinion, what long-term effects can divorce have on families? Freewrite for a few minutes about this issue.

Build Background

In Japan, as in many other Asian countries, parents traditionally arranged marriages. Marriage was viewed as an institution that served to satisfy family needs, and love was not considered a requirement. In this system, the wife devoted herself to caring for her husband's family under the direction of her mother-in-law. Since the 1920s, the traditional arranged marriage has become less common in Japanese culture.

Set Purposes for Reading

Big Idea Family and Tradition

As you read, ask yourself, How do Yoshiko's early family relationships influence her present life?

Literary Element Conflict

The central struggle between two opposing forces in a literary work is **conflict**. An **external conflict** arises when a character struggles against some outside force, such as nature, society, fate, or another person. An **internal conflict** takes place within the mind of a character who is torn between opposing feelings, desires, or goals. As you read "The Jay," ask yourself, Does the story resolve the conflicts it presents?

Reading Strategy Review

When you **review** a text, you reexamine what you've read to note what was important, and you organize your ideas so you can recall them later. You can also review background material to clarify a work's context. As you read, ask yourself, How do the events in the story unfold?

Tip: Chart Sequence Draw a simple timeline to chart the sequence of events in this story. Use Yoshiko's age or any other time markers you find convenient.

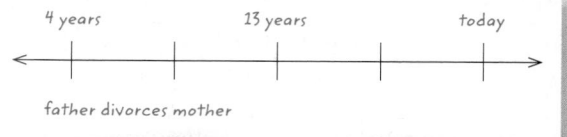

Learning Objectives

For pages 753–760

In studying this text, you will focus on the following objectives.

Literary Sutdy: Analyzing conflict.

Reading: Reviewing.

Vocabulary

furtively (fər′tiv lē) *adv.* in a secret manner; p. 755 *Furtively, the thieves cut the wires to the burglar alarm and forced open the door of the store.*

intransigence (in tran′sə jənts) *n.* the state of being uncompromising; p. 757 *My uncle's intransigence on money matters drives my aunt crazy.*

assiduously (ə sij′wəs lē) *adv.* in an attentive or busy manner; p. 758 *The host of the small inn assiduously set about making sure we had everything we needed.*

plaintively (plān′tiv lē) *adv.* in a manner expressing suffering or woe; p. 758 *As Sam left on his business trip, his small daughter called plaintively after him.*

Tip: Word Origins *Etymology* is the study of a word's history and origins. A word's etymology may give clues to its spelling and meaning. *Furtive*, for example, is related to the Greek words *phōr* and *pherein*, meaning "thief" and "to carry."

Reading Practice

Chart Sequence Tell students that much of this story is told in flashback, a technique in which the author inserts past events into the chronological sequence of the story. Some students may become confused regarding which events in the story happen in the present and which happen in the past.

Have students divide a sheet of paper into two columns, headed "Past" and "Present." Have them list the events of the story that are flashbacks in the "Past" column and the present events in the "Present" column.s

754

The Jay

Yasunari Kawabata

Translated by Lane Dunlop and
J. Martin Holman

Kobo Daishi (Kukai) as a Child, Kamakura period (1185–1333). Anonymous. Hanging scroll with ink and color on silk, 86.7 x 48.9 cm. Gift of the Joseph and Helen Regenstein Foundation. The Art Institute of Chicago, IL. ★

Since daybreak, the jay had been singing noisily.

When they'd slid open the rain shutters, it had flown up before their eyes from a lower branch of the pine, but it seemed to have come back. During breakfast, there was the sound of whirring wings.

"That bird's a nuisance." The younger brother started to get to his feet.

"It's all right. It's all right." The grandmother stopped him. "It's looking for its child. Apparently the chick fell out of the nest yesterday. It was flying around until late in the evening. Doesn't she know where it is? But what a good mother. This morning she came right back to look."

"Grandmother understands well," Yoshiko said.

Her grandmother's eyes were bad. Aside from a bout with nephritis[1] about ten years ago, she had never been ill in her life. But, because of her cataracts,[2] which she'd had since girlhood, she could only see dimly out of her left eye. One had to hand her the rice bowl and the chopsticks. Although she could grope her way around the familiar interior of the house, she could not go into the garden by herself.

Sometimes, standing or sitting in front of the sliding-glass door, she would spread out her hands, fanning out her fingers against the sunlight that came through the glass, and gaze out. She was concentrating all the life that was left to her into that many-angled gaze.

At such times, Yoshiko was frightened by her grandmother. Though she wanted to call out to her from behind, she would **furtively** steal away.

---

1. *Nephritis* is an acute or a chronic inflammation of the kidneys.

2. *Cataracts* are a clouding of the lenses of the eyes.

Vocabulary

furtively (fər′ tiv lē) *adv.* in a secret manner

YASUNARI KAWABATA **755**

1 Conflict *How do the brother and the grandmother view the jay's cry? Is there a conflict in the making?*

Advanced Learners/Pre-AP

DIFFERENTIATED INSTRUCTION

Report on Arranged Marriages To students raised in Western traditions, the prospect of an arranged marriage may seem unfair. Yet to those in cultures where marriages are arranged, Western traditions may seem disrespectful of parents. Have students research and report on attitudes in cultures that advocate arranged marriages.

English Learners

DIFFERENTIATED INSTRUCTION

Advanced The entire class can benefit from learning about other cultures. Have students from other countries tell the class about the marriage practices in their native lands. They can talk about the process of engagement, the ceremonies, the role of the family, or anything else they deem worth sharing.

Teach

Literary Element   1

Conflict **Answer:** *There is potential conflict, because the brother views the jay's cry as a nuisance, while the grandmother views it as a searching call for the jay's missing chick.*

Big Idea   2

Family and Tradition
Ask: What internal conflict do Yoshiko's actions illustrate with regard to her grandmother? *(Yoshiko feels as if she should respect and love her grandmother, but she is also afraid of her and wants to escape her.)*

View the Art ★

In this scroll, the Buddhist cleric Kūkai is shown as a child, seated on a lotus-flower throne. In medieval Buddhist paintings such as this, events in the life of a religious founder were recalled. The calligraphy is a quotation from Kūkai describing a blissful childhood dream in which he was transported on a lotus flower to a heavenly place where he spoke with several Buddhas.

 For an audio recording of this selection, use Listening Library Audio CD-ROM.

Readability Scores
Dale-Chall: 6.2
DRP: 54
Lexile: 720

Learning Objectives
Analyzing conflict. (SE)
Charting sequence of events. (TE)

Teach

Big Idea   1

Family and Tradition

Answer: *She explains the appearance of her nails with modern scientific knowledge as opposed to traditional folklore.*

(**ADVANCED**) Ask advanced students what other instances of contrast between traditional and modern elements they find in the story. *(Yoshiko's parents are divorced, a contemporary problem, yet her father arranges a marriage for Yoshiko in the traditional way.)*

Literary Element   2

Conflict Answer: *It suggests that the marital conflicts were not resolved. The father is still very angry.*

(**ADVANCED**) Ask advanced students what they infer might have caused Yoshiko's parents to divorce. *(Answers may vary. Many will guess that Yoshiko's mother was having an affair.)*

 For additional literary element practice, see Unit 4 Teaching Resources Book, p. 144.

This nearly blind grandmother, simply from having heard the jay's voice, spoke as if she had seen everything. Yoshiko was filled with wonder.

When, clearing away the breakfast things, Yoshiko went into the kitchen, the jay was singing from the roof of the neighbor's house.

In the back garden, there was a chestnut tree and two or three persimmon trees. When she looked at the trees, she saw that a light rain was falling. It was the sort of rain that you could not tell was falling unless you saw it against the dense foliage.

The jay, shifting its perch to the chestnut tree, then flying low and skimming the ground, returned again to its branch, singing all the while.

The mother bird could not fly away. Was it because her chick was somewhere around there?

Worrying about it, Yoshiko went to her room. She had to get herself ready before the morning was over.

In the afternoon, her father and mother were coming with the mother of Yoshiko's fiancé.

Sitting at her mirror, Yoshiko glanced at the white stars under her fingernails. It was said that, when stars came out under your nails, it was a sign that you would receive something, but Yoshiko remembered having read in the newspaper that it meant a deficiency of vitamin C or something. The job of putting on her makeup went fairly pleasantly. Her eyebrows and lips all became unbearably winsome.[3] Her kimono,[4] too, went on easily.

---

3. *Winsome* means "charming."
4. A *kimono* is a long robe with wide sleeves and a broad sash, traditionally worn in Japan.

1 **Family and Tradition** *How do Yoshiko's thoughts here defy traditional folkloric knowledge?*

She'd thought of waiting for her mother to come and help with her clothes, but it was better to dress by herself, she decided.

Her father lived away from them. This was her second mother.

When her father had divorced her first mother, Yoshiko had been four and her younger brother two. The reasons given for the divorce were that her mother went around dressed in flashy clothes and spent money wildly, but Yoshiko sensed dimly that it was more than that, that the real cause lay deeper down.

Her brother, as a child, had come across a photograph of their mother and shown it to their father. The father hadn't said anything but, with a face of terrible anger, had suddenly torn the photograph to bits.

When Yoshiko was thirteen, she had welcomed the new mother to the house. Later, Yoshiko had come to think that her father had endured his loneliness for ten years for her sake. The second mother was a good person. A peaceful home life continued.

When the younger brother, entering upper school, began living away from home in a dormitory, his attitude toward his stepmother changed noticeably.

"Elder sister, I've met our mother. She's married and lives in Azabu. She's really beautiful. She was happy to see me."

Hearing this suddenly, Yoshiko could not say a word. Her face paled, and she began to tremble.

From the next room, her stepmother came in and sat down.

"It's a good thing, a good thing. It's not bad to meet your own mother. It's only natural. I've known for some time that this day would come. I don't think anything particular of it."

Conflict *What does this action suggest about the relationship between the mother and the father?* **2**

Grammar Practice

Use Demonstrative Pronouns Remind students that demonstrative pronouns (*this, that, these, those*) point out specific persons, places, or things. A demonstrative pronoun may come before or after its antecedent. An antecedent may be understood. Write this sentence on the board: <u>This</u> was her second <u>mother</u>. Note that the pronoun is *this* and its antecedent is *mother*.

Ask students to write four sentences, one to illustrate the correct use of each of the demonstrative pronouns. Have students exchange sentences and check one another's work for accuracy.

756

But the strength seemed to have gone out of her stepmother's body. To Yoshiko, her emaciated stepmother seemed pathetically frail and small.

Her brother abruptly got up and left. Yoshiko felt like smacking him.

"Yoshiko, don't say anything to him. Speaking to him will only make that boy go bad." Her stepmother spoke in a low voice.

Tears came to Yoshiko's eyes.

Her father summoned her brother back home from the dormitory. Although Yoshiko had thought that would settle the matter, her father had then gone off to live elsewhere with her stepmother.

It had frightened Yoshiko. It was as if she had been crushed by the power of masculine indignation and resentment. Did their father dislike even them because of their tie to their first mother? It seemed to her that her brother, who'd gotten to his feet so abruptly, had inherited the frightening male **intransigence** of his father.

And yet it also seemed to Yoshiko that she could now understand her father's sadness and pain during those ten years between his divorce and remarriage.

And so, when her father, who had moved away from her, came back bringing a marriage proposal, Yoshiko had been surprised.

"I've caused you a great deal of trouble. I told the young man's mother that you're a girl with these circumstances and that, rather than treating you like a bride,[5] she

5. *". . . rather than treating you like a bride"* refers to the fact that brides in arranged marriages were traditionally treated harshly by the husband's mother.

3 **Family and Tradition** *How is Yoshiko's father fulfilling his traditional family role, even though he lives apart from his children?*

Vocabulary

intransigence (in tran′ sə jənts) *n.* the state of being uncompromising

Japanese Grey robe decorated with flowers and birds. Leeds Museums and Art Galleries, UK..

should try to bring back the happy days of your childhood."

When her father said this kind of thing to her, Yoshiko wept.

If Yoshiko married, there would be no woman's hand to take care of her brother and grandmother. It had been decided that the two households would become one. With that, Yoshiko had made up her mind. She had dreaded marriage on her father's account, but, when it came down to the actual talks, it was not that dreadful after all.

When her preparations were completed, Yoshiko went to her grandmother's room.

"Grandmother, can you see the red in this kimono?"

YASUNARI KAWABATA **757**

Teach

Big Idea **3**

Family and Tradition
Answer: *He is arranging a marriage for her, albeit without his first wife's input.*

APPROACHING Ask students approaching level how they react to the father's moving out and leaving Yoshiko and her brother living with their grandmother. *(Many students may find it strange or surprising.)*

Learning Objectives
Analyzing conflict. (SE)
Using demonstrative pronouns. (TE)

English Learners

DIFFERENTIATED INSTRUCTION

Beginning English learners might not be familiar with some of the descriptive words in "The Jay," such as *chestnut, persimmon,* and *foliage.* Have them write down unfamiliar words and look them up in a dictionary. Then have them search for images, online or in a library, that illustrate these words. They should print out or make copies of these images, which they can keep as references while they read.

Advanced Learners/Pre-AP

DIFFERENTIATED INSTRUCTION

Write a Haiku Kawabata's style has often been compared to the traditional Japanese haiku, a form of poetry that is short and spare, and relies heavily on nature imagery and the power of suggestion. Have advanced students take an image from "The Jay," such as the light rain on the trees or the bird flying through the garden, and write a haiku about it. Remind them that a haiku is a three-line poem that consists of seventeen syllables. The first and third lines contain five syllables each, and the second line contains seven. Have students share their haiku in small groups.

Teach

Reading Strategy | 1

Review **Answer:** *At the beginning of the story, the mother jay's song prompts the grandmother to claim that the bird is looking for her lost chick.*

(ADVANCED) Ask advanced students how the character of the blind grandmother contributes to the meaning of the story. *(For Yoshiko, who has been deserted by both her mother and father, her grandmother's presence seems connected to the jay's search for its chick. She represents tradition and devotion to family.)*

Literary Element | 2

Conflict **Answer:** *Possible response: Yoshiko hopes it might, but her father's anger is so deep that he would probably misunderstand the significance of the bird's actions.*

Cultural History ☆

Japanese Gardens Traditional Japanese gardens are very different from European-inspired flower gardens or formal gardens. They are carefully designed according to age-old principles and design elements. Inspired by and emulating natural scenery, Japanese gardens use symbolism to represent a landscape, such as a mountain or a lake, on a smaller scale.

> To check students' understanding of the selection, see Unit 4 Teaching Resources Book, p. 149.

"I can faintly make out some red over there. Which is it, now?" Pulling Yoshiko to her, the grandmother put her eyes close to the kimono and the sash.

"I've already forgotten your face, Yoshiko. I wish I could see what you look like now."

Yoshiko stifled a desire to giggle. She rested her hand lightly on her grandmother's head.

Wanting to go out and meet her father and the others, Yoshiko was unable just to sit there, vaguely waiting. She went out into the garden. She held out her hand, palm upward, but the rain was so fine that it didn't wet the palm. Gathering up the skirts of her kimono, Yoshiko **assiduously** searched among the little trees and in the bear-grass bamboo thicket. And there, in the tall grass under the bush clover, was the baby bird.

Her heart beating fast, Yoshiko crept nearer. The baby jay, drawing its head into its neck feathers, did not stir. It was easy to take it up into her hand. It seemed to have lost its energy. Yoshiko looked around her, but the mother bird was nowhere in sight.

Running into the house, Yoshiko called out, "Grandmother! I've found the baby bird. I have it in my hand. It's very weak."

"Oh, is that so? Try giving it some water." Her grandmother was calm.

When she ladled some water into a rice bowl and dipped the baby jay's beak in it, it drank, its little throat swelling out in an appealing way. Then—had it recovered?— it sang out, "Ki-ki-ki, Ki-ki-ki . . ."

The mother bird, evidently hearing its cry, came flying. Perching on the telephone wire, it sang. The baby bird, struggling in Yoshiko's hand, sang out again, "Ki-ki-ki . . ."

"Ah, how good that she came! Give it back to its mother, quick," her grandmother said.

Yoshiko went back out into the garden. The mother bird flew up from the telephone wire but kept her distance, looking fixedly toward Yoshiko from the top of a cherry tree.

As if to show her the baby jay in her palm, Yoshiko raised her hand, then quietly placed the chick on the ground.

As Yoshiko watched from behind the glass door, the mother bird, guided by the voice of its child singing **plaintively** and looking up at the sky, gradually came closer. When she'd come down to the low branch of a nearby pine, the chick flapped its wings, trying to fly up to her. Stumbling forward in its efforts, falling all over itself, it kept singing.

Still the mother bird cautiously held off from hopping down to the ground.

Soon, however, it flew in a straight line to the side of its child. The chick's joy was boundless. Turning and turning its head, its outspread wings trembling, it made up to its mother. Evidently the mother had brought it something to eat.

Yoshiko wished that her father and stepmother would come soon. She would like to show them this, she thought. ∾

---

1 **Review** *In the story, where is the baby bird first mentioned? What are the circumstances?*

Vocabulary
assiduously (ə sij′wəs lē) *adv.* in an attentive or busy manner

2 **Conflict** *In your opinion, would such an action resolve the larger conflict? Explain.*

Vocabulary
plaintively (plān′tiv lē) *adv.* in a manner expressing suffering or woe

---

Grammar Practice

Identify Participial Phrases **Write on the board:** "Running into the house, Yoshiko called out." Tell students that a participle is a verb form that can function as an adjective. A participial phrase contains a participle plus any complements and modifiers. Present participles always end in *-ing*. Have students identify the present participle *(Running)*, the participial phrase *(Running into the house)*, and the word it describes or modifies *(Yoshiko)*.

Have students identify and explain the function of three more participial phrases in the story. Check students' work for accuracy.

After You Read

Respond and Think Critically

Respond and Interpret

1. What questions linger in your mind after reading this story?

2. (a)At the beginning of the story, how does the grandmother explain the jay's singing? (b)How does Yoshiko **characterize** her grandmother at this point?

3. (a)Who is Yoshiko preparing to meet? Why is she meeting this person? (b)How does Yoshiko feel about her future?

4. (a)What happens with Yoshiko and the jays at the end of the story? (b)In your opinion, why does Yoshiko want to show the jays to her father and stepmother?

Analyze and Evaluate

5. An **implied comparison** is one in which the similarities or the differences between two things are suggested but not directly stated. What implied comparison is made in this story?

6. Do you think the father is right or wrong to discourage contact between the children and their mother? Explain.

Connect

7. **Big Idea** **Family and Tradition** Do traditional family values seem to win out over personal choices in this story? Explain.

8. **Connect to the Author** Kawabata is known for writing stories in which the characters are emotionally distant from one another. How is that idea reflected in "The Jay"?

You're the Critic

Different Viewpoints

Kawabata is known for his melancholy, symbolic fiction that incorporates imagery reminiscent of haiku. His stories often lack clear-cut, traditional elements of fiction. Read the quotations below about Kawabata's style.

"Just as a haiku may contain a richness rivaling that of a longer poem, so these stories, in the plenitude of their content, the complexity of their psychology, and the sharpness of their observation of human life, rival longer prose fictions."
—Lane Dunlop and J. Martin Holman

"Stylistically he is known as an elliptical, even surrealistic, writer whose work is governed more by a desire to evoke mood than by an interest in plot, structure, logical development, and so many of the other features often associated with the writing of fiction."
—Van C. Gessel

Group Activity Discuss the following questions with your classmates.

1. How do the critics seem to feel about Kawabata's lack of traditional fictional elements in his stories?

2. Based on your reading of "The Jay," which quotation do you agree with more? Explain.

Figure of Bodhidharma, 1496. Chinese school. Bronze. Private collection.

You're the Critic

1. Dunlop and Holman seem to admire Kawabata's style and feel that his stories are rich and skillfully crafted. Gessel, on the other hand, seems more objective, merely describing Kawabata's style as nontraditional.

2. Answers will vary. Some students may not appreciate the unresolved nature of "The Jay" and will therefore agree more with the second quotation. Other students may appreciate Kawabata's psychological insights and will agree with the first quotation.

After You Read

Assess

1. Answers will vary.

2. (a) The grandmother says the jay is looking for her lost chick. (b) She thinks her grandmother is perceptive and impressive.

3. (a) She is preparing to meet her future mother-in-law because her father has arranged a marriage. (b) She seems resigned to it and even moderately happy.

4. (a) She finds the chick, cares for it, and returns it to its mother. (b) She hopes it represents her family's reunion.

5. The behavior of the mother jay, which will not give up on finding her chick, is contrasted with the behavior of Yoshiko's mother, who seems to accept her separation from her children.

6. Answers will vary. Students may feel he is wrong because a child should have access to both parents.

7. Family and tradition take precedence over personal choice, yet Yoshiko doesn't seem to have any other preferences and is not being prevented from making any other choice.

8. Yoshiko's father is essentially estranged from the rest of the family. Yoshiko has no contact with her biological mother. There is also tension between Yoshiko's brother and their stepmother.

 For additional selection assessment, see Assessment Resources, pp. 153–154.

After You Read

Assess

Literary Element

1. (a) Yoshiko is caught between her father's anger toward her mother and her brother's desire to see her mother. (b) Nothing is quite resolved.

2. (a) Yoshiko's relationships with her grandmother and her stepmother are comfortable. However, she does not have a real relationship with her mother. (b) Her relationships with her father and her brother are stressful.

3. (a) The characters don't talk about their feelings. One example is when Yoshiko's father silently tears apart the picture of her mother. (b) This makes it difficult to resolve conflicts.

Review: Mood

1. Students may describe the mood as pensive or restless.

2. Answers will vary depending on how students described the mood.

Reading Strategy

A is the correct answer. Yoshiko's father and stepmother are bringing the mother of her fiancé to meet Yoshiko.

Progress Check

Can students review text?

If No → See Unit 4 Teaching Resources Book, p. 145.

760

Literary Element Conflict

Conflict is the struggle that lies at the center of a story's plot. In a story that has a standard plot structure, the central conflict reaches a climax and is resolved at the end. "The Jay," however, does not follow this typical plot development. Instead, the story portrays a slice of family life and leaves several conflicts unresolved.

1. (a) What conflicts exist between Yoshiko and the men in this story? (b) Are any of these conflicts resolved? Explain.

2. (a) How would you characterize the relationships between Yoshiko and the women in the story? (b) How do these relationships compare with those Yoshiko has with the men in her family?

3. (a) How do the characters in this story deal with their feelings? Give specific examples. (b) How does this affect the resolution or lack of resolution of the conflicts?

Review: Mood

As you learned on page 713, **mood** is the emotional quality of a literary work. An author's choice of language, subject matter, setting, and tone, as well as certain sound devices, contributes to a work's mood. Kawabata's stories are respected for their focused and subtle mood, which often recalls the tightness of Japanese poetic forms such as the **tanka** (see pages 712–715) and **haiku** (see pages 738–742).

Partner Activity Meet with a classmate and discuss the following questions.

1. How would you describe the mood of "The Jay"?

2. What details in the story contribute to this mood?

LOG ON ▶ **Literature** Online

Selection Resources For Selection Quizzes, eFlashcards, and Reading-Writing Connection activities, go to glencoe.com and enter QuickPass code GLW6053u4.

Reading Strategy Review

ACT Skills Practice

What is Yoshiko waiting for when the story occurs?

A. Her father and stepmother's arrival

B. Her reunion with her mother

C. Her meeting with her fiancé

D. The return of her brother

Vocabulary Practice

Practice with Word Origins Create a word map like the one below for each boldfaced vocabulary word. Use a dictionary for help.

furtively   intransigence
assiduously   plaintively

EXAMPLE:

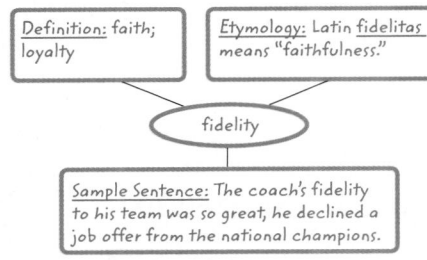

Definition: faith; loyalty

Etymology: Latin _fidelitas_ means "faithfulness."

fidelity

Sample Sentence: The coach's fidelity to his team was so great, he declined a job offer from the national champions.

Academic Vocabulary

*Yoshiko deserves some **credit** for considering her family's welfare in deciding to marry.*

Credit has many meanings. Synonyms include *commendation, recognition,* and *acclaim.* Using context clues, try to figure out the meaning of *credit* in each of the following sentences and explain the difference between the meanings.

1. Though I helped my sister with her science fair project, she didn't give me **credit** for it.

2. Because I overpaid my library fines, I have an outstanding **credit** of five dollars.

For more on academic vocabulary, see pages 36–37 and R83–R85.

Vocabulary

Sample responses:

furtively: Definition: in a secret manner; Etymology: Latin furtum means "theft"; Sample sentence: The tiger moved furtively through the tall grass.

intransigence: Definition: the state of being uncompromising; Etymology: Latin in- + transigere means "not agree"; Sample sentence: The determined leader showed intransigence.

Academic Vocabulary

1. In this sentence, *credit* means "recognition."

2. In this sentence, *credit* means "a sum of money owed."

Respond Through Writing

Evaluate Style At the end of "The Jay" the reader doesn't know precisely why Yoshiko wants her father and stepmother to see the birds. Kawabata often ends his stories like this, without a clear resolution. In an expository essay, evaluate how effectively his style contributes to the ambiguous ending of this story.

Understand the Task When you **evaluate** a story, you make a reasoned judgment or form an opinion about it. Something that is **ambiguous** has more than one possible meaning.

Prewrite To help organize your essay, select categories you want to use to assess elements of Kawabata's style, such as word choice, imagery, or mood. Rank his performance in each category using the numbered scale below—one being the lowest and five being the highest—and take notes about your judgments. Use these notes to shape your thesis.

Draft In your essay, offer examples of Kawabata's style. You might use a sentence frame like these to help you:

Some examples of _____ in the story are _____, _____, and _____.

Images such as _____ and _____ contribute to Kawabata's style by _____.

Evaluate how well Kawabata's style contributes to the ambiguous ending of the story. Did it add to or detract from your experience? Did it make the ending more or less ambiguous than it might otherwise have been? Use a timeline like the one on page 754 to sequence your essay properly.

Revise Trade papers with a classmate and critique one another's essays. Check that the details your partner cites support his or her evaluation. If an aspect of the essay isn't working, offer alternative suggestions.

Edit and Proofread Proofread your paper, correcting any errors in spelling, grammar, and punctuation. Review the Grammar Tip in the side column for information about using coordinating conjunctions.

Learning Objectives

In this assignment, you will focus on the following objectives:

Writing: Writing an expository essay.

Grammar: Understanding coordinating conjunctions.

> ## Grammar Tip

Coordinating Conjunctions

Use coordinating conjunctions such as *and, but, or, so, nor, yet,* and *for* to combine two sentences that contain equally important ideas. This can make your sentences more varied and fluid.

Original: *The ending left me confused. The image of the birds presents an interesting comparison.*

Combined: *The ending left me confused, but the image of the birds presents an interesting comparison.*

After You Read

Assess

Respond Through Writing

Students' essays should:

- express an opinion about whether Kawabata's style enhanced the story's ambiguity
- have a clear organizational plan
- use specific examples from the text to support that opinion

A student who meets all of these criteria should receive the equivalent of a 4-point response.

A student who fully meets two and partially meets the third of these criteria should receive the equivalent of a 3-point response.

A student who fully meets one and partially meets a second of these criteria, or who partially meets all three criteria, should receive the equivalent of a 2-point response.

A student who partially fully meets one or partially meets two of these criteria should receive the equivalent of a 1-point response.

 For grammar practice, see Unit 4 Teaching Resources Book, p. 148.

 To create custom assessments online, go to Progress Reporter Online Assessment.

 To create custom assessments using software, use ExamView Assessment Suite.

Focus

Beside a Chrysanthemum

Korea

Bellringer Options

Daily Language Practice Transparency 68

Or ask: How do you view the passing of the seasons, particularly the coming of autumn? Some students might welcome autumn's arrival, finding its changes beautiful. Others might be sad because it means that summer is over and winter is coming.

Literary History ☆

Baudelaire In his time, Baudelaire became notorious when, of the hundred poems in his first published collection, thirteen were labeled offensive to morality and religion. Six of them deemed "obscene" were removed from the book. After his death, however, Baudelaire became recognized as an important artist who influenced poets such as Arthur Rimbaud, Rainer Maria Rilke, and T. S. Eliot, as well as Sŏ Chŏngju.

Meet **Sŏ Chŏngju**

(1915–2000)

When Sŏ Chŏngju's poetry first appeared in the late 1930s, it shocked readers with its bold imagery. When he died in 2000, Sŏ was the most famous contemporary poet in Korea, known for literary works that explored settings ranging from the sensual natural world to a mythical Buddhist kingdom.

Political Turmoil Sŏ was born in southern Korea five years after Japan annexed the country. The years of Japanese occupation were difficult for the Korean people, yet Korean literature blossomed during this time. Early twentieth-century Korean poetry reflects both an interest in experimentation and a growing feeling of nationalism. However, after Japan invaded China in 1937, Japanese authorities put strict wartime restrictions on the people of Korea. This led to widespread poverty and the repression of literature. In Sŏ's famous poem "Self-Portrait," the speaker candidly portrays his poor family background, describing his father as "a serf" who "never came home, even late at night." In 1945, Korea was liberated from Japanese rule. It divided into North Korea and South Korea in 1948.

Bold and Famous After attending Central Buddhist College, Sŏ published his first collection, *Flower Snake*, in 1941. His bold, sensual poems, influenced by French poet Charles Baudelaire, scandalized many readers. However, the collection was widely admired for its use of vivid imagery and natural spoken language. Sŏ's *Selected Poems*, which includes "Beside a Chrysanthemum," was published in 1953, the last year of the Korean War. Throughout the

> *Some read a convict in my eyes, some an idiot in my mouth, but I will repent nothing.*
>
> —Sŏ Chŏngju

country, Koreans memorized and recited "Beside a Chrysanthemum," which is perhaps Sŏ's most famous poem. It became a sort of anthem during a time of national division.

Ancient Influences In many of his later poems, Sŏ found inspiration in ancient spiritual legends. His *Shilla Sketch*, published in 1961, depicts an ancient Buddhist kingdom known for its beautiful art and architecture. He wrote that his poetry was "a poetic reconciliation of the present with the eternal." He was nominated for the Nobel Prize in Literature several times and won the Republic of Korea Academy of Arts Award in 1967. Sŏ's poetry remains admired for its deep sense of spiritual longing and its beautiful use of the Korean language.

 Literature Online

Author Search For more about Sŏ Chŏngju, go to glencoe.com and enter QuickPass code GLW6053u4.

Selection Skills

Literary Elements
- Simile (SE pp. 763–765)
- Imagery (TE p. 764)

Beside a Chrysanthemum

Writing Skills/Grammar
- Letter (SE p. 765)
- Apostrophe (TE p. 764)

Reading Skills
- Analyze Speaker (SE pp. 763, 765)

Literature and Reading Preview

Connect to the Poem

What aspects of nature have special meaning for you? Discuss this question with a small group.

Build Background

The chrysanthemum, an autumn-blooming flower in the daisy family, permeates East Asian literature, symbolizing ideas such as perfection, fidelity, and longevity. One of the four Chinese "noble plants," the chrysanthemum has been cultivated since the fifteenth century B.C. in China, where it was associated with the nobility and believed to cure a variety of ailments. In the eighth century A.D., the flower was introduced into Japan, where the imperial family adopted it as its official symbol. It remains the unofficial national seal of Japan today.

Set Purposes for Reading

Big Idea Moments of Reflection

As you read, ask yourself, How do the speaker's observations of nature connect to reflections on the passage of time and the fragility of beauty?

Literary Element Simile

A **simile** is a figure of speech that uses *like* or *as* to compare seemingly unlike things. Poets use similes to make it easier for the reader to grasp what is being described. As you read, ask yourself, What simile does Sŏ use to connect the speaker's reflections on nature to larger concerns about human life?

Reading Strategy Analyze Speaker

When you **analyze** a **speaker**, you examine the details in a poem to determine what they reveal about the voice that is speaking. Sometimes the speaker's voice is that of the poet, sometimes that of a fictional person or even a thing. As you read, ask yourself, What details help you draw conclusions about the speaker?

Tip: Track Details In a chart like the one below, list details and what they reveal about the speaker.

Detail	What It Reveals About Speaker
The speaker looks at a chrysanthemum and thinks of thunder and black clouds.	

Learning Objectives

For pages 762–765

In studying this text, you will focus on the following objectives:

Literary Study: Analyzing simile.

Reading: Analyzing speaker.

Writing: Writing a letter.

One panel of an eight-fold screen depicting birds and flowers. Korean School. Natural pigments on paper. Gahoe Museum, Jongno-gu, South Korea.

SŎ CHŎNGJU **763**

Before You Read

Focus

Summary

The speaker attributes the beauty of a chrysanthemum to the autumnal events that have led to its blooming. The flower is also compared to the speaker's sister, who has returned from an absence. The night before, the speaker did not sleep due to a frost.

 For summaries in languages other than English, see Unit 4 Teaching Resources Book, pp. 151–156.

Cultural History ☆

Chinese and Japanese Influence Korea has long been influenced, culturally and politically, by both China and Japan. In 1894, their competition for control of Korea led to the Sino-Japanese War. The Japanese won the war, thereby establishing Japanese rule over Korea. During its rule, Japan deprived Koreans of many of their basic freedoms, including freedoms of speech and the press. Colonial schools, where only Japanese was taught, were established to replace many Korean schools.

Approaching Level

DIFFERENTIATED INSTRUCTION

 Choose Images Point out to students approaching level how greatly Sŏ Chŏngju's choice of imagery affects this poem's atmosphere. Tell them that when they write, their choice of images is important in creating their desired atmosphere. They should consider, when choosing an image to include in their writing, what its connotations are and what associations it might bring up in the mind of the reader. Divide students into small groups. Have each group choose a type of atmosphere they would like to create. For instance, a group might choose to create a relaxed atmosphere. They should then brainstorm a list of images that would establish a relaxed atmosphere, such as "breeze through the trees" or "rippling water."

Each student should contribute at least one image to the group. Make sure that the groups accept everyone's ideas. Students can respond to an idea by saying that, for them, a particular image might have associations that do not fit with the atmosphere their group is creating, but no idea should be labeled "wrong."

Teach

Literary Element 1

Imagery Ask: What connotations are attached to this imagery? How would you describe the atmosphere this image creates? *(Black clouds and thunder usually have negative connotations. It is a dark, ominous atmosphere.)*

ENGLISH LEARNERS Ask English learners to name other words they might associate with this image. *(Possible answers: lightning, rain, storm)*

Literary Element 2

Simile Answer: *It applies the speaker's ideas about the natural world to the human world as well.*

 For additional literary element practice, see Unit 4 Teaching Resources Book, p. 157.

 To check students' understanding of the selection, see Unit 4 Teaching Resources Book, p. 159.

Beside a Chrysanthemum

Sŏ Chŏngju

Translated by David R. McCann

To bring one chrysanthemum
to flower, the cuckoo has cried
since spring.

To bring one chrysanthemum to bloom,
5 thunder has rolled
1 through black clouds.

Flower, like my sister returning
from distant, youthful byways°
of throat-tight longing
10 to stand by the mirror:

for your yellow petals to open,
last night such a frost fell,
and I did not sleep.

Bridal panel, 19th century. Korean school. Red satin. Victoria and Albert Museum, London.

8 Byways: small, infrequently traveled roads.

---

2 Simile *How does this comparison expand the meaning of the poem?*

Writing Practice

SPIRAL REVIEW 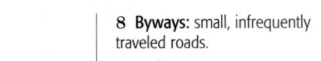 **Apply Apostrophe** An apostrophe is a figure of speech in which a speaker addresses an inanimate object, an idea, or an absent person as if it were present and capable of understanding. In poetry, apostrophe is often used with personification and helps a poet to achieve a sense of emotional immediacy.

Have students write a short passage, consisting of a sentence or two, which includes an instance of apostrophe. Then pair students up and have them share their sentences with their partners.

After You Read

Respond and Think Critically

Respond and Interpret

1. What images did you find most striking? Explain.

2. (a)What three things had to happen for the chrysanthemum to bloom? (b)What might these things have in common?

3. (a)What can you infer about the time of year from line 12? (b)What might be the significance of the chrysanthemum's blooming at this time?

4. (a)Why might the speaker not have slept the night before? (b)What does this suggest about the connection between the human and natural worlds?

Analyze and Evaluate

5. (a)Why might the chrysanthemum remind the speaker of his or her sister? (b)What emotional effects do lines 8–9 create?

6. What is the connection between the chrysanthemum and the other natural phenomena the speaker describes?

Connect

7. **Big Idea** **Moments of Reflection** How does the poet use nature to convey a message about the connection between beauty and pain?

8. **Connect to the Author** What do you think Sŏ Chŏngju would have thought about the haiku you studied earlier (pages 738–741)?

Literary Element Simile

Similes help readers make connections between things that at first may seem dissimilar.

1. (a)What two things are compared in the third stanza? (b)What do you think are the "distant, youthful byways / of throat-tight longing"?

2. Why might the speaker connect the chrysanthemum to these "distant, youthful byways"?

Reading Strategy Analyze Speaker

Refer to the chart you made on page 763.

1. What can you infer about the speaker's relationship with nature?

2. Addressing an inanimate object or an idea is called **apostrophe.** What does the use of apostrophe in the last two stanzas suggest about the speaker's attitude toward the chrysanthemum?

Literature Online

Selection Resources For Selection Quizzes, eFlashcards, and Reading-Writing Connection activities, go to glencoe.com and enter QuickPass code GLW6053u4.

Academic Vocabulary

*Sŏ **reverses** chronology by starting with the blooming chrysanthemum and then describing the natural phenomena that preceded it.*

Reverse is a word often used in academic contexts. In more casual usage, you might say someone put a car in **reverse** to back out of a parking space. To further explore the meaning of this word, answer this question: What is an example of a court case in which a legal act or ruling has been **reversed**?

For more on academic vocabulary, see pages 36–37 and R83–R85.

Writing

Write a Letter Have the speaker and his sister had a falling out, or do they get along well? Write a letter from the speaker to his sister. Include details that suggest the speaker's personality and a simile to connect the details to larger issues.

SŎ CHŎNGJU **765**

Literary Element

1. (a) The speaker compares the chrysanthemum to his or her sister. (b) The feelings of longing he or she experienced in his or her own youth or that he or she imagines the sister experienced.

2. Both evoke pain as well as beauty, or the flower has, like the speaker's sister, been "away"—not blooming.

Reading Strategy

1. He or she has an impassioned and close connection with nature.

2. Possible interpretations: the speaker is angry that the flower is ignorant of the larger world. He or she may also be in awe of the interconnectedness of the natural world.

After You Read

Assess

1. Answers will vary.

2. (a) A cuckoo had to cry from spring through fall, thunder had to roll through black clouds, and a frost had to fall. (b) They are all processes of change, each associated with pain or struggle.

3. (a) The frost in line 12 indicates it is autumn. (b) It would seem the chrysanthemum's beauty is fleeting and coexists with the death of other natural things.

4. (a) The speaker was emotionally or physically disturbed, perhaps by the frost. (b) The speaker is deeply affected by and connected to natural processes.

5. (a) Perhaps because she is young and beautiful, or perhaps her absence and return are like the chrysanthemum's annual blooming. (b) The words evoke a sense of memory and loss.

6. The other natural phenomena have led to autumn, the flowering season for chrysanthemums.

7. The poet uses the chrysanthemum to show how all of nature—the beautiful and the painful—is connected.

8. Answers will vary.

Academic Vocabulary

Students might mention a case such as the landmark 1966 case *Miranda* v. *Arizona*.

Writing

Students' letters should

- be written in the voice of the speaker of "Beside a Chrysanthemum"
- include similes
- use details to develop the characters of the speaker and the sister

Focus

Before You Read

Bellringer Options

Selection Focus
Transparency 47
Daily Language Practice
Transparency 69

Or ask: What are the advantages and disadvantages of having a daily routine? Students should say that the advantages are efficiency and productivity; the disadvantages are monotony and no spontaneity.

Literary History ☆

The Misty Poets Toward the end of China's Cultural Revolution, a group of writers used poetry to express their disillusionment with communism. Fearing censorship, the poets avoided direct statements and instead used figurative language to condemn the lack of individual freedoms in communism. Shu Ting was among the group branded "The Misty Poets" by opponents attempting to minimize the poets' influence.

Selection Skills

Assembly Line

China

Meet **Shu Ting**
(born 1952)

Writing in the wake of China's Cultural Revolution, Shu Ting (shōō′ ting′) is known for defying communist ideals by composing poems charged with compassion. According to Shu Ting, "Today, what people urgently require is respect, trust and warmth. As far as possible, I would like to express my concern for 'humanity' through my poetry."

Interrupted Education Shu Ting was born in Fujian province a few years after the communist takeover of China. From a young age, her relatives exposed her to foreign literature. When she was in junior secondary school, however, Chinese leader Mao Tse-tung launched the Cultural Revolution, a movement that resulted in the abuse of many intellectuals and the elderly. Shu Ting's father, a bank official, was labeled a "nonconformist" by communist authorities and was banished to a remote area. Shu Ting's education was cut short in 1966 when Mao shut down China's schools.

A Displaced Generation Mao organized millions of urban youths into militant groups called the Red Guards, which protested authorities and perpetrated widespread violence. These actions disrupted daily life in Chinese cities, however, and the government eventually urged the Red Guards to disband. When the schools reopened in 1968, there was not enough room for all the urban youth who had fallen behind in their education. In 1969, Shu Ting became one of about seventeen million young people who were sent to the countryside to work with peasants. However, once they arrived in the countryside, they received little support from the government and were often resented by locals. Many were unable to make a living either in the country or the cities. The generation that had originally embraced the ideals of the communist government was confronted with alienation and disillusionment.

From Odd Jobs to Poetry In 1973, Shu Ting was allowed back to the city of Xiamen (shä′ men), where she held a variety of jobs. She also began to write highly personal poems charged with strong emotions. For the emotional quality of her writing, Shu Ting has been linked with a like-minded group known as the Misty Poets. Although the communist government criticized her poems, Shu Ting won China's National Poetry award in 1981 and 1983 and is celebrated for her poems about love and sorrow.

> "[Ting's] poems search the emotional life for signs of what lies beneath and beyond the self."
>
> —J. D. McClatchy, editor

LOG ON ▶ **Literature** Online

Author Search For more about Shu Ting, go to glencoe.com and enter QuickPass code GLW6053u4.

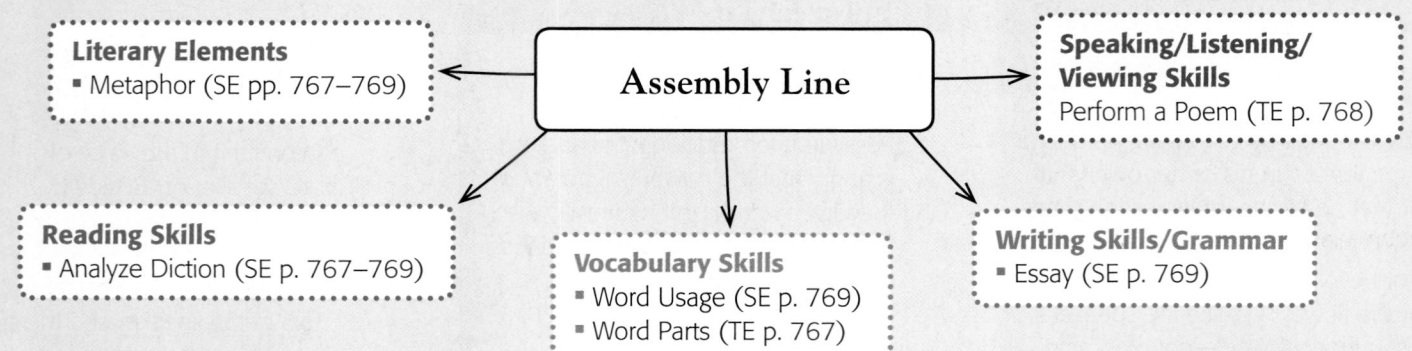

Literary Elements
- Metaphor (SE pp. 767–769)

Assembly Line

Speaking/Listening/ Viewing Skills
Perform a Poem (TE p. 768)

Reading Skills
- Analyze Diction (SE p. 767–769)

Vocabulary Skills
- Word Usage (SE p. 769)
- Word Parts (TE p. 767)

Writing Skills/Grammar
- Essay (SE p. 769)

Literature and Reading Preview

Connect to the Poem

What makes certain types of work more rewarding than others? Freewrite for a few minutes about different kinds of work.

Build Background

The assembly-line system dates back to the Industrial Revolution of the nineteenth century. A pioneer of the modern assembly line was Henry Ford, who in 1913 introduced the world to his automobile factory's use of it. This increased productivity by allowing workers to stand in one place and concentrate on a single task. Assembly-line production quickly spread throughout various industries despite the arguments of some who believed this type of labor dehumanized workers.

Set Purposes for Reading

Big Idea Virtue and Wisdom

According to communist ideals, work is virtuous and fulfilling because it benefits society. As you read "Assembly Line," ask yourself, How does the speaker feel about performing his or her duty for the state?

Literary Element Metaphor

A **metaphor** is a figure of speech that compares two unlike things without using the word *as* or *like*. Metaphors can be only a few words long or can extend throughout a paragraph, stanza, or literary work. As you read, ask yourself, How does Shu Ting develop the idea of the assembly line as a metaphor for the speaker's life?

Reading Strategy Analyze Diction

When you **analyze diction**, you examine how an author's words work together to create meaning in a piece of literature. Often, an author will use a series of words that suggest a particular feeling. For example, an author might use scientific vocabulary to create a feeling of rigidity and formality. As you read, ask yourself, What do the poet's words tell you about the speaker's experiences?

Tip: Track Word Choice In a chart like the one below, list key words and what they suggest about the speaker's outlook.

Word	Suggests
presses	suffocating, oppressive life

SHU TING **767**

Learning Objectives

For pages 766–769

In studying this text, you will focus on the following objectives:

Literary Study: Analyzing metaphor.

Reading: Analyzing diction.

Writing: Writing an essay.

Vocabulary

monotony (mə not'ən ē) *n.* tiresome sameness; p. 768 *The monotony of the ticking clock made me sleepy.*

tempo (tem'pō) *n.* pattern or rate of movement; p. 768 *The orchestra played an exciting piece with a quick tempo.*

Tip: Word Usage When you encounter a new word, you might want to ask yourself a question about it to help you understand it further. For example, does the music you like generally have a fast *tempo* or a slow one?

Before You Read

Focus

Summary

In "Assembly Line," poet Shu Ting expresses the monotony and demoralization associated with executing one's duty to a communist state. Through the use of repetition and word choice, she exposes the ramifications of monotony in all facets of life and the universe, including nature. Her loss of individuality and fulfillment is most evident in the last lines "I'm unable to show concern / For my own manufactured fate."

 For summaries in languages other than English, see Unit 4 Teaching Resources Book, pp. 161–166.

Vocabulary

Word Parts Ask students to brainstorm words with the prefix *mono-* (*monopoly, monologue, monotone*). **Ask:** What does the prefix *mono-* mean? *(one)*

Say: The word *tempo* comes from the Latin word *tempus*, which means "time." What words related to *tempo* can you think of? *(temporary, temporal, temporize)*

 For additional vocabulary practice, see Unit 4 Teaching Resources Book, p. 169.

English Learners

DIFFERENTIATED INSTRUCTION

SMALL GROUP

Intermediate Help English learners improve their understanding of the poem through visualization. Remind students that imagery is a set of words that paints a picture in the reader's mind. Have small groups of students read the poem aloud first, and discuss images that came to mind. Have them underline examples of imagery in the poem, particularly the imagery exhibited in the first and second stanzas, such as:

- "In line as we march towards home."
- "Over our heads in a row / The assembly line of stars / stretches across the sky"
- "The little trees are all sick, / Choked on smog and monotony, / Stripped of their color and shape."

Then ask students to draw a picture on their own and share it with their group.

Teach

Literary Element 1

Metaphor **Answer:** *"Time's assembly line" is a metaphor for life. It moves along mechanically and is indifferent to people's suffering.*

 For additional literary element practice, see Unit 4 Teaching Resources Book, p. 167.

Reading Strategy 2

Analyze Diction **Answer:** *The word* numb *suggests her life is unfulfilling and boring.*

(**APPROACHING**) For students who may be struggling with the reading strategy, elaborate on the concept of numb by giving real-world examples, such as having numb hands after being in the cold too long, or having numb legs after sitting cross-legged for a long period. Work with students to circle other examples of precise words and discuss their meaning and purpose in the poem.

 For additional practice using the reading skill or strategy, see Unit 4 Teaching Resources Book, p. 168.

Cultural History ☆

The Assembly Line Henry Ford famously declared "Nothing is particularly hard if you divide it into small jobs." Based on this premise, Ford's engineers created a manufacturing process called an assembly line. In an assembly line, items move down a conveyor belt, and each worker assembles a discrete part that the next worker then builds on. This process dramatically reduced the time it took to build vehicles, thus making them more affordable.

768

ASSEMBLY LINE ☆

Shu Ting
Translated by Carolyn Kizer

Smoke rises from chimneys at the Chongqing Iron and Steel Factory. Photograph. Chongqing Municipality, China.

In time's assembly line
Night presses against night.
We come off the factory night-shift
In line as we march towards home.
5 Over our heads in a row
The assembly line of stars
Stretches across the sky.
Beside us, little trees
Stand numb in assembly lines.

10 The stars must be exhausted
After thousands of years
Of journeys which never change.
The little trees are all sick,

15 Choked on smog and **monotony**,
Stripped of their color and shape.
It's not hard to feel for them;
We share the same **tempo** and rhythm.

Yes, I'm numb to my own existence
As if, like the trees and stars
20 —perhaps just out of habit
—perhaps just out of sorrow,
I'm unable to show concern
For my own manufactured fate.

Analyze Diction *What do the speaker's words suggest about her life?* **2**

Vocabulary

monotony (mə not′ ən ē) *n.* tiresome sameness
tempo (tem′ pō) *n.* pattern or rate of movement

1 Metaphor *What is "time's assembly line"?*

768 UNIT 4 EAST ASIA

Skills Practice

 Perform a Poem Have students work in small groups to read aloud the poem "Assembly Line" to the class. Encourage them to make a plan to:

- Decide which lines each student will read or which lines they will read chorally.
- Annotate lines and words to emphasize.

- Devise body language. For example, students may want to stand in an "assembly line," and look downtrodden as they read the poem in a monotone.

Review how to read poems with the class. Remind students that they should use punctuation, not line breaks, as their guide for pausing. Then have each group perform their poem for the class as other students listen attentively.

After You Read

Respond and Think Critically

Respond and Interpret

1. How did you feel after reading this poem?

2. (a)Which images from nature are described in terms of an assembly line? (b)Why does the speaker see nature in these terms?

3. (a)What sensations does the speaker ascribe to the stars and trees? (b)What does the speaker mean by "we share the same tempo and rhythm"?

4. (a)What has made the speaker numb to his or her own existence? (b)How do you interpret the phrase "my own manufactured fate"?

Analyze and Evaluate

5. How does the speaker extend the idea of an assembly line beyond factory walls?

6. (a)Shu Ting uses the phrase "assembly line" twice in the first stanza. How does this repetition reinforce the meaning of the poem? (b)Where else in the poem does Shu Ting use repetition effectively? Explain.

7. (a)Why do you think Shu Ting uses the pronoun *we*, rather than *I*, in the first two stanzas? (b)What is the effect of the pronoun *I* in the final stanza?

Connect

8. **Big Idea** **Virtue and Wisdom** In this poem, how does the speaker's work affect her?

9. **Connect to Today** Do you think the feelings expressed in "Assembly Line" apply only to people in China, or are they universal? Explain.

Literary Element Metaphor

In contrast to a simile, a **metaphor** implies a comparison instead of stating it directly.

1. What does the metaphor "assembly line of stars" in line 6 suggest about the stars?

2. How does Shu Ting develop the assembly-line metaphor in the second stanza?

Reading Strategy Analyze Diction

Review the chart you made on page 767 and then answer the following questions.

1. (a)What words does the speaker use to describe the trees in lines 13–15? (b)What do these words suggest about the speaker's own experience?

2. Would you describe Shu Ting's diction in "Assembly Line" as complex or simple? Explain.

 Literature Online

Selection Resources For Selection Quizzes, eFlashcards, and Reading-Writing Connection activities, go to glencoe.com and enter QuickPass code GLW6053u4.

Vocabulary Practice

Practice with Usage Respond to these statements to help you explore the meanings of the vocabulary words from the poem.

1. Describe something that is an example of **monotony**.

2. What type of **tempo** do you prefer in music? Name a song you like that demonstrates this tempo.

Writing

Write an Essay "Assembly Line" suggests the relationship between work and life—a topic explored by many authors. For instance, Henry Wadsworth Longfellow wrote, "Taste the joy / That springs from labor," while Alfred, Lord Tennyson stated, "Ah, why should life / all labor be?" With which quote do you agree more? Write a brief essay that explores your response. Include a **metaphor** in your essay.

SHU TING **769**

Literary Element

1. the repetition and routine of nature

2. She describes how the stars, like members of an assembly line, are exhausted from their long, unchanging journey and how the trees, like assembly line workers, are sick and have been stripped of their individuality.

Reading Strategy

1. (a) The speaker uses words such as *little, sick, choked,* and *stripped* to describe the trees. (b) This suggests the speaker feels helpless and stifled.

2. Her diction is fairly simple. She uses concrete words such as *sick, smog,* and *numb* to convey her meaning.

After You Read

Assess

1. Answers will vary.

2. (a) stars and trees (b) Factory work has deprived the speaker of vitality and individuality so that even nature seems like an assembly line.

3. (a) exhaustion and boredom (b) The speaker feels their lives are just as monotonous and repetitive as the speaker's.

4. (a) The speaker is numb out of habit and sorrow. (b) The speaker does not control his or her life.

5. The speaker sees everything around him or her, including nature, as regimented.

6. (a) It mimics the repetitive nature of assembly line work. (b) line 2; lines 20 and 21; lines 9 and 18

7. (a) The use of *we* emphasizes the common experience of the workers. (b) The use of *I* creates a more personal tone and places the speaker within the scene she has created.

8. It destroys the speaker's individuality and sense of personal fulfillment.

9. The stress of boring, repetitive work is universal; however, some societies provide more satisfying rewards for such work.

Vocabulary

1. waiting for a long period of time

2. Answers will vary.

Writing

Students' essays should
- respond to the quotations
- express their views on work
- include a metaphor

Focus

Summary

In the 1960s, Kitakyushu, an industrial city, was one of the most polluted places in Japan. In response to the hazardous conditions, the city's housewives arranged experiments to quantify the city's pollution and its effects on citizens. Politicians responded to the alarming data. This led to the city's winning the United Nations Environmental Program's Global 500 Award. Now Kitakyushu uses its experience to help other developing become more environment-friendly.

 For summaries in languages other than English, see Unit 4 Teaching Resources Book, pp. 172–177.

 For an audio recording of this selection, use Listening Library Audio CD-ROM.

Readability Scores

Dale-Chall: 8.1
DRP: 62
Lexile: 1180

770

Learning Objectives

For pages 770–773

In studying this text, you will focus on the following objectives:

Reading:
Using text features.
Analyzing informational text.
Identifying problem and solution.

Set a Purpose for Reading

Read to learn about how the citizens of Kitakyushu, Japan, improved their environment. Consider how this relates to the problems of industrialization detailed in Shu Ting's poem "Assembly Line."

Preview the Article

1. Read the deck—the brief text beneath the article's title—and scan the photographs in this article. What do you think it is about?

2. Skim the first paragraph. What essential facts do you learn?

Reading Strategy

Identify Problem and Solution

When you **identify problem and solution**, you uncover the structure and purpose of an article. As you read this article, ask yourself, What problems and solutions does it present? Use a chart like the one below to record your findings.

Problems	Solutions

770 UNIT 4 EAST ASIA

A New Day
DAWNS

An industrial city that was among the most polluted in Japan has become an environmental role model.

By **BRYAN WALSH**

AS HE BEGAN HIS DAILY COMMUTE, YOICHI Kaminaga could look down the mountainside on which he lived and see the layer of smoky red, black, and brown air that hid the city of Kitakyushu below. It was the 1960s, and smoke soared from hundreds of factories in this western Japanese city that produced raw materials for the country's manufacturing boom. But if the impact of rapid industrial growth on the environment was already visible in Kitakyushu, that didn't mean it was understood. "I had to go down through the smoke when I was coming to work, and it smelled awful," says Kaminaga, who worked at a brick factory. "But we didn't feel it was dangerous. It meant for us that we were producing a lot for the country. Now I realize that we were destroying the environment."

By the 1960s, Kitakyushu, one of the nation's main industrial centers, was possibly Japan's most polluted city, at a time when the country was an environmental nightmare. But Kitakyushu was also one of the first major Japanese cities to clean itself up, when local housewives debated, protested, and shamed officials and companies into controlling the pollution. Step out of Kitakyushu's new international airport today and you'll see blue sky and clean water next to factories that puff smoke as gently as a professor's pipe.

Across Japan, urban pollution has been controlled to a remarkable degree. Kitakyushu stands out among the country's success stories. The city's effort to reduce

---

Vocabulary Practice

Recognize Adjectives Point out to students that adjectives help make informational texts more effective by adding vivid details and color that strengthen description. **Ask:** What adjectives do you find in the first paragraph? *(daily, smoky, red, black, brown, western, Japanese, raw, manufacturing, rapid, visible, understood, awful, brick, dangerous)*

Have students to reread the paragraph, leaving the adjectives out. **Ask:** How is the paragraph different without adjectives? *(There is not as much information given; it is less specific and less compelling.)*

pollution is an example of Japan's path to becoming environmentally aware and an antipollution experience for other Asian cities to follow. "We want to help those cities before they suffer as much as we did," says Koichi Sueyoshi, Kitakyushu's long-time mayor. "I believe [other cities] can clean up because we were able to do it, and we can be the role model."

Kitakyushu wasn't always a model to follow. A documentary produced by one of the city's women's groups in 1965 shows the city's factories, charcoal-polluted skies, filthy apartment buildings, and children who looked like chimney cleaners. When the film was made, some 100 tons of dust fell per sq km some months in Kitakyushu's most polluted districts. The narrator of the documentary declares: "Industrial development should not take place at the cost of the people."

It was a simple but revolutionary statement that would inspire the changes to come. In the 1950s and '60s, the housewives of Kitakyushu—organized into numerous women's associations across the city—were the first to recognize the damage uncontrolled development brought to their families. "They could never get their laundry white from all the soot," says Yoshiko Misumi, the president of an organization that has studied the women's movement in Kitakyushu. "Their children would get sick. That's what pushed them."

Because most of the women were married to factory workers or executives, they were in the awkward position of protesting the very businesses that put food on their tables. So rather than dem-

At the Kitakyushu industrial center, industry and housing vie for space. Heavy pollution plagues the people who live nearby.

Greg Davis/OnAsia Images

onstrating in the streets, they began to carefully gather evidence. Working with supportive university professors, the women spent months calculating the pollution with homemade experiments. They measured how much soot dust accumulated on drying bedsheets and recorded how often children were absent from school with illnesses caused by breathing polluted air. They even tossed a live goldfish into a bowl of water taken from Kitakyushu's industrial Dokai Bay, otherwise known as the "Sea of Death." (The fish died instantly.)

Led by resourceful women like Akiko Mori, a teacher recognized decades later by the United Nations for her work to improve the environment, the Kitakyushu's

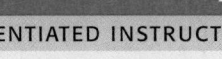

TIME

Teach

Big Idea   1

Virtue and Wisdom Remind students that Confucius taught that the key to life is to behave in harmony with the principle of order in the universe. He also said that rulers governed by a "Mandate of Heaven," and that if they did not govern properly, it was reflected in the state of the region over which they had authority. Ask students if Confucius would think, based on the incident of the goldfish, that Kitakyushu was being governed properly. *(He would not.)*

Learning Objectives
Identifying problem and solution. (SE)
Capitalizing proper nouns. (TE)

English Learners

DIFFERENTIATED INSTRUCTION

Intermediate The opening paragraph of this piece is highly visual, but it might prove difficult to picture for English learners. Suggest that students take the time to see all of the images Walsh describes. Have students close their eyes and then read descriptions from the text aloud to help them create a clear picture in their mind of what Kitakyushu looked like in the 1960s.

Advanced Learners/Pre-AP

DIFFERENTIATED INSTRUCTION

Debate Have advanced students gather in small groups. Divide each group in half, assigning one side the role of the factory owners and managers and the other side the role of the women's group members. Each side should take up their role's argument as to whether industry should or should not be restricted. Some students might find it difficult to argue for the side they are assigned to, but make clear to them that they are not expressing their *own* opinion but their assigned *group's* side of the debate.

TIME

Text Element　1

Capitalization　Have students identify the capitalized nouns in this sentence. *(Kitakyushu, Japanese, United Nations Environmental Program, Global 500 Award)* Have them explain why each is capitalized. *(They are all considered proper nouns because they fit in the following categories, and are thus capitalized:* Kitakyushu *is a geographical term;* Japanese *is a national group;* UNEP *is the name of an organization; and the* Global 500 Award *is an award.)*

View the Photograph ★

Ask students to compare the photos on this page and the previous page and indicate which view of the city they think would be a more inspiring setting for a poet. *(Most students will say the cleaner city.)*

Tetsuya Miura for Time

★ **GREEN FUTURE** Kitakyushu's once-polluted Dokai Bay area as it appears today.

women's associations took their research data to city officials and industry executives and demanded action. One factory manager dismissed the movement, saying, "Citizens should endure a certain degree of pollution." But the women knew better, and by the mid-'60s public opinion, in Kitakyushu and elsewhere, began to swing their way. "They said it was in everyone's interest to do something, because the pollution was affecting everyone," says Beverly Yamamoto, a professor at Osaka University who has studied the movement. "They backed that up with hard data."

If industry was slow to respond at first, city politicians were quicker. They knew the women's

groups were planning to turn pollution into an issue during upcoming elections. Shortly after the national government passed Japan's first real pollution laws in 1967, Kitakyushu began establishing even tougher regulations. Factories there installed over 1,000 air cleaners between 1967 and 1978, and in the early 1970s they switched to fuels that created less smog.

In 1972 the city began to clean the bottom of Dokai Bay, which had been seriously contaminated with mercury. Equally important, the local government strictly enforced regulations to control pollution. One policy required companies to reduce the amount of smog-causing sulfur dioxide pro-

duced by their factories by 20–40% on days when weather conditions made smog formation likely.

The citizens of Kitakyushu also began to use less coal. As a result, dust levels fell nearly 75% from 1970–75. Kitakyushu's pioneering housewives had made the difference. "If there had been no women's movement, our work to reduce pollution would have been significantly delayed," says Reiji Hitsumoto, an environmental official with the city government.

In 1990, Kitakyushu became 1 the first Japanese city to win the United Nations Environmental Program's (UNEP) Global 500 Award. The award recognizes the environmental achievements of individuals and organizations

772　UNIT 4　EAST ASIA

Writing Practice

SPIRAL REVIEW　**Research Report**　Have students research an environmental problem of their choice. Students should present evidence of the problem and discuss possible solutions. They should summarize their findings in a two-page report. Remind students to cite their sources. Ask volunteers to share their research with the class in a brief oral presentation.

around the world. Kitakyushu's concerned citizens had learned that if they express their views, they could save even the most polluted city.

Kitakyushu is sharing that lesson with developing cities struggling with the effects of industrialization on the environment. Since 1980 Kitakyushu, with the help of the Japan International Cooperation Agency, has sent environmental consultants to developing countries. The consultants help local governments plan and practice anti-pollution measures based on the Kitakyushu model. Thousands of environmental officers from abroad have also visited Kitakyushu to be trained in pollution control methods. They learn everything from how to dispose of garbage and other waste to insuring cleaner industrial production.

The results can be seen in Dalian, a city in northeastern China that was once a carbon copy of the polluted Kitakyushu of the 1960s. Over the past 15 years, Kitakyushu has trained factory managers from Dalian, refitted plants there with cleaner industrial technology and conducted a survey that helped the local government to develop a model environmental zone. The cooperation has paid off. Under Kitakyushu's guidance Dalian joined the UNEP's honor roll in 2001. Officials in Dalian hope their success will be a model for other Chinese cities to follow.

The transformation of Kitakyushu and Dalian is powerful proof that even cities that once measured their success solely by how well industries performed can discover the importance of environmental-friendly economic growth. "Combining environmental efforts with economic benefits has become

a vital international issue," says Hiro Mizoguchi, the director of Kitakyushu's Office for International Environmental Cooperation. "I definitely think it can be accomplished, and our effort is part of that."

For Kitakyushu, this commitment to a cleaner future is now an important part of its character. The city that once accepted pollution as an ordinary part of urban life now even boasts its own environment museum, where former factory workers like Kaminaga teach schoolchildren about the importance of a clean environment. "People here feel about the environment the way they used to about production," he says. "I'm proud of my city."

— **With reporting by Yuki Oda/ Kitakyushu Updated 2007.**

Respond and Think Critically

Respond and Interpret

1. Write a brief summary of the main ideas in this article before you answer the following questions. For help in writing a summary, see page 1147.

2. (a) Who led the environmental movement in Kitakyushu? (b) How did they influence public opinion?

3. (a) What problems did pollution create for the citizens of Kitakyushu? (b) Why might it have taken so long for anti-pollution efforts to take hold?

4. (a) How did the city's industries and government reduce pollution? (b) What does this suggest about the potential for efforts to control pollution in other places?

Analyze and Evaluate

5. (a) How did the activists in Kitakyushu organize themselves? (b) What does their example suggest about grassroots organizations?

6. (a) How does Kitakyushu serve as a role model to Dalian, China, and the world? (b) Is it important to have a global discussion about environmental pollution? Why or why not?

Connect

7. What similarities do you see between the pollution in Kitakyushu and the pollution described in Shu Ting's poem "Assembly Line"?

A NEW DAY DAWNS **773**

Assess

1. Answers will vary, but summaries should address the seriousness of Kitakyushu's 1960s pollution, the women's groups that helped find solutions to the problem, and the city's current assistance to other cities that face pollution problems.

2. (a) A range of women's groups—largely consisting of housewives—based in Kitakyushu led the movement. (b) They collected data (and soot) to prove their point.

3. (a) The air and bodies of water were full of pollution. Fish were dying, and children were becoming ill. (b) People may have felt pollution was a necessary part of prosperity or that pollution was not harmful.

4. (a) Factories installed air cleaners, switched to low-sulfur fuel, and cut emissions; the government created tougher environmental regulations. (b) When industry and government collaborate on preventive measures and stricter environmental regulations, pollution can be reduced.

5. (a) The activists founded women's associations, gathered information, and demanded action from industries and local government. (b) Grassroots organization may be a way to change industry and government. In order to be successful, activists need to implement a strategy and follow through with it.

6. (a) Kitakyushu, along with the Japan International Cooperation Agency, sent consultants to help Dailan improve its environment. They also have shown citizens can quickly improve a severely polluted city. (b) Students should support their answers.

7. Similarities include pollution coming from factories, smog, and sickened living things (in the poem, trees are mentioned).

Focus

Bellringer Options

**Daily Language Practice
Transparency 70**

Or write on the board:

Indochina

Point out that this was the name of the French colony that consisted of the modern Southeast Asian countries of Vietnam, Laos, and Cambodia. **Ask:** What two geographical names are combined in this term? *(India and China)* **Ask:** What might this term indicate about the culture of Southeast Asia? *(It has strong influences from India and China.)*

View the Art ★

The Australian painter David Dridan depicts the characteristic landscapes of South Australia, the part of the country where he makes his home. **Ask:** What does this landscape indicate about South Australia? *(It has a desert climate.)*

Ⓐ Mt. Egmont and Lake Mangamahoe. Douglas Pearson. Egmont National Park, New Zealand.

Ⓑ *Betty Bon Cordillo, Australia.* David Clyde Dridan. Private collection. ★

Literature Online

Literature and Reading For more about the history and literature of this period, go to glencoe.com and enter QuickPass code GLW6053u4.

774

Part Introduction Skills

Reading Skills
- Analyze Graphic Information (SE p. 777)
- Analyze Cultural Context (SE p. 782; TE p. 776)
- Compare and Contrast (SE p. 783)
- Analyze Cause-and-Effect Relationships (SE p. 784)

Part 2 Introduction

Speaking/Listening/Viewing Skills
- Visual Literacy (SE p. 785)
- Panel Discussion (SE p. 785)
- Analyze Art (TE pp. 775, 776, 778)

Vocabulary Skills
- Context Clues (TE p. 778)

Writing Skills/Grammar
- Consistent Verb Tenses (TE p. 782)

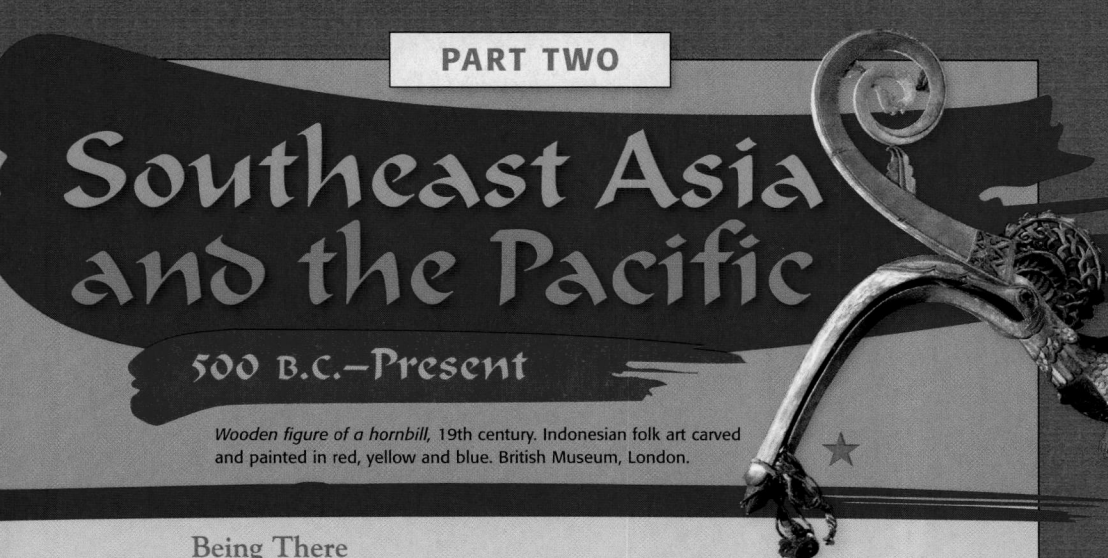

PART TWO

Southeast Asia and the Pacific

500 B.C.–Present

Wooden figure of a hornbill, 19th century. Indonesian folk art carved and painted in red, yellow and blue. British Museum, London.

Being There

Southeast Asia has two geographical regions: the mainland, extending southward from the Chinese border to the tip of the Malay Peninsula, and a chain of islands, most of which are part of present-day Indonesia or the Philippines. To the east and south of these regions lie the vast continent of Australia, the smaller and wetter islands of New Zealand, and the thousands of islands scattered across the Pacific Ocean.

Looking Ahead

China and India strongly influenced the cultures of Southeast Asia and the Pacific. The Pacific islands, now almost all grouped into independent republics, are still inhabited by descendants of the people who migrated there from Southeast Asia centuries ago. The majority of the inhabitants of Australia and New Zealand, on the other hand, are descendants of European settlers.

Keep the following questions in mind as you read:

How did political conflict and war influence Southeast Asian literature?

What responses to the natural environment does the literature of the Pacific islands reflect?

How does the literature of Australia and New Zealand reflect this region's colonization by Europeans?

775

Focus
Summary

This introduction gives an overview of the complex cultural forces that shaped Southeast Asia and the Pacific Islands, including the rise of Southeast Asian kingdoms, the spice trade, and colonialism. The introduction also describes Southeast Asian architecture, performing arts, and music, and the art of the Pacific island cultures.

Reading Strategy | 1

Question **Ask:** How is Australia's geography different from that of the rest of this region? *(Australia is largely desert.)*
ENGLISH LEARNERS English learners may need help with geographical terms such as *mainland, peninsula, desert,* and *continent.*

> For additional support for English Learners, see Unit 4 Teaching Resources Book, p. 182.

View the Art

The Iban are one group of the Dyaks (or Dayaks), a general term for the non-Muslim native peoples who live in the interior region of the island of Borneo. The tropical bird known as the hornbill is a frequent subject of Iban art.
Ask: What words would you use to describe the artistic style of this carving? *(Students might use such words as decorative, abstract, or elaborate.)*

Approaching Level

DIFFERENTIATED INSTRUCTION

Purpose for Reading Point out to students that the questions at the bottom of page 775 are intended to help guide their reading of the Part 2 introduction. Work with small groups of students to create other purpose-setting questions, such as the following:

- How did India and China influence the cultures of Southeast Asia?

- What are the countries of Southeast Asia like today?
- How do the Pacific island cultures differ from those of mainland Southeast Asia?

Have students write down their questions and answer them as they read the introduction to Part 2.

Teach

Reading Strategy | 1

Analyze Cultural Context

Ask: What evidence does the timeline offer of Chinese political and cultural influence in Southeast Asia? *(after 111 B.C.—Chinese writing system is introduced into Vietnam; 111 B.C.—China conquers what is now northern Vietnam)*

ADVANCED Ask: How long was Vietnam under Chinese control? *(1,050 years; from 111 B.C. until A.D. 939)*

View the Art ★

The easternmost of the Polynesian islands, Easter Island is famous for its huge stone statues. Carved from volcanic rock, most of the statues range from 10 to 20 feet in height, though a few are far larger. **Ask:** What do you think these statues were intended to depict? *(Students might mention gods or ancestors.)* **Ask:** What mood is created by these statues? *(Students might feel that the statues create a mood of mystery or timelessness.)*

776

Timeline 500 B.C.–Present

SOUTHEAST ASIAN AND PACIFIC LITERATURE | 1

| 500 B.C. | A.D. 1 | | A.D. 1000 |

after 111
Chinese writing system is introduced into Vietnam

c. 870
Javanese version of the *Ramayana* is composed

◄ **1113**
Earliest surviving text in the Burmese language is carved in stone

c. 1250
Earliest surviving Thai literature is written

1380
Nguyen Trai is born in Vietnam

SOUTHEAST ASIAN AND PACIFIC EVENTS | 2

| 500 B.C. | A.D. 1 | | A.D. 1000 |

c. 500
Dong Son culture is established in northern Vietnam

c. 250
First Buddhist missionaries arrive in Southeast Asia

111
China conquers what is now northern Vietnam

c. 100
Funan, the first great Southeast Asian kingdom, is established in Cambodia

c. 400
Easter Island is settled ▼

c. 800
First Maori arrive in New Zealand

802
Khmer state is founded in Cambodia

939
Vietnam regains independence from China

c. 1150
Construction of Angkor Wat is completed in Cambodia

1238
First Thai kingdom is founded

★

WORLD EVENTS

| 500 B.C. | A.D. 1 | |

490
Greeks defeat Persians at the Battle of Marathon

c. 483
Siddhārtha Gautama, founder of Buddhism, dies

c. 1
Bantu people begin to migrate east and south from Central Africa

711
Islamic armies invade Spain

800
Charlemagne is crowned Holy Roman Emperor

c. 900
Rise of Toltec civilization in Mexico

▲
c. 985
First Viking settlements are established in Greenland

1275–1292
Marco Polo visits China

1492
Christopher Columbus reaches America

LOG ON ▶ **Literature** Online

Literature and Reading To explore the Interactive Timeline, go to glencoe.com and enter QuickPass code GLW6053u4.

Reading Practice

SPIRAL REVIEW **Use Graphic Organizers** Explain that a timeline is one kind of chart that presents a sequence of events. Another kind of diagram that serves this function is a flow chart. To construct a flow chart, arrange events in order. Then draw arrows between these events to show how one event flows into another.

Dutch explorer Tasman is first European to sight New Zealand *(3)*
First Maori arrive in New Zealand *(1)*
Dutch East India Company is formed *(2)*

A.D. 1500

1651
Roman alphabet for writing the Vietnamese language is introduced

1765
Nguyen Du, author of Vietnamese epic *The Tale of Kieu*, is born ☆

1922
Katherine Mansfield's *The Garden Party* is published

1973
Patrick White becomes the first Australian to win the Nobel Prize in Literature

1991
Pro-democracy activist Aung San Suu Kyi of Myanmar wins the Nobel Peace Prize

NATIONAL LEAGUE FOR DEMOCRACY

◄ **1642**
Dutch explorer Tasman is first European to sight New Zealand

1779 ►
Explorer Captain James Cook dies after fruitless search for the Northwest Passage

1602
Dutch East India Company is formed

1788
British establish prison colony in New South Wales, Australia

Captain Cook's Tiki, 18th Century

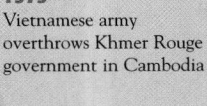

1858–1893
France takes control of Indochina

1979
Vietnamese army overthrows Khmer Rouge government in Cambodia

A.D. 1500

1789
French Revolution begins

1869
Suez Canal is completed

1912
Last Chinese emperor abdicates

1957
Soviet Union launches *Sputnik I* satellite

Reading Check

Analyze Graphic Information About how many years after the death of Siddhārtha Gautama did Buddhist missionaries begin arriving in Southeast Asia?

INTRODUCTION **777**

Advanced Learners/Pre-AP

DIFFERENTIATED INSTRUCTION

SMALL GROUP

Maori Society Point out to students that the Maori of New Zealand have a unique social organization that helped them avoid the fate of other indigenous peoples (such as the Aborigines of neighboring Australia). The Maori fought a series of guerrilla wars against British rule in the mid-1800s and later succeeded in gaining representation in the New Zealand parliament. Today many Maori live in rural areas and maintain their cultural traditions. Have students work in small groups to research Maori history and culture, looking particularly for features that allowed them to remain independent. Have each group present its conclusions to the class.

UNIT FOUR
PART 2

Teach
Reading Check

Answer: *Buddhist missionaries began arriving in Southeast Asia about 233 years after the death of Siddhartha Gautama.*

Reading Strategy | 2

Analyze Graphic Information Ask: Were the Maori present on New Zealand when the Dutch explorer Tasman sighted the islands? *(yes)*

APPROACHING If students have trouble answering, have them scan the timeline for the word *Maori*. **Ask:** When did the Maori arrive in New Zealand? *(in about A.D. 800)*

Literary History ☆

Nguyen Du and *The Tale of Kieu* Often described as the father of Vietnamese literature, Nguyen Du wrote *The Tale of Kieu*, a long tale in verse of doomed love. The tale also explores differences between Confucian values and Buddhist values. Popular with Vietnamese people from all walks of life, *The Tale of Kieu* is the masterpiece of Vietnamese literature.

Learning Objectives
Analyzing graphic information. (SE)
Analyzing cultural context. (TE)
Using graphic organizers. (TE)

777

Teach

Reading Strategy   1

Determine Main Idea

Ask: What is the topic sentence of this paragraph? (*The religions of Southeast Asia and the Pacific Islands often combine many layers of cultural influences.*)

ADVANCED **Ask:** What is another region of the world where traditional animistic beliefs coexist with world religions? (*Students might mention Africa, where animism coexists with Islam and Christianity.*)

View the Art ★

Located in the delta of the Red River near the Gulf of Tonkin, Haiphong is Vietnam's largest seaport. A key element in the French campaign to colonize Vietnam was taking control of the Red River delta.
Ask: What seems to have been the purpose of this print? (*to create a diagram giving an overview of the French occupation of this area*)

Learning Objectives

For pages 774–785

In studying this text, you will focus on the following objectives:

Literary Study: Analyzing literary periods.

Reading: Evaluating historical influences.
Connecting to the literature.

Southeast Asia and the Pacific
500 B.C.–Present

Historical, Social, and Cultural Forces

A Complex Region

Southeast Asia is a complex region reflecting a rich mixture of peoples, cultures, and religions. The earliest settlers arrived from the north and west thousands of years ago, traveling down through Indochina and eventually spreading as far east as Polynesia. Mountain ranges and river valleys divide the nations of Southeast Asia. These geographical barriers may explain why the region was never unified under a single government. Instead, distinctive cultures with different languages and religions developed.

A Mixture of Faiths   1

The religions of Southeast Asia and the Pacific islands often combine many layers of cultural influences. The oldest beliefs are animistic, requiring the performance of ceremonies and rituals to communicate with gods, spirits, and ancestors. Later, Indian missionaries and merchants carried both Buddhist and Hindu traditions to Indonesia. In Myanmar, Thailand, Laos, and Cambodia, most people practice a variety of Buddhism that is in many ways close to the Buddha's original teachings. In Vietnam, the influence of Confucian thought has been strong.

In the thirteenth century, Arab traders played a large part in converting Malaysia and most of Indonesia to Islam. Today, only the people of Bali retain a form of Hinduism, but Indian traditions are still very evident throughout Indonesian music, dance, theater, and textile arts. (See "The *Mahabharata* as Shadow Play," pages 574–575.) Christianity, introduced by European missionaries, is widespread in the Philippines and the Pacific islands.

Buddha Park, 1958. Bunleua Sulilat. Vientiane, Laos.

Vocabulary Practice

SPIRAL REVIEW

Use Context Clues Remind students that they can often figure out the meaning of an unfamiliar word by examining the clues present in its context, which consists of the words and sentences that surround it. Point out that a common type of context clue is an example. Draw students' attention to the following sentence in the paragraph at the bottom of page 779.

"This situation changed dramatically in the late nineteenth century, however, when the "new imperialism" resulted in the European colonization of much of Southeast Asia." **Ask:** What example is given of the effect of imperialism? (*widespread colonization*) **Ask:** What might you infer is the meaning of *imperialism?* (*a policy of establishing colonies*)

Have students write the definitions of the underlined words in the following sentences, based on the context.

1. The people's religion was <u>animism</u> and they worshipped spirits and ancestors. (*worship of spirits and ancestors*)

2. The <u>sultan</u> ruled a kingdom that engaged in the spice trade. (*ruler*)

3. The <u>repressive</u> government denied the right of free speech to its citizens. (*tyrannical*)

Ancient Kingdoms

Before A.D. 1500, a number of states developed in Southeast Asia, adapting political models from India and China. The Vietnamese were one of the first peoples in Southeast Asia to develop their own state. After the Chinese conquered Vietnam in 111 B.C., they tried for centuries to make it part of China. The Vietnamese clung to their own identity, however, and in A.D. 939 they finally overthrew Chinese rule.

> *"How dare you bandits trespass on our soil?*
> *You shall meet your undoing at our hands."*
>
> —Traditional Vietnamese poem

In the ninth century A.D., the kingdom of Angkor arose in what is now Cambodia. This kingdom was formed when a powerful ruler named Jayavarman united the Khmer (kə mer´) people and established his capital at Angkor Thom. Although surrounded by enemies, Angkor, or the Khmer Empire, remained the most powerful state in Southeast Asia for several centuries.

The Spice Trade

Some Southeast Asian states, such as the Sultanate of Melaka (located in present-day Malaysia and Indonesia), supported themselves chiefly through trade. During the Middle Ages, the demand for spices enriched these trading states. Merchant fleets from India, the Arabian Peninsula, and, later, Europe sailed to the Indonesian islands. There they bought cloves, pepper, nutmeg, cinnamon, and precious woods, such as teak and sandalwood, which wealthy Chinese and Europeans desired.

Western Imperialism [2]

For centuries, the European presence in Southeast Asia was confined to a few trading and missionary outposts. This situation changed dramatically in the mid-nineteenth century, however, when the

Arrival of the French in the Bay of Haiphong, 1884. Vietnamese school. Private collection.

"new imperialism" resulted in the European colonization of much of Southeast Asia. From 1858 to 1893, France gained control of Vietnam, Cambodia, and Laos, creating French Indochina. After World War II, Vietnamese nationalists under communist leader Ho Chi Minh fought against the French. In 1954, France withdrew from Vietnam, and the country was divided into communist North Vietnam and noncommunist South Vietnam, which soon waged civil war. The United States intervened in support of South Vietnam, but eventually withdrew its troops. By 1975, the communists ruled all of Vietnam.

Postcolonial Southeast Asia ☆

Many colonies in Southeast Asia achieved independence after World War II. In 1946, the United States granted independence to the Philippines. Two years later, Burma (now Myanmar), a British colony, became independent. In 1949, the Netherlands recognized the independence of Indonesia. Malaya, another British colony, became independent in 1957 (and became part of Malaysia in 1963). Many of these nations, however, have been plagued by ethnic and religious conflicts, political corruption, and repressive governments. For example, the military government in Myanmar has repressed free speech. Moreover, it continues to keep under house arrest Aung San Suu Kyi, an activist for democracy and the winner of the 1991 Nobel Peace Prize.

INTRODUCTION **779**

UNIT FOUR
PART 2

Teach

Reading Strategy | 2

Compare and Contrast
Ask: How did the "new imperialism" differ from previous European presence in Southeast Asia? *(The early European presence had been limited to trade; the new imperialism involved turning many nations of Southeast Asia into European colonies.)*

Cultural History ☆

Thailand Thailand (formerly Siam) was one of the few countries in Southeast Asia that did not fall under colonial rule in the 1800s, largely due to the diplomacy of King Mongkut (Rama IV) and his son Chulalongkorn (Rama V). Mongkut was interested in Western ideas and invited European advisers to help him modernize his kingdom. Mongkut was the model for the king in the Broadway musical *The King and I,* which was based on Margaret Langdon's book *Anna and the King of Siam.*

Approaching Level

DIFFERENTIATED INSTRUCTION 🐾

Religion Chart Students might find it easier to retain the information on the region's religions if they organized it in a table like the one started below.

Country	Religion
Indonesia	Buddhism, Hinduism

Learning Objectives
Analyzing historical influences. (SE)
Using context clues. (TE)

779

Teach

Vocabulary   **1**

Context Clues   **Ask:** What process does the architecture of Borobodur describe? *(the passage of a soul toward enlightenment)*

[APPROACHING] **Ask:** How does this outline of the process of salvation in Buddhism provide context for the meaning of *exposition*? *(The outline explains the word exposition.)*

Political History ☆

Suryavarman II The builder of Angkor Wat was a religious reformer who promoted the worship of the Hindu gods Vishnu and Shiva, and ceased the royal patronage of Buddhism begun by his predecessors. Sculpted as Vishnu on the walls of Angkor Wat, Suryavarman is shown carrying out various duties as king, such as reviewing his troops or holding audiences.

Architecture

Borobudur, on the Indonesian island of Java, and Angkor Wat, in Cambodia, rank among the world's great architectural monuments. Borobudur, built over a period of decades around A.D. 800, is both a Buddhist temple and an exposition in stone of the Buddhist faith. As pilgrims circle the temple's nine levels, they symbolically move from the material world toward spiritual enlightenment—shown as an only partially visible figure of the Buddha. Angkor Wat, a twelfth-century Hindu temple, is the crowning achievement of the temple-building Khmers. Angkor Wat, which covers about 500 acres and is the largest religious structure in the world, was conceived as an image of the sacred mountain that was believed to be the source of all creation. It was also built as a royal tomb; it is the resting place of Suryavarman II, who was king when the temple was built.

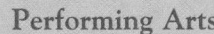

> *"It is grander than anything left to us by Greece and Rome ... "*
>
> —Henri Mouhot,
> early French visitor to Angkor Wat

Entrance to Angkor Wat. Bob Krist. Angkor Wat, Cambodia. ☆

Performing Arts

Southeast Asian theater combines music, song, dance, drama, mime, and narrative. Performers often wear masks or have heavily painted faces, and they wear rich, gold-decorated fabrics. Tales from the two Indian epics, the *Mahabharata* and the *Ramayana*, are popular even in non-Hindu countries; episodes from these classical tales are often interwoven with local legends and histories.

Although each nation has its own individual style, classical dance characteristics include the following:

- Dancers perform close to the ground.
- They use extensive, controlled arm and hand gestures.
- Dancers maintain composed faces.
- Dance tempos are slow, except for the vigorous battle scenes.

Dancer at the Royal Palace. Gian Berto Vanni. Ubud, Bali, Indonesia. ★

Reading Practice

SPIRAL REVIEW   **Determine Main Idea and Supporting Details** Remind students that the main idea of a paragraph will be the thought that organizes that paragraph and around which all the other sentences are built. Some writers directly state the main idea in a topic sentence, while others imply the main idea with examples and other clues. Draw students' attention to the paragraph under the heading "Gong Orchestras."

Ask: Is the topic sentence directly stated or implied? *(stated)* **Ask:** What is the topic sentence? *("The gongs differ in material, number, size, the way they are played, and the sounds they produce.")* **Ask:** What supporting details does the paragraph present? *(different types of gong orchestras in various regions of Southeast Asia)*

Have students identify the topic sentence and the supporting details in the paragraph under the heading "Art of the Pacific Islands." *(topic sentence: "The kind of art produced in the Pacific islands often depends on what resources are available." supporting details: different materials used on various Pacific islands)*

◀ Playing a Trompong in a Gamelan Orchestra. Christine Osborne. Bali, Indonesia.

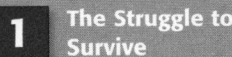 gongs and may also include wood instruments, such as xylophones with bamboo resonators. In Thailand, Laos, and Cambodia, families of instruments—gongs, xylophones, reeds, and drums—play different parts of the music. In Malaysia, parts of Indonesia, and the Philippines, suspended gongs produce a deep, booming sound. The gong orchestras often accompany dance dramas, masked and shadow plays, and religious ceremonies.

Art of the Pacific Islands

The kind of art produced in the Pacific islands often depends on what resources are available. In New Zealand, raw materials are abundant; carved wooden gateways and jade sculptures were made there. In eastern Polynesia, art has ranged from the monumental stone sculptures of Easter Island to the feather capes and headdresses of Hawaii. On the small islands, where raw materials are few, artists and craftspeople concentrate on making everyday objects as simple and elegant as possible.

Gong Orchestras

The use of gong orchestras is a characteristic common to most Southeast Asian music. The gongs differ in material, number, size, the way they are played, and the sounds they produce. In Java and Bali, gamelan (ga′ mə lan) orchestras are popular; they use an array of different types of

PREVIEW **Big Ideas** of Southeast Asia and the Pacific **3**

1 The Struggle to Survive	**2** Place and Identity	**3** Cultures in Conflict
The peoples of Southeast Asia often have struggled for freedom and even survival. In modern times, the Vietnamese faced colonization, occupation, and civil war. Cambodians suffered savage brutality under the radical communist rule of the Khmer Rouge. **See page 782**	The Chinese poetic ideal of a simple rural life away from the world's bustle deeply influenced traditional Vietnamese poetry. The geographic isolation of the Pacific islands stimulated their literature, which expresses a profound reverence for the ocean. **See page 783**	Colonists journeyed to Australia and New Zealand to build a new life, but they also brought British values and their familiar class system with them. This spurred conflict with native peoples. **See page 784**

Advanced Learners/Pre-AP

DIFFERENTIATED INSTRUCTION

SMALL GROUP

Culture Map To help the class appreciate the richness and variety of the cultures of the Southeast Asia and the Pacific, have a small group of interested students collaborate on a regional map illustrated with images of examples of the traditional arts of each area.

To get students started on their research, suggest these examples:

- Cambodia (temple sculptures)
- New Zealand (wood carving)
- Australia (rock art)
- Bali (masks)
- Indonesia (shadow puppets)
- Easter Island (monumental sculptures)
- Hawaii (featherwork)

When students have completed their maps, have them present the maps to the class.

Teach

Reading Strategy **2**

Question **Ask:** What do you think the purpose of a resonator is? *(to increase the sound of a musical instrument)*

Text Element **3**

Boxes Remind students that the three boxed features on page 781 summarize key characteristics of Southeast Asia and the Pacific that will be developed in the three succeeding pages. **Ask:** How was the experience of British settlers in Australia and New Zealand like that of American pioneers? *(The settlers' British values conflicted with the values of native peoples.)*

View the Art ★

Some Balinese dance dramas combine theatrical performance with ritual reenactments of an eternal battle between good and evil spirits. **Ask:** What performance qualities do you think contribute to the enduring popularity of these dance dramas? *(Students might mention such qualities as music, costuming, the skills of the dancers, or the appeal of the stories.)*

Learning Objectives
Analyze historical influences. (SE)
Determine main idea and supporting details. (TE)

Teach

Reading Check

Answer: *The heroic status given to the Trung sisters reflects the Vietnamese values of independence and resistance to foreign domination.*

Reading Strategy | **1**

Analyze Tone **Ask:** What attitude toward the Trung sisters do these lines express? *(great reverence for their heroism)*

Ask: What other women in history might be regarded in much the same way as the Trung sisters? *(Students might mention such national heroines as Joan of Arc, Queen Elizabeth I, Boadicea, Rani Lakshmibai, Aung San Suu Kyi, and Rosa Parks.)* ADVANCED

Big Idea 1
The Struggle to Survive

How might the history of some Southeast Asian nations, marked by repeated struggles for independence, have helped shape their national characters?

Vietnamese Nationalism

In 111 B.C., China's powerful Han emperor Wu-Ti conquered what is now northern Vietnam. Attempts to impose Chinese culture on the Vietnamese, however, soon met with determined resistance. In A.D. 39, two noblewomen, Trung Trac and her sister Trung Nhi, organized a revolt against local Chinese rulers. At first successful, the sisters eventually were defeated by a Han army, after which China tightened its control over Vietnam. Still, the Trung sisters were regarded as national heroes and are still celebrated today. Even after regaining independence in A.D. 939, Vietnam endured periodic Chinese invasions. These centuries of struggle against a foreign power helped shape the Vietnamese national character. It is marked by a fierce streak of independence and a staunch refusal to yield to foreign rule.

> "To slay the people's foe and wreak revenge,
> Two sisters lifted arms for their just cause . . .
> While streams and hills endure, their shrine shall stand:
> A monument to peerless womanhood."
>
> —Traditional Vietnamese poem

1

Children Caught up in the Fall of Saigon, April 29, 1975. Jacques Pavlovsky. South Vietnam.

The Khmer Rouge

In 1975, the Khmer Rouge, a radical communist faction, used guerrilla warfare to seize control of Cambodia. It installed its military leader, Pol Pot, as prime minister and enacted a series of measures designed to bring about a classless society. Under the Khmer Rouge, more than one million Cambodians died from execution, torture, disease, or starvation. In 1979, Vietnamese forces ousted the Khmer Rouge from power. Pin Yathay describes the sufferings inflicted by the Khmer Rouge in Cambodia in *Stay Alive, My Son* (see pages 819–827). After Pol Pot's death in 1998, the last remnants of the Khmer Rouge disbanded.

Literature of Southeast Asia

A consistent theme in contemporary Southeast Asian literature is the struggle of the author to express a personal identity amid social and political change. Important modern authors include novelist Pramoedya Ananta Toer of Indonesia and democracy activist Aung San Suu Kyi of Myanmar, winner of the Nobel Peace Prize.

Reading Check

Analyze Cultural Context What Vietnamese cultural values does the heroic status of the Trung sisters reflect?

Writing Practice

SPIRAL REVIEW **Keep Verb Tenses Consistent** Remind students to avoid shifting or changing tenses when two or more events occur at the same time. Draw students' attention to the underlined verbs in this sentence:

The Khmer Rouge <u>seized</u> control of Cambodia and <u>install</u> Pol Pot as prime minister.

Point out that both actions described by the verbs occur at the same time, but *seized* is in the past tense and *install* is in the present tense. Have students determine whether the verbs in the following sentences are consistent in tense. If they are, write "correct"; if not, rewrite the sentence to make the tenses consistent.

1. The Trung sisters organized a revolt and defeat a Chinese military commander. *(The Trung sisters organized a revolt and defeated a Chinese military commander.)*

2. The sisters captured many fortresses and proclaimed themselves queens of an independent state. *(correct)*

3. Untrained Vietnamese forces are no match for Chinese troops, however, and were later defeated. *(Untrained Vietnamese forces were no match for Chinese troops, however, and were later defeated.)*

Big Idea 2
Place and Identity

2 The idea of remoteness, of "getting away from it all," may call to mind an array of images, such as a country landscape with a still pond reflecting the stars, or a mysterious island with huge waves battering its shores. The literatures of Southeast Asia and the Pacific often express remoteness, exploring connections between place and identity.

Fields and Gardens

Chinese literature distinguished different types of remoteness. Some poets wrote about "fields and gardens," describing a gentle, familiar rural world. Others portrayed the wilder, more distant landscapes of "mountains and water." The poets of the "fields and gardens" tradition often celebrated the joys of retiring to a place close to nature and far from the city. This tradition influenced Vietnamese authors such as Nguyen Trai, whose "Bamboo Hut" (see pages 786–789) describes a simple rural refuge.

> "My life
> to begin where the nightmare ended
> and crosses stand like islands:
> Upolu, Savii, Apolima, and
>   Manono
> are scented with morning."
>
> —Albert Wendt

Island Worlds

The Pacific Ocean covers a third of the Earth's surface. Scattered across its millions of square miles are groups of tiny islands—tens of thousands of them, including the islands of Melanesia, Micronesia, and Polynesia, a region known as

Threadfin Butterfly Fish Swimming. Stuart Westmorlan. Fakarava Atoll, French Polynesia.

Oceania. In spite of the distances separating these islands, their languages, social structures, and beliefs are remarkably consistent. Oceania was settled by Asian voyagers who came in open canoes. Navigating by the stars and other natural features, they populated almost all the scattered islands of the vast ocean. Until about 500 years ago, Oceania was isolated from most of the outside world. As a result, its cultures developed their own identities and perspectives. Its literature often evokes a distinct type of remoteness, conveying an attitude toward nature that combines   reverence and fear. Kauraka Kauraka of the Cook Islands (see pages 829–833) expresses this attitude in describing "the waves that destroy us / the waves that create new lands." Oceanic literature also draws upon rich oral traditions in which different animals symbolize places. Authors such as Albert Wendt (see pages 829–833) celebrate the uniqueness of Pacific island culture.

Reading Check

Compare and Contrast How does the Chinese "fields and gardens" approach to nature differ from that of the literature of the Pacific islands?

Teach
Reading Check

Answer: *"Fields and gardens" literature portrays nature as gentle and comforting, while the literatures of the Pacific Islands portray nature as powerful and potentially threatening.*

Reading Strategy 2

Connect to Personal Experiences Ask: What images do you connect to the expression "getting away from it all"? *(Students may mention recreational activities and vacation destinations.)*
[ENGLISH LEARNERS] English learners may need some help with the English expression "getting away from it all." Explain that the "it" can be a daily routine, work, social obligations, and whatever else an individual finds burdensome. Ask if there are equivalent expressions in their native languages for taking a break from everyday tasks and routines.

Learning Objectives
Analyzing cultural context. (SE)
Comparing and contrasting. (SE)
Keeping verb tenses consistent. (TE)

English Learners

DIFFERENTIATED INSTRUCTION

Intermediate Point out to students that the word *remote* has several uses and that these different uses may sometimes carry connotations. Offer these three common uses of *remote:*

- "distant in space" or "far away"; for example, "a remote village" This use of *remote* can have positive or negative connotations.
- "distant in time"; for example, "a remote period of history" This use of *remote* can

have positive or negative connotations.
- "emotionally distant" or "reserved"; for example, "a remote personality" This use of remote often carries a negative connotation.

Have students evaluate the use of *remote* in the following sentences as positive, negative, or neutral.

1. The cabin house was remote and provided a lot of privacy. *(positive)*

2. Her manner was cold and remote. *(negative)*

3. The decisions we make now on global warming could affect even our remote descendents. *(neutral)*

4. The community was so remote that it was difficult to get supplies. *(negative)*

5. In this remote period of the past, human life was brutal and often short. *(negative)*

783

Teach

Reading Check

Answer: *The hardships of frontier life led to works of literature that expressed homesickness for Britain, as well as those that expressed a love for rugged exploration.*

Reading Strategy | 1

Activate Prior Knowledge
Ask: How does the settlement of Australia resemble the settlement of the United States? *(As in the United States, early settlement in Australia was confined to a coastal region until pioneers crossed the mountains and moved westward.)*

View the Art ★
James Cook was killed in a skirmish with Hawaiians that was prompted by the theft of a long-boat from one of the ships under his command. **Ask:** How does this painting emphasize Cook's heroism? *(by having him facing the advancing Hawaiians alone)*

Big Idea 3
Cultures in Conflict

Death of Captain James Cook at Kealakekua Bay, Hawaii, in 1779. John the Younger Cleveley. ★

The first European colonists in America viewed the region in different ways. Some considered it an idyllic garden to be cultivated; others, a frightening wilderness to be tamed. Similarly, the British and other Europeans who settled parts of Southeast Asia had different views of this part of the world.

A Pioneer Society

Australia has interior regions of arid grassland and desert. Before Europeans arrived, it was sparsely populated by nomadic peoples later called Aborigines. In 1770, British explorer Captain James Cook landed in southeastern Australia and claimed it for England. Eighteen years later, Britain began shipping convicts to prison colonies in Australia, a practice that continued well into the nineteenth century. After a few years, free men and women also began arriving, and by 1860 more than a million people had settled there. Settlers originally were concentrated on the temperate east coast, but more and more of them moved westward across the Great Dividing Range and into a dry, treeless region known as the bush or the Outback. These pioneers who braved the hardships and dangers of the frontier considered themselves a breed apart from those who remained safely behind. **1**

> "... through our blood there runs
> The vagabonding love of change
> That drove us westward of
>   the range
> And westward of the suns."
>
> —A. B. "Banjo" Paterson,
> from *The Man from Snowy River*

Australian and New Zealand Literature

The earliest published writing from Australia often conveyed a sense of homesickness for the British Isles; many were "convict novels," written by or about people shipped to the prison colonies. Australian outlaws (the "bushrangers") such as Ned Kelly were popular subjects for folktales and songs. Later novelists examined the Australian national character. Among them was Patrick White, who was awarded the Nobel Prize in Literature in 1973. New Zealand literature established an international reputation because of the fame of authors such as Katherine Mansfield (see pages 790–801) and Janet Frame. Since the late 1940s, more indigenous people—the Aborigines in Australia and the Maori in New Zealand—have been writing, usually in English. One of the best known is poet Hone Tuwhare, who also writes in the Maori language. Among the themes explored by authors such as Oodgeroo of the tribe Noonuccal (see pages 806–809) is the destruction of the traditional ways of life.

Reading Check

Analyze Cause-and-Effect Relationships How did the experience of frontier life in the Outback affect the development of literature in Australia?

Skills Practice

Distinguish Fact from Opinion Remind students that a fact is a statement that can be proved true by direct observation or by consulting an authoritative source, such as a reference book. Provide the following example: *Captain James Cook landed in southeastern Australia in 1770.* Point out that this fact can be verified by going to an encyclopedia or a biographical dictionary.

An *opinion* is a statement that often expresses an attitude. Provide the following example: *Captain James Cook was a great hero.* Point out that, unlike a fact, an opinion cannot be proved true; however, an opinion can be supported by facts.

Have students identify one fact and one opinion on pages 784–785. *(Possible fact: "The driest of the continents, Australia has interior regions of arid grassland and desert." Possible opinion: Captain Cook was a "great British explorer.")*

Wrap-Up

John Lennon and Yoko Ono with "War Is Over" Sign, December 22, 1969. Montreal, Canada.

Legacy of the Periods

For centuries, foreign nations—particularly China—dominated the countries of Southeast Asia politically and culturally. This circumstance has left a complex legacy. The region's religious, artistic, and literary traditions reflect the influences of China, India, the Islamic world, and Europe. From the earliest times, however, resistance to foreign rule has influenced cultural values, especially in Vietnam.

The landscape of the Pacific islands has given its cultures a deep awareness of the power of nature and its relation to humans. **2**

Since the late 1700s, colonization helped shape the societies and cultures of Australia and New Zealand. As in America, this process generated a new class of pioneers, displaced native peoples, and affected the environment. The colonial societies imported British values and prejudices and Britain's class system. Because of these influences, the literature of Australia and New Zealand often explored topics such as the challenges of frontier life and the loss of native traditions.

Cultural and Literary Links

- The cultures of the Pacific islands have attracted many outsiders, including American author Herman Melville, who jumped ship in the Marquesas Islands and later celebrated them in his first novel, *Typee.*

- With her psychological insights and distinctive style, New Zealand-born author Katherine Mansfield influenced the development of the modern short story.

- The United States' involvement in Vietnam was a watershed event in American history. From this struggle emerged a war literature that includes Michael Herr's memoir *Dispatches* and Tim O'Brien's novel *The Things They Carried.*

LOG ON ▶ **Literature** Online

Unit Resources For additional skills practice, go to glencoe.com and enter QuickPass code GLW6053u4.

Activities

Use what you have learned about the periods to do one of these activities.

1. Follow Up Go back to the Looking Ahead on page 775 and answer the questions.

2. Contrast Historical Influences Working with other students, research the history of the settlement of Australia and then hold a panel discussion comparing and contrasting this process with the settlement of the United States.

3. Build Visual Literacy Create a visual display highlighting some of the important forms of Southeast Asian and Pacific art, including Buddhist and Hindu temple architecture, Indonesian puppet theater, Balinese dancing,

gamelan music, Maori visual arts (including tattooing), and the sculptures of Easter Island.

4. Take Notes You might try using this graphic organizer to note questions you have about the literary works in this part.

FOLDABLES
Study Organizer

LAYERED-LOOK BOOK

| Reader's Questions |
| Who? |
| What? |
| Where? |
| When? |
| Why? |

Advanced Learners/Pre-AP

DIFFERENTIATED INSTRUCTION

Biographical Sketch Point out to students that Ned Kelly is a most famous Australian bushranger, or outlaw. The robberies that he and his gang committed captured the public's imagination, and he became seen by many Australians as a working-class hero fighting against big landowners. His position as a folk hero in Australian legend might be compared to American outlaws such as Jesse James,

Gregorio Cortez, and Pretty-Boy Floyd. Have interested students research Ned Kelly's career and legend and write a biographical sketch about him.

Assess

Reading Strategy | 2

Connect to Contemporary Issues Ask: Why might global warming be a particularly important issue for the peoples of Oceania? *(Rising sea levels caused by melting polar ice could threaten Pacific islands.)*

Literary History ☆

Typee Herman Melville's first novel, *Typee,* was very popular, going through four editions in the three years after it was published. Melville himself was less enthusiastic about his early success, fearing that he would be known to posterity only as a "man who lived among cannibals."

Activities

1. **Follow Up** Students should support their answers with details from this introduction.

2. **Contrast Historical Influences** Students may notice similarities between the devastating effects of European settlement on indigenous peoples in Australia and the United States, as well as similarities between the settlers' desires for freedom and adventure.

3. **Build Visual Literacy** Students should explain how the examples of art they have chosen reflect Southeast Asian and Pacific cultural values.

4. **Take Notes** After students finish each selection, have them list questions in the Foldable.

Before You Read

Focus

Bellringer Options

**Selection Focus
   Transparency 48
Daily Language Practice
   Transparency 71**
Or ask: How would you define
"the simple life"? What appeal
does this lifestyle have for
you? (*Students may say that a
simple life is one that is quiet,
with little stress and commotion. Some may equate it with
rural living.*) Invite volunteers
to share their definitions and
opinions with the class. Explain
that "The Bamboo Hut" is about
a person who enjoys a simple
life in the country.

Cultural History ☆

A Hero's Shrine On the 560th
anniversary of Nguyen Trai's death
(August 16, 2002), a temple
to honor the poet was formally
opened to the public. The temple
is located in the Vietnamese
village of Con Son, the place Trai
considered his home.

Before You Read

Vietnam

The Bamboo Hut

Meet **Nguyen Trai**
(1380–1442)

Nguyen Trai (noo yin´trī) led a life full
enough for several people. He excelled
as a soldier, politician, historian, geog-
rapher, scholar, and poet.

Nguyen's childhood was marked by the loss of
his mother when he was five years old. He then
lived with his maternal grandfather, who died
a short time later. Despite his difficult life,
Nguyen earned his master's degree at the age
of twenty. He was serving as the deputy head
provincial administrator of Ha Dong province
when Vietnam was invaded by China in 1407.
In 1418, he joined the Vietnamese resistance
under the general Le Loi.

> *"Better conquer hearts than citadels."*
> —Nguyen Trai

Soldier, Statesman, and Poet Nguyen's skill
as a military strategist helped his people achieve
a decisive victory that restored Vietnamese
independence. According to legend, he used
honey to write the message "Le Loi for the
people, Nguyen Trai for Le Loi" on the leaves
of trees. When ants ate the parts of the leaves
covered in honey, they carved out the message.
The enemy, however, assumed supernatural
forces had inscribed it.

Following his heroics in helping Vietnam
achieve independence, Nguyen Trai was
appointed to a high government position. He
wrote a famous poetic account of the war, titled

Phoenix Ewer, 14th-15th
century. Vietnamese school.
Stoneware with underglaze
cobalt blue decoration,
H. 11 1/2 in. The Metropolitan
Museum of Art, NY.

the *Proclamation of Victory over the Chinese.*
The Chinese invaders had destroyed books
and works of art in an attempt to wipe out
Vietnamese culture. After the occupation, the
entire culture had to be rebuilt. At the forefront
of this effort, Nguyen Trai wrote poetry in
chu nom (choo´nôm´), a written form of the
Vietnamese language based on Chinese characters. By using *chu nom,* he hoped to create a
national literature in simple, direct language
everyone in his country could understand.

Fall from Power After fighting to free
Vietnam from foreign domination and then to
rebuild its culture, Nguyen Trai retired to a
simple life in the country. Still, he served as an
adviser to the king, and some members of the
court were jealous of his influence. Accused
of planning to kill the king, Nguyen Trai was
executed along with his entire family. Today
he is honored as a hero in Vietnam. ☆

Literature Online

Author Search For more about Nguyen Trai, go to
glencoe.com and enter QuickPass code GLW6053u4.

Selection Skills

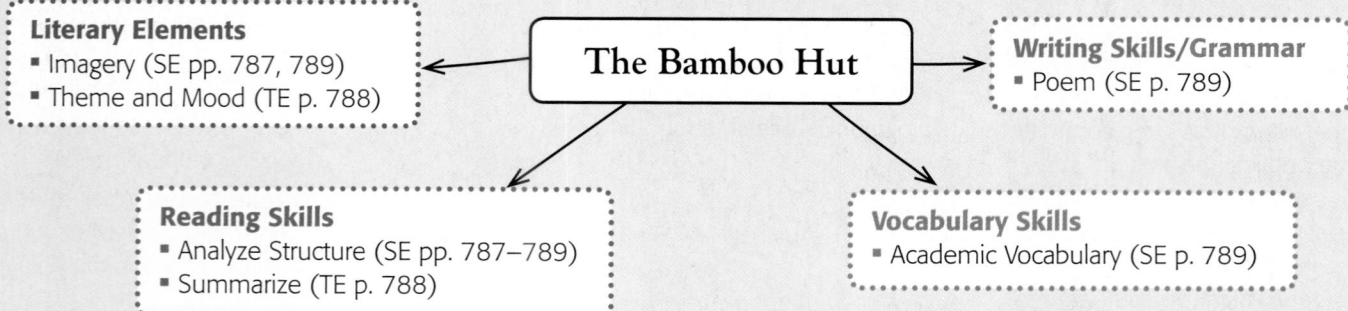

Literary Elements
- Imagery (SE pp. 787, 789)
- Theme and Mood (TE p. 788)

The Bamboo Hut

Writing Skills/Grammar
- Poem (SE p. 789)

Reading Skills
- Analyze Structure (SE pp. 787–789)
- Summarize (TE p. 788)

Vocabulary Skills
- Academic Vocabulary (SE p. 789)

Literature and Reading Preview

Connect to the Poem

Where do you go when you want to get away from the world? Write a journal entry describing an ideal place to be alone with your thoughts.

Build Background

Bamboo—a tall, treelike plant that is actually a grass—has long been praised in the literature and art of East and Southeast Asia. Bamboo grows in hollow, jointed stalks. The sturdy and fast-growing bamboo stems provide an ideal material for building. They are used to make houses and rafts, scaffoldings for construction sites, and a variety of smaller items ranging from furniture to walking sticks.

Set Purposes for Reading

Big Idea Place and Identity

The Chinese poetic ideal of living a simple rural life away from the world's bustle deeply influenced traditional Vietnamese poetry. As you read, ask yourself, How does this poem reflect that influence?

Literary Element Imagery

Imagery is the word pictures that help evoke an emotional response. In creating images, authors use sensory details or descriptions that appeal to one or more of the five senses. As you read, ask yourself, What do the images in the poem reveal about the speaker's life?

Reading Strategy Analyze Structure

When you **analyze structure**, you identify the pattern of oranization an author uses to present his or her ideas. "The Bamboo Hut" is made up of four two-line sentences. As you read, ask yourself, Why did the poet choose this structure?

Tip: Take Notes In a chart like the one below, write down an analysis of each sentence in this poem.

Sentence	Structure	Main Idea	Supporting Details
1	Two-part sentence divided by dash; first part gives physical details		

Learning Objectives

For pages 786–789

In studying this text, you will focus on the following objectives:

Literary Study: Analyzing imagery.

Reading: Analyzing structure.

Writing: Writing a poem.

Bamboo, Momoyama Period, ca.1568-1615. Japanese school. Ink on paper. Private collection.

Before You Read

Focus

Summary

The speaker describes the place where he finds peace and inspiration—a simple bamboo hut surrounded by a plum tree bower, a pond, and flowers.

> **For summaries in languages other than English, see Unit 4 Teaching Resources Book, pp. 183–188.**

Literary History ☆

National Style Remind students that "The Bamboo Hut" is translated from Vietnamese, a lyrical, tonal language. It is written using ideograms, characters that stand for more than the phonetic sounds of words. Nguyen followed the conventions of Chinese poetry, but he also allowed his poems to reflect the rhythm of his native language.

Learning Objectives
Understanding imagery. (SE)
Analyzing structure. (SE)
Summarizing. (TE)
Researching information. (TE)

Approaching Level

DIFFERENTIATED INSTRUCTION

Summarize Some students may find it difficult to separate the main idea from the details in the poem. Guide students to summarize the main idea of lines 2–3 for their charts. *(Possible answer: simple living is better than an extravagant lifestyle)* Have students work in pairs to summarize the last two couplets.

Advanced Learners/Pre-AP

DIFFERENTIATED INSTRUCTION

SMALL GROUP

Research Chinese Poetry Traditional Vietnamese poetry is modeled on the structures and conventions of Chinese poetry developed during the Tang dynasty. Have interested students work in small groups to research the rules of Chinese poetry and present their finding to the class.

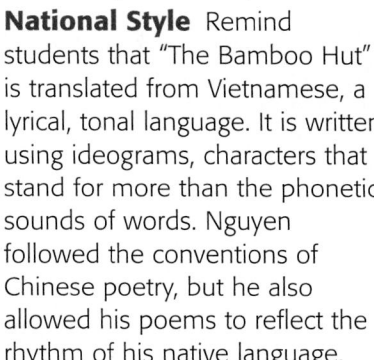

Teach

Reading Strategy   1

Analyze Structure Answer:
This line echoes line 2: "That's where I spend my days, far from the world's talk."

[APPROACHING] Invite a volunteer to read lines two and eight aloud. **Ask:** Why do you think the poet uses the phrases *"That's where I"* and *"That's when I."* (*to emphasize the importance of the setting*)

> For additional practice using the reading skill or strategy, see Unit 4 Teaching Resources Book, p. 190.

> For an audio recording of this selection, use Listening Library Audio CD-ROM.

View the Art ★

This watercolor represents literati painting, a style within the tradition of Chinese landscape painting.

Plum Blossoms, 1972. Guan Tianying (Bonnie Kwan Huo). Watercolor, 37.5 x 15 cm. Private collection. ★

The Bamboo Hut

Nguyen Trai

**Translated by Nguyen Ngoc Bich
with Burton Raffel and W. S. Merwin**

A bamboo hut and a plum tree bower—[1]
That's where I spend my days, far from the world's talk.
For meals, only some pickled cabbage,
But I've never cared for the life of damask[2] and silk.
There's a pool of water for watching the moon,
And land to plough into flower beds.
Sometimes I feel inspired on snowy nights—
That's when I write my best poems, and sing.

---

1. A *bower* (bou′ər) is a shelter (as in a garden) made with tree boughs.
2. *Damask* (dam′əsk) is a rich, patterned fabric.

1   Analyze Structure *What line in the poem does this line echo?*

Literary Element Practice

Present an Illustration Have students review the section under the heading "Fields and Gardens," on page 783 (Big Idea 2 essay) of the Part 2 Introduction. **Say:** During the seventh through the early thirteenth centuries, similar Buddhist, Taoist, and Confucian philosophies influenced the development of Chinese and Vietnamese landscape painting. Traditionally these elegant landscapes had a soft, mystic quality that reflected the idea of spiritually connecting to the natural world.

Have students create an illustration that evokes the theme or mood of "The Bamboo Hut," using any medium or style they choose. Students might paint a picture in a realistic or an abstract style to capture the mood of the poem, or they might create a collage of images that express the theme of the poem. Have volunteers share their illustrations with the class.

After You Read

Respond and Think Critically

Respond and Interpret

1. Can you identify with the speaker's feelings in this poem? Explain.

2. (a)Where does the speaker spend his days? (b)What does the speaker like about this place?

3. What can you infer about the speaker's view of work from the last four lines?

Analyze and Evaluate

4. Do you think the poet is the speaker in this poem? Why or why not?

---

5. The **theme** of a literary work is its main idea. What do you think is the theme of this poem?

Connect

6. **Big Idea** **Place and Identity** How would you describe the relationship between the speaker and nature in this poem?

7. **Connect to Today** (a)What might be the modern-day equivalents of a bamboo hut? of a life of damask and silk? (b)Do you think most Americans would choose "a bamboo hut and a plum tree bower" over a life of luxury? Explain.

Literary Element Imagery

Authors use **imagery** to convey how things look, taste, feel, sound, and smell. Nguyen's imagery helps the reader picture the speaker's surroundings.

1. Based on the imagery in the poem, what kind of life does the speaker live?

2. What images help you picture the speaker's environment and lifestyle? Explain.

Reading Strategy Analyze Structure

The **structure** of "The Bamboo Hut" is four sentences, each of which is two lines long. Review the chart you made on page 787. Then answer the following questions.

1. How would you state the main idea of the second sentence?

2. (a)What structural similarities can you find in the first and fourth sentences? (b)What does the contrast between the words "talk" and "sing" suggest?

Literature Online

Selection Resources For Selection Quizzes, eFlashcards, and Reading-Writing Connection activities, go to glencoe.com and enter QuickPass code GLW6053u4.

Academic Vocabulary

*Trai's poem suggests that a simple lifestyle that fosters creativity is **sufficient** for happiness.*

Sufficient is an academic word. In more familiar usage, you might say that a piece of fruit is often a **sufficient** snack. To study this word, fill out a graphic organizer like the one below.

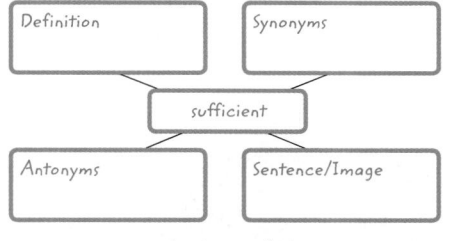

For more on academic vocabulary, see pages 36–37 and R83–R87.

Writing

Write a Poem Write a poem about an ideal spot "far from the world's talk." Include imagery and figures of speech to describe the kind of life you would lead in your ideal spot. Share your poem with your classmates.

After You Read

Assess

1. Answers will vary. Many students will identify with the need for solitude.

2. (a) He spends his days in the country, in a bamboo hut near plum trees, open land, and a pool of water. (b) He likes the isolation, the beauty of nature, and the snowy nights.

3. The speaker values writing poetry more than doing practical farm chores.

4. Since the speaker is a poet, it is likely there is a close identification between the speaker and the author.

5. Possible response: People can find happiness living simply, in harmony with nature.

6. The speaker lives in harmony with nature. The natural world is his source of peace and joy.

7. (a) The American equivalent of a bamboo hut might be a small country home. A life of damask and silk might be a luxurious house in an upper-class neighborhood. (b) Answers will vary.

Literary Element

1. The speaker lives a simple, happy life surrounded by nature.

2. The "plum tree bower," "pool of water for watching the moon," "flower beds," and "snowy nights" all indicate the speaker lives in a rural area without amenities. He survives on "only some pickled cabbage."

Writing

Students' poems should

- describe the kind of life they would lead in an ideal spot
- contain imagery and figures of speech

Reading Strategy

1. A life of simplicity is preferable to one of luxury.

2. (a) Both sentences have two parts separated by a dash and are parallel in structure. (b) The contrast suggests the bustle of a sophisticated lifestyle as opposed to the peace of a simple, natural one.

Academic Vocabulary

Possible answer:

Definition: *Enough as is needed*

Synonyms: *enough, adequate*

Antonyms: *inadequate, insufficient*

Sentence/image: *I had sufficient funds in my account to buy four CDs.*

Before You Read

Focus

Bellringer Options

Daily Language Practice Transparency 72
Or ask: What factors influence one's social status in school? Is social status important? Why?

Find out if students think that money, styles of clothing, possessions, academic or sports expertise, in-group acceptance, or conformity affect their attitudes toward classmates and friends.

Literary History ☆
Autobiographical Influences
Tell students that "The Doll's House" is one of several Mansfield stories that draws upon the author's bittersweet memories of family life in New Zealand. In "The Doll's House," Kezia, the central character, is intended to represent Mansfield as a child.

Before You Read

The Doll's House

New Zealand

Meet **Katherine Mansfield**
(1888–1923)

Katherine Mansfield lived only 34 years, but in her short life she became one of the greatest short story authors and an innovator in the form. Although she lived in Europe as an adult, she often returned to her childhood home in New Zealand in her fiction.

Born Kathleen Mansfield Beauchamp (bē′chəm), she grew up in Karori, a rural New Zealand village not far from the nation's capital, Wellington. The daughter of a wealthy banker, she nevertheless attended local New Zealand schools, rubbing elbows with children from families far less privileged than her own.

> "I want to write about my own country till I simply exhaust my store."
>
> —Katherine Mansfield

Setbacks and Success Independent from childhood, she moved to London at nineteen to start a writing career. Her life there got off to a rough start. She married hastily and left her husband after only a few days, then became increasingly disillusioned. In 1911 her life improved—Mansfield published her first book and met her future second husband, John Middleton Murry, editor of two magazines that published her stories.

The death of her soldier brother in 1915 affected Mansfield deeply. Dedicating herself to preserving her memories of him and their shared childhood, she wrote a series of short stories that beautifully portray her family life in New Zealand. Regarded today as masterpieces of the short story form, they were published in 1920 in the collection *Bliss and Other Stories*. ☆

Illness and Critical Acclaim Mansfield contracted tuberculosis in her late twenties. Despite her illness, she continued to write, producing some of her best works while desperately seeking a cure for her illness. During this period she published the critically acclaimed collection *The Garden Party*. She completed her last story only months before her death in France.

Mansfield revolutionized the concept of the short story, moving it away from the strictures of plot and external action. She was able to capture the meaning of a relationship, illuminating the inner truth of a character's life. Her stories have been called delicate and profound. "I choose not only the length of every sentence, but even the sound of every sentence," she wrote. "I choose the rise and fall of every paragraph."

 **Literature** Online

Author Search For more about Katherine Mansfield, go to glencoe.com and enter QuickPass code GLW6053u4.

Selection Skills

Literary Elements
- Symbol (SE pp. 791, 793, 795, 800)
- Point of View (SE p. 800)
- Character (TE p. 794)

Reading Skills
- Analyze Sensory Details (SE pp. 791, 793, 795, 796, 798, 800)
- Analyze Sensory Details (TE p. 793)
- Interpret Imagery (TE p. 794)

The Doll's House

Writing Skills/Grammar
- Short Story (SE p. 801)
- Essay (TE p. 798)

Speaking/Listening/Viewing Skills
- Analyze Art (SE p. 797)

Vocabulary Skills
- Context Clues (SE pp. 791, 800)
- Academic Vocabulary (SE p. 800)
- Matching Game (TE p. 791)
- Understand Multiple-Meaning Words (TE p. 797)

Literature and Reading Preview

Connect to the Story

How much does a person's social class affect his or her status in your school or community? Write a journal entry in response to this question.

Build Background

During the late 1800s, class differences in New Zealand were far more pronounced than they are today. Because there were few schools in rural areas, wealthy New Zealanders sent their children to the same schools the poor attended. However, the wealthy still made harsh judgments based on social status.

Set Purposes for Reading

Big Idea **Cultures in Conflict**

As you read, ask yourself, What conflicts does the class system in the story create?

Literary Element **Symbol**

A **symbol** is a person, a place, or a thing that stands for itself and something beyond itself, often an abstract quality or idea. For example, a red heart is a common symbol for love; a dove is a common symbol for peace. As you read, ask yourself, What symbols support this story's message, or theme?

Reading Strategy **Analyze Sensory Details**

In creating effective images, authors use **sensory details**, or descriptions that appeal to one or more of the five senses: sight, hearing, touch, taste, and smell. As you read, ask yourself, How do the sensory details influence the tone and meaning?

Tip: Make a Chart In a chart like the one below, keep track of the sensory appeal of the details in "The Doll's House."

Detail	Sense	Effect
"A dark, oily spinach green, picked out with bright yellow"	Sight; also perhaps taste and touch	Helps the reader visualize and emotionally respond to the doll's house.

Learning Objectives

For pages 790–800

In studying this text, you will focus on the following objectives:

Literary Study: Identifying symbol.

Reading: Analyzing sensory details.

Vocabulary

congealed (kən jēld´) *adj.* thickened; changed from a liquid to a solid state; p. 793 *As the temperature dropped, it was difficult to stir the congealed paint.*

marvelous (märv´ə ləs) *adj.* extraordinary; causing wonder; p. 793 *Her marvelous performance exceeded my expectations.*

flag (flag) *v.* to decline in interest or attraction; p. 796 *After a few hours at the carnival, the children's excitement began to flag.*

titter (ti´tər) *v.* to laugh nervously; p. 796 *The guests tittered at their host's little joke.*

imploring (im plôr´ing) *adj.* begging or beseeching; p. 798 *With an imploring look, the prisoner pleaded for mercy.*

Tip: Context Clues When you come upon an unfamiliar term, examine the surrounding words to determine its possible meaning. For example, in the sentence *With an imploring look, the prisoner pleaded for mercy, imploring* must mean "entreating" because the prisoner is pleading for mercy.

KATHERINE MANSFIELD **791**

Advanced Learners/Pre-AP

DIFFERENTIATED INSTRUCTION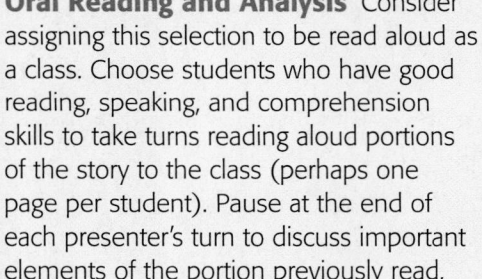

Oral Reading and Analysis Consider assigning this selection to be read aloud as a class. Choose students who have good reading, speaking, and comprehension skills to take turns reading aloud portions of the story to the class (perhaps one page per student). Pause at the end of each presenter's turn to discuss important elements of the portion previously read, asking presenters to comment on details such as tone, point of view, the emotional impact of word choices, symbols, and other elements of the author's style as appropriate. Amend or amplify presenters' comments as needed. The oral reading and discussion should help students complete the After You Read activities that follow "The Doll's House."

Before You Read

Focus

Summary

When the three Burnell sisters receive a spectacular doll's house as a gift, they are allowed to invite their friends over in groups of two to see it. But they do not invite the Kelvey sisters, whose mother is a washerwoman and whose father is reputed to be in prison. One evening the youngest Burnell sister notices the Kelvey sisters walking near her house; she invites them in to see the doll's house, but their enjoyment is interrupted by Aunt Beryl, who rudely drives Lil and Else away.

 For summaries in languages other than English, see Unit 4 Teaching Resources Book, pp. 193–198.

Vocabulary

Matching Game Group students in pairs. Distribute a list of vocabulary words to one partner in each pair. Distribute a list of definitions to the other partner. Tell students with the word lists to read aloud a word and have the partner read aloud the correct definition. That student should then read aloud another definition and have the partner read aloud the correct vocabulary word. Pairs should continue alternating in this manner until all words and definitions have been supplied. Then have them trade lists and repeat the process.

 For additional vocabulary practice, see Unit 4 Teaching Resources Book, p. 201.

 Interactive Read and Write
Other options for teaching this selection can be found in Interactive Read and Write for On-Level Learners, pp. 197–210.

Teach

Reading Strategy | 1

Analyze Sensory Details

Ask: What details in the first paragraph suggest that the Burnell family is well-off or privileged? *(Entertaining a house guest, receiving a lavish thank-you gift, consigning the doll's house to the courtyard to keep paint fumes out of the house, and Aunt Beryl's condescending, superior tone all suggest a family of means.)*

 For an audio recording of this selection, use Listening Library Audio CD-ROM.

Readability Scores

Dale-Chall: 6.2
DRP: 54
Lexile: 620

Suffragette's House. Tirzah Ravilious (1908–1951). Private collection.

TIRZAH GARWOOD

The Doll's House

••❧••━━━━❧•❦❧•━━━━••❧••

Katherine Mansfield

Listening and Speaking Practice

SPIRAL REVIEW

Present an Oral Interpretation Invite volunteers to read aloud the first paragraph of the story. Have them monitor and adjust their inflections to match the tone of the passage. Point out key phrases to which students should pay special attention: "dear old Mrs. Hay," "For, really, the smell of paint," "Sweet of . . . and generous!" "quite enough."

After several students have presented the passage, have the class discuss the tone. **Ask:** How does hearing the passage help you react more clearly to Aunt Beryl? How does the tone reinforce your opinion of Aunt Beryl? *(Hearing Aunt Beryl's superior-sounding, gratuitous, and dismissive comments on Mrs. Hays and her gift spoken aloud makes her*

unpleasantness come to life, confirming students' opinions of her.)

1 When dear old Mrs. Hay went back to town after staying with the Burnells she sent the children a doll's house. It was so big that the carter and Pat carried it into the courtyard, and there it stayed, propped up on two wooden boxes beside the feed room door. No harm could come to it: it was summer. And perhaps the smell of paint would have gone off by the time it had to be taken in. For, really, the smell of paint coming from that doll's house ("Sweet of old Mrs. Hay, of course; most sweet and generous!")—but the smell of paint was quite enough to make anyone seriously ill, in Aunt Beryl's opinion. Even before the sacking was taken off. And when it was . . .

There stood the Doll's house, a dark, oily, spinach green, picked out with bright yellow. Its two solid little chimneys, glued on to the roof, were painted red and white, and the door, gleaming with yellow varnish, was like a little slab of toffee. Four windows, real windows, were divided into panes by a broad streak of green. There was actually a tiny porch, too, painted yellow, with big lumps of **congealed** paint hanging along the edge.

But perfect, perfect little house! Who could possibly mind the smell. It was part of the joy, part of the newness.

"Open it quickly, someone!"

The hook at the side was stuck fast. Pat pried it open with his penknife, and the whole house front swung back, and—there you were, gazing at one and the same moment into the drawing room and dining room, the kitchen and two bedrooms. That is the way for a house to open! Why don't all houses open like that? How much more exciting than peering through the slit of a door into a mean little hall with a hatstand and two umbrellas! That is—isn't it?—what you long to know about a house when you put your hand on the knocker. Perhaps it is the way God opens houses at the dead of night when He is taking a quiet turn with an angel . . .

"O-oh!" The Burnell children sounded as though they were in despair. It was too **marvelous**; it was too much for them. They had never seen anything like it in their lives. All the rooms were papered. There were pictures on the walls, painted on the paper, with gold frames complete. Red carpet covered all the floors except the kitchen; red plush chairs in the drawing room, green in the dining room; tables, beds with real bedclothes, a cradle, a stove, a dresser with tiny plates and one big jug. But what Kezia liked more than anything, what she liked frightfully, was the lamp. It stood in the middle of the dining room table, an exquisite little amber lamp with a white globe. It was even filled all ready for lighting, though, of course, you couldn't light it. But there was something inside that looked like oil and moved when you shook it.

The father and mother dolls, who sprawled very stiff as though they had fainted in the drawing room, and their two little children asleep upstairs, were really too big for the doll's house. They didn't look as though they belonged. But the lamp

---

2 Analyze Sensory Details *To what senses does this passage appeal?*

Vocabulary
congealed (kən jēld′) *adj.* thickened; changed from a liquid to a solid state

---

Symbol *Why does the little lamp attract Kezia's attention?* **3**

Vocabulary
marvelous (märv′ə ləs) *adj.* extraordinary; causing wonder

KATHERINE MANSFIELD **793**

English Learners

DIFFERENTIATED INSTRUCTION

 SMALL GROUP **Intermediate** Several words in this story are used in unusual ways, reflecting British usage, unfamiliar meanings, or metaphorical intents. Write these phrases on the board: "They <u>burned</u> to tell everybody," "<u>Burning</u> with shame," "What a little <u>guy</u> she looked." Ask students to use context clues to determine what each of the underlined words means. (burned: "became excited; yearned ardently;" burning: "being inflamed with feelings such as anger, passion, disgust, etc.," guy: "a person of grotesque appearance") Have students work in small groups to find other examples of unusual usages. Tell them to debate possible meanings and then look the words up in a dictionary. Groups can share what they learn with the class. (Some possibilities: carter, feed room, frightfully, mutton, pinafore, thieved)

Teach

Reading Strategy **2**

Analyze Sensory Details
Answer: *It appeals primarily to the sense of sight and perhaps also to the senses of taste and touch.*

 For additional practice using the reading skill or strategy, see Unit 4 Teaching Resources Book, p. 200.

Literary Element **3**

Symbol Answer: *The lamp seems perfect—as if it were real.*

ADVANCED Ask advanced students what they infer about Kezia from her admiration of the lamp. (*She is an observant and discerning child. She notices beauty and can distinguish it from its surroundings.*)

Learning Objectives
Identifying symbol. (SE)
Analyzing sensory details. (SE)
Presenting an oral interpretation. (TE)

Teach

Character Direct attention to the sentence in the second column beginning "She held quite a court. . . ." Ask students to explain what is taking place. Who is the center of attention? Why? What does her behavior suggest about her? *(Isabel is the center of attention. She has hinted that she has something important to tell them, so they press close to her, in an attempt to curry her favor. Isabel's earlier insistence that, as the eldest of the sisters, she was given the privilege of telling about the doll's house suggests that she is probably savoring this moment.)*

Cultures in Conflict

Answer: *Societies sometimes establish boundaries, identifying a lowest level whose members are not "fit" to associate with the rest of the people. The Kelvey girls, by the circumstance of their birth, have been assigned that status by the rest of the village society.*

Cultural History ☆

Afternoon Tea The narrator's observation that the Burnell girls were allowed to invite friends to view the doll house but "not to stay for tea, of course" is a reference to the English practice of taking an afternoon break for tea—sometimes shared with neighbors or other acquaintances.

---

was perfect. It seemed to smile at Kezia, to say, "I live here." The lamp was real.

The Burnell children could hardly walk to school fast enough the next morning. They burned to tell everybody, to describe, to—well—to boast about their doll's house before the school-bell rang.

"I'm to tell," said Isabel, "because I'm the eldest. And you two can join in after. But I'm to tell first."

There was nothing to answer. Isabel was bossy, but she was always right, and Lottie and Kezia knew too well the powers that went with being eldest. They brushed through the thick buttercups at the road edge and said nothing.

"And I'm to choose who's to come and see it first. Mother said I might."

For it had been arranged that while the doll's house stood in the courtyard they might ask the girls at school, two at a time, to come and look. Not to stay to tea, of course, or to come traipsing[1] through the house. But just to stand quietly in the courtyard while Isabel pointed out the beauties, and Lottie and Kezia looked pleased . . .

Visual Vocabulary
Palings are the stakes or pickets that form a fence.

But hurry as they might, by the time they had reached the tarred palings of the boys' playground the bell had begun to jangle. They only just had time to whip off their hats and fall into line before the roll was called. Never mind. Isabel tried to make up for it by looking very important and mysterious and by whispering behind

---

1. *Traipsing* means "walking around idly or aimlessly."

794   UNIT 4   SOUTHEAST ASIA AND THE PACIFIC

---

her hand to the girls near her, "Got something to tell you at playtime."

Playtime came and Isabel was surrounded. The girls of her class nearly fought to put their arms round her, to walk away with her, to beam flatteringly, to be her special friend. She held quite a court under the huge pine trees at the side of the playground. Nudging, giggling together, the little girls pressed up close. And the only two who stayed outside the ring were the two who were always outside, the little Kelveys. They knew better than to come anywhere near the Burnells.   **1**

For the fact was, the school the Burnell children went to was not at all the kind of place their parents would have chosen if there had been any choice. But there was none. It was the only school for miles. And the consequence was all the children of the neighborhood, the Judge's little girls, the doctor's daughters, the storekeeper's children, the milkman's, were forced to mix together. Not to speak of there being an equal number of rude, rough little boys as well. But the line had to be drawn somewhere. It was drawn at the Kelveys. Many of the children, including the Burnells, were not allowed even to speak to them. They walked past the Kelveys with their heads in the air, and as they set the fashion in all matters of behavior, the Kelveys were shunned by everybody. Even the teacher had a special voice for them, and a special smile for the other children when Lil Kelvey came up to her desk with a bunch of dreadfully common-looking flowers.

They were the daughters of a spry, hard-working little washerwoman, who went

---

Cultures in Conflict *What conflict does this general attitude toward the Kelvey girls suggest?*   **2**

Reading Practice

SPIRAL REVIEW ⊙ **Interpret Imagery** Point out that among short story writers, Katherine Mansfield is known for her attention to detail. The fact that she singles out the tiny lamp in the doll's house for description ought to be a signal to readers that the lamp will play a significant role in the action of the story. Review with students the first mention of the lamp on page 793. Have them pay close attention to each subsequent mention of the lamp.

What does the narrator say about it? What do the children say and think about it? When is it mentioned? Why is it mentioned? When students have completed the story, they should be prepared to discuss the lamp's symbolic significance.

about from house to house by the day. This was awful enough. But where was Mr. Kelvey? Nobody knew for certain. But everybody said he was in prison. So they were the daughters of a washerwoman and a jailbird. Very nice company for other people's children! And they looked it. Why Mrs. Kelvey made them so conspicuous was hard to understand. The truth was they were dressed in "bits" given to her by the people for whom she worked. Lil, for instance, who was a stout, plain child, with big freckles, came to school in a dress made from a green art-serge tablecloth of the Burnells', with red plush sleeves from the Logans' curtains. Her hat, perched on top of her high forehead, was a grown-up woman's hat, once the property of Miss Lecky, the postmistress. It was turned up at the back and trimmed with a large scarlet quill. What a little guy[2] she looked! It was impossible not to laugh. And her little sister, our Else, wore a long white dress, rather like a nightgown, and a pair of little boy's boots. But whatever our Else wore she would have looked strange. She was a tiny wishbone of a child, with cropped hair and enormous solemn eyes—a little white owl. Nobody had ever seen her smile; she scarcely ever spoke. She went through life holding on to Lil, with a piece of Lil's skirt screwed up in her hand. Where Lil went, our Else followed. In the playground, on the road going to and from school, there was Lil marching in front and our Else holding on behind. Only when she wanted anything, or when she was out of breath, our Else gave Lil a tug, a twitch, and Lil stopped and turned round. The Kelveys never failed to understand each other.

Now they hovered at the edge; you couldn't stop them listening. When the little girls turned round and sneered, Lil, as usual, gave her silly, shamefaced smile, but our Else only looked.

And Isabel's voice, so very proud, went on telling. The carpet made a great sensation, but so did the beds with real bedclothes, and the stove with an oven door.

When she finished Kezia broke in. "You've forgotten the lamp, Isabel."

"Oh, yes," said Isabel, "and there's a teeny little lamp, all made of yellow glass, with a white globe that stands on the dining room table. You couldn't tell it from a real one."

"The lamp's best of all," cried Kezia. She thought Isabel wasn't making half enough of the little lamp. But nobody paid any attention. Isabel was choosing the two who were to come back with them that afternoon and see it. She chose Emmie Cole and Lena Logan. But when the others knew they were all to have a chance, they couldn't be nice enough to Isabel. One by one they put their arms round Isabel's waist and walked her off. They had something to whisper to her, a secret. "Isabel's *my* friend."

Only the little Kelveys moved away forgotten; there was nothing more for them to hear.

Days passed, and as more children saw the doll's house, the fame of it spread. It became the one subject, the rage. The one question was, "Have you seen Burnells' doll's house? Oh, ain't it lovely!" "Haven't you seen it? Oh, I say!"

---

2. In British slang, a *guy* is an ugly, shabbily dressed person.

 Analyze Sensory Details *What effect does this description of Lil create?*

Symbol *What does the doll's house represent to the Burnells' classmates?*

Reading Strategy 3

Analyze Sensory Details Answer: *This description depicts Lil as an impoverished and unfashionable outsider; her clothes are stitched together from handouts.*

Literary Element 4

Symbol Answer: *The doll's house represents social respectability. Simply having been asked to view the house indicates social acceptance by the Burnell sisters—whose family are the elite members of this society.*

Learning Objectives
Analyzing sensory details. (SE)
Analyzing character. (TE)
Interpreting imagery. (TE)
Identifying symbols. (TE)

Approaching Level

DIFFERENTIATED INSTRUCTION

Chart the Lamp References Provide struggling readers with a chart that shows the sequence of references to the lamp. Discuss the information the narrator provides in each reference.

Lamp References
page 793: "But what Kezia liked . . ."
page 795: "'Oh, yes,' said Isabel . . ." and "'The lamp's best of all . . .'"
page 798: "'I seen the little lamp . . .'"

Advanced Learners/Pre-AP

DIFFERENTIATED INSTRUCTION

Identify Symbols Challenge advanced learners to find other details that might have symbolic significance. Have them share their examples. *(doll's house: social status; gleaming paint: ostentation, superficiality; courtyard: the Burnells' superior opinion of themselves; Aunt Beryl: intolerance; Lil's grown-up hat: motherly responsibility; Else's dress: innocence; the children's lunches: privilege and poverty)*

795

Teach

Reading Strategy   1

Analyze Sensory Details
Answer: *The Burnell girls and others enjoy nourishing lunches with meat and a dessert, which shows they are well-off. The Kelvey girls have meager jam sandwiches wrapped in newspaper, which shows they are poor.*

Vocabulary   2

Multiple Meaning Words
Direct attention to the footnote for *sell*. **Ask:** Why is Lena's effort viewed as a "sell"? *(She failed to get the reaction she expected.)*

Even the dinner hour was given up to talking about it. The little girls sat under the pines eating their thick mutton sandwiches and big slabs of johnny cake[3] spread with butter. While always, as near as they could get, sat the Kelveys, our Else holding on to Lil, listening too, while they chewed their jam sandwiches out of a newspaper soaked with large red blobs.

"Mother," said Kezia, "can't I ask the Kelveys just once?"

"Certainly not, Kezia."

"But why not?"

"Run away, Kezia; you know quite well why not."

At last everybody had seen it except them. On that day the subject rather **flagged**. It was the dinner hour. The children stood together under the pine trees, and suddenly, as they looked at the Kelveys eating out of their paper, always by themselves, always listening, they wanted to be horrid to them. Emmie Cole started the whisper.

"Lil Kelvey's going to be a servant when she grows up."

"O-oh, how awful!" said Isabel Burnell, and she made eyes at Emmie.

Emmie swallowed in a very meaning way and nodded to Isabel as she'd seen her mother do on those occasions.

"It's true—it's true—it's true," she said.

Then Lena Logan's little eyes snapped. "Shall I ask her?" she whispered.

"Bet you don't," said Jessie May.

"Pooh, I'm not frightened," said Lena.

---

3. A *johnny cake* is a flat, crisp cake made of cornmeal.

> **1** Analyze Sensory Details *What does the contrast in the little girls' lunches suggest about their class differences?*

> **Vocabulary**
> **flag** (flag) *v.* to decline in interest or attraction

Suddenly she gave a little squeal and danced in front of the other girls. "Watch! Watch me! Watch me now!" said Lena. And sliding, gliding, dragging one foot, giggling behind her hand, Lena went over to the Kelveys.

Lil looked up from her dinner. She wrapped the rest quickly away. Our Else stopped chewing. What was coming now?

"Is it true you're going to be a servant when you grow up, Lil Kelvey?" shrilled Lena.

Dead silence. But instead of answering, Lil only gave her silly, shamefaced smile. She didn't seem to mind the question at all. What a sell[4] for Lena! The girls began to **titter**.

Lena couldn't stand that. She put her hands on her hips; she shot forward. "Yah, yer father's in prison!" she hissed, spitefully.

This was such a marvelous thing to have said that the little girls rushed away in a body, deeply, deeply excited, wild with joy. Someone found a long rope, and they began skipping. And never did they skip so high, run in and out so fast, or do such daring things as on that morning.

In the afternoon Pat called for the Burnell children with the buggy and they drove home. There were visitors. Isabel and Lottie, who liked visitors, went upstairs to change their pinafores. But Kezia thieved out at the back. Nobody was about; she began to swing on the big white gates of the courtyard. Presently, looking along the road, she saw two little dots. They grew bigger, they were coming towards her. Now she could see that one was in front and one

---

4. In British slang, a *sell* is a great disappointment.   **2**

> **Vocabulary**
> **titter** (ti′ tər) *v.* to laugh nervously

Writing Practice

Use Indirect Objects Remind students that indirect objects, like direct objects, are complements—they complete the meaning of a verb. Indirect objects answer the question *to whom, for whom, to what,* or *for what.* They only occur in sentences that contain direct objects and always appear after the verb and before the direct object. **Write this sentence on the board:** "Kezia showed the Kelveys the doll's house." Point out that *The doll's house* is the direct object; it answers the question *what? The Kelveys* is the indirect object; it answers the question *to whom?*

Tell students that indirect objects can be expressed differently by turning them into prepositional phrases using *to* or *for:* "Kezia showed the doll's house to the Kelveys."

Ask students to summarize the story using sentences with indirect objects; have them underline the indirect objects.

Big Idea　　3

Cultures in Conflict

Answer: *Lil understands that Mrs. Burnell regards the Kelvey family as so inferior she even warned Mrs. Kelvey that Kezia was not allowed to associate with her children. Lil and Else have come to accept social exclusion as a way of life.*

View the Art ★

Answer: *The soft look of the painting seems to suggest a more serene mood than the story.*

The Road to the school on Edam. Max Liebermann.Oil on canvas. Pushkin Museum, Moscow.

 View the Art Liebermann was an important German Impressionist. He often focused on light and color in his paintings. How does the mood of this painting compare with the mood of the story? ★

close behind. Now she could see that they were the Kelveys. Kezia stopped swinging. She slipped off the gate as if she was going to run away. Then she hesitated. The Kelveys came nearer, and beside them walked their shadows, very long, stretching right across the road with their heads in the buttercups. Kezia clambered back on the gate; she had made up her mind; she swung out.

"Hullo," she said to the passing Kelveys.

They were so astounded that they stopped. Lil gave her silly smile. Our Else stared.

"You can come and see our doll's house if you want to," said Kezia, and she dragged one toe on the ground. But at that Lil turned red and shook her head quickly.

"Why not?" asked Kezia.

Lil gasped, then she said, "Your ma told our ma you wasn't to speak to us."

Cultures in Conflict *What does Lil understand about social tensions in the community?*　**3**

KATHERINE MANSFIELD　**797**

Learning Objectives
Analyzing sensory details. (SE)
Analyzing art. (SE)
Using indirect objects. (TE)
Understanding multiple-meaning words. (TE)

Advanced Learners/Pre-AP

DIFFERENTIATED INSTRUCTION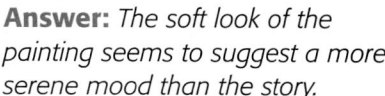

Connect to Personal Experience
Mansfield spends a good deal of time in this story documenting the feelings and behavior of children. Ask students to relate the behavior of the children in the story to their own behavior (or the behavior of others) when they were younger and to their behavior now as teens. How accurate is Mansfield's portrayal of how the children treat the Kelvey sisters? of how Isabel interacts with her younger sisters? of the ways in which Isabel's classmates attempt to gain her favor? Have students outgrown these behaviors now as teens, or are such behaviors still in evidence, perhaps demonstrated in more subtle ways? Tell students to prepare a brief oral report explaining their views.

Teach

Big Idea   1

Cultures in Conflict
Answer: *Aunt Beryl's scolding words to Kezia reflect the opinion of the entire community. The Kelveys have no place in the Burnells' yard, just as they have no place in society. They are outcasts, and Aunt Beryl reminds them of it.*

Reading Strategy   2

Analyze Sensory Details
Answer: *The setting is pastoral; the Burnells' house is in the countryside, set amid working farms.*

(ADVANCED) Ask advanced students why they think Mansfield chose to place Lil and Else in this setting at the end of the story? *(Possible answer: Mansfield might be suggesting that Lil and Else belong here, among down-to-earth working families and, by extension, that the Burnell family are the real outsiders, seeing themselves as above others in the community.)*

To check students' understanding of the selection, see Unit 4 Teaching Resources Book, p. 204.

"Oh, well," said Kezia. She didn't know what to reply. "It doesn't matter. You can come and see our doll's house all the same. Come on. Nobody's looking."

But Lil shook her head still harder.

"Don't you want to?" asked Kezia.

Suddenly there was a twitch, a tug at Lil's skirt. She turned round. Our Else was looking at her with big, **imploring** eyes; she was frowning; she wanted to go. For a moment Lil looked at our Else very doubtfully. But then our Else twitched her skirt again. She started forward. Kezia led the way. Like two little stray cats they followed across the courtyard to where the doll's house stood.

"There it is," said Kezia.

There was a pause. Lil breathed loudly, almost snorted; our Else was still as stone.

"I'll open it for you," said Kezia kindly. She undid the hook and they looked inside.

"There's the drawing room and the dining room, and that's the—"

"Kezia!"

Oh, what a start they gave!

"Kezia!"

It was Aunt Beryl's voice. They turned round. At the back door stood Aunt Beryl, staring as if she couldn't believe what she saw.

"How dare you ask the little Kelveys into the courtyard?" said her cold, furious voice. "You know as well as I do, you're not allowed to talk to them. Run away, children, run away at once. And don't come back again," said Aunt Beryl. And she stepped into the yard and shooed them out as if they were chickens.

"Off you go immediately!" she called, cold and proud.

They did not need telling twice. Burning with shame, shrinking together, Lil huddling along like her mother, our Else dazed, somehow they crossed the big courtyard and squeezed through the white gate.

"Wicked, disobedient little girl!" said Aunt Beryl bitterly to Kezia, and she slammed the doll's house to.

The afternoon had been awful. A letter had come from Willie Brent, a terrifying, threatening letter, saying if she did not meet him that evening in Pulman's Bush, he'd come to the front door and ask the reason why! But now that she had frightened those little rats of Kelveys and given Kezia a good scolding, her heart felt lighter. That ghastly pressure was gone. She went back to the house humming.

When the Kelveys were well out of sight of Burnells', they sat down to rest on a big red drainpipe by the side of the road. Lil's cheeks were still burning; she took off the hat with the quill and held it on her knee. Dreamily they looked over the hay paddocks, past the creek, to the group of wattles [5] where Logan's cows stood waiting to be milked. What were their thoughts?

Presently our Else nudged up close to her sister. But now she had forgotten the cross lady. She put out a finger and stroked her sister's quill; she smiled her rare smile.

"I seen the little lamp," she said, softly.

Then both were silent once more. ∾

---

1 **Cultures in Conflict** *How does Aunt Beryl serve as a spokesperson for the entire community?*

Vocabulary

imploring (im plôr´ ing) *adj.* begging or beseeching

5. *Wattles* are branches or poles woven together to make walls.

Analyze Sensory Details *What do these details suggest about the setting of the final scene?*   2

Writing Practice

Write an Essay Have students write a brief essay on one of the topics described below. Select a few essays on each topic to be read aloud and discussed.

- Identify the narrator's attitude toward Aunt Beryl, Isabel, Kezia, Lil, Else, and Lena. Cite words the narrator uses to describe each character, and tell what tone the words convey.

- In "The Doll's House," Lena taunts Lil about growing up to become a servant. Does a person's social class affect his or her status in our society? Are one's opportunities today determined by social class or status? Use your journal entry on status as a foundation for offering your opinions on these questions.

After You Read

Respond and Think Critically

Respond and Interpret

1. What was your reaction to the way the Kelvey girls are treated?

2. (a)Describe the Burnells' doll's house. Why does it remain outside? (b)What do the Burnell children think of their new doll's house?

3. (a)Under what conditions are the girls' school friends allowed to see the doll's house? (b)Why do the Burnells set such strict conditions?

4. (a)What rule must the Burnell girls obey regarding the Kelvey sisters? Why? (b)What effect do adult prejudices have on the Burnell girls and some of the other girls at school?

Analyze and Evaluate

5. (a)How is Kezia different from her family? Support your answer with details from the story.

(b)What do you think Kezia will be like when she grows up? Why?

6. What is significant about Else's statement at the end of the story?

7. The **theme**, or main idea, of a story can often be expressed as a general statement. How would you express the theme of this story?

Connect

8. **Big Idea** **Cultures in Conflict** What does the story suggest about the way economic or class differences can affect people?

9. **Connect to Today** The children in this story yield to peer pressure in their admiration of Isabel and their rejection of the Kelvey sisters. What qualities must a young person have to resist peer pressure in today's world?

Daily Life & Culture

Society in Miniature

Like their clothes, children's toys may reflect the socioeconomic class of their owners, as suggested in Mansfield's story. In the 1800s, children of wealth enjoyed dolls with finely detailed heads and hands of bisque (unglazed china), porcelain, or molded wax. Doll's houses

were also indicative of status. Well-to-do children might play with elaborate doll's houses beautifully furnished. As with children's dolls, many of these houses were meant for show rather than play. Poor children, needless to say, seldom, if ever, had the luxury of playing with doll's houses.

Group Activity Discuss the following questions.

1. Does the doll's house in this story seem intended as a toy or as a display piece? Explain.

2. The doll's house in this story is described on p. 793 as a "perfect little house." In your opinion, is it perfect? Explain.

Daily Life & Culture

1. The doll's house seems intended as a display piece. In the story, the little girls look at it but do not play with it.

2. Students may agree it is less than perfect due to the "big lumps of congealed paint."

8. They can create great unhappiness and injustice.

9. Students may say a young person must have insight to recognize peer pressure and courage to do what is right rather than to conform.

Assess

1. Many students will be disturbed by the treatment the girls receive.

2. (a) The doll's house is large; it has all the details of a real house, and it opens in the middle so you can view the entire inside at once. It is kept outside in the courtyard because it smells of paint. (b) They think it is the most wonderful thing they have ever seen. Kezia likes the little lamp best of all because it looks so real.

3. (a) They may come two at a time to view the doll's house, but they cannot stay for tea or come inside. (b) The Burnells will not tolerate the noise or mess children might create in their house.

4. (a) They are not allowed to invite the Kelvey sisters over or even to speak to them because they are the daughters of a washerwoman and a "jailbird." (b) Adult prejudices are adopted by the children and cause them to behave badly.

5. (a) Kezia feels some sympathy for the Kelvey sisters and wants to invite them to see the doll's house. Like our Else, she has an appreciation for the little lamp. (b) Some students might think Kezia will retain her independence; others might think she will lose her innocence and respect the class distinctions of her society.

6. The statement shows Else, like Kezia, appreciates wonderful things. Mansfield is making the point that despite class distinctions Kezia and Else are not so different in their feelings.

7. Possible response: A class system can be used to justify malicious behavior.

After You Read

Assess

Literary Element

1. (C) is the correct answer. The lamp represents a genuine truth that cuts across class divisions.

2. (D) is the correct answer. An invitation to the Burnells symbolizes social acceptance.

Progress Check

Can students identify symbols?

If No → See Unit 4 Teaching Resources Book, p. 199.

Review: Point of View

It is told from the third-person omniscient point of view because the narrator describes the thoughts and emotions of several characters. The nature of the feelings expressed suggests the narrator is reflecting the enthusiasm of the children.

Reading Strategy

1. Students may say visual images are most frequent.

2. Answers will vary.

Literary Element Symbol

SAT Skills Practice

1. In this story, the little lamp symbolizes the abstract qualities of

  (A) struggle and justice

  (B) knowledge and persistence

  (C) genuineness and truth

  (D) love and creativity

  (E) spirituality and faith

2. Mrs. Burnell prohibits Kezia from inviting the Kelvey girls to their home because that action would represent the Burnells'

  (A) desire to set positive role models for the Kelveys

  (B) enjoyment of the girls' unfussy demeanor

  (C) goal of converting the girls to Christianity

  (D) acceptance of the Kelveys as social equals

  (E) lack of other playmates

Review: Point of View

As you learned on page 497, **point of view** is the relationship of the narrator to the story.

- **First-person:** the narrator is a character in the story and uses the words *I* and *me*

- **Third-person omniscient:** the narrator knows everything about the characters and events

- **Third-person limited:** the narrator describes events as only one character perceives them

Partner Activity With a partner, determine the point of view of this story. Then reread the passage on page 793 beginning "The hook at the side was stuck fast . . . ." Do you think the narrator is expressing her own thoughts or those of one of the characters? Explain.

LOG ON ▶ **Literature** Online

Selection Resources For Selection Quizzes, eFlash-cards, and Reading-Writing Connection activities, go to glencoe.com and enter QuickPass code GLW6053u4.

Reading Strategy Analyze Sensory Details

The author's use of **sensory details** helps you imagine the characters, the setting, and the action. Look back at the chart you made on page 791 and then answer these questions.

1. What types of sensory details does Mansfield use most often?

2. Which of the sensory details do you find most striking or effective? Explain.

Vocabulary Practice

Practice with Context Clues Look back through the story to find context clues for the vocabulary words below. Record your findings in a graphic organizer like the one shown.

congealed marvelous flag titter imploring

EXAMPLE:

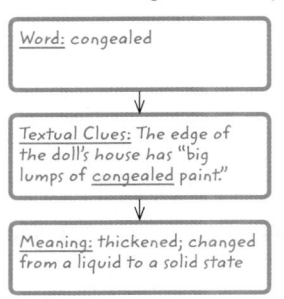

> Word: congealed
>
> ↓
>
> Textual Clues: The edge of the doll's house has "big lumps of congealed paint."
>
> ↓
>
> Meaning: thickened; changed from a liquid to a solid state

Academic Vocabulary

*To the Kelvey sisters, the doll's house is beyond reach; it therefore is a **simulation** of the larger society that excludes them.*

Simulation is an academic word with a variety of uses. For example, astronauts use flight **simulation** to train for space missions. To further explore the meaning of this word, complete the sentence below.

A simulation of life in medieval Europe might include _____, _____, and _____.

For more on academic vocabulary, see pages 36–37 and R83–R85.

Vocabulary

marvelous <u>Textual Clues</u>: The doll's house is "too much" for the children to comprehend. "They had never seen anything like it in their lives." <u>Meaning</u>: extraordinary; causing wonder

flagged <u>Textual Clues</u>: "At last everybody had seen it …" suggests that seeing the doll's house is a thing of the past. Thus, as a topic of conversation ("subject"), it no longer engages interest; <u>Meaning</u>: to decline in interest or attraction

titter <u>Textual Clues</u>: "The girls began to titter" suggests they reacted in some way. "Lena couldn't stand that!" suggests that the titters embarrassed her; <u>Meaning</u>: to laugh nervously

imploring <u>Textual Clues</u>: "Our Else was looking at her with big imploring eyes; she wanted to go." Eyes opened wide often suggest surprise, wonder, or earnestness. "She wanted to go" suggests that Else is begging Lil through her facial expression; <u>Meaning</u>: begging or beseeching

Academic Vocabulary

Answers should be associated with medieval Europe, such as horses, knights, castles, minstrels, or peasants.

Respond Through Writing

Short Story

Apply Symbolism In "The Doll's House," Mansfield created realistic characters and developed rich symbols to explore class distinctions and the problems they can cause. Using this story as a model, write your own story to explore a social issue in your community. Use a symbol to reinforce the theme.

Understand the Task A **symbol** is a person, a place, or a thing that represents something beyond its literal meaning.

Prewrite Plan a sequence of events for your story, and choose an effective point of view (see the Review on page 800). Then brainstorm a list of possible symbols, and create a web like the one below to explore their meaning. Then choose a symbol to support the theme.

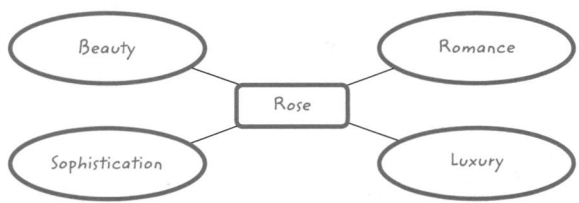

Draft Outline your story to include the elements of an engaging plot (see Literary Terms Handbook p. R13). Make sure to provide details that develop your chosen symbol. As you write, show how various characters relate to the symbol. What does it signify to each character, and how does each character feel about it?

Revise Make sure you have included concrete sensory details to describe the specific actions, movements, gestures, and feelings of the characters. Refer to the chart you made on page 791 to help in your evaluation. Use the rubric on page 158 of the Writing Workshop on short stories to check other elements of your story.

Edit and Proofread Proofread your paper, correcting any errors in grammar, spelling, and punctuation. Use the Grammar Tip in the side column to help you with sentence fragments.

Learning Objectives

In this assignment, you will focus on the following objectives:

Writing: Writing a short story.

Grammar: Using sentence fragments for effect.

> ### Grammar Tip
>
> **Sentence Fragments for Effect**
>
> In formal writing, avoid using sentence fragments—an incomplete sentence that may lack either a subject or a verb, or both. But in creative writing, you can use fragments to capture realistic dialogue, as Mansfield does with this fragment from the story:
>
> *"Wicked, disobedient little girl!"*
>
> As you write your story, incorporate sentence fragments for emphasis or dialogue. Use them sparingly lest you dilute the effect.

After You Read

Assess

Respond Through Writing

Students' stories should

- include a setting made clear through vivid sensory details
- include all the elements of plot
- include a central symbol to help convey the story's meaning
- show how the symbol relates to various characters

A student who meets all of these criteria should receive the equivalent of a 4-point response.

A student who fully meets three and partially meets the fourth of these criteria should receive the equivalent of a 3-point response.

A student who fully meets two of these criteria, or who partially meets three criteria, should receive the equivalent of a 2-point response.

A student who partially fully meets one or partially meets two of these criteria should receive the equivalent of a 1-point response.

 For grammar practice, see Unit 4 Teaching Resources Book, p. 203.

 To create custom assessments online, go to Progress Reporter Online Assessment.

 To create custom assessments using software, use ExamView Assessment Suite.

Approaching Level

DIFFERENTIATED INSTRUCTION

Model Story-Writing Steps Provide struggling writers with a checklist of steps to follow. Explain each step, modeling a sample story plan on the board.

Checklist

- Choose an issue of importance to you.
- Decide what point you want to make. This will be your theme.
- Create a brief, two- or three-sentence story idea that illustrates the theme.
- Choose a person, place, or thing to serve as a symbol—an abstract idea that is important to the plot or theme.
- Create a sequence of plot events.
- Draft the story, using specific, concrete nouns; strong, action verbs; and vivid adjectives.
- Revise and proofread your draft.

Before You Read

Focus

Rainforest and *River Bend*

Australia

Bellringer Options

Selection Focus
Transparency 49
Daily Language Practice
Transparency 73

Or ask: In what ways does your environment impact your life? Answers will vary. Elicit examples of how students' environments affect their lives on a daily basis and, in turn, how they affect their environment (recycling, littering, etc.).

Cultural History ☆

Aborigines When the British began settling in Australia in 1788, they brought cultural values that clashed with those of the Aborigines. Expansion of European settlements disregarded Aboriginal land tenure, economy, and sacred sites. War and disease killed many Aboriginies and survivors were treated as second class citizens. Today there is a strong campaign to revive and respect Aboriginal culture.

Meet **Judith Wright**
(1915–2000)

"The true function of an art and a culture," Australian poet Judith Wright once wrote, "is to interpret us to ourselves, and to relate us to the country and society in which we live." She carried out this sentiment in her poetry, her commitment to the environment, and her involvement in politics.

Love for the Land Wright was born into a family that had lived in Australia since the nineteenth century. Her connection to the natural world was formed during her childhood on a ranch in the mountains of New South Wales. For Wright, it was not family but the land itself that would become the greatest influence on her life.

The Poet Emerges As a young child, Wright was educated at home, but when she began her studies at the New England Girls' School, one of her teachers recognized and encouraged her talent for writing. During her last year at school, she broke her pelvis in a riding accident. When doctors told her she would be unable to have children, Wright remembered one of her favorite childhood books, *My Brilliant Career*, which describes a young woman who decides not to get married so she can maintain her independence. Wright knew she could have a fulfilling life as an author. In the mid-1940s Wright began to compose poetry and was published in several literary journals, including *Meanjin Papers*. Tired of the old "literature of nostalgia," she believed the time had come to make Australia a spiritual and literary home for its people.

Artist and Activist Wright's beautifully crafted, lyrical poems present a world in which humans and nature are bonded together, but she was also aware of the connection between art

"As a poet you have to imitate somebody, but as I had a beautiful landscape outside that I loved so much and was in so much . . . it was my main object from the start."

—Judith Wright

and politics. She was an outspoken opponent of uranium mining and nuclear power. She devoted much of her time to advocating for the rights of Aboriginal people of Australia and for the protection of natural resources. Some of Wright's critics claimed her politics began to overshadow the artistic merits of her poetry, but she insisted the two were not separate. She was one of the first to deliver a scholarly paper analyzing the work of Aboriginal writers. Her final public act came just before her death when she led a march across the Sydney Harbor Bridge during bitterly cold winter weather. She and the other marchers were demonstrating for reconciliation for Australia's Aboriginal population. ☆

Literature Online

Author Search For more about Judith Wright, go to glencoe.com and enter QuickPass code GLW6053u4.

Selection Skills

Literary Elements
- Meter and Rhythm (SE pp. 803, 805; TE p. 804)

Reading Skills
- Clarify Meaning (SE pp. 803–805)

Rainforest *and* River Bend

Writing Skills/Grammar
- Proposal (SE p. 805)
- Predicate Nominatives and Adjectives (TE p. 804)

Vocabulary Skills
- Word Usage (SE pp. 803, 805)
- Pantomime (TE p. 803)

Literature and Reading Preview

Connect to the Poems

To what aspects of the natural world do you think people are most strongly connected? Discuss this question with a small group. Consider the power and strength of nature, as well as its subtle characteristics.

Build Background

The Aborigines of Australia lived off the land without adversely affecting it. But since the arrival of Europeans, much of the land has been cleared for lumbering or farming. In Wright's native state of New South Wales, the forest that was once prevalent now covers only 10 percent of the land.

Set Purposes for Reading

Big Idea Place and Identity

As you read the poems, ask yourself, How do the poems show that humans, animals, and plants are interconnected?

Literary Element Meter and Rhythm

Meter is a regular pattern of stressed (marked ´) and unstressed (marked ˘) syllables that give a line of poetry a **rhythm**, or pattern of beats. The basic metrical unit is called the **foot**, which usually consists of one stressed syllable and one or more unstressed syllables. As you read the poems, ask yourself, How do meter and rhythm create a musical effect?

Reading Strategy Clarify Meaning

When you **clarify meaning**, you examine difficult sections of text to clear up what is confusing. As you read, ask yourself, Do I understand the ideas in each part of the text? If your answer is "no," ask yourself questions about the text, reread more slowly, and look up unfamiliar words in a dictionary.

Tip: Take Notes Use a chart like the one below to record your interpretations of excerpts from Wright's poems.

Excerpt	Questions	My Interpretation
"We cannot understand that call <u>unless we move into his dream</u>, where all is one and one is all and <u>frog and python are the same.</u>"	What does it mean to "move into" the frog's dream? How can a frog and a python be the same?	We need to enter a mindset in which we can see the unity of all creatures.

JUDITH WRIGHT **803**

Learning Objectives

For pages 802–805

In studying these texts, you will focus on the following objectives:

Literary Study: Analyzing meter and rhythm.

Reading: Clarifying meaning.

Writing: Writing a proposal.

Vocabulary

mutter (mut´ər) *v.* to speak in a low voice or indistinctly with lips partially closed; p. 804 *Andrea saw the grade written on her test and began to mutter behind her hand.*

forage (fôr´ij) *v.* to hunt or search for food; p. 804 *The raccoons like to forage for scraps near the garbage cans.*

perpetual (pər pech´o͞o əl) *adj.* everlasting; eternal; p. 804 *The forest of giant redwoods seems to exist in perpetual silence.*

Tip: Word Usage When you encounter a new word, it might help you to answer a specific question about the word. For example, When might you **mutter** a comment as opposed to saying it clearly?

Before You Read

Focus

Summary

In "Rainforest," Judith Wright uses figurative language to illustrate nature's beauty while denouncing humans' destruction of the rainforest. In "River Bend," Wright contrasts the agelessness of nature with the mortality of animals and humans, namely Aborigines. This poem touches upon one of Wright's lifelong causes, that of preserving the Aborigine population.

 For summaries in languages other than English, see Unit 4 Teaching Resources Book, pp. 206–211.

Vocabulary

Pantomime Ask students to work with a partner to act out the vocabulary terms *mutter* and *forage*. Encourage them to act them out in different ways. Their partner must guess the correct vocabulary term. You may also ask them to draw a picture of these terms on flashcards and write the term on the back of the card. Have them use the flashcards to quiz their partner. Students should review and discuss any terms they guess incorrectly.

 For additional vocabulary practice, see Unit 4 Teaching Resources Book, p. 214.

Approaching Level

DIFFERENTIATED INSTRUCTION

Line Breaks Remind students that when reading poetry they should use punctuation, not line breaks, to guide their pauses. Have students circle the punctuation in the poems and read them twice, once using punctuation as a guide and once using line breaks as their guide. Ask students to discuss how the different readings affected the rhythm of the poems and their understanding of them.

Advanced Learners/Pre-AP

DIFFERENTIATED INSTRUCTION

Research Suggest that students look into the history and development of Australia in the mid-twentieth century when Wright was writing. Have students research social movements that could have caused Wright to put such stress on the state of the environment and the interaction of humans within it.

Teach

Literary Element   1

Meter and Rhythm As a class, mark the stressed and unstressed syllables. **Ask:** How would you mark the meter in this stanza, and what effect does it have on the rhythm? *(Students should note that the meter creates a regular rhythm.)*

Reading Strategy   2

Clarify Meaning Answer: *The rainforest is equated with the simple call of a tree-frog.*

ENGLISH LEARNERS To assist English learners, **ask:** What images do you see in the first stanza? Have students underline specific text details and use them to draw a picture. Discuss students' pictures and have them explain the mood and message that the imagery creates.

 For additional practice using the reading skill or strategy, see Unit 4 Teaching Resources Book, p. 213.

Big Idea   3

Place and Identity Answer: *The three entities, or voices, are those of a dog, a woman, and the river. The first two voices represent mortality and impermanence, but the river's voice represents the eternity of nature.*

Rainforest
Judith Wright

The forest drips and glows with green.
The tree-frog croaks his far-off song.
His voice is stillness, moss and rain
drunk from the forest ages long.   **1**

5 We cannot understand that call
unless we move into his dream,
where all is one and one is all
and frog and python are the same.

We with our quick dividing eyes
10 measure, distinguish and are gone.
The forest burns, the tree-frog dies,
yet one is all and all are one.

River Bend
Judith Wright

What killed that kangaroo-doe, slender skeleton
tumbled above the water with her long shanks[1]
cleaned white as moonlight?
Pad-tracks in sand where something drank fresh blood.

5 Last night a dog howled somewhere,
a hungry ghost in need of sacrifice.

Down by that bend, they say, the last old woman,
thin, black and **muttering** grief,
foraged for mussels, all her people gone.

10 The swollen winter river
curves over stone, a wild **perpetual** voice.

---

1. *Shanks* are the part of the leg from knee to ankle.

2 Clarify Meaning *In this stanza, what small thing does the poet equate with the majesty of the rainforest?*

3 Place and Identity *What are the three entities, or voices, mentioned in this poem, and what does each represent?*

Vocabulary

mutter (mut′ ər) *v.* to speak in a low voice or indistinctly with lips partially closed
forage (fôr′ ij) *v.* to hunt or search for food
perpetual (pər pech′ ōō əl) *adj.* everlasting; eternal

804 UNIT 4 SOUTHEAST ASIA AND THE PACIFIC

Grammar Practice

SPIRAL REVIEW **Predicate Nominatives and Adjectives** Remind students that a predicate nominative is a noun that follows a subject and a linking verb and identifies or renames the subject. A predicate adjective follows a linking verb and points back to the subject and describes it.

Write this sentence on the board:
His voice is <u>stillness, moss, and rain</u>.

Explain to students that the underlined words are predicate nominatives.

Write this sentence on the board:
Her hair is <u>long</u>.

Point out that the underlined word is a predicate adjective. Have each student write a paragraph on the themes of Wright's poems. The paragraph should contain two sentences with predicate nominatives and two with predicate adjectives.

After You Read

Respond and Think Critically

Respond and Interpret

1. Which images in these poems did you find particularly powerful? Why?

2. (a)According to the speaker in "Rainforest," what must we do to understand the tree-frog's call? (b)What is the central message of this poem?

3. (a)In "Rainforest," to whom does Wright refer when she writes, "We with our quick dividing eyes"? (b)What is the significance of this description?

4. (a)What question does the speaker pose in lines 1–3 of "River Bend"? (b)What does the speaker suggest is the answer to this question?

Analyze and Evaluate

5. (a)Identify the metaphor in the first stanza of "Rainforest." (b)Do you find this metaphor effective? Explain.

6. (a)In "River Bend," who is the "last old woman"? (b)How might her fate be related to that of the kangaroo-doe?

Connect

7. **Big Idea** **Place and Identity** Wright often contrasts ageless elements of nature and transitory life. How is this true of "River Bend"?

8. **Connect to Today** What aspects of today's environment do you feel should be protected?

Literary Element **Meter and Rhythm**

To **scan** a poem means to note the stressed (´) and unstressed (˘) syllables and to divide the line into its **feet**. Poems with consistent meter have a predictable **rhythm**, but can still contain variations.

1. Mark the scansion in each line of "Rainforest." Does the poem have a regular meter? Explain.

2. Is the meter in "Rainforest" the same in every line, or does it vary? Explain.

Reading Strategy **Clarify Meaning**

Refer to the chart you made on page 803 and answer the following questions.

1. If you did not know "Rainforest" and "River Bend" were written by the same poet, what clues might lead you to that conclusion?

2. Do you think the poet intended "River Bend" to be a sad poem? Explain.

LOG ON **Literature** Online

Selection Resources For Selection Quizzes, eFlashcards, and Reading-Writing Connection activities, go to glencoe.com and enter QuickPass code GLW6053u4.

Vocabulary Practice

Practice with Word Usage Respond to these statements to help you explore the meanings of vocabulary words from the poems.

1. Describe a possible mindset of someone who often **mutters** to herself.

2. Give an example of an animal that **forages**.

3. Name something that is—or seems—**perpetual**.

Writing

Write a Proposal Wright's nature poetry makes a compelling argument for preserving the natural world. Think about some aspect of your school or community that could be more environmentally friendly. Write a proposal explaining how to make these changes a reality. In your proposal, include vivid images of nature to inspire your audience. Make sure to present your ideas clearly; first present the problem, then outline a plan for solving it.

JUDITH WRIGHT **805**

After You Read

Assess

1. Answers will vary.

2. (a) We must participate in his dream of unity. (b) the importance of the unity of all things

3. (a) She refers to humans. (b) Humans don't think of all creatures existing in a delicate balance; we like to categorize, divide, and individualize.

4. (a) The speaker asks what killed the kangaroo-doe. (b) the dog

5. (a) The voice of the tree-frog is compared with stillness, moss and rain. (b) Answers will vary.

6. (a) She is most likely an Aborigine. (b) She is on the verge of death herself.

7. She contrasts the ageless river to the dead kangaroo-doe and to the old woman, the last of her people. The river's voice is "perpetual," unlike the muttering voice of the old woman.

8. Students may mention the air and water supply and specific endangered species of animals.

Literary Element

1. The poem has a regular meter. It is written in iambic tetrameter—a line consisting of four iambic feet, or sets of one unstressed and one stressed syllable.

2. The meter varies. For example, line 1 is regular and line 10 is not.

Progress Check

Can students analyze rhythm?

If No → See Unit 4 Teaching Resources Book, p. 212.

Reading Strategy

1. Both poems show reverence for all creatures and the myster of nature.

2. Students should support answers.

Writing

Students' proposals should present an action to help the environment, clearly outline what can be done to achieve this goal, and include vivid nature imagery.

Vocabulary

1. Students will likely name a negative mindset, such as distraction, aggression, or depression.

2. Students might identify a squirrel, bird, or other animal.

3. Students should express an understanding that the word perpetual means "ongoing or eternal."

Before You Read

Focus

Bellringer Options

Daily Language Practice Transparency 74

Or ask: Who are some activist poets in the United States that have challenged traditional thought? As students respond, elicit specific examples of what these poets believed in and how they influenced the world. Explain that Oodgeroo Noonuccal fought for Aboriginal rights and ask students to draw parallels between her fight and the examples they gave of poets. Encourage students to think about the characteristics of a good leader—what makes one person persevere in history and others fade away.

Cultural History ☆

Aboriginal Activism Although the Aboriginal culture was repressed during British colonialism, the culture began reviving in the mid-1900s. Efforts to promote civil rights, land rights, and equal wages continue to this day.

Before You Read

Municipal Gum

Meet **Oodgeroo of the tribe Noonuccal**
(1920–1993)

Oodgeroo of the tribe Noonuccal (ōōd′jer ōō nōō′noo kəl) adopted her tribal name in 1988 to protest bicentennial celebrations of the European settlement in Australia. She characterized the 200 years of settlement as years of destruction and carnage, writing, "From the Aboriginal point of view, what is there to celebrate?"

Early Life Noonuccal was born Kathleen (Kath) Ruska, a member of the Noonuccal tribe of Stradbroke Island, Queensland, in northeastern Australia. When she was thirteen, financial pressures forced her to leave school and take a job as a servant. She wrote that, for an Aborigine at that time, "there wasn't the slightest possibility of getting 'a better job' [even] if you stayed on at school." During World War II, she worked for the Australian Women's Army Service. She was promoted to corporal, but had to resign from the service because of chronic middle ear infections. In 1942, she married Bruce Walker, with whom she had a son in 1946.

Aboriginal Voice After the war, Noonuccal began to gain wide recognition for her poetry and for her celebration of her heritage. With her first book, *We Are Going* (1964), she became the first Aboriginal poet ever published. It became one of the best-selling poetry collections in Australian history. She wrote of the collection, "I felt poetry would be the breakthrough for the Aboriginal people because they were storytellers and song-makers, and I thought poetry would appeal to them more than anything else. It was more of a book of their voices that I was trying to bring out, and I think I succeeded in doing this."

"Change is the law. The new must oust the old."

—Oodgeroo of the tribe Noonuccal

Tireless Activist In addition to writing, Noonuccal worked as a political and environmental activist throughout her life. In the 1960s, she served as the Queensland State Secretary of the Federal Council for the Advancement of Aborigines and Torres Strait Islanders, a group created to combat racism and ensure citizenship and voting rights for indigenous people. In 1970, she returned to her homeland of Minjerriba on Stradbroke Island and purchased property that became an open air classroom for Aboriginal culture and society. That same year, she was appointed a Member of the Order of the British Empire for her work advancing Aboriginal rights. However, she returned the honor in 1987 to protest Australia's bicentennial celebration. She is famous for poetry that expresses anger over European-Australian racism and conveys nostalgia for the lost Aboriginal ways of life. ☆

 LOG ON ▶ **Literature** Online

Author Search For more about Oodgeroo of the tribe Noonuccal, go to glencoe.com and enter QuickPass code GLW6053u4.

Selection Skills

Literary Elements
- End Rhyme (SE pp. 807–809)

← **Municipal Gum** →

Speaking/Listening/Viewing Skills
- Oral Interpretation (TE p. 808)

Reading Skills
- Connect to Personal Experience (SE pp. 807, 809; TE p. 808)

Vocabulary Skills
- Denotation and Connotation (SE pp. 807, 809)
- Collages (TE p. 808)

Writing Skills/Grammar
- Internal Monologue (SE p. 809)

Literature and Reading Preview

Connect to the Poem

How can something change when it is taken out of its natural habitat? Write a journal entry about this question.

Build Background

When Europeans arrived in Australia in the late eighteenth century, they encountered one of the world's oldest cultures, dating back at least 42,000 years. The Aborigines (ab´ə rij´ə nēs) are hunter-gatherers who perform rituals to honor the earth and who live in close connection with Australia's animal and plant species. These include the native gum tree, or euca-lyptus, which remains a symbol of the country and its people.

Set Purposes for Reading

Big Idea Cultures in Conflict

As you read, ask yourself, How have colonization and urbanization affected the Australian landscape?

Literary Element End Rhyme

Rhyme is the repetition of sound in words that appear close to one another. **End rhyme** occurs at the ends of lines. As you read, ask yourself, What are the patterns of end rhymes in the poem? Read the poem out loud and consider how the end rhyme contributes to the poem's emotional impact.

Reading Strategy Connect to Personal Experience

When you **connect to personal experience**, you make con-nections between details in a literary work and your life to help you understand the work. As you read, ask yourself, How do the ideas in "Municipal Gum" relate to my experiences?

Tip: Make a Web Use a web like the one below to record your thoughts as you read.

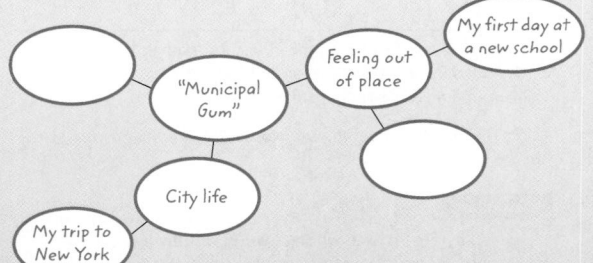

Learning Objectives

For pages 806–809

In studying this text, you will focus on the following objectives:

Literary Study: Analyzing end rhyme.

Reading: Connecting to personal experience.

Writing: Writing an internal monologue.

Vocabulary

listless (list´lis) *adj.* showing disinterest; spiritless; p. 808 *Stuck indoors on a rainy day, Laura grew listless.*

dolorous (dō´lər əs) *adj.* marked by sadness or grief; p. 808 *The dolorous love song had the audience in tears.*

Tip: Denotation and Connotation A word's denotation is its literal meaning, while its connotations are its implied meanings. For example, the word *listless* literally means "dis-interested," but it has a stronger con-notation than the word *disinterested*.

English Learners

DIFFERENTIATED INSTRUCTION

Intermediate English learners may have a difficult time understanding the purpose and use of personification in this poem. Explain to students that the "you" is an address to the tree, which allows the tree to possess human characteristics. Ask them to comment on the effect this personifica-tion has on the poem.

Advanced Learners/Pre-AP

DIFFERENTIATED INSTRUCTION

Debate Ask advanced learners to identify whether they agree or disagree with the displacement of trees into cities. Have them write at least three specific reasons to support their view, such as giving an example of one of the benefits of instilling nature into urban areas. Divide supporters and dissenters into two groups and have them debate in front of the class. Encourage other students to participate.

Before You Read

Focus

Summary

In the poem "Municipal Gum," Oodgeroo of the tribe Noonuccal uses powerful word choice and figurative language to describe the displacement of a tree to an urban environment. She describes the displacement as incredibly cruel, and she compares the tree's tragedy to the displacement of Aborigines from their land. Noonuccal employs personification by addressing the tree as "you."

> For summaries in languages other than English, see Unit 4 Teaching Resources Book, pp. 218–223.

Vocabulary

SMALL GROUP

Collages Have stu-dents use pictures from magazines and newspapers to create two collages, one that illustrates *listlessness* and the other that shows something *dolorous*. Ask students to present their collages in small groups and discuss their picture choices. **(APPROACHING)** For students having difficulty under-standing the vocabulary terms, ask them to use a thesaurus to look up synonyms for the words and make a list of them. Reinforce that synonyms may have different connotations. Have them underline the synonyms they found that have the closest connotations to the vocabulary terms.

> For additional vocabulary practice, see Unit 4 Teaching Resources Book, p. 226.

Teach

Reading Strategy 1

Connect to Personal Experience Ask students to recall times they have felt a sense of hopelessness. **Ask:** Based on your experiences with hopelessness, why might the author have subscribed this feeling to the tree? (*Students should say that the poet sees nature's and the Aborigine's futures as bleak.*)

> For additional practice using the reading skill or strategy, see Unit 4 Teaching Resources Book, p. 225.

Literary Element 2

End Rhyme Answer: *It creates an insistent rhythm that enhances the feeling of anger and despair.*

> For additional literary element practice, see Unit 4 Teaching Resources Book, p. 224.

Cultural History

Eucalyptus Trees Gum trees, otherwise known as eucalypti, are prominent in Australia. The tree consists of leathery leaves and fruit that contain small seeds. The oil from eucalypti trees is used for medical purposes, such as for inhalants. The wood is used extensively for fuel and construction, and is a source for papermaking.

Municipal Gum

Oodgeroo of the tribe Noonuccal
(Kath Walker)

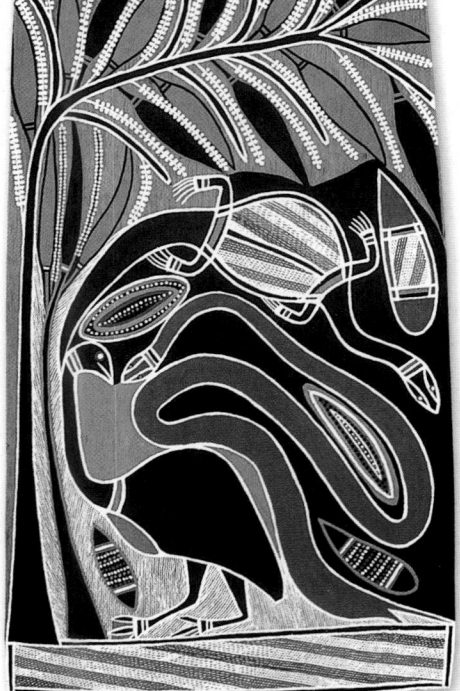

The Tree of Life and His Totems. David Malangi (b. 1934). Bark painting Aham Land, Northern Territory, Australia.

Gumtree in the city street,
Hard bitumen[1] around your feet,
Rather you should be
In the cool world of leafy forest halls
5 And wild bird calls.
Here you seem to me
Like that poor cart-horse
Castrated,[2] broken, a thing wronged,
Strapped and buckled, its hell prolonged,
10 Whose hung head and **listless** mien[3] express **1**
Its hopelessness.
Municipal gum, it is **dolorous**
To see you thus
Set in your black grass of bitumen—
15 O fellow citizen,
What have they done to us?

---

1. *Bitumen* (bī tōō′mən) can mean "tar" or "asphalt."
2. *Castrated* means "impotent" or "lacking in vitality."
3. *Mien* (mēn) is a person's manner or appearance.

End Rhyme *How does the use of end rhyme enhance your sense of the speaker's emotions?* **2**

Vocabulary

listless (lĭst′lĭs) *adj.* showing disinterest; spiritless
dolorous (dō′lər əs) *adj.* marked by sadness or grief

Speaking and Listening Practice

 SMALL GROUP

Perform an Oral Interpretation Remind students that one way to interact with a text is to read it aloud. Arrange students in groups of four or five and instruct them to produce an oral reading of the poem that emphasizes the message within the text. Encourage students to include acting, dance, or other forms of expression that better the students' understanding of the poem.

As an alternative, pass out copies of the poem, double-spaced, and tell students to cut up the poem by lines and re-order it. Explain that while the poem presents a logical order of progression, it is possible to reorder the lines and come to understand the text in another way. Have students do this individually and then read their "found" poems aloud in a meaningful way.

After You Read

Respond and Think Critically

Respond and Interpret

1. What images from this poem did you find the most memorable? Explain.

2. (a)How does the speaker contrast the life of a city gum tree and that of a gum tree in the forest? (b)What does this suggest about the Noonuccal tribe's beliefs?

3. (a)What might the gum tree and cart-horse represent? (b)How would you state the **theme**, or message, of this poem?

Analyze and Evaluate

4. (a)What **metaphor** does the author use in line 14? (b)How does this metaphor reinforce the poem's theme?

5. What can you infer about the speaker's relationship with, and attitude toward, the natural world? Explain.

6. (a)What do the last two lines of the poem suggest? (b)How effective do you find these two lines? Explain.

Connect

7. **Big Idea** **Cultures in Conflict** How does this poem illustrate the conflict between Aboriginal values and European values?

8. **Connect to the Author** Noonuccal changed her name to reflect her culture. What kinds of things do people do today to celebrate their heritage and define themselves?

Literary Element | End Rhyme

Poets use **end rhyme** to create rhythm, to stress particular ideas, or to amuse their audiences.

1. What idea does the poet express through the end rhymes in lines 8–9?

2. How does the end rhyme add to the overall effect of the poem?

Reading Strategy | Connect to Personal Experience

Connecting to personal experience allows you to better understand pieces of literature.

1. (a)Describe a situation in which you felt out of place. (b)What aspects of the situation were most uncomfortable?

2. To what extent were the emotions you experienced similar to those in the poem?

LOG ON **Literature** Online

Selection Resources For Selection Quizzes, eFlashcards, and Reading-Writing Connection activities, go to glencoe.com and enter QuickPass code GLW6053u4.

Vocabulary Practice

Practice with Denotation and Connotation
Each of the boldfaced vocabulary words below is listed with a word that has a similar denotation. Choose the word that has the stronger connotation.

1. **listless**   bored

2. **dolorous**   miserable

✍ Writing

Write an Internal Monologue Write an internal monologue from the point of view of the tree in "Municipal Gum." If the tree had a voice, what do you think it would say about being displaced? As you plan, think about your experiences observing the overlap of urban and rural features, such as strip malls along country roads. Consult your web on page 807 for ideas and use sensory details to capture how the tree experiences its environment.

OODGEROO OF THE TRIBE NOONUCCAL   **809**

After You Read

Assess

1. Answers will vary.

2. (a) The life of a city tree is imprisoning and unnatural; the life of a forest tree is free and natural. (b) The Noonuccals prefer life in nature to life in the city.

3. (a) The gum tree and cart-horse may represent city dwellers in general and Aborigines in particular. (b) The theme might be that city life and colonialism are oppressive and imprisoning.

4. (a) The bitumen is compared with "black grass." (b) The metaphor is ironic because the bitumen is a non-living substance. It emphasizes the unfavorable contrast of city life with the natural world.

5. The speaker is closely connected to the natural world. She views the gum tree and cart-horse as fellow creatures.

6. (a) They suggest the Aborigines, like the gum tree, have been mistreated, displaced, and denied their natural rights. (b) Answers will vary.

7. The coming of Europeans has led to the rise of modern cities in Australia, which have destroyed the Aborigines' more traditional ways of life.

8. Answers will vary.

Literary Element

1. She suggests the mistreatment of the horse, and of the Aborigines, has gone on too long.

2. The end rhyme is surprising. Just as the tree is out of place in the city, and the speaker does not belong, a singsong rhyme is jolting in a poem of lament.

Reading Strategy

1. Answers will vary.

2. Answers will vary.

Vocabulary Practice

1. listless

2. miserable

✍ Writing

Students' internal monologues should
- give accounts of the tree's experience from the tree's point of view
- make a comparison between rural and urban environments
- use sensory details

Before You Read

Focus

Bellringer Options

Daily Language Practice Transparency 75

Or ask: Have you ever been in a situation when you had the opportunity to help a person less fortunate than you, but did not? Encourage students to discuss their reasons for declining to help, and whether or not they feel they were justified.

Literary History ☆

Dallas's Style Dallas has an abiding interest in Asian philosophies and religions, such as Buddhism, and her work exhibits the influence of both Chinese poetry and Japanese haiku. Her poems, some of which are written in the haiku form, often present peaceful, detached meditations on works of art or natural objects. Of this introspective tendency, Dallas writes, "I don't like excitement. I like calm."

Before You Read

Clouds on the Sea

Meet **Ruth Dallas**
(born 1919)

Ruth Dallas, whose working-class settler family owned a gas station in Southland, New Zealand, comments that she began writing "in an environment where I knew no one who was interested in poetry." She attributes her unique poetic style, which incorporates her passion for New Zealand's landscape and her interest in Buddhist philosophy, to her lack of formal literary training. "There were no walls to break down," she writes, "and I was able to pass as freely into one culture as into another."

A Complex Background Ruth Mumford took the pen name Dallas from her grandmother, who came to New Zealand from Scotland in the late 1800s. Dallas was fascinated by this period of New Zealand's history, during which European settlers met—and often clashed with—the Maori people, who had inhabited the island since about A.D. 800. Dallas portrayed this culture clash in a well-known series of children's books, beginning with *The Children in the Bush* (1969). This series, inspired by her mother's childhood, depicts the adventures of a pioneer family in the 1890s.

A Poetry of Place Dallas began writing poetry at an early age, and her poems were first published in the *Southland Daily News* when she was still a child. Later, she was encouraged to write by the editor and critic M. H. Holcroft, who published her poems in the *Southland Times* in 1946. Dallas then published her first collection, *Country Road and Other Poems, 1947–1952*, in 1953. This collection established her reputation as a nature poet, deeply attuned to the processes of Southland's rural life. *The Turning Wheel*, published in 1961, showed the increasing

"We enjoyed the solitary peace of the earth, where the sheer magnitude of the sky and sun seemed to dwarf human beings to insignificance."

—Ruth Dallas

influence of Chinese and Japanese poetry on Dallas's work. She received a New Zealand Book Award in 1977 for *Walking in the Snow*, and has been awarded numerous other honors, including an Order of the British Empire in 1989. Both her fiction and poetry are characterized by their striking descriptions of New Zealand's natural beauty. This quality led the author James Bertram to comment, "She is one of the most independent and unfashionable of New Zealand writers, but her purity of diction and clear singing note seem likely to preserve her work when more aggressively modern verse is forgotten."

Literature Online

Author Search For more about Ruth Dallas, go to glencoe.com and enter QuickPass code GLW6053u4.

Selection Skills

Literary Elements
- Speaker (SE pp. 811, 813; TE p. 812)
- Rhyme (TE p. 811)

← **Clouds on the Sea** →

Writing Skills/Grammar
- Essay (SE p. 813)

Reading Skills
- Summarize (SE pp. 811–813)
- Respond to Tone (TE p. 812)

Vocabulary Skills
- Academic Vocabulary (SE p. 813)

Literature and Reading Preview

Connect to the Poem

Why do some people have so much, while others have so little? Freewrite about how modern technology offers opportunities to some people, while others are left behind.

Build Background

The government of New Zealand funds health care, higher education, and low-income housing, and the nation has one of the world's oldest social security systems. Despite these conditions, however, social and economic inequalities persist between New Zealanders of European descent and the Maori. The Maori have gained acceptance in many areas, but they continue to assert their traditional land and fishing rights and work actively to preserve their language and cultural heritage.

Set Purposes for Reading

Big Idea Cultures in Conflict

As you read, ask yourself, How has New Zealand addressed its social class divisions?

Literary Element Speaker

The **speaker** in a poem is the voice that talks to the reader. You should not assume the speaker is the same as the poet. As you read, ask yourself, What details in the poem tell the reader about the speaker's background?

Reading Strategy Summarize

When you **summarize**, you check your comprehension by stating in your own words the main ideas of a literary work in the order in which they appear. As you read the poem, ask yourself these questions to help you summarize it: Who is mentioned? What is the poem about? Where and when does the poem take place? How is the subject described?

Tip: Make a 5 Ws and an H Chart As you read, keep track of the poem's details and main ideas in a chart like the one below.

Who	Children
What	
Where	New Zealand
Why	
When	
How	

Learning Objectives

For pages 810–813

In studying this text, you will focus on the following objectives:

Literary Study: Analyzing speaker.

Reading: Summarizing.

Writing: Writing an essay.

A carved wood Maori head with inlaid shell eyes. Wood, shell. Auckland Institute and Museum, New Zealand.

RUTH DALLAS   **811**

In the poem "Clouds on the Sea," Ruth Dallas explores social and economic inequality in her native New Zealand. The speaker in the poem lists benefits that contribute to a high quality of life for those New Zealanders with "tall bones…and pink faces": access to good education, clothing, food, and domestic comfort. The final stanza depicts a poor woman trailing reapers to collect fallen grain, a sharp reminder that the privileges described earlier in the poem are not available to everyone. Looking for an explanation to justify this disparity, the speaker admits that "no satisfactory answer has been found."

> **For summaries in languages other than English, see Unit 4 Teaching Resources Book, pp. 229–234.**

Cultural History

Maori The Maori, Polynesian New Zealanders, have inhabited New Zealand for hundreds of years. Their lands and culture were greatly jeopardized by the influx of European settlers following the British takeover of New Zealand in 1840. After decades of fighting, the Maori had lost much of their former land, and their society was irreparably damaged. Although they moved to urban areas and married European New Zealanders, they still suffered economic disadvantages, mostly due to a systematic lack of education. In 1961, the Maori Education Foundation began to address this issue. Cultural revival flourished, and Maori was made an official language in 1987.

Approaching Level

DIFFERENTIATED INSTRUCTION

Rhyme Explain to students the various kinds of rhyme that often appear in poetry:

Internal Rhyme occurs within lines of poetry.

End Rhyme occurs at the end of lines

Half/Slant Rhymes are words that sound similar, but do not rhyme exactly (jackal/buckle.)

Read the poem aloud to the class, demonstrating the correct pronunciation of each word. Then read the poem again, asking students to repeat after each line. Have students identify the rhyme scheme in the poem by going through the text line by line and assigning each rhyme with a letter, starting with "A," *(for example, lines 2 and 4 would be labeled "B").*

Teach

Literary Element 1

Repetition Explain to students that writers often use repetition to emphasize an idea or influence the poem's rhythm.

[ADVANCED] **Ask:** Why might the author have repeated "In my country?" How does this relate to the theme? Students should respond that the use of repetition reinforces the theme of wide disparity between the living conditions of European New Zealanders and those of the Maori.

Reading Strategy 2

Summarize Answer: *The people of New Zealand live in material comfort.*

[ENGLISH LEARNERS] Ask English learners to compare the disparity depicted in New Zealand with a form of social division in their home country.

 For additional practice using the reading skill or strategy, see Unit 4 Teaching Resources Book, p. 236.

Big Idea 3

Cultures in Conflict
Answer: *There is a huge division between the living conditions of the wealthy (European) and the poor (Maori).*

Clouds on the Sea

Ruth Dallas

Lowry Bay, New Zealand, 1954. Roland Wakelin. Oil on board. Private collection.

I walk among men with tall bones,
With shoes of leather, and pink faces;
I meet no man holding a begging
    bowl;
All have their dwelling places.

5 In my country
Every child is taught to read and
    write,
Every child has shoes and a warm
    coat,
Every child must eat his dinner,
No one must grow any thinner;
10 It is considered remarkable and not
    nice
To meet bed-bugs or lice.
Oh we live like the rich
With music at the touch of a switch,

Light in the middle of the night,
15 Water in the house as if from a spring.
Hot, if you wish, or cold, anything
For the comfort of the flesh,
In my country. Fragment
Of new skin at the edge of the world's
    ulcer.

20 For the question
That troubled you as you watched the
    reapers
And a poor woman following,
Gleaning the ears on the ground,
*Why should I have grain and this
    woman none?*
25 No satisfactory answer has been
    found.

2 **Summarize** *How would you summarize the main idea of this stanza?*

Cultures in Conflict *What do these lines tell you about class divisions in New Zealand?* **3**

Reading Practice

Respond to Tone An important part of this poem is the author's attitude, or tone, towards the subject. Explain that authors establish tone through the details they include and, more notably, through their word choice. Review connotations with students and emphasize that different words provoke distinct feelings. Authors choose their words carefully in order to provoke the exact feeling they want in their reader.

Read the poem aloud to the class and ask students to note the words that provoke a strong emotional response. Have students to identify the kinds of emotions that are portrayed through the poem. Make sure students identify specific text details that cause them to draw these conclusions.
Ask: How would you categorize the overall tone of the poem? *(The tone of the poem is bitter and cynical.)*

After You Read

Respond and Think Critically

Respond and Interpret

1. Which lines in the poem were most surprising to you? Explain.

2. (a)Describe the appearance of the men in lines 1–2. (b)Based on this description, what can you infer about their identity?

3. (a)According to the second stanza, what is life like in New Zealand? (b)How does this description contrast with that of the woman in the third stanza?

4. (a)What question troubles the "you" in the final stanza? (b)Who do you think the "you" is?

Analyze and Evaluate

5. How would you contrast the **mood** of the second stanza with that of the final stanza?

6. (a)How do you interpret the **metaphor** in lines 18–19? (b)What effect does this metaphor create?

Connect

7. **Big Idea** Cultures in Conflict How does the situation described in this poem reflect a culture clash in New Zealand?

8. **Connect to Today** Is the situation described by Dallas relevant only to New Zealand, or does it apply to contemporary American society? Explain.

Literary Element Speaker

A poet can express his or her ideas and opinions through a **speaker**. You can find clues about a speaker's identity and attitudes when you pay attention to elements such as tone and diction.

1. How would you describe the speaker's **tone** (the attitude he or she takes toward the subject)?

2. Do you think Dallas shares the speaker's views? Explain.

Reading Strategy Summarize

Refer to the chart you made on page 811 and then answer the following questions.

1. Summarize what the adults and children of New Zealand have, according to the poem.

2. How would you summarize the **theme** expressed in the final stanza?

LOG ON ▶ **Literature** Online

Selection Resources For Selection Quizzes, eFlashcards, and Reading-Writing Connection activities, go to glencoe.com and enter QuickPass code GLW6053u4.

Academic Vocabulary

The speaker in "Clouds on the Sea" makes a clear **differentiation** *between the rich and the poor, but she struggles to find an underlying reason for the gap between these two groups.*

Differentiation is an academic word. Identical twins may look alike, but the **differentiation** in their personalities marks them as individuals. The word *differentiation* is also used in biology. Use context clues to figure out the meaning of *differentiation* in the following sentence.

During **differentiation**, the cells of an embryo develop into separate and specific tissues.

For more on academic vocabulary, see pages 36–37 and R83–R85.

Writing

Write an Essay Using "Clouds on the Sea" as a springboard, research policies that address social and economic inequality in New Zealand. Present your findings in a brief expository essay. In one of your body paragraphs, compare New Zealand's policies with similar ones in the United States.

RUTH DALLAS **813**

After You Read

Assess

1. Answers will vary.

2. (a) The men are tall and have pink faces. (b) They are New Zealanders of European descent.

3. (a) Europeans live a life of material prosperity and comfort. (b) She lives a life of poverty.

4. (a) "Why should I have grain and this woman none?" (b) Answers will vary. The "you" may be Europeans.

5. The mood of the second stanza is cheerful, while the mood of the final stanza is one of sadness and confusion.

6. (a) "Fragment of new skin" might refer to the "new" European New Zealanders; the "world's ulcer" might refer to the past and present problems of the world. (b) The metaphor is a shocking, vivid image of suffering that contrasts with the material comforts described earlier.

7. Social and economic divisions still exist.

8. The situation involves disparities between ethnic groups, which does apply to American society.

Literary Element

1. The tone is sarcastic and troubled.

2. Because Dallas is also a New Zealander, it is likely she shares some of the views. However, while the speaker's initial outlook is positive, Dallas is likely more skeptical.

Progress Check

Do students understand the concept of speaker?

If No → See Unit 4 Teaching Resources Book, p. 235.

Reading Strategy

1. The adults have homes, music, electricity and running water; the children have books, shoes, coats and food.

2. The theme is that although the speaker's world is comfortable, she is troubled by other people's hardships.

Academic Vocabulary

Students should note that in this scientific process, tissues become distinct and separate from one another.

Writing

Students' expository essays should
- present evidence from research
- present similarities and differences in manifestations of social inequality

Before You Read

Focus

Bellringer Options

Selection Focus
Transparency 50
Daily Language Practice
Transparency 76

Or ask: What would you miss most about your life if you had to move to a new region or country? Encourage students to consider the physical and emotional aspects of being separated from their home or loved ones. Have students list people or aspects of their lives they would miss and share their list with a partner.

Language History ☆

The Land Between Rivers

The name *Hanoi* means "the land between rivers." Hanoi is located in the fertile Red River delta, on the banks of the Red River. Other rivers, such as the Duong, Nhue, and Day Rivers, also flow through Hanoi.

Before You Read

Thoughts of Hanoi

Meet **Nguyen Thi Vinh**
(born 1924)

For much of her life, Nguyen Thi Vinh (noo yin′ tī vin′) has lived in the presence of war. She is known for writing fiction and poetry that movingly depict the pain of Vietnamese citizens during her country's division from 1954–1975.

Childhood Turmoil Nguyen's surname comes from one of the two ruling families of Vietnam's history. The Nguyen dynasty was the last to rule Vietnam before French forces occupied the country in the late nineteenth century. In 1930, when Nguyen was six, the people of northwestern Vietnam, near the capital of Hanoi, staged an unsuccessful revolt against French colonial forces. Ten years later, Japanese troops occupied Vietnam and controlled the country until 1945. Then, from 1946 to 1954, communist Ho Chi Minh led the Viet Minh in a bloody war for independence from France. During this period, Nguyen wrote her first and most famous work of fiction, *Two Sisters* (1953).

A Divided Country The year Nguyen Thi Vinh turned 30, Vietnamese forces overthrew the French, and an international conference on the fate of Vietnam followed. The conference resulted in the division of the country into two nations: communist North Vietnam and democratic South Vietnam. For 300 days after the conference, people were allowed to pass from one zone to the other. This migration sometimes divided families, friends, and business associates who found themselves on different sides of what Nguyen calls "a frontier of hatred." Some were even forced to confront loved ones in battle during the Vietnam War (1954–1975).

Gunners, 1965. Quang Tho. Oil on canvas. Private collection.

> "How can this happen to us
> my friend
> my foe?"
>
> —Nguyen Thi Vinh

Versatile Writer During the war, Nguyen watched as conflict between South Vietnamese communist rebels and the South Vietnamese government turned friends into bitter enemies. Until the Vietnam War ended, she was active in the literary community of Saigon (the former capital of South Vietnam, now called Ho Chi Minh City), working as an editor and contributing to magazines and journals. In 1973, North and South Vietnam agreed to a cease-fire, and two years later, North Vietnam took over South Vietnam. After the fall of Saigon in April 1975, Nguyen remained in South Vietnam, though she no longer played a prominent public role. In 1983, she emigrated to Norway to join the rest of her family.

 Literature Online

Author Search For more about Nguyen Thi Vinh, go to glencoe.com and enter QuickPass code GLW6053u4.

Selection Skills

Literary Elements
- Flashback (SE pp. 815, 817, 818)

Reading Skills
- Activate Prior Knowledge (SE pp. 815, 816, 818)
- Visualize (TE p. 816)

Thoughts of Hanoi

Vocabulary Skills
- Synonyms (SE pp. 815, 818)

Speaking/Listening/Viewing Skills
- Analyze Art (TE p. 816)

Writing Skills/Grammar
- Letter (SE p. 818)

Literature and Reading Preview

Connect to the Poem

Have you ever had a friend or relative from whom you were separated? Write a journal entry about this experience.

Build Background

Founded nearly 1,000 years ago by Emperor Ly Thai To, Hanoi (ha nôi') is the capital of Vietnam. Hanoi was the capital of French Indochina (Vietnam, Laos, and Cambodia) during the years of French rule and remained an important administrative center during the Japanese occupation, from 1940 to 1945. During the Vietnam War, the United States bombed Hanoi, causing severe damage. Today, Hanoi is a center of industry, agriculture, and government.

Set Purposes for Reading

Big Idea **The Struggle to Survive**

As you read, ask yourself, What kind of unique struggles must a nation face during a civil war?

Literary Element **Flashback**

A **flashback** interrupts a literary work to relate a scene from an earlier time. In "Thoughts of Hanoi," Nguyen uses this device when she presents a picture of Hanoi before the war. As you read, ask yourself, How does Nguyen use flashback to emphasize the differences between her nation's past and present?

Reading Strategy **Activate Prior Knowledge**

When you **activate prior knowledge**, you create meaning by combining what you know from previous reading and experience with what you find in a literary work. Using your knowledge of people, places, and history can help you comprehend what is on the page and what is suggested by a text.

Tip: Take Notes As you read "Thoughts of Hanoi," ask yourself, What prior knowledge do I have that can help me interpret details in the poem? Use a graphic organizer like the one below.

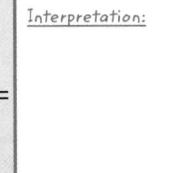

| Details: Speaker says "I dream of Hanoi." Reference to "ten years of separation." | + | Prior Knowledge: Vietnam was divided into North and South Vietnam in 1954, and many people left their homes and friends. | = | Interpretation: |

Learning Objectives

For pages 814–818

In studying this text, you will focus on the following objectives:

Literary Study: Analyzing flashback.

Reading: Activating prior knowledge.

Writing: Writing a letter.

Vocabulary

yearn (yurn) *v.* to desire or long; p. 816 *Hiking through the desert, we yearned for water.*

lush (lush) *adj.* luxuriant; thick with vegetation; p. 816 *The rain forest was so lush that we had trouble making our way through the trees.*

ruddy (rud'ē) *adj.* having a rosy or reddish complexion; p. 816 *Claire had been skiing all day, and her cheeks had a ruddy glow.*

jubilant (jōō'bə lənt) *adj.* joyful; rejoicing; p. 817 *Upon winning the race, Steven gave a jubilant shout.*

obsolete (ob'sə lēt') *adj.* outdated; no longer in use; p. 817 *The invention of DVDs means VCRs will soon be obsolete.*

Tip: Synonyms Synonyms are words with similar meanings. For example, *obsolete* and *outdated* are synonyms.

NGUYEN THI VINH **815**

Forced to leave Hanoi after a civil war, the speaker dreams longingly of his home and wonders how the city and those who stayed behind have changed. The first stanza describes the speaker's pleasant childhood memories at great length. The second stanza reveals how the division of Vietnam separated families and friends, turning them into enemies. From this stanza through the last one, the speaker sadly contemplates the divisive, destructive nature of war and expresses a hope for reconciliation.

 For summaries in languages other than English, see Unit 4 Teaching Resources Book, pp. 239–244.

Vocabulary

Act It Out Write each of the vocabulary words on index cards. Invite volunteers to draw a card and act out a scene that suggests the meaning of the word they chose. Have the rest of the class identify the vocabulary word that best applies to the scene.

 For additional vocabulary practice, see Unit 4 Teaching Resources Book, p. 247.

English Learners

DIFFERENTIATED INSTRUCTION

Intermediate Have English learners look up the meaning of the word *root* in the dictionary prior to reading the poem. Discuss the various meanings of *root*. Guide students to predict what meaning might apply to a poem about being separated from one's home and loved ones. *(the meaning that refers to "the personal connections to a place, including the culture or people, that make the place one's home")*

Advanced Learners/Pre-AP

DIFFERENTIATED INSTRUCTION

Synonyms Invite students to choose one or more vocabulary words and find at least two synonyms for each word. Challenge students to create sentences that demonstrate the connotative meaning of each word and its synonyms. Invite volunteers to read their sentences to the class or display them for others to read.

Teach

Reading Strategy | 1

Activate Prior Knowledge
Answer: *Vietnam has been divided into two parts for ten years. The "frontier of hatred" refers to the border between North and South Vietnam.*

[ENGLISH LEARNERS] Before discussing the question, check to make sure that English learners understand that a *frontier* is a "borderland" and that the word connotes an area that is unsettled.

> For additional practice using the reading skill or strategy, see Unit 4 Teaching Resources Book, p. 246.

View the Art ★

Explain that during the Vietnam War, Hanoi artist and teacher Vu Giang Huong volunteered with her students to accompany army units. They drew soldiers' activities, used their art to boost morale, and helped rebuild roads on the Ho Chi Minh Trail. This woodcut on rice paper is based on drawings the artist made at Ham Rong Bridge. **Ask: How does this scene relate to the poem?** *(The scene relates to the theme of repairing and reestablishing severed communications.)*

Thoughts of Hanoi

Nguyen Thi Vinh
Translated by Nguyen Ngoc Bich with Burton Raffel and W. S. Merwin

The night is deep and chill
as in early autumn. Pitchblack,
it thickens after each lightning flash.
I dream of Hanoi:
5 Co-ngu° Road
ten years of separation
the way back sliced by a frontier of hatred.
I want to bury the past
to burn the future
10 still I **yearn**
still I fear
those endless nights
waiting for dawn.

Brother,
15 how is Hang Dao° now?
How is Ngoc Son° temple?
Do the trains still run
each day from Hanoi
to the neighboring towns?
20 To Bac-ninh, Cam-giang, Yen-bai,°
the small villages, islands
of brown thatch in a **lush** green sea?
The girls
    bright eyes
25   **ruddy** cheeks
    four-piece dresses
        raven-bill scarves
    sowing harvesting
        spinning weaving
30   all year round,
the boys
    ploughing
        transplanting
    in the fields

5 Co-ngu: (kō´ əng)

15 Hang Dao: (hän dou)
16 Ngoc Son: (nyok´ sun)

20 Bac-ninh: (bäk´ nĕn);
Cam-giang: (käm´ yē än); Yen-bai: (yin´ bī)

---

 1 | Activate Prior Knowledge *In light of what you know about Vietnam's history, how do you interpret these lines?*

Vocabulary

yearn (yurn) *v.* to desire or long
lush (lush) *adj.* luxuriant; thick with vegetation
ruddy (rud´ ē) *adj.* having a rosy or reddish complexion

Reading Practice

Visualize Remind students that to visualize is to "picture a writer's ideas or descriptions in your mind's eye." **Ask: What details in lines 1–4 help you visualize the opening setting?** *("deep and chill," "early autumn," "Pitchblack," "thickens," "lightning flash").*

Have students work in pairs to identify other details from the poem that help them visualize the people or places that hold fond memories for the speaker. Invite interested students to use these details to illustrate the speaker's memories of a happier time. Ask volunteers to share the words and phrases that inspired their drawings. Guide students to conclude that visualizing can be a helpful strategy for understanding poetry.

35   in their shops
      running across
         the meadow at evening
      to fly kites
         and sing alternating songs.

40   Stainless blue sky,
         jubilant voices of children
      stumbling through the alphabet,
         village graybeards strolling to the temple,
      grandmothers basking in twilight sun,
45   chewing betel° leaves
      while the children run—

      Brother,
      how is all that now?
      Or is it **obsolete**?
50   Are you like me,
      reliving the past,
      imagining the future?
      Do you count me as a friend
      or am I the enemy in your eyes?
55   Brother, I am afraid
      that one day I'll be with the
         March-North Army°
      meeting you on your way to the South.
      I might be the one to shoot you then
      or you me
60   but please
      not with hatred.

      For don't you remember how it was,
      you and I in school together,
      plotting our lives together?
65   Those roots go deep!

      Brother, we are men,
      conscious of more
      than material needs.
      How can this happen to us
70   my friend
      my foe?

---

45 betel (bē′təl) **leaves:** a mild stimulant from a type of pepper tree; the habit of chewing them, although diminishing, is still widespread in southeast Asia.

56 March-North Army: the South Vietnamese army at the time of the Vietnam War.

Ham Rong Bridge, 1970. Vu Giang Huong. Woodcut on rice paper, 12 x 16 7/8 in. Collection of the Artist. ★

2 Flashback *Why are the speaker's memories of Hanoi so idyllic?*

3 The Struggle to Survive *How are the speaker's values in conflict with the demands of the war?*

Vocabulary

jubilant (jo͞o′bə lənt) *adj.* joyful; rejoicing
obsolete (ob′sə lēt′) *adj.* outdated; no longer in use

NGUYEN THI VINH   **817**

Literary Element **2**

Flashback Answer: *The speaker's memory of the time before the war is idyllic when compared with the current pain and destruction. In general, we often idealize our childhoods or pasts.*

ENGLISH LEARNERS Be sure that English learners understand the meaning of *idyllic.* Provide a synonym, such as *carefree.* **Ask: Why are people's memories of childhood often idyllic?** *(because people typically have fewer responsibilities at that time in life)*

Big Idea **3**

The Struggle to Survive
Answer: *The speaker values deep personal relationships, but the war forces him or her to ignore these and focus on "material needs."*

ADVANCED Challenge students to speculate about what the poet is saying in lines 66–68 about the affects of war on people or a society. (Possible answer: *War destroys not only cities, but also communities. It forces people to adopt an untrusting, survivalist mentality.*)

Approaching Level

DIFFERENTIATED INSTRUCTION

Clarify Meaning Explain that phrasing refers to how words are grouped for meaning. Help students use proper phrasing to increase their understanding of the poem. Invite volunteers to read lines 1–4 of the poem aloud, first line-by-line and then using punctuation marks as cues to meaning.

Remind students that in poetry, the arrangement of the words can also be a clue to meaning. Work with students to experiment with the phrasing of lines 5–13. Discuss

alternative interpretations, asking where students would pause for sense and why. Help students see that while the period in line 13 signals the end of a thought, reading lines 8–13 without pausing would be confusing. (*Students may suggest pausing at the end of lines 9, line 10, and line 13.*)

As students work through the rest of the poem, ask them how phrasing improved their comprehension.

Learning Objectives
Activating prior knowledge. (SE)
Understanding flashback. (SE)
Visualizing. (TE)

817

Assess

1. Answers will vary.

2. (a) how things are in Hanoi and whether trains still run (b) girls sowing, harvesting, spinning and weaving; boys plowing fields, running, and flying kites; elderly people strolling and enjoying the sun

3. (a) The speaker wonders if Brother sees the speaker as a friend or enemy, and if he remembers their time in school together. (b) hatred

4. (a) It may represent the explosions of bombs during war. (b) The image contrasts with the flashbacks of beauty and peace.

5. The style is conversational.

6. The unanswered questions emphasize the speaker's despair and uncertainty.

7. One painful aspect of a civil war is that friends and relatives may be on different sides. The speaker and Brother are simultaneously "friends" and "foes."

8. Answers will vary.

Literary Element

1. She wanted to contrast a pre-war, peaceful Hanoi with a war-torn Vietnam, and thereby call attention to the horrors of war.

2. The flashback's tone is joyful and nostalgic; the rest of the poem's tone is sad, puzzled, and angry.

Progress Check

Can students identify flashback?

If No → See Unit 4 Teaching Resources Book, p. 245.

818

After You Read

Respond and Think Critically

Respond and Interpret

1. How would you answer the final question if you were the speaker's friend?

2. (a) What questions about Hanoi does the speaker ask the person addressed as "Brother"? (b) What scenes from his past does the speaker recall?

3. (a) In lines 50–64, what does the speaker wonder about Brother? (b) What emotion frightens the speaker?

Analyze and Evaluate

4. (a) Nguyen begins "Thoughts of Hanoi" with an image of a dark, lightning-filled sky. What do you think this image might represent?

(b) Why might the poem begin with such an image?

5. How would you describe the **style**—the expressive qualities, including word choice and sentence arrangement—of this poem?

6. What is the effect of the poet's use of a series of unanswered questions?

Connect

7. **Big Idea** **The Struggle to Survive** How does this poem illustrate how civil war affects individuals?

8. **Connect to Today** What recent conflicts in the world have caused divisions among people?

Literary Element Flashback

Authors often use **flashbacks** to provide background information, to create tension, or to create a contrast with the present situation being described.

1. Why might Nguyen have wanted to paint a picture of Hanoi before the war?

2. How does the tone of the flashback differ from the tone of the rest of the poem?

Reading Strategy Activate Prior Knowledge

Consult the chart you made on page 815 and then answer the following questions.

1. (a) What situations have you heard of in which former friends became enemies? (b) How could such a change of feelings be prevented?

2. Discuss what you know about the Vietnam War. How might this knowledge help you understand and connect to the poem?

 Literature Online

Selection Resources For Selection Quizzes, eFlashcards, and Reading-Writing Connection activities, go to glencoe.com and enter QuickPass code GLW6053u4.

Vocabulary Practice

Practice with Synonyms With a partner, match each boldfaced vocabulary word below with its synonym. Use a thesaurus or dictionary to check your answers.

1. yearn
2. lush
3. ruddy
4. jubilant
5. obsolete

a. archaic
b. flushed
c. crave
d. euphoric
e. flourishing

Writing

Write a Letter Write a letter to the speaker in "Thoughts of Hanoi" in which you answer the question posed at the end of the poem as if you are the "Brother." Activate your prior knowledge about the Vietnam War and personal experiences of separation from loved ones to stimulate your thinking. In your letter, use **flashbacks** to show how you (as the "Brother") felt about the speaker in the past and how you remember life before the war.

Reading Strategy

1. (a) Answers will vary. (b) Some will say that ongoing communication may help to prevent such breaks.

2. The feelings of hopelessness and disillusionment many Americans experienced during the Vietnam War resemble those expressed by the poem's speaker.

Vocabulary

1. c 2. e 3. b 4. d 5. a

Writing

Students' letters should

- answer the question from the poem
- be written from the point of view of the "Brother" in the poem
- contain flashbacks

Before You Read

Feeding the Fire of Enmity
from *Stay Alive, My Son*

Cambodia

Meet Pin Yathay

(born 1953)

When he was in his early twenties, Pin Yathay (pin yä′tī) worked as an engineer in Cambodia's Ministry of Public Works. In April 1975, communist guerrillas known as the Khmer Rouge (kə mer′roozh) took control of Phnom Penh (pə näm′pen′), the capital of Cambodia. At first, Thay (the short version of his name) welcomed them because he hoped they would restore order to his nation. Thay's hopes for an improved Cambodia, however, soon turned into a nightmare.

False Promises Claiming a U.S. bombing of Phnom Penh was imminent, the Khmer Rouge ordered three million people, including those in hospitals, out of the country's cities, promising them they could soon return to their homes. Instead, they were transported to rural labor camps, where they were forced to do hard labor for at least twelve hours a day, digging canals and building irrigation systems. Rations were limited to about a half a pound of rice a day for eight people. Malnourished and exhausted, many died.

Others were taken to detention centers, where many were killed if they knew a second language, were educated, or even wore glasses. The Khmer Rouge sought to eradicate the intellectuals and rebuild Cambodia as a classless peasant society where all resources would be shared equally. In pursuit of this goal, the Khmer Rouge changed schools and places of worship into labor and re-education camps. Singing, dancing, and praying were outlawed. Being immodest or stealing was punishable by death. Banks, money, and private property were abolished. All religions were outlawed. Estimates

"Through our suffering, I want . . . my readers to see how fine-sounding ideals of justice and equality can be perverted by fanatics to create brutal oppression. . ."

—Pin Yathay

vary, but it is believed that between one and three million people died, or about one third of the population of Cambodia. Yathay himself lost seventeen members of his family. The atrocities continued until Vietnam invaded Cambodia in 1979, ending the Khmer Rouge dictatorship.

A Father's Directive Among the family members Yathay lost during the Khmer Rouge's reign of terror was his father. Lying on his deathbed, Yathay's father said to him, "Stay alive, my son." These words, which Yathay later spoke to his own son, became the title of his memoir.

Literature Online

Author Search For more about Pin Yathay, go to glencoe.com and enter QuickPass code GLW6053u4.

PIN YATHAY **819**

Before You Read

Focus

Bellringer Options

Selection Focus
   Transparency 51

Daily Language Practice
   Transparency 77

Or ask: If you were forced into hard labor each day by people who placed no value on your life, what would your plan be for staying alive? Discuss whether a strategy of perfect obedience would be the best strategy. Have students predict what strategy they will read about.

Political History ☆

The Khmer Rouge Pol Pot and other leaders of the Khmer Rouge were filled with idealistic notions about the virtues of the simple life of farming, the end of exploitation by the rich and powerful, and a Marxist-inspired economic equality for all. Along with these ideals, however, they instituted slave labor and the extermination of all dissidents and other perceived enemies, including almost every Buddhist monk.

Selection Skills

Literary Elements
- Protagonist and Antagonist (SE pp. 820, 822, 825, 826)
- Author's Purpose (SE p. 826)

Reading Skills
- Question (SE pp. 820, 822, 824, 826, 827)
- Synthesize (TE p. 820)

Feeding the Fire of Enmity

Vocabulary Skills
- Word Parts (SE p. 820, 827)

Speaking/Listening/Viewing Skills
- Performance (SE p. 827)

Writing Skills/Grammar
- Adverbs (TE p. 822)
- News Story (TE p. 824)

Before You Read

Focus

Summary

Confined to a Khmer Rouge work camp, Yathay is caught with an illegal portion of rice and turned over to his group leader, Run. The crime is punishable by death, but Yathay reminds Run about antibiotics that he obtained for Run's wife. Fearing for his own life, Run gives Yathay another chance.

 For summaries in languages other than English, see Unit 4 Teaching Resources Book, pp. 251–256.

Vocabulary

Word Parts Place students in groups of four, and have each student write one of these words, as underlined, on a sheet of paper: frant**ically**, **pre**lude, ac**com**plice, and plaus**ible**. Ask students to spend one minute listing words with the same word part and then to pass the paper to their right four times. Each group member should make an effort to contribute to all four lists. Then have students discuss the meaning of each word part, the part of speech it may create, and its relative usefulness to them in understanding new words.

 For additional vocabulary practice, see Unit 4 Teaching Resources Book, p. 259.

 For an audio recording of this selection, use Listening Library Audio CD-ROM.

Readability Scores

Dale-Chall: 6.5
DRP: 57
Lexile: 780

Literature and Reading Preview

Connect to the Memoir

Have you ever felt you were treated unjustly by someone in a position of authority? Discuss this question with a partner.

Build Background

From 1970 to 1975, Cambodia was ruled by an army general named Lon Nol, who had seized power from the previous ruler, Prince Sihanouk, in a *coup* (kü′)—a sudden, violent overthrow of the government. In 1975, the Khmer Rouge overthrew Lon Nol's regime with the support of the North Vietnamese and the exiled Prince Sihanouk. In 1976, a Khmer Rouge leader named Pol Pot became prime minister of Cambodia. Under his leadership, the country's entire population was forced to live and work as peasants in rural camps. Those who disobeyed orders or behaved in a "counterrevolutionary" way were killed.

Set Purposes for Reading

Big Idea The Struggle to Survive

As you read, ask yourself, How does the narrator cope with the constant threat of death?

Literary Element Protagonist and Antagonist

The **protagonist** is the central character in a literary work, the one around whom the action revolves. The **antagonist** is the person or force that works against the protagonist. As you read, ask yourself, What details influence my feelings about the protagonist and antagonist?

Reading Strategy Question

Skilled readers **ask questions** to deepen their understanding of a text. When a detail of setting, a bit of dialogue, or even a vocabulary word puzzles you, ask questions about what it means. As you read, ask yourself questions such as "Why is this idea important?"

Tip: Make a KWL Chart Use a KWL chart to record your questions and answers.

What I Know	What I Want to Know	What I Learned
Rice is an important food staple in Southeast Asia.	How did people survive when their food rations were insufficient?	They were forced to obtain rice illegally.

Learning Objectives

For pages 819–827

In studying this text, you will focus on the following objectives:

Literary Study: Analyzing protagonist and antagonist.

Reading: Questioning.

Listening and Speaking: Performing a scene.

Vocabulary

frantically (fran′tik lē) *adv.* in a manner marked by fast and nervous activity; p. 823 *Helen frantically tried to pick up all the marbles before someone slipped on them and fell.*

prelude (prel′ūd) *n.* an event preceding and preparing for a more important matter; p. 823 *The appetizers were a prelude to the feast.*

accomplice (ə kom′plice) *n.* a participant in a crime or wrongdoing; p. 824 *The robber's accomplice stayed in the car and kept the motor running.*

plausible (plô′zə bəl) *adj.* appearing worthy of belief; p. 824 *Late for class for the third time that week, Mike did not have a plausible excuse.*

taint (tānt) *v.* to contaminate morally; to corrupt; p. 825 *"Your actions taint our society," said the judge.*

Tip: Word Parts Knowledge of word parts can help you understand unfamiliar words. Knowing that the prefix *pre-* in *prelude* means "before" can help you understand the entire word.

Reading Practice

Synthesize Remind students to make full use of the Before You Read information to help them understand the selection. Have students summarize information by following these steps

Say: Summarize the "Build Background" information on this page. (*Lon Nol seized power in 1975; the Khmer Rouge overthrew him in 1976. The Khmer Rouge's leader Pol Pot forced everyone into labor camps and absolute obedience.*)

Say: Relate the information back to "Meet Pin Yathay" on page 819. **Ask:** What does Yathay's story have to do with the Khmer Rouge and labor camps? (*Yathay suffered greatly during the period when the Khmer Rouge was in power. He was sent to a work camp; many of his family members died.*)

FEEDING THE FIRE OF ENMITY

from
Stay Alive, My Son

Pin Yathay

Boys in the Field, 1991. Monirith Chhea. Oil on canvas, 58x 48 in. Collection of the artist.

---

1 For the first couple of months in Leach[1]—November and December 1976—we survived as we had in Veal Vong,[2] by supplementing our rations buying rice on the black market,[3] with the occasional addition of sugar, fruit and fish. Though our hoard of spare clothing and jewelry inherited from my family was running low, I still had dollars, and these were valued in Leach. A hundred dollars bought fifteen cans of rice (a hundred-dollar bill being once again the basic unit of currency).

My job was clearing trees, along with a hundred other men. Our first assignment involved a scheme that was typical of the way the Khmer Rouge did things. We were marched off to a rice field in which grew a scattering of fruit trees and bushes. It looked like a perfectly serviceable rice field

to me, perhaps better than most because it supported the fruit trees as well, mostly rather fine mangoes and tamarinds.

Our leader, Comrade Run, explained our task with obvious pride. Apparently, at harvest time the place was infested with sparrows that gorged themselves on the rice. The sparrows nested in the fruit trees. Eager to display true revolutionary initiative, to apply the sacred spirit of self-sufficiency that Angkar[4] demanded, Comrade Run planned an assault on the sparrows. How? By destroying their nests. And how again? By cutting down the fruit trees. While people were dying of hunger a mile away, we were out chopping down fruit trees. The damage wrought by the

---

4. According to the author, *Angkar* (ang´kär), represents "the faceless all-pervading authority" of the new government. ☆

Protagonist and Antagonist *Who is the antagonist? What clues in this passage indicate this?* **2**

---

1. *Leach* (le´ich)
2. *Veal Vong* (vil vong)
3. The *black market* is illegal trade in goods and foods.

PIN YATHAY **821**

English Learners

DIFFERENTIATED INSTRUCTION

Intermediate Encourage English learners to use cognates to help them understand the text. Have students find and list cognates on this page and note how many of them are nouns or naming words. *(For Spanish speakers: November—noviembre, December—diciembre; survive—sobrevivir; supplement—suplir; rations—raciónes; rice—arroz; market—mercado; sugar—azúcar; fruit—fruta; family—familia; dollars—dólares; basic—básico)*

Have students exchange their lists with a partner and check them to be sure they make sense.

Teach

Big Idea | 1

The Struggle to Survive
Ask: How did people manage to survive in circumstances like Yathay's? *(They had to find ways to add to the food they were given, which was not enough to survive on.)*

[ADVANCED] **Ask:** What can you infer about Yathay's past and present based on these opening details? *(He may have been more privileged than others were; he was willing to risk illegal trading; taking risks was part of staying alive for him.)*

Literary Element | 2

Protagonist and Antagonist
Answer: *Comrade Run is the antagonist. He is enthusiastic about a ridiculous project, he doesn't think things through, and he has no regard for the people who are starving nearby.*

Political History ☆

Angkar Angkar was the government of the Khmer Rouge. The word means "organization." Note the varying perspective provided by the author in the footnote.
Ask: What does the author mean when he calls Angkar "faceless and all-pervading"? *(He suggests that there is no one person or leader to whom everyone answers, but a unified force called Angkar, which controls everything and is everywhere.)*

Learning Objectives
Analyzing antagonist and protagonist. (SE)
Synthesizing information. (TE)

Teach

Reading Strategy   1

Question Answer: *This would have given them personal freedom, something the Khmer Rouge authorities were determined to eliminate.*

 For additional practice using the reading skill or strategy, see Unit 4 Teaching Resources Book, p. 258.

Reading Strategy   2

Question Answer: *He realizes people in desperate situations are not always kind to one another, and their generosity in such a difficult time is an extraordinary gesture.*

sparrows was nothing compared to the damage we did to Leach's fruit harvest.

After that notable objective was achieved, we were turned loose on the forest to make new clearings. We were divided into ten groups. I belonged to a group of twelve who were considered the best workers and thus designated Group No. 1. In the morning, we walked in columns to the work site. At noon, there was an hour's break for lunch, then we returned to work until six p.m. At night, when the moon shone, we worked up until ten or eleven p.m. We would return to the village every tenth day to rest, but also to attend a political meeting.

There was, however, another unofficial side to our lives. Out in our forest camp, I and two others hung our hammocks a little apart from the rest, in the hope of having some peace, away from constant supervision. Sometimes, when our comrades and our group leader were fast asleep, we would sneak away two at a time to go back to the village. The third always stayed in his hammock to tell any snooping Khmer Rouge that the other two had gone into the forest to relieve themselves. On these trips, I would pass through a number of Leach's other subsidiary camps, each one a collection of eight foot by ten foot bamboo huts, thatched with palm leaves and raised on stilts. It was on these occasions I was able to continue making exchanges. I would make a deal on the way in with a broker—as in Veal Vong, the brokers were well-known to the New People[5]—go home to see Any,[6] collect clothing, jewelry, or dollars, and pick up the extra cans of rice on my way back. Any was the focus of this activity. Seeing her and talking with her was my only pleasure, my only strength.

We were life itself to each other, each other's only hope.

We were forbidden to have extra food, but we managed. Though not allowed to cook rice, we could boil water, so when we saw our group leader, Run, coming, we would snatch up a water can, and put it on the fire, whipping away any rice that was cooking and hiding it in the bushes. Thus, whenever it was my turn to go back to the village, I could take cooked rice to Any, returning to the forest camp before dawn, so that on waking up no one noticed my absence.

One rest day, I decided to stay in my hut rather than go to the political meeting. It was foolhardy, but all I had to do was remain out of sight until I heard the gong, which rang to call the children to eat—an hour or so before the adults' meal—and also signified the end of the meeting. Then it would take the men about an hour to get back to camp. It would be easy for me to drift back in time for the communal meal.

When I left, I took with me in my scarf one can's worth of newly bought raw rice which I intended to cook that evening. At the campsite, however, I found to my surprise that everyone had eaten. Apparently, the meeting had been shorter than usual and my workmates had returned and eaten early. For a moment I was taken aback, thinking I was about to go hungry, until I saw that they had kept some rice aside for me. I was touched—in those harsh conditions, it was more than I would have expected. Eager for food, I unthinkingly put my scarf containing the rice into the nearest hammock and sat down to eat about twenty yards away.

---

5. The *New People* refers to former urban dwellers like Pin Yathay.
6. *Any* is the author's wife.

Question *Why do you think the workers were not allowed to cook rice?*   **1**

Question *Why is Yathay so moved by his comrades' generosity?*   **2**

Writing Practice

Use Adverbs Remind students that an adverb is a word that modifies a verb, an adjective, or another adverb by making it more specific. **Write this sentence on the board:** "Not me," I said <u>innocently</u>. *(The underlined adverb modifies the verb* said *and answers the question* how?*)* Point out that most, but not all, adverbs end in the suffix *-ly.*

Read the sentences below aloud. Point out the adverbs, which are underlined, and the words they modify, which are italicized.

Modifying verbs: <u>Never</u> *disobey* Comrade Run.

Modifying adjectives: The day was <u>very</u> *hot* and <u>too</u> *long.*

Modifying adverbs: Run spoke <u>quite</u> *loudly.*

To What Degree?: I was <u>very</u> sorry.

Have students identify ten adverbs in this selection and indicate what each modifies in the sentence and whether it modifies a verb, adjective, or another adverb. Sample answers:

(It looked like a <u>perfectly</u> serviceable rice field to me… [perfectly modifies serviceable, which is an adjective])

(Apparently, the meeting had been shorter than usual and my workmates had returned and eaten <u>early</u>. [Early modifies eaten, which is a verb])

Just then, the owner of the hammock, a friend of mine called Chorn, came back, went to lie down, and sat right on the bundle of rice. He jumped up in surprise, and prodded the scarf. His jaw dropped. "Rice!" he said, in an appalled voice. Possessing extra rice was a major offense, and here was a whole bundle of it in his hammock. In panic, he held the scarf up and shouted, "But it's not mine! This rice doesn't belong to me! Who left rice in my hammock?"

You would have thought he was holding a bomb. I flapped my hand and mouthed **frantically** at him to attract his attention. Too late—the camp chief, the boss of the whole operation, was already on his way across to us. Seeing him, Chorn protested even more loudly: "It's not my rice! It's not my rice!" He kept repeating the words over and over, as if they were some sort of incantation.

"Whose is it then?" the chief asked. "And whose scarf is it? You're sure they're not yours?"

"No! I found them under me when I lay in my hammock."

The chief turned to the rest of us. "Whose rice is this?" he asked, his gaze wandering from one to another.

Everyone knew the scarf was mine. Sooner or later the truth would come out.

I stood up. "Comrade, the rice is mine."

Then Run, my immediate supervisor, the group leader, whose responsibility it was to deal with the situation, stepped forward. It would, in normal circumstances, have been the **prelude** to my death. Fortunately, however, Run and I were not complete strangers.

Two weeks before I had seen Run sitting in front of his house, looking utterly crushed. When I asked him what the matter was, he said, "It's my wife, Thay. She's very sick. She's in such pain she sometimes screams for relief."

"Have you no medicine for her?" I asked.

"I've tried our medicines, but they're not effective," he said. He was obviously a very worried man, for he had tried everything available to a Khmer Rouge. At once, I saw there was a chance here to get some extra rations, for I knew someone who could obtain some tetracyclin, an antibiotic.[7] There were doctors among the New People who still did what they could for us. They brought their medicines into the black market, as others provided food, clothing, jewelry, or watches. One tablet of tetracyclin was worth a can of rice. I would ask two cans—one for me, one for my supplier. But I had to proceed cautiously.

"Comrade, have you tried foreign medicine?" It was a harmless way to suggest the idea. If he disapproved of foreign medicine, I wouldn't be trapped. But he leaped at it.

"Comrade, do you happen to have any? Do you know where to get any?"

"Not me," I said innocently, placing my hand on my heart. "I don't want to be mixed up in anything illegal. I have never seen any foreign medicines, but I've heard about them in the camp."

He couldn't care less about my guilt or innocence. He just wanted his wife to be free of the pain. "Try to do something for me, Thay! My wife cries all the time. I don't know what to do. I'm desperate."

I said I would do my best.

The next day, having done precisely nothing, I told him that, despite the risks involved, I had contacted a man who had two tablets of tetracyclin. Not, of course, that I could guarantee a complete cure . . .

7. An *antibiotic* is a medicine derived from a microorganism that inhibits or kills another microorganism.

Vocabulary

frantically (fran′tik lē) *adv.* in a manner marked by fast and nervous activity

prelude (prel′ūd) *n.* an event preceding and preparing for a more important matter

---

Question **Why is Yathay so cautious with Run after it is clear Run is willing to disobey the law?**

Teach

Reading Strategy | 3

Question **Answer:** *He wants to protect himself and his sources.*

Learning Objectives
Questioning. (SE)
Using adverbs. (TE)
Conducting research and synthesizing. (TE)

Advanced Learners/Pre-AP

DIFFERENTIATED INSTRUCTION

Research and Synthesize Have students develop a research strategy for defining and understanding the operation of a black market. Require the use of a variety of reference materials that include print as well as nonprint sources. Have students evaluate each source not only for its reliability but also for facts, information, and perspectives that are relevant to this selection. Ask students to communicate their findings on this topic in a unique way, such as with a detailed poster or flow chart or the creation of a Web page or Webcast.

Teach

Big Idea   1

The Struggle to Survive
Answer: *It is his only power over Run because it refers to Run's own problems. Yathay plans to blackmail Run with this knowledge and earn his life.*

Reading Strategy   2

Identify Sequence **Say:**
Yathay abandons chronological order to use a flashback. **Ask:** Where does the flashback begin? (at the bottom of the first column on page 823) **Ask:** Where does the flashback end? (at the break in the copy on page 824). Remind students to use print concepts such as extra lines of space to aid comprehension; note that such devices often denote shifts in time and place. Discuss why Yathay uses this technique and how it enhances the selection.

Literary Element   3

Protagonist and Antagonist
Answer: *Yathay's friends are worried for him—causing the reader also to feel sympathy.*

"How can I get them?"

"The man wants two cans' worth of rice for one tablet. I can arrange that for you."

"Come back tomorrow. I'll find the rice. Don't let me down."

So we became **accomplices**. I found him the tablets, and he gave me the rice. The two of us shared a secret. If one of us betrayed his promise, in the eyes of the authorities we would both be guilty.

Now here was Run, bombarding me with questions as he had to in the presence of the camp leader and a whole crowd of others. "The rice is yours? Where did it come from? Why did you leave the rice in your comrade's hammock? Do you want to eat more than others? You're a counterrevolutionary, is that it?"

I was on a knife-edge. Run had the power of life and death over me, and nobody would have reproached him for having me killed. He had reason enough—theft and black-marketeering were capital offenses.[8] Moreover, I knew he had another reason to show himself as an intransigent[9] leader—by having me killed, he could get rid of a witness to his own crime. "Who sold you the rice?" he shouted. "You must denounce the person who sold it to you!"

I certainly didn't want to do that. The only thing I could do was make up something **plausible** and then somehow turn the conversation to my advantage. "A soldier," I said. "I exchanged a pair of trousers for it with a soldier who was passing on his bicycle." No, I had no idea of his name. I had

never seen him before. "Anyway, comrade, the rice was not for me."

Run was taken aback. "I don't understand. Why did you bring the rice here then?"

"I was going to trade it to find medicine for my *wife*," I said, looking him in the eye.

There was the briefest of pauses.

"She's getting worse," I went on. "Angkar's medicines have not cured her. I have to find some tablets. You know how it is."

I could see that he did.

"But why did you bring the rice to the worksite?"

"I told you: I thought perhaps one of us had medicine."

"Who then?"

"Oh! I didn't have anybody special in mind, comrade. I—"

At this point, the camp leader interrupted. "This is a serious crime, comrades! Comrade Run, it is up to you to decide how to punish Comrade Thay."

Run tied my elbows behind my back, and led me away. From their terrified expressions, it was obvious my friends thought I was going to my death.

Run pushed me towards his hammock, away from the others, and told me to squat down in front of him. He sat back and began to lecture me. I would have expected nothing less, and lowered my head, playing my role as the ritual phrases of condemnation poured over me. "Thay, you are a counterrevolutionary . . . you participated in exchanges . . . you don't know how to get rid of individualist leanings . . . you

---

8. *Capital offenses* are crimes punishable by death.
9. *Intransigent* means "unwilling to compromise or come to an agreement."

Vocabulary

accomplice (ə kom′plice) *n.* a participant in a crime or wrongdoing

plausible (plô′ zə bəl) *adj.* appearing worthy of belief

The Struggle to Survive *Why does Yathay make up the story about planning to trade the rice for medicine? How does he think it will help save his life?*   **1**

Protagonist and Antagonist *What details in this passage indicate Yathay is the protagonist?*   **3**

Writing Practice

Write a News Story Have students imagine themselves as journalists hiding in the jungle when the confrontation over the rice takes place between Run and Yathay. Have students write what they observe as a news report.

Suggest these steps:

- Prewrite by creating a who, what, when, where, and why organizer. Remember that a journalist could not know everything that Run and Yathay know.

- Create a draft that is like a news story. Begin with a lead, tell events in order of interest and importance, and maintain as much objectivity as possible.

- Revise for clarity and for all the traits of good writing. Focus especially on tone, which should be objective and serious, and on point of view, which should be third person limited.

- Proofread for grammar, mechanics, usage, and spelling, but pay special attention to the correct use of quotation marks in dialogue.

<u>taint</u> our group . . . you've been in reeducation for more than a year and a half, yet you have remained a counterrevolutionary . . ." and on and on for an hour or more.

It occurred to me as he talked that he seemed to be so taken up with the need to show himself as strong that he was in danger of forgetting the favor I'd done him. If he went on like that, he would leave himself no other course but to have me cudgeled to death in the forest or sent off to a reeducation camp. I thought I'd better take action.

As he drew breath, I said in a low voice, "Comrade, remember your sick wife. Remember my efforts to help you. If you hurt me, I will denounce you." I looked up at him, so there could be no doubt about my seriousness. "If I die, you die."

His eyes widened, and the color drained from his face, and I knew I had a chance.

In a second or two, he resumed the look of an austere and inflexible leader, his face impassive.[10] For another quarter of an hour, he continued his harangue,[11] his voice growing louder and louder. It became clear to me that he was putting on a show for everyone to hear, especially the camp leader. I began to relax, wondering how he could retract his accusations without loss of face.

"Thay, you are a counterrevolutionary, but fortunately for you, you are a good worker." Then he began to praise me, still talking in a loud voice—"I have noticed you are the first to wake in the mornings and that you are the best worker," and on and on he went about how I gave every-

Seven Women in the Field, 1990. Monirith Chhea. Oil on canvas, 58 x 64 in. Collection of the artist.

<u>View the Art</u> Like Pin Yathay, Monirith Chhea is haunted by his memories of Cambodia during the Khmer Rouge regime. How does the artist use different shapes to create a mood in this painting? How is this mood present in the memoir?

thing I had to my work. It was such an astonishing performance that I could hardly believe our undeclared conspiracy would not be discovered. Never had the most assiduous[12] Khmer Rouge, the most perfect revolutionary, been garlanded with such praise. An hour before I was criminal scum; now Comrade Run found it hard to do justice to my merits. And he concluded: "As a result, this time—and only this time—I will ask the chief to give you a warning so that you can cleanse yourself. It will be a serious warning, Thay. The next time, you will become fertilizer on our rice fields."

After that, it only remained for the camp leader to give me a brief, formal warning—"Don't do it again! Next time, you'll be fertilizer"—and I was saved. ✎

---

10. An *impassive* face is calm and shows no emotion.
11. A *harangue* is a long, blustering, noisy, or scolding speech.

4 Question *Why is Yathay worried that Run feels a need to prove his strength?*

Vocabulary

<u>taint</u> (tānt) *v.* to contaminate morally; to corrupt

---

12. *Assiduous* means "busy, diligent, or persevering."

PIN YATHAY **825**

Approaching Level

DIFFERENTIATED INSTRUCTION

Write a Summary Help students summarize the story by having them fill out a graphic organizer like this one:

Who?
What?
When?
Where?
Why/How?

Suggest this strategy for moving from prewriting to drafting.

1. Write a first sentence that tells the name of the work, the author, and something about the main character (who) and the time or place (where and when). For example, use this sentence starter: In _____ by _____, _____.

2. Write additional sentences to tell only the main events (what) and to supply only the most basic ideas about how they relate to each other, the main character, or the time and place (why/how).

3. End the summary with the final event. For example, use this sentence starter. At the end of _____, . . .

Teach

Reading Strategy | **4**

Question **Answer:** *Yathay may fear Run will begin to believe his own rhetoric and will sentence him to death.*

<u>View the Art</u> ★

Answer: *The elongated shapes in the painting create a surreal effect that conveys the distortion and nightmarish quality of the lives of Yathay and the Cambodian people.*

Dressed in the uniforms of the Khmer Rouge, seven women work under the hot sun in a labor camp field. The artist used seven to symbolize the days of the week during which people at this time labored from sunrise to sunset. He used thick impasto and bold colors to create an intensity of emotion and to evoke the dry, hot setting of the labor camp.

Learning Objectives
Identifying antagonist and protagonist. (SE)
Questioning. (SE)
Analyzing art. (TE)
Writing a news story. (TE)

After You Read

Assess

1. Students may say they felt sympathy for Yathay and were outraged by the Khmer Rouge.

2. (a) Because the sparrows eat rice, the soldiers plan to cut down the fruit trees that hold their nests. (b) This will destroy even more food while people are starving.

3. (a) Yathay clears the forest. (b) They live in spare conditions with simple hammocks, and are forbidden to cook their own rice.

4. (a) He wants Yathay to identify the source of the rice, labels Yathay a counter-revolutionary, but praises his hard work. (b) Yathay threatens to expose Comrade Run if he doesn't help him.

5. The tone is bitter and critical.

6. (a) He would have been executed had he been caught, but his efforts brought him extra rice and some power over Run. (b) Most will think this was a good decision because it later helped him to stay alive.

7. (a) their own individual survival (b) It was not an ideal commune; instead, the conditions forced people to take desperate actions to ensure survival.

8. Some may say they would have pardoned Yathay more readily; others may say Run had to maintain his authority.

Literary Element

1. **A** is the correct answer. **C** is incorrect because Comrade Run is an antagonist, and **B** and **D** are minor figures, neither protagonists nor antagonists.

2. **J** is the correct answer. **I** is incorrect because, although Comrade Run is the main antagonist, the camp leader and the Khmer Rouge also oppose Yathay.

826

After You Read

Respond and Think Critically

Respond and Interpret

1. How did you feel as you read about Yathay's experiences in the labor camp? Explain.

2. (a)Why do the Khmer Rouge want to eliminate the sparrows, and what is their plan for destroying the birds? (b)Why is Yathay critical of the Khmer Rouge's plan?

3. (a)What is Yathay's work after the sparrows are eliminated, and where is this work done? (b)Describe the workers' living quarters.

4. (a)Summarize what Comrade Run says to Yathay in response to his crime. (b)How does Yathay use the favor he has done for Comrade Run to his advantage?

Analyze and Evaluate

5. **Tone** is the attitude an author takes toward his or her subject. How would you describe the tone of this excerpt?

6. (a)What were the risks and advantages to Yathay for helping Comrade Run find medicine for his wife? (b)Do you think Yathay made a good decision when he did this? Explain.

Connect

7. **Big Idea** **The Struggle to Survive** (a)Are the characters in the excerpt primarily concerned with their own individual survival, with the survival of the group, or with both? Explain. (b)What does this tell you about life in communist Cambodia?

8. **Connect to Today** If you had been in Comrade Run's place, what would you have done about the narrator's law-breaking?

Literary Element Protagonist and Antagonist

ACT Skills Practice

1. Who is the protagonist of this excerpt?

   A. Pin Yathay

   B. Chorn

   C. Comrade Run

   D. Any

2. Which of the following functions as an antagonist in the excerpt?

   I. Comrade Run

   II. The camp leader

   III. The Khmer Rouge

   F. I only

   G. II only

   H. I and III only

   J. I, II, and III

826 UNIT 4 SOUTHEAST ASIA AND THE PACIFIC

Review: Author's Purpose

As you learned on page 402, an **author's purpose** is his or her main reason for writing a particular work. Authors write for many different reasons, such as to persuade, to inform, to explain, to entertain, or to describe. Sometimes an author might have a general and a specific purpose. For example, the general purpose might be to inform, while the specific purpose might be to explain how the Khmer Rouge showed their ignorance by cutting down fruit trees.

Partner Activity With a classmate, discuss Yathay's purpose for writing this work. Complete a chart like the one below. Write the author's purpose, and list details that support that purpose.

Author's Purpose:		
Supporting Detail	Supporting Detail	Supporting Detail

Progress Check

Can students identify protagonist and antagonist?

If No → See Unit 4 Teaching Resources Book, p. 257.

Review: Author's Purpose

Author's Purpose: to inform readers of horrors and hardships under the rule of the Khmer Rouge.

Supporting Detail: The Khmer Rouge destroyed food when people were hungry.

Supporting Detail: Medicines were only available on the black market. Dealing with the black market could mean death.

Reading Strategy Question

By asking questions as you read, you can improve your comprehension of a literary work, even if you don't find the answers to your specific questions. For example, in this excerpt we never learn how large a can of rice is, but we do learn how valuable it is to the people who don't have enough of it. Review the chart you made on page 820 and then respond to the following items.

1. List four questions you have about the story. Answer as many of these as you can.

2. Explain how these questions help you understand the story better.

Vocabulary Practice

Practice with Word Parts For each bold-faced vocabulary word in the left column, identify the related word with a shared word part in the right column. Use a dictionary to look up the meaning of the related word. Then explain how it is related to the vocabulary word.

1. frantically   ludicrous
2. prelude   plaudit
3. accomplice   frenetic
4. plausible   tincture
5. taint   complicate

Academic Vocabulary

When Yathay skips the meeting, he **estimates** *that he has one hour between the ringing of the bell and the return of the men for their meal.*

Estimate is an academic word. If you have to guess how many pizzas you need to order to feed ten of your friends, you have to **estimate** the number. To further explore the meaning of this word, answer the following question:

When have you had to **estimate** something? Describe the process.

Listening and Speaking

 Performance

Assignment Perform a section of this memoir that features Pin Yathay and Comrade Run. You might start with "Two weeks before . . ." (p. 823). Supplement the text with dramatic elements, imagined dialogue, and an additional scene in which Comrade Run explains his behavior to Yathay.

Prepare Consider how you want to portray Yathay and Run, and use their movements and gestures to help convey their thoughts. Make sure your new material matches the tone of the rest of the memoir—the characters and dialogue should remain consistent. Create a chart like the one below to help move from the text to a working script.

Text	Dramatic Elements	Spoken Dialogue
Two weeks before I had seen Run sitting in front of his house, looking utterly crushed. . . . (page 823)	Run is sitting slumped against the wall of his house. He sighs and rubs his face worriedly.	Yathay: What's the matter, Comrade? Run: It's my wife, Thay. She's in such pain she sometimes screams.

Perform Try to embody the scene as fully as possible, using all the tools at your disposal—setting, dialogue, body language, tone of voice—to re-create the mood of the piece.

Evaluate Write a paragraph evaluating your dramatic performance. Do you think your understanding of the work translated to the audience? Did performing this part make you empathize with the characters? Did your view of the characters change after you performed this piece?

 Literature Online

Selection Resources For Selection Quizzes, eFlash-cards, and Reading-Writing Connection activities, go to glencoe.com and enter QuickPass code GLW6053u4.

PIN YATHAY **827**

Listening and Speaking

Students' performances should
- portray the characters faithfully, vocally and physically
- display an understanding of the work
- include a new scene in keeping with Yathay's memoir

Academic Vocabulary

Students should relate an instance of having to calculate something approximately, using their reasoning and information at hand. They might mention estimating how many hours they will have to babysit in order to buy a new computer or how far a car can go before it runs out of gas.

After You Read

Assess

Reading Strategy

1. Possible responses: How did Yathay manage to hide his hoard of spare clothing and jewelry he had inherited from his family? (Answer not provided in text.) Why was the hundred-dollar bill the basic unit of currency? (We can infer that prices had become inflated.) What was the purpose of clearing trees out of the jungle? (We can infer that it was to create more farming land.) Why is the author's wife still in town and not in the fields working? (Answer not provided in text.)

2. Answers will vary.

Progress Check

Can students use questioning to enhance their understanding of the memoir?

If No → See Unit 4 Teaching Resources Book, p. 258.

Vocabulary

1. frenetic; Both come from the Middle English *frenetik*, meaning "insane."

2. ludicrous; Both come from the Latin *ludus*, meaning "play."

3. complicate; Both come from the Latin *complicare*, "to fold together."

4. plaudit; Both come from the Latin *plaudere*, meaning "to applaud."

5. tincture; Both come from Latin *tingere*, meaning "to dye."

Focus

Advertisements

Read several advertisements to the class, and point out loaded words such as *best, premier, deluxe,* and *extraordinary.* **Ask:** What connotations do these words have? *(They have positive connotations.)* **Ask:** What is the intended effect of these loaded words? *(They are meant to persuade the reader or listener to buy a product.)*

Teach

Bias and Hyperbole

Advise students to keep an eye out for bias and hyperbole when they read, particularly when reading persuasive documents such as articles, essays, or advertisements. Tell them to be wary of instances wherein writers use loaded words in place of factual evidence. This is a technique used to appeal to readers' emotions instead of logic.

Assess

1. Loaded words: *scheme, marched.* Persuasive techniques: bias
2. Loaded words: *counterrevolutionary, individualist, taint.* Persuasive techniques: propaganda and bias
3. Loaded words: *cleanse, fertilizer on our rice fields.* Persuasive techniques: propaganda, positive bias, and hyperbole

828

Learning Objectives

In this workshop, you will focus on the following objectives:

Vocabulary: Understanding denotation and connotation. Understanding bias, hyperbole, and propaganda.

Loaded Words

Loaded words express strong connotations and emotions. Some reveal **bias**, or a one-sided point of view, while others use **hyperbole**, or exaggeration, to make a point. **Propaganda** is persuasive language that may distort the truth.

Test-Taking Tip

When you read a text, ask yourself, "What is the author's purpose?" Once you have determined the author's purpose, look for words or phrases that are used to make you think or feel a certain way.

Literature Online

Vocabulary For more vocabulary practice, go to glencoe.com and enter QuickPass code GLW6053u4.

Vocabulary Workshop

Denotation and Connotation

Literature Connection In this passage from *Stay Alive, My Son* by Pin Yathay, a leader refers to the Cambodian workers as "comrades."

> *"At this point, the camp leader interrupted. 'This is a serious crime, comrades! Comrade Run, it is up to you to decide how to punish Comrade Thay.'"*

The **denotation**, or dictionary definition, of *comrade* is "friend, companion, or associate," but in this context it has a charged, political **connotation**, or association. The Khmer Rouge used the word to describe citizens of their communist society and to convey a sense of equality. The word took on different connotations, however, when it was used to help justify the Khmer Rouge's brutal policies. Pin Yathay uses the word to contrast the ideal definition with reality. Because words with strong connotations can be used to distort reality, it is important to recognize how they can be used. Bias, hyperbole, and propaganda all make use of connotations.

Language that expresses a one-sided point of view demonstrates **bias**. Try substituting *stood up to* for *betrayed* in the following sentence. Notice how *stood up to* produces a positive bias, while *betrayed* produces a negative one.

> *The soldier betrayed his superiors by refusing to fight.*

Hyperbole is exaggerated language used to make a point.

> *A shift in political power would mean <u>the death of all our freedoms</u>.*

Language used to influence public opinion is called **propaganda**.

> *In our <u>glorious</u> city, citizens live as <u>harmoniously</u> as <u>brothers and sisters</u>.*

Practice For each passage, underline words that have strong connotations and determine the persuasive techniques.

1. "Our first assignment involved a scheme that was typical of the way the Khmer Rouge did things. We were marched off to a rice field…"
2. "'Thay, you are a counterrevolutionary . . . you participated in exchanges . . . you don't know how to get rid of individualist leanings . . . you taint our group . . .'"
3. "'I will ask the chief to give you a warning so that you can cleanse yourself. It will be a serious warning, Thay. The next time, you will become fertilizer on our rice fields.'"

Vocabulary Practice

Analyze Loaded Language Guide students to consider words with the same denotation but different connotations, such as *untidy, messy,* and *sloppy.* Have students create sentence strings, placing the words with the most positive connotations with *I,* neutral connotations with *you,* and negative connotations with *they.* An example would be "I am firm, you are strict and they are harsh."

Meet Kauraka Kauraka and Albert Wendt

The Pacific Islands have a strong tradition of oral literature. So strong, in fact, its written literature didn't truly begin to blossom until the 1960s. During the 1970s, such authors as Albert Wendt began to react against the European image of their culture: "Up to now, most literature about us [the Pacific Islanders] has been written by outsiders—much of it superficial and distorted and over romantic and racist. We now want to examine ourselves and our way of life ourselves."

Albert Wendt (born 1939) The person most responsible for the emergence of Pacific Island written literature is Wendt, a novelist and poet from the republic of Western Samoa. Wendt blends Polynesian oral traditions with European literary heritage to portray islanders and their way of life. According to Wendt, at the heart of indigenous writing are "the techniques of oral storytelling . . . and indigenous philosophies and visions." Much of his writing responds to colonialism and the injustices the Pacific Islanders have continued to face long after their independence. His work addresses the feelings of exile—due to both geography and culture—they have experienced because of other people's ideas and myths about their way of life.

Wendt and other Pacific Island authors believe they should write about islanders and for islanders, and thus value the importance of integrating the oral tradition of their culture into their work. These myths, legends, songs, chants, and tales of magic allow them to express their way of life. While this literature is written in English, which allows the authors to speak to a wide audience, its language reflects the influence of Pacific culture and spoken literature.

Kauraka Kauraka (1951–1997) Born in Rarotonga, the main island of the Cook Islands, Kauraka Kauraka was one of the best known Pacific Island authors. The Cooks, consisting of fifteen volcanic islands, form a self-governing state in the South Pacific. Previously controlled by New Zealand, the Cook Islands—like much of the Pacific—are home to a culture shaped by the intersection of local tradition and colonial rule. Through his verse and his work as an anthropologist with the Ministry of Cultural Development, Kauraka studied and brought attention to the people of the Cook Islands and their rich oral traditions. He published stories, nonfiction, and six poetry collections in both English and the Cook Islands Maori language. His writings are renderings of myths and legends about the land, the sea, and the gods, as well as original works. Kauraka's poems often convey a profound sense of loss, while simultaneously expressing great pride in his homeland.

> "I belong to Oceania . . . and it nourishes my spirit, helps to define me, and feeds my imagination."
>
> —Albert Wendt

Literature Online

Author Search For more about Albert Wendt and Kauraka Kauraka, go to glencoe.com and enter QuickPass code GLW6053u4.

KAURAKA KAURAKA AND ALBERT WENDT **829**

Before You Read

Focus

Bellringer Options

Daily Language Practice Transparency 78

Or ask: What are examples of landscapes that may provoke strong feelings? Students may suggest that rough mountainsides can provoke fear because they're dangerous to traverse. Others may point to popular landscapes, such as the Grand Canyon, which provokes awe in its visitors.

Political History ☆

Colonial Rule In the late 1700s, the Pacific Islands' location made it a profitable area for traders, who tried to change economic policies and cultural attitudes to protect their economic interests. Some native chiefs resisted traders, tensions rose, and the traders' governments intervened. From 1842 until 1900, almost all of the islands were controlled by Europe and the United States. By 1980, through the efforts of the United Nations, most of the Pacific Islands had achieved independence.

Selection Skills

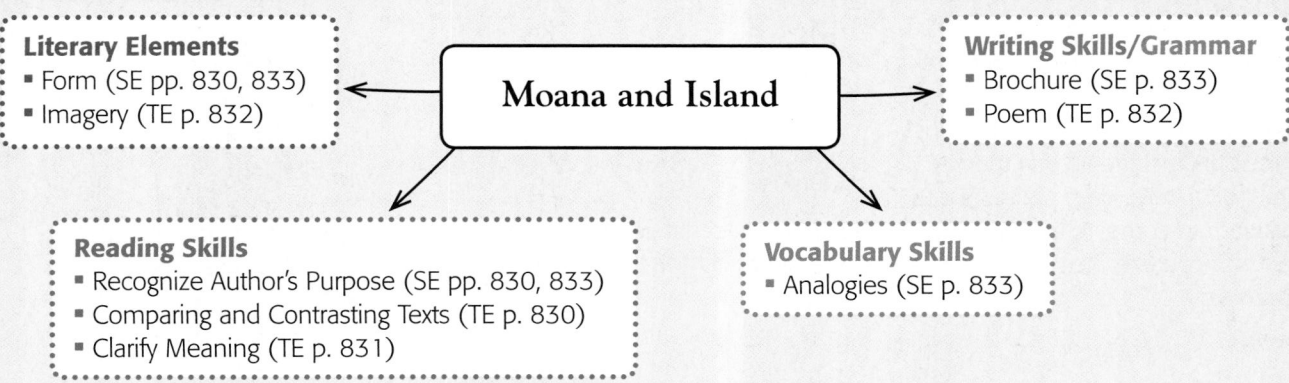

Literary Elements
- Form (SE pp. 830, 833)
- Imagery (TE p. 832)

Moana and Island

Writing Skills/Grammar
- Brochure (SE p. 833)
- Poem (TE p. 832)

Reading Skills
- Recognize Author's Purpose (SE pp. 830, 833)
- Comparing and Contrasting Texts (TE p. 830)
- Clarify Meaning (TE p. 831)

Vocabulary Skills
- Analogies (SE p. 833)

Before You Read

Focus

Summary

"Moana" praises the Pacific Ocean and establishes it as a mysterious god with the power to give life and take it away.

"Island" suggests that nature, namely the ocean and a volcano, gave birth to the island, and therefore to human life.

 For summaries in languages other than English, see Unit 4 Teaching Resources Book, pp. 264–269.

Vocabulary   1

 Word Associations
Have students work in small groups to play a word association game. Have them take turns providing a verbal clue about one of the vocabulary words. For instance, for the word *graceful*, students can provide a synonym such as *refined* or an example, such as *ballerina*. The first student to guess the correct word wins a point.

 For additional vocabulary practice, see Unit 4 Teaching Resources Book, p. 272.

Literature and Reading Preview

Connect to the Poems

What do you think of when you hear the words *island* and *ocean*? Freewrite for a few minutes about the images that appear in your mind when you think about these words.

Build Background

The Pacific island nations occupy some 34,000 square miles of land spread over millions of square miles of ocean. Their inhabitants came from Asia by way of Indonesia thousands of years ago. The more than 10,000 islands include two general types. Volcanos usually produced mountainous, forested islands. Islands that grew from coral reefs are usually smaller and lower, with sparse vegetation and limited fresh water.

Set Purposes for Reading

Big Idea Place and Identity

As you read, ask yourself, How are the poetry and the authors influenced by the landscape?

Literary Element Form

A poem's **form**—or structure—contributes to its theme and reflects its subject. Pacific island poets and many other modern authors use loosely structured poetic forms, or free verse. They vary line length, stanzas, rhythm, rhyme, repetition, and word placement to emphasize their ideas and emotions and convey meaning. As you read, ask yourself, How does the form of these poems contribute to their themes and subjects?

Reading Strategy Recognize Author's Purpose

An **author's purpose** is his or her reason for writing. Authors typically write to persuade, to inform, to explain, to entertain, or to describe. The purpose is often revealed in the title, form, word choice, tone, and content. As you read, ask yourself, What clues reveal the author's purpose?

Tip: Cluster Details Use a cluster diagram like the one below to help you determine the poets' purposes.

Learning Objectives

For pages 829–833

In studying these texts, you will focus on the following objectives:

Literary Study: Analyzing form.

Reading: Recognizing author's purpose.

Writing: Creating a brochure.

Vocabulary

graceful (grās′fəl) *adj.* showing effortless beauty or movement; p. 831 *The dancer's movements were graceful and fluid.*

frail (frāl) *adj.* easily broken or damaged; fragile; p. 832 *The hikers carefully inched across the frail bridge, hoping it would not snap under their weight.*

Tip: Analogies When you read an analogy question, you should read it as a sentence that shows the relationship between two words. For example, in the analogy *dancer : graceful :: scholar : _____*, the sentence showing the relationship is "A dancer is graceful." To complete the analogy, you would read "A scholar is _____."

Reading Practice

Compare and Contrast Poems Have students compare and contrast the two poems. Tell students that comparing and contrasting texts helps improve their understanding of a theme, topic, genre, or culture. Have students use a Venn diagram to compare and contrast both poems. Encourage them to look at aspects such as:

- length
- form
- topic
- theme
- style
- literary elements
- purpose

As a class, discuss what their comparisons revealed about the Pacific Island cultures.

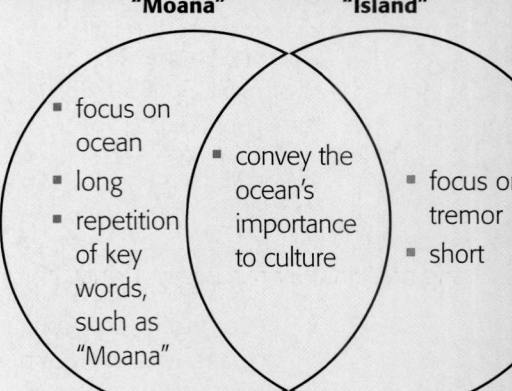

830

Moana

Kauraka Kauraka

Name of the Great Ocean
the dark blue sea
the mysterious
Moana-Nui-o-Kiva
5   Moana-Vai-a-Vare[1] **2**
mysterious ocean
Moana our daughter
graceful rider through space
from Havaiki[2]
10   today you have earned
the keys to enter
the four rooms
of the mysterious
ocean of life
15   many will call upon
your name for guidance
for interpretation
of these mysteries
Moana our sister
20   you were born and raised
in the mysterious ocean
we look to you for understanding
of the fish we eat
the waves that destroy us
25   the waves that create new lands **3**
for us
Moana our daughter
Moana our sister
Moana our mother

Seashells on the Seashore. Brian Kere (Solomon Islands, b. 1960). Mixed media, 90 x 64 cm. The International Museum of 20th Century Arts, Laguna Beach, CA.

---

1. Lines 4–5 refer to the Pacific Ocean.
2. *Havaiki* (hä vä ē′ kē) is the legendary homeland of the Maori. Cook Islanders are considered a branch of the Maori people.

4   Place and Identity *What can you infer about the ocean from each comparison?*

Vocabulary

graceful (grās′ fəl) *adj.* showing effortless beauty or movement

Teach

Literary Element   2

Repetition Tell students that poets may repeat key words or phrases within a poem to emphasize an idea or affect the poem's form. **Ask:** What might be the poet's purpose for repeating the word *Moana*? *(The poet might want to emphasize Moana's importance or give the poem a chant-like rhythm to follow his culture's oral tradition.)*

Reading Strategy   3

Clarify Meaning Explain that, since poetry is full of implied meaning, students should clarify meaning as they read. Encourage students to paraphrase every few lines to check that they understand their meaning. **Ask:** What do these lines reveal about Moana? *(They reveal that Moana has omniscient powers, like a god, who can create life and death.)*

Big Idea   4

Place and Identity Answer: *The ocean is like a daughter who needs the protection of people; the ocean is like a sister who is an equal and living being; the ocean is like a mother who confers life and provides sustenance.*

English Learners

DIFFERENTIATED INSTRUCTION

Beginning Ask English learners to recall key landscape features from their native countries and make a list of how these features impacted their culture, way of life, literature, traditions, and so on. Have students draw a picture of the landscape and present their pictures in a small group.

Approaching Level

DIFFERENTIATED INSTRUCTION

Question Make sure students understand the poems' key ideas. Encourage them to make a list of questions they have about the poem. Then discuss their questions as a class. For example, students may ask about the cause of the tremor in the "Island" poem or may need to further discuss the importance of the ocean in "Moana."

Learning Objectives
Recognizing author's purpose. (SE)
Identifying form. (SE)
Comparing and contrasting. (TE)
Clarifying meaning. (TE)

831

Teach

Literary Element

Imagery Explain to students that imagery is the use of words to create pictures in a reader's mind. **Ask:** What picture does this imagery paint in your mind? What does it tell you about how the author views the ocean? Students should say that, through the use of words such as *stingrays, dark,* and *threat,* the imagery evokes a frightening, mysterious scene. The author may see the ocean as powerful and mystifying.

 For additional practice using the reading skill or strategy, see Unit 4 Teaching Resources Book, p. 271.

Cultural History ☆

Samoa Samoa had been under foreign power for over a century, with New Zealand controlling it from World War I until 1962. It was that year that Samoa became the first Polynesian nation to regain independence in the twentieth century.

ISLAND

Albert Wendt

This island was a **frail** tremor snared
in stingray seas dark with threat of storm.
The tremor was strong enough
to give us birth.

Vocabulary

frail (frāl) *adj.* easily broken or damaged; fragile

Lava pouring into ocean, Volcanoes Nat'l Park, Big Island, Hawaii. Art Wolfe. Photograph.

832   UNIT 4   SOUTHEAST ASIA AND THE PACIFIC

Writing Practice

Write a Poem Say: Both poems are deeply influenced by the landscape— the relationships of the land to the vast ocean. Many literary works place great symbolic value on the surrounding landscape. For example, Walt Whitman highlights America's "wide open spaces" in his work, and Henry David Thoreau spent two years at Walden Pond interacting with landscape.

Ask: What distinctive features of the local landscape mean something to you? With the class, brainstorm some features, such as the streets of the city, the greenery of suburbia, a span of desert, a patch of forest, or a stretch of field. Have students create a web with the feature in the middle and details in the surrounding circles. Then have students use their web to write a poem. Encourage students to share their poems with the class.

832

After You Read

Respond and Think Critically

Respond and Interpret

1. What feelings did you experience while reading these poems? Explain.

2. (a)Who or what is Moana? (b)Why do you think the speaker of "Moana" repeatedly refers to Moana as "mysterious"?

3. (a)The **speaker** of a poem is the voice that talks to the reader. What do the speaker of "Moana" and the people expect from Moana? (b)How would you describe the relationship between the people and Moana?

4. What does the speaker in "Island" say the island once was?

Analyze and Evaluate

5. What does Wendt's description of the ocean as "stingray seas" suggest about the region?

6. (a)What examples of **alliteration** can you find in "Island"? (b)How does alliteration contribute to the poem's overall effect?

7. (a)How are "Moana" and "Island" similar as creation stories? (b)How do they differ?

Connect

8. **Big Idea** **Place and Identity** What does the Moana myth tell of the culture that created it?

9. **Connect to Today** How do people in your community feel about local geography? Explain.

Literary Element Form

The **form** of a poem is the way it is arranged on a page, such as the placement of words and phrases, the length of lines, and the shape of stanzas.

1. Explain the form of "Moana." How does the form relate to the meaning of the poem?

2. How does the form of "Moana" reflect the culture and ideas of the Pacific islands? Explain.

Reading Strategy Recognize Author's Purpose

Use the diagram you made on page 830 to help you answer the following questions.

1. Consider Kauraka's word choice in "Moana." How do the words convey his purpose?

2. How does the length of "Island" relate to the author's purpose?

LOG ON **Literature** Online

Selection Resources For Selection Quizzes, eFlash-cards, and Reading-Writing Connection activities, go to **glencoe.com** and enter QuickPass code GLW6053u4.

Vocabulary Practice

Practice with Analogies Identify the pair of words that best expresses the relationship in the original pair.

1. graceful : fluid ::
a. stars : night   c. adult : baby
b. adventure : explore   d. peaceful : tranquil

2. frail : sturdy ::
a. delightful : unpleasant c. lamb : sheep
b. excitement : joy   d. cook : stove

✍ Writing

Create a Brochure Using the library and the Internet, research the role the ocean plays in the daily life of Pacific islanders. As you research, note essential facts and interesting information about the ocean. Then create a brochure summarizing your findings. You might format your brochure with a three-column layout, include photographs, and present some of your information in bulleted lists.

KAURAKA KAURAKA AND ALBERT WENDT **833**

After You Read

Assess

1. Answers will vary.
2. (a) the Pacific Ocean
   (b) because the ocean is so deep, vast, and unknowable
3. (a) guidance and understanding (b) They are very close, like family members.
4. a volcanic eruption, or "a frail tremor snared in stingray seas"
5. It is lively, dark, dangerous, and full of mysterious life.
6. (a) The *s* sound is in "snared," "stingray seas," "storm," and "strong." (b) It may represent the hissing of lava as it enters the sea and may suggest the beginnings of the island.
7. (a) Both present the ocean as the mysterious source of all life. (b) "Island" portrays a violent springing from the Earth; "Moana" portrays the presence of a personified deity.
8. It suggests a closeness to the natural world and an examination of the oral tradition.
9. Answers will vary.

Literary Element

1. The poem is written in a loose style and does not follow strict line lengths or stanzas. The form illustrates the ocean's power and mystery.
2. The form reflects the subject of nature and the creation of the world. Nature is free and cannot be contained by humans, just as the lines cannot be contained by poetic conventions.

Progress Check

Do students understand form?

If No → See Unit 4 Teaching Resources Book, p. 270.

Reading Strategy

1. He repeats the words *mystery* and *mysterious*. These words reveal that his purpose is to explain the vastness of the ocean and the inability of humans to control it.

2. The brevity of the poem emphasizes the suddenness of the island's creation.

Academic Vocabulary

1. d   2. a

✍ Writing

Students' brochures should
- contain educational facts about the Pacific Ocean and the Islanders
- include photos and bulleted lists

Focus

Bellringer Options

Daily Language Practice
Transparency 79

Or ask: What are some issues that have caused controversy in this school or in the larger community? Elicit students' responses. Make a list of the issues they mention on the board. **Say:** In this workshop, you will learn to write and deliver a persuasive speech on a topic that is important to you. Have students identify issues listed on the board which would be strong topics for a persuasive speech. Advise them that a strong topic for a persuasive speech is one that has compelling arguments to be made on either side.

Summary

In this workshop students will write and present a persuasive speech. Students will follow the stages of the writing process: prewriting, drafting, revising, and editing. In addition, mini-lessons on using evidence and parallelism are provided.

Workshop Resources

Print Materials

- Unit 4 Teaching Resources pp. 277–278
- Writing Kit
- Success in Writing: Research and Reports

Technology

- Literature Online: Writing Resources and Grammar Resources, glencoe.com
- Online Essay Grader, glencoe.com
- Student Presentation Builder on Student-Works Plus CD-ROM
- Media Workshop DVD
- Online Student Edition

Learning Objectives

For pages 834–841

In this workshop, you will focus on the following objectives:

Writing:
Writing a persuasive speech using the writing process.

Understanding how to elaborate on ideas with evidence.

Grammar: Understanding how to use parallelism.

> ### Writing Process
>
> At any stage of a writing process, you may think of new ideas. Feel free to return to earlier stages as you write.
>
> **Prewrite**
>
> **Draft**
>
> **Revise**
>
> Focus Lesson: Evidence
>
> **Edit and Proofread**
>
> Focus Lesson: Parallelism
>
> **Present**

 **Literature** Online

Writing and Research For prewriting, drafting, and other revising tools, go to glencoe.com and enter QuickPass code GLW6053u4.

Writing Workshop

Persuasive Speech

Literature Connection In the following passage from the *Analects,* Confucius makes a point about the state of family relationships by using a memorable comparison and a powerful rhetorical question.

> *"'Filial sons' nowadays are people who see to it that their parents get enough to eat. But even dogs and horses are cared for to that extent. If there is no feeling of respect, wherein lies the difference?"*

In a persuasive speech, you use such rhetorical devices, along with well-reasoned arguments, to convince an audience to take your side on a particular issue. To write an effective persuasive speech, you will need to study the goals and strategies listed below.

Rubric

Goals	Strategies
To present a clearly stated opinion on an issue	☑ Give background information on the issue. ☑ State your opinion at the beginning of the speech.
To explain and support your opinion	☑ Give reasons for your opinion in a logical order. ☑ Use facts and examples to support your reasons.
To convince and engage your audience	☑ Use logical, emotional, and ethical appeals. ☑ Use rhetorical devices. Persuade your audience to act.
To anticipate and address counterarguments	☑ Describe other points of view. ☑ Respond to these points of view with reasoned arguments.

Assignment: Present a Viewpoint

Write a persuasive speech of at least 1,000 words about an issue in your community that you feel strongly about. As you move through the stages of writing, keep your audience and purpose in mind.

Audience: your school or community

Purpose: to use logical arguments and detailed evidence to persuade an audience to act

Real-World Connection

At various points in your life, you will need to use persuasive skills to ensure that your voice is heard in your community. To influence a local project, policy, or problem, you must be able to articulate and defend your opinions clearly.

Analyze a Professional Model

In the following persuasive speech, given in 1969, former congresswoman Shirley Chisholm urges the House of Representatives to spend government money on social programs in the United States rather than on the Vietnam War. Pay close attention to the comments in the margin. They point out features you might want to include in your own persuasive speech.

from *"The Business of America Is War"*
by Shirley Chisholm

Mr. Speaker, on the same day President Nixon announced he had decided the United States will not be safe unless we start to build a defense system against missiles, the Head Start program[1] in the District of Columbia was cut back for the lack of money.

As a teacher, and as a woman, I do not think I will ever understand what kind of values can be involved in spending nine billion dollars—and more, I am sure—on elaborate, unnecessary and impractical weapons when several thousand disadvantaged children in the nation's capital get nothing.

When the new administration took office, I was one of the many Americans who hoped it would mean that our country would benefit from the fresh perspectives, the new ideas, the different priorities of a leader who had no part in the mistakes of the past. Mr. Nixon has said things like this:

Ethical Appeal

Appeal to your audience's sense of right and wrong.

---

1. *Head Start* is a program, run by the U.S. Department of Health and Human Services, that provides services to children from low-income families.

WRITING WORKSHOP **835**

Teach

Big Idea   1

The Struggle to Survive

Have students read the professional model. **Ask:** What other speeches do you know of that have had an effect on a political struggle? (*Students might mention Patrick Henry's "Give me liberty or give me death" speech, Abraham Lincoln's Gettysburg Address, or Martin Luther King Jr.'s "I Have a Dream" speech.*)

ADVANCED Encourage interested students to read some of these famous political speeches and to incorporate the persuasive techniques they encounter into their own speeches.

Writing Skills

Quotation Point out that people giving persuasive speeches often use quotations to provide expert opinions that support their points. However, Chisholm used the quotation from President Nixon for quite a different purpose—to show Congress that the president failed to keep his word. Encourage students to look for contradictory or hypocritical statements from opponents as they research their topics. They may be able to use these quotations to strengthen their own positions.

English Learners

DIFFERENTIATED INSTRUCTION

Advanced Politicians often use idioms and jargon that may be difficult for English learners to understand. Before students read the professional model, explain the meanings and connotations of the terms *Capitol Hill, good guys, black America, white America,* and *right side up.* Encourage students to write down any other terms that they do not understand as they read, and then to look up these terms in a dictionary. Inform students that, in addition to providing formal definitions of words, many dictionaries also provide casual and idiomatic definitions.

Learning Objectives
Analyzing a professional model. (SE)
Using quotations. (TE)

Writing Workshop

Teach

Writing Skills

Humor

Say: Humor can be a powerful persuasive technique, because it leads people to see things in new ways. Point out that Chisholm's discussion of the delayed social programs is humorous because it plays on the multiple meanings of the word *launch*, slyly calling attention to what she believes to be the illogical nature of the government's actions. Encourage students to incorporate humor into their own speeches where appropriate.

[ENGLISH LEARNERS] Make sure that English learners understand that *launch* means both "to release (a weapon)" and "to initiate (a program)."

Writer's Technique ☆

The Word *I* For other formal writing assignments, students may have been discouraged from using the words *I* and *my*, because these pronouns make a writer's stance seem subjective, rather than objective. First-person pronouns can sometimes be effective in a persuasive speech, however. Chisholm not only frequently uses the word *I* but also makes her personal connection to the topic clear from the start, identifying herself as both "a teacher" and "a woman." This sense of personal investment strengthens the emotional appeal of her speech.

Quotation

Use quotations from experts and well-known figures.

Shirley Chisholm Addressing National Press Club, April 20, 1972, Washington, DC.

Supporting Evidence

Use specific facts and examples to illustrate your points.

Logical Appeal

Appeal to your audience's sense of reason.

Counterarguments

To strengthen your position, refute objections.

Conclusion

End your speech by powerfully restating your position and calling your audience to action.

Rhetorical Devices

Use devices such as parallelism, repetition, and rhetorical questions.

"If our cities are to be livable for the next generation, we can delay no longer in launching new approaches to the problems that beset them and to the tensions that tear them apart." . . .

Apparently launching those new programs can be delayed for a while, after all. It seems we have to get some missiles launched first...

Secretary of Defense Melvin Laird came to Capitol Hill . . . Mr. Laird talked of being prepared to spend at least two more years in Vietnam . . .

We Americans have come to feel that it is our mission to make the world free. We believe that we are the good guys, everywhere—in Vietnam, in Latin America, wherever we go. We believe we are the good guys at home, too. When the Kerner Commission[2] told white America what black America had always known, that prejudice and hatred built the nation's slums, maintain them and profit by them, white America would not believe it. But it is true. Unless we start to fight and defeat the enemies of poverty and racism in our own country and make our talk of equality and opportunity ring true, we are exposed as hypocrites in the eyes of the world when we talk about making other people free.

I am deeply disappointed at the clear evidence that the number-one priority of the new administration is to buy more and more weapons of war, to return to the era of the cold war, to ignore the war we must fight here—the war that is not optional. . .

For this reason, I intend to vote "No" on every money bill that comes to the floor of this House that provides any funds for the Department of Defense. Any bill whatsoever, until the time comes when our values and priorities have been turned right side up again, until the monstrous waste and the shocking profits in the defense budget have been eliminated and our country starts to use its strength, its tremendous resources, for people and peace, not for profits and war.

---

2. The *Kerner Commission* was a group appointed to investigate urban riots in the 1960s.

Reading-Writing Connection Think about the writing techniques you just encountered and try them out in the persuasive speech you write.

Writing Practice

Support a Thesis Remind students that they should choose speech topics that have two strong opposing sides. If they choose to argue against very weak opposition, there will be no need for persuasion, since their audience will probably already be in agreement with them.

Once students have chosen a topic, have them map out the sides. Strong topics will have several good reasons listed on both the *yes* and *no* sides. Have students choose whether to take the *yes* or *no* position in their speech.

Prewrite

Choose an Issue What issues in your school or community are important to you? Choose an issue in which you have a personal stake and make sure it has two strong opposing sides that can be argued. The more current and controversial the issue, the more likely it will hold your audience's attention.

Gather Reasons To clarify your own position on the issue, you will need to identify specific logical, ethical, or emotional reasons for supporting either side. Think about the arguments that could be made for both sides. If necessary, conduct research to learn more about the issue.

State Your Thesis After you have decided which side of the issue you support, write a thesis statement that sums up your position. As you write, remember your purpose. Your thesis statement should be not only a statement of opinion but also a call for your audience to do something.

Make an Outline Make a plan for your essay. Your introduction should grab your audience's attention and clearly state your thesis, while your conclusion should restate your thesis and call for action. Your body paragraphs should use logical analyses and well-crafted appeals to relate specific pieces of evidence to your thesis. Below are two possible ways of organizing your body paragraphs.

Body Paragraph Structure

Reason: most important reason to accept proposed schedule change is to help keep students safe

↓

Evidence: sleep deprivation puts teens at a higher risk for depression, social problems, etc.

↓

Analysis and Appeal: Need to ask ourselves whether we can afford to keep depriving overstressed students of sleep. If pushing back starting time can make students happier and healthier, we should accept costs

OR

Counterargument: Several of the most vocal objectors have been coaches, who argue that later starting time would interfere with after-school sports

↓

Refutation: new schedule could actually strengthen sports at Franklin High

↓

Evidence: coaches complain about team members being tired during practices.

↓

Analysis: Just as an extra hour of sleep has been shown to improve students' attendance and alertness in class, it is bound to improve their performance in sports as well.

Types of Appeals

Consider using these types of appeals in your speech.

Logical appeals reach an audience through reasoned arguments.

Emotional appeals rouse the audience's feelings.

Ethical appeals reach the audience's sense of right and wrong.

Avoid Plagiarism

Your speech will be strengthened by the use of direct quotes, paraphrases, and testimonies from expert witnesses to support your thesis. Copying the words of another writer is wrong, however, unless you give proper credit. Be sure to note where you found your supporting evidence and give credit to each source.

Writing Workshop

Persuasive Speech

Teach

Writing Skills

Gather Evidence Advise students to look for as many different types of evidence as possible to support their arguments. These might include firsthand observations by themselves or others, informed opinions from experts, examples that demonstrate more general points, logical reasons, and facts.

Cultural History ☆

The Sophists Throughout history, the art of persuasive speech has been used for a variety of purposes. In their writings, both Plato and Aristotle criticize the sophists, a class of professional teachers and debaters who were more concerned with winning arguments than with discovering truth. Specifically, Plato condemns their use of rhetorical techniques that made weaker arguments seem stronger. Today, the term *sophist*, which originally simply meant "wise," connotes someone who argues for the sake of argument and who uses false reasoning.

Approaching Level
DIFFERENTIATED INSTRUCTION

Choose a Topic Some students may have difficulty selecting an appropriately narrow topic for their persuasive speech. Provide these students with a list of topics affecting the school or community, such as implementing a dress code or extending the school day. Then ask them questions about their feelings on these topics. Work with them to choose a topic about which they have strong feelings and could take a "yes" or "no" position.

Advanced Learners/Pre-AP
DIFFERENTIATED INSTRUCTION

Explore a National or International Issue Some students may enjoy the challenge of writing a persuasive speech on a national or international issue, rather than simply focusing on their school or community. Have them look in current newspapers and magazines for ideas.

Encourage them to read editorials for ideas on how to structure and defend their arguments.

Learning Objectives
Analyzing a persuasive speech. (SE)
Prewriting. (SE)
Supporting a thesis. (TE)

Teach

Writing Skills

Thesis Statement **Answer:** *It acknowledges that the topic has been controversial and encourages the audience to reconsider the facts.*

Counterarguments
Answer: *The writer undermines the counterargument by showing that it is unscientific and offers his or her own argument as a logical alternative.*

Writing Frames

As you read the workshop model, think about the writer's use of the following persuasive writing frames.

What these objectors fail to realize is _____.

Studies have shown that _____.

Try using these kinds of frames to offer counterarguments to those who may disagree with your ideas.

Thesis Statement

How does the writer's thesis statement appeal to those who are not yet convinced?

Counterarguments

How does the writer strengthen his or her position by addressing this counterargument?

Draft

Develop Your Tone Following your outline, draft your speech from start to finish. Use a formal and respectful tone.

Analyze a Workshop Model

Here is a final draft of a persuasive speech. Read the speech and answer the questions in the margin. Use the answers to these questions to guide you as you write.

Sleepy Students: Waking Up to the Solution

Walk into almost any Franklin High classroom in the first few hours of the day, and you'll see students struggling to keep their eyes open. A survey taken last year showed that Franklin High students sleep an average of 6.5 hours per night—2.5 hours less than the recommended amount for teenagers. In light of research showing that people need a good night's sleep to think and learn properly, these findings are disturbing. However, many members of this community have decried a proposed measure to address these issues. The measure, which would change Franklin High's starting time from 7:00 A.M. to 8:00 A.M., would give students an extra hour of sleep and could significantly improve their lives.

Opponents of the later starting time have blamed students' sleep habits, rather than Franklin High's current schedule, for the fact that students are so sleepy. Several community members have argued that we should focus on teaching students to go to bed earlier. While it is true that students need to be taught good sleep habits, studies have shown that teenagers actually remain alert later at night than adults. In addition, they continue producing melatonin, the chemical responsible for sleepiness, far longer into the morning than adults. These findings explain why Franklin High's current schedule doesn't work. Pushing back the starting time is the only way to truly address the problem.

Writing Practice

SMALL GROUP
Use Rhetorical Devices
Write: Walk into almost any Franklin High classroom in the first few hours of the day, and you'll see students struggling to keep their eyes open. Explain that this is an effective opening sentence because it offers a vivid, specific illustration of the problem that the speech will address. Students will need to begin their persuasive speeches with a similar "hook" that will capture the audience's attention. This sentence might inform the audience of a problem, provide a mental picture, or ask a thought-provoking question. Have students write three possible opening sentences for their persuasive essays. Encourage them to use the following sentence frames:

Imagine that _____.

Recently in our community, _____.

We can no longer ignore the problem of _____.

Then divide students into pairs. Have students choose which of their partner's sentences would be the most effective opener.

Pushing back Franklin's starting time would also sharpen students' minds and promote learning. Educational researcher Kyla Wahlstrom conducted a four-year study of two Minneapolis school districts, both of which pushed back their starting times by about an hour. Students reported they were going to bed at the same time as they had before the change and so were getting an extra hour of sleep each night. The extra hour made a difference: teachers at the schools reported that "students were more alert and ready for learning." These findings are consistent with research showing we need sleep to retrieve long-term memories, to learn new material, and to perform complex mental tasks. They make it clear that a later starting time could have a significant academic benefit for Franklin High.

Several of the most vocal objectors to the proposed schedule change have been coaches, who argue that the later starting time would interfere with after-school sports. What these objectors fail to realize is that the new schedule could actually strengthen sports. Every season, Franklin High coaches complain about team members being tired during practices. Just as an extra hour of sleep has been shown to improve students' attendance and alertness in class, it is bound to improve their performance in sports as well.

Perhaps the most important reason to accept the proposed schedule change is that it would help keep students safe. Studies have shown that sleep deprivation puts teenagers at a higher risk for depression and other behavior issues. However, students report less depression when their schools introduce later starting times. As U.S. Rep. Zoe Lofgren of California states, later starting times "could do more to improve education and reduce teen accidents and crime than many more expensive initiatives." If pushing back Franklin High's starting time can make students happier and healthier, it is our duty to accept the costs.

Let's put aside our fear of change and embrace this simple measure that could benefit students, teachers, coaches, and parents alike.

Persuasion

Logical Appeal
How does the writer appeal to the audience's reason here?

Supporting Evidence
How does the writer use facts to support his or her position?

Rhetorical Devices
How do the writer's rhetorical questions help support his or her point?

Conclusion
How does the writer tailor the conclusion to his or her audience?

Writing Workshop

Persuasive Speech

Teach

Writing Skills

Logical Appeal Answer: *The writer applies scientific findings to the situation to clarify what is going on and why his or her solution will work.*

Supporting Evidence Answer: *The writer uses positive results from schools that made a similar change and argues that his or her own school could have the same positive results.*

Rhetorical Devices Answer: *The answers to these questions would be obvious to the writer's audience, so the audience would be compelled to agree with the writer.*

Conclusion Answer: *The writer identifies each group in the community that would benefit from the measure.*

Learning Objectives
Analyzing a persuasive speech. (SE)
Using the writing process. (SE)
Using rhetorical devices. (TE)

Approaching Level

DIFFERENTIATED INSTRUCTION

Previewing Some students may have difficulty following the complex arguments presented in the workshop model. Have them preview the speech by reading the entire first paragraph, and then the first and last sentences of each body paragraph.
Then ask: What do you predict will be the main points of this speech? Based on their responses, create an outline on the board similar to the one below:

I. Biology, not student behavior, is to blame for sleepiness

II. Later start time would increase learning

III. Later start time would help, not hurt, student athletics

Say: As you read each sentence of the workshop model, ask yourself: Which of the main points on the board does this sentence support?

Persuasive Speech

Teach

✍ Writing Skills

Revise Remind students that it can be tempting to make exaggerated, illogical, or untrue claims when trying to persuade someone of something. For example, a student might try to draw a conclusion about an entire group of people based on the opinions of only one member of that group. Have students exchange speeches with a partner and check one another's work for any of the following errors in logic:

- Stereotyping
- False analogies
- Overgeneralizations
- False or oversimplified cause-and-effect relationships

Traits of Strong Writing

Follow these traits of strong writing to express your ideas effectively.

Ideas

Organization

Voice

Word Choice

Sentence Fluency

Conventions

Presentation

For more information on using the Traits of Strong Writing, see pages R28–R30.

Word Choice

This academic vocabulary word appears in the student model.

complex (kəm pleks´) *adj.* intricate; complicated; *Students have trouble absorbing complex concepts when they're tired.*

Using academic vocabulary may help strengthen your writing. Try to use one or two academic vocabulary words in your essay. See the complete list on pages R83–R85.

LOG ON ▶ **Literature** Online

Writing and Research For editing and publishing tools, go to glencoe.com and enter QuickPass code GLW6053u4.

Revise

When you have finished writing, use the checklist below to evaluate your persuasive speech.

Checklist

☑ Do you introduce a controversial issue and present a clear thesis and call to action?

☑ Do you present specific reasons with supporting evidence?

☑ Do your arguments appeal to your audience's reason, emotions, and ethics?

☑ Do you use rhetorical devices to strengthen your arguments?

☑ Do you present and respond to counterarguments?

▶ **Focus Lesson**

Evidence

To make your reasons convincing, you must back them up with evidence such as statistics, examples, and explanations. Below is a sentence from the Workshop Model followed by three kinds of supporting evidence—facts, examples, and an expert opinion—that you may want to use in your persuasive speech.

Draft:

Perhaps the most important reason to accept the proposed schedule change is that it would help keep students safe.

Revision:

Perhaps the most important reason to accept the proposed schedule change is that it would help keep students safe. Studies have shown that sleep deprivation puts teenagers at a higher risk for depression and other behavior issues. However, students report less depression when their schools introduce later starting times. [1] *As U.S. Rep. Zoe Lofgren of California states, later starting times "could do more to improve education and reduce teen accidents and crime than many more expensive initiatives."* [2]

[1]: **Facts and Examples** [2]: **Expert Opinion**

Writing Practice

Vary Sentence Structure Write on the board: What these objectors fail to realize is that the new schedule could actually strengthen sports at Franklin High. Every season, Franklin High coaches complain about team members skipping practices. How often have we, as students, heard our friends say they are skipping practice because they are "just too tired"?

Point out that this passage is a good model for how to vary one's sentence structure throughout a speech. The writer varies the structure of the second sentence by beginning with a phrase ("Every season"). Then, in the third sentence, the writer uses a rhetorical question, which adds interest and variety.

Have students go through their drafts and make sure that at least one sentence in every paragraph begins with an introductory phrase. Have them make sure that they have used at least one rhetorical question in their draft.

Edit and Proofread

Get It Right When you have completed the final draft of your persuasive speech, proofread it for errors in grammar, usage, mechanics, and spelling. Refer to the Language Handbook, pages R40–R59, as a guide.

> ## Focus Lesson
> ### Parallelism
>
> Parallelism is the use of the same grammatical form to express ideas similar in content and function. For example, in a sentence with a list, all the items must be the same part of speech or the same type of phrase or clause. Parallelism can also be used across several sentences to clarify and reinforce a particular point.
>
> **Original:** Three items in a list are not grammatically parallel.
>
> *These findings are consistent with research showing that we need sleep for <u>long-term memories</u>, <u>performing complex mental tasks</u>, and <u>to learn new material</u>.*
>
> **Improved:** Make the items parallel by balancing grammatical forms.
>
> *These findings are consistent with research showing that we need sleep <u>to retrieve long-term memories</u>, <u>to learn new material</u>, and <u>to perform complex mental tasks</u>.*

Present/Publish

Style Your Speech Once you have finished reviewing your work, check that it meets the length requirement. Ask your teacher if you are required to hand in a hard copy; if so, be sure to write it neatly or type it. If you use secondary sources, you may also be required to hand in a works-cited list. Check with your teacher for specific presentation guidelines.

Peer Review Tips

As you revise, ask a partner to point out places where you could add transitional words and phrases—such as *first, second, finally, more important,* and *moreover*—to show the logical progression of ideas within and between paragraphs. Transitional words and phrases strengthen your arguments by showing a clear line of thinking.

Word-Processing Tip

Type your speech using a word processing program and adjust your spacing, margins, and font size so you can easily read it aloud.

Writer's Portfolio

Place a clean copy of your persuasive speech in your portfolio to review later.

Advanced Learners/Pre-AP
DIFFERENTIATED INSTRUCTION

Publishing Interested students may wish to take their speeches a step further by submitting them to school or local newspapers. Encourage them to conduct research to determine the government agencies that deal with their chosen issues, and have them send their speeches to these agencies as well.

English Learners
DIFFERENTIATED INSTRUCTION

Beginning English learners may find it daunting to present their speeches to the class in English. Offer them the opportunity to rehearse their speeches for you in private, and encourage them to ask you questions about word meanings and pronunciations. These students may feel more comfortable presenting their final speeches in small groups, or even in a private meeting with you.

Teach

Writing Skills

Editing and Proofreading
Remind students that a fresh set of eyes can be invaluable during the editing and proofreading process. Have them work in pairs to check one another's drafts for errors in grammar, usage, mechanics, and spelling. Students should write neatly on one another's drafts and use standard proofreading symbols.

Presenting Say: Your delivery will affect whether or not you convince others to agree with you. The right pacing and tone can give your arguments more impact. Have students use colored pens and highlighters to mark parts of their speech where they want to add emphasis, pause, or use a certain tone of voice. **Say:** If you become nervous and begin to rush while presenting, these marks will serve as visual reminders to slow down and speak with conviction.

Learning Objectives
Writing a persuasive speech. (SE)
Using the writing process. (SE)
Varying sentence structure. (TE)

Focus

Summary

In this workshop, students will learn techniques for planning, rehearsing, and delivering a persuasive presentation to the class.

Teach

Use Models Play videos and audio recordings of famous persuasive speeches for the class, such as Martin Luther King Jr.'s *I Have a Dream* speech. Alternatively, play recordings of political debates or news programs in which politicians, experts, or "pundits" debate current events. Have students listen carefully and take notes on the speakers' rhetorical styles. Encourage them to pay attention to how the speakers use gestures, tone, pauses, and repetition.

Learning Objectives

For pages 842–843
In this workshop, you will focus on the following objective:

Listening and Speaking: Delivering a persuasive presentation.

Speaking Frames

As you prepare your speech, think about using some of the following frames to get started.

- My own view is that _____, because _____.
- For example, _____ shows that _____.
- For these reasons, _____ should be _____.

Hook Your Audience

Your arguments are more likely to convince audience members if your topic interests them. Rather than launching directly into your thesis statement, look for a particular anecdote or fact in your written speech that will grab your audience's attention. Use this "hook" to open your speech.

Speaking, Listening, and Viewing Workshop

Persuasive Presentation

Literature Connection Confucius delivered all his teachings orally. Only after his death did his followers attempt to capture his clever rhetorical devices and powerful delivery in writing. In this workshop, you will do the opposite: you will translate your persuasive writing into engaging spoken language. To do this, you will need to streamline your writing into concise statements and use techniques such as tone and gestures to enhance your arguments.

> **Assignment** **Deliver a Persuasive Speech** Adapt a persuasive essay into a speech and present it to an audience, using nonverbal techniques such as eye contact, body language, voice, and gestures for emphasis.

Plan Your Presentation

In writing your persuasive speech, you clarified your thinking and created logical, ordered arguments. Now your goal is to develop an engaging speaking style to present your viewpoint. Follow these steps to prepare your persuasive speech for oral delivery.

- Read your speech aloud several times. Take note of sections where you stumble and think about how you might revise them using simpler, more straightforward language.
- Use a highlighter to note the thesis and the main arguments of your speech. Use a different color highlighter to highlight the key pieces of evidence that support your arguments. Cross out details that are not persuasive enough or that would be unnecessary for a speech.
- Write your main arguments and pieces of evidence on note cards. Refer to the note cards as you rehearse. Your goal is to become familiar enough with your material that you will be arguing from your own expertise, rather than reading from your note cards, in your final presentation.

Speaking and Listening Practice

Evaluate Evidence Encourage students to use as many different types of evidence as possible in their persuasive presentations. **Say:** Each piece of evidence you use strengthens your thesis. Your thesis will be more strongly supported if you use a variety of types of evidence. Have students listen for the following types of evidence in one another's presentations:

- Firsthand observations
- Informed opinions
- Appropriate examples
- Logical reasons
- Provable facts

You may want to convert the above list into a checklist for students to use when evaluating one another. After students have identified the types of evidence used in their classmates' presentations, encourage them to think about whether the evidence was used appropriately and how well it supported the speaker's main points. Remind students to watch out for personal opinions, speculations, or faulty reasoning that may be presented by their classmates as "evidence."

Create Visual Aids

Visual aids add interest to your persuasive speech and can serve as evidence. The types of visual aids you use will depend on the types of appeals you make. A graph or a chart might best enhance a logical argument based on scientific data, while a powerful photograph might best strengthen an emotional appeal. Limit yourself to one or two visual aids that directly support your main arguments. Use a chart like the one below to brainstorm ideas.

Argument	Visual Aid	Purpose of Visual Aid
Starting school an hour later would have academic benefits	Graph showing improved attendance at other schools	To show that attendance could also improve at our school

Rehearse

Take turns rehearsing speeches with a partner. Use the following techniques to assess one another's speeches.

- Identify the thesis and the main arguments. If you are unable to identify these, work with your partner to find clearer ways of stating his or her main points.

- Ask questions and offer additional counterarguments. Your partner's presentation will be stronger if he or she has prepared responses to many possible objections.

- Evaluate the effectiveness of your partner's speech. How convincing were the arguments? Which rhetorical devices were most powerful?

Finally, keep in mind the following verbal and nonverbal delivery techniques while rehearsing.

Techniques for Delivering a Persuasive Speech

Verbal Techniques	Nonverbal Techniques
☑ **Tone** Vary your tone to draw attention to important points.	☑ **Eye Contact** Look directly at your audience.
☑ **Enunciation** Speak clearly.	☑ **Posture** Avoid leaning or slouching.
☑ **Emphasis** Stress important ideas.	☑ **Gestures** Use gestures to emphasize your points.
☑ **Pace** Speak slowly.	☑ **Visual Aids** Do not block your visual aids.

Presentation Tips

Use the following checklist to evaluate your presentation.

- Did you vary the tone of your presentation, adding emphasis where needed?
- Did you make eye contact with the audience?
- Did you remember not to block the visuals?
- Did you face the audience and not the visuals?

 Literature Online

Speaking, Listening, and Viewing For project ideas, templates, and presentation tips, go to glencoe.com and enter QuickPass code GLW6053u4.

Advanced Learners/Pre-AP

DIFFERENTIATED INSTRUCTION

Take Action Encourage interested students to take their presentations a step further and try to spur real change in the community. Have them deliver their persuasive presentations at school assemblies or community meetings.

Approaching Level

DIFFERENTIATED INSTRUCTION

Visual Persuasion Students who have difficulty speaking in front of the class may wish to create a persuasive poster, advertisement, or cartoon about a favorite topic or activity. Show them advertisements and political cartoons to help them get ideas. Have them briefly present their work to the class and explain the point that they have tried to convey.

Teach

Active Listening Remind students that active listening requires making connections to what they already know. **Say:** As you listen to your classmates' speeches, think about what you already know about the topic and how it relates to your own persuasive speech topic. However, you should listen with an open mind. Do not let your own biases affect your evaluations of your classmates' presentations.

Eye Contact Remind students that making eye contact will keep their audience engaged and interested. Advise them to make eye contact with many different audience members during their presentation.

(APPROACHING) Some students may be uncomfortable with making eye contact. Advise them to try looking at the spaces directly between their classmates' eyes instead. It will appear that they are making eye contact, and they will be less likely to become distracted and lose their train of thought.

 For help with creating presentations, see Student Presentation Builder on StudentWorks Plus.

 For Speaking, Listening, and Viewing Rubric, see Unit 4 Teaching Resources, pp. 279–282.

Learning Objectives
Delivering a persuasive presentation. (SE)
Evaluating evidence. (TE)

843

Focus

Summary

This workshop provides strategies for distinguishing between propaganda and objective reporting in the media. It includes a focus lesson on logical fallacies. It also asks students to identify the reasoning strategies used in two primary documents: a propaganda poster and a radio news transcript.

Teach

Literary History ☆

An Early Media Critic The nineteenth-century English satirist Samuel Butler is known for his witty criticisms of many Victorian institutions, including the mainstream news press. Share with students the following quotation by Butler: "The most important service rendered by the press and the magazines is that of educating people to approach printed matter with distrust."

 For video presentations related to this workshop, see Media Workshop DVD.

Learning Objectives

For pages 844–847

In this workshop, you will focus on the following objectives:

Media Literacy:

Distinguishing between propaganda and ethical reasoning strategies in print and nonprint media.

Explaining how text features, such as captions and illustrations, aid the reader's understanding.

The *Little Red Book,* a collection of Mao Tse-tung's ideas, spread propaganda about the Chinese Communist Party during Mao's rule.

Media Workshop

Analyze Media Messages

Literature Connection Bei Dao's poem "Answer" questions the authority of China's ruling Communist Party. One key difference between a communist and a democratic country is freedom of the press—a freedom guaranteed in the First Amendment to the U.S. Constitution. Communist countries like China (and the former Soviet Union) control the press—one way in which governments can control information and shape the beliefs of their people.

Forms of Media

Everyday you encounter different types of media messages. **Print media,** such as newspapers, magazines, books, and billboards, convey their messages through the printed word and still images. **Electronic media,** such as radio, television, CDs, DVDs, movies, videotapes, documentary films, and the Internet, rely on the power of moving images and sound to convey their messages.

The type of media helps determine the message and the way it will affect you as a reader, listener, or viewer. Think of the difference between reading an ad in a magazine for an amazing new product and then watching a TV commercial of the product in action. Imagine reading a brochure about a political candidate and then hearing her speak on the radio. Each type of media has specific characteristics that are used to elicit specific reactions from its intended audience.

Media Strategies

Propaganda is a form of communication that distorts facts or presents misleading information in order to promote the ideas of an organization or a government. Creators of propaganda use images, words, sounds, and moving images to attempt to shape the audience's attitude. **Objective reporting**—the goal of responsible news journalism—is a presentation of the known facts that allow the audience to make reasoned decisions about a subject. However, even in objective reporting, the news creators' viewpoints affect their choice of images, text, and sound. Refer to the media strategy checklist to help you analyze, or deconstruct, media messages you encounter.

844 UNIT 4 EAST ASIA AND THE PACIFIC

Writing Practice

 Write an Advertising Slogan Explain to students that advertising slogans are memorable "catchphrases," such as Nike's "Just do it." Point out that these phrases are often vague and sometimes have very little to do with the product itself, but they are usually clever or emotionally affecting. Ask students to recall and share slogans associated with specific products. Then pass around slips of paper with types of products written on them, such as "soft drink," "car," or "shampoo." Have each student write a slogan to advertise the product they have been assigned. Encourage them to use at least one of the logical fallacies described on page 845. Have them present their slogans to the class and explain why they think they would appeal to a particular audience.

Strategy		Questions to Ask Yourself
source	☑	Who created the media message? How does the source affect what you see or do not see?
purpose	☑	What is the goal for creating the media message? To inform? To persuade? To entertain?
word choice	☑	How do the creators of the media use language to express their message to the audience? Do they use figurative language? Technical language? How does the word choice affect the intended message?
cultural elements	☑	Does the message transmit cultural values or beliefs? Are the creators of the message trying to reflect the beliefs of a particular group or nation?
symbols	☑	Does the message use symbols or cultural icons? How are those symbols intended to affect the viewer?
target audience	☑	How do the creators of the message tailor the content to the intended audience? Are stereotypes of people used to sway the audience?
design elements and/ or film techniques	☑	How have the creators visually composed the message? Do visual elements such as color, line, shape, or texture enhance the message? Are film techniques or special effects used to manipulate a viewer's response?

> **Focus Lesson**

Persuasive Techniques: Logical Fallacies

Many media messages use persuasive techniques to urge readers, viewers, or listeners to agree with a viewpoint or to take action. Sometimes media creators use logical fallacies, or errors in reasoning, to sway audiences. Propagandists rely heavily on ideas or arguments that *sound* logical but are not supported with actual facts or proof. Try to spot the following types of logical fallacies in all forms of media:

- *ad hominem* shifting attention away from a person's views by attacking the person
- **false cause** inaccurately drawing a cause-and-effect relationship between two events that follow one after another
- **red herring** dodging an issue by changing the subject
- **overgeneralization** making a sweeping statement without solid supporting evidence
- **bandwagon** urging the audience to think or act like everyone else
- **either-or fallacy** presenting only two possible sides or solutions instead of showing a broader range of choices

> **Activity**
>
> **Examine Media Strategies**
>
> Use the Media Strategies chart to examine a magazine or TV ad. Write a one-paragraph summary explaining how the ad used some of the strategies to convey its message.

Media Workshop

Analyze Media Messages

Teach

Reading Strategy | 1

Connect to Personal Experience Explain to students that ad hominem appeals try to distract audiences by attacking a person's character, rather than focusing on his or her actual actions or positions. **Ask:** In what type of media have you seen this strategy used? (*Students may mention commercials for political campaigns.*) Explain that, just as an individual's reputation can be used by propagandists to create negative associations with a product or idea, it can also be used to create positive associations.

Activity

Summaries should include specific details from the ad, cite at least four media strategies from the chart, and explain how they are used in the ad.

Learning Objectives
Examining media strategies. (SE)
Writing an advertising slogan. (TE)
Comparing and contrasting. (TE)
Connecting to personal experience. (TE)

Write an Advertising Slogan Students who are struggling with the Writing Practice activity on page 844 may benefit from a more limited, structured assignment. Place these students in a homogeneous group and have them all write slogans for the same type of product. Assign each individual student a different approach to use in their slogan: ad hominem, false cause, red herring, overgeneralization, bandwagon, or either-or fallacy. Show them advertisements that are examples of each of these approaches. Encourage students to model their slogans on these examples.

Reflect on Advertising After advanced learners have written their advertising slogans, encourage them to discuss the role advertising plays in society. Ask students if they can think of situations in which the logical fallacies listed above have been used for noble or beneficial purposes. (*Students may mention that political activists have often used these same techniques to get their points across.*)

Teach

Viewing Skills

Identify Audience Remind students that all media, whether they include words, sounds, or images, have been created to appeal to a specific audience. **Ask:** Who is the intended audience for this poster? Explain. *(Students will probably say that the intended audience is China's youth, because the poster portrays a group of happy, attractive young people.)*

Activity

1. Students may say that Mao Zedong is a magnetic leader and teacher who captivates Chinese youth with his wisdom.

2. Many students may use descriptive words such as light, pale, airy, or muted.

3. Many students may say bandwagon because Mao is the center of attention and is surrounded by worshipping admirers—both young men and young women: "Everybody loves Mao and you should too."

4. The seaside setting, where Mao and a group of young people gather near the shore, reinforces the figurative meaning of "strong winds and strong waves."

Media Impact: **Propaganda Poster**

Build Background Propaganda posters are usually very simple. They are intended to convey one clear idea. In this poster from the 1960s, Chairman Mao Tse-tung, one of the key leaders of the communist revolution in China, is celebrated as the center of Chinese life. Mao adapted Soviet Union-style communism to his own purposes in China.

Activity

Listening and Speaking

Meet in a small group to discuss the following questions:

1. What is the basic message of this propaganda poster?

2. How would you describe the colors the artist used in this poster?

3. Review the list of logical fallacies on page 845. Which fallacy do you think best applies to the message in this poster? Explain your choice.

4. How does the image reflect the caption of the poster?

Design Element

Mao is the focal point here. Notice how brightly the sun is shining on his yellow shirt.

Symbol

Mao, the great teacher, is surrounded by young people, who symbolize China's future. They are eagerly listening to his every word. Notice how most of them are looking at the seated Mao.

Design Element

The backdrop is an open space near water. Notice the warm colors of the ground and the brightness of the beautiful blue sky that surrounds Mao and his students.

紧跟毛主席　在大风大浪中锻炼成长

Closely following Chairman Mao, let us train and develop in strong winds and strong waves.

Text Feature

The caption uses metaphors—"strong winds and strong waves"—to suggest Mao's powerful influence on shaping young minds.

 **Literature** Online

Media Literacy For project ideas, templates, and media analysis guides, go to glencoe.com and enter QuickPass code GLW6053u4.

Speaking and Listening Practice

Analyze Media Coverage Divide students into groups and assign each group a current event or political issue that is receiving national media attention. Have the group members divide the responsibility of gathering newspaper and magazine articles, videotapes or notes on television reports, and Internet accounts of the event or issue. Then have the groups compare and critique the media coverage using the strategies described in this workshop. Have the groups decide which source has the best coverage, and which has the worst. Then have them present their choice and an explanation to the rest of the class.

Media Impact: **News Transcript**

Build Background In the past two decades, China not only has become one of the most powerful economic forces in the world, but also has developed one of the largest militaries in the world. In this radio news report, broadcast the week before China celebrated the 80th anniversary of the founding of the People's Liberation Army by men like Mao Tse-tung, a National Public Radio reporter visited Beijing's Military Museum to see an exhibit of China's newest weaponry and military technology.

TRANSCRIPT

REPORTER ANTHONY KUHN: The exhibit features *Top Gun*-style videos showing China's latest military hardware in action. Out in the parking lot are tanks, fighter jets, and a vehicle that looks an awful lot like a Hum-Vee. The videos of new submarines and missiles highlight the Chinese military's shifting emphasis from fighting defensive wars on its own turf to projecting power beyond its borders.

[Short quote of Chinese soldier explaining a new technology in Chinese]

KUHN: One young soldier shows off China's advances in military satellite technology. With a few touches on a large screen, the view zooms in from miles above down to a Chinese city with clearly marked buildings and streets. So how accurate is the map, I ask, and when did the military start using these things?

[Short quote of soldier answering Kuhn's question in Chinese]

KUHN: "It's not convenient for me to say," he replies. It's not clear from the exhibit just how much of China's army, known as the PLA, actually has such advanced weaponry and information technology. Experts say that while some elite units have it, much of China's military lags behind the U.S. by a generation or more.

Activity

Listening and Speaking

Take notes as you watch a local TV newscast about a political event. Then respond to the following questions:

1. What visual images did you find striking? Why?

2. Did anyone shown on the newscast use propaganda? If so, give examples.

3. Was the news report objective? Why or why not?

Cultural Perspective

The reporter uses a reference to an American military movie to describe the style of the videos.

Sound Reasoning

The reporter makes a reasonable statement about the purpose of the exhibit based on the facts he has learned.

Objective Reporting

The soldier's answer to the reporter's question reveals the tight control the Chinese government maintains over its citizens.

Sources

The reporter cites experts in Chinese military history to add validity to his report.

Teach

Political History

The Peoples Liberation Army
With more than two million members, the Peoples Liberation Army (PLA) is the world's largest army. Founded during a 1927 communist uprising against the Nationalists, the PLA was originally called the Red Army. In recent years, China has taken steps to depoliticize and professionalize the PLA, forming a college-based training corps and reducing the amount of political education its members must undergo. However, the PLA still retains strong ties to its political roots.

Activity

1. Answers will vary. Students should cite specific visual images from the newscast, describe the images, and explain their impact.

2. Answers will vary. Students should cite specific examples (either images or spoken words) from the newscast and provide reasonable support for their interpretations of propaganda.

3. Answers will vary. Students should note if the news report was fair, balanced, and factual.

English Learners

DIFFERENTIATED INSTRUCTION

Advanced Distinguishing shades of meaning among synonyms may be difficult for English learners. In reviewing news sources for the Speaking and Listening Practice activity on page 846, they may see such sentences as *The mayor refused to comment on the issue* (hints that the mayor may have had something to hide) or *The mayor declined to comment on the issue* (uses the more neutral declined to suggest that the mayor had nothing to say).

Have English learners work in pairs with native English speakers to select words from their news accounts whose synonyms might have slanted the story differently. Have them use the words in sentences and discuss how they change the meanings of the sentences.

Learning Objectives
Analyzing propaganda. (SE)
Analyzing a newscast. (SE)
Analyzing media coverage. (TE)

Focus

Summary

The purpose of this feature is to interest students in reading additional literature by East Asian, Southeast Asian, and Pacific writers. Classic fiction and nonfiction by modern writers of the regions are represented in the profiled works.

Teach

Literary History ☆

In the Author's Words

JoAn D. Criddle said of her desire to aid Cambodian refugees, "My husband and I, along with four other couples, knew that we could do little to relieve the suffering of the thousands upon thousands of Southeast Asians seeking aid. But we could make a difference in the life of at least one refugee by becoming sponsors. Teeda But Mam and her family arrived in Davis, California, in March 1980. In August, her family of thirteen moved into our home." Hearing their stories of living in Cambodia under Communist rule prompted Criddle to write *To Destroy You Is No Loss.*

Independent Reading

Literature of the Region

THE LITERATURE OF EAST ASIA AND THE PACIFIC SHOWS THE ENDURING influence of traditions such as Confucian ethics and Buddhist spirituality. These works often detail the virtues of leadership and family ties, the meditative power of nature and rural life, and the intrigue of romance and court life. Many contemporary authors from this region explore the adaptability of traditional values to the modern age. Others detail the ravaging effects of war and oppression.

A Healing Family

Kenzaburo Oe

Although doctors urged Oe and his wife to let their disabled baby die, Oe refused. In this memoir, the Nobel Prize–winning novelist explores his life raising a special-needs child. Despite severe disabilities, Hikari, Oe's son, has become an accomplished composer of classical music. Oe writes, "The central theme of my work . . . has been the way my family has managed to live with this handicapped child. Indeed, . . . the very ideas that I hold about society and the world at large . . . are based on and learned through living with him."

To Destroy You Is No Loss: The Odyssey of a Cambodian Family

JoAn D. Criddle

In 1975, Pol Pot led the Khmer Rouge to victory in a Cambodian civil war and soon began a reign of terror. All residents of cities were evacuated to the countryside to live in labor camps and work in collective agriculture. Teeda Butt Mam, then fifteen, and her family were among those who endured four years of oppression, torture, killings, and starvation. The author narrates their efforts to stay alive and their frightening escape from war and famine, finding their way to a refugee camp in Thailand and then to a new life in California.

Reading Practice

Analyze Tone As they read independently, have students think about the writers' intentions and motivations in creating the works. Were they meant to

- inform?
- entertain?
- persuade?

Have them also consider the tone of each work. Does it convey

- humor?
- anguish?
- sarcasm?
- romance?

Tell students to think of a word that describes the tone of each work and place that word in the middle of a word web. Students should complete the web by writing words or phrases from the work that help communicate the tone.

Fallen Angels

Walter Dean Myers

Myers describes the horrors of the Vietnam War through the eyes of Richie Perry, a young, confused American GI who enters combat when he is only seventeen years old. On the front lines, Perry fights to stay alive and struggles to understand why he and his comrades are there at all.

GLENCOE
LITERATURE
LIBRARY

Picture Bride

Yoshiko Uchida

A young woman travels from her home in Japan to San Francisco, California, to marry a man she has never met. In America, she faces hard work, prejudice, and difficult circumstances with courage and dignity. She and her husband deal with the sometimes hostile conditions of their new land and find comfort in the warmth and closeness of the Japanese community.

CRITICS' CORNER

"Lady Murasaki invented the modern novel almost a thousand years ago. In [The Tale of Genji's] portrayal of complex, three-dimensional characters in a fully developed social and historical context . . . she has anticipated Henry James, Marcel Proust, Virginia Woolf, and other novelists of the modern sensibility."

—M. Thomas Inge, from "Lady Murasaki and the Craft of Fiction"

The Tale of Genji

Murasaki Shikibu

The Tale of Genji, generally considered the world's first novel, consists of a series of tales about Genji, a handsome and talented prince who is unable to succeed his father as emperor because of his mother's inferior status at court. The novel follows Genji's artistic and romantic pursuits, painting a picture of the social norms, moral codes, and gender relations of the day.

 Write a Review

Read one of the books listed here and write a review of it for your classmates. Include reasons why your classmates might enjoy the book as well as suggestions on how they might overcome difficulties in reading it. Present your review to your classmates.

Independent Reading

Teach

Glencoe Literature Library

Glencoe Literature Library offers an extensive collection of hardcover books that help you encourage your students to read independently. Choose among the more than 120 full-length literary works—novels, novellas, plays, and nonfiction. Each book includes related readings from a broad range of genres. Go to glencoe.com for more information.

> For access to all study guides for the Glencoe Literature Library, see the Literature Library Teacher Resources CD-ROM.

> To create customized reading lists from a database of more than 30,000 titles, use BookLink K-12 CD-ROM.

Assess

Write a Review

Students' reviews should

- present an assessment of the book
- include reasons why classmates would enjoy the book
- include suggestions on how one might overcome difficulties in reading the book

Approaching Level

DIFFERENTIATED INSTRUCTION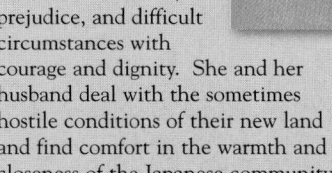

Analyze Character To help less proficient readers better comprehend the works they read, have them write character sketches, describing each of the major characters from their books. Remind students to describe each character's appearance, personality, and role in the story. Also have students note how cultural forces from the novel's historical period, such as political climate and national identity, may have affected the characters. These sketches may help students better understand and predict characters' actions in the works.

Learning Objectives
Reading literature independently. (SE)
Writing a review. (SE)
Analyzing tone. (TE)

Focus

Have students think of past exams in which they did not perform as well as they had hoped. **Ask:** What did you learn from these exams? What did you do differently to perform better on the next one? *(Possible answers: Study well in advance versus cramming; read directions thoroughly; stay calm.)*

Teach

Assessment

Tell students that this Assessment section will provide reinforcement in general test-taking strategies and will test them in the skills and vocabulary taught in this unit. Students will read a fiction selection and will answer context, comprehension, and inference questions. Then they will choose answers for ten sentence-completion items and ten paragraph-improvement items. Lastly, they will be asked to write a short essay based on a prompt.

Reading Practice

Skimming Explain that skimming involves looking over an entire selection quickly to get a general idea of what the piece is about. Skimming gives the reader a general idea of a selection's content. An effective way to practice skimming is to read, as quickly as possible, the first sentence and the last sentence of every paragraph. The more students practice this method, the easier it will become, as students will learn to look for key verbs and nouns. Suggest that students practice this technique using magazine or newspaper articles.

Assessment

English–Language Arts

Reading: Fiction

Carefully read the following passage. Use context clues to help you define any words with which you are unfamiliar. Pay close attention to **themes, cultural context, author's purpose,** and the use of **literary devices.** Then, on a separate sheet of paper, answer the questions on pages 851–852.

"Peach-Blossom Spring" by T'ao Ch'ien
Translated by David Hinton

During the T'ai-yüan years [376–397 A.D.] of the Chin Dynasty, there was a man in Wu-ling who caught fish for a living. One day he went up a stream, and soon didn't know how far he'd gone. Suddenly, he came upon a peach orchard in full bloom. For hundreds of feet, there was nothing but peach
5　trees crowding in over the banks. And in the confusion of fallen petals, there were lovely, scented flowers. The fisherman was amazed. Wanting to see how far the orchard went, he continued on.

　　The trees ended at the foot of a mountain, where a spring fed the stream from a small cave. It seemed as if there might be a light inside, so the fisher-
10　man left his boat and stepped in. At first, the cave was so narrow he could barely squeeze through. But he kept going and, after a few dozen feet, it opened out into broad daylight. There, on a plain stretching away, austere houses were graced with fine fields and lovely ponds. Dikes and paths crossed here and there among mulberries and bamboo. Roosters and dogs
15　called back and forth. Coming and going in the midst of all this, there were men and women tending the fields. Their clothes were just like those worn by the people outside. And whether they were old with white hair or children in pigtails, they were all happy and of themselves content.

　　When they saw the fisherman, they were terribly surprised and asked
20　where he had come from. Once he had answered all their questions, they insisted on taking him back home. And soon, they had set out wine and killed chickens for dinner. When the others in the village heard about this man, they all came to ask about him. They told him how, long ago, to escape those years of turmoil during the Ch'in Dynasty [221–207 B.C.], the village
25　ancestors gathered their wives and children, and with their neighbors came to this distant place. And never leaving, they'd kept themselves cut-off from the people outside ever since. So now they wondered what dynasty it was. They'd never heard of the Han [203 B.C.–A.D. 220], let alone Wei [A.D. 386–535] or Chin. As the fisherman carefully told them everything he knew,

30 they all sighed in sad amazement. Soon, each of the village families had
    invited him to their house, where they also served wine and food.
        After staying for some days, the fisherman prepared to leave these people.
    As he was going, they said *There's no need to tell the people outside*. He
    returned to his boat and started back, careful to remember each pace along
35 the way.
        When he got back home, he went to tell the prefect what had happened,
    and the prefect sent some men to retrace the route with him. They tried to
    follow the landmarks he remembered, but they were soon lost and finally
    gave up the search.
40   Liu Tzu-chi, who lived in Nan-yang, was a recluse of great honor and
    esteem. When he heard about this place, he joyfully prepared to go there.
    But before he could, he got sick and passed away. Since then, no one's asked
    the Way.

1. What is the author's primary purpose in
    describing the peach orchard in lines 3–7?
    A. to show the danger of being drawn in by
        beauty
    B. to comment on the joys of cultivating
        plants
    C. to set a mood of confusion and distress
    D. to create an atmosphere of mystery and
        beauty

2. Why does the fisherman enter the small cave?
    F. He thinks he sees a light inside.
    G. He is enticed by the lovely, scented
        flowers.
    H. He is amazed.
    J. He wants to see the extent of the
        orchard.

3. Where does the fisherman find the village?
    A. in the middle of a peach orchard
    B. at the top of a mountain
    C. inside a large cave at the beginning of a
        stream
    D. past the peach orchard, through a small
        cave at the beginning of the stream

4. From the second paragraph, what can be
    inferred about the author's view of nature?
    F. The author sees nature as a constant
        threat to humans.
    G. The author thinks humans should live in
        harmony with nature.
    H. The author believes that humans
        inevitably destroy nature.
    J. The author finds humans more interesting
        than nature.

5. As it is used in line 18, the word *content* most
    nearly means:
    A. subject matter.
    B. satisfied.
    C. substance.
    D. ignorant.

6. At what point do the villagers set out wine
    and kill chickens?
    F. after they insist on taking the fisherman
        back home
    G. after the fisherman leaves
    H. before the fisherman answers all of their
        questions
    J. before they see the fisherman

ASSESSMENT **851**

1. **D** is the correct answer. The
   story does not address the
   themes in **A** and **B**, so both are
   incorrect. **C** does not accurately
   describe the mood of the story,
   so it is incorrect. `DOK 2`

2. **F** is the correct answer. **G, H,** and
   J are all reasons the fisherman
   continues his journey, but **F** is
   why he enters the cave. `DOK 1`

3. **D** is the correct answer. The
   fisherman travels upstream,
   through the orchard, to the head
   of the stream. There he finds a
   small cave leading to the village.
   `DOK 1`

4. **G** is the correct answer. The images
   in the second paragraph, such as
   "fine fields and lovely ponds" and
   "men and women tending the
   fields," suggest peace and harmony with nature. `DOK 4`

5. **B** is the correct answer. The
   context implies that *happy* and
   content have similar meanings.
   `DOK 2`

6. **F** is the correct answer. The
   villagers set out wine and kill
   chickens after the fisherman
   answered all of their questions
   and after they insisted on taking
   him back home. `DOK 1`

Approaching Level

DIFFERENTIATED INSTRUCTION

Monitor Comprehension Tell students
that the reading-comprehension questions on the ACT measure their ability to
understand and interpret what they read.
Remind them that they should try to read
each passage quickly and spend most of
their time on answering questions. They
can return to the passage to find the specific details they need in order to answer
questions. For the ACT, they should leave

themselves a little time at the end of the
section to review their answers and fill
in any they have skipped with their best
guesses.

Advanced Learners/Pre-AP

DIFFERENTIATED INSTRUCTION

Handling Recall Questions Advanced
students might be misled by questions on
standardized tests asking them to recall
information. Remind students that, although
they may wish to make their own interpretations of passages, some questions will
probably concern only the details explicitly
stated. With such questions, students
should merely answer the question using
only the literal information from the text.

Assessment

English-Language Arts

Assess

7. A is the correct answer. The villagers "were terribly surprised and asked where he had come from." [DOK 1]

8. H is the correct answer. The author explicitly states that the village ancestors wanted to escape turmoil. [DOK 1]

9. A is the correct answer. The villagers do not wish they had not left the outside world, so **B** is incorrect. The villagers are not frustrated or melancholy, so **C** and **D** are incorrect. [DOK 4]

10. J is the correct answer. Based on the villagers' disapproval of the outside world, it can be inferred they think such contact would harm their society. [DOK 4]

11. B is the correct answer. The context implies that the prefect has authority over the men. [DOK 2]

12. J is the correct answer. The ancestors' escape during the Ch'in (or Qin) Dynasty is explained in lines 29–33. [DOK 1]

13. C is the correct answer. Lines 48–50 suggest that the village and its inhabitants remain a mystery. It is possible but not certain that the fisherman imagined, dreamed, or fabricated the village. [DOK 2]

14. H is the correct answer. The passage contrasts the outside world with the peaceful lifestyle of the village and emphasizes the difficulty of "returning" to the village. [DOK 2]

---

7. How do the people in the village react when the fisherman arrives?
   A. They are frightened and confused.
   B. They treat him irreverently and ridicule him.
   C. They are intrigued and ask him many questions.
   D. They immediately begin telling him the story of their escape from the outside world.

8. The residents of the village cut themselves off from the outside world because:
   I. they wanted to explore uncharted lands.
   II. they were banished by the leaders of the Ch'in Dynasty.
   III. they wanted to escape turmoil.
   F. I only
   G. II only
   H. III only
   J. II and III

9. According to the passage, the phrase "sad amazement" (line 30) implies that:
   A. the villagers are surprised and disappointed at their lack of knowledge about the outside world.
   B. the villagers wholeheartedly regret having left the outside world.
   C. the villagers are frustrated with their own ignorance about the outside world.
   D. the villagers are melancholy by nature.

10. What is the most likely explanation for the villagers' warning that "there's no need to tell the people outside" (line 33)?
    F. They think outsiders already know about their society.
    G. They are afraid they will be punished for fleeing if they are discovered.
    H. They are ashamed of their simple way of life.
    J. They fear that contact with the outside world would destroy their way of life.

11. As it is used in line 36, the word *prefect* most nearly means:
    A. monk
    B. high official
    C. fisherman
    D. servant

12. At what point did the ancestors of the villagers escape to the secret place?
    F. During the T'ai-yüan years of the Chin Dynasty
    G. After the Han Dynasty
    H. After the Wei Dynasty
    J. During the Ch'in Dynasty

13. What is the main insight suggested by the statement in lines 37–39 ("They tried... search")?
    A. The people from outside are uninterested in the past.
    B. The men are unable to trace the route because the village does not exist.
    C. The place the men are searching for remains a mystery.
    D. The fisherman dreams up the village and its inhabitants and tells the prefect in order to gain respect.

14. Which of the following best states the theme of this story?
    F. Cutting oneself off from society leads to sadness and ignorance.
    G. True adventurers do not need plans or directions to guide them.
    H. Society has lost its connection to the peaceful, harmonious lifestyle of the past.
    J. We are actually not so different from those we view as outsiders.

 To create custom assessments online, go to Progress Reporter Online Assessment.

Vocabulary Skills: Sentence Completion

For each item in the Vocabulary Skills section, choose the word or words that best complete the sentence. Write your answers on a separate sheet of paper.

1. Although Confucius's _____ for moral behavior are strict, they are not yet _____, for many people still follow them today.
   A. extents...undulant
   B. accomplices...glittering
   C. reprisals...perpetual
   D. dictates...obsolete

2. Zen masters teach their students to _____ long periods of meditation.
   F. endure
   G. flag
   H. banish
   J. chastise

3. Although he had served as a statesman and a soldier, Nguyen Trai was accused of being a(n) _____ in a murder plot against the king.
   A. accomplice
   B. intransigence
   C. prelude
   D. tempo

4. Samurai _____ follow a training regimen, refrain from pursuing their own pleasures, and show allegiance only to their lords.
   F. assiduously
   G. frantically
   H. plaintively
   J. furtively

5. Because of a severe shortage of food, citizens under the rule of the Khmer Rouge often had to _____ to stay alive.
   A. detest
   B. tamper
   C. forage
   D. trample

6. Bei Dao _____ for freedom, so he resigned from the Red Guards and joined the pro-democracy movement.
   F. banished
   G. foraged
   H. tainted
   J. yearned

7. Because of China's _____ economic growth in recent years, experts _____ that the country's economy will soon surpass that of Germany.
   A. trivial...flag
   B. vigorous...anticipate
   C. glittering...gesticulate
   D. congealed...yearn

8. The Maori, the indigenous people of New Zealand, paid _____ to their gods by decorating their bodies and faces with tattoos.
   F. prelude
   G. homage
   H. extent
   J. tempo

9. A trek through one of New Zealand's national parks is not for the _____, but strong hikers will enjoy exploring the majestic volcanoes and _____ rain forests.
   A. docile...imploring
   B. frail...lush
   C. marvelous...ruddy
   D. inquisitive...congealed

10. Outback Australia, a brutal expanse of desert, is _____ visited by city dwellers.
    F. frantically
    G. plaintively
    H. seldom
    J. assiduously

To create custom assessments using software, use ExamView Assessment Suite.

Assessment
English-Language Arts

Assess

1. **D** is the correct answer. "Many people still follow them today" is another way of saying they are "not obsolete." DOK 2

2. **F** is the correct answer. Zen masters teach their students to *endure,* or sit through, long periods of meditation. DOK 2

3. **A** is the correct answer. Nguyen Trai was accused of being an *accomplice,* or assistant, in a murder plot. DOK 2

4. **F** is the correct answer. Samurai *assiduously,* or diligently, follow a training regimen. DOK 2

5. **C** is the correct answer. Because of a severe shortage of food, citizens under the rule of the Khmer Rouge had to *forage,* or scrounge, for food. DOK 2

6. **J** is the correct answer. Bei Dao *yearned* for, or strongly desired, freedom. DOK 2

7. **B** is the correct answer. China's *vigorous,* or high-paced, economic growth has caused analysts to *anticipate,* or forecast, that the country's economy will soon surpass that of Germany. DOK 2

8. **G** is the correct answer. The Maori paid *homage,* or tribute, to their gods by decorating their bodies with tattoos. DOK 2

9. **B** is the correct answer. Trekking through national parks is not for the *frail,* or weak. Hikers will enjoy the *lush,* or thriving, rain forests. DOK 2

10. **H** is the correct answer. City dwellers *seldom,* or infrequently, visit outback Australia. DOK 2

Assess

1. **B** is the correct answer. *For* is the correct preposition. (DOK 1)

2. **H** is the correct answer. The adjective *wasted*, not the gerund *wasting*, should modify *potential*. The verb form *means* should be changed to *mean*, so **G** is incorrect. (DOK 1)

Grammar and Writing Skills: Paragraph Improvement

Read carefully through the following passage from the first draft of a student's essay. Choose the best answer to each question or the best alternative for each word or phrase that is underlined and numbered. If you think the original version is best, choose "NO CHANGE." Write your answers on a separate sheet of paper.

Though teenagers make up only 6.4 percent of all drivers in the United States, they account <u>by</u> 14
₁
percent of all drivers in fatal accidents (Allstate 1). <u>Traffic deaths of these mean wasting</u> potential and
₂
devastation to families. Preventing these deaths should be a top priority in our state. However, lawmakers have proposed a misguided solution to this many-layered problem: raising the driving age from 16 to 18. This law would not reduce <u>the</u>
₃
<u>number of fatal crashes, and it would only</u> create a new set of obstacles for teenagers trying to achieve independence.

Of course, lawmakers are right to draw our attention to the high teen accident rate. "Teen drivers ages 16 to 19 are four times more likely than older drivers to crash" (Insurance Institute for Highway Safety 2005). However, it does not make sense to attribute this higher incidence of crashes to immaturity. <u>Two thirds of teens killed in car crashes</u>
₄
in 2003 were males (Allstate 2). People become good drivers not because they are mature but
₅
because they <u>extensively</u> have practiced.
₆
<u>So</u> raising the driving age would only cause there to be more inexperienced drivers, who would be just as likely to crash as their younger counterparts. Instead of taking away a 16-year-old's chance to drive, authorities would be better off requiring he or she to spend extra hours behind the wheel with an instructor's supervision before obtaining a license.**7**
₈
[1] Students with working parents often <u>needed</u> to provide their own after-school transportation. [2] Raising the driving age would also place unfair constraints on teenagers' activities. [3] Without the ability to drive, they would be forced to give up their activities. [4] Many high school students live in areas without reliable public transportation, but
₉
<u>enjoy participating in after-school clubs, working part time, or to play sports.</u>

1. **A.** NO CHANGE
    B. for
    C. into
    D. to

2. **F.** NO CHANGE
    G. These deaths in traffic means wasted
    H. These traffic deaths mean wasted
    J. Traffic deaths of these sorts mean wasting

Writing Practice

Avoid Unnecessary Words Remind students that the clearest and most effective writing is simple and direct. A sentence should most often contain only necessary words; a paragraph, only necessary sentences. In paragraph improvement segments, editing often includes cutting out unnecessary words. Practice with identifying excessive words will help students achieve higher scores on the paragraph improvement section of standardized tests.

Write the following phrases on the board, instructing students to rephrase the underlined portions to eliminate unnecessary words:

<u>He is a man who</u> swims every day. *(He swims every day.)*

Sheila refuses to swim <u>for the reason that</u> she is afraid of the water. *(Sheila refuses to swim because she is afraid of the water.)*

The lifeguard, <u>in a rapid manner</u>, dove into the pool. *(The lifeguard rapidly dove into the pool.)*

<u>Owing to the fact that</u> it's raining, the pool is closed. *(Since/Because it's raining, the pool is closed.)*

3. **A.** NO CHANGE
   B. the number of fatal crashes, would only
   C. the number of fatal crashes; it would only
   D. the number of fatal crashes; and it would only

4. **F.** NO CHANGE
   G. Two-thirds of car crashes in 2003 involved male teens (Allstate 2).
   H. Male teens accounted for about two thirds of teen car crash victims in 2003.
   J. OMIT the underlined portion

5. **A.** NO CHANGE
   B. (Place after *because*)
   C. (Place after *practiced*)
   D. (Place after *have*)

6. **F.** NO CHANGE
   G. (Begin new paragraph) To summarize,
   H. (Begin new paragraph) In addition,
   J. (Do NOT begin new paragraph) So

7. Suppose the writer changed the verb *taking* in the preceding sentence to *snatching*. This change would make the sentence more:
   A. biased
   B. straightforward
   C. positive
   D. ambiguous

8. **F.** NO CHANGE
   G. will be needed
   H. needing
   J. need

9. **A.** NO CHANGE
   B. enjoy participating in after-school clubs, work part time, or to play sports
   C. enjoy participating in after-school clubs, working part time, or sports
   D. enjoy participating in after-school clubs, working part time, or playing sports

10. Which is the logical sequence of sentences in Paragraph 4?
    F. 4, 3, 2, 1
    G. 2, 1, 4, 3
    H. 3, 4, 1, 2
    J. 1, 2, 4, 3

Essay

In the *Tao Te Ching*, Lao-Tzu writes, "Do you want to improve the world? / I don't think it can be done / . . . If you tamper with it, you'll ruin it." Write a brief persuasive essay in which you argue for or against Lao-Tzu's claim. Be sure to include real-life examples to support your position. As you write, keep in mind that your essay will be evaluated for **ideas, organization, voice, word choice, sentence fluency, conventions, and presentation.**

Checklist for Your Writing

This checklist will help you do your best work. Make sure you do the following:

☑ Read the essay prompt carefully.

☑ Organize your writing with an introduction, a body, and a conclusion.

☑ Use specific evidence and logical reasoning to support your ideas.

☑ Use precise language that is appropriate for your audience and purpose.

☑ Edit for sentence fluency and conventions.

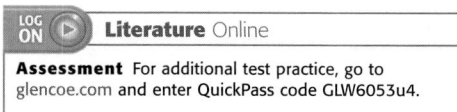

LOG ON ▶ **Literature** Online

Assessment For additional test practice, go to glencoe.com and enter QuickPass code GLW6053u4.

9. **D** is the correct answer. Only **D** is parallel in construction. DOK 4

10. **G** is the correct answer. Sentence 2 should be first because it is the main idea that the other sentences in the paragraph support. Sentence 1 introduces the idea that teens with working parents need to drive to after-school activities. Because Sentences 3 and 4 echo this idea, Sentence 1 should be second. Sentence 4 builds on the information provided in Sentence 1, so it should come third. Sentence 3 recapitulates the information in the paragraph, so it should be last. DOK 4

Assessment
English-Language Arts

Assess

3. **C** is the correct answer. A semicolon is used here to emphasize the connection between the two thoughts expressed in this sentence. DOK 1

4. **J** is the correct answer. The information in the underlined sentence is irrelevant to the debate. It should be omitted. DOK 1

5. **C** is the correct answer. The adverb *extensively* modifies the verb *practiced* and should immediately follow it. DOK 1

6. **J** is the correct answer. The sentence in question supports the argument from the preceding sentence. It does not begin a new argument or introduce a new main idea, so it should not begin a new paragraph. DOK 1

7. **A** is the correct answer. *Snatching* has a negative connotation, so changing the verb from *taking* to *snatching* would show that the writer is biased against the lawmakers and would jeopardize the writer's credibility. DOK 4

8. **J** is the correct answer. Students with working parents continue to provide their own after-school transportation, so the present-tense *need* makes the most sense. DOK 2

Essay

Students should support their opinions with specific examples and address counterarguments. Remind students that, although their persuasive essays will not be read aloud, they will still need to present their arguments using persuasive language and rhetorical devices. DOK 3

855

Skills Scope and Sequence

Readability Scores Key: Dale-Chall/DRP/Lexile

PART 1: Early Europe A.D. 400–1650

Selections and Features	Literary Elements
Part Introduction pp. 856–869	Literary Periods **SE** p. 868
Myth Ragnarok: The Twilight of the Gods, *from* **The Prose Edda,** by Snorri Sturluson, translated by Jean I. Young **5.8**/**56**/**1070** pp. 870–875	Description **SE** p. 871
Vocabulary Workshop p. 876	
Epic *from* **The Song of Roland,** translated by Frederick Goldin pp. 877–885	Epic **SE** p. 878
Poem Bisclavret: The Lay of the Werewolf, by Marie de France, translated by Robert Hanning and Joan Ferrante pp. 886–897	Suspense **SE** p. 887 Motivation (review) **SE** p. 896
Poem *from* **The Inferno,** *from* **The Divine Comedy,** by Dante Alighieri, translated by John Ciardi pp. 898–914	Allegory **SE** p. 899 Form (review) **SE** p. 913
Literary Perspective *from* **The Divine Comedy,** *from* **Seven Nights,** by Jorge Luis Borges, translated by Eliot Weinberger **7.6**/**59**/**970** pp. 915–917	
Comparing Literature Laura from **Canzionere** (sonnet), by Petrarch, translated by Morris Bishop **Sonnet 8** (sonnet), by Louise Labé, translated by Willis Barnstone **Secretly I am building in the heart** (sonnet), by Julia Alvarez pp. 918–925	Theme **SE** p. 918 Petrarchan Sonnet **SE** p. 920 Enjambment **TE** p. 921 Personification **TE** p. 923

Reading Skills and Strategies	Vocabulary	Writing / Grammar	Speaking, Listening, Viewing
Evaluate Historical Influences **SE** p. 862 Connect to the Literature **SE** p. 869	Context Clues **TE** p. 862 Word Parts **TE** p. 864	Write an Expository Paragraph **TE** p. 856 Create a Graphic Organizer **TE** p. 860 Ordinal Numbers with Dates **TE** p. 862 Create a Glossary **TE** p. 866 Parentheses **TE** p. 868 Take Notes **SE** p. 869	Panel Discussion **SE** p. 869 Visual Display **SE** p. 869
Summarize **SE** p. 871 Identify Sequence **TE** p. 872	Word Usage **SE** p. 875	Write a Retelling **TE** p. 874 Write a Description **SE** p. 875	View the Art **TE** p. 872
	Word Origins **SE** p. 876 Word Parts **TE** p. 876		
Evaluate Characters **SE** p. 878 Analyze Structure **TE** p. 878 Analyze Epic Hero **TE** p. 882	Word Origins **SE** p. 897 Analogies **TE** p. 884	Write a Character Sketch **SE** p. 885	Oral Interpretation **TE** p. 880 View the Art **SE** p. 881
Monitor Comprehension **SE** p. 887 Draw Conclusions About Culture **TE** p. 890	Context Clues **SE** p. 887 Academic Vocabulary **SE** p. 897	Semicolons **TE** p. 888 Write a Persuasive Argument **TE** p. 892 Write a Skit **SE** p. 897 Write an Evaluation **SE** p. 897	View the Art **TE** p. 888 Debate **TE** p. 894 Performance **SE** p. 897
Analyze Sound Devices **SE** p. 899 Visualize **TE** p. 900 Recognize Author's Purpose **TE** p. 908	Synonyms **SE** p. 913 Academic Vocabulary **SE** p. 913	Write a Research Report **TE** p. 904 Capitalization **TE** p. 910 Write an Expository Essay **SE** p. 914 Quotations in Text **SE** p. 914 Write an Allegory **TE** p. 914	Oral Report **TE** p. 902 View the Art **SE** p. 906 Oral Interpretation **TE** p. 906 Discussion **SE** p. 912
Determine Main Idea and Supporting Details **SE** p. 915 Analyze Theme **TE** p. 916		Write a Summary **SE** p. 917	
Compare Historical Context **SE** p. 918 Interpret Imagery **SE** p. 920	Synonyms **SE** p. 922	Research Art **TE** p. 920 Write a Sonnet **SE** p. 923 Write a Comparison-Contrast Essay **SE** p. 925	Discussion **SE** pp. 924, 925 Recitation **TE** p. 924 Visual Display **SE** p. 925

Readability Scores Key: Dale-Chall/DRP/Lexile

PART 1: Early Europe A.D. 400–1650 *(continued)*

PART 2: Modern Europe 1650–Present

Readability Scores Key: Dale-Chall/DRP/Lexile

PART 2: Modern Europe 1650–Present *(continued)*

Selections and Features	Literary Elements
Short Story How Much Land Does a Man Need? by Leo Tolstoy, translated by Louise and Aylmer Maude **7.8/55/860** pp. 983–999	Structure **SE** p. 984 Foreshadowing **TE** p. 996 Irony (review) **SE** p. 998
Grammar Workshop p. 1000	
Short Story The Bet, by Anton Chekhov, translated by Constance Garnett **6/59/940** pp. 1001–1011	Character **SE** p. 1002 Mood (review) **SE** p. 1010
Literary History The Symbolist Poets pp. 1012–1013	Literary Periods **SE** p. 1012 Literary Genres **SE** p. 1012
Short Story First Sorrow, by Franz Kafka, translated by Willa and Edwin Muir **9.9/62/1590** pp. 1014–1020	Tone **SE** p. 1015 Theme (review) **SE** p. 1019
Poem Lot's Wife, by Anna Akhmatova, translated by Richard Wilbur pp. 1021–1024	Rhyme Scheme **SE** p. 1022
Short Story War, by Luigi Pirandello, translated by Samuel Putnam **8/57/1170** pp. 1025–1031	Dialogue **SE** p. 1026 Characterization (review) **SE** p. 1030
Memoir Two Memories of Sido *from* **Earthly Paradise,** by Colette, translated by Una Vincenzo Troubridge and Enid McCleod **8.1/56/1020** pp. 1032–1040	Autobiography **SE** p. 1033 Repetition (review) **SE** p. 1039

Reading Skills and Strategies	Vocabulary	Writing Grammar	Speaking, Listening, and Viewing

Make Inferences About Theme
   SE p. 984
	Context Clues **SE** p. 998
	Academic Vocabulary
	   SE p. 998
		Write a Summary **TE** p. 984
		Write a Comparison-Contrast
		   Essay **TE** p. 992
		Active and Passive Voice
		   TE p. 994
		Write a Persuasive Essay
		   SE p. 999
		Sentence Structure **SE** p. 999
			View the Art **SE** p. 988
			Performance **TE** p. 990
			Discussion **SE** p. 997

		Main and Subordinate
		   Clauses **SE** p. 1000
		Punctuate Adverb Clauses
		   TE p. 1000	

Analyze Cause-and-Effect
   Relationships **SE** p. 1002
Monitor Comprehension **TE** p. 1004
Analyze Figurative Language
   TE p. 1006
Analyze theme **TE** p. 1008
	Connotation and Denotation
	   SE p. 1010
	Academic Vocabulary
	   SE p. 1010
		Write an Anecdote
		   TE p. 1002
		Write a Summary **SE** p. 1011
		Absolute Phrases **SE** p. 1011
			View the Art **SE** p. 1005
			Discussion **SE** p. 1009

Evaluate Historical Influences
   SE p. 1013
Connect to the Literature **SE** p. 1013
			Analyze Symbolist Art
			   TE p. 1012

Respond to Characters **SE** p. 1015	Word Usage **SE** p. 1020
	Academic Vocabulary
	   SE p. 1020
		Apply Tone in a Short Story
		   SE p. 1020
			Debate **TE** p. 1018

Connect to Personal
   Experience **SE** p. 1022
	Academic Vocabulary
	   SE p. 1024
		Write a Response **TE** p. 1022
		Write a Character Sketch
		   SE p. 1024	

Recognize Author's Purpose
   SE p. 1026
Analyze Characters **TE** p. 1026
	Word Parts **SE** p. 1031
	Academic Vocabulary
	   SE p. 1031
		Write an Interior
		   Monologue **TE** p. 1028
		Apply Dialogue in a
		   Short Story **SE** p. 1031
			View the Art **TE** p. 1027

Analyze Characterization **SE** p. 1033
Evaluate Dialogue **TE** p. 1034
	Antonyms **SE** p. 1039
	Academic Vocabulary
	   SE p. 1039
		Hyphens **TE** p. 1036
		Write a Biographical Narrative
		   SE p. 1040
		Idioms **SE** p. 1040
			View the Art **SE** p. 1036
			Discussion **SE** p. 1038

PART 2: Modern Europe 1650–Present *(continued)*

Selections and Features	Literary Elements
Poem The Guitar, by Federico García Lorca, translated by Robert Bly pp. 1041–1044	Sound Devices **SE** p. 1042
Poem Encounter, by Czesław Miłosz, translated by the author and Lillian Vallee pp. 1045–1048	Title **SE** p. 1046
Poem The World, My Friends, My Enemies, You, and the Earth, by Nazim Hikmet, translated by Randy Blasing and Mutlu Konuk pp. 1049–1053	Free Verse **SE** p. 1050
The Art of Translation The Dream of a Common Language pp. 1054–1055	
Essay The Myth of Sisyphus, by Albert Camus, translated by Justin O'Brien **9.2/60/890** pp. 1056–1062	Persuasion **SE** p. 1057 Symbol (review) **SE** p. 1061
Memoir *from* **Night,** by Elie Wiesel, translated by Marion Wiesel **5.5/45/380** pp. 1063–1071	Memoir **SE** p. 1064 Conflict (review) **SE** p. 1070
Poem Freedom to Breathe, by Aleksandr Solzhenitsyn, translated by Michael Glenny pp. 1072–1075	Prose Poetry **SE** p. 1073
Informational Text TIME: 60 Years of Risk Takers, by Yuri Zarakhovich pp. 1076–1081	
Writing Workshop pp. 1082–1091	
Speaking, Listening, and Viewing Workshop pp. 1092–1095	
Independent Reading pp. 1096–1097	
Assessment pp. 1098–1103	

Reading Skills and Strategies	Vocabulary	Writing Grammar	Speaking, Listening, and Viewing
Analyze Style **SE** p. 1042 Respond to Theme **TE** p. 1042	Academic Vocabulary **SE** p. 1044	Write a Song **SE** p. 1044	Performance **SE** p. 1044
Interpret Imagery **SE** p. 1046	Academic Vocabulary **SE** p. 1048	Write a Description **TE** p. 1046 Write a Dramatic Scene **SE** p. 1048	
Monitor Comprehension **SE** p. 1050 Analyze Structure **TE** p. 1050	Word Usage **SE** p. 1052 Context Clues **TE** p. 1050	Write a Letter **TE** p. 1052 Write a Poem **SE** p. 1053	
Analyze Cultural and Historical Context **SE** p. 1054 Understand the Nature of Language **SE** p. 1055			Debate **TE** p. 1054
Determine Main Idea and Supporting Details **SE** p. 1057 Identify Genre **TE** p. 1058	Word Origins **SE** p. 1062 Academic Vocabulary **SE** p. 1062	Apply Symbolism in an Essay **SE** p. 1062	Multimedia Presentation **TE** p. 1060
Evaluate Characters **SE** p. 1064 Make Inferences **TE** p. 1064	Synonyms **SE** p. 1071 Academic Vocabulary **SE** p. 1071	Write a Personal Response **TE** p. 1064 Conduct Internet Research **SE** p. 1071 Write Notes **SE** p. 1071	Oral Report **SE** p. 1071
Visualize **SE** p. 1073	Academic Vocabulary **SE** p. 1075	Write a Prose Poem **SE** p. 1075	Speech **TE** p. 1074
Evaluate Historical Influences **SE** p. 1076 Evaluate Evidence **TE** p. 1080	Context Clues **TE** p. 1076	Write a Summary **SE** p. 1081	Discussion **TE** p. 1078
	Prewrite **SE** p. 1083	Write a Biographical Investigation **SE** p. 1091	
Compare and Contrast **TE** p. 1094	Draft **SE** p. 1085	Write an Outline **SE** p. 1093 Create a Storyboard **SE** p. 1094	Multimedia Presentation **SE** p. 1095
Read Literature Independently **SE** p. 1096		Write an Interview **SE** p. 1097	Performance **SE** p. 1097
		Write an Essay **SE** p. 1103	Read Aloud **TE** p. 1102

Focus

Bellringer Option

**Literature Launcher
    Pre-Reading Video Unit 5**
**Daily Language Practice
    Transparency 80**

Or say: Among the continents, Europe is very small; only Australia is smaller. One country, Russia, is far larger than Europe, and several other countries, including Canada and the United States, are nearly as large. How do you think the size of Europe's influence on world history and culture has compared with its geographical size? Help students grasp that Europe has had an influence on the rest of the world far out of proportion to its size, resulting in an extraordinary spread of European languages and literatures, art and ideas, science and technology, and governmental and legal systems.

 *View the Art* ★

Answers will vary. Students might say the birds represent freedom or rebirth.

 For school-to-home activities, see Unit 5 Teaching Resources Book, pp. 5–11.

 For students who would profit from independent novel study, see Novel Companion, pp. 207–250.

Le Trait d'Union, 1942. René Magritte. Oil on Canvas, 60 x 150 cm. Private collection. © ARS, NY.

View the Art Magritte is known for his Surrealist paintings. What might the birds in this painting represent?

Writing Practice

Write an Expository Paragraph Have students select a European language, work of literature or work of art, scientific or philosophical idea, or some other product of Europe, and write a paragraph explaining why they think it is one of the most important of Europe's contributions to world history and culture. Students may wish to consult history books, the encyclopedia, or the Internet to generate topics. Remind students to follow these guidelines in writing their paragraphs:

- Create a topic sentence that clearly expresses an opinion.
- Offer logical, convincing reasons in support of the opinion.
- Use effective transitional words and phrases.
- End with a strong conclusion.

EUROPE

A.D. 400–PRESENT

Nel mezzo del camin di nostra vita, mi ritrovai
per una selva oscura, che la diritta via era smarrita.

Midway in our life's journey, I went astray from
the straight road and woke to find myself alone in
a dark wood.

—Dante, from the *Inferno*

PART ONE
Early Europe...................................pages 858–947

PART TWO
Modern Europe............................pages 948–1103

857

Focus

Summary

Unit Five is divided into two sections. Part 1 covers early Europe, from the Middle Ages through the Renaissance; Part 2 covers modern Europe, from the Enlightenment to the present. The introduction for Part 1 is on pages 858–869; the introduction for Part 2 is on pages 948–959.

Reading Strategy | 1

Analyze Metaphor **Ask:** What does Dante compare to a road? *(the virtuous way of life)*

 For diagnostic and end-of-unit assessment, see Assessment Resources, pp. 25–30, 261–262.

Unit Resources

Print Materials
- Unit 5 Teaching Resources, pp. 1–348
- Interactive Read and Write, On Level
- Novel Companion, pp. 207–250
- Bellringer Option Transparencies: Selection Focus 52–68; Daily Language Practice 80–104
- Literary Element Transparencies
- Assessment Resources, Unit Assessment, pp. 261–262

- Assessment Resources, Selection Assessment, pp. 175–218

Technology
- TeacherWorks Plus CD
- StudentWorks Plus CD
- Literature Launchers: Pre-Reading Videos DVD
- Literature Online
- Listening Library CD-ROM

- ExamView CD-ROM
- Skill Level Up! CD-ROM

Reading Strategy | 1

Analyze Graphic Information Point out that Europe has been called a peninsula of peninsulas. Remind students that a peninsula is a body of land surrounded on three sides by water. **Ask:** Which regions of Europe are peninsulas? *(Greece, Italy, Spain, and Brittany and Normandy in France)*

ADVANCED **Ask:** What advantages and disadvantages would societies located on peninsulas have? *(easy access to water for fishing and trade; vulnerability to invasion by sea)*

View the Art ★

A book of hours was a medieval illuminated manuscript consisting of a collection of Christian texts, prayers, and songs. Most were written in Latin. The books were intended for Christians who wished to incorporate elements of monasticism into their daily lives. The Playfair Book of Hours was created in the French city of Rouen, the site of a famous cathedral.

A Neuschwanstein Castle in autumn, Bavaria, Germany.

B *June: Hay harvest.* Playfair Book of Hours. France (Rouen), late 15th c. Victoria and Albert Museum, London. ★

LOG ON ▶ **Literature** Online

Literature and Reading For more about the history and literature of this period, go to glencoe.com and enter QuickPass code GLW6053u5.

858

Part Introduction Skills

Text Elements
- Headings (TE p. 860)
- Boxes (TE p. 865)

Part 1 Introduction

Speaking/Listening/Viewing Skills
- Panel Discussion (SE p. 869)
- Visual Literacy (SE pp. 869)

Reading Skills
- Analyze Graphic Information (SE p. 861; TE pp. 858, 860, 861)
- Analyze Cause-and-Effect Relationships (SE p. 866; TE p. 863)
- Make Generalizations (SE p. 867)

Vocabulary Skills
- Word Parts (TE p. 864)
- Context Clues (TE pp. 862, 864)

Writing Skills/Grammar
- Expository Paragraph (TE p. 856)
- Parentheses (TE p. 868)

EARLY EUROPE

A.D. 400–1650

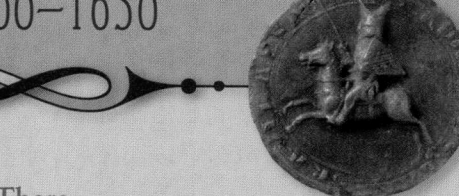

Seal of Landgrave Johann, 14th century AD. Wax. Germanisches Nationalmuseum, Nuremberg, Germany.

Being There

On a world map, Europe is little more than a peninsula on the northwest corner of Asia. A band of fertile plains stretches through the center, from the Atlantic Ocean to Russia. The region to the north is rugged and chilly. The central plains and the north were the home of Celtic and Germanic peoples. The region to the south, which has a mild climate, runs along the coast of the Mediterranean Sea and provided the setting for the classical Greek and Roman civilizations.

Looking Ahead

2 When the Western Roman Empire collapsed in the 400s, few people in Europe identified themselves as Europeans. Their languages, religious beliefs, and ways of life defined them from their neighbors. By the year 1000, however, a European civilization had begun to emerge from the traditions of the Germanic and Celtic peoples, the legacy of Roman civilization, and Christianity.

Keep the following questions in mind as you read:

- What did Germanic and Celtic traditions contribute to the development of medieval romance?

- How did Christianity shape medieval civilization?

- How did the Renaissance change the direction of European civilization?

859

Focus

Summary

This introduction gives an overview of historical, social, and cultural forces in early Europe, including the development, flowering, and decline of medieval civilization and the rise and spread of the Renaissance. The introduction concludes with a survey of three Big Ideas that shaped early Europe: the blending of cultural traditions in medieval civilization, the influence of Christianity on the Middle Ages, and the nature of Renaissance humanism.

Reading Strategy | 2

Analyze Cultural Context

Ask: What cultural elements contributed to the development of the European civilization of the Middle Ages? *(the traditions of the Germanic and Celtic peoples, the legacy of Roman civilization, and Christianity)*

 For additional support for English Learners, see Unit 5 Teaching Resources Book, p. 20.

Advanced Learners/Pre-AP

DIFFERENTIATED INSTRUCTION

American Pilgrimage Sites Point out to students that just as early European culture can be better understood by examining its pilgrimage sites, so can modern American culture. Have small groups of students (1) brainstorm a list a modern American pilgrimage sites, (2) discuss the merits of these sites as reflective of modern American culture, and (3) vote to determine a "Top Ten" list of American

pilgrimage sites. Have the different groups present their lists to the class.

Remind the groups of the following guidelines for effective participation in a discussion:

- Speak clearly and distinctly.
- Give reasons for your opinions.
- Answer questions that others ask about your opinions.
- Be ready to summarize or repeat your ideas if asked to.
- Listen politely to others' opinions and ask follow-up questions.

Headings Direct students' attention to the timeline sub-headings. **Ask:** Into what broad categories is the information organized? *(Early European Literature; Early European Events; World Events)*

ADVANCED Have students skim the various events in the timeline. **Ask:** What other categories could these events be organized into? *(Students might mention such categories as Christianity, warfare, education, government, art, and exploration.)*

Analyze Graphic Information Point out that both Clovis and Charlemagne ruled the kingdom of the Franks. **Ask:** Which king ruled first? *(Clovis)* **Ask:** Approximately how many years separated the reigns of these two Frankish kings? *(nearly 300 years)*

Reading Practice

Use a Graphic Organizer Point out to students that the information in the timeline is already organized into broad categories. Have students create a table like the one started here and use different categories—such as Christianity, Government and Warfare, or Education—to reorganize the timeline information and give it different emphases.

TIMELINE A.D. 400–1650

EARLY EUROPEAN LITERATURE   1

400

c. 405
Vulgate (Latin) translation of the Bible is completed

c. 750
Beowulf is composed

780s–790s
Charlemagne encourages revival of learning

900

1222–1223
Snorri Sturluson writes the *Prose Edda* in Iceland

c. 1314
Dante completes the *Divine Comedy* in Italy   3

c. 1353
Boccaccio completes the *Decameron* in Italy

EARLY EUROPEAN EVENTS

400

496 ☆
Clovis, king of the Franks, converts to Christianity

732
Christians stop Arab expansion northward into France

c. 790
Viking raids begin in Western Europe

900

1054
East-West Schism divides Roman and Byzantine Christians

1066 ▶
French-speaking Normans conquer England

1215
King John signs the Magna Carta in England

1241
Mongols invade central Europe   4

WORLD EVENTS

400

300–900
Maya civilization flourishes in Central America

900

c. 1000
Vikings reach North America

1095
Christians launch the First Crusade against Muslims

c. 1150
Temple of Angkor Wat completed in Cambodia

LOG ON ▶ **Literature** Online

Literature and Reading To explore the Interactive Timeline, go to glencoe.com and enter QuickPass code GLW6053u5.

Viking bridle mount

Christianity	Government and Warfare	Education
c. 405 Vulgate (Latin) translation of the Bible is completed	**c. 790** Viking raids begin in Western Europe	**780s–790s** Charlemagne encourages revival of learning

1400

c. 1445
Gutenberg develops the first printing press in Europe

1485
Sir Thomas Malory's *Le Morte d'Arthur* is published

1513 ▶
Machiavelli writes *The Prince* in Italy

1516
Sir Thomas More's *Utopia* is published

1605
Part 1 of Cervantes's *Don Quixote* is published in Spain

1623
First Folio of Shakespeare is published in England

1668–1694
French poet Jean de La Fontaine publishes the *Fables*

1400

c. 1478
Moscow gains freedom from Mongol control

1517
Martin Luther ignites the Protestant Reformation

1526
Ottoman Turks conquer Hungary

1543 ▲
Copernicus publishes his theory of the sun-centered universe

1588
English navy defeats the Spanish Armada

c. 1600
Italian musicians create the first operas

1626
St. Peter's Basilica completed in Rome

1400

1411–1413
Chinese ships begin traveling to Arabia and Africa

1492
Christopher Columbus makes his first voyage to America

c. 1500
Songhay Empire reaches its peak in Africa

1526
Mogul dynasty under Babur begins in India
▼

c. 1600 ▲
Japanese dramatists create the Kabuki form of theater

c. 1650
Taj Mahal is completed in India

Reading Check

Analyze Graphic Information Which of the following authors' works first appeared before the invention of printing, and which first appeared after? (a)Shakespeare; (b)Dante; (c)Cervantes; (d)Boccaccio; (e)Machiavelli

Advanced Learners/Pre-AP

DIFFERENTIATED INSTRUCTION

Charlemagne's Cultural Legacy Point out that in A.D. 800, Pope Leo III, the head of the Christian Church, crowned Charlemagne as the new Roman emperor. This brought together the Germanic, Roman, and Christian cultures. Charlemagne's successors established the Holy Roman Empire, which lasted for about 850 years and became the basis for European civilization during that time.

Have advanced learners select from the following topics to research for a report to the class on Charlemagne's cultural legacy:

- palace school and revival of learning
- preservation of classical texts
- creation of monastic schools
- Carolingian minuscule script
- "matter of France," *chanson de geste*, and *The Song of Roland*

Teach

Reading Check

Answer: *before: (b) and (d); after: (a), (c), and (e)*

Reading Strategy | 3

Analyze Graphic Information Ask: Who were three Italian writers who lived during the period covered by this timeline? *(Dante, Boccaccio, and Machiavelli)*

Reading Strategy | 4

Analyze Graphic Information Ask: What were three peoples who tried to invade areas of Europe during the period covered by this timeline? *(Arabs, Vikings, and Mongols)*

ADVANCED Have advanced learners research where each of these groups came from. *(the Arabs from Spain in the south, the Vikings from northern Europe, and the Mongols from Asia)*

Cultural History ☆

Clovis The Franks were a Germanic-speaking people. Invading the Roman Empire during the A.D. 400s, the Franks settled in what is now northern France and western Germany. Their name survives in the word *France*. Clovis became king of the Franks in A.D. 481. He later became the first Germanic ruler to accept Christianity.

Learning Objectives
Analyzing graphic information. (SE)
Analyzing text elements. (TE)
Using graphic organizers. (TE)

Teach

Analyze Cultural Context
Ask: How did the Frankish kingdom differ from the other Germanic states? *(The Frankish kingdom survived, but the Germanic states did not.)*

ADVANCED **Ask:** Recalling the material from the timeline, what might have contributed to the success of the Frankish kingdom? *(the conversion of Clovis to Christianity)*

Context Clues **Ask:** What is feudalism? *(a system of social organization in which land is granted in exchange for military service)* **Ask:** What two types of context clues are provide for the meaning of *feudalism?* *(appositive: "system of social organization"; example: "granting them land in exchange for military service.")*

Learning Objectives

For pages 858–869

In studying this text, you will focus on the following objectives:

Literary Study: Analyzing literary periods.

Reading: Evaluating historical influences. Connecting to the literature.

EARLY EUROPE

A.D. 400–1650

Historical, Social, and Cultural Forces

The Early Middle Ages

Germanic peoples had begun to move into the lands of the Western Roman Empire by the third century. In A.D. 476, a date often seen as the fall of the Western Empire, the Germanic ruler Odaacer deposed the Roman emperor. (The Eastern, or Byzantine Empire, based in Constantinople, would survive until 1453.) Over the next few centuries, a series of Germanic states rose and fell in Western Europe, but only the kingdom of the Franks endured. The most powerful Frankish ruler was Charlemagne, who greatly expanded his territory and created the Carolingian Empire. At its height in the early 800s, his empire covered much of western and central Europe. Charlemagne's political strength was matched by his desire to promote learning throughout his kingdom. His efforts led to a revival of education and culture called the Carolingian Renaissance.

The High Middle Ages

By the eleventh and twelfth centuries, a medieval civilization had developed that combined the traditions of the Germanic and Celtic peoples, the heritage of Roman civilization, and the institutions of the Christian Church. The church shaped every aspect of people's lives, providing predictable rituals that gave medieval life its structure. The church also established monasteries where men dedicated themselves to lives of work, prayer, and study. Monasteries became centers

Glorification of the Virgin (detail) North Rose Window, Chartres Cathedral, France.

Reading Practice

Use Ordinal Numbers with Dates
Draw students' attention to the following sentence: "Germanic peoples had begun to move into the lands of the Western Roman Empire by the third century." **Ask:** What is a date in the middle of the third century? *(possible date: 250)* Point out the dates in the third century—either B.C. or A.D.—are nearly all in the 200s. To be exact, the third century B.C. began in 300 B.C. and ended in 201 B.C. The third

century A.D. began in A.D. 201 and ended in A.D. 300. Point out that both the first century B.C. and A.D. are the "tens" dates. For example:

Julius Caesar was assassinated in the first century B.C. (44 B.C.).

The Great Fire of Rome took place in the first century A.D. (A.D. 64).

Have students give the century for each of the following dates.

1. A.D. 1066 *(eleventh century A.D.)*
2. A.D. 1492 *(fifteenth century A.D.)*
3. 399 B.C. *(fourth century B.C.)*
4. A.D. 476 *(fifth century A.D.)*
5. 31 B.C. *(first century B.C.)*

of learning in which schools were established and books were copied by hand. Another fundamental medieval institution was feudalism. This system of social organization was useful in a time of frequent warfare. Nobles maintained private armies of knights by granting them land in exchange for military service.

The Decline of Medieval Civilization

Beginning in the fourteenth century, a series of events shattered medieval civilization. In 1347, an outbreak of bubonic plague, called "the Black Death," spread throughout Europe, killing perhaps a third of the population before it ended. Between 1337 and 1453 England and France fought the Hundred Years' War, devastating parts of France and draining both countries economically. Finally, the Great Schism, a struggle over the leadership of the church that began in 1378, divided Europe and weakened the church's authority.

The Rise of the Renaissance

As medieval civilization declined, however, a new cultural revolution known as the Renaissance began to reshape Europe. The Renaissance emerged in Italian city-states in the mid-1300s and spread throughout Europe in the decades to come. A major factor that contributed to the rise of this movement, and to the philosophy known as humanism, was a renewed interest in the classical civilizations of ancient Greece and Rome. Humanists believed humanity held a central place in the divine order and asserted that there were no limits to what individuals could accomplish.

> "Men can do all things if they will."
> —Leon Battista Alberti

The Spread of the Renaissance

One of the most important factors in the spread of Renaissance ideas was the development of printing. In the mid-1400s, Europeans learned how to print with movable metal type. Johannes Gutenberg played a crucial role in this process. The Gutenberg Bible, printed around 1455, was the first European book produced from movable type. By 1500, there were more than 1,000 printers in Europe, and almost 40,000 titles had been published. The printing of books encouraged scholarly research and increased the public's desire for knowledge, impacting European society and literacy.

Portrait of a Lady as the Magdalen,
c. 1490 - c. 1540. Master of the Female Half Lengths. Flemish tempera on panel. Sotheby's, London.

Reading Strategy　3

Analyze Cause-and-Effect Relationships　Ask: What encouraged the spread of feudalism in the Middle Ages? *(frequent warfare)*

ADVANCED　Ask: Are there other historical societies with which you are familiar that might be described as feudal? *(Students might mention Japan under the shoguns, where the relationship between a daimyo and his samurai was similar to that of a European feudal lord and his knights.)*

Reading Strategy　4

**Analyze Cultural Context
Ask:** What events contributed to the decline of medieval civilization? *(the Black Death, the Hundred Years' War, and the Great Schism)*

Learning Objectives
Evaluate historical influences. (SE)
Use context clues. (TE)
Use ordinal numbers with dates. (TE)

Approaching Level
DIFFERENTIATED INSTRUCTION

Ordinal Numbers with Dates If students have trouble with the Reading Practice, draw a timeline on the board from 500 B.C. to A.D. 500. Divide the timeline into ten 100-year sections, labeled with their ordinal designations. Also indicate the dates of each century: 500 B.C. –401 B.C., and so on. Give students specific dates and have them respond with the correct century designations.

Advanced Learners/Pre-AP
DIFFERENTIATED INSTRUCTION

Report on a Century Point out that historians often choose a century as a focus for study. Historian Barbara Tuchman, for example, wrote a popular narrative history of the late Middle Ages titled *A Distant Mirror: The Calamitous Fourteenth Century.* Have interested students select a particular century and research its events for a brief report. Have them focus on several events that seem to share a certain quality and give their century a qualifying word or phrase that expresses this quality. For example, if the student chose the thirteenth century and focused on events related to cathedrals, the report might be titled "The Gothic Century" or "The Century of the Builders."

Reading Strategy | 1

Compare and Contrast

Ask: How did Romanesque and Gothic buildings differ? *(Romanesque buildings had rounded forms and arches and massive walls to support their weight; Gothic buildings had pointed arches and high, thin walls with exterior bracing.)*

Vocabulary | 2

Context Clues **Ask:** What does *minstrel* mean? *(a traveling entertainer who performed songs)*

ENGLISH LEARNERS If English learners have difficulty, point to the context clues *traveling* and *sang.* Have students use these clues to create a definition of *minstrel.*

Cultural History ☆

Sermons in Stone In an age when few people could read, medieval builders and artisans turned medieval churches into "sermons in stone," visual tools for learning the Christian religion. The ground plan of most churches was laid out in the shape of a cross. Sculptures and stained-glass windows graphically depicted stories from the Bible, the lives of the saints, and other moral tales. They also vividly displayed the rewards of heaven and the punishments of hell.

Architecture 1

Most of the great achievements of medieval and Renaissance architecture were religious buildings. Romanesque architecture, dominant from about 1000 to about 1150, emphasized rounded forms and arches. Large buildings in this style needed massive walls to support their weight. Builders in the Gothic style, which succeeded Romanesque, developed pointed arches and exterior bracing that allowed them to erect much higher, thinner walls that often featured magnificent stained glass windows. The Gothic style of architecture created an overall impression of extraordinary lightness. Medieval cathedral builders adorned both Romanesque and Gothic buildings with carvings, usually illustrating biblical stories. They also sought inspiration from ancient Roman and Greek models. Churches and other buildings in the Renaissance style frequently included Doric or Corinthian columns (see page 185) and other classical elements in their decoration.

Music

During the Middle Ages and the Renaissance, European music became increasingly varied, complex, and secular. Originally developed around 600, Gregorian chant was the dominant form of

> "It is fitting that the body, simultaneously with the soul, repeatedly sings praises to God through the voice."
> —Hildegard of Bingen

medieval music. Chants were religious music, often sung by monks. Performers sang in unison or with simple harmonies and used few instruments. Composers remained anonymous, and tunes evolved from one performance to the next. One exception to the anonymity of medieval composers was the German nun Hildegard of Bingen, who wrote about 80 musical works. By the 1200s, minstrels traveling from one noble's court to another sang about love, war, and other worldly themes. A century later, musicians played instruments, such as the lute, independently, rather than solely to accompany a singer. By the 1500s, individual composers, such as Italian Giovanni Palestrina, were becoming popular.

Duomo Cathedral, Florence, Italy

Vocabulary Practice

Use Word Parts Draw students' attention to this sentence: "The church shaped every aspect of people's lives, providing predictable rituals that gave medieval life its structure." **Ask:** What does *predictable* mean? *(capable of being predicted; known in advance)* **Ask:** How is *predictable* formed? *(the root word* predict *plus the suffix* -able*)* Point out that the suffix *-able* (and its variant form *-ible*) mean "capable of," "worthy of," or "inclined to."

Have students give the meanings of the italicized words in the following sentences.

1. She was moody, with a very *changeable* personality. *(likely to change)*
2. The castle on the cliff was easily *defensible*. *(capable of being defended)*
3. Would you have found the silence of a medieval monastery *endurable*? *(capable of being tolerated)*
4. They found trouble locating *affordable* housing. *(capable of being afforded)*

Boy playing the lute. Michelangelo Merisi da Caravaggio. Hermitage, St. Petersburg, Russia.

Renaissance Painting

Prior to the Renaissance, painting was a minor art in Europe, often used to illustrate books. Medieval artists usually created biblical and other religious images that were colorful but flat. Renaissance painters explored new subject matter and artistic techniques. For example, they revived the classical tradition of portraiture, painting vivid, revealing images of their subjects' faces—and sometimes of their own. Renaissance artists also revolutionized painting by rediscovering the techniques of perspective. Using these techniques, Renaissance painters arranged forms and colors to create the appearance of depth on a flat surface.

Annunciation. Hans Vredeman de Vries 1598. Oak, 221 x 140 cm. Kunsthistorisches Museum, Vienna, Austria.

PREVIEW **Big Ideas** of Early Europe **4**

1 From Myth to Romance

After the collapse of the Western Roman Empire, a new civilization took shape in Western Europe that combined elements of Christianity, Roman heritage, and Germanic and Celtic heroic traditions. Literature of this period often celebrates the courageous adventures and chivalric virtues of knights.

See pages 866

2 The Vision of Faith

After the fall of Rome, the Christian Church became the greatest power in Europe. The church controlled every aspect of medieval life and culture. Medieval literature expressed the beliefs and values of Christianity, and sought to harmonize scientific reason with religious faith.

See page 867

3 The Renaissance and Humanism

With the decline of medieval civilization in the mid-1300s, a new cultural spirit known as the Renaissance reshaped European civilization. Developing in Italy and spreading throughout Europe, Renaissance literature expressed a cultural outlook called humanism, which celebrated human freedom and the joys of this world.

See page 868

INTRODUCTION **865**

Approaching Level

DIFFERENTIATED INSTRUCTION

Perspective Diagram Students may grasp the idea of visual perspective better if you provide them with a diagram. You might draw a simple sketch on the board to demonstrate basic techniques of linear perspective; for example, a road with its boundaries drawing together in the distance to meet at a vanishing point. If you are comfortable drawing, you could add stylized trees or buildings on either side, making those in the foreground larger.

Advanced Learners/Pre-AP

DIFFERENTIATED INSTRUCTION

Visual Presentation Interested students might gather some examples of Renaissance art displaying linear perspective and do a visual presentation for the class. Possible examples include Sandro Botticelli, *The Annunciation;* Raphael, *Marriage of the Virgin* or *The School of Athens;* Andrea Mantegna, *The Dead Christ* or *Saint James Led to His Execution;* Parmigianino, *Self-Portrait in a Convex Mirror.*

Teach

Reading Strategy 3

Compare and Contrast
Ask: How did medieval and Renaissance painting differ? *(Medieval painting was largely religious and presented flat surfaces; Renaissance painting used new subject matter, such as portraits, and perspective technique to give the appearance of depth.)*
ADVANCED **Ask:** How does the Renaissance interest in portraits reflect the ideas of humanism? *(Students may feel that humanism's focus on individuals and their potential would encourage an interest in portraits.)*

Text Element 4

Boxes Remind students that the three boxed features on page 863 summarize key characteristics of medieval and Renaissance literature and culture that will be developed on the three succeeding pages. **Ask:** How did medieval literature address divisions between faith and reason? *(It sought to harmonize faith and reason.)*
ADVANCED **Ask:** In which subject area of high school does reason play the most important role? *(Some students may say science; others may argue for mathematics.)*

Learning Objectives
Comparing and contrasting. (TE)
Using word parts. (TE)

Teach

Reading Check

Answer: *The bond of loyalty between a Germanic warrior and his lord helped shape the institution of feudalism.*

Reading Strategy | 1

Connect to Contemporary Issues Ask: What do you think the image of the knight has come to mean today? *(Students may mention a variety of associations for the image of the knight, drawn from movies, television, fiction, comic books, video games, and other forms of popular culture.)*

Vocabulary | 2

Word Usage Point out that, in medieval usage, the word *vassal* described an honorable relationship. Today, *vassal* has come to mean "servant," "follower," or even "flunky" or "stooge." **Ask:** Why do you think the usage of *vassal* has changed? *(Students may feel that in modern democratic societies the idea of swearing homage to another person has come to seem more submissive.)*

Language History ☆

Chivalry The term *chivalry* comes from the French word *chevalier*, meaning "horseman" or "knight." The code of chivalry called for knights to be brave in battle, fight fairly, keep promises, defend the Church, and treat women of noble birth in a courteous manner. Chivalry eventually became the standard of good manners in Western society.

Big Idea 1
From Myth to Romance

The knight in armor is the most familiar symbol of the Middle Ages. Some of the basic features of the culture of knighthood expressed in medieval epics and romances came from the traditions of the Celtic and Germanic peoples of Europe.   **1**

Celtic and Germanic Peoples

Before its collapse, the Western Roman Empire was home to a variety of peoples who spoke Celtic and Germanic languages. The Celts originally inhabited wide areas of western and central Europe. Conquered first by the Romans and later by Germanic groups, they survived only in regions at the edge of Europe, including Ireland, Scotland, Wales, and Brittany. Germanic peoples, particularly the Franks, eventually occupied much of the former territory of the Western Roman Empire.

> *"Franks are good men; like vassals brave they'll stand. . ."*
>
> —from the *Song of Roland*

Lords and Vassals   **2**

Among the most enduring contributions of the Germanic peoples to the emerging civilization of the Middle Ages was the idea of honor. The bond of loyalty between a warrior and his lord, even in times of struggle, represented a commitment to an ideal vision of nobility, pride, and courage. Early Norse myths such as *Ragnarok* (see pages 870–875), for example, celebrated the devotion to heroism in spite of a guaranteed loss. In Germanic society, warriors swore an oath of loyalty to their leaders, who rewarded them with gold, weapons, horses, and other prized gifts. This idea of loyalty between a warrior and his lord survived in the medieval institution of feudalism. To become a

Two knights fighting, c1415. Their armour includes scale, mail and plate, which in the case of the man on the right, has proved inadequate. Shelfmark ID: Cotton Nero E ii part 1. Folio No: 1. British Library, London.

vassal, a knight performed an act of homage to his lord. In feudal society, loyalty to one's lord was the chief virtue. This relationship can be seen in the greatest medieval epic, the *Song of Roland* (see pages 877–885).

The Rise of Romance

One of the principal Celtic contributions to later medieval culture was the legend of King Arthur. Although he may have been a Celtic chieftain in Britain who briefly withstood invading Germanic peoples in the early 500s, the legend of Arthur grew over the centuries until he was portrayed as a great leader. The tales of King Arthur and his knights of the Round Table were one of the principal cycles of medieval romance, a literary form that developed in France during the 1100s. In prose or verse, the medieval romance related stories of knights in combat and in love. These stories exhibited the ideals of chivalry, the knightly code that required courage, loyalty, and honor. Medieval romances also presented the values of courtly love, which celebrated romantic passion and the unswerving devotion of a knight to his lady.

Reading Check

Analyze Cause-and-Effect Relationships How did Germanic values contribute to the development of feudalism?

Reading Practice

Create a Glossary Point out to students that one of the most important types of content in historical background material, such as this introduction, is the specialized vocabulary presented. Draw their attention to the following terms presented on pages 866–867: *knight, epic, romance, Celtic, Germanic, vassal, homage, chivalry, pope, abbot, Crusade, relic, scholasticism.*

Have students create a glossary for the historical and cultural terms presented in this introduction. Point out that in many cases an appositive definition is provided. (As examples, point out the appositive definition provided for *romance* in the paragraph under "The Rise of Romance.") If they cannot get the meaning of the word from context, have them use a dictionary.

Big Idea 2
The Vision of Faith

Adoration of the Magi, detail from one of four tabernacle reliquaries. Fra Angelico. Museo di S. Marco, Florence.

The tall spires of Gothic cathedrals that soared above many towns in the Middle Ages are apt symbols of the domination of medieval life by the Christian Church.

The Power of the Church

By the end of the 300s, Christianity had become the supreme religion of the Roman Empire. As the Western Roman Empire fell apart in 476, the church played an increasingly important role in the growth of European civilization. As feudalism developed, church officials were often feudal lords who held worldly as well as spiritual power. One of the most extraordinary expressions of Christianity's power in the world was the Crusades. In 1095, Pope Urban II launched the first of a long series of Christian military expeditions to regain the Holy Land of Palestine from the Muslims. Though this goal ultimately failed, the extensive efforts of Christian crusaders demonstrate the strength of the church's leadership in medieval Europe.

Christian Belief

In the Middle Ages, the sacraments of the church were a crucial part of ordinary people's lives from birth to death. The sacraments were seen as the principal means for receiving God's grace and therefore necessary for salvation. Only the clergy could administer the sacraments, so every Christian depended on the clergy to achieve salvation. Other religious practices were widespread, including the veneration of Christian saints. Relics, or bones of saints or objects connected with them, were used to heal people or produce other miracles. Pilgrimages to sacred Christian shrines were also widespread.

> "But now was turning my desire
>   and will,
> Even as a wheel that equally
>   is moved,
> The Love which moves the sun and
>   the other stars."
>   —Dante, from the *Paradiso*

Christian Thought

Through its control of education and the copying of books, the church shaped the development of intellectual life in the Middle Ages. Theology was the most highly regarded area of study at medieval universities. One of the most influential intellectual traditions in the Middle Ages was scholasticism, which sought to reconcile faith and reason—to show that what was accepted on faith was in harmony with what could be learned through reason and experience. In his religious epic the *Divine Comedy* (see pages 898–914), the Italian poet Dante expressed this medieval attempt to reconcile the world of faith with the world of experience.

Reading Check
Make Generalizations How did the Christian Church dominate European life in the Middle Ages?

INTRODUCTION **867**

Advanced Learners/Pre-AP

DIFFERENTIATED INSTRUCTION

Courtly Love Tell students that the ideal of courtly love was codified during the Middle Ages, with rules established to govern the proper conduct of a knight toward his lady. One set of rules was created by Andreas Capellanus (Latin for "Andrew the Chaplain"), who may have been a chaplain at one of the French courts. In his *Book on the Art of Loving Nobly,* Andreas presents observations such as "It is well known that love is always increasing or decreasing." Have students research medieval rules of courtly love and present a report to the class.

UNIT FIVE
PART 1

Teach
Reading Check

Answer: *The Christian Church dominated European life religiously, politically, socially, and culturally.*

Reading Strategy | 3

Question **Ask:** Why do you think medieval Church officials came to hold worldly power? *(Students may feel that the Church's assumption of worldly power reflected its importance in medieval society.)*

ADVANCED **Ask:** How does the U.S. system of government guard against the overlapping of religious and secular authority? *(The First Amendment of the U.S. Constitution allows for freedom of religion, which implies that the government cannot make laws that give official status to any particular religion—that is, laws that would establish a national religion.)*

Reading Strategy | 4

Connect to Contemporary Issues Point out that the words *crusade* and *crusader* have very different connotations in Western and Islamic countries. In Western countries the terms have generally positive connotations; in Islamic countries, strongly negative. **Ask:** Why do you think the term *crusader* would have strongly negative connotations in Islamic countries? *(Students may say that the negative connotations result from Islamic resentment toward what they see as Western aggression.)*

Learning Objectives
Analyzing cause-and-effect relationships. (SE)
Making generalizations. (SE)
Creating a glossary. (TE)

867

Teach

Reading Check

Answer: *Students may feel the humanists' interest in education stemmed from their belief in the greatness of human potential.*

Reading Strategy | 1

Analyze Figurative Language Ask: What does Leonardo see as the proper functions of iron, of water, and of the human mind? *(Iron should function as a tool or weapon, water should flow, and the human mind should think.)*

Cultural History ☆

Leonardo's Notebooks

Throughout his career, Leonardo kept a record of his thoughts and observations in his many volumes of notebooks. Written in a reverse script that has to be held up to a mirror to be read and including many drawings, Leonardo's notebooks, like his paintings, show a fierce dedication to his lifelong goal of "knowing how to see."

Big Idea 3
The Renaissance and Humanism

Television, computers, the Internet, cell phones—these electronic media have created a revolution in communications, the biggest in the last 500 years. An earlier revolution took place during the Renaissance when the invention of the printing press changed the way people got their information.

The Growth of the Renaissance

The word *renaissance* means "rebirth." A number of people who lived in Italy between 1350 and 1550 believed they were witnessing a rebirth of the ancient Greek and Roman worlds. Living in prosperous urban societies where their increasing wealth brought about new possibilities for the enjoyment of material things, these people developed a secular, or worldly, outlook. A new, optimistic view of human beings and individual potential began to emerge. The well-rounded, universal individual, or "Renaissance man," was seen as capable of achievements in many areas. One of the greatest examples of this new ideal was Leonardo da Vinci, who was a painter, a sculptor, an architect, an inventor, and a mathematician.

Self-Portrait (playing a musical instrument). Lavinia Fontana. Uffizi, Florence.

> *"Iron rusts from disuse, stagnant water loses its purity, and in cold weather becomes frozen: even so does inaction sap the vigors of the mind."* **1**
>
> —Leonardo da Vinci, from the *Notebooks*

Humanism

Secularism and an emphasis on the individual characterized the Renaissance. These characteristics are reflected in humanism, a key intellectual movement of the Renaissance. Humanism was based on the study of the classics, the literary works of ancient Greece and Rome. The Italian scholar and poet Petrarch (see pages 919–922) did more than any other individual to foster the early development of humanism. He looked for forgotten Latin manuscripts and set in motion a search for similar manuscripts in monastic libraries throughout Europe. Petrarch also perfected the fourteen-line poem known as the sonnet.

The humanist movement had a profound effect on education. Renaissance humanists believed education could dramatically improve human beings. At the core of humanist schools were liberal studies (what we today call the liberal arts), which they believed enabled individuals to reach their full potential.

Reading Check

Interpret Why do you think Renaissance humanists took such an active interest in education?

Writing Practice

Use Parentheses Remind students that parentheses are used to set off supplemental material. Tell them to always place a comma, a semicolon, or a colon after the closing parenthesis. For example:

One example of Renaissance versatility was Leonardo da Vinci (1452–1519); another was the artist, architect, and poet Michelangelo (1475–1564).

Have students rewrite the following sentences to correct the use of parentheses with other punctuation. If the sentence has no errors, have them write "correct."

1. A major figure was the scholar and poet Petrarch (sometimes called "the father of humanism)"; he recovered forgotten Latin manuscripts. *(A major figure was the scholar and poet Petrarch (sometimes called "the father of humanism"); he recovered forgotten Latin manuscripts.)*

2. Leonardo was interested in engineering, anatomy (the physical structure of plants and animals,) and flight. *(Leonardo was interested in engineering, anatomy (the physical structure of plants and animals), and flight.*

3. One of Michelangelo's best-loved statues, the *Pietà* (Italian for *pity*), depicts the Virgin Mary holding the body of the dead Christ. *(correct)*

WRAP-UP

Don Quixote. 1955. Pablo Picasso © ARS, NY. Musee d'Art et d'Histoire, St. Denis, France.

2 Legacy of the Period

Although Europe is geographically small, its influence has been significant. The laws and government of the United States have their roots in Europe, and European books, ideas, and art have affected ways of life around the world.

Basic rights that protect Americans today, such as trial by jury, were established when King John of England was forced to sign the Magna Carta in 1215. The first universities, such as the University of Paris, appeared during the Middle Ages.

Modern educational systems and mass media would not exist without the invention of the printing press. The discoveries of Renaissance scientists such as Copernicus and Galileo reshaped our view of the universe and the place of the Earth in it.

Cultural and Literary Links

 Many famous painters have illustrated scenes from Dante's *Divine Comedy,* including the Italian artist Sandro Botticelli, the English artist William Blake, and the French artist Eugène Delacroix.

 The form of the sonnet developed by Petrarch (known as the Italian or Petrarchan sonnet) was used by many subsequent authors, including the English poets William Wordsworth and John Keats.

Cervantes's comic characters Don Quixote and Sancho Panza have directly or indirectly influenced many subsequent fictional characters, including Mr. Pickwick and his servant Sam Weller from Charles Dickens's picaresque novel *The Pickwick Papers.*

LOG ON ▶ **Literature** Online

Unit Resources For additional skills practice, go to glencoe.com and enter QuickPass code GLW6053u5.

Activities

 Choose one of the following activities to explore and develop as you read this part.

1. **Follow Up** Go back to the Looking Ahead on page 859 and answer the questions.

2. **Contrast Historical Influences** In the modern world, with its emphasis on specialization, does it make more sense to strive for excellence in a single area or is the ideal of the "Renaissance man" still valid? Hold a panel discussion to explore this question.

3. **Build Visual Literacy** Research different illustrations for Dante's *Divine Comedy,* including those by Botticelli, Blake, Delacroix, Henry Fuseli, Gustave Doré, Salvador Dali, and others.

Prepare a visual display showing the range of styles.

4. **Take Notes** Use this graphic organizer to keep track of the three big ideas in this part.

FOLDABLES Study Organizer   **THREE-POCKET BOOK**

Big Idea 1   Big Idea 2   Big Idea 3

Advanced Learners/Pre-AP

DIFFERENTIATED INSTRUCTION

Profile a Renaissance Individual

Point out to students that one of the significant cultural legacies of the Renaissance period was the ideal of the multifaceted person who pursues achievement in a variety of fields. Have interested students select a contemporary person that they feel personifies the "Renaissance individual" and create a profile of this person for the class.

English Learners

DIFFERENTIATED INSTRUCTION

Advanced Encourage students from other countries to create a profile of some person from their homeland who they feel personifies the multisided achievements of the "Renaissance individual."

Reading Strategy | 2

Connect to Contemporary Issues Ask: How might the Renaissance be linked to the creation of today's global economy? *(The Renaissance development of economies based on buying and selling, coupled with the worldwide expansion of European influence as a result of the Age of Discovery, helped lay the foundations for the modern global economy.)*

APPROACHING If students have trouble, draw a simple flow chart on the board, linking the two factors mentioned above. **Ask:** How might these two factors have helped lead to a global economy? *(by spreading the European economic system worldwide)*

Assess

Activities

1. **Follow Up** The Germanic and Celtic traditions contributed to the idea of feudalism; Christianity shaped nearly every aspect of medieval civilization, including religious, political, and artistic life; the Renaissance contributed humanism, the printing press, and increasing exploration and trade.

2. **Contrast Historical Influences** Students should describe what skills they would associate with a contemporary "Renaissance man."

3. **Build Visual Literacy** Students should describe how the images they present emphasize different themes in Dante's work.

4. **Take Notes** Students should note key points from the part introduction.

Before You Read

Focus

Bellringer Options

Daily Language Practice Transparency 81

Or ask: What would motivate someone to fight a battle he or she could not win? *(Students may say that a person would fight for personal or family honor, out of loyalty to another person or to one's country, for an ideal, to prove oneself, or to make the future better for one's children or for future generations.)*

Literary History ☆

How-To Handbook The *Prose Edda* consists of three parts: a retelling of the ancient Norse myths; lists of traditional *heiti* (poetic substitutions for everyday nouns) and kennings (metaphorical compound words or phrases) and instructions for writing poetry; and a poem of more than one hundred stanzas written to honor and curry favor with King Haakon IV.

Before You Read

Ragnarok: The Twilight of the Gods

Meet **Snorri Sturluson**
(1179–1241)

Chess piece king and queen, 12th century BC. Walrus ivory. Isle of Lewis, Outer Hebrides.

The apocalyptic story of "Ragnarok: The Twilight of the Gods" includes a series of vicious winters, an era of moral chaos, and an epic battle between giants and gods. The myth is part of an anonymous collection of heroic poems called the *Poetic Edda* originally compiled in writing around the tenth century. The *Poetic Edda* reflects the pagan values of its Nordic audience and was a main source for Snorri Sturluson's *Prose Edda*. In this work written three centuries later for Christian readers, Sturluson aims to teach his fellow writers about the older style and expression of early Icelandic *skalds* (court poets) and to bring contemporary relevance to ancient myths. It is fitting, therefore, that this excerpt from Sturluson's Christian retelling of the pagan Ragnarok myth describes a turning point in history. In the battle, as in medieval Iceland, one world ends as another begins.

Political Intrigue Snorri Sturluson was born in western Iceland to a politically active family. He grew up in Oddi in the home of Iceland's most powerful chieftain. Sturluson married an heiress in 1199, moved to Reykjaholt in 1206, and later became president of the Icelandic high court. During this period, he forged a political relationship with King Haakan IV of Norway to further his own political ambitions in Iceland. This maneuver proved to be Sturluson's undoing, as the Norwegian king became suspicious of Sturluson's motives and had him assassinated.

The *Eddas* Though his personal and political life was turbulent, Sturluson had a celebrated literary career as a poet and historian. In addition to the *Prose Edda*, he is credited with writing the *Heimskringla*, a massive work chronicling the history of the kings of Norway from ancient times to the late twelfth century. He also authored *Egil's Saga*, a biography of the tenth-century poet Egill Skallagrimsson, an ancestor of Sturluson's. The *Prose Edda*, however, represents Sturluson's most significant literary contribution. Written at a time long after Christianity had superseded pagan beliefs in Western Europe, it includes a prologue in which the author advises his readers on how to approach the myths:

> "Remember, these tales . . . must be revered as ancient tradition, but are neither to be believed nor to be tampered with."
>
> —Snorri Sturluson

Scholars theorize that Sturluson may have included this advice to protect himself from criticism by the clergy—who were determined to eliminate any influence of pagan beliefs on Icelandic society—while at the same time promoting a respect and love for the myths.

LOG ON **Literature** Online

Author Search For more about Snorri Sturluson, go to glencoe.com and enter QuickPass code GLW6053u5.

870 UNIT 5 EARLY EUROPE

Selection Skills

Literary Elements
- Description (SE pp. 871, 874, 875)

Reading Skills
- Summarize (SE p. 871, 873–875)
- Preview (TE p. 872)
- Identify Sequence (TE p. 872)

← **Ragnarok: The Twilight of the Gods** →

Writing Skills/Grammar
- Description (SE p. 875)
- Retelling (TE p. 874)

Vocabulary Skills
- Word Usage (SE p. 875)
- Word Origins (TE p. 871)

Literature and Reading Preview

Connect to the Myth

What other stories have you read about the end of the world? Discuss these stories with a partner. Consider how they are similar to and different from "Ragnarok: The Twilight of the Gods."

Build Background

The universe of Norse mythology was composed of three realms. Asgard, the home of the gods (the Aesir), was at the top; Midgard, the home of men, was in the middle; and Niflheim, the home of the dead, was at the bottom. The gods and human heroes of Norse myths fought in vain against the forces of evil (giants and monstrous creatures), anticipating the rise of a new world that would follow the destruction of the old world.

Set Purposes for Reading

Big Idea From Myth to Romance

As you read "Ragnarok," ask yourself, What details reveal characteristics of mythology?

Literary Element Description

Description is a detailed portrayal of a person, a place, an object, or an event. Good descriptive writing includes imagery that appeals to the senses. As you read, ask yourself, Which descriptions are especially vivid and powerful?

Reading Strategy Summarize

When you **summarize**, you state the main ideas and events of a text in your own words and in a logical sequence. Summarizing helps you determine whether you've understood what the text is about. As you read, ask yourself, What happened in each paragraph and section?

....

Tip: Take Notes As you read, answer these questions to help you summarize.

- ☑ Who are the characters?
- ☑ What are they doing?
- ☑ When and where do they do it?
- ☑ How and why do they do it?

Learning Objectives

For pages 870–875

In studying this text, you will focus on the following objectives:

Literary Study: Analyzing description.

Reading: Summarizing.

Writing: Writing a description.

Vocabulary

misery (miz′ər ē) *n.* unhappy state of mind; great distress; wretchedness; p. 873 *Everyone who endured the hurricane experienced misery and suffering.*

sever (sev′ər) *v.* cut or break apart; separate; divide; p. 873 *The worker severed the cord that bound the stack of wheat, freeing up the sheaves.*

writhe (rīth) *v.* twist the body violently; contort; p. 874 *The wounded man writhed in pain, twisting and turning uncontrollably on the ground.*

asunder (ə sun′dər) *adv.* into parts; into different pieces; p. 874 *Displeased with what she had written, the author tore the manuscript asunder and threw away the pieces.*

....

Tip: Word Usage When you encounter a new word, you can gain a better understanding of it by asking yourself a question. For example, What might cause someone to feel *misery*?

Approaching Level

DIFFERENTIATED INSTRUCTION

Mythic Characteristics To help students respond to the Big Idea, discuss myths they have read. Guide them in using their knowledge to compile a list of the characteristics of myths, such as:

- gods as characters
- tell about a golden age
- describe struggles between good and evil

- creation stories
- explanations of some aspect of human life or of how something in nature came to be
- include magical events
- describe deaths of gods
- characters that return from the dead

Before You Read

Focus

Summary

In this excerpt, a Norse god tells of a prophecy describing the end of the world. Terrible winters occur. Men kill one another. A great upheaval occurs on Earth and monstrous creatures are set free. The forces of evil—including giants, evil gods, and beasts—gather and march to the home of the gods to destroy them. The gods fight the evil forces on a vast plain. After most of the combatants on both sides are killed, the world is destroyed by fire.

 For summaries in languages other than English, see Unit 5 Teaching Resources Book, pp. 21–26.

Vocabulary

Derivation Detectives

Have students work in pairs to match each vocabulary word with its origins and to explain how the older word and its derivative relate in meaning. **Ask:** Which word is derived from

- the Latin word *miser,* meaning "wretched"? *(misery)*
- the Old Norse word *ritha,* meaning "twist"? *(writhe)*
- the Sanskrit word *sanutar,* meaning "away"? *(asunder)*
- the Latin prefix *se-,* meaning "apart," and the word *parare,* meaning "to prepare" or "get ready"? *(sever)*

 For additional vocabulary practice, see Unit 5 Teaching Resources Book, p. 29.

Teach

Reading Strategy | 1

Preview Have students study the names and descriptions before they read the selection. Provide help with pronunciations as needed.

[APPROACHING] Some students may find the quantity of names and relationships overwhelming. Instruct these students to create a three-column chart, using these heads: "Force of Good", "Force of Evil", "Place". Have students write each name in the appropriate column and add brief notes beside each entry to jog their memories as they read.

Writer's Technique ☆

Dramatic Dialogue The myths in the *Prose Edda* were woven into a story of the Swedish king Gylfi's visit to Asgard, the home of the gods. The story was presented as a dramatic dialogue. In this excerpt, a god named the High One relates the prophecy that has been made about the end of the world—and the end of the reign of the gods.

View the Art ★

Valhalla is the hall of Odin, the leader of the Norse gods. It is located in the realm of Asgard. The hall is reserved for warriors who have died nobly in battle. Today, the term *Valhalla* is also used to refer to a paradise-like destination.

Readability Scores

Dale-Chall: 5.8
DRP: 56
Lexile: 1070

872

Ragnarok: The Twilight of the Gods

from The Prose Edda

Snorri Sturluson
Translated by Jean I. Young

Valhalla and the Midgard Serpent (detail), 1680. Icelandic School. Arni Magnusson Institute, Reykjavik, Iceland.

Skills Practice

Identify Sequence Say: Writers use transitional words and phrases, such as *first* and *when*, to signal the order of events in a story. What transitional words and phrases can you find in this selection? (*Possible answers:* "First," "before that," "then," "At that time," "so," "when these things are happening," "Immediately afterwards," "Thereupon")
Point out that like the *Iliad*, "Ragnarok" comes from the oral tradition of poetry.

To illustrate, read one or more passages aloud, emphasizing the transitional words and phrases. **Ask:** What purpose might these transitional words and phrases have had in poetry designed for performance? (*They helped performers remember the order of events and perhaps added a bit of drama. They clarified the sequence of events for the audience.*) Tell students to watch for these signal words when they read.

midgards Ormurin

FENRIR A monstrous wolf bound in chains by the gods until Ragnarok; offspring of Loki

MIDGARD SERPENT A sea serpent encircling Midgard in the waters surrounding it and so large he bites his own tail; offspring of Loki

NAGLFAR Ship that transports the giants to the final conflict

HRYM (also called Thrym) leader of the frost giants

MUSPELL A southern region of fire

SONS OF MUSPELL Fire giants who live in Muspell

SURT Giant who guards Muspell; leader of the sons of Muspell

BIFROST A rainbow bridge connecting Midgard to Asgard

VIGRID A vast plain on which the final conflict takes place

LOKI Considered a god, but born of two giants; father of Fenrir and the Midgard Serpent; evil mischief maker bound by the gods until Ragnarok

HEL (also called Niflheim) The underworld or land of the dead presided over by an evil goddess of the same name who is an offspring of Loki

HEIMDALL Watchman of the gods who guarded the entry to Asgard

ODIN (also called Wodan, Woden, and Wotan) Leader of the gods; protector of heroes in his hall Valhalla; god of poetry

MIMIR God of wisdom whose head and speech were preserved after he was killed by rival gods

MIMIR'S WELL Well or spring of wisdom located at the roots of Yggdrasil and guarded by Mimir's head

AESIR Collective name for the group of gods who live in Asgard

EINHERJAR Dead warriors who reside in Valhalla within Asgard

YGGDRASIL The World Tree; a giant ash tree that supports the universe

THOR God of thunder, second only to Odin in rank; son of Odin and guardian of the gods

FREY God of fertility; ruler of the sun and rain

SKIRNIR Frey's messenger or servant

GARM A monstrous hound bound in chains

GNIPAHELLIR A cave at the entrance to Hel

TYR God of war, considered the bravest of the gods; son of Odin

VIDAR Son of Odin; a survivor of the final conflict

"First will come the winter called Fimbulvetr. Snow will drive from all quarters, there will be hard frosts and biting winds; the sun will be no use. There will be three such winters on end with no summer between. Before that, however, three other winters will pass accompanied by great wars throughout the whole world. Brothers will kill each other for the sake of gain, and no one will spare father or son in manslaughter. As it says in the *Sibyl's Vision*:

> Brothers will fight
> and kill each other,
> men will know **misery,**
> an axe-age, a sword-age,
> shields will be cloven,
> a wind-age, a wolf-age,
> before the world's ruin.

"Then will occur what will seem a great piece of news, the wolf will swallow the sun and that will seem a great disaster to men. Then another wolf will seize the moon and that one too will do great harm. The stars will disappear from heaven. Then this will come to pass, the whole surface of the earth and the mountains will tremble so [violently] that trees will be uprooted from the ground, mountains will crash down, and all fetters and bonds will be snapped and **severed.** The wolf Fenrir will get loose then. The sea will lash against the land

---

Summarize What events will take place during the first set of winters before the end of the world?

Vocabulary

misery (miz'ər ē) *n.* unhappy state of mind; great distress; wretchedness

sever (sev'ər) *v.* cut or break apart; separate; divide

SNORRI STURLUSON **873**

English Learners

DIFFERENTIATED INSTRUCTION

Intermediate The idea of fate and of prophesized events is important to this myth. Call attention to the word *sibyl* in paragraph one. Explain that a *sibyl* is a prophetess. Have students tell about the role seers and fortunetellers play in their traditional tales and cultures.

Advanced Learners/Pre-AP

DIFFERENTIATED INSTRUCTION

Symbols Invite advanced learners to research the meanings of symbols commonly used in Norse literature, such as wolves, the ash tree Yggdrasil, fire, and the number nine. Have them create a book or poster that incorporates their findings.

Teach

Literary Element 2

Description Ask: To what senses do the images in these lines appeal? *(to sight, touch, and sound)*

(APPROACHING) Help students comprehend the level of destruction described in the passage by connecting to their knowledge of natural disasters. **Ask:** What forces of nature cause the kinds of destruction described in this passage? *(earthquakes, landslides and mudslides, volcanic eruptions)* Have students describe images they have seen of New Orleans, Pompeii, or other places that have experienced such destruction.

> For additional literary element practice, see Unit 5 Teaching Resources Book, p. 27.

Reading Strategy 3

Summarize Answer: *Great wars will take place and everyone will suffer.*

> For additional practice using the reading skill or strategy, see Unit 5 Teaching Resources Book, p. 28.

> **Interactive Read and Write**
> Other options for teaching this selection can be found in Interactive Read and Write for On-Level Learners, pp. 211–220.

Learning Objectives
Summarizing. (SE)
Previewing. (TE)
Identifying sequence. (TE)

Teach

Literary Element | 1

Description Answer: *The wolf has an enormous open mouth and fiery eyes and nostrils. The serpent spatters the sky and sea with poison.*

[APPROACHING] Have students skim the second paragraph and describe Surt. *(He is the one who rides out first, surrounded by fire, with a sword brighter than the sun.)*

Big Idea | 2

From Myth to Romance
Answer: *Odin is the leader of the gods who consults with Mimir because Mimir is the god of wisdom.*

[APPROACHING] Suggest that students consult this selection's glossary in order to answer this question.

Reading Strategy | 3

Summarize Answer: *Surt kills Frey; Garm and Tyr kill each other; Thor and the Midgard Serpent kill each other; the wolf kills Odin; Vidar kills the wolf; Loki and Heimdall kill each other.*

---

because the Miðgarð Serpent is **writhing** in giant fury trying to come ashore. At that time, too, the ship known as Naglfar will become free. It is made of dead men's nails, so it is worth warning you that, if anyone dies with his nails uncut, he will greatly increase the material for that ship which both gods and men devoutly hope will take a long time building. In this tidal wave, however, Naglfar will be launched. The name of the giant steering Naglfar is Hrym. The wolf Fenrir will advance with wide open mouth, his upper jaw against the sky, his lower on the earth (he would gape more widely still if there were room) and his eyes and nostrils will blaze with fire. The Miðgarð Serpent will blow so much poison that the whole sky and sea will be spattered with it; he is most terrible and will be on the other side of the wolf.

"In this din the sky will be rent **asunder** and the sons of Muspell ride forth from it. Surt will ride first and with him fire blazing both before and behind. He has a very good sword and it shines more brightly than the sun. When they ride over Bifröst, however—as has been said before—that bridge will break. The sons of Muspell will push forward to the plain called Vígríð and the wolf Fenrir and the Miðgarð Serpent will go there too. Loki and Hrym with all the frost giants will also be there by then, and all the family of Hel will accompany Loki. The sons of Muspell, however, will form a host in themselves and that a very bright one. The plain Vígríð is a hundred and twenty leagues in every direction.

"When these things are happening, Heimdall will stand up and blow a great blast on the horn Gjöll and awaken all the gods and they will hold an assembly.

Then Óðin will ride to Mímir's spring and ask Mímir's advice for himself and his company. The ash Yggdrasil will tremble and nothing in heaven or earth will be free from fear. The Æsir and all the Einherjar will arm themselves and press forward on to the plain. Óðin will ride first in a helmet of gold and a beautiful coat of mail and with his spear Gungnir, and he will make for the wolf Fenrir. Thór will advance at his side but will be unable to help him, because he will have his hands full fighting the Miðgarð Serpent. Frey will fight against Surt and it will be a hard conflict before Frey falls; the loss of the good sword that he gave to Skírnir will bring about his death. Then the hound Garm, which was bound in front of Gnipahellir, will also get free; he is the worst sort of monster. He will battle with Týr and each will kill the other. Thór will slay the Miðgarð Serpent but stagger back only nine paces before he falls down dead, on account of the poison blown on him by the serpent. The wolf will swallow Óðin and that will be his death. Immediately afterwards, however, Víðar will stride forward and place one foot on the lower jaw of the wolf. On this foot he will be wearing the shoe which has been in the making since the beginning of time; it consists of the strips of leather men pare off at the toes and heels of their shoes, and for this reason people who want to help the Æsir must throw away these strips. Víðar will take the wolf's upper jaw in one hand and tear his throat asunder and that will be the wolf's death. Loki will battle with Heimdall and each will kill the other. Thereupon Surt will fling fire over the earth and burn up the whole world. ∾

---

1 **Description** *Describe Fenrir and the Midgard Serpent.*

Vocabulary

writhe (rīth) *v.* twist the body violently; contort
asunder (ə sun′dər) *adv.* into parts; into different pieces

874 UNIT 5 EARLY EUROPE

From Myth to Romance *Who is Odin, and why will he ask Mimir for advice?* **2**

Summarize *Beginning with this sentence and continuing to the myth's end, briefly summarize the outcomes of the individual battles.* **3**

Writing Practice

Write a Retelling Have students use the Internet or the library to research other stories or poems about the death (and resurrection) of the world. For example, students might research the Aztec "Legend of the Five Suns" or the story of the Apocalypse described in the Book of Revelation. Instruct students to choose one story to retell. Encourage them to read and compare several versions of the story, noting common characters, events, and symbols.

Instruct students to draws on their research in describing the setting, the characters, and the key events in their story. Remind them to use sensory language and concrete details to make the stories come alive. Invite students to read their accounts to the class, to a partner, or privately to you.

Students' stories should

- reflect the values and beliefs of the culture from which the story originated
- incorporate key characters and plot elements from the original account
- use sensory language and concrete details effectively
- use transitional words and phrases to present a clear sequence of events

After You Read

Respond and Think Critically

Respond and Interpret

1. What part of this myth made the strongest impression on you? Explain.

2. (a)Identify the beings that roam the land during the upheaval on Earth. (b)Do they represent forces of good or evil? Explain. (Use information from the glossary on page 873 to support your answer.)

3. (a)On what battlefield does the final conflict take place? (b)Where is this battlefield located? How do you know?

Analyze and Evaluate

4. (a)What is the battle's final outcome? (b)Based on what you've learned about Norse mythology, why was this outcome inevitable?

5. Based on what you know about other mythologies (Greek and Roman, for example), why is it significant that gods die in this myth?

6. What might evil's triumph over good in this myth indicate about the ancient Norse outlook on life?

Connect

7. **Big Idea** **From Myth to Romance** How are the characters, events, and ideas in this myth similar to and different from myths of other cultures with which you are familiar?

8. **Connect to Today** This myth uses Icelandic winters and local creatures such as wolves to represent destructive forces. What images of destruction might exist in a modern end of the world story?

Literary Element Description

Description involves a detailed portrayal of a person, a place, an object, or an event.

1. What is particularly menacing about Fenrir and the Midgard Serpent?

2. (a)Which individual battle do you think is described most graphically? (b)Do you think the description is effective? Why or why not?

Reading Strategy Summarize

A **summary** is a boiled-down, distilled, and refined statement of the key details in a text.

1. Identify the characters and places in this myth.

2. In your own words, briefly summarize the plot of this myth. Use your notes from page 871.

LOG ON ▶ **Literature** Online

Selection Resources For Selection Quizzes, eFlashcards, and Reading-Writing Connection activities, go to glencoe.com and enter QuickPass code GLW6053u5.

Vocabulary Practice

Practice with Word Usage Respond to these statements to help you explore the meanings of the vocabulary words from the myth.

1. Identify an event that has caused **misery**.

2. Explain how you might **sever** something.

3. Name something that makes you **writhe**.

4. Explain how you might put two things **asunder**.

Writing

Write a Description Write your own description about an event that would mark a dramatic turning point in history. Set your description in the future, but make it resemble an event that could really happen. Be sure to use details to paint a picture of the event and appeal to all the senses as Sturluson does.

SNORRI STURLUSON **875**

After You Read

Assess

1. Answers will vary.

2. (a) The wolf Fenrir, the Midgard Serpent, giants led by Hrym, the sons of Muspell led by Surt, and the forces of Hel led by Loki (b) They all represent forces of evil.

3. (a) On a vast plain called Vigrid (b) In Asgard, the home of the gods; the invaders from Midgard cross Bifrost to get to the plain.

4. (a) Surt destroys the world with fire. (b) Norse myths emphasize the futility of the struggle against evil.

5. Gods are usually immortal. That they die in this myth makes them more like human beings.

6. It suggests that they did not believe that the power of good could overcome the power of evil or that any all-powerful benevolent force existed.

7. Similarities include a variety of gods with individual responsibilities; terrifying beasts and giants; and the display of courage. Differences include the mortality of gods, the superiority of evil over good, and a general pessimism about life.

8. Students may mention the threat of nuclear war, uncontrolled epidemics, or global warming.

Literary Element

1. The wolf stalks the earth with a gaping mouth and eyes and nostrils that blaze fire. The serpent agitates the sea, writhing violently as he struggles to reach land.

2. (a) Answers will vary. (b) Have students identify specific images that support their opinions.

Reading Strategy

1. Instruct students to distinguish characters by individual traits.

2. For a sample summary, see page 871 of this teacher's edition.

Vocabulary Practice

Accept all responses that demonstrate an understanding of the numbered statements and the vocabulary words.

Writing

Students' descriptions should

▪ focus on a major event, set in the future

▪ use details to describe many aspects of the event and paint a broad picture

▪ use descriptive language to appeal to all the senses

Vocabulary Workshop

Words from Norse Myth

Focus

Write on the board: In the prophecy about Ragnarok, brothers <u>slaughter</u> one another, gods <u>die</u>, and monsters <u>take</u> control of the earth. Point out to students that all the verbs in this sentence are derived from Norse words.

Say: Many English words are derived from the Norse language. This lesson shows the origins of some of these words.

Teach

Etymology Make sure that students understand how to look up the etymology of a word. The etymology of a word is usually given in brackets [ ] after the definition. Older forms of the word are separated by the symbol >, which means "derived from." Abbreviations for the word's languages of origin, such as *ON* for Old Norse, are also included.

Assess

Practice

1. d **2.** c **3.** e **4.** a **5.** b

Vocabulary Practice

Understand Word Parts Write the following words, which all have roots derived from Old Norse, on the board:

lowering

uplifted

unwanted

Have students identify the meanings of the prefixes and suffixes in the words. Then have them use a dictionary to find the etymologies of the Norse roots. Finally,

have them use each word correctly in a sentence. *(Lowering: the suffix -er denotes the comparative form of an adjective, the suffix -ing forms the present participle of a verb, the root* low *is derived from the Old Norse* lagr. *Uplifted: the prefix* up- *means "upward," the suffix -ed means "characterized by," the root* lift *is derived from the Old Norse* lypta. *Unwanted: the prefix* un- *means "not," the suffix -ed means*

"characterized by," the root want *is derived from the Old Norse* vanta.)

Learning Objective

In this workshop, you will focus on the following objective:

Vocabulary: Understanding word origins.

Word Origins

Word origins, or etymologies, are the history and development of words. **Word roots** are the part of the word from which the core meaning is derived.

Test-Taking Tip

When you do not know the meaning of a word, consider its root and origin. Thinking about how a word was derived can help you understand its meaning.

LOG ON ▶ **Literature** Online

Vocabulary For more vocabulary practice, go to glencoe.com and enter QuickPass code GLW6053u5.

Vocabulary Workshop

Words from Norse Myth

Literature Connection Though Odin, leader of the Norse gods, met his end in the final conflict of Ragnarok, we still pay tribute to him on our calendar. The English word *Wednesday* comes from the Old English word *Wodnesdaeg,* which means "Woden's day" (Odin's day). In addition, our words *Tuesday, Thursday,* and *Friday* are named for the Norse deities Tyr, Thor, and Freya/Frigg.

Tracing the etymology, or origin, of a word can help you understand how words from other cultures enter our language. Modern English has its roots in Old English, the language of the Anglo-Saxons who lived in England during the early Middle Ages. The development of Old English was influenced in part by the Scandinavian Vikings who invaded and settled the British Isles. Thus, it is not surprising that many English words can be traced directly or through Old English to Norse origins. For example, the word "berserk" comes from the Norse word meaning "bear shirt." Below is a chart of English words and their definitions, along with their etymologies showing the Norse words from which they were derived.

English Word	Etymology
skill *n.* ability gained by practice; expertise	from Middle English *skil,* meaning "cause, reason"; from Old Norse *skil,* "knowledge, distinction"
husband *n.* a married man	from Old English *husbonda,* meaning "master of the house"; from Old Norse *husbondi,* meaning "householder, peasant who owns land"
ski *n.* one of a pair of long, flat, thin pieces of wood, plastic, or metal used for gliding over snow	from Norwegian *ski* (same meaning); from Old Norse *skith,* meaning "stick of wood"

Practice Match the English words below with their meanings from their Norse origins. Use a dictionary to check your answers.

1. sky   **a.** whip

2. gape   **b.** butcher's meat

3. stagger   **c.** open the mouth wide

4. fling   **d.** cloud

5. slaughter   **e.** push

Before You Read

from the *Song of Roland*

The *Song of Roland*, often called the national epic of France, is the earliest known example of the genre of medieval French poetry called *chansons de geste*, or "songs of deeds." The poem, whose authorship is unknown, was composed around the year 1100, but is based on a historical event from centuries earlier that grew into a legend passed down from one generation to the next.

The Empire Charlemagne (shär´ lə mān´), or Charles the Great, was king of the Franks (an early Germanic tribe) from 768 to 814. After years of campaigning against various warring kings and city-states, he managed to establish a unified state in Western Europe, an area roughly equivalent to the ancient Roman Empire. In 800, Pope Leo III crowned Charlemagne as the first emperor in the West since the fall of Rome. He was a civilized king instrumental in spreading Christianity, art, and learning throughout Western Europe. His domain later became known as the Holy Roman Empire, and in one form or another, it lived on until 1806.

The Story Behind the Epic In Charlemagne's time, Arab Muslims ruled Spain. Agreeing to intercede between two of their warring factions, Charlemagne led a siege on the Spanish city of Saragossa in 778. But his Spanish campaign was a disaster, and he was forced to retreat. With his army, he crossed the Pyrenees Mountains that divide France and Spain. There, in the narrow pass at Roncevaux (rawns voh´), his rear guard was attacked and destroyed by local mountaineers known as Basques. One of the soldiers killed in this battle was a commander named Roland.

The Legend Grows Approximately 300 years later, in the eleventh century, Roland was celebrated in an epic poem. During this time, Europe was in the throes of the Crusades, the series of holy wars fought by Christians hoping to reclaim the city of Jerusalem from the Muslims and restore it as a center of Christianity. Feelings against Muslims ran high throughout Europe. In the legend of Roland, the attackers were no longer Christian Basques, but Muslims—the pagan "Saracens" referred to in the poem. Their force had grown from a small local band of mountaineers to a fierce army 400,000 strong. The conflict itself had swollen into an epic battle between Christianity and Islam, reflecting the large-scale battles fought during the Crusades. Roland, who had played only a minor role in the actual Spanish expedition, was now Charlemagne's nephew, his most valiant chieftain—and a legendary epic hero.

> "'The end! The end of the world is upon us!' . . . it is the worldwide grief for the death of Roland."
>
> —from the *Song of Roland*

Olifant, 1st 1/2 11th century. Musee Paul Dupuy, Toulouse, France.

SONG OF ROLAND **877**

Before You Read

Focus

Bellringer Options

Selection Focus Transparency 52

Daily Language Practice Transparency 82

Or ask: To what extent is perfection required from a hero? Point out that for all their bravery and goodness, heroes are also often flawed. Ask why these flaws might prove more endearing than off-putting to generations of listeners. *(They make the heroes more human, so the audience can identify with them.)*

Literary History ☆

Chansons de geste *Chansons de geste* were probably composed by wandering musicians. Performers called *jongleurs* sang them to the accompaniment of a bowed, stringed instrument. The audience for a *chanson de geste*, which could range in length from about 1,000 words to 20,000 words, were pilgrims who were on their way to the holy places where the heroes of the tales were said to be buried.

Selection Skills

Literary Elements
- Epic (SE pp. 878–882, 885)

from the **Song of Roland**

Speaking/Listening/Viewing Skills
- Oral Interpretation (TE p. 880)

Reading Skills
- Evaluate Characters (SE p. 878, 880, 883, 885)
- Analyze Structure (TE p. 878)
- Draw Conclusions (TE p. 882)

Vocabulary Skills
- Word Origins (SE p. 885; TE p. 878)
- Analogies (TE p. 884)

Writing Skills/Grammar
- Character Sketch (SE p. 885)
- Analyze Epic Hero (TE p. 882)

Before You Read

Focus

Summary

Roland, a military commander, and his troops are in a desperate situation in the midst of the battle of Roncevaux. When Roland is finally ready to sound the horn to call for help from the main army, an angry Oliver upbraids Roland for having placed them in this situation because of his pride. The archbishop steps in to stop their quarrel and urges them to at least die nobly. Although Roland sounds the horn, the treacherous Ganelon discourages the king from responding. Roland dies, and angels bear his soul to Paradise.

 For summaries in languages other than English, see Unit 5 Teaching Resources Book, pp. 34–39.

Vocabulary

Word Origins Divide the class into groups of five, and have each student find the etymology of one of the vocabulary words. Have them focus on and copy all the abbreviations in the etymology, or the portion of the entry that details the word's origins. When students have finished, have them compile a list of abbreviations and symbols that students need in order to read etymologies in the dictionary. For example, students might list and explain *OE, AF, L,* and *fr.,* as well as the use of brackets to enclose etymologies.

 For additional vocabulary practice, see Unit 5 Teaching Resources Book, p. 42.

Literature and Reading Preview

Connect to the Epic

Which of these two qualities do you think is more valuable in a leader: the ability to set an example through individual excellence, or the ability to make sure the whole team functions smoothly as a unit? Discuss this question with a partner.

Build Background

Ganelon, Roland's stepfather, became furious because Roland had recommended him for the dangerous job of Charlemagne's ambassador to the Saracen king Marsilion. Turning traitor, Ganelon encouraged Marsilion to attack the rear guard of Charlemagne's army, and also persuaded Charlemagne to place Roland in command of that rear guard. As this excerpt opens, Roland, his loyal friend Oliver, and a small detachment of troops are trapped in a mountain pass at Roncevaux, under surprise attack by the Saracen army.

Set Purposes for Reading

Big Idea From Epic to Romance

As you read, ask yourself, What medieval values does Roland represent?

Literary Element Epic

An **epic** is a long narrative poem that describes the adventures of a larger-than-life hero. Medieval epics include characteristics such as formal speeches, supernatural elements, battle descriptions, and repetition of key words. As you read, ask yourself, What epic conventions are apparent in this work?

Reading Strategy Evaluate Characters

When you **evaluate characters,** you judge their qualities and compare them with those of other characters in a literary work. As you read, ask yourself, What details can help me assess each character?

Tip: Sort Details In a chart like the one below, list details about Roland. Then decide which qualities those details suggest.

Details	Qualities
Roland earlier refused to blow the horn.	pride; foolhardiness
Roland tries to break his sword so that pagans cannot use it.	

878 UNIT 5 EARLY EUROPE

Learning Objectives

For pages 877–885

In studying this text, you will focus on the following objectives:

Literary Study: Analyzing epic.

Reading: Evaluating characters.

Writing: Writing a character sketch.

Vocabulary

refuge (ref′ūj) *n.* shelter or protection from danger; p. 879 *As the floodwaters rose, townspeople sought refuge by fleeing to higher ground.*

torment (tôr′ment) *n.* great pain or suffering; p. 879 *Psychologists say people who inflict torment on animals are emotionally troubled.*

exult (ig zult′) *v.* to rejoice greatly; p. 881 *Our team exulted after defeating a strong opponent.*

strut (strut) *v.* to walk in a proud manner; p. 882 *The player who scored the touchdown strutted in the end zone.*

feign (fān) *v.* to make a false show of; pretend; p. 882 *Did you feign being sick so you could skip school and avoid that math test?*

Tip: Word Origins Etymologies trace a word's development from its language of origin to its current meaning and usage. For example, *feign* ultimately derives from the Latin *fingere,* meaning "to form, shape, or alter."

Reading Practice

Analyze Structure Have students scan the selection to get some idea of the scope of the *Song of Roland* and the way in which this selection extracts some consecutive and some nonconsecutive portions of the text.

Ask: What is the structure of this "song"? **or** What is this song composed of? *(The song consists of stanzas of varying lengths.)* **Ask:** Why do you think the stanzas vary in length? *(Students may* conjecture that the song was not written as a single, unified work but created over the years by its many performers.)*

878

from the
Song of Roland

Charlemagne battling the Neapolitans. French Illumination from the History of Emperors. Bibliotheque de l'Arsenal, Paris.

Translated by
Frederick Goldin

❧ 110 ❧

The battle is fearful and full of grief.
Oliver and Roland strike like good men,
the Archbishop°, more than a thousand blows,
and the Twelve Peers° do not hang back, they strike!
5 the French fight side by side, all as one man.
The pagans die by hundreds, by thousands:
whoever does not flee finds no **refuge** from death,
like it or not, there he ends all his days.
And there the men of France lose their greatest arms;
10 they will not see their fathers, their kin again,
or Charlemagne, who looks for them in the passes.
Tremendous **torment** now comes forth in France,
a mighty whirlwind, tempests of wind and thunder,
rains and hailstones, great and immeasurable,
15 bolts of lightning hurtling and hurtling down:
it is, in truth, a trembling of the earth.
From Saint Michael-in-Peril to the Saints,
from Besançon to the port of Wissant,°
there is no house whose veil of walls does not crumble.

Epic *What details in this stanza suggest that this battle is one of epic proportions?*

Vocabulary

refuge (ref′ ūj) *n.* shelter or protection from danger
torment (tôr′ ment) *n.* great pain or suffering

---

3 Archbishop: Turpin, archbishop of Reims and chaplain for Charlemagne's forces.

4 Twelve Peers: Charlemagne's top military leaders.

17–18 Saint Michael . . . Wissant: By naming cities in various parts of France, the song suggests the battle's far-reaching impact.

SONG OF ROLAND **879**

Teach

Literary Element

Epic **Answer:** *Every element is larger-than-life: the Archbishop strikes "more than a thousand blows," soldiers die "by hundreds, by thousands," and the weather is freakishly bad.*

View the Art ★

This illustration comes from an illuminated manuscript, a hand-written book that includes vividly colored illustrations and highly detailed decorations, often incorporating actual gold. **Ask: What makes Charlemagne's army seem formidable or unstoppable?** *(It is huge. Its soldiers can be seen far into the distance. The soldiers are on horseback, while the enemy is trampled underfoot. The soldiers have full suits of armor, swords, and lances.)*

 For an audio recording of this selection, use Listening Library Audio CD-ROM.

Learning Objectives
Analyzing epic. (SE)
Evaluating characters. (SE)
Finding word origins. (TE)

Approaching Level

DIFFERENTIATED INSTRUCTION

Analyze Structure Call attention to the blue numbers that appear before stanzas. **Ask: What does the number 110 tell you at the very beginning of the selection?** *(This is the 110th stanza in the poem; much has already happened.)* Remind students that whenever they are reading an excerpt, they should refer to Build Background to help them understand what is happening. For example, the background information tells where Oliver and Roland are and what is happening as the selection opens. **Say:** Preview the text structure by turning to pages 880–881. **Ask: What do the numbers 130, 131, 132, and 134 tell you on these pages?** *(The story has jumped ahead from the stanza 110, but now several stanzas are being retold as in the original version.)* Point out that the selection students are reading will continue to leave out portions of the original, and that students may need to fill in some gaps as they read.

Teach

Epic Answer: *The claim that grief for Roland's death is "world-wide" emphasizes his importance.*

(ADVANCED) **Ask:** What other clues in this first stanza would lead you to categorize this work as an epic? *(The author emphasizes the magnitude of the battle by using terms such as* fearful *and* full of grief *and by referring to people dying by the hundreds and thousands. There are also extraordinary natural or supernatural phenomena, such as the eclipse and the trembling of the earth.)*

Reading Strategy | **2**

Evaluate Characters
Answer: *On the basis of Oliver's claims, one can say Roland lacks judgment and restraint and it is his fault that so many have died in this surprise attack.*

Cultural History

Oliphants Modern musical horn instruments that are made out of metal had their beginnings in oliphants. Oliphants were end-blown horns used by the military and the nobility in medieval Europe. The horns, usually made from valuable elephant tusks or ox horns, were often as intricately carved as pieces of art.

880

---

20 A great darkness at noon falls on the land,
    there is no light but when the heavens crack.
    No man sees this who is not terrified,
    and many say: "The Last Day! Judgment Day!
    The end! The end of the world is upon us!"
25 They do not know, they do not speak the truth:
    it is the worldwide grief for the death of Roland.°

❧ 130 ❧

    And Roland says: "We are in a rough battle.
    I'll sound the olifant,° Charles will hear it."
    Said Oliver: "No good vassal would do it.
30 When I urged it, friend, you did not think it right.
    If Charles were here, we'd come out with no losses.
    Those men down there—no blame can fall on them."
    Oliver said: "Now by this beard of mine,
    If I can see my noble sister, Aude,°
35 once more, you will never lie in her arms!"

❧ 131 ❧

    And Roland said: "Why are you angry at me?"
    Oliver answers: "Companion, it is your doing.
    I will tell you what makes a vassal good:
            it is judgment, it is never madness;
40 restraint is worth more than the raw nerve of a fool.
    Frenchmen are dead because of your wildness.
    And what service will Charles ever have from us?
    If you had trusted me, my lord would be here,
    we would have fought this battle through to the end,
45 Marsilion would be dead, or our prisoner.
    Roland, your prowess—had we never seen it!°
            And now, dear friend, we've seen the last of it.
    No more aid from us now for Charlemagne,
    a man without equal till Judgment Day,
50 you will die here, and your death will shame France.
    We kept faith, you and I, we were companions;
            and everything we were will end today.
    We part before evening, and it will be hard."

> **Epic** *How does the narrator emphasize Roland's importance?* | **1**

> **Evaluate Characters** *What judgment can you make about Roland's character based on Oliver's claims?* | **2**

26 death of Roland: Roland has not died at this point, but the narrative suggests that the natural world is already mourning his coming death.

28 olifant (also spelled *oliphant*): a horn made of an elephant's tusk.

34 Aude: Oliver's sister, is engaged to marry Roland.

41–46 Frenchmen . . . seen it: When Roland's troops were ambushed, Oliver had begged Roland to sound his horn and call for help immediately, but out of pride Roland had refused.

Speaking and Listening Practice

Present an Oral Interpretation With death near, Oliver does not mince words as he speaks to Roland. Turpin responds with great emotion and urgency. Have students work in groups of three to prepare dramatic readings of stanzas 130–132. Remind students that they must capture all the passion and gravity of three men who are about to die and to whom honor and their king are everything. Suggest these steps:

1. Read the text again for sense.
2. Script parts using the exact words of the text wherever possible.
3. Analyze each part to determine tone of voice, gestures, body language, changes in volume, and pauses.
4. Rehearse. If possible, get feedback.
5. Perform for the class.

❧ 132 ❧

Turpin the Archbishop hears their bitter words,
55 digs hard into his horse with golden spurs
and rides to them; begins to set them right:
"You, Lord Roland, and you, Lord Oliver,
I beg you in God's name do not quarrel.
To sound the horn could not help us now, true,
60 but still it is far better that you do it:
let the King come, he can avenge us then—
these men of Spain must not go home **exulting!**
Our French will come, they'll get down on
       their feet,
and find us here—we'll be dead, cut to pieces.
65 They will lift us into coffins on the backs of mules,
and weep for us, in rage and pain and grief,
and bury us in the courts of churches;
and we will not be eaten by wolves or pigs or dogs."
Roland replies, "Lord, you have spoken well."

❧ 134 ❧

70 And now the mighty effort of Roland the Count:
he sounds his olifant; his pain is great,
and from his mouth the bright blood comes
       leaping out,
and the temple bursts in his forehead.
That horn, in Roland's hands, has a mighty voice:
75 King Charles hears it drawing through the passes.
Naimon° heard it, the Franks listen to it.
And the King said: "I hear Count Roland's horn;
he'd never sound it unless he had a battle."
Says Ganelon: "Now no more talk of battles!
80 You are old now, your hair is white as snow,
the things you say make you sound like a child.
You know Roland and that wild pride of his—
what a wonder God has suffered it so long!
Remember? he took Noples without your command:

76 **Naimon:** one of Charlemagne's
dukes.

Epic *Why might Roland's blowing of the horn be considered heroic?*   **3**

Vocabulary

exult (ig zult´) *v.* to rejoice greatly

***Charlemagne (Charles the Great) in his
coronation robes,*** 16th century. after
Albrecht Dürer. Oil on Canvas, 213 x 113
cm. Kunsthistorisches Museum, Vienna.

View the Art Charlemagne brought
order and Christian culture to the
western part of the former Roman
Empire. How has the artist tried to give
a sense of the emperor's personality?

SONG OF ROLAND   **881**

Teach

Literary Element   **3**

Epic Answer: *He continues to
sound the horn in spite of the pain
it causes him and in spite of the
knowledge that he may be causing
his own death.*

View the Art ★

Answer: *Charlemagne appears
regal, and the sword held in his
right hand and the cross in his left
hand suggest the importance he
placed on political power and on
religion.*

Albrecht Dürer was commissioned
to paint a portrait of Charlemagne
in 1513 by the city of Nuremberg,
which possessed Charlemagne's
sword, crown, and robes. He created an idealized image. The arms
of Germany and France can be
seen at the top of the painting.

Learning Objectives
Analyzing epic. (SE)
Evaluating characters. (SE)
Analyzing art. (TE)
Presenting an oral interpretation. (TE)

English Learners

DIFFERENTIATED INSTRUCTION

Intermediate Before students prepare
their oral interpretation, review the use of
context clues. Practice using context clues
to figure out the meaning of *restraint* in
stanza 131. (Judgment *may be a synonym;*
madness *may be an antonym*). Ask pairs
of students to isolate context clues for these
words and to discuss what they think each
means: stanza 130: *vassal;* stanza 131:
prowess; stanza 132: *avenge* and *exulting*.

Advanced Learners/Pre-AP

DIFFERENTIATED INSTRUCTION

Explore Point of View Divide advanced
students into groups of four. Based on
stanzas 130–132, have three students take
on the characters of Roland, Oliver, and
Turpin, with the fourth taking on the role
of narrator. Students should discuss their
characters' depictions, complimenting or
complaining about how the narrator presents them. Each character should suggest
some additions or deletions to the text that
will improve the text from his or her point
of view. The narrator should defend the
text.

Teach

Draw Conclusions Have students reread Ganelon's words beginning at line 82. **Say:** Recall what you read in Build Background and other details in the epic so far. Then draw conclusions about Ganelon's motivations and his credibility in this passage. *(Ganelon is motivated by envy; nevertheless, Oliver's words suggest the same kind of imprudence and pride that Ganelon displays here. Ganelon, however, is more hyperbolic and nasty about Roland's weaknesses, as evidenced by word choices such as* strutting *and* bragging.*)*

Epic Answer: *Despite his oncoming death, Roland prays for his soldiers as well as for himself; then he walks as far as he can, to die removed from public view.*

ADVANCED **Ask:** Does Roland fear death? *(He appears not to. His actions suggest that he is living up to a code—"there must be no reproach"— that he believes will ensure his honor before both man and God. Students may ask why it would be necessary for Roland to pray for himself if he did not fear death or feel the need somehow to commend himself.)*

---

85   the Saracens rode out, to break the siege;
     they fought with him, the great vassal Roland.
     Afterwards he used the streams to wash the blood
     from the meadows: so that nothing would show.
     He blasts his horn all day to catch a rabbit,
90   he's **strutting** now before his peers and bragging—
     who under heaven would dare meet him on the field?
     So now: ride on! Why do you keep on stopping?
     The Land of Fathers° lies far ahead of us."

1

93 Land of Fathers: Ganelon is referring to France.

⟨168⟩

     Now Roland feels that death is very near.
95   His brain comes spilling out through his two ears;
     prays to God for his peers: let them be called;
     and for himself, to the angel Gabriel;°
     took the oliphant: there must be no reproach!
     took Durendal his sword in his other hand,
100 and farther than a crossbow's farthest shot
     he walks toward Spain, into a fallow° land,
     and climbs a hill: there beneath two fine trees
     stand four great blocks of stone, all are of marble;
     and he fell back, to earth, on the green grass,
105 has fainted there, for death is very near.

97 Gabriel: The archangel Gabriel served as God's messenger.

101 fallow: plowed but not sown with seed.

⟨169⟩

     High are the hills, and high, high are the trees;
     there stand four blocks of stone, gleaming of marble.
     Count Roland falls fainting on the green grass,
     and is watched, all this time, by a Saracen:
110 who has **feigned** death and lies now with the others,
     has smeared blood on his face and on his body;
     and quickly now gets to his feet and runs—
     a handsome man, strong, brave, and so crazed with pride
     that he does something mad and dies for it:
115 laid hands on Roland, and on the arms of Roland,

Epic *Read the rest of this stanza. How does Roland continue to prove himself a true epic hero?*   **2**

Vocabulary

strut (strut) *v.* to walk in a proud manner
feign (fān) *v.* to make a false show of; pretend

Writing Practice

Analyze Epic Hero Review the definition of *epic hero* with students. Then have students work in pairs to isolate and identify each of Roland's words, thoughts, and actions in stanzas 169 and 170 as characteristic or not characteristic of an epic hero. *(Stanza 169: Roland falls dying to the ground—not characteristic; "the Count begins to come round"—characteristic because the Count has high social status and his action is legendary.*

Stanza 170—characteristic because shouting "you aren't one of ours" and "you nobody" embodies the ideals of his people and sending "two eyes flying out of his head" is a legendary action.)

Have students draft an essay analyzing stanzas 169 and 170 for their portrayal of an epic hero. Remind them to present a thesis in their opening paragraph and to explain and support that thesis in their body paragraphs.

and cried: "Conquered! Charles's nephew conquered!
I'll carry this sword home to Arabia!"
As he draws it, the Count begins to come round.

⊰170⊱

Now Roland feels: *someone taking his sword!*
120 opened his eyes, and had one word for him:
"I don't know you, you aren't one of ours";
grasps that olifant that he will never lose,
strikes on the helm° beset with gems in gold,
shatters the steel, and the head, and the bones,
125 sent his two eyes flying out of his head,
dumped him over stretched out at his feet dead;
and said: "You nobody! how could you dare
lay hands on me—rightly or wrongly: how?
Who'll hear of this and not call you a fool?
130 Ah! the bell-mouth of the olifant is smashed,
the crystal and the gold fallen away."

⊰173⊱

Roland the Count strikes down on a dark rock,
and the rock breaks, breaks more than I can tell,
and the blade grates, but Durendal will not break,
135 the sword leaped up, rebounded toward the sky.
The Count, when he sees that sword will not be broken,
softly, in his own presence, speaks the lament:
"Ah Durendal, beautiful, and most sacred,
the holy relics in this golden pommel!
140 Saint Peter's tooth and blood of Saint Basile,
a lock of hair of my lord Saint Denis,
and a fragment of blessed Mary's robe:
your power must not fall to the pagans,
you must be served by Christian warriors.
145 May no coward ever come to hold you!
It was with you I conquered those great lands

123 **helm:** helmet.

Evaluate Characters *What does Roland's interaction with the Saracen in this stanza indicate about his character?* **3**

From Epic to Romance *What does Roland fear will happen to Durendal? What might his attitude toward his sword reveal about medieval values?* **4**

Teach

Reading Strategy   3

Evaluate Characters
Answer: *Even though Roland is near death, he is quick-witted and agile when confronted by the Saracen. He shows no pity for the enemy and is easily angered.*

Progress Check

Can students evaluate characters?

If No → See Unit 5 Teaching Resources Book, p. 41.

Big Idea   4

From Epic to Romance
Answer: *He feels his sword will be sullied in the hands of his enemies. Students may feel his devotion to the sword's religious connections shows piety; others may feel it shows an intolerance for others' beliefs.*

Learning Objectives
Analyzing epic. (SE)
Evaluating characters. (SE)
Drawing conclusions. (TE)
Analyzing epic hero. (TE)

Advanced Learners/Pre-AP

DIFFERENTIATED INSTRUCTION

Analyze Imagery, Figurative Language, and Allusion Have students analyze how, in stanzas 169 and 170, imagery, figurative language, and allusion contribute to Roland's characterization as an epic hero. (*Students may mention visual and auditory images, such as grating blades; hyperbole such as the high hills, the flying eyes, the shattered rock; personification of Durendal; and allusions to Christian relics.*)

Visualize Before students write, read stanzas 169 and 170 aloud and ask students to visualize what is happening, forming a picture of the action in their mind. You might also ask students to identify the sounds they hear and compare their visualizations.

Teach

Literary Element · 1

Epic **Ask:** In what ways does this ending reflect the characteristics of a medieval epic?

(Students should identify the supernatural elements of angels, saints, and Paradise.)

Progress Check

Can students analyze epic?

If No → See Unit 5 Teaching Resources Book, p. 40.

Big Idea · 2

From Epic to Romance
Answer: *His confession and his prayer reaffirm the importance of the church during this time.*

View the Art ★

Death of Roland By the fifteenth century, artists were using later versions of the legend, as in this detail from the so-called Pseudo-Turpin chronicle, which shows Baldwin, Roland's half-brother, kneeling over the figure of the dead hero while the battle rages in the background. Next to Roland's body is his sword, Durendal. **Ask:** What other detail in the foreground is at odds with the version of the story that you just read? *(The original version says that Roland smashed the oliphant against the head of a Saracen, but in this painting, it lies unscathed next to the body of Roland.)*

To check students' understanding of the selection, see Unit 5 Teaching Resources Book, p. 45.

Death of Roland during the Battle in the Valley of Roncevalles, 15th century. Attributed to Jean Fouquet. Illumination from Les grandes chroniques des rois de France. Bibliotheque Nationale, Paris. ★

that Charles has in his
    keeping, whose beard
    is white,
the Emperor's lands, that
    make him rich and strong."

⁂176⁂

Count Roland lay stretched out beneath a pine;
150 he turned his face toward the land of Spain,
began to remember many things now:
how many lands, brave man, he had conquered;
and he remembered: sweet France, the men of his line,
remembered Charles, his lord, who fostered him:°
155 cannot keep, remembering, from weeping, sighing;
but would not be unmindful of himself:
he confesses his sins, prays God for mercy:
"Loyal Father, you who never failed us,
who resurrected Saint Lazarus from the dead,
160 and saved your servant Daniel° from the lions:
now save the soul of me from every peril
for the sins I committed while I still lived."
Then he held out his right glove to his Lord:
Saint Gabriel took the glove from his hand.
165 He held his head bowed down upon his arm, **1**
he is gone, his two hands joined, to his end.
Then God sent him his angel Cherubin
and Saint Michael, angel of the sea's Peril;°
and with these two there came Saint Gabriel:
170 they bear Count Roland's soul to Paradise.

154 Charles . . . him: Roland was brought up in the household of Charlemagne, his uncle.

160 Daniel: According to the Bible, Daniel was thrown into a den of lions as punishment for praying to God rather than to King Darius of Babylon. God kept the lions from harming Daniel.

167–168 Cherubin . . . Peril: The poet here depicts the cherubim—a group of angels whose function is to praise God—as Cherubin, a single angel. St. Michael the Archangel is the patron saint of sailors.

From Epic to Romance *How does Roland's piety relate to medieval culture?* **2**

884 UNIT 5 EARLY EUROPE

Vocabulary Practice

Understand Analogies Provide test-taking and vocabulary skills practice by assigning these analogies or working through them together as a class.

1. profanity : irreverence : : prayer :
a. blasphemy
b. answer
c. piety

2. carpenter : build : : farmer :
a. raze
b. grow
c. compose

3. illogic : fallacy : : bargain :
a. discount
b. reason
c. indulge

*(Answers: **1.** c **2.** b **3.** a)*

After You Read

Respond and Think Critically

Respond and Interpret

1. Do you think Roland is a hero because he dies for his king and his country? Explain.

2. (a)What causes the quarrel between Roland and Oliver, and what reasoning does Turpin use to resolve it? (b)Why do you think Roland rejected Oliver's advice until it was too late?

3. (a)What is Roland's last action in life? (b)How does this contribute to his stature as a hero?

Analyze and Evaluate

4. A **symbol** is something that stands for itself and something in addition to itself. How does Roland's sword, Durendal, function as a symbol?

5. Roland dies from sounding the horn to call for help, not from a wound suffered in battle. What do you think the poet means to imply by this?

6. Identify two examples of **repetition** in this poem and comment on their effectiveness.

7. What are some reasons that might justify the poet's alteration of historical facts in this poem?

Connect

8. **Big Idea** **From Epic to Romance** What insights into medieval culture can you gain from this excerpt from the *Song of Roland*?

9. **Connect to Today** If these events had taken place in modern times, do you think Roland would be celebrated as a hero? Why or why not?

Literary Element Epic

The *Song of Roland* is an epic that stems from an oral tradition that combines history with myth and reflects the cultural values of medieval society.

1. Name three character traits that qualify Roland as an epic hero.

2. Identify two supernatural elements in the epic.

Reading Strategy Evaluate Characters

You can **evaluate characters** based on their speech, motivations, and actions. Review the chart you made on page 878 and then answer these questions.

1. How would you evaluate the character of Oliver?

2. How would you evaluate Ganelon, Roland's stepfather?

LOG ON  **Literature** Online

Selection Resources For Selection Quizzes, eFlashcards, and Reading-Writing Connection activities, go to glencoe.com and enter QuickPass code GLW6053u5.

Vocabulary Practice

Practice with Word Origins Studying the etymology of a word can help you better explore its meaning. Create a word map for each boldfaced vocabulary word.

refuge   torment   exult   strut   feign

EXAMPLE:

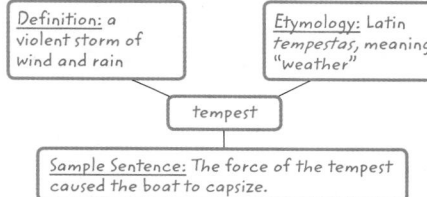

Definition: a violent storm of wind and rain

Etymology: Latin *tempestas*, meaning "weather"

tempest

Sample Sentence: The force of the tempest caused the boat to capsize.

Writing

Write a Character Sketch Write a character sketch of someone you know who has some of Roland's qualities. Describe the positive and negative aspects of your subject's personality.

SONG OF ROLAND **885**

Vocabulary

Sample sentences will vary; other sample answers:

refuge—Definition: shelter or protection from danger; Etymology: L. *refugere* "to escape." **torment**—great pain or suffering; L. *tormentum* "torture." **exult**—To rejoice exceedingly; L. *exsilio* "to leap up." **strut**—to walk in a proud manner; O.E. *strutian* "to stand out stiffly."

feign—to make a false show of; pretend; L. *fingere* "to form, shape, or alter."

Writing

Students' character sketches should

- make connections between Roland and someone the student knows
- include details about the person's traits and actions

After You Read

Assess

1. Answers will vary.

2. (a) Oliver accuses Roland of waiting too long to call for help. Turpin agrees but urges Roland to call anyway so others can avenge their deaths. (b) Roland may have misjudged his enemy.

3. (a) He asks for forgiveness of his sins, his soul, and his soldiers' souls. (b) Piety and concern for others add to his stature.

4. Roland calls his sword "sacred," suggesting that it does holy deeds.

5. The poet may imply that this is Roland's punishment for pride.

6. Repeated references to Judgment Day (stanza 110) and the end of the world and to the idea that "death is very near" (stanza 168) help create the elegiac tone.

7. The poet may have wanted to emphasize Christian heroism.

8. Students may mention the importance of duty to one's lord, bravery in battle, accepting death in battle, and religious piety.

9. Answers will vary.

Literary Element

1. He makes long, formal speeches, fights great battles, and calls on supernatural forces.

2. The storm and Durendal, the unbreakable sword, are examples.

Reading Strategy

1. Oliver knows Roland well enough to be critical of his pride.

2. Ganelon proves himself a true villain by persuading Marsilion to attack the Christians, by persuading the king not to help Roland, and by characterizing Roland as proud and vain.

Before You Read

Bisclavret: The Lay of the Werewolf

Bellringer Options

**Selection Focus
Transparency 53**

**Daily Language Practice
Transparency 83**

Ask: Why do you think stories of werewolves arose and were preserved in the oral tradition? Talk about the pleasure that readers, listeners, and viewers take, even today, in a great horror story. Lead students to discuss the qualities of wolves, such as preying on mammals and traveling in packs, that would have been especially terrifying to people living in isolated huts or small villages at the edge of forests.

Meet **Marie de France**

(late twelfth century)

Marie de France, the earliest known French woman poet, is considered one of the finest poets of her century. Although little is known about her life, historians believe she was aristocratic and knew several languages, including French, English, and Latin. She likely spent many years in England, and may have been the half-sister of Henry II, who ruled from 1154 to 1189.

A Preserver of Culture Although it was customary at the time for authors to remain anonymous, Marie's name appears on three works of twelfth-century French literature. These works are the *Lais*, from which this poem is taken; the *Fables*, a collection of fables translated from English into Old French; and *St. Patrick's Purgatory*, the life of a saint translated from Latin into French. Without Marie's work, these tales would not have survived.

A Keen Observer Marie is best known for her twelve *lais*, short narrative poems written in rhyming couplets and intended to be sung. In these "lays," whose subjects range from love to adventure, Marie presents details of twelfth-century western European court life, including descriptions of the speech and behavior of noble men and women.

A Noble Purpose Marie's purpose in writing these lays was to preserve the oral literature sung by the minstrels who came from Brittany. She explains that she "called to mind those lays I had heard so often . . . I would not that they should perish, forgotten, by the roadside. In my turn, therefore, I have made of them a song, rhymed as well as I am able, and often has their shaping kept me sleepless in my bed."

> "He to whom God has granted wisdom and eloquence in speech ought not to hide these gifts in silence, but gladly to make use of them."
>
> —Marie de France

Ahead of Her Time Everyday women in medieval Europe were generally regarded as inferior to men, but the "courtly love" tradition idealized the concept of femininity. The lover, smitten by the beauty and virtue of his lady, worshipped her from afar. Marie de France wrote within this tradition, but she gave it a new twist by portraying female characters who possess their own personalities. For her, a relationship between a man and a woman should be based on genuine affection. In an age when most marriages were based on economics or politics, this attitude set her apart from the norm.

Literature Online

Author Search For more about Marie de France, go to glencoe.com and enter QuickPass code GLW6053u5.

Literary History ☆

Lays Lays are short romances, or stories written in verse. This translation does not preserve the traditional form of a Medieval French lay, which has a tight poetic structure with uniform stanzas. Each line consists of eight syllables. The earliest source of this poem was likely Celtic legend.

Selection Skills

Literary Elements
- Suspense (SE pp. 887, 891, 893, 896)
- Motivation (SE p. 896)
- Plot (TE p. 894)

← **Bisclavret: The Lay of the Werewolf** →

Speaking/Listening/ Viewing Skills
- Performance (SE p. 897)
- Conduct a Debate (TE pp. 894)

Reading Skills
- Monitor Comprehension (SE pp. 887, 889, 890, 895, 897)
- Draw Conclusions about Culture (TE pp. 890, 892)

Vocabulary Skills
- Context Clues (SE p. 897; TE p. 887)

Writing Skills/Grammar
- Semicolons (TE p. 888)
- Persuasive Argument (TE p. 892)

Literature and Reading Preview

Connect to the Poem

Have you ever known or read about a person who had a hidden side to his or her personality? Write a journal entry that describes how you might react if you discovered a hidden personality trait in someone you were close to.

Build Background

In "Bisclavret," a wife's discovery that her husband is a werewolf causes serious problems in their marriage. In folklore, a werewolf is a human being who turns into a wolf at times and devours animals or people. Legends about werewolves were common in European folklore. Medieval intellectuals dismissed werewolves as creatures of the imagination, but common people believed such creatures were real.

Set Purposes for Reading

Big Idea From Myth to Romance

As you read "Bisclavret," ask yourself, How do medieval superstitions, customs, and traditions form the background of the tale?

Literary Element Suspense

Suspense is the tension or excitement a reader feels about what will happen next in a story. Authors often create a feeling of suspense by putting the central character in a threatening or dangerous situation and raising questions in the reader's mind about what will happen next. As you read the poem, ask yourself, What specific details help create suspense?

Reading Strategy Monitor Comprehension

When you **monitor comprehension,** you pause during reading to determine if you fully understand what is happening in a text. As you pause, you might make predictions, ask questions, paraphrase, and summarize. If you find you cannot complete any of these tasks satisfactorily, go back and reread the parts that are giving you trouble. As you read, ask yourself, What can I do to improve my understanding of the text?

Tip: Take Notes Use a chart like the one below to ask yourself questions about the plot and answer those questions with evidence from the text.

Question	Answer
Why is the wife upset?	Her husband is gone for three days a week, and she doesn't know where he goes.

Learning Objectives

For pages 886–897

In studying this text, you will focus on the following objectives:

Literary Study: Analyzing suspense.

Reading: Monitoring comprehension.

Listening and Speaking: Performing a skit.

Vocabulary

savage (sav′ij) *adj.* wild; untamed, and often fierce; p. 888 *After the savage attack by the dog, Alicia had to undergo several surgeries.*

rational (rash′ən əl) *adj.* able to reason; p. 892 *Despite the chaotic surroundings, Denise remained rational.*

grudge (gruj) *n.* a feeling of hatred or resentment; p. 894 *Simon had a grudge against Kathy for years because of her cruelty toward him when they were children.*

Tip: Context Clues When you read an unfamiliar word, pay close attention to the context, or setting, in which it appears. One type of context clue is an explanation, such as "This beast is rational—he has a mind" (page 892). This sentence indicates that the beast is able to reason.

English Learners

DIFFERENTIATED INSTRUCTION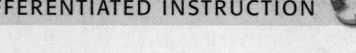

Beginning Tell students that "Bisclavret" is about a wife who discovers that her husband is a werewolf.

- Explain the term *werewolf*, using pictures or verbal explanation.
- Ask students what they think will happen. After students predict, tell them that the wife will trick her husband, who is a true and noble knight.

- Explain the term *knight* using pictures or verbal information.
- Ask students revise their predictions on the basis of what they know about the husband and the wife.

Then have students read to find out what happens between the husband and wife.

Before You Read

Focus

Summary

Bisclavret's habit of disappearing for several days a week so mystifies his wife that she draws from him the details of his secret life: He is a werewolf. With the aid of a knight who loves her, she betrays her husband so that he is unable to revert to human form. The king to whom Bisclavret owes his loyalty finds him and spares his life. When the wolf attacks both Bisclavret's wife and the knight who betrayed him, the king's men conclude that the wolf is Bisclavret and help restore him to human form.

 For summaries in languages other than English, see Unit 5 Teaching Resources Book, pp. 47–52.

Vocabulary

Context Clues Note that context clues can be synonyms, antonyms, definitions, restatements, examples, and more. Have students work in pairs to brainstorms lists of possible context clues for each of the four vocabulary words and to identify the types of clues. Provide this word from the selection as an example: <u>fury</u>

synonym: rage

antonym: calmness

definition: state of intense anger

restatement: a fit of angry displeasure

examples: lashing out verbally and delivering physical blows

 For additional vocabulary practice, see Unit 5 Teaching Resources Book, p. 55.

Teach

Reading Strategy   1

Analyze Structure Ask: Why is there a stanza break after line 14? *(The first fourteen lines are an introduction to the history and content of the poem; the narrative begins with line 15.)*

Big Idea   2

From Myth to Romance
Answer: *These lines tell that in medieval tradition, a werewolf is considered evil. It is described as a furious creature that is likely to eat people and do "much harm."*

View the Art ★

This illustration from an Italian illuminated manuscript presents a dapper knight whose overall appearance suggests the pursuit of pleasure, not war. The code of chivalry followed by knights demanded the virtues of piety, honor, valor, courtesy, and chastity, as well as loyalty to God, his king and master, and his lady.
Ask: How does the painting show that knights enjoyed a privileged status in medieval times? *(The knight has a horse, a pet falcon, an embroidered tunic and a fancy hat; the horse is also adorned richly.)*

For an audio recording of this selection, use Listening Library Audio CD-ROM.

BISCLAVRET
The Lay of the Werewolf

Marie de France
Translated by Robert Hanning and Joan Ferrante

Since I am undertaking to compose *lais*,
I don't want to forget Bisclavret;°
In Breton,° the *lai's* name is *Bisclavret*—
the Normans° call it *Garwaf* [*The Werewolf*].
5   In the old days, people used to say—
and it often actually happened—
that some men turned into werewolves
and lived in the woods.
A werewolf is a **savage** beast;
10   while his fury is on him
he eats men, does much harm,
goes deep in the forest to live.
But that's enough of this for now:
I want to tell you about the Bisclavret. **1**

15   In Brittany there lived a nobleman
whom I've heard marvelously praised;
a fine, handsome knight
who behaved nobly.
He was close to his lord,
20   and loved by all his neighbors.
He had an estimable wife,
one of lovely appearance;
he loved her and she him,
but one thing was very vexing to her:
25   during the week he would be missing
for three whole days, and she didn't know
what happened to him or where he went.

Knight in Blue Tunic on Green Horse. From *Capodilista Codex.* Italian illuminated Manuscript. Bilbioteca Civica, Padua, Italy. ★

2 **Bisclavret:** (bēs′ klä vrā′)

3 **Breton:** (bret′ an) the language spoken by the people of Brittany in northwest France.

4 **Normans:** people who lived just northeast of Brittany.

---

2 **From Myth to Romance** *What do these lines reveal about medieval beliefs about werewolves?*

Vocabulary
savage (sav′ ij) *adj.* wild; untamed, and often fierce

Writing Practice

Use Semicolons Point out to students how frequently semicolons appear at the end of lines in this romance. Have students identify how they function. *(In most cases, a semicolon joins two groups of words that could be sentences on their own. In a few cases, it joins an independent clause and additional words that relate to it.)*

Have students analyze the use of semicolons throughout the narrative and develop a theory about why they are used in many places where a period might have been used instead. *(They help speed the narrative along; they do not create the same final stop that a period would create.)*

Nor did any of his men know anything about it.
One day he returned home
30 happy and delighted;
she asked him about it.
"My lord," she said, "and dear love,
I'd very much like to ask you one thing—
if I dared;
35 but I'm so afraid of your anger
that nothing frightens me more."
When he heard that, he embraced her,
drew her to him and kissed her.
"My lady," he said, "go ahead and ask!
40 There's nothing you could want to know,
that, if I knew the answer, I wouldn't tell you."
"By God," she replied, "now I'm cured!
My lord, on the days when you go away from me
I'm in such a state—
45 so sad at heart,
so afraid I'll lose you—
that if I don't get quick relief
I could die of this very soon.
Please, tell me where you go,
50 where you have been staying.
I think you must have a lover,
and if that's so, you're doing wrong."
"My dear," he said, "have mercy on me, for God's sake!
Harm will come to me if I tell you about this,
55 because I'd lose your love
and even my very self."
When the lady heard this
she didn't take it lightly;
she kept asking him,
60 coaxed and flattered him so much,
that he finally told her what happened to him—
he hid nothing from her.
"My dear, I become a werewolf:
I go off into the great forest,
65 in the thickest part of the woods,
and I live on the prey I hunt down."
When he had told her everything,
she asked further
whether he undressed or kept his clothes on

> *Harm will come to me if I tell you about this, because I'd lose your love and even my very self.*

Monitor Comprehension *Why do you think the knight kept this secret for so long? Was this the right choice? Explain.* **3**

889

Teach

Reading Strategy 3

Monitor Comprehension
Answer: *He felt he would lose her love, as he did. Some students may argue he might have won his wife's sympathy if he had told her earlier.*

Cultural History ☆

Werewolves In the Middle Ages, people lived in fear of wolves, which preyed on livestock and occasionally attacked people. The wolf began to assume mythological status as a symbol of evil and was hunted ruthlessly. The word *werewolf* comes from the Old English word *wer*, meaning "man" and *wulf*, meaning "wolf." The word *wer* is related to the Latin word *vir*, from which derive such words as *virility* and *virtue*, designations of two manly traits of a medieval knight.

Learning Objectives
Monitoring comprehension. (SE)
Analyzing structure. (TE)
Using semicolons. (TE)

Approaching Level
DIFFERENTIATED INSTRUCTION

Use Semicolons as Separators
Remind students that they can use semicolons, as well as colons, as devices for dividing text into manageable units. For example, one good strategy for reading is to break long sentences down into smaller parts. Use the first four lines of the selection as a model for dividing two distinct parts of a sentence. Have students paraphrase the meaning of both portions of the sentence.

Advanced Learners/Pre-AP
DIFFERENTIATED INSTRUCTION

Compare Uses of Punctuation
Ask advanced students to determine similarities and differences in the use of colons, dashes, and semicolons. *(All appear frequently at the ends of lines. The semicolon tends to join phrases and clauses and other units of discourse, linking ideas and making for a smoother narrative. The colon and dash tend to separate clauses and other units of discourse, creating dramatic pauses or emphasizing information.)*

Teach

Reading Strategy   1

Monitor Comprehension

Answer: *Students may explain that early impressions of her as a loyal and loving wife change when she quickly decides to "get rid of" Bisclavret.*

[APPROACHING] **Say:** I am going to review what happened. The wife has just learned that her husband is a werewolf. What does she decide to do once she learns this information? *(to get rid of him)*

[when he became a werewolf].

70   "Wife," he replied, "I go stark naked."
     "Tell me, then, for God's sake, where your clothes are."
     "That I won't tell you;
     for if I were to lose them,
     and then be discovered,
75   I'd stay a werewolf forever.
     I'd be helpless
     until I got them back.
     That's why I don't want their hiding place to be known."
     "My lord," the lady answered,
80   "I love you more than all the world;
     you mustn't hide anything from me
     or fear me in any way:
     that doesn't seem like love to me.
     What wrong have I done? For what sin of mine
85   do you mistrust me about anything?
     Do the right thing and tell me!"
     She harassed and bedeviled him so,°
     that he had no choice but to tell her.
     "Lady," he said, "near the woods,
90   beside the road that I use to get there,
     there's an old chapel
     that has often done me good service;
     under a bush there is a big stone,
     hollowed out inside;
95   I hide my clothes right there
     until I'm ready to come home."
     The lady heard this wonder
     and turned scarlet from fear;
     she was terrified of the whole adventure.
100   Over and over she considered
     how she might get rid of him;
     she never wanted to sleep with him again.
     There was a knight of that region
     who had loved her for a long time,
105   who begged for her love,
     and dedicated himself to serving her.
     She'd never loved him at all,
     nor pledged her love to him,
     but now she sent a messenger for him,
110   and told him her intention.
     "My dear," she said, "cheer up!"

87 **harassed and bedeviled:** exhausted by persistent questioning.

> *What wrong have I done? For what sin of mine do you mistrust me about anything?*

---

1   Monitor Comprehension *What do you think of the wife at this point? Has your opinion changed since she was first introduced? Explain.*

Reading Practice

Draw Conclusions About Culture
Have students draw at least three conclusions about the culture of knights and their ladies, which forms the backdrop of this tale. *(The knights appear drawn to the lady for her looks and do not assess her motives or her virtue; the woman both fears her husband's anger and also exercises considerable power over the men who love her; people believe in werewolves; knights can adore a married woman; codes of monogamous virtue do not appear to be strong; the king has ultimate privilege and authority.)*

        I shall now grant you without delay
        what you have suffered for;
        you'll meet with no more refusals—
115   I offer you my love and my body;
        make me your mistress!"
        He thanked her graciously
        and accepted her promise,
        and she bound him to her by an oath.
120   Then she told him
        how her husband went away and what happened to him;
        she also taught him the precise path
        her husband took into the forest,
        and then she sent the knight to get her husband's clothes.
125   So Bisclavret was betrayed,
        ruined by his own wife.
        Since people knew he was often away from home
        they all thought
        this time he'd gone away forever.
130   They searched for him and made inquiries
        but could never find him,
        so they had to let matters stand.
        The wife later married the other knight,
        who had loved her for so long.
135   A whole year passed
        until one day the king went hunting;
        he headed right for the forest
        where Bisclavret was.
        When the hounds were unleashed,
140   they ran across Bisclavret;
        the hunters and the dogs
        chased him all day,
        until they were just about to take him
        and tear him apart,
145   at which point he saw the king
        and ran to him, pleading for mercy.
        He took hold of the king's stirrup,
        kissed his leg and his foot.
        The king saw this and was terrified;
150   he called his companions.
        "My lords," he said, "come quickly!
        Look at this marvel—
        this beast is humbling itself to me.
        It has the mind of a man, and it's begging me for mercy!

Wolf-Beast from December: Book of Hours, 15th century. Workshop of the Bedford Master, French illuminated manuscript. The Huntington Library, San Marino, CA.

Suspense *How does this passage create a feeling of suspense?* **2**

MARIE DE FRANCE **891**

Approaching Level

DIFFERENTIATED INSTRUCTION

Make a Chart To draw conclusions about culture, suggest that students create a two-column chart like this one and try to list two or more bits of evidence from the lay for each conclusion they draw.

Evidence	Conclusion About the Culture

Advanced Learners/Pre-AP

DIFFERENTIATED INSTRUCTION

Compare and Contrast Have students compare and contrast the cultural values expressed in this lay with those expressed in the excerpt from the *Song of Roland,* pages 879–884, and "Federigo's Falcon," pages 928–932. *(Students may focus on expressions of faith and loyalty in the Song of Roland and "Bisclavret"; they may focus on love and marriage in "Federigo's Falcon" and "Bisclavret.")*

Teach

Literary Element 2

Suspense Answer: *This passage leads the reader to the realization that the king will discover Bisclavret; knowing the king has dogs makes the reader worry for Bisclavret's safety.*

View the Art ★

This detail from a fifteenth-century illuminated manuscript shows a wolf being held at bay by a dog and a man with a stick. Discuss how the scene is less than convincing by modern standards of figure painting. *(Both dog and wolf have odd and unconvincing shapes; the dog and the man are too close to the wolf to be realistic. The movement is stilted and unnatural.)* **Ask:** How does this work express the universal theme of untamed nature versus civilization? *(The man and dog are in the light and clearing; the wolf comes out of the darkness of the forest.)*

Learning Objectives
Analyzing suspense. (SE)
Monitoring comprehension. (SE)
Drawing conclusions about culture. (TE)

Teach

Reading Strategy 1

Draw Conclusions About Culture Say: Here, the story-teller reflects the shared culture of her audience. **Ask:** What does this statement show about the storyteller and her audience? *(They know the value and importance of staying "close to the king"; that a knight can never leave, or forsake, his king; and that a knight is best protected by his king.)*

Big Idea 2

From Myth to Romance
Answer: *The word* listen *reminds the reader of the story's oral tradition. It also creates a connection between the author and her audience.*

155 Chase the dogs away,
and make sure no one strikes it.
This beast is **rational**—he has a mind.
Hurry up: let's get out of here.
I'll extend my peace to the creature;°

160 indeed, I'll hunt no more today!"
Thereupon the king turned away.

1 Bisclavret followed him;
he stayed close to the king, and wouldn't go away;
he'd no intention of leaving him.

165 The king led him to his castle;
he was delighted with this turn of events,
for he'd never seen anything like it.
He considered the beast a great wonder
and held him very dear.

170 He commanded all his followers,
for the sake of their love for him, to guard Bisclavret well,
and under no circumstances to do him harm;
none of them should strike him;
rather, he should be well fed and watered.°

175 They willingly guarded the creature;
every day he went to sleep
among the knights, near the king.
Everyone was fond of him;
he was so noble and well behaved

180 that he never wished to do anything wrong.
Regardless of where the king might go,
Bisclavret never wanted to be separated from him;
he always accompanied the king.
The king became very much aware that
the creature loved him.

185 Now listen to what happened next.
The king held a court;
to help him celebrate his feast
and to serve him as handsomely° as possible,
he summoned all the barons

190 who held fiefs° from him.
Among the knights who went,
and all dressed up in his best attire,
was the one who had married Bisclavret's wife.

159 **extend my peace:** grant royal protection.

> *This beast is rational—*
> *he has a mind.*

174 **watered:** given water to drink.

188 **handsomely:** abundantly or richly.

190 **fiefs:** parcels of land granted by a king to nobles (barons) under the feudal system of medieval Europe. In return, the nobles pledged to support and serve the king.

2 **From Myth to Romance** *Why do you think the author addresses the reader directly? How does this reflect the literary tradition of the time?*

Vocabulary
rational (rash′ ən əl) *adj.* able to reason

Writing Practice

Write a Persuasive Argument What kind of miniseries would "Bisclavret" make? Have students imagine themselves as writers or agents who are trying to pitch this story to television studio executives. Ask them to craft a persuasive argument that lists dramatic elements of the tale and tells how they would appeal to a modern audience. Remind students to use persuasive techniques such as rhetorical questions, repetition, and effective word choice. Suggest this essay structure:

- Attention-grabbing opener
- Clear, forceful statement of claim or position
- Most important reason, followed by support
- Second most important reason, followed by support
- Least important reason, followed by support
- Acknowledgement and rebuttal of counterarguments
- Call to action (studio)

He neither knew nor suspected
195 that he would find Bisclavret so close by.
As soon as he came to the palace
Bisclavret saw him,
ran toward him at full speed,
sank his teeth into him, and started to drag him down.
200 He would have done him great damage
if the king hadn't called him off,
and threatened him with a stick.
Twice that day he tried to bite the knight.
Everyone was extremely surprised,
205 since the beast had never acted that way
toward any other man he had seen.
All over the palace people said
that he wouldn't act that way without a reason:
that somehow or other, the knight had mistreated Bisclavret,
210 and now he wanted his revenge.
And so the matter rested
until the feast was over
and until the barons took their leave of the king
and started home.
215 The very first to leave,
to the best of my knowledge, ☆
was the knight whom Bisclavret had attacked.
It's no wonder the creature hated him.
Not long afterward,
220 as the story leads me to believe,
the king, who was so wise and noble,
went back to the forest
where he had found Bisclavret,
and the creature went with him.
225 That night, when he finished hunting,
he sought lodging out in the countryside.
The wife of Bisclavret heard about it,
dressed herself elegantly,
and went the next day to speak with the king,
230 bringing rich presents for him.
When Bisclavret saw her coming,
no one could hold him back;
he ran toward her in a rage.
Now listen to how well he avenged himself!
235 He tore the nose off her face.
What worse thing could he have done to her?

> When Bisclavret saw her coming,
> no one could hold him back;
> he ran toward her in a rage.

Suspense *What does the reader know at this point that the wife does not? How does this contribute to the suspense?* **3**

Teach

Literary Element 3

Suspense Answer: *The reader knows Bisclavret is with the king. After the attack on the knight, the reader anticipates there will be another attack, this time on the wife.*

Writer's Technique ☆

Shift in Point of View Note how Marie de France mainly employs the third person to tell the story, but occasionally shifts the point of view to insert her own commentary and perspective. This is most notable in lines 1–14, and students have also seen this occur on page 892. **Ask:** Where does the storyteller break the narrative flow and either shift point of view or insert editorial commentary on this page? *(lines 216, 218, 220, 234, 236)* **Ask:** Why do you think she does this? *(She may do this to engage listeners or to be playful.)* Note that many authors have used this convention and continue to use it even in postmodern literature.

Learning Objectives
Analyzing suspense. (SE)
Drawing conclusions about culture. (TE)
Writing a persuasive argument. (TE)

English Learners

DIFFERENTIATED INSTRUCTION

Advanced Write these sentence frames on the board to help students in the persuasive writing assignment on page 892.

To make a claim:
- We must _____.
- My own view is that _____, because _____.

To give reasons:
- The most important reason why we should _____ is that _____.
- Another key reason for making this choice is _____.

To address a counterclaim or counterargument:
- Although I agree that _____, I still maintain that _____.

- The claim that _____ is contradicted by _____.

To end effectively:
- For all these reasons, let's _____ now.
- The need for _____ is demonstrated by _____.

Teach

Literary Element | 1

Plot **Ask:** Is the action rising or falling? How do you know? *(The action is still rising; the climax occurs when the knight finally returns to human form.)*

(ADVANCED) **Ask:** To what degree does the plot continue to be suspenseful? *(Students may say it is no longer suspenseful at all; the audience can anticipate the outcome.)*

View the Art ★

Relate this painting from the 1400s to the discussion of perspective on page 865. Point out that this image lacks perspective: the mounted hunters at the top look as if they are flying above those on foot below. Discuss with students how the painting could be made to look more realistic.

Now men closed in on him from all sides;
they were about to tear him apart,
when a wise man said to the king,
240 "My lord, listen to me!
This beast has stayed with you,
and there's not one of us
who hasn't watched him closely,
hasn't traveled with him often.
245 He's never touched anyone,
or shown any wickedness,
except to this woman.
By the faith that I owe you,
he has some **grudge** against her,
250 and against her husband as well.
This is the wife of the knight
whom you used to like so much,
and who's been missing for so long—
we don't know what became of him.
255 Why not put this woman to torture°
and see if she'll tell you
why the beast hates her?
Make her tell what she knows!
We've seen many strange things
260 happen in Brittany!"
The king took his advice;
he detained the knight.
At the same time he took the wife
and subjected her to torture;
265 out of fear and pain
she told all about her husband:
how she had betrayed him
and taken away his clothes;
the story he had told her
270 about what happened to him and where he went;
and how after she had taken his clothes
he'd never been seen in his land again.
She was quite certain
that this beast was Bisclavret.
275 The king demanded the clothes; **1**
whether she wanted to or not
she sent home for them,
and had them brought to Bisclavret.

Wolf hunt, 15th century. French school. Vellum. Bibliotheque Nationale, Paris. ★

255 torture: during this time, an acceptable means of gathering information. Sometimes testimony was not considered acceptable in court unless the witness had been tortured.

Vocabulary

grudge (gruj) *n.* a feeling of hatred or resentment

---

894 UNIT 5 EARLY EUROPE

Speaking and Listening Practice

SMALL GROUP **Conduct a Debate** Is "Bisclavret: The Lay of the Were-wolf," as some critics maintain, a piece of misogynist, or anti-woman, literature? Form two teams of two, four, or six students. Choose one side of this question and develop a list of reasons to support it. To support your argument, rely not only on textual evidence but also on your understanding of the culture, the time period, and the purpose of telling the lay.

Also, develop arguments that will rebut your opponent's point of view.

Keep these listening strategies in mind as you focus on your opponent's argument and prepare to respond to it:

- Identify the argument and the evidence.
- Listen for ways to challenge the quality, quantity, or credibility of the evidence.
- Listen for faulty reasoning, and dismiss arguments that present distractions,

use false reasoning, claim false causes, rely on overgeneralizations, or employ bandwagon techniques.

When they were put down in front of him
280 he didn't even seem to notice them;
the king's wise man—
the one who had advised him earlier—
said to him, "My lord, you're not doing it right.
This beast wouldn't, under any circumstances,
285 in order to get rid of his animal form,
put on his clothes in front of you;
you don't understand what this means:
he's just too ashamed to do it here.
Have him led to your chambers
290 and bring the clothes with him;
then we'll leave him alone for a while.
If he turns into a man, we'll know about it."
The king himself led the way
and closed all the doors on him.
295 After a while he went back,
taking two barons with him;
all three entered the king's chamber.
On the king's royal bed
they found the knight asleep.
300 The king ran to embrace him.
He hugged and kissed him again and again.
As soon as he had the chance,
the king gave him back all his lands;
he gave him more than I can tell.
305 He banished the wife,
chased her out of the country.
She went into exile with the knight
with whom she had betrayed her lord.
She had several children
310 who were widely known
for their appearance:
several women of the family
were actually born without noses,
and lived out their lives noseless.

315 The adventure that you have heard
really happened, no doubt about it.
The *lai* of Bisclavret was made
so it would be remembered forever.

> *On the king's royal bed they found the knight asleep.*

Monitor Comprehension *What aspect of Bisclavret's character leads to the story's outcome?*

MARIE DE FRANCE **895**

Teach

Reading Strategy	2

Respond to Tone Ask: What tone do you sense here in the storyteller's voice? *(Students may hear playfulness or verbal irony.)*
Ask: How do you respond to the tone of these final lines? *(Amusement is the most likely response.)*
(ADVANCED) **Ask:** Is the tone at the end of the romance consistent with the tone of the romance as a whole? *(Students may say that it is, and that the whole tale is a lighthearted entertainment that mocks not only the evildoing wife but also the naive husband, as well as, perhaps, legends of werewolves. Some may say that the tale is not so playful as the ending makes it appear to be.)*

Reading Strategy	3

**Monitor Comprehension
Answer:** *His loyalty to the king wins him his life and enables him to return to human form.*

To check students' understanding of the selection, see Unit 5 Teaching Resources Book, p. 57.

Advanced Learners/Pre-AP

DIFFERENTIATED INSTRUCTION

Research Have students research and report on the criticisms of "Bisclavret" as a misogynist work. Ask them to print out or photocopy at least two articles, and to annotate them to show the points with which they agree or disagree, as well as to show where they question the writer's logic or assertions. Ask students to synthesize what they learned in an essay or an oral report to the class.

Approaching Level

DIFFERENTIATED INSTRUCTION

Identify and Analyze Ask students to begin preparing for their debate by finding examples in the text of the wife's words and actions. Have students list these details in the left-hand column of a two-column chart. In the right-hand column, have them note their reaction by responding to these questions: Are these words or actions negative or positive? Do they seem to suggest stereotypes about women in general, or do they seem specific to this character?

Learning Objectives
Monitoring comprehension. (SE)
Analyzing plot. (TE)
Conducting a debate. (TE)
Responding to tone. (TE)

After You Read

Assess

1. Students may express surprise, concern, or amusement.

2. (a) The wife proclaims her love, threatens to die, and implies her husband has a lover. (b) She is determined to get her way.

3. (a) She takes a lover and tells him to hide Bisclavret's clothes so Bisclavret cannot return to his human form. (b) She is horrified at the thought of being married to a werewolf.

4. (a) Bisclavret attacks his wife and her new husband. (b) The wise man observes that because the wolf's attack is directed only toward one man and one woman, it must have a grudge against them.

5. (a) Lines 9–12 and 66 describe the savagery of werewolves, and lines 97–99 describe the wife's fear. (b) Answers will vary.

6. (a) The king initially hunts him down, but then gives him mercy. (b) Students may find the king acted wisely and fairly. They may, however, object to his use of torture to extract a confession.

7. People were becoming less interested in tales about epic heroes and more interested in tales of a more personal nature.

8. Honesty and trust are important in marriage.

Literary Element

1. Some may say that interrupting the narrative flow slows down the story and decreases suspense; others may say it increases suspense by creating a dramatic pause and foreshadowing.

2. Readers have to wait to learn the king's judgment and Bisclavret's fate.

3. Some students may think the

896

After You Read

Respond and Think Critically

Respond and Interpret

1. How did you react to the changes Bisclavret underwent throughout the poem?

2. (a) What arguments does the wife use in lines 32–52 to persuade her husband to divulge his secret? (b) What do you think these arguments reveal about her character?

3. (a) How does the wife betray her husband? (b) Why do you think she does this?

4. (a) How does Bisclavret punish his unfaithful wife? (b) In what way do Bisclavret's actions lead to the wise man's advice to the king in lines 240–260?

Analyze and Evaluate

5. (a) Which lines in the poem might justify the wife's actions? (b) In your opinion, is the wife's punishment just, or is it too severe? Explain.

6. (a) How does the king treat Bisclavret, both before and after finding out who he really is? (b) Would you describe the king as a wise and fair ruler? Explain.

Connect

7. **Big Idea** **From Myth to Romance** How does this poem reflect the changing interests of the time in which it was written?

8. **Connect to Today** Does this poem convey a theme or message for people today? If so, what is it?

Literary Element **Suspense**

With one type of **suspense,** readers do not know what will happen next. With a second type, readers either know the plot or can make a reliable prediction about the outcome, but they still wonder *how* the events will unfold.

1. At several points in the poem, the narrator interrupts the story to address the reader directly (line 185, for example). In your opinion, do these intrusions help or hinder the suspense? Explain.

2. Does the wise man's speech in lines 240–260 create suspense? If so, how?

3. In your opinion, what is the most suspenseful moment in the poem? Explain.

Review: Motivation

As you learned on page 93, a character's **motivation** is the set of reasons he or she acts in a certain way. Authors can state a character's motivation directly, or they can imply motivation through a character's words and actions.

Partner Activity Meet with a classmate and discuss the motivations of the three main characters: Bisclavret, his wife, and the king. Working with your partner, complete a chart like the one below. Fill it in with a description of each character's motivations. Whose motivations are most praiseworthy? Whose are most blameworthy? Support your answers with specific details from the poem.

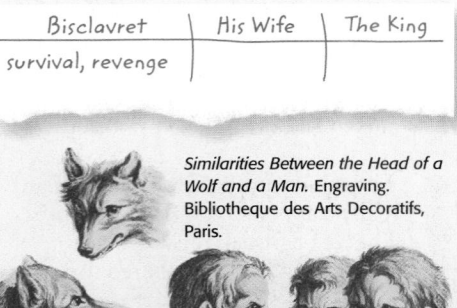

Bisclavret	His Wife	The King
survival, revenge		

Similarities Between the Head of a Wolf and a Man. Engraving. Bibliotheque des Arts Decoratifs, Paris.

---

most suspenseful moment is when Bisclavret attacks his wife and her second husband because the reader does not know if the king will punish him for it.

Review: Motivation

Bisclavret: desire for survival, revenge

His Wife: fear

The King: a desire to be fair and to reward loyal subjects

Students may find any one of the characters to be most realistic or believable. Only the king has praiseworthy motives. Both Bisclavret and his wife can be both praised and blamed for their actions.

Reading Strategy — Monitor Comprehension

ACT Skills Practice

Why does Bisclavret's wife decide to "get rid of" her husband?

A. She is in love with another knight.

B. Bisclavret threatens to kill her if she ever reveals his secret.

C. She is fearful of her husband and disgusted by the fact that he is a werewolf.

D. She is tired of Bisclavret's frequent absences.

Vocabulary Practice

Practice with Context Clues Look back at pages 888–895 to find context clues for the boldfaced vocabulary words below. For each, record the word, the context clues that suggest its meaning, and the meaning of the word.

savage   rational   grudge

EXAMPLE:

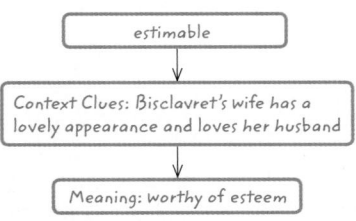

Academic Vocabulary

*Bisclavret's **phase** as a werewolf prompts the betrayal that is central to this tale.*

Phase is an academic word. The word *phase* can have different meanings in different subject areas. Using context clues, try to figure out its meaning in the following sentence: The computer manufacturer decided to gradually **phase** in a new microprocessor.

For more on academic vocabulary, see pages 36–37 and R83–R85.

Listening and Speaking

Performance

Assignment Create and perform an original, modern "lay" using de France's poem as a model. Style your performance as a skit that examines modern society as "Bisclavret" examines medieval court life.

Prepare Consult your question and answer chart on page 887 and brainstorm ideas for characters you want to include in your skit. To refine your ideas, collect images of people and settings you think would exemplify the aspect of modern society you want to examine. As you rehearse your drama, be sure to use vocal tones and body language that suit each character.

Perform Create a stage diagram for your skit. Make the best use of the features of your performance space, and make the space interesting for and visible to your audience. Draw an overhead view of your set, labeling the important features, such as rooms and furniture. Make sure the actors are familiar with the stage diagram, and know where in the space each event takes place.

Perform your skit for the class, using only body language and vocal tones that are in keeping with the mood you want to create and the comment you wish to make about modern life. Stay in character throughout the skit.

Evaluate Write an evaluation of your classmates' performances. Style your evaluation as a theater review. Did you understand the skits? What could have helped you understand them better? Be sure to comment on what you admired in your classmates' work and offer suggestions for improvement.

 Literature Online

Selection Resources For Selection Quizzes, eFlashcards, and Reading-Writing Connection activities, go to glencoe.com and enter QuickPass code GLW6053u5.

MARIE DE FRANCE **897**

 For additional selection assessment, see Assessment Resources, pp. 179–180.

 To create custom assessments online, go to Progress Reporter Online Assessment.

 To create custom assessments using software, use ExamView Assessment Suite.

Listening and Speaking

Students' performances should

- involve an original skit that contains plot elements from "Bisclavret" (betrayal, suspense) and critiques modern life
- include a stage diagram that all could understand, and use the space well for their performance
- include vocal tones and body language appropriate to the characters

---

After You Read

Assess

Reading Strategy

C is the correct answer. Bisclavret's wife is faithful to her husband until he finally shares his secret with her. Then she "turned scarlet from fear" and "never wanted to sleep with him again."

Progress Check

Can students successfully monitor their comprehension?

If No → See Unit 5 Teaching Resources Book, p. 54.

Vocabulary

Sample answer:

savage Context Clues: "A werewolf is a savage beast" that "goes deep in the forest to live." Meaning: wild; untamed

rational Context Clues: "This beast is rational—he has a mind." Meaning: able to reason

grudge Context Clues: "He has some grudge against her"; "the beast hates her." Meaning: a feeling of hatred or resentment usually in response to a past deed

Academic Vocabulary

Possible answer:

Here, **phase** is a verb meaning to introduce something gradually over a period of time.

Bellringer Options

**Selection Focus
   Transparency 54**
**Daily Language Practice
   Transparency 84**

Or: Have students work in small groups to discuss *how* punishments should be determined for various crimes in society.
Ask: Who should decide? What criteria should be applied? Have groups report their conclusions to the class.

Literary History ☆

The Muses Beatrice is called a "source of literary inspiration" for Dante. Tell students that the term *muse* is used to refer to one who inspires an artist. In Greek mythology, the Muses were the patron goddesses of the arts. There were nine: Calliope, epic poetry and eloquence; Euterpe, lyric poetry; Erato, love poetry; Polyhymnia, oratory or sacred poetry; Clio, history; Melpomene, tragedy; Thalia, comedy; Terpsichore, choral song and dance; and Urania, history.

Meet **Dante Alighieri**
(1265–1321)

I n *La Vita Nuova* (The New Life), a collection of poems joined by autobiographical prose commentaries, the young Dante Alighieri describes the one true love of his life. Historians believe this love was Beatrice Portinari, the daughter of a wealthy Florentine banker. Dante first encountered her at a party when he was only nine and she a year younger. He recalls being overwhelmed by her beauty and gentle manner. He met her again nine years later, but she did not share his romantic feelings, and his inferior social position precluded any realistic possibility of marriage. She became instead a source of literary inspiration, embodying his ideal of spiritual perfection. In *Il Paradiso* (Paradise), the last section of Dante's epic the *Divine Comedy*, it is Beatrice who guides the poet in the final stage of his journey to salvation and Heaven.

Personal History Born in Florence, a European center of wealth and culture, Dante received an excellent education in classic literature and religious studies. When he was about eighteen, he married Gemma Donati, fulfilling a marriage contract his father had arranged when Dante was twelve. As a young man, Dante was active in Florence's political life, serving in the military and holding public office. When a rival political faction assumed power in 1301, Dante was banished. He never returned to the city, and it is not known whether he ever saw his wife and family again. For the remaining twenty years of his life, Dante lived in various other parts of Italy, accepting the hospitality of friends and patrons. He died at the home of a friend in Ravenna after contracting malaria.

"Consider your origin; you were not born to live like brutes, but to follow virtue and knowledge."

—Dante Alighieri

Literary History Dante wrote the *Divine Comedy* during his exile. He composed the poem in modern Italian instead of Latin, which most major contemporary authors used. In doing so, he made the poem accessible to many Italians and established Italian as a literary language. In the *Divine Comedy*, Dante strove to persuade readers to live better lives through faith by showing them the consequences of evil and the rewards of salvation. He titled the epic *La Commedia*, not because it was humorous but rather because it had a happy ending. After his death, Dante's literary reputation steadily grew, and he became known throughout Italy as the *divino poeta* (divine poet). Today, the *Divine Comedy* is considered one of the masterpieces of Western literature.

LOG ON ▶ **Literature** Online

Author Search For more about Dante Alighieri, go to glencoe.com and enter QuickPass code GLW6053u5.

Selection Skills

Literary Elements
- Allegory (SE pp. 899, 901, 904, 908, 911, 913)
- Form (SE p. 913)

Reading Skills
- Analyze Sound Devices (SE pp. 899, 902, 904, 908, 911, 913)
- Recognize Author's Purpose (TE p. 908)

from the Inferno

Vocabulary Skills
- Synonyms (SE p. 913)
- Academic Vocabulary (SE p. 913)

Speaking/Listening/Viewing Skills
- Analyze Art (SE p. 906)
- Oral Report (TE p. 902)
- Oral Interpretation (TE p. 906)

Writing Skills/Grammar
- Expository Essay (SE p. 914)
- Research Report (TE p. 904)
- Capitalization (TE p. 910)

Literature and Reading Preview

Connect to the Poem

In your opinion, how should people be punished for wrong-doing? Freewrite for a few minutes about this question.

Build Background

The *Divine Comedy* is divided into three parts—*Inferno* (Hell), *Purgatorio* (Purgatory), and *Paradiso* (Paradise). Dante used a verse form called *terza rima*—three-line stanzas in which the first and third lines rhyme and the second line rhymes with the first line of the next stanza. The episodes you are about to read are from the *Inferno*. Dante's vision of Hell includes nine levels, each level for different kinds of sinners. The First Circle is Limbo, for unbaptized spirits. The next four circles punish those who committed the lesser sins of lust, gluttony, avarice, and wrathfulness. With the Sixth Circle, the extreme torments begin for heretics, murderers, seducers, thieves, hypocrites, liars, and finally (frozen in the ice of the Ninth Circle) betrayers.

Set Purposes for Reading

Big Idea The Vision of Faith

As you read, ask yourself, Which details represent the beliefs and values of Christianity in medieval Italy?

Literary Element Allegory

In an **allegory,** actions, objects, and people represent moral qualities, universal struggles, or abstract ideas such as love or virtue. A popular allegorical motif is the journey or quest. As you read, ask yourself, What is Dante's allegorical purpose?

Reading Strategy Analyze Sound Devices

Poets use **sound devices** such as **rhythm** (meter), **rhyme, alliteration** (repetition of consonant sounds at the beginnings of words), **consonance** (repetition of consonant sounds, typically at the end of non-rhyming words), and **assonance** (repetition of the same or similar vowel sounds in stressed syllables) to create mood or reinforce meaning. As you read, ask yourself, What do these devices contribute to the poem?

Tip: Group Details In a chart like the one below, list examples of sound devices and describe their effects.

Example of Sound Device	Effect on Mood or Meaning
Line 4—alliteration: "grinning, grotesque"	The "gr" sound reinforces the fearsome sight of Minos.

DANTE ALIGHIERI **899**

Learning Objectives

For pages 898–913

In studying this text, you will focus on the following objectives:

Literary Study: Analyzing allegory.

Reading: Analyzing sound devices.

Vocabulary

verdict (vur′dikt) *n.* decision; judgment; p. 901 *My teacher's verdict was proof she doubted my excuse.*

anguish (ang′gwish) *n.* severe physical or mental pain; suffering; p. 902 *Though she affected a stiff upper lip, our aunt could not hide the anguish of her loss.*

reel (rēl) *v.* stand or move unsteadily; sway from a blow or shock; p. 905 *The stunned boxer reeled from the force of his opponent's punches.*

nimble (nim′bəl) *adj.* sure-footed; light and quick; p. 909 *The hikers crossed the shallow creek with nimble steps, treading lightly on the exposed rocks.*

Tip: Synonyms Words that have the same or nearly the same meaning are synonyms. For example, the words *verdict* and *judgment* are synonyms. Synonyms are always the same part of speech.

Before You Read

Focus

Summary

In the Second Circle of Hell, an eternal whirlwind swirls the damned about the heads of Dante and the poet Virgil, who is Dante's guide. In this circle are the souls of the carnal, those who abandoned themselves to physical passion. Dante is allowed to speak to one of the souls and feels such great pity that he faints. In the Ninth Circle, which is the last depth, they see Satan himself. In this circle are those who were treacherous to their masters, but the poets cannot speak to them. Instead, they observe the horrors of Satan himself. Finally Virgil leads Dante back to his own world.

 For summaries in languages other than English, see Unit 5 Teaching Resources Book, pp. 59–64.

Vocabulary

 Flash Cards Have students write each vocabulary word on an index card. On the other side of each card, tell them to draw a sketch or visual representation of the word's definition. Then have them work in small groups to have classmates guess the vocabulary word represented by the picture on each card.

 For additional vocabulary practice, see Unit 5 Teaching Resources Book, p. 67.

Advanced Learners/Pre-AP

DIFFERENTIATED INSTRUCTION

Connect to Contemporary Culture
Point out that the *Inferno* is the first part of a three-part work. **Ask:** What other works can you think of—novels, movies, music, or other kinds of works—that come in threes? *(Remind students that Greek tragedies were presented in trilogies. Students might cite Tolkien's* Lord of the Rings, *the* Matrix *movies, and the original* Star Wars *movies.)*

Ask: Why do you think artists like to work in threes? *(There is no one answer to the question. One possibility is that the parts reflect the beginning, middle, and end of all good storytelling. Point out that Dante's artistic choice of a three-part structure reflects the medieval Catholic view of the afterlife—hell, purgatory, and heaven.)*

Teach

Vocabulary 1

Discover Meaning Point out the reference to Purgatory in the caption on page 900. **Ask:** Do you know what Purgatory is? How can you find out? *(According to Roman Catholic doctrine, it is the intermediary state in which souls may become fit for Heaven. It is sometimes used generically to mean "a place of temporary suffering." A dictionary would be a good place to look for a simple definition.)*

View the Art ★

The manuscript painting shows Virgil, Dante, and Statius passing through the fire of the seventh terrace of Purgatory, in which the lustful are purged of their sin. At the top of the mountain is the Earthly Paradise.

For an audio recording of this selection, use Listening Library Audio CD-ROM.

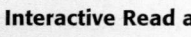

Interactive Read and Write

Other options for teaching this selection can be found in Interactive Read and Write for On-Level Learners, pp. 221–232.

---

from the Inferno
from the Divine Comedy

Dante Alighieri
Translated by John Ciardi

1 *Inferno, Purgatory and Paradise with the Poets,* 14th century. Illumination from *Dante's Divine Comedy.* British Museum, London. ★

Reading Practice

Visualize Explain that Dante sees the *Inferno* as a series of concentric circles, each smaller and lower than the last. To help students visualize this, draw a diagram on the board or on poster board. An apt comparison might be a circular sports arena, with tiers rising upward and outward from a central circle.

As an alternative, have volunteers draw nine concentric circles on cardboard, cut them out, and then affix them to a stiff cardboard background. Then point out that the entrance to the Inferno is on the top level. Dante and his guide descend the levels one by one, finally to encounter Satan at the center of the bottom level.

Canto V

CIRCLE TWO..*The Carnal*

The Poets enter the Second Circle. Here sits Minos, the dread and
semi-bestial judge of the damned who assigns to each soul its
eternal torment. They find themselves on a dark ledge swept by a
great whirlwind, which spins within it the souls of the Carnal, whose
sin was to abandon themselves to the tempest of their passions.

> So we went down to the second ledge alone;
>   a smaller circle of so much greater pain
>   the voice of the damned rose in a bestial° moan.
>
> There Minos sits, grinning, grotesque, and hale.°
> 5   He examines each lost soul as it arrives
>   and delivers his **verdict** with his coiling tail. **2**
>
> That is to say, when the ill-fated soul
>   appears before him it confesses all,
>   and that grim sorter of the dark and foul
>
> 10   decides which place in Hell shall be its end,
>   then wraps his twitching tail about himself
>   one coil for each degree it must descend.
>
> The soul descends and others take its place:
>   each crowds in its turn to judgment, each confesses,
> 15   each hears its doom and falls away through space.
>
> "O you who come into this camp of woe,"
>   cried Minos when he saw me turn away
>   without awaiting his judgment, "watch where you go
>
> once you have entered here, and to whom you turn!
> 20   Do not be misled by that wide and easy passage!"°
>   And my Guide° to Him: "That is not your concern;

3 **bestial:** animal-like.

4 **hale:** healthy and vigorous—an ironic description, given the character of the place where Minos judges.

20 **wide and easy passage:** This phrase is a reference to the Book of Matthew in the Bible where Jesus warns that "wide is the gate, and broad is the way, that leadeth to destruction."

21 **Guide:** the Roman poet Virgil, also referred to as the poet and the Master.

Allegory *What is Dante literally preparing to do? What warning does Minos give, and what is the allegorical meaning of this warning?* **3**

Vocabulary

verdict (vur′dikt) *n.* decision; judgment

DANTE ALIGHIERI   **901**

Teach

Vocabulary | 2

Improvise Have a pair of students play the parts of a judge and a juror in a trial, to portray the meaning of the word *verdict*. (They can model their lines after popular TV shows about the justice system.) The judge should ask the juror if the jury has reached its verdict, and the juror should state whether the jury has found the accused guilty or not guilty.

Literary Element | 3

Allegory Answer: *Dante is standing at a wide entranceway to Hell, preparing to enter. Minos warns him to be careful. This warning echoes the biblical admonition that the path to destruction is a wide and easy one. The allegorical meaning of the warning is that the entrance to the Second Circle, though easy, may likewise lead to destruction.*

English Learners

DIFFERENTIATED INSTRUCTION

Intermediate Explain to students that the translation they are reading is by a twentieth-century American poet and translator, John Ciardi. While trying to preserve the form and style of Dante's writing, Ciardi also writes in accessible, modern English.

Encourage students not to be intimidated by the poetic form of the work. Have individual volunteers read portions of the poem aloud, reading in sentences rather than stanzas. That is, tell them not to stop at the end of a line or a stanza if there is no period. Some examples of sentences are lines 7–12, 16–19, and 21–24.

Learning Objectives
Analyzing allegory. (SE)
Discovering meaning of vocabulary. (TE)
Visualizing. (TE)

901

Teach

Vocabulary   1

Construct a Web Have a volunteer construct a web on the board with *anguish* in a center circle and *physical* and *mental* in connected circles. Have students suggest situations in which a person might feel anguish, while the volunteer adds them to the web.

Reading Strategy   2

Analyze Sound Devices
Answer: *The words* war *and* winds *demonstrate alliteration. The "w" sound beginning these words suggests the whooshing roar of a gust of wind.*

it is his fate to enter every door.
   This has been willed where what is willed must be,
   and is not yours to question. Say no more."

25 Now the choir of **anguish**, like a wound, **1**
   strikes through the tortured air. Now I have come
   to Hell's full lamentation,° sound beyond sound.

I came to a place stripped bare of every light
   and roaring on the naked dark like seas
30   wracked by a war of winds. Their hellish flight

of storm and counterstorm through time foregone,°
   sweeps the souls of the damned before its charge.
   Whirling and battering it drives them on,

and when they pass the ruined gap of Hell
35   through which we had come, their shrieks begin anew.
   There they blaspheme° the power of God eternal.

And this, I learned, was the never ending flight
   of those who sinned in the flesh, the carnal° and lusty
   who betrayed reason to their appetite.

40 As the wings of wintering starlings bear them on
   in their great wheeling° flights, just so the blast
   wherries° these evil souls through time foregone.

Here, there, up, down, they whirl and, whirling, strain
   with never a hope of hope to comfort them,
45   not of release, but even of less pain.

As cranes go over sounding their harsh cry,
   leaving the long streak of their flight in air,
   so come these spirits, wailing as they fly.

And watching their shadows lashed by wind, I cried:
50   "Master, what souls are these the very air
   lashes with its black whips from side to side?"

27 **lamentation:** wailing out of grief and pain.

31 **time foregone:** time past.

36 **blaspheme** (blas fēm´): to insult or show a lack of reverence for God.

38 **carnal:** interested only in physical pleasure.

41 **wheeling:** to fly around in circles.

42 **wherries:** transports quickly, as in a light, low rowboat.

2 Analyze Sound Devices *What example of alliteration here suggests the sound of roaring mentioned in line 29? How is this effect achieved?*

Vocabulary

anguish (ang´gwish) *n.* severe physical or mental pain; suffering

Speaking Practice

Present an Oral Report Explain that Satan has appeared as a character in many plays and novels, especially those inspired by the Faust legend. These works have in turn inspired a number of musical and dramatic pieces. Suggest that students research and report on one of these works.

If possible, have students read a scene from a play or story about a satanic character or play a selection from a musical work about such a character. (Possible sources include *Faust,* by Charles Gounod; "The Devil and Daniel Webster," both a short story by Stephen Vincent Benét and an opera by Douglas Moore; and *Damn Yankees,* by Douglass Wallop and George Abbott.)

"The first of these whose history you would know,"
   he answered me, "was Empress of many tongues.
   Mad sensuality corrupted her so

55   that to hide the guilt of her debauchery°
      she licensed all depravity alike,
      and lust and law were one in her decree.

   She is Semiramis° of whom the tale is told
      how she married Ninus and succeeded him
60   to the throne of that wide land the Sultans° hold.

   The other is Dido;° faithless to the ashes
      of Sichaeus, she killed herself for love.
      The next whom the eternal tempest lashes

   is sense-drugged Cleopatra. See Helen° there,
65   from whom such ill arose. And great Achilles,°
      who fought at last with love in the house of prayer.

   And Paris. And Tristan."° As they whirled above
      he pointed out more than a thousand shades
      of those torn from the mortal life by love.

70   I stood there while my Teacher one by one
      named the great knights and ladies of dim time;
      and I was swept by pity and confusion.

   At last I spoke: "Poet, I should be glad
      to speak a word with those two swept together°
75   so lightly on the wind and still so sad."

   And he to me: "Watch them. When next they pass,
      call to them in the name of love that drives
      and damns them here. In that name they will pause."

   Thus, as soon as the wind in its wild course
80   brought them around, I called: "O wearied souls!
      if none forbid it, pause and speak to us."

   As mating doves that love calls to their nest
      glide through the air with motionless raised wings,
      borne by the sweet desire that fills each breast—

The Vision of Faith *Why do you think Dante includes historical and
literary characters from antiquity in his description of Hell?*

55 debauchery: excessive
indulgence in sensual pleasures;
behavior lacking virtue or morality

58 Semiramis (sə mir′ə mis):
According to legend, Semiramis built
Babylon. Her sin was her love affair
with her own son.

60 Sultans: Muslim rulers of the
area that was Babylon in Dante's day.

61 Dido: The queen of Carthage,
unfaithful to the memory of her
dead husband Sichaeus, fell in love
with Aeneas; when he abandoned
her, she killed herself.

64 Helen: the queen of Sparta.
Helen left her husband Menelaus for
Paris (line 67), the prince of Troy.

65 Achilles: In the Trojan War, the
Greek hero Achilles fell so deeply
in love with Polyxena, a Trojan, that
he planned to switch sides. On his
way to marry Polyxena, he was
killed by Paris.

67 Tristan: In a famous love story
of the Middle Ages, Tristan loved
and died with Isolde, the wife of his
uncle, King Mark.

74 those two swept together: The
narrator sees Paolo and Francesca
suffering together and wants to
speak to them. In 1275 Francesca
entered into a political marriage with
Giovanni Malatesta. She fell in love
with Giovanni's younger brother,
Paolo, who was himself married.
Their affair continued for several
years, until Giovanni discovered
them together and killed them.

Teach

Big Idea   3

The Vision of Faith
Answer: *His audience would
have been familiar with these
sinners and with their sins.*

Literary History ☆
Comedy Students may be
confused to see this material
entitled *comedy*. Explain that one
definition of *comedy* is "a narrative
that ends happily." Despite the
suffering in the *Divine Comedy*, the
poet's fate is not tragic. The term
comedy also applies to literature
that deals with serious matters in
a satirical manner—that is, holding
up human vices to scorn, which
Dante does in this work.

Learning Objectives
Analyzing sound devices. (SE)
Constructing a vocabulary web. (TE)
Presenting an oral report. (TE)

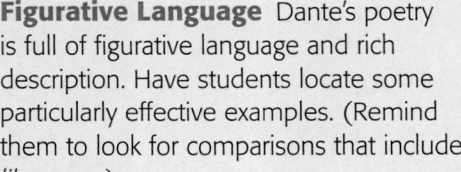

Advanced Learners/Pre-AP

DIFFERENTIATED INSTRUCTION

Figurative Language Dante's poetry
is full of figurative language and rich
description. Have students locate some
particularly effective examples. (Remind
them to look for comparisons that include
like or *as*.)

Ask: What similes do you find on these
pages? *(Some examples: "like a wound,"
line 25; "like seas wracked by a war of
winds," lines 29–30; "As the wings of*

*wintering starlings . . . ," lines 40–41; "As
cranes . . . ," lines 46–47)*

Ask: What is being compared? *(In most
cases, the souls are compared to birds
in flight.)*

Extend this activity by having students
locate metaphors and other descriptive
phrases. *(Some examples: "naked dark,"
line 29; "the very air lashes with its*

*black whips," lines 50–51; "torn sky," line
85; "sick night," line 89)* Tell students to
watch for further examples of such uses of
language as they continue to read.

Teach

Reading Strategy　　1

Analyze Sound Devices

Answer: *The double "o" vowel sound in "s<u>oo</u>nest," "bl<u>oo</u>m," and "d<u>oo</u>m" demonstrates assonance. The produced "oo" sound suggests the swooning of lovers, which echoes the content here.*

View the Art ★

Paolo Malatesta and Francesca da Rimini, placed in Hell by Dante for consummating their illicit love, had great appeal for writers and artists of the nineteenth-century Romantic movement. Hallé, the son of French immigrants living in England, was influenced by Ingres and Rossetti, both of whom had also painted Paolo and Francesca. In his sympathetic portrait, Hallé has chosen to depict the pair in a fond embrace at the moment their intimacy began. The book that led them astray, containing the account of Lancelot's similarly illicit love for Guinevere, can be seen lying on the floor by their feet.

85　　Just so those spirits turned on the torn sky
　　　　from the band where Dido whirls across the air;
　　　　such was the power of pity in my cry.

　　　"O living creature, gracious, kind, and good,
　　　　going this pilgrimage through the sick night,
90　　　visiting us who stained the earth with blood,

　　　were the King of Time° our friend, we would pray His peace
　　　　on you who have pitied us. As long as the wind
　　　　will let us pause, ask of us what you please.

　　　The town where I was born lies by the shore
95　　　where the Po° descends into its ocean rest
　　　　with its attendant streams in one long murmur.

　　　Love, which in gentlest hearts will soonest bloom
　　　　seized my lover with passion for that sweet body
　　　　from which I was torn unshriven° to my doom.

100　　Love, which permits no loved one not to love,
　　　　took me so strongly with delight in him
　　　　that we are one in Hell, as we were above.

　　　Love led us to one death. In the depths of Hell
　　　　Caïna° waits for him who took our lives."
105　　This was the piteous tale they stopped to tell.

　　　And when I had heard those world-offended lovers
　　　　I bowed my head. At last the Poet spoke:
　　　　"What painful thoughts are these your lowered brow
　　　　　covers?"

　　　When at length I answered, I began: "Alas!
110　　What sweetest thoughts, what green and young desire
　　　　led these two lovers to this sorry pass."

　　　Then turning to those spirits once again,
　　　　I said: "Francesca, what you suffer here
　　　　melts me to tears of pity and of pain.

91 King of Time: God.

95 Po: Italy's longest river. It empties into the ocean at the northern end of the Adriatic Sea.

99 unshriven: In Roman Catholic belief, to die unshriven—without confessing one's sins and receiving God's forgiveness—means that the soul carries its sins into the afterlife.

104 Caïna: the ring of Hell reserved for people who commit treachery against their relatives.

Analyze Sound Devices *Find an example of assonance in this stanza. How is the sound appropriate to the content of the stanza?*　　1

Writing Practice

Write a Research Report Students who are used to the notion that Hell is a place of eternal flames might be surprised at Dante's description of it as a "frozen shell" (Canto 34, line 3). In truth, Hell has been many things to many people over the centuries.

Suggest that students do Internet research and write a one-or-two-page research report on one aspect of their findings. In addition to a description of the place of punishment and what goes on there, students should include the culture that developed this particular notion. Tell students to cite their research carefully and to be sure to use quotation marks appropriately if they use any direct quotations.

115 But tell me: in the time of your sweet sighs
       by what appearances found love the way
       to lure you to his perilous paradise?"

   And she: "The double grief of a lost bliss
       is to recall its happy hour in pain.
120   Your Guide and Teacher knows the truth of this.

   But if there is indeed a soul in Hell
       to ask of the beginning of our love
       out of his pity, I will weep and tell:

   On a day for dalliance° we read the rhyme
125   of Lancelot,° how love had mastered him.
       We were alone with innocence and dim time.

   Pause after pause that high old story drew
       our eyes together while we blushed and paled;
       but it was one soft passage overthrew

130 our caution and our hearts. For when we read
       how her fond smile was kissed by such a lover,
       he who is one with me alive and dead

   breathed on my lips the tremor of his kiss.
       That book, and he who wrote it, was a pander.°
135   That day we read no further." As she said this,

   the other spirit, who stood by her, wept
       so piteously, I felt my senses **reel**   **2**
       and faint away with anguish. I was swept

   by such a swoon as death is, and I fell,
140   as a corpse might fall, to the dead floor of Hell.

Paolo and Francesca. Edward Charles Hallé
(1846-1919). Oil on canvas, 73 1/2 x 48 1/4
in. Private collection. ★

124 dalliance: wasting time in
mindless pleasure; here, it means
romantic love-making.

125 Lancelot: chief among the
knights of the Round Table, he fell in
love with King Arthur's wife.

134 pander: one who deliberately
appeals to people's self-indulgent
side.

The Vision of Faith *What excuse does Francesca offer for her transgressions? What is ironic about her excuse?*   **3**

Vocabulary

reel (rēl) *v.* stand or move unsteadily; sway from a blow or shock

---

Teach

Vocabulary   **2**

Pantomime Have one or two
students work singly to pantomime
the word *reel:* They should reel
across the front of the room.

Big Idea   **3**

The Vision of Faith
Answer: *She claims Lancelot
and Guinevere's passion tempted
her. This is ironic because she and
Paolo conveniently ignored the
legend's moral lesson.*

Cultural History ☆

Banned Books Francesca
blames Paolo's and her downfall
on the book they were reading.
The notion that reading about
improper behavior can cause
people to behave improperly is
an old one, and it has led, over
the centuries, to calls for banning
any number of literary works. Have
students do brief Internet research
on banned books and report
on one title each, including the
reason(s) for its banning.

Learning Objectives
Analyzing sound devices. (SE)
Analyzing art. (SE)
Writing a research report. (TE)

English Learners

DIFFERENTIATED INSTRUCTION

Intermediate Read the last sentence
of Canto V aloud ("I was swept . . . dead
floor of Hell," lines 138–140). **Ask:** What
happens to the poet? *(He swoons.)*
What does it mean to swoon? *(to faint,
or lose consciousness)* What sorts of
experiences usually cause a person to
faint? *(dehydration, lack of blood to the
brain, intense emotions)*

What causes the poet's swoon here?
*(He is overcome with emotion at the
story Francesca tells.)* Look for similes,
or comparisons using the word *as*
or *like.* *("such a swoon as death is";
"as a corpse might fall")* What is being
compared here? *(The poet's swoon is
compared to death; his fall is compared
to that of a corpse.)*

Approaching Level

DIFFERENTIATED INSTRUCTION

Clarify Meaning You might adapt this
activity for approaching-level students
by discussing the causes and effects of
fainting. Have them supply synonyms for
fainting, along with instances when they or
someone they knew fainted or situations in
which one might faint.

905

Teach

Reading Strategy | 1

Make Judgments Ask: Why do you think the poet considers those who have been treacherous to their masters to be the worst sinners? Do you agree? Why or why not? *(The poet apparently values loyalty to one's leaders, or masters, above all else and condemns disloyalty—like Judas's to Jesus, or Satan's to God—as the foulest of sins. Many students will disagree.)*

View the Art ★

Answer: *It seems that this artist wanted to portray Satan as a ruthless and voracious half-man, half-beast because he is attacking many sinners at once.*

This anonymous Flemish artist has departed from Dante's graphic description of Satan. The batlike wings are visible; but instead of the three ravenous heads, we are shown one grotesque head with horns, fangs, and sow's ears. Other bestial features of "The Emperor of the Universe of Pain" include claws, a hairy body, and a tail.

Canto XXXIV

NINTH CIRCLE: COCYTUS................*Compound Fraud*
ROUND FOUR: JUDECCA...................*The Treacherous to Their Masters*

THE CENTER..*Satan*

As the Poets face the last depth, they see Satan in the distance, his great wings beating like a windmill. It is their beating that is the source of the icy wind of Cocytus, the exhalation of all evil. All about him in the ice are strewn the sinners of the last round. These are the **1** *Treacherous to Their Masters*. It is impossible to speak to them, and the poets move on to observe Satan.

Hell (The Inferno), 15th century. Flemish School. Oil on wood panel. Correr Civic Museum, Venice.

View the Art The Flemish style of art, which was inspired by manuscript illumination, was known for its attention to detail and superior technique. What qualities of Satan did this artist seek to portray? ★

906 UNIT 5   EARLY EUROPE

Speaking Practice

SMALL GROUP
Present an Oral Interpretation Point out that interest in translating Dante into English and other languages continues even today, centuries after the poet's death. Since so much of poetry is about sound—rhythm, rhyme, alliteration, assonance, and consonance—translators face many challenges in their work.

Suggest that students find other translations of the *Inferno* and locate the cantos from the textbook. Have volunteers read the same section aloud from each work as classmates listen. Invite listeners to comment on the similarities and differences in the poets' styles and state their preferences. Robert Pinsky, the ninth poet laureate of the United States, is one contemporary poet who has translated Dante.

"On march the banners of the King of Hell,"
   my Master said. "Toward us. Look straight ahead:
   can you make him out at the core of the frozen shell?"

5   Like a whirling windmill seen afar at twilight,
   or when a mist has risen from the ground—
   just such an engine° rose upon my sight

stirring up such a wild and bitter wind
   I cowered for shelter at my Master's back,
   there being no other windbreak I could find.

10   I stood now where the souls of the last class
   (with fear my verses tell it) were covered wholly;
   they shone below the ice like straws in glass.

Some lie stretched out; others are fixed in place
   upright, some on their heads, some on their soles;
15   another, like a bow, bends foot to face.

When we had gone so far across the ice
   that it pleased my Guide to show me the foul creature
   that once had worn the grace of Paradise,°

he made me stop, and, stepping aside, he said:
20   "Now see the face of Dis!° This is the place
   where you must arm your soul against all dread."

Do not ask, Reader, how my blood ran cold
   and my voice choked up with fear. I cannot write it:
   this is a terror that cannot be told.

25   I did not die, and yet I lost life's breath:
   imagine for yourself what I became,
   deprived at once of both my life and death.

The Emperor of the Universe of Pain
   jutted his upper chest above the ice;
30   and I am closer in size to the great mountain

6 engine: machine.

17–18 foul creature . . . Paradise: According to the Bible, Satan originally was the highest ranking and most beautiful of God's angels. (See also lines 34–35.)

20 Dis: Satan.

2

3

The Vision of Faith *What punishment do sinners suffer at the bottom of Hell?*

DANTE ALIGHIERI **907**

Teach

Literary Element 2

Imagery Have students discuss the images used to describe the Ninth Circle. **Ask:** To what sense or senses do these images appeal? *(The images in the Ninth Circle are mostly visual, dealing with the size and ugliness of Satan. The poet also refers to great cold.)*

Big Idea 3

The Vision of Faith
Answer: *The sinners are completely immobilized—frozen in ice.*

Cultural History ☆

Dis It is natural for Virgil, a Roman, to speak of Dis, also known as Dis Pater, who was the Roman god of the dead and ruled the Underworld. Dis is the counterpart of the Greek god Hades. **Ask:** What other names do you know that have been used in various cultures to refer to Satan? *(Possible responses: Devil, Lucifer, Beelzebub, Mephistopheles, Old Scratch, Baal, Pluto, Prince of Darkness)*

Advanced Learners/Pre-AP

DIFFERENTIATED INSTRUCTION

SMALL GROUP

Connect to Contemporary Issues Dante's *Divine Comedy* is an allegory, or extended metaphor, for the spiritual journey each person takes. By imagining a modern-day Inferno, students might better understand Dante's motivation for writing.

Encourage students to learn more about how Dante saw the afterlife and then work together to apply that knowledge to develop a contemporary Inferno. Suggest that they first decide on the levels of Hell and the criteria for one's being placed in each level. Then have students suggest literary characters or contemporary personalities that they might see there. Have groups share their conclusions with the class.

Learning Objectives
Analyzing art. (SE)
Making judgments. (TE)
Analyzing imagery. (TE)
Presenting an oral interpretation. (TE)

Analyze Sound Devices

Answer: *The hissing sound of a snake occurs in the words "wing*s*," "ro*s*e," "*s*pan," "*s*o gro*ss*," and "*s*aw *s*uch *s*ails . . . *s*ea."*

---

the Titans° make around the central pit,
    than they to his arms. Now, starting from this part,
    imagine the whole that corresponds to it!

35   If he was once as beautiful as now
    he is hideous, and still turned on his Maker,
    well may he be the source of every woe!

With what a sense of awe I saw his head
    towering above me! for it had three faces:
    one was in front, and it was fiery red;

40   the other two, as weirdly wonderful,°
    merged with it from the middle of each shoulder
    to the point where all converged at the top of the skull;

the right was something between white and bile;°
    the left was about the color one observes
45   on those who live along the banks of the Nile.

Under each head two wings rose terribly,
    their span proportioned to so gross° a bird:
    I never saw such sails upon the sea.

They were not feathers—their texture and their form
50   were like a bat's wings—and he beat them so
    that three winds blew from him in one great storm:

it is these winds that freeze all Cocytus.
    He wept from his six eyes, and down three chins
    the tears ran mixed with bloody froth and pus.

55   In every mouth he worked a broken sinner
    between his rake-like teeth. Thus he kept three
    in eternal pain at his eternal dinner.

For the one in front the biting seemed to play
    no part at all compared to the ripping: at times
60   the whole skin of his back was flayed° away.

31 Titans: according to Greek mythology, a race of giants who ruled the earth until they were overthrown by Zeus and the other gods of Olympus. The speaker says that Satan is so huge that next to him the Titans look smaller than a human being would look next to a Titan.

40 wonderful: here, literally filling a person with wonder or amazement.

43 bile: a fluid secreted by the liver, yellow or yellowish-green in color.

47 gross: of both large size and distasteful character.

60 flayed: having the skin ripped from it.

---

1   **Analyze Sound Devices** *What sound accompanies this description of Satan's wings?*

Reading Practice

Recognize Author's Purpose
Remind students that the "characters" in Dante's *Inferno* were based on real people, some of whom were still alive at the time he wrote. Students can surmise, from the fact that Dante was writing about old political enemies, that part of his motivation was revenge. But was that his only purpose?

Ask students to reread parts of the text that mention specific people and then to break into small groups to discuss what the author's purpose may have been in describing those people's sins. Suggest that, to imagine the purpose of Dante's having exposed the sins of living people, students consider what it would be like to see a work that features contemporary politicians, religious leaders, and celebrities.

"That soul that suffers most," explained my Guide,
  "is Judas Iscariot,° he who kicks his legs
  on the fiery chin and has his head inside.

Of the other two, who have their heads thrust forward,
65 the one who dangles down from the black face
  is Brutus:° note how he writhes without a word.

And there, with the huge and sinewy arms, is the soul
  of Cassius.—But the night is coming on
  and we must go, for we have seen the whole."

70 Then, as he bade, I clasped his neck, and he,
  watching for a moment when the wings
  were opened wide, reached over dexterously

and seized the shaggy coat of the king demon;
  then grappling matted hair and frozen crusts
75 from one tuft to another, clambered down.

When we had reached the joint where the great thigh°
  merges into the swelling of the haunch,
  my Guide and Master, straining terribly,

turned his head to where his feet had been
80 and began to grip the hair as if he were climbing;
  so that I thought we moved toward Hell again.

"Hold fast!" my Guide said, and his breath came shrill
  with labor and exhaustion. "There is no way
  but by such stairs to rise above such evil."

85 At last he climbed out through an opening
  in the central rock, and he seated me on the rim;
2 then joined me with a **nimble** backward spring.

---

62 Judas Iscariot: one of Jesus's disciples. For a payment of 30 pieces of silver, he betrayed his master, showing the authorities where Jesus could be found and captured. Later, remorseful for this act, he hanged himself.

66 Brutus: a praetor (magistrate) in Rome. He and **Cassius** (line 68), once a general in the Roman army, led the plot to assassinate Julius Caeser in 44 B.C.

76 great thigh: The travelers are at Satan's hip.

Allegory *What are Dante and Virgil literally doing? What is the allegorical significance of their actions?*

Vocabulary

nimble (nim′bəl) *adj.* sure-footed; light and quick

Teach

Vocabulary 2

Examples Have students suggest people they have seen—and the activities they were engaged in—that could be described as nimble (for example, gymnasts, acrobats, clowns, dancers).

Literary Element 3

Allegory Answer: *They are literally climbing down the body of Satan. Allegorically, this shows that resisting temptation is as challenging as confronting Satan himself.*

Learning Objectives
Analyzing sound devices. (SE)
Analyzing allegory. (SE)
Giving examples of vocabulary. (TE)

English Learners

DIFFERENTIATED INSTRUCTION

Advanced Have students describe, as vividly as they can, the scenes in which Virgil and Dante encounter Satan and then climb down his hairy body to emerge upside down on the other side. You might want to combine this activity with the English Learners activity on page 911. In that case, encourage students to use the diagram to illustrate their paraphrases.

Approaching Level

DIFFERENTIATED INSTRUCTION

Paraphrase Students having difficulty with the poetic language might have particular trouble understanding this passage. Choose ten to twelve lines on pages 908–911 and write your own paraphrase of them. Have the students choose their own lines and read them aloud. Then the students can paraphrase the lines they chose, accompanied by the diagram described in the English Learners

activity on page 911. Encourage students to ask questions about words, phrases, or descriptions they don't understand

909

Teach

Reading Strategy   1

Question **Ask:** Why does the speaker have difficulty understanding the location of the Inferno? Do you understand Virgil's explanation? Explain it in your own words. *(The speaker cannot understand how they could have been climbing down the fiend and then have found themselves climbing back up. Virgil explains that they have passed through the center of the Earth, into the Southern Hemisphere.)*

Reading Strategy   2

Activate Prior Knowledge Point out line 111: "the point to which all gravities are drawn." **Say:** Think about the shape of the Earth and what you know about gravity. **Ask:** What point would be the center of all gravity? *(the very center; the core of the Earth)*

Literary Element   3

Allegory Answer: *The sky represents paradise (Heaven).*

I looked up, thinking to see Lucifer°
    as I had left him, and I saw instead
90   his legs projecting high into the air.

Now let all those whose dull minds are still vexed
    by failure to understand what point it was
    I had passed through, judge if I was perplexed.

"Get up. Up on your feet," my Master said.
95   "The sun already mounts to middle tierce,°
    and a long road and hard climbing lie ahead."

It was no hall of state we had found there,
    but a natural animal pit hollowed from rock
    with a broken floor and a close and sunless air.

100 "Before I tear myself from the Abyss,"°
    I said when I had risen, "O my Master, **1**
    explain to me my error in all this:

where is the ice? and Lucifer—how has he
    been turned from top to bottom: and how can the sun
105   have gone from night to day so suddenly?"

And he to me: "You imagine you are still
    on the other side of the center where I grasped
    the shaggy flank of the Great Worm of Evil

which bores through the world—you were while I climbed
      down,
110   but when I turned myself about, you passed
2   the point to which all gravities are drawn.

You are under the other hemisphere where you stand;
    the sky above us is the half opposed
    to that which canopies the great dry land.

115 Under the midpoint of that other sky
    the Man° who was born sinless and who lived
    beyond all blemish, came to suffer and die.

88 Lucifer: light-bearer. The name is a reminder that Satan once had a place of honor among the angels of Heaven.

95 middle tierce: The Roman Catholic Church divided the day into canonical hours. Tierce (or terce) named the period from 6:00 A.M. to 9:00 A.M., so middle tierce would be about 7:30 A.M. As they have crossed Satan, the travelers have moved ahead half a day (it was twilight in line 68; see also line 120).

100 Abyss (ə bis´): a very deep gulf or pit. The Bible uses the term more specifically to refer to the hellish depths of the earth.

116 Man: Jesus. Virgil is also explaining that they now are on the other side of the world from Jerusalem, the city in which Jesus was crucified.

---

3   Allegory *What does "the sky above us" represent?*

Writing Practice

 Capitalization Point out that the translator uses capital letters for such nouns as *Hell, Fiend, Image, Evil,* and *Stars,* as well as the adjective *Heavenly.* Explain that these examples represent an older, more formal style of capitalization than that which is now used, one in which certain words were capitalized to emphasize their significance. You may point out that, in German, nouns are still capitalized.

Have students brainstorm a list of the uses of capital letters in modern-day English. The list may include the names of individuals, the titles of individuals, the names of ethnic groups and national groups, the names of languages, certain religious terms, the names of school courses, and the titles of works. Suggest that students give examples for each category.

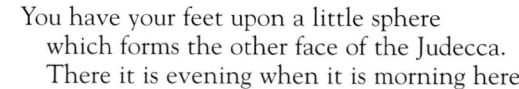

You have your feet upon a little sphere
    which forms the other face of the Judecca.
120   There it is evening when it is morning here.

4 And this gross Fiend and Image of all Evil
    who made a stairway for us with his hide
    is pinched and prisoned in the ice-pack still.

    On this side he plunged down from heaven's height,
125   and the land that spread here once hid in the sea
    and fled North to our hemisphere for fright;

    and it may be that moved by that same fear,
    the one peak° that still rises on this side
    fled upward leaving this great cavern here."

130 Down there, beginning at the further bound
    of Beelzebub's° dim tomb, there is a space
    not known by sight, but only by the sound

    of a little stream° descending through the hollow
    it has eroded from the massive stone
135   in its endlessly entwining lazy flow."

    My Guide and I crossed over and began
    to mount that little known and lightless road
    to ascend into the shining world again.

    He first, I second, without thought of rest
140   we climbed the dark until we reached the point
    where a round opening brought in sight the blest

    and beauteous shining of the Heavenly cars.°
    And we walked out once more beneath the Stars.

128 one peak: the Mount of Purgatory. In Roman Catholic belief, souls spend a time of suffering in Purgatory and thus are cleansed to enter Heaven.

131 Beelzebub: another name of Satan—literally, lord of the flies.

133 little stream: This may refer to the river Lethe (lē′thē), the stream from which souls drank to forget the sorrows of their earthly lives. If so, Virgil may be suggesting that the stream carries memories of sin away from purified souls and into Hell.

142 cars: chariots; figuratively, Dante is referring to the planets and stars.

Analyze Sound Devices *Identify the sound device in this line and explain its effect.*   **5**

DANTE ALIGHIERI **911**

English Learners

DIFFERENTIATED INSTRUCTION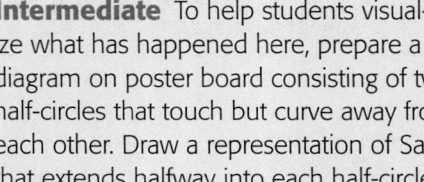

Intermediate To help students visualize what has happened here, prepare a diagram on poster board consisting of two half-circles that touch but curve away from each other. Draw a representation of Satan that extends halfway into each half-circle. Start with Satan right side up. Have a volunteer place a pointer at the bottom of that curve alongside Satan's middle. Explain that this is where the poets stand when

they look up at Satan towering above them (line 38).

Now review the poets' climb down Satan's body (lines 73–75). Have the volunteer follow with the pointer. Now turn the diagram upside down and point out how Satan's feet now point up (line 90). Finally, have the volunteer trace a line up the curve that represents the poets' climb up and out to see the starry sky (lines 140–143).

Teach

Literary Element **4**

Characterization Point out "Image of all Evil" in line 121 and comment that Dante uses many such *epithets*, or descriptive words and phrases, throughout the work to refer to Satan. Have students scan Canto Nine and list the various names by which Satan is called. **Ask:** What do these descriptions reveal about Satan's character? *(Epithets such as "Emperor of the Universe of Pain," "king demon," and "Great Worm of Evil" reveal Satan to be thoroughly loathsome, evil, and powerful.)*

Reading Strategy **5**

Analyze Sound Devices
Answer: *The sound device is alliteration. The explosive "p" sounds in "pinched," "prisoned," and "ice-pack" suggest punches or blows directed at Satan.*

 To check students' understanding of the selection, see Unit 5 Teaching Resources Book, p. 69.

Progress Check

Can students analyze sound devices?

If No → See Unit 5 Teaching Resources Book, p. 66.

Learning Objectives
Analyzing allegory. (SE)
Analyzing sound devices. (SE)
Questioning. (TE)
Analyzing characterization. (TE)
Understanding capitalization. (TE)

911

After You Read

Assess

1. Students should cite explicit examples from the text and explain how they were affected by those examples.

2. (a) They move in an unending whirlwind that represents the chaos of their uncontrolled lust. (b) He feels pity for them, as in lines 137–140, when the sight of Paolo weeping causes Dante to faint.

3. (a) They are freezing in an icy wind as punishment for betraying their masters. (b) Because the traitors were cold and unfeeling to their masters, they now suffer from a lack of warm and comforting human contact.

4. (a) Judas Iscariot, Brutus, and Cassius; they all betrayed their masters. (b) Because Dante was a religious man, he may have equated betrayal of a leader with disloyalty to God.

5. Encourage students to discuss and debate how Dante suited the punishments to the sins.

6. Answers will vary. Students may note that public figures have always been the objects of satire.

7. Students may suggest the book may have encouraged the two lovers, but they are responsible for their own actions.

8. Students will probably say his message was that people should avoid temptation because they will be punished.

9. Students may refer to the position of traitors in the deepest circle of hell as evidence of Dante's personal experiences.

After You Read

Respond and Think Critically

Respond and Interpret

1. How did you react to the descriptions of the suffering sinners? Which description made the most vivid impression on you? Explain.

2. (a) In Canto V, what punishment do the souls suffer? For what sin do they suffer? (b) What is Dante's attitude toward the sinners in Canto V? Support your answer with evidence from the text.

3. (a) At the beginning of Canto XXXIV, how are the sinners punished? For what sin are they punished? (b) How might this punishment be appropriate?

4. (a) Who are the three sinners trapped in the mouths of Lucifer and what do they have in common? (b) Why do you think Dante considered their sin to be so terrible?

Analyze and Evaluate

5. Do you think the punishments described in these excerpts are just? Explain.

6. In your opinion, is Dante being unfair by including historical characters among the damned? Explain.

7. Paolo and Francesca blame their downfall on a book. Is this a good excuse? Explain.

Connect

8. **Big Idea** **The Vision of Faith** Dante wrote the *Divine Comedy* for a European, Christian audience in the fourteenth century. What message or theme did he intend for that audience?

9. **Connect to the Author** Dante included many of his real-life enemies in the different circles of Hell. How does knowing he experienced betrayal help you understand the poem?

Primary Source Quotation

An Overpowering Love

In the quotation below from *La Vita Nuova*, Dante describes his initial impression of Beatrice when the two first met as children.

"The moment I saw her I say in all truth that the vital spirit, which dwells in the inmost depths of the heart, began to tremble so violently that I felt the vibration alarmingly in all my pulses, even the weakest of them. As it trembled, it uttered these words: Ecce deus fortior me, qui veniens domitiabitur mihi. [Behold a god more powerful than I who comes to rule over me.] At this point, . . . [the brain] . . . made this pronouncement: Apparuit iam beatitudo vestra. [Now your source of joy has been revealed.]"

Dante Alighieri and Beatrice in Paradise.
Biblioteca Nazionale, Marciana, Venice.

Group Activity Discuss the questions below with your classmates.

1. What does the statement beginning "Behold a god …" imply about Beatrice's effect on Dante?

2. Explain how the painting reproduced here illustrates Dante's attitude toward Beatrice.

Primary Source Quotation

1. She has a supernatural power over him.

2. In the painting, Dante is looking adoringly at Beatrice. She, in turn, is gesturing for him to join her as she points to Heaven.

 For additional selection assessment, see Assessment Resources, pp. 181–182.

Literary Element | Allegory

SAT Skills Practice

1. In allegorical terms, Dante's character represents

   (A) paganism
   (B) everyman
   (C) spiritual perfection
   (D) sin
   (E) God

2. As an allegorical figure, Virgil represents

   (A) spiritual perfection
   (B) Christian faith
   (C) sin
   (D) reason
   (E) Satan

Review: Form

As you learned on page 739, **form** is the structure of a poem. As explained in the Build Background on page 899, Dante Alighieri composed the *Divine Comedy* in terza rima—three-line stanzas in which the first and third lines rhyme and the second line rhymes with the first line of the next stanza.

Partner Activity Meet with another classmate to discuss the form of John Ciardi's translation of the poem. Working together, answer the following questions.

1. (a)What aspects of terza rima does Ciardi reproduce? (b)What aspect is notably missing?

2. Many lines in Ciardi's translation follow iambic pentameter. Describe this rhythmic pattern and cite examples of lines that exhibit it.

3. Some stanzas end in near rhymes rather than exact ones. Why might Ciardi have done this? Cite an example to support your answer.

LOG ON ⟩ **Literature** Online

Selection Resources For Selection Quizzes, eFlashcards, and Reading-Writing Connection activities, go to glencoe.com and enter QuickPass code GLW6053u5.

Reading Strategy | Analyze Sound Devices

When you read a poem aloud, the sounds of the words can help you picture a scene more vividly. Review the chart you made on page 899. Then answer the following questions.

1. (a)Cite one example of **alliteration, assonance,** and **consonance** from the poem. (b)Describe how the sound adds to your understanding of the setting, characters, or action.

2. Cite one example of a line or lines in which the **meter** contributes to the meaning.

3. Cite one example of a stanza in which the **rhyme** contributes to the meaning.

Vocabulary Practice

Practice with Synonyms A synonym is a word that has the same or nearly the same meaning as another word. With a partner, brainstorm three synonyms for each boldfaced vocabulary word below. Then discuss your choices with your classmates.

verdict   **anguish**   **reel**   **nimble**

EXAMPLE: cadaverous

Synonyms: gaunt, emaciated, skeletal

Academic Vocabulary

In the Inferno*, Dante encounters characters who endure physical and **mental** suffering.*

Mental is an academic word. In another usage, you might say a psychic claimed to have **mental** powers, but without proof many people did not believe her. To further explore this word, answer the following question:

What has been your toughest **mental** exercise? Explain.

For more on academic vocabulary, see pages 36–37 and R83–R85.

DANTE ALIGHIERI **913**

Literary Element

1. B
2. D

Review: Form

1. (a) He writes in three-line stanzas and rhymes the first and third line of each stanza. (b) He does not rhyme the second line of each stanza with the first line of the next stanza.

2. Iambic pentameter consists of five feet. Each foot is composed of an unstressed syllable followed by a stressed syllable. Lines 13 and 46 of Canto V are examples.

3. It is likely he wanted to draw attention to certain lines. In lines 7 and 9 of Canto V, the near rhyme of *foul* and *soul* reinforces the distasteful nature of Minos's task and the sins he assesses.

Progress Check

Can students analyze allegory?

If No → See Unit 5 Teaching Resources Book, p. 65.

Vocabulary

Possible synonyms:

verdict—*judgment, decision, opinion;* **anguish**—*pain, suffering, torment;* **reel**—*stagger, stumble, totter;* **nimble**—*quick, spry, agile*

Explanations will vary.

Academic Vocabulary

Students should describe their "toughest mental exercise" and explain why they characterize it as a *mental* activity.

Reading Strategy

1. Students should be able to cite and explain examples from their lists and/or recall examples covered in the Reading Strategy questions that appear with the selection.

2. Possible answer: Line 4 of Canto V. The iambic pentameter completely breaks down in this line. The four stresses in the first five syllables emphasize the imposing presence of Minos. Suggest students look for other places where the rhythm breaks down and for possible reasons that it departs from what is expected.

3. Possible answer: lines 97 and 99 of Canto V. By rhyming *bloom* and *doom* Ciardi connects them in a cause-effect relationship. The blooming of the couple's love is the source of their doom.

913

After You Read

Assess

Respond Through Writing

Students' essays should

- compare and contrast the effects of the two methods of expression—allegorical and literal—in achieving specific goals
- use evidence from the selection to support their arguments
- use transitions to signal comparisons and contrasts

A student who meets all of these criteria should receive the equivalent of a 4-point response.

A student who fully meets two and partially meets the third of these criteria should receive the equivalent of a 3-point response.

A student who fully meets one and partially meets a second of these criteria, or who partially meets all three criteria, should receive the equivalent of a 2-point response.

A student who partially fully meets one or partially meets two of these criteria should receive the equivalent of a 1-point response.

Respond Through Writing

Expository Essay

Evaluate Theme In the *Inferno*, Dante expresses his theme about salvation through an allegorical journey. Would his expression of this theme be more powerful or less powerful if he had presented it literally? In an essay of 1,500 words or more, evaluate the effectiveness of Dante's expression of his theme through allegory, including the major ideas and the nuances of the work.

Understand the Task When you **evaluate** something, you make a judgment based on evidence. A **nuance** is a subtle quality or variation.

Prewrite Before you begin to write, create a web like the one below to help you evaluate the effects Dante's use of allegory has on the expression of his theme.

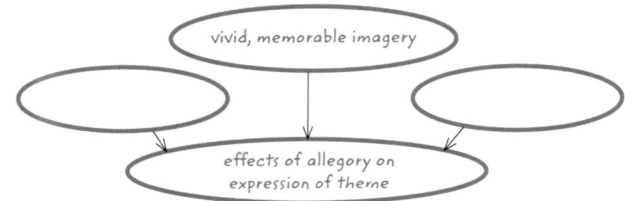

vivid, memorable imagery

effects of allegory on expression of theme

Then create a similar web in which you describe what the effects might have been had Dante presented his theme literally. When you have completed your two webs, review them and decide which mode of presentation—allegorical or literal—would produce a more powerful effect. This can serve as the basis of your thesis.

Draft Formulate a clear thesis supported with credible, valid, and relevant evidence. Develop an engaging introduction and include transitions, a body, and a conclusion. Make sure your body paragraphs compare and contrast the effectiveness of an allegorical and a literal presentation.

Revise Identify and address complexities.. For example, you may need to account for instances in which the method you defend is less successful than the other.

Edit and Proofread Proofread your paper, correcting any errors in spelling, grammar, and punctuation. Review the Grammar Tip in the side column for information on embedding quotations in text.

Learning Objectives

In this assignment, you will focus on the following objectives:

Writing: Writing an expository essay.

Grammar: Understanding quotations in text.

Grammar Tip

Quotations in Text

When you quote a passage from Dante's *Inferno* to support your thesis, keep the following points in mind:

Use double quotation marks at the beginning and end of the quotation.

Use ellipses to indicate lines you have left out.

Use slashes to show line breaks. For example: "Midway through life's journey, I went astray / from the straight road / . . ."

If your passage includes speech or dialogue, use single quotes to indicate this. For example:

"And she: 'The double grief of a lost bliss / is to recall its happy hour in pain.'"

Literary Element Practice

Allegory Students may be better able to write about Dante's allegory if they have a more personal experience of how allegory works. Suggest that students construct their own allegories. They can follow these steps:

- Create a human protagonist who is symbolic of an abstract quality (such as truth, greed, loyalty, etc.).
- Create an antagonist who is symbolic of an abstract quality that is in opposition to, or detrimental to, that of the protagonist.
- Create a dramatic situation in which the protagonist and antagonist enter into conflict, either physical or mental. The situation should have a beginning, middle, and end.
- Consider the outcome of the dramatic situation. Describe it in one sentence, first using the characters' names. (For example: Kate wins out over Hannah in a foot race.)
- Now rewrite the description, substituting the characters' symbolic qualities. (For example: In life, good sportsmanship wins out over dirty tricks.)

Explain to students that this last description can be considered the theme, or meaning, of this allegory.

FROM THE

Divine Comedy

Jorge Luis Borges
Translated by Eliot Weinberger

National Book Critics Circle Award Winner

Literary Perspective

on the *Inferno*
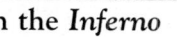

Focus

Summary

Borges writes that the characters in the Divine Comedy are eternal—they have been captured forever in brief, powerful images. He focuses on Paolo and Francesca, who take on a "heroic grandeur" in the text because they refuse to repent for their sin of lust. Borges speculates that Dante may have felt both sympathy and envy for Paolo and Francesca, because, while they could be together in Hell, he himself was separated from Beatrice, the woman he loved.

Teach

Learning Objectives

For pages 915–917

In studying this text, you will focus on the following objectives:

Reading:
Determining main idea and supporting details.
Making connections across literature.
Analyzing informational text.

Set a Purpose for Reading

Read to discover one author's view of the significance of characters in the *Inferno*.

Build Background

Many critics have commented on the deep sympathy Dante shows for the lustful in the *Inferno*. This sympathy may stem from the poet's own unrequited love for Beatrice Portinari, who was married to another man and died at an early age. In the *Paradiso*, the third book of the *Divine Comedy*, Dante ascends to heaven and is reunited with Beatrice. Guided by her beauty and goodness, he rises to the highest realm of paradise. In the following excerpt from the collection of lectures *Seven Nights*, Argentine author Jorge Luis Borges (bôr´hez) explores the importance the lovers in the *Inferno* may have held for Dante.

Reading Strategy | **Determine Main Idea and Supporting Details**

When you **determine** the **main idea** of a text, you find the most important idea in a paragraph or text that is developed through the use of **supporting details**, such as examples, reasons, facts, or descriptions. As you read, ask yourself, How does Borges use details to support his main points?

Dante and Beatrice rise towards the sphere of the sun which is radiating dazzling shafts of golden light on the earth beneath. British Library, London.

A contemporary novel requires five or six hundred pages to make us know somebody, if it ever does. For Dante a single moment is enough. In that moment a person is defined forever. Dante unconsciously sought that central moment. I have wanted to do the same in many stories, and I have been admired for a discovery which actually belongs to Dante in the Middle Ages: that of presenting a moment as a cipher[1] of a life. In Dante we have characters whose lives may consist of only a few tercets,[2] and yet their lives are eternal. They live in a word, in a gesture; they need do nothing more. They are merely part of a canto,[3] but that part is eternal. They keep living and renewing themselves in the memory and in the imagination of men. . . .

---

1. In this context, *cipher* means "a representation in code."
2. A *tercet* is a group of three lines with a set rhyme scheme.
3. A *canto* is a section of a long poem, similar to a chapter in a novel. The *Inferno* is divided into 34 cantos.

JORGE LUIS BORGES **915**

Literary History ☆

A Worldly Writer Jorge Luis Borges grew up reading books written in both English and Spanish. His award-winning fiction, which blends reality and fantasy, makes wide-ranging allusions to the literature of Europe and the Americas. The critic Peter Witonski writes that Borges's "grasp of world literature is one of the fundamental elements of his art."

For activities related to this selection, see Unit 5 Teaching Resources Book, pp. 71–79.

English Learners

DIFFERENTIATED INSTRUCTION

Intermediate Point out to students the following sentence in the text: *Amor condusse noi ad una morte*.

Write on the board:

Spanish: muerte
Italian: morte
English: mortality

Then say: Cognates are words in different languages that are descended from the same root. In this case, the words are all descended from the Latin root *mort*, which means "death."

Explain that if students know the Spanish word *muerte* or the Italian word *morte*, they could probably figure out the meaning of the English word *mortality*. Encourage students to use cognates as clues to meaning as they read informational text.

Readability Scores

Dale-Chall: 7.6
DRP: 59
Lexile: 970

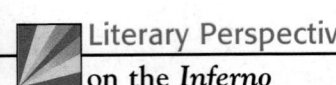

Literary Perspective
on the *Inferno*

Teach

Big Idea | **1**

The Vision of Faith **Ask:** Is
Borges more interested in giving
a theological interpretation of
Dante's *Inferno* or a literary one?
Explain. Suggest to students that
Borges is more interested in
how Francesca and Paolo are
developed as characters than in
the moral implications of their
actions.

Language History ☆

Romance Languages Some
of the Italian words in the selection bear resemblance to Spanish
and English words with which
students may be familiar. Both
the Italian and Spanish languages
are part of the Romance language
group, which also includes French
and Portuguese. The Romance
languages share one key trait:
they are all derived directly from
the Latin that was spoken in
the Roman Empire. The English
language, while it includes many
Latin roots, is actually more closely
related to the languages of
Germany and the Netherlands.

---

1 Let us recall two examples. First, the best-known episode of the *Inferno*, the story of Paolo and Francesca in the fifth canto. I would not presume to summarize what Dante has said—it would be irreverent for me to say in other words what Dante has said for always in his Italian—but I'd like simply to recall the circumstances.

Dante and Virgil arrive at the second circle. There they see the whirlwind of souls and smell the stench of sin, the stench of punishment. There is Minos,[4] twining his tail around himself to indicate to which circle the condemned must descend. It is physically disagreeable, delib-erately ugly, because it is understood that in Hell nothing can be beautiful.

In that circle where the lustful are punished there are great, illustrious names. I say "great names" because Dante, when he began the canto, had not yet reached the perfection of his art, the point where the characters became something more than their names. But halfway through the canto, Dante makes his great discovery: the possibility of a dialogue between the souls of the dead and Dante himself, who will respond and judge in his fashion. No, he will not judge them. He knows that he is not the Judge, that the Judge is the Other, the third speaker, the Divinity.

Well then: there are Helen, Achilles, Paris, Tristan, and other luminaries.[5] But Dante sees two whom he does not know, less illustrious, and who belong to the con-temporary world: Paolo and Francesca. He knows that they have both died as adulterers. He calls to them and they

come, "*quali colombe dal disio chiamate.*"[6] Here we have two sinners, and Dante com-pares them to two doves called by desire, because sensuality must also be the essence of the scene. They draw near, and Francesca, who is the only one to speak—Paolo cannot—thanks him for calling them and speaks these pathetic words: "*Se fosse amico il Re dell'universo/ noi pregheremmo lui per la tua pace,*" if we were friends of the King of the universe—she cannot say God, because that name is forbidden in Hell and Purgatory—we would pray for your peace, since you have taken pity on our misfortune.

Francesca tells her story, and she tells it twice. The first time she tells it in a reserved fashion, but she insists that she is still in love with Paolo. Repentance is for-bidden in Hell. She knows she has sinned and must continue to be faithful to her sin, which gives her a heroic grandeur. It would be terrible if she repented, if she denied what happened. Francesca knows the punishment is just; she accepts it, and continues to love Paolo.

Dante is curious about one thing. "*Amor condusse noi ad una morte*": Paolo and Francesca were executed together. Dante is not interested in adultery, nor in the way they were discovered and brought to jus-tice. What interests him is something more intimate, and that is how they knew they were in love, how they fell in love, how they reached the time of the sweet sighs. He asks them. . . .

This is what Dante wants to know; he wants them to tell him how it happened. She tells how, to entertain themselves one day, they were reading about Lancelot and

---

4. Minos is a mythological Greek king. Dante presents him as a monster who points each sinner toward the proper circle of Hell.
5. A *luminary* is an admired or inspirational person.

6. *Quali colombe dal disio chiamate* means "As doves, called onward by desire."

Reading Practice

Analyze Theme After reading Borges's interpretation of the *Inferno*, students may have developed quite a positive and sym-pathetic view of the souls in the circle of the lustful. Have students ask themselves why Dante might have considered lust to be one of the mildest, least reprehensible sins. Why might he have portrayed these sinners, in particular, as pitiable or even noble?

(Students may say that lust is something succumbed to, rather than chosen willfully, which makes it less reprehensible than sins like malice or heresy. Others may say that Dante himself may have been guilty of lust, and so may have tried to portray it sympathetically. He seems also to have viewed romantic love as something that could lead to spiritual growth, as evidenced by his devotion to Beatrice.)

how he complained of love. They were alone and suspected nothing. They did not suspect they were in love. And they were reading a story from the *Matière de-Bretagne*, one of those books conceived by the British in France after the Saxon invasion—one of those books that fed the madness of Alonso Quijano[7] and revealed their guilty love to Paolo and Francesca. Well: Francesca states that at times they blushed. Then, "*quando leggemmo il disiato riso*,"[8] when we read how the longed-for smile was kissed by such a lover, this one, who will never be separated from me, kissed my mouth, *tutto tremante*.[9]

There is something that Dante does not say, but which one feels at a distance from the episode and perhaps gives it its virtue. Dante relates the fate of the two lovers with an infinite pity, and we sense that he envies their fate. Paolo and Francesca are in Hell and he will be saved, but they have loved and he never won the love of the woman he loved, Beatrice. There is a certain injustice to this, and Dante must feel it as something terrible, now that he is separated from her. In contrast, these two sinners are together. They cannot speak to each other, they turn in the black whirlwind without hope, yet they are together. When she speaks, she says "we," speaking for the two of them, another form of being together. They are together for eternity; they share Hell—and that, for Dante, must have been a kind of Paradise.

We know that he is quite moved. He then collapses as though he were dead. ∾

---

7. In Miguel de Cervantes's *Don Quixote,* the character Alonso Quijano avidly reads chivalric romances, becoming so engaged in them he confuses reality and fantasy and starts to regard himself as a great knight.
8. *Quando leggemmo il disiato riso* means "When we read about the longed-for mouth."
9. *Tutto tremante* means "all trembling."

Respond and Think Critically

Respond and Interpret

1. Write a brief summary of the main ideas in this essay before you answer the following questions. For help on writing a summary, see page 1147.

2. (a)What emotions does Borges say Dante shows toward the lovers? (b)Why does Borges believe Dante feels this way?

Analyze and Evaluate

3. (a)According to Borges, how are Paolo and Francesca heroic or noble? (b)How does this relate to what Borges says is unique about Dante's writing?

4. (a)Why is Paolo and Francesca's Hell "a kind of Paradise" to Dante? (b)How does this relate to his vision of Paradise, discussed in the background information on page 898?

5. (a)How did reading this essay deepen or change your understanding of the *Inferno*? (b)Do you think it is fair to assume biographical information about Dante can contribute to a reader's understanding of his writings? Explain.

Connect

6. How does Dante's love for Beatrice compare with the love between Paolo and Francesca?

JORGE LUIS BORGES **917**

Advanced Learners/Pre-AP

DIFFERENTIATED INSTRUCTION

A Cipher of Life In the text, Borges writes that in his own fiction he has sought a goal that "actually belongs to Dante in the Middle Ages: that of presenting a moment as a cipher of life." Have advanced learners read selections from Borges's anthology of short stories *Ficciones* (1935–1944). Then have them write a paragraph reflecting upon whether or not they think Borges achieves this goal in these stories.

Assess

1. Answers will vary. Students should mention (1) the idea that Dante's characters live eternally and (2) for Dante, Paolo and Francesca's being together in Hell is better than being apart.

2. (a) He says Dante feels pity and envy. (b) Dante envies the sinners because, although he will be saved, he is separated from Beatrice, the woman he loves.

3. (a) They are noble because they remain in love and stay "faithful" to their sin. (b) Borges says Dante's writing is unique because it creates characters whose lives are eternal. Paolo and Francesca are eternal—and heroic—because of the steadfastness of their love.

4. (a) It is a kind of Paradise because the lovers are together forever. (b) In the *Paradiso*, Dante portrays heaven as a place in which he is reunited with his beloved Beatrice.

5. (a) Students may realize Dante's feelings toward sinners were complex and often conflicted. (b) Some students may say one cannot assume Dante the character is identical to Dante the author. Most will agree, however, that Dante's relationship with Beatrice heavily influenced the *Divine Comedy*.

6. It is similar because it is all-consuming. However, Dante's love for Beatrice was unrequited and developed into a source of artistic inspiration and salvation.

Focus

Bellringer Options

Selection Focus
Transparencies 55–56
Daily Language Practice
Transparency 85

Say: In every time and in every culture, the most popular topic for writing has probably been love. **Ask:** What kinds of writing about love are you familiar with? *(Students may mention poetry, romance novels, young adult novels, and diaries.)*

Compare Literature About Love

Ask: What makes a love poem different from a love letter? *(Students may say that a love poem is more romantic, is more difficult to write, or requires certain conventions of structure. They may also suggest that a love poem may be addressed to a fictional beloved, while a love letter almost always has an intended recipient.)*

Compare Literature About Love

For centuries, love has been a popular inspiration for authors, but people define love in many ways. These sonnets by Francesco Petrarch (pē´trärk), Louise Labé (lä bā´), and Julia Alvarez give contrasting views of love.

Laura from Canzoniere by Petrarch...........................sonnet............ 919
ITALY, c. 1340

Sonnet 8 by Louise Labé ....sonnet............ 923
FRANCE, 1555

Secretly I am building in the heart
by Julia Alvarez ....sonnet............ 924
UNITED STATES, 1984

COMPARE THE Big Idea **The Renaissance and Humanism**

Humanist authors of the Renaissance put the pleasures and pains of everyday life at the center of their works. They also painstakingly studied the styles and ideas of classical authors. Petrarch's love sonnets embody these developments. Louise Labé injected a strong female point of view into the Petrarchan tradition. Julia Alvarez provides a novel view of love. As you read, ask yourself, How do these authors describe personal emotions?

COMPARE Sonnets

A **sonnet** is a fourteen-line poem written in **iambic pentameter.** Each line has five metric units consisting of an unstressed syllable followed by a stressed syllable. Sonnets have a fixed rhyme scheme and a two-part structure. Since Petrarch popularized the sonnet in the 1300s, many poets have used the form. As you read, ask yourself, How does each poet use the sonnet structure to share his or her ideas?

COMPARE Responses to Love

The speaker in a sonnet frequently conveys a distinct attitude toward love. Petrarch's sonnets feature a male speaker who loves an idealized, unattainable woman. Labé offers a similar response from a woman's perspective. Alvarez presents a different vision of love. As you read, ask yourself, What details in each sonnet reveal the poet's attitude toward love?

Self portrait with Isabella Brandt, his first wife, in the honeysuckle bower, c.1609. Peter Paul Rubens. Oil on canvas. Alte Pinakothek, Munich.

 Literature Online

Author Search For more about Petrarch, Louise Labé, and Julia Alvarez, go to glencoe.com and enter QuickPass code GLW6053u5.

Learning Objectives

For pages 918–925
In studying these texts, you will focus on the following objectives:

Literary Study: Comparing themes.
Analyzing Petrarchan sonnet.
Interpreting imagery.

Reading: Comparing historical context.

Writing Writing a sonnet.

Literary Elements
- Sonnet (SE pp. 918, 920, 922)
- Enjambment (TE p. 921)
- Personification (TE p. 923)

Speaking/Listening/Viewing Skills
- Visual Display (SE p. 925)
- Art Research (TE p. 920)
- Recite a Sonnet (TE p. 924)

Comparing Literature

Reading Skills
- Interpret Imagery (SE pp. 920–922)
- Analyze Historical Context (TE p. 919)

Vocabulary Skills
- Synonyms (SE pp. 920, 922)
- Create a Story (TE p. 920)

Writing Skills/Grammar
- Sonnet (SE p. 922)
- Essay on Form (SE p. 925)

Before You Read

Laura from *Canzoniere*

 Italy

Meet **Petrarch**

(1304–1374)

On Easter 1341, Petrarch was crowned poet laureate of Rome. The huge ceremony was said to be the first celebration of its size in more than 1,000 years. The magnitude of the event illustrates the monumental status of Petrarch, who is known as both the founder of modern humanism and one of the world's greatest love poets.

A Passion for Literature Francesco Petrarca, known in English as Petrarch, was born in Arezzo in central Italy, but he was raised near the papal court in Avignon, France. Bowing to family pressure, Petrarch studied law in France and Italy until his father's death in 1326. He then moved to the household of Cardinal Giovanni Colonna until 1337, writing and participating in the fashionable lifestyle of the city of Avignon.

Scholar and Sonneteer Petrarch, along with his friend Giovanni Boccaccio (see pages 926–934), played a key role in the Renaissance revival of ancient Greek and Roman literature. Petrarch was an authority on classical authors and used their writing styles and philosophical insights in many of his own writings. Petrarch was also famous for his sonnets, many of which focus on a mysterious woman named Laura.

Blending Two Worlds Petrarch is credited with founding humanism, a movement that sought to dignify people by focusing on their earthly achievements. In his writing, however, he often blends the sacred and the secular. One work that embodies this effort is *De viris illustribus*, a collection of biographies of famous men

> "*To be able to say how much you love is to love but little.*"
>
> —Petrarch

from the Old Testament through Roman and Christian history. Another piece—*Secretum meum*—reflects Petrarch's personal struggle with spirituality and earthly experiences. It concludes that a spiritual life is still possible even among the distractions of the world.

As Petrarch grew more committed to his faith, he drew back from his preoccupation with Laura, viewing it as a symptom of earthly attachment. Petrarch grew to love solitude and nature, living for many years in the isolation of France's Vaucluse region. *De vita solitaria* (1346), describes the value of a solitary life. Throughout his diverse works, Petrarch powerfully combines a love of the ancient world with a yearning for inner peace.

PETRARCH **919**

Comparing Literature

Before You Read

Focus

Reading Strategy   1

Analyze Historical Context Draw students' attention to Petrarch's having been crowned Poet Laureate of Rome at a huge ceremony. **Ask:** What kind of society would have a huge ceremony for a new poet laureate? (*Students will say that Roman society at this time must have valued poetry very much. Some students will point out that Italy during the Renaissance celebrated its poets and artists.*)

Literary History

Who Was Laura? Many of Petrarch's sonnets in *Canzoniere* are about the poet's love for a mysterious and unattainable woman named Laura, who causes him joy and despair in life and grief following her death. Laura remains a mystery. She may have been a married woman; she may not even have existed. Even if she existed only in Petrarch's imagination, however, she is more realistically portrayed than the conventional lady of the courtly love tradition, and she is more human and down-to-earth than Dante's angelic and idealized Beatrice.

English Learners

DIFFERENTIATED INSTRUCTION

Intermediate Be aware that speakers of Spanish, Italian, or Portuguese will recognize that the title of Petrarch's book, *Canzoniere*, is likely to mean *song* or *songs* because the Spanish cognate for *song* is *cancion*. Elicit this information from English learners and have them share the information with the rest of the class. **Ask:** Does it change your expectations about the sonnets to know this? (*Students may say that they expect the sonnets to be highly lyrical and songlike.*)

Comparing Literature

Before You Read

Focus

Summary

In the first octave, the speaker describes Laura as having been both beautiful and joyful in the past, but implies that she is less so in the present. The speaker imagines or remembers a moment in the past when Laura seemed to look on him with pity, but perhaps with only false pity. The speaker says his love for Laura was a fire raging inside him that burned fiercely. In the closing six lines the speaker describes Laura as having been angelic, almost divine. In the last two lines it becomes clear that the speaker addresses someone who has told him Laura has changed, but the speaker declares his feelings for her are still very strong.

 For summaries in languages other than English, see Unit 5 Teaching Resources Book, pp. 81–86.

Vocabulary

Create a Story Have students volunteer possible story topics suggested to them by the vocabulary words: *tangle, pity, dreary*. Record the topics on the board. Then have students choose one of the topics and write a short story about the topic. For instance, for *pity* a student might suggest for a story about a student undergoing a public embarrassment for which others *pity* him. Students should use the suggested topic as a starting point; encourage them to depart from it if they feel the desire to.

 For work with vocabulary strategies, see Unit 5 Teaching Resources Book, p. 89.

920

Literature and Reading Preview

Connect to the Poem

How does time affect our feelings for someone we love? Freewrite for a few minutes about this question.

Build Background

Many of the sonnets in Petrarch's collected poems, the *Canzoniere,* are about Petrarch's love for a mysterious woman named Laura. The *Canzoniere* is organized to show the conflicted emotions Petrarch experienced while Laura lived and the grief he felt following her death.

Set Purposes for Reading

Big Idea **The Renaissance and Humanism**

As you read, ask yourself, Which descriptions of Laura represent a blending of the sacred and the secular?

Literary Element **The Petrarchan Sonnet**

The **Petrarchan,** or **Italian,** sonnet is divided into a group of eight lines, called the octave, and a group of six lines, called the sestet, with a turn between the two parts. The **octave** describes a problem or a situation and has the rhyme scheme *abba, abba.* The **turn** is the shift from the problem to the resolution. The problem or situation is resolved in the **sestet,** which can have varying rhyme schemes, such as *cde cde, cde dce,* or *cdc dcd.*

Reading Strategy **Interpret Imagery**

When you **interpret imagery,** you use your knowledge of the world to find meaning in images beyond the literal level. As you read, ask yourself, What are the literal and symbolic meanings of the poem's images?

Tip: Use a Web As you read, use a web to record images from the poem and note your interpretations.

speaker has great reverence for Laura

golden hair

Vocabulary

pity (pit´ē) *n.* sympathy for another's suffering; p. 921 *I felt pity for the stray dog whimpering outside my door.*

dreary (drēr´ē) *adj.* dull or sorrowful; p. 921 *After the third rainy day of our camping trip, we were all in a dreary mood.*

Tip: Synonyms Synonyms are words with the same or similar meanings. For example, *tangle, twist,* and *snarl* express differently the idea of combining in a messy way. Authors often choose from among several synonyms, each with its own shade of meaning, to express their ideas accurately.

Viewing Practice

 SMALL GROUP **Research Art** Explore what students already know about Renaissance artwork, and briefly address the significance of the period's innovations in painting, sculpture, and architecture. Ask them to form small groups to research the painting, sculpture, and architecture of the Renaissance.

Students may use photocopies of illustrations in library reference works and art history magazines, as well as online resources from the Internet, to compose a Renaissance portfolio.

Ask students to share their work with the class as a whole, perhaps by posting the pictures in the classroom and conducting a gallery walk.

You might suggest the following artists as suitable subjects for research: Giotto, Masaccio, Botticelli, Raphael, Titian, Donatello, and Michelangelo.

Young woman at Her Toilet, 1515 (detail). Giovanni Bellini. Oil on panel. Kunsthistorisches Museum, Vienna.

Laura
from Canzoníere

Petrarch
Translated by Morris Bishop

She used to let her golden hair fly free
    For the wind to toy and tangle and molest;
    Her eyes were brighter than the radiant west.
    (Seldom they shine so now.) I used to see
5 **Pity** look out of those deep eyes on me.
    ("It was false pity," you would now protest.)
    I had love's tinder° heaped within my breast;
    What wonder that the flame burned furiously?
  She did not walk in any mortal way,
10   But with angelic progress;° when she spoke,
    Unearthly voices sang in unison.
  She seemed divine among the **dreary** folk
    Of earth. You say she is not so today?
    Well, though the bow's unbent,° the wound bleeds on.

Canzoníere (kan zō nē′ ər): the Italian word for songs.

7 tinder: material used to start a fire.

10 progress: here, a forward movement.

14 unbent: An archer bends a bow into a curve before firing an arrow.

2   **Interpret Imagery** *To what does the speaker compare Laura's eyes? What might this image symbolize?*

Vocabulary

pity (pit′ē) *n.* sympathy for another's suffering
dreary (drēr′ē) *adj.* dull or sorrowful

PETRARCH **921**

Comparing Literature

Literary Element   1

Enjambment Point out the enjambment in lines 4 and 5. Remind students that enjambment is the continuation of a sentence from one line of a poem to another without pause. Students should note that most of the lines in "Laura" have end-stopped lines, so the use of enjambment here and between lines 1 and 2 draws the reader's attention to these lines in particular. **Ask:** How does enjambment enhance these lines? (*It highlights the word "Pity" and preserves the poem's rhyme scheme.*)

Reading Strategy   2

Interpret Imagery Answer: *The speaker compares Laura's eyes to a bright sunset. The brilliance of her eyes might symbolize her perfection.*

 For additional practice using the reading skill or strategy, see Unit 5 Teaching Resources Book, p. 88.

Learning Objectives
Interpret imagery. (SE)
Research art. (TE)
Analyze enjambment. (TE)

Advanced Learners/Pre-AP

DIFFERENTIATED INSTRUCTION

Compare Octave and Sestet Review **octave** (the first eight lines of a sonnet, in which the problem or situation is described) and **sestet** (the last six lines of a sonnet, in which the problem or situation is resolved) with advanced students. Point out that the speaker describes Laura differently in the octave than he does in the sestet. Direct students to focus on the turn (lines 8 and 9, in which the poem switches from problem to resolution).

Encourage students to consider why Petrarch phrases line 8 as a question. (*Students should note that in the octave Laura is described as a radiant young woman, and in the sestet she is described as having qualities of the divine and as a woman who has changed.*) Note that the speaker also hints at how he himself has changed. Suggest that students make charts to compare what Laura was like when the speaker first knew her and what he sees now.

Then have them compare what the speaker was like when he first knew Laura and how he has changed since then. (*Students' charts should show that Laura has lost the otherworldliness that the speaker once saw in her. He has a more realistic view of her, but still loves her.*)

After You Read

Assess

1. Answers will vary.

2. (a) Her eyes do not shine as they used to. (b) She is older and may no longer be happy.

3. (a) *bow* and *wound* (b) "The wound bleeds on" means he still loves and suffers from it.

4. (a) the wind (b) They vividly suggest Laura was a free spirit.

5. (a) They show Laura as she is now. (b) They suggest that circumstances have changed.

6. (a) True love survives aging and even death. (b) Students should cite details from the poem to support their answers.

7. (a) Both. In the past, the speaker thought she looked divine compared with ordinary people. Though he now sees her as mortal, he still loves her. (b) It embraces romance and finds divinity in earthly love.

8. Today's readers can relate to the agony of unrequited love, the beauty of loved ones, and the effects of the passage of time.

Literary Element

1. (a) *abbaabba*. (b) It changes to *cdedce*.

2. In the octave the poet is reliving the past and explaining why he fell in love with the idealized Laura. In the sestet he accepts her as mortal.

Progress Check

Can students recognize a Petrarchan sonnet?

If No ➔ See Unit 5 Teaching Resources Book, p. 87.

922

After You Read

Respond and Think Critically

Respond and Interpret

1. What image of Laura did you find most memorable? Explain.

2. (a) According to lines 1–4, how has Laura's appearance changed? (b) What caused this change?

3. (a) The last line contains an **allusion** to Cupid, the god of love who shoots lovers with arrows. Which words in line 14 make the allusion? (b) Explain the metaphor in that line.

Analyze and Evaluate

4. (a) What is being personified in lines 1–2? (b) How effective are these lines in describing Laura's personality? Explain.

5. (a) What is the function of the comments enclosed within parentheses in lines 4 and 6? (b) Do they achieve this goal? Explain.

6. (a) What does this poem say about love, aging, and death? (b) Do you agree or disagree with the speaker's sentiments? Explain.

Connect

7. **Big Idea** **The Renaissance and Humanism** (a) Is Laura depicted as human, divine, or both? Explain. (b) How does this poem exemplify the concerns of Renaissance humanism?

8. **Connect to Today** How does this poem's theme have meaning for today's readers?

Literary Element **The Petrarchan Sonnet**

In the **Italian sonnet**, or **Petrarchan sonnet**, the octave usually presents a single **theme**, or message, and the sestet expands or develops it.

1. (a) What is the rhyme scheme of the octave? (b) How does it change in the last six lines?

2. What is the main idea expressed in the octave? in the sestet?

Reading Strategy **Interpret Imagery**

Look at the web you made on page 920 and then answer the following questions.

1. (a) What picture does line 3 create? (b) What does this image suggest about Laura?

2. (a) Identify the metaphor in lines 7–8. (b) What does it tell you about the speaker's love?

LOG ON ▶ **Literature** Online

Selection Resources For Selection Quizzes, eFlashcards, and Reading-Writing Connection activities, go to glencoe.com and enter QuickPass code GLW6053u5.

922 UNIT 5 EARLY EUROPE

Vocabulary Practice

Practice with Synonyms With a partner, match each boldfaced vocabulary word below with its synonym. Use a thesaurus or dictionary to check your answers. You will not use all the answer choices.

1. pity   **a.** sympathy   **d.** dismal

2. dreary   **b.** snarl   **e.** sorrow

     c. unravel

✍ Writing

Write a Sonnet Petrarch wrote this sonnet to describe how he and Laura had changed. Think of a person you know who has changed since you have known him or her, or a situation that is different now than when it began. Write a sonnet about this person or situation, using the rhyme scheme and structure of the Petrarchan sonnet. Include figurative language, such as metaphors and similes.

Reading Strategy

1. (a) The reader might picture a brilliant sunset. (b) The image suggests she is joyful, beautiful, and full of life.

2. (a) Love is compared to a fire. (b) It is fierce and passionate.

Vocabulary Practice

1. a   **2.** d

✍ Writing

Students' sonnets should

- focus on a subject that has changed
- follow the octave-sestet format and the meter and rhyme scheme of a Petrarchan sonnet
- use figurative language

Build Background

The French poet Louise Labé (c. 1524–1566) wrote within the Petrarchan tradition, but she provided her own perspective. In the typical Petrarchan love sonnet, the male speaker yearns for an idealized, aloof, and inaccessible lady. The lady's beauty is praised in extravagant terms, but she is portrayed as a prized object rather than as a thinking and feeling subject. Using a female speaker with a male beloved, Louise Labé challenged these conventions. In the dedication to her single volume of poetry, she made the revolutionary move of urging women to set aside their domestic activities, fine clothes, and jewelry, in order to study literature and culture.

Sonnet 8

Louise Labé
Translated by Willis Barnstone

I live, I die, I burn myself and drown.
I am extremely hot in suffering cold:
my life is soft and hardness
   uncontrolled.
When I am happy, then I ache
   and frown.

5 Suddenly I am laughing while I cry
and in my pleasure I endure
   deep grief:
my joy remains and slips out
   like a thief.
Suddenly I am blooming and turn dry.
So Love inconstantly leads me
   in vain

10 and when I think my sorrow has
   no end
unthinkingly I find I have no pain.
But when it seems that joy is in
   my reign
and an ecstatic hour is mine to spend,
He comes and I, in ancient
   grief, descend.

1

The Pained Heart or *Sigh No More, Ladies,* 1868. Arthur Hughes (England 1832-1915). Oil on canvas, 94 x 110 cm. The Maas Gallery, London.

Quickwrite

How does Labé describe the experience of being in love? How do you think her experience is affected by the fact she is a woman? Based on your knowledge of the Petrarchan sonnet and the portrayal of women in Renaissance literature and art, how might this poem be evidence that Labé was a feminist in the context of her time?

LOUISE LABÉ   **923**

In this sonnet, the beloved is male and the speaker is female. In the octave, the speaker describes her experience of love entirely in terms of contradictory and conflicting physical sensations—extremes of hot and cold, pleasure and pain, sorrow and joy, laughter and tears. After this tumult, in the sestet the speaker finds herself paradoxically calm just when her torment seems endless; yet when the beloved arrives, the speaker is once more thrown into a state of chaotic emotion.

Teach

Literary Element   **1**

Personification Remind students that personification is a figure of speech in which human qualities are attributed to objects, animals, or ideas. **Say:** Labé uses personification in lines 7 and 9. What abstract ideas are given human qualities in these lines? *(Joy in line 7, and love in line 9)*

Quickwrite

Students' responses should

- discuss the idea that love is burdensome and confusing
- address Labé's choice to write about a thinking and feeling person, rather than creating an idealized image
- cite evidence from the sonnet to support their conclusions about Labé's feminism

Learning Objectives
Analyze author's purpose. (SE)
Understand personification. (TE)

English Learners

DIFFERENTIATED INSTRUCTION

Intermediate Students may recognize many simple words in this sonnet—words such as *live, die, hot, cold*—which are commonly taught in newcomers' curricula. Be aware, however, that this familiarity with certain words cannot help students understand the poem's oppositional structure and may even confuse them. Draw students' attention to how words with conflicting meanings appear in the speaker's statements: *live* and *die, burn* and *drown.* Help students to recognize that statements of this kind are not to be understood literally but as exaggerated descriptions of what it feels like to be in love.

Focus

Summary

The speaker addresses the reader and describes her efforts to build a "delicate structure" in her heart, laboriously piecing together an unnamed object that she characterizes as made from the ruins of another earlier effort. The speaker never explicitly names what it is he or she is working on, but tells the reader that this work is done out of love.

Teach

Writer's Technique ☆

Julia Alvarez Alvarez once said, "I write to find out what I'm thinking. I write to find out who I am. I write to understand things."
Ask: What do you think Alvarez means when she says she writes to find out what she's thinking? *(Students may say that the process of writing often reveals the state of the writer's mind, even to the writer, and helps to clarify thinking.)*

Discussion Starter

Students should recognize the speaker is "building" poetry. Her "love" in this poem is a love for the inner life and for creative work. The speaker's references to modern objects suggest that in her poetic craft she is creating contemporary works of art. The statement "I've / labored with my heart to outlast the heart" suggests her creations will survive after her death. Students may say this displays a humanist belief in the importance of human endeavors on earth.

Build Background

Born in New York City in 1950 and raised in the Dominican Republic, the award-winning author Julia Alvarez is known for writing poems and novels that probe the qualities of identity. In *Homecoming* (1984), which contains the sonnet you are about to read, Alvarez explores her identity as a woman and her fascination with traditional verse forms. One of her goals is to write sonnets that portray women as independent voices rather than "love objects." As Alvarez writes, "My idea of traditional forms is that as women much of our heritage is trapped in them. But the cage can turn into a house if you housekeep it the right way." To this end, Alvarez varies the traditional conventions of the sonnet, experimenting with loose rhythms and slant rhyme. ☆

Secretly
I am building in the heart

Julia Alvarez

Secretly I am building in the heart
a delicate structure like one of those
cardhouses or Popsicle palaces
kids build, patiently piecing each part
5 together, fingers pinching a small tube
of glue, eyes straining to perceive what
new thing I am making that takes so
   much time
   to finish if there's finish in these
   things.
And making it out of nothing but what
10 are ruins from an earlier effort
and tempted constantly to believe that
a readymade is better, and yet I've
labored with my heart to outlast the
   heart
with this thing I'm creating out of love.

Portrait of Joan Salvat-Papasseit, 1918. Rafael Perez Barradas. Collection of Gustau Camps, Barcelona.

> **💬 Discussion Starter**
>
> Although this sonnet refers to traditional subjects such as "love" and the "heart," the object of the speaker's love is very different from the usual beloved. What is the speaker "building"? What does she mean when she says she has "labored with my heart to outlast the heart"? Discuss these questions with a group.

Speaking Practice

Recite a Sonnet Have students memorize and recite a sonnet. You might make this an assignment for the whole class, or you may wish to allow some students the option of reciting the sonnets they have chosen in a small group setting. Tell students they may choose any sonnet by any poet they wish. You might encourage students to memorize former Poet Laureate Billy Collins's humorous poem entitled *Sonnet,* which describes the sonnet structure within the poem's text, and also mentions Petrarch and Laura.

Wrap-Up: Comparing Literature

Across Time and Place

- *Laura* from *Canzoniere* by Petrarch

- *Sonnet 8* by Louise Labé

- *Secretly I am building in the heart* by Julia Alvarez

COMPARE THE Big Idea **The Renaissance and Humanism**

Visual Display During the Renaissance, details and experiences of everyday life moved to the forefront of art and literature. How do Renaissance depictions of such worldly subjects as work, love, and marriage compare with contemporary illustrations? Using Internet and print sources, create a collage of images from the cultures of Petrarch (Renaissance Italy), Labé (Renaissance France), and Alvarez (present-day United States) that celebrate love in the context of everyday life. Present your display to the class and discuss the similarities and differences between the images and the cultural values they suggest. Make sure you give proper credit to your sources.

COMPARE Sonnets

Writing Write a brief essay comparing the three poets' use of the sonnet form. Consider elements such as meter, rhyme, and the turn between the octave and the sestet. In addition, consider the authors' style, tone, and diction. Be sure to address how Alvarez both adheres to and breaks from the traditional sonnet form, and discuss passages in the poem that might explain her reasons for these artistic decisions.

COMPARE Responses to Love

Group Activity With a small group, answer the following questions. Cite evidence from the poems to defend your points.

1. What motivates each speaker to write?

2. In your opinion, how would each speaker define "love"?

3. How can you apply the background information (see pages 920, 923, and 924) to help you understand the speakers' views of love?

Lovers with Daisies (Les Amoreux aux Marguerites), 1949-1950. Marc Chagall. Private collection.© ARS, NY.

 Literature Online

Author Search For information about Francesco Petrarch, Louise Labé, and Julia Alvarez, go to glencoe.com and enter QuickPass code GLW6053u5.

COMPARING LITERATURE **925**

Assess

Compare the Big Idea

Students' displays should

- use images from appropriate time periods and relate the images to their historical context

- clearly explain how the images reflect ideas in the poems, such as the idealization of the beloved, the pain of being in love, and the joys of introspection and creativity

- identify and explain similarities and differences between the cultures' depictions of love

Compare Sonnets

Students' essays should discuss how both Petrarch and Labé use rhyme and meter to structure their poems. They should include Labé's use of the octave to describe the "symptoms" of her love and the sestet to analyze the situation, as well as Alvarez's use of loose slant rhyme; her use of iambic pentameter; and her description of her "project" in the octave and reflections on it in the sestet. Students should also discuss passages such as *a delicate structure, ruins from an earlier effort,* and *a readymade is better* as they relate to Alvarez's desire to carefully preserve the sonnet form while making it her own as a female author.

Compare Responses to Love

1. An unrequited love for Laura motivates Petrarch's speaker; the intermittent joy and pain of being in love motivates Labé's speaker; a dedication to work motivates Alvarez's speaker.

2. Possible answers: Petrarch: an unyielding feeling for a beloved; Labé: an emotion that inevitably leads to pain; Alvarez: a passion for what one creates.

3. Students should mention Petrarch's real-life love for Laura; Labé's desire to present women as rounded, independent characters; and Alvarez's desire to celebrate the everyday lives of women.

Before You Read

Focus

Bellringer Options

**Selection Focus
   Transparency 57**
**Daily Language Practice
   Transparency 86**

Or ask: What things would you be willing to sacrifice for someone you love? Students may suggest social standing, wealth, professional advancement, or personal goals. **Or ask:** Do people control their own destinies? Students will probably agree that people's actions, decisions, and goals determine their destinies but that circumstances beyond their control may also affect what happens to them.

Literary History ☆

The *Decameron* The title *Decameron* means "ten days' work" and refers to the ten days of storytelling that form the book's structure. Each day is devoted to a specific kind of story: adventure, love, comic trickery, and so on. On the last day, the themes from the previous days are brought together.

Before You Read

Federigo's Falcon

Meet **Giovanni Boccaccio**
(1313–1375)

Giovanni Boccaccio has been called the father of modern fiction because he was one of the first authors to write prose stories in a modern language. With a life full of ups and downs, he had a rich store of experience to draw upon for his writings.

Early Life Boccaccio spent his early life in the city-state of Florence, which later became part of Italy. Drawn toward the literary arts when he was quite young, Boccaccio found himself at odds with his business-conscious father. After a rather unhappy boyhood, Boccaccio was sent to Naples to study business and law in 1328. There he was exposed to the wealth and relative ease of the middle and upper classes and spent time with members of the intellectual elite of the court. He wrote a great deal and soon grew to revere the works of another Italian author, Petrarch (see page 919). This comfortable life soon came to an end, however, when the company Boccaccio and his father worked for went bankrupt around 1340. Boccaccio was called back to Florence where he got his first—but not his last—taste of financial hardship.

An Artist in Full Bloom The fifteen years following Boccaccio's return to Florence were the most prolific of his life as an author. He remained in Florence when the deadly bubonic plague struck the city, killing thousands. During this difficult time, Boccaccio penned his masterpiece, ☆ the *Decameron*, which was to become one of the most famous and best-loved literary works of all time. Most of the book's 100 stories address either love or the corruption of church officials.

> "To take pity on people in distress is a human quality which every man and woman should possess."
>
> —Giovanni Boccaccio

Historians believe Boccaccio wrote the *Decameron* from 1348 to 1353. During that time, he served as an ambassador for the city of Florence and traveled widely. In 1350 he met Petrarch, the author whose work he had so admired years earlier. The two men became friends, inspired each other's writing, and together helped pave the way for Renaissance humanism in Europe. Both men wrote in Italian, not Latin, which elevated the literary status of the vernacular, or common, language.

In many ways, Boccaccio embodied the Renaissance man. He studied and translated the classics and held his own work to classical standards of accomplishment. Having spent time with the wealthy elite, but having lived most of his days in poverty, he understood life from an unusually varied set of perspectives. This understanding of the complexities of the human struggle is perhaps what makes his work just as relevant today as it was more than six centuries ago.

 Literature Online

Author Search For more about Giovanni Boccaccio, go to glencoe.com and enter QuickPass code GLW6053u5.

Selection Skills

Literary Elements
- Theme (SE pp. 927, 928, 932, 933)
- Irony (SE pp. 933)
- Character (TE p. 930)

Reading Skills
- Analyze Plot (SE pp. 927, 929, 931, 934)
- Apply Background Information (TE p. 928)
- Analyze Cultural Context (TE p. 928)

Federigo's Falcon

Vocabulary Skills
- Word Usage (SE p. 934)
- Academic Vocabulary (SE p. 934)
- Create Sentences (TE p. 927)

Speaking/Listening/Viewing Skills
- Analyze Art (SE p. 932)
- Oral Report (SE p. 934)

Writing Skills/Grammar
- Research Report (TE p. 930)
- Adjective Clauses (TE p. 932)

Literature and Reading Preview

Connect to the Story

What role do you think chance or luck plays in a person's happiness? Discuss this question with a partner.

Build Background

In 1348, the city of Florence suffered from an outbreak of the bubonic plague. To avoid this deadly disease, many fled to the countryside, as do the ten young people in the *Decameron*. To entertain each other during their ten-day retreat, each member of the group takes a turn playing the role of king or queen and directs the others to tell stories. "Federigo's Falcon" is one tale told by the "queen."

Set Purposes for Reading

Big Idea The Renaissance and Humanism

As you read "Federigo's Falcon," ask yourself, What are the author's views on free will versus individual choice?

Literary Element Theme

The **theme** is the central message about life in a literary work. The theme is different from the topic. The *topic* of a work might be love; the *theme* is what the author says about love—that it is painful, wonderful, or both, for example. As you read the story, ask yourself, What is the topic and the theme?

Reading Strategy Analyze Plot

When you **analyze** the **plot** of a literary work, you examine its various sections to see how the parts fit together to create the whole. As you read this story, ask yourself, How does each element of the plot contribute to my understanding of the text?

Tip: Use a Diagram You can use a diagram like the one below to track and connect the story's events.

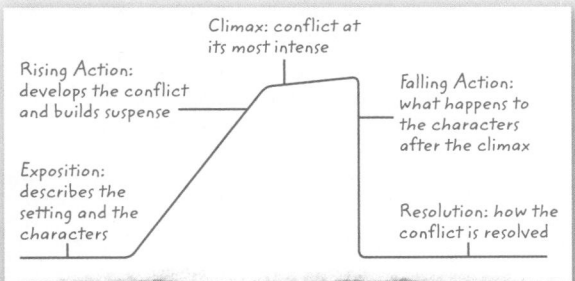

Climax: conflict at its most intense

Rising Action: develops the conflict and builds suspense

Falling Action: what happens to the characters after the climax

Exposition: describes the setting and the characters

Resolution: how the conflict is resolved

Learning Objectives

For pages 926–934

In studying this text, you will focus on the following objectives:

Literary Study: Analyzing theme.

Reading: Analyzing plot.

Listening and Speaking: Presenting an oral report.

Vocabulary

revered (ri vērd′) *adj.* regarded as worthy of great honor; p. 929 *My friend found out her uncle is a revered political figure in the Czech Republic.*

chaste (chāst) *adj.* innocent; pure; p. 929 *Fairy tales are full of magic, handsome princes, and chaste kisses.*

penuriously (pi noor′ē əs lē) *adv.* marked by severe poverty; p. 929 *The elderly couple lived penuriously in a tiny apartment.*

presumption (pri zump′shən) *n.* attitude or conduct that oversteps the bounds of propriety or courtesy; p. 931 *The landlady had the presumption to enter our apartment without our permission.*

contrary (kon′trer ē) *adj.* unfavorable; p. 931 *The judge gave a contrary ruling, which disappointed the defendants.*

Before You Read

Focus

Summary

Federigo squanders his estate in a futile attempt to win the love of Monna Giovanna. With little left but one magnificent falcon, he retires to the country. When the widowed Monna retires to a nearby estate, her son strikes up a friendship with Federigo and delights in the falcon. When the boy falls ill, he asks for the bird as the one thing that would make him better. Monna goes to Federigo reluctantly. When she finally brings up the reason for her visit, it is too late. Federigo confesses that in honor of her visit he killed the falcon and served it for dinner. Soon afterward Monna's son dies. When her brothers urge Monna to remarry, she chooses Federigo, remembering his selfless generosity.

 For summaries in languages other than English, see Unit 5 Teaching Resources Book, pp. 92–97.

Vocabulary

Create Sentences Read the vocabulary words and their definitions aloud. After each one, ask several volunteers to use the vocabulary word in a sentence. To conclude the exercise, tell students to write new sentences for each vocabulary word.

 For additional vocabulary practice, see Unit 5 Teaching Resources Book, p. 100.

English Learners

DIFFERENTIATED INSTRUCTION

Intermediate Preview the selection, focusing on Boccaccio's writing style. Point out that the introduction and asides reflect his observance of literary conventions of the time, which favored courtly expression, ornate diction and syntax. If students have trouble following the storyline, encourage them to simplify passages by removing embellishments such as unnecessary phrases, compliments, and courtesies.

Approaching Level

DIFFERENTIATED INSTRUCTION

Clarify Structure For students who have trouble separating the frame story from the story itself, point out the following:

- Paragraph 1—The storyteller is identified.
- Paragraph 2—She explains the kind of story she will tell and the lesson to be learned from it.
- Paragraph 3—She reveals who told her the story.
- Paragraph 4—Story begins.

Teach

Reading Strategy | 1

Apply Background Information **Ask:** Who is the queen, and why is it her turn to tell a story? *(She is the member of the group who is presiding over the storytelling on this particular day. It is her turn because all the other members have told their stories except Dioneo, who owns the privilege of being the last storyteller.)*

Literary Element | 2

Theme **Answer:** *The theme may be that people must sometimes take control of their lives instead of allowing Fortune to dictate events.*

View the Art ★

Dosso Dossi was a prominent, sixteenth-century artist in the court of the dukes of the Italian city-state of Ferrara. Dramatic landscapes, rich colors, and effective use of light are characteristic elements of his paintings. *Melissa*, one of his most famous works, depicts a magical scene from a poem by Ariosto about an enchantress who frees victims of sorcery who have been transformed into animals and trees.

 For an audio recording of this selection, use Listening Library Audio CD-ROM.

Readability Scores

Dale-Chall: 7.9
DRP: 58
Lexile: 1200

928

Melissa (detail), c.1523. Dosso Dossi (Italy, 1479-1542). Oil on canvas. Galleria Borghese, Rome. ★

Federigo's Falcon

from the DECAMERON

Giovanni Boccaccio
Translated by Richard Aldington

1 Filomena had ceased speaking, and the queen, seeing that nobody was left to speak except Dioneo (who had his privilege)[1] and herself, began cheerfully as follows:

It is now my turn to speak, dearest ladies, and I shall gladly do so with a tale similar in part to the one before, not only that you may know the power of your beauty over the gentle heart, but because you may learn yourselves to be givers of rewards when fitting, without allowing Fortune[2] always to dispense them, since Fortune most often bestows them, not discreetly but lavishly.

You must know then that Coppo di Borghese Domenichi, who was and

---

1. *Dioneo* (dē ō nā′ō) had the right to tell the last story in each day's group of stories.

2. *Fortune* means "fate" or "destiny."

Theme *What do the queen's opening remarks imply about the theme of the story?* **2**

928 UNIT 5 EARLY EUROPE

Reading Practice

Analyze Cultural Context Point out that the plot revolves around the characters' desire to follow the etiquette of entertaining, which is reflected in the narrative's language, action, and dialogue.

Have students skim the story to find examples of the courteous style used for entertaining. *(Examples may include "courteously saluted her," "do honor to the lady," "desire to honor the lady," "served it with the greatest devotion," "'in your graciousness,'" "'honor you with the best food.'")*

perhaps still is one of our fellow citizens, a man of great and **revered** authority in our days both from his manners and his virtues (far more than from nobility of blood), a most excellent person worthy of eternal fame, and in the fullness of his years delighted often to speak of past matters with his neighbors and other men. And this he could do better and more orderly and with a better memory and more ornate speech than anyone else.

Among other excellent things, he was wont[3] to say that in the past there was in Florence a young man named Federigo, the son of Messer Filippo Alberighi, renowned above all other young gentlemen of Tuscany[4] for his prowess in arms and his courtesy. Now, as most often happens to gentlemen, he fell in love with a lady named Monna Giovanna, in her time held to be one of the gayest[5] and most beautiful women ever known in Florence. To win her love, he went to jousts and tourneys, made and gave feasts, and spent his money without stint. But she, no less **chaste** than beautiful, cared nothing for the things he did for her nor for him who did them.

Now as Federigo was spending far beyond his means and getting nothing in, as easily happens, his wealth failed and he remained poor with nothing but a little farm, on whose produce he lived very **penuriously**, and one falcon which was

among the best in the world. More in love than ever, but thinking he would never be able to live in the town any more as he desired, he went to Campi where his farm was. There he spent his time hawking,[6] asked nothing of anybody, and patiently endured his poverty.

Now while Federigo was in this extremity it happened one day that Monna Giovanna's husband fell ill, and seeing death come upon him, made his will. He was a very rich man and left his estate to a son who was already growing up. And then, since he had greatly loved Monna Giovanna, he made her his heir in case his son should die without legitimate children; and so died.

Monna Giovanna was now a widow, and as is customary with our women, she went with her son to spend the year in a country house she had near Federigo's farm. Now the boy happened to strike up a friendship with Federigo, and delighted in dogs and hawks. He often saw Federigo's falcon fly, and took such great delight in it that he very much wanted to have it, but did not dare ask for it, since he saw how much Federigo prized it.

While matters were in this state, the boy fell ill. His mother was very much grieved, as he was her only child and she loved him extremely. She spent the day beside him, trying to help him, and often asked him if there was anything he wanted, begging him to say so, for if it were possible to have it, she would try to get it for him. After she had many times made this offer, the boy said:

"Mother, if you can get me Federigo's falcon, I think I should soon be better."

---

3. *Wont* (wōnt) means "accustomed."
4. *Tuscany* is an area in central Italy; its chief city is Florence.
5. *Gayest* means "liveliest, most high-spirited."

3 The Renaissance and Humanism *How does Federigo's behavior reflect Renaissance attitudes toward material things?*

Vocabulary

revered (ri vērd´) *adj.* regarded as worthy of great honor
chaste (chāst) *adj.* innocent; pure
penuriously (pi noor´ ē əs lē) *adv.* marked by severe poverty

---

6. To go *hawking* is to hunt birds with a trained hawk (falcon).

Analyze Plot *What parts of the exposition help explain who or what is responsible for the loss of Federigo's fortune?* **4**

GIOVANNI BOCCACCIO **929**

Teach

Big Idea	**3**

The Renaissance and Humanism Answer: *During the Renaissance, increasing wealth led people to place more emphasis on material things.*

Reading Strategy	**4**

Analyze Plot Answer: *"To win her love, he went to jousts and tourneys, made and gave feasts, and spent his money without stint"* and *"Federigo was spending far beyond his means"* indicate that Federigo himself is responsible for the loss of his fortune. His love for Monna causes him to spend all his money to entertain and impress her.

Learning Objectives
Identifying theme. (SE)
Analyzing plot. (SE)
Applying background knowledge. (TE)
Analyzing cultural context. (TE)

Advanced Learners/Pre-AP

DIFFERENTIATED INSTRUCTION

 SMALL GROUP **Federigo's Character** Assign several of your most advanced students to work together to analyze Federigo's character. Tell the group to track descriptions of his attitudes and behavior throughout the story. Instruct them to prepare and present a report in which they answer the following questions:

What are Federigo's strengths and weaknesses? *(Strengths: generosity, devotion, courteousness; Weaknesses: acting foolishly, squandering his fortune)* In what ways does he change during the course of the story? *(Poverty forces him to live modestly. He reforms his spending habits after marrying Monna.)*

What is the group's overall assessment of his character? *(Federigo can be viewed as both foolish and admirable, a character whose decency is rewarded despite his foolishness.)*

929

Teach

Literary Element　1

Character　Ask: What character traits does Monna display here, as she ponders what to do, and later, when she visits Federigo? *(She displays love for her child, concern for taking advantage of Federigo, and embarrassment at her dilemma. At Federigo's cottage she is polite, courteous, and candid.)*

Reading Strategy　2

Predict Ask students if they were able to predict at this point how Federigo would resolve his problem. *(Some students might guess that he will pawn his falcon to buy food. Others might reason that the only expedient solution is the one that he eventually chooses.)*

Cultural History ☆

Falconry Hawking, also called falconry, involves training hawks, falcons, or eagles to dive through the air and kill birds and other small animals that have been flushed out of undergrowth or wooded areas. In the 1500s, the sport was popular throughout Europe. The type of hawk or falcon an individual owned signified his social rank. Peregrine falcons and gyrfalcons, the two most prized species, were reserved for the nobility and royalty. Serfs hunted with goshawks.

The lady paused a little at this, and began to think what she should do. She knew that Federigo had loved her for a long time, and yet had never had one glance from her, and she said to herself:

"How can I send or go and ask for this falcon, which is, from what I hear, the best that ever flew, and moreover his support in life? How can I be so thoughtless as to take this away from a gentleman who has no other pleasure left in life?"

 Although she knew she was certain to have the bird for the asking, she remained in embarrassed thought, not knowing what to say, and did not answer her son. But at length love for her child got the upper hand and she determined that to please him in whatever way it might be, she would not send, but go herself for it and bring it back to him. So she replied:

"Be comforted, my child, and try to get better somehow. I promise you that tomorrow morning I will go for it, and bring it to you."

The child was so delighted that he became a little better that same day. And on the morrow the lady took another woman to accompany her, and as if walking for exercise went to Federigo's cottage, and ☆ asked for him. Since it was not the weather for it, he had not been hawking for some days, and was in his garden employed in certain work there. When he heard that Monna Giovanna was asking for him at the door, he was greatly astonished, and ran there happily. When she saw him coming, she got up to greet him with womanly charm, and when Federigo had courteously saluted her, she said:

"How do you do, Federigo? I have come here to make amends for the damage you have suffered through me by loving me more than was needed. And in token of this, I intend to dine today familiarly with you and my companion here."

"Madonna," replied Federigo humbly, "I do not remember ever to have suffered any damage through you, but received so much good that if I was ever worth anything it was owing to your worth and the love I bore it. Your generous visit to me is so precious to me that I could spend again all that I have spent; but you have come to a poor host."

Visual Vocabulary
Madonna is an Italian term of respect once used to address a lady. The term is also used as a name for the Virgin Mary.

So saying, he modestly took her into his house, and from there to his garden. Since there was nobody else to remain in her company, he said:

"Madonna, since there is nobody else, this good woman, the wife of this workman, will keep you company, while I go to set the table."

Now, although his poverty was extreme, he had never before realized what necessity 　2 he had fallen into by his foolish extravagance in spending his wealth. But he repented of it that morning when he could find nothing with which to do honor to the lady, for love of whom he had entertained vast numbers of men in the past. In his anguish he cursed himself and his fortune and ran up and down like a man out his senses, unable to find money or anything to pawn.[7] The hour was late and his desire to honor the lady extreme, yet he would not apply to anyone else, even to his own workman; when suddenly his eye fell upon his falcon, perched on a bar in the sitting room. Having no one to whom he could

---

7. To *pawn* something is to deposit it with someone as security for a loan.

Writing Practice

Write a Research Report Boccaccio does not describe Federigo's falcon in detail. **Ask:** What kind of falcon might Federigo have owned? *(perhaps a peregrine falcon or gyrfalcon)* What clue in the text suggests this possibility? *(The storyteller says it was among the best in the world.)*

Have students use the library or Internet to find more information about the features (physical appearance, habitat, and characteristics) of either a peregrine falcon or gyrfalcon. Tell them to use what they learn to write a brief, detailed description of the species they have researched.

appeal, he took the bird, and finding it plump, decided it would be food worthy such a lady. So, without further thought, he wrung its neck, made his little maid servant quickly pluck and prepare it, and put it on a spit to roast. He spread the table with the whitest napery,[8] of which he had some left, and returned to the lady in the garden with a cheerful face, saying that the meal he had been able to prepare for her was ready.

The lady and her companion arose and went to table, and there together with Federigo, who served it with the greatest devotion, they ate the good falcon, not knowing what it was. They left the table and spent some time in cheerful conversation, and the lady, thinking the time had now come to say what she had come for, spoke fairly[9] to Federigo as follows:

"Federigo, when you remember your former life and my chastity, which no doubt you considered harshness and cruelty, I have no doubt that you will be surprised at my **presumption** when you hear what I have come here for chiefly. But if you had children, through whom you could know the power of parental love, I am certain that you would to some extent excuse me.

"But, as you have no child, I have one, and I cannot escape the common laws of mothers. Compelled by their power, I have come to ask you—against my will, and against all good manners and duty—for a gift, which I know is something especially dear to you, and reasonably so, because I

know your straitened[10] fortune has left you no other pleasure, no other recreation, no other consolation. This gift is your falcon, which has so fascinated my child that if I do not take it to him, I am afraid his present illness will grow so much worse that I may lose him. Therefore I beg you, not by the love you bear me (which holds you to nothing), but by your own nobleness, which has shown itself so much greater in all courteous usage than is wont in other men, that you will be pleased to give it to me, so that through this gift I may be able to say that I have saved my child's life, and thus be ever under an obligation to you."

When Federigo heard the lady's request and knew that he could not serve her, because he had given her the bird to eat, he began to weep in her presence, for he could not speak a word. The lady at first thought that his grief came from having to part with his good falcon, rather than from anything else, and she was almost on the point of retraction. But she remained firm and waited for Federigo's reply after his lamentation. And he said:

"Madonna, ever since it has pleased God **5** that I should set my love upon you, I have felt that Fortune has been **contrary** to me in many things, and have grieved for it. But they are all light in comparison with what she has done to me now, and I shall never be at peace with her again when I reflect that you came to my poor house, which you never deigned to visit when it was rich, and asked me for a little gift, and Fortune has so acted that I cannot give it to you. Why this cannot be, I will briefly tell you.

---

8. *Napery* is another word for table linens–tablecloths, napkins, and so on.
9. Here, *fairly* describes a pleasant, charming way of speaking.

3 Analyze Plot *How does this part of the rising action develop the conflict and build suspense?*

Vocabulary
presumption (pri zump′shən) *n.* attitude or conduct that oversteps the bounds of propriety or courtesy

---

10. *Straitened*, here, alludes to Federigo's fortune being almost used up.

Analyze Plot *What is this part of the plot called? Why?* **4**

Vocabulary
contrary (kon′trer ē) *adj.* unfavorable

GIOVANNI BOCCACCIO **931**

Teach

Reading Strategy | **3**

Analyze Plot **Answer:** *The eating of the falcon develops the conflict and builds suspense because it is now unclear how Monna Giovanna will fulfill her son's wish to have the falcon. The reader wonders how the conflict can be resolved happily.*

Reading Strategy | **4**

Analyze Plot **Answer:** *This is the climax, because it shows the conflict at its most intense point.*

Reading Strategy | **5**

Analyze Plot **Ask:** What clue does the storyteller provide at the beginning of this selection to indicate how the conflict will be resolved? *(At the beginning, the storyteller advises her listeners "to be givers of rewards when fitting," which suggests that Federigo's good intentions might still lead to a happy resolution.)*

Learning Objectives
Analyzing plot. (SE)
Analyzing character. (TE)
Writing a research report. (TE)

Advanced Learners/Pre-AP

DIFFERENTIATED INSTRUCTION

Prepare Plot Diagrams Have students prepare plot diagrams to track and connect the story's events. Select an exceptionally good example of a plot diagram. Ask the student who created it to reproduce it on the board and to explain to the class how each plot stage is connected to the next one. Then ask the class to comment on their assessment of the plot. *(Discussion should focus on how effec-* *tively or believably each stage is connected to the next and how the stages lead to a satisfying conclusion.)*

Approaching Level

DIFFERENTIATED INSTRUCTION

Review Plot Diagrams Pair students who have successfully completed their diagrams with students who have struggled to complete theirs. Have pairs work together to identify and correct incomplete or inaccurate information.

931

Teach

Literary Element   1

Theme **Possible answer:**
People should be concerned with the welfare of others even at the expense of one's own welfare.

(ADVANCED) Ask students to cite several ways in which this theme is illustrated. *(Federigo squanders his fortune to honor Monna. Monna attempts to fulfill her child's request even though it embarrasses her to do so. Federigo sacrifices his last pleasure in life in order to honor Monna.)*

View the Art ★

Answer: *The scene is rural like the location of Federigo's farm and Monna Giovanna's country home.*

Simon Bening, a Flemish painter, was best known for his miniatures. He was described by a contemporary, Francisco de Hollanda, as "the most agreeable colorist among the Flemings and the best for trees and distances."

 To check students' understanding of the selection, see Unit 5 Teaching Resources Book, p. 103.

April, from *Da Costa Book of Hours,* 1515. Simon Bening. Illuminated manuscript. The Pierpont Morgan Library, NY

View the Art Simon Bening was best known for his miniatures. How does the scene in the painting reflect the setting of the story? ★

"When I heard that you in your graciousness desired to dine with me and I thought of your excellence and your worthiness, I thought it right and fitting to honor you with the best food I could obtain; so, remembering the falcon you ask me for and its value, I thought it a meal worthy of you, and today you had it roasted on the dish and set forth as best I could. But now I see that you wanted the bird in another form, it is such a grief to me that I cannot serve you that I think I shall never be at peace again."

And after saying this, he showed her the feathers and the feet and the beak of the bird in proof. When the lady heard and saw all this, she first blamed him for having killed such a falcon to make a meal for a woman; and then she inwardly commended his greatness of soul which no poverty could or would be able to abate. But, having lost all hope of obtaining the falcon, and thus perhaps the health of her son, she departed sadly and returned to the child. Now, either from disappointment at not having the falcon or because his sickness must inevitably have led to it, the child died not many days later, to the mother's extreme grief.

Although she spent some time in tears and bitterness, yet, since she had been left very rich and was still young, her brothers often urged her to marry again. She did not want to do so, but as they kept on pressing her, she remembered the worthiness of Federigo and his last act of generosity, in killing such a falcon to do her honor.

"I will gladly submit to marriage when you please," she said to her brothers, "but if you want me to take a husband, I will take no man but Federigo degli Alberighi."

At this her brothers laughed at her, saying:

"Why, what are you talking about, you fool? Why do you want a man who hasn't a penny in the world?"

But she replied:

"Brothers, I know it is as you say, but I would rather have a man who needs money than money which needs a man."

Seeing her determination, the brothers, who knew Federigo's good qualities, did as she wanted, and gave her with all her wealth to him, in spite of his poverty. Federigo, finding that he had such a woman, whom he loved so much, with all her wealth to boot, as his wife, was more prudent with his money in the future, and ended his days happily with her. ∾

Theme *What is the theme of this story?*   **1**

Adjective Clauses **Write on the board:** "Now Federigo had the woman <u>whom he had loved so much.</u>"

Tell students that the underlined words are an adjective clause that modifies the noun *woman.* Draw an arrow from the clause to the noun. Explain that an adjective clause is a subordinate clause that modifies a noun or pronoun. Remind students that a subordinate clause (also called a dependent clause) cannot stand alone, but must be attached to a main, or independent, clause.

Write the following sentences from the story on the board and, for each, have students underline the adjective clause and draw an arrow to the noun or pronoun it modifies:

- "The lady asked me for a gift <u>that she knew was dear to me.</u>" *(Arrow should go from adjective clause to "gift.")*

- "The choice was one <u>that I did not hesitate to make.</u>" *(Arrow should go from adjective clause to "one.")*

- "I made the only choice <u>that was fair.</u>" *(Arrow should go from adjective clause to "choice.")*

Respond and Think Critically

Respond and Interpret

1. Do you think Federigo acted wisely or foolishly? Explain.

2. (a)How and why does Federigo squander his wealth? (b)How did your response to Federigo's actions change over the course of the story?

3. (a)Why is killing his prized possession such a great sacrifice for Federigo? (b)What is ironic about his action?

Analyze and Evaluate

4. How might the outcome of the story be different if Monna had told Federigo at the beginning of her visit that she wanted the falcon?

5. From her final decision and her behavior throughout the story, what values would you say are most important to Monna?

Connect

6. **Big Idea** **The Renaissance and Humanism** To what extent do you think the outcome of the story is due to fortune, and to what extent is it due to the characters' ability to control their own destinies?

7. **Connect to the Author** How does your knowledge of Boccaccio's financial problems contribute to your understanding of Federigo's troubles?

Literary Element Theme

A work's **theme** is the central message it conveys about life. Some works have a **stated theme,** which the author expresses directly. More often there is an **implied theme,** which the author reveals gradually through the story's details. Many literary works have more than one theme. Consult the plot diagram you made on page 927 for clues to the story's theme.

1. The narrator states one theme of "Federigo's Falcon" in the second paragraph. What is this lesson?

2. Through Federigo's experiences, what theme is implied about a person's ability to control his or her own fate?

Review: Irony

As you learned on page 291, **irony** is a discrepancy between appearance and reality. At what points in "Federigo's Falcon" are the characters' actions ironic? How do these ironic actions help

further the theme of the story? Analyze Boccaccio's use of irony in a brief essay, using details from "Federigo's Falcon" to support your ideas. Before you begin, gather your thoughts in a chart like the one below.

Irony	How Irony Furthers Theme

Partner Activity When you have completed your essay, trade with a partner and read each other's work aloud. Listen carefully to hear whether your points and ideas are clear. Make sure you have adequately addressed the story's irony and how it connects to the theme. Revise your work if necessary.

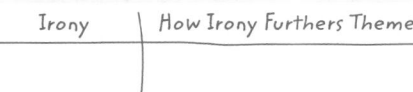

LOG ON ▶ **Literature** Online

Selection Resources For Selection Quizzes, eFlashcards, and Reading-Writing Connection activities, go to glencoe.com and enter QuickPass code GLW6053u5.

GIOVANNI BOCCACCIO **933**

Literary Element

1. The narrator states one must reward loyalty and love and not always wait for fortune to do so.

2. Federigo's experiences suggest a person of good character may overcome the vagaries of fate.

Progress Check

Can students determine theme?

If No → See Unit 5 Teaching Resources Book, p. 98.

After You Read

Assess

1. Students may feel Federigo acted both wisely and foolishly and should support their answers with examples from the story.

2. (a) He spends it on jousts, tourneys, and feasts trying to impress Monna. (b) Many students will respond they grew to like Federigo more as his generosity is revealed.

3. (a) It is the only thing of true value he has left. (b)The irony is that it is the one thing Monna wants.

4. The falcon probably would have lived, and Monna's son might also have survived.

5. Monna appears to value loyalty and generosity.

6. Possible response: The story implies that even though fate can bring unhappiness, we have the power to change our destinies for good or bad.

7. Knowing Boccaccio had financial problems creates sympathy for Federigo. It also makes his challenges seem more believable and authentic.

> For additional assessment, see Assessment Resources, pp. 185–186.

Review: Irony

Students' essays will vary. Students may see two ironies: The bird Federigo serves to impress Monna is the very bird she needs to save her son's life, while her son's death leads her to marry Federigo. Both instances of irony further the theme that, in the end, love and loyalty are rewarded.

After You Read

Assess

Reading Strategy

(D) is the correct answer. When Monna's brothers urge her to marry again, she remembers Federigo's act of selfless generosity and refuses to marry any other.

Progress Check

Can students analyze plot?

If No → See Unit 5 Teaching Resources Book, p. 99.

Vocabulary Practice

Sample responses:

1. A revered person might be respected, admired, and even worshipped by others.

2. Nuns, priests, and others who have vowed to live a holy life are chaste.

3. To live penuriously is to live with a minimum of worldly goods.

4. You might make a presumption he or she is going to harm you.

5. Answers will vary. Students should explain what they expected and how this expectation was not met.

Academic Vocabulary

Possible answer:

<u>Meaning</u>: of central or fundamental importance

<u>Context Clues</u>: most people, honesty and integrity, values

---

Reading Strategy Analyze Plot

ACT Skills Practice

Why does Monna decide to marry Federigo at the end of the story?

A. Federigo threw lavish banquets and spent all his money trying to woo her.

B. She pities Federigo because he has loved her for so long and not received so much as a glance from her.

C. She is grateful to Federigo because he saved her son's life.

D. Federigo showed tremendous generosity in killing his prized falcon to honor her.

Vocabulary Practice

Practice with Word Usage Respond to these questions and statements to help you explore the meanings of the vocabulary words from the story.

1. Describe someone who is universally **revered**.

2. What type of people live a **chaste** life?

3. What does it mean to live **penuriously**?

4. What is a **presumption** you might make about a stranger?

5. How might someone behave if he or she is being **contrary**?

Academic Vocabulary

*The story of Federigo's falcon expresses a **core** humanistic value—the belief in the power of goodwill to overcome obstacles.*

Core is an academic word with a variety of uses. For example, someone might say most people believe honesty and integrity are **core** values. Using context clues, figure out the meaning of the word *core* in the sample sentence above. Check your guess in a dictionary.

For more on academic vocabulary, see pages 36–37 and R83–R85.

Listening and Speaking

Oral Report

Assignment Early in this story, the queen says Fortune does not distribute rewards evenly. At one point, Federigo adds, "I have felt that Fortune has been contrary to me in many things, and have grieved for it." Present an oral report in which you compare medieval and Renaissance ideas about fate and human potential, and describe how these ideas are evident in the story.

Prepare Identify electronic and print resources you can use to research this topic. Before you begin your research, generate some questions. Here are some examples:

- How did ideas about fate affect people's daily lives during the Middle Ages?

- Why did the humanists create new theories about fate and human potential?

- Who was the goddess Fortuna, and what was the "Wheel of Fortune"?

The Wheel of Fortune. Chretien Legouais. Ovid Moralise. 14th century BC. Bibliotheque Municipale, Rouen, France.

As you research, take notes that address your questions. Rehearse your speech several times and check for coherence. Does your report flow well? If not, try switching the order in which you present ideas. Practice using body language and hand gestures to emphasize your main points.

Report Present your report to the class. Focus on communicating effectively through ideas, voice, and body language. Consider using visual aids like the one above.

Evaluate Write a paragraph in which you assess your oral report's effectiveness.

Listening and Speaking

Students' oral reports should:

- compare and contrast the opposing views about fate
- generate research questions and use several resources for information
- relate the information to the selection

 For grammar practice, see Unit 5 Teaching Resources Book, p. 102.

from *Don Quixote*

Spain

Meet **Miguel de Cervantes**
(1547–1616)

Soldier, slave, civil servant, satirist—Miguel de Cervantes (mē gel′ dā sər vän′ tāz) was all these things—and the most celebrated author in Spanish literature. He was born in Alcalá, near Madrid, the fourth of seven children. His family was of minor nobility, but poor, and the family moved frequently as the father traveled looking for work. However, young Cervantes became an enthusiastic reader and published his first poems at age 21.

☆ **Soldier, Slave** In 1570 Cervantes enlisted as a soldier with Spanish military forces stationed in Italy. Fighting valiantly against the Turks in the battle of Lepanto, he was wounded in the chest and permanently lost the use of his left hand. Returning by sea to Spain with letters of commendation to the king, he was captured by Barbary pirates and sold into slavery. He tried to escape several times.

Civil Servant, Novelist Eventually his high ransom was paid, and Cervantes returned to Spain. He married and found a job as purchasing agent for the navy. During this period he had a number of plays produced, but none brought him the fame and fortune he desired. At this time, he was also at work on a book-length fictional prose narrative in what was then a new literary form, the novel. Part I of *Don Quixote* was published in 1605 and was an immediate success. Since he had sold the publishing rights, however, Cervantes made no more financial profit. By the time Part II was published in 1615, the first part had seen many subsequent editions. Together the two parts of the work became the world's most frequently published novel, and Cervantes was one of the world's most esteemed authors.

> "It can be said that all prose fiction is a variation on the theme of *Don Quixote*."
>
> —Lionel Trilling

His Great Work The Spanish philosopher Miguel de Unamuno has remarked that Cervantes's novel embodies the spirit and genius of the Spanish people. *Don Quixote* is also one of the world's great parodies. The work is structured as a series of adventures that bring its hero into contact with a wide variety of human types and situations. This structure allowed Cervantes to mock old-fashioned notions of chivalry and to explore the unstable boundaries between reality and imagination, between sanity and insanity. Is Quixote mad, as the narrator claims? Or is he a simple, pure soul who attempts to make the world a better place by following his own vision of reality? Readers have been debating that question for centuries.

 Literature Online

Author Search For more about Miguel de Cervantes, go to glencoe.com and enter QuickPass code GLW6053u5.

MIGUEL DE CERVANTES **935**

Before You Read

Focus

Bellringer Options

Selection Focus
 Transparency 58

Daily Language Practice
 Transparency 87

Or ask: Have you ever dreamed about pursuing a daring adventure? What was it and what motivated your choice? Students might mention space exploration, military combat, travel to exotic places, among others.

Literary History ☆

The Captive's Tale During the battle of Lepanto, Cervantes suffered two gunshots to his chest and one to his left hand. He lost the use of his left hand permanently. Scattered accounts indicate that he acted courageously both in battle and during his captivity. His experiences in this military campaign and later as a prisoner are recounted in the captive's tale, which takes up several chapters in *Don Quixote*.

Selection Skills

from **Don Quixote**

Literary Elements
- Parody (SE pp. 936, 941, 942, 944, 946)
- Plot (SE p. 946; TE pp. 938, 943)
- Irony (TE p. 944)

Reading Skills
- Make Inferences About Theme (SE pp. 936, 938, 943, 946)
- Analyze Tone (TE p. 936)
- Predict (TE p. 940)

Vocabulary Skills
- Word Parts (SE pp. 936; 946)
- Academic Vocabulary (SE p. 946)
- Idioms (TE p. 940)

Speaking/Listening/Viewing Skills
- Analyze Art (SE p. 940)
- Narrative Presentation (TE p. 938)

Writing Skills/Grammar
- Reflective Essay (SE p. 947)
- Concrete and Abstract Nouns (TE p. 942)

Before You Read

Focus

Summary

A middle-aged man of La Mancha, steeped in the lore of knight-errantry, transforms himself into Don Quixote de la Mancha. His first challenge is to destroy a brood of wicked giants. The giants are really windmills, however, and they nearly destroy Quixote. Believing the giants have been turned into windmills by an evil force, Don Quixote remounts and sets off for more adventures.

 For summaries in languages other than English, see Unit 5 Teaching Resources Book, pp. 105–110.

Vocabulary

Identify Word Parts Read the vocabulary words aloud. Ask students to supply definitions without consulting their texts. Then focus attention on one of the words, identifying and defining its parts (root, prefix, and/or suffix). Ask students to supply other words that contain some of the same word parts and to explain how the definitions of those parts help explain the meaning of the words.

Literature and Reading Preview

Connect to the Story

Have you ever seen a friend do something you knew was fool-hardy? To what extent did you feel responsible for your friend's behavior? Write a journal entry that describes what you thought and did.

Build Background

Chivalry is based on a code of honor whereby a knight swears an oath that binds him to God and king, to his love, and to a life of serving victims of oppression. By Cervantes's time, this tradition lived on only in literature. Cervantes's original intent was to mock the absurdities of the romances of his day, but his narrative broadened to include the serious themes and complex character development of the modern novel.

Set Purposes for Reading

Big Idea The Renaissance and Humanism

As you read, ask yourself, How does Don Quixote's idealism, in his quest to right the wrongs of the world, drive the story?

Literary Element Parody

A **parody** is a humorous imitation of a particular writing style. As you read, ask yourself, What characteristics of the medieval romance does Cervantes parody in the story?

Reading Strategy Make Inferences About Theme

A **theme** is a central message of a literary work. Some works have a stated theme. More often, a work has an implied theme that is revealed gradually through events, dialogue, or descriptions. In such cases, a reader must **infer**, or make a reasonable guess about, the meaning of the work based on the author's words. As you read, ask yourself, What can I infer about Cervantes's themes?

Tip: Watch for Clues To make inferences, you must often interpret clues. Take notes and organize them in a chart like this.

Reference:	Don Quixote thinks:	I think:
"The reason for the unreason . . ."	The words are "more valuable than pearls."	It sounds very romantic, but it's meaningless.

Vocabulary

abstinence (ab´stə nəns) *n.* the act of doing without food, drink, or other pleasures; p. 937 *Paul declared that total abstinence from chocolate was the only way he was going to lose weight.*

decipher (di sī´fər) *v.* to translate; figure out; p. 938 *Dad squinted at the postcard, trying to decipher his cousin's scrawled message.*

renown (ri noun´) *n.* a state of being widely acclaimed; p. 939 *She was one of those stars who seem to achieve renown without actually doing anything to earn it.*

discourteous (dis kur´tē əs) *adj.* impolite; p. 942 *Veronica frowned at her little brother for being so discourteous when he refused to share the playground swing.*

enmity (en´mə tē) *n.* hatred or ill will; p. 944 *Although she was filled with enmity toward the man who had crashed into her car, Sarah spoke to him politely.*

Reading Practice

Analyze Tone Don Quixote's naïve idealism is exposed by the ironic tone of sarcasm—the use of bitter or caustic language to point out shortcomings or flaws—that the narrator uses to mock Quixote's futile endeavors. Remind students that irony is a contrast or discrepancy between what is expected and what actually happens. Ask students to reread the selection, noting examples of this sarcastic tone. *(The narrator mentions Quixote's love of "clarity"* in writing, citing nonsensical examples; notes that he "undid in a moment what it had taken him a week to create"; calls his horse "the foremost nag in all the world"; and so on.)*

Then have students write a short essay analyzing the effect this tone has on the reader. Does it make the reader judge Don Quixote more harshly? Does the reader feel sympathy for Don Quixote?

Is the reader amused? Make sure the students cite examples from the text to support their opinion.

from Don Quixote

Miguel de Cervantes
Translated by
Edith Grossman

Don Quichote, im Lehnstuhl lesend (Don Quixote Reading in his Easy Chair), 1834. Adolf Schroedter (German, 1805-1875) Oil on canvas, 54.5 x 46 cm. National Gallery, Berlin.

CHAPTER I
Which describes the condition and profession of the famous gentleman Don Quixote of La Mancha

1 Somewhere in La Mancha,[1] in a place whose name I do not care to remember, a gentleman lived not long ago, one of those who has a lance and ancient shield on a shelf and keeps a skinny nag and a greyhound for racing. An occasional stew, beef more often than lamb, hash most nights, eggs and **abstinence** on Saturdays, lentils on Fridays, sometimes squab[2] as a treat on Sundays—these consumed three-fourths of his income. The rest went for a light woolen tunic and velvet breeches and hose of the same material for feast days, while weekdays were honored with dun-

---

1. *La Mancha* is a region in south-central Spain.

2. A *squab* is a young pigeon.

> **Vocabulary**
>
> **abstinence** (ab′stə nəns) *n.* the act of doing without food, drink, or other pleasures

MIGUEL DE CERVANTES **937**

English Learners

DIFFERENTIATED INSTRUCTION

Beginning The first paragraph of this story includes a variety of details that relate to Spanish culture. Invite students of Spanish ancestry to offer their own observations on details with which they are familiar—for example, traditional foods, clothing, or pastimes. In what ways does their Spanish ancestry influence their family life? Are they familiar with any contemporary cultural references to Cervantes and *Don Quixote?* Encourage students to volunteer information pertaining to Spanish culture and *Don Quixote*.

Teach

Literary Element **1**

Tone **Ask:** What does the phrase "in a place whose name I do not care to remember" suggest about the narrator's attitude toward his subject? *(It suggests casual indifference or condescension.)* **Then ask:** What other words or phrases in the first sentence reinforce this tone? *("one of those" and "skinny nag")*

View the Art ★

Adolph Schroedter, who specialized in historical and literary subjects, found his greatest inspiration in *Don Quixote*. His painting adheres closely to Cervantes's text, portraying the Don as "scrawny" and "gaunt." The facial features and expression suggest the monomania that led to lack of sleep and the loss of his wits.

 For an audio recording of this selection, use Listening Library Audio CD-ROM.

 Interactive Read and Write
Other options for teaching this selection can be found in Interactive Read and Write for On-Level Learners, pp. 233–242.

Readability Scores

Dale-Chall: 7.5
DRP: 63
Lexile: 1250

Learning Objectives
Identifying word parts. (TE)
Analyzing tone. (TE)

Teach

Reading Strategy ‖ 1

Make Inferences About Theme Answer: *The tone is sarcastic; the story is, after all, fiction, and it contains outlandish descriptions of farcical actions.*

[ADVANCED] **Ask:** What literary device does the narrator employ in this statement? *(The narrator is using irony to make a point. He means exactly the opposite of what he says.)*

Literary Element ‖ 2

Plot Ask: What stage of the plot is signaled in this paragraph? *(This paragraph marks the beginning of the rising action. Up to this point, the story has focused on exposition—a description of Quixote's personality and situation. Now, having lost his mind, Quixote makes a decision to take action.)*

 For additional literary element practice, see Unit 5 Teaching Resources Book, p. 111.

colored coarse cloth. He had a housekeeper past forty, a niece not yet twenty, and a man-of-all-work who did everything from saddling the horse to pruning the trees. Our gentleman was approximately fifty years old; his complexion was weathered, his flesh scrawny, his face gaunt, and he was a very early riser and a great lover of the hunt. Some claim that his family name was Quixada, or Quexada, for there is a certain amount of disagreement among the authors who write of this matter, although reliable conjecture seems to indicate that his name was Quexana. But this does not matter very much to our story; in its telling there is absolutely no deviation from the truth.

And so, let it be said that this aforementioned gentleman spent his times of leisure—which meant most of the year—reading books of chivalry with so much devotion and enthusiasm that he forgot almost completely about the hunt and even about the administration of his estate; and in his rash curiosity and folly he went so far as to sell acres of arable land in order to buy books of chivalry to read, and he brought as many of them as he could into his house; and he thought none was as fine as those composed by the worthy Feliciano de Silva,[3] because the clarity of his prose and complexity of his language seemed to him more valuable than pearls, in particular when he read the declarations and missives of love, where he would often find written: *The reason for the unreason to which my reason turns so weakens my reason that with reason I complain of thy beauty.* And also when he

read: . . . *the heavens on high divinely heighten thy divinity with the stars and make thee deserving of the deserts thy greatness deserves.*

With these words and phrases the poor gentleman lost his mind, and he spent sleepless nights trying to understand them and extract their meaning, which Aristotle[4] himself, if he came back to life for only that purpose, would not have been able to **decipher** or understand. Our gentleman was not very happy with the wounds that Don Belianís gave and received, because he imagined that no matter how great the physicians and surgeons who cured him, he would still have his face and entire body covered with scars and marks. But, even so, he praised the author for having concluded his book with the promise of unending adventure, and he often felt the desire to take up his pen and give it the conclusion promised there; and no doubt he would have done so, and even published it, if other greater and more persistent thoughts had not prevented him from doing so. He often had discussions with the village priest—who was a learned man, a graduate of Sigüenza—regarding who had been the greater knight, Palmerín of England or Amadís of Gaul; but Master Nicolás, the village barber, said that none was the equal of the Knight of Phoebus, and if any could be compared to him, it was Don Galaor, the brother of Amadís of Gaul, because he was moderate in everything: a knight who was not affected, not as weepy as his brother, and incomparable in questions of courage.

In short, our gentleman became so

---

3. *Feliciano de Silva* was the author of several novels of chivalry. The names of the authors and heroes that follow in this paragraph are all typical of the romantic literature of the period.

4. The Greek philosopher *Aristotle* (384–322 B.C.) was considered to possess one of the greatest minds of the ancient world.

 Make Inferences About Theme *What kind of tone does the narrator use here?*

Vocabulary

decipher (di sī′fər) *v.* to translate; figure out

Listening and Speaking Practice

Deliver a Narrative Presentation
Direct attention to the passage at the end of page 939, beginning "And the first thing he did" and ending "and accepted it as an extremely fine sallet," which describes Quixote's attempt to fashion a helmet for himself. Have a proficient reader present the passage orally, and ask students to picture in their minds the humor of the scene. After the presentation, discuss students' impressions, focusing on the

physical details that add to the humor. As an alternative to class discussion, have students write a paragraph describing the picture that the description evokes.

caught up in reading that he spent his nights reading from dusk till dawn and his days reading from sunrise to sunset, and so with too little sleep and too much reading his brains dried up, causing him to lose his mind. His fantasy filled with everything he had read in his books, enchantments as well as combats, battles, challenges, wounds, courtings, loves, torments, and other impossible foolishness, and he became so convinced in his imagination of the truth of all the countless grandiloquent[5] and false inventions he read that for him no history in the world was truer. He would say that El Cid Ruy Díaz had been a very good knight but could not compare to Amadís, the Knight of the Blazing Sword, who with a single backstroke cut two ferocious and colossal giants in half. He was fonder of Bernardo del Carpio because at Roncesvalles he had killed the enchanted Roland by availing himself of the tactic of Hercules when he crushed Antaeus, the son of Earth, in his arms.[6] He spoke highly of the giant Morgante because, although he belonged to the race of giants, all of them haughty and lacking in courtesy, he alone was amiable and well-behaved. But, more than any of the others, he admired Reinaldos de Montalbán, above all when he saw him emerge from his castle and rob anyone he met, and when he crossed the sea and stole the idol of Mohammed made all of gold, as recounted in his history. He would have traded his housekeeper, and even his niece, for the chance to strike a blow at the traitor Guenelon.

5. *Grandiloquent* language is high-flown and overwrought.
6. *tactic of Hercules . . . in his arms.* The Roman hero Hercules defeated the giant Anteus, who derived his strength from his contact with the earth, by holding him up in the air.

The truth is that when his mind was completely gone, he had the strangest thought any lunatic in the world ever had, which was that it seemed reasonable and necessary to him, both for the sake of his honor and as a service to the nation, to become a knight errant[7] and travel the world with his armor and his horse to seek adventures and engage in everything he had read that knights errant engaged in, righting all manner of wrongs and, by seizing the opportunity and placing himself in danger and ending those wrongs, winning eternal **renown** and everlasting fame. The poor man imagined himself already wearing the crown, won by the valor of his arm, of the empire of Trebizond at the very least; and so it was that with these exceedingly agreeable thoughts, and carried away by the extraordinary pleasure he took in them, he hastened to put into effect what he so fervently desired. And the first thing he did was to attempt to clean some armor that had belonged to his great-grandfathers and, stained with rust and covered with mildew, had spent many long years stored and forgotten in a corner. He did the best he could to clean and repair it, but he saw that it had a great defect, which was that instead of a full sallet[8] helmet with an attached neckguard, there was only a simple headpiece; but he compensated for this with his industry, and out of pasteboard he fashioned a kind of half-helmet that, when attached

7. A *knight errant* traveled about in search of adventure.
8. A *sallet* was a type of light helmet with or without a visor and a piece over the neck.

The Renaissance and Humanism *How does Don Quixote plan to contribute to humankind?*

Vocabulary

renown (ri noun′) *n.* a state of being widely acclaimed

Big Idea

The Renaissance and Humanism Answer: *He is setting forth to right "all manner of wrongs."*

Language History ☆

Knights and Chivalry Point out that the word *knight* comes from Old English *cniht*, which was the word the English used to describe French mounted soldiers at the time of the Norman conquest. Similarly, the word *chivalry* (from Old French *chevalerie*) originally meant "mounted men at arms" during the Middle Ages. Over time, *knight* came to refer to the special class of warrior dedicated to championing virtuous causes for his king, his country, and his lady, and *chivalry* came to refer to the gallant behavior and deeds characteristic of a knight.

Approaching Level
DIFFERENTIATED INSTRUCTION

Make a Sketch Students who struggle to express themselves verbally might enjoy visually conveying their reaction to Quixote's attempt to dress like a knight. Suggest that they draw a picture of how they visualize one part of this episode. Discuss physical details that they might include (rusty armor, pasteboard, sword, hacked up pieces, strips of iron, and so on). Display the completed drawings.

Advanced Learners/Pre-AP
DIFFERENTIATED INSTRUCTION

Draw an Abstract Representation Gifted or advanced students might enjoy creating an abstract or surreal drawing, using geometric shapes and exaggerated or distorted elements to convey the humor of this episode. Have students present their drawings to the class, explaining the logic behind their interpretations.

Learning Objectives
Making inferences about theme. (SE)
Analyzing plot. (TE)
Delivering a narrative presentation. (TE)
Predicting. (TE)

Teach

Reading Strategy | 1

Predict **Say:** Compare what Quixote believes about himself and his horse with the reality of the situation. **Ask:** Based on the evidence, how successful do you think he will be at "righting all manner of wrongs" in the world? *(Quixote is convinced that he is a famous knight who owns an excellent steed. The reality of the situation—a witless man and a scrawny nag—suggests that he will fail miserably.)*

View the Art ★

Answer: *This Sancho Panza does not look like he aspires to anything but laziness, eating, and drinking.*

Sir John Gilbert, a book and newspaper illustrator, was also a historical-genre painter in the Victorian tradition. The portrait of Sancho Panza on this page emphasizes the squire's role as a foil, or contrast, to Don Quixote. The Don is thin, abstemious, and addicted to romantic dreaming; the Sancho Panza depicted in this painting is corpulent, red-nosed, very fond of food and drink, and (literally and figuratively) down to earth.

to the headpiece, took on the appearance of a full sallet. It is true that in order to test if it was strong and could withstand a blow, he took out his sword and struck it twice, and with the first blow he undid in a moment what it had taken him a week to create; he could not help being disappointed at the ease with which he had hacked it to pieces, and to protect against that danger, he made another one, placing strips of iron on the inside so that he was satisfied with its strength; and not wanting to put it to the test again, he designated and accepted it as an extremely fine sallet.

Then he went to look at his nag, and though its hooves had more cracks than his master's pate and it showed more flaws than Gonnella's horse, that *tantum pellis et ossa fuit*,[9] it seemed to him that Alexander's Bucephalus and El Cid's Babieca[10] were not its equal. He spent four days thinking about the name he would give it; for—as he told himself—it was not seemly that the horse of so famous a knight, and a steed so intrinsically excellent, should not have a worthy name; he was looking for the precise name that would declare what the horse had been before its master became a knight errant and what it was now; for he was determined that if the master was changing his condition, the horse too would change its name to one that would win the fame and recognition its new position and profession deserved; and so, after many names that he shaped and discarded, subtracted from and added to, unmade and remade in his memory and imagination, he finally decided to call the horse *Rocinante*, a name, in his opinion, that was noble, sonorous, and reflective of what it had been when it was a

---

9. The Latin phrase *tantum pellis et ossa fuit* means "was nothing but skin and bones."
10. *Bucephalus* was the favorite horse of Alexander the Great (356–323 B.C.). *Babieca* was the horse of El Cid (Rodrigo Diaz de Vivar, 1040–1099), Spain's national hero.

nag, before it was what it was now, which was the foremost nag in all the world.

Having given a name, and one so much to his liking, to his horse, he wanted to give one to himself, and he spent another eight days pondering this, and at last he called himself *Don Quixote*, which is why, as has been noted, the authors of this absolutely true history determined that he undoubtedly must have been named Quixada and not Quexada, as others have claimed. In any event, recalling that the valiant Amadís had not been content with simply calling himself Amadís but had added the name of his kingdom and realm in order to bring it fame, and was known as Amadís of Gaul, he too, like a good knight, wanted to add the name of his birthplace

Sancho Panza, 1859. Sir John Gilbert. Oil on canvas, 77 x 64 cm. Harris Museum and Art Gallery, Preston, Lancashire, UK.

View the Art Sir John Gilbert, a prolific artist and illustrator in England during the nineteenth century, illustrated many classic works, including *Don Quixote*. Does Sancho Panza look like "a young man of noble birth aspiring to knighthood"? Why or why not? ★

Vocabulary Practice

Understand Idioms Ask students the meaning of the expression "to tilt at windmills" *(to combat imaginary foes or dangers).* Explain that this expression became popular after the publication of *Don Quixote*. Knowing the connection between the idiom and its source is helpful in appreciating the aptness of the idiom's meaning. Ask students to identify or guess the meaning of these idioms and

their origins: Achilles' heel *(a vulnerable spot: Achilles, in Homer's Iliad, was mortally vulnerable only in his heel)* and take a rain check *(request that an invitation be extended again at a later date: from the practice of issuing a special ticket to a fan at a baseball game postponed by rained—the special ticket allowed the fan to attend a later game for free).* What other idioms can students suggest?

(throw a curve ball, jump the gun, in mint condition, break a leg, get one's act together, and so on).

940

to his own, and he called himself *Don Quixote of La Mancha*, thereby, to his mind, clearly stating his lineage and country and honoring it by making it part of his title.

Having cleaned his armor and made a full helmet out of a simple headpiece, and having given a name to his horse and decided on one for himself, he realized that the only thing left for him to do was to find a lady to love; for the knight errant without a lady-love was a tree without leaves or fruit, a body without a soul. He said to himself:

"If I, because of my evil sins, or my good fortune, meet with a giant somewhere, as ordinarily befalls knights errant, and I unseat him with a single blow, or cut his body in half, or, in short, conquer and defeat him, would it not be good to have someone to whom I could send him so that he might enter and fall to his knees before my sweet lady, and say in the humble voice of surrender: 'I, lady, am the giant Caraculiambro, lord of the island Malindrania, defeated in single combat by the never sufficiently praised knight Don Quixote of La Mancha, who commanded me to appear before your ladyship, so that your highness might dispose of me as you chose'?"

Oh, how pleased our good knight was when he had made this speech, and even more pleased when he discovered the one he could call his lady! It is believed that in a nearby village there was a very attractive peasant girl with whom he had once been in love, although she, apparently, never knew or noticed. Her name was Aldonza Lorenzo, and he thought it a good idea to call her the lady of his thoughts, and, searching for a name that would not differ significantly from his and would suggest and imply that of a princess and great lady, he decided to call her *Dulcinea of Toboso*, because she came from Toboso, a name, to his mind, that was musical and beautiful and filled with significance, as were all the others he had given to

himself and everything pertaining to him.

In spite of the arguments of his family and friends, Don Quixote is determined to live out his dream. A squire—a young man of noble birth aspiring to knighthood—accompanied most knights errant in books. Don Quixote's squire is slightly different.

CHAPTER VII
Regarding the second sally of our good knight Don Quixote of La Mancha

---

During this time, Don Quixote approached a farmer who was a neighbor of his, a good man—if that title can be given to someone who is poor—but without much in the way of brains. In short, he told him so much, and persuaded and promised him so much, that the poor peasant resolved to go off with him and serve as his squire. Among other things, Don Quixote said that he should prepare to go with him gladly, because it might happen that one day he would have an adventure that would gain him, in the blink of an eye, an ínsula,[11] and he would make him its governor. With these promises and others like them, Sancho Panza, for that was the farmer's name, left his wife and children and agreed to be his neighbor's squire.

Then Don Quixote determined to find some money, and by selling one thing, and pawning another, and undervaluing everything, he managed to put together a reasonable sum. He also acquired a round shield, which he borrowed from a friend, and doing the best he could to repair his broken helmet, he informed his squire of the day and time he planned to start out so

---

11. An *ínsula* is a Latinate—therefore, high-flown—term for "island."

Parody *How does Sancho Panza compare to his master?*

MIGUEL DE CERVANTES **941**

Teach

Literary Element   1

Parody Answer: *Sancho Panza and Don Quixote are both dreamers willing to leave their homes and families in pursuit of greatness. Quixote dreams of doing great deeds. Sancho Panza, who is poor and more practical-minded, dreams of personal gain.*

Learning Objectives
Analyzing parody. (SE)
Analyzing art. (SE)
Understanding idioms. (TE)

Advanced Learners/Pre-AP

DIFFERENTIATED INSTRUCTION

Chivalry Students who are especially interested in medieval chivalry might enjoy researching this topic further. Suggest that they narrow their focus to a specific aspect of the subject: the history of chivalry; characteristics, dress, training, or duties of a knight; jousting tournaments; or a specific literary work about the adventures of a knight (for example, *The Song of Roland*, Marie de France's *Lanval*, or one of the retellings of the Arthurian legend). Ask students to prepare a brief written or oral report of what they learn to present to the class. If time permits, consider assigning a range of specific topics to individual students and devote a class period to exploring the subject in depth.

Teach

Parody **Answer:** *Sancho Panza sees the windmills for what they are; Don Quixote sees them as giant monsters. One would expect the knight to be more experienced, level-headed, and realistic than his squire.*

that Sancho could supply himself with whatever he thought he would need. He ordered him in particular to bring along saddlebags, and Sancho said he certainly would bring them and also planned to take along a donkey he thought very highly of because he wasn't one for walking any great distance. As for the donkey, Don Quixote had to stop and think about that for a while, wondering if he recalled any knight errant who had with him a squire riding on a donkey, and none came to mind, yet in spite of this he resolved to take Sancho along, intending to obtain a more honorable mount for him at the earliest opportunity by appropriating the horse of the first **discourteous** knight he happened to meet. He furnished himself with shirts and all the other things he could, following the advice the innkeeper had given him; and when this had been accomplished and completed, without Panza taking leave of his children and wife, or Don Quixote of his housekeeper and niece, they rode out of the village one night, and no one saw them, and they traveled so far that by dawn they were certain they would not be found even if anyone came looking for them.

Sancho Panza rode on his donkey like a patriarch,[12] with his saddlebags, and his wineskin, and a great desire to see himself governor of the ínsula his master had promised him. Don Quixote happened to follow the same direction and route he had followed on his first sally, which was through the countryside of Montiel, and he rode there with less difficulty than he had the last time, because at that hour of the morning the sun's rays fell obliquely and did not tire them.

> ### CHAPTER VIII
> *Regarding the good fortune of the valorous Don Quixote in the fearful and never imagined adventure of the windmills, along with other events worthy of joyful remembrance*

As they were talking, they saw thirty or forty of the windmills found in that countryside, and as soon as Don Quixote caught sight of them, he said to his squire:

"Good fortune is guiding our affairs better than we could have desired, for there you see, friend Sancho Panza, thirty or more enormous giants with whom I intend to do battle and whose lives I intend to take, and with the spoils we shall begin to grow rich, for this is righteous warfare, and it is a great service to God to remove so evil a breed from the face of the earth."

"What giants?" said Sancho Panza.

"Those you see over there," replied his master, "with the long arms; sometimes they are almost two leagues[13] long."

"Look, your grace," Sancho responded, "those things that appear over there aren't giants but windmills, and what looks like their arms are the sails that are turned by the wind and make the grindstone move."

"It seems clear to me," replied Don Quixote, "that thou art not well-versed in the matter of adventures: these are giants; and if thou art afraid, move aside and start to pray whilst I enter with them in fierce and unequal combat."

And having said this, he spurred his horse, Rocinante, paying no attention to

---

12. A *patriarch* is the oldest and most respected member of a family.

Vocabulary

discourteous (dis kur′tē əs) *adj.* impolite

---

13. A *league* is a measure of distance of about three miles.

Parody *How does Sancho Panza's advice parody the traditional relationship between a knight and his squire?* **1**

Grammar Skills

Concrete and Abstract Nouns

Remind students that a concrete noun names an object recognized by the senses and that an abstract noun names an idea, quality, or characteristic. Direct attention to the dialogue on page 942 that begins "Good fortune is guiding our affairs." Read the paragraph and identify the concrete and abstract nouns in it. *(Concrete: friend, Sancho Panza, giants, battle, spoils, face, earth; Abstract: for-*

tune, affairs, lives, warfare, service, breed)

Select another passage from the story and ask students to copy it, double-spaced, on a sheet of paper. Have them label each noun as abstract *(a)* or concrete *(c)*. Review students' answers in class, calling on volunteers to identify each noun.

Don Quixote and the Windmill. Francisco J. Torromé (Spainish fl.1890-1908) Bonhams, London. ★

the shouts of his squire, Sancho, who warned him that, beyond any doubt, those things he was about to attack were windmills and not giants. But he was so convinced they were giants that he did not hear the shouts of his squire, Sancho, and could not see, though he was very close, what they really were; instead, he charged and called out:

"Flee not, cowards and base creatures, for it is a single knight who attacks you."

Just then a gust of wind began to blow, and the great sails began to move, and, seeing this, Don Quixote said:

"Even if you move more arms than the giant Briareus, you will answer to me."

And saying this, and commending himself with all his heart to his lady Dulcinea, asking that she come to his aid at this critical moment, and well-protected by his shield, with his lance in its socket, he
2 charged at Rocinante's full gallop and attacked the first mill he came to; and as he thrust his lance into the sail, the wind

moved it with so much force that it broke the lance into pieces and picked up the horse and the knight, who then dropped to the ground and were very badly battered. Sancho Panza hurried to help as fast as his donkey could carry him, and when he reached them he discovered that Don Quixote could not move because he had taken so hard a fall with Rocinante.

"God save me!" said Sancho. "Didn't I tell your grace to watch what you were doing, that these were nothing but windmills, and only somebody whose head was full of them wouldn't know that?"

"Be quiet, Sancho my friend," replied Don Quixote. "Matters of war, more than any others, are subject to continual change; moreover, I think, and therefore it is true, that the same Frestón the Wise who stole my room and my books has turned these giants into windmills in order to deprive

---

Make Inferences About Theme *How does this statement contribute to your understanding of the story's theme?* **3**

MIGUEL DE CERVANTES **943**

Teach

Literary Element 2

Plot **Say:** Explain how Don Quixote's attack on the windmills represents both an external conflict and an internal conflict. *(The conflict is external in the sense that Quixote believes he is fighting against an outside force [giants]; it is internal in the sense that these giants exist only in his mind. Internally, he has created the foe he is fighting.)*

Reading Strategy 3

Make Inferences About Theme **Possible Answer:** *Don Quixote's monomania will likely lead him to continue to misinterpret reality and to try to fix nonexistent problems.*

View the Art ★

Torromé, a Spanish contemporary of Picasso, has captured the moment that the Don and his horse are knocked to the ground by one of the windmills. Splinters of his lance fly through the air, and Rocinante convulses in terror. Sancho Panza holds his hands to his head in dismay at his master's suffering from a head full of windmills.

Approaching Level

DIFFERENTIATED INSTRUCTION

Make Predictions After students have completed the selection, remind them that what they have read is only a small part of a much longer work. Point out the clues on page 944 that indicate there will be more adventures: "he could not fail to find many diverse adventures," "I shall do such great deeds that you will consider yourself fortunate for deserving to see them," and "he did not consider it work but sheer pleasure to go around seeking adventures."

Have students reread this page and then tell partners what they think will happen next to Don Quixote and Sancho Panza and why they think so. *(The two will probably have more ridiculous adventures. Sancho Panza will probably have to rescue Don Quixote again. Clues indicate that even though Don Quixote has lost his lance, he will fight with a tree limb.)*

Learning Objectives
Understanding parody. (SE)
Making inferences about theme. (SE)
Analyzing plot. (TE)
Analyzing mood. (TE)
Identifying concrete and abstract nouns. (TE)

Teach

Big Idea | **1**

The Renaissance and Humanism Answer: *They are enjoying the freedom of travel. They hope to find more adventures and to right the wrongs of the world.*

Literary Element | **2**

Parody Answer: *Sancho Panza complains about every small feeling and Don Quixote ignores his serious injury. A traditional knight would be more stoic than Sancho Panza and more realistic than Don Quixote.*

Literary Element | **3**

Irony Ask: What is ironic about Don Quixote's laughing at his squire's simplemindedness? *(He fails to see the practicality of his squire's attitude toward pain and is blind to his own simplemindedness.)*

To check students' understanding of the selection, see Unit 5 Teaching Resources Book, p. 116.

me of the glory of defeating them: such is the **enmity** he feels for me; but in the end, his evil arts will not prevail against the power of my virtuous sword."

"God's will be done," replied Sancho Panza.

He helped him to stand, and Don Quixote remounted Rocinante, whose back was almost broken. And, talking about their recent adventure, they continued on the road to Puerto Lápice, because there, said Don Quixote, he could not fail to find many diverse adventures since it was a very heavily trafficked place; but he rode heavy-hearted because he did not have his lance; and expressing this to his squire, he said:

"I remember reading that a Spanish knight named Diego Pérez de Vargas, whose sword broke in battle, tore a heavy bough or branch from an oak tree and with it did such great deeds that day, and thrashed so many Moors, that he was called Machuca,[14] the Bruiser, and from that day forward he and his descendants were named Vargas y Machuca. I have told you this because from the first oak that presents itself to me I intend to tear off another branch as good as the one I have in mind, and with it I shall do such great deeds that you will consider yourself fortunate for deserving to see them and for being a witness to things that can hardly be believed."

"It's in God's hands," said Sancho. "I believe everything your grace says, but sit a little straighter, it looks like you're tilting,

14. The name *Machuca* comes from the Spanish verb *machucar*, "to crush."

1 **The Renaissance and Humanism** *What freedoms are these companions enjoying? What do they hope to accomplish?*

Vocabulary

enmity (en′ mə tē) *n.* hatred or ill will

it must be from the battering you took when you fell."

"That is true," replied Don Quixote, "and if I do not complain about the pain, it is because it is not the custom of knights errant to complain about any wound, even if their innards are spilling out because of it."

"If that's true, I have nothing to say," Sancho responded, "but God knows I'd be happy if your grace complained when something hurt you. As for me, I can say that I'll complain about the smallest pain I have, unless what you said about not complaining also applies to the squires of knights errant."

Don Quixote could not help laughing at **3** his squire's simplemindedness; and so he declared that he could certainly complain however and whenever he wanted, with or without cause, for as yet he had not read anything to the contrary in the order of chivalry. Sancho said that it was time to eat. His master replied that he felt no need of food at the moment, but that Sancho could eat whenever he wished. With this permission, Sancho made himself as comfortable as he could on his donkey, and after taking out of the saddlebags what he had put into them, he rode behind his master at a leisurely pace, eating and, from time to time, tilting back the wineskin with so much gusto that the most self-indulgent tavernkeeper in Málaga might have envied him. And as he rode along in that manner, taking frequent drinks, he did not think about any promises his master had made to him, and he did not consider it work but sheer pleasure to go around seeking adventures, no matter how dangerous they might be. ∾

Parody *How do Sancho Panza's and Don Quixote's attitude toward pain compare with a traditional knight's bravery and stamina?* **2**

Writing Practice

Write an Episode What do students think will happen next to Don Quixote and Sancho Panza? What adventures will they have? What dangers will they face? Ask students to try their hand at creating a new episode about Don Quixote and his squire. Encourage them to be creative, and suggest that they need not concern themselves with matters of historical accuracy or period detail. They might choose to depict Don Quixote encountering foreign invaders, aliens from outer space, pirates, or other outlandish imaginary foes.

Regardless of the situation and conflict they choose, students' stories should reflect the humorous spirit and satirical point of view of the selection they have read. Select several well-written stories to share with the class.

After You Read

Respond and Think Critically

Respond and Interpret

1. (a)How did you react to the character of Don Quixote? (b)List three adjectives you would use to describe his personality.

2. (a)Why does Don Quixote lose his wits? (b)Why does he decide to become a knight errant?

3. (a)How does Don Quixote persuade Sancho Panza to become his squire? (b)How would you describe Sancho Panza's philosophy of life?

4. (a)Summarize the windmill episode. (b)What two ways of looking at the world might Don Quixote and Sancho represent?

Analyze and Evaluate

5. (a)A **symbol** stands for something else in addition to itself. What might the windmills symbolize? (b)What might the code of chivalry, as portrayed in the novel, symbolize?

6. (a)What is the tone of *Don Quixote*? (b)Do you think the narrator likes Don Quixote and Sancho Panza? Explain.

7. Through Don Quixote, what might Cervantes be suggesting about people who "live in the past"?

Connect

8. **Big Idea** **The Renaissance and Humanism** How does Don Quixote represent an emphasis on human values and relationships to the world?

9. **Connect to Today** Do you think a serious code of chivalry could be drawn up for modern life? What ideals would you include in your code?

You're the Critic: Point/Counterpoint

Is *Don Quixote* Only a Parody?

Does *Don Quixote* present a parody of knights and chivalry, or are there other interpretations of the novel? Each of the following quotations offers a different view.

"If Don Quixote had been nothing but a satire and knock-about burlesque of the fading romances of chivalry, it would have been dying by 1650, dead by 1700, and forgotten by the time it actually set so many good eighteenth-century novelists writing."

—J. B. Priestly, from *Literature and Western Man*

"Don Quixote, in basic conception, is a parody of Spanish romances of chivalry. It concerns an hidalgo, a member of the minor gentry, from a village somewhere in La Mancha. His lifestyle, described on the memorable opening page, conforms to that of familiar type, associated with threadbare frugality, hunting, the relics of honorable ancestry, parochial seclusion. In short, a very prosaic backdrop for the delusions of grandeur about to fill the stage."

—A. J. Close, from *Don Quixote*

Group Activity Discuss the following questions with your classmates.

1. How would you respond to Close's viewpoint?

2. Why do you think Priestly has a problem with critics who label the novel as only a satire?

You're the Critic

 For additional selection assessment, see Assessment Resources, pp. 187–188.

1. Some students will agree the novel is a parody of chivalry based on its setting and plot.

2. He argues that accepting Cervantes' claim that the novel is simply a satire limits a reader's experience. Books that stand the test of time have multiple interpretations.

After You Read

Assess

1. (a) Answers will vary. (b) Possible responses: foolish, impractical, romantic, unrealistic, idealistic, brave, foolhardy

2. (a) He deprives himself of sleep by staying up all night to read tales of knight-errantry. (b) He wants to increase his renown and serve society by redressing wrongs.

3. (a) He promises Sancho Panza the governorship of his own island. (b) Possible answer: Sancho Panza is concerned mainly with the basics of life, such as food and comfort.

4. (a) Don Quixote thinks the windmills are giant monsters; he runs at them with his lance but is caught up in a sail and is unhorsed. (b) Don Quixote represents the idealistic and impractical view, and Sancho Panza represents the practical, unimaginative view.

5. (a) The windmills may symbolize problems that people blow out of proportion. (b) The code of chivalry might represent an unrealistic worldview or a concept of a "Golden Age" that never did exist in real life.

6. (a) The tone is humorous and somewhat ironic. (b) Students should support their answers.

7. He may be suggesting the past is not an answer to the problems of the present and that the glories of the past may never have existed.

8. Don Quixote is a common man, albeit one with lofty ideals about service to society, and he is willing to put himself in danger to help others.

9. Students should give reasons to support their ideas.

After You Read

Assess

Literary Element

1. The language in the quotations from de Silva is unlike that of Cervantes' own book, and the quotations themselves make no sense.

2. He appears to be satirizing the whole concept of knight-errantry and those who hold chivalry as an ideal.

Review: Plot

Characters: Don Quixote, Sancho Panza

Setting: Southwest Spain in the early 1600s

Situation: Don Quixote is an impoverished gentleman who devotes himself to reading novels of chivalry at the expense of his run-down estate.

Rising Action: Don Quixote loses his wits through too much reading and decides to embark on a life of knight-errantry.

Reading Strategy

(A) is the correct answer. Cervantes is poking fun at a past that was probably always romanticized and bore little resemblance to reality.

Progress Check

Are students able to make inferences about the theme?

If No → See Unit 5 Teaching Resources Book, page 112.

Literary Element Parody

A **parody** is a humorous imitation of a literary work that aims to point out the work's shortcomings. A parody may imitate the plot, characters, or style of another work. Parody often goes hand in hand with **satire**, or writing that comments humorously on human flaws, ideas, social customs, or institutions in order to change them.

1. How can you tell Cervantes is parodying the style of Feliciano de Silva?

2. What is the target of Cervantes's satire when the narrator describes Don Quixote's lofty goals?

Review: Plot

As you learned on page 84, **plot** refers to the sequence of events in a story. Because this literary work is an excerpt of a long novel, you do not have access to the entire plot. You do, however, have a substantial amount of the **exposition**, which introduces the story's characters, setting, and situation, as well as a portion of what is called the **rising action**.

Partner Activity Work with a classmate to summarize these elements in the exposition of *Don Quixote.* You can create a chart like this one to help organize your thoughts.

> Characters:
>
> Setting:
>
> Situation:
>
> Rising Action:

Literature Online

Selection Resources For Selection Quizzes, eFlashcards, and Reading-Writing Connection activities, go to glencoe.com and enter QuickPass code GLW6053u5.

Reading Strategy Make Inferences About Theme

SAT Skills Practice

Based on his parody of chivalric romances, what can you infer about Cervantes's theme?

(A) Chivalric romances idealize a past that may never have existed.

(B) Chivalry is worth preserving.

(C) Chivalric romances are a realistic portrayal of life.

(D) Chivalry needs to be updated if it is to survive in the future.

(E) Chivalry is an important means to equal rights for women.

Vocabulary Practice

Practice with Word Parts For each boldfaced vocabulary word in the left column, identify the related word with a shared word part in the right column. Write each word and underline the part they have in common. Use a printed or online dictionary to look up the meaning of the related word. Then explain how it is related to the vocabulary word.

1. abstinence   renew
2. decipher   abstain
3. renown   decode
4. discourteous   discredit
5. enmity   enemy

Academic Vocabulary

In Don Quixote, *Cervantes introduces a fake* **quotation** *from a writer of chivalric romances to parody the absurd literary style of these works.*

Quotation is an academic term. To further explore the meaning of this word, answer the following question: How might you use a **quotation** in a biographical sketch? in an editorial?

For more on academic vocabulary, see pages 36–37 and R83–R85.

Vocabulary

1. **abstinence**, ab̲s̲tain. One who practices abstinence abstains from various activities.

2. **decipher**, de̲c̲ode. Deciphering and decoding involve figuring out something cryptic or puzzling.

3. **renown**, re̲n̲ew. Someone who is renowned is beyond famous; when one renews something it is continued.

4. **discourteous**, discredit. Both words involve taking away something (courtesy and credit).

Academic Vocabulary

A quotation might be used as support or evidence.

Respond Through Writing

Reflective Essay

Explore Theme What theme do you think Cervantes is expressing through the character of Don Quixote? Explore this question in a 1,500-word reflective essay, in which you reference *Don Quixote* and your own experience.

Understand the Task In a **reflective essay,** you examine details from your experience and reading to present a thought about life.

Prewrite Before you draft your essay, create a concept map like the one below to organize your ideas about Don Quixote. Then identify experiences of your own that seem to link with those of Don Quixote and add them to your concept map. You might derive these experiences from a variety of sources, including brainstorming, journals, and discussions. As you plan, use the graphic organizer you filled out on page 936.

- *Don Quixote—courageous but foolish*
- *Me—trying to be an actor*

Don Quixote—hero or lunatic?

Draft Formulate a clear thesis statement, relating Cervantes's theme to your own experiences. In your body paragraphs, make reference to Don Quixote and your own experience. Your conclusion should restate your thesis and provide closure by using Cervantes's theme and your own experience as the basis for a reflection on life.

Revise Use the following checklist in revising your essay.

- Does my thesis clearly state how Cervantes expresses his theme and how it relates to my own experience?
- Do I use details from *Don Quixote* and my own experience?
- Does my conclusion link Cervantes's theme and my own experience?

Edit and Proofread Proofread your paper, correcting any errors in spelling, grammar, and punctuation. Use your computer's word count feature to check that your essay is about 1,500 words. Review the Grammar Tip in the side column for information on using hyphens.

MIGUEL DE CERVANTES **947**

Learning Objectives

In this assignment, you will focus on the following objectives:

Writing: Writing a reflective essay.

Grammar: Understanding how to use hyphens.

> ### Grammar Tip
>
> #### Hyphens
>
> One common use of hyphens is to separate compound words, such as *good-bye.*
>
> Hyphens are also used to join two modifying words into a single compound modifier, such as *lean-faced.* Remember that expressions consisting of an adverb ending in –*ly* and an adjective— such as *extravagantly worded*—are not hyphenated.

 # After You Read

Assess

Respond Through Writing

Students' essays should

- show how Cervantes uses the character of Don Quixote to express his theme
- link this theme to their own experiences
- use hyphens correctly

A student who meets all of these criteria should receive the equivalent of a 4-point response.

A student who fully meets two and partially meets the third of these criteria should receive the equivalent of a 3-point response.

A student who fully meets one and partially meets a second of these criteria, or who partially meets all three criteria, should receive the equivalent of a 2-point response.

A student who partially fully meets one or partially meets two of these criteria should receive the equivalent of a 1-point response.

 For grammar practice, see Unit 5 Teaching Resources Book, p. 115.

 To create custom assessments online, go to Progress Reporter Online Assessment.

 To create custom assessments using software, use ExamView Assessment Suite.

English Learners

DIFFERENTIATED INSTRUCTION

Advanced Provide students learning English with this activity to aid understanding of new vocabulary.

Write on the board:

Choose the one word in each list that is a synonym for the underlined vocabulary word.

<u>abstinence:</u> enjoyment, avoidance, anger

<u>decipher:</u> interpret, destroy, confuse

<u>renown:</u> knowledge, courtesy, fame

<u>discourteous:</u> daring, amiable, unchivalrous

<u>enmity:</u> cleverness, hostility, promise

(avoidance, interpret, fame, unchivalrous, hostility)

Focus

Bellringer Options

Daily Language Practice Transparency 88

Say: The word *modern* has a number of meanings. It can refer to a formal literary movement of the early 1900s, any historical era after the Middle Ages, or the present. In Unit Five, Part 2 you will encounter European authors grappling with what it means to be "modern." Their works confront the massive changes that have affected Europe over the past several hundred years.

Ask: How might modern literature differ from traditional literature? *(Students may mention the form and themes of different literary genres.)*

View the Photograph ★

Tossa de Mar is a resort on Spain's famous Costa Brava, which lies along the Mediterranean Sea. The section of medieval wall at the center dates to the 1100s.

A Tossa de Mar, Spain ★

B A customer receives his change from a grocer at an open air market along Rue Mouffetard in Paris, France.

LOG ON ▶ **Literature** Online

Literature and Reading For more about the history and literature of this period, go to glencoe.com and enter QuickPass code GLW6053u5.

948

Part Introduction Skills

Text Elements
- Timeline (TE p. 950)
- Numbering (TE p. 955)

Part 2 Introduction

Speaking/Listening/Viewing Skills
- Panel Discussion (SE p. 959)

Reading Skills
- Analyze Graphic Information (SE p. 951; TE p. 950)
- Compare and Contrast (SE p. 956)
- Make Generalizations (SE p. 957)
- Interpret (SE p. 958)

Vocabulary Skills
- Word Parts (TE p. 949)
- Academic Vocabulary (TE p. 953)

Writing Skills/Grammar
- Cultural Contrast (SE p. 959)
- Summary (TE p. 952)

MODERN EUROPE

1650–PRESENT

The Future of Statues, ca. 1937. René Magritte. Tate Gallery, London. © ARS, NY.

Being There

1 From the Arctic edges of Russia to the beaches of Spain, Europe presents an array of geography and cultures. This relatively small peninsula launched many of the ideas and technologies that changed the modern world. During the twentieth century, fierce nationalism took hold in many European nations, leading to invasions and wars that climaxed in the bloodshed of World War I and World War II.

Looking Ahead

The development of European literature since the Renaissance includes a number of distinct literary movements—the Enlightenment, Romanticism, Realism, and Modernism. During the twentieth century, World War I and World War II created generations of authors who looked outside tradition to find new meanings of life in a world suddenly left in rubble.

Keep the following questions in mind as you read:

 How did the ideas of the Enlightenment influence intellectual and political thought in Europe?

 How did the Industrial Revolution affect trends in art and literature?

 How did World War I and World War II impact European literature?

949

Focus

Summary

This introduction gives an overview of historical, social, and cultural forces in Europe between 1650 and the present. It discusses the influence of the Enlightenment, the Industrial Revolution, nationalism, and the two world wars on the development of European literature. Important cultural developments, including modern films, music, and painting, are also discussed. The introduction concludes with a survey of three Big Ideas that shaped modern Europe: the progression of ideas from the Enlightenment to Romanticism, the influence of Realism and Modernism, and the impact of World War II.

Vocabulary   **1**

Understand Word Parts

Ask: What is a peninsula? *(an area of land almost completely surrounded by water)* Explain that the word derives from the Latin prefix *paene-* ("almost") and root *insula* ("island.")

 For additional support for English Learners, see Unit 5 Teaching Resources Book, p. 119.

Approaching Level

DIFFERENTIATED INSTRUCTION

Track Cause-and-Effect Relationships Have students try to answer the three purpose-setting questions on this page as they read the Part 2 introduction. Demonstrate a method for doing so by drawing a two-column chart on the board. Label one column *Causes* and the other *Effects*. Then, in the *Causes* column, write the three events listed in the questions—the Enlightenment, the Industrial Revolution, and the world wars. As students read, have them fill out the *Effects* column in their own chart. In this column, students should note how each of these three forces affected the literature and thought of the time.

Advanced Learners/Pre-AP

DIFFERENTIATED INSTRUCTION

Research Cause-and-Effect Relationships Have advanced learners select a specific European invention of the time period whose introduction was a turning point in industry, medicine, communications, or agriculture. Have them conduct independent research on the effects of the invention. Suggest that they focus on the broader effects of the invention and how it changed European culture.

Teach

Text Element   1

Timeline **Ask:** Into what intervals of time is the timeline divided? *(The intervals are 100 years long, except for the first interval, which is 50 years long.)* Point out the importance of noting the specific dates of the events listed in a single interval. They may have occurred simultaneously or anywhere from one year to one hundred years apart.

APPROACHING Suggest that students who are having difficulty select a small portion of the timeline (for example, the period from 1800 to 1900 in the European Literature category) and create a more detailed timeline. The physical distances on students' timelines should be proportional to the actual amounts of time between events.

Reading Strategy   2

Analyze Graphic Information **Ask:** How long after the Spanish colonies in the Americas began to win independence did the Greeks begin their own war for independence? *(13 years)*

Reading Practice

SMALL GROUP

Monitor Comprehension To aid comprehension, have students divide the events on each of the three timelines into larger categories and then list examples of items in each category. Draw the following partial example for the Modern European Literature timeline on the board:

Poetry	Fiction	Drama	Nonfiction
1827: Heinrich Heine publishes *The Book of Songs* in Germany	1759: French author Voltaire publishes *Candide*	1666: French playwright Molière's *The Misanthrope* is first performed	1947: *The Diary of Anne Frank* is published

Have students work in groups to determine the categories of events on the Modern European Events and World Events timelines. *(Inventions, Leaders,* *Wars, Policies, Disasters)* Then have them create charts with examples of items from each category.

TIMELINE 1650–PRESENT 1

EUROPEAN LITERATURE

1650

1666
French playwright Molière's *The Misanthrope* is first performed

1750

1759 ▶
French author Voltaire publishes *Candide*

1827
Heinrich Heine publishes *The Book of Songs* in Germany

1832
German author Goethe publishes *Faust, Part II*

1850

1862
French author Victor Hugo publishes *Les Misérables*

1865–1869
Russian author Leo Tolstoy publishes *War and Peace*

1879
Henrik Ibsen's *A Doll's House* is first performed

EUROPEAN EVENTS

1650

1661
Louis XIV begins a massive renovation of the Palace of Versailles in France

c. 1668
Anton van Leeuwenhoek develops simple microscope

1707
England and Scotland unite as Great Britain

1750

1762
Catherine the Great becomes ruler of Russia

1804
Napoleon Bonaparte becomes emperor of France

1821
Greeks begin war for independence

1845
Potato blight starts a five-year famine in Ireland
▼

1850

1861
Russian Czar Alexander II frees the serfs

1918
World War I ends

1919–1920
European countries establish the League of Nations ☆

WORLD EVENTS

1650

c. 1650
Taj Mahal completed in India

c. 1697
Ashanti Empire formed in Africa

1752 ▲
Ben Franklin invents the lightning rod

1775
American Revolution begins

1808
Spanish colonies in the Americas begin winning independence 2

1825
Java War begins between Indonesians and Dutch colonialists

1850

1853
First railroad line in India is completed

1903
The Wright brothers fly the first airplane

1910
The Mexican Revolution begins

LOG ON ▶ **Literature** Online

Literature and Reading To explore the Interactive Timeline, go to glencoe.com and enter QuickPass code GLW6053u5.

1950

1900–1903
French author Colette publishes her *Claudine* novels

1904
Anton Chekhov's *The Cherry Orchard* is first performed

1907 ▶
Anna Akhmatova begins writing poetry in Russia

1973
The first parts of Aleksandr Solzhenitsyn's *The Gulag Archipelago* are published

▲
2006
Turkish author Orhan Pamuk wins the Nobel Prize in Literature

1945
World War II ends

THE VICTORY OF THE UNITED NATIONS IS ASSURED

1955
Eastern European countries sign the Warsaw Pact

1957
Soviet Union launches *Sputnik I*, the first artificial satellite

▲
1989
Germany opens the Berlin Wall

1991
Soviet Union dissolves into separate republics **3**

1993
The European Union is formed

1999
Eleven European countries adopt a single currency

2005
Terrorist bombings in London claim more than 50 lives

1950

1918–1919
Worldwide influenza epidemic kills 20 million people

1957
African colonies win independence

1956
Cuban Revolution begins

1969
Apollo XI lands on the moon

1978
Israel and Egypt sign a peace treaty

1994 ▶
Nelson Mandela is elected president of South Africa

2003
War in Iraq begins

Reading Check

Analyze Graphic Information How many years separate the first plane flight and the first landing on the moon?

Approaching Level

DIFFERENTIATED INSTRUCTION

SMALL GROUP

Make a Timeline Those students who have difficulty comprehending the significance of the events on the timeline may benefit from creating a timeline of events with which they are more familiar. Have them work in groups with more advanced students to brainstorm a list of important world events that have taken place in the past year. Then have them construct a timeline of these

events. After they have done so, have them discuss which event on their timeline seems to be the most significant—which one will, in their opinion, have the most lasting consequences. Monitor these discussions to ensure that each student takes time both to speak and to listen quietly. Then have each group present a rationale for its selection to the class.

Teach

Reading Check

Answer: *Sixty-six years elapsed between the Wright brothers' flight and the landing of Apollo XI.*

Reading Strategy   3

Analyze Graphic Information   Ask: How long before the dissolution of the Soviet Union was the first part of *The Gulag Archipelago* published? (*18 years*)

Political History ☆

The League of Nations
The League of Nations was a predecessor of the United Nations. Set up in the wake of the devastation caused by World War I, it was intended to ensure that such conflicts would never again arise. But it was often divided in its counsels, and the authoritarian governments that arose in the 1920s and 1930s simply ignored its decisions. Still, simply by establishing the principle that the nations of the world should work together, it made an important contribution.

Learning Objectives
Analyzing graphic information. (SE)
Analyzing timeline. (TE)
Monitoring comprehension. (TE)

Predict Before students begin reading, write the four heads from these two pages on the board: The Enlightenment, The Industrial Revolution, Nationalism, The Two World Wars. Prompt students to share their prior knowledge of these terms and predict what the section will be about based on that knowledge. Students may have heard of the Industrial Revolution and the two world wars, but may be less familiar with the terms *Enlightenment* and *Nationalism*.

APPROACHING Point out that they can use the parts of each of these words to make predictions about their meanings. (*Enlightenment* contains the word *enlighten*, so it probably has to do with the discovery of knowledge; *Nationalism* contains the word *nation*, so it probably involves a belief about a nation.)

Learning Objectives

For pages 948–959
In studying this text, you will focus on the following objectives:

Literary Study: Analyzing literary periods.

Reading: Evaluating historical influences.
Connecting to the literature.

MODERN EUROPE

1650–PRESENT

Historical, Social, and Cultural Forces

The Enlightenment

The Enlightenment dominated philosophy and literature in the late 1600s and 1700s. Faith in human reason and skepticism toward traditional religion characterized this broad movement. Also referred to as Rationalism and "The Age of Reason," the Enlightenment stimulated an outburst of scientific and intellectual inquiry that included Denis Diderot's monumental *Encyclopédie* and Sir Isaac Newton's investigation into the laws of motion. The Enlightenment also shook the political establishment in challenging the "divine right" of kings. These ideas laid the foundation for a modern worldview based on secularism and the rights of the individual. The arguments of such Enlightenment figures as John Locke and Jean-Jacques Rousseau helped shape the ideals behind the American Revolution, the Declaration of Independence, and the French Revolution.

The Industrial Revolution

In the 1700s and 1800s, Europeans began to radically change the way they made goods. Instead of making them by hand and with simple tools, they increasingly used power-driven machines. This change, called the Industrial Revolution, affected

people's lives in many ways. The mass production of such goods as shoes, clothes, and furniture gave people more products they could afford. This new technology came at a human cost, however, as factory workers, including children, endured brutal conditions and long workdays. In the late 1700s, authors associated with the literary movement known as Romanticism began to respond to this change by turning toward nature and the imagination. In the mid-1800s, Realist authors brought attention to the problems of the working class.

A Forge, 1893. Fernand Corman. Oil on canvas. Musee d'Orsay, Paris.

Write a Summary Point out to students that summarizing is a helpful way to review and understand what they have read. **Say:** Summarizing means writing down the main ideas of what you have just read, without including any extra information.
A summary omits specific details and examples.

Write on the board the following one-sentence summary of the paragraph under "The Enlightenment": The Enlightenment, an eighteenth-century movement that emphasized scholarship and reason, spurred scientific progress and the development of new political systems in Europe.

Point out to students that a good summary of a historical topic will often include terms such as *caused*, *led to*, or *resulted in*. Have them write one-sentence summaries of the three remaining sections of text on pages 952 and 953. Urge them to include only absolutely crucial information—what, why, where, when, and how.

2 Nationalism

In the 1800s, political borders rarely matched cultural borders. Europe, like most of the world, consisted of tiny kingdoms and sprawling multi-ethnic empires. For example, German-speaking people lived throughout 300 states, while the vast Austrian Empire included Hungarians, Poles, Czechs, Serbs, and other ethnic groups. Europeans felt more loyal to their region or their ruler than to their nationality or ethnic background. However, the idea of nationalism, which comprises a sense of devotion to a nation and a feeling everyone who shares a language and a culture should be in a single separate state, was spreading. Politicians began to exploit ethnic rivalries. People began to embrace, and to even kill and die for, their national identity. These developments propelled Napoleon Bonaparte's drive to conquer Europe in the name of France. During the Napoleonic Wars between 1792 and 1815, France staged a series of invasions, including a failed attempt to conquer Russia. Despite Napoleon's defeat, the trend of nationalism spread throughout Europe. Germany, Italy, and Russia each developed strong dictatorships fueled by nationalist sentiment.

> "What is the throne?—a bit of wood gilded and covered with velvet. I am the state—I alone am the representative of the people."
>
> —Napoleon

The Two World Wars

A complex system of alliances led to the outbreak of World War I (1914–1918). This war pitted the Allies (Britain, France, Russia, Italy, Japan, and the United States) against the Central Powers (Germany, Austria-Hungary, and the Turkish Ottoman Empire). During World War I, armies unleashed new technologies—such as machine guns, tanks, and poisonous gas—that contributed to the deaths of more than 20 million people.

French troops stand guard along the trenches. Undated photograph, ca. 1914-1919. ★

The peace that followed the "Great War" was short-lived, as poor economic conditions in Germany caused by World War I contributed to Adolf Hitler's rise to power. His *blitzkrieg* ("lightning war") invasions of Poland, Belgium, The Netherlands, and France propelled Europe into World War II. Fought between 1939 and 1945, this conflict further devastated Europe. The Axis Powers—Italy, Germany, and Japan—overwhelmed much of the world before the Allies—led by Britain, Russia, and the United States—eventually thwarted them. In World War II, gas chambers, conventional bombs, and atomic weapons killed more than 50 million people. World War II included the Holocaust, one of the darkest periods in European history, as Hitler's Nazi party used racist ideology to justify the systematic killing of six million Jews.

Since World War II, Europe has worked to heal its wounds and prevent future conflicts through political diplomacy. This spirit has created a range of groups, including the United Nations (UN), the European Economic Community (EEC), and the European Union (EU), which was established in 1993 and absorbed the EEC. Today, European countries are moving toward standardizing currencies and other government functions across the continent while maintaining their distinct ethnic traditions.

INTRODUCTION **953**

English Learners

DIFFERENTIATED INSTRUCTION

Intermediate English learners may have difficulty following the sequence of causes and effects described on these pages. Urge them to scan each section of the text before they read and look for signal words that will help them predict the types of events or conflicts that will be described. Examples of signal words include *loyal, devotion, kill, die, conquer* and *defeat*.

Advanced Learners/Pre-AP

DIFFERENTIATED INSTRUCTION

Research and Report This introduction alludes to many different ideologies—such as capitalism, democracy, and nationalism—that arose in Europe and then went on to influence societies around the world. Have advanced learners choose one such ideology and then write a brief report tracing its rise and spread.

Teach

Reading Strategy 2

Connect to Contemporary Issues Ask: How do you see nationalism exhibited in the United States today? *(Many people fly American flags at their homes and are proud to identify themselves as Americans. The events of September 11, 2001, also caused an outpouring of American nationalism and patriotism.)*

ADVANCED Ask: What are some ideologies that might be seen as competing with nationalism? *(Students may mention loyalty to a specific ethnic group or a desire to maintain one's distinct cultural identity.)*

View the Photograph ★

Explain to students that trench warfare was a key feature of World War I. On the Western Front in France, huge armies needed to be protected from the deady fire of machine guns and from exploding shells from long-range artillery. Trenches provided this needed defense, and when used in combination with barbed wire, they could also provide a strong defensive position from which to slow enemy offensives.

Learning Objectives
Analyzing historical influences. (SE)
Writing a summary. (TE)
Predicting. (TE)

Teach

Reading Strategy · 1

Analyze Historical Influences **Ask:** How was classical music influenced by European nationalism?

(Nationalism inspired composers to incorporate folk melodies, which imparted a sense of national history and pride, into their compositions.)

ADVANCED Encourage musically inclined students to listen to and write descriptions of classical compositions that incorporate folk themes. Examples include the works of Czech composers Antonin Dvořák and Bedřich Smetana, who used folk melodies to convey a feeling of national pride.

View the Art ★

Russian painter Wassily Kandinsky (1866–1944) was a pioneer in modern abstract art. Self-taught, he was heavily influenced by folk art and the French impressionists. He often compared painting to composing music.

Modern Films

Motion pictures developed in the late 1800s, following the work of British photographer Eadweard Muybridge, who rigged a row of separate cameras to take a series of photographs of a running horse. Muybridge attached strings to the shutters of the cameras, and as the horse ran by it broke the strings, triggering the shutters in succession. The result was the first motion picture. Inventors in other countries soon developed more portable devices to make films. The Lumière brothers—famous for their early motion picture cameras and projectors—showed their first motion picture in Paris in 1895. Since the 1950s, movie directors such as Italy's Federico Fellini and France's François Truffaut have created films that demonstrate the enduring appeal of great art.

Modern Music

1 Inspired by the nationalism spreading through Europe, many composers in the 1800s and 1900s incorporated folk styles into their music to celebrate the histories of their countries. Often, they challenged listeners with new harmonies, scales, and rhythms. In 1913, Russian composer Igor Stravinsky's score for the ballet *The Rite of Spring* proved too much for some audiences. The driving rhythms and jarring harmonies outraged many listeners, who responded with boos and catcalls, pushing, shoving, and even fistfights. One critic called the score "the most irritating friction and squeaking that can be imagined." Yet European composers continued to push avant-garde boundaries. The French composer Pierre Boulez incorporated serialism (repeating patterns) into his music, while the Austrian composer Arnold Schoenberg invented twelve-tone music and created atonal works that purposely lacked harmony.

Modern Painting **2**

During the first half of the 1800s, European painters continued to develop the styles and methods they inherited from earlier generations. The

Improvisation Painting, 1914. Wassily Kandinsky. ★

Galloping Horse, plate 628 from *Animal Locomotion,* 1887. Eadweard Muybridge.

> "To listen is an effort, and just to hear is no merit. A duck hears also."
>
> —Igor Stravinsky

Reading Practice

Analyze Cause-and-Effect Relationships Point out to students that many of the cultural developments described on these pages follow a common formula: the rejection of an older style or idea in favor of a new, and often opposite, style or idea. Draw the following chart on the board as an example:

Who:	Rejected:	Result:
Modern composers	Classical rhythms and harmonies	Jarring, atonal music

Then have students fill out similar charts for the other cultural developments described in the introduction, including contemporary music, Impressionism, Picasso's art, abstract art, the Enlightenment, and Romanticism.

middle of the century, however, saw the rise of the Impressionists. These artists, including Claude Monet and Pierre Auguste Renoir, rejected the importance of traditional subject matter and artistic practices. Instead, they brought their painting outdoors and aimed to manipulate color, texture, and tone in new ways. In the early 1900s artists made even more revolutionary efforts. Pablo Picasso, for example, rejected the traditional emphasis on portraying an object's surface. Instead of showing an object from a single perspective, he showed it from several angles in the same painting. One critic described Marcel Duchamp's 1912 painting *Nude Descending a Staircase* as "an explosion in a shingle factory." While such painters as Picasso and Duchamp shocked viewers by what they showed, other painters shocked people by what they left out of their work. Vassily Kandinsky and Piet Mondrian created nonrepresentational, abstract paintings—works that combined colors, lines, and forms without portraying any particular real-world object.

Nude Descending a Staircase, No.2, 1912. Marcel Duchamp. Oil on canvas. Philadelphia Museum of Art, Pennsylvania.

PREVIEW **Big Ideas** of Modern Europe **3**

1 From the Enlightenment to Romanticism	**2** Realism and Modernism	**3** Postwar Europe
The Enlightenment marked an outburst of intellectual freedom and scientific inquiry in the late 1600s. By the late 1700s, a new cultural movement known as Romanticism emphasized nature, passion, and the imagination. **See page 956**	By the mid-1800s, Realism, a reaction to Romanticism, changed the shape of literature. Realist authors sought to re-create the texture of everyday life and address the problems of ordinary people. In the late 1800s and early 1900s, Modernist authors broke tradition with experimental techniques and an interest in the unpredictable side of human nature. **See page 957**	World War II resulted in millions of deaths and left much of Europe in ruins. The horrors of the Holocaust and the threat of nuclear war seemed to challenge all traditional values. Postwar European authors responded in a variety of ways to these events, from expressions of hope to celebrations of human absurdity. **See page 958**

INTRODUCTION **955**

Advanced Learners/Pre-AP

DIFFERENTIATED INSTRUCTION

Art and Music Advanced learners may be interested to know that composers and artists have often purposely reflected the themes or settings of others' artistic works. An example is the composition "Pictures at an Exhibition" by Modest Mussorgsky (1839–1881), which gives a musical rendition of ten pictures by the Russian artist Victor Hartmann. Have interested students locate a reproduction of a work by a modern artist and a musical composition that seems to capture the same feeling. For example, the driving rhythms and jarring harmonies of Stravinsky's work suggest certain works by Picasso. Have students write an analysis of the links between the two compositions.

Teach

Reading Strategy | 2

Identify Assumptions Have students read the paragraph under "Modern Painting." **Ask:** Based on this paragraph, what do you think were the assumptions underlying early nineteenth-century painting? *(Artists assumed paintings should portray traditional subjects in a realistic way.)* **Then ask:** How did modern painters challenge these assumptions? *(Modern painters created works that were nonrealistic and even nonrepresentational.)*

Text Element | 3

Numbering Have students read the numbered subheads and text under Big Ideas of Modern Europe. **Ask:** Why are the three Big Ideas presented in this order? *(They are presented in the chronological order of the literary movements they discuss.)*

View the Art ★

This painting by Marcel Duchamp (1887–1968) was controversial when first released. It has been compared to superimposed frames of a motion picture.

Learning Objectives
Analyzing historical influences. (SE)
Analyzing cause-and-effect relationships. (TE)
Identifying assumptions. (TE)
Understanding text structures. (TE)

Teach

Reading Check

Answer: *Enlightenment authors believed in the power of reason; Romantics believed in the power of the imagination.*

Reading Strategy | 1

Compare and Contrast

Point out to students that the ideas of Enlightenment thinkers such as John Locke influenced the drafting of the Declaration of Independence. **Ask:** What similarities do you see between the ideals of the Enlightenment and those of the U.S. Founding Fathers? *(Similarities include the idea that men are born equal, the idea that they are fit to govern themselves, and the belief that human beings possess certain individual rights.)*

View the Art ★

Caspar David Friedrich (1774–1840) was a leading German Romantic artist. He was especially well-known for his paintings of lone figures contemplating harsh landscapes.

Reading Practice

Compare and Contrast Point out to students that, while Enlightenment authors and Romantic authors differed in many ways, they also shared many of the same beliefs. Have students create a Venn diagram that illustrates the similarities and differences between the two movements. An example is at the right. Suggest that students create similar diagrams for Realism and Modernism after they have read the introductory material on Big Idea 2.

Big Idea 1

From the Enlightenment to Romanticism

The balance of logic and passion in literature shifted dramatically during the eighteenth century. Enlightenment authors in the late 1600s and 1700s crafted logical arguments on subjects ranging from politics to happiness. Romantic authors in the early 1800s created daring works of imagination and expressed an abiding vision of the artist as an outsider—brooding, mysterious, and dangerous.

The Enlightenment Thinkers

The Enlightenment challenged the power wielded by the upper class, the monarchy, and the church. John Locke, an influential Enlightenment philosopher, believed humans were born as a "blank slate," without predisposition to evil and worthy of the chance to govern themselves. France's Jean-Jacques Rousseau argued that society corrupted the goodness of the individual and that common people had a right to revolt against unjust governments. While the French Enlightenment author Voltaire (see pages 960–969) disagreed with much of the political optimism embedded in these claims, he applied Enlightenment thinking in his cutting satires. In 1750, Voltaire served as an adviser to the Prussian king Frederick the Great, who enacted an ambitious plan to reform society. Voltaire transformed this experience into his philosophical novel *Candide*, which satirizes the goal of creating a perfect society.

The Romantic Imagination

While Rousseau's championing of the individual paved the way for the rise of Romanticism, the Romantics sharply disagreed with the Enlightenment's skeptical attitude and faith in scholarship. The late-eighteenth-century German literary movement *Sturm und Drang* ("Storm and Stress") stimulated the transition between these ways of thinking. Led by the author Johann Wolfgang von Goethe, this movement sought to replace the trend of scholarship with a renewed interest in the power of the imagination and individual experience.

The Wanderer above the Sea of Fog, 1818. Caspar David Friedrich. Oil on canvas. Hamburger Kunsthalle, Hamburg, Germany. ★

> *"Genius develops in the quiet places, Character out in the full current of human life"*
> —Johann Wolfgang von Goethe

During the 1800s, Romantics such as Heinrich Heine (see pages 972–975) explored the power of desire, the lure of history, and the dignity of people considered "outsiders." Victor Hugo (see pages 976–982) wrote drama and poetry, including works exploring the rise and fall of Napoleon Bonaparte. In his plays, Hugo created characters that find value in both sides of a contradiction.

Reading Check

Compare and Contrast What differentiated Enlightenment authors from Romantic authors?

Enlightenment Authors
- were skeptical toward faith
- believed in scholarship

Both
- championed the individual
- challenged the upper class

Romantic Authors
- believed in the imagination
- explored the dignity of "outsiders"

Big Idea 2
Realism and Modernism

Woman with violin. ca. 1921. Henri Matisse. Musee de l'Orangerie, Paris.© ARS, NY.

Do you think a factual report best represents reality, or do people lead an inner life that can only be represented in abstract ways? Since the late 1800s, artists and scholars have pondered this question.

> "Art is not handicraft, it is the transmission of feeling the artist has experienced."
>
> —Leo Tolstoy

Realist and Naturalist Concerns

The literary movement known as Realism reacted against Romanticism in seeking to depict life as it really happens. This meant stripping away the idealism that shaped Romantic works. Realists often moved away from nature to focus on the struggles of the urban working class. Realist Leo Tolstoy (see pages 983–999) wrote novels that explored the moral structure of society and such social ills as greed. Anton Chekhov (see pages 1001–1011) emerged as a major dramatist and master of the short story. His works feature "slices of life" that detail the motives of characters.

Naturalist authors, expanding on the ideas of Realism, argued grimly that heredity, social class, and the environment govern the lives of individuals. Naturalists wrote austerely objective works inspired by social Darwinism, a liberal application of Charles Darwin's scientific theory about the evolution of species through natural selection. The French authors Émile Zola and Guy de Maupassant spearheaded the rise of Naturalism in fiction.

The Modernist Revolution

By the late 1800s and early 1900s, Modernism revolutionized the way people saw the world. Many critics refer to Norwegian dramatist Henrik

Ibsen's play *A Doll's House* as the first Modern drama. When it was first performed in 1879, it sent shock waves through the audience. At the time, theatergoers were used to seeing plays with traditional dramatic conventions, romantic plots, and tidy resolutions. Ibsen created a play about marital conflict that ends with the sound of a door slamming and questions left unanswered. Its realistic detail and psychological insight combine the innovations of both Realism and Modernism.

Modernists, such as the Symbolist poets of France (see pages 1012–1013) and the Spanish poet Federico García Lorca (see pages 1041–1044), pushed the boundaries of form and style. They also found inspiration in the works of Sigmund Freud, the creator of psychoanalysis, and Albert Einstein, who showed the relativity of time and space. This turbulent period also witnessed the horrors of World War I, which compelled authors to turn from tradition in a world suddenly left in shambles. The era created an anxiety reflected in such Modernist masterpieces as Franz Kafka's *The Metamorphosis*, in which the character Gregor Samsa wakes up one morning to find himself transformed into a monstrous insect.

Reading Check

Make Generalizations What are some assumptions Modernism makes about the individual's experience of the world?

Teach

Reading Check

Answer: *Reality is unstable and each individual perceives it differently.*

View the Art

Henri Matisse (1869–1954) is considered one of the most important European artists of the 1900s. He led a movement called Fauvism, in which paint was applied straight from paint tubes to create bursts of color. This domestic scene is typical of Matisse's work. **Ask:** What is modern about the theme of this painting? *(The violinist is shown contemplating the painter rather than playing the violin.)*

Cultural History ☆

Charles Darwin From 1831 to 1836, Charles Darwin served as a naturalist on a British scientific expedition aboard the HMS *Beagle*. As the ship traveled around the world, Darwin was able to study plants and animals at every stop. Those studies convinced Darwin that the primary mechanism for evolution was a process called natural selection. In 1859 he published his startling theories in a book called *On the Origin of Species by Means of Natural Selection.*

Learning Objectives
Comparing and contrasting. (SE)
Making generalizations. (SE)
Questioning. (TE)

English Learners

DIFFERENTIATED INSTRUCTION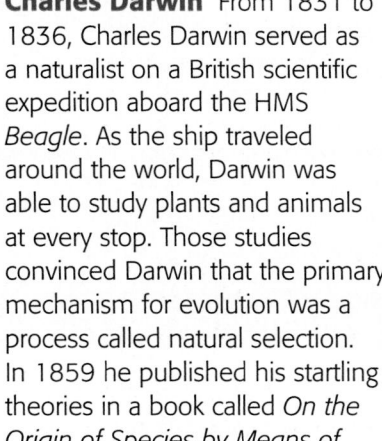

Intermediate English learners may gain a better understanding of these two movements by further exploring the words themselves. Explain that to *enlighten* literally means to "shed light upon"—in other words, to impart intellectual or spiritual knowledge. The word *Romanticism* comes from the word *romantic*, whose most literal definition is "in language derived from that of the

Romans." In literary criticism, the word *romantic* has a variety of meanings. It can refer to medieval adventure stories, to any literature that emphasizes the powers of emotion and the imagination, or to the specific European movement of the late 1700s. Emphasize that the word does not necessarily mean "relating to love," as it does in its most common usage.

957

Teach

Reading Check

Answer: *It reminds the world of this tragic period in history so that future generations will avoid such atrocities.*

Literary History ☆

The Diary of Anne Frank

Originally published in Dutch as *The Diary of a Young Girl*, *The Diary of Anne Frank* is an enduring classic of world literature. Discovered by a family friend after the Frank family had been captured by the Nazis, it reveals young Anne's emotional development during her years in hiding. Though it tells the story of only one person, it has come to symbolize the suffering of the millions of voiceless victims of the Holocaust. It is particularly memorable for the hope, strength, and insight exhibited by the teenage Anne Frank. At one point she writes, "In spite of everything I still believe that people are really good at heart."

Big Idea 3
Postwar Europe

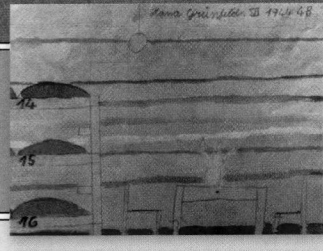

Drawings by Jewish children while at Terezin ghetto: both later died at Auschwitz concentration camp.

War often spurs dramatic changes in literature. The collective exhaustion that Europeans felt following World War II led many to lose faith in traditional ideas.

> "Everything had to be reassessed because everything had changed. With one stroke, mankind's achievements seemed to have been erased."
> —Elie Wiesel

Holocaust Literature

Elie Wiesel's response to the atrocities of the Nazi death camp Auschwitz echoes the concerns of many post–World War II authors. The Holocaust represented the Nazis' "final solution to the Jewish question" (as phrased by the Nazis) and led to the killing of six million Jews. Postwar authors detailed the horrors of the Holocaust to give voice to the voiceless victims of the period and to ensure the world would never forget the tragedy. Elie Wiesel (see pages 1063–1071) has documented the horrors of the Holocaust through both nonfiction and fiction. Engraved in the U.S. Holocaust Memorial Museum are his words: "For the dead and the living, we must bear witness."

☆ *The Diary of Anne Frank* (originally published in 1947) is another masterpiece of Holocaust literature. Frank was a young Jewish girl who recorded her experiences while hiding from Nazi forces in The Netherlands. Frank eventually died in a concentration camp only weeks before Allied forces liberated the camp. The graphic novelist Art Spiegelman, born in Poland to Jewish parents who survived Auschwitz, created *Maus* (published from 1980 to 1985), a pivotal work in the rise of the graphic novel and a poignant telling of the Holocaust.

Gulags, Existentialism, and the Absurd

Following World War II, tense political conditions persisted in many parts of Europe. The Cold War that emerged between nuclear superpowers Russia and the United States caused many people to live in daily fear of nuclear attack. In Russia, Joseph Stalin's Communist Party created the Gulag political prisons and restricted the freedom of authors such as Aleksandr Solzhenitsyn (see pages 1072–1075), whom they viewed as a threat to authority.

Existentialism, a philosophy that investigates the meaning of existence, reflected the anxiety of this period. Many Existentialists concluded life was essentially meaningless and absurd. A related movement in drama called "Theater of the Absurd" flourished in the 1950s and 60s. It presented confused and anxious characters wandering through a meaningless world. The French author Albert Camus (see pages 1056–1062) emerged as the spokesman for these complex responses to the world. However, rather than describing a world of bottomless despair, Camus argued that once people realize the underlying meaninglessness of the world they can begin to make choices that give meaning to their lives.

Reading Check

Interpret How does Holocaust literature honor those who died in Nazi concentration camps?

958 UNIT 5 MODERN EUROPE

Reading Practice

Make an Outline To help students take notes and study the Big Ideas on pages 956–958, have them write outlines using the titles and headings on the pages. Below is a partial example outline for Big Idea 3:

Postwar Europe

I. Holocaust Literature
   A. Authors detailed Nazi atrocities
      1. Elie Wiesel's writings
      2. *The Diary of Anne Frank*
      3. Art Spiegelman's *Maus*

WRAP-UP

Legacy of the Period

The literary movement of Romanticism contributed to European and American culture a belief in the spiritual power of nature, the importance of the imagination, and the dignity of the artist. Realism extended Romantic ideals and inspired such social changes as better working conditions. Modernists wanted people to see life in a new way—they strove to break away from traditional forms and often explored the power of the subconscious. The Modernist desire to experiment remains alive in literature today.

Cultural and Literary Links

 Many famous American authors, including Ernest Hemingway and Gertrude Stein, moved to Paris at the beginning of the twentieth century. These authors drew from modern European art and literature. For example, Stein applied the innovations of Cubist painting to her groundbreaking poems.

Portrait of Gertrude Stein, 1906. Pablo Picasso. Oil on canvas. Metropolitan Museum of Art, NY.

 Anton Chekhov wrote more than 600 short stories in his lifetime. When interviewed in 1987, ten well-known authors, including Eudora Welty, Nadine Gordimer, and Raymond Carver, cited him as a key influence.

> **LOG ON** ▶ **Literature** Online
>
> **Unit Resources** For additional skills practice, go to glencoe.com and enter QuickPass code GLW6053u5.

Activities

 Use what you have learned about the period to do one of these activities.

1. Follow Up Go back to the Looking Ahead on page 949 and answer the questions.

2. Contrast Cultures The literature of modern Europe takes many forms, including short stories, novels, and poetry. Write several paragraphs in which you select one of these forms and contrast it with the same form in another culture you have studied in this book. Consider such literary elements as theme, form, and diction.

3. Speaking/Listening With classmates, organize a panel discussion with representatives from the Enlightenment, the Romantic, Realism, and Modernism periods, and postwar Europe. Choose a moderator to lead the discussion and have each

representative explain his or her views on subjects such as war, the nature of good and evil, or reality.

4. Take Notes Use this graphic organizer to record your responses to the literary works in this part.

FOLDABLES
Study Organizer

BOUND BOOK

INTRODUCTION **959**

Teach

Reading Strategy | 1

Question Ask: How might a piece of realist literature bring about social change? Suggest to students that literature can both inform and persuade. For example, a novel could show privileged readers the true difficulties faced by the working poor. These readers might then be inspired to take political action in order to change working conditions.

Assess

Activities

1. Follow Up They brought scientific knowledge to the forefront and questioned religious faith; Romantic writers turned to nature for inspiration and Realist writers portrayed working class people; Authors clung to hope or described the absurdity of modern life.

2. Contrast Cultures Students should support their ideas with evidence from the selections they examine.

3. Speaking/Listening Students should remain in character during the discussion and should respond appropriately to the moderator's questions.

4. Take Notes Students should include their personal responses to the literary works.

Advanced Learners/Pre-AP

DIFFERENTIATED INSTRUCTION

Research and Report Some students may be interested in learning more about American Modernist authors who chose to relocate to Europe. They were known as expatriates, a word taken from the Latin *expatriare*, meaning to leave one's own country. Point out that expatriation was also a trend among American writers of later generations. Suggest that students research American expatriate authors

from several generations, comparing and contrasting their reasons for choosing to leave the United States. Have them present their findings in a brief written report.

Before You Read

Focus

Bellringer Options

Daily Language Practice Transparency 89

Or ask: Is a perfect society ever possible? Students will likely agree that a perfect society is not possible, largely because the conditions for such a society (selflessness, generosity, lack of corruption) are difficult to establish and maintain in any group of people.

Readability Scores

Dale-Chall: 9
DRP: 61
Lexile: 1010

Before You Read

from *Candide*

France

Meet **Voltaire**

(1694–1778)

Voltaire (vol tār′) spent his life fighting the injustices of the legal system, the cruelties of war, the intolerance of religions, and the callousness of society toward its poor. To this day, he remains one of France's most influential thinkers.

Jailed for Satire Known by his pen name Voltaire, he was born François-Marie Arouet to middle-class parents. In college Voltaire became interested in literature, theater, and fashionable Parisian society, and he soon became popular among Paris intellectuals with the publication of several short satirical poems. After King Louis XIV died in 1715, his five-year-old great-grandson acceded to the throne as Louis XV, with the Duc d'Orléans serving as regent, or acting ruler. Voltaire was accused of satirizing the regent and was imprisoned in the Bastille. While there he wrote a tragic drama, *Oedipe,* which was staged in Paris upon his release and became a great success.

Jail and Exile Voltaire continued to criticize the behavior of the nobility, which earned him a second jail term and exile to England. He thrived within the more permissive environment of England, a country whose intellectuals proved to be more tolerant of free thought than his countrymen. Voltaire admired the works of the scientist Sir Isaac Newton and the social philosopher John Locke and enjoyed the company of satirical authors Jonathan Swift and Alexander Pope. When he returned to Paris, Voltaire wrote *Lettres philosophiques,* which embodies eighteenth-century rationalism. He argued that the purpose of life is not to achieve heaven through penitence, but rather to bring happiness to all people through advancements in

"Let us work without arguing... it's the only way to make life endurable."

—Voltaire

the arts and sciences. Because he praised England so enthusiastically, his French contemporaries were again displeased. His *Essay on the Morals and the Spirit of the Nations* was banned and Voltaire was sent into a second exile.

Famed as a "Saint of Reason" Although he stayed away from Paris for most of his remaining years, Voltaire's outspoken criticism of social injustices brought him trouble wherever he lived. After extensive travels throughout Europe, Voltaire retired to an estate near Geneva, Switzerland, and another in Tourney, France, just over the border; by crossing the border he could escape either country's authorities. He continued to write about multiple subjects in various genres, earning both praise and criticism from important literary and political figures. His satirical novel *Candide,* published in 1759, became his most famous work. At age 83, just before his death, Voltaire returned to Paris in triumph for the production of his last play. Years after his death and after the French Revolution of 1789—a revolution influenced in part by Voltaire's ideas for social reform—his body was interred in the Panthéon in Paris, a site of honor reserved for France's most famous figures.

 Literature Online

Author Search For more about Voltaire, go to glencoe.com and enter QuickPass code GLW6053u5.

Selection Skills

Literary Elements
- Satire (SE pp. 961, 963–965, 968)
- Narrator (SE p. 968)
- Allusion (TE p. 966)

Reading Skills
- Apply Background Knowledge (SE pp. 961, 964, 968)
- Distinguish Fact and Opinion (TE p. 962)

Candide

Vocabulary Skills
- Understand Word Origins (SE pp. 961, 968)
- Understand Similes (TE p. 961)

Writing Skills/Grammar
- Expository Essay (SE p. 969)
- Editorial (TE p. 964)
- Autobiographical Narrative (TE p. 966)

Literature and Reading Preview

Connect to the Novel

Have you ever felt yourself the victim of injustice? How did you react? Discuss these questions with a small group.

Build Background

Candide is Voltaire's response to the ideas of German philosopher Gottfried Wilhelm Leibniz (līb′nits), who was the model for Dr. Pangloss, the tutor of Candide (kon dēd′) and Cunegonde (koo′nə gond). The students initially accept Dr. Pangloss's pronouncement that "all is for the best . . . in this best of all possible worlds," and consequently endure every imaginable humiliation. Candide and Cunegonde grow more realistic as Votaire ridicules Dr. Pangloss's optimistic philosophy.

Set Purposes for Reading

Big Idea From the Enlightenment to Romanticism

As you read the excerpt from *Candide,* ask yourself, How does Voltaire's novel both represent and satirize eighteenth-century Enlightenment ideas and intellectual inquiry?

Literary Element Satire

Writing that comments on human flaws, ideas, social customs, or institutions is called **satire.** Often humorous, sometimes biting, satire often promotes reform. As you read, ask yourself, Whom or what does Voltaire satirize in this work?

Reading Strategy Apply Background Knowledge

Sometimes **background knowledge** helps a reader understand the historical context or the implied message of a work. For example, knowing that Dr. Pangloss is based on a real person can enhance your enjoyment. As you read, ask yourself, What was happening in the world when this novel was written?

Tip: Record Influences Review the part introduction on pages 948–959 to get a sense of the context of the novel. Record your notes for easy reference as you read.

Background	Candide
Constant warring in Europe	Candide conscripted for Bulgarian army

Vocabulary

candor (kan′dər) *n.* honesty or frankness; openness; p. 963 *With the candor of a child, my little sister told me how strange my outfit looked.*

pensive (pen′siv) *adj.* thoughtful; p. 964 *I think Leon's pensive look is from worrying about exams.*

vivacity (vi vas′ə tē′) *n.* liveliness; animation; p. 964 *There's a charming vivacity in the voice of the play's main actor.*

consternation (kon′stər nā′ shən) *n.* great fear or shock; upset; p. 964 *The smoke coming through the window caused much consternation among the shoppers.*

clemency (klem′ən sē) *n.* mercy; leniency, especially toward an enemy; p. 966 *The judge was determined to show little clemency toward the convicted robbers.*

Tip: Word Origins Word origins, or etymologies, may give clues to a word's meaning. The word *vivacity,* for example, comes from a Latin word that refers to life. Knowing this etymology can help you determine the word's meaning.

VOLTAIRE **961**

Before You Read

Focus

Summary

Candide is a satirical philosophical novel that follows naïve and optimistic Candide on a series of adventures. This excerpted selection introduces Candide, who has been brought up in the noble castle of Baron Thunder-ten-tronckh. But Candide is eventually banished from the castle, recruited into military service, and punished severely for escaping. The King of the Bulgarians recognizes Candide's naïveté, however, and spares him.

 For summaries in languages other than English, see Unit 5 Teaching Resources Book, pp. 120–125.

Vocabulary

Satirical Similes Remind students that a simile is a comparison that shows similarities between things, using the word *like* or *as.* Similes usually explain something unfamiliar by comparing it to something more familiar. Have students use the vocabulary words and a satirical tone to create humorous analogies describing an odious character. *(Example: The lying ogre has as much candor as a taunted wolverine has charm.)*

 For additional vocabulary practice, see Unit 5 Teaching Resources Book, p. 128.

Approaching Level

DIFFERENTIATED INSTRUCTION

Identify Tone Point out to students the light, satiric, sometimes humorous tone of the selection. Explain that the narrator's words are not meant to be taken at face value. Rather, they often ridicule human flaws, customs, and ideas. Have students to record examples from the text that suggest a satiric or humorous tone in one column of a two-column chart. In the second column, have students explain what makes the example satiric or humorous.

Example	Explanationn

Teach

Cultural History ☆

Optimism and *Candide*

In his novel *Candide*, Voltaire satirizes optimism, a prevailing philosophical attitude of his time. Optimism is the general belief that the world is a positive place and people are inherently good. In the novel, Candide's tutor, Doctor Pangloss, follows the philosophy of Gottfried Wilhelm Leibniz, a German philosopher and contemporary of Voltaire's. According to Leibniz, this world is the best of all possible worlds, with God at the center and man acting in God's likeness.

Interactive Read and Write
Other options for teaching this selection can be found in Interactive Read and Write for On-Level Learners, pp. 243–252.

Eltz Castle. Domenico Quaglio II (1787–1837). Oil on canvas. Hamburger Kunsthalle, Hamburg, Germany.

Reading Practice

Distinguish Fact and Opinion Have students describe the language and details the narrator provides about the castle and its inhabitants so far *(extremely positive and complimentary, hyperbolic, satiric)*. Cue students to extreme expressions such as "most powerful" and "in every respect." Have students work together in pairs to review the selection so far and distinguish factual details from the narrator's opinions. Students can create two-column charts, listing *Facts* on one side and *Opinions* on the other. Help students recognize the faulty conclusions the narrator comes to and the opinions inherent in such statements. For example, "The Baroness weighed about three hundred fifty pounds, was therefore greatly respected . . ." While the Baroness's large size may be a fact, her size is not necessarily the reason she is respected.

from CANDIDE ☆

Voltaire
Translated by Richard Aldington

CHAPTER I

How Candide Was Brought Up in a Noble Castle and How He Was Expelled from the Same

In the castle of Baron Thunder-ten-tronckh in Westphalia[1] there lived a youth, endowed by Nature with the most gentle character. His face was the expression of his soul. His judgment was quite honest and he was extremely simple-minded; and this was the reason, I think, that he was named Candide. Old servants in the house suspected that he was the son of the Baron's sister and a decent honest gentleman of the neighborhood, whom this young lady would never marry because he could only prove seventy-one quarterings,[2] and the rest of his genealogical tree[3] was lost, owing to the injuries of time. The Baron was one of the most powerful lords in Westphalia, for his castle possessed a door and windows. His Great Hall was even decorated with a piece of tapestry. The dogs in his stableyards formed a pack of hounds when necessary; his grooms were his huntsmen; the village curate was his Grand Almoner.[4] They all called him "My Lord," and laughed heartily at his stories. The Baroness weighed about three hundred and fifty pounds, was therefore greatly respected, and did the honors of the house with a dignity which rendered her still more respectable. Her daughter Cunegonde, aged seventeen, was rosy-cheeked, fresh, plump and tempting. The Baron's son appeared in every respect worthy of his father. The tutor Pangloss was the oracle[5] of the house, and little Candide followed his lessons with all the **candor** of his age and character. Pangloss taught metaphysico-theologo-cosmolonigology. He proved admirably that there is no effect without a cause and that in this best of all possible worlds, My Lord the Baron's castle was the best of castles and his wife the best

---

1. *Baron Thunder-ten-tronckh* (bar′ən thun′dər ten träk) is a nobleman in *Westphalia* (west fä′lē ə), a region in northwestern Germany.
2. *Quarterings* are divisions in a coat of arms that symbolize connections among noble families. *Seventy-one quarterings* is an impossibly high number.
3. A *genealogical tree* is a family tree, a diagram showing family ancestry.

4. A *Grand Almoner* is the person charged with distributing *alms*, or charity, among the poor.
5. An *oracle* (ôr′ə kəl) here means a person of great knowledge or wisdom.

> **From the Enlightenment to Romanticism** *What Enlightenment value might a live-in tutor represent?* **2**

> **Vocabulary**
> **candor** (kan′dər) *n.* honesty or frankness; openness

> **Satire** *This castle is later called "very noble" and "the best of castles." What details reveal the truth about the castle's importance?*

1

VOLTAIRE **963**

Teach

Literary Element | 1

Satire Answer: *The castle has "a door and windows . . . [and] a piece of tapestry." In truth, the castle is not very important or noble.*

Big Idea | 2

From the Enlightenment to Romanticism Answer:
During the Enlightenment, education was revered and a live-in tutor was probably a fixture in most estates.

Language History ☆

The Persistence of Pangloss Pangloss, the tutor of Candide and Cunegonde, follows an extreme form of optimism, which he in turn teaches to his students. The adjective *Panglossian* entered the English lexicon in 1831 and means "blindly or naively optimistic."

Learning Objectives
Analyzing satire. (SE)
Distinguishing fact and opinion. (TE)

English Learners

DIFFERENTIATED INSTRUCTION

SMALL GROUP
Intermediate Have English learners form small groups and summarize what they have read. Have each student take turns summarizing the important traits of the characters and the setting. *(Students should recognize Candide's simplemindedness, innocence, attraction to Cunegonde and devotion to Pangloss; Cunegonde's beauty; and Pangloss's optimism and faulty logic. The castle grounds are noble, but ordinary, despite the exaggerated description.)*

Advanced Learners/Pre-AP

DIFFERENTIATED INSTRUCTION

Analyze Diction Have students identify examples of diction that reflect the noble characters and the time period in which the story is set *(baron, baroness, curate, lady, gentleman, tapestry, waiting-maid, quarterings, spectacles, breeches).*

Teach

Literary Element | 1

Satire Answer: *Pangloss comes to the obvious conclusion that there is no effect without a cause. His claim for a cause is ridiculous, however; bad eyesight led to the creation of eyeglasses, or spectacles, not the presence of an appendage to support them.*

Reading Strategy | 2

Apply Background Knowledge Answer: *The Baron does not want his daughter "corrupted" by becoming involved with a member of the lower classes. Perhaps the Baron is mindful of his own sister's experience with the illegitimate birth of Candide.*

 For additional practice using the reading skill or strategy, see Unit 5 Teaching Resources Book, p. 127.

of all possible Baronesses. " 'Tis demonstrated," said he, "that things cannot be otherwise; for, since everything is made for an end, everything is necessarily for the best end. Observe that noses were made to wear spectacles; and so we have spectacles. Legs were visibly instituted to be breeched, and we have breeches.[6] Stones were formed to be quarried and to build castles; and My Lord has a very noble castle; the greatest Baron in the province should have the best house; and as pigs were made to be eaten, we eat pork all the year round; consequently, those who have asserted that all is well talk nonsense; they ought to have said that all is for the best." Candide listened attentively and believed innocently; for he thought Mademoiselle Cunegonde extremely beautiful, although he was never bold enough to tell her so. He decided that after the happiness of being born Baron of Thunder-ten-tronckh, the second degree of happiness was to be Mademoiselle Cunegonde; the third, to see her every day; and the fourth to listen to Doctor Pangloss, the greatest philosopher of the province and therefore of the whole world. One day when Cunegonde was walking near the castle, in a little wood which was called The Park, she observed Doctor Pangloss in the bushes, giving a lesson in experimental physics to her mother's waiting-maid, a very pretty and docile[7] brunette. Mademoiselle Cunegonde had a great inclination for science and watched breathlessly the reiterated[8] experiments she witnessed; she observed clearly the Doctor's sufficient

reason, the effects and the causes, and returned home very much excited, **pensive**, filled with the desire of learning, reflecting that she might be the sufficient reason of young Candide and that he might be hers. On her way back to the castle she met Candide and blushed; Candide also blushed. She bade[9] him good morning in a hesitating voice; Candide replied without knowing what he was saying. Next day, when they left the table after dinner, Cunegonde and Candide found themselves behind a screen; Cunegonde dropped her handkerchief, Candide picked it up; she innocently held his hand; the young man innocently kissed the young lady's hand with remarkable **vivacity**, tenderness and grace; their lips met, their eyes sparkled, their knees trembled, their hands wandered. Baron Thunder-ten-tronckh passed near the screen, and, observing this cause and effect, expelled Candide from the castle by kicking him in the backside frequently and hard. Cunegonde swooned;[10] when she recovered her senses, the Baroness slapped her in the face; and all was in **consternation** in the noblest and most agreeable of all possible castles.

---

6. *Breeches* are pants or trousers.
7. *Docile* means "easy to manage or teach."
8. *Reiterated* means "repeated."

1 **Satire** *What kind of logical argument does Voltaire satirize here?*

---

9. *Bade* is the past tense of *bid*, in the sense of "to give, express, or declare."
10. *Swooned* means "fainted."

Apply Background Knowledge *Why does the Baron expel Candide from his castle?* | 2

Vocabulary

pensive (pen´siv) *adj.* thoughtful
vivacity (vi vas´ə te´) *n.* liveliness; animation
consternation (kon´stər nā´shən) *n.* great fear or shock; upset

Writing Practice

Write an Editorial Remind students about the techniques of persuasive writing, including logical and emotional appeals, and rhetorical devices such as parallelism, repetition, and rhetorical questions. In addition, note the need to avoid logical fallacies and propaganda techniques such as circular thinking and the use of broad generalizations.

Have students write an editorial from the perspective of Cunegonde to the *Westphalia Press*. In the editorial, briefly explain the events leading up to Candide's banishment from the castle, and request the Baron to take him back. Make sure students use the persuasive techniques to make their argument effective. Encourage students to match the character, voice, and perspective of Cunegonde as closely as possible when writing.

Encourage students to be as authentic as possible in their editorial. Allow them to use the type of reasoning with which Cunegonde would be most familiar (including emotional appeals and circular reasoning).

CHAPTER II

What Happened to Candide Among the Bulgarians[11]

Candide, expelled from the earthly paradise, wandered for a long time without knowing where he was going, turning up his eyes to Heaven, gazing back frequently at the noblest of castles which held the most beautiful of young Baronesses; he lay down to sleep supperless between two furrows in the open fields; it snowed heavily in large flakes. The next morning the shivering Candide, penniless, dying of cold and exhaustion, dragged himself toward the neighboring town, which was called Waldberghoff-trarbk-dikdorff. He halted sadly at the door of an inn. Two men dressed in blue noticed him. "Comrade," said one, "there's a well-built young man of the right height." They went up to Candide and very civilly invited him to dinner. "Gentlemen," said Candide with charming modesty, "you do me a great honor, but I have no money to pay my share." "Ah, sir," said one of the men in blue, "persons of your figure and merit never pay anything; are you not five feet five tall?" "Yes, gentlemen," said he, bowing, "that is my height." "Ah, sir, come to table; we will not only pay your expenses, we will never allow a man like you to be short of money; men were only made to help each other." "You are in the right," said Candide, "that is what Doctor Pangloss was always telling me, and I see that everything is for the best." They begged him to accept a few crowns,[12] he took them and wished to give them an I O U; they refused to take it and all sat down to table. "Do you not love tenderly . . ." "Oh, yes," said he. "I love Mademoiselle Cunegonde tenderly." "No," said one of the gentlemen. "We were asking if you do not tenderly love the King of the Bulgarians." "Not a bit," said he, "for I have never seen him." "What! He is the most charming of Kings, and you must drink his health." "Oh, gladly, gentlemen." And he drank. "That is sufficient," he was told. "You are now the support, the aid, the defender, the hero of the Bulgarians; your fortune is made and your glory assured." They immediately put irons on his legs and took him to a regiment.[13] He was made to turn to the right and left, to raise the ramrod[14] and return the ramrod, to take aim, to fire, to double up, and he was given thirty strokes with a stick; the next day he drilled not quite so badly, and received only twenty strokes; the day after, he only had ten and was looked on as a prodigy[15] by his comrades. Candide was completely mystified and could not make out how he was a hero. One fine spring day he thought he would take a walk, going straight ahead, in the belief that to use his legs as he pleased was a

---

11. *The Bulgarians* here refers to Frederick the Great's Prussian army.

12. *Crowns* are coins of various worth in different countries.
13. Candide is being forced into military service, in a Bulgarian *regiment*, or army unit.
14. A *ramrod* is a rod used to force (ram) gunpowder and ammunition into the barrel of a musket or firearm.
15. A *prodigy* is a person of unusual talent or genius.

> **Satire** *What kind of military recruiting practices do the two men in blue demonstrate in this passage?* **3**

Literary Element 3

Satire Answer: *They claim that, by drinking to the king's health, Candide has pledged allegiance to him. Actually, they are conscripting him, forcing him unwillingly—and unwittingly—into military service, a practice often done during that time.*

Progress Check

Can students identify satire?

If No → See Unit 5 Teaching Resources Book, p. 126.

Political History ☆

Seven Years' War Voltaire published *Candide* in 1759, in the middle of the Seven Years' War. The war took place between 1756 and 1763, and involved all the major forces of Europe. It began when Austria attempted to win back the province of Silesia from Prussia. Austria aligned with France and Russia, and Great Britain aligned with Prussia. During the European war, conflict extended outside Europe as well, as France and others fought Britain for colonial control in India and North America. Ultimately, Austria and its allies gave up the fight for Silesia, and Britain became the dominant colonial power overseas.

English Learners

DIFFERENTIATED INSTRUCTION

 Advanced Check that students understand why the Bulgarians take in Candide and offer him food and drink. *(They are conscripting him to serve for Bulgaria.)* In groups, have students paraphrase the events in Chapter II as necessary, using details in the text to infer what is happening to Candide. For example, the detail "two men dressed in blue" suggests that the men are in uniform. They describe Candide as a "well-built young man of the right height," suggesting that he meets a physical requirement. When they tell him "You are now the . . . defender, the hero of the Bulgarians," it becomes clear that Candide now has a noble responsibility to Bulgaria.

Learning Objectives
Analyzing satire. (SE)
Applying background knowledge. (SE)
Writing an editorial. (TE)

Teach

Big Idea · 1

From the Enlightenment to Romanticism **Answer:** *He claims to have free will, an Enlightenment ideal. That ideal is turned against him, however, when he is told his "liberty" is to choose between two unfavorable outcomes.*

Literary Element · 2

Allusion **Ask:** Why do you think the surgeon used ointments recommended by Dioscorides? *(Dioscorides was a physician from the first century who was a leading expert in his field.)*

Big Idea · 3

From the Enlightenment to Romanticism **Answer:** *Enlightenment scholars studied classical Greece and Rome; it is not surprising the doctor is reviving one of the old (and therefore, proven) remedies.*

 To check students' understanding of the selection, see Unit 5 Teaching Resources Book, p. 131.

Prelude. Oil on canvas. Boilly, Louis Leopold (1761-1845). Pushkin Museum, Moscow.

privilege of the human species as well as of animals. He had not gone two leagues[16] when four other heroes, each six feet tall, fell upon him, bound him and dragged him back to a cell. He was asked by his judges whether he would rather be thrashed thirty-six times by the whole regiment or receive a dozen lead bullets at once in his brain. Although he protested that men's wills are free and that he wanted neither one nor the other, he had to make a choice; by virtue of that gift of God which is called *liberty*, he

---

16. A *league* is a measure of distance roughly equivalent in some countries to three miles.

1 **From the Enlightenment to Romanticism** *How does Candide demonstrate his belief in Dr. Pangloss's version of Enlightenment philosophy?*

determined to run the gauntlet[17] thirty-six times and actually did so twice. There were two thousand men in the regiment. That made four thousand strokes which laid bare the muscles and nerves from his neck to his backside. As they were about to proceed to a third turn, Candide, utterly exhausted, begged as a favor that they would be so kind as to smash his head; he obtained this favor; they bound his eyes and he was made to kneel down. At that moment the King of the Bulgarians came by and inquired the victim's crime; and as this King was possessed of a vast genius, he perceived from what he learned about Candide that he was a young metaphysician[18] very ignorant in worldly matters, and therefore pardoned him with a **clemency** which will be praised in all newspapers and all ages. An honest surgeon healed Candide in three weeks with the ointments recommended by Dioscorides.[19] He had already regained a little skin and could walk when the King of the Bulgarians went to war with the King of the Abares.[20] ❧

---

17. In being forced to *run the gauntlet,* Candide must run between two rows of men who will beat him as he passes.
18. A *metaphysician* is a person who studies metaphysics, or the nature of reality.
19. *Dioscorides* (dī′əs kor ē dəs) was a Greek physician and pharmacologist of the first century A.D.
20. *Abares* here refers to the French.

From the Enlightenment to Romanticism *Why would this doctor treat Candide with ancient Greek remedies?* **3**

Vocabulary

clemency (klem′ən sē) *n.* mercy; leniency, especially toward an enemy

Writing Practice

Write an Autobiographical Narrative Remind students that an autobiography is a story of a person's life written by that person. Have students write an autobiographical narrative from the perspective of Candide, imagining that they have experienced everything he has experienced in the selection. Have students keep in mind Candide's naïveté as well as the optimistic worldview he learned from Doctor Pangloss. Have students use chronological order and vivid sensory details to recount the main events.

In addition, students should add personal thoughts and feelings Candide would have felt as the story events transpired. Have students include any insights Candide may have gained by the end of the selection, noting, in particular, whether his Panglossian worldview is still as unshakeable.

After You Read

Respond and Think Critically

Respond and Interpret

1. What surprised you most about this excerpt? Why?

2. (a)What is Candide's status at Baron Thunder-ten-tronckh's castle? (b)Summarize the circumstances that cause Candide to be expelled from the castle.

3. (a)How does Dr. Pangloss prove that "everything is made for an end"? (b)What conclusion does he draw from these examples?

4. (a)Why do the two men in blue comment on Candide's height? (b)Why do they want to meet him?

5. (a)Why can't Candide walk away from the Bulgarian regiment? (b)What are his options, and what is his choice?

Analyze and Evaluate

6. (a)How does the setting of this excerpt affect the plot? (b)Could the story take place in another time or place? Explain.

7. (a)Are Voltaire's characters three-dimensional and believable? Explain. (b)Why do you think Voltaire might have drawn his characters with the amount of detail he did?

Connect

8. **Big Idea** **From the Enlightenment to Romanticism** How does Dr. Pangloss demonstrate that he is a product of the Enlightenment? Explain.

9. **Connect to the Author** Voltaire, like Candide, suffered for his beliefs. How do you think the author's personal experiences might have affected his attitude toward his main character?

Primary Source Quotation

The Real Pangloss

Candide's tutor, Dr. Pangloss, is a satirical portrait of Gottfried Wilhelm Leibniz (1646–1716), a German philosopher, mathematician, metaphysician, historian, political adviser, and logician. One of his major areas of investigation involved the question of good and evil: Why does God allow horrible events such as murders, wars, and natural disasters? He concluded that:

"God has chosen the best of all possible worlds."

Humans who object that this cannot be the best of worlds because of the suffering in it are merely shortsighted, he argues; there is no way for us to know what may be the greatest good for all creation, and what seems to us to be evil may in fact be necessary on the cosmic scale. In *Candide*, Voltaire satirizes Leibniz's philosophy as simplistic, and to prove his point, he brutalizes his characters, kills them off, and brings them back to life, as if to say, "*Now* what do you think of your 'best of all possible worlds'?"

Gottfried Wilhelm von Leibniz.

Group Activity Discuss the following questions with your classmates.

1. How might you prove this is the best of all possible worlds?

2. How might you prove this is *not* the best of all possible worlds?

---

6. (a) The political and cultural setting contribute to the plot. (b) The story could occur anywhere class and intellectual snobbery and brutal military tactics were prevalent.

7. (a) The characters are comparatively shallow, two-dimensional, and not totally believable. They are types rather than well-rounded personalities. (b) Voltaire focused less on characterization than on proving his point.

8. Dr. Pangloss describes many respected Enlightenment philosophies, specifically Leibniz's widespread "best of all possible worlds" idea.

9. Because Voltaire suffered imprisonment and exile for his opinions, he might have been more understanding of Candide's problems. His experiences might also have made him impatient for Candide to learn more about the world so he could disprove Dr. Pangloss's optimism.

After You Read

Assess

1. Answers will vary.

2. (a) His status is undefined. He is simply allowed to live there, probably because he is the Baron's sister's illegitimate son. (b) Inspired by having seen Dr. Pangloss making love to the waiting-maid, Cunegonde flirts with Candide, and he responds. The Baron finds Candide and Cunegonde kissing behind a screen, and, fearful she might be "corrupted," he expels Candide.

3. (a) He uses the examples of noses, legs, stones, and pigs as causes for spectacles, pants, castles, and pork dinners. (b) He concludes that "everything is necessarily for the best end," and that this is the "best of all possible worlds."

4. (a) They may be noting that he has the physical attributes of a soldier, or that he will fit the army's uniforms. (b) They want to force him into military service.

5. (a) Candide is unwittingly deserting the army, an offense often punishable by death. (b) He is given the choice between execution or running the gauntlet, a brutally punishing sentence. He chooses the gauntlet.

Primary Source Quotation

1. Answers will vary; students may regard Leibniz's proof that an all-knowing, all-powerful god would not allow anything less as a compelling proof.

2. Answers will vary; students may point out many instances of seemingly needless suffering—the route Voltaire has chosen in writing *Candide*.

After You Read

Assess

Literary Element

(C) is the correct answer. We see Candide's character developing when he uses reason to argue before his judges.

Review: Narrator

1. third-person omniscient
2. The narrator's diction is formal and his tone superior; there is little feeling of concern for the characters.
3. The narrator makes fun of the characters instead of empathizing with them.

Reading Strategy

1. He doesn't understand what they want and believes what they say, thinking "men were only made to help each other."
2. He is given the "liberty" of two deadly choices, a perversion of the true meaing of the word.

Academic Vocabulary

Students' examples may involve poverty, prejudice, health care, or the environment.

Literary Element Satire

SAT Skills Practice

The primary satirical purpose of Chapter II is to

(A) illustrate the brutality of the Bulgarians
(B) show the punishment for desertion
(C) show that Candide adheres to what he has learned and what he knows to be true
(D) introduce the King of the Bulgarians
(E) question the concept of heroism

Review: Narrator

As you learned on page 637, a **narrator** is the person who tells a story. The narrator may be a character in the story or remain outside the story. The narrator's **point of view** may have a great effect on the story and the impressions it creates.

Narrative Points of View	
First Person	Narrator a character in story; uses *I* and *me*
Third-Person Omniscient	Narrator all-knowing; tells thoughts and feelings
Third-Person Limited	Narrator describes events as only one character perceives them

Partner Activity Work with a classmate to answer the following questions.

1. From what point of view is *Candide* told?
2. Describe the narrator's voice in terms of diction, tone, and concern for the characters and events.
3. In your opinion, what effect does Voltaire's use of the narrator have on his satirical effect?

 **Literature** Online

Selection Resources For Selection Quizzes, eFlashcards, and Reading-Writing Connection activities, go to glencoe.com and enter QuickPass code GLW6053u5.

Reading Strategy Apply Background Knowledge

Use your background knowledge to answer these questions. Consult the chart you made on page 961.

1. Why does Candide readily accept the hospitality of the "two men dressed in blue"?
2. How does "liberty" figure in Candide's having to run the gauntlet?

Vocabulary Practice

Practice with Word Origins Studying the etymology, or origin and history, of a word can help you better understand and explore its meaning. Create a word map like the one below for each boldfaced vocabulary word from the novel. Use a dictionary for help.

candor   pensive   vivacity
consternation   clemency

EXAMPLE:

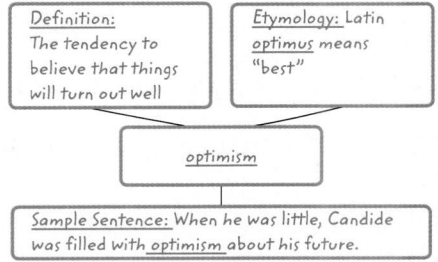

Academic Vocabulary

In Candide, *Voltaire uses the misadventures of his innocent hero to* **demonstrate** *the defects of European society.*

Demonstrate is an academic term meaning "to clearly show the nature of something by using examples." To further explore the meaning of this word, answer this question: What examples would you use to **demonstrate** flaws in society today?

For more on academic vocabulary, see pages 36–37 and R83–R85.

Vocabulary

candor
Definition: honesty or frankness; Etymology: Latin <u>candor</u> means "sincerity"; Sample Sentence: She noted the candidate's candor once others sidestepped the issue.

pensive
Definition: thoughtful; Etymology: Anglo-Norman <u>pensif</u> means "thoughtful";

Sample Sentence: He had a pensive look after the final exam, because he knew he hadn't done well.

vivacity
Definition: liveliness and high spirits; Etymology: Latin <u>vivicitas</u> means "natural vigor"; Sample Sentence: The child's vivacity was apparent, though he had played for hours.

consternation
Definition: great fear or shock; upset

Etymology: Latin <u>consterno</u> means "to throw into confusion"; <u>Sample Sentence</u>: The fans' consternation was apparent when their team lost.

clemency
Definition: mercy; leniency, especially toward an enemy; Etymology: Latin <u>clementia</u> means "mildness"; <u>Sample Sentence</u>: The president showed clemency in pardoning criminals.

Respond Through Writing

Expository Essay

Analyze Cause and Effect In *Candide*, Voltaire uses cause-and-effect relationships as one of his satirical strategies. For example, the Baroness is widely respected because she weighs 350 pounds. In a 1,500-word expository essay, explain how Voltaire uses cause and effect in Chapters 1 and 2 of *Candide* and analyze how this contributes to the overall tone of his fiction.

Understand the Task The **tone** of a literary work is the attitude an author takes toward the audience, a subject, or a character.

Prewrite Use a graphic organizer like the one below to get started. Then plan a sequence for presenting these details within your essay.

> *Cause:* The Baron's castle has a door and windows
>
> *Effect:* He is one of the most powerful lords in Westphalia
>
> *Relation to Tone:* Here Voltaire pokes fun at Westphalia by saying that simply having a castle with a door and windows makes the Baron one of Westphalia's most powerful lords. This exemplifies Voltaire's satiric tone.

Draft Structure your body paragraphs so that each presents a separate example of Voltaire's use of cause and effect. Include supporting evidence from the text to back up your ideas and explain how this evidence is meaningful.

Revise Review your draft to make sure you look beyond the literal meaning of the events in *Candide* in considering how causes and effects reflect a particular tone. Review the text as well as the background material on pages 960–961 to see if you left out any essential ideas. Before handing in your work, consider including a visual element within your essay. For example, you might create a map of Candide's travels annotated with various causes and effects and their meanings.

Edit and Proofread Proofread your paper, correcting any errors in spelling, grammar, and punctuation. Use the word count feature on a computer to determine that your paper is at least 1,500 words. Review the Grammar Tip in the side column for information on active and passive voice.

VOLTAIRE **969**

Learning Objective

In this assignment, you will focus on the following objectives:

Writing: Writing an expository essay.

Grammar: Understanding active and passive voice.

▶ Grammar Tip

Active and Passive Voice

An action verb is in the **active voice** when the subject of the verb performs the action. It is in the **passive voice** when its action is performed on the subject.

Voltaire attacked the social evils of his time. [active]

The social evils of his time were attacked by Voltaire. [passive]

The active voice usually creates a stronger impression than the passive. Passive voice can be effective when you do not want to call attention to who performed the action.

After You Read

Assess

Respond Through Writing

Students' expository essays should

- clearly state a thesis about how Voltaire's use of cause and effect contributes to the tone of *Candide*
- present examples of Voltaire's use of cause and effect in support of a thesis
- use active and passive voice correctly

 For grammar practice, see Unit 5 Teaching Resources Book, p. 130.

 To create custom assessments online, go to Progress Reporter Online Assessment.

 To create custom assessments using software, use ExamView Assessment Suite.

Advanced Learners/Pre-AP

DIFFERENTIATED INSTRUCTION

Analyze Active and Passive Voice
Have advanced students reread and analyze the following passage from page 964:

"'. . . since everything is made for an end, everything is necessarily for the best end. Observe that noses were made to wear spectacles; and so we have spectacles. Legs were visibly instituted to be breeched, and we have breeches…consequently, those who have asserted that all is well talk nonsense; they ought to have said that all is for the best.'" Have students note which parts of the passage are in passive voice and which are in active voice and analyze the overall effect. *(Each example follows the same pattern of a clause in passive voice followed by a clause in active voice. This parallelism emphasizes the examples and gives them the sound of a rational argument.*)

Focus

Learning Objectives

For pages 970–971

In studying this text, you will focus on the following objectives:

Literary Study: Analyzing literary periods.

Reading:
Evaluating historical influences.
Connecting to the literature.

Literary History

The Faust Legend

YOU HAVE PROBABLY HEARD THE EXPRESSIONS "SELL YOUR SOUL" OR "make a deal with the devil." These sayings originate with the Faust (foust) legend, a medieval tale in which a man trades his soul for knowledge. The legend of Faust (also called Faustus or Doctor Faustus) has been retold for more than four centuries.

Bellringer Option

Ask: Have you ever heard people say that they would sell their souls for something? **Say:** This expression is an idiom that has roots in the oldest of European folklore traditions. The story of Faust is from this tradition. Then **ask:** Is there anything you think would be worth making such a deal? *(Students might say that achieving wealth and fame, being given great talents, or being granted immortality would be worth selling their souls. Others will say nothing could be worth such a thing.)*

"Fate has given this man a spirit
Which is always pressing onwards, beyond control,
And whose mad striving overleaps
All joys of the earth between pole and pole.
Him shall I drag through the wilds of life
And through the flats of meaninglessness,
I shall make him flounder and gape and stick
And to tease his insatiableness
Hang meat and drink in the air before his watering lips;
In vain he will pray to slake his inner thirst,
And even had he not sold himself to the devil
He would be equally accursed."

—Mephistopheles, from *Faust* by Johann Wolfgang von Goethe

Faust and Mephistopheles, 1826-1827. (Ferdinand Victor) Eugene Delacroix. Wallace Collection, London, UK.

Rise of Faust

A real person in Germany, about whom little is known inspired the Faust legend. Several public documents and letters from the early sixteenth century mention a boastful wandering magician named George Faust, and accounts from several decades later tell of a Johannes Faust—probably the same man—who called the devil his "brother-in-law." By the mid-sixteenth century, people had begun to tell fantastical stories of a magician who had been given magical powers by the devil. In 1587, the earliest printed collection of these tales appeared. Known as the *Faustbuch*, or "Faust Book," it portrays Faust as a bold and selfish man who desires superhuman powers and knowledge. With the

aid of a devil named Mephistopheles (mef´ ə stof´ ə lēz´) (also known as Mephisto), Faust performs astounding feats of magic until he plunges to hell. Using dark humor, the *Faustbuch* stresses Christian values and warns of the consequences of a sinful life.

The first major literary adaptation of the legend was *The Tragical History of Doctor Faustus,* written in 1589 by the English dramatist Christopher Marlowe. The play portrays Faust as a "Renaissance man," obsessed with worldly knowledge and experience. The play retains the humor, sorcery, and final punishment found in the original tales. However, Marlowe's Doctor Faustus is an admirable man corrupted by power, rather than the power-hungry Faust depicted in the original.

Vocabulary Practice

Analyze Connotation Have students reread the display quote on page 970. Tell them to make a list of they key words they find in the quote, such as "fate," and "spirit." Begin by having them look at the key words from the first four lines of the quote. **Ask:**

1. What is the connotation of these words? *(Fairly positive)*

2. What kind of a picture do they paint of Faust? *(Faust seems to be an ambitious achiever.)*

Then have them look at the key words in the remaining lines of the quote. **Ask:**

1. What is the connotation of these words? *(Negative)*

2. What kind of tone do they create in the second portion of the passage?

(It seems menacing and cruel.)

Goethe's *Faust*

Johann Wolfgang von Goethe (gur′tə) embraced the heroic aspects of the Faust legend in his poetic drama *Faust* (1808–1832), which is considered the legend's greatest retelling. Growing up in Frankfurt am Main, Germany, in the mid-eighteenth century, Goethe became fascinated by the Faust legend after seeing it performed as a puppet play. An early version of Goethe's *Faust* reflects the ideas of the *Sturm und Drang*, or "Storm and Stress," movement. This movement spurred German Romanticism, which embraced the values of individualism and imagination. Goethe cast his Faust as a Romantic hero: idealistic, emotional, and hungry for knowledge.

Goethe's *Faust* transformed the traditionally bleak ending of the legend. A merciful God praises Faust's quest for knowledge and saves him from the fires of hell. The work also portrays the devil Mephistopheles in a new light—he is ironic, witty, and cynical. Part epic and part drama, Goethe's *Faust* includes an impressive range of verse forms, and critics view it as an ironic comment on the goals and limits of the Western intellectual tradition.

Modern Adaptations

The most highly regarded twentieth-century retelling of the Faust legend is the 1947 novel *Doctor Faustus* by the German author Thomas Mann. Narrating the life of a composer who makes a pact with the devil, the novel also serves as an allegory for the intellectual decline of Germany in the period before World War II.

In modern times, the Faust legend has been the basis for comic books, orchestral compositions, and films, including a famous 1926 version by the German director F. W. Murnau.

Opera Poster advertising Faust, 1875. T. Laval. Lithograph from engraving.

 Literature Online

Literature and Reading For more about the Faust legend, go to glencoe.com and enter QuickPass code GLW6053u5.

Respond and Think Critically

1. How did the Faust legend reinforce religious beliefs in the Middle Ages?

2. How did Romanticism influence Goethe's version of the legend?

3. What makes Goethe's version unique?

4. Why do you think the Faust legend continues to captivate people?

English Learners

DIFFERENTIATED INSTRUCTION

Advanced Ask English learners if they are aware of any similar myths or tales from their cultures, wherein a character gives up something very important in exchange for something they greatly desire. Have students share these stories with the class or write them in a journal that they can share later.

Advanced Learners/Pre-AP

DIFFERENTIATED INSTRUCTION

Create a Dialogue Christopher Marlowe wrote the Faust legend in the form of a drama. Have advanced students write short, one- to two-page dialogues in which a character makes a deal with a devil. The "devil" can be an actual demon, or it could be any figure of temptation. Make sure they give the Faust character a compelling reason to make such a deal.

Teach

Big Idea | 1

From the Enlightenment to Romanticism Ask: How do you think the depiction of Faust would have been different were it written during the Enlightenment? *(Students might note the following: his depiction would have been more negative; his dealing with the devil would have signaled corruption and seemed less forgivably human; the story might have focused on Faust as a member of society more than as an individual; he might have been shown as a seeker of knowledge who was corrupted and therefore flawed.)*

Assess

1. It warned people to behave piously and not to overstep the bounds of human knowledge.

2. Romanticism contributed to the vision of Faust as an individualistic man who was heroic in his imaginative pursuits.

3. It combines multiple genres, verse forms, and literary influences; it portrays Faust as a hero; it ends with Faust going to heaven instead of hell; and it presents Mephistopheles as an ironic, witty character.

4. Possible answers: The basic plot has many possible meanings and interpretations; the idea of having to make a difficult choice is universal and relevant to everyday life.

Before You Read

Focus

Bellringer Options

Selection Focus
   Transparency 59

Daily Language Practice
   Transparency 90

Or ask: Have you encountered a person or had an experience that you found both dangerous and irresistible? Guide students to describe what makes a person or an experience irresistible. Have students discuss what threshold they have for danger, and if danger can at times make someone or something more attractive.

Or ask: What are the most memorable representations of sadness you've encountered in literature or film? Suggest students discuss both portrayals of characters and depictions of symbolic images, such as a desolate landscape.

Before You Read

The Lorelei

Meet **Heinrich Heine**

(1797–1856)

Historians are not entirely sure when German poet Heinrich Heine (hīn´rikн hī´nə) was born, mostly because Heine refused to either confirm or deny the birth date most often attributed to him. This is just one of many controversies surrounding a poet whose work has remained popular over the course of nearly two centuries.

School Days Historians believe Heine was born into a Jewish family in Düsseldorf, one of four children. His family expected him to go into business, so in 1814 he enrolled in business school and later worked as an accountant. However, Heine was not cut out for such a career. His family soon decided he would be better off studying law. In 1819 he dutifully enrolled in the University of Bonne, but transferred to the University of Göttingen because of its reputation as a top law school. Heine never fit in with the students or faculty at Göttingen, and was expelled for engaging in a duel with a fellow student. He was allowed to return and finish his degree a few years later, but by that time he had found a publisher for his first volume of poems.

The Poet Emerges Heine began to win notoriety for his writing, but financial stability did not come with this praise. He traveled a great deal, searching in vain for a career option that would both suit him and pay his bills. In 1828 he took the only regularly paid job he would ever have—as editor of a magazine. He resigned after only six months. Yet even as he struggled to make a living, Heine was becoming a force on the German literary scene. By 1830, he had become a famous author. But he was plagued by the German government's censors, who disapproved of his moral and political views. In the spring of 1831, fearing he might be imprisoned, he emigrated to Paris where he received a warm welcome in French literary circles. He grew to love Paris and lived there the remainder of his life.

Set to Music "The Lorelei," a literary ballad about a supernatural creature, has been set to music by more than 25 composers. The poem became so popular that the anti-Semitic Nazis, who controlled Germany during the 1930s and early 1940s, did not remove the song from schoolbooks after they banned Heine's works along with those of other Jewish authors. Instead, editors described it as "a popular folk song, author unknown."

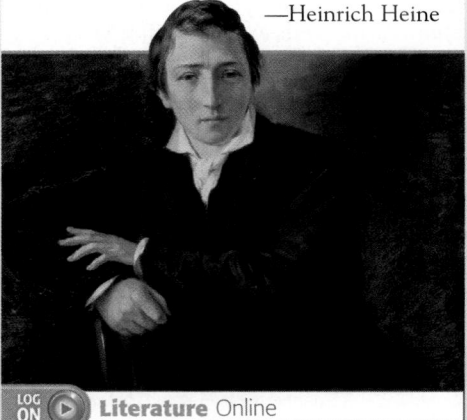

"Poetry hardly bears the process of exportation. To be rightly esteemed it needs to be enjoyed in the land of its birth, like tropical fruits."

—Heinrich Heine

LOG ON ▶ **Literature** Online

Author Search For more about Heinrich Heine, go to glencoe.com and enter QuickPass code GLW6053u5.

Selection Skills

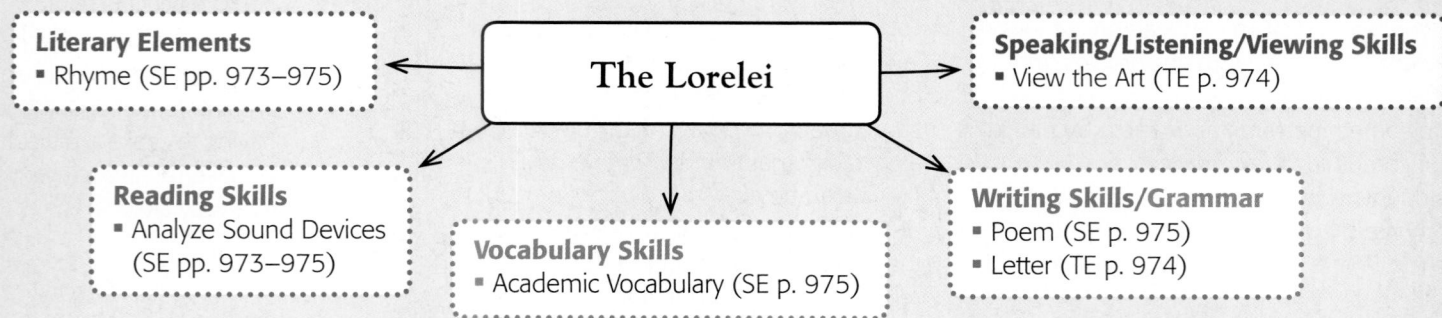

Literary Elements
- Rhyme (SE pp. 973–975)

The Lorelei

Speaking/Listening/Viewing Skills
- View the Art (TE p. 974)

Reading Skills
- Analyze Sound Devices (SE pp. 973–975)

Vocabulary Skills
- Academic Vocabulary (SE p. 975)

Writing Skills/Grammar
- Poem (SE p. 975)
- Letter (TE p. 974)

Literature and Reading Preview

Connect to the Poem

Have you ever experienced a sight or sound so beautiful it made you lose track of what was going on around you? Freewrite for a few minutes about this experience.

Build Background

The Lorelei, on the bank of the Rhine River, is a large rock that has always presented a danger to ships passing through the area. This danger, combined with an eerie echo produced by wind blowing through the rock, no doubt gave rise to the persistent stories about the spirit of a woman who would lure boatmen to their deaths with her beautiful singing. The first mention of this myth was not in Heine's poem, but rather in a ballad written by the German Romantic poet Clemens Maria Brentano.

Set Purposes for Reading

Big Idea From the Enlightenment to Romanticism

As you read "The Lorelei," ask yourself, How is Heine's poem an example of Romantic ideals of nature, passion, and imagination?

Literary Element Rhyme

Rhyme is a term that applies to several kinds of sound repetition. **End rhyme** occurs at the ends of lines of poetry. **Internal rhyme** occurs within a single line. **Slant rhyme** occurs when words include sounds that are similar but not identical. As you read, ask yourself, What kinds of rhyme does Heine use?

Reading Strategy Analyze Sound Devices

When you analyze the **sound devices** in a poem, you listen for the repetition of certain sounds. For example, **assonance** is the repetition of the same or similar vowel sounds in stressed syllables that end with different consonant sounds. **Consonance** is the repetition of consonant sounds at the ends of stressed syllables. **Alliteration** is the repetition of consonant sounds at the beginnings of words. As you read, ask yourself, What kinds of sound devices help me understand the events in the poem?

Tip: Track Details You can take notes to identify and analyze examples of various kinds of rhyme.

Passage	Sound Device	Effect
"A girl sits high up there; Her golden jewelry glistens ..."	alliteration	The repeated g sound creates a lilting song-like feeling.

Learning Objectives

For pages 972–975

In studying this text, you will focus on the following objectives:

Literary Study: Analyzing rhyme.

Reading: Analyzing sound devices.

Writing: Writing a poem.

River Rhine and legendary Rock of Loreley near Goarshausen, Germany.

Before You Read

Focus

Summary

The speaker is troubled by the following fable: as night falls, a boatman is lured off course by a mysterious woman's beautiful song, leading him to ignore the perilous rocks in the Rhine, thereby sinking his boat.

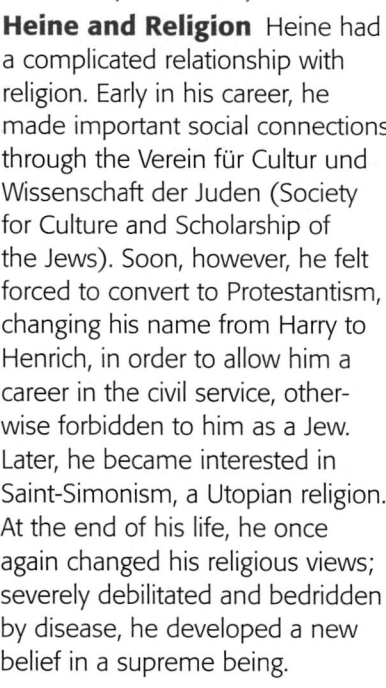 For summaries in languages other than English, see Unit 5 Teaching Resources Book, pp. 135–140.

Literary History ☆

Heine and Religion Heine had a complicated relationship with religion. Early in his career, he made important social connections through the Verein für Cultur und Wissenschaft der Juden (Society for Culture and Scholarship of the Jews). Soon, however, he felt forced to convert to Protestantism, changing his name from Harry to Henrich, in order to allow him a career in the civil service, otherwise forbidden to him as a Jew. Later, he became interested in Saint-Simonism, a Utopian religion. At the end of his life, he once again changed his religious views; severely debilitated and bedridden by disease, he developed a new belief in a supreme being.

English Learners

DIFFERENTIATED INSTRUCTION

Intermediate To help students comprehend the plot, have them work though the poem by picking out the events that occur in the text. *(Students may understand the poem in its simplest form: A girl is sitting on a rock next to the river combing her hair and singing a song when a boatman sails by and is mesmerized by her voice. He ignores the rocks in the water, is swallowed by the waves, cries out, and drowns)*

Advanced Learners/Pre-AP

DIFFERENTIATED INSTRUCTION

Analyze Theme Ask students to think creatively about the theme of the poem. Suggest that the theme is probably larger than a simple moral. Discuss this in a large group, allowing the discussion to turn in various directions. **Ask:** Based on this poem, what conclusion can you draw about Heine's Romanticism? *(Some students might think he embraces and glorifies nature and beauty; others might think he warns against embracing them.)*

Teach

Literary Element

Rhyme Answer: *There and hair are examples of true rhyme; vision and glisten are examples of slant rhyme.*

Reading Strategy

**Analyze Sound Devices
Answer:** *The long "o" sounds in the repetition of the words* comb, gold, *and* golden *create assonance. The assonance creates a hollow sound that recalls an echo, and this effect helps the reader perceive the Lorelei as a haunting, omnipresent spirit.*

 For additional practice using the reading skill or strategy, see Unit 5 Teaching Resources Book, p. 142.

 To check students' understanding of the selection, see Unit 5 Teaching Resources Book, p. 143.

View the Art ★

Mythical Women The Sirens (described in Homer's *Odyssey*), like the Lorelei, sang songs to lure sailors to their deaths. Charles Landelle painted this draped Siren in his characteristic soft, pale style.
Ask: How does this painting embody your understanding of the Lorelei? *(Answers will vary, but students might say the Siren is portrayed as a mesmerizing and beautiful woman like the poem's Lorelei.)* **Then ask:** How is this Siren like the Lorelei? *(Both are ideally beautiful, and both lure sailors to their destruction. Both seem to suggest certain kinds of beauty may be dangerous. Both are magical creatures.)*

The Lorelei

Heinrich Heine
Translated by Aaron Kramer

I cannot explain the sadness
That's fallen on my breast.
An old, old fable haunts me,
And will not let me rest.

5 The air grows cool in the twilight,
And softly the Rhine flows on;
The peak of a mountain sparkles
Beneath the setting sun.

More lovely than a vision,
10 A girl sits high up there;
Her golden jewelry glistens,
She combs her golden hair.

With a comb of gold she combs it,
And sings an evensong;[1]
15 The wonderful melody reaches
A boat, as it sails along.

The boatman hears, with an anguish
More wild than was ever known;
He's blind to the rocks around him;
20 His eyes are for her alone.

—At last the waves devoured
The boat, and the boatman's cry;
And this she did with her singing,
The golden Lorelei.

---

1. *Evensong* is a prayerful song sung late in the afternoon or in the evening.

Rhyme *What examples of true and slant rhyme can you find in this stanza?*

Analyze Sound Devices *Identify the assonance in lines 11–13. How does it add to the poem?*

The Siren, 1879. Charles Landelle (French 1821-1908). Oil on canvas. Russell-Cotes Art Gallery and Museum, Bournemouth, UK. ★

Writing Practice

Write a Letter In this poem, the boatman dies because the beautiful Lorelei's singing enchants him. Have students write an advice column to sailors, suggesting ways to avoid the Lorelei's spell. Or, if students prefer, have them write a letter to the Lorelei that informs her of the effect she has on sailors. Then suggest that they write a few paragraphs from the Lorelei's point of view, explaining her actions.

After You Read

Respond and Think Critically

Respond and Interpret

1. Which images from this poem linger in your mind? Share your response with the class.

2. (a)What is the "old, old fable" that has been troubling the speaker? (b)Why do you think he is troubled by this?

3. (a)What does the girl in the legend do? (b)Do you think she is a real person? Explain.

Analyze and Evaluate

4. (a)In creating the image of the girl, which features does the poet emphasize? (b)Why do you think he uses this imagery?

5. (a)How is the ending of the poem ironic, or unexpected? (b)How does this irony connect to the poem's theme?

Connect

6. **Big Idea** From the Enlightenment to Romanticism (a)What do you think the girl's singing symbolizes? (b)In what way does this reflect the ideals of the Romantic period?

7. **Connect to Today** Does "The Lorelei" remind you of any contemporary poems or songs you know? Explain.

Literary Element Rhyme

When words sound similar but do not rhyme exactly (like *alone* and *belong*), they are called **half-rhymes** or **slant rhymes**. A poem's rhyme scheme can be expressed by letters indicating the pattern of rhymes that occur at the ends of lines (for example, *aabb* or *abab*).

1. What is the rhyme scheme of "The Lorelei"?

2. Identify two examples of half-rhyme in this translation of the poem.

Reading Strategy Analyze Sound Devices

An unstressed syllable at the end of a line is called a feminine ending, while a stressed syllable at the end of a line is known as a masculine ending.

1. Read the poem aloud to yourself. Which lines have feminine endings?

2. Identify an example of consonance in line 7 and of assonance in lines 18–20.

LOG ON **Literature** Online

Selection Resources For Selection Quizzes, eFlashcards, and Reading-Writing Connection activities, go to glencoe.com and enter QuickPass code GLW6053u5.

Academic Vocabulary

"More lovely than a vision, / A girl sits high up there"

—Heinrich Heine, "The Lorelei"

Vision is an academic word. In more casual conversation, you might say you have 20/20 **vision** if you have perfect eyesight. To explore this word further, write and answer a question about "The Lorelei" using the word *vision*.

For more on academic vocabulary, see pages 36–37 and R83–R85.

Writing

Write a Poem Heine uses sound devices to make "The Lorelei" pleasing to the ear. Using Heine's style as a model, write a poem about an experience you've had with something beautiful. Refer to the chart you made on page 973 about sound devices in "The Lorelei" for devices to use in your own poem.

HEINRICH HEINE **975**

Academic Vocabulary

Questions and answers will vary.

Writing

Students' poems should
- have "beauty" as a subject
- use sound devices such as assonance, consonance, alliteration, or rhyme

Reading Strategy

1. Students should recognize the first and third lines have feminine endings.

2. The "k" sounds in *peak* and *sparkles* in line 7 offer an example of consonance. The long "i" sounds in *wild*, *blind*, and *eyes* in lines 18–20 form an example of assonance.

After You Read

Assess

1. Answers will vary.

2. (a) It is the legend of the Lorelei. (b) The legend ends in tragedy, and the speaker is deeply affected by the pathos of the scene.

3. (a) She sits on the mountain, combing her golden hair and singing an enchanting song. (b) The poem suggests she is not real, being "more lovely than a vision."

4. (a) He compares her jewelry, hair, and comb to gold. (b) The gleaming of the gold suggests the last rays of the sun and also suggests the elements of a fairy tale.

5. (a) It is ironic that something so wondrously beautiful causes destruction. (b) Beauty and passion have a dark side and can lead to ruin.

6. (a) It may symbolize hopeless love or a consuming passion. (b) Poets of the Romantic period praised passion, nature, and the power of the imagination. This poem touches on all three elements.

7. Students should cite examples of the similarities between "The Lorelei" and other poems and songs they have heard or read.

Literary Element

1. *abcb*

2. *on/sun, vision/glistens*

Progress Check

Can students identify slant rhymes?

If No → See Unit 5 Teaching Resources Book, p. 141.

Before You Read

Focus

Bellringer Options

Daily Language Practice Transparency 91

Or ask: How is war portrayed through literary or other mediums? Have students brainstorm a list of movies, television shows, and books that depict war. Then have them consider how war is depicted there.

Cultural History ☆

Napoleon in Russia When Napoleon's forces first entered Russia in June of 1812, they numbered 600,000. After reaching Moscow, however (most of which was destroyed in a fire the same day), Napoleon was unable to corner the Russian army. Forced to retreat, the French army was caught in an unusually early winter. By the time the forces crossed the Berezina River in November of 1812, fewer than 10,000 soldiers were left to fight.

Before You Read

France

Russia 1812 from *The Expiation*

Meet **Victor Hugo**
(1802–1885)

In an age marked by political and cultural upheaval, Victor Hugo became one of France's most famous poets, novelists, playwrights, and statesmen—a creative genius with an unforgettable personality. As a leader of the Romantic movement, which emphasized emotion and imagination rather than reason, Hugo introduced important innovations in French poetry and mixed what he called "the grotesque" with the sublime.

The "Prince of Poets" Hugo's father was a major and later a general in Napoleon Bonaparte's army. Hugo, his mother, and two older brothers traveled extensively, following their father's posting to different locations such as Madrid, Spain and Naples, Italy. It was during these trips abroad that Hugo first witnessed the poverty and suffering of the lower and middle classes. These experiences would leave a lasting impression on the young author, and his views of the ruling class's hold on the lower and middle classes became a familiar topic in many of his literary works.

It was not until his mother settled the family in Paris that Hugo began to hone his writing style. With his mother's support, Hugo published his first literary magazine, the *Conservateur Litteraire* (1819–1821). Hugo soon made friends with other authors who shared similar beliefs and found an outlet for his liberal views in the Romantic movement. Using his work as a platform to express his political and social views, he quickly emerged as a champion of social and political free thought. In 1831, he published his most famous work, *The Hunchback of Notre Dame*—a novel that described the problems and sufferings of the poor.

"What is said about men often has as much influence upon their lives, and especially upon their destinies, as what they do."

—Victor Hugo

A National Hero Hugo's creative genius was soon rewarded with political posts—until Louis Napoleon (later Napoleon III) seized power. Hugo's opposition to Napoleon's rule drove him into exile in 1851, but not into silence. During his nearly twenty years abroad, he continued to challenge the authoritarian hold on his homeland by publishing works that spread his liberal views to the masses. In exile he wrote some of his most famous works, including his protest novel *Les Misérables* and *The Expiation*, a narrative poem about the career of Napoleon I. Hugo was welcomed back to France when a new republican government came to power in 1870. Fifteen years later, his funeral was attended by two million people, including delegates from every European country. As fellow French poet Charles Baudelaire claimed, "No artist is more universal than he."

 **Literature** Online

Author Search For more about Victor Hugo, go to glencoe.com and enter QuickPass code GLW6053u5.

Selection Skills

Literary Elements
- Antagonist (SE pp. 977, 979–981)
- Metaphor (SE p. 981)
- Mood (TE p. 979)

Reading Skills
- Visualize (SE pp. 977–979, 982)
- Analyze Plot (TE p. 978)

Russia 1812

Vocabulary Skills
- Synonyms (SE pp. 977, 982)
- Academic Vocabulary (SE p. 982)

Speaking/Listening/Viewing Skills
- Oral Interpretation (SE p. 982)
- Analyze Art (SE p. 980)

Writing Skills/Grammar
- Infinitives (TE p. 980)

Literature and Reading Preview

Connect to the Poem

Can a leader suffer a loss and still be considered a hero? Discuss this question with a partner.

Build Background

☆ Napoleon I controlled much of Europe at the time he invaded Russia in 1812. He expected a quick victory against Czar Alexander I, but the Russians retreated, luring the French deeper into their territory. Napoleon entered Moscow, which the Russians had abandoned, in mid-September. The fierce winter and attacks from the Russians nearly destroyed Napoleon's Grand Army. The defeat marked the beginning of the end for Napoleon, as it emboldened his enemies and forced him to abdicate and go into exile within two years. Hugo saw Napoleon as both a tyrant and a hero. In the following poem, he shows how the emperor's eventual downfall paid for, or "expiated," his political crime of seizing power illegally.

Set Purposes for Reading

Big Idea From the Enlightenment to Romanticism

As you read, ask yourself, How does Hugo's description of war relate to Romantic ideals?

Literary Element Antagonist

In a literary work, the **antagonist** is the person, group of people, or force (such as nature or society) opposing the protagonist, or main character. As you read "Russia 1812," ask yourself, How does the weather affect the soldiers and Napoleon?

Reading Strategy Visualize

When you **visualize** you form pictures in your mind. By using your imagination to visualize an author's details, you can understand the characters, actions, and setting more deeply. As you read, ask yourself, How do the speaker's images help readers experience the misery felt by the retreating men?

....

Tip: Classify Details As you read, use a chart like the one below to track details about Napoleon, the soldiers, and the weather.

Napoleon	Weather	Soldiers
Bowed his head for the first time.	"Snow rained down in blizzards."	

Learning Objectives

For pages 976–982

Literary Study: Analyzing antagonist.

Reading: Visualizing.

Listening and Speaking: Presenting an oral interpretation.

Vocabulary

solitude (sol′ə tōōd′) *n.* state of being alone; isolation; p. 979 *The prisoner sat in solitude, isolated from the other inmates.*

obsessed (əb sesd′) *adj.* having an excessive concern; p. 979 *The general was obsessed with the idea that there was a spy in his camp.*

....

Tip: Synonyms Synonyms are words that have the same or similar meanings. Identifying the meaning of one synonym in a sentence can help you recognize the meaning of the other. In the first sample sentence above, *solitude* and *isolated* are synonyms.

Before You Read

Focus
Summary

In this excerpt, Hugo describes the retreat from Moscow of Napoleon's once-proud army. He recalls the savagery of the weather, the Cossacks who badger the army, and the soldiers' struggle to survive. Yet through it all, the army remains loyal to Napoleon, who calls out to God, asking whether this is the end, and receives the reply "No, Napoleon."

 For summaries in languages other than English, see Unit 5 Teaching Resources Book, pp. 145–150.

Vocabulary

Tell a Story Divide students into small groups. Write the list of vocabulary words on the board. Instruct them to go around in a circle and tell a story, each telling one sentence at a time. Each sentence, however, must correctly use one of the vocabulary words. Give them three minutes in which to tell their stories.

 For additional vocabulary practice, see Unit 5 Teaching Resources Book, p. 153.

Advanced Learners/Pre-AP

DIFFERENTIATED INSTRUCTION

Research Suggest that interested students do some outside research on Russia in 1812 and Napoleon's invasion. Have students consider the following questions: What was going on in the early nineteenth century that caused such an invasion? In what ways was Napoleon a good leader? Why were his troops so loyal? Have students summarize their findings and deliver an oral presentation.

English Learners

DIFFERENTIATED INSTRUCTION

Intermediate Have English learners work with partners as they read the poem. Suggest that, after reading every nine or ten lines, they take turns telling one another what happened in that section. Encourage them to use the footnotes to interpret unfamiliar terms. When students are comfortable with the content of the poem, suggest they take turns reading it aloud to one another.

Teach

Vocabulary 1

Borrowed Words Remind students that English has "borrowed" many words from other languages. For example, point out that *vanguard* (line 9) derives from a French term, *avant-garde*, and that many military terms still in use in English were adopted from French. Have students look up the origins of the following terms in a dictionary: *aide-de-camp, bivouac, cadet, caisson, echelon, liaison, lieutenant, reveille, sortie.*

Reading Strategy 2

Visualize Answer: *The white of the snow predominates. The effect is chilling and distressing.*

(APPROACHING) Ask approaching level students to think about how color functions in writing. How does it help the reader grasp ideas? *(It helps the reader visualize and experience the poem physically.)*

RUSSIA 1812

Napoleon's Retreat From Moscow. Adolf Northen (German, 1828–1876) Private collection.

from THE EXPIATION

Victor Hugo
Translated by Robert Lowell

The snow fell, and its power was multiplied.
For the first time the Eagle° bowed its head—
dark days! Slowly the Emperor returned—
behind him Moscow! Its onion domes° still burned.
5　The snow rained down in blizzards—rained and froze.
Past each white waste a further white waste rose.
None recognized the captains or the flags.
Yesterday the Grand Army, today its dregs!
1 No one could tell the vanguard from the flanks.°
10　The snow! The hurt men struggled from the ranks,
hid in the bellies of dead horse, in stacks
of shattered caissons. By the bivouacs,°
one saw the picket° dying at his post,

---

2 Eagle: Napoleon, who took the eagle as his standard. Napoleon required his troops to swear by this standard that they would conquer or die.

4 onion domes: domes of Eastern Orthodox churches.

9 vanguard: the front division of an army. flanks: an army's sides.

12 caissons (kā′sənz): chests that hold ammunition or carts for ammunition. bivouacs: temporary encampments.

13 picket: here, a sentry.

---

2 Visualize *What is the predominant color in this description? What emotions does this scene evoke?*

Reading Practice

Analyze Plot "Russia 1812" is an example of a narrative poem, meaning it tells a story. One characteristic of a story is that it has a beginning, a middle, and an end. A story usually has a climax, the point of greatest interest or emotional tension in a literary work, sometimes referred to as the "turning point."

Have pairs of students take turns reading the poem aloud to each other, focusing on the places in the poem that elicit an emotional response. Read the poem aloud twice to the class. The first time, just have them listen closely to the poem. The second time, however, have students raise their hands when they think they hear the climax.

still standing in his saddle, white with frost,
15   the stone lips frozen to the bugle's mouth!

3 Bullets and grapeshot° mingled with the snow,
that hailed . . . The Guard, surprised at shivering, march
in a dream now; ice rimes° the gray mustache.
The snow falls, always snow! The driving mire
20   submerges; men, trapped in that white empire,
have no more bread and march on barefoot—gaps!
They were no longer living men and troops,
but a dream drifting in a fog, a mystery,
mourners parading under the black sky.
25   The **solitude**, vast, terrible to the eye,
was like a mute avenger everywhere,
as snowfall, floating through the quiet air,
buried the huge army in a huge shroud.°
Could anyone leave this kingdom? A crowd—
30   each man, **obsessed** with dying, was alone.
Men slept—and died! The beaten mob sludged on,
ditching the guns to burn their carriages.
Two foes. The North, the Czar. The North was worse.
In hollows where the snow was piling up,
35   one saw whole regiments fallen asleep.
Attila's dawn, Cannaes of Hannibal!°
The army marching to its funeral!
Litters,° wounded, the dead, deserters—swarm,
crushing the bridges down to cross a stream.
40   They went to sleep ten thousand, woke up four.°
Ney,° bringing up the former army's rear,
hacked his horse loose from three disputing Cossacks . . .
All night, the *qui vive?*° The alert! Attacks;
retreats! White ghosts would wrench away our guns,
45   or we would see dim, terrible squadrons,
circles of steel, whirlpools of savages,
rush sabering through the camp like dervishes.°
And in this way, whole armies died at night.

The Emperor was there, standing—he saw.
50   This oak already trembling from the axe,
watched his glories drop from him branch by branch:

---

16 **grapeshot:** small metal balls fired from cannons.

18 **rime:** to cover with ice.

28 **shroud:** a sheet in which a corpse is wrapped before burial.

36 **Attila:** ruler of the Huns (c. 406–453). Called "the Scourge of God," he plagued both the Roman and Byzantine empires. **Hannibal:** the Carthaginian general (247–183 B.C.) also fought against Rome. Hugo suggests that the winter (the North) gave Napoleon as much trouble as Attila and Hannibal gave ancient Rome.

38 **Litters:** stretchers.

40 **ten thousand, woke up four:** Napoleon's losses during this trek might have been as many as 500,000 soldiers (in an army of 600,000 to 700,000).

41 **Ney** (nā): Napoleon's second in command during this campaign.

43 *qui vive* (kē vēv): "long live who?" is the challenge of a sentry in French (similar to "who goes there?").

47 **dervishes:** a sect of Islam that is known for the whirling dances performed (sometimes with sabers, or swords) in religious ceremonies.

---

4 Antagonist *How does Hugo describe the snow? How has it become the men's antagonist?*

5 Visualize *What has happened to these men? How do you visualize them?*

Vocabulary

solitude (sol′ə to̅o̅d′) *n.* state of being alone; isolation

obsessed (əb sesd′) *adj.* having an excessive concern

VICTOR HUGO **979**

Teach

Literary Element 3

Mood **Ask:** What kind of a mood does Hugo create here? *(confusing, suspenseful, dangerous)*

Literary Element 4

Antagonist **Answer:** *"Mute avenger" and "huge shroud" are metaphors used to describe the snow. The men seem to be lost in the freezing, empty landscape. The snow and cold have replaced their human enemy.*

ENGLISH LEARNERS Point out these lines to English learners: "Two foes. The North, the Czar. The North was worse." Explain that this is an example of personification, where a non-human element is given human characteristics; here, the winter weather ("The North") is the foe against which the soldiers struggle.

Reading Strategy 5

Visualize **Answer:** *They have died. They welcome death as a sleep to end their suffering.*

Learning Objectives
Visualizing. (SE)
Identifying the antagonist. (SE)
Analyzing borrowed words. (TE)
Analyzing plot. (TE)

Advanced Learners/Pre-AP

DIFFERENTIATED INSTRUCTION

Write a Letter Ask students to imagine they are French soldiers in the war. Have them draft letters to friends or family members explaining the conditions of war and how they feel fighting under Napoleon. Tell them that they should use the poem as a jumping-off point and that they need not worry too much about the historical or textual accuracy of their letters.

For students who are interested in French history and/or literature, suggest they read Victor Hugo's famous *Les Miserables*. While they read, suggest that they note places in the text that are of particular interest. Invite them to share these passages with the class, if they are relevant to the selection.

Teach

Literary Element   1

Antagonist Answer: *He remains a symbol of strength and hope. In spite of their suffering, they believe he can lead them safely home.*

 To check students' understanding of the selection, see Unit 5 Teaching Resources Book, p. 154.

View the Art

Answer: *The mood of both painting and poem is gloomy, picturing relentless snow, deprivation, and death.*

This painting of French soldiers may arouse sympathy in contemporary viewers, but the artist probably strove for a different response. Many nineteenth-century Europeans regarded the memory of Napoleon with hostility. **Ask:** How does this painting depict the actual event? *(The painting depicts the hardships that resulted from the intolerable weather and lack of resources.)*

The Remains of the Grande Armee on the Retreat from Russia 1812, 1890. Carl Röchling. Color print after a gouache.

View the Art The lack of supplies and the frigid Russian winter inflicted unspeakable suffering on Napoleon's troops. How would you describe the mood of this painting? How is it similar to the mood of the poem at this point? ★

chiefs, soldiers. Each one had his turn and chance—
they died! Some lived. These still believed his star,
and kept their watch. They loved the man of war,
55 this small man with his hands behind his back,
whose shadow, moving to and fro, was black
behind the lighted tent. Still believing, they
accused their destiny of *lèse-majesté.*°
His misfortune had mounted on their back.
60 The man of glory shook. Cold stupefied
him, then suddenly he felt terrified.
Being without belief, he turned to God:
"God of armies, is this the end?" he cried.
And then at last the expiation came,
65 as he heard someone call him by his name,
someone half-lost in shadow, who said, "No,
Napoleon." Napoleon understood,
restless, bareheaded, leaden, as he stood
before his butchered legions in the snow.

58 **lèse-majesté** (lez´ ma´zhes tā´): the crime of insulting a ruler. Here, it is the weather that has committed the crime against Napoleon.

1 Antagonist *Why do the soldiers remain loyal to Napoleon even though he has brought them to certain death?*

Grammar Practice

Infinitives Remind students that an infinitive is the word *to* plus the base form of a verb: *to play, to study*. Good writers usually avoid putting words between the word *to* and the verb to avoid awkwardness. For example, "They had to stop frequently on the long march," instead of "They had to frequently stop on the long march."

Write the following sentences on the board and have the students identify the infinitive in each:

1. The exhausted soldiers struggled to move on. *(to move)*

2. The snow continued to come down, covering everything in sight. *(to come)*

3. It was impossible to distinguish the vanguard from the flanks. *(to distinguish)*

After You Read

Respond and Think Critically

Respond and Interpret

1. How did you feel about Napoleon and the soldiers? Explain.

2. (a)What is happening as the poem begins? (b)What does this suggest about the situation?

3. (a)Whose thoughts and feelings are described in the poem? (b)Whose thoughts and feelings are omitted?

4. How do you interpret Napoleon's reaction to the voice that says this is not the end?

Analyze and Evaluate

5. **Tone** is the attitude a speaker takes toward the audience, the subject, or a character. What is the speaker's tone in "Russia 1812"?

Literary Element Antagonist

SAT Skills Practice

1. Snow is a major antagonist in the poem. Which trait best describes the snow?

   (A) powerless

   (B) kindly

   (C) gentle

   (D) mysterious

   (E) malevolent

2. Refer to lines 60–69. How does the speaker feel about the campaign and retreat?

   (A) The Russians were sadistic in burning their fields before Napoleon's army arrived.

   (B) Napoleon deserved this disaster.

   (C) Napoleon was a great leader who stood boldly in the worst of circumstances.

   (D) God chose to ruin Napoleon.

   (E) Napoleon's campaign was a tragedy.

6. (a)Which images in the poem suggest extreme cold? (b)Why might Hugo have chosen to repeat the word *snow* so many times in the poem?

7. Is Hugo's portrait of Napoleon sympathetic or unsympathetic? Explain.

8. Do you think Hugo glamorizes war? Give examples from the poem to support your answer.

Connect

9. **Big Idea** From the Enlightenment to Romanticism (a)How does Hugo emphasize nature and passion in this poem? (b)What is the effect of this emphasis?

10. **Connect to Today** What kind of weather might challenge soldiers in a modern war?

Review: Metaphor

As you learned on page 767, a **metaphor** is a figure of speech that compares two seemingly unlike things without using the word *like* or *as*. In contrast to a simile, a metaphor implies the comparison instead of stating it directly.

Partner Activity Hugo uses metaphors throughout "Russia 1812" to capture the extreme hardships the soldiers endure.

"The snow falls, always snow! The driving mire submerges; men, trapped in that white empire, have no more bread and march on barefoot—
gaps!
They were no longer living men and troops, but a dream drifting in a fog, a mystery, mourners parading under the back sky."

1. Identify each metaphor in the excerpt above.

2. In the poem, what metaphor describes Napoleon as his army is being destroyed?

After You Read

Assess

1. Answers will vary.

2. (a) Napoleon's army is retreating from Moscow in the winter of 1812. (b) The once-proud Napoleon is getting his first taste of a major defeat.

3. (a) those of the French army (b) those of the Russian army

4. The dejected Napoleon seems to believe that he has reason to continue fighting.

5. mournful and solemn

6. (a) the repeated mention of snow falling and covering everything; men hiding in the bellies of dead horses (b) The repetition mimics the endless falling of the snow and the accumulation of hardship.

7. Answers will vary. Students should support their answers.

8. Students may say he does not glamorize war because he emphasizes suffering rather than acts of heroism.

9. (a) Hugo uses vivid imagery and sensory details to describe the horrible weather and the men's loyalty to Napoleon. (b) The poem becomes more about the harsh reality of war.

10. Students may point to conflicts in the Middle East with desert conditions of heat and wind.

Literary Element

1. **(E)** is the correct answer. The snow is powerful and seems to have a malicious intention toward Napoleon's army. The snow "buried the huge army in a huge shroud."

2. **(B)** is the correct answer. The title of the poem implies that what is described is Napoleon's punishment.

Progress Check

Can students identify an antagonist?

If No → See Unit 5 Teaching Resources Book, p. 151.

Review: Metaphor

1. "white empire"; "dream drifting in a fog, a mystery"; "mourners parading"

2. He is compared to an oak whose branches are being chopped off one by one.

After You Read

Assess

Reading Strategy

1. (a) They show the seriousness of the situation and the loyalty and fear of the men. (b) They show the total failure of the campaign.

2. (a) The theme is that the crimes of the ruling class are often paid for by the masses. Napoleon illegally gained control of France, and his tyranny cost the lives of thousands. (b) The details of the men's struggle show how loyal followers paid for their leader's crimes.

Progress Check

Can students visualize?

If No → See Unit 5 Teaching Resources Book, p. 152.

Vocabulary

1. b 2. c

Reading Strategy Visualize

"Russia 1812" is a narrative poem, or a poem that tells a story. Hugo uses descriptive language to help the reader **visualize** the setting, the characters, and the action.

1. (a)What do the descriptions help you "see" and understand about the men and the war? (b)What do the details suggest about the war?

2. (a)What is the theme of the poem? (b)How do the details help you understand the theme?

Vocabulary Practice

Practice with Synonyms A synonym is a word that has the same or nearly the same meaning as another word. With a partner, match each boldfaced vocabulary word below with its synonym. Use a thesaurus or dictionary to check your answers. You will not use all the answer choices.

1. solitude   a. dismal

2. obsessed   b. isolation

                c. preoccupied

                d. comradeship

Academic Vocabulary

*Hugo presents key **aspects** of Napoleon's character, including his stubborn pride, even in the face of defeat.*

Aspects is an academic word with a variety of uses. One of the many **aspects** of writing a good story is character development. Write and answer a question about "Russia 1812" using this word.

For more on academic vocabulary, see pages 36–37 and R83–R85.

Listening and Speaking

 Oral Interpretation

Assignment Present an oral interpretation of "Russia 1812" to convey Hugo's attitude toward Napoleon and the war.

Prepare As you review Hugo's narrative poem, use the following checklist to develop your interpretation of the poem:

- What is the historical background of "Russia 1812"?
- Who is the speaker?
- What type of imagery predominates?
- What metaphors are used?

Familiarize yourself with the sound devices and rhythm in the poem. Practice your oral interpretation a few times, experimenting with different tones, volumes, speeds, and other vocal devices. Use facial expressioons and gestures to reflect the meaning of your words. Try to increase your fluency, or ease with which you read, each time you read the poem. You may wish to record your practice readings.

You may want to introduce visual effects into your oral interpretation (such as art depicting the retreat from Moscow). If you do, be sure these effects do not overshadow your presentation. Refer to the graphic organizer you filled out on page 977 as you consider how you want your listener to visualize your interpretation.

Perform Present your interpretation in front of the class, varying the tone of your voice to keep your audience's attention.

Evaluate Write a paragraph in which you assess the effectiveness of your oral interpretation. Use the rubric on page 167 to help in this self-evaluation.

LOG ON ▶ **Literature** Online

Selection Resources For Selection Quizzes, eFlashcards, and Reading-Writing Connection activities, go to glencoe.com and enter QuickPass code GLW6053u5.

Academic Vocabulary

Possible answer:

Question: What **aspect** of the retreat is worst for Napoleon's soldiers?

Answer: I think the snow is the worst **aspect** for the soldiers, because they have difficulty moving through the snow and it is so cold that many freeze to death.

Listening and Speaking

Students' oral interpretations should

- indicate a close reading of the poem
- present an interpretation of the poem
- incorporate effective verbal and nonverbal techniques

 For additional selection assessment, see Assessment Resources, pp. 193–194.

 To create custom assessments online, go to Progress Reporter Online Assessment.

 To create custom assessments using software, use ExamView Assessment Suite.

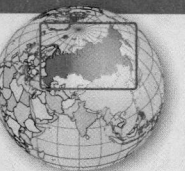

Before You Read

How Much Land Does a Man Need?

Meet **Leo Tolstoy**
(1828–1910)

When he was an old man, Leo Tolstoy sometimes made visitors uncomfortable; it often seemed as if he could read their minds. His profound psychological insight is also apparent in his fiction. One of Russia's greatest novelists, Tolstoy was a master at portraying people's thoughts and feelings.

Life on the Estate Tolstoy came from an aristocratic family. His parents died before he was ten, and he lost his grandmother and a beloved aunt within the next few years. Even so, he always remembered a "blissful" early life under the care of another aunt and a favorite cousin. He inherited the family's 2,000-acre estate when he was nineteen, and he wrote his first two books while serving as an officer in the Russian army.

At age 34, Tolstoy married the eighteen-year-old daughter of family friends, settling down on his estate. Within fifteen years, he wrote his two masterpieces, the novels *War and Peace* and *Anna Karenina*. Shortly after finishing *Anna Karenina*, a spiritual crisis led him to renounce these novels. For a while, he wrote only nonfiction works about religion and morality. Eventually he returned to fiction, producing moral tales written in a simplified style. By the end of his life, Tolstoy was revered throughout the world as an artist and a philosopher.

Sudden Prophet Inspired by the religious faith of Russian peasants, Tolstoy underwent a spiritual awakening in his early fifties. He eventually rejected the doctrines of the Russian Orthodox Church and was excommunicated. In a series of essays, Tolstoy set forth a new system of beliefs based on the New Testament Gospels. He stressed the importance of pacifism, simple living, and self-improvement through physical work. He eventually gave up all claim to his land holdings, believing it was wrong to own property. His son Ilya described the effect of Tolstoy's spiritual crisis: "From the fun-loving, lively head of our family he was transformed before our eyes into a stern, accusatory prophet." Tolstoy's ideas of civil disobedience influenced the young Mahatma Gandhi, who used them to lead the people of India to independence from Great Britain.

Unhappiness at home led Tolstoy to flee on October 28, 1910, and he died of pneumonia a few days later. The quest of his life was captured in his last words: "To seek, always to seek . . ." .

> "An artist is an artist because he sees things not as he wishes to see them but as they really are."
>
> —Leo Tolstoy

LOG ON ▶ **Literature** Online

Author Search For more about Leo Tolstoy, go to glencoe.com and enter QuickPass code GLW6053u5.

LEO TOLSTOY **983**

Before You Read

Focus

Bellringer Options

Selection Focus Transparency 60

Daily Language Practice Transparency 92

Or ask: Do any circumstances justify acquiring much more of something than you really need? If so, what are they? If not, why not?

Find out if students think that accumulating wealth and material goods is an appropriate use of a person's time and energy.

Literary History ☆
Tolstoy's Masterpiece
Tolstoy's novel *War and Peace* tells about several Russian families during the wars against Napoleon in the early 1800s. In this book, Tolstoy argues that history is shaped not by the ideas and plans of great men, but by the seemingly small decisions made by ordinary people.

Selection Skills

Literary Elements
- Structure (SE pp. 984–986, 989, 991, 994, 998)
- Irony (SE p. 998)
- Foreshadowing (TE p. 986)

Reading Skills
- Make Inferences About Theme (SE pp. 984, 985, 988, 990, 991, 993, 995, 996, 998)
- Visualize (TE p. 991)

Vocabulary Skills
- Context Clues (SE pp. 984, 998)
- Academic Vocabulary (SE p. 998)

How Much Land Does a Man Need?

Speaking/Listening/Viewing Skills
- Analyze Art (SE p. 988)
- Create a Business Plan (TE p. 988)
- Improvise Dialogue (TE p. 990)

Writing Skills/Grammar
- Persuasive Essay (SE p. 999)
- Summary (TE p. 984)
- Active and Passive Voice (TE p. 994)

Before You Read

Focus

Summary

Pakhom, a shrewd peasant, thinks that if he just had enough land, he would not fear even the Devil. Unbeknownst to him, the Devil hears his boast and plans to use Pakhom's desire for land to corrupt the man's soul. Pakhom acquires land, but it is not enough. He hears about a prairie of virgin soil in the land of the Bashkirs and sets out to acquire some. His obsession to obtain more land leads to his demise.

 For summaries in languages other than English, see Unit 5 Teaching Resources Book, pp. 156–161.

Vocabulary

Word Clues Have students write on separate index cards a context sentence for each vocabulary word, substituting an underlined nonsense word for the vocabulary word. On the back of the card, they should write a synonym or antonym of the word. Pairs then trade cards and try to determine what the missing vocabulary word is. They get two points for getting it through the context sentence alone, and one point if they have to check the other side of the card for a second clue.

 For additional vocabulary practice, see Unit 5 Teaching Resources Book, p. 164.

Literature and Reading Preview

Connect to the Story

How can you tell the difference between what you want and what you need? Discuss this question with a small group. Consider why people often want much more than they need.

Build Background

Until 1861, when Czar Alexander II emancipated the peasants, millions worked on Russian farms under a system called serfdom. Serfs lived in virtual slavery and were tied to the land; if a landowner sold a section of property, the serfs working that area were also sold. Serfs had few legal rights—they could not leave, change jobs, or marry without the landowner's permission—and they were often beaten or sent to serve in the army. After the abolition of serfdom, they were supposed to receive land, but landowners and local authorities often gave them the smallest or least productive plots.

Set Purposes for Reading

Big Idea Realism and Modernism

As you read, ask yourself, How does Tolstoy describe the everyday lives and problems of his ordinary characters?

Literary Element Structure

Structure is the order or pattern an author uses to present ideas. The most common structure for a narrative is chronological order, in which events are told in the order they happen. Other kinds of writing, such as persuasive or expository writing, might use a cause-and-effect or problem-solution structure. As you read the story, ask yourself, How does Tolstoy's structure contribute to the story's message?

Reading Strategy Make Inferences About Theme

When you **make inferences about theme,** you look for clues that suggest the author's message about life. Those clues can be found in the events, dialogue, and descriptions that make up the story. As you read, ask yourself, What details point to clues about the author's message?

Tip: Note Details As you read, note details that contribute to the theme in a chart like the one below.

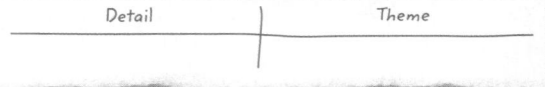

Detail	Theme

Learning Objectives

For pages 983–998

In studying this text, you will focus on the following objectives:

Literary Study: Analyzing structure.

Reading: Making inferences about theme.

Vocabulary

disparage (dis par′ ij) *v.* speak badly of; p. 985 *Eve disparaged my contribution to the potluck dinner.*

discord (dis′ kôrd) *n.* angry or quarrelsome disagreement; lack of harmony; p. 986 *Discord between the two sisters disrupted the happiness of the family reunion.*

trespass (tres′ pəs) *v.* illegally enter property; p. 987 *The guard's yell stopped them from trespassing.*

arable (ar′ə bəl) *adj.* fit for growing crops; p. 989 *Hoping to raise corn, hay, and lettuce, the Potter family bought twenty acres of arable land.*

disperse (dis purs′) *v.* scatter or spread in many directions; p. 993 *After the party, the guests dispersed to their own homes.*

Tip: Context Clues When you read an unfamiliar word, pay close attention to the context, or setting, in which it appears. One type of context clue is a contrast, such as "The younger sister . . . disparaged the life of a tradesman, and stood up for that of a peasant."

Writing Practice

Write a Summary Point out to students that when sellers advertise land, they often describe the likely use of the land—agricultural, residential, industrial, or mixed. In many communities, the use of the land is determined by zoning laws that permit or prohibit certain activities, depending on how an area is zoned. Have students research the laws in their communities to learn what, if any, zoning laws are in effect. Suggest that they obtain details on what kinds of zones are possible and what kinds of building are allowed in each one. Have students write summaries of what they learn.

How Much Land Does a Man Need?

Leo Tolstoy
Translated by Louise and Aylmer Maude

Ploughing the Field, 1871. Mikhail Konstantinovich Klodt von Juergensburg. Oil on canvas. State Russian Museum, Moscow.

I

An elder sister came to visit her younger sister in the country. The elder was married to a tradesman in town, the younger to a peasant in the village. As the sisters sat over their tea talking, the elder began to boast of the advantages of town life: saying how comfortably they lived there, how well they dressed, what fine clothes her children wore, what good things they ate and drank, and how she went to the theater, promenades, and entertainments.

The younger sister was piqued, and in turn **disparaged** the life of a tradesman, and stood up for that of a peasant.

---

1 Make Inferences About Theme *After reading the title and the first two sentences, what theme do you think might develop in this story?*

Vocabulary

disparage (dis par′ ij) *v.* speak badly of

"I would not change my way of life for yours," said she. "We may live roughly, but at least we are free from anxiety. You live in better style than we do, but though you often earn more than you need, you are very likely to lose all you have. You know the proverb, 'Loss and gain are brothers twain.' It often happens that people who are wealthy one day are begging their bread the next. Our way is safer. Though a peasant's life is not a fat one, it is a long one. We shall never grow rich, but we shall always have enough to eat."

The elder sister said sneeringly:

"Enough? Yes, if you like to share with the pigs and the calves! What do you know of elegance or manners! However much your goodman may slave, you will die as you are living—on a dung heap—and your children the same."

---

2 Structure *How does Tolstoy use a compare-contrast structure to present the two sisters' opposing views of life?*

LEO TOLSTOY **985**

Teach

Reading Strategy　1

Make Inferences About Theme **Answer:** *The theme might relate to the difference between country and city values. It might also have something to do with the foolishness of pursuing materialistic goals.*

（ENGLISH LEARNERS） Point out that this same argument about country versus city values is made in Aesop's fable about the country mouse and the city mouse. Ask English learners if the cultures they come from have a similar tale.

Literary Element　2

Structure **Answer:** *One sister praises the benefits of city living and disparages country living, and the other praises the benefits of country living and disparages city living.*

View the Art　★

After serfdom was abolished in 1861, many Russians took a greater interest in rural life. Realistic paintings of peasants and the landscape, like this one, became increasingly popular. This painting shows the physical attributes of the Russian steppes, which are flat, largely treeless plains similar to the American prairies.

English Learners

DIFFERENTIATED INSTRUCTION

Beginning English learners may be confused by words that have several functions. Write the following pairs of sentences on the board, and point out the part of speech of the underlined word.

1. "We will have a <u>tussle</u>," he thought. *(noun)*

   Pakhom <u>tussled</u> with his problem. *(verb)*

2. A cow <u>strayed</u> into her garden. *(verb)*

   The family's dog was a <u>stray</u>. *(noun)*

3. All the cows were in the <u>stable</u>. *(noun)*

   The cows had to be <u>stabled</u>. *(verb)*

Point out that many words can be nouns, verbs, and sometimes adjectives. Explain that these forms usually have similar meanings. Have students read and explain each sentence, identifying the part of speech of each underlined word.

Readability Scores

Dale-Chall: 7.8
DRP: 55
Lexile: 860

Learning Objectives
Making inferences about theme. (SE)
Analyzing structure. (SE)
Writing a summary. (TE)

Teach

Literary Element 1

Foreshadowing Have students speculate about what this statement by the Devil might foreshadow. *(This statement hints that the Devil has a plan to use Pakhom's greed and materialistic values to destroy him.)*

Literary Element 2

Structure Answer: *Tolstoy begins a new section to show time has passed. This division creates suspense when the Devil's comments and Pakhom's ambitious plans are put aside temporarily.*

Political History ☆

Russia After 1861 Draw students' attention to paragraph 3 in Section 2. **Say:** After the Russian serfs received their freedom in 1861, most of them stayed where they were. Their well-being, therefore, depended to a great extent on who owned the land. They would naturally be worried about a new owner who might treat them worse than the previous one had.

"Well, what of that?" replied the younger. "Of course our work is rough and coarse. But, on the other hand, it is sure, and we need not bow to any one. But you, in your towns, are surrounded by temptations; today all may be right, but tomorrow the Evil One[1] may tempt your husband with cards, wine, or women, and all will go to ruin. Don't such things happen often enough?"

Pakhom, the master of the house, was lying on the top of the stove and he listened to the women's chatter.

"It is perfectly true," thought he. "Busy as we are from childhood tilling mother earth, we peasants have no time to let any nonsense settle in our heads. Our only trouble is that we haven't land enough. If I had plenty of land, I shouldn't fear the Devil himself!"

The women finished their tea, chatted a while about dress, and then cleared away the tea-things and lay down to sleep.

But the Devil had been sitting behind the stove, and had heard all that was said. He was pleased that the peasant's wife had led her husband into boasting, and that he had said that if he had plenty of land he would not fear the Devil himself.

 "All right," thought the Devil. "We will have a tussle. I'll give you land enough; and by means of that land I will get you into my power."

II

Close to the village there lived a lady, a small landowner who had an estate of about three hundred acres. She had always lived on good terms with the peasants until she engaged as her steward an old soldier,

---

1. The *Evil One* is the Devil.

2 Structure *Why does Tolstoy begin a new section of the story here? How does this division help develop the plot?*

986 UNIT 5 MODERN EUROPE

---

who took to burdening the people with fines. However careful Pakhom tried to be, it happened again and again that now a horse of his got among the lady's oats, now a cow strayed into her garden, now his calves found their way into her meadows—and he always had to pay a fine.

Pakhom paid up, but grumbled, and going home in a temper, was rough with his family. All through that summer, Pakhom had much trouble because of this steward, and he was even glad when winter came and the cattle had to be stabled. Though he grudged the fodder when they could no longer graze on the pasture-land, at least he was free from anxiety about them.

In the winter the news got about that the lady was going to sell her land and that the keeper of the inn on the high road was bargaining for it. When the peasants heard this they were very much alarmed.

"Well," thought they, "if the innkeeper gets the land, he will worry us with fines worse than the lady's steward. We all depend on that estate."

So the peasants went on behalf of their commune,[2] and asked the lady not to sell the land to the innkeeper, offering her a better price for it themselves. The lady agreed to let them have it. Then the peasants tried to arrange for the commune to buy the whole estate, so that it might be held by them all in common. They met twice to discuss it, but could not settle the matter; the Evil One sowed **discord** among them and they could not agree. So they decided to buy the land individually, each according to his means; and the lady agreed to this plan as she had to the other.

---

2. In some rural areas, farmers organize into *communes* for mutual support. Members of the commune also may own or use property or equipment in common.

Vocabulary

discord (dis´kôrd) n. angry or quarrelsome disagreement; lack of harmony

---

Grammar Practice

Punctuate Dialogue Remind students of these rules for punctuating dialogue:

- Use double quotation marks to enclose direct quotations.
- Use single quotation marks to enclose a quotation within a quotation.
- When quoting conversations, begin a new paragraph for each speaker.

- Separate interrupted quoted material from the identification of the speaker with a comma (if the thought is incomplete) or a period (if the thought is complete). Examples: "Hey, Joey," said Louise, "let's go inside. It's getting cold out here." (Note the comma after *Louise*.)

  "Let's go inside," said Louise. "It's getting cold out here." (Note the period after *Louise*.)

- Place commas and periods inside quotation marks.
- Place dashes, question marks, and exclamation points inside quotation marks only if they belong to the quotation.

Have students find in the story one example of each rule in use.

986

Presently Pakhom heard that a neighbor of his was buying fifty acres, and that the lady had consented to accept one half in cash and to wait a year for the other half. Pakhom felt envious.

"Look at that," thought he, "the land is all being sold, and I shall get none of it." So he spoke to his wife.

"Other people are buying," said he, "and we must also buy twenty acres or so. Life is becoming impossible. That steward is simply crushing us with his fines."

So they put their heads together and considered how they could manage to buy it. They had one hundred rubles laid by.

Visual Vocabulary
The *ruble* is the basic unit of Russian currency.

They sold a colt and one half of their bees, hired out one of their sons as a laborer and took his wages in advance; borrowed the rest from a brother-in-law, and so scraped together half the purchase money.

Having done this, Pakhom chose out a farm of forty acres, some of it wooded, and went to the lady to bargain for it. They came to an agreement, and he shook hands with her upon it and paid her a deposit in advance. Then they went to town and signed the deeds; he paying half the price down, and undertaking to pay the remainder within two years.

So now Pakhom had land of his own. He borrowed seed, and sowed it on the land he had bought. The harvest was a good one, and within a year he had managed to pay off his debts both to the lady and to his brother-in-law. So he became a landowner, ploughing and sowing his own land, making hay on his own land, cutting his own trees, and feeding his cattle on his own pasture. When he went out to plough his fields, or to look at his growing corn, or at his grass-meadows, his heart would fill with joy. The grass that grew and the flowers that bloomed there seemed to him unlike any that grew elsewhere. Formerly, when he had passed by that land, it had appeared the same as any other land, but now it seemed quite different.

III

So Pakhom was well-contented, and everything would have been right if the neighboring peasants would only not have **trespassed** on his corn-fields and meadows. He appealed to them most civilly, but they still went on: now the communal herdsmen would let the village cows stray into his meadows, then horses from the night pasture would get among his corn. Pakhom turned them out again and again, and forgave their owners, and for a long time he forbore[3] to prosecute any one. But at last he lost patience and complained to the district court. He knew it was the peasants' want of land, and no evil intent on their part, that caused the trouble, but he thought:

"I cannot go on overlooking it or they will destroy all I have. They must be taught a lesson."

So he had them up, gave them one lesson, and then another, and two or three of the peasants were fined. After a time Pakhom's neighbors began to bear him a grudge for this, and would now and then let their cattle on to his land on purpose. One peasant even got into Pakhom's wood at night and cut down five young lime trees

---

3. *Forbore* means "refrained from or held back."

Vocabulary

trespass (tres′pas) *v.* illegally enter property

4 Realism and Modernism *What do Pakhom's words reveal about his family's daily struggles?*

Reading Strategy | 3

Question Draw students' attention to this sentence and to the beginning of Section III. **Ask:** How does Pakhom feel owning his own land and tending to his own animals? What happens to change his feelings? *(At first his heart fills with joy. Then he starts having trouble with trespassing neighbors and finds himself fining them just as he was fined before.)*

Big Idea | 4

Realism and Modernism
Answer: *They show his family has financial troubles because they don't own the land they farm.*

Language History ☆

Etymology The word *want* can be used as a noun or a verb. In this case, it is used as a noun, meaning "lack." The word comes from an Old Norse word, *vant*, meaning "lacking" or "missing." As used here, the word has a similar meaning in the expression "a state of want," which means "poverty or destitution." That sense of the word suggests a lack that may threaten life.

Approaching Level

DIFFERENTIATED INSTRUCTION

SMALL GROUP **Read and Discuss** Students having difficulty following the story may benefit from working with a small group and listening while others take turns reading sections aloud. Following each paragraph or so, groups should work together to paraphrase what they have just read and discuss what is happening in the story.

Advanced Learners/Pre-AP

DIFFERENTIATED INSTRUCTION

Research Farming Costs Advanced learners might find it interesting to what it would cost for a farmer in the United States to do what Pakhom did: buy forty acres, plow the land, plant wheat and corn, harvest the crops, and take care of cattle. Would it be possible to pay for the land within two years, as Pakhom did? Suggest that they prepare a report on the subject and present it to the class.

Learning Objectives
Analyzing foreshadowing. (SE)
Analyzing structure. (SE)
Questioning meaning. (TE)
Understanding punctuation. (TE)

Teach

Reading Strategy | 1

Respond to Characters
Have students respond to the thought Pakhom expresses in this paragraph. **Ask:** Do you think he is being selfish and greedy? *(He seems to be thinking only of himself and how he can benefit from his neighbors' losses.)*

Reading Strategy | 2

Make Inferences About Theme Answer: *They are affecting his life negatively. The more he owns, the more paranoid and belligerent he becomes.*

View the Art ★

Answer: *Students may say the peasants live simple but hard lives, just as the peasants in the story do.*
Sinaida Serebryakova loved to paint scenes of rural life. Although she was a rising star in St. Petersburg before the Russian Revolution, she chose to live in the countryside to be close to her favorite subjects. In many paintings, she showed peasants at work or enjoying a moment of leisure.

for their bark. Pakhom passing through the wood one day noticed something white. He came nearer and saw the stripped trunks lying on the ground, and close by stood the stumps where the trees had been. Pakhom was furious.

"If he had only cut one here and there it would have been bad enough," thought Pakhom, "but the rascal has actually cut down a whole clump. If I could only find out who did this, I would pay him out."[4]

He racked his brains as to who it could be. Finally he decided: "It must be Simon—no one else could have done it." So he went to Simon's homestead to have a look round, but he found nothing, and only had an angry scene. However, he now felt more certain than ever that Simon had done it, and he lodged a complaint. Simon was summoned. The case was tried, and retried, and at the end of it all Simon was acquitted, there being no evidence against him. Pakhom felt still more aggrieved, and let his anger loose upon the elder and the judges.

"You let thieves grease your palms," said he. "If you were honest folk yourselves you would not let a thief go free."

So Pakhom quarrelled with the judges and with his neighbors. Threats to burn his building began to be uttered. So though Pakhom had more land, his place in the commune was much worse than before.

About this time a rumor got about that many people were moving to new parts.

1 "There's no need for me to leave my land," thought Pakhom. "But some of the others might leave our village and then there would be more room for us. I would take over their land myself and make my estate a bit bigger. I could then live more

---

4. To *pay him out* means that Pakhom wants to hurt the person for the wrong he has done.

2 Make Inferences About Theme *What does this passage suggest about how Pakhom's possessions are affecting his life?*

The Wheat Harvest, 1914. Sinaida Yewgenyevna Serebryakova. Oil sketch. Private collection.

View the Art Serebryakova spent much of her youth at her family's country estate, Neskuchnoye. It was there that she first became captivated by the life of peasants. What do you think these peasants' lives are like? How might they be similar to the lives of the peasants in the story? ★

at ease. As it is, I am still too cramped to be comfortable."

One day Pakhom was sitting at home when a peasant, passing through the village, happened to call in. He was allowed to stay the night, and supper was given him. Pakhom had a talk with this peasant and asked him where he came from. The stranger answered that he came from beyond the Volga,[5] where he had been working. One word led to another, and the man went on to say that many people were settling in those parts. He told how some people from his village had settled there. They had joined the commune, and had had twenty-five acres per man granted them. The land was so good, he said, that the rye

---

5. The *Volga* is a river in western Russia.

Speaking and Listening Practice

SMALL GROUP

Create a Business Plan
Explain to students that one way of planning any venture is to create a business plan that can act as a guideline. Have students work in groups to make plans for business ventures. Suggest that each group begin by discussing possible business ventures and agreeing on one to pursue. Once that is decided, they can determine how much they will be able to spend, how much they would like to earn during a five-year period, and what their expenses are likely to be. They can figure out how long it might take to pay back any loans they needed to get the venture started. Remind them that profit will be the money left after expenses. Have each group present their plans to the class. They might want to create a chart to use as a visual aid.

sown on it grew as high as a horse, and so thick that five cuts of a sickle made a sheaf. One peasant, he said, had brought nothing with him but his bare hands, and now he had six horses and two cows of his own.

Pakhom's heart kindled with desire. He thought:

"Why should I suffer in this narrow hole, if one can live so well elsewhere? I will sell my land and my homestead here, and with the money I will start afresh over there and get everything new. In this crowded place one is always having trouble. But I must first go and find out all about it myself."

Towards summer he got ready and started. He went down the Volga on a steamer to Samara,[6] then walked another three hundred miles on foot, and at last reached the place. It was just as the stranger had said. The peasants had plenty of land: every man had twenty-five acres of communal land given him for his use, and any one who had money could buy, besides, at two shillings an acre as much good freehold[7] land as he wanted.

Having found out all he wished to know, Pakhom returned home as autumn came on, and began selling off his belongings. He sold his land at a profit, sold his homestead and all his cattle, and withdrew from membership of the commune. He only waited till the spring, and then started with his family for the new settlement.

3

IV

As soon as Pakhom and his family reached their new abode, he applied for admission into the commune of a large village. He

---

6. *Samara* is a city on the Volga.
7. Pakhom could purchase and then sell *freehold* land to anyone he liked.

4 Realism and Modernism *How does this passage reflect economic changes during this period in Russia?*

---

stood treat to the elders[8] and obtained the necessary documents. Five shares of communal land were given him for his own and his sons' use: that is to say—125 acres (not all together, but in different fields) besides the use of the communal pasture. Pakhom put up the buildings he needed, and bought cattle. Of the communal land alone he had three times as much as at his former home, and the land was good cornland. He was ten times better off than he had been. He had plenty of **arable** land and pasturage, and could keep as many head of cattle as he liked.

At first, in the bustle of building and settling down, Pakhom was pleased with it all, but when he got used to it he began to think that even here he had not enough land. The first year, he sowed wheat on his share of the communal land and had a good crop. He wanted to go on sowing wheat, but had not enough communal land for the purpose, and what he had already used was not available; for in those parts wheat is only sown on virgin soil or on fallow land.[9] It is sown for one or two years, and then the land lies fallow till it is again overgrown with prairie grass. There were many who wanted such land and there was not enough for all; so that people quarrelled about it. Those who were better off wanted it for growing wheat, and those who were poor wanted it to let to dealers, so that they might raise money to pay their taxes. Pakhom wanted to sow more wheat, so he rented land from a

---

8. When Pakhom *stood treat to the elders,* he treated the elder members of the council to food and drink.
9. *Virgin soil* is land that has never been farmed; *fallow land* is land that is being rested after producing a harvest.

Structure *What pattern of behavior is Pakhom beginning to exhibit? What problems might this cause later?* **5**

Vocabulary

arable (ar′ ə bəl) *adj.* fit for growing crops

LEO TOLSTOY **989**

Teach

Reading Strategy **3**

Review Have students review what has happened so far in the story and look over their predictions. **Ask:** How would you revise your predictions on the basis of story events? *(Students' summaries should refer not only to what Pakhom has done but also to the title and to the Devil's vow to entrap Pakhom.)*

Big Idea **4**

Realism and Modernism
Answer: *It reflects the new opportunities for former serfs to improve their lives through their own efforts.*

Literary Element **5**

Structure Answer: *Pakhom is initially pleased with his success but eventually wants more. This pattern will prevent Pakhom from ever being happy.*

Learning Objectives
Making inferences about theme. (SE)
Analyzing art. (SE)
Analyzing structure. (SE)
Creating a business plan. (TE)

Approaching Level

DIFFERENTIATED INSTRUCTION

Track Sequence of Events Some students might have trouble following the sequence of events in Pakhom's life from the time he first becomes a landowner. If so, instruct them to review the text from that point on. Each time Pakhom makes a decision about his land, they should write it down in a bulleted list. When finished, they can look over their lists and review the sequence of events in Pakhom's downfall.

Advanced Learners/Pre-AP

DIFFERENTIATED INSTRUCTION

Conduct Internet Research In Russian, tea is called *chai.* The word is pronounced like the first syllable of *China,* which, as a tea-producing country, is the source of the Russian word. Have advanced students conduct research to find more information about tea, such as what countries are the biggest producers, what kinds of tea exist, and what climate is best for growing tea. Have students present their findings in written reports.

Teach

Reading Strategy 1

Make Inferences About Theme Answer: *Some students may say it is the Devil working within Pakhom, while others may suggest that discontent is a common human trait.*

Reading Strategy 2

Make Inferences About Theme Answer: *Pakhom would probably not recognize the irony of the question because his craving for more land is never satisfied.*

dealer for a year. He sowed much wheat and had a fine crop, but the land was too far from the village—the wheat had to be carted more than ten miles. After a time Pakhom noticed that some peasant-dealers were living on separate farms and were growing wealthy; and he thought:

"If I were to buy some freehold land and have a homestead on it, it would be a different thing altogether. Then it would all be nice and compact."

The question of buying freehold land recurred to him again and again.

He went on in the same way for three years, renting land and sowing wheat. The seasons turned out well and the crops were good, so that he began to lay money by. He might have gone on living contentedly, but he grew tired of having to rent other people's land every year, and having to scramble for it. Wherever there was good land to be had, the peasants would rush for it and it was taken up at once, so that unless you were sharp about it you got none. It happened in the third year that he and a dealer together rented a piece of pasture land from some peasants; and they had already ploughed it up, when there was some dispute and the peasants went to law about it, and things fell out so that the labor was all lost.

"If it were my own land," thought Pakhom, "I should be independent, and there would not be all this unpleasantness."

So Pakhom began looking out for land which he could buy; and he came across a peasant who had bought thirteen hundred acres, but having got into difficulties was willing to sell again cheap. Pakhom bargained and haggled with him, and at last they settled the price at 1,500 rubles, part in cash and part to be paid later. They had all but clinched the matter when a passing

dealer happened to stop at Pakhom's one day to get a feed for his horses. He drank tea with Pakhom and they had a talk. The dealer said that he was just returning from the land of the Bashkirs,[10] far away, where he had bought thirteen thousand acres of land, all for 1,000 rubles. Pakhom questioned him further, and the tradesman said:

"All one need do is to make friends with the chiefs. I gave away about one hundred rubles worth of silk robes and carpets, besides a case of tea, and I gave wine to those who would drink it; and I got the land for less than a penny an acre." And he showed Pakhom the title-deeds, saying:

"The land lies near a river, and the whole prairie is virgin soil."

Pakhom plied him with questions, and the tradesman said:

"There is more land there than you could cover if you walked a year, and it all belongs to the Bashkirs. They are as simple as sheep, and land can be got almost for nothing."

"There now," thought Pakhom, "with my one thousand rubles, why should I get only thirteen hundred acres, and saddle myself with a debt besides? If I take it out there, I can get more than ten times as much for the money."

Pakhom inquired how to get to the place, and as soon as the tradesman had left him, he prepared to go there himself. He left his wife to look after the homestead, and started on his journey taking his man[11]

---

10. The *Bashkirs* (bäsh´kērs) are a nomadic people of western Russia.
11. Pakhom's *man* is his male servant.

---

1 Make Inferences About Theme *What causes Pakhom's discontent?*

Make Inferences About Theme *The title of this story is a question. How might Pakhom answer it at this point?* **2**

Speaking and Listening Practice

Improvise Dialogue Point out that the author gives readers only a general idea of what was said during the conversation between Pakhom and the Bashkirs. Despite this, there is enough information for readers to be able to understand the mood and tone of the discussion. Have students study the description of the conversation and then work in groups to improvise the scene up through the arrival of the chief. Remind students of what is

involved in improvisation:

- acting without a script
- reacting to the environment created by the other actors
- quickly responding to what others say and do
- staying "in character" no matter what happens

Allow each group time to present their improvisation to the class.

with him. They stopped at a town on their way and bought a case of tea, some wine, and other presents, as the tradesman had advised. On and on they went until they had gone more than three hundred miles, and on the seventh day they came to a place where the Bashkirs had pitched their tents. It was all just as the tradesman had said. The people lived on the steppes,[12] by a river, in felt-covered tents. They neither tilled the ground, nor ate bread. Their cattle and horses grazed in herds on the steppe. The colts were tethered behind the tents, and the mares were driven to them twice a day. The mares were milked, and from the milk kumiss[13] was made. It was the women who prepared kumiss, and they also made cheese. As far as the men were concerned, drinking kumiss and tea, eating mutton, and playing on their pipes, was all they cared about. They were all stout and merry, and all the summer long they never thought of doing any work. They were quite ignorant, and knew no Russian, but were good-natured enough.

As soon as they saw Pakhom, they came out of their tents and gathered round their visitor. An interpreter was found, and Pakhom told them he had come about some land. The Bashkirs seemed very glad; they took Pakhom and led him into one of the best tents, where they made him sit on some down cushions placed on a carpet, while they sat round him. They gave him some tea and kumiss, and had a sheep killed, and gave him mutton to eat. Pakhom took presents out of his cart and

distributed them among the Bashkirs, and divided the tea amongst them. The Bashkirs were delighted. They talked a great deal among themselves, and then told the interpreter to translate.

"They wish to tell you," said the interpreter, "that they like you, and that it is our custom to do all we can to please a guest and to repay him for his gifts. You have given us presents, now tell us which of the things we possess please you best, that we may present them to you."

"What pleases me best here," answered Pakhom, "is your land. Our land is crowded and the soil is exhausted; but you have plenty of land and it is good land. I never saw the like of it."

The interpreter translated. The Bashkirs talked among themselves for a while. Pakhom could not understand what they were saying, but saw that they were much amused and that they shouted and laughed. Then they were silent and looked at Pakhom while the interpreter said:

"They wish me to tell you that in return for your presents they will gladly give you as much land as you want. You have only to point it out with your hand and it is yours."

The Bashkirs talked again for a while and began to dispute. Pakhom asked what they were disputing about, and the interpreter told him that some of them thought they ought to ask their chief about the land and not act in his absence, while others thought there was no need to wait for his return.

VI

While the Bashkirs were disputing, a man in a large fox-fur cap appeared on the scene. They all became silent and rose to

---

12. *Steppes* are vast land areas and are usually level and treeless.
13. *Kumiss* (koo´mis) is a beverage made from fermented horse milk.

> **3** **Structure** *Here and elsewhere in section V, Tolstoy describes a way of life very different from Pakhom's. How does Tolstoy use the compare-contrast structure to develop the story?*
> **4**

> **Make Inferences About Theme** *Describe the Bashkirs' attitude toward land ownership.* **5**

Teach

Reading Strategy   3

Visualize Have students describe the lifestyle and landscape of the Bashkirs. **Ask:** Is land important to them? *(They live on the steppes, which are like prairies. They are mainly nomadic herders, raising cattle and horses. They do not raise crops; land is important to them as pasture, but they do not think in terms of owning it in individual parcels.)*

Literary Element   4

Structure **Answer:** *Tolstoy contrasts the Bashkirs' way of life with Pakhom's. Unlike Pakhom, the Bashkirs enjoy life, they don't work constantly to acquire wealth, and they are generous to strangers.*

Reading Strategy   5

Make Inferences About Theme **Answer:** *They are not obsessed with owning land; they share what they have.*

Learning Objectives
Making inferences about theme. (SE)
Analyzing structure. (SE)
Visualizing. (TE)
Improvising dialogue. (TE)

Approaching Level

DIFFERENTIATED INSTRUCTION

Focus on Imagery Help students improve their reading comprehension skills by encouraging them to use visual imagery. The writing in this selection is rich with images for them to visualize. Have students close their eyes as you read aloud the first paragraph of Section V of the story. Pause and ask them to picture in their minds the sentences they have just heard. Call on students to describe their mental pictures. Continue by reading the next paragraph. Finish the section this way and then ask students to briefly summarize what has taken place.

Advanced Learners/Pre-AP

DIFFERENTIATED INSTRUCTION

Oral Report Have students research the Bashkirs. Suggest that they look for answers to these questions:

- How old is the Bashkir culture?
- Where do most Bashkirs live?
- What kind of work do they do?
- What are their marriage customs?

Have students report to the class, using visual aids such as maps and photographs.

991

Teach

Literary Element   1

Characterization Remind students that one method of indirect characterization is to reveal a character through what others think about him/her. **Ask:** How does Tolstoy introduce the character of the chief to show how important a man he is? (*All the men stop talking and rise to their feet when the chief appears.*)

View the Art ★

Ilya Ostroukhov was a landscape painter who sought to capture the particular mood of the Russian countryside in his works. Ostroukhov was not only an artist but a collector. His home in Moscow was filled with paintings of all genres, styles, and periods. His collection included works of Russian and European masters.

Landscape. I.S. Ostroukhov (Russiaian, 1858-1929). Oil on Canvas, 17 1/2 x 23 in. Private collection. ★

---

1 their feet. The interpreter said, "This is our chief himself."

Pakhom immediately fetched the best dressing-gown and five pounds of tea, and offered these to the chief. The chief accepted them, and seated himself in the place of honor. The Bashkirs at once began telling him something. The chief listened for a while, then made a sign with his head for them to be silent, and addressing himself to Pakhom, said in Russian:

"Well, let it be so. Choose whatever piece of land you like; we have plenty of it."

"How can I take as much as I like?" thought Pakhom. "I must get a deed to make it secure, or else they may say, 'It is yours,' and afterwards may take it away again."

"Thank you for your kind words," he said aloud. "You have much land, and I only want a little. But I should like to be sure which bit is mine. Could it not be measured and made over[14] to me? Life and death are in God's hands. You good people give it to me, but your children might wish to take it away again."

"You are quite right," said the chief. "We will make it over to you."

"I heard that a dealer had been here," continued Pakhom, "and that you gave him a little land, too, and signed title-deeds to that effect. I should like to have it done in the same way."

The chief understood.

---

14. Here, *made over* means "legally changed from one owner to another."

Writing Practice

Write a Compare-and-Contrast Essay Point out that the Bashkirs' attitude toward land is very different from Pakhom's. Pakhom, in turn, appears to have a point of view different from that of the commune members. Have students compare and contrast the three views concerning land ownership: Pakhom's, the Bashkirs', and the commune members'. Their comparisons should answer the following questions:

- What commonalities are there among the three?
- What differences are there?
- How do the differences affect Pakhom's fate?

To help organize their thoughts, students might want to complete a three-way Venn diagram like this one:

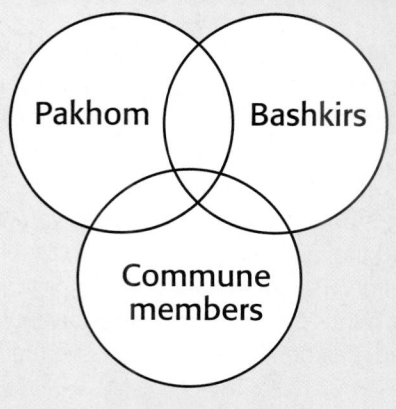

"Yes," replied he, "that can be done quite easily. We have a scribe,[15] and we will go to town with you and have the deed properly sealed."

"And what will be the price?" asked Pakhom.

"Our price is always the same: one thousand rubles a day."

Pakhom did not understand.

"A day? What measure is that? How many acres would that be?"

"We do not know how to reckon it out," said the chief. "We sell it by the day. As much as you can go round on your feet in a day is yours, and the price is one thousand rubles a day."

Pakhom was surprised.

"But in a day you can get round a large tract of land," he said.

The chief laughed.

"It will all be yours!" said he. "But there is one condition: If you don't return on the same day to the spot whence you started, your money is lost."

"But how am I to mark the way that I have gone?"

"Why, we shall go to any spot you like, and stay there. You must start from that spot and make your round, taking a spade with you. Wherever you think necessary, make a mark. At every turning, dig a hole and pile up the turf; then afterwards we will go round with a plough from hole to hole. You may make as large a circuit as you please, but before the sun sets you must return to the place you started from. All the land you cover will be yours."

Pakhom was delighted. It was decided to start early next morning. They talked a while, and after drinking some more kumiss

---

15. Here, a *scribe* is an official secretary or recorder of legal documents.

3 Make Inferences About Theme *What bargain does the chief strike with Pakhom? How do you think Pakhom will respond?*

and eating some more mutton, they had tea again, and then the night came on. They gave Pakhom a feather bed to sleep on, and the Bashkirs **dispersed** for the night, promising to assemble the next morning at daybreak and ride out before sunrise to the appointed spot.

VII

Pakhom lay on the feather bed, but could not sleep. He kept thinking about the land.

"What a large tract I will mark off!" thought he. "I can easily do thirty-five miles in a day. The days are long now, and within a circuit of thirty-five miles what a lot of land there will be! I will sell the poorer land, or let it to peasants, but I'll pick out the best and farm it. I will buy two ox teams, and hire two more laborers. About a hundred and fifty acres shall be ploughland, and I will pasture cattle on the rest."

Pakhom lay awake all night, and dozed off only just before dawn. Hardly were his eyes closed when he had a dream. He thought he was lying in that same tent and heard somebody chuckling outside. He wondered who it could be, and rose and went out, and he saw the Bashkir chief sitting in front of the tent holding his sides and rolling about with laughter. Going nearer to the chief, Pakhom asked: "What are you laughing at?" But he saw that it was no longer the chief, but the dealer who had recently stopped at his house and had told him about the land. Just as Pakhom was going to ask, "Have you been here long?" he saw that it was not the dealer, but the peasant who had come up from the Volga, long ago, to Pakhom's old home. Then he saw that it was not the peasant

Vocabulary

disperse (dis purs′) *v.* scatter or spread in many directions

LEO TOLSTOY **993**

Teach

Reading Strategy | 2

Connect to Personal Experience Ask students how many miles they can walk in one hour. Then point out that the average pace for a person walking on flat ground is 3.5 miles per hour. At that pace, it would take 10 hours to walk 35 miles. But Pakhom is tired from lack of sleep, he will be walking over somewhat rough land, he has to dig a hole at every turn, and he needs to rest every now and then. **Ask:** Can Pakhom finish 35 miles by sunset? *(Students may say it sounds extremely difficult.)*

Reading Strategy | 3

Make Inferences About Theme Answer: *In exchange for one thousand rubles, Pakhom can keep as much land as he wants if he can walk the distance and return by the end of the day. If he fails, he will lose his money and the land. Pakhom will probably continue to be greedy and try to get as much land as he can.*

Learning Objectives
Making inferences about theme. (SE)
Connecting to personal experience. (TE)
Writing a compare-and-contrast essay. (TE)

English Learners

DIFFERENTIATED INSTRUCTION

Intermediate Remind students that an idiom is an expression that has a meaning different from the meanings of the individual words in it. Write these idioms from the story on the board:

- put their heads together
- pay him out
- racked his brains
- grease your palms
- lay money by
- fell out
- high time

Have English learners discuss the meanings of these expressions with partners who are fluent in English. Then ask students to use each expression in an original sentence.

Teach

Literary Element　1

Structure Answer: *The dream is a warning that predicts Pakhom's future. It foreshadows the Devil's presence during his walk and the consequences of Pakhom's greed.*

Writer's Technique ☆

Description Point out the simile Tolstoy uses to describe the land: "as black as the seed of a poppy." The color of the soil and the fact that different kinds of grasses are growing "breast high" indicates that the soil is quite fertile.

2 either, but the Devil himself with hoofs and horns, sitting there and chuckling, and before him lay a man barefoot, prostrate on the ground, with only trousers and a shirt on. And Pakhom dreamt that he looked more attentively to see what sort of a man it was that was lying there, and he saw that the man was dead, and that it was himself! He awoke horror-struck.

"What things one does dream," thought he.

Looking round he saw through the open door that the dawn was breaking.

"It's time to wake them up," thought he. "We ought to be starting."

He got up, roused his man (who was sleeping in his cart), bade him harness; and went to call the Bashkirs.

"It's time to go to the steppe to measure the land," he said.

The Bashkirs rose and assembled, and the chief came too. Then they began drinking kumiss again, and offered Pakhom some tea, but he would not wait.

"If we are to go, let us go. It is high time," said he.

VIII

The Bashkirs got ready and they all started: some mounted on horses, and some in carts. Pakhom drove in his own small cart with his servant and took a spade with him. When they reached the steppe, the morning red was beginning to kindle. They ascended a hillock (called by the Bashkirs a *shikhan*) and dismounting from their carts and their horses, gathered in one spot. The chief came up to Pakhom and stretching out his arm towards the plain;

---

1 **Structure** *The author reveals an essential element of the story through a dream sequence. What is revealed? How is it important?*

"See," said he, "all this, as far as your eye can reach, is ours. You may have any part of it you like."

Pakhom's eyes glistened: it was all virgin soil, as flat as the palm of your hand, as black as the seed of a poppy, and in the hollows different kinds of grasses grew breast high.

The chief took off his fox-fur cap, placed it on the ground and said:

"This will be the mark. Start from here, and return here again. All the land you go round shall be yours."

Pakhom took out his money and put it on the cap. Then he took off his outer coat, remaining in his sleeveless undercoat. He unfastened his girdle[16] and tied it tight below his stomach, put a little bag of bread into the breast of his coat, and tying a flask of water to his girdle, he drew up the tops of his boots, took the spade from his man, and stood ready to start. He considered for some moments which way he had better go—it was tempting everywhere.

"No matter," he concluded, "I will go towards the rising sun."

He turned his face to the east, stretched himself, and waited for the sun to appear above the rim.

"I must lose no time," he thought, "and it is easier walking while it is still cool."

The sun's rays had hardly flashed above the horizon, before Pakhom, carrying the spade over his shoulder, went down into the steppe.

Pakhom started walking neither slowly nor quickly. After having gone a thousand yards he stopped, dug a hole, and placed pieces of turf one on another to make it more visible. Then he went on; and now that he had walked off his stiffness he quickened his pace. After a while he dug another hole.

---

16. Here, a *girdle* is a length of cloth used as a belt or back support.

Grammar Practice

Active and Passive Voice
Write on the board:

- He annoyed me.
- I was annoyed by him.

Point to the first sentence and **say:** A verb is in the active voice when the subject of the sentence performs the action.

Point to the second sentence and **say:** A verb is in the passive voice when the action is performed on the subject. Tell students that the active voice is generally stronger, and grammarians recommend it for use in most writing. Then write the following sentences on the board:

1. The people on the hill could hardly be seen by Pakhom.

2. They were puzzled by Pakhom's attitude.

3. Pakhom was tempted by the promise of cheap land.

Have students change the passive verbs into active verbs. (*Pakhom could hardly see the people on the hill. Pakhom's attitude puzzled them. The promise of cheap land tempted Pakhom.*)

Pakhom looked back. The hillock could be distinctly seen in the sunlight, with the people on it, and the glittering tyres of the cartwheels. At a rough guess Pakhom concluded that he had walked three miles. It was growing warmer; he took off his undercoat, flung it across his shoulder, and went on again. It had grown quite warm now; he looked at the sun, it was time to think of breakfast.

"The first shift is done, but there are four in a day, and it is too soon yet to turn. But I will just take off my boots," said he to himself.

He sat down, took off his boots, stuck them into his girdle, and went on. It was easy walking now.

"I will go on for another three miles," thought he, "and then turn to the left. This spot is so fine, that it would be a pity to lose it. The further one goes, the better the land seems."

He went straight on for a while, and when he looked round, the hillock was scarcely visible and the people on it looked like black ants, and he could just see something glistening there in the sun.

"Ah," thought Pakhom, "I have gone far enough in this direction, it is time to turn. Besides I am in a regular sweat, and very thirsty."

He stopped, dug a large hole, and heaped up pieces of turf. Next he untied his flask, had a drink, and then turned sharply to the left. He went on and on; the grass was high, and it was very hot.

Pakhom began to grow tired: he looked at the sun and saw that it was noon.

"Well," he thought, "I must have a rest."

He sat down, and ate some bread and drank some water; but he did not lie down, thinking that if he did he might fall asleep. After sitting a little while, he went on again. At first he walked easily: the food had strengthened him; but it had become terribly hot and he felt sleepy, still he went on, thinking: "An hour to suffer, a lifetime to live."

He went a long way in this direction also, and was about to turn to the left again, when he perceived a damp hollow: "It would be a pity to leave that out," he thought. "Flax would do well there." So he went on past the hollow, and dug a hole on the other side of it before he turned the corner. Pakhom looked towards the hillock. The heat made the air hazy: it seemed to be quivering, and through the haze the people on the hillock could scarcely be seen.

"Ah!" thought Pakhom, "I have made the sides too long; I must make this one shorter." And he went along the third side, stepping faster. He looked at the sun: it was nearly halfway to the horizon, and he had not yet done two miles of the third side of the square. He was still ten miles from the goal.

"No," he thought, "though it will make my land lopsided, I must hurry back in a straight line now. I might go too far, and as it is I have a great deal of land."

So Pakhom hurriedly dug a hole, and turned straight towards the hillock.

IX

Pakhom went straight towards the hillock, but he now walked with difficulty. He was done up with the heat, his bare feet were cut and bruised, and his legs began to fail. He longed to rest, but it was impossible if he meant to get back before sunset. The sun waits for no man, and it was sinking lower and lower.

"Oh dear," he thought, "if only I have not blundered trying for too much! What if I am too late?"

Make Inferences About Theme *Why does Pakhom keep changing his plans?*

Literary Element | 2

Archetype Remind students that an archetype is a symbol, image, or story pattern that recurs throughout the literary works of different eras and cultures. The idea of a character either making a bargain with the Devil or being controlled by the Devil is an archetype. Other examples of this archetype can be found in Marlowe's *Doctor Faustus,* Goethe's *Faust,* and in the 1997 movie *The Devil's Advocate.*

Reading Strategy | 3

Make Inferences About Theme Answer: *Initially, he wants to get all the good plots of land. Later, he realizes the plot has a strange shape so he takes a different path. Finally, he realizes he is running out of time and changes his route again.*

Progress Check

Can students make infrerences about theme?

If No → See Unit 5 Teaching Resources Book, p. 163.

Learning Objectives
Analyzing structure. (SE)
Making inferences about theme. (SE)
Using active voice. (TE)
Analyzing archetype. (TE)

Approaching Level
DIFFERENTIATED INSTRUCTION

Reread and Paraphrase Some students may be having trouble following the story. If so, have small groups work together to reread the sections that are difficult. Have them take turns reading paragraphs aloud and then restating in their own words what each paragraph means.

English Learners
DIFFERENTIATED INSTRUCTION

Beginning Tell students that some nouns in English are formed by adding a suffix to a verb, an adjective, or even some adverbs. Write these nouns on the board, pointing out the underlined noun-forming suffix in each one:

- stiff<u>ness</u>
- direct<u>ion</u>
- difficult<u>y</u>

Other noun-forming suffixes include *-ity* (as in *possibility*), *-ism* (as in *nationalism*), *-ation* (as in *imagination*), and *-eer* (as in *profiteer*). Suggest that students collect words with noun-forming suffixes and list them in their notebooks.

Teach

Literary Element | 1

Dramatic Irony Remind students that dramatic irony is a situation in which the reader knows something that the character does not. **Ask:** What does Pakhom finally understand about his actions that the reader already knows? With what internal conflict does he still struggle? *(He realizes he has tried for too much land and that his greed may kill him. Yet he worries that people will call him a fool if he stops.)*

Reading Strategy | 2

Make Inferences About Theme Answer: *No land is enough for a man who is greedy. But in the end, even a greedy man needs only six feet of land for his grave.*

(ADVANCED) Ask advanced learners how they would answer the question in the title of the story.

To check students' understanding of the selection, see Unit 5 Teaching Resources Book, p. 167.

1 He looked towards the hillock and at the sun. He was still far from his goal, and the sun was already near the rim.

Pakhom walked on and on; it was very hard walking but he went quicker and quicker. He pressed on, but was still far from the place. He began running, threw away his coat, his boots, his flask, and his cap, and kept only the spade which he used as a support.

"What shall I do?" he thought again, "I have grasped too much and ruined the whole affair. I can't get there before the sun sets."

And this fear made him still more breathless. Pakhom went on running, his soaking shirt and trousers stuck to him and his mouth was parched. His breast was working like a blacksmith's bellows, his heart was beating like a hammer, and his legs were giving way as if they did not belong to him. Pakhom was seized with terror lest he should die of the strain.

Though afraid of death, he could not stop. "After having run all that way they will call me a fool if I stop now," thought he. And he ran on and on, and drew near and heard the Bashkirs yelling and shouting to him, and their cries inflamed his heart still more. He gathered his last strength and ran on.

The sun was close to the rim, and cloaked in mist looked large, and red as blood. Now, yes now, it was about to set! The sun was quite low, but he was also quite near his aim. Pakhom could already see the people on the hillock waving their arms to hurry him up. He could see the fox-fur cap on the ground and the money on it, and the chief sitting on the ground holding his sides. And Pakhom remembered his dream.

"There is plenty of land," thought he, "but will God let me live on it? I have lost my life, I have lost my life! I shall never reach that spot!"

Pakhom looked at the sun, which had reached the earth: one side of it had already disappeared. With all his remaining strength he rushed on, bending his body forward so that his legs could hardly follow fast enough to keep him from falling. Just as he reached the hillock it suddenly grew dark. He looked up—the sun had already set! He gave a cry: "All my labor has been in vain," thought he, and was about to stop, but he heard the Bashkirs still shouting, and remembered that though to him, from below, the sun seemed to have set, they on the hillock could still see it. He took a long breath and ran up the hillock. It was still light there. He reached the top and saw the cap. Before it sat the chief laughing and holding his sides. Again Pakhom remembered his dream, and he uttered a cry: his legs gave way beneath him, he fell forward and reached the cap with his hands.

"Ah, that's a fine fellow!" exclaimed the chief. "He has gained much land!"

Pakhom's servant came running up and tried to raise him, but he saw that blood was flowing from his mouth. Pakhom was dead!

The Bashkirs clicked their tongues to show their pity.

His servant picked up the spade and dug a grave long enough for Pakhom to lie in, and buried him in it. Six feet from his head to his heels was all he needed. ∾

Make Inferences About Theme **How does the title of the story relate to the theme?** **2**

Literary Practice

Foreshadowing Tell students that an important element of "How Much Land Does a Man Need?" is foreshadowing, or an author's use of clues to prepare readers for events that will happen later in a story. Have students review the story and identify clues that set the stage for the final scenes. Then ask the following questions.

1. In Section I, how do the words of Pakhom's sister-in-law foreshadow what will happen to Pakhom? *(She predicts that her sister and her sister's family will die as they have lived—in an undignified way. That is exactly what happens to Pakhom.)*

2. How do the Devil's thoughts in Section I foreshadow Pakhom's fate? *(The Devil sets out to get Pakhom in his power, and that is what happens.)*

3. Explain how the dream sequence in Section VII and Pakhom's thoughts in Section IX provide additional foreshadowing. *(In the dream sequence in Section VII, Pakhom sees himself as dead, and in Section IX, Pakhom "was seized with terror lest he should die of the strain." Later, he thinks, "I have lost my life, I have lost my life!")*

After You Read

Respond and Think Critically

Respond and Interpret

1. Did you feel sorry for Pakhom at the end of this story? Explain.

2. (a)Summarize the philosophies of the sisters at the beginning of the story. (b)How does their conversation **foreshadow,** or give advance warning of, Pakhom's end?

3. (a)What does Pakhom boast at the beginning of the story? (b)How does this boast lead to his downfall?

4. (a)What dream does Pakhom have in the land of the Bashkirs? (b)What does the dream mean?

5. (a)What does the Bashkir chief offer Pakhom? (b)Why does this arrangement lead to Pakhom's death?

Analyze and Evaluate

6. (a)In your opinion, is Pakhom a good man or a bad man, or a little of both? Explain. (b)How well does Tolstoy develop Pakhom's character?

7. What kind of audience do you think Tolstoy was trying to reach with this story?

Connect

8. **Big Idea** **Realism and Modernism** (a)Which elements of this story are fantastic and which ones are realistic? (b)Would the story have been better if it were entirely realistic or entirely fantastic? Explain.

9. **Connect to the Author** As he grew older, Tolstoy came to believe that private ownership of property was evil. How is this view reflected in the story?

Primary Source Quotation

What Is Art?

Read what Tolstoy has to say about the definition and purpose of art.

"Nothing is more common than to hear it said of reputed works of art that they are very good but very difficult to understand. We are quite used to such assertions, and yet to say a work of art is good but incomprehensible to the majority of men, is the same as saying of some kind of food that it is very good but most people can't eat it. . . .

Art is differentiated from activity of the understanding, which demands preparation and a certain sequence of knowledge (so that one cannot learn trigonometry before knowing geometry), by the fact that it acts on people independently of their state of development and education, that the charm of a picture, of *sounds, or of forms, infects any man whatever his plane of development.*

The business of art lies just in this: to make that understood and felt which in the form of an argument might be incomprehensible and inaccessible."

Group Activity Discuss the following questions with your classmates.

1. In your own words, what is Tolstoy's attitude about art and its purposes?

2. Do you think "How Much Land Does a Man Need?" fits Tolstoy's definition of art and fulfills his ideas of art's purpose? Explain, citing evidence from the story.

LEO TOLSTOY **997**

Primary Source Quotation

1. Art should be simple to understand. It should communicate thoughts and feelings difficult to understand if presented in another way.

2. Most will agree Tolstoy's story fits his definition of art, since it is easy to understand and it communicates his ideas about land ownership.

portrayed realistically. (b) Students should explain their opinions with examples from the text.

9. Tolstoy implies that people who have no interest in property ownership (the Bashkirs) are happier, while people who are greedy (Pakhom) lose everything.

After You Read

Assess

1. Answers will vary.

2. (a) The elder sister believes that city living is more fulfilling and exciting, while the younger sister believes that country living is better because it is free from the anxiety of losing what they have. (b) The older sister's words imply that ultimately Pakhom's efforts will result in nothing.

3. (a) He boasts that even the Devil could not harm him if he had enough land. (b) The Devil decides to "have a tussle" to regain power over Pakhom

4. (a) He sees the Bashkir chief, the dealer, the peasant, and the Devil as part of the same creature. He also sees his body lying before the Devil. (b) It reveals the Devil's involvement in Pakhom's inevitable fate.

5. (a) an opportunity to have all the land he can claim (b) His greed for land causes him to ignore his physical problems. He dies of exhaustion.

6. (a) Students should support their answers. (b) Some students will say Tolstoy develops Pakhom's character well; others will say because Pakhom functions as a limited character in a parable he is more like a symbol than a developed character.

7. The upper classes might have become more sympathetic to the serfs after reading the story. The serfs who were gaining more material success might also have been part of the audience. Tolstoy might have wanted to caution them.

8. (a) Students may say the Devil's involvement is fantastic. Pakhom's logic and his relationships with other peasants are

After You Read

Assess

Literary Element

1. C is the correct answer. Pakhom reaches the hillock and sees the chief holding his sides, as in the dream. Then Pakhom utters a cry and dies.

Progress Check

Can students analyze structure?

If No → See Unit 5 Teaching Resources Book, p. 162.

Review: Irony

Possible answer: In Section I, Pakhom's wife says, "Our way is safer," yet she is the one who loses her husband later in the story. This is an example of situational irony.

Reading Strategy

1. The Bashkirs represent a life free of the compulsion to acquire material goods; Pakhom represents greed.

2. Happiness does not come in the form of material goods, but rather in the enjoyment of simple pleasures.

Vocabulary Practice

Possible answers:

disparage <u>Clues</u>: The younger sister disparages her sister's lifestyle and defends her own;
<u>Meaning</u>: to speak badly of; to belittle; to dishonor

discord <u>Clues</u>: The Evil One sows discord among the peasants;
<u>Meaning</u>: an angry or quarrelsome disagreement, lack of harmony;

998

Literary Element Structure

ACT Skills Practice

When does Pakhom know he will die and never use the land he worked so hard to gain?

A. when the dealer tells him about the Bashkirs

B. when the chief tells him he can have the land he can walk around in a day

C. when he is running toward the hillock and remembers his dream

D. when the Bashkirs wave at him to hurry back

Review: Irony

As you learned on page 291, **irony** is a contrast between appearance and reality or between expectation and outcome. **Situational irony** occurs when something happens that is different from what the characters, readers, or audience expect. **Dramatic irony** occurs when the reader or audience knows something a character does not.

Partner Activity Meet with a classmate and discuss the use of irony in this story. Working together, complete a chart like the one below. Fill it in with examples of irony. Then tell what type of irony each one is and explain how you know.

Example	Type	Explanation
The Devil overhears Pakhom's boast.	Dramatic	The reader knows about it, but Pakhom does not.
Pakhom dies just as he reaches his goal.		

LOG ON ▶ **Literature** Online

Selection Resources For Selection Quizzes, eFlashcards, and Reading-Writing Connection activities, go to glencoe.com and enter QuickPass code GLW6053u5.

Reading Strategy Make Inferences About Theme

This story is an **allegory**, a story in which the characters, settings, and events represent ideas or qualities beyond themselves. The theme of this story is the answer to the question posed in the title. Review the chart you made on page 984.

1. What do the Bashkirs represent? What does Pakhom represent?

2. What values do you think Tolstoy is trying to teach?

Vocabulary Practice

Practice with Context Clues Look back at pages 985–996 to find context clues for the boldfaced vocabulary words below. Record your findings in a chart like the one here.

disparage   discord   trespass
arable   disperse

EXAMPLE:

<u>Word</u>: anxiety

↓

<u>Textual Clues</u>: The younger sister says country life is free from anxiety, unlike city life.

↓

<u>Meaning</u>: nervousness or agitation

Academic Vocabulary

*In this short story, Tolstoy makes an **assessment** about the destructive power of greed.*

Assessment is an academic term. A synonym for *assessment* is *evaluation*. To further explore the meaning of this word, answer the following question: What might a teacher look for when doing an assessment of a student's writing?

For more on academic vocabulary, see pages 36–37 and R83–R85.

---

trespass <u>Clues</u>: It bothers Pakhom when his neighbors trespass on his land;
<u>Meaning</u>: to illegally enter property

arable <u>Clues</u>: Pakhom is well-off because he has plenty of arable land;
<u>Meaning</u>: fit for growing crops

disperse <u>Clues</u>: Pakhom goes to bed, and the Bashkirs disperse for the night;
<u>Meaning</u>: scatter or spread in many directions

Academic Vocabulary

organization, focus, correct use of grammar and punctuation, correct spelling

 For additional selection assessment, see Assessment Resources, pp. 195–196.

Respond Through Writing

Persuasive Essay

Argue a Position "How Much Land Does a Man Need?" has the effect of a parable, a story that teaches a moral lesson. The lesson of Pakhom's fate seems to be about the danger of greed. However, some readers might see him as ambitious and independent. Write a 1,500-word persuasive essay that supports or challenges Tolstoy's lesson.

Understand the Task A **persuasive essay** expresses a writer's opinion and tries to make readers agree and perhaps even take action.

Prewrite Before you draft your essay, use a chart like the one below to organize arguments for and against the lesson of Tolstoy's story. Then, decide which position seems stronger.

Arguments for Tolstoy's Lesson	Arguments Against Tolstoy's Lesson
Ambitious individuals often create envy and resentment that damages community life.	Without ambitious individuals, the economic life of a community stagnates.

Draft To persuade your audience that your position is valid, provide reasons in your body paragraphs and support them with evidence. In your conclusion, summarize your position and end with a call to action.

Revise In your revision, you may want to strengthen your arguments with appeals to ethics or emotions. For example, you might ask readers to think about how the pioneer spirit affected American history:

What would have happened to the future of the United States if Americans had just stopped at the Mississippi River, unwilling to face the challenges of the prairies, mountains, and deserts?

Use the rubric on page 834 of the Writing Workshop on persuasive speeches to check other elements of your review.

Edit and Proofread Proofread your paper, correcting any errors in spelling, grammar, and punctuation. Use the word count feature on your computer to check that your essay is 1,500 words. Review the Grammar Tip in the side column for information on sentence structure.

Learning Objectives

In this assignment, you will focus on the following objectives:

Writing: Writing a persuasive essay.

Grammar: Understanding sentence structure.

Grammar Tip

Sentence Structure

Varying the types of sentences you use will make your writing more interesting and effective.

A **simple sentence** has a single main clause: *Tolstoy's story teaches the danger of ambition.*

A **compound sentence** has two or more main clauses: *Pakhom acquires more land, but his neighbors resent him for his success.*

A **complex sentence** has a main clause and one or more subordinate clauses: *He and his family move to a less-settled region, where Pakhom is able to get even more land.*

After You Read

Assess

Respond Through Writing

Students' persuasive essays should

- clearly state a position for or against the story's lesson
- develop logical arguments in support of a position
- offer evidence in support of arguments
- make references to the story to defend a position

A student who meets all of these criteria should receive the equivalent of a 4-point response.

A student who fully meets three and partially meets the fourth of these criteria should receive the equivalent of a 3-point response.

A student who fully meets two of these criteria, or who partially meets three criteria, should receive the equivalent of a 2-point response.

A student who partially fully meets one or partially meets two of these criteria should receive the equivalent of a 1-point response.

 For grammar practice, see Unit 5 Teaching Resources Book, p. 166.

 To create custom assessments online, go to Progress Reporter Online Assessment.

 To create custom assessments using software, use ExamView Assessment Suite.

Advanced Learners/Pre-AP

DIFFERENTIATED INSTRUCTION

Research Have students research modern Russian agriculture to find out what has changed since Tolstoy's time. They can look for answers to these questions:

- What is different about crops?
- How has livestock care changed?
- In what ways does technology help?
- How is land ownership different?

Suggest that students make a chart to display the similarities and differences between the time periods. Have them present their findings to the class in an oral report.

Focus

Write these sentences on the board:

- Ashley walked home after she was done with rehearsal.
- Before she got home, it began to rain.

Say: Identify the independent and dependent clauses in each sentence. *(Ashley walked home—independent; after she was done with rehearsal—dependent. Before she got home—dependent; it began to rain—independent.)*

Teach

Subordinating Conjunctions

An adverb clause modifies a verb, an adjective, or an adverb in another clause. Adverb clauses begin with subordinating conjunctions, such as *after, although, because, if, since, when,* and *where.*

Assess

1. Main clause: *Pakhom was proud of his way of life*
   Subordinate clause: *who lived in the village* (adjective clause)
2. Main clause: *Pakhom started to walk faster*
   Subordinate clause: *When he saw the sun beginning to sink* (adverb clause)
3. Main clause: *Greedy people often lose what they have*
   Subordinate clause: *what they have* (noun clause)

 For additional grammar practice, see Unit 5 Teaching Resources Book, p. 169.

1000

Learning Objectives

In this workshop, you will focus on the following objective:

Grammar: Understanding main and subordinate clauses.

Main and Subordinate Clauses

A **main clause** contains a subject and predicate and can stand alone as a complete sentence. A **subordinate clause** contains a subject and predicate but does not express a complete thought.

Tip

You can identify a subordinate clause by looking for a subordinating conjunction or a relative pronoun followed by a subject and a predicate.

Subordinating Conjunctions	Relative Pronouns
after	that
as	whatever
because	which
before	whichever
since	who
unless	whom
until	whoever
when	whose

Language Handbook

For more on **main and subordinate clauses,** see Language Handbook, pp. R40–R59.

 **Literature** Online

Grammar For more Grammar practice, go to glencoe.com and enter QuickPass code GLW6053u5.

Grammar Workshop

Main and Subordinate Clauses

Literature Connection The following sentence by Leo Tolstoy uses both a main and a subordinate clause: "While the Bashkirs were disputing, a man in a large fox-fur cap appeared on the scene."

A **main clause** contains a subject and a predicate, expresses a complete thought, and can stand alone as a sentence. A **subordinate clause** contains a subject and a predicate, but does not express a complete thought and cannot stand alone as a sentence. In the sentence above, *a man in a large fox-fur cap appeared on the scene* is the main clause. *While the Bashkirs were disputing* is the subordinate clause. Three types of subordinate clauses are described below.

Adverb Clauses An adverb clause modifies a verb, adjective, or another adverb from the main clause. Adverb clauses are usually signaled by **subordinating conjunctions,** such as *because, until,* and *when.*

> *Because he wanted all of the land,* Pakhom walked as far as he could.

[The underlined adverb clause modifies the verb *walked*.]

Adjective Clauses An adjective clause modifies a noun or pronoun from the main clause of the sentence. Adjective clauses are usually signaled by relative pronouns, such as *who, what,* or *that.*

> The eldest sister, *who lived in the city,* bragged about her life.

[The underlined adjective clause modifies the noun *sister*.]

Noun Clauses A noun clause is a special kind of subordinate clause that functions as a noun *within* a main clause. Noun clauses are usually signaled by relative pronouns.

> *What Pakhom did* was foolish.

[The underlined noun clause is the subject of the verb *was*.]

Proofread Identify the main and subordinate clauses in each of the following sentences. Then identify whether the subordinate clause is an adverb clause, an adjective clause, or a noun clause.

1. Pakhom, who lived in the village, was proud of his way of life.
2. When he saw the sun beginning to sink, Pakhom started to walk faster.
3. Greedy people often lose what they have.

Grammar Practice

Punctuate Adverb Clauses Have students keep the following in mind:

- A dependent clause depends on an independent clause to complete its meaning.
- If a dependent clause comes before an independent clause, a comma must appear after the dependent clause.

Have students review the following sentences to determine if commas are necessary in them. If so, instruct students to insert the necessary punctuation:

- After she had gone to bed Ashley remembered she hadn't brushed her teeth. *(comma after* bed*)*
- Her sleepiness made her ambivalent before she finally got out of bed. *(no comma)*

Before You Read

The Bet

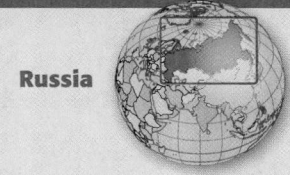

Russia

Meet **Anton Chekhov**
(1860–1904)

☆ *"The artist is not meant to be a judge of his characters and what they say; his only job is to be an impartial witness."*

—Anton Chekhov

As a doctor, the Russian author Anton Chekhov (chek′ôf) saw many sides of the human experience in his brief life. His stories and plays reveal not only what life was like during his lifetime, but what it means to be human in any era.

A Childhood Without Childhood "The father of the modern short story," Anton Pavlovich Chekhov was born in a seaport town in southern Russia. Chekhov recalls his father as a stern figure who tyrannized young Anton and his two older brothers. Chekhov's mother, on the other hand, was a wonderful storyteller who passed along to him her gift for words. The family struggled financially for years, and Chekhov's father fled to Moscow in 1875 to escape his debts. Chekhov stayed behind with his mother and younger siblings to finish his schooling. Before long, his mother lost the house to an unscrupulous local bureaucrat and

joined her husband in Moscow. Chekhov eked out a living by tutoring younger pupils at his school. Life was difficult; as he wrote later, "There was no childhood in my childhood." His luck improved, however, when he won a scholarship to study medicine at Moscow University.

Writing from Necessity While he was still a student, Chekhov published a series of short fictional sketches in humor magazines. He wrote less out of love for the craft than to ease the financial hardship of his family. However, it was in these short pieces that some of his lifelong subjects began to emerge. His stories often feature the petty tyranny of government bureaucrats and other authority figures, the suffering of the poor, and the ironies inherent in human relationships. Chekhov became wildly popular as a humorist. Though continuing his medical practice, Chekhov gradually became more comfortable with his literary work. Medicine eventually took a back seat to writing.

A Man of the Theater In 1887 Chekhov began working on a play that he later titled *Ivanov*. It was produced to great acclaim later the same year. Chekhov responded to this latest success with characteristic modesty—he left town. Over the next seventeen years, however, he penned the four masterworks that would make him famous: *The Seagull* (1896), *Uncle Vanya* (1897), *Three Sisters* (1901), and *The Cherry Orchard* (1904). Chekhov also fell in love with an actress, Olga Knipper. They were married in 1901, even though Chekhov had tuberculosis. His illness worsened over the next three years and finally took his life, silencing one of Russia's literary giants.

Literature Online

Author Search For more about Anton Chekhov, go to glencoe.com and enter QuickPass code GLW6053u5.

Before You Read

Focus

Bellringer Options

Selection Focus
Transparency 61

Daily Language Practice
Transparency 93

Or ask: Imagine if you were forced to stay alone inside a small room for many years. You would be denied human contact, but your food and items such as books and music would be passed to you through a window. What would you do to pass the time? Elicit students' opinions. Then have them read to discover why a man must live in this way.

Writer's Technique ☆

Aphorisms Discuss the meaning of the display quotation on page 1001. *(A writer should let his characters develop naturally.)* The quote is an *aphorism*—a short, pointed sentence expressing a clever observation. Explain that Chekhov, like Mark Twain and other witty writers, often offered aphorisms.

Selection Skills

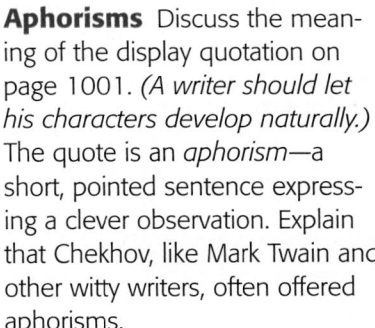

Literary Elements
- Character (SE pp. 1002, 1004, 1006, 1007, 1010)
- Mood (SE pp. 1010)
- Figurative Language (TE p. 1008)

The Bet

Speaking/Listening/Viewing Skills
- Analyze Art (SE p. 1005)
- Group Discussion (SE p. 1009)

Reading Skills
- Analyze Cause-and-Effect Relationships (SE pp. 1002, 1004, 1008, 1010)
- Make and Verify Predictions (TE pp. 1003, 1007)
- Make Connections (TE p. 1008)

Vocabulary Skills
- Denotation and Connotation (SE p. 1010)

Writing Skills/Grammar
- Summary (SE p. 1011)

Before You Read

Focus

Summary

An old banker recalls a party fifteen years before at which, in the course of a heated debate over whether the death penalty or life imprisonment was more humane, the banker bet a rash young lawyer two million rubles that the lawyer could not spend fifteen years in solitary confinement. Now the lawyer is nearing the end of his voluntary imprisonment, and the banker realizes that he will be bankrupt if he must pay. He plans to kill the lawyer; however, when he enters the prisoner's lodge, he finds a letter in which the lawyer renounces the money, the world, and its values. Only hours before his term would have been completed, the lawyer disappears. The banker is free of his obligation but filled with self-contempt.

> For summaries in languages other than English, see Unit 5 Teaching Resources Book, pp. 170–175.

Vocabulary

Categories Discuss the vocabulary words, their definitions, and the example sentences. Then write on the board: *humane acts, compulsory items, acting indiscriminately, emaciated animals, ethereal feelings.* Challenge students to suggest words that fit each category. For example, humane acts might include taking care of a sick person or adopting a kitten from an animal shelter.

> For additional vocabulary practice, see Unit 5 Teaching Resources Book, p. 178.

Literature and Reading Preview

Connect to the Story

Have you ever spent a long period of time alone? How is isolation good and bad for a person? Write a journal entry that describes your thoughts during your period of isolation.

Build Background

Chekhov achieved great fame and popularity in Russia, but by the 1880s many critics began to rebuke him for his failure to espouse a political point of view. Although he was the grandson of serfs, Chekhov never became a political writer. He preferred to explore the details of human experience. As his writing matured, his themes encompassed more humanitarian issues, such as starvation or marital and child abandonment.

Set Purposes for Reading

Big Idea Realism and Modernism

As you read "The Bet," ask yourself, How do Chekhov's ordinary characters reveal the complexities of human behavior?

Literary Element Character

A **character** is a person portrayed in a literary work. A **main character** is central to the story and is typically fully developed. A **minor character** displays few personality traits. As you read "The Bet," ask yourself, Why does the author never give names to the two main characters?

Reading Strategy Analyze Cause-and-Effect Relationships

A **cause-and-effect relationship** always deals with the question "Why?" Sometimes a cause-and-effect relationship can have a single cause and a single effect. Other times, an effect causes other effects in a **causal chain.** Identifying these relationships can help you better understand what you read. As you read, ask yourself, Why did each event happen?

Tip: Use a Graphic Organizer Use a graphic organizer like the one below to track the chain of causes and effects as you read.

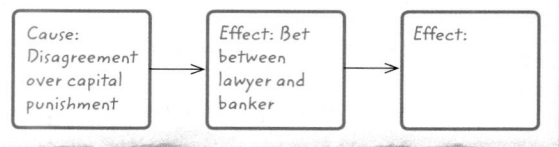

Cause: Disagreement over capital punishment → Effect: Bet between lawyer and banker → Effect:

> **Learning Objectives**
>
> *For pages 1001–1011*
>
> In studying this text, you will focus on the following objectives:
>
> **Literary Study:** Analyzing character.
>
> **Reading:** Analyzing cause-and-effect relationships.

Vocabulary

humane (hū mān´) *adj.* marked by compassion, sympathy, or consideration for humans or animals; p. 1003 *Annie is very humane; she treats all animals kindly.*

compulsory (kəm pul´sər ē) *adj.* mandatory; enforced; p. 1004 *To graduate to the next level, students took a compulsory test.*

indiscriminately (in´dis krim´ə nit lē) *adv.* randomly; haphazardly; p. 1006 *In trying to get the driver's attention, the police officer waved her arms indiscriminately.*

emaciated (i mā´shē āt id) *adj.* thin and feeble; p. 1007 *The elderly man was so emaciated he looked like a skeleton.*

ethereal (i thēr´ē əl) *adj.* otherworldly; p. 1008 *Her pale face looked ethereal in the moonlight.*

Tip: Connotation and Denotation The **connotation** of a word is its suggested or implied meaning. The **denotation** is its literal definition. For example, *thin* means *emaciated,* but *emaciated* has a stronger connotation than *thin.*

Writing Practice

Write an Anecdote Following your discussion of aphorisms, write these Chekhov aphorisms on the board:

People don't notice whether it is winter or summer when they are happy.

We learn about life not from pluses alone, but from minuses as well.

You must trust and believe in people or life becomes impossible.

Review with students that an **anecdote** is a brief account that illustrates a point by giving one or more examples. Have each student select one of the aphorisms above and write an original anecdote to illustrate its central point.

The Bet

Anton Chekhov
Translated by Constance Garnett

The Artist's Dinner Party, 1903. Viggo Johansen. Oil on canvas. National Museum, Stockholm, Sweden.

I

1 **2** It was a dark autumn night. The old banker was walking up and down his study and remembering how, fifteen years before, he had given a party one autumn evening. There had been many clever men there, and there had been interesting conversations. Among other things they had talked of capital punishment. The majority of the guests, among whom were many journalists and intellectual men, disapproved of the death penalty.

They considered that form of punishment out of date, immoral, and unsuitable for Christian States. In the opinion of some of them the death penalty ought to be replaced everywhere by imprisonment for life.

"I don't agree with you," said their host the banker. "I have not tried either the death penalty or imprisonment for life, but if one may judge à *priori*,[1] the death penalty is more moral and more **humane** than imprisonment for life. Capital punishment kills a man at once, but lifelong imprisonment kills him slowly. Which executioner is the more humane, he who kills you in a few minutes or he who drags the life out of you in the course of many years?"

"Both are equally immoral," observed one of the guests, "for they both have the same object—to take away life. The State is not God. It has not the right to take away what it cannot restore when it wants to."

---

1. *À priori* (ä′ prī ôr′ī) is a Latin term referring to reasoning based on ideas assumed to be true.

> **Vocabulary**
>
> **humane** (hū mān′) *adj.* marked by compassion, sympathy, or consideration for humans or animals

ANTON CHEKHOV **1003**

Approaching Level

DIFFERENTIATED INSTRUCTION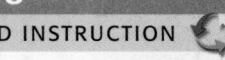

Verb Tenses If students have difficulty recognizing the flashback clues, call attention to the use of past progressive and past perfect tense verbs. The past progressive tense *(was walking)* is used to describe an ongoing action that took place in the past; the past perfect tense verbs *(had given, had talked,* etc.*)* describe past actions that occurred prior to other past actions being described.

English Learners

DIFFERENTIATED INSTRUCTION

Advanced Looking for context clues is a valuable tool for determining the meanings of unfamiliar words.

Write these words on the board: frivolous, reckoning, caprice, obligation, audible. Guide students to use context clues to figure out the meaning of each one. Have them check their definitions in a dictionary. Then call on volunteers to use each word in an original sentence.

Teach

Reading Strategy   1

Make and Verify Predictions Ask students to read the first paragraph of the story to predict what the subject of the bet will be. Then have them read the following page to verify or revise their predictions.

Literary Element   2

Flashback Remind students that a *flashback* is a portion of the story that looks back at events that happened in the past. Have them look for clues that indicate that Chekhov is employing a flashback. *(The dark autumn night is in the present. The banker is looking back fifteen years earlier, when the dinner party took place.)*

View the Art

This painting of a dinner party at his home reflects Viggo Johansen's keen interest in the effects of light.

> For an audio recording of this selection, use Listening Library Audio CD-ROM.

Readability Scores
Dale-Chall: 6.0
DRP: 59
Lexile: 940

Learning Objectives
Making and verify predictions. (TE)
Identifying flashback. (TE)

Teach

Literary Element | 1

Motivation Ask: Why do you think the lawyer suggests an imprisonment of fifteen years when the banker originally suggested five? *(Students may say the lawyer wants to prove his point beyond a doubt.)*

APPROACHING Then ask: If you were in his place, would you have suggested a longer imprisonment? Why or why not? *(Most students will say they would have taken the shorter imprisonment because they would not wish to be in solitary confinement any longer than they had to.)*

Reading Strategy | 2

Analyze Cause-and-Effect Relationships Answer: *The cause is each man's desire to prove his point.*

Literary Element | 3

Character Answer: *He is proud, spoiled, rich, and competitive. He is used to getting his way.*

 For additional literary element practice, see Unit 5 Teaching Resources Book, p. 176.

Reading Strategy | 4

Analyze Cause-and-Effect Relationships Answer: *The banker hopes the lawyer's need for human contact will cause him to give up his solitary confinement and lose the bet.*

Among the guests was a young lawyer, a young man of five-and-twenty. When he was asked his opinion, he said:

"The death sentence and the life sentence are equally immoral, but if I had to choose between the death penalty and imprisonment for life, I would certainly choose the second. To live anyhow is better than not at all."

A lively discussion arose. The banker, who was younger and more nervous in those days,[2] was suddenly carried away by excitement; he struck the table with his fist and shouted at the young man:

☆ "It's not true! I'll bet you two millions you wouldn't stay in solitary confinement for five years."

1 "If you mean that in earnest," said the young man, "I'll take a bet, but I would stay not five but fifteen years."

"Fifteen? Done!" cried the banker. "Gentlemen, I stake two millions!"

"Agreed! You stake your millions and I stake my freedom!" said the young man.

And this wild, senseless bet was carried out! The banker, spoiled and frivolous, with millions beyond his reckoning, was delighted at the bet. At supper he made fun of the young man, and said:

"Think better of it, young man, while there is still time. To me two millions are a trifle, but you are losing three or four of the best years of your life. I say three or four, because you won't stay longer. Don't forget either, you unhappy man, that voluntary confinement is a great deal harder to bear

---

2. Even as he grew old, however, the banker continued to take risks with his money.

2 Analyze Cause-and-Effect Relationships *If the effect of the exchange between the lawyer and the banker is the bet itself, what is the cause?*

3 Character *Based on his opinion and the way he speaks, what assumptions can you make about the banker?*

1004 UNIT 5 MODERN EUROPE

than **compulsory**. The thought that you have the right to step out in liberty at any moment will poison your whole existence in prison. I am sorry for you."

And now the banker, walking to and fro, remembered all this, and asked himself: "What was the object of that bet? What is the good of that man's losing fifteen years of his life and my throwing away two millions? Can it prove that the death penalty is better or worse than imprisonment for life? No, no. It was all nonsensical and meaningless. On my part it was the caprice of a pampered man, and on his part simple greed for money. . . ."

Then he remembered what followed that evening. It was decided that the young man should spend the years of his captivity under the strictest supervision in one of the lodges in the banker's garden. It was agreed that for fifteen years he should not be free to cross the threshold of the lodge, to see human beings, to hear the human voice, or to receive letters and newspapers. He was allowed to have a musical instrument and books, and was allowed to write letters, to drink wine, and to smoke. By the terms of the agreement, the only relations he could have with the outer world were by a little window made purposely for that object. He might have anything he wanted—books, music, wine, and so on—in any quantity he desired by writing an order, but could only receive them through the window. The agreement provided for every detail and every trifle that would make his imprisonment strictly solitary, and bound the young

---

Analyze Cause-and-Effect Relationships *What single cause does the banker assume will bring about the lawyer's losing the bet?*

Vocabulary

compulsory (kəm pul′sər ē) *adj.*mandatory; enforced

Reading Practice

Monitor Comprehension Lead students to understand that the paragraph beginning "And now the banker, walking to and fro, remembered . . ." represents a break in the flashback. Discuss the clues that Chekhov embedded in the text to help readers recognize the shift. *(He reminds readers that the banker began the story by walking back and forth in his study as he remembered the events of fifteen years ago.)* Then have them reread the final paragraph on the page. **Ask:** In what time frame does this paragraph take place? Have students identify the clues that Chekhov used to help them recognize the shift.

Evening in the Ukraine, 1878. Arkhip Ivanovich Kuindzhi. Oil on canvas, 81 x 163 cm. State Russian Museum, St. Petersburg.

 View the Art Arkhip Kuindzhi, a nineteenth-century landscape painter, was fascinated by the almost concrete effects of light. How might the setting of this painting be similar to the setting of the story? ★

man to stay there *exactly* fifteen years, beginning from twelve o'clock of November 14, 1870, and ending at twelve o'clock of November 14, 1885. The slightest attempt on his part to break the conditions, if only two minutes before the end, released the banker from the obligation to pay him two millions.

5 For the first year of his confinement, as far as one could judge from his brief notes, the prisoner suffered severely from loneliness and depression. The sounds of the piano could be heard continually day and night from his lodge. He refused wine and tobacco. Wine, he wrote, excites the desires, and desires are the worst foes of the prisoner; and besides, nothing could be more dreary than drinking good wine and seeing no one. And tobacco spoilt the air of his room. In the first year the books he

sent for were principally of a light character; novels with a complicated love plot, sensational and fantastic stories, and so on.

In the second year the piano was silent in the lodge, and the prisoner asked only for the classics. In the fifth year music was audible again, and the prisoner asked for wine. Those who watched him through the window said that all that year he spent doing nothing but eating and drinking and lying on his bed, frequently yawning and angrily talking to himself. He did not read books. Sometimes at night he would sit down to write; he would spend hours writing, and in the morning tear up all that he had written. More than once he could be heard crying.

In the second half of the sixth year the prisoner began zealously studying languages, philosophy, and history. He threw himself

ANTON CHEKHOV **1005**

Approaching Level

DIFFERENTIATED INSTRUCTION

Summarize To ensure comprehension, work with students to review the terms of the bet. You might ask such leading questions as the following to guide them. **What was the bet?** *(If the lawyer spent fifteen years in solitary confinement, the banker would pay him 2 million rubles.)* **Where was he imprisoned?** *(in a small cottage, or lodge, on the banker's estate)*

What was he allowed to have? *(musical instruments, books, food, wine, and tobacco)* **Was he allowed human contact?** *(no)* **Was he allowed to leave the lodge?** *(If he crossed the threshold, he forfeited the bet.)*

Teach

Reading Strategy	5

Identify Sequence Have students make charts or time lines to summarize, compare, and contrast the lawyer's circumstances as his confinement progresses. For example, on this page have them summarize and compare his activities, moods, and interests in the first and second year.

Cultural History ☆

Rubles The wager is two million rubles, the Russian unit of currency dating from the thirteenth century. At the time of this story (1870), two million rubles was a sizeable fortune. However, during the Russian Revolution (1917), inflation made it almost worthless. Under Soviet rule, the ruble's value often changed dramatically overnight. Inflation continued to plague the ruble after the fall of the Soviet Union. In 1998, one ruble was worth about 15 cents (American); in 1999, it was worth only 4 cents. That value remained fairly consistent over the next decade.

View the Art ★

Answer: *Students might imagine the young man living in an isolated cottage like this one.* In *Evening in the Ukraine,* fading sunlight brings out the beauty of simple village houses.

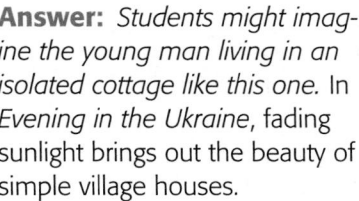

Learning Objectives
Analyzing character. (SE)
Analyzing cause-and-effect relationships. (SE)
Connecting. (TE)
Monitoring comprehension. (TE)
Identifying sequence. (TE)

1005

Teach

Literary Element **1**

Character **Answer:** *He is intelligent, tenacious, and curious.*

Literary Element **2**

Flashback Lead students to understand that the flashback is now over. Chekhov uses the Roman numeral, as well as the lead-in "The old banker remembered . . ." to signal the shift.

Big Idea **3**

Realism and Modernism
Answer: *The banker's behavior shows that he is all too human—he is the victim of the powerful forces of his own will and vanity. This reflects Realism's preoccupation with the foibles and inconsistencies of human nature.*

[APPROACHING] Students may benefit from a review of the principles of Realism. Point out that its goal is to show ordinary, "real" people experiencing "real" and believable feelings. By showing the banker's feelings of greed and vanity, Chekhov makes the character full and dynamic. The banker is not merely a "bad" character. He is human.

Literary History ☆
Reading "Indiscriminately"
Point out that Chekhov includes great examples of the lawyer's random and varied choices of reading material. He reads books about the natural sciences (biology, geology, botany) and then asks for books by the Romantic poet Byron and by Shakespeare. He then moves on to chemistry, medicine, fiction, philosophy, and theology.

eagerly into these studies—so much so that the banker had enough to do to get him the books he ordered. In the course of four years some six hundred volumes were procured at his request. It was during this period that the banker received the following letter from his prisoner:

"My dear Jailer, I write you these lines in six languages. Show them to people who know the languages. Let them read them. If they find not one mistake I implore you to fire a shot in the garden. That shot will show me that my efforts have not been thrown away. The geniuses of all ages and of all lands speak different languages, but the same flame burns in them all. Oh, if you only knew what unearthly happiness my soul feels now from being able to understand them!" The prisoner's desire was fulfilled. The banker ordered two shots to be fired in the garden.

Then after the tenth year, the prisoner sat immovably at the table and read nothing but the Gospel. It seemed strange to the banker that a man who in four years had mastered six hundred learned volumes should waste nearly a year over one thin book easy of comprehension. Theology and histories of religion followed the Gospels.

In the last two years of his confinement the prisoner read an immense quantity of books quite **indiscriminately**. At one time he was busy with the natural sciences, then he would ask for Byron or Shakespeare. There were notes in which he demanded at the same time books on chemistry, and a manual of medicine, and a novel, and some treatise on philosophy or theology. His

  1 | Character *What does the lawyer's mastery of languages reveal about his character?*

Vocabulary

indiscriminately (in´ dis krim´ ə nit lē) *adv.* randomly; haphazardly

reading suggested a man swimming in the sea among the wreckage of his ship, and trying to save his life by greedily clutching first at one spar and then at another.

◆ II ◆

The old banker remembered all this, **2** and thought:

"Tomorrow at twelve o'clock he will regain his freedom. By our agreement I ought to pay him two millions. If I do pay him, it is all over with me: I shall be utterly ruined."

Fifteen years before, his millions had been beyond his reckoning; now he was afraid to ask himself which were greater, his debts or his assets. Desperate gambling on the Stock Exchange, wild speculation, and the excitability which he could not get over even in advancing years, had by degrees led to the decline of his fortune, and the proud, fearless, self-confident millionaire had become a banker of middling rank, trembling at every rise and fall in his investments. "Cursed bet!" muttered the old man, clutching his head in despair. "Why didn't the man die? He is only forty now. He will take my last penny from me, he will marry, will enjoy life, will gamble on the Exchange; while I shall look at him with envy like a beggar, and hear from him every day the same sentence: 'I am indebted to you for the happiness of my life, let me help you!' No, it is too much! The one means of being saved from bankruptcy and disgrace is the death of that man!"

It struck three o'clock, the banker listened; everyone was asleep in the house, and nothing could be heard outside but the

Realism and Modernism *How does Chekhov's description of the banker's behavior and motivations reflect the overall sensibilities of Realism?* **3**

Reading Practice

 **Analyze Figurative Language**
Discuss Chekhov's use of figurative language in the passage regarding the lawyer's "indiscriminate" reading. Have students work with partners or in small groups to analyze this figurative language and to tell, in specific terms, why Chekhov might have chosen to compare the lawyer to a drowning man, and

whether or not they feel that the image is effective. **Ask:** What other comparisons might Chekhov have used to describe the lawyer's situation and state of mind? Provide time for partners or groups to share their opinions with the class.

rustling of the chilled trees. Trying to make no noise, he took from a fireproof safe the key of the door which had not been opened for fifteen years, put on his overcoat, and went out of the house.

It was dark and cold in the garden. Rain was falling. A damp cutting wind was racing about the garden, howling and giving the trees no rest. The banker strained his eyes, but could see neither the earth nor the white statues, nor the lodge, nor the trees. Going to the spot where the lodge stood, he twice called the watchman. No answer followed. Evidently the watchman had sought shelter from the weather, and was now asleep somewhere either in the kitchen or in the greenhouse.

"If I had the pluck to carry out my intention," thought the old man, "suspicion would fall first upon the watchman."

He felt in the darkness for the steps and the door, and went into the entry of the lodge. Then he groped his way into a little passage and lighted a match. There was not a soul there. There was a bedstead with no bedding on it, and in the corner there was a dark cast-iron stove. The seals on the door leading to the prisoner's rooms were intact.

When the match went out the old man, trembling with emotion, peeped through the little window. A candle was burning dimly in the prisoner's room. He was sitting at the table. Nothing could be seen but his back, the hair on his head, and his hands. Open books were lying on the table, on the two easy chairs, and on the carpet near the table.

Five minutes passed and the prisoner did not once stir. Fifteen years' imprisonment had taught him to sit still. The banker tapped at the window with his finger, and the prisoner made no movement whatever in response. Then the banker cautiously broke the seals off the door and put the key in the keyhole. The rusty lock gave a grating sound and the door creaked. The banker expected to hear at once footsteps and a cry of astonishment, but three minutes passed and it was as quiet as ever in the room. He made up his mind to go in.

At the table a man unlike ordinary people was sitting motionless. He was a skeleton with the skin drawn tight over his bones, with long curls like a woman's, and a shaggy beard. His face was yellow with an earthy tint in it, his cheeks were hollow, his back long and narrow, and the hand on which his shaggy head was propped was so thin and delicate that it was dreadful to look at it. His hair was already streaked with silver, and seeing his **emaciated**, aged-looking face, no one would have believed that he was only forty. He was asleep. . . . In front of his bowed head there lay on the table a sheet of paper on which there was something written in fine handwriting.

"Poor creature!" thought the banker, "he is asleep and most likely dreaming of the millions. And I have only to take this half-dead man, throw him on the bed, stifle him a little with the pillow, and the most conscientious expert would find no sign of a violent death. But let us first read what he has written here. . . ."

The banker took the page from the table and read as follows:

"Tomorrow at twelve o'clock I regain my freedom and the right to associate with other men, but before I leave this room and see the sunshine, I think it necessary to say a few words to you. With a clear conscience I tell you, as before God, who beholds me, that I despise freedom and life and health, and all that in your books is called the good things of the world.

Vocabulary

emaciated (i mā′shē āt id) *adj.* thin and feeble

ANTON CHEKHOV **1007**

Teach

Reading Strategy 4

Make and Verify Predictions After students have read this paragraph, ask them to predict what the banker plans to do *(kill the lawyer)*. Then have them read on to verify or revise their predictions.

(APPROACHING) If students have difficulty inferring his plans through the thoughts he expresses, remind them of his fears of bankruptcy.

Ask: How might preventing the lawyer from collecting the money solve the banker's problem?

Literary Element 5

Character Discuss how the lawyer's letter proves that he is a dynamic character, and that imprisonment has caused him to change dramatically.

Learning Objectives
Analyzing character. (SE)
Identifying flashback. (TE)
Making and verifying predictions. (TE)
Analyzing figurative language. (TE)

Approaching Level

DIFFERENTIATED INSTRUCTION

Make a Timeline For students who have trouble keeping track of past and present events in this story, have them keep a timeline as they read, placing events to reflect how time has passed between them. Instruct students to mark the point on the timeline at which the story begins. *(Students should mark the day before the lawyer is to be released and receive his reward.)*

English Learners

DIFFERENTIATED INSTRUCTION

Intermediate Students may have difficulty understanding the meanings of the words and phrases below. Work with them to use context clues to unlock the meanings. Then have them use each word in an original sentence.

- *If I had the **pluck**:* "If I had the nerve" or "If I dared"
- ***peeped** through the little window:* "peeked" or "carefully looked"

- ***stifle** him:* "smother him"
- ***flood** the sky:* "fill the sky [with color]"
- ***cleaving** the storm clouds:* "splitting" or "separating"

Teach

Literary Element | 1

Figurative Language
Discuss the meanings of the simile and metaphor in this paragraph *(like a mirage; as though you were no more than mice burrowing under the floor).*

Reading Strategy | 2

Make Connections Discuss with students how the lawyer's reflections on what he has read are similar to their own experiences of reading adventure stories, tall tales, nonfiction articles about geography, and other diverse forms of literature.

Reading Strategy | 3

Analyze Cause-and-Effect Relationships Answer: *He has learned that money and life—the things he valued earlier—are meaningless.*

 To check students' understanding of the selection, see Unit 5 Teaching Resources Book, p. 181.

"For fifteen years I have been intently studying earthly life. It is true I have not seen the earth nor men, but in your books I have drunk fragrant wine, I have sung songs, I have hunted stags and wild boars in the forests, have loved women. . . . Beauties as **ethereal** as clouds, created by the magic of your poets and geniuses, have visited me at night, and have whispered in my ears wonderful tales that have set my brain in a whirl. In your books I have climbed to the peaks of Elburz and Mont Blanc, and from there I have seen the sun rise and have watched it at evening flood the sky, the ocean, and the mountaintops with gold and crimson. I have watched from there the lightning flashing over my head and cleaving the storm clouds. I have seen green forests, fields, rivers, lakes, towns. I have heard the singing of the sirens, and the strains of the shepherds' pipes; I have touched the wings of comely devils who flew down to converse with me of God. . . . In your books I have flung myself into the bottomless pit, performed miracles, slain, burned towns, preached new religions, conquered whole kingdoms. . . .

"Your books have given me wisdom. All that the unresting thought of man has created in the ages is compressed into a small compass in my brain. I know that I am wiser than all of you.

"And I despise your books, I despise wisdom and the blessings of this world. It is all worthless, fleeting, illusory, and deceptive, like a mirage. You may be proud, wise, and
1 fine, but death will wipe you off the face of the earth as though you were no more than mice burrowing under the floor, and your posterity, your history, your immortal

geniuses will burn or freeze together with the earthly globe.

"You have lost your reason and taken the wrong path. You have taken lies for truth, and hideousness for beauty. You would marvel if, owing to strange events of some sorts, frogs and lizards suddenly grew on apple and orange trees instead of fruit, or if roses began to smell like a sweating horse; so I marvel at you who exchange heaven for earth. I don't want to understand you.

"To prove to you in action how I despise all that you live by, I renounce the two millions of which I once dreamed as of paradise and which now I despise. To deprive myself of the right to the money I shall go out from here five hours before the time fixed, and so break the compact. . . ."

When the banker had read this he laid the page on the table, kissed the strange man on the head, and went out of the lodge, weeping. At no other time, even when he had lost heavily on the Stock Exchange, had he felt so great a contempt for himself. When he got home he lay on his bed, but his tears and emotion kept him **2** for hours from sleeping.

Next morning the watchmen ran in with pale faces, and told him they had seen the man who lived in the lodge climb out of the window into the garden, go to the gate, and disappear. The banker went at once with the servants to the lodge and made sure of the flight of his prisoner. To avoid arousing unnecessary talk, he took from the table the writing in which the millions were renounced, and when he got home locked it up in the fireproof safe. ∾

Vocabulary

ethereal (i thēr′ē əl) *adj.* otherworldly

Analyze Cause-and-Effect Relationships *How is the overall effect of the lawyer's confinement a kind of death sentence?* **3**

Reading Practice

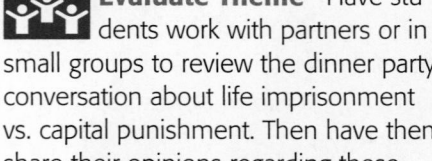 **SMALL GROUP Evaluate Theme** Have students work with partners or in small groups to review the dinner party conversation about life imprisonment vs. capital punishment. Then have them share their opinions regarding these questions:

Did the lawyer prove his point that "To live anyhow is better than not at all"?

Who won the bet?

Why did the banker keep the lawyer's letter and lock it up in a fireproof safe?

Provide time for partners or groups to share their opinions with the class.

After You Read

Respond and Think Critically

Respond and Interpret

1. Were you surprised by the outcome of the story? Explain.

2. (a)What issue do the guests debate at the banker's party? (b)Why does the banker bait the lawyer into making the bet?

3. (a)What are the terms of the lawyer's imprisonment? (b)How is the banker also imprisoned?

Analyze and Evaluate

4. (a)According to the banker's remarks about the death penalty, what does he value most in life? (b)Does he change his point of view by the end of the story? Explain.

5. (a)In your opinion, which is the most difficult period of the lawyer's imprisonment? Explain. (b)Which is the least difficult? Explain.

6. (a)Why does the lawyer choose to stay in solitary confinement until the last day? (b)In your opinion, did the lawyer truly find wisdom during his imprisonment? Explain.

Connect

7. [Big Idea] **Realism and Modernism** What statement does Chekhov make about the realities of power and money?

8. **Connect to Today** Maximum-security prisons exist all over the United States. In these facilities, prisoners are kept in solitary confinement for nearly the entire day. (a)Why do you think prisons use solitary confinement? (b)Do you think it is effective? Explain.

Daily Life & Culture

Journey to Sakhalin

In 1890, Chekhov traveled to remote Sakhalin Island on the eastern edge of Russia to study a real prison colony. He detailed the geography and moral and social structure of the colony—including the often-brutal living conditions of prisoners. He allegedly made 10,000 census cards, which he used to thoroughly survey the colony. In 1895 he published his findings as *The Island of Sakhalin*. In it he added that the compulsion to escape incarceration is unavoidable: "Unless he is a philosopher who can live anywhere and under any conditions, he simply cannot prevent himself from desiring to escape. . ."

Group Activity With a small group of classmates, discuss the following questions.

1. How does the lawyer defy Chekhov's conclusion about the desire for escape?

2. How does this information about Chekhov's journey help you understand "The Bet"?

Riveting the heavy chains on a Russian convict on the Siberian prison island of Sakhalin.

ANTON CHEKHOV **1009**

Daily Life & Culture

1. The lawyer willingly incarcerates himself, thereby going against basic human nature.

2. It gives the story a more realistic view of prison life, the moral implications of imprisonment, and an insight as to why the lawyer doesn't escape his confinement even though he can.

7. Chekhov's story shows that neither money nor enforced withdrawal from society will lead to a satisfying life.

8. (a) Students may note that solitary confinement is used to protect or punish prisoners. (b) Some may understand the need for protection, and others may point out the damaging psychological effects of long-term isolation.

After You Read

Assess

1. Some students may have been surprised, given the fact that the lawyer could have left his "prison" at any time.

2. (a) They discuss the morality of the death penalty. (b) The banker assumes that, like himself, no one could spend those years alone. Consequently, he feels sure he will win.

3. (a) If the lawyer stays in solitary confinement for fifteen years, the banker will pay him two million rubles. (b) As time passes, the banker worries about losing his money.

4. (a) The banker values freedom; he believes that a quick death would be better than prison. (b) Many students will say the banker feels disgusted with himself at the end of the story, but they may also believe that he has not really changed.

5. (a) Students may note that in the fifth year, the lawyer drinks wine, gives up reading, and becomes depressed and bored. (b) Students may say that the year the lawyer learned six languages was the easiest because he was committed to a goal.

6. (a) He may have wanted to prove to the banker that he was not giving up out of weakness. (b) Students may respond that true wisdom might have led the lawyer to leave earlier or to understand better how to live in an imperfect world.

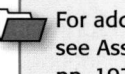 For additional assessment, see Assessment Resources, pp. 197–198.

After You Read

Literary Element

1. He is round because he reveals pride, confidence, fear, and guilt.

2. He is dynamic because he changes significantly during his imprisonment.

3. The guests at the dinner party and the watchmen who keep an eye on the lawyer's cottage are all minor characters.

Review: Mood

Students' should see that the quotation evokes a mood of excitement and desperation.

Reading Strategy

(E) is the correct answer. The banker squandered away his money. Paying the man would ruin him financially. He believed the only solution was to kill the man. Answers A, B, C, and D are not supported by details in the story.

Progress Check

Can students analyze cause-and-effect relationships?

If No → See Unit 5 Teaching Resources Book, p. 177.

Vocabulary Practice

Possible answers:

Vocabulary word: *humane* Similar word: gentle Explanation: *Humane* has the stronger connotation. *Gentle* implies a nature in general, while *humane* implies a response to a situation.

Vocabulary word: *compulsory* Similar word: necessary Explanation: *Compulsory* has the stronger connotation. *Compulsory* implies that whatever must be done will be enforced, while something might be necessary but not enforced.

1010

Literary Element Character

A **flat character** has only one or two dominant traits. **Round characters** are more fully developed; like real people, there are many sides to their personalities. Characters who change significantly as the plot unfolds are called **dynamic characters**. **Static characters** remain essentially the same, even though their outward circumstances might change. For example, a character who experiences great hardship but remains cheerful throughout a story is a static character.

1. Is the banker a flat or round character? Explain.

2. Is the lawyer a static or dynamic character? Explain.

3. Who are the story's minor characters?

Review: Mood

As you learned on page 713, **mood** is the overall feeling of a literary work. An author's choice of language, subject matter, setting, and tone contribute to the mood. In Chekhov's stories and plays, it often seems that not much is happening. But he creates a strong sense of mood as he explores the inner worlds of his characters and the way they think and live.

Partner Activity With a partner, read the following quotation from the story. Discuss the mood it evokes.

> *"What was the object of that bet? What is the good of a man's losing fifteen years of his life and my throwing away two millions? Can it prove that the death penalty is better or worse than imprisonment for life? No, no. It was all nonsensical and meaningless."*

LOG ON ▶ **Literature** Online

Selection Resources For Selection Quizzes, eFlash-cards, and Reading-Writing Connection activities, go to glencoe.com and enter QuickPass code GLW6053u5.

Reading Strategy Analyze Cause-and-Effect Relationships

SAT Skills Practice

Why did the banker plan to kill the man in the cell?

(A) The banker had to prove that long imprisonment does kill a man.

(B) The banker took out a life insurance policy on the man and needed the money.

(C) The banker was wary of the man's wisdom, gained from years of reading and solitude.

(D) The banker was afraid the man would kill him.

(E) The banker's fortunes had failed in the last fifteen years, and paying his bet would bankrupt him.

Vocabulary Practice

Practice with Denotation and Connotation
Denotation is the dictionary meaning of a word. **Connotation** is its implied meaning. Complete a graphic organizer like this one for each boldfaced vocabulary word.

humane   compulsory   emaciated
ethereal   indiscriminately

EXAMPLE:

| Vocabulary word: zealous | → | Similar word: eager |

↓

Explanation: Zealous has the stronger connotation. A zealous person is very enthusiastic about one thing, and an eager person might not be as enthusiastic.

Academic Vocabulary

*The young man in "The Bet" agrees to be **isolated** from the world for fifteen years.*

Isolated is an academic word with a variety of uses. For example, in chemistry an **isolated** substance is something that has been separated from a mixture. To further explore this word, answer the following question: Have you ever felt **isolated** from other people? Explain.

For more on academic vocabulary, see pages 36–37 and R83–R85.

Vocabulary word: *emaciated* Similar word: thin Explanation: *Emaciated* has the stronger connotation because it is a shocking thinness.

Vocabulary word: *ethereal* Similar word: airy Explanation: *Ethereal* has the stronger connotation because it refers to the celestial realm. *Airy* could merely refer to physical ventilation or a lightness of being.

Vocabulary word: *indiscriminately* Similar word: randomly Explanation: *Indiscriminately* has the stronger connotation because it can involve thought, whereas *randomly* implies chance.

Academic Vocabulary

Students might describe a time they felt distanced from others because of an argument or a difference of opinion.

Respond Through Writing

Summary

Report Story Events To fully grasp "The Bet," you need to be able to summarize the events of the story. A **summary** is a short retelling of events in chronological order. Write a summary of "The Bet," telling the main events of the story in proper sequence. Your summary should be about 100 words and should not include your personal feelings, just the facts. Be sure to report the cause-and-effect relationships in the story.

Understand the Task In a **plot summary**, you report the main story events and explain the main conflicts and their resolutions.

Prewrite To help you get organized before you write, refer to the chart you made on page 1002. Then make a cause-and-effect chain to review the key events of the story.

Draft Use your chain to create a time-based structure in your summary. Keep in mind that a summary includes only important details. For instance, you could say that the banker lacks money to pay the bet, but not that he lost money on the Stock Exchange. Here is a summary of Katherine Mansfield's "The Doll's House" (see pages 790–801).

The Burnell sisters receive an exquisite dollhouse, which must be kept in the courtyard. The youngest sister, Kezia, especially loves a tiny lamp in the house. The only girls from school who are not invited to see the dollhouse are the Kelveys, who are shunned because of their low social class. One day when Kezia is alone in the courtyard, the Kelveys come walking down the road. Kezia invites them to look at the dollhouse. While they are looking, Kezia's aunt yells at the children and the Kelveys leave. The younger Kelvey sister, Else, says she saw the lamp Kezia loves.

Revise When you finish your draft, get feedback from someone who has read the story and someone who has not. The person who has read the story should check for inaccuracies in your summary. The person who has not read the story should understand the basic story from your summary. Revise your summary to reflect your readers' comments.

Edit and Proofread Proofread your paper, correcting any errors in spelling, grammar, and punctuation. Review the Grammar Tip in the side column for ideas on using absolute phrases.

> **Grammar Tip**

Absolute Phrases

An absolute phrase modifies an entire sentence, rather than a specific word. These phrases have no grammatical relation to the rest of the sentence, and they consist of nouns or pronouns along with participles and related modifiers. In the following example, the absolute phrase is underlined:

His money depleting, the banker worries how he can pay if he loses the bet.

The lawyer turned to books, his mind reeling in solitude.

In some absolute phrases, the participle *being* is understood rather than stated: *The jail sentence* [being] *over, the lawyer could have claimed his money.*

After You Read

Assess

Respond Through Writing

Students' summaries should

- present the facts of the story in chronological order
- highlight cause-and-effect relationships
- be free of personal opinions

<u>Sample Summary for "The Bet":</u>

At a party, men debate over which is worse, life imprisonment or capital punishment. A young man says that he would rather be in solitary confinement for fifteen years than die, and a banker bets him that he could not last that long. The man reads many books during his confinement. The night before the bet is up, the banker decides he must kill the man because he can no longer afford to pay him. The banker finds the man sleeping and reads a letter that he has written. It says that the man will end the bet because he has renounced the world. The man leaves the next morning, and the banker is filled with self-contempt.

For grammar practice, see Unit 5 Teaching Resources Book, p. 180.

Advanced Learners/Pre-AP

DIFFERENTIATED INSTRUCTION

Analyze Author's Purpose Have interested students review the information regarding Anton Chekhov on pages 1001 and 1002. Then have them discuss the following: *Critics once rebuked Chekhov for not espousing strong political points of view. In "The Bet," did he espouse a strong political point of view on the issue of capital punishment versus life imprisonment?*

Approaching Level

DIFFERENTIATED INSTRUCTION

Summarize Before students begin drafting their story summaries, point out that their task is to compress a lengthy story into just 100 words, which is about five or six sentences. Therefore, stress that a summary should contain only the main ideas, the main characters, and only the most important details. To stimulate thought and provide an example, you might work with them to write an opening sentence, such

as: *At a party, men debate over which is worse, life imprisonment or capital punishment.*

Focus

Bellringer Option

Read this quote aloud to students: "Written poetry is worth reading once, and then should be destroyed. Let the dead poets make way for others. Then we might even come to see that it is our veneration for what has already been created, however beautiful and valid it may be, that petrifies us." Explain to students that these are the words of Antonin Artaud, a writer who was much influenced by the Symbolists. Artaud felt that excessive study of older poetry would prevent contemporary poets from producing innovative works. **Ask:** Do you agree or disagree with Artaud's statement? (*Some students may agree that the exemplary poetry of the past may paralyze the contemporary poet. Others may feel that contemporary poets should learn all they can from poets of the past.*)

Learning Objectives

For pages 1012–1013
In studying this text, you will focus on the following objectives:

Literary Study:
Analyzing literary periods.
Analyzing literary genres.

Reading:
Evaluating historical influences.
Connecting to the literature.

The Symbolist Poets

IN THE LATE NINETEENTH CENTURY, A GROUP OF FRENCH POETS CREATED daring, emotional poems rich with symbols, or details with both literal and figurative meanings. Known as the Symbolists, these authors revolutionized poetry with their experimental rejection of strict forms and classical subjects.

Baudelaire and Mallarmé

The writings of Charles Baudelaire (bō də lär´) mark a turning point from the Romanticism that dominated poetry in the early 1800s and the emergence of Symbolism later in the century. Like the Romantics, Baudelaire (1821–1867) wrote emotionally charged poetry. However, he disliked Romanticism's direct statement of emotions and its focus on nature. Inspired by the American author Edgar Allan Poe's use of symbols, Baudelaire created rich images to suggest, rather than directly state, the harshness of urban life. Although critics today consider Baudelaire one of the finest nineteenth-century poets, his work appalled many

of his contemporaries. When his collection *The Flowers of Evil* was published in 1857, six of the poems were banned, and Baudelaire was accused of obscenity and blasphemy.

One of the few poets of the day to embrace Baudelaire's sordid urban landscapes was Stéphane Mallarmé (mal´ är mā), who emerged as a leader of the Symbolists. In such works as *Divagations* (1897), Mallarmé (1842–1898) bends language into lines of poetry without clear meaning. Through the use of fantastic images and musical sound patterns, Mallarmé believed poets could give their readers glimpses of deep emotional and mental realities that could not be described directly. He said "To *name* an object is to take away three-fourths of the pleasure given by a poem. The pleasure consists in guessing little by little: to *suggest* it, that is the ideal."

Rimbaud and Verlaine

An arrogant and volatile genius from a young age, Arthur Rimbaud (rom bō´) (1854–1891) saw himself as a poetic "seer," or prophet. Along with his friend Paul Verlaine (vār len), he wanted to break free of the conventional ways poets described the world. Rimbaud created brilliant free verse and prose poems in his teenage years that matched his brash vision. However, Rimbaud left poetry behind before the age of twenty, and in 1875 he began a series of adventures as a merchant and gunrunner in Africa. The following poem exemplifies Rimbaud's use of symbolism.

Seated portrait of symbolist poet Stephane Mallarme.
Nadar. Photograph.

Viewing Practice

Analyze Symbolist Art Draw students' attention to the painting on page 1013, by the French artist Pierre Puvis de Chavannes (1824–1898). Inform them that Puvis de Chavannes, who was considered a Symbolist painter, used evocative images and rejected traditional rules of perspective in his paintings.

Ask: What do you think makes this painting a work of Symbolist art? (*Students may note that the painting* suggests the fisherman as a Christ figure but does not spell this out for the viewer. The fisherman wears a wreath that suggests a crown of thorns, and the woman and child could be seen as a Madonna.)

Then ask: Why is the figure in the boat ambiguous and not obviously a Christ figure? (*Students should point out that that the figure of the fisherman does not have any of the usual accoutrements of an image of Christ, such as a wound in his* side. The scene is curiously idyllic and still.)

Ask: How does looking at this painting make you feel? How is this different from your response to other works of art? (*Answers will vary. Students should support their answers. Students may say that other works of art have more obvious ways of provoking the viewer into responding with a particular emotion or idea.*)

1 My Bohemia
A Fantasy

Arthur Rimbaud
Translated by Wyatt Mason

And so off I went, fists thrust in the torn pockets
Of a coat held together by no more than its name.
O Muse, how I served you beneath the blue;
And oh what dreams of dazzling love I dreamed!

My only pair of pants had a huge hole.
—Like some dreaming Tom Thumb, I sowed
Rhyme with each step. My inn was the Big Dipper.
—My stars rustled in the sky.

Roadside on warm September nights
I listened as drops of dew fell
On my forehead like fortifying wine;

And there, surrounded by streaming shadows,
I rhymed
Aloud, and as if they were lyres, plucked the laces
Of my wounded shoes, one foot beneath my heart.

Like Rimbaud, Paul Verlaine (1844–1896) began his career by imitating contemporary forms. Soon, however, he began exploring the musical properties of language. This impulse led to the 1874 collection *Songs Without Words.* Rimbaud's stormy friendship with Verlaine ended violently in 1873, when, in a fit of rage, Verlaine shot and wounded Rimbaud. Verlaine served two years in prison for the act. In 1886, under the mistaken belief his friend had died, Verlaine published Rimbaud's collection *Illuminations,* which was written during their travels together. This image-rich collection of prose poems made Rimbaud famous.

The Symbolist Legacy

Spurred by the innovations of Mallarmé, Rimbaud, and Verlaine, Symbolism gained momentum in the 1880s, when many Symbolist journals and magazines began to appear. Although the movement declined around the turn of the century, it laid the foundations for modern British and American poetry. Imagism— an American poetic movement of the early twentieth century led by Ezra Pound—applied Symbolist principles to the presentation of images. The work of William Butler Yeats, T. S. Eliot, and Virginia Woolf was also influenced by the Symbolist poets.

The Poor Fisherman, 1881. Pierre Puvis de Chavannes. Oil on canvas. Musee d'Orsay, Paris.

 **Literature** Online

Literature and Reading For more about the Symbolist poets, go to glencoe.com and enter QuickPass code GLW6053u5.

Respond and Think Critically

1. How does Baudelaire's poetry differ from that of the Romantics?

2. (a)What poetic techniques did the Symbolists embrace? (b)What poetic conventions did they reject?

3. (a)What role does the imagination play in the life of the speaker of "My Bohemia"? (b)What does this tell you about the concerns of the Symbolists?

4. Do the images in "My Bohemia" appeal more to emotion or to logic? Explain.

Advanced Learners/Pre-AP

DIFFERENTIATED INSTRUCTION

Parnassianism Advanced learners may be interested to know that another French poetic movement, Parnassianism, occurred between Romanticism and Symbolism.

Have advanced students conduct research on the Parnassians. In an oral presentation, have them discuss whether they prefer the poetry of the Romantics, the Parnassians, or the Symbolists, providing specific reasons for their choices.

Teach

Big Idea   1

From the Enlightenment to Romanticism Have students reread the beginning of Victor Hugo's "Russia 1812" (page 978). Have them compare the style of that poem to the style of "My Bohemia." **Ask:** If you did not know who had written these two poems, would it be possible to assume they were written by the same author? Why or why not? *(Some students will say yes, because both are written in a similarly emotional, expressive style. Others will say no, because Hugo's poem contains a concrete narrative, while Rimbaud's is composed of whimsical—and even nonsensical—images.)*

Assess

1. It uses images to suggest emotions, rather than stating them directly. It also focuses on urban life rather than nature.

2. (a) the use of symbolic images, loose forms, and musical language (b) classical forms and direct expressions of emotions

3. (a) The imagination brings joy and richness to the speaker's meager life. (b) They were interested more in abstractions than in real-world observations or experiences.

4. The images appeal more to emotion. Phrases such as "My inn was the Big Dipper" and "one foot beneath my heart" do not make sense literally, but they evoke a sense of mystery and beauty.

Before You Read

Bellringer Options

Daily Language Practice Transparency 94

Or ask: Have you ever tried to help someone deal with deep anxiety or alienation? Explain. Allow students to discuss their responses. Encourage them to discuss the complexity of the issue and the value of empathy.

Literary History ☆

Alienation in the Modern World During the late 1800s and early 1900s, great changes in Europe such as the Industrial Revolution and World War I shattered established traditions and values, challenging people's understanding of their place in the world. The characters in much of Modernist fiction, including the fiction of Kafka, must confront a threatening, confusing, and possibly meaningless society. They often deal with personal anxiety and alienation as a result.

First Sorrow

Austria/Czech Republic

Meet **Franz Kafka**
(1883–1924)

Franz Kafka's fiction presents the most unusual events as completely commonplace. In "The Metamorphosis," for example, a young man wakes up to discover he has been transformed into an insect. Kafka's fictional world is full of such occurrences—nightmares that capture what he saw as the anxiety of modern life. His characters—ordinary, rational beings—must cope with a world they no longer understand, a world inspired by Kafka's own anxieties and insecurities.

Strained Family Life Kafka was born to a German-speaking Jewish family in Prague, which was then under the control of the Austro-Hungarian Empire and is now the capital of the Czech Republic. His father, a successful merchant, was a domineering authority figure who often bragged of his humble working-class background. Though Kafka lived at home for most of his life, he did not enjoy a satisfying relationship with his parents, neither of whom took his writing aspirations seriously. His relationship with his father was especially problematic. Kafka's ambivalence toward his father—simultaneously seeking his approval and being intimidated by his bullying tactics—haunted the author throughout his life and had a powerful influence on his work.

A Reclusive Professional In 1901, Kafka began university studies in law, German literature, and art history. He graduated in 1906 with a degree in law and began working for an Italian insurance company the following year. A year later he joined the Workers' Accident Insurance Institute and balanced his work with writing and socializing. His small circle of friends regarded him as charming, intelligent, and kind

"We need the books that affect us like a disaster, that grieve us deeply.... A book must be the axe for the frozen sea inside us."
—Franz Kafka

but also reserved, insecure, and increasingly isolated. Kafka's sense of isolation can be explained in part as the result of a lack of social identity. As a German-speaking Jew—who did not practice Judaism—living in a city with a Czech majority, Kafka felt estranged from each social group around him. He became involved in several serious relationships and was engaged three times (twice to the same woman), but he never married. Plagued by a frail constitution since childhood, Kafka spent much of his time in hospitals to treat a tubercular condition.

Many of his stories and novels remained unpublished during his lifetime, in part because of his own insecurities regarding their worth. When he realized he was dying, Kafka left instructions with his literary executor to destroy all of his writings. Fortunately, those instructions were ignored. After his death, some of his best work was published—including the novels *The Trial*, *The Castle*, and *America*.

 **Literature** Online

Author Search For more about Franz Kafka, go to glencoe.com and enter QuickPass code GLW6053u5.

Selection Skills

Literary Elements
- Tone (SE pp. 1015, 1017, 1019)
- Theme (SE p. 1019)
- Character (TE p. 1016)

First Sorrow

Writing Skills/Grammar
- Apply Tone (SE p. 1020)

Reading Skills
- Respond to Characters (SE pp. 1015, 1017, 1018, 1020)

Vocabulary Skills
- Word Usage (SE pp. 1015, 1020)
- Academic Vocabulary (TE p. 1020)

Speaking/ Listening/Viewing Skills
- Debate (TE p. 1018)

Literature and Reading Preview

Connect to the Story

Have you ever wanted to isolate yourself from your friends or family? Where would you go to be alone? Freewrite for a few minutes about these questions.

Build Background

☆ Kafka's works influenced Jean Paul Sartre and Albert Camus (see page 1056), leaders of the Existentialist movement in France. Existentialism is a philosophy that posits the belief that life has no meaning, purpose, or value other than that which individuals give to their own lives. It developed as a pragmatic response to the alienation and confusion many people believed defined contemporary life.

Set Purposes for Reading

Big Idea Realism and Modernism

Modernist works share a variety of characteristics, including a focus on the mundane realities of modern life and a preoccupation with themes such as uncertainty, alienation, and ambiguity. As you read "First Sorrow," ask yourself, What details portray the mundane nature of an isolated modern life?

Literary Element Tone

Tone is an author's attitude toward his or her subject matter or the audience. Tone is conveyed through elements such as word choice, punctuation, sentence structure, dialogue, and figurative language. As you read "First Sorrow," ask yourself, How does the author's tone contribute to your response to the story?

Reading Strategy Respond to Characters

Kafka's stories and novels have been described as "open parables" whose meanings are somewhat ambiguous. An effective way to respond to this ambiguity is to focus on your response to the characters and their actions. As you read, ask yourself, How do the characters' actions affect you?

....

Tip: Compile Details As you read, use a chart to compile a list of what happens. Next to each item, respond to the characters' actions. Later, you can use your responses to help you interpret the meaning of the story.

What Happens	My Response
First paragraph: "he never came down from his trapeze by night or day"	This seems odd. Why does he do this?

Learning Objectives

For pages 1014–1020

In studying this text, you will focus on the following objectives:

Literary Study: Analyzing tone.

Reading: Responding to characters.

Writing: Applying tone.

Vocabulary

modest (mod′ist) *adj.* unassuming; plain; simple; p. 1017 *To avoid being overdressed, we changed into more modest clothes.*

seclusion (si klo̅o̅′zhən) *n.* solitude; privacy; isolation; p. 1017 *The hermit lived in seclusion, totally isolated from society.*

prolong (prə lông′) *v.* lengthen in time or space; draw out; p. 1017 *The master of ceremonies prolonged his introduction, citing all the speaker's honors.*

distressed (dis tres′d) *adj.* anxious; anguished; upset; p. 1018 *The distressed doctor felt even worse when she saw the villagers' suffering firsthand.*

furrows (fur′ōs) *n.* grooves or tracks cut in the earth by a plow; wrinkles; p. 1018 *The speaker tried to appear calm, but the furrows on his brow revealed his nervousness.*

....

Tip: Word Usage When you encounter a new word, ask yourself a question about it. For example, What might cause furrows on someone's forehead?

FRANZ KAFKA **1015**

Approaching Level

DIFFERENTIATED INSTRUCTION

Write an Informational Document
Have approaching–level students research a topic related to the history of the circus or acrobatics. Topics might include the Wallendas, the Ringling Brothers, Chinese acrobats, or the Cirque du Soleil. Have students write a brief informational document, such as a brochure. Ask interested students to read their documents to the class or discuss any interesting facts they noted in their research.

Advanced Learners/Pre-AP

DIFFERENTIATED INSTRUCTION

Write a News Story Have advanced students research a specific topic or event related to the circus that is suited for a news article. Have students include *who, what, where, when, why,* and *how* in their articles, a catchy headline, and an engaging lead-in. For historical topics, have students write as if the event occurred recently. Articles should include researched information, as well as tone and voice appropriate to the genre and topic.

Before You Read

Focus

Summary

While working in a theater, a trapeze artist arranges his life so that he never has to descend from his trapeze. He requests two trapezes for his act instead of one. The manager assents readily, but the trapeze artist breaks down and sobs, because suddenly the idea of having only one trapeze seems unbearable. The manager finally consoles the trapeze artist, but he realizes that the trapeze artist will only continue to be haunted by this and similar sorrows.

 For summaries in languages other than English, see Unit 5 Teaching Resources Book, pp. 185–190.

Vocabulary

Synonym Substitution

Have students write a brief scene or character sketch using all of the vocabulary words. Then have students form pairs and trade papers. Each student should try to choose appropriate synonyms for each vocabulary word as quickly as possible. In addition, encourage students to read the most interesting sketches or scenes aloud and have students, as a class, choose additional synonyms.

 For additional vocabulary practice, see Unit 5 Teaching Resources Book, p. 193.

Teach

Cultural History ☆

Existentialism Have students review Build Background from page 1015. Explain that Existentialism includes the belief that human existence is individual and constituted by possibility. At any moment, individuals are confronted with infinite possibilities or choices. In a meaningless or absurd world, an individual's choices are the only way he or she can create meaning. The outcome of any choice is never guaranteed, however, so possibility is always surrounded by anxiety. Kafka himself described human existence as the attempt to find a secure and stable reality that is never within reach.

For an audio recording of this selection, use Listening Library Audio CD-ROM.

Readability Scores

Dale-Chall: 9.9
DRP: 62
Lexile: 1590

In the Circus, 1932. Lill Tschudi. Linocut. Private collection.

FIRSTSORROW

Franz Kafka
Translated by Willa and Edwin Muir

Literary Element Practice

Analyze Character Have students record details from the story that are clues to the trapeze artist's character. Remind students that writers create characters by describing a character's appearance; describing the character's thoughts, words, and actions; and by describing what other characters say or think about the character. Have students create a three-column chart to organize details that are clues to the trapeze artist's character. Then have students create brief, two- to three-sentence summaries about the trapeze artist's character so far.

Character: The Trapeze Artist

Physical Traits	Thoughts, Words, Actions	Others' Thoughts and Words
Summary:		

A trapeze artist—this art, practiced high in the vaulted domes of the great variety theaters, is admittedly one of the most difficult humanity can achieve—had so arranged his life that, as long as he kept working in the same building, he never came down from his trapeze by night or day, at first only from a desire to perfect his skill, but later because custom was too strong for him. All his needs, very **modest** needs at that, were supplied by relays of attendants who watched from below and sent up and hauled down again in specially constructed containers whatever he required. This way of living caused no particular inconvenience to the theatrical people, except that, when other turns were on the stage, his being still up aloft, which could not be dissembled, proved somewhat distracting, as also the fact that, although at such times he mostly kept very still, he drew a stray glance here and there from the public. Yet the management overlooked this, because he was an extraordinary and unique artist. And of course they recognized that this mode of life was no mere prank, and that only in this way could he really keep himself in constant practice and his art at the pitch of its perfection.

Besides, it was quite healthful up there, and when in the warmer seasons of the year the side windows all around the dome of the theater were thrown open and sun and fresh air came pouring irresistibly into the dusky vault, it was even beautiful. True, his social life was somewhat limited, only sometimes a fellow acrobat swarmed up the ladder to him, and then they both sat on the trapeze, leaning left and right against the supporting ropes, and chatted, or builders' workmen repairing the roof exchanged a few words with him through an open window, or the fireman, inspecting the emergency lighting in the top gallery, called over to him something that sounded respectful but could hardly be made out. Otherwise nothing disturbed his **seclusion**; occasionally, perhaps, some theater hand straying through the empty theater of an afternoon gazed thoughtfully up into the great height of the roof, almost beyond eyeshot, where the trapeze artist, unaware that he was being observed, practiced his art or rested.

The trapeze artist could have gone on living peacefully like that, had it not been for the inevitable journeys from place to place, which he found extremely trying. Of course his manager saw to it that his sufferings were not **prolonged** one moment more than necessary; for town travel, racing automobiles were used, which whirled him, by night if possible or in the earliest hours of the morning, through the empty streets at breakneck speed, too slow all the same for the trapeze artist's impatience; for railways journeys, a whole compartment was reserved, in which the trapeze artist, as a possible though wretched alternative to his usual way of living, could pass the time up on the luggage rack; in the next town on their circuit, long before he arrived, the trapeze was already slung up in the theater and all the doors leading to the stage were flung wide open, all corridors kept free— yet the manager never knew a happy moment until the trapeze artist set his foot

1 Respond to Characters *What type of person is the trapeze artist?*

2 Tone *What is ironic about the narrator's observation? What is the narrator's attitude?*

Vocabulary

modest (mod′ ist) *adj.* unassuming; plain; simple

Vocabulary

seclusion (si klōō′ zhən) *n.* solitude; privacy; isolation
prolong (prə lông′) *v.* lengthen in time or space; draw out

FRANZ KAFKA **1017**

Teach

Reading Strategy   1

Respond to Characters
Answer: *The trapeze artist seems to be an obsessive perfectionist.*

Literary Element   2

Tone Answer: *The narrator's observation is a gross understatement. The trapeze artist has virtually no social life. The narrator's attitude seems to be one of casual indifference. The word* true *suggests the observation is an afterthought and somewhat suggests minimal concern for the artist's isolation.*

 For additional literary element practice, see Unit 5 Teaching Resources Book, p. 191.

Learning Objectives
Responding to characters. (SE)
Analyzing tone. (SE)
Analyzing character. (TE)

Approaching Level

DIFFERENTIATED INSTRUCTION

Make and Verify Predictions Have students record their predictions about what they think will happen next. Their answers will vary. Have students verify their predictions as they finish the story.

Teach

Reading Strategy   **1**

Respond to Characters
Answer: *The journeys interrupt his routine. His irritation seems inappropriate.*

Big Idea   **2**

Realism and Modernism
Answer: *He wants to keep the innocent and fragile trapeze artist from suffering. The sentences that follow suggest the manager does not think this is possible; he worries about the consequences.*

on the rope ladder and in a twinkling, at long last, hung aloft on his trapeze.

Despite so many journeys having been successfully arranged by the manager, each new one embarrassed him again, for the journeys, apart from everything else, got on the nerves of the artist a great deal.

Once when they were again traveling together, the trapeze artist lying on the luggage rack dreaming, the manager leaning back in the opposite window seat reading a book, the trapeze artist addressed his companion in a low voice. The manager was immediately all attention. The trapeze artist, biting his lips, said that he must always in future have two trapezes for his performance instead of only one, two trapezes opposite each other. The manager at once agreed. But the trapeze artist, as if to show that the manager's consent counted for as little as his refusal said that never again would he perform on only one trapeze, in no circumstances whatever. The very idea that it might happen at all seemed to make him shudder. The manager, watchfully feeling his way, once more emphasized his entire agreement, two trapezes were better than one, besides it would be an advantage to have a second bar, more variety could be introduced into the performance. At that the trapeze artist suddenly burst into tears. Deeply **distressed,** the

manager sprang to his feet and asked what was the matter, then getting no answer climbed up on the seat and caressed him, cheek to cheek, so that his own face was bedabbled by the trapeze artist's tears. Yet it took much questioning and soothing endearment until the trapeze artist sobbed: "Only the one bar in my hands—how can I go on living!" That made it somewhat easier for the manager to comfort him; he promised to wire from the very next station for a second trapeze to be installed in the first town on their circuit; reproached himself for having let the artist work so long on only one trapeze; and thanked and praised him warmly for having at last brought the mistake to his notice. And so he succeeded in reassuring the trapeze artist, little by little, and was able to go back to his corner. But he himself was far from reassured, with deep uneasiness he kept glancing secretly at the trapeze artist over the top of his book. Once such ideas began to torment him, would they ever quite leave him alone? Would they not rather increase in urgency? Would they not threaten his very existence? And indeed the manager believed he could see, during the apparently peaceful sleep which had succeeded the fit of tears, the first **furrows** of care engraving themselves upon the trapeze artist's smooth, childlike forehead. ∾

---

1   Respond to Characters *Why do journeys bother the trapeze artist? Does his irritation seem reasonable? Explain.*

Vocabulary

distressed (dis tres′d) *adj.* anxious; anguished; upset

Realism and Modernism *Why does the manager want to comfort the trapeze artist? Support your answer with evidence from the story.*   **2**

Vocabulary

furrows (fur′ ōs) *n.* grooves or tracks cut in the earth by a plow; wrinkles

Speaking and Listening Practice

Debate Say: Throughout the story, the manager responds to the trapeze artist's every need. The manager allows him to remain on the trapeze indefinitely, makes traveling as comfortable as possible, comforts him when he is upset, and fulfills his requests. The relationship between the artist and manager is much like that between a child and parent.

Have students debate the following question: Is the manager's approach ultimately helpful or hurtful to the trapeze artist?

Have students take sides depending on their opinions and participate in a class debate. One side should give a point in support of their argument, allowing time for the other side to form a rebuttal. Sides should take turns. Allow enough time

for each side to form their points, and allow any students who want to speak the chance to do so. *(Possible responses: Students may argue that in a threatening world, the trapeze artist depends on the compassion of his manager for survival. Others may argue that the manager's well-intentioned efforts cause the artist to become more isolated.)*

After You Read

Respond and Think Critically

Respond and Interpret

1. Do you sympathize or identify more with the trapeze artist or his manager? Explain.

2. (a)Why does the trapeze artist stay on his trapeze night and day? (b)Does this make him happy? Support your answer with evidence from the story.

3. (a)What request does the trapeze artist make of his manager during one journey? (b)Why does he make this request?

4. (a)Why is the manager worried at the end of the story? (b)What prompts him to have this thought?

Analyze and Evaluate

5. At the end of the story, is the manager concerned only for the trapeze artist, or might he also be concerned for himself? Explain.

6. (a)What is the significance of the story's title? (b)What moment in the story does it describe?

7. Why do you think Kafka chose to refer to his characters by what they do ("the artist" and "the manager") rather than by actual names?

Connect

8. **Big Idea** **Modernism and Realism** (a)How is the trapeze artist's way of life and his request to the manager a metaphor for the uncertainties of modern life? (b)Explain the significance of the story's last four sentences.

9. **Connect to the Author** Kafka continually focused on the estrangement of the individual from society in his works. How is this topic reflected in "First Sorrow"?

Literary Element | Tone

Authors deliberately write with a certain tone to convey particular impressions, moods, or ideas. Sometimes a work can have more than one tone.

1. (a)What is the narrator's attitude toward the trapeze artist's situation? (b)What words or phrases help convey the narrator's tone?

2. Tone often influences a work's **mood**, or overall feeling. What mood is created by the change in tone in the story's last paragraph?

Review: Theme

As you learned on page 927, **theme** is the message about life in a literary work. In some works, such as fables and folk tales, the theme is directly stated, usually in the form of a moral at the end. In most works, however, the theme is implied. The reader is responsible for analyzing what happens in order to identify the message the author wishes to convey.

Partner Activity Meet with another classmate to discuss the theme of "First Sorrow."

1. (a)What might the trapeze artist's enjoyment of his craft and his dislike of traveling symbolize? (b)What might the artist's request and the manager's concern represent?

2. What is the theme of "First Sorrow"?

Programme for the Cirque Rancy, 19th century. Tamagno. Colour lithograph. Musee de la Ville de Paris, Musee Carnavalet, Paris.

FRANZ KAFKA **1019**

Literary Element

1. (a) He seems unconcerned and detached. (b) The phrase "caused no particular inconvenience" downplays the situation, as does the word "somewhat" in "proved somewhat distracting" and the phrase "drew a stray glance from the public."

2. The tone becomes serious and unsettling, which creates an anxious, almost ominous mood.

Review: Theme

1. (a) Isolation might represent comfort away from unpleasant realities. Traveling might represent confronting those realities. (b) The artist's request symbolizes humanity's urge to strive for more. The manager's concern represents the desire to protect innocence.

2. Modern life is filled with uncertainties that force individuals to cope or survive as necessary.

After You Read

Assess

1. Answers will vary.

2. (a) Initially, he does this to perfect his craft. Later, he does it out of habit. (b) He is happier on the trapeze than during other times.

3. (a) He asks for a second trapeze. (b) Practicing on one trapeze has become unbearable.

4. (a) The manager worries he will be unable to comfort the artist and keep him happy. (b) He sees the beginning of a wrinkle on the artist's face, indicating stress and a loss of innocence.

5. He is worried that the artist will suffer but also that he will be unable to ensure the artist's happiness.

6. (a) On a literal level, it refers to the trapeze artist's realization he is not content with only one trapeze. On a symbolic level, the "first sorrow" refers to a loss of innocence. (b) The trapeze artist experiences his first discontent when he begins to find the thought of only one trapeze unbearable.

7. This makes them representative of a universal condition.

8. (a) The artist's way of life represents the isolated life of a modern individual who seeks relief from the harsh realities of life. When he asks for a second trapeze, he might be beginning on a journey of dissatisfaction and anxiety. (b) The manager fears the artist will be consumed by more desires that will threaten his ability to cope with life.

9. The trapeze artist is isolated by his profession and by his own desire to be alone, which eventually causes him great distress.

After You Read

Assess

Reading Strategy

1. D is the correct answer. In the last sentence, the manager sees "the first furrows of care" on the artist's face.

Progress Check

Can students respond to characters?

If No → See Unit 5 Teaching Resources Book, p. 192.

Vocabulary

1. Students should describe someone who is humble rather than showy.

2. Students might describe spending time alone in a quiet place.

3. Students should describe an event they wished did not have to end.

4. Encourage students to describe what was distressing about the occurrence.

5. Students should describe a narrow groove, and may allude to gardening or to a wrinkled face.

Reading Strategy Respond to Characters

ACT Skills Practice

How does the trapeze artist change by the end of the story?

A. He does not want to stay on his trapeze all the time.

B. He will only perform on one trapeze.

C. He refuses to travel anymore.

D. He has begun to worry about things.

Vocabulary Practice

Practice with Word Usage Respond to these statements to help you explore the meanings of the vocabulary words from the story.

1. Describe the behavior of a **modest** person.

2. Explain what you would do if you wanted **seclusion**.

3. Name an experience you've had that you wished you could **prolong**.

4. Identify something that has recently caused you to be **distressed**.

5. Explain what a **furrow** looks like.

Academic Vocabulary

*At the end of the story, the **aggregate** of the trapeze artist's thoughts and actions reveal a man struggling to cope with himself.*

Aggregate is an academic word. More familiar words that are similar in meaning are *total*, *whole*, and *collection*. To further explore the meaning of *aggregate*, answer the following question: What is the **aggregate** of your experience in school this year?

For more on academic vocabulary, see pages 36–37 and R83–R85.

Write with Style

Apply Tone

Assignment The term *Kafkaesque* refers to a nightmarishly complex, bizarre, or illogical situation. Invent a Kafkaesque situation and create a character, such as the trapeze artist in "First Sorrow," who exists in this situation and has an internal life hidden from most people. Write a story about this character, applying the tone Kafka used in "First Sorrow."

Get Ideas You might scan newspaper articles or observe people in public to choose the subject of your story. Choose someone to be your main character who piques your interest so you can invent a life for him or her. Create a chart like the one you filled out on page 1015 to help you respond to your character.

Give It Structure Many modern short stories, including Kafka's "First Sorrow," include an **epiphany**, or sudden revelation, as the climax of the story. Consider building your narrative around an epiphany that relates to the theme of the story. You can diagram your ideas about the epiphany, as in the example below.

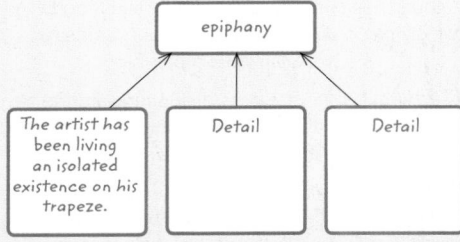

Look at Language Evaluate the tone of your story and check the tone against that of "First Sorrow."

 Literature Online

Selection Resources For Selection Quizzes, eFlashcards, and Reading-Writing Connection activities, go to glencoe.com and enter QuickPass code GLW6053u5.

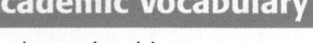

Academic Vocabulary

Students should attempt to convey the total outcome of their academic, artistic, athletic, and social activities related to school.

 For additional selection assessment, see Assessment Resources, pp. 199–200.

Write with Style

Students' stories should

- focus on one character
- display a Kafkaesque situation
- include an epiphany

 For grammar practice, see Unit 5 Teaching Resources Book, p. 195.

To create custom assessments online, go to Progress Reporter Online Assessment.

To create custom assessments using software, use ExamView Assessment Suite.

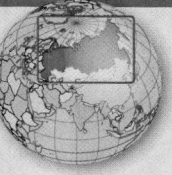

Before You Read

Lot's Wife

Meet **Anna Akhmatova**

(1888–1966)

Portrait of Anna Akhmatova, 1914. Natan Isaevic Altman. The State Russian Museum.

> "*I'm not of those who left their country For wolves to tear it limb from limb.*"
>
> —Anna Akhmatova

Anna Akhmatova (uk mä′tə və) has been called the greatest woman poet to hail from the former Soviet Union. Highly regarded for her intimate yet sophisticated poems about life, love, and politics, Akhmatova suffered greatly under communism. She said, "Fate did not leave anything out for me. Everything anyone could possibly experience fell to my lot."

A New Voice Akhmatova began writing poetry at age eleven. She published her first poem in 1907 in a literary magazine founded by the poet Nikolai Gumilyov. In 1910, after repeated proposals, Akhmatova married Gumilyov, who soon emerged as the leader of the Acmeists. This small group of early twentieth-century Russians believed that poets were not mystics but rather patient craftspeople building their art word by word. Rejecting the principles of French Symbolism and its metaphorical language, the Acmeists focused on human emotions and aesthetic beauty. Akhmatova was an active member of the group and soon garnered fame with the 1912 publication of her collection of poems, *Vecher*. For many, her simplistic approach to exploring the intimacy of love, jealousy, parting, and death captured the tragic spirit of the time. However, other critics defined her poetic voice as a combination of "a harlot and a nun."

Surrounded by Totalitarianism In 1914, with the start of World War I, the world—and Akhmatova's poetic voice—began to change. Surrounded by totalitarianism and tragedy, her themes became less personal and feminine and increasingly prophetic. In her poem "Molitva," the speaker pleads with God for peace: "This I pray at your liturgy / After so many tormented days, / So that the stormcloud over darkened Russia / Might become a cloud of glorious rays."

In 1921, the Communists executed Gumilyov and later imprisoned her son. Although she remained loyal to her country through these trials (even taking a firm stance against emigration), she became politically suspect because her works focused on love and God, subjects that were taboo to Communists. Her works were censored, and she published nothing in the Soviet Union from 1923 until 1940. When she wrote about Stalin's reign of terror in a cycle of poems called *Requiem*, she and a few trusted friends memorized passages because writing them down would have been too dangerous. *Requiem* was finally published in Russia in 1989. Following Stalin's death in 1953, Akhmatova slowly began to publish her poems, translations, and essays, and the years preceding her death brought a renewed interest in her work.

LOG ON ▶ **Literature** Online

Author Search For more about Anna Akhmatova, go to glencoe.com and enter QuickPass code GLW6053u5.

ANNA AKHMATOVA **1021**

Before You Read

Focus

Bellringer Options

Daily Language Practice Transparency 95

Or ask: What lessons can we learn from ancient narratives? What messages about loss and grief do they teach? (*Encourage students to discuss how many human emotions are universal and have been explored in narratives.*)

Cultural History ☆

Stalin's Collectivism In the late 1920s, Joseph Stalin began to move aggressively against private farming in an attempt to create a socialist economy by force. He began a mass campaign to make farms into collectively organized land cooperatives. By the early 1930s, Stalin had forced unwilling farmers to give up their land, and punished whole communities if they did not meet the state's grain quotas.

Selection Skills

Literary Elements
- Rhyme Scheme (SE pp. 1022, 1024)

Lot's Wife

Writing Skills/Grammar
- Character Sketch (SE p. 1024)

Reading Skills
- Connect to Personal Experience (SE pp. 1022, 1024)
- Make Inferences (TE p. 1022)

Vocabulary Skills
- Academic Vocabulary (SE p. 1024)

Before You Read

Focus

Summary

As she turns for one last look at her home, Lot's Wife is transformed to a pillar of salt and cemented to the ground. The italicized phrases in the poem are her own "wild" expressions of grief, a grief that drove her to turn around and look at the burning city.

> For summaries in languages other than English, see Unit 5 Teaching Resources Book, pp. 198–203.

Language History

Cyrillic Alphabet The Russian version of "Lot's Wife" on page 1023 appears in the Cyrillic alphabet. The alphabet was developed by the Christian missionary St. Cyril in the ninth century. It was based on the Greek alphabet, but many letters were added or changed to reflect the different sounds of the Slavic languages.

Literature and Reading Preview

Connect to the Poem

How would you react if you were forced to leave your home? List several objects, people, or places you might miss most.

Build Background

According to the biblical story, God sent angels to Sodom after hearing of the town's wickedness. They found only one virtuous man living there—Lot. The angels told him to flee with his family, warning them to avert their eyes from Sodom. However, Lot's wife looked back at the burning city and was turned into a pillar of salt. Akhmatova wrote the poem "Lot's Wife" sometime between 1922 and 1924. During this period, she sometimes used biblical and literary allusions to suggest themes that could not be discussed openly. Although she suffered greatly under communism, she had strong feelings for her homeland. On the following page, "Lot's Wife" appears both in English and in the original Russian.

Set Purposes for Reading

Big Idea Realism and Modernism

As you read, ask yourself, What does this poem suggest about the Soviet people and the choices they had to make?

Literary Element Rhyme Scheme

The **rhyme scheme** is the pattern that end rhymes form in a stanza or poem. You can mark the rhyme scheme by assigning a different letter to each new rhyme. For example, the first four lines of "Lot's Wife" have an *abab* rhyme scheme. As you read, ask yourself, What is the rhyme scheme of each stanza of this poem?

Reading Strategy Connect to Personal Experience

When you **connect to personal experience,** you link what you read to events in your own life or to your personal beliefs or feelings. Connecting literature to your own experiences and knowledge can help you understand the meaning and purpose of a work. As you read, ask yourself, How would I feel if I were forced to leave my home and never return?

Tip: **Categorize Details** In a chart like the one below, list details from the poem and connect them to your own experiences.

Detail	My Experience
Lot is ordered to leave his home.	

Learning Objectives

For pages 1021–1024

In studying this text, you will focus on the following objectives:

Literary Study: Analyzing rhyme scheme.

Reading: Connecting to personal experience.

Writing: Writing a character sketch.

Lot Fleeing from Sodom, 1810. Benjamin West. Oil on panel. The Detroit Institute of Arts, MI.

Writing Practice

Respond to Speaker In Akhmatova's poem the speaker enters the mind of Lot's wife. Readers are therefore able to sympathize with her. The last stanza of the poem complicates this by implying that a woman who would gaze back in sorrow at Sodom is not worth tears. As the stanza goes on it seems to address readers who have also been grieved by similar sorrows: "is she not the least of our losses?"

Ask: Should Lot's wife command our sympathy?

Ask students to write a few paragraphs in answer to this question from Akhmatova's point of view. Before they write, remind students to consider what kind of place Sodom was. In addition, remind students that Anna Akhmatova criticized Russians who emigrated after the revolution because she felt it was more patriotic to stay and try to resist tyranny. Tell students that while this information can help them interpret the poem, the poet and the speaker are not the same, so they should also refer to textual evidence from the work in crafting their response.

1022

LOT'S Wife

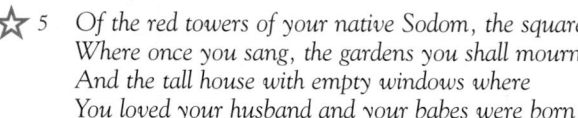

Anna Akhmatova

Translated by Richard Wilbur

The just man followed then his angel guide
Where he strode on the black highway, hulking
   and bright;
But a wild grief in his wife's bosom cried,
Look back, it is not too late for a last sight

☆ 5 *Of the red towers of your native Sodom, the square*
Where once you sang, the gardens you shall mourn,
And the tall house with empty windows where
You loved your husband and your babes were born.

1 10 She turned, and looking on the bitter view
Her eyes were welded shut by mortal pain;
Into transparent salt her body grew,
And her quick feet were rooted in the plain.

Who would waste tears upon her? Is she not
The least of our losses, this unhappy wife?
15 Yet in my heart she will not be forgot
Who, for a single glance, gave up her life.

☆ И праведник шел за посланником Бога,
Огромный и светлый, по черной горе.
Но громко жене говорила тревога:
Не поздно, ты можешь еще посмотреть

5 На красные башни родного Содома,
На площадь, где пела, на двор, где пряла,
На окна пустые высокого дома,
Где милому мужу детей родила.

Взглянула—и, скованы смертною болью,
10 Глаза ее больше смотреть не могли;
И сделалось тело прозрачною солью,
И быстрые ноги к земле приросли.

Кто женщину эту оплакивать будет?
Не меньшей ли мнится она из утрат?
15 Лишь сердце мое никогда не забудет
Отдавшую жизнь за единственный взгляд.

Lot and His Daughters Leaving Sodom, 17th century. Louis de Caullery (Flemish, 1580-1621). Oil on canvas. Rafael Valls Gallery, London.

2   **Realism and Modernism** *What idea does this stanza express? How is it different from the first three stanzas?*

English Learners

DIFFERENTIATED INSTRUCTION

Intermediate English learners may struggle with the subtle use of imagery in the poem. While the poem does not outwardly label Lot's wife in a particular way, conclusions can be drawn about her character, or the disposition that the speaker wants to convey. **Ask:** How is Lot's wife portrayed in the poem? *(as an ordinary, happy, and sentimental person who sang and loved her garden and her family)*

Advanced Learners/Pre-AP

DIFFERENTIATED INSTRUCTION

Research Suggest that advanced students research the surrounding passages from the Bible's book of Genesis. Have them note important passages that help them understand the location and meaning behind the story of Sodom and Gomorrah. Ask students to do research into how people from this period in history tended to regard their neighbors. Were there other places that were regarded as similarly evil?

Teach

Reading Strategy   1

Make Inferences **Ask:** What evidence is there in the poem that Lot's wife was turned to salt not by the angel but by her grief and pain in leaving her home? *(Students should note that the poem reads, "Her eyes were welded shut" and she was turned to salt "by mortal pain.")* Have students discuss whether or not they think that Akhmatova is suggesting that Lot's wife's grief and loss literally turned her to stone.

 For additional practice using the reading skill or strategy, see Unit 5 Teaching Resources Book, p. 205.

Big Idea   2

Realism and Modernism
Answer: *This stanza expresses the beliefs and feelings of the speaker. It is different because the other stanzas tell the story. This last stanza captures the meaning and purpose of the poem.*

Cultural History ☆

Sodom and Gomorrah In the Book of Genesis in the Old Testament, Sodom and Gomorrah are twin sinful cities. The Bible says they were destroyed by God because of their evil. Though not destroyed, the cities were devastated in 1900 B.C. by an earthquake in the Great Rift Valley.

Learning Objective
Making inferences. (TE)

After You Read

Assess

1. Answers will vary.
2. (a) She is moved by her memories of the places that are important to her. (b) Her memories are happy ones.
3. (a) She turns into a pillar of salt. (b) immediately
4. (a) The speaker will remember her because of her strong feelings for her homeland. (b) The speaker relates to the wife and might feel the same way about being forced to leave her home.
5. (a) reflective, nostalgic, and melancholy (b) sympathetic, admiring, and sorrowful; The speaker identifies with Lot's wife's suffering and understands her choice to look back.
6. Images of towers, garden, and house show Lot's wife's attachment to Sodom.
7. It reflects her concern over the rights of the individual that are stifled by tyrannical governments. It also highlights the challenge of finding a place of belonging within the isolation of the modern world.
8. Possible answers: political persecution, war, natural disaster.

 For additional selection assessment, see Assessment Resources, pp. 201–202.

After You Read

Respond and Think Critically

Respond and Interpret

1. Which lines from this poem did you find most interesting or moving? Explain.
2. (a) According to the speaker, what motivates Lot's wife to look back at Sodom? (b) Do you think her memories are mostly positive or negative? Explain.
3. (a) What happens to Lot's wife when she looks back at Sodom? (b) How quickly does this happen?

Analyze and Evaluate

4. (a) Why will the speaker never forget Lot's wife? (b) How does the speaker view Lot's wife's experience?

5. (a) **Tone** is the attitude an author takes toward the audience or subject. What is the speaker's tone in the second stanza? (b) What tone does the speaker use in discussing Lot's wife? Why?
6. How does the poem's imagery help the reader understand Lot's wife's feelings about her homeland?

Connect

7. **Big Idea** **Realism and Modernism** How does the story of Lot's wife and Sodom express Akhmatova's Modernist beliefs about the conditions of life in the Soviet Union?
8. **Connect to Today** What events in the world today force individuals to flee their homelands as Lot and his wife did?

Literary Element **Rhyme Scheme**

Each stanza in "Lot's Wife" is a **quatrain**—four lines—in which the first and third lines rhyme, as do the second and fourth lines.

1. What is the main idea of each quatrain?
2. What is the rhyme scheme of the entire poem?

Reading Strategy **Connect to Personal Experience**

As you read a poem, look for similarities between your own experiences and those of the characters or speaker.

1. Could you relate to Lot's wife or to the speaker? How?
2. How did your connections help you understand the poem?

 Literature Online

Selection Resources For Selection Quizzes, eFlashcards, and Reading-Writing Connection activities, go to glencoe.com and enter QuickPass code GLW6053u5.

Academic Vocabulary

Lot's wife's **commitment** to Sodom and her life there causes her to look back even though she was warned not to.

Commitment is an academic word. If someone has an appointment at a certain time, he or she has a commitment. To explore this word further, write and answer a question about "Lot's Wife" using the word commitment.

For more about academic vocabulary, see pages 36–37 and R83–R85.

Writing

Write a Character Sketch Akhmatova writes that Lot's wife "for a single glance, gave up her life." Refer to the chart you made on page 1022 about your experiences in relation to the poem. Think of someone who has made a sacrifice. Write a character sketch of this person, highlighting the similarities and differences between him or her and Lot's wife.

1024 UNIT 5   MODERN EUROPE

Literary Element

1. First stanza: Lot and his wife leave Sodom, but her grief demands that she look back. Second stanza: She recalls her former happiness. Third stanza: She looks back and is destroyed. Fourth stanza: The speaker reacts to Lot's wife's fate.
2. *abab cdcd efef ghgh*

Reading Strategy

1. Responses will vary, but students should explain their connections.
2. They should have helped students understand the importance of home and of how difficult it is to leave one's home. Even at the risk of death, Lot's wife could not leave without one last look.

Academic Vocabulary

Questions and answers will vary. Accept reasonable responses.

Writing

Students' character sketches should
- focus on someone who has made a sacrifice
- compare and contrast this figure with the character of Lot's wife

1024

Before You Read

War

Meet **Luigi Pirandello**
(1867–1936)

Luigi Pirandello was one of Italy's most famous playwrights and modern authors. His work is known for its atmosphere of mystery and tension, along with the questions he raises about the "fictions we create for ourselves."

A Sicilian Youth Born in Sicily in 1867, Pirandello became interested in literature at a young age. He wrote his first play at the age of twelve with the support of siblings and friends. His father, however, enrolled Pirandello at a technical college. He later transferred to an academic secondary school to study oratory and literature. Despite this act of rebellion, Pirandello did agree to marry Antoinetta Portulano, the daughter of his father's business associate. After he earned his doctorate in Romance philosophy, he married and moved to Rome, where he began publishing poetry and short stories.

Personal Setbacks In 1903, Pirandello was financially devastated when his family's sulfur mine was destroyed. His wife suffered an emotional breakdown and was institutionalized in 1919 after battling mental illness for years. To escape his troubles, Pirandello immersed himself in writing. Though best known for his 1918 play, *Six Characters in Search of an Author,* he became a playwright only when asked to dramatize one of his stories. He later invented "grotesco," a form of theatrical expressionism that sacrifices realism in order to portray psychological experience.

⭐ **A Master Illusionist** The conflict between reality and illusion informs Pirandello's work. His characters often deceive themselves and nurture illusions to avoid troubling realities.

The tone, often mysterious or ironic, becomes tragic when characters are forced to face the truth. Pirandello stated, "My works of art . . . *are* images, often very vivid images of life, which, fostered by the labors of my mind, assume universal significance quite on their own, through the formal unity of art."

In his day, Pirandello's work was viewed as controversial. Some critics suggested that his observations of his wife's mental illness deepened his interest in the problem of identity. In 1934 he was awarded the Nobel Prize in Literature. Today, his work is still provocative, strongly influencing playwrights who explore life's ironies and paradoxes.

> "Life is full of endless absurdities, which, boldfaced as they may be, do not even have to appear plausible, since they are true."
>
> —Luigi Pirandello

Literature Online

Author Search For more about Luigi Pirandello, go to glencoe.com and enter QuickPass code GLW6053u5.

LUIGI PIRANDELLO **1025**

Before You Read

Focus

Bellringer Options

Selection Focus
   Transparency 62
Daily Language Practice
   Transparency 96

Ask: What do parents feel when they send their children to fight a war? *(In addition to worry and loss, parents often feel an intense sense of patriotism. In some cases, however, parents question the cause for which their child's life might be sacrificed.)*

Literary History ☆
The Subconscious Mind
Pirandello's interest in Realism was not confined to realistic details of time and place. He was also fascinated by the concept of the subconscious mind. Following on the heels of Freud, who pioneered ideas about repressed thoughts and feelings at the start of the twentieth century, Pirandello explored this phenomenon through characters such as the fat man and the woman in mourning in this story.

Selection Skills

Literary Elements
- Dialogue (SE pp. 1026, 1028, 1030)
- Characterization (SE p. 1030)

War

Writing Skills/Grammar
- Apply Dialogue (SE p. 1031)
- Interior Monologue (TE p. 1028)

Reading Skills
- Recognize Author's Purpose (SE pp. 1026, 1029, 1031)
- Analyze Characters (TE p. 1026)

Vocabulary Skills
- Word Parts (SE pp. 1026, 1031)

Before You Read

Focus

Summary

A woman in deep mourning enters a railroad carriage with her husband. They are going to Rome to see their son, a soldier, before he leaves for the front. The couple begins talking with other passengers and each reveals how he or she has been affected by the war.

 For summaries in languages other than English, see Unit 5 Teaching Resources Book, pp. 208–213.

Vocabulary

Word Parts Ask students to work in groups of three or four to underline familiar word parts in each of the vocabulary words and then to make lists of familiar words with the same word parts whose meanings can help them understand the vocabulary words.

 For additional vocabulary practice, see Unit 5 Teaching Resources Book, p. 216.

Literary and Reading Preview

Connect to the Story

How do you deal with grief or loss? Write a journal entry in response to this question.

Build Background

Turning against its German and Austro-Hungarian allies, Italy joined World War I on the side of Britain, France, and Russia. Italy's wartime efforts proved unsuccessful. During its three-year involvement in World War I, an estimated 650,000 Italians died, and nearly one million were wounded. Italy eventually surrendered to German forces and withdrew its troops from the war. Pirandello was personally aware of the anguish the war caused many families—his own son was a prisoner of war.

Set Purposes for Reading

Big Idea **Realism and Modernism**

As you read, ask yourself, How does Pirandello focus on the problems of ordinary people in this story?

Literary Element **Dialogue**

Dialogue is conversation between characters. In "War," Pirandello uses dialogue to illustrate various attitudes of parents toward their children. Each passenger speaks philosophically about his or her personal tragedy. As you read, ask yourself, How does Pirandello use dialogue to show how the characters cope with their losses?

Reading Strategy **Recognize Author's Purpose**

Authors typically write for one or more reasons: to persuade, to inform, to explain, to entertain, and to describe. As you read, ask yourself, What was Pirandello's purpose for writing "War"?

Tip: Chart Details In a chart like the one below, list details about the characters in the story. Then use your notes to draw a conclusion about Pirandello's position on the war.

Woman's Husband	Man with Two Sons	Fat Man	Woman in Mourning
He claims the world is nasty and tells the passengers about their son.	Explains that a father loves his children equally and therefore his suffering is double.		

Learning Objectives

For pages 1025–1031

In studying this text, you will focus on the following objectives:

Literary Study: Analyzing dialogue.

Reading: Recognizing author's purpose.

Writing: Applying dialogue.

Vocabulary

console (kən´sōl´) *v.* to alleviate a person's grief, sense of loss, or trouble; to comfort; p. 1028 *Nothing could console her after her husband died.*

disillusion (dis´i lōō´zhən) *n.* the state of being freed from misleading images or naïve trust; p. 1029 *His friend's betrayal filled him with sadness and disillusion.*

distorted (dis tôr´tid) *adj.* twisted out of normal or original shape or condition; p. 1029 *His distorted face and swollen eyes were signs of grief.*

Tip: Word Parts Use your knowledge of word parts to figure out the meanings of new words. Two vocabulary words—*disillusion* and *distorted*—for example, have the prefix *dis-*, meaning "two" or "apart." When you look at a word, check to see if there is a root word and any affixes—prefixes or suffixes.

Literary Element Practice

Analyze Characters Have students analyze the character of the woman in mourning. Begin by having them look closely at the first details that describe her. Ask students what Pirandello is saying about this character who must be hoisted into the car, appears as a "shapeless bundle," and is identified as "in mourning." Ask students to record every detail that Pirandello selects in creating her character, and to analyze what those details suggest.

Have them consider these questions:

- Is the woman really in mourning? Why is she characterized that way? *(She may be in mourning for someone who is not her son; Pirandello perhaps uses this characterization to emphasize lifelessness about her.)*

- Does the woman change? *(She comes out of her sleep or shapelessness to assume a pivotal role in the story; she awakens to an understanding of sorts.)*

- Why does she remain silent so long? How does she finally seem to awaken? *(She is aware and convinced only of her own suffering; she thinks others cannot understand her. She awakens to the idea that there may be both meaning and some consolation of immortality in losing a son in the war, only to have this theory discredited by the reaction of the fat man.)*

1026

WAR

Luigi Pirandello
Translated by Samuel Putnam

The Railway Carriage-Blackout. Kenneth Rowntree (1915-1997). Watercolour on paper. Fry Art Gallery, Saffron Walden, Essex, UK.

The passengers who had left Rome by the night express had had to stop until dawn at the small station of Fabriano in order to continue their journey by the small old-fashioned "local" joining the main line with Sulmona.

At dawn, in a stuffy and smoky second-class carriage in which five people had already spent the night, a bulky woman in deep mourning, was hoisted in—almost like a shapeless bundle. Behind her— puffing and moaning, followed her husband—a tiny man, thin and weakly, his face death-white, his eyes small and bright and looking shy and uneasy.

Having at last taken a seat he politely thanked the passengers who had helped his wife and who had made room for her; then he turned round to the woman trying to pull down the collar of her coat and politely inquired:

"Are you all right, dear?"

The wife, instead of answering, pulled up her collar again to her eyes, so as to hide her face.

"Nasty world," muttered the husband with a sad smile.

And he felt it his duty to explain to his traveling companions that the poor woman was to be pitied for the war was taking away from her her only son, a boy of twenty to whom both had devoted their entire life, even breaking up their home at Sulmona to follow him to Rome where he had to go as a student, then allowing him to volunteer for war with an assurance, however, that at least for six months he would not be sent to the front, and now, all of a sudden, receiving a wire saying that he was due to leave in three days' time and asking them to go and see him off.

The woman under the big coat was twisting and wriggling, at times growling like a wild animal, feeling certain that all those explanations would not have aroused even a shadow of sympathy from those people who—most likely—were in the same plight as herself. One of them, who had been listening with particular attention, said:

"You should thank God that your son is only leaving now for the front. Mine has been sent there the first day of the war. He has already come back twice wounded and been sent back again to the front."

LUIGI PIRANDELLO **1027**

---

1 Realism and Modernism *Why does Pirandello describe the setting this way? What does it tell you about the characters?*

English Learners

DIFFERENTIATED INSTRUCTION

Beginning Read the first sentence aloud. Then help students visualize the action: A couple enters a smoky, stuffy car with five other passengers. The woman needs help and looks like a big bundle. Her thin, weak husband does not seem well.

Paraphrase: The first thing he says is his wife should be pitied because her only son is going off to war.

Advanced Learners/Pre-AP

DIFFERENTIATED INSTRUCTION

Research and Synthesize Challenge students to look up Freud's ideas about repression of fundamental thoughts, memories, and feelings and to analyze one of the characters from a Freudian perspective.

Teach

Big Idea | 1

Realism and Modernism
Answer: *The description makes it realistic. The claustrophobic setting represents the passengers' feelings of wartime stress.*

View the Art ★

The work of Kenneth Rowntree is characterized by the repetition of geometric shapes, as evidenced here in the pattern of windows and panels. In this painting, however, it is not the geometry but the face-lessness of the carriage occupants that is most arresting. **Ask:** What statements about identity might the artist be making? *(Each individual is deeply separate. Even the couple whose arms are joined appear to have different thoughts or perspectives based on the direction of their glance. The facelessness suggests a general opacity—or the blackout of the title: the passengers are unknow-able to each other, and perhaps to themselves as well.)*

 For an audio recording of this selection, use Listening Library Audio CD-ROM.

Readability Scores
Dale-Chall: 8.0
DRP: 57
Lexile: 1170

Learning Objectives
Analyzing word parts. (SE)
Analyzing characters. (TE)

Teach

Literary Element 1

Dialogue Answer: *Each character feels his or her situation is worse than the others' situations.*

 For additional literary element practice, see Unit 5 Teaching Resources Book, p. 214.

Literary Element 2

Dialogue Answer: *He wants to show how the children's actions are similar to how the parents would have acted when they were young. Also, he wants to show how his son's life was happy—even if it was cut short.*

"What about me? I have two sons and three nephews at the front," said another passenger.

"Maybe, but in our case it is our *only* son," ventured the husband.

"What difference can it make? You may spoil your only son with excessive attentions, but you cannot love him more than you would all your other children if you had any. Paternal love is not like bread that can be broken into pieces and split amongst the children in equal shares. A father gives *all* his love to each one of his children without discrimination, whether it be one or ten, and if I am suffering now for my two sons, I am not suffering half for each of them but double. . . ."

"True . . . true . . ." sighed the embarrassed husband, "but suppose (of course we all hope it will never be your case) a father has two sons at the front and he loses one of them, there is still one left to **console** him . . . while . . ."

"Yes," answered the other, getting cross, "a son left to console him but also a son left for whom he must survive, while in the case of the father of an only son if the son dies the father can die too and put an end to his distress. Which of the two positions is the worse? Don't you see how my case would be worse than yours?"

"Nonsense," interrupted another traveler, a fat, red-faced man with bloodshot eyes of the palest gray.

He was panting. From his bulging eyes seemed to spurt inner violence of an uncontrolled vitality which his weakened body could hardly contain.

"Nonsense," he repeated, trying to cover his mouth with his hand so as to hide the two missing front teeth. "Nonsense. Do we give life to our children for our own benefit?"

The other travelers stared at him in distress. The one who had had his son at the front since the first day of the war sighed: "You are right. Our children do not belong to us, they belong to the Country. . . ."

"Bosh," retorted the fat traveler. "Do we think of the Country when we give life to our children? Our sons are born because . . . well, because they must be born and when they come to life they take our own life with them. This is the truth. We belong to them but they never belong to us. And when they reach twenty they are exactly what we were at their age. We too had a father and mother, but there were so many other things as well . . . girls, cigarettes, illusions, new ties . . . and the Country, of course, whose call we would have answered—when we were twenty—even if father and mother had said no. Now, at our age, the love of our Country is still great, of course, but stronger than it is the love for our children. Is there any one of us here who wouldn't gladly take his son's place at the front if he could?"

There was a silence all round, everybody nodding as to approve.

"Why then," continued the fat man, "shouldn't we consider the feelings of our children when they are twenty? Isn't it natural that at their age they should consider the love for their Country (I am speaking of decent boys, of course) even greater than the love for us? Isn't it natural that it should be so, as after all they must look upon us as upon old boys who cannot move any more and must stay at home? If Country exists, if Country is a natural necessity like bread, of which each of us must eat in order not to die of hunger, somebody must go to defend it. And our sons go, when they are twenty, and they

1 Dialogue *What do you learn about the characters through this conversation?*

Vocabulary

console (kən′sōl′) *v.* to alleviate a person's grief, sense of loss, or trouble; to comfort

Dialogue *What is the main idea of the fat man's arguments?* **2**

Writing Practice

Write an Interior Monologue

Pirandello raises several philosophical questions in this brief story:

- Does dying for one's country make death easier, happier, or better?
- When a child dies, does a parent of an only child suffer more than a parent who has more than one child?

- To what extent are the losses of parents in war time more grievous or just as grievous as the loss of the soldiers themselves?
- Can one person understand or alleviate another's suffering, especially when it seems so similar, at least on the surface?

Have students choose one of these questions or another question raised by the selection and write an interior monologue in which one of the characters, or an occupant of the carriage who does not speak in this selection, muses on the answer to the question.

don't want tears, because if they die, they die inflamed and happy (I am speaking, of course, of decent boys). Now, if one dies young and happy, without having the ugly sides of life, the boredom of it, the pettiness, the bitterness of **disillusion** . . . what more can we ask for him? Everyone should stop crying: everyone should laugh, as I do . . . or at least thank God—as I do—because my son, before dying, sent me a message saying that he was dying satisfied at having ended his life in the best way he could have wished. That is why, as you see, I do not even wear mourning. . . ."

He shook his light fawn[1] coat as to show it; his livid lip over his missing teeth was trembling, his eyes were watery and motionless and soon after he ended with a shrill laugh which might well have been a sob.

"Quite so . . . quite so . . ." agreed the others.

The woman who, bundled in a corner under her coat, had been sitting and listening had—for the last three months—tried to find in the words of her husband and her friends something to console her in her deep sorrow, something that might show her how a mother should resign herself to send her son not even to death but to a probable danger of life. Yet not a word had she found amongst the many which had been said . . . and her grief had been greater in seeing that nobody—as she thought—could share her feelings.

But now the words of the traveler amazed and almost stunned her. She suddenly realized that it wasn't the others who were wrong and could not understand her but herself who could not rise up to the same height of those fathers and mothers willing to resign themselves, without cry-

ing, not only to the departure of their sons but even to their death.

She lifted her head, she bent over from her corner trying to listen with great attention to the details which the fat man was giving to his companions about the way his son had fallen as a hero, for his King and his Country, happy and without regrets. It seemed to her that she had stumbled into a world she had never dreamed of, a world so far unknown to her and she was so pleased to hear everyone joining in congratulating that brave father who could so stoically[2] speak of his child's death.

Then suddenly, just as if she had heard nothing of what had been said and almost as if waking up from a dream, she turned to the old man, asking him:

"Then . . . is your son really dead?"

Everybody stared at her. The old man, too, turned to look at her, fixing his great, bulging, horribly watery light gray eyes, deep in her face. For some little time he tried to answer, but words failed him. He looked and looked at her, almost as if only then—at that silly, incongruous question—he had suddenly realized at last that his son was really dead . . . gone forever . . . forever. His face contracted, became horribly **distorted**, then he snatched in haste a handkerchief from his pocket and, to the amazement of everyone, broke into harrowing,[3] heart-rending, uncontrollable sobs.

---

2. *Stoically* means "indifferently to emotional pain."
3. *Harrowing* means "extremely distressing; agonizing."

Recognize Author's Purpose *What does this description suggest about people's attitude toward the war?* `3`

---

1. This coat would be pale grayish-brown in color.

Vocabulary

disillusion (dis'i lōō´zhən) *n.* the state of being freed from misleading images or naïve trust

Vocabulary

distorted (dis tôr´id) *adj.* twisted out of normal or original shape or condition

LUIGI PIRANDELLO **1029**

Teach

Reading Strategy | 3

Recognize Author's Purpose **Answer:** *Many people have not yet accepted the reality of the war's devastation.*

Political History ☆

Nationalism Along with alliances and militarism, nationalism is one of the most frequently cited causes of World War I. By the end of the nineteenth century, nationalism had become a widespread and overwhelming force in Europe. People glorified the state because they believed it acted in accordance with the collective will and for the collective good of the people. In nationalist thinking, the aims and goals of the country come before those of the individual.

Learning Objectives
Analyzing dialogue. (SE)
Recognizing author's purpose. (SE)
Writing an interior monologue. (TE)

Approaching Level

DIFFERENTIATED INSTRUCTION

Build Background Review the term *interior monologue*. Remind students that *interior* means "inside." Explain that an interior monologue consists of the thoughts going on inside one character's head, and that these thoughts are not spoken; there are no speaker tags as in dialogue, such as "he said" or "she asked." Note that a monologue uses the first person (the pronouns *I, me, my, myself,*

and *mine*). Provide these sentence frames to help students structure their interior monologues.

When <a different character's name> said _____, I thought/felt/wondered _____.

My own feeling is/was _____.

This struck me as _____ because _____.

I realized that _____.

After You Read

Assess

1. Answers will vary.

2. (a) They are going to see their son before he leaves for battle. (b) She is worried and anxious about her son.

3. (a) He feels they should not complain. (b) He claims his son died happy and ended his life in a good way.

4. (a) She wonders if she should resign herself to her son's departure. (b) Possible response: Unlike the others, he has already lost his son. He expresses himself so rationally that she can hardly believe his son has been killed.

5. Answers will vary. Many students will say the fat man has the true epiphany because he suddenly and fully acknowledges his son's death.

6. The tone is matter-of-fact and almost comical for much of the story, but it turns serious and sympathetic toward the end.

7. This statement describes the fat man. To reconcile his personal feelings with the needs of the country, he adopts the mask of a father proud to have a son who died for his country. When the man finally faces the reality of his son's death, the mask comes off and his real feelings come to the surface.

8. (a) the conditions in the carriage and the realistic dialogue (b) It offers unflattering details about their physical appearances and honestly portrays their reactions to the other characters' suffering.

9. The fat man has deluded himself—a symptom of insanity. When he meets the wife, however, he confronts reality and shows himself to be sane.

1030

After You Read

Respond and Think Critically

Respond and Interpret

1. Were you surprised by the fat man's reaction at the end of the story? Explain.

2. (a) Why are the husband and wife traveling to Sulmona? (b) Why does the wife wriggle under her coat as the husband explains their situation?

3. (a) How does the fat man feel about the debate between the husband and the other passengers? (b) Why hasn't the fat man mourned the death of his son?

4. (a) What effect does the fat man's speech have on the woman? (b) Why do you think she reacts as she does to the fat man's speech?

Analyze and Evaluate

5. An **epiphany** is a sudden, unexpected moment of insight. Who do you think has the epiphany in this story, the woman or the fat man? Explain.

6. **Tone** is the attitude a narrator takes toward a subject or character. Do you think the narrator's tone remains consistent in this story? Explain.

7. According to one critic, Pirandello created characters who "adopt multiple identities, or 'masks,' in an effort to reconcile social demands with personal needs." Do you think this statement describes the characters in "War"? Explain.

Connect

8. **Big Idea** **Realism and Modernism** (a) Which details of the setting contribute to the story's realism? (b) What is realistic about the portrayal of the characters?

9. **Connect to the Author** Pirandello's wife suffered from mental illness for years, and many of his literary works deal with the relationship between madness and sanity. Do you think he saw the fat man as sane or insane? Explain.

Literary Element | Dialogue

The conversations between characters, or **dialogue,** can contribute to characterization, create mood, advance the plot, and develop theme. Dialogue should be convincing; what a character says must be appropriate to his or her personality, background, and intelligence. In "War," Pirandello uses dialogue to present a realistic exchange of ordinary people's ideas and opinions about war and its costs. Consult your chart about author's purpose on page 1026 and consider how the dialogue reveals Pirandello's purpose.

1. (a) What does their dialogue reveal about the personalities of the two men who have sons at the front? (b) Is their dialogue natural? Explain.

2. How does the dialogue in "War" serve as an exchange of ideas?

Review: Characterization

As you learned on page 608, the methods an author uses to reveal the personality of a character is called **characterization.** Authors may describe a character and make explicit statements about him or her. They may also reveal a character through his or her words, thoughts, and actions and through what other characters think and say about the character.

Partner Activity Work with a partner to analyze Pirandello's characterization of the fat man and the woman.

1. (a) What does Pirandello's description of the fat man reveal about the character? (b) What do the fat man's actions reveal about his feelings?

2. (a) How does Pirandello describe the woman? (b) What do her actions reveal about her feelings and opinions? (c) How does Pirandello signal her change in mood?

Literary Element

1. (a) They both lack sympathy for the couple. (b) Yes, each is argumentative and feels most pitiable.

2. Possible response: Pirandello uses a conversation between a group of people on a train to present different opinions about family, nationalism, and war.

Review: Characterization

1. (a) His appearance shows his internal emotions and the external violence these emotions may reflect. (b) His agitated appearance and laugh contradict his seemingly calm resignation.

2. (a) Bulky and silent, she barely looks at anyone. Instead, she huffs, moans, hides, and growls. (b) Her actions show her suffering, selfishness, and inability to cope. (c) She lifts her head.

Reading Strategy · Recognize Author's Purpose

SAT Skills Practice

Pirandello uses the fat man's apparent resignation to his son's death to show that

(A) He never loved his son.

(B) Many people do not understand the effects of the war.

(C) He believes his country will win the war.

(D) People do not support the war.

(E) He is trying to keep his son's death a secret.

Vocabulary Practice

Practice with Word Parts For each bold-faced vocabulary word in the left column, identify the related word with a shared word part in the right column. Write each word and underline the part they have in common. Use a printed or online dictionary to look up the meaning of the related word. Then explain how it is related to the vocabulary word.

1. console   consolidate
2. disillusion   distract
3. distorted   illusory

Academic Vocabulary

The husband and wife in "War" are **persistent** *in following their son.*

Persistent is an academic word. Similar words include *stubborn, determined,* and *resolute.* Complete a four-square organizer like the one below for *persistent.*

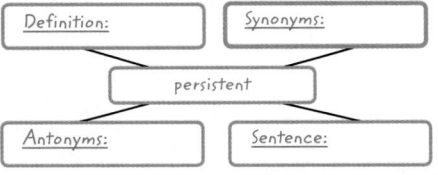

For more on academic vocabulary, see pages 36–37 and R83–R85.

Write with Style

Apply Dialogue

Assignment Dialogue drives the narration and characterization in "War." We find out most details about characters and their circumstances through their words. Apply Pirandello's use of dialogue in a 1,000-word story about a group of strangers.

Get Ideas Choose a controversial topic. Then create a group of characters and list details about them. You can use real people for inspiration.

Give It Structure Determine your purpose for writing the story. How do you want to affect your readers? Present the dialogue in a sequence that allows your ideas to flow in a dramatic way. Also explain the setting and context of your story.

EXAMPLE:

> Gabriel and Greta stopped when they reached the bus stop. "Did we miss it?"
>
> "I don't think so," said Gabriel.
>
> While they caught their breath, they noticed an older man sitting on the bench. This was Mr. Brown.
>
> "Excuse me, are you waiting for Bus 52?" asked Greta. Gabriel wondered why she would ask a stranger.
>
> "I am," said Mr. Brown. "It's late."
>
> The three waited for some time. Gabriel wrung his hands. "We have to go. We should have gone before. Let's get a taxi."
>
> "I don't know," said Greta. "We're already here, and we probably have some time." Gabriel looked at her. "Let's just wait a little longer."
>
> "What if it never comes? Ever think of that? Are we just going to wait here?"
>
> "It all comes, if you wait long enough," said Mr. Brown.
>
> And so they stood in the afternoon sun.

Look at Language Read your story aloud. Does the dialogue sound real? Check your attribution tags and the punctuation. Remember to begin a new paragraph and use a new set of quotation marks every time the speaker changes.

LOG ON **Literature** Online

Selection Resources For Selection Quizzes, eFlashcards, and Reading-Writing Connection activities, go to glencoe.com and enter QuickPass code GLW6053u5.

LUIGI PIRANDELLO **1031**

Write with Style

Students' stories should

- use dialogue to advance the narration
- include characterization
- demonstrate correct punctuation and attribution tags of dialogue

For grammar practice, see Unit 5 Teaching Resources Book, p. 218.

After You Read

Reading Strategy

(B) is the correct answer. Many people do not grasp the devastating effects of the war.

Progress Check

Can students recognize the author's purpose?

If No → See Unit 5 Teaching Resources Book, p. 215.

Vocabulary Practice

1. <u>con</u>sole, <u>con</u>solidate. When someone is consoled, they are brought relief and when things are consolidated, they are brought together.
2. dis<u>illus</u>ion, <u>illus</u>ory. Disillusion involves the stripping away of innocence and an awareness of possible deception. When something is illusory, it is deceptive.
3. <u>dist</u>orted, <u>dist</u>ract. When something is distorted, it's shape is changed or taken away. When someone distracts someone else, they change the focus of that person's attention.

Academic Vocabulary

persistent

<u>Definition:</u> continuing in a belief or action despite difficulty, opposition, or failure

<u>Synonyms:</u> unrelenting, continual, determined

<u>Antonyms:</u> feeble, weak, ineffectual

<u>Sentence:</u> I had a persistent feeling I'd forgotten something, so I went back to my car and discovered I'd left the lights on.

Before You Read

Focus

Bellringer Options

Daily Language Practice Transparency 97

Ask: How does it affect a grown child to see a parent who carries on with vigor and enthusiasm up until the very end of his or her life? Mention the range of emotions such behavior elicits, including pride and admiration, as well as what resolutions or thoughts it might inspire in the grown child about his or her own life.

Literary History ☆

Feminism Colette was an early voice of feminism in France, where her ideas about independence, gender roles, and traditional behavior for women were in opposition to those embraced by mainstream French society. Her typical heroine was a strong, robust woman with a formidable life force and keen sense of independence—much as Colette's mother is portrayed in this excerpt.

Before You Read

France

Two Memories of Sido

Meet **Colette**
(1873–1954)

Sidonie-Gabrielle Colette (kô let´), known simply as Colette, grew up in a small village in the Burgundy region of France. Her much-loved mother taught her to appreciate the sights, sounds, tastes, textures, and colors of the French countryside. Her skill at sensual description is one of the distinguishing aspects of her writing.

First Marriage At age twenty, Colette married the author and critic Henri Gauthier-Villars (gō´ tē ā ve yär), better known as "Willy." Fifteen years older, he soon recognized her literary talent and encouraged—some say forced—her to write salacious stories based on her childhood. These novels center on the fortunes of a young heroine named Claudine and were so popular that they inspired many commercial products, such as Claudine clothing, soap, perfume, and haircuts (matching Colette's). There was even a musical based on the character. In spite of this success, Colette did not benefit financially from her work. Her husband published the stories under his own name and kept the royalties.

Moving On After leaving Willy, Colette found herself on shaky financial ground. She performed in music halls and continued to write fiction and journalism. A second marriage also ended in divorce, but her third husband, Maurice Goudeket, proved to be a faithful and loving companion. Her happiness turned to despair, however, when Goudeket was arrested and imprisoned by the Nazis during World War II. Colette also endured crippling arthritis, which eventually confined her to her Paris apartment.

Finding Her Voice Colette is widely admired for her precise style, her evocative descriptions of nature, and her insight into relations between men and women. She also wrote several memoirs about her life, using diverse experiences—from hairdressing to performing as a mime—as sources for her work. In many of these autobiographical writings, her mother took on a larger-than-life role. Although her writing and life were controversial, Colette received high honors from the French literary establishment. At her death in 1954, she was given a state funeral, an unprecedented honor at the time for a female French author. Her literary reputation continues to grow, supported by her more than 50 novels and novellas along with an even greater number of short stories.

> "The day necessity put a pen in my hand, and in return for my written pages I was given a little money, I realized that every day thereafter I would slowly, tractably, patiently have to write …"
>
> —Colette

LOG ON ▶ **Literature** Online

Author Search For more about Colette, go to glencoe.com and enter QuickPass code GLW6053u5.

Selection Skills

Literary Elements
- Autobiography (SE pp. 1033, 1037, 1039)
- Repetition (SE p. 1039)

Two Memories of Sido

Speaking/Listening/Viewing Skills
- Analyze Art (SE p. 1036; TE p. 1035)

Reading Skills
- Analyze Characterization (SE pp. 1033–1036, 1039)
- Evaluate Dialogue (TE p. 1034)

Vocabulary Skills
- Antonyms (SE pp. 1033, 1039)
- Academic Vocabulary (SE p. 1039)

Writing Skills/Grammar
- Biographical Narrative (SE p. 1040)
- Use Hyphens (TE p. 1036)

Literature and Reading Preview

Connect to the Story

What do you think you will be like when you are elderly? Discuss this question with a partner.

Build Background

Colette's memoirs offer an endearing portrait of her mother, Sidonie, who showed a deep respect for everything that "germinates, blossoms, or flies." Sido (sē dō′), as Colette called her, was not a typical country wife. Her unconventional views about religion and morality had a great influence on Colette. Sido taught Colette how to read before the age of three and supported her writing throughout her life.

Set Purposes for Reading

Big Idea Realism and Modernism

As you read, ask yourself, How does the narrator weave the texture of everyday life and the problems of ordinary people into the text?

Literary Element Autobiography

An **autobiography** is a person's account of his or her own life. Told from the first-person point of view, autobiographies can offer revealing insights into a person's view of himself or herself. Colette's autobiography also incorporates elements of a **biography,** or an account of a person's life written by someone else. As you read, ask yourself, How does Colette reveal information about her own values as she portrays her mother?

Reading Strategy Analyze Characterization

When you **analyze characterization,** you consider the ways an author reveals a character's personality. An author can build characterization through a character's actions, words, and habits or through imagery and other literary elements. As you read, ask yourself, How does Colette reveal her mother's character?

....

Tip: Use a Graphic Organizer Use a chart to keep track of how the author reveals her mother's character.

Method	Example	What It Reveals
Dialogue	"Too quickly? What do you call too quickly? I was going down quickly. Have I time to go downstairs majestically like the Sun King?"	She's always busy.

Learning Objectives

For pages 1032–1039

In studying this text, you will focus on the following objectives:

Literary Study: Analyzing autobiography.

Reading: Analyzing characterization.

Vocabulary

elasticity (i las′tis′ə tē) *n.* the quality of being easily adaptable or adjustable, so as to fit changes or new circumstances; p. 1035 *Sharon, with her usual elasticity, was able to fit the new activities into her already packed schedule.*

undaunted (un dôn′tid) *adj.* courageously firm or resolute, especially in the face of danger or difficulty; not discouraged; p. 1036 *Carlos was undaunted by the rough terrain, so he continued running.*

respites (res′pits) *n.* periods of temporary relief, rest, or delay; p. 1036 *The hikers required frequent respites on their four-day hike.*

....

Tip: Antonyms Antonyms are words that have opposite or nearly opposite meanings. For example, the words *defiance* and *submission* are antonyms.

COLETTE **1033**

Before You Read

Focus

Summary

The author recalls the last years of her mother's life when, frail and with failing faculties, Sido struggles stubbornly against her infirmities. Throughout this period Sido maintains her zest for life, rising early to welcome the day, even giving up a visit to her beloved daughter so that she can stay home to watch her cactus bloom. The writer promises herself that she will never forget her mother's example.

 For summaries in languages other than English, see Unit 5 Teaching Resources Book, pp. 221–226.

Vocabulary

Antonyms Have students work in pairs with a thesaurus to generate a list of antonyms or near antonyms for one of the vocabulary words and then to make word crosses for another pair to solve. For example, students might write *undaunted* in connected boxes across the page, and then supply blank boxes that connect on the first *n* (for spelling out the antonym *uncertain*); on the *a* (for *cowardly*), on the second *n* (for *apprehensive*), and on the *e* (for *irresolute*).

English Learners

DIFFERENTIATED INSTRUCTION

Beginning Remind students to use cognates as they read to help them understand vocabulary. For example, students whose first language is Spanish will find that the first paragraph contains the cognate *occasion (ocasión),* and the fourth paragraph contains the cognate *innocence (inocencia).* Warn students, however, that some words look similar to English words but have very different meanings. *Embar-* *rassed* in paragraph 4 is an example; it does not mean *embarazada* in Spanish, or "pregnant"; instead it means "a state of discomfort or difficulty" often stemming from actions one regrets.

Among the cognates students may list from the first two pages of the story are *imagine (imaginar), furiously (furiosamente), object (objeto), expression (expresión), passionate (apasionado), devotion (devoción), tem-* *porary (temperero/temperario), opposite (opuesto), chocolate (chocolate), coffee (café), hours (horas), colors (colores),* and *fruits (frutas).* After students have compiled their lists, ask them to exchange them with a partner and check to be sure that each word makes sense.

Teach

Literary Element | 1

Autobiography Answer:
The person is Sido, the author's aging mother. Her final years are described.

[ADVANCED] **Ask:** What can you infer about the biographer or the biographer's attitude toward her subject? *(The biographer knows her subject well; she knows her inner feelings or can interpret her response to her aging.)*

Reading Strategy | 2

Analyze Characterization
Answer: *The use of imagery shows Sido's desire for independence despite her increasing weakness.*

 For an audio recording of this selection, use Listening Library Audio CD-ROM.

Readability Scores

Dale-Chall: 8.1
DRP: 56
Lexile: 1020

Two Memories of Sido
from EARThly pARADiSE

Colette
Translated by Una Vincenzo Troubridge and Enid McCleod

ThE TiME CAME . . .

The time came when all her strength left her. She was amazed beyond measure and would not believe it. Whenever I arrived from Paris to see her, as soon as we were alone in the afternoon in her little house, she had always some sin to confess to me. On one occasion she turned up the hem of her dress, rolled her stocking down over her shin, and displayed a purple bruise, the skin nearly broken.

"Just look at that!"

"What on earth have you done to yourself this time, Mother?"

She opened wide eyes, full of innocence and embarrassment.

"You wouldn't believe it, but I fell downstairs!"

"How do you mean—'fell'?"

"Just what I said. I fell, for no reason. I was going downstairs and I fell. I can't understand it."

"Were you going down too quickly?"

"Too quickly? What do you call too quickly? I was going down quickly. Have I time to go downstairs majestically like the Sun King?[1] And if that were all . . . But look at this!"

On her pretty arm, still so young above the faded hand, was a scald forming a large blister.

"Oh goodness! Whatever's that!"

"My footwarmer."

"The old copper footwarmer? The one that holds five quarts?"

"That's the one. Can I trust anything, when that footwarmer has known me for forty years? I can't imagine what possessed it, it was boiling fast, I went to take it off the fire, and crack, something gave in my wrist. I was lucky to get nothing worse than the blister. But what a thing to happen! After that I let the cupboard alone. . . ."

She broke off, blushing furiously.

"What cupboard?" I demanded severely.

My mother fenced, tossing her head as though I were trying to put her on a lead.

---

1. Louis XIV (1638–1715), King of France, was known as the *Sun King*.

---

1 Autobiography *Who is described in the first paragraph? What period in the person's life is described?*

2 Analyze Characterization *How does Colette's use of imagery help you understand her mother?*

1034 UNIT 5 MODERN EUROPE

Reading Practice

Evaluate Dialogue Ask students to work in pairs or small groups and reread the dialogue to evaluate it for two qualities:

- how natural or credible the dialogue sounds
- how well it fulfills the function of revealing character

Among the criteria students may use to evaluate credibility or naturalness is whether the word choices, sentence structures, and sentence lengths approximate spoken, rather than written, language; and whether the tone of the dialogue seems realistic in view of the situation or information it conveys.

To evaluate how well the dialogue reveals characters, students should make inferences about what each bit of dialogue reveals about both characters; they should use several of those inferences, along with their knowledge of how characters are revealed, to make an evaluation. *(Students should find that the dialogue is natural and well-crafted, approximating speech, and that it reveals both Sido's personality and the relationship between mother and daughter.)*

1034

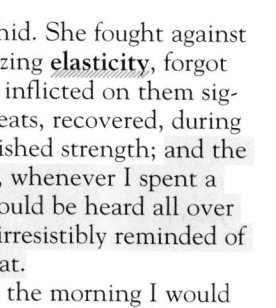

At the Cafe, 1949. Tsuguharu Foujita. Oil oncanvas, 76 x 64 cm. Musee National d'Art Moderne, Paris. Licensed by ARS, NY.

"Oh, nothing! No cupboard at all!"

"Mother! I shall get cross!"

"Since I've said, 'I let the cupboard alone,' can't you do the same for my sake? The cupboard hasn't moved from its place, has it? So, shut up about it!"

The cupboard was a massive object of old walnut, almost as broad as it was high, with no carving save the circular hole made by a Prussian bullet that had entered by the right-hand door and passed out through the back panel.

"Do you want it moved from the landing, Mother?"

An expression like that of a young she-cat, false and glittery, appeared on her wrinkled face.

"I? No, it seems to me all right there—let it stay where it is!"

All the same, my doctor brother and I agreed that we must be on the watch. He saw my mother every day, since she had followed him and lived in the same village, and he looked after her with a passionate

devotion which he hid. She fought against all her ills with amazing **elasticity**, forgot them, baffled them, inflicted on them signal if temporary defeats, recovered, during entire days, her vanished strength; and the sound of her battles, whenever I spent a few days with her, could be heard all over the house till I was irresistibly reminded of a terrier tackling a rat.

At five o'clock in the morning I would be awakened by the clank of a full bucket being set down in the kitchen sink immediately opposite my room.

"What are you doing with that bucket, Mother? Couldn't you wait until Josephine arrives?"

And out I hurried. But the fire was already blazing, fed with dry wood. The milk was boiling on the blue-tiled charcoal stove. Nearby, a bar of chocolate was melting in a little water for my breakfast, and, seated squarely in her cane[2] armchair, my mother was grinding the fragrant coffee which she roasted herself. The morning hours were always kind to her. She wore their rosy colors in her cheeks. Flushed with a brief return to health, she would gaze at the rising sun, while the church bell rang for early Mass, and rejoice at having tasted, while we still slept, so many forbidden fruits.

The forbidden fruits were the overheavy bucket drawn up from the well, the firewood split with a billhook on an oaken block, the spade, the mattock, and above all the double steps propped against the gable

---

2. *Cane* furniture is made by weaving the hollow woody stems of reeds.

Analyze Characterization How does Sido react to her various ailments? How does her daughter react? What do their reactions reveal about each of them? **3**

Vocabulary

elasticity (i las′tis′ə tē) n. the quality of being easily adaptable or adjustable, so as to fit changes or new circumstances

COLETTE **1035**

Teach

Reading Strategy **3**

Analyze Characterization
Answer: *Sido refuses to accept the changes and is surprised by the accidents. Instead of seeing her own body aging, she blames the objects. Her daughter tries to protect her but admires her mother's spirit. Both characters are strong and resilient.*

View the Art

Tsuguharu Foujita was raised in Japan but lived much of his adult life in France. The white skin tone of the woman writing a letter in a café is characteristic of some of his portrait paintings. **Ask:** Is this woman consistent with your image of the author who records her memories of her mother? Why or why not? (*Students may say that her contemplative expression and her dramatic choice of dress make her consistent with the woman whose voice they hear. They might also respond to the whiteness of her skin as evocative of Sido, viewing it as an emblem of someone suspended between life and death, or of someone china-like or breakable superimposed on aspects of a more credible reality.*)

Approaching Level

DIFFERENTIATED INSTRUCTION

Evaluate Dialogue For students having difficulty with the Reading Practice activity on page 1034, suggest that they begin to evaluate dialogue by reading it aloud to each other. Students should ask:

- Who said it?

- Why would she say that? What is her motive? What else might she have said?

- Are the sentences of the dialogue short? Do the words seem like everyday words?

Advanced Learners/Pre-AP

DIFFERENTIATED INSTRUCTION

Write Dialogue Challenge advanced students to write additional dialogue that takes place between Colette and her mother on the subject of Sido's everyday activities. Require students to match the style of the dialogue that Colette created.

Learning Objectives
Analyze autobiography. (SE)
Analyze characterization. (SE)
Evaluate dialogue. (TE)
Analyze art. (TE)

Teach

Reading Strategy   1

Analyze Characterization
Answer: *Her will and curiosity are her greatest strengths, but they sometimes lead her to undertake things she is no longer capable of doing.*

Progress Check

Can students analyze characteristics?

If No → See Unit 5 Teaching Resources Book, p. 228.

View the Art ★

Answer: *The woman in the painting seems thoughtful and busy. She may be attending to personal correspondence, like Sido's letter of regret.*

Anna Ancher, one of the few professional female Danish artists of her time, enjoyed popularity and critical success. She is best known for her paintings of domestic interiors. In this work, she creates a strong contrast between the remote, solitary figure in a dark dress and the brilliant sunlight shining through the window. **Ask:** What do the woman's position and posture indicate about her? *(She is intent on her work; she is bending fully to the task and absorbed by it. She is not distracted by the brilliant sunshine outside. She may be working with intensity or energy.)* Note that the painting may have been chosen to evoke an image of either Colette or her mother.

A Woman Sitting at Her Writing Desk. Anna Ancher. Oil on canvas, 48.5 x 39.5 cm. Private collection.

View the Art Archer was known for her paintings of domestic interiors. How might this woman remind you of Colette or Sido? ★

The forbidden fruits were the overheavy bucket drawn up from the well, the firewood split with a billhook on an oaken block, the spade, the mattock, and above all the double steps propped against the gable window of the woodhouse. There were the climbing vine whose shoots she trained up to the gable windows of the attic, the flowery spikes of the too-tall lilacs, the dizzy cat that had to be rescued from the ridge of the roof. All the accomplices of her old existence as a plump and sturdy little woman, all the minor rustic[3] divinities who once obeyed her and made her so proud of doing without servants, now assumed the appearance and position of adversaries. But they reckoned without that love of combat

---

3. The narrator describes the plants and the cat as being almost godlike in importance in this country (*rustic*) setting.

1036   UNIT 5   MODERN EUROPE

which my mother was to keep till the end of her life. At seventy-one, dawn still found her **undaunted**, if not always undamaged. Burnt by the fire, cut with the pruning knife, soaked by melting snow or spilled water, she had always managed to enjoy her best moments of independence before the earliest risers had opened their shutters. She was able to tell us of the cats' awakening, of what was going on in the nests, of news gleaned,[4] together with the morning's milk and the warm loaf, from the milkmaid and the baker's girl, the record in fact of the birth of a new day.

It was not until one morning when I found the kitchen unwarmed, and the blue enamel saucepan hanging on the wall, that I felt my mother's end to be near. Her illness knew many **respites**, during which the fire flared up again on the hearth, and the smell of fresh bread and melting chocolate stole under the door together with the cat's impatient paw. These respites were periods of unexpected alarms. My mother and the big walnut cupboard were discovered together in a heap at the foot of the stairs, she having determined to transport it in secret from the upper landing to the ground floor. Whereupon my elder brother insisted that my mother should keep still and that an old servant should sleep in the little house. But how could an old servant prevail against a vital energy so youthful and mischievous that it contrived to tempt and lead astray a

---

4. *Gleaned* means "gathered."

Analyze Characterization *What are Sido's greatest strengths—and how do they sometimes backfire?*   **1**

Vocabulary

undaunted (un dôn′tid) *adj.* courageously firm or resolute, especially in the face of danger or difficulty; not discouraged

respites (res′pits) *n.* periods of temporary relief, rest, or delay

Writing Practice

Use Hyphens Remind students that a common use of a hyphen is to join compound adjectives that precede a noun, as in the following examples: *wind-whipped snow, well-educated woman*. Also review when a hyphen is not used: when the compound adjective follows the noun or if the expression is made up of an adverb ending in *-ly* and an adjective: *The woman is well educated; a happily married couple.*

Write the following sentences on the board.

Then have students place hyphens correctly.

1. There are clear cut issues to decide. *(clear-cut)*

2. A widely known authority will speak. *(widely known)*

3. The second speaker is also well liked. *(well liked)*

4. There'll be an up to date analysis. *(up-to-date)*

body already half fettered[5] by death? My brother, returning before sunrise from attending a distant patient, one day caught my mother red-handed in the most wanton[6] of crimes. Dressed in her nightgown, but wearing heavy gardening sabots,[7] her little gray septuagenarian's plait of hair[8] turning up like a scorpion's tail on the nape of her neck, one foot firmly planted on the crosspiece of the beech trestle, her back bent in the attitude of the expert jobber,[9] my mother, rejuvenated by an indescribable expression of guilty enjoyment, in defiance of all her promises and of the freezing morning dew, was sawing logs in her own yard.

"SIR, YOU ASK ME..."

"Sir,

"You ask me to come and spend a week with you, which means I would be near my daughter, whom I adore. You who live with her know how rarely I see her, how much her presence delights me, and I'm touched that you should ask me to come and see her. All the same I'm not going to accept your kind invitation, for the time being at any rate. The reason is that my pink cactus is probably going to flower. It's a very rare plant I've been given, and I'm told that in our climate it flowers only once every four years. Now, I am already a very old woman, and if I went away when my pink cactus is about to flower, I am certain I shouldn't see it flower again.

"So I beg you, sir, to accept my sincere thanks and my regrets, together with my kind regards."

---

5. *Fettered* means "chained" or "shackled."
6. Anything done in a *wanton* way displays mischief—and, sometimes, cruelty.
7. *Sabots* (sa bōz´) is French for wooden shoes.
8. A *septuagenarian* (sep´tōō ə jə nār´ē ən) is a person in his or her seventies; a *plait of hair* is a braid.
9. The mother would bend in the position of an expert woodcutter, one foot braced on the horizontal piece of a bench made of beech wood.

2 Realism and Modernism *How does this passage reflect the early twentieth-century issue of independence and women's rights?*

This note, signed "*Sidonie Colette, née*[10] *Landoy*," was written by my mother to one of my husbands, the second. A year later she died, at the age of seventy-seven.

Whenever I feel myself inferior to everything about me, threatened by my own mediocrity, frightened by the discovery that a muscle is losing its strength, a desire its power, or a pain the keen edge of its bite, I can still hold up my head and say to myself: "I am the daughter of the woman who wrote that letter—that letter and so many more that I have kept. This one tells me in ten lines that at the age of seventy-six she was planning journeys and undertaking them, but that waiting for the possible bursting into bloom of a tropical flower held everything up and silenced even her heart, made for love. I am the daughter of a woman who, in a mean, close-fisted, confined little place, opened her village home to stray cats, tramps, and pregnant servant girls. I am the daughter of a woman who many a time, when she was in despair at not having enough money for others, ran through the wind-whipped snow to cry from door to door, at the houses of the rich, that a child had just been born in a poverty-stricken home to parents whose feeble, empty hands had no swaddling clothes[11] for it. Let me not forget that I am the daughter of a woman who bent her head, trembling, between the blades of a cactus, her wrinkled face full of ecstasy over the promise of a flower, a woman who herself never ceased to flower, untiringly, during three quarters of a century."

---

10. *Née* (nā) is French for "born" and is used to identify a married woman's maiden name.
11. *Swaddling clothes* are narrow strips of cloth wrapped around an infant to restrict its movement.

Autobiography *What lesson does Colette learn from her mother's life?* **3**

COLETTE **1037**

Teach

Big Idea   2

Realism and Modernism
Answer: *It shows the strength of women and their ability to continue in spite of adversities. The author's portrayal of her mother is also an example of a positive female role model.*

Literary Element   3

Autobiography Answer:
She learns that life should be lived to the fullest and that every moment should be cherished.

(**ADVANCED**) **Ask:** How is a hierarchy of value conveyed through this observation? (*Students may discern a poet's or naturalist's sensibilities taking precedence over action. They may say the mother's intense inner life was the only thing more powerful than her outward energy.*)

To check students' understanding of the selection, see Unit 5 Teaching Resources Book, p. 232.

Learning Objectives
Analyze characterization. (SE)
Analyze art. (SE)
Analyze autobiography. (SE)
Use hyphens. (TE)

Approaching Level

DIFFERENTIATED INSTRUCTION

Compound Words Review the three types of compound words: closed, such as *teacup;* open, such as *food web;* and hyphenated, such as *merry-go-round.* Writers also create hyphenated compounds, such as "*blue-tiled* charcoal stove." Have students distinguish between standard hyphenated compounds that appear in the dictionary and situational hyphenated compounds that are based only on context.

1. Tim placed the article on the editor-in-chief's desk. (*standard; this compound is always hyphenated*)
2. Ana loved cross-country skiing. (*standard; several words with* cross *are hyphenated*)
3. The self-righteous man droned on. (*standard; words with* self *are always hyphenated*)
4. An icy chill seeped through the paper-thin walls. (*situational or context driven*)

Advanced Learners/Pre-AP

DIFFERENTIATED INSTRUCTION

Use Hyphens Challenge students to recast three or more of Colette's descriptive sentences to incorporate hyphenated compound adjectives. Students may introduce new words or vary the wording somewhat in order to use hyphenated compounds that are consistent with Colette's sensory language and imagery.

After You Read

Assess

1. Possible answers: *determined/ stubborn; strong/overambitious; enthusiastic, vivacious* and *unrealistic.* Students may use adjectives that have both positive and negative connotations.

2. (a) "for no reason" (b) She is not in good health and was walking too quickly.

3. (a) She answers, "No, it seems to me all right there—let it stay where it is!" (b) She wants to maintain her independence and move the cupboard by herself.

4. (a) These objects are "forbidden fruits." (b) Sido treasures these tasks, and they tempt her even though she knows she should not be doing them.

5. (a) when Sido fails to do her morning chores (b) The author thinks nothing but death could stop Sido from doing her work.

6. Some students will say Colette idealizes her mother, always showing her to be strong-willed and caring. Others may argue that Colette was realistic about her mother's strengths and flaws.

7. (a) Some may say restricting Sido would have limited her enjoyment of life. Others may say it would have made no difference because Sido was so independent. (b) It reveals that they respected their mother's wishes and wanted her to be happy.

8. Each time Colette repeats the phrase, she cites an example of her mother's strength, generosity, and love of nature. This reflects the spirit of the times, in which a respect for independence and the rights of women were beginning to emerge.

After You Read

Respond and Think Critically

Respond and Interpret

1. What adjectives come to mind when you think of Sido?

2. (a)According to Sido, why did she fall? (b)What is another interpretation of the reason for her fall?

3. (a)When her daughter asks whether she wants the cupboard moved from the landing, what is Sido's response? (b)How do her words contradict her wishes?

4. (a)What collective term does Colette use to describe the bucket, firewood, and other objects used in Sido's labor? (b)What does Colette mean by this?

5. (a)When does Colette feel her mother is close to dying? (b)Why does she feel this way?

Analyze and Evaluate

6. Do you think Colette idealizes Sido? Explain.

7. (a)Do you think Colette and her brother should have taken stronger measures to protect Sido from injury? Explain. (b)What does their decision to let Sido make her own decisions reveal about the family's relationship?

Connect

8. **Big Idea** **Realism and Modernism** Colette repeats the phrase "I am the daughter of a woman who . . ." How does her pride in her mother reflect the spirit of the times?

9. **Connect to the Author** In writing this autobiography, Colette makes a significant change to the facts of the cactus incident. In the real letter, her mother mentions the blooming flower, but agrees to visit her daughter. (a)Why do you think Colette chose to make this change? (b)What does this reveal about an author's freedom to alter history?

Primary Source Quotation

Delight in the Ordinary

Colette said her journals and memoirs were closer to random groupings of observations and reflections than a strict chronological retelling.

"I do not possess the knack of writing a proper journal. The art of selection, of noting things of mark, retaining the unusual while discarding the commonplace, has never been mine, since most of the time I am stimulated and quickened by the ordinary."

Colette, 1896. Jacques Fernand Humbert. Oil on canvas. Private collection.

Group Activity

Think about the quotation by Colette in relation to "Two Memories of Sido." Then answer these questions with a group.

1. What details in "Two Memories of Sido" might be considered "commonplace"?

2. Do you think these details make the work more or less appealing? Explain.

---

9. (a) Colette's goal was to show her mother as a strong character. Portraying her as someone who would stick to her principles over a small event such as a flower's blooming contributes to this goal. (b) This shows an author is free to alter details to serve a larger purpose.

Primary Source Quotation

1. Answers will vary. Students may note some of the tasks Sido takes upon herself.

2. Answers will vary. Many students may feel these details help characterize the mother and add to Colette's unique descriptive style.

Literary Element Autobiography

ACT Skills Practice

1. How does the author feel about Sido?

   A. Sido should give up making breakfast.

   B. Sido is too old to live alone.

   C. Sido does not let her illness and old age hinder her ambitions.

   D. Sido can do everything she used to do, if she tries hard enough.

2. Colette is proud of her mother because she:

   F. lives life to the fullest.

   G. is utterly dependent on her.

   H. is deeply religious.

   J. obeys all her instructions.

Review: Repetition

As you learned on page 79, **repetition** is the recurrence of sounds, words, phrases, lines, or stanzas in a speech or literary work.

Partner Activity With a partner, complete a diagram like the one below. Fill it in with examples that complete the repeated phrase "I am the daughter of a woman who . . ." Then, discuss the effect of this repetition on the reader. How does it reveal the author's feelings about her mother?

I am the daughter of a woman who . . .

LOG ON ▶ **Literature** Online

Selection Resources For Selection Quizzes, eFlashcards, and Reading-Writing Connection activities, go to glencoe.com and enter QuickPass code GLW6053u5.

Reading Strategy Analyze Characterization

An author can use **direct characterization** by simply telling the reader what the character is like. More often, however, authors use **indirect characterization** by describing a character's behavior or physical appearance, telling what the character says and thinks, revealing what other characters say and think about the character, and showing a character's effect on other people.

1. (a)Why does Sido describe her mother's expression as "guilty enjoyment" when she is discovered sawing logs? (b)How effective is this image as a way of characterizing Sido? Explain.

2. List three additional examples of indirect characterization. Explain how each example reveals something about Sido and about Colette's attitude toward her.

Vocabulary Practice

Practice with Antonyms With a partner, brainstorm three antonyms for each boldfaced vocabulary word below. Then discuss your choices with your classmates. Be prepared to explain why you chose your words.

elasticity   undaunted   respites

EXAMPLE: majestic

Antonyms: humble, modest, unimposing
Explanation: A majestic person would make a show of descending the stairs, but a humble person would not.

Academic Vocabulary

*Colette suggests there are spiritual **dimensions** to Sido's personality, as Sido's accomplices are "rustic divinities" and her face is "full of ecstasy."*

Dimensions is an academic word. In more casual conversation, someone might say they had to measure the **dimensions** of a room to see if new furniture would fit. To further explore this word, answer the following question: What are the **dimensions** of your personality?

For more on academic vocabulary, see pages 36–37 and R83–R85.

COLETTE **1039**

Literary Element

1. C is the correct answer. Sido has accidents when she tries to do tasks beyond her declining ability, but she still does what she wants to do.

2. F is the correct answer. Sido cherishes every moment of life.

Progress Check

Can students analyze autobiography?

If No → See Unit 5 Teaching Resources Book, p. 227.

Review: Repetition

Possible response:

- wrote about the importance of a flowering cactus and was planning trips at age 76
- opened her village home to stray cats, tramps, and pregnant servant girls
- begged for money to help a poor family
- never ceased to flower, untiringly, during three-quarters of a century

Repetition helps reveal the author's admiration for her mother's energy and love of life.

Reading Strategy

1. (a) Sido enjoys remaining active but feels guilty about defying her children. (b) It shows rather than tells that Sido was energetic and independent.

2. Sido's morning activities, such as warming milk, melting chocolate, or rescuing a cat, reveal her energy and independence and how much Colette admired her.

Vocabulary

Possible answers:

elasticity—Antonyms: inflexibility, rigidness, firmness; Explanation: Something that has elasticity is flexible.

undaunted—Antonyms: worried, scared, disturbed; Explanation: Someone who is undaunted is not worried.

respite—Antonym: continuation, prolongation, extension; Explanation: A respite is a pause, rather than a continuation.

Academic Vocabulary

In describing dimensions of their personalities, students should describe a range of characteristics and explore how their personalities change around different groups of people.

After You Read

Respond Through Writing

Students' profiles should

- focus on one person the student admires
- use figurative language and imagery
- use direct and indirect characterization

A student who meets all of these criteria should receive the equivalent of a 4-point response.

A student who fully meets two or partially meets three of these criteria should receive the equivalent of a 3-point response.

A student who fully meets one or partially meets two of these criteria should receive the equivalent of a 2-point response.

A student who partially meets one of these criteria should receive the equivalent of a 1-point response.

 For grammar practice, see Unit 5 Teaching Resources Book, p. 231.

Respond Through Writing

Biographical Narrative

Apply Characterization Colette describes her mother, Sido, as her role model because she does not allow old age and illness to dampen her vitality. Write a 500-word profile of someone whose example you would like to follow. You might choose someone you know personally, someone famous, a fictional character, or a historical figure. Your profile should include both direct and indirect characterization.

Understand the Task A **profile** is an abridged biography, or a short descriptive article about someone.

Prewrite Research to learn about your subject. If you know the person, you might interview him or her. If you do not know your subject, you might use the Internet to conduct research. Organize your information in a storyboard like the one below. In the top panels draw pictures related to key ideas you want to include in your profile. In the bottom panels include a caption that explains the relevance of the image.

Draw an early memory of your subject	Draw an example of your subject in action.	Draw an example of your subject among others.
Note how this memory has affected you.	Note how this action relates to the reason your subject is a good role model.	Note how your subject has affected the lives of others.

Draft As you write, refer to the chart you made about methods of characterization on page 1033. Use figurative language and imagery to describe your subject's character and behavior. Include specific details about places and events.

Revise Check your draft against the storyboard you created. Is the sequence of events correct? Do you shift tone when appropriate, and are transitions clear? Do you effectively convey information to the reader?

Edit and Proofread Proofread your paper, correcting any errors in spelling, grammar, and punctuation. Use the word count feature on your computer to check that your profile is 500 words. Review the Grammar Tip in the side column for information on using idioms.

Learning Objective

In this assignment, you will focus on the following objectives:

Writing: Writing a biographical narrative.

Grammar: Understanding idioms.

> **Grammar Tip**
>
> **Idioms**
>
> An **idiom** is a word or phrase that has a different figurative meaning from its literal meaning. The phrase *out of the question* is so familiar to most English speakers that they know immediately it means "not to be considered" or "impossible." (However, someone who is not fluent in English might interpret the phrase literally.)
>
> Some idioms cannot be interpreted so easily: *stuck up, happy as a clam, in a pickle, cost an arm and a leg.* In these cases, context clues can be helpful. In your narrative, try using familiar idioms that match your subject.

Writing Practice

Apply Figurative Language Suggest students try out this step-by-step method for creating similes and metaphors to use in their biographical narrative.

- Choose a subject (for example, a tropical plant).
- Focus on an outstanding or central characteristic of the subject (for example, the plant's huge leaves).

- Choose an unrelated subject with a similar central characteristic or quality (for example, a blanket).
- Write a metaphor or simile that compares or equates the subject with something fresh and new by incorporating the shared central quality or characteristic (for example, *The banana leaves were soft, green*

blankets under which colonies of insects slept or *The banana leaf was like a soft, green blanket under which thousands of insects seemingly slept).*

1040

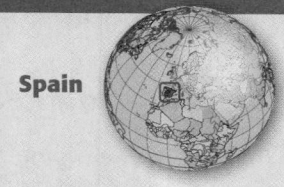
Meet **Federico García Lorca**

(1898–1936)

Federico García Lorca's life was cut short by tragedy. Yet during his brief but brilliant career, he became one of Spain's preeminent modern authors.

Musical Roots The first of four children, García Lorca was born into a wealthy family in Andalusia, a rural region in southern Spain. Although his family moved to the city of Granada when García Lorca turned ten, his heart remained in the Andalusian countryside. García Lorca was not a successful student—he took nine years to obtain his bachelor's degree at the University of Granada—but he thrived as a musician. He particularly excelled at composing and playing the piano. While still in his teens, he began to experiment with poetry and drama. He soon developed a style all his own, juxtaposing genres with a strong sense of musicality.

> "I have a huge storehouse of childhood recollections in which I can hear the people speaking. This is poetic memory, and I trust it implicitly."
>
> —Federico García Lorca

Life in Madrid In 1919, García Lorca relocated to Madrid and moved into the Residencia de Estudiantes. There he met a group who would one day include the best-known artists of their generation, such as surrealist painter Salvador Dalí and filmmaker Louis Buñuel. It was at this time García Lorca established himself as a member of Madrid's literary elite, specifically the "Generation of 1927." García Lorca became notorious for purposely holding up publication of his books. He preferred to perform his own plays and poetry, and his florid style of presentation won him many admirers.

Success and a Tragic End In 1928, García Lorca published *Gypsy Ballads*, a collection of poems inspired by traditional Spanish songs. It was his first unqualified literary success, but fame did not suit García Lorca's personality. He was a private person, and the spotlight robbed him of his solitude during an especially difficult period in his personal life. His relationship with Dalí disintegrated and he experienced a spiritual crisis and depression. A visit to the United States and Cuba in 1929 improved his spirits; he returned to Spain with renewed energy in 1930, took over as head of the theater company La Barraca, and wrote a play (*Once Five Years Pass*, 1931). Other plays soon followed, including the tragedies *Blood Wedding* and *The House of Bernarda Alba*.

In 1936, the Spanish Civil War broke out. Within the first few months of the war, García Lorca, a liberal intellectual with a controversial personal life, was labeled a radical. He was arrested and, without benefit of a trial, shot to death by Nationalist soldiers. His death stunned the world, especially since his poetry had never been obviously political. Fifty years later, Spain erected a monument at the site of the assassination to commemorate García Lorca's accomplishments.

LOG ON ▶ **Literature** Online

Author Search For more about Federico García Lorca, go to glencoe.com and enter QuickPass code GLW6053u5.

FEDERICO GARCÍA LORCA **1041**

Before You Read

Focus

Bellringer Options

Selection Focus Transparency 63

Daily Language Practice Transparency 98

Or ask: What role does music play in your life? Encourage students to think about how music has affected their lives.

Or: Play a recording of a guitar selection by a Spanish composer, such as Albeniz or Tarrega, and ask students to write about how they feel while listening to the music. Inform them that a similar kind of music inspired Lorca to write "The Guitar."

Political History ☆

War Times From 1936 to 1939, Spain was involved in a brutal civil war between the wealthy Nationalists, who were supported by Italian Fascists and German Nazis, and the middle-class Republicans, who were backed by the Soviet Union. Casualties from the war are estimated between 500,000 and 1 million.

Selection Skills

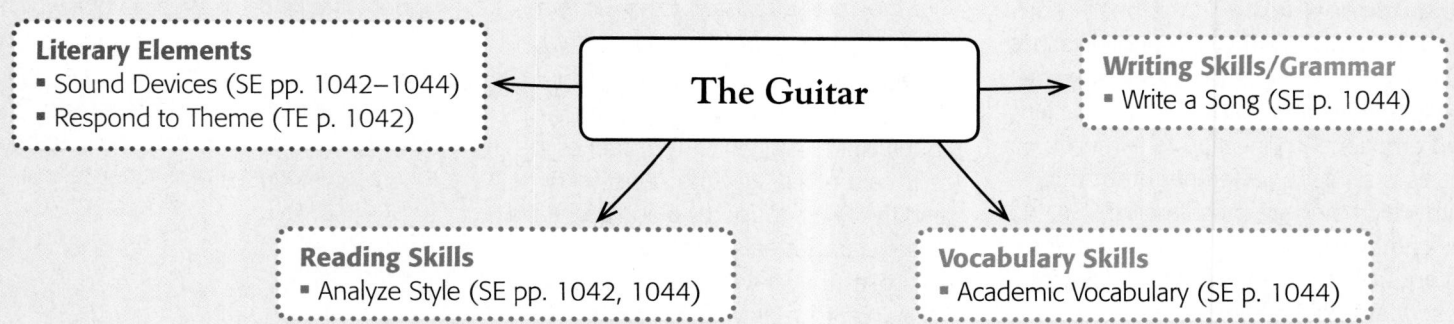

Literary Elements
- Sound Devices (SE pp. 1042–1044)
- Respond to Theme (TE p. 1042)

The Guitar

Writing Skills/Grammar
- Write a Song (SE p. 1044)

Reading Skills
- Analyze Style (SE pp. 1042, 1044)

Vocabulary Skills
- Academic Vocabulary (SE p. 1044)

Before You Read

Focus

Summary

In "The Guitar," Lorca compares the sound of a guitar to a human cry of pain. This idea becomes a refrain in the poem. Lorca ends the poem with a direct address to the instrument.

> For summaries in languages other than English, see Unit 5 Teaching Resources Book, pp. 234–239.

Cultural History ☆

The History of Flamenco

Though flamenco is still vibrant today, the height of its popularity was between 1780 and 1845. Initially, the movement highlighted singing, but after Silverio Franconetti opened a flamenco café, the emphasis shifted to music and dance. Lorca was among others who strove to restore flamenco to its original form through competitions which started in 1922.

Literary and Reading Preview

Connect to the Poem

What kind of music evokes strong emotions for you? Write a journal entry that describes how the beat of the music, the sound of the instruments, or the rhythm of the lyrics affect your mood.

Build Background

☆ García Lorca wrote a book of poetry entitled *Poem of the Deep Song*. In it, he sought to capture the emotional power of the native Andalusian flamenco music of his boyhood. While some flamenco music is festive, García Lorca preferred the more somber aspects of the form *cante jondo* (kän te hōn′dō) ("deep song"). The guitar, an instrument associated with Spain and Spanish culture for centuries, plays a central role in this music. Most of the poems in García Lorca's collection are written in short, irregular lines that echo the forceful energy of flamenco.

Set Purposes for Reading

Big Idea Realism and Modernism

As you read, ask yourself, How does the poet use the memory of a musical style to evoke the complexity of human passion?

Literary Element Sound Devices

Sound devices are poetic techniques that appeal to the ear. Authors use sound devices to create a sense of rhythm, to emphasize particular sounds, or to add to the musical quality of their writing. As you read "The Guitar" aloud, ask yourself, What rhythm and musicality do I hear?

Reading Strategy Analyze Style

When you **analyze** an author's **style**, you examine the combination of unique expressive qualities such as word choice and the use of figurative language and imagery. Style can reveal an author's attitude and purpose. As you read, ask yourself, What elements of the poem contribute to García Lorca's style?

Tip: Compare Words As you read, consider the concrete words and phrases García Lorca uses in place of less specific ones. Create a chart like the one below.

Ineffective	Effective
General: weapons	Specific: five swords
Abstract: injured	Concrete: gravely wounded

Learning Objectives

For pages 1041–1044

In studying this text, you will focus on the following objectives:

Literary Study: Analyzing sound devices.

Reading: Analyzing style.

Writing: Writing a song.

Guitar and Flowers, 1912. Juan Gris. Oil on canvas, 44 1/8 x 27 5/8 in. Bequest of Anna Erickson Levene, in memory of her husband Dr. Phoebus Aaron Theodor Levene. The Museum of Modern Art, NY.

Literary Element Practice

Respond to Theme In this poem, Lorca tries to capture the rhythms and emotions associated with flamenco music. Ask students to think about how Lorca's reaction and emotional connection to flamenco music is similar or different from music with which they are most familiar. (*Students may mention classical or popular compositions that evoke similar feelings of sadness and longing. Some may say*

that they prefer to listen to music that makes them feel happy or peaceful.)

Ask each student to bring in a sample of music, lyrics from a song, or a poem about music with which they feel especially connected. Play the selection or read the lyrics or poems aloud and have students pay attention to the emotional responses they have to each selection. Ask students to draw conclusions

about what kinds of music evoke which emotions. (*Students may say that slower, more melodic songs and songs in minor keys evoke feelings of sadness and longing. The may say that quick, upbeat songs and songs in major keys evoke feelings of joy.*)

The Guitar

Federico García Lorca
Translated by Robert Bly

El Jaleo, 1882 John Singer Sargent. Isabella Stewart Gardner Museum, Boston.

1 The crying of the guitar
starts.
The goblets[1]
of the dawn break.
5 The crying of the guitar
starts.
No use to stop it.
It is impossible
to stop it.
10 It cries repeating itself
as the water cries,
as the wind cries
over the snow.

It is impossible
15 to stop it.
It is crying for things
far off.
The warm sand of the South
that asks for white camellias.[2]
20 For the arrow with nothing to hit,
the evening with no dawn coming,
and the first bird of all dead
on the branch.
Guitar!
25 Heart wounded, gravely,
by five swords.

---

1. A *goblet* is a drinking glass with a stem.

2. The *camellia* (kə mēl′yə) is an evergreen shrub or tree with sweet-smelling flowers.

2 Sound Devices *What effect does this repetition create? How does it affect the mood of the poem?*

Realism and Modernism *These lines cry out in pain and yet they reflect the poet's joy in the music. How does this reflect the contradictory themes of the Modernist movement?* **3**

FEDERICO GARCÍA LORCA **1043**

Teach

Literary Element 1

Free Verse Remind students that free verse is a style of poetry that is written without a strict metrical pattern or rhyme scheme. Tell students that "The Guitar" is written in free verse. **Ask:** How does Lorca create a sense of rhythm in this poem without using rhyme or meter? *(He creates a sense of rhythm by using repetition and enjambment, both of which add a lilting, musical quality to the poem.)*

Literary Element 2

Sound Devices Answer: *The repetition creates a musical effect and creates a melancholy mood by stressing the weeping.*

Big Idea 3

Realism and Modernism Answer: *The poem focuses on deeply human emotions but uses a nontraditional form to experiment with rhythm and mimic another genre, flamenco music.*

Learning Objectives
Analyze sound devices. (SE)
Respond to theme. (TE)
Analyze free verse. (TE)

Approaching Level

DIFFERENTIATED INSTRUCTION

Monitor Comprehension Ask students to carefully reread the poem and think about whether it was written by a musician. **Ask**: What clues are given in the poem to make you think that the author was or was not a musician? *(The poem seems to show an understanding of the way a musical composition is constructed, so a musician or someone who understands the way music is composed could have written it.)*

Advanced Learners/Pre-AP

DIFFERENTIATED INSTRUCTION

Apply Criticism Talk to students about New Criticism, a mid-twentieth-century school of criticism which argued that a work of literature should be analyzed in isolation, without reference to an author's biography or time period. Ask students to comment on whether they agree with this theory, and have them apply it to Lorca's poem. **Ask:** How would your understanding of the poem change if you knew nothing about Lorca's political background or about flamenco music? *(Some students may say that the poem would still be powerful to a reader with no background knowledge, because the poem evokes universal feelings through vivid imagery. Others may say that this background knowledge is required for one to appreciate the poem's underlying meaning.)*

1043

After You Read

Assess

1. Answers will vary.

2. (a) Lines 3–4 mention how the silence is shattered like goblets breaking. (b) The poem is delivered in short bursts that allow the reader to imagine a quiet place suddenly erupting with sound.

3. (a) The sound of the guitar is compared to wind and water. (b) The similes show how the music of the guitar is as timeless as wind and water.

4. (a) Examples include the guitar, the water, and the wind crying and the sand asking for camellias. (b) Answers will vary. Students may note that personifying inanimate objects that cannot weep or make requests makes them more real.

5. (a) The speaker's emotions are wounded by the sound of the guitar. (b) The five swords refer to the guitarist's fingers.

6. Realism focuses on everyday details (flamenco). Modernism experiments with ideas and form (experimental rhythm).

7. Examples might include "Killing Me Softly (With His Song)" or The Beatles' "While My Guitar Gently Weeps."

 For additional assessment, see Assessment Resources, pp. 207–208.

After You Read

Respond and Think Critically

Respond and Interpret

1. What emotions did this poem evoke in you? Explain.

2. (a) Which lines suggest the attention-getting beginning of a piece of guitar music? (b) How does the poet achieve this musicality?

3. (a) Find two **similes** in the poem. What is being compared? (b) How do these similes contribute to your understanding of the poem?

Analyze and Evaluate

4. (a) How do you interpret the last two lines of the poem? (b) What do you think the "five swords" represent?

5. (a) Identify an example of **personification** in "The Guitar." (b) In your opinion, how effective is this use of personification? Support your answer with examples from the poem.

Connect

6. **Big Idea** **Realism and Modernism** How does "The Guitar" embody Realist and Modernist principles?

7. **Connect to Today** Can you think of a contemporary poem, song, or story that addresses the emotional impact or quality of a particular kind of music or musical instrument? Explain.

Literary Element **Sound Devices**

García Lorca wrote "The Guitar" using **free verse,** which has no regular pattern of rhythm, rhyme, or line breaks. However, he did use sound devices such as repetition to create a musical rhythm.

1. How does García Lorca's repetition of the guitar's constant crying help you understand the point of the poem?

2. What emotions does the poem's staccato rhythm highlight?

Reading Strategy **Analyze Style**

Consult the chart you made on page 1042 and then complete the following activity.

Partner Activity Work with a partner to compile song lyrics that you both enjoy. Compare the rhythm and emotional effect of these lyrics with that of "The Guitar." Present your findings to the class.

 LOG ON **Literature** Online

Selection Resources For Selection Quizzes, eFlashcards, and Reading-Writing Connection activities, go to glencoe.com and enter QuickPass code GLW6053u5.

Academic Vocabulary

*Flamenco music is the **foundation** of García Lorca's poem.*

Foundation is an academic word with several definitions. For example, you might say a building had to be demolished because its **foundation** was cracked. Using context clues, figure out the meaning of the word as it is used in the following sentence: A large donation helped the **foundation** pursue a broad array of projects.

For more on academic vocabulary, see pages 36–37 and R83–R85.

Writing

Write a Song Poetry and music share many qualities. For example, the repetition and rhythm in "The Guitar" echo the flamenco songs that inspired García Lorca. Choose an object important to you and write a song about it, applying García Lorca's use of sound devices to your lyrics. If you play an instrument, set your lyrics to music and perform it for the class.

Literary Element

1. He produces a mournful sound that echoes the poem's concept of beauty and unfulfilled desire or yearning.

2. The rhythm highlights deep sorrow and excitement or pain.

Reading Strategy

Students should focus on rhythm and emotional effect of the lyrics.

Progress Check

Do students understand sound devices?

If No → See Unit 5 Teaching Resources Book, p. 240.

Academic Vocabulary

Here, *foundation* means "an institution that pursues research, education, and the arts."

Writing

Students' songs should focus on one object and its significance and include sound devices.

Before You Read

Encounter

Meet Czesław Miłosz

(1911–2004)

The renowned Nobel Prize–winning poet and novelist Czesław Miłosz lived through some of the most turbulent times in history, and he used the gift of his poetry to give voice to the dangers he saw overtaking the world.

The Catastrophists Miłosz was born in the Lithuanian town of Sateiniai and spent much of his early life in czarist Russia where his father was employed as a civil engineer. Shortly after World War I ended, however, Miłosz and his family settled in Vilna, which had become a part of Poland. Miłosz was only in his early twenties when he published his first volume of poetry. While enrolled at the University of Vilna, he became a part of a literary group known as the Catastrophists. This company of student writers became well known for their belief that the world was about to be taken over by a global war that would decimate nations and break down all cultural values. When World War II broke out, Miłosz and his fellow Catastrophists believed their prophecies were coming true to some extent. By now, Miłosz was living in Nazi-occupied Warsaw, Poland. He began to publish anti-Nazi poetry and worked as a writer and a translator for the Polish resistance forces.

Toward the Pacific Coast At the close of World War II, Miłosz began working as a cultural ambassador for the Polish communist government. But it was not long before the authoritarian leanings of this government began to disturb Miłosz deeply. In 1951 he defected from Poland and moved to Paris. The Polish government responded by declaring Miłosz a "nonperson" and banned his work within Poland for the next 30 years. But Miłosz continued to live and write in Paris, and in 1960 he

> "In a room where people unanimously maintain a conspiracy of silence, one word of truth sounds like a pistol shot."
>
> —Czesław Miłosz

was invited to join the faculty of the University of California at Berkeley. Miłosz settled there and became a professor emeritus of literature at Berkeley in 1978. His time in the San Francisco Bay Area was reflected in his poetry of that period, which often contrasts images of the Pacific Coast with those of the Lithuanian landscape of his youth.

The poems of Czesław Miłosz have been praised for their concentrated, clear expression of complex ideas. In 1980 Miłosz was awarded the Nobel Prize in Literature. In his acceptance speech he said: ". . . by choosing solitude and giving myself to a strange occupation, that is, to writing poems in Polish while living in France or America, I tried to maintain a certain ideal image of a poet, who, if he wants fame, he wants to be famous only in the village or the town of his birth."

 LOG ON ▶ **Literature** Online

Author Search For more about Czesław Miłosz, go to glencoe.com and enter QuickPass code GLW6053u5.

Before You Read

Focus

Bellringer Options

Selection Focus Transparency 64

Daily Language Practice Transparency 99

Or ask: Have you ever had a random encounter that gave you a new perspective on your own life? Encourage students to discuss personally meaningful encounters and how the encounters affected them. Many will describe instances in which they encountered a way of doing things that was drastically different from their own. Suggest to them that encountering the surprising or the unfamiliar often leads to growth and insight.

Or ask: What makes encounters in nature a source of wonder? *(Possible response: because many elements in nature are living, but indifferent to the rules and logic of humans, the natural world is often a source of mystery, intrigue, and wonder for humans.)*

Selection Skills

Literary Elements
- Analyze Title (SE pp. 1046, 1048)
- Analyze Parallelism (TE p. 1047)

Encounter

Writing Skills/Grammar
- Dramatic Scene (SE p. 1048)
- Description (TE p. 1046)

Reading Skills
- Interpret Imagery (SE pp. 1046–1048)

Before You Read

Focus

Summary

In the poem, the speaker recalls a past encounter while riding with a companion through a frozen field in a wagon. A bird took flight, and the speaker's companion pointed to a hare running across the road. The speaker reflects that neither the companion nor the hare are still alive. He recalls the sights and sounds of the encounter, and he asks, out of wonder, where both are, and where they are going.

 For summaries in languages other than English, see Unit 5 Teaching Resources Book, pp. 244–249.

Literary History ☆

Milosz on Nature For Milosz, nature could be beautiful but was not synonymous with beauty. In one discussion, he even said that nature was "pure horror." Though nature became a frequent subject of his work, Milosz refused to romanticize nature or treat it sentimentally.

 For an audio recording of this selection, use Listening Library Audio CD-ROM.

1046

Literature and Reading Preview

Connect to the Poem

Have you ever witnessed a natural phenomenon—a sunset, a deer in the woods—that made you consider your place in the world? Freewrite for a few minutes about how a moment in nature gave you a new perspective on your own life.

Build Background

☆ Czesław Miłosz wrote many descriptions of landscapes. As a boy, he wanted to become a naturalist, and this interest carried over into his poetry. As he once claimed: "The forests, the valleys and the rivers which I saw in my childhood possess for me a strong evocative force." Unlike many poets, however, Miłosz refused to idealize nature in his work. He said American authors tend to emphasize the beauty of nature, whereas he felt, "nature is extremely cruel, or at least indifferent."

Set Purposes for Reading

Big Idea **Postwar Europe**

Miłosz's poem "Encounter" takes the form of a memory of a lost event in a lost location. As you read the poem, ask yourself, How does the passage of time affect the speaker's relationship with the "encounter" in the poem?

Literary Element **Title**

The **title** is the name of a literary work. A title can help explain a setting, provide insight into the theme, or describe the action that will take place in the work. As you read, ask yourself, What kind of feeling does the word "encounter" connote to me?

Reading Strategy **Interpret Imagery**

Imagery is the "word pictures" authors create to evoke an emotional response in readers. To create effective imagery, authors use **sensory details,** or descriptions that appeal to one or more of the five senses. As you read, ask yourself, What details are clues that guide me to the work's meaning?

Tip: Note Details Use a chart like the one below to note details that appeal to your sense of sight (visual) and to your sense of hearing (aural).

Visual	Aural
frozen fields, dawn, red wing, darkness...	

Learning Objectives

For pages 1045–1048

In studying this text, you will focus on the following objectives:

Literary Study: Analyzing title.

Reading: Interpreting imagery.

Writing: Writing a dramatic scene.

Winter Sunday in Dalecarlia, 1899. Gustaf Ankarcrona (Swedish, 1869-1933). Oil on canvas, 64 x 109 cm. Private collection.

Writing Practice

Write a Description Have students consider a time in their own lives when they experienced a moving or unsettling encounter with the natural world. If students prefer, they can imagine such an encounter instead. Then, have students write a descriptive paragraph in which they describe the encounter and reveal its significance. Remind them to include the following in their descriptions:

- sensory details
- vivid verbs
- personal thoughts and feelings

Note to students that the encounters they write about need not be extreme or life-changing. A small, seemingly insignificant encounter may provide more insight than a dramatic one. Encourage students to use a tone similar to that of Milosz in "Encounter." In particular, have students try to refrain from sentimentalizing or romanticizing nature.

Winter landscape, 1905. Stanislaw Wyspianski. Pastel on paper. National Museum in Cracow, Poland.

Encounter

Czesław Miłosz
Translated by the author and Lillian Vallee

We were riding through frozen fields in a wagon at dawn.
A red wing rose in the darkness.

And suddenly a hare ran across the road.
One of us pointed to it with his hand.

That was long ago. Today neither of them is alive,
Not the hare, nor the man who made the gesture.

O my love, where are they, where are they going.
The flash of a hand, streak of movement, rustle of pebbles.
I ask not out of sorrow, but in wonder.

Jechaliśmy przed świtem po zamarzłych polach,
Czerwone skrzydło wstawało, jeszcze noc.

I zając przebiegł nagle tuż przed nami,
A jeden z nas pokazał go ręką.

To było dawno. Dzisiaj już nie żyją
Ni zając, ani ten co go wskazywał.

Miłości moja, gdzież są, dokąd idą
Błysk ręki, linia biegu, szelest grud—
Nie z żalu pytam, ale z zamyślenia.

2 Interpret Imagery *To which sense do these images appeal? Which words convey the images?*

3 Postwar Europe *How does the tone of this poem reflect the cultural outlook of post–World War II Europe?*

CZESŁAW MIŁOSZ **1047**

English Learners

DIFFERENTIATED INSTRUCTION

Intermediate After English learners have written their descriptive paragraph (page 1046, bottom), have them form groups and switch papers for a peer review. Students should include positive feedback as well as noting areas for improvement during their review. After students revise their paragraphs, have them practice reading their paragraphs aloud alone, then with a partner, until they are comfortable. Then have students read their paragraphs in small groups or in front of the class, depending on their fluency and confidence. Check for general fluency and encourage students to adjust their tone, volume, and pacing accordingly as they read aloud.

Literary Element 1

Parallelism **Ask:** What makes these phrases parallel? What is the effect of the parallelism? *(Each phrase has the same structure. The parallelism emphasizes each element, giving it a similar "weight" or importance as the other two. It also creates a unique rhythm.)*

APPROACHING Have students find an example of repetition of words or phrases in the poem and describe the effect. *(The statement "where are they" is repeated. The repetition suggests an urgency or insistence in the question.)*

For additional literary element practice, see Unit 5 Teaching Resources Book, p. 250.

Reading Strategy 2

Interpret Imagery **Answer:** *Images appeal to the sense of sight. The description of the dawn, the running hare, and the raised hand convey the images.*

Big Idea 3

Postwar Europe **Answer:** *The speaker reflects on the passage of time. The hare and the speaker's companion have died and he wonders where they have gone. After the death and destruction of World War II, Europe was also faced with a changed world and a sense of wonder about the past and future.*

Learning Objectives
Interpret imagery. (SE)
Write a description. (TE)
Analyze parallelism. (TE)

After You Read

Assess

1. Students should voice their thoughts honestly.

2. (a) It happened years earlier. (b) Both the hare and the speaker's companion have died.

3. (a) What happens after death (b) Either wonder or sadness

4. (a) The running hare and the man's hand (b) The contrast between these memories and reality cause wonder.

5. (a) Many students will say the encounter has become significant only with the passage of time. (b) He may be the speaker's father or an older relative.

6. (a) Students may conclude the speaker is filled with regret for the transience of life. (b) Encourage students to discuss whether the speaker feels sorrowful or is, as he asserts, only filled with wonder.

7. The death and suffering caused by the war led many to question the meaning of existence.

8. They make past events feel immediate. The speed of modern communication might also change our ability to comment on events in the past.

 For additional assessment, see Assessment Resources, pp. 209–210.

After You Read

Respond and Think Critically

Respond and Interpret

1. What were your thoughts as you finished reading this poem? Explain.

2. (a) When did the encounter in the poem take place? (b) What has happened since then?

3. (a) In the last stanza, what is the speaker asking about "in wonder"? (b) Based on this, what is the poem's main emotion?

4. (a) What things cause the speaker to wonder? (b) What larger question does the speaker consider after seeing these things?

Analyze and Evaluate

5. (a) Do you think the encounter in the poem was important to the speaker as it occurred? Explain.

(b) What would you guess is the relationship between the speaker and the man who made the gesture? Explain.

6. Scholars Leonard Nathan and Arthur Quinn assert that "Encounter" is "full of the very regret that the speaker tries to deny." (a) What is that regret? (b) Do you agree that the speaker tries to deny it? Explain.

Connect

7. **Big Idea** **Postwar Europe** How do the poem's mood and tone reflect the world's state after World War II?

8. **Connect to Today** How might television, video journals, blogs, or instant messages affect how memories are preserved today?

Literary Element Title

You can recall a work's **title** as you read to see how it resonates within the work.

1. Describe the encounter referenced in the poem's title.

2. A dictionary might define "encounter" as (a) a meeting between hostile factions or (b) a chance meeting. How might Miłosz's poem embody these definitions?

Reading Strategy Interpret Imagery

Miłosz uses imagery to capture the passage of time and the fleeting nature of existence.

Partner Activity With a partner, read through the poem line by line and discuss each image in the poem. What **mood** do these images create?

 Literature Online

Selection Resources For Selection Quizzes, eFlash-cards, and Reading-Writing Connection activities, go to glencoe.com and enter QuickPass code GLW6053u5.

Academic Vocabulary

*The speaker in "Encounter" recalls **physical** details, such as the "flash of a hand," as he contemplates the mysteries of life and death.*

*Physical is an academic word. In more familiar conversation, you might say that soccer is a **physical** game. To further explore the meaning of this word, answer the following question: What aspects of **physical** activities do you prefer over mental activities?*

For more on academic vocabulary, see pages 36–37 and R83–R85.

Writing

Write a Dramatic Scene Think of a memorable encounter you have had with an animal, a person, or a situation. Write a dramatic scene about this encounter. Refer to the chart about visual and aural details you made on page 1046 to help brainstorm imagery for your scene, and give it an engaging title that will grab your readers' attention.

Literary Element

1. While riding in a wagon, the speaker and a companion encounter a hare running across the road.

2. The hare and the hawk are enemies, and the human beings and the animals might present a danger to each other. The meeting of all these creatures takes place by chance on a cold morning in the distant past.

Reading Strategy

Students will probably say the mood is melancholy, nostalgic, or sorrowful. Students might point to the "frozen fields."

Progress Check

Can students interpret imagery?

If No → See Unit 5 Teaching Resources Book, p. 251.

Academic Vocabulary

Students should make a distinction between physical exertion, such as running, and mental exertion, such as reading.

Writing

Students' scenes should

- focus on a memorable encounter
- use sensory details
- include an engaging title

1048

Before You Read

The World, My Friends,
My Enemies, You, and the Earth

Meet **Nazim Hikmet**

(1902–1963)

B anned in his homeland for much of his lifetime, the writings of Nazim Hikmet (nä zēm´ hēkн´met) bore witness to the fall of the ancient Ottoman Empire and the birth of the Turkish Republic. These experiences formed the backbone of his visionary writing.

Politics and Poetry Hikmet was born in Salonika, Greece, the son of an Ottoman Turkish government official. After going to school in the European part of Turkey, Hikmet worked for a short time as a teacher in the Asian part of Turkey known as Anatolia. He published his first poems when he was only fifteen years old; many of these works were eloquent meditations on his affinity for the people of Anatolia's peasant class. After World War I, Turkey's Ottoman Empire collapsed, and Hikmet joined the fight for Turkish nationalism.

In 1921 he went to Russia to study at a college in Moscow. The radical political theories he learned there eventually led him back to his homeland to join the Turkish Communist Party. He published essays, plays, and poetry that spoke out against the injustices he saw overtaking his country. In 1925, his writing got him into legal trouble for the first (but certainly not the last) time. The sentence for this first offense was harsh—fifteen years in prison. Rather than serve his sentence, Hikmet fled to Russia. He returned to Turkey in 1928 and worked at a progressive magazine called *Pictorial Monthly*. The authoritarian Turkish government monitored his activities, however, and his radical views and incendiary writing repeatedly landed him in jail—he would spend nearly 30 years of his life either behind bars or under government surveillance. These experiences inspired many of his finest poems.

> "I want to write poems that both talk only about me and address just one other person and call out to millions."
>
> —Nazim Hikmet

Prison and a New Country The charges against Hikmet were not always clear, and government officials tended to contradict themselves when discussing his various sentences. Regardless of the specific charges, in 1938 he was sentenced to 35 years in prison. The sentence may have been due to his part in inciting a riot among young members of the military. It might also have resulted from a poem he wrote against fascism called "At the Gates of Madrid." Hikmet served twelve years of the sentence before leading international intellectuals organized a protest campaign and gained his release in 1950—the same year he won the prestigious International Peace Prize. Assuming it would not be wise for him to remain in Turkey, Hikmet returned to Russia and spent the rest of his life in exile.

 Literature Online

Author Search For more about Nazim Hikmet, go to glencoe.com and enter QuickPass code GLW6053u5.

NAZIM HIKMET **1049**

Before You Read

Focus

Bellringer Options

Selection Focus
Transparency 65

Daily Language Practice
Transparency 100

Or ask: What role do politics play in the lives of everyday people today? Many people feel that political passion and desire for social justice has dissipated in contemporary society. Ask students to think about and comment on how politics and social reforms play a role in the lives of today's youth.

Cultural History ☆

Pan-Turkism Prior to and following World War I, there was a surge of Turkish nationalism known as Pan-Turkism. The goal of this political movement was to unite all Turkish speakers across the Ottoman Empire, including those in Russia, China, Iran, and Afghanistan. Through Turkish newspapers and prominent Turkish authors, the movement gained momentum between 1913 and 1918 and was officially supported by the Ottoman government.

Selection Skills

Literary Elements
- Free Verse (SE pp. 1050, 1052, 1053)

Reading Skills
- Monitor Comprehension (SE pp. 1050, 1052, 1053)
- Analyze Text Structure (TE p. 1050)

The World, My Friends, My Enemies, You, and the Earth

Writing Skills/Grammar
- Poem (SE p. 1053)
- Letter (TE p. 1052)

Vocabulary Skills
- Vocabulary Preview (SE p. 1050)
- Word Usage (SE p. 1053)
- Context Clues (TE p. 1050)

Before You Read

Focus

Summary

The speaker of the poem says he is happy to have been born into such a beautiful, varied world. Although he has never traveled beyond his homeland, he feels that he is united by common dreams and desires with people all across the earth. He ends the poem by expressing his commitment to social change. Without this commitment, he says, neither the beauty of his love nor that of the earth can satisfy him.

 For summaries in languages other than English, see Unit 5 Teaching Resources Book, pp. 254–259.

Vocabulary

Context Clues Ask students to read the sentences that contain the vocabulary words and draw conclusions from the surrounding information about the definitions of the words. If students are already familiar with the words, tell them it is important to be able to identify and understand the parts of sentences that can help define words that they may not know in the future. For extra practice, write three sentences on the board using the words *pedantry, hastiness, and lucidity.* Have students use context clues to guess their meanings.

 For additional vocabulary practice, see Unit 5 Teaching Resources Book, p. 262.

Literature and Reading Preview

Connect to the Poem

In what ways are you connected to people around the world? Discuss this question with a small group.

Build Background

In 1938 the Turkish government accused Hikmet of using his poetry to promote disloyalty and sentenced him to prison. While serving his sentence, he produced a large body of work, including "The World, My Friends, My Enemies, You, and the Earth." He enclosed poems in letters to friends and relatives who then circulated them in manuscript form. Although an international protest campaign helped win Hikmet's release, his poetry was not published in Turkey until after his death.

Set Purposes for Reading

Big Idea Modernism and Realism

Like many Modernist authors, Hikmet wrote poems that were at once personal and public. As you read, ask yourself, How does the speaker illustrate this idea of public and private in the poem?

Literary Element Free Verse

Free verse is a form of poetry that has no fixed pattern of meter, rhyme, line length, or stanza arrangement. Although poets who write free verse ignore traditional rules, they use techniques such as repetition and alliteration to create musical patterns. As you read, ask yourself, How do the line breaks and punctuation help you understand the poem's meaning?

Reading Strategy Monitor Comprehension

When you **monitor comprehension,** you check in with yourself as you read to see if you fully grasp the ideas in a literary work. To do this, you will find it helpful to divide the work into sections and pause to ask questions after reading each one. If necessary, reread the section. As you read, ask yourself, What is the main idea and emotion in each section?

Tip: Chart Questions In a chart like the one below, list your questions and answers as you read Hikmet's poem.

Question: Who is the speaker in the poem?	Question:	Question:
Answer: The poet himself	Answer:	Answer:

Reading Practice

 Analyze Text Structure
Hikmet's poem presents an eclectic structure, which may generate questions from students. Ask students to analyze the poem by retyping it and placing line breaks and stanza breaks where they seem appropriate. Tell students to pay attention to the poem as they type, noting how the form affects the meaning. For example, if the first line were broken after "happy," then it would take on a new meaning, indicating general happiness, rather than the speaker's specific happiness at having "[come] into the world." Ask students to print out their newly formatted poems and, in small groups, discuss their reasons for formatting the poems as they did. Have them present both their agreements and disagreements to the rest of the class.

Learning Objectives

For pages 1049–1053
In studying this text, you will focus on the following objectives:

Literary Study: Analyzing free verse.

Reading: Monitoring comprehension.

Writing: Writing a poem.

Vocabulary

dimension (di men′shən) *n.* a measure of physical form or proportion; p. 1051 *Given the dimensions of the boat, it was clear it would seat only three people.*

mere (mēr) *adj.* being nothing more or less than; p. 1052 *Though it was a mere three miles to town, it was farther than we were willing to walk.*

nautical (nô′ti kəl) *adj.* of or relating to sailors or ships; p. 1052 *The restaurant features a nautical theme—from its all-seafood menu to the servers' sailor caps.*

Tip: Word Usage When you encounter a new word, ask yourself a question about it to help you understand what it means. For example, you might ask, What are the dimensions of my bedroom?

The World, My Friends, My Enemies, You, and the Earth

Nazim Hikmet

Translated by Randy Blasing and Mutlu Konuk

Parana, Brazil I, 1995.
Deirdre Kelly. Screenprint
and collage, 75 x 72 cm.
Hardware Gallery, London.

I'm wonderfully happy I came into the world,
I love its earth, its light, its struggle, and its bread.
Even though I know its **dimensions** from pole to pole to the
                                          centimeter,

> **Vocabulary**
>
> **dimension** (di men′shən) *n.* a measure of physical form or proportion

---

Teach

Reading Strategy   1

Predict Ask students to predict, on the basis of the title, what they will learn about the speaker's personality. *(Students may think that the speaker is someone who is gregarious, enjoys people and ideas, and has a sense of humor.)*

> For an audio recording of this selection, use Listening Library Audio CD-ROM.

Learning Objectives
Analyze free verse. (SE)
Understand context clues. (TE)
Analyze structure. (TE)

English Learners

DIFFERENTIATED INSTRUCTION

Advanced Explain to English learners that in English, it is considered ungrammatical to use negatives to reinforce one another, as in "I haven't seen nobody"; the literal meaning is the opposite of that intended. However, an expression such as Hikmet's "not unaware" is acceptable, since its literal and intended meaning is the same—the speaker is aware that the earth is smaller than the sun.

Have English learners rewrite the following sentences to eliminate the double negatives:

1. He didn't have no idea what had happened. *(He didn't have any . . . He had no . . .)*

2. I won't answer no questions. *(I won't answer any . . . I'll answer no . . .)*

3. You shouldn't never have come. *(You should never . . . You should not have . . .)*

Teach

Literary Element `1`

Free Verse **Answer:** *It captures the natural rhythm of casual, intimate conversation.*

[APPROACHING] Explain that, unlike poetry with strict syllabic requirements, free verse can include line breaks where a person would naturally pause when speaking. Have students identify such pauses in lines 8–13. *(Possible answers: "However, / I made my…" and "Me and our corner grocer, / we're both…")*

Reading Strategy `2`

Monitor Comprehension
Answer: *"Friends" are those who agree with him or wish him well; "enemies" are those who disagree with him or wish him to be silent.*

 For additional practice using the reading skill or strategy, see Unit 5 Teaching Resources Book, p. 261.

 To check students' understanding of the selection, see Unit 5 Teaching Resources Book, p. 264.

and while I'm not unaware that it's a **mere** toy next to the sun,
5 the world for me is unbelievably big.
I would have liked to go around the world
and see the fish, the fruits, and the stars that I haven't
                                                    seen.

However,
I made my European trip only in books and pictures.
10 In all my life I never got one letter
                with its blue stamp canceled in Asia.
Me and our corner grocer,
we're both mightily unknown in America.
Nevertheless,
15 from China to Spain, from the Cape of Good Hope to Alaska,
in every **nautical** mile, in every kilometer, I have friends
                                                    and enemies.

Such friends that we haven't met even once—
we can die for the same bread, the same freedom, the same
                                                    dream.
And such enemies that they're thirsty for my blood,
20   I am thirsty for their blood.
My strength
is that I'm not alone in this big world.
The world and its people are no secret in my heart,
                no mystery in my science.
25 Calmly and openly
                I took my place
                                in the great struggle.
And without it,
                you and the earth
30   are not enough for me.
And yet you are astonishingly beautiful,
                the earth is warm and beautiful.

`1` **Free Verse** *How does the free verse form contribute to the poem's tone?*

`2` **Monitor Comprehension** *What does the speaker mean by "friends and enemies"?*

Vocabulary

mere (mēr) *adj.* being nothing more or less than
nautical (nô′ti kəl) *adj.* of or relating to sailors or ships

Writing Practice

Write a Letter Ask students to write a letter to the speaker of the poem. This letter might be in the voice of one of the people mentioned in the poem: perhaps a "friend" from another part of the world, an "enemy," or even the speaker's love. Alternatively, students might choose to write in the voice of one of Hikmet's former jail mates, or simply in their own voices. Students' poems should express a response to the way Hikmet's speaker views the world. Encourage them to take issue with the speaker's views, and even challenge them directly. Alternatively, they may wish to describe an experience that confirms the speaker's beliefs. No matter what position they take, students should try to imitate Hikmet's casual, conversational tone in their letters.

After You Read

Respond and Think Critically

Respond and Interpret

1. Which lines in this poem made the biggest impression on you? Explain.

2. (a)What is the speaker's overall impression of the world? (b)How has he formed this impression?

3. (a)What is the "great struggle" the poet mentions? (b)What has the speaker gained from his involvement in that struggle?

Analyze and Evaluate

4. A **symbol** is any object, person, place, or experience that stands for something else, usually something abstract. What do you think bread symbolizes in this poem?

5. What adjective would you use to describe the speaker? Why?

6. Do you agree with how the speaker seems to view the world? Explain.

Connect

7. **Big Idea** **Realism and Modernism** Like other Modernists, Hikmet's work broke with convention. Considering he wrote this poem in jail, what is surprising about his perspective?

8. **Connect to Today** Hikmet's speaker notes several similarities between himself and his enemies. Can you think of any modern-day enemies that have more in common than they think? Explain.

Literary Element Free Verse

Because **free verse** has no fixed pattern of meter, poets use other techniques to create rhythm. Reread the poem to find examples of repeated words and phrases.

1. (a)What is the poem's tone? (b)How does the poet's use of free verse intensify that tone?

2. Describe a technique that Hikmet uses to create shifts in the rhythm of his poem. Point out specific examples.

Reading Strategy Monitor Comprehension

Comprehending poetry requires more than simply understanding the words and images. Readers must also think about the overall meaning, or **theme,** of the poem. Reread the poem. Then use the question-and-answer chart you created on page 1050 to help you answer these questions.

1. What is the poet's message to his love? What is the message to his readers?

2. (a)In one sentence, state the theme of Hikmet's poem. (b)How does the poem's title shed light on its theme?

Vocabulary Practice

Practice with Word Usage Respond to these statements to help you explore the meanings of the vocabulary words from the poem.

1. Estimate the **dimensions** of the room you are in.

2. Describe something that is a "**mere** toy" next to something else.

3. List things you might see on a **nautical** trip.

Writing

Write a Poem Hikmet writes about his relationship with the world, even those places he has never seen. Write a poem in free verse about your relationship with the world, using the theme and style of Hikmet's poem as a model. Try including sound devices such as alliteration and repetition.

LOG ON **Literature** Online

Selection Resources For Selection Quizzes, eFlashcards, and Reading-Writing Connection activities, go to glencoe.com and enter QuickPass code GLW6053u5.

NAZIM HIKMET **1053**

After You Read

Assess

1. Answers will vary. Students may volunteer to read their responses to the class.

2. (a) The world is beautiful and large. (b) He has formed this impression through books and pictures.

3. (a) The struggle is the ongoing political challenge to treat working people fairly. (b) It has given his life meaning.

4. Possible answers: sustenance; food and other things needed for life.

5. Possible answers: idealistic, confident, hopeful.

6. Students should support their opinions with logical arguments.

7. It is surprising that the speaker focuses on the beauty in the world while he is in prison.

8. Students should identify specific countries or groups of people who are in conflict but who also share a common language, heritage, or geography.

Writing

Students' poems should
- focus on the student's relationship with the rest of the world
- use free verse and literary devices

Literary Element

1. (a) The tone is joyous. (b) The use of free verse captures the natural rhythm of casual, high-spirited conversation among friends.

2. Students may point out repeated words such as *world* in lines 5–6, *blood* in lines 19–20, and *beautiful* in lines 31–32.

Reading Strategy

1. The message to his love is that personal love is not enough without love of country and community. The message to his readers is that there is no need to pity him—the struggle is worthwhile.

2. (a) The world is a wonderful place for those who embrace life and fight against hunger and oppression. (b) The title stresses the all-embracing attitude expressed in the poem.

Vocabulary

1. Students should provide a numerical answer.

2. Students may describe a tugboat and a yacht.

3. Students may describe things familiar to an ocean, river, or lake.

1053

Focus

Bellringer Options

Ask: If someone told you in Spanish that you were *bizarro,* would you take it as a compliment? Because of the word's similarity to the English word *bizarre,* English speakers might assume that the person was calling them odd or strange, and be insulted. However, Spanish speakers will know that *bizarro* actually means "brave" or "gallant."

Teach

Text Element	1

Organization Point out that the author ends each of the first two paragraphs with a question. **Ask:** Why has the author included these two questions? What organizational purpose do they serve? *(To pique the reader's interest and introduce the dilemmasinthe essay.)*

View the Art ★

This poster advertises a 1930 meeting of the Sennacieca Asocio Tutmonda (SAT), or the World Non-National Association, a global organization that aims to unite workers of all countries though the use of Esperanto. SAT holds a congress in a different part of the world each year, and publishes Esperanto pamphlets, brochures, and dictionaries.

1054

Learning Objectives

For pages 1054–1055

In studying this text, you will focus on the following objectives:

Reading: Analyzing cultural and historical context. Understanding the nature of language.

The Dream of a Common Language

MOST OF THE EUROPEAN UNION HAS BEEN ABLE TO ADOPT A SINGLE currency, but it still has 23 official languages, a record-keeper's nightmare. At the United Nations, every word spoken at an official meeting must be translated and printed in six langages, at an estimated cost of hundreds of millions of dollars a year. Why can't Europe—and the rest of the world—agree on a single language for all communication?

For centuries, many people have promoted the idea of adopting one language for use in international communication. Simple, easy-to-learn languages have been invented for that purpose, with Esperanto, a phonetic language derived from Romance language roots, being the best known. But nations cannot agree on a single international language, either an existing one or a new one. Why do Europeans—and the rest of the world—resist a proposal that could save time, effort, money, and misunderstanding?

Welcome

Albanian	*Misardhje*
Basque	*Ongi-etorri*
Bulgarian	Добрè дошъл
Danish	*Velkommen*
Dutch	*Welkom*
Esperanto	*Bonveno*
French	*Bienvenue*
German	*Willkommen*
Hungarian	*Isten hozott*
Irish Gaelic	*Fáilte*
Italian	*Benvenuto*
Norweigian	*Velkommen*
Polish	*Witajcie*
Portuguese	*Bem-vindo*
Russian	Добрó пожáловать
Serbian	*Dobro si dosao*
Slovenian	*Dobrodôsel*
Spanish	*Bienvenido*
Swedish	*Välkommen*

The Politics of Language

Europe is a small continent—not much larger than the United States—but its people are divided into many nations and speak about 60 different languages. The political and cultural differences among Europeans have played a part in igniting the two world wars of the twentieth century. Not surprisingly, Europe has been the center of the Esperanto movement, whose proponents believe that international understanding and tolerance would be furthered if everyone spoke the same language.

Although Esperanto has been the most successful language invented for international use, it has failed to catch on. In the twentieth century, as nationalism grew in Europe, many governments viewed the Esperanto movement as a threat to their national identity and goals. Esperanto faced competition from national languages as well as other invented languages.

Since World War II, English has become the international language of commerce, science, and technology because English-speakers have dominated those fields. Even so, the world's nations have not adopted English as the single official language for international forums. Many governments equate adopting a language with allowing one culture to dominate others. According to this view, language equals control.

European currency: one Euro coin

Speaking and Listening Practice

Participate in a Debate The text presents several arguments both for and against the adoption of Esperanto as an international language. Divide students into two teams, and conduct a debate on this topic. Students may wish to conduct additional Internet research on Esperanto and other invented languages to prepare for the debate. Remind students to listen carefully to the opposing side so that they can refute the arguments they hear with counterarguments. They should use specific evidence and examples to back up their points.

LEARN ESPERANTO & MEET WORKERS FROM FORTY COUNTRIES AT THE S.A.T. CONGRESS 3–7 AUG. 1930 CONWAY HALL LONDON

SECRETARY JOEL SULSKY 19 LEYTON RD HARPENDEN

Learn Esperanto and Meet Workers from Forty Countries, 1930. Poster.

The issue of cultural domination would seem to strengthen the case for adopting a neutral, invented language; however, many people object to invented languages on principle. They claim that invented languages lack the richness, vitality, and expressiveness that existing languages have accumulated over time. They resist giving up a "natural" language for an "artificial" one.

Language and National Pride

Each of the world's languages has evolved over a long period of time, and each reflects the history and the culture of its speakers. Each language contains many words and expressions that have gained associations and feelings (connotations) specific to a given culture. Such aspects of a language cannot be easily translated or imported into an invented language.

Many English words, for example, have connotations that either are lacking or are different in other languages. Take the word *red,* for instance. In English, the word is associated with blood, passion, and anger, as in the expression "seeing red." In Russian, on the other hand, the word connotes beauty, and the name *Red Square* suggests beautiful architecture. In Russian, a "red girl" is a beautiful girl. In Chinese, the word *red* is associated with joy and celebration.

English, like other languages, contains thousands of culture-specific idioms that are difficult, if not impossible, to translate. An **idiom** is an expression that has a meaning other than its literal one, such as "barking up the wrong tree." An idiom such as this would be meaningless if translated literally into another language.

Each language has so many culture-specific elements that help to define its speakers to the world and to themselves. Take away a people's language, and you take away part of their being. A Welsh proverb expresses this idea: "A nation without a language is a nation without a heart."

LOG ON ▶ **Literature** Online

Literature and Reading For more about common language and the translators in this book, go to glencoe.com and enter the QuickPass code GLW6053u5.

Respond and Think Critically

1. (a) How many official languages are spoken in Europe? (b) How does this affect political relations between nations?

2. (a) What is Esperanto? (b) Why are some Europeans reluctant to speak it?

3. What idioms do you use that might be difficult to translate into another language?

4. Which do you think is a better solution to the international language problem—using an existing language or an invented one? Explain.

THE ART OF TRANSLATION **1055**

Advanced Learners/Pre-AP

DIFFERENTIATED INSTRUCTION

Common Origins Advanced learners may be interested in researching the common origins of modern European languages. Have them look at the chart on page 1054 and group together the languages that seem to have similar origins, based on similarities between the words for "Welcome." Then have students conduct research on origins and families of languages and see if their guesses were correct.

Teach

Big Idea **2**

Postwar Europe **Ask:** How Esperanto advocates seem similar to those of the speaker in "The World, My Friends, My Enemies, You, and the Earth?" *(Both want to emphasize the commonality between all peoples and create ways for them to connect and communicate..)* **Ask:** Are there any "universal languages" in the modern world? *(Computer codes, Morse code, universal symbols, numerical systems, and music)*

Assess

1. (a) There are 23 official languages. (b) Many official documents need to be translated into a variety of languages. Translators are a necessity at United Nations meetings.

2. (a) Esperanto is the best-known language that was developed expressly for the purpose of becoming an international language. (b) Many European nations link their language with their identity and interpret Esperanto as a threat to their national goals.

3. Encourage English language learners to share examples from their first languages. Examples from English might include "I'd give my eyeteeth for that" and "Don't lead with your chin."

4. Students should support their opinions with well-reasoned arguments.

Before You Read

Focus

Bellringer Options

Selection Focus
Transparency 66

Daily Language Practice
Transparency 101

Say: Think of an adult you know who does the same job every day, day in and day out, but never seems to get anywhere in the job. **Ask:** Why do you think that person keeps doing the task? (*Students may mention economic necessities and the need for routines.*)

Literary History ☆

Literature as Philosophy
Philosophy draws heavily on logic, analysis, and science. For the French in the 1900s, its genesis was often literary. Among the great French literary philosophers of the 1900s were Henri-Louis Bergson, who influenced Marcel Proust's concept of time; Jean-Paul Sartre, the novelist who launched existentialism; and Camus.

Before You Read

France

The Myth of Sisyphus

Meet **Albert Camus**
(1913–1960)

N ovelist, playwright, moralist, and political activist, Albert Camus was regarded by many as the spokesman of his generation.

An Impoverished Childhood Albert Camus (al bār ka mōō) was born and raised near Mondovi, Algeria, then a French territory. His father was killed in World War I, and to supplement her small pension as a war widow, his illiterate and hearing-impaired mother worked as a cleaning woman. She and her two sons lived near poverty with her widowed mother and a paralyzed uncle in a small, two-room apartment. Based on his academic achievement in primary school, Camus won a scholarship to the Grand Lycée, one of two high schools in Algiers. In school he enjoyed soccer, swimming, and boxing, but a diagnosis of tuberculosis at age seventeen put an end to his sports activities. Nevertheless, this severe illness—at the time incurable and barely treatable—did not stop him from studying the works of the ancient Greeks and the philosophers Kierkegaard, Heidegger, and Nietzsche at the University of Algiers.

Literary Career For a few years in the 1930s, Camus' concern for the plight of Algerian Muslims led him to become involved in the Algerian Communist Party, where he became a leading figure among the left-wing intellectuals. In addition, he acted, wrote, and produced plays with the Workers' Theater, working in a genre he considered to be the ultimate artistic form of expression. Moving to Paris, he wrote for several newspapers, including the anti-Nazi underground newspaper, *Combat*, where he became friends with the Existentialist author

> "*The remarkable thing in man is not that he despairs, but that he overcomes or forgets despair.*"
>
> —Albert Camus

and philosopher Jean-Paul Sartre. By the end of World War II, Camus was famous for his first novel, *The Stranger*; for a collection of philosophical essays titled *The Myth of Sisyphus*; and for his plays.

Spokesman for His Generation By the 1950s, Camus was a controversial spokesman for his generation. His work described the meaninglessness of modern life, but also offered a type of optimism that irritated Existentialist contemporaries such as Sartre and Simone de Beauvoir. In 1957 Camus received the Nobel Prize in Literature, an award that made him more of a public figure but caused alienation from his old friends. In 1960, he was driving with friends back to Paris from the south of France when he was killed instantly in a car crash.

 **Literature** Online

Author Search For more about Albert Camus, go to glencoe.com and enter QuickPass code GLW6053u5.

1056 UNIT 5 MODERN EUROPE

Selection Skills

Literary Elements
- Persuasion (SE pp. 1057, 1060, 1061)
- Symbol (SE p. 1061)

Reading Skills
- Determine Main Idea and Supporting Details (SE pp. 1057, 1059, 1062)
- Identify Genre (TE p. 1058)
- Identify Ambiguities (TE p. 1058)

The Myth of Sisyphus

Vocabulary Skills
- Word Origins (SE pp. 1057, 1062)

Speaking/Listening/Viewing Skills
- Deliver a Multimedia Presentation (SE p. 1060)

Writing Skills/Grammar
- Apply Symbolism (SE p. 1062)
- Advice Column (TE p. 1062)

Literature and Reading Preview

Connect to the Essay

Have you ever thought about the meaning of your life? Freewrite for a few minutes about what makes life meaningful for you.

Build Background

In "The Myth of Sisyphus," Camus addresses the problems that arise from the concept of the absurd, a philosophical term referring to the idea that human life has no inherent meaning. Camus argues that the absurd does not justify despair. Once people recognize that the world is essentially meaningless, they can begin to make choices that give meaning to their lives. In this essay, Camus interprets a Greek myth about a man who offends the gods. Sisyphus was an ancient Greek trickster figure who chained up Death when it came for him. Eventually, he was condemned forever to push a huge stone up a hill, only to have it roll back every time he neared the top.

Set Purposes for Reading

Big Idea Postwar Europe

As you read, ask yourself, How does Camus challenge traditional values of religion and philosophy and find some dignity in the absurd?

Literary Element Persuasion

Persuasion is an attempt to convince readers to think or act a certain way. An author often attempts to persuade by applying logic to a number of pieces of evidence or by appealing to emotions, patriotism, or other states of mind. As you read, ask yourself, What kind of persuasion is Camus using in this essay?

Reading Strategy Determine Main Idea and Supporting Details

The **main idea** is the most important idea in a paragraph or text. **Supporting details** contribute to or prove the main idea. As you read, ask yourself, What details support the main idea?

Tip: Make an Outline As you read, determine which statement, if any, may serve as the organizing idea of the paragraphs in the essay.

> I. Main Idea
>   A. Supporting Detail 1: Sisyphus
>   B. Supporting Detail 2: Oedipus
>   C. Supporting Detail 3: Kirilov

Learning Objectives

For pages 1056–1062

In studying this text, you will focus on the following objectives:

Literary Study: Analyzing persuasion.

Reading: Determining main idea and supporting details.

Writing: Applying symbolism.

Vocabulary

prudent (prōōd′ənt) *adj.* sensible; sound in judgment; p. 1058 *Vic thought it would be prudent not to ask for more allowance while his father was still upset over his report card.*

scorn (skôrn) *n.* disrespect; contempt; p. 1059 *Marilou didn't hide her scorn for the embarrassingly crude jokes her brother was telling.*

myriad (mir′ē əd) *adj.* countless; of a very great number of persons or things; p. 1060 *My uncle has myriad funny anecdotes to tell about his travels around the world.*

fidelity (fi del′ə te) *n.* faithfulness; p. 1060 *The dog pulled his owner from the burning building in a show of fidelity.*

negate (ni gāt′) *v.* to make ineffectual or powerless; p. 1060 *John fumed over Courtney's attempts to negate his suggestions for vacation destinations.*

ALBERT CAMUS **1057**

Before You Read

Focus

Summary

In this essay, Camus draws on the story of Sisyphus because he feels this mythical trickster is the epitome of the absurd hero. Until he is finally forced into his endless task of rolling a rock up a hill, only to have it roll down again, Sisyphus has stood up to the gods, mocking and scorning them. At last, he recognizes—as an absurd hero must—the meaninglessness of his task and of life itself. It is this recognition that brings him happiness. As Sisyphus descends the hill to begin his task yet again, he enjoys a moment of private victory.

 For summaries in languages other than English, see Unit 5 Teaching Resources Book, pp. 266–271.

Vocabulary

 SMALL GROUP **Word Origins** Have students work in teams of two or three to preview the vocabulary list and make predictions based on prior knowledge about origins for each of the words. Encourage students to think of other words with similar roots (such as *neg*); similar spellings, such as *sc* (or the variant *sk*) or *yr;* or exposure to other similar words or terms, such as *Myrmidons,* to help them with his task. Explain that students will verify their predictions by completing an exercise after they have read the selection

For additional vocabulary practice, see Unit 5 Teaching Resources Book, p. 274.

English Learners

DIFFERENTIATED INSTRUCTION

Beginning Build background and have students connect to the reading by repeating a meaningless task, such as pushing an eraser up the edge of the chalkboard with one finger until you can no longer push it and it falls. Do this several times, emphasizing the idea of doing a useless task over and over.

Write the word *absurd,* and tell students that Camus uses this term to describe

the action of a man named Sisyphus who pushes a heavy rock up a hill over and over and over.

Use and write the word *meaningless* as a synonym for *absurd,* emphasizing the use of the suffix *-less* to decode the term as "without meaning."

Explain that Camus is writing, in part, to answer the question of whether human life is absurd and meaningless.

Teach

Reading Strategy   1

Identify Ambiguities Ask:
How well do the ideas in this paragraph appear to support the contention that Sisyphus was the wisest and most prudent of mortals? *(The details do not support the topic sentence; the paragraph is ambiguous. Sisyphus takes extraordinary and seemingly very unwise risks, making bargains with the gods and defying mortality itself. Camus glorifies that risk-taking as wisdom.)*

View the Art ★

Ask: How does the painter convey the enormity of the task Sisyphus faces? *(He makes Sisyphus' body very powerful and muscular, yet shows how greatly this powerful man must strain in order to roll the rock. He also merges the rock with Sisyphus' body, making it an extension of his very identity; head, chest, and knee all bend inward toward the rock.)*

For an audio recording of this selection, use Listening Library Audio CD-ROM.

Interactive Read and Write
Other options for teaching this selection can be found in Interactive Read and Write for On-Level Learners, pp. 253–264.

Readability Scores

Dale-Chall: 9.2
DRP: 60
Lexile: 890

The MYTH of SISYPHUS

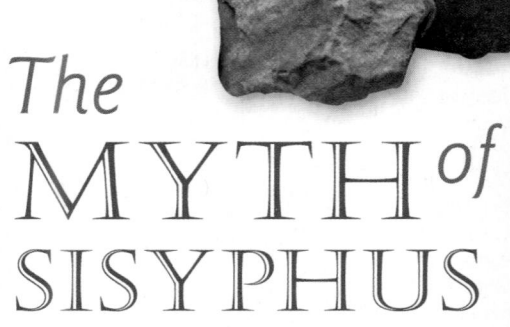

Albert Camus
Translated by Justin O'Brien

Sisyphos, 1547-1548. Titian (Tiziano Vecellio). Canvas, 237 x 216 cm. Museo del Prado, Madrid. ★

The gods had condemned Sisyphus to ceaselessly rolling a rock to the top of a mountain, whence the stone would fall back of its own weight. They had thought with some reason that there is no more dreadful punishment than futile and hopeless labor.

1 If one believes Homer, Sisyphus was the wisest and most **prudent** of mortals. According to another tradition, however, he was disposed to practice the profession of highwayman. I see no contradiction in this. Opinions differ as to the reasons why he became the futile laborer of the underworld. To begin with, he is accused of a certain levity[1] in regard to the gods. He stole their secrets. Aegina, the daughter of Aesopus, was carried off by Jupiter. The father was shocked by that disappearance and complained to Sisyphus. He, who knew of the abduction, offered to tell about it on condition that Aesopus would give water to the citadel of Corinth.[2] To the celestial thunderbolts he preferred the benediction[3] of water. He was punished for this in the underworld. Homer tells us also that Sisyphus had put Death in chains. Pluto could not endure the sight of his deserted, silent empire. He dispatched the god of war, who liberated Death from the hands of her conqueror.

It is said also that Sisyphus, being near to death, rashly wanted to test his wife's love. He ordered her to cast his unburied body into the middle of the public square. Sisyphus woke up in the underworld. And there, annoyed by an obedience so contrary to human love, he obtained from Pluto permission to return to earth in order to chastise his wife. But when he had seen again the face of this world, enjoyed water and sun, warm stones and the sea, he no longer wanted to go back to the infernal darkness.

---

1. *Levity*, a lack of seriousness, borders on mocking disrespect.

Vocabulary

prudent (prōōd′ənt) *adj.* sensible; sound in judgment

---

2. According to Greek mythology, Sisyphus was the king of the city of *Corinth*; a *citadel* is a city's most important fort.
3. Here, *benediction* is something that causes goodness or well-being.

1058 UNIT 5 MODERN EUROPE

Reading Practice

Identify Genre Note that Camus's central purpose is not to retell the myth of Sisyphus, which would result in a fictional narrative. Instead, he uses portions of the myth in order to achieve his own persuasive purpose.

Have students identify the genre of this work *(nonfiction/persuasive essay)* and explain how they know it is nonfiction. *(One clue is the shift between paragraph one and two from retelling the action to commenting on the action. Other clues in the second paragraph include the discussion of varying opinions, including the author's own. In paragraph two and elsewhere, various modes of nonfiction or expository writing are also employed, including cause-effect analysis and personal reflection.)*

Recalls, signs of anger, warnings were of no avail. Many years more he lived facing the curve of the gulf, the sparkling sea, and the smiles of earth. A decree of the gods was necessary. Mercury came and seized the impudent man by the collar and, snatching him from his joys, led him forcibly back to the underworld, where his rock was ready for him.

You have already grasped that Sisyphus is the absurd hero. He *is*, as much through his passions as through his torture. His **scorn** of the gods, his hatred of death, and his passion for life won him that unspeakable penalty in which the whole being is exerted toward accomplishing nothing. This is the price that must be paid for the passions of this earth. Nothing is told us about Sisyphus in the underworld. Myths are made for the imagination to breathe life into them. As for this myth, one sees merely the whole effort of a body straining to raise the huge stone, to roll it and push it up a slope a hundred times over; one sees the face screwed up, the cheek tight against the stone, the shoulder bracing the clay-covered mass, the foot wedging it, the fresh start with arms outstretched, the wholly human security of two earth-clotted hands. At the very end of his long effort measured by skyless space and time without depth, the purpose is achieved. Then Sisyphus watches the stone rush down in a few moments toward that lower world whence he will have to push it up again toward the summit. He goes back down to the plain.

It is during that return, that pause, that Sisyphus interests me. A face that toils so close to stones is already stone itself! I see that man going back down with a heavy yet measured step toward the torment of which he will never know the end. That hour like a breathing space which returns as surely as his suffering, that is the hour of consciousness. At each of those moments when he leaves the heights and gradually sinks toward the lairs of the gods, he is superior to his fate. He is stronger than his rock.

If this myth is tragic, that is because its hero is conscious. Where would his torture be, indeed, if at every step the hope of succeeding upheld him? The workman of today works every day in his life at the same tasks, and this fate is no less absurd. But it is tragic only at the rare moments when it becomes conscious. Sisyphus, proletarian[4] of the gods, powerless and rebellious, knows the whole extent of his wretched condition: it is what he thinks of during his descent. The lucidity that was to constitute his torture at the same time crowns his victory. There is no fate that cannot be surmounted by scorn.

If the descent is thus sometimes performed in sorrow, it can also take place in joy. This word is not too much. Again I fancy Sisyphus returning toward his rock, and the sorrow was in the beginning. When the images of earth cling too tightly to memory, when the call of happiness becomes too insistent, it happens that melancholy rises in man's heart: this is the rock's victory, this is the rock itself. The boundless grief is too heavy to bear. These are our nights of Gethsemane.[5] But crushing truths perish

---

4. A *proletarian* is an industrial wage-earner.
5. According to the Bible, *Gethsemane* (geth sem′ ə nā) is the olive grove where Jesus Christ contemplated his possible death on the eve of his arrest.

Determine Main Idea and Supporting Details *How does this detail support the main idea?*

Postwar Europe *How does Camus connect Greek myths to the conditions in postwar Europe?* **3**

Vocabulary

scorn (skôrn) *v.* disrespect; show contempt for

Teach

Reading Strategy   2

Determine Main Idea and Supporting Details
Answer: *The image of Sisyphus choosing to return to his unending toil and the comparison of Sisyphus' strength to the rock supports the main idea that human beings have the power to give their own lives meaning.*

Big Idea   3

Postwar Europe **Answer:**
Workers during and after the war, like Sisyphus, may have thought their jobs absurd and meaningless because the war itself seemed absurd and meaningless. Their deliberate choice to continue resembles the efforts of Sisyphus.

Learning Objectives
Determine main idea and supporting details. (SE)
Identify genre. (TE)
Analyze art. (TE)

Approaching Level

DIFFERENTIATED INSTRUCTION

Establish Chronology Help students see how Camus uses the myth, or story, of Sisyphus as a jumping-off point. Note that Camus begins with Sisyphus' ultimate, or final, fate: rolling the rock forever. In order to help students understand the myth of Sisyphus, have them order its details chronologically:

- He steals the secrets of the gods.
- The gods punish him by sending him to the underworld, a kind of hell.
- Sisyphus puts Death in chains.
- Sisyphus tests his wife's love and returns to Earth.
- Sisyphus is returned to the underworld, where he must forever roll the rock uphill.

Emphasize that it is the final episode of Sisyphus' story, the eternal rolling of the rock, that most interests Camus.

Advanced Learners/Pre-AP

DIFFERENTIATED INSTRUCTION

Analyze Style and Voice Although this is a persuasive—and philosophical—essay, it has a strong personal voice and obvious literary qualities. Have students identify aspects of style that contribute to the voice of the essay. *(Students may identify stylistic choices ranging from poetic diction and parallelism to the use of varying sentence lengths for added interest, fluidity, and grace.)*

Teach

Literary Element 1

Persuasion Answer: *Oedipus and Kirilov are usually thought of as bound by their fates. Camus rewrites this interpretation and instead chooses to make them absurd heroes just like Sisyphus.*

 For additional literary element practice, see Unit 5 Teaching Resources Book, p. 272.

Literary Element 2

Persuasion Possible Answer: *Some students will accept Camus's argument based on his logic and the act of reinventing the way Sisyphus is usually seen, while others will question the author's reasoning.*

[ADVANCED] **Say:** Identify the reasons that support the argument. *(Possible responses include Sisyphus' consciousness of his task and his return to it; the ancient examples of triumph over absurdity; the inseparability of happiness and absurdity, as well as the comingling of contradictions [for example, sun and shadow] in all life.)*

Reading Strategy 3

Analyze Rhetorical Devices Ask: What rhetorical devices do you find in the final paragraph of this essay? *(Devices include repetition: "One always," "One must"; balance and parallelism: "Each atom," "each mineral flake"; and richly connotative word choice: "night-filled mountain")*

 To check students' understanding of the selection, see Unit 5 Teaching Resources Book, p. 277.

1060

from being acknowledged. Thus, Oedipus[6] at the outset obeys fate without knowing it. But from the moment he knows, his tragedy begins. Yet at the same moment, blind and desperate, he realizes that the only bond linking him to the world is the cool hand of a girl. Then a tremendous remark rings out: "Despite so many ordeals, my advanced age and the nobility of my soul make me conclude that all is well." Sophocles' Oedipus, like Dostoyevsky's Kirilov,[7] thus gives the recipe for the absurd victory. Ancient wisdom confirms modern heroism.

One does not discover the absurd without being tempted to write a manual of happiness. "What! by such narrow ways—?" There is but one world, however. Happiness and the absurd are two sons of the same earth. They are inseparable. It would be a mistake to say that happiness necessarily springs from the absurd discovery. It happens as well that the feeling of the absurd springs from happiness. "I conclude that all is well," says Oedipus, and that remark is sacred. It echoes in the wild and limited universe of man. It teaches that all is not, has not been, exhausted. It drives out of this world a god who had come into it with dissatisfaction and a preference for futile sufferings. It makes of fate a human matter, which must be settled among men.

All Sisyphus' silent joy is contained therein. His fate belongs to him. His rock is his thing. Likewise, the absurd man, when he contemplates his torment, silences all

the idols. In the universe suddenly restored to its silence, the **myriad** wondering little voices of the earth rise up. Unconscious, secret calls, invitations from all the faces, they are the necessary reverse and price of victory. There is no sun without shadow, and it is essential to know the night. The absurd man says yes and his effort will henceforth be unceasing. If there is a personal fate, there is no higher destiny, or at least there is but one which he concludes is inevitable and despicable. For the rest, he knows himself to be the master of his days. At that subtle moment when man glances backward over his life, Sisyphus returning toward his rock, in that slight pivoting he contemplates that series of unrelated actions which becomes his fate, created by him, combined under his memory's eye and soon sealed by his death. Thus, convinced of the wholly human origin of all that is human, a blind man eager to see who knows that the night has no end, he is still on the go. The rock is still rolling.

I leave Sisyphus at the foot of the mountain! One always finds one's burden again. But Sisyphus teaches the higher **fidelity** that **negates** the gods and raises rocks. He too concludes that all is well. This universe henceforth without a master seems to him neither sterile nor futile. Each atom of that stone, each mineral flake of that night-filled mountain, in itself forms a world. The struggle itself toward the heights is enough to fill a man's heart. One must imagine Sisyphus happy. ∾

---

6. **Oedipus** is a character from Greek mythology who fulfilled a prophesy by unknowingly killing his father and marrying his mother. The Greek dramatist Sophocles wrote a series of plays about him (see pages 250–318).

7. Russian author Fyodor *Dostoyevsky* (dos´tə yef´skē) wrote about a character named Kirilov who commits suicide in an attempt to prove that there is no God to control his actions.

1 Persuasion *How do these additional examples strengthen the persuasiveness of Camus' argument?*

Persuasion *In your opinion, has Camus successfully proved his point? Explain.* **2**

Vocabulary

myriad (mir´ē əd) *adj.* countless; of a very great number of persons or things

fidelity (fi del´ə tē) *n.* faithfulness

negate (ni gāt´) *v.* to make ineffectual or powerless

Speaking and Listening Practice

Multimedia Presentation Have students prepare a computer slideshow or other presentation that combines sounds and images to present both Sisyphus' story and Camus's view of it. One option is to present the episodes of the myth in chronological order, with Camus acting as the narrator who tells what is happening and comments on its meaning. Students may also add sound effects or music to help in the telling of the story.

Suggest that students follow these steps to prepare:

- Consider the availability of equipment including cameras, screens, projectors, hardware, and software before determining the presentation's form.
- Create a storyboard of the episodes to create a logical order.
- Rehearse several times to be sure all elements are timed correctly, and elicit feedback from peers.

After You Read

Respond and Think Critically

Respond and Interpret

1. (a)What surprised you most about Camus' interpretation of the myth of Sisyphus? (b)What question would you ask Camus about his philosophy?

2. (a)What explanations does Camus offer for Sisyphus's punishment in the second and third paragraphs? (b)How does Camus summarize these explanations in his declaration that Sisyphus is the absurd hero?

3. (a)What opportunity becomes available to Sisyphus when the stone rolls down the slope? (b)Why does Camus feel that Sisyphus's descent down the slope can be joyous?

Analyze and Evaluate

4. (a)What does Camus mean by his statement "Happiness and the absurd are two sons of the same earth"? (b)Do you agree with his assertion? Explain.

5. (a)According to Camus, what raises torture or even dreary, absurd tasks to the level of tragedy? (b)What must Sisyphus or any human do to achieve victory and surmount fate?

6. (a)What evidence is there that Camus has rejected religion in his philosophy? (b)In your opinion, are Camus' ideas incompatible with a religious view of the world? Explain.

Connect

7. **Big Idea** **Postwar Europe** "The Myth of Sisyphus" was first published in 1942. Why might Camus have written an essay like this during World War II?

8. **Connect to Today** Are Camus' ideas still relevant today? Explain.

Literary Element Persuasion

Persuasion is an attempt to convince readers to think or act a certain way. Philosophical essays generally appeal to the reader's intellect through logic and evidence. Other forms of persuasive writing, such as political speeches and advertisements, may rely more on emotional appeals to win over the reader.

1. What does Camus want his readers to think or do?

2. In your opinion, which part of Camus' argument is most effective, and which part is least effective? Explain.

Review: Symbol

As you learned on page 791, a **symbol** is an object or action that stands for something in addition to itself.

Partner Activity Meet with a classmate to discuss Camus' use of symbolism in "The Myth of Sisyphus." Then answer the following questions.

1. What might the rock symbolize in Camus' interpretation of the myth?

2. Is Sisyphus a symbol? If so, what does he symbolize?

3. Can you find any other instances of symbolism in this essay? Explain.

Literary Element

1. He wants them to examine their own lives and find meaning in their struggles.

2. Students should explain their answers.

Review: Symbol

1. Possible answers: the ceaseless struggles of life; our endless search for answers to life's mysteries

2. Possible answer: As the absurd hero, Sisyphus is "everyman," or a representative of every human.

3. Possible answer: The mountain might be seen as the sheer magnitude of life's difficulties.

After You Read

Assess

1. (a) Students may have been surprised by the author's saying happiness and the absurd are one. (b) Answers will vary.

2. (a) He revealed the secret that Jupiter had abducted a woman, he put Death in chains, and he left the underworld after dying and refused to return. (b) "His scorn of the gods, his hatred of death, and his passion for life" bring about his punishment. Through his punishment, he recognizes his whole being accomplishes nothing.

3. (a) He has time to consider his situation. (b) At this time, Sisyphus chooses to give his own meaning to his fate rather than accept the gods' meaning.

4. (a) Happiness and the absurd have the same origin, so it follows that the two are linked. (b) Answers will vary

5. (a) Camus says, "It is tragic only at the rare moments when it becomes conscious." (b) One must scorn his or her fate.

6. (a) The statement "It makes of fate a human matter, which must be settled among men" implies that supreme beings do not control fate and punishment. (b) Answers will vary.

7. He may have wanted to comfort or support people who felt despair because of the war.

8. Some students might see Camus's ideas as relevant only in his historical context. Others might connect to Camus because they feel that their own lives lack direction, meaning, and sense.

 For additional selection assessment, see Assessment Resources, pp. 213–214.

After You Read

Assess

Reading Strategy

(D) is the correct answer. By continuing to push the rock up the mountain, Sisyphus controls his own fate.

Progress Check

Can students determine the main idea and supporting details?

If No → See Unit 5 Teaching Resources Book, p. 273.

Vocabulary

Possible answers:

prudent <u>D</u>: sensible; <u>E</u>: Latin *prudens* means "knowing"; <u>SS</u>: They decided to bring whatever they needed for the night, as it was not prudent to return home.

scorn <u>D</u>: show contempt for; <u>E</u>: Middle Dutch *schernen* means "to ridicule"; <u>SS</u>: After getting a new toy, the boy scorned his friends because they did not have it.

myriad <u>Definition</u>: countless; of a very great number of persons or things; <u>Etymology</u>: Greek *myriades* means "plural"; <u>Sample Sentence</u>: Because he has collected them for years, my friend has a myriad of stamps.

fidelity <u>D</u>: faithfulness; <u>E</u>: Latin *fidelitas* means "faithfulness"; <u>SS</u>: Many political prisoners die out of fidelity to their cause.

negate <u>D</u>: to make ineffectual or powerless; <u>E</u>: Latin *negatio* means "denying"; <u>SS</u>: The Magna Carta was designed to negate the power of the sovereign and increase the power of the aristocracy.

1062

Reading Strategy Determine Main Idea and Supporting Details

SAT Skills Practice

What is the meaning of the last line, "One must imagine Sisyphus happy"?

(A) Sisyphus hopes he will finish his task soon.

(B) Sisyphus is happy because he chastised his wife.

(C) Sisyphus will be rewarded for his devotion.

(D) Sisyphus is actually master of his own fate.

(E) Sisyphus will never realize his own absurdity, and so lives in blissful ignorance.

Vocabulary Practice

Practice with Word Origins Studying the origin and history of a word can help you better understand its meaning. Using a dictionary, create a word map for each vocabulary word.

prudent   scorn   myriad   fidelity   negate

EXAMPLE:

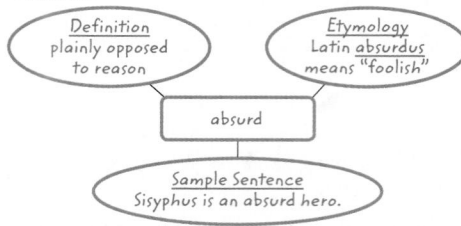

Academic Vocabulary

*In this essay, Camus presents a **justification** for the plight of Sisyphus: that pushing the rock gives meaning to Sisyphus's life.*

Justification is an academic word that often occurs in writing related to current events. For example, an editorial might say an unprovoked attack creates a **justification** for going to war. To further explore the meaning of this word, complete the following statement.

_____ is my justification for _____.

For more on academic vocabulary, see pages 36–37 and R83–R85.

1062 UNIT 5   MODERN EUROPE

Write with Style

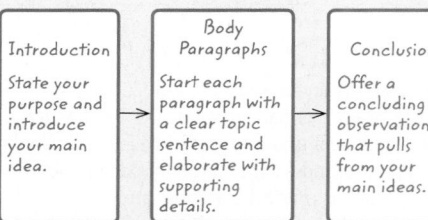 **Apply Symbolism**

Assignment Review the way Camus uses symbolism and allusion to argue that even an absurd life has meaning. With this strategy in mind, write an essay to persuade your readers to change their perspective on an issue of your choosing.

Get Ideas Page through your journal or brainstorm to find a topic about which you think many people should alter their perspective. Consider what you think is wrong with most people's view, and make a list of things that could change their minds. When you begin to compile ideas, sort them into a main idea and supporting details chart. Use the chart you filled out on page 1057 as a model. After organizing your ideas, create a plan for your essay that addresses purpose, audience, and the time frame you have to complete the essay.

Give It Structure Refer to your prewriting notes as you draft your essay. Use an organizer like the one below to structure your essay.

Introduction	Body Paragraphs	Conclusion
State your purpose and introduce your main idea.	Start each paragraph with a clear topic sentence and elaborate with supporting details.	Offer a concluding observation that pulls from your main ideas.

Look at Language While modeling your own writing on Camus' style, remember to maintain your own voice. Try developing your unique style by using sentence variety and combining short sentences into longer, more complex ones (see pages 90–91).

 Literature Online

Selection Resources For Selection Quizzes, eFlashcards, and Reading-Writing Connection activities, go to glencoe.com and enter QuickPass code GLW6053u5.

Academic Vocabulary

Possible answer: Working late on weekdays is my justification for sleeping in on Saturdays.

Write with Style

Students' essays should

- show a grasp of Camus's symbolism
- attempt to persuade an audience
- include clear topic sentences that express main ideas
- include supporting details for the main ideas

Before You Read

from *Night*

Meet **Elie Wiesel**

(born 1928)

Elie Wiesel (el′ ē vē zel′) lived in Sighet, Romania, until 1944, when Nazi soldiers rounded up the town's Jews for extermination. Until that day, the residents of Sighet had been relatively insulated from the outside world, living lives of prayer and contemplation, and had no idea of the horrors to come.

Peace Before the Holocaust Wiesel recalls his early childhood as happy. Synagogues, day schools, and Jewish newspapers flourished in the community of Sighet. Wiesel started *kheder* (religious elementary school) when he was three years old. He studied secular subjects, played the violin, and eventually found a local scholar with whom he could study Kabbalah, a mystical interpretation of Hebrew scriptures. He recalls that in Sighet, he and the other inhabitants "spoke Yiddish among ourselves, responded to others in Romanian or Hungarian or Ruthenian, and we prayed in Hebrew."

> "We must always take sides. Neutrality helps the oppressor, never the victim."
>
> —Elie Wiesel

 Auschwitz When he was fifteen, Wiesel, his parents, and his three sisters were deported to Auschwitz, a concentration camp in Poland. His mother and younger sister were gassed to death immediately. He and his father were sent to the slave-labor division of Auschwitz, and eight months later were part of a death march to Buchenwald. His father died just a few months before liberation in April 1945. The American military evacuated Wiesel, along with other child survivors, and brought them to France. He was sent to a home for Jewish child survivors and was later reunited with his two older sisters.

Giving Voice to Memory After liberation, Wiesel vowed to keep silent about the horrors he had witnessed. He continued his education at the Sorbonne in France. While studying in Paris, he began work as a journalist, writing stories for the Yiddish newspaper *Zion in Kamf* and the Israeli newspaper *Yedi'ot Akharonot*. Journalism put him in contact with a critical figure, French writer François Mauriac. In 1954, at Mauriac's behest, Wiesel broke his silence and finally gave voice to his memories. Wiesel wrote and published his Yiddish memoir, *Un Di Velt Hot Geshvign* ("And the World Kept Silent"), in 1956. Under Mauriac's guidance, Wiesel revised the text and translated it into French under the title *La Nuit* in 1958; in 1960 this seminal work was translated into English as *Night*.

Wiesel moved to the United States in 1956 and was naturalized as a citizen in 1963. As a result of his prolific writing and lecturing, Wiesel has become one of the most visible and renowned Holocaust survivors, eventually winning the Nobel Peace Prize in 1986.

> **LOG ON** ▶ **Literature** Online
>
> **Author Search** For more about Elie Wiesel, go to glencoe.com and enter QuickPass code GLW6053u5.

ELIE WIESEL **1063**

Before You Read

Focus

Bellringer Options

Selection Focus
Transparency 67

Daily Language Practice
Transparency 102

Or say: This excerpt from *Night* is set in a German concentration camp during the Holocaust. What do you know about the Holocaust? Working in small groups, have students record what they know. Allow time for group presentations.

Political History ☆

Concentration Camps During World War II, large numbers of concentration camps were established across Europe. Most were used as prisons, forced-labor camps, or detention centers. Less fortunate prisoners were sent to Auschwitz-Birkenau, Belzec, Chelmno, Treblinka, Sobibor, and Majdanek, death camps located in remote areas of Poland under German control. Today, many of these camps are memorials to the millions of people who died there.

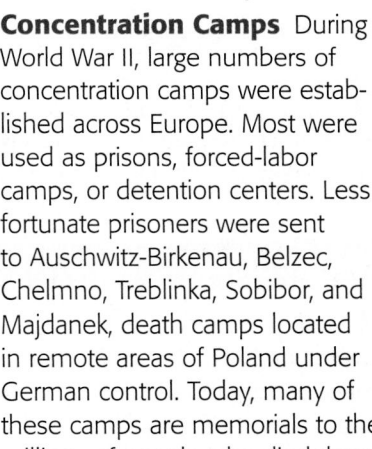

Selection Skills

Literary Elements
- Memoir (SE pp. 1064, 1065, 1068–1070)
- Conflict (SE p. 1070)

Reading Skills
- Evaluate Characters (SE pp. 1064–1071)
- Make Inferences (TE p. 1064)

Vocabulary Skills

- Synonyms (SE p. 1071; TE p. 1064)

Research/Study Skills
- Internet Research (SE p. 1071)

Night

Speaking/Listening/Viewing Skills
- Present an Oral Report (SE p. 1071)

Writing Skills/Grammar
- Response to Quotation (TE p. 1064)
- Response to Theme (TE p. 1066)

Before You Read

Focus

Summary

When fifteen-year-old Eliezer Wiesel and his father arrive at Buchenwald concentration camp, the father is in a pitiful state. The youth does all he can to help his father even though he understands that the situation is hopeless. Torn between trying to survive and remaining faithful to his father, Eliezer stays with his father in a section set aside for invalids. The last thing he hears from his father is his own name being called. He does not respond because he fears the officer who smashed his father's head will hurt him, too. When Eliezer wakes in the morning, his father is gone, and he cannot even weep for him.

 For summaries in languages other than English, see Unit 5 Teaching Resources Book, pp. 279–284.

Vocabulary

Concentration Write these words on index cards: *plaintive, rivet, spasmodically, mournful, woeful, transfix, grip, fitfully, jerkily*.

Prepare two sets of cards. Next divide students into two groups, and split each group into two teams. Give each group one set of cards to arrange face down in rows. **Say:** The teams will take turns. Each team, will turn over three cards. Your goal is to find three words that have nearly the same meaning. If the words you choose are synonymous, your team keeps the cards. If not, return them, face down, to their places. The team with the most cards wins. Allow students to look up the meanings of unfamiliar words.

1064

Literature and Reading Preview

Connect to the Memoir

What would you give up to prolong another person's life? Write a journal entry that responds to this question.

Build Background

Unlike Auschwitz, Buchenwald did not have gas chambers for killing prisoners. However, many of the prisoners at Buchenwald died from disease, exhaustion, beatings, and executions. As the United States army neared Buchenwald in April 1945, the prisoners rose up in revolt and liberated the camp. In *Night,* Wiesel said when he first had a chance to look at himself in a mirror, he was shocked to see a corpse gazing back at him.

Set Purposes for Reading

Big Idea Postwar Europe

As you read, ask yourself, How did the horrors of the Holocaust affect the author?

Literary Element Memoir

A **memoir** is a first-person narrative that presents the story of a specific period in the author's life. Unlike an **autobiography,** which describes the events of a person's entire life, a memoir often focuses on just one meaningful experience. A memoir emphasizes the author's thoughts and feelings, personal relationships, or the impact of historical events on his or her life. As you read, ask yourself, What does Wiesel say about himself and the events he witnesses?

Reading Strategy Evaluate Characters

When you **evaluate characters,** you analyze their attitudes, actions, words, and motivations. For example, when you read about someone who steals bread from a sick man, you can assess this action. Does it mean that the thief is unspeakably cruel or desperate to save his or her own life? As you read, ask yourself, What motivates the characters' actions?

Tip: Track Attitudes In a chart like the one below, use a question-and-answer format to track your evaluations.

Question	Answer
Why does Elie's father sit down in the snow?	He has given up. He is ready to die.
Why does Elie continue to argue with his father?	He has hope they will survive.

1064 UNIT 5 MODERN EUROPE

Learning Objectives

For pages 1064–1071

In studying this text, you will focus on the following objectives:

Literary Study: Analyzing memoir.

Reading: Evaluating characters.

Research: Using the Internet.

Vocabulary

plaintive (plān′tiv) *adj.* expressive of suffering or distress; p. 1066 *The cat's plaintive cry was the first clue that he was sick.*

elude (i lōōd′) *v.* to avoid or escape; p. 1067 *The child eluded his mother by hiding under the bed.*

rivet (riv′it) *v.* fixed firmly; completely engrossed; p. 1068 *Ben's attention was riveted to the screen, which displayed a slide show of the class reunion photos.*

Tip: Synonyms Words that have the same or nearly the same meaning are **synonyms.** For example, synonyms of *plaintive* are *mournful* and *sad.* Synonyms are always the same part of speech.

Writing Practice

Respond to a Quotation Discuss Elie Wiesel's reasons for writing *Night,* focusing on his belief in the "mystical power of memory." Display the following quotes from "Hope, Despair, and Memory," a lecture Wiesel gave after winning the Nobel Peace Prize. **Write** on the board: 1. "The memory of evil will serve as a shield against evil . . . the memory of death will serve as a shield against death." 2. "Remembering is a noble and necessary act."

Say: Write a personal response in which you explain your thoughts on one of the quotes.

A successful response will identify the quote and its author, clearly state your reaction to the quote, include supporting details and quotations, and summarize the significance of the quote to you or apply it to today's world

from Night

Elie Wiesel

Translated by
Marion Wiesel

We Are the Living. Alfred Tibor (Hungarian, b. 1920). Marble, height: 48 in. The Columbus Museum of Art, OH.

At the entrance to the camp, SS officers[1] were waiting for us. We were counted. Then we were directed to the *Appelplatz.* The orders were given over the loudspeakers:

"Form ranks of fives! Groups of one hundred! Five steps forward!"

I tightened my grip on my father's hand. The old, familiar fear: not to lose him.

Very close to us stood the tall chimney of the crematorium's[2] furnace. It no longer impressed us. It barely drew our attention.

A veteran of Buchenwald told us that we would be taking a shower and afterward be sent to different blocks. The idea of a hot shower fascinated me. My father didn't say a word. He was breathing heavily beside me.

"Father," I said, "just another moment. Soon, we'll be able to lie down. You'll be able to rest . . ."

He didn't answer. I myself was so weary that his silence left me indifferent. My only wish was to take the shower as soon as possible and lie down on a cot.

Only it wasn't easy to reach the showers. Hundreds of prisoners crowded the area. The guards seemed unable to restore order. They were lashing out, left and right, to no avail. Some prisoners who didn't have the strength to jostle, or even to stand, sat down in the snow. My father wanted to do the same. He was moaning:

"I can't anymore . . . It's over . . . I shall die right here . . ."

He dragged me toward a pile of snow from which protruded human shapes, torn blankets.

"Leave me," he said. "I can't go on any-more . . . Have pity on me . . . I'll wait here

---

1. *SS officers* were a unit of Nazi soldiers in charge of policing the concentration camps, among other things.
2. A *crematorium* is a place containing a furnace for burning dead bodies.

Memoir *What does this section reveal about the previous experiences of Wiesel and his father?*

ELIE WIESEL **1065**

Teach

Reading Strategy   1

Predict After reading the first few paragraphs, ask students what they think the selection will be about. *(It will be about the author's experiences in a concentration camp.)*

Literary Element   2

Memoir Answer: *It reveals they have already experienced such horror that they are almost immune to it. They know they are powerless to stop the death that surrounds them.*

📁 For additional literary element practice, see Unit 5 Teaching Resources Book, p. 285.

💿 For an audio recording of this selection, use Listening Library Audio CD-ROM.

Readability Scores
Dale-Chall: 5.5
DRP: 45
Lexile: 380

Learning Objectives
Analyzing a memoir. (SE)
Responding to a quote. (TE)

English Learners

DIFFERENTIATED INSTRUCTION

Intermediate Discuss the meanings of *block,* both as a noun and a verb. Help students use context clues to determine that, in paragraph five, *block* refers to "a large rectangular building that is divided into rooms that resemble prison cells."

Advanced Learners/Pre-AP

DIFFERENTIATED INSTRUCTION

Predict Ask students how the image of the young man holding his father's hand may foreshadow upcoming events in the selection. *(These lines suggest that the two have a very close relationship. Students may predict that the son loses or fears losing his father.)*

Teach

Big Idea 1

Postwar Europe Answer:
After the Holocaust, many people did not want to look to the past, and Wiesel feels the need to make them see the truth.

[APPROACHING] Some students may not understand the deeper, symbolic meaning of these lines. **Ask:** What point is the author trying to make? *(Possible answers: that the struggle to survive was too much for some people to bear; war takes a terrible toll on humanity)*

Reading Strategy 2

Evaluate Character
Answer: *Wiesel's will to live is very strong, but he feels unable to escape the responsibility of caring for his dying father. The passage shows that he is ashamed of these feelings.*

Writer's Technique ☆

Dialogue Point out that Wiesel's extensive use of dialogue adds life and emotional depth to his memoir, as if he is "seeing" incidents that are still living his mind.

---

until we can go into the showers . . . You'll come and get me."

I could have screamed in anger. To have lived and endured so much; was I going to let my father die now? Now that we would be able to take a good hot shower and lie down?

"Father!" I howled. "Father! Get up! Right now! You will kill yourself . . ."

And I grabbed his arm. He continued to moan:

"Don't yell, my son . . . Have pity on your old father . . . Let me rest here . . . a little . . . I beg of you, I'm so tired . . . no more strength . . ."

He had become childlike: weak, frightened, vulnerable.

"Father," I said, "you cannot stay here."

I pointed to the corpses around him; they too had wanted to rest here.

☆ "I see, my son. I do see them. Let them sleep. They haven't closed an eye for so long . . . They're exhausted . . . exhausted . . ."

His voice was tender.

I howled into the wind:

"They're dead! They will never wake up! Never! Do you understand?"

This discussion continued for some time. I knew that I was no longer arguing with him but with Death itself, with Death that he had already chosen.

The sirens began to wail. Alert. The lights went out in the entire camp. The guards chased us toward the blocks. In a flash, there was no one left outside. We were only too glad not to have to stay outside any longer, in the freezing wind. We let ourselves sink into the floor. The cauldrons at the entrance found no takers. There were several tiers of bunks. To sleep was all that mattered.

1 **Postwar Europe** *How does Wiesel's statement indicate his purpose in writing about his experiences in the Holocaust?*

When I woke up, it was daylight. That is when I remembered that I had a father. During the alert, I had followed the mob, not taking care of him. I knew he was running out of strength, close to death, and yet I had abandoned him.

I went to look for him.

Yet at the same time a thought crept into my mind: If only I didn't find him! If only I were relieved of this responsibility, I could use all my strength to fight for my own survival, to take care only of myself . . . Instantly, I felt ashamed, ashamed of myself forever.

I walked for hours without finding him. Then I came to a block where they were distributing black "coffee." People stood in line, quarreled.

A **plaintive** voice came from behind me: "Eliezer, my son . . . bring me . . . a little coffee . . ."

I ran toward him.

"Father! I've been looking for you for so long . . . Where were you? Did you sleep? How are you feeling?"

He seemed to be burning with fever. I fought my way to the coffee cauldron like a wild beast. And I succeeded in bringing back a cup. I took one gulp. The rest was for him.

I shall never forget the gratitude that shone in his eyes when he swallowed this beverage. The gratitude of a wounded animal. With these few mouthfuls of hot water, I had probably given him more satisfaction than during my entire childhood . . .

He was lying on the boards, ashen, his lips pale and dry, shivering. I couldn't stay

---

Evaluate Characters *What does this passage reveal about Wiesel's character and his inner conflict? How does he react to his feelings?* **2**

Vocabulary

plaintive (plān′tiv) *adj.* expressive of suffering or distress

---

Writing Practice

Respond to Theme Say: Elie Wiesel wrote *Night* as a testament to his experiences during the Holocaust, but also to share his insights about life and the human experience. Some of these themes, or messages, can be found in this excerpt. To identify a theme, answer these questions.

Write on the board:

▪ What happened in this account?

▪ What lessons did the author learn?

▪ What details help me know this?

▪ What did the author want to teach me about life, death, relationships, or survival?

Guide students in using the bulleted questions to identify themes, such as *The bonds between a parent and a child endure forever; Human beings will do what they need to do to survive; Sometimes death is a welcome release.* Have students write a brief response

about one of the selection's themes. Tell students to include both textual evidence and their own opinions in their response.

with him any longer. We had been ordered to go outside to allow for cleaning of the blocks. Only the sick could remain inside.

We stayed outside for five hours. We were given soup. When they allowed us to return to the blocks, I rushed toward my father:

"Did you eat?"

"No."

"Why?"

"They didn't give us anything . . . They said that we were sick, that we would die soon, and that it would be a waste of food . . . I can't go on . . ."

I gave him what was left of my soup. But my heart was heavy. I was aware that I was doing it grudgingly.

Just like Rabbi Eliahu's[3] son, I had not passed the test.

Every day, my father was getting weaker. His eyes were watery, his face the color of dead leaves. On the third day after we arrived in Buchenwald, everybody had to go to the showers. Even the sick, who were instructed to go last.

When we returned from the showers, we had to wait outside a long time. The cleaning of the blocks had not been completed.

From afar, I saw my father and ran to meet him. He went by me like a shadow, passing me without stopping, without a glance. I called to him, he did not turn around. I ran after him:

"Father, where are you running?"

He looked at me for a moment and his gaze was distant, otherworldly, the face of a stranger. It lasted only a moment and then he ran away.

---

3. Earlier, Eliezer had witnessed *Rabbi Eliahou's* son purposefully leaving his father behind to die. Eliezer had prayed for the strength never to betray his own father in this way.

 Evaluate Characters *What does this action reveal about Wiesel's character?*

Father and Child, 1946. Ben Shahn. Tempera on cardboard, 39 7/8 x 30 in. Gift of James Thrall Soby. The Museum of Modern Art, NY.© VAGA, NY.

Suffering from dysentery, my father was prostrate on his cot, with another five sick inmates nearby. I sat next to him, watching him; I no longer dared to believe that he could still **elude** Death. I did all I could to give him hope.

All of a sudden, he sat up and placed his feverish lips against my ear:

"Eliezer . . . I must tell you where I buried the gold and silver . . . In the cellar . . . You know . . ."

And he began talking, faster and faster, afraid of running out of time before he could tell me everything. I tried to tell him that it was not over yet, that we would be going home together, but he no longer wanted to listen to me. He *could* no longer listen to me. He was worn out. Saliva mixed with blood was trickling from his lips. He had closed his eyes. He was gasping more than breathing.

Vocabulary

elude (i lo͞od′) *v.* to avoid or escape

ELIE WIESEL **1067**

Reading Strategy 3

Evaluate Characters
Answer: *It reveals that even though Eliezer wants to be free of caring for his father, he is still a loyal son.*

Reading Strategy 4

Draw Conclusions Explain that before the Nazi soldiers took the Wiesels from their home, the family members buried their valuables. **Ask:** What does the father's need to tell his son about the gold reveal about the father's condition? *(That the father is critically ill and knows he will die soon.)*

Learning Objectives
Evaluating characters. (SE)
Drawing conclusions. (TE)
Responding to theme. (TE)

Approaching Level
DIFFERENTIATED INSTRUCTION

Present a Monologue Remind students that in a memoir, readers learn about events from only the author's point of view. Invite students to perform a monologue in which they retell a part of the selection from the point of view of the father or of the head of the block. As students develop their monologues, have them consider how that person might interpret Eliezer's actions and attitudes.

Advanced Learners/Pre-AP
DIFFERENTIATED INSTRUCTION

Draw Conclusions Have students write a paragraph in response to the following prompt. **Write** on the board: Wiesel attempts to keep his father alive in the face of extreme difficulties. What does this indicate about Wiesel and why he managed to survive? Support your opinion with details from the text. *(These efforts suggest that Wiesel was by nature optimistic and hopeful. Even when he saw the worst, he clung to the hope that somehow things would be better. Those who give up hope are not likely to survive.)*

Teach

Literary Element **1**

Memoir Answer: *The doctor's words reveal that the prisoners were treated horribly, that the Nazis felt that the prisoners were barely human, and that the Nazis regarded them as worthless unless they could work.*

Reading Strategy **2**

Evaluate Characters
Answer: *It indicates they have lost the human feelings of compassion for the weak and the sick; they are putting their own will to live above the welfare of another person.*

For a ration of bread I was able to exchange cots to be next to my father. When the doctor arrived in the afternoon, I went to tell him that my father was very ill.

"Bring him here!"

I explained that he could not stand up, but the doctor would not listen. And so, with great difficulty, I brought my father to him. He stared at him, then asked curtly:

"What do you want?"

"My father is sick," I answered in his place . . . "Dysentery . . ."

"That's not my business. I'm a surgeon. Go on. Make room for the others!"

My protests were in vain.

"I can't go on, my son . . . Take me back to my bunk."

I took him back and helped him lie down. He was shivering.

"Try to get some sleep, Father. Try to fall asleep . . ."

His breathing was labored. His eyes were closed. But I was convinced that he was seeing everything. That he was seeing the truth in all things.

Another doctor came to the block. My father refused to get up. He knew that it would be of no use.

In fact, that doctor had come only to finish off the patients. I listened to him shouting at them that they were lazy good-for-nothings who only wanted to stay in bed . . . I considered jumping him, strangling him. But I had neither the courage nor the strength. I was **riveted** to my father's agony. My hands were aching, I was clenching them so hard. To strangle the

---

1 **Memoir** *What do the doctor's words reveal about the Nazis' treatment of the prisoners?*

Vocabulary

rivet (riv´it) *v.* fixed firmly; completely engrossed

1068 UNIT 5 MODERN EUROPE

---

doctor and the others! To set the whole world on fire! My father's murderers! But even the cry stuck in my throat.

On my return from the bread distribution, I found my father crying like a child:

"My son, they are beating me!"

"Who?" I thought he was delirious.

"Him, the Frenchman . . . and the Pole . . . They beat me . . ."

One more stab to the heart, one more reason to hate. One less reason to live.

"Eliezer . . . Eliezer . . . tell them not to beat me . . . I haven't done anything . . . Why are they beating me?"

I began to insult his neighbors. They mocked me. I promised them bread, soup. They laughed. Then they got angry; they could not stand my father any longer, they said, because he no longer was able to drag himself outside to relieve himself.

The following day, he complained that they had taken his ration of bread.

"While you were asleep?"

"No. I wasn't asleep. They threw themselves on me. They snatched it from me, my bread . . . And they beat me . . . Again . . . I can't go on, my son . . . Give me some water . . ."

I knew that he must not drink. But he pleaded with me so long that I gave in. Water was the worst poison for him, but what else could I do for him? With or without water, it would be over soon anyway . . .

"You, at least, have pity on me . . ."

Have pity on him! I, his only son . . .

A week went by like that.

"Is this your father?" asked the *Blockälteste*.

"Yes."

Evaluate Characters *What does this passage reveal about the prisoners who were abusing Eliezer's father?* **2**

Reading Practice

Make Inferences Say: As a reader, you must use both what you know and the details that you are given in order to figure out, or infer, what the author wants you to understand.

Have students reread the last three paragraphs of the selection. **Say:** Wiesel does not use many descriptive phrases in these lines. He understates what he feels yet his words are full of meaning.

Discuss what the author is saying about himself in each of these paragraphs. *(The author is shocked to know that his father had died. He is reproving himself for not at least bearing witness or bidding farewell to his father. He is numbed by the experience.)*

Focus students' attention on the last sentence. **Ask:** Who is "free at last"? *(Wiesel seems to acknowledge that deep*

down he was relieved to be free of the burden of caring for his father.)

1068

"He is very sick."

"The doctor won't do anything for him."

He looked me straight in the eye:

"The doctor *cannot* do anything more for him. And neither can you."

He placed his big, hairy hand on my shoulder and added:

"Listen to me, kid. Don't forget that you are in a concentration camp. In this place, it is every man for himself, and you cannot think of others. Not even your father. In this place, there is no such thing as father, brother, friend. Each of us lives and dies alone. Let me give you good advice: stop giving your ration of bread and soup to your old father. You cannot help him anymore. And you are hurting yourself. In fact, you should be getting *his* rations . . ."

I listened to him without interrupting. He was right, I thought deep down, not daring to admit it to myself. Too late to save your old father . . . You could have two rations of bread, two rations of soup . . .

It was only a fraction of a second, but it left me feeling guilty. I ran to get some soup and brought it to my father. But he did not want it. All he wanted was water.

"Don't drink water, eat the soup . . ."

"I'm burning up . . . Why are you so mean to me, my son? . . . Water . . ."

I brought him water. Then I left the block for roll call. But I quickly turned back. I lay down on the upper bunk. The sick were allowed to stay in the block. So I would be sick. I didn't want to leave my father.

All around me, there was silence now, broken only by moaning. In front of the block, the SS were giving orders. An officer passed between the bunks. My father was pleading:

"My son, water . . . I'm burning up . . .

My insides . . ."

"Silence over there!" barked the officer.

"Eliezer," continued my father, "water . . ."

The officer came closer and shouted to him to be silent. But my father did not hear. He continued to call me. The officer wielded his club and dealt him a violent blow to the head.

I didn't move. I was afraid, my body was afraid of another blow, this time to *my* head.

My father groaned once more, I heard:

"Eliezer . . ."

I could see that he was still breathing— in gasps. I didn't move.

When I came down from my bunk after roll call, I could see his lips trembling; he was murmuring something. I remained more than an hour leaning over him, looking at him, etching his bloody, broken face into my mind.

Then I had to go to sleep. I climbed into my bunk, above my father, who was still alive. The date was January 28, 1945.

I woke up at dawn on January 29. On my father's cot there lay another sick person. They must have taken him away before daybreak and taken him to the crematorium. Perhaps he was still breathing . . .

No prayers were said over his tomb. No candle lit in his memory. His last word had been my name. He had called out to me and I had not answered.

I did not weep, and it pained me that I could not weep. But I was out of tears. And deep inside me, if I could have searched the recesses of my feeble conscience, I might have found something like: Free at last! . . . ∾

---

3 | Evaluate Characters **What does this passage reveal about the head of the block?**

Memoir **Think about the way Wiesel chooses to reveal his father's death. How does this indirect description affect you?** **4**

Teach

Reading Strategy | 3

Evaluate Characters
Answer: *The passage reveals that the head of the block is more jaded and realistic than Eliezer, who still hopes to help his father. Some students may say that the man's words to Eliezer show that he is also sympathetic or caring.*

Literary Element | 4

Memoir Answer: *The indirect description offers no specific details and allows the reader to imagine the worst.*

 To check students' understanding of the selection, see Unit 5 Teaching Resources Book, p. 290.

Learning Objectives
Evaluating characters. (SE)
Analyzing a memoir. (SE)
Making inferences. (TE)

English Learners

DIFFERENTIATED INSTRUCTION

Advanced Point out that persecution and discrimination like those described in this memoir still exist. Students who have lived in other countries may know of such incidents. **Ask:** How do your experiences help you to understand Wiesel's story? In what ways can such experiences change a person? Encourage a discussion that draws on students' observations.

Approaching Level

DIFFERENTIATED INSTRUCTION

Analyze Details Say: Memoirs often include historical information that can teach you about the history of the period in which the memoir takes place. Skim the selection for details Wiesel provides about life in Buchenwald. Based on these details, what was life like in a World War II concentration camp? Have students write a brief summary of their findings and present their findings to you or to a partner.

Point out to struggling readers that the simple language and dialogue in this selection make it a good choice for practicing reading fluency. Have students choose a passage to prepare for reading aloud. Instruct them to read the passage quietly to themselves a few times before reading it aloud to a partner. Suggest that the pair discuss ways the reader could improve his or her accuracy and expression.

After You Read

Assess

1. Answers will vary.
2. (a) He lies down in the snow and tells Eliezer to go without him. (b) He fears his father will die if he stays in the snow.
3. (a) They hit him and steal his food. (b) They are starving. The brutal camp has made the inmates themselves brutal.
4. (a) He tells Eliezer to think of himself and to take his father's rations. (b) For a moment Eliezer agrees and considers taking his father's rations.
5. (a) Eliezer suspects that his father may have still been breathing when he was carried off to the crematory. (b) Fearing the officer would also beat him, he remained silent when his father called to him.
6. (a) Possible answers: his lying down among the corpses; the "ghostly" way he walks. (b) This foreshadowing is effective.
7. Most students will say they are not justified because he could not have helped his father more.
8. These events suggested that values such as human life and belief in the kindness of God might be unfounded.
9. The message is relevant today in a world where ethnic cleansing, prejudice, injustice, and fanaticism still cause suffering.

Literary Element

1. It might not reveal as much about Wiesel's thoughts and feelings.
2. To bear witness to the Holocaust, preserve the memory of his father, and to explore his feelings
3. Wiesel's writing is extremely powerful, and is corroborated by photographs and other physical evidence.

1070

After You Read

Respond and Think Critically

Respond and Interpret

1. What detail or incident in this excerpt did you find most disturbing? Explain.
2. (a) How does Wiesel's father react when he hears about the hot showers? (b) Why does Wiesel insist that his father follow him to the showers?
3. (a) How do the other inmates treat the father after he comes down with dysentery? (b) Why do the other inmates behave this way?
4. (a) What advice does the head of the block offer Wiesel? (b) Why does Wiesel feel guilty after hearing this advice?
5. (a) How does Wiesel's father die? (b) Why does Wiesel say that his father's last word was a call he did not answer?

Analyze and Evaluate

6. (a) **Foreshadowing** occurs when an author provides hints about what will happen later in a text. What details foreshadow the death of Wiesel's father? (b) How well does the foreshadowing prepare you for what happens?
7. Do you think Wiesel's guilty feelings about his father are justified? Why or why not?

Connect

8. **Big Idea** Postwar Europe How did the events Wiesel describes lead him and other authors to question basic values that most people take for granted?
9. **Connect to Today** Do you think the message of Wiesel's memoir is still relevant today? Explain.

Literary Element Memoir

Traditionally, autobiography has been distinguished from **memoir,** but the two types of writing are closely related. A memoir is a type of autobiographical writing that usually focuses on the author's involvement in historically or culturally significant events, either as an eyewitness or a participant. Consult the chart you made on page 1064 then answer the following questions.

1. How might this memoir differ if it were written by someone other than Wiesel?
2. Based on this excerpt from *Night,* what was Wiesel's purpose in writing the book?
3. Some people deny the Holocaust ever occurred. How might you use Wiesel's writing to respond to that view?

 Literature Online

Selection Resources For Selection Quizzes, eFlashcards, and Reading-Writing Connection activities, go to glencoe. com and enter QuickPass code GLW6053u5.

1070 UNIT 5 MODERN EUROPE

Review: Conflict

As you learned on page 754, **conflict** is the central struggle between two opposing forces in a literary work. It can be **external,** when a character struggles against an outside force. It can also be **internal,** when the struggle takes place within the mind of a character torn between opposing feelings, desires, or goals.

Partner Activity Meet with a classmate and discuss the external and internal conflicts Wiesel experiences. Working with your partner, complete a chart like the one below.

When?	Conflict	External or Internal
Day of arrival at Buchenwald		
Morning after arrival at Buchenwald		

Review: Conflict
Possible answer:

Row 1: Day of arrival at Buchenwald, Argument with father about resting in the snow, External; Row 2: Morning after arrival at Buchenwald, Feeling he'd rather not find his father, Internal

 For additional assessment, see Assessment Resources, pp. 215–216.

For grammar practice, see Unit 5 Teaching Resources Book, p. 289.

Reading Strategy · Evaluate Characters

SAT Skills Practice

What does Eliezer's reaction to the advice from the head of the block reveal about him?

(A) He is selfish and stingy.

(B) He is trusting and cooperative.

(C) He is easily shocked.

(D) He listens to his elders.

(E) He is compassionate and selfless.

Vocabulary Practice

Practice with Synonyms A synonym is a word that has the same or nearly the same meaning as another word. With a partner, match each boldfaced vocabulary word below with its synonym. Use a thesaurus or dictionary to check your answers. You will not use all the answer choices.

1. plaintive   **a.** fasten
2. elude   **b.** mournful
3. rivet   **c.** fitfully
                d. hinge
                e. escape

Academic Vocabulary

Wiesel's humanitarian work promotes an ***ideology*** *of justice and equality.*

Ideology is an academic word with which you may be familiar from social studies classes. In the sentence above, *ideology* means "a set of principles and thoughts that guide an individual or a group." To further explore the meaning of this word, answer the following question: Do you hold any **ideologies?** If so, what are they?

For more on academic vocabulary, see pages 36–37 and R83–R85.

Research and Report

 Internet Connection

Assignment Use the Internet to research Wiesel's impact on the world through his humanitarian efforts related to the Holocaust. Deliver an oral report on your findings.

Get Ideas Create questions to guide your research. Through your research questions, generate key words that will lead to specific results and give you reliable information to include in your report.

Research Question	Key Word
What was life like at Buchenwald prison camp, where Eliezer and his father were sent?	"Buchenwald camp"
How has Elie Wiesel promoted education about the Holocaust?	"Elie Wiesel" AND "Holocaust education"

Use Boolean search techniques, which offer different ways to combine words. Searching for "Holocaust memorials" tells the computer to find every book or articles with exactly those words. By removing the quotation marks, you will get documents where the words "Holocaust" and "memorials" appear, but not necessarily together. Use AND to link search items and NOT to exclude others. For example, searching Wiesel AND "Nobel Prize" will produce documents in which both "Wiesel" and "Nobel Prize" appear. Searching Wiesel AND "Nobel Prize" NOT Holocaust will produce documents in which "Wiesel" and "Nobel Prize" appear, and "Holocaust" does not.

Research Evaluate the reliability of your sources and take careful notes. Then organize them in relation to your key words. Place Wiesel, his writings, and his humanitarian work in context, such as the creation of Holocaust memorials. Also address criticism of Wiesel and his work.

Report Use effective eye contact, tone, and body language to express yourself. Offer your own analysis of what you found in your Internet sources.

ELIE WIESEL **1071**

Reading Strategy

(E) is the correct answer. The advice to take his dying father's food rations instead of giving his father his own food is sound, but Eliezer cannot follow it because his compassion for his father is too strong.

Progress Check

Can students evaluate characters?

If No → See Unit 5 Teaching Resources Book, p. 286

Vocabulary Practice

1. b **2.** e **3.** a

Academic Vocabulary

Students should describe any clear principles that guide their lives. Encourage students to consider how societal norms, cultural background, and other affiliations could create an ideology.

Research and Report

Students' oral reports should

- include evidence from Internet research
- show a grasp of key words and research questions used for research
- include their own analysis as well as sourced information

English Learners

DIFFERENTIATED INSTRUCTION

Intermediate For students not yet fluent in English, the idea of giving a presentation may be daunting. Have these students focus on researching, making sure they look up any unfamiliar words they come across and ask questions if they do not understand a piece of information. It may help them to conduct their initial research in their native language.

Then you can meet with students one-on-one and have them tell you about their findings. Allow them to bring notated printouts with them to which they can refer. For beginning English learners, this summarizing can constitute the presentation. For more advanced English learners, you can suggest ways to shape their data into an oral report. You can also offer help with their pronunciation and delivery. They can then give their presentation to the class.

Before You Read

Focus

Bellringer Options

Selection Focus
Transparency 68
Daily Language Practice
Transparency 103

Or say: Imagine that you have been in jail for many years and are being released. You open the door to sunlight and green grass. What would you feel? *(Possible responses: joy, a sense of freedom)* Ask students to list freedoms they enjoy that they would be denied in a tightly controlled environment like prison.

Political History ☆

Stalin In 1924, Joseph Stalin (1879–1953) established a ruthless dictatorship in Russia. Stalin ranks with Hitler as one of the biggest mass murderers in history. During the "Great Purge" (1934–1938) he executed and imprisoned thousands of people he deemed to be traitors.

Before You Read

Freedom to Breathe

Russia

Meet **Aleksandr Solzhenitsyn**
(born 1918)

When Aleksandr Solzhenitsyn was awarded the Nobel Prize, he did not accept the award in person, fearing he would not be allowed to return home. However, he prepared an acceptance speech in which he stated that world literature can help nations discover "the true history of another" and spare it "from repeating the same cruel mistakes."

Childhood and Education Solzhenitsyn was born in Kislovodsk, Russia, one year after the outbreak of the Russian Revolution. His father died before Solzhenitsyn was born. Solzhenitsyn grew up in Rostov, where his mother earned a modest living as a stenographer. Though he was interested in literature, family and financial circumstances led him to pursue studies in mathematics and physics at the University of Rostov. During World War II, he served in the military, rising to the rank of captain of artillery.

Imprisonment and Exile Late in the war, Solzhenitsyn was arrested for writing letters in which he criticized Soviet leader Joseph Stalin. After eight years in prison, he was exiled to southern Kazakhstan for three years, where he worked as a teacher and began to write.

After emerging from exile in 1956, Solzhenitsyn continued teaching and writing. In 1961, when the new Soviet leader Nikita Khrushchev launched an attack on Stalinism and established a more open policy toward artistic expression, Solzhenitsyn took a chance. He arranged to have his novel *One Day in the Life of Ivan Denisovich* published in *Novy Mir* (*New World*), a prestigious literary and political journal. When it appeared in 1962, it quickly became a success, but also generated much controversy. The inner

"Lies can prevail against much in this world, but never against art."

Aleksandr Solzhenitsyn

executive committee of the Communist Party openly criticized and harassed Solzhenitsyn and strongly objected to his grim depictions of Soviet oppression. After Khrushchev's fall from power, the attacks intensified. In 1965, the secret police seized Solzhenitsyn's papers, and later, Soviet authorities tried to ban his work from being published in foreign countries.

Solzhenitsyn was expelled from Russia in 1974, shortly after parts of *The Gulag Archipelago*, his historical account of the horrors of the Stalin-era Soviet labor camps, were published in Paris. After living briefly in Switzerland, he settled in Vermont. In 1989, influenced by Mikhail Gorbachev's policy of *glasnost* (openness), *Novy Mir* published government-approved excerpts from *The Gulag Archipelago*. In 1990, Soviet authorities reinstated Solzhenitsyn's citizenship. Four years later Solzhenitsyn returned to his homeland, having outlasted the Soviet regime.

 Literature Online

Author Search For more about Aleksandr Solzhenitsyn, go to glencoe.com and enter QuickPass code GLW6053u5.

Selection Skills

Literary Elements
- Prose Poetry (SE pp. 1073, 1074, 1075)
- Imagery (TE p. 1074)

Reading Skills
- Visualize (SE pp. 1073, 1074, 1075)

Freedom to Breathe

Vocabulary Skills
- Academic Vocabulary (SE p. 1075)

Speaking/Listening/Viewing
- Deliver a Speech (TE p. 1074)

Writing Skills/Grammar
- Prose Poem (SE p. 1075)

Literature and Reading Preview

Connect to the Poem

What images do you associate with the word *freedom*? List several descriptive words or phrases that come to mind.

Build Background

Solzhenitsyn spent the last days of his imprisonment in a Gulag labor camp in a bitterly cold area of northern Kazakhstan. In *The Gulag Archipelago*, he describes his release and journey into exile. Although officially he was a free man, his activities were still restricted. The night of his release, having not yet obtained lodging, he stayed at MGB headquarters (department of safeguard), and the guards allowed him to spend the night outside. The poem "Freedom to Breathe," which he wrote later, appears in his book *Stories and Prose Poems*, first published in English in 1971.

Set Purposes for Reading

Big Idea **Postwar Europe**

As you read, ask yourself, How does Solzhenitsyn respond to political conditions in the post–World War II Soviet Union?

Literary Element **Prose Poetry**

A **prose poem** is a short prose composition that uses rhythm, imagery, figurative language, and other poetic devices to express an idea or emotion. Unlike metrical and free verse, prose poetry does not have line breaks; instead, the sentences appear in standard paragraph form. As you read "Freedom to Breathe," ask yourself, Which poetic devices does Solzhenitsyn use to express his feelings about freedom?

Reading Strategy **Visualize**

Poets use sensory language (words that appeal to sight, sound, taste, smell, and touch) to help readers picture an idea or feeling they want to convey. In "Freedom to Breathe," Solzhenitsyn creates a variety of pictures which, taken together, help the reader visualize his ideas about freedom. As you read, ask yourself, What images help me visualize Solzhenitsyn's experience?

··

Tip: **Track Sensory Language** As you read the poem, use a chart to jot down words or groups of words that appeal to the senses. By each example, describe the picture the words create.

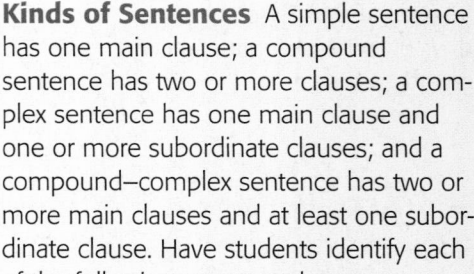

Example of Sensory Language	Picture It Creates
apple tree in blossom, grass glistens with moisture, sweet fragrance pervades the air	pleasant, satisfying images of nature

Learning Objectives

For pages 1072–1075

In studying this text, you will focus on the following objectives:

Literary Study: Analyzing prose poetry.

Reading: Visualizing.

Writing: Writing a prose poem.

L'Envol, 1968-1971. Marc Chagall (Russian, 1887–1985). Oil on canvas ,125 x 90 cm. Private collection. ©ARS

Before You Read

Focus

Summary

This prose poem highlights the euphoria of freedom, noting that one often does not realize the value of an intangible thing, such as freedom, until it is taken away. Solzhenitsyn employs descriptive imagery, which appeals to the senses and helps to transport the reader to a similar natural setting. The perspective shifts from the first person "I" in the beginning of the poem to the third-person "we" in the end. The theme of freedom is drawn from Solzhenitsyn's ten-year imprisonment as a political prisoner in Siberia, during which he wrote this and many other pieces.

 For summaries in languages other than English, see Unit 5 Teaching Resources Book, pp. 292–297.

Political History ☆

Gulag Gulag is a Russian acronym that refers to the forced labor camps where both political prisoners and ordinary criminals were housed from the 1920's to the 1950's. The publication of Solzhenitsyn's *The Gulag Archipelago* brought the term to the West, where it had been relatively unknown. At their peak, in 1936, the camps held up to 5 million people. The prisoners were forced to engage in huge building projects, such as constructing canals or dams, or in industries such as mining. Prisoners were sometimes threatened and often lived in inhumane conditions. The camps began to be dismantled following Stalin's death in 1953.

Approaching Level

DIFFERENTIATED INSTRUCTION

Kinds of Sentences A simple sentence has one main clause; a compound sentence has two or more clauses; a complex sentence has one main clause and one or more subordinate clauses; and a compound–complex sentence has two or more main clauses and at least one subordinate clause. Have students identify each of the following sentences by type:

1. Words cannot describe the sweet fragrance that pervades the air. *(complex)*

2. I stand under an apple tree in blossom and I breathe. *(compound)*

3. It rained during the night and now dark clouds drift across the sky, after it looked as if it was going to clear up. *(compound–complex)*

4. I cease to hear the motorcycle backfiring. *(simple)*

Teach

Literary Element 1

Imagery Have students discuss the central image that expresses the sense of freedom throughout the piece: breathing. **Ask:** How do you think breathing is a form of freedom? *(Students may say that breath is a symbol of life.)* How does the image capture the essence of freedom? *(Solzhenitsyn uses it as a way to exemplify his freedom, his ability to go out into the world and be nurtured by it.)*

Reading Strategy 2

Visualize Answer: *The speaker is standing under an apple tree, probably in the early morning. There are dark clouds from the previous night's rain and moisture is on the grass. The speaker smells the fragrance of the apple blossoms and grass. The images appeal to sight and smell.*

 For additional practice using the reading skill or strategy, see Unit 5 Teaching Resources Book, p. 299.

Literary Element 3

Prose Poetry Answer: *In the final paragraph, the first sentence contains the simile "like cages in a zoo." The second sentence includes the onomatopoeic words "whining" and "burble." The simile likens the five-story houses to cages in a zoo. The onomatopoeic words describe intrusive sounds.*

 For additional literary element practice, see Unit 5 Teaching Resources Book, p. 298.

Aleksandr Solzhenitsyn

Translated by Michael Glenny

Apple Trees in Bloom, 1904. Kazimir Severinovich Malevich (Russian, 1878-1935). Oil on canvas, 55 x 70 cm. State Russian Museum, St. Petersburg.

A shower fell in the night and now dark clouds drift across the sky, occasionally sprinkling a fine film of rain.

I stand under an apple tree in blossom and I breathe. Not only the apple tree but the grass round it glistens with moisture; words cannot describe the sweet fragrance that pervades the air. I inhale as deeply as I can, and the aroma invades my whole being; I breathe with my eyes open, I breathe with my eyes closed—I cannot say which gives me the greater pleasure. **1**

This, I believe, is the single most precious freedom that prison takes away from us: the freedom to breathe freely, as I now can. No food on earth, no wine, not even a woman's kiss is sweeter to me than this air steeped in the fragrance of flowers, of moisture and freshness.

No matter that this is only a tiny garden, hemmed in by five-story houses like cages in a zoo. I cease to hear the motorcycles backfiring, radios whining, the burble of loud-speakers. As long as there is fresh air to breathe under an apple tree after a shower, we may survive a little longer.

Visualize *Describe the scene. To what senses do the images appeal?* **2**

Prose Poetry *What examples of figurative language can you find in this paragraph? Describe each example.* **3**

Speaking Practice

Deliver a Speech Have students compose and deliver a speech on the topic of personal freedoms. Ask them to think about the ways in which they are free. Ask them to think about the generations that came before them and how the sense of freedom has changed over the years. Have students create a web with different ideas that come to mind when they think about freedom. Tell them that their speech can go in various directions and be tangential to the actual discussion of freedom. Emphasize the importance of eye contact and confidence when presenting a speech.

After You Read

Respond and Think Critically

Respond and Interpret

1. The speaker describes a setting that gives him great pleasure. What memories of pleasurable moments from your own experience did his description evoke?

2. (a)How would you describe the setting at the beginning of "Freedom to Breathe"? (b)Why might Solzhenitsyn have included the setting's details in the last paragraph?

3. (a)What does the sweet fragrance of the flowers and the grass inspire the speaker to do? (b)What might Solzhenitsyn be suggesting about a person's connection to nature?

4. (a)According to the speaker, what is the most precious freedom prison takes away? (b)What, in your opinion, does this statement mean?

Analyze and Evaluate

5. What can you infer has happened to the speaker in the past?

6. **Tone** is a speaker's attitude toward the subject. What is the tone of "Freedom to Breathe"?

7. In the last sentence of the poem, what does the speaker imply about freedom?

Connect

8. **Big Idea** **Postwar Europe** What might the speaker's reverence for freedom imply about prison conditions in the Russian Gulag?

9. **Connect to the Author** (a)What biographical connection can you make between the speaker in the poem and Solzhenitsyn? (b)How would you interpret the last sentence of the poem?

Literary Element Prose Poetry

A **prose poem** allows a poet to express poetical ideas without following the usual rules of poetic form.

1. (a)Identify one example of parallel structure in the poem. (b)What purpose does it serve?

2. (a)Read the last paragraph aloud at a moderate speed. What rhythm is created? (b)What purpose might this rhythm serve?

Reading Strategy Visualize

When you **visualize**, you picture an author's ideas or descriptions in your mind.

1. (a)Identify examples of imagery that appeal to sight. (b)To which ones does the speaker seem to respond favorably? To which unfavorably?

2. (a)What images in the last paragraph appeal to hearing? (b)What might they represent?

 Literature Online

Selection Resources For Selection Quizzes, eFlashcards, and Reading-Writing Connection activities, go to glencoe.com and enter QuickPass code GLW6053u5.

Academic Vocabulary

Solzhenitsyn writes about the **bond** *between nature and people.*

Bond is an academic word. In more casual conversation, you might talk about the **bond** among friends or family members. Using context clues, figure out the meaning of *bond* in the sentence above. Check your guess in a dictionary.

For more on academic vocabulary, see pages 36–37 and R83–R85.

Writing

Write a Prose Poem Think of a time when doing something simple, like breathing, gave you great pleasure. Write a prose poem about that experience, using "Freedom to Breathe" as a model. Use sensory language and poetic devices to convey your feelings. Refer to the chart you made on page 1073 to help create original details for your poem.

ALEKSANDR SOLZHENITSYN **1075**

After You Read

Assess

1. Answers will vary.

2. (a) The speaker is standing under an apple tree on a damp morning. (b) Freedom can inspire beauty anywhere.

3. (a) It inspires him to breathe deeply. (b) Perhaps he is saying nature allows people to breathe.

4. (a) the freedom to breathe freely (b) Prisoners cannot breathe freely because they are always in fear; they cannot breathe fresh air, only prison air.

5. He was probably in prison.

6. Possible answers: joyous, reverent, awestruck.

7. Freedom, regardless of one's circumstances, gives one hope.

8. Students may say prison conditions were harsh and did not allow for even basic pleasures in life, such as breathing fresh air.

9. (a) Both the speaker and Solzhenitsyn were imprisoned. (b) After his release from prison, Solzhenitsyn was harrassed by Soviet authorities for years. He might be saying his freedom gave him the strength to endure the harassment.

> For additional assessment, see Assessment Resources, pp. 217–218.

Academic Vocabulary

Students should recognize that *bond* means "connection."

Writing

Students' prose poems should
- focus on a moment of joy
- use sensory language and poetic devices
- follow the conventions of a prose poem

Literary Element

1. (a) "I breathe with my eyes open, I breathe with my eyes closed" (b) reinforces joy of breathing freely

2. (a) Slight pauses occur naturally throughout the paragraph. (b) The pauses join the thoughts of each sentence, reveal a progression of thought, and lead to the final line: "we may survive a little longer."

Reading Strategy

1. Favorable images: a fine film of rain, grass glistening with moisture, and the apple tree. Unfavorable images: the tiny garden and cages in a zoo.

2. (a) Motorcycles backfiring, radios whining, and the burble of loud-speakers (b) They represent intrusions and the realities of life that the speaker endures.

Focus

Summary

This article gives short biographies of individuals who have emerged from the turbulence of the past sixty years to make significant contributions to the world. Those discussed in the article are: Aleksandr Solzhenitsyn, Jacques-Yves Cousteau, King Juan Carlos, Mother Teresa, John Lydon, and Linus Torvalds.

Teach

Literary History ☆

Solzhenitsyn Imprisoned

Solzhenitsyn served the first year of his sentence in regular prison camps. In 1946, however, due to his mathematical skills, he was transferred to a *sharashka* (scientific research institute) to help develop a device for telephone encryption. The conditions were relatively privileged, but in 1950 he was sent to one of the new and harsh "special camps" intended for political prisoners only.

Learning Objectives

For pages 1076–1081

In studying this text, you will focus on the following objectives:

Reading: Evaluating historical influences.
Using text features.
Analyzing informational text.

Set a Purpose for Reading

Read to learn about six people who have revolutionized politics, the arts, science, and technology. Consider how their lives relate to the drastic changes that have occurred in postwar Europe.

Preview the Article

1. Scan the headings of the paragraphs. What do you already know about the people discussed in this article?

2. Skim the photos and their captions. What is similar and what is different about the people in the images?

Reading Strategy Evaluate Historical Influences

As you read, assess how the people profiled in this article created turning points in history, and trace how their actions affected others. Use a chart like the one below.

Person	Turning Point	Influence
King Juan Carlos	Spoke Catalan	Spread democratic ideals

---

60 Years of Risk Takers

O VER THE PAST 60 YEARS, MANY EXTRAORDINARY people have emerged from the turmoil, creativity, and chaos of a period that witnessed the aftermath of world war, the collapse of communism, the failure of old certainties, and the rise of new fears.

Some fought battles against repression and prejudice. Others tapped into the energies of the era to produce new technologies and innovative art forms. Still others introduced us to exciting new worlds and environments. Many of these agents of change took risks—with ideas, with conventions, sometimes with life itself. All of them changed our world for the better.

Aleksandr Solzhenitsyn

His powerful account of life in the Soviet Union's Gulag gave a voice to victims of oppression. ☆

By YURI ZARAKHOVICH

His is a story about the power of the written word. In 1945, Aleksandr Solzhenitsyn was sentenced to eight years in the labor camps for criticizing the Soviet Union's dictator Joseph Stalin in letters to a friend. Seventeen years later, he turned his experience into *One Day in the Life of Ivan Denisovich*, the first literary work to describe the brutalities of prison under Stalin.

The book propelled Solzhen-itsyn to fame, but after the praise came persecution. Solzhenitsyn's books were banned and the writer was watched by the KGB, the Soviet intelligence agency. Yet he still kept writing, secretly sending novels abroad where they could be published. The first part of his epic three-volume work, *The Gulag Archipelago*, was published in Paris in 1973. It enraged the Soviet government and Solzhenitsyn was exiled abroad, which for a Russian writer, he said, amounted to a spiritual death.

That death was to last for 20 years. Now back home after the collapse of the communist government in 1991, Solzhenitsyn is still unwilling to stay quiet. He turned down new Russia's highest state award to protest "the all-out

---

Vocabulary Practice

Context Clues On the board, **write:** the failure of old certainties. Point out that this phrase is in the first sentence of the article. Have students use dictionaries to find the two meanings of *certainty*. ("the state of being certain" or "something certain; an assured fact") Have a volunteer write both meanings on the board. Explain that to determine which meaning is intended, one must look at the context. **Say:** The word *failure* is a key clue to the intended meaning of *certainties*. **Ask:** Which word in the two definitions could be something that would fail during a time of turmoil? *(fact)* How can facts "fail"? *(Statements that were true at one time are no longer true at a later time.)* How does the word *old* in the phrase support this conclusion? *(It shows that the certainties were something from the past.)* As students continue reading, have them jot down examples of certainties that failed. *(A writer is allowed to return to a country that banished him for his views; the creator of popular films and television programs becomes a father of the environmental movement; a king leads his country to democracy; a young nun who teaches social studies becomes a saint; a sickly child turns into a singer who turns the music world upside down; a 21-year-old writes a revolutionary computer program and distributes it for free.)*

plundering of the country" he felt had been condoned by the regime that followed the Soviets.

But he doesn't believe in blaming bad government for all ills. On Feb. 12, 1974, the same day the KGB broke into his apartment to arrest him, *Live Not by Lies* was published. It was a roadmap on how to fight oppression: "It is not they who are to blame for everything—we are to blame ourselves, we alone . . . And the simplest key to liberation is this: personal nonparticipation in lies." It's a philosophy that is today just as relevant in his homeland—and in the wider world—as it was in Russia's totalitarian past.

Jacques-Yves Cousteau

Pioneering filmmaker and environmentalist, he showed the world the wonders of the deep.

By CATHERINE MAYER

Sailors tell tales of a magical world beneath the sea. Until Jacques-Yves Cousteau developed the aqualung SCUBA diving equipment, that world was off-limits to all but submariners and professional divers in clunky suits and helmets, sucking on air delivered by hosepipe. But with his self-contained breathing equipment and body-hugging wet suit, Cousteau became a "manfish" and was soon sending reports from this gloriously strange environment.

His many films, books, and long-running TV series—including *The Undersea World of Jacques Cousteau*—entranced people across the world. His 1956 film *Le Monde du Silence* (The Silent

Jacques Cousteau, French undersea explorer and oceanographer, shown in 1971 photo.

Bettmann/Corbis

World) won an Academy Award and was the first documentary to win the Palme d'Or award at the Cannes Film Festival. The documentary is hardly an advertisement for environmental best practices—the captain and his crew from the good ship *Calypso* are shown taking rides on turtles and casually killing sharks. Nevertheless, when Cousteau died, aged 87, in 1997, he was widely regarded as one of the fathers of environmentalism for his work as an oceanographer and vocal opposition to France's nuclear test program.

His was a life seemingly destined for greatness. Long before rising to public attention, Cousteau had already received France's top award, the Légion d'Honneur (the

Legion of Honor), for aiding the anti-Nazi French Resistance during World War II. His enduring legacy was to make the world aware of the beauty and fragility of the sea. "I spent my life amazed by nature and dazzled by the experiences of life," he said. And his achievements continue to amaze and dazzle.

King Juan Carlos

Groomed to take over from a dictator, he used his power to transform Spain into a democracy.

By JAMES GRAFF

European royalty has struggled to stay relevant in the modern age.

60 YEARS OF RISK TAKERS **1077**

Teach

Reading Strategy 1

Respond **Ask:** What element of this article about Jacques-Yves Cousteau did you find most interesting or surprising? *(Answers will vary: many students will be surprised that he developed scuba gear.)*

For activities related to this selection, see Unit 5 Resources Book, pp. 302–310.

Readability Scores

Dale-Chall: 8.8
DRP: 61
Lexile: 1120

Learning Objectives
Evaluate historical influences. (SE)
Use context clues to determine meanings. (TE)

English Learners

DIFFERENTIATED INSTRUCTION

SMALL GROUP
Intermediate It is very important that English learners understand the rest of the opening paragraph of this piece, in addition to the phrase discussed in the Skills Practice on the previous page. The paragraph provides the theme of the article, as well as the connection between the people discussed in it. English learners will probably encounter unfamiliar and difficult words

in this paragraph. Place English learners of various fluency levels in small groups and have them compile a list of words from the opening that are unfamiliar to any of the groups' members. Then have the students work together to look up the words' definitions in a dictionary. Have more fluent English learners help explain the words' meanings to those who are less proficient.

Approaching Level

DIFFERENTIATED INSTRUCTION

Postwar Europe Make sure approaching level students recall the meaning of the term *Postwar Europe*. **Ask:** What is meant by the word *postwar? (The time after World War II, which ended in 1945.)* **Ask:** What might be meant by the title of this article, "60 Years of Risk"? *(The period from 1945 to 2005 was a dangerous time.)*

TIME

Teach

Reading Strategy   1

Respond to an Anecdote
Ask: What is your response to the anecdote detailing the author's first interaction with Mother Teresa? *(Answers will vary. Some may find the story touching or inspiring, others may be surprised that she would command a stranger like that.)*

ADVANCED Ask advanced students to use information in this section to find a connection between Mother Teresa and Modern Europe, the source of the literature for this part of the textbook. *(This section mentions that Mother Teresa was Albanian, and Albania is a country in Europe.)*

One monarch who succeeded is King Juan Carlos of Spain, whose sure sense of personal and national destiny helped his country turn itself into a democracy.

That happy result was hardly predestinated. Juan Carlos was born in exile in 1938. His father gave up control of his son's education to General Francisco Franco, the dictator who succeeded the royals after years of civil war, hoping this would encourage Franco to restore the crown. Juan Carlos was named Franco's eventual successor in 1969, but democrats had no great expectations of him. They realized their mistake once he took the throne upon Franco's death in 1975. Within four months he created a sensation by speaking Catalan, a language Franco had repressed. He then worked hard to have a centrist Prime Minister selected and began to introduce democratic reforms at a rapid pace. Spain's democratic constitution was ratified in 1978.

There was another test to come. After a series of terrorist bombings by Basques, an ethnic group that wants to secede from Spain, a conservative faction in the military tried to take control of the government in 1981. Many of them believed they were acting on the King's behalf. But Juan Carlos ordered military units back to their barracks, and without his support, the attempt collapsed. Four days later, 3 million people marched in cities throughout Spain in support of democracy. Their slogan, almost universally, was *"¡Viva el Rey!"* (Long live the King). That sentiment has persisted, more quietly, ever since.

Nobel peace prize winner Mother Teresa of Calcutta embraces nine month old Christina Ott

Reuters/CORBIS

Mother Teresa

The Saint of Calcutta spread her love to the unwanted, the homeless, and the abandoned.

By DOMINIQUE LAPIERRE

My first sight of her was in her hospice of the Pure Heart in Calcutta, India decades ago. She was on her knees feeding, with a spoon and a plate of rice, a man who looked more like a corpse than a human being. Suddenly, she sensed my presence behind her. She turned around and abruptly handed me her plate: "Go on feeding this man," she said, "and love him." Those words—and actions—reflect Mother Teresa's message. To love those who have never been loved. To love the unwanted, the homeless, the abandoned, as if each one were Jesus Christ himself. For nearly 40

years, the Saint of Calcutta spread her message throughout India and the rest of the world.

And yet, from her arrival in Calcutta in 1929 as a young Albanian nun of the Loreto missionary order, her life had begun in a very different way. For years, she taught history and geography in Loreto schools in Calcutta and elsewhere. But on Sept. 10, 1946, she experienced a calling while on a train taking her to a retreat in Darjeeling at the foot of the Himalayas. The inner voice told her to give up the comfort of her surroundings, and to go share the life of the inhabitants of the nearest slum. She wrote to the Vatican for permission, and went to the bazaar to buy a cheap piece of white cotton cloth bordered with blue. This humble sari was to become the uniform of the exceptional group she then set up to serve the poorest of the poor, wherever they

Speaking and Listening Practice

Participate in a Discussion Have students reread the first paragraph of the selection. Based on this introduction, discuss as a class the role of risk takers as agents for change. Begin by reviewing effective techniques for participating in a discussion:

- Prepare to listen by clearing your mind of other thoughts and focus on the speaker.
- Remain quiet until it is your turn to speak.
- Use nonverbal communication such as

nodding and eye contact to show you understand what the speaker is saying.

- When it is your turn to talk, speak in a clear voice to all members of the group.
- Avoid repeating ideas needlessly.
- State opinions and ask questions in a thoughtful and respectful manner.

Encourage students to discuss other individuals who have risk-taking qualities similar to the people profiled in the selection. Each student should support

his or her choice with examples of the individual's achievements and contributions to humanity. Be aware that some students may struggle with organizing or presenting their ideas orally. Write the following sentence frame on the board and instruct students to use it in presenting their ideas to the class:

I would profile _____ because he/she _____.

were: the homeless, the hungry, lepers, unwanted babies, AIDS victims. In 1979, she was awarded the Nobel Peace Prize.

Today, Mother Teresa's Missionaries of Charity carry on her ideal of compassion to all suffering human beings—with the same message I heard from her lips the very first day I met her in Calcutta: "Love them."

John Lydon

As the frontman of the ultimate British punk band the Sex Pistols, he inspired a new generation—and terrified an old one. **2**

By HUGH PORTER

Londoners watching a local early-evening TV talk show dropped their forks. It was 1976 and they had expected the usual, easily digestible broadcast. Instead, they were served up musical revolution with their beans on toast. "They are punk rockers. The new craze, they tell me," announced the host Bill Grundy of his guests, the Sex Pistols. Grundy couldn't hide his

John Lydon, a.k.a. Johnny Rotten, is shown in a head shoulders photo

Lynn Goldsmith/CORBIS

TIME

Teach

Text Element **2**

Deck Point out the sentence beneath the subheading, or the "deck." Also point out that there is one deck for each subheading. **Ask:** How do the decks help you understand the article? *(The decks offer a preview of the biographical segment the reader is about to encounter, familiarizing the reader with the subject and his or her importance to the world.)*
ADVANCED Ask advanced students why a musician who "terrified" an old generation might be included in an article about extraordinary people. *(as an example of someone involved in major cultural changes)*

Advanced Learners/Pre-AP

DIFFERENTIATED INSTRUCTION

Research a Historical Figure Instruct advanced students to research one of the people they thought of during the discussion on page 1078. They should use reliable Internet sources or a library to find an article about their chosen individual's life. Have them read the article and take notes; afterwards, they should jot down a list of the achievements they would discuss if they were to write an article about this historical figure.

English Learners

DIFFERENTIATED INSTRUCTION

Advanced Ask English Learners to choose a person from their native culture who would make a good subject for this article. Emphasize that the person must be someone from the postwar period. Have them write a paragraph summarizing the key achievements of the person they chose.

Teach

Reading Strategy 1

Evaluate Historical Influences Ask volunteers who are knowledgeable about computers to explain the function of an operating system. *(An operating system controls the basic operations of a computer and directs the processing of programs. A new computer comes with an operating system already installed.)* **Ask:** Why might the creator of a free operating system have more historical influence the creator of other types of software programs? *(Without an operating system, other types of software cannot be run. A free operating system could make computers less expensive.)*

contempt, pushing the band to respond outrageously. Viewers were witnessing a clash of generations, but the Pistols challenged not only their conservative elders but mainstream rock and its enduring hippie influences.

As the Pistols' lead singer, John Lydon—a.k.a. Johnny Rotten—wore the very heart of punk on his torn sleeve. He meant it then. He still does. Britain in the mid-1970s was strike-ridden and divided, and happy songs about love and sunshine seemed hopelessly out of tune with the times. The country needed punk, and it couldn't have happened without Lydon. He had the attitude and the look, and he was also articulate. His lyrics, delivered with a snarl, were social commentaries, often witty, often nasty. It made him as threatening to some as he was inspiring to others.

Always the outsider, Lydon was born to Irish parents in a north London slum, surviving the illness spinal meningitis as a 7-year-old and then enduring a strict Catholic schooling. In August 1975, now a scrawny youth with green locks, he was spotted on London's King's Road and asked to audition for a pop band. Lydon became Rotten, the TV clash guaranteed fame, and terrified town councils forbid the Pistols from performing. By the summer of 1977, they had taken on Britain's head of state. Their alternative anthem, God Save the Queen—with its reference to "her fascist regime" and "no future" refrain—was released as the country celebrated the 25th anniversary of Queen Elizabeth II's reign. "We had declared war on the entire country—without meaning to," said Lydon.

> **"His lyrics, delivered with a snarl, were social commentaries, often witty, often nasty."**
>
> —Hugh Porter

Six months later it was all over: the Pistols had split up and punk was beginning to be adopted by the mainstream. "It became acceptable and absorbed back into the system," said Lydon. He instantly rejected his insider status by forming a new band, Public Image Ltd, whose post-punk experimentation with new sounds and genres was massively influential and produced eight albums over 14 years. These days Lydon, perhaps inspired by his early encounter with Grundy, is a frequent TV presence, his gift for controversy undimmed by the passing years.

Linus Torvalds

By giving away his software, the Finnish programmer earned a place in history.

By PETER GUMBEL

Linus Torvalds was just 21 when he changed the world. Working out of his family's apart-

ment in Finland's capital, Helsinki, in 1991, he wrote the beginnings of a new computer operating system called Linux. He then posted the system for free on the Internet—and invited anyone interested to help improve it. Today Linux powers everything from supercomputers to mobile phones around the world, and Torvalds has achieved fame as the godfather of the open-source movement. Followers believe software code should be shared and developed in a collaborative, or group, effort rather than being kept locked up by a single owner.

Some of Torvalds' supporters portray him as a sort of anti-Bill Gates, but the significance of Linux is much bigger than merely a criticism of Microsoft. Sharing core technologies could lead to a huge reduction in some business costs, freeing up money for more innovative investments elsewhere.

Torvalds continues to keep a close eye on Linux's development and has made some money from two companies that use the system in their products. But his success isn't just measured in dollars. There's an asteroid named after him, as well as an annual software festival. Torvalds' parents were student radicals in the 1960s and his father, a communist, even spent a year studying in Moscow. But it's their son who has turned out to be the real revolutionary.

—from TIME Atlantic

Reading Practice

Evaluate Evidence Have students decide which of these historical figures they believe to be the most significant, based on the evidence presented in the article. Each student should write down on a sheet of paper which person he or she chooses, as well as the reasoning behind that belief. Students can use the following sentence frame to help them develop their reasoning.

Write on the board:

_____ is the most significant of these historical figures because he/she _____.

Then divide students into pairs and have them share their sentences and discuss their reasoning with one another.

Linus Torvalds Holding Laptop Computer

Jim Sugar/Corbis

Respond and Think Critically

Respond and Interpret

1. Write a brief summary of the main ideas in each profile before you answer the following questions. For help on writing a summary, see page 1147.

2. (a)What punishment did Aleksandr Solzhenitsyn face in the Soviet Union? (b)Do you think people must face such obstacles to initiate change? Why or why not?

3. (a)Compare and contrast Mother Teresa's early life with her later life in India. (b)Mother Teresa believed she had to "give up the comfort of her surroundings." Do you think this is necessary in order to give to those less fortunate than yourself? Why or why not?

4. (a)What was unique about the way in which Torvalds developed Linux? (b)What quality does this reveal about Torvalds's character?

Analyze and Evaluate

5. (a)What was contradictory about Jacques-Yves Cousteau's work? (b)Is it possible to still be highly regarded for your achievements despite your faults? Explain.

6. (a)How is John Lydon's story different from the other profiles in this article? (b)Does it surprise you that his achievements were included in the article? Explain.

Connect

7. After World War II in Europe, many people lost faith in traditional ideals. Which of these risk takers may have been affected by this kind of change?

60 YEARS OF RISK TAKERS **1081**

Approaching Level

DIFFERENTIATED INSTRUCTION

Gathering Evidence Ask: What text element can you use to help with question 1? *(the decks in purple type)* **Say:** To answer question 3, consider how Mother Teresa's life changed. **Ask:** What did she do when she was a young nun? *(She taught history and geography.)* What group did she set up after she experienced a calling in 1946? (the Missionaries of Charity) **Say:** To answer question

5, look for contradictory information in the Cousteau section. Look for words such as *but, despite, nevertheless,* and *although.* **Ask:** Which of these words appears in the section? *(nevertheless)* Which information follows this word? *(Cousteau was widely regarded as a father of environmentalism.)* Which information precedes it? *(He took rides on turtles and killed sharks.)*

TIME

Assess

1. Students should provide complete summaries.

2. (a) eight years in labor camps. (b) Some may think people learn from obstacles. Others may think leaders can also develop through positive experiences.

3. (a) Mother Teresa lived a comfortable life in Albania and was trained as a missionary. Later, she chose to share her life with those living in slums in Calcutta. (b) Some may think sacrifice is required in order to give to others. Others may think giving can take place no matter how much comfort a person experiences.

4. (a) He invited Internet users to improve his system. (b) He is open-minded and confident.

5. (a) He was an environmentalist, yet his divers once killed sharks. (b) Some may think leaders should be accountable for all of their actions. Others may think a person should be regarded for his or her entire body of work.

6. (a) He was a leader of a countercultural movement and openly criticized. (b) Some students may think a punk musician should not be included. Others may appreciate an artist's role in changing society.

7. Most wanted to change society. Solzhenitsyn wanted to change his oppressive government. Cousteau fought in the anti-Nazi resistance movement. King Juan Carlos changed the image of the Spanish monarchy. Mother Teresa helped people without regard to their religious faith. Lydon opposed the monarchy in England.

Writing Workshop

Biographical Investigation

Focus

For pages 1082–1091

Learning Objectives

In this workshop, you will focus on the following objectives:

Writing: Writing a biographical investigation using the writing process. Understanding how to develop coherent paragraphs.

Grammar: Understanding how to use commas correctly.

Writing Workshop

Biographical Investigation

Literature Connection Dante casts himself as the main character of the *Divine Comedy*, indirectly linking many details in the poem to emotions and experiences from his life.

> *"Then turning to those spirits once again,*
> *I said: 'Francesca, what you suffer here*
> *melts me to tears of pity and of pain . . .'"*

Researching Dante's life can give you a context for understanding his portrayal of Hell. Learning about authors' lives can reveal insights into their writing, because authors often use their real-life experiences as sources for their work. One function of a **research report** is to investigate how an author's historical period, beliefs, and personal experiences affected his or her work. To write this kind of report, use the strategies below.

Bellringer Options

Daily Language Practice Transparency 104

Or write on the board: "Write what you know." **Then ask:** Have you ever heard this expression? What does it mean? *(It is an encouragement to writers to write about topics and experiences that are familiar to them. It implies that their writing will be better and more meaningful if they do so.)*

Summary

In this workshop, students will write and present a biographical investigation. Students will follow the stages of the writing process: prewriting, drafting, revising, and editing. In addition, two mini-lessons, one on creating coherent paragraphs and one on using commas, are provided.

 For Writing Workshop graphic organizer and rubric, see Unit 5 Teaching Resources Book, pp. 312–314.

Writing Process

At any stage of a writing process, you may think of new ideas. Feel free to return to earlier stages as you write.

Prewrite

Draft

Revise

Focus Lesson: Coherent Paragraphs

Edit and Proofread

Focus Lesson: Commas

Present

LOG ON **Literature** Online

Writing and Research For prewriting, drafting, and revising tools, go to glencoe.com and enter QuickPass code GLW6053u5.

Rubric

Goals	Strategies
To present a clear thesis	☑ Narrow and clarify the focus of your essay. ☑ Revise your thesis statement as needed.
To support your thesis with historical evidence	☑ Make connections between the author's life and the literary text.
To organize your research logically	☑ Structure your essay with a clear introduction, body, and conclusion. ☑ Organize your evidence into paragraphs with clear topic sentences.
To use evidence effectively and correctly	☑ Take notes on a variety of sources. ☑ Quote, paraphrase, and summarize information and credit sources.
To present your own ideas on the topic	☑ Comment on experts' ideas. ☑ Present your own insights.

Workshop Resources

Print Materials

- Unit 5 Teaching Resources Book, pp. 312–314
- Writing Kit
- Success in Writing: Research and Reports

Transparencies

- Writing Workshop Transparencies

Technology

- Literature Online: Writing Resources and Grammar Resources, www.glencoe.com
- Online Essay Grader, www.glencoe.com
- Student Presentation Builder on StudentWorks Plus CD-ROM
- Media Workshop DVD
- Online Essay Grader, www.glencoe.com

Assignment: Connect an Author's Life and Work

Write a research paper of at least 1,000 words in which you investigate the relationship between an author's life and his or her work. As you move through the stages of writing, keep your audience and purpose in mind.

Audience: peers, classmates, and teacher

Purpose: research an author's life and make connections with his or her work

Prewrite

Narrow Your Topic Review the literary works in this unit and think about which authors' lives intrigue you. Depending on the author you choose and the amount of research available, you may want to narrow your focus to a particular theme or element of a single work or a specific aspect of the author's life. To help narrow your focus, make a list of questions and choose one or two of them. For example, if you choose to write about the connection between Dante's life and his poetry, you might ask questions like these:

1 ▶ Was Beatrice modeled on a woman in Dante's life?

▶ How did Dante know so much about different aspects of human experience?

▶ Is Dante himself the main character in the *Divine Comedy*?

Gather Information Identify a variety of sources, including books, reputable Internet sites, and encyclopedias (see page R32 for more on reliable sources). A **primary source** is an original document from the time period you are researching. Autobiographies or letters written by your author or by people who knew the author are particularly useful primary sources. A **secondary source** is a document, such as an encyclopedia entry, by a person who had no personal involvement in the events you are writing about.

As you research, think about your paper's **thesis,** or central idea. Look for patterns and contradictions in your sources, and think about what conclusions you can draw about your topic.

Take Notes As you investigate your topic, take notes on four different kinds of note cards. Color-code or label them so you know exactly what type of information—bibliography, summary, paraphrase, or quotation—appears on each note card. Be sure to record page numbers to indicate where you found the information. This will help you manage the information you gather. (For more on how to use note cards effectively, see page R32–R33.)

Real-World Connection

Many activities in life require the ability to gather research, take notes, and synthesize information. Whether you are investigating a career or choosing a college, your ability to evaluate information will help you make informed decisions.

Avoid Plagiarism ☆

As you research, you might come across a phrase or sentence that says exactly what you want to say. If this happens, be sure to show your readers the source of your ideas. Plagiarizing, or presenting someone else's words or ideas as your own, is dishonest. It is important to distinguish between a paraphrase, a quote, or a summary when you take notes. Include quotation marks to indicate direct quotes. If you summarize or paraphrase, you must give the author due credit.

English Learners

DIFFERENTIATED INSTRUCTION

Advanced English learners who may lack the self-confidence to produce a research paper independently will benefit from discussing their progress and difficulties with other students. Consider pairing English learners with English-proficient students. Suggest that the two discuss each stage of their work—that is, prewriting, drafting, and so forth—and share what they have done, including the difficulties they have overcome.

Advanced Learners/Pre-AP

DIFFERENTIATED INSTRUCTION

Work in Groups Students who are interested in the same author or in similar topics may wish to meet in groups to discuss their ideas. Encourage them to write on complementary topics—perhaps different aspects of the same author's life—that could be presented together. After they have written their papers, have them give a group presentation to the class that synthesizes their various researched areas of expertise.

Writing Workshop

Biographical Investigation

Teach

Writing Process

Prewriting Emphasize to students that choosing an appropriately limited topic is one key to writing a successful research paper. Encourage them to look through books and other sources to get a sense of the breadth of their topic, which subtopics it might be narrowed down to, and how much information is available on the topic.

APPROACHING Have struggling students present you with a list of their research questions at this point. Review these lists and redirect those students whose questions are too broad or vague, or encourage them to pursue the questions which seem most promising.

Big Idea　　　1

The Vision of Faith Point out to students that the sample research questions draw several parallels between Dante's life and the events in the *Divine Comedy*. **Ask:** Do you think the primary purpose of the *Divine Comedy* is to tell an autobiographical tale or to provide religious instruction? Point out that the text can be interpreted on a variety of levels that are not mutually exclusive. Dante may have ultimately been seeking to teach moral lessons, but he may have done so by drawing from the richness and immediacy of his personal experience.

Learning Objectives
Write a biographical investigation. (SE)
Use the writing process. (SE)

Biographical Investigation

Teach

Writing Skills

Avoid Bias Say: Before you use a source, it is important to evaluate it for bias. Ask yourself: What is the author's background and reputation? Does the author back up the claims he or she makes with evidence? Are the views of this author often disputed by others? Have students go through their bibliography note cards and eliminate any sources which seem biased.

Language History ☆

Kidnapping Words Plagiarizing—presenting someone else's writing as one's own—is quite literally a form of theft. In fact, the word *plagiarist* comes from the Latin word *plagiarus*, meaning "kidnapper."

Cite Your Sources

As you write your draft, indicate each source with parenthetical citations. Typically, parenthetical citations include the author's last name and the page number **(Stade 411)**. If you mention the author's name in a sentence, you only need to cite the page number. For sources with no author listed, give a shortened version of the title in parentheses. (For more about citations and creating a works-cited list, see pages R34–R37.)

▶ **Bibliography note cards** Write the complete publishing information for each source on a separate card.

▶ **Summary note cards** Write the author's last name and the source's title, and then write down the source's main ideas.

▶ **Paraphrase note cards** Write the author's last name and the source's title, and then retell information from the source in your own words.

▶ **Quotation note cards** Write the author's last name and the source's title, and then copy the passage exactly.

Create an Outline Use your note cards to create an outline for your paper. Your outline is a plan for the body of your paper, which should expand upon and provide support for a main idea. Organize note cards with similar topics into groups, and arrange the groups in a logical order. Use each group as a main topic in your outline. Once you have created a general outline, insert specific evidence from your note cards to support each main topic. Cite the sources as in the example below.

Outline Form

I. Main topic	I. Dante's pain over lost love
A. Subtopic	A. Falls in love with Beatrice, whose premature death causes Dante enormous grief
1. Evidence	1. "Dante called her Beatrice, the bringer of blessings, the one who brought bliss to all who looked upon her" (Stade 411).
B. Subtopic	B. After Beatrice's death, embarks on a period of intense study and learning
C. Subtopic	C. Love of Beatrice transforms into love of philosophy, which influences the *Divine Comedy*
II. Main topic	II. Dante's political disappointments
A. Subtopic	A. Enters public life during period of political strife between Black and White Guelfs
B. Subtopic	B. Develops deep hatred for policies of Pope Boniface VIII
III. Main topic	III. Dante's exile from Florence
A. Subtopic	A. Experiences loneliness and difficulty
B. Subtopic	B. Benefits from exile

Develop a Thesis Statement Once you have organized your research into an outline, write your thesis statement—the central idea you will prove in your paper. Your thesis statement should be a one- or two-sentence synthesis of the main topics in your outline.

Writing Practice

Narrow a Topic Emphasize to students the importance of selecting a topic that is appropriately limited. If students select a topic that is too broad, they will have difficulty creating a focused thesis; however, if they select a topic that is too narrow, they will have difficulty finding enough source material. Write the following possible research topics on the board. Have students decide whether the topics are too general, too limited, or appropriately limited for a biographical investigation.

1. The life of Francesco Petrarch *(too general)*
2. Boccaccio's first meeting with Petrarch in 1350 *(too limited)*
3. The influence of Victor Hugo's exile on his poetry *(appropriately limited)*

☆ Draft

Create Structure As you draft, use your outline to guide your writing. Write at least one paragraph for each main topic in your outline. Include a topic sentence and supporting details in each paragraph. Your conclusion should restate your thesis in a different way, recount your main points, or provide a final thought-provoking idea.

Analyze a Workshop Model

Here is a final draft of a biographical investigation. Read the essay and answer the questions in the margin. Use your answers to these questions to guide you as you write.

Suffering and Creativity: The Life of Dante Alighieri

The hardships and triumphs of authors' lives often become the foundations for their fiction. Dante Alighieri experienced great tragedy and change during his life, including a deeply felt heartache over a lost love, political betrayals, and exile from his home in Florence, Italy. Narrating in the first person and casting himself as the protagonist, Dante translated his experiences into the *Divine Comedy*, one of the greatest works in Western literature.

When he was just nine years old, Dante fell in love with the daughter of the noble Florentine Folco Portinari. George Stade explains that Dante called this girl Beatrice, meaning "the bringer of blessings, the one who brought bliss to all who looked upon her" (411). Beatrice was perhaps the most powerful force in Dante's life and art, but his love for her was never returned— Beatrice married another man. Although Dante eventually married as well, he continued to idealize Beatrice throughout his life. Her premature death caused him enormous grief.

Exposition

Writing Frames

As you read the workshop model, think about the following persuasive frames.

• The writer's argument that _____ is supported by _____ _____, and _____.

• The writer argues _____, and I agree, because _____.

Try using frames like these as you write your paper.

Thesis Statement

What makes this thesis statement effective?

Citations

Why does the writer include only the page number in this parenthetical citation?

 Writing Workshop

Biographical Investigation

Teach

Writing Skills

Thesis Statement Answer: *It provides a concise explanation of the connection between Dante's life and the* Divine Comedy.

Writer's Technique ☆

A Solid Introduction After conducting their research and organizing their notes, students may have difficulty knowing how to begin their introductions. Many writers cross this hurdle by simply writing the body paragraphs first, and then going back and writing the introduction last. Writing the body paragraphs first helps to develop the main ideas, thus clarifying what needs to be included in the introduction.

Learning Objectives
Write a biographical investigation. (SE)
Use the writing process. (SE)
Narrow a topic. (TE)

English Learners

DIFFERENTIATED INSTRUCTION

Intermediate English learners might have difficulty comprehending the workshop model. These students might benefit from reading in pairs. Have them work with a reading partner, stopping every two or three paragraphs to discuss the main ideas and details of what they have read so far. Have them help each other clarify any confusing facts or unfamiliar words the writer uses.

Advanced Learners/Pre-AP

DIFFERENTIATED INSTRUCTION

Art and Suffering Encourage advanced learners to keep the following general question in mind as they read the workshop model: Is it necessary to have a difficult life in order to produce great art? Some students may feel that that an author's suffering can lend emotional depth and sympathy to his or her work. Others may say that happiness and well-being are more conducive to producing art. Urge

students to keep this question in mind as they research the lives of their chosen authors, as well.

Writing Workshop

Teach

Writing Skills

Citations Answer: *The author is noted at the beginning of the sentence.*

Block Quotations Answer: *The quotation uses Dante's own words to explain the complicated effect that Beatrice had on him.*

Explanations Answer: *The sentence summarizes the quotation and connects it to the main idea of the paragraph.*

Block Quotations

Why might the writer have chosen to include a quotation of this length?

Explanations

Why is this sentence an effective way to transition from the block quotation to the next sentence?

Secondary Sources

How does this secondary source help reinforce the writer's point?

Main Ideas

Which sentence in this paragraph states the main idea?

The loss of Beatrice influenced Dante's religious and philosophical development, eventually leading him to the vision of Heaven he presents in his last work, the *Divine Comedy*. Searching for comfort after the death of Beatrice, Dante turned away from the love poetry he had written in his youth and embarked on a period of intense study and learning. He read the work of the Greek political philosopher Cicero and the medieval philosopher Boethius. Dante admits in the *Convivio*, a philosophical work published sometime between 1304 and 1307, that this reading was very difficult for him at first. Still, he kept at it. Also in the *Convivio*, he writes:

> And as it may happen that a man looking for silver accidentally hits on gold . . . so I, seeking consolation, found not only a remedy for my sorrow but the language of authors and sciences and books; reflecting on which I judged that philosophy—the lady of these authors and sciences and books—was a very great thing. And I imagined it as a noble lady, whom I could not represent to myself in any attitude but one of compassion; with the result that my sense of truth was so drawn to her that I could not take my eyes off her. (qtd. in Foster 45)

This quotation describes how Dante's early romantic love of Beatrice transformed into a love of philosophy, which would become the driving force behind his later poetry. Reynolds remarks that, in his maturity, Dante portrayed Beatrice not as "the scornful young woman" of the early poems, but as a figure who led him to higher philosophical truths (112). Dante's intellectual development, she explains, "led him to create a new Beatrice [in the *Divine Comedy*], beatified and invested with the divine qualities he had already associated with her but which formerly he had not understood" (112).

Well before Dante wrote the *Divine Comedy,* however, he became involved in the political life of Florence. Florence was a thriving economic, artistic, and political center in Dante's time, and the poet felt a deep love for his city, despite the feuding and conspiracies that characterized public life. In 1295, he sought

---

Writing Practice

Write a Thesis Statement Remind students that their thesis statements should reflect the purpose of their writing. For example, they might be writing in order to contrast an author's life with his or her works. Or they might be writing to show a cause-effect relationship between an author's life experiences and his or her works. Suggest that they use the following sentence frames from the workshop model to write their thesis statements.

[Author] translated [his/her] experiences into _____.

Although [author] _____, [he/she] nonetheless _____.

Like [author's] life, [work of literature] describes _____.

1086

public office as a member of the physician's guild. However, his timing was disastrous. The Guelfs, the ruling party in Florence, had recently divided into two warring factions: the Blacks, who supported papal rule, and the Whites, who felt that religious and political rule should remain separate. Dante, a White Guelf, felt deep distress over this state of affairs—a distress he expresses memorably in Canto 26 of the *Inferno*, where he writes that Florence's political unrest is so well-known that the city's name is spread "throughout Hell" (Alighieri 220). On May 1, 1300, the turmoil reached a boiling point, and violence broke out between the Black and White Guelfs. As a result, many of Dante's fellow White Guelfs were exiled. Dante makes these devastating events the backdrop for the *Divine Comedy*, setting his epic during Easter Week of 1300 (Reynolds 36).

The pain and bitterness Dante felt at this time come through most obviously in his hate-filled portrayal of Pope Boniface VIII in the *Divine Comedy*. Elected in 1294, Boniface helped the Black Guelfs stage a 1301 coup of Florence; he was also accused by Dante and others of simony, or selling religious titles for profit (Reynolds 41). As Ricardo J. Quinones points out, Dante hated Boniface because his actions defied one of Dante's primary beliefs: that politics and religion must be kept separate to preserve the purity of the church (Quinones 80). In the *Inferno*, Dante goes out of his way to criticize Boniface's behavior, having one soul mention that the pope is expected in Hell. He even has St. Peter rail against Boniface in the *Paradiso* (Reynolds 384–385). Dante was a devout Christian and hated Boniface for corrupting the title of pope. However, there was another, more personal cause for his feelings. He seems to have seen Boniface as directly responsible for his next major misfortune: his devastating exile from Florence.

Exposition

Paraphrase

Why is a direct quotation not necessary here?

The graceful Cathedral of Santa Maria del Fiore, and its baptistery and campanile, form the heart of Florence, Italy.

Writing Workshop

Biographical Investigation

Teach

Writing Skills

Secondary Sources Answer: *It provides a detailed interpretation of the figure of Beatrice in the* Divine Comedy, *supporting the writer's idea that Dante's experiences shaped his work.*

Main Ideas Answer: *The first sentence states the main idea.*

Paraphrase Answer: *The author's original words are not needed to convey these facts.*

Learning Objectives
Write a biographical investigation. (SE)
Use the writing process. (SE)
Write a thesis statement. (TE)

Approaching Level

DIFFERENTIATED INSTRUCTION

Using Quotations "Dropped quotes" are a common problem in student research papers. Many students have difficulty understanding the correct way to integrate quotations into their own sentences.
Say: When writing a story, an author cannot simply include a piece of dialogue on its own. The author must also include a speech tag, such as "he said" or "she said," so the reader will know

who is speaking. Similarly, in a research paper, direct quotations usually need to be accompanied by a phrase, such as "he writes that" or "she explains," in addition to a parenthetical citation.

Have students look for other techniques that the writer of the workshop model uses to incorporate quotations into his or her own sentences. Encourage them to use these techniques in their own papers.

Teach

⚡ Writing Skills

Primary Sources Answer:
Using Dante's own words creates a more memorable, poetic impression than simply noting that he was unhappy.

Synthesize Answer: *The writer contributes the idea that the "dark wood" represents Dante's feelings about exile.*

Paragraph Structure Answer:
To support the idea that Dante's experiences in exile provided much of the material for his **Divine Comedy,** *the writer provides details about the exile and connects them to several passages from the work.*

Primary Sources

Why might the writer have chosen to use a direct quotation here rather than paraphrasing?

Synthesize

What original ideas does the writer offer?

Paragraph Structure

How does the writer use details to support the main idea of this paragraph?

Dante's exile, a pivotal event in his life, provided much of the spiritual and creative inspiration for the *Divine Comedy*. Following Boniface's Black Guelf takeover, Dante was banished on charges of political corruption. If he returned to Florence, he would risk being captured and burned alive. At first, Dante was able to find comfort in a community of fellow exiles, but after quarrelling with them over failed attempts at regaining power, he was left on his own (Reynolds 49). He then began a lonely and difficult period of travel in northern Italy, "fulfilling diplomatic assignments, when he could find them, on behalf of lords who received him grudgingly and those who really opened their doors to him" (*Dante: His Life* 19–20). Of this period, Dante himself remarked, "Truly I have been a ship without a sail and without a rudder, driven to many ports and river mouths and shores by the dry wind of miserable poverty . . ." (qtd. in *Dante: His Life* 5). The "dark wood" Dante finds himself in at the beginning of the *Inferno* may represent the sense of despair and uncertainty he felt in exile—he did not know, at the time of writing, whether he would ever be allowed to return to Florence.

Though Dante's exile was painful, it led to several positive developments in his life. First, the solitude afforded him the opportunity to resume his writing. By most accounts, he began writing the *Comedy* to sustain and comfort himself in the first years of his exile. Then, from 1312 on, he found patronage in the courts of several noblemen (Hollander 6), a turn of events that provided him with a new level of stability and security. When he wrote the joyful final canto of the *Paradiso* just before his death in 1321, he was probably living under some of the happiest conditions of his life (Hollander 6).

Like Dante's life, the *Divine Comedy* describes a difficult journey that has more than its share of disappointments, hardships, and revelations. In fact, Dante's difficult experiences were his primary motivation for pursuing philosophy and writing. If Dante had not experienced the pain of lost love, the bitterness of political betrayal, and the longing for home, he may never have achieved such poetic

---

Writing Practice

Freewrite After spending many days researching their topic, students may feel overwhelmed and unsure of how to begin writing. Choose a class day when students will already have spent a good deal of time researching their topics, but will be unlikely to have started drafting. Have them put away all their books and other materials, leaving only a pen and a few sheets of paper on their desks. Then have them freewrite about their topic for fifteen minutes, drawing purely from memory. Remind them that they can go back and check specific facts later. This exercise will help them clarify their focus, and it will also suggest to them a natural, logical order in which to present their ideas.

greatness. His *Divine Comedy* demonstrates that personal difficulties can often be translated into works of supreme beauty.

Works Cited

Alighieri, Dante. <u>Inferno</u>. Trans. John Ciardi. New Brunswick: Rutgers UP, 1954.

"Dante." <u>Encyclopedia Britannica</u>. 2007. Encyclopedia Britannica Online. 23 Jan. 2007 <http://www.britannica.com/eb/article-22147>.

"Florence." <u>Encyclopedia Britannica</u>. 2007. Encyclopedia Britannica Online. 19 Jan. 2007 <http://www.britannica.com/eb/article-22454>.

Foster, Kenelm. "The Mind in Love: Dante's Philosophy." <u>Dante: A Collection of Critical Essays</u>. Ed. John Freccero. Englewood Cliffs: Prentice-Hall, 1965. 43–60.

"Guelf and Ghibelline." <u>Encyclopedia Britannica</u>. 2007. Encyclopedia Britannica Online. 23 Jan. 2007 <http://www.britannica.com/eb/article-9038359>.

Hollander, Robert. <u>Dante: A Life in Works</u>. New Haven: Yale UP, 2001.

Quinones, Ricardo J. <u>Dante Alighieri</u>. Updated ed. Twayne's World Authors Series. New York: Simon & Schuster Macmillan, 1998.

Reynolds, Barbara. <u>Dante: The Poet, the Political Thinker, the Man</u>. Emeryville: Shoemaker & Hoard, 2006.

Salvadori, Giuseppina T., and Bernice L. Lewis, trans. <u>Dante: His Life, His Times, His Works</u>. New York: American Heritage, 1968.

Stade, George, ed. "Dante Alighieri." <u>European Writers: Selected Authors</u>. Vol. 1. New York: Scribner, 1992. 411–415.

Exposition

Conclusion
What makes this conclusion effective?

Variety of Sources
How might this encyclopedia entry have been helpful to the writer?

Reliable Sources
What indicates that this source is reliable?

Writing Workshop

Biographical Investigation

Teach

Writing Skills

Conclusion Possible answer: *The conclusion is effective because it restates the idea that the difficulties Dante experienced in his life influenced the* **Divine Comedy,** *and it ends with a general insight about the relationship between suffering and creativity.*

Variety of Sources Answer: *Encyclopedias provide background information on unfamiliar topics—in this case, the city of Florence.*

Reliable Sources Answer: *It is written by a scholar and appears in an anthology from a reputable publisher.*

Learning Objectives
Write a biographical investigation. (SE)
Use the writing process. (SE)
Freewrite. (TE)

Advanced Learners/Pre-AP

DIFFERENTIATED INSTRUCTION

Primary Sources Point out that the writer of the workshop model uses an additional primary source by Dante, the *Convivio*, to support the points that he or she makes about the *Divine Comedy*. Encourage advanced learners to take a similar approach, reading widely in their chosen author's body of works. They may find that other works provide insight into the author's life that will help students understand the primary work they are researching. They may also find interesting contrasts or contradictions among the author's works, which might help them develop a thesis for their paper.

Writing Workshop

Teach

Writing Skills

Revising Ask students to work in pairs and to identify parts of each other's papers that are confusing or unclear. **Say:** If your partner is confused by a concept in your paper, try explaining it to him or her orally. Have your partner jot down what you say. This will help you clarify your own ideas and provide you with simpler phrasing to use in your paper.

Writer's Technique ☆

Transitions The workshop model exemplifies how a writer can use transitions to guide readers from one idea to the next. Nearly every paragraph in the model begins by referencing an idea mentioned in the previous paragraph—sometimes to explore another aspect of that idea and sometimes to create a point of contrast for a new idea. These transitions serve as guideposts to show where the essay has been and where it is going.

Traits of Strong Writing

Include these traits of strong writing to express your ideas effectively.

Ideas

Organization

Voice

Word Choice

Sentence Fluency

Conventions

Presentation

For more information on using the Traits of Strong Writing, see also pages R28–R30.

Word Choice

This academic vocabulary word appears in the workshop model.

primary (prī'mer´ē) *adj.* first or greatest in importance; *Dante's primary inspiration was his love for Beatrice.* Using academic vocabulary may help strengthen your writing. Try to use one or two academic vocabulary words in your paper. See the complete list on pages R83–R85.

LOG ON ▶ **Literature** Online

Writing and Research For editing and publishing tools, go to glencoe.com and enter QuickPass code GLW6053u5.

Revise

Peer Review Have a peer review your draft to identify its strengths and weaknesses. Use the checklist below to evaluate your own writing.

Checklist

☑ Do you begin with a well-defined thesis statement?

☑ Do you connect information about the author's life to his or her writing?

☑ Do you include direct quotations and cite sources accurately?

☑ Do you provide your own insights on the topic?

▶ Focus Lesson

Coherent Paragraphs

As you revise, delete unimportant details, rearrange the order of ideas, or improve transitions to make a paragraph flow better.

Draft:

By most accounts, Dante began writing the *Comedy* to sustain and comfort himself in the first years of his exile. *Though his exile was painful, it led to several positive developments in his life. The solitude afforded him the opportunity to resume his writing.* From 1312 on, he found patronage in the courts of several noblemen (Hollander 6), a turn of events that provided him with a new level of stability and security. . . . *Dante's death, at the age of 56, was caused by malarial fever (Hollander 4).*

Revision:

Though Dante's exile was painful, it led to several positive developments in his life. First,[1] the solitude afforded him the opportunity to resume his writing.[2] By most accounts, he began writing the *Comedy* to sustain and comfort himself in the first years of his exile. *Then,[1]* from 1312 on, he found patronage in the courts of several noblemen (Hollander 6), a turn of events that provided him with a new level of stability and security. . . . ~~Dante's death, at the age of 56, was caused by malarial fever (Hollander 4).[3]~~

1: Link ideas with transitional phrases   **2: Improve the flow of ideas**   **3: Delete unrelated details**

Writing Practice

Use Apostrophes with Possessives

Write the following sentences from the workshop model on the board:

The loss of Beatrice influenced Dante's religious and philosophical development.

The hardships and triumphs of authors' lives often become the foundations for their fiction.

Remind students that they should use an apostrophe and an *s* to form the possessive of any singular noun—even a singular noun that ends with an *s*. (Some sources make an exception for classical names, such as Odysseus and Sisyphus.) However, they should use an apostrophe alone to form the possessive of a plural noun that ends in *s*. For practice, have them correct the following sentences:

Miguel de Cervantes' works are still read today. *(Miguel de Cervantes's works are still read today.)*

Leo Tolstoys' story is about a peasant named Pakhom. *(Leo Tolstoy's story is about a peasant named Pakhom.)*

Many poet's life experiences influence their writing. *(Many poets' life experiences influence their writing.)*

Then have students go through their own papers and correct any errors with apostrophes.

Edit and Proofread

Get It Right When you have completed the final draft of your research report, proofread it for errors in grammar, usage, mechanics, and spelling. Refer to the Language Handbook, pages R40–R59, as a guide.

> **Focus Lesson**

Commas

Commas are often used to separate transitional words and phrases. Use commas after introductory expressions (at the beginning of a sentence) and on either side of interrupters (in the middle of a sentence).

Original: *Like Dante's life* is an introductory transitional phrase.

Like Dante's life the Divine Comedy describes a difficult journey that has more than its share of disappointments, hardships, and revelations.

Improved: Add a comma after the introductory transitional phrase.

Like Dante's life, the Divine Comedy describes a difficult journey that has more than its share of disappointments, hardships, and revelations.

Original: The transitional word *however* is an interrupter.

Well before Dante wrote the Divine Comedy however, he became involved in the political life of Florence.

Solution: Add another comma before the interrupter.

Well before Dante wrote the Divine Comedy, however, he became involved in the political life of Florence.

Present/Publish

Final Check Before turning in your paper, check that it is at least 1,000 words. Make sure all your in-text citations are in the proper format and include an alphabetical works cited list with full bibliographic information for each of your sources (see pages R35–R37). You may wish to bind your research report in a folder with a cover sheet that gives the title of the paper and your name. Check with your teacher for additional presentation guidelines, such as page numbering and margins.

Exposition

Peer Review Tips

If you review a classmate's essay, look for their thesis, main points, and supporting details.

- Circle his or her thesis statement in pencil.
- Use sticky notes to point out the topic sentence in each paragraph.
- Underline the supporting details for each main point.

Word-Processing Tip

If you are typing your essay on a computer, use a professional font style. Make sure it is properly sized and easy to read. Many creative fonts are appropriate for large posters, but can be difficult to read in smaller sizes.

Writer's Portfolio

Place a clean copy of your research report in your portfolio to review later.

 Writing Workshop

Biographical Investigation

Teach

Writing Skills

Editing and Proofreading
Write on the board: Try to avoid miss spelling worlds. **Ask:** What is wrong with this sentence? *(The word* misspelling *is written incorrectly as two words; the word "words" is written incorrectly as* worlds.*)* **Say:** The spell-check feature in a word processing program would find no errors in this sentence, because miss, spelling, and worlds are all spelled correctly. This is an example of the importance of careful proofreading.

Presenting Encourage students to include relevant visual aids with their final paper. These might include timelines, photographs, or maps. Remind them that any visuals they include should be accompanied by a caption that explains the visuals' meaning and relevance.

Learning Objectives
Write a biographical investigation. (SE)
Use the writing process. (SE)
Use apostrophes with possessives. (TE)

Approaching Level
DIFFERENTIATED INSTRUCTION

 Peer Review Less proficient readers may lack the self-confidence to offer helpful criticism to their peers. Encourage them to be confident in their abilities. Explain that they can judge the clarity of any research paper by how well they understand it. Group students of varied reading abilities. Have them read their reports out loud to each other and offer suggestions on the parts that need clarification.

Advanced Learners/Pre-AP
DIFFERENTIATED INSTRUCTION

Reflection The Peruvian writer Mario Vargas Llosa has said that even the most inventive writers can only tell stories based on their own stories. After students have handed in the final draft of their paper, some of them may be interested in reflecting upon whether or not their research supports Llosa's statement. Have them write their ideas in a brief paragraph.

Focus

Summary

In this workshop, students will learn techniques for planning, rehearsing, and delivering a multimedia presentation to the class.

Teach

Incorporate Technology Advise students not to use a higher level of technology than that with which they are comfortable. Struggling with technology may distract them from developing the spoken component of their presentations. Remind them that a low-tech presentation, if done well, can be just as impressive as a high-tech one.

 For help with creating presentations, see Student Presentation Builder on StudentWorks Plus.

 For Speaking, Listening, and Viewing activities and rubric, see Unit 5 Teaching Resources Book, pp. 315–318.

Learning Objectives

For pages 1092–1095

In this workshop, you will focus on the following objectives:

Listening and Speaking: Selecting print and nonprint media for the purpose, occasion, and audience to develop into a formal presentation. Selecting and using appropriate available technologies to enhance communication and achieve a purpose.

Workshop Model

In this workshop, note the examples used from a multimedia presentation titled "Suffering and Creativity: The Life of Dante Alighieri." You might try out some of the techniques shown in the multimedia presentation you create.

Real-World Connection

Many museums present multimedia exhibits. Try visiting a virtual or online museum for ideas and inspiration before you begin your presentation.

Speaking, Listening, and Viewing Workshop

Multimedia Presentation

Literature Connection The *Divine Comedy* endures as a classic partly because of its sights and sounds: Paolo and Francesca swirling through a whirlwind; Satan silently beating his wings; Beatrice radiating beauty. In this workshop, you will select and combine sights and sounds to transform your biographical investigation report into a multimedia presentation.

Assignment

Plan and deliver a multimedia presentation of your biographical investigation report. As you develop your presentation, keep your audience and purpose in mind.

Audience: classmates and teacher

Purpose: to inform and describe; to engage

Plan Your Presentation

A multimedia presentation combines text, sound, and images (art, photos, video clips, animation, and print). Multimedia presentations include narrated slide or transparency presentations, Web sites, and Web casts.

The first step in planning your presentation is finding out what kind of equipment is available at your school. The answers to the following questions will help you decide what are some possibilities for your presentation:

- Does your school have digital or video cameras, screens, or projectors available for student use?
- Are there computers available? Do they have sufficient memory for video or large graphics programs?
- What kinds of software are available? For example, are there photo, animation, or multimedia authorship programs?
- Will the equipment be available for sufficient preparation and practice time? Will the equipment be available on the date of your presentation?

The chart on the next page shows some options for your presentation and the types of equipment each requires.

Speaking, Listening, and Viewing Practice

Select Media Remind students that multimedia presentations incorporate three types of media: text, sound, and images. Draw a three-column chart like this one on the board:

Text	Sound	Images

Then have students list examples of media that fit into each of the three categories. (*Possible answers: Text: bulleted lists, captions, quotations; Sound: music, sound effects, audio clips of interviews; Images: photographs, paintings, maps.*) Encourage students to use a variety of types of media from each category in their presentations. However, caution students that different types of media can also distract from or contradict one another if combined carelessly.

Ways to Create a Multimedia Presentation

	Equipment	Application
Low-tech	Camera, slide or overhead projector, and tape recorder	Use 35-mm slides or overhead transparencies for the visuals—images or text, or images with text.
	Computer with speakers, monitor, and microphone	Use presentation software to create a computer-based slide show combining text, graphics, images, and sound.
High-tech	Computer with speakers, monitor, microphone, digital camera, video camera, and scanner	Use a hypertext program to combine text, graphics, images, and sounds to create a series of "cards" containing hyperlinks that make different sequences possible.

Choose Your Media

Once you decide on a type of presentation, reread your biographical investigation report. Return to your outline. Add ideas to it for ways to present the information or enhance the information by means of images and sound.

I. Introduction
  Dramatic reading of my introduction
  Display thesis statement

II. Dante's pain over lost love
  A. Beatrice as cause of grief
    Fine art rendering of Beatrice
    Religious music of the 14th century?
  B. After Beatrice's death, intense period of study and learning
    Images of study, book learning
    Illuminated manuscript from c. 1300?
  C. Love of Beatrice becomes love of philosophy

III. Dante's political disappointments
  A. Strife between Black and White Guelfs
  B. Hatred of Pope Boniface's policies
    Drawing of Pope Boniface
    Minor chords or dissonant sounds

IV. Dante's exile from Florence
  A. Loneliness and difficulty
  B. Benefits from exile
    Map showing Florence and exile

V. Conclusion

Select Appropriate Media

To write your biographical investigation report, you used criteria to select only objective, reliable, and valid sources. Subject your media to the same careful evaluation. Determine whether the writer or sponsor is an authority and why the work was created. Look for clues that tell you the work was checked carefully or edited before posting, publication, or release.

Find Media

Use search engines and databases to find your sounds and images. Check with your school and public librarians to learn about subscription databases or other sources of free, downloadable audio and video.

 Literature Online

Speaking, Listening, and Viewing For project ideas, templates, and presentation tips, go to glencoe.com and enter QuickPass code GLW6053u5.

Teach

Logical Order Say: The student in the model has chosen to present ideas in the same order in which they appear in his or her biographical investigation paper. You may find that a different order better suits your purpose. Encourage students to begin their presentations with a memorable anecdote or image and to present their ideas in an order that makes sense thematically, even if it is not the same order they follow in their papers.

Learning Objectives
Select appropriate media for a presentation. (SE)
Use logical order. (TE)

Approaching Level
DIFFERENTIATED INSTRUCTION

Using Media Struggling students may find it overwhelming to incorporate many different types of media into a single presentation. These students may benefit from a more limited assignment. Suggest that they choose just one type of media—for example, music or photographs—to accompany the spoken portion of their presentations. Then work with them to select media that are appropriate for their purposes.

Advanced Learners/Pre-AP
DIFFERENTIATED INSTRUCTION

Analyzing Media Effects Remind students of the power of technology to sway audiences. Encourage advanced students to reflect upon the following questions as they prepare their presentations: How can combinations of text, sound, and images be manipulative? How might such combinations be used to mislead or even deceive viewers? Explain to students that it is important to

consider such questions when creating a multimedia presentation, regardless of if its purpose is to inform, to entertain, or to persuade.

Teach

Transitions Caution students using slide projectors or pre-sentation software to avoid long stretches of silence between slides. They should instead use transi-tional sentences to help guide the audience from one slide to the next. Remind them that transitional narration can also help disguise any delays or minor technical glitches they may encounter.

Cultural History ☆

Medieval Music Medieval music, like medieval literature, was heavily influenced by the traditions of the Christian church. One of the most important musical developments of the Middle Ages was that of polyphony—the sounding of two or more tones at the same time. This development grew out of the chants that were performed during the Catholic mass.

Skills Practice

SMALL GROUP

Compare and Contrast Have each student select a small por-tion of his or her presentation (perhaps a single slide) and substitute new sounds for the old ones. Then have students divide into small groups and share the new and old versions with their peers. Have students discuss how the new sounds change the meaning. For example, playing triumphant, cheerful music while discussing Dante's attitude toward Pope

1094

Avoid Plagiarism
Correctly credit each image, video clip, and sound, along with all your print sources, in your Works Cited list. (See pages R34–37 for standardized citation styles.)

Develop Your Presentation

Follow these steps to build your presentation.

- *Focus on your purpose.* Your main purpose is to inform. All the sounds and images should clearly and accurately present main ideas that explain your thesis and give strong support to back it up.

- *Make your thesis clear.* Because your thesis is the most important idea you will present, consider displaying your thesis at the beginning of your presentation and restating it at the end.

- *Remember the audience and occasion.* Think about other ways to help your audience understand and follow your presentation. If you are using unfamiliar or technical terms, think about explaining them. Consider using diagrams, maps, graphs, or charts.

- *Write your narration.* Remember that, in most cases, your images and sounds will not speak for themselves. Create a narration that clearly conveys your main ideas and helps your audience make links between the different parts of your presentation.

- *Edit for conciseness.* Add interest and information where needed. Delete unnecessary or distracting ideas, images, and sounds.

Organize Your Presentation

Next, create a storyboard. Draw one frame of the storyboard for each slide, card, or transparency you will use. Begin with a title and author frame, and end with a Works Cited frame that includes all your research sources, as well all your visual and sound sources. In the remainder of the storyboard frames, list in order the ideas for the images, sounds, and text you will use.

• title • Gustav Doré illustration <u>Medieval religious music</u> ☆	• thesis <u>bring music down</u> • image of Dante	• image of Beatrice • dramatic reading—quote from Stade tell main idea and details <u>Medieval religious music</u>	• page from an illuminated manuscript • dramatic reading—quote from *Convivio* tell main idea and details
• picture of Boniface or Guelfs <u>clashing sounds/minor chords</u> tell main idea/details	• title page of *Divine Comedy* narrate main idea and details <u>glorious/celebratory religious music c. 1300</u>	• dramatic reading of quotation from *Dante: His Life* • map showing exile tell main idea and details	• thesis • Works Cited <u>music from opening frame</u>

Boniface would convey quite a different impression than playing minor chords and dissonant sounds. Have students discuss which combination of media seems more appropriate in each case.

Here are two examples of slides based on ideas mapped out in the model storyboard.

"Suffering and Creativity" The Life of Dante Alighieri

by Silvia Diaz

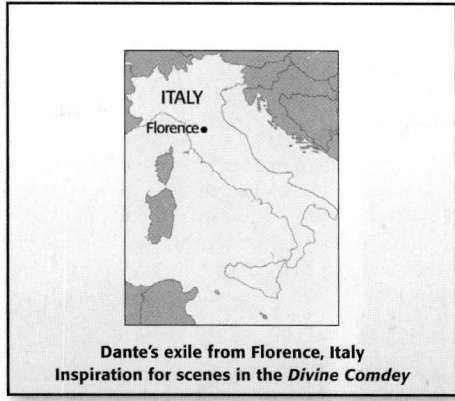

Dante's exile from Florence, Italy
Inspiration for scenes in the *Divine Comdey*

Rehearse and Deliver Your Presentation

A successful multimedia presentation depends, in large part, on timing. Rehearse several times in order to be sure that all your images, sound, and narration work smoothly together. Once you have the timing down, give your presentation to one or two classmates or family members. Find out whether they can state your thesis and the main ideas that support it. Use their feedback to help you make adjustments to your pace, to your volume, or to specific slides.

As you rehearse and deliver your presentation, keep the presentation techniques below in mind. When you are an audience member, keep the listening and viewing techniques in mind.

Techniques for Delivering a Multimedia Presentation

Presentation Techniques	Listening and Viewing Techniques
☑ **Pace** Because your audience is not familiar with your research or your images, allow more time to convey information.	☑ **Posture** Show your enthusiasm in the presentation by sitting upright in your seat and keeping your head up. Try not to doodle, tap, or fidget.
☑ **Volume** Your audience must be able to hear you at all times. Be sure your music and sound effects do not drown out or overpower your words.	☑ **Movement and Facial Expression** Maintain a look on your face that says, "I'm interested." As appropriate, use subtle movements such as a nod to show you are engaged.

Evaluation Checklist

☑ Does the presentation flow smoothly and keep you interested from beginning to end?

☑ Is the thesis clear? Are the main ideas that support it clear?

☑ Do the images and sounds work well to convey or complement the thesis and main ideas?

☑ Does the presentation reflect careful editing and rehearsing?

SPEAKING, LISTENING, AND VIEWING WORKSHOP **1095**

English Learners

DIFFERENTIATED INSTRUCTION

Beginning English learners may wish to prerecord themselves speaking and incorporate this audio into their presentations, rather than actually speaking in front of the class. Prerecording will reduce some of the anxiety associated with presenting, and will allow students multiple chances to get pronunciations right in a low-pressure setting. Offer these students assistance with word meanings and pronunciations before they make their recordings.

Advanced Learners/Pre-AP

DIFFERENTIATED INSTRUCTION

Presenting Encourage students who are proficient with technology to upload their presentations to your school's website. Alternatively, have them contribute an electronic copy of their presentation to the school library to serve as a resource for other students.

Teach

Active Listening and Viewing

Have each student write a brief paragraph evaluating his or her performance as an audience member. Have students refer to the Listening and Viewing Techniques checklist on this page when evaluating themselves.

[APPROACHING] Those students who have difficulty focusing on their peers' presentations may benefit from having their teacher convert the Presentation Techniques checklist into a feedback form that they can fill out. For each of the techniques on the list, have them assign their peers a rating between 1 and 5. This will help them focus on a purpose for listening and viewing.

Authenticity
Remind students to evaluate the images and sounds they use for historical authenticity. A student focusing on an author from the Renaissance, for example, should avoid using medieval music or art in his or her presentation unless there is a specific justification for doing so. Likewise, a student focusing on an author who lived two hundred years ago should avoid using video footage that contains distracting contemporary objects.

Learning Objectives
Select appropriate media for a presentation. (SE)
Use transitions. (TE)
Compare and contrast. (TE)
Listen actively. (TE)
Evaluate historical authenticity of media. (TE)

Independent Reading

Literature of the Region

T HE LITERATURE OF MODERN EUROPE PRESENTS SHARP CRITIQUES OF SOCIETY AND poignant responses to war. From the mid-1600s through the 1700s, authors such as the French playwright Molière mocked the elitism of the upper classes. In the eighteenth and nineteenth centuries, authors responded to the rise of industrial cities and a range of political turmoil and revolutions. The greatest turning points in the literature of modern Europe, however, were formed by World War I and World War II. To mirror the effects of the wars, authors such as Primo Levi wrote with gritty realism. Postwar European authors abandoned tradition and experimented with form.

The Misanthrope and Other Plays

☆ **Molière**

The Misanthrope (1666), a social satire, tells the story of Célimène and her many fickle and insecure suitors. Love triangles abound, and like many comedies, it ends with the announcement of a marriage. Commissioned by King Louis XIV of France, Molière wrote plays performed for the royal court. He borrowed from the Italian *commedia dell'arte* of the sixteenth century. Based on improvisations, *commedia* used masked characters in stock situations. In many of the plays in this compilation, readers will come across familiar characters in familiar situations.

A Doll's House

Henrik Ibsen

A Doll's House (1879) tells the story of a bank manager named Torvald Helmer, his wife Nora, and their three young children. Nora secretly borrows money to save her husband's life and another character, Nils Krogstad, threatens to expose her. When Torvald learns of the loan, he scolds Nora and expresses his concern for his own reputation. Overwhelmed by Torvald's lack of faith in her, Nora leaves him and their children. The early productions of Ibsen's play shocked audiences and reflected a sharp break with tradition. Its realistic details and presentation of both a marital conflict and an independent woman has led many critics to call *A Doll's House* the first Modern drama.

Reading Practice

Evaluate As students read literature independently, tell them to pay attention to the opinions they form about the author's message and purpose, the characters' likeability, and the credibility of the plot. Remind students that making judgments involves evaluating the work critically; encourage students to keep notes about their judgments and the reasons for them. Point out that they may revise their judgments as they continue reading.

Focus

Summary

The purpose of this feature is to interest students in reading additional literature by European writers. Classic fiction, nonfiction, and drama by writers of the region are represented in the profiled works.

Teach

Literary History ☆

Molière's Death Molière's final play was called *The Imaginary Invalid*. In the play Molière acted the role of the hypochondriac. On February 17, 1673, while on stage for the play's fourth performance, Molière, coughing up blood, collapsed. After being carried home, he died of a pulmonary embolism. Since he had not received the sacraments before dying and never formally renounced his profession as an actor, a direct appeal had to be made to the king in order to allow his burial in a cemetery, even without a religious ceremony to accompany his burial.

To create customized reading lists from a database of more than 30,000 titles, use BookLink K-12 CD-ROM.

GLENCOE LITERATURE LIBRARY

Jane Eyre

Charlotte Brontë

Brontë meshes elements of Romanticism and Realism in this romantic tale of a poor, orphaned governess and her wealthy, brooding employer.

The Brothers Karamazov

Fyodor Dostoyevsky

The Brothers Karamazov is a tale of romance, murder, and exile involving Fyodor Karamozov and his four sons.

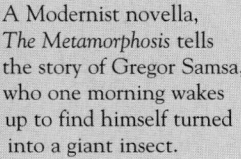

The Metamorphosis

Franz Kafka

A Modernist novella, *The Metamorphosis* tells the story of Gregor Samsa, who one morning wakes up to find himself turned into a giant insect.

CRITICS' CORNER

"Levi's more outstanding virtue is his compassionate understanding of how in these conditions men cease to be men, either give up the struggle or in devious ways win it, usually at the expense of their fellow men."

—G. F. Seddon

Survival in Auschwitz

Primo Levi

Italian-Jewish author Primo Levi survived life in a Nazi concentration camp, and related his experiences in his memoir *Survival in Auschwitz* (1947). When Nazi troops overtook Italy, Levi joined the resistance movement. Captured and deported to Auschwitz, he was forced into slave labor working in a synthetic rubber factory. In this memoir, he takes a detached approach to life under the Nazi regime.

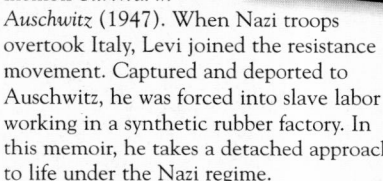 **Interview an Author**

Read one of the books on these pages and prepare a hypothetical interview with the author. Be sure to prepare a list of questions based on the characters, themes, or imagery in the book. You can also ask questions about experiences in the author's life that might have influenced his or her writing. Finally, do some research on the Internet or at a library to find answers to your questions. Perform your interview for your class, asking a partner to play the role of the author.

Approaching Level

DIFFERENTIATED INSTRUCTION

Visualize Setting To help less proficient readers better visualize the works they are reading, have them pay special attention to the memoir's, play's, and novel's settings. Remind them that a work of literature's setting is its time and place and that the setting can be important to the plot. Encourage each student to draw a picture of one important setting from the work he or she has chosen.

Advanced Learners/Pre-AP

DIFFERENTIATED INSTRUCTION

Research Setting Have advanced learners do some historical research about the time period in which their works of literature are set. Each should research the cultural and historical setting of his or her chosen work. Researching a piece's setting will help students understand the characters' environment and social milieu.

Independent Reading

Teach

Interview an Author

Students' interviews should

- include a list of questions that draw attention to issues in the author's life and works
- include appropriate research to answer those questions

Literary History ☆

Brontë's Failures For Charlotte Brontë, the path to success was not an easy one. Her first published work was a collection of poetry she and her sisters Emily and Anne—both of whom were later well-reputed novelists—wrote. Only two copies were sold. The following year, the sisters set out to publish a three-volume collection containing a novel by each. A firm agreed to publish Anne and Emily's novels, but refused Charlotte's novel, *The Professor.* It was never published in her lifetime.

Glencoe Literature Library

Glencoe Literature Library offers an extensive collection of hardcover books that help you encourage your students to read independently. Choose among more than 120 full-length literary works—novels, novellas, plays, and nonfiction. Each book includes related readings from a broad range of genres. Go to glencoe.com for more information.

 For access to all study guides for the Glencoe Literature Library, see the Literature Library Teacher Resources CD-ROM.

1097

Assessment

English-Language Arts

Focus

Bellringer Options

Daily Language Practice
Transparency 105

Or say: "No matter how hard you study as a student, if you don't know how to go about taking a test, whether multiple choice or essay, you won't score the highest possible mark." Have students brainstorm a list of key test-taking strategies that can help them on tests. *(Possible answers include: skimming passages, determining main ideas, eliminating distracters, and making educated guesses)*

Teach

Assessment

Tell students that the Assessment feature will provide reinforcement in general test-taking strategies and will test them on many of the skills and vocabulary words taught in this unit. Students will read a fiction selection and will answer context, comprehension, and inference questions. Then they will choose answers for ten sentence-completion items and ten sentence-improvement items. Finally, they will respond to a short analytical essay prompt.

 To create custom assessments online, go to Progress Reporter Online Assessment.

 To create custom assessments using software, use ExamView Assessment Suite.

1098

Assessment

English–Language Arts

Reading: Fiction

Carefully read the following passage. Use context clues to help you define any words with which you are unfamiliar. Pay close attention to **themes, cultural context, author's purpose,** and the use of **literary devices**. Then, on a separate sheet of paper, answer the questions on page 1100.

from *Crime and Punishment* by Fyodor Dostoevsky

Towards the end of a sultry afternoon early in July a young man came out of his little room in Stolyarny Lane and turned slowly and somewhat irresolutely in the direction of Kamenny Bridge.

5 He had been lucky enough to escape an encounter with his landlady on the stairs. His little room, more like a cupboard than a place to live in, was tucked away under the roof of the high five-storied building. The landlady, who let him the room and provided him with dinners and service,

10 occupied a flat on the floor below, and every time he went out he was forced to pass the door of her kitchen, which nearly always stood wide open. He went past each time with an uneasy, almost frightened, feeling that made him frown with shame. He was heavily in debt to his landlady

15 and shrank from meeting her.

It was not that he was a cowed or naturally timorous person, far from it; but he had been for some time in an almost morbid state of irritability and tension. He had cut himself off from everybody and withdrawn so completely

20 into himself that he now shrank from every kind of contact. He was crushingly poor, but he no longer felt the oppression of his poverty. For some time he had ceased to concern himself with everyday affairs. He was not really afraid of any landlady, whatever plots he might think she

25 was hatching against him, but to have to stop on the stairs and listen to all her chatter about trivialities in which he refused to take any interest, all her complaints, threats, and insistent demands for payment, and then to have to extricate himself, lying and making excuses—no, better to

30 creep downstairs as softly as a cat and slip out unnoticed.

Reading Practice

Daily Practice Tell students that reading a little every day not only helps build their vocabulary but also sharpens their critical-thinking skills. Remind them that this daily reading practice will give them excellent preparation for the type of reading passages they'll encounter on the SAT and ACT. Tell students that one of the best ways to improve their writing is to read the works of great writers, such as Chinua Achebe and Katherine Mansfield, as well as a variety of periodicals.

This time, however, he reached the street feeling
astonished at the intensity of his fear of his landlady.
'To think that I can contemplate such a terrible act
and yet be afraid of such trifles,' he thought, and he smiled
35   strangely. 'Hm…yes…a man holds the fate of the world in
his two hands, and yet, simply because he is afraid, he just lets
things drift—that is a truism…I wonder what men are
most afraid of…Any new departure, and especially a *new
word*—that is what they fear most of all…But I am talking
40   too much. That's why I don't act, because I am always
talking. Or perhaps I talk so much just because I can't act. I
have got into a habit of babbling to myself during this last
month, while I have been lying in a corner for days on end,
thinking…fantastic nonsense. And why have I come out
45   now? Can I really be capable of *that*? Am I really serious?
No, of course I'm not serious. So I am just amusing myself
with fancies, children's games? Yes, perhaps I am only
playing a game.'
The heat in the streets was stifling. The stuffiness,
50   the jostling crowds, the bricks and mortar, scaffolding and
dust everywhere, and that peculiar summer stench so
familiar to everyone who cannot get away from St.
Petersburg into the country, all combined to aggravate the
disturbance of the young man's nerves. The intolerable
55   reek from the public houses, so numerous in that part of the
city, and the sight of the drunken men encountered at every
turn, even though this was not a holiday, completed the
mournfully repellant picture. An expression of the deepest
loathing passed across the young man's delicate features.
60   (He was, by the way, a strikingly handsome young man,
with fine dark eyes, brown hair, and a slender well-knit
figure, taller than the average.) Soon, however, he relapsed
again into profound thought, or rather into a sort of
abstraction, and continued on his way in complete and
65   willful unconsciousness of his surroundings. Once or twice
he muttered something to himself in a manner that, as he
had just confessed, had grown habitual with him. He
himself realized that at times his thoughts were confused
and that he was very weak; he had eaten practically nothing
70   for two days.

Reading Strategy

Close Reading In reading
comprehension sections, students
may be tempted to hurry through
a selected passage in order to get
to the questions more quickly. Tell
students that slowing down to
read a passage carefully will help
them to absorb information more
effectively. When they reach the
questions that pertain to the passage they've read, they will be better prepared and more confident in
choosing answers.

Approaching Level

DIFFERENTIATED INSTRUCTION

Manage Your Time Tell students that on
the SAT, all of the questions are worth the
same number of points. Students should
not take a lot of time on any one question
because doing so might leave them with
insufficient time to finish the test. Instead,
they should skip any question that takes too
much time and return to it if they have extra
time at the end of the test. It is better to
miss one question and finish the test than

it is to spend lots of time figuring out one
question, thereby risking missing multiple
questions at the test's end.

Tell students they should be sure to mark
any questions they have skipped so that
they can, with any extra time, efficiently go
back to these questions. Also, tell them it is
very important to check their answer sheets
periodically to make sure that their answer
corresponds to the correct question.

Assessment

English-Language Arts

Assess

1. D is the correct answer. There is no evidence that the man is cruel, so **A** is incorrect. While the author states the young man is poor, there is no evidence he recently lost money, so **B** is incorrect. The author states he was not "a cowed or naturally timorous person," so **C** is incorrect. The young man's shyness is a result of an unsettling change in his mental state, so **E** is incorrect. `DOK 4`

2. B is the correct answer. The context connects the word *timorous* to the young man having "cut himself off from everybody." `DOK 2`

3. E is the correct answer. This statement shows the young man's fear had reached a new pinnacle. `DOK 1`

4. D is the correct answer. The young man feels he is pathetic for being afraid of the insignificant prospect of meeting his landlady, and consequently feels self-pity. The young man's strange smile and the contradiction between his fear of his landlady and his capacity for contemplating "a terrible act" show the irony of the situation. `DOK 4`

1. What does the young man's behavior toward his landlady suggest?
   - **(A)** That he is a cruel and intolerant man
   - **(B)** That he has recently lost a great deal of money
   - **(C)** That he is antisocial by nature
   - **(D)** That there has been an unsettling change in his mental state
   - **(E)** That he is painfully shy

2. In line 16, "timorous" most nearly means
   - **(A)** outgoing
   - **(B)** fearful
   - **(C)** dishonest
   - **(D)** emotional
   - **(E)** depraved

3. The statement in lines 31–32 serves primarily to
   - **(A)** show that the young man has been steadily going crazy
   - **(B)** suggest that the intensity of his fear of his landlady is a positive force in his life
   - **(C)** justify the young man's actions
   - **(D)** portray the young man in a negative light
   - **(E)** show that this particular instance was especially frightening for the young man

4. The young man's comment in lines 33–34 ("To think…trifles") has a tone of
   - **(A)** playful surprise
   - **(B)** total detachment
   - **(C)** strict formality
   - **(D)** ironic self-pity
   - **(E)** utter despair

5. According to the young man, what do men fear most?
   - **(A)** A new word
   - **(B)** Truisms
   - **(C)** People who babble to themselves
   - **(D)** Fantastic nonsense
   - **(E)** Death

6. The primary purpose of the fifth paragraph is to
   - **(A)** show the abysmal conditions in which the young man lived
   - **(B)** offer details that will encourage the reader to sympathize with the young man
   - **(C)** show the young man's interior monologue, which is an example of his feverish mind at work
   - **(D)** prove that the young man has completely lost his mind
   - **(E)** suggest that the landlady's strict demeanor has driven the young man mad

7. What is the main idea in lines 49–54 ("The heat…nerves")?
   - **(A)** The streets of St. Petersburg are stiflingly hot.
   - **(B)** Many inhabitants of St. Petersburg do not have enough money to leave during the summer.
   - **(C)** The summer stench and dust are unbearable.
   - **(D)** The bricks, mortar, and scaffolding show there is construction in St. Petersburg.
   - **(E)** The heat, stuffiness, crowds, bricks and mortar, scaffolding and dust, and stench combine to further irritate the young man's nerves.

8. The author's use of a parenthetical statement in lines 60–62 ("He was…average") serves primarily to
   - **(A)** show that the protagonist is very popular
   - **(B)** contrast the protagonist's attractive appearance with his confused mental state
   - **(C)** suggest that the protagonist is on the path to recovery
   - **(D)** emphasize the protagonist's flair for drama
   - **(E)** de-emphasize the protagonist's reveries

5. A is the correct answer. In lines 37–39, the young man says, "I wonder what men are most afraid of…Any new departure, and especially a new word— that is what they fear most." `DOK 1`

6. C is the correct answer. In the fifth paragraph, the young man mutters to himself. This interior monologue gives the reader an example of what the author has already explained—that the young man is in "an almost morbid state of irritability and tension." `DOK 2`

7. E is the correct answer. The main idea of these lines is that all of the problems in St. Petersburg, such as the stench and the jostling crowds, exacerbate the young man's irritability and stress level. `DOK 2`

8. B is the correct answer. The young man is not popular, so **A** is incorrect.

Nothing in the parenthetical statement suggests that the young man is on the path to recovery, so **C** is incorrect. The parenthetical statement comments on the young man's appearance, not his demeanor, so **D** is incorrect. The statement does not emphasize or de-emphasize the young man's reveries, so **E** is incorrect. `DOK 2`

Vocabulary Skills: Sentence Completion

For each item in the Vocabulary Skills section, choose the word or words that best complete the sentence. Write your answers on a separate sheet of paper.

1. Crying out in _____, the souls of the lustful drift through a whirlwind in Dante's *Inferno*.
   - **(A)** grudge
   - **(B)** torment
   - **(C)** respites
   - **(D)** scorn
   - **(E)** solitude

2. When he began to see Laura as a _____ earthly distraction, Petrarch stopped presenting her as a _____, goddess-like figure in his poetry.
   - **(A)** contrary…discourteous
   - **(B)** nautical…obsessed
   - **(C)** savage…rational
   - **(D)** mere…revered
   - **(E)** myriad…plaintive

3. Knights swore never to be _____, but to show politeness and _____ to their lords.
   - **(A)** rational…elasticity
   - **(B)** discourteous…fidelity
   - **(C)** chaste…solitude
   - **(D)** prudent…vivacity
   - **(E)** distorted…consternation

4. Because they were only given the least _____, most undesirable plots of land, Russian peasants had to live quite _____ for many years.
   - **(A)** arable…penuriously
   - **(B)** nimble…indiscriminately
   - **(C)** prudent…clemency
   - **(D)** contrary…distressed
   - **(E)** compulsory…asunder

5. Europe is home to _____ cultural groups, and there has often been strife and _____ between them.
   - **(A)** nimble…disillusion
   - **(B)** humane…presumption
   - **(C)** myriad…discord
   - **(D)** modest…elasticity
   - **(E)** compulsory…renown

6. Dante was _____ with Beatrice for many years, as evidenced by the repeated references to her in his work.
   - **(A)** obsessed
   - **(B)** plaintive
   - **(C)** undaunted
   - **(D)** compulsory
   - **(E)** discourteous

7. After he was deported from Russia for _____ the communist government, Aleksandr Solzhenitsyn sought _____ in the United States.
   - **(A)** reeling…abstinence
   - **(B)** consoling…seclusion
   - **(C)** negating…furrows
   - **(D)** disparaging…refuge
   - **(E)** deciphering…renown

8. Marie de France has received great _____ and praise for her well-crafted poems.
   - **(A)** anguish
   - **(B)** renown
   - **(C)** seclusion
   - **(D)** verdict
   - **(E)** discord

Assessment
English-Language Arts

Assess

1. **B** is the correct answer. **A, C, D,** and **E** make no sense in the context. `DOK 2`

2. **D** is the correct answer. The phrase *goddess-like figure* suggests that Laura was an object of worship. `DOK 2`

3. **B** is the correct answer. *Discourteousness* is the opposite of politeness. `DOK 2`

4. **A** is the correct answer. The word *undesirable* indicates the land was not very fertile. This would have caused poverty for the peasants who farmed it. `DOK 2`

5. **C** is the correct answer. **A, B, D,** and **E** make no sense in the context. The word *strife* indicates the ethnic groups have clashed. `DOK 2`

6. **A** is the correct answer. **B, C, D,** and **E** make no sense in the context. Dante was *obsessed*, or preoccupied, with Beatrice. `DOK 2`

7. **D** is the correct answer. Solzhenitsyn made *disparaging*, or negative, remarks about the government, and sought *refuge*, or safety in the United States. `DOK 2`

8. **B** is the correct answer. Marie de France has received great *renown*, or praise, for her well-crafted poems. `DOK 2`

Approaching Level

DIFFERENTIATED INSTRUCTION

Sentence Completion As students approach the sentence completion section on a test, they should consider the following tips in choosing an answer:

1. Predict: Before looking at the answer options, read the sentence and determine what sort of word could successfully fill the blank space.

2. Make your choice: Decide which answer choice best fits the blank or blanks. If you've already made a prediction based on the sentence, look to see if any of the answers matches your prediction or expresses the same idea as your prediction.

3. Read the sentence back: Check your answer by reading the sentence aloud with your word choice in place.

Assessment
English-Language Arts

Assess

1. **A** is the correct answer. Only **A** uses the past tense and places the adverb in the correct position. (DOK 1)

2. **C** is the correct answer. The verb form *has been* should be changed to *have been* in order to correspond with the subject. (DOK 1)

3. **E** is the correct answer. The nonessential appositive phrase should be set off with commas. (DOK 1)

4. **A** is the correct answer. The sentence is correct as written. (DOK 1)

5. **D** is the correct answer. The helping verb *is* should be changed to *are* to correspond with the subject of the sentence. (DOK 1)

6. **C** is the correct answer. In this sentence, a comma should separate only the adjectives *small* and *furry*. (DOK 1)

Grammar and Writing Skills:
Sentence Improvement

Read the following sentences carefully. Pay close attention to the writer's **sentence structure**, **transitions**, and use of **punctuation**. Then, on a separate sheet of paper, write the letter of the answer that correctly fixes each underlined portion.

1. Rosie the Riveter, an image that appeared on posters during World War II, quickly became a cultural icon.
   - **(A)** quickly became a cultural icon
   - **(B)** became quickly a cultural icon
   - **(C)** quickly become a cultural icon
   - **(D)** have become quickly a cultural icon
   - **(E)** quickly becoming a cultural icon

2. Many different portable audio devices has been used to play music over the years, including cassette players, CD players, and MP3 players.
   - **(A)** has been used to play music
   - **(B)** been used to play music
   - **(C)** have been used to play music
   - **(D)** should be used to play music
   - **(E)** is used to play music

3. The Golden Gate Bridge the second longest suspension bridge in the United States, connects San Francisco to Marin County.
   - **(A)** The Golden Gate Bridge the second longest suspension bridge in the United States,
   - **(B)** The Golden Gate Bridge the second, longest suspension bridge in the United States,
   - **(C)** The Golden Gate Bridge the second longest suspension bridge, in the United States,
   - **(D)** The Golden, Gate Bridge the second longest suspension bridge, in the United States,
   - **(E)** The Golden Gate Bridge, the second longest suspension bridge in the United States,

4. Wolfgang Amadeus Mozart wrote over 600 compositions before dying at the age of 35.
   - **(A)** before dying at the age of 35.
   - **(B)** before the age of 35 when he had been dying.
   - **(C)** dying before the age of 35.
   - **(D)** at the age of 35 dying.
   - **(E)** at the age of 35 when he had died.

5. Many different types of hot breakfast cereals, such as oatmeal, grits, and porridge, is eaten around the world.
   - **(A)** is eaten around the world.
   - **(B)** should be eaten around the world.
   - **(C)** has eaten around the world.
   - **(D)** are eaten around the world.
   - **(E)** have eaten around the world.

6. The Lhasa apso is a small furry dog originally bred in Tibet and now very popular in the United States.
   - **(A)** a small furry dog originally bred in Tibet and now very popular
   - **(B)** a small, furry dog, originally bred in Tibet and now very popular
   - **(C)** a small, furry dog originally bred in Tibet and now very popular
   - **(D)** a small furry dog, originally bred in Tibet and now very popular
   - **(E)** a small furry dog originally bred in Tibet, and now very popular

Speaking and Listening Practice

Read Aloud Have students read the sentences in this segment aloud to themselves. Then have them substitute each possible answer into the sentence, reading each variation aloud. They will often find that they can tell which answer is correct simply by noting how the sentences feel and sound when read aloud. Students should, when reading aloud, pay special attention to punctuation, which will dictate how the sentences are read.

Have five students read one of the sentences from this portion aloud, one reading the original sentence and the rest substituting in the possible answers B, C, D, and E. Have their classmates individually write down which sentence variation sounds correct to them. Then go over which is correct, explaining to the students why it is so.

7. Although salmon is not a traditional Japanese food, many American sushi chefs serve the fish in their maki rolls and <u>as sashimi; a slice of raw fish</u> accompanied by condiments.
   (A) as sashimi; a slice of raw fish
   (B) as sashimi, a slice of raw fish
   (C) as sashimi a slice of raw fish
   (D) like sashimi, a slice of raw fish
   (E) like sashimi; a slice of raw fish

8. Because fixed gear bicycles do not have a free wheel, riders do not have the luxury of <u>coasting; instead, they must pedal all the time.</u>
   (A) coasting; instead, they must pedal all the time.
   (B) coasting—instead they must pedal all the time.
   (C) coasting, instead they must be pedaling all the time.
   (D) coasting, instead; they must pedal all the time.
   (E) coasting; instead they must pedal all the time.

9. Swedish filmmaker Ingmar Bergman, perhaps best known for his stark portrayal of medieval Europe in "The Seventh Seal," <u>has died in 2007 at the age of 89.</u>
   (A) has died in 2007 at the age 89.
   (B) in 2007 has died at the age of 89.
   (C) dying at 89 in 2007.
   (D) died in 2007 at the age of 89.
   (E) at the age of 89, in 2007, had died.

10. The sticky note was created by accident when Dr. Spencer Silver made a <u>weak adhesive whose glue did not leave a residue.</u>
    (A) a weak adhesive whose glue did not leave a residue.
    (B) a weak adhesive which did not leave a glue.
    (C) a weak adhesive that did not leave a residue.
    (D) a weak adhesive that leave no residue.
    (E) a weak adhesive which leaves no residue.

Essay

Think carefully about the following excerpt and the writing assignment below.

"Too late to save your old father . . . You could have two rations of bread, two rations of soup . . .
   It was only a fraction of a second, but it left me feeling guilty. I ran to get some soup and brought it to my father."

—Elie Wiesel, from *Night*

Write an essay in which you analyze Elie Wiesel's internal conflict in *Night*. What factors cause his conflict? What values does the conflict illustrate? How is the conflict resolved, or is it left unresolved? Be sure to include specific examples from the text in your essay. As you write, keep in mind that your essay will be evaluated for **ideas, organization, voice, word choice, sentence fluency, conventions,** and **presentation**.

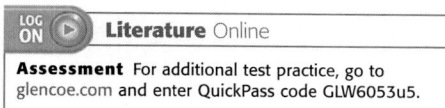

LOG ON ▶ **Literature** Online

Assessment For additional test practice, go to glencoe.com and enter QuickPass code GLW6053u5.

ASSESSMENT **1103**

Advanced Learners/Pre-AP

DIFFERENTIATED INSTRUCTION

Get Organized Tell students that, during a standardized test, they will have to organize themselves in order to write a successful essay. Advanced learners might have difficulties synthesizing their knowledge into a concise essay as well as determining which of their insights should be used and which should not. Making an outline will help students clarify and focus their essays. First, students should carefully read the question. Then, they should take notes on their ideas. They can use these notes to craft a thesis and make an outline of their essay. They should refer back to this outline as they write to make sure that they are staying on topic, proving their point, and using all the evidence at their disposal.

Assessment
English-Language Arts

Assess

7. **B** is the correct answer. "A slice of raw fish accompanied by condiments" is an appositive phrase that modifies *sashimi*. It should be separated from the word it modifies by a comma. If the appositive phrase completes a sentence, then a period or a semicolon would be necessary. ⬚ DOK 1

8. **A** is the correct answer. The sentence is correct as written. The second sentence, which begins with *instead*, builds on the idea presented in the first sentence, so separating them with a semicolon is correct. ⬚ DOK 1

9. **D** is the correct answer. The past tense should be used. ⬚ DOK 1

10. **C** is the correct answer. Use of the word *glue* is repetitive because *glue* and *adhesive* have the same meaning, so **A** and **B** are incorrect. The verb form *leaves*, not *leave*, corresponds with "a weak adhesive," so **D** is incorrect. "Leave no residue" is essential to the meaning of the sentence, so it should be introduced by the relative pronoun *that*, so **E** is incorrect. ⬚ DOK 1

Essay

Students' essays should
- analyze Wiesel's internal conflict
- include clearly stated main ideas with supporting evidence
- follow the conventions of standard English ⬚ DOK 3

Skills Scope and Sequence

Readability Scores Key: Dale-Chall/DRP/Lexile

PART 1: The Early Americas 3000 B.C.–A.D. 1900

Selections and Features	Literary Elements
Part Introduction pp. 1104–1117	Literary Periods **SE** p. 1114
The Art of Translation Cracking the Maya Code pp. 1118–1119	
Sacred Text *from* **The Popul Vuh,** translated by Dennis Tedlock **8.8/61/1120** pp. 1120–1129	Myth **SE** p. 1121 Imagery (review) **SE** p. 1128
Grammar Workshop p. 1130	
Folktale Coyote Finishes His Work, retold by Barry Lopez **4.4/53/860** pp. 1131–1135	Motif **SE** p. 1132
Journal *from* **The Voyage of Christopher Columbus,** by Christopher Columbus, translated by John Cummins **7.2/59/1160** pp. 1136–1147	Journal **SE** p. 1137 Setting (review) **SE** p. 1146
History *from* **The Broken Spears: The Aztec Account of the Conquest of Mexico,** edited by Miguel Leon-Portilla, translated by Lysander Kemp **6/56/810** pp. 1148–1160	Setting **SE** p. 1149 Point of View (review) **SE** p. 1159
Vocabulary Workshop p. 1161	
Literary History Literature of the Conquest Era pp. 1162–1163	Literary Genres **SE** p. 1162

Reading Skills and Strategies	Vocabulary	Writing Grammar	Speaking, Listening, Viewing
Evaluate Historical Influences **SE** p. 1110 Connect to the Literature **SE** p. 1117		Write a Short Story **TE** p. 1114 Write a Comparison-Contrast Essay **SE** p. 1117	View the Art **SE** p. 1104 Panel Discussion **SE** p. 1117
Understand Cultural and Historical Context **SE** p. 1118 Understand the Nature of Translation **SE** p. 1119			
Clarify Meaning **SE** p. 1121 Analyze Sensory Details **TE** p. 1122 Analyze Cultural Context **TE** p. 1124	Context Clues **SE** p. 1129 Academic Vocabulary **SE** p. 1129	Conduct Internet Research **SE** p. 1129 Write a Research Report **SE** p. 1129	View the Art **SE** p. 1126 Oral Report **SE** p. 1129
		Misplaced and Dangling Modifiers **SE** p. 1130	
Draw Conclusions About Culture **SE** p. 1132	Word Parts **SE** p. 1135	Write a Graphic Story **SE** p. 1135	
Recognize Bias **SE** p. 1137 Distinguish Fact and Opinion **TE** p. 1142	Word Usage **SE** p. 1146 Academic Vocabulary **SE** p. 1146	Write a Summary **SE** p. 1147 Commas with Appositives **SE** p. 1147	View the Art **SE** p. 1141 Discussion **SE** p. 1145
Analyze Cultural Context **SE** p. 1149 Analyze Sensory Details **TE** p. 1154	Analogies **SE** p. 1160 Academic Vocabulary **SE** p. 1160	Write Questions **SE** p. 1160 Write an Evaluation **SE** p. 1160 Write a Movie Scene **TE** p. 1158	View the Art **SE** p. 1153 Interview **SE** p. 1160
	Denotation and Connotation **SE** p. 1161		
Evaluate Historical Influences **SE** p. 1163 Connect to the Literature **SE** p. 1163			

Readability Scores Key: Dale-Chall/DRP/Lexile

PART 1: The Early Americas 3000 B.C.–A.D. 1900 *(continued)*

Selections and Features	Literary Elements
Poem Sonnet 145, by Sor Juana Inés de la Cruz, translated by Margaret Sayers Peden pp. 1164–1168	Metaphor **SE** p. 1165 Petrarchan Sonnet (review) **SE** p. 1167
Poem Two Countries, by José Martí, translated by Elinor Randall pp. 1169–1172	Juxtaposition **SE** p. 1170 Figurative Language **TE** p. 1170
Informational Text TIME: Who Were the First Americans? by Michael D. Lemonick and Andrea Dorfman 10/68/1280 pp. 1173–1177	

PART 2: The Modern Americas 1800–Present

Part Introduction pp. 1178–1189	Literary Periods **SE** p. 1184 Metaphor **TE** p. 1188
Short Story A Canary's Ideas, by Joaquim Maria Machado de Assis, translated by Jack Schmitt and Lorie Ishimatsu 6.3/59/1030 pp. 1190–1198	Narrator **SE** p. 1191 Setting **TE** p. 1192 Anthropomorphism (review) **SE** p. 1197
Short Story The Luck of Teodoro Méndez Acúbal, by Rosario Castellanos, translated by Myralyn F. Allgood 8/57/860 pp. 1199–1208	Plot **SE** p. 1200 Irony (review) **SE** p. 1207
Comparing Literature **Horses** (poem), by Pablo Neruda, translated by Alastair Reid **The Panther** (poem), by Rainer Maria Rilke, translated by Stephen Mitchell **The Iguana** *from* **Out of Africa** (nonfiction), by Isak Dinesen 6.5/59/1100 **The Red Cockatoo** (poem), by Po Chü-i, translated by Arthur Waley pp. 1209–1219	Alliteration **SE** p. 1211 Oxymoron **TE** p. 1212
Poem Fable, by Octavio Paz, translated by Eliot Weinberger pp. 1220–1223	Style **SE** p. 1221
Short Story When Greek Meets Greek, by Samuel Selvon 5.3/50/750 pp. 1224–1229	Dialect **SE** p. 1225 Aside **TE** p. 1226
Short Story The Night Face Up, by Julio Cortázar, translated by Paul Blackburn 8/61/1070 pp. 1230–1241	Point of View **SE** p. 1231 Setting and Mood **TE** p. 1234 Style (review) **SE** p. 1240

Reading Skills and Strategies	Vocabulary	Writing Grammar	Speaking, Listening, Viewing

Paraphrase **SE** p. 1165
Clarify Meaning **TE** p. 1166
	Synonyms **SE** p. 1168
	Academic Vocabulary
	    SE p. 1168
		Apply Metaphor in a Poem
		    SE p. 1168	

Analyze Figures of Speech **SE** p. 1170	Word Usage **SE** p. 1172	Write a Reflective Essay **SE** p. 1172	
Determine Main Idea and Supporting Details **SE** p. 1173 Identify Author's Purpose **TE** p. 1174		Write a Poem **TE** p. 1176 Write a Summary **SE** p. 1177	

Reading Skills and Strategies	Vocabulary	Writing Grammar	Speaking, Listening, Viewing

Evaluate Historical Influences
    SE p. 1182
Connect to the Literature **SE** p. 1189
	Denotation and Connotation
	    TE p. 1182
		Write a Comparison-Contrast
		    Essay **SE** p. 1189
			Oral Interpretation **TE** p. 1186
			Radio or TV Broadcast
			    SE p. 1189

Synthesize **SE** p. 1191
Identify Sequence **TE** p. 1194
	Denotation and Connotation
	    SE p. 1198
	Academic Vocabulary
	    SE p. 1198
		Write a Research Report
		    SE p. 1198
		Conduct Internet Research
		    TE p. 1198
			View the Art **SE** p. 1195
			Multimedia Presentation
			    SE p. 1198

Preview and Review **SE** p. 1200
Set a Purpose for Reading **TE** p. 1200
Analyze Characters **TE** p. 1202
	Synonyms **SE** p. 1208
	Academic Vocabulary
	    SE p. 1208
		Write Questions **SE** p. 1208
		Write a Reflective Essay
		    SE p. 1208
		Write an Evaluation
		    SE p. 1208
			View the Art **SE** p. 1202
			Interview **SE** p. 1208

Monitor Comprehension **TE** p. 1210
Evaluate Figurative Language
    SE p. 1211
Analyze Tone **TE** p. 1218
	Word Usage **SE** p. 1214	Write a Poem **SE** p. 1214
		Main and Subordinate
		    Clauses **TE** p. 1216
		Write a Comparison-Contrast
		    Essay **SE** p. 1219
			Discussion **SE** pp. 1217, 1219
			Collage **SE** p. 1219

Interpret Imagery **SE** p. 1221
Analyze Figurative Language
    TE p. 1222
	Academic Vocabulary
	    SE p. 1223
		Write an Expository Essay
		    SE p. 1223	

Make Inferences About Characters
    SE p. 1225
	Analogies **SE** p. 1225	Write a Short Story
		    SE p. 1229	

Identify Sequence **SE** p. 1231
Visualize **TE** p. 1232
Analyze Conflict **TE** p. 1236
	Antonyms **SE** p. 1240
	Academic Vocabulary
	    SE p. 1240
		Write a Review **SE** p. 1241
		Transitional Phrases
		    SE p. 1241
			Discussion **SE** p. 1239

Readability Scores Key: Dale-Chall/DRP/Lexile

PART 2: The Modern Americas 1800–Present *(continued)*

Selections and Features	Literary Elements
Vocabulary Workshop p. 1242	
Short Story The Handsomest Drowned Man in the World, by Gabriel García Márquez, translated by Gregory Rabassa and J. S. Bernstein **n/a/58/1480** pp. 1243–1251	Hyperbole **SE** p. 1244 Symbol **TE** p. 1246 Theme (review) **SE** p. 1250
Short Story Bishop Berkeley or Mariana of the Universe, by Liliana Heker, translated by Alberto Manguel **4.4/48/490** pp. 1252–1260	Allusion **SE** p. 1253 Antagonist and Protagonist **TE** p. 1254 Dialogue (review) **SE** p. 1259
Literary Perspective *from* **My Invented Country**, by Isabel Allende, translated by Margaret Sayers Peden **8.4/57/1320** pp. 1261–1263	
Short Story Day of the Butterfly, by Alice Munro **5.8/57/720** pp. 1264–1275	Dialect and Idiom **SE** p. 1265 Symbol (review) **SE** p. 1274
Grammar Workshop p. 1276	
Novel Excerpt A Walk to the Jetty, *from* **Annie John,** by Jamaica Kincaid **5.1/55/1180** pp. 1277–1286	Foreshadowing and Flashback **SE** p. 1278 Conflict (review) **SE** p. 1285
Poem Fishing, by Joy Harjo pp. 1287–1291	Voice **SE** p. 1288 Metaphor **TE** p. 1288
Writing Workshop pp. 1292–1299	
Speaking, Listening, and Viewing Workshop pp. 1300–1301	
Independent Reading pp. 1302–1303	
Assessment pp. 1304–1309	

Reading Skills and Strategies	Vocabulary	Writing / Grammar	Speaking, Listening, and Viewing
	Multiple-Meaning Words **SE** p. 1242		
Question **SE** p. 1244	Context Clues **SE** p. 1251 Academic Vocabulary **SE** p. 1251	Apply Hyperbole in a Persuasive Essay **SE** p. 1251	View the Art **SE** p. 1249
Analyze Conflict **SE** p. 1253 Analyze Mood **TE** p. 1256 Question **TE** p. 1258	Denotation and Connotation **SE** p. 1260 Academic Vocabulary **SE** p. 1260	Write an Essay **TE** p. 1260 Write an Evaluation **SE** p. 1261	View the Art **SE** p. 1257 Literature Group **SE** p. 1261
Analyze Philosophical Assumptions **SE** p. 1261		Write a Summary **SE** p. 1263	
Analyze Characterization **SE** p. 1265 Analyze Historical Context **TE** p. 1270	Word Usage **SE** p. 1275 Academic Vocabulary **SE** p. 1275	Write Literary Criticism **SE** p. 1275 Write an Evaluation **SE** p. 1275	View the Art **SE** p. 1267 Oral Presentation **SE** p. 1275
		Semicolons **SE** p. 1276 Conjunctions and Conjunctive Adjectives **SE** p. 1276	
Make and Verify Predictions **SE** p. 1278 Identify Sequence **TE** p. 1280 Make Inferences **TE** p. 1284	Connotation and Denotation **SE** p. 1286	Write a Description **TE** p. 1282 Apply Flashback in a Short Story **SE** p. 1286	View the Art **TE** p. 1281
Summarize **SE** p. 1288 Activate Prior Knowledge **TE** p. 1290	Antonyms **SE** p. 1291	Write a Letter **SE** p. 1291	
		Prewrite **SE** p. 1295 Draft **SE** p. 1296 Revise **SE** p. 1298 Write a Literary Analysis **SE** p. 1299	
		Write a Thesis **SE** p. 1300 Create a Visual Aid **SE** p. 1301	Monitor Tone **TE** p. 1300 Critical Review **SE** p. 1301
Read Literature Independently **SE** p. 1302			Panel Discussion **SE** p. 1303
Summarize **TE** p. 1304 Analyze Text Structure **TE** p. 1306		Write a Comparison-Contrast Essay **SE** p. 1309	

Focus

View the Art ★

Answer: *Students may say this mural conveys a peaceful and joyful mood.*

Diego Rivera (1886–1957) studied art in Europe for 12 years but spent most of his life in his native land, Mexico. The influence of the Spanish master El Greco can be seen in Rivera's 1913 painting *The Well of Toledo* (also called *At the Fountain of Toledo)*. Rivera was also heavily influenced by the work of the French painter Paul Cezanne.

 For school-to-home activities, see Unit 6 Teaching Resources Book, pp. 5–11.

 For students who would profit from independent novel study, see Novel Companion, pp. 251–294.

The Well of Toledo (La fuente de Toledo). Diego Rivera © Banco de Mexico Trust. Fundacion Dolores Olmedo, Mexico City, D.F., Mexico.

View the Art Diego Rivera was a famous mural painter. What mood does this mural convey?

Reading Practice

Analyze the Quotation Ask a volunteer to read aloud the quotation from Pablo Neruda. Lead a discussion about what Neruda may be saying. Use the following questions to spark student responses:

- How might ancient America be like a bride?
- How is a bridal veil similar to the sea?
- What does the word "jungle" imply about ancient America?

THE AMERICAS

3000 B.C. – PRESENT

Antigua América, novia sumergida. . .
al salir del la selva hacia el alto vacío de los dioses. . .

Ancient America, bride in her veil of sea. . .
from the jungle's edges to the rare height of gods. . .

—Pablo Neruda

PART ONE

PART TWO

1105

Reading Strategy

Make Inferences Read aloud the quotation. **Ask:** Based on this quotation, what kinds of themes or topics do you think you will be exploring in Unit 6? *(Students may suggest that they will read stories about new experiences and exploration.)*

[APPROACHING] Point out to approaching-level students that a bride starts a new life with her husband. Then, have them answer the question above.

For diagnostic and end-of-unit assessment, see Assessment Resources, pp. 31–36, 263–264.

Unit Resources

Print Materials
- Unit 6 Teaching Resources, pp. 1–298
- Interactive Read and Write, On Level
- Novel Companion, pp. 251–294
- Bellringer Option Transparencies: Selection Focus 69–84; Daily Language Practice 106–126
- Literary Element Transparencies
- Assessment Resources, Unit Assessment, pp. 263–264

- Assessment Resources, Selection Assessment, pp. 219–252

Technology
- TeacherWorks Plus CD
- StudentWorks Plus CD
- Literature Launchers: Pre-Reading Videos DVD
- Literature Online
- Listening Library CD-ROM

- ExamView CD-ROM
- Skill Level Up! CD-ROM

UNIT SIX

PART 1

Focus

Bellringer Options

Literature Launcher
  Pre-Reading Videos DVD
  Unit Launcher: Unit 6

Daily Language
  Transparency 105

Or, on the board, write: The
New World. **Ask:** What do you
know about the exploration and
colonization of the New World?
What do you know about the
ancient civilizations that were
in existence in the New World?
*(Students may list the names of
European explorers, such as Cortés, or what the explorers did when
they landed in the New World.
Students may mention the Aztec's
civilization and their culture).*

 For additional support for English
Learners, see Unit 6 Teaching
Resources Book, p. 20.

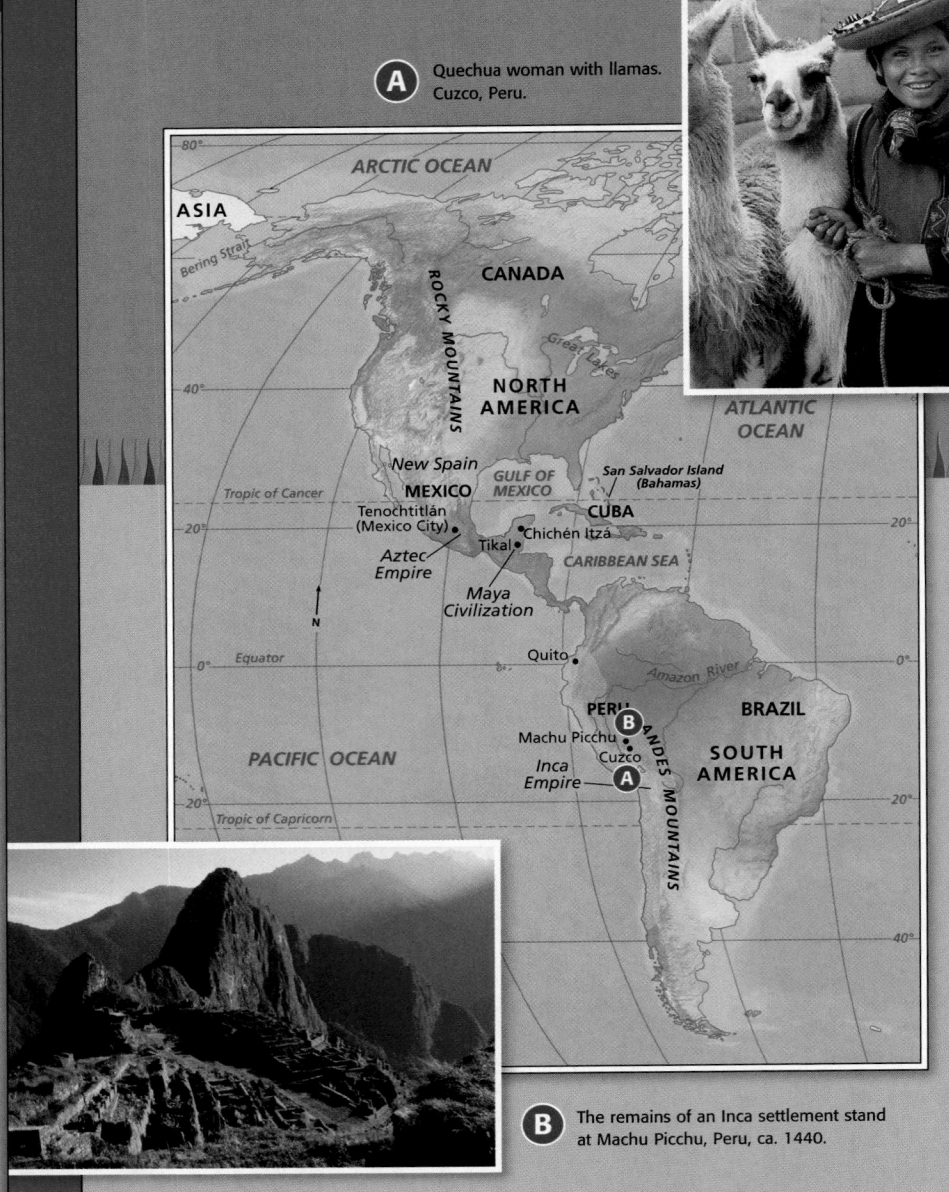

A Quechua woman with llamas.
Cuzco, Peru.

B The remains of an Inca settlement stand
at Machu Picchu, Peru, ca. 1440.

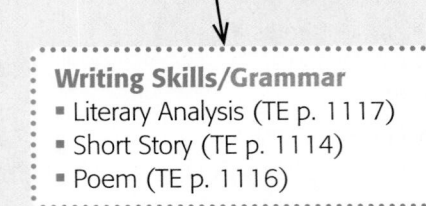 **Literature** Online

Literature and Reading For more about the history
and literature of this period, go to glencoe.com and
enter QuickPass code GLW6053u6.

1106

Part Introduction Skills

Reading Skills
- Analyze Graphic Information
  (SE p. 1109; TE p. 1108)
- Make Generalizations (SE p. 1114)
- Analyze Cause-and-Effect Relationships
  (SE p. 1115)
- Compare and Contrast (SE p. 1116)
- Paraphrase (TE p. 1112)

Part 1 Introduction

Speaking/Listening/Viewing Skills
- Analyze Art (SE p. 1104)
- Panel Discussion (SE p. 1117)

Writing Skills/Grammar
- Literary Analysis (TE p. 1117)
- Short Story (TE p. 1114)
- Poem (TE p. 1116)

THE EARLY AMERICAS

3000 B.C.– A.D. 1900

Mask, representing the God Quetzalcoatl or Tonatiuh, c.1500. Aztec school. Turquoise and shell on wood. British Museum, London.

Being There

The two connecting continents of North and South America stretch nearly 10,000 miles from north to south. The first settlers arrived in the Americas perhaps 30,000 years ago. With the domestication of crops such as corn and potatoes, the cultures of the original settlers, who were hunters and gatherers, gradually developed into advanced civilizations, culminating in the Aztec and Inca empires. The Spanish conquistadors overthrew these empires in the early 1500s.

Looking Ahead

In the centuries following the Spanish conquest, Native American and European elements blended in the cultures of the Americas. Native American oral and written records were preserved in the Spanish language. European soldiers and settlers wrote accounts of their experiences in the New World. Colonial writers adapted European literary forms such as the epic and the sonnet.

Keep the following questions in mind as you read:

- What role did storytelling have in Native American tradition?
- Why did Native Americans and European settlers come into conflict?
- How did European literature develop in the Americas?

1107

Focus

Summary

This introduction gives an overview of life in the Americas from 3000 B.C. to A.D. 1900. It describes the early civilizations and culture of the Maya, the Aztec, and the Incas. The introduction also describes European exploration, conquest, and colonization of Native Americans in the Americas. These conquests led to Latin American revolutions. The Europeans did bring some improvements to the Americas, but they also brought disease and treated the Native Americans cruelly. The introduction describes the art, architecture, music, dance, and literature of the Early Americans. It explains how European culture and literary trends influenced literature of the Native Americans.

View the Art ★

Often referred to as a feathered snake, Quetzalcoatl was the Aztec god of creation and the sky. Several Aztec rulers took this god's name as their own when they came to power.

Approaching Level

DIFFERENTIATED INSTRUCTION

Text Features Remind students that the information in this introduction is organized by headings and subheadings. Explain that these text features help organize writing and make information easier to find. Ask students to locate the headings and subheadings on this page. Ask what key information is conveyed. *(This part covers the Americas up until 1900. The page* *contains information to guide the reader through the rest of this section.)*

Teach

Reading Strategy | 1

Using the Timeline **Ask:**
How do the genres of literature used in the 15th and 16th centuries reflect events during that time? *(The genre of letters reflects the exploration of the time period. Explorers wanted to report their discoveries to their patrons.)*

Literary History ☆

Bernal Díaz Bernal Díaz (1495–1584) was a Spanish soldier and author. He visited Cuba in 1514 and later accompanied Hernán Cortés to Mexico. Feeling that he, as a first-hand observer, could best describe the expeditions of the Spanish in the Americas, Díaz wrote *The True History of the Conquest of Mexico.* His work serves as a record of history as well as a source for idiomatic expressions of 16th century Spanish.

TIMELINE 3000 B.C.–A.D.1900

LITERATURE OF THE EARLY AMERICAS

3000 B.C.   **A.D. I**

c. 300–200
Maya develop writing

The Destruction of the land of Mu
from Maya Codex Troano

EVENTS OF THE EARLY AMERICAS

3000 B.C.   **A.D. I**

c. 3000
Inuit live in the Arctic

c. 1500
Permanent villages
forming in Mesoamerica

c. 1200
Olmec civilization begins
in Mexico

c. 400
Olmec civilization declines

c. 150
Pyramid of the Sun
constructed at
Teotihuacán, Mexico

c. 200
Hopewell period begins
in North America

▲ c. 250
Classic Maya period begins
in Mexico

c. 750
Teotihuacán is abandoned

c. 900s
Legendary Toltec ruler
Quetzalcoatl reigns

WORLD EVENTS

3000 B.C.   **A.D. I**

c. 3000
Mesopotamians develop
cuneiform writing

c. 1500
Indo-European tribes
occupy northern India

330
Alexander the Great
conquers the Persian Empire

27
Augustus becomes first
Roman emperor

476
Last Roman emperor in
the west deposed

622
Muhammad's Hegira marks
beginning of Islam

Augustus, 63 BC-14 AD,
Roman Emperor from 27 BC

LOG ON ▶ Literature Online

Literature and Reading To explore the Interactive Timeline, go to glencoe.com and enter QuickPass code GLW6053u6.

Reading Practice

Analyze Graphic Information Remind students that a timeline is a useful tool for showing the sequence of events during a time period. Use the following questions to give students practice using a timeline:

- What event in world history happened during the time when the Aztec found Tenochtitlán? *(The Black Death killed many people in Europe.)*

- What event in world history happened not long after the Declaration of Independence was signed? (The French Revolution began.)
- What types of literature were being produced in the 17th century Americas? *(Histories and historical accounts were being produced.)*

Have students create their own questions based on the timeline. Have them switch their questions with a partner. Tell partners to answer one another's questions.

Hernando Cortés

A.D. 1000

1493
[1] Columbus's letter proclaims the success of his first voyage

1519–1526
Hernán Cortés writes five letters to Charles V about the conquest of Mexico

1554–1558
Mayan mythology is preserved in the Popol Vuh

1585
The Florentine Codex, a Spanish translation of Aztec records, is published

1632
Bernal Díaz del Castillo's *True History of the Conquest of New Spain* is published ☆

1667
Sor Juana Inés de la Cruz begins her life as a nun

1810
Father Miguel Hidalgo delivers the *Grito de Dolores* ("Cry of Dolores"), a call for Mexican independence

1815
Bolívar's "The Letter from Jamaica" outlines a vision of a unified Latin America

Portrait of Sor Juana Inéz de la Cruz.

A.D. 1000

c. 1000
Leif Eriksson leads first European landing in North America

c. 1325–1350 ▶
Aztecs found Tenochtitlán (now Mexico City)

Head of serpent on the Temple of the Eagles and Jaguar.

1492 ▶
Christopher Columbus reaches America

1521
[2] Spanish conquistador Hernán Cortés defeats the Aztecs

1776
American Declaration of Independence is signed

1821
Mexico wins independence from Spain

1898
Spanish-American War is fought ☆

A.D. 1000

1347
The Black Death begins to ravage Europe

1453
Ottoman Turks capture Constantinople

1789
French Revolution begins

1816–1828 ▶
Shaka establishes Zulu kingdom in Africa

1868
Meiji Restoration begins modernization of Japan

c. 1885 ▶
German inventors develop the first automobile

Inventor Karl Benz with his assistant Josef Brecht seated on the 1885 Benz Motorwagen.

Reading Check

Analyze Graphic Information How many years after Father Miguel Hidalgo's *Grito de Dolores* did Mexico achieve its independence?

INTRODUCTION **1109**

Advanced Learners/Pre-AP

DIFFERENTIATED INSTRUCTION

Research an Event Have students select one event from each timeline to research. Tell them to use print and Internet resources to discover more information on the event. If students use the Internet, make sure they use reliable sites. For example, sites ending in *.edu, .gov,* and *.org* are generally reliable. You may want to suggest that they stay away from *.coms.*

Have students write brief summaries of their findings. Then, have them share their findings with the class. Lead a discussion about similarities and differences between the events researched. Note any connections between events in the early Americas and events in the rest of the world. Tell students to retain this information as they read the selections in this part.

They may find the background information useful in understanding the context of the selections.

Teach

Reading Check

Answer: *Eleven years separate the two events.*

Reading Strategy   2

Make Inferences Ask: Based on the items appearing on the Events of Early Americas timeline and on the World Events timeline, what can you say about life from the 16th to the 18th centuries? *(Cultural and political upheaval took place during this time period both in the Early Americas and elsewhere in the world.)*

Political History ☆

Spanish-American War During 1898, Spain and the United States fought a war over the Spanish colonial presence in the Americas. Cuba's struggle to gain independence from Spain spurred the start of the war. Newspapers in the United States printed sensational accounts of Spain's brutal treatment of the Cuban people. Eventually the United States decided to declare war on Spain. In the end, the United States defeated Spain. As part of the peace agreement, Puerto Rico and Guam were given to the United States and Spain renounced its claim to Cuba. The United States also gained control of the Philippines.

Learning Objectives
Analyzing graphic information. (SE)
Using a timeline. (TE)
Making inferences. (TE)

Reading Strategy | **1**

Monitor Comprehension

Ask: Summarize the changes in lifestyle that occurred as a result of agricultural advancements. *(As a result of agricultural advancements, Native Americans changed from leading nomadic lives to creating permanent homes.)*

Reading Strategy | **2**

Make Inferences **Ask:**

What do the Maya's and Aztec's achievements in architecture reveal about them? *(Their achievements reveal that they were resourceful and intelligent.)*

APPROACHING Point out to approaching-level students that the Maya and the Aztec did not have the technological advantages that we do today. Have them consider how this would have made building structures much more difficult. Then have them answer the question above.

Cultural History ☆

Mayan Culture The Mayan culture was characterized by technological, intellectual, and artistic advancements. For example, they developed advanced techniques in agriculture. Some of these techniques include terracing and irrigation systems. The Maya also developed a system of writing. They wrote their hieroglyphs on paper made from the bark of wild fig trees.

Learning Objectives

For pages 1106–1117
In studying this text, you will focus on the following objectives:

Literary Study: Analyzing literary periods.

Reading: Evaluating historical influences.
Connecting to the literature.

THE EARLY AMERICAS

3000 B.C.–1900

Historical, Social, and Cultural Forces

Hunters and Farmers

The oldest and most widespread lifestyle found among Native Americans was that of nomadic hunters. In North America, groups moved with the seasons, following bison and caribou or traveling to lake areas to trap migrating ducks and geese. In winter, people lived on dried food. Along the northwest coast, where fish were abundant, people were able to establish permanent settlements, leading to the artistic achievements of groups including the Haida and Tlingit.

The domestication of vegetables such as corn, squash, and beans led to the rise of farming-based societies. With the growth of farming, more groups established permanent towns and villages—although hunting remained an important food resource for most groups. Permanent homes and a more secure food supply allowed peoples such as the Natchez to develop complex societies and artistic forms. From about 900 to 1200, the Mississippians erected huge mounds at a site known as Cahokia in what is now Illinois. **1**

City Builders ☆

The Maya, Aztec, and Inca are the best known of the urban-oriented civilizations of early America. Other groups included the Olmec, the Toltec, and the Zapotec. At sites such as Chichén Itzá and Palenque, in present-day Mexico, and Tikal in present-day Guatemala, the ancient Maya erected plazas, temples, and huge pyramids—symbolic sacred mountains—where thousands gathered for religious ceremonies and festivals. The Aztec capital Tenochtitlán (tā nōch tē′tiahn), which may have included about 400,000 inhabitants at its height in 1519, rivaled other great cities of that period in size

Mayan Stone Relief of Xoc Performing a Blood-Letting Ritual. ca. 8th century.

Writing Practice

Research Revolutions Have students research one of the people mentioned in the "Latin American Revolutions" section. Students can look for birth/death dates, hometowns, family information, and actions or achievements. Have students find or draw an image of their selected person. Tell them to write the information they found around the image. Then, have them share their images and findings with the class.

and magnificence. From their capital city of Cuzco, located in the Andes in what is now Peru, the Incas ruled an empire that extended more than 2,500 miles along the Pacific coast of South America.

Religion and Sacrifice

Religion dominated these advanced civilizations. Mayan kings were spiritual, as well as political, leaders. They performed rituals and ceremonies to appease the gods. Like the ancient Greeks, the Maya believed that the movements of the sun, moon, and planets were journeys undertaken by the gods. Because the gods controlled nature, charting the movements of the heavenly bodies was crucial. To do so, Mayan priests learned to excel at mathematics and astronomy. Images on temples, sacred objects, and pottery provide clues about ancient Mayan beliefs and practices.

Religion motivated the Aztecs to wage war and offer sacrifice. Borrowing beliefs from the Maya and the Toltecs, the Aztecs held that human sacrifice was necessary to propitiate the gods and prevent natural disasters. Like the Aztecs, Inca priests sometimes offered human victims to their gods.

> "I found very many islands peopled with inhabitants beyond number."
>
> —Christopher Columbus, in a 1493 letter

Exploration, Conquest, and Colonization

After Christopher Columbus's fleet reached the islands of the Caribbean in 1492, European nations turned their attention to the Western Hemisphere. Eager for fame and gold, Spanish soldier-explorers known as *conquistadors* overthrew the empires of the Aztec and the Inca within a few decades. By the 1600s, Spain's empire in the New World included much of North and South America. Under Spanish rule, Native American peoples declined rapidly because of disease and mistreatment. To replace a

Battle With Natives in the Early French and Portuguese Colonization of Brazil, 1562. Theodor de Bry. Service Historique de la Marine, Chateau de Vincennes, France.

dwindling labor force, the Spanish introduced enslaved Africans to their colonies.

Over time, the merging of Native American, European, and African peoples in Spain's American colonies gave rise to a new culture. The center of this new culture was Mexico City, the capital of New Spain, which had been erected on the ruins of the Aztecs' Tenochtitlán. At its peak in the 1700s, this colonial capital contained many elegant homes and public buildings as well as splendid churches and convents.

Latin American Revolutions

In the early 1800s, region after region in Latin America rebelled against Spanish colonial rule. Military leaders such as Venezuela's Simón Bolívar and Argentina's José de San Martín led liberation movements, and by 1825 most of the modern-day nations of Latin America had won their independence from Portugal and Spain. An exception was Cuba, which—despite a series of uprisings in the late 1800s—did not become an independent republic until 1902. One of the Cuban rebel leaders was the poet José Martí (see pages 1169–1172), who in 1895 was killed fighting for independence from Spain.

Approaching Level

DIFFERENTIATED INSTRUCTION

Read Aloud with Fluency Use the text on this page to give students practice in reading fluently. Explain to students that, when reading prose, it is important to read slowly, pause when necessary, and read expressively.

First, read the page aloud for students, modeling proper phrasing and fluency. Be sure to show students how to pause after punctuation and before new paragraphs.

Then, re-read the first paragraph aloud to students. Have them read the same paragraph aloud, mimicking your fluency. Continue in this fashion until you and the students have read each paragraph on the page. If time allows, have several volunteers read the page aloud. Compliment students on their ability to speak fluently and pause correctly while reading.

Teach

Reading Strategy | 3

Make Inferences Ask: Based on the information in this paragraph, how do you think the Native Americans viewed the Spanish? *(The Native Americans may have viewed the Spanish as cruel and frightening.)*

Reading Strategy | 4

Determine Main Idea Ask: What is the main idea of this paragraph? *(The main idea is that the cultures of the Native Americans, Europeans, and Africans blended together to create a new culture.)*

Reading Strategy | 5

Make Predictions Ask: What kind of literature do you think may have been produced as a result of the Latin American revolutions? *(Students may say that turbulent times often produce literature with topics such as revolution, independence, and conquest.)*

Reading Strategy | 6

Make Inferences Ask: What does Martí's involvement in the revolution reveal about him? *(His involvement reveals that he was brave and was loyal to his country and his ideals.)*

Learning Objectives
Making inferences. (TE)
Researching historical figures. (TE)
Determining main idea. (TE)

1111

Teach

Reading Strategy | **1**

Determine Main Idea and Supporting Details **Ask:**

What are two details in this paragraph that support the main idea that pottery making is an old tradition? *(Known examples of pottery date back to 3200 B.C. The Moche culture made vessels in the shapes of animals and human heads.)*

Cultural History

Ancient Markets The marketplace was a center of pre-Columbian Indian life. Trade among the Maya, Aztec, and Inca empires linked together far-flung groups. Lowland Maya traded handicrafts and jaguar pelts to highland Maya for jade, volcanic glass, and feathers. The greatest Aztec markets drew as many as sixty thousand visitors daily.

Pottery and Ceramics 1

The tradition of pottery-making in the Americas is more than 5,000 years old; the earliest known examples, from Ecuador, date from about 3200 B.C. Most pottery was made by the coil method and shaped into bowls, vases, and spouted jars. The Moche (mō′cheh) culture, which flourished on the north coast of Peru from the first to the eighth centuries, excelled at making vessels in the shape of animals and human heads. These portrait jars, some of them depictions of Moche rulers, were executed with exceptional skill.

Architecture

Ceremonial pyramids topped by temples were constructed throughout Central and South America. Some of the most elaborate were built by the Maya, who rank among history's greatest builders. The Maya had little technology—they built their cities using only stone and bone tools—but great ingenuity. Many Mayan temples were built on top of artificial mounds. Each building consisted of a massive base, a series of terraces or stairs, and a single-storied temple on top. In later years, sometimes a palace occupied the place of the temple. The entire building was covered with white stucco and brilliantly decorated. Often the interior was painted with frescoes.

The Aztecs of Mexico built their capital, Tenochtitlán, on artificial islands connected by causeways to the shore. In 1521, when the Spaniards under Hernán Cortés first glimpsed this city with its plazas and pyramids, soldiers such as Bernal Díaz del Castillo were stunned by its size and beauty. In the Andes Mountains, the Inca built entire cities from huge blocks of granite, fitting the stones together so skillfully that a knife blade could not fit between them. Even in ruins, the temples and palaces of the Aztec and the Inca remain among the wonders of the world.

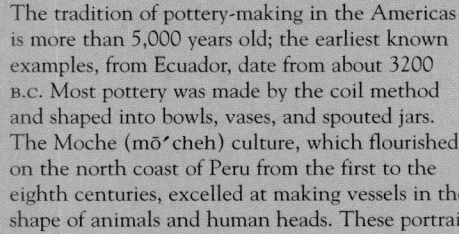

A Mochica vase depicting a warrior stands in a museum in Peru.

The figure of a Chac-Mool, ready to receive the hearts of victims of human sacrifice, gazes at Kukulcan Pyramid. Height of the Pyramid 30 m. Chichen Itza, Yucatan, Mexico.

1112 UNIT 6   THE EARLY AMERICAS

Reading Practice

SMALL GROUP

Paraphrase Remind students that, when they paraphrase, they put the text in their own words. Unlike summarizing, paraphrasing includes all of the text—not just the main idea and supporting details.

Organize students into small groups. Have each group member paraphrase one of the paragraphs on the page. Make sure students are putting the language into their own words.

After group members have finished, have them share their paraphrases with the group. Tell group members to check that each member has paraphrased all of the text from his or her paragraph. Also have students point out any instances where a group member has paraphrased something incorrectly. After groups are satisfied with their paraphrases, have a volunteer group share their paraphrases with the class.

Music and Dance

2 Early American music and dance share many characteristics, despite distinctive regional variations. Dances were commonly associated with planting and harvesting ceremonies, hunting trips, war, and religious ceremonies. Other common dance characteristics included:

- a two-part rhythm, alternating between a strong and a weak beat
- dancers assuming a slightly bent-over posture, with raised knees
- flat-footed movements

Percussion instruments included a variety of drums and rattles made of deer hoofs or turtle shells. Wind instruments included conch-shell trumpets, used in religious ceremonies, and many types of flutes, the best known of which are the panpipes used in the Andes. Native American peoples were quick to adopt the stringed instruments introduced by Europeans, developing their own traditions of guitar, violin, and harp playing.

Ballet Folklorico de Mexico Performance in Mexico City. ▶

Textiles **3**

In 1925, archaeologists excavating a cemetery on the south coast of Peru found hundreds of funeral bundles, with the remains of the dead wrapped in magnificent cloths. It became clear that these belonged to the Paracas culture, which thrived in the region from 900 B.C. to A.D. 400. The 2,000-year-old textiles had survived because of the desert-like conditions of the region. Many of the cloths were cloaks, embroidered with representations of animals and plants, real and imaginary. This visual imagery was a means of communicating among people who had no written language.

PREVIEW | Big Ideas of The Early Americas

1 Gods and Mortals

The early Americas were home to hundreds of native civilizations, from the tribal groups of North America to the Maya, Aztec, and Inca civilizations of Central and South America. The oral and written literature of these peoples explores the origin of humanity and tells of the interrelations between people, animals, and gods.

See page 1114

2 Cultures in Conflict

The voyages of Christopher Columbus in the 1490s inaugurated an era of European exploration and conquest that reshaped the Americas. Written accounts of the initial encounters between natives and explorers reflect the striking contrasts between their values and ways of living.

See page 1115

3 Transplanting Traditions

A complex mixture of indigenous and European elements shaped Latin American culture. Authors transplanted such European traditions as the sonnet and Romanticism into literature that expressed new perspectives on gender, identity, and displacement, including the effects of exile.

See page 1116

Reading Strategy | 2

Make Generalizations Ask: Based on the information in this paragraph, what generalization can you make about Native Americans and music? *(Music played an important role in all aspects of Native American life.)*

Reading Strategy | 3

Make Inferences Ask: What do the cloths found with the dead reveal about the Paracas? *(Students may suggest that the cloths reveal the Paracas's respect for the dead. The cloths may also be evidence of a religious ritual.)*

Learning Objectives
Determining main idea and supporting details. (TE)
Analyzing simile. (TE)
Paraphrasing text. (TE)
Making generalizations. (TE)

INTRODUCTION **1113**

Approaching Level
DIFFERENTIATED INSTRUCTION

Create an Organizer To help students organize the information on this page, have them create a graphic organizer to record their notes; for example, they may want to create a two-column chart, using the section subheads as heads in the chart. Then they can record details from each section in the appropriate column. Encourage students to create an organizer that works for them.

Advanced Learners/Pre-AP
DIFFERENTIATED INSTRUCTION

Write a Journal Entry Have students imagine they are one of the early Americans. Tell them to describe a day when dance was used to accompany a ceremony, such as a harvest or religious ceremony. They can describe the reason for the dance, who was involved, and what the music was like.

Teach

Reading Check

Answer: *Such figures, combining both animal and human characteristics, might reflect the Native American sense of kinship with the natural world.*

Reading Strategy | 1

Monitor Comprehension
Say: Summarize the Maya creation myth. *(The Maya believed that a creator god wanted to make creatures with the ability to worship the gods. After destroying several failures, the god made human beings out of corn.)*

Reading Strategy | 2

Make Inferences **Ask:** How might an oral tradition affect the tales that are passed down? *(The oral tradition may result in changes or additions to stories as they are passed down.)*

Cultural History ☆

Shamans In Native American cultures, a shaman is a person thought to be able to communicate with and influence natural forces. The most important part of a shaman's powers is the ability to heal the sick, which led early European settlers to refer to them as "medicine men" (although women also often filled this role). This ability is not simply mythical; knowledge of the healing powers of plants and herbs, and a considerable understanding of psychology, often make a shaman an effective healer.

Big Idea 1
Gods and Mortals

Quetzalcoatl with black beard rising from the jaws of earth. Museo Nacional de Antropologia e Historia, Mexico City, D.F., Mexico.

The myths told throughout the world share character types and story patterns, known as archetypes. For example, a creator god is a character archetype. A series of worlds existing before the present one is a plot pattern archetype. These archetypes also appear in the mythologies of the early Americas.

> *"Here is the story of the beginning, when there was not one bird, not one fish, not one mountain."*
> —from the Popol Vuh

Creators and Nature Gods ☆

The Maya creation myth was preserved in the Popol Vuh (see pages 1120–1129), or "Council Book," a collection of Maya myths recorded soon after the Spanish Conquest. The Maya believed that the creator god had tried several times to make creatures capable of worshipping the gods. After destroying creatures made from mud and wood, the creator god finally formed humans out of corn. According to the ancient Aztecs, several previous worlds, or "suns," had perished because of flood, fire, wind, or supernatural beasts. The Aztecs believed the present world would be destroyed by earthquake.

The mythologies of the Maya, Aztecs, and Incas included a large number of gods and goddesses, many of which embodied forces of nature. For example, the Maya god Huracan was both the creator and the god of storms. (His name is the basis for the word *hurricane*.) The Aztec god Quetzalcoatl was associated with winds, rain, and the planet Venus. The central Inca god was Inti, the divine sun, who was believed to be the ancestor of the Inca rulers.

Oral Traditions

Although the Maya and the Aztecs had well-developed systems of writing, most Native American peoples did not. To preserve their myths, histories, and legends, they had to transmit them orally from one generation to the next, telling and retelling them at tribal ceremonies. In Native American oral traditions, the trickster is a character archetype that appears in many tales. Frequently depicted as an animal with speech and other human traits, this figure is not only troublesome but also clever and creative. Two prominent Native American tricksters are Coyote and Raven. | **2**

Reading Check

Make Generalizations What might tricksters such as Coyote and Raven reveal about the Native American attitude toward nature?

Writing Practice

Write a Short Story Have students write a short story containing a trickster archetype. Tell them they can use any animal they want to be their trickster. Point out that their tricksters could create trouble or perform actions that are clever and creative. Encourage students to think about their characters, plot, and setting before they begin writing.

After students have finished writing, have them proofread their stories for errors in spelling, punctuation, and grammar. You may have students exchange papers to check for errors. Then, have volunteers share their trickster tales, explaining how their main character fits the trickster archetype. Tell students to keep their stories in mind as they read the trickster tale in Part One.

Big Idea 2
Cultures in Conflict

The European exploration, conquest, and settlement of the Americas had both positive and negative consequences for the cultures of the native peoples. For one thing, it led to the founding of new nations. Moreover, the reintroduction of the horse—exterminated by early American hunters—revolutionized transportation. The production of furs and other raw materials expanded, as people sought items to trade for European manufactured goods. European colonization, however, was also the prologue to the destruction of many Native American societies. Spain had two goals for its overseas empire—**3** to acquire wealth and to spread Christianity. These goals proved disastrous for native peoples.

Cruelty and Disease

Under the *encomienda* system, a brutal type of forced labor established by Spanish rulers in their American colonies, landowners had the right to use Native Americans as enslaved workers. Many of those enslaved later died from mistreatment or overwork. Deadly diseases introduced from Europe also took a terrible toll. Exposed to smallpox and measles for the first time, millions of Native Americans died during the first 50 years of Spanish rule. The Spanish priest Bartolomé de Las Casas, who had firsthand knowledge of Spain's brutal colonial policies, protested the abuses of Native Americans in his *Brief Report on the* **4** *Destruction of the Indies.*

> "Long before they heard the word Spaniard, *the Indians had properly organized states, wisely ordered by excellent laws, religion, and custom.*"
>
> —Bartolomé de Las Casas, from *The Destruction of the Indies*

Destruction of Records **5**

The Spanish also destroyed much of the culture of the Maya and the Aztecs, including written records contained in painted books known as *codices.* Written largely in pictographic scripts, these books were the property of priests, nobles, and rulers. They contained information on mythic and secular histories, genealogies, and tax and tribute accounts. They also provided information on when to plant and harvest, and when and how to conduct rituals. During the Spanish Conquest, religious authorities ordered the destruction of hundreds of codices, condemning them as pagan relics. The few codices that survived provide a vital record of Aztec and Maya civilizations.

American Indians Carrying Goods for the Conquerors. From Diego Duran's History of the American Indians, 1579. Manuscript, fol. 204v. Biblioteca Nacional, Madrid.

Reading Check

Analyze Cause-and-Effect Relationships How did the Spanish goal of Christianizing Native Americans contribute to the destruction of their written records?

INTRODUCTION **1115**

English Learners
DIFFERENTIATED INSTRUCTION

Intermediate Have students from other cultures compare the influence of outside groups on the development of their own culture. Point out that the introduction includes details about the Europeans' influence on early American civilization. Have students describe any similar events—such as the arrival of foreign customs, technology, or health care practices—that had an impact on the development of their own culture.

Advanced Learners/Pre-AP
DIFFERENTIATED INSTRUCTION

Research Diseases Have students research information on smallpox and measles. Tell them to use Internet and print sources to research the diseases. Have them look for information on the diseases' histories and cures and then create a poster that contains information that they have discovered about smallpox and measles. Encourage them to present their posters to the class.

Teach
Reading Check

Answer: *Christian missionaries destroyed Maya codices because the missionaries viewed these records as relics of paganism.*

Reading Strategy   **3**

Monitor Comprehension
Ask: What were the positive effects of European settlement in America? *(The horse revolutionized transportation. The production of furs and other raw materials expanded due to trading opportunities.)*

Reading Strategy   **4**

Make Inferences   Ask: Based on the information in this paragraph, what qualities did Las Casas possess? *(He was outspoken, but he was sympathetic to the plight of the Native Americans.)*

Reading Strategy   **5**

Connect to Personal Experience   Ask: How would you feel if someone destroyed items that were important to you? *(Students may suggest that they would be angry or hurt.)*

ADVANCED Lead a discussion about whether students think destruction of personal property by an invader would be an effective means of controlling a country.

Learning Objectives
Making generalizations. (SE)
Analyzing cause-and-effect relationships. (SE)
Writing a story. (TE)

Teach

Reading Check

Answer: *Bernal Díaz wrote a factual account of Cortés's campaign in Mexico, while Alonso de Ercilla created an epic about the Spanish war against the Mapuche in Chile.*

Reading Strategy | 1

Monitor Comprehension

Ask: How did European literature influence the writing of Alonso de Ercilla? *(He used the European epic style in his writing.)*

View the Art ★

The children depicted in the art on this page are mestizos, a term that refers to a mixed ancestry consisting of European and Native American peoples. After the Spanish settled in the Americas, some of the Spanish men began intermarrying with Native American women. This intermarrying has continued for centuries, so that today millions of Latin Americans are mestizos to some degree.

Writing Practice

Write a Poem Have students use the information from the introduction as inspiration for a poem. For example, students could write a poem about the influences of European culture on the Native Americans; or, they could write a poem about Spain's treatment of the Native Americans. Encourage students to use poetic devices, such as sound devices (such as alliteration, rhythm, and rhyme), imagery, and figurative language in their poems.

After students have finished their poems, have them write out the poems on a clean sheet of paper. Then, tell students to illustrate their poems with pictures or borders. Allow them to be creative. Finally, have students share their poems with the class. After a volunteer has read his or her poem, have students determine the inspiration for the poem.

Big Idea 3
Transplanting Traditions

Although the Europeans converted many Native Americans to Christianity, elements of ancient practices have survived in some areas. For example, according to legend, Our Lady of Guadalupe, the patron saint of Mexico, first appeared to an Aztec in 1531, but elements of pre-Columbian earth and moon worship have been incorporated into the festivities and pilgrimages honoring her.

The virgin of Guadalupe with mixed couples and their mestizo-children. Luis de Mena. Museo de America, Madrid. ★

> *"One of the chief idols of the Inca kings and their subjects was the imperial city of Cuzco which the Indians worshipped as a sacred thing."*
>
> —Garcilaso de la Vega, from *Royal Commentaries of the Incas*

Early Spanish-American Literature

Official letters from explorers to their royal patrons constitute the earliest European literature written in the Americas. Among the most famous are the 1493 letter from Columbus to King Ferdinand and Queen Isabella of Spain and the series of five letters from Cortés to Spanish Emperor Charles V. Besides the official accounts of battles and explorations, the early Spaniards in America produced other kinds of work. In 1568, nearly 50 years after the defeat of the Aztecs, Bernal Díaz del Castillo, one of Cortés's soldiers, wrote about the sufferings of the common soldier in his *True History of the Conquest of New Spain.* Garcilaso de la Vega, the son of an Inca princess and a Spanish soldier, chronicled both the history of the Inca empire and the early years of Spanish rule in *Royal Commentaries of the Incas.*

Poetry also took root in the Americas. The Spanish soldier Alonso de Ercilla y Zúniga used the European epic style to write of the wars between Spaniards and Native Americans in southern Chile. In *La Araucana,* published between 1569 and 1589, he praised the courageous resistance of the Mapuche (or Araucana) people to Spanish rule. In *Mexico's Grandeur,* published in 1604, the poet Bernardo de Balbuena described the beauties of the colonial city of Mexico. The first great lyric poet of colonial America was Sor Juana Inés de la Cruz, who adapted the literary conventions of Renaissance European poetry (see pages 1164–1168).

Reading Check

Compare and Contrast Both Bernal Díaz del Castillo and Alonso de Ercilla y Zúniga wrote about Spain's wars in the Americas. How did their approaches differ?

WRAP-UP

Legacy of the Period

Many native cultures flourished in the early Americas. These cultures created rich oral traditions and mythologies that influenced modern literature. Trickster figures in Native American traditions, such as Raven and Coyote, continue to teach and delight modern readers. The relationship between gods and humans depicted in early literature of South America influenced magic realism, a literary movement in twentieth-century Latin America.

The arrival of Europeans forever altered the Americas and destroyed many native cultures. Surviving writings of the Spaniards' exploration and conquest of present-day Mexico include first-hand accounts, describing both the exploits of the conquistadors and the plight of the conquered.

Cultural and Literary Links

 Magic realist authors such as Gabriel García Márquez drew on early American cultures' worldviews, which accept the presence of fantastical forces as part of everyday life.

Conchero Dancers in Traditional Headdresses. Hugh Sitton. Mexico.

 Columbus Day, declared an American national holiday in 1937, has come under scrutiny recently as more people have become sensitive to the plight of Native Americans under European colonization.

 In 1522, after being conquered by the Spaniards, the Chichimec tribe of Mexico began performing ritual dances called concheros to preserve their pre-Columbian religious rituals. Still performed today, the members of *concheros* dance chiefly at four sites, which are north, south, east, and west of Mexico City.

LOG ON ▶ **Literature** Online

Unit Resources For additional skills practice, go to glencoe.com and enter QuickPass code GLW6053u6.

Activities

Use what you have learned about the period to do one of these activities.

1. **Follow Up** Go back to the Looking Ahead on page 1107 and answer the questions.

2. **Contrast Literary Periods** In a brief essay, contrast one or more creation hymns from the Americas (such as the Popol Vuh) with a creation myth from another culture, such as Mesopotamia or ancient Greece.

3. **Speaking/Listening** Conduct a panel discussion on whether Columbus Day should be celebrated as a national holiday.

4. **Take Notes** You might try using this graphic organizer to keep track of the three Big Ideas in this part.

FOLDABLES Study Organizer   **THREE-POCKET BOOK**

Big Idea 1   Big Idea 2   Big Idea 3

INTRODUCTION   **1117**

Teach

Legacy of the Period

Direct students' attention to the first paragraph. **Ask:** Have you read any stories or seen any movies that contained a version of the trickster archetype? *(Students may suggest stories or movies that have clever characters who easily trick people.)*

Cultural and Literary Links

As students read Part One, have them look for European influences on the literature and culture of Native Americans.

Assess

Activities

1. **Follow Up** Students should support their answers with details from this introduction.

2. **Contrast Literary Periods** Students' essays should contrast a creation myth from the Americas with a creation myth from another culture.

3. **Speaking/Listening** Encourage students to support their opinion with specific examples from the unit introduction, as well as to consider what the celebration means to various cultures: Latin American, North American, Spanish, and Italian.

4. **Take Notes** After students finish each selection, have them list details in the graphic organizer that relate to the selection's Big Idea.

Advanced Learners/Pre-AP

DIFFERENTIATED INSTRUCTION

Write a Compare-and-Contrast Essay
Have students write an essay, using what they have learned in the introduction, to compare and contrast the cultures of Native Americans and Europeans. Encourage students to do further research to aid their essays. Remind students that their essays should contain a thesis statement, supporting details, and a clear form of organization.

Suggest to students that they first record their thoughts in a graphic organizer. This will help them organize the details they want to compare and contrast in their essays.

After students have finished, have them share their essays with a small group. Have students pay attention to details that they did not know before. This information will help their understanding of selections in the unit.

Focus

Summary

For many years, people believed that Mayan hieroglyphics represented entire words. They ignored the possibility that the hieroglyphs stood for sounds. Yuri Knorosov changed this point of view by realizing that the glyphs stood for sounds as well as ideas. This way of thinking helped crack the code to understanding Mayan hieroglyphics. Egyptian hieroglyphics were cracked in a similar way.

Teach

Reading Strategy | 1

Analyze Cultural Context

Ask: Mayan writing was reserved for members of the elite and the priesthood. How might this have affected what was recorded? *(The recorded information could have been biased by the beliefs of those groups.)*

Learning Objectives

For pages 1118–1119
In studying this text, you will focus on the following objectives:

Reading: Understanding cultural and historical context. Understanding the nature of translation.

Cracking The Maya Code

CRACKING THE CODE OF MAYA HIEROGLYPHIC WRITING IS AMONG THE great achievements of the late twentieth century. But why, given the nearly 200-year history of Maya archaeology, did the code take so long to crack? The answer lies in the difficulty of deciphering an ancient script and in mistaken assumptions made about its nature.

The Mystery of the Maya

1 Among the peoples of pre-Columbian America, only the Maya developed a complete script or system of writing. To the Maya, writing was a sacred gift from the great creator god Itzamná. Knowledge of this gift belonged exclusively to members of the **2** Maya elite and the priesthood, many of whom were scribes. Educated in both painting and writing, these artist-authors drew hieroglyphs on pottery, walls, and sculptures and in painted books called codices (the plural of *codex*). They also carved these writings into stone buildings and on stelae (stē′le)—commemorative stone slabs or pillars. Near the glyphs, they often created artistic scenes that serve as illustrations of the text.

By the time the Spaniards conquered Maya territory in the early 1500s, Maya civilization was in decline and the population was dispersed. However, the deserted Maya centers remained full of hieroglyphs.

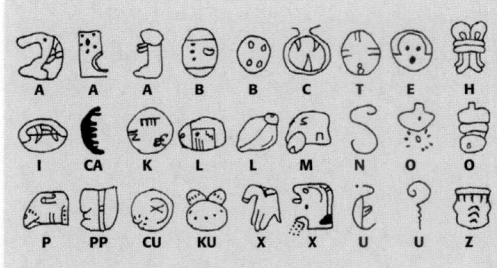

The Spanish Bishop Diego de Landa used these to create an "alphabet" of Maya writing, in which he paired one or more hieroglyphs with a letter or consonant-vowel combination. He published his findings in a book called *Account of the Affairs of Yucatán*. This book disappeared until 1862, but even when it was rediscovered, scholars paid little attention to it.

Mayan hieroglyphic text panel, Palenque Mayan ruins, Chiapas, Mexico. Classic Period, 750 AD.

1118 UNIT 6 THE EARLY AMERICAS

Reading Practice

SMALL GROUP

Identify Problem and Solution Organize students into small groups. Tell them to identify the problem or problems in this feature. Then have them explain the solution or solutions given in the feature. Encourage students to use a graphic organizer similar to the one shown here to record the problems and solutions. Tell students they can add or eliminate boxes from the organizer as needed.

After students finish, have them share their organizers with the class. Make sure students understand how the writer organized the material in a problem-solution format.

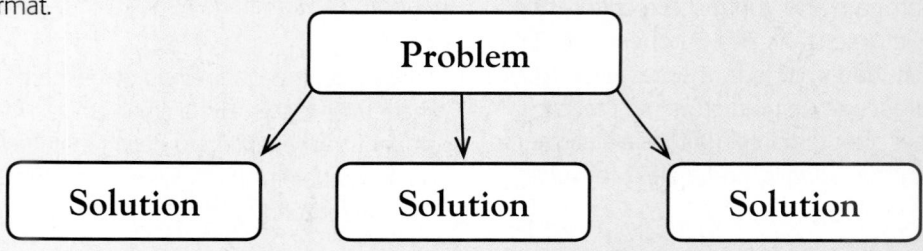

Cracking the Code

Why was Landa's "alphabet" ignored for so long? The field of Maya studies was dominated by a few scholars who insisted Maya writing was primarily "picture writing." That is, they viewed each hieroglyph as a picture representing a particular word or idea. They didn't believe the glyphs had any relation to the Mayan language. But in 1952, a Russian scholar named Yuri Knorosov, who had never even seen a Maya ruin, showed that Maya writing reflects spoken language. Using Landa's "alphabet" and modern Maya dictionaries, Knorosov showed that the Maya script consists of both symbols that express ideas and symbols that express sounds.

Besides using the alphabetic system shown on the opposite page, the Maya combined symbols in a number of ways. These characters illustrate five different ways to write the Maya word for "jaguar."

The ancient scribes organized the glyphs into blocks placed in horizontal and vertical rows. In each block, they wrote one or more glyphs. As the example on the left shows, a block might include a logogram (a glyph that represents a whole word, in this case *jaguar*) combined with phonetic signs (signs representing the sounds of syllables), or just phonetic signs.

Since Knorosov's discovery, scholars have unlocked the meaning of many more glyphs. In so doing, they have disproved the belief that the glyphs primarily record astronomical and mythological events. Many actually describe the history of the Maya kings—their birth, accession to the throne, marriages, children, military conquests, participation in bloodletting rites and human sacrifice, and deaths. This new information shattered the long-cherished view of the ancient Maya as a peaceful, star-gazing people. They were, we now know, constantly at war and capable of great cruelty toward their enemies. Yet they also developed a very rich and sophisticated culture.

Deciphering Other Ancient Scripts

Maya hieroglyphic writing is not the only script that long eluded scholars. Egyptian hieroglyphic writing—a complex script with many similarities to Maya writing—also proved difficult to crack (see pages 34–35). As ancient Egyptian culture died out, and with it knowledge of Egyptian writing (the last example of ancient Egyptian writing is from A.D. 394), people began entertaining the mistaken notion that it was picture writing. This belief persisted until 1822, when a young Frenchman named Jean François Champollion proved the glyphs are largely phonetic, or based on the sounds of the spoken language. In so doing, he paved the way for the breaking of other early scripts, which scholars now realize all have phonetic components.

Respond and Think Critically

1. What steps might you take in trying to figure out an inscription in an unknown language?

2. (a) What is your impression of the glyphs used to spell the word *jaguar*? (b) What, in your opinion, are the strengths and weaknesses of each type of glyph?

3. Compare Maya hieroglyphic writing with the Egyptian writing on pages 34–35. Which script do you think would be most difficult to decipher? Why?

THE ART OF TRANSLATION **1119**

Teach

Big Idea | 2

Gods and Mortals **Ask:** How did the Mayan system of writing reveal the Maya's connection to the gods? *(The system of writing allowed the Maya to show their religious beliefs. They believed that writing was a gift from a god.)*

Assess

1. Students may respond that a first step might be to look for repeated symbols and to examine the contexts in which the repeated symbols appear.

2. (a) Students may be puzzled by the glyphs but may note that all but the last include a representation of a jaguar's head. Some students may speculate that glyphs took on conventional meanings to users, just as alphabetic letters do.
   (b) Answers will vary.

3. Students should discuss the relationship between symbols and referents in both systems of writing.

Advanced Learners/Pre-AP

DIFFERENTIATED INSTRUCTION

Cracking Codes Students might be interested in exploring the similarities between archaeologists' cracking a writing code and governments' cracking a code used by enemies in communicating with field commanders, ships at sea, and the like during war.

Have students investigate Great Britain's cracking of the Enigma code, used by the German high command, early in World War II.

Have students present their findings to the class. They should give an overview of how the code was cracked and the effects of this knowledge on the course of the war. Also have students explain the similarities and differences between cracking a system of hieroglyphic writing and cracking a communication code. Allow students to use any necessary visual aids in their presentations.

Bellringer Options

Selection Focus
   Transparency 69
Daily Language
   Transparency 106

Or ask: Why do you think people want to know where they came from? *(Students may say that people want to know where they came from to understand the history of human beings and learn more about themselves in the process.)* Discuss with students what people can learn from reading myths about the origins of different peoples.

Before You Read

from the *Popol Vuh*

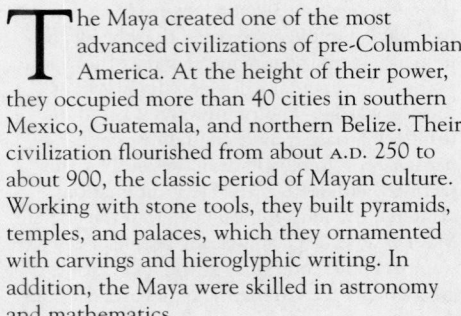

The Maya created one of the most advanced civilizations of pre-Columbian America. At the height of their power, they occupied more than 40 cities in southern Mexico, Guatemala, and northern Belize. Their civilization flourished from about A.D. 250 to about 900, the classic period of Mayan culture. Working with stone tools, they built pyramids, temples, and palaces, which they ornamented with carvings and hieroglyphic writing. In addition, the Maya were skilled in astronomy and mathematics.

> *"Here we shall inscribe . . . the Ancient Word . . . how things were put in shadow and brought to light ..."*
>
> —from the Popol Vuh

Mayan Civilization The earliest Mayan settlements, established about 1500 B.C., were small farming communities that grew mainly corn, beans, and squash. By the time of the classic period, however, these communities had been transformed into a network of magnificent cities that featured ceremonial buildings, public plazas, and sports facilities. At its peak, Mayan civilization may have numbered two million people.

The remains of temples and other artifacts provide evidence of an artistic culture unequaled by any other Native American people. Mayan art is strikingly narrative, rich in color and detail. Hieroglyphic texts reveal astonishing intellectual achievements. The Maya developed a complex calendar based on astronomical calculations that enabled them to chart the positions of heavenly bodies and to predict solar eclipses. The calendar includes both an eighteen-month solar year (with each month containing twenty days) and a 260-day sacred year.

Religion was important to ancient Mayan culture. The Maya worshipped a variety of deities, including nature gods and goddesses. Each day of the sacred calendar was associated with a god or goddess. The Maya fasted, prayed, and offered ritual sacrifices—both animal and human—to seek divine favor.

Relic from a Lost Civilization Tragically, the Maya abandoned their magnificent cities by the year 900 and retired to the countryside. Why they did so remains a mystery. By the middle of the 1500s, Spanish forces had completely conquered the Maya.

Fortunately, the Popol Vuh (pō pəl vu′), a sacred text of the ancient Maya, survived the Spanish Conquest and the burning of Mayan books. Some Christian-trained Maya wrote down the Popol Vuh in the Roman alphabet. Around 1700 a friar named Francisco Ximénez copied this version and translated it into Spanish. Modern editions of the Popol Vuh are based on his copy.

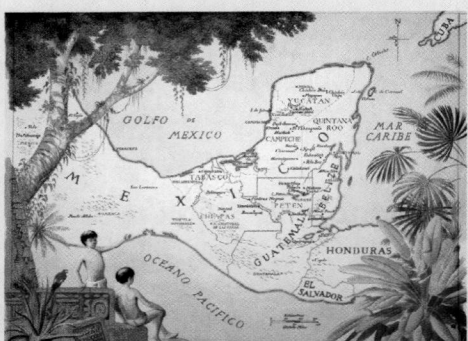

Map of the Maya Area. Nigel Hughes. Watercolour on paper. Private collection.

Literary Elements
- Myth (SE pp. 1121, 1123, 1127, 1128)

from the Popul Vuh

Speaking/Listening/Viewing Skills
- Analyze Art (SE p. 1126)

Reading Skills
- Clarify Meaning (SE pp. 1121, 1124, 1126, 1129; TE pp. 1122, 1125)
- Analyze Sensory Details (TE p. 1122)
- Analyze Cultural Context (TE p. 1124)

Vocabulary Skills
- Context Clues (SE pp. 1121, 1129)

Writing Skills/Grammar
- Research and Report (SE p. 1129)
- Movie Scene (TE p. 1126)

Literature and Reading Preview

Connect to the Sacred Text

What stories have you heard about the creation of human beings? Discuss this question with a small group.

Build Background

The Popol Vuh, or "Council Book," is an important source of information about ancient Mayan culture and history. It was written in Quiché (kē chā'), a language a Mayan group in Guatemala spoke. The Quiché people believed that the Popol Vuh enabled their leaders to see into the future. The book contains stories about mythological heroes and an account of creation. It also relates the history of the Quiché people up to the Spanish Conquest, around 1550.

Set Purposes for Reading

Big Idea Gods and Mortals

The literature of the peoples of the early Americas explored the origin of humanity and the relationship between humans and the gods. As you read, ask yourself, What does this creation myth reveal about the Maya?

Literary Element Myth

A **myth** is a traditional story that explains some aspect of human society or the natural world. Creation myths explain the origin of the world and its inhabitants. As you read, ask yourself, What mythic elements appear in this excerpt from the Popol Vuh?

Reading Strategy Clarify Meaning

When you **clarify meaning**, you apply a variety of comprehension strategies to help you understand difficult passages of a text. These strategies include rereading confusing sections, reading slowly and carefully, drawing on personal background, questioning, predicting, summarizing, paraphrasing, and constructing graphic organizers. As you read, ask yourself, Which strategies help clarify the meaning of this creation myth?

Tip: Apply Comprehension Strategies Use a chart like the one below to clarify the meaning of difficult passages.

Difficult Passage	Simplified Meaning
The face of the earth is not clear.	The Earth does not yet exist.

Learning Objectives

For pages 1120–1129

In studying this text, you will focus on the following objectives:

Literary Study: Analyzing myth.

Reading: Clarifying meaning.

Research: Presenting an oral report.

Vocabulary

conception (kən sep'shən) *n.* thought; idea; design; plan; p. 1123 *The old plan for the stadium is better known than the new conception.*

edible (ed'ə bəl) *adj.* fit to eat; p. 1126 *Even though the mushrooms looked safe to eat, they were not edible.*

Tip: Context Clues When you come across an unfamiliar word, pay close attention to the surrounding words and try to determine a possible meaning. For example, in the sentence *Even though the mushrooms looked safe to eat, they were not edible, edible* must mean "safe to eat," the phrase that describes the mushrooms' appearance.

POPOL VUH **1121**

Before You Read

Focus

Summary

In this creation myth, the gods meet to create the earth, mountains, and waterways. They then create animals to populate the earth but are disappointed that the animals cannot speak and praise their names. After turning their attention to humankind, the gods eventually find a way to create human beings of flesh and blood who can pray to and praise the gods. The gods are pleased with their creations but regret giving human beings complete understanding and knowledge. To ensure their eternal superiority to their creation, the gods limit the human ability to think and understand.

 For summaries in languages other than English, see Unit 6 Teaching Resources Book, pp. 21–26.

Vocabulary

Context Clues Have students copy the sentences that use the vocabulary words. For each sentence, have students circle the context clues that relate to the meaning of the vocabulary word. Then, in pairs, have students compare their work and discuss how the text they circled hints at the meanings of the vocabulary words.

 For additional vocabulary practice, see Unit 6 Teaching Resources Book, p. 29.

Advanced Learners/Pre-AP

DIFFERENTIATED INSTRUCTION

 Exploring Creation Myths Have students meet in small groups to discuss creation myths they have read or heard before. Tell groups to brainstorm a list of myths and then discuss similarities and differences among them. For example, students might consider the questions these myths try to answer. Suggest that some of these questions are the same from culture to culture; only the answers are different.

Have groups list the similarities and differences they determine in chart form. Then, have students add to their charts as they read the excerpt from the Popul Vuh. After reading, have students discuss whether creation myths are relevant today. What can we learn from them? What do they teach us about humanity?

Teach

Reading Strategy   1

Clarify Meaning Remind students that rereading can help them clarify confusing passages. Have students reread the bracketed paragraphs. **Ask:** What elements currently exist in this setting? What elements are missing? *(The only elements in the setting are the sky and water. Missing are any people, animals, plants, or physical landforms.)*

 For additional practice using the reading skill or strategy, see Unit 6 Teaching Resources Book, p. 28.

Literary Element   2

Myth Answer: *They are gods. They take the form of light.*

(APPROACHING) Some students might expect the creation myth to have one god. Point out that this creation myth portrays a group of gods who work together to create different elements of the universe. For example, the Heart of Sky and the Sovereign Plumed Serpent join forces to create the earth.

 For an audio recording of this selection, use Listening Library Audio CD-ROM.

Readability Scores

Dale-Chall: 6.3
DRP: 55
Lexile: 700

The Creation of Man, page from *Popol Vuh*. Diego Rivera. Watercolor on paper. Museo Casa Diego Rivera (INBA), Guanajuato, Mexico.

from the

POPOL VUH

Translated by Dennis Tedlock

Reading Practice

Analyze Sensory Details Remind students that sensory details appeal to the senses of sight, sound, touch, taste, and smell. Explain that sensory details help readers experience and relate to images and events in a story. Point out the sentence "Only the sea alone is pooled under all the sky." Explain why the image appeals to the sense of sight.

Have students scan these two pages for other sensory details. Ask volunteers to write examples on the board, and then discuss each example with the class. To what sense(s) does the image appeal? How does the detail help readers envision or experience what is being described? Help students determine the overall effect of the details.

his is the beginning of the Ancient Word, here in this place called Quiché. Here we shall inscribe, we shall implant the Ancient Word, the potential and source for everything done in the citadel[1] of Quiché, in the nation of Quiché people. . . .

This is the account, here it is:

Now it still ripples, now it still murmurs, ripples, it still sighs, still hums, and it is empty under the sky.

Here follow the first words, the first eloquence:

1 There is not yet one person, one animal, bird, fish, crab, tree, rock, hollow, canyon, meadow, forest. Only the sky alone is there; the face of the earth is not clear. Only the sea alone is pooled under all the sky; there is nothing whatever gathered together. It is at rest; not a single thing stirs. It is held back, kept at rest under the sky.

Whatever there is that might be is simply not there: only the pooled water, only the calm sea, only it alone is pooled.

Whatever might be is simply not there: only murmurs, ripples, in the dark, in the night. Only the Maker, Modeler alone, Sovereign Plumed Serpent, the Bearers, Begetters are in the water, a glittering light. They are there, they are enclosed in quetzal feathers, in blue-green.

Thus the name, "Plumed Serpent."

Visual Vocabulary

A *quetzal* (ket säl′) is a Central American bird, brilliantly colored, with long, flowing tail feathers. It is the national bird of Guatemala.

---

1. A *citadel* is a fortress that commands a city or a stronghold.

2 Myth *Who are these characters? What form do they take?*

Feathered Serpent. Postclassical. Stone. Museo Nacional de Antropología e Historia, Mexico City, D.F.

They are great knowers, great thinkers in their very being.

And of course there is the sky, and there is also the Heart of Sky. This is the name of the god, as it is spoken.

3 And then came his word, he came here to the Sovereign Plumed Serpent, here in the blackness, in the early dawn. He spoke with the Sovereign Plumed Serpent, and they talked, then they thought, then they worried. They agreed with each other, they joined their words, their thoughts. . . .

"Let it be this way, think about it: this water should be removed, emptied out for the formation of the earth's own plate and platform, then should come the sowing, the dawning of the sky-earth. But there will be no high days and no bright praise for our work, our design, until the rise of the human work, the human design," they said. **4**

And then the earth arose because of them, it was simply their word that brought it forth. For the forming of the earth they said "Earth." It arose suddenly, just like a cloud, like a mist, now forming, unfolding. Then the mountains were separated from the water, all at once the great mountains came forth. By their genius alone, by their cutting edge alone they carried out the **conception** of the mountain-plain, whose face grew instant groves of cypress and pine.

Vocabulary

conception (kən sep′shən) *n.* thought; idea; design; plan

POPOL VUH **1123**

Teach

Big Idea | 3

Gods and Mortals Point out that the two gods—Heart of Sky and Sovereign Plumed Serpent—discuss their ideas about the universe. Eventually, they "join" their "words [and] thoughts." **Ask:** What might this description reveal about Maya values? *(Students may say the description reveals that the Maya valued working together and respecting others.)*

Literary Element | 4

Myth Have the students review the Popul Vuh up to this point. **Ask:** What do the gods agree will be their most worthy task? *(Their most worthy task will be creating human beings.)* **Ask:** Why might this task be more challenging than the gods' other creations? *(Students may point out that human beings would be more complicated because they have great mental and emotional capacities; landforms and animals would be simpler to design.)*

Learning Objectives
Analyzing myth. (SE)
Clarifying meaning. (SE)
Analyzing sensory details. (TE)

English Learners

DIFFERENTIATED INSTRUCTION

Advanced Remind students that in a simile two or more objects are compared by means of the word *like* or *as*. Write the following simile on the board: "[The Earth] arose suddenly, just like a cloud, like a mist, now forming, unfolding." Underline the subject of the comparison: *Earth*. Then circle what the Earth is being compared to: *cloud* and *mist*.

Discuss with students characteristics of clouds and mist. Point out that both can start out light and transparent and can seem to arise from nowhere; however, they can quickly grow larger and thicker and spread across an area. Have pairs discuss what the comparison suggests about the formation of the Earth.

Approaching Level

DIFFERENTIATED INSTRUCTION

Understanding Repetition Point out the repetition of different versions of the phrase "What there is that might be is simply not there." Discuss how the repetition emphasizes what is to come in the creation. Explain that, at first, the scene is empty other than the ocean and the sky; however, "what might be" exists in "murmurs" of the gods. Clarify that "what might be" is the universe and its inhabitants.

Teach

Reading Strategy   1

Clarify Meaning Tell students that asking themselves questions as they read can help improve their comprehension. **Ask:** Why do the gods tell the deer and birds to "multiply" and "scatter"? *(They want the deer and birds to fill the entire earth with their presence.)* Encourage students to ask themselves other questions about the text on this page.

Reading Strategy   2

Clarify Meaning Possible answer: *The Earth came into being only because the gods thought of it.*

[ADVANCED LEARNERS] For advanced learners, **Ask:** Are the names of the creators—Heart of Sky and Heart of Earth—appropriate? Why or why not? *(Students may say the names are appropriate because the two gods created both elements; as such, they represent the heart, or life, or the sky and the earth.)*

Big Idea   3

Gods and Mortals Answer: *The gods are displeased because the animals have not spoken their names (that is, offered praise to the gods).*

And the Plumed Serpent was pleased with this:

"It was good that you came, Heart of Sky, Hurricane, and Newborn Thunderbolt, Sudden Thunderbolt. Our work, our design will turn out well," they said.

And the earth was formed first, the mountain-plain. The channels of water were separated; their branches wound their ways among the mountains. The waters were divided when the great mountains appeared.

Such was the formation of the earth when it was brought forth by the Heart of Sky, Heart of Earth, as they are called, since they were the first to think of it. The sky was set apart, and the earth was set apart in the midst of the waters.

Such was their plan when they thought, when they worried about the completion of their work. . . .

And then they gave out homes to the deer and birds:

"You, the deer: sleep along the rivers, in the canyons. Be here in the meadows, in the thickets, in the forests, multiply yourselves. You will stand and walk on all fours," they were told. So then they estab-

Man standing on a turtle, The Creator of the World. Mayan. Earthenware. Private collection.

2 Clarify Meaning *How would you paraphrase this sentence?*

1124 UNIT 6   THE EARLY AMERICAS

lished the nests of the birds, small and great:

"You, precious birds: your nests, your houses are in the trees, in the bushes. Multiply there, scatter there, in the branches of trees, the branches of bushes," **1** the deer and birds were told.

When this deed had been done, all of them had received a place to sleep and a place to stay. So it is that the nests of the animals are on the earth, given by the Bearer, Begetter. Now the arrangement of the deer and birds was complete.

And then the deer and birds were told by the Maker, Modeler, Bearer, Begetter:

"Talk, speak out. Don't moan, don't cry out. Please talk, each to each, within each kind, within each group," they were told—the deer, birds, puma, jaguar, serpent.

"Name now our names, praise us. We are your mother, we are your father. Speak now:

'Hurricane,
Newborn Thunderbolt, Sudden Thunderbolt,
Heart of Sky, Heart of Earth,
Maker, Modeler,
Bearer, Begetter,'

speak, pray to us, keep our days,"[2] they were told. But it didn't turn out that they spoke like people: they just squawked, they just chattered, they just howled. It wasn't apparent what language they spoke; each one gave a different cry. When the Maker, Modeler heard this:

"It hasn't turned out well, they haven't spoken," they said among themselves. "It hasn't turned out that our names have been named. Since we are their mason and

---

2. *Keep our days* refers to the Mayan sacred calendar. Each day was associated with one of the gods. The Maya consulted the calendar to guide their worship.

Gods and Mortals *Why are the gods displeased?*   **3**

Reading Practice

Analyze Cultural Context Remind students that a myth explains to a culture some aspect of society or the natural world. A creation myth explains how people came into being. This creation explains the motivations of the Maya gods in creating the earth, animals, and people.

Have students review the selection to find example of the motives of the Maya gods, in particular what problem they are trying to solve—first in creating the animals and then in creating various versions of humankind. In a class discussion, have students comment on what this problem-solving format reveals about the attitude of the Maya culture toward its gods.

sculptor, this will not do," the Bearers and Begetters said among themselves. So they told them:

"You will simply have to be transformed. Since it hasn't turned out well and you haven't spoken, we have changed our word:

"What you feed on, what you eat, the places where you sleep, the places where you stay, whatever is yours will remain in the canyons, the forests. Although it turned out that our days were not kept, nor did you pray to us, there may yet be strength in the keeper of days, the giver of praise whom we have yet to make. Just accept your service, just let your flesh be eaten.

"So be it, this must be your service," they were told when they were instructed—the animals, small and great, on the face of the earth.

And then they wanted to test their timing again, they wanted to experiment again, and they wanted to prepare for the keeping of days again. They had not heard their speech among the animals; it did not come to fruition and it was not complete.

And so their flesh was brought low: they served, they were eaten, they were killed—the animals on the face of the earth.

After informing the animals what their function on earth will be, the gods attempt to create humans. Working with earth and mud, they sculpt a body, but it keeps separating, loosening, and dissolving. Discouraged, the gods decide to carve humans out of wood. The woodcarvings look and talk like humans but are empty-headed and have no hearts. They neither remember nor praise the gods. Discouraged again, the gods destroy the woodcarvings—crushing and pulverizing them—and set out to discover the right ingredients for making humans.

And here is the beginning of the conception of humans, and of the search for the ingredients of the human body. So they spoke, the Bearer, Begetter, the Makers, Modelers named Sovereign Plumed Serpent:

"The dawn has approached, preparations have been made, and morning has come for the provider, nurturer, born in the light, begotten in the light. Morning has come for humankind, for the people of the face of the earth," they said. It all came together as they went on thinking in the darkness, in the night, as they searched and they sifted, they thought and they wondered.

And here their thoughts came out in clear light. They sought and discovered what was needed for human flesh. It was only a short while before the sun, moon, and stars were to appear above the Makers and Modelers. Split Place, Bitter Water Place[3] is the name: the yellow corn, white corn came from there.

And these are the names of the animals who brought the food: fox, coyote, parrot, crow. There were four animals who brought the news of the ears of yellow corn and white corn. They were coming from over there at Split Place, they showed the way to the split.

And this was when they found the staple[4] foods.

And these were the ingredients for the flesh of the human work, the human design, and the water was for the blood. It became human blood, and corn was also used by the Bearer, Begetter.

And so they were happy over the provisions of the good mountain, filled with sweet things, thick with yellow corn, white corn, and thick with pataxte and cacao,

---

3. *Split Place, Bitter Water Place* refers to a high mountain in Guatemala near the Mexican border. Those who live near it today believe corn originated there.
4. *Staple* means "primary."

Gods and Mortals *According to Mayan belief, what symbolizes human flesh? What symbolizes blood?* **5**

Reading Strategy | 4

Clarify Meaning Point out the references to light and darkness in the bracketed paragraph. Have students draw on their own personal experiences to answer these questions: What do light and darkness usually symbolize? *(Students may suggest that light and darkness symbolize good and evil, respectively.)* How are light and darkness used in this paragraph? *(Darkness is used to illustrate the period of questioning and wondering; light is used to illustrate the period of clarity and new ideas.)*

[APPROACHING] If students struggle to answer the questions, encourage them to think how the concepts of daytime and nighttime are portrayed in books, in movies, and on television. During what period do most people struggle? During what period do most people find peace and hope?

Big Idea | 5

Gods and Mortals Answer: *Corn symbolizes flesh. Water symbolizes blood.*

Learning Objectives
Analyzing myth. (SE)
Clarifying meaning. (SE)
Analyzing cultural context. (TE)

Advanced Learners/Pre-AP

DIFFERENTIATED INSTRUCTION

Applications to Daily Life Ask: What aspect of the universe does the text on this page explain? *(It explains the place of animals in the hierarchy; it explains why animals can be killed and eaten.)* How might the Maya have applied this information to their daily lives? *(Students may suggest the Maya used the text to justify eating meat or justify human superiority over animals.)*

Have students review the selection for other practical applications. For example, students might consider what the selection implies or directly teaches about human behaviors and attitudes. Remind students that the selection might also instruct on what human beings should avoid doing. Have students list their findings and then share them in a class discussion.

Teach

Literary Element | 1

Myth Point out that this part of the Popul Vuh explains the origins of human beings. **Ask:** How were the first people different from the animals the gods had created? *(The first people spoke with words, they walked upright, and they had an understanding of the world.)* How are the first people different from people today? *(Students may point out that the first people had perfect understanding of their surroundings; they seemed to possess more knowledge than people do today.)*

Reading Strategy | 2

Clarify Meaning Answer: *Human beings did not come from the womb of any woman, including that of a goddess. The phrases "simply made and modeled," "no mother and no father," and "by genius alone" provide clues.*

View the Art ★

Answer: *Students may mention the vacant eyes, the ritual dress, and the positioning of the hands.*

Young Maize God, c. 775 Honduras. Height 89.7 cm. British Museum, London.

View the Art Since corn, or maize, was the Maya's most important food, it is not surprising that the maize god was of great importance in Mayan culture. How does the artist suggest that this sculpture depicts a god? ★

countless zapotes, anonas, jocotes, nances, matasanos,[5] sweets—the rich foods filling up the citadel named Split Place, Bitter Water Place. All the **edible** fruits were there: small staples, great staples, small plants, great plants. The way was shown by the animals.

And then the yellow corn and white corn were ground, and Xmucane did the grinding nine times. Food was used, along with the water she rinsed her hands with,[6]

---

5. *Pataxte and cacao, . . . nances, matasanos:* Pataxte and cacao are seeds used to make cocoa and chocolate. Zapotes, anonas, jocotes, nances, and matasanos are all tropical fruits.
6. *Xmucane . . . rinsed her hands with:* Xmucane is one of the two seers the gods consult earlier in the story. Women ground corn to make corn cakes. They would rinse off the particles of corn meal that stuck to their hands during the grinding.

Vocabulary
edible (edʹə bəl) *adj.* fit to eat

1126 UNIT 6 THE EARLY AMERICAS

for the creation of grease; it became human fat when it was worked by the Bearer, Begetter, Sovereign Plumed Serpent, as they are called.

After that, they put it into words:

> the making, the modeling of our first mother-father,
> with yellow corn, white corn alone for the flesh,
> food alone for the human legs and arms,
> for our first fathers, the four human works.

It was staples alone that made up their flesh.

These are the names of the first people who were made and modeled.

This is the first person: Jaguar Quitze.
And now the second: Jaguar Night.
And now the third: Not Right Now.
And the fourth: Dark Jaguar.

And these are the names of our first mother-fathers. They were simply made and modeled, it is said; they had no mother and no father. We have named the men by themselves. No woman gave birth to them, nor were they begotten by the builder, sculptor, Bearer, Begetter. By sacrifice alone, by genius alone they were made, they were modeled by the Maker, Modeler, Bearer, Begetter, Sovereign Plumed Serpent. And when they came to fruition, they came out human:

They talked and they made words.
They looked and they listened.
They walked, they worked.

They were good people, handsome, with looks of the male kind. Thoughts came into existence and they gazed; their vision came all at once. Perfectly they saw, perfectly they knew everything under the sky, **1** whenever they looked. The moment they turned around and looked around in the

---

Clarify Meaning *What does this sentence mean? What clues help clarify the meaning?* **2**

Writing Practice

SMALL GROUP **Write a Movie Scene** Suggest to students that myths are well suited for adapting into movies because they often contain supernatural elements, such as godlike characters and talking animals. Explain that a scene is an unbroken piece of narrative that takes place in one setting. For example, the creation of the earth is one scene; the gods' interaction with animals is another scene.

Organize students into groups, and have each group choose a scene from the Popul Vuh to adapt into a script for a movie. Members should discuss how they can bring the scene to life on film, including how they will handle the setting, characters, conflict, and dialogue. Encourage students to use their creativity to elaborate on the basic information set forth in the Popul Vuh.

Provide students with a format to follow as they write their scripts; for example, suggest that they begin the script with a cast of characters and include detailed scene descriptions as needed. Remind students to think in terms of sound—not just dialogue, but also sound effects that might occur. Allow groups to describe their movie scenes to the class.

1126

sky, on the earth, everything was seen without any obstruction. They didn't have to walk around before they could see what was under the sky; they just stayed where they were.

As they looked, their knowledge became intense. Their sight passed through trees, through rocks, through lakes, through seas, through mountains, through plains. Jaguar Quitze, Jaguar Night, Not Right Now, and Dark Jaguar were truly gifted people.

And then they were asked by the builder and mason:

"What do you know about your being? Don't you look, don't you listen? Isn't your speech good, and your walk? So you must look, to see out under the sky. Don't you see the mountain-plain clearly? So try it," they were told.

And then they saw everything under the sky perfectly. After that, they thanked the Maker, Modeler:

"Truly now,
double thanks, triple thanks
that we've been formed, we've been given
our mouths, our faces,
we speak, we listen,
we wonder, we move,
our knowledge is good, we've understood
what is far and near,
and we've seen what is great and small
under the sky, on the earth.
Thanks to you we've been formed,
we've come to be made and modeled,
our grandmother, our grandfather,"

they said when they gave thanks for having been made and modeled. They understood everything perfectly, they sighted the four sides, the four corners in the sky, on the earth, and this didn't sound good to the builder and sculptor:

"What our works and designs have said is no good:

'We have understood everything, great and small,' they say." And so the Bearer, Begetter took back their knowledge:

"What should we do with them now? Their vision should at least reach nearby, they should see at least a small part of the face of the earth, but what they're saying isn't good. Aren't they merely 'works' and 'designs' in their very names? Yet they'll become as great as gods, unless they procreate, proliferate at the sowing, the dawning, unless they increase."

"Let it be this way: now we'll take them apart just a little, that's what we need. What we've found out isn't good. Their deeds would become equal to ours, just because their knowledge reaches so far. They see everything," so said

the Heart of Sky, Hurricane,
Newborn Thunderbolt, Sudden Thunderbolt,
Sovereign Plumed Serpent,
Bearer, Begetter,
Xpiyacoc, Xmucane,
Maker, Modeler,

as they are called. And when they changed the nature of their works, their designs, it was enough that the eyes be marred by the Heart of Sky. They were blinded as the face of a mirror is breathed upon. Their vision flickered. Now it was only from close up that they could see what was there with any clarity.

And such was the loss of the means of understanding, along with the means of knowing everything, by the four humans. The root was implanted.

And such was the making, modeling of our first grandfather, our father, by the Heart of Sky, Heart of Earth. ❧

Myth *What limitation does this turn of events help explain?* **3**

Gods and Mortals *What do the gods do to impair the understanding of the first people?* **4**

English Learners

DIFFERENTIATED INSTRUCTION

Intermediate Point out the word *vision* on this page. Tell students *vision* can mean more than just the ability to see; *vision* can also refer to the ability to understand or imagine. Ask students to explain how both definitions of the word *vision* apply to the first people. *(The first people were able to see the world around them and understand and imagine it.)*

Advanced Learners/Pre-AP

DIFFERENTIATED INSTRUCTION

Analyze Symbolism Point out to students that the names of three of the four "first people" contain the word *jaguar*. Ask students to use print and online resources to research jaguars and their significance in Maya civilization. What characteristics of the jaguar might the Maya have admired or feared? Why might jaguars have appeared in the Maya creation myth? Have students briefly summarize their findings.

Teach

Literary Element | **3**

Myth Answer: *The limitation of human knowledge is explained. The gods decided it was not good for human beings to "understand everything perfectly."* **Ask:** Is this outcome similar to or different from other creation myths you have read or heard? Explain. *(Students will likely find the outcome similar; most creation myths emphasize a nonhuman power that is all-powerful and all-knowing.)*

Big Idea | **4**

Gods and Mortals Answer: *The gods mar their vision, clouding it in a manner similar to the way that breath fogs a mirror.* **Ask:** How might the Maya hearing the creation myth have taken comfort in this outcome? *(Students may suggest the Maya might have found comfort in trusting that only the gods possessed a thorough understanding of the world and that human beings did not have this ability.)*

To check students' understanding of the selection, see Unit 6 Teaching Resources Book, p. 31.

Learning Objectives
Analyzing myth. (SE)
Clarifying meaning. (SE)
Writing a movie scene. (TE)

After You Read

Assess

1. Students may wonder whether the Maya explained how the gods finally created the human beings that exist today.

2. (a) It is dark, near dawn. Only sky and pooled water exist. (b) The gods are in the water. The Maya would think this an appropriate place because they associated water with the gods.

3. (a) They say "Earth," and land arises from the water. (b) They worry because they have not yet formed human beings.

4. (a) They change their plan because the animals cannot speak or praise them. (b) The gods have a need to be worshipped as creators.

5. No; the gods' actions explain that the Maya exist to realize that they are the creation of the gods and to praise them for it.

6. Possible answer: The Maya felt that religious worship was important and that human beings should not seek to emulate the gods.

7. This story reflects the beliefs that the gods created human beings, the gods need to be worshipped, and human beings should serve this function.

8. Students may respond that the Maya, instead of experimenting with nature, regard it as sacred.

After You Read

Respond and Think Critically

Respond and Interpret

1. What thoughts went through your mind as you finished reading this myth?

2. (a)Describe the setting at the beginning of the story. (b)Where are the gods? According to Mayan religious practices, why might this be considered an appropriate place for the gods?

3. (a)How do the gods create Earth? (b)Why do they worry about the completion of their plan?

4. (a)Why do the gods change their plan for the animals? (b)Why do the gods need human beings?

Analyze and Evaluate

5. To a neutral observer, the gods in this story might appear to be vain, selfish, or cruel. Do you think the Maya viewed them this way? Why or why not?

6. What does this myth reveal about the values of the ancient Maya?

Connect

7. **Big Idea** Gods and Mortals Myths reflect a culture's perception of the deepest truths about humans and the gods. What Mayan beliefs does this story reflect?

8. **Connect to Today** How does the Mayan view of nature and humankind's place in it differ from the modern scientific view of the natural world?

Literary Element Myth

ACT Skills Practice

1. This literary work is classified as a myth because it explains:

   I. the origin of the world.

   II. the meaning of existence.

   III. the nature and feats of heroes.

   A. I only

   B. I and II only

   C. I and III only

   D. I, II, and III

2. In this myth, the Creators first make human beings because:

   F. they are lonely.

   G. they need laborers to build temples to them.

   H. they need to destroy the animals.

   J. the animals cannot speak to praise them.

Review: Imagery

As you learned on page 787, **imagery** refers to the "word pictures" that evoke emotional responses. To create images, authors use **sensory details**—descriptions that appeal to one or more of the five senses: sight, hearing, touch, taste, and smell.

Partner Activity Meet with a classmate to identify and analyze images in the Popol Vuh. Use a chart like the one below to list examples of images. When you finish filling in your chart, discuss the effect achieved by the images that describe the setting before the creation of Earth.

Image	Sensory Appeal	Effect
Only murmurs, ripples, in the dark, in the night	sight and hearing	Suggests an unseen presence

 **Literature** Online

Selection Resources For Selection Quizzes, eFlashcards, and Reading-Writing Connection activities, go to glencoe.com and enter QuickPass code GLW6053u6.

Literary Element

1. **B** is the correct answer. **C** and **D** are incorrect because, although other sections of the Popul Vuh include tales of the nature and feats of heroes, this section does not.

2. **J** is the correct answer. **H** is incorrect because, even though the Creators proclaim that human beings are to sacrifice and eat animals, this is not the primary reason human beings were created.

Progress Check

Can students analyze myth?

If No → See Unit 6 Teaching Resources Book, p. 27.

Review: Imagery

Images of darkness, rippling, murmuring sounds, and pooled water evoke a sense of mystery and anticipation.

For additional selection assessment, see Assessment Resources, pp. 219–220.

Reading Strategy Clarify Meaning

Rereading a passage that appears unclear at first can often unlock its meaning. However, it also helps to identify parts of the text that seem clear, so you can weigh your interpretations of difficult sections against them.

Partner Activity With a partner, look back at the chart you made on page 1121, choose a passage that was unclear at first, and reexamine it in relation to parts of the myth that seem clear. What is your interpretation of the difficult passage now?

Vocabulary Practice

Practice with Context Clues Look back at pages 1122–1127 to find context clues for the boldfaced vocabulary words below. Record your findings in a chart like the one shown.

conception   edible

EXAMPLE:

Word: sift

Textual Clues: The creators "searched and they sifted, they thought and they wondered" for a long time, so they must have been considering their ideas very carefully.

Meaning: sort out; examine very carefully

Academic Vocabulary

In the Popol Vuh, the gods create the human **design** *by using corn for flesh and water for blood.*

Design is an academic word. In more familiar usage, the phrase **graphic design** refers to the process of planning and creating visual information. To further explore the word *design*, answer the following items.

1. What materials might an architect use to create a **design** for a house?

2. Use the word *design* in a sentence of your own describing a project you once worked on.

For more on academic vocabulary, see pages 36–37 and R83–R85.

Connect to *Social Studies*

Research and Report

Assignment In another section of the Popol Vuh, twin brothers avenge the deaths of the Maize (corn) Gods, who were killed by the gods of the underworld while playing a game called Pitz. The object of this game is to bounce a ball through stone hoops, without using one's hands. Research this ancient Mayan game, using library resources and the Internet. Then present an oral report to share your findings.

Investigate First, list possible sources of information, how to access them, and their likely reliability. Remember that copyright laws require you to credit your sources. Take notes on what you learn from each source, recording information and ideas accurately and coherently. A helpful strategy is to write your notes in a web organized by main topics, like the one shown below.

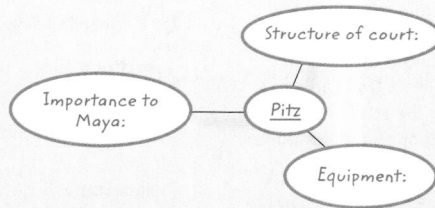

Create Organize your notes coherently and then prepare an introduction, a middle section, and a conclusion. In the middle section of your report, connect your research to contemporary life by drawing parallels between the importance of sports in Mayan and modern cultures. Use props, visual aids, graphs, and electronic media to enhance the appeal of your presentation. Prepare a bibliography of reference materials to provide as a handout.

Report As you present your report, use effective and interesting language as well as appropriate eye contact, body movements, and voice register. Then have a partner provide feedback on whether you have synthesized, organized, and presented your information carefully.

After You Read

Assess

Reading Strategy

Encourage students to identify passages that they were able to clarify by comparing the confusing passages to ones that were already clear.

Vocabulary Practice

Possible answers:

Word: *conception*

Textual Clues: The creators "agreed with each other, they joined their words, their thoughts…Then the mountains were separated from the water, all at once the great mountains came forth." In other words, they came up with a plan and used it to create the world.

Meaning: thought; idea; design; plan

Word: *edible*

Textual Clues: The "edible fruits" appear in the list of "foods," so *edible* must mean "able to be eaten."

Meaning: fit to eat

> For grammar practice, see Unit 6 Teaching Resources Book, p. 30.

Academic Vocabulary

1. Students might list drafting paper, pencils, and measuring tools.
2. Students should describe the planning stages of the project.

Connect to *Social Studies*

Students' reports should

- present information in an accurate and interesting way
- connect their research to contemporary life
- effectively use verbal and nonverbal delivery techniques, such as eye contact and body language

 To create custom assessments online, go to Progress Reporter Online Assessment.

 To create custom assessments using software, use ExamView Assessment Suite.

Grammar Workshop

Misplaced and Dangling Modifiers

Focus

Write on the board:

Pass me behind you the sugar.

Walking by the park, the leaves on the trees were changing colors.

Remind students that modifiers are words or phrases that describe something. Point to the two sentences on the board and ask students whether these sentences make sense. Then, underline the modifier in each sentence ("behind you," "walking by the park"). Explain to students that the first sentence contains a misplaced modifier and the second sentence contains a dangling modifier. Work with students to correct the problems in the sentences.

Teach

Identifying Misplaced and Dangling Modifiers
When writing, tell students to underline modifiers and circle the words they modify. This will help them determine if they have any misplaced or dangling modifiers.

 For additional grammar practice, see Unit 6 Teaching Resources Book, p. 33.

Assess

Possible rewrites:
1. Enclosed in quetzal feathers, the Serpent, the Bearers, and Begetters are in the water.
2. Emptied out of the earth, the water was not to be found.
3. The waters parted the mountains into two divisions.
4. Devoured, the animals were gone.

1130

Modifiers

A **misplaced modifier** is a word or a phrase that makes a sentence unclear because the modifier is in the wrong place. A **dangling modifier** doesn't modify anything in a sentence.

Tip

To avoid misplaced and dangling modifiers, think about the meaning of the sentence. Draw an arrow from the modifier to the word or phrase it modifies.

Language Handbook

For more about **modifers,** see Language Handbook, p. R40.

LOG ON ▶ **Literature** Online

Grammar For more grammar practice, go to glencoe.com and enter QuickPass code GLW6053u6.

Grammar Workshop

Misplaced and Dangling Modifiers

Literature Connection A **misplaced modifier** is a word or phrase appearing in the wrong place in a sentence. Read the sentence below from the Popol Vuh.

> *"The dawn has approached, preparations have been made, and morning has come for the provider, nurturer, born in the light, begotten in the light."*

If the modifier *born in the light, begotten in the light* were moved to the beginning of the sentence, it would read: *Born in the light, begotten in the light, the dawn has approached . . .* The phrase would then incorrectly modify the word *dawn*, instead of *nurturer*. A sentence may also have a **dangling modifier**, which seems logically to modify no word at all. For example in the sentence *Bare and silent, there was no life*, "bare and silent" is dangling.

PROBLEM 1 A misplaced modifier
Separated from the water, the Makers formed mountains.

SOLUTION Place the modifier as close as possible to the word it modifies.
The Makers formed mountains separated from the water.

PROBLEM 2 A dangling modifier
Blinded, their understanding was now limited.

SOLUTION Supply a word that the dangling modifier can sensibly modify.
Blinded, the humans now had limited understanding.

Revise Rewrite the following sentences on a separate piece of paper to correct misplaced or dangling modifiers. If a sentence needs no revision, write *correct*.

1. Enclosed in quetzal feathers, The Serpent, the Bearers, and Begetters are in the water.
2. Emptied out of the earth, now there was no water to be found.
3. Into two divisions, the waters parted the mountains.
4. Devoured, gone were the animals.

1130 UNIT 6 THE EARLY AMERICAS

Writing Practice

Write a Description To give students more practice with misplaced and dangling modifiers, have them write a short description of a setting or experience. For example, they could write about a time they went on vacation. Tell students to include modifiers in their descriptions. Also, have them include several misplaced and dangling modifiers in their descriptions.

After students have finished, have them exchange their descriptions with a partner. Have students underline all of the modifiers in the description. Then, have them circle the misplaced and dangling modifiers. Have partners work together to correct the modifier errors. Invite volunteers to share their corrected descriptions with the class.

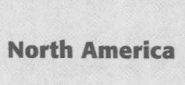
Coyote Finishes His Work

Meet **Barry Lopez**
(born 1945)

Author and photographer Barry Lopez finds many of the subjects for his writing in nature and the environment. He has written about the desert in *Desert Notes: Reflections in the Eye of a Raven* (1976) and the Arctic vastness in *Arctic Dreams* (1986). In 1978 he published the best-selling *Of Wolves and Men*. Two works of fiction, *River Notes: The Dance of Herons* (1979) and *Winter Count* (1981), have also been well received. In addition to his nature writing, Lopez is acclaimed for his retellings of Native American tales.

Influence of Nature Lopez grew up primarily in rural southern California. Living near the desert, he developed a keen interest in nature. Lopez recalls that "encounters with coyotes, jackrabbits, and even rattlesnakes were not unusual." In college, Lopez began to merge his interest in nature with his passion for literature.

Reteller of Folktales While attending the University of Oregon, Lopez met Professor Barre Toelken. Toelken introduced him to the study of natural history and geography as well as to a number of creative people including "senior Native American men, itinerant Asian poets, black jazz musicians, and translators." Native American culture particularly impressed Lopez because of the close relationship it fostered between humanity and nature.

"Coyote Finishes His Work" is from Lopez's collection *Giving Birth to Thunder, Sleeping with His Daughter: Coyote Builds North America* (1977). According to Lopez, "Coyote is a creature of *oral* literature and mutable." In other words, because the original coyote folktales were

> "If I were asked what I want to accomplish as a writer, I would say it's to contribute to a literature of hope."
>
> —Barry Lopez

not written down, they were subject to alteration as one generation passed them down orally to the next. Stories about coyote were told "all over North America—in Cheyenne tipis, Mandan earth lodges, Inupiak igloos, Navajo hogans and Sia pueblos—with much laughter and guffawing and with exclamations of surprise and awe." In his Native American folktale retellings, Lopez strives to preserve the stories' connections to tribal identity, their entertainment values, and their reinforcement of moral beliefs.

 Literature Online

Author Search For more about Barry Lopez, go to glencoe.com and enter QuickPass code GLW6053u6.

Before You Read

Focus

Bellringer Options

Daily Language Transparency 107

Or ask: What stories or movies have you read or watched in which animals acted like human beings? *(Students may suggest Aesop's Fables or examples of children's literature. Students may mention cartoons or movies.)* Lead a discussion about why students think the writers of these stories and movies choose to tell their tales through walking and talking animals.

Selection Skills

Literary Elements
- Analyze Motif (SE p. 1132, 1134, 1135; TE p. 1132)

Reading Skills
- Draw Conclusions About Culture (SE pp. 1132, 1134, 1135)

Coyote Finishes His Work

Vocabulary Skills
- Word Parts (SE p. 1132, 1135)

Speaking/Listening/Viewing Skills
- Create a Folktale (TE p. 1134)

Writing Skills/Grammar
- Graphic Story (SE p. 1135)

Before You Read

Focus

Summary

The Creator sends Coyote around the world—to sort people into tribes; teach them different languages; show them how to hunt, dress, and dance; and play tricks on them. Then the Creator comes to Earth and sends Coyote to a special place, saying that the people will not see Coyote again until the earth is old and ready for its final transformation.

 For summaries in languages other than English, see Unit 6 Teaching Resources Book, pp. 34–39.

Vocabulary

Word Parts Tell students to write the words *habitat* and *revival* on a sheet of paper. Have them underline the parts of these words that are similar to *inhabit* and *revive*. Then tell students to look up the meanings of *habitat* and *revival* in a dictionary. Have them explain how the words are similar to the vocabulary words.

 For additional vocabulary practice, see Unit 6 Teaching Resources Book, p. 42.

Literary Element Practice

Analyze Motif Before students begin reading "Coyote Finishes His Work," suggest they compile a list of questions or create a graphic organizer to help them record details about the story's motif—a trickster figure. You may want to allow students to work with a partner to devise these questions or organizers.

Here are some questions that students may suggest to help them track details of motif:

- Who is the trickster figure in the story?
- How does this trickster break rules or create trouble?
- How does the trickster outwit people or gods?
- What characteristics does the trickster possess?

Students may suggest graphic organizers such as webs or charts to track the actions and characteristics of the trickster.

Literature and Reading Preview

Connect to the Folktale

What qualities do you associate with coyotes? Discuss this question with a group.

Build Background

Whether creator, teacher, hero, or trickster, Coyote appears in a number of stories throughout the folklore traditions of the North American Plains Indians. In these stories, Coyote displays a variety of traits (foolishness, cleverness, playfulness, wisdom, strength, resourcefulness), all of which he uses—sometimes accidentally—to set the world right.

Set Purposes for Reading

Big Idea Gods and Mortals

Native American literature tells of the interrelations between people, animals, and gods. As you read, ask yourself, What do these interrelations suggest about Native American values?

Literary Element Motif

A **motif** is an element that recurs throughout a work or several works and is related to its theme. In most folklore traditions, the **trickster figure** (see pages 38–51) is a motif. Tricksters represent that part of human nature that wants to break rules and stir up trouble. As you read, ask yourself, How does the motif of the trickster help shape this folktale?

Reading Strategy Draw Conclusions About Culture

When you **draw conclusions about culture,** you make broad statements about the culture the work reflects, using clues found in the dialogue, the narrator's commentary, and the details of the plot. As you read, ask yourself, What can I conclude about the cultural background of this folktale?

Tip: Take Notes In a graphic organizer like the one below, write down details and a broad statement about the culture.

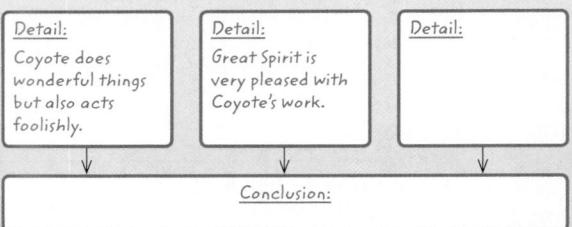

Learning Objectives

For pages 1131–1135

In studying this text, you will focus on the following objectives:

Literary Study: Analyzing motif.

Reading: Drawing conclusions about culture.

Writing: Writing a graphic story.

Vocabulary

inhabit (in hab′ it) *v.* to reside or live in; p. 1133 *A rare species of finches inhabits the island.*

revive (ri vīv′) *v.* to recover; to come back to life; p. 1134 *After several days in a coma, Jacob revived and began to speak.*

Tip: Word Parts Knowing a word's derivation often provides a clue to its meaning. For example, knowing the word *revive* is composed of the Latin prefix *re-*, which means "again," and the verb *vivere,* which means "to live," may help you remember that *revive* means "to recover" or "to live again."

COYOTE ☆
FINISHES HIS WORK

Retold by Barry Lopez

Brush Poppers, 1984. Jaune Quick-to-See Smith
Flathead/Shoshone/Cree Tribes. Pastel on paper, 30 x
22 in. Marilyn Butler Gallery, Sante Fe, NM.

From the very beginning, Coyote was traveling around all over the earth. He did many wonderful things when he went along. He killed the monsters and the evil spirits that preyed on the people. He made the Indians, and put them out in tribes all over the world because Old Man Above wanted the earth to be **inhabited** all over, not just in one or two places.

He gave all the people different names and taught them different languages. This is why Indians live all over the country now and speak in different ways.

He taught the people how to eat and how to hunt the buffalo and catch eagles. He taught them what roots to eat and how to make a good lodge and what to wear. He taught them how to dance.

Vocabulary

inhabit (in hab′it) *adj.* to reside or live in

Gods and Mortals *What do these details suggest about the interrelations between people and animals?* **1**

BARRY LOPEZ **1133**

Teach

Big Idea   1

Gods and Mortals Answer: *These details suggest the dependence of Native Americans on an animal for their tribal identities and languages.*

Literary History ☆

Coyote Tales There are hundreds of tales in North American Indian mythology and folklore that involve Coyote. In one tale, Porcupine seeks revenge on Coyote because Coyote tricked Porcupine out of some meat. In another tale, Coyote and Skunk reveal their inability to hunt.

 For an audio recording of this selection, use Listening Library Audio CD-ROM.

Readability Scores

Dale-Chall: 4.4
DRP: 46
Lexile: 550

Learning Objectives
Analyzing motif. (SE)
Drawing conclusions about culture. (SE)

English Learners

DIFFERENTIATED INSTRUCTION

Intermediate Write the following excerpts from the story on the board: "He gave all the people different names" (past tense), "Indians live all over the country now and speak in different ways" (present tense), "I will send messages to the earth" (future tense).

Point out to students that each underlined verb is in a different tense. Each refers to a different time during which the action of the verb is taking place. Explain fiction writers often change tenses as the needs of a story dictate. Have students write a three-paragraph story, with the first relating to past events, the second moving to the present, and the third to the future. Ask students to exchange stories with partners and check partners' work for accurate verb tense.

Teach

Literary Element   1

Motif **Answer:** *The trickster figure is ambivalent; his actions sometimes belie his wisdom and strength.*

> For additional literary element practice, see Unit 6 Teaching Resources Book, p. 40.

Reading Strategy   2

Draw Conclusions About Culture **Answer:** *Students may say that Native Americans view supernatural beings as actively participating in natural and human events.*

APPROACHING To help approaching level students answer this question, have them consider what Coyote does for and to human beings in this story. You may have them write a list of Coyote's actions. Then have them answer the question.

> For additional practice using the reading skill or strategy, see Unit 6 Teaching Resources Book, p. 41.

> To check students' understanding of the selection, see Unit 6 Teaching Resources Book, p. 44.

Sometimes he made mistakes, and even though he was wise and powerful, he did many foolish things. But that was his way.

Coyote liked to play tricks. He thought about himself all the time, and told everyone he was a great warrior, but he was not. Sometimes he would go too far with some trick and get someone killed. Other times, he would have a trick played on himself by someone else. He got killed this way so many times that Fox and the birds got tired of bringing him back to life. Another way he got in trouble was trying to do what someone else did. This is how he came to be called Imitator.

Coyote was ugly too. The girls did not like him. But he was smart. He could change himself around and trick the women. Coyote got the girls when he wanted.

One time, Coyote had done everything he could think of and was traveling from one place to another place, looking for other things that needed to be done. Old Man saw him going along and said to himself, "Coyote has now done almost everything he is capable of doing. His work is almost done. It is time to bring him back to the place where he started."

So Great Spirit[1] came down and traveled in the shape of an old man. He met Coyote. Coyote said, "I am Coyote. Who are you?"

Old Man said, "I am Chief of the earth. It was I who sent you to set the world right."

"No," Coyote said, "you never sent me. I don't know you. If you are the Chief, take that lake over there and move it to the side of that mountain."

"No. If you are Coyote, let me see you do it."

Coyote did it.

"Now, move it back."

Coyote tried, but he could not do it. He thought this was strange. He tried again, but he could not do it.

Chief moved the lake back.

Coyote said, "Now I know you are the Chief."

Old Man said, "Your work is finished, Coyote. You have traveled far and done much good. Now you will go to where I have prepared a home for you."

Then Coyote disappeared. Now no one knows where he is anymore.

Old Man got ready to leave, too. He said to the Indians, "I will send messages to the earth by the spirits of the people who reach me but whose time to die has not yet come. They will carry messages to you from time to time. When their spirits come back into their bodies, they will **revive** and tell you their experiences.

"Coyote and myself, we will not be seen again until Earth-woman[2] is very old. Then we shall return to earth, for it will require a change by that time. Coyote will come along first, and when you see him you will know I am coming. When I come along, all the spirits of the dead will be with me. There will be no more Other Side Camp.[3] All the people will live together. Earth-mother will go back to her first shape and live as a mother among her children. Then things will be made right."

Now they are waiting for Coyote. ∾

---

1. *Great Spirit* is the creator; in this case, it is Old Man Above.

1 Motif *What can you infer about the trickster figure?*

2 Draw Conclusions About Culture *What can you conclude about the Native American view of the supernatural?*

2. *Earth-woman* is Earth personified as a woman and, figuratively, the mother of all people.
3. *Other Side Camp* is a place where the spirits of the dead reside.

Vocabulary

revive (ri vīv′) *v.* to recover; to come back to life

1134 UNIT 6   THE EARLY AMERICAS

Speaking Practice

Create a Tale Many Native American folktales include a wise figure, animals, and/or elements of nature as characters. In small groups, have students create an original folktale aloud. Each student will take turns adding sentences to the story until it is complete. Their folktales should teach a moral, or valuable lesson and should include an animal and/or elements of nature as characters. Students should discuss what makes their folktale interesting or unique. Then have each group share their folktale with the class. Discuss how the folktale may have changed from the original version. Remind students that original coyote folktales were not written down but were passed down through oral tradition.

After You Read

Respond and Think Critically

Respond and Interpret

1. Which details or incidents in this folktale did you find most interesting? Explain.

2. (a)How was Coyote foolish? (b)On whom did he depend for rescue when his foolishness went too far?

3. (a)How does Old Man prove to Coyote that he is the Chief of the earth? (b)Why does Old Man decide to send Coyote away from the world?

Analyze and Evaluate

4. (a)What does the incident of the mountain and the lake suggest about Coyote's power? (b)To what extent does Old Man guide Coyote's actions throughout the tale?

---

5. Tales such as "Coyote Finishes His Work" were originally passed down orally rather than in written form. How does the author's style suggest the oral nature of this tale?

Connect

6. **Big Idea** Gods and Mortals Based on this folktale, what values do you think are important to Native Americans?

7. **Connect to Today** (a)What trickster figures can you identify in modern literature or in popular culture? (b)Do these figures serve a useful function in society? Explain.

Literary Element Motif

In Native American folklore, the **trickster motif** is most commonly found in the character of Coyote. Although Coyote never shows concern for others, his actions often end up benefiting them.

1. What elements of the trickster motif does Coyote embody in this story?

2. Overall, do you think Coyote is a force for good or for evil? Explain.

Reading Strategy Draw Conclusions About Culture

Look back at the chart you made on page 1132, and then answer the following questions.

1. What conclusions can you draw about the spiritual belief system presented in this myth?

2. Which details support your conclusions?

 Literature Online

Selection Resources For Selection Quizzes, eFlash-cards, and Reading-Writing Connection activities, go to glencoe.com and enter QuickPass code GLW6053u6.

Vocabulary Practice

Practice with Word Parts For each vocabulary word in the left column, identify the related word with a shared part in the right column. Write each word and underline the part they have in common. Use a printed or online dictionary to look up the meaning of the related word. Then explain how it is related to the vocabulary word.

1. inhabit   revitalize

2. revive   habitation

EXAMPLE: disconsolate, solace

Solace means "comfort." A disconsolate person is one who cannot be comforted.

Writing

Write a Graphic Story How do you imagine people might receive Coyote when he returns to usher in the Earth's final transformation? Create a graphic story of three or four panels that tells the story of Coyote's return as you imagine it. If possible, use dialogue in your story.

BARRY LOPEZ **1135**

Literary Element

1. Coyote is selfish, foolish, and mischievous, but he is also a powerful creator.

2. Some students may focus on Coyote's tricks and deception; others may focus on his role as a teacher of the people.

Reading Strategy

1. Possible answer: The belief system includes supernatural beings and an afterlife.

2. The mention of Other Side Camp and the characters of Coyote and Old Man support these conclusions.

After You Read

Assess

1. Students should give reasons for their choices.

2. (a) He played tricks that hurt himself and others. (b) Fox and the birds

3. (a) He prevents Coyote from moving the lake and then moves it himself. (b) Coyote has accomplished almost all of his work.

4. (a) The incident suggests that Old Man is the source of Coyote's power and can take it away if he wants. (b) He guides Coyote's work, but he allows Coyote to play tricks on people and do other foolish things.

5. The author uses simple diction, short sentences, and simple sentence structures. Also, he briefly summarizes events that take place over a long period of time.

6. Possible answers: the importance of creativity and experimentation

7. (a) Students may mention Bugs Bunny or Road Runner cartoons. (b) Answers will vary.

Vocabulary

1. inhabit, habitation
   Inhabit means "to dwell" and a *habitation* is a dwelling place.

2. revive; revitalize
   Both words involve rejuvenation.

Writing

Students' graphic stories should

- reflect an understanding of Native American culture
- remain true to the characters in the folktale

Before You Read

Focus

Bellringer Options

Selection Focus
Transparency 70

Daily Language
Transparency 108

Or ask: What can we learn from people from other cultures? (*Students may say we can learn new ways of doing things and new ways of viewing the world.*) Point out that in the past, people often viewed other cultures as strange or frightening. Instead of valuing the differences between cultures, people wanted to make other cultures more like their own. Discuss with students what people can learn from cultural differences.

Before You Read
from *The Voyage of Christopher Columbus*

Meet **Christopher Columbus**
(1451–1506)

Christopher Columbus was not the first European to reach the Americas; the Vikings arrived there 500 years earlier. However, he began an age of exploration, conquest, and cultural exchange that changed the world.

A native of the Italian port city of Genoa, Columbus went to sea at a young age. After surviving a shipwreck, he went to live with his brother Bartholomew in Lisbon, Portugal. Employed as a chart maker, he studied mathematics and astronomy. In 1479 he married and also became captain of a merchant ship. Columbus developed a proposal for reaching Asia by sailing west from Europe instead of sailing south around Africa, a shortcut that—if successful—would greatly facilitate trade with the Far East.

Historic Voyage After the Portuguese king turned down Columbus's proposal, King Ferdinand and Queen Isabella of Spain kept him waiting for seven years before they agreed to fund an expedition. His fleet set sail across the Atlantic Ocean on August 3, 1492: the *Niña*, the *Pinta*, and the flagship *Santa Maria*, with Columbus as admiral. The ships finally sighted land on October 12—a small island in the Bahamas that Columbus christened San Salvador. Columbus continued to explore several Caribbean islands. The following January he set sail to return to Spain, leaving behind 39 men in a stockade named *La Navidad* and taking with him parrots, spices, a small amount of gold, a number of islanders, and the first tobacco plants Europe had ever seen.

Christopher Columbus. Sebastiano del Piombo (Italian, 1485-1547) Metropolitan Museum of Art, NY.

Later Voyages News of his discoveries quickly spread throughout Europe. Honored by the Spanish court, Columbus planned his next voyage. The second expedition was on a much larger scale: Columbus commanded seventeen ships with between 1,200 and 1,500 men, including a group of friars. When he returned to *La Navidad*, however, he found it in ruins, the Spanish defenders slaughtered. Columbus nevertheless went on to establish settlements and reached the mainland of South America. After making a third and a fourth voyage across the Atlantic Ocean, Columbus lost royal support, perhaps for having failed to find gold, perhaps for having failed to find a route to the East.

 **Literature** Online

Author Search For more about Christopher Columbus, go to glencoe.com and enter QuickPass code GLW6053u6.

Selection Skills

Literary Elements
- Journal (SE pp. 1137, 1140, 1144, 1146; TE p. 1139)
- Setting (SE p. 1146)

from The Voyage of Christopher Columbus

Speaking/Listening/Viewing Skills
- Analyze Art (SE p. 1141)

Reading Skills
- Recognize Bias (SE pp. 1137, 1138, 1140, 1142, 1143, 1146)
- Identify Assumptions (TE p. 1138)

Vocabulary Skills
- Word Usage (SE pp. 1137, 1146)
- Academic Vocabulary (SE p. 1146)

Writing Skills/Grammar
- Summary (SE p. 1147)
- News Story (TE p. 1138)
- Infinitives (TE p. 1144)

Literature and Reading Preview

Connect to the Journal

What is your opinion of Columbus's achievement? Discuss this question with a small group.

Build Background

Columbus did not set out to "prove that the Earth was round"—all educated Europeans of his time knew it was. Columbus's great achievement as an explorer was in setting straight out across the ocean to see what was there. It is hard to say for certain what drove Columbus to make the voyage. Certainly he expected to make money, but his religious faith was an important factor as well. Toward the end of his life, he came to believe that he had been divinely appointed to spread Christianity and that his voyages were bringing him ever closer to "the rivers of Paradise."

Set Purposes for Reading

Big Idea Cultures in Conflict

Written accounts of the initial encounters between native peoples and explorers reflect the striking contrasts between their values and ways of living. As you read, ask yourself, What contrasts does Columbus describe in this excerpt from his journal?

Literary Element Journal

A **journal** is a personal record of experiences, ideas, and reflections that is kept on a regular basis. Although many people use journals as a way of privately exploring their feelings, some journals are intended for publication or to be read by a specific audience. As you read, ask yourself, What audience did Columbus have in mind when he wrote his journal?

Reading Strategy Recognize Bias

When you **recognize bias,** you identify statements that are prejudiced or that strongly support only one side of an issue. You can sometimes detect bias by identifying statements with emotionally charged words or those that suggest oversimplification. As you read, ask yourself, What examples of bias can I identify?

Tip: Take Notes In a chart like the one below, record examples of bias in this journal.

Example of Bias	Explanation
"They must be good servants" (p. 1141)	oversimplification

Learning Objectives

For pages 1136–1146

In studying this text, you will focus on the following objectives:

Literary Study: Analyzing journal.

Reading: Recognizing bias.

Vocabulary

stray (strā) *v.* to wander away; to go off course; p. 1138 *Don't stray too far from the cabin; it's easy to get lost in these woods.*

solemn (sol′əm) *adj.* serious; gravely important; p. 1140 *The girls swore a solemn vow not to disclose the secrets of their Mystic Sisterhood.*

coercion (kō ur′shən) *n.* force; repression; p. 1140 *Many parents prefer to use coaxing rather than coercion with their children.*

tedious (tē′dē əs) *adj.* tiresome because of length or dullness; boring; p. 1141 *Listening to the tedious lecture, Anita tried to keep herself from dozing off.*

veer (vēr) *v.* to change direction or course; p. 1144 *Mom veered her car sharply to avoid hitting the child who had steered his bike in our path.*

Tip: Word Usage When you encounter a new word, it might help you to answer a specific question about it. For example, What **solemn** moments are depicted in recent films you have seen?

Before You Read

Focus

Summary

As Columbus nears the new world, he and his crew see objects floating in the water that suggest they are near land. They go ashore on the island of San Salvador, which Columbus claims for King Ferdinand and Queen Isabella of Spain. Columbus describes the island and the islanders. In the days that follow, he and his crew explore other nearby islands, engaging in trade with the inhabitants and taking islanders captive to teach them Spanish and to learn where gold can be found.

 For summaries in languages other than English, see Unit 6 Teaching Resources Book, pp. 46–51.

Vocabulary

Word Usage Organize students in pairs. Have each pair practice using the vocabulary words by asking each other questions that involve the words. For example: "Which television programs do you find **tedious**?"

 For additional vocabulary practice, see Unit 6 Teaching Resources Book, p. 54.

English Learners

DIFFERENTIATED INSTRUCTION

Intermediate Help students connect to what they are about to read by leading a discussion about exploration. Ask students to imagine that they are explorers in unfamiliar territory, such as on the sun or the deepest part of the ocean. Have students consider the following questions:

- Would you keep a journal of your experiences? Why or why not?

- What feelings might you have during your explorations?
- How might you view objects, plants, animals, or people that are different from those in your homeland?

As students discuss the questions, write key words on the board, such as *excited, frightened, awe, unknown, unchartered, curious,* and *interpret.* Ask students to help you come up with definitions for the words.

Encourage students to copy the words and definitions into their notebooks for reference as they read and discuss the selection. Tell students to add relevant words to the list as they read.

Teach

Reading Strategy   1

Recognize Bias Answer:
Columbus attributes the success of the voyage thus far to divine favor.
Ask: What does this bias reveal about Columbus? *(Students might suggest that it reveals Columbus's strong religious convictions.)*

📁 For additional practice using the reading skill or strategy, see Unit 6 Teaching Resources Book, p. 53.

💿 For an audio recording of this selection, use Listening Library Audio CD-ROM.

Readability Scores

Dale-Chall: 7.2
DRP: 59
Lexile: 1160

FROM THE VOYAGE OF
CHRISTOPHER COLUMBUS

CHRISTOPHER COLUMBUS
TRANSLATED BY JOHN CUMMINS

THURSDAY, 11 OCTOBER. Course wsw.[1] A heavy sea, the roughest in the whole voyage so far. We saw petrels,[2] and a green reed close to the ship, and then a big green fish of a kind which does not **stray** far from the shoals.[3] On the Pinta they saw a cane and a stick, and they picked up another little piece of wood which seemed to have been worked with an iron tool; also a piece of cane and another plant which grows on land, and a little board. On the Niña too they saw signs of land, and a thorn branch laden with red fruits, apparently newly cut. We were all filled with joy and relief at these signs. Sailed twenty-eight and a half leagues before sunset. After sunset I resumed our original course westward, sailing at about nine knots. By two o'clock in the morning we had sailed about sixty-eight miles, or twenty-two and a half leagues.

When everyone aboard was together for the *Salve Regina*,[4] which all seamen say or sing in their fashion, I talked to the men about the grace which God had shown us by bringing us in safety, with fair winds and

1. *WSW* is the abbreviation for West-South-West, one point on a mariner's compass.
2. *Petrels* (peʹtrəlz) are seabirds that can fly far from land.
3. *Shoals* (shōlz) are sandbanks or sandbars that make the water shallow.

4. *Salve Regina* (Latin for "Hail Holy Queen") is a prayer addressed to Mary, the mother of Jesus.

Vocabulary

stray (strā) *v.* to wander away; to go off course

Recognize Bias *How do Columbus's religious views influence his interpretation of events?*   1

Reading Practice

Identify Assumptions Tell students that assumptions are beliefs that are based only partially on facts or not based on facts at all. Explain that it is important to identify assumptions when reading to evaluate a text accurately. For example, when evaluating Columbus's description of the land and people he encounters, readers should consider his assumptions to determine the validity of his statements.

Have students consider the following questions as they continue reading: What assumptions might Columbus hold because of his culture? His intellect? His personal belief system? Have pairs review the background information about Columbus to think of how his assumptions may have been influenced by his childhood, his gender, his age, his education, and the time period and country in which he lived.

Then have pairs identify assumptions in the excerpt from Columbus's journal. Encourage students to speculate on the reasons Columbus held each assumption. Finally ask pairs to write a brief summary of their findings, including how identifying assumptions affected their comprehension and interpretation of the text.

Santa Maria, 1939. Andre Bauchant. Oil on canvas, 73 x 100 cm. Private collection.

Journal Point out the reference to "Your Majesties" in the bracketed passage. **Ask:** What does this reveal about Columbus's audience and purpose for writing? *(Columbus is writing the journal not for himself or future explorers but for the king and queen of Spain.)* Remind students that the king and queen of Spain are financing Columbus's expedition. **Ask:** How might Columbus's audience influence the information he includes in his journal? *(Students might suggest that he will include only information that paints the expedition and crew in a positive light.)*

 For additional literary element practice, see Unit 6 Teaching Resources Book, p. 52.

no obstacles, and by comforting us with signs which were more plentiful every day. I urged them to keep a good watch and reminded them that in the first article of the sailing instructions issued to each ship in the Canaries[5] I gave orders not to sail at night after we had reached a point seven hundred leagues from there; I was sailing on because of everyone's great desire to sight land. I warned them to keep a good lookout in the bows and told them that I would give a silk doublet[6] to the man who first sighted land, as well as the prize of 10,000 *maravedis*[7] promised by Your Majesties.

I was on the poop deck[8] at ten o'clock in the evening when I saw a light. It was so indistinct that I could not be sure it was land, but I called Pedro Gutiérrez, the Butler of the King's Table, and told him to look at what I thought was a light. He looked, and saw it. I also told Rodrigo Sánchez de Segovia, Your Majesties' observer on board, but he saw nothing because he was standing in the wrong place. After I had told them, the light appeared once or twice more, like a wax candle rising and falling. Only a few people thought it was a sign of land, but I was sure we were close to a landfall.

---

5. The *Canaries* are the Canary Islands. Owned by Spain, the Canaries are located in the Atlantic Ocean about 70 miles west of North Africa.
6. A *doublet* ia a man's close-fitting jacket.
7. A *maravedi* (mä rä vä′dē) was a Spanish gold coin.
8. A *poop deck* is a short deck above the main deck at the stern of a boat or ship.

CHRISTOPHER COLUMBUS **1139**

Learning Objectives
Recognizing bias. (SE)
Analyzing journal. (TE)
Identifying assumptions. (TE)

English Learners

DIFFERENTIATED INSTRUCTION

Beginning You may want to teach English learners compass points in English. Call students' attention to the first line of the selection. Point out that "wsw" is an abbreviation for "west-southwest." Ask a volunteer to read the line aloud with the correct pronunciation. Then ask volunteers to write on the board the names and abbreviations of the four cardinal directions.

Continue the activity by introducing the terms and abbreviations for *northeast (ne), northwest (nw), southeast (se),* and *southwest (sw).* Give students a visual depiction of each direction by drawing a compass on the board and labeling it with the four cardinal directions. Draw different arrows coming from the compass. As you draw each arrow, have students identify the direction in which you are "traveling."

Teach

Literary Element | 1

Journal Answer: *The Spanish king and queen, as sponsors of the expedition, will demand a thorough account of where the explorers went, what they found, and what they did. This journal serves, in effect, as a record of information that Columbus can use later to support his report and to encourage his royal patrons to finance future explorations. Columbus hopes that the king and queen will be pleased to hear of his taking possession of the island in their names.*

Big Idea | 2

Cultures in Conflict

Answer: *No; he is trying to buy their friendship with worthless trinkets.*

Reading Strategy | 3

Recognize Bias Answer: *Columbus bases his judgment of wealth on possession of land and material goods—the European norm—and interprets the islanders' lack of clothing and personal possessions as proof of poverty.*

Then the Pinta, being faster and in the lead, sighted land and made the signal as I had ordered. The first man to sight land was called Rodrigo de Triana. The land appeared two hours after midnight, about two leagues away. We furled all sail except the *treo*, the mainsail with no bonnets, and jogged off and on until Friday morning, when we came to an island. We saw naked people, and I went ashore in a boat with armed men, taking Martín Alonso Pinzón and his brother Vicente Yáñez, captain of the Niña. I took the royal standard, and the captains each took a banner with the Green Cross which each of my ships carries as a device, with the letters F and Y, surmounted by a crown, at each end of the cross.

Visual Vocabulary
A *device* is a symbolic design, or emblem, often accompanied by a motto. Heralds—official messengers—carried a device to identify the noble family they represented.

When we stepped ashore we saw fine green trees, streams everywhere and different kinds of fruit. I called to the two captains to jump ashore with the rest, who included Rodrigo de Escobedo, secretary of the fleet, and Rodrigo Sánchez de Segovia, asking them to bear **solemn** witness that in the presence of them all I was taking possession of this island for their Lord and Lady the King and Queen, and I made the necessary declarations which are set down at greater length in the written testimonies.

Soon many of the islanders gathered round us. I could see that they were people who would be more easily converted to our Holy Faith by love than by **coercion**, and wishing them to look on us with friendship I gave some of them red bonnets and glass beads which they hung round their necks, and many other things of small value, at which they were so delighted and so eager to please us that we could not believe it. Later they swam out to the boats to bring us parrots and balls of cotton thread and darts, and many other things, exchanging them for such objects as glass beads and hawk bells. They took anything, and gave willingly whatever they had.

However, they appeared to me to be a very poor people in all respects. They go about as naked as the day they were born, even the women, though I saw only one, who was quite young. All the men I saw were quite young, none older than thirty, all well built, finely bodied and handsome in the face. Their hair is coarse, almost like a horse's tail, and short; they wear it short, cut over the brow, except a few strands of hair hanging down uncut at the back.

Some paint themselves with black, some with the color of the Canary Islanders, neither black nor white, others with white, others with red, others with whatever they can find. Some have only their face painted, others their whole body, others just their eyes or nose. They carry no weapons, and are ignorant of them; when I showed them some swords they took them by the blade and cut themselves. They have no iron; their darts are just sticks without an iron head, though some of them have a fish tooth or something else at the tip.

---

1 | Journal *How might this information be useful later in Columbus's official report at court?*

Vocabulary

solemn (sol′əm) *adj.* serious; gravely important

Cultures in Conflict *Does Columbus show respect for the islanders here? Explain.* | **2**

Recognize Bias *What criterion does Columbus use to judge the wealth of the islanders?* | **3**

Vocabulary

coercion (kō ur′shən) *n.* force; repression

1140 UNIT 6 THE EARLY AMERICAS

Writing Practice

Write a News Story Have students write a news story about Columbus's encounter with the islanders on Thursday, October 11. Tell students they may write the article for an audience of Columbus and his crew, or for an audience of islanders. Provide students with copies of news articles to examine as you review the following points.

- News stories should answer the questions *who, what, when, where, why,* and *how.* Students should provide the basic answers to these questions at the start of the story and then add details in the body.
- To keep readers' interest, news stories should provide a mix of facts, background information, and quotations. Suggest that students imagine they have interviewed one or more of the people involved.

- A news story should contain an appealing headline that attracts readers' attention and makes them want to read the article.
- News writing should be objective, or without bias. Remind students that they are reporting on the event, not giving their opinions on it.

Ask volunteers to share their news stories with the class.

Landing of Columbus, ca. 1893. Albert Bierstadt. Oil on canvas, 72 x 121 in. The Newark Museum, NJ.

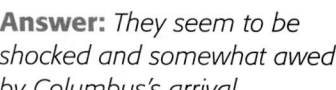 Bierstadt was known for his dramatic landscape paintings. How do the Native Americans in this painting react to Columbus's arrival? ★

They are all the same size, of good stature, dignified and well formed. I saw some with scars on their bodies, and made signs to ask about them, and they indicated to me that people from other islands nearby came to capture them and they defended themselves. I thought, and still think, that people from the mainland come here to take them prisoner. They must be good servants, and intelligent, for I can see that they quickly repeat everything said to them. I believe they would readily become Christians; it appeared to me that they have no religion. With God's will, I will take six of them with me for Your Majesties when I leave this place, so that they may learn Spanish.

I saw no animals on the island, only parrots.

SATURDAY, 13 OCTOBER. In the early morning many of the islanders came to the beach, all young, as I have said, tall and handsome, their hair not curly, but flowing and thick, like horsehair. They are all broader in the forehead and head than any people I have ever seen, with fine, large eyes. None of them is black; they are rather the same color as the folk on the Canary Islands, which is what one might expect, this island being on the same latitude as Hierro in the Canaries, which lies due E. Their legs are very straight, and they are all the same height, not stout in the belly but

well shaped. They came out to the ship in *almadías* made from a tree trunk, like a long boat, all of a piece, wonderfully shaped in the way of this land, some big enough to carry forty or fifty men, others smaller, with only one man. They row them with paddles like a baker's shovel, very swiftly, and if the boat overturns they all jump into the sea to turn it over again and bale it out with gourds. They brought us balls of cotton thread and parrots and darts and other little things which it would be **tedious** to list, **4** and exchanged everything for whatever we offered them.

I kept my eyes open and tried to find out if there was any gold, and I saw that some of them had a little piece hanging from a hole in their nose. I gathered from their signs that if one goes south, or around the south side of the island, there is a king with great jars full of it, enormous amounts. I tried to persuade them to go there, but I saw that the idea was not to their liking.

I decided to wait until tomorrow and then to set off to the southwest, for many of them seemed to be saying that there is land to the s and sw and NW, and that the people from the NW often come to attack them, and continue to the sw in search of gold

Vocabulary

tedious (tē′dē əs) *adj.* tiresome because of length or dullness; boring

CHRISTOPHER COLUMBUS **1141**

Teach

Big Idea	4

Cultures in Conflict Ask: What do the islanders' gifts reveal about their culture? *(Possible answer: The gifts reveal that the islanders value practical items.)* **Ask:** How does Columbus view the islanders' gifts? How can you tell? *(Columbus dismisses the gifts as having little or no value; he calls them "little things.")* Discuss with students how this treatment reveals differences in the two cultures.

View the Art ★

Answer: *They seem to be shocked and somewhat awed by Columbus's arrival*

Learning Objectives
Recognizing bias. (SE)
Analyzing journal. (SE)
Writing a news story. (TE)

Approaching Level

DIFFERENTIATED INSTRUCTION

Mapping Columbus's Voyage Some students may respond better to visual representations of what they are reading than they do to the text alone—particularly when they are trying to imagine something as unfamiliar as a sea voyage from the past. Have students locate Europe, the Atlantic Ocean, and the West Indies (where Columbus landed) on a globe or a map. Then organize students into pairs. Have

the pairs chart the approximate path of Columbus's voyage—from Spain to the Canary Islands (west of Africa) to San Salvador. Students may then make their own maps of the islands, based on Columbus's statements about direction and distance.

Advanced Learners/Pre-AP

DIFFERENTIATED INSTRUCTION

Write a Journal Entry Have students compose a "new" entry to Columbus's journal. Students might describe the landscape, daily life on the ship, or encounters with islanders. Point out to students that even though Columbus is "reporting" on his experience, he includes such literary elements as suspense and figurative language. Encourage students to follow his example.

Teach

Recognize Bias Answer:
Although Columbus calls the islanders "intelligent" (p. 1141), he is referring to their ability to mimic his language and to their possible use as servants. He certainly does not consider them intelligent when he describes their bargaining for "pieces of broken plate and broken glasses."

Big Idea · 2

Cultures in Conflict
Answer: *Columbus believes that the islanders regard the Spaniards as gods.*

APPROACHING Explain that Columbus's opinion reveals his belief in the superiority of Europeans. Point out that despite the quotation in Columbus's journal, the islanders do not speak the same language as Columbus. The quotation is Columbus's interpretation of the islanders' words and actions.

---

and precious stones. This island is large and very flat, with green trees and plenty of water; there is a large lake in the middle, no mountains, and everything is green and a delight to the eye. The people are very gentle; they are so eager for our things that if we refuse to give them something without getting something in exchange they seize what they can and jump into the water with it. But they will give whatever they have for anything one gives them; they even bargained for pieces of broken plate and broken glasses. I saw them take three Portuguese *ceotís,* the equivalent of one Castilian *blanca,*[9] for sixteen balls of cotton which must have contained more than an *arroba*[10] of thread. I had forbidden anyone to take this, except that I had given orders to take it all for Your Majesties if it was in sufficient quantity. It grows on this island, though in the little time available I could not swear to this, and the gold they wear hanging from their noses is also from the island, but so as not to waste time I wish to set off to see if I can reach the island of Cipango.

It is now after nightfall and they have all gone ashore in their *almadías.*

SUNDAY, 14 OCTOBER. I gave orders at daybreak for the small boat of the Santa María and the boats of the two caravels to be got ready, and went along the coast to the northeast to examine the eastward part of the island, and the villages, of which I saw two or three. The people kept coming down to the beach, calling to us and giving thanks to God. Some brought us water, some food; others, seeing that I did not

wish to go ashore, swam out to us, and we understood them to be asking if we had come from Heaven. One old man climbed into the boat, and the others, men and women, kept shouting, "Come and see the men who have come from Heaven; bring them food and drink."

Many men and women came, each bringing something and giving thanks to God, throwing themselves on the ground and raising their hands in the air. They called to us to go ashore, but I was afraid of a great reef which encircles the whole island, though between it and the shore there is a deep harbor big enough to hold every ship in Christendom, with a very narrow entrance channel. There are certainly shoals within this reef, but the sea inside it is as calm as a millpond.

I bestirred myself to explore all this this morning so as to be able to give Your Majesties a description of it all, and also of a possible site for a fort. I saw a piece of land which is virtually an island; there are six houses on it, and it could be converted into an island with a couple of days' work, although I do not see the necessity. These people have little knowledge of fighting, as Your Majesties will see from the seven I have had captured to take away with us so as to teach them our language and return them, unless Your Majesties' orders are that they all be taken to Spain or held captive on the island itself, for with fifty men one could keep the whole population in subjection and make them do whatever one wanted.

Near the islet I have described there are groves of the most beautiful trees I ever saw; so green, with their leaves like those in Castile in April and May. There is also plenty of water. I explored the whole harbor, and then returned to the ship and set

---

9. *Ceotís* (thā ō tēs′) and *blanca* (blän′kä) are coins. *Castilian,* often used as a synonym for "Spanish," refers to Castile, a large region of central Spain.
10. An *arroba* (ä rō′bä) is a unit of measurement equal to about 25 pounds.

1 **Recognize Bias** *Does Columbus consider the islanders intelligent? Explain.*

2 **Cultures in Conflict** *How do the islanders regard the Spanish sailors?*

Reading Practice

Distinguish Fact from Opinion Point out to students that, throughout his journal, Columbus records both factual information and opinion. Remind students that facts are statements of truth; they can be proved by evidence. Opinions, however, are statements of belief; they show how someone feels about a subject and are not based on evidence.

Have student pairs create two-column charts labeled "Facts" and "Opinions" and then fill out the charts with examples from the selection. Give students the following two examples to get them started: *Fact—The islanders brought the crew food. Opinion—The islanders were giving thanks to God.* As pairs identify examples from the selection, ask them to discuss how they can distinguish fact from opinion.

sail. I saw so many islands that I could not decide which to go to first. The men I had captured told me by signs that there are so many that they cannot be counted; they gave me the names of over a hundred. I therefore looked for the largest, and decided to sail for it, which is what I am doing now. It must be about five leagues from this island of San Salvador.[11] Some of the others are nearer, some further away. They are all very flat and fertile, with no mountains, and they are all populated and make war on one another, though these people are very simple, and very finely made.

MONDAY, 15 OCTOBER. Last night I lay to[12] for fear of approaching land to anchor before morning, not knowing if the coast was free from shoals, and intending to increase sail at dawn. The distance was more than five leagues, nearer seven, and the tide set us back, so that it would be around noon when I reached the island. I found that the arm of the island nearest San Salvador runs N–S, and is five leagues long, and the other, along which I sailed, runs E–W for over ten leagues.

From this island I sighted another larger one to the west, so I increased sail to press on all day until nightfall, for otherwise I could not have reached the western cape. I named this island Santa María de la Concepción. I anchored off the western cape just before sunset to find out if there was any gold there. The prisoners I took on San Salvador kept telling me that the people of this island wore great gold bracelets and legbands, but I thought it was all invention to enable them to escape. However, my intention being not to pass by

11. *San Salvador* (sän säl′və dor) is one of the islands of the Bahamas in the Caribbean Sea. It is believed to be the place where Columbus first landed, on October 12, 1492.
12. *Lay to* means "kept the ship in place at sea with the front facing toward the wind."

3 Recognize Bias *Why does Columbus think his captives are lying about the gold?*

any island without taking possession of it, although taking possession of one might be taken to serve for them all, I anchored and remained there until today, Tuesday.

At daybreak I armed the boats and went ashore. There were numerous people, naked and similar to those on San Salvador. They let us go about on the island and gave us whatever I asked for. The wind was strengthening from the southeast, so I decided not to linger, but set off to return to the ship. A large *almadía* was alongside the Niña, and one of the men from San Salvador who was aboard the caravel jumped into the sea and went off in it (another had jumped overboard the previous night). Our boat set off after the *almadía*, which paddled away so fast that no boat ever built could have outpaced it, even with a considerable start. Anyway, it reached the shore and they abandoned it. Some of my men landed in pursuit, and the islanders all fled like chickens. The *almadía* was taken back on board the Niña.

By now another small *almadía* was approaching the Niña from a different headland with one man in it who had come to barter a ball of cotton. He did not want to come aboard, so some of the sailors jumped into the sea and captured him. I saw all this from the deck of the sterncastle,[13] so I sent for him; I gave him a red bonnet and put a few little green glass beads on his arm and hung two bells from his ears. I had him put back in his *almadía*, which had also been taken aboard the ship's boat, and sent him back ashore. I then made sail to go to the other large island which I could see to the westward, and I ordered the other *almadía* which the Niña was towing astern[14] to be set adrift.

13. The *sterncastle* is part of the upper deck toward the stern, or rear of a ship.
14. Here, *astern* means "behind."

CHRISTOPHER COLUMBUS **1143**

Teach

Reading Strategy | 3

Recognize Bias **Answer:**
Columbus thinks his captives are lying about the presence of gold in order to induce him to spend more time searching the islands, since the longer it takes Columbus to search for gold, the more opportunities the captives will have to escape.

APPROACHING **Ask:** Why do you think Columbus does not believe the prisoners? (*Students may suggest that the concept of ordinary people wearing gold bracelets and leg bands is so foreign to Columbus that he assumes the prisoners are lying.*)

Learning Objectives
Recognizing bias. (SE)
Distinguishing fact from opinion. (TE)

Advanced Learners/Pre-AP

DIFFERENTIATED INSTRUCTION

Effects of European Exploration
Have students use print and online resources to develop an oral presentation on one of the long-term effects of European exploration. Share the following topic ideas with students:

- **Diseases** Tell students native groups had lived in relative isolation until their contact with Europeans. They did not have immunity to such diseases as measles and smallpox and were thus devastated by the exposure.
- **Food** Tell students that many of the foods they eat today came became popular as the result of European explorations. For example, Europeans introduced bananas to the Americas; the New World introduced corn and potatoes to the Europeans.
- **Christianity** As evidenced by statements in Columbus's journal, part of Spain's mission was to spread Christianity to other parts of the world by conquering native populations and converting them.

Encourage students to include visuals, such as charts, graphs, and maps, with their presentations. Allow listeners to ask questions after the presentations.

1143

Teach

Big Idea 1

Cultures in Conflict
Answer: *Columbus wants to project a good image of the Spaniards so that the natives will trust future explorers.*

Literary Element 2

Journal Answer: *He intends to persuade Ferdinand and Isabella that his explorations have been successful so that they will be more likely to sponsor further voyages.*

Progress Check

Can students analyze journals?

If No → See Unit 6 Teaching Resources Book, p. 52.

When the man to whom I had given gifts, refusing his ball of cotton, reached the shore I saw that all the others came up to him. He was amazed and thought that we were good people and that the other who had escaped was being taken with us because he had done us some harm. That was my purpose in giving him presents and letting him go: to make them think well of us, so that when Your Majesties send someone else here he may be well received. All the things I gave him would not be worth four *maravedis* if you put them together.

I set sail, then, at about ten o'clock with the wind SE, **veering** southerly, to cross to this other island. It is very large, and all the men from San Salvador tell me by signs that there is a lot of gold, which the people wear as bracelets and legbands, and in their ears and noses, and round their necks.

From the island of Santa María to this new one is nine and a half leagues, almost due W, and all this part of the island runs from NW to SE. There appears to be at least thirty leagues of coast on this side, very flat, without a hill anywhere, like San Salvador and Santa María. There are sandy beaches all the way, except that there are some underwater rocks near the shoreline, making it necessary to take care when anchoring and not to anchor close inshore, although the water is very clear and one can see the bottom. Two lombard[15] shots from shore all around these islands one can find no bottom.

The islands are very green and lush, with sweet breezes, and there may be many things here which I do not know about, because rather than lingering I wish to explore and investigate many islands in search of gold. As these people tell me by signs that the folk wear it on their arms and legs—and it is gold they mean, for I showed them some pieces of my own—with God's help I cannot fail to find the source of it.

Halfway between these two islands, Santa María and this larger one which I am calling Fernandina, we found a man alone in an *almadía* making the same crossing as ourselves. He had a piece of bread as big as his fist, a calabash[16] of water, a piece of red earth, powdered and kneaded, and a few dried leaves which must be something of importance to these people, because they brought me some in San Salvador. He also had a small basket with a little string of glass beads and two *blancas*, so I knew that he had come from San Salvador and called at Santa María on his way to Fernandina. He came alongside the ship and I let him come aboard at his request. I also made him bring his *almadía* on board with him. I let him keep all the things he had with him, and ordered him to be given bread and honey, and something to drink. I am going to take him to Fernandina and give him all his possessions so that he will give a good report of us, in order that when Your Majesties, with the grace of God, send men back to this place they will be received with honor, and we will be given whatever the island has to offer. ❧

---

15. A *lombard* was a type of cannon.

1 Cultures in Conflict *Why does Columbus try to manipulate the islanders?*

Vocabulary
veer (vēr) *v.* to change direction or course

---

16. A *calabash* is a dried gourd used as a container.

Journal *Whom does Columbus intend to persuade by using such language?* **2**

Grammar Practice

Infinitive Phrases On the board, write the following sentence from the second paragraph on this page:

I set sail, then, at about ten o'clock with the wind SE, veering southerly, <u>to cross to this other island</u>.

Remind students that an infinitive is a verb form that consists of the word *to* plus the first-person singular form of a verb. Point out the phrase "to cross," in the underlined text above, as an example.

Tell students that an infinitive phrase consists of an infinitive plus its complements and modifiers. Explain that in the underlined text, the prepositional phrase "to this other island" is a modifier for the infinitive "to cross." Taken together, all of the underlined words form a phrase that serves as an adverb modifying the verb "set." The phrase explains why Columbus set sail.

Have students locate another infinitive in the first paragraph of the second column. *("to explore and investigate many islands in search of gold")* Ask them which word the phrase modifies. *("wish")*

Then have them find another infinitive phrase in this same paragraph and the word it modifies. *("to find the source of it" modifies "fail")*

After You Read

Respond and Think Critically

Respond and Interpret

1. What thoughts went through your mind as you finished reading this journal?

2. (a)What leads Columbus to believe he is nearing land? (b)Why do you think Columbus shares this belief with his men?

3. (a)What is the first thing Columbus does when he lands on San Salvador? (b)What do his actions suggest about his intentions regarding the islanders?

Analyze and Evaluate

4. (a)Why does Columbus give presents to some islanders? (b)What does Columbus's explanation of his giving presents to the islanders reveal about his character?

5. **Motivation** is the reason or reasons behind a character's action. Which of the reasons behind Columbus's actions do you find most admirable, and which do you find least admirable? Explain.

6. Do you think Columbus gives a fair and accurate portrayal of the islanders? Explain your response.

Connect

7. **Big Idea** **Cultures in Conflict** These journal entries describe the first encounters between Spaniards and Native Americans. What future conflicts do these entries foreshadow?

8. **Connect to Today** How might a modern audience's evaluation of Columbus's treatment of the islanders differ from his audience's evaluation at the time?

You're the Critic: Point/Counterpoint

Was Columbus a Hero or a Tyrant?

In the centuries since his voyages, Columbus has been subject to both praise and blame. Read the two opposing views of his achievements.

Here was a man greedy in large ways, and in small ways—to the point where he took for himself the reward for first sighting land from the Pinta lookout. Cruel in petty things, as when he set a dying monkey with two paws cut off to fight a wild pig, cruel on a continental scale, as when he set in motion what Las Casas called 'the beginning of the bloody trail of conquest across the Americas.'"

—Hans Koning

" . . . [h]e was desirous of . . . civilizing the natives, of . . . subjecting every thing to the control of law, order and religion, and thus of founding regular and prosperous empires."

—Washington Irving

Group Activity Discuss the following questions with your classmates. Refer to the quotations and cite evidence from *The Voyage of Christopher Columbus* for support.

1. Washington Irving wrote in 1828, and Hans Koning wrote in 1976. How might this account for some of the differences in their viewpoints?

2. In your opinion, does evidence of Columbus's greed and cruelty detract from his accomplishments as an explorer? Explain.

CHRISTOPHER COLUMBUS **1145**

You're the Critic

1. Possible answer: Irving was writing some fifty years after the birth of the United States and may have been exhibiting patriotic fervor for the discoverer of America. Koning, writing 150 years later, makes use of detailed historical evidence and takes what we might call a psychological approach to history.

2. Possible answer: Columbus's flaws do not detract from his discoveries but seriously compromise his status as a hero.

 For additional assessment, see Assessment Resources, pp. 223–224.

After You Read

Assess

1. Students may be struck by Columbus's combination of wonder and practicality.

2. (a) He sees pieces of wood that have been worked with tools and a branch bearing fruit. (b) Possible answers: He wants them to be alert; he wants them to remain hopeful and not to lose faith in his leadership.

3. (a) He plants the royal standard and declares that he is taking possession of the island for the Spanish king and queen. (b) He plans to trade with them.

4. (a) He wants them to say good things about him so that other Spaniards who come to the island will be welcome. (b) Possible answers: He is a shrewd and calculating person who is not above using deception to further his ends.

5. Answers will vary.

6. He seems reasonably objective in his description of their physical appearance and behavior, but he makes incorrect assumptions, such as his belief that they have no religion, because of his lack of background knowledge.

7. Possible answer: Although Columbus's discoveries led to cultural exchanges of foods, animals, minerals, and other items, they also introduced deadly diseases to the islanders. His discoveries also led to waves of colonization that all but destroyed the civilizations of many indigenous peoples in both North and South America.

8. A modern audience might criticize Columbus's treatment of the islanders.

1145

After You Read

Literary Element

1. (B) is correct. Ferdinand and Isabella were the financial sponsors of the voyage, so he wrote for them.

2. (D) is correct. He mainly wanted to make his patrons believe that they had invested wisely in him and that the voyage would prove profitable.

Review: Setting

1. Possible answers: "green trees, streams everywhere and different kinds of fruit"; "no animals on the island, only parrots"; "groves of the most beautiful trees"; "very flat and fertile."

2. Possible answer: The Spaniards must be self-sufficient and must fish, hunt, or gather what food they can. The distance and isolation prevent easy communication with home; they must make their own decisions about where to go and how to treat the natives they encounter.

3. Possible answer: Columbus's point of view is Eurocentric —he and his men represent Spain, one of the dominant naval forces of the world; they have the power to lay claim to new lands and to take whatever resources those lands may offer.

Literary Element Journal

SAT Skills Practice

1. Columbus's intended audience for his journal entries was

  (A) the Italian clergy

  (B) King Ferdinand and Queen Isabella of Spain

  (C) his brother Bartholomew in Lisbon

  (D) the upper classes of Europe

  (E) his wife and son

2. Columbus's main purpose for writing these journal entries was to

  (A) document events for the historical record

  (B) finally prove himself a success

  (C) convince the church to send missionaries to convert the natives

  (D) assure his patrons that their investment was worthwhile

  (E) establish himself as an author

Review: Setting

As you learned on page 108, **setting** is the time and place in which the events of a literary work occur.

Partner Activity Discuss the following questions with a classmate.

1. List some of the details Columbus provides to describe the landscape.

2. How do the great distance of the Bahamas from Spain and the islands' relative isolation influence the events described in the journal?

3. What is the cultural context of Columbus's point of view and his actions?

LOG ON ▶ **Literature** Online

Selection Resources For Selection Quizzes, eFlashcards, and Reading-Writing Connection activities, go to glencoe.com and enter QuickPass code GLW6053u6.

Reading Strategy Recognize Bias

Review the chart you filled in on page 1137. Then answer the following items.

1. Cite some descriptions of the islanders that seem objective and neutral.

2. In one sentence, summarize Columbus's bias as reflected in these journal entries.

Vocabulary Practice

Practice with Word Usage Respond to these statements to help explore the meanings of the vocabulary words from the text.

1. Explain what might happen if you **strayed** off course while hiking in the woods.

2. Describe a **solemn** event.

3. Relate a situation in which you observed someone using **coercion** to get his or her way.

4. Give three examples of tasks you find **tedious**.

5. Name things that might cause a driver to **veer** while driving down a street.

Academic Vocabulary ▶

New information about Columbus's treatment of Native Americans has forced many readers to make **adjustments** *to their perspectives on his voyages.*

Adjustment is a word that has many meanings. Using context clues, figure out the meaning of *adjustment* in each sentence below. Then explain the difference between the two meanings.

1. After the insurance company made an **adjustment**, the doctor sent a bill to the patient for the remaining cost of her services.

2. Some economists predicted a market **adjustment** even before the dot-com bubble burst.

For more on academic vocabulary, see pages 36–37 and R83–R85.

Reading Strategy

1. Possible answer: Columbus describes the islanders as young, well-built, with straight legs, not overweight.

2. Possible answer: The New World islanders, although attractive, are an inferior race that will offer the Spaniards little resistance either in accepting their religion or in becoming their slaves.

Vocabulary

Possible answers:

1. You would get lost in the woods.

2. an event that is solemn and serious

3. Students' responses should demonstrate that they understand that *coercion* means "force."

4. homework, chores, or waiting in line

5. a large object falling from a vehicle onto the road

Academic Vocabulary

1. Since the patient received a bill for the "remaining cost," an *adjustment* must be the process of determining what percentage of costs will be covered by an insurance company.

2. The reference to the dot-com bubble suggests that an *adjustment* is a rapid plunge in stock prices.

Respond Through Writing

Summary

Report Main Ideas and Events When you write a summary of a nonfiction work, you restate the main ideas or events. In about 100 words, summarize the first entry from Columbus's journal.

Understand the Task When you **restate**, you retell written or spoken text in your own words without stating opinions.

Prewrite Note answers to the questions *who? what? when? where? why?* and *how?* in a chart. The chart below was created to summarize the excerpt from *Stay Alive, My Son* on pages 821–825.

Who	Pin Yathay
What	the memoir <u>Stay Alive, My Son</u>
When	1987
Where	a Cambodian work camp
Why	to show the brutality of the Khmer Rouge by relating his own experiences
How	

Draft Draw upon the answers to the six questions as you draft your summary. Below is a summary of the excerpt from *Stay Alive, My Son*.

In this excerpt from Stay Alive, My Son, Pin Yathay describes his experiences in a Cambodian work camp to show the brutality and ineffectiveness of the Khmer Rouge. Yathay recounts a time when he was ordered to cut down fruit trees that could have provided food for the hungry workers. He then describes how he was caught with an illegally obtained can of rice and turned over to his group's leader, Run. Facing punishment by death, Yathay reminded Run that he had helped him obtain antibiotics illegally two weeks earlier. Run then spared Yathay because he feared for his own life.

Revise Have a partner read your summary and ask him or her to circle the answers to the six questions listed above. If your partner cannot find the answers to all the questions, revise your summary accordingly.

Edit and Proofread Proofread your paper, correcting any errors in grammar, spelling, and punctuation. Use the Grammar Tip in the side column for help with using commas with appositives.

Learning Objectives

In this assignment, you will focus on the following objectives:

Writing: Writing a summary.

Grammar: Understanding commas with appositives.

► Grammar Tip

Commas with Appositives

An appositive is a noun or a pronoun that is placed next to another noun or pronoun to identify it or give additional information about it. In the sentence *The group leader, Run, asks Yathay for help,* the name *Run* is an appositive. It is set off by commas because it gives information that is not essential to the meaning of the sentence. Usually an appositive follows the noun or pronoun it identifies or explains.

After You Read

Assess

Respond Through Writing

Students' summaries should

- answer the questions *who? what? when? where? why?* and *how?*
- define unfamiliar technical and cultural terms
- reflect an understanding of the main ideas and events of the journal entry

A student who meets all of these criteria should receive the equivalent of a 4-point response.

A student who fully meets two and partially meets the third of these criteria should receive the equivalent of a 3-point response.

A student who fully meets one and partially meets a second of these criteria, or who partially meets all three criteria, should receive the equivalent of a 2-point response.

A student who partially fully meets one or partially meets two of these criteria should receive the equivalent of a 1-point response.

 For grammar practice, see Unit 6 Teaching Resources Book, p. 56.

 To create custom assessments online, go to Progress Reporter Online Assessment.

 To create custom assessments using software, use ExamView Assessment Suite.

Approaching Level

DIFFERENTIATED INSTRUCTION

Help with Summarizing Tell students that, when summarizing, they should first read the passage in its entirety to gain an understanding of it as a whole and avoid focusing on individual sentences or phrases. Once students feel they comprehend the passage, they can go back and take notes on key ideas.

You may wish to assist students with their summaries by providing them with copies of the graphic organizer with the information already filled in. Students can then focus on developing and paraphrasing the information, rather than on finding the answers to the six questions.

1147

Before You Read

Focus

Bellringer Options

Daily Language Transparency 109

Or ask: In what positive and negative ways do people react to new people, places, or ideas? *(Students may suggest that people may react with kindness and excitement, welcoming new experiences. Other people react to new people, places, or ideas with fear or the desire to hold on to what is comfortable.)* Discuss with students how they themselves react to new people, ideas, or experiences.

Before You Read

from *The Broken Spears: The Aztec Account of the Conquest of Mexico*

For hundreds of years, historians based their understanding of the Spanish Conquest of the Aztec Empire almost exclusively on accounts provided by the Spanish explorer Hernán Cortés and his soldier Bernal Díaz del Castillo. Then in 1962, *The Broken Spears: The Aztec Account of the Conquest of Mexico* told the story of the conquest from the Aztecs' perspective.

The Spanish Conquest By the early 1500s, just before the Spanish invasion, the Aztec Empire rivaled the empires of the other great Meso-American cultures that had preceded it. From Tenochtitlán (tae nōch´tēt län´), the Aztec capital city, Motecuhzoma II (ruled an advanced agricultural and trading society of nearly six million people.

Then in 1519, Cortés and his forces landed on the east coast of Mexico and made their way to the Aztec capital. These invaders demolished Tenochtitlán, leveling temples and burning many

> "Broken spears lie in the roads;
> we have torn our hair in grief.
> The houses are roofless now, and their walls
> are red with blood."
>
> from *The Broken Spears*

of the Aztec codices (hieroglyphic texts). The conquerors considered it their Christian duty to destroy all artifacts of the Aztecs' pagan religion. Some Spanish missionaries, however, managed to salvage a few codices. They then taught an alphabetic version of Nahuatl (nä wä´təl), the Aztec language, to the conquest's survivors. Working together, the Spanish missionaries and their Aztec pupils recorded accounts of the Spanish invasion as well as native songs, poems, and narratives.

The Broken Spears *The Broken Spears,* compiled by Miguel Leon-Portilla, contains excerpts from several of the more than 40 Aztec manuscripts that survived the conquest. The first thirteen chapters present chronological accounts, beginning with the arrival of the Spanish and ending with the destruction of Tenochtitlán. Chapter Fourteen is a brief summary of the conquest taken from a single source that provides information not found anywhere else. The last chapter contains "songs of sorrow," elegies written by post-conquest survivors lamenting the fall of their city.

The excerpts from *The Broken Spears* that follow are divided into two parts. Part I describes the Aztecs' reaction to the arrival of the Spanish; Part II describes the battles leading to the fall of Tenochtitlán.

Aztec Empire located on an Island in the Lake of Texcoco. Franz Hogenbergh and Georg Braun. Colored engraving. Biblioteca Marciana, Venice.

1148 UNIT 6 THE EARLY AMERICAS

Selection Skills

Literary Elements
- Setting (SE pp. 1149, 1151, 1154, 1159)

from **The Broken Spears**

Speaking/Listening/Viewing Skills
- Analyze Art (SE p. 1153)
- Conduct an Interview (SE p. 1160)

Reading Skills
- Analyze Cultural Context (SE pp. 1149, 1152, 1154, 1157, 1158, 1160)
- Analyze Sensory Details (TE p. 1154)

Vocabulary Skills
- Analogies (SE p. 1160; TE p. 1149)

Writing Skills/Grammar
- Character Sketch (TE p. 1152)
- Movie Scene (TE p. 1158)

Literature and Reading Preview

Connect to the History

What accounts about exploration and conquest have you read? Discuss this question with a small group.

Build Background

The Aztecs were the last of a series of nomadic groups to migrate to the fertile Valley of Mexico. They founded Tenochtitlán in 1325 on an island in Lake Texcoco (tes kō′kō), the site of present-day Mexico City. Gradually, the Aztecs expanded and consolidated their power through alliances with or conquests of other groups, including the forced annexation of Tlatelolco (tlä tə lōl′kō), a nearby commercial center that became part of the capital.

Set Purposes for Reading

Big Idea Cultures in Conflict

Written accounts of the initial encounters between native peoples and explorers reflect the striking contrasts between their values and ways of living. As you read, ask yourself, What are the contrasts between the Spanish explorers and the Aztecs?

Literary Element Setting

The **setting** is the time and place in which the events of a literary work occur. Setting includes not only the physical surroundings, but also the ideas, customs, values, and beliefs of a particular time and place. As you read, ask yourself, How does the setting influence the conflict between the Spaniards and the Aztecs?

Reading Strategy Analyze Cultural Context

When you **analyze cultural context,** you determine how the values and beliefs of the people living in a particular time and place affect the work. As you read, ask yourself, How do the Aztecs' values and beliefs influence their response to events?

Tip: Track Events In a chart like the one below, list events, the Aztecs' response, and the reason for their response.

Event	Aztecs' Response	Reason for Response
The Aztecs sight a ship offshore.	They assume the ship is a mountain.	They have seen mountains before but not a ship.

Learning Objectives

For pages 1148–1160

In studying this text, you will focus on the following objectives:

Literary Study: Analyzing setting.

Reading: Analyzing cultural context.

Listening and Speaking: Conducting an interview.

Vocabulary

haste (hāst) *n.* quickness of action or movement; hurry; p. 1151 *Arriving late at the airport, we proceeded to the gate with great haste.*

humility (hū mil′ə tē) *n.* modesty; meekness; p. 1152 *With deep humility, the performer bowed to acknowledge the applause.*

straggler (strag′lər) *n.* one who lags behind or strays from a group; p. 1156 *The stragglers trailed the other runners by several blocks.*

epidemic (ep′ə dem′ik) *n.* rapid spread of disease affecting many people; p. 1157 *A flu epidemic made many students miss school.*

sustenance (sus′tə nəns) *n.* food; nourishment; means of support; p. 1157 *Lost, the camper desperately sought water and sustenance.*

Advanced Learners/Pre-AP

DIFFERENTIATED INSTRUCTION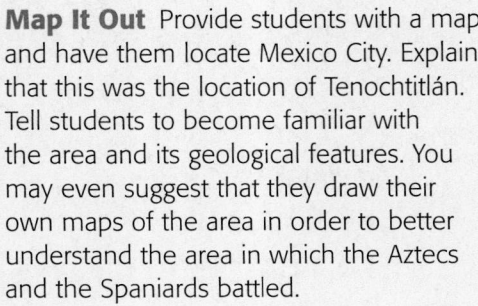

Map It Out Provide students with a map and have them locate Mexico City. Explain that this was the location of Tenochtitlán. Tell students to become familiar with the area and its geological features. You may even suggest that they draw their own maps of the area in order to better understand the area in which the Aztecs and the Spaniards battled.

Before You Read

Focus

Summary

In this excerpt, the narrator describes the first glimpse the Aztecs have of the Spaniards. The Aztecs see what they think are mountains floating in the water. Motecuhzoma sends men to discover what the Aztecs have seen. The men bring news of the Spaniards' activities. When Cortés arrives, Motecuhzoma sends messengers to greet Cortés and bring him gifts. Cortés leaves the area, putting Don Pedro de Alvarado in charge. In Cortés's absence, Alvarado begins attacking the Aztecs. The Spaniards continue to push the Aztecs away from their homes, destroying cities and lives. The Aztecs eventually end up in Amaxac, starving and homeless.

 For summaries in languages other than English, see Unit 6 Teaching Resources Book, pp. 59–64.

Vocabulary

Analogies Explain to students that the trick to analogies involves discovering the relationship between the word pairs. Often the word pairs are synonyms or antonyms. Have students use a dictionary or a thesaurus to find synonyms and antonyms for the vocabulary words. Tell them to color-code the words so they know which are antonyms and which are synonyms. For example, they could write the synonyms in green and the antonyms in blue.

For additional vocabulary practice, see Unit 1 Teaching Resources Book, p. 67.

Teach

View the Art ★

This shield dates from around the time of the Spanish Conquest. The feathers and fangs in this image are characteristic of the feathered serpents of Aztec mythology. **Ask:** How might this shield make an Aztec warrior feel? *(The fierceness of the creature depicted might give a warrior courage.)*

For an audio recording of this selection, use Listening Library Audio CD-ROM.

Readability Scores

Dale-Chall: 6
DRP: 56
Lexile: 810

Reading Practice

Activating Prior Knowledge Have students create a list of pieces of information they have learned about the Aztecs or Spanish exploration. You may wish to have them reread the Part 1 Introduction or other selections in this part. If students have trouble writing the list, allow them to write the list in their native language or draw pictures to represent the pieces of information.

1150

Shield, c.1500. Aztec. Feathers, sheet-gold, agave paper, leather, and reed. Museum fur Volkerkunde, Vienna.

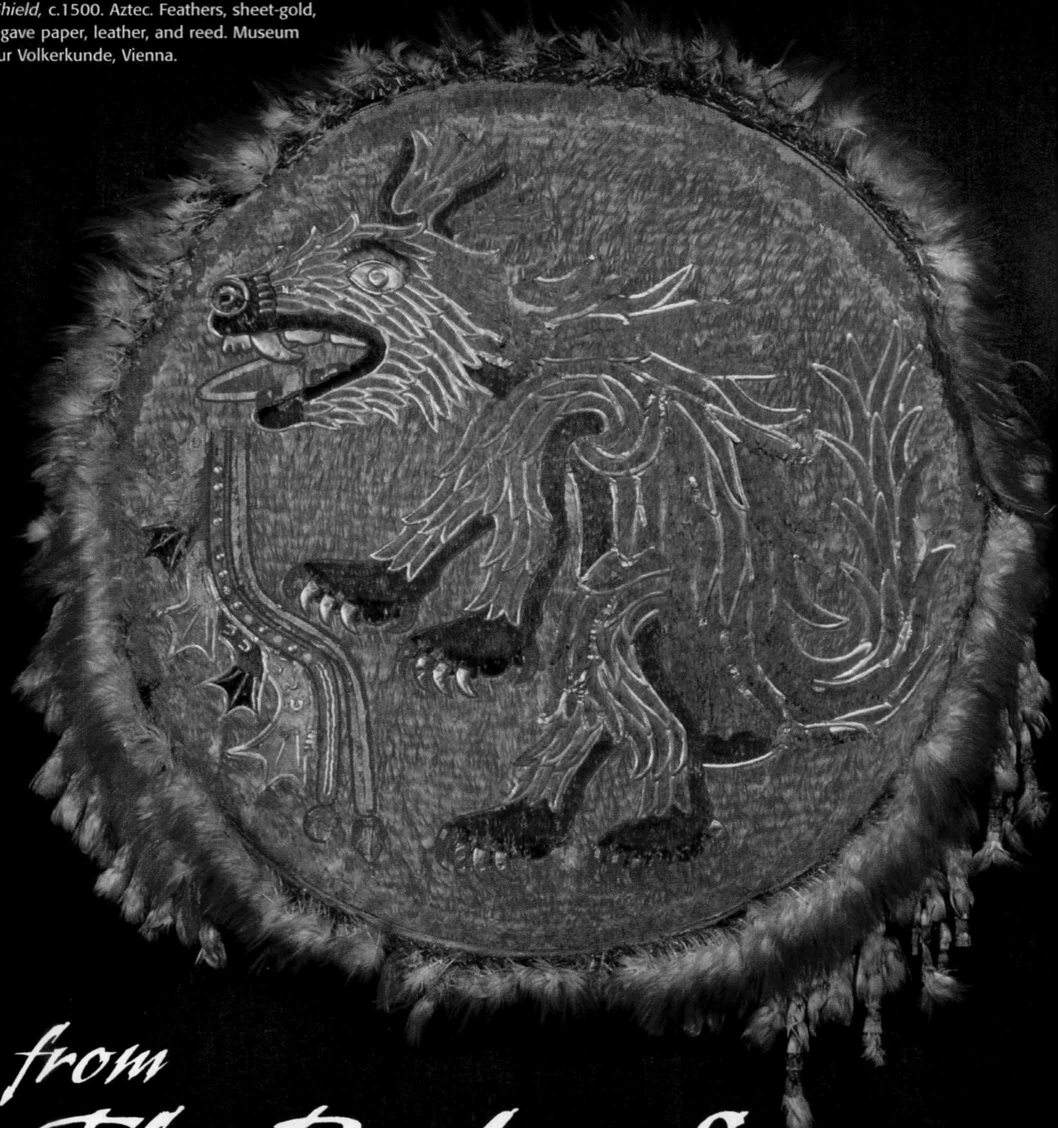

from The Broken Spears

Edited by Miguel Leon-Portilla
Translated by Lysander Kemp

When the Spanish explorer Hernán Cortés and his troops arrived in Mexico, they first landed at Tabasco on the southeastern coast, where they made contact with local Indians. They then sailed up the coast, landing at what is now Veracruz. From there, they marched west into the interior of Mexico toward Tenochtitlán. Along the way, Cortés enlisted the aid of Indian groups who had been conquered by the Aztecs and resented their control, most notably the Tlaxcala nation. The conquest of the Aztec Empire took three years and was complicated by internal strife on both sides. The excerpts in Part I describe the Aztecs' reaction to the arrival of strangers in their land.

I.

A Macehual Arrives from the Gulf Coast

A few days later a *macehual* [common man] came to the city from Mictlancuauhtla. No one had sent him, none of the officials; he came of his own accord. He went directly to the palace of Motecuhzoma and said to him: "Our lord and king, forgive my boldness. I am from Mictlancuauhtla. When I went to the shores of the great sea,[1] there was a mountain range or small mountain floating in the midst of the water, and moving here and there without touching the shore. My lord, we have never seen the like of this, although we guard the coast and are always on watch."

Motecuhzoma thanked him and said: "You may rest now."

Motecuhzoma said to his *petlacalcatl:*[2] "Take him to the prison, and guard him well." Then he called for a *teuctlamacazqui*

---

1. *The great sea* is the Gulf of Mexico in the Atlantic Ocean.
2. A *petlacalcatl* was the king's head steward or servant.

---

1 Setting *What detail in the setting frightens the commoner?*

[priest] and appointed him his grand emissary. He said to him: "Go to Cuetlaxtlan, and tell the official in charge of the village that it is true, strange things have appeared on the great sea. Tell him to investigate these things himself, so as to learn what they may signify. Tell him to do this as quickly as he can, and take the ambassador Cuitlalpitoc with you."

When they arrived in Cuetlaxtlan, the envoys spoke with the official in charge there, a man named Pinotl. He listened to them with great attention and then said: "My lords, rest here with me, and send your attendants out to the shore." The attendants went out and came back in great **haste** to report that it was true: they had seen two towers or small mountains floating on the waves of the sea. The grand emissary said to Pinotl: "I wish to see these things in person, in order to learn what they are, for I must testify to our lord as an eyewitness. I will be satisfied with this and will report to him exactly what I see." Therefore he went out to the shore with Cuitlalpitoc, and they saw what was floating there, beyond the edge of the water. They also saw that seven or eight of the strangers had left it in a small boat and were fishing with hooks and lines.

The grand emissary and Cuitlalpitoc climbed up into a broad-limbed tree. From there they saw how the strangers were catching fish and how, when they were done, they returned to the ship in their small boat. The grand emissary said: "Come, Cuitlalpitoc." They climbed down from the tree and went back to the village, where they took hasty leave of Pinotl. They returned as swiftly as possible to the great city of Tenochtitlan, to report to Motecuhzoma what they had observed. **2**

Vocabulary

haste (hāst) *n.* quickness of action or movement; hurry

THE BROKEN SPEARS **1151**

Teach

Literary Element **1**

Setting **Answer:** *The commoner sees what he interprets as a mountain range floating in the great sea.*

Literary Element **2**

Setting Have the students reread the passage. **Ask:** How do the grand emissary and Cuitlalpitoc use the setting to their advantage? *(They climb a tree in order to better observe the men in the boats.)*

ADVANCED LEARNERS **Ask:** What do the emissary and Cuitlalpitoc's actions reveal about their relationship with the setting? *(Their actions reveal a connection to and understanding of their setting.)*

Learning Objectives
Analyzing setting. (SE)
Activating prior knowledge. (TE)
Analyzing art. (TE)

Approaching Level

DIFFERENTIATED INSTRUCTION

Activating Prior Knowledge To help students with the Reading Practice activity on page 1150, have them focus on the following basic questions: Who were the Aztecs? During what time period did the Aztec civilization exist? Where did they live? Encourage students to build on these questions to discover additional details about ancient Aztec society. You may wish to have them search the Internet for images of art or architecture to give them a visual context for the selection.

Teach

Reading Strategy | 1

Analyze Cultural Context **Answer:** *The emissary likens the color of the Spaniards' jackets to a particular Aztec outer garment and their hats to a common Aztec baking dish.*

Reading Strategy | 2

Analyze Cultural Context **Answer:** *According to the Aztec legend and calendar, the time of the strangers' arrival coincides with a time favorable for the return of Quetzalcoatl.*

Cultural History ☆

Aztec Calendar The Aztec calendar was similar to the Mayan calendar. It consisted of 260 days a year and a 52-year time cycle. The ritual cycle, the 260-day cycle, had two smaller cycles within it. The first smaller cycle contained an ordered sequence of 20 named days. The other smaller cycle consisted of a sequence of days numbered from 1–13; this cycle was important for religious purposes.

When they reached the city, they went directly to the king's palace and spoke to him with all due reverence and **humility**: "Our lord and king, it is true that strange people have come to the shores of the great sea. They were fishing from a small boat, some with rods and others with a net. They fished until late and then they went back to their two great towers and climbed up into them. There were about fifteen of these people, some with blue jackets, others with red, others with black or green, and still others with jackets of a soiled color, very ugly, like our *ichtilmatli*.[3] There were also a few without jackets. On their heads they wore red kerchiefs, or bonnets of a fine scarlet color, and some wore large round hats like small *comales*,[4] which must have been sunshades. They have very light skin, much lighter than ours. They all have long beards, and their hair comes only to their ears."

Motecuhzoma was downcast when he heard this report, and did not speak a word.

Motecuhzoma Instructs His Messengers

Motecuhzoma then gave orders to Pinotl of Cuetlaxtlan and to other officials. He said to them: "Give out this order: a watch is to be kept along all the shores at Nauhtla, Tuztlan, Mictlancuauhtla, wherever the strangers appear." The officials left at once and gave orders for the watch to be kept.

Motecuhzoma now called his chiefs together: Tlilpotonque, the serpent

woman,[5] Cuappiatzin, the chief of the house of arrows, Quetzalaztatzin, the keeper of the chalk,[6] and Hecateupatiltzin, the chief of the refugees from the south. He told them the news that had been brought to him and showed them the objects he had ordered made. He said: "We all admire these blue turquoises, and they must be guarded well. The whole treasure must be guarded well. If anything is lost, your houses will be destroyed and your children killed, even those who are still in the womb."

The year 13-Rabbit now approached its end. And when it was about to end, they appeared, they were seen again. The report of their coming was brought to Motecuhzoma, who immediately sent out messengers. It was as if he thought the new arrival was our prince Quetzalcoatl.[7] ☆

This is what he felt in his heart: *He has appeared! He has come back! He will come here, to the place of his throne and canopy, for that is what he promised when he departed!*

Motecuhzoma sent five messengers to greet the strangers and to bring them gifts. They were led by the priest in charge of the sanctuary of Yohualichan. The second was from Tepoztlan; the third, from Tizatlan; the fourth, from Huehuetlan; and the fifth, from Mictlan the Great. He said to them: "Come forward, my Jaguar Knights, come

---

3. An *ichtilmatli* was an outer garment made from the fibers of maguey, a desert plant characterized by clusters of fleshy leaves.
4. *Comales* are wide, flat dishes used for baking tortillas.

1 | **Analyze Cultural Context** *How does the emissary draw upon his cultural background in describing the Spaniards?*

Vocabulary

humility (hū mil′ə tē) *n.* modesty; meekness

---

5. *Serpent woman* was a title given to the king's chief adviser.
6. The *keeper of the chalk* was the official responsible for the colors priests used for painting their bodies when performing rituals.
7. *Quetzalcoatl* was the god of learning. According to Aztec legend, a rival god expelled him from Mexico. In one version, Quetzalcoatl sailed away and disappeared beyond the eastern horizon, promising to return. According to the Aztec calendar, the year in which Cortés arrived in Mexico was considered to be a favorable one for Quetzalcoatl's return.

Analyze Cultural Context *Based on the footnote about Quetzalcoatl, explain why Motecuhzoma considers the time of the strangers' arrival important.* | **2**

Writing Practice

Write a Character Sketch Have students write a character sketch of Motecuhzoma. Explain that a character sketch is a brief glimpse at what a character is like. The sketch may include details about the character's appearance, occupation, thoughts, actions, or values. Encourage students to reread this page before they begin their sketches.

Allow students enough time to finish their sketches. Make sure that they are writing no more than one or two paragraphs. After they have finished, have them share their sketches with a partner. Tell partners to point out any important details that students may have missed in their sketches. Encourage students to add to or rework their sketches as they continue reading the selection.

Meeting of Montezuma and Hernan Cortez. Artist unknown. Painting. Private collection.

View the Art How does the meeting of Cortés (Cortez) and Motecuhzoma (Montezuma) in this painting compare with the description of their meeting in *The Broken Spears*? ★

forward. It is said that our lord has returned to this land. Go to meet him. Go to hear him. Listen well to what he tells you; listen and remember."

Motecuhzoma Awaits Word from the Messengers

3 While the messengers were away, Motecuhzoma could neither sleep nor eat, and no one could speak with him. He thought that everything he did was in vain, and he sighed almost every moment. He was lost in despair, in the deepest gloom and sorrow. Nothing could comfort him, nothing could calm him, nothing could give him any pleasure.

He said: "What will happen to us? Who will outlive it? Ah, in other times I was contented, but now I have death in my heart! My heart burns and suffers, as if it were drowned in spices . . . ! But will our lord come here?"

Then he gave orders to the watchmen, to the men who guarded the palace: "Tell me, even if I am sleeping: 'The messengers have come back from the sea.' " But when they went to tell him, he immediately said: "They are not to report to me here. I will receive them in the House of the Serpent. Tell them to go there." And he gave this order: "Two captives are to be painted with chalk." **3**

The messengers went to the House of the Serpent, and Motecuhzoma arrived. The

THE BROKEN SPEARS **1153**

Literary Element	3

Setting Have students reread the section where Motecuhzoma Instructs His Messengers. **Ask:** How does the setting deceive Motecuhzoma about what is really coming? *(Motecuhzoma's belief that it was time for Quetzalcoatl's return deceives him and leaves him unprepared for what is really coming to his city.)*

Interactive Read and Write

Other options for teaching this selection can be found in Interactive Read and Write for On-Level Learners, pp. 265–276.

View the Art ★

Answer: *In the painting, Cortés appears to be giving Motecuhzoma gifts whereas in the excerpt, Motecuhzoma gives Cortés gifts.*

Learning Objectives
Analyzing cultural context. (SE)
Analyzing art. (SE)
Writing a character sketch. (TE)

Advanced Learners/Pre-AP

DIFFERENTIATED INSTRUCTION

Write a Journal Entry Have students imagine that they are Motecuhzoma and they are excited about the possible return of Quetzalcoatl. In a journal entry, tell students to record their thoughts about the return of the strange people. Have them explain their preparations and feelings about the possible return. After they have finished, ask volunteers to share their entries with the class.

Teach

Reading Strategy   **1**

Analyze Cultural Context
Answer: *The Aztecs would have considered being in the presence of the gods a great honor and would have felt compelled to acknowledge it with offerings to the gods.*

Literary Element   **2**

Setting Answer: *They report the roar of cannons, stone balls shooting sparks and fire, the odor of smoke, the splitting of a mountain and the shattering of trees into splinters.*

Big Idea   **3**

Cultures in Conflict
Answer: *Believing that the Spaniards are gods, he likely interprets what the messengers have seen as proof of the gods' powers and may despair over what they plan to do.*

two captives were then sacrificed before his eyes: their breasts were torn open, and the messengers were sprinkled with their blood.[8] This was done because the messengers had completed a difficult mission: they had seen the gods, their eyes had looked on their faces. They had even conversed with the gods!

The Messengers' Report

When the sacrifice was finished, the messengers reported to the king. They told him how they had made the journey, and what they had seen, and what food the strangers ate. Motecuhzoma was astonished and terrified by their report, and the description of the strangers' food astonished him above all else.

He was also terrified to learn how the cannon roared, how its noise resounded, how it caused one to faint and grow deaf. The messengers told him: "A thing like a ball of stone comes out of its entrails: it comes out shooting sparks and raining fire. The smoke that comes out with it has a pestilent odor, like that of rotten mud. This odor penetrates even to the brain and causes the greatest discomfort. If the cannon is aimed against a mountain, the mountain splits and cracks open. If it is aimed against a tree, it shatters the tree into splinters. This is a most unnatural sight, as if the tree had exploded from within."

---

8. *The two captives . . . with their blood:* The captives were slaves captured in war for the purpose of being used for ritual sacrifices. Human sacrifices were an important element of the Aztecs' religion. They believed that the gods needed the blood from sacrifices to make them strong.

1   Analyze Cultural Context *Why does the king think it necessary to offer human sacrifices?*

2   Setting *What unfamiliar sights, sounds, and smells do the messengers report in this paragraph?*

The messengers also said: "Their trappings and arms are all made of iron. They dress in iron and wear iron casques[9] on their heads. Their swords are iron; their bows are iron; their shields are iron; their spears are iron. Their deer[10] carry them on their backs wherever they wish to go. These deer, our lord, are as tall as the roof of a house.

"The strangers' bodies are completely covered, so that only their faces can be seen. Their skin is white, as if it were made of lime. They have yellow hair, though some of them have black. Their beards are long and yellow, and their moustaches are also yellow. Their hair is curly, with very fine strands.

"As for their food, it is like human food. It is large and white, and not heavy. It is something like straw, but with the taste of a cornstalk, of the pith of a cornstalk. It is a little sweet, as if it were flavored with honey; it tastes of honey, it is sweet-tasting food.

"Their dogs are enormous, with flat ears and long, dangling tongues. The color of their eyes is a burning yellow; their eyes flash fire and shoot off sparks. Their bellies are hollow, their flanks long and narrow. They are tireless and very powerful. They bound here and there, panting, with their tongues hanging out. And they are spotted like an ocelot."

Visual Vocabulary
An *ocelot* is a medium-sized wildcat.

When Motecuhzoma heard this report, he was filled with terror. It was as if his heart had fainted, as if it had shriveled. It was as if he were conquered by despair.

---

9. A *casque* is a helmet.
10. *Deer* refers to the troops' horses. The messenger mistakes them for deer because he has never seen a horse.

Cultures in Conflict *Why do you think Motecuhzoma is filled with terror after hearing the messengers' report?*   **3**

Reading Practice

Analyze Sensory Details Explain to students that sensory details are descriptions that appeal to a reader's five senses—sight, sound, taste, touch, and smell. Writers use sensory details to make a piece of writing come alive. Sensory details help readers visualize what they are reading. Point out that the writer uses many sensory details in the paragraphs describing the strangers' appearance, their food, and even their dogs.

Have students identify the sensory details in "The Messengers' Report." Tell them to organize the examples by the senses to which they appeal. Invite students to share their examples with the class. Lead a discussion about how the sensory details can aid the students to view the strangers from the Aztec perspective. *(Students may suggest the following sensory details: "skin is white, as if it were made of lime"; "yellow hair";*

"beards are long and yellow"; "hair is curly"; "large and white, not heavy"; "something like straw"; "tastes of honey"; "flat ears and long, dangling tongues"; "flanks long and narrow"; "panting, with their tongues hanging out.")

Aztec Bird God. Gold. Private collection.

> The excerpts in Part II describe Cortés's initial arrival in Tenochtitlán and subsequent events. It is told by survivors of the Tlaltelolco district of the city and, as such, reflects the local pride and bias that influenced their descriptions of the conflict.

II.

The Arrival of Cortés

Year 1-Canestalk. The Spaniards came to the palace at Tlayacac. When the Captain[11] arrived at the palace, Motecuhzoma sent the Cuetlaxteca to greet him and to bring him two suns as gifts. One of these suns was made of the yellow metal, the other of the white.[12] The Cuetlaxteca also brought him a mirror to be hung on his person, a gold collar, a great gold pitcher, fans and ornaments of quetzal[13] feathers and a shield inlaid with mother-of-pearl.

The envoys made sacrifices in front of the Captain. At this, he grew very angry. When they offered him blood in an "eagle dish," he shouted at the man who offered it and struck him with his sword. The envoys departed at once.

All the gifts which the Cuetlaxteca brought to the Captain were sent by Motecuhzoma. That is why the Cuetlaxteca went to meet the Captain at Tlayacac: he was only performing his duties as a royal envoy.

Then the Captain marched to Tenochtitlan. He arrived here during the month called Bird, under the sign of the day 8-Wind. When he entered the city, we

---

11. *Captain* refers to Cortés.
12. *Yellow metal, the other of the white* means "gold and silver."
13. A *quetzal* (ket säl´) is a Central American bird, brilliantly colored, with long, flowing tail feathers.

Cultures in Conflict *Why might the sacrifices offend Cortés?*   4

THE BROKEN SPEARS   **1155**

Learning Objectives
Analyzing cultural context. (SE)
Analyzing setting. (SE)
Analyzing sensory details. (TE)

Approaching Level

DIFFERENTIATED INSTRUCTION

Sequence Chart Have students create a sequence of events chart for this excerpt from *The Broken Spears*. Suggest that they use the subheadings as an aid to structuring their charts. Point out that they will need to determine the main events of the narrative as they create their charts.

Teach

Big Idea   1

Cultures in Conflict

Answer: *The Spaniards might assert that their attack is just punishment for the pagan rituals taking place.*

APPROACHING Before you ask Approaching Level students this question, make sure they understand that the Aztecs' religious practices were different from those of the Spaniards. Point out that differences in religious beliefs can often create conflict.

Literary Element   2

Setting Have students reread "The Massacre in the Main Temple." **Ask:** Why might the setting of the killings make the Aztecs more upset and angry about them? *(The religious setting of the killings makes the killings seem even more cruel and unjust.)*

Political History ☆

Spanish Politics Cortés left Don Pedro de Alvarado in charge because he heard that Pánfilo Narváez was coming to take away his command. Narváez was the leader of a Spanish group from Cuba. Cortés defeated Narváez, enlisting the army for his own forces.

---

gave him chickens, eggs, corn, tortillas and drink. We also gave him firewood, and fodder for his "deer." Some of these gifts were sent by the lord of Tenochtitlan, the rest by the lord of Tlatelolco.

Later the Captain marched back to the coast, leaving Don Pedro de Alvarado—The Sun—in command.

The Massacre in the Main Temple

During this time, the people asked Motecuhzoma how they should celebrate their god's fiesta. He said: "Dress him in all his finery, in all his sacred ornaments."

During this same time, The Sun commanded that Motecuhzoma and Itzcohuatzin, the military chief of Tlatelolco, be made prisoners. The Spaniards hanged a chief from Acolhuacan named Nezahualquentzin. They also murdered the king of Nauhtla, Cohualpopocatzin, by wounding him with arrows and then burning him alive.

For this reason, our warriors were on guard at the Eagle Gate. The sentries from Tenochtitlan stood at one side of the gate, and the sentries from Tlatelolco at the other. But messengers came to tell them to dress the figure of Huitzilopochtli.[14] They left their posts and went to dress him in his sacred finery: his ornaments and his paper clothing.

When this had been done, the celebrants began to sing their songs. That is how they celebrated the first day of the fiesta. On the second day they began to sing again, but without warning they were all put to death. The dancers and singers were completely unarmed. They brought only their embroidered cloaks, their turquoises,

their lip plugs, their necklaces, their clusters of heron feathers, their trinkets made of deer hooves. Those who played the drums, the old men, had brought their gourds of snuff and their timbrels.[15]

The Spaniards attacked the musicians first, slashing at their hands and faces until they had killed all of them. The singers—and even the spectators—were also killed. This slaughter in the Sacred Patio went on for three hours. Then the Spaniards burst into the rooms of the temple to kill the others: those who were carrying water, or bringing fodder for the horses, or grinding meal, or sweeping, or standing watch over this work.

The king Motecuhzoma, who was accompanied by Itzcohuatzin and by those who had brought food for the Spaniards, protested: "Our lords, that is enough! What are you doing? These people are not carrying shields or *macanas*.[16] Our lords, they are completely unarmed!"

The Sun treacherously murdered our people on the twentieth day after the Captain left for the coast. We allowed the Captain to return to the city in peace. But on the following day we attacked him with all our might, and that was the beginning of the war. **2**

The Night of Sorrows

The Spaniards attempted to slip out of the city at night, but we attacked furiously at the Canal of the Toltecs, and many of them died. This took place during the fiesta of Tecuilhuitl. The survivors gathered first at Mazatzintamalco and waited for the **stragglers** to come up.

---

14. *Huitzilopochtli* was the Aztec god of war, and the special protector of the people of Tenochtitlán.

 1 Cultures in Conflict *How might the Spaniards justify their slaughter of those at the festival?*

15. A *timbrel* is a small drum.
16. *Macanas* are clubs or cudgels.

Vocabulary

straggler (strag′lər) *n.* one who lags behind or strays from a group

---

Reading Practice

 SMALL GROUP

Analyze Cause-and-Effect Relationships Remind students that a cause is what makes something happen; what happens is the effect. Explain that by looking at cause-and-effect relationships, readers can see how events are connected. Organize students into small groups and have them identify the cause-and-effect relationships in the text.

Suggest that students create a list or some kind of organizer in which to record these relationships. This will help them keep their ideas organized. After students have finished, have them share their lists with the class. Be sure to point out any causes or effects that students may have missed.

Year 2-Flint. This was the year in which Motecuhzoma died.[17] Itzcohuatzin of Tlatelolco died at the same time.

The Spaniards took refuge in Acueco, but they were driven out by our warriors. They fled to Teuhcalhueyacan and from there to Zoltepec. Then they marched through Citlaltepec and camped in Temazcalapan, where the people gave them hens, eggs and corn. They rested for a short while and marched on to Tlaxcala.

Soon after, an **epidemic** broke out in Tenochtitlan. Almost the whole population suffered from racking coughs and painful, burning sores.

The Siege of Tenochtitlan

Now the Spaniards began to wage war against us. They attacked us by land for ten days, and then their ships appeared. Twenty days later, they gathered all their ships together near Nonohualco, off the place called Mazatzintamalco. The allies from Tlaxcala and Huexotzinco set up camp on either side of the road.

Our warriors from Tlatelolco immediately leaped into their canoes and set out for Mazatzintamalco and the Nonohualco road. But no one set out from Tenochtitlan to assist us: only the Tlatelolcas were ready when the Spaniards arrived in their ships. On the following day, the ships sailed to Xoloco.

---

17. *Motecuhzoma died:* The circumstances of Motecuhzoma's death are not known. Historians theorize that he may have died of injuries sustained during the Aztec rebellion.

3 Analyze Cultural Context *What might this statement suggest about the relationship between the Tlatelolcas and the other residents of Tenochtitlán?*

Vocabulary

epidemic (ep′ə dem′ik) *n.* rapid spread of disease affecting many people

---

The fighting at Xoloco and Huitzillan lasted for two days. While the battle was under way, the warriors from Tenochtitlan began to mutiny. They said: "Where are our chiefs? They have fired scarcely a single arrow! Do they think they have fought like men?" Then they seized four of their own leaders and put them to death. The victims were two captains, Cuauhnochtli and Cuapan, and the priests of Amantlan and Tlalocan. This was the second time that the people of Tenochtitlan killed their own leaders.

The Flight to Tlatelolco

The Spaniards set up two cannons in the middle of the road and aimed them at the city. When they fired them, one of the shots struck the Eagle Gate. The people of the city were so terrified that they began to flee to Tlatelolco. They brought their idol Huitzilopochtli with them, setting it up in the House of the Young Men. Their king Cuauhtemoc[18] also abandoned Tenochtitlan. Their chiefs said: "Mexicanos! Tlatelolcas! All is not lost! We can still defend our houses. We can prevent them from capturing our storehouses and the produce of our lands. We can save the **sustenance** of life, our stores of corn. We can also save our weapons and insignia, our clusters of rich feathers, our gold earrings and precious stones. Do not be discouraged; do not lose heart. We are Mexicanos! We are Tlatelolcas!"

The Fighting Is Renewed

The Spaniards made ready to attack us, and the war broke out again. They assembled

---

18. *Cuauhtemoc* became king of the Aztecs after the death of Motecuhzoma.

Vocabulary

sustenance (sus′tə nəns) *n.* food; nourishment; means of support

THE BROKEN SPEARS **1157**

Teach

Reading Strategy   **3**

Analyze Cultural Context
Answer: *It might suggest that tension, resentment, or jealousy existed between the two groups even before the landing of the Spaniards.*

Learning Objectives
Analyzing cultural context. (SE)
Analyzing setting. (TE)
Analyzing cause-and-effect relationships. (TE)

Advanced Learners/Pre-AP

DIFFERENTIATED INSTRUCTION

Create a Diagram Have students use print or Internet sources to determine the locations of the battles fought in the text. After they have located the positions of the battles, tell them to create a diagram or map that shows the battle locations. Provide them with paper, markers, colored pencils, or any other items they may need. Encourage students to create legends for their diagrams or maps that use color-coded symbols to represent the Aztecs and the Spaniards. Have them develop a system for pointing out who won each battle. After they have finished, have students display their diagrams and maps in the classroom. Refer to these drawings as you continue to read the selection. You may have students add to their diagrams and maps as they read.

Teach

Reading Strategy | 1

Analyze Cultural Context
Answer: *It reveals the Aztecs most likely saw women and men as equals.*

Literary Element | 2

Setting **Ask:** What emotional effect does the setting in this poem create? *(The setting creates emotions of fear and despair.)*

Big Idea | 3

Cultures in Conflict
Answer: *They probably realized they were outmatched by the Spanish and the battle could not continue indefinitely.*

[ADVANCED] Lead a discussion about how students think the Aztecs must have felt when they decided to give up the fight. Tell them to use details from the text to support their responses. *(Students may suggest that the Aztecs felt frustrated, disappointed, or angry about having to give up the fight. They fought long to try to preserve what was theirs. This loss must have been disappointing.)*

To check students' understanding of the selection, see Unit 6 Teaching Resources Book, p. 70.

their forces in Cuepopan and Cozcacuahco. A vast number of our warriors were killed by their metal darts. Their ships sailed to Texopan, and the battle there lasted three days. When they had forced us to retreat, they entered the Sacred Patio, where there was a four-day battle. Then they reached Yacacolco.

The Tlatelolcas set up three racks of heads in three different places. The first rack was in the Sacred Patio of Tlilancalco [Black House], where we strung up the heads of our lords the Spaniards. The second was in Acacolco, where we strung up Spanish heads and the heads of two of their horses. The third was in Zacatla, in front of the temple of the earth-goddess Cihuacoatl, where we strung up the heads of Tlaxcaltecas.

The women of Tlatelolco joined in the fighting. They struck at the enemy and shot arrows at them; they tucked up their skirts and dressed in the regalia of war.

The Spaniards forced us to retreat. Then they occupied the market place. The Tlatelolcas—the Jaguar Knights, the Eagle Knights, the great warriors—were defeated, and this was the end of the battle. It had lasted five days, and two thousand Tlatelolcas were killed in action. During the battle, the Spaniards set up a canopy for the Captain in the market place. They also mounted a catapult on the temple platform.

Epic Description of the Besieged City

And all these misfortunes befell us.
We saw them and wondered at them;
we suffered this unhappy fate.

2 Broken spears lie in the roads;
we have torn our hair in our grief.

The houses are roofless now, and their walls are red with blood.

Worms are swarming in the streets and plazas, and the walls are splattered with gore.
The water has turned red, as if it were dyed, and when we drink it,
it has the taste of brine.

We have pounded our hands in despair against the adobe walls,
for our inheritance, our city, is lost and dead.
The shields of our warriors were its defense, but they could not save it.

We have chewed dry twigs and salt grasses;
we have filled our mouths with dust and bits of adobe;
we have eaten lizards, rats and worms. . . .

The City Falls

Cuauhtemoc said to the fortune tellers: "Please come forward. What do you see in your books?"

One of the priests replied: "My prince, hear the truth that we tell you. In only four days we shall have completed the period of eighty days. It may be the will of Huitzilopochtli that nothing further shall happen to us. Let us wait until these four days have passed."

But then the fighting broke out again. The captain of Huitznahuac—the same Huasteco who had brought in Xochitl— renewed the struggle. The enemy forced us to retreat to Amaxac. When they also attacked us there, the general flight began. The lake was full of people, and the roads leading to the mainland were all crowded.

Thus the people of Tenochtitlan and Tlatelolco gave up the struggle and abandoned the city. We all gathered in Amaxac. We had no shields and no *macanas*, we had nothing to eat and no shelter. And it rained all night. ∾

1 Analyze Cultural Context *What does this reveal about the Aztecs' attitude toward women?*

Cultures in Conflict *Why do you think the Aztecs gave up the fight?* **3**

Writing Practice

Write a Movie Scene Tell students to select one of the scenes from the selection and turn it into a movie scene. Encourage them to select a scene that they understand well. Have them consider cast members, costumes, setting, props, music, and dialogue. Point out that movies rely more on visuals than dialogue.

If students have problems visualizing their scenes, suggest they draw pictures of the scenes or act the scenes out. This may help them better visualize how they want the scene to look. After they have finished their scenes, ask them to share the scenes with the class. Lead a discussion about the choices that students made in their scenes.

After You Read

Respond and Think Critically

Respond and Interpret

1. What details about the Aztecs or the conquest impressed you most? Why?

2. (a)When the messengers confirm the sighting of strangers, what objects does Motecuhzoma order to be made? (b)What might he want to do with them?

3. (a)Why do you think the narrator refers to Don Pedro de Alvarado as "The Sun"? (b)How do you think the narrator regards The Sun after he murders Aztecs?

4. (a)What do the citizens of Tenochtitlán do when Cortés returns to the city? (b)Why does the narrator say this moment "was the beginning of the war"?

Analyze and Evaluate

5. (a)Why do you think Cortés was able to receive assistance from Indian groups within the Aztec Empire? (b)What does this suggest about the power of the Aztecs?

6. How does the tone of the poem on page 1158 differ from the tone of the prose sections of the narrative? Support your response with evidence from the text.

Connect

7. **Big Idea** Cultures in Conflict (a)Why do you think Cortés and his troops were able to defeat the Aztecs? (b)Under what circumstances might the Aztecs have been victorious?

8. **Connect to Today** Why is it important for modern readers to understand the Aztecs' perspective on the Spanish Conquest?

Literary Element Setting

ACT Skills Practice

1. "The great sea" is significant in the narrative because it is:

    I. the route by which the Spaniards arrived.

    II. the location of the first Spaniard sightings.

    III. the route Quetzalcoatl used to leave Mexico.

    A. II only

    B. I and II only

    C. I and III only

    D. I, II, and III

2. The details of setting in the poem at the end of the narrative suggest a feeling of:

    F. exhilaration.

    G. mystery.

    H. devastation.

    J. prosperity.

Review: Point of View

As you learned on page 497, **point of view** is the relationship of the narrator to the literary work. Though the narrators of this historical account occasionally use first-person pronouns, the excerpts are told mainly from the **third-person** point of view. At times, the narrator is omniscient or all-knowing, as when describing Motecuhzoma's reaction to the messengers' report.

Partner Activity Working with a partner, discuss the following questions.

1. What cultural limitations affected the Aztec narrators' descriptions of the Spaniards?

2. The account in Part II is told by different Tlatelolco narrators. What details reveal a point of view specific to them?

After You Read

Assess

1. Answers will vary.

2. (a) turquoise ornaments (b) He intends to give the ornaments to the strangers.

3. (a) The Sun is a designation associated with the gods. The narrators believe that the Spaniards are gods. (b) He probably feels horribly betrayed.

4. (a) The citizens drive out Cortés and his troops. (b) It was the first time the Aztecs launched a major counterattack against the massacring Spaniards.

5. (a) Many of these groups had been conquered by the Aztecs and resented their control. (b) Cortés's ability to enlist the aid of subject Indian tribes suggests that Aztec power was maintained through fear and that, given the right circumstances, subject tribes would rebel against that power.

6. The poem is more despairing and grief-stricken, whereas the rest of the narrative seems detached and reportorial.

7. (a) He had superior weapons and assistance from other Indian groups. He also was able to intimidate the Aztecs. (b) If the Aztecs had more positive relationships with their subject tribes, they might have been able to overwhelm the Spaniards with sheer numbers.

8. to get a more complete picture of the Spanish Conquest; to understand its violent nature

Progress Check

Can students identify setting?

If No ➔ See Unit 6 Teaching Resources Book, p. 65.

Review: Point of View

1. The Aztecs were describing people they had never seen before. Nothing in their native culture prepared them for their encounter with the Spaniards.

2. Details include their criticism of the people from other parts of Tenochtitlán and the pride reflected in their claim that only they fought against the Spaniards.

Literary Element

1. **D** is the correct answer. All three of these factors contribute to the great sea's significance.

2. **H** is the correct answer. The details include broken spears in the roads, roofless houses, blood-spattered walls, worms in streets, and bits of adobe.

After You Read

Assess

Reading Strategy

1. Examples include religious beliefs that allowed them to view the Spaniards as gods, social and religious practices such as gift-giving and the offering of sacrifices, and a limited world view that prevented them from understanding the Spaniards' intentions. Students may offer specific examples within these categories.

2. It led them to put misplaced trust in the Spaniards. Students may offer specific examples.

Progress Check

Can students analyze cultural context?

If No → See Unit 6 Teaching Resources Book, p. 66.

Vocabulary

1. b 2. c 3. a 4. b 5. b

Academic Vocabulary

Students should describe a time when they reached an incorrect conclusion and explain some of the factors that swayed them the wrong way.

Listening and Speaking

Students' reports should
- provide well-supported assessments of the validity of the subjects' statements
- include effective oral delivery techniques

 For grammar practice, see Unit 6 Teaching Resources Book, p. 69.

1160

Reading Strategy Analyze Cultural Context

Analyzing the cultural context of a text helps you identify the values and beliefs that influenced the work. Look back at the chart you made on page 1149, and then answer the following questions.

1. How did the cultural beliefs and practices of the Aztecs influence their treatment of the Spaniards? Cite examples from the text.

2. How did the Aztecs' view of the world work to their disadvantage in their dealings with the Spaniards?

Vocabulary Practice

Practice with Analogies Choose the word that best completes each analogy. Use a dictionary if you need help.

1. haste : speed :: hurry :
   a. politeness **b.** swiftness **c.** sensibleness

2. humility : pomposity :: envy :
   a. scorn **b.** timidity **c.** admiration

3. straggler : stray :: achiever :
   a. succeed **b.** withdraw **c.** criticize

4. epidemic : outbreak :: offense :
   a. defense **b.** insult **c.** delight

5. sustenance : starvation :: wealth :
   a. excess **b.** poverty **c.** luxury

Academic Vocabulary

The legend of the return of Quetzalcoatl influenced the Aztecs' **interpretation** *of the Spaniards' arrival.*

Interpretation is an academic word. In the justice system, lawyers and judges use their **interpretations** of laws to determine which actions are crimes. To further explore the meaning of this word, describe a time when your **interpretation** of an event or a literary character was inaccurate, and explain why.

For more on academic vocabulary, see pages 36–37 and R83–R85.

Listening and Speaking

 Interview

Assignment *The Broken Spears* is a compilation of several firsthand accounts of the conquest of Mexico. These primary sources changed the perspectives of many readers who had been familiar only with secondhand accounts. Conduct interviews with your peers and others in your community to determine what they know about the Spanish Conquest of the Aztec Empire. Then write a report based on the interviews.

Prepare Write a list of relevant questions phrased in mature, sensitive, and respectful language. Questions should reflect your understanding of the topic. Leave space under each for answers.

Interview Take notes on your subjects' responses to your questions. Follow these tips:

- Allow your subject to respond completely; don't interrupt.
- Make frequent eye contact.
- Adjust your tone of voice or body language in response to your subject.
- If necessary, ask further questions to clarify information.
- Review your subject's statements as a final check.
- Thank your subject for his or her cooperation.

Report Organize your interview notes to compile information for a short report. In your report, include your own reflections on the validity and reliability of each of your subjects' statements. Point out any contradicting information from interview subjects.

Evaluate Write a paragraph reflecting on your performance as an interviewer and outlining ideas for how to extract more in-depth answers if you were to re-interview your subjects.

 Literature Online

Selection Resources For Selection Quizzes, eFlashcards, and Reading-Writing Connection activities, go to glencoe.com and enter QuickPass code GLW6053u6.

 For additional selection assessment, see Assessment Resources, pp. 225–226.

To create custom assessments online, go to Progress Reporter Online Assessment.

 To create custom assessments using software, use ExamView Assessment Suite.

Vocabulary Workshop

Denotation and Connotation

Literature Connection In the excerpts from *The Broken Spears*, the narrator recounts Motecuhzoma's reaction to the news of the arrival of the Spanish conquistadors: "He was filled with terror. It was as if his heart had fainted, as if it had shriveled. It was as if he were conquered by despair." The narrator could have used words other than *terror*. For instance, he could have spoken of *trepidation* or *anxiety*—after all, those words have a meaning similar to *terror*. But they also have subtle differences. Words can have similar **denotations** (dictionary definitions) but different **connotations** (suggested ideas, images, or feelings).

A semantic chart like the one below can help you look more closely at the similarities, differences, and shades of meaning of the words *terror*, *trepidation*, and *anxiety*. Follow these instructions to complete the chart.

- Write the words you will analyze in the first column.
- Check a dictionary to find the definition for each word. Write the definitions in the second column.
- In the third column, record ideas, images, or feelings you associate with each word. For example, you may associate *terror* with acts of violence carried out by subversive groups. Such associations are a word's connotations.

Word	Denotation	Connotation
terror		
trepidation		
anxiety		

Practice Use what you have learned about denotation and connotation to complete the activities below.

1. Complete this semantic chart on a separate sheet of paper. With your classmates, discuss the denotations and connotations of the three words. Why do you think the narrator chose to describe Motecuhzoma's reaction as *terror* and not as *trepidation* or *anxiety*?

2. Find three or four similar words used to describe a character's reaction in another literary work in Unit 6, Part 1. Create a semantic chart for these words. Share your completed charts with your classmates.

Learning Objectives

In this workshop, you will focus on the following objective:

Vocabulary: Understanding denotation and connotation.

Denotation and Connotation

The **denotation** of a word is its literal meaning; the **connotation** of a word is its implied meaning.

Test-Taking Tip

If you are asked a word's denotation on a test, think about how you would define the word to someone else. To identify the word's connotations, think about the images and ideas the word brings to mind.

Literature Online

Vocabulary For more vocabulary practice, go to glencoe.com and enter QuickPass code GLW6053u6.

Advanced Learners/Pre-AP

DIFFERENTIATED INSTRUCTION

Denotation and Connotation Have students write short stories in which they choose words whose denotations and connotations make their writing come alive for readers. When students select a verb or adjective, have them check a thesaurus or dictionary for other words that may better express what they want to say.

Explain that a word's connotation can add a deeper level of meaning to a story. Connotations can help readers better understand a character's personality and his or her actions. After students have finished writing, have them share their stories with the class. Point out examples where a word's connotation adds meaning to the story.

Focus

Activity

Write the following phrases on the board: *rummaged through the closet; a slender woman; fumbled the ball* **Ask:** What do the words *rummaged, slender,* and *fumbled* mean? Point out that the definitions of these words are their denotations. Then explain the meaning of connotation. Lead a discussion about the connotations of each word. (rummaged: *clumsiness or swiftness;* slender: *positive, healthy;* fumbled: *clumsy, uncoordinated*)

Teach

Denotation and Connotation

To help students remember the difference between denotation and connotation, have them connect the word denotation with dictionary. You can find a word's denotation in a dictionary.

Assess

1. *Terror* conveys intense fear. *Trepidation* conveys fearful agitation. *Anxiety* conveys a sense of uneasiness about the future. The narrator was trying to convey Motecuhzoma's feelings of dread at the messenger's report.

2. Students might find similar words in the excerpts from the *Popul Vuh* (pages 1122–1127) and *The Voyage of Christopher Columbus* (pages 1138–1144). Answers should reflect an understanding of the denotations and connotations of the words selected.

Focus

Learning Objectives

For pages 1162–1163

In studying this text, you will focus on the following objectives:

Literary Study: Analyzing literary genres.

Reading: Evaluating historical influences.

Connecting to the literature.

Literary History

Literature of the Conquest Era

MUCH OF THE INFORMATION WE HAVE ABOUT THE SPANISH Conquest of the Americas was written by the conquerors themselves. However, a few accounts are told from a Native American point of view.

Bellringer Options

Daily Language Transparency 110

Or ask: What problems arise when you only hear one side of a story? *(Students may suggest that only hearing one side of a story may result in a biased perception of an event.)* Discuss the importance of hearing both sides of a story before forming an opinion or judgment about what occurred.

Aztec Records

For hundreds of years following the Spanish Conquest of the Aztecs, the only version of this tragic history was that of the victors. The Aztecs left two types of documentary records, however. The first are the pictographic books known as *codices*. The Aztec codices created before the Spanish Conquest are entirely pictorial and largely devoted to religious ritual. Later codices were created under Spanish supervision; some of these were copies of pre-Conquest records that are now lost. These post-Conquest codices sometimes include Spanish commentary as well as pictographs and contain important information on Aztec history and culture. The second type of Aztec records are books written in Nahuatl, the language of the Aztecs, but using the Latin alphabet the Spanish had taught the Native Americans. In these books, the Aztecs preserved poems, songs, histories, and other traditions they had memorized in their own schools prior to the Spanish Conquest.

Teach

For activities related to this selection, see Unit 6 Teaching Resources Book, pp. 72–73.

Aztec feather artisan, mid 16th century. Bernardino de Sahagun. Illustration. Biblioteca Medicea-Laurenziana, Florence.

important primary sources about the Spanish Conquest of what is now Mexico.

Another important source is the account written by one of Cortés's men, Bernal Díaz del Castillo. He began writing *The True History of the Conquest of New Spain* in the early 1550s, but it was only after reading another account of the conquest, with which he disagreed, that he became motivated to complete his own. Díaz believed his personal involvement as a member of the expedition made him better qualified to describe it.

Hernán Cortés and Bernal Díaz del Castillo

In 1519, long before his forces had completed their conquest of the Aztec Empire, Hernán Cortés began sending reports to Spain in the form of lengthy letters to the Spanish ruler, Charles V. Cortés was an excellent writer, and his letters present a vivid, detailed, and carefully constructed version of the events of his expedition, designed to heighten his own achievements and silence his political enemies. The five letters of Cortés are among the most

Bartolomé de Las Casas

In the years following the Spanish Conquest, many people began to protest against the brutality of the

1162 UNIT 6   THE EARLY AMERICAS

Analyze Tone Remind students that tone is the writer's attitude toward his or her subject; for example, a tone can be formal, informal, admiring, or sarcastic. Ask students to analyze the tone used on this page. Tell them that a writer's word choice can often reveal his or her tone. *(Students may suggest that the tone is formal, objective, or informative.)*

Have students imagine that the writer used a sorrowful or disapproving tone. Ask them how this change in tone would affect their understanding of the lack of Aztec accounts. Would they feel more sorry for the Aztecs? Would they feel angry at the victors? Lead a class discussion about students' responses to the questions above.

Help students understand that writers can use tone to convey messages or to persuade readers. If time allows, have students rewrite a paragraph from this page. Tell them to write the paragraph in a new tone. Have volunteers share their paragraphs with the class. Point out how the choice of tone changes the feel of the passage.

encomienda system through which Spanish colonists exacted forced labor from Native Americans. One prominent advocate for native peoples was Bartolomé de Las Casas, Bishop of Chiapas, an "Apostle of the Indies." As a young man on the Caribbean island of Hispaniola, Las Casas was horrified by Spanish mistreatment of Native Americans. He later wrote several books describing their destruction. His books were read throughout Europe, creating pressure on the Spanish government to change their policies.

> "Surely God will wreak his fury and anger against Spain some day for the unjust wars waged against the Indians."
>
> —Bartolomé de Las Casas

Hernando Cortez. Museo Ciudad Mexico.

Garcilaso de La Vega

Between 1532 and the early 1570s, the Spanish conquered the Inca Empire, destroying much of Inca civilization in the process. The source for much of what is known about the early history of the Incas is Garcilaso de la Vega's *Royal Commentaries of the Incas*, published between 1608 and 1617. Born in Peru in 1539, de la Vega, later known as "El Inca," was the son of an Inca princess and a Spanish conquistador. He grew up hearing his mother's relatives and friends retelling the ancient myths and legends of the Incas, which became the basis for his account. *The Royal Commentaries* is divided into two parts: the first deals with Inca history and civilization, the second with the Spanish conquest of Peru.

Alonso de Ercilla y Zúñiga

Born in Spain in 1533, Alonso de Ercilla y Zúñiga arrived in South America in 1555 and served with the Spanish in their long struggle against the Araucanian (or Mapuche) people of southern Chile and Argentina. The Native Americans were led by a brave, skillful warrior named Lautaro, who successfully resisted the Spanish until he was defeated and killed. He is one of the main characters in *La Araucana*, an epic poem in which Ercilla describes the Spanish campaigns in which he fought. Although Ercilla believed the Native Americans were wrong to resist Spanish authority once they had accepted it, his epic presents a sympathetic account of their struggle.

 Literature Online

Literature and Reading For more about the literature of the Conquest Era, go to glencoe.com and enter QuickPass code GLW6053u6.

Respond and Think Critically

1. If you could ask one of these writers a question, who would it be and what would you ask?

2. How did the Aztec codices created before the Spanish Conquest differ from those produced after it?

3. (a) What seems to be the most characteristic form of Spanish literature of the Conquest Era? (b) Why do you think this was so?

LITERARY HISTORY **1163**

Advanced Learners/Pre-AP

DIFFERENTIATED INSTRUCTION

Research Indians in Chile The Spanish determined there were three separate populations of Araucanian peoples—the Mapuche, the Picunche, and the Huilliche. Organize students into small groups, and have them select one of the populations to research. Make sure that each population is being researched.

Have students present their findings in the form of a poster. Students may include visuals on the poster, such as pictures of the people or a map of where the people lived. Tell students the information on the posters should be easy to follow and read. After they have finished, have groups share their findings with the class.

Literary History

Teach

Big Idea 1

Cultures in Conflict Ask: Why do you think literature is often created during times of conflict? *(Times of conflict create great emotion. Writers use literature as outlets for these emotions.)*

Cultural History ☆

Araucanians The Araucanians lived in the middle valleys of south-central Chile. These Native Americans were hunters, fishermen, and farmers. They grew many types of vegetables. Unlike other native peoples in Chile, the Araucanians resisted Spanish conquerors. They organized alliances with other villages and used horses in battle to combat Spanish troops.

Assess

1. Responses will vary.

2. The Aztec codices created before the Spanish conquest are exclusively pictographic and deal largely with ritual; those created after the conquest include Spanish commentary as well as Aztec pictographs and present material on a variety of subjects.

3. (a) The most characteristic form seems to be historical writing of various kinds. (b) Students may feel that the overwhelming events of the Spanish Conquest would lead writers to focus on narrative history.

Focus

Sonnet 145

Bellringer Options

Selection Focus
   Transparency 71

Daily Language
   Transparency 111

Or ask: Which personal characteristics can be captured by photography? Which cannot? *(Students may say that photography can capture a person's physical characteristics and expression; however, photography cannot capture nuances of a person's character, such as his or her voice, laugh, tone, and beliefs.)* Discuss with students whether they feel that photographs, such as school or family pictures, accurately represent them.

Meet **Sor Juana Inés de la Cruz** (1651–1695)

Sor Juana Inés de la Cruz (sôr hwä′nä ē nās′ dā lä kruz′) was the first major author of European descent born in Latin America. She always maintained that women were intellectually equal to men—a controversial view at the time.

Child Prodigy Born in a village outside Mexico City, Sor Juana began reading at age three. Using her grandfather's extensive library, she taught herself Latin, literature, science, theology, and foreign languages. She was so eager to learn that when she was eight she asked her parents to let her disguise herself as a boy so she could attend the University of Mexico. Unfortunately, women had little opportunity to pursue education in colonial Mexico.

Conflict with Church Authorities When she was about seventeen, she decided to become a nun so that she could concentrate on her studies. For about two decades in the convent, Sor Juana wrote religious, philosophical, and love poems as well as plays. She also read widely and performed scientific experiments. Then her life took a sudden turn.

In 1690, the Bishop of Puebla invited Sor Juana to write an essay explaining her theological criticisms. Sor Juana obliged but insisted her essay should not be made public. The bishop, however, published the work, which many people found offensive. In response, Sor Juana wrote a passionate treatise defending a woman's right to pursue knowledge and learning. This treatise set some prominent church figures against her. Although she defended both her opinions and her right to express them with vigor, criticism continued. Angered by the

"Have [women] not a rational soul as men do? Well, then, why cannot a woman profit by the privilege of enlightenment as they do?"

—Sor Juana Inés de la Cruz

authorities' unyielding opposition, Sor Juana decided to stop writing altogether. She sold her books and research materials—more than 4,000 volumes, considered the largest library in Mexico—and gave the money to the poor. Then she devoted herself to caring for the sick. She died while nursing the victims of an epidemic.

 **Literature** Online

Author Search For more about Sor Juana Inés de la Cruz, go to glencoe.com and enter QuickPass code GLW6053u6.

Selection Skills

Literary Elements
- Metaphor (SE pp. 1165, 1167)
- Petrarchan Sonnet (SE p. 1167)

Sonnet 145

Writing Skills/Grammar
- Write a Poem (TE p. 1168)

Reading Skills
- Paraphrase (SE pp. 1165, 1166, 1168)
- Clarify Meaning (TE p. 1166)

Vocabulary Skills
- Synonyms (SE pp. 1165, 1168)
- Academic Vocabulary (SE p. 1168)

Literature and Reading Preview

Connect to the Poem

Have you ever felt surprised or uncomfortable about your own image in a photograph? Write a journal entry explaining why you think your image made you feel that way.

Build Background

Sor Juana wrote a number of poems about portraits. In Sonnet 145, she addresses a painting of herself. Her modesty is reflected in the poem's full title: "She attempts to minimize the praise occasioned by a portrait of herself inscribed by truth, which she calls passion."

Set Purposes for Reading

Big Idea Transplanting Traditions

Colonial Latin American authors adapted traditional European forms such as the sonnet to express their perspectives. As you read, ask yourself, What perspectives does the speaker express in this sonnet?

Literary Element Metaphor

A **metaphor** is a figure of speech that compares two seemingly unlike things. Unlike a **simile**, a metaphor implies the comparison rather than stating it directly, so there is no use of a connective word such as *like* or *as*. As you read, ask yourself, What metaphors can I identify in this sonnet?

Reading Strategy Paraphrase

When you **paraphrase,** you put something you have read or heard into your own words. Paraphrasing is a useful strategy for breaking down difficult text and making it easier to understand. As you read, ask yourself, What passages can I clarify by paraphrasing them?

Tip: Take Notes In a chart like the one below, note difficult passages and your paraphrases of them.

Passages	My Paraphrases
"colorful deceit, / that so immodestly displays art's favors."	This portrait reflects not the truth but the artist's trickery.

Learning Objectives

For pages 1164–1168

In studying this text, you will focus on the following objectives:

Literary Study: Analyzing metaphor.

Reading: Paraphrasing.

Writing: Applying metaphor.

Vocabulary

fallacious (fə lā′shəs) *adj.* erroneous; p. 1166 *The research paper received a failing grade because it had several fallacious references.*

mitigate (mit′ə gāt′) *v.* to lessen; p. 1166 *The darkening clouds increased, rather than mitigated, our fear that a tornado was coming.*

artifice (är′tə fis) *n.* ingenious deception; p. 1166 *The celebrity used dark glasses, a wide-brimmed hat, and other artifices to escape detection.*

ploy (ploi) *n.* a trick or tactic; p. 1166 *He used a ploy to get me to invest in that wild scheme.*

Tip: Synonyms Synonyms are words that have nearly the same meaning. To determine whether two words are synonyms, see if one word can replace the other in a sentence. For example, in the sentence *The research paper received a failing grade because it had several fallacious references,* the word *misleading* can replace *fallacious*. Therefore, *misleading* and *fallacious* are synonyms.

SOR JUANA INÉS DE LA CRUZ **1165**

Before You Read

Focus

Summary

In this sonnet, the author disagrees with the way she has been portrayed in a portrait. She claims the image focuses on the superficial, hides signs of her age, and gives no indication of her spirit.

 For summaries in languages other than English, see Unit 6 Teaching Resources Book, pp. 74–79.

Vocabulary

Find the Synonym Have students work in pairs to write multiple-choice questions about the vocabulary words and their possible synonyms. For example:

The doctor hoped the medication would <u>mitigate</u> the patient's pain.

A exaggerate	C respect
B clarify	D lessen

Have pairs exchange work and complete each other's questions. Encourage students to use different synonyms than those listed in their textbook.

 For additional vocabulary practice, see Unit 6 Teaching Resources Book, p. 82.

Advanced Learners/Pre-AP

DIFFERENTIATED INSTRUCTION

Exploring Portraits of Historical Figures Point out to students that the author of this poem takes offense at seeing what she considers a physically flattering yet empty portrait of herself. Discuss with students other historical portraits they have viewed. (You might spark the discussion by showing students portraits of historical figures from an online art gallery.) How do they think most subjects of portraits wanted to be seen as and thought of? Use students' responses as a point of comparison. Are they surprised by the author's reaction to her portrait? Given her gender and the time period, is her reaction common or unusual? What does her reaction tell students about her beliefs and values? Have students read the poem to see what else they can learn about the author.

Teach

Reading Strategy | 1

Paraphrase **Answer:** *The painting has omitted all signs of its subject's aging, in order to suggest that she has managed to escape the inevitability of growing older.*

(APPROACHING) Remind students that paraphrasing means to put something in their own words. Suggest that when students struggle to find "their own words," they should imagine explaining the text to a friend or family member.

> For additional practice using the reading skill or strategy, see Unit 6 Teaching Resources Book, p. 81.

Literary Element | 2

Metaphor Point out the last line of the poem. **Ask:** What is the poet comparing here? *(She is comparing her portrait to a dead body, ashes, a shadow, and a void.)* **Ask:** What does she mean to convey about her portrait through these metaphors? *(Students may suggest that she means to emphasize the emptiness of her portrait; the portrait does not show her soul or character, just the outer shell of her person.)*

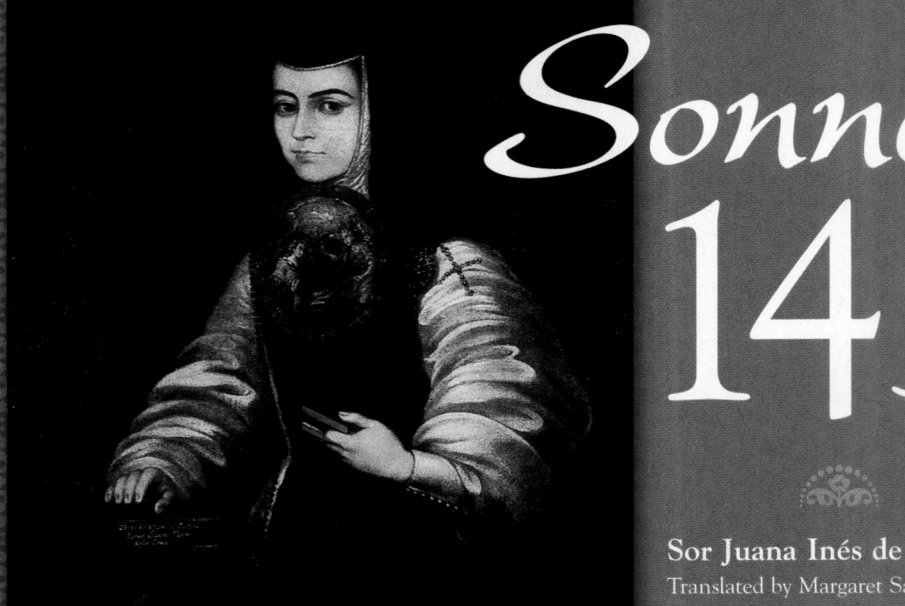

Sonnet 145

Sor Juana Inés de la Cruz
Translated by Margaret Sayers Peden

Portrait of Sor Juana Inez de la Cruz. Unknown artist. Oil on canvas, 41½ x 32½ in. Philadelphia Museum of Art, PA.

> This that you gaze on, colorful deceit,
> that so immodestly displays art's favors,°
> with its **fallacious** arguments of colors
> is to the senses cunning counterfeit,
> 5   this on which kindness practiced to delete
> from cruel years accumulated horrors,
> constraining time to **mitigate** its rigors,
> and thus oblivion and age defeat,
>   is but an **artifice,** a sop° to vanity,
> 10 is but a flower by the breezes bowed,
> is but a **ploy** to counter destiny,
>   is but a foolish labor, ill-employed,
> is but a fancy, and, as all may see,
> is but cadaver, ashes, shadow, void. **2**

2 art's favors: here, applied decorations of little value.

9 sop: a bribe.

1 Paraphrase *How would you paraphrase this passage?*

Vocabulary

fallacious (fə lā′shəs) *adj.* erroneous
mitigate (mit′ə gāt′) *v.* to lessen
artifice (är′tə fis) *n.* ingenious deception
ploy (ploi) *n.* a trick or tactic

Reading Practice

SMALL GROUP
Clarify Meaning Clarify the meaning of the poem by asking groups of students the following questions:

- In line 1, who is the "you" that the author is referring to? *(She is referring to anyone who looks at her portrait.)*
- How has the artist deceived the author? *(The artist has painted an overly flattering image of the author.)*

- What "kindness" has the artist "practiced"? *(The artist has made the author look younger.)*
- How does the portrait attempt to bribe the author's vanity? *(By making the author appear more beautiful than she truly is.)*
- The destiny of every human is to grow old and die. How does the portrait try to "counter" this destiny? *(The portrait preserves the author in life, and shows her younger than she really is.)*
- Why does the author say that making the portrait was "a foolish labor"? *(She is unhappy with the portrait and anyone who knows her will see that it is inaccurate.)*

Have students pose additional questions about the poem and try to answer them in their groups.

After You Read

Respond and Think Critically

Respond and Interpret

1. What ideas or insights did you gain from reading the poem? Share them with the class.

2. (a)What does the phrase "fallacious arguments of colors" in line 3 refer to? (b)What does this statement imply about the speaker?

3. (a)According to lines 5–8, what elements have been left out of the portrait? (b)Why might the artist have chosen to leave them out?

Analyze and Evaluate

4. Why do you think Sor Juana refers to the portrait as a "ploy to counter destiny"?

Literary Element Metaphor

SAT Skills Practice

1. The speaker compares her portrait to a flower to emphasize its

   (A) beauty

   (B) bright colors

   (C) fragility

   (D) grace

   (E) smallness

2. What common qualities do the speaker's comparisons in the last line share?

   (A) ugliness

   (B) darkness

   (C) sadness

   (D) emptiness

   (E) lightness

Review: The Petrarchan Sonnet

As you learned on page 920, a **sonnet** consists of fourteen lines with a rhyme scheme that varies depending on the type of sonnet. Sor Juana's

5. **Tone** is the attitude a speaker takes toward the audience, a subject, or a character. How would you describe the speaker's tone toward the painting? Support your answer with details from the poem.

Connect

6. **Big Idea** **Transplanting Traditions** What perspective on women does Sor Juana express?

7. **Connect to Today** How might a modern-day celebrity react to the speaker's attitude toward her image?

Sonnet 145 is a **Petrarchan sonnet**, which uses the rhyme scheme favored by fourteenth-century Italian poet Petrarch. Complete the rhyme scheme of Sor Juana's poem.

> Lines 1, ___, ___, and ___ form the *a* rhymes.

> Lines ___, 3, ___, and ___ form the *b* rhymes.

> Lines ___, ___, and ___ form the *c* rhymes.

> Lines ___, ___, and 14 form the *d* rhymes.

Partner Activity Work with a partner to compare Sonnet 145 with a European sonnet written during the Renaissance period. You might like to use Petrarch's "Laura" on page 921 of this book. Discuss the style and theme of each poem. When you are finished, share your conclusions with the class.

After You Read

Assess

1. Students should support their answers.

2. (a) The phrase refers to the superficial and misleading effect of the painted surface. (b) It implies that the painting creates a flattering rather than a realistic picture of her.

3. (a) the effects of aging, which change the appearance of the poet (b) in order to curry favor with the subject or someone else

4. The poet's destiny is to age and die, which the portrait tries to overcome by preserving her image.

5. Students may say the tone is critical, objective, scornful, or disapproving. Students may say that phrases such as "colorful deceit," "cunning counterfeit," and "foolish labor" suggest the poet's tone.

6. Sor Juana expresses the perspective that women, who confront realities such as aging and death, should not be idealized as simply beautiful.

7. Students may say that a modern-day celebrity may have difficulty understanding the attitude of a woman who prefers the real person to a flattering image.

Literary Element

1. **(C)** is the correct answer. The comparison to a flower bent by the breeze emphasizes fragility.

2. **(D)** is the correct answer. **(A)** applies only to *cadaver*; **(B)** only to *shadow*; **(E)** only to *ashes*. **(C)** doesn't directly apply to any of the metaphors.

Progress Check

Can students analyze metaphor?

If No → See Unit 6 Teaching Resources Book, p. 80.

Review: The Petrarchan Sonnet

a rhymes: 4, 5, and 8

b rhymes: 2, 6, and 7

c rhymes: 9, 11, and 13

d rhymes: 10 and 12

Partner Activity Students should select a sonnet from a European Renaissance writer and focus on style and theme.

After You Read

Reading Strategy

1. *colorful: vivid, bright, eye-catching; deceit: lie, fake, trick; cunning: clever, sneaky, mischievous.*

2. Students should use the paraphrasing techniques they have learned in the lesson.

Vocabulary

1. c   **2.** d   **3.** a   **4.** e

Academic Vocabulary

Students' responses should reflect an understanding of either the academic or casual meaning of the word *comment*.

Write with Style

Students' poems should
- express how they think others see them
- use a variety of metaphors
- develop these metaphors with additional details

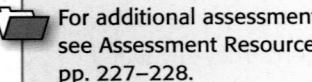
For additional assessment, see Assessment Resources, pp. 227–228.

Reading Strategy   Paraphrase

When you **paraphrase**, you restate ideas in your own words. Look back at the chart you made on page 1165, and then answer the following questions.

1. Think about the connotations of the words *colorful* (line 1), *deceit* (line 1), and *cunning* (line 4). Write at least three words you might use to paraphrase each of these words.

2. How would you paraphrase the first six lines of the poem?

Vocabulary Practice

Practice with Synonyms A synonym is a word that has the same or nearly the same meaning as another word. With a partner, match each boldfaced vocabulary word below with its synonym. Use a thesaurus or dictionary to check your answers. You will not use all the answer choices.

1. **fallacious**   a. trickery
2. **mitigate**   b. learned
3. **artifice**   c. misleading
4. **ploy**   d. soften
                  e. stratagem
                  f. strengthen

Academic Vocabulary

Critical **comments** *about Sor Juana often focus on her feminist ideals.*

Comment is an academic word. The word is also used in more casual settings—for example, an online message-board posting is called a **comment**. To further explore the meaning of this word, describe a time when a peer's **comment** pleased you, and explain why.

For more on academic vocabulary, see pages 36–37 and R83–R85.

Write with Style

Apply Metaphor

Assignment In Sonnet 145, Sor Juana uses metaphors, such as a flower and a corpse, to express the emptiness she sees in a portrait of herself. Write a poem in which you use a variety of metaphors to express the different ways the people in your life seem to regard you.

Get Ideas Create a web like the one below in which you identify the people in your life. Try to imagine how each one sees you. Then create a metaphor to express that person's view.

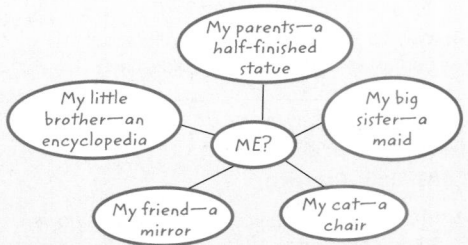

Give It Structure Once you have created metaphors expressing how the people in your life see you, begin assembling these metaphors into a poem.

Look at Language In revising your draft, strengthen your metaphors by creating precision and interest through supporting details. Use language in natural, fresh, and vivid ways.

EXAMPLE:
To my parents, I'm a half-done statue they've struggled to mold for years.

Just can't get the features right; something's still wrong with the ears.

LOG ON   **Literature** Online

Selection Resources For Selection Quizzes, eFlashcards, and Reading-Writing Connection activities, go to glencoe.com and enter QuickPass code GLW6053u6.

Writing Practice

Drafting a Poem Share the following tips with students before they begin writing their poems:

- Poetry can take many different forms (for example, free verse, lyric, haiku, and sonnet). Encourage students to experiment with different forms in their rough draft.

- Write first and edit later. Tell students that once they get down the basic idea they want to convey, they can go back and experiment with different words and phrases.

- Pause occasionally and read the words aloud. Students may find that certain versions have a better rhythm or sound than others.

- Avoid using metaphors that are clichéd, or overused. Ask students to review their poems to make sure the metaphors are unique to their poem—not something students have heard or read before.

- Use different literary devices. Review common devices with students, and suggest they incorporate at least one of them into their poems. For example, students might use rhyme, repetition, or alliteration.

Before You Read

Two Countries

Cuba

Meet **José Martí**

(1853–1895)

Born in Havana, Cuba, José Martí (hō zā′mär tē′) devoted his life to Cuba's struggle for independence from Spain. When he was sixteen, he became a political prisoner, and the colonial government in Cuba sentenced him to hard labor at the quarries in Havana for his political activities. After he was released, he spent almost all of his adult life in exile, living in various countries in Europe and Latin America. In 1881 he moved to New York City, where he wrote poetry and worked as a journalist. He continued to write articles for Latin American journals, chronicling events such as the building of the Brooklyn Bridge. Through these writings he sought to help Latin Americans develop their understanding of the United States. While in New York, he also helped form the Cuban Revolution Party.

Revolutionary Hero Though uprooted from his homeland, Martí always remained true to the cause of Cuban independence. In 1891, he published "Nuestra America," a provocative essay that called for an alliance of the middle class, working class, and peasantry against Spanish landholders in Cuba and American-based businesses that profited there. A passionate speaker, he rallied support for Cuban emancipation, organized political groups in the United States and Central America, and fostered Cuban patriotism and pride. In April 1895, he took part in the Cuban Revolutionary Party's military invasion of Cuba. He died a month later on the battlefield—seven years before his dream of Cuban independence became a reality.

"What matters in poetry is to feel, regardless of whether it resembles what others have felt; and what is felt anew, is new."

—José Martí

Suffering Artist Martí believed that art grows out of suffering. He wrote that pain "matures poetry . . . Man needs to suffer. When he lacks real pain, he creates it. Pain purifies and prepares." Critics have praised his imagery, which he said came to him through visions. His innovative prose style greatly influenced Latin American authors in the twentieth century.

LOG ON ▶ **Literature** Online

Author Search For more about José Martí, go to glencoe.com and enter QuickPass code GLW6053u6.

Before You Read

Focus

Bellringer Options

Selection Focus
 Transparency 72
Daily Language
 Transparency 112

Or ask: How do people react to hardships? *(Students may suggest that people become upset or depressed when hardships befall them.)* Discuss with students positive ways that people can deal with hardships. *(Students may suggest outlets such as exercising or writing.)*

Interactive Read and Write
Other options for teaching this selection can be found in Interactive Read and Write for On-Level Learners, pp. 277–282.

Selection Skills

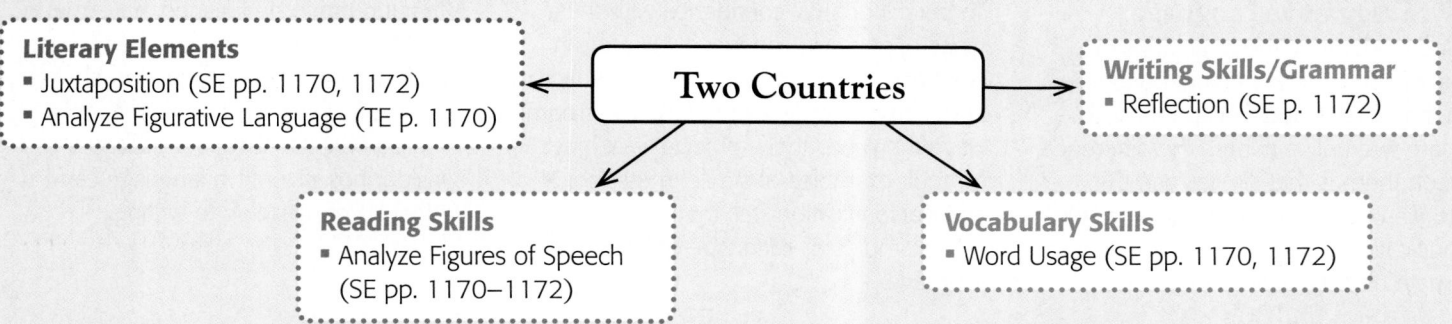

Literary Elements
- Juxtaposition (SE pp. 1170, 1172)
- Analyze Figurative Language (TE p. 1170)

Two Countries

Writing Skills/Grammar
- Reflection (SE p. 1172)

Reading Skills
- Analyze Figures of Speech (SE pp. 1170–1172)

Vocabulary Skills
- Word Usage (SE pp. 1170, 1172)

Before You Read

Focus

Summary

In this poem, the speaker tells of his despair over the state of Cuba and over his exile. Because of his great sense of loss, the speaker feels it is time to die.

 For summaries in languages other than English, see Unit 6 Teaching Resources Book, pp. 86–91.

Vocabulary

Word Usage Write the following sentences and questions on the board:

- Describe how a leaf may **flutter** to the ground.
- When might you see a scene of nature's **majesty?**
- How might a teacher **commence** a class?
- Describe an experience when a **hindrance** stopped you from reaching your goal.

Have students write their answers on a sheet of paper.

 For additional vocabulary practice, see Unit 6 Teaching Resources Book, p. 94.

Literary Practice

Analyze Figurative Language

Remind students of the definitions of simile, metaphor, and personification. Tell them that similes and metaphors both compare two unlike things. The difference between them is that similes use the words *like* or *as* to make the comparison. Personification gives human qualities to inanimate objects, events, or places.

To build students' confidence with these types of figurative language, have them write their own examples. Tell students to select six objects in or near the classroom. Have them use these objects as subjects for their examples of simile, metaphor, and personification. Tell them to write two examples of each type of figurative language.

After students have finished, have them share their examples of figurative language with the class. Lead a discussion about how figurative language helps readers visualize objects. Also have students consider how figurative language can add levels of meaning to writing.

1170

Literature and Reading Preview

Connect to the Poem

How might you react if tragedy befell your homeland? Discuss this question with a partner.

Build Background

After Columbus's arrival in 1492, Cuba became a Spanish colony. By the mid-nineteenth century, however, many Cubans resented the Spanish colonial government. A bitter struggle for independence broke out in 1868 and lasted ten years. A second conflict erupted in 1895. Then in 1898, the United States declared war on Spain, and at the war's end Spain withdrew from Cuba. The last U.S. troops left the island in 1902, when the Republic of Cuba was declared.

Set Purposes for Reading

Big Idea Transplanting Traditions

Latin American authors transplanted European traditions to express new perspectives. As you read, ask yourself, How would you describe the author's vision of his homeland?

Literary Element Juxtaposition

Juxtaposition refers to the placing of two or more distinct elements of a literary work—for example, words, phrases, images, lines, or passages—next to or close to one another. For example, in line 1 of "Two Countries," Martí uses this technique to emphasize his plight of living in exile: "I have two countries: Cuba and the night." As you read, ask yourself, What other examples of juxtaposition can I identify?

Reading Strategy Analyze Figures of Speech

When you **analyze figures of speech,** you look critically at types of figurative language such as metaphor, personification, or simile. By analyzing figures of speech, you can better explore the theme and tone of a poem. As you read, ask yourself, what figures of speech does Martí use to support his theme?

Tip: Chart Figures of Speech In a chart like the one below, record your interpretations of the figures of speech in this poem.

Figure of Speech	Interpretation
Simile: "Cuba . . . appears as a sad and silent widow"	Cuba is bereft of her beloved patriots who suffer in exile.

Learning Objectives

For pages 1169–1172

In studying this text, you will focus on the following objectives:

Literary Study: Identifying juxtaposition.

Reading: Analyzing figures of speech.

Writing: Writing a reflection.

Vocabulary

majesty (maj′is tē) *n.* greatness or magnificence of quality or nature; splendor; p. 1171 *When we stood at the foot of the mountain, we truly appreciated its majesty.*

commence (kə mens′) *v.* to begin; p. 1171 *The luncheon commenced with the introduction of the guests of honor.*

hindrance (hin′drəns) *n.* a thing that presents a challenge, struggle, or delay to someone or something; obstacle; p. 1171 *Inexperience and lack of education were hindrances in his job search.*

flutter (flut′ər) *v.* move with uneven or trembling motion; p. 1171 *The first leaves fluttered to the ground, marking the beginning of fall.*

Tip: Word Usage Try answering a specific question to explore the meaning of a new word. For example, How can fear become a **hindrance** to success?

Two
Countries

José Martí

Translated by Elinor Randall

Peasants, Havana. Eduardo Abela. Havana, Cuba.

I have two countries: Cuba and the night.
Or are both one? No sooner does the sun
Withdraw its **majesty,** than Cuba,
With long veils and holding a carnation,
5   Appears as a sad and silent widow.
I know about that bloodstained carnation
That trembles in her hand! My breast
Is empty, destroyed and empty
Where the heart lay. Now is the time
10 To **commence** dying. Night is a good time
To say farewell. Light is a **hindrance**
As is the human word. The universe
Talks better than man.
                              Like a flag
That calls to battle, the candle's
15 Red flame **flutters.** I feel a closeness
And open windows. Crushing the carnation's
Petals silently, widowed Cuba passes by
Like a cloud that dims the heavens. . . . **1**

Analyze Figures of Speech *Why does the speaker personify the universe?*   **2**

Vocabulary

majesty (maj′is tē) *n.* greatness or magnificence of quality or nature; splendor

commence (kə mens′) *v.* to begin

hindrance (hin′drəns) *n.* a thing that presents a challenge, struggle, or delay to someone or something; obstacle

flutter (flut′ər) *v.* move with uneven or trembling motion

JOSÉ MARTÍ   **1171**

Teach

Big Idea   1

Transplanting Traditions
Point out to students that Romanticism focused on the power of Nature. Romantic poets looked to nature for inspiration and guidance. **Ask:** How do the images in this poem reveal the influence of Romanticism? *(Students may suggest that the images of the carnation and the cloud shading the heavens reveal the influence of Romanticism.)*

Reading Strategy   2

Analyze Figures of Speech Answer: *The speaker suggests that for someone in exile, communication with others is unsatisfying and incomplete. The universe communicates more deeply with the speaker than does any other human being.*

For additional practice using the reading skill or strategy, see Unit 6 Teaching Resources Book, p. 93.

Learning Objectives
Analyzing figures of speech. (SE)
Analyzing figurative language. (TE)

English Learners

DIFFERENTIATED INSTRUCTION

Intermediate Write the first line of "Two Countries" on the board: "I have two countries: Cuba and the night." Point out to students that the colon introduces a list (even if the list consists of only one or two items). Explain that colons should not follow a verb in a sentence or interrupt prepositional phrases.

Write the following sentences on the board. Tell students to identify which sentence uses the colon correctly.

- The gardeners worked with: hoes, shovels, and picks. *(This sentence is incorrect because the colon is interrupting a prepositional phrase. No colon is necessary.)*

- The students read two poems in Unit Six: "Sonnet 145" and "Two Countries." *(This sentence is correct because a list follows the colon.)*

After You Read

Assess

1. Answers will vary.

2. (a) Cuba appears to him as a sad and silent widow. (b) The speaker feels anguish and despair after the sun sets.

3. (a) Most students will say that the speaker is somewhere outside Cuba because Cuba appears to him at night, in a strange vision. (b) The poet is saddened by the oppression of his homeland and the pain of his exile.

4. (a) Possible answer: the heart missing from the speaker's breast; war-torn Cuba. (b) The approach of death is symbolized.

5. Possible answer: The ellipses suggest interruption of the speaker's thoughts, perhaps by death.

6. Martí's vision of his homeland is that of a woman bereft of her husband through violence.

7. Students may say that a modern Cuban exile likely would empathize more deeply with the speaker's sufferings.

Literary Element

1. The speaker reinforces the image of Cuba as a widow who endures the loss of a beloved in silence.

2. It suggests that the speaker's feelings are numbed after undergoing a terrible misfortune.

Reading Strategy

1. (a) the approach of death. (b) With its suggestions of death, this simile reinforces the despairing and melancholic tone of this poem.

2. Cuba is personified as a widow; the universe is said to talk; a flag calls to battle.

After You Read

Respond and Think Critically

Respond and Interpret

1. Which line or passage in this poem made the strongest impression on you? Explain.

2. (a) According to the speaker, what happens when the sun sets? (b) How is this related to the speaker's emotions in lines 7–9?

3. (a) Do you think this poem is set in Cuba, or is the speaker somewhere else? Explain. (b) What point is the author making about Cuba?

Analyze and Evaluate

4. A **symbol** is an object or action that stands for something else in addition to itself. (a) What might the bloodstained carnation symbolize? (b) What does the crushing of the carnation's petals symbolize?

5. **Ellipses points** are a mark of punctuation (. . .) indicating that words have been left out in a quotation. Outside a quotation, ellipses points indicate an unfinished or implied thought. Why might Martí have chosen to end his poem with ellipses points?

Connect

6. **Big Idea** **Transplanting Traditions** What vision of Cuba does Martí share in this poem?

7. **Connect to Today** After Fidel Castro led communist revolutionaries to seize control of Cuba in 1959, thousands of middle-class and professional Cubans fled to the United States. How might one of these modern Cuban exiles react to Martí's poem?

Literary Element **Juxtaposition**

By using **juxtaposition**, poets can create unexpected pairings and stunning contrasts.

1. In line 5, what effect does the poet create by juxtaposing the words *sad* and *silent*?

2. In line 8, what does the phrase "destroyed and empty" suggest about the speaker?

Reading Strategy **Analyze Figures of Speech**

A **simile** is a comparison, using the words *like* or *as*, of two things that have something in common. **Personification** is a figure of speech that gives human characteristics to nonhuman things.

1. (a) What does the simile in lines 13–15 suggest? (b) How does it support the poems' tone?

2. Identify two examples of personification.

 Literature Online

Selection Resources For Selection Quizzes, eFlashcards, and Reading-Writing Connection activities, go to glencoe.com and enter QuickPass code GLW6053u6.

Vocabulary Practice

Practice with Usage Respond to these statements to help you explore the meanings of the vocabulary words from the poem.

1. Describe a time you witnessed a display of nature's **majesty**.

2. Explain how a typical weekday **commences** for you.

3. Give an example of an event that might prove to be a **hindrance** to a relationship.

4. List some animals that move by **fluttering**.

Writing

Write a Reflection Write a brief reflective essay in which you express what a particular place means to you. This could be the place where you now live, or another place you feel attached to. In your essay, use figures of speech to make your descriptions come alive. Refer to the chart you made on page 1170 for ideas.

Vocabulary

1. Students should describe an impressive natural phenomenon, such as a mountain or waterfall.

2. Students might mention rising from bed, eating breakfast, and other morning activities.

3. Students may mention geographical distance.

4. Students might list birds and butterflies.

Writing

Students' reflections should

- explain what the place means to them personally
- use figurative language

 For additional selection assessment, see Assessment Resources, pp. 229–230.

Learning Objectives

For pages 1173–1177

In studying this text, you will focus on the following objectives:

Reading:
Determining main ideas and supporting details.
Using text features.
Analyzing informational text.

Set a Purpose for Reading

Read to learn about the scientific and ethical debates that followed the discovery of an ancient skeleton.

Preview the Article

"Who Were the First Americans?" describes how new archaeological evidence is challenging conventional theories about the earliest humans in the Americas.

1. Read the **subheads,** or smaller headlines within the article. What controversies might this article address?

2. Briefly skim the entire article. What types of evidence do you think the authors will use to support their claims?

Reading Strategy

Determine Main Idea and Supporting Details

The **main idea** is the most important thought in a paragraph or a text. **Supporting details** are pieces of evidence that back up the main idea, including examples, reasons, facts, or descriptions. As you read, ask yourself, What are the main ideas and supporting details?

TIME

Who Were the First AMERICANS?

They may have been a lot like Kennewick Man, whose hotly disputed bones are helping rewrite our earliest history.

By **MICHAEL D. LEMONICK** and **ANDREA DORFMAN**

IT WAS CLEAR FROM THE MOMENT JIM CHATTERS FIRST SAW the partial skeleton that no crime had been committed—none recent enough to be prosecutable, anyway. Chatters, a forensic anthropologist, had been called in by the coroner of Benton County, Washington, to consult on some bones found by two college students on the banks of the Columbia River, near the town of Kennewick. The bones were obviously old, and when the coroner asked for an opinion, Chatters' first guess, based on the skull's superficially Caucasian-like features, was that they probably belonged to a settler from the late 1800s. Then a CT scan revealed a stone spear point set in the skeleton's pelvis, so Chatters sent a bit of finger bone off to the University of California at Riverside for radiocarbon dating. When the results came back, it was clear that his estimate was dramatically off the mark. The bones weren't 100 or even 1,000 years old. They belonged to a man who had walked the banks of the Columbia more than 9,000 years ago.

In short, the remains that came to be known as Kennewick Man were almost twice as old as the celebrated Iceman discovered in 1991 in an Alpine glacier, and among the oldest and most complete skeletons ever found in the Americas. Plenty of archaeological sites date back that far, or nearly so, but scientists have found only about 50 skeletons from such ancient times, most of them fragmentary. Any new find can thus add crucial

WHO WERE THE FIRST AMERICANS? **1173**

TIME

Focus

Summary

In 1996, in Kennewick, Washington, two college students discovered a partial skeleton. Upon investigation, scientists discovered that the skeleton was more than 9,000 years old. The Kennewick Man, as the skeleton came to be called, opened a door for scientists who had been looking for an answer to questions such as where the first Americans came from, when they arrived, and how they got there. The bones revealed that the Kennewick Man was 5 feet 9 inches tall, that he hunted and fished, that he may have been around thirty-eight years old, and that he was deliberately buried. The discovery of the Kennewick Man has put into question who the real first Americans were.

 For activities related to this selection, see Unit 6 Teaching Resources Book, pp. 98–106.

 Interactive Read and Write
Other options for teaching this selection can be found in Interactive Read and Write for On-Level Learners, pp. 283–300.

Advanced Learners/Pre-AP

DIFFERENTIATED INSTRUCTION

SMALL GROUP
Researching the Iceman Organize students into small groups, and have them use Internet and print sources to discover more information about the Iceman. Students can research how the remains were dated, where the body was found, and what additional information was discovered about the body. Make sure that students use credible sites if they are using the Internet.

After groups have finished their research, have them give oral presentations on their findings to the class and encourage them to use visual aids; for example, they could use pictures of the Iceman or a map to show where he was discovered. Make sure that each group member participates in the presentation.

Readability Scores
Dale-Chall: 10
DRP: 68
Lexile: 1280

1173

TIME

Teach

Big Idea ⬛1

Cultures in Conflict **Ask:**
How have cultural conflicts affected the life of Douglas Owsley? *(Cultural conflicts have increased the demand for Owsley's professional skills.)*

Reading Strategy ⬛2

Main Idea and Supporting Details **Ask:** What details in this paragraph support the main idea that studying the Kennewick Man would reveal important information about the time he lived? *(The discovery of his height and build reveal information about the size and activities of the people during the time period.)*

Reading Strategy ⬛3

Main Idea and Supporting Details **Ask:** What is the main idea of this paragraph? *(The main idea is that the scientists had to work within the restraints placed on them by the U.S. Army Corps of Engineers.)*

insight into the ongoing mystery of who first colonized the New World—the last corner of the globe to be populated by humans. Kennewick Man could cast some much-needed light on the difficult questions of when that migration took place, where the first Americans originally came from and how they got here.

U.S. government researchers examined the bones, but it would take almost a decade for independent scientists to get a good look at the skeleton. Although it was found in the summer of 1996, the local Umatilla Indians and four other Columbia Basin tribes almost immediately claimed it as ancestral remains under the Native American Graves Protection and Repatriation Act, demanding that the skeleton be reburied without the violation of scientific study. A group of researchers sued, starting a legal tug-of-war and negotiations that ended in 2005, with the scientists getting their first extensive access to the bones. And now, for the first time, we know the results of that examination.

What the Bones Revealed
It was clearly worth the wait. The scientific team that examined the skeleton was led by forensic anthropologist Douglas Owsley of the Smithsonian Institution's National Museum of Natural History. (Forensic anthropologists analyze skeletal remains and help identify individuals who died in mass disasters, wars, or due to homicide, suicide, or accidental death.) Owsley has worked with thousands of historic and pre-historic skeletons, including those

of Jamestown colonists, Plains Indians and Civil War soldiers. He helped identify remains from the 9/11 attack on the Pentagon and mass graves in Croatia. ⬛1

In this case, Owsley and his team were able to nail down or make strong guesses about Kennewick Man's physical attributes. He stood about 5' 9" tall and was fairly muscular. He was clearly right-handed: the bones of the right arm are markedly larger than those of the left. In fact, says Owsley, "the bones are so robust that they're bent," the result, he speculates, of muscles built up during a lifetime of hunting and spear fishing. ⬛2

An examination of the joints showed that Kennewick Man had arthritis in the right elbow, both knees, and several vertebrae but that it wasn't severe enough to be crippling. He had suffered plenty

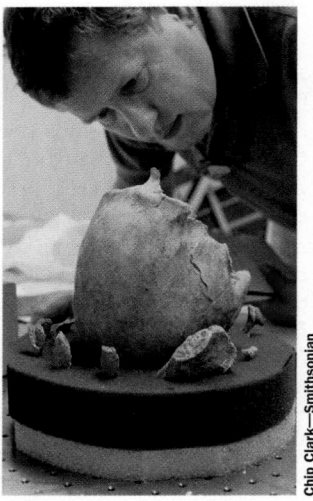

Forensic anthropologist Owsley takes one last look at the pieces of Kennewick Man's skull before having them scanned for posterity.

Chip Clark—Smithsonian

of trauma as well. "One rib was fractured and healed," says Owsley, "and there is a depression fracture on his forehead and a similar indentation on the left side of the head." None of those fractures were fatal, though, and neither was the spear jab. "The injury looks healed," says Owsley. Previous estimates had Kennewick Man's age as 45 to 55 when he died, but Owsley thinks he may have been as young as 38. Nothing in the bones reveals what caused his death.

But that's just the beginning of ⬛3 an impressive catalog of information that the scientists have added to what was already known—all the more impressive given the limitations placed on the team by the U.S. Army Corps of Engineers. The Corps is responsible for the skeleton because it has jurisdiction over the federal land on which it was found. The researchers had to do nearly all their work at the University of Washington's Burke Museum, where Kennewick Man has been housed in a locked room since 1998, under the watchful eyes of representatives of both the Corps and the museum. And they had to follow a strict schedule that had to be submitted in advance. "We only had 10 days to do everything we wanted to do," says Owsley. "It was like a choreographed dance."

Perhaps the most remarkable discovery: Kennewick Man had been buried deliberately. By looking at concentrations of calcium carbonate, a colorless or crystal-like compound, left behind as underground water collected on the underside of the bones and then evaporated, scientists can tell

Reading Practice

Analyze Author's Purpose Remind students that an author's purpose is his or her reason for writing. An author's purpose may be to entertain, to persuade, to describe, to explain, or to inform. Point out that an author's tone and word choice can act as clues to his or her purpose for writing. The title of a piece of writing may also act as a clue. Have students look at the title and reread the text they have read so far. Ask them what they think the author's purpose is for writing. Point out that an author may have more than one purpose. Write students' responses on the board. After they have finished reading the article, return to their responses. Have students note whether they changed their minds or if their responses are still the same. Then have them give reasons for their final decisions.

that he was lying on his back with his feet rolled slightly outward and his arms at his side, the palms facing down—a position that could hardly have come about by accident. And there was no evidence that animal scavengers had been at the body.

The researchers could also tell that Kennewick Man had been buried parallel to the Columbia, with his left side toward the water: the bones were ground down on that side by water that eroded the bank and eventually dumped him out. It probably happened no more than six months before he was discovered, says team member Thomas Stafford, a research geochemist based in Lafayette, Colorado. "It wouldn't have been as much as a year," he says. "The bones would have been more widely dispersed."

4 The deliberate burial makes it especially frustrating for scientists that the Corps in 1998 dumped hundreds of tons of boulders, dirt and sand on the discovery site— officially as part of a project to combat erosion along the Columbia River, although some scientists suspect it was also to avoid further conflict with the local tribes. Kennewick Man's actual burial pit had already been washed away by the time Stafford visited the site in December 1997, but a careful survey might have turned up objects that could have been buried with him. And if his was part of a larger burial plot, there's now no way for archaeologists to locate any contemporaries who might have been buried close by.

Still, the bones have more secrets to reveal. They were never

fossilized, and a careful analysis of their carbon and nitrogen makeup, yet to be performed, should reveal plenty about Kennewick Man's diet. Says Stafford: "We can tell if he ate nothing but plants, predominantly meat or a mixture of the two." The researchers may be able to determine whether he preferred meat or fish. It's even possible that DNA could be extracted and analyzed someday.

While the Corps insisted that most of the bones remain in the museum, it allowed the researchers to send the skull fragments and the right hip, along with its spear point, to a lab in Lincolnshire, Illinois, for ultrahigh-resolution CT scanning. The process produced virtual slices just 0.39 mm (about 0.02") thick—"much more detailed than the ones made of ancient Egypt's King Tut's mummy," says Owsley. The slices were then digitally recombined into 3-D computer images that were used to make exact copies out of plastic. The replica of the skull has already enabled scientists to clear up a popular misconception that dates back to the initial reports of the discovery.

Was Kennewick Man Caucasian? **5**

Thanks to Chatters' mention of Caucasian-like features back in 1996, the myth that Kennewick Man might have been European never quite died out. The reconstructed skull confirms that he was not—and Chatters never seriously thought otherwise. "I tried my hardest to curtail that business about Caucasians in America early," he says. "I'm not talking about today's Caucasians.

Map of multiple human migrations.

I'm saying they had 'Caucasoid-like' characteristics. There's a big difference." Says Owsley: "[Kennewick Man] is not North American looking, and he's not tied in to Siberian or Northeast Asian populations (or groups of people). He looks more Polynesian or more like the Ainu [an ethnic group that is now found only in northern Japan but in prehistoric times lived throughout coastal areas of eastern Asia] or southern Asians."

That assessment will be tested more rigorously when researchers compare Kennewick Man's skull with databases of several thousand other skulls, both modern and ancient. But for the time being, at least, the evidence fits in with a revolutionary new picture that over the past decade has utterly transformed anthropologists' long-held theories about the colonization of the Americas.

English Learners

DIFFERENTIATED INSTRUCTION

Beginning Many of the words on this page may be difficult or unfamiliar to students. Have students make a list of words they are unfamiliar with and look them up in a dictionary. Tell students to record the definition next to each word in their list and then suggest that they use this list as a reference for reading the rest of the selection.

Approaching Level

DIFFERENTIATED INSTRUCTION

Creating an Organizer Students are given a great deal of information in this article. For the section "Was Kennewick Man Caucasian?" have students create a graphic organizer that organizes the information.

TIME

Teach

| Big Idea | 4 |

Cultures in Conflict
Remind students that the conflict between the Corps and local tribes made the retrieval of the Kennewick Man difficult. **Ask:** Based on the information in this paragraph, how can cultural conflicts affect society? *(Cultural conflicts can affect the advancement of scientific knowledge.)*

| Text Element | 5 |

Subheads **Ask:** Why do you think the authors divided their article with subheads? *(Students may suggest that the subheads break up the information and make it easier to locate.)* Do you think the subheads effectively help the authors achieve their purpose? *(Students may suggest that the subheads help the authors achieve their purpose of informing.)*

Cultural History ☆

Mummies A mummy is a dead body that is preserved by embalming. In Egypt, mummification was related to religious beliefs. Egyptians felt that preserving the body would keep the fate of a person's soul safe. Mummification was at first reserved for kings; however, it was later used for the king's attendants and sacred animals.

Learning Objectives
Determining main ideas and supporting details. (SE)
Analyzing author's purpose. (TE)

1175

Teach

Reading Strategy | 1

Main Idea and Supporting Details **Ask:** What is the main idea of this paragraph? *(The theory of the first Americans told in textbooks is wrong.)* What are two details that support this main idea? *(Sites found in North and South America predated the Clovis culture. Studies of skulls revealed that people in South America had different ancestors from people in North America.)*

APPROACHING Suggest that approaching–level students show the main idea and supporting details in a web. For example, they could record the main idea in the center circle and the supporting details in the outer circles. A visual representation of the paragraph may help them better grasp the concept of main idea and supporting details.

Cultural History ☆

Clovis Culture The Clovis are a group of Paleo-Indians. Artifacts, such as chipped flint points, reveal that the Clovis hunted and killed big game; for example, some of their flint points were found with the remains of mammoths.

Informational Text

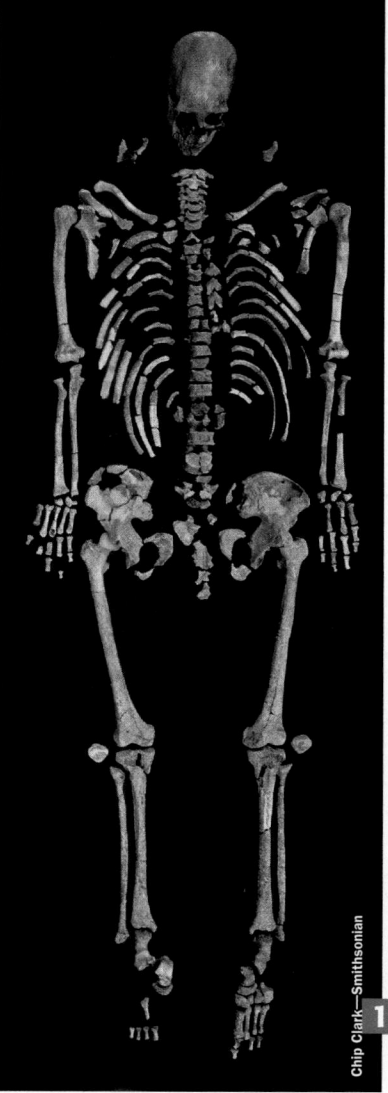

Chip Clark—Smithsonian

Skeleton of Kennewick Man

Who Really Discovered America? ☆

The conventional answer to that question dates to the early 1930s, when stone projectile points—typically used as dart or arrow points—that were nearly identical began to turn up at sites across the American Southwest. They suggested a single cultural tradition that was christened Clovis, after an 11,000-year-old-plus site near Clovis, New Mexico. And because no older sites were known to exist in the Americas, scientists assumed that the Clovis people were the first to arrive. They came, according to the theory, no more than 12,000 years B.P. (before the present), walking across the dry land that connected modern Russia and Alaska at the end of the last ice age, when sea level was hundreds of feet lower than it is today. From there, the earliest immigrants would have made their way south through an ice-free corridor that geologists know cut through what are now the Yukon and Mackenzie river valleys. They then traveled along the eastern flank of the Canadian Rockies to the continental United States and on to Latin America.

That's the story textbooks told for decades—and it's almost certainly wrong. The first cracks in the theory began appearing in the 1980s, when archaeologists discovered sites in both North and South America that seemed to predate the Clovis culture. Then came genetic and linguistic analyses suggesting that Asian and Native American populations diverged not 12,000 years ago but closer to 30,000 years ago. Studies of ancient skulls hinted that the earliest Americans in South America had different ancestors from those in the North. Finally, it began to be clear that artifacts from Northeast Asia dating from just before the Clovis period and South American artifacts of comparable age didn't have much in common with Clovis artifacts.

Those discoveries led to all sorts of competing theories, but few archaeologists or anthropologists took them seriously until 1997. In that year, a prestigious panel of researchers took a hard look at evidence presented by Tom Dillehay, then at the University of Kentucky, from a site he had been excavating in Monte Verde, Chile. After years of skepticism, the panel finally affirmed his claim that the site proved humans had lived there 12,500 years ago. "Monte Verde was the turning point," says David Meltzer, a professor of prehistory at Southern Methodist University in Dallas who was on the panel. "It broke the Clovis barrier."

Why? Because if people were living in southern Chile 12,500 years ago, they must have crossed over from Asia considerably earlier, and that means they couldn't have used the ice-free inland corridor; it didn't yet exist. "You could walk to Fairbanks," says Meltzer. "It was getting south from Fairbanks that was a problem." Instead, many scientists now believe, the earliest Americans traveled down the Pacific coast—possibly even using boats. The idea has been around for a long time, but few took it seriously before Monte Verde.

Writing Practice

Write a Poem Have students write a poem that is inspired by the information in the article. Suggest that they try a traditional poetic form, such as a sonnet, or write in free verse. Remind students that poems often contain sound devices or figurative language. Review the definitions of alliteration, onomatopoeia, simile, metaphor, and personification with them. Ask that they include at least one poetic element in their poems. After students'

have finished, have volunteers share their poems with the class. Ask them to share the inspiration for their poems.

Multiple Migrations

Even if the earliest Americans traveled down the coast, that doesn't mean they couldn't have come through the interior as well. Could there have been many waves of migration along a variety of different routes? One way scientists have tried to get a handle on that question is through genetics. Their studies have focused on two different types of evidence extracted from the cells of modern Native Americans: mitochondrial DNA, which resides outside the nuclei of cells and is passed down only through the mother; and the Y chromosome, which is passed down only from father to son. Since DNA changes subtly over the generations, it serves as a sort of molecular clock,

and by measuring differences between populations, you can gauge when they were part of the same group.

Or at least you can try. Those molecular clocks are still rather crude. "The mitochondrial DNA signals a migration up to 30,000 years ago," says research geneticist Michael Hammer of the University of Arizona. "But the Y suggests that it occurred within the last 20,000 years." That's quite a discrepancy. Nevertheless, Hammer believes that the evidence is consistent with a single, or primary pulse of migration.

Theodore Schurr, director of the University of Pennsylvania's Laboratory of Molecular Anthropology, thinks there could have been many migrations. "It

looks like there may have been one primary migration, but certain genetic markers are more prevalent in North America than in South America," Schurr explains, suggesting secondary waves. At this point, there's no definitive proof of either idea, but the evidence and logic lean toward multiple migrations. "If one migration made it over," Dillehay, now at Vanderbilt University, asks rhetorically, "why not more?"

—With reporting by Dan Cray/Los Angeles
From TIME, Updated 2007

Assess

1. Summaries should reflect the main ideas of the article.
2. (a) They are more than 9,000 years old. (b) He was about 5 feet 9 inches tall, he was right-handed, and he had suffered several injuries in his lifetime.
3. (a) The Corps did not allow the researchers to remove the remains from the museum where they had been placed and gave the researchers only ten days to complete their work. (b) Local Native American groups originally demanded that the skeleton be reburied without scientific study.
4. (a) They found that Kennewick Man had been buried deliberately. (b) They examined deposits of calcium carbonate to determine that he had been placed deliberately on his back, and they found that no animal scavengers had attacked the body. They also used the fact that the bones of his left side were worn down by water to determine that he had been buried parallel to the Columbia River.

Respond and Think Critically

Respond and Interpret

1. Write a brief summary of the main ideas in this article before you answer the following questions. For help on writing a summary, see page 1147.
2. (a)How old are the remains of the Kennewick Man? (b)What are some physical characteristics of Kennewick Man?
3. (a)What restrictions did the U.S. Army Corps of Engineers place on scientific study of Kennewick Man's remains? (b)What did local Native American groups originally demand?

Analyze and Evaluate

4. (a)What "remarkable discovery" did the researchers make about Kennewick Man's burial? (b)What evidence led them to this discovery?

5. (a)Until the 1980s, what was the accepted theory about the origin of the first Americans? (b)How did archaeological evidence from Monte Verde, Chile, prove this theory wrong?
6. (a)Why might local Native American groups have considered scientific study of Kennewick Man's remains as a kind of "desecration"? (b)In your opinion, was it appropriate for scientists to study the remains? Explain.

Connect

7. How does the conflict between scientists and Native American groups described in this article relate to the conflicts you have read about in Unit 6, Part 1?

5. (a) The accepted theory was that people came to the Americas no more than 12,000 years ago by way of a land bridge between Russia and Alaska, later traveling south via an inland corridor. (b) The evidence proved that humans had lived in Monte Verde 12,500 years ago. They could not have used an inland corridor to travel south from Alaska because such a corridor did not exist at that time.

6. (a) Possible answer: Local Native American groups may have held beliefs about the sanctity of human remains that conflicted with the procedures the scientists wanted to perform. (b) Some students may say that the information the scientists uncovered justified their procedures. Others may say that the end does not justify the means.

7. Some students may say that both the scientists' analysis of the remains of Kennewick Man and the Corps' decision to lock the remains in a museum violated the sanctity of Native American burial rites. Students may say that these actions show the same spirit of disrespect that was displayed by the early European explorers, who disparaged or disregarded native traditions.

1178

Bellringer Options

Daily Language Practice Transparency 113

Or ask: What comes to mind when you think of South America, Central America, and the Caribbean in modern times? *(Students may list places such as Mexico and Jamaica, and things such as Mexican food, llamas, and rainforests.)*

Or ask: What do you know about any connections between the histories of South and Central America and the Caribbean islands? *(Students may say they know that many South and Central American countries and Caribbean islands were colonies of European nations in the past.)*

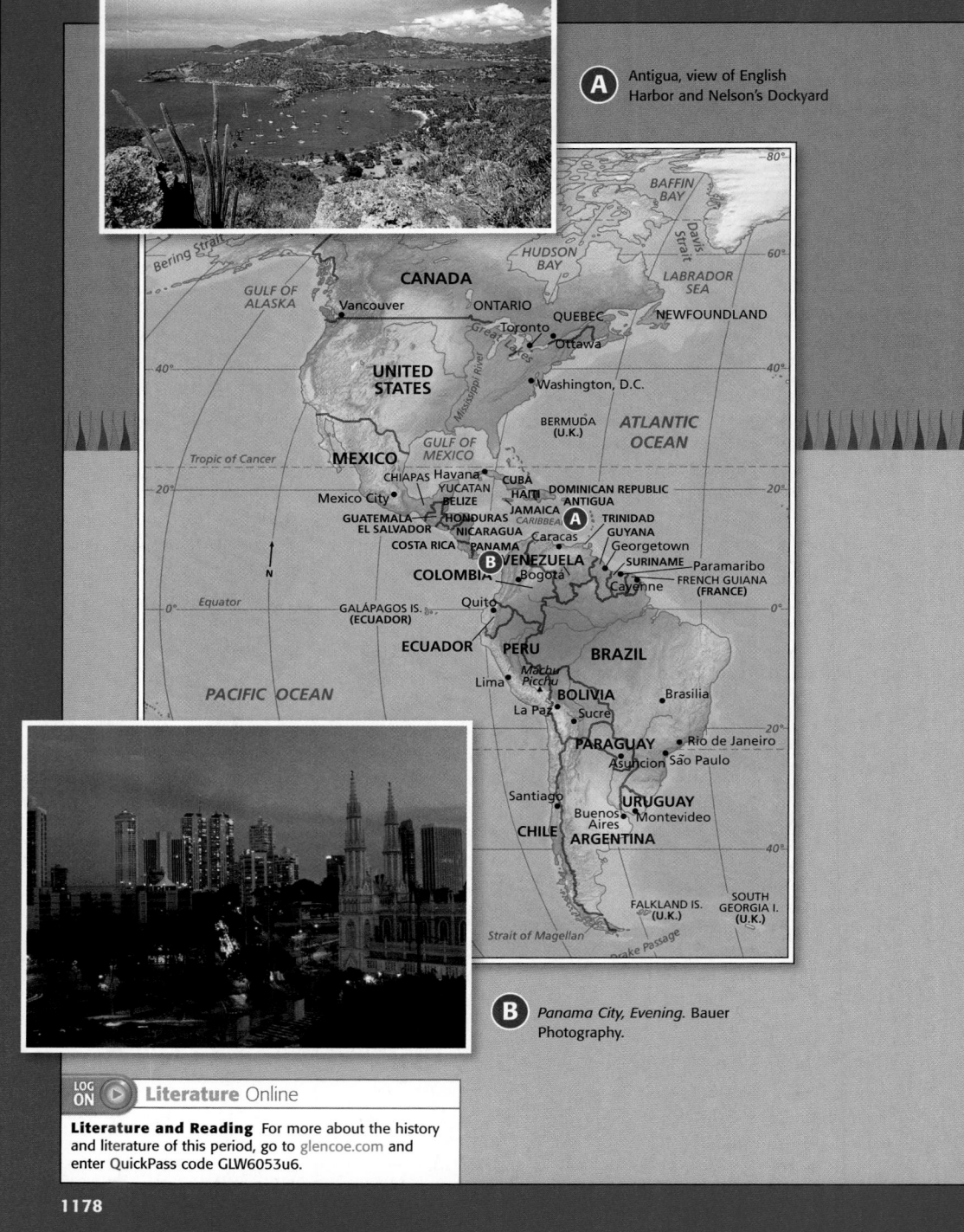

A Antigua, view of English Harbor and Nelson's Dockyard

B *Panama City, Evening.* Bauer Photography.

LOG ON ▶ **Literature** Online

Literature and Reading For more about the history and literature of this period, go to glencoe.com and enter QuickPass code GLW6053u6.

1178

Part Introduction Skills

Reading Skills
- Analyze Graphic Information (SE p. 1181)
- Analyze Cause and Effect Relationships (SE p. 1186; TE p. 1183)
- Compare and Contrast (SE p. 1187)
- Apply Background Knowledge (SE p. 1188)

Part 2 Introduction

Speaking/Listening/Viewing Skills
- Persuasive Broadcast (SE p. 1189)

Writing Skills/Grammar
- Comparison Essay (SE p. 1189)

Vocabulary
- Understand Denotation and Connotation (TE p. 1182)

THE MODERN AMERICAS

1800–PRESENT

Storyteller. Helen Cordero (b.1915). Ceramic. Fred Jones Jr. Museum of Art, University of Oklahoma.

Being There

The Americas have undergone great changes over the past two centuries. Between 1776 and 1867, most countries in the Americas won their independence from England, Spain, and Portugal. In their short histories, many of these countries have faced severe problems, including civil wars, dictatorships, poverty, and overpopulation. In recent times, people in the Americas have been increasingly concerned about the environment, as the tropical rain forests are destroyed and natural disasters have ravaged many communities.

Looking Ahead

Authors in the Americas have responded to these sweeping changes by creating styles, such as magic realism, that fuse traditional and contemporary elements. Some authors of the region have drawn on local geography and folklore to explore the continuity of the past and present, while others have explored the contradictions of life in postcolonial society.

Keep the following questions in mind as you read:

- How did colonialism shape the modern Americas?
- What is the relationship between dreams and reality?
- How do geography and nature influence a community?

1179

UNIT SIX

PART 2

Focus

Summary

This introduction gives an overview of the history, culture, art, and literature of Modern America, including South and Central America and the Caribbean islands, from 1800 to the present. It describes the politics of colonialism and subsequent revolutions, military coups, and human rights violations as well as improvements that globalization has brought to the area. The art, music, and dance of the area and their influences are also described.

> For additional support for English Learners, see Unit 6 Teaching Resources Book p. 108.

Approaching Level

DIFFERENTIATED INSTRUCTION

Preview Approaching Level students may benefit from previewing and reviewing text before being introduced to the Big Ideas. First, have students preview the rest of the introduction by looking at page headings, subheads, illustrations and photographs. **Ask:** What earlier sections in the introduction connect to the title of each Big Idea? *(Students should connect The Legacy of Colonialism to "Politics in* the Americas"; they may connect "Magic Realism" and "Nature and the Imagination" to "Mexican Muralists" and "Music of the Americas.")*

Teach

Reading Strategy | 1

Using the Timeline Have students examine the timeline and relate any key events in modern American literature to the history of the Americas and the world. Explain that this part of the unit covers two centuries defined by revolution and the movement of people. **Ask:** What can you assume from the closeness in time of the dates of independence of Mexico, Central America, Peru, and Brazil? *(Students can assume that one area inspired another to declare independence.)*

Political History ☆

Benito Juárez Known for being impeccably honest, Benito Juárez dedicated his life to politics. A liberal in a conservative country run by landowning elites and the clergy, he was exiled for his ideas and briefly sought refuge in the United States before returning to Mexico with the goal of creating equality for the Mexican people. His reforms included the abolition of courts for the rich and powerful and the nationalizing of most church property to effectively separate religion from government.

1180

TIMELINE 1800–PRESENT

MODERN AMERICAN LITERATURE

1800

1830
Emily Dickinson is born in Amherst, Massachusetts

1839
Joaquim Maria Machado de Assis is born in Rio de Janeiro, Brazil

1850

1855
Walt Whitman publishes *Leaves of Grass*

1888 ▶
Rubén Darío publishes *Azul*, initiating the Modernismo movement

AMERICAN EVENTS

1800

1804
Haiti becomes first independent nation in the West Indies ▼

▲
1821 **1**
Mexico and Central America win independence from Spain; Peru proclaims independence from Spain

1822
Brazil declares independence from Portugal

1836
Texas declares independence from Mexico

1850

1861 ☆
Benito Juarez becomes President of Mexico

1865
American Civil War ends

1867
British establish the Dominion of Canada

1876
Porfirio Díaz takes power in Mexico

1888
Brazil abolishes slavery

WORLD EVENTS

1800

1821
Electric motor is developed in Great Britain

1837 ▶
Queen Victoria is crowned Queen of Great Britain

1845–1849
Potato famine strikes Ireland

1861
Italians establish a united kingdom

1877
Samurai revolt against abolition of feudalism in Japan

LOG ON ▶ **Literature** Online

Literature and Reading To explore the Interactive Timeline, go to glencoe.com and enter QuickPass code GLW6053u6.

1180 UNIT 6 THE MODERN AMERICAS

Reading Practice

Timeline Explain to students that a timeline is a chart that shows a sequence of events. These pages show three timelines that illustrate how events in three categories have overlapped. Invite students to point out relationships between events from one timeline to the next. **Ask:** How many years passed between Mexico's winning independence and the Mexican Revolution? *(89 years)*

Encourage students to note that the "Americas" portion of the time line is devoted primarily to nations declaring their independence from European nations or from each other. Have students discuss how this may have affected living conditions during that time. Ask students to compare the Americas of the 1800s with recent history in the former Soviet Union and the nations of Eastern Europe.

1900 2

1900
José Enrique Rodó publishes *Ariel*

1924
Pablo Neruda publishes *Twenty Love Poems and a Song of Despair*

▲
1945
Gabriela Mistral becomes first Latin American to win the Nobel Prize in Literature

1950

1963
Martin Luther King Jr. writes his letter from Birmingham jail

1968
Alice Munro wins Canada's prestigious Governor General's Literary Award for fiction for the first time

2001
Trinidadian author Sir V. S. Naipaul wins the Nobel Prize in Literature

2003
Isabel Allende publishes *My Invented Country*
▼

1900

1910
Mexican Revolution begins

1912
European immigrants to Argentina surpass 300,000

1921 ☆
Diego Rivera begins work on his first mural in Mexico

1950

1959
Fidel Castro establishes communist government in Cuba

1969
Canada passes Official Languages Act

1970s
Major oil deposits are discovered in Gulf of Mexico

2005
Hurricane Katrina causes devastation in the United States' Gulf Coast

1900

1904
Russia completes the first Trans-Siberian Railroad

1914–1918
World War I

1931
Japan invades China

1936
First regular television broadcasts begin in Great Britain

1948
State of Israel is formed
▼

▲
1961
Yuri Gagarin, a Russian, becomes the first human to orbit Earth

1975
Vietnam War ends

1991
Soviet Union collapses

Reading Check
Analyze Graphic Information How long after Fidel Castro took power in Cuba did the Soviet Union collapse?

INTRODUCTION **1181**

Teach

Reading Check

Answer: *Thirty-two years separated the two events.*

Reading Strategy 2

Using the Timeline **Ask:** In the timeline, how many Modern American writers who won Nobel Prizes for Literature are included in the 1900s? *(two)*

Cultural History ☆

Diego Rivera Trained in Mexico City and Europe and inspired by the Mexican Revolution, Diego Rivera painted frescoes depicting the people, culture, and natural landscapes of Mexico. One of his most controversial pieces was a mural intended for Rockefeller Center in New York City in 1933. Rivera brought his leftist politics to the piece by including an image of Vladimir Lenin—the Communist leader of the Russian Revolution—in the mural. When he refused to remove Lenin's face, the painting was destroyed.

English Learners

DIFFERENTIATED INSTRUCTION 🐟

Advanced Invite students to create a timeline of their own, setting world and national events on one line and significant events from their own lives on another. If the students are recent arrivals to the United States, encourage them to use events from their native countries in their timelines and to note the year they left their country to come to the United States.

Advanced Learners/Pre-AP

DIFFERENTIATED INSTRUCTION 🐟

Research Invite students to find out more about the events in the timeline. Challenge students to find connections between events and literature. **Ask:** Does literature influence people to change their societies or political structures? Or, does a change in society or political power influence a change in the literature of a country? Encourage students to share their responses with the class.

Learning Objectives
Analyzing graphic information. (SE)
Using a timeline. (TE)

Teach

Draw Conclusions Ask:
What conclusion can you draw about the influence of the U.S. independence on the other countries of North and South America? *(Students may say that based on the events in Canada, Latin America, and Mexico, the United States' independence may have influenced revolutions in bordering countries.)*

Learning Objectives

For pages 1178–1189
In studying this text, you will focus on the following objectives:

Literary Study: Analyzing literary periods.

Reading: Evaluating historical influences.
Connecting to the literature.

THE MODERN AMERICAS
1800–PRESENT

Historical, Social, and Cultural Forces

Diversity in the Americas

Modern societies in the Americas reflect a diversity of cultural traditions and ethnic heritages. This multiculturalism stems from the traditions of the native people who first inhabited the Americas as well as from colonialism, slavery, and immigration.

Politics in the Americas 1

As the nineteenth century began, the United States was adjusting to its newfound indepen-

dence, while Canada and many Latin American countries remained under colonial rule. As the century continued, most of these countries gained their independence; however, power in many Latin American countries remained concentrated among elite landowners. In 1867, the British North American Act established Canada as a Dominion of Britain, though it was run primarily as an independent state. (The British Parliament's authority was transferred to the Canadian Parliament in 1982.) In Mexico, guerrilla armies waged war against the dictatorship of Porfirio Díaz in 1910 and 1920, finally establishing a constitutional republic. The new Mexican constitution became a model for many other countries in the region.

In 1959, Fidel Castro overthrew Cuba's dictator and installed a communist government. The United States took many steps to prevent similar uprisings in other Latin American countries, including giving support to military dictatorships throughout the region in the 1980s. The end of the twentieth century saw a return to democracy in some Latin American countries.

Effective vote - No Re-election (Sufragio effectivo - no reeleccion), detail with marching peasants. Juan O'Gorman. Mural. Museo Nacional de Historia, Castillo de Chapultepec, Mexico City, D.F.

Vocabulary Practice

Denotation and Connotation Draw students' attention to the use of the word *elite* when describing landowners. Have students look up the denotations, or definitions, of the word. *(The elite are the best in a class or the group that holds power in a society.)* Explain to students that the connotation is the emotional feeling a word evokes; connotation is often described as positive, negative, or neutral.

Ask: Does the word *elite* have a positive, negative, or neutral connotation in its context in the text? Explain. *(Students may say the word has a negative connotation because it is used to describe the landowners who held the power, suggesting inequality among the population.)* Write the following sentence on the board: These breakthroughs in heart surgery are the result of research at elite hospitals.

Ask: What connotation does the word *elite* have here? Explain. *(Students are likely to say that elite has a positive connotation here as it is describing specialists who are working hard to cure disease and help people.)* Encourage students to consider the connotation of specific words in their reading.

Checking Voting Rolls Alongside Hindu Deities

Human Rights ☆

Human rights in the Americas have improved greatly since the beginning of the nineteenth century. At that time, slavery was still legal in the United States, and indigenous groups on both continents endured removal from their ancestral lands and the loss of their cultural identities. The human rights abuses against these groups continued well into the twentieth century, fueling the civil rights movement in the United States and a number of movements by indigenous peoples in other countries in the Americas.

In the twentieth century, Latin Americans also fought for freedom from abuse under military regimes, and similar human rights struggles continue today. Many people from Mexico and Central America have sought better opportunities in the United States. In 1962, Cesar Chavez, a former farmworker and the son of Mexican immigrants, founded the National Farm Workers Association to advocate for the rights of migrant workers. It became the first successful union of its kind in the country. As Hispanic immigration to the United States increases, Americans continue to confront related issues, such as questions about ethnic diversity and bilingual education in schools.

> "We are Europeans yet we are not Europeans. What are we then? It is difficult to define what we are, but our works speak for us."
>
> —Mexican author Octavio Paz, in his Nobel lecture

Globalization 2

Recent political and economic changes in the Americas reflect the increasingly interconnected global landscape of the twenty-first century. In 1994, Mexico joined Canada and the United States in the North American Free Trade Agreement (NAFTA), which removed trade barriers between countries in the region. Improvements in road transportation, literacy, and technology continue to decrease the isolation of rural Latin Americans. In an increasingly global culture, the people of the Americas continue to reinvent themselves while remaining connected to their diverse backgrounds and regional traditions.

UNIT SIX
PART 2

Teach

Reading Strategy   2

Analyze Cause and Effect Have students consider the changes in Latin America described in the text. Encourage students to consider what these changes will cause down the road. **Ask:** What is an expected effect of increased literacy in rural Latin America? *(Students may say that increased literacy in Latin America will result in less isolation in rural areas and will likely result in more literature and writers from these areas.)*

Political History ☆

Indigenous Peoples Over the centuries, many of the indigenous peoples of South America were wiped out due to war, disease, and the destruction of their environment. The late 1900s saw a surge of activity directed at preserving the rights and cultures of the indigenous peoples who remained. The first official international attention to the issue was the Declaration of Barbados, which called for the recognition and protection of indigenous peoples in 1971.

English Learners

DIFFERENTIATED INSTRUCTION

Beginning English learners may relate to the description on this page about the movement of people into the United States. Ask for volunteers to share their stories and explain why their families have come to the United States. Explain that in the past, people in other countries thought of the United States as a country where the "streets were paved with gold." Ask students to describe the perception of the United States in their native countries.

Advanced Learners/Pre-AP

DIFFERENTIATED INSTRUCTION

Human Rights Violations Invite students to research a current example of human rights violations in the Americas. Encourage students to connect the violations to the political, religious, or social institution that is its source and to describe the groups that are working on solving the problem. Invite students to share their research with the class.

Learning Objectives
Drawing conclusions about historic events. (TE)
Using denotation and connotation. (TE)
Analyzing cause and effect. (TE)

1183

Reading Strategy 1

Draw Conclusions **Ask:**
What conclusion can you draw about Mexican culture and art from the location of Mayan and early twentieth century murals? *(Students may say that because the murals are on the walls of public buildings, this culture considers art a public pursuit for public consumption and enjoyment.)*

APPROACHING Explain to approaching-level students that a conclusion is a statement supported by details from a text. Turn the question around and **ask:** What supports the conclusion that Mayan and Mexican art are public pursuits? *(The ancient Maya and early twentieth century Mexican artists painted murals on public walls.)*

Mexican Muralists 1

Murals have been an important form of Mexican art since the wall paintings of the ancient Maya. In the early 1900s, Mexican artists sought to synthesize the events of Mexico's present with indigenous styles of expression. Artists such as Diego Rivera, David Siqueiros, and José Orozco created murals depicting the Mexican Revolution on the walls of public buildings. These expressive paintings of workers, soldiers, peasants, and revolutionary leaders such as Emiliano Zapata captured the excitement and fervor of the time. An equally important artist of this era was Frida Kahlo, who married Rivera. In her vivid self-portraits, Kahlo used symbolic images to depict her physical and mental struggles.

> "I never painted dreams. I painted my own reality."
>
> —Frida Kahlo

Self Portrait with Velvet Dress, 1926. Frida Kahlo. Oil on canvas. Private collection.

Music of the Americas

Tango dancers in Plaza Dorrego, San Telmo.

The Americas have produced some of the most famous musical styles in the world, including blues, jazz, salsa, rock and roll, and reggae. The influence of African musical traditions in North America has been especially notable, beginning with the slave songs of the nineteenth century. The call-and-response pattern common in many blues songs can be traced to African musical roots. Jazz, which developed at the beginning of the twentieth century, combines improvisation with African rhythms and European harmonies. Reggae—Jamaica's best known cultural export—originated there in the late 1960s, not long after Jamaica gained independence from Britain. Reggae musicians combine heavy rhythmic music with lyrics that decry oppression and social injustice.

Indian, European, and African influences in Latin America gave rise to the Brazilian samba, the Cuban salsa, and other dance music that has become popular throughout the world. One of the most influential of these dances is the tango. This expressive dance developed in the poor areas of Buenos Aires, Argentina, in the late 1800s. Later, Cuban dances such as the mambo and the rhumba became popular. In recent years, salsa dancing has marked the resurgence of a characteristically Latin style.

1184 UNIT 6 THE MODERN AMERICAS

Reading Practice

Determine Supporting Details
Explain to students that a main idea of a paragraph is often, but not always, found in its topic sentence. Have students reread the section Music of the Americas. **Ask:** What is the main idea of this section? *(Students may say that music in the Americas was influenced by music from other continents, most notably Africa.)*

Have students list the details that support this main idea. *(Students should list the African influence on blues, jazz, and reggae and the various influences on dance music in Latin America.)* Explain that sometimes the supporting details in a paragraph or passage may also contain smaller details. Point out the author's descriptions of the unique characteristics

of blues, jazz, and reggae. These descriptions of specific kinds of music provide additional support for the author's main idea. Remind students that when they are confused by a passage, they can work backwards and identify details in order to determine the main idea.

Carnival

On the West Indian island of Trinidad and in Rio de Janeiro, Brazil, internationally famous events called Carnival mark the beginning of Lent—the 40-day period of fasting and reflection before Easter that some Christians observe. In these two places, more than a million people join in the street festivities—singing, dancing, parading in fantastic costumes, and engaging in masquerade and band competitions. The origins of Carnival are obscure, but the celebration probably originated in pre-Christian nature festivals and was brought from Europe to the Americas by Catholics. Many of the musical instruments, rhythms, and dances of Carnival have influenced popular music worldwide. The steel drums and rhythmic calypso of Trinidad and the samba dances of Brazil were first heard and seen on the streets at Carnival.

Colorful costume from Parade of Bands during Carnival- Port of Spain, Trinidad.

PREVIEW **Big Ideas** of The Modern Americas

1 The Legacy of Colonialism	**2** Magic Realism	**3** Nature and the Imagination
Colonialism had both positive and negative consequences for the people of the Americas. Authors have responded to this legacy by exploring the injustices of colonial societies, the relationship between homeland and identity, and the multiculturalism produced by immigration. **See page 1186**	One of the dominant literary styles in modern Latin American literature is magic realism, which features fantastic, supernatural events that occur in narratives with realistic elements. This literature meshes local folklore with Surrealist imagery to explore the relationship between perception and reality. **See page 1187**	Nature remains a vital subject in literature from North and South America, where authors explore connections between the natural world and a range of social issues. Modern Latin and Native American poets create lush nature imagery that reflects the importance of geography and the power of sensory experience. **See page 1188**

INTRODUCTION **1185**

Advanced Learners/Pre-AP
DIFFERENTIATED INSTRUCTION

Carnival Invite students to find out more about Carnival and its cousin in the United States, Mardi Gras. Students can investigate the history of each, the possible influences of each upon the other, and the differences in how each is celebrated. Have students bring illustrations or other visual aids to class that show the differences or similarities.

UNIT SIX
PART 2

Teach

Reading Strategy 2

Question Before the class reads the Carnival section, explain that asking questions before and during reading is part of actively participating in reading. **Ask:** What questions do you have about Carnival's origin and place in Latin American life? *(Possible questions: How did Carnival start in Latin America? Why is it important?)* After students finish reading the section, **ask:** Where can you find more detailed answers to your questions? *(Students may say that they can find answers in other parts of the text, on the Internet, or in an encyclopedia.)*

Cultural History
Combining Religions Haiti provides a good example of the blend of European and native religions that is common throughout the Americas. On July 16 of each year, people from all over Haiti descend on the village of Ville-Bonheur to celebrate the *saut d'eau,* or "waterfall." Here the Virgin Mary is reported to have appeared in the nineteenth century. Pilgrims stand under the waterfall to pray to the Virgin Mary—and to offer prayers to the voodoo (or *vodun*) deities.

Learning Objectives
Drawing conclusions about culture. (TE)
Identifying main idea and details. (TE)
Asking questions about a text. (TE)

1185

Teach

Reading Check

Answer: *The lack of economic development and the concentration of power among wealthy landowners contributed to inequality.*

Reading Strategy   1

Analyze Tone Discuss with students the tragic situations described in this page. **Ask:** How does the author present this information? Is it highly emotional? Explain. *(Students are likely to say that the information is presented evenly; the author is providing information rather than trying to rally people to a cause.)*

Cultural History ☆

Religion in the Americas One distinctive aspect of religious activity in the modern Americas is the general repudiation of the concept of "state religion." Under the colonial governments, people were expected—sometimes obligated—to worship at the official church. Weddings and funerals often had to be presided over by members of the established clergy. The official church often controlled education. Sometimes churches were the best-organized force in a newly independent country, and some leaders maintained their official status for that reason. However, the trend in all countries since independence is toward religious freedom.

Big Idea 1

The Legacy of Colonialism 1

Almost every region in North and South America and the Caribbean has been influenced by European colonialism. In South America and the Caribbean, these years of oppression left wounds that were difficult to heal, even after countries had gained independence.

Colonial Ideology ☆

The Spanish and Portuguese in South America had two goals: to increase the wealth of their home countries and to convert native peoples to Christianity. These settlers claimed huge plots of land for themselves, displacing indigenous peoples who had been there for generations. Native Americans were forced to work on colonial farms, and many died of European diseases.

Inspired by the American Revolution, Latin Americans successfully fought for independence in the early 1800s. But independence did not fundamentally change the colonial structure of Latin American societies. The region continued to export agricultural raw materials and import consumer goods as it had during colonial times, a practice that ensured continued economic dependence on Europe. As a result, power remained concentrated in the hands of elite estate owners. Vast inequality, reinforced by sharp class distinctions, persisted through much of the next century.

Latin American authors have addressed the legacy of colonialism in a variety of ways. In the nineteenth century, some authors reflected on the contrast between the European-based life of the elite and the rural cultures of Native Americans. These works sought to overthrow the racial ideology that supported colonialism in Latin America. Twentieth-century authors such as Rosario Castellanos (see pages 1199–1208) wrote about the class prejudices that remain embedded in society.

> "The colonial experience of my generation was almost wholly without violence . . . It was a terror of the mind."
>
> —George Lamming, West Indian novelist

Identity and Homeland

Many contemporary Latin American and Caribbean authors continue to explore the effects of colonialism on their homelands, often addressing issues such as discrimination, identity, and exile. Some, like Antiguan author Jamaica Kincaid (see pages 1277–1286), portray both the nurturing and restricting power of homeland. In her novel *Annie John*, Kincaid's protagonist struggles with ambivalent feelings as she leaves Antigua to pursue her dream in England.

Coffee, 1935. Candido Portinari. Oil on canvas.
Museu Nacional Belas Artes, Rio de Janeiro, Brazil.

Reading Check

Analyze Cause-and-Effect Relationships What factors contributed to continuing social inequality in Latin America following independence?

Speaking and Listening Practice

Present an Oral Interpretation Many prominent Latin American writers have protested the authoritarian regimes that have ruled their respective countries. Have students locate English translations of the work of one or more of these writers. These works should focus on the writers' protest against undemocratic governments. Students can assemble several works (or excerpts from them) and present an oral interpretation of the works, accompanied by commentary on each writer and the social/political conditions that gave rise to the protest.

Big Idea 2
Magic Realism

2 In the mid-twentieth century, Latin American authors developed a unique form of expression called magic realism. Many Latin American authors believe this style best expresses the unique history and hopes of the Latin American people.

> "The fantastic is something that one must never say goodbye to lightly."
>
> —Julio Cortázar

From Folklore to Surrealism

Works of magic realism include strong, realistic narratives that incorporate elements of local folklore and myth. Through this combination of styles, magic realist authors seek to mesh avant-garde literary trends, such as Surrealism, with their unique regional identities. In addition to exploring the world of dreams and fantasy, these authors also address social and political ills. In addition to fantastic elements, these works often include humor and exaggeration and present distorted views of time and identity.

The method of storytelling in works of magic realism focuses on the flexibility of reality when viewed from different perspectives. The most famous example of the genre is Gabriel García Márquez's (see pages 1243–1251) 1967 novel *One Hundred Years of Solitude*. The novel is set in the fictional town of Macondo, where local events slip back and forth between reality and fantasy. For example, villagers are unsurprised when a local priest rises into the air and floats. However, when these same villagers are introduced to magnets, telescopes, and magnifying glasses, they are dumbfounded by what they see as magic. Narratives such as this suggest that reality is subjective rather than objective.

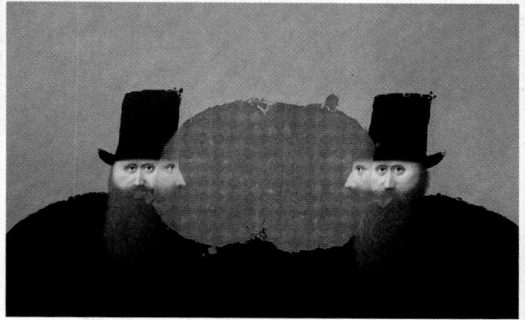

El secreto compartido, 1999. Alfredo Castañeda (b. 1938). Oil on canvas, 80 x 110 cm. Private collection.

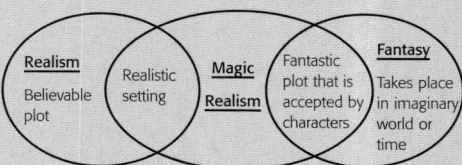

| **Realism** | | **Magic** | | **Fantasy** |
| Believable plot | Realistic setting | **Realism** | Fantastic plot that is accepted by characters | Takes place in imaginary world or time |

The Latin American Boom

Argentine author Jorge Luis Borges and Cuban author Alejo Carpentier developed the magic realist style in the 1940s. In the decades that followed, a so-called boom of Latin American fiction brought international fame to authors such as Márquez, Julio Cortázar (see pages 1230–1241), Carlos Fuentes, and Mario Vargas Llosa. In the 1980s and 1990s, many female magic realist voices emerged, including the Chilean novelist Isabel Allende (see pages 1261–1263). Though many consider the style to be unique to Latin America, it has influenced literature around the world. Such diverse authors as American novelist Toni Morrison, German novelist Günter Grass, and Indian author Salman Rushdie have produced works containing elements of magic realism.

Reading Check

Compare and Contrast How are fantasy and magic realism alike, and how do they differ?

INTRODUCTION **1187**

UNIT SIX
PART 2

Teach
Reading Check

Answer: *Both contain magical and fantastic elements accepted by characters; however, magic realism stories usually take place in believable settings, while fantasy stories usually take place in imaginary worlds or different times.*

Reading Strategy **2**

Distinguish Fact from Opinion Ask: What opinion do some Latin American authors have of magic realism? *(They believe that magic realism best expresses the Latin American people's hopes and history.)* **Ask:** Which word indicates that this statement is an opinion? *(the word* believe*)* **Ask:** Which facts about magic realism does the author present? *(This style combines realistic and fantastic elements; it was developed in the mid-twentieth century.)*

English Learners

DIFFERENTIATED INSTRUCTION

Intermediate English learners may be exposed to unfamiliar terms and concepts in this unit introduction. Have students start a log of terms, listing magic realism, folklore, avant-garde, Surrealism, and supernatural among others. Then have students use a dictionary or other resource to look up definitions of these terms. Finding examples of Surrealist art may also assist in students' comprehension.

Advanced Learners/Pre-AP

DIFFERENTIATED INSTRUCTION

Connect Literature to Art Have students research surrealistic and other art of the early- to mid-twentieth century in the Americas that deals with the fantastic and supernatural. Invite students to present examples of the art in class and describe the artists' backgrounds as well as their inspiration or the school of art that spawned their creative outlook.

Learning Objectives
Analyzing cause and effect relationships. (SE)
Comparing and contrasting. (SE)
Presenting an oral interpretation. (TE)
Distinguishing fact and opinion. (TE)

1187

Reading Check

Possible Answer: *Many Latin Americans are descended from these peoples, and these poets probably view them as an important part of their history.*

Personification Review with students the definition of personification. **Ask:** What is personified in this quote, and how does it reflect the Big Idea? *(The Earth is personified—it keeps on "talking." This quote connects to the importance of nature in the Big Idea by describing nature as stronger and longer-lasting than humans.)*

Cultural History ☆

Machu Picchu Likely a retreat for Inca royalty, Machu Picchu was occupied during the fifteenth and sixteenth centuries, but the reason for its abandonment is still a mystery. It was "discovered" in 1911 by a Yale professor and in 1983 became a UNESCO World Heritage site.

Big Idea 3
Nature and the Imagination

For centuries, people have been captivated by the rugged beauty of the Americas. Modern literature of the region often explores the beauty and power of nature and the tensions between nature and civilization.

Geography and Myth

Many contemporary Latin American poets explore the link between physical landscape and cultural identity. Octavio Paz (see pages 1220–1223) and Pablo Neruda (see pages 1210–1214), the foremost poets of the Latin American *vanguardia*, or avant-garde, movement sought to illuminate the past by exploring local geography. In poems such as "Hymn Among Ruins," Paz meditates on the passage of time by describing ancient architectural relics. His works draw from European traditions such as Surrealism and Romanticism as well as local folk traditions. ☆

Neruda also found inspiration in the geography of his homeland. In "Heights of Machu Picchu," one of his most famous works, he evokes the glory of the ancient Incas in describing a majestic ruin. In his later poems, Neruda shifted his focus toward the simple and the commonplace. These poems seek to illuminate the richness beneath everyday items, such as an artichoke or a piece of wood.

Nature as Metaphor

The works of contemporary North American authors, such as the Native American poet Joy Harjo (see pages 1287–1291), often reflect an appreciation and understanding of nature. In many North American works, nature and natural elements serve as metaphors for events or problems. American and Canadian essayists, poets, and novelists have often explored the influence of regional landscapes on local communities. These authors—including Henry David Thoreau, Willa Cather, Eudora Welty, and Jack London—are connected in the national

Turtle Sounds, 1986. David Dawangyumptewa. Watercolor, 23 x 30 in. Coconino Center for the Arts, Flagstaff, AZ.

> And we go on, keep giving birth
>   and watch
> ourselves die, over and over.
> And the ground spinning beneath us
> goes on talking.
>
> —Joy Harjo, from "For Alva Benson, and
> For Those Who Have Learned to Speak"

consciousness with the regional landscapes they depicted. In her richly detailed short stories, Canadian author Alice Munro (see pages 1264–1275) evokes the physical surroundings of her small-town Ontario characters as she explores the cultural values that both define and limit them.

Reading Check

Apply Background Knowledge Why might the ruins of the ancient Maya and Inca be so meaningful to Latin American poets?

Literary Element Practice

Metaphor Explain to students that in poetry and prose, a metaphor is the comparison of two unlike things, often by using the word *is*; one thing is said to be something else. An extended metaphor compares two unlike things throughout a poem's stanza or a paragraph of prose, or even an entire text. Discuss with students images of nature in media.

Ask: What in nature, including animals and images of the landscape, can be used to represent the human experience? *(Students may list beauty, youth, violence, or a human's isolation in the world.)* **Ask:** Why might nature be used as a metaphor for events or problems? *(Students may say that nature encompasses the good and evil of life, giving writers unlimited material.)*

Supply a variety of poetry or prose that contains metaphors. Have students identify the metaphors and identify the two unlike things being compared. Then encourage students to try their hand at writing a metaphor using nature.

WRAP-UP

Legacy of the Period

The cultural heritage of the Americas is very diverse, drawn from its indigenous peoples and the colonists, slaves, and immigrants who settled there. In the United States, literary movements such as Transcendentalism reflected European influences while expressing a distinctly American perspective. In Canada, the writings of immigrants such as Michael Ondaatje, from Sri Lanka, and Rohinton Mistry, from India, show the influence of their South Asian heritage.

Latin American authors have won five Nobel Prizes since 1945. Poets such as Pablo Neruda and novelists such as Isabel Allende have inspired readers throughout the world through their intriguing imagery and their use of magic realism.

Among Native Americans, the oral storytelling tradition remains vital in contemporary life. Leslie Marmon Silko has preserved the stories and cadences of Native American oral traditions. Silko, N. Scott Momaday, and Louise Erdrich have also explored the effects of white culture on Native American identity.

Four Mexican Musicians, Mexico.

Cultural Links

 Magic realism has influenced authors such as Salman Rushdie and Nobel Prize winners Toni Morrison and Günter Grass.

Gabriel García Márquez and other Latin American novelists were inspired by American authors, including William Faulkner and Ernest Hemingway.

Music from the Americas such as blues, jazz, hip-hop, and rock and roll has influenced musicians throughout the world, including The Rolling Stones and Led Zeppelin.

 **Literature** Online

Unit Resources For additional skills practice, go to glencoe.com and enter QuickPass code GLW6053u6.

Activities

Use what you have learned about the period to do one of these activities.

1. Follow Up Go back to the Looking Ahead on page 1179 and answer the questions.

2. Contrast Literary Periods Works of magic realism sometimes resemble Greek myths. In the myth of Echo and Narcissus, for example, an extraordinary transformation occurs. Select a Greek myth and write a short essay, comparing its elements with those of magic realism.

3. Speaking/Listening Research a contemporary issue in Latin America. Then create a radio or TV broadcast in which you take sides on the issue and present supporting evidence.

4. Take Notes Use this organizer to keep track of the Big Ideas in this part.

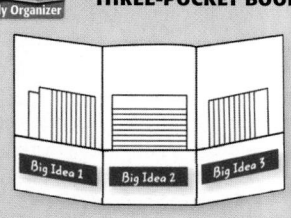

THREE-POCKET BOOK

INTRODUCTION **1189**

Assess

Activities

1. **Follow Up** Students should answer questions with specific facts from the text.

2. **Contrast Literary Periods** Students' essays should reflect an understanding of the myth they selected. Their comparisons and contrasts should be supported with evidence from the text and should reflect a basic grasp of magic realism.

3. **Speaking/Listening** Students should use the knowledge of Latin American history they have gained to support their points.

4. **Note Taking** Students' Foldables should be well organized and their notes should relate to the Big Ideas.

Study Organizer

Have students make and label the Three-Pocket Book Foldable. They can put note cards about each Big Idea in each pocket.

Approaching Level

DIFFERENTIATED INSTRUCTION

Support Have approaching-level students use their Foldable to record author information. Students should connect authors to a Big Idea by listing their names in the correct section of the foldable. This will give students a quick reference when working on their literary analysis at the end of the unit.

Advanced Learners/Pre-AP

DIFFERENTIATED INSTRUCTION

Literary Influence Students will notice that many Modern American authors have been influenced by European literary movements. Invite students to research these movements and create a chart listing the movement, its identifying characteristics, the authors influenced by each movement, and the work from each author found in this unit. Students will be able to use this information as they analyze literary works in this unit and in future literature courses. This chart will encourage students to make the connections between literary movements, cultures, and authors.

Before You Read

A Canary's Ideas

Brazil

Daily Language Practice Transparency 114

Or ask: What would you like to believe in that has not yet been scientifically proven to exist? *(Responses will vary. Students may say that they'd like to believe in ghosts, UFOs, or magic.)* **Ask:** Do you think believing in these things is a sign of imagination or immaturity? *(Students may say that believing in things that are possible—such as life on other planets—isn't immature at all but shows imagination. Other students may say believing in things that have no scientific basis, such as magic, is a sign of immaturity.)*

Meet **Joaquim Maria Machado de Assis**

(1839–1908)

Joaquim Maria Machado de Assis once belonged to a liars' club. Everything said in the club had to be a lie. Because the best lies closely resemble the truth, this was no doubt excellent training for an author who would break new ground in the shadowy terrain between the real and the fantastic.

A Brazilian Sensation The grandchild of freed slaves, Machado de Assis—also known simply as Machado—was born to workers on an estate in Rio de Janeiro, Brazil, much like the one described in the final scene of "A Canary's Ideas." He had only an elementary formal education and was orphaned as a teenager. By the age of seventeen, he was making a living by working in a printing shop. In addition to all these challenges, Machado's problems with stuttering, vision, and epilepsy plagued him as an adult.

Machado began his writing career in the same way many authors do—by writing in the established ways or according to the popular conventions of their time. For Machado, that meant writing Romantic poetry. Most critics deemed his first poems genuinely awful; nevertheless, they were Machado's first steps on the path to finding his own voice. As he practiced his craft, he showed increasing aptitude for many forms, including essays, drama, and better poetry. His work gained him recognition and largely ceremonial government posts that enabled him to spend the majority of his time writing. He became a critical success and an important figure in the literary world of Rio de Janeiro and a national sensation in Brazil.

> "I myself am missing, and this lack is essential."
>
> —Machado des Assis

Early Magic Realist Today, Machado's fame rests on his short stories and his novels. These works helped lay the foundations of magic realism, one of the dominant literary styles of modern Latin American literature. Works of magic realism layer the fantastic and the surreal with otherwise realistic detail; they also embrace ambiguity. You can experience that ambiguity and absurdity in the quotation above, which is uttered by the narrator of Machado's novel *Dom Casmurro*. Notice how these words turn literary convention upside down by presenting the book's narrator missing in action. This quote also shows Machado's sense of humor.

Machado began to publish witty, although pessimistic, novels and short stories like *Dom Casmurro* after he turned 40. In a historical period dominated by the optimistic belief that humans were moving forward in the world, he explored the irrational nature of human behavior and the absurdity of life. Machado's work influenced many twentieth-century authors such as Jorge Luis Borges and Carlos Fuentes.

 Literature Online

Author Search For more about Joaquim Maria Machado de Assis, go to glencoe.com and enter QuickPass code GLW6053u6.

Selection Skills

Literary Elements
- Analyze Narrator (SE pp. 1191, 1192, 1194, 1197; TE 1196)
- Anthropomorphism (SE p. 1197)

Reading Skills
- Synthesize (SE pp. 1191, 1194–1196, 1198; TE pp. 1192,1193)
- Identify Sequence (TE p. 1194)

A Canary's Ideas

Vocabulary Skills
- Denotation and Connotation (SE p. 1198)
- Synonyms (TE p. 1191)

Listening/Speaking/Viewing Skills
- Analyze Art (SE p. 1195)

Writing Skills/Grammar
- Research Report (SE p. 1198)
- Character Sketch (TE p. 1196)

Literature and Reading Preview

Connect to the Story

How do you know what is real and what is imaginary? Discuss this question with a small group.

Build Background

In this story, Machado points his witty pessimism at science. The central character is Macedo, an ornithologist (a scientist who studies birds). Although his knowledge should surely dissuade him from leaping to the conclusion that a canary can talk and discuss philosophy, he eagerly initiates detailed observation and study of the bird in the hopes of astounding the world.

Set Purposes for Reading

Big Idea Magic Realism

As you read, ask yourself, How are fantastic events interwoven with realistic people, places, and things?

Literary Element Narrator

A **narrator** is the person who tells the events in a work of fiction. A narrator can be unreliable and offer a faulty or distorted vision of events. As you read, ask yourself, What does the narrator know and not know, and what shapes his view of reality?

Reading Strategy Synthesize

When you **synthesize**, you combine existing ideas to create something new. That is, you begin with information you read, but you examine and rearrange it to arrive at a richer, more complete understanding. As you read, ask yourself, What appears to be unusual, strange, or surprising?

Tip: Record Questions To navigate a work of magic realism and synthesize meaning from it, record questions about anything that strikes you as surreal, fantastic, contradictory, or ambiguous.

Text	My Questions
Paragraphs 1 and 2	• Why does the narrator say no one took Macedo seriously but then retell Macedo's narrative in a serious way? • Why does the narrator speak in the first person, as if he were Macedo?

JOAQUIM MARIA MACHADO DE ASSIS   **1191**

Learning Objectives

For pages 1190–1198

In studying this text, you will focus on the following objectives:

Literary Study: Analyzing narrator.

Reading: Synthesizing.

Writing: Connecting to science.

Vocabulary

austere (ôs tēr′) *adj.* stern or severe in appearance or manner; p. 1192 *The austere greeting contained no hint of welcome.*

banal (bān′əl) *adj.* lacking originality; commonplace; p. 1193 *Keira's sonnet was just a banal repetition of the model poem, without any fresh images.*

phenomenon (fə nom′ə non′) *n.* an observable fact or subject of scientific study; a remarkable event or occurrence; p. 1194 *The spread of the beetle to higher elevations was a phenomenon several scientists had recorded.*

presumptuous (pri zump′chōō əs) *adj.* excessively bold or arrogant; taking liberties; p. 1195 *Steven made the presumptuous move of entering the house before he was invited.*

cursory (kur′sə rē) *adj.* hasty and not thorough; superficial; p. 1196 *The woman disliked the artist's works, so she gave his new painting only a cursory glance.*

Before You Read

Focus

Summary

Macedo discovers a canary in a secondhand shop. When he asks for the bird's definition of the world, the canary answers that it is a secondhand shop. Astonished, Macedo buys the bird and takes it home. This time when Macedo asks the canary its view of the world, the bird replies that the world is a veranda. Macedo becomes so obsessed with studying the bird that he makes himself ill, and the bird flies away. Later when Macedo chances upon the bird in a tree, its view of the world is the infinite blue sky. It has never heard of a secondhand shop.

For summaries in languages other than English, see Unit 6 Teaching Resources Book, pp. 109–114.

Vocabulary

Synonyms Have students use a dictionary and thesaurus to find at least three synonyms for each vocabulary word. Then have students draw a continuum line for each vocabulary word with *Negative* on one end, *Positive* on the other, and *Neutral* in the middle. Finally have students place each synonym on the line according to its connotation.

For additional vocabulary practice, see Unit 6 Teaching Resources Book, p. 117.

English Learners

DIFFERENTIATED INSTRUCTION

Beginning Explain to English learners that the first scene of this story takes place in a secondhand shop. These students may be unfamiliar with this type of store. Explain the purpose of a secondhand shop, and ask students to contribute anything they know about such shops. When students finish reading the scene in the secondhand shop, ask them to list unfamiliar objects from the shop's description.

Have them look up the meanings of each of these words in a dictionary. To demonstrate their understanding of the terms and to help them remember their meanings in the future, have students arrange a collage of pictures that represent the objects they listed.

Teach

Reading Strategy   1

Synthesize **Ask:** What do you learn about Macedo's own worldview from this passage? *(Macedo has the ability to see the "stories" behind the items in the shop, but he is unable to create a story for the shop owner.)*

Literary Element   2

Analyze Narrator **Answer:** *The third-person narrator begins to tell the story in the first-person as if the narrator were Macedo.*

[APPROACHING] Direct approaching–level students to the use of *his* in the last line of the first paragraph. Explain that this indicates that the information in this paragraph is told from the third-person point of view. **Ask:** What does the use of *I* in the second paragraph indicate? *(The story is told from the first-person point of view.)*

View the Art ★

Following the Surrealist idea of mixing fantasy with realism, Rouillard reveals his own version of Reality: a hand reaching toward a perched canary that acts as the connection between the harsh room in which the hand exists and the sunlit existence displayed within the frame.

For an audio recording of this selection, use Listening Library Audio CD-ROM.

Readability Scores

Dale-Chall: 6.3
DRP: 59
Lexile: 1030

1192

A Canary's Ideas

Joaquim Maria Machado de Assis
Translated by
Jack Schmitt and Lorie Ishimatsu

Reality, 1986. Andre Rouillard. Acrylic on canvas.

A man by the name of Macedo, who had a fancy for ornithology, related to some friends an incident so extraordinary that no one took him seriously. Some came to believe he had lost his mind. Here is a summary of his narration.

At the beginning of last month, as I was walking down the street, a carriage darted past me and nearly knocked me to the ground. I escaped by quickly side-stepping into a secondhand shop. Neither the racket of the horse and carriage nor my entrance stirred the proprietor, dozing in a folding chair at the back of the shop. He was a man of shabby appearance: his beard was the color of dirty straw, and his head was covered by a tattered cap which probably had not found a buyer. One could not guess that there was any story behind him, as there could have been behind some of the objects he sold, nor could one sense in him that **austere,** disillusioned sadness inherent in the objects which were remnants of past lives.

The shop was dark and crowded with the sort of old, bent, broken, tarnished, rusted articles ordinarily found in secondhand shops, and everything was in that state of semidisorder befitting such an establishment. This assortment of articles, though

Vocabulary

austere (ôs tēr′) *adj.* stern or cold in appearance or manner

---

Narrator *What shift does the narrator make between the first and second paragraphs?*

1192 UNIT 6   THE MODERN AMERICAS

Literary Element Practice

Setting Review with students the definition of setting. Then explain that time, place, and other physical qualities of a story's setting make up a story's atmosphere. The atmosphere can, in turn, influence the story's mood, or the feeling that a literary work creates for its readers. **Ask:** What is the setting at the beginning of the story? What are its physical qualities? *(The beginning of the story is set in a secondhand shop. The shop is dark, crowded,* *and full of old, dusty, and broken items.)* **Ask:** How do the setting's physical qualities contribute to the atmosphere? *(Students may say that the setting gives the story a mysterious atmosphere.)* **Ask:** How would you describe the mood of the story so far? *(Students may describe a mood of possibility; they, and the narrator, aren't sure what to expect.)*

Visual Vocabulary
A *fencing foil* is a light sword used in the sport of fencing.

banal, was interesting. Pots without lids, lids without pots, buttons, shoes, locks, a black shirt, straw hats, fur hats, picture frames, binoculars, dress coats, a fencing foil, a stuffed dog, a pair of slippers, gloves, nondescript vases, epaulets, a velvet satchel, two hatracks, a slingshot, a thermometer, chairs, a lithographed portrait by the late Sisson, a backgammon board, two wire masks for some future Carnival[1]—all this and more, which I either did not see or do not remember, filled the shop in the area around the door, propped up, hung, or displayed in glass cases as old as the objects inside them. Further inside the shop were many objects of similar appearance. Predominant were the large objects—chests of drawers, chairs, and beds—some of which were stacked on top of others which were lost in the darkness.

I was about to leave, when I saw a cage hanging in the doorway. It was as old as everything else in the shop, and I expected it to be empty so it would fit in with the general appearance of desolation. However, it wasn't empty. Inside, a canary was hopping about. The bird's color, liveliness, and charm added a note of life and youth to that heap of wreckage. It was the last passenger of some wrecked ship, who had arrived in the shop as complete and happy as it had originally been. As soon as I looked at the bird, it began to hop up and

down, from perch to perch, as if it meant to tell me that a ray of sunshine was frolicking in the midst of that cemetery. I'm using this image to describe the canary only because I'm speaking to rhetorical people, but the truth is that the canary thought about neither cemetery nor sun, according to what it told me later. Along with the pleasure the sight of the bird brought me, I felt indignation regarding its destiny and softly murmured these bitter words:

"What detestable owner had the nerve to rid himself of this bird for a few cents? Or what indifferent soul, not wishing to keep his late master's pet, gave it away to some child, who sold it so he could make a bet on a soccer game?"

The canary, sitting on top of its perch, trilled this reply:

"Whoever you may be, you're certainly not in your right mind. I had no detestable owner, nor was I given to any child to sell. Those are the delusions of a sick person. Go and get yourself cured, my friend . . ."

"What?" I interrupted, not having had time to become astonished. "So your master didn't sell you to this shop? It wasn't misery or laziness that brought you, like a ray of sunshine, to this cemetery?"

"I don't know what you mean by 'sunshine' or 'cemetery.' If the canaries you've seen use the first of those names, so much the better, because it sounds pretty, but really, I'm sure you're confused."

"Excuse me, but you couldn't have come here by chance, all alone. Has your master always been that man sitting over there?"

"What master? That man over there is my servant. He gives me food and water every day, so regularly that if I were to pay him for his services, it would be no small sum, but canaries don't pay their servants.

---

1. *Carnival,* traditionally, is a festival held before Lent, the season of penitence observed by some Christian denominations. Carnivals include feasting, dances, and masquerades.

Vocabulary

banal (bā′nəl) *adj.* lacking originality; commonplace

Magic Realism *What real and fantastic elements does Machado combine in this passage?* **4**

Teach

Reading Strategy **3**

Synthesize Ask: What is the canary's opinion of Macedo? *(The canary thinks that Macedo is mentally unstable.)* **Ask:** What do the canary's comments indicate about its worldview? *(Students may say that the canary's assessment that Macedo is crazy is due to Macedo coming up with a back story of the canary's early life. This indicates that the canary takes things literally and has no imagination.)*

Big Idea **4**

Magic Realism Answer: *It seems logical that a bird would not think the way the narrator does, but it is a fantastic element that the bird talks.*

Literary History ☆

Indianista Novels Although his later writing lacks any description of the natural world, Machado de Assis began his literary career writing Romantic poetry. A related genre particular to Brazil is the Indianista novel, which romanticizes the life of the South American Indian. Often nostalgic and melancholy, this form became popular in the mid 1800s.

English Learners

DIFFERENTIATED INSTRUCTION

Intermediate Direct English learners' attention to the author's use of *wreckage* and *wrecked.* Have students look up the base word *wreck.* Instruct students to look up the definitions and parts of speech for *wreck, wreckage,* and *wrecked.* **Ask:** What is the "heap of wreckage"? *(the shop full of dusty, broken, old things)* Explain that the author is using a metaphor in the next sentence to say that the canary is the "last passenger" on a "wrecked ship."

Advanced Learners/Pre-AP

DIFFERENTIATED INSTRUCTION

Metaphor Direct students' attention to the author's use of a metaphor: "It was the last passenger of some wrecked ship. . . ." Remind students that a metaphor compares two unlike things, often by using the word *is.* **Ask:** What is the author comparing here? *(The canary is compared to a shipwreck survivor and the shop is compared to a shipwreck.)* Have students write metaphors to describe the shopkeeper and Macedo.

Learning Objectives
Analyzing narrator. (SE)
Analyzing setting. (TE)

Teach

Reading Strategy | 1

Synthesize Answer: *The canary thinks it is the center of the world and the reason for others' existence. The canary believes the world belongs to canaries.*

Literary Element | 2

Narrator Answer: *The narrator's astonishment and his desire for external validation make him believable. He is suspect because he believes he is in the presence of a talking canary and because he thinks the canary wants him to speak.*

Literary Element | 3

Narrator Answer: *He is untrustworthy because he thinks a canary can speak, because he corrects his observations, and because he is not clear about what the bird communicates.*

 For additional literary element practice, see Unit 6 Teaching Resources Book, p. 115.

Literary History ☆

A Changing Style An illness was the catalyst for a change in Machado de Assis's writing. His 1881 novel "The Posthumous Memoirs of Brás Cubas" is revolutionary, telling of one man's fictionalized memoirs in numerous short chapters in a free-flowing, often nonlinear, narrative.

In fact, since the world belongs to canaries, it would be extravagant for them to pay for what is already in the world."

Astonished by these answers, I didn't know what to marvel at more—the language or the ideas. The language, even though it entered my ears as human speech, was uttered by the bird in the form of charming trills. I looked all around me so I could determine if I were awake and saw that the street was the same, and the shop was the same dark, sad, musty place. The canary, moving from side to side, was waiting for me to speak. I then asked if it were lonely for the infinite blue space …

"But, my dear man," trilled the canary, "what does 'infinite blue space' mean?"

"But, pardon me, what do you think of this world? What is the world to you?"

"The world," retorted the canary, with a certain professorial air, "is a secondhand shop with a small rectangular bamboo cage hanging from a nail. The canary is lord of the cage it lives in and the shop that surrounds it. Beyond that, everything is illusion and deception."

With this, the old man woke up and approached me, dragging his feet. He asked me if I wanted to buy the canary. I asked if he had acquired it in the same way he had acquired the rest of the objects he sold and learned that he had bought it from a barber, along with a set of razors.

"The razors are in very good condition," he said.

"I only want the canary."

I paid for it, ordered a huge, circular cage of wood and wire, and had it placed on the veranda of my house so the bird could see the garden, the fountain, and a bit of blue sky.

It was my intention to do a lengthy study of this **phenomenon,** without saying anything to anyone until I could astound the world with my extraordinary discovery. I began by alphabetizing the canary's language in order to study its structure, its relation to music, the bird's appreciation of aesthetics,[2] its ideas and recollections. When this philological[3] and psychological analysis was done, I entered specifically into the study of canaries: their origin, their early history, the geology and flora of the Canary Islands, the bird's knowledge of navigation, and so forth. We conversed for hours while I took notes, and it waited, hopped about, and trilled.

As I have no family other than two servants, I ordered them not to interrupt me, even to deliver a letter or an urgent telegram or to inform me of an important visitor. Since they both knew about my scientific pursuits, they found my orders perfectly natural and did not suspect that the canary and I understood each other.

Needless to say, I slept little, woke up two or three times each night, wandered about aimlessly, and felt feverish. Finally, I returned to my work in order to reread, add, and emend.[4] I corrected more than one observation, either because I had misunderstood something or because the bird had not expressed it clearly. The definition of the

---

2. *Aesthetics* (es thet′iks) is a branch of philosophy dealing with the nature of beauty and art, as well as their creation and appreciation.
3. *Philological* (fil′ə loj′i kəl) means "of or relating to philology, the comparative study of languages, including their origins, developments, and interrelationships."
4. To *emend* is to correct a text.

Narrator How trustworthy is the narrator? | **3**

Vocabulary

phenomenon (fə nom′ə non′) *n.* an observable fact or subject of scientific study; a remarkable event or occurrence

---

1 **Synthesize** *What do the canary's comments here reveal about its worldview?*

2 **Narrator** *In this paragraph, what makes the narrator believable? What makes him suspect?*

Reading Practice

Identify Sequence Relating steps in a process is one way writers sequence ideas. Macedo's narration involves a brief but thorough explanation of his process for studying the canary. Have students list the steps Macedo follows, including the purpose of each step. Encourage students to keep the outline in a logical order. *(First he states the nature of the process: "It was my intention. . . ." Then he relates how he began the process: "I began by alphabetizing. . . ." Next he states he "entered specifically into the study of canaries. . . ." Finally he says how he did it: We conversed for hours. . . .")*

Ask: What words in the passage give you clues about the sequence of events? *(The words* began *and* when *are clues.)*

Teach

Paisaje (Landscape). Juan Cárdenas (Columbian, b. 1939). Oil on linen, 50 x 65 cm. Private collection.

<u>View the Art</u> The figure in the painting may be Cárdenas, who often paints incidents from his own life. What kind of mood did he create in this painting? How does it remind you of the story?

Reading Strategy 4

Synthesize Answer: *There is increased fantasy as the canary is able to express more than one worldview, yet keep part of it consistent. Here it becomes clear that the canary's worldview is based on its location and perspective, so readers may begin to ask whether the whole story is an examination of how individual perception affects reality.*

<u>View the Art</u> ★

Answer: *The mood is intense and threatening. The painting may remind students of the main character's mood at the end of the story--lost and isolated.*

---

world was one of these. Three weeks after the canary's entrance into my home, I asked it to repeat to me its definition of the world.

"The world," it answered, "is a sufficiently broad garden with a fountain in the middle, flowers, shrubbery, some grass, clear air, and a bit of blue up above. The canary, lord of the world, lives in a spacious cage, white and circular, from which it looks out on the rest of the world. Everything else is illusion and deception."

4 | **Synthesize** *How do the similarities and differences between the canary's past and present worldview contribute to the sense of ambiguity or fantasy?*

The language of my treatise[5] also suffered some modifications, and I saw that certain conclusions which had seemed simple were actually **presumptuous.** I still could not write the paper I was to send to the National Museum, the Historical Institute, and the German universities, not due to a lack of material but because I first had to

---

5. A *treatise* (trē′tis) is a book or an essay that examines a topic thoroughly and systematically.

Vocabulary

presumptuous (pri zump′chōō əs) *adj.* excessively bold or arrogant; taking liberties

JOAQUIM MARIA MACHADO DE ASSIS **1195**

Learning Objectives
Analyzing narrator. (SE)
Synthesizing. (SE)
Identifying sequence. (TE)

Approaching Level

DIFFERENTIATED INSTRUCTION

Cause and Effect Relationship
Approaching-level students may have difficulty understanding Macedo's explanation of the trouble he has finishing his paper. Explain that although we tend to think of cause and effect as linear, or moving in a direct line, the author has explained the effect before describing the cause. Direct students' attention to the passage that begins "I still could not write the paper. . . ."

Have students rewrite the sentence in three smaller sentences. The first explains Macedo couldn't write the paper, the second shows Macedo had enough material, and the third demonstrates Macedo had to put together his observations and test them. Point out the author's use of the word *first* and explain that this is a clue to the order of the cause-and-effect relationship in this situation.

Teach

Literary Element   **1**

Narrator **Ask:** What does Macedo assume about the bird? What does this say about Macedo? *(Macedo assumes that the bird talks only to those who are smart enough to understand it; he assumes that the bird is intelligent. This shows that Macedo considers himself worthy of the bird's attention.)*

Reading Strategy   **2**

Synthesize **Answer:** *The bird appears to control reality by allowing Macedo to find it, starting up the conversation, and suggesting that it was Macedo who disappeared.*

Big Idea   **3**

Magic Realism **Answer:** *These words suggest that reality is based entirely on the present.*

 To check students' understanding of the selection, see Unit 6 Teaching Resources Book, p. 120.

---

put together all my observations and test their validity. During the last few days, I neither left the house, answered letters, nor wanted to hear from friends or relatives. The canary was everything to me. One of the servants had the job of cleaning the bird's cage and giving it food and water every morning. The bird said nothing to him, as if it knew the man was completely lacking in scientific background. Besides, the service was no more than **cursory,** as the servant was not a bird lover.

   One Saturday I awoke ill, my head and back aching. The doctor ordered complete rest. I was suffering from an excess of studying and was not to read or even think, nor was I even to know what was going on in the city or the rest of the outside world. I remained in this condition for five days. On the sixth day I got up, and only then did I find out that the canary, while under the servant's care, had flown out of its cage. My first impulse was to strangle the servant—I was choking with indignation and collapsed into my chair, speechless and bewildered. The guilty man defended himself, swearing he had been careful, but the wily bird had nevertheless managed to escape.

   "But didn't you search for it?"

   "Yes, I did, sir. First it flew up to the roof, and I followed it. It flew to a tree, and then who knows where it hid itself? I've been asking around since yesterday. I asked the neighbors and the local farmers, but no one has seen the bird."

   I suffered immensely. Fortunately, the fatigue left me within a few hours, and I was soon able to go out to the veranda and the garden. There was no sign of the canary. I ran everywhere, making inquiries and posting announcements, all to no avail. I had already gathered my notes together to write my paper, even though it would be disjointed and incomplete, when I happened to visit a friend who had one of the largest and most beautiful estates on the outskirts of town. We were taking a stroll before dinner when this question was trilled to me:

   "Greetings, Senhor Macedo, where have you been since you disappeared?"

   It was the canary, perched on the branch of a tree. You can imagine how I reacted and what I said to the bird. My friend presumed I was mad, but the opinions of friends are of no importance to me. I spoke tenderly to the canary and asked it to come home and continue our conversations in that world of ours, composed of a garden, a fountain, a veranda, and a white circular cage.

   "What garden? What fountain?"

   "The world, my dear bird."

   "What world? I see you haven't lost any of your annoying professorial habits. The world," it solemnly concluded, "is an infinite blue space, with the sun up above."

   Indignant, I replied that if I were to believe what it said, the world could be anything—it had even been a secondhand shop …

   "A secondhand shop?" it trilled to its heart's content. "But is there really such a thing as a secondhand shop?" ❧

Vocabulary

cursory (kur′sə rē) *adj.* hasty and not thorough; superficial

---

Synthesize *Who appears to control reality?*   **2**

Magic Realism *What do the canary's final words suggest about reality?*   **3**

Writing Practice

Character Sketch Have students write a one- to two-page character sketch of Macedo, using what they learned about him through his dialogue and actions, both with the canary and others. Encourage students to draw conclusions about Macedo. Encourage students to describe his mental state. **Ask:** Is he crazy? Explain using details from the story. *(Students may say that he has to be crazy to think that a canary is speaking to him. Other students may say that, as a person who studies birds, he is likely the only person who could understand them.)* **Ask:** If you believe that Macedo is crazy, how do you explain the canary's worldview? How do you explain its view if you think that Macedo is sane? *(Students may say that the canary's worldview is part of his insanity; Macedo cannot imagine the world beyond his own immediate surroundings. Students may say that if Macedo is sane, perhaps he is using the canary's ideas as a way of explaining other worldviews.)* Discuss students' character sketches and conclusions as a class.

After You Read

Respond and Think Critically

Respond and Interpret

1. What questions do you have about the canary or about Macedo?

2. (a)Where does Macedo find the canary? (b)Why is he surprised to find it there?

3. (a)How does the canary initially define the world? (b)How does this idea conflict with Macedo's assumptions about the canary?

4. (a)What new idea of the world does the canary express in Macedo's home? (b)How is the canary's new idea consistent with its former idea?

Analyze and Evaluate

5. How does this story satirize or ridicule scientific observation?

6. (a)Does the canary regard itself as a master or a servant? Explain. (b)How does this relationship contribute to the contradiction or ambiguity in the story?

Connect

7. **Big Idea** **Magic Realism** How does the canary take over reality?

8. **Connect to Today** What message about science and reality might this story offer to a modern reader? Explain.

Literary Element | Narrator

A **narrator** tells a story. Some narrators are **unreliable** because their account of events is faulty or distorted in some way. Some unreliable narrators intentionally mislead readers, while others fail to understand the true meaning of the events they describe. Many stories with unreliable narrators are written in the first person.

1. This story is a narration of a narration. Does that make the narrator unreliable? Explain.

2. Do you think first-person narration is a better choice for this story than third-person narration? Explain.

3. When Macedo becomes physically ill, how does his physical state reflect his ability to accurately and objectively retell and interpret events?

Review: Anthropomorphism

As you learned on page 39, **anthropomorphism** is the assignment of human characteristics to gods, animals, or inanimate objects.

Partner Activity Work with a classmate to find examples of anthropomorphism in the story and to identify the human qualities each conveys. Complete a chart like the one below. When you are done, decide how anthropomorphism is used in "A Canary's Ideas" to suggest a philosophy of human or animal life. Also consider what it contributes to the magic realism of the story.

Quotation	Human Qualities

After You Read

Assess

1. Answers will vary.

2. (a) He finds it in a secondhand shop. (b) The canary's energy and color contrasts with the shop's age and filth.

3. (a) It defines the world as a secondhand shop ruled by the canary. (b) He assumes that the canary longs for freedom, but it is entirely content in its cage.

4. (a) The canary now says the world consists of a veranda and a garden, its new environment. (b) The canary's idea of reality is based on the present.

5. In spite of his notes and observations, the professor knows little about reality and thinks he can learn about it from a canary. He constantly changes his observations, which an objective scientist should never do, and becomes emotionally attached to his subject.

6. (a) The canary thinks of itself as a master and those around it (the shopkeeper) as his servants. It talks to Macedo as if it were superior. (b) The canary's ideas become more important than the human's; the canary seems to be in control; it is "everything" to Macedo. This is a fantastic reversal of reality.

7. It has the last word, it erases the past, it defines reality based on its present experience, it turns Macedo into a servant, and it subverts science.

8. A modern reader might question his or her perception of reality and the power of scientific knowledge to define reality.

 For additional assessment, see Assessment Resources, pp. 231–232.

Literary Element

1. Some may say yes, because the story is already secondhand.

2. A third-person narration implies objectivity; a first-person narration is subjective. This increases the sense of the irrational and emphasizes the theme of individual perception.

3. The physical illness is a metaphor for his mental breakdown.

Review: Anthropomorphism

Students may say anthropomorphism helps to show how both humans and animals create their worldview based on their experience and limited perception. They may say it adds to the magic realism by introducing fantastic elements into believable settings.

After You Read

Assess

Reading Strategy

(A) is the correct answer. The other options are factors the canary takes into account when forming its ideas.

Progress Check

Can students synthesize?

If No → See Unit 6 Teaching Resources Book, p. 116.

Vocabulary Practice

Possible answers:

Vocabulary word: *austere*

Similar word: *formal*

Explanation: *Austere* has the stronger connotation. *Formal* could simply imply politeness, while *austere* usually implies strictness and severity.

Vocabulary word: *banal*

Similar word: *vapid*

Explanation: *Vapid* has the stronger connotation. *Banal* implies commonness, while *vapid* implies extreme dullness.

Vocabulary word: *phenomenon*

Similar word: *miracle*

Explanation: *Miracle* has the stronger connotation. *Phenomenon* implies an interesting occurrence, while *miracle* implies an amazing or supernatural one.

Vocabulary word: *presumptuous*

Similar word: *smug*

Explanation: *Smug* has the stronger connotation. *Presumptuous* implies forwardness and boldness, while *smug* implies outright arrogance.

Vocabulary word: *cursory*

Similar word: *careless*

Explanation: *Careless* has the stronger connotation. *Cursory*

1198

SAT Skills Practice

Unlike Macedo, the canary develops its ideas without regard for

(A) the scientific method

(B) firsthand observations

(C) individual instincts

(D) the natural environment

(E) the present moment

Vocabulary Practice

Practice with Denotation and Connotation
Denotation is the literal meaning of a word. **Connotation** is its implied meaning. For example, the words *sad* and *despairing* have a similar denotation—"unhappy" —but *despairing* has a stronger connotation. Work with a partner to complete a graphic organizer like the one below for each vocabulary word. Include the vocabulary word in one box and a word that has a similar denotation in another. Explain which word has the stronger connotation.

austere	banal	phenomenon
presumptuous	cursory	

EXAMPLE:

Vocabulary word: *despairing* — Similar word: *sad*

Explanation: *Despairing* has the stronger connotation. *Sad* implies general unhappiness, while *despairing* implies desperation.

Academic Vocabulary

*Machado's story shows how, for the canary, reality is a matter of **individual** perception.*

Individual is an academic word. To further explore its meaning, describe a situation in which you saw a group of people combine their **individual** talents to achieve success.

For more on academic vocabulary, see pages 36–37 and R83–R85.

1198 UNIT 6   THE MODERN AMERICAS

---

implies a quick or preliminary action, while *careless* implies outright negligence or sloppiness.

Academic Vocabulary

Students might describe a sports team's victory.

Connect to *Science*

Research and Report

Assignment In Machado's story, the canary concludes that the world "is an infinite blue space, with the sun up above." Research the cognition of birds and their ability to communicate, and create a multimedia presentation based on your findings.

Investigate Use print and online sources to research how and why birds communicate, as well as why only certain birds can "talk," or mimic human speech. To guide your research, create a K-W-L chart like the one below.

What I Know	What I Want to Know	What I Learned
Some birds can mimic human speech.	Can they actually comprehend the meaning of the words?	

As you take notes, be sure to annotate unfamiliar scientific terms, such as *ornithology* (the study of birds). Then synthesize the information in your K-W-L chart into a few general ideas you want to present. To review the synthesis process, consult the chart you made on page 1191.

Create Create a multimedia oral report that incorporates imagery, speech, and sound. You may wish to use presentation software or a slide projector to show images of birds as you speak. Alternately, you might present video or audio recordings of birds "talking." Remember that the media components you choose are meant to enhance, rather than replace, your presentation's oral component.

Report In your oral report, be sure to attribute information to the proper sources and clearly explain scientific terms. Rehearse your presentation several times to maximize the effectiveness of your multimedia aids and resolve any technical difficulties that might arise.

 Literature Online

Selection Resources For Selection Quizzes, eFlashcards, and Reading-Writing Connection activities, go to glencoe.com and enter QuickPass code GLW6053u6.

Connect to *Science*

Students' reports should

- present clear, organized information about bird cognition and communication
- use effective media aids to enhance the presentation
- use effective verbal and nonverbal delivery techniques

 For grammar practice, see Unit 6 Teaching Resources Book, p. 119.

Before You Read

The Luck of Teodoro Méndez Acúbal

Meet **Rosario Castellanos**
(1925–1974)

Lola Alverez Bravo

Being born into a society that expected little more of its female members than to marry and have children can be a significant obstacle to any young woman who has other ambitions. Rosario Castellanos (rō sä′rē ō kä stä yä′nōs) overcame this obstacle and more to become one of the most important twentieth-century Mexican woman authors.

Growing Up in Chiapas Born into a wealthy family, Castellanos spent time with her native Maya nanny and other household workers on her father's plantations in the Chiapas region of southern Mexico. Her relationships with these people provided the warmth she never received from her parents, who preferred her younger brother. When he died suddenly, her devastated parents said the "wrong child" had died. During the late 1930s, agrarian reform affected Castellanos's family when the government seized its land and redistributed it among the peasants. This change in fortune led the family to move to Mexico City when Castellanos was sixteen. There, she completed her secondary education and enrolled in college. In 1948, her parents died within weeks of each other. This sudden loss put her in a state of crisis, but she recognized she was now free to pursue her own ambitions.

Spearheading Feminism In 1950, Castellanos received her master's degree in philosophy and published her thesis, "On Feminine Culture." This work is generally regarded as the starting point for the feminist movement in Mexico. In it, Castellanos criticized the patriarchal nature of Mexican society for the fact that women rarely participated in cultural activities. A year later, she returned to Chiapas where she studied the

> "Laughter is the most immediate form of freeing ourselves from that which oppresses us the most, of distancing ourselves from that which imprisons us!"
>
> —Rosario Castellanos

culture of the Maya Chamula group. In her later fiction, Castellanos often focused on relations between the Chamulas and the landowners. She believed that Mexican women and the Chamulas suffered from similar forms of oppression.

Later Years During the 1960s, Castellenos lectured at universities in the United States and Mexico. In 1971, she was appointed Mexico's ambassador to Israel. While carrying out her diplomatic responsibilities, she continued to write and teach. When she was only 49, she died in a household accident. She is buried in the Rotunda of Illustrious Men in Mexico City, one of only two women so honored.

 Literature Online

Author Search For more about Rosario Castellanos, go to glencoe.com and enter QuickPass code GLW6053u6.

ROSARIO CASTELLANOS **1199**

Before You Read

Focus

Bellringer Options

Selection Focus
Transparency 73

Daily Language Practice
Transparency 115

Or ask: Do you believe in luck or coincidence? Are some people luckier than others, or is luck all a matter of perception? *(Students may say they believe in luck and some people are luckier than others. Some students may say they do not believe in luck, and some people just seem lucky. Others may say what is lucky to one person may be unlucky to another.)* Discuss with students how what is "lucky" can be relative depending on a person's situation.

Selection Skills

Literary Elements
- Plot (SE pp. 1200, 1202, 1203, 1205–1207; TE pp. 1201, 1204)
- Irony (SE p. 1207)

Reading Skills
- Preview and Review (SE pp. 1200, 1201, 1205, 1206, 1208)
- Set a Purpose for Reading (TE p. 1200)
- Analyze Characters (TE p. 1202)

The Luck of Teodoro Méndez Acúbal

Vocabulary Skills
- Synonyms (SE p. 1208)
- Academic Vocabulary (SE p. 1208)

Speaking/Listening/Viewing Skills
- Analyze Art (SE p. 1202)
- Interview (SE p. 1208)

Writing Skills/Grammar
- Dialogue (TE p. 1204)
- Avoid Sentence Fragments (TE p. 1206)

Before You Read

Focus

Summary

When Teodoro finds a silver coin on the street, he is fearful because he is of the lowest social class in his town, but excited because he has finally had a stroke of good fortune. He wants to spend his coin on a clay figurine of the Virgin Mary in the store of Don Agustín Velasco. Don Agustín is disturbed and feels threatened by the sight of an Indian outside his shop. Secretly worried about his own social status, Don Agustín believes he can gain respect in the community by accusing Teodoro of being a thief. When Teodoro finally comes into the store and reaches for the coin, Don Agustín believes he is reaching for a weapon and summons the police. Teodoro is arrested and sent to jail without trial.

 For summaries in languages other than English, see Unit 6 Teaching Resources Book, pp. 122–127.

Vocabulary

Prefixes Have students study each vocabulary word for a prefix and list the suspected prefixes. *(Students may list ir–, pro–, con–, and dis–.)* Then, have students use a dictionary to look up each word and prefix and ascertain whether any of the words is using a prefix. *(Students will find that only ir– is a prefix.)*

 For additional vocabulary practice, see Unit 6 Teaching Resources Book, p. 130.

Literature and Reading Preview

Connect to the Story

How might the acquisition of a lot of money change someone? List the possible effects of suddenly coming into wealth.

Build Background

"The Luck of Teodoro Méndez Acúbal" is set in Chiapas, once a center of Mayan civilization. Many of its inhabitants are descended, either completely or partly, from the Maya. Over the centuries, conflicts have broken out between the Maya and landowners in Chiapas. Ethnic, class, and language barriers have made it difficult for many Maya to achieve an adequate standard of living.

Set Purposes for Reading

Big Idea **The Legacy of Colonialism**

As you read, ask yourself, How does the multicultural legacy of the area affect its poorest inhabitants?

Literary Element **Plot**

The **plot** is the sequence of events in a story. Most plots develop around a **conflict,** a struggle between opposing forces, and begin with **exposition,** which introduces the characters, setting, and situation. The **rising action** adds **complications** that culminate in the **climax,** the point of highest tension. The climax gives way rapidly to its logical result in the **falling action,** and finally to the **resolution,** in which the final outcome is revealed. As you read, ask yourself, Where does each plot element occur?

Reading Strategy **Preview and Review**

When you **preview** a literary work, you look at the title, the art, and the opening paragraph to get an idea of what the work is about. When you **review,** you reread sections of text. Before you read, ask yourself, How can the title, the art, and the first paragraph help me understand the story?

Tip: Scan the Text In a chart like the one below, note various text features and what each suggests.

Feature	What It Suggests
Title: "The Luck of Teodoro Méndez Acúbal"	Luck has a role—is it good luck or bad luck?
Opening art	

Reading Practice

Set a Purpose for Reading Explain that while authors have at least one purpose for writing a text, such as to inform, entertain, or persuade, readers also have a purpose for reading. Setting a purpose for reading before beginning to read will help students use their time wisely, and they will be able to get the most out of the reading material.

Ask: What is your purpose for reading this story? *(Students are likely to say they are reading the story to complete an assignment or to learn about Modern American literature.)* Explain to students that having a purpose for reading will affect how they read a text.

Learning Objectives

For pages 1199–1208

In studying this text, you will focus on the following objectives:

Literary Study: Analyzing plot.

Reading: Previewing and reviewing.

Listening and Speaking: Conducting an interview.

Vocabulary

irrevocable (i rev′ə kə bəl) *adj.* incapable of being brought back, undone, or changed; p. 1203 *After the house was sold, the decision to move was irrevocable.*

propriety (prə prī′ə tē) *n.* conformity to what is acceptable in conduct or speech; p. 1204 *Cara's sense of propriety prevented her from wearing shorts to the wedding.*

condescending (kon′di sen′ ding) *adj.* characterized by an air of superiority or smugness; p. 1205 *Armando's condescending attitude made it unpleasant for Justine to be around him.*

disdain (dis dān′) *n.* an attitude of scorn or contempt for something considered inferior; p. 1205 *Her disdain for Harry prompted her to regard his comments as "silly and idiotic."*

diligence (dil′ə jəns) *n.* persistent hard work; p. 1206 *Erin's diligence was rewarded when she finally learned to play the piece flawlessly.*

The Luck of **Teodoro Méndez Acúbal**

Rosario Castellanos
Translated by Myralyn F. Allgood

Union (La union), July 1923-early 1924. Diego Rivera © Banco de Mexico Trust. Mural, 2.06 x 1.33 m. Secretaria de Educacion Publica, Mexico City, D.F.

Walking along the streets of Jobel (with his eyes cast downward as custom dictates for those of his humble station), Teodoro Méndez Acúbal spotted a coin. All but lost in the dust, caked with mud, worn from years of use, it had been ignored by the white *caxlanes*.[1] For the *caxlanes* walk with their heads held high. Moved by pride, they contemplate from afar the important matters that absorb them.

Teodoro stopped, more out of disbelief than greed. Kneeling as if to fasten one of his sandals, he waited until no one was looking to pick up what he had found. He hid it quickly in the folds of his sash.

He stood again, swaying, overcome by a kind of dizziness. Weak-kneed and dry-mouthed, his eyes blurred as he felt his heart pounding, pulsing between his eyebrows.

Staggering from side to side as if in a drunken stupor, Teodoro began to make his way down the street. From time to time the passersby had to push him aside to avoid bumping into him. But Teodoro's spirit was too troubled to be bothered by what was going on around him. The coin, hidden in his sash, had transformed him into another man—a stronger man than before, it is true. But also more fearful.

---

1. *Caxlanes* (käs lä´näs) are the dominant socioeconomic class in Chiapas, which has a large Mayan population.

Preview and Review *Based on the title and this first paragraph, what can you predict about the story?*

The Legacy of Colonialism *What details here and earlier in the story suggest differences between the social classes?* **3**

ROSARIO CASTELLANOS **1201**

Teach

| **Literary Element** | 1 |

Plot Ask: What have we learned so far in this exposition of the story? *(Teodoro, a man from the lower class in Mexican society, has found a coin.)*

| **Reading Strategy** | 2 |

Preview and Review
Answer: *The story will probably have something to do with how finding the coin changes Teodoro's luck. The story may address the relationships between people of different classes.*

📁 For additional practice using the reading skill or strategy, see Unit 6 Teaching Resources Book, p. 129.

| **Big Idea** | 3 |

The Legacy of Colonialism
Answer: *The different ways of walking, Teodoro's caution, and Teodoro's strange movements demonstrate how the two classes behave differently. The lower classes are poor and mistreated; upper classes are detached from the problems of the poor.*

💿 For an audio recording of this selection, use Listening Library Audio CD-ROM.

English Learners

DIFFERENTIATED INSTRUCTION

Beginning Direct English learners' attention to the parenthesis in the first sentence. Explain that sometimes writers use parentheses to add explanatory information to a sentence. Tell students that when they encounter parentheses in this sentence, they may read around it and then read the information within it. This will help students process both pieces of information separately before seeking the connection that links them.

Advanced Learners/Pre-AP

DIFFERENTIATED INSTRUCTION

Predict Challenge students to predict what will happen to Teodoro as a result of finding the coin. Remind students that predictions are based on personal knowledge and experience paired with clues from the text. Students should consider what they already know about Teodoro and the *caxlanes*. They should also consider the story's title.

Readability Scores
Dale-Chall: 8.0
DRP: 57
Lexile: 860

Learning Objectives
Previewing and reviewing. (SE)
Analyzing plot. (SE)
Setting a purpose for reading. (TE)

Teach

Plot **Answer:** *Teodoro is experiencing an internal conflict about the coin. On the one hand, he feels entitled to keep it a secret, but on the other hand, he feels guilty about it.*

View the Art ★

Students may say goodness, chastity, or piety.

Cultural History ☆

Coinage of Mexico The peso, originally introduced to Spain in 1497, became the basis for silver coinage in Spanish holdings in the late eighteenth century. Simultaneously, Charles III directed that the peso be minted in a style similar to gold pieces, with the bust of the reigning monarch on one side and a coat of arms on the other.

He stepped off the path that led to his village and sat down on a fallen log. Could this be all a dream? Pale with anxiety, Teodoro's hands felt his sash. Yes, there it was—firm and round—the precious coin. Teodoro unwrapped it, moistened it with his breath and saliva and rubbed it against his clothing. On the metal (it had to be silver, judging from its whitish color) the outline of a profile appeared. Majestic. And around the edge, letters, numbers, and signs. Calculating its weight, testing it with his teeth, listening to its ring, Teodoro was able—at last—to determine its value.

And so, with this stroke of fortune, he had become rich. Richer than the owner of great flocks of sheep or vast stretches of cornfields. He was as rich as . . . as a *caxlán*. And Teodoro was amazed that the color of his skin had not changed.

The images of the members of his family (his wife, his three children, his aging parents) struggled to invade Teodoro's reverie. But he dispelled them with an air of displeasure. He saw no reason to tell anyone about his discovery, much less share it. He worked to maintain his household. That's as it should be; it's the custom, an obligation. But as for this stroke of fortune, it was his. Exclusively his.

And so, when Teodoro arrived at his hut and sat down by the fire to eat, he did not speak. His own silence made him uncomfortable, as if being quiet were a way of mocking everyone else. To punish himself he allowed his feelings of loneliness to grow within him, along with his shame. Teodoro was a man set apart, stifled by his secret. Moreover, this anguish produced physical discomfort—a cramp in the pit of his stomach, a chill deep in the marrow of his bones. Why suffer all this, when with a word the pain would disappear? To keep himself from

Virgin of Guadalupe, c. 19th century. Artist Unknown. Mexico.
View the Art It is believed that the Virgin of Guadalupe appeared to Juan Diego in 1531, miraculously imprinting her image on his cape. What values do you think the Virgin of Guadalupe might represent? ★

uttering it, Teodoro grasped his sash and felt the lump there, made by the metal.

During the sleepless night, Teodoro talked to himself: what shall I buy? Before now he had never wanted things. So convinced was he that they were beyond his reach that he passed them by without a thought, without the slightest curiosity. And now he wasn't about to consider necessities—a blanket, a machete, a hat. No. These are things to be bought with wages. But Méndez Acúbal had not earned this coin. It was his luck, an outright gift. It was given to him so he could play with it, so he could waste it, so he could have something impractical and beautiful.

Teodoro had no idea about prices. On his next trip to Jobel, he began to notice the dealings of buyers and sellers. Both appeared to be calm. The one feigning lack of interest, the other the desire to please, they spoke of pesos and centavos,[2] of pounds and

---

 Plot *What conflict is Teodoro experiencing?*

2. *Pesos and centavos* (sen tä′vōs) are coins used as currency in some Latin American countries. One hundred centavos equal one peso. ☆

Reading Practice

Analyze Characters Explain that analyzing a character's thoughts and actions can help students gain insight into a character's life. By recording information about Teodoro both before and after he finds the coin, students can better understand how finding the money has changed the character. Have students complete a three-column chart like the one shown.

(Students are likely to record the following opinions Teodoro has of himself: he considers himself humble before finding the coin; afterward he feels that he is a stronger man, becomes fearful, and wonders why his skin hasn't changed color. Students are likely to record the following actions: Teodoro walks with his head down and is a hard worker before finding the coin; after finding the coin, Teodoro then becomes unfriendly and silent with his family and thinks only about the coin.)

	Before Finding Coin	**After Finding Coin**
Opinion of Self		
Actions		

measures, of many other things that whirled about in Teodoro's head, making no sense at all.

Exhausted, Teodoro abandoned the struggle and took refuge in a delightful notion: with his silver coin he could buy anything he wanted.

Months went by before Teodoro made his **irrevocable** selection. It was a clay figurine, a small statue of the Virgin.[3] It was also a real find, because the figure lay in the midst of a clutter of objects that decorated the window of a store. From that time on, Teodoro hovered around it like a lover. Hours and hours went by. And always he was there, standing like a sentinel beside the window.

Don Agustín Velasco, the merchant, watched him with his tiny squinting eyes (eyes of a hawk, his mother would say) from inside the store.

Even before Teodoro acquired the custom of appearing in front of his establishment, the Indian's features had attracted the attention of Don Agustín. No Ladino[4] could help but notice a Chamula[5] walking on the sidewalks (reserved for the *caxlanes*), and less so when he walked as slowly as if out for a stroll. It was unusual for this to happen, and Don Agustín had not even considered it possible. But he now had to admit that things might go further: an

---

3. *Virgin* refers to Mary, the mother of Jesus.
4. *Ladino*, in the dialect of Chiapas, refers to an individual of mixed Mayan and Spanish heritage. Ladinos make up the middle class.
5. *Chamula* (chä mōō′lä) are a group of pure Mayan heritage, who make up the least privileged socioeconomic class.

---

2 **The Legacy of Colonialism** *How does this passage highlight the injustices and the racial prejudices that exist in this colonial society?*

Vocabulary

irrevocable (i rev′ə kə bəl) *adj.* incapable of being brought back, undone, or changed

---

Indian was also capable of daring to stand before a window contemplating the display, not just with the assurance of one who can appreciate it, but with the bold insolence of one who comes to buy.

Don Agustín's thin, yellowish face grimaced in a gesture of scorn. For an Indian to go to Guadalupe Street to shop for candles for his saints, or whiskey for his festivals, or tools for his work is acceptable. The people who deal with them have neither illustrious lineage nor family names; they have no fortunes and therefore work at demeaning jobs. For an Indian to enter a pharmacy to ask for healing powders or liquid potions or miraculous ointments can be tolerated. After all, pharmacists belong to the middle-class families that wish to move upward and mingle with their betters, and that is why it's good for the Indians to humble them by frequenting their places of business.

But for an Indian to position himself so firmly in front of a jewelry store—no ordinary jewelry store at that, but the one belonging to Don Agustín Velasco, descendant of conquistadors, well received in the best circles, appreciated by his colleagues—was, at the very least, unfathomable. Unless . . .

A terrible thought began to gnaw at him. What if the boldness of this Chamula was based on the strength of his tribe? It wouldn't be the first time, the salesman admitted bitterly. Rumors . . . where had he heard rumors of revolt? Quickly Don Agustín tried to recall the places he had visited in the past few days: the Bishop's Palace, the Casino, the meeting at Doña Romelia Ochoa's house.

What foolishness! Don Agustín smiled, silently laughing at himself. How right

---

Plot *Notice that the point of view has shifted from that of Teodoro to that of Don Agustín. Why do you think this shift has taken place, and how do you think it will affect the plot?* **4**

Big Idea **2**

The Legacy of Colonialism
Answer: *The injustice extends even to people's right to walk on the sidewalks. It shows that the lower classes are not even allowed the luxury of a leisurely stroll in town.*

Literary Element **3**

Plot **Ask:** What "interaction" between Teodoro and Don Agustín provides tension to the rising action of the story? *(Teodoro hovers outside the shop, which upsets Don Agustín, adding to the tension in the story.)*

Literary Element **4**

Plot **Answer:** *The author wants to explore the irrational fears that Don Agustín develops about Teodoro. These fears will lead to the climax of the story.*

Learning Objectives
Analyzing plot. (SE)
Analyzing art. (SE)
Analyzing characters. (TE)

Approaching Level

DIFFERENTIATED INSTRUCTION

Point of View Explain to students that the narrator's description of more than one character's thoughts and feelings indicates that that this story is told from the omniscient third-person point of view. Point out that the author's first use of Don Agustín's name indicates a point of view shift from Teodoro to Don Agustín. Tell students to look for this clue again later in the story.

English Learners

DIFFERENTIATED INSTRUCTION

Intermediate Direct students' attention to the author's use of the idiom "eyes of a hawk." (Explain that the usual English usage is "eyes like a hawk.") **Ask:** Using context clues, what do you think this means? *(Students should say that it means that Don Agustín sees everything that happens around him.)* Explain that many English idioms use animal characteristics to describe humans; for example,

someone may be described as "strong as a bull," "weak as a kitten," or "eating like a bird." Ask students to share any animal-related idioms from their native languages.

Teach

Literary Element | 1

Plot **Ask:** What internal conflict does Don Agustín face? *(He fears an Indian uprising.)*

Big Idea | 2

The Legacy of Colonialism

Ask: How does Don Agustín's idea of loss in this passage reflect the inequality of the classes? *(Don Agustín's idea of the "losses" that the caxlanes face in an uprising—the loss of land and material goods that were likely earned through conquest in the first place—belittles the loss the lower classes have suffered at the hands of the upper class and the risk the lower classes are willing to take to make themselves heard.)*

Bishop Manuel Oropeza had been when he said that every sin has its punishment. And Don Agustín, who rigorously abstained from alcohol, tobacco, and women, was still a slave to one bad habit: gossip.

Slyly he made himself a part of conversations in doorways, in the market, even in the Cathedral. Don Agustín was the first to hear a rumor, to sniff out the scandals, and he longed for shared confidences, for secrets to guard and for intrigues to plot.

And at night, after supper (of thick chocolate provided by his anxious, worn-out mother), Don Agustín made a habit of attending a gathering of some sort. There they talked and entertained each other with stories. About love affairs, feuds over inheritances, sudden and unexplained fortunes, duels. For several nights the conversation had revolved around one topic: Indian uprisings. Everyone present had been witness, participant, victim, or victor in one or another. They recalled details of those they had seen. Terrible images that made Don Agustín tremble: fifteen thousand

Visual Vocabulary
In Latin America, a *hacienda* generally refers to a large ranch, farm, or plantation, especially to the main building or owner's residence.

Chamulas ready for war, besieging Ciudad Real.[6] Haciendas plundered, men killed, women (no, no, we must not think of these things), women . . . in the end, violated.

Victory always fell on the side of the *caxlanes* (anything else would have been inconceivable), but at such a price, such loss.

Is experience worth anything? Judging by the Indian standing at the window of his jewelry store, no. The inhabitants of Ciudad Real, caught up in their daily routines and interests, forgot the past, which should serve

---

6. *Ciudad Real* (sü däd′rä äl′) is a city in Chiapas.

1204 UNIT 6 THE MODERN AMERICAS

as a lesson to them, and went about their business as if no danger threatened. Don Agustín was horrified by such an irresponsible attitude. The security of his life was so fragile that all it took was the face of a Chamula, seen through a glass, to shatter it completely.

Don Agustín looked out again into the street hoping to find the Indian no longer present. But Méndez Acúbal remained there still, motionless and attentive.

The passersby walked near him without any sign of surprise or alarm. This consoling fact (and the familiar sounds that came from the back of the house) restored Don Agustín's sense of tranquility. He could no longer justify his fears. Events like the one at Cancuc, like Pedro Díaz Cuscat's siege of Jobel, and Pajarito's threats[7]—those couldn't happen again. These were different times, more secure for decent people.

And besides, who was going to provide arms, who was going to lead the rebels? The Indian who was here, with his nose pressed against the window of the jewelry store, was alone. And if things got out of hand, no one was to blame but the townspeople themselves. No one was going to respect them if they themselves were not worthy of respect. Don Agustín disapproved of his fellow citizens' conduct, as if he had been betrayed by them.

They say that some—not many, thank God—even shake hands with the Indians. Indians—what a race of thieves!

The thought left a peculiarly painful taste in Don Agustín's mouth. Not only from a sense of **propriety,** as entrenched in him as in anyone else in his profession, but from a special circumstance.

---

7. *[Cancuc . . . Pajarito's threats]* are references to conflicts involving Maya and people of European descent.

Vocabulary

propriety (prə prī′ə tē) *n.* conformity to what is acceptable in conduct or speech

---

Writing Practice

PARTNERS **Dialogue** The author describes the conversations Don Agustín has about Indian uprisings when he is out at gatherings. Have pairs of students write an imagined one-page dialogue between Don Agustín and another caxlane based on the description the author provides. Tell students to remember to use tags to identify each speaker and to try to show each speaker's emotions through his or her words rather than describing them in the tags. To get students started, **ask** the following questions: **Is Don Agustín trying to convince people that the Indians will revolt? Are the others as afraid? What is their biggest fear? What action will they suggest, or are these plans all talk? Does everyone just want to share stories and gossip rather than gather facts and plan?**

Invite student pairs to share their dialogues with the class with each student reading a speaker's part.

Ranchos Orilleros, 1932. José Cúneo. Oil on burlap, 24 1/4 x 36 in. Private collection.

Don Agustín did not have the courage to admit it, but what tormented him was the suspicion that he was himself insignificant. And to make matters worse, his mother confirmed his suspicions in many ways. Her attitude toward this, her only child (son of Saint Anne,[8] she used to say), born when he was more a bother than a comfort, was one of Christian resignation. The "boy"—his mother and the servants continued to call him that in spite of the fact that Don Agustín was past forty—was very shy, cowardly, and passive. How many business deals had slipped through his fingers! And how many of those he did make resulted in nothing but failure! The Velasco fortune had dwindled considerably since Don Agustín took charge of things. And as for the prestige of the firm, it was maintained with great difficulty, and only because of the respect his late father, still mourned by mother and son, instilled in everyone.

But what could one expect from a wimp, an "overgrown child"? Don Agustín's mother shook her head sighing. And she kept on with her wheedling, her prudery, her **condescending** comments, for this was her way of expressing **disdain.**

Instinctively, the shopkeeper knew that he had before him the opportunity to prove his courage to others and himself. His zeal, his keen insight, would be evident to everyone. One simple word—thief—had given him the clue: the man with his nose pressed against the glass of his jewelry store was a thief. No doubt about it. Besides, the case was not uncommon. Don Agustín

4

Preview and Review *What information does the author provide here and earlier about Don Agustín?* **3**

Vocabulary

condescending (kon′ di sen′ding) *adj.* characterized by an air of superiority or smugness
disdain (dis dān′) *n.* an attitude of scorn or contempt for something considered inferior

---

8. *Saint Anne* was the mother of Mary, mother of Jesus.

ROSARIO CASTELLANOS **1205**

Teach

Reading Strategy **3**

Preview and Review
Answer: *He is shy, cowardly, passive, and unsuccessful; his mother sees him as a "bother" and despises him as a "wimp."*

Big Idea **4**

The Legacy of Colonialism
Ask: What are the Indians subjected to because of their race? *(They are suspected of being thieves without any proof or without even having committed a crime.)*

Learning Objectives
Analyzing plot. (SE)
Previewing and reviewing. (SE)
Writing dialogue. (TE)

Advanced Learners/Pre-AP

DIFFERENTIATED INSTRUCTION

Prejudice and Fear In the short story, Don Agustín reacts to Teodoro out of fear born of prejudice. He sees Teodoro as a "lowly" Indian. He also believes himself responsible for protecting his own higher class of citizens from people like Teodoro—all because Teodoro is looking in his shop window, contemplating a purchase. Have students pair up to investigate prejudice in contemporary society.

Have students find articles in newspapers, magazines, or on the Internet detailing incidents that have occurred because of prejudice. Invite pairs to create an oral and/or visual presentation on a particular incidence of prejudice that has taken place in one location. Have students comment on whether they believe attitudes have improved in the past decade, or whether prejudices have shifted from focusing on

one type of people to another, based on race, social standing, gender, sexual orientation, or another issue.

Teach

Literary Element   1

Plot **Answer:** *These details are part of the rising action.*

Literary Element   2

Plot **Answer:** *The climax occurs when Teodoro reaches into his sash to get his coin and Don Agustín thinks he is reaching for a weapon.*

Reading Strategy   3

Preview and Review
Answer: *It is ironic because Teodoro is not leading a revolt, and he is as frightened about coming into the store as Don Agustín is to have him there.*

Big Idea   4

The Legacy of Colonialism Ask: What does the resolution of the story say about the effect of colonialism on the Indians of Mexico? *(Students may say that the story shows that colonialism hurt the native peoples of Mexico.)*

ADVANCED **Ask:** What similarities does the resolution have with the way people behave in the real world? *(Students may say that the resolution of the story shows that inside people are afraid of the unknown and that the differences between people may be based on arbitrary ideas of ancestry and material wealth.)*

 To check students' understanding of the selection, see Unit 6 Teaching Resources Book, p. 133.

1206

---

could think of countless anecdotes of robberies and even worse crimes attributed to the Indians.

Satisfied with his deductions, Don Agustín didn't settle for merely preparing a defense. His sense of racial, class, and professional solidarity obliged him to share his suspicions with the other merchants, and together they went to the police. The neighborhood was prepared, thanks to the **diligence** of Don Agustín.

But the person responsible for those precautions suddenly disappeared from sight. After a few weeks he appeared again in his customary spot and in the same posture: standing guard. Because Teodoro didn't dare go in. No Chamula had ever attempted such a bold act. If he were to risk being the first, surely they would throw him out into the street before his lice had a chance to escape into the establishment. But, if by remotest chance they didn't eject him, and if they allowed him to remain inside the store long enough to discuss the matter, Teodoro wouldn't know how to express his desires. He could neither understand nor speak Spanish. And so, to unclog his ears, to loosen his tongue, he had been drinking Indian whiskey. The liquor had instilled in him a sense of power. His blood flowed, hot and fast, through his veins. The ease with which he moved his muscles dictated his actions. As if in a dream, he crossed the threshold of the jewelry store. But the cool dampness and the still, musty air inside brought him abruptly back to reality with a shock of terror. From a jewelry case the flashing eye of a diamond stared at him threateningly.

"May I help you, Chamula? What would you like?"

By repeating such pleasantries, Don Agustín sought to gain time. At the same time his hands searched for the gun he kept in the counter drawer. The Indian's silence frightened him more than any threat. He dared not raise his eyes until he had the gun in his hand.

The look he encountered paralyzed him. A gaze of surprise, of reproach. Why was the Indian staring at him like that? Don Agustín wasn't the one at fault. He was an honest man, he had never harmed anyone. And it appeared that he would be the first victim of these Indians who had suddenly set themselves up as judges! Here was his executioner, coming toward him with his fingers searching the folds of his sash, soon to draw forth who knows what instrument of death.

Don Agustín clutched the gun but could not fire. He cried out to the police for help.

When Teodoro tried to get away, he couldn't, because a crowd had gathered in the doorway of the store blocking his path. Shouts, gestures, angry faces. The police seized the Indian, questioned him, searched him. When the silver coin appeared in the folds of his sash, a shout of triumph arose from the crowd. Don Agustín excitedly held up the coin for all to see. The shouting exhilarated him. "Thief, thief!"

Teodoro Méndez Acúbal was taken to jail. Since the charges against him were not unusual, no one was in a hurry to gather the facts of the case. His file grew yellow with age on the shelves of the police department.   **4**

---

1 Plot *What part of the plot do these details represent?*

Vocabulary
diligence (dil′ ə jəns) *n.* persistent hard work

Plot *The climax is the moment of greatest tension, where the story can resolve itself in one or more ways. Identify the climax of this story.* **2**

Preview and Review *Is this story ironic? Explain.* **3**

1206 UNIT 6 THE MODERN AMERICAS

Grammar Practice

Avoid Sentence Fragments Explain to students that they should avoid using sentence fragments in academic writing. However, once students learn how to recognize and correct fragments, they can practice using them for artistic effect in their creative writing. **Write** on the board: The look he encountered paralyzed him. A gaze of surprise, of reproach. Point out to students that the fragment is missing a subject and a verb.

Ask: What does this fragment emphasize? *(The fragment emphasizes the look that Teodoro gives Don Agustín.)* Have students reread the paragraph that begins "When Teodoro tried to get away" and note the fragment it contains. Then, have students rewrite the paragraph and insert two of their own fragments for artistic effect. Students should explain their choices and what the fragments emphasize in the text.

After You Read

Respond and Think Critically

Respond and Interpret

1. (a)How did you react to the story's ending? (b)Why do you think you responded that way?

2. (a)According to the narrator, why does Teodoro find a coin that the *caxlanes* failed to notice? (b)What does this explanation suggest about relations between Chamulas and *caxlanes* in Jobel?

3. (a)What does Teodoro decide to purchase with the coin? (b)What does this decision suggest about him?

4. (a)Why does Don Agustín grow suspicious of Teodoro? (b)How does Don Agustín's family background influence his feelings regarding the Chamulas?

5. (a)What happens when Teodoro finally goes into the store? (b)How does Don Agustín misunderstand Teodoro's actions?

Analyze and Evaluate

6. What, if anything, did you find humorous in this story? Explain.

7. Do you think Teodoro is idealized in the story or portrayed realistically? Explain.

Connect

8. **Big Idea** **The Legacy of Colonialism** What do you think Castellanos is saying about colonial society in places like Jobel?

9. **Connect to Today** Do the social and justice systems in this story relate to modern-day class struggles in the United States? Explain.

Literary Element Plot

ACT Skills Practice

1. When does Don Agustín first begin to grow wary of Teodoro?

  A. Even before Teodoro begins to position himself in front of the shop.

  B. After Teodoro begins to position himself in front of the shop.

  C. After Teodoro enters the shop.

  D. After Teodoro reaches into his sash for the coin.

2. The resolution of the story occurs when Teodoro:

  F. finds the coin.

  G. decides to buy the clay figurine.

  H. enters the shop.

  J. goes to jail.

Review: Irony

As you learned on page 291, **irony** is a discrepancy between appearance and reality. **Dramatic irony** occurs when the reader or the audience of a literary work knows something a character does not know. It can be used for comic effect, to generate suspense, or to increase our sympathy for a character who is about to make a fateful error.

Partner Activity Meet with a classmate and discuss the dramatic irony in "The Luck of Teodoro Méndez Acúbal." Consider these questions in your discussion.

1. What dramatic irony develops from Don Agustín's fear of Teodoro?

2. (a)What dramatic irony occurs at the end of the story? (b)How does this irony affect your response to the ending? Explain.

Literary Element

1. **A** is the correct answer. The author states, "Even before Teodoro acquired the custom of appearing in front of his establishment, the Indian's features had attracted the attention of Don Agustín."

2. **J** is the correct answer. This is the point after the highest tension in the story.

Review: Irony

1. The irony is that Don Agustín's fear comes from his misinterpretation of Teodoro's own fearful actions.

2. (a) The reader knows that Teodoro found the coin he is accused of stealing. (b) Possible answer: This irony makes the ending more powerful because what seemed like good luck has brought Teodoro bad luck.

After You Read

Assess

1. (a) The ending may surprise students. (b) Students may mention the unfairness with which Teodoro is treated.

2. (a) He walks with his eyes cast down, while the *caxlanes* hold their heads high as they walk. (b) There is a sharp divide between the Chamulas and the *caxlanes*.

3. (a) a small clay statue of the Virgin Mary (b) He is religious.

4. (a) Teodoro stands at the window of the jewelry store. (b) He claims to be descended from conquistadors, who conquered the native peoples.

5. (a) Don Agustín has him arrested. (b) He mistakes Teodoro's reaching for the coin as reaching for a weapon.

6. Teodoro's finding the coin, the description of Don Agustín, and his relationship with his mother are all humorous.

7. He is not idealized. Castellanos describes his fearful behavior, his keeping the coin secret from his family, and his getting drunk before entering the store.

8. It is in dire need of reform to raise the living standards and the educational level of the lower classes.

9. Students will probably say that both systems exhibit inequities in the treatment of the upper and lower classes, but that in the United States the situation is not as bad because everyone has rights, including the right to legal representation and the right to a speedy trial; furthermore, the divisions between classes are less rigid in the United States than in Jobel.

 For additional assessment, see Assessment Resources, pp. 233–234.

After You Read

Reading Strategy

1. The art and the information in the first paragraph suggest that Jobel is a diverse place.

2. The title is ironic because Teodoro's luck turns out to be bad luck. The art is ironic because the image of diverse people living together contrasts with the story's reality of racial and class divisions.

Vocabulary Practice

Sample answers:

irrevocable <u>Synonyms</u>: permanent, irreversible, changeless

<u>Sample explanation</u>: Something irrevocable, like something irreversible, cannot be changed.

propriety <u>Synonyms</u>: decorum, respectability, suitability

<u>Sample explanation</u>: Someone who exhibits decorum, like someone who exhibits propriety, conforms to an accepted set of manners.

condescending <u>Synonyms</u>: arrogant, superior, scornful

<u>Sample explanation</u>: Both a condescending person and a scornful person would look down on others, although the connotations of *scornful* are slightly stronger.

disdain <u>Synonyms</u>: contempt, hatred, derision

<u>Sample explanation</u>: Both contempt and disdain are forms of hatred, but *contempt* implies more passionate engagement than *disdain*.

diligence <u>Synonyms</u>: persistence, assiduousness, constancy

<u>Sample explanation</u>: Someone who shows diligence would work consistently, as would someone who shows persistence.

Reading Strategy Preview and Review

You can deepen your understanding and enjoyment of a work when you **preview** it before you begin reading and then **review** it after you have finished. Previewing includes considering the title, looking at the art and trying to guess its relationship to the text, and skimming the first paragraph or two. Later, reviewing the text is a way to verify the accuracy of the predictions you made during your preview.

1. How do the art on the opening page and the information in the first paragraph give you a clue as to what the story is about?

2. In reviewing the story, what seems ironic about the title and the opening art?

Vocabulary Practice

Practice with Synonyms With a partner, brainstorm three synonyms for each boldfaced vocabulary word below. Then discuss your choices with your classmates.

irrevocable	propriety	condescending
disdain	diligence	

EXAMPLE: complacent

Synonyms: contented, serene, happy

Sample explanation: Both serene and complacent mean "contented," though complacent has more negative connotations.

Academic Vocabulary

The **structure** of the society in Castellanos's story consists of an upper class and a lower class.

Structure is an academic word often used to refer to the relations or hierarchies between different groups in a society. To further explore the meaning of this word, complete the following sentence.

_____ could be one advantage of living in a society with a rigid structure.

For more on academic vocabulary, see pages 36–37 and R83–R85.

Listening and Speaking

 Interview

Assignment Imagine you are an international reporter who has come to Jobel to write an article about the incident at the jewelry store. With a partner, role-play a 750-word interview with Teodoro or Don Agustín about their encounter that day.

Prepare Review the graphic organizer you filled out on page 1200. Using that information as a starting point, discuss the interview subject's character traits and motivation with your partner. Also discuss what facts may have been overlooked in other reports of the incident. If you are the reporter, prepare a list of probing questions that would help you uncover the truth about the incident. Remember that your questions should reflect an objective stance.

If you are the interviewee, prepare to role-play by reviewing your character's behavior in the story. Think about what questions the reporter might ask and imagine how your character would respond.

Interview If you are the reporter, take careful notes on your subject's responses. Allow your subject to respond completely to each question, ask further questions to clarify information, and check to make sure you have recorded your subject's statements correctly. If you are the interviewee, remember to stay in your role, speaking as your character rather than expressing your own ideas and opinions.

Report Write a brief reflection on how role-playing helped you better understand the themes of the story. If you are the interviewee, you may wish to comment on what was frustrating about playing your character.

Evaluate Write a paragraph evaluating your partner's performance in the interview.

 Literature Online

Selection Resources For Selection Quizzes, eFlashcards, and Reading-Writing Connection activities, go to glencoe.com and enter QuickPass code GLW6053u6.

Academic Vocabulary

Possible answer: A sense of certainty about one's identity could be one advantage of living in a society with a rigid structure.

 For grammar practice, see Unit 6 Teaching Resources Book, p. 132.

Listening and Speaking

Students' interviews should

- be based on the characterization in the story
- include objective and respectful questions
- include written reflections that show an understanding of the story's themes

Comparing Literature
Across Time and Place

Compare Literature About Animals

The beauty and the mystery of animal life continue to inspire authors and readers in today's technological age. The following literary works by Pablo Neruda (pä´blō nā rōō´dä), Rainer Maria Rilke (rī nər mä rē´ä ril´kə), Isak Dinesen (ē säk dē´nə sən), and Po Chü-i demonstrate how animals spark our imaginations and influence our lives.

Horses by Pablo Neruda...poem 1210
CHILE, 1958

The Panther by Rainer Maria Rilke...............................poem 1215
AUSTRIA / CZECH REPUBLIC, 1906

The Iguana from
Out of Africa by Isak Dinesen...............................nonfiction 1216
DENMARK, 1937

The Red Cockatoo by Po Chü-i...................................poem 1218
CHINA, c. 800

COMPARE THE Big Idea **Nature and the Imagination**

Humans have drastically altered the earth's natural landscape in the process of developing their societies. This process of change provides the backdrop for these four literary works, each of which takes place in a region where plants and animals have been put in captivity or otherwise impacted by humans. As you read, ask yourself, How does each author show the relationship between people and animals?

COMPARE Portrayals of Animals

Wild or domestic, common or exotic, animals serve many purposes in literature. To some authors, animals are relatable figures with tendencies much like our own. To others, animals symbolize qualities that are frightening, inspiring, or even sublime. As you read, ask yourself, What do the animals in these works represent for the authors?

COMPARE Styles

An author's established style often shapes the subject of his or her work. Neruda, Rilke, Dinesen, and Po Chü-i have distinct styles that make comparing their work a productive way to see how a similar subject can be treated in a variety of ways. As you read, ask yourself, What are the similarities and differences between these authors' styles?

Learning Objectives

For pages 1209–1219
In studying these texts, you will focus on the following objectives:

Literary Study: Analyzing alliteration.

Reading:
Evaluating figurative language.
Comparing cultural contexts.
Comparing themes.

Writing: Writing a poem.

Horse and a Youth in Blue, 1905-1906. Pablo Picasso. Watercolour and gouache on paper, 49.8 x 32.1 cm. Tate Gallery, London. © ARS, NY.

 Literature Online

Author Search For more about Pablo Neruda, Rainer Maria Rilke, Isak Dinesen, and Po Chü-i, go to glencoe.com and enter QuickPass code GLW6053u6.

COMPARING LITERATURE **1209**

Comparing Literature
Across Time and Place

Focus

Bellringer Options

Selection Focus
Transparencies 74–76
Daily Language Practice
Transparency 116

Ask: What are your favorite animal stories or films? *(Students' responses will vary.)* Why do you think animals inspire artists and writers as well as fascinate readers and viewers? *(Students may say animals inspire artists because of their "otherness" and their nature as soft and cute, or wild and dangerous. Students may say animals inspire readers and viewers because they share the same fascination as those who create the art.)*

Connect to the Reading Selections

Have students discuss any experience they have had with the four types of animals described in the selection titles. Students may describe the emotions each type of animal inspires in them.

Selection Skills

Literary Elements
- Alliteration (SE pp. 1211, 1213, 1214)
- Oxymoron (TE p. 1212)

Reading Skills
- Evaluate Figurative Language (SE pp. 1211, 1213, 1214; TE pp. 1215, 1216)
- Monitor Comprehension Using Graphic Organizer (TE p. 1210)

Comparing Literature

Vocabulary Skills
- Practice with Word Usage (SE p. 1214)

Writing/Grammar Skills
- Write a Poem (SE p. 1214)
- Literary Analysis (SE p. 1219)
- Use Main and Subordinate Clauses (TE p. 1216)
- Quickwrite (SE pp. 1215, 1218)

Before You Read

Focus

Summary

In this poem, the speaker describes watching horses from a window on a cold winter day in Berlin. The horses are so vibrant and alive that the memory of their beauty has erased the essence of the cold winter.

> For summaries in languages other than English, see Unit 6 Teaching Resources Book, pp. 136–141.

Before You Read

Chile

Horses

Meet **Pablo Neruda**
(1904–1973)

A s a shy, lonely boy growing up in southern Chile, Pablo Neruda immersed himself in literature and the natural world. "Nature there went to my head like a strong whiskey," he commented. "I was barely ten at the time, but already a poet." At age fifteen, Neruda began publishing his work, and by his early twenties, he was one of Chile's most popular authors.

Early Fame Neruda was born Neftalí Ricardo Reyes Basoalto. However, because his father disapproved of his literary aspirations, the poet published his first collection of poems using the pen name Pablo Neruda. Later, he changed his name legally. His second collection, *Twenty Love Poems and a Song of Despair*, achieved instant popularity when it was published in 1924; even so, Neruda was unable to earn a living by writing. To earn money, he entered Chile's diplomatic service, beginning a life of travel and adventure.

Travel, Politics, and Poetry Neruda took diplomatic positions in Asia, South America, and Europe, drawing poetic inspiration from the places he saw and the people he met. In 1933, he published the collection *Residence on Earth*, in which he moved beyond his earlier lyrical poems to a more experimental technique and a darker, surrealist vision. During his subsequent involvement with the Spanish Civil War, Neruda grew deeply committed to left-wing politics. In the poems in *Spain in My Heart* (1937), he expressed socialist ideals in impassioned verse.

In 1940, Neruda took a post as a consul in Mexico, where he studied that country's ancient civilizations. After returning to Chile, he joined

> "If you ask what my poetry is, I must confess that I don't know; but if you'll ask my poetry, it will tell you who I am."
>
> —Pablo Neruda

the Communist Party and won election to the Senate. After harshly criticizing the president, however, he was forced to move abroad. He left Chile on horseback, crossing the Andes mountains by night. For the next several years, Neruda traveled through the Soviet Union, Poland, Hungary, and Mexico.

The Voice of a Continent In 1952, Neruda returned to his beloved Chile. In 1971, he was awarded the Nobel Prize in Literature. When presenting the prize, Swedish Academy member Karl Ragnar Gierow emphasized that, while Neruda's body of work has universal appeal, it speaks particularly to the people of Latin America. "In [Neruda's] work," he commented, "a continent awakens to consciousness."

Reading Practice

Monitor Comprehension Students should compare the authors' works and styles at the end of this section, monitoring their comprehension by filling in a chart as they read.

Author	Genre	Tone	Message/Theme
Neruda			
Rilke			
Dinesen			
Po Chu-i			

Have students record information for each selection after they finish reading. Remind students that tone is the attitude an author shows toward the subject of a literary work, and the theme is sometimes a message or lesson on how to live. Encourage Approaching Level and English learners to work in pairs if necessary.

(Possible answers: Neruda: poetry; awe; the beauty of nature can change one's outlook. Rilke: poetry; concern; caging animals paralyzes their wild nature. Dinesen: nonfiction prose; disappointment or curiosity; killing something beautiful kills what makes it beautiful. Po Chu-i: poetry; disgust; people will try to possess what they cannot understand.)

Literature and Reading Preview

Connect to the Poem

What qualities do you associate with horses? Discuss this question with a partner. Consider the size, strength, and appearance of real horses and horses you know from movies or books.

Build Background

Pablo Neruda wrote about 50 volumes of poetry in a career that spanned half a century. Some of his poems are dense, highly experimental works; others are simple and direct. Uniting the different phases of his career are his love for the people and the landscape of Chile, his exuberance, and the freshness of his imagery.

Set Purposes for Reading

Big Idea Nature and the Imagination

As you read, ask yourself, How does the natural world function as a source of meaning in the Latin American literary tradition?

Literary Element Alliteration

Alliteration is the repetition of consonant sounds at the beginnings of words. Poets often use alliteration to emphasize a particular line by making it more memorable, or to echo the mood or the action of a poem. As you read, ask yourself, Where and why does Neruda use alliteration?

Reading Strategy Evaluate Figurative Language

Figurative language is language used for descriptive effect to convey ideas or emotions. Metaphors, similes, and personification are figurative language. When you **evaluate figurative language**, you identify these expressions and judge how effective they are. As you read, ask yourself, How effective is Neruda's use of figurative language to evoke an idea or a feeling?

Tip: Use a Graphic Organizer As you read the poem, assess Neruda's figurative language using a diagram like this one.

Passage	Type of Figurative Language	Evaluation
"The air white like a moistened loaf."	Simile	Effective because it gives the reader the physical sensation of a damp, bleak winter day

Vocabulary

sheer (shēr) *adj.* unmixed; pure; p. 1213 *Alex felt sheer joy as he held his newborn daughter for the first time.*

disgruntled (dis grən′təld) *adj.* unhappy; grumpy; p. 1213 *After yet another customer treated him rudely, the disgruntled waiter announced he was quitting.*

unwitting (un wit′ing) *adj.* not knowing; unaware; p. 1213 *The vendor assured the unwitting tourist that the sunglasses he was selling were designer brands.*

obliterate (ə blit′e rāt′) *v.* to erase from memory; to destroy all traces of; p. 1213 *Maureen sought to obliterate her unsuccessful past by moving to another city and starting a new career.*

Tip: Word Usage When you encounter a new word, it might help you to answer specific questions about the word. For example, Do you know someone who is frequently **disgruntled**? How does this person behave?

PABLO NERUDA **1211**

Comparing Literature

Before You Read

Focus

Vocabulary

Word Origins Have students look up vocabulary words in the dictionary to determine the original source of each word. Then, have students compare each word's source to see if any of the words share origins (sheer *and* disgruntled *both come from Middle English,* obliterate *is from Latin, and* unwitting *comes from Old English*).

 For additional vocabulary practice, see Unit 6 Teaching Resources Book, p. 144.

Literary History ☆

Chilean Connections Gabriela Mistral, author of a collection of work highlighted in the Independent Reading section of this unit, encouraged young Pablo Neruda to write. As an adult, Neruda traveled the world and experienced other countries with similar colonial backgrounds to Chile, influencing his leftist political leanings. Later in life he supported Salvador Allende, president of Chile and uncle to Isabel Allende, the author of "My Invented Country" that is excerpted in this unit.

Approaching Level

DIFFERENTIATED INSTRUCTION

Reading Poetry Prepare students to read poetry by reviewing a poetry selection from earlier in the book. Remind them that poems often use inverted sentence structure, requiring students to rearrange the clauses and phrases in the sentence for comprehension. Also remind students that they should follow the punctuation in a poem, pause at commas, and stop at periods rather than at the end of lines.

Advanced Learners/Pre-AP

DIFFERENTIATED INSTRUCTION

Comparing Neruda's Work Invite students to find one of Pablo Neruda's poems that describes an everyday item, such as "Ode to My Socks." Have students write a short essay comparing his use of imagery, tone, and figurative language in "Horses" to that in the other poem. Challenge students to consider their attitude toward the poems and explain which poem they prefer and why.

Teach

Reading Strategy   1

Evaluate Figurative Language Ask: What does the simile in line 4 compare? What does this use of figurative language evoke? *(The simile compares the air to a moist loaf of bread. The comparison evokes the image of moist, squishy air, full of the condensation from the exhaling of people and animals.)*

 For additional practice using the reading skill or strategy, see Unit 6 Teaching Resources Book, p. 143.

Horses

Pablo Neruda
Translated by Alastair Reid

The Small Yellow Horses, 1912. Franz Marc. Germany Staatsgalerie, Stuttgart.

It was from the window I saw the horses.

I was in Berlin, in winter. The light
was without light, the sky skyless.

1 The air white like a moistened loaf.

Literary Element Practice

Oxymoron Explain to students that an oxymoron is a statement of contradictory terms. Direct students' attention to lines 2–3 of the poem. **Ask:** What oxymorons do you find in these lines? *(The speaker says that the "light was without light" and the "sky skyless.")* Discuss poetry's use of figurative language to describe everyday things in a new way. **Ask:** Why might a poet use an oxymoron? *(Students may say that an oxymoron will cause readers to stop their reading and try to imagine what the poet is really trying to describe.)* **Ask:** What do you visualize when you think of "light … without light" and a "skyless" sky? *(Responses will vary. Students may say the description causes them to imagine a sky so bright that it has no edges.)*

Have students write an oxymoron to describe an item they use everyday, such as a backpack or pair of shoes. Encourage students to share their samples with the class.

5 From my window, I could see a deserted arena,
a circle bitten out by the teeth of winter.

All at once, led out by a man,
ten horses were stepping into the snow.
Emerging, they had scarcely rippled into existence
10 like flame, than they filled the whole world of my eyes,
empty till now. Faultless, flaming,
they stepped like ten gods on broad, clean hooves,
their manes recalling a dream of pure grace.

Their rumps were globes, were oranges.

15 Their color was amber and honey, was on fire.

Their necks were towers
carved from the stone of pride,
and in their furious eyes, **sheer** energy
showed itself, a prisoner inside them.

20 And there, in the silence, at the midpoint of the day, in a dirty, **disgruntled** winter,
the horses' intense presence was blood,
was rhythm, was the beckoning Grail° of being.

I saw, I saw, and, seeing, I came to life.
25 There was the **unwitting** fountain, the dance of gold,
the sky,
the fire that sprang to life in beautiful things.

I have **obliterated** that gloomy Berlin winter.

I shall not forget the light from these horses.

23 **Grail:** in legend, the cup used by Jesus at the Last Supper. It was sought by Arthurian knights during a long, difficult quest.

---

2 Evaluate Figurative Language *Does the poet's use of personification enhance your sense of the setting? Explain.*

3 Nature and the Imagination *What do the horses represent to the speaker?*

Alliteration *How does the use of alliteration contribute to the meaning of these lines?* **4**

Vocabulary

sheer (shēr) *adj.* unmixed; pure
disgruntled (dis grən′təld) *adj.* unhappy; grumpy
unwitting (un wit′ing) *adj.* not knowing; unaware
obliterate (ə blit′e rāt′) *v.* to erase from memory; to destroy all traces of

PABLO NERUDA **1213**

Reading Strategy	**2**

Evaluate Figurative Language Answer: *The personification enhances the setting because it gives the sense of bitter, cold weather.*

Big Idea	**3**

Nature and the Imagination Answer: *They represent life and perhaps divinity.*
Review simile with students. **Ask: What is the speaker comparing in line 12?** *(the horses and gods)*
APPROACHING Ask: What does this comparison say about how the speaker feels about the horses? *(Students may say the speaker thinks the horses are amazing or larger than life.)*

Literary Element	**4**

Alliteration Answer: *The repetition of the "b" sound in* blood, beckoning, *and* being *creates an intense rhythm, similar to the "rhythm" mentioned in line 23.*

English Learners
DIFFERENTIATED INSTRUCTION

Advanced Point out to English learners the verbs Neruda uses in "Horses." Explain that an action verb is a word that describes physical or mental action. **(Example: The cat *swiped* at the yarn.)** Have students identify action verbs in the poem. *(Students may identify* saw, stepped, recalling, showed, sprang, *and* obliterated, *among others.)*

Advanced Learners/Pre-AP
DIFFERENTIATED INSTRUCTION

Visual Presentation Pablo Neruda describes the horses using words associated with art. Have students find pictures of statues in Berlin, Germany, that feature horses. Have students write a short essay comparing Neruda's description to the horses depicted in stone or bronze. Students may consider whether the artists have captured a horse's energy as Neruda has. Encourage students to present their ideas and show the pictures they have found to the class.

Learning Objectives
Evaluating figurative language. (SE)
Analyzing alliteration. (SE)
Analyzing oxymoron. (TE)

After You Read

Assess

1. Answers will vary.
2. (a) They are probably being trained or exercised. (b) The presence of the horses suggests the essential elements of life.
3. (a) They make the speaker feel alive again. (b) The speaker's response to the horses has made him forget the weather.
4. (a) Neruda may be describing an actual experience, or wish to contrast city with nature. (b) Cold contrasts with the warmth of the horses' presence.
5. (a) gloomy, depressing, or somber (b) It begins to change in line 7 as the horses emerge.
6. (a) Answers will vary. (b) Students should give specific reasons for their opinions.
7. The speaker is part of an urban world but connects to the natural world through the horses.
8. Some will argue that nature still has an ability to connect people to something greater than themselves. Others may point out that people are less connected to nature than they have been in past generations.

 For additional assessment, see Assessment Resources, pp. 235–236.

Literary Element

1. The repetition of the "f" sound emphasizes the horses' movement.
2. It gives a rhythm to the lines and increases their emotional impact.

After You Read

Respond and Think Critically

Respond and Interpret

1. What emotions did you feel as you finished reading this poem? Explain.
2. (a) Why do you think the horses are being led outside? (b) In your opinion, what do lines 22 and 23 of the poem mean?
3. (a) How do the horses affect the speaker? (b) What does the speaker mean by "I have obliterated that gloomy Berlin winter" (line 27)?

Analyze and Evaluate

4. (a) Why might Neruda have set this poem in a city rather than the countryside? (b) Why might Neruda have set this poem in winter?

5. (a) **Mood** is the overall feeling of a literary work. What mood is established early in the poem? Explain. (b) When does the mood change, and how does Neruda achieve this effect?
6. **Style** is an author's distinctive manner of expression—not *what* is said, but *how* it is said. (a) What aspects of Neruda's style stood out to you? (b) How effective is Neruda's style? Explain.

Connect

7. **Big Idea** **Nature and the Imagination** How is the speaker in this poem both separated from and connected to the natural world?
8. **Connect to Today** Is Neruda's message of the power of nature still relevant for readers today? Explain.

Literary Element Alliteration

Alliteration, the repetition of consonant sounds, can emphasize rhythm and convey emotion.

1. Explain the cumulative effect of the alliteration in lines 10 and 11.
2. Why do you think alliteration is used in lines 20–26?

Reading Strategy Evaluate Figurative Language

Evaluating figurative language means assessing an author's use of devices such as simile, metaphor, and personification.

Partner Activity With a partner, discuss how the use of personification in line 21 contributes to the poem.

 Literature Online

Selection Resources For Selection Quizzes, eFlashcards, and Reading-Writing Connection activities, go to glencoe.com and enter QuickPass code GLW6053u6.

Vocabulary Practice

Practice with Word Usage Respond to these statements to explore the vocabulary words.

1. Describe a moment when you felt **sheer** terror.
2. List things that might cause an employee to become **disgruntled**.
3. Explain an incident when someone was **unwitting**.
4. Name a natural phenomenon that could **obliterate** a city.

Writing

Write a Poem Write a poem describing an experience you have had with nature that reminds you of the speaker's experience. For example, you might write about an encounter with an animal. Use alliteration to enhance the emotional effects of your poem and figurative language to make it more vivid. For ideas, refer to the chart you filled out on page 1211.

Reading Strategy

The personification of winter as "dirty" and "disgruntled" gives insight into the speaker's mental and emotional state.

Vocabulary Practice

1. Answers will vary.
2. Students might list poor working conditions, unequal treatment, or unfair pay.
3. Student's explanations will vary.

4. Students might mention earthquakes, hurricanes, or tsunamis.

Writing

Students' poems should
- describe an emotional encounter with the natural world
- use alliteration
- use figurative language

Build Background

In 1902, Austrian-Czech author Rainer Maria Rilke (1875–1926) went to Paris, France, to write a book about French sculptor Auguste Rodin. The artist's ability to capture the essence of a being or an object impressed Rilke. In *dinggedichte* ("thing-poems"), Rilke attempted a similar focus and offered exacting descriptions of animals, landscapes, works of art, and physical objects. The speaker's feelings are usually left unstated, yet Rilke suggested them by focusing on the visible world. "The Panther" describes a caged animal in a Paris park.

The Panther

Rainer Maria Rilke
Translated by Stephen Mitchell

☆ *In the Jardin des Plantes, Paris*

His vision, from the constantly passing bars
has grown so weary that it cannot hold
anything else. It seems to him there are
a thousand bars; and behind the bars, no
world.

5 As he paces in cramped circles, over and
   over,
1 the movement of his powerful soft strides
is like a ritual dance around a center
in which a mighty will stands paralyzed.

Only at times, the curtain of the pupils
10 lifts, quietly—. An image enters in,
rushes down through the tensed, arrested
   muscles,
plunges into the heart and is gone.

Last Refuge. Yvonne Delvo. Oil on canvas.
Private collection.

 Quickwrite

The poet W. H. Auden wrote that Rilke conveys ideas with "physical rather than intellectual symbols . . . Rilke thinks of the human in terms of the nonhuman." What idea about humankind might Rilke be conveying through the image of the panther? Write a few paragraphs addressing this question.

RAINER MARIA RILKE **1215**

Advanced Learners/Pre-AP

DIFFERENTIATED INSTRUCTION

Research Explain to students that in centuries past, monarchs and other rulers often collected animals from conquered lands; in some cases, the animals were given as good-will gestures from the rulers of far-away countries and considered entertainment for the public, who flocked to see the exotic and unusual. Invite students to research this practice in France, especially in the seventeenth and eighteenth centuries.

Have students find out what types of animals could be found in the parks and zoos of the time and where they came from. Encourage students to share their discoveries with the class.

Comparing Literature

Before You Read

Focus

Summary

In this poem, the speaker describes a panther pacing in a small cage in a Parisian park. The panther only sees the bars as it constantly circles; every so often, something catches its eye but is gone just as quickly, leaving no lasting impression.

Teach

Reading Strategy **1**

Evaluate Figurative Language Ask: What does the simile in lines 5–8 describe? *(The simile compares the panther's pacing to a ritual dance done around a "mighty will" that is paralyzed.)*

Literary History ☆

Worpswede School Rilke was a member of an artists' group in Worpswede, Germany, in the late 1880s and 1890s. Rilke found inspiration with the group and wrote about the artists and the landscape that influenced their romantic paintings.

 **Quickwrite**

Rilke uses clear diction and imagery that is surprising, arresting, powerful, and evocative. He may be conveying the idea that people need to live freely in order to perceive the world with clarity.

Learning Objective
Evaluating figurative language. (TE)

1215

Comparing Literature

Before You Read

Focus

Summary

In this excerpt from *Out of Africa*, Dinesen describes her attraction to the beautiful colors of an iguana's skin. She describes what happened when she killed one of the lizards: its skin lost its color in death. When Dinesen sees a native girl wearing a bracelet that reminds her of the iguana, she buys it from the girl only to find that it loses its luster on her own arm. In the hopes of encouraging people to value what is alive, she implores the settlers of East Africa not to shoot iguanas.

Teach

Reading Strategy | 1

Evaluate Figurative Language **Ask:** What figurative language does Dinesen use in this passage? *(a simile)* How does the simile indicate an iguana's worth? *(By comparing an iguana to precious stones or a stained glass window, Dinesen shows the value of the lizard.)*

Build Background

Before becoming an author, Isak Dinesen (1885–1962) studied painting; later she said this training taught her how to observe nature. Dinesen, whose legal name was Karen Blixen, was born into an upper-class Danish family and moved to Africa after her marriage. Seven years later, when her marriage had fallen apart, she stayed in Africa to run a large coffee plantation near Nairobi, Kenya. Her 1937 memoir, *Out of Africa*, portrays incidents that occurred on the plantation, her friendships with Africans and colonists, and her relationship with English hunter Denys Finch-Hatton. The book also reflects her deep love for Africa.

THE IGUANA
from Out of Africa Isak Dinesen

I n the Reserve I have sometimes come upon the Iguana, the big lizards, as they were sunning themselves upon a flat stone in a riverbed. They are not pretty in shape, but nothing can be imagined more beautiful than their coloring. They shine like a heap of **1** precious stones or like a pane cut out of an old church window. When, as you approach, they swish away, there is a flash of azure, green and purple over the stones, the color seems to be standing behind them in the air, like a comet's luminous tail.

Guana, plate from *Brehms Tierleben Allgemeine Kunde des Tierreichs*, 1892. Colour lithograph. Private collection.

1216 UNIT 6 THE MODERN AMERICAS

Grammar Practice

Use Main and Subordinate Clauses Review with students the difference between a main and a subordinate clause. A main, or independent clause, is a sentence that can stand by itself. A subordinate clause, although it has a subject and verb, cannot stand alone. It often begins with conjunctions such as *because, as if, which,* and *while,* and it shows relationships in time, contrast, result, and condition, as well as giving other information.

Ask students to identify the main and subordinate clauses in this sentence and identify the relationship the subordinate clause describes:

When you approach, they swish away. (When you approach *is the subordinate clause;* they swish away *is the main clause; the subordinate clause begins with* when *and describes relationship of time*).

Have students create a complex sentence that contains a main and subordinate clause from these sentences. "Once I shot an Iguana. I thought that I should be able to make some pretty things from his skin." *(Possible response: Once I shot an Iguana because I thought that I should be able to make some pretty things from his skin.)*

Once I shot an Iguana. I thought that I should be able to make some pretty things from his skin. A strange thing happened then, that I have never afterwards forgotten. As I went up to him, where he was lying dead upon his stone, and actually while I was walking the few steps, he faded and grew pale, all color died out of him as in one long sigh, and by the time that I touched him he was gray and dull like a lump of concrete. It was the live impetuous blood pulsating within the animal, which had radiated out all that glow and splendor. Now that the flame was put out, and the soul had flown, the Iguana was as dead as a sandbag.

Often since I have, in some sort, shot an Iguana, and I have remembered the one of the Reserve. Up at Meru I saw a young Native girl with a bracelet on, a leather strap two inches wide, and embroidered all over with very small turquoise-colored beads which varied a little in color and played in green, light blue and ultramarine. It was an extraordinarily live thing; it seemed to draw breath on her arm, so that I wanted it for myself, and made Farah buy it from her. No sooner had it come upon my own arm than it gave up the ghost.[1] It was nothing now, a small, cheap, purchased article of finery. It had been the play of colors, the duet between the turquoise and the "nègre,"—

So sad did it seem that I remembered the saying of the hero in a book that I had read as a child:"I have conquered them all, but I am standing amongst graves."

that quick, sweet, brownish black, like peat[2] and black pottery, of the Native's skin,—that had created the life of the bracelet.

In the Zoological Museum of Pietermaritzburg, I have seen, in a stuffed deep-water fish in a showcase, the same combination of coloring, which there had survived death; it made me wonder what life can well be like, on the bottom of the sea, to send up something so live and airy. I stood in Meru and looked at my pale hand and at the dead bracelet, it was as if an injustice had been done to a noble thing, as if truth had been suppressed. So sad did it seem that I remembered the saying of the hero in a book that I had read as a child: "I have conquered them all, but I am standing amongst graves."

In a foreign country and with foreign species of life one should take measures to find out whether things will be keeping their value when dead. To the settlers of East Africa I give the advice: "For the sake of your own eyes and heart, shoot not the Iguana." ◊

2

---

2. *Peat* is a plant-based fuel source.

💬 **Discussion Starter**

Dinesen compares the experience of shooting an iguana with that of buying a beaded bracelet from a young girl. Do you think this comparison is appropriate or effective? Explain. How does this comparison reflect the larger issue of European colonialism in Africa? Discuss these issues in a small group.

---

1. In this context, *gave up the ghost* means "became lifeless."

ISAK DINESEN **1217**

Comparing Literature

Teach

Big Idea 2

Nature and the Imagination Ask: How has Dinesen's imagination altered her view of nature? *(Students may say that Dinesen's imagination turns the situation with the iguana into a life-altering moment in which she realizes that capturing or killing something doesn't let you possess it.)*

Discussion Starter

Some may say that this comparison shows that trying to possess beautiful objects ruins their value. Others may find the comparison inappropriate because it compares killing a living thing to buying an inanimate object. Dinesen's main idea—that some victors destroy what they conquer—may be a criticism of the European domination of African peoples.

Learning Objectives
Evaluating figurative language. (TE)
Using main and subordinate clauses. (TE)

Approaching Level

DIFFERENTIATED INSTRUCTION

Flashbacks Review with students that a flashback is an interruption in a narrative to describe something that happened before the current action. Instruct students to reread the paragraph that begins "In the Zoological Museum...." **Ask:** What clue has the author given to help you understand that this is a flashback? *(The place of the action has changed from the Reserve to a museum.)*

Explain to students that flashbacks are often used to help readers better understand the current action or situation of a story. **Ask:** What does this flashback help explain? *(The flashback helps contrast the author's experience with the iguana, which loses its color in death, to an observation she made when viewing a dead deep-water fish, which still had its beautiful coloring.)*

English Learners

DIFFERENTIATED INSTRUCTION

Intermediate Discuss with English learners the colors that Dinesen uses to describe the iguana's skin and the beads on the bracelet. Have students identify colors they recognize and look up those with which they aren't familiar. Encourage students to do an Internet search for the colors so that they may see the colors as well as read a description. *(Students are likely to look up azure, turquoise, and ultramarine.)*

Before You Read

Focus

Summary

This poem describes a gift of a bird. In addition to describing its colorful plumage and ability to talk, the speaker comments that the bird shares the fate of intelligent people—to be caged.

Teach

Big Idea

Nature and the Imagination **Ask:** What comment is the speaker making about freedom and imagination? *(The speaker suggests that one may only be imaginative if one is free and that those without imagination wish to punish those who have it.)*

Quickwrite

Po's red cockatoo symbolizes how society often "cages" people. Some may say the problem persists in modern society; others may feel today's world is more accepting and diverse.

Build Background

Poet Po Chü-i (772–846) devoted his life to uniting literature with social protest. Born to a poor family in China's Henan province, Po began writing poems at the age of five. As an adult, he worked as a government official and became highly critical of the corrupt, decadent lifestyle of China's upper class. In 814, he was exiled for slandering members of the court. Po also became an outspoken critic of the courtly poetry that dominated Chinese literature at the time. For Po, the elegant nature poetry of the court only demonstrated that literature had become divorced from its moral and social functions. "The work of literature," he wrote, "must truthfully reflect the life of the people." To this end, Po wrote satirical and allegorical poems based on the forms of traditional folk ballads. In these poems, he criticized the greed of public officials and portrayed the hardships of China's oppressed peasant class.

THE *Red* COCKATOO

Po Chü-i
Translated by Arthur Waley

Sent as a present from Annam—
A red cockatoo.
Colored like the peach-tree blossom,
Speaking with the speech of men.
And they did to it what is always done
To the learned and eloquent.
They took a cage with stout bars
And shut it up inside.

Quickwrite

Po Chü-i wrote poems that were allegories of the problems he saw in courtly society. What problem is he responding to in this poem? How does he use the red cockatoo to address it? Do similar problems exist in contemporary society? Write a paragraph addressing these questions.

Birds of Asia. John Gould. Coloured lithograph. Christie's Images.

Reading Practice

Analyze Tone Discuss with students the process of analyzing tone, or the author's attitude toward the subject matter of a literary work. Explain that word choice, figures of speech, and even punctuation and sentence structure can all convey tone. Have students reread "The Red Cockatoo" and then answer the following questions. **Ask:** How does the poem's sentence structure help convey tone? *(Students may say the short lines and the direct, to-the-point sentences help convey a disappointed, angry tone.)* How does figurative language in the poem help convey the tone? *(Students may say the description of the bird's beautiful colors contrasted with the description of the strong cage help convey a tone of disgust that someone could do something so cruel to the animal.)* How does the poet's word choice help convey tone? *(Students may say the use of "what is always done" and "shut it up" express a negative attitude toward people who would stifle beauty or creativity; the use of "learned and eloquent," which are creative ways to describe a talking bird, make the bird's imprisonment that much more unthinkable.)*

Wrap-Up: Comparing Literature

Across Time and Place

- *Horses* by Pablo Neruda
- *The Panther* by Rainer Maria Rilke
- *The Iguana from Out of Africa* by Isak Dinesen
- *The Red Cockatoo* by Po Chü-i

COMPARE THE `Big Idea` Nature and the Imagination

Visual Display The literary works by Neruda, Rilke, Dinesen, and Po Chü-i demonstrate the influence of setting on our lives. Using works of art from the authors' cultures (contemporary Latin America, early-twentieth-century Europe, late colonial Africa, and Tang dynasty China), create a collage that illustrates the relationship between the natural world and human society that these works suggest. Share your display with your classmates.

COMPARE Portrayals of Animals

Group Activity The authors here use animals for a variety of purposes. In a small group, discuss the following questions. Cite evidence from the texts to support your points.

1. In these literary works, animals function as rounded characters, objects of another character's reflections, and symbols. Which of these categories best applies to the animal(s) in each of the works? Explain.

2. Where is the speaker or the narrator located in relation to the animal(s) in each of the works? Does he or she take part in the action described?

3. Which portrayals of animals most resemble one another in these works? Explain.

COMPARE Styles

Writing Four distinct styles differentiate these works: "Horses" is written in free verse, "The Panther" is written in four quatrains of iambic pentameter, "The Iguana" is prose nonfiction, and "The Red Cockatoo" is written in the simple style of a folk ballad. Consider the elements that contribute to each author's style, such as diction and figurative language. Then write a brief essay in which you compare two of the authors' styles, reflecting on how each style reinforces a specific theme.

Black panther. Francois Pompon. Bronze. Private collection.

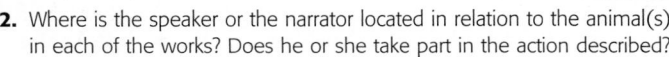

LOG ON ▶ **Literature** Online

Selection Resources For Selection Quizzes, eFlashcards, and Reading-Writing Connection activities, go to glencoe.com and enter QuickPass code GLW6053u6.

COMPARING LITERATURE **1219**

Compare Styles

Students' essays should reflect an appreciation of
- Neruda's use of separated, uneven stanzas of free verse to embody the free-flowing, emotional quality of his reflections
- Rilke's use of regular meter and stanza structure to create a precise, detailed representation
- Dinesen's use of an associative nonfiction style to connect several experiences and convey a direct lesson
- Po's use of straightforward, precise lines to create a simple metaphor

Assess

Compare the Big Idea

Students' displays should
- use images from the appropriate cultures and time periods
- clearly explain how the images reflect the visions of nature and society in the literary works
- identify and explain similarities and differences in the cultures' depictions of the natural world

Compare Portrayals of Animals

1. The horses are objects of reflection because they prompt the speaker's emotional transformation; the panther is a nuanced character with a complex inner life (and possibly also an object of reflection); the iguanas symbolize the danger of trying to possess beautiful objects; the cockatoo symbolizes the fate of outspoken individuals in society.

2. Neruda's speaker watches the horses through a window and takes part in the action (the "action" is that of the speaker's own mental and emotional transformations); Rilke's speaker is omniscient and not part of the action; Dinesen is the main character and part of the action; Po's speaker is omniscient and not part of the action.

3. "The Panther" and "The Red Cockatoo" portray the fate of animals in captivity; "Horses" and "The Iguana" describe an individual's encounter with the mysterious beauty of nature.

Before You Read

Focus

Bellringer Options

Selection Focus
  Transparency 77
Daily Language Practice
  Transparency 117

Or draw four columns on the board and label them *YOUTH, BRAVERY, HAPPINESS,* and *PATRIOTISM.* Add any other ideas. **Ask:** What types of images from nature are used in advertisements, films, and television to represent these ideas? *(Students may say that images such as blooming flowers and sprouting seeds are used to represent youth; lions and other large animals, bravery; a shining sun and birds singing, happiness; and a soaring eagle, patriotism.)* Discuss ways that nature and animals are used to symbolize other ideas and characteristics.

Before You Read

Fable

Meet **Octavio Paz**
(1914–1998)

Opposites, conflicts, contraries: these ideas and images, which so often trouble readers, were the building blocks of Octavio Paz's work. In apparent contradictions, such as Paz's favorite image of "burnt water," the poet saw a kind of transcendent union, or what he called "a higher synthesis." This sense of opposites is present in the following lines from one of Paz's most well-known poems, "Between What I See and What I Say . . .":

> *"poetry*
> *comes and goes*
>   *between what is*
> *and what is not.*
>   *It weaves*
> *and unweaves reflections."*
>
> —Octavio Paz

Politics Meets Poetry Born in 1914 in Mexico City, Paz was immediately influenced by politics. His father had been active in the revolution of 1911, and Paz's family had to flee briefly to Los Angeles, California. Home again in Mexico City, Paz composed poetry and short stories at an early age; his first volume of poetry was published when he was nineteen. He attended law school for a brief period and maintained a lifelong interest in politics. He supported the leftists in the Spanish Civil War in their fight against the Fascists, and when he returned home to Mexico, he brought the cause with him.

At the same time that he wrote volumes of prose and poetry, he worked as a Mexican diplomat in Europe, India, the United States, and Japan, and spoke out about causes around the world. In fact, his diplomatic career ended when he protested the Mexican government's crackdown on student demonstrators in Mexico City.

Turning to the Maya Paz's concern with politics was not limited to contemporary issues or conflicts. Deeply influenced by a journey he took as a young man to study the Mayan ruins of the Yucatán, Paz became concerned with the indigenous cultures of Mexico and the period of the Spanish Conquest, a time that stood out for him as a fundamental moment in Mexico's history. Some readers interpret "Fable" as an expression of that fateful moment when the conquistadors displaced the great civilization of the Maya. Others see one or more of Paz's three great subjects in the poem: time, history, and the political reality in which we all live.

During his lifetime, Paz was a leading figure in the careers of other authors, whom he nurtured and showcased in his many literary journals and reviews. Influential and respected for decades, Paz received many honors, including the Nobel Prize in Literature in 1990.

 Literature Online

Author Search For more about Octavio Paz, go to glencoe.com and enter QuickPass code GLW6053u6.

Selection Skills

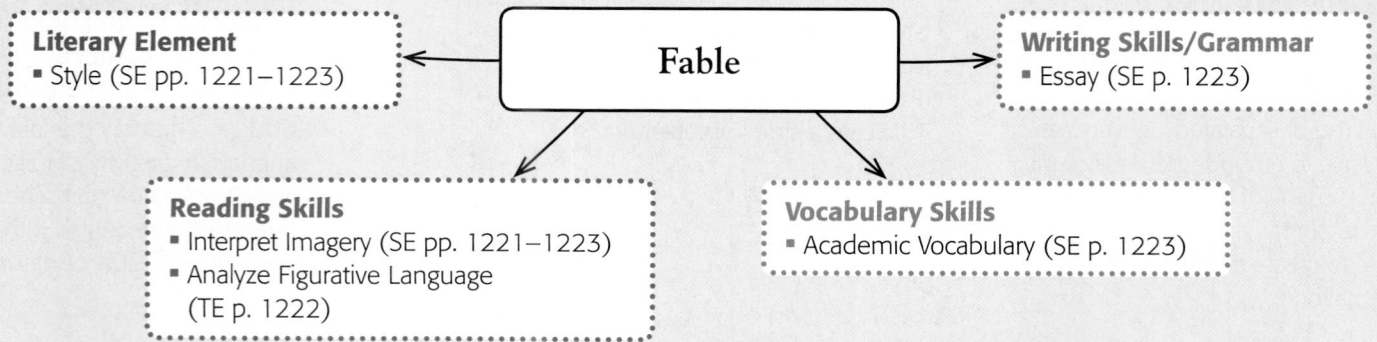

Literary Element
  ▪ Style (SE pp. 1221–1223)

Fable

Writing Skills/Grammar
  ▪ Essay (SE p. 1223)

Reading Skills
  ▪ Interpret Imagery (SE pp. 1221–1223)
  ▪ Analyze Figurative Language (TE p. 1222)

Vocabulary Skills
  ▪ Academic Vocabulary (SE p. 1223)

Literature and Reading Preview

Connect to the Poem

Have you ever had a dream in which impossibly strange things happened, things that could never happen in your real life? Write a journal entry that describes this dream and its significance.

Build Background

As a young writer, Paz was deeply attracted to a new movement in literature and the visual arts called Surrealism. This movement, which developed in Europe in the 1920s, sought to reveal the unconscious mind in dreamlike images. It relied on fantastic images and combined things in irrational ways. For example, a tree growing out of a hand is surreal. That is, it could happen only in a dream or a dreamlike vision, or it is an image created by the subconscious mind.

Set Purposes for Reading

Big Idea **Nature and the Imagination**

As you read the poem, ask yourself, How does the speaker transform images from nature into something different?

Literary Element **Style**

Style is the author's choice and arrangement of words and sentences in a literary work. Style can reveal an author's purpose in writing and his or her attitude toward a subject or audience. As you read "Fable," ask yourself, How does the poet's style reveal information about the poem's central message?

Reading Strategy **Interpret Imagery**

When you **interpret imagery,** you come up with associations, suggestions, and meanings for the sensory details in a literary work. You might also decide how a particular image affects you as a reader.

···

Tip: Record Reactions Because Surrealist imagery is irrational, a good starting point for interpreting it is by deciding how it makes you feel. As you read "Fable," ask yourself, Does each image strike you as positive, negative, or neutral? Record your reactions in a chart like this one.

Positive	Negative	Neutral
youth of water	broken mirrors	fire and air

Learning Objectives

For pages 1220–1223
In studying this text, you will focus on the following objectives:

Literary Study: Analyzing style.

Reading: Interpreting imagery.

Writing: Writing an essay.

Imaginary Flowers, 1944. Juan O'Gorman. Christies, London.

Before You Read

Focus

Summary

Octavio Paz's poem describes the beginning of the world as a surreal place of water, heat, insects, trees, and birds. The end of this paradise comes with the creation of language, which works to separate everyone from nature and one another.

> For summaries in languages other than English, see Unit 6 Teaching Resources Book, pp. 148–153.

Literary History ☆

Vanguardia The French avant-garde movement of the early twentieth century influenced the Latin American avant-garde movement known as vanguardia. Vangardista poetry experimented with new forms and themes, and focused on what had before been considered ugly or unworthy of poetic attention: the everyday.

Approaching Level
DIFFERENTIATED INSTRUCTION

Paraphrase Approaching Level students may have difficulty following the surreal images in Paz's poem. Explain that paraphrasing, or restating the poet's words using their own words, can help them better understand the poem. Students should read the poem through once. Then, as they read it a second time, have them stop and write a paraphrase of each line in their own words.

English Learners
DIFFERENTIATED INSTRUCTION

Beginning Explain to English learners that some poets do not use standard punctuation, and others do not use any punctuation at all. Have students preview "Fable" and note the absence of any punctuation. Tell students to pause at the end of each line when there is no punctuation and to consider each line a separate statement.

Advanced Learners/Pre-AP
DIFFERENTIATED INSTRUCTION

Surrealism Invite students to research the surrealist art movement of the twentieth century. Encourage students to choose one artist and investigate his or her work and influences. Then, tell students to choose one piece of work from that artist and create an oral presentation that introduces the art to the class. Students should explain the images in the piece and what makes them surreal.

Teach

Big Idea   1

Nature and the Imagination
Ask: What is the speaker's "fable"
that explains the source of birds?
How does the surreal description
connect to real-life images? *(In the
speaker's story, the origin of birds is
the tree's singing and fortune-telling;
in real life, a tree "sings" when its
leaves move in the wind, causing
birds to take flight.)*

Literary Element   2

Style Answer: *They suggest
some kind of movement, perhaps
from some time or some place to
another time or location.*

> For additional literary element
> practice, see Unit 6 Teaching
> Resources Book, p. 154.

Reading Strategy   3

Interpret Imagery Answer:
*The broken mirrors suggest
an intensely negative change:
destruction that cannot be
repaired, fragmentation, and
disunion.*

> For additional practice using the
> reading skill or strategy, see Unit 6
> Teaching Resources Book, p. 155.

FABLE

Octavio Paz
Translated by Eliot Weinberger

El pollito (The Chick), 1945.
Frida Kahlo. Oil on masonite,
28 x 20 cm. Fundacion
Dolores Olmedo, Mexico City.

Ages of fire and of air
Youth of water
From green to yellow
           From yellow to red
From dream to watching
           From desire to act
5   It was only one step and you took it so lightly
Insects were living jewels
The heat rested by the side of the pond
Rain was a willow with unpinned hair
A tree grew in the palm of your hand
10 And that tree laughed, sang, prophesied
1 Its divinations[1] filled the air with wings
There were simple miracles called birds
Everything was for everyone
           Everyone was everything
There was only one huge word with no back to it
15 A word like a sun
One day it broke into tiny pieces
They were the words of the language we now speak
Pieces that will never come together
Broken mirrors where the world sees itself shattered

---

1. *Divinations* are prophecies or premonitions of future events that are
arrived at by supernatural means.

2   Style *What does the repetition of the words* from *and to in these lines
suggest? Explain.*

3   Interpret Imagery *What kind of change do the broken mirrors
suggest? Explain.*

Reading Practice

Analyze Figurative Language Review
with students the differences between
similes and metaphors, two types of
figurative language. Explain that a simile
compares two unlike things using *like*
or *as*; a metaphor, two unlike things by
saying one thing *is* another. Have students make a two-column chart with the
headings *SIMILES* and *METAPHORS*. Then,
have students re-read the poem, looking
for examples of these kinds of figurative
language and recording them in their
charts. *(Students should find metaphors
in lines 6, 8, 12, and 14, as well as a
simile in line 15.)* **Ask:** How does the
figurative language affect your understanding of the poem? *(Students may
say that the metaphors create almost
concrete images; they can imagine
insects that look like jewels and rain that
looks like a weeping willow. Students
may say that the simile in line 15 helps*
*them understand how overwhelming the
concept of a word, or language, is in this
visual world.)*

After You Read

Respond and Think Critically

Respond and Interpret

1. Which line or lines do you find most difficult to understand in this poem? Explain.

2. (a)Which lines in the poem are about beginnings? (b)What is the speaker's attitude toward these beginnings?

3. (a)How does line 5 signal that a change is taking place? (b)Up to this point, what is the speaker's attitude toward the change?

4. (a)Which line suggests harmony between all people and all things? (b)To what single idea, image, or concept is this harmony related?

5. (a)To what does the speaker compare the word? (b)What does the comparison suggest?

Analyze and Evaluate

6. What kind of event does this poem describe? Cite evidence from the poem to support your answer.

7. This fable has no talking animals nor a stated lesson (both common features of fables). Why do you think the poet called the poem "Fable"?

Connect

8. **Big Idea** **Nature and the Imagination** How does the poem personify nature?

9. **Connect to the Author** Paz was interested in his country's history. How might this poem be read as a fable about the Spanish conquest of the native peoples of the Yucatan?

Literary Element Style

Although Paz avoids traditional rhyme and meter in "Fable," he nevertheless uses poetic devices.

1. Do you think the free verse form of the poem is effective? Explain.

2. (a)Identify examples of repetition and parallelism in the poem. (b)What is their effect?

Reading Strategy Interpret Imagery

Examine the chart you created on page 1221 of positive, negative, and neutral reactions to the imagery in the poem. Use this information to interpret the poem.

1. Explain how the imagery changes throughout the poem from positive to neutral to negative.

2. Look back at the color imagery in lines 3–4. What kind of shift might it suggest?

Literature Online

Selection Resources For Selection Quizzes, eFlashcards, and Reading-Writing Connection activities, go to glencoe.com and enter QuickPass code GLW6053u6.

Academic Vocabulary

*Paz's poem describes a **transformation**: the world goes from having only one "word" to having many languages and realities.*

Transformation is an academic word. In an everyday setting, a person who dramatically altered his or her appearance might be said to have gone through a physical **transformation**. To further explore the meaning of this word, answer the following question. What is a story you have read in which a person undergoes a dramatic inner **transformation**?

For more on academic vocabulary, see pages 36–37 and R83–R85.

Writing

Write an Essay Scholar Jason Wilson suggests that the lack of punctuation in "Fable" supports Paz's portrayal of paradise as a place where "everybody belong[s] to the world and . . . all flows." Do you agree with this interpretation? Write an expository essay presenting your opinion, citing quotations from the poem to support it.

OCTAVIO PAZ **1223**

After You Read

Assess

1. Answers will vary.

2. (a) Lines 1–2 suggest beginnings by referencing fundamental elements and youth. Lines 3–5 signaling change. (b) The speaker seems happy about beginnings.

3. (a) Line 5 refers to taking a step. (b) Change was easy.

4. (a) Line 13 (b) the "one huge word with no back to it"

5. (a) a sun (b) All revolves around and is balanced by the word.

6. the process of creation and destruction, or unity and division. Creation is described with nature images; destruction with the image of the broken mirror.

7. The poem resembles a myth, yet the word *fable* implies "fabulous." Paz's surrealist poem may be a new fable that breaks with traditional definitions.

8. The poem shows heat resting; a willow with unpinned hair; and a tree that laughs, sings, and prophesies. It may be referring to the universe, nature, or act of creation by means of the personal pronoun *you* and the possessive pronoun *your*.

9. The story reflects a Paradise that has its unity broken. This represents the effects of colonialism on an indigenous people's traditions and language.

Literary Element

1. Students may think it is effective because the poem deals with abstractions such as time and history that do not fit into regular patterns.

2. (a) The "from . . . to" phrases in lines 3–4 and the "everything was" phrases in line 13 are examples of parallelism. (b) They emphasize transition and balance, or harmony.

Reading Strategy

1. It begins with elements, colors, abstractions, and dreams, which are positive or neutral; it moves on to mainly positive images of nature; it ends with negative images of rupture and chaos.

2. possible answers: from plants to animals; from coolness to warmth; from passivity to action

Academic Vocabulary

Students should name a story in which a person's character or values change significantly.

Writing

Students' essays should

- include a clear thesis stating whether they agree with Wilson's interpretation
- use quotations to support their points

1223

Before You Read

Focus

Bellringer Options

Selection Focus
  Transparency 78
Daily Language Practice
  Transparency 118

Or write: "It's all Greek to me" on the board. **Say:** This saying is usually used to mean that you can see something but you just cannot understand it, as if it were written in Greek.
Ask: What do you do when you are faced with a situation in which you're unsure what to do, such as in a foreign country or even at a service for a religion other than your own? Do you pretend to know what you're doing, or do you admit ignorance? *(Students may say that they watch others and try to emulate them; others may say that they tell a close friend or relative that they're unsure of how to proceed.)*

Before You Read

Trinidad

When Greek Meets Greek

Meet **Samuel Selvon**
(1923–1994)

Born in Trinidad to an Indian father and an Indian-Scottish mother, Samuel Selvon experienced life under colonialism firsthand. He served as a radio operator for the British Royal Naval Reserve during World War II and moved to London after the war. Within a few years, he was writing full-time. Using his own experiences and observations, he exposed racial prejudices in England and Trinidad. Known for his use of Trinidadian dialect, vibrant descriptions, and informal tone, Selvon makes serious issues accessible.

Island Setting Selvon published his first novel, *A Brighter Sun*, in 1952. The story focuses on a young East Indian couple who struggle to survive World War II and search to find their place in Trinidad's racially segregated colonial society. Several other works, including *I Hear Thunder* and *An Island Is a World*, are also set in Trinidad and focus on the world Selvon and so many West Indians tried to escape—only to find they weren't accepted in Britain either. Selvon regarded *An Island Is a World* as his favorite and most personal work.

London Setting After living in London for six years and witnessing the prejudice and poverty immigrants faced, Selvon published *The Lonely Londoners*. The novel deals with racial misconceptions, including the belief in white supremacy and blacks' inability to succeed. Like *A Brighter Sun*, *The Lonely Londoners* was critically acclaimed. Reviewer Whitney Balliett called *The Lonely Londoners* "a nearly perfect work of its kind . . . This is the blessedly balanced realism that skirts completely the depressing passion of the naturalist novelist—the romance of total misery."

Market Scene. Jean-Pierre (1914-1979). Private collection.

> "If I have anything significant to say on an issue it is to be found inside my novels and short stories."
>
> —Samuel Selvon

Selvon found both humor and sympathy for his fellow man. Unlike some authors, he was more concerned with "the translation of emotions, feelings, and situations," rather than creating an "epic or saga," claiming "there is more than enough history and drama here for others to do more comprehensive and detailed studies." He published ten novels, two collections of short stories, nearly twenty radio plays, and numerous articles for the BBC and weekly and monthly newspapers including *London Magazine, New Statesman, Nation,* and *The Sunday Times.* His work greatly contributed to the growth of West Indian fiction, and critics claim that even if he had only written *A Brighter Sun* and *The Lonely Londoners,* he would still be considered an important and extremely influential author.

 Literature Online

Author Search For more about Samuel Selvon, go to glencoe.com and enter QuickPass code GLW6053u6.

Selection Skills

Literary Elements
- Dialect (SE p. 1225, 1226, 1229; TE p. 1228)
- Identify Asides (TE p. 1226)

When Greek Meets Greek

Writing Skills/Grammar
- Story (SE p. 1229)

Reading Skills
- Make Inferences about Characters (SE pp. 1225, 1227–1229; TE p. 1226)

Vocabulary Skills
- Analogies (SE p. 1229)
- Synonyms (TE p. 1225)

Literature and Reading Preview

Connect to the Story

If you moved to another country, would you seek other Americans or try to meet others? Discuss this in a small group.

Build Background

After World War II many people from the West Indies, Africa, and Asia moved to Britain in search of a better life. By the mid-1950s, more than 25,000 West Indians were arriving in Britain every year. They often settled and formed communities in particular neighborhoods, and their increasing numbers aroused hostility from some British people. Parliament's efforts to control immigration had little effect.

Set Purposes for Reading

Big Idea **The Legacy of Colonialism**

As you read, ask yourself, How does Selvon use humor to expose the racial tensions between the British and the West Indians?

Literary Element **Dialect**

Dialect is the version of a language spoken by members of a regional or social group. Dialects may differ from the standard form of a language in vocabulary, pronunciation, or grammatical form. Much of "When Greek Meets Greek" is written in a Caribbean-English dialect. As you read, ask yourself, How does Selvon use dialect to make his story more realistic?

Reading Strategy **Make Inferences About Characters**

When you **make inferences about characters,** you draw conclusions about them based on their traits, beliefs, actions, and motivations. Making inferences helps you look more deeply at the characters and leads you toward the story's theme. Look for clues about the characters in descriptions, dialogue, events, and relationships. As you read, ask yourself, What can I infer about the characters from Selvon's use of dialogue and details?

Tip: Take Notes Use a chart like the one below to track details and dialogue that reveal information about each character. Then use that information to make an inference about the characters.

Character	Details	Dialogue
Ram	"most of the time his eyes colliding up with _No Colors, Please,_ or _Sorry, No Kolors._"	

Learning Objectives

For pages 1224–1229

In studying this text, you will focus on the following objectives:

Literary Study: Analyzing dialect.

Reading: Making inferences about characters.

Writing: Writing a story.

Vocabulary

collide (kə līd´) _v._ to run into accidentally; to come together with direct impact; p. 1226 _Not paying attention to where she was going, the woman collided with me and nearly knocked me over._

menace (men´is) _n._ a person or thing that is a threat or danger; p. 1228 _That aggressive dog is a menace to the neighborhood._

perusal (pə rōō´zəl) _n._ the act of reading in detail or examining carefully; examination p. 1228 _After my lawyer's perusal of the lease, I signed it and wrote the landlord a check._

Tip: Analogies Analogies are comparisons based on relationships between words and ideas. In the analogy _menace : threat :: animosity : hostility,_ both pairs of words are synonyms.

SAMUEL SELVON **1225**

Before You Read

Focus

Summary

Ram is a West Indian looking for a room to rent in England, but he is having trouble because many prejudiced landlords won't rent to West Indians who have African backgrounds. He encounters a friend, Fraser, who suggests that he pose as an immigrant from India, as many landlords will rent to Indians. Employing this ruse, Ram finds a room in a boarding house, but his life is complicated by another boarder, Chan, who Ran believes is actually from India. Worrying that he will be exposed, Ram tries to get rid of Chan by complaining to the landlord that Chan is a troublemaker. The plan backfires and Ram is evicted from his room, only to learn that Chan is not really from India but from Jamaica.

 For summaries in languages other than English, see Unit 6 Teaching Resources Book, pp. 158–163.

Vocabulary

Synonyms Have students use a dictionary and a thesaurus to look up common synonyms of the vocabulary words. Students can then create quizzes to test one another on identifying the vocabulary words from their synonyms.

 For additional vocabulary practice, see Unit 6 Teaching Resources Book, p. 166.

English Learners

DIFFERENTIATED INSTRUCTION

Advanced Explain to English learners that "When Greek Meets Greek" involves a situation in which a landlord is prejudiced against a man on the basis of the man's ethnic background; however, the landlord isn't educated enough to realize that he is mistaken in his assumption of the man's background at first. **Ask:** Have you ever been in a situation in which someone has incorrectly assumed what your ethnic background is? Explain. _(Student responses will differ.)_ Discuss with students the ways in which people make assumptions about those from other backgrounds or cultures. **Ask:** What is the one thing about your background or culture that you wish everyone knew? _(Responses will vary.)_

Teach

Reading Strategy   1

Make Inferences About Characters **Ask:** What can you infer of Ram's attitude from the song he sings? *(He doesn't seem to be offended by the discriminatory signs he reads.)*

> For additional practice using the reading skill or strategy, see Unit 6 Teaching Resources Book, p. 165.

Literary Element   2

Dialect **Answer:** *They use non-standard English.*

Point out to English learners that ENGLISH LEARNERS Fraser's dialogue is missing the word *is*, and the narration uses shifting verb forms and tenses.

> For additional literary element practice, see Unit 6 Teaching Resources Book, p. 164.

> For an audio recording of this selection, use Listening Library Audio CD-ROM.

Readability Scores

Dale-Chall: 5.3
DRP: 50
Lexile: 750

Alegría-Alegría! Antonio Seguí (Argentina, b. 1934). Oil on canvas, 65.4 x 81.3 cm. Private collection.

When Greek Meets Greek
Samuel Selvon

One morning Ramkilawansingh (after this, we calling this man Ram) was making a study of the notice boards along Westbourne Grove what does advertise rooms to let. Every now and then he writing down an address or a telephone number, though most of the time his eyes **colliding** up with *No Colors, Please,* or *Sorry, No Kolors.*

> **Vocabulary**
>
> **collide** (kə līd′) *v.* to run into accidentally; to come together with direct impact

"Red, white and blue, all out but you," **1** Ram was humming a little ditty what children say when they playing whoop. Just as he get down by Bradley's Corner he met Fraser.

"You look like a man who looking for a place to live," Fraser say.

"You look like a man who could tell me the right place to go," Ram say.

Dialect *What do you notice about the way the characters talk?*   **2**

Literary Element Practice

Identify Asides Explain to students that an aside is a literary element that they will usually encounter in drama when a character's speech is meant to be heard only by the audience. It breaks down the invisible wall between a character and an audience. In "When Greek Meets Greek," the narrator inserts asides to explain that the characters will be called by shorter names throughout the rest of the story.

Ask: What's noticeable about the language of the asides? *(Students are likely to say that the language in the asides is similar in diction to that of the rest of the story.)* What effect do the asides have on the story's mood? *(Students may say that the asides add humor and familiarity to the relationship between the narrator and the readers.)*

"You try down by Ladbroke Grove?" Fraser ask.

"I don't want to go down in that criminal area," Ram say, "at least, not until they find the man who kill Kelso."

"Then you will never live in the Grove," Fraser say.

"You are a contact man,"[1] Ram say, "which part you think I could get a room, boy?"

Fraser scratch his head. "I know of a landlord up the road who vow that he ain't ever taking anybody who come from the West Indies. But he don't mind taking Indians. He wouldn't know the difference when he see you is a Indian . . . them English people so foolish they believe every Indian come from India."

"You think I stand a chance?" Ram ask.

"Sure, you stand a chance. All you have to do is put on a turban."

"I never wear a turban in my life; I am a born Trinidadian, a real Creole. All the same, you best hads give me the address, I will pass around there later."

So Fraser give him the address, and Ram went on reading a few more boards, but he got discourage after a while and went to see the landlord.

The first thing the landlord ask him was: "What part of the world do you come from?"

"I am an Untouchable[2] from the heart of India," Ram say. "I am looking for a single

---

1. A *contact man* is someone who has useful information that is not common knowledge.
2. An *Untouchable* is a member of the lowest caste (hereditary social group) in India.

Make Inferences About Characters *What can you infer about Ram's attitude toward his heritage from this description?*

The Legacy of Colonialism *Why is this the first thing the landlord asks? What can you infer about the relationship between West Indians and the British?*

---

room. I dwelt on the banks of the Ganges. Not too expensive."

"But you are not in your national garments," the landlord say.

"When you are in Rome," Ram say, making it sound like an original statement, "do as the Romans do."

While the landlord sizing up Ram, an Indian tenant come up the steps to go inside. This fellar was Chandrilaboodoo (after this, we calling this man Chan) and he had a big beard with a hair net over it, and he was wearing a turban. When he see Ram, he clasp his hands with the palms touching across his chest by way of greeting.

The old Ram catch on quick and do the same thing.

"*Acha, Hindustani,*"[3] Chan say.

"*Acha, pilau, papadom, chickenvindaloo,*"[4] Ram say desperately, hoping for the best.

Chan nod his head, say good morning to the landlord and went inside.

"That was a narrow shave," Ram thought, "I have to watch out for that man."

"That was Mr. Chan," the landlord say, "he is the only other Indian tenant I have at the moment. I have a single room for two pounds. Are you a student?"

"Who is not a student?" Ram say, getting into the mood of the thing. "Man is for ever studying ways and means until he passes into the hands of Allah."

Well, to cut a long story short, Ram get a room on the first floor, right next door to Chan, and he move in that same evening.

---

3. *Acha Hindustani* (ä′chä hin′dōō stä′nē) is a traditional greeting.
4. *Pilau* (pi′lou), *papadom* (pä′pä dom), and *chicken vindaloo* (vin′də lōō) are three traditional Indian foods.

SAMUEL SELVON **1227**

Visual Vocabulary
The *Ganges* (gan′jēz) is India's major river. It is sacred to followers of the Hindu religion.

English Learners

DIFFERENTIATED INSTRUCTION

Intermediate Students will find idiomatic expressions in this story. Have students guess their meanings using context:

1. "a narrow shave" (*a situation in which someone is nearly caught*)
2. "passes into the hands" (*dies and joins his or her god*)
3. "cat-and-mouse" (*running and hiding from someone who you think is "toying" with you*)

Advanced Learners/Pre-AP

DIFFERENTIATED INSTRUCTION

Research Invite students to find out more about the untouchables of India, the Ganges and its place in the Hindu religion, the "national garments" of India and the rules of wearing a turban, and the importance of Islam (Allah) in Indian life. Have students create a short presentation in which they explain how Ram has confused things while pretending to be Indian.

Teach

Big Idea 3

The Legacy of Colonialism
Ask: What is ironic about the situation at the boarding house? (The landlord is prejudiced against people from the West Indies, but he does not know the difference between someone from the West Indies and someone from India.)

Reading Strategy 4

Make Inferences About Characters **Answer:** *He is proud of his heritage and does not want to pretend to be Indian.*

Big Idea 5

The Legacy of Colonialism
Answer: *The landlord classifies people by their heritage. This indicates that some of the British are hostile toward West Indians and do not want them in Britain.*

Cultural History ☆

Trinidad Over the years, Trinidad has had its share of immigrants, a result of which is a population with genetic ties to England, France, Spain, Africa, India, and China. Of course, this also means that the islands' four Creole languages are a mixture of those of the colonizing countries; furthermore, the islands boast a variety of religions, including Roman Catholicism, several types of Protestantism, Hinduism, and Islam.

Learning Objectives
Analyzing dialect. (SE)
Making inferences about characters. (SE)
Identifying and analyzing asides. (TE)

1227

Teach

Big Idea   1

The Legacy of Colonialism
Answer: *The humor gives the story a comedic tone. It makes the serious subject matter easier to relate to and understand.*

Literary Element   2

Dialect **Ask:** Does Ram's dialect actually change here, or is it the same as it was before? Explain. (Students may say that once Ram is caught, he is less formal with the landlord and calls him "old man"; however, his dialect sounds grammatically the same as it did before.)

Reading Strategy   3

Make Inferences About Characters Answer: *Chan knows the landlord is prejudiced; therefore he is willing to pretend to be from India to keep his apartment.*

 To check students' understanding of the selection, see Unit 6 Teaching Resources Book, p. 169.

But as the days going by, Ram had to live like cat-and-mouse with Chan. Every time he see Chan, he have to hide in case this man start up this Hindustani talk again, or start to ask him questions about Mother India. In fact, it begin to get on Ram nerves, and he decide that he had to do something.

"This house too small for the two of we," Ram say to himself, "one will have to go."

So Ram went down in the basement to see the landlord.

"I have the powers of the Occult,"[5] Ram say, "and I have come to warn you of this man Chan. He is not a good tenant. He keeps the bathroom dirty, he does not tidy up his room at all, and he is always chanting and saying his prayers loudly and disturbing the other tenants."

"I have had no complaints," the landlord say.

"But I am living next door to him," Ram say, "and if I concentrate my powers I can see through the wall. That man is a **menace**, and the best thing you can do is to give him notice. You have a good house here and it would be a pity to let one man spoil it for the other tenants."

"I will have a word with him about it," the landlord say.

Well, the next evening Ram was in his room when he hear a knock at the door. He run in the corner quick and stand upon his head, and say, "Come in."

The landlord come in.

"I am just practicing my yogurt," Ram say.

---

5. *Powers of the Occult* are supernatural abilities to reveal secret knowledge.

The Legacy of Colonialism *Ram's mispronunciation of yoga is an example of humor. Why do you think Selvon uses humor here?*   1

Vocabulary

menace (men′is) *n.* a person or thing that is a threat or danger

---

> *That man is a menace, and the best thing you can do is to give him notice.*

"I have had a word with Mr. Chan," the landlord say, "and I have reason to suspect that you have deceived me. You are not from India, you are from the West Indies."

Ram turn right-side up. "I am a citizen of the world," he say.

"You are flying false colors,"[6] the landlord say. "You do not burn incense like Mr. Chan, you do not dress like Mr. Chan, and you do not talk like Mr. Chan."

"Give me a break, old man," Ram say, falling back on the good old West Indian dialect.   2

"It is too late. You have already started to make trouble. You must go."

Well, the very next week find Ram out scouting again, giving the boards a **perusal**, and who he should chance to meet but Fraser.

He start to tell Fraser how life hard, how he had to keep dodging from this Chan fellar all the time, and it was pure torture.

"Listen," Fraser say, "you don't mean a big fellar with a beard, and he always wearing a turban?"

"That sound like him," Ram say. "You know him?"

"Know him!" Fraser say. "Man, that is a fellar from Jamaica who I send to that house to get a room!" ∽

---

6. *Flying false colors* means engaging in deception.

Make Inferences About Characters *What conclusions can you draw about Chan? Why do you think he acts and dresses like he's from India?*   3

Vocabulary

perusal (pə roo′zəl) *n.* the act of reading in detail or examining carefully; examination

---

Reading Practice

Identify Assumptions Discuss with students the dangers of making assumptions or taking the truth for granted. Explain that while being aware of a writer's assumptions in nonfiction texts can help readers identify bias, identifying assumptions in works of fiction can help readers gain insight into a character's beliefs and feelings. **Ask:** What does the landlord assume about Ram when they first meet? *(The landlord assumes that Ram is from India.)* **Ask:** What does the landlord base his assumption on? *(He bases it on Ram's interaction with Chan.)* **Ask:** What do you know about the accuracy of Ram's interaction with Chan? *(Ram doesn't know what he is doing.)* Discuss what this line of reasoning illuminates about the landlord. **Ask:** What can you conclude that the landlord knows or doesn't know? And what does this say about the landlord's prejudice? *(Students are likely to say that the landlord does not know the difference between an Indian and a West Indian, which means that his prejudice is based on false ideas and ignorance.)*

After You Read

Respond and Think Critically

Respond and Interpret

1. Were you surprised by the ending? Explain.

2. (a)Why has Ram had difficulty finding a place to live? (b)What advice does Fraser offer Ram? (c)How does Ram respond to this advice?

3. (a)What happens when Ram meets Chan? (b)Why does Ram feel threatened by Chan?

4. (a)Why does Ram try to get Chan kicked out of the house? (b)Does Ram's plan work? Explain.

Analyze and Evaluate

5. Did you find Ram to be a sympathetic character? Explain.

6. **Situational irony** exists when the outcome of a situation is unexpected. Identify an example of situational irony and explain why it is ironic.

7. **Tone** is the attitude a narrator takes toward the reader, a subject, or a character. How would you describe the narrator's tone?

Connect

8. **Big Idea** **The Legacy of Colonialism** How does the story's theme relate to the legacy of colonialism?

9. **Connect to Today** What kinds of prejudice and ignorance exist in the United States today? How do people use humor to deal with them?

Literary Element Dialect

Dialects often differ in pronunciation, vocabulary, and grammar. The dialect in the story often uses nonstandard progressive forms—"We calling this man Ram" instead of "We will call this man Ram."

1. Identify an example of dialect in the story that differs in grammar from Standard English.

2. (a)Why might Selvon have chosen to use dialect in this story? (b)What is its effect?

Reading Strategy Make Inferences About Characters

When you **make inferences about characters,** you use clues from the text and your own experiences to determine what the author implies about characters. Consult your chart from page 1225.

1. Why do you think Ram feels compelled to play a "cat-and-mouse" game with Chan?

2. Based on the landlord's actions and dialogue, what can you infer about his beliefs?

 Literature Online

Selection Resources For Selection Quizzes, eFlashcards, and Reading-Writing Connection activities, go to glencoe.com and enter QuickPass code GLW6053u6.

Vocabulary Practice

Practice with Analogies Choose the word that best completes the relationship expressed in the original pair of words.

1. collide : crash :: sprint :
   a. trickle   c. stroll
   b. dash   d. pause

2. menace : threat :: conclusion :
   a. finale   c. start
   b. assumption   d. draft

3. perusal : examination :: difference :
   a. distinction   c. variety
   b. similarity   d. occasion

Writing

Write a Story Think of a familiar setting in which a case of mistaken identity could occur. Write a story about this situation, choosing whether to make your readers aware of the mistake early or reveal it in a surprise ending. Use **dialect** in either your dialogue or narration. If your character is hiding his or her identity, show his or her motivations.

SAMUEL SELVON **1229**

After You Read

Assess

1. Answers will vary.

2. (a) Racism has kept him out of more desirable neighborhoods. (b) He tells Ram to see a landlord who accepts Indian tenants and to tell the landlord he is Indian. (c) He agrees but refuses to wear a turban.

3. (a) Chan greets Ram with the traditional Hindu greeting, and Ram pretends to understand. (b) Ram fears that Chan will reveal Ram's secret.

4. (a) He wants to protect his false identity. (b) Ram's plan fails because Chan tells the landlord Ram is not from India. The landlord evicts Ram.

5. Answers will vary

6. Ram thinks Chan is a real Indian, but Chan is actually Jamaican. This is ironic because it is unexpected.

7. comical, familiar, and ironic

8. Ram represents the experience of many West Indian immigrants who have endured prejudice, and the landlord represents British people who discriminated against West Indians.

9. One way racism and ignorance of other cultures exist in the United States today is in the form of stereotypes. People often use movies, songs, or television shows to deal with these issues in a humorous way.

Writing

Students' stories should
- include a case of misidentification that is revealed at some point in the story
- reveal their characters' motivations
- use dialect

Literary Element

1. Examples: "notice boards…what does advertise"; "Just as he get down."

2. (a) Possible answers: He might have wanted to add local color, to offer an authentic portrayal of the characters' speech, or to enhance the story's humor. (b) It makes the story more realistic and easier to connect with the characters and their situations.

Reading Strategy

1. He fears that too much contact with Chan will expose him as a fraud.

2. He believes West Indians are inferior to him. He is racist and prejudiced.

Vocabulary Practice

1. b 2. a 3. a

Before You Read

Focus

Bellringer Options

Selection Focus Transparency 79

Daily Language Practice Transparency 119

Or ask: What do you believe is the purpose of dreams? *(Students may say that dreams are a way for the subconscious to process what the mind has experienced in a given day; others may say that dreams help people make decisions or show people what they really want.)* Bring a dream dictionary to class, and tell students that some people believe that particular items, animals, events, or people they dream about are symbols. Ask for volunteers to describe something they have dreamed about and encourage a discussion of dream symbolism.

Before You Read

Argentina

The Night Face Up

Meet **Julio Cortázar**

(1914–1984)

Julio Cortázar (hōō´lē ō kôr tä´sär) was born in Brussels, Belgium, when his Argentine parents were there on a business trip shortly before World War I. They waited out the war in Europe, returning to Argentina in 1918. A short time later, his father abandoned the family, and Cortázar and his younger sister were raised by their mother, aunt, and grandmother in a suburb of Buenos Aires. He later described his early years as a time of great sadness that he escaped by reading fantasy and poetry.

A Varied Career Early in Cortázar's career, he taught school and—although he had to leave college for financial reasons—continued his studies on his own, reading foreign literature and writing poetry. In 1944 and 1945, he taught French literature at the university level but resigned in 1946 after being briefly imprisoned for political demonstrations against Juan Perón, the president of Argentina. Cortázar left the country in 1951 to move to Paris, France, where he resided the rest of his life. He worked as a United Nations translator a few months a year and wrote and traveled the rest of the year.

Cortázar published his first collection of short stories the year he left Argentina. He soon won acclaim as a novelist as well as a short story writer. Cortázar loved using experimental literary techniques. His narratives often shift back

> "No one can retell the plot of a Cortázar story; each one consists of determined words in a determined order. If we try to summarize them, we realize that something precious has been lost."
>
> —Jorge Luis Borges

and forth through time and space, challenging the laws of nature and logic.

The Anti-Novel *Hopscotch*, which Cortázar published in 1963, is one of the most important modern Latin American novels. Described as an open-ended anti-novel, it is divided into three sections: 36 chapters set in Paris, twenty chapters set in Buenos Aires, and 99 short pieces called "Expendable Chapters." The reader is invited to rearrange the material in an activity resembling hopscotch, jumping back and forth through the volume. This experimental technique is not exclusive to *Hopscotch*; Cortázar played with time sequences and the perception of reality in many other works.

A True Humanitarian Cortázar was passionately involved in the political issues of his day. Throughout the 1970s and up to the time of his death, he was committed to the cause of justice in Latin America. He campaigned tirelessly in favor of human rights and against the atrocities of the military regime in Argentina. He died in Paris of leukemia.

LOG ON **Literature** Online

Author Search For more about Julio Cortázar, go to glencoe.com and enter QuickPass code GLW6053u6.

Selection Skills

Literary Elements
- Point of View (SE pp. 1231–1233, 1235, 1238, 1240; TE p. 1236)
- Style (SE p. 1240)

Reading Skills
- Identify Sequence (SE pp. 1231, 1233, 1234, 1236, 1240; TE p. 1235)
- Visualize (TE p. 1232)
- Analyze Conflict (TE p. 1236)

The Night Face Up

Vocabulary Skills
- Antonyms (SE p. 1240; TE p. 1231)

Speaking/Listening/Viewing Skills
- Primary Visual Artifact (SE p. 1239)
- Analyze Art (TE p. 1235)

Writing Skills/Grammar
- Review (SE p. 1241)
- Short Story (TE p. 1238)

Literature and Reading Preview

Connect to the Story

Have you ever had a dream that felt like it was really happening? Write a journal entry in which you describe the details of the dream.

Build Background

In "The Night Face Up," Cortázar explores a frightening aspect of the Aztec culture. When the Aztecs dominated what is now central and southern Mexico, their religion included the ritual sacrifice of humans. In one form of sacrifice, priests cut out the beating hearts of victims on temple altars. Most of the sacrificial victims were prisoners of war or from groups the Aztecs had conquered.

Set Purposes for Reading

Big Idea **Magic Realism**

As you read, ask yourself, When do realistic elements mesh with fantastic, unbelievable events?

Literary Element **Point of View**

Point of view is the perspective from which a story is told. In **third-person limited** point of view, the narrator reveals the thoughts of one character. In **third-person omniscient** point of view, the narrator knows what all characters are thinking. As you read the story, ask yourself, How does the author use point of view to offer different perspectives?

Reading Strategy **Identify Sequence**

When you **identify sequence,** you look for clues that will help you determine the order in which events occur. Such clues might include sequence words such as *first, next,* and *then.* They might also include references to the time of day, indications of light and darkness, and terms that refer to time, such as *now, three days,* and *twenty minutes later.* As you read, ask yourself, Where does each event fit in the timeline of events?

Tip: Use Matrices Use a matrix like this one to keep track of the sequence of events. In your matrix, compare both settings.

	Reality?	Dream?
First	Accident	Battle
Second	Taken by ambulance to hospital	Taken by Aztec captors to temple

JULIO CORTÁZAR **1231**

Learning Objectives

For pages 1230–1240

In studying this text, you will focus on the following objectives:

Literary Study: Analyzing point of view.

Reading: Identifying sequence.

Vocabulary

solace (sol′is) *n.* a source of relief; mental or spiritual comfort; p. 1233 *For solace in his time of grief, he turned to the music they had both enjoyed.*

lucid (loo′sid) *adj.* having full use of one's mental abilities; clearheaded; p. 1233 *His senile father often has lucid intervals.*

supplication (sup′lə ka′shən) *n.* a humble entreaty; a prayer of request; p. 1235 *The governor pardoned the prisoner after hearing the inmate's mother give her supplication.*

beneficent (bə nef′ə sənt) *adj.* doing or producing good; p. 1235 *The beneficent work of Mother Teresa improved the lives of many people.*

Tip: Antonyms Words that have opposite meanings are antonyms. For example, *lucid* and *confused* are antonyms. Like synonyms, antonyms are always the same part of speech.

Before You Read

Focus

Summary

One morning an unnamed man mounts his motorcycle and rides it through the streets of a city. After he unavoidably runs into a jay-walking pedestrian and is injured, he is taken to a hospital. There he alternates between sleep and consciousness. While sleeping, he has a nightmare in which he is a Moteca Indian fleeing from Aztec warriors who want to capture him and offer him as a blood sacrifice. Eventually the reader learns that the dream and reality are reversed. The man is actually a captured Moteca Indian; his experiences on the motorcycle and in the hospital are the dream.

> For summaries in languages other than English, see Unit 6 Teaching Resources Book, pp. 171–176.

Vocabulary

Antonyms Have students read the definitions and sentences supplied with the vocabulary words. Then, have students write an antonym for each word based on the definition given. For example, part of the definition of *solace* is *relief*; students could list *anxiety* as an antonym. Challenge students to write more than one antonym for each word without looking in the dictionary.

> For additional vocabulary practice, see Unit 6 Teaching Resources Book, p. 179.

> **Interactive Read and Write**
> Other options for teaching this selection can be found in Interactive Read and Write for On-level Learners, pp. 301–314.

1231

English Learners

DIFFERENTIATED INSTRUCTION

Intermediate Important elements of "The Night Face Up" are sleeping, waking, and dreaming. English learners may have difficulty understanding related idiomatic terms such as "drift off." Have students record unfamiliar terms as they encounter them in the story, looking up difficult terms in the dictionary. Students may also list terms separately in a three-column chart labeled *Waking, Sleeping,* and *Dreaming.*

Advanced Learners/Pre-AP

DIFFERENTIATED INSTRUCTION

Research Explain to students that there was more to the Aztec culture than war and human sacrifice. Encourage students to research the contributions the Aztec culture made to the world. Students may investigate Aztec building and engineering, including the development of Aztec cities, how Aztec society was organized and run, and the Aztecs' knowledge of astronomy.

Teach

Literary Element | 1

Point of View Answer:
third person; unclear whether it is limited or omniscient.

[APPROACHING] Review with Approaching Level readers the differences between limited and omniscient third-person point of view. Point out that readers cannot be sure whether the point of view is limited or omniscient because only one character has been introduced so far.

Cultural History ☆

The Aztecs The Aztec culture became powerful because of its success with agriculture, reclaiming swampland for crops, and designing irrigation systems provided food for a growing population. Before the Aztec nation was defeated in 1521, it had a population of nearly six million spread across 80,000 square miles.

 For an audio recording of this selection, use Listening Library Audio CD-ROM.

Readability Scores

Dale-Chall: 5.6
DRP: 57
Lexile: 970

The Night Face Up

Julio Cortázar
Translated by Paul Blackburn

Fire and Destruction, 1985. Juri Palm. Oil on canvas. Art Museum of Estonia, Tallinn.

Halfway down the long hotel vestibule,[1] he thought that probably he was going to be late, and hurried on into the street to get out his motorcycle from the corner where the next-door superintendent let him keep it. On the jewelry store at the corner he read that it was ten to nine; he had time to spare. The sun filtered through the tall downtown buildings, and he—because for himself, for just going along thinking, he did not have a name— he swung onto the machine, savoring the idea of the ride. The motor whirred between his legs, and a cool wind whipped his pants legs.

He let the ministries[2] zip past (the pink, the white), and a series of stores on the main street, their windows flashing. Now he was beginning the most pleasant part of the run, the real ride: a long street bordered with trees, very little traffic, with spacious villas[3] whose gardens rambled all the way down to the sidewalks, which were barely indicated by low hedges. A bit inattentive perhaps, but tooling along on the right side of the street, he allowed himself to be carried away by the freshness, by the weightless contraction of this hardly begun day.

---

1. A *vestibule* (ves′tə būl′) is a small passage or hall between the outer door and the interior of a building.

1 Point of View *What point of view does Cortázar use here?*

1232 UNIT 6 THE MODERN AMERICAS

---

2. *Ministries,* here, are government office buildings.
3. *Villas* are urban homes with a yard and garden space.

Reading Practice

Visualize Explain to students that visualizing is using an author's descriptions to form a mental picture of scenes, characters, and events. Explain that visualization is usually based on what can be seen, but if an author has used imagery that appeals to more than the sense of sight, students may be able to add layers to their visualization.

Ask: What time of day do you visualize? What is the weather like? *(Students are likely to visualize early morning light and a slight breeze.)* **Ask:** How do you visualize the character's motorcycle ride? *(Students are likely to describe pink and white buildings, trees, and gardens speeding by.)* Now encourage students to add layers to their visualizations.

Ask: What can you "visualize" with your other senses? *(Students may say that they can feel the wind rushing by and the motorcycle vibrating. They may describe hearing the motorcycle's engine and the rush of air. They may also discuss the smell of the flowers in the gardens and car exhaust.)* Encourage students to note detailed descriptions and to visualize the action as they continue to read.

This involuntary relaxation, possibly, kept him from preventing the accident. When he saw that the woman standing on the corner had rushed into the crosswalk while he still had the green light, it was already somewhat too late for a simple solution. He braked hard with foot and hand, wrenching himself to the left; he heard the woman scream, and at the collision his vision went. It was like falling asleep all at once.

He came to abruptly. Four or five young men were getting him out from under the cycle. He felt the taste of salt and blood, one knee hurt, and when they hoisted him up he yelped, he couldn't bear the pressure on his right arm. Voices which did not seem to belong to the faces hanging above him encouraged him cheerfully with jokes and assurances. His single **solace** was to hear someone else confirm that the lights indeed had been in his favor. He asked about the woman, trying to keep down the nausea which was edging up into his throat. While they carried him face up to a nearby pharmacy, he learned that the cause of the accident had gotten only a few scrapes on the legs. "Nah, you barely got her at all, but when ya hit, the impact made the machine jump and flop on its side . . ." Opinions, recollections of other smashups, take it easy, work him in shoulders first, there, that's fine, and someone in a dustcoat giving him a swallow of something soothing in the shadowy interior of the small local pharmacy.

Within five minutes the police ambulance arrived, and they lifted him onto a cushioned stretcher. It was a relief for him to be able to lie out flat. Completely **lucid,** but realizing that he was suffering the effects

of a terrible shock, he gave his information to the officer riding in the ambulance with him. The arm almost didn't hurt; blood dripped down from a cut over the eyebrow all over his face. He licked his lips once or twice to drink it. He felt pretty good, it had been an accident, tough luck; stay quiet a few weeks, nothing worse. The guard said that the motorcycle didn't seem badly racked up. "Why should it," he replied. "It all landed on top of me." They both laughed, and when they got to the hospital, the guard shook his hand and wished him luck. Now the nausea was coming back little by little; meanwhile they were pushing him on a wheeled stretcher toward a pavilion[4] further back, rolling along under trees full of birds, he shut his eyes and wished he were asleep or chloroformed.[5] But they kept him for a good while in a room with that hospital smell, filling out a form, getting his clothes off, and dressing him in a stiff, grayish smock. They moved his arm carefully, it didn't hurt him. The nurses were constantly making wisecracks, and if it hadn't been for the stomach contractions he would have felt fine, almost happy.

They got him over to X ray, and twenty minutes later, with the still-damp negative lying on his chest like a black tombstone, they pushed him into surgery. Someone tall and thin in white came over and began to look at the X rays. A woman's hands were arranging his head, he felt that they were moving him from one stretcher to another.

---

4. A *pavilion*, here, is an extension of a main building, such as a hospital.
5. *Chloroformed* (klôr′ə fôrmd) means "rendered unconscious through the use of chloroform, a sweet-smelling, colorless liquid."

Point of View *In this passage, how does the narrator reveal the character's thoughts?* **3**

Identify Sequence *List the events that have occurred in the story so far in chronological order.* **4**

JULIO CORTÁZAR **1233**

Vocabulary

solace (sol′is) *n.* a source of relief; mental or spiritual comfort

lucid (loo′sid) *adj.* having full use of one's mental abilities; clearheaded

Teach

Reading Strategy   2

Identify Sequence Ask: What two things happen simultaneously? *(The man is carried, and he finds out what has happened to the woman.)* **Ask:** What word indicates sequence here? *(While)*

 For additional practice using the reading skill or strategy, see Unit 6 Teaching Resources Book, p. 178.

Literary Element   3

Point of View Answer: *The narrator describes the character's physical injuries with sensory images.*

Reading Strategy   4

Identify Sequence Answer: *The narrator had a motorcycle accident and was taken to the hospital. He joked with some of the attendants, started experiencing nausea and stomach contractions, was X-rayed, and was pushed into surgery.*

Learning Objectives
Analyzing point of view. (SE)
Identifying sequence. (SE)
Visualizing story details. (TE)

English Learners

DIFFERENTIATED INSTRUCTION

Intermediate Because sentences often rely on word order for meaning, English learners may have some difficulty with placing adverbs because the same adverb can appear in more than one position in a sentence. Write the following sentences on the board and ask students to identify the adverb in each sentence. **He came to abruptly. They moved his arm carefully.** *(abruptly, carefully)*

Explain that because these sentences are simple, or without dependent clauses, the adverb in each may be moved without changing the sentence's meaning. Have students rewrite each sentence, moving the adverb to create a different, but still grammatically correct, sentence. *(Revisions: Abruptly, he came to. Carefully they moved his arm.)*

Explain to students that moving adverbs in complex sentences is more difficult, especially when there is more than one adverb. Write this example on the board: He came to abruptly and groggily asked what had happened. Explain that the adverb must be kept near the verb it modifies. Show students this incorrect revision: Groggily, he came to abruptly and asked what had happened.

Teach

Big Idea   1

Magic Realism Ask: What is the first indication that the realistic and the fantastic are combined in this story? (*The man is dreaming of smells, and he has never dreamed smells before.*)

Reading Strategy   2

Identify Sequence Answer: *The story appears to have shifted from "real life" to a dream set in a Mexican forest during the time of Aztec rule.*

Big Idea   3

Magic Realism Ask: How do reality and fantasy combine here? (*He jumps in his dream and in his bed at the same time.*)

The man in white came over to him again, smiling, something gleamed in his right hand. He patted his cheek and made a sign to someone stationed behind.

1 It was unusual as a dream because it was full of smells, and he never dreamed smells. First a marshy smell, there to the left of the trail the swamps began already, the quaking bogs from which no one ever returned. But the reek lifted, and instead there came a dark, fresh composite fragrance, like the night under which he moved, in flight from the Aztecs. And it was all so natural, he had to run from the Aztecs who had set out on their manhunt, and his sole chance was to find a place to hide in the deepest part of the forest, taking care not to lose the narrow trail which only they, the Motecas,[6] knew.

What tormented him the most was the odor, as though, notwithstanding the absolute acceptance of the dream, there was something which resisted that which was not habitual, which until that point had not participated in the game. "It smells of war," he thought, his hand going instinctively to the stone knife which was tucked at an angle into his girdle of woven wool. An unexpected sound made him crouch suddenly stock-still and shaking. To be afraid was nothing strange, there was plenty of fear in his dreams. He waited, covered by the branches of a shrub and the starless night. Far off, probably on the other side of the big lake, they'd be lighting the bivouac[7] fires; that part of the sky had a reddish glare. The sound was not repeated. It had been like a broken limb. Maybe an animal

that, like himself, was escaping from the smell of war. He stood erect slowly, sniffing the air. Not a sound could be heard, but the fear was still following, as was the smell, that cloying[8] incense of the war of the blossom. He had to press forward, to stay out of the bogs and get to the heart of the forest. Groping uncertainly through the dark, stooping every other moment to touch the packed earth of the trail, he took a few steps. He would have liked to have broken into a run, but the gurgling fens lapped on either side of him. On the path and in darkness, he took his bearings. Then he caught a horrible blast of that foul smell he was most afraid of, and leaped forward desperately. **3**

"You're going to fall off the bed," said the patient next to him. "Stop bouncing around, old buddy."

He opened his eyes and it was afternoon, the sun already low in the oversized windows of the long ward. While trying to smile at his neighbor, he detached himself almost physically from the final scene of the nightmare. His arm, in a plaster cast, hung suspended from an apparatus with weights and pulleys. He felt thirsty, as though he'd been running for miles, but they didn't want to give him much water, barely enough to moisten his lips and make a mouthful. The fever was winning slowly and he would have been able to sleep again, but he was enjoying the pleasure of keeping awake, eyes half-closed, listening to the other patients' conversation, answering a question from time to time. He saw a little white pushcart come up beside the bed, a blond nurse rubbed the front of his thigh with alcohol and stuck him with a fat needle connected to a tube which ran up to a bottle filled with a milky, opalescent[9] liquid.

---

6. *Motecas* are another Native American culture of central Mexico.

7. A *bivouac* (biv′ ō̅o̅ ak′) is a temporary military encampment.

2 Identify Sequence *What shift in time and place seems to have taken place in this section?*

8. *Cloying* means "causing weariness by too much of anything pleasant."

9. *Opalescent* means "having a play of colors like that of an opal, a translucent gemstone."

Literary Element Practice

Setting and Mood Explain that specific details in a setting will often help a reader immediately know what kind of story he or she will be reading. **Ask:** What kind of story is usually set in a haunted house? (*a horror story*) on a battlefield? (*a war story*) on another planet? (*a science-fiction story*) Then, discuss the link between setting and mood.

Ask: What mood do you immediately identify with a story set in a haunted house? (*Students are likely to answer scary, depressing, morose, or anxious.*) Explain that sometimes authors will place unusual events in normal, everyday settings to create a more powerful effect.
Ask: What effect does the contrast between the hospital and the forest setting have on the mood of the story?

(*Students are likely to say that the strange dream is even more strange when contrasted with the clean and quiet hospital.*) Encourage students to consider the contrast in setting as they continue the story.

Jungle with Branches (Selva con rama). María Eugenia Terrazas. Watercolor, 70 x 60 cm. Private collection.

A young intern arrived with some metal and leather apparatus which he adjusted to fit onto the good arm to check something or other. Night fell, and the fever went along dragging him down softly to a state in which things seemed embossed as through opera glasses,[10] they were real and soft and, at the same time, vaguely distasteful; like sitting in a boring movie and thinking that, well, still, it'd be worse out in the street, and staying.

A cup of a marvelous golden broth came, smelling of leeks, celery and parsley. A small hunk of bread, more precious than a whole banquet, found itself crumbling little by little. His arm hardly hurt him at all, and only in the eyebrow where they'd taken stitches a quick, hot pain sizzled occasionally. When the big windows across the way turned to smudges of dark blue, he thought it would not be difficult for him to sleep. Still on his back so a little uncomfortable, running his tongue out over his hot, too-dry lips, he tasted the broth still, and with a sigh of bliss, he let himself drift off.

10. *Opera glasses* are small, lightweight binoculars.

First there was a confusion, as of one drawing all his sensations, for that moment blunted or muddled, into himself. He realized that he was running in pitch darkness, although, above, the sky crisscrossed with treetops was less black than the rest. "The trail," he thought, "I've gotten off the trail." His feet sank into a bed of leaves and mud, and then he couldn't take a step that the branches of shrubs did not whiplash against his ribs and legs. Out of breath, knowing despite the darkness and silence that he was surrounded, he crouched down to listen. Maybe the trail was very near, with the first daylight he would be able to see it again. Nothing now could help him to find it. The hand that had unconsciously gripped the haft[11] of the dagger climbed like a fen scorpion up to his neck where the protecting amulet[12] hung. Barely moving his lips, he mumbled the **supplication** of the corn which brings about the **beneficent** moons, and the prayer to Her Very Highness,[13] to the distributor of all Motecan possessions. At the same time he felt his ankles sinking deeper into the mud, and the waiting in the darkness of the obscure grove of live oak grew intolerable to him. The war of the blossom had started at the beginning of the moon and had been going on for three days and three nights now. If he managed to hide in the depths of the forest, getting off the trail further up

---

11. The *haft* of a dagger is its handle.
12. An *amulet* is an object worn to bring good fortune or to protect against disease or misfortune.
13. *Her Very Highness* is an apparent reference to a Motecan deity.

Point of View *How does the point of view contribute to the confused and fearful mood of the story?* **5**

Vocabulary

supplication (sup′lə kā′shən) *n.* a humble entreaty; a prayer of request
beneficent (bə nef′ə sənt) *adj.* doing or producing good

JULIO CORTÁZAR **1235**

Teach

Reading Strategy | **4**

Identify Sequence **Ask:** What happens before the "confusion"? *(He eats and then goes to sleep in the hospital.)* What happens right after the "confusion"? *(He realizes that he has lost the trail.)*

Literary Element | **5**

Point of View **Answer:** *The third-person point of view allows the narrator to describe the protagonist's passing from sleep to wakefulness, the confusion of his flight through the forest, and the sense of uncertainty about what is really occurring in the story.*

View the Art ★

María Eugenia Terrazas used soft outlines in this painting, making the foliage barely distinguishable from the pools of light on the jungle floor. **Ask:** How does this painting appeal to the senses? Does the story appeal in a similar way? *(The painting may appeal to students visually, with its lush colors. The story might appeal additionally to senses of touch, smell, or hearing, because of the narrator's description.)*

Advanced Learners/Pre-AP

DIFFERENTIATED INSTRUCTION

Make Predictions Challenge students to make predictions about the text. Explain that predictions are based on clues in the text and a reader's experience or knowledge. Explain that making predictions about stories that use magic realism, however, can be tricky because of the nature of the genre. Remind students that it is difficult to know what is "real" and what is "fantasy" in magic realism.

Before finishing the story, have students write predictions about what will happen to the man in the hospital bed and what will happen to the man in his dreams. Tell students to support their predictions with clues from the text and their own knowledge. After they finish the story and verify their predictions, students may share what they learned about magic realism with the class.

Learning Objectives
Analyzing point of view. (SE)
Identifying sequence. (SE)
Analyzing setting and mood. (TE)

1235

Teach

Reading Strategy　1

Identify Sequence Answer:
The knife links the dream and real life. The protagonist, his hunters, and the doctor have knives. Other devices that link the sequence of events are the protagonist's thirst and the sense that the doctors and nurses begin to resemble the Aztec priests.

APPROACHING Instruct Approaching Level students to reread the previous dream sequence and write a list of items and events found there. Then, students can use this list to understand the similarities among dream sequences before investigating the similarities these items have to those in the hospital setting.

Literary Element　2

Analyze Point of View

Ask: How do the character's thoughts in this passage contribute to the narrow perspective of the story? *(Students may say that the character's fear of the nightmare and his thoughts of amusing himself enhance the feeling of being inside one person's head without any other perspective.)*

Detail from Aztec Codex, early 16th century AD. Manuscript on paper, 39 x 40 cm. Bibliotheque de l'Assemblee Nationale, Paris.

past the marsh country, perhaps the warriors wouldn't follow his track. He thought of the many prisoners they'd already taken. But the number didn't count, only the consecrated period. The hunt would continue until the priests gave the sign to return. Everything had its number and its limit, and it was within the sacred period, and he on the other side from the hunters.

He heard the cries and leaped up, knife in hand. As if the sky were aflame on the horizon, he saw torches moving among the branches, very near him. The smell of war was unbearable, and when the first enemy jumped him, leaped at his throat, he felt an almost-pleasure in sinking the stone blade flat to the haft into his chest. The lights were already around him, the happy cries. He managed to cut the air once or twice, then a rope snared him from behind.

---

1 Identify Sequence *How does the image of the knife help connect the events? What other elements link the sequence of events?*

"It's the fever," the man in the next bed said. "The same thing happened to me when they operated on my duodenum.[14] Take some water, you'll see, you'll sleep all right."

Laid next to the night from which he came back, the tepid[15] shadow of the ward seemed delicious to him. A violet lamp kept watch high on the far wall like a guardian eye. You could hear coughing, deep breathing, once in a while a conversation in whispers. Everything was pleasant and secure, without the chase, no . . . But he didn't want to go on thinking about the nightmare. There were lots of things to amuse himself with. He began to look at the cast on his arm, and the pulleys that held it so comfortably in the air. They'd left a bottle of mineral water on the night table beside him. He put the neck of the bottle to his mouth and drank it like a precious liqueur. He could now make out the different shapes in the ward, the thirty beds, the closets with glass doors. He guessed that his fever was down, his face felt cool. The cut over the eyebrow barely hurt at all, like a recollection. He saw himself leaving the hotel again, wheeling out the cycle. Who'd have thought that it would end like this? He tried to fix the moment of the accident exactly, and it got him very angry to notice that there was a void there, an emptiness he could not manage to fill. Between the impact and the moment that they picked him up off the pavement, the passing out or what went on, there was nothing he could see. And at the same time he had the feeling that this void, this nothingness, had lasted an eternity. No, not even time, more as if, in this void, he had passed across something, or

2

---

14. The *duodenum* (dōō′ ə dē′ nəm) is part of the small intestine.
15. *Tepid* means "moderately or slightly warm."

Reading Practice

 SMALL GROUP

Analyze Conflict Review with students the differences between internal and external conflict. Internal conflict is a struggle that characters have within themselves, while external conflict is a struggle characters have with an outside force such as another character. **Ask:** What internal conflict is the character in the hospital having? *(He is having nightmares and wants them to stop.)*

Ask: What external conflict is the character in the dream having? *(He is hunted and caught by Aztecs.)* In small groups, have students discuss the possibility of characters sharing conflicts, or of one character's conflict having an impact on another character's conflict. **Ask:** In what way does each character share the other's conflict? How does this link between conflicts affect the story?

(Student groups may say that the man in the hospital bed shares the prisoner's external conflict because he cannot get out of bed or move; he is being held prisoner. The prisoner shares the patient's internal conflict because he is afraid and has no control over what is happening. The sharing of these conflicts adds to the heightened feeling of captivity and imminent danger.)

had run back immense distances. The shock, the brutal dashing against the pavement. Anyway, he had felt an immense relief in coming out of the black pit while the people were lifting him off the ground. With pain in the broken arm, blood from the split eyebrow, contusion on the knee; with all that, a relief in returning to daylight, to the day, and to feel sustained and attended. That was weird. Someday he'd ask the doctor at the office about that. Now sleep began to take over again, to pull him slowly down. The pillow was so soft, and the coolness of the mineral water in his fevered throat. The violet light of the lamp up there was beginning to get dimmer and dimmer.

As he was sleeping on his back, the position in which he came to did not surprise him, but on the other hand the damp smell, the smell of oozing rock, blocked his throat and forced him to understand. Open the eyes and look in all directions, hopeless. He was surrounded by an absolute darkness. Tried to get up and felt ropes pinning his wrists and ankles. He was staked to the ground on a floor of dank, icy stone slabs. The cold bit into his naked back, his legs. Dully, he tried to touch the amulet with his chin and found they had stripped him of it. Now he was lost, no prayer could save him from the final . . . From afar off, as though filtering through the rock of the dungeon, he heard the great kettledrums of the feast. They had carried him to the temple, he was in the underground cells of Teocalli itself, awaiting his turn.

He heard a yell, a hoarse yell that rocked off the walls. Another yell, ending in a moan. It was he

Visual Vocabulary
Teocalli was the chief temple in Tenochtitlán, the Aztec capital.

who was screaming in the darkness, he was screaming because he was alive, his whole body with that cry fended off what was coming, the inevitable end. He thought of his friends filling up the other dungeons, and of those already walking up the stairs of the sacrifice. He uttered another choked cry, he could barely open his mouth, his jaws were twisted back as if with a rope and a stick, and once in a while they would open slowly with an endless exertion, as if they were made of rubber. The creaking of the wooden latches jolted him like a whip. Rent, writhing, he fought to rid himself of the cords sinking into his flesh. His right arm, the strongest, strained until the pain became unbearable and he had to give up. He watched the double door open, and the smell of the torches reached him before the light did. Barely girdled by the ceremonial loincloths, the priests' acolytes[16] moved in his direction, looking at him with contempt. Lights reflected off the sweaty torsos and off the black hair dressed with feathers. The cords went slack, and in their place the grappling of hot hands, hard as bronze; he felt himself lifted, still face up, and jerked along by the four acolytes who carried him down the passageway.

The torchbearers went ahead, indistinctly lighting up the corridor with its dripping walls and a ceiling so low that the acolytes had to duck their heads. Now they were taking

16. *Acolytes* (ak′ə līts′) are individuals who assist a priest at religious services.

Magic Realism *What details in this passage emphasize the overlap of the two worlds the narrator experiences?* **3**

Big Idea 3

Magic Realism Answer: *Day and night overlap, the character feels the same pain in his arm in both states, he sees similar lights, and he feels like he is bound or restrained in both states.*

Cultural History

Aztec Calendar The Aztec culture had an elaborate calendar system of a 365-day civil cycle and a 260-day ritual cycle. Every 52 years, the New Fire Ceremony was held to celebrate the day when the two calendars matched. After everyone let their fires burn out, priests reignited home and ritual fires from a fire lit on the breast of a human sacrifice.

Approaching Level

DIFFERENTIATED INSTRUCTION

SMALL GROUP

Summarize As the action in the dream sequences becomes more frantic, struggling readers may have difficulty with comprehension because of the author's use of sentence fragments and comma splices. To improve students' comprehension, have them work in small groups to individually read a portion of the scene in which the prisoner wakes up in the cell.

As students read, they should try to mentally complete sentence fragments and create two sentences out of comma splices. Then, have the groups convene and write a summary of their individual portions of the scene. Encourage students to assist one another with comprehension. Finally, students should compile their summaries of smaller sections into a comprehensive summary.

Learning Objectives
Identifying sequence. (SE)
Analyzing point of view. (TE)
Analyzing conflict. (TE)

Teach

Big Idea 1

Magic Realism Ask: How is fantasy beginning to take over reality? *(The patient cannot stay in the hospital; he is unable to "wake up" and leave his dream behind.)*

Literary Element 2

Point of View Answer: *In the beginning, the narrator seemed to take the motorcycle, the city, the traffic lights, and the ambulance for granted. Here, however, we realize he didn't really understand those things and they were just part of a fantastic dream.*

 To check students' understanding of the selection, see Unit 6 Teaching Resources Book, p. 182.

him out, taking him out, it was the end. Face up, under a mile of living rock which, for a succession of moments, was lit up by a glimmer of torchlight. When the stars came out up there instead of the roof and the great terraced steps rose before him, on fire with cries and dances, it would be the end. The passage was never going to end, but now it was beginning to end, he would see suddenly the open sky full of stars, but not yet, they trundled him along endlessly in the reddish shadow, hauling him roughly along and he did not want that, but how to stop it if they had torn off the amulet, his real heart, the life-center.

In a single jump he came out into the hospital night, to the high, gentle, bare ceiling, to the soft shadow wrapping him round. He thought he must have cried out, but his neighbors were peacefully snoring. The water in the bottle on the night table was somewhat bubbly, a translucent shape against the dark azure shadow of the windows. He panted, looking for some relief for his lungs, oblivion for those images still glued to his eyelids. Each time he shut his eyes he saw them take shape instantly, and he sat up, completely wrung out, but savoring at the same time the surety that now he was awake, that the night nurse would answer if he rang, that soon it would be daybreak, with the good, deep sleep he usually had at that hour, no images, no nothing . . . It was difficult to keep his eyes open, the drowsiness was more powerful than he. He made one last effort, he sketched a gesture toward the bottle of water with his good hand and did not manage to reach it, his fingers closed again on a black emptiness, and the passageway went on endlessly, rock after rock, with momentary ruddy flares, and face up he choked out a dull moan because the roof was about to end, it rose, was opening like a mouth of shadow, and the acolytes straightened up,

and from on high a waning[17] moon fell on a face whose eyes wanted not to see it, were closing and opening desperately, trying to pass to the other side, to find again the bare, protecting ceiling of the ward. And every time they opened, it was night and the moon, while they climbed the great terraced steps, his head hanging down backward now, and up at the top were the bonfires, red columns of perfumed smoke, and suddenly he saw the red stone, shiny with the blood dripping off it, and the spinning arcs cut by the feet of the victim whom they pulled off to throw him rolling down the north steps. With a last hope he shut his lids tightly, moaning to wake up. For a second he thought he had gotten there, because once more he was immobile in the bed, except that his head was hanging down off it, swinging. But he smelled death, and when he opened his eyes he saw the blood-soaked figure of the executioner-priest coming toward him with the stone knife in his hand. He managed to close his eyelids again, although he knew now he was not going to wake up, that he was awake, that the marvelous dream had been the other, absurd as all dreams are—a dream in which he was going through the strange avenues of an astonishing city, with green and red lights that burned without fire or smoke, on an enormous metal insect that whirred away between his legs. In the infinite lie of the dream, they had also picked him up off the ground, someone had approached him also with a knife in his hand, approached him who was lying face up, face up with his eyes closed between the bonfires on the steps. ❧

1

---

17. *Waning* means "diminishing in size, strength, or brightness."

Point of View *What does this passage reveal about the narrator's perception of the events at the beginning of the story?* 2

Writing Practice

Short Story Because "The Night Face Up" is told from the third-person point of view, readers never hear directly from the protagonist when he is a patient or a prisoner. The character's reactions, thoughts, and emotions are all communicated by the narrator. Invite students to choose a scene in the story and rewrite it from first-person point of view.

Challenge students to choose a scene in which the patient sleeps and "dreams" the prisoner or vice versa. Once students choose a scene, **ask** the following questions to get them started: What extra information can you add to the scene if it is told from first-person point of view? What emotions and thoughts is the character experiencing?

What can the character see, feel, smell, hear, or taste, and how will the character describe it from his point of view? Encourage students to share their rewritten scenes with the class.

After You Read

Respond and Think Critically

Respond and Interpret

1. Which images in this story linger in your mind? Explain.

2. (a)Describe the motorcycle accident. (b)Which symptoms resulting from the accident may affect the rider's perception of reality?

3. (a)What happens to the rider after the accident? (b)What is the rider's impression of the hospital? Use details from the story to support your response.

4. (a)What are the two settings of the story? (b)What parallels exist between these two settings?

5. (a)Why is the Moteca man running through the forest? (b)Until the last paragraph, what does the narrator lead us to believe about the scenes involving the Moteca man?

Analyze and Evaluate

6. (a)What plot twist occurs at the end of the story? (b)Do you think the ending can be explained logically? Why or why not?

7. (a)**Irony** is a contrast between what is expected or believed to be true and what actually occurs or exists. Describe the most important irony of the story. (b)Were you satisfied with the ending? Explain.

8. (a)How would you explain the title of the story? (b)Do you think the title is effective? Explain.

Connect

9. **Big Idea** Magic Realism (a)What details does Cortázar use to convey the sensation of waking from a dream? (b)How do these details contribute to the sense that perception and reality are often two different things?

10. Connect to Today What kinds of books, movies, or television shows do you know that blur the line between fantasy and reality?

Primary Visual Artifact

Aztec Customs

Aztec religion emphasized the god of the sun, who died each evening and was born anew the next morning. At dawn, he began his struggle, driving away the stars and the moon with a shaft of light. The Aztecs believed the sun god needed human nourishment to maintain his strength for this important task. The Aztecs viewed war, therefore, as a religious endeavor that provided victims for sacrifice.

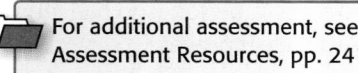

The knife shown here, with a mosaic handle and a stone blade, was made for use in those ceremonial sacrifices.

Group Activity Discuss the following questions with your classmates. Refer to the art and cite evidence from "The Night Face Up" to support your answers.

1. Explain the connection between the art and various descriptions in "The Night Face Up."

2. Notice the intricate detail of the mosaic on the handle of the knife. What might this level of artistry suggest about Aztec culture?

JULIO CORTÁZAR **1239**

Primary Visual Artifact

1. The art shows the sacrificial altar, the priest's acolytes, the priest, and some of the victims at the Aztec temple/pyramid—all details of the forest scenes.

2. Students may say that the level of artistry suggests that the Aztecs took pride in their work and were accomplished in many different areas.

📁 For additional assessment, see Assessment Resources, pp. 241–242.

After You Read

Assess

1. Answers will vary.

2. (a) The man riding a motorcycle collides with a woman who has stepped into a crosswalk. (b) The rider's head injuries, blood loss, and fever may have altered his perception.

3. (a) He is taken to a pharmacy and later transported to a hospital. (b)The rider focuses on sensory details of the hospital.

4. (a) One is an unnamed modern city; the other is a forest in Mexico hundreds of years before. (b) In both, the subject awakes stunned and confused. Overlapping elements: a knife, feeling of being bound, pain in his arm, and various lights.

5. (a) He is trying to escape from Aztec warriors. (b) that the Aztec scenes are a dream

6. (a) The forest scene is real, and the motorcycle accident is the dream. (b) Answers will vary.

7. (a) the ending, which subverts the reader's expectations about reality and fantasy (b) Answers will vary.

8. (a) The title may refer to the position of the rider during surgery and the Moteca man during the sacrifice. (b) Most will agree that the title is effective because it represents the inversion of reality and fantasy.

9. (a) The author uses details and sensations that cross between the two settings; for example, the Moteca man feels bound by ropes, which may be the tubes or restraints used in a hospital. (b) These details show that perception is unreliable.

10. Students might mention books, movies, or shows that deal with time travel, science fiction, or fantasy.

After You Read

Assess

Literary Element

D is the correct answer. The story is told in the third person, but it is limited to the perceptions of the protagonist.

Review: Style

Additional example of fragment might include the following:

- "Another yell, ending in a moan."

Additional example of comma splices might include the following:

- "The man in white came over to him again, smiling, something gleamed in his right hand."

Students might mention that the fragments and splices contribute to the sense of confusion the narrator is experiencing—his thoughts, like his sentences, are disjointed and confused.

Progress Check

Can students analyze point of view?

If No → See Unit 6 Teaching Resources Book, p. 177.

Reading Strategy

1. (a) his realization in the city that he's about to have a motorcycle accident (b) The protagonist's capture and movement to the temple correspond to his being taken by the ambulance attendants to the hospital.
2. It causes the reader to be as confused as the protagonist.

Vocabulary Practice

Sample answers:

solace Antonyms: uneasiness, distress Explanation: Unlike a per-

1240

Literary Element Point of View

ACT Skills Practice

From which point of view is "The Night Face Up" told?

A. First person.

B. Second person.

C. Third-person omniscient.

D. Third-person limited.

Review: Style

As you learned on page 1221, **style** is the expressive qualities that distinguish an author's work. Elements of style include sentence length and variety, diction, organization, and use of figurative language, dialect, or rhythmic devices.

Partner Activity With a classmate, discuss how Cortázar plays with sentence structure conventions. Consider the fact that poets and fiction writers frequently violate the rules of sentence structure to create specific literary effects. In "The Night Face Up," Cortázar uses both sentence fragments and comma splices (clauses joined by commas, often in combination with fragments). Work with your partner to complete a chart like the one below. Then consider this question: How does Cortázar's use of sentence fragments and comma splices convey a sense of confusion and rapid action?

Sentence Type	Examples
Fragment	The shock, the brutal dashing against the pavement.
Comma splice	They had carried him to the temple, he was in the underground cells of Teocalli itself, awaiting his turn.

LOG ON ▶ **Literature** Online

Selection Resources For Selection Quizzes, eFlashcards, and Reading-Writing Connection activities, go to glencoe.com and enter QuickPass code GLW6053u6.

Reading Strategy Identify Sequence

In "The Night Face Up," the author jumps back and forth in time. Yet within each time frame, the sequence of events is clear. If you **identify sequence** as you read, you can keep the events organized in your mind. Consult your chart from page 1231 and then answer the following questions.

1. (a)Which event in the city sequence corresponds to the narrator's realization that he's "gotten off the trail" in the Aztec sequence? (b)Which city event matches the narrator's being captured and taken to the temple?

2. How does the movement from one sequence to another add to the mystery of the story?

Vocabulary Practice

Practice with Antonyms Antonyms are words that have opposite meanings. With a partner, brainstorm three antonyms for each boldfaced vocabulary word below. Then discuss your choices with your classmates. Be prepared to explain why you chose your words.

solace   lucid   supplication   beneficent

EXAMPLE: zealous
Antonyms: indifferent, apathetic, uninterested
Sample explanation: A zealous person would show great enthusiasm, but an apathetic person would not.

Academic Vocabulary

In "The Night Face Up," Cortázar creates an **analogous** relationship between the sensations experienced when dreaming and those experienced when awake.

Analogous is an academic word. For example, one might say that the relationship between the body and the brain is *analogous* to the relationship between a car and driver. To further explore this word, complete the following sentence.

The feeling Cortázar's protagonist has when riding his motorcycle is analogous to the feeling I have when ____.

For more on academic vocabulary, see pages 36–37 and R83–R85.

---

son in distress, a person who had found solace would feel peaceful.

lucid Antonyms: confused, muddled, incoherent Explanation: A person who is lucid would think clearly; a person who is confused would not.

supplication Antonyms: refusal, rejection Explanation: A supplication is a request for something; a grant is given in response to a request.

beneficent Antonyms: harmful, malevolent, malicious Explanation: A beneficent person would help others, while a malevolent person would harm others.

Academic Vocabulary

Students should describe an activity that is relaxing and enjoyable to them.

Respond Through Writing

Review

Convince an Audience When deciding whether to read a book, people often consult reviews. Write a 500-word critical review of Cortázar's story. Include your opinions about both the effectiveness of the point of view and the sequence of events. Your audience is a group of peers who like literature.

Understand the Task In a **review**, a writer presents his or her well-supported opinions about a work of literature or nonfiction.

Prewrite Read book and film reviews for ideas on how to express your own opinions and format your review. Pay attention to the language these critics use, and think about how to use similar words and phrases.

Next, reread the story and determine your controlling idea. To help you plan your review, fill out a pro-and-con chart like the one below.

"The Night Face Up"	
Pros	Cons
Alternating between two stories keeps the reader interested	The story is frustratingly inconclusive

Draft As you draft your review, make sure you back up your points with evidence from the story. Make sure you cite all quotations correctly. Try to anticipate disagreements your audience might have and address these in your paper. You can make your analysis more convincing by using rhetorical strategies that professional reviewers use, such as

- **Glittering generalities**—emotionally charged words, such as *heroism* or *love,* that are associated with deeply valued concepts

- **Rhetorical questions**—questions posed to prove a point rather than to get an answer

Revise After you have drafted your review, check it for logic. Do your examples support your opinion? Exchange with a partner and review each other's work. Incorporate your partner's comments in your draft.

Edit and Proofread Proofread your paper, correcting any errors in spelling, grammar, and punctuation. Use the word-count feature on your computer to make sure your review is 500 words. Review the Grammar Tip in the side column to help you with transitional phrases.

JULIO CORTÁZAR **1241**

Learning Objectives

In this assignment, you will focus on the following objectives:

Writing: Writing a review.

Grammar: Understanding how to use transitional phrases.

> **Grammar Tip**

Transitional Phrases

Transitional phrases clarify the relationship between two ideas. They often include transitional words such as *however, next,* and *therefore.* Transitional words express relationships based on sequence (*when, before, soon, first, second*), space (*beyond, farther, in front of*), and importance (*in fact, especially, above all*). Look at the following sentence:

"The Night Face Up" is an entertaining read. More important, it is a story that challenges readers' beliefs about reality.

More important is a transitional phrase. It makes the relationship between the two sentences clearer.

After You Read

Assess

 ## Respond Through Writing

Students' reviews should

- express a clear opinion about the story and back it up with specific evidence
- use a logical organizational strategy, including an introduction, a body, and a conclusion
- address the audience's potential disagreements with the student's opinion
- use a variety of rhetorical strategies, such as glittering generalities, rhetorical questions, and bandwagon statements

 For grammar practice, see Unit 6 Teaching Resources Book, p. 181.

To create custom assessments online, go to Progress Reporter Online Assessment.

 To create custom assessments using software, use ExamView Assessment Suite.

English Learners

DIFFERENTIATED INSTRUCTION

Intermediate Some English learners may be confused by an assignment that gives them free rein to state and support an opinion about literature. Ask students whether giving a personal opinion in a public forum or even reviewing literature, film, or other art is something that is considered acceptable for young people in their native country.

Explain to English learners that while people are entitled to a personal opinion on any subject, analysis and support are necessary in a review. Encourage students to read reviews about American media to understand how the reviewer supports his or her opinion.

Advanced Learners/Pre-AP

DIFFERENTIATED INSTRUCTION

Explore Other Works Encourage students to find, read, and review another of Cortazar's short stories. Have students compare his use of magic realism in "The Night Face Up" with that in the other tale. Students can present their reviews to class, describing the story's use of magic realism and explaining why other students might or might not like the story.

Focus

Activity

Write the following sentences on the board:

Theresa made the game-winning _____ before the final buzzer.

We packed a _____ for our trip to the park.

Ask: What word will work in both of these sentences? *(basket)*

Teach

Parts of Speech

Remind students that multiple-meaning words share the same part of speech. For example, the word *stage* can be a verb or a noun; however, the noun *stage* has several different meanings, making it a multiple-meaning word. Tell students in order to understand the meaning of a multiple-meaning word, they should determine how the word is being used in its context.

Assess

1. b
2. b

Vocabulary Practice

Learning Objectives

In this workshop, you will focus on the following objective:

Vocabulary: Understanding multiple-meaning words.

Multiple-meaning Words

A **multiple-meaning word** is a word that has several related definitions listed in a single dictionary entry.

Test-Taking Tip

To determine the intended use of a multiple-meaning word, look for context clues.

LOG ON ▶ Literature Online

Vocabulary For more vocabulary practice, go to glencoe.com and enter QuickPass code GLW6053u6.

Vocabulary Workshop

Multiple-Meaning Words

Literature Connection In the following sentence from Julio Cortázar's "The Night Face Up," *right* means "situated to the side of the body that is east when one is facing north."

> *"A bit inattentive perhaps, but tooling along on the right side of the street, he allowed himself to be carried away by the freshness, by the weightless contraction of this hardly begun day."*

Right can also mean "correct," "appropriate," and "having its axis perpendicular to the base." *Right* is a **multiple-meaning word,** or a word that has several related definitions listed within a single dictionary entry. Multiple-meaning words are different from homographs, which are words that are spelled alike but different in meaning or derivation or pronunciation. Homographs have separate dictionary entries that are usually designated by superscript numerals.

Here are two groups of sentences in which multiple-meaning words are used differently according to context.

The test results came back <u>positive</u>.
She always had a <u>positive</u> attitude.
I'm <u>positive</u> I saw him in the store.

He is the <u>object</u> of my affection.
That is an oddly shaped <u>object</u>.
The <u>object</u> of this class is to learn about world literature.

Practice Read each of the sentences below. On a separate piece of paper, write the letter of the best definition for the underlined word. Use a dictionary if you need help.

1. I put little <u>stock</u> in his word because he's been wrong before.
  a. a portion of financial capital in a corporation
  b. confidence or faith
  c. the descendants of one individual

2. Studying for the test will be the <u>key</u> to success.
  a. an instrument by which the bolt of a lock is turned
  b. something that provides a solution
  c. one of the levers of a keyboard instrument

Understand Multiple-Meaning Words Understanding the difference between multiple-meaning words and homographs can be confusing for students of all levels. Remind students that a word that has multiple meanings can be a homograph, but that if one form of the word has more than one definition, that form of the word is a multiple-meaning word. For example, the verb *present* is pronounced differently than the noun,

making it a homograph. Yet, the verb *present* has multiple definitions, making it a multiple-meaning word, but the noun form of *present* that means *gift* is not.

Have students use a dictionary to identify each of the following words as a homograph or multiple-meaning word: *tone* (noun), *cut* (verb), *kid* (adjective). Then, students should use the multiple-meaning word(s) to write two sentences, using these words differently in each

sentence. *(Sentences will vary. Students should write two sentences using the noun* tone, *meaning a musical sound, a manner of expression, or the tint or shade of a color; they should also use the verb* cut, *meaning to slice, to hurt someone's feelings, or to make an abrupt transition, among other definitions. The adjective* kid *is not a multiple-meaning word; its most common usage is in the phrase "kid brother.")*

Before You Read

The Handsomest Drowned Man in the World

Meet **Gabriel García Márquez**
(born 1928)

> "In the Caribbean, we are capable of believing anything."
>
> —Gabriel García Márquez

Born to a poor family in Aracataca, Colombia, Gabriel García Márquez spent the first eight years of his life living with his grandparents "in an enormous house, full of ghosts." Later, García Márquez would model many of his characters on his grandparents "because I knew how they talked, how they behaved." His grandmother shared local legends with the boy, while his grandfather, a retired colonel, told him stories of the fierce civil war that Colombians call the War of a Thousand Days (1899–1902).

The Fantastic Epicenter García Márquez's childhood home, near the Caribbean coast of Colombia, is the epicenter of his fictional universe. Many of his early novels and stories are set in Macondo, a fictional version of his hometown. His native region provided him with material for his writing and a way of viewing the world that included a taste for the fantastic.

García Márquez was a gifted student and serious about his studies—until he enrolled in college to study law, as his parents wished. García Márquez wanted to be a writer instead. He focused on writing nonfiction during his college years but also began to write fiction. He became a journalist and soon abandoned the study of law to devote himself to writing full time.

One Hundred Years of Solitude The novel that catapulted García Márquez to fame was published in 1967. *One Hundred Years of Solitude* placed characters in Macondo, where anything, it seemed, was possible. International acclaim followed; so, too, did a new respect for the style of writing known as magic realism. Although García Márquez was not the first author to employ this style, he was the author, more than any other, who validated the style and made it an international sensation.

García Márquez has continued to write rich literary works, including *The Autumn of the Patriarch*, a political work about a dictator; and *Love in the Time of Cholera*, a fictional remembrance of love. In 1982, García Márquez received the Nobel Prize in Literature. Since then, he has continued to publish novels, short stories, and some works of nonfiction.

LOG ON ▶ **Literature** Online

Author Search For more about Gabriel García Márquez, go to glencoe.com and enter QuickPass code GLW6053u6.

GABRIEL GARCÍA MÁRQUEZ **1243**

Before You Read

Focus

Bellringer Options

Selection Focus
Transparency 80

Daily Language Practice
Transparency 120

Or ask: Do you think that our society has a healthy attitude toward death? *(Responses will vary.)* Discuss with students the rituals involved in mourning loved ones as well as those we never meet but whose death is national news.

Or ask: How does our attitude toward people change when they die? *(Students may say that after someone dies he or she is remembered for all of the good things he or she did.)*

Selection Skills

Literary Elements
- Hyperbole (SE pp. 1244, 1246, 1249, 1250)
- Theme (SE p. 1250)

The Handsomest Drowned Man in the World

Speaking/Listening/Viewing Skills
- Analyze Art (SE p. 1249)

Reading Skills
- Question (SE pp. 1244, 1246, 1247, 1249, 1251)

Vocabulary Skills
- Practice with Context Clues (SE p. 1251)
- Academic Vocabulary (SE p. 1251)

Writing Skills/Grammar
- Apply Hyperbole (SE p. 1251)
- Main and Subordinate Clauses (TE p. 1248)

Before You Read

Focus

Summary

A drowned man washes up on a village beach and is taken to the nearest house. There the village women clean up the man's body and discover he is the largest, handsomest man any of them has ever seen. They name him Estaban and begin to wonder about what sort of man he was. The villagers prepare a funeral, mourn greatly, and then give him a burial at sea. After the funeral, the villagers are inspired to beautify their village.

 For summaries in languages other than English, see Unit 6 Teaching Resources Book, pp. 184–189.

Vocabulary

Related-Words Crossword Puzzle Have students use a dictionary to find words related to the vocabulary words. The related words will have similar definitions but represent different parts of speech. Then, have students create a crossword puzzle using definitions of the related and vocabulary words as clues. Students can try to solve one another's puzzles. (*Students should find* frivolous, improvisation, *and* discretion.)

Literary Element Practice

Identify Genre The story the students are about to read contains magic realism. While students may be unfamiliar with this literary term, they are likely to be familiar with fantasy and science fiction. Organize the class into four small groups, and assign each group one of the following genres: science fiction, fantasy, fairy tale, realistic fiction. Instruct students to work together to compile a list of elements that each genre contains. Students should

consider types of characters, settings, time periods, and situations. Also have students consider which elements in the genre are "fantastic" and "realistic." **Ask:** Are there elements in fantastical fiction that are realistic? Are there fantastical elements in realistic fiction? (*Student groups' lists will differ.*) As a class, come together to discuss the similarities and differences in each genre.

Then ask: Where does magic realism fall in this list of genres? Is it closer to fantasy? Or is it more realistic than fantastic? (*Students may say that it is a combination of the two.*) Discuss with students the designation of genre categories using books with which the students are familiar.

Literature and Reading Preview

Connect to the Story

What motivates people to make a new start? Discuss this question with a partner. Consider both positive and negative events that could serve as motivation.

Build Background

García Márquez has explained that he knows the art of "saying incredible things with a completely undisturbed face." Authors who use magic realism often blur the lines between reality and fantasy by treating extraordinary events as typical occurrences. The settings in these stories are usually realistic locations, but the characters and events take on a bizarre quality. Some critics have explained this dual nature as an outgrowth of colonialism. Countries composed of multiple cultures, such as Latin American countries, must make sense of more than one reality at a time. Magic realism allows space for the reality of the conquerors and the conquered, as well as the everyday and the fantastic.

Set Purposes for Reading

Big Idea **Magic Realism**

As you read the story, ask yourself, What is real and what is fantastic?

Literary Element **Hyperbole**

Hyperbole is a figure of speech that uses exaggeration to express strong emotion, make a point, or evoke humor. As you read the story, ask yourself, Why does the author use hyperbole?

Reading Strategy **Question**

When you **question,** you participate actively in your reading by investigating the story. As you read, ask yourself questions such as: What is going on here? What does this mean? or Why did the character say, do, or think that? Then find details in the story that might answer your questions.

··········

Tip: Take Notes Use a chart to keep track of your questions and answers.

My Question	My Answer
How big could he possibly be? How small are the villagers' homes?	He could be bloated by having been in the sea; the villagers might live in tiny homes. The villagers may be small people; the man might be a giant only by comparison.

Learning Objectives

For pages 1243–1251

In studying this text, you will focus on the following objectives:

Literary Study: Analyzing hyperbole.

Reading: Questioning.

Writing: Applying hyperbole.

Vocabulary

haggard (hag′ərd) *adj.* worn or wasted, as from hunger; p. 1246 *Leah was haggard after having spent two days lost on Mount Spenser.*

frivolity (fri vol′ə tē) *n.* silliness; p. 1247 *The adults, who had work to do, could not take part in their children's frivolity.*

improvise (im′prə vīz′) *v.* to create to meet an unexpected need; p. 1247 *Chuck did not have packing tape, so he had to improvise in order to seal the package.*

·········

Tip: Context Clues When you come across an unfamiliar term, pay close attention to its context. For example, you can figure out that *improvise* means "to create to meet an unexpected need" in the sentence above because the clue "did not have packing tape" lets you know Chuck has to seal the package in another way.

The Handsomest Drowned Man in the World

Gabriel García Márquez
Translated by Gregory Rabassa and J. S. Bernstein

Regreso del lunauta (Return of the Astronaut), 1969. Raquel Forner. Oil on canvas, 160 x 120 cm. National Air and Space Museum, Smithsonian Institution, Washington, DC.

The first children who saw the dark and slinky bulge approaching through the sea let themselves think it was an enemy ship. Then they saw it had no flags or masts and they thought it was a whale. But when it was washed up on the beach, they removed the clumps of seaweed, the jellyfish tentacles, and the remains of fish and flotsam,[1] and only then did they see that it was a drowned man.

They had been playing with him all afternoon, burying him in the sand and digging him up again, when someone chanced to see them and spread the alarm in the village. The men who carried him to the nearest house noticed that he weighed more than any dead man they had ever known, almost as much as a horse, and they said to each other that maybe he'd been floating too long and the water had got into his bones. When they laid him on the floor they said he'd been taller than all other men because there was barely enough room for him in the house,

but they thought that maybe the ability to keep on growing after death was part of the nature of certain drowned men. He had the smell of the sea about him and only his shape gave one to suppose that it was the corpse of a human being, because the skin was covered with a crust of mud and scales.

They did not even have to clean off his face to know that the dead man was a stranger. The village was made up of only twenty-odd wooden houses that had stone courtyards with no flowers and which were spread about on the end of a desertlike cape. There was so little land that mothers always went about with the fear that the wind would carry off their children and the few dead that the years had caused among them had to be thrown off the cliffs. But the sea was calm and bountiful and all the men fit into seven boats. So when they found the drowned man they simply had to look at one another to see that they were all there.

Magic Realism *What does this detail tell you about the villagers and their beliefs?* **2**

---

1. *Flotsam* is the floating wreckage of a ship or its cargo.

GABRIEL GARCÍA MÁRQUEZ **1245**

Teach

Literary Element 1

Hyperbole Ask: What is hyperbole in this passage? *(The dead man weighed almost as much as a horse.)* What does this example of hyperbole evoke? *(Students are likely to say that it evokes humor.)*

Big Idea 2

Magic Realism Answer: *They are naïve, imaginative, and able to accept other versions of reality.*

 For an audio recording of this selection, use Listening Library Audio CD-ROM.

Readability Scores

Dale-Chall: 7.5
DRP: 58
Lexile: 1480

Learning Objectives
Identifying hyperbole. (TE)
Analyzing genre. (TE)

English Learners

DIFFERENTIATED INSTRUCTION

SMALL GROUP

Advanced Many countries have stories about figures larger than life. Students more familiar with a literary heritage other than English may be able to enlighten other students about the tall tales of their cultures. Ask the class to name some well-known tall tales. Then have English learners describe any mythic stories about giants or other hero types from their own cultures. Student groups can compare the stories to note similarities and differences among literary traditions.

Advanced Learners/Pre-AP

DIFFERENTIATED INSTRUCTION

SMALL GROUP

Compare Sea Stories Stories and myths about the sea abound in cultures from coastal areas and islands, such as Hawaii and Ireland. Instruct student pairs to find a myth or legend from another culture that features the sea. Have students write a short essay that compares the plot, tone, mood, and other elements of Márquez's story with those of the story they found.

1245

Teach

Vocabulary　1

Using Word Parts Direct students' attention to the use of the prefix *en–* in *entangled.* Explain that the prefix takes on different meanings depending on whether it's joined with a verb or a noun. Have students look up the prefix and determine its meaning when joined with the verb *tangle.* *(The prefix means "thoroughly.")*

Literary Element　2

Hyperbole Answer: *It suggests that his size is so immense that it cannot be comprehended even when looking at him.*

Reading Strategy　3

Question Possible Answer: *Why are the women selecting such valuable or costly items for the burial of a stranger, even one who is handsome?*

Literary History

Nobel Speech In his 1982 acceptance speech for the Nobel Prize, Gabriel García Márquez describes the tragedies of a postcolonial Latin America and expresses a wish that the qualities that make Latin American literature unique should be those same qualities that can make it a utopia and end its "one hundred years of solitude."

That night they did not go out to work at sea. While the men went to find out if anyone was missing in neighboring villages, the women stayed behind to care for the drowned man. They took the mud off with grass swabs, they removed the underwater stones entangled in his hair, and they scraped the crust off with tools used for scaling fish. As they were doing that they noticed that the vegetation on him came from faraway oceans and deep water and that his clothes were in tatters, as if he had sailed through labyrinths of coral.[2] They noticed too that he bore his death with pride, for he did not have the lonely look of other drowned men who came out of the sea or that **haggard,** needy look of men who drowned in rivers. But only when they finished cleaning him off did they become aware of the kind of man he was and it left them breathless. Not only was he the tallest, strongest, most virile, and best built man they had ever seen, but even though they were looking at him there was no room for him in their imagination.

They could not find a bed in the village large enough to lay him on nor was there a table solid enough to use for his wake. The tallest men's holiday pants would not fit him, not the fattest ones' Sunday shirts, nor the shoes of the one with the biggest feet. Fascinated by his huge size and his beauty, the women then decided to make him some pants from a large piece of sail and a shirt from some bridal brabant[3] linen so that he could continue through his death with dignity. As they sewed, sitting

---

2. *Coral,* formed from the skeletal deposits of marine animals, can form reefs that extend for hundreds of miles.
3. *Brabant* is a region in western Europe known for its textiles. Here, the word is used as an adjective.

2 Hyperbole *Why is this an example of hyperbole?*

3 Question *What question might you ask about these details that describe the man's burial clothing?*

in a circle and gazing at the corpse between stitches, it seemed to them that the wind had never been so steady nor the sea so restless as on that night and they supposed that the change had something to do with the dead man. They thought that if that magnificent man had lived in the village, his house would have had the widest doors, the highest ceiling, and the strongest floor, his bedstead would have been made from a midship frame held together by iron bolts, and his wife would have been the happiest woman. They thought that he would have had so much authority that he could have drawn fish out of the sea simply by calling their names and that he would have put so much work into his land that springs would have burst forth from among the rocks so that he would have been able to plant flowers on the cliffs. They secretly compared him to their own men, thinking that for all their lives theirs were incapable of doing what he could do in one night, and they ended up dismissing them deep in their hearts as the weakest, meanest, and most useless creatures on earth. They were wandering through that maze of fantasy when the oldest woman, who as the oldest had looked upon the drowned man with more compassion than passion, sighed:

"He has the face of someone called Esteban."[4]

It was true. Most of them had only to take another look at him to see that he could not have any other name. The more stubborn among them, who were the youngest, still lived for a few hours with the illusion that when they put his clothes on and he lay among the flowers in patent

---

4. *Esteban* is the Spanish equivalent of Steven, which derives from the Greek for "crown."

Vocabulary

haggard (hag′ərd) *adj.* worn or wasted, as from hunger

Literary Element Practice

Symbol Review with students the definition of symbol; a symbol is something that stands for something else, including an idea, belief, or quality. **Ask:** What ideas or qualities do beautiful things or people often symbolize in advertisements or the media? *(Students may list goodness, fertility, or wealth.)*

Ask: Based on the women's musings about the dead man, what can you conclude about their lives? *(Students may say the women's lives are drab and difficult.)* What could the dead man symbolize to the women? Explain. *(Students may say he symbolizes physical strength because they imagine him building a strong house. He may symbolize strength of personality because they imagine him charming fish out of the sea.)*

leather shoes his name might be Lautaro.[5] But it was a vain illusion. There had not been enough canvas, the poorly cut and worse sewn pants were too tight, and the hidden strength of his heart popped the buttons on his shirt. After midnight the whistling of the wind died down and the sea fell into its Wednesday drowsiness. The silence put an end to any last doubts: he was Esteban. The women who had dressed him, who had combed his hair, had cut his nails and shaved him were unable to hold back a shudder of pity when they had to resign themselves to his being dragged along the ground. It was then that they understood how unhappy he must have been with that huge body since it bothered him even after death. They could see him in life, condemned to going through doors sideways, cracking his head on crossbeams, remaining on his feet during visits, not knowing what to do with his soft, pink, sea lion hands while the lady of the house looked for her most resistant chair and begged him, frightened to death, sit here, Esteban, please, and he, leaning against the wall, smiling, don't bother, ma'am, I'm fine where I am, his heels raw and his back roasted from having done the same thing so many times whenever he paid a visit, don't bother, ma'am, I'm fine where I am, just to avoid the embarrassment of breaking up the chair, and never knowing perhaps that the ones who said don't go, Esteban, at least wait till the coffee's ready, were the ones who later on would whisper the big boob finally left, how nice, the handsome fool has gone. That was what the women were thinking beside the body a little before dawn. Later, when they covered his face with a handkerchief so that the light would not bother him, he looked so forever dead, so defenseless, so much like their men that

---

5. *Lautaro* is an allusion to a native South American hero who fought against the Spanish.

the first furrows of tears opened in their hearts. It was one of the younger ones who began the weeping. The others, coming to, went from sighs to wails, and the more they sobbed the more they felt like weeping, because the drowned man was becoming all the more Esteban for them, and so they wept so much, for he was the most destitute, most peaceful, and most obliging man on earth, poor Esteban. So when the men returned with the news that the drowned man was not from the neighboring villages either, the women felt an opening of jubilation in the midst of their tears.

"Praise the Lord," they sighed, "he's ours!"

The men thought the fuss was only womanish **frivolity.** Fatigued because of the difficult nighttime inquiries, all they wanted was to get rid of the bother of the newcomer once and for all before the sun grew strong on that arid, windless day. They **improvised** a litter with the remains of foremasts and gaffs,[6] tying it together with rigging so that it would bear the weight of the body until they reached the cliffs. They wanted to tie the anchor from a cargo ship to him so that he would sink easily into the deepest waves, where fish are blind and divers' die of nostalgia,[7] and bad currents would not bring him back to shore, as had happened with other bodies. But the more they hurried, the more the women thought of ways to waste time. They walked about like startled hens,

---

6. *Gaffs* are hooks for lifting heavy fish.
7. Here, *nostalgia* refers to the effects that changes in atmospheric pressure may have on deep-sea divers; symptoms include depression and disorientation.

Question *What question might you ask about this detail, or any of the other details in this paragraph?* **5**

Vocabulary

frivolity (fri vol′ə tē) *n.* silliness
improvise (im′prə vīz′) *v.* to create to meet an unexpected need

GABRIEL GARCÍA MÁRQUEZ **1247**

Teach

Literary Element | **4**

Hyperbole **Ask:** What effect does the hyperbole in this passage have? (*Students may say that describing Esteban's buttons popping because of his heart evokes an emotional response.*)

Reading Strategy | **5**

Question **Possible Answer:** *Why are the men's reactions so different from those of the women?*

Learning Objectives
Using questioning. (SE)
Identifying and analyzing hyperbole. (SE)
Understanding word parts. (TE)
Analyzing symbol. (TE)

English Learners

DIFFERENTIATED INSTRUCTION

Beginning Direct students' attention to the use of *ma'am* in the story. Explain that *ma'am* is an abbreviation of *madam* and is used as a polite form of address for a woman, just as *sir* is used for a man. Ask students to share titles of address from their native languages.

Advanced Learners/Pre-AP

DIFFERENTIATED INSTRUCTION

Research Have students note the detail about the rituals of burial in this village (the sewing of clothes for the wake, the covering of the face with a handkerchief, the carrying of the corpse to the cliffs for a sea burial). Point out that all cultures ritualize death and burial, although these rites have differed greatly over time and throughout cultures. As an example, mention the elaborate burial procedures of pharaohs of ancient Egypt.

Have students research historical burial traditions of a country or religion of their choosing. Have volunteers share the information with the class.

Teach

Magic Realism Possible
Answer: *The men begin to make a myth themselves to explain the drowned man's personality and emotions.*

[APPROACHING] Direct Approaching Level students to the shift in point of view from *he* to *I*. Explain that this shift doesn't indicate that Esteban is actually speaking but that the men are imagining what he would say.

Language History ☆

Charm The word *charm* is used in the context of the story to describe a small talisman or amulet believed to have magic or lucky powers. The word originates from the Latin *carmen*, meaning "incantation"; a charm is also a song or chant believed to have magic powers. The earliest examples of written literature include charms, including an Old English charm against dwarves.

☆

Visual Vocabulary
A *scapular* is a pair of small cloth squares joined by shoulder tapes worn under the clothing as a sacramental badge.

pecking with the sea charms on their breasts, some interfering on one side to put a scapular of the good wind on the drowned man, some on the other side to put a wrist compass on him, and after a great deal of *get away from there, woman, stay out of the way, look, you almost made me fall on top of the dead man*, the men began to feel mistrust in their livers and started grumbling about why so many main-altar decorations for a stranger, because no matter how many nails and holy-water jars he had on him, the sharks would chew him all the same, but the women kept piling on their junk relics, running back and forth, stumbling, while they released in sighs what they did not in tears, so that the men finally exploded with *since when has there ever been such a fuss over a drifting corpse, a drowned nobody, a piece of cold Wednesday meat*. One of the women, mortified by so much lack of care, then removed the handkerchief from the dead man's face and the men were left breathless too.

He was Esteban. It was not necessary to repeat it for them to recognize him. If they had been told Sir Walter Raleigh,[8] even they might have been impressed with his gringo accent, the macaw on his shoulder, his cannibal-killing blunderbuss,[9] but there could be only one Esteban in the world and there he was, stretched out like a sperm whale, shoeless, wearing the pants of an undersized child, and with those stony nails

that had to be cut with a knife. They only had to take the handkerchief off his face to see that he was ashamed, that it was not his fault that he was so big or so heavy or so handsome, and if he had known that this was going to happen, he would have looked for a more discreet place to drown in, seriously, I even would have tied the anchor off a galleon[10] around my neck and staggered off a cliff like someone who doesn't like things in order not to be upsetting people now with this Wednesday dead body, as you people say, in order not to be bothering anyone with this filthy piece of cold meat that doesn't have anything to do with me. There was so much truth in his manner that even the most mistrustful men, the ones who felt the bitterness of endless nights at sea fearing that their women would tire of dreaming about them and begin to dream of drowned men, even they and others who were harder still shuddered in the marrow of their bones at Esteban's sincerity.

That was how they came to hold the most splendid funeral they could conceive of for an abandoned drowned man. Some women who had gone to get flowers in the neighboring villages returned with other women who could not believe what they had been told, and those women went back for more flowers when they saw the dead man, and they brought more and more until there were so many flowers and so many people that it was hard to walk about. At the final moment it pained them to return him to the waters as an orphan and they chose a father and mother from among the best people, and aunts and uncles and cousins, so that through him all the inhabitants of the village became kinsmen.

---

8. *Sir Walter Raleigh* was a British sailor who explored South America in the sixteenth century.
9. A *blunderbuss* is a short rifle with a broad muzzle.

---

10. A *galleon* is a large sailing ship.

Magic Realism *What do these lines show about the men's changing view of the drowned man?* | **1**

Grammar Practice

Use Main and Subordinate Clauses
Márquez uses many long sentences. Direct students' attention to the sentence that begins "They walked about like startled hens" and ends with "a piece of cold Wednesday meat." Point out that although this sentence is long, it is not a run-on sentence because it contains a series of independent clauses connected appropriately with coordinating conjunctions separated by commas.

Review with students the differences between a main or independent clause (a clause that can stand alone as a full sentence) and a subordinate or dependent clauses (a clause that cannot stand alone).

Ask students to identify each independent clause in the story's sentence, ignoring the clauses within the italicized type. *(Students should find the following independent clauses: They walked . . . pass him on; the*

men began . . . a stranger; the sharks . . . the same; the women kept . . . meat.)

Some sailors who heard the weeping from a distance went off course and people heard of one who had himself tied to the mainmast, remembering ancient fables about sirens.[11] While they fought for the privilege of carrying him on their shoulders along the steep escarpment[12] by the cliffs, men and women became aware for the first time of the desolation of their streets, the dryness of their courtyards, the narrowness of their dreams as they faced the splendor and beauty of their drowned man. They let him go without an anchor so that he could come back if he wished and whenever he wished, and they all held their breath for the fraction of centuries the body took to fall into the abyss. They did not need to look at one another to realize that they were no longer all present, that they would never be. But they also knew that everything would be different from then on, that their houses would have wider doors, higher ceilings, and stronger floors so that Esteban's memory could go everywhere without bumping into beams and so that no one in the future would dare whisper the big boob finally died, too bad, the handsome fool has finally died, because they were going to paint their house fronts gay colors to make Esteban's memory eternal and they were going to break their backs digging for springs among the stones and planting flowers on the cliffs so that in future years at dawn the passengers on great liners would awaken, suffocated by the smell of gardens on the high seas, and the captain would have to come down from the bridge in his dress uniform, with his astrolabe,[13] his pole star, and his row of war medals and, pointing to the promontory of roses on the horizon, he would say in fourteen languages, look there, where the wind is so peaceful now that it's gone to sleep beneath the beds, over there, where the sun's so bright that the sunflowers don't know which way to turn, yes, over there, that's Esteban's village. ∿

Women in Procession from For Complete Social Security of All Mexicans. David Alfaro Siqueiros. Mural. Hospital de la Raza, Mexico City © Estate of David Alfraro Siqueiros. ©ARS, NY.

View the Art Siqueiros's murals are known for their force and energy. How do these women remind you of the women in the story? ★

---

11. [*Tied . . . sirens*] refers to the *Odyssey*, in which Odysseus has himself tied to the mast so he can navigate safely past the Sirens (mythical enchantresses whose singing charmed sailors into jumping overboard).
12. An *escarpment* is a steep slope.

2 Hyperbole *Explain the hyperbole in this passage.*

---

13. An *astrolabe* (as′trə lāb′) is a device used to observe and calculate the position of celestial bodies.

Question *Ask a question about how the drowned man has affected the villagers.* **4**

GABRIEL GARCÍA MÁRQUEZ **1249**

Advanced Learners/Pre-AP

DIFFERENTIATED INSTRUCTION

Superstitions Márquez's story describes a population that is superstitious. (They're afraid of sirens and the women wear "sea charms.") Challenge students to find out about other superstitions related to working on or living near the sea. Have students evaluate the influence of the sea on imagination in a short essay. Invite students to share their discoveries with the class.

Teach

Literary Element   2

Hyperbole Answer: *The sailors go off course as a result of hearing the villagers' weeping.*

Progress Check

Can students identify hyperbole?

If No → See Unit 6 Teaching Resources Book, p. 190.

Big Idea   3

Magic Realism Ask: How is the line between fantasy and reality blurred in this passage? What does it indicate about the villagers' beliefs? *(The villagers bury Esteban at sea without an anchor so that he may return to them, which indicates a belief in a sort of afterlife.)*

Reading Strategy   4

Question Possible Answers: *Did the villagers really change their village? Did Esteban's "magic" end with his return to the sea?*

View the Art ★

Answers: *The women in the painting seem to be on a mission, much like the women in the story.*

Learning Objectives
Identifying and analyzing hyperbole. (SE)
Using questioning. (SE)
Analyzing art. (SE)
Using main and subordinate clauses. (TE)

After You Read

Assess

1. Humor and seriousness mingle in this story. Students should support their opinions.

2. (a) They think it is an enemy ship or a whale. (b) The children treat him as a plaything; the adults treat him with awe.

3. (a) He is the tallest, best-built, and handsomest man the villagers have ever seen. (b) It is fantastic: Esteban's size and beauty are not described realistically, and he seems to continue growing after death.

4. (a) his house and land, his wife's happiness, and his awkwardness when visiting other people's homes (b) They may be bored with their lives; they may have active imaginations.

5. (a) They want to plant gardens and make their houses larger and brighter. (b) The story describes their plans but does not indicate whether these plans were completed.

6. Possible answers: The allusion to Odysseus and the sirens brings to mind mythical creatures; the allusion to Lautaro suggests heroism in battle.

7. The absence of names makes the story seem more like folklore. Because the villagers have no names, the reader sees them more as a group than as individuals.

8. Students may see either gentle mockery or compassion. They may cite the humor, focus on the people's rich imaginations, and their willingness to believe, or point to delusion, which begins in the first sentence and ends only at the last one.

9. Possible answer: People might call the police or scientists, or try to explain the event in more rational terms.

After You Read

Respond and Think Critically

Respond and Interpret

1. Did you find this story to be humorous or serious? Explain.

2. (a) What do the children think when they first notice Esteban's body? (b) How is the children's reaction to Esteban different from the adults' reaction?

3. (a) What is unusual about Esteban's appearance? (b) Is the description of Esteban's face and body realistic or fantastic? Explain.

4. (a) What do the women think about as they sew Esteban's clothes? (b) What do the women's thoughts suggest about them?

5. (a) What changes do the villagers want to make in honor of Esteban? (b) Have the villagers actually changed as a result of their experience with Esteban? Explain.

Analyze and Evaluate

6. An **allusion** is a reference to a well-known person, place, or event from history, literature, or religion. Identify an allusion in the story and explain what it suggests to you.

7. Why might García Márquez have decided not to name the village and its inhabitants?

Connect

8. **Big Idea** Magic Realism Does the author's creation of fantasy tend to mock the characters and their world or to celebrate them? Explain.

9. **Connect to Today** If this story were to occur in a village or a city in the United States, how might people react?

Literary Element Hyperbole

ACT Skills Practice

1. Which of the following is *not* an example of hyperbole?

   A. Some sailors who heard the weeping of the villagers went off course.

   B. The women thought Esteban could have called fish out of the sea.

   C. The strength of Esteban's heart popped the buttons on his shirt.

   D. The women thought that the drowned man's name must be Esteban.

2. Which of the following passages offers the strongest example of hyperbole?

   F. "he would have put so much work into his land that springs would have burst forth from among the rocks"

   G. "They only had to take the handkerchief off his face to see that he was ashamed"

   H. "The tallest men's holiday pants would not fit him"

   J. "mothers always went about with the fear that the wind would carry off their children"

Review: Theme

As you learned on page 927, a **theme** is the central message about life in a literary work. Most works, like this one, have an implied theme.

Partner Activity Meet with a classmate to discuss the theme that is implied in the description of the changes that will be made in the village. Then discuss the theme that is implied when the villagers return the drowned man's body to the sea.

Literary Element

1. **D** is the correct answer. **A, B,** and **C** are all exaggerations.

2. **F** is the correct answer. **G** and **H** are not hyperbole; **J,** while hyperbole, is less exaggerated than **F.**

Review: Theme

Students may say that the theme is that anything idealized can inspire people to set goals and improve their lives. Another theme is that life is cyclical; odd occurrences or seeming gifts from the sea or nature return to their sources.

Reading Strategy | Question

Review the chart of questions you made on page 1244. As you answer the questions below, consider what you know and what you do not from the details presented in the story.

1. What is the best answer you can give to the question of who the drowned man is? Cite details from the story to support your answer.

2. List two other questions that the story does not answer fully.

Vocabulary Practice

Practice with Context Clues Look back at the story to find context clues for the boldfaced vocabulary words below. Record your findings in a graphic organizer like the one shown.

haggard   frivolity   improvise

EXAMPLE:

> Word: haggard

> Textual Clues:
> He doesn't have a "needy look," so he doesn't seem to have suffered from poverty or want.

> Meaning: worn or wasted as from hunger

Academic Vocabulary

In Marquez's story, the villagers **channel** *their need for a hero into the elaborate myth they create about the drowned man.*

Channel is an academic word. The word is also used in many everyday contexts. For example, an executive might **channel** information to employees by having those directly below her pass information on to those below them. To explore the meaning of the word further, answer the following question: When might you send a complaint through official **channels**?

For more on academic vocabulary, see pages 36–37 and R83–R85.

Write with Style

 Apply Hyperbole

Assignment The use of hyperbole in "The Handsomest Drowned Man in the World" contributes to the story's magic realism. In nonfiction writing, such as a persuasive essay, exaggeration can also be employed in a variety of ways. Write a persuasive essay of 750 words in which you use hyperbole to stimulate interest or appeal to emotion.

Get Ideas Generate ideas for your persuasive essay from multiple sources, including brainstorming, journals, and print and electronic media. To help determine whether there is sufficient difference of opinion on a potential issue to make it an interesting subject, use a chart to diagram arguments for and against the issue. You should be able to support each side with two or three reasons. If the balance leans too heavily one way or the other, it's likely that most people have already made up their minds on the issue.

Give It Structure One of the most effective ways to organize a persuasive essay is by order of importance, presenting your arguments and evidence from the most important to the least important. As you draft your essay, decide how to introduce hyperbole effectively. One way is to make an exaggerated statement in your introduction to add a touch of humor or to hook your audience. Another is to use hyperbole as an emotional appeal to motivate your audience to take action on an issue.

Look at Language Be judicious in your use of hyperbole: a little exaggeration goes a long way. Unwisely used, hyperbole can weaken the effect of the arguments and the evidence that are the foundation of your case.

LOG ON ▶ **Literature** Online

Selection Resources For Selection Quizzes, eFlashcards, and Reading-Writing Connection activities, go to glencoe.com and enter QuickPass code GLW6053u6.

GABRIEL GARCÍA MÁRQUEZ   **1251**

 For additional selection assessment, see Assessment Resources, pp. 243–244.

 For grammar practice, see Unit 6 Teaching Resources Book, p. 194.

Write with Style

Students' persuasive essays should

- argue an issue on which there is sufficient difference of opinion
- use a clear method of organization, such as order of importance
- use hyperbole to engage readers or strengthen a call to action

Reading Strategy

1. He may be a large foreign man whose features seem exotic to the villagers.

2. Possible answer: Why are the women so eager to "own" the handsome man? Why do the men participate in the women's myth when earlier they were skeptical?

Progress Check

Can students use questioning?

If No → See Unit 6 Teaching Resources Book, p. 191.

Vocabulary Practice

Sample responses:

frivolity Clue: the men thought "the fuss was only womanish frivolity"; Meaning: worn or wasted

improvise Clue: "improvised a litter with the remains of foremasts and gaffs"; Meaning: silliness

discreet Clue: "a more discreet place to drowned in . . . in order not to be upsetting people"; Meaning: to create to meet an unexpected need

Academic Vocabulary

Sample response:

When you have a disagreement with a government worker.

Bellringer Options

Selection Focus
   Transparency 81
Daily Language Practice
   Transparency 121

Or write *cogito, ergo sum* on the board. **Say:** When translated from Latin, this means "I think, therefore I am." **Ask:** How can you prove, or disprove, this statement? *(Responses will vary. Students may say thinking proves they exist. Other students may say that thinking itself cannot be proven, so neither can existence.)*

Before You Read

Bishop Berkeley or Mariana of the Universe

Meet **Liliana Heker**
(born 1943)

Many of Liliana Heker's (hāk´ər) protagonists are young women trying to find their place in the world. In the story you are about to read, at least one of the two female main characters seems far too young to argue as intelligently and articulately as she does. This character trait is just one of the ways Heker challenges your perception of reality.

At Home in Argentina Heker grew up in Buenos Aires, Argentina. She began writing professionally at the age of seventeen with the help of Abelardo Castillo, a writer and an editor of a literary magazine. When Heker was 23, she published her first collection of short stories, *Those Who Beheld the Burning Bush*. The book established Heker as one of the most promising Argentinean writers of her generation. Soon afterward, she became chief editor of the literary journal *El escarabajo de oro (The Golden Scarab)*. In 1977, she cofounded *El Ornitorrinco (The Platypus)*, a literary magazine that published the work of local and foreign writers and provided an important leftist forum. Through directorship of these journals, she influenced literary ideas in her country for more than twenty years.

When Argentina fell under a military dictatorship in 1966, Heker decided not to follow other authors into exile. Instead, she remained in her country and continued to write. Over the years, Heker published more short stories, including *The Stolen Party: And Other Stories* and *The Edges of the Real*. Heker also went on to publish novels, the first of which won a major literary prize. More recently, she has published several essays, including the collection *Las hermanas de Shakespeare (Shakespeare's Sisters)*, a study of women authors.

Realism Without Magic In the 1970s, political life in Argentina grew more volatile, a military junta seized power, and the process of national reorganization—popularly known as the Dirty War—began. During these years, as the world gradually came to realize later, people were imprisoned, tortured, and finally "disappeared." Not surprisingly, much of Heker's work from this period took a political turn, and she has continued to write in a political vein since then. Her most well-known novel is *El fin de la historia (The End of History)*, published in 1996. It portrays the cruel realities of 1970s Argentina. Yet it remains a work of fiction, one in which Heker says she "tried to blur the border between documentation and fiction."

In 1980, Heker published a collection of interviews with famous people on the topic of life and death. More than twenty years later, she enlarged and reissued the work. The volume offers countless insights, big and small, including some of Heker's own, such as this one:

"In the end, no artist, and no human being, wants to disappear without leaving footprints."

—Liliana Heker

 Literature Online

Author Search For more about Liliana Heker, go to glencoe.com and enter QuickPass code GLW6053u6.

Selection Skills

Literary Elements
- Allusion (SE pp. 1253, 1256, 1259)
- Dialogue (SE p. 1259)
- Mood (TE p. 1256)

Reading Skills
- Analyze Conflict (SE pp. 1253, 1255, 1257, 1258, 1260)
- Question (TE p. 1258)

Bishop Berkeley or Mariana of the Universe

Vocabulary Skills
- Denotation and Connotation (SE p. 1260)

Speaking/Listening/Viewing Skills
- Literature Groups (SE p. 1260)
- Analyze Art (SE p. 1257)

Writing Skills/Grammar
- Dialogue (TE p. 1258)

Literature and Reading Preview

Connect to the Story

What is the loneliest situation you can imagine? Discuss this question in a small group.

Build Background

The title of Heker's story refers to the eighteenth-century philosopher George Berkeley (bär´klē). He argued that the existence of physical things is dependent on perception. A chair, for example, consists of a group of qualities such as shape, color, and weight. In Berkeley's view, these qualities are ideas. Since ideas must exist in the mind, the chair exists only if it can be perceived. Berkeley realized that his theory could be misinterpreted to support views opposed to common sense. Such misinterpretation is at the heart of Heker's story.

Set Purposes for Reading

Big Idea Magic Realism

In this story, the lines between theory and reality seem to blur. As you read, ask yourself, How does one character manipulate the other's sense of reality?

Literary Element Allusion

An **allusion** is a reference in a work of literature to a character, a place, or a situation from history, literature, music, or art. As you read, ask yourself, Why does the title of this story allude to Bishop Berkeley?

Reading Strategy Analyze Conflict

The basis of a story's plot is conflict—a struggle between opposing forces. An **external conflict** exists when a character struggles against some outside force, such as another character, a force of nature, or society. An **internal conflict** is a struggle within a character. When a character struggles to make a difficult decision, for example, he or she is experiencing internal conflict. Stories often involve more than one kind of conflict. As you read, ask yourself, What kinds of conflicts do the characters experience?

....

Tip: Sort Information Record and classify the conflicts in a chart like this one.

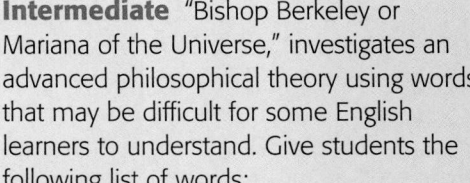

Internal Conflict	External Conflict
Mariana has conflicting visions of Lucia.	

LILIANA HEKER **1253**

Learning Objectives

For pages 1252–1260

In studying this text, you will focus on the following objectives:

Literary Study: Analyzing allusion.

Reading: Analyzing conflict.

Listening and Speaking: Participating in a literature group.

Vocabulary

pounce (pouns) *v.* to swoop down on and quickly seize upon or take advantage of something; p. 1255 *Amit would pounce on any error his opponent made and turn it to his advantage.*

mediocre (mē´dē ō´kər) *adj.* of moderate or low quality; undistinguished; p. 1255 *Although Diego was talented, he viewed his latest work as only mediocre and did not want others to see it.*

resignation (rez´ig nā´shən) *n.* unresisting acceptance; p. 1256 *Some workers responded to the news of the factory closing with anger; others, however, accepted the news with resignation.*

gravely (grāv´lē) *adv.* in a serious or dignified manner; p. 1256 *Mr. Watkins spoke gravely as he described the damage done by the storm.*

Before You Read

Focus

Summary

When Mariana asks her older sister when their mother will come home, Lucia expounds on the philosophical theory that what people perceive exists only in their imagination. Lucia tries to convince Mariana that what she believes to be real is instead imaginary. Mariana becomes agitated, thinking that the entire universe may not really exist.

 For summaries in languages other than English, see Unit 6 Teaching Resources Book, pp. 197–202.

Vocabulary

Related Words Flash Cards

Have students use a dictionary to find words that have similar meanings to the vocabulary words listed. *(Students may find mediocrity [n.], resign [v.], gravity [n.], and grave [adj.].)* Then, have students create flash cards with the vocabulary words and the newly found words. They should place the word on one side, and its part of speech and definition on the other. Students can test one another to guess the words and their definitions.

English Learners

DIFFERENTIATED INSTRUCTION

Intermediate "Bishop Berkeley or Mariana of the Universe," investigates an advanced philosophical theory using words that may be difficult for some English learners to understand. Give students the following list of words:

exist, philosophy, imagine, meditate, theory

Have students use a dictionary to look up each word and learn its definition; if necessary, encourage students to use a native-language dictionary to assist in their comprehension. Students should keep their definitions nearby while reading the story.

Advanced Learners/Pre-AP

DIFFERENTIATED INSTRUCTION

Research Presentation Challenge students to research the philosophy described in this story and create a presentation that simplifies ideas about knowledge and experience. Tell students to limit their presentations to ten minutes and to use visual aids. Doing so allows students to focus on an easy-to-understand explanation of a complex theory for their classmates.

Teach

Literary History ☆

Argentinean Literature

Literature in Argentina in the later years of the twentieth century is marked by experimentation and a focus on political and social issues. Jorge Luis Borges, one of the most famous and influential Argentinean writers, is known for fantastical works that describe a vibrant and complex dream world as well as others that investigate an individual's inner life.

For an audio recording of this selection, use Listening Library Audio CD-ROM.

Readability Scores

Dale-Chall: 4.4
DRP: 48
Lexile: 490

Bishop Berkeley or Mariana of the Universe

Liliana Heker

Translated by
Alberto Manguel

La nina con mascara de la muerte (Girl with a Death Mask), 1938 Frida Kahlo. Oil on tin, 14.9 x 11 cm. Private collection.

"How much longer till Mom comes home?"

It's the fourth time Mariana has asked that same question. The first time, her sister Lucia answered that she'd be back real soon; the second, how the heck was she to know when Mom would be back; the third time she didn't answer, she just raised her eyebrows and stared at Mariana. That was when Mariana decided that things weren't going all that well and that the best thing to do was not to ask any more questions.

Anyhow, she asked herself, *Why do I want Mom to come back, if I'm here with Lucia . . . ?* She corrected herself: *Why do I want Mom to come back, if I'm here with my big sister?* She blinked, deeply moved by the thought. *Big sisters look after little sisters,* she told herself as if she were reciting a poem. *How lucky to have a big sister.* Lucia, with large guardian-angel wings, hovered for a second over Mariana's head. But in a flash the winged image was

1254 UNIT 6   THE MODERN AMERICAS

Literary Element Practice

Antagonist and Protagonist Remind students the difference between a protagonist and antagonist; a protagonist is the character around whom the main conflict revolves and with whom the audience is supposed to sympathize, while the antagonist is the person or force that opposes the protagonist. Explain that modern literature doesn't always follow strict literary rules. **Ask:** Who is the protagonist? the antagonist? Explain.

(Students are likely to say that Mariana is the protagonist because although the story is told from third-person point of view, readers get to see inside her head. Students may say that Lucia is the antagonist because Mariana imagines that her sister is strangling her.)

Ask: What effect does being unsure of the role of each character create? *(Students may say that being unsure of whom to sympathize with creates confusion.)* Encourage students to consider whether their answers change as they continue the story, and have students decide at the end which character, if either, is the protagonist and which is the antagonist.

replaced by another, one which returned every time their mother left them on their own: Lucia, eyes bulging out of their sockets, hair in a furious tangle, was pointing a gun at her. Sometimes there was no gun. Lucia would **pounce** on her, trying to rip Mariana's eyes out with her nails. Or strangle her. The reason was always the same: Lucia had gone mad.

It is a well-known fact that mad people kill normal people, which meant that if Lucia went mad when they were alone together, she'd kill Mariana. That was obvious. Therefore Mariana decides to abandon her good intentions and asks again, for the fourth time, "How much longer till Mom comes home?"

Lucia stops reading and sighs.

"What I'd like to know," she says (and Mariana thinks, *She said "I'd like to know"; does one say "I would like to know" or "I should like to know"?*) "What I'd like to know is why in God's name do you always need Mom around?"

"No." *Now she'll ask me, "No what?" She always manages to make things difficult.* But Lucia says nothing, and Mariana continues, "I was just curious, that's all."

"At twelve."

"What do you mean, at twelve!" Mariana cries. "But it's only ten to nine now!"

"I mean at twelve, six and six," Lucia says.

1 Analyze Conflict *What kind of conflict is expressed in the opening paragraphs?*

2 Magic Realism *How does the author manipulate time or reality in these first three paragraphs?*

Vocabulary

pounce (pouns) *v.* to swoop down on and quickly seize upon or take advantage of something

Mariana howls with laughter at the joke; she laughs so hard that for a moment she thinks she'll die laughing. To tell the truth, she can't imagine anyone else on earth could be as funny as her sister. *She's the funniest, nicest person in the world, and she'll never go mad. Why should she go mad, she, who's so absolutely terrific?*

"Lu," she says adoringly, "Let's play something, okay? Let's, okay?"

"I'm reading."

"Reading what?"

"**Mediocre** Man."

"Ah." *I bet now she'll ask me if I know what mediocre man means, and I won't know, and she'll say then, "Why do you say 'Ah,' you idiot?"* Quickly she asks, "Lu, I can't remember, what does Mediocre Man mean?"

"The Mediocre Man is the man who has no ideals in life."

"Ah." This lays her mind at rest, because she certainly has ideals in life. She always imagines herself already grown up, all her problems over, everyone understands her, things turn out fine, and the world is wonderful. That's having ideals in life.

"Lu," she says, "we, I mean, you and I, we're not mediocre, are we?"

"A pest," Lucia says, "That's what you are."

"Lucia, why is it that you're so unpleasant to everyone, eh?"

"Listen, Mariana. Do you mind just letting me read in peace?"

"You're unpleasant to everyone. That's terrible, Lucia. You fight with Mom, you fight with Dad. With *everyone*." Mariana

Vocabulary

mediocre (mē′ dē ō′ kər) *adj.* of moderate or low quality; undistinguished

LILIANA HEKER **1255**

Reading Strategy 1

Analyze Conflict **Answer:**
Mariana has an internal conflict between deeply distrusting her sister and wanting to be protected by her.

Big Idea 2

Magic Realism **Answer:**
She states that the question has been asked four times, and then she has Mariana ask the question for the fourth time.

(**APPROACHING**) Direct Approaching Level students to reread the beginning of the story and compare it to the highlighted passage. Point out that a majority of the information in the long second paragraph happens after Mariana asks the question for the third time.

Learning Objectives
Analyzing conflict. (SE)
Analyzing antagonist and protagonist. (TE)

Approaching Level

DIFFERENTIATED INSTRUCTION

Internal Thoughts Explain to Approaching Level students that writers sometimes use italicized text to differentiate a character's internal thoughts from narration. Tell students that even though this story is told from a limited third-person point of view, the author has shown Mariana's thoughts in the first-person point of view. Direct students to look for an identifying tag such as "he thought" or "she thinks" with the first

instance of the italicized text to determine when a character is sharing his or her thoughts. Further explain that an author usually won't use an identifying tag on subsequent instances of internal thought; italicized text itself will tip off readers that the words are thoughts. **Ask:** Why might the author have shown us Mariana's thoughts instead of just describing what she was thinking?

(Students may say by showing Mariana's thoughts, the author has allowed readers to feel more intimately connected to Mariana. Readers can better relate to her because they, too, talk to themselves.)

Teach

Allusion Answer: *Using an allusion that is too specific would distract readers who are unfamiliar with Berkeley. By not mentioning him, the author also stimulates curiosity about the title.*

Literary History ☆

Bishop George Berkeley
Berkeley's philosophical quests began when he was still a young man; he first questioned the existence of material substance in his early twenties and published his ideas in *Arithmetica and Miscellanea Mathematica* (1707). Soon after, he revised his theory of subjectivity to explain the difference in perception between the subject perceiving an object and the object being perceived. Not concerned with just philosophical study, Berkeley also published political sermons, essays, travel diaries, a rejection of Newton's scientific theories, and even a plan for the education of Native Americans.

---

lets out a deep sigh. "You give your parents nothing but trouble, Lucia."

"Mariana, I wish you'd just drop dead, okay?"

"You're horrible, Lucia, horrible! You don't say to anyone that you wish they would drop dead, not to your worst enemy, and certainly not to your own sister."

"That's it, now start to cry, so that afterwards they will scream at me and say that I torture you."

"Afterwards? When afterwards? Do you know exactly *when* Mom will be back?"

"Just afterwards." Lucia has gone back to reading *Mediocre Man*. "Afterwards is afterwards." She lifts her eyes and frowns as if she were meditating on something very important. "The future, I mean."

"What future? You said Mom would be back very soon."

Lucia shakes her head in **resignation** and goes back to her book.

"Yes, of course, she'll be back very soon."

"No. Yes, of course, no. Is she coming back very soon or isn't she coming back very soon?"

Lucia glares at Mariana; then she seems to remember something and smiles briefly.

"And anyway what does it matter?" She shrugs her shoulders.

"What do you mean, what does it matter? You don't know what you're saying, do you? If someone comes home very soon, it means she comes home very soon, doesn't it?"

"*If* someone comes home, yes."

"What?"

"I just said that *if* someone comes home, then yes. Will you please let me read?"

"You're a cow, that's what you are! What you really want is for Mom never to come home again!"

Vocabulary

resignation (rez´ig nā´shən) *n.* unresisting acceptance

Lucia closes the book and lays it down on the bed. She sighs.

"It has nothing to do with my wanting it or not," she explains. "What I'm saying is that it simply doesn't matter if Mom is here or there."

"What do you mean, there?"

"Just there; anywhere; it's all the same."

"Why the same?"

Lucia rests her chin on both her hands and stares **gravely** at Mariana.

"Listen, Mariana," she says, "I've got something to tell you. Mom doesn't exist."

Mariana jumps.

"Don't be stupid, okay?" she says, trying to look calm. "You know Mom doesn't like you saying stupid things like that."

"They're not stupid things. Anyway, who cares what Mom says, if Mom doesn't exist?"

"Lu, I'm telling you for the last time: I-don't-like-you-say-ing-stu-pid-things, okay?"

"Look, Mariana," Lucia says in a tired tone of voice. "I'm not making it up; there's a whole theory about it, a book."

"What does it say, the book?"

"What I just said. That nothing really exists. That we imagine the world."

"*What* do we imagine about the world?"

"Everything."

"You just want to frighten me, Lucia. Books don't say things like that. What does it say, eh? For real."

"I've told you a thousand times. The desk, see? There isn't really a desk there, you just imagine there's a desk. Understand? You, now, this very minute, imagine that you're inside a room, sitting

---

☆ **Allusion** *Why do you think the story never mentions Bishop Berkeley except in the title?*   **1**

Vocabulary

gravely (grāv´lē) *adv.* in a serious or dignified manner

Literary Element Practice

Mood Explain to students that mood is the overall feeling that a literary work creates for readers. In stories with descriptions of time and place, the author creates an atmosphere that contributes to mood; however, in this story readers only have dialogue and some descriptions of facial expressions and internal thoughts with which to determine mood. Have groups discuss the elements that contribute to the mood of the story.

Ask: How would you describe Mariana's and Lucia's emotions during their conversation? *(Students may say that Mariana is anxious and confused; Lucia is annoyed.)* How would you describe the mood of the story? *(Students are likely to say anxious, nervous, confused, or even fearful.)* Have student groups present their findings and encourage a discussion of contrasting ideas among groups.

on the bed, talking to me, and you imagine that somewhere else, far away, is Mom. That's why you want Mom to come back. But those places don't really exist, there is no here or far away. It's all inside your head. You are imagining it all."

"And you?"

"I what?"

"There's you, see?" Mariana says with sudden joy. "You can't imagine the desk in the same exact place that I imagine it, can you?"

"You've got it all wrong, Mariana sweetheart. You just don't understand, as usual. It's not that both of us imagine that the desk is in the same place: it's that *you imagine* that both of us imagine that the desk is in the same place."

"No, no, no, no. *You got* it all wrong. Each of us doesn't imagine things on our own, and one can't guess what the other is imagining. You *talk* about what you imagine. I say to you: how many pictures are there in this room? And I say to myself: there are three pictures in this room. And at exactly the same time you tell me that there are three pictures in this room. That means that the three pictures are here, that we see them, not that we imagine them. Because two people can't imagine the same thing at the same time."

"Two can't, that's true."

"What do you mean?"

"I'm saying that *two* people can't."

"I don't understand what you're saying."

"I'm saying that you are also imagining *me*, Mariana."

"You're lying, you're lying! You're the biggest liar in the whole world! I hate you, Lucia. Don't you see? If I'm imagining you, how come you know I'm imagining you?"

Hace mucho tiempo (Having Too Much Time), 1995. Alicia Carletti. Oil on canvas, 100 x 80 cm, Zurbaran Galeria, Buenos Aires, Argentina.

View the Art Like magic realist authors, Alicia Carletti combines the everyday and the bizarre in her art. What character in the story does this girl remind you of? Explain. ★

"I *don't* know, I don't *anything*. You are just making me up, Mariana. You've made up a person called Lucia, who's your sister, and who knows you've made her up. That's all."

"No, come on, Lu. Say it's not true. What about the book?"

"What book?"

"The book that talks about all this."

"That talks about what?"

"About things not really existing."

"Ah, the book . . . The book is also imagined by you."

"That's a lie, Lucia, a lie! I could never imagine a book like that. I never know

2 **Analyze Conflict** *Describe the conflict between Mariana and Lucia.*

Magic Realism *In this passage, how does the author play with the nature of reality?* 3

LILIANA HEKER **1257**

Teach

Reading Strategy   2

Analyze Conflict Answer: *Mariana is trying to explain her point, but Lucia remains condescending toward her younger sister. This debate is an external conflict over the nature of reality.*

Big Idea   3

Magic Realism Possible Answer: *Some may say that the author presents a philosophy that suggests that reality is based on perception. Others may point out that a real conversation is taking place between people who, according to Lucia, don't exist.*

View the Art ★

Answer: *Students may be reminded of either Mariana or Lucia; both resemble this pensive-looking girl, who could be dreaming about the universe or a way to frighten her sister.*

Learning Objectives
Analyzing conflict. (SE)
Analyzing allusion. (SE)
Analyzing mood. (TE)

English Learners

DIFFERENTIATED INSTRUCTION

Intermediate Explain that an interjection is a word or group of words tacked onto a sentence to express feeling. Identify the interjections *okay, eh,* and *see* in these examples: "Don't be stupid, okay?" "What does it say, eh?" "There's you, see?"

Explain that some interjections, such as *like* and *you know,* have become overused and can confuse what a student is trying to express.

Advanced Learners/Pre-AP

DIFFERENTIATED INSTRUCTION

SMALL GROUP

Problem Solving This story takes a philosophical theory—that all reality is a product of the imagination—and pushes it to an absurd extreme. However, the reality in which people perceive can be the result of their own thought processes. Ask students to discuss how their perceptions of the following might be influenced by imagination or other mental processes so that their picture of reality might be confused: A new student at school seems aloof to some, but shy to others; A teacher assigns a low grade on an assignment on which the student has spent many hours; The public is divided about the truthfulness or integrity of a public official. Ask students how they might reconcile these problems in their experiences with or thoughts about others.

Teach

Literary Element   1

Allusion **Ask:** What categories of things does Lucia allude to here? *(She alludes to concepts such as history and math as well as inventions such as airplanes and medicine.)* What do these things have to do with her explanation? *(She is saying that everything—from academic topics, ideas in books, medicine, and inventions—are all imaginary.)*

Reading Strategy   2

Analyze Conflict **Answer:** *Mariana accuses her sister of lying and at other times thinks Lucia is "mad" and likely to murder her; at the same time, she thinks her sister is funny and looks up to her. The reader never really knows what motivates Lucia or what she is like except through Mariana's eyes.*

Big Idea   3

Magic Realism **Answer:** *She is afraid and confused. She believes what Lucia has told her, and she feels alone and uncertain. She believes she has created her universe.*

 To check students' understanding of the selection, see Unit 6 Teaching Resources Book, p. 208.

about things like that, don't you understand, Lu? I could never imagine something as complicated as that."

1 "But my poor Mariana, that book is nothing compared to the other things you've imagined. Think of History and the Law of Gravity and Maths and all the books ever written in the world and Aspirins, and the telegraph and planes. Do you realize what you've done?"

"No, Lucia, no, please. Everyone knows about those things. Look. If I bring a lot of people into this room, and I say when I count up to three, we all point to the radio at the same time, then you'll see. We'll all point in the same direction. Let's play at that, Lu, please, come on; let's play at pointing at things. Please."

"But are you stupid or what? I'm telling you that *you* are the one who's imagining all the people in the world."

"I don't believe you. You say that just to frighten me. I can't imagine all the people in the world. What about Mom? What about Dad?"

"Them too."

"Then I'm all alone, Lu!"

"Absolutely. All alone."

"That's a lie, that's a lie! Say that you're lying! You're just saying that to frighten me, right? Sure. Because everything's here. The beds, the desk, the chairs. I can see them, I can touch them if I want to. Say yes, Lu. So that everything's like before."

"But why do you want me to say yes, if anyway it will be *you* imagining that *I* am saying yes?"

"Always me? So there's no one but *me* in the world?"

---

2 **Analyze Conflict** *What is the connection between Mariana's reaction to Lucia's philosophical theory and her conflicting attitudes toward her older sister?*

"Right."

"And you?"

"As I said, you're imagining me."

"I don't want to imagine any more, Lu. I'm afraid. I'm really frightened, Lu. How much longer till Mom comes home?"

Mariana leans out of the window. Mom, come back soon, she begs. But she no longer knows to whom she's begging, or why. She shuts her eyes and the world disappears; she opens them, and it appears again. Everything, everything, everything. If she can't think about her mother, she won't have a mother any more. And if she can't think about the sky, the sky . . . And dogs and clouds and God. Too many things to think about all at once, all on her own. And why she, alone? Why *she* alone in the universe? When you know about it, it's so difficult. Suddenly she might forget about the sun or her house or Lucia. Or worse, she might remember Lucia, but a mad Lucia coming to kill her with a gun in her hand. And now she realizes at least how dangerous all this is. Because if she can't stop herself thinking about it, then Lucia will really be like that, crazy, and kill her. And then there won't be anyone left to imagine all those things. The trees will disappear and the desk and thunderstorms. The color red will disappear and all the countries in the world. And the blue sky and the sky at night and the sparrows and the lions in Africa and the earth itself and singing songs. And no one will ever know that, once, a girl called Mariana invented a very complicated place to which she gave the name of Universe. ◐

---

3 **Magic Realism** *What is Mariana's state of mind at the end of the story?*

Writing Practice

Writing Dialogue Ask students to imagine what happens when Mariana's and Lucia's mother comes home, especially the conversation they have about the philosophy lesson Lucia gave to Mariana. Tell students to write the conversation in voices that resemble those of Mariana and Lucia in the story.

After You Read

Respond and Think Critically

Respond and Interpret

1. What would you like to say to Mariana? What would you like to say to Lucia?

2. (a)What question does Mariana keep asking Lucia? (b)Why do you think the author gives Mariana this piece of dialogue?

3. (a)How does Lucia react to Mariana's question? (b)What motivates Lucia to react this way?

4. (a)In what two ways does Mariana imagine Lucia in her mind? (b)What do these images suggest about Mariana's attitude toward her older sister?

5. (a)What theory does Lucia present about the girls' mother? (b)How does Mariana respond to Lucia's theory?

Analyze and Evaluate

6. (a)How old do Lucia and Mariana seem to you? Cite evidence from the story to support your answer. (b)Why do you think the reader learns almost nothing about the characters that goes beyond the present event?

7. Do you think Lucia is really trying to offer an accurate version of Berkeley's ideas about existence? Explain.

8. How well does the title reflect the content of the story?

Connect

9. **Big Idea** **Magic Realism** How is this story an example of magic realism?

10. **Connect to the Author** Heker remained in Argentina during one of the country's most oppressive periods—a time when civilians were kidnapped from their homes, tortured, and killed. How might these experiences have affected her desire to play with the nature of reality in this short story?

Literary Element | Allusion

SAT Skills Practice

The author of this story alludes to Bishop Berkeley's philosophy in order to

(A) logically disprove it

(B) push it to an absurd extreme

(C) praise its genius

(D) show a contrast between the ideas of children and adults

(E) highlight a difference between old and new ways of thinking

Review: Dialogue

As you learned on page 1026, **dialogue** is conversation between characters in a literary work. Dialogue helps reveal characters, suggest the theme, and advance the plot.

1. Does "Bishop Berkeley or Mariana of the Universe" depend more on narration or dialogue to advance the plot? Explain.

2. How does dialogue function as the device for presenting the philosophical idea that underpins the story?

3. What makes the dialogue an ideal device for exposing and intensifying the main external conflict?

LOG ON ▶ **Literature** Online

Selection Resources For Selection Quizzes, eFlashcards, and Reading-Writing Connection activities, go to glencoe.com and enter QuickPass code GLW6053u6.

LILIANA HEKER **1259**

After You Read

Assess

1. Students may want to reassure Mariana and admonish Lucia for being cruel to her younger sister.

2. (a) "When will Mom be back?" (b) It shows Mariana's youth and vulnerability.

3. (a) She is annoyed and begins spouting her misconception of Bishop Berkeley's theory. (b) She wants to stop Mariana's annoying questions, to control her sister, and to be cruel.

4. (a) as a winged guardian angel and a violent attacker (b) Her attitude is conflicted.

5. (a) She claims that their mother does not exist and that Mariana is only imagining the world. (b) She tries very hard to refute it; she says she and Lucia can't both imagine the same thing.

6. (a) Students should provide support for their answers. (b) The characters are used only to present a philosophical idea.

7. Most students will feel that Lucia is deliberately distorting Berkeley's theory to tease her sister.

8. Answers will vary. Students may say that the story is about Bishop Berkeley's ideas or that it distorts his theory and therefore is mistitled. They may say that "Mariana of the Universe" is appropriate based on the story's conclusion. They may say that the word *or* in the title suggests a choice that is at the heart of the story.

9. The story deals with the nature of reality, manipulates the concept of time, and places otherworldly concepts within an everyday situation.

10. The mother has "disappeared" temporarily, Lucia is torturing her younger sister mentally, and neither sister has a firm grip on reality.

Literary Element

(B) is correct. The philosophy is pushed to the extreme; it is suggested that all reality is a product of the imagination.

Progress Check

Can students identify allusions?

If No → See Unit 6 Teaching Resources Book, p. 203.

Review: Dialogue

1. It relies almost completely on dialogue; there is almost no narration.

2. As the characters argue, the philosophy is explained (and distorted).

3. It shows the sisters squaring off on two sides of the issue.

1259

After You Read

Reading Strategy

1. Mariana wants Lucia to play with her and to reassure her, but Lucia wants to read a book and to control Mariana.

2. Possible answers: Mariana struggles to reconcile the conflicting images of her sister; she worries about her mother; she is tormented by the implications of the idea that she has imagined the universe.

Progress Check

Can students analyze conflict?

If No → See Unit 6 Teaching Resources Book, p. 204.

Vocabulary Practice

1. *Pounce* has the more negative connotation.
2. *Mediocre* has the more negative connotation.
3. *Submissiveness* has the more negative connotation.
4. *Gravely* has the more negative connotation.

Academic Vocabulary

In addition to collecting quantitative data such as the number of people living in a household and their ages, a census taker might also collect qualitative data such as the individuals' professions and ethnic backgrounds.

 For additional selection assessment, see Assessment Resources, pp. 245–246.

 For grammar practice, see Unit 6 Teaching Resources Book, p. 207.

Reading Strategy Analyze Conflict

In this story the central conflict between the sisters is transformed into a conflict of ideas. Review the chart you made on page 1253 and then respond to the following items.

1. Describe an external conflict in "Bishop Berkeley or Mariana of the Universe."

2. Describe an internal conflict in the story.

Vocabulary Practice

Practice with Denotation and Connotation
Denotation is the literal, or dictionary, meaning of a word. **Connotation** is the implied, or cultural, meaning of a word.

Next to each vocabulary word below is a word that has a similar denotation. Choose the word that has the more negative connotation.

1. pounce   leap

2. mediocre   moderate

3. resignation   submissiveness

4. gravely   seriously

Academic Vocabulary

*Lucia makes the **qualitative** observation that people imagine their own realities.*

Qualitative is an academic word. In making a diagnosis, a doctor would assess **qualitative** data, such as a patient's description of his or her symptoms, along with quantitative (numerical) data, such as the patient's temperature and blood pressure. To study this word further, answer the following question: What types of **qualitative** data might be collected by a person taking a census?

For more on academic vocabulary, see pages 36–37 and R83–R85.

Listening and Speaking

 Literature Groups

Assignment With a small group, discuss whether you believe "reality" is real or imagined. Consider the gray areas that emerge in the distinction between reality and the imagination. Use specific arguments to back up your points.

Prepare To prepare for the discussion, review the information on page 1187, noting the philosophical assumptions that underpin magic realist works. Make charts like the one below to organize arguments from the story and your own opinions.

Argument	Evaluation
Passage: "…two people can't imagine the same thing at the same time."	Response: I don't agree, though the argument seemed convincing at first.
Meaning: Things must exist outside of our imaginations.	Counterargument: As Lucia says, Mariana is forgetting that she might also be imagining the existence of other people.
Logic, Reasons, or Evidence: Both Mariana and Lucia would see three pictures in the room without consulting one another, so the pictures must be real.	

Discuss During the discussion, listen carefully to your peers and build off their ideas. Take notes on what is said. When you want to introduce a different idea, try using a transitional statement like the one below.

So far, we have been talking about _____. But I think the real issue is _____.

Report Use your notes to create a short oral report on your discussion and the consensus—if any—that your group reached. Conclude the report by synthesizing ideas from the discussion into a few remaining questions. Create a visual aid such as a flowchart to illustrate the progression of ideas in your discussion.

Evaluate Write a paragraph in which you assess the effectiveness of your discussion.

Listening and Speaking

Students should

- communicate respectfully, follow up on one another's ideas, and offer counterarguments
- make sure everyone gets an equal chance to speak
- use effective oral delivery techniques and visual aids

 To create custom assessments online, go to Progress Reporter Online Assessment.

To create custom assessments using software, use ExamView Assessment Suite.

Literary Perspective

on Magic Realism

from
My Invented Country

Isabel Allende
Translated by
Margaret Sayers Peden

American Book Award Winner

Learning Objectives

For pages 1261–1263

In studying this text, you will focus on the following objectives:

Reading: Analyzing philosophical assumptions. Making connections across literature. Analyzing informational text.

Set a Purpose for Reading

Read to understand how one author's experiences and beliefs shaped her magic realist fiction.

Build Background

 In 1973, Isabel Allende's cousin, the president of Chile, was assassinated in a brutal coup. Allende and her family soon found life too dangerous in Chile and moved to Caracas, Venezuela, where Allende began her first novel, *The House of the Spirits.* Allende wrote the novel in a magic realist style, endowing each of the characters with magical qualities and including spirits of the dead who speak to the living. In the following excerpt from her memoir, Allende reflects on the role her imagination has played in shaping her memories and her writing.

Reading Strategy Analyze Philosophical Assumptions

When you **analyze philosophical assumptions,** you look for clues to what an author believes. Assumptions may be stated directly or may be implied in the conclusions the author draws. As you read, take notes on Allende's beliefs about subjectivity, reality, and the imagination.

F rom the instant I crossed the cordillera[1] of the Andes one rainy winter morning, I unconsciously began the process of inventing a country. I have flown over those mountains many times since, and I am always deeply moved because the memory of that morning assaults me full-force as I look down on the magnificent spectacle of the mountains. The infinite solitude of those white peaks, those dizzying abysses, the blue depths of the sky, symbolizes my farewell to Chile. I never imagined I would be gone for so long. Like all Chileans—except the military—I was convinced that given our tradition, the soldiers would soon return to their barracks, there would be a new election, and we would have a democratic government again. I must have intuited something in regard to the future, however, because I spent my first night in Caracas crying inconsolably in a borrowed bed. Deep down, I sensed that something had ended forever, and that my life was taking a new direction. I have felt the pangs of nostalgia ever since that first night, and they did not lessen for many

1. A *cordillera* is a system of mountain ranges.

ISABEL ALLENDE **1261**

English Learners

DIFFERENTIATED INSTRUCTION

Advanced English learners may not be familiar with the names of government systems or political parties. Explain the term *democratic* refers to a system of government in which the population votes for its representatives. Encourage students to share information with the class about government systems or political parties from their native countries.

Advanced Learners/Pre-AP

DIFFERENTIATED INSTRUCTION

Research Encourage students to research other memoirs or autobiographies about this tumultuous time in Chilean history. Challenge them to find out whether there is a wide selection of such material from Chilean writers. Ask students whether the coup d'etat and the changes in social and political life influenced a surge of writing from "survivors." Encourage students to share their findings with the class.

Before You Read

Focus

Summary

In this excerpt, Isabel Allende describes how her years of exile from Chile led to the development of an imagined place. She explains her memories of the country. Allende realizes these memories, along with her lost family members, supersede reality.

For activities related to this selection, see Unit 6 Teaching Resources Book, pp. 210–218.

Teach

Political History ☆

General Augusto Pinochet

Pinochet became the president of Chile after a military takeover in 1973. For the next 16 years, any opposing parties were either suppressed or dissolved. The standard of living declined for many. In the early 1980s, an opposition began to form against Pinochet for his mishandling of the country and reports of human rights violations. The free election in 1989 resulted in a new president, but Pinochet retained his hold on the military until 1998. Also in 1998, Pinochet came under scrutiny for his role in the disappearances of those who dared to oppose his leadership. In 2005 and 2006 he was indicted on a variety of charges, but he died before he could be brought to trial.

Readability Scores

Dale-Chall: 8.4
DRP: 57
Lexile: 1320

Teach

Big Idea | 1

Magic Realism Review the Big Idea with students. **Ask:** How has Allende purposely blurred the line between reality and fantasy? *(Allende has chosen to create memories of her country and family that she knows are not accurate.)*

Reading Strategy | 2

Analyze Philosophical Assumptions **Ask:** What does Allende assume that everyone else does? *(She assumes that everyone remembers things that did not happen.)* How does this assumption fit in with her ideas about memory? *(She says that the process of imagining and remembering are nearly identical, so she has no problem with people making up memories.)*

View the Photograph ★

The capital of Chile, Santiago was founded by the Spanish in 1541. After the War of Independence in the early nineteenth century, Santiago grew to become the center of Chilean industry. **Ask:** How do the past and the future coexist in this photograph? *(The photograph shows a modern skyscraper towering over a cathedral that is obviously hundreds of years old, indicating a city that holds onto its past wile looking toward the future.)*

★

years—until the dictatorship fell and I again stood on the soil of my country. Through the intervening years, I lived with my eyes turned south, listening to the news, waiting for the moment I could go back, as I selected my memories, altered some events, exaggerated or ignored others, refined my emotions, and so gradually constructed the imaginary country in which I have sunk my roots.

I have constructed an idea of my country the way you fit together a jigsaw puzzle, by selecting pieces that fit my design and ignoring the others. My Chile is poetic and poor, which is why I discard the evidence of a modern, materialistic society in which a person's value is measured by wealth, fairly acquired or otherwise, and insist on seeing signs everywhere of my country of old. I have also created a version of myself that has no nationality, or, more accurately, many nationalities. I don't belong to one land, but to several, or perhaps only to the ambit[2] of the fiction I write. I can't pretend to know what part of my memory is reliable and how much I've invented, because the job of defining the line between them is beyond my ability. My granddaughter

Andrea wrote a composition for school in which she said that she liked her "grandmother's imagination." I asked her what she was referring to, and without hesitation she replied, "You remember things that never happened." Don't we all do that? I have read that the mental process of imagining and that of remembering are so much alike that they are nearly indistinguishable. Who can define reality? Isn't everything subjective? If you and I witness the same event, we will recall it and recount it differently. Comparing the versions of our childhood that my brothers tell, it's as if each of us had been on a different planet. Memory is conditioned by emotion; we remember better, and more fully, things that move us, such as the joy of a birth, the pleasure of a night of love, the pain of a loved one's death, the trauma of a wound. When we call up the past, we choose intense moments—good or bad—and omit the enormous gray area of daily life.

If I had never traveled, if I had stayed on, safe and secure in the bosom of my family, if I had accepted my grandfather's vision and his rules, it would have been impossible for me to recreate or embellish my own existence, because it would have been defined by others and I would merely be one link more in a long family chain. Moving about has forced me, time after time, to readjust my story, and I have done that in a daze, almost without noticing, because I have been too preoccupied with the task of surviving. Most of our lives are similar, and can be told in the tone used to read the telephone directory—unless we decide to give it a little oomph, a little

2. *Ambit* means "bounds" or "scope."

Reading Practice

Draw Conclusions About Author's Beliefs Explain that a conclusion is a general statement combining reason and experience with clues from a text. **Ask:** What conclusions can you draw about Allende's political beliefs and her opinions of social classes, progress, and patriotism? What clues in the text help you draw these conclusions? *(Students can draw the conclusion that Allende has democratic beliefs because she hoped for elections and the return to a democratic government, and she did not return to Chile until the dictatorship fell. From her description of "her" Chile as "poetic and poor" and her negative description of a materialistic society, students can draw the conclusions that Allende believes a preoccupation with attaining wealth is not progress. She does not look down on "lower" classes, but embraces their contributions.)*

color. In my case, I have tried to polish the details and create my private legend, so that when I am in a nursing home awaiting death I will have something to entertain the other senile old folks with.

I wrote my first book by letting my fingers run over the typewriter keys, just as I am writing this, without a plan. I needed very little research because I had it all inside, not in my head but in that place in my chest where I felt a perpetual knot. I told about Santiago in the time of my grandfather's youth, just as if I'd been born then; I knew exactly how a gas lamp was lit before electricity was installed in the city, just as I knew the fate of hundreds of prisoners in Chile during that same period. I wrote in a trance, as if someone was dictating to me, and I have always attributed that favor to the ghost of my grandmother, who was whispering into my ear. Only one other time have I been gifted with a book dictated from that other dimension, and that was when I wrote my memoir *Paula* in 1993. I have no doubt that in writing that book I received help from the benign spirit of my daughter.[3]

---

3. Allende named the memoir *Paula* after her daughter, who died in 1992 at the age of 28. The book focuses on her daughter's illness and death.

Who, really, are these and the other spirits who live with me? I haven't seen them floating around the hallways of my home, wrapped in white sheets, nothing as interesting as that. They are simply memories that come to me and that from being caressed so often gradually acquire flesh. That happens with people, and also with Chile, that mythic country that from being missed so profoundly has replaced the real country. That country inside my head, as my grandchildren describe it, is a stage on which I place and remove objects, characters, and situations at my whim. Only the landscape remains true and immutable; I am not a foreigner to the majestic landscape of Chile. My tendency to transform reality, to invent memory, disturbs me, I have no idea how far it may lead me. Does the same thing happen with people? If, for example, I saw my grandparents or my daughter for an instant, would I recognize them? Probably not, because in looking so hard for a way to keep them alive, remembering them in the most minimal details, I have been changing them, adorning them with qualities they may not have had. I have given them a destiny much more complex than the ones they lived. ॐ

Respond and Think Critically

Respond and Interpret

1. Write a brief summary of the main ideas in this excerpt before you answer the following questions. For help in writing a summary, see page 1147.

2. (a)What is the meaning of the title of Allende's memoir? (b)What facts about Chile does she say she chooses to ignore?

3. (a)How does Allende say she would be different if she had not left Chile? (b)In what way does she say her exile has influenced her writing?

Analyze and Evaluate

4. (a)What assumption does Allende make about subjectivity? (b)Do you agree with this assumption? Explain.

5. (a)What does Allende believe about the nature of memory? (b)Do her beliefs about memory seem to distress her? Explain.

Connect

6. What insights into magic realism did you gain from reading this excerpt?

ISABEL ALLENDE **1263**

Advanced Learners/Pre-AP

DIFFERENTIATED INSTRUCTION

Imagined Memoir Encourage students to write a short "memoir" of a created memory about an ancestor or close family member. Students may choose a particular event or situation, such as a wedding, the start of a war, or other national event. Challenge students to use period details when setting the scene of their "memory." Ask volunteers to share their memoirs with the class.

After You Read

Assess

1. Answers will vary, but summaries should deal with Allende's ideas about imaginations being like memory, about re-creating her own existence, and about her tendency to transform reality.

2. (a) Allende says Chile is an "invented country" for her because she has been selective in the way she chooses to remember it, altering and even making up places and events. (b) She says she chooses to ignore the evidence that Chile has become a modern, materialistic society.

3. (a) She says she would have accepted her grandfather's vision of the world and would not have created and embellished the story of her own existence. (b) Exile has caused her to "transform reality" in her writing.

4. (a) Allende assumes that "everything" is subjective and that no one can define reality because everyone perceives the world differently. (b) Students should give specific reasons for their opinions.

5. (a) Allende believes that memory is conditioned by emotion, that it leaves out many details, and that it transforms reality. (b) She mentions that her tendency to transform reality disturbs her; however, she seems to appreciate it and see it as a source of creativity.

6. Students may say they gained a better understanding of how an author's subjective experiences could shape a work of magic realism.

Selection Focus
    Transparency 82
Daily Language Practice
    Transparency 122

Ask: What makes someone a friend? What's the most important thing you can do for a friend? *(Students may say that a friend is someone who treats you right, respects you, and wants to spend time with you. They may also say the most important things someone can do for friends are to stick up for them, to be there for them, and to help them get through rough times.)* As students volunteer elements of friendship, list them on the board and encourage the class to rate them in order of importance.

Interactive Read and Write

Other options for teaching this selection can be found in Interactive Read and Write, On Level, pp. 315–330.

Before You Read

Day of the Butterfly

Meet **Alice Munro**

(born 1931)

Most of Alice Munro's short stories are set among the Scotch-Irish settlers of southern Ontario, and she gained international recognition for her finely drawn depictions of these rural and small-town Canadians.

A Farmer's Daughter The eldest of three children, she was born Alice Laidlaw in the small farming community of Wingham, Ontario. Her father was a poultry farmer who for a time raised silver foxes for fur; her mother was a schoolteacher who was ambitious for her daughter. Munro began writing in her teens, hiding in a locked schoolroom to do so because writing was considered an "odd" activity. She left home in 1949 to attend the University of Western Ontario, where she helped support herself with various odd jobs and began writing in earnest. She published her first short story while she was at school.

A Wife and a Mother She left the university after two years to marry James Munro. The couple moved to British Columbia, where they opened a bookstore and raised three children. She found, however, that her literary ambitions often conflicted with family responsibilities. During this time she led, she says, "two completely different lives—the real and absolutely solitary life and the life of appearances." Although she went through periods of depression, her "incredible stubbornness" allowed her to continue writing. Her first collection of stories, *Dance of the Happy Shades*, was published in 1968, winning the Governor General's Literary Award, Canada's highest literary prize—one of three such awards she

> "*I'm not an intellectual writer. I'm very, very excited by what you might call the surface of life.*"
>
> —Alice Munro

would win. Her marriage to Munro broke up in 1972, and she moved back to Ontario, where she later remarried. She lives with her second husband on a farm twenty miles from Wingham.

A Regional Author Although Munro's stories are rooted in a rural setting, she achieves universality through her telling details of characters and setting. "I love the landscape so much—more than love it. It's something I know so thoroughly I don't want to detach from it." Known for her realistic descriptions, Munro believes it is important "to get at the exact tone or texture of how things are." Many of her stories are about misfits or people who feel isolated in some way. Several of her short stories have been adapted as radio and television dramas. In 1990, she won the Canada Council Molson prize for her "outstanding lifetime contribution to the cultural and intellectual life of Canada."

LOG ON ▶ **Literature** Online

Author Search For more about Alice Munro, go to glencoe.com and enter QuickPass code GLW6053u6.

Selection Skills

Literary Elements
- Dialect and Idiom (SE pp. 1265, 1266, 1269–1271, 1273, 1274)
- Symbol (SE p. 1274)

Reading Skills
- Analyze Characterization (SE pp. 1265, 1266, 1268, 1269, 1273, 1275)
- Analyze Historical Context (TE p. 1270)

Day of the Butterfly

Vocabulary Skills
- Word Usage (SE p. 1275)
- Crossword (TE p. 1265)

Speaking/Listening/Viewing Skills
- Analyze Art (SE p. 1267)

Writing Skills/Grammar
- Literary Criticism (SE p. 1275)
- Avoid Run-On Sentences (TE p. 1266)
- Interior Monologue (TE p. 1268)

Literature and Reading Preview

Connect to the Story

What are the most important factors that have influenced your choice of friends? Discuss this question with a partner.

Build Background

Most of Alice Munro's stories are set in the rolling farmland of southern Ontario—where her family has lived since the 1840s. She remembers the residents of Wingham as practical people who considered reading a waste of time. Even now, Munro says, many of her relatives generally consider her writing "a very meaningless, useless type of work."

Set Purposes for Reading

Big Idea **Nature and the Imagination**

As you read, ask yourself, How does the setting influence the attitudes and the actions of the characters?

Literary Element **Dialect and Idiom**

A **dialect** is a variation of a language spoken in a particular region or by a particular class. Dialects may differ from the standard forms of a language in vocabulary, pronunciation, or grammatical form. An **idiom** is an expression whose meaning differs from its literal meaning. For example, a character in this story says Myra has to *look after* her little brother, meaning she must take care of him. If you see unusual language as you read, ask yourself, Is this an example of dialect or an idiom?

Reading Strategy **Analyze Characterization**

Characterization refers to the methods an author uses to reveal a character's personality. Describing personality traits—for example, stating that a character is lazy—is **direct characterization**. **Indirect characterization** lets readers draw their own conclusions about characters—based on such things as the characters' words, thoughts, and actions.

Tip: Compile Details Use a chart like the one below to record details of characterization, both direct and indirect.

Character	Detail	Type
Gladys	"Oh she [Myra] washes it in cod-liver oil..."	indirect
Myra	cryptically uncommunicative	direct

Learning Objectives

For pages 1264–1275

In studying this text, you will focus on the following objectives:

Literary Study: Analyzing dialect and idiom.

Reading: Analyzing characterization.

Listening and Speaking: Reporting on literary criticism.

Vocabulary

cryptically (krip′tik lē) *adv.* secretly or mysteriously; p. 1267 *"The proof of a pudding is in the eating," Mother said cryptically.*

self-possessed (self′pə zest′) *adj.* in control of oneself; p. 1268 *She was a very self-possessed young woman and refused to be rattled by the comments of the construction workers.*

supplementary (sup′lə men′tər ē) *adj.* extra or additional; p. 1271 *The supplementary income Mark brought home from his second job helped his family a great deal.*

Tip: Word Usage When you encounter a new word, try asking yourself a question about it to help you remember its meaning. For example, What is the difference between someone who is **self-possessed** and someone who is insecure?

Advanced Learners/Pre-AP

DIFFERENTIATED INSTRUCTION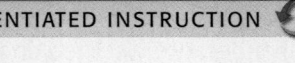

Survey Discuss with students the information about Alice Munro's early writing life and her family's attitude about her art. Have students do a survey of classmates, friends, family members, and other acquaintances to discover their opinions on reading and writing. Students should compile a set of at least five questions asking for descriptive answers to their questions. They may also compose a set of five to ten statements about reading and writing that require those being surveyed to answer or rate their agreement with the statement. One example is *I believe that literature is more important than films and television.* Have students draw conclusions about society's attitude toward writing and reading and share their survey results with the class.

Before You Read

Focus

Summary

The story's narrator, Helen, recalls a girl in her school, Myra Sayla, and Myra's younger brother, Jimmy. Myra is an unpopular girl; she keeps to herself and the other girls make fun of her. One morning Helen walks with Myra and Jimmy to school, and she strikes up a friendship with Myra, offering her Cracker Jacks and the prize in the box, a brooch in the shape of a butterfly. Weeks later, Myra is no longer in school, and the students learn that she is in the hospital. At the urging of the teacher, the students plan a birthday party for Myra in her hospital room. Many of the girls attend, but Myra focuses on Helen, who is glad to be "set free" when the party ends.

 For summaries in languages other than English, see Unit 6 Teaching Resources Book, pp. 219–224.

Vocabulary

Crossword Puzzle Have students create a crossword puzzle with the vocabulary words, using the definition and part of speech in the clue. Have students complete one another's crossword puzzle.

 For additional vocabulary practice, see Unit 6 Teaching Resources Book, p. 227.

Teach

Reading Strategy | 1

Analyze Characterization
Answer: *It is direct characteriza-tion: the narrator describes the teacher's appearance and charac-ter traits.*

Literary Element | 2

Dialect and Idiom Answer:
The teacher considers Myra's description too direct and offensive and gives her a substitute descrip-tion that is euphemistic (neutral and socially acceptable).

(**ENGLISH LEARNERS**) Explain to Eng-lish learners that a *euphemism* is a term used to replace an embar-rassing, offensive, or unpleasant term. Give students the example "passed away," which is used instead of "died."

 For an audio recording of this selection, use Listening Library Audio CD-ROM.

Readability Scores

Dale-Chall: 5.8
DRP: 57
Lexile: 720

Day of the Butterfly

Alice Munro

I do not remember when Myra Sayla came to town, though she must have been in our class at school for two or three years. I start remembering her in the last year, when her little brother Jimmy Sayla was in Grade One. Jimmy Sayla was not used to going to the bathroom by him-self and he would have to come to the Grade Six door and ask for Myra and she would take him downstairs. Quite often he would not get to Myra in time and there would be a big dark stain on his little button-on cotton pants. Then Myra had to come and ask the teacher: "Please may I take my brother home, he has wet himself?"

That was what she said the first time and everybody in the front seats heard her—though Myra's voice was the lightest singsong—and there was a muted giggling which alerted the rest of the class.

Our teacher, a cold gentle girl who wore glasses with thin gold rims and in the stiff solicitude of certain poses resembled a giraffe, wrote something on a piece of paper and showed it to Myra. And Myra recited uncertainly: "My brother has had an acci-dent, please, teacher."

Everybody knew of Jimmy Sayla's shame and at recess (if he was not being kept in, as he often was, for doing something he shouldn't in school) he did not dare go out on the school grounds, where the other lit-tle boys, and some bigger ones, were waiting to chase him and corner him against the back fence and thrash him with tree branches. He had to stay with Myra. But at

---

Analyze Characterization *Is this an example of direct or indirect characterization? Explain.* **1**

Dialect and Idiom *Why does the teacher insist that Myra use this phrase instead of her own words?* **2**

Grammar Practice

Avoid Run-on Sentences Explain to students that there are two kinds of run-on sentences: a comma splice and a fused sentence. A comma splice occurs when two independent clauses are joined by a comma but missing a coordinating conjunction. A fused sentence occurs when two or more independent clauses are run together without commas or conjunctions.

Write the following sentences on the board: **I need to take my brother home, he is not feeling well.** **Ask:** Is this a fused sentence or a comma splice? (*a comma splice*) How could you rewrite this to avoid a run-on? (*Revision exam-ple: I need to take my brother home? He is not feeling well.*)

Explain that because we often do not speak in grammatically correct sentences, writers often have their characters speak in the same way. Have students find at least three other comma splices or fused sentences in the story and rewrite them.

1266

our school there were the two sides, the Boys' Side and the Girls' Side, and it was believed that if you so much as stepped on the side that was not your own you might easily get the strap. Jimmy could not go out on the Girls' Side and Myra could not go out on the Boys' Side, and no one was allowed to stay in the school unless it was raining or snowing. So Myra and Jimmy spent every recess standing in the little back porch between the two sides. Perhaps they watched the baseball games, the tag and skipping and building of leaf houses in the fall and snow forts in the winter; perhaps they did not watch at all. Whenever you happened to look at them their heads were slightly bent, their narrow bodies hunched in, quite still. They had long smooth oval faces, melancholy and discreet—dark, oily, shining hair. The little boy's was long, clipped at home, and Myra's was worn in heavy braids coiled on top of her head so that she looked, from a distance, as if she was wearing a turban too big for her. Over their dark eyes the lids were never fully raised; they had a weary look. But it was more than that. They were like children in a medieval painting, they were like small figures carved of wood, for worship or magic, with faces smooth and aged, and meekly, **cryptically** uncommunicative.

Most of the teachers at our school had been teaching for a long time and at recess they would disappear into the teachers' room and not bother us. But our own teacher, the young woman of the fragile gold-rimmed glasses, was apt to watch us from a window and sometimes come out, looking brisk and uncomfortable, to stop a fight among the little girls or start a running game among the big ones, who had been huddled together

Vocabulary

cryptically (krip′tik lē) *adv.* secretly or mysteriously

Still Closer, 1995. Daniel Nevins. Oil, acrylic, collage on wood, 51 x 39 in. Private collection.

View the Art Nevins has said that he strives to convey stories through his paintings. What scene or characters from this story does this painting remind you of?

playing Truth or Secrets. One day she came out and called, "Girls in Grade Six, I want to talk to you!" She smiled persuasively, earnestly, and with dreadful unease, showing fine gold rims around her teeth. She said, "There is a girl in Grade Six called Myra Sayla. She *is* in your grade, isn't she?"

We mumbled. But there was a coo from Gladys Healey. "Yes, Miss Darling!"

"Well, why is she never playing with the rest of you? Every day I see her standing in the back porch, never playing. Do you think she looks very happy standing back

ALICE MUNRO **1267**

Teach

Reading Strategy | 3

Analyze Characterization
Ask: What do you learn about Myra and Jimmy from the description in these lines? *(They are shy, lonely, scared, and quiet.)* Is this direct or indirect characterization? Explain. *(The narrator describes the children's physical characteristics; therefore, this passage is indirect characterization.)*

View the Art ★

Answer: *Students may be reminded of the girls talking about Myra behind her back.*

Learning Objectives
Analyzing dialect and idiom. (SE)
Analyzing characterization. (SE)
Avoiding run-on sentences. (TE)

English Learners

DIFFERENTIATED INSTRUCTION

Beginning English learners may have difficulty with indefinite pronouns because many indefinite pronouns seem to refer to groups but require singular verbs, for example, *everybody, anybody, nobody, anyone,* and *somebody.* Ask students to write five sentences, each using one of the pronouns listed above. Check students' work for correct subject–verb agreement.

Approaching Level

DIFFERENTIATED INSTRUCTION

Physical Description Approaching Level students may have some difficulty understanding the descriptions of Myra and Jimmy. Have students create a four-column chart for each character. The column labels are as follows: Hair, Eyes, Faces, and Body Language. Students should fill in their charts with information from the story, taking note of the mood the author creates with her descriptions of the characters.

Advanced Learners/Pre-AP

DIFFERENTIATED INSTRUCTION

Art Research The narrator describes Myra and Jimmy as looking like "children in a medieval painting." Challenge students to do some research on medieval paintings and find a visual representation showing aspects of the narrator's description. The painting does not necessarily have to be of children, but it should showcase a person painted with an oval face and melancholy mien.

Teach

Reading Strategy | 1

Analyze Characterization
Ask: How does the characterization of the teacher help you characterize the narrator? *(Students may say that by describing Miss Darling as clueless and a bit pathetic, the narrator shows that she believes herself to be superior to her teacher.)*

Reading Strategy | 2

Analyze Characterization
Answer: *Gladys is mocking Miss Darling for her attempts to make the girls be kind to Myra. Her action suggests that Gladys has a superiority complex, as well as a bit of a mean streak.*

Literary Element | 3

Dialect and Idiom **Ask:** What does the word *kept* mean in this context? *(It means "owned or ran.")*

Big Idea | 4

Nature and the Imagination **Answer:** *This is a rural setting, and the school is in a small town. This suggests that everyone knows everyone else and, perhaps, looks down on students from outlying farms.*

Cultural History ☆

Dry Goods Traditionally, dry goods stores sold mostly clothing and household goods—or "dry" items—rather than groceries. Two of the most well-known dry goods companies of the early 1900s were Levi Strauss and J. C. Penney.

there? Do you think you would be very happy, if *you* were left back there?"

Nobody answered; we faced Miss Darling, all respectful, **self-possessed,** and bored with the unreality of her question. Then Gladys said, "Myra can't come out with us, Miss Darling. Myra has to look after her little brother!"

"Oh," said Miss Darling dubiously. "Well you ought to try to be nicer to her anyway. Don't you think so? Don't you? You will try to be nicer, won't you? I *know* you will." Poor Miss Darling! Her campaigns were soon confused, her persuasions turned to bleating and uncertain pleas.

When she had gone Gladys Healey said softly, "You will try to be nicer, won't you? I *know* you will!" and then drawing her lip back over her big teeth she yelled exuberantly, "I don't care if it rains or freezes." She went through the whole verse and ended it with a spectacular twirl of her Royal Stuart tartan skirt. Mr. Healey ran a Dry Goods and Ladies' Wear, and his daughter's leadership in our class was partly due to her flashing plaid skirts and organdy blouses and velvet jackets with brass buttons, but also to her early-maturing bust and the fine brutal force of her personality. Now we all began to imitate Miss Darling.

Visual Vocabulary
Tartan is a plaid wool cloth woven in the particular pattern of a Scottish clan.

---

2 Analyze Characterization *What does Gladys's action suggest about her character?*

Vocabulary

self-possessed (self′ pə zest′) *adj.* in control of oneself

1268 UNIT 6 THE MODERN AMERICAS

We had not paid much attention to Myra before this. But now a game was developed; it started with saying, "Let's be nice to Myra!" Then we would walk up to her in formal groups of three or four and at a signal, say together, "Hel-lo Myra, Hello My-ra!" and follow up with something like, "What do you wash your hair in, Myra, it's so nice and shiny, My-ra." "Oh she washes it in cod-liver oil, don't you, Myra, she washes it in cod-liver oil, can't you smell it?"

And to tell the truth there was a smell about Myra, but it was a rotten-sweetish smell as of bad fruit. That was what the Saylas did, kept a little fruit store. Her father sat all day on a stool by the window, with his shirt open over his swelling stomach and tufts of black hair showing around his belly button; he chewed garlic. But if you went into the store it was Mrs. Sayla who came to wait on you, appearing silently between the limp print curtains hung across the back of the store. Her hair was crimped in black waves and she smiled with her full lips held together, stretched as far as they would go; she told you the price in a little rapping voice, daring you to challenge her and, when you did not, handed you the bag of fruit with open mockery in her eyes.

One morning in the winter I was walking up the school hill very early; a neighbor had given me a ride into town. I lived about half a mile out of town, on a farm, and I should not have been going to the town school at all, but to a country school nearby where there were half a dozen pupils and a teacher a little demented since her change of life. But my mother, who was an ambitious woman, had prevailed on the town trustees to accept me and my father to pay the extra tuition, and I went to

---

Nature and the Imagination *How does this natural setting influence the actions of the characters?* **4**

Writing Practice

SMALL GROUP

Interior Monologue So far, students have learned about Myra from the narrator's point of view. Explain to students that an interior monologue is a character's internal narrative, describing what a character is thinking and feeling as events take place around him or her. Have students write a one- to two-page interior monologue from Myra's point of view.

Tell students to re-read the narrator's descriptions of Myra, as well as the events surrounding her. In small groups, students can discuss the following questions before they write their monologues: **Does Myra understand what is going on? How does she feel about the school? about Miss Darling? about the other girls?** Encourage students to share their monologues with their groups.

1268

school in town. I was the only one in the class who carried a lunch pail and ate peanut-butter sandwiches in the high, bare, mustard-colored cloakroom, the only one who had to wear rubber boots in the spring, when the roads were heavy with mud. I felt a little danger, on account of this; but I could not tell exactly what it was.

> *A role was shaping up for me that I could not resist playing. I felt a great pleasurable rush of self-conscious benevolence. . . .*

I saw Myra and Jimmy ahead of me on the hill; they always went to school very early—sometimes so early that they had to stand outside waiting for the janitor to open the door. They were walking slowly, and now and then Myra half turned around. I had often loitered in that way, wanting to walk with some important girl who was behind me, and not quite daring to stop and wait. Now it occurred to me that Myra might be doing this with me. I did not know what to do. I could not afford to be seen walking with her, and I did not even want to—but, on the other hand, the flattery of those humble, hopeful turnings was not lost on me. A role was shaping for me that I could not resist playing. I felt a great pleasurable rush of self-conscious benevolence; before I thought what I was doing I called, "Myra! Hey, Myra, wait up, I got some Cracker Jack!" and I quickened my pace as she stopped.

Myra waited, but she did not look at me; she waited in the withdrawn and rigid attitude with which she always met us. Perhaps she thought I was playing a trick on her, perhaps she expected me to run past and throw an empty Cracker Jack box in her face. And I opened the box and held it out to her. She took a little. Jimmy ducked behind her coat and would not take any when I offered the box to him.

"He's shy," I said reassuringly. "A lot of little kids are shy like that. He'll probably grow out of it."

"Yes," said Myra.

"I have a brother four," I said. "He's awfully shy." He wasn't. "Have some more Cracker Jack," I said. "I used to eat Cracker Jack all the time but I don't any more. I think it's bad for your complexion."

There was a silence.

"Do you like Art?" said Myra faintly.

"No. I like Social Studies and Spelling and Health."

"I like Art and Arithmetic." Myra could add and multiply in her head faster than anyone else in the class.

"I wish I was as good as you. In Arithmetic," I said, and felt magnanimous.

"But I am no good at Spelling," said Myra. "I make the most mistakes, I'll fail maybe." She did not sound unhappy about this, but pleased to have such a thing to say. She kept her head turned away from me staring at the dirty snowbanks along Victoria Street, and as she talked she made a sound as if she was wetting her lips with her tongue.

"You won't fail," I said. "You are too good in Arithmetic. What are you going to be when you grow up?"

She looked bewildered. "I will help my mother," she said. "And work in the store."

"Well I am going to be an airplane hostess," I said. "But don't mention it to anybody. I haven't told many people."

---

5 Analyze Characterization *What does this admission reveal about the narrator's character?*

6

---

7 Dialect and Idiom *What does the narrator mean by this?*

Teach

Reading Strategy 5

Analyze Characterization
Answer: *The narrator is subjected to peer pressures and afraid that her classmates will ridicule her for even being seen with Myra. Yet she is basically a decent person who feels she should at least be nice to Myra—and she can't resist this opportunity to be looked up to, even by Myra.*

Reading Strategy 6

Analyze Characterization
Ask: How does the narrator's lie fit in with her "self-conscious benevolence?" *(The narrator is trying to make Myra feel good.)*

Literary Element 7

Dialect and Idiom **Answer:** *"I have a brother who is four years old."*

Learning Objectives
Analyzing dialect and idiom. (SE)
Analyzing characterization. (SE)
Writing an interior monologue. (TE)

English Learners

DIFFERENTIATED INSTRUCTION

Intermediate Point out the author's use of *self-conscious* to English learners. Explain that when *self* is attached to another word with a hyphen, it creates a compound word in which the action of the second word reflects back on the user. For example, *self-respect* is respect given to oneself; *self-isolation* is to isolate oneself from others.

Advanced Learners/Pre-AP

DIFFERENTIATED INSTRUCTION

Make Predictions Have students make predictions about what they suspect will happen between the narrator and Myra, based on the scene when they talk on the way to school. **Ask:** What usually happens when people who are not friends suddenly find that they have a lot in common? What do you expect the narrator really feels? What do you think Myra believes is going on?

(Students may say that when people share interests, a common bond forms. They may say that the narrator actually likes Myra but is afraid of others' opinions. They may also say that Myra is probably suspicious but too desperate for a friend to reject the narrator.) Tell students to base their predictions on clues in the text, as well as on their own experiences and knowledge.

Teach

Literary Element | 1

Dialect and Idiom Answer:
It is an idiom meaning that who-ever finds something first gets to keep it.

Literary History ☆

Alice Munro Several of Munro's novels and short stories feature a female protagonist's search for identity. Her collection *Dance of the Happy Shades* is considered to be partially autobiographical, and *The Lives of Girls and Women* follows one woman's attempt to understand the world. *A Wilderness Station* uses "historical documents" from the nineteenth and twentieth century to tell the story of an orphan sent to the wilderness to be a bride.

Vegetation. Tamas Galambos. Oil on canvas. Private collection.

"No, I won't," said Myra. "Do you read Steve Canyon in the paper?"

"Yes." It was queer to think that Myra, too, read the comics, or that she did anything at all, apart from her role at the school. "Do you read Rip Kirby?"

"Do you read Orphan Annie?"

"Do you read Betsy and the Boys?"

"You haven't had hardly any Cracker Jack," I said. "Have some. Take a whole handful."

Myra looked into the box. "There's a prize in there," she said. She pulled it out. It was a brooch,[1] a little tin butterfly, painted gold with bits of colored glass stuck onto it to look like jewels. She held it in her brown hand, smiling slightly.

I said, "Do you like that?"

Myra said, "I like them blue stones. Blue stones are sapphires."

"I know. My birthstone is sapphire. What is your birthstone?"

"I don't know."

"When is your birthday?"

"July."

"Then yours is ruby."

"I like sapphire better," said Myra. "I like yours." She handed me the brooch.

"You keep it," I said. "Finders keepers."

Myra kept holding it out, as if she did not know what I meant. "Finders keepers," I said.

"It was your Cracker Jack," said Myra, scared and solemn. "You bought it."

"Well you found it."

"No—" said Myra.

"Go on!" I said. "Here, I'll *give* it to you." I took the brooch from her and pushed it back into her hand.

---

1. A *brooch* (brōch) is an ornamental pin.

Dialect and Idiom *Is this phrase an example of dialect or idiom? What does it mean?* **1**

Reading Practice

Analyze Historical Context Explain to students that analyzing descriptions of clothing or household items can give readers an indication of the time period or historical context of a text. An important element to the narrator in this story is clothing. **Ask:** What types of clothing does the narrator describe? *(plaid skirts, organdy blouses, velvet jackets, rubber boots, serge tunics, and taffeta and crepe dresses)*

Have students look up the fabrics online or in another visual reference source.
Ask: What materials are your school clothes made of? *(Students are likely to answer cotton, denim, flannel, and other easy-care fabrics.)* Discuss the differences in the clothes mentioned in the story from those worn by the students in class.
Ask: What can you conclude about the historical context from the clothing descriptions?

(Students may say, based on Myra's oddly formal attire, the story takes place sometime in the mid-twentieth century, when children dressed more formally for school.)

We were both surprised. We looked at each other; I flushed but Myra did not. I realized the pledge as our fingers touched; I was panicky, but *all right*. I thought, I can come early and walk with her other mornings. I can go and talk to her at recess. Why not? *Why not?*

Myra put the brooch in her pocket. She said, "I can wear it on my good dress. My good dress is blue."

I knew it would be. Myra wore out her good dresses at school. Even in midwinter among the plaid wool skirts and serge tunics, she glimmered sadly in sky-blue taffeta, in dusty turquoise crepe, a grown woman's dress made over, weighted by a big bow at the v of the neck and folding empty over Myra's narrow chest.

And I was glad she had not put it on. If someone asked her where she got it, and she told them, what would I say?

It was the day after this, or the week after, that Myra did not come to school. Often she was kept at home to help. But this time she did not come back. For a week, then two weeks, her desk was empty. Then we had a moving day at school and Myra's books were taken out of her desk and put on a shelf in the closet. Miss Darling said, "We'll find a seat when she comes back." And she stopped calling Myra's name when she took attendance.

Jimmy Sayla did not come to school either, having no one to take him to the bathroom.

In the fourth week or the fifth, that Myra had been away, Gladys Healey came to school and said, "Do you know what— Myra Sayla is sick in the hospital."

It was true. Gladys Healey had an aunt who was a nurse. Gladys put up her hand in the middle of Spelling and told Miss Darling. "I thought you might like to know," she said. "Oh yes," said Miss Darling. "I do know."

"What has she got?" we said to Gladys.

And Gladys said, "Akemia,[2] or something. And she has blood transfusions." She said to Miss Darling, "My aunt is a nurse."

So Miss Darling had the whole class write Myra a letter, in which everybody said, "Dear Myra, We are all writing you a letter. We hope you will soon be better and be back to school, Yours truly. . . ." And Miss Darling said, "I've thought of something. Who would like to go up to the hospital and visit Myra on the twentieth of March, for a birthday party?"

I said, "Her birthday's in July."

"I know," said Miss Darling. "It's the twentieth of July. So this year she could have it on the twentieth of March, because she's sick."

"But her *birthday* is in July."

"Because she's sick," said Miss Darling, with a warning shrillness. "The cook at the hospital would make a cake and you could all give a little present, twenty-five cents or so. It would have to be between two and four, because that's visiting hours. And we couldn't all go, it'd be too many. So who wants to go and who wants to stay here and do **supplementary** reading?"

We all put up our hands. Miss Darling got out the spelling records and picked out the first fifteen, twelve girls and three boys. Then the three boys did not want to go so

---

2. *Akemia* is a mispronounciation of *leukemia,* which is a form of cancer that affects the blood.

Nature and the Imagination *How is nature intruding on the everyday lives of the children?* 3

Vocabulary

supplementary (sup′lə men′tər ē) *adj.* extra or additional

ALICE MUNRO **1271**

2 Dialect and Idiom *What does it mean that the dress has been "made over"? How does this fact contribute to Myra's characterization?*

Teach

Literary Element   2

Dialect and Idiom Answer:
Myra's dress has been cut down and re-sewn from a woman's dress—probably her mother's. This suggests that Myra's family is too poor to afford new clothes for her. Poverty may contribute to her strange behavior.

Big Idea   3

Nature and the Imagination Answer: *A life-threatening disease such as leukemia is a harsh reality for children to have to deal with.*

English Learners

DIFFERENTIATED INSTRUCTION

Intermediate Draw students' attention to the use of *-ness* in the words *shrillness* and *heaviness*. Explain that the suffix *-ness* means condition, quality, or degree. For example, loudness is a degree of volume. Have students use the suffix to create five more words; then, have them provide a definition of each word. Invite students to use a dictionary to check their work.

Advanced Learners/Pre-AP

DIFFERENTIATED INSTRUCTION

Research Students can infer from the teacher's insisting on having a party that Myra is very ill. Invite students to do some research on leukemia, including rates of the disease in childhood. Encourage students to investigate mortality rates now compared with those of the time period during which this story takes place. Have students share their discoveries with the class.

Learning Objectives
Analyzing dialect and idiom. (SE)
Analyzing historical context. (TE)

Teach

Literary Element   1

Dialect and Idiom Ask:
What is meant by this statement? *(The hospital is staffed by nuns.)*

Reading Strategy   2

Analyze Characterization
Ask: What is revealed about Myra from this characterization? *(Students may say that she knows that she is the center of attention and is acting "queenly.")*

Big Idea   3

Nature and the Imagination **Answer:** *She may have a vague idea, but she does realize that her illness and all the attention it brings her place her in a kind of superior position.*

she picked out the next three girls. And I do not know when it was, but I think it was probably at this moment that the birthday party of Myra Sayla became fashionable.

Perhaps it was because Gladys Healey had an aunt who was a nurse, perhaps it was the excitement of sickness and hospitals, or simply the fact that Myra was so entirely, impressively set free of all the rules and conditions of our lives. We began to talk of her as if she were something we owned, and her party became a cause; with womanly heaviness we discussed it at recess, and decided that twenty-five cents was too low.

We all went up to the hospital on a sunny afternoon when the snow was melting, carrying our presents, and a nurse led us upstairs, single file, and down a hall past half-closed doors and dim conversations. She and Miss Darling kept saying, "Sh-sh," but we were going on tiptoe anyway; our hospital demeanor was perfect.

At this small country hospital there was no children's ward, and Myra was not really a child; they had put her in with two gray old women. A nurse was putting screens around them as we came in.

Myra was sitting up in bed, in a bulky stiff hospital gown. Her hair was down, the long braids falling over her shoulders and down the coverlet. But her face was the same, always the same.

She had been told something about the party, Miss Darling said, so the surprise would not upset her; but it seemed she had not believed, or had not understood what it was. She watched us as she used to watch in the school grounds when we played.

"Well, here we are!" said Miss Darling. "Here we are!"

And we said, "Happy birthday, Myra! Hello, Myra, happy birthday!" Myra said, "My birthday is in July." Her voice was lighter than ever, drifting, expressionless.

"Never mind when it is, really," said Miss Darling. "Pretend it's now! How old are you, Myra?"

"Eleven," Myra said. "In July."

Then we all took off our coats and emerged in our party dresses, and laid our presents, in their pale flowery wrappings, on Myra's bed. Some of our mothers had made immense, complicated bows of fine satin ribbon, some of them had even taped on little bouquets of imitation roses and lilies of the valley. "Here Myra," we said, "here Myra, happy birthday." Myra did not look at us, but at the ribbons, pink and blue and speckled with silver, and the miniature bouquets; they pleased her, as the butterfly had done. An innocent look came into her face, a partial, private smile.

"Open them, Myra," said Miss Darling. "They're for you!"

Myra gathered the presents around her, fingering them, with this smile, and a cautious realization, an unexpected pride. She said, "Saturday I'm going to London[3] to St. Joseph's Hospital."

"That's where my mother was at," somebody said. "We went and saw her. They've got all nuns there." **1**

"My father's sister is a nun," said Myra calmly.

She began to unwrap the presents, with an air that not even Gladys could have bettered, folding the tissue paper and the ribbons, and drawing out books and puzzles and cutouts as if they were all prizes she had won. Miss Darling said that maybe she should say thank you, and the person's name with every gift she opened, to make sure she knew whom it was from, and so Myra said, "Thank you, Mary Louise, thank **2**

---

3. *London* is a city in southern Ontario, Canada.

Nature and the Imagination *Do you think Myra realizes how dangerously ill she is? Explain.* **3**

Writing Practice

Description Discuss with students the importance of clear description to help readers create a mental picture of a scene. Explain that one way of writing description is to use visual imagery, as Munro does when describing Myra in the hospital bed, as well as the wrapping on the birthday presents. Have students choose an item, a place, a person, or an animal to be described in two paragraphs.

Before students write, have them imagine that they are describing the item to someone who has never seen it before. **Ask: What is the most important, colorful, or unusual thing about this item? What small details might a casual observer overlook?** Encourage students to use imagery that appeals to the five senses.

Also, encourage them to use precise adjectives and adverbs. Have students share their descriptions with their classmates.

2 you, Carol," and when she came to mine she said, "Thank you, Helen." Everyone explained their presents to her and there was talking and excitement and a little gaiety, which Myra presided over, though she was not gay. A cake was brought in with *Happy Birthday Myra* written on it, pink on white, and eleven candles. Miss Darling lit the candles and we all sang Happy Birthday to You, and cried, "Make a wish, Myra, make a wish—" and Myra blew them out. Then we all had cake and strawberry ice cream.

Myra said, "I got too many things. You take something."

At four o'clock a buzzer sounded and the nurse took out what was left of the cake, and the dirty dishes, and we put on our coats to go home. Everybody said, "Good-bye, Myra," and Myra sat in the bed watching us go, her back straight, not supported by any pillow, her hands resting on the gifts. But at the door I heard her call; she called, "Helen!" Only a couple of the others heard; Miss Darling did not hear, she had gone out ahead. I went back to the bed.

Myra said, "I got too many things. You take something."

"What?" I said. "It's for your birthday. You always get a lot at a birthday."

"Well you take something," Myra said. She picked up a leatherette case with a mirror in it, a comb and a nail file and a natural lipstick and a small handkerchief edged with gold thread. I had noticed it before. "You take that," she said.

"Don't you want it?"

"You take it." She put it into my hand. Our fingers touched again.

"When I come back from London," Myra said, "you can come and play at my place after school."

"Okay," I said. Outside the hospital window there was a clear carrying sound of somebody playing in the street, maybe chasing with the last snowballs of the year. This sound made Myra, her triumph and her bounty, and most of all her future in which she had found this place for me, turn shadowy, turn dark. All the presents on the bed, the folded paper and ribbons, those guilt-tinged offerings, had passed into this shadow, they were no longer innocent objects to be touched, exchanged, accepted without danger. I didn't want to take the case now but I could not think how to get out of it, what lie to tell. I'll give it away, I thought, I won't ever play with it. I would let my little brother pull it apart.

The nurse came back, carrying a glass of chocolate milk.

"What's the matter, didn't you hear the buzzer?"

So I was released, set free by the barriers which now closed about Myra, her unknown, exalted, ether-smelling hospital world, and by the treachery of my own heart. "Well thank you," I said. "Thank you for the thing. Good-bye."

Did Myra ever say good-bye? Not likely. She sat in her high bed, her delicate brown neck, rising out of a hospital gown too big for her, her brown carved face immune to treachery, her offering perhaps already forgotten, prepared to be set apart for legendary uses, as she was even in the back porch at school.

---

4 Analyze Characterization *What does this gesture reveal about Myra's character?*

5 Dialect and Idiom *What does Helen want here? Why?*

ALICE MUNRO **1273**

Reading Strategy | **4**

Analyze Characterization
Answer: *Myra can also be generous, but only when she is in a position to be. Her gift further suggests that she doesn't forget a friendly gesture and wants to repay Helen for her attention.*

Literary Element | **5**

Dialect and Idiom **Answer:** *Helen finds herself embarrassed, unsure of how she should respond or how much commitment she is accepting. She wishes she could be removed from the situation.*

Progress Check

Can students identify dialect and idiom?

If No → See Unit 6 Teaching Resources Book, p. 225.

 To check students' understanding of the selection, see Unit 6 Teaching Resources Book, p. 230.

Learning Objectives
Analyzing dialect and idiom. (SE)
Analyzing characterization. (SE)
Writing a description. (TE)

English Learners

DIFFERENTIATED INSTRUCTION

Advanced Draw students' attention to *guilt-tinged* and *ether-smelling*. Explain that these are compound modifiers, or a pair of words that collectively modify a noun. Further explain that *ether* and *smelling* alone cannot describe the hospital, but together they describe the hospital's smell. Have students create compound modifiers to describe an item in the classroom.

Approaching Level

DIFFERENTIATED INSTRUCTION

Connecting to the Literature Explain to students that connecting to literature means responding personally to characters, situation, and events. **Ask: Whom do you connect with more at the end of the story, Myra or Helen?** *(Students who connect more with Myra may say that they understand her loneliness. Students who connect more with Helen may understand why she wants the other girls to like her.)*

Advanced Learners/Pre-AP

DIFFERENTIATED INSTRUCTION

Rethink the Ending Students may be unsatisfied with the ending of the story, as there is no clear resolution of Myra's situation. Invite students to add one or two pages to the end of the story explaining what happens to Myra, her brother, the narrator, and the other children. Challenge students to describe how Myra's either returning to school or not returning to school affects the others.

After You Read

Assess

1. Answers will vary.
2. (a) She is withdrawn, is unfashionable, and comes from a poor family lacking social prestige. (b) They resent Miss Darling's insistence that they be kind to Myra.
3. (a) Helen is flattered by Myra's wanting to speak with her. (b) Helen is also an outsider because she lives on a farm instead of in town.
4. (a) a butterfly from a Cracker Jack box (b) Helen wants to be kind but is afraid of what her classmates would think about such a friendship.
5. (a) She becomes mysterious and interesting. (b) She may believe Myra will never return.
6. Miss Darling tries to make the students behave nicely toward Myra, but her efforts lead them to tease Myra instead.
7. (a) first person (b) to draw readers into the story; to make Helen more sympathetic
8. Illness and possible death drive the plot. Myra's illness leads the others to treat her differently.
9. Myra is isolated. Helen may also be a misfit, although more accepted by her classmates. Miss Darling seems awkward, expecting better behavior from her students than she should.

Literary Element

1. be punished by being hit with a strap
2. assist, as a clerk assists a customer
3. stay there until I am with you
4. stop that form of behavior when he becomes older

For additional assessment, see Assessment Resources, pp. 247–248.

1274

After You Read

Respond and Think Critically

Respond and Interpret

1. Did your feelings for the narrator, Helen, change during the story? Explain.
2. (a) Why is Myra unpopular with the other girls at school? (b) Why do Myra's classmates begin to tease her after ignoring her for so long?
3. (a) Why does Helen start a conversation with Myra on the way to school? (b) Why might Helen be more sympathetic toward Myra than the other girls?
4. (a) What gift does Helen give to Myra? (b) Do you think Helen has decided to become Myra's friend when she gives her the gift? Why or why not?
5. (a) How does Myra's reputation in class change after she goes into the hospital? (b) Why do you think Miss Darling makes up an excuse for the students to visit Myra in the hospital?

Analyze and Evaluate

6. **Irony** is a contrast between what is believed or expected and what actually exists or occurs. Identify an example of irony in the story.
7. (a) From what **point of view** is the story told? (b) What effect does this point of view have on your impression of the characters?

Connect

8. **Big Idea** **Nature and the Imagination** How do nature and the cycle of life influence the characters in the story?
9. **Connect to the Author** Many of Munro's characters are isolated people or misfits. Which characters in this story, if any, fit that description?

Literary Element **Dialect and Idiom**

A **dialect** is a language variation spoken in a particular part of a country or by a particular class. An **idiom** is an expression whose meaning differs from its literal meaning. Idioms are often specific to members of a particular society or culture and may not be understood by outsiders. What do these idiomatic expressions from "Day of the Butterfly" mean?

1. "get the strap" (p. 1267)
2. to "wait on" a person (p. 1268)
3. "wait up" (p. 1269)
4. "grow out of it" (p. 1269)

Review: Symbol

As you learned on page 791, a **symbol** is a person, a place, or a thing that has meaning in itself and also stands for something beyond itself. One way to recognize a symbol is by noting that something is especially important to one or more characters. In this story, the title calls attention to a possible symbol.

Partner Activity Meet with a classmate to discuss these questions.

1. What does the butterfly pin seem to symbolize to Myra?
2. What does the butterfly seem to symbolize to Helen?
3. How is Myra like a butterfly?

Review: Symbol

1. It represents beauty, and, as Myra appropriates the sapphire as her birthstone, that beauty belongs to her.
2. Helen recognizes the brooch as the simple, cheap thing it is, but she sees that it makes Myra happy, so she gives it to her as a way of providing Myra some pleasure.
3. Possible answer: Just as a drab caterpillar changes into a colorful butterfly, so the oft-rejected Myra becomes the center of attention as she sits surrounded by the colorful wrappings of her presents. However, a butterfly is also fragile and short-lived, and Myra and her friendship with Helen seem similarly destined to be brief.

Reading Strategy

SAT Skills Practice

Myra's calm acceptance of the gifts from her classmates (page 1272) serves primarily to suggest that

(A) she is not an emotional person

(B) she does not value material objects

(C) she does not understand that she is ill

(D) she fears her classmates

(E) she has changed since her classmates last saw her

Vocabulary Practice

Practice with Word Usage Respond to these questions to help you explore the meanings of the vocabulary words from the story.

1. If someone said something to you **cryptically**, would it be easy to understand? Explain.

2. How might someone who is **self-possessed** behave?

3. If you are given **supplementary** information about something, what type of information is it?

Academic Vocabulary

*Helen's perspective **shifts** from the beginning of the story to the end: she begins to see Myra as "legendary" rather than pitiable.*

Shift is an academic word. In more casual conversation, someone might say that moving an automobile from one gear to another is called *shifting gears*. To further explore the meaning of this word, answer this question: What accounts for the sudden **shift** in Helen's behavior on the day she gives Myra the tin butterfly?

For more on academic vocabulary, see pages 36–37 and R83–R85.

Research and Report

 Literary Criticism

Assignment Munro has said "I'm very, very excited by what you might call the surface of life." What lies beneath the surface in her writing? Search for literary criticism about Munro's work and give an oral presentation in which you evaluate how various critics describe her work.

Prepare Scholar Coral Ann Howells points out that in Munro's early stories, there is "always the sense of ordinary surfaces covering over some secret or scandal which threatens to collapse them." Look for more criticism in books about Munro, anthologies of criticism, scholarly journals, and online databases. Write down statements from the critics and find details from the story that support them.

Review the graphic organizer on page 1265 and think about how the details you recorded fit the critics' comments. When you find critical statements you disagree with, cite examples from the story that disprove them. Be sure to define unfamiliar terms you come across. Remember also to rehearse your report so it flows naturally.

Report When you give your report, make eye contact, speak loudly and clearly, and maintain good posture. Modify your tone of voice and use a variety of gestures to help convey your opinions.

Evaluate Use a chart like the one below to evaluate your research and delivery.

	Research	Delivery
Strength	Used criticism from a wide variety of sources	Used logical organization
Weakness	Didn't use evidence to support my disagreements with critics	Didn't vary my tone or gestures

LOG ON **Literature** Online

Selection Resources For Selection Quizzes, eFlashcards, and Reading-Writing Connection activities, go to glencoe.com and enter QuickPass code GLW6053u6.

ALICE MUNRO **1275**

Approaching Level

Reviews and Criticism Approaching learners are likely to find literary criticism daunting. Encourage students to start by first reading reviews of Munro's work in online journals and magazines, such as *The New York Review of Books, The Atlantic Monthly, Powells.com,* and *The New York Times.* Explain that reviews may introduce students to authors that write criticisms of and scholarly articles about literature.

After You Read

Assess

Reading Strategy

(E) is the correct answer. All the changes in Myra's behavior combine to suggest she has become "immune to treachery" and even "legendary."

Progress Check

Can students analyze characterization?

If No → See Unit 6 Teaching Resources Book, p. 226.

Vocabulary Practice

1. It would not be easy to understand, as it would be mysterious and secretive.
2. Students should describe the behavior of someone who is confident or proud.
3. additional information

Academic Vocabulary

Her behavior shifts, and she is kind to Myra because she enjoys the feeling of "self-conscious benevolence" it gives her.

Research and Report

Students should

- draw from a wide variety of criticism
- use evidence from the story to back up their evaluations of the criticism
- use effective oral delivery techniques in their presentations

 For grammar practice, see Unit 6 Teaching Resources Book, p. 229.

Focus

Activity

Say: Using a semicolon gives emphasis to the idea that links two independent clauses. Write the following pair of sentences on the board: I've always wanted to be an opera singer. My voice isn't strong enough.

Explain that the second sentence lacks force when on its own, but adding a semicolon and a conjunctive adverb such as *however* will emphasize the idea completed by the second sentence. Write the new version on the board.

Teach

Combining Sentences

Write the following sentences on the board: I've taken my cat to the vet. He'll come home tomorrow. Explain that adding a semicolon and a coordinating conjunction like *and* won't work: I've taken my cat to the vet; and he'll come home tomorrow. However, explain that students can simply use a semicolon to combine the two sentences: I've taken my cat to the vet; he'll come home tomorrow.

Assess

Possible rewrites:

1. Alice Munro is a Canadian author; it took her twelve years to write her first volume of short stories.
2. Her story "Day of the Butterfly" is entertaining; however, it focuses on a young girl with leukemia.
3. The story is told through a first-person narrator; she is Myra's classmate.

1276

Conjunctions and Conjunctive Adjectives

A **conjunction** is a word, such as *and, or,* or *but,* that joins single words or groups of words. A **conjunctive adjective** is used to clarify the relationship between clauses of a compound sentence. Some examples include the words *therefore, however, consequently,* and *furthermore.*

Tip

When deciding whether to use a semicolon, first determine if the sentence has at least two clauses that express complete thoughts.

Language Handbook

For more about semicolons, see Language Handbook, p. R40.

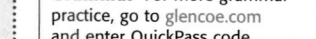

Literature Online

Grammar For more grammar practice, go to glencoe.com and enter QuickPass code GLW6053u6.

Grammar Workshop

Semicolons

Literature Connection In this sentence from "Day of the Butterfly," Alice Munro uses a semicolon to link related ideas.

"Perhaps they watched the baseball games, the tag and skipping and building of leaf houses in the fall and snow forts in the winter; perhaps they did not watch at all."

A **semicolon** can connect two or more main, or independent, clauses into one sentence. For example, you can connect the closely related clauses "Jimmy Sayla was not used to going to the bathroom by himself" and "He would have to come to the Grade Six door and ask Myra to take him" with a semicolon to form the following sentence: "Jimmy Sayla was not used to going to the bathroom by himself; he would have to come to the Grade Six door and ask Myra to take him."

SITUATION To replace a comma and a coordinating conjunction in a compound sentence

Myra and Jimmy went to school very early, and the janitor was the only one there.

Myra and Jimmy went to school very early; the janitor was the only one there.

SITUATION To use a semicolon before a conjunctive adverb in a compound sentence

The students thought Myra smelled of cod-liver oil, however, she smelled like her father's fruit market.

The students thought Myra smelled of cod-liver oil; however, she smelled like her father's fruit market.

Revise Rewrite the following sentences using a semicolon.

1. Alice Munro is a Canadian author, and she took twelve years to write her first volume of short stories.
2. Her story, "Day of the Butterfly," is entertaining, however, it focuses on a young girl with leukemia.
3. The story is told through a first-person narrator. She is Myra's classmate.

Grammar Practice

Use Semicolons Explain to students that semicolons can be used in certain kinds of lists. Write the following paragraph on the board:

To win the grand prize at the cake-baking contest, contestants must create an original recipe; submit the recipe, a sample of the cake, and an essay explaining how he or she created the recipe; and bake the cake on-site at the state fair.

Point out to students that when an item in a list includes commas, all of the items should be set off with semicolons.

Challenge students to correctly punctuate the following sentence:

Letters from pen pals came from Las Vegas, Nevada, Honolulu, Hawaii, Jacksonville, Florida, and as far away as Tokyo, Japan. (*Students should place semicolons after* Nevada, Hawaii, *and* Florida.)

Meet **Jamaica Kincaid**

(born 1949)

"Everyone thought I had a way with words," Jamaica Kincaid once wrote, "but it came out as a sharp tongue. No one expected anything from me at all." Smart and rebellious, Kincaid didn't let others' expectations stand in her way. She turned her way with words into a thriving career.

A Young Troublemaker Born Elaine Potter Richardson, Kincaid grew up on the Caribbean island of Antigua. When she was nine years old, the first of her three brothers was born, causing her to feel estranged from her mother. As a result, she became an avid reader, often ducking out of family and social obligations to spend more time reading. Once, when she was supposed to be babysitting, she instead sneaked off by herself to read. Her mother became so irate over the incident that she doused all of Kincaid's books with kerosene and set them ablaze.

> "I think life is difficult. I am interested in pursuing a truth, and the truth often seems to be not happiness but its opposite."
>
> —Jamaica Kincaid

Possessed of both a sharp mind and a sharp tongue, Kincaid was often dubbed a troublemaker by her teachers. However, they also recognized her extraordinary intellectual abilities and at one point suggested she was worthy of a scholarship to further her education. Despite this encouragement, Kincaid's mother insisted her young daughter was needed at home. As years went by, Kincaid felt more and more trapped by the vast sea that surrounded Antigua. But her troubled early years on the island provided a rich cultural backdrop—one to which she would return over and over in her writing.

Breaking into Magazines When Kincaid was seventeen, her family's financial situation took a turn for the worse, and she was sent to New York to work as a nanny. She was determined to write, however, and she applied repeatedly to various fashion magazines published in New York City. Finally, she wrote an article that was published in *Ingenue* magazine. The article was so successful that the magazine hired Kincaid to write a series. Her confidence grew as one literary success followed another. Kincaid eventually became first a staff writer for and then a regular contributor to the prestigious *New Yorker* magazine.

Kincaid writes with great emotion and insight about family and culture. From her lonely and difficult childhood, she has charted her own course to become an internationally renowned author.

 Literature Online

Author Search For more about Jamaica Kincaid, go to glencoe.com and enter QuickPass code GLW6053u6.

JAMAICA KINCAID **1277**

Bellringer Options

Selection Focus Transparency 83

Daily Language Practice Transparency 123

Or ask: What memories do you have of yourself at five years old? At seven? At nine? *(Responses will vary.)* Discuss with students the ability of outside forces, such as tastes and smells, to trigger memories. **Ask:** What triggers your memories of yourself at a young age? *(Students should describe situations that cause them to recall their younger days.)*

Selection Skills

Literary Elements
- Foreshadowing and Flashback (SE pp. 1278, 1280, 1281, 1285)

A Walk to the Jetty

Speaking/Listening/Viewing Skills
- Analyze Art (TE p. 1281)

Reading Skills
- Make and Verify Predictions (SE pp. 1278–1280, 1282–1284, 1286)
- Connect to Personal Experience (TE p. 1278)
- Identify Sequence (TE p. 1280)
- Make Inferences (TE p. 1284)

Vocabulary Skills
- Denotation and Connotation (SE p. 1286)

Writing Skills/Grammar
- Apply Flashback (SE p. 1286)
- Description (TE p. 1282)

Before You Read

Focus

Summary

A teenage girl, Annie, describes walking with her father and mother through town to the jetty where she will board a ship bound for England. Annie, now seventeen, is leaving home to study for a nursing career. During the walk she recalls numerous details from her life: her apprenticeship as a seamstress, the first time she walked on the road alone, her church, school, stores, the library, and the times she walked to the jetty with her father. After the family arrives at the jetty, the group is taken in a launch to the ship, where Annie says good-bye to her parents.

> For summaries in languages other than English, see Unit 6 Teaching Resources Book, pp. 233–238.

Vocabulary

Synonym Round-Robin
In small groups, each member takes a turn to provide a synonym for *loom*. The student who cannot provide a synonym for *loom* must provide one for *scorn*, and so on down the list. The student who cannot provide a synonym for *stupor* may return to *loom*. The game ends when group members have run out of synonyms for all the vocabulary words.

> For additional vocabulary practice, see Unit 6 Teaching Resources Book, p. 241.

1278

Literature and Reading Preview

Connect to the Story

How do you think you would feel if you were about to leave home forever? Respond to this question in your journal.

Build Background

The work you are about to read is from the last chapter of *Annie John,* a coming-of-age novel about a girl growing up on the small (108 square miles) eastern Caribbean island of Antigua. After she turns seventeen, Annie decides to move to England and study for a career in nursing. In "A Walk to the Jetty" (a *jetty* is a landing pier), Kincaid portrays Annie's confused feelings about her departure.

Set Purposes for Reading

Big Idea The Legacy of Colonialism

The island of Antigua was a British colony. As you read, ask yourself, How would you describe the relationship between homeland and identity experienced by the protagonist?

Literary Element Foreshadowing and Flashback

Authors use **foreshadowing** to present clues about events that will occur later in a story. In a **flashback,** the narrator interrupts the action of a literary work to present a scene that took place at an earlier time. As you read the story, ask yourself, What are examples of foreshadowing and flashback?

Reading Strategy Make and Verify Predictions

One way to get the most from your reading is to **make predictions,** or educated guesses, about what will happen later in a work. Base your predictions on details the author provides about time, place, situation, and characters. You then **verify predictions** by looking for evidence that confirms their accuracy. As you read, ask yourself, What predictions can I make about events and their outcomes?

Tip: Take Notes Use a chart like the one below to make and verify predictions.

Passage	Notes	Prediction
"My mother had arranged with a stevedore to take my trunk to the jetty."	The narrator's mother is sending a trunk ahead. The narrator will take a trip.	This story may be about a person leaving home.

1278 UNIT 6 THE MODERN AMERICAS

Learning Objectives

For pages 1277–1286

In studying this text, you will focus on the following objectives:

Literary Study: Analyzing foreshadowing and flashback.

Reading: Making and verifying predictions.

Writing: Applying flashback.

Vocabulary

loom (lōōm) *v.* to come into sight in enlarged or distorted form; p. 1279 *In the carnival's haunted house, a face loomed out of the darkness.*

guffaw (gu fô´) *n.* a loud or boisterous burst of laughter; p. 1283 *The comedian made each person break into a guffaw.*

shrivel (shriv´əl) *v.* to become wrinkled as a result of lack of moisture; p. 1283 *If a grape shrivels, it becomes a raisin.*

stupor (stōō´pər) *n.* a dulled mental state, often as a result of shock or stress; a daze; p. 1284 *The young man sat in a stupor after the car accident.*

Tip: Connotation and Denotation
A word's denotation is its literal, or dictionary, meaning. Each word, however, has a different connotation, the feeling or the impression it suggests. For example, *scorn* and *dislike* have similar denotations, but the connotation of *scorn* is more negative and hostile.

Reading Practice

Connect to Personal Experience The Build Background section explains that "A Walk to the Jetty" is about a teenager leaving home. Students can think about their personal experiences with leaving home and family behind, either for an overnight stay at a friend's house or a longer trip with a school or church group. **Ask:** What emotions did you experience when leaving? How did your parents or close friends act before you left? How did it fee to return? *(Responses will vary. Students may say they felt excited to be going on a trip but apprehensive about leaving familiar people or surroundings. They may say that parents and friends acted sad when they left but returning home was a happy occasion.)*

Tell students to pause when reading the story to consider how their thoughts and emotions might be similar to Annie's in the same situation.

Village Life. Victor Collector. Oil on canvas. Private collection.

A Walk to the Jetty *from* **Annie John**

Jamaica Kincaid

My mother had arranged with a stevedore[1] to take my trunk to the jetty ahead of me. At ten o'clock on the dot, I was dressed, and we set off for the jetty. An hour after that, I would board a launch that would take me out to sea, where I then would board the ship. Starting out, as if for old time's sake and without giving it a thought, we lined up in the old way: I walking between my mother and my father. I **loomed** way above

my father and could see the top of his head. We must have made a strange sight: a grown girl all dressed up in the middle of a morning, in the middle of the week, walking in step in the middle between her two parents, for people we didn't know stared at us. It was all of half an hour's walk from our house to the jetty, but I was passing through most of the years of my life. We passed by the house where Miss Dulcie, the seamstress that I had been apprenticed to for a time, lived, and just as I was passing by, a wave of bad feeling for her came over me, because I suddenly remembered that

1. A *stevedore* (stē′vǝ dôr′) is one who works at or is responsible for loading and unloading ships in port.

Vocabulary

loom (lo͞om) *v.* to come into sight in enlarged or distorted form

Make and Verify Predictions *Based on this sentence, what do you predict will be the focus of this story?*

JAMAICA KINCAID **1279**

Teach

Reading Strategy   1

Make and Verify Predictions Answer: *Students may predict that the story will record the narrator's memories as she is about to leave her home country.*

📁 For additional practice using the reading skill or strategy, see Unit 6 Teaching Resources Book, p. 240.

Literary Element   2

Foreshadowing and Flashback Ask: What is your first indication that a flashback is about to occur? *(The narrator says, "I was passing through most of the years of my life.")*

💿 For an audio recording of this selection, use Listening Library Audio CD-ROM.

Readability Scores

Dale-Chall: 5.1
DRP: 55
Lexile: 1180

Learning Objectives
Analyzing foreshadowing and flashback. (SE)
Making and verifying predictions. (SE)
Connecting to personal experience. (TE)

English Learners

DIFFERENTIATED INSTRUCTION

Intermediate English learners may be puzzled by the use of the word *would* in a past-tense narration. Explain that Kincaid frequently uses this past tense of the auxiliary verb *will* to indicate that something occurred repeatedly in the past. Ask students to rewrite the following sentences, using the word *would* to convey the same idea.

1. My friends and I frequently played outdoors. (My friends and I would frequently play outdoors.)
2. The boys often teased me because I was so tall. (The boys would often tease me because I was so tall.)

Advanced Learners/Pre-AP

DIFFERENTIATED INSTRUCTION

Research The narrator goes to the chemist's (pharmacy) to buy medicinal plants rather than the things we usually buy at a drug store, such as aspirin or cough medicine. Invite students to research the plants mentioned in the story to find their medicinal applications. Have students share their findings with the class and, if possible, show illustrations of the plants.

1279

Teach

Literary Element   1

Foreshadowing and Flashback **Answer:** *The narrator has recalled the time she spent as a seamstress's apprentice.*

Reading Strategy   2

Make and Verify Predictions **Answer:** *Answers will depend on students' predictions.*

(APPROACHING) Instruct approaching-level students that if their predictions have not been correct, they should record the new information in their charts and then make new predictions.

Literary Element   3

Foreshadowing and Flashback **Ask:** Where can you guess that the next flashback will take place? What clues help you follow the narrator's flashbacks? *(The next flashbacks will take place at church and at a friend's house. The flashbacks are related to the buildings the narrator passes.)*

the months I spent with her all she had me do was sweep the floor, which was always full of threads and pins and needles, and I never seemed to sweep it clean enough to please her. Then she would send me to the store to buy buttons or thread, though I was only allowed to do this if I was given a sample of the button or thread, and then she would find fault even though they were an exact match of the samples she had given me. And all the while she said to me, "A girl like you will never learn to sew properly, you know." At the time, I don't suppose I minded it, because it was customary to treat the first-year apprentice with such scorn, but now I placed on the dustheap of my life Miss Dulcie and everything that I had had to do with her.

We were soon on the road that I had taken to school, to church, to Sunday school, to choir practice, to Brownie meetings, to Girl Guide meetings, to meet a friend. I was five years old when I first walked on this road unaccompanied by someone to hold my hand. My mother had placed three pennies in my little basket, which was a duplicate of her bigger basket, and sent me to the chemist's shop[2] to buy a pennyworth of senna leaves, a pennyworth of eucalyptus leaves, and a pennyworth of camphor.[3] She then instructed me on what side of the road to walk, where to make a turn, where to cross, how to look carefully before I crossed, and if I met anyone that I knew to politely pass greetings and keep on my way. I was wearing a freshly ironed yellow dress that had printed on it scenes of

acrobats flying through the air and swinging on a trapeze. I had just had a bath, and after it, instead of powdering me with my baby-smelling talcum powder, my mother had, as a special favor, let me use her own talcum powder, which smelled quite perfumy and came in a can that had painted on it people going out to dinner in nineteenth-century London and was called Mazie. How it pleased me to walk out the door and bend my head down to sniff at myself and see that I smelled just like my mother. I went to the chemist's shop, and he had to come from behind the counter and bend down to hear what it was that I wanted to buy, my voice was so little and timid then. I went back just the way I had come, and when I walked into the yard and presented my basket with its three packages to my mother, her eyes filled with tears and she swooped me up and held me high in the air and said that I was wonderful and good and that there would never be anybody better. If I had just conquered Persia,[4] she couldn't have been more proud of me.

We passed by our church—the church in which I had been christened and received and had sung in the junior choir. We passed by a house in which a girl I used to like and was sure I couldn't live without had lived. Once, when she had mumps, I went to visit her against my mother's wishes, and we sat on her bed and ate the cure of roasted, buttered sweet potatoes that had been placed on her swollen jaws, held there by a piece of white cloth. I don't know how, but my mother

---

2. A *chemist's* shop is a pharmacy, in British usage.
3. *Senna leaves, eucalyptus* (ū kə lip′ təs) *leaves* and *camphor* are plant products used for medicinal purposes.

1   **Foreshadowing and Flashback** *This is just one in a series of flashbacks. What other flashback has occurred in the story so far?*

4. The phase *conquered Persia* means " accomplished and extraordinary feat." The allusion is to Alexander the Great, who vanquished the Persian Empire in the fourth century B.C.

Make and Verify Predictions *Have your predictions of what the story would be about been verified so far? If so, explain why. If not, how does the story differ?*   **2**

Reading Practice

Identify Sequence Point out to students that "A Walk to the Jetty" blends two sequences of events. One involves Annie's walk to the jetty, which is arranged in chronological order. The other involves the sequence of her memories.

Ask students to make two timelines of the reading selection: one for the sequence of events that takes place in the "present" and the other to include the events that Annie remembers.

When students finish their timelines, **ask: How do Annie's emotions during the walk affect her attitude toward her memories?** *(Students may say because she is nervous about leaving, Annie feels free to feel hatred for Miss Dulcie; furthermore, her good memories—like that of her walk to the chemist's—become more poignant.)*

Encourage students to continue to fill in their timelines as they read the story and to consider connections between the two threads of sequence.

found out about it, and I don't know how, but she put an end to our friendship. Shortly after, the girl moved with her family across the sea to somewhere else. We passed the doll store, where I would go with my mother when I was little and point out the doll I wanted that year for Christmas. We passed the store where I bought the much-fought-over shoes I wore to church to be received in. We passed the bank. On my sixth birthday, I was given, among other things, the present of a sixpence. My mother and I then went to this bank, and with the sixpence I opened my own savings account. I was given a little gray book with my name in big letters on it, and in the balance column it said "6d." Every Saturday morning after that, I was given a sixpence—later a shilling, and later a two-and-sixpence piece—and I would take it to the bank for deposit. I had never been allowed to withdraw even a farthing[5] from my bank account until just a few weeks before I was to leave; then the whole account was closed out, and I received from the bank the sum of six pounds ten shillings and two and a half pence.

We passed the office of the doctor who told my mother three times that I did not need glasses, that if my eyes were feeling weak a glass of carrot juice a day would make them strong again. This happened when I was eight. And so every day at recess I would run to my school gate and meet my mother, who was waiting for me with a glass of juice from carrots she had

Tartane, Martinique. Claude Salez. Oil on canvas. Private collection.

just grated and then squeezed, and I would drink it and then run back to meet my chums. I knew there was nothing at all wrong with my eyes, but I had recently read a story in *The Schoolgirl's Own Annual* in which the heroine, a girl a few years older than I was then, cut such a figure to my mind with the way she was always adjusting her small, round, horn-rimmed glasses that I felt I must have a pair exactly like them. When it became clear that I didn't need glasses, I began to complain about the glare of the sun being too much for my eyes, and I walked around with my hands shielding them—especially in my mother's presence. My mother then bought for me a pair of sunglasses with the exact horn-rimmed frames I wanted, and how I enjoyed the gestures of blowing on the lenses, wiping them with the hem of my uniform, adjusting the glasses when they slipped down my nose, and just removing them from their case and putting them on. In three weeks, I grew tired of them and they found a nice resting place in a drawer, along with some other things that at one time or another I couldn't live without. **5**

---

5. A *sixpence,* a *shilling,* and a *farthing* are former monetary units in various British Commonwealth countries. A shilling was worth twelve pence (pennies) or one-twentieth of a pound; a farthing was worth one-fourth of a penny.

 Foreshadowing and Flashback *You may note that, so far, almost all the events in this story take place in the past. What do you think the author is building up to?*

Literary Element | 4

Foreshadowing and Flashback Answer: *All the mundane memories that build up in Annie's mind will culminate with her leaving the island.*

Literary Element | 5

Foreshadowing and Flashback Ask: What opinion does Annie seem to have of her younger self? Explain. *(Students may say that Annie's flashbacks show that she knows that she was silly when she was younger, but that she seems matter-of-fact about it rather than disdainful.)*

View the Art

Ask: What might this scene represent for a typical Western viewer? How does this differ from the way someone from a tropical island might view it? *(Students may say that boats on a beautiful beach represent vacation to Western viewers but work or everyday existence to an islander.)*

Learning Objectives
Analyzing foreshadowing and flashback. (SE)
Making and verifying predictions. (SE)
Identifying sequence. (TE)

Approaching Level
DIFFERENTIATED INSTRUCTION

Long Sentences A characteristic of Kincaid's style is lengthy paragraphs of long, complex sentences, which can present a challenge for approaching-level students. Explain to students that breaking down paragraphs and sentences into their parts will help them better understand Kincaid's descriptions. Direct students to make a photocopy of the story and then visually highlight each sentence in a paragraph in a different color.

Tell students to then identify each independent clause's subject and verb. Students can then link clauses and phrases with the word or words they modify.

English Learners
DIFFERENTIATED INSTRUCTION

Intermediate Direct students' attention to the author's use of *heroine,* the feminine form of *hero.* Further, explain gender-neutral words in English were often feminized when applied to a woman, although this practice has been a subject of scorn for recent generations of women in the United States. For example a female comedian used to be called a *comedienne,* and a female aviator an *aviatrix.*

Teach

Reading Strategy · 1

**Make and Verify
Predictions Answer:**
*Students may predict that by the
end of the story, reality will set in
for the narrator.*

Literary Element · 2

**Foreshadowing and
Flashback Ask:** What
happens when Annie focuses
on her fear in the present time?
*(She slips back into another
flashback.)*

ADVANCED Ask: How are Annie's
memories a coping mechanism?
*(Annie uses her memories to dis-
tract herself from her anxiety and
fear about leaving home.)*

Literary History ☆
Literature of the Caribbean
The narrator's father and his friend
discuss cricket, a British sport,
because Antigua was a British
island. In the early twentieth century, writers on Spanish and French
Caribbean islands began to seek
a voice of their own. Writers in the
British Caribbean islands, inspired
by their neighbors, followed in the
1940s.

We passed the store that sold only
grooming aids, all imported from England.
This store had in it a large porcelain dog—
white, with black spots all over and a red
ribbon of satin tied around its neck. The
dog sat in front of a white porcelain bowl
that was always filled with fresh water, and
it sat in such a way that it looked as if it
had just taken a long drink. When I was a
small child, I would ask my mother, if ever
we were near this store, to please take me
to see the dog, and I would stand in front
of it, bent over slightly, my hands resting
on my knees, and stare at it and stare at it.
I thought this dog more beautiful and more
real than any actual dog I had ever seen or
any actual dog I would ever see. I must
have outgrown my interest in the dog, for
when it disappeared I never asked what
became of it. We passed the library, and if
there was anything on this walk that I
might have wept over leaving, this most
surely would have been the thing. My
mother had been a member of the library
long before I was born. And since she took
me everywhere with her when I was quite
little, when she went to the library she
took me along there, too. I would sit in her
lap very quietly as she read books that she
did not want to take home with her. I
could not read the words yet, but just the
way they looked on the page was interesting to me. Once, a book she was reading
had a large picture of a man in it, and
when I asked her who he was she told me
that he was Louis Pasteur[6] and that the
book was about his life. It stuck in my
mind, because she said it was because of
him that she boiled my milk to purify it
before I was allowed to drink it, that it was
his idea, and that that was why the process
was called pasteurization. One of the things

---

6. *Louis Pasteur* was a nineteenth-century French chemist
   who invented the process known as pasteurization.

1282 UNIT 6 THE MODERN AMERICAS

I had put away in my mother's old trunk in
which she kept all my childhood things was
my library card. At that moment, I owed
sevenpence in overdue fees.

As I passed by all these places, it was as
if I were in a dream, for I didn't notice the
people coming and going in and out of
them, I didn't feel my feet touch ground,
I didn't even feel my own body—I just saw
these places as if they were hanging in the
air, not having top or bottom, and as if
I had gone in and out of them all in the
same moment. The sun was bright; the sky
was blue and just above my head. We then
arrived at the jetty.

My heart now beat fast, and no matter
how hard I tried, I couldn't keep my mouth
from falling open and my nostrils from
spreading to the ends of my face. My old
fear of slipping between the boards of the
jetty and falling into the dark-green water
where the dark-green eels lived came over
me. When my father's stomach started to
go bad, the doctor had recommended a
walk every evening right after he ate his
dinner. Sometimes he would take me with
him. When he took
me with him, we usu-
ally went to the jetty,
and there he would sit
and talk to the night
watchman about
cricket or some other
thing that didn't
interest me, because it
was not personal; they
didn't talk about their
wives, or their chil-
dren, or their parents, or about any of their
likes and dislikes. They talked about things

Visual Vocabulary
Cricket is a bat-
and-ball game ☆
popular throughout
the West Indies.

· 2

Make and Verify Predictions *What prediction can you
make about Annie's state of mind based on her description
of her dreamlike state?* · 1

Writing Practice

Description Writers frequently use
descriptions to help readers picture what
might otherwise be unfamiliar to them
or to help readers understand how a
character thinks. Kincaid often compares
her state of mind with something more
familiar to readers. Direct students' attention to this sentence in the story: "I was
always sorry when we got to the jetty and
saw that the night watchman on duty was
the one he enjoyed speaking to; it was

like being locked up in a book filled with
numbers and diagrams and what-ifs."
Ask: Why doesn't Annie like this night
watchman? *(When he and her father
speak, they only talk about things that
confuse or do not interest Annie.)*
Have students write their own descriptions
of how they might feel in each of the
following situations: The first time I asked
someone to dance it felt as if _____.
When I get a bad (or good) grade in an

assignment, I feel as though _____.
To me, going camping is like _____.
Encourage students to share their
descriptions with the class.

in such a strange way, and I didn't see what they found funny, but sometimes they made each other laugh so much that their **guffaws** would bound out to sea and send back an echo. I was always sorry when we got to the jetty and saw that the night watchman on duty was the one he enjoyed speaking to; it was like being locked up in a book filled with numbers and diagrams and what-ifs. For the thing about not being able to understand and enjoy what they were saying was I had nothing to take my mind off my fear of slipping in between the boards of the jetty.

Now, too, I had nothing to take my mind off what was happening to me. My mother and my father—I was leaving them forever. My home on an island—I was leaving it forever. What to make of everything? I felt a familiar hollow space inside. I felt I was being held down against my will. I felt I was burning up from head to toe. I felt that someone was tearing me up into little pieces and soon I would be able to see all the little pieces as they floated out into nothing in the deep blue sea. I didn't know whether to laugh or cry. I could see that it would be better not to think too clearly about any one thing. The launch was being made ready to take me, along with some other passengers, out to the ship that was anchored in the sea. My father paid our fares, and we joined a line of people waiting to board. My mother checked my bag to make sure that I had my passport, the money she had given me, and a sheet of paper placed between some pages in my Bible on which were written the names of

the relatives—people I had not known existed—with whom I would live in England. Across from the jetty was a wharf, and some stevedores were loading and unloading barges. I don't know why seeing that struck me so, but suddenly a wave of strong feeling came over me, and my heart swelled with a great gladness as the words "I shall never see this again" spilled out inside me. But then, just as quickly, my heart **shriveled** up and the words "I shall never see this again" stabbed at me. I don't know what stopped me from falling in a heap at my parents' feet.

When we were all on board, the launch headed out to sea. Away from the jetty, the water became the customary blue, and the launch left a wide path in it that looked like a road. I passed by sounds and smells that were so familiar that I had long ago stopped paying any attention to them. But now here they were, and the ever-present "I shall never see this again" bobbed up and down inside me. There was the sound of the seagull diving down into the water and coming up with something silverish in its mouth. There was the smell of the sea and the sight of small pieces of rubbish floating around in it. There were boats filled with fishermen coming in early. There was the sound of their voices as they shouted greetings to each other. There was the hot sun, there was the blue sea, there was the blue sky. Not very far away, there was the white sand of the shore, with the run-down houses all crowded in next to each other, for in some places only poor people lived near the shore. I was seated in the launch between

---

2

3 **Make and Verify Predictions** *Do you think Annie will get on the boat, given her reservations about leaving? Explain.*

 Vocabulary

guffaw (gu fô´) *n.* a loud or boisterous burst of laughter

---

4 **The Legacy of Colonialism** *What internal conflict does Annie experience about leaving her homeland?*

 **Vocabulary**

shrivel (shriv´əl) *v.* to become wrinkled as a result of lack of moisture

Reading Strategy | **3**

Make and Verify Predictions **Answer:** *Most students will probably say she will get on the boat despite her reservations. Some may think she will somehow avoid leaving.*

ENGLISH LEARNERS Explain to English learners that *reservations* in this context means "doubt."

Big Idea | **4**

The Legacy of Colonialism
Answer: *She experiences a longing to leave and a longing to stay at the same time.*

APPROACHING Review with approaching-level students the differences between internal and external conflict. **Ask:** What type of conflict is Annie experiencing here? *(internal conflict)*

Learning Objectives
Making and verifying predictions. (SE)
Analyzing foreshadowing and flashback. (TE)
Writing a description. (TE)

Approaching Level
DIFFERENTIATED INSTRUCTION

Sensory Details Kincaid uses several layers of sensory details in her description of the launch ride to the ship. Have students create a five-column chart with the headings "Sight," "Smell," "Hearing," "Taste," and "Touch." Students can use the chart to record the sensory details that Annie experiences on the ride. Encourage students to imagine other details, such as what the launch boat sounded like.

Advanced Learners/Pre-AP
DIFFERENTIATED INSTRUCTION

Write a Description Challenge students to write a one- to two-page description of what it would be like for them to take a ride to the airport, knowing that they wouldn't be home again for a long time. Tell students to consider the day-to-day sights, sounds, and smells that they barely notice but that would become the focus of the trip. Encourage students to try to emulate Kincaid's style of building detail in

free-flowing descriptions. Ask for volunteers to share their descriptions with the class.

Teach

Reading Strategy   1

Make and Verify Predictions Answer:
Students may feel that Annie will be sad but that she will get through her departure successfully because she realizes she has to.

Reading Strategy   2

Make and Verify Predictions Ask: How do you predict Annie's parents will act at her final departure? *(Students may say that the final good-byes will be quiet because her parents haven't said anything so far and because the captain says that they must be quick.)*

Cultural History ☆

Migration to England The twentieth century saw the arrival of many immigrants in the British Isles. People from the West Indies began to arrive in large numbers in the 1950s, and by the late twentieth century, the West Indian population in Britain was its second largest ethnic minority population.

To check students' understanding of the selection, see Unit 6 Teaching Resources Book, p. 244.

my parents, and when I realized that I was gripping their hands tightly I glanced quickly to see if they were looking at me with scorn, for I felt sure that they must have known of my never-see-this-again feelings. But instead my father kissed me on the forehead and my mother kissed me on the mouth, and they both gave over their hands to me, so that I could grip them as much as I wanted. I was on the verge of feeling that it had all been a mistake, but I remembered that I wasn't a child anymore, and that now when I made up my mind about something I had to see it through. At that moment, we came to the ship, and that was that.

2 The good-byes had to be quick, the captain said. My mother introduced herself to him and then introduced me. She told him to keep an eye on me, for I had never gone this far away from home on my own. She gave him a letter to pass on to the captain of the next ship that I would board in ☆ Barbados.[7] They walked me to my cabin, a small space that I would share with someone else—a woman I did not know. I had never before slept in a room with someone I did not know. My father kissed me good-bye and told me to be good and to write home often. After he said this, he looked at me, then looked at the floor and swung his left foot, then looked at me again. I could see that he wanted to say something else, something that he had never said to me before, but then he just turned and walked away. My mother said, "Well," and then she threw her arms around me. Big tears streamed down her face, and it must have been that—for I could not bear to see my mother cry—which started me crying, too. She then tightened her arms around me

and held me to her close, so that I felt that I couldn't breathe. With that, my tears dried up and I was suddenly on my guard. "What does she want now?" I said to myself. Still holding me close to her, she said, in a voice that raked across my skin, "It doesn't matter what you do or where you go, I'll always be your mother and this will always be your home."

I dragged myself away from her and backed off a little, and then I shook myself, as if to wake myself out of a **stupor.** We looked at each other for a long time with smiles on our faces, but I know the opposite of that was in my heart. As if responding to some invisible cue, we both said, at the very same moment, "Well." Then my mother turned around and walked out the cabin door. I stood there for I don't know how long, and then I remembered that it was customary to stand on deck and wave to your relatives who were returning to shore. From the deck, I could not see my father, but I could see my mother facing the ship, her eyes searching to pick me out. I removed from my bag a red cotton handkerchief that she had earlier given me for this purpose, and I waved it wildly in the air. Recognizing me immediately, she waved back just as wildly, and we continued to do this until she became just a dot in the matchbox-size launch swallowed up in the big blue sea.

I went back to my cabin and lay down on my berth. Everything trembled as if it had a spring at its very center. I could hear the small waves lap-lapping around the ship. They made an unexpected sound, as if a vessel filled with liquid had been placed on its side and now was slowly emptying out. ✑

---

7. *Barbados* (bär bāʹdōz) is the easternmost island of the West Indies in the Caribbean Sea.

1 Make and Verify Predictions *How do you think Annie will handle her departure?*

1284 UNIT 6   THE MODERN AMERICAS

Vocabulary

stupor (stōōʹpər) *n.* a dulled mental state, often as a result of shock or stress; a daze

Reading Practice

Make Inferences Explain to students that an inference is a guess based both on details in a text and on one's own knowledge. Have students make inferences about Annie's feelings about her parents. **Ask:** What can you infer about Annie's feelings for her father? Explain. *(Students may say that while Annie likely loves her father, she feels distant from him. Students may base their inferences on the fact that he does not speak when she thinks he* has something important to say to her, and she does not push him to disclose his feelings.) **Ask:** What can you infer about Annie's feelings toward her mother? Explain. *(Students may say that Annie has a loving relationship with her mother but, at the same time, has a desire to leave home. Although Annie grasps her mother's hand while on the launch, she pushes her mother away when her mother says that "this will always be your home.")*

Respond and Think Critically

Respond and Interpret

1. What memories of yours were stirred as you read this story?

2. (a)How have Annie's feelings about Miss Dulcie changed since she was her apprentice? (b)What does this change in her feelings suggest about Annie?

3. (a)What happened when Annie returned from her first unaccompanied walk on the road? (b)From Annie's description of that walk, how would you describe the relationship between Annie and her mother when Annie was little?

4. (a)What does Annie recall about her walks to the jetty as a child? (b)What parallel does Annie draw between her trips to the jetty as a child and the present moment?

Analyze and Evaluate

5. Why do you think Annie notices things she had long ignored as she rides on the launch? Support your answer with details from the story.

6. (a)Why does Annie think her parents might be looking at her with scorn on the launch? (b)What conflicting emotions does Annie experience on the launch?

7. (a)Why does Annie become wary of her mother when they are saying good-bye? (b)What does this tell you about the nature of their relationship?

Connect

8. **Big Idea** The Legacy of Colonialism In an analysis of *Annie John*, scholar Laura Niesen de Abruna suggests that the daughter's relationship with the mother is similar to the daughter's relationship with her "motherland," or homeland. Do you agree? Explain.

9. **Connect to the Author** Kincaid left Antigua for the United States when she was seventeen. Do you think this experience influenced *Annie John*? Explain.

Literary Element Foreshadowing and Flashback

ACT Skills Practice

Kincaid includes the flashback that describes Annie's walks to the jetty with her father (page 1282) primarily to:

A. clarify the tensions between Annie and her father.

B. provide an enjoyable diversion from the main action.

C. draw a parallel between Annie's childhood fear of falling and her fear of leaving home.

D. illustrate Annie's desire for independence from her family.

Review: Conflict

As you learned on page 754, an **internal conflict** is a struggle within the mind of a character torn between opposing feelings, desires, or goals.

Partner Activity With a partner, create a chart like the one below to identify internal conflicts in "A Walk to the Jetty."

Text	Conflict
"I could see that he wanted to say something else, something that he had never said to me before, but then he just turned and walked away."	Internal conflict of Annie's father: he wants to tell his daughter something but cannot find the words to do so.

JAMAICA KINCAID **1285**

Literary Element

C is the correct answer. Both the flashback and the present situation cause Annie to fear the unknown.

Review: Conflict

Students should list internal conflicts and provide evidence from the story.

Progress Check

Can students analyze foreshadowing and flashblack?

If No → See Unit 6 Teaching Resources Book, p. 239.

Assess

1. Students' responses will vary.

2. (a) She did not resent Miss Dulcie's treatment of her when she was an apprentice, but now she does. (b) It implies she has a stronger sense of self-worth than she did when she was a child.

3. (a) Her mother praised her extravagantly. (b) They had a warm and loving relationship.

4. (a) She remembers her fear of slipping between the boards of the jetty and her boredom during her father's conversations with the watchman. (b) Just as she had no interesting conversation to distract her from her fear of falling, she now has nothing to distract her from her fear of leaving home.

5. They suddenly seem important to her because she knows she is experiencing them for the last time and from a different perspective. Details will vary.

6. (a) She feels they may interpret her happiness about leaving as a rejection of them. She thinks they might feel she has betrayed them by leaving the island. (b) She feels both joy and sadness.

7. (a) She may fear that her mother will try to dissuade her from leaving, or she may fear that she will be overcome by her mother's emotion. (b) They love and deeply care for each other.

8. Most students will probably agree that both Annie's mother and her homeland have nurtured and protected her and that Annie feels fear and sorrow at leaving both behind.

9. Students will probably guess that the novel is somewhat autobiographical.

After You Read

Assess

Reading Strategy

1. Annie's memories, which are often bittersweet, offer a means to predict her bittersweet response to leaving home.
2. Students should state their initial predictions and explain how they were or were not verified.

Vocabulary Practice

Possible answers:

Vocabulary word: *loom*

Similar word: *approach*

Explanation: *Loom* has the stronger connotation. *Approach* simply suggests that something is about to happen, while *loom* suggests that something frightening or terrible is about to happen.

Vocabulary word: *guffaw*

Similar word: *giggle*

Explanation: *Guffaw* has the stronger connotation. *Guffaw* implies loud, riotous laughter, while *giggle* implies quieter, more restrained laughter.

Vocabulary word: *shrivel*

Similar word: *dry*

Explanation: *Shrivel* has the stronger connotation. *Dry* is a general word for the losing of moisture, while *shrivel* implies withering.

Vocabulary word: *stupor*

Similar word: *dullness*

Explanation: *Stupor* has the stronger connotation. *Dullness* implies a subdued mental state, but *stupor* implies a dazed trance.

> For additional selection assessment, see Assessment Resources, pp. 249–250.

Reading Strategy Make and Verify Predictions

Have you ever read or watched a detective story, decided who committed the crime, and then changed your mind as more clues emerged? You were adjusting your prediction. Did you exclaim, "I knew it!" when the murderer was revealed? You were verifying your prediction. Review the chart you made on page 1278 and then answer the following questions.

1. How did Annie's memories of her past help you make predictions about the present events in the story?
2. (a)What did you predict about the narrator's emotional response at the end of the story? (b)Could you verify this prediction? Explain.

Vocabulary Practice

Practice with Denotation and Connotation
Denotation is the literal, or dictionary, meaning of a word. **Connotation** is the implied, or cultural, meaning of a word. For example, the words *amusing* and *hilarious* have a similar denotation, "funny," but they have different connotations:

Weaker	Stronger
amusing	hilarious

Work with a partner to complete a graphic organizer like the one below for each bold-faced vocabulary word. Include the vocabulary word in one box and a word that has a similar denotation in another. Then explain which word has the stronger connotation.

loom   guffaw   shrivel   stupor

EXAMPLE:

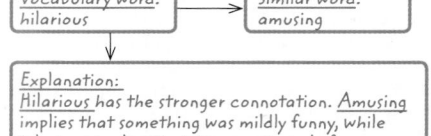

Write with Style

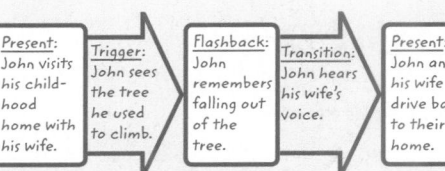 **Apply Flashback**

Assignment In this excerpt from Kincaid's novel, Annie recalls a number of details from her life as she walks toward a ship bound for her new life across the Atlantic Ocean. Write a short story in which you use flashbacks to illuminate the significance of the present, as Kincaid does.

Get Ideas You will most likely need to go through several drafts to integrate the flashbacks smoothly into your story. Once you have come up with some ideas, think about the complexity of the task and then make a schedule for yourself. Working backward from the assignment's due date, set deadlines for yourself that will allow you enough time to take a break between each stage of drafting and revising.

Give It Structure Remember that you will need to use logical transitions to show how the flashbacks relate to the main action. Come up with details in the present that would trigger memories for the characters. Then brainstorm transitional sentences that could guide readers back into the present at the end of the flashbacks. Organize your ideas in a diagram like the one below.

Look at Language As you revise, replace vague adjectives with more precise, vivid ones. Work to establish a distinctive voice and a personal style. If you use a thesaurus, be aware of the different shades of meaning contained within the different synonyms you find. Use a variety of sentence patterns to maintain the reader's interest.

> **LOG ON** ▶ **Literature** Online
>
> **Selection Resources** For Selection Quizzes, eFlash-cards, and Reading-Writing Connection activities, go to glencoe.com and enter QuickPass code GLW6053u6.

Write with Style

Students' stories should

- include flashbacks that are significant to the present action of the story
- use effective transitions between flashbacks and the present action
- use vivid, precise adjectives

 For grammar practice, see Unit 6 Teaching Resources Book, p. 243.

 To create custom assessments online, go to Progress Reporter Online Assessment.

 To create custom assessments using software, use ExamView Assessment Suite.

Before You Read

Fishing

United States

Meet **Joy Harjo**
(born 1951)

Born into the Muskogee (Creek) Indian tribe, Joy Harjo knew at an early age she was going to be an artist. Since her childhood in Tulsa, Oklahoma, she has immersed herself in painting, theater, music, film, and the written word.

Native American Roots The daughter of a Cherokee-French mother and a Creek father, Harjo is descended from a long line of tribal leaders and orators. She describes this heritage as the foundation of her writing: "I know when I write that there is an old Creek within me that often participates."

Harjo studied painting and theater at the Institute of American Indian Arts in Santa Fe, New Mexico, and the University of New Mexico in Albuquerque. In 1970, she adopted her paternal grandmother's surname and became known as Joy Harjo.

Making Magic from Words At the age of 22, Harjo heard Simon Ortiz's work at a poetry reading. His poems, steeped in the mood and the voice of the familiar Southwest, inspired her. She studied Native American, African American, and Latino authors and soon began to write her own poems. She switched her major to poetry, claiming that her own poetry was "taking on more magical qualities than my painting. I could say more when I wrote." Besides Ortiz, her influences came to include Leslie Marmon Silko, James Wright, Pablo Neruda, and Meridel Le Sueur. After finishing her bachelor's degree, she went on to receive her master of fine arts in creative writing from the University of Iowa in 1978. She has taught at a number of educational institutions, includ-

> "Writing helped me give voice to turn around a terrible silence that was killing me."
>
> —Joy Harjo

ing the Institute of American Indian Arts, the University of Colorado, the University of Arizona, the University of New Mexico, and the University of California, Los Angeles.

Much of Harjo's poetry—as well as the song lyrics she writes for her band—focuses on the history and contemporary problems of Native Americans. Although she does not identify herself as a political author, she has worked tirelessly to use her art as a means to spread awareness about Native American culture. Her poems often reflect her strong ties to the landscape and the people of the American Southwest. Harjo has escaped her "terrible silence" to become a compelling literary voice in the United States and beyond.

LOG ON ▶ **Literature** Online

Author Search For more about Joy Harjo, go to glencoe.com and enter QuickPass code GLW6053u6.

JOY HARJO **1287**

Before You Read

Focus

Bellringer Options

Selection Focus
   Transparency 84
Daily Language Practice
   Transparency 124

Or discuss with students the role water plays in mythology and folklore. **Ask:** What do bodies of water, especially rivers, symbolize in familiar myths and stories? (*Students may say that rivers often symbolize the divide between life and death, or the land of the living and the land of the dead, such as the River Styx. Students may also describe the ocean as symbolizing danger or the depths of the unknown.*)

Selection Skills

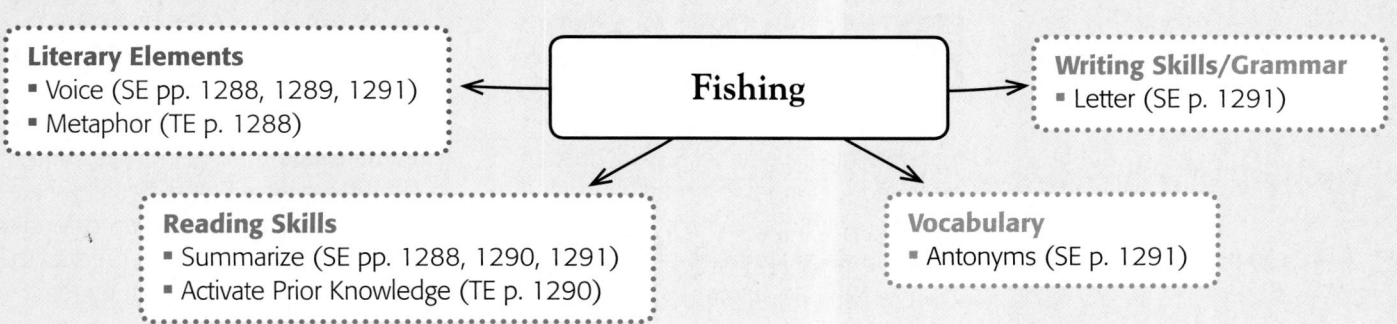

Literary Elements
- Voice (SE pp. 1288, 1289, 1291)
- Metaphor (TE p. 1288)

Fishing

Writing Skills/Grammar
- Letter (SE p. 1291)

Reading Skills
- Summarize (SE pp. 1288, 1290, 1291)
- Activate Prior Knowledge (TE p. 1290)

Vocabulary
- Antonyms (SE p. 1291)

Before You Read

Focus

Summary

In this prose poem, the speaker goes to a favorite fishing spot on an Oklahoma river to remember a late friend, her fellow poet Louis Oliver. Using descriptions of fishing and the wiliness of the fish, the speaker muses on life, death, and the sacred in this poem to a greatly missed friend.

 For summaries in languages other than English, see Unit 6 Teaching Resources Book, pp. 246–251.

Vocabulary

Parts of Speech Have students use a dictionary to look up the vocabulary words to discover how each one can be used as a different part of speech or as a part of a different word. *(Students should find the verb* relent, *the noun* muster, *the verb* profane, *and the noun* profanity.) Have students write out new definitions of these terms and consider their connection to the definition of each vocabulary word.

 For additional vocabulary practice, see Unit 6 Teaching Resources Book, p. 254.

1288

Literature and Reading Preview

Connect to the Poem

What do you do to remember absent friends or relatives? Freewrite for a few minutes about how these activities make you feel.

Build Background

Until the early nineteenth century, the Muskogee, or Creek, people lived in settled agricultural towns in the southern areas of present-day Georgia and Alabama. In the 1830s, most of the Muskogee were forced to move to Indian Territory in present-day Oklahoma. Harjo sees Oklahoma as "my mother, my motherland. I am connected psychically; there is a birth cord that connects me. But I don't live there and don't know that I ever will. It's too familiar and too painful."

Set Purposes for Reading

Big Idea Nature and the Imagination

As you read "Fishing," ask yourself, How does the speaker use nature images to make a statement about life and death?

Literary Element Voice

Voice is the distinctive use of language that conveys the author's or narrator's personality to the reader. It is determined by elements of style such as word choice and tone. As you read, ask yourself, What is distinctive about Harjo's voice?

Reading Strategy Summarize

Summarizing, or reducing large sections of text to their key ideas and main points, can help you get more from what you read. One way to accomplish this is to look for words and phrases that capture the essence of a section of text. As you read, ask yourself, Which words and phrases can I write down or underline to help me remember the main idea?

Tip: Adjust Your Reading Rate If you don't understand what you're reading, it's important to slow down. Use a chart like the one below to help you understand the prose poem.

Text	I wonder:	She might mean:
Paragraph 1	What might the poet mean when she mentions "the Illinois River or a similar river in the same place"?	All rivers everywhere

---

Learning Objectives

For pages 1287–1291

In studying this text, you will focus on the following objectives:

Literary Study: Analyzing voice.

Reading: Summarizing.

Writing: Writing a letter.

Vocabulary

relentless (ri lent′lis) *adj.* showing or promising no lessening of severity or intensity; p. 1289 *A relentless, cold wind howled at our backs.*

muster (mus′tər) *v.* to cause to gather; p. 1290 *The early American pioneers needed all the courage they could muster.*

profane (prō fān′) *adj.* not concerned with religious purposes; p. 1290 *The relationship between what is sacred and what is profane has fascinated poets and philosophers for hundreds of years.*

Tip: Antonyms Words that have opposite meanings are antonyms. For instance, *profane* and *sacred* are antonyms. Like synonyms, antonyms are always the same part of speech.

Literary Element Practice

SPIRAL REVIEW Metaphor Explain to students that a metaphor is a type of figurative language in which two unlike things are compared. A metaphor asserts that one thing *is* another. Explain that an extended metaphor is a metaphorical comparison throughout a paragraph, a stanza, or an entire piece of literature.

Discuss fishing with students. **Ask: What is the act of trying to catch fish similar to in the "real world"?** *(Students may say that fishing is like making new friends, trying to attract someone of the opposite sex, or trying to trick someone into doing something for you.)* As students share their responses, write their ideas on the board. Explain that "Fishing" could be read as an extended metaphor, and encourage students to consider this possibility as they read.

Fishing

Joy Harjo

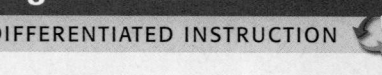

Kwahu (Eagle). Kachina Loren Phillips. Hopi paint on carved cottonwood root. Gallery 10, Carefree, AZ.

This is the longest day of the year, on the Illinois River or a similar river in the same place. Cicadas[1] are part of the song as they praise their invisible ancestors while fish blinking back the **relentless** sun in Oklahoma circle in the muggy river of life. They dare the fisher to come and get them.

---

1. *Cicadas* (si ka′ dəz) are large insects that make a loud, shrill, buzzing sound.

Voice *What does the author's word choice reveal about her view of the relationship between humans and other creatures?*　　**1**

Vocabulary

relentless (ri lent′lis) *adj.* showing or promising no lessening of severity or intensity

JOY HARJO　**1289**

English Learners

DIFFERENTIATED INSTRUCTION

Beginning Explain to English learners that the word *ancestor* comes from the Latin word *antecessor*, meaning "one who comes before," and refers to a person from whom someone is descended. **Ask:** Whose ancestors does the poet mention? *(the cicadas' and the fish's)* Introduce students to the terms *family tree* and *roots* as they relate to genealogy. Invite students to start their own family trees and describe their ancestors.

Advanced Learners/Pre-AP

DIFFERENTIATED INSTRUCTION

Rewrite Poetry Explain to students that this is a prose poem. Unlike free verse, which lacks strict meter and rhyme but is usually formatted to look like traditional poetry, prose poetry is composed of paragraphs in regular prose form. Challenge students to rewrite "Fishing" in free verse or even traditional poetic form. They may change some of of the words to create rhythm and rhyme, but they need to keep the concept of the poem the same.

Teach

| Literary Element | 1 |

Voice　Answer: *The word* dare *implies that the fish and the fisher are involved in a natural battle.*

ENGLISH LEARNERS Explain to English learners that *dare* can be either a verb or a noun; to dare is to challenge someone to perform a certain action, usually as a way to prove courage.

 For additional literary element practice, see Unit 6 Teaching Resources Book, p. 252.

Cultural History ☆

Midsummer Ritual "Fishing" takes place on the "longest day of the year;" this day is the summer solstice, also called midsummer. In Creek culture, midsummer is the day of the Green Corn ceremony. Important in many southeastern Native American cultures, this ceremony marks a time of renewal in the community, ritualized by the rekindling of the sacred fire.

 For an audio recording of this selection, use Listening Library Audio CD-ROM.

Readability Scores
Dale-Chall: 6.3
DRP: 55
Lexile: 960

Learning Objectives
Analyzing voice. (SE)
Analyzing metaphor. (TE)

Teach

Reading Strategy　　1

Summarize　Answer:
Students should mention *only place, promise,* and *inside a poem.*

APPROACHING　Remind approaching-level students that when selecting key words in a sentence, they may eliminate most articles (such as *a, an,* and *the*) and pronouns (such as *this* and *that*) to help them to more easily see important terms.

Progress Check

Can students summarize?

If No → See Unit 6 Teaching Resources Book, p. 253.

Literary Element　　2

Voice　Ask: What is the tone of the poet's voice in this passage? Explain. *(Students are likely to say that the tone is humorous because the poet describes the silliness and embarrassment of trying to die but being unable to.)*

Big Idea　　3

Nature and the Imagination　Answer: *"The struggle of the universe . . . in the sport"* and *"with the right pole, the right place"* both conjure the battles and choices in life.

 To check students' understanding of the selection, see Unit 6 Teaching Resources Book, p. 256.

Fish too anticipate the game of fishing. Their ancestors perfected the moves, sent down stories that appear as electrical impulses when sunlight hits water. The hook carries great symbology in the coming of age, and is crucial to the making of warriors. The greatest warriors are those who dangle a human for hours on a string, break sacred water for the profanity of air, then snap fiercely back into pearly molecules that describe fishness.

They smell me as I walk the banks with fishing pole, night crawlers[2] and a promise I made to that old friend Louis to fish with him this summer. This is the only place I can keep that promise, inside a poem as familiar to him as the banks of his favorite fishing place. I try not to let the fish see me see them as they look for his tracks on the soft earth made of fossils and ashes. I hear the burble of fish talk: *When is that old Creek coming back? He was the one we loved to tease most, we liked his songs and once in a while he gave us a good run.*

Last night I dreamed I tried to die. I was going to look for Louis. It was rather comical. I worked hard to **muster** my last breath, then lay down in the summer, along the banks of the last mythic river, my pole and tackle box next to me. What I thought was my last breath floated off as a cloud making an umbrella of grief over my relatives. How embarrassing when the next breath came, and then the next. I reeled in one after another, as if I'd caught a bucket

of suckers[3] instead of bass. I guess it wasn't my time, I explained, and went fishing anyway as a liar and I know most fishers to be liars most of the time. Even Louis when it came to fishing, or even dying.

The leap between the sacred and **profane** is as thin as fishing line, and is part of the mystery on this river of life, as is the way our people continue to make warriors in the strangest of times. I save this part of the poem for the fish camp next to the oldest spirits whose dogs bark to greet visitors. It's near Louis's favorite spot, where the wisest and fattest fish laze. I'll meet him there.

A few weeks before he died I wrote my friend the Muscogee poet, Louis Oliver, a promise that I would go fishing with him in Oklahoma that summer. Fishing to Louis was holy communion.

The struggle of the universe is exemplified in the sport. Yet it's possible to find the answer to every question with the right pole, the right place on the river.

As I mailed the letter I had a strange feeling the letter would never reach him. That cloud of illogic hovered over me for a few days.

When I was informed of his death I knew I had to keep that promise.

This is how I kept it.

---

2. *Night crawlers* are large earthworms found on the soil surface after dark. They are prized as fish bait.

1　**Summarize** *In this sentence, which key words would you underline to remember in a summary?*

Vocabulary

muster (mus′tər) *v.* to cause to gather

3. *Suckers* are a group of toothless freshwater fish, not valued by fishers.

Nature and the Imagination *What imagery does the author use to support ideas about the relationship between fishing and life?*　**3**

Vocabulary

profane (prō fān′) *adj.* not concerned with religious purposes

Reading Practice

SPIRAL REVIEW　**Activate Prior Knowledge**
Explain that drawing on their prior knowledge can help students understand "Fishing." With students, brainstorm a list of things they know about fishing—equipment, bait, places to fish, techniques, reasons for fishing—and list the things on the board. After students finish reading the selection, ask them the following question: **How did your prior knowledge deepen or enrich your understanding of the** selection? *(Students may say that their prior knowledge helped them relate to the poet's description of the trickiness of fish and the smell and feel of a day on the water. They may also say that an understanding of fishing helped them better understand how the poet uses it to ponder the secrets of life and death.)* If any students that had little or no prior knowledge, ask what they learned about fishing from the selection.

After You Read

Respond and Think Critically

Respond and Interpret

1. What insights did you gain from reading this poem? Write a few sentences in your journal to answer this question. Then share your response with a classmate.

2. (a)What has the speaker promised Louis? (b)Why does the speaker have to write a poem to keep this promise?

3. (a)Why did the speaker try to die in her dream? (b)What makes the dream comical?

Analyze and Evaluate

4. (a)Is the poem set in a real or an imaginary place? (b)What does the river symbolize in this poem?

5. (a)In your opinion, could this poem stand on its own, without the italicized sentences that explain the background? Explain. (b)How does the italicized ending affect the emotional quality of the poem?

Connect

6. **Big Idea** **Nature and the Imagination** According to Harjo, the fisher's hook plays a role in the coming of age of the fish. What do you think the hook might symbolize in terms of the life and the coming of age of a human?

7. **Connect to the Author** Harjo's poem is a personal message to her friend, yet she connects his death to the "river" of life. Why do you think she puts this single event into a larger context?

Literary Element | Voice

Harjo uses metaphor and personification to create a tribute to an old friend in her moving prose poem "Fishing."

1. What does the description of the dream reveal about the speaker's personality?

2. Why do you think the speaker believes that the fish enjoyed Louis's visits?

Reading Strategy | Summarize

Underlining key words and phrases or taking notes can test your recall before you write a summary.

Partner Activity With a partner, discuss the main idea of each section and decide which key words and phrases you would use in a summary. Consult the chart you made on page 1288. Summarize each section, then summarize the whole poem.

 Literature Online

Selection Resources For Selection Quizzes, eFlashcards, and Reading-Writing Connection activities, go to glencoe.com and enter QuickPass code GLW6053u6.

Vocabulary Practice

Practice with Antonyms With a partner, brainstorm three antonyms for each boldfaced vocabulary word below. Then discuss your choices with your classmates. Be prepared to explain your choices.

relentless   muster   profane

EXAMPLE: thwart
Antonyms: aid, help, assist
Sample explanation: A person who thwarts something prevents it from happening; a person who aids something helps it happen.

Writing

Write a Letter In "Fishing," the speaker writes that she sent a letter to her friend Louis Oliver just before he died, though she "had a strange feeling the letter would never reach him." What do you imagine she wrote in this letter? Write a letter to Louis Oliver, pretending you are the speaker. Do your best to imitate her voice throughout.

JOY HARJO **1291**

After You Read

Assess

1. Answers will vary.

2. (a) The speaker has promised to go fishing with her friend in Oklahoma in the summer. (b) Because he died, a poem is the only way she can communicate with him and keep her promise.

3. (a) To be close to Louis (b) The speaker hopes that each breath will be her last, but instead she takes one breath after another.

4. (a) The speaker's fishing trip is imagined but is full of vivid images. (b) The river symbolizes the eternal cycles of life.

5. (a) Answers will vary. (b) Many students will feel especially moved by the final explanation offered in the italicized end of the poem.

6. The hook might symbolize life's daily struggles.

7. Because it connects her to nature and the cycles of life and death, the image of the river is comforting. The river continues, just as life continues even when people die.

Vocabulary Practice

Sample answers:
relentless: intermittent, yielding, brief; Something relentless goes on without stopping; something intermittent stops and starts.
muster: disperse, scatter, spread out; Mustering is gathering up, which is the opposite of scattering.
profane: sacred, holy, religious; Profane means "not sacred" or "not holy."

> For additional selection assessment, see Assessment Resources, pp. 251–252.

Literary Element

1. It reveals she can mourn her friend's death and also gain perspective.

2. The fish's response to Louis mirrors the speaker's own feelings.

Reading Strategy

Students should use each section of the poem as a key idea in the overall summary they present.

Writing

Students' letters should

- be written in the speaker's voice
- reflect an understanding of the themes of the poem
- include a proper greeting, body, and closing

Writing Workshop

Literary Analysis

Focus

Bellringer Options

Daily Language Practice Transparency 125

Or bring copies of book reviews to class to share with students. Discuss how the reviewers support their opinions about whether they liked the piece of work. **Ask:** How do the reviewers describe literary elements in the review? *(Students' responses will vary.)* Point out to students the differences between a reviewer's opinion and an analysis of the reviewed work.

Summary

In this workshop, students will write a literary analysis in which they will analyze a short story from this unit. They will follow the stages of the writing process, including prewriting, drafting, revising, editing, and presenting. Two mini-lessons on sentence openers and avoiding run-on sentences are also provided.

Learning Objectives

For pages 1292–1299

In this workshop, you will focus on the following objectives:

Writing: Writing a literary analysis using the writing process. Understanding how to use sentence openers.

Grammar: Understanding how to avoid run-on sentences.

Writing Process

At any stage of a writing process, you may think of new ideas. Feel free to return to earlier stages as you write.

Prewrite

Draft

Revise

Focus Lesson:
Sentence Openers

Edit and Proofread

Focus Lesson:
Run-on Sentences

Present

 **Literature** Online

Writing and Research For prewriting, drafting, and revising tools, go to glencoe.com and enter QuickPass code GLW6053u6.

Writing Workshop

Literary Analysis

Literature Connection As evidenced in the following sentence, Julio Cortázar uses vivid sensory details to create suspense and terror in "The Night Face Up."

"But he smelled death, and when he opened his eyes he saw the blood-soaked figure of the executioner-priest coming toward him with the stone knife in his hand."

A **literary analysis** is a type of essay in which you examine specific literary or stylistic elements, such as imagery, in a story or a poem in order to better understand the work as a whole. Literary analysis fits under the larger category of **literary criticism,** which involves the study, the interpretation, and the evaluation of literature. To write an effective literary analysis, you will need to become familiar with the goals and the strategies listed below.

Rubric

Goals	Strategies
To present a concise explanation of the meaning of a work	☑ In your introduction, present a thesis that states your interpretation of the work's meaning. ☑ In your conclusion, restate your thesis and summarize your main points.
To analyze specific literary elements of the work	☑ Show how elements such as plot, tone, style, and figurative language contribute to the work's meaning.
To support your analysis with evidence	☑ Present direct quotations and concrete examples from the work. ☑ Draw your own conclusions about the meaning of these examples. ☑ Explain how your evidence relates to your thesis.
To present your ideas in a logical order	☑ Include a clear introduction and conclusion. ☑ Use each body paragraph to develop one main idea. ☑ Use transitions between ideas and sections of your essay.

Workshop Resources

Print Materials

- Unit 6 Teaching Resources Book, pp. 259–261
- Writing Kit
- Success in Writing: Research and Reports

Transparencies

- Writing Workshop Transparencies

Technology

- Literature Online: Writing Resources and Grammar Resources, glencoe.com
- Online Essay Grader, glencoe.com
- Student Presentation Builder on StudentWorks Plus CD-ROM
- Media Workshop DVD
- Online Essay Grader, glencoe.com

Assignment: Analyze a Short Story

Write an analysis of a short story, using evidence to support your thesis. As you move through the stages of writing, keep your audience and purpose in mind.

Audience: peers, classmates, and teachers who are familiar with the story

Purpose: to present an interpretation of the story's meaning and an analysis of the effects that create that meaning

Analyze a Professional Model

In the following essay on Gabriel García Márquez's story "The Handsomest Drowned Man in the World," scholar Rena Korb argues that the reason the drowned man in the story has such a profound effect on the villagers is that they are willing to accept fantastic events in their daily lives. As you read, pay close attention to the comments in the margin. They point out features you might want to include in your own literary analysis.

An Analysis of "The Handsomest Drowned Man in the World" by Rena Korb

In addition to *One Hundred Years of Solitude*, García Márquez's short story "The Handsomest Drowned Man in the World" highlights his talents at using magic realism to draw the reader into a world unlike one in which most people dwell . . . In the story, García Márquez presents a tiny coastal town filled with people who seem unremarkable in any way except for their ability to accept the fantastic and thus enrich their own lives. . . .

Because the villagers naturally accept the fantastic, an enormous drowned man who washes upon their shore does not frighten them nor do they reject him. Instead of being freakish for his size, he is "the tallest, strongest, most virile and best built man they had ever seen." The drowned man, whom they come to call Esteban, has more ideal qualities than just the physical. He is compassionate,

Exposition

Real-World Connection

To convince others that your opinion about a book or a film is valid, you must first demonstrate that you understand the work. Professional reviewers and critics are experienced at describing how authors and filmmakers use stylistic devices to achieve their effects.

Introduction

In your introduction, mention the title of the work and the author, and capture your reader's attention.

Thesis

Summarize your interpretation in one sentence.

Main Points

Begin each body paragraph with a main point that relates to your thesis.

⚡ Writing Workshop

Literary Analysis

Teach

Big Idea | 1

Magic Realism Remind students that in this unit they have read selections inspired by magic realism, a genre of Latin American literature that combines fantastic and realistic elements. Students' literary analyses might explore how authors' use of magic realism reflects, as well as comments on, their culture.

⚡ Writing Skills

Thesis Remind students that a thesis should usually be narrower, or more focused, than they might at first think. Point out the thesis in the professional model and explain that "their ability to accept the fantastic and thus enrich their own lives" is the main point of the thesis; in a short essay, the writer cannot explain every single element of the story.

Learning Objectives
Writing a literary analysis of a short story. (SE)
Narrowing the focus of a thesis. (TE)

Approaching Level
DIFFERENTIATED INSTRUCTION 🐟

Organization Approaching-level students may benefit from using visual aids when organizing their research, analysis, and writing. Students can keep track of the various elements of an analysis by writing ideas, notes, and quotations on sticky notes or note cards. The cards can then be physically laid out and moved around, allowing students to see the layout of the analysis and to change its order more easily.

English Learners
DIFFERENTIATED INSTRUCTION 🐟

Intermediate Some English learners may have difficulty with the concept of analysis. Explain that although their essays will contain small sections of text summary, a literary analysis is part breaking down and part reader response. Encourage students to understand the assignment as a way to describe how an author's use of literary elements, such as setting and mood, affect a reader's understanding.

Writing Workshop

Teach

Writing Skills

Literary Elements Ask students to define *myth*. (*A myth is a traditional story that deals with gods, heroes, and supernatural forces; some cultures use myths to explain customs or forces of nature.*) Remind students that many of the stories they've read have had supernatural elements, which could be connected to the mythology of Central and South America, Canada, or the Caribbean. By making this type of connection, students can strengthen their literary analysis.

Cultural History ☆

Estevanico In addition to being the first African many Indians had seen, Estevanico traveled with Franciscan friar Marcos de Niza in the early 1500s to what is now New Mexico. The pair searched for the "Seven Golden Cities of Cibola," rumored to be full of gold, silver, and other wealth.

Evidence

Support your main points with direct quotations from the text.

Analysis

Explain how your textual evidence supports your thesis.

Literary Elements

Focus on specific literary elements and explain how these elements contribute to the story's meaning.

Context

Explain allusions or context to help the reader better understand the text.

Conclusion

Restate your thesis and include a few final, thought-provoking comments.

---

recognizing the anxiety that his size causes and possessing the artful knowledge that "the lady of the house looked for her most resistant chair and begged him, frightened to death, sit here" . . .

Because the villagers do not spend their time wondering how Esteban came to exist, they can concentrate on what is important: the man. Looking in his face they see that "he did not have the lonely look of other drowned men who came out of the sea or that haggard, needy look of men who drowned in rivers." When they realize that he will have to be dragged to his funeral (no one can carry him), they understand the shame and awkwardness his size caused him in life. Not only do they understand how Esteban feels, but they begin to understand a bit more about their own lives. As the women sit up all night, sewing an outfit for Esteban, "it seemed to them that the wind had never been so steady nor the sea so restless . . . and they supposed that the change had something to do with the dead man." Already their lives, fed by the "calm and bountiful" sea, are changing. . . .

The use of another element of magic realism helps justify the monumental effect Esteban had: the mythic. In the personage of Esteban are shades of heroes from different cultures and time periods. His very name, Spanish for Stephen, invokes St. Stephen, the first Christian martyr. Esteban also may recall Estevanico (a diminutive form of the name), an African slave who explored Florida and the Southwest United States in the 1500s. He was the first African many Indians had ever seen, and they thought he might be a god and gave him many gifts. As with Esteban, his appearance led him to be revered as something more than an ordinary man; just as the villagers would strive "to make Esteban's memory eternal," legends were passed down for generations, right until the present day, about Estevanico. . . .

The story may best be seen as presenting the multiple realities that are inherent to magic realism. Just as the villagers have to be open to possibilities in order to reap the benefits of Esteban's visit, so must readers suspend their disbelief.

Reading-Writing Connection Think about the writing techniques you just encountered and try them in your literary analysis.

Writing Practice

Write a Paragraph Explain that the number of sentences in a paragraph is not as important as the paragraph's structure and effect. Express to students the importance of a topic sentence in each paragraph. Writers want to lead readers through their essays, and topic sentences are a good way to inform readers what paragraphs will be about, as well as being a good way for writers to keep track of what they're saying. Have students write a paragraph that describes their trip to school that morning. For the sake of the assignment, have students write five to six sentences. Students should write a topic sentence that lets readers understand what information the paragraph will contain. The paragraph should also contain a concluding sentence that sums up the information. Encourage students to use transitional words and phrases in their paragraph to lead the reader through the events of the morning.

Prewrite

Explore a Story What short story from Unit 6 was particularly interesting to you? Carefully reread the story, writing down passages that embody the author's themes and writing style.

Choose a Focus After you have reread the story, look over your notes. Consider which literary elements and stylistic devices contribute to the story's meaning. Then choose a particular aspect as your focus. For example, you could focus on how an author uses figurative language to develop a story's theme.

Analyze the Elements Make a chart like the one below to examine how the author uses specific literary and stylistic elements.

Julio Cortázar's "The Night Face Up"

Element	Passages	Effect
Sensory Details	"the damp smell, the smell of oozing rock"	Lends reality and immediacy
Transitions	"'You're going to fall off the bed,' said the patient next to him."	Creates a jarring feeling

Develop a Working Thesis Review your chart and think about what your details say about the story as a whole. Then write a one-sentence working thesis that explains how the author uses literary devices to develop the story's meaning.

Create a Structure Think about the main points you want to make in your essay and the order in which you will make them. Then create an outline for each of your body paragraphs, including quotations and ideas from your analysis chart as support. Use the format below to organize each of your body paragraphs.

Main Point: Cortázar presents the ancient setting of the dream as a self-contained world with its own rituals and customs.	→	Evidence: The protagonist takes note of the "quaking bogs from which no one ever returned"; later, he refers to "the supplication of the corn which brings about the beneficent moons."	→	Analysis: These are details specific to the Moteca world, which the contemporary protagonist could not know; however, they are presented in such a matter-of-fact manner that readers accept them.

Exposition

Persuasion Versus Analysis

Remember that the goal of a literary analysis is different from that of a persuasive essay. Although you want your audience to agree with your interpretation of the text, your goal in a literary analysis is to explain *how* the author achieves certain effects rather than to offer your opinion about the merit of the work.

Avoid Plagiarism

Give credit to all of your sources, even if your only source is your short story. If you paraphrase sections of the story or include a direct quote, refer to the relevant page number. If you quote directly from the story, make sure you write the quote accurately.

WRITING WORKSHOP **1295**

Teach

Writing Process

Prewrite After students have chosen a short story and reread it a few times, have them freewrite to determine which element of the story they feel most comfortable analyzing. They can choose a couple of topics, such as mood and figurative language, and freewrite for as long as possible on each, making sure to write down ideas they have about those elements. Express to students the fact that prewriting means that ideas don't have to be completely thought out—they don't even have to be complete sentences.

Writing Skills

Avoiding Plagiarism Explain that, in an essay of this length, students will likely embed shortened quotations from the story into their sentences. Tell them to be sure to write around these truncated quotations so that they fit in as parts of the sentences. Students should include a page number in parenthesis at the end of each sentence containing a quotation. If students use sources other than the story, direct them to a resource that will help them compose in-text citations and a Works Cited list.

Learning Objectives
Analyzing a literary model. (SE)
Understanding features of literary analysis. (SE)
Prewriting a literary analysis. (SE)
Writing a well-organized paragraph. (TE)
Avoiding plagiarism. (TE)

Advanced Learners/Pre-AP

DIFFERENTIATED INSTRUCTION

Context Encourage students to do a deep reading of their chosen story and write down anything that sparks their interest, such as place names, character names, historic events, or references to other works. Then tell students to take a little time to research the author's life and background to see if anything in the story can be explained or better understood by learning more about the author. Encourage students to consider context when writing their analyses. However, express to students the idea that a connection between historic context or the author's life and a short story does not necessarily mean that a story is autobiographical. Encourage students to understand the difference between an author's inspiration and his or her intent.

Teach

⚡ Writing Skills

Introduction Answer: *It introduces a discussion of the realistic nature of the story's contemporary and ancient settings.*

Thesis Answer: *It lists three literary elements—the fluid style, sensory details, and the plot structure—and then explains that these draw in and orient the reader.*

Literary History ☆

Magic Realism The term *magic realism* was coined in the 1940s by the writer Alejo Carpentier. Although other cultures have been known to combine fantastic elements with realistic ones, magic realism is considered by some as similar to postcolonial writing.

Writing Frames

As you read the workshop model, think about the writer's use of the following literary analysis frames.

- Having finished the story, some readers may wonder _____; however, _____.

- By presenting _____ Cortázar leads readers to _____

Try using these kinds of frames to present your analysis to readers.

Introduction

Why does the writer include this information at the beginning of the introduction?

Thesis

How does the writer's thesis connect the literary elements to the text's broader meaning?

Draft

Stay in the Present Draft your essay from start to finish, using the present tense (also known as the literary present) when referring to events in the text.

Analyze a Workshop Model

Here is a final draft of a literary analysis. Read the essay and answer the questions in the margin. Use the answers to these questions to guide you as you write.

Competing Realities: Julio Cortázar's "The Night Face Up"

The protagonist in Julio Cortázar's "The Night Face Up" moves fluidly between two realities. Lying in a hospital bed after a motorcycle accident, he has a recurring dream in which he is a Moteca Indian escaping from Aztecs who want to offer him as a sacrifice. This dream becomes increasingly vivid until the narrator reveals that it is real, and that the contemporary setting has been the dream. The author uses a fluid style, sensory details, and a jarring plot structure to draw readers into both the contemporary setting and the ancient one, refusing to present either as more "real" than the other. This creates a disorienting effect that challenges readers' assumptions about fiction and reality.

Cortázar narrates in such a matter-of-fact style that it is easy to accept both the dream and the contemporary setting on their own terms. One example comes at the beginning of the story, when Cortázar's unnamed protagonist is "late" for some event, but there is no sense of urgency. Instead, the protagonist enjoys a motorcycle ride through an environment that seems familiar to him. Cortázar uses long sentences to describe this scene: buildings "zip past (the pink, the white)," and the protagonist calmly "allow[s] himself to be carried away by the freshness, by the weightless contraction of the hardly begun day." Cortázar's calm tone and flowing style make the setting seem natural and believable.

Grammar Practice

Commas with Nonessential Sentence Elements Students often misuse *that* and *which* in their writing, leading to incorrect comma usage. Explain to students that *that* introduces a restrictive clause, giving information that is necessary to the sense. **I took the bike that was leaning against the tree.** In this case, the clause introduced by *that* identifies the exact bike that was taken.

The word *which* introduces a nonrestrictive clause, giving information that isn't essential to an understanding of the sentence. **The bike, which was blue, was leaning against a tree.** In this sentence, the color of the bike is not important to the point of the sentence. Explain that nonrestrictive clauses, like other nonessential sentence elements, are set off with commas.

Have students use the following sentences to create new sentences containing restrictive and nonrestrictive clauses that correctly use commas.
Restrictive: I need the math book. The math book was on the table. (*I need the math book that was on the table.*)
Nonrestrictive: Samantha's new puppy is asleep. The puppy is in a box. (*Samantha's new puppy, which is in a box, is asleep.*)

Similarly, Cortázar presents the ancient setting of the dream as a self-contained world with its own rituals and customs. The protagonist takes note of the "quaking bogs from which no one ever returned"; later, he refers to "the supplication of the corn which brings about the beneficent moons." These are details specific to the Moteca world, which the contemporary protagonist could not know; however, they are presented in such a matter-of-fact manner that readers accept them. Cortázar also employs vivid imagery to lend a sense of reality to details in both settings. For example, there is a "damp smell, the smell of oozing rock"; similarly, in the hospital, a "blond nurse rub[s] the front of [the protagonist's] thigh with alcohol." Such sensory details suggest a knowledge of both time periods, so it is difficult to dismiss either setting as fantasy.

Because both settings seem so thoroughly real, the transitions between them create jarring interruptions. For instance, Cortázar shifts from the first two dream sequences by inserting abrupt comments from the patient in the hospital bed next to the protagonist. This creates a jolting effect; readers must reorient themselves to the new setting after each shift. Readers can no better understand what is "real" than the protagonist can.

In the end, Cortázar chooses the opposite of the comfortable, expected conclusion, which would state that the ancient Moteca sequences were "only a dream." Instead, he forces readers to see something far more disturbing: that the "dream" in the story is every bit as real as the "reality," and that both are in fact "absurd as all dreams are." By presenting two equally convincing worlds, Cortázar leads readers to recognize their reliance on literary conventions and their willingness to accept fiction at face value. Like other magic realist authors, he draws attention to the fine line between reality and fantasy by presenting the simultaneous existence of two different realities in a natural way. His story shows how easily the illusion of reality can be created or pulled away.

Exposition

Literary Elements
How does the writer's discussion of sensory details help support the thesis?

Evidence
Why does the writer include both of these quotations in the same sentence?

Conclusion
What makes this conclusion effective?

Literary Analysis

Teach

🖋 Writing Skills
Literary Elements
Answer: *The writer explains that sensory details help make both settings seem more real.*

Evidence Answer: *They are both examples of sensory details.*

Conclusion Answer: *It restates the thesis and comments on the broader significance of the story as a work of magic realism.*

View the Art ★

This curved serpent with turquoise inlaid mosaic represents an important figure to the Aztecs. Although turquoise mosaics are most commonly found at Mixtec sites, the serpent form symbolizes the gods of the Aztec religion and was used to denote ceremonial Aztec locations. Ask: How does this ornament's design reflect the "compting realities" described in the essay? (Students may say that the two heads of the snake represent the two "realities" experienced by the same character in the story.)

Approaching Level
DIFFERENTIATED INSTRUCTION 🐾

Outlines Approaching-level students may benefit from making an outline of the model essay on these pages. Have students summarize the essay's thesis and then list the supporting evidence found in each paragraph. Have students complete their outlines by listing the plot elements the writer describes. Encourage students to do the same when organizing their own essays.

English Learners
DIFFERENTIATED INSTRUCTION 🐾

Transitional Terms English learners can benefit from creating lists of transitional words and phrases. Have students use resources in this text or others to compile lists of such expressions and of ways they're used. For example, *on the other hand* and *similarly* can be used in compare-and-contrast situations, *because* and *due to* in cause-and-effect situations, and *first, next,* and *finally* in chronological descriptions.

Learning Objectives
Analyzing features of a literary analysis. (SE)
Using commas with nonessential sentence elements. (TE)

1297

Teach

🔲 Writing Process

Revise Students often draw back from the idea of rewriting a paper, usually because they're unsure exactly how to improve on what they've already written. Have students take turns reading their drafts to partners. As one student reads, the other should use the revision checklist to take notes on aspects of the essay that need improvement. Encourage students to take their partner's criticism constructively and to think of the writing process as a collaborative effort.

🔲 Writing Skills

Word Choice Encourage students to use a thesaurus to find synonyms and antonyms of words they use often. However, tell students to check a word's definition in the dictionary, as there may be nuances of meaning that will render the new word inaccurate in the context of a student's essay. Also, stress to students not to use words because they sound important but to use only those that they understand.

Traits of Strong Writing

Follow these traits of strong writing to express your ideas effectively.

Ideas

Organization

Voice

Word Choice

Sentence Fluency

Conventions

Presentation

For more information on using the Traits of Strong Writing, see pages R28–R30.

Word Choice

This academic vocabulary word appears in the Workshop model.

environment (in vī′rən mənt) *n.* the circumstances, the objects, or the conditions by which one is surrounded; *Instead, the protagonist enjoys a motorcycle ride through an environment that seems familiar to him.*

Using academic vocabulary may help strengthen your writing. Try to use one or two academic vocabulary words in your essay. See the complete list on pages R83–R85.

Revise

When you have finished writing, use the checklist below to evaluate your literary analysis.

Checklist

- ☑ Do you provide a concise thesis statement that includes your interpretation of the theme or the effect to be analyzed?
- ☑ Do you show how specific literary elements in the story contribute to its overall meaning?
- ☑ Do you present quotations from the story along with analysis that supports your main points?
- ☑ Do you present your points in a logical, effective order?

▶ Focus Lesson

Sentence Openers

To improve the flow of your paragraphs, open your sentences with different words. Avoid beginning every sentence with a pronoun, a noun, or the word *the*. Instead, try starting some sentences with a transitional or descriptive word (such as *therefore* or *finally*), a phrase (such as *after the accident* or *during the dream*), or a clause (such as *before the man arrives* or *because he is frightened*).

Draft:

He is lying in a hospital bed after a motorcycle accident when he has a recurring dream in which he is a Moteca Indian escaping from Aztecs who want to offer him as a sacrifice.

Revision:

Lying in a hospital bed after a motorcycle accident,[1] he has a recurring dream in which he is a Moteca Indian escaping from Aztecs who want to offer him as a sacrifice.

1: Opens with a clause

Grammar Practice

Avoid Dangling Modifiers A common mistake in students' academic writing is misplaced modifiers. As well as encouraging them to use clauses and phrases to vary sentence structure, supply them with activities that support their understanding of modifiers and where they should go. Explain that a dangling modifier is a phrase that logically modifies a word that doesn't appear in the sentence, causing confusion for readers.

Write on the board: Lounging on the beach, the dog ran up and licked my face. **Ask:** Who is lounging, the speaker or the dog? *(Students are likely to say that the speaker is lounging.)* **Say:** Although it's understood that the speaker is lounging, the speaker is not referred to directly in the sentence. Hence, there's no word for "lounging on the beach" to modify.

Ask: How could you rewrite this sentence to avoid the dangling modifier? *(Possible rewrites: While I was lounging on the beach, a dog came up and licked my face. Lounging on the beach, I was licked on the face by a dog.)* Have students reread their drafts to find any dangling modifiers that they may need to correct.

Edit and Proofread

Get It Right When you have completed the final draft of your literary analysis, proofread it for errors in grammar, usage, mechanics, and spelling. Refer to the Language Handbook, pages R40–R59, as a guide.

> **Focus Lesson**

Run-on Sentences

A run-on sentence joins two independent clauses (groups of words that could stand alone as sentences) using a comma or no punctuation. Below is an example of a run-on sentence from an early draft of the Workshop model, along with two possible corrections.

Original: The following is a run-on sentence. Two independent clauses (highlighted) are separated by a comma.

This creates a jolting effect, readers must reorient themselves to the new setting after each shift.

Improved: Use a semicolon to separate the two independent clauses.

This creates a jolting effect; readers must reorient themselves to the new setting after each shift.

Improved: Use a comma and a coordinating conjunction to join the independent clauses.

This creates a jolting effect, and readers must reorient themselves to the new setting after each shift.

Present/Publish

Follow Conventions Once you have finished reviewing your work, read through it again to make sure you have included quotation marks around any text quoted directly from the story. Then check to see that you have written the titles of works in the proper format. Short story titles should be in quotation marks, while book titles should be italicized or underlined. Check that your essay meets any length requirements and is neatly presented in handwriting or typed form.

Exposition

Peer Review Tips

As you revise, ask a partner to point out places where you could add transitional words and phrases—such as *first, second, finally, more important*, and *moreover*—to show the logical progression of ideas within and between paragraphs. Transitional words and phrases strengthen your points by showing a clear line of thinking.

Word-Processing Tip

Type your analysis on a computer and adjust your spacing, margins, and font size so that it is easy to read.

Writer's Portfolio

Place a clean copy of your literary analysis in your portfolio to review later.

LOG ON ▶ **Literature** Online

Writing and Research For editing and publishing tools, go to glencoe.com and enter QuickPass code GLW6053u6.

Teach

⚡ Writing Process

Proofreading Explain to students that proofreading is the final step before handing in a paper. One way for students to catch mistakes is to read their essay one line at a time, using two pieces of paper to block out the text before and after the line being read. This way, students have to focus only on the words directly in front of them. Also encourage students not to depend solely on their word processor's spell checker, as it will not find mistakes where the wrong word is spelled correctly (*too, two, to*).

Learning Objectives
Examining the writing stages of revising, editing, proofreading, and presenting. (SE)
Understanding how to use sentence openers. (SE)
Understanding how to avoid run-on sentences. (SE)
Avoiding dangling modifiers. (TE)

Approaching Level
DIFFERENTIATED INSTRUCTION

Confusing Words Have students reread their essays to look for words that are often misused, such as *affect/effect* and *lay/lie*. Instruct students to use dictionaries or other resources to find the definitions and correct uses of these words and to review their use of the words in their essays. Encourage students to seek extra assistance if they have difficulty understanding the correct way to use these words.

Advanced Learners/Pre-AP
DIFFERENTIATED INSTRUCTION

Literary Criticism Students may be curious to learn more about literary criticism and its relationship to analysis. Encourage students to find introductions to literary criticism, such as texts employed in introductory college courses. Students may find some literary theories, such as "new historicism," easier to comprehend than others, such as deconstructionism; but encourage them to familiarize themselves

with the concepts used in theorizing about literature.

This will help students prepare for the higher analytical thinking they will be required to do in college.

Focus

Summary

In this workshop, students will learn techniques for writing, rehearsing, and presenting a critical review of a literary text.

Teach

Speaking Skills

Supporting an Opinion Show students a video recording or play an audio recording of a review of a popular film or book. After you've played the review, discuss with students how the speaker supported his or her opinion of the author's or filmmaker's work. **Ask:** What reasons did the reviewer give to support his or her opinion? *(Answers will vary.)* How did the support for the reviewer's opinion explain more about the reviewed work than it did about the reviewer? *(Students should describe details about the review that are based on the work's merits rather than the reviewer's personal likes and dislikes.)*

Encourage students to be sure to analyze the elements of the text they're reviewing rather than their personal attitudes toward the work.

 For help with creating presentations, see Student Presentation Builder on StudentWorks Plus.

Learning Objectives

For pages 1300–1301

In this workshop, you will focus on the following objective:

Listening and Speaking: Delivering a critical review.

Writing Frames

As you prepare your review, think about using some of the following frames to get started.

- My own view is that _____, because _____.

- Of course, some might disagree with my claim and say that _____.

Speaking, Listening, and Viewing Workshop

Critical Review

Literature Connection Literary analyses are often published in scholarly journals geared toward specialized audiences. A more widely read form of literary criticism is the **critical review**. Critical reviews feature thoughtful analysis, but they also take a firm stand on the merits of a work—often praising or panning it.

> **Assignment** Plan and orally deliver a critical review of a literary work from the unit.

Develop Your Opinion

In a critical review, you present your opinion of a work and back it up with evidence. Follow these steps to plan the content of your presentation.

- Use a chart like the one in the Unit 6 Writing Workshop (see page 1295) to examine significant passages from the text. If you review the same story you analyzed for the Writing Workshop, you will have already examined the literary elements, and you probably have an opinion of the work.

- Think about how the passages you analyze contribute to the work as a whole. Does the author achieve the desired literary effects? How convincingly does the author develop the theme?

- Write a one- or two-sentence summary of your opinion. This will serve as your thesis. It should include descriptive words about the work, along with a statement of the effectiveness of the author's use of literary and stylistic devices. This thesis can be more subjective than one for an analytical essay.

- Write down your supporting arguments and quotations. Choose vivid, attention-grabbing quotations that will be memorable.

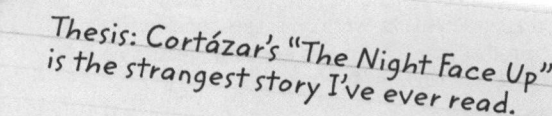

Thesis: Cortázar's "The Night Face Up" is the strangest story I've ever read.

Speaking and Listening Practice

PARTNERS **Tone** Discuss tone of voice with students. Explain that tone is especially important when students are presenting and supporting personal opinions. Students need to have firm opinions, but not ones so forceful that they are obnoxious; on the other hand, they shouldn't be apologetic about their opinions, either. Have students work in pairs, delivering their presentation openings to each other.

Students should rate their partner's delivery on a scale of one to ten; one is too meek and unsure, and ten is too pompous. Tell students to try to have an even but sure tone somewhere around five or six. Encourage students to pay attention to how many times a partner says *I* and *me*. Have students share their ratings with one another and use the constructive criticism when rehearsing their presentations.

Prepare Your Presentation

Once you have formed your opinion of the work, follow these steps to plan your oral presentation:

- Listen to the language used by book and film critics on television. They often deliver their opinions in a colloquial, casual style but use formal, analytical language to back up their ideas.

- As you listen to these samples, think of words and phrases that you could use to spice up your own main points. Replace dry language with colorful, descriptive phrases wherever possible.

- Create a visual aid that will help reinforce your evaluation of the work. One possibility is to write out quotations in large lettering on a piece of poster board so that you can refer to them as you speak.

Rehearse

Rehearse your presentation for a friend or a family member. Ask this person to comment on how well you analyze evidence to support your opinion of the work. Also ask for feedback on the language and the style of your presentation, and have your partner evaluate your use of the following techniques.

Techniques for Delivering an Oral Presentation

Verbal Techniques	Nonverbal Techniques
☑ **Pace** Pause after important ideas.	☑ **Gestures** Make natural hand gestures that emphasize your points.
☑ **Tone** Adjust your tone to emphasize important points.	☑ **Eye Contact** Look at your audience.
☑ **Pronunciation** Speak each word clearly.	☑ **Display** Point to your visual aids when appropriate.
☑ **Volume** Speak loudly enough so that everyone can hear you.	☑ **Posture** Stand tall and be proud of your work.

Use the First Person
Unlike a literary analysis, a critical review includes your personal response to a literary work. In a critical review, it is appropriate to use the word *I* and to discuss your opinion about the work.

Presentation Tips
Use the following checklist to evaluate your presentation.

- Did you vary your tone and use natural gestures?
- Did you make eye contact with the audience?
- Did you face the audience and not the visuals?

Teach

Viewing Skills

Using Visual Aids as Support

Explain that when using visual aids in a presentation, students want to be sure to use the aids effectively but not to depend too much on them or to let them sit without explanation. Remind students to write visual aids into their presentation notes. Students can draw a star or other symbol on note cards to remind themselves to turn to their illustrations or charts.

Listening Skills: Peer Assessment

Responding Ask students to evaluate their classmates' performance according to the following criteria:

- Did the speaker present a clear thesis and support his or her thesis with evidence and examples from the text?
- Did the speaker vary his or her pace, volume, and tone during the presentation?
- Did the speaker use nonverbal techniques to effectively communicate with the audience?

Approaching Level
DIFFERENTIATED INSTRUCTION

Vocalized Pauses Encourage students to avoid using "um" or colloquialisms such as "you know" or "like." Explain these will not only interrupt a smooth delivery, but will also distract their listeners from their review. Students are often unaware that they are using these vocalized pauses; if possible, tape-record their rehearsals of speeches for them to listen to privately. Give students time to practice their delivery before or after class.

English Learners
DIFFERENTIATED INSTRUCTION

Pronunciation Have English learners practice the pronunciation of more difficult words—especially proper names and multi-syllabic words. Encourage students to seek out correct pronunciations of unfamiliar or difficult words in a dictionary or from a trusted classmate. Give students time to practice their delivery before or after class so they may receive pronunciation corrections.

Learning Objectives
Developing an opinion. (SE)
Preparing a presentation. (SE)
Rehearsing a presentation. (SE)
Supporting an opinion. (TE)
Practicing tone. (TE)
Using visual aids. (TE)
Responding. (TE)

Focus

Summary

The purpose of this feature is to encourage students to read novels and collections of short stories and poetry about the history of the Americas and its contemporary society. Doing so enables students to build on the knowledge they have gained from this unit.

Teach

Literary History ☆

Gabriela Mistral "Gabriela Mistral" was the pen name of the Chilean poet Lucila Godoy Alcayaga (1889–1957). A teacher at 15 and a noted poet by 25, she also served as diplomat in Madrid and Nice. The titles of some of her poetry collections—*Desolation, Tenderness*, and *Destruction*—indicate their themes, and some of her work has been translated into English by such popular authors as Langston Hughes and Ursula K. Le Guin.

Reading Practice

Analyze Historical Context Remind students to consider, as they read novels, short stories, and poetry independently, the texts' historical contexts. Explain that a writer's environment, culture, and experience will influence his or her work. Further explain that students must use some knowledge of historical events depicted in a text when analyzing historical context.

Independent Reading

Literature of the Region

THE EUROPEAN COLONIZATION OF THE AMERICAS LED TO FIERCE CULTURAL CONFLICTS AND THE blending of traditions. This legacy is evident in a variety of works from the region, which often combine local mythology with European styles. In their works, modern authors of the Americas frequently explore the effects of contemporary political struggles, the power of memory and personal experience, and the importance of love and community.

True History of the Conquest of New Spain

Bernal Díaz del Castillo

Combining elements of autobiography, history, and fiction, *True History of the Conquest of New Spain* describes Díaz's firsthand experience as a soldier and conquistador during the Spanish settlement of the Americas. Frustrated by other Spanish accounts of discovery, which he felt were biased and incomplete, Díaz set out to tell the story of the foot soldiers who risked their lives in the conquest. Díaz's narrative is notable for its colloquial writing style; its intricate, realistic portrayals of his comrades; and its relative sympathy toward the indigenous peoples of the Americas.

A Gabriela Mistral Reader

Gabriela Mistral ☆

This collection by the first Latin American author to receive the Nobel Prize in literature contains poems and other works of love, pain, and hope. Much of Mistral's poetic inspiration stemmed from the tragic death of her fiancé at a young age, and her works are frequently infused with a sense of loss and spiritual struggle. For more poetry by Mistral, look for *Selected Poems of Gabriela Mistral*, translated by American author Doris Dana, who was awarded Chile's Order of Merit (the country's highest honor) for her work.

Encourage students to research the historical context of their text. Have students ask themselves these questions: What event is the author describing? What influence did this event have on the author's life? How has the author shown his or her opinion or perspective on this event in the text?

Explain that the last question may require students to make inferences or draw conclusions from textual clues.

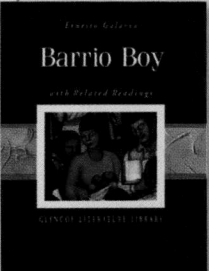

Barrio Boy
Ernesto Galarza

Caught between opposing forces of the Mexican Revolution, a family sets out from a small mountain village hoping to find safety and a new life in Sacramento, California.

... And the Earth Did Not Devour Him
Tomás Rivera

This compilation of short stories and vignettes follows one year's painful events for a boy in a community of migrant workers in the United States.

The Bridge of San Luis Rey
Thornton Wilder

The collapse of Peru's most famous bridge in 1714 is the catalyst for this Pulitzer Prize-winning novel, which explores the workings of fate and divine intervention.

CRITICS' CORNER

"As best exemplified by One Hundred Years of Solitude, *García Márquez's* ingenious mixture of realism and fantasy has resulted in the creation of a total fictional universe in which the commonplace takes on an aura of magic and the impossible is made believable. His penetrating insights into the ambiguities of human nature are enhanced by a rich vein of anecdotes and leitmotifs [recurring themes] he taps from his private mythology."

—George R. McMurray

One Hundred Years of Solitude
Gabriel García Márquez

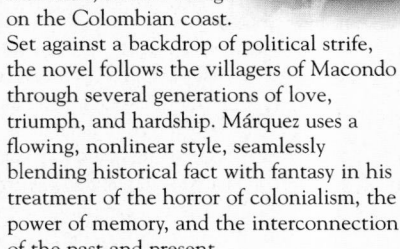

Considered to be García Márquez's masterpiece, this novel tells the story of the fictional town of Macondo, a small village on the Colombian coast. Set against a backdrop of political strife, the novel follows the villagers of Macondo through several generations of love, triumph, and hardship. Márquez uses a flowing, nonlinear style, seamlessly blending historical fact with fantasy in his treatment of the horror of colonialism, the power of memory, and the interconnection of the past and present.

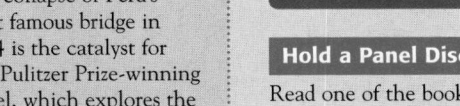

Hold a Panel Discussion

Read one of the books listed here and form a group with students who have read other books on the list. Hold a panel discussion in which you compare the books' treatments of a common subject, such as colonialism, tradition, or love.

Teach

Panel Discussion
Groups should focus on a common subject.

Literary History
Gabriel García Márquez
Marquez published the first volume of a planned three-part autobiography, *Living to Tell the Tale,* in 2004. García Márquez explains that his adoption of magic realism can be traced back to the stories his female relatives told. Readers familiar with his novels will discover secrets, such as the real-life influence for the fictional town of Macondo in *One Hundred Years of Solitude.*

Glencoe Literature Library
Glencoe Literature Library offers an extensive collection of hardcover books that help you encourage your students to read independently. Choose among more than 120 full-length literary works—novels, novellas, plays, and nonfiction. Each book includes related readings from a broad range of genres. Go to glencoe.com for more information.

> **For access to all study guides for the Glencoe Literature Library,** see the Literature Library Teacher Resources CD-ROM.

> **To create customized reading lists from a database of more than 30,000 titles,** use BookLink K-12 CD-ROM.

Approaching Level

DIFFERENTIATED INSTRUCTION

Chain of Events Less-proficient readers may have difficulty following the chain of events of novels or stories that contain magic realism. To help students better comprehend the sequence of the story, have them keep a log. Students should first describe the main event of the story, such as an important move, a migration, or a war. Then students can list the smaller events as they happen. Encourage students having acute difficulty to record the names of the main characters and list each character's actions chapter by chapter. Tell students to reread sections of the story that contain magic realism. Have students ask themselves how the fantastical events fit in with the events of the rest of the story.

Assessment

English-Language Arts

Focus

Bellringer Options

Daily Language Practice Transparency 126

Or ask: What steps can you take to prepare yourselves for test success? *(Students may say study, take notes, pay attention in class, and practice with partners or study groups.)* Discuss with students other things that they can do to prepare for a test, such as getting a good night's sleep, studying over a period of time instead of cramming the night before, and eating a balanced meal.

Teach

Assessment

Explain to students that this Assessment feature is intended to reinforce their general test-taking strategies, as well as to test the skills and vocabulary covered in the unit. They will first be asked to read a fiction selection and a nonfiction selection and answer comprehension, context-clue, tone, and characterization questions. Then, they will be asked to answer ten sentence-completion exercises and ten paragraph-improvement questions. Finally, they will be asked to write a short essay comparing and contrasting the styles of two short stories in this unit.

 To create custom assessments online, go to Progress Reporter Online Assessment.

 To create custom assessments using software, use ExamView Assessment Suite.

1304

Assessment

English–Language Arts

Reading: Fiction and Informational Text

Carefully read the following passage. Use context clues to help you define any words with which you are unfamiliar. Pay close attention to the author's **tone** and use of **characterization**. Then, on a separate sheet of paper, answer questions 1–5 on page 1306.

from *The House of the Spirits* by Isabel Allende
Translated by Magda Bogin

That was Marcos's longest trip. He returned with a shipment of enormous boxes that were piled in the far courtyard, between the chicken coop and the woodshed, until the winter was over. Marcos spent two weeks assembling the contents according to an instruction manual written in English, which he was
5 able to decipher thanks to his invincible imagination and a small dictionary. When the job was finished, it turned out to be a bird of prehistoric dimensions, with the face of a furious eagle, wings that moved, and a propeller on its back. It caused an uproar. The police, on horseback and carrying lances, had trouble keeping the crowds far enough away from the center of the park, where Marcos
10 waited dressed in mechanic's overalls, with huge racer's goggles and an explorer's helmet. He was also equipped with a compass, a telescope, and several strange maps that he had traced himself based on various theories of Leonardo da Vinci and on the polar knowledge of the Incas. Against all logic, on the second try the bird lifted off without mishap and with a certain elegance, accompa-
15 nied by the creaking of its skeleton and the roar of its motor. It rose flapping its wings and disappeared into the clouds, to a send-off of applause, whistlings, handkerchiefs, drumrolls, and the sprinkling of holy water. All that remained on earth were the comments of the amazed crowd below and a multitude of experts, who attempted to provide a reasonable explanation of the miracle. Clara
20 continued to stare at the sky long after her uncle had become invisible. She thought she saw him ten minutes later, but it was only a migrating sparrow. After three days the initial euphoria that had accompanied the first airplane flight in the country died down and no one gave the episode another thought, except for Clara, who continued to peer at the horizon.
25 After a week with no word from the flying uncle, people began to speculate that he had gone so high that he had disappeared into outer space, and the ignorant suggested he would reach the moon. With a mixture of sadness and relief, Severo decided that his brother-in-law and his machine must have fallen into some hidden crevice of the cordillera, where they would never be found.
30 Nívea wept disconsolately and lit candles to San Antonio, patron of lost objects.

Reading Practice

Summarize Remind students that a summary is a restatement of the main idea and important details of a selection. Explain to students that summarizing test selections will help them comprehend and retain information, which in turn will help them succeed on the test. Tell students to write their summaries on scrap paper or along the margins of the test, if allowed. Further explain that in a test-taking situation, students should usually write a one-sentence summary for each paragraph in a selection. For longer paragraphs, like those in the Allende excerpt, students can mentally break down the information into two or three smaller parts. Summaries for paragraphs of this length should be two or three short sentences.

Severo opposed the idea of having masses said, because he did not believe in them as a way of getting into heaven, much less of returning to earth, and he maintained that masses and religious vows, like the selling of indulgences, images, and scapulars, were a dishonest business. Because of his attitude, Nívea
35 and Nana had the children say the rosary behind their father's back for nine days. Meanwhile, groups of volunteer explorers and mountain climbers tirelessly searched peaks and passes, combing every accessible stretch of land until they finally returned in triumph to hand the family the mortal remains of the deceased in a sealed black coffin. The intrepid traveler was laid to rest in a gran-
40 diose funeral. His death made him a hero and his name was on the front page of all the papers for several days. The same multitude that had gathered to see him off the day he flew away in his bird paraded past his coffin. The entire family wept as befit the occasion, except for Clara, who continued to watch the sky with the patience of an astronomer. One week after he had been buried, Uncle
45 Marcos, a bright smile playing behind his pirate's mustache, appeared in person in the doorway of Nívea and Severo del Valle's house. Thanks to the surreptitious prayers of the women and children, as he himself admitted, he was alive and well and in full possession of his faculties, including his sense of humor. Despite the noble lineage of his aerial maps, the flight had been a failure. He
50 had lost his airplane and had to return on foot, but he had not broken any bones and his adventurous spirit was intact. This confirmed the family's eternal devotion to San Antonio, but was not taken as a warning by future generations, who also tried to fly, although by different means.

Informational Reading Carefully read the following announcement, playing close attention to details and specific instructions. Then answer questions 6–8 on page 1306.

Recall Alert

Product: Joe's Airplanes Company has announced a recall of 2,000 rechargeable battery packs for toy airplanes. The recall affects battery packs included with Intrepid III toy airplanes sold worldwide between June 1, 2005 and February 1, 2007. The code MARCOS857 is printed near the top of affected battery packs.
5 Battery packs imprinted with DELVALLES858 are not affected by the recall.
Problem: The battery cells may overheat and pose a fire hazard.
What to do: All consumers should stop using the battery packs immediately and email recall@joesairplanes.com (U.S. consumers) or intcustserv@joesairplanes.com (international consumers) for information about obtaining free
10 replacement battery packs.

ASSESSMENT **1305**

Teach

Reading Strategy

Establish a Purpose for Reading In this Assessment section, students read two different types of text. When students are reading from materials of varied types, it is important that they establish a purpose for reading each. Have them preview each reading passage. **Ask:** If you were reading this passage on your own and not for a test, what might be your purpose for reading it? *(Students may say that they would read the first passage for enjoyment and the second to obtain necessary information and instructions.)*

English Learners
DIFFERENTIATED INSTRUCTION

Advanced The excerpt contains a number of references to religious items, concepts, and rituals. Explain that students do not need to specifically understand what an indulgence or a scapular is, but by using the context clues *heaven* and *religious vows*, they may gain a general idea that the passage is describing the difference between Nívea's and Severo's opinions about religion.

Approaching Level
DIFFERENTIATED INSTRUCTION

Understanding Euphemisms
Some students may have difficulty understanding that expressions such as "mortal remains," "the deceased," and "intrepid traveler" refer to Marco. Explain that a euphemism is an expression used to replace an offensive or unpleasant one. Advise students to pause in their reading to identify which character is being referred to and what the euphemism stands for.

Assess

1. C is the correct answer. The context suggests that Nívea is the mother of the children, and the author refers to Severo as the children's father. `DOK 4`

2. F is the correct answer. The author writes that Severo thinks masses and religious vows are a dishonest business but Nívea has the children pray behind their father's back. `DOK 2`

3. D is the correct answer. Nívea weeps disconsolately and lights candles to San Antonio at about the time Severo becomes convinced Marcos must have fallen into a *cordillera*, which is a week after Marcos disappeared. `DOK 1`

4. H is the correct answer. "Behind their father's back" in line 36 is a clue that *surreptitious* means "stealthy" or "secretive." `DOK 2`

5. C is the correct answer. The passage refers to Marcos's "invincible imagination" and "adventurous spirit." `DOK 2`

6. H is the correct answer. The announcement states that the code is "printed near the top of affected battery packs." `DOK 1`

7. D is the correct answer. The announcement promises "information about obtaining free replacement battery packs." `DOK 1`

8. G is the correct answer. The consumer purchased a toy airplane between June 1, 2005, and February 1, 2007, and its battery pack bears the code of the affected packs, so she needs to contact the company. Because she lives outside the United States, she should e-mail intcustserv@joesairplanes.com. `DOK 1`

1306

Items 1–5 apply to the passage from *The House of the Spirits*.

1. Which of the following can you infer about the relationship between Severo and Nívea del Valle?
   - **A.** They are casual acquaintances.
   - **B.** They are brother and sister.
   - **C.** They are husband and wife.
   - **D.** They are mother and son.

2. What is the main source of the tension between Severo and Nívea del Valle?
   - **F.** a disagreement over religious practices
   - **G.** a disagreement over the whereabouts of the missing Marcos
   - **H.** a long-standing disagreement over child-rearing methods
   - **J.** a disagreement over how to dispose of the remains of the dead

3. At what point does Nívea weep disconsolately and light candles to San Antonio?
   - **A.** during Marcos's funeral
   - **B.** after the groups of volunteers return the mortal remains of the deceased
   - **C.** before Marcos takes off on his adventure
   - **D.** after a week with no word from Marcos

4. As it is used in lines 47–48, the word *surreptitious* most nearly means:
   - **F.** persistent
   - **G.** obvious
   - **H.** stealthy
   - **J.** insincere

5. From information in the passage, which of the following best describes the character of Marcos?
   - **A.** He is outgoing and universally loved.
   - **B.** He is cautious.
   - **C.** He is adventurous and imaginative.
   - **D.** He has trouble making decisions.

Items 6–8 apply to "Recall Alert."

6. Where should consumers look for the code MARCOS857?
   - **F.** on the Web site joesairplanes.com
   - **G.** on the side of Intrepid III toy airplanes
   - **H.** near the top of their battery packs
   - **J.** in an e-mail sent to consumers by Joe's Airplanes Company

7. What action does Joe's Airplanes Company plan to take to assist consumers affected by the recall?
   - **A.** reclaim all affected Intrepid III toy airplanes
   - **B.** sell replacement battery packs at a reduced rate
   - **C.** provide refunds on purchases of the Intrepid III
   - **D.** provide free replacement battery packs

8. What action should be taken by a consumer who lives in Mexico and possesses a battery pack with the code MARCOS857 that she purchased in 2006?
   - **F.** She should e-mail recall@joesairplanes.com.
   - **G.** She should e-mail intcustserv@joesairplanes.com.
   - **H.** She should contact Joe's Airplanes Company by phone.
   - **J.** She should take no action.

1306 UNIT 6 THE AMERICAS

Reading Practice

Analyze Text Structure Explain that the purpose of nonfiction—to inform or persuade—influences the structure of the text **Ask: How does the structure of the recall notice affect readers' understanding?** (*Students may say that having an identifying run-in heading before each part of the text might lead readers to keep in mind the information expressed in each part.*)

Explain to students that considering text structure during a test will help their comprehension and will help them find answers to test questions more quickly.

Vocabulary Skills: Sentence Completion

For each item in the Vocabulary Skills section, choose the word or words that best complete the sentence. Write your answers on a separate sheet of paper.

1. Racial and class barriers are often a _____ to the many Maya who wish to achieve a higher standard of living.
   A. conception
   B. ploy
   C. solace
   D. hindrance

2. Pablo Neruda _____ from traditional subject matter in his odes, writing about ordinary, rather than _____, objects.
   F. strays…exalted
   G. improvises…haggard
   H. veers…lucid
   J. collides…mediocre

3. Despite their commonplace subject matter, Neruda's odes avoid _____ by revealing the great beauty and majesty of everyday objects.
   A. supplication
   B. frivolity
   C. resignation
   D. haste

4. In Neruda's poem "Horses," the vibrant presence of the horses helps _____ the effects of a monotonous winter day.
   F. revive
   G. improvise
   H. mitigate
   J. muster

5. Many consecrated Native American religious sites have sustained _____ damage by development.
   A. irrevocable
   B. austere
   C. banal
   D. fallacious

6. Magic realist authors often combine two distinct elements: precise realism and _____ fantasy.
   F. sheer
   G. haggard
   H. supplementary
   J. unwitting

7. Corn was the primary source of _____ for the prehistoric peoples who _____ the Mississippi region of North America.
   A. sustenance…inhabited
   B. coercion…commenced
   C. humility…fluttered
   D. diligence…pounced

8. In the early years of European settlement, deadly _____ claimed the lives of Native Americans, who lacked immunity to European diseases.
   F. stragglers
   G. epidemics
   H. guffaws
   J. stupors

9. Christopher Columbus often presented a/an _____ and demeaning view of native peoples he encountered.
   A. irrevocable
   B. condescending
   C. tedious
   D. edible

10. In Alice Munro's "Day of the Butterfly," the students' attempts to "be nice" to Myra are _____ because the students are actually mocking her.
    F. fallacious
    G. edible
    H. relentless
    J. presumptuous

English Learners

DIFFERENTIATED INSTRUCTION

Intermediate Encourage students to look for clues in vocabulary test questions that can help them determine that the missing word is an antonym of another word in the sentence. Explain that words such as *rather* and *despite* indicate an opposition in the sentence. Students should then figure out what concepts or ideas are being contrasted so they may choose the correct vocabulary word.

Advanced Learners/Pre-AP

DIFFERENTIATED INSTRUCTION

Expanding Vocabulary Explain that most college entrance exams test advanced vocabulary. Encourage students to keep a list of unfamiliar words they come across in their reading. Students should look up each word and write it, along with its definition, in a log. Then, to practice using the words, students can pick one word a day and try to use the word naturally in a sentence.

Assessment
English-Language Arts

Assess

1. **D** is the correct answer. The use of *barriers* suggests that the Maya are being prevented or blocked from achieving success. DOK 2

2. **F** is the correct answer. *Exalted* is the only word that works as the opposite of *ordinary* in this context. DOK 2

3. **B** is the correct answer. "Commonplace subject matter" suggests that the poems could be light or trivial, so *frivolity* is the only noun that makes sense in this context. DOK 2

4. **H** is the correct answer. The fact that the horses' presence is *vibrant* suggests they will lessen the effects of the winter day, so *mitigate* is the only verb that makes sense in this context. DOK 2

5. **A** is the correct answer. The other choices make no sense in this context, so **B, C,** and **D** are all incorrect. DOK 2

6. **F** is the correct answer. **G, H,** and **J** do not make sense in this context. DOK 2

7. **A** is the correct answer. **B, C,** and **D** do not make sense in this context. DOK 2

8. **G** is the correct answer. *Epidemics* is the only option that makes sense given the mention of "European diseases."

9. **B** is the correct answer. The context clue *demeaning* indicates that Columbus considered native peoples to be inferior. DOK 2

10. **F** is the correct answer. That the students are mocking Myra suggests that their attempts are deceptive. DOK 2

Assessment
English-Language Arts

Assess

1. C is the correct answer. The original sentence contains an error in verb tense. No other option corrects this problem without introducing a new error or changing the meaning of the sentence.
DOK 1

2. G is the correct answer. The original sentence uses the incorrect form of the verb *believe*. The verb acts as a noun in this sentence, so the gerund form is required. Only **G** corrects this problem without introducing a new error or changing the meaning of the sentence. **DOK 1**

3. C is the correct answer. The original sentence contains a series of three items that need to be separated by commas. **DOK 1**

4. J is the correct answer. The original sentence incorrectly includes a parenthetical citation within the quotation marks. Only **J** corrects this problem without introducing new errors. **DOK 1**

Grammar and Writing Skills: Paragraph Improvement

In the following excerpt from a student's first draft of a persuasive essay, numbers appear beneath underlined parts. The numbers correspond to items below that provide options for replacing or ask questions about the underlined parts. Numbers that appear in boxes within the essay refer to questions about specific paragraphs or about the essay as a whole. On a separate sheet of paper, record the letter of the best option in each item. If you think the original should not be changed, choose "NO CHANGE." Read the passage through once before you begin to answer the questions. As you read, pay close attention to the writer's use of **commas, verb tenses,** and **quotations**.

[1]

In Pablo Neruda's poem "Horses," the speaker described a transition from a deadened emotional
¹
state to one of renewed hope. The poem is written in highly irregular free verse, which could trick a
²
reader into believe that Neruda gave little thought to poetic forms or conventions. This is not the case. The poem's formal characteristics, on the contrary, are essential to its meaning. Specifically, Neruda uses irregular stanzas enjambment and sound
³
devices to reinforce the poem's theme of emotional transformation.

[2]

Neruda's short, irregular stanzas add to the poem's meaning in several ways. First, they create dramatic pauses during which the reader can fully absorb the poem's images. For example, Neruda includes a two-line stanza in lines 2–3: "I was in Berlin in winter. The light / was without light, the sky skyless." This is followed by a vivid one-line stanza: "The air
white like a moistened loaf (line 3)." The pauses
⁴
after each of these stanzas reinforces the silence and
⁵

emptiness of the scene. The short stanzas also echo the natural movement of the speaker's thoughts, readers are able to follow the speaker's observations
⁶
as though they were experiencing the scene themselves.

[3]

Irregular enjambment also proves essential to the emotional power of "Horses." Using line breaks to create dramatic pauses in his sentences Neruda
⁷
gives the poem a vigorous rhythm. In lines 20–21, Neruda inserts a line break in the middle of the word *midpoint,* added unexpected energy and drama
⁸
to its words. This formal move echoes the vitality of
⁹
the horses in the poem. Neruda also uses rich personification in the poem. **10**

1. **A.** NO CHANGE
    B. the speaker describing a transition
    C. the speaker describes a transition
    D. the speaker in describing a transition

2. **F.** NO CHANGE
    G. trick a reader into believing that
    H. trick a reader believing that
    J. trick a believing reader that

Grammar Practice

Subject-Verb Agreement Explain to students that correct subject-verb agreement can be tricky when a plural subject is "hidden" behind a singular indefinite pronoun, such as *each, anyone, everyone,* or *everybody*. Write the following sentences on the board:

1. Either of the umbrellas is fine with me.

2. The snacks provided for everyone cover two tables.

Explain that in sentence 1 *either* is both the subject of the sentence and a singular indefinite pronoun; the singular verb *is* agrees with it. In sentence 2 the plural verb *cover* agrees with the subject *snacks*; the indefinite pronoun *everyone* is part of a participial phrase and is not the subject.

Have students choose the correct verb forms in the following sentences:

1. Neither of Amelia's cats (has, have) eaten since the storm. (*has*)

2. During the graduation ceremony, the families of each student (want, wants) a clear view of the stage. (*want*)

Assessment
English-Language Arts

3. **A.** NO CHANGE
   B. irregular stanzas enjambment, and sound devices
   C. irregular stanzas, enjambment, and sound devices
   D. irregular stanzas: enjambment and sound devices

4. **F.** NO CHANGE
   G. "The air white like a moistened loaf (line 3)".
   H. "The air white like a moistened loaf," line 3.
   J. "The air white like a moistened loaf" (line 3).

5. **A.** NO CHANGE
   B. The pauses after each of these stanzas reinforce the silence
   C. The pauses after each of these stanzas, reinforce the silence
   D. The pauses after each of these stanzas reinforced the silence

6. **F.** NO CHANGE
   G. thoughts, readers are able to follow. The speaker's observations as though
   H. thoughts, so readers are able to follow the speaker's observations as though
   J. thoughts, readers are able to follow the speaker's observations, as though

7. **A.** NO CHANGE
   B. in his sentences, Neruda
   C. in his sentences. Neruda
   D. in his sentences

8. **F.** NO CHANGE
   G. adds
   H. adding
   J. had been adding

9. **A.** NO CHANGE
   B. our
   C. his
   D. those

10. Which sentence should be deleted from the final paragraph?
    F. the second sentence
    G. the third sentence
    H. the fourth sentence
    J. the fifth sentence

Essay

Write an essay comparing and contrasting the styles of two short stories from this unit. Discuss how stylistic elements such as figurative language, tone, and imagery contribute to the meaning of each story. Be sure to include specific examples from the texts in your essay. As you write, keep in mind that your essay will be evaluated for **ideas, organization, voice, word choice, sentence fluency,** and **grammar and spelling conventions.**

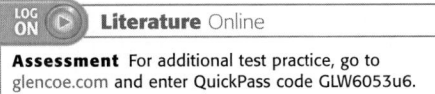

LOG ON **Literature** Online

Assessment For additional test practice, go to glencoe.com and enter QuickPass code GLW6053u6.

Approaching Level
DIFFERENTIATED INSTRUCTION

Reusing Graphic Organizers
Encourage students to review the graphic organizers they used to analyze the elements of the short stories in this unit. By revisiting their notes, students can identify similarities and differences between stories more easily. Have students use the information in the organizers to create a new graphic organizer that will help them visualize the details they will cover in their essays.

Advanced Learners/Pre-AP
DIFFERENTIATED INSTRUCTION

Revisit Big Ideas
Tell students to avoid giving a running list of similarities and differences between their selected stories. Encourage students to revisit the big idea associated with each story and to investigate how the authors' styles differ in accordance with the stories' themes or overriding literary elements. Students may find that the authors approach colonialism similarly or differ in their underlying purpose when using magic realism.

Assess

5. **B** is the correct answer. The subject of the sentence is *pauses*, but the writer incorrectly uses the singular present-tense form of the verb *reinforce*. Only **B** corrects this problem without introducing new errors. **DOK 1**

6. **H** is the correct answer. The original sentence is a run-on. Only **H** corrects this problem without introducing new errors. **DOK 1**

7. **B** is the correct answer. The introductory participial phrase "Using line breaks . . . sentences" needs to be followed by a comma. Only **B** corrects this problem without introducing new errors. **DOK 1**

8. **H** is the correct answer. The present participle *adding* is needed here. **DOK 1**

9. **C** is the correct answer. The pronoun should be changed to *his* because it refers to Neruda. **DOK 1**

10. **J** is the correct answer. Neruda's use of personification is irrelevant to this paragraph, which focuses on his use of enjambment. **DOK 4**

Essay

Students' essays should
- clearly state main ideas and support them with evidence from the text
- use effective voice, word choice, and sentence variety
- show attention to grammar and spelling conventions **DOK 3**

Reference Section

Literary Terms Handbook

A

Absurd, Theater of the See *THEATER OF THE ABSURD.*

Act A major unit of a drama or play. Modern dramas generally have one, two, or three acts. Older dramas typically have five acts. Acts may be divided into one or more scenes.

See also *DRAMA, SCENE.*

Allegory The use of events, actions, objects, and persons in a narrative to represent moral qualities, universal struggles, or abstract ideas such as love, fear, or virtue. An allegory may be as brief as a metaphor, or it may be the basis for an entire novel. Virgil's *Aeneid* contains a number of allegorical episodes.

See pages 93 and 899.

See also *METAPHOR.*

Alliteration The repetition of consonant sounds at the beginnings of words. For example, in line 13 of Léopold Sédar Senghor's "Night of Sine," the *s* sound is repeated:

> What do they <u>s</u>ay <u>s</u>o <u>s</u>ecretly to the stars?

See page 1211.

See also *SOUND DEVICES.*

Allusion A reference to a well-known person, place, or event from history, literature, or religion. Allusions enrich the reading experience by adding another dimension of meaning. *Lautaro,* one of the names suggested for the drowned man in Gabriel García Márquez's "The Handsomest Drowned Man in the World," is an allusion to a great native South American hero who fought against the Spanish.

See page 1253.

Ambiguity The state of having more than one meaning. The richness of literary language lies in its ability to evoke multiple layers of meaning. The red glow in Khalida Asghar's "The Wagon" is an intentionally ambiguous detail.

Analogy A comparison that shows similarities between two things that are otherwise dissimilar. An analogy often explains something unfamiliar or abstract by comparing it with something familiar or concrete. In "Jade Flower Palace," Tu Fu draws an analogy between the inevitable effect of time on the palace and its effect on human life.

See page 620.

Anecdote A brief story giving an amusing, insightful look at a single incident or event.

Antagonist In a literary work, the person or force opposing the protagonist, or central character. The antagonist may be an individual, a group of people, a force of nature, or a social force such as racial or class prejudice. The reader is generally not meant to sympathize with the antagonist. In Bessie Head's story, "The Prisoner Who Wore Glasses," Warden Hannetjie is the antagonist.

See pages 820 and 977.

See also *PROTAGONIST.*

Anthropomorphism The assignment of human characteristics to gods, animals, or inanimate objects. It is a key element in fables and folktales, in which the main characters are often animals. Coyote in "Coyote Finishes his Work," as retold by Barry Lopez, is an example of anthropomorphism.

See page 39.

See also *FABLE, FAIRY TALE, FOLKLORE, FOLKTALE.*

Antithesis The balanced contrast of two phrases or ideas. Through antithesis, authors help emphasize important ideas, as in "Creation Hymn" from the Rig-Veda:

> Their cord was extended across. Was there below?
>
> Was there above? There were seed-placers;
>
> there were powers. There was impulse
>
> beneath; there was giving-forth above.

See page 492.

Archetype A symbol, character, image, or story pattern that is common to human experience across cultures and throughout the world and evokes strong responses, often based on unconscious memory. In their purest form, archetypes occur in the oral tradition, but they also appear in written works of literature. The story of an ancient divine ruler such as Osiris, who teaches his people the essential skills of civilization, is an example of the archetype of the culture hero. Archetypes can be divided into the following categories:

Character archetype: Includes familiar individuals such as the wise leader, the rebel, the damsel in distress, and the traitor.

Image archetype: Objects or places that have a universal symbolism. For example, a lily can be a symbol of purity.

Plot pattern archetype: Stories that occur in many cultures. Making the long journey home, completing the "impossible" task, and outwitting the formidable enemy are all archetypal plots.

Theme archetype: Ideas that occur wherever people tell stories. The ideas that good can overcome evil, that people can redeem themselves, and that an underworld exists are all archetypal themes.

See page 17.

See also *FOLKLORE, MYTH, ORAL TRADITION, STOCK CHARACTER, SYMBOL.*

Argument A type of persuasive writing in which logic and reason are used to try to influence a reader's ideas or actions. In Sophocles' *Oedipus the King,* Creon's speech in which he defends himself against accusations of treason is an example of argument.

See page 321.

See also *RHETORICAL DEVICES.*

Aphorism See *MAXIM.*

Aside In a play, a comment that a character makes to the audience that other characters onstage do not hear. The speaker turns to one side—or "aside"— away from the action onstage. Asides, which are rare in modern drama, reveal what a character is thinking or feeling.

See also *DRAMA, DRAMATIC CONVENTION, SOLILOQUY.*

Assonance The repetition of similar vowel sounds, especially in a line of poetry. The repeated *a* sound in "the flash of a hand" from Czesław Miłosz's poem "Encounter" is an example of assonance.

See also *SOUND DEVICES.*

Atmosphere The dominant emotional feeling of a literary work that contributes to the mood. Authors create atmosphere primarily through details of setting such as time, place, and weather.

See also *MOOD, SETTING.*

Author's purpose An author's reasons for creating a literary work. These may include a desire to entertain, inform, or explain, or to express feelings, impressions, and opinions. The author's purpose in the Egyptian poem "The Immortality of Writers" is to emphasize the lasting importance of literature.

See page 402.

Autobiography The story of a person's life written by that person. Since autobiographies generally stress the author's personal views, they are often not as objective as other forms of nonfiction, such as history books. Some fictional works, such as Jamaica Kincaid's "A Walk to the Jetty," are partially autobiographical.

See pages 626 and 1033.

See also *BIOGRAPHY, DIARY, JOURNAL, MEMOIR, NONFICTION.*

B

Bias An inclination toward a certain opinion or position on a topic.

Biography A nonfiction narrative of a person's life written by someone other than that person. Colette's "Two Memories of Sido" is a memoir but contains elements of biography.

See also *MEMOIR.*

C

Cadence The rhythmic rise and fall of language when it is spoken or read aloud.

See also *FREE VERSE, METER.*

Caesura A pause in a line of poetry, usually near the middle of a line, with two stressed syllables before and two after, creating a strong rhythm. A caesura is used to produce variations in meter and to draw attention to certain words. Some pauses are indicated by punctuation, others by phrasing or meaning.

Canto From the Italian word for song, a subdivision in a long poem such as Dante's *Divine Comedy.*

Carpe diem A Latin phrase meaning "seize the day"; in other words, "make the most of each moment." In *carpe diem* poems, the speaker emphasizes the shortness of life—usually to persuade a young woman to yield to love while she still has her youth and beauty.

Character A person, an animal, or a presence in a literary work. Characters may be major or minor depending on their importance to the work. Characters can be described as flat or round. A flat character reveals only one personality trait, whereas a round character shows varied and sometimes contradictory traits. In Bessie Head's "The Prisoner Who Wore Glasses," Brille is a round character; his children are flat characters. Characters may also be classified as static or dynamic. A static character remains the same throughout the story. A dynamic character changes. In Head's story, Martha is a static character; Hannetjie is a dynamic character.

See pages 125 and 1002.

Characterization The methods an author uses to develop the personality of a character. With direct characterization, the author makes direct statements about a character's personality, simply stating that a character is, for example, shy or selfish. Indirect characterization requires that readers draw their own conclusions about a character based on evidence from the story. This evidence might include the character's appearance, words, thoughts, or actions, and other characters' thoughts and comments on that character.

See page 608.

Chorus A performer or group of performers whose function is to comment on the action that has just occurred in a drama and to sing and dance between scenes. The chorus serves as a bridge between the actors and the audience. Often an element in ancient Greek drama, the chorus is also found in other dramatic traditions, such as Japanese Noh drama.

See page 251.

See also *NOH.*

Climax The point of greatest interest or emotional intensity in a literary work. Also called the turning point, the climax usually comes near the end of a story or drama. For example, the climax of Rosario Castellanos's "The Luck of Teodoro Méndez Acúbal" occurs when Teodoro reaches into his sash for the coin and Don Augustín pulls a gun on him.

See also *DRAMATIC STRUCTURE, PLOT.*

Colloquialism Informal language used in everyday conversation, but not in formal writing or speech. In Alice Munro's "Day of the Butterfly," a child, speaking colloquially, says, "That's where my mother was at . . . They've got all nuns there."

See also *DIALECT, VERNACULAR.*

Comedy A type of drama or story that is humorous and often has a happy ending. Miguel de Cervantes's *Don Quixote* is a comedy. Comedy can be divided into two categories: high and low. High comedy makes fun of human behavior in a witty, sophisticated manner. Low comedy involves physical humor and simple, often vulgar, wordplay.

See also *DRAMA, HUMOR, PARODY, SATIRE, WIT.*

Conflict A struggle between two opposing forces in the plot of a story. An external conflict exists when a character struggles against an outside force, such as another person, nature, society, or fate. An internal conflict occurs within the mind of a character who is torn between opposing feelings or goals. Many characters experience both external and internal conflicts.

See pages 583 and 754.

Connotation The unspoken or unwritten meanings associated with a word beyond its literal definition, or denotation. Paying attention to the connotations of words is often helpful in understanding literature that deals with abstract concepts or includes many abstract words. Words such as *peered* and *blood-red* in Khalida Asghar's "The Wagon" have an eerie and foreboding connotation.

See also *DENOTATION.*

Consonance The repetition of consonant sounds within or at the ends of nonrhyming words. For example, notice the *l* sounds in this line of Horace's "Better to Live, Licinius":

> to take in sail when it swells in a wind
> that's a little too kind

See also *SOUND DEVICES.*

Couplet Two consecutive rhymed lines of poetry that follow the same rhythmic pattern.

D

Denotation The literal, or dictionary, meaning of a word.

See also *CONNOTATION.*

Description Writing that creates a clear image of an appearance, feeling, or action. Good descriptive writing appeals to the senses through imagery. The use of figurative language and precise verbs, adjectives, and adverbs can also help make a description vivid.

See pages 150 and 871.

See also *IMAGERY, SENSORY DETAILS.*

Dialect A version of a language spoken by people in a particular region or social group. For example, Cockney is an English dialect spoken by working-class residents of East London. Dialects of the same language may differ from one another in pronunciation, vocabulary, and grammar.

See page 1225.

Dialogue Written conversation between characters in a literary work. Dialogue brings characters to life by revealing their personalities and by showing what they are thinking and feeling as they interact with other characters. Dialogue can also create mood, advance the plot, and develop theme. Plays are composed almost completely of dialogue.

See pages 1026 and 1265.

See also *MOOD, PLOT, THEME.*

Diary A work in which a person keeps an informal record of events in his or her life. Unlike a journal, a diary is most often a simple, spontaneous account of daily life. Sei Shōnagon's *The Pillow Book* is a diary.

See page 717.

See also *AUTOBIOGRAPHY, JOURNAL, MEMOIR, NONFICTION.*

Diction An author's choice of words and the way they are arranged; an important element in the author's voice or style. Diction can be described in any number of ways, such as formal or informal, old-fashioned or modern, friendly or detached, plain or ornate, depending on vocabulary and style. Skilled authors choose their words carefully to convey a particular meaning or feeling.

See page 525.

See also *AUTHOR'S PURPOSE, CONNOTATION, STYLE, TONE, VOICE.*

Drama A story intended to be acted out in front of an audience, also called a play or stage play. The script of a dramatic work often includes the author's instructions to the actors and the director, known as stage directions. A drama may be divided into acts, which may also be broken up into scenes, indicating changes in location or the passage of time. Sophocles' *Oedipus the King* is a drama.

See pages 248 and 736..

See also *ACT, DRAMATIC CONVENTION, DRAMATIC STRUCTURE, NOH, PROP, SCENE, STAGE DIRECTIONS, TRAGEDY.*

Dramatic convention An unrealistic device that a playwright uses to present a story on stage, which the audience accepts as realistic. For example, audiences at Noh plays accept the convention of male actors playing female roles. They also accept unrealistic shifts in time.

Dramatic structure The way information is presented in a play. Common elements in dramatic structure are exposition, or revelation of important background information; rising action, which adds complications to the plot; climax (also called turning point or crisis), the moment of greatest emotional intensity or suspense; falling action, which unravels the complications; and resolution, which resolves them or brings them to a close.

See also *CLIMAX, EXPOSITION, FALLING ACTION,*

E

Elegy A poem dealing with loss, sadness, or human mortality and the emotional consequences. Nāzik al-Malāʾikah's "Elegy for a Woman of No Importance" is a modern example of this ancient poetic form.

End rhyme The repetition of sounds in the syllables at the ends of lines that appear close to one another in a poem. The following lines from Oodgeroo of the tribe Noonuccal's "Municipal Gum" contain end rhyme.

> **In the cool world of leafy forest <u>halls</u>**
>
> **And wild bird <u>calls</u>.**

See page 807.

See also *RHYME.*

End-stopped line A line of poetry that contains a complete thought and is thus punctuated at the end. The following example from the Egyptian poem "So small are the flowers of Seamu" is an end-stopped line:

> **Your voice gives life, like nectar.**

See also *ENJAMBMENT.*

Enjambment The continuation of a sentence from one line of a poem to the next, also called a run-on line. Enjambment enables poets to express a thought or image within the structure of the line, as well as to extend it to the next line(s), while still maintaining unity of thought. Enjambment occurs in the following lines from Heinrich Heine's "The Lorelei."

> **The wonderful melody reaches**
>
> **A boat, as it sails along.**

See page 521.

See also *END-STOPPED LINE, RUN-ON LINE.*

Enlightenment A European philosophical and literary movement characterized by faith in human reason and skepticism toward traditional religion. This movement is sometimes referred to as "The Age of Reason" or Rationalism, a related movement. The Enlightenment worldview stimulated an outburst of scientific inquiry and intellectual freedom, which laid the foundation for a modern worldview based on rationalism, secularism, and the rights of the individual. These ideas shook established ways of seeing the world; the arguments of such Enlightenment thinkers as John Locke and Jean-Jacques Rousseau helped shape the ideals of the American Revolution and the Declaration of Independence.

Epic A long narrative poem about a larger-than-life hero who embodies the values of his or her people. Many early epics, such as *Gilgamesh,* were composed orally and preserved by storytellers before being written down. Such oral epics, or folk epics, may be developed in different versions as they are passed along from generation to generation. Literary epics, such as Virgil's *Aeneid,* are composed as written texts, although they are often modeled on oral epic poetry. Many epics share standard characteristics known as epic conventions. These include an invocation, or formal plea to a deity for inspiration; epithets, something like nicknames, such as "the swift runner Achilles"; epic similes, which are longer and more elaborate than typical similes; and a set rhythm or metrical structure.

See page 58 and 879.

See also *EPIC HERO, EPITHET, FOLKLORE, FOLKTALE, MYTH, ORAL TRADITION.*

Epic hero A legendary, larger-than-life figure whose adventures form the core of an epic.

See pages 193, 449, and 564.

See also *EPIC, EPITHET, FOLKLORE, FOLKTALE, MYTH, ORAL TRADITION.*

Epigram See *MAXIM.*

Epigraph A quotation from another work or source that occurs at the beginning of a literary work and highlights a theme or main idea of the work at hand. "The Lion-Makers" from the *Panchatantra* begins with an epigraph.

Epiphany A sudden, unexpected moment of insight. A key element of many modern short stories, epiphany is often employed in the stories of Katherine Mansfield, author of "The Doll's House."

Epithet A word or brief phrase used to characterize a person, place, or thing. In the *Iliad,* for instance, the epithet "breaker of horses" is used to identify Hector.
See also *EPIC.*

Essay A short piece of literary nonfiction devoted to a single topic from a limited viewpoint. Essays may be classified as formal or informal. Formal essays include expository essays, which offer information about a topic, and persuasive essays, which promote a specific opinion or position. Informal essays include personal essays, such as the memoir or the reflective essay, which explores the meaning and effect of a personal observation or experience from the author's life.
See also *NONFICTION.*

Exaggeration An overstatement for the purpose of emphasis.
See also *HYPERBOLE.*

Existentialism A philosophy that seeks the meaning of existence itself. Existentialists believe that life is empty of any purpose or value other than that which individuals give to their own lives. Existentialism developed as a pragmatic response to the alienation and confusion that many people believed defined contemporary life. Many Existentialists came to the conclusion that life was essentially meaningless and absurd. Along with the French philosopher Jean-Paul Sartre, Albert Camus emerged as a spokesman for these complex responses to the world. However, rather than describing a world of bottomless despair, Camus argued that when people can see the underlying meaninglessness in the world, they can begin to make choices that give meaning to their lives.
See also *THEATER OF THE ABSURD.*

Exposition An author's introduction of the characters, setting, and conflict at the beginning of a story, novel, or play.
See also *PLOT.*

Extended metaphor A metaphor that compares two unlike things in various ways throughout a paragraph, stanza, or an entire literary work.
See also *METAPHOR.*

F

Fable A brief folktale, often featuring animals or inanimate objects as characters, told to teach a specific lesson or moral. In some fables, such as those of Aesop, the lesson or moral is stated explicitly. In other fables, the reader must infer the lesson based on what happens in the story.
See also *ANTHROPOMORPHISM.*

Fairy tale A type of folktale that features supernatural elements, such as spirits, talking animals, and magic.
See also *ANTHROPOMORPHISM, FABLE, FOLKLORE, FOLKTALE, LEGEND, MYTH.*

Falling action The action that follows the climax in a play or story. The falling action may show the results of the climax. It may also include the denouement, a French word meaning "unknotting." The denouement, or resolution, explains the plot or unravels the mystery.
See also *CLIMAX, DRAMATIC STRUCTURE, PLOT.*

Fantasy A story that takes place in an unreal world and features incredible characters and events.

Farce A type of comedy with stereotyped characters in ridiculous situations. Anton Chekhov often wrote farces.
See also *COMEDY, HUMOR, PARODY, SATIRE.*

Fiction A narrative written in prose in which the situations and characters are invented by the writer. Novels, short stories, folktales, fairy tales, fables, and other forms of made-up stories are types of fiction.
See also *FABLE, FAIRY TALE, FOLKTALE, NOVEL, SHORT STORY.*

Figurative language Language used for descriptive effect in order to convey ideas or emotions. Figurative expressions, while not literally descriptive, express an aspect of the subject beyond the literal level.

See page 749.

See also *FIGURES OF SPEECH.*

Figures of speech Language that uses expressions that are not literally true, but express some truth beyond the literal level. Types of figures of speech include hyperbole, metaphor, personification, simile, and understatement. Pablo Neruda's poem "Horses" contains several figures of speech. "The air white like a moistened loaf" is a simile, "they filled the whole world of my eyes" is a metaphor, and the reference to "the teeth of winter" is personification.

See also *HYPERBOLE, IMAGERY, METAPHOR, OXYMORON, PERSONIFICATION, SIMILE, SYMBOL, UNDERSTATEMENT.*

Flashback An interruption in the chronological order of a narrative to relate a scene from an earlier time. An author may use this device to give the reader background information or to create tension or contrast. In "A Walk to the Jetty," the narrator has many flashbacks while walking with her mother to the jetty, including memories of her apprenticeship as a seamstress and her friend's case of the mumps.

See pages 815 and 1278.

Flat character See *CHARACTER.*

Foil A character whose personality traits are unlike, and best understood in contrast to, another character's. Often a foil is a minor character who serves, through contrast, to emphasize the distinctive characteristics of the main character. Through the use of a foil, a writer calls attention to the strengths or weaknesses of a character. In Alice Munro's "Day of the Butterfly," Gladys Healey, the prime antagonist, is a foil for Helen, the narrator.

Folklore The traditional beliefs, customs, stories, songs, and dances of a culture. Folklore is based on the concerns of ordinary people and is passed down through oral traditions.

See also *EPIC, FABLE, FAIRY TALE, FOLKTALE, LEGEND, MYTH, ORAL TRADITION.*

Folktale A story that has been passed down from one generation to the next by word of mouth. Folktales do not have a known author, although they are often retold by authors for audiences of different times and cultures. They generally reflect the values of the societies that preserve them. Most folktales are simple narratives told for entertainment, although they might also teach moral values. Folktales include animal stories, trickster stories, fairy tales, myths, legends, and tall tales. "Coyote Finishes His Work" is a Native American folktale.

See also *EPIC, FABLE, FAIRY TALE, FOLKLORE, LEGEND, MYTH, ORAL TRADITION.*

Foot The basic unit in the measurement of rhythm in poetry. A foot usually contains one stressed syllable and one or more unstressed syllables.

See also *METER, RHYTHM, SCANSION.*

Foreshadowing The use of clues by the author to prepare readers for events that will happen later in a story. Foreshadowing helps build suspense and draws the reader into the plot. In Leo Tolstoy's story "How Much Land Does a Man Need?", Pakhom's dream foreshadows the danger in his accepting the Bashkir chief's deal.

See page 1278.

Form The arrangement of words and lines in a poem. Many modern authors use loosely structured forms instead of following traditional or formal patterns. These poets vary the lengths of lines and stanzas, relying on emphasis, rhythm, pattern, and the placement of words and phrases to convey meaning. *Form* can also be used as a synonym for *genre.*

See pages 739 and 830.

Formal speech A speech whose main purpose is to persuade, although it may also inform and entertain. There are four main types of formal speech: legal, political, ceremonial, and religious.

See page 335.

Frame story A plot structure that includes the telling of a story within a story. The frame is the outer story, which usually precedes and follows the inner, more important story. This technique is common in both ancient and modern writing. Some literary works, such as Giovanni Boccaccio's *Decameron,* have frames that bind together many different stories.

Free verse Poetry that does not follow a regular meter or rhyme scheme. Although poets who write free verse ignore traditional rules, they use techniques such as sound devices and cadence to create musical patterns in their poems.

See page 1050.

See also *CADENCE, SOUND DEVICES.*

G

Genre A category or type of literature. Examples of genres include poetry, drama, short story, essay, and epic. The term also refers to subcategories of literature. For example, fantasy, magic realism, mystery, romance, and science fiction are subgenres of fiction.

H

Haiku A Japanese poetry form consisting of seventeen syllables arranged in three lines. The first and third lines have five syllables each, and the middle line has seven. Because they are so short, haiku rely heavily on the power of suggestion. Words in haiku are chosen for the associations they create in the reader's mind. Usually about nature, a traditional haiku uses striking and often contrasting imagery to evoke an insight or capture a mood. The haiku existed originally as a subset of a type of poetry called the renga, but was developed into its own form by the Japanese haiku master Bashō and his contemporaries.

See also *TANKA.*

Hero The chief character in a literary work, typically one whose qualities or deeds arouse admiration. For example, Gilgamesh is the hero of *Gilgamesh.* Although the word *hero* is applied only to males in traditional usage—*heroine* being the term used for females—modern usage applies the term to either gender.

See also *EPIC HERO.*

Historical context The time and place in which a literary work was written, including the traditions, customs, beliefs, and values of that time and place. Miguel de Cervantes's *Don Quixote,* for example, is set in sixteenth-century Spain and contrasts the chivalry idealized in literature with the reality of that time.

Historical fiction Fiction that sets characters against a backdrop of events from a past time period that actually existed. Some works of historical fiction include actual historical figures along with fictitious characters.

History A factual account of real events that occurred in the past. Typically, a history is arranged chronologically and seeks to provide an objective description of what took place.

Humor The quality of a literary work intended to be funny or amusing, although it can also be an important tool of persuasion. There are three basic types of humor. Humor of situation develops from the plot of a literary work, which may contain exaggerated or unexpected events. Humor of character uses exaggerated personalities to make us laugh at the flaws of human nature. Humor of language may include wordplay, verbal irony, exaggeration, or sarcasm. Humorous writing can be equally effective in fiction and nonfiction.

See also *PARODY, SARCASM, SATIRE, WIT.*

Hymn A lyric poem or song addressed to a divine being. The term is also applied to a section of a longer religious poem. The excerpt in this book from the Maya text the *Popol Vuh* is a hymn.

Hyperbole A figure of speech that uses intentional exaggeration to express strong emotion, make a point, or create humor. Notice the hyperbole in this line from "The Handsomest Drowned Man in the World".

> **the hidden strength of his heart popped the buttons on his shirt.**

See page 1244.

See also *EXAGGERATION, FIGURES OF SPEECH.*

I

Idiom An expression whose meaning is different from its literal meaning. Phrases such as "catch his eye," "turn the tables," and "over the hill" are idiomatic expressions in English. Idioms can add realism to dialogue in a story and contribute to characterization.

See page 1265.

See also *DIALECT.*

Imagery Descriptive language that appeals to one or more of the five senses: sight, hearing, touch, taste, and smell. The use of sensory details helps create an emotional response in the reader. Most imagery is visual, but imagery can also help readers hear sounds, feel textures, taste foods, and smell aromas (as in this portion of Aleksandr Solzhenitsyn's "Freedom to Breathe").

> **No food on earth, no wine, not even a woman's kiss is sweeter to me than this air steeped in the fragrance of flowers, of moisture and freshness.**

See pages 30, 121, 242, 377, 704, and 787.

Implied comparison A comparison that is suggested rather than directly stated. An implied comparison is conveyed by connecting images in a new or unexpected way rather than by indicating that the one image *is* the other (metaphor) or is *like* the other (simile). For instance, in his haiku, Kobayashi Issa links the image of melting snow to that of children.

In medias res Latin phrase meaning "in the middle of things." A work of literature is said to start in medias res when the story begins in the middle of the action. A work of literature that starts in medias res skips the exposition and moves directly to the rising action.

Inversion The reversal of the usual word order in a prose sentence or a line of poetry. Writers use inversion to maintain rhyme scheme or meter, to vary sentence structure, or to emphasize certain words or phrases. In this passage from Li Po's "The River-Merchant's Wife: A Letter," the verb (*played*) comes before the subject (*I*), a reversal of the usual order.

> While my hair was still cut straight across my forehead
>
> <u>Played</u> <u>I</u> about the front gate, pulling flowers.

Irony A contrast or discrepancy between expectation and reality, or between what is expected and what actually happens. Dramatic irony occurs when the reader or audience knows something that a character does not know. For instance, in "The Story of Pyramus and Thisbe" by Ovid, the reader knows that Thisbe is merely hiding when Pyramus believes that she is dead. Situational irony occurs when what actually happens is the opposite of what is expected or appropriate. In Giovanni Boccaccio's "Federigo's Falcon," the hero serves his prized falcon to the lady as a meal, not knowing she has come to ask for it as a gift for her son. Verbal irony occurs when a writer or speaker says one thing but really means the opposite. It might occur when a person responds to a disappointment with an expression such as "That's great."

See pages 52 and 291.

J

Journal A personal record of experiences, ideas, and reflections that is kept on a regular basis. A journal is often begun with the intention of keeping a record of a significant time or series of events. Like letters, journals are a form of autobiographical or personal writing, but are usually less intimate than a diary and emphasize events rather than emotions.

See page 1137.

See also *AUTOBIOGRAPHY, DIARY, MEMOIR, NONFICTION.*

Juxtaposition The placement of two or more distinct things side by side in order to contrast or compare them. It is commonly used to evoke an emotional response in the reader.

See page 1170.

K

Kabuki A theater created for the common people that arose around 1600, eventually replacing Noh as Japan's most popular dramatic form. A group of female performers originated the style. However, the government viewed Kabuki as excessively provocative and banned women from performing it in 1629. Today, Kabuki, like Noh, exists as an all-male art form. Unlike Noh plays, Kabuki plays are extravagant and unrestrained. They usually have a historical or domestic focus, and feature lower-class heroes who resist oppression by the nobility. Like Noh, Kabuki makes use of dance, music, and stylized gestures. However, Kabuki performers wear no masks and constantly interact with their audience.

See page 736.

See also *NOH.*

L

Legend A traditional story handed down from past generations and believed to be based on historical fact. Legends usually celebrate the heroic qualities of a national or cultural leader. Because legends are the stories of the people, they are often expressions of the values or character of a nation.

See also *EPIC, FABLE, FOLKLORE, HERO, MYTH, ORAL TRADITION.*

Legendary heroes Idealized figures, sometimes based on real people, who embody qualities admired by the cultural group to which they belong. The adventures and accomplishments of these heroes are preserved in legends or tales that are handed down from generation to generation. Achilles is a legendary hero.

See also *EPIC HERO, HERO, LEGEND, MYTH.*

Line The basic unit of poetry. A line consists of a word or a row of words. In metered poems, lines are measured by the number of feet they contain.

See also *FOOT, STANZA.*

Lyric poetry Poetry in which the speaker expresses personal thoughts and feelings. Lyric poems are usually short and musical. While the subject of a lyric poem might be an object, a person, or an event, the emphasis of the poem is on the experience of emotion rather than telling a story.

See also *ELEGY, ODE, POETRY, SONNET.*

M

Magic realism A prose fiction style that originated in Europe and is now especially associated with Latin American authors, such as Gabriel García Márquez, Julio Cortázar, and Liliana Heker. In a magic realist work, figures from history, mythology, literature, and dreams may appear and play a part in everyday life. The rules of everyday life itself change: characters may suddenly travel great distances in space or time. Magic realism differs from surrealism in its emphasis on the intrusion of fantastic elements into normal life.

Maxim A short saying that contains a general truth or gives practical advice. Philosophers have often used maxims to share advice, particularly about mortality and behavior, as Lao-tzu does in the *Tao Te Ching.* A maxim is also known as an adage or aphorism.

See pages 512 and 685.

Memoir A type of narrative nonfiction that presents the story of a period in the author's life and is usually written from the first-person point of view. A memoir often emphasizes the author's thoughts and feelings, his or her relationships with other people, or the impact of significant historical events on his or her life. Isak Dinesen's *Out of Africa* is a memoir.

See page 1064.

See also *AUTOBIOGRAPHY, DIARY, JOURNAL.*

Metaphor A figure of speech that makes a comparison between two seemingly unlike things without using the words *as* or *like*. An extended metaphor compares two unlike things point by point throughout a paragraph, a stanza, or an entire piece of writing.

See pages 767 and 1165.

See also *FIGURES OF SPEECH, SIMILE.*

Meter or **Metrical structure** A regular pattern of stressed and unstressed syllables that gives a line of poetry a predictable rhythm. The unit of meter within the line is the foot. A particular meter is named for the type of foot and the number of feet per line.

See page 803.

See also *FOOT, RHYTHM.*

Metonymy A figure of speech in which a word or phrase is substituted for another thing that is related. For example, the executive branch of the British government is often referred to as "Downing Street," where the prime minister lives in London.

See also *SYNECHDOCHE.*

Modernism A literary style developed in the late nineteenth century that reflected a break with existing tradition. In addition to technical experimentation, Modernist authors and artists in the first half of the twentieth century were interested in the irrational or inexplicable, as well as in the workings of the unconscious mind. Liliana Heker's "Bishop Berkeley or Mariana of the Universe" displays Modernist characteristics.

Monologue A long speech or written expression of thoughts by a character in a literary work.

Mood The overall feeling or emotional quality that a work of literature creates for readers. An author's choice of language, subject matter, setting, diction, and tone, as well as sound devices such as rhyme, rhythm, and meter, can help create mood. Mood is a broader term than tone, which refers specifically to the attitude of the speaker or narrator. It also differs from atmosphere, which is concerned mainly with the physical qualities that contribute to mood, such as time, place, and weather.

See page 713.

See also *ATMOSPHERE, TONE.*

Moral A practical lesson about right and wrong conduct, often found in an instructive story such as a fable or parable. "The Lion-Makers" from the *Panchatantra* has a moral at the end.

See page 596.

See also *FABLE.*

Motif A significant word, phrase, character, image, metaphor, idea, or other element that recurs throughout a work or several works of literature and is related to the theme.

See page 1132.

Motivation The reason or reasons behind a character's actions. A character's motivation may be stated directly, or the reader may have to infer motivation from details in the story. Characters are often motivated by a combination of factors that can include external circumstances, internal morals, or emotional impulses.

See page 93.

Myth A traditional story that explains some aspect of human life or the natural world. Myths reflect the religious beliefs of a particular people. They often depict the actions of gods or heroes. Ovid's *Metamorphoses* retells a number of Greek and Roman myths. Creation myths explain the origin of the world and its inhabitants.

See page 1121.

See also *FOLKLORE, FOLKTALE, LEGEND, ORAL TRADITION.*

N

Narrative Any writing or speech that tells a story. Narratives may be fiction or nonfiction, prose or poetry. Driven by a conflict or problem, a narrative unfolds event by event and leads to a resolution. The story is narrated, or told, by a narrator and can take the form of a novel, an essay, a poem, or a short story.

See also *AUTOBIOGRAPHY, BIOGRAPHY, ESSAY, MEMOIR.*

Narrative poetry Verse that tells a story. Narrative poems are usually contrasted with lyric poems. Ballads, epics, and romances are all types of narrative poetry. Ovid's "The Story of Pyramus and Thisbe" is an example of a narrative poem. Epics, such as Homer's *Iliad* and Virgil's *Aeneid,* are long narrative poems that recount the deeds of an epic hero.

See page 369.

See also *EPIC, LYRIC POETRY, NARRATIVE.*

Narrator The character who tells a story. The narrator may be a character in the story, as in "A Walk to the Jetty" by Jamaica Kincaid, or outside the story, as in "The Night Face Up" by Julio Cortázar. Narrators are not always truthful; a narrator in a work of literature may be reliable or unreliable. Some unreliable narrators intentionally mislead readers. Others fail to understand the true meaning of the events they describe. Most stories with unreliable narrators are written in the first person.

See pages 637 and 1191.

See also *NARRATIVE, POINT OF VIEW, SPEAKER.*

Noh A highly stylized form of Japanese drama that originated in the Middle Ages, growing out of Zen Buddhist religious festivals. The traditional theater of the nobility, Noh developed its permanent form in the fourteenth century. It retains a strong spiritual element, using powerful gestures and meditative silences to tell stories. A Noh play (also spelled *No*) usually tells the tale of a restless ghost and typically has only three or four roles, all performed by men. The stage is small and bare. The actors, in contrast, wear elaborate costumes and masks. Throughout the play, a chorus echoes the words of the main characters, who dance and gesture to the music of a flute player and drummers. Most action in a Noh play is symbolic. For example, a character may take only a few steps to indicate that he is on a long journey.

See page 736.

See also *CHORUS, KABUKI.*

Nonfiction Literature about real people, places, and events. The broadest category of literature, nonfiction includes autobiographies, biographies, journals, memoirs, diaries, essays, letters, speeches, travelogues, news articles, reports, and many other types of writing.

Novel A long fictional prose narrative containing a plot, or ordered sequence of events that takes place in a specific setting and is concerned with character development and statement of theme, or message. Miguel de Cervantes's *Don Quixote* is generally considered the first modern novel in European literature.

O

Ode A lengthy lyric poem with an elevated style and an exalted or enthusiastic tone. Some odes follow the form's original intent of glorifying a public figure or commemorating an important event, but the Roman poet Horace developed an ode that was more personal and meditative. Odes are traditionally written in three stanzas and include rhyme.

See page 364.

See also *LYRIC POETRY.*

Onomatopoeia The use of a word or phrase that imitates or suggests the sound of what it describes, for example *hiss, swoosh,* or *crackle.*

See also *SOUND DEVICES.*

Oral tradition The passing of literature by word of mouth from one generation to the next. Oral literature was a way of recording the past, glorifying leaders, and teaching morals and traditions to young people. Literature in most of the world began in this way. In West Africa the *griot*—or professional storyteller—committed stories and family histories to memory and recited verses to music, acting out dramatic parts.

See also *EPIC, FABLE, FOLKLORE, FOLKTALE.*

Oratory The art of effective public speaking, or the use of persuasive skills when speaking. Oratory is common in politics, law, and religion. Today, oratory is usually called "public speaking."

Oxymoron A term made of two words that contradict each other, for example, *jumbo shrimp.*

P

Parable A simple story that teaches a moral or religious lesson. It differs from a fable in that the characters are people instead of animals. The New Testament of the Bible contains many of Jesus' parables.

See pages 487 and 731.

See also *FABLE.*

Paradox A situation or statement that appears to be contradictory but is actually true, either in fact or in a figurative sense. For example, one of Catullus's poems contains this paradox:

> I couldn't like you if you were the best of women,
>
> or stop loving you, no matter what you do.

See page 559.

Parallelism The use of a series of words, phrases, or lines that have similar grammatical form. Authors employ this technique to emphasize an idea or emotion, to create a sense of unity or balance in a literary work, or for musical effect. Lao-tzu uses parallelism in the following lines from the *Tao Te Ching:*

> There is a time for being ahead,
>
> a time for being behind;
>
> a time for being in motion,
>
> a time for being at rest;

See pages 477 and 690.

Parody The humorous imitation of a particular writing style or literary work, often intended as a criticism but sometimes done simply for humor. *Don Quixote* is a parody of chivalry and stories about knight-errantry.

See page 936.

See also *HUMOR, SARCASM, SATIRE, WIT.*

Persona The character created by the author to tell the story. Whether the story is told by an omniscient narrator or by one of the characters, the author of the work often adopts a persona—a personality different from his or her real one. The attitudes and beliefs of the persona may differ from those of the author.

See also *NARRATOR, POINT OF VIEW, SPEAKER, VOICE.*

Personification A figure of speech in which human qualities are attributed to an animal. Poets use this device to highlight an idea or to create striking descriptions. In "Two Countries," José Martí uses personification to describe Cuba:

> . . . Cuba,
>
> With long veils and holding a carnation,
>
> Appears as a sad and silent widow.

See pages 134 and 517.

Persuasion Writing, usually nonfiction, which attempts to convince readers to think or act in a certain way. Philosophical essays sometimes appeal to the reader's intellect through logic and evidence and—as in Confucius's *Analects*—sometimes by giving rules and examples. Political speeches and advertisements may rely more on emotional appeals.

See page 1057.

See also *ARGUMENT, RHETORICAL DEVICES.*

Petrarchan sonnet A sonnet, also called an Italian sonnet, divided into a group of eight lines, called the octave, and a group of six lines, called the sestet. The rhyme scheme of the octave is *abba, abba.* The sestet may follow a number of different rhyme schemes. Among the most common patterns are *cde cde, cde dcd,* and *cdc dee.* The octave usually presents a single theme, or main idea, and the sestet expands, contradicts, or develops it.

See page 920.

See also *SONNET.*

Plot The sequence of events in a narrative work. Most plots develop around a conflict, a struggle between opposing forces. Exposition introduces the story's characters, setting, and conflict. Rising action develops the conflict with complications. The climax is the emotional high point of the story. Falling action shows what happens after the climax. The resolution shows how the conflict is resolved.

See pages 84 and 1200.

Poetry A form of literary expression that differs from prose in emphasizing the line, rather than the sentence, as the unit of composition. The traditional characteristics of poetry include emotional, imaginative language; employment of figures of speech; division into stanzas; and the use of rhyme and regular meter.

See also *FIGURATIVE LANGUAGE, PROSE, RHYME, STANZA.*

Point of view The perspective from which a story is told. In a story with first-person point of view, the narrator is a character in the story and uses the words *I* and *me* to tell the story, as in Jamaica Kincaid's "A Walk to the Jetty." In a story with third-person point of view, the narrator is someone who stands outside the story and describes the characters and action. In a story with third-person limited point of view, the narrator reveals the thoughts, feelings, and observations of only one character, to referred to in the third person. Julio Cortázar's "The Night Face Up" is told from a third-person limited point of view. In a story with third-person omniscient point of view, the narrator knows everything that goes on—including the thoughts and feelings of every character, as in Rosario Castellanos's story, "The Luck of Teodoro Méndez Acúbal."

See pages 497 and 1231.

See also *NARRATOR, PERSONA, SPEAKER.*

Postmodernism A broad contemporary movement in art, music, film, literature, and other cultural areas that is viewed as growing out of or replacing Modernism. Many of the characteristic features of Postmodernist literature extend or exaggerate tendencies of Modernism. For example, Modernist writers turned away from the apparent objectivity of Realism; Postmodernists go further, introducing a frankly artificial, self-conscious playfulness into their works.

See also *MODERNISM.*

Propaganda Written or spoken material designed to bring about a change or damage a cause through the use of emotionally charged words, name-calling, or other techniques.

Props A theater term (a shortened form of *properties*) for the objects and elements of the scenery used in a stage play, movie, or television show.

See also *DRAMA, STAGE DIRECTIONS.*

Prose Literature that is written in sentences and paragraphs (as distinguished from poetry, which is arranged in lines and stanzas). Essays, short stories, novels, magazine articles, and most plays are examples of prose.

Prose poem A short prose composition that uses rhythm, imagery, and other poetic devices to express an idea or emotion. Unlike metrical and free verse, prose poetry does not have line breaks; instead, the sentences appear in standard paragraph form. A prose poem allows the writer to express a poetic idea without following the usual rules of poetic form. "Fishing" by Joy Harjo is a prose poem.

See page 1073.

See also *POETRY, PROSE.*

Protagonist The central character in a literary work around whom the main conflict revolves. Generally, the reader or audience is meant to sympathize with the protagonist. Brille is the protagonist of Bessie Head's "The Prisoner Who Wore Glasses."

See page 820.

See also *ANTAGONIST, CHARACTER, CONFLICT, HERO, TRAGEDY*

R

Realism A literary movement of late-nineteenth- and early-twentieth-century authors that sought to re-create the texture of everyday life and address the problems of ordinary people. The Realists sought to depict life objectively as it is really lived, without sentimentality or idealization; they usually focused on the problems of middle- and lower-class people. Their work is often filled with details based on careful observation of everyday life. Anton Chekhov and Leo Tolstoy are considered Realists.

Repetition The recurrence of sounds, words, phrases, lines, or stanzas in a literary work. Authors may use repetition to help unify their work, to create a musical or rhythmic effect, or to emphasize an idea. Rhyme, parallelism, and alliteration are types of repetition. Note the repetition in this passage from Léopold Sédar Senghor's "Night of Sine":

> <u>Listen</u> to its song, <u>listen</u> to our dark blood beat, <u>listen</u>
>
> To the deep pulse of Africa beating in the mist of forgotten villages.

See page 79.

See also *SOUND DEVICES.*

Resolution See *DRAMATIC STRUCTURE, PLOT.*

Rhetorical devices Persuasive techniques used by public speakers and authors of literary works, especially those written to persuade. Rhetorical devices include repetition, parallelism, analogy, logic, and the skillful use of connotation and anecdote. Effective rhetoric often appeals to logic, emotion, morality, or authority. A rhetorical question is a question to which no answer is expected or the answer is obvious.

See also *ANALOGY, ANECDOTE, ARGUMENT, CONNOTATION, PARALLELISM, PERSUASION, REPETITION.*

Rhyme The repetition of sounds in words that appear close to each other in a poem. Words rhyme when their accented vowels and all the letters that follow sound the same. For example, the word *borrow* rhymes with *tomorrow,* and the word *sincere* rhymes with *fear.* Internal rhyme occurs within lines of poetry. End rhyme occurs at the ends of lines. When words sound similar but do not rhyme exactly (like *pain* and *again*), they are called half rhymes or slant rhymes.

See page 973.

See also *RHYME SCHEME.*

Rhyme scheme The pattern of end rhyme, designated by letters. A different letter of the alphabet signals each new rhyme (for example *aabbcc* or *ababcdcd*). Notice the rhyme scheme (*aaba*) in the following lines from Omar Khayyám's *Rubáiyát*:

> Awake! for Morning in the Bowl of <u>Night</u>
>
> Has flung the Stone that puts the Stars to <u>Flight</u>:
>
> And Lo! the Hunter of the East has <u>caught</u>
>
> The Sultán's Turret in a Noose of <u>Light.</u>

See pages 506 and 1022.

See also *FORM, RHYME.*

Rhythm The pattern of beats created by the arrangement of stressed and unstressed syllables in a line, especially in poetry. Rhythm gives poetry a musical quality and can add emphasis to certain words or ideas to help convey meaning. Rhythm can be regular or irregular. Meter is a regular pattern of stressed and unstressed syllables that sets the overall rhythm of certain poems. The basic unit in measuring rhythm is the foot, which usually contains one stressed syllable and one or more unstressed syllables. Free verse, which does not have a regular meter, often follows the rhythm of natural speech.

See page 803.

Romanticism An artistic movement that began in Europe in the 1800s and emphasized imagination, nature, passion, and feeling over intellect and reason. The works of William Wordsworth, Samuel Taylor Coleridge, Lord Byron, and John Keats represent the height of Romantic poetry.

Ruba'i A Persian word meaning "quatrain," or four-line verse.

Run-on line See *ENJAMBMENT.*

S

Sacred Text Writings such as the Tanakh, the Qur'an, or the Rig-Veda that are revered as holy or are closely linked to religion or religious rituals. These texts, which are sometimes called scriptures, are often regarded as divine revelations, directly communicated from God to human beings on a specific occasion.

See page 456.

Sarcasm The use of bitter or caustic language to point out shortcomings or flaws.

See also *IRONY, SATIRE.*

Satire Writing that uses humor to comment on human flaws, ideas, social customs, or institutions in order to change them. The purpose of satire is to persuade, although satires can only be effective if they are also entertaining. In order to get his or her point across, a satirist might use such literary techniques as irony, exaggeration, parody, and understatement. For example, Cervantes's *Don Quixote* satirizes stories that idealize chivalry.

See pages 142 and 961.

Scansion The analysis of the meter of a line of verse. To scan a line of poetry means to note the stressed and unstressed syllables and to divide the line into its feet, or rhythmic units.

See also *FOOT, METER, RHYTHM*

Scene A subdivision of an act in a play.

Sensory details Evocative words or phrases that convey sensory experiences—seeing, hearing, tasting, touching, and smelling. Sensory details make writing come alive by helping readers imagine what is being described.

See also *IMAGERY.*

Setting The time and place in which the events of a literary work occur. The elements of setting may include geographical location, historical period, season of the year, time of day, and the beliefs and customs of a society. Setting can help establish the atmosphere and mood of a story. It can also influence the way characters think and behave.

See pages 108 and 1149.

See also *ATMOSPHERE, HISTORICAL CONTEXT, MOOD.*

Short story A short, fictional prose narrative that generally includes the following major elements: setting, characters, plot, point of view, and theme.

See also *FICTION, NOVEL, PLOT.*

Simile A figure of speech that uses the words *like* or *as* to compare two seemingly unlike things. R.K. Narayan's "Like the Sun" contains the following simile:

> **Truth, Sekhar reflected, is like the sun. I suppose no human being can ever look it straight in the face without blinking or being dazed.**

An epic simile is a long, elaborate comparison that continues for several lines. It is a feature of epic poems, but is found in other poems as well.

See pages 210, 529, and 763.

See also *ANALOGY, FIGURES OF SPEECH, METAPHOR.*

Soliloquy In drama, a long speech by a character who is alone on the stage. A soliloquy reveals the private thoughts and emotions of that character.

Sonnet A fourteen-line lyric poem developed in Italy during the Renaissance. A Shakespearean sonnet, sometimes called an English sonnet, has three quatrains (groups of four lines), which are followed by a rhymed couplet of two lines. The rhyme scheme is as follows: *abab, cdcd, efef, gg.* A Shakespearean sonnet retains the break in thought between octave and sestet, but forcefully states the theme, or sometimes inverts the theme, in the concluding couplet. A Petrarchan sonnet has an eight-line octave and a six-line sestet.

See also *PETRARCHAN SONNET and RHYME SCHEME.*

Sound devices Techniques used to emphasize particular sounds in writing. Authors use sound devices, such as alliteration, consonance, assonance, and onomatopoeia, to underscore the meaning of certain words, enhance the rhythm of a piece, or add a musical quality to the work.

See page 1042.

See also *ALLITERATION, ASSONANCE, CONSONANCE, ONOMATOPOEIA, RHYME, RHYTHM.*

Speaker The voice that communicates with the reader of a poem, similar to the narrator in a work of prose. Sometimes the speaker's voice is that of the poet, but in some poems the speaker has a distinct identity, perhaps of a fictional person or even an inanimate object, so one should never assume that the speaker and the poet are identical. A speaker who is clearly different from the writer, as in Li Po's "The River-Merchant's Wife: A Letter," is called a persona.

See pages 359 and 811.

See also *NARRATOR, PERSONA.*

Stage directions Notes in the text of a play that describe the appearance and movements of the characters, as well as the sets, costumes, and lighting. Stage directions serve primarily as instructions for the cast and crew of a theatrical production, but they also help readers imagine the action of the play.

Stanza A group of lines forming a unit in a poem or song. A stanza in a poem is similar to a paragraph in prose. Typically, stanzas are separated in a poem by a line of space.

See also *LINE.*

Stereotype A generalization about a group of people that is made without regard for individual differences. In literature, this term is often used to describe a conventional or flat character who conforms to an expected, fixed pattern of behavior. Stereotypes are used to make or reflect broad generalizations about a group of people.

See also *STOCK CHARACTER.*

Stock character A character who represents a type that is recognizable as belonging to a particular genre. For example, cruel stepmothers or charming princes are often found in fairy tales. Valiant knights and heroes are found in legends and myths. The hard-boiled detective is found in detective stories. Stock characters have conventional traits and mannerisms shared by all members of their type.

See also *ARCHETYPE, CHARACTER, STEREOTYPE.*

Structure The particular order or pattern an author uses to present ideas. Narratives commonly follow a chronological order, while the structure of persuasive or expository writing may vary. Listing detailed information, using cause and effect, or describing a problem and offering a solution are some other ways an author can structure a text. Poetic structure—more commonly known as form—refers to the organization of words, lines, and images as well as ideas.

See page 984.

See also *FORM, PLOT.*

Style The expressive qualities that distinguish an author's work, including word choice and the length and arrangement of sentences, as well as the use of figurative language and imagery. Style can reveal an author's attitude and purpose in writing.

See page 1221.

See also *AUTHOR'S PURPOSE, FIGURATIVE LANGUAGE, IMAGERY, TONE.*

Subject The topic of a literary work.

Surprise ending An unexpected plot twist at the end of a story. The ending might surprise readers because the author provides ambiguous clues or withholds important information. A surprise ending is most effective when it adds to the meaning of a story rather than merely overturns the reader's expectation.

Surrealism A literary and artistic style that originated in Europe in the 1920s. Typically, surrealist works feature ordinary people and objects brought together in strange and unexpected ways, or bizarre and impossible events treated as if they were normal, as in Naguib Mahfouz's "Half a Day." Surrealism differs from magic realism in its emphasis on what surrealists see as the strangeness in everyday life.

Suspense The tension or excitement that a reader feels about what will happen next in a story. Authors often create suspense by raising questions in the reader's mind about the outcome of a plot. Suspense is especially important in the plot of an adventure or mystery story.

See page 887.

See also *FORESHADOWING.*

Symbol A person, place, or thing that exists on a literal level but represents something else on a figurative level. Some literary symbols have meanings that are widely understood. A rushing river, for example, often symbolizes the passing of time, just as sunrise often symbolizes rebirth or hope. In "Fishing," Joy Harjo uses fishing as a symbol for the struggle of the universe.

See pages 533 and 791.

Symbolist poetry A kind of poetry that emphasizes suggestion and inward experience instead of explicit description. Symbolist poets such as Arthur Rimbaud, Paul Verlaine, and Stéphane Mallarmé influenced twentieth-century authors such as T.S. Eliot and Ezra Pound.

See also *MODERNISM.*

Synecdoche A figure of speech in which a part is used for the whole or a whole is used for a part. In this line from the book of Revelation in the Bible, "All nations, and kindreds, and people, and tongues," *tongues* (a part) is used for the whole (languages).

See also *FIGURATIVE LANGUAGE, METONYMY.*

T

Tanka An unrhymed Japanese verse form that consists of five lines. The first and third lines have five syllables each; the other lines have seven syllables each.

See also *HAIKU.*

Theater of the Absurd Drama that does not tell a story but instead presents a series of scenes in which the characters, confused and anxious, seem to exist in a meaningless world. The movement, spearheaded by Thomas Beckett, flourished in the 1950s and 1960s.

See also *DRAMA.*

Theme The main idea or message about life that a poem, story, novel, or play conveys. All the details of a literary work point to the theme, which is usually an insight into human experience. Sometimes a theme is directly stated, either by a narrator or by another character. More often, a theme is implied or suggested. The reader must figure out the theme from the work's details. Themes and subjects are different. The subject of a work might be love; the theme would be what the author says about love— for example, love is cruel, love is wonderful, or love is fleeting. Many literary works have more than one theme.

See pages 471 and 927.

See also *AUTHOR'S PURPOSE, MORAL.*

Thesis The main idea of an essay or other work of nonfiction. The thesis may be implied but is usually stated directly.

See also *ESSAY, NONFICTION.*

Tone The attitude that an author takes toward the audience, a subject, or a character. Tone is conveyed through elements such as word choice, punctuation, sentence structure, and figures of speech. An author's tone may convey a variety of attitudes, such as sympathy, seriousness, irony, sadness, bitterness, or humor.

See pages 25, 695, and 1015.

See also *ATMOSPHERE, AUTHOR'S PURPOSE, DICTION, MOOD, NARRATOR, SPEAKER, STYLE, VOICE.*

Tragedy A play in which the main character, or tragic hero, is brought to ruin or suffers a great sorrow as a result of a fatal character flaw, errors in judgment, or forces beyond human control, such as fate. Traditionally, the tragic hero is a person of high rank who, out of an exaggerated sense of power and pride, violates a human, natural, or divine law. By breaking the law, the hero poses a threat to society and causes the suffering or death of family members, friends, and associates. In the last act of a traditional Greek tragedy, these wrongs are set right when the tragic hero is punished or dies and order is restored. According to the Greek philosopher Aristotle, the purpose of tragedy is to arouse pity (through identification with the main character) and fear (through dread at the possibility of sharing the main character's tragic flaw) in the audience as the tragic hero's terrible fate unfolds. Oedipus is the tragic hero of Sophocles' *Oedipus the King.*

See page 274.

See also *DRAMA.*

Tragic hero See *TRAGEDY.*

Trickster figures Characters that represent that part of human nature that wants to break rules and cause trouble. Tricksters try to outwit people, animals, and even gods. Although they are generally self-centered, we may admire them for their cunning and ability to overcome obstacles. Trickster figures are most commonly depicted in animal form. Almost every folklore tradition has its own trickster figures, such as West Africa's Anansi.

See also *ANTHROPOMORPHISM, ARCHETYPES, FOLKLORE.*

Turning point See *DRAMATIC STRUCTURE.*

U

Understatement Language that emphasizes the importance of something by treating it as unimportant.

See also *HYPERBOLE.*

Unreliable narrator See *NARRATOR.*

V

Vernacular Ordinary speech of a particular country or region. Vernacular is more casual than cultivated, formal speech. Slang, dialect, and idiom are commonly included as part of vernacular. Authors often employ vernacular to enhance the realism of their narrative or dialogue.

See also *DIALECT, IDIOM.*

Voice The distinctive use of language that conveys the author's or narrator's personality to the reader. Voice is determined by elements of style such as word choice and tone.

See page 1287.

See also *DICTION, NARRATOR, PERSONA, SPEAKER, STYLE, TONE.*

Verse paragraph A group of lines in a poem that form a unit. Unlike a stanza, a verse paragraph does not have a fixed number of lines. Many contemporary poems are made up of verse paragraphs. Verse paragraphs help to organize a poem into thoughts, as paragraphs help to organize prose.

See also *FREE VERSE, PROSE POEM, STANZA.*

Wit A type of humor that relies on cleverness, especially on innovative observation and deft wordplay.

See also *COMEDY, HUMOR, PARODY, SARCASM, SATIRE.*

Word choice See *DICTION.*

 # Reading and Thinking with Foldables®
by Dinah Zike, M.Ed., Creator of Foldables®

Using Foldables® Makes Learning Easy and Enjoyable

Anyone who has paper, scissors, and maybe a stapler or some glue can use Foldables in the classroom. Just follow the illustrated step-by-step directions. Check out the following samples:

 **Reading Objective:** to understand how one character's actions affect other characters in a short story

Use this Foldable to keep track of what the main character does and how his or her actions affect the other characters.

 **Step ❶** Place a sheet of paper in front of you so that the short side is at the top. Fold the paper in half from top to bottom.

 **Step ❷** Fold in half again, from side to side, to divide the paper into two columns. Unfold the paper so that the two columns show.

 **Step ❸** Draw a line along the column crease. Then, through the top layer of paper, cut along the line you drew, forming two tabs.

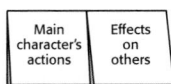 **Step ❹** Label the tabs *Main character's actions* and *Effects on others.*

Step ❺ As you read, record the main character's actions under the first tab. Record how each of those actions affects other characters under the second tab.

 Short Story

Reading Objective: to analyze a short story on the basis of its literary elements

As you read, use the following Foldable to keep track of five literary elements in the short story.

 Step ❶ Stack three sheets of paper with their top edges about a half-inch apart. Be sure to keep the side edges straight.

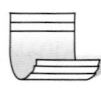 **Step ❷** Fold up the bottom edges of the paper to form six tabs, five of which will be the same size.

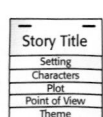 **Step ❸** Crease the paper to hold the tabs in place and staple the sheets together along the crease.

Step ❹ Turn the sheets so that the stapled side is at the top. Write the title of the story on the top tab. Label the five remaining tabs *Setting, Characters, Plot, Point of View,* and *Theme.*

Step ❺ Use your Foldable as you read the short story. Under each labeled tab, jot down notes about the story in terms of that element.

You may adapt this simple Foldable in several ways.

• Use it with dramas, longer works of fiction, and some narrative poems—wherever five literary elements are present in the story.

• Change the labels to focus on something different. For example, if a story or a play has several settings, characters, acts, or scenes, you could devote a tab to each one.

 **Drama**

Reading Objective: to understand conflict and plot in a drama

As you read the drama, use the following Foldable to keep track of conflicts that arise and ways that those conflicts are resolved.

 Step ❶ Place a sheet of paper in front of you so that the short side is at the top. Fold the paper in half from side to side.

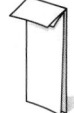 **Step ❷** Fold the paper again, one inch from the top as shown here.

 **Step ❸** Unfold the paper and draw lines along all of the folds. This will be your chart.

Step ❹ At the top, label the left column *Conflicts* and the right column *Resolutions*.

Step ❺ As you read, record in the left column the various conflicts that arise in the drama. In the right column, explain how each conflict is resolved by the end of the drama.

You may adapt this simple Foldable in several ways.
- Use it with short stories, longer works of fiction, and many poems—wherever conflicts and their resolutions are important.
- Change the labels to focus on something different. For example, you could record the actions of two characters, or you could record the thoughts and feelings of a character before and after the story's climax.

 **Lyric Poem**

Reading Objective: to interpret the poet's message by understanding the speaker's thoughts and feelings

As you read the poem, use the following Foldable to help you distinguish between what the speaker *says* and what the poet *means*.

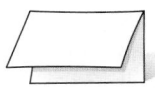 **Step ❶** Place a sheet of paper in front of you so that the short side is at the top. Fold the paper in half from top to bottom.

 **Step ❷** Fold the paper in half again from left to right.

 **Step ❸** Unfold and cut through the top layer of paper along the fold line. This will make two tabs.

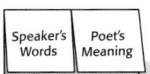 **Step ❹** Label the left tab *Speaker's Words*. Label the right tab *Poet's Meaning*.

Step ❺ Use your Foldable to jot down notes on as you read the poem. Under the left tab, write down key things the speaker says. Under the right tab, write down what you think the poet means by having the speaker say those things.

You may adapt this simple Foldable in several ways.
- Use it to help you visualize the images in a poem. Just replace *Speaker's Words* with *Imagery* and replace *Poet's Meaning* with *What I See.*
- Replace the label *Speaker's Words* with *Speaker's Tone* and under the tab write adjectives that describe the tone of the speaker's words.
- If the poem you are reading has two stanzas, you might devote each tab to notes about one stanza.

Functional Documents

Functional documents are specialized forms of expository writing that serve specifc purposes. Functional documents are an everyday part of business, school, and even home life. They must be clear, concise, accurate, and correct in style and usage.

Letter of Application

A letter of application is a form of business writing. It can be used when applying for a job, an internship, or a scholarship. In most cases, the letter is intended to accompany a résumé or an application. Because detailed information is usually included in the accompanying form, a letter of application should provide a general overview of your qualifications and the reasons you are submitting an application. A letter of application should be concise. You should clearly state which position you are applying for and then explain why you are interested and what makes you qualified. The accompanying material should speak for itself.

❶ The optional subject line indicates the topic of the letter.

❷ In a business letter, the greeting is followed by a colon.

❸ The writer states her purpose directly and immediately.

❹ The writer comments briefly on her qualifications.

❺ The writer makes reference to the accompanying material.

32 South Street
Austin, Texas 78746
May 6, 2009

Melissa Reyes
City Life Magazine
2301 Davis Avenue
Austin, Texas 78764

❶ Re: Internship

❷ Dear Ms. Reyes:

I am a junior at City High School and editor of the City High Herald. I am
❸ writing to apply for your summer internship at City Life magazine. As a journalism student and a longtime fan of your magazine, I feel that an internship with your magazine would provide me with valuable experience in the field of journalism. I believe that my role with the City High Herald has
❹ given me the skills necessary to be a useful contributor to your magazine this summer. In addition, my enclosed application shows that I am also a
❺ diligent worker.

I thank you for considering my application for your summer internship, and I hope to be working with you in the coming months.

Sincerely,
Anne Moris
Anne Moris

Activity

Choose a local business where you might like to work. Write a letter of application for an internship at that business. Assume that you will be submitting this letter along with a résumé or an internship application that details your experience and qualifications.

Résumé

The purpose of a résumé is to provide the employer with a comprehensive record of your background information, related experience, and qualifications. Although a résumé is intended to provide a great deal of information, the format is designed to provide this information in the most efficient way possible.

❶ Jane Wiley
909 West Main Street, Apt. #1
Urbana, Illinois 61802
(217) 555-0489 • jane@internet.edu

Goal
Seeking position in television news production

❷ **Education**
Junior standing in the College of Communications at the University of
    Illinois, Urbana-Champaign
2005 Graduate of City High School

Honors
Member of National Honor Society

Activities
❸ Member, Asian American Association: 2005–Present
Environmental Committee Chairperson, Asian American Association:
    August 2006–May 2007

Work Experience
❹ Radio Reporter, WPGU, 107.1 FM, Champaign, Illinois: May 2007–Present
❺ • Rewrote and read stories for afternoon newscasts
• Served as field reporter for general assignments

Cashier, Del's Restaurant, Champaign, Illinois: May 2006–August 2006
• Responsible for taking phone orders
• Cashier for pickup orders

Assistant Secretary, Office of Dr. George Wright, Woodstock, Illinois:
May 2005–August 2005
• Answered phones
• Made appointments

❶ The header includes all important contact information.

❷ All important education background is included.

❸ Related dates are included for all listed activities.

❹ The job title is included along with the place of employment.

❺ Job responsibilities are briefly listed, with a parallel structure used in each bulleted item.

Activity
Create an outline that lists the information that you would want to include in a résumé. Use a word processor to help format your outline.

Job Application

When applying for a job, you usually need to fill out a job application. When you fill out the application, read the instructions carefully. Examine the entire form before beginning to fill it out. If you fill out the form by hand, make sure that your handwriting is neat and legible. Fill out the form completely, providing all information directly and honestly. If a question does not apply to you, indicate that by writing *n/a,* short for "not applicable." Keep in mind that you will have the opportunity to provide additional information in your résumé, in your letter of application, or during the interview process.

❶ **Please type or print neatly in blue or black ink.**

❷ **Name:** _____ **Today's date:** _____

Address: _____

Phone #: _____ **Birth date:** _____ **Sex:** __ **Soc. Sec. #:** ___

✳✳✳

❸ **Job History** (List each job held, starting with the most recent job.)

1. Employer: _____ Phone #:_____

Dates of employment: _____

Position held: _____

❹ Duties: _____

2. Employer: _____ Phone #:_____

Dates of employment: _____

Position held: _____

Duties: _____

✳✳✳

Education (List the most recent level of education completed.)

_____

_____

✳✳✳

Personal References:

1. Name: _____ Phone #:_____

Relationship: _____

2. Name: _____ Phone #:_____

Relationship: _____

❶ The application provides specific instructions.

❷ All of the information requested should be provided in its entirety.

❸ The information should be provided legibly and succinctly.

❹ Experience should be stated accurately and without embellishment.

Activity

Pick up a job application from a local business or use the sample application shown. Complete the application thoroughly. Fill out the application as if you were actually applying for the job. Be sure to pay close attention to the guidelines mentioned above.

Memos

A memorandum (memo) conveys precise information to another person or a group of people. A memo begins with a leading block. It is followed by the text of the message. A memo does not have a formal closing.

TO: All Employees
FROM: Jordan Tyne, Human Resources Manager
❶ SUBJECT: New Human Resources Assistant Director
DATE: November 3, 2009

❷ Please join me in congratulating Daphne Rudy on her appointment as assistant director in the Human Resources Department. Daphne comes to our company with five years of experience in the field. Daphne begins **❸** work on Monday, November 10. All future general human resource inquiries should be directed to Daphne.

Please welcome Daphne when she arrives next week.

❶ The topic of the memo is stated clearly in the subject line.

❷ The announcement is made in the first sentence.

❸ All of the important information is included briefly in the memo.

Business E-mail

E-mail is quickly becoming the most common form of business communication. While e-mail may be the least formal and most conversational method of business writing, it shouldn't be written carelessly or too casually. The conventions of business writing—clarity, attention to your audience, proper grammar, and the inclusion of relevant information—apply to e-mail.

An accurate subject line should state your purpose briefly and directly. Use concise language and avoid rambling sentences.

To: LiamS@internet.com
From: LisaB@internet.com
CC: EricC@internet.com
Date: January 7, 8:13 a.m.
❶ Subject: New Product Conference Call

Liam,

❷ I just wanted to make sure that arrangements have been made for next week's conference call to discuss our new product. The East Coast sales team has already scheduled three sales meetings at the end of the month with potential buyers, so it's important that our sales team is prepared to talk about the product. Please schedule the call when the manufacturing director **❸** is available, since he will have important information for the sales team.

Lisa

❶ Subject line clearly states the topic.

❷ The purpose is stated immediately and in a conversational tone.

❸ Important details are included in a brief, direct fashion.

Activity
Write an e-mail to your coworkers. Inform them of a change in company procedure that will affect them.

Travel Directions

When planning an event or a social occasion, it is often necessary to provide people with detailed directions to the location. These directions must be clear enough to enable those who are unfamiliar with the surrounding area to easily find their way. Creating a map that shows the route with clearly labeled streets can also be a great help.

Directions to Darien High School's Graduation Ceremony

From I-95 North, take Exit 11. ❶

Turn Left onto Post Road (Route 1).

At the first light, turn Left onto Samuel Avenue. Travel 2.5 miles. ❷

Turn Right onto Cherry Hill Road.

Turn Left onto High School Lane. ❸

Follow signs to Visitor Parking.

❶ Begins at a point from which most people will be coming

❷ Offers travel distances to help travelers locate streets

❸ Gives the name of each street along the route

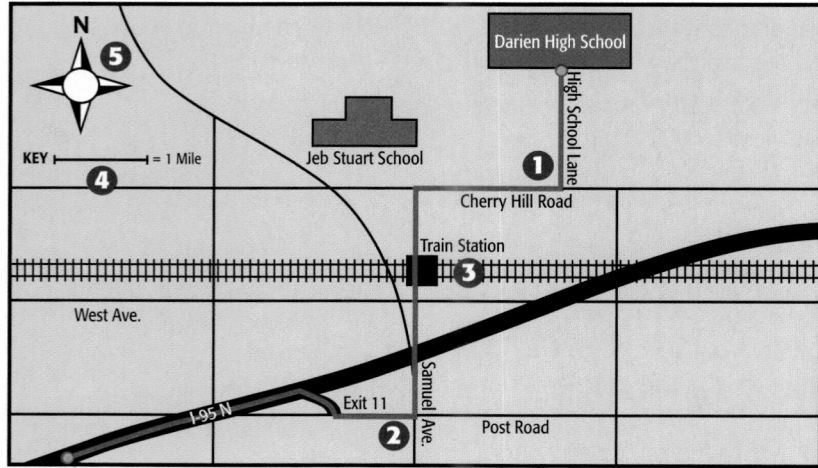

❶ Clearly labels all streets to be traveled

❷ Labels major cross streets so the traveler can keep better track of his or her progress

❸ Includes landmarks to help identify the area

❹ Includes legend to show scale

❺ Includes compass rose to help orient the traveler

Activity

Write directions and draw an accompanying map to a location in your town. Be sure to include enough details and give clear enough directions to enable even someone who is unfamiliar with the area to find the destination.

Technical Writing

Technical writing involves the use of very specific vocabulary and a special attention to detail. The purpose of technical writing is to describe a process clearly enough so that the reader can perform the steps and reach the intended goal, such as installing software, connecting a piece of equipment, or programming a device.

Instructions for Connecting DVD Player to HDTV

❶ Your DVD player can be connected to an HDTV using RCA cables or, for best picture quality, an HDMI cable.

Connecting with RCA Cables:

❷ **Step 1:** Insert the ends of the red, white, and yellow cables into the jacks labeled "AUDIO/VIDEO OUT." Be sure to match the colors of the cable with the colors of the jack.

Step 2: Insert the other ends of the RCA cables into the jacks labeled "AUDIO/VIDEO IN" on your HDTV. These are usually located on the side or the back of the television. Again, be sure to match the colors of the cables with the colors of the jacks.

Connecting with HDMI Cable:

Step 1: Insert one end of the HDMI cable into the HDMI port located on the back of the DVD player.

Step 2: Insert the other end of the HDMI cable into the HDMI port on your HDTV.

❸ **Note:** Your HDTV may have more than one HDMI port. If so, be sure that you set your HDTV to the correct input when viewing.

❶ Uses specific language to clearly describe the process

❷ Lists each step individually

❸ Directs attention to possible variations the reader may encounter

Activity

Choose a device that you own or have access to, such as an MP3 player or a cell phone. Write brief step-by-step directions on how to perform a specific function on the device, so that someone else can follow your instructions and perform the function successfully.

Writing Handbook

Using the Traits of Strong Writing

What are some basic terms you can use to discuss your writing with your teacher or class-mates? What should you focus on as you revise and edit your compositions? Check out the following terms, or traits, that describe the qualities of strong writing. Learn the meaning of each trait and find out how using the traits can improve your writing.

Ideas

The message or the theme and the details that develop it

Writing is clear when readers can grasp the meaning of your ideas right away. Check to see whether you're getting your message across.

- ☑ Does the title suggest the theme of the composition?

- ☑ Does the composition focus on a single narrow topic?

- ☑ Is the thesis—the main point or central idea—clearly stated?

- ☑ Do well-chosen details elaborate your main point?

Organization

The arrangement of main ideas and supporting details

An effective plan of organization points your readers in the right direction and guides them easily through your composition from start to finish. Find a structure, or order, that best suits your topic and writing purpose. Check to see whether you've ordered your key ideas and details in a way that keeps your readers on track.

- ☑ Are the beginning, middle, and end clearly linked?

- ☑ Is the internal order of ideas easy to follow?

- ☑ Does the introduction capture your readers' attention?

- ☑ Do sentences and paragraphs flow from one to the next in a way that makes sense?

- ☑ Does the conclusion wrap up the composition?

Voice

A writer's unique way of using tone and style

Your writing voice comes through when your readers sense that a real person is communicating with them. Readers will respond to the **tone** (or attitude) that you express toward a topic and to the **style** (the way that you use language and shape your sentences). Read your work aloud to see whether your writing voice comes through.

- ☑ Does your writing sound interesting?
- ☑ Does your writing reveal your attitude toward your topic?
- ☑ Does your writing sound like you—or does it sound like you're imitating someone else?

Word Choice

The vocabulary a writer uses to convey meaning

Words work hard. They carry the weight of your meaning, so make sure you choose them carefully. Check to see whether the words you choose are doing their jobs well.

- ☑ Do you use lively verbs to show action?
- ☑ Do you use vivid words to create word pictures in your readers' minds?
- ☑ Do you use precise words to explain your ideas simply and clearly?

Sentence Fluency

The smooth rhythm and flow of sentences that vary in length and style

The best writing is made up of sentences that flow smoothly from one sentence to the next. Writing that is graceful also sounds musical—rhythmical rather than choppy. Check for sentence fluency by reading your writing aloud.

- ☑ Do your sentences vary in length and structure?
- ☑ Do transition words and phrases show connections between ideas and sentences?
- ☑ Does parallelism help balance and unify related ideas?

Conventions

Correct spelling, grammar, usage, and mechanics

A composition free of errors makes a good impression on your readers. Mistakes can be distracting, and they can blur your message. Try working with a partner to spot errors and correct them. Use this checklist to help you.

- ☑ Are all words spelled correctly?
- ☑ Are all proper nouns—as well as the first word of every sentence—capitalized?
- ☑ Is your composition free of sentence fragments?
- ☑ Is your composition free of run-on sentences?
- ☑ Are punctuation marks—such as apostrophes, commas, and end marks—inserted in the right places?

Presenting and Publishing

The formatting of writing for various purposes

For many writers, the writing process is not complete until they present their work to an audience. This can mean submitting your writing for publication in a school paper or a national magazine, or it can simply mean preparing your writing in a neat and presentable format. For readers to fully appreciate your writing, it is very important that you present it neatly, effectively, and according to professional standards.

Format

- The standard typeface setting for most writing submissions is Courier 12 point.

- Double-space your work so that it is easy to read.

- Leave one-inch margins on all sides of every page.

- Italicize titles or when using terms from other languages. You may also italicize words to add emphasis, but do this only when it is necessary to make your point clear. (If you are submitting your writing to a professional publication, underline words that should appear in italics.)

- Most word processing programs make it easy to set the page number to appear in the upper right-hand corner of each page. Include your last name before each page number after the first page.

- If you are including charts, graphs, maps, or other visual aids, consider setting them on their own page. This will allow you to show the graphic at a full size that is easy to read.

Organization

- On a separate sheet of paper, center your name under the title of your work. If you are submitting your writing for publication, include the total number of words in the upper right-hand corner, and your name and address in the upper left-hand corner.

- The body of your work follows immediately.

- End your presentation with your list of works cited.

Research Paper Writing

More than any other types of papers, research papers are the product of a search—a search for data, for facts, for informed opinions, for insights, and for new information.

Selecting a topic

- If a specific topic is not assigned, choose a topic. Begin with the assigned subject or a subject that interests you. Read general sources of information about that subject and narrow your focus to some aspect of it that interests you. Good places to start are encyclopedia articles and the tables of contents of books on the subject. A computerized library catalog will also display many subheads related to general topics. Find out if sufficient information about your topic is available.

- As you read about the topic, develop your paper's central idea, which is the purpose of your research. Even though this idea might change as you do more research, it can begin to guide your efforts. For example, if you were assigned the subject of the Civil War, you might find that you're interested in women's roles during that war. As you read, you might narrow your topic down to women who went to war, women who served as nurses for the Union, or women who took over farms and plantations in the South.

Conducting a broad search for information

- Generate a series of researchable questions about your chosen topic. Then research to find answers to your questions.

- Among the many sources you might use are the card catalog, the computer catalog, the *Readers' Guide to Periodical Literature* (or an electronic equivalent), newspaper indexes, and specialized references such as biographical encyclopedias.

- If possible, use primary sources as well as secondary sources. A **primary source** is a firsthand account of an event—for example, the diary of a woman who served in the army in the Civil War is a primary source. **Secondary sources** are sources written by people who did not experience or influence the event. Locate specific information efficiently by using the table of contents, indexes, chapter headings, and graphic aids.

Developing a working bibliography

If a work seems useful, write a **bibliography card** for it. On an index card, write down the author, title, city of publication, publisher, date of publication, and any other information you will need to identify the source. Number your cards in the upper right-hand corner so you can keep them in order.

Following are model bibliography, or source, cards.

Book

1 Settle, Mary Lee   **2** 6

    3 <u>All the Brave Promises.</u>

    4 Columbia: University of

      South Carolina Press,

5 1995.

6 Evanston Public Library   **7** D810.W754

1 Author   **5** Date of publication
2 Source number   **6** Location of source
3 Title   **7** Library call number
4 City of publication/ Publisher

Periodical

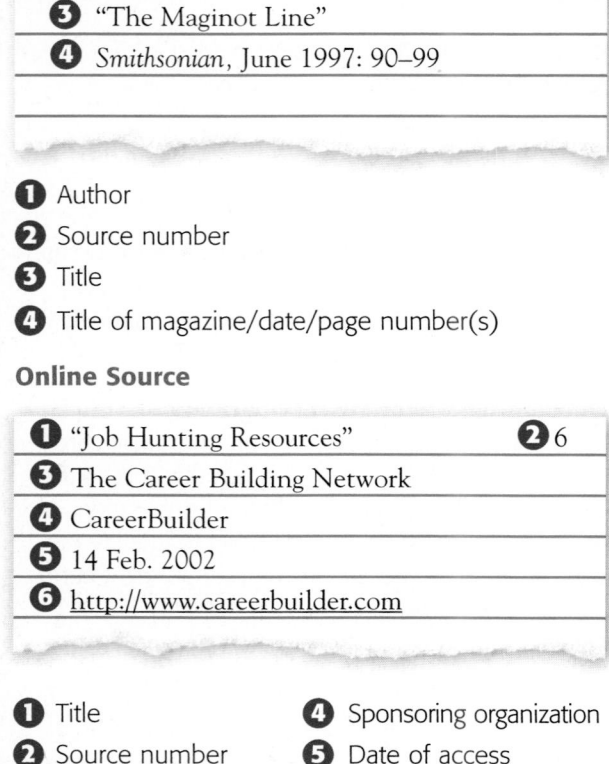

❶ Author

❷ Source number

❸ Title

❹ Title of magazine/date/page number(s)

Online Source

❶ Title   ❹ Sponsoring organization

❷ Source number   ❺ Date of access

❸ Title of database   ❻ URL

Evaluating your sources

Your sources should be **a**uthoritative, **r**eliable, **t**imely, and **s**uitable **(arts)**.

- The source should be **authoritative.** The author should be well-known in the field. An author who has written several books or articles about a subject or who is frequently quoted may be considered an authority. You might also consult *Book Review Index* and *Book Review Digest* to find out how other experts in the field have evaluated a book or an article.

- The source should be **reliable.** If possible, avoid material from popular magazines in favor of that from more scholarly journals. Be especially careful to evaluate material from online sources. For example, the Web site of a well-known university is more reliable than that of an individual. (You might also consult a librarian or your instructor for guidance in selecting reliable online sources.)

- The source should be **timely.** Use the most recent material available, particularly for subjects of current importance. Check the publication date of books as well as the month and year of periodicals.

- The source should be **suitable,** or **appropriate.** Consider only material that is relevant to the purpose of your paper. Do not waste time on books or articles that have little bearing on your topic. If you are writing on a controversial topic, you should include material that represents more than one point of view.

Compiling and organizing note cards

Careful notes will help you to organize the material for your paper.

- As you reread and study sources, write useful information on index cards. Be sure that each note card identifies the source (use the number of the bibliography card that corresponds to each source).

- In the lower right-hand corner of the card, write the page number on which you found the information. If one card contains several notes, write the page number in parentheses after the relevant material.

- Three helpful ways to take notes are paraphrasing, summarizing, and quoting directly.

  1. **Paraphrase** important details that you want to remember; that is, use your own words to restate specific information.
  2. **Summarize** main ideas that an author presents. When you summarize several pages, be sure to note the page on which the material begins and the page on which it ends—for example, 213–221.
  3. **Quote** the exact words of an author only when the actual wording is important. Be careful about placing the author's words in quotation marks.

- Identify the subject of each note card with a short phrase written in the upper left.

See the sample note card below, which includes information about careers and goals from three pages.

Careers and goals	12
Many people "crave work that will spark . . . excitement and energy." (5) Sher recognizes that a career does not necessarily satisfy a person's aim in life. (24) She also offers tips on how to overcome obstacles that people experience in defining their goals. (101)	

- Organize your note cards to develop a **working outline.** Begin by sorting them into piles of related cards. Try putting the piles together in different ways that suggest an organizational pattern. (If, at this point, you discover that you do not have enough information, go back and do further research.) Many methods of organization are possible. You might also combine methods of organization.

Developing a thesis statement

A thesis statement tells what your topic is and what you intend to say about it—for example, "World War II changed the lives of African Americans and contributed to the rise of the civil rights movement."

- Start by examining your central idea.
- Refine it to reflect the information that you gathered in your research.
- Next, consider your approach to the topic. What is the purpose of your research? Are you proving or disproving something? illustrating a cause-and-effect relationship? offering a solution to a problem? examining one aspect of the topic thoroughly? predicting an outcome?
- Revise your central idea to reflect your approach.
- Be prepared to revise your thesis statement if necessary.

Drafting your paper

Consult your working outline and your notes as you start to draft your paper.

- Concentrate on getting your ideas down in a complete and logical order.
- Write an introduction and a conclusion. An effective introduction creates interest, perhaps by beginning with a question or a controversial quotation; it should also contain your thesis statement. An effective conclusion will summarize main points, restate your thesis, explain how the research points to important new questions to explore, and bring closure to the paper.

Avoiding plagiarism

Plagiarism is the act of presenting an author's words or ideas as if they were your own. This is not only illegal, but also unethical. You must credit the source not only for material directly quoted but also for any facts or ideas obtained from the source.

Consider this example:

From the original SparkNotes study guide by Melissa and Stephanie Martin

> Throughout the novel, Twain depicts the society that surrounds Huck as little more than a collection of degraded rules and precepts that defy logic. This faulty logic appears early in the novel, when the new judge in town allows Pap to keep custody of Huck.

Plagiarized usage

> Twain's depiction of society is as a collection of illogical rules and principles. A good example of this is when Pap is awarded custody of Huck.

Simply rewording the original passage is not enough. In order to legally and ethically use the words or ideas of another writer you must credit the writer of the original or rework the original into your own new idea.

Using material without plagiarizing

1. **Quote the original directly and credit the author.**

   As Melissa and Stephanie Martin note in their SparkNotes study guide, Huck lives in a society that is "little more than a collection of degraded rules and precepts that defy logic." They offer the example of Pap being awarded custody of Huck.

2. **Paraphrase the original and credit the author.**

   In their SparkNotes study guide, Melissa and Stephanie Martin note that Twain depicts society as a collection of illogical rules and principles. A good example of this is when Pap is awarded custody of Huck.

3. **Use the information in the original to create your own idea.**

   It is hard to blame Huck for wanting to escape from a world where he is forced to follow arbitrary rules, and where he is forced to live with an abusive father.

Crediting your source is not only fair to the writer of the original source; it is also the law. Plagiarism is a serious offense and can result in failing grades, expulsion, and even legal action.

- In addition to citing books and periodicals from which you take information, cite song lyrics, letters, and excerpts from literature.

- Also credit original ideas that are expressed graphically in tables, charts, and diagrams, as well as the sources of any visual aids you may include, such as photographs.

- You do not need to cite the source of any information that is common knowledge, such as "John F. Kennedy was assassinated in 1963 in Dallas, Texas."

In-text citations The most common method of crediting sources is with parenthetical documentation within the text. Generally a reference to the source and page number is included in parentheses at the end of each quotation, paraphrase, or summary of information borrowed from a source. An in-text citation points readers to a corresponding entry in your **works-cited list**—a list of all your sources, complete with publication information, that will appear as the final page of your paper. The Modern Language Association (MLA) recommends the following guidelines for crediting sources in text. You may wish to refer to the *MLA Handbook for Writers of Research Papers* by Joseph Gibaldi for more information and examples.

- Put in parentheses the author's last name and the page number where you found the information: An art historian has noted, "In Wood's idyllic farmscapes, man lives in complete harmony with Nature; he is the earth's caretaker" (Corn 90).

- If the author's name is mentioned in the sentence, put only the page number in parentheses: Art historian Wanda Corn has noted, "In Wood's idyllic farmscapes, man lives in complete harmony with Nature; he is the earth's caretaker" (90).

- If no author is listed, put the title or a shortened version of the title in parentheses. Include a page number if you have one: Some critics believe that Grant Wood's famous painting *American Gothic* pokes fun at small-town life and traditional American values ("Gothic").

Compiling a list of works cited

At the end of your text, provide an alphabetized list of published works or other sources cited.

- Include complete publishing information for each source.

- For magazine and newspaper articles, include the page numbers. If an article is continued on a different page, use + after the first page number.

- For online sources, include the date accessed.

- Cite only those sources from which you actually use information.

- Arrange entries in alphabetical order according to the author's last name. Write the last name first. If no author is given, alphabetize by title.

- For long entries, indent five spaces every line after the first.

How to cite sources

On the next three pages, you'll find sample style sheets that can help you prepare your list of sources—the final page of the research paper. Use the one your teacher prefers.

MLA Style

MLA style is most often used in English and social studies classes. Center the title *Works Cited* at the top of your list.

Source	Style
Book with one author	Isaacson, Walter. *Einstein: His Life and Universe.* New York: Simon & Schuster, 2007.
Book with two or three authors	Mortenson, Greg, and Relin, David Oliver. *Three Cups of Tea: One Man's Mission to Promote Peace…One School at a Time.* New York: Penguin Books, 2006. [If a book has more than three authors, name only the first author and then write "et al." (Latin abbreviation for "and others").]
Book with editor(s)	Lehman, David, and McHugh, Heather, eds. *The Best American Poetry 2007.* New York: Scribner, 2007.
Book with an organization or a group as author or editor	Adobe Creative Team. *Adobe Photoshop CS3 Classroom in a Book.* Berkeley: Adobe Press, 2007.
Work from an anthology	Kilmer, Joyce. "Trees." *The Poetry Anthology, 1912–2002.* Ed. Joseph Parisi. Chicago: Ivan R. Dee, 2004. 7
Introduction in a published book	Jackson, Peter. Introduction. *The Making of* Star Wars: *The Definitive Story Behind the Original Film.* By J. W. Rinzler. New York: Del Rey, 2007. iii.
Encyclopedia article	"Jazz." *Encyclopedia Britannica.* 15th ed. 2007.
Weekly magazine article	Sacks, Oliver. "A Bolt from the Blue." *The New Yorker.* 23 July 2007: 38–42.
Monthly magazine article	Plotnikoff, David. "Hungry Man." *Saveur.* July 2007: 35–36.
Newspaper article	Long, Ray, and Meitrodt, Jeffrey. "Some Budget Progress Made." *Chicago Tribune.* 26 July 2007: B3. [If no author is named, begin the entry with the title of the article.]
Internet	"Americans Embracing 'Green' Cleaning." *ABC News.* 30 January 2006. ABC News Internet Ventures. 1 August 2007 <http://abcnews.go.com/Technology/Business/story?id=1544322>.
Online magazine article	Parks, Bob. "Robot Buses Pull In to San Diego's Fastest Lane." *Wired Magazine.* 15.08 (July 2007). 25. Oct. 2007 <http://www.wired.com/cars/futuretransport/magazine/15-08/st_robot>.
Radio or TV program	"Jungles." *Planet Earth.* Animal Planet. Discovery Channel. 25 July 2007.
Videotape or DVD	Guggenheim, David, dir. *An Inconvenient Truth.* DVD. Paramount, 2006. [For a videotape (VHS) version, replace "DVD" with "Videocassette."]
Interview	Campeche, Tanya. E-mail interview. 25 Feb. 2004. [If an interview takes place in person, replace "E-mail" with "Personal"; if it takes place on the telephone, use "Telephone."]

CMS Style

CMS style was created by the University of Chicago Press to meet its publishing needs. This style, which is detailed in *The Chicago Manual of Style* (CMS), is used in a number of subject areas. Center the title *Bibliography* at the top of your list.

Source	Style
Book with one author	Isaacson, Walter. *Einstein: His Life and Universe.* New York: Simon & Schuster, 2007.
Book with two or three authors	Mortenson, Greg, and David Oliver Relin. *Three Cups of Tea: One Man's Mission to Promote Peace…One School at a Time.* New York: Penguin Books, 2006. [If a book has more than ten authors, name only the first seven and then write "et al." (Latin abbreviation for "and others").]
Book with editor(s)	Lehman, David, and Heather McHugh, eds. *The Best American Poetry 2007.* New York: Scribner, 2007.
Book with an organization or a group as author or editor	Adobe Creative Team. *Adobe Photoshop CS3 Classroom in a Book.* Berkeley: Adobe Press, 2007.
Work from an anthology	Kilmer, Joyce. "Trees." *The Poetry Anthology, 1912–2002.* Ed. Joseph Parisi, 7. Chicago: Ivan R. Dee, 2004.
Introduction in a published book	Rinzler, J. W. *The Making of* Star Wars: *The Definitive Story Behind the Original Film.* Introduction by Peter Jackson. New York: Del Rey, 2007.
Encyclopedia article	[Credit for encyclopedia articles goes in your text, not in your bibliography.]
Weekly magazine article	Sacks, Oliver. "A Bolt from the Blue." *The New Yorker,* July 23, 2007, 38–42.
Monthly magazine article	Plotnikoff, David. "Hungry Man." *Saveur,* July 2007, 35–36.
Newspaper article	Long, Ray and Jeffrey Meitrodt. "Some Budget Progress Made." *Chicago Tribune.* July 26, 2007, B3. [Credit for unsigned newspaper articles goes in your text, not in your bibliography.]
Internet	ABC News Internet Ventures. "Americans Embracing 'Green' Cleaning." *ABC News,* 2006, http://abcnews.go.com/Technology/Business/story?id=1544322.
Online magazine article	Parks, Bob. "Robot Buses Pull In to San Diego's Fastest Lane." *Wired Magazine.* 15.08 (July 2007). http://www.wired.com/cars/futuretransport/magazine/15-08/st_robot.
Radio or TV program	[Credit for radio and TV programs goes in your text, not in your bibliography.]
Videotape or DVD	Guggenheim, David, dir. *An Inconvenient Truth.* Paramount, 2006. DVD. [For a videotape (VHS) version, replace "DVD" with "Videocassette."]
Interview	[Credit for interviews goes in your text, not in your bibliography.]

APA Style

The American Psychological Association (APA) style is commonly used in the sciences. Center the title *References* at the top of your list.

Source	Style
Book with one author	Isaacson, Walter. (2007). *Einstein: His life and universe.* New York: Simon & Schuster.
Book with two or three authors	Mortenson, Greg and Relin, David Oliver. *Three cups of tea: One man's mission to promote peace...One school at a time.* New York: Penguin Books, 2006. [If a book has more than ten authors, name only the first seven and then write "et al." (Latin abbreviation for "and others").]
Book with editor(s)	Lehman, David and McHugh, Heather. (Eds.). (2007). *The best American poetry 2007.* New York: Scribner.
Book with an organization or a group as author or editor	Adobe Creative Team. (2007). *Adobe Photoshop CS3 Classroom in a Book.* Berkeley: Adobe Press.
Work from an anthology	Kilmer, Joyce. "Trees." *The Poetry Anthology, 1912–2002.* Ed. Joseph Parisi, 7. Chicago: Ivan R. Dee, 2004.
Introduction in a published book	[Credit for introductions goes in your text, not in your references.]
Encyclopedia article	Jazz. (2007). In *Encyclopedia Britannica.* (Vol. 6, pp. 519). Chicago: Encyclopedia Britannica.
Weekly magazine article	Sacks, Oliver. (2007, July 23). A bolt from the blue. *The New Yorker,* 38–42.
Monthly magazine article	Plotnikoff, David. (2007, July). Hungry man. *Saveur,* 103, 35–36.
Newspaper article	Long, Ray and Meitrodt, Jeffrey. (2007, July 26). Some budget progress made. *Chicago Tribune,* p. B3. [If no author is named, begin the entry with the title of the article.]
Internet	ABC News Internet Ventures. (2006, January 30). *ABC News.* "Americans Embracing 'Green' Cleaning." Retrieved August 1, 2007, from http://abcnews.go.com/Technology/Business/story?id=1544322.
Online magazine article	Parks, Bob. (2007, July). Robot buses pull in to San Diego's fastest lane." *Wired Magazine.* 15.08. Retreived July 25, 2007, from http://www.wired.com/cars/futuretransport/magazine/15-08/st_robot.
Radio or TV program	Jungles. (2007, July 25). *Planet Earth* [Television series episode]. Animal Planet. Silver Spring, MD: Discovery Channel.
Videotape or DVD	Guggenheim, David (Director). (2006). *An inconvenient truth.* DVD. Paramount, 2006. [For a videotape (VHS) version, replace "DVD" with "Videocassette."]
Interview	[Credit for interviews goes in your text, not in your bibliography.]

Reading Handbook

Reading Handbook

Being an active reader is a crucial part of being a lifelong learner. It is also an ongoing task. Good reading skills are recursive; that is, they build on each other, providing the tools you'll need to understand text, to interpret ideas and themes, and to read critically.

Understanding Text Structure

To follow the logic and message of a selection and to remember it, analyze the **text structure,** or organization of ideas, within a writer's work. Recognizing the pattern of organization can help you discover the writer's purpose and will focus your attention on important ideas in the selection. **Look for signal words** to point you to the structure.

- **Spatial sequence** uses words or phrases such as *nearby, to the left, above,* and *behind* to show the physical arrangement of people and objects in an area.

- **Order of importance** will use words such as *most important* and *least necessary* to compare the importance of things or ideas.

- **Chronological order** often uses such words as *first, then, after, later,* and *finally* to show a sequence of events in time.

- **Cause-and-effect order** discusses chains of events using words or phrases such as *therefore, because, subsequently,* or *as a result.*

- **Comparison-contrast order** may use words or phrases such as *similarly, in contrast, likewise,* or *on the other hand.*

- **Problem-solution order** presents a problem and then offers one or more solutions. A problem-solution structure may incorporate other structures such as order of importance, chronological order, or comparison-contrast order.

Comprehension Strategies

Because understanding is the most critical reading task, lifelong learners use a wide variety of reading strategies before, during, and after reading to ensure their comprehension.

Determining the Main Idea

The **main idea** of a selection is the writer's purpose in writing the selection. As you read, it will be helpful to determine the main idea not only of the entire piece, but also of each paragraph. After identifying the important details in each paragraph, pause and ask yourself

- What is the main point of this selection?

- What do these details add up to?

- What is the writer trying to communicate?

Summarizing

A summary is a short restatement of the main ideas and important details of a selection. Summarizing what you have read is an excellent tool for understanding and remembering a passage. To summarize a selection:

- Identify the **main ideas.**

- Determine the essential **supporting details.**

- Relate all the main ideas and essential details in a **logical sequence.**

- **Paraphrase**—that is, restate the selection in your own words.

- Answer **who, what, where, when,** and **why** questions.

The best summaries can easily be understood by someone who has not read the selection. If you're not sure whether an idea is a main idea or a supporting detail, try taking it out of your summary. Does your summary still sound complete?

Distinguishing between fact and opinion

It is always important to be able to tell whether the ideas in a selection are facts or the writer's opinions.

- **Facts** can be proven or measured; you can verify them in reference materials. Sometimes you can observe or test them yourself.

  Example: Chicago is about 800 miles from New York City.

- **Opinions** are often open to interpretation and contain phrases such as "I believe" or "from my point of view."

  Example: Chicago to New York is too far to drive.

As you read a selection, evaluate any facts as well as any opinions you find. Ask yourself:

- Are the facts relevant? Are they actually true?
- Are the opinions well informed and based on verifiable facts? Are they persuasive?

Drawing inferences and supporting them

An **inference** involves using your reason and experience to come up with an idea based on what a writer implies or suggests but does not directly state.

- **Drawing a conclusion** is making a general statement you can explain with reason or with supporting details from the text.
- **Making a generalization** is generating a statement that can apply to more than one item or group.

What is most important when inferring is to be sure that you have accurately based your thoughts on supporting details from the text as well as on your own knowledge.

Making a prediction

A **prediction** is an educated guess as to what a text will be about, based on initial clues a writer provides. You can also make predictions about what will happen next in a story as you read.

- Take breaks during your reading and **ask yourself questions** about what will happen next, such as, "How will this character react to this news?"
- **Answer these questions for yourself,** supporting your answers with evidence from the text. For example, "Sam will be jealous when he hears the news, because he is in love with Antonia."
- As you continue reading, **verify** your predictions.

Reading silently for sustained periods

When you read for long periods of time, your task is to avoid distractions. Check your comprehension regularly by summarizing what you've read so far. Using study guides or graphic organizers can help you get through difficult passages. Take regular breaks when you need them and vary your reading rate with the demands of the task.

Keep in mind:

Whichever strategies you choose to use while reading, it will always be helpful to:

- Read slowly and carefully.
- Reread difficult passages.
- Take careful notes.

Also, when reading more difficult material, consider these steps to modify or change your reading strategies when you don't understand what you've read.

- Reread the passage.
- Consult other sources, including text resources, teachers, and other students.
- Write comments or questions on another piece of paper for later review or discussion.

Language Handbook

Grammar Glossary

This glossary will help you quickly locate information on parts of speech and sentence structure.

A

Absolute phrase. *See* Phrase.

Abstract noun. *See* Noun chart.

Action verb. *See* Verb.

Active voice. *See* Voice.

Adjective A word that modifies a noun or pronoun by limiting its meaning. Adjectives appear in various positions in a sentence. (The *gray* cat purred. The cat is *gray*.)

Many adjectives have different forms to indicate degree of comparison. (short, shorter, shortest)

The positive degree is the simple form of the adjective. (easy, interesting, good)

The comparative degree compares two persons, places, things, or ideas. (easier, more interesting, better)

The superlative degree compares more than two persons, places, things, or ideas. (easiest, most interesting, best)

A predicate adjective follows a linking verb and further identifies or describes the subject. (The child is happy.)

A proper adjective is formed from a proper noun and begins with a capital letter. Many proper adjectives are created by adding these suffixes: *-an, -ian, -n, -ese,* and *-ish.* (Chinese, African)

Adjective clause. *See* Clause chart.

Adverb A word that modifies a verb, an adjective, or another adverb by making its meaning more specific. When modifying a verb, an adverb may appear in various positions in a sentence. (Cats *generally* eat less than dogs. *Generally,* cats eat less than dogs.) When modifying an adjective or another adverb, an adverb appears directly before the modified word. (I was *quite* pleased that they got along so well.) The word *not* and the contraction

-n't are adverbs. (Mike *wasn't* ready for the test today.) Certain adverbs of time, place, and degree also have a negative meaning. (He's *never* ready.)

Some adverbs have different forms to indicate degree of comparison. (soon, sooner, soonest)

The comparative degree compares two actions. (better, more quickly)

The superlative degree compares three or more actions. (fastest, most patiently, least rapidly)

Adverb clause. *See* Clause chart.

Antecedent. *See* Pronoun.

Appositive A noun or a pronoun that further identifies another noun or pronoun. (My friend *Julie* lives next door.)

Appositive phrase. *See* Phrase.

Article The adjective *a, an,* or *the.*

Indefinite articles (*a* and *an*) refer to one of a general group of persons, places, or things. (I eat *an* apple *a* day.)

The definite article (**the**) indicates that the noun is a specific person, place, or thing. (*The* alarm woke me up.)

Auxiliary verb. *See* Verb.

B

Base form. *See* Verb tense.

C

Clause A group of words that has a subject and a predicate and that is used as part of a sentence. Clauses fall into two categories: *main clauses,* which are also called *independent clauses,* and *subordinate clauses,* which are also called *dependent clauses.*

A main clause can stand alone as a sentence.

Types of Subordinate Clauses			
Clause	**Function**	**Example**	**Begins with . . .**
Adjective clause	Modifies a noun or a pronoun	Songs *that have a strong beat* make me want to dance.	A relative pronoun such as *which, who, whom, whose,* or *that*
Adverb clause	Modifies a verb, an adjective, or an adverb	*Whenever Al calls me,* he asks to borrow my bike.	A subordinating conjunction such as *after, although, because, if, since, when,* or *where*
Noun clause	Serves as a subject, an object, or a predicate nominative	*What Philip did* surprised us.	A word such as *how, that, what, whatever, when, where, which, who, whom, whoever, whose,* or *why*

There must be at least one main clause in every sentence. (*The rooster crowed,* and *the dog barked.*)

A subordinate clause cannot stand alone as a sentence. A subordinate clause needs a main clause to complete its meaning. Many subordinate clauses begin with subordinating conjunctions or relative pronouns. (**When Geri sang her solo,** the audience became quiet.) The chart on this page shows the main types of subordinate clauses.

Collective noun. *See* Noun chart.

Common noun. *See* Noun chart.

Comparative degree. *See* Adjective; Adverb.

Complement A word or phrase that completes the meaning of a verb. The four basic kinds of complements are *direct objects, indirect objects, object complements,* and *subject complements.*

A direct object answers the question *What?* or *Whom?* after an action verb. (**Kari found a dollar.** Larry saw *Denise.*)

An indirect object answers the question *To whom? For whom? To what?* or *For what?* after an action verb. (**Do** *me* **a favor.** She gave the *child* a toy.)

An object complement answers the question *What?* after a direct object. An object complement is a noun, a pronoun, or an adjective that completes the meaning of a direct object by identifying or describing it. (**The director made me the**

understudy **for the role. The little girl called the puppy** *hers.*)

A subject complement follows a subject and a linking verb. It identifies or describes a subject. The two kinds of subject complements are *predicate nominatives* and *predicate adjectives.*

A predicate nominative is a noun or pronoun that follows a linking verb and tells more about the subject. (**The author of "The Raven" is** *Poe.*)

A predicate adjective is an adjective that follows a linking verb and gives more information about the subject. (**Ian became** *angry* **at the bully.**)

Complex sentence. *See* Sentence.

Compound preposition. *See* Preposition.

Compound sentence. *See* Sentence.

Compound-complex sentence. *See* Sentence.

Conjunction A word that joins single words or groups of words.

A coordinating conjunction *(and, but, or, nor, for, yet, so)* joins words or groups of words that are equal in grammatical importance. (**David** *and* **Ruth are twins. I was bored,** *so* **I left.**)

Correlative conjunctions *(both . . . and, just as . . . so, not only . . . but also, either . . . or, neither . . . nor, whether . . . or)* work in pairs to join words and groups of words of equal importance. (**Choose** *either* **the muffin** *or* **the bagel.**)

(Choose *either* the muffin *or* the bagel.)

A subordinating conjunction *(after, although, as if, because, before, if, since, so that, than, though, until, when, while)* joins a dependent idea or clause to a main clause. (Beth acted *as if* she felt ill.)

Conjunctive adverb An adverb used to clarify the relationship between clauses of equal weight in a sentence. Conjunctive adverbs are used to replace *and (also, besides, furthermore, moreover)*; to replace *but (however, nevertheless, still)*; to state a result *(consequently, therefore, so, thus)*; or to state equality *(equally, likewise, similarly)*. (Ana was determined to get an A; *therefore,* she studied often.)

Coordinating conjunction. *See* Conjunction.

Correlative conjunction. *See* Conjunction.

D

Declarative sentence. *See* Sentence.

Definite article. *See* Article.

Demonstrative pronoun. *See* Pronoun.

Direct object. *See* Complement.

E

Emphatic form. *See* Verb tense.

F

Future tense. *See* Verb tense.

G

Gerund A verb form that ends in *-ing* and is used as a noun. A gerund may function as a subject, the object of a verb, or the object of a preposition. (*Smiling* uses fewer muscles than *frowning.* Marie enjoys *walking.*)

Gerund phrase. *See* Phrase.

I

Imperative mood. *See* Mood of verb.

Imperative sentence. *See* Sentence chart.

Indicative mood. *See* Mood of verb.

Indirect object. *See* Complement.

Infinitive A verb form that begins with the word *to* and functions as a noun, an adjective, or an adverb. (No one wanted *to answer.*) Note: When *to* precedes a verb, it is not a preposition but instead signals an infinitive.

Infinitive phrase. *See* Phrase.

Intensive pronoun. *See* Pronoun.

Interjection A word or phrase that expresses emotion or exclamation. An interjection has no grammatical connection to other words. Commas follow mild ones; exclamation points follow stronger ones. (*Well,* have a good day. *Wow!*)

Interrogative pronoun. *See* Pronoun.

Intransitive verb. *See* Verb.

Inverted order In a sentence written in *inverted order,* the predicate comes before the subject. Some sentences are written in inverted order for variety or special emphasis. (Up the beanstalk *scampered Jack.*) The subject also generally follows the predicate in a sentence that begins with *here* or *there.* (*Here* was the solution to his problem.) Questions, or interrogative sentences, are generally written in inverted order. In many questions, an auxiliary verb precedes the subject, and the main verb follows it. (*Has* anyone *seen* Susan?) Questions that begin with *who* or *what* follow normal word order.

Irregular verb. *See* Verb tense.

L

Linking verb. *See* Verb.

M

Main clause. *See* Clause.

Mood of verb A verb expresses one of three moods: indicative, imperative, or subjunctive.

The indicative mood is the most common. It makes a statement or asks a question. (We *are* out of bread. *Will* you *buy* it?)

The imperative mood expresses a command or makes a request. (*Stop* acting like a child! Please *return* my sweater.)

Types of Nouns		
Noun	Function	Examples
Abstract noun	Names an idea, a quality, or a characteristic	capitalism, terror
Collective noun	Names a group of things or persons	herd, troop
Common noun	Names a general type of person, place, thing, or idea	city, building
Compound noun	Is made up of two or more words	checkerboard, globe-trotter
Noun of direct addrress	Identifies the person or persons being spoken to	*Maria,* please stand.
Possessive noun	Shows possession, ownership, or the relationship between two nouns	my *sister's* room
Proper noun	Names a particular person, place, thing, or idea	Cleopatra, Italy, Christianity

The subjunctive mood is used to express, indirectly, a demand, suggestion, or statement of necessity **(I demand that he *stop* acting like a child. It's necessary that she *buy* more bread.)** The subjunctive is also used to state a condition or wish that is contrary to fact. This use of the subjunctive requires the past tense. **(If you *were* a nice person, you *would return* my sweater.)**

N

Nominative pronoun. *See* Pronoun.

Noun A word that names a person, a place, a thing, or an idea. The chart on this page shows the main types of nouns.

Noun clause. *See* Clause chart.

Noun of direct address. *See* Noun chart.

Number A noun, pronoun, or verb is *singular* in number if it refers to one; *plural* if it refers to more than one.

O

Object. *See* Complement.

P

Participle A verb form that can function as an adjective. Present participles always end in *-ing.* **(The** woman comforted the *crying* child.) Many past participles end in *-ed.* **(We bought the beautifully *painted* chair.)** However, irregular verbs form their past participles in some other way. **(Cato was Caesar's *sworn* enemy.)**

Passive voice. *See* Voice.

Past tense. *See* Verb tense.

Perfect tense. *See* Verb tense.

Personal pronoun. *See* Pronoun; Pronoun chart.

Phrase A group of words that acts in a sentence as a single part of speech.

An absolute phrase consists of a noun or pronoun that is modified by a participle or participial phrase but has no grammatical relation to the complete subject or predicate. (*The vegetables being done,* we finally sat down to eat dinner.)

An appositive phrase is an appositive along with any modifiers. If not essential to the meaning of the sentence, an appositive phrase is set off by commas. (Jack plans to go to the jazz concert, *an important musical event.*)

A gerund phrase includes a gerund plus its complements and modifiers. (*Playing the flute* is her hobby.)

An infinitive phrase contains the infinitive plus its complements and modifiers. (It is time *to leave for school.*)

A participial phrase contains a participle and any modifiers necessary to complete its meaning. (**The woman** *sitting over there* **is my grandmother.**)

A prepositional phrase consists of a preposition, its object, and any modifiers of the object. A prepositional phrase can function as an adjective, modifying a noun or a pronoun. (**The dog** *in the yard* **is very gentle.**) A prepositional phrase may also function as an adverb when it modifies a verb, an adverb, or an adjective. (**The baby slept** *on my lap.*)

A verb phrase consists of one or more auxiliary verbs followed by a main verb. (**The job** *will have been completed* **by noon tomorrow.**)

Positive degree. *See* Adjective.

Possessive noun. *See* Noun chart.

Predicate The verb or verb phrase and any objects, complements, or modifiers that express the essential thought about the subject of a sentence.

A simple predicate is a verb or verb phrase that tells something about the subject. (**We** *ran.*)

A complete predicate includes the simple predicate and any words that modify or complete it. (**We** *solved the problem in a short time.*)

A compound predicate has two or more verbs or verb phrases that are joined by a conjunction and share the same subject. (**We** *ran to the park and began to play baseball.*)

Predicate adjective. *See* Adjective; Complement.

Predicate nominative. *See* Complement.

Preposition A word that shows the relationship of a noun or pronoun to some other word in the sentence. Prepositions include *about, above, across, among, as, behind, below, beyond, but, by, down, during, except, for, from, into, like, near, of, on, outside, over, since, through, to, under, until, with.* (**I usually eat breakfast** *before* **school.**)

A compound preposition is made up of more than one word. (**according to, ahead of, as to, because of, by means of, in addition to, in spite of, on account of**) (**We played the game** *in spite of* **the snow.**)

Prepositional phrase. *See* Phrase.

Present tense. *See* Verb tense.

Progressive form. *See* Verb tense.

Pronoun A word that takes the place of a noun, a group of words acting as a noun, or another pronoun. The word or group of words that a pronoun refers to is called its antecedent. (**In the following sentence,** *Mari* **is the antecedent of** *she. Mari likes Mexican food, but she doesn't like Italian food.*)

A demonstrative pronoun points out specific persons, places, things, or ideas. *(this, that, these, those)*

An indefinite pronoun refers to persons, places, or things in a more general way than a noun does. *(all, another, any, both, each, either, enough, everything, few, many, most, much, neither, nobody, none, one, other, others, plenty, several, some)*

An intensive pronoun adds emphasis to another noun or pronoun. If an intensive pronoun is omitted, the meaning of the sentence will be the same. (**Rebecca** *herself* **decided to look for a part-time job.**)

An interrogative pronoun is used to form questions. *(who? whom? whose? what? which?)*

A personal pronoun refers to a specific person or thing. Personal pronouns have three cases: nominative, possessive, and objective. The case depends upon the function of the pronoun in a sentence. The first chart on the next page shows the nominative and objective forms.

A reflexive pronoun reflects back to a noun or pronoun used earlier in the sentence, indicating that the same person or thing is involved. (**We told** *ourselves* **to be patient.**)

A relative pronoun is used to begin a subordinate clause. *(who, whose, that, what, whom, whoever, whomever, whichever, whatever)*

Proper adjective. *See* Adjective.

Proper noun. *See* Noun chart.

R

Reflexive pronoun. *See* Pronoun.

Relative pronoun. *See* Pronoun.

S

Sentence A group of words expressing a complete thought. Every sentence has a subject and a predicate. Sentences can be classified by function or by structure. The second chart on this page shows the categories by function; the following subentries describe the categories by structure. *See also* Subject; Predicate; Clause.

A simple sentence has only one main clause and no subordinate clauses. *(Alan found an old violin.)* A simple sentence may contain a compound subject or a compound predicate or both. *(Alan and Teri found an old violin. Alan found an old violin and tried to play it. Alan and Teri found an old violin and tried to play it.)* The subject and the predicate can be expanded with adjectives, adverbs, prepositional phrases, appositives, and verbal phrases. As long as the sentence has only one main clause, however, it remains a simple sentence. *(Alan, rummaging in the attic, found an old violin.)*

A compound sentence has two or more main clauses. Each main clause has its own subject and predicate, and these main clauses are usually joined by a comma and a coordinating conjunc-

tion. *(Cats meow, and dogs bark, but ducks quack.)* Semicolons may also be used to join the main clauses in a compound sentence. *(The helicopter landed; the pilot had saved four passengers.)*

A complex sentence has one main clause and one or more subordinate clauses. *(Since the movie starts at eight, we should leave here by seven-thirty.)*

A compound-complex sentence has two or more main clauses and at least one subordinate clause. *(If we leave any later, we may miss the previews, and I want to see them.)*

Simple predicate. *See* Predicate.

Simple subject. *See* Subject.

Subject The part of a sentence that tells what the sentence is about.

A simple subject is the main noun or pronoun in the subject. *(Babies crawl.)*

A complete subject includes the simple subject and any words that modify it. *(The man from New Jersey won the race.)* In some sentences, the simple subject and the complete subject are the same. *(Birds fly.)*

Personal Pronouns			
Case	Singular Pronouns	Plural Pronouns	Function in Sentence
Nominative	I, you, she, he, it	we, you, they	subject or predicate nominative
Objective	me, you, her, him, it	us, you, them	direct object, indirect object, or object of a preposition

Types of Sentences			
Sentence Type	Function	Ends with . . .	Examples
Declarative sentence	Makes a statement	A period	I did not enjoy the movie.
Exclamatory sentence	Expresses strong emotion	An exclamation point	What a good writer Consuela is!
Imperative sentence	Makes a request or gives a command	A period or an exclamation point	Please come to the party. Stop!
Interrogative sentence	Asks a question	A question mark	Is the composition due?

A compound subject has two or more simple subjects joined by a conjunction. The subjects share the same verb. (**Firefighters** and **police officers** protect the community.)

Subjunctive mood. *See* Mood of verb.

Subordinate clause. *See* Clause.

Subordinating conjunction. *See* Conjunction.

Superlative degree. *See* Adjective; Adverb.

T

Tense. *See* Verb tense.

Transitive verb. *See* Verb.

V

Verb A word that expresses action or a state of being. *(cooks, seem, laughed)*

An action verb tells what someone or something does. Action verbs can express either physical or mental action. (**Crystal** *decided* to *change* **the tire herself.**)

A transitive verb is an action verb that is followed by a word or words that answer the question *What?* or *Whom?* (**I** *held* **the baby.**)

An intransitive verb is an action verb that is not followed by a word that answers the question *What?* or *Whom?* (**The baby** *laughed.*)

A linking verb expresses a state of being by linking the subject of a sentence with a word or an expression that identifies or describes the subject. (**The lemonade** *tastes* **sweet. He** *is* **our new principal.**) The most commonly used linking verb is *be* in all its forms *(am, is, are, was, were, will be, been, being).* Other linking verbs include *appear, become, feel, grow, look, remain, seem, sound, smell, stay, taste.*

An auxiliary verb, or helping verb, is a verb that accompanies the main verb to form a verb phrase. (**I** *have been* **swimming.**) The forms of *be* and *have* are the most common auxiliary verbs: *(am, is, are, was, were, being, been; has, have, had, having).* Other auxiliaries include *can, could, do, does, did, may, might, must, shall, should, will, would.*

Verbal A verb form that functions in a sentence as a noun, an adjective, or an adverb. The three kinds of verbals are gerunds, infinitives, and participles. *See* Gerund; Infinitive; Participle.

Verb tense The tense of a verb indicates when the action or state of being occurs. All the verb tenses are formed from the four principal parts of a verb: a base form *(talk),* a present participle *(talking),* a simple past form *(talked),* and a past participle *(talked).* A regular verb forms its simple past and past participle by adding *-ed* to the base form. *(climb, climbed)* An irregular verb forms its past and past participle in some other way. *(get, got, gotten)*

In addition to present, past, and future tenses, there are three perfect tenses.

The present perfect tense expresses an action or a condition that occurred at some indefinite time in the past. This tense also shows an action or a condition that began in the past and continues into the present. (**She** *has played* **the piano for four years.**)

The past perfect tense indicates that one past action or condition began *and* ended before another past action started. (**Andy** *had finished* **his homework before I even began mine.**)

The future perfect tense indicates that one future action or condition will begin *and* end before another future event starts. Use *will have* or *shall have* with the past participle of a verb. (**By tomorrow, I** *will have finished* **my homework, too.**)

The progressive form of a verb expresses a continuing action with any of the six tenses. To make the progressive forms, use the appropriate tense of the verb *be* with the present participle of the main verb. (**She** *is swimming.* **She** *has been swimming.*)

The emphatic form adds special force, or emphasis, to the present and past tense of a verb. For the emphatic form, use *do, does,* or *did* with the base form. (**Toshi** *did want* **that camera.**)

Voice The voice of a verb shows whether the subject performs the action or receives the action of the verb.

A verb is in the active voice if the subject of the sentence performs the action. (**The referee** *blew* **the whistle.**)

A verb is in the passive voice if the subject of the sentence receives the action of the verb. (**The whistle** *was blown* **by the referee.**)

Troubleshooter

The Troubleshooter will help you recognize and correct errors that you might make in your writing.

Sentence Fragment

Problem: A fragment that lacks a subject
The grass is wet. Can't be mowed now.

Solution: Add a subject to the fragment to make it a complete sentence.
The grass is wet. It can't be mowed now.

Problem: A fragment that lacks a complete verb
We enjoyed our dinner. Beans, rice, and salad.
The storm was fierce. The wind blowing hard.

Solution A: Add either a complete verb or a helping verb to make the sentence complete.
We enjoyed our dinner. Beans, rice, and salad make a good meal.
The storm was fierce. The wind was blowing hard.

Solution B: Combine the fragment with another sentence.
We enjoyed our dinner of beans, rice, and salad.
The storm was fierce with the wind blowing hard.

Problem: A fragment that is a subordinate clause
We went to the park. Where we had often gone before.
Jan won the swimming medal. Which she gave to her parents.

Solution A: Combine the fragment with another sentence.
We went to the park, where we had often gone before.
Jan won the swimming medal, which she gave to her parents.

Solution B: Rewrite the fragment as a complete sentence, eliminating the subordinating conjunction or the relative pronoun and adding a subject or other words necessary to make a complete thought.
We went to the park. We had often gone there before.
Jan won the swimming medal. She gave it to her parents.

Problem: A fragment that lacks both a subject and a verb
The birds woke us with their songs. At six in the morning.

Solution: Combine the fragment with another sentence.
The birds woke us with their songs at six in the morning.

Rule of Thumb: Sentence fragments can make your writing hard to understand. Make sure every sentence has a subject and a verb.

Note: In almost all of the writing you do, especially for school, you should avoid sentence fragments. However, sentence fragments can be used to create special effects, such as adding emphasis or conveying realistic dialogue.
"Not again!" she cried.
The pizza was gone. All of it.

Run-On Sentence

Problem: Comma splice—two main clauses separated only by a comma
The sky is pitch black, there is no moon.

Solution A: Replace the comma with an end mark of punctuation, such as a period or a question mark, and begin the new sentence with a capital letter.
The sky is pitch black. There is no moon.

Solution B: Place a semicolon between the two main clauses.
The sky is pitch black; there is no moon.

Solution C: Add a coordinating conjunction after the comma.
The sky is pitch black, and there is no moon.

Problem: Two main clauses with no punctuation between them
We picked the apples then we made pies.

Solution A: Separate the main clauses with an end mark of punctuation, such as a period or question mark, and begin the second sentence with a capital letter.
We picked the apples. Then we made pies.

Solution B: Separate the main clauses with a semicolon.
We picked the apples; then we made pies.

Solution C: Add a comma and a coordinating conjunction between the main clauses.
We picked the apples, and then we made pies.

Problem: Two main clauses with no comma before the coordinating conjunction
Elephants still live in the wild but they are endangered.

Solution: Add a comma before the coordinating conjunction to separate the two main clauses.
Elephants still live in the wild, but they are endangered.

Rule of Thumb: It often helps to have someone else read your longer sentences to see if they are clear. Since you know what the sentences are supposed to mean, you might miss the need for punctuation.

Lack of Subject-Verb Agreement

Problem: A subject that is separated from the verb by an intervening prepositional phrase
Ten pieces of the puzzle is on the floor.
The shoe department in each of our stores are closing.

Solution: Make the verb agree with the subject, which is never the object of a preposition.
Ten pieces of the puzzle are on the floor.
The shoe department in each of our stores is closing.

Problem: A predicate nominative that differs in number from the subject
Hamburgers is tonight's dinner.
Tonight's dinner are hamburgers.

Solution: Ignore the predicate nominative, and make the verb agree with the subject of the sentence.
Hamburgers are tonight's dinner.
Tonight's dinner is hamburgers.

Problem: A subject that follows the verb
On my desk is two letters from my dad.
Here is my answers to them both.

Solution: In an inverted sentence look for the subject after the verb. Then make sure the verb agrees with the subject.
On my desk are two letters from my dad.
Here are my answers to them both.

Rule of Thumb: Reversing the order of an inverted sentence may help you decide on the verb form to use: "My answers to them both are here."

Problem: A collective noun as the subject
The cross country team are in first place.
The team gathers at the captain's house after each meet.

Solution A: If the collective noun refers to a group as a whole, use a singular verb.
The cross country team is in first place.

Solution B: If the collective noun refers to each member of a group individually, use a plural verb.
The team gather at the captain's house after each meet.

Problem: A noun of amount as the subject
Five bushels are a great many tomatoes.
Three marbles is in my pocket.

Solution: Determine whether the noun of amount refers to one unit and is therefore singular or whether it refers to a number of individual units and is therefore plural.
Five bushels is a great many tomatoes.
Three marbles are in my pocket.

Problem: A compound subject that is joined by *and*
The hill and the lake makes a lovely setting for a picnic.
Spaghetti and meatballs are her favorite dinner.

Solution A: If the parts of the compound subject do not belong to one unit or if they refer to different people or things, use a plural verb.
The hill and the lake make a lovely setting for a picnic.

Solution B: If the parts of the compound subject belong to one unit or if both parts refer to the same person or thing, use a singular verb.
Spaghetti and meatballs is her favorite dinner.

Problem: A compound subject that is joined by *or* or *nor*
Neither those trees nor that shrub are healthy.

Solution: Make the verb agree with the subject that is closer to it.
Neither those trees nor that shrub is healthy.

Problem: A compound subject that is preceded *by many a, every,* or *each*
Many a dog and cat ends up in an animal shelter or a pound.

Solution: When *many a, every,* or *each* precedes a compound subject, the subject is considered singular. Use a singular verb.
Many a dog and cat end up in an animal shelter or a pound.

Problem: A subject that is separated from the verb by an intervening expression
That issue, as well as several others, are bothering me.

Solution: Certain expressions, such as those beginning with *as well as, in addition to,* and *together with,* do not change the number of the subject. Ignore an intervening expression between a subject and its verb, and make the verb agree with the subject.
That issue, along with several others, is bothering me.

Problem: An indefinite pronoun as the subject
Neither of the boys are on time.

Solution: Determine whether the indefinite pronoun is singular or plural, and make the verb agree. Some indefinite pronouns are singular—*another, anyone, everyone, one, each, either, neither, anything, everything, something,* and *somebody.* Some are plural—*both, many, few, several,* and *others.* Some can be singular or plural—*some, all, any, more, most,* and *none.* In these cases, find the noun to which the pronoun refers to determine which verb form to use.
Neither of the boys is on time.

Lack of Pronoun-Antecedent Agreement

Problem: A singular antecedent that can be either male or female.
A climber must check his equipment carefully.

Solution A: Traditionally, a masculine pronoun has been used to refer to an antecedent that may be either male or female. This usage ignores or excludes females. Reword the sentence to use *he or she, him or her,* and so on.
A climber must check his or her equipment carefully.

Solution B: Reword the sentence so that both the antecedent and the pronoun are plural.
Climbers must check their equipment carefully.

Solution C: Reword the sentence to eliminate the pronoun.
A climber must check the equipment carefully.

Rule of Thumb: Although you may see the masculine forms used exclusively in older literature, they are not acceptable in contemporary writing.

Problem: A second-person pronoun that refers to a third-person antecedent
Juan likes sitcoms that make you think as well as laugh.

Solution A: Use the appropriate third-person pronoun.
Juan likes sitcoms that make him think as well as laugh.

Solution B: Use an appropriate noun instead of a pronoun.
Juan likes sitcoms that make people think as well as laugh.

Problem: A singular indefinite pronoun as an antecedent
Each of the volumes has their own index.

Solution: *Each, every, either, neither,* and *one* are singular and therefore require singular personal pronouns even when followed by a prepositional phrase that contains a plural noun.
Each of the volumes has its own index.

Rule of Thumb: To help you remember that *each, either,* and *neither* are singular, think *each one, either one,* and *neither one.*

Lack of Clear Pronoun Reference [Unclear Antecedent]

Problem: A pronoun reference that is weak or vague
We spent several weeks at the farm this summer, and it was exciting.
The label says to shake it before pouring a serving.

Solution A: Rewrite the sentence, adding a clear antecedent for the pronoun.
We spent our vacation at the farm this summer, and it was exciting.

Solution B: Rewrite the sentence, substituting a noun for the pronoun.
The label says to shake the bottle of salad dressing before pouring a serving.

Problem: A pronoun that could refer to more than one antecedent
Lauren and Abby wrote six songs, and she recorded them all.
Don't buy a car from that dealership: it will let you down.

Solution A: Rewrite the sentence, substituting a noun for the pronoun.
Lauren and Abby wrote six songs, and Abby recorded them all.

Solution B: Rewrite the sentence, making the antecedent of the pronoun clear.
A car from that dealership will let you down; don't buy one there.

Problem: The indefinite use of *you* or *they*
You just have to laugh at that scene in the movie.
They say the weather will be clear tomorrow.

Solution A: Rewrite the sentence, substituting a noun for the pronoun.
The audience just has to laugh at that scene in the movie.

Solution B: Rewrite the sentence, eliminating the pronoun entirely.
According to the forecast, the weather will be clear tomorrow.

Shift in Pronoun

Problem: An incorrect shift in person between two pronouns
Lynn likes the front seat, where you are most comfortable.
The Chins planted a maple on the south side of the house, where you need shade the most.

Solution A: Replace the incorrect pronoun with a pronoun that agrees with its antecedent.
Lynn likes the front seat, where she is most comfortable.

Solution B: Replace the incorrect pronoun with an appropriate noun.
The Chins plants a maple on the south side of the house, where the house needs shade the most.

Shift in Verb Tense

Problem: An unnecessary shift in tense.
The children will give their mother flowers, and they kiss her.
After the party ended, we go home.

Solution: When two or more events occur at the same time, be sure to use the same verb tense to describe each event.
The children will give their mother flowers, and they will kiss her.
After the party ended, we went home.

Problem: A lack of correct shift in tenses to show that one event precedes or follows another
By the time the concert ended, we sat for four hours.

Solution: When two past events being described have occurred at different times, shift from the past tense to the past perfect tense to indicate that one action began and ended before another past action began. Use the past perfect tense for the earlier of the two actions.
By the time the concert ended, we had sat for four hours.

Rule of Thumb: When you need to use several verb tenses in your writing, it may help to first jot down the sequence of events you're writing about. Be clear in your mind what happened first, next, last.

Incorrect Verb Tense or Form

Problem: An incorrect or missing verb ending
When I began taking lessons, I learn about quarter, half, and whole notes.
I had start the lessons two months ago.

Solution: Add *–ed* to a regular verb to form the past tense and the past participle.
When I began taking lessons, I learned about quarter, half, and whole notes.
I had started the lessons two months ago.

Problem: An improperly formed irregular verb
James brung the book back to the library.
Catherine has writed six pages on that topic.

Solution: Irregular verbs form their past and past participles in some way other than by adding *–ed*. Memorize these forms, or look them up.
James brought the book back to the library.
Catherine has written six pages on that topic.

Problem: Confusion between the past form and the past participle
We have ate too many apples.
She had swam the Chesapeake last July.

Solution: Use the past participle form of an irregular verb, not the past form, when you use the auxiliary verb *have*.
We have eaten too many apples.
She had swum the Chesapeake last July.

Problem: Improper use of the past participle
The catcher thrown several runners out.
The DiCaprios done a fine job rearing those children.

Solution A: The past participle of an irregular verb cannot stand alone as a verb. Add a form of the auxiliary verb *have* to the past participle to form a complete verb.
The catcher had thrown several runners out.
The DiCaprios have done a fine job rearing those children.

Solution B: Replace the past participle with the past form of the verb.
The catcher threw several runners out.
The DiCaprios did a fine job rearing those children.

Misplaced or Dangling Modifier

Problem: A misplaced modifier
The children were swimming in the photograph.
Swooping down on a fish, I spotted the gull.
I saw a man at the movies eating popcorn.

Solution: Modifiers that modify the wrong word or seem to modify more than one word in a sentence are called misplaced modifiers. Move the misplaced phrase as close as possible to the word or words it modifies.
The children in the photograph were swimming.
I spotted the gull swooping down on a fish.
I saw a man eating popcorn at the movies.

Problem: Incorrect placement of the adverb *only*
Tricia only has enough money to buy a pencil.

Solution: Place the adverb *only* immediately before the word or group of words it modifies.
Only Tricia has enough money to buy a pencil.
Tricia has enough money to buy only a pencil.
Tricia has only enough money to buy a pencil.

Rule of Thumb: Note that each time *only* is moved, the meaning of the sentence changes. Check to be sure your sentence says what you mean.

Problem: A dangling modifier
Croaking loudly, I listened to the sounds of the frogs in the bog.
Stealing home, the game was won for the Pirates.

Solution: Dangling modifiers do not seem to logically modify any word in the sentence. Rewrite the sentence, adding a noun to which the dangling phrase clearly refers. Often you will have to add other words too.
I listened to the sounds of the frogs croaking loudly in the bog.
Stealing home, Layla won the game for the Pirates.

Missing or Misplaced Possessive Apostrophe

Problem: Singular nouns
The womans child loved the circus trapeze artists.

Solution: Use an apostrophe and *–s* to form the possessive of a singular noun, even one that ends in *s*.
The woman's child loved the circus's trapeze artists.

Problem: Plural nouns ending in *– s*
The hikers cars were parked at the base of the trail.

Solution: Use an apostrophe alone to form the possessive of a plural noun that ends in *–s*.
The hikers' cars were parked at the base of the trail.

Problem: Plural nouns not ending in *–s*
Did Brian join the mens group?

Solution: Use an apostrophe and *–s* to form the possessive of a plural noun that does not end in *–s*.
Did Brian join the men's group?

Problem: Pronouns
Everyones contribution helps.
These pencils are your's, and those pencils are their's.

Solution A: Use an apostrophe and *–s* to form the possessive of a singular indefinite pronoun.
Everyone's contribution helps.

Solution B: Do not use an apostrophe with any of the possessive personal pronouns.
These pencils are yours, and those pencils are theirs.

Problem: Confusion between *its* and *it's*
Will you tell me when its ten o'clock?
The cat licked it's fur.

Solution: Do not use an apostrophe to form the possessive of *it.* Use an apostrophe to form the contraction of *it is.*
Will you tell me when it's ten o'clock?
The cat licked its fur.

Missing Commas with Nonessential Element

Problem: Missing commas with nonessential participles, infinitives, and their phrases
Pounding hard on the roof the rain awakened me.
The whole set of cups chipped from many years of use was discarded.
To answer your question this software package is worth the price.

Solution: Determine whether the participle, infinitive, or phrase is essential to the meaning of the sentence. If it is not essential, set off the phrase with commas.
Pounding hard on the roof, the rain awakened me.
The whole set of cups, chipped from many years of use, was discarded.
To answer your question, this software package is worth the price.

Problem: Missing commas with nonessential adjective clauses
My mother who is a very generous woman gave us investment tips.

Solution: Determine whether the clause is essential to the meaning of the sentence. If it is not essential, set off the clause with commas.
My mother, who is a very generous woman, gave us investment tips.

Problem: Missing comas with nonessential appositives
John the lead-off batter singled on a line drive

Solution: Determine whether the appositive is essential to the meaning of the sentence. If it is not essential, set off the appositive with commas.
John, the lead-off batter, singled on a line drive.

Rule of Thumb: To determine whether a word or phrase is essential, try reading the sentence without it.

Problem: Missing commas with interjections and parenthetical expressions
Wow what a great cat that is!
On Saturdays as a rule we sleep late.

Solution: Set off the interjection or parenthetical expression with commas.
Wow, what a great cat that is!
On Saturdays, as a rule, we sleep late.

Missing Commas in a Series

Problem: Missing commas in a series of words, phrases, or clauses
Alicia Nirupam and Matt made the honor roll.
Mark made the dough kneaded it and left it to rise.
The firefighter carries the child out of the apartment down the stairs and into the arms of her mother.
Joe pitched the tent Meg gathered firewood and Bud unloaded the truck.

Solution: When there are three or more elements in a series, use a comma after each element that precedes the conjunction.
Alicia, Nirupam, and Matt made the honor roll.
Mark made the dough, kneaded it, and left it to rise.
The firefighter carries the child out of the apartment, down the stairs, and into the arms of her mother.
Joe pitched the tent, Meg gathered firewood, and Bud unloaded the truck.

Rule of Thumb: When you're having difficulty with a rule of usage, try rewriting the rule in your own words. Then check with your teacher to be sure you have grasped the concept.

Mechanics

This section will help you use correct capitalization, punctuation, and abbreviations in your writing.

Capitalization

This section will help you recognize and use correct capitalization in sentences.

Rule: Capitalize the first word in any sentence, including direct quotations and sentences in parentheses unless they are included in another sentence.

Example: *She said, "Come back soon."*

Example: *Emily Dickinson became famous only after her death. (She published only six poems during her lifetime.)*

Rule: Always capitalize the pronoun *I* no matter where it appears in the sentence.

Example: *Some of my relatives think that I should become a doctor.*

Rule: Capitalize proper nouns, including
a. names of individuals, and titles used in direct address that precede a name or describing a relationship.
Example: *George Washington; Dr. Morgan; Aunt Margaret*

b. names of ethnic groups, national groups, political parties and their members, and languages.
Example: *Italian Americans; Aztec; the Republican Party; a Democrat; Spanish*

c. names of organizations, institutions, firms, monuments, bridges, buildings, and other structures.
Example: *Red Cross; Stanford University; General Electric; Lincoln Memorial; Tappan Zee Bridge; Chrysler Building; Museum of Natural History*

d. trade names and names of documents, awards, and laws.
Example: *Microsoft; Declaration of Independence; Pulitzer Prize; Sixteenth Amendment*

e. geographical terms and regions or localities.
Example: *Hudson River; Pennsylvania Avenue; Grand Canyon; Texas; the Midwest*

f. names of planets and other heavenly bodies.
Example: *Venus; Earth; the Milky Way*

g. names of ships, planes, trains, and spacecraft.
Example: *USS Constitution; Spirit of St. Louis; Apollo 11*

h. names of most historical events, eras, calendar items, and religious names and items.
Example: *World War II; Age of Enlightenment; June; Christianity; Buddhists; Bible; Easter; God*

i. titles of literary works, works of art, and musical compositions.
Example: *"Why I Live at the P.O."; The Starry Night; Rhapsody in Blue*

j. names of specific school courses.
Example: *Advanced Physics; American History*

Rule: Capitalize proper adjectives (adjectives formed from proper nouns).

Example: *Christmas tree; Hanukkah candles; Freudian psychology; American flag*

Punctuation

This section will help you use these elements of punctuation correctly.

Rule: Use a period at the end of a declarative sentence or a polite command.

Example: *I'm thirsty.*
Example: *Please bring me a glass of water.*

Rule: Use an exclamation point to show strong feeling or after a forceful command.

Example: *I can't believe my eyes!*
Example: *Watch your step!*

Rule: Use a question mark to indicate a direct question.

Example: *Who is in charge here?*

Rule: Use a colon
a. to introduce a list (especially after words such as *these*, *the following*, or *as follows*) and to introduce material that explains, restates, or illustrates previous material.

Example: *The following states voted for the amendment: Texas, California, Georgia, and Florida.*
Example: *The sunset was colorful: purple, orange, and red lit up the sky.*

b. to introduce a long or formal quotation.
Example: *It was Mark Twain who stated the following proverb: "Man is the only animal that blushes. Or needs to."*

c. in precise time measurements, biblical chapter and verse references, and business letter salutations.
Example: 3:35 P.M.   7:50 A.M.
          Gen. 1:10–11   Matt. 2:23
          Dear Ms. Samuels: Dear Sir:

Rule: Use a semicolon
a. to separate main clauses that are not joined by a coordinating conjunction.
Example: *There were two speakers at Gettysburg that day; only Lincoln's speech is remembered.*

b. to separate main clauses joined by a conjunctive adverb or by *for example* or *that is.*
Example: *Because of the ice storm, most students could not get to school; consequently, the principal canceled all classes for the day.*

c. to separate the items in a series when these items contain commas.
Example: *The students at the rally came from Senn High School, in Chicago, Illinois; Niles Township High School, in Skokie, Illinois; and Evanston Township High School, in Evanston, Illinois.*

d. to separate two main clauses joined by a coordinating conjunction when such clauses already contain several commas.
Example: *The designer combined the blue silk, brown linen, and beige cotton into a suit; but she decided to use the yellow chiffon, yellow silk, and white lace for an evening gown.*

Rule: Use a comma
a. between the main clauses of a compound sentence.
Example: *Ryan was late getting to study hall, and his footsteps echoed in the empty corridor.*

b. to separate three or more words, phrases, or clauses in a series.
Example: *Mel bought carrots, beans, pears, and onions.*

c. between coordinate modifiers.

Example: *That is a lyrical, moving poem.*

d. to set off parenthetical expressions, interjections, and conjunctive adverbs.
Example: *Well, we missed the bus again.*
Example: *The weather is beautiful today; however, it is supposed to rain this weekend.*

e. to set off nonessential words, clauses, and phrases, such as:
   —adverbial clauses
Example: *Since Ellen is so tall, the coach assumed she would be a good basketball player.*
   —adjective clauses
Example: *Scott, who had been sleeping, finally woke up.*
   —participles and participial phrases
Example: *Having found what he was looking for, he left.*
   —prepositional phrases
Example: *On Saturdays during the fall, I rake leaves.*
   —infinitive phrases
Example: *To be honest, I'd like to stay a while longer.*
   —appositives and appositive phrases
Example: *Ms. Kwan, a soft-spoken woman, ran into the street to hail a cab.*

f. to set off direct quotations.
Example: *"My concert," Molly replied, "is tonight."*

g. to set off an antithetical phrase.
Example: *Unlike Tom, Rob enjoys skiing.*

h. to set off a title after a person's name.
Example: *Margaret Thomas, Ph.D., was the guest speaker.*

i. to separate the various parts of an address, a geographical term, or a date.
Example: *My new address is 324 Indian School Road, Albuquerque, New Mexico 85350.*
Example: *I moved on March 13, 1998.*

j. after the salutation of an informal letter and after the closing of all letters.
Example: *Dear Helen,   Sincerely,*

k. to set off parts of a reference that direct the reader to the exact source.
Example: *You can find the article in the* Washington Post, *April 4, 1997, pages 33–34.*

l. to set off words or names used in direct address and in tag questions.

Example: *Yuri, will you bring me my calculator?*
Lottie became a lawyer, didn't she?

Rule: Use a dash to signal a change in thought or to emphasize parenthetical material.

Example: *During the play, Maureen—and she'd be the first to admit it—forgot her lines.*

Example: *There are only two juniors attending—Mike Ramos and Ron Kim.*

Rule: Use parentheses to set off supplemental material. Punctuate within the parentheses only if the punctuation is part of the parenthetical expression.

Example: *If you like jazz (and I assume you do), you will like this CD. (The soloist is Miles Davis.)*
Example: *The upper Midwest (which states does that include?) was hit by terrible floods last year.*

Rule: Use brackets to enclose information that you insert into a quotation for clarity or to enclose a parenthetical phrase that already appears within parentheses.

Example: *"He serves his [political] party best who serves the country best."—Rutherford B. Hayes*
Example: *The staircase (which was designed by a famous architect [Frank Lloyd Wright]) was inlaid with ceramic tile.*

Rule: Use ellipsis points to indicate the omission of material from a quotation.

Example: *". . . Neither an individual nor a nation can commit the least act of injustice against the obscurest individual. . . ." —Henry David Thoreau*

Rule: Use quotation marks
a. to enclose a direct quotation, as follows:
Example: *"Hurry up!" shouted Lisa.*

When a quotation is interrupted, use two sets of quotation marks.

Example: *"A cynic," wrote Oscar Wilde, "is someone who knows the price of everything and the value of nothing."*

Use single quotation marks for a quotation within a quotation.

Example: *"Did you say 'turn left' or 'turn right'?" asked Leon.*

In writing dialogue, begin a new paragraph and use a new set of quotation marks every time the speaker changes.

Example: *"Do you really think the spaceship can take off?" asked the first officer.*
"Our engineer assures me that we have enough power," the captain replied.

b. to enclose titles of short works, such as stories, poems, essays, articles, chapters, and songs.
Example: *"The Lottery"* [short story]
"Provide, Provide" [poem]
"Civil Disobedience" [essay]

c. to enclose unfamiliar slang terms and unusual expressions.
Example: *The man called his grandson a "rapscallion."*

d. to enclose a definition that is stated directly.
Example: *Gauche is a French word meaning "left."*

Rule: Use italics
a. for titles of books, lengthy poems, plays, films, television series, paintings and sculptures, long musical compositions, court cases, names of newspapers and magazines, ships, trains, airplanes, and spacecraft. Italicize and capitalize articles (*a, an, the*) at the beginning of a title only when they are part of the title.
Example: *E.T.* [film]; *The Piano Lesson* [play]
The Starry Night [painting]
the *New Yorker* [magazine]
Challenger [spacecraft]
The Great Gatsby [book]
the *Chicago Tribune* [newspaper]

b. for foreign words and expressions that are not used frequently in English.
Example: *Luciano waved good-bye, saying, "Arrivederci."*

c. for words, letters, and numerals used to represent themselves.
Example: There is no *Q* on the telephone keypad.
Example: Number your paper from *1* through *10*.

Rule: Use an apostrophe

a. for a possessive form, as follows:

Add an apostrophe and *s* to all singular nouns, plural nouns not ending in *s*, singular indefinite pronouns, and compound nouns. Add only an apostrophe to a plural noun that ends in *s*.

Example: *the tree's leaves*
the man's belt
the bus's tires
the children's pets
everyone's favorite
my mother-in-law's job
the attorney general's decision
the baseball player's error
the cats' bowls

If two or more persons possess something jointly, use the possessive form for the last person named. If they possess something individually, use the possessive form for each one's name.

Example: *Ted and Harriet's family*
Ted's and Harriet's bosses
Lewis and Clark's expedition
Lewis's and Clark's clothes

b. to express amounts of money or time that modify a noun.

Example: *two cents' worth*
Example: *three days' drive (You can use a hyphenated adjective instead: a three-day drive.)*

c. in place of omitted letters or numerals.

Example: *haven't [have not]*   *the winter of '95*

d. to form the plural of letters, numerals, symbols, and words used to represent themselves. Use an apostrophe and *s*.

Example: You wrote two *5's* instead of one.
Example: How many *s's* are there in Mississippi?
Example: Why did he use three *!'s* at the end of the sentence?

Rule: Use a hyphen

a. after any prefix joined to a proper noun or proper adjective.

Example: *all-American   pre-Columbian*

b. after the prefixes *all-, ex-,* and *self-* joined to any noun or adjective; after the prefix *anti-* when it joins a word beginning with *i;* after the prefix *vice-* (except in some instances, such as *vice president*); and to avoid confusion between words that begin with *re-* and look like another word.

Example: *ex-president*
self-important
anti-inflammatory
vice-principal
re-creation of the event
recreation time
re-pair the socks
repair the computer

c. in a compound adjective that precedes a noun.
Example: *a bitter-tasting liquid*

d. in any spelled-out cardinal or ordinal numbers up to *ninety-nine* or *ninety-ninth,* and with a fraction used as an adjective.
Example: *twenty-three   eighty-fifth*
one-half cup

e. to divide a word at the end of a line, between syllables.
Example: *air-port   scis-sors*
fill-ing   fin-est

Abbreviations

Abbreviations are shortened forms of words.

Rule: Use only one period if an abbreviation occurs at the end of a sentence. If the sentence ends with a question mark or an exclamation point, use the period and the second mark of punctuation.

Example: *We didn't get home until 3:30 A.M.*
Example: *Did you get home before 4:00 A.M.?*
Example: *I can't believe you didn't get home until 3:30 A.M.!*

Rule: Capitalize abbreviations of proper nouns and abbreviations related to historical dates.

Example: *John Kennedy Jr.   P.O. Box 333*
800 B.C.   A.D. 456   1066 C.E.

Use all capital letters and no periods for most abbreviations of organizations and government agencies.
Example: *CBS   CIA   FBI*
IBM   NFL
MADD   GE

Spelling

The following basic rules, examples, and exceptions will help you master the spellings of many words.

Forming plurals

English words form plurals in many ways. Most nouns simply add *s*. The following chart shows other ways of forming plural nouns and some common exceptions to the pattern.

General Rules for Forming Plurals		
If the word ends in	**Rule**	**Example**
ch, s, sh, x, z	add *es*	glass, glasses
a consonant + *y*	change *y* to *i* and add *es*	caddy, caddies
a vowel + *y* or *o*	add only *s*	cameo, cameos monkey, monkeys
a consonant + *o* common exceptions	generally add *es* but sometimes add only *s*	potato, potatoes cello, cellos
f or *ff* common exceptions	add *s* change *f* to *v* and add *es*	cliff, cliffs hoof, hooves
lf	change *f* to *v* and add *es*	half, halves

A few plurals are exceptions to the rules in the previous chart, but they are easy to remember. The following chart lists these plurals and some examples.

Special Rules for Forming Plurals	
Rule	**Example**
To form the plural of most proper names and one-word compound nouns, follow the general rules for plurals.	Cruz, Cruzes Mancuso, Mancusos crossroad, crossroads
To form the plural of hyphenated compound nouns or compound nouns of more than one word, make the most important word plural.	sister-in-law, sisters-in-law motion picture, motion pictures
Some nouns have unusual plural forms.	goose, geese child, children
Some nouns have the same singular and plural forms.	moose scissors pants

Adding prefixes

When adding a prefix to a word, keep the original spelling of the word. Use a hyphen only when the original word is capitalized or with prefixes such as *all-, ex-,* and *self-* joined to a noun or an adjective.

co + operative = cooperative
inter + change = interchange
pro + African = pro-African
ex + partner = ex-partner

Suffixes and the silent *e*

Many English words end in a silent letter *e.* Sometimes the *e* is dropped when a suffix is added. When adding a suffix that begins with a consonant to a word that ends in silent *e,* keep the *e.*

like + ness = likeness sure + ly = surely
COMMON EXCEPTIONS awe + ful = awful;
judge + ment = judgment

When adding a suffix that begins with a vowel to a word that ends in silent *e,* usually drop the *e.*

believe + able = believable
expense + ive = expensive
COMMON EXCEPTION mile + age = mileage

When adding a suffix that begins with *a* or *o* to a word that ends in *ce* or *ge,* keep the *e* so the word will retain the soft *c* or *g* sound.

notice + able = noticeable
courage + ous = courageous

When adding a suffix that begins with a vowel to a word that ends in *ee* or *oe,* keep the final *e.*

see + ing = seeing   toe + ing = toeing

Drop the final silent *e* after the letters *u* or *w.*

argue + ment = argument
owe + ing = owing

Keep the final silent *e* before the suffix *-ing* when necessary to avoid ambiguity.

singe + ing = singeing

Suffixes and the final *y*

When adding a suffix to a word that ends in a consonant + *y,* change the *y* to *i* unless the suffix begins with *i.* Keep the *y* in a word that ends in a vowel + *y.*

try + ed = tried   fry + ed = fried
stay + ing = staying   display + ed = displayed
copy + ing = copying joy + ous = joyous

Adding *ly* and *ness*

When adding *ly* to a word that ends in a single *l,* keep the *l,* but when the word ends in a double *l,* drop one *l.* When the word ends in a consonant + *le,* drop the *le.* When adding *-ness* to a word that ends in *n,* keep the *n.*

casual + ly = casually
practical + ly = practically
dull + ly = dully
probable + ly = probably
open + ness = openness
mean + ness = meanness

Doubling the final consonant

Double the final consonant in words that end in a consonant preceded by a single vowel if the word is one syllable, if it has an accent on the last syllable that remains there even after the suffix is added, or if it is a word made up of a prefix and a one-syllable word.

stop + ing = stopping
admit + ed = admitted
replan + ed = replanned

Do not double the final consonant if the accent is not on the last syllable, or if the accent shifts when the suffix is added. Also do not double the final consonant if the final consonant is *x* or *w.* If the word ends in a consonant and the suffix begins with a consonant, do not double the final consonant.

benefit + ed = benefited
similar + ly = similarly
raw + er = rawer
box + like = boxlike
friend + less = friendless
rest + ful = restful

Forming Compound Words

When joining a word that ends in a consonant to a word that begins with a consonant, keep both consonants.

> out + line = outline
> after + noon = afternoon
> post + card = postcard
> pepper + mint = peppermint

ie and *ei*

Learning this rhyme can save you many misspellings: "Write *i* before *e* except after *c,* or when sounded like *a* as in *neighbor* and *weigh.*" There are many exceptions to this rule, including *seize, seizure, leisure, weird, height, either, neither, forfeit.*

-*cede*, -*ceed*, and -*sede*

Because of the relatively few words with *sēd* sounds, these words are worth memorizing.

> These words use -*cede:* **accede, precede, secede.**
> One word uses -*sede:* **supersede.**
> Three words use -*ceed:* **exceed, proceed, succeed.**

Logic and Persuasion Handbook

Persuasion

Propositions

One of the main reasons people write and talk is to persuade each other. Persuasive writing and speaking attempts to convince someone of the truth of a **proposition,** that is, a statement or claim. There are four basic types of proposition:

- A proposition of **fact** is a claim that certain information is correct.
  Candidate Wilkins comes from Illinois.

- A proposition of **value** is a statement that a feeling or judgment is valid.
  Candidate Wilkins is a friendly woman.

- A proposition about a **problem** combines fact and judgment.
  Candidate Wilkins is not qualified to run.

- A proposition of **policy** is a claim that someone should do something.
  Everyone should vote for candidate Wilkins.

A proposition may be **true** or **false.** In evaluating persuasive speaking and writing, you need to know which type of proposition is being made so that you can decide whether it is true or false.

Evidence and Arguments

Persuasive writing and speaking usually includes **evidence,** that is, reasons why someone should accept a proposition. Together, a proposition and a reason for accepting it make up an **argument.**

Everyone should vote for candidate Wilkins, because she is the most qualified.

An argument may be **valid** or **invalid,** that is, reasonable or unreasonable.

Appeals

Arguments are meant to appeal to certain beliefs, values, or feelings belonging to the reader or listener. Most reasons given in support of a proposition make at least one of four types of **appeal:**

- An **appeal to logic** is a claim based on fact and reason.
  Wilkins is unqualified, because she does not meet the age requirement.

- An **appeal to ethics or values** is a claim based on shared values or judgments.
  Wilkins is best, because she is the most honest and caring.

- An **appeal to authority** is a claim based on sources believed to be reliable.
  Wilkins is best, because the Metropolitan Bar Association supports her.

- An **appeal to emotion** is a claim based on shared feelings.
  Wilkins is best, because she has overcome hardship.

In evaluating arguments, you need to know which type of appeal is being made so that you can decide whether it is valid or invalid. Note that an argument may involve more than one type of appeal.

Exercise: Analyzing an Argument

Read the following statements. For each statement, identify the type of proposition made and the type of appeal used to support it..

1. If we want clean beaches, then we need to provide trash cans and arrange for garbage removal in the summer.

2. It is our responsibility as human beings to keep ocean ecosystems healthy by polluting them as little as possible or not at all.

3. According to eminent marine biologists, we have a lot to learn about the animals that live in the ocean depths.

4. Restricting owners of beachfront property from building wherever they want to on their property is highly unfair.

Statement	Proposition	Appeal
1	about a problem	
2		
3		
4		to ethics or values

Logic

Inductive Reasoning

Inductive reasoning involves putting facts together to come up with a generalized statement as a conclusion.

Specific facts:

> **Fact 1.** *Star Wars* is the second-biggest money-maker of all time.

> **Fact 2.** The number one movie at the box office in 2004 was *Shrek 2.*

> **Fact 3.** *Spider-Man* broke many box office records in 2002.

Generalization: Science fiction and fantasy films do very well at the box office.

Errors In Inductive Reasoning

To avoid errors in inductive reasoning, be sure you use a large enough sample of specific facts, and of course, make sure your facts are accurate. Assuming you have a large enough sample of accurate facts, make sure that your generalization is logical.

For example, it would be illogical to conclude from the facts above that movies whose titles begin with the letter *S* do well at the box office.

Deductive Reasoning

Deductive reasoning is essentially the opposite of inductive reasoning. With deductive reasoning you start with a generalization to come to a conclusion about a specific case.

Generalization: Paul can only eat vegetarian food.

Specific fact: The Glory Diner offers vegetarian food.

Conclusion: Paul can eat at the Glory Diner.

Syllogisms

A syllogism is a formal statement of a deductive argument. It consists of a **major premise,** or general statement; a **minor premise,** or related fact; and a **conclusion** based on the two.

Major premise: People who travel between countries need a passport.

Minor premise: Jody is flying from the United States to Spain.

Conclusion: Jody needs a passport.

Errors In Deductive Reasoning

Errors in deductive reasoning result from faulty construction of the argument. Make sure the major premise is a universal statement, that both premises are true, and that the conclusion follows logically from the premises.

Note: A syllogism is *valid* if it follows the rules of deductive reasoning. A syllogism is *true* if the statements are factually accurate. Therefore, a perfectly valid syllogism can be untrue. For example:

Major premise: All voters are good citizens. [There is more to good citizenship than voting.]

Minor premise: My parents are voters.

Conclusion: Therefore, my parents are good citizens.

This conclusion is valid according to the premises; however, it isn't necessarily true because the major premise is flawed.

Exercise: Analyzing Logical Reasoning

For each argument below, identify whether inductive or deductive reasoning is used. Evaluate whether the conclusion is valid or invalid and explain your evaluation.

1. An epic poem is a serious, long narrative poem centered on the life of a cultural or national hero or heroine. *El Cid* is an epic poem. In more than 30,000 lines, it celebrates the life and accomplishments of a Spanish military and political leader who lived in the eleventh century.

2. If a computer can play compact discs, the computer must have been built before 1985. This computer can play CDs. This computer must have been built before 1985.

3. Many humorists use puns. Mark Twain used puns in his writing and his speeches. Ogden Nash used puns in his poems. Woody Allen uses puns in his movies.

Exercise: Using Logical Reasoning

Write a short essay arguing a proposition. In your argument, use at least two examples each of valid inductive and deductive reasoning.

Logical Fallacies

A **logical fallacy** is a particular type of faulty reasoning. Fallacies often seem reasonable at face value, so they are often used, both intentionally and unintentionally. Some fallacies are so common that they have names.

To identify fallacies in the writing and speaking of others and to avoid them in your own persuasive communication, you need to be able to identify fallacies and to understand why they are illogical.

- **Ad Hominem**
  Don't listen to what Smyth says about the election; he spent time in prison.
  An ad hominem argument (literally, an argument "against the person") implies that a defect in a person's character or behavior is evidence that what he says is unreliable. Note that the ad hominem fallacy contains a hidden premise: *People who have spent time in prison cannot have valid opinions.* Because this premise is untrue, the argument about Smyth is untrue also.

- **Non Sequitur or False Causality**
  This shirt is unlucky: every time I wear it, something bad happens.
  Non sequitur literally means "it doesn't follow." Just because two events occur together, it doesn't follow logically that one caused the other.

- **Glittering Generalities**
  If you love freedom, vote for Jack.
  Glittering generalities are words with overwhelmingly positive connotations, used to make it seem impossible to disagree with an idea. How can you argue against the idea of freedom? A listener's initial reaction to this statement might be, "Freedom is a good thing, so I must vote for Jack."

- **Overgeneralization and Stereotype**
  Tall people make excellent basketball players.
  An overgeneralization is any conclusion that may be accurate about a small group, but is inaccurate when applied to a much larger group. An overgeneralization about a group of people is called a stereotype.

- **Argument from Authority and Celebrity Endorsement**
  Four out of five doctors recommend Pumpidox for most heart conditions.
  Argument from authority is the quoting of an alleged expert on a certain topic. As a logical fallacy, arguments from authority rely solely on the mention of the word "expert," and give no clear facts from the expert. Companies often hire celebrities to appear in commercials for their products in the hope that audiences will respond to the likability of the famous person, even if that person has no real expert knowledge about the product.

- **The Bandwagon Effect**
  Choose America's favorite toothpaste!
  The term "jumping on the bandwagon" means doing or thinking something because everyone else is doing it or thinking it. This type of reasoning provides no evidence to support a decision or viewpoint.

- **Card Stacking**
  Senator Porter voted against childcare laws and recycling programs. It's time for new leadership!
  Card stacking involves piling on evidence that supports one side of an argument while ignoring or suppressing valid evidence supporting the other side. Saying that a politician voted against positive-sounding programs does not mean that he or she didn't have good reason to, or that the opposition has a better record.

Ethical Reasoning and Propaganda

Propaganda

Propaganda is the process of persuading by deliberately misleading or confusing an audience. Through the use of combinations of logical fallacies, propaganda can appeal to ethics or values, authority, or emotion, but they do so in a way that is unsupported or inappropriate.

Political propaganda

A vote for Marmelard is a vote for the enemy!
America: You're with us or against us!

Advertising

Be the best parent you can be: Serve your kids Super Goody cereal.
The most successful people shop at Blorland's Department Store.

Ethical Reasoning

Reasoning that persuades by helping its intended audience make informed decisions is called **ethical reasoning.** As a writer or speaker, you have the responsibility to use ethical reasoning and avoid propaganda. This means that you must gather complete information about a topic, check your facts for accuracy, and make sure that your reasoning includes no errors in logic or false conclusions. You should address opposing evidence with clear and accurate argumentation. Using ethical reasoning in your persuasive writing or speeches will strengthen your positions as your audience sees that you have logically addressed all sides of an idea.

Identifying Unethical Persuasive Techniques

The following essay contains several examples of faulty reasoning. Read through the entire text once, then go back and look for logical fallacies, invalid arguments, and manipulative appeals. For each example you find, make an entry in a chart like the one shown. Then write a paragraph evaluating the essay's argument.

Passage	Type(s) of Appeals	Why Invalid
"Principal Spaly"	Appeal to logic	Card stacking

Don't Take Away Our Freedom

The school board recently announced plans to remove all vending machines from our schools' cafeterias. They say that candy, snacks, and cola are bad for students. But is starvation good for students? Is taking away freedom to choose good for students?

Every expert on nutrition agrees that it is not healthy for kids to go for hours between meals without some sort of snack in between to tide them over. If the school board has its way, students will be passing out at their desks from hunger and dehydration. Principal Spaly claims that students are more likely to pass out from a "sugar crash." This is the same Principal Spaly who recently showed what he thought of students when he denied sophomores the right to park at the high school.

We are taught in these very schools that America is a land of democracy, freedom, and liberty. It is clear that the school board has forgotten this. Any student who loves his or her school will write to the school board and let them know how we feel.

Glossary/Glosario

This glossary lists the vocabulary words found in the selections in this book. The definition given is for the word as it is used in the selection; you may wish to consult a dictionary for other meanings of these words. The key below is a guide to the pronunciation symbols used in each entry.

Pronunciation Key

a	**a**t	ō	h**o**pe	ng	si**ng**
ā	**a**pe	ô	f**o**rk, **a**ll	th	**th**in
ä	f**a**ther	oo	w**oo**d, p**u**t	th	**th**is
e	**e**nd	ōō	f**oo**l	zh	trea**s**ure
ē	m**e**	oi	**oi**l	ə	**a**go, tak**e**n, penc**i**l,
i	**i**t	ou	**ou**t		lem**o**n, circ**u**s
ī	**i**ce	u	**u**p	′	primary stress
o	h**o**t	ū	**u**se	´	secondary stress

English

A

abate (ə bāt′) v. to lessen or reduce in force or intensity; **p. 474**

abhor (ab hôr′) v. to detest; **p. 494**

abstinence (ab′ stə nəns) n. the act of doing without food, drink, or other pleasures; **p. 937**

accomplice (ə kom′ plice) n. a participant in a crime or wrongdoing; **p. 824**

acquittal (ə kwit′ əl) n. setting free from a criminal charge by verdict, sentence, or other legal process; **p. 336**

acrid (ak′ rid) adj. strong, bitter, and often unpleasant in smell or taste; **p. 81**

affront (ə frunt′) n. a deliberate insult; **p. 61**

aggravate (ag′ rə vāt′) v. to make something worse; **p. 122**

anguish (ang′ gwish) n. severe physical or mental pain; suffering; **p. 902**

Español

A

abate/amainar v. bajar o disminuir; **p. 474**

abhor/aborrecer v. detestar; **p. 494**

abstinence/abstinencia s. vivir sin comida, bebida u otros placeres; **p. 937**

accomplice/cómplice s. participante en un delito o crimen; **p. 824**

acquittal/absolución s. liberación de una acusación criminal mediante veredicto, sentencia u otro proceso legal; **p. 336**

acrid/acre: adj. sabor o olor fuerte, amargo y a menudo desagradable; **p. 81**

affront/afrenta s. insulto hecho a propósito; **p. 61**

aggravate/agravar v. empeorar o hacer peor; **p. 122**

anguish/angustia s. fuerte dolor físico o mental; sufrimiento; **p. 902**

animosity (an′ ə mos′ i tē) *n.* ill will or resentment; **p. 135**

anticipate (an tis′ ə pāt′) *v.* expect; consider in advance; **p. 734**

antidote (an′ ti dōt′) *n.* something that relieves, prevents, or counteracts; **p. 462**

appease (ə pēz′) *v.* to make peace with concessions; to satisfy insistent demands; **p. 193**

arable (ar′ ə bəl) *adj.* fit for growing crops; **p. 984**

arid (ar′ id) *adj.* excessively dry; **p. 608**

artifice (är′ tə fis) *n.* ingenious deception; **p. 1166**

assailant (ə sā′ lənt) *n.* attacker; **p. 54**

assertion (ə sur′ shən) *n.* a forceful or confident statement of fact or belief; **p. 514**

assertive (ə sur′ tiv) *adj.* bold; forceful in a confident way; **p. 127**

assiduously (ə sij′ wəs lē) *adv.* attentively or busily; **p. 758**

asunder (ə sun′ dər) *adv.* into parts; into different pieces; **p. 873**

attainment (ə tān′ mənt) *n.* accomplishment; **p. 597**

austere (ôs tēr′) *adj.* stern or cold in appearance or manner; **p. 1192**

austerity (ôs ter′ ə tē) *n.* a morally strict act; **p. 566**

avail (ə vāl′) *n.* use or advantage; **p. 86**

avarice (av′ ər is) *n.* greed; **p. 569**

B

banal (bə nal′) *adj.* lacking originality, freshness, or novelty; **p. 1193**

banish (ban′ ish) *v.* to drive away or remove by authority; **p. 721**

banquet (bang′ kwit) *n.* an elaborate, ceremonial meal; **p. 19**

barbaric (bär bar′ ik) *adj.* crude; wild in taste, style, or manner; **p. 222**

bedlam (bed′ ləm) *n.* a state of uproar or confusion; **p. 128**

animosity/animosidad *s.* mala voluntad o resentimiento; **p. 135**

anticipate/anticipar *v.* esperar o consider con antelación; **p. 734**

antidote/antídoto *s.* algo que alivia, impide o contrarresta; **p. 462**

appease/apaciguar *v.* hacer paz con concesiones; satisfacer exigencias; **p. 193**

arable/arable *adj.* capaz de ser cultivado; **p. 984**

arid/árido *adj.* excesivamente seco; **p. 608**

artifice/artificio *s.* decepción ingeniosa; **p. 1166**

assailant/agresor *n.* atacante **p. 54**

assertion/afirmación *s.* declaración de hecho o creencia con firmeza o confianza; **p. 514**

assertive/autoritario *adj.* audaz; fuerte pero con confianza; **p. 127**

assiduously/diligentemente *adv.* atenta o aplicadamente; **p. 758**

asunder/partido *adv.* dividido violentamente por la mitad o en dos; **p. 873**

attainment/consecución *s.* logro; **p. 597**

austere/austero *adj.* severo o frío en apariencia o forma; **p. 1192**

austerity/austeridad *s.* un acto moralmente restringido; **p. 566**

avail/provecho *s.* uso o ventaja; **p. 87**

avarice/avaricia *s.* codicia; **p. 569**

B

banal/banal *adj.* carente de originalidad, frescura o novedad; **p. 1193**

banish/desterrar *v.* hacer exiliar o salir por autoridad; **p. 721**

banquet/banquete *s.* comida ceremonial elaborada; **p. 19**

barbaric/bárbaro *adj.* rudimentario; salvaje en sabor, estilo o forma; **p. 222**

bedlam/manicomio *s.* un estado de confusión o ánimo; locura; **p. 128**

beneficent (bə nef′ ə sənt) *adj.* doing or producing good; **p. 1235**

bereft (bi reft′) *adj.* deprived or robbed; **p. 213**

C

candor (kan′ dər) *n.* honesty or frankness; openness; **p. 963**

censure (sen′ shər) *v.* to find fault with and criticize; **p. 338**

chaste (chāst) *adj.* innocent; pure; **p. 929**

chastise (chas tīz′) *v.* to punish, reprimand, or discipline severely; **p. 721**

chide (chīd) *v.* to scold; **p. 494**

clandestine (klan des′ tin) *adj.* kept secret for an illicit reason; **p. 534**

clemency (klem′ ən sē) *n.* mercy; leniency, especially toward an enemy; **p. 966**

coax (kōks) *v.* to persuade by means of gentle urging or flattery; **p. 112**

coercion (kō ur′ shən) *n.* force; repression; **p. 1140**

coincide (kō′ in sīd′) *v.* to occupy the same place in space or time; **p. 151**

collide (kə līd′) *v.* to run into accidentally; to come together with direct impact; **p. 1226**

commandeer (kom′ ən dēr′) *v.* to take arbitrary or forceful possession of; **p. 198**

commence (kə mens′) *v.* to begin; **p. 1171**

commiserate (kə miz′ ə rāt′) *v.* sympathize with; pity; **p. 329**

compassion (kəm pash′ ən) *n.* sympathetic awareness of another's distress; **p. 522**

compulsory (kəm pul′ sər ē) *adj.* mandatory; enforced; **p. 1004**

conception (kən sep′ shən) *n.* thought; idea; design; plan; **p. 1123**

condescending (kon′ di sen′ ding) *adj.* characterized by an air of superiority or smugness; **p. 1205**

beneficent/beneficioso *adj.* hacer o producir bien; **p. 1235**

bereft/desprovisto *adj.* deprivado o robado de algo; **p. 213**

C

candor/franqueza *s.* honestidad o transpariencia; **p. 963**

censure/censurar *v.* criticar y reprobar; **p. 338**

chaste/casto *adj.* inocente; puro; **p. 929**

chastise/reprender *v.* castigar o disciplinar; **p. 721**

chide/reprobar *v.* reprender o castigar; **p. 494**

clandestine/clandestino *adj.* mantener en secreto por razones ilícitas; **p. 534**

clemency/clemencia *s.* merced; indulgencia, especialmente hacia un enemigo; **p. 966**

coax/engatusar *v.* persuadir con halagos o exhortación suave; **p. 112**

coercion/coacción *s.* fuerza, represión; **p. 1140**

coincide/coincidir *v.* ocupar el mismo lugar en espacio o tiempo; **p. 151**

collide/colisionar *v.* chocar con por accidente o con impacto directo; **p. 1226**

commandeer/requisar *v.* apropriarse con fuerza o de modo arbitrario; **p. 198**

commence/comenzar *v.* empezar; **p. 1171**

commiserate/compadecer *v.* simpatizar con; sentir lástima; **p. 329**

compassion/compasión *s.* conciencia simpática del dolor de otro; **p. 522**

compulsory/obligatorio *adj.* mandatorio, forzoso; **p. 1004**

conception/concepción *s.* pensamiento, idea; diseño, plan; **p. 1123**

condescending/condescendiente *adj.* caracterizado por un aire de superioridad o arrogancia; **p. 1205**

confound (kən found´) *v.* to confuse or bewilder; **p. 499**

congealed (kən jēld´) *adj.* thickened; changed from a liquid to a solid state; **p. 793**

consecrate (kon´ sə krāt´) *v.* to elevate into a sacred position through a religious rite; **p. 110**

considerably (kən sid´ ər ə blē) *adv.* greatly; by a large amount; **p. 526**

console (kən sōl´) *v.* to alleviate a person's grief, sense of loss, or trouble; to comfort; **p. 1028**

conspire (kən spīr´) *v.* to join in agreement; to plot; **p. 508**

consternation (kon´ stər nā´ shən) *n.* great fear or shock; upset; **p. 964**

constituency (kən stich´ oo ən se) *n.* voters in a district; a group of supporters; **p. 95**

consummation (kon´ sə mā´ shən) *n.* end; completion; **p. 327**

contrary (kon´ trer ē) *adj.* unfavorable; **p. 931**

corrupt (kə rupt´) *adj.* morally unsound; evil; **p. 472**

covenant (kuv´ ə nənt) *n.* an agreement; a pact **p. 473**

crucial (kroo´ shəl) *adj.* essential; decisive; **p. 287**

cryptically (krip´ tik lē) *adv.* secretly or mysteriously; **p. 1267**

cunningly (kun´ ing lē) *adv.* cleverly; sneakily; **p. 130**

cursory (kur´ sə rē) *adj.* hasty and not thorough; superficial; **p. 1196**

D

decay (di kā´) *v.* to rot or decompose; **p. 31**

decipher (di sī´ fər) *v.* to translate; figure out; **p. 938**

deem (dēm) *v.* to regard in a certain way; **p. 514**

defiance (di fī´ əns) *n.* a refusal to recognize or obey someone or something; **p. 97**

confound/confundir *v.* desconcertar o frustrar; **p. 499**

congealed/cuajado *adj.* espesado, cambiado de un estado líquido a sólido; **p. 793**

consecrate/consecrar *v.* elevar a una posición sagrada mediante un rito religioso; **p. 110**

considerably/considerablemente *adv.* bastante; por una cantidad enorme; **p. 526**

console/consolar *v.* aliviar el dolor, sentido de pérdida o problema de una persona; confortar; **p. 1028**

conspire/conspirar *v.* tramar; acordarse; **p. 508**

consternation/consternación *s.* gran miedo o choque; upset; **p. 964**

constituency/electores *s.* votantes potenciales en un distrito electoral; grupo de partidarios; **p. 95**

consummation/consumación *s.* finalización, terminación; **p. 327**

contrary/contrario *adj.* desfavorable; **p. 931**

corrupt/corrupto *adj.* malo; moralmente impuro; **p. 472**

covenant/alianza *s.* cláusula, pacto o promesa; **p. 473**

crucial/crucial *adj.* esencial; decisivo; **p. 287**

cryptically/ocultamente *adv.* enigmática o misteriosamente; secretamente; **p. 1267**

cunningly/astutamente *adv.* ingeniosamente; disimuladamente; **p. 130**

cursory/somero *adj.* rápido y superficial; **p. 1196**

D

decay/decaer *v.* pudrirse o descomponer; **p. 31**

decipher/descifrar *v.* traducir; deducir; **p. 938**

deem/estimar *v.* creer o percibir de cierta manera; **p. 514**

defiance/desafío *s.* cuando se niega a reconocer o obeír a alguien o algo; **p. 97**

defile (di fīl′) *v.* to make unclean; **p. 386**

demolition (dem′ ə lish′ ən) *n.* an act of tearing down or breaking to pieces; destruction; **p. 405**

demonstrate (dem′ ən strāt′) *v.* to participate in a public display of group opinion; to rally or march; **p. 539**

demur (di mur′) *n.* a hesitation or an objection; **p. 611**

denizen (den′ ə zən) *n.* an inhabitant; **p. 114**

denounce (di nouns′) *v.* to inform against; accuse publicly; **p. 262**

depraved (di prāvd′) *adj.* marked by evil; **p. 406**

derisively (di rī′ siv lē) *adv.* using ridicule or scorn to show contempt; **p. 61**

desist (di zist′) *v.* to cease; to stop; **p. 136**

detect (di tekt′) *v.* discover or determine something; **p. 370**

detest (di test′) *v.* dislike intensely; hate; **p. 691**

detractor (di trak′ tər) *n.* one who speaks ill of someone or something; **p. 336**

devoted (di vō′ tid) *adj.* dedicated; feeling strong attachment; **p. 536**

dictates (dik′ tāts) *n.* principles that must be followed; **p. 687**

dignity (dig′ nə tē) *n.* worthiness; the quality of being worthy of honor; **p. 254**

diligence (dil′ ə jəns) *n.* persistent hard work; alertness; **p. 1206**

dimension (di men′ shən) *n.* a measure of physical form or proportion; **p. 1051**

dire (dīr) *adj.* terrible; bad enough to arouse dread; **p. 265**

discord (dis′ kôrd) *n.* angry or quarrelsome disagreement; lack of harmony; **p. 986**

discourteous (dis kur′ tē əs) *adj.* impolite; **p. 942**

discreetly (dis krēt′ lē) *adv.* unnoticeably; **p. 61**

disdain (dis dān′) *n.* an attitude of scorn or contempt for those considered inferior; **p. 1205**

defile/defilar *v.* ensuciar; **p. 386**

demolition/demolición *s.* acto de derrumbar o romper en trozos; destrucción; **p. 405**

demonstrate/manifestarse *v.* participar en una exhibición pública de opinión colectiva; reunirse y andar; **p. 539**

demur/reparo *s.* vacilación u obyección; **p. 611**

denizen/morador *s.* habitante; **p. 114**

denounce/denunciar *v.* acusar públicamente; informar en contra; **p. 262**

depraved/depravado *adj.* marcado por el malo; **p. 406**

derisively/de burla *adv.* usando ridículo o desdén para mostrar menosprecio; **p. 61**

desist/desistir *v.* cesar, abstenerse, parar; **p. 136**

detect/detectar *v.* descubrir o notar algo; **p. 370**

detest/detestar *v.* caerle intensamente mal; odiar; **p. 691**

detractor/detractor *s.* uno que habla mal de algo o de alguien; **p. 336**

devoted/devoto *adj.* dedicado, unido, vinculado fuertemente; **p. 536**

dictates/dictámenes *s.* principios que deben ser seguidos; **p. 687**

dignity/dignidad *s.* valor; la qualidad de ser digno de honor; **p. 254**

diligence/diligencia *s.* trabajo persistente; estado de alerta; **p. 1206**

dimension/dimensión *s.* medida de forma física o proporción; **p. 1051**

dire/funesto *adj.* terrible; nefasto; suficientement malo para incitar miedo; **p. 265**

discord/discordia *s.* falta de armonía; desacuerdo antipático o peleador; **p. 986**

discourteous/descortés *adj.* falta de cortesía, maleducado; **p. 942**

discreetly/discretamente *adv.* sin percibir; **p. 61**

disdain/desdén *s.* una actitud de menosprecio para los que se consideran inferiores; **p. 1205**

disgruntled (dis grən′ təld) *adj.* unhappy; grumpy; **p. 1213**

disillusion (dis′ i loo′ zhən) *n.* the state of being freed from misleading images or naïve trust; **p. 1029**

disparage (dis par′ ij) *v.* speak badly of; **p. 985**

dispel (dis pel′) *v.* to drive off; **p. 27**

disperse (dis purs′) *v.* scatter or spread in many directions; **p. 993**

dissension (di sen′ shən) *n.* disagreement; discord; **p. 54**

distinguishing (dis ting′ gwish ing) *adj.* marking as different; characterizing; **p. 560**

distorted (dis tôr′ tid) *adj.* twisted out of normal or original shape or condition; **p. 1029**

distressed (dis tres′ d) *adj.* anxious; anguished; upset; **p. 1018**

diversified (di vur′ sə fīd) *adj.* varied; **p. 19**

docile (dos′ əl) *adj.* easily taught; obedient; **p. 687**

dolorous (dō′ lər əs) *adj.* expressing sadness or causing pain; **p. 808**

dreary (drēr′ ē) *adj.* dull or sorrowful; **p. 921**

droves (drōvz) *n.* large numbers of animals or people, moving along together; crowds; **p. 195**

dubious (doo′ bē əs) *adj.* of a questionable nature; **p. 122**

dupe (doop) *v.* to deceive or delude; **p. 381**

E

edible (ed′ ə bəl) *adj.* fit to eat; **p. 1126**

elasticity (i las′ tis′ ə tē) *n.* the quality of being easily adaptable or adjustable, so as to fit changes or new circumstances; **p. 1035**

elude (ē loo′d) *v.* to avoid or escape; **p. 1067**

emaciated (i mā′ shē āt id) *adj.* thin and feeble; **p. 1006**

disgruntled/contrariado *adj.* infeliz, descontento; **p. 1231**

disillusion/desilusión *s.* estado de liberación de imágenes engañosas o confianza ingénua; **p. 1029**

disparage/menospreciar *v.* hablar mal de; **p. 985**

dispel/disipar *v.* hacer desparecer o desvanecer; **p. 27**

disperse/dispersar *v.* esparcir o tirar en muchas direcciones; **p. 993**

dissension/disensión *s.* desacuerdo; discordia; **p. 54**

distinguishing/distintivo *adj.* característico, marcando una diferencia; **p. 560**

distorted/distorsionado *adj.* retorcido en contraste con su forma o condición natural o normal; **p. 1029**

distressed/afligido *adj.* ansioso; angustiado; descontento; **p. 1018**

diversified/diversificado *adj.* variado; **p. 19**

docile/dócil *adj.* fácilmente instruido; obediente; **p. 687**

dolorous/doloroso *adj.* expresando tristeza o causando dolor; **p. 808**

dreary/lóbrego *adj.* deprimente o sombrío; **p. 921**

droves/hordas *s.* un número grande de animales o personas, moviendo en grupo; muchedumbre o manada; **p. 195**

dubious/dudoso *adj.* de una naturaleza discutible o sospechosa; **p. 122**

dupe/embaucar *v.* engañar o deludir; **p. 381**

E

edible/comestible *adj.* apto para ser comido; **p. 1126**

elasticity/elasticidad *s.* la qualidad de ser flexible y adaptarse a cambios o nuevas circunstancias; **p. 1035**

elude/eludir *v.* evitar o escapar; **p. 1067**

emaciated/emaciado *adj.* delgado y débil; **p. 1006**

endorse (en dôrs′) *v.* to inscribe with one's signature to show legal or official approval; **p. 145**

endure (en door′) *v.* continue to exist; last; **p. 692**

enlist (en list′) *v.* to join or give help; convince (someone) to join or to give help; **p. 203**

enmity (en′ mə tē) *n.* hatred or ill will; **p. 944**

epidemic (ep′ ə dem′ ik) *n.* rapid spread of disease affecting many people; **p. 1157**

ethereal (i thēr′ ē əl) *adj.* otherworldly; **p. 1007**

extent (iks tent′) *n.* amount or distance; **p. 687**

exult (ig zult′) *v.* to rejoice greatly; **p. 881**

F

fallacious (fə lā′ shəs) *adj.* erroneous; **p. 1166**

fasten (fas′ ən) *v.* to attach firmly; **p. 245**

fatuous (fach′ o͞o əs) *adj.* silly; foolish; **p. 569**

feign (fān) *v.* to make a false show of; pretend; **p. 882**

fettered (fe′ tərd) *adj.* chained; tied up; **p. 613**

fidelity (fi del′ ə tē) *n.* faithfulness; **p. 1060**

flag (flag) *v.* to decline in interest or attraction; **p. 796**

flout (flout) *v.* to treat with disdain or contempt; scoff at; **p. 137**

flutter (flut′ ər) *v.* move with uneven or trembling motion; **p. 1171**

forage (fôr′ ij) *v.* to hunt or search for food; **p. 804**

foreboding (fôr bō′ ding) *n.* a feeling that something bad or harmful will happen; **p. 285**

formidable (fôr′ mi də bəl) *adj.* tending to inspire awe, wonder, or alarm; **p. 612**

frail (frāl) *adj.* easily broken or damaged; fragile; **p. 832**

frantically (fran′ tik lē) *adv.* in a manner marked by fast and nervous activity; **p. 823**

frivolity (fri vol′ ə tē) *n.* silliness; **p. 1247**

endorse/endosar *v.* firmar para aprobar legal o oficialmente; **p. 145**

endure/perdurar *v.* continuar existiendo; durar; **p. 692**

enlist/alistar *v.* unirse para ayudar; reclutar; convencerle a alguien a aliarse; **p. 203**

enmity/enemistad *s.* odio o mala voluntad; **p. 944**

epidemic/epidemia *s.* diseminación rápida de enfermedad que afecta a mucha gente; **p. 1157**

ethereal/etéreo *adj.* de otro mundo; **p. 1007**

extent/extensión *s.* amplitud; alcance; distancia; **p. 687**

exult/exultarse *v.* regocijarse enormemente; **p. 881**

F

fallacious/falaz *adj.* erróneo; **p. 1166**

fasten/sujetar *v.* atar o abrochar firmemente; **p. 245**

fatuous/fátuo *adj.* tonto; ridículo; **p. 569**

feign/fingir *v.* hacer una impresión falsa; disimular; **p. 882**

fettered/encadenado *adj.* atado, puesto en grillos; **p. 613**

fidelity/fidelidad *s.* sentido de fe; lealtad; **p. 1060**

flag/decaer *v.* perder o disminuir en interés o atracción; **p. 796**

flout/desacatar *v.* desobedecer; tratar con desdén y menosprecio; **p. 137**

flutter/revolotear *v.* mover tremblando o con gestos irregulares o discontinuos; **p. 1171**

forage/forrajear *v.* buscar comida; **p. 804**

foreboding/aprensión *s.* sentimiento o premonición que algo malo o dañoso occurirá; **p. 285**

formidable/formidable *adj.* lo que inspira asombro, preocupación o maravilla.; **p. 612**

frail/endeble *adj.* fácilmente roto o dañido; frágil; **p. 832**

frantically/fránticamente *adv.* marcado por actividad rápida y nerviosa; **p. 823**

frivolity/frivolidad *s.* tontería; **p. 1247**

fruitless (fro͞ot′ lis) *adj.* unproductive; useless; sure to end in failure; **p. 499**

fumble (fum′ bəl) *v.* to grope or handle clumsily; **p. 147**

furrows (fur′ ōs) *n.* grooves or tracks cut in the earth by a plow; wrinkles; **p. 1018**

furtively (fər′ tiv lē) *adv.* in a secret manner; **p. 755**

futile (fū′ til) *adj.* useless; worthless; ineffectual; **p. 371**

G

gauge (gāj) *v.* to estimate; judge; **p. 286**

gesticulate (jes tik′ yə lāt′) *v.* to make gestures, especially when speaking; **p. 719**

glean (glēn) *v.* gather after reapers; gather slowly, bit by bit; discover or find out slowly; **p. 479**

glistening (glis′ən′ ing) *adj.* glittering; twinkling; **p. 216**

glittering (glit′ ər ing) *adj.* marked by a sparkling quality or brilliance; **p. 751**

gloat (glōt) *v.* to regard with malignant satisfaction; **p. 224**

graceful (grās′ fəl) *adj.* showing effortless beauty or movement; **p. 831**

gratitude (grat′ ə to͞od′) *n.* thankfulness; **p. 95**

gravely (grāv′ lē) *adv.* in a serious or dignified manner; **p. 1252**

grudge (gruj) *n.* a feeling of hatred or resentment; **p. 894**

guffaw (gu fô′) *n.* loud or boisterous burst of laughter; **p. 1283**

H

haggard (hag′ ərd) *adj.* worn or wasted, as from hunger; **p. 1246**

haste (hāst) *n.* quickness of action or movement; hurry; **p. 1151**

fruitless/infructuoso *adj.* inútil; no productivo; lo que acabará en fracaso; **p. 499**

fumble/buscar a tientas *v.* hurgar o revolver torpemente; **p. 147**

furrows/surcos *s.* vías o ranuras abiertas en la tierra por un arado; arrugas; **p. 1018**

furtively/furtivamente *adv.* de manera secreta; **p. 755**

futile/inútil *adj.* sin valor, incapaz; **p. 371**

G

gauge/calcular *v.* evaluar, medir; **p. 286**

gesticulate/gesticular *v.* hacer gestos, especialmente mientras habla; **p. 719**

glean/cosechar *v.* recoger después de la cosecha; recoger lentamente, poco a poco, o descubrir lentamente; **p. 479**

glistening/centelleante *adj.* brillante, relumbrante; **p. 216**

glittering/resplandesciente *adj.* marcado por una qualidad de luz o brillo; **p. 751**

gloat/regodearse *v.* ver con satisfacción maligna; **p. 224**

graceful/grácil *adj.* mostrando belleza o movimiento sin esfuerzo; **p. 831**

gratitude/gratitud *s.* sentido de agradecimiento; **p. 95**

gravely/gravemente *adv.* de manera seria o digna; **p. 1252**

grudge/rencilla *s.* un sentido de odio o resentimiento; **p. 894**

guffaw/carcajada *s.* una risa alta y ruidosa; **p. 1283**

H

haggard/demacrado *adj.* cansado o emaciado, como de hambre; **p. 1246**

haste/apuro *s.* prisa; rapidez de acción o movimiento; **p. 1151**

heedless (hēd′ lis) *adj.* inconsiderate; thoughtless; **p. 62**

hindrance (hin′ drəns) *n.* a thing that presents a challenge, struggle, or delay to someone or something; obstacle; **p. 1171**

homage (hom′ ij) *n.* the honor or respect that is shown to another person; **p. 687**

horde (hôrd) *n.* a teeming crowd or throng; **p. 87**

horrendous (hô ren′dəs) *adj.* horrible; frightful; **p. 310**

hover (huv′ ər) *v.* to hang in the air; **p. 26**

humane (hū mān′) *adj.* marked by compassion, sympathy, or consideration for humans or animals; **p. 1003**

humility (hū mil′ ə tē) *n.* modesty; meekness; **p. 1152**

I

ignominious (ig′ nə min′ ē əs) *adj.* marked or characterized by disgrace or shame; **p. 205**

impartial (im pär′ shəl) *adj.* treating everyone or everything in an equal way; **p. 122**

impel (im pel′) *v.* to urge forward as if through moral pressure; **p. 384**

impervious (im pur′ vē əs) *adj.* not easily affected or disturbed; **p. 639**

imploring (im plôr′ ing) *adj.* begging or beseeching; **p. 798**

improvise (im′ prə vīz′) *v.* to create to meet an unexpected need; **p. 1247**

impulse (im′ puls) *n.* a sudden desire or feeling that makes one want to act; **p. 560**

incessant (in ses′ ənt) *adj.* continuing without interruption; **p. 139**

incomprehensible (in′ kom pri hen′ sə bəl) *adj.* unintelligible; indiscernible; not understood; **p. 629**

incredulous (in krej′ ə ləs) *adj.* doubting; skeptical; **p. 323**

heedless/hecho caso omiso *adj.* sin prestar atención o pensar; **p. 62**

hindrance/estorbo *s.* obstáculo; algo que presenta un desafío, pelea o demora; **p. 1171**

homage/homenaje *s.* el honor o respeto dado a otro; **p. 687**

horde/horda *s.* una multitud animada o muchedumbre; **p. 87**

horrendous/horrendo *adj.* horrible, miedoso; **p. 310**

hover/cernerse *v.* sostenerse en el aire; **p. 26**

humane/humanitario *adj.* marcado por compasión, simpatía o consideración para humanos o animales; **p. 1003**

humility/humildad *s.* modestia; docilidad; **p. 1152**

I

ignominious/ignominioso *adj.* marcado o caracterizado por desgracia o vergüenza; **p. 205**

impartial/imparcial *adj.* tratar a todo y a todo el mundo de manera igual; **p. 122**

impel/impeler *v.* pedirle a alguien con insistencia y con presión moral; **p. 384**

impervious/impermeable *adj.* no influido o perturbado fácilmente; **p. 639**

imploring/implorante *adj.* rogante o suplicante; **p. 798**

improvise/improvisar *v.* crear para responder a una necesidad no anticipada; **p. 1247**

impulse/impulso *s.* un deseo o sentimiento repentino que inspira a uno a actuar; **p. 560**

incessant/incesante *adj.* continuar sin cesar o interrumpir; **p. 139**

incomprehensible/incomprensible *adj.* no comprendido; imperceptible; ininteligible; **p. 629**

incredulous/incrédulo *adj.* dudoso; escéptico; **p. 323**

increment (ing′ krə mənt) *n.* something gained or added in a series, usually at regular intervals; **p. 623**

incur (in kur′) *v.* to bring upon oneself; **p. 494**

indiscriminately (in′ dis krim′ ə nit lē) *adv.* randomly; haphazardly; **p. 1006**

inexorable (i nek′ sər ə bəl) *adj.* relentless; unyielding; **p. 639**

inflict (in flikt′) *v.* to give or cause; **p. 305**

inhabit (in hab′ it) *adj.* to reside or live in; **p. 1133**

inordinate (in ôr′ də nit) *adj.* excessive; **p. 568**

inquisitive (in kwiz′ ə tiv) *adj.* curious about the world or the affairs of others; **p. 720**

insular (in′ sə lər) *adj.* isolated; narrow-minded; **p. 628**

intermittently (in′ tər mit′ ənt lē) *adv.* on and off again; coming at intervals; **p. 588**

intersection (in′ tər sek′ shən) *n.* a place where roads cross one another; **p. 731**

intimation (in tə mā′ shən) *n.* an indirect suggestion; **p. 338**

intransigence (in tran′ sə jənts) *n.* the state of being uncompromising; **p. 757**

irrevocable (i rev′ ə kə bəl) *adj.* incapable of being brought back, undone, or changed; **p. 1203**

J

jubilant (jōō′ bə lənt) *adj.* joyful; rejoicing; **p. 817**

L

lament (lə ment′) *v.* to mourn or express grief for; **p. 19**

listless (list′ lis) *adj.* showing disinterest; spiritless; **p. 808**

loom (lōōm) *v.* to come into sight in enlarged or distorted form; **p. 1279**

lucid (lōō′ sid) *adj.* having full use of one's faculties; clear-headed; **p. 1233**

---

increment/incremento *s.* algo ganado o añadido en una serie, generalmente por entregas; **p. 623**

incur/incurrir en *v.* provocar o buscarse algo; **p. 494**

indiscriminately/indiscriminadamente *adv.* hecho caprichosamente o al azar; **p. 1006**

inexorable/inexorable *adj.* sin rendir; **p. 639**

inflict/afligir *v.* dar o causar; **p. 305**

inhabit/habitar *adj.* vivir o residir en; **p. 1133**

inordinate/exorbitante *adj.* excesivo; **p. 568**

inquisitive/inquisitivo *adj.* curioso sobre el mundo o los asuntos de otros; **p. 720**

insular/insular *adj.* aislado; cerrado mentalmente; **p. 628**

intermittently/intermitente *adv.* llegando por intérvalos irregulares; **p. 588**

intersection/intersección *s.* un lugar donde los caminos se entrecruzan; **p. 731**

intimation/indicio *s.* una sugestión indirecta; **p. 338**

intransigence/intransigencia *s.* estado de no comprometerse; **p. 757**

irrevocable/irrevocable *adj.* incapaz de ser recuperado, cambiado o deshecho; **p. 1203**

J

jubilant/de júbilo *adj.* exultante, feliz; **p. 817**

L

lament/lamentar *v.* expresar pena por o llorar la pérdida de alguien; **p. 19**

listless/apático *adj.* mostrando desinterés; lánguido; **p. 808**

loom/avecinarse *v.* acercarse o aparecer en forma distorsionada o ampliada; **p. 1279**

lucid/lúcido *adj.* estado de tener uso completo de las facultades; mentalidad clara; **p. 1233**

lush (lush) *adj.* luxuriant; thick with vegetation; **p. 816**

M

magnitude (mag′ nə to͞od′) *n.* great size or importance; **p. 585**

majesty (maj′ is tē) *n.* greatness or magnificence of quality or nature; splendor; **p. 1171**

malicious (mə lish′ əs) *adj.* marked by a desire to cause pain, injury, or distress to another; **p. 522**

marvelous (marv′ ə ləs) *adj.* extraordinary; causing wonder; **p. 793**

mediocre (mē′ dē ō′ kər) *adj.* of moderate or low quality; undistinguished; **p. 1251**

menace (men′ is) *n.* a person or thing that is a threat or danger; **p. 1228**

mere (mēr) *adj.* being nothing more or less than; **p. 1052**

mesmerize (mez′ mə rīz′) *v.* to hypnotize; spellbind; **p. 97**

misery (miz′ ər ē) *n.* unhappy state of mind; great distress; wretchedness; **p. 873**

mitigate (mi′ tə gāt′) *v.* to lessen; **p. 1166**

moderation (mod′ ə rā′ shən) *n.* avoiding or limiting excesses or extremes; self-control; **p. 365**

modest (mod′ ist) *adj.* unassuming; plain; simple; **p. 1017**

monotony (mə not′ ən ē) *n.* tiresome sameness; **p. 768**

munificence (mū nif′ ə səns) *v.* great generosity; **p. 406**

murmur (mər′ mər) *v.* to say something in an indistinct voice; to say something quietly and cautiously; **p. 518**

muster (mus′ tər) *v.* to cause to gather; **p. 1290**

mutter (mut′ ər) *v.* to speak in a low voice or indistinctly with lips partially closed; **p. 804**

myriad (mir′ ē əd) *adj.* countless; of a very great number of persons or things; **p. 1060**

lush/exuberante *adj.* lleno de vegetación; abundante; **p. 816**

M

magnitude/magnitud *s.* gran tamaño o importancia; **p. 585**

majesty/majestad *s.* esplendor; magnificencia de calidad o naturaleza; **p. 1171**

malicious/malicioso *adj.* marcado por el deseo de causar dolor o herir a otro; **p. 522**

marvelous/maravilloso *adj.* extraordinario; causando asombro; **p. 793**

mediocre/mediocre *adj.* de calidad moderada o baja; sin distinguir; **p. 1251**

menace/amenaza *s.* una persona o cosa que es un peligro; **p. 1228**

mere/mero *adj.* ser nada más o menos que; **p. 1052**

mesmerize/cautivar *v.* hipnotizar; fascinar; **p. 97**

misery/miseria *s.* un estado mental infeliz; gran angustia; desgracia; **p. 873**

mitigate/mitigar *v.* disminuir; **p. 1166**

moderation/moderación *s.* evitar o limitar lo excesivo o lo extremo; control sobre sí mismo; **p. 365**

modest/modesto *adj.* sin pretensión; simple; sencillo; **p. 1017**

monotony/monotonía *s.* repetición tediosa; **p. 768**

munificence/munificencia *v.* gran generosidad; **p. 406**

murmur/murmurar *v.* decir algo en una voz suave; decir algo calladamente con prudencia; **p. 518**

muster/llamar a asambea *v.* reunir; lograr a formar; **p. 1290**

mutter/refunfuñar *v.* hablar en una voz baja o indistinta o hablar entre dientes; **p. 804**

myriad/millar de *adj.* de un gran número de personas o cosas; **p. 1060**

N

nautical (nô′ ti kəl) *adj.* of or relating to sailors or ships; **p. 1052**

negate (ni gāt′) *v.* to make ineffectual or powerless; **p. 1060**

nimble (nim′ bəl) *adj.* sure-footed; light and quick; **p. 909**

nonentity (non en′ tə tē) *n.* a person or a thing of little or no importance; **p. 95**

nullity (nul′ ə tē) *n.* a mere nothing; something insignificant; **p. 598**

O

obliterate (ə blit′ e rāt′) *v.* to erase from memory; to destroy all traces of; **p. 1213**

oblivion (ə bliv′ ē ən) *n.* state of having been forgotten; **p. 304**

obscure (əb skyoor′) *v.* to hide from view; **p. 126**

obsessed (əb sesd′) *adj.* having an excessive concern; **p. 979**

obsolete (ob′ sə lēt′) *adj.* outdated; no longer in use; **p. 817**

P

pensive (pen′ siv) *adj.* thoughtful; **p. 964**

penuriously (pi noor′ ē əs lē) *adv.* marked by severe poverty; **p. 929**

perish (per′ ish) *v.* to die or cease to exist; **p. 31**

perpetual (pər pech′ o͞o əl) *adj.* everlasting; eternal; **p. 804**

perusal (pə ro͞o′ zəl) *n.* the act of reading in detail or examining carefully; examination; **p. 1228**

pester (pes′ tər) *v.* to harass or annoy with petty irritations; **p. 145**

phenomenon (fə nom′ ə non′) *n.* an observable fact or subject of scientific study; a remarkable event or occurrence; **p. 1194**

pity (pit′ ē) *n.* sympathy for another′s suffering; **p. 921**

N

nautical/naútico *adj.* relacionado con marineros o barcos; **p. 1052**

negate/negar *v.* hacer ineficaz o rendir sin poder; **p. 1060**

nimble/hábil *adj.* ligero y rápido; de pie firme; **p. 909**

nonentity/don nadie *s.* persona insignificante o cosa de poca importancia; **p. 95**

nullity/nulidad *s.* una cosa trivial; algo insignificante; **p. 598**

O

obliterate/arrasar *v.* destruir todos los rastros de; borrar de la memoria; **p. 1213**

oblivion/olvido *s.* estado de haber sido olvidado; **p. 304**

obscure/ocultar *v.* esconder de la vista; **p. 126**

obsessed/obsesionado *adj.* preocupado excesivamente; **p. 979**

obsolete/obsoleto *adj.* anticuado; ya no usado; **p. 817**

P

pensive/meditabundo *adj.* pensativo; **p. 964**

penuriously/penuriamente *adv.* marcado por pobreza severa; **p. 929**

perish/perecer *v.* morir o cesar a existir; **p. 31**

perpetual/perpétuo *adj.* eterno; imperecedero; **p. 804**

perusal/examinación *s.* el actor de leer cuidadosa o detenidamente; **p. 1228**

pester/importunar *v.* molestar o fastidiar con irritaciones triviales; **p. 145**

phenomenon/fenómeno *s.* hecho o tema de estudio científico que se puede observar; evento o acontecimiento notable; **p. 1194**

pity/lástima *s.* simpatía por el sufrimiento de otro; **p. 921**

plaintively (plān′ tiv lē) *adv.* in a manner expressing suffering or woe; **p. 758**

plausible (plô′ zə bəl) *adj.* appearing worthy of belief; **p. 824**

plight (plīt) *n.* a situation that is hard to manage or resolve; **p. 122**

ploy (ploi) *n.* a trick or tactic; **p. 1166**

poignancy (poin′ yən sē) *n.* the quality of painfully affecting one's feelings; **p. 567**

pounce (pouns) *v.* to swoop down on and quickly seize upon or take advantage of something; **p. 1251**

precipitous (pri sip′ ə təs) *adj.* having very steep sides; **p. 405**

prelude (prel′ ūd) *n.* an event preceding and preparing for a more important matter; **p. 823**

presumption (pri zump′ shən) *n.* attitude or conduct that oversteps the bounds of propriety or courtesy; **p. 931**

presumptuous (pri zump′ chōō əs) *adj.* excessively bold or arrogant; taking liberties; **p. 1195**

prevail (pri vāl′) *v.* to gain ascendancy through strength or superiority; to triumph; **p. 459**

primordial (prī môr′ dē əl) *adj.* original; existing from the beginning; **p. 589**

pristine (pris′ tēn′) *adj.* pure; unspoiled; **p. 590**

proclaim (prə klām′) *v.* to announce publicly; to make known; to declare; **p. 561**

profane (prō fān′) *adj.* not concerned with religious purposes; **p. 1290**

prolong (prə lông′) *v.* lengthen in time or space; draw out; **p. 1017**

propriety (prə prī′ ə tē) *n.* conformity to what is acceptable in conduct or speech; **p. 1204**

prosperity (pros per′ ə tē) *n.* the state of being successful; **p. 514**

provincial (prə vin′ shəl) *adj.* belonging or peculiar to a particular province; local; lacking sophistication or polish; **p. 628**

plaintively/lastimeramente *adv.* en una manera que expresa lástima o pena; **p. 758**

plausible/verosímil *adj.* lo que aparenta ser creíble; **p. 824**

plight/apuro *s.* situación difícil de resolver o negociar; **p. 122**

ploy/treta *s.* un engaño o táctica; **p. 1166**

poignancy/lo conmovido *s.* la calidad de afectar dolorosamente las emociones de uno; **p. 567**

pounce/saltar *v.* lanzarse sobre algo para captarlo o aprovecharse; **p. 1251**

precipitous/precípito *adj.* con lados empinados; **p. 405**

prelude/preludio *s.* un evento que precede y que prepara para un evento importante; **p. 823**

presumption/presunción *s.* actitud o conducta que va más allá de las fronteras de la cortesía o del decoro; **p. 931**

presumptuous/presuntuoso *adj.* excesivamente audaz o arrogante; tendencia a tomarse libertades; **p. 1195**

prevail/prevalecer *v.* ascender mediante fuerza o superioridad; triunfar; **p. 459**

primordial/primordial *adj.* original; que existe desde del comienzo; **p. 589**

pristine/inmaculado *adj.* puro; impoluto; **p. 590**

proclaim/proclamar *v.* anunicar públicamente; hacerlo saber; declarar; **p. 561**

profane/profano *adj.* no relacionado con propósitos religiosos; **p. 1290**

prolong/prolongar *v.* extender en tiempo o espacio; alargar; **p. 1017**

propriety/decoro *s.* conformidad con lo que se acepta en conducta o habla; **p. 1204**

prosperity/prosperidad *s.* el estado de tener éxito; **p. 514**

provincial/provincial *adj.* perteneciente a o particular de una provincia específica; local; carente de sofisticación o pulcro; **p. 628**

prudent (pro͞od′ ənt) *adj.* sensible; sound in judgment; **p. 1058**

pungent (pun′ jənt) *adj.* having a sharp or stinging quality, especially affecting the sense of taste or smell; **p. 643**

R

radiant (rā′ dē ənt) *adj.* glowing; beaming; **p. 26**

random (ran′ dəm) *n.* lack of careful choice or plan; **p. 294**

range (rānj) *n.* the full extent over which something moves or is seen, heard, effective, etc.; scope; **p. 526**

rare (rār) *adj.* distinctive or seldom seen; **p. 522**

rational (rash′ ən əl) *adj.* able to reason; **p. 892**

ravaged (rav′ ijd) *adj.* devastated; ruined; **p. 454**

rebuke (ri bu̅k′) *v.* to criticize sharply; **p. 110**

redeem (ri dēm′) *v.* buy back, as with property; **p. 482**

reel (rēl) *v.* stand or move unsteadily; sway from a blow or shock; **p. 905**

refuge (ref′ ūj) *n.* shelter or protection from danger; **p. 879**

refuse (ref′ ūs) *n.* trash; garbage; **p. 87**

relentless (ri lent′ lis) *adj.* showing or promising no lessening of severity or intensity; **p. 1289**

renown (ri noun′) *n.* a state of being widely acclaimed; **p. 939**

reprisal (ri prī′ zəl) *n.* the act of using force in retaliation for damage or loss suffered; **p. 750**

resignation (rez′ ig nā′ shən) *n.* unresisting acceptance; **p. 1252**

respites (res′ pits) *n.* periods of temporary relief, rest, or delay; **p. 1036**

retaliation (ri tal′ ē ā′ shən) *n.* revenge; **p. 116**

retort (ri tôrt′) *v.* to reply in kind, especially with anger or with a witty or an insulting response; **p. 54**

prudent/prudente *adj.* sensible; sensato en los juicios; **p. 1058**

pungent/acre *adj.* tener un qualidad fuerte o mordaz, que afecta especialmente el sentido de sabor o olfato; **p. 643**

R

radiant/radiante *adj.* resplandeciente; brillante; **p. 26**

random/al azar *s.* falta de selección o plan meticuloso; **p. 294**

range/ámbito *s.* la esfera entera por la que algo se mueve, es oído o tiene alcance; campo; **p. 526**

rare/raro *adj.* distinto o poco visto; **p. 522**

rational/racional *adj.* capaz de razonar; **p. 892**

ravaged/asolado *adj.* devastado; arruinado; **p. 454**

rebuke/reprender *v.* criticar fuertemente; **p. 110**

redeem/desempeñar *v.* comprar de nuevo, como con propiedad; **p. 482**

reel/tambalearse *v.* estar de pie o moverse inestablemente; moverse en respuesta a un golpe o choque; **p. 905**

refuge/refugio *s.* sanctuario o protección de peligro; **p. 879**

refuse/desperdicios *s.* residuos; basura; **p. 87**

relentless/incesante *adj.* lo que aparenta o promete no disminuir en severidad o intensidad; **p. 1289**

renown/renombre *s.* estado de ser ampliamente aclamado; **p. 939**

reprisal/represalia *s.* el acto de usar fuerza en venganza por daño sufrido; **p. 750**

resignation/resignación *s.* aprobación o aceptación sin resistencia; **p. 1252**

respites/respiros *s.* periodos breves de descanso, alivio o demora; **p. 1036**

retaliation/represalias *s.* venganza; **p. 116**

retort/réplica *v.* responder con ira o con contestación humorosa o ofensiva; **p. 54**

retract (ri trakt´) v. take back or deny; **p. 287**

revered (ri vērd´) adj. regarded as worthy of great honor; **p. 929**

revive (ri vīv´) v. to recover; to come back to life; **p. 1134**

rivet (riv´ it) v. fixed firmly; completely engrossed; **p. 1068**

ruddy (rud´ ē) adj. having a rosy or reddish complexion; **p. 816**

rustle (rus´ əl) v. to make a succession of soft crackling sounds; **p. 80**

S

savage (sav´ ij) adj. wild; untamed, and often fierce; **p. 888**

scholarship (skol´ ər ship´) n. academic achievement or knowledge; **p. 597**

scorn (skôrn) v. disrespect; show contempt for; **p. 1059**

scrutinize (skrōōt´ ən īz´) v. to examine with close attention to detail; **p. 623**

seclusion (si klōō´ zhən) n. solitude; privacy; isolation; **p. 1017**

sedately (si dāt´ lē) adv. in a dignified or serious manner; calmly; solemnly; **p. 631**

seldom (sel´ dəm) adv. rarely; **p. 734**

self-possessed (self´ pə zest´) adj. in control of oneself; **p. 1268**

sever (sev´ ər) v. cut or break apart; separate; divide; **p. 873**

sheer (shēr) adj. unmixed; pure; **p. 1213**

shirk (shurk) v. to evade or avoid one's duty; **p. 622**

shrill (shrill) adj. high-pitched; **p. 518**

shrivel (shriv´ əl) v. to become wrinkled as a result of lack of moisture; **p. 1283**

retract/retirar v. negar o retractarse; **p. 287**

revered/venerado adj. visto como digno de gran honor; **p. 929**

revive/resucitar v. recubrir, reanimarse; **p. 1134**

rivet/remachar v. atado firmemente; completamente fascinado; **p. 1068**

ruddy/rubicundo adj. tener una complexión rosada; **p. 816**

rustle/susurrar v. hacer una sucesión de sonidos suaves o crujientes; **p. 80**

S

savage/salvaje adj. feroz, sin domar, agreste; **p. 888**

scholarship/investigación s. estudio o conocimiento académico; **p. 597**

scorn/desdén v. falta de respeto; menospreciar; **p. 1059**

scrutinize/escudriñar v. examinar detenidamente; **p. 623**

seclusion/reclusión s. soledad; privacidad; aislamiento; **p. 1017**

sedately/reposadamente adv. tranquilamente; solemnemente; de manera dignificada o seria; **p. 631**

seldom/pocas veces adv. rara vez, raramente; **p. 734**

self-possessed/sereno adj. dueño de sí mismo; **p. 1268**

sever/cercenar v. cortar o romper; separar; dividir; **p. 873**

sheer/puro adj. sin mezclar con otra cosa; **p. 1213**

shirk/rehuir v. evitar o eludir la responsabilidad; **p. 622**

shrill/estridente adj. agudo; **p. 518**

shrivel/marchitarse v. encogerse y arrugarse por falta de humedad; **p. 1283**

sinister (sin′ is tər) *adj.* singularly evil; menacing; **p. 406**

sly (slī) *adj.* clever; wily; secretive; **p. 371**

sojourn (sō′ jurn) *v.* stay or reside temporarily; **p. 478**

solace (sol′ is) *n.* a source of relief; mental or spiritual comfort; **p. 1233**

solemn (sol′ əm) *adj.* serious; gravely important; **p. 1140**

solitary (sol′ ə ter′ ē) *adj.* characterized by loneliness or lack of companions; lonely; **p. 526**

solitude (sol′ ə tood′) *n.* state of being alone; isolation; **p. 979**

sordid (sôr′ did) *adj.* dirty; squalid; wretched; **p. 614**

splendid (splen′ did) *adj.* grand; magnificent; **p. 19**

stern (sturn) *adj.* harsh or severe in manner; firm or unyielding; **p. 365**

stifled (stī′ fəld) *adj.* muffled or repressed; **p. 153**

straggler (strag′ lər) *n.* one who lags behind or strays from a group; **p. 1156**

stray (strā) *v.* to wander away; to go off course; **p. 1138**

strut (strut) *v.* to walk in a proud manner; **p. 882**

stupefied (stoo′ pə fīd) *adj.* stupid, groggy, or insensible; **p. 623**

stupor (stoo′ pər) *n.* a dulled mental state, often as a result of shock or stress; a daze; **p. 1284**

submerge (səb murj′) *v.* to go under water; **p. 153**

subtle (sut′ əl) *adj.* hard to detect; **p. 243**

sullen (sul′ ən) *adj.* showing resentment and ill humor by sulky withdrawal; **p. 280**

supplementary (sup′ lə men′ tər ē) *adj.* extra or additional; **p. 1271**

sinister/siniestro *adj.* singularmente malo; amenazante; **p. 406**

sly/ladino *adj.* listo, astuto, secreto; **p. 371**

sojourn/residir por una temporada *v.* quedar provisionalmente o durante una estadía breve; **p. 478**

solace/solaz *s.* una fuente de alivio mental o espíritual; **p. 1233**

solemn/solemne *adj.* serio; gravemente importante; **p. 1140**

solitary/solitario *adj.* caracterizado por soledad o falta de compañeros; solo; **p. 526**

solitude/soledad *s.* estado de estar solo; aislamiento; **p. 979**

sordid/sórdido *adj.* sucio; esquálido; desdichado; **p. 614**

splendid/espléndido *adj.* grandioso; magnífico; **p. 19**

stern/severo *adj.* agresivo o duro en actitud; firme o sin rendir; **p. 365**

stifled/sofocar *adj.* reprimido o ahogado; **p. 153**

straggler/rezagado *s.* uno que se queda atrás o se aparta de un grupo; **p. 1156**

stray/extraviarse *v.* apartarse; alejarse del camino; **p. 1138**

strut/pavonearse *v.* caminar de modo orgulloso; **p. 882**

stupefied/estupefacto *adj.* estúpido, insensible o atontado; **p. 623**

stupor/estupor *s.* un estado mental atontado muchas veces como resultado de choque o estrés; **p. 1284**

submerge/sumergir *v.* descender bajo agua; **p. 153**

subtle/sútil *adj.* difícil de detectar; **p. 243**

sullen/hosco *adj.* mostrando resentimiento al retirarse malhumorado; **p. 280**

supplementary/suplementario *adj.* extra o adicional; **p. 1271**

suppliant (sə′ plē′ ənt) *n.* one who asks humbly and earnestly; **p. 386**

supplication (sup′ lə kā′ shən) *n.* humble entreaty; prayer of request; **p. 1235**

suppress (sə pres′) *v.* keep in or hold back; **p. 370**

surge (surj) *n.* a strong, sudden increase or flow; **p. 648**

surpass (sər pas′) *v.* to exceed; **p. 244**

sustenance (sus′ tə nəns) *n.* food; nourishment; means of support; **p. 1157**

swell (swel) *v.* to increase in size or volume; expand; **p. 365**

T

taint (tānt) *v.* to contaminate morally; to corrupt; **p. 825**

tamper (tam′ pər) *v.* meddle improperly; **p. 692**

tangible (tan′ jə bəl) *adj.* real; actual; definite; **p. 326**

taut (tôt) *adj.* having no give or slack; tightly drawn; **p. 152**

tedious (tē′ dē əs) *adj.* tiresome because of length or dullness; boring; **p. 1144**

tempo (tem′pō) *n.* pattern or rate of movement; **p. 768**

tepid (tep′ id) *adj.* lukewarm; halfhearted; **p. 631**

thicket (thik′ it) *n.* a dense growth of shrubs, underbrush, or small trees; **p. 498**

throng (throng) *n.* a crowd of many people; **p. 86**

titter (ti′ tər) *v.* to laugh nervously; **p. 796**

toil (toil) *n.* fatiguing work or effort; **p. 54**

torment (tôr′ ment) *n.* great pain or suffering; **p. 879**

torrent (tôr′ ənt) *n.* a powerful flood or outpouring; **p. 81**

suppliant/suplicante *s.* uno que pide con humildad y seriedad; **p. 386**

supplication/súplica *s.* ruego humilde; oración de petición; **p. 1235**

suppress/suprimir *v.* guardar o retener; **p. 370**

surge/subida *s.* un aumento o flujo repentino y fuerte; **p. 648**

surpass/superar *v.* exceder; **p. 244**

sustenance/sustento *s.* comida, alimento; apoyo; **p. 1157**

swell/hincharse *v.* aumentar en tamaño o volumen; expandir; **p. 365**

T

taint/mancillar *v.* contaminar moralmente; corrumpir; **p. 825**

tamper/alterar *v.* tocar o cambiar incorrectamente; **p. 692**

tangible/tangible *v.* real; definido; palpable; **p. 326**

taut/tirante *adj.* no ser flojo; tenso; **p. 152**

tedious/tedio *adj.* cansado debido a la extensión o falta de interés; aburrido; **p. 1144**

tempo/tempo *s.* pauta o ritmo de movimiento; **p. 768**

tepid/tibio *adj.* poco cálido; poco entusiasta; **p. 631**

thicket/matorral *s.* crecimiento denso de plantas, arbustos o árboles pequeños; **p. 498**

throng/muchedumbre *s.* multitud de muchas personas; **p. 86**

titter/reírse disimuladamente *v.* reirse nerviosamente con risitas ahogadas; **p. 796**

toil/labor *s.* gran esfuerzo o trabajo duro; **p. 54**

torment/tormento *s.* gran dolor o sufrimiento; **p. 879**

torrent/torrente *s.* gran flujo o desahogo; **p. 81**

trample (tram´ pəl) *v.* to walk upon and damage by crushing or bruising; to stomp; **p. 750**

tranquil (trang´ kwəl) *adj.* calm; peaceful; **p. 32**

treacherous (trech´ ər əs) *adj.* hazardous; dangerous; **p. 458**

trespass (tres´ pəs) *v.* illegally enter property; **p. 987**

trivial (triv´ ē əl) *adj.* commonplace; of little importance; **p. 720**

tumult (tōō´ məlt) *n.* commotion or noisy confusion; **p. 501**

U

undaunted (un dôn´ tid) *adj.* courageously firm or resolute, especially in the face of danger or difficulty; not discouraged; **p. 1036**

undulant (un´ jə lənt) *adj.* having a wavy form or motion; **p. 750**

unwitting (un wit´ ing) *adj.* not knowing; unaware; **p. 1213**

V

vague (vāg) *adj.* unclear; without form; indistinct; **p. 518**

veer (vēr) *v.* to change direction or course; **p. 1144**

vengeance (ven´ jəns) *n.* revenge; the return of a harmful deed for a harmful deed; **p. 255**

verdict (vur´ dikt) *n.* decision; judgment; **p. 901**

versatility (vər´ sə ti´ lə tē) *n.* ability to do many things well; **p. 326**

vigorously (vig´ ər əs lē) *adv.* energetically; **p. 143**

vivacity (vi vas´ ə tē´) *n.* liveliness; animation; **p. 964**

vulnerable (vul´ nər ə bəl) *adj.* weak; unable to defend oneself; **p. 314**

trample/pisotear *v.* caminar por encima y hacer daño aplastando; **p. 750**

tranquil/tranquilo *adj.* calmado; pacífico; **p. 32**

treacherous/traicionero *adj.* peligroso, arriesgado; **p. 458**

trespass/traspasar *v.* entrar en propiedad ajena ilegalmente; **p. 987**

trivial/trivial *adj.* común; de poca importancia; **p. 720**

tumult/tumulto *s.* conmoción o confusión ruidosa; **p. 501**

U

undaunted/impertérrito *adj.* firme o resoluto con coraje, especialmente ante peligro o dificultad; difícil de desanimar; **p. 1036**

undulant/ondulante *adj.* con forma de olas o que hace movimientos en forma de olas; **p. 750**

unwitting/involuntario *adj.* sin saber; inconsciente; **p. 1213**

V

vague/vago *adj.* poco claro; sin forma; indistinto; **p. 518**

veer/virar *v.* cambiar rumbo o sentido; **p. 1144**

vengeance/venganza *s.* hacer una hazaña dañina a cambio de otra hazana dañina; **p. 255**

verdict/veredicto *s.* decisión; juicio; **p. 901**

versatility/versatilidad *s.* capacidad de hacer muchas cosas; **p. 326**

vigorously/vigurosamente *adv.* con mucha energía; **p. 143**

vivacity/vivacidad *s.* entusiasmo; animación; **p. 964**

vulnerable/vulnerable *adj.* débil; incapaz de defenderse; **p. 314**

W

waive (wāv) *v.* to reject, decline, or give up; p. 507

winnow (win′ ō) *v.* to remove by exposing to air currents; free from lighter particles; to sift; to separate; p. 480

writhe (rīth) *v.* twist the body violently; contort; p. 873

Y

yearn (yurn) *v.* to desire or long; p. 816

W

waive/renunciar *v.* rechazar, no exigir, rehusar; p. 507

winnow/aventar *v.* echar en el aire para esparcir; separar; diseminar en partículos; tamizar; p. 480

writhe/retorcerse *v.* mover el cuerpo violentamente, contorsionarse; p. 873

Y

yearn/anhelar *v.* desear o ansiar; p. 816

Academic Word List

To succeed academically in high school and prepare for college, it is important to know academic vocabulary—special terms used in classroom discussion, assignments, and tests. These words are also used in the workplace and among friends to share information, exchange ideas, make decisions, and build relationships. Research has shown that the words listed below, compiled by Averil Coxhead in 2000, are the ones most commonly used in these ways. You will encounter many of them in the Glencoe Language Arts program. You will also focus on specific terms in connection with particular reading selections.

Note: The lists are ordered by frequency of use from most frequent to least frequent.

List One

analysis
approach
area
assessment
assume
authority
available
benefit
concept
consistent
constitutional
context
contract
create
data
definition
derived
distribution
economic
environment
established
estimate
evidence
export
factors
financial
formula
function
identified
income
indicate
individual
interpretation
involved
issues
labor
legal
legislation
major
method
occur
percent
period
policy
principle
procedure
process
required
research
response
role
section
sector
significant
similar
source
specific
structure
theory
variables

List Two

achieve
acquisition
administration
affect
appropriate
aspects
assistance
categories
chapter
commission
community
complex
computer
conclusion
conduct
consequences
construction
consumer
credit
cultural
design
distinction
elements
equation
evaluation
features
final
focus
impact
injury
institute
investment
items
journal
maintenance
normal
obtained
participation
perceived
positive
potential
previous
primary
purchase
range
region
regulations
relevant
resident
resources
restricted
security
select
site
sought
strategies
survey
text
traditional
transfer

List Three

alternative
circumstances
comments
compensation
components
consent
considerable
constant
constraints
contribution
convention
coordination
core
corporate
corresponding
criteria
deduction
demonstrate
document
dominant
emphasis
ensure
excluded
framework
funds
illustrated
immigration
implies
initial

instance
interaction
justification
layer
link
location
maximum
minorities
negative
outcomes
partnership
philosophy
physical
proportion
published
reaction
registered
reliance
removed
scheme
sequence
sex
shift
specified
sufficient
task
technical
techniques
technology
validity
volume

List Four

access
adequate
annual
apparent
approximated
attitudes
attributed
civil
code
commitment
communication

concentration
conference
contrast
cycle
debate
despite
dimensions
domestic
emerged
error
ethnic
goals
granted
hence
hypothesis
implementation
implications
imposed
integration
internal
investigation
job
label
mechanism
obvious
occupational
option
output
overall
parallel
parameters
phase
predicted
principal
prior
professional
project
promote
regime
resolution
retained
series
statistics
status

stress
subsequent
sum
summary
undertaken

List Five

academic
adjustment
alter
amendment
aware
capacity
challenge
clause
compounds
conflict
consultation
contact
decline
discretion
draft
enable
energy
enforcement
entities
equivalent
evolution
expansion
exposure
external
facilitate
fundamental
generated
generation
image
liberal
license
logic
marginal
medical
mental
modified
monitoring

network
notion
objective
orientation
perspective
precise
prime
psychology
pursue
ratio
rejected
revenue
stability
styles
substitution
sustainable
symbolic
target
transition
trend
version
welfare
whereas

List Six

abstract
accurate
acknowledged
aggregate
allocation
assigned
attached
author
bond
brief
capable
cited
cooperative
discrimination
display
diversity
domain
edition
enhanced

estate
exceed
expert
explicit
federal
fees
flexibility
furthermore
gender
ignored
incentive
incidence
incorporated
index
inhibition
initiatives
input
instructions
intelligence
interval
lecture
migration
minimum
ministry
motivation
neutral
nevertheless
overseas
preceding
presumption
rational
recovery
revealed
scope
subsidiary
tapes
trace
transformation
transport
underlying
utility

List Seven

adaptation
adults
advocate
aid
channel
chemical
classical
comprehensive
comprise
confirmed
contrary
converted
couple
decades
definite
deny
differentiation
disposal
dynamic
eliminate
empirical
equipment
extract
file
finite
foundation
global
grade
guarantee
hierarchical
identical
ideology
inferred
innovation
insert
intervention
isolated
media
mode
paradigm
phenomenon
priority
prohibited

publication
quotation
release
reverse
simulation
solely
somewhat
submitted
successive
survive
thesis
topic
transmission
ultimately
unique
visible
voluntary

List Eight

abandon
accompanied
accumulation
ambiguous
appendix
appreciation
arbitrary
automatically
bias
chart
clarity
commodity
complement
conformity
contemporary
contradiction
crucial
currency
denote
detected
deviation
displacement
dramatic
eventually
exhibit

exploitation
fluctuations
guidelines
highlighted
implicit
induced
inevitably
infrastructure
inspection
intensity
manipulation
minimized
nuclear
offset
paragraph
plus
practitioners
predominantly
prospect
radical
random
reinforced
restore
revision
schedule
tension
termination
theme
thereby
uniform
vehicle
via
virtually
visual
widespread

List Nine

accommodation
analogous
anticipated
assurance
attained
behalf
bulk

ceases
coherence
coincide
commenced
concurrent
confined
controversy
conversely
device
devoted
diminished
distorted
duration
erosion
ethical
format
founded
incompatible
inherent
insights
integral
intermediate
manual
mature
mediation
medium
military
minimal
mutual
norms
overlap
passive
portion
preliminary
protocol
qualitative
refine
relaxed
restraints
revolution
rigid
route
scenario
sphere

subordinate
supplementary
suspended
team
temporary
trigger
unified
violation
vision

List Ten

adjacent
albeit
assembly
collapse
colleagues
compiled
conceived
convinced
depression
encountered
enormous
forthcoming
inclination
integrity
intrinsic
invoked
levy
likewise
nonetheless
notwithstanding
odd
ongoing
panel
persistent
posed
reluctant
so-called
straightforward
undergo
whereby

Index of Skills

Reading and Critical Thinking

Research, Test-Taking, and Study Skills

Interdisciplinary Activities

Index of Authors and Titles

Acknowledgments

Unit 1

From "the Harper's Song for Inherkhawy" from *Ancient Egyptian Literature: An Anthology,* translated by John L. Foster. Copyright © 2001. By permission of the University of Texas Press.

"Pleasant Songs: Part II" ("So Small Are the Flowers of Seamu") edited by Ezra Pound, translated by Noel Stock, from *Love Poems of Ancient Egypt,* copyright © 1962 by Noel Stock. Reprinted by permission of New Directions Publishing Corp.

"Coyote Steals Fire" from *American Indian Trickster Tales* by Richard Erdoes and Alphonso Ortiz, copyright © 1998 by Richard Erdoes & The Estate of Alphonso Ortiz. Used by permission of Viking Penguin, a division of Penguin Group (USA) Inc.

"Master Cat Or Puss in Boots" by Charles Perrault, translated by Maria Tatar, from *The Annotated Classic Fairy Tales,* edited by Maria Tatar. Copyright © 2002 by Maria Tatar. Used by permission of W.W. Norton & Company, Inc.

"Edju and the Two Friends" from Radin, Paul; *African Folktales.* Copyright © by Bollingen Foundation, Inc., New York, NY, revised 1964. First Princeton/Bollingen Paperback printing, 1970. Reprinted by permission of Princeton University Press.

"The Lion's Awakening" from *Sundiata: An Epic of Old Mali, 2nd Edition,* by D.T. Niane. Copyright © 1965 by Longmans, Green & co. Reprinted by permission of Pearson Education Limited.

"Half a Day", translated by Denys Johnson-Davis, copyright © 1991 by American University in Cairo Press, from *The Time and the Place & Other Stories* by Naguib Mahfouz. Used by permission of Doubleday, a division of Random House, Inc.

"The Voter" from *Girls at War and Other Stories* by Chinua Achebe, copyright © 1972, 1973 by Chinua Achebe. Used by permission of Doubleday, a division of Random House, Inc.

From *No Future Without Forgiveness* by Desmond Tutu, copyright © 1999 by Desmond Tutu. Used by permission of Doubleday, a division of Random House, Inc.

"The Prisoner Who Wore Glasses," copyright © Bessie Head, from *Tales of Tenderness and Power,* Ad. Donker, 1989.

From *Things Fall Apart* by Chinua Achebe. Copyright © 1959 by Chinua Achebe. Reprinted by permission of Harcourt Education.

From *Ake: The Years of Childhood* by Wole Soyinka, copyright © 1981 by Wole Soyinka. Used by permission of Random House, Inc.

Unit 2

"The Death of Hector," by Homer, "The Rage of Achilles," by Homer from *The Iliad* by Homer, translated by Robert Fagles, copyright © 1990 by Robert Fagles. Used by permission of Viking Penguin, a division of Penguin Group (USA) Inc.

From "Echoes of the Heroic Age" by Caroline Alexander, *National Geographic,* December 1999. Copyright © 1999 The National Geographic society. Reprinted by permission.

Excerpt from *Sappho: Poems and Fragments,* translated by Stanley Lombardo. Copyright © 2002 by Hackett Publishing Company. Reprinted by permission of Hackett Publishing Company, Inc. All rights reserved.

"Oedipus the King," by Sophocles, from *Three Theban Plays* by Sophocles, translated by Robert Fagles, copyright © 1982 by Robert Fagles. Used by permission of Viking Penguin, a division of Penguin Group (USA) Inc.

From *The History of the Peloponnesian War* by Thucydides, translated by Rex Warner, with an introduction and notes by M.I. Finley (Penguin Classics 1954, Revised Edition 1972). Translation copyright © Rex Warner, 1954. Introduction and Appendices copyright © M.I. Finley, 1972. Reprinted by permission.

From *The Dialogues of Plato* by William Chase Greene, editor, from the translation of Benjamin Jowett. Copyright 1927 by Horace Liveright, Inc., renewed 1954 by Liveright Publishing Corporation. Used by permission of Liveright publishing Corporation.

"Better to Live, Licinius" from *Odes and Epodes of Horace: A Modern English Verse Translation,* by Joseph P. Clancy. Copyright © 1960 by The University of Chicago. Reprinted by permission.

"The Story of Piramus and Thisbe" from *Metamorphoses* by Ovid, translated by Rolfe Humphries. Copyright © 1955 Indiana University Press. Reprinted by permission of Indiana University Press.

"Book Two: The Final Hours of Troy" from *Virgil: The Aeneid* by Virgil, translated by Robert Fagles, copyright © 2006 by Robert Fagles. Used by permission of Viking Penguin, a division of Penguin Group (USA) Inc.

From *The Annals of Imperial Rome* by Tacitus, translated with an introduction by Michael Grant (Penguin Classics 1956, Sixth revised edition 1989). Copyright © Michael Grant Publications Ltd, 1956, 1959, 1971, 1973, 1975, 1977, 1989.

Excerpt from *The Bells of Nagasaki* by Takashi Nagai, translated by William Johnston. Copyright © 1984 by Kodansha International Ltd. Reprinted by permission.

From *The Lives of the Twelve Caesars* by Suetonius, translated by Joseph Garvorse, copyright 1931 and renewed 1959 and 1967 by Modern Library, a division of Random House, Inc. Used by permission of Modern Library, a division of Random House, Inc.

Unit 3

Reprinted and edited with the permission of The Free Press, a division of Simon & Schuster Adult Publishing Group, from *Gilgamesh: A New English Version* by Stephen Mitchell. Copyright © 2004 by Stephen Mitchell. All rights reserved.

Reprinted with the permission of Simon & Schuster Adult Publishing Group from *The Bible Designed To Be Read As Living Literature: the Old and New Testaments in the King James Version,* edited by Ernest Sutherland Bates. Copyright 1936 by Simon & Schuster, Inc. Copyright renewed © 1964 by Simon & Schuster Inc.

"The Exordium" and "Daylight" from *The Koran,* translated by N.J. Dawood (Penguin Classics 1956, Fifth revised edition 1990). Copyright © N.J. Dawood, 1956, 1959, 1966, 1968, 1974, 1990, 1993, 1997, 1999, 2003. Reprinted by permission of Penguin Group (UK)

"The Second Voyage of Sinbad the Sailor" from *Tales from the Thousand and One Nights,* translated by N.J. Dawood, wood engravings by William Harvey (Penguin Classics 1954, Revised edition 1973). Translation copyright © N.J. Dawood, 1954, 1973.

"The Counsels of the Bird" reprinted with permission from *Teachings of Rumi: The Masnavi* (Octagon Press Ltd., London).

From "Love Song for Words" by Nazik Al-Malaika, translated by Matthew

Sorenson and Christopher Middleton, from *Modern Arabic Poetry,* copyright © 1991 Columbia University Press. Reprinted by permission.

"The Sound of Birds at Noon" by Dahlia Ravikovitch, translated by Chana Bloch and Ariel Bloch, from *The Window.* Reprinted by permission of Chana Bloch.

"The Diameter of the Bomb" from *The Selected Poetry of Yehuda Amichai,* by Yehuda Amichai, edited and translated by Chana Bloch and Stephen Mitchell. Copyright © 1966 The Regents of the University of California. Published by the University of California Press. Reprinted by permission.

"Butterflies" by Fawziyya Abu Khalid, from *The Literature of Modern Arabia,* copyright © 1988 by the King Saud University. Reprinted by permission of Kegan Paul International.

"Poem" by Fawziyya Abu Khalid, translated by Salwa Jabsheh and John Heath-Stubbs, from from *Modern Arabic Poetry,* copyright © 1991 Columbia University Press. Reprinted by permission.

"The Letter" translated by Mattias Ripa & Blake Ferris, from *Persepolis: The Story of a Childhood,* by Marjane Satrapi, translated by Mattias Ripa & Blake Ferris, copyright © 2003 by L'Associaiton, Paris, France. Used by permission of Pantheon Books, a division of Random House, Inc.

"Creation Hymn" from *The Rig Veda: An Anthology of One Hundred and Eight Hymns,* selected, translated and annotated by Wendy Doniger O'Flaherty (Penguin Classics 1981). Copyright © Wendy Doniger O'Flaherty, 1981.

"Hundred Questions" from *The Mahabharata* by R.K. Narayan. Copyright © 1978 by R.K Narayan. Used by permission of the Wallace Literary Agency, Inc.

From "Homer in India" by William Dalrymple, copyright William Dalrymple, 2006. Reprinted by permission of David Goodwin Associates on behalf of the author.

"Rama and Ravana in Battle" from *The Ramayana* by R.K. Narayan, copyright © 1972 by R.K. Narayan. Used by permission of Viking Penguin, a division of Penguin Group (USA) Inc.

"The Lion-Makers" from *The Panchatantra,* translated from the Sanskrit by Arthur W. Ryder. Copyright © 1956 by Mary E. and Winifred Ryder. Reprinted by permission of The University of Chicago Press.

"The Oak and the Reed" from *La Fontaine: Selected Fables,* translated by James Michie, introduction by Geoffrey Grigson (Allen Lane 1979, Penguin Classics, 1982). Translation copyright © James Michie, 1979. Introduction copyright © Geoffrey Grigson, 1979.

"The Elephant Who Changed the World" from *Fables for Our Time,* copyright © 1956 by James Thurber. Copyright © renewed 1984 by Rosemary A. Thurber. Reprinted by arrangement with Rosemary A. Thurber and The Barbara Hogenson Agency, Inc.

"Like the Sun" by R.K. Narayan, from *Under the Banyan Tree* by R.K. Narayan, copyright © 1985 by R.K. Narayan. Used by permission of Viking Penguin, a division of Penguin Group (USA) Inc.

"By Any Other Name" from *Gifts of Passage* by Santha Rama Rau. Copyright 1951 by Santha Rama Rau. Copyright renewed © 1979 by Santha Rama Rau. Reprinted by permission of HarperCollins Publishers. "By Any Other Name" originally appeared in The New Yorker.

"The Taj Mahal" from *Step Across This Line* by Salman Rushdie, copyright © 2002 by Salman Rushdie. Used by permission of Random House, Inc.

Unit 4

Reprinted with the permission of Scribner, an imprint of Simon & Schuster Adult Publishing Group, from *The Analects of Confucius,* by Arthur Waley, translator. Copyright © 1938 by George Allen & Unwin Ltd. All rights reserved.

29, 31, 33 from *Tao Te Ching by Lao Tzu, A New English Version, with Foreward and Notes* by Stephen Mitchell. Translation copyright © 1988 by Stephen Mitchell. Reprinted by permission of HarperCollins Publishers.

"The River-Merchant's Wife: A Letter" by Ezra Pound, from *Personae,* copyright © 1926 by Ezra Pound. Reprinted by permission of New Directions Publishing Corp.

Excerpts from "The Southern Emperor Rules the Land" and "Homage to the Trung Queens" from *Heritage of Vietnamese Poetry,* edited and translated by Huynh Sanh Thong. Repritned by permission of Yale University Press.

"Jade Flower Palace" by Tu Fu, translated by Kenneth Rexroth, from *One Hundred Poems from the Chinese,* copyright © 1971 by Kenneth Rexroth. Reprinted by permission of New Directions Publishing Corp.

"Huzun," translated by Maureen Freely, from *Istanbul: Memories and the City* by Orhan Pamuk, translated by Maureen Freely, copyright © 2004 by Alfred A. Knopf, a division of Random House, Inc. Used by permission of Alfred A. Knopf, a division of Random House, Inc.

Excerpts from *The Pillow Book of Sei Shōnagon,* translated by Ivan Morris. Copyright © 1991 Columbia University Press. Reprinted by permission.

"Four Views of Spring Rain" by Yosa Buson, from *The Penguin Book of Japanese Verse,* translated by Geoffrey Bownas and Anthony Thwaite (Penguin Books, 1964). Reprinted by permission.

"A World of Dew and Melting Snow" by Kobayashi Issa, from *The Penguin Book of Japanese Verse,* translated by Geoffrey Bownas and Anthony Thwaite (Penguin Books, 1964). Reprinted by permission.

"Poverty's Child" and "The Sun's Way" by Basho, from An Introduction to Haiku by Harold G. Henderson, copyright © 1958 by Harold G. Henderson. Used by permission of Doubleday, a division of Random House, Inc.

Three haiku from Introduction (p. xi) by Bashō, Buson and Issa, from *The Essential Haiku: Versions of Bashō, Buson & Issa, Edited and With an Introduction* by Robert Hass. Introduction and selection copyright © 1994 by Robert Hass. Unless otherwise noted, all translations copyright © 1994 by Robert Hass. Reprinted by permission of HarperCollins Publishers.

"Rainforest" and "River Bend" from *A Human Pattern: Selected Poems* by Judith Wright. (ETT Imprint, Sydney, 1996) Reprinted by permission.

"Municipal Gum" by Oodgeroo of the tribe Noonuccal, from *My People, 3rd Edition,* The Jacaranda Press, 1990, reproduced by permission of John Wiley & Sons Australia.

"Clouds on the Sea" by Ruth Dallas, from *Fire in the Sea,* edited by Sue Cowing. Copyright © 1996 University of Hawaii Press. Reprinted by permission of the University of Hawaii Press.

From Pin Yathay: *Stay Alive, My Son.* Copyright © 1987, 2000 by Pin Yathay. Used by permission of the publisher, Cornell University Press.

"Moana" by Kauraka Kauraka, from *Fire in the Sea,* edited by Sue Cowing. Copyright © 1996 University of Hawaii Press. Reprinted by permission of the University of Hawaii Press.

"Island" by Albert Wendt, from *Fire in the Sea,* edited by Sue Cowing. Copyright © 1996 University of Hawaii Press. Reprinted by permission of the University of Hawaii Press.

From *The Selected Poems of T-ao Ch'ien,* translation copyright © 1993 by David Hinton. Reprinted by permission of Copper Canyon Press.

Unit 5

From *The Prose Edda: Tales from Norse Mythology,* by Snorri Sturluson, translated by Jean I. Young, copyright © 1964 by The Regents of the University of Califonia. Repritned by permission of the University of California Press.

From *The Song of Roland,* translated by Frederick Goldin. Copyright © 1978 by W.W. Norton & Company, Inc. Used by permission of W.W. Norton & Company, Inc.

From *The Divine Comedy* by Dante Alighieri, translated by John Ciardi. Copyright 1954, 1957, 1959, 1960, 1961, 1965, 1967, 1970 by the Ciardi Family Publishing Trust. Used by permission of W.W. Norton & Company, Inc.

"The Divine Comedy" by Jorges Luis Borges, translated by Eliot Weinberger, from *Seven Nights,* copyright © 1984 by Eliot Weinberger. Reprinted by permission of New Directions Publishing Corp.

"33" ("Secretly I am building in the heart…") from *Homecoming.* Copyright © 1984, 1996 by Julia Alvarez. Published by Plume, an imprint of Penguin Group (USA); originally published by Grove Press. Reprinted by permission of Susan Bergholz Literary Services, New York. All rights reserved.

"Federigo's Falcon- 9th Tale" from *The Decameron,* translated by Richard Aldington. Copyright © Estate of Richard Aldington, 1957, 1985. Reprinted by permission of Rosica Colin Limited.

Excerpts from *Don Quixote* by Miguel de Cervantes, a new translation by Edith Grossman. Introduction by Harold Bloom. Translation copyright © 2003 by Edith Grossman; introduction copyright © 2003 by Harold Bloom. Reprinted by permission of HarperCollins Publishers.

"The Lorelei" from *Poetry and Prose of Heinrich Heine,* by Heinrich Heine, edited by Frederic Ewen. Copyright © 1948, 1976 by Citadel Press. All rights reserved. Reprinted by arrangement with Citadel Press/Kensington Publishing Corp. www.kensingtonbooks.com.

"My Bohemia" translated by Wyatt Mason, from *Rimbaud Complete* by Arthur Rimbaud, translated by Wyatt Mason, copyright © 2002 by Wyatt Mason. Used by permission of Modern Library, a division of Random House, Inc.

"First Sorrow" from *The Penal Colony* by Franz Kafka, translated by Edwin & Willa Muir, copyright 1948 and renewed 1976 by Schocken Books. Used by permission of Schocken Books, a division of Random House, Inc.

"Lot's Wife," translation by Richard Wilbur, from *Walking to Sleep: New Poems and Translations,* copyright © 1969 and renewed 1997 by Richard Wilbur, reprinted by permission of Harcourt, Inc.

"War" from *The Medals and Other Stories* by Luigi Pirandello. Copyright © 1939 by E.P. Dutton & Co. Reprinted by permission of the Pirandello Estate and Toby Cole, agent.

"The Guitar" from *Lorca and Jimenez: Selected Poems,* copyright © 1973, 1997 by Robert Bly. Reprinted by permission.

"Encounter" from *Bells in Winter* by Czeslaw Milosz. Copyright © 1974, 1977, 1978 by Czeslaw Milosz. Reprinted by permission of HarperCollins Publishers.

"The World, My Friends, My Enemies, You and the Earth" from *Poems of Nazim Hikmet,* translated by Randy Blasing and Mutlu Konuk. Translation copyright © 2994, 2002 by Randy Blasing and Mutlu Konuk. Reprinted by permission of Persea Books, Inc. (New York).

Excerpt from *Crime and Punishment* by Feodor Dostoevsky, translated and edited by Jessie Coulson. Reprinted by permission of Oxford University Press.

Unit 6

Reprinted with the permission of Simon & Schuster Adult Publishing Group from *Popol Vuh* by Dennis Tedlock. Copyright © 1985, 1996 by Dennis Tedlock.

From *The Broken Spears* by Miguel Leon-Portilla. Copyright © 1962, 1990 by Miguel Leon-Portilla. Expanded and Updated edition © 1992 by Miguel Leon-Portilla. Reprinted by permission of Beacon Press, Boston.

"Sonnet 145" reprinted by permission of the publisher from *Sor Juana* by Octavio Paz, translated by Margaret Sayers Peden, p. 299, Cambridge, Mass: The Belknap Press of Harvard University Press, copyright © 1988 by the President and Fellows of Harvard College.

"A Canary's Ideas" from *The Devil's Church and Other Stories* by Joaquim Maria Machado de Assis, translated by Jack Schmitt and Lori Ishimatsu, copyright © 1977. By permission of the University of Texas Press.

"The Luck of Teodoro Mendez Acubal" from *Another Way to Be: Selected Works of Rosario Castellanos,* by Rosario Castellanos, foreword by Edward D. Terry. Copyright © 1990 by The University of Georgia Press. Reprinted by permission.

"Horses" from *A New Decade,* by Pablo Neruda. English translation copyright © 1969 by Alistair Reid. Used by permission of Grove/Atlantic, Inc.

"The Panther," copyright © 1982 by Stephen Mitchell, from *The Selected Poetry of Rainer Maria Rilke* by Rainer Maria Rilke, translated by Stephen Mitchell. Used by permission of Random House, Inc.

"The Iguana" from *Out of Africa* by Isak Dinesen, copyright 1937 by Random House, Inc. and renewed 1965 by Rungstedlundfonden. Used by permission of Random House, Inc.

"The Red Cockatoo," by Po Chu-yi, from *Anthology of Chinese Literature,* edited by Cyril Birch. Copyright © 1995 by Grove Press, Inc. Used by permission of Grove/Atlantic, Inc.

"Fable" by Octavio Paz, translated by Muriel Rukeyser, from *Early Poems 1935-1955,* copyright © 1973 by Octavio Paz and Muriel Rukeyser. Reprinted by permission of New Directions Publishing Corp.

From "Between What I See and What I Say…" by Octavio Paz, translated by Eliot Weinberger, from *Collected Poems 1957-1987,* copyright © 1986 by Octavio Paz and Eliot Weinberger. Reprinted by permission of New directions Publishing Corp.

"The Handsomest Drowned Man in the World" from *Leaf Storm and Other Stories* by Gabriel García Márquez. Copyright © 1971 by Gabriel García Márquez. Reprinted by permission of HarperCollins Publishers.

"Bishop Berkley or Mariana of the Universe" by Liliana Heker is reprinted with permission from the publisher of *Short Stories by Latin American Women,* edited by Celia Correas de Zapata (© 1990 Arte Publico Press-University of Houston).

From *My Invented Country: A Nostalgic Journey Through Chile* by Isabel Allende. Translated by Margaret Sayers Peden. Copyright © 2003 by Isabel Allende. Translation copyright © 2003 by HarperCollins Publishers Inc. Reprinted by permission of HarperCollins Publishers.

"Fishing" from *The Woman Who Fell From the Sky* by Joy Harjo. Copyright © 1994 by Joy Harjo. Used by permission of W.W. Norton & Company, Inc.

From "For Alva Benson, and for Those Who Have Learned to Speak" by Joy Harjo. Reprtined by permission of the author.

From Rena Korb's article on Gabriel García Márquez, from *Short Stories for Students, Presenting Analysis, Context and Criticism on Commonly Studied Short Stories* by Kathleen Wilson. Reprinted with permission of Thomson Learning: www.thomsonrights.com. FAX: 800-730-2215.

From *House of the Spirits* by Isabel Allende, translated by Magda Bogin, copyright © 1985 by Alfred A. Knopf, A Division of Random House Inc. Used by permission of Alfred A. Knopf, a division of Random House, Inc.

Photography

Cover Erich Lessing/Art Resource, NY (bkgd) Farinaz Taghavi/Getty Images **T6** (t)Private Collection, Photo ©Bonhams, London, UK/Bridgeman Art Library, (b) Hugh Sitton/zefa/CORBIS; **T7** Christie's Images/Bridgeman Art Library; **T8** Brooklyn Museum of Art, New York, USA, Frank L. Babbott Fund /Bridgeman Art Library; **T9** Christie's Images; **T10** Erich Lessing/Art Resource, NY; **T11** Brooklyn Museum/CORBIS; **T12** Photodisc/PunchStock; **T13** (t)Scala/Art Resource, NY, (b)Reed Kaestner/CORBIS; **T14** (t)Scala/Art Resource, NY, (b)Christie's Images; **T15** Gianni Dagli Orti/CORBIS; **T16** akg-images; **T17** Jason Horowitz/zefa/CORBIS; **T18** Private Collection/Bridgeman Art Library; **T19** Tomb of Qin shi Huang Di, Xianyang, China/Bridgeman Art Library; **T20** China Photos/Getty Images; **T21** (t)Erich Lessing/Art Resource, NY, (b)Indochina Arts Partnership; **T22** Germanisches Nationalmuseum, Nuremberg, Germany/Bridgeman Art Library; **T23** SuperStock, Inc.; **T24** The Art Archive/Musée du Louvre Paris/Gianni Dagli Orti; **T25** Digital Image ©The Museum of Modern Art/Licensed by SCALA/Art Resource, NY; **T26** (t)British Museum, London/Bridgeman Art Library, (b)Museum fur Volkerkunde, Vienna, Austria/Bridgeman Art Library; **T27** Private Collection, Photo ©Boltin Picture Library/Bridgeman Art Library; **T28** Art Museum of Estonia, Tallinn/Bridgeman Art Library; **T41** Digital Vision/Getty Images; **T60** David Schmidt/Masterfile; **2** Bridgeman Art Library/Getty Images; **4** (t)Digital Vision/PunchStock, (b)Michel Gounot/Godong/CORBIS; **5** Christie's Images; **6** (tl)HIP/Art Resource, NY; (tr)Boltin Picture Library/Bridgeman Art Library; (c)Erich Lessing/Art Resource, NY; (b)The Art Archive/Museo Capitolino Rome/Alfredo Dagli Ort; **7** (tl)Werner Forman/Art Resource, NY; (tr)British Library, London/Bridgeman Art Library; (cl)Museo Nacional de Antropologia, Mexico City/Giraudon/Bridgeman Art Library; (cr)Martin Gray/National Geographic Image Collection; (b)HIP/Art Resource, NY; **8** The Art Archive/Bibliothèque Musée du Louvre/Gianni Dagli Orti; **9** Boltin Picture Library/Bridgeman Art Library; **10** (l)Glen Allison/Getty Images; (r)Horniman Museum, London/Heini Schneebeli/Bridgeman Art Library; **11** Werner Forman/CORBIS; **12** The Art Archive/Ragab Papyrus Institute Cairo/Gianni Dagli Orti; **13** Private Collection/Heini Schneebeli/Bridgeman Art Library; **14** Private Collection, Paul Freeman/Bridgeman Art Library; **15** Scala/Art Resource, NY; **18** HIP/Art Resource, NY; **20** Erich Lessing/Art Resource, NY; **21** Comstock/PunchStock; **24** Erich Lessing/Art Resource, NY; **26** Gianni Dagli Orti/CORBIS; **28** Bildarchiv Preussischer Kulturbesitz/Art Resource, NY; **31** Valley of the Kings, Thebes, Egypt, Held Collection/Bridgeman Art Library; **32** Werner Forman/Art Resource, NY; **34** British Museum, London/Bridgeman Art Library; **35** The Art Archive/Dagli Orti; **38** The Metropolitan Museum of Art/Art Resource, NY; **39** Private Collection, Photo ©Bonhams, London, UK/Bridgeman Art Library; **40** Private Collection, Photo ©Boltin Picture Library/Bridgeman Art Library; **42** Private Collection, Photo ©Heini Schneebeli/Bridgeman Art Library; **44** Museo Nacional de Antropologia, Mexico City/Michel Zabe/AZA/Bridgeman Art Library; **47** Private Collection, Roger Perrin/Bridgeman Art Library; **48** Private Collection/Bridgeman Art Library; **51 53** C.A.A.C - The Pigozzi Collection, Geneva; **56–57** (t)Authors Image/Alamy Images; Jason Lauré; **60** Musee Barbier-Mueller, Geneva/Heini Schneebeli/Bridgeman Art Library; **61** Andy Crawford/Getty Images; **62** Brooklyn Museum/CORBIS;

64 (t)Private Collection/Bridgeman Art Library; (b)Joseph Van Os/Stone/Getty Images; **67** Indianapolis Museum of Art, IN, Gift of Mr and Mrs Harrison Eiteljorg/Bridgeman Art Library; **68** (t)mary Evans/The Womens Library; (c)Private Collection/Michael Graham-Stewart/Bridgeman Art Library; (bl)Imperial War Museum, London/Bridgeman Art Library; (br)Private Collection/Bridgeman Art Library; **69** (t)Ulf Andersen/Getty Images; (c)AP Images; (b)AFP/Getty Images; **70** Private Collection/Michael Graham-Stewart/Bridgeman Art Library; **71** Alain DeJean/Sygma/CORBIS; **72** (l)Rick D'Elia/CORBIS; (r)Atlantide Phototravel/CORBIS; **73** Lindsay Hebberd/CORBIS; **74** The Newark Museum/Art Resource, NY; **75** Bernard Bisson/CORBIS SYGMA; **76** Louise Gubb/CORBIS SABA; **77** Schomburg Center/Art Resource, NY; **78** Felix Man/Stringer/Getty Images; **80** Held Collection/Bridgeman Art Library; **83** Reza; Webstan/CORBIS; **85** David A. Land/Jupiter Images; **87** Robert Harding Picture Library Ltd/Alamy Images; **92** AFP/Getty Images; **94** Private Collection/Bridgeman Art Library; **96** J.Garcia/photocuisine/CORBIS; **98** Contemporary African Art Collection Limited/CORBIS; **103 105** David Turnley/CORBIS; **107** John Newcomb/SuperStock; **109** Private Collection/Bridgeman Art Library; **113** (t)Christie's Images; (b)Frans Lemmens/Alamy Images; **115** Wendy L. Goldberg-Hammon/Stock Illustration RF/Getty Images; **117** (l c)Getty Images; (r)Ulf Andersen/Getty mages; **122** Ariadne Van Zandbergen/Alamy Images; **124** George Hallett; **126** Photodisc/PunchStock; **128** Private Collection/Michael Graham-Stewart/Bridgeman Art Library; **129** Heini Schneebeli/Bridgeman Art Library; **133** Graham Jepson/Writer Pictures; **135** Jeffrey L. Rotman/CORBIS; **137** Bettmann/CORBIS; **138** C.A.A.C. - The Pigozzi Collection, Geneva; **141** Private Collection/Bridgeman Art Library; **146** Angelo Cavalli/Getty Images; **149** Private Collection, Curwen Gallery/Bridgeman Art Library; **151** Collection of HM King Hussein of Jordan/Bridgeman Art Library; **152** Brand X Pictures/JupiterImages; **156** Khali Mazraawl/AFP/GETTY; **159** Darren Greenwood/Design Pics/CORBIS; **163** Stockbyte/PunchStock; **168** (l)Lindsey Gable/The McGraw-Hill Companies; (r)Grey Villet/Time & Life Pictures/Getty Images; **169** (l)The McGraw-Hill Companies; Eliot Elisofon/Time & Life Pictures/Getty Images; Jacques Langevin/CORBIS SYGMA; **178** (t)Reed Kaestner/CORBIS; (b)Schmitz-Söhnigen/zefa/CORBIS; **179** Erich Lessing/Art Resource, NY; **180** (tl)Nationalmuseet, Copenhagen/Bridgeman Art Library; (tr)Nimatallah/Art Resource, NY; (cl)Scala/Art Resource, NY; (cr)Erich Lessing/Art Resource, NY; (b)Snark/Art Resource, NY; **181** (tr tl)Scala/Art Resource, NY; (bl)Borromeo/Art Resource, NY; (bc br)Erich Lessing/Art Resource, NY; **182** Réunion des Musées Nationaux/Art Resource, NY; **183** British Museum, London/Bridgeman Art Library; **184** (t)Scala/Art Resource, NY; (b)Erich Lessing/Art Resource, NY; **185** (t)Bettmann/CORBIS; (b)Bridgeman Art Library; **186** Erich Lessing/Art Resource, NY; **187** Bildarchiv Preussischer Kulturbesitz/Art Resource, NY; **188** Scala/Art Resource, NY; **189** Mike Blake/Reuters/CORBIS; **190** The Metropolitan Museum of Art/Art Resource, NY; **191** Ashmolean Museum, University of Oxford/Bridgeman Art Library; **192** The Art Archive/Museo Capitolino Rome/Alfredo Dagli Orti; **194** Giraudon/Art Resource, NY; **197** Scala/Art Resource, NY; **199** Christie's Images; **204 206 211** Scala/Art Resource, NY; **214** Erich Lessing/Art Resource, NY; **219** Philip Harrington/The National Museum, Athens/National Geographic Society; **220** Giraudon/Art Resource, NY; **222** Museum of Fine Arts, Boston, Massachusetts, William Francis Warden Fund/Bridgeman Art Library; **226** Fitzwilliam Museum, University of Cambridge,/Bridgeman Art Library; **228** Christie's Images; **229** Getty Images; **232** (b)Galleria degli Uffizi, Florence, Italy/Bridgeman Art Library; **232-233** (t)Claudio H. Artman/Alamy Images; **233** (b)akg London; **234** The Art Archive/National Archaeological Museum Athens/Gianni Dagli Orti; **234** Victoria & Albert Museum, London/Bridgeman Art Library; **236** National Geographic; **237** Erich Lessing/Art Resource, NY; **238** The Art Archive/Archaeological Museum Delphi/Gianni Dagli Orti; **239** National Geographic; **241** Scala/Art Resource, NY; **244** Victoria & Albert Museum, London/Bridgeman Art Library; **248** Sheridan/Ancient Art & Architecture Collection; **249** Paul A. Souders/CORBIS; **250** Gianni Dagli

Orti/CORBIS; **252** The Israel Museum, Jerusalem, ©DACS/Vera & Arturo Schwarz Collection of Dada and Surrealist Art/Bridgeman Art Library; **255** ©1998 Kate Rothko-Prizel & Christopher Rothko/Artists Rights Society, New York/Art Resource, NY; **256** Staatliche Museen, Berlin/Bridgeman Art Library; **261** Arte & Immagini srl/CORBIS; **262** C.M.Dixon/Ancient Art & Architecture Collection Ltd; **267** Tate Gallery, London/Art Resource, NY; **272** Christie's Images; **281** SuperStock; **288** Erich Lessing/Art Resource, NY; **295** Christie's Images; **300** Donald Cooper/Photostage; **305 315** Erich Lessing/Art Resource, NY; **316** (l c)Getty Images; **316** (b)The Art Archive/Museo Nazionale Taranto/Gianni Dagli Orti; **320 322** Erich Lessing/Art Resource, NY; **327** INTERFOTO Pressebildagentur/Alamy Images; **328** The Detroit Institute of Arts, Founders Society Purchase/Bridgeman Art Library; **329** Vanni/Art Resource, NY; **334** Réunion des Musées Nationaux/Art Resource, NY; **337** Alinari/Art Resource, NY; **343** Karen Moskowitz; **344** HIP/Art Resource, NY; **346** (t)Anthony Cassidy/JAI/CORBIS; (b)Alessandro Saffo/Grand Tour/CORBIS; **347** Bildarchiv Preussischer Kulturbesitz/Art Resource, NY; Giraudon/Art Resource, NY; **348** (tl)Musee National du Bardo, Le Bardo, Tunisia/Giraudon/Bridgeman Art Library; (tr cl cr br)Scala/Art Resource, NY; (bl)Liu Liqun/CORBIS; **349** (t)Louvre, Paris/Bridgeman Art Library; (bl)Metropolitan Museum of Art, New York/Bridgeman Art Library; (br)Werner Forman/Art Resource, NY; **350** Bibliotheque Nationale, Paris/Bridgeman Art Library; **351** Private Collection, Alinari/Bridgeman Art Library; **352** (l)British Museum, London/Bridgeman Art Library; (r)Atlantide Phototravel/CORBIS; **353** Scala/Art Resource, NY; **354** The Art Archive/Musée Archéologique Naples/Alfredo Dagli Orti; **355** Scala/Art Resource, NY; **356** Gianni Dagli Orti/CORBIS; **357** Mitchell Gerber/CORBIS; **358** The Granger Collection; **359** Scala/Art Resource, NY; **360** Bradford City Art Gallery and Museum, England/SuperStock; **363** Scala/Art Resource, NY; **365** Museo della Civilta Romana, Rome, Italy/Bridgeman Art Library; **368** Scala/Art Resource, NY; **373** De Morgan Foundation, London/SuperStock; **376** Roger Wood/CORBIS; **378** National Gallery, London/SuperStock; **381** The De Morgan Centre, London/Bridgeman Art Library; **385** San Diego Museum of Art/Bridgeman Art Library; **393** Christie's Images; **396** (tl tc)Getty Images; (b)Bildarchiv Preussischer Kulturbesitz/Art Resource, NY; **400** Ashmolean Museum, University of Oxford, UK/Bridgeman Art Library; **401** akg-images; **403** Buddy Mays/CORBIS; **404** Giraudon/Art Resource, NY; **405** Royalty-Free/CORBIS; **410** Underwood & Underwood/CORBIS; **412** Bettmann/CORBIS; **413** Private Collection, England & Co. Gallery, London/Bridgeman Art Library; **415** Bettmann/CORBIS; **418** Boltin Picture Library/Bridgeman Art Library; **421** Held Collection/Bridgeman Art Library; **424** Ancient Art and Architecture Collection Ltd./Bridgeman Art Library; **426** (l)Time & Life Pictures/Getty Images; (r)Museo Capitolino, Rome, Italy/Bridgeman Art Library; **427** (l)The McGraw-Hill Companies; (c)Lindsey Gable/The McGraw-Hill Companies; (r)Museo Archeologico Nazionale, Naples/Bridgeman Art Library; **436** (t)Jose Fuste Raga/CORBIS; (t)Peter Horree/Alamy Images; (c)Gary J. Antonetti, Ortelius Design, Inc.; (b)Gary Braasch/CORBIS; **438** (c)Gianni Dagli Orti/CORBIS; (bl)Bettmann/CORBIS; (br)Museum of Fine Arts, Houston, TX, Museum purchase funded by 'One Great Night in November 1988'/Bridgeman Art Library; **439** (t)The Trustees of the Chester Beatty Library, Dublin/Bridgeman Art Library; (c)Sandro Vannini/CORBIS; (c)West Semitic Research/Dead Sea Scrolls Foundation/CORBIS; **440** Kazuyoshi Nomachi/CORBIS; **441** Louvre, Paris/Bridgeman Art Library; **442** (l)Ashmolean Museum, University of Oxford, UK/Bridgeman Art Library; (r)Hans Georg Roth/CORBIS; **443** Murat Taner/zefa/CORBIS; **444** Instituto da Biblioteca Nacional, Lisbon, Portugal/Bridgeman Art Library; **445** Victoria & Albert Museum, London/Art Resource, NY; **446** Israel Museum, Jerusalem/Bridgeman Art Library; **447** Private Collection, ©DACS /Roger Perrin/Bridgeman Art Library; **448** Erich Lessing/Art Resource, NY; **450** Louvre, Paris, France, Peter Willi/Bridgeman Art Library; **452** Michael Holford; **455** Mary Evans Picture Library; **456** Victoria & Albert Museum, London/Art Resource, NY; **457** akg-images; **461** Museo Archeologico Prenestino, Palestrina,

Italy, Roger-Viollet, Paris/Bridgeman Art Library; **462** Erich Lessing/Art Resource, NY; **464** (l c)Getty Images; (b)Reuters/CORBIS; **467** HIP/Art Resource, NY; **469** Victoria & Albert Museum, London/Art Resource, NY; **470** The Jewish Museum, NY/Art Resource, NY; **472** San Marco, Venice, Italy, Lauros/Giraudon/Bridgeman Art Library; **481** Southampton City Art Gallery, Hampshire, UK/Bridgeman Art Library; **483** (l c)Getty Images; (b)Scala/Art Resource, NY; **486** British Library Board. All Rights Reserved/Bridgeman Art Library; **487** Cameraphoto Arte, Venice/Art Resource, NY; **489** Erich Lessing/Art Resource, NY; **491** Bibliotheque Nationale, Paris/Bridgeman Art Library; **493 494** Giraudon/Art Resource, NY; **496** Private Collection, Roger Perrin/Bridgeman Art Library; **498** Freer Gallery of Art, Smithsonian Institution, Washington D.C.; **499** Goodshoot/Fotosearch; **500 502** Freer Gallery of Art, Smithsonian Institution, Washington D.C.; **505** The Fine Art Society, London/Bridgeman Art Library; **507** Chehel Sotun, or 'The 40 Columns', Isfahan, Iran, Giraudon/Bridgeman Art Library; **508** Bonhams, London/Bridgeman Art Library; **511** akg London; **513** Art Resource, NY; **518** Private Collection/Bridgeman Art Library; **520** Haaratz/Writer Pictures; **522** Martin Harvey; Gallo Images/CORBIS; **524** peitschphoto.com/Writer Pictures; **526 528** Private Collection/Bridgeman Art Library; **529** age_fotostock/SuperStock; **530** Private Collection/Bridgeman Art Library; **532** Eric Robert/VIP Production/CORBIS; **534-540** Marjane Satrapi; **543** Khalil Mazraawi/AFP/Getty Images; **544** ©2002 Tom Stoddart; **546** (t)Ric Ergenbright/CORBIS; (c)Gary J. Antonetti, Ortelius Design, Inc.; (b)Sheldan Collins/CORBIS; **547** Jason Horowitz/zefa/CORBIS; **548** (tl)Bibliotheque Nationale, Paris, Archives Charmet/Bridgeman Art Library; (tr)Redlink/CORBIS; (c)Victoria & Albert Museum, London/Bridgeman Art Library; (b)The Granger Collection, New York; **549** (t)CORBIS SYGMA; (cr)Hulton-Deutsch Collection/CORBIS; (cr)Private Collection, The Stapleton Collection/Bridgeman Art Library; (b)Musee Conde, Chantilly, France/Bridgeman Art Library; (ct)Stapleton Collection/CORBIS; **550** National Museum of Karachi, Pakistan/Bridgeman Art Library; **551** Ashmolean Museum, University of Oxford, UK/Bridgeman Art Library; **552** (l)Horniman Museum, London/Photo ©Heini Schneebeli/Bridgeman Art Library; (r)Stapleton Collection, UK/Bridgeman Art Library; **553** Dinodia Photo Library/Brand X/CORBIS; **554** Victoria & Albert Museum, London,The Stapleton Collection/Bridgeman Art Library; **555** Reuters/CORBIS; **556** Thierry Prat/Sygma/CORBIS; **557** Robbie Jack/CORBIS; **558** Freud Museum, London/Bridgeman Art Library; **560** National Museum of India, New Delhi/Bridgeman Art Library; **561** Werner Forman/Art Resource, NY; **563** National Museum of India, New Delhi/Bridgeman Art Library; **565** Réunion des Musées Nationaux/Art Resource, NY; **567** Private Collection, The Stapleton Collection/Bridgeman Art Library; **568** Surya Temple, Somnath, Mumbai, India, Dinodia/Bridgeman Art Library; **570** The Pierpont Morgan Library/Art Resource, NY; **571** Getty Images; **574** Free Agents Limited/CORBIS; **574–575** (t) Iconotec/Alamy Images; **575** (b)Owen Franken/CORBIS; **576** ©Raghu Rai/Magnum Photos; **579** The Metropolitan Museum of Art/Art Resource, NY; **580** Jeffrey L. Rotman/CORBIS; **582** ©British Museum/Art Resource, NY; **584** Erich Lessing/Art Resource, NY; **587** HIP/Art Resource, NY; **588** Photodisc/PunchStock; **591** Private Collection, Archives Charmet/Bridgeman Art Library; **594** The Pierpont Morgan Library/Art Resource, NY; **595** Giraudon/Art Resource, NY; **597** The Metropolitan Museum of Art/Art Resource, NY; **598** Christie's Images/Bridgeman Art Library; **601** akg-images; **603** Bridgeman Art Library/SuperStock; **606** Private Collection, Archives Charmet/Bridgeman Art Library; **607** E.O. Hoppé/CORBIS; **609** Private Collection/Bridgeman Art Library; **611** Author's Image; **613** BananaStock/PunchStock; **615** Bradford Art Galleries and Museums, West Yorkshire, UK/Bridgeman Art Library; **616** (l c)Getty Images; (b)Alinari Archives/CORBIS; **621** Fry Art Gallery, Saffron Walden, Essex/Bridgeman Art Library; **623** Private Collection/Bridgeman Art Library; **625** Hulton Archive/Getty Images; **627** Private Collection/Bridgeman Art Library; **629** arabianEye FZ LLC/Alamy Images; **630** Private Collection/Bridgeman Art Library; **636** Neil McAllister/Alamy Images; **638** Ignacio Auzike/ArtBox Images/Getty

Images; **640** Edward North/Alamy Images; **641** Private Collection/ Bridgeman Art Library; **643** Arts Council Collection, Hayward Gallery, London/Bridgeman Art Library; **644** Private Collection, Will's Art Warehouse, London/Bridgeman Art Library; **647** Bill Lyons Photography; **649** Chris Rainier/CORBIS; **653** Will & Deni McIntyre/ CORBIS; **656** Dan Guravich/CORBIS; **660 661** Bob Sciarrino/Star Ledger/CORBIS; **662** (l)Royal Asiatic Society, London/Bridgeman Art Library; (r)The McGraw-Hill Companies; **663** (t c b)The McGraw-Hill Companies; **672** (t)Bruno Levy/zefa/CORBIS; **672** (b)Keren Su/Getty Images; **673** Tomb of Qin shi Huang Di, Xianyang, China/Bridgeman Art Library; **674** (t)Lee & Lee Communications/Art Resource, NY; (cl)Asian Art & Archaeology, Inc./CORBIS; (cr)Tomb of Qin shi Huang Di, Xianyang, China/Bridgeman Art Library; (b)Danny Lehman/CORBIS; **675** (tl)The Art Archive; (tr)Micheline Pelletier/CORBIS; (cl)Werner Forman/Art Resource, NY; (cr)Hans Gedda/Sygma/CORBIS; (b)Private Collection, ©Michael Graham-Stewart/Bridgeman Art Library; **676** Scala/Art Resource, NY; **677** Private Collection/Bridgeman Art Library; **678** (t)Stapleton Collection, UK/Bridgeman Art Library; (b)Marc Garanger/CORBIS; **679** Frank Leather; Eye Ubiquitous/CORBIS; |**680** Oriental Museum, Durham University, UK/Bridgeman Art Library; **681** HIP/Art Resource, NY; **682** British Library, London/©British Library Board. All Rights Reserved/Bridgeman Art Library; **683** Brooklyn Museum of Art, New York, USA/Bridgeman Art Library; **684** Vanni/Art Resource, NY; **685** Bibliotheque Nationale, Paris/Bridgeman Art Library; **689** Bibliotheque Nationale, Paris, Archives Charmet/Bridgeman Art Library; **690** Erich Lessing/Art Resource, NY; **691** Art Institute of Chicago; **694** Erich Lessing/Art Resource, NY; **695** Brooklyn Museum of Art, New York, Gift of Anna Ferris /Bridgeman Art Library; **696** The Cleveland Museum of Art; **699** HIP/Art Resource, NY; **700–701** (t)Photodisc/PunchStock; (b)Private Collection, Photo ©Christie's Images/Bridgeman Art Library; **702** David Forbert/ SuperStock; **704** Private Collection, Giraudon/Bridgeman Art Library; **705** Christie's Images; **707** Roger Wood/CORBIS; **709** Underwood & Underwood/CORBIS; **711** Dave Bartruff/CORBIS; **712** Victoria & Albert Museum, London/Art Resource, NY; **713** UCL Art Collections, University College London/Bridgeman Art Library; **714** Katsushika Hokusai/Bridgeman Art Library/Getty Images; **716** Musee des Beaux-Arts, Angers, Giraudon/Bridgeman Art Library; **719** British Library Board. All Rights Reserved/Bridgeman Art Library; **721** Private Collection/ Bridgeman Art Library; **723** Dean Conger/CORBIS; **725** The Stapleton Collection/Bridgeman Art Library; **726** Asian Art & Archaeology, Inc./ CORBIS; **726** Getty Images; **730** Artkey/CORBIS; **733** Mary Evans Picture Library; **736** Guthrie/Art Resource, NY; **737** Reuters/CORBIS; **738** Snark/Art Resource, NY; **739** Victoria & Albert Museum, London/ Bridgeman Art Library; **740** The Art Institute of Chicago; **742** The Trustees of the Chester Beatty Library, Dublin/Bridgeman Art Library; **745** Brooklyn Museum of Art, New York, Frank L. Babbott Fund / Bridgeman Art Library; **746** The Trustees of the Chester Beatty Library, Dublin/Bridgeman Art Library; **748** Ann Arbor/Writer Pictures; **751** Jacques Langevin/CORBIS SYGMA; **753** AGIP RA/Lebrecht Music & Arts; **755** The Art Insititute of Chicago; **757** Leeds Museums and Art Galleries (City Museum) UK/Bridgeman Art Library; **759** (t)Getty Images; (b)Private Collection, Paul Freeman/Bridgeman Art Library; **762** AGIP RA/Lebrecht Music & Arts; **763** Gahoe Museum, Jongno-gu, South Korea/Bridgeman Art Library; **764** Victoria & Albert Museum, London/Art Resource, NY; **766** ChinaStock; **768** China Photos/Getty Images; **771** Greg Davis/OnAsia Images; **772** Tetsuya Miura; **774** (t)Douglas Pearson/CORBIS; **774** (b)Private Collection, ©Agnew's, London/Bridgeman Art Library; **775** Erich Lessing/Art Resource, NY; **776** (t)LonelyPlanetImages; (b)Wolfgang Kaehler/CORBIS; (bl)The Art Archive/Mireille Vautier; **777** (tl)Private Collection/Bridgeman Art Library; (tr)David Van Der Veen/epa/CORBIS; (c)Commonwealth Institute, London/Bridgeman Art Library; (b)Ray Moreton/Hulton Archive/GettyImages; **778** Jose Fuste Raga/CORBIS; **779** The Art Archive/Private Collection/Marc Charmet; **780** (l)Bob Krist/CORBIS; (r)Gian Berto Vanni/CORBIS; **781** Christine Osborne/CORBIS; **782** Jacques Pavlovsky/Sygma/CORBIS; **783** Stuart Westmorland/

CORBIS; **784** The Art Archive; **785** Bettmann/CORBIS; **786** ©The Metropolitan Museum of Art/Art Resource, NY; **787** Private Collection, Photo ©Boltin Picture Library/Bridgeman Art Library; **788** SuperStock; **790** Bettmann/CORBIS; **792** Private Collection, ©DACS/Bridgeman Art Library; **794** Photodisc/PunchStock; **797** Pushkin Museum, Moscow/ ©DACS/Bridgeman Art Library; **799** (l c)Getty Images; (b)Victoria & Albert Museum, London/Art Resource, NY; **802** NLA/Writer Pictures; **804** Digital Vision/PunchStock; **806** Oliver Strewe/CORBIS; **808** Penny Tweedie/CORBIS; **810** Courtesy of The Otago Daily Times; **811** Werner Forman/Art Resource, NY; **814** Private Collection/ Bridgeman Art Library; **817** Indochina Arts Partnership; **819** Sophie Bassouls/CORBIS SYGMA; **821 825** Courtesy of Monirith Chhea; **829** Courtesy of Albert Wendt; **831** TIMOTCA, Laguna Beach, CA; **832** Art Wolfe; **836** Bettmann/CORBIS; **838** Lisa Pines/GettyImages; **843** Bruce Laurance/GettyImages; **844** Ryan Pyle/None/CORBIS; **846** Private Collection/Bridgeman Art Library; **848** (l)Ulla Montan/ Writer Pictures; (r)R.S. Criddle/Cover: Jeanne K. Pietrzak; **849** (t b)The McGraw-Hill Companies; (r)Courtesy Penguin Books; **856** Photothèque R. Magritte-ADAGP/Art Resource, NY; **858** (t)Herbert Spichtinger/zefa/ CORBIS; (b)Victoria & Albert Museum, London/Art Resource, NY; **859** Germanisches Nationalmuseum, Nuremberg/ Bridgeman Art Library; **860** (tl b)Werner Forman/Art Resource, NY; (tr)Private Collection, Lauros/Giraudon/Bridgeman Art Library; (cl cr)Erich Lessing/Art Resource, NY; **861** (t)Palazzo Vecchio (Palazzo della Signoria) Florence/Bridgeman Art Library; (cl)Erich Lessing/Art Resource, NY; (cr)Tokyo Fuji Art Museum, Japan/Bridgeman Art Library; (b)British Library, London/Bridgeman Art Library; **862** SuperStock; **863** Sotheby's Picture Library, London/Bridgeman Art Library; **864** SuperStock; **865** (l)Scala/Art Resource, NY; (r)Erich Lessing/Art Resource, NY; **866** HIP/Art Resource, NY; **867** Erich Lessing/Art Resource, NY; **868 869** Scala/Art Resource, NY; **872** Arni Magnusson Institute, Reykjavik/Bridgeman Art Library; **877** Giraudon/Art Resource, NY; **879** Scala/Art Resource, NY; **881** Germanisches Nationalmuseum, Nuremberg/Bridgeman Art Library; **884** akg-Images; **886** Writer Pictures; **888** SuperStock; **891** Huntington Library/SuperStock; **894** Bibliotheque Nationale, Paris/Bridgeman Art Library; **896** Bibliotheque des Arts Decoratifs, Paris, Archives Charmet/ Bridgeman Art Library; **900** British Museum, London/Bridgeman Art Library; **905** Christie's Images; **906** SuperStock; **912** (t)Getty Images; (b)The Art Archive/Biblioteca Nazionale Marciana Venice/Alfredo Dagli Orti; **915** HIP/Art Resource, NY; **918** Alte Pinakothek, Munich, Giraudon/Bridgeman Art Library; **919** Alinari/Art Resource, NY; **921** Kunsthistorisches Museum, Vienna/Bridgeman Art Library; **923** The Maas Gallery, London/Bridgeman Art Library; **924** Collection of Gustau Camps, Barcelona/Bridgeman Art Library; **925** Art Resource, NY; **926** Erich Lessing/Art Resource, NY; **928** SuperStock; **930** Pushkin Museum of Fine Arts, Moscow/SuperStock; **932** The Pierpont Morgan Library/Art Resource, NY; **934** Giraudon/Art Resource, NY; **935** Private Collection, Ken Welsh/Bridgeman Art Library; **937** akg-Images; **940** Harris Museum and Art Gallery, Preston, Lancashire/Bridgeman Art Library; **943** Bonhams, London/ Bridgeman Art Library; **945** Getty Images; **948** (b)Paul Almasy/CORBIS; (t)Jose Fuste Raga/CORBIS; **949** Tate, London/Art Resource, NY; **950** (t)The Art Archive/Musée du Louvre Paris/Gianni Dagli Orti; (c)Timothy McCarthy/Art Resource, NY; (b)Pennsylvania Academy of the Fine Arts/Bridgeman Art Library; **951** (t)SOPHIE BASSOULS/CORBIS SYGMA; (cl)HIP/Art Resource, NY; (c)Snark/Art Resource, NY; (cr)Stephen Ferry/Getty Images; (b)Bettmann/CORBIS; (br)Philippe Wojazer/Reuters/CORBIS; **952** Musee d'Orsay, Paris, Giraudon/Bridgeman Art Library; **953** Bettmann/CORBIS; **954** (l)Stapleton Collection, UK/Bridgeman Art Library; (r)Geoffrey Clements/CORBIS; **955** Philadelphia Museum of Art, Pennsylvania, PA©DACS/Bridgeman Art Library; **956** Hamburger Kunsthalle, Hamburg/Bridgeman Art Library; **957** Erich Lessing/Art Resource, NY; **958** THE GRANGER COLLECTION; **959** Metropolitan Museum of Art, New York ©DACS/Bridgeman Art Library; **960** Bridgeman-Giraudon/Art Resource, NY; **966** Pushkin Museum, Moscow, Giraudon/Bridgeman Art Library; **967** (b)Bildarchiv

Preussischer Kulturbesitz/Art Resource, NY; (t)Getty Images; **970** Wallace Collection, London/Bridgeman Art Library; **971** Bibliotheque de l'Opera Garnier, Paris, Joseph Martin/Bridgeman Art Library; **972** Bildarchiv Preussischer Kulturbesitz/Art Resource, NY; **973** nagelestock.com/Alamy Images; **974** Russell-Cotes Art Gallery and Museum, Bournemouth/Bridgeman Art Library; **976** Stapleton Collection/CORBIS; **978** Sotheby's Picture Library, London; **980** akg-images; **983** Adoc-photos/Art Resource, NY; **985** State Russian Museum, Moscow/Scala/Art Resource, NY; **987** Chris Hammond/Alamy Images; **988** akg-images; **992** Christie's Images; **997** (b)CORBIS; (t)Getty Images; **1001** Bettmann/CORBIS; **1003** Nationalmuseum, Stockholm ©DACS/Bridgeman Art Library; **1005** State Russian Museum, St. Petersburg, Russia/Bridgeman Art Library; **1009** (l c)Getty Images; (b)Underwood & Underwood/CORBIS; **1012** Bettmann/CORBIS; **1013** Musee d'Orsay, Paris, Lauros/Giraudon/Bridgeman Art Library; **1014** Private Collection, Archives Charmet/Bridgeman Art Library; **1016** The Fine Art Society, London/Bridgeman Art Library; **1019** Musee de la Ville de Paris, Musee Carnavalet, Paris, Archives Charmet/Bridgeman Art Library; **1021** The State Russian Museum/CORBIS; **1022** The Detroit Institute of Arts, Founders Society Purchase, R.H. Tannahill Foundation fund/Bridgeman Art Library; **1023** Rafael Valls Gallery, London/Bridgeman Art Library; **1025** Bettmann/CORBIS; **1027** Fry Art Gallery, Saffron Walden, Essex, UK/Bridgeman Art Library; **1032** Musee d'Art Moderne Richard Anacreon, Granville, France, Archives Charmet/Bridgeman Art Library; **1035** (l)CNAC/MNAM/Dist. Réunion des Musées Nationaux/Art Resource, NY; **1035** (r)Photodisc/GettyImages; **1036** Sotheby's Picture Library, London; **1038** (t)Getty Images; (b)Private Collection, Archives Charmet/Bridgeman Art Library; **1041** Geraint Lewis/Writer Pictures; **1042** The Museum of Modern Art/Licensed by SCALA/Art Resource, NY; **1043** Isabella Stewart Gardner Museum, Boston/Bridgeman Art Library; **1045** Sophie Bassouls/CORBIS SYGMA; **1046** National Museum in Cracow, Poland/Bridgeman Art Library; **1046** Sotheby's Picture Library, London; **1049** Courtesy Persea Books; **1051** Hardware Gallery, London/Bridgeman Art Library; **1054** DigitalVision/Getty Images; **1054-1055** Iconotec/Alamy Images; **1055** Swim Ink 2, LLC/CORBIS; **1056** Roger Viollet/Getty Images; **1058** (l)Getty Images; (r)Erich Lessing/Art Resource, NY; **1063** Eddie Adams/Sygma/CORBIS; **1065** Courtesy Alfred Tibor; **1067** Digital Image ©The Museum of Modern Art/Licensed by SCALA/Art Resource, NY; **1072** Tim Brakemeier/dpa/CORBIS; **1073** ©1999 Artists Rights Society (ARS)/ADAGP, Paris/Sotheby's Picture Library, London; **1074** State Russian Museum, St. Petersburg/Bridgeman Art Library; **1077** Bettmann/CORBIS; **1078** Reuters/CORBIS; **1079** Lynn Goldsmith/CORBIS; **1080** Jim Sugar/CORBIS; **1085** Newport Museum and Art Gallery, South Wales/Bridgeman Art Library; **1087** Royalty-Free/CORBIS; **1095** (l)Archivo Iconografico, S.A./CORBIS; (r)Lindsey Gable/The McGraw-Hill Companies; **1096** (l)Réunion des Musées Nationaux/Art Resource, NY; (r)Hulton-Deutsch Collection/CORBIS; **1097** (t cl b)The McGraw-Hill Companies; (cr)AGIP RA/Lebrecht Music & Arts; **1104** Schalkwijk/Art Resource, NY; **1106** (t)Wolfgang Kaehler Photography; (b)Charles & Josette Lenars/CORBIS; (c)Gary J. Antonetti, Ortelius Design, Inc.; **1107** British Museum, London/Bridgeman Art Library; **1108** (t)The Art Archive/Antochiw Collection Mexico/Mireille Vautier; (b)The Art Archive/British Museum/Harper Collins Publishers; **1109** (t)Museo Nacional de Historia, Mexico City/Bridgeman Art Library; (cl)The Art Archive/Manuel Cohen; (c)The Art Archive/Monastery of the Rabida, Palos, Spain/Gianni Dagli Orti; (cr)The Art Archive/American Museum Madrid; (bl)Private Collection, Photo ©Heini Schneebeli/Bridgeman Art Library; (br)Bettmann/CORBIS; **1110** Bettmann/CORBIS; **1111** Archivo Iconografico, S.A./CORBIS; **1112** (t)Charles & Josette Lenars/CORBIS; (b)Erich Lessing/Art Resource, NY; **1113** Lindsay Hebberd/CORBIS; **1114** Michel Zabe/Art Resource, NY; **1115** Giraudon/Art Resource, NY; **1116** Erich Lessing/Art Resource, NY; **1117** Hugh Sitton/zefa/CORBIS; **1118** (c)Jami Woy/The McGraw-Hill Companies; **1118–1119** (t)brianlatino/Alamy Images; **1119** Jami Woy/The McGraw-Hill Companies; **1120** Private Collection/Bridgeman Art Library; **1122** Museo Casa Diego Rivera (INBA), Guanajuato, Mexico, Index/he Bridgeman Art Library; **1123** (r)Erich Lessing/Art Resource, NY; (l)Kevin Schafer/Getty Images; **1124** Private Collection, Photo ©Boltin Picture Library/Bridgeman Art Library; **1126** British Museum/Werner Forman Archive/Topham/The Image Works; **1131** Galen Rowell/CORBIS; **1133** Jerry Jacka Photography; **1136** SuperStock; **1138** Adam Woolfitt/CORBIS; **1139** ©1999 Artists Rights Society (ARS)/ADAGP, Paris/Christie's Images; **1140** Mary Evans Picture Library; **1141** The Newark Museum/Art Resource, NY; **1145** Getty Images; **1148** Bildarchiv Preussischer Kulturbesitz/Art Resource, NY; **1150** Museum fur Volkerkunde, Vienna/Bridgeman Art Library; **1153** Michel Zabe/Art Resource, NY; **1154** SuperStock/Alamy Images; **1155** Private Collection, Photo ©Boltin Picture Library/Bridgeman Art Library; **1162** Biblioteca Medicea-Laurenziana, Florence/Bridgeman Art Library; **1163** The Art Archive/Museo Ciudad Mexico/Alfredo Dagli Orti; **1164** Erich Lessing/Art Resource, NY; **1166** Philadelphia Museum of Art/CORBIS; **1169** Bettmann/CORBIS; **1171** Snark/Art Resource, NY; **1174** CHIP CLARK-SMITHSONIAN; **1175** Time Inc.; **1176** CHIP CLARK-SMITHSONIAN; **1178** (t)Wolfgang Kaehler Photography; (b)Bauer Photography ©2007; **1179** Fred Jones Jr. Museum of Art, University of Oklahoma, USA, Gift of Dr. and Mrs. R. E. Mansfield, 2003/Bridgeman Art Library; **1180** (tl)Private Collection, Photo ©Boltin Picture Library/Bridgeman Art Library; (tr)Nik Wheeler/CORBIS; (c)Jean Pierre Amet/CORBIS SYGMA; (b)Private Collection/Bridgeman Art Library; **1181** (t)Time & Life Pictures/Getty Images; (cl)Chihuahua City Museum, Mexico, Sean Sprague/Mexicolore/Bridgeman Art Library; (c)Rykoff Collection/CORBIS; (cr)Penni Gladstone/CORBIS; (b)Atlantide Phototravel/CORBIS; **1182** Schalkwijk/Art Resource, NY; **1183** Steve Raymer/CORBIS; **1184** (t)Jon Hicks/CORBIS; (b)Private Collection/Photo: Jorge Contreras Chacel/Bridgeman Art Library; **1185** Wolfgang Kaehler Photography; **1186** Museu Nacional Belas Artes, Rio de Janeiro, Giraudon/Bridgeman Art Library; **1187** Christie's Images; **1188** Jerry Jacka Photography; **1189** Hugh Sitton/zefa/CORBIS; **1190** Nettie Lee Benson Latin American Collection, University of Texas at Austin; **1193** JUPITERIMAGES/Comstock Images/Alamy Images; **1195** Christie's Images; **1199** Lola Alverez Bravo/Writer Pictures; **1201** Schalkwijk/Art Resource, NY; **1202** SuperStock; **1204** Chlaus Lotscher/Peter Arnold; **1205** Christie's Images/SuperStock; **1209** Tate, London/Art Resource, NY; **1210** SuperStock, Inc./SuperStock; **1212** Erich Lessing/Art Resource, NY; **1215–1216** Private Collection/Bridgeman Art Library; **1218** Christie's Images/Bridgeman Art Library; **1219** Private Collection, ©DACS/Bridgeman Art Library; **1220** Time & Life Pictures/Getty Images; **1221** Christie's Images/CORBIS; **1222** INBA/Schalkwijk/Art Resource, NY; **1224** Private Collection/Bridgeman Art Library; **1226** Christie's Images; **1227** Mark Downey/Getty Images; **1230** Ulla Montan/Writer Pictures; **1232** Art Museum of Estonia, Tallinn/Bridgeman Art Library; **1235** Kactus Foto, Santiago/SuperStock; **1236** Bridgeman-Giraudon/Art Resource, NY; **1237** (l)Bridgeman-Giraudon/Art Resource, NY; (r)Historical Picture Archive/CORBIS; **1239** (tl tc)Getty Images; (b)©British Museum/Art Resource, NY; **1243** Colita/CORBIS; **1245** National Air and Space Museum, Smithsonian Institution. NASM 5008, CAT NO 1975-0095.; **1249** Schalkwijk/Art Resource, NY; **1252** Emiliano Lasalvia/Eniefoto/Writer Pictures; **1254** INBA/Christie's Images; **1257** Zurbaran Galeria, Buenos Aires/SuperStock; **1261** William J Hebert/Getty Images; **1262** TongRo Image Stock/Alamy Images; **1264** Paul Hawthorne/AP Images; **1267** Daniel Nevins/SuperStock; **1268** colinspics/Alamy Images; **1270** Bridgeman Art Library/SuperStock; **1277** Jeremy Bembaron/CORBIS SYGMA; **1279 1281** Private Collection/Bridgeman Art Library; **1282** ImageSource/PunchStock; **1287** Paul Abdoo/Writer Pictures; **1289** Jerry Jacka Photography; **1293** Carl & Ann Purcell/CORBIS; **1297** Werner Forman/Art Resource, NY; **1300** Michael Newman/PhotoEdit; **1302** Bettmann/CORBIS; **1303** (t c b)The McGraw-Hill Companies; (cl)Colita/CORBIS.